Rand McNally

The

Revised and Updated

Comprehensive World Atlas

LONGMEADOW
PRESS

Contents

Using the Atlas _____ iii - iv
Sequence of the Maps
Getting the Information
  Finding Places, Measuring Distances,
  Determining Directions, Understanding
  Map Symbols

The Earth _____ v - xvi
The Earth and the Universe _____ v
The Earth in the Solar System _____ vi
Earth, Satellites, and Mapping _____ viii
The Earth's Land _____ x
The Earth's Oceans _____ xii
The Earth's Habitats _____ xiv
World Time Zones _____ xvi

Reference Maps _____ 1-128
Map Symbols _____ 1
The World and
  Special Regions _____ 2-7
The World _____ 2
Polar Map of the World _____ 4
Atlantic Ocean _____ 5
Pacific Ocean _____ 6
Antarctica _____ 7

Europe _____ 8-29
Europe and Western Asia _____ 8
British Isles _____ 10
Ireland _____ 11
England and Wales _____ 12
Scotland and Northern England _____ 13
Norway, Sweden and Finland _____ 14
Denmark and Northern Germany _____ 15
France and the Low Countries _____ 16
Belgium, Netherlands, Luxembourg
  and Western Germany _____ 17
Germany, Austria and Switzerland _____ 18
Central Germany _____ 19
Alpine Regions _____ 20
Switzerland _____ 21
Spain and Portugal _____ 22
Italy _____ 23

Yugoslavia, Hungary, Romania
  and Bulgaria _____ 24
Greece, Albania and Western Turkey _____ 25
Poland and Czechoslovakia _____ 26
Western Soviet Union _____ 27
South Central Soviet Union _____ 28
Soviet Union _____ 29

Asia _____ 30-41
Asia _____ 30
China, Mongolia, Korea,
  Japan and Taiwan _____ 31
Northeastern China _____ 32
Japan and Korea _____ 33
Indonesia and the Philippines _____ 34
Kampuchea (Cambodia), Laos, Vietnam,
  Thailand and Malaysia _____ 35
India, Pakistan, Bangladesh, Burma
  and Sri Lanka _____ 36
Central India and Nepal _____ 37
Middle East _____ 38
Iran and Afghanistan _____ 39
Turkey, Cyprus, Syria, Jordan,
  Israel and Lebanon _____ 40
Israel and Northern Egypt _____ 41

Africa _____ 42-49
Africa _____ 42
Northeast Africa _____ 43
Northwest Africa _____ 44
West Africa _____ 45
Equatorial Africa _____ 46
East Africa _____ 47
Central Africa _____ 48
Southern Africa _____ 49

Australia and Oceania _____ 50-52
Australia _____ 50
Southeastern Australia
  and New Zealand _____ 51
Pacific Islands _____ 52

South America _____ 53-60
South America _____ 53
Central and Southern Argentina
  and Chile _____ 54
Bolivia, Paraguay, Northern Argentina
  and Chile _____ 55
Uruguay and Southern Brazil _____ 56
Eastern Brazil _____ 57
Peru and Ecuador _____ 58
Guyana, Suriname, French Guiana
  and Northern Brazil _____ 59
Colombia and Venezuela _____ 60

North America _____ 61-127
North America _____ 61
Central America _____ 62
Mexico _____ 63
West Indies _____ 64
Caribbean Islands _____ 65
Canada _____ 66
Alberta _____ 68
British
  Columbia _____ 69
Manitoba _____ 70
Maritime
  Provinces _____ 71
Newfoundland _____ 72
Ontario _____ 73
Quebec _____ 74
Saskatchewan _____ 75

United States of America _____ 76
Alabama _____ 78
Alaska _____ 79
Arizona _____ 80
Arkansas _____ 81
California _____ 82
Colorado _____ 83
Connecticut _____ 84
Delaware _____ 85
Florida _____ 86
Georgia _____ 87
Hawaii _____ 88
Idaho _____ 89
Illinois _____ 90
Indiana _____ 91
Iowa _____ 92
Kansas _____ 93
Kentucky _____ 94
Louisiana _____ 95
Maine _____ 96
Maryland _____ 97
Massachusetts _____ 98
Michigan _____ 99
Minnesota _____ 100
Mississippi _____ 101
Missouri _____ 102
Montana _____ 103
Nebraska _____ 104
Nevada _____ 105
New Hampshire _____ 106
New Jersey _____ 107
New Mexico _____ 108
New York _____ 109
North Carolina _____ 110
North Dakota _____ 111
Ohio _____ 112
Oklahoma _____ 113
Oregon _____ 114
Pennsylvania _____ 115
Rhode Island _____ 116
South Carolina _____ 117
South Dakota _____ 118
Tennessee _____ 119
Texas _____ 120
Utah _____ 121
Vermont _____ 122
Virginia _____ 123
Washington _____ 124
West Virginia _____ 125
Wisconsin _____ 126
Wyoming _____ 127

North Polar Regions _____ 128

Index to World
  Reference Maps _____ 129-224
Introduction to the Index
  and List of Abbreviations _____ 129
Index to World Reference Maps _____ 130

The Comprehensive World Atlas

Copyright © 1991 by Rand McNally & Company

Pages iii, iv, xvi, and 1 to 224 from Cosmopolitan World Atlas,
Copyright © 1991 by Rand McNally & Company.
Pages v to xv from Illustrated Atlas of the World,
Copyright © 1985 by Rand McNally & Company.

Published by Longmeadow Press
  201 High Ridge Road
  Stamford, CT 06304

Printed in the United States of America
ISBN 0-681-41176-7

0 9 8 7 6 5 4 3 2 1

Using the Atlas

Sequence of the Maps

The world is made up of seven major land-masses: the continents of Europe, Asia, Africa, Australia, South America, North America, and Antarctica (figure 5). To allow for the inclusion of detail, each continent is broken down into a series of maps, and this grouping is arranged so that as consecutive pages are turned, a continuous and successive part of the continent is shown. Larger-scale maps are used for regions of greater detail (having many cities, for example) or for areas of global significance.

The continental sequence of the maps is as follows: Europe (traditionally first in atlases), Asia (connected to Europe and forming the Eurasian landmass), Africa, Australia and Oceania, South America, and North America.

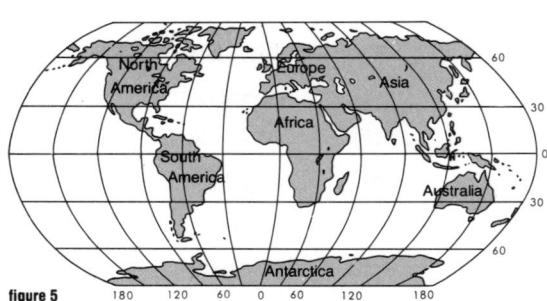

figure 5

Getting the Information

An atlas can be used for many purposes, from planning a trip to finding hot spots in the news and supplementing world knowledge. But to realize the full potential of an atlas, the user must be able to:

1. Find places on the maps
2. Measure distances
3. Determine directions
4. Understand map symbols

Finding Places

One of the most common and important tasks facilitated by an atlas is finding the *location* of a place in the world. A river's name in a book, a city mentioned in the news, or a vacation spot may prompt your need to know where the place is located. The illustrations and text below explain how to find Benguela, Angola.

1. Look up the place-name in the index at the back of the atlas. Benguela, Angola, can be found on the map on page 48, and it can be located on the map by the letter-number key *D1* (figure 6).

Benevento, Italy	D5	23
Benevolence, Ga., U.S.	E2	87
Benewah, co., Id., U.S.	B2	89
Benezett, Pa., U.S.	D5	115
Benfeld, Fr.	A3	20
Bengal, Ok., U.S.	C6	113
Bengal, hist reg., Asia	D8	36
Bengal, Bay of, b., Asia	F8	36
Ben Gardane, Tun.	C7	44
Bengbu, China	E8	31
Benghazi (Banghāzī), Libya	C4	43
Bengkalis, Indon.	E2	34
Bengkalis, i., Indon.	L5	35
Bengkulu, Indon.	F2	34
Bengo, dept., Ang.	C1	48
Bengough, Sk., Can.	H3	75
Benguela, Ang.	D1	48
Benguela, dept., Ang.	D1	48
Benham, Ky., U.S.	D7	94
Ben Hill, co., Ga., U.S.	E3	87
Beni, Nig.	D7	45
Beni, Zaire	A4	48
Beni, dept., Bol.	B2	55
Beni, stm., Bol.	B2	55
Béni Abbas, Alg.	C4	44

Benzonia, MI., U.S.		
Beo, Indon.		
Béoumi, I.C.		
Beowawe, Nv., U.S.		
Beppu, Japan		
Beqa, i., Fiji		
Beqa Passage, strt., Fiji		
Bequia, i., St. Vin.		
Berach, stm., India		
Berati, Alb.		
Berau, F.R.Ger.		
Berau Bay, b., Indon.		
Berbera, Som.		
Berbérati, Cen. Afr. Rep.		
Berbice, stm., Guy.		
Berceto, Italy		
Bercher, Switz.		
Berchogur, Sov. Un.		
Berchtesgaden, F.R.Ger.		
Berck, Fr.		
Berclair, Tx., U.S.		
Berdichev, Sov. Un.		
Berdsk, Sov. Un.		
Berdyansk, Sov. Un.		
Berea, Ky., U.S.		

figure 6

2. Turn to the map of Central Africa on page 48. Note that the letters A through E and the numbers 1 through 7 appear in the margins of the maps.
3. To find Benguela on the map, place your left index finger on D and your right index finger on 1. Move your left finger across the map and your right finger into the map. Your fingers will meet in the area in which Benguela is located (figure 7).

figure 7

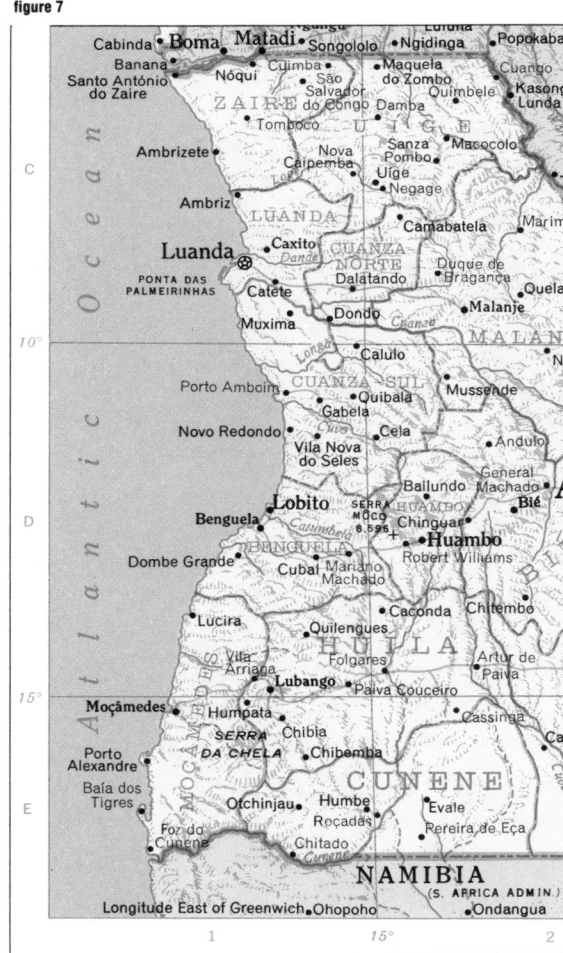

Measuring Distances

In planning trips, determining the distance between two places is essential, and an atlas can help in travel preparation. For instance, to determine the approximate distance between Paris and Rouen, France, follow these three steps:

1. Lay a slip of paper on the map on page 16 so that its edge touches the two cities. Adjust the paper so one corner touches Rouen. Mark the paper directly at the spot where Paris is located (figure 8).

figure 8

2. Place the paper along the scale of statute miles beneath the map. Position the corner at 0 and line up the edge of the paper along the scale. The pencil mark on the paper indicates Rouen is between 50 and 75 miles from Paris (figure 9).
3. To find the exact distance, move the paper to the left so that the pencil mark is at 50 on the scale. The corner of the paper stands in the fourth 5-mile unit on the scale. This means that the two towns are 50 miles plus 15 miles plus 2 miles, or 67 miles, apart (figure 10).

figure 9

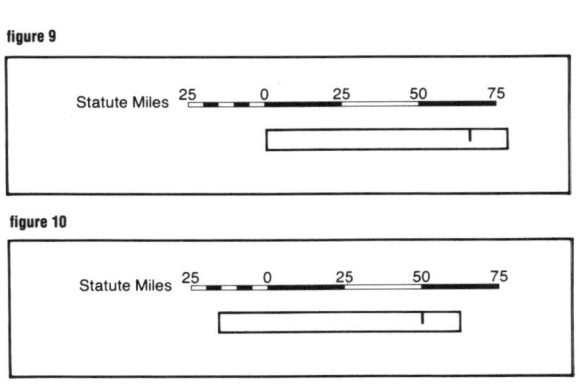

figure 10

The scale relationship of the map to the earth may also be expressed as a ratio, for example, 1:1,000,000 (one to one million). The map unit in the ratio is always given as one, and the number of similar units the map unit represents on the earth's surface is written after the colon. Thus for a 1:1,000,000 map, 1 inch on the map represents 1,000,000 inches on the earth's surface. In order to determine how many miles on the earth 1 inch on the map represents, divide 63,360 (the number of inches in one mile) into 1,000,000. This results in the written scale for a 1:1,000,000 map being stated as, 1 inch (on the map) = 16 miles (on the earth).

Determining Directions

Most of the maps in the atlas are drawn so that when oriented for normal reading north is at the top of the map, south is at the bottom, west is at the left, and east is at the right. Most maps have a series of lines drawn across them — the lines of latitude and longitude. Lines of latitude, or parallels of latitude, are drawn east and west. Lines of longitude, or meridians of longitude, are drawn north and south (figure 11).

Parallels and meridians appear as either curved or straight lines. For example, in the section of the map of Europe in figure 12, the parallels of latitude appear as curved lines. The meridians of longitude are straight lines that come together toward the top of the map.

Latitude and longitude lines help locate places on maps. Parallels of latitude are numbered in degrees north and south of the *Equator*. Meridians of longitude are numbered in degrees east and west of a line called the *Prime Meridian,* running through Greenwich, England, near London. Any place on earth can be located by the latitude and longitude lines running through it.

To determine directions or locations on maps, you must use the parallels and meridians. For example, suppose you want to know which city is farther north, Bergen, Norway, or Stockholm, Sweden. The map in figure 12 shows that Stockholm is south of the 60° parallel of latitude and Bergen is north of it. This means that Bergen is farther north than Stockholm. By looking at the meridians of longitude, you can determine which city is farther east. Bergen is approximately 5° east of the 0° meridian (Prime Meridian), and Stockholm is almost 20° east of it. This means that Stockholm is farther east than Bergen.

Understanding Map Symbols

In a very real sense, the whole map is a symbol, representing the world or a part of it. It is a reduced representation of the earth; each of the world's features — cities, rivers, etc. — is represented on the map by a symbol. Map symbols may take the form of points, such as dots or stars (often used for cities, capital cities, or points of interest), or lines (roads, rivers, railroads). Symbols may also occupy an area, showing extent of coverage (states, forests, deserts). They seldom look like the feature they represent and therefore must be identified and interpreted. For instance, the maps in this atlas show and differentiate political units (countries, states) with color. The political units are further defined by a heavy line depicting their boundaries. Neither the colors nor the boundary lines are actually found on the surface of the earth, but because countries and states are such important political components of the world, strong symbols are used to represent them.

The legend on page 1 identifies the symbols used in this atlas.

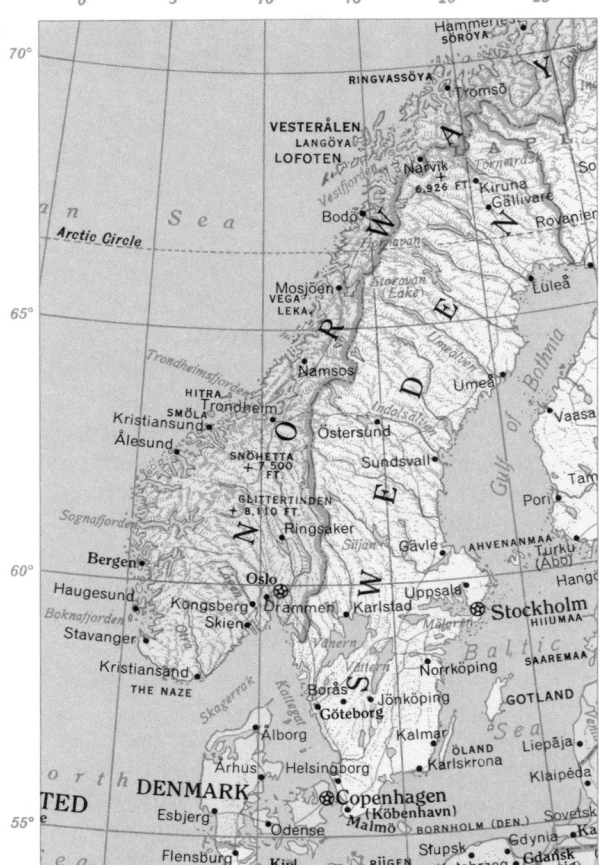

figure 12

figure 11

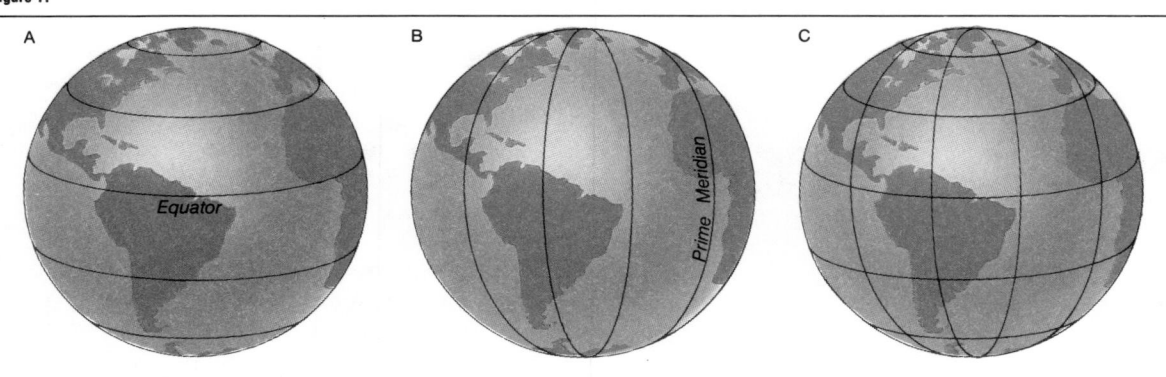

The Earth and The Universe

Most astronomers believe that the universe began in a great explosion of matter and energy about 15,000 million years ago – the "Big Bang". This event was implied by Einstein's theory of general relativity, as well as by more recent astronomical observations and calculations. But the clinching evidence came in 1965, when two American radio astronomers discovered a faint, uniform, background radiation which permeated all space. This they identified as the remnants of the Big Bang.

The generally accepted explanation for the so-called "cosmic microwave" background, detected by American astronomers Arno Penzias and Robert Wilson, is indeed that it is the echo of the Big Bang itself, the radio noise left over from the fireball of creation. In recognition of their discovery, Penzias and Wilson shared a Nobel Prize in 1978.

The Big Bang has also been identified by astronomers in other ways. All the evidence shows that the universe is expanding, and its constituent parts — clusters of galaxies, each containing thousands of millions of stars like our Sun — are moving away from each other at great speeds. From this and other evidence scientists deduce that long ago the galaxies must have been closer together, in a superdense phase, and that at some time in the remote past all the material in the universe must have started spreading out from a single point. But this "single point" includes not only all three-dimensional matter and space but also the dimension of time, as envisioned in Einstein's revolutionary concept of space-time. Einstein's theory of relativity describes the phenomenon, not in terms of galaxies moving through space in the expansion, but as being carried apart by the expansion of space-time itself. Space-time may be imagined as a rubber sheet speckled with paint blobs (galaxies), which move apart as the rubber sheet expands.

Galaxies consist of star systems, dust clouds and gases formed from the hot material exploding outward from the original cosmic fireball. Our own Milky Way system, the band of light that stretches across the night sky, is typical of many galaxies, containing millions of stars slowly rotating around a central nucleus.

The evidence of just why these huge explosions occur is often hard to obtain, because the exploding galaxies may be so far away that light from them takes millions of years to reach telescopes on Earth. But it is becoming increasingly accepted by astronomers that such violent events may be associated with the presence of black holes at the centers of some galaxies.

These black holes are regions in which matter has become so concentrated that the force of gravity makes it impossible for anything — even light itself — to escape. As stars are pulled into super-massive black holes they are torn apart by gravitational forces, and their material forms into a swirling maelstrom from which huge explosions can occur. Collapse into black holes, accompanied by violent outbursts from the maelstrom, may be the ultimate fate of all matter in the universe. For our own Solar System, however, such a fate is far in the future: the Sun in its present form is believed to have enough "fuel" to keep it going for at least another 5,000 million years.

Stars vary enormously in size, temperature and luminosity. The largest, so-called red giants like Antares (1)—the biggest yet known—or Aldebaran (2), are nearing the end of their lives: diminishing nuclear "fuel" causes their thinning envelopes to expand. Rigel (3) is many times brighter than our Sun (4)—a middle-aged star—but both are so-called main-sequence stars. Epsilon Eridani (5) is rather like the Sun. Wolf 359 (6) is a red dwarf.

The Big Bang theory above, of the origin of the universe envisages all matter originating from one point in time and space — a point of infinite density. In the intensely hot Big Bang all the material that goes to make up the planets, stars and galaxies that we see now began to expand outward in all directions. This expansion has been likened to someone blowing up a balloon on which spots have been painted. As the air fills and expands the balloon, the spots get farther away from each other. Likewise, clusters of galaxies that formed from the original superdense matter began, and continue, to move away from neighboring clusters.

The Earth in The Solar System

Nuclear reactions in the Sun's core maintain a temperature of some 15,000,000°C and this heat prevents the star from shrinking. The surface temperature is comparatively much lower —a mere 6,000°C. Thermonuclear energy-generating processes cause the Sun to "lose" mass from the center at the rate of four million tonnes of hydrogen every second. This mass is turned into energy (heat), and each gram of matter "burnt" produces the heat equivalent of 100 trillion electric fires. The Sun's total mass is so great, however, that it contains enough matter to continue radiating at its present rate for several thousand million years before it runs out of "fuel."

The Sun's retinue

The Solar System emerged from a collapsing gas cloud. In addition to the Sun there are at least nine planets, their satellites, thousands of minor planets (asteroids), comets and meteors. Most stars occur in pairs, triplets or in even more complicated systems, and the Sun is among a minority of stars in being alone except for its planetary companions. It does seem, however, that a single star with a planetary system offers the greatest potential for the development of life. When there are two or more stars in the same system, any planets are likely to have unstable orbits and to suffer from wide extremes of temperature.

The Solar System's structure is thought to be typical of a star that formed in isolation. As the hot young Sun threw material outward, inner planets (Mercury, Venus, Earth and Mars) were left as small rocky bodies, whereas outer planets (Jupiter, Saturn, Uranus and Neptune) kept their lighter gases and became huge "gas giants." Jupiter has two and a half times the mass of all the other planets put together. Pluto, a small object with a strange orbit, which sometimes carries it within the orbit of Neptune, is usually regarded as a ninth planet, but some astronomers consider it to be an escaped moon of Neptune or a large asteroid.

Planetary relations

Several planets are accompanied by smaller bodies called moons or satellites. Jupiter and Saturn have at least 17 and 22 respectively, whereas Earth has its solitary Moon. Sizes vary enormously, from Ganymede, one of Jupiter's large, so-called Galilean satellites, which has a diameter of 5,000 km (3,100 miles), to Mars' tiny Deimos, which is only 8 km (5 miles) across.

The Earth's Moon is at an average distance of 384,000 km (239,000 miles) and has a diameter of 3,476 km (2,160 miles). Its mass is $\frac{1}{81}$ of the Earth's. Although it is referred to as the Earth's satellite, the Moon is large for a secondary body. Some astronomers have suggested that the Earth/Moon system is a double planet. Certain theories of the origins of the Moon propose that it was formed from the solar nebula in the same way as the Earth was and very close to it. The Moon takes 27.3 days to orbit the Earth—exactly the same time that it takes to rotate once on its axis. As a result, it presents the same face to the Earth all the time.

Our planet's orbit around the Sun is not a perfect circle but an ellipse and so its distance from the Sun varies slightly. More importantly, the Earth is tilted, so that at different times of the year one pole or another "leans" toward the Sun. Without this tilt there would be no seasons. The angle of tilt is not constant: over tens of thousands of years the axis of the Earth "wobbles" like a slowly spinning top, so that the pattern of the seasons varies over the ages. These changes have been linked to recent ice ages, which seem to occur when the northern hemisphere has relatively cool summers.

Patterns of time

The Earth's movements on its axis and around the Sun give us our basic measurements of time—the day and the year—as well as setting the rhythm of the seasons and the ice ages. One rotation of the Earth on its axis—the time from one sunrise to the next—originally defined the day, and the time taken for one complete orbit around the Sun defined the year. Today, however, scientists define both the day and the year in terms of time units "counted" by precision instruments called atomic clocks.

A third basic rhythm is set not by the Sun but by the Moon, which runs through a cycle of phases $29\frac{1}{2}$ days long. This is the basis of the calendar month. But just as the modern calendar cannot cope with months $29\frac{1}{2}$ days long, so too it would have trouble with the precise year, which is, inconveniently, just less than $365\frac{1}{4}$ days long. This is the reason for leap years, by means of which an extra day is added to the month of February every fourth year.

Even this system does not keep the calendar exactly in step with the Sun. Accordingly, the leap year is left out in the years which complete centuries, such as 1900, but retained when they divide exactly by 400. The year 2000 will, therefore, be a leap year. With all these corrections, the average length of the calendar year is within 26 seconds of the year defined by the Earth's movements around the Sun. Thus the calendar will be one day out of step with the heavens in the year 4906.

Cosmic rubble

The other planets are too small and too far away to produce noticeable effects on the Earth, but the smallest members of the Sun's family, the asteroids, can affect us directly. Some of them have orbits that cross the orbit of the Earth around the Sun. From time to time they penetrate the Earth's atmosphere: small fragments burn up high in the atmosphere as meteors, whereas larger pieces may survive to strike the ground as meteorites. These in fact provide an echo of times gone by. All the planets, as the battered face of the Moon shows, suffered collisions from many smaller bodies in the course of their evolution from the collapsing pre-solar gas cloud.

Eclipses occur because the Moon, smaller than the Sun, is closer to Earth and looks just as big. This means that when all three are lined up the Moon can blot out the Sun, causing a solar eclipse. When the Earth passes through the main shadow cone, or umbra, the eclipse is total; in the area of partial shadow, or penumbra, a partial eclipse is seen. A similar effect is produced when Earth passes between the Moon and the Sun, causing a lunar eclipse. At most full moons, eclipses do not occur; the Moon passes either above or below the Earth's shadow, because the Moon's orbit is inclined at an angle of 5° to the orbit of the Earth.

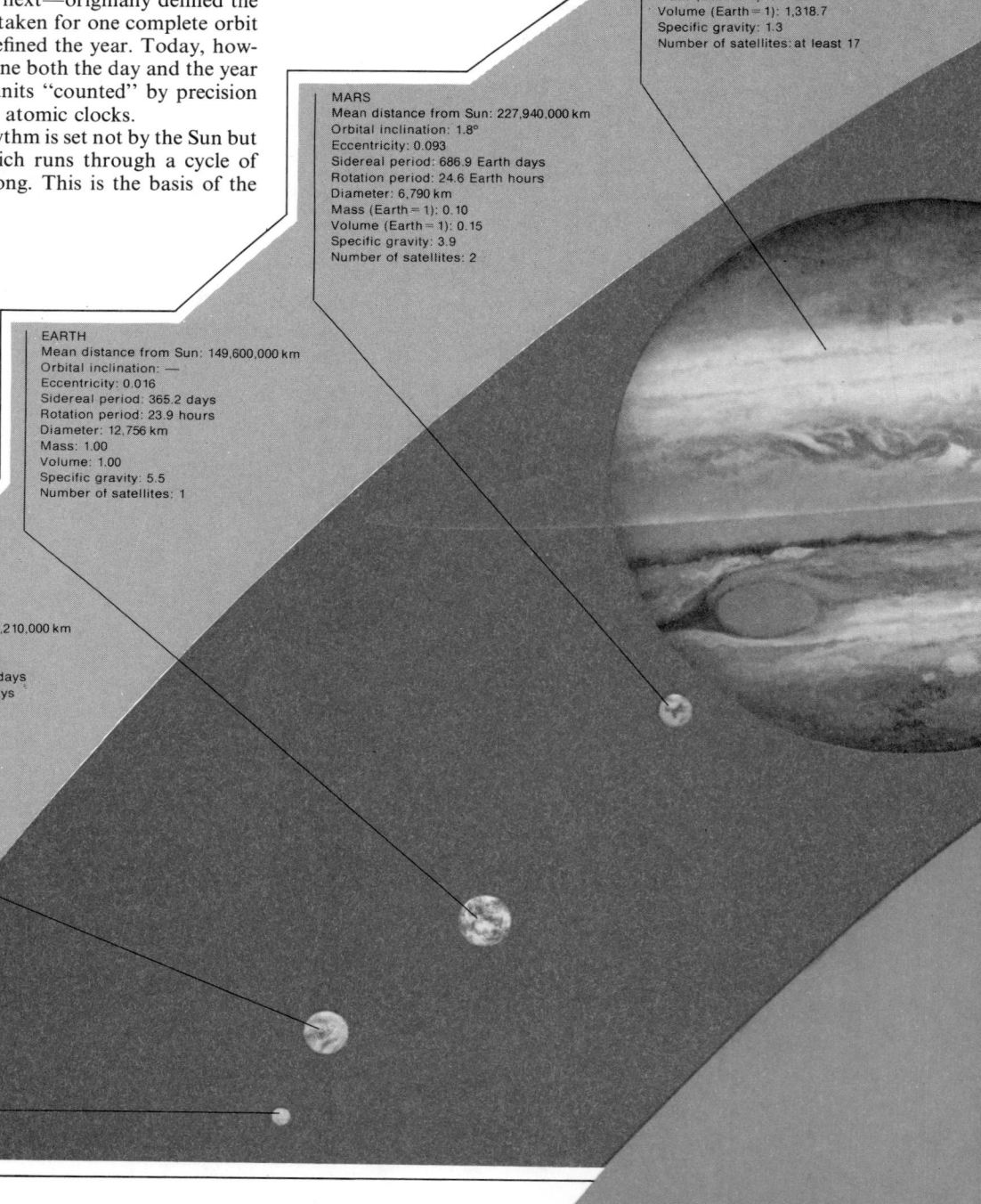

JUPITER
Mean distance from Sun: 778,340,000 km
Orbital inclination: 1.3°
Eccentricity: 0.048
Sidereal period: 11.8 Earth years
Rotation period: 9.8 Earth hours
Diameter: 142,800 km
Mass (Earth = 1): 317.89
Volume (Earth = 1): 1,318.7
Specific gravity: 1.3
Number of satellites: at least 17

MARS
Mean distance from Sun: 227,940,000 km
Orbital inclination: 1.8°
Eccentricity: 0.093
Sidereal period: 686.9 Earth days
Rotation period: 24.6 Earth hours
Diameter: 6,790 km
Mass (Earth = 1): 0.10
Volume (Earth = 1): 0.15
Specific gravity: 3.9
Number of satellites: 2

EARTH
Mean distance from Sun: 149,600,000 km
Orbital inclination: —
Eccentricity: 0.016
Sidereal period: 365.2 days
Rotation period: 23.9 hours
Diameter: 12,756 km
Mass: 1.00
Volume: 1.00
Specific gravity: 5.5
Number of satellites: 1

MEMBERS OF THE SOLAR SYSTEM

The Sun has nine planetary attendants. They are best compared in terms of orbital data (distance from the Sun, inclination of orbit to the Earth's orbit, and eccentricity, which means the departure of a planet's orbit from circularity); planetary periods (the time for a planet to go around the Sun—sidereal periods, and the time it takes for one axial revolution—the rotation period); and physical data (equatorial diameter, mass, volume and density or specific gravity—the weight of a substance compared with the weight of an equal volume of water).

VENUS
Mean distance from Sun: 108,210,000 km
Orbital inclination: 3.3°
Eccentricity: 0.006
Sidereal period: 224.7 Earth days
Rotation period: 243 Earth days
Diameter: 12,100 km
Mass (Earth = 1): 0.81
Volume (Earth = 1): 0.85
Specific gravity: 5.2
Number of satellites: 0

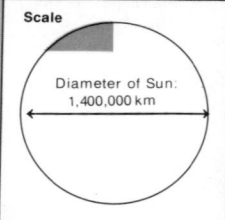

Scale

Diameter of Sun:
1,400,000 km

MERCURY
Mean distance from Sun: 57,910,000 km
Orbital inclination: 7°
Eccentricity: 0.205
Sidereal period: 87.9 Earth days
Rotation period: 58.7 Earth days
Diameter: 4,870 km
Mass (Earth = 1): 0.05
Volume (Earth = 1): 0.05
Specific gravity: 5.5
Number of satellites: 0

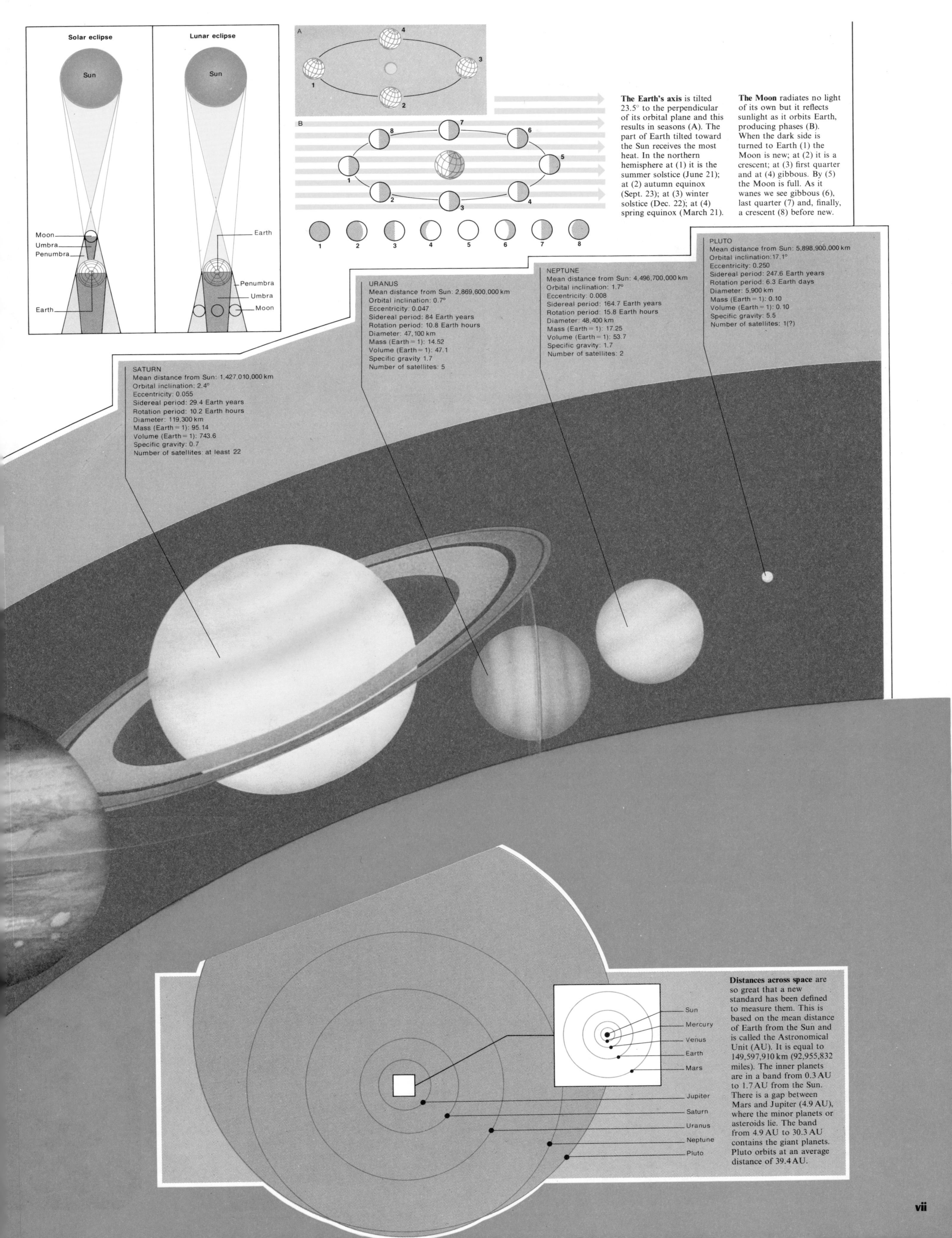

Solar eclipse

Lunar eclipse

Sun

Sun

Moon
Umbra
Penumbra

Earth

Earth

Penumbra
Umbra
Moon

A

B

The Earth's axis is tilted 23.5° to the perpendicular of its orbital plane and this results in seasons (A). The part of Earth tilted toward the Sun receives the most heat. In the northern hemisphere at (1) it is the summer solstice (June 21); at (2) autumn equinox (Sept. 23); at (3) winter solstice (Dec. 22); at (4) spring equinox (March 21).

The Moon radiates no light of its own but it reflects sunlight as it orbits Earth, producing phases (B). When the dark side is turned to Earth (1) the Moon is new; at (2) it is a crescent; at (3) first quarter and at (4) gibbous. By (5) the Moon is full. As it wanes we see gibbous (6), last quarter (7) and, finally, a crescent (8) before new.

PLUTO
Mean distance from Sun: 5,898,900,000 km
Orbital inclination:17.1°
Eccentricity: 0.250
Sidereal period: 247.6 Earth years
Rotation period: 6.3 Earth days
Diameter: 5,900 km
Mass (Earth = 1): 0.10
Volume (Earth = 1): 0.10
Specific gravity: 5.5
Number of satellites: 1(?)

NEPTUNE
Mean distance from Sun: 4,496,700,000 km
Orbital inclination: 1.7°
Eccentricity: 0.008
Sidereal period: 164.7 Earth years
Rotation period: 15.8 Earth hours
Diameter: 48,400 km
Mass (Earth = 1): 17.25
Volume (Earth = 1): 53.7
Specific gravity: 1.7
Number of satellites: 2

URANUS
Mean distance from Sun: 2,869,600,000 km
Orbital inclination: 0.7°
Eccentricity: 0.047
Sidereal period: 84 Earth years
Rotation period: 10.8 Earth hours
Diameter: 47,100 km
Mass (Earth = 1): 14.52
Volume (Earth = 1): 47.1
Specific gravity 1.7
Number of satellites: 5

SATURN
Mean distance from Sun: 1,427,010,000 km
Orbital inclination: 2.4°
Eccentricity: 0.055
Sidereal period: 29.4 Earth years
Rotation period: 10.2 Earth hours
Diameter: 119,300 km
Mass (Earth = 1): 95.14
Volume (Earth = 1): 743.6
Specific gravity: 0.7
Number of satellites: at least 22

Sun
Mercury
Venus
Earth
Mars
Jupiter
Saturn
Uranus
Neptune
Pluto

Distances across space are so great that a new standard has been defined to measure them. This is based on the mean distance of Earth from the Sun and is called the Astronomical Unit (AU). It is equal to 149,597,910 km (92,955,832 miles). The inner planets are in a band from 0.3 AU to 1.7 AU from the Sun. There is a gap between Mars and Jupiter (4.9 AU), where the minor planets or asteroids lie. The band from 4.9 AU to 30.3 AU contains the giant planets. Pluto orbits at an average distance of 39.4 AU.

Earth, Satellites and Mapping

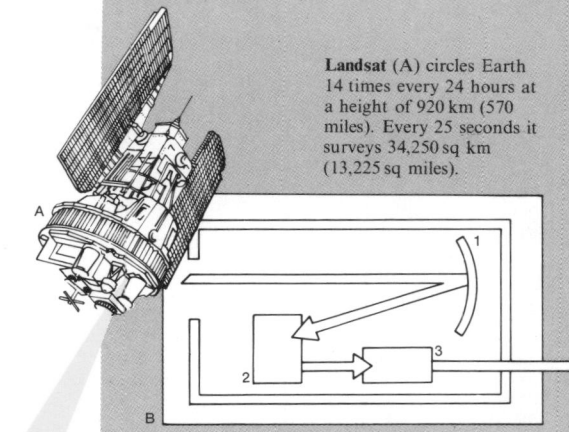

Landsat (A) circles Earth 14 times every 24 hours at a height of 920 km (570 miles). Every 25 seconds it surveys 34,250 sq km (13,225 sq miles).

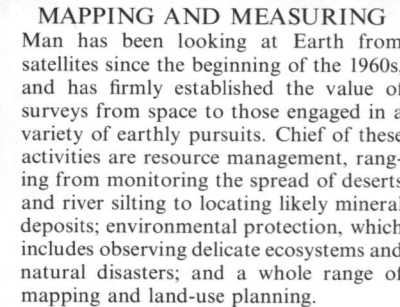

MAPPING AND MEASURING

Man has been looking at Earth from satellites since the beginning of the 1960s, and has firmly established the value of surveys from space to those engaged in a variety of earthly pursuits. Chief of these activities are resource management, ranging from monitoring the spread of deserts and river silting to locating likely mineral deposits; environmental protection, which includes observing delicate ecosystems and natural disasters; and a whole range of mapping and land-use planning.

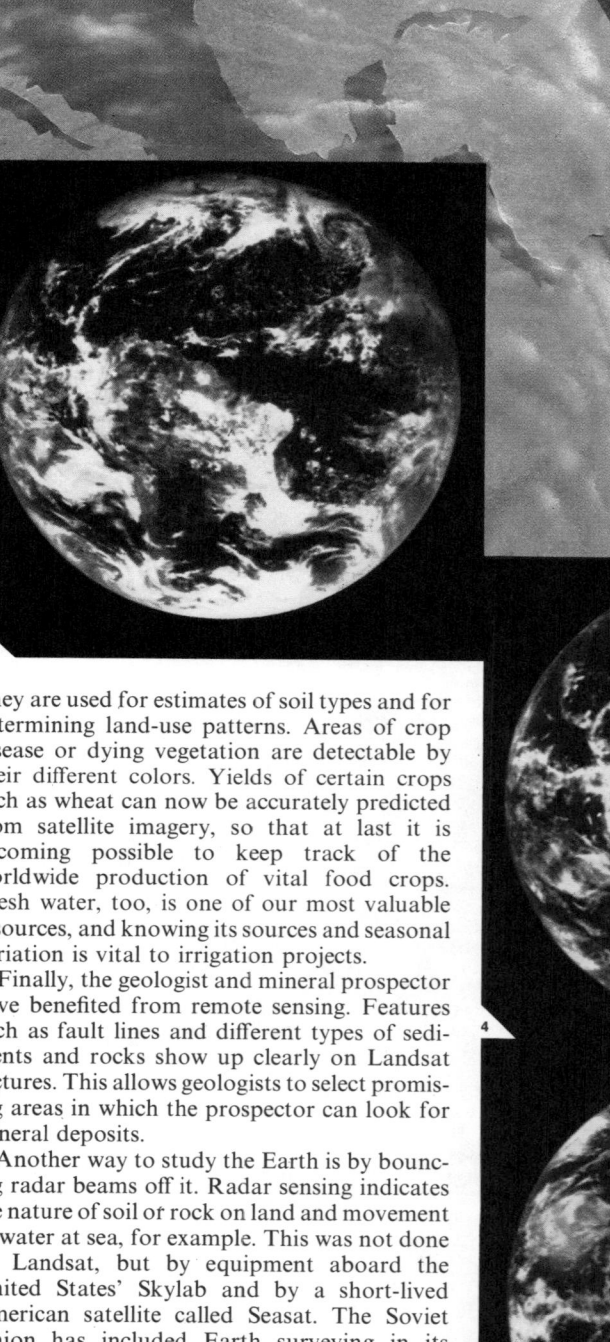

Satellites give us a greater overview of numerous aspects of life on Earth than any earthbound eye could see.

Of all the information gleaned from satellites, accurate weather forecasts are of particular social and economic value. The first weather satellite was Tiros 1 (Television and Infrared Observation Satellite), launched by the United States in 1960. By the time Tiros 10 ceased operations in 1967, the series had sent back more than half a million photographs, firmly establishing the value of satellite imagery.

Tiros was superseded by the ESSA (Environmental Science Services Administration) and the NOAA (National Oceanic and Atmospheric Administration) satellites. These orbited the Earth from pole to pole, and they covered the entire globe during the course of a day. Other weather satellites, such as the European Meteosat, are placed in geostationary orbit over the Equator, which means they stay in one place and continually monitor a single large region.

Watching the weather

In addition to photographing clouds, weather satellites monitor the extent of snow and ice cover, and they measure the temperature of the oceans and the composition of the atmosphere. Information about the overall heat balance of our planet gives clues to long-term climatic change, and includes the effects on climate of human activities such as the burning of fossil fuels and deforestation.

Infrared sensors allow pictures to be taken at night as well as during the day. The temperature of cloud tops, measured by infrared devices, is a guide to the height of the clouds. In a typical infrared image, high clouds appear white because they are the coldest, lower clouds and land areas appear gray, and oceans and lakes are black. Information on humidity in the atmosphere is provided by sensors tuned to wavelengths between 5.5 and 7 micrometers, at which water vapor strongly absorbs the radiation.

To "see" inside clouds, where infrared and visible light cannot penetrate, satellites use sensors tuned to short-wavelength radio waves (microwaves) around the 1.5 centimeter wavelength. These sensors can reveal whether or not clouds will give rise to heavy rainfall, snow or hail. Microwave sensors are also useful for locating ice floes in polar regions, making use of the different microwave reflections from land ice, sea ice and open water.

Satellites that send out such pictures are in relatively low orbits, at a height of about 1,000 km (620 miles), and they pass over each part of the Earth once every 12 hours. But to build up a global model of the Earth's weather and climate, meteorologists need continual information on wind speed and direction at various levels in the atmosphere, together with temperature and humidity profiles. This data is provided by geostationary satellites. Cloud photographs taken every half-hour give information on winds, and computers combine this with temperature and humidity soundings to give as complete a model as is possible of the Earth's atmosphere.

Increasing attention is also being paid to the Earth's surface, notably by means of a series of satellites called Landsat (originally ERTS or Earth Resource Technology Satellites), the first of which was launched by the United States in 1972. The third and current Landsat is in a similar pole-to-pole orbit as the weather satellites, but its cameras are more powerful and they make more detailed surveys of the Earth. Landsat rephotographs each part of the Earth's surface every 18 days.

How to map resources

The satellite has two sensor systems: a television camera, which takes pictures of the Earth using visible light; and a device called a multispectral scanner, which scans the Earth at several distinct wavelengths, including visible light and infrared. Data from the various channels of the multispectral scanner can be combined to produce so-called false-color images, in which each wavelength band is assigned a color (not necessarily its real one) to emphasize features of interest.

An important use of Landsat photographs is for making maps, particularly of large countries with remote areas that have never been adequately surveyed from the ground. Several countries, including Brazil, Canada and China, have set up ground stations to receive Landsat data directly. Features previously unknown or incorrectly mapped, including rivers, lakes and glaciers, show up readily on Landsat images. Urban mapping and hence planning are aided by satellite pictures that can distinguish areas of industry, housing and open parkland.

Landsat photographs have also proved invaluable for agricultural land-use planning. They are used for estimates of soil types and for determining land-use patterns. Areas of crop disease or dying vegetation are detectable by their different colors. Yields of certain crops such as wheat can now be accurately predicted from satellite imagery, so that at last it is becoming possible to keep track of the worldwide production of vital food crops. Fresh water, too, is one of our most valuable resources, and knowing its sources and seasonal variation is vital to irrigation projects.

Finally, the geologist and mineral prospector have benefited from remote sensing. Features such as fault lines and different types of sediments and rocks show up clearly on Landsat pictures. This allows geologists to select promising areas in which the prospector can look for mineral deposits.

Another way to study the Earth is by bouncing radar beams off it. Radar sensing indicates the nature of soil or rock on land and movement of water at sea, for example. This was not done by Landsat, but by equipment aboard the United States' Skylab and by a short-lived American satellite called Seasat. The Soviet Union has included Earth surveying in its Salyut program, and resource mapping is also a feature of the spacelab aboard the American space shuttle. All these activities help man to manage the limited resources on our planet and to preserve the environment.

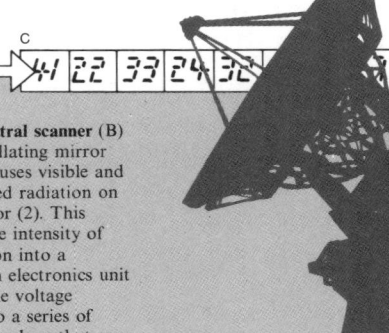
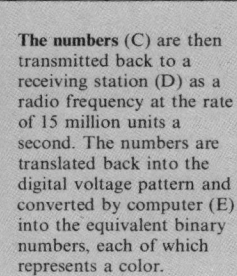

A multispectral scanner (B) has an oscillating mirror (1) that focuses visible and near infrared radiation on to a detector (2). This converts the intensity of the radiation into a voltage. An electronics unit (3) turns the voltage pattern into a series of digitized numbers that can be fed into a computer.

The numbers (C) are then transmitted back to a receiving station (D) as a radio frequency at the rate of 15 million units a second. The numbers are translated back into the digital voltage pattern and converted by computer (E) into the equivalent binary numbers, each of which represents a color.

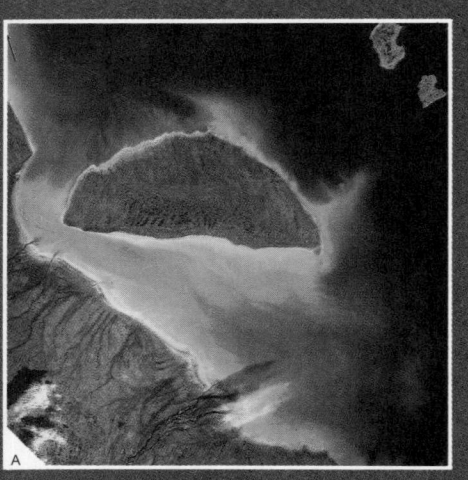
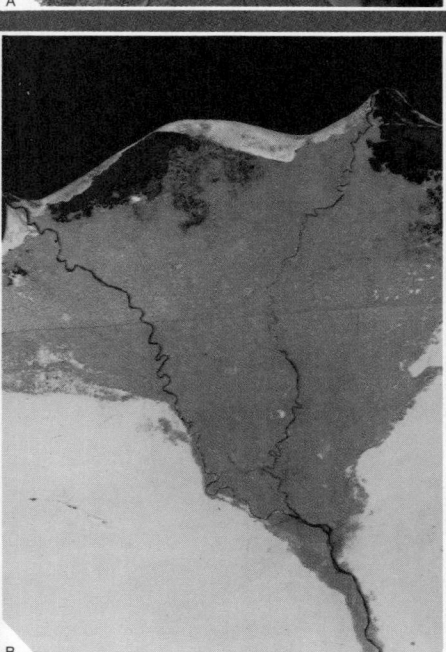

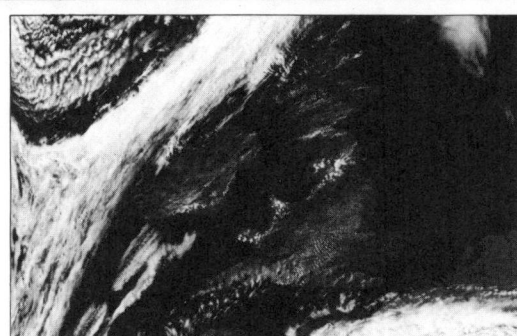
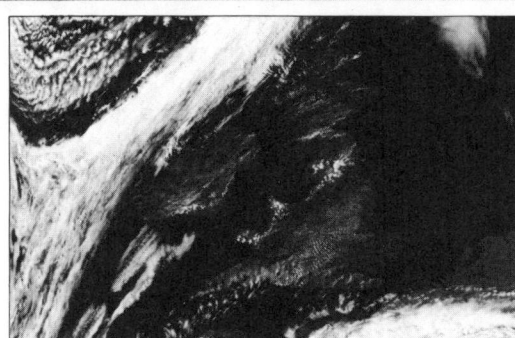

A Landsat image is made up of very many points, each of which is obtained by means of the procedure described above. Each number in the image (F) represents the radiation from a small area of land, or pixel, 0.44 hectares (1.1 acres) in size. A computer then translates the numbers into different colors, or different shades of one color, which are projected on to a TV screen (G) and the image is seen for the first time. Finally, photographs of this false-color image are produced (H). This picture, showing a forest fire in the Upper Peninsula, Michigan, is of use to those engaged in forest management. Other satellite data of use in forestry include types of trees, patterns of growth and the spread of disease.

Observation of waterways and coastal areas (above) shows pollution and deposition of sediments. This is of importance to the fishing industry. Fish congregate in areas where upwelling brings nutrients to the surface, for example. The large yellow-orange halo around Akimiski Island in James Bay (A)— a southern extension of Hudson Bay in Canada— is fine sediment resulting from wave action on a silty shore. Seeing the sediment in this way helps to determine current patterns in the Bay. In a predominantly desert area, the Nile delta (B) stands out dramatically. The red is an intensively cultivated area: cotton is the main crop. The larger irrigation canals can be seen on the photograph. Thermal imagery, or heat capacity mapping, is used to identify rocks, to study the effects of urban "heat islands," to estimate soil moisture and snow melt,

and to map shallow ground water. In this photograph of the northeast coast of North America (C) purple represents the coldest temperatures—in Lakes Erie and Ontario. The coldest parts of the Atlantic Ocean are deep blue, whereas warmer waters near the coast are light blue. Green is the warmer land, but also the Gulf Stream in the lower right part of the image. Brown, yellow and orange represent successively warmer land surface areas. Red is hot regions around cities and coal-mining regions found in eastern Pennsylvania (to the upper left of center in the picture); and, finally, gray and white are the very hottest areas—the urban heat islands of Baltimore, Philadelphia and New York City. Black areas in the upper left are cold clouds. The temperature range of the image is about 30°C (55°F).

Weather satellite imagery can save lives and property by giving advance warning of bad weather conditions, as well as providing day-to-day forecasts. This Tiros image (left) shows a cold

front moving west of Ireland with low-level wave clouds over southern and central England. There are low-pressure systems over northern France and to the northwest of Ireland.

The Earth seen from space shows phases just like the Moon, Mercury and Venus do to us. These dramatic photographs were taken from a satellite moving at

35,885 km (22,300 miles) above South America at 7.30 am (1), 10.30 am (2), noon (3), 3.30 pm (4) and at 10.30 pm (5), and clearly show the Earth in phase.

LANDSAT AND THE FARMER

| sown | grows | dormant | grows | ripe | harvest |

| Sep | Oct | Nov | Dec | Jan | Feb | Mar | Apr | May | Jun | Jul | Aug |

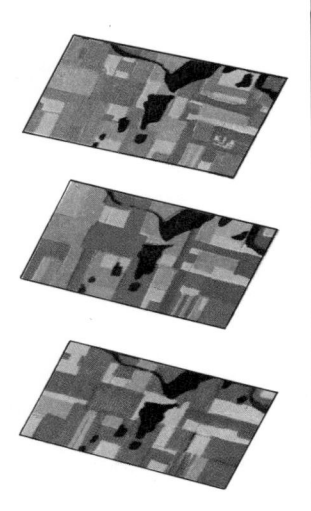

Agriculturists benefit from "multitemporal analysis" by satellites (left). This is the comparison of data from the same field recorded on two or more dates. It is also able to differentiate crops, which may have an identical appearance, or signature, on one day, but on another occasion exhibit different rates of growth. The pattern of growth is different for small grains than most other crops. A "biowindow" is the period of time in which vegetation is observed. These three biowindows (right) show the emergence and ripening (light blue to red to dark blue) of wheat in May, July and August.

The Earth's Land

THE DYNAMIC EARTH
As early as the 17th century, the English philosopher Francis Bacon noted that the coasts on either side of the Atlantic were similar and could be fitted together like pieces of a jigsaw puzzle. Three hundred years later Alfred Wegener proposed the theory of continental drift, but no one would believe the Earth's rigid crust could move. Today, geological evidence has provided the basis for the theory of plate tectonics, which demonstrates that the Earth's crust is slowly but continually moving.

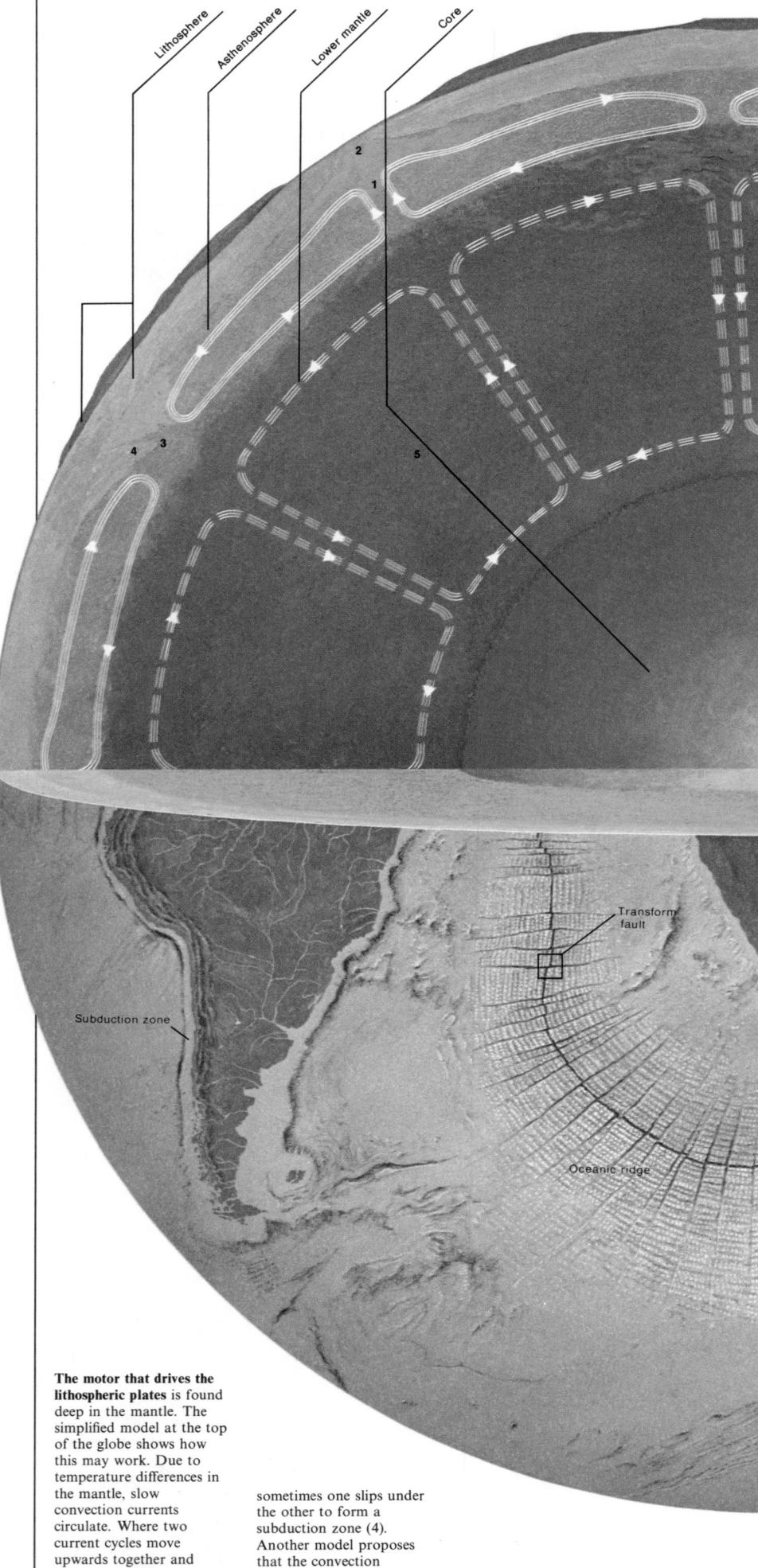

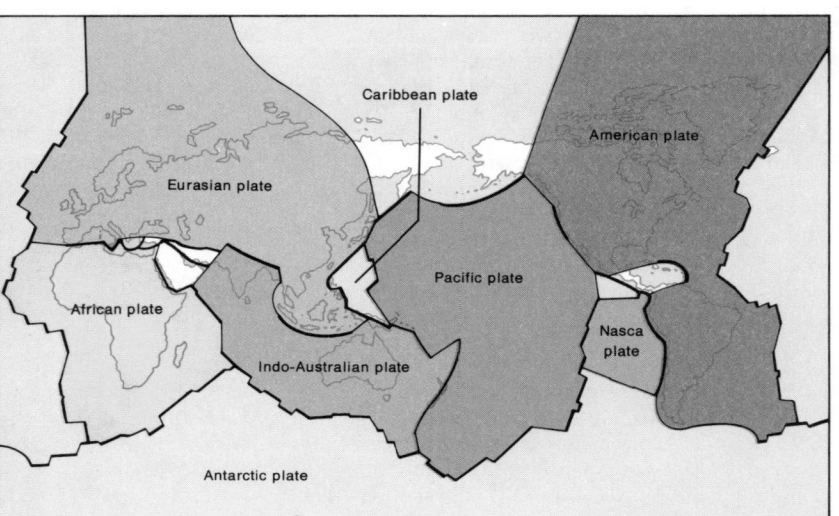

Earth's lithosphere—the rocky shell, or crust—is made up of six major plates and several smaller platelets, each separated from each other by ridges, subduction zones or transcurrent faults. The plates grow bigger by accretion along the mid-ocean ridges, are destroyed at subduction zones beneath the trenches, and slide beside each other along the transcurrent faults. The African and Antarctic plates have no trenches along their borders to destroy any of their crust, so they are growing bigger. This growth is compensated by the subduction zone that is developing to the north of the Tonga Islands and subduction zones in the Pacific. Conversely, the Pacific and Indo-Australian plates are shrinking. Along the plate boundaries magma wells up from the mantle to form volcanoes. Here, too, are the origins of earthquakes as the plates collide or slide slowly past each other.

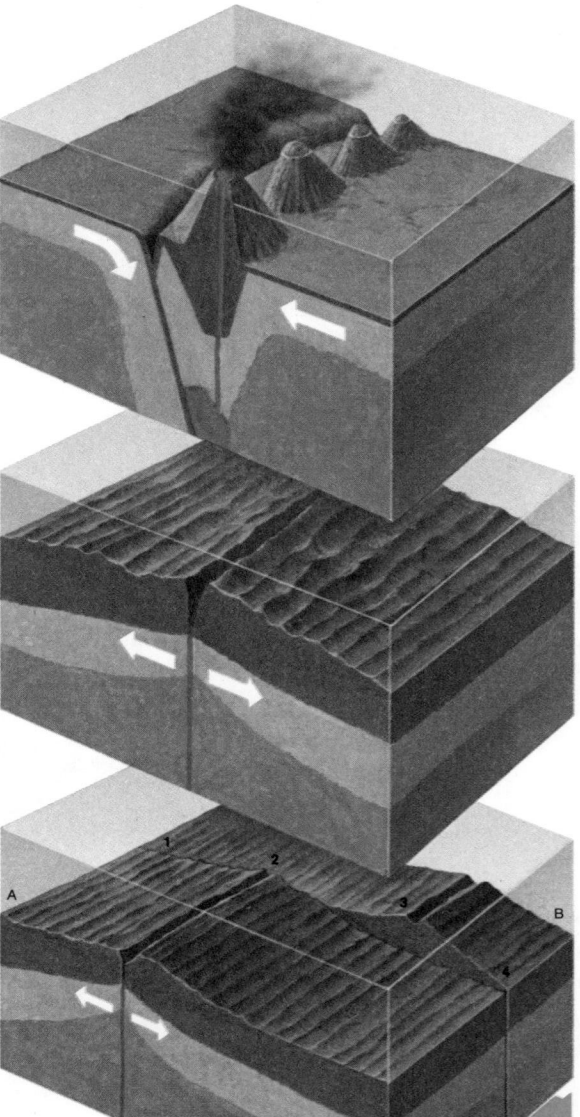

Subduction zones are the sites of destruction of the ocean crust. As one plate passes beneath another down into the mantle, the ocean floor is pulled downward and a deep ocean trench is formed. The movement taking place along the length of the subduction zone causes earthquakes, while melting of the rock at depth produces magma that rises to create the volcanoes that form island arcs.

An oceanic ridge is formed when two plates move away from each other. As they move, molten magma from the mantle forces its way to the surface. This magma cools and is in turn injected with new magma. Thus the oceanic ridge is gradually forming the newest part of Earth's crust.

Transform, or transcurrent, faults are found where two plates slide past each other. They may, for example, link two parts of a ridge (A, B). A study of the magnetic properties of the seabed may suggest a motion shown by the white arrows, but the true movements of the plates are shown by the red arrows. The transform fault is active only between points (2) and (3). Between points (1) and (2) and between (3) and (4) the scar of the fault is healed and the line of the fault is no longer a plate boundary.

The motor that drives the lithospheric plates is found deep in the mantle. The simplified model at the top of the globe shows how this may work. Due to temperature differences in the mantle, slow convection currents circulate. Where two current cycles move upwards together and separate (1), the plates bulge and move apart along mid-ocean ridges (2). Where there is a downward moving current (3), the plates move together and sometimes one slips under the other to form a subduction zone (4). Another model proposes that the convection currents are found deep in the mantle (5). Only time and more research, however, will reveal the true mechanism of plate movement.

The early evidence for continental drift was gathered by Alfred Wegener, a German meteorologist. He noticed that the coastlines on each side of the Atlantic Ocean could be made to fit together, and that much of the geological history of the flanking continents—shown by fossils, structures and past climates—also seemed to match. Wegener compared the two sides of the Atlantic with a sheet of torn newspaper and reasoned that if not just one line of print but 10 lines match then there is a good case for arguing that the two sides were once joined. Yet for 50 years continental drift was generally considered to be a fanciful dream.

Seafloor spreading
In the 1950s the first geological surveys of the oceans began, and a 60,000 km (37,200 mile) long chain of mountains was discovered running down the center of the Atlantic Ocean, all round the Antarctic, up to the Indian Ocean, into the Red Sea and up the Eastern Pacific Ocean into Alaska. Along the axis of this mid-ocean ridge system there was often a narrow, deep rift valley. In places this ridge was offset along sharp fractures in the ocean floor.

The breakthrough in developing the global plate tectonic theory came with the first large-scale survey of the ocean floor. Magnetometers, which were developed during World War II for tracking submarines, showed the ocean floor to be magnetically striped. The ocean floor reveals magnetic characteristics because the ocean crust basalts are full of tiny crystals of the magnetic mineral magnetite. As the basalt cooled, the magnetic field of these crystals aligned itself with the Earth's magnetic field. This would be insignificant if it were not for the fact that the magnetic pole of the Earth has switched from north to south at different times in the past. Half the magnetite compasses of the ocean floor point south rather than north.

In the middle 1960s, two Cambridge geophysicists, Drummond Matthews and Fred Vine, noticed that the pattern of stripes was symmetrical around the mid-ocean ridge. Such an extraordinary and unlikely symmetry could mean only one thing—any two matching stripes must have originally been formed together at the mid-ocean ridge and then moved away from each other as newer crust formed between them to create new stripes. It was soon calculated that the North Atlantic Ocean was growing wider by about 2 cm (¾ in) a year. At last, drifting continents was accepted.

Consumption of the seafloor
Seafloor spreading soon became included in an even more sensational model—plate tectonics. If the oceans are growing wider, then either the whole planet is expanding or the spreading ocean floor is consumed elsewhere. In the late 1950s a global network of seismic stations had been set up to monitor nuclear explosions and earthquakes. For the first time the positions of all earthquakes could be accurately defined.

It was found that the zones of earthquake activity were predominantly narrow, following the mid-ocean ridges and extending along the rim of the Pacific, beneath the island arcs of the

West Pacific and beneath the continental margins in the East Pacific as well as underlying the Alpine-Himalayan Mountain Belt. The seismic zones around the Pacific dipped away from the ocean and continued to depths as great as 700 km (430 miles). They intercepted the surface at the curious arc-shaped deep-ocean trenches. It had been known for 20 years that the pull of gravity over these trenches is strangely reduced, so to survive they must continually be dragged downwards. Here was the site of ocean-floor consumption—now known as a subduction zone. Subduction zones must be efficient at consuming ocean crust because no known ocean crust is older than 200 million years—less than five percent of Earth's lifetime.

The oceanic lithosphere (the Earth's rocky crust) is extraordinarily rigid. Even where the oceanic lithosphere becomes consumed within subduction zones it still maintains its rigidity. As it bends down into the Earth it tends to corrugate, forming very long folds. These corrugations give rise to the pattern of chains of deep-ocean trenches and chains of volcanic islands formed above the subduction zone.

As oceanic lithosphere grows older it cools, contracts and sinks. From the depth of the ocean floor it is possible to make an accurate estimate of the age of the crust beneath. Even the steepness of the subduction zone is a function of the age, and therefore the density, of the lithosphere. The oldest crust provides the strongest downward pull and hence the steepest angle of dip of the subduction zone.

As well as the spreading ridges (constructive margins) and the subduction zones (destructive margins) there is another kind of plate boundary (conservative margins), where the plates slip past one another along a major fault such as the San Andreas Fault of California.

The past positions of the continents
Continental drift is thus the result of the creation and destruction of oceanic lithosphere, but only the continents can record the oceanic plate motions taking place more than 200 million years ago. The discovery of ancient lines of subduction zone volcanoes can testify to the destruction of long-gone oceans. One particularly important technique for finding the positions of the continents is to study the magnetism of certain rocks, particularly lavas, that record the position of the north–south magnetic poles at the time when the rock cooled. If the rock "compass" points, for example, west, then the continent must have rotated by 90°. The vertical dip of the rock compass can reveal the approximate latitude of the rock at its formation (the dip increases from horizontal at the Equator to vertical at the magnetic poles).

As longitude is entirely arbitrary (defined on the position of Greenwich) one can only hope to gain the relative positions of the continents with regard to one another. The best additional information is provided by studies of fossils—if the remains of shallow-water marine organisms are very different they must have been separated by an ocean. The full impact of continental drift on the development of land animals and plants is only beginning to be realized.

THE DRIFTING CONTINENTS
It is now accepted that the continents have changed their positions during the past millions of years, and by studying the magnetism preserved in the rocks the configuration of the continents has been plotted for various geological times. The sequence of continental drifting, illustrated below, begins with one single landmass—the so-called supercontinent Pangaea—and the ancestral Pacific Ocean, called the Panthalassa Ocean. Pangaea first split into a northern landmass called Laurasia and a southern block called Gondwanaland, and subsequently into the continents we see today. The maps illustrate the positions of the continents in the past, where they are now and their predicted positions in 50 million years' time.

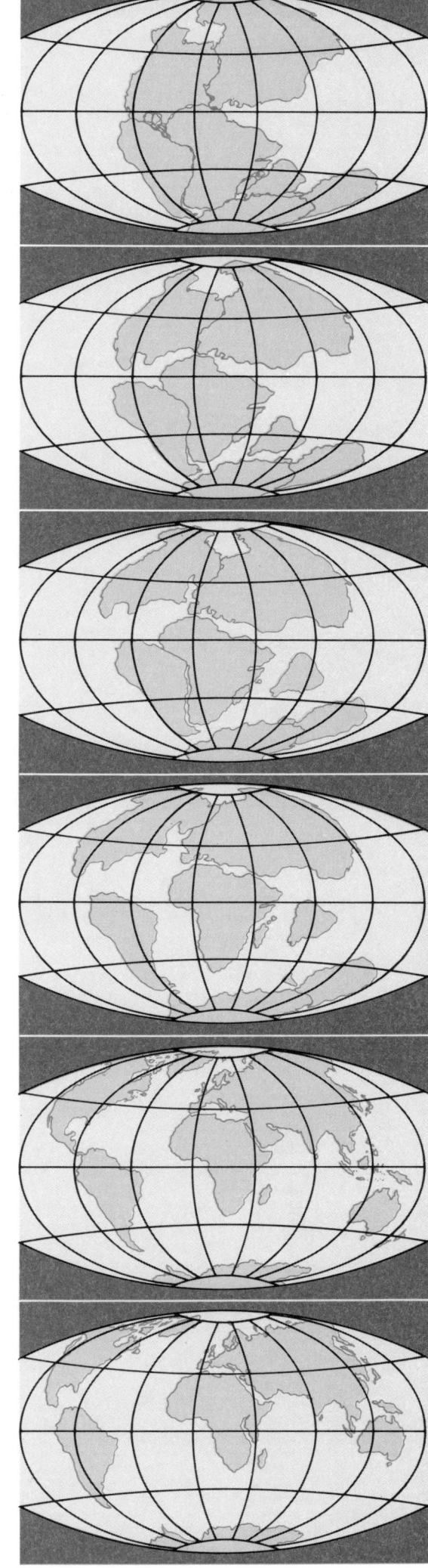

225 million years ago one large landmass, the supercontinent Pangaea, exists and Panthalassa forms the ancestral Pacific Ocean. The Tethys Sea separates Eurasia and Africa and forms an ancestor of the Mediterranean Sea.

180 million years ago Pangaea splits up, the northern block of continents, Laurasia, drifts northwards and the southern block, Gondwanaland, begins to break up. India separates and the South American–African block divides from Australia–Antarctica. New ocean floor is created between the continents.

135 million years ago the Indian plate continues its northward drift and Eurasia rotates to begin to close the eastern end of the Tethys Sea. The North Atlantic and the Indian Ocean have opened up and the South Atlantic is just beginning to form.

65 million years ago Madagascar has split from Africa and the Tethys Sea has closed, with the Mediterranean Sea opening behind it. The South Atlantic Ocean has opened up considerably, but Australia is still joined to the Antarctic and India is about to collide with Asia.

The present day: India has completed its northward migration and collided with Asia, Australia has set itself free from Antarctica, and North America has freed itself from Eurasia to leave Greenland between them. During the past 65 million years (a relatively short geological span of time) nearly half of the present-day ocean floor has been created.

50 million years in the future, Australia may continue its northward drift, part of East Africa will separate from the mainland, and California west of the San Andreas Fault will separate from North America and move northwards. The Pacific Ocean will become smaller, compensating for the increase in size of both the Atlantic and Indian oceans. The Mediterranean Sea will disappear as Africa moves to the north.

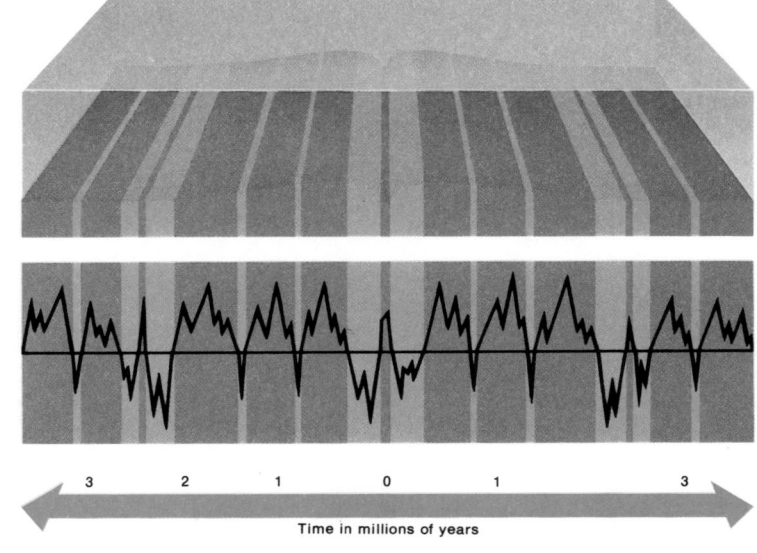

Magnetic surveys of the seabed helped build the plate tectonics theory. Research vessels equipped with magnetometers sailed back and forth over a mid-ocean ridge and recorded the varying magnetism of the seabed. The Earth's magnetic pole has switched from north to south at different times in the past, and this mapping revealed a striped magnetic pattern on the seabed. It was noticed that the stripes on either side of the ridge were symmetrical. The explanation was that the matching stripes must have formed together and moved apart as more crust was injected between them—a notion that was subsequently supported by dating of the seafloor.

3   2   1   0   1   3

Time in millions of years

The Earth's Oceans

No topographic map of the Earth can be drawn unless there is some kind of base line from which to measure depths and heights. This base line has always been taken as the level of the sea, yet the sea is perpetually changing level. One can choose some kind of average to call "sea level," but even today different countries have defined that base line in different ways. The currents found within the sea itself can also give the water surface a slope—the calm Sargasso Sea off the northern coast of South America is, for example, about 1.5 m (5 ft) higher than the water to the west adjacent to the Gulf Stream.

Waves

The changes in the level of the sea, at its surface, provide the most familiar image of motion within the waters. Various changes take place over many different time periods, but the most rapid are those that we call waves.

Waves are produced by the wind moving over the water and catching on the surface. They can move at between 15 and 100 km/hr (10–60 mph) and wave crests may be separated by up to 300 m (1,000 ft) in the open ocean. In general, the greater the wavelength, the faster the wave's speed and the farther the distance traveled by the wave. Waves that have traveled a long way from the winds that created them are known as swell. Without the wind continually pushing them they become symmetrical and smooth. Wind waves produce spilling breakers more like the rapids of a mountain torrent, whereas swell produces giant plunging breakers.

A combination of strong winds and low atmospheric pressure associated with storms can cause yet another kind of wave, known as a storm surge. A storm surge is formed by the water being driven ahead of the wind, and rising as the atmospheric pressure weighing down on the water decreases. Where storms drive water into funnel-shaped coasts, the water can rise more than 10 m (33 ft) above normal sea level, flooding large areas of low-lying land at the head of the bay. Venice, the Netherlands and Bangladesh have been particularly subject to destructive storm surges. Other catastrophic changes in sea level have their origins in the seabed. These are tsunamis (Japanese for "high-water in the harbor") and are generally triggered by underwater earthquakes that suddenly raise or lower large areas of the seafloor.

Tides

As the Earth orbits around the Sun the water in the oceans experiences a changing pull of gravity from both the Moon and the Sun. The Sun is overhead once a day, and because the Moon is itself orbiting the Earth, it is overhead once every 24 hours 50 minutes. The pull of gravity from the Sun is less than half that from the Moon, and so it is the Moon that sets the rhythm of the water movements we call tides. The variation in gravitational pull from the Moon is extremely small, however, and even if the whole of the Earth were covered with deep water a tide of only about 30 cm (12 in) would be produced, rushing around the world keeping

pace with the circling Moon. Yet the tides in shallow coastal regions are often very much higher than this—for example, up to 18 m (60 ft) in the Bay of Fundy, Canada. The seas and bays with the highest tides are located where the whole mass of water is resonating—rebounding backwards and forwards like water in a bath, as the smaller tides in the outlying oceans push it twice each day.

The Bay of Fundy experiences a particularly high tidal range because it happens to have a resonant frequency—a range of movement—very close to the 12½-hour frequency between tides. Large enclosed seas such as the Mediterranean have very small tides because there is no outside push from an ocean to set them resonating. In contrast, where water movement associated with the tides passes through a narrow channel it can produce tidal currents of up to 30 km/hr (19 mph), such as the famous maelstrom of northern Norway.

After these relatively short-lived disturbances the sea returns to its normal, or at least to its average, level again. When the total volume of free water at the Earth's surface alters, or when the shapes of the ocean basins vary, the sea level itself may start to wander.

How does the volume of water vary? It can be buried in rocks—but the steam clouds above volcanoes return such water so it is normally recycled rather than lost. Some vapor can be broken down through radiation in the upper atmosphere and the hydrogen lost to outer space, but this is relatively insignificant. Or it can be frozen and stacked up on land in the form of ice—this is significant as we are still living in an ice age. The lowest ice-age sea levels produced beaches at about 130 m (430 ft) below present sea level, and the low-lying coastal regions of that period have now become flooded to form the continental shelves.

The salt content of the oceans

Average ocean water contains about 35 parts per 1,000 of salts which include 14 elements in concentrations greater than 1 part per million—the most abundant being sodium and chlorine. Where there is considerable surface evaporation, for example in enclosed seas such as the Dead Sea, the salt concentration builds up and the water becomes denser. Where the sea-surface is turning to ice the salt also becomes concentrated in the water.

The coldest, saltiest ocean water comes from the Antarctic. As it is also the densest it hugs the ocean bottom as it flows northwards, reaching as far as the latitudes of Spain. A similar current from the Arctic is slightly lighter and therefore rides above it—but traveling southwards, as far as the southern Atlantic. A second slightly lighter body of Antarctic water rides above the Arctic water—again traveling northwards. Where these water movements meet each other they rise up, bringing to the surface oxygenated water that can support a profusion of life in oceans that have been compared to a desert because of their lack of biological activity. Unlikely as it seems, it is the icy, stormy, polar waters that provide the lungs of the oceans.

Depth in meters
0 1 2 3 4 5 6 7 8

Earth
Sun
Moon
1
Neap tide

Moon
Sun
Earth
2
Spring tide

Moon
Sun
Earth
3
Neap tide

Moon
Sun
Earth
4
Spring tide

Both the Sun and the Moon exert gravitational pull on the water in the oceans, but the pull of the Sun is less than half that of the Moon. It is the Moon, therefore, that sets the rhythm of the tides. Because the Moon orbits the Earth every 24 hours and 50 minutes, the time of high or low tide advances approximately an hour each day. When the Moon is in its first and last quarters (1, 3) it forms a right angle with the Earth and the Sun and the gravitational fields are opposed, thus causing only a small difference between high and low tide. These are called neap tides. When the Sun, Moon and Earth lie in a straight line (2, 4), at the full and the new Moon, then the high tides become higher and the low tides lower. These are the spring tides. The graph illustrates tidal range over a period of a month.

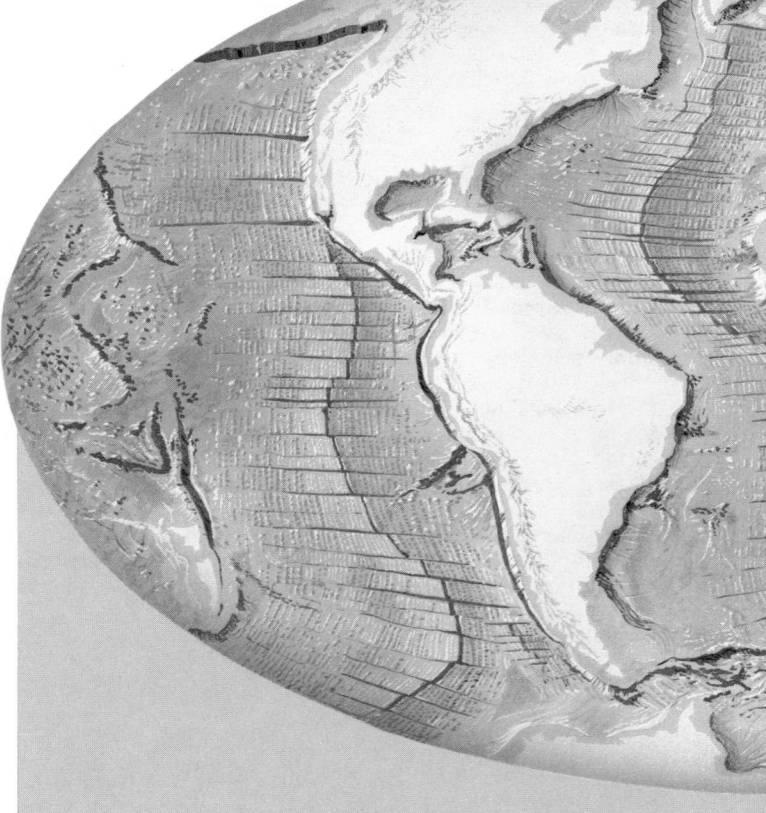

Depth in meters

1	Continent
2	Continental shelf
3	Continental slope
4	Continental rise
5	Submarine canyon
6	Abyssal plain
7	Abyssal hills
8	Mid-ocean ridge
9	Oceanic trench
10	Island arc
11	Continental sea

Depth in meters

0
1,000
2,000
3,000
4,000
5,000
6,000
7,000
8,000

THE CHANGING OCEANS

Nearly two-thirds of the Earth's surface is covered by the seas and oceans and this great expanse of water is continually in movement. The most familiar movements are waves formed by the wind and the rising and falling tides that respond to the position of the Moon. But even greater movements take place. Currents driven by prevailing winds form whirlpools an ocean in width, and below the surface flow great rivers of colder water. Sea level is also rising as ice melts from the polar caps.

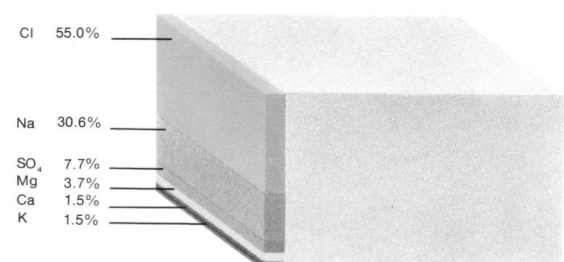

Cl	55.0%
Na	30.6%
SO₄	7.7%
Mg	3.7%
Ca	1.5%
K	1.5%

Seawater is about 96% pure water and the rest is made up of dissolved salts. Many elements are present in minute quantities, but only chlorine (Cl), sodium (Na), sulphate (SO₄), magnesium (Mg), calcium (Ca) and potassium (K) appear in concentrations of more than 1% of the total dissolved salts.

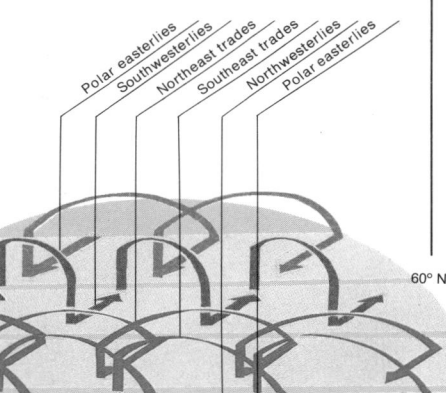

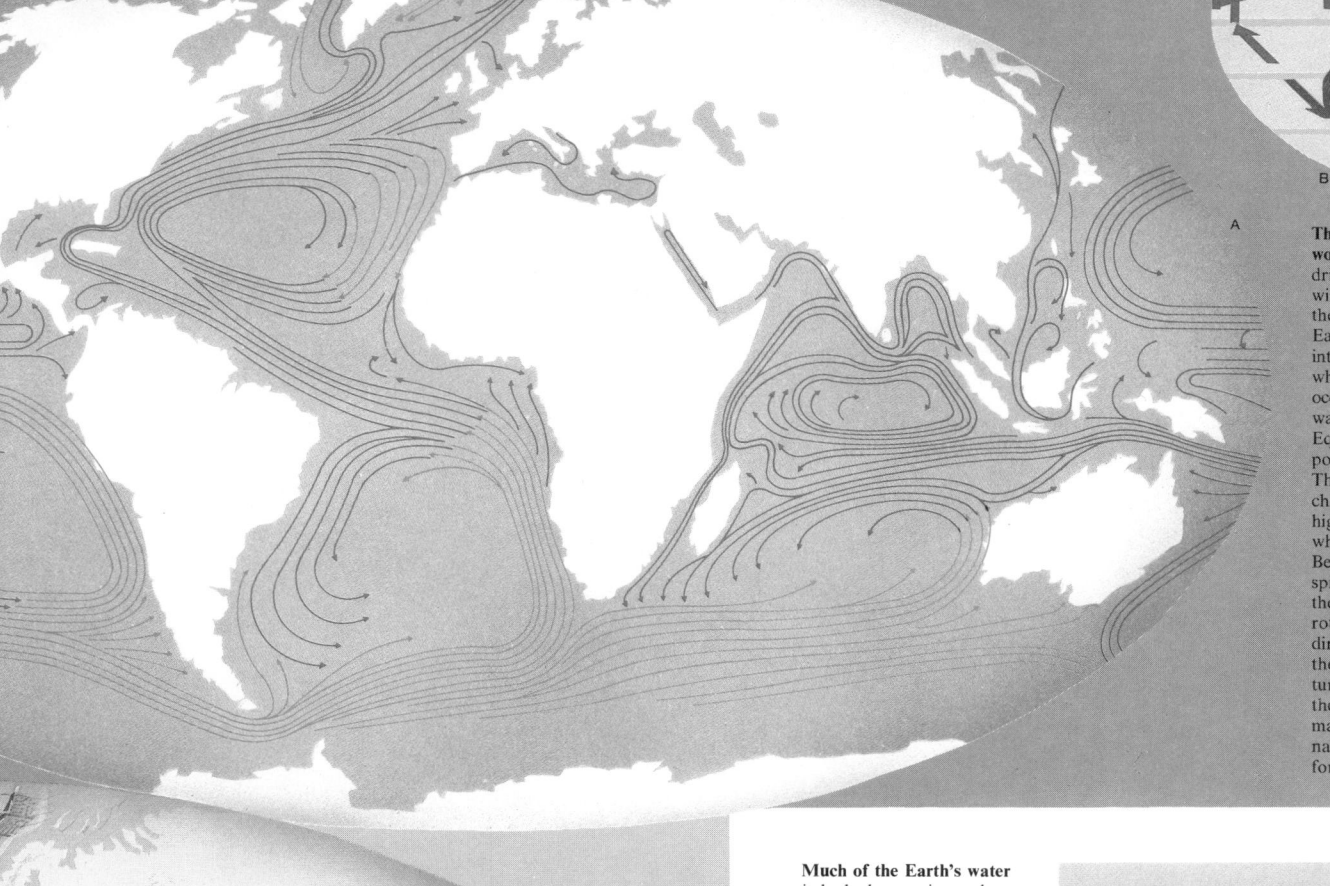

The surface currents of the world's oceans (A) are driven by the prevailing winds (B). The winds and the spinning motion of the Earth drive the currents into gyres—massive whirlpools the width of an ocean. These gyres draw warm water away from the Equator and pull cold polar waters towards it. The centers of gyres are characterized by areas of high pressure, around which winds circulate. Because the Earth is spinning, gyres formed in the northern hemisphere rotate in a clockwise direction, whereas those of the southern hemisphere turn anticlockwise. In all, there are five major gyres, made up of the 38 major named currents. The formation of warm (red) and cold (blue) surface currents is not difficult to understand, given the regions from which they flow. However, even in temperate and subtropical regions, the warm waters of the oceans' surfaces have a permanent layer of cold water beneath them. This cold layer has been formed in the polar regions, where, as the ocean waters have been chilled, they have sunk and then spread out into all the other major ocean basins of the world. The warm subtropical and temperate waters float like an oil slick, from 10 m to 550 m (33–1,900 ft) thick, on top of this cold layer. There is very little mixing between the two layers because the warm water is lighter than the cold water.

Much of the Earth's water is locked up as ice and stacked on the land. As the ice melts the sea level rises. Only 20,000 years ago the sea level was a full 100 m (330 ft) lower than it is today, and the continental shelves were dry land. About 10,000 years ago the sea level was rising as fast as 3 cm (1 in) each year. Today the melting ice is causing the sea level to rise about 1 mm (0.04 in) each year: only a small increment, but if all the ice melted, the sea level would rise by about 60 m (197 ft) and would flood many of the world's major cities.

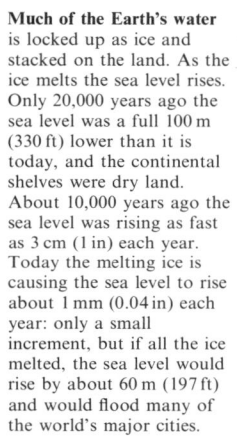

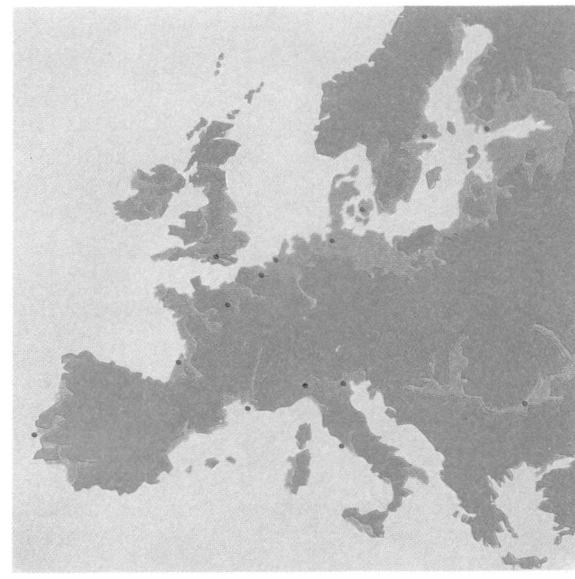

- ● < 60 m
- • > 60 m
- · Major cities

The seabed, more uniform than the land surface, also contains a landscape of underwater features that resemble the plains, valleys and mountains of the continents. Off the edge of continents lie the flat, shallow continental shelves, which are bounded by the steeper incline of the continental slope, which meets the true ocean floor at the continental rise. Here deep submarine canyons may be found. These seem to be in a process of continual erosion from turbidity currents. River water pouring into major estuaries and carrying sediment can also scour out the slope—especially during periods of low sea level. The abyssal plain is rarely interrupted by volcanic hills and mountains. The largest chains are at the mid-ocean ridge, where two crustal plates are moving apart and new ocean floor is being created. At some ocean margins deep trough-shaped valleys or trenches are the sites of ocean floor consumption at a subduction zone. The volcanic island arcs that form behind it sometimes isolate a continental sea.

TSUNAMIS

Tsunamis are generated by massive underwater earthquakes (A) and are common around the Pacific. They can travel at more than 700 km/hr (435 mph) and individual waves may occur at intervals of 15 minutes, or 200 km (125 miles). Low-lying atolls of the Pacific have extremely steep sides underwater, and are generally unharmed, but the gently shelving islands such as Hawaii slow down the tsunami and build it into a giant wave 30 m (100 ft) or more in height. This map plots the hourly position of a tsunami that originated south of Alaska.

The Earth's Habitats

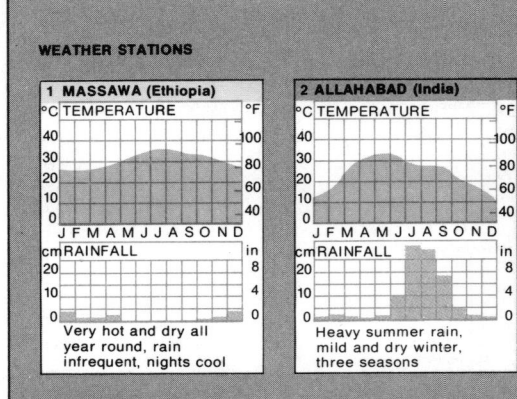

WEATHER STATIONS
1 MASSAWA (Ethiopia)
°C TEMPERATURE °F
40 30 20 10 0
100 80 60 40
J F M A M J J A S O N D
cm RAINFALL in
20 10 0
8 4 0
Very hot and dry all year round, rain infrequent, nights cool
2 ALLAHABAD (India)
°C TEMPERATURE °F
J F M A M J J A S O N D
cm RAINFALL in
Heavy summer rain, mild and dry winter, three seasons

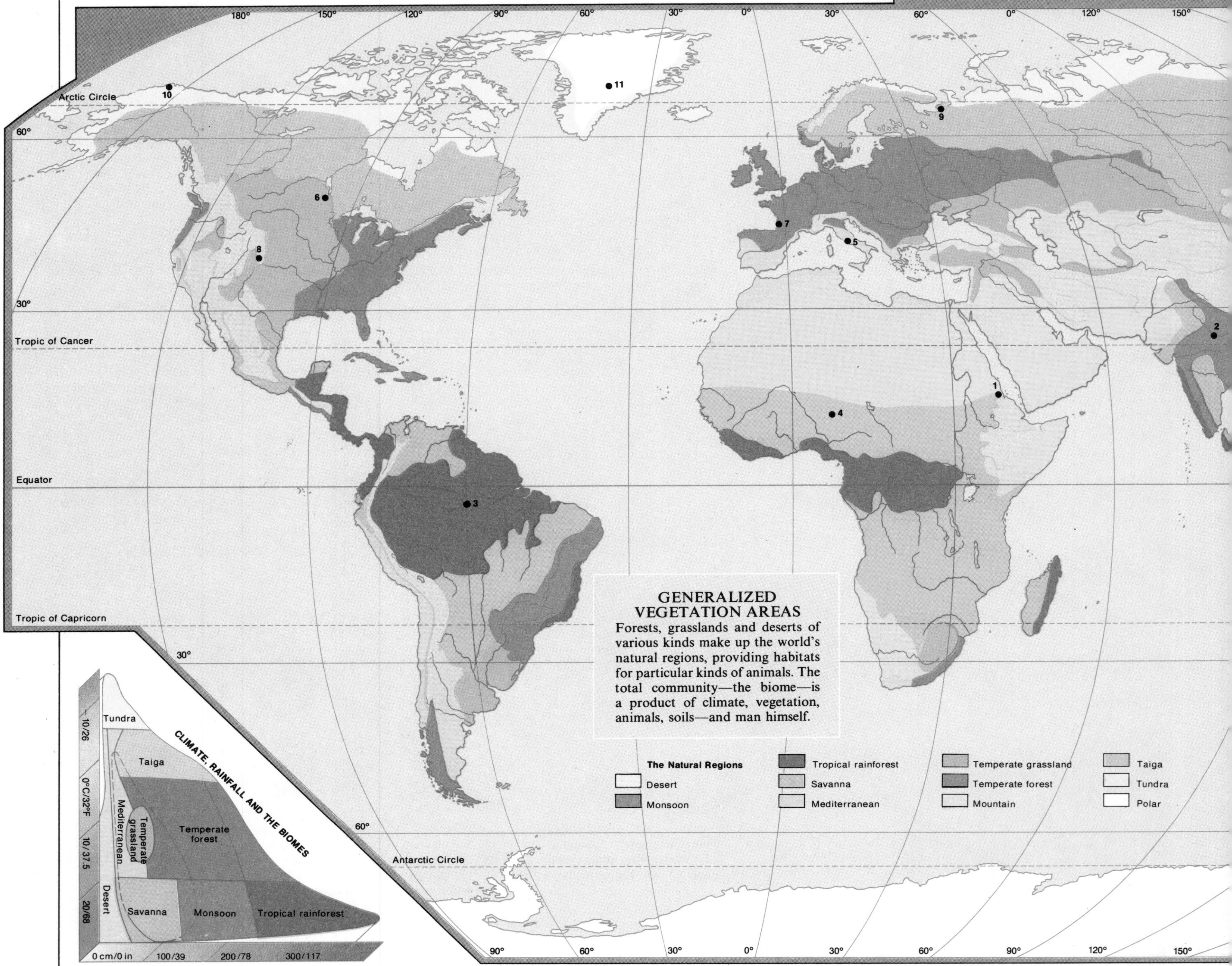

180° 150° 120° 90° 60° 30° 0° 30° 60° 90° 120° 150°
Arctic Circle
60°
30°
Tropic of Cancer
Equator
Tropic of Capricorn
30°
60°
Antarctic Circle
1 2 3 4 5 6 7 8 9 10 11
GENERALIZED VEGETATION AREAS
Forests, grasslands and deserts of various kinds make up the world's natural regions, providing habitats for particular kinds of animals. The total community—the biome—is a product of climate, vegetation, animals, soils—and man himself.
The Natural Regions
Desert
Monsoon
Tropical rainforest
Savanna
Mediterranean
Temperate grassland
Temperate forest
Mountain
Taiga
Tundra
Polar
CLIMATE, RAINFALL AND THE BIOMES
Tundra
Taiga
Temperate grassland
Mediterranean
Temperate forest
Desert
Savanna
Monsoon
Tropical rainforest
-10/26
0°C/32°F
10/37.5
20/68
0 cm/0 in
100/39
200/78
300/117

Temperature and rainfall (above) govern the world's zones of plant and animal life. Dryness prevents tree growth both in icy tundra and in hot deserts. Wetter conditions cause savannas and grasslands to yield to forest biomes, tropical or temperate (the dotted line indicates zones within which variations occur).

A broad correlation (below) between soil types, climate and vegetation areas shows the interconnections that define the biomes. The soil of the biome is related to climatic conditions and is also modified by plant and animal activity, but soil types are not necessarily confined to any one particular biome.

1 Gley
Grasses/shrubs
Waterlogged soil
Clay, silt, sand, rock fragments
Permafrost
2 Podsol
Needle layer
Acid humus
Rapid leaching of oxides
Iron pan
Oxides deposited
Bedrock
3 Gray-brown
Thick leaf debris
Humus
Less rapid decomposition
Soil animals flourish
Weathered material
Tree roots
Bedrock
4 Chernozem
Thick sod cover
Soil animals flourish
Upward movement of soil solution
Nodules of calcium carbonate
Calcium carbonate
5 Ferruginous
Light debris
Wet season
Dry season
Soil solution rises
Silica removed
Some silica
Kaolinitic material over igneous rocks
6 Ferralitic
Plentiful debris
Soil animals very active. Rapid organic decomposition
Dissolved salts quickly percolate away. Silica removed
Some silica
Bedrock

Soil profiles (above) from surface to bedrock reflect the influence of climate and vegetation on the rock. Depths vary from 1 m in the tundra to 30–40 m at the Equator. Waterlogged gley (1) may form above tundra permafrost. Podsol (2) is typical of taiga forests, where spring snow-melt is heavily leached through a needle layer, sometimes forming an iron "pan." Gray-brown forest soil (3) has rich, organic humus, as has chernozem (4), the typical temperate grassland soil. Ferruginous soils (5) occur in dry-season tropical climates (monsoon, savanna), and ferralitic soils (6) where there is constant rainfall.

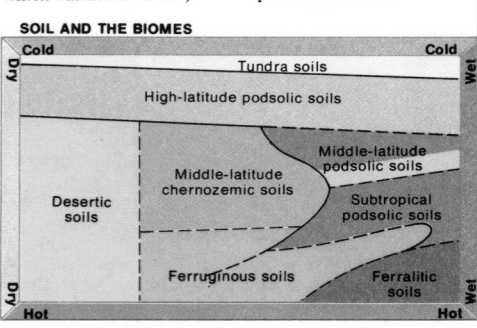

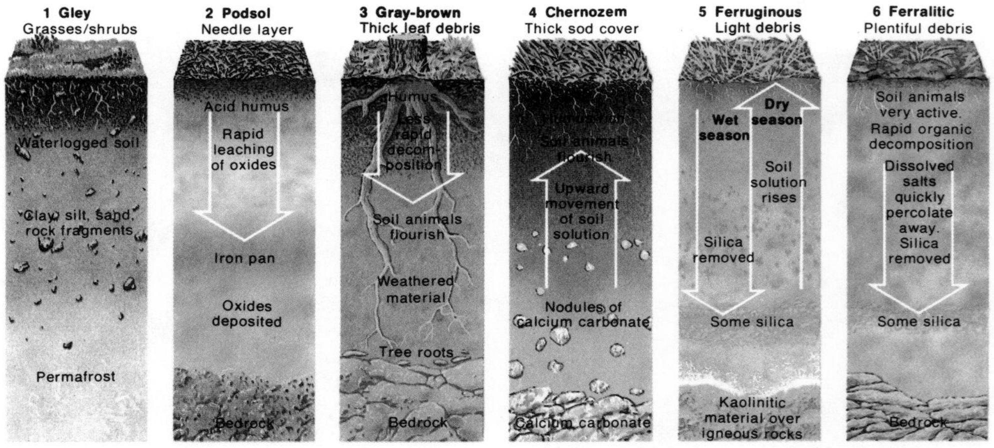

SOIL AND THE BIOMES
Cold
Cold
Dry
Wet
Tundra soils
High-latitude podsolic soils
Desertic soils
Middle-latitude chernozemic soils
Middle-latitude podsolic soils
Subtropical podsolic soils
Ferruginous soils
Ferralitic soils
Dry
Wet
Hot
Hot

ECOSYSTEM DYNAMICS

An ecosystem consists of a group of organisms and its physical environment. A marshland ecosystem from North America (right) shows the dynamic interactions between plant and animal communities and their habitats, which include climate, soil and water. The energy and food in the system initially derive from the Sun—the main energy source for living things, notably plants. Plants are food for herbivores, on land and in water; herbivores are food for carnivores; decomposers (bacteria and fungi) nourish plants, breaking down dead bodies into compounds.

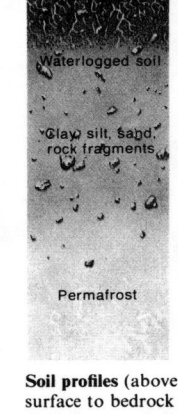

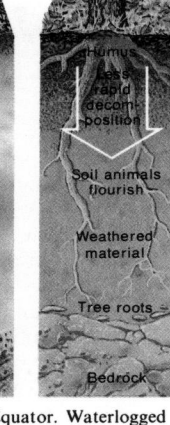

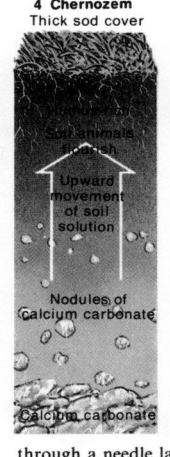

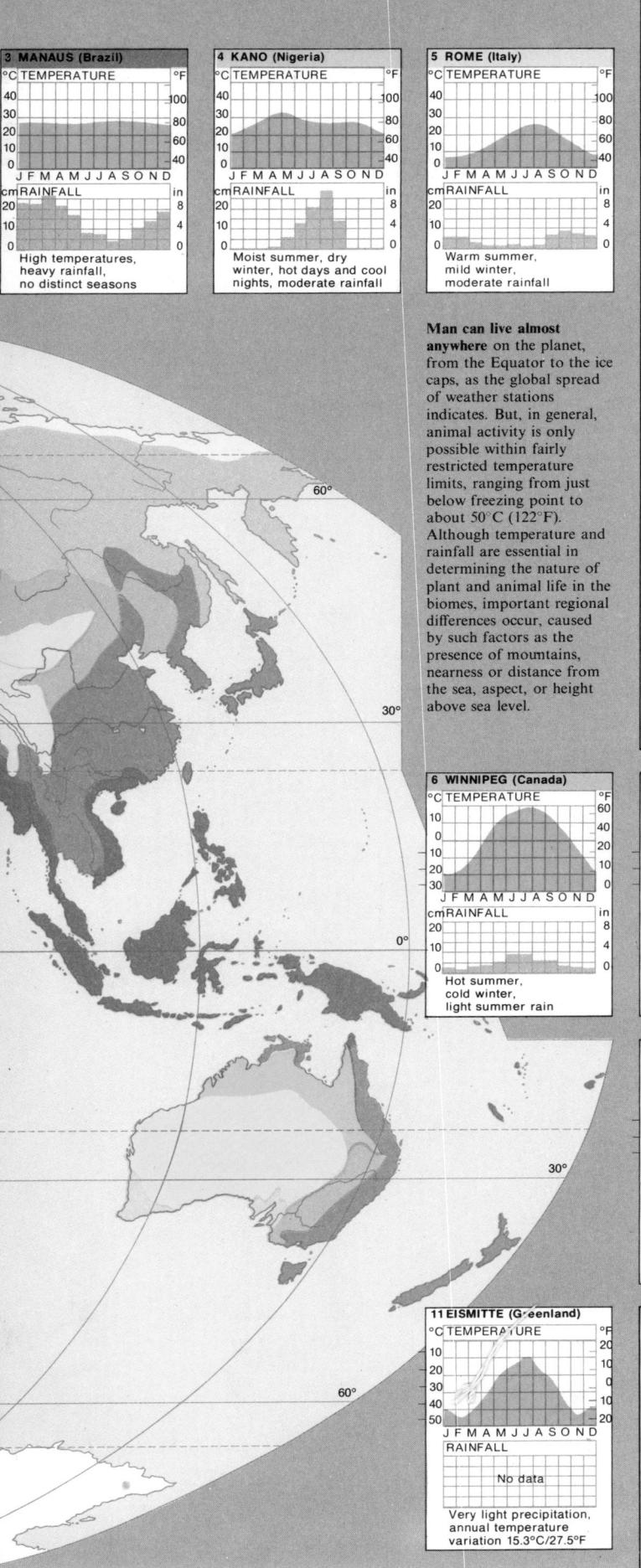

3 MANAUS (Brazil)
TEMPERATURE °C / °F
RAINFALL cm / in
High temperatures, heavy rainfall, no distinct seasons

4 KANO (Nigeria)
TEMPERATURE °C / °F
RAINFALL cm / in
Moist summer, dry winter, hot days and cool nights, moderate rainfall

5 ROME (Italy)
TEMPERATURE °C / °F
RAINFALL cm / in
Warm summer, mild winter, moderate rainfall

6 WINNIPEG (Canada)
TEMPERATURE °C / °F
RAINFALL cm / in
Hot summer, cold winter, light summer rain

7 BORDEAUX (France)
TEMPERATURE °C / °F
RAINFALL cm / in
Warm summer, mild winter, four distinct seasons

8 PIKE'S PEAK (USA)
TEMPERATURE °C / °F
RAINFALL cm / in
4,300 m (14,111 ft)
Temperature decreases with increasing altitude

9 ARKHANGELSK (USSR)
TEMPERATURE °C / °F
RAINFALL cm / in
Short summer, long and cold winter, light summer rain

10 BARROW (Alaska)
TEMPERATURE °C / °F
RAINFALL cm / in
Brief summer, very long and cold winter, very light rainfall

11 EISMITTE (Greenland)
TEMPERATURE °C / °F
RAINFALL
No data
Very light precipitation, annual temperature variation 15.3°C/27.5°F

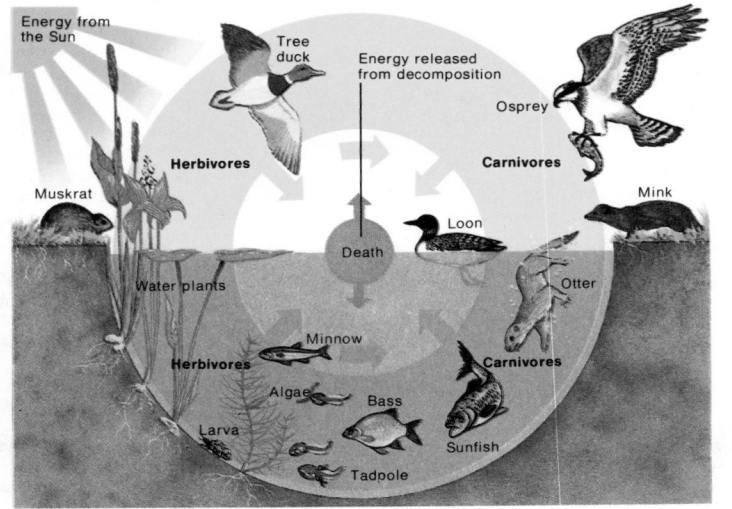

Energy from the Sun · Tree duck · Energy released from decomposition · Osprey · Herbivores · Carnivores · Muskrat · Mink · Loon · Water plants · Death · Otter · Minnow · Herbivores · Carnivores · Algae · Bass · Larva · Sunfish · Tadpole

Man can live almost anywhere on the planet, from the Equator to the ice caps, as the global spread of weather stations indicates. But, in general, animal activity is only possible within fairly restricted temperature limits, ranging from just below freezing point to about 50°C (122°F). Although temperature and rainfall are essential in determining the nature of plant and animal life in the biomes, important regional differences occur, caused by such factors as the presence of mountains, nearness or distance from the sea, aspect, or height above sea level.

Natural Regions

Divisions according to climate were first suggested by the Greek philosopher Aristotle, and his ideas were still in use until about 100 years ago. Aristotle posited a number of climatic zones—called torrid, temperate and frigid—defined by latitude. But with time it became increasingly apparent that the complex distribution of atmospheric pressure, winds, rainfall and temperature could not be related to such a simple frame. Nineteenth-century scientists divided the world into 35 climatic provinces. Then in 1900 the German meteorologist Wladimir Köppen produced a more sophisticated climatic classification based on temperature and moisture conditions related to the needs of plants. At about the same time other scientists studied the distribution of vegetation types throughout the world. These studies together provided the basis for much of the later work on climatic regions.

An important step forward was made in 1904 by the British geographer A. J. Herbertson. He argued that subdivision of physical environments should take into account the distribution of the various phenomena as they related to each other. He conceived the idea of *natural regions*, each with "a certain unity of configuration (relief), climate and vegetation." His final classification contained four groups or regions: Polar Types, Cool Temperate Types, Warm Temperate Types and Tropical Hot Lands. Herbertson's scheme, controversial at first, was later much used for teaching geography.

Ecology

Meanwhile the study of environmental problems had been advanced by the idea of *ecology*, the relationship of living things between each other and their surroundings. The term was first used in 1868 by Ernst Haeckel, the German biologist, but it was not until the end of the nineteenth century that scientists really began to study life forms in relation to their habitat. In addition to the central ideas of interdependence between the members of plant and animal communities and between the community and the physical environment, there now came the suggestion that communities develop in a sequence that leads to a "climax"—a final step of equilibrium or balance. Their climax stage depends on conditions of climate or soil.

Later the British botanist A. G. Tansley, a leading exponent of ecological thinking, introduced the term *ecosystem* to describe a group of living organisms and its effective environment. Tansley's definition of 1935 referred to the whole system, including "not only the organism complex, but also the whole complex of physical factors forming what we call the environment of the biome." The idea became very influential and has been used in the social sciences as well as in the natural ones. But it is difficult to apply in practice, partly because of the highly complex and often diverse interactions that take place in different parts of the ecosystem.

Ecologists have developed special methods and have given particular attention to the ways in which energy is transferred within the system. The term *biome* refers to the whole complex of organisms, both animals and plants, that live together naturally as a society. By *environment* is meant all the external conditions that affect the life and development of an organism.

Biomes

The biomes shown on the map are broadly drawn generalizations. They should be regarded as idealized regions, within which many local variations may exist—for example, of climate or soil conditions. On a larger scale such features as mountain ranges may cause variations at a regional level. Scientists have tried to work out "hierarchies" that include many levels or orders of scale leading to the major climatic-vegetation realms or biomes. These realms give a broad picture that is useful at the world level of scale, and which forms a starting point for further analysis. Any map of the biomes has to have lines to indicate the boundaries of each region, but these too are generalizations. Although climate and vegetation do sometimes change abruptly from place to place, more often there are transitional zones, and the boundaries on the maps give the broad locations of these.

Herbertson's concept of natural regions attempted also to take account of the influence of man as an important factor in the environment. But he was not totally successful in including man in his analysis, no doubt because of the complexity of the problems involved and because of the immense influence that man has had upon the natural vegetation of the world. The cutting of forests, the drainage and reclamation of land, the introduction, use and spread of cultivated plants, the domestication of animals, the development of sophisticated systems of agriculture and many other actions all create, over large areas of the biomes, landscapes that are more man-made than natural.

Resource systems

An idea that clarifies the study of the interrelations of societies and environments, and the ways in which these change with the passage of time, is that of the *resource system*. This is a model of a population of human beings and their social and economic characteristics, including their technical skills and resources, together with those aspects of the natural environment that affect them and which they influence. The model includes the sequences by which natural materials are obtained, transformed and used. It tries to show how societies are organized according to their natural resources, the effects of that use, and the ways in which natural conditions limit or expand the life and work of the society. But it is easier to apply such a model to societies that have direct relations with natural conditions, through farming, fishing or forestry, than to great urban–industrial complexes.

The sections that follow present a picture of the diversity of habitats from ice caps to equatorial forests, the principal ways man has modified the environment and the problems of maintaining healthy resource systems.

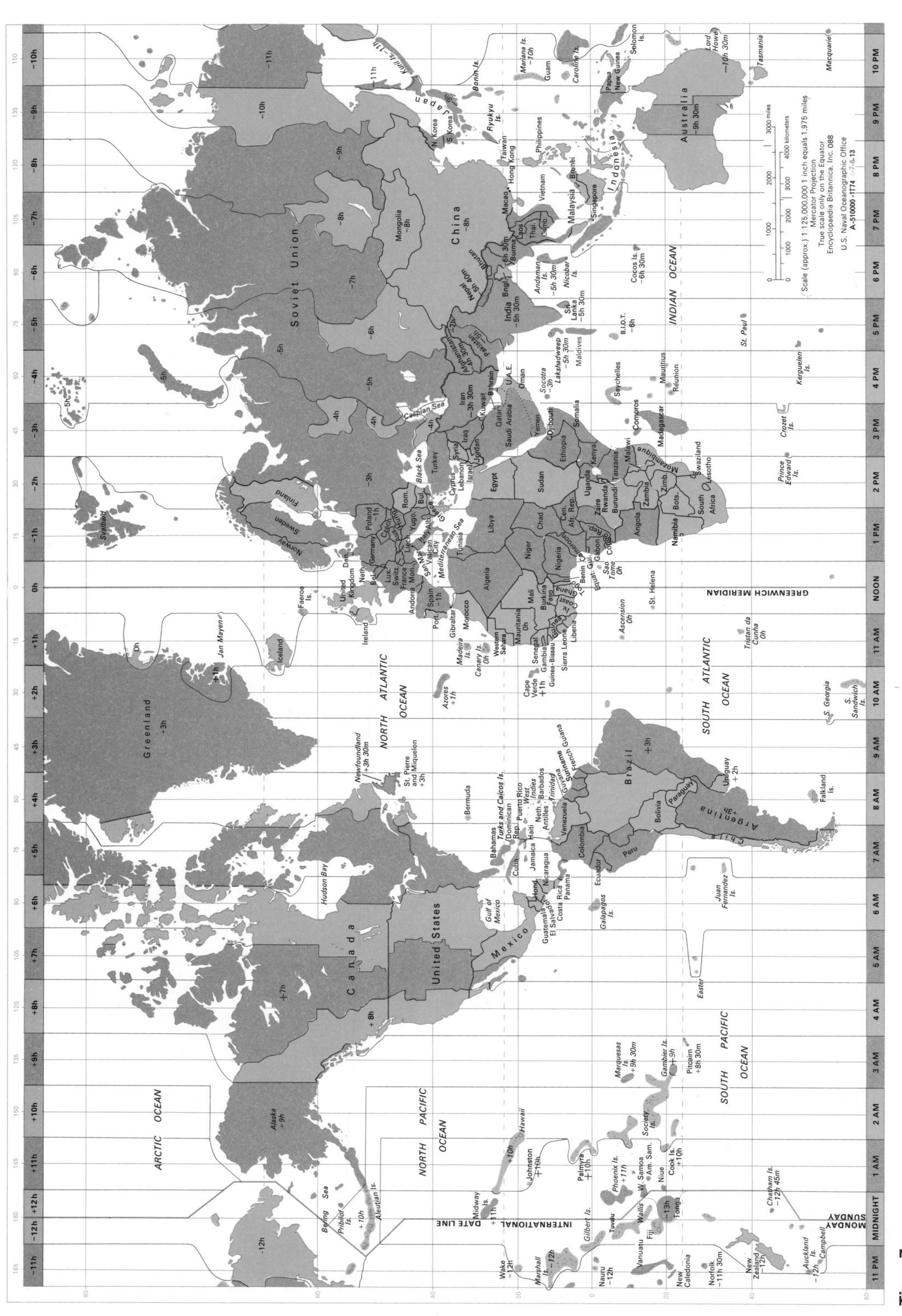

Time Zones

Standard time zone of even-numbered hours from Greenwich time

Standard time zone of odd-numbered hours from Greenwich time

Time varies from the standard time zone by half an hour

Time varies from the standard time zone by other than half an hour

[h m] hours, minutes

The standard time zone system, fixed by international agreement and by law in each country, is based on a theoretical division of the globe into 24 zones of 15° longitude each. The mid-meridian of each zone fixes the hour for the entire zone. The zero time zone extends 7½° east and 7½° west of the Greenwich meridian, 0° longitude. Since the earth rotates toward the east, time zones to the west of Greenwich are earlier, to the east, later. Plus and minus hours at the top of the map are added to or subtracted from local time to find Greenwich time. Local standard time can be determined for any area in the world by adding one hour for each time zone counted in an easterly direction from one's own, or by subtracting one hour for each zone counted in a westerly direction. To separate one day from the next, the 180th meridian has been designated as the international date line. On both sides of the line the time of day is the same, but west of the line it is one day later than it is to the east. Countries that adhere to the international zone system adopt the zone applicable to their location. Some countries, however, establish time zones based on political boundaries, or adopt the time zone of a neighboring unit. For all or part of the year some countries also advance their time by one hour, thereby utilizing more daylight hours each day.

Scale (approx.) 1:125,000,000 1 inch equals 1,975 miles
Mercator Projection
True scale only on the Equator
Encyclopædia Britannica, Inc. 088
U.S. Naval Oceanographic Office
A-510000-1T74   -7-5-13

Reference Maps

MAP SYMBOLS

CULTURAL FEATURES

Political Boundaries

▬▬▬	International
▬▬▬	Secondary (State, province, etc.)
▬▬▬	County

Populated Places

Cities, towns, and villages

· · • • ● ●   Symbol size represents population of the place

Type size represents relative importance of the place.

Corporate area of large U.S. and Canadian cities and urban area of other foreign cities

Major Urban Area
Area of continuous commercial, industrial, and residential development in and around a major city

○ Community within a city
⊛ Capital of major political unit
☆ Capital of secondary political unit
◎ Capital of U.S. state or Canadian province
○ County Seat
▲ Military Installation
⊙ Scientific Station

Miscellaneous

National Park
National Monument
Provincial Park
Indian Reservation
△ Point of Interest
∴ Ruins
■ ♠ Buildings
⬭ Race Track
▬▬▬ Railroad – International Maps
┤├ Tunnel
▭▭▭ Underground or Subway
Dam
Bridge
Dike

▬▬▬ Highway – U.S. and Canadian Maps
▬▬▬ Railroad – U.S. and Canadian Maps

LAND FEATURES

Ranges →
Peaks →
Passes →
     LITTLE PASS
Point of Elevation above sea level   8,520 FT +
Escarpments, Bluffs, Cliffs, and Plateaus
     PLATEAU
Glaciers →
Volcanoes →
Lava Flows →
Sand Dunes →
Deserts →

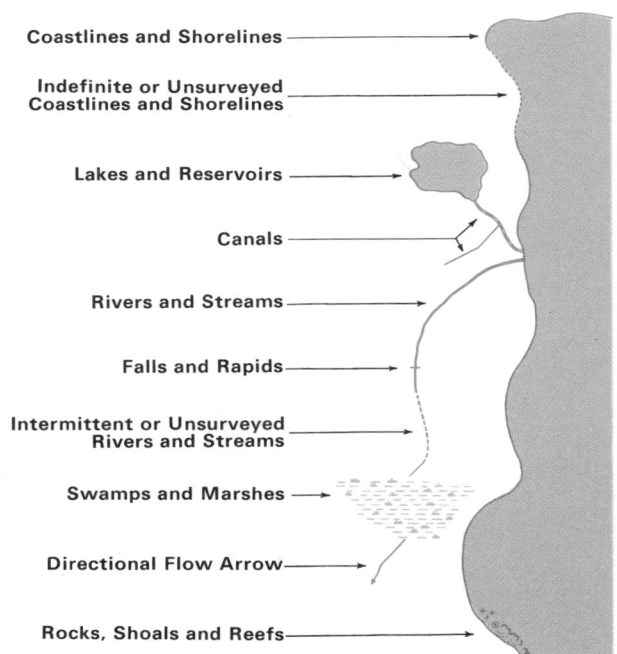

WATER FEATURES

Coastlines and Shorelines →
Indefinite or Unsurveyed Coastlines and Shorelines →
Lakes and Reservoirs →
Canals →
Rivers and Streams →
Falls and Rapids →
Intermittent or Unsurveyed Rivers and Streams →
Swamps and Marshes →
Directional Flow Arrow →
Rocks, Shoals and Reefs →

TYPE STYLES USED TO NAME FEATURES

ASIA	Continent	PANTELLERIA (ITALY)	Country of which unit is a dependency in parentheses	UINTA DESERT	Major Terrain Features
DENMARK CANADA	Country, State, or Province	SRI LANKA (CEYLON)	Former or alternate name	MT. MORIAH	Individual Mountain
		Rome (Roma)	Local or alternate city name	STROMBOLI NUNIVAK	Island or Coastal Feature
BÉARN	Region, Province, or Historical Region	Naval Air Station	Military Installation	Ocean Lake River Canal	Hydrographic Features
CROCKETT	County	MESA VERDE SAN XAVIER	National Park or Monument, Provincial Park, Indian Res.,		

Note: Size of type varies according to importance and available space. Letters for names of major features are spread across the extent of the feature.

THE INDEX REFERENCE SYSTEM

Place	Location	Index Key	Page
Cadillac, Que., Can	*h11	73
Cadillac, Sask., Can	H2	70
Cadillac, Fr	E3	14
Cadillac, Wexford, Mich	B4	90
Cadiz, San Bernardino, Calif.	E6	82
Cadiz, Trigg, Ky.	D2	94
Cadron, creek, Ark	B3	81
Caen, Fr.	C3	14
Caetité, Braz.	D2	57
Calcutta, India	D8	39
Cambridge, Eng.	D8	12
Catania, It.	F5	21
Ceará, state, Braz.	D2	57
Chamblee, DeKalb, Ga.	h8	87
Chambly, Que., Can.	D4	73
Chambord, Que., Can.	A5	73
Champagne, former prov., Fr.	C5	14
Champaign, Champaign, Ill.	B4	90
Champdore, lake, Que., Can.	g8	75
Champerico, Guat.	C2	62
Champéry, Switz.	D2	19
Champex, Switz.	D3	19
Champigneulles, Fr.	F6	15
Champion, Chase, Nebr.	D4	103
Champlain, co., Que., Can.	B4	73
Champlain, lake, N.Y., Vt.	B2	120
Champoton, Mex.	D6	63
Changchou, China	E8	34
Chanthaburi, Thai.	F5	38
Chaparral, Col.	C2	60
Charleville-Mézières, Fr.	C6	14
Chatham, Eng.	C8	12
Chiapa de Corzo, Mex.	D6	63
Chiapas, state, Mex.	D6	63
Chiba, Jap.	I10, n19	37
Chiba, pref., Jap.	*I10	37
Chibemba, Ang.	E1	48
Chibougamau, Que., Can.	k12	73
Chicago, Cook, Ill.	B4	90
Chichaoua, Mor.	C3	44
Chichen Itzá, ruins, Mex.	C7	63
Chichester, Eng.	D7	12
Chickasaw, co., Iowa	A5	92
Chiclana, Sp.	D2	20
Chiclayo, Peru	C2	58
Columbus, Franklin, Ohio	C3	111

The indexing system used in this atlas is based upon the conventional pattern of parallels and meridians used to indicate latitude and longitude. The index samples beside the map indicate that the cities of *Chicago, Cadillac,* and *Champaign* are all located in *B4.* Each index key letter, *in this case "B,"* is placed between corresponding degree numbers of latitude in the vertical borders of the map. Each index key number, *in this case "4,"* is placed between corresponding degree numbers of longitude in the horizontal borders of the map. Crossing of the parallels above and below the index letter with the meridians on each side of the index number forms a confining "box" in which the given place is certain to be located. It is important to note that location of the place may be anywhere in this confining "box."

Insets on many foreign maps are indexed independently of the main maps by separate index key letters and figures. All places indexed to these insets are identified in the index key. A diamond-shaped symbol in the margin of the map is used to separate the insets from the main map and also to separate key letters and numbers where the spacing of the parallels and meridians is great.

Place-names are indexed to the location of the city symbol. Political divisions and physical features are indexed to the location of their names on the map.

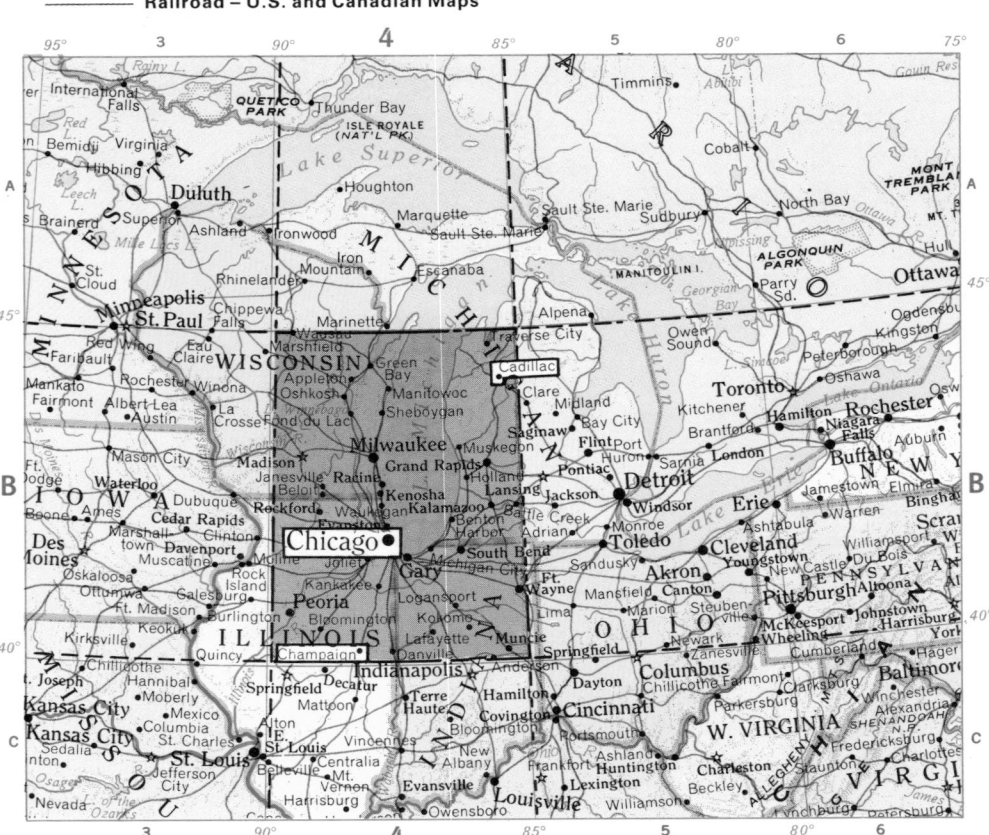

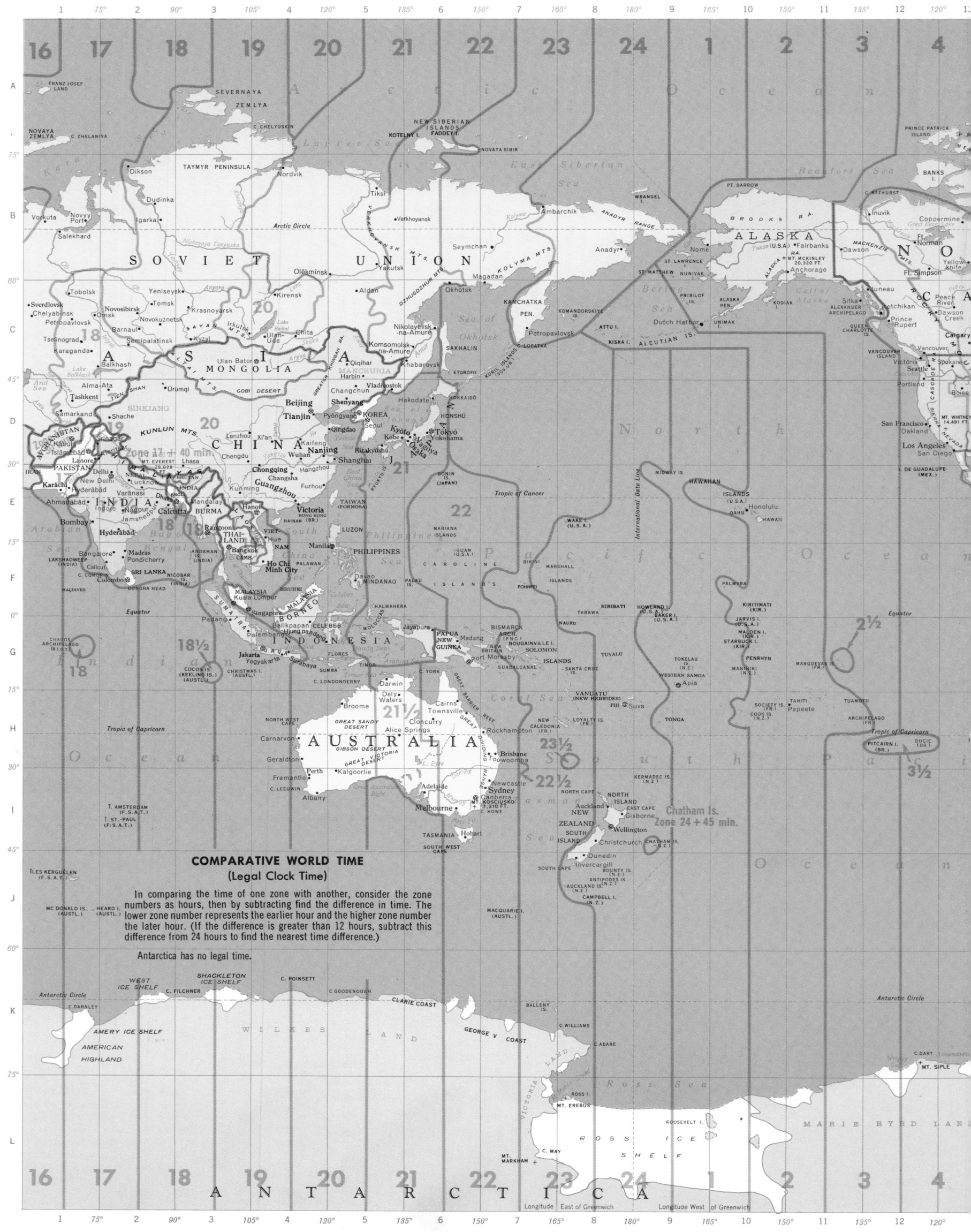

COMPARATIVE WORLD TIME
(Legal Clock Time)

In comparing the time of one zone with another, consider the zone numbers as hours, then by subtracting find the difference in time. The lower zone number represents the earlier hour and the higher zone number the later hour. (If the difference is greater than 12 hours, subtract this difference from 24 hours to find the nearest time difference.)

Antarctica has no legal time.

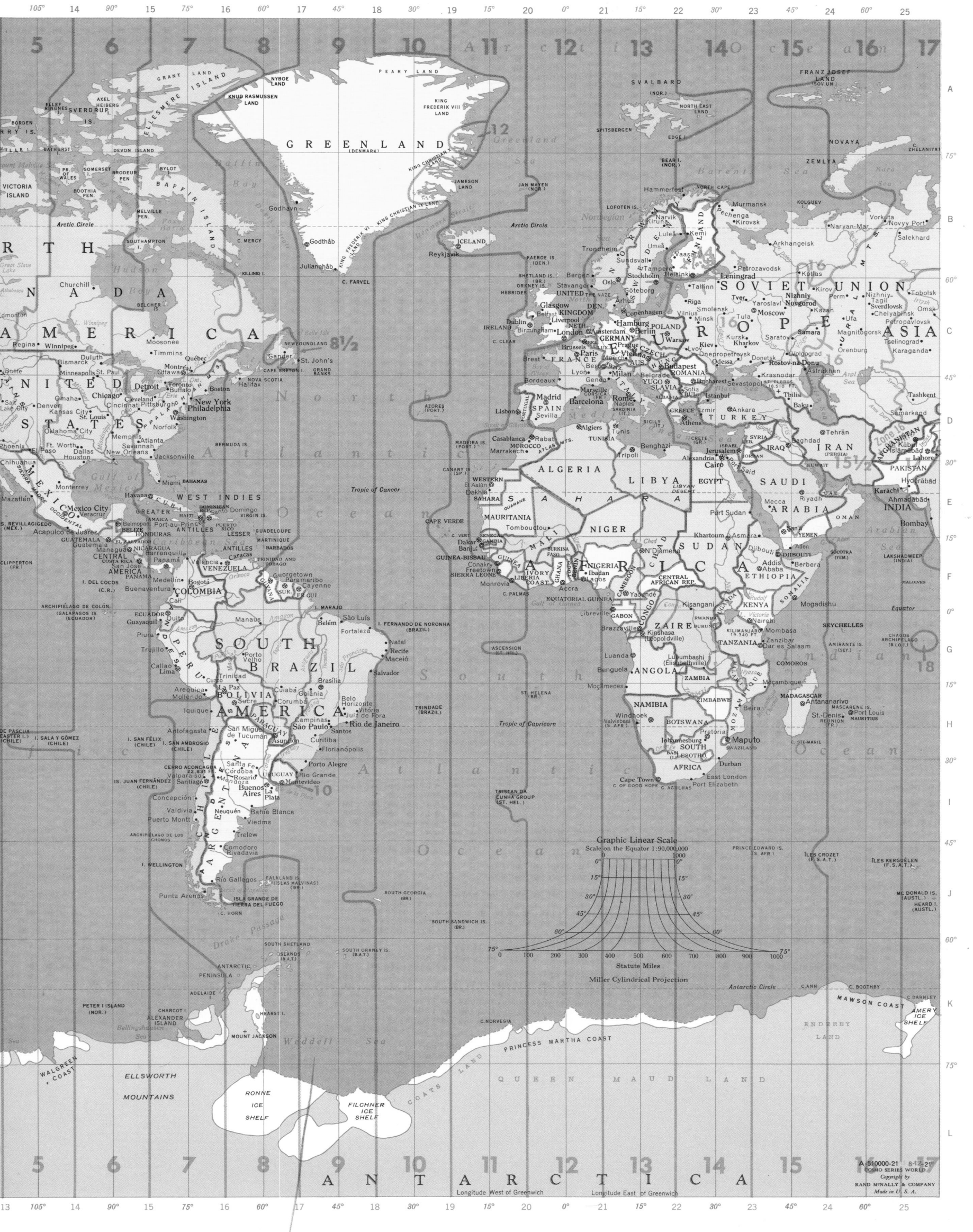

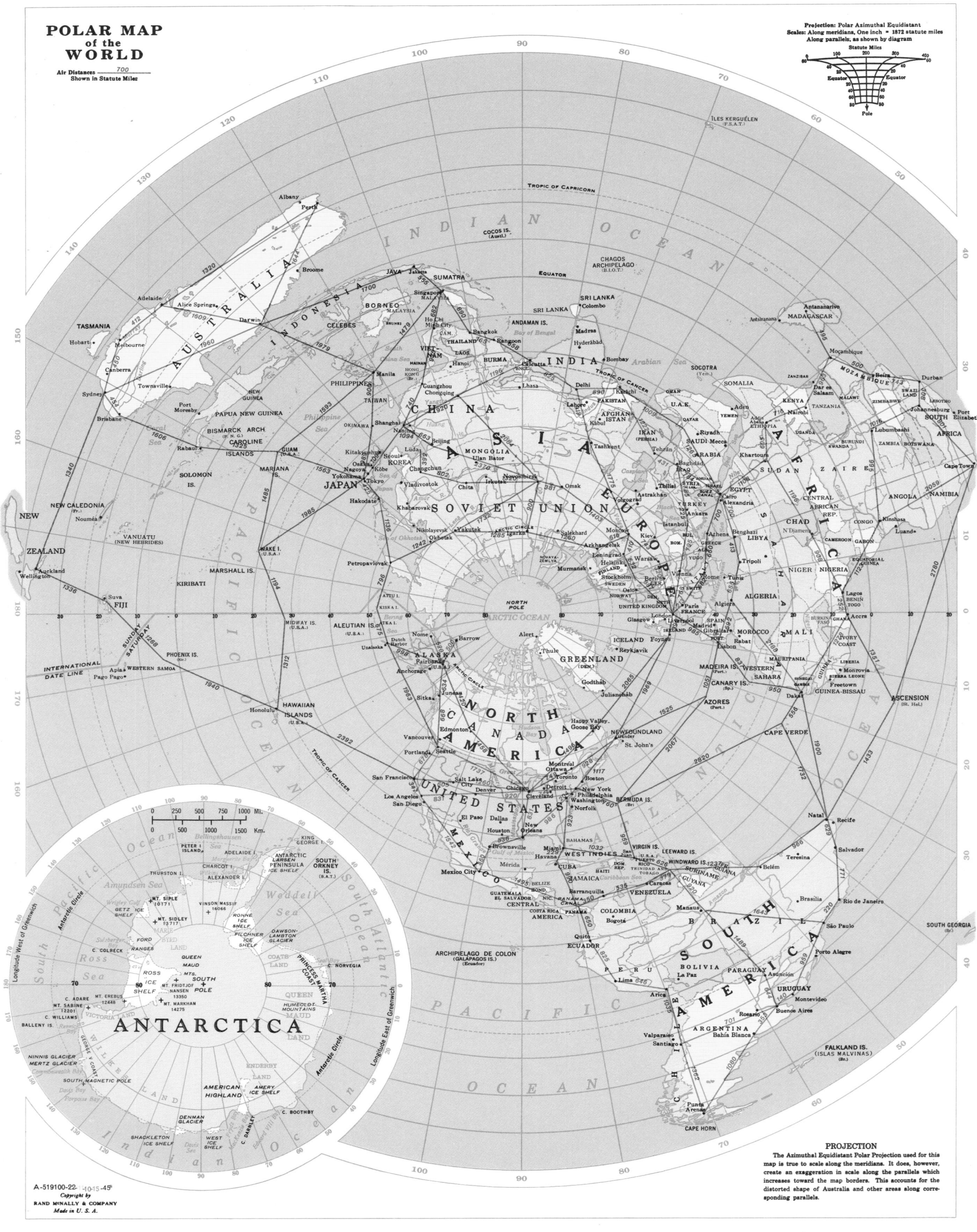

POLAR MAP
of the
WORLD

Air Distances —— 700
Shown in Statute Miles

Projection: Polar Azimuthal Equidistant
Scales: Along meridians, One inch = 1872 statute miles
Along parallels, as shown by diagram

PROJECTION

The Azimuthal Equidistant Polar Projection used for this map is true to scale along the meridians. It does, however, create an exaggeration in scale along the parallels which increases toward the map borders. This accounts for the distorted shape of Australia and other areas along corresponding parallels.

A-519100-22- 40-15-45°
Copyright by
RAND McNALLY & COMPANY
Made in U. S. A.

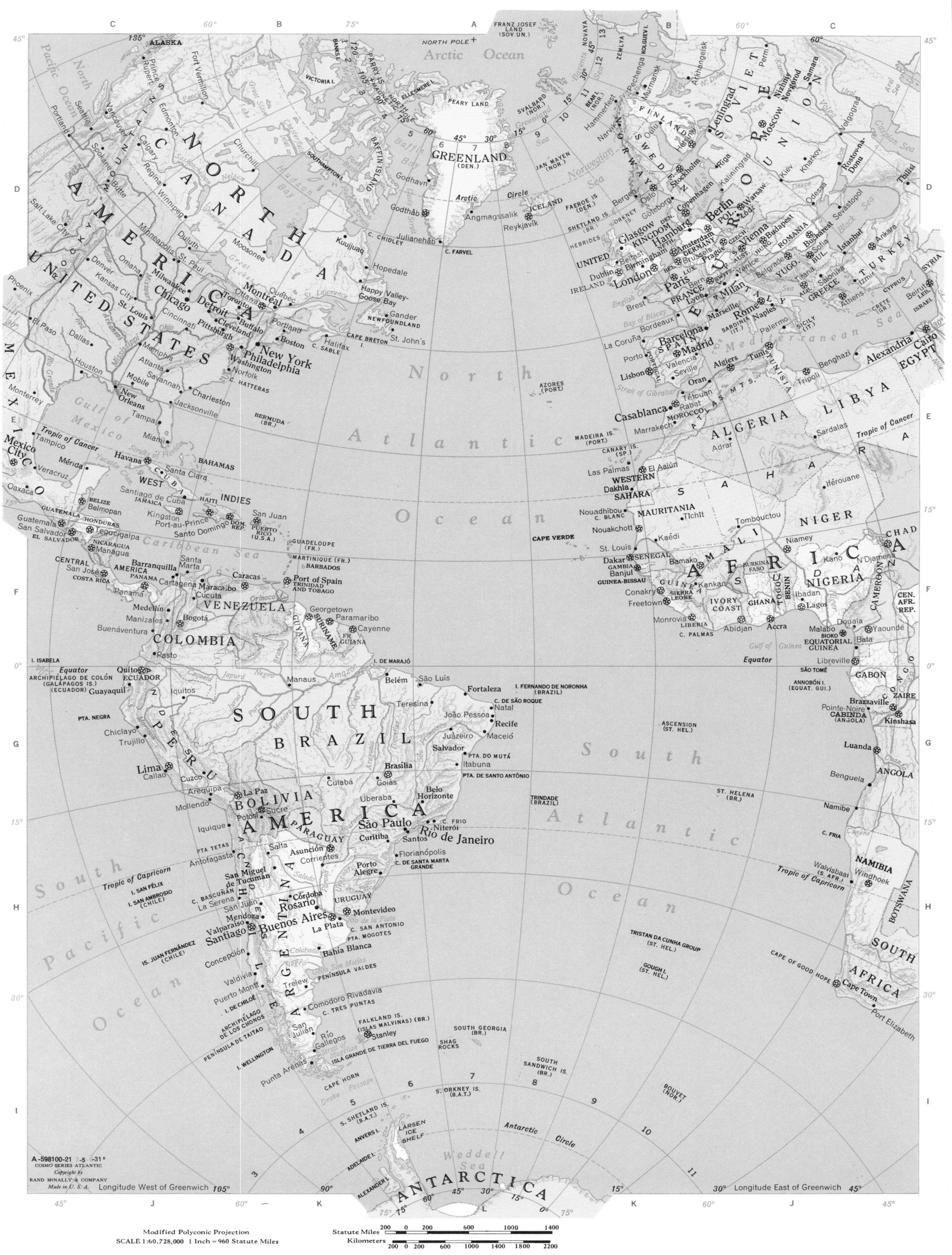

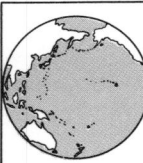

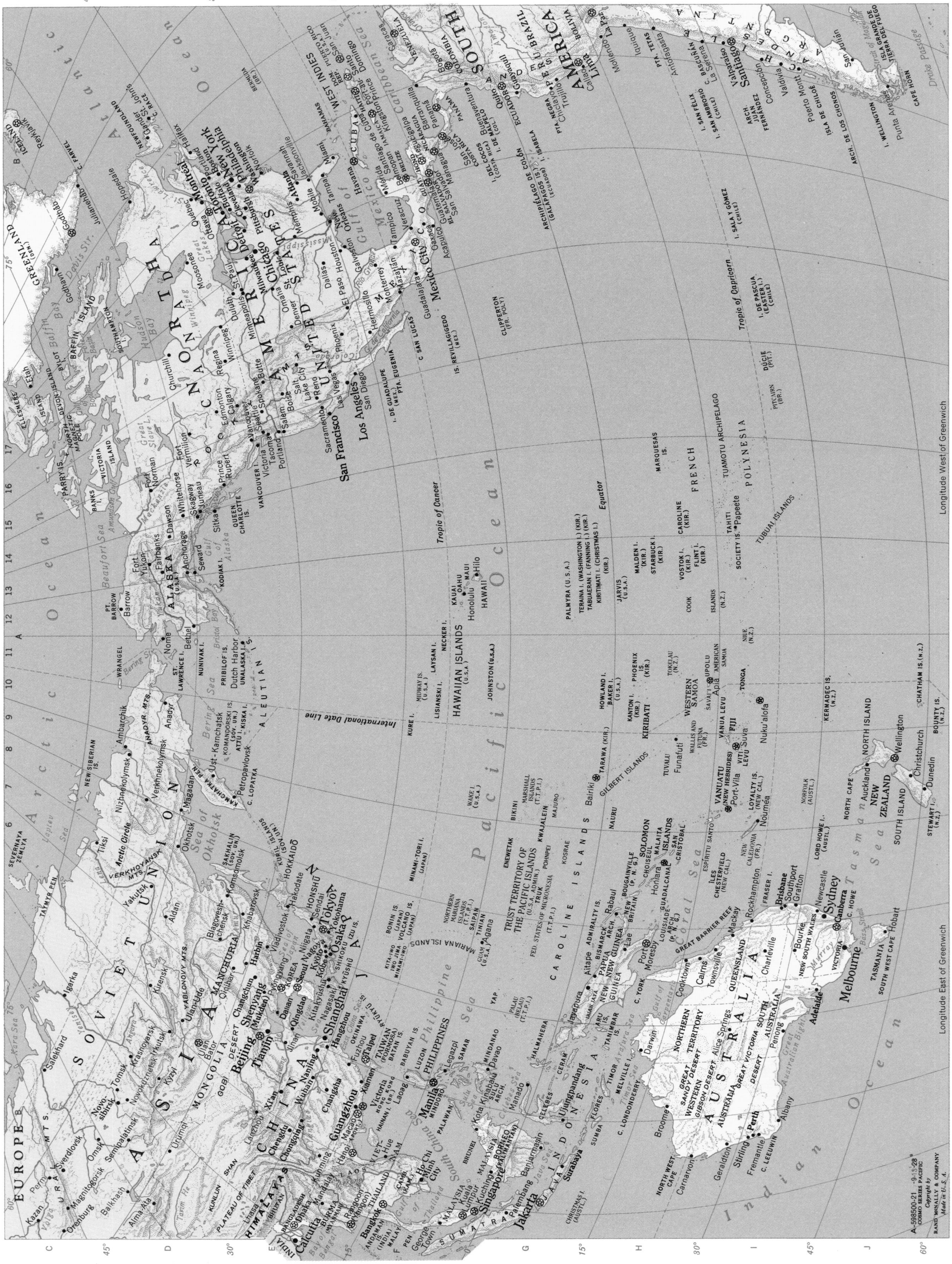

Modified Secant Conic Projection
SCALE 1:66,800,000 1 Inch = 1,040 Statute Miles

Statute Miles
200 0 200 600 1000 1400

Kilometers
200 0 200 600 1000 1400 1800 2200

Modified Secant Conic Projection
SCALE 1:66,800,000 1 Inch = 1,040 Statute Miles

A-59B500-21 -91-15-28*
RAND M?NALLY & COMPANY
Copyright by
RAND M?NALLY & COMPANY
Made in U.S.A.

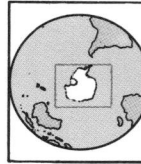

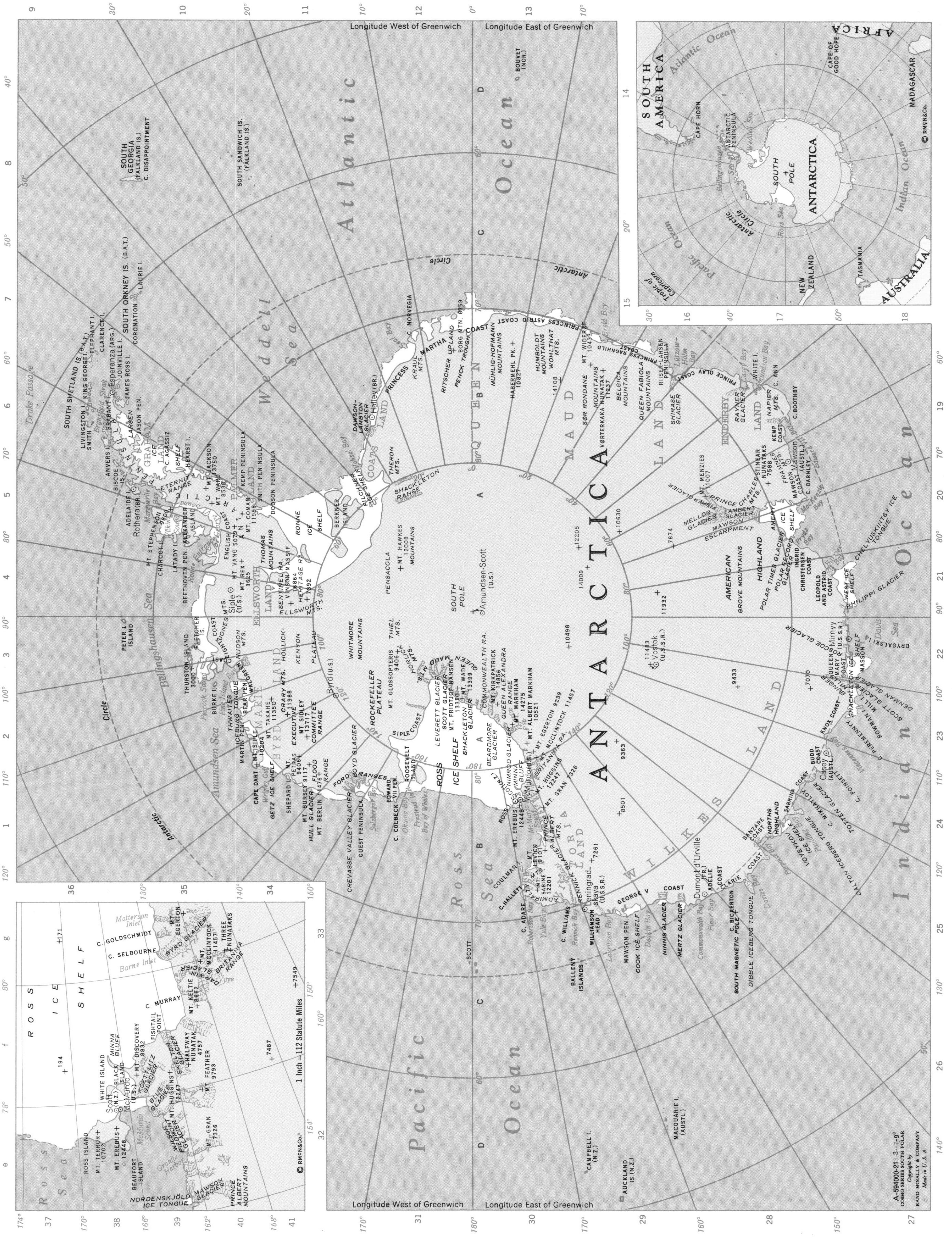

Main Map

Longitude West of Greenwich | Longitude East of Greenwich

ANTARCTICA

SOUTH POLE
Amundsen-Scott (U.S.)

Atlantic Ocean
Indian Ocean
Pacific Ocean

Weddell Sea
Ross Sea
Amundsen Sea
Bellingshausen Sea
Drake Passage

Antarctic Circle

QUEEN MAUD LAND
ENDERBY LAND
WILKES LAND
VICTORIA LAND
MARIE BYRD LAND
ELLSWORTH LAND
COATS LAND
PALMER LAND
GRAHAM LAND
PRINCESS MARTHA COAST
PRINCESS ASTRID COAST
PRINCE OLAV COAST

SOUTH GEORGIA (FALKLAND IS.)
C. DISAPPOINTMENT
SOUTH SANDWICH IS. (FALKLAND IS.)
SOUTH ORKNEY IS. (B.A.T.)
CORONATION IS. LAURIE I.
SOUTH SHETLAND IS. (B.A.T.)
ELEPHANT I. CLARENCE I.
KING GEORGE I. JOINVILLE I. JAMES ROSS I.
LIVINGSTON I. SMITH I.
SNOW HILL I.
ESPERANZA (ARG.)
JASON PEN.
LARSEN ICE SHELF
BRABANT I.
ANVERS I.
BISCOE IS.
ADELAIDE I.
Rothera (BR.)
Stephenson (BR.)
Marguerite Bay
ALEXANDER ISLAND
CHARCOT I.
PETER I Ø ISLAND
THURSTON ISLAND
FLETCHER IS.
BERKNER ISLAND
RONNE ICE SHELF
FILCHNER ICE SHELF
SHACKLETON RANGE
THERON MTS.
PENSACOLA MOUNTAINS
THIEL MTS.
WHITMORE MOUNTAINS
ELLSWORTH MTS.
SENTINEL RA.
SIPLE (U.S.)
BYRD (U.S.)
ROCKEFELLER PLATEAU
EXECUTIVE COMMITTEE RANGE
ROOSEVELT ISLAND
ROSS ICE SHELF
EDWARD VII PEN.
BAY OF WHALES
MT. EREBUS 12448
MT. MARKHAM 14275
MT. KIRKPATRICK 14856
BEARDMORE GLACIER
QUEEN ALEXANDRA RANGE
COMMONWEALTH RA.
C. ADARE
C. HALLETT
BALLENY ISLANDS
Dumont d'Urville (FR.)
ADÉLIE COAST
MACQUARIE I. (AUST.)
CAMPBELL I. (N.Z.)
AUCKLAND IS. (N.Z.)
MAWSON (AUST.)
Casey (AUST.)
Vostok (U.S.S.R.) 11483
BOUVET (NOR.)
MÜHLIG-HOFMANN MOUNTAINS
HUMBOLDT MOUNTAINS
SØR RONDANE MOUNTAINS
BELGICA MOUNTAINS
WOHLTHAT MTS.
LAMBERT GLACIER
PRINCE CHARLES MTS.
AMERICAN HIGHLAND
POLAR TIMES GLACIER
NORTHS HIGHLAND
SHACKLETON ICE SHELF
WEST ICE SHELF
AMERY ICE SHELF
SOUTH MAGNETIC POLE

Inset Map (Upper Right)

SOUTH AMERICA
AFRICA
AUSTRALIA
NEW ZEALAND
TASMANIA
MADAGASCAR
ANTARCTICA
ANTARCTIC PENINSULA
SOUTH POLE
CAPE HORN
CAPE OF GOOD HOPE
Atlantic Ocean
Pacific Ocean
Indian Ocean
Weddell Sea
Ross Sea
Bellingshausen Sea
Arctic Circle
Tropic of Capricorn
© RM&N Co.

Inset Map (Lower Left)

ROSS ICE SHELF
ROSS SEA
Matterson Inlet
C. GOLDSCHMIDT
C. SELBOURNE
Barne Inlet
BYRD GLACIER
THREE NUNATAKS
C. MURRAY
HALFWAY NUNATAK
WHITE ISLAND
BLACK ISLAND
MINNA BLUFF
Scott (N.Z.)
McMurdo (U.S.)
MT. DISCOVERY
MT. EREBUS 12448
MT. TERROR 10702
ROSS ISLAND
BEAUFORT ISLAND
McMurdo Sound
PRINCE ALBERT MOUNTAINS
NORDENSKJÖLD ICE TONGUE
MAWSON GLACIER
1 Inch = 112 Statute Miles
© RM&N Co.

Lambert Azimuthal Equal Area Projection
SCALE 1:28,000,000   1 Inch = 442 Statute Miles

Statute Miles 100 0 100 200 300 400 500
Kilometers 100 0 100 300 500 700

A-594000-21 13-7-9
COMBINED BEARING SOUTH POLAR
Copyright by
RAND MCNALLY & COMPANY
Made in U.S.A.

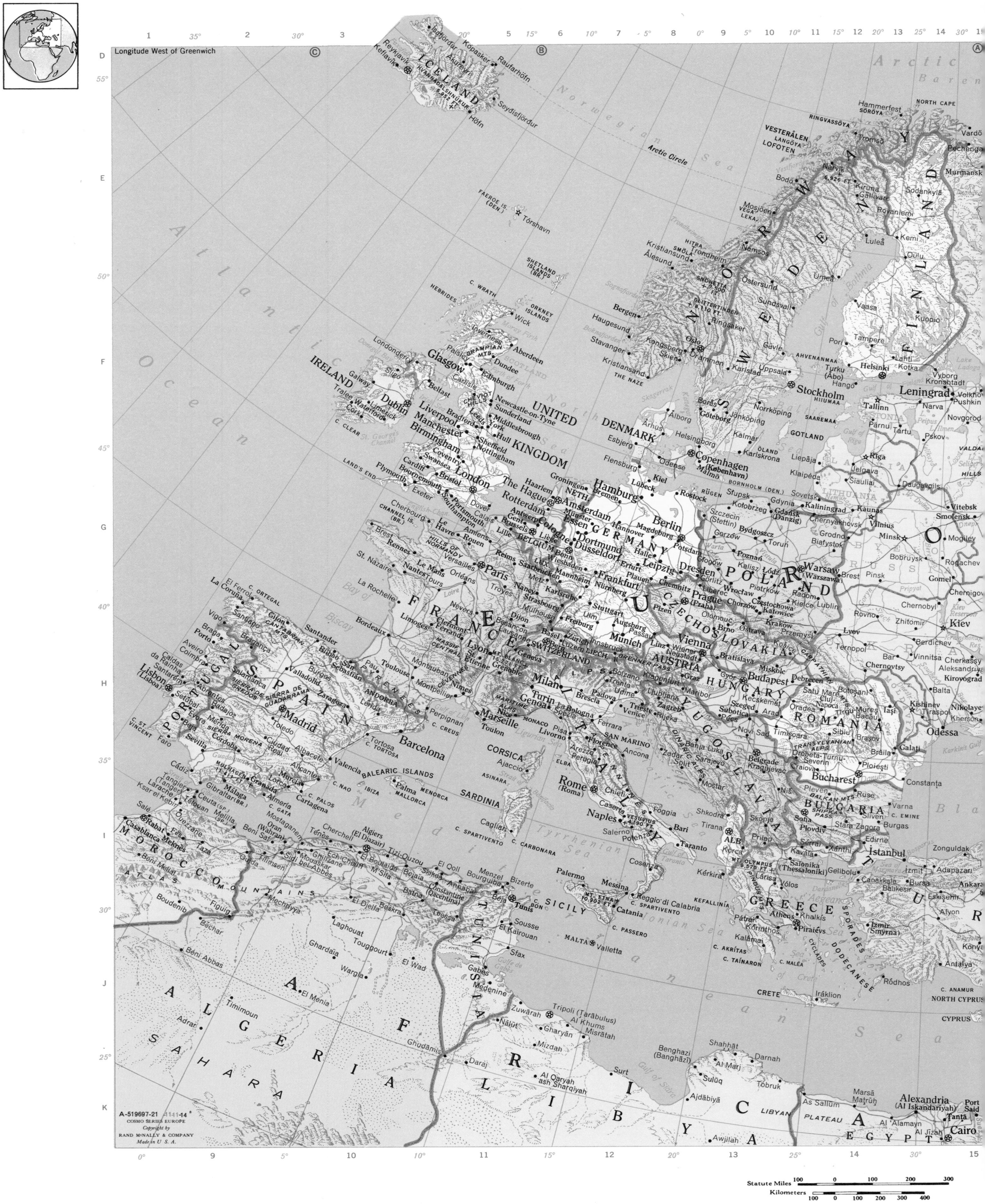

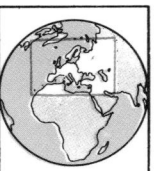

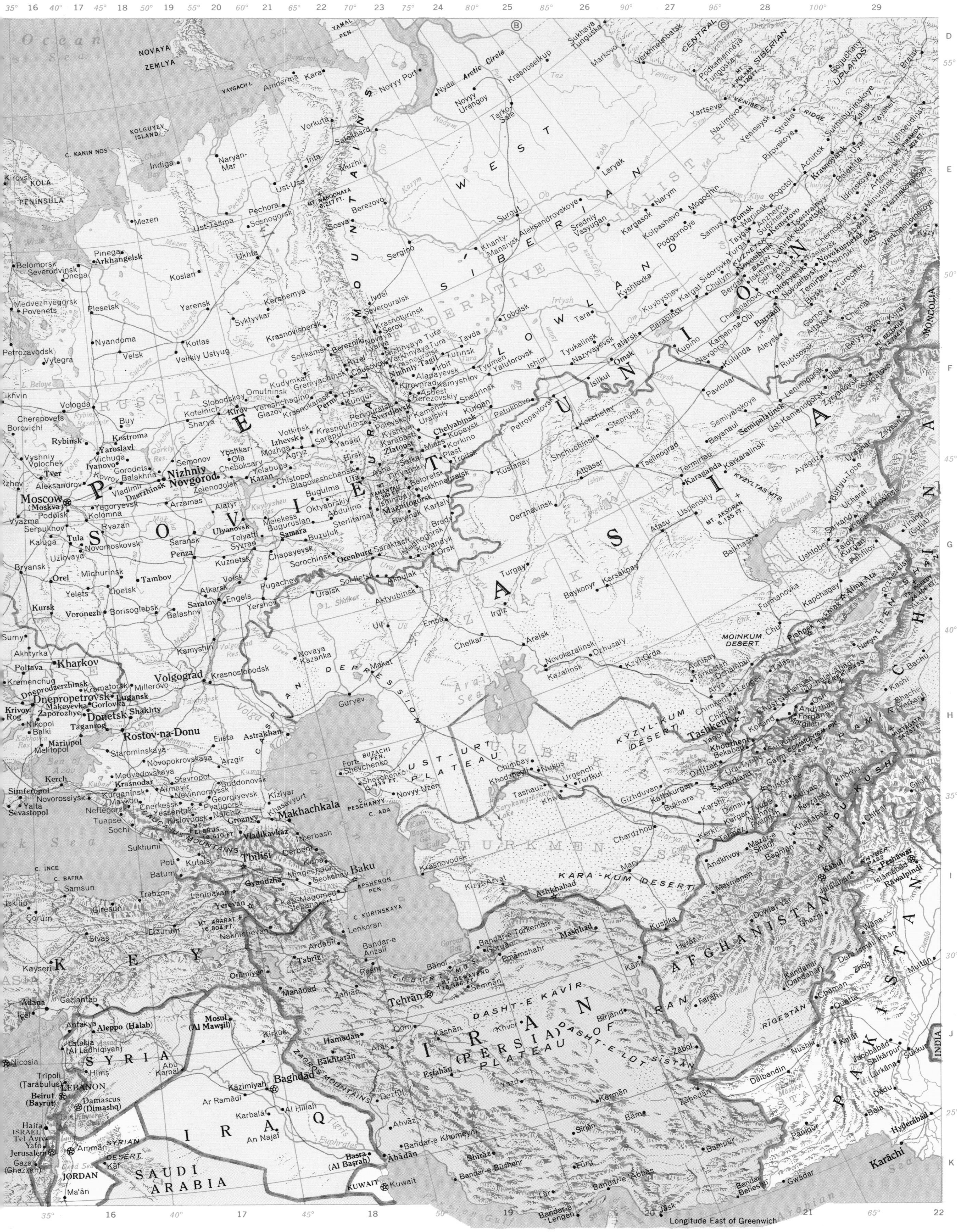

Map — Soviet Union and surrounding regions

Top border longitude/latitude markings:
35° 16 40° 17 45° 18 50° 19 55° 20 60° 21 65° 22 70° 23 75° 24 80° 25 85° 26 90° 27 95° 28 100° 29

Major country / region labels:
SOVIET FEDERATIVE SOCIALIST REPUBLIC
RUSSIAN SOVIET FEDERATIVE SOCIALIST REPUBLIC
UNION
WEST SIBERIAN LOWLAND
CENTRAL SIBERIAN UPLANDS
KAZAKHSTAN S.S.R.
UZBEK S.S.R.
TURKMEN S.S.R.
IRAN (PERSIA)
AFGHANISTAN
PAKISTAN
INDIA
CHINA
MONGOLIA
IRAQ
SYRIA
SAUDI ARABIA
JORDAN
LEBANON
ISRAEL
TURKEY

Seas / bodies of water:
Ocean Sea
Kara Sea
White Sea
Aral Sea
Caspian Sea
Black Sea
Sea of Azov
Persian Gulf
Baydaratskaya Bay
Pechora Bay

Deserts / physical:
DASHT-E KAVÎR
DASHT-E LÛT
KARA-KUM DESERT
KYZYL-KUM DESERT
MOINKUM DESERT
RIGESTAN
USTYURT PLATEAU
PLATEAU OF IRAN
ZAGROS MOUNTAINS
HINDU KUSH
CAUCASUS MOUNTAINS
TIAN SHAN
NOVAYA ZEMLYA

Selected cities (west to east, north to south):
Moscow (Moskva), Nizhniy Novgorod, Yaroslavl, Ivanovo, Tver, Vologda, Kirov, Perm, Izhevsk, Kazan, Ulyanovsk, Samara, Saratov, Penza, Tambov, Voronezh, Kursk, Orel, Tula, Ryazan, Vladimir
Arkhangelsk, Naryan-Mar, Vorkuta, Syktyvkar, Ukhta, Pechora
Sverdlovsk, Chelyabinsk, Magnitogorsk, Nizhniy Tagil, Tyumen, Kurgan, Omsk, Novosibirsk, Tomsk, Kemerovo, Barnaul, Krasnoyarsk, Kyzyl
Kharkov, Dnepropetrovsk, Donetsk, Rostov-na-Donu, Volgograd, Astrakhan
Krasnodar, Stavropol, Grozny, Makhachkala, Vladikavkaz, Tbilisi, Baku, Yerevan, Sukhumi, Batumi
Orenburg, Uralsk, Aktyubinsk, Guryev, Kzyl-Orda, Karaganda, Tselinograd, Semipalatinsk, Pavlodar, Ust-Kamenogorsk, Alma-Ata, Tashkent, Samarkand, Bukhara, Ashkhabad, Chardzhou
Tehrān, Mashhad, Eşfahān, Shīrāz, Tabrīz, Hamadān, Qom, Kermān, Zāhedān, Abādān, Ahvāz
Kabul, Herāt, Qandahār, Mazār-e Sharīf
Baghdad, Basra (Al Başrah), Mosul (Al Mawşil), Karbalā, An Najaf
Damascus (Dimashq), Aleppo (Halab), Beirut (Bayrūt), Tripoli (Ṭarābulus), Jerusalem, Tel Aviv, Amman, Nicosia
Kuwait, Rawalpindi, Islāmābād, Peshāwar, Karachi, Hyderabad, Quetta

Mountain elevations:
MT. NARODNAYA 6,217 FT.
MT. ARARAT 16,804 FT.
ELBRUS 18,510 FT.
MT. AKSORAN 5,135 FT.

Arctic Circle

Bottom:
Longitude East of Greenwich

Conic Projection
SCALE 1:16,000,000   1 Inch = 252 Statute Miles

9

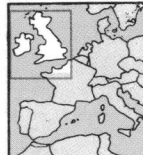

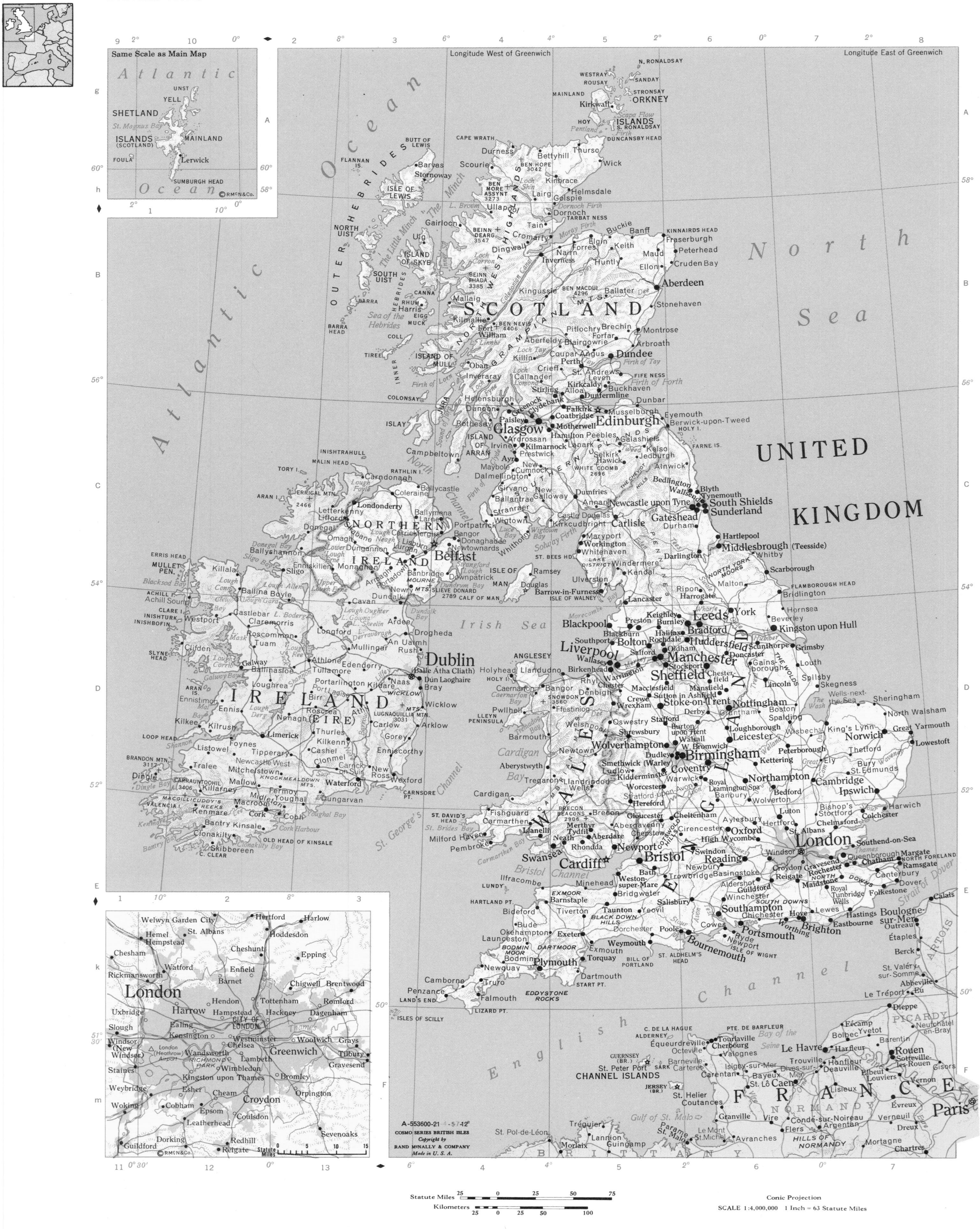

Same Scale as Main Map
Atlantic Ocean
SHETLAND ISLANDS (SCOTLAND)
UNST
YELL
MAINLAND
St. Magnus Bay
FOULA
Lerwick
SUMBURGH HEAD
Longitude West of Greenwich
Longitude East of Greenwich
Atlantic Ocean
North Sea
UNITED KINGDOM
SCOTLAND
IRELAND (EIRE)
NORTHERN IRELAND
WALES
ENGLAND
FRANCE
NORMANDY
BRITTANY
PICARDY
ARTOIS
ORKNEY ISLANDS
N. RONALDSAY
WESTRAY
ROUSAY
SANDAY
STRONSAY
MAINLAND
Kirkwall
HOY
S. RONALDSAY
Scapa Flow
Pentland Firth
DUNCANSBY HEAD
CAPE WRATH
BUTT OF LEWIS
FLANNAN IS.
ISLE OF LEWIS
OUTER HEBRIDES
Barvas
Stornoway
The Minch
The Little Minch
NORTH UIST
SOUTH UIST
BARRA
BARRA HEAD
ISLAND OF SKYE
Uig
CANNA
RHUM
EIGG
MUCK
COLL
TIREE
Sea of the Hebrides
ISLAND OF MULL
INNER HEBRIDES
COLONSAY
ISLAY
JURA
Durness
Scourie
Thurso
Wick
Bettyhill
BEN HOPE 3042
BEN MORE ASSYNT 3273
Kinbrace
Helmsdale
Lairg
Golspie
Ullapool
L. Broom
Dornoch
Dornoch Firth
TARBAT NESS
Tain
Gairloch
BEINN DEARG 3547
Cromarty
Moray Firth
Dingwall
Inverness
Nairn
Forres
Elgin
Buckie
Banff
KINNAIRDS HEAD
Fraserburgh
Peterhead
Keith
Huntly
Maud
Ellon
Cruden Bay
Aberdeen
Stonehaven
Loch Ness
Caledonian Canal
NORTHWEST HIGHLANDS
GRAMPIAN MTS.
BEINN BHADA 3385
Kingussie
BEN MACDUI 4296
Ballater
Dee
Mallaig
Kilmallie
BEN NEVIS 4406
Fort William
Linnhe
Pitlochry
Brechin
Montrose
Forfar
Arbroath
Aberfeldy
Blairgowrie
Coupar Angus
Dundee
Firth of Tay
Perth
Killin
Loch Tay
Oban
Firth of Lorn
Crieff
St. Andrews
Leven
FIFE NESS
Firth of Forth
Inveraray
Callander
Loch Lomond
Kirkcaldy
Buckhaven
Stirling
Alloa
Dunfermline
Dunbar
Helensburgh
Dunoon
Greenock
Clydebank
Falkirk
Coatbridge
Musselburgh
Eyemouth
Edinburgh
Berwick-upon-Tweed
HOLY I.
Rothesay
Paisley
Glasgow
Motherwell
Hamilton
Peebles
Galashiels
Ardrossan
Lanark
Kelso
Jedburgh
FARNE IS.
ISLAND OF ARRAN
Irvine
Kilmarnock
SOUTHERN UPLANDS
Selkirk
Hawick
Ayr
Prestwick
Campbeltown
Maybole
New Cumnock
WHITE COOMB 2696
THE CHEVIOT HILLS
Alnwick
Dalmellington
Girvan
Ballantrae
Stranraer
Dumfries
Annan
Newton Stewart
New Galloway
Castle Douglas
Kirkcudbright
Wigtown
Whithorn
Luce Bay
Wigtown Bay
Solway Firth
Bedlington
Blyth
Wallsend
Tynemouth
South Shields
Sunderland
Newcastle upon Tyne
Gateshead
Carlisle
Durham
Hartlepool
Middlesbrough (Teesside)
Whitby
Darlington
INISHTRAHULL
MALIN HEAD
TORY I.
RATHLIN I.
ARAN I.
ERRIGAL MTN. 2466
Carndonagh
Lough Foyle
Coleraine
Ballycastle
North Channel
Londonderry
Letterkenny
Lifford
Ballymena
Larne
Donegal
Strabane
Lough Neagh
Carrickfergus
Portpatrick
Bangor
Donaghadee
Newtownards
Omagh
Dungannon
Lisburn
Lurgan
Belfast
Donegal Bay
Ballyshannon
Sligo Bay
Enniskillen
Monaghan
Lower Lough Erne
Upper Lough Erne
Strangford Lough
Armagh
Portadown
Banbridge
MOURNE MTS.
Downpatrick
Dundrum Bay
SLIEVE DONARD 2789
Newry
Dundalk
Dundalk Bay
ISLE OF MAN
Ramsey
Douglas
CALF OF MAN
ERRIS HEAD
MULLET PEN.
Killala
Blacksod Bay
Lough Conn
Lough Allen
Sligo
Ballina
Boyle
ACHILL HEAD
Achill Sound
Lough Mask
Lough Gara
CLARE I.
INISHTURK
INISHBOFIN
Westport
Castlebar
Claremorris
L. Boderg
Cavan
Lough Oughter
L. Gowna
L. Sheelin
Longford
Ardee
Drogheda
Roscommon
Tuam
Mullingar
Lough Derravaragh
An Uaimh
Rush
SLYNE HEAD
Clifden
Lough Corrib
Lough Ree
Galway
Athlone
Ballinasloe
Tullamore
Edenderry
Dublin (Baile Átha Cliath)
Dún Laoghaire
Bray
Galway Bay
Loughrea
Portarlington
Kildare
Naas
WICKLOW MTS.
Wicklow
ARAN IS.
Ennistimon
Ennis
Lough Derg
Birr
Roscrea
Nenagh
Athy
Carlow
LUGNAQUILLIA MTN. 3031
Arklow
Kilkee
Kilrush
Shannon
LOOP HEAD
Limerick
Thurles
Kilkenny
Gorey
Foynes
Tipperary
Cashel
Listowel
Enniscorthy
BRANDON MTN. 3117
Tralee
Newcastle West
Mitchelstown
Clonmel
Carrick on Suir
New Ross
Wexford
Dingle
Dingle Bay
CARRAUNTOOHIL 3406
Killarney
Mallow
KNOCKMEALDOWN MTS.
Waterford
CARNSORE PT.
MACGILLICUDDY'S REEKS
VALENCIA I.
Fermoy
Youghal
Dungarvan
Macroom
Kenmare
Cork
Youghal Bay
Cobh
Cork Harbour
Bantry
Kinsale
Bantry Bay
Clonakilty
Clonakilty Bay
OLD HEAD OF KINSALE
Skibbereen
C. CLEAR
St. George's Channel
Irish Sea
ST. BEES HD.
Maryport
Workington
Whitehaven
LAKE DISTRICT
Windermere
Kendal
Ulverston
Barrow-in-Furness
ISLE OF WALNEY
Morecambe Bay
PENNINES
Lancaster
Ripon
Harrogate
NORTH YORK MOORS
Malton
Scarborough
FLAMBOROUGH HEAD
Bridlington
York
Blackpool
Preston
Keighley
Burnley
Leeds
Bradford
Beverley
Hornsea
Kingston upon Hull
Humber
Blackburn
Halifax
Rochdale
Huddersfield
Southport
Bolton
Oldham
Liverpool
Wallasey
Salford
Manchester
Scunthorpe
Grimsby
Doncaster
THE WOLDS
Birkenhead
Stockport
Sheffield
Gainsborough
Louth
ANGLESEY
Holyhead
Llandudno
HOLY I.
Rhyl
Chester
Warrington
Chesterfield
Macclesfield
Mansfield
Lincoln
Spilsby
Skegness
Caernarfon
Caernarfon Bay
Bangor
Denbigh
Crewe
Sutton in Ashfield
SNOWDON 3560
Wrexham
Stoke-on-Trent
Nottingham
Wells-next-the-Sea
The Wash
Sheringham
Festiniog
Derby
Grantham
Boston
North Walsham
Pwllheli
LLEYN PENINSULA
Tremadog Bay
Oswestry
Stafford
Spalding
King's Lynn
Great Yarmouth
Barmouth
Welshpool
Shrewsbury
Burton upon Trent
Loughborough
Leicester
Wisbech
Norwich
Lowestoft
Walsall
W. Bromwich
Wolverhampton
Cardigan Bay
Newtown
Dudley
Birmingham
Peterborough
Thetford
Aberystwyth
Smethwick (Warley)
Coventry
Kettering
Bury St. Edmunds
Ely
Ludlow
Kidderminster
Northampton
Cambridge
Tregaron
CAMBRIAN MTS.
Llandrindod Wells
Worcester
Warwick
Royal Leamington Spa
Bedford
Ipswich
Cardigan
Stratford-upon-Avon
Banbury
Wolverton
Harwich
Hereford
Luton
Bishop's Stortford
Colchester
ST. DAVID'S HEAD
St. Brides Bay
Fishguard
Carmarthen
BRECON BEACONS 2906
Brecon
Gloucester
Cheltenham
COTSWOLD HILLS
Aylesbury
Hertford
St. Albans
Chelmsford
Milford Haven
Pembroke
Llanelli
Merthyr Tydfil
Abergavenny
Cirencester
Oxford
High Wycombe
London
Southend-on-Sea
Neath
Aberdare
Chepstow
Swindon
Windsor
Thames
Margate
Carmarthen Bay
Swansea
Rhondda
Cardiff
Newport
Bristol
Reading
Queenborough
NORTH FORELAND
Ramsgate
Bristol Channel
Bath
Newbury
Croydon
Gravesend
Chatham
Rochester
Canterbury
Dover
Strait of Dover
Ilfracombe
Weston-super-Mare
Trowbridge
Basingstoke
Reigate
NORTH DOWNS
Maidstone
Folkestone
LUNDY
Minehead
EXMOOR
Bridgwater
Aldershot
Guildford
Royal Tunbridge Wells
Calais
HARTLAND PT.
Barnstaple
Bideford
Salisbury
Winchester
SOUTH DOWNS
Lewes
Hastings
Boulogne-sur-Mer
Tiverton
Taunton
Yeovil
Southampton
Chichester
Hove
Brighton
Eastbourne
Outreau
Bude
BLACK DOWN HILLS
Avon
Cowes
Worthing
Okehampton
Dorchester
Poole
Portsmouth
Étaples
Launceston
Exeter
Ryde
Newport
ISLE OF WIGHT
BODMIN MOOR
DARTMOOR
Weymouth
Bournemouth
Berck
Bodmin
Exmouth
Torquay
BILL OF PORTLAND
ST. ALDHELM'S HEAD
Newquay
Plymouth
Dartmouth
St. Valéry-sur-Somme
Abbeville
Camborne
START PT.
Penzance
Truro
LAND'S END
Falmouth
Le Tréport
Eu
EDDYSTONE ROCKS
LIZARD PT.
English Channel
Dieppe
ISLES OF SCILLY
Fécamp
Neufchâtel-en-Bray
C. DE LA HAGUE
PTE. DE BARFLEUR
Bay of the Seine
Yvetot
Bolbec
ALDERNEY
Équeurdreville
Tourlaville
Cherbourg
Valognes
Le Havre
Harfleur
Barentin
Rouen
Octeville
Sotteville-lès-Rouen
GUERNSEY (BR.)
St. Peter Port
SARK
Barneville-Carteret
Isigny-sur-Mer
Trouville
Honfleur
Deauville
Dives-sur-Mer
Elbeuf
Louviers
Gisors
Vernon
CHANNEL ISLANDS
Carentan
Bayeux
St. Lô
Caen
Lisieux
JERSEY (BR.)
St. Helier
Coutances
Évreux
Gulf of St. Malo
Granville
Vire
Condé-sur-Noireau
Verneuil
Dreux
Paris
Tréguier
Argentan
Flers
St. Pol-de-Léon
Lannion
Paramé
St. Malo
Le Mont St. Michel
Avranches
HILLS OF NORMANDY
Mortagne
Chartres
Morlaix
Guingamp
Welwyn Garden City
Hertford
Harlow
St. Albans
Hemel Hempstead
Hoddesdon
Cheshunt
Chesham
Epping
Watford
Enfield
Rickmansworth
Barnet
Chigwell
Brentwood
London
Hendon
Tottenham
Romford
Harrow
Uxbridge
Hampstead
Hackney
Dagenham
Ealing
CITY OF LONDON
Slough
Kensington
Westminster
Windsor (New Windsor)
London (Heathrow) Airport
Chelsea
Woolwich
Grays
Wandsworth
Greenwich
Tilbury
RICHMOND PARK
Lambeth
Gravesend
Staines
Wimbledon
Kingston upon Thames
Bromley
Weybridge
Esher
Cheam
Croydon
Orpington
Woking
Cobham
Epsom
Coulsdon
Leatherhead
Sevenoaks
Dorking
Redhill
Guildford
Reigate
Statute Miles 0 5 10 15
©RMcN&Co.
A-553600-21 -5-7-12
COSMO SERIES BRITISH ISLES
Copyright by RAND McNALLY & COMPANY
Made in U. S. A.
Statute Miles 25 0 25 50 75
Kilometers 25 0 25 50 100
Conic Projection
SCALE 1:4,000,000 1 Inch = 63 Statute Miles

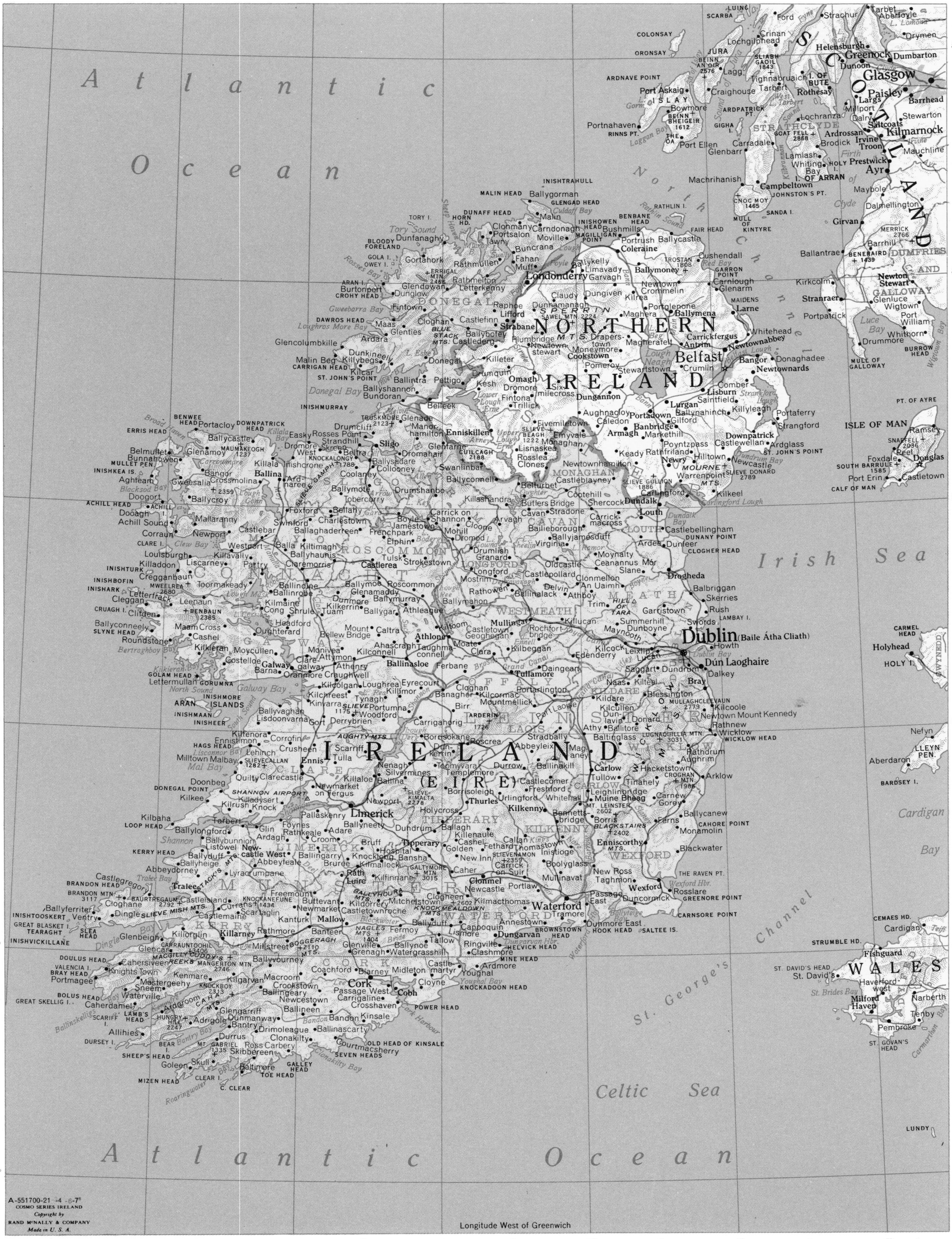

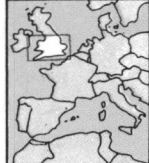

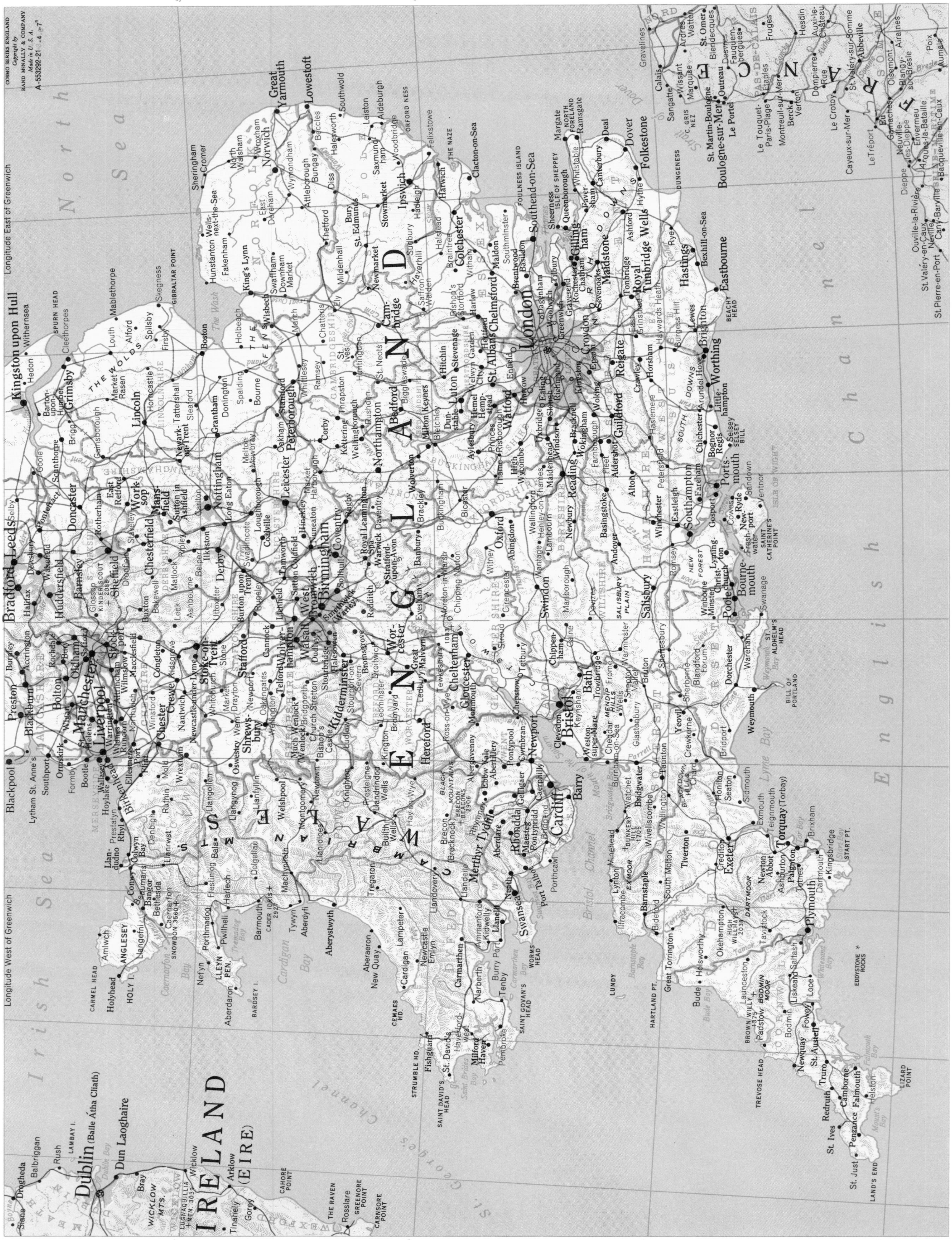

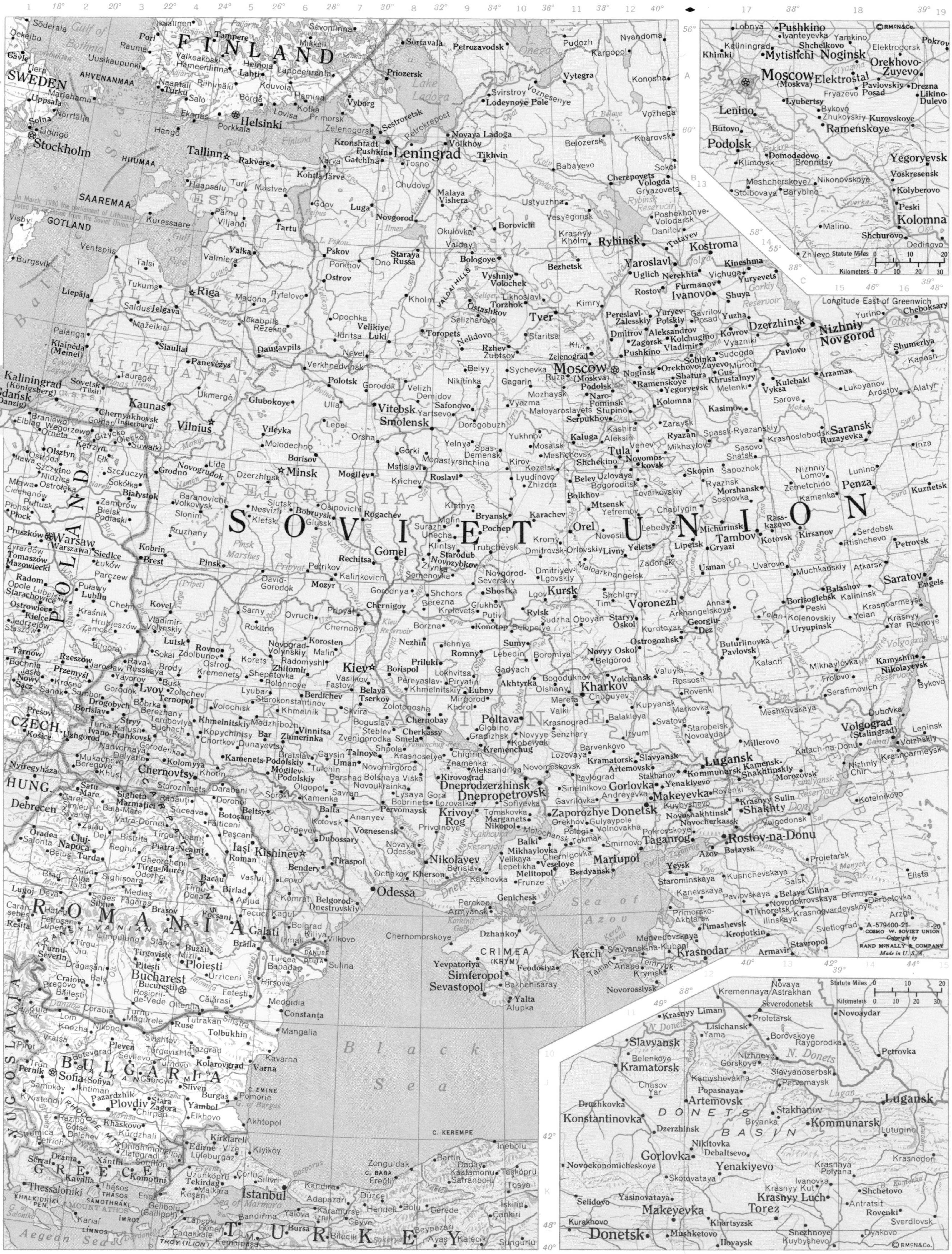

Statute Miles 50 0 50 100 150 200 250

Kilometers 50 0 50 100 150 200 250 300

Sinusoidal Projection

SCALE 1: 11,400,000   1 Inch = 180 Statute Miles

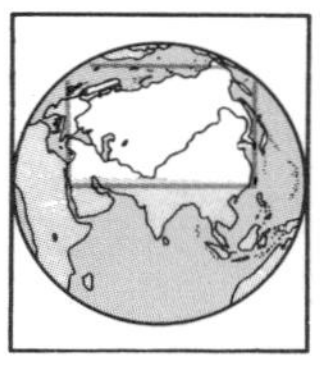

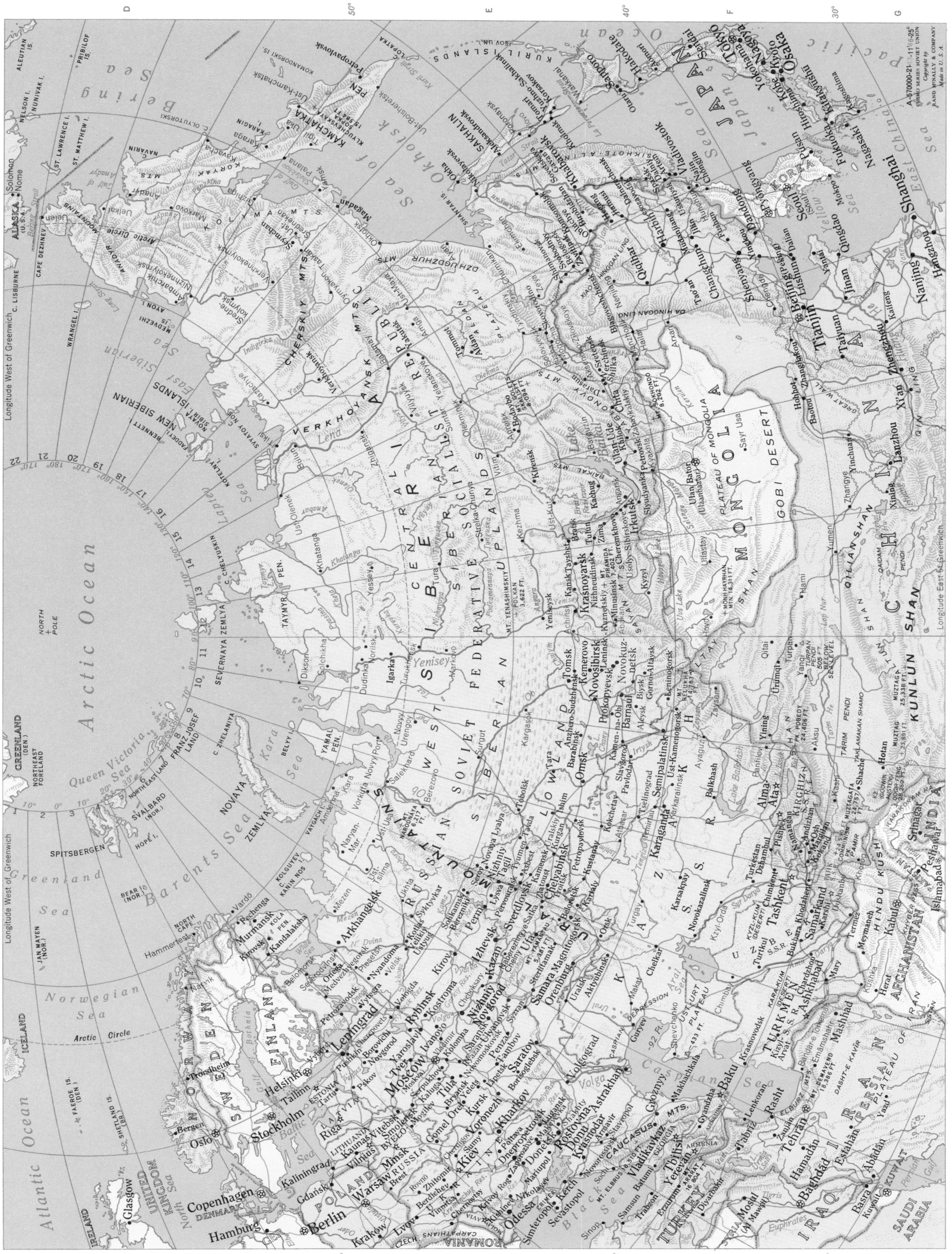

Lambert Azimuthal Equal Area Projection
SCALE 1:28,000,000 1 Inch = 442 Statute Miles

Statute Miles 100 0 100 200 300 400 500
Kilometers 100 0 100 300 500 700

Arctic Ocean
NORTH POLE
Pacific Ocean
Indian Ocean
Atlantic Ocean
Mediterranean Sea
Arabian Sea
Bay of Bengal
South China Sea
Sea of Japan
Sea of Okhotsk
Bering Sea
Caspian Sea
Black Sea
Red Sea
SOVIET UNION
ASIA
EUROPE
AFRICA
CHINA
MONGOLIA
INDIA
PAKISTAN
AFGHANISTAN
IRAN
IRAQ
SAUDI ARABIA
TURKEY
SYRIA
JORDAN
ISRAEL
YEMEN
OMAN
UNITED ARAB EMIRATES
JAPAN
KOREA
BURMA
THAILAND
LAOS
VIETNAM
CAMBODIA
MALAYSIA
INDONESIA
PHILIPPINES
BANGLADESH
NEPAL
BHUTAN
SRI LANKA (CEYLON)
EGYPT
LIBYA
SUDAN
ETHIOPIA
SOMALIA
KENYA
TANZANIA
Tropic of Cancer
Equator
Arctic Circle
Longitude West of Greenwich
Longitude East of Greenwich
A-519695-21 -4-4-4-8
COSMO SERIES EURASIA
Copyright by RAND McNALLY & COMPANY
Made in U.S.A.
Statute Miles 100 0 100 300 500 700 900
Kilometers 100 0 100 300 700 1100
Lambert Azimuthal Equal Area Projection
SCALE 1:42,000,000 1 Inch = 663 Statute Miles

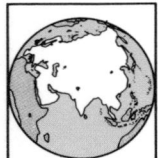

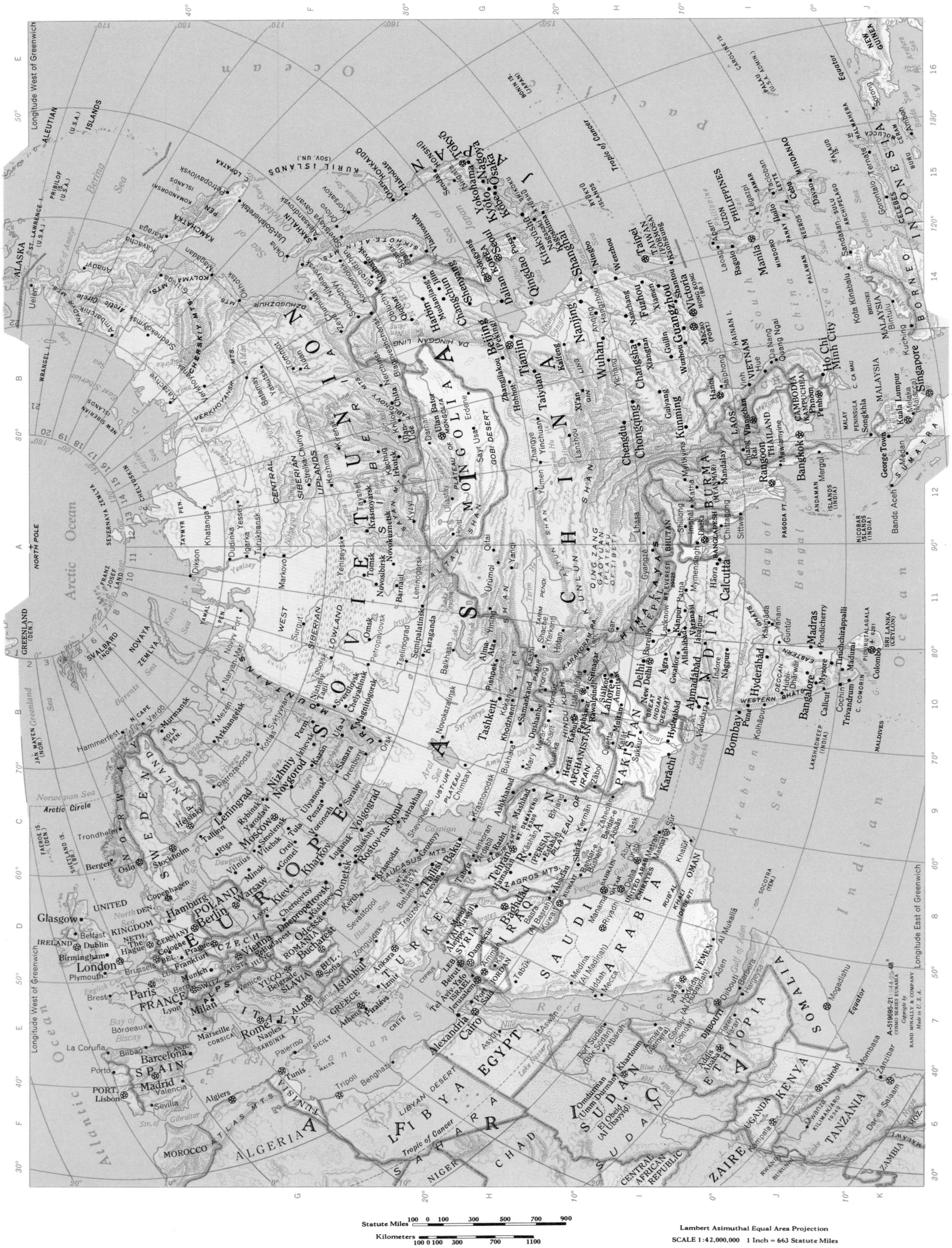

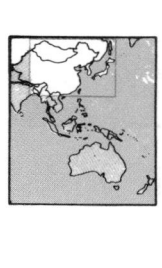

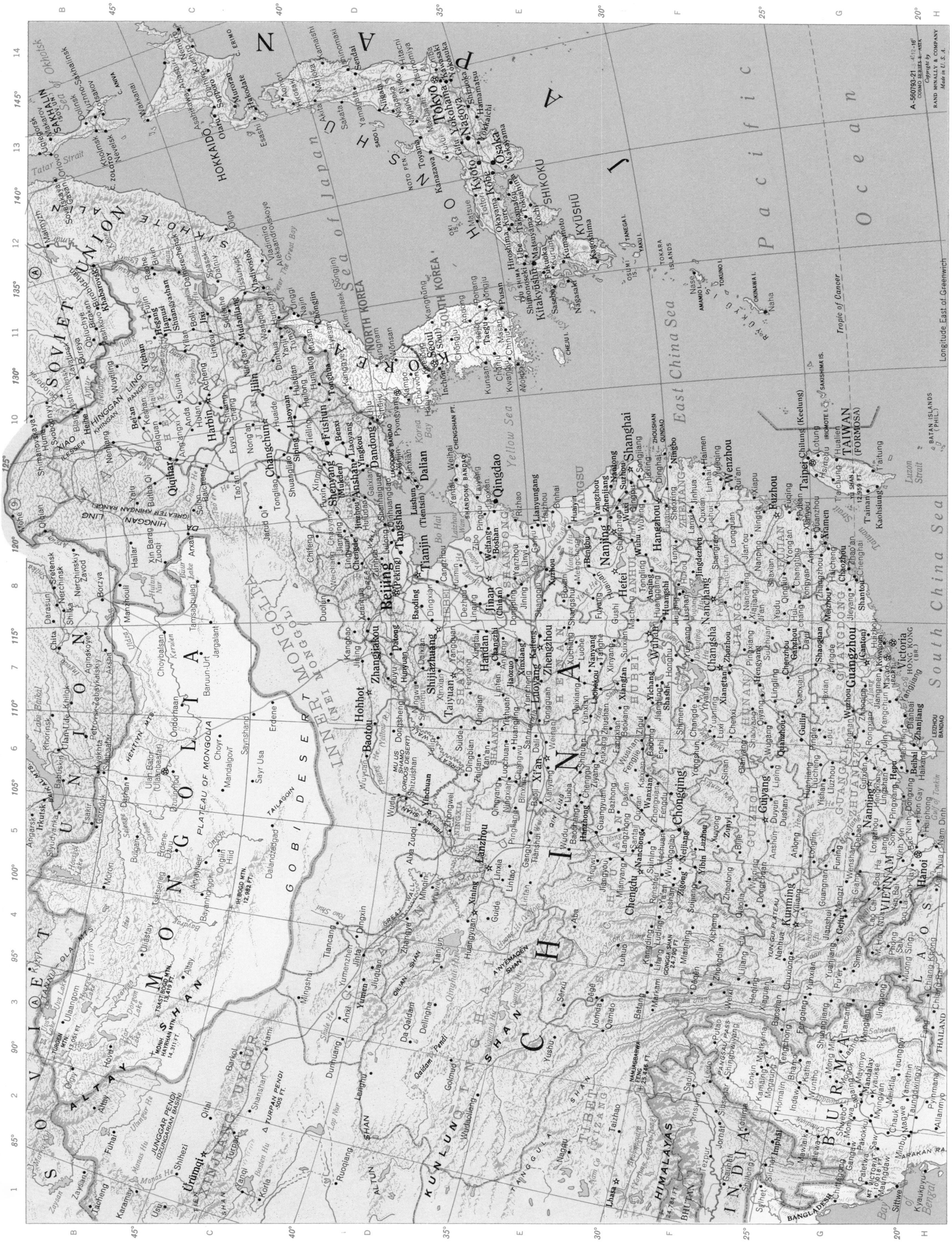

Polyconic Projection

SCALE 1:16,000,000 1 Inch = 252 Statute Miles

Statute Miles 100 0 100 200 300

Kilometers 100 0 100 200 300 400

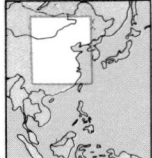

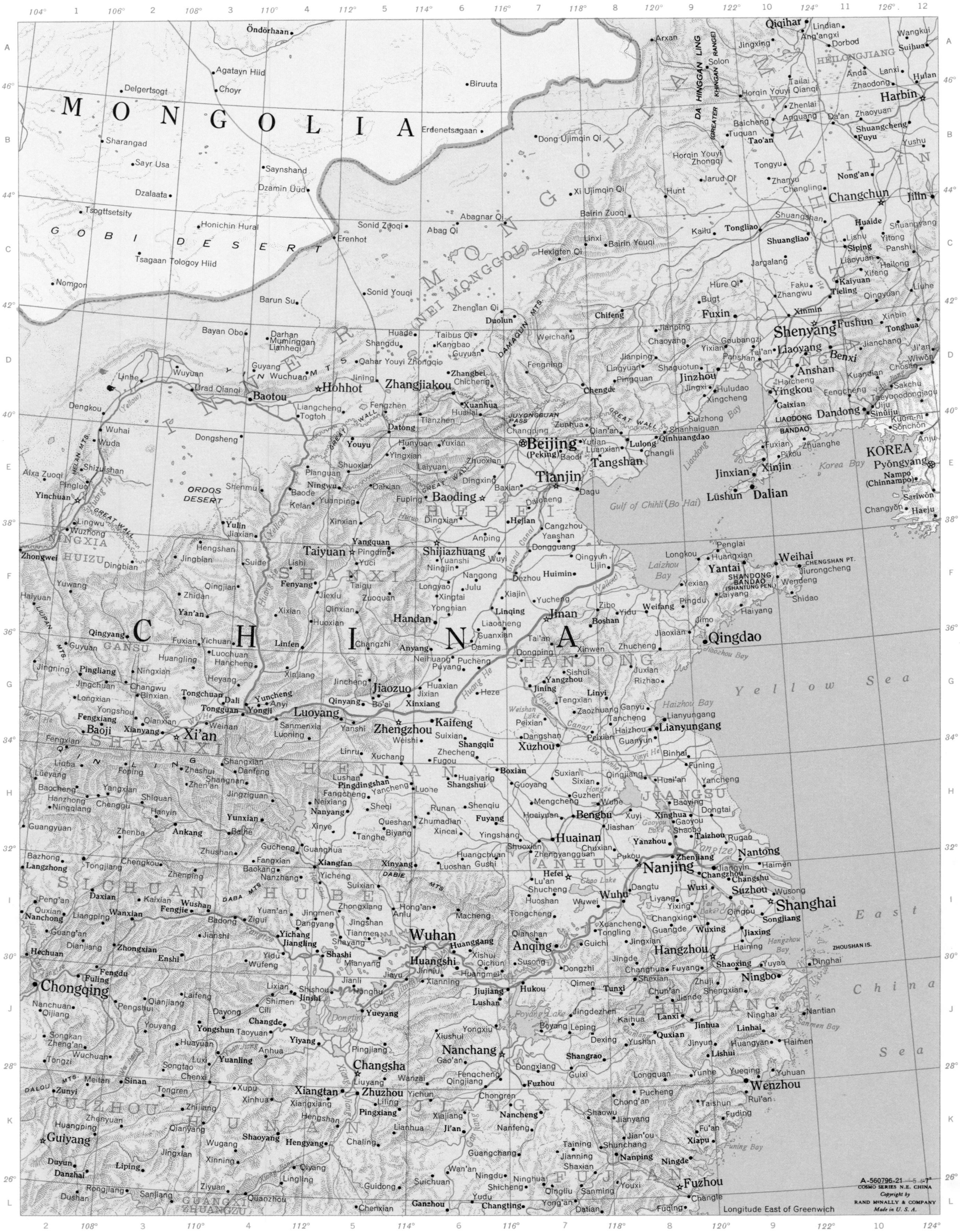

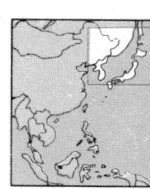

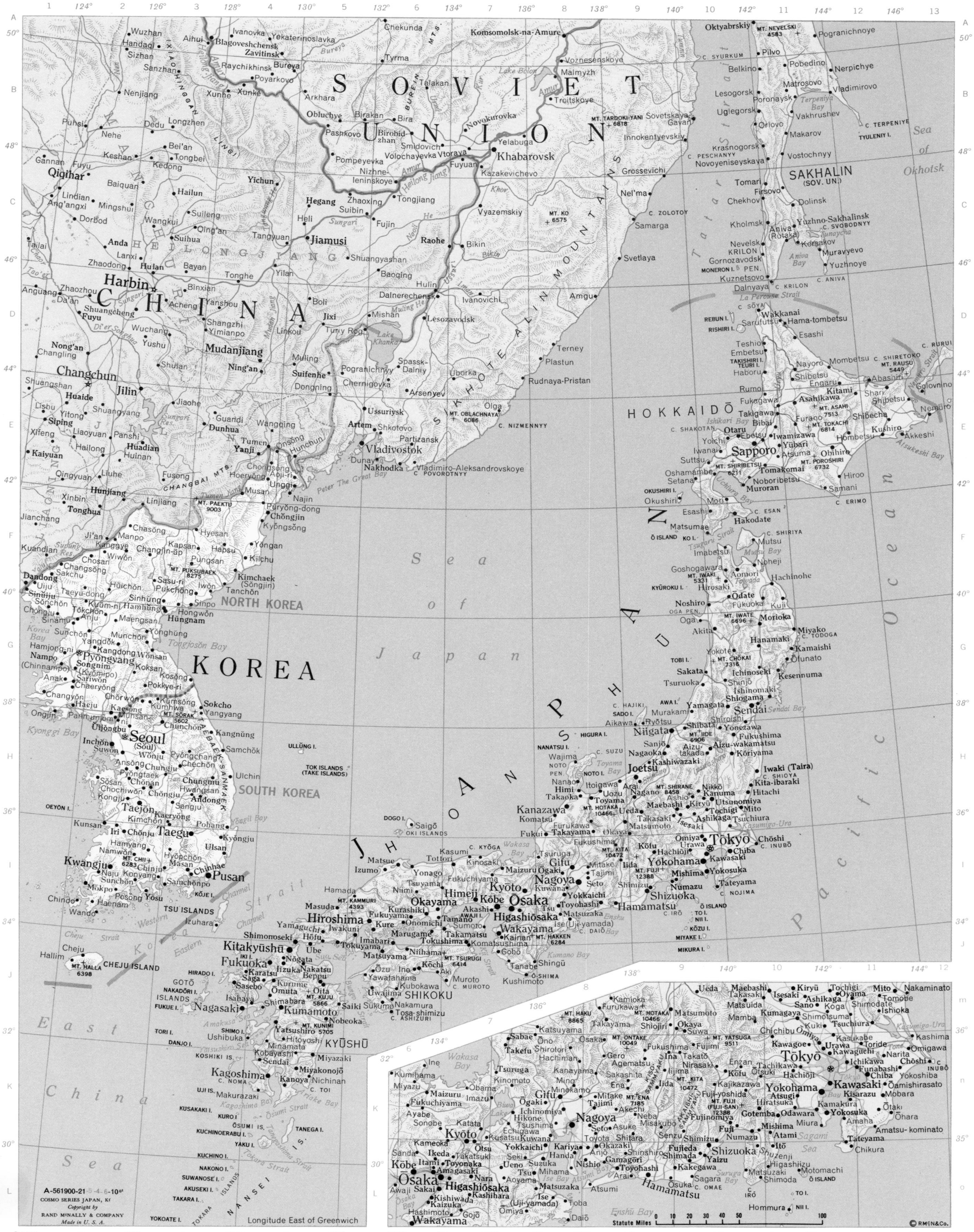

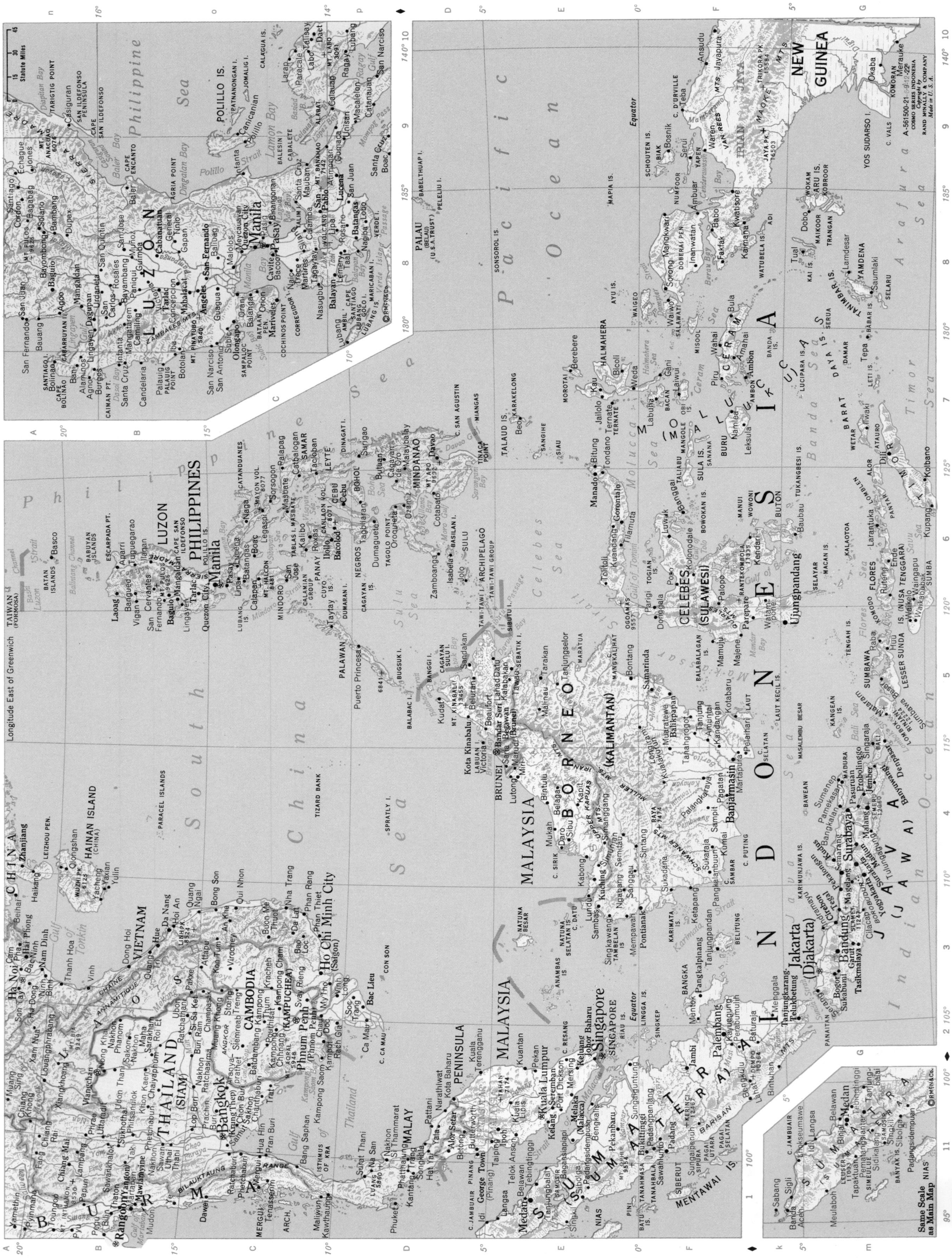

Statute Miles 100 0 100 200 300
Kilometers 100 0 100 200 300 400

Polyconic Projection
SCALE 1:16,000,000 1 Inch = 252 Statute Miles

Same Scale as Main Map

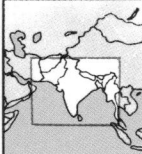

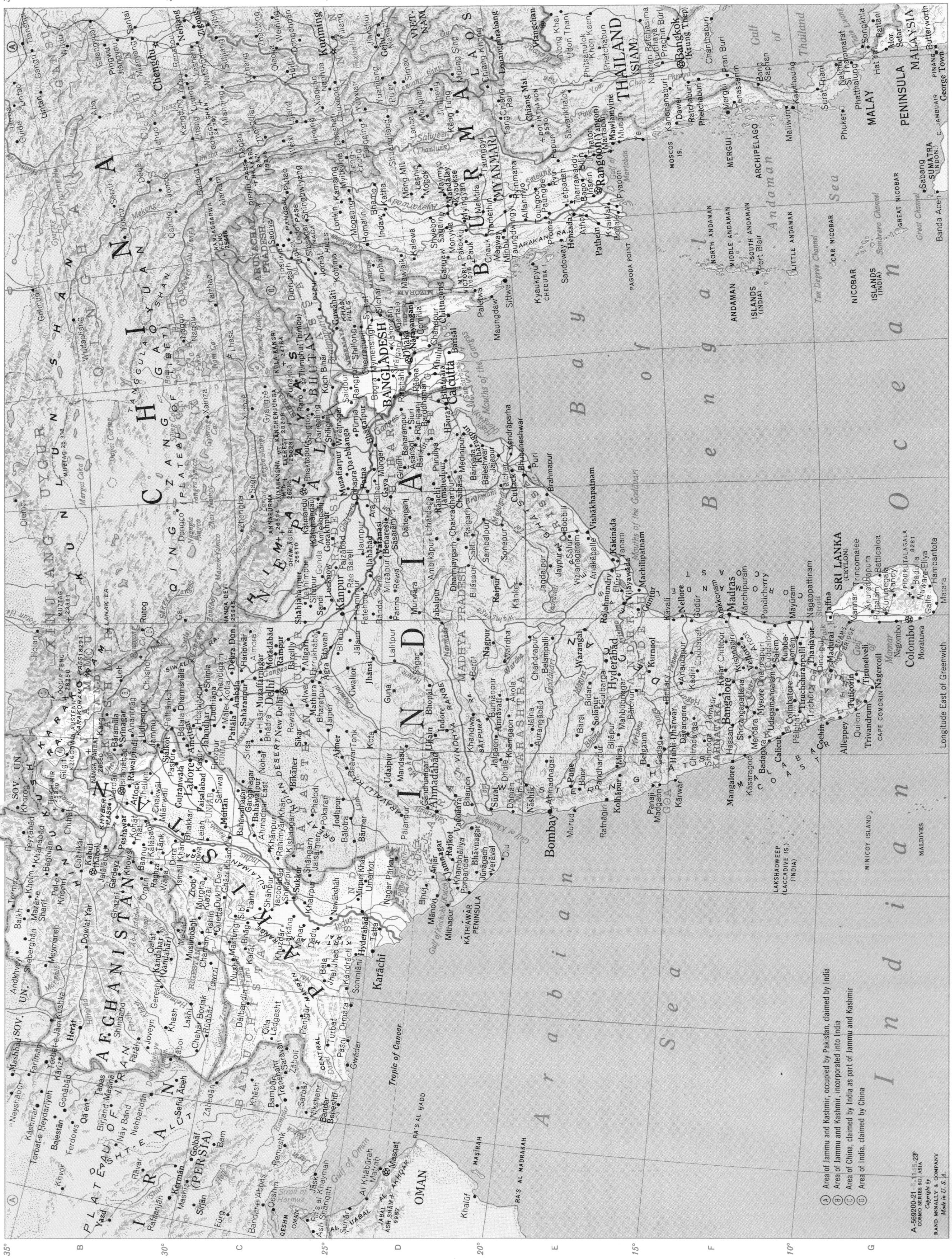

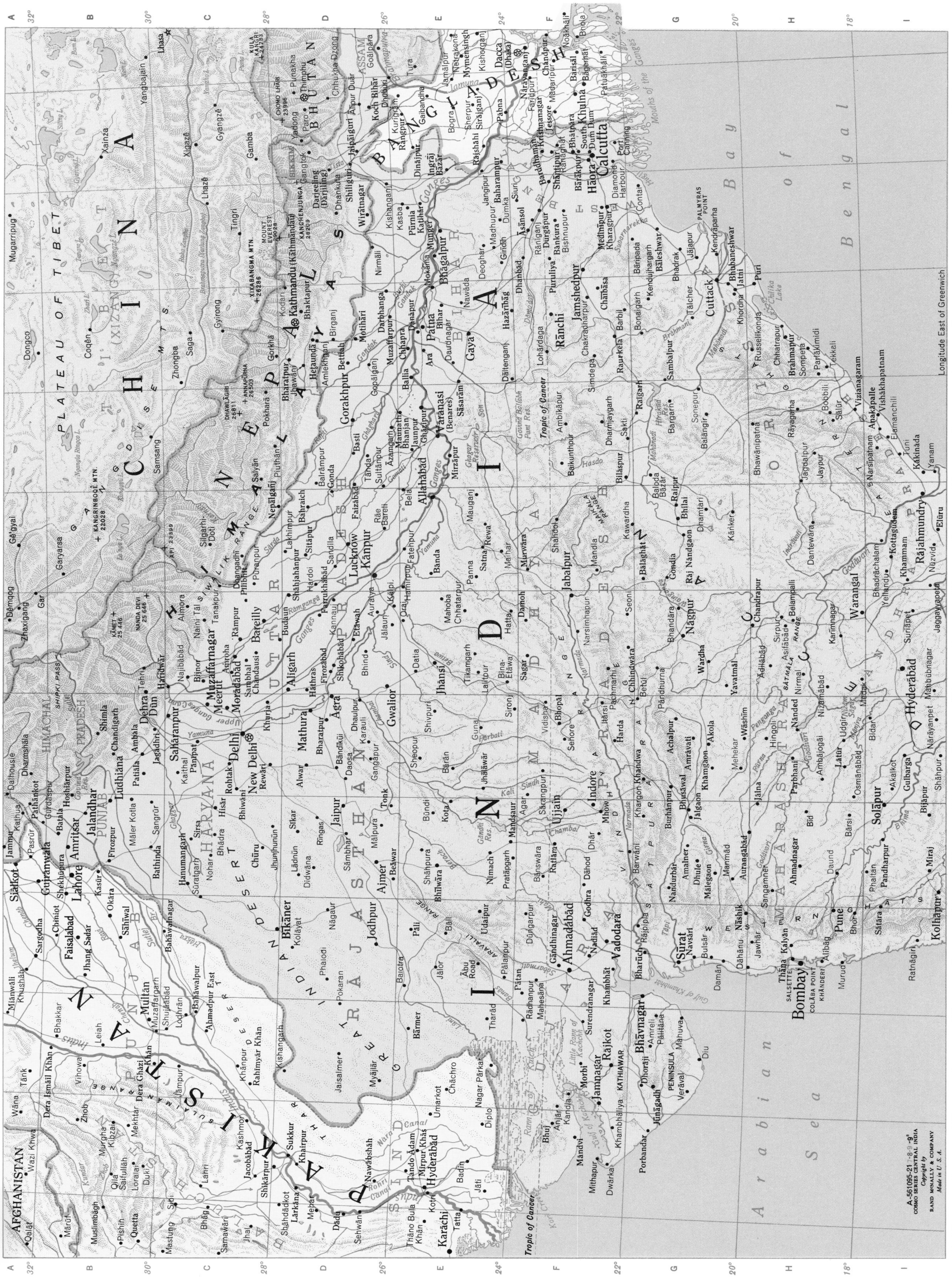

Lambert Conformal Conic Projection
SCALE 1 : 8,000,000   1 Inch = 126 Statute Miles

Statute Miles   50   0   50   100   150
Kilometers   50   0   50   100   200

A-561095-21-ⁱ-8ⁱ-9ⁱ
COSMO SERIES CENTRAL INDIA
Copyright by
RAND M⁰NALLY & COMPANY
Made in U. S. A.

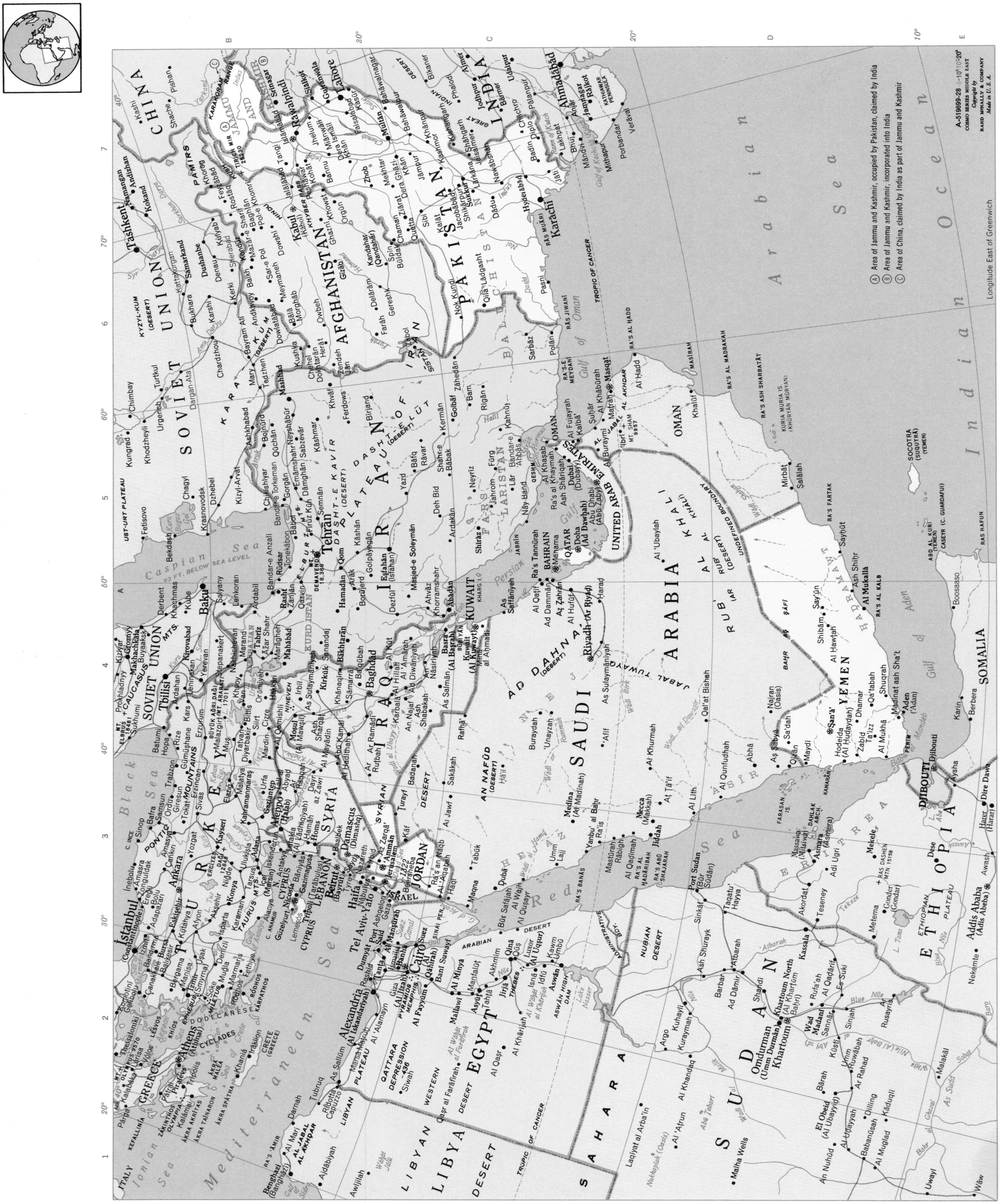

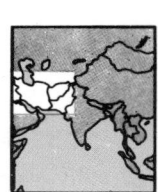

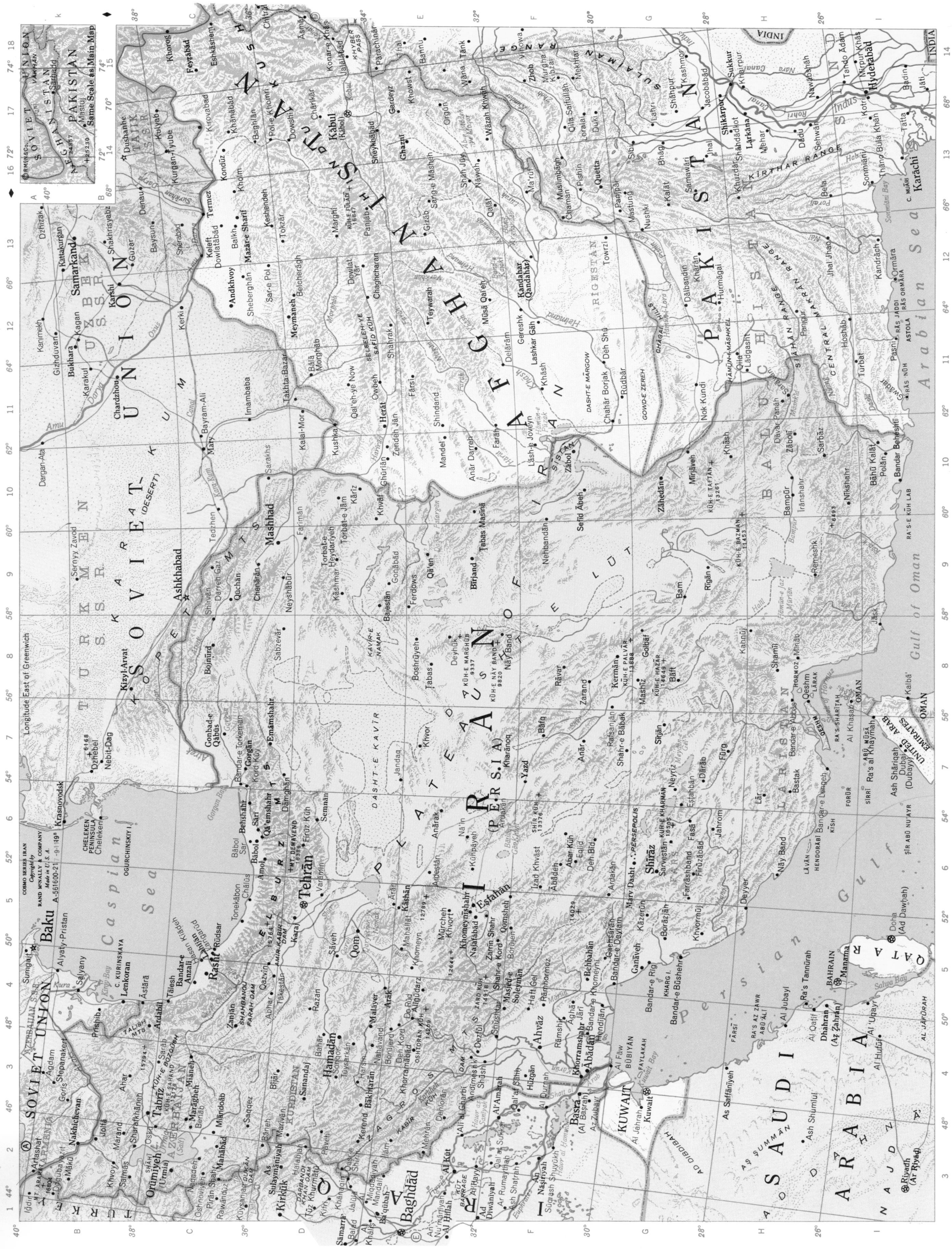

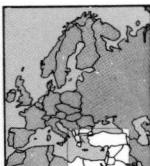

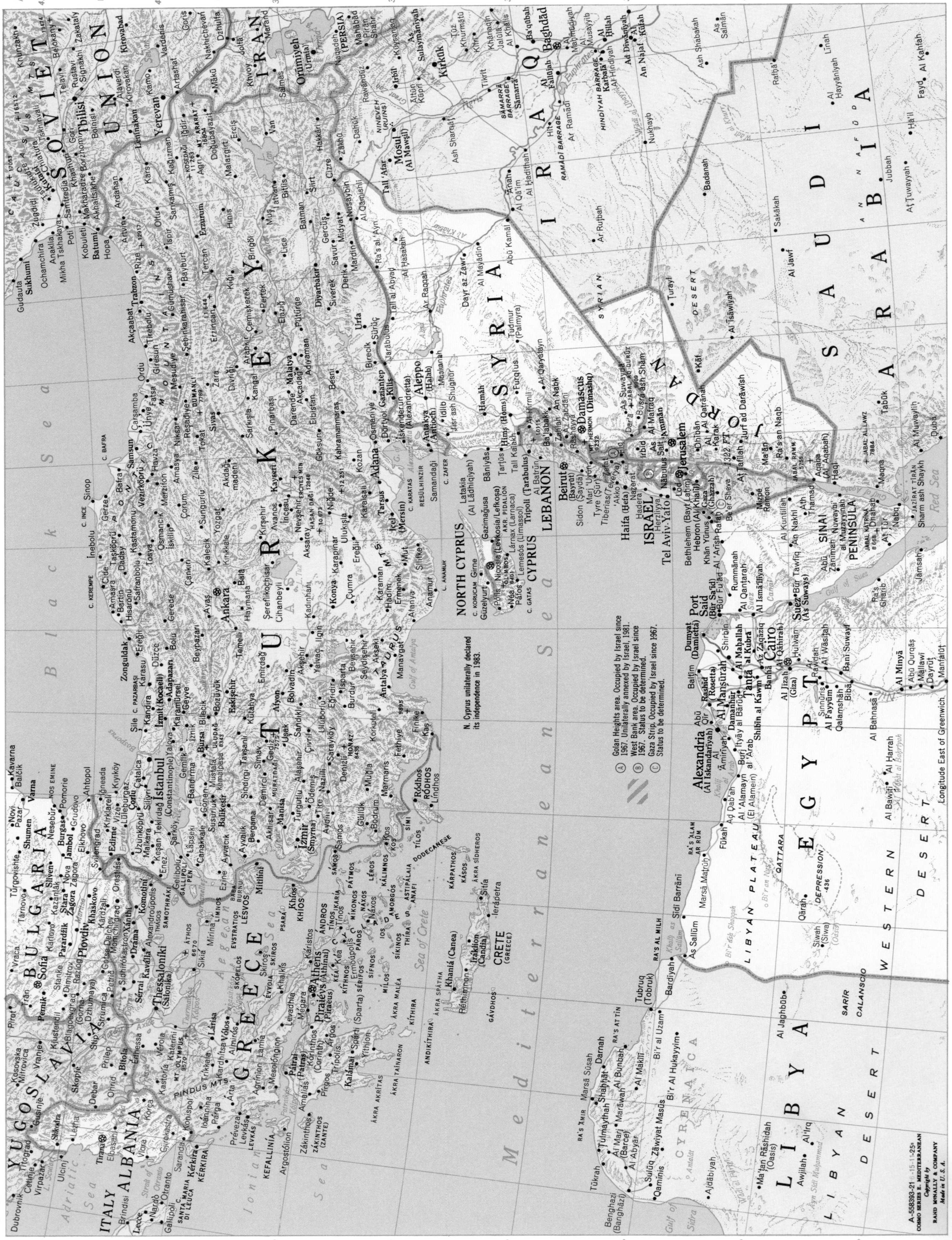
SOVIET UNION
TURKEY
CYPRUS
NORTH CYPRUS
SYRIA
LEBANON
ISRAEL
JORDAN
IRAQ
IRAN
SAUDI ARABIA
EGYPT
LIBYA
GREECE
BULGARIA
YUGOSLAVIA
ALBANIA
ITALY
Black Sea
Mediterranean Sea
Aegean Sea
Ionian Sea
Sea of Crete
Red Sea
N. Cyprus unilaterally declared its independence in 1983.
Ⓐ Golan Heights area. Occupied by Israel since 1967. Unilaterally annexed by Israel, 1981.
Ⓑ West Bank area. Occupied by Israel since 1967. Status to be determined.
Ⓒ Gaza Strip. Occupied by Israel since 1967. Status to be determined.
Longitude East of Greenwich
A-558393-21 -15-11-25-
COMMO SERIES E. MEDITERRANEAN
Copyright by RAND McNALLY & COMPANY
Made in U. S. A.

Statute Miles 50 0 50 100 150

Kilometers 50 0 50 100 200

Lambert Conformal Conic Projection

SCALE 1 : 8,000,000 1 Inch = 126 Statute Miles

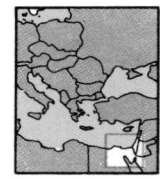

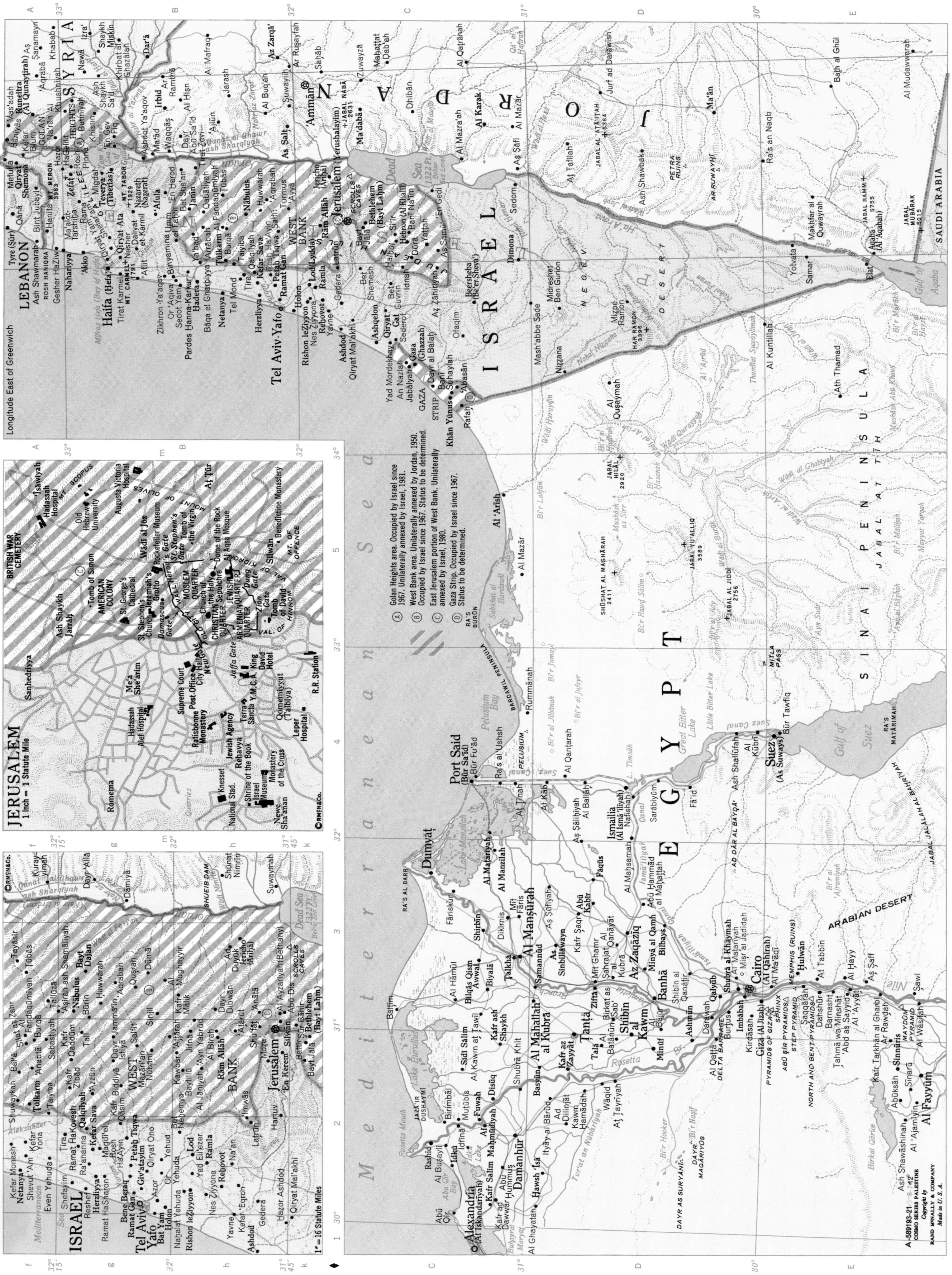

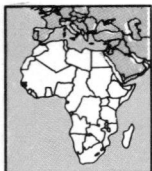

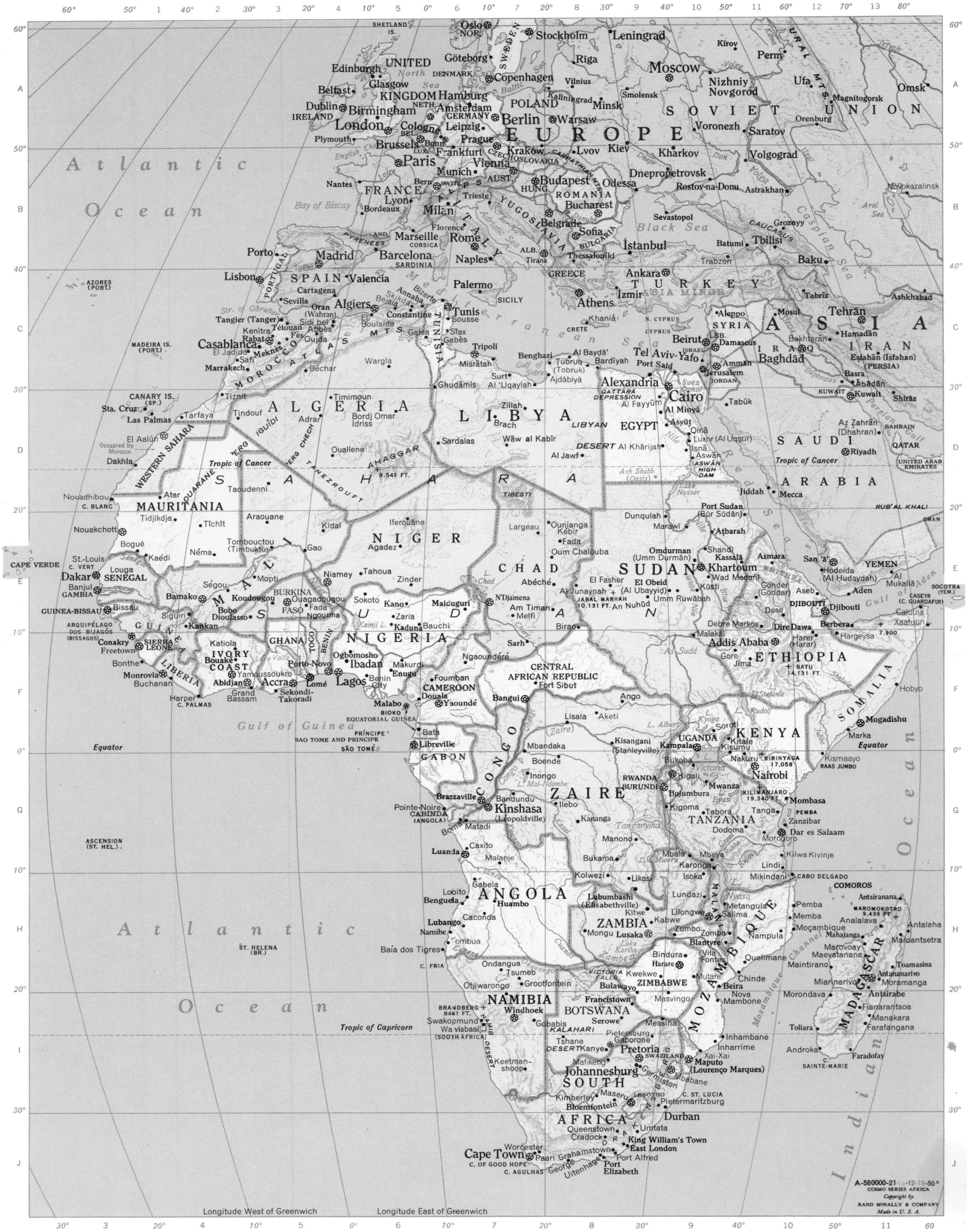

Statute Miles 100 0 100 300 500 700 900

Kilometers 100 0 100 300 500 700 900 1100 1300

Sinusoidal Projection
SCALE 1:36,313,000 1 Inch = 565 Statute Miles

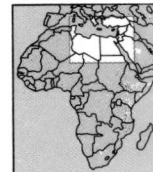

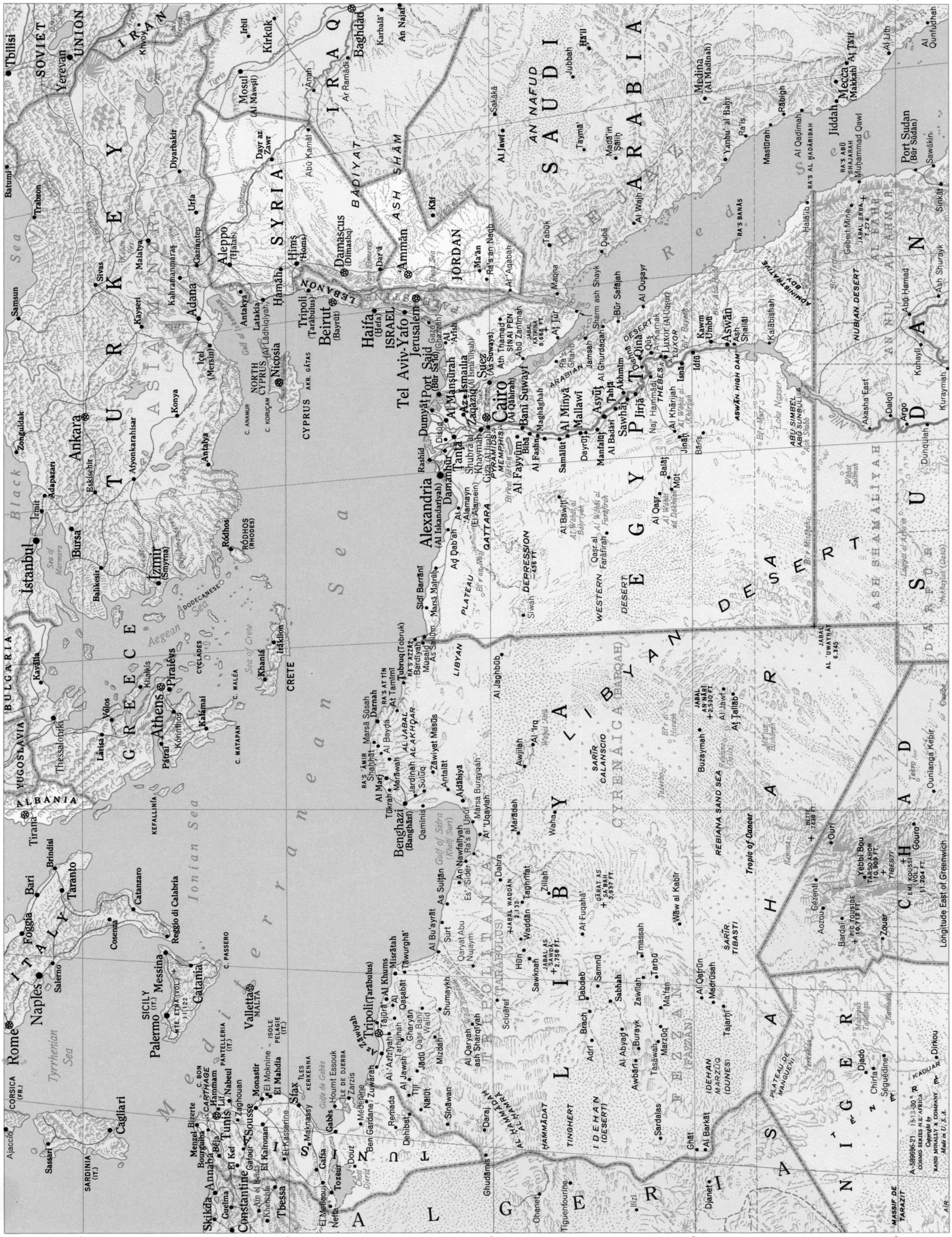

Sinusoidal Projection
SCALE 1 : 11,400,000   1 Inch = 180 Statute Miles

Statute Miles
50 0 50 100 150 200 250
50 0 50 100 150 200 250 300

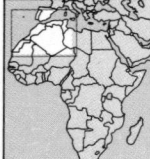

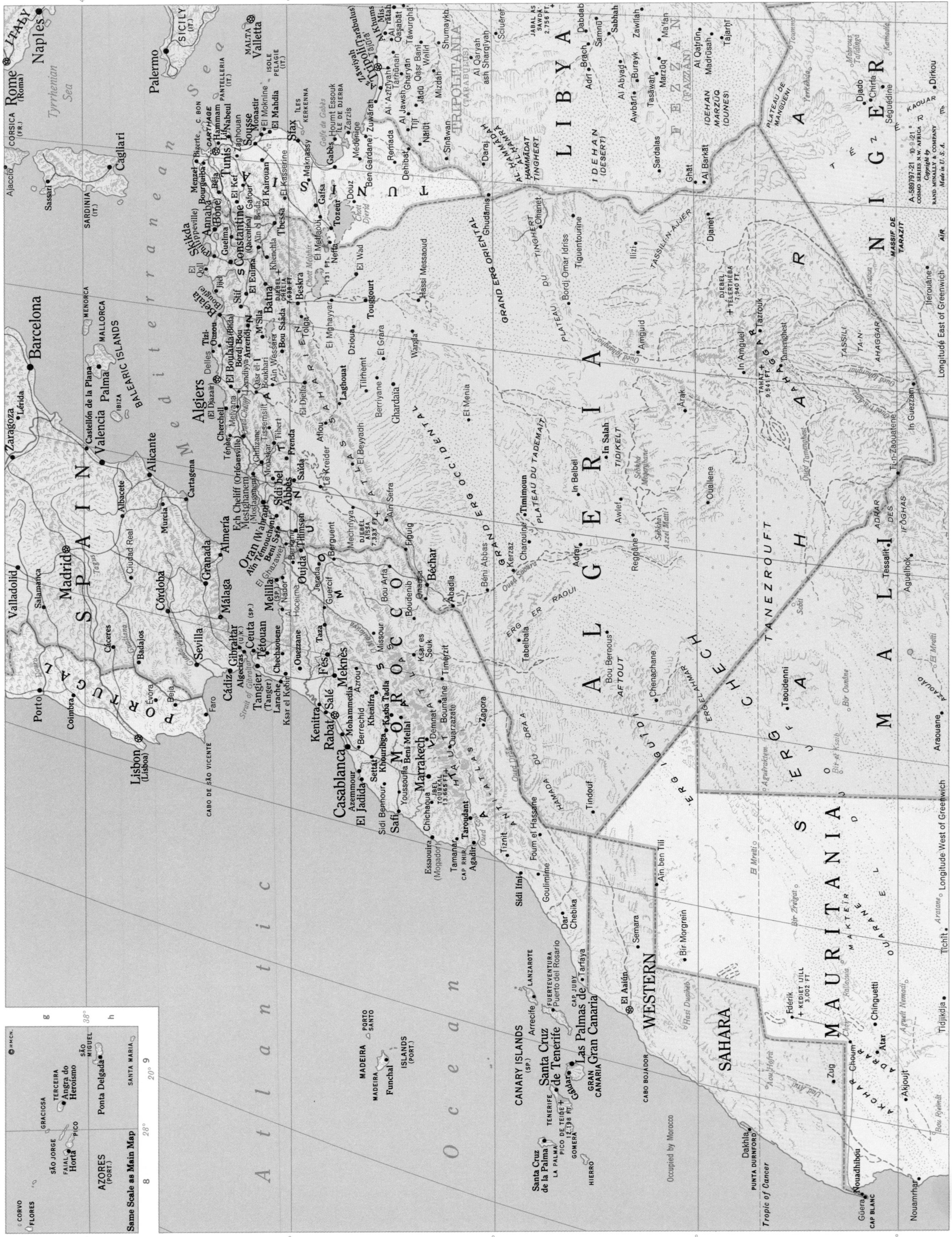

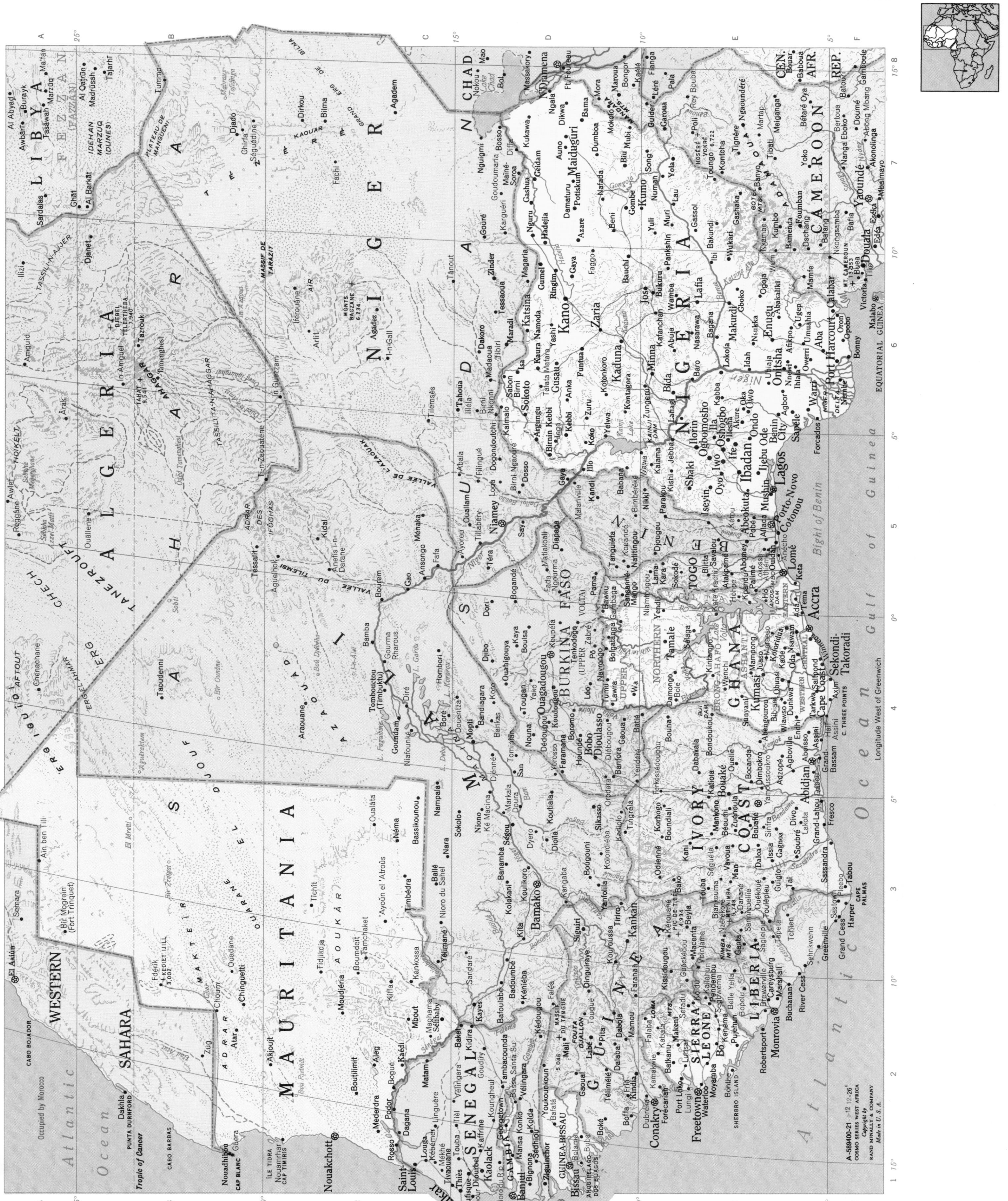

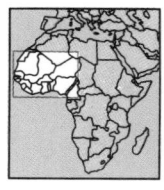

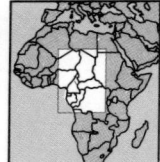

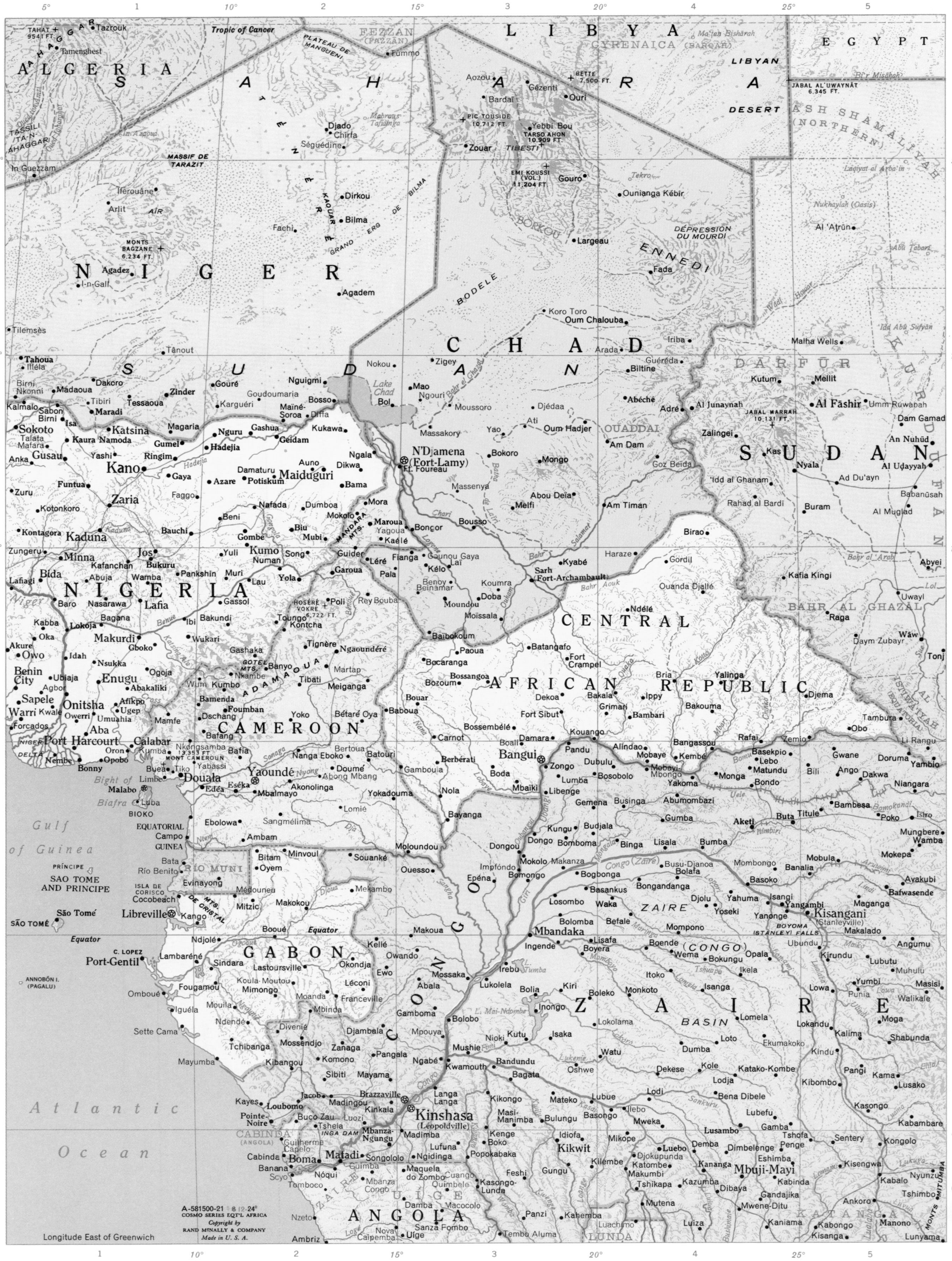

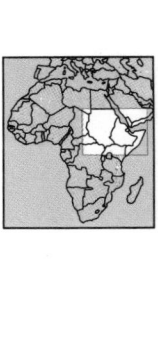

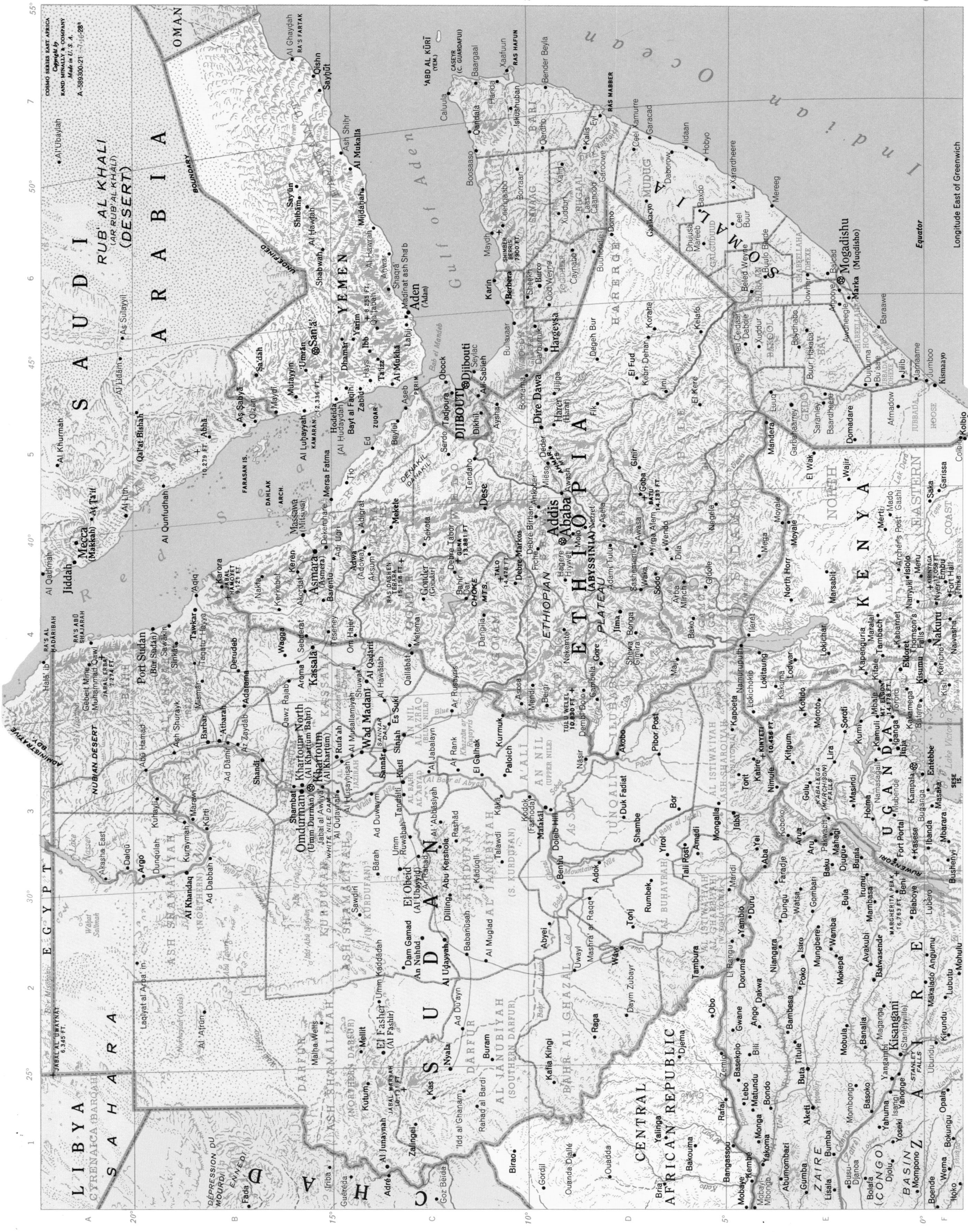

Sinusoidal Projection
SCALE 1 : 11,400,000   1 Inch = 180 Statute Miles

Statute Miles 50 25 0 50 100 150 200 250
Kilometers 50 0 50 100 150 200 250 300

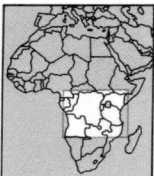

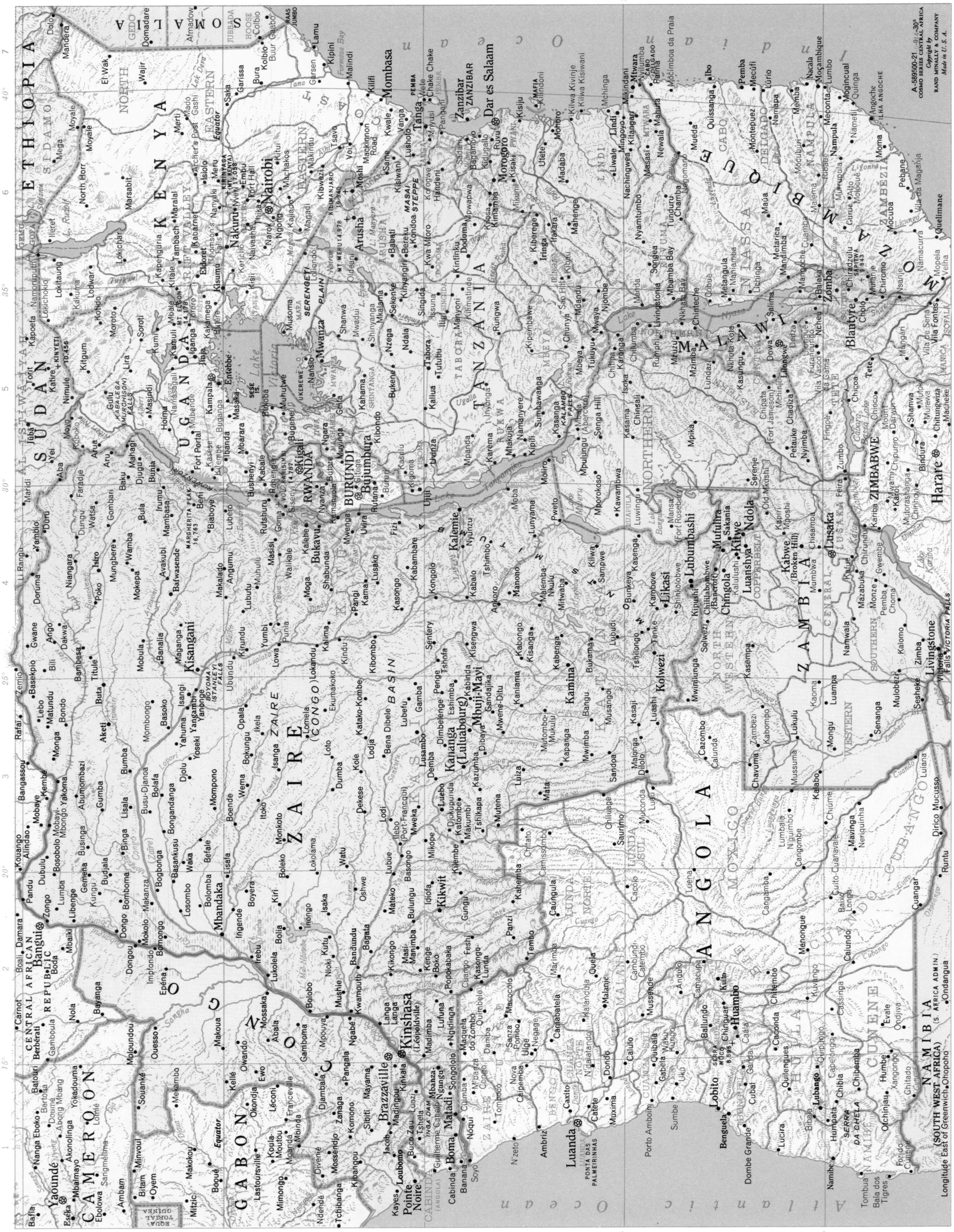

Statute Miles 50 0 50 100 150 200 250

50 0 50 100 150 200 250 300

Sinusoidal Projection

SCALE 1 : 11,400,000   1 Inch = 180 Statute Miles

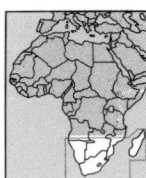

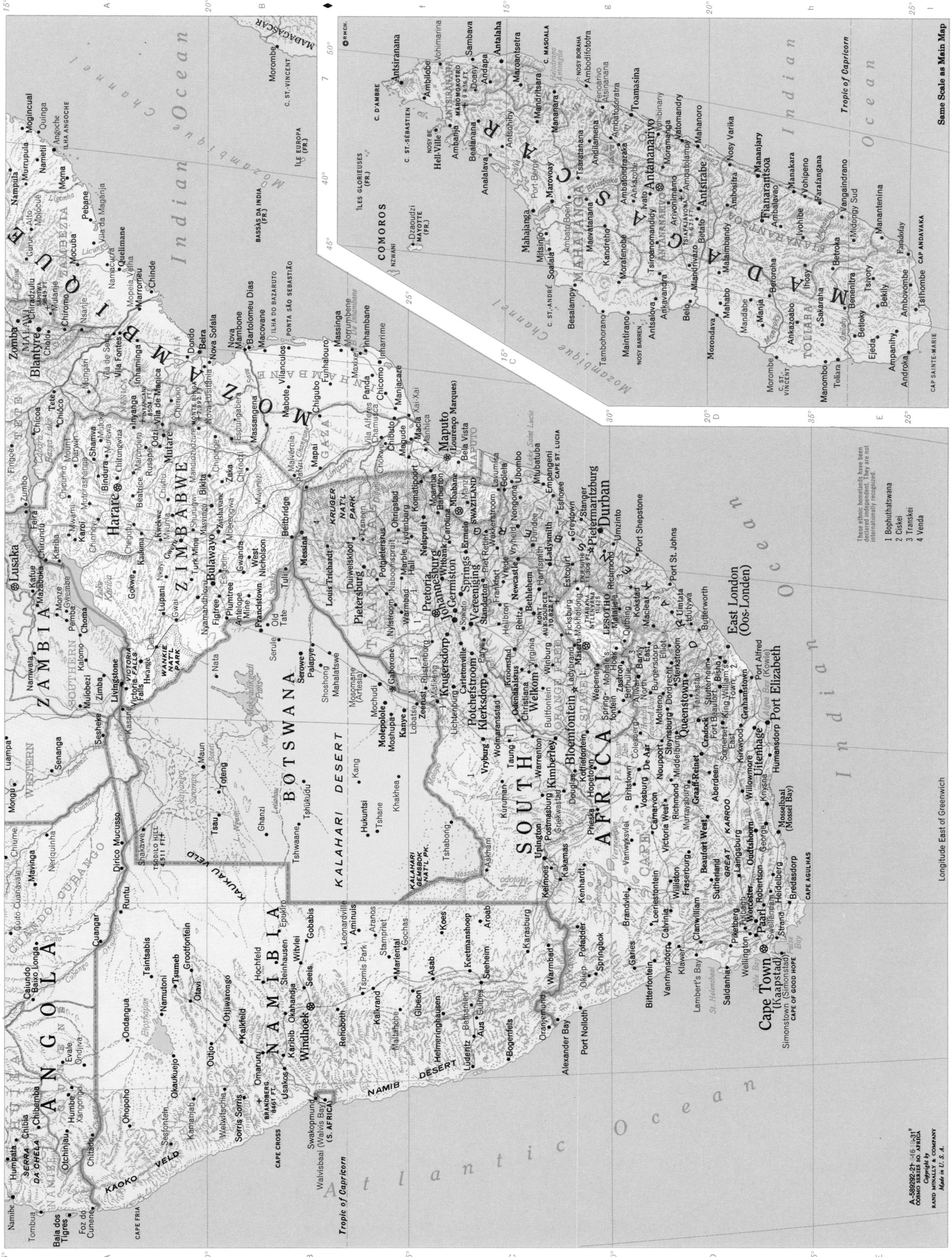

ANGOLA
NAMIBIA
BOTSWANA
ZAMBIA
ZIMBABWE
MOZAMBIQUE
SOUTH AFRICA
LESOTHO
SWAZILAND
MALAWI
MADAGASCAR
COMOROS
KALAHARI DESERT
NAMIB DESERT
Atlantic Ocean
Indian Ocean
Mozambique Channel
Tropic of Capricorn
These ethnic homelands have been declared independent. They are not internationally recognized.
1 Bophuthatswana
2 Ciskei
3 Transkei
4 Venda
Same Scale as Main Map
Longitude East of Greenwich
A-589292-21- -16 -31
COSMO SERIES SO. AFRICA
Copyright by RAND McNALLY & COMPANY
Made in U. S. A.

Sinusoidal Projection
SCALE 1: 11,400,000 1 Inch = 180 Statute Miles

Statute Miles 50 25 0 50 100 150 200 250
Kilometers 50 0 50 100 150 200 250 300

Statute Miles 100 0 100 200 300

Kilometers 100 0 100 200 300 400

Lambert Azimuthal Equal Area Projection

SCALE 1:16,000,000 1 Inch = 252 Statute Miles

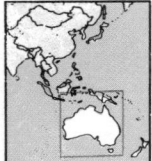

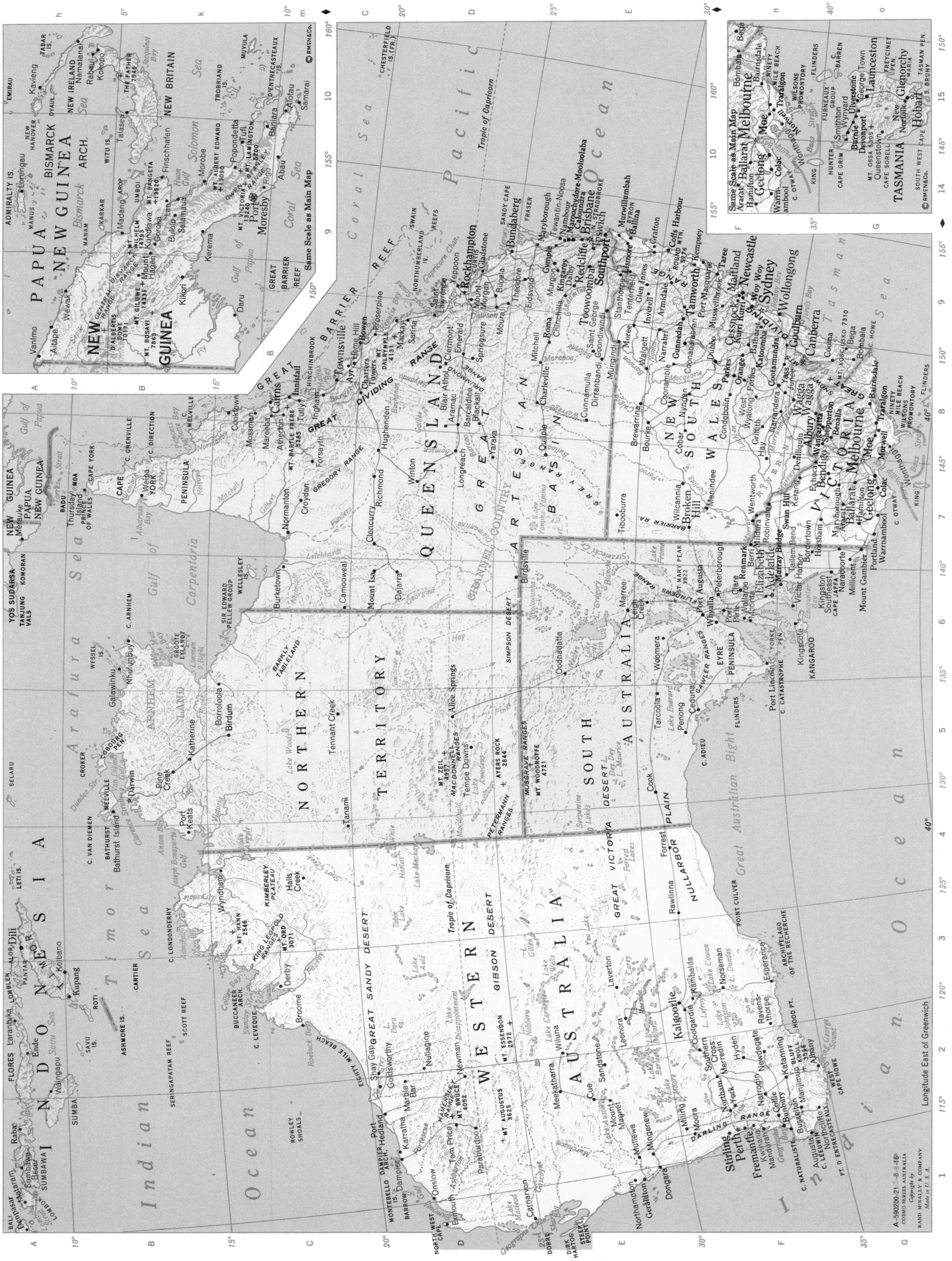

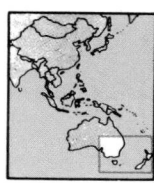

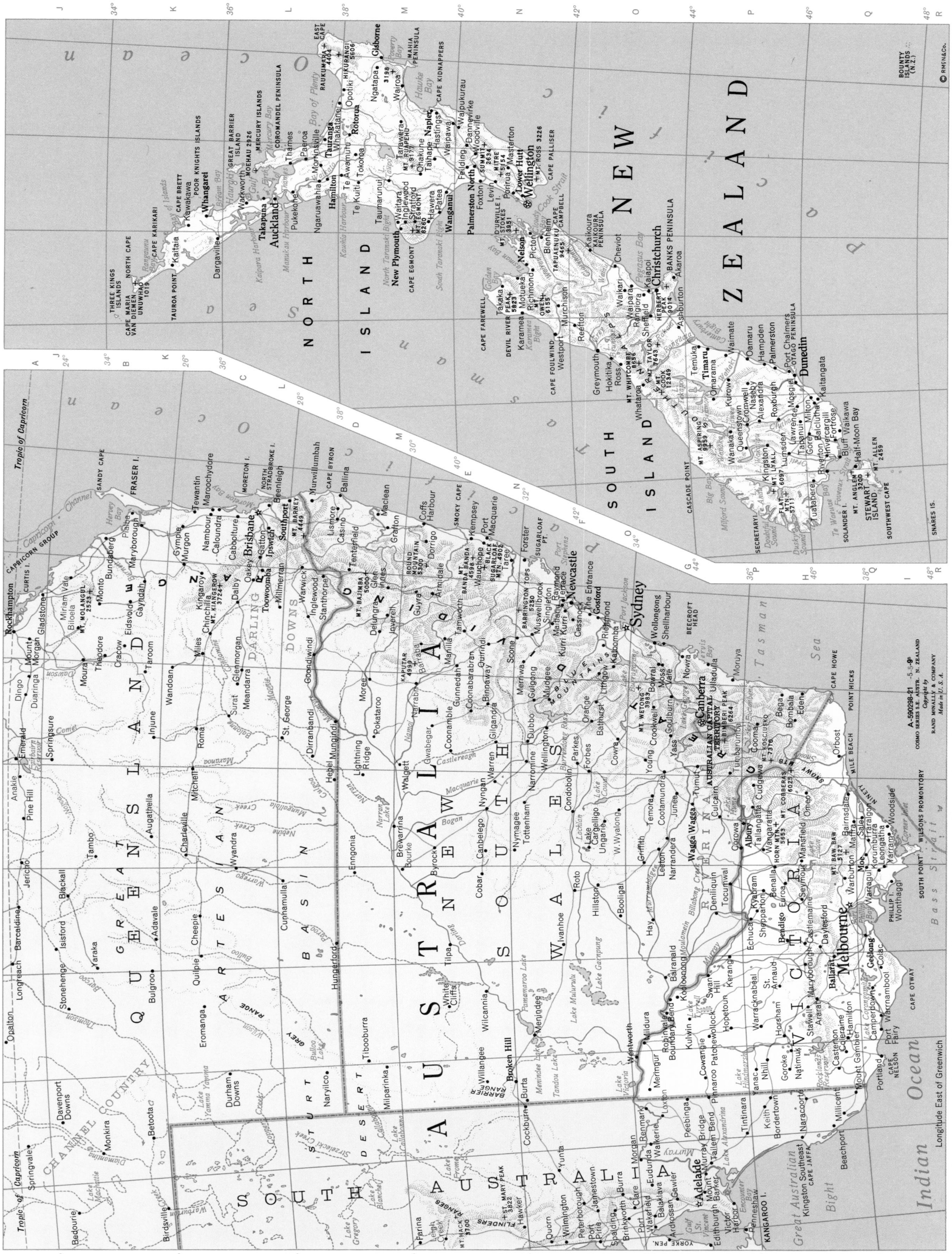

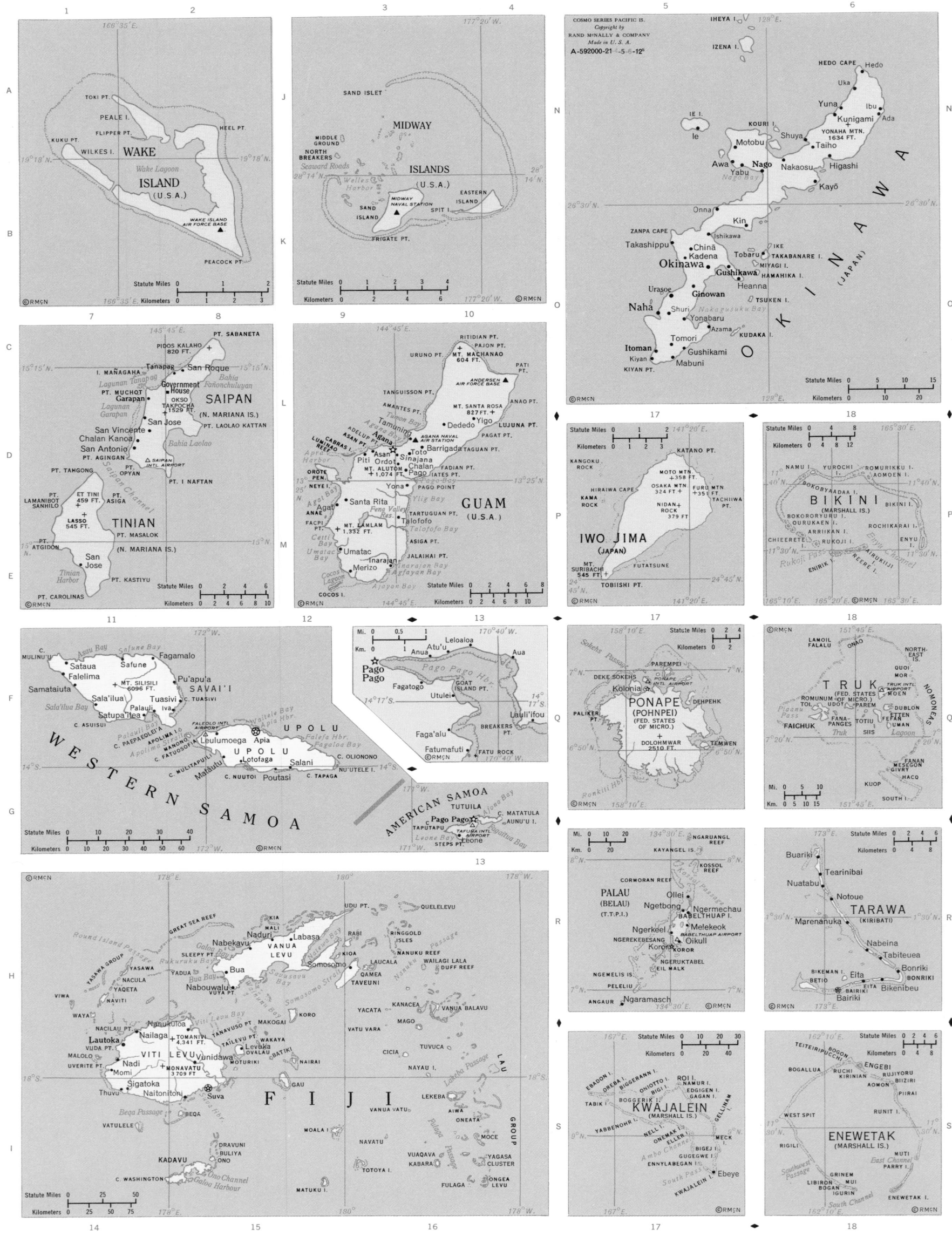

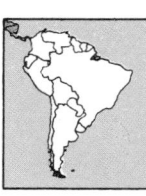

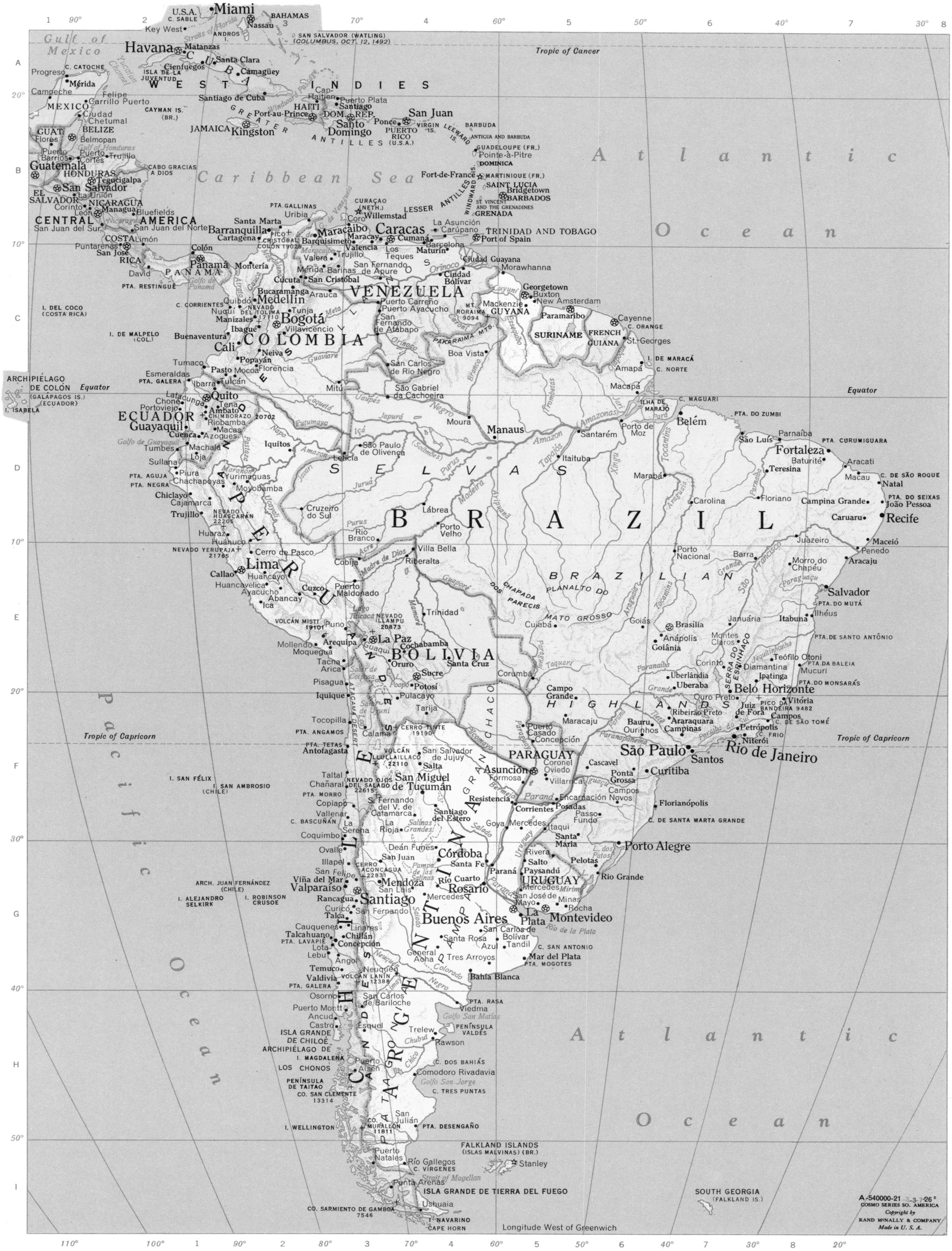

Sinusoidal Projection
SCALE 1: 29,465,000 1 Inch = 465 Statute Miles

Statute Miles 100 0 100 300 500 700
Kilometers 100 0 100 300 500 700 900 1100

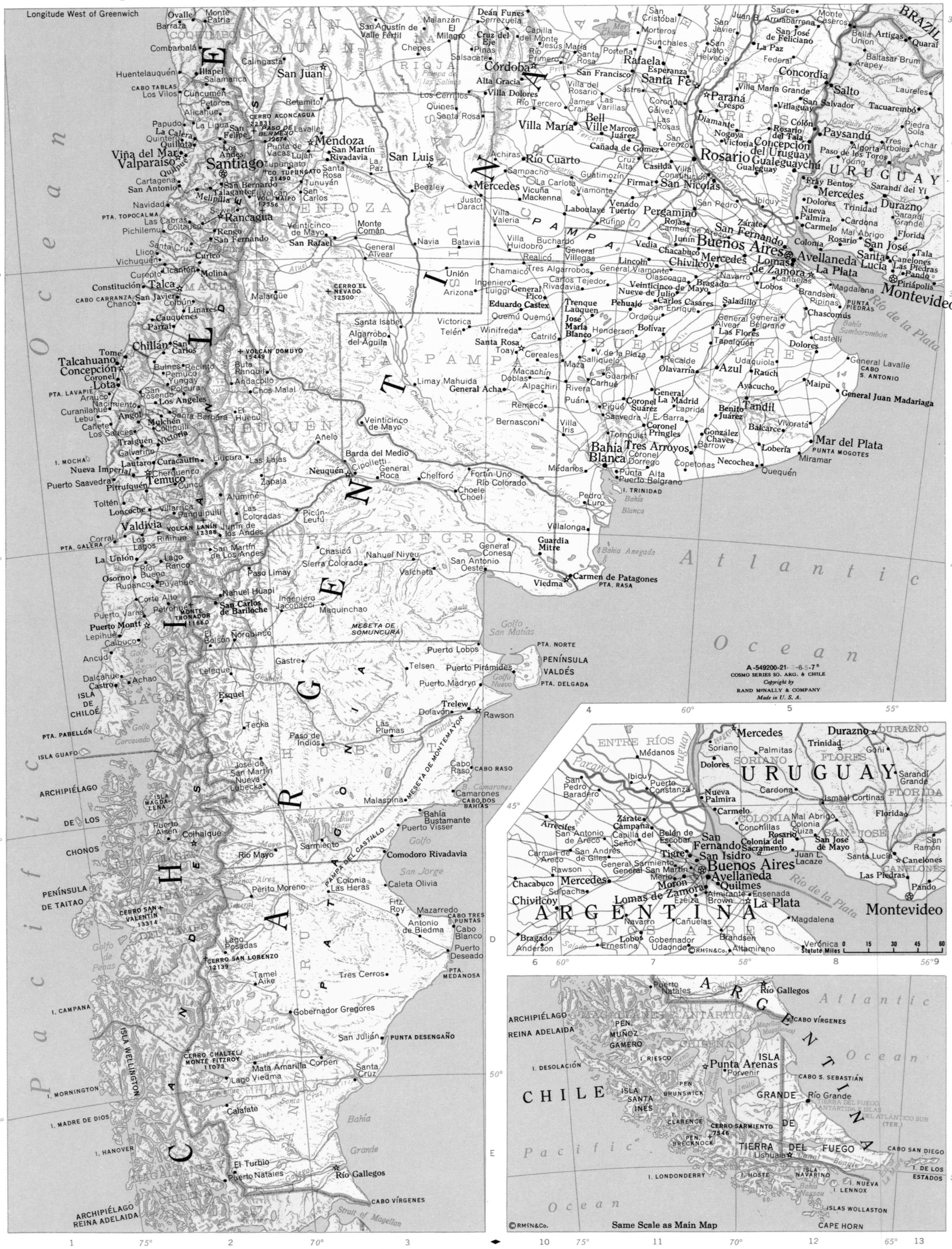

CENTRAL AND SOUTHERN ARGENTINA AND CHILE

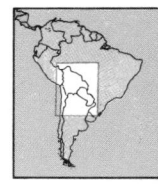

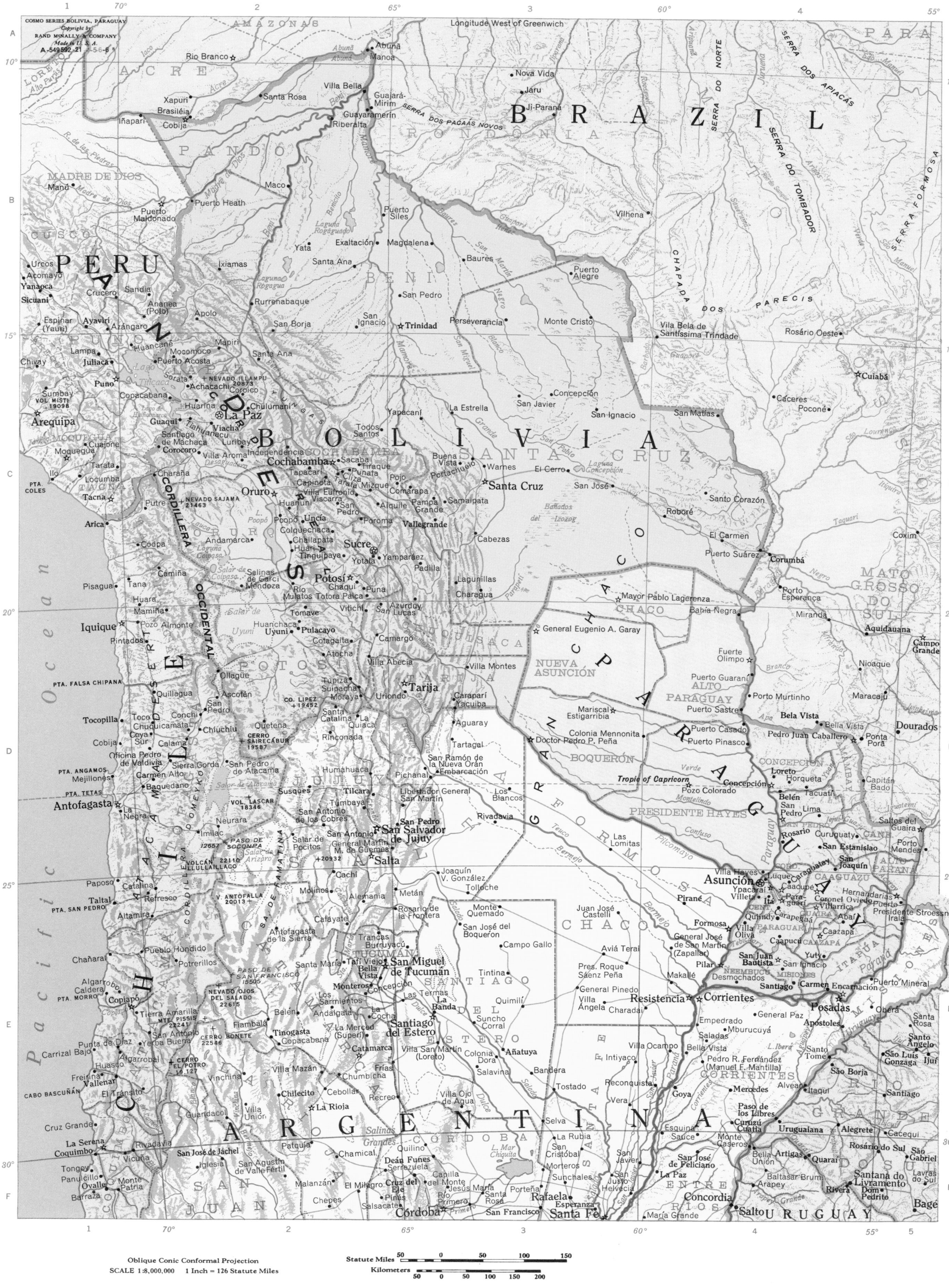

Oblique Conic Conformal Projection
SCALE 1:8,000,000 1 Inch = 126 Statute Miles

Statute Miles 50 0 50 100 150
Kilometers 50 0 50 100 150 200

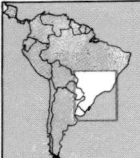

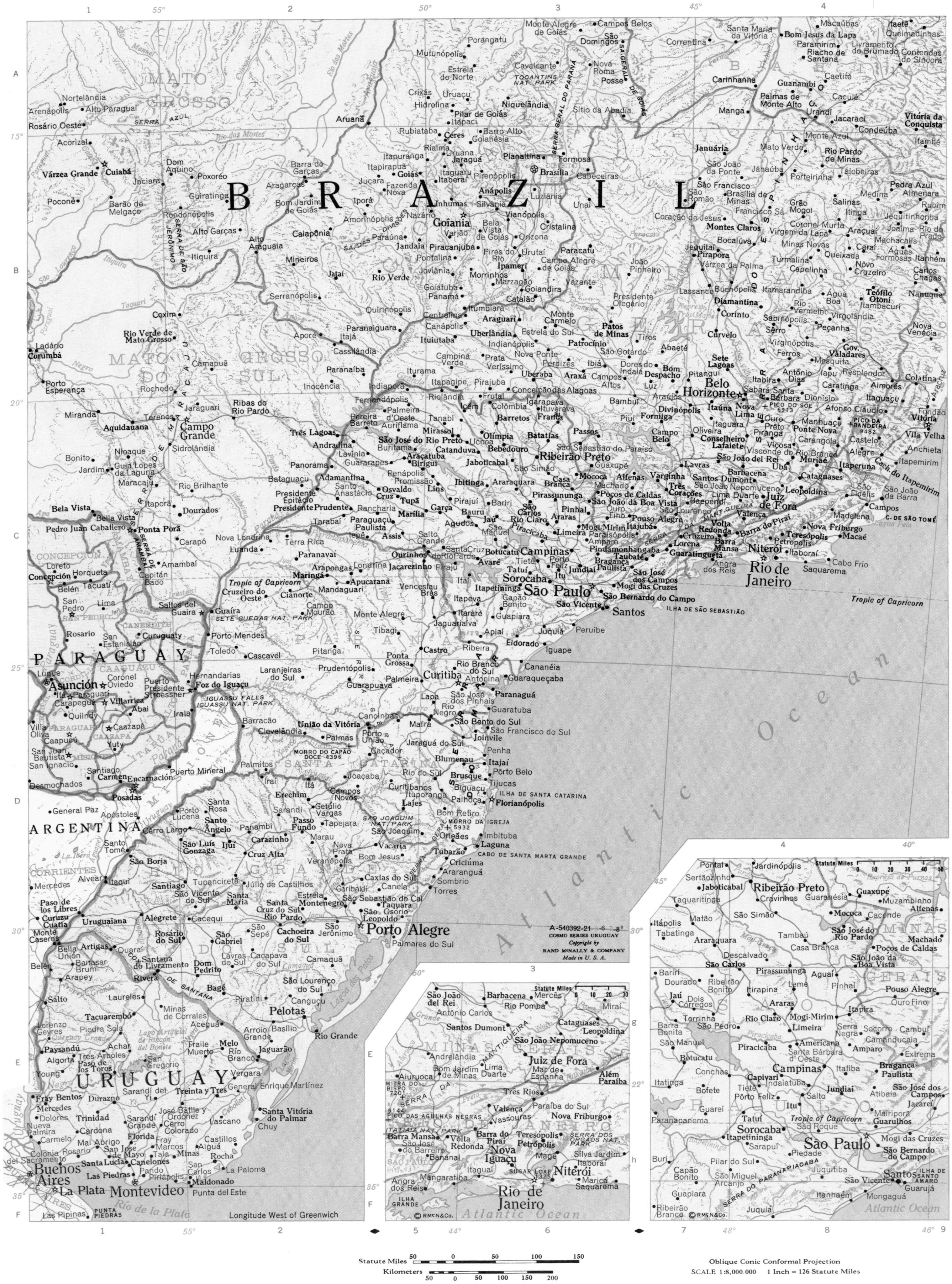

BRAZIL
PARAGUAY
ARGENTINA
URUGUAY
MATO GROSSO
MATO GROSSO DO SUL
PARANÁ
SANTA CATARINA
RIO GRANDE DO SUL
MINAS GERAIS
SÃO PAULO
Atlantic Ocean
Tropic of Capricorn
Cuiabá
Várzea Grande
Brasília
Goiânia
Anápolis
Belo Horizonte
Campo Grande
Corumbá
Asunción
Encarnación
Posadas
Foz do Iguaçu
Curitiba
Florianópolis
Porto Alegre
Pelotas
Rio Grande
Montevideo
Buenos Aires
La Plata
Punta del Este
São Paulo
Santos
Campinas
Rio de Janeiro
Niterói
Juiz de Fora
Ribeirão Preto
Uberlândia
Londrina
Maringá
Ponta Grossa
Joinvile
Blumenau
Caxias do Sul
Santa Maria
Paysandú
Salto
Rivera
A-540392-21 -6 -8
COSMO SERIES URUGUAY
Copyright by RAND McNALLY & COMPANY
Made in U. S. A.
Longitude West of Greenwich
Statute Miles 50 0 50 100 150
Kilometers 50 0 50 100 150 200
Oblique Conic Conformal Projection
SCALE 1:8,000,000 1 Inch = 126 Statute Miles
© RMcN&Co.

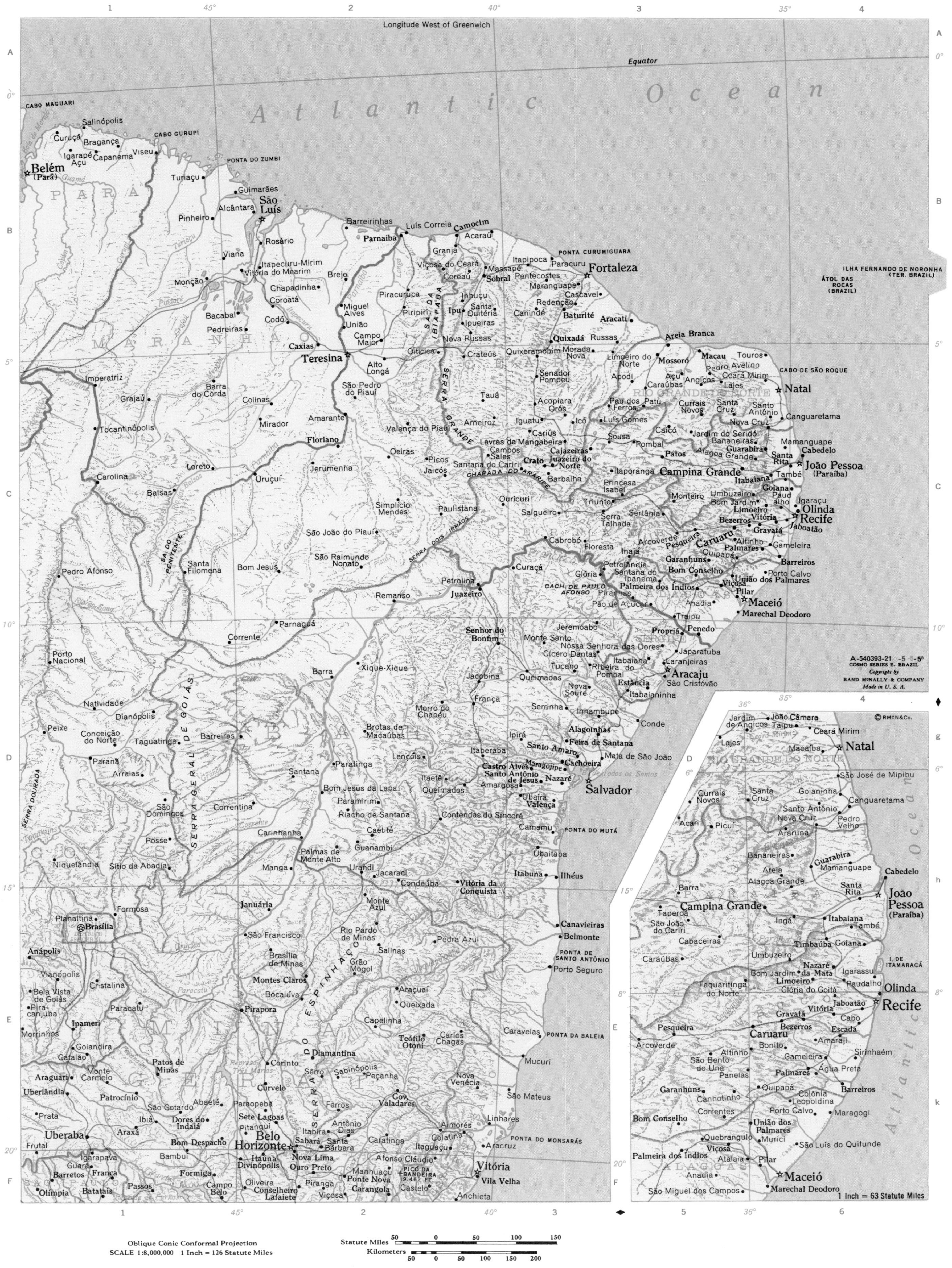

Longitude West of Greenwich

A t l a n t i c   O c e a n

Equator

A-540393-21 -5 -5-5ª
COSMO SERIES E. BRAZIL
Copyright by
RAND McNALLY & COMPANY
Made in U. S. A.

Oblique Conic Conformal Projection
SCALE 1:8,000,000   1 Inch = 126 Statute Miles

Statute Miles
Kilometers

1 Inch = 63 Statute Miles

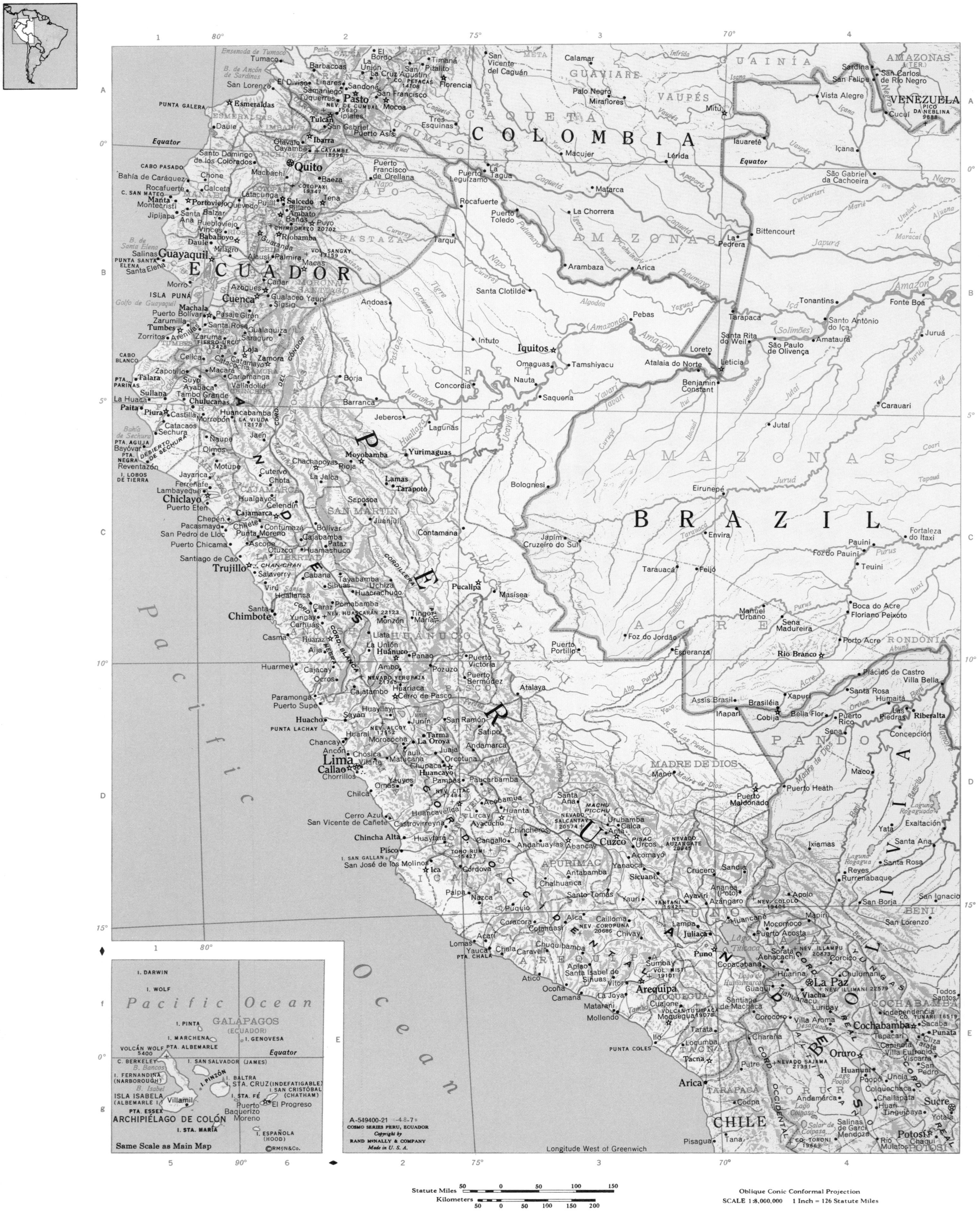

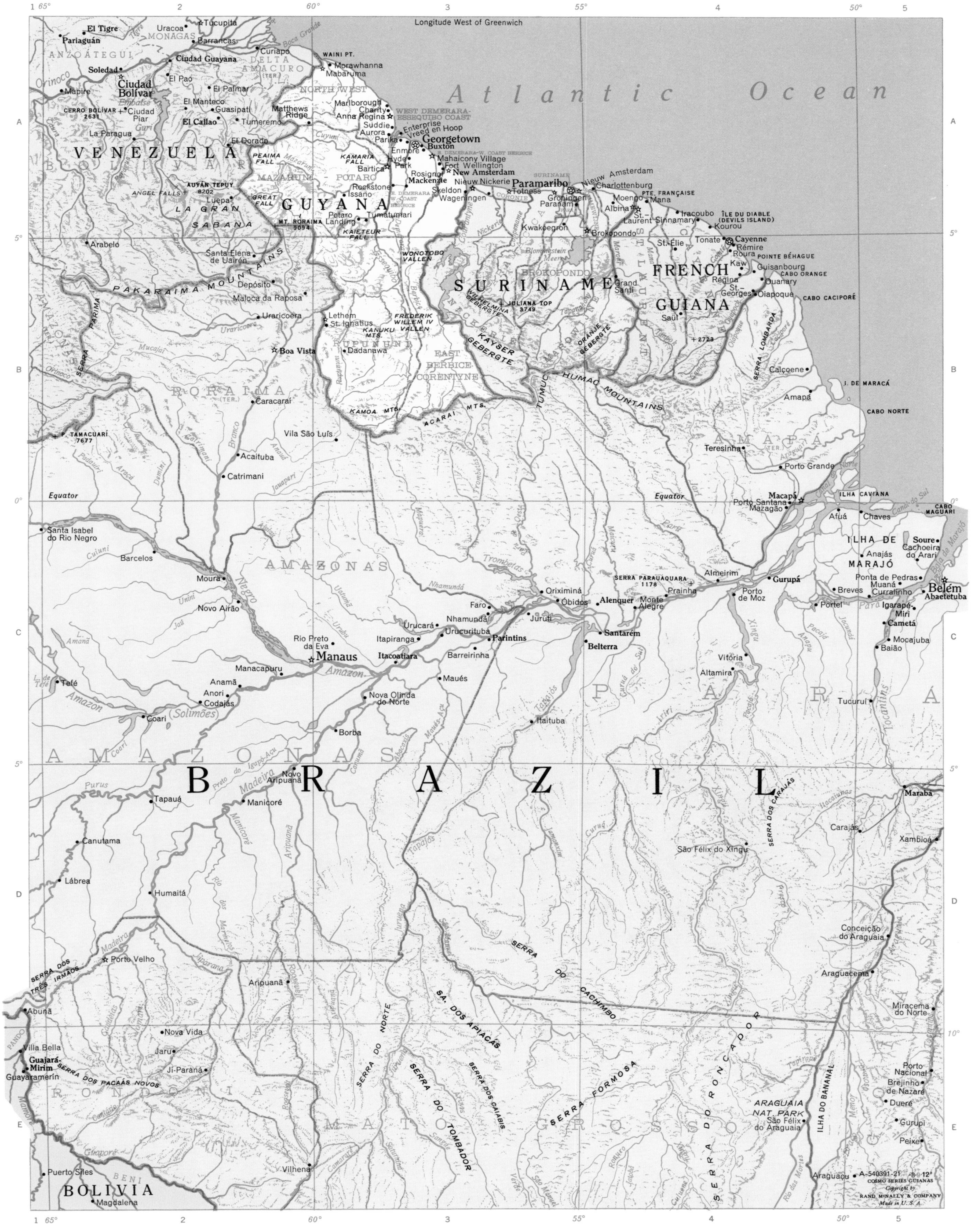

Longitude West of Greenwich

Atlantic Ocean

VENEZUELA

GUYANA

SURINAME

FRENCH GUIANA

BRAZIL

BOLIVIA

Oblique Conic Conformal Projection
SCALE 1:8,000,000   1 Inch = 126 Statute Miles

Statute Miles   50   0   50   100   150

Kilometers   50   0   50   100   150   200

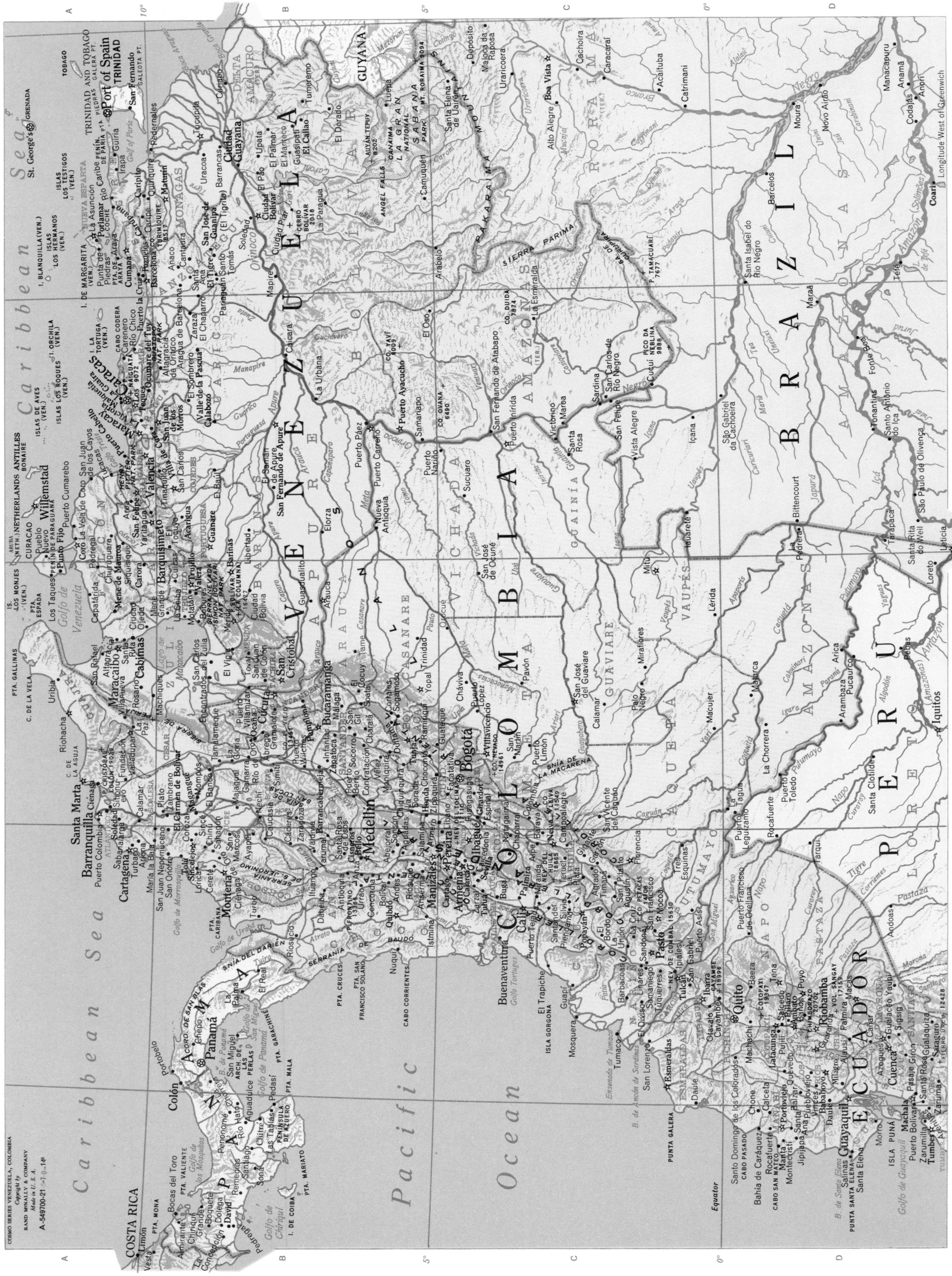

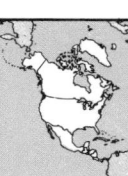

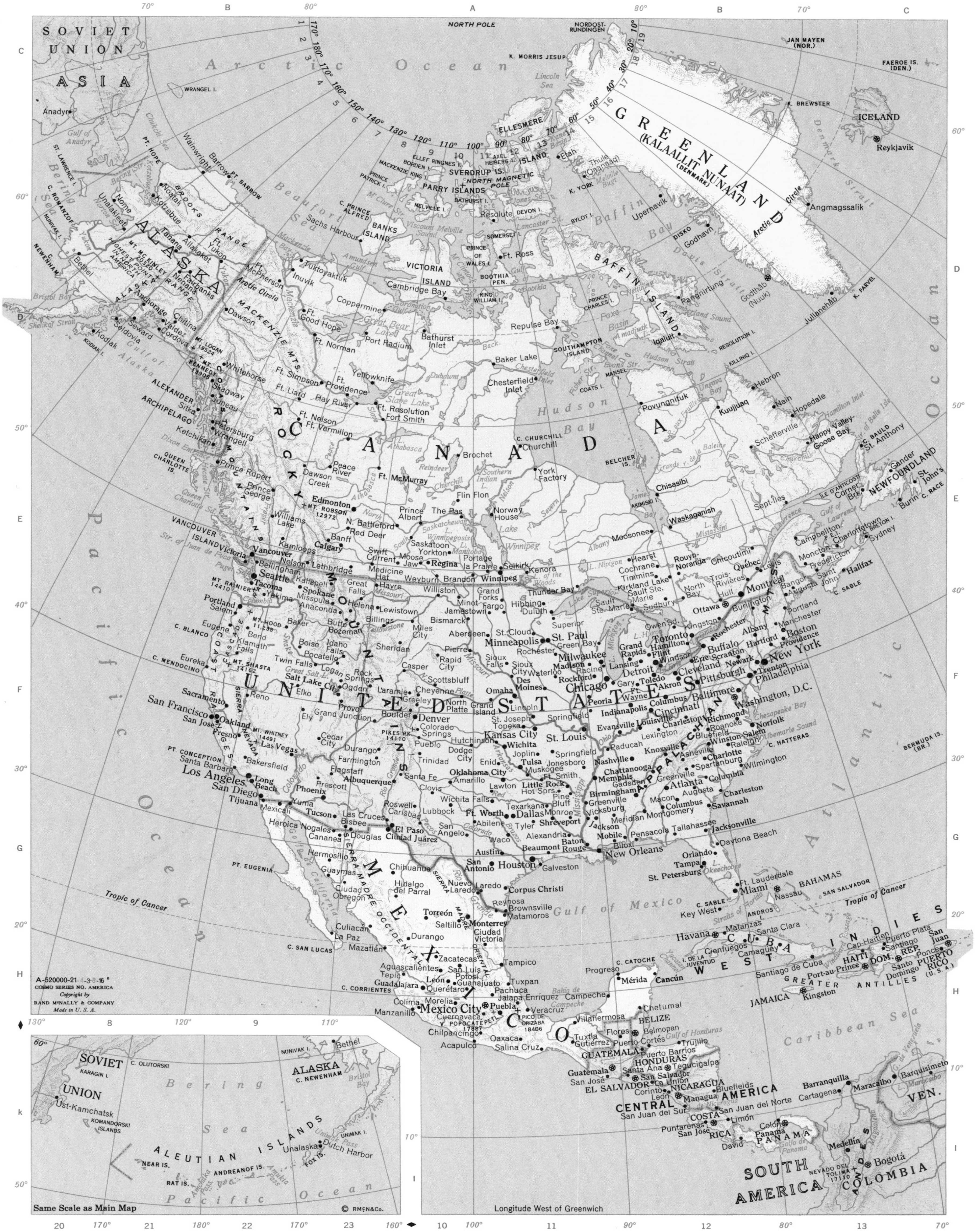

Lambert Azimuthal Equal Area Projection
SCALE 1:31,977,000 1 Inch = 490 Statute Miles

Statute Miles 100 0 100 200 300 400 500 600 700 800

Kilometers 100 0 100 200 400 600 800 1000

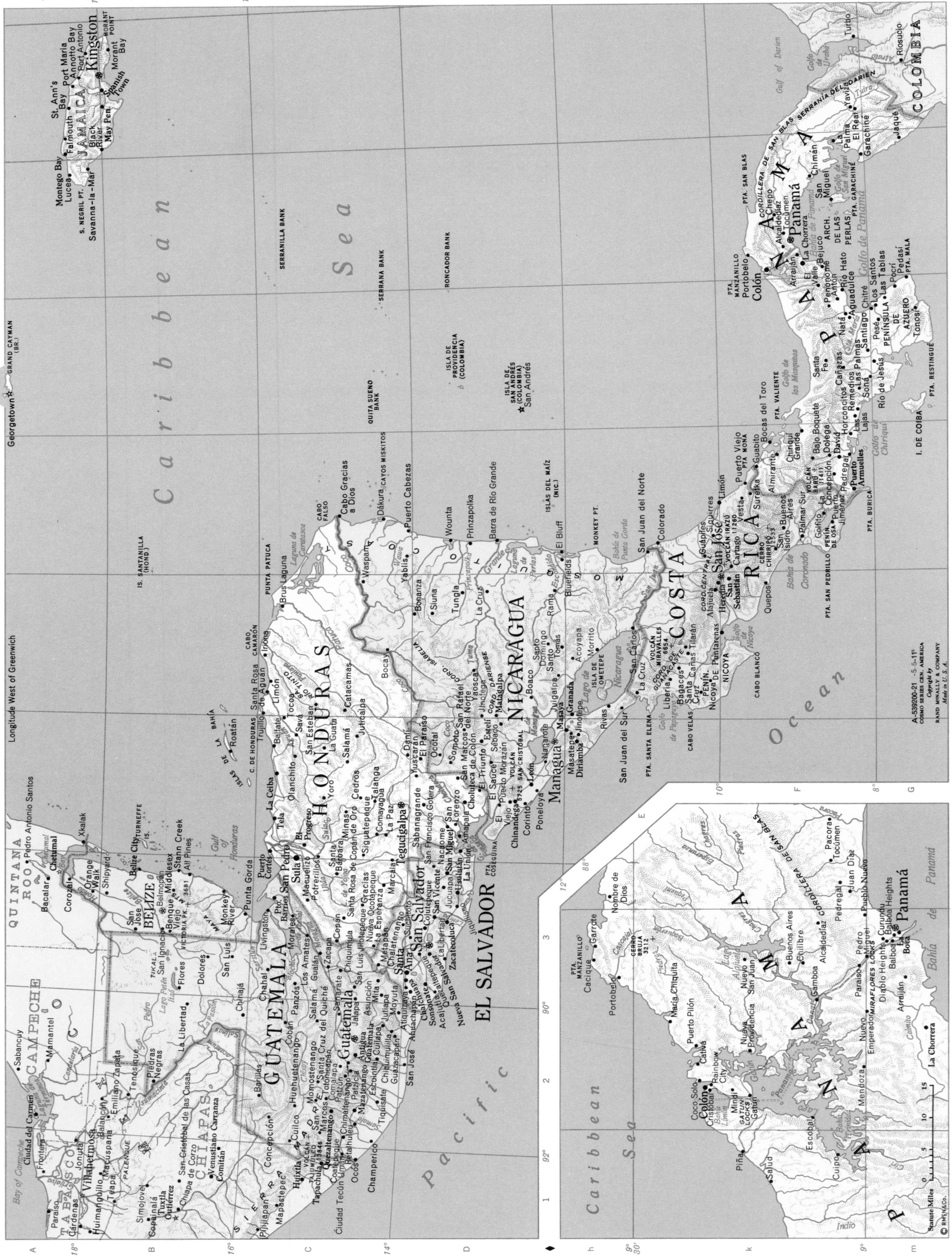

Statute Miles 25 0 25 75 125
Kilometers 25 0 25 75 125 175

Oblique Conic Conformal Projection
SCALE 1:6,000,000 1 Inch = 95 Statute Miles

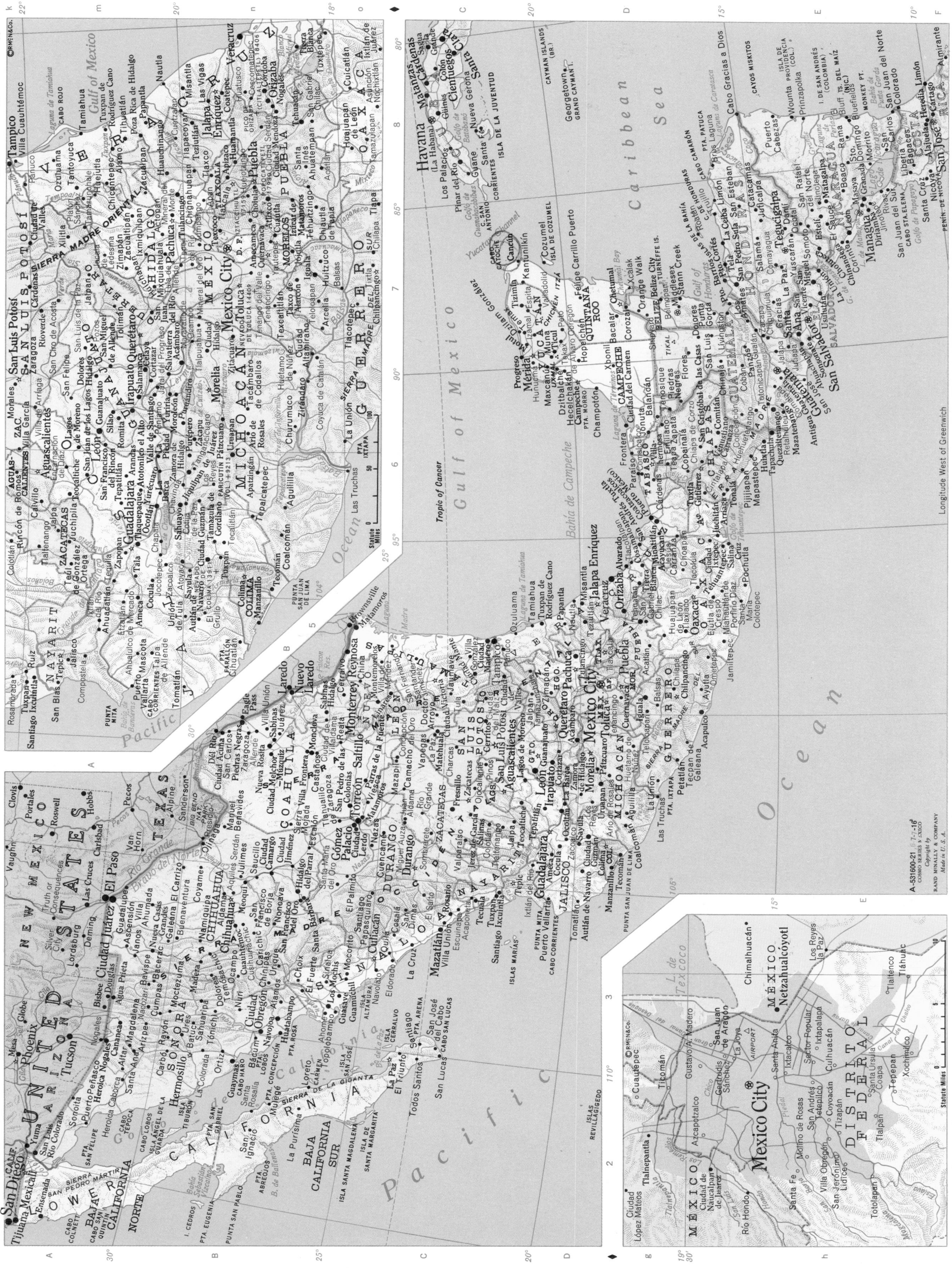

Oblique Conic Conformal Projection
SCALE 1:12,000 000 1 Inch ≈ 189 Statute Miles

Statute Miles
50 25 0   50   100   150   200   250

Kilometers
50 0   100   200   300

A-53I600-21 ʌ.7.-16ᵈ
COSMO SERIES ᴄ.XSCO
Rand McNally & Company
Made in U.S.A.

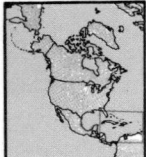

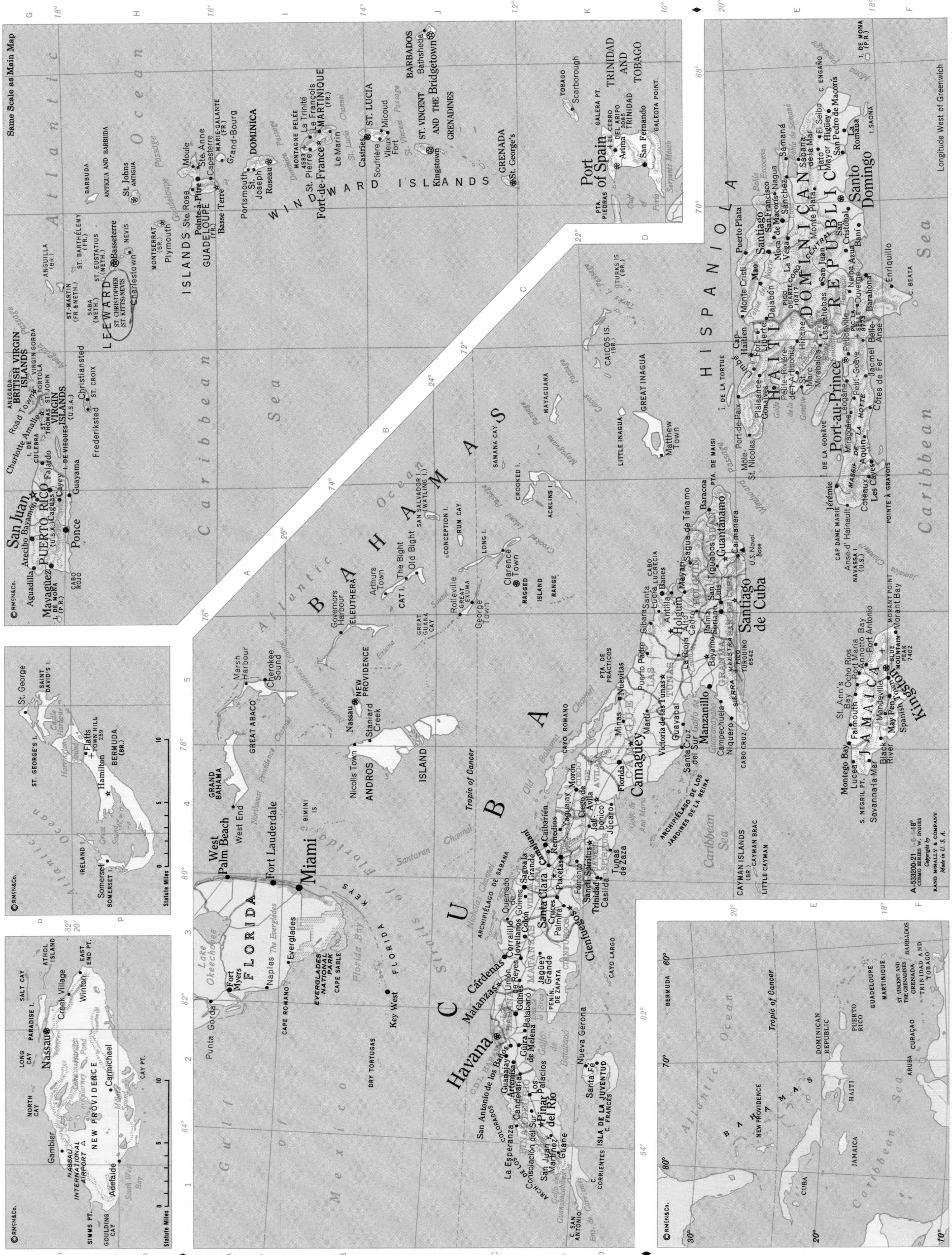

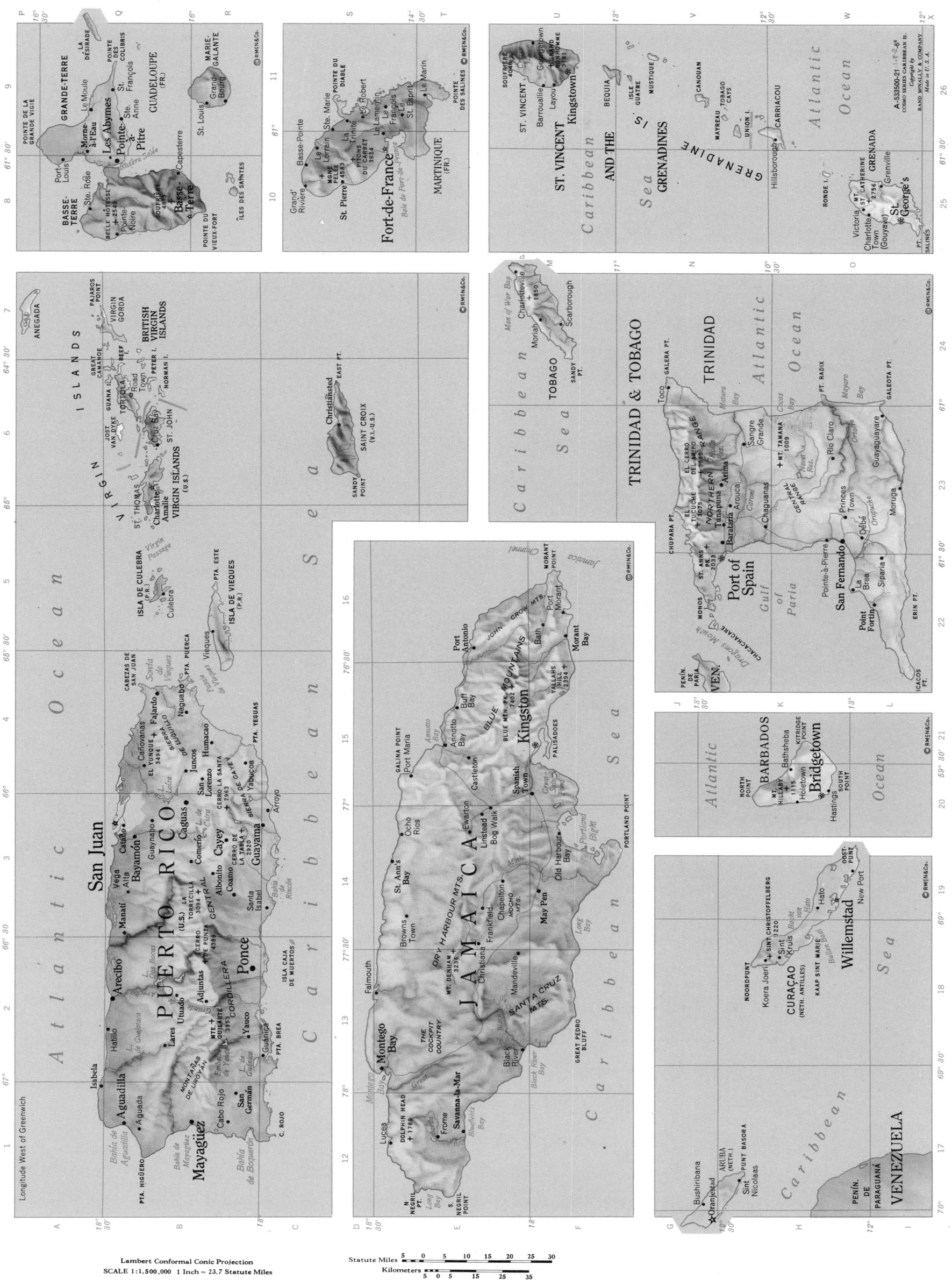

Lambert Conformal Conic Projection
SCALE 1:1,500,000 1 Inch = 23.7 Statute Miles

Statute Miles
5 0 5 10 15 20 25 30

Kilometers
5 0 5 15 25 35

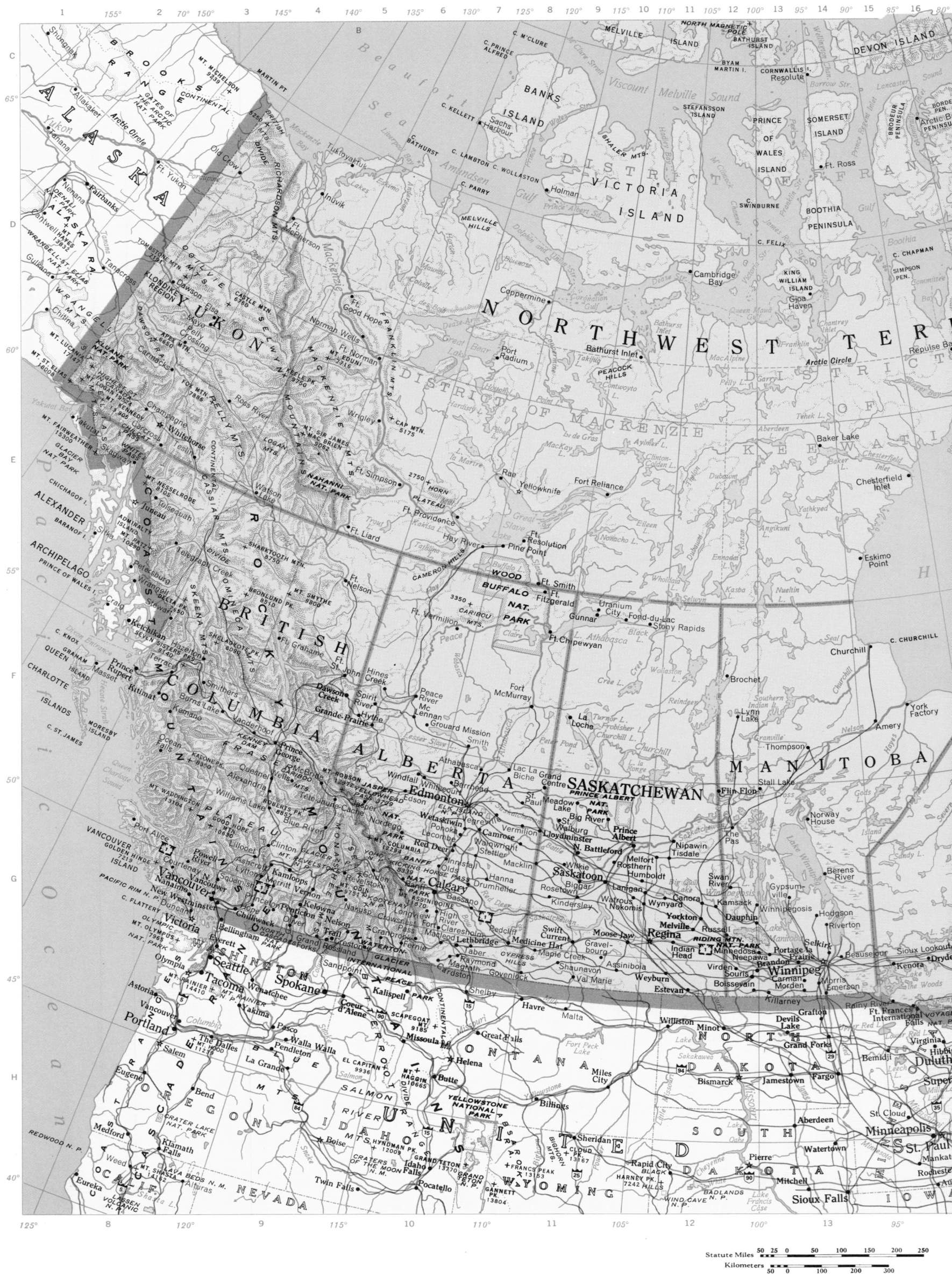

Lambert Conformal Conic Projection
SCALE 1:12,000,000   1 Inch = 189 Statute Miles

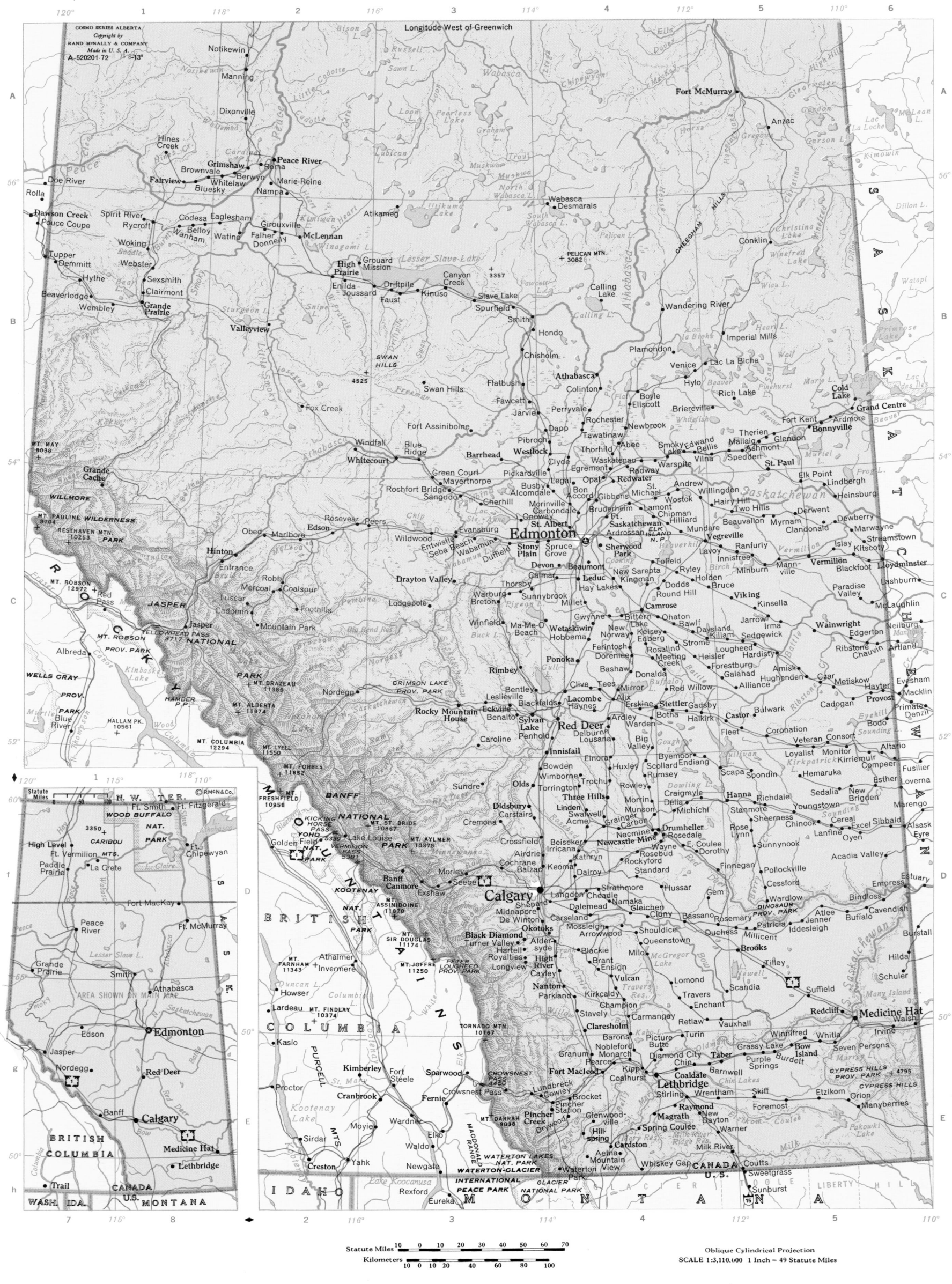

Statute Miles 10 0 10 20 30 40 50 60 70
Kilometers 10 0 10 20 40 60 80 100

Oblique Cylindrical Projection
SCALE 1:3,110,000 1 Inch = 49 Statute Miles

Oblique Cylindrical Projection
SCALE 1:4,255,000   1 Inch = 67 Statute Miles

Statute Miles 10 0 10 20 30 40 50 60 70 80 90 100

Kilometers 10 0 10 20 40 60 80 100 120 140

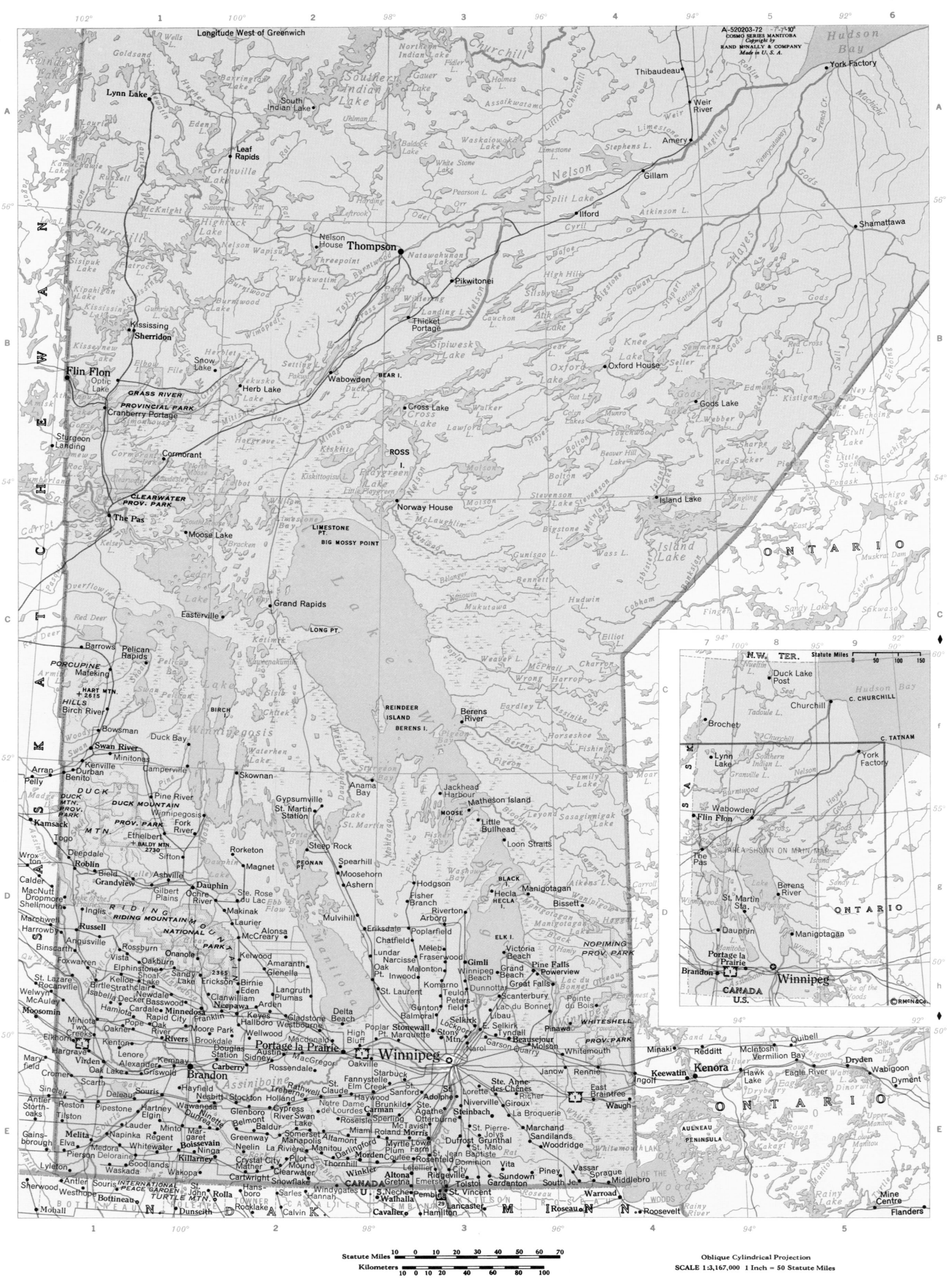

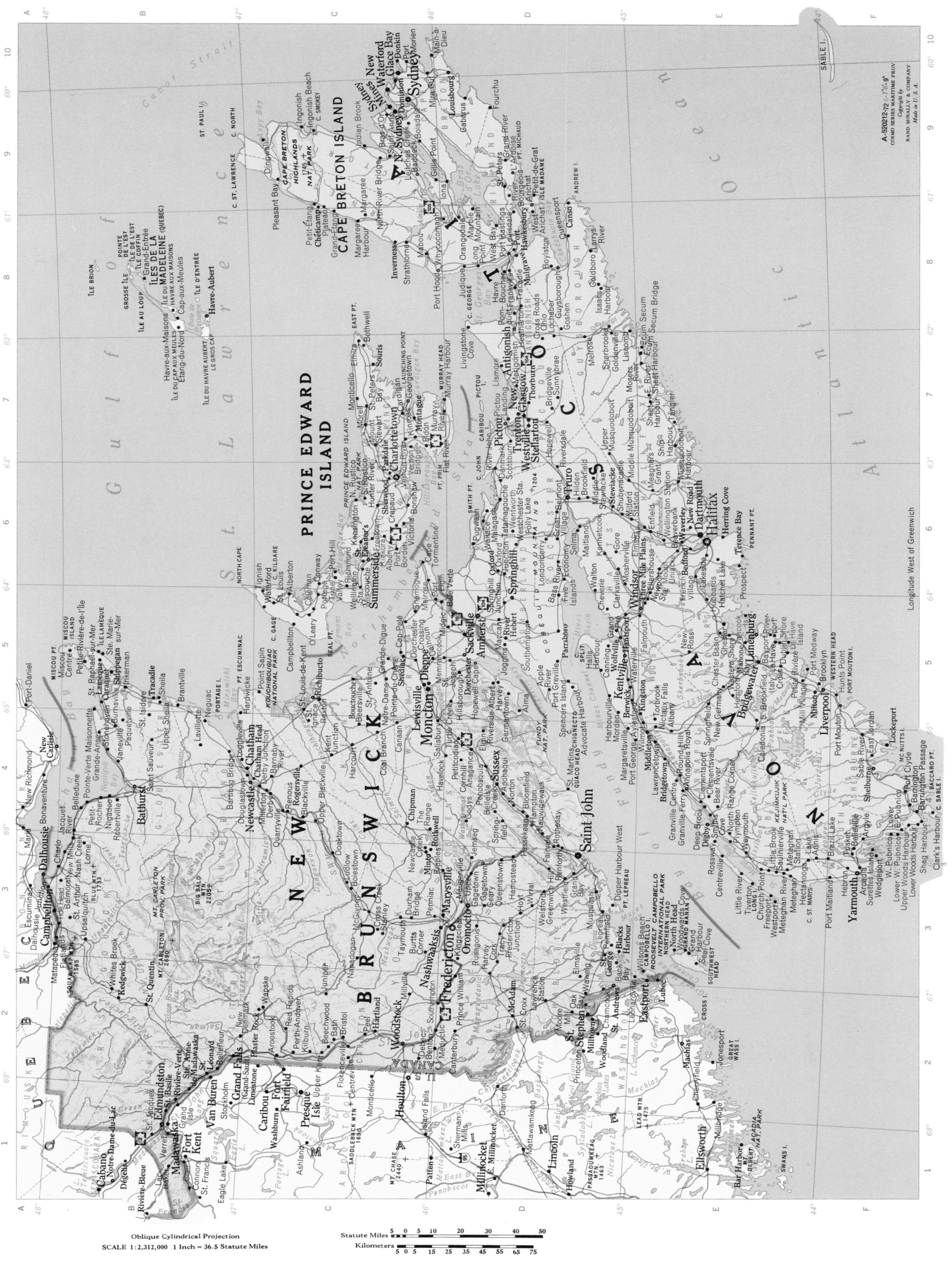

Oblique Cylindrical Projection
SCALE 1:2,312,000   1 Inch = 36.5 Statute Miles

Statute Miles
5 0 5   10   20   30   40   50

Kilometers
5 0 5 15   25   35   45   55   65   75

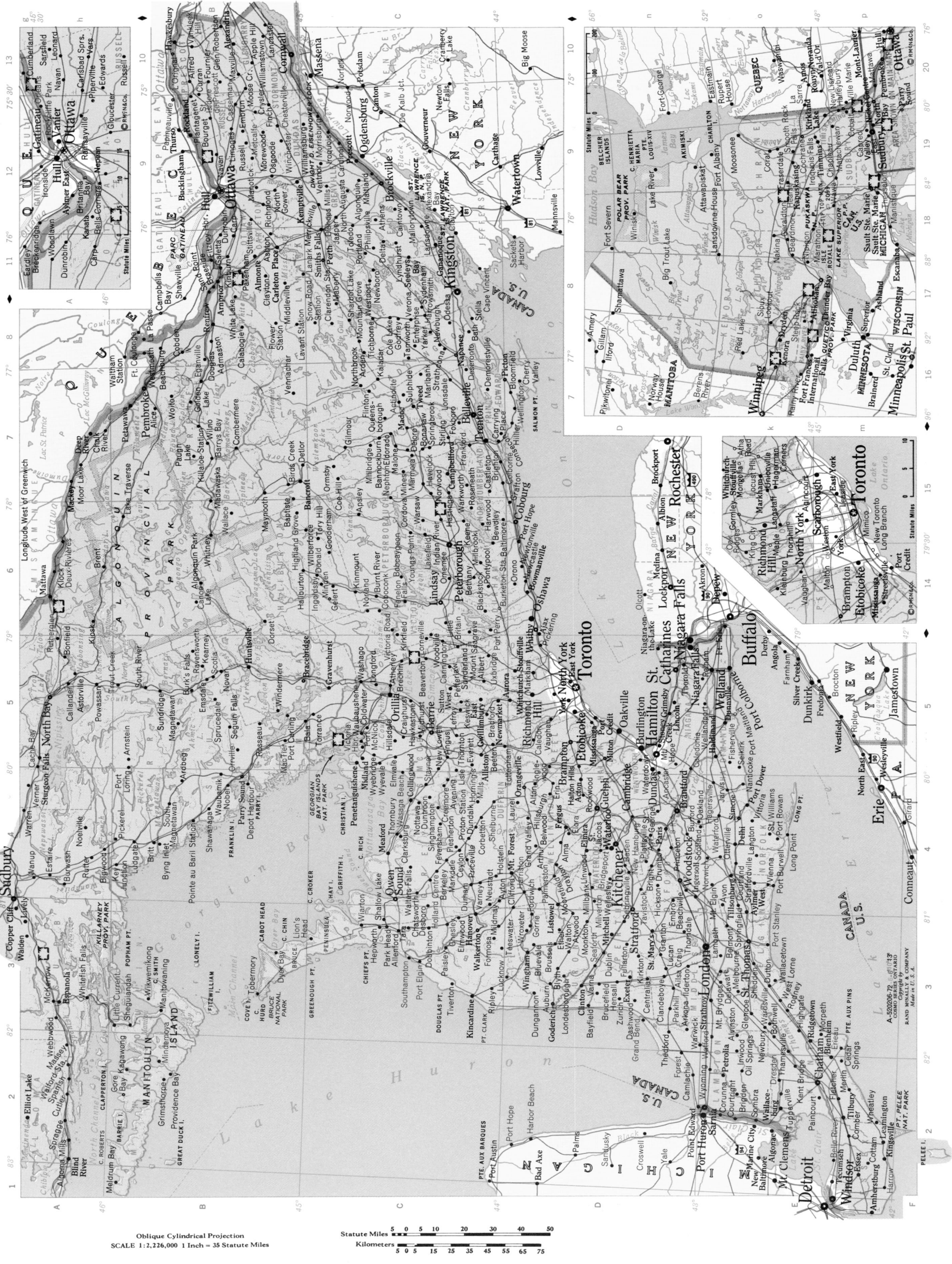

Oblique Cylindrical Projection
SCALE 1:2,226,000 1 Inch = 35 Statute Miles

Statute Miles
Kilometers

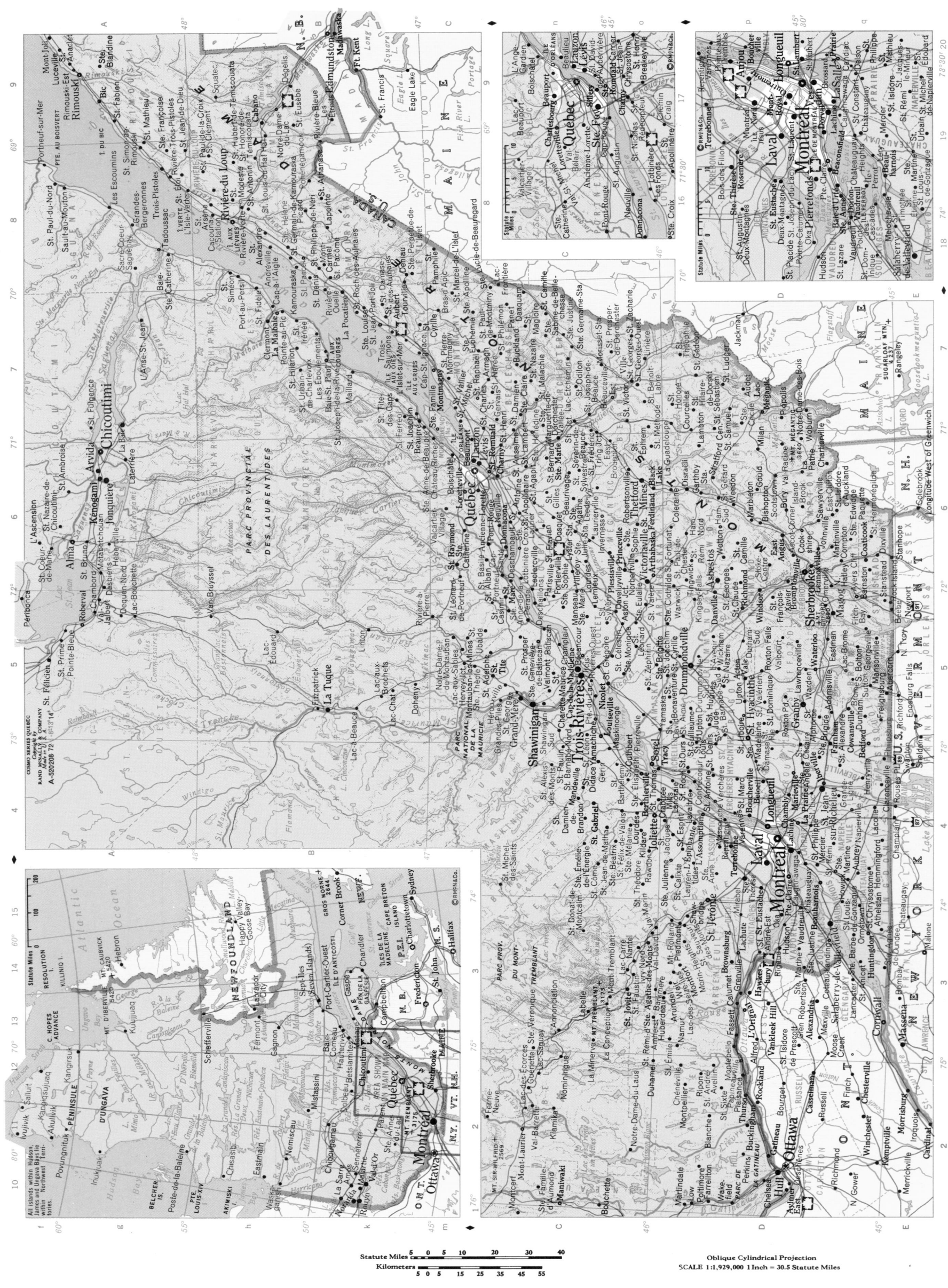

Statute Miles 5 0 5 10 20 30 40
Kilometers 5 0 5 15 25 35 45 55

Oblique Cylindrical Projection
SCALE 1:1,929,000 1 Inch = 30.5 Statute Miles

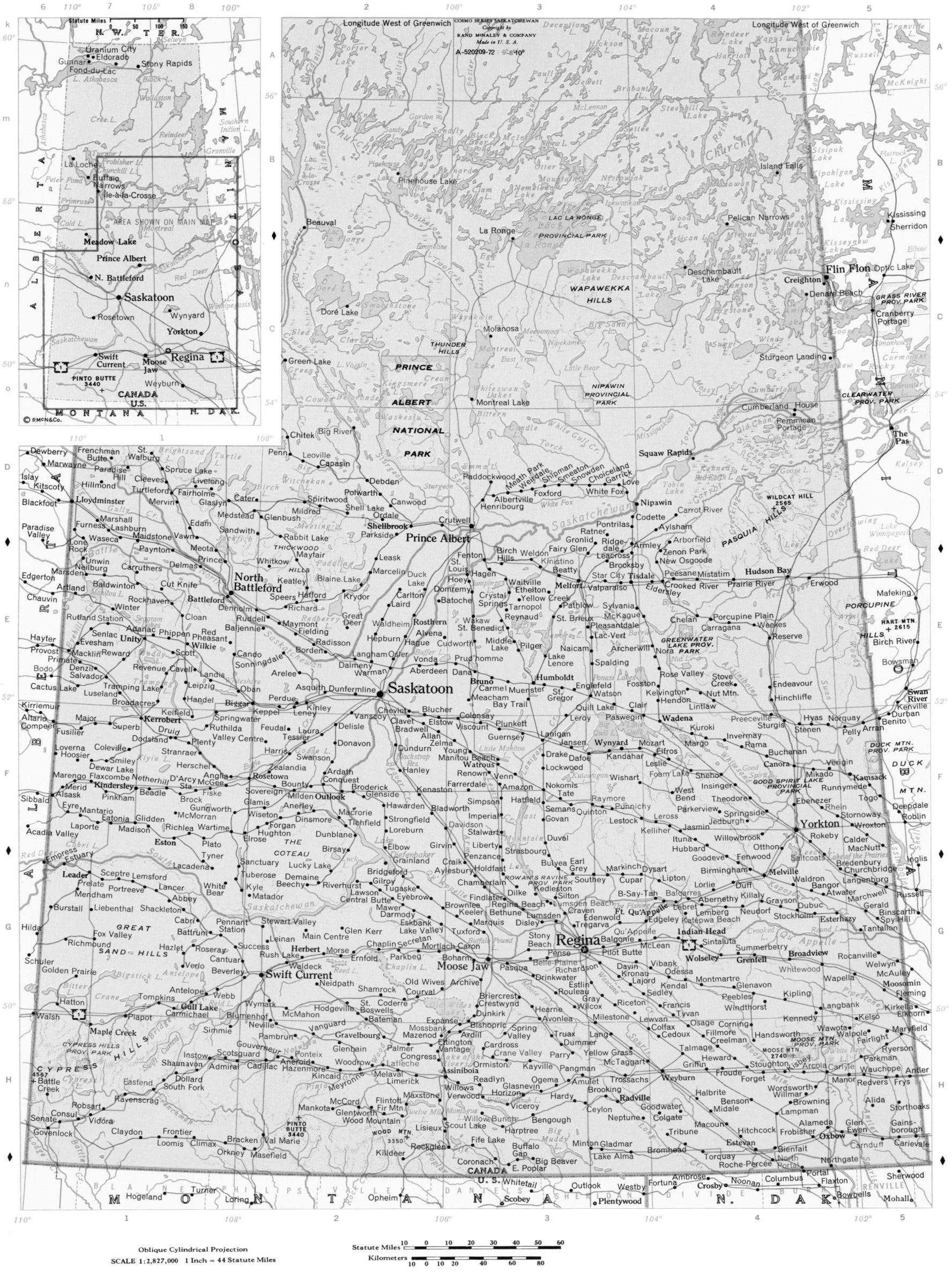

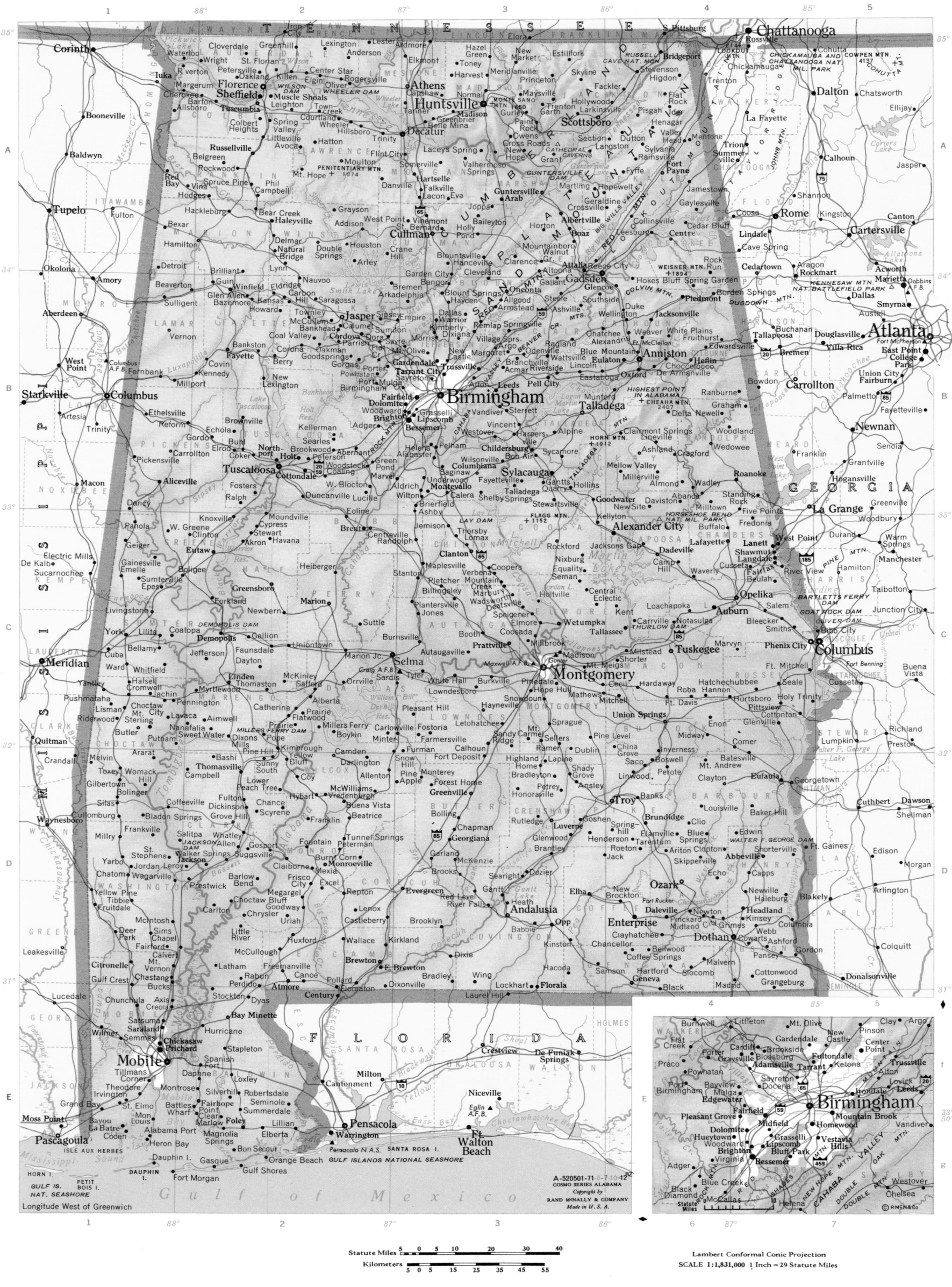

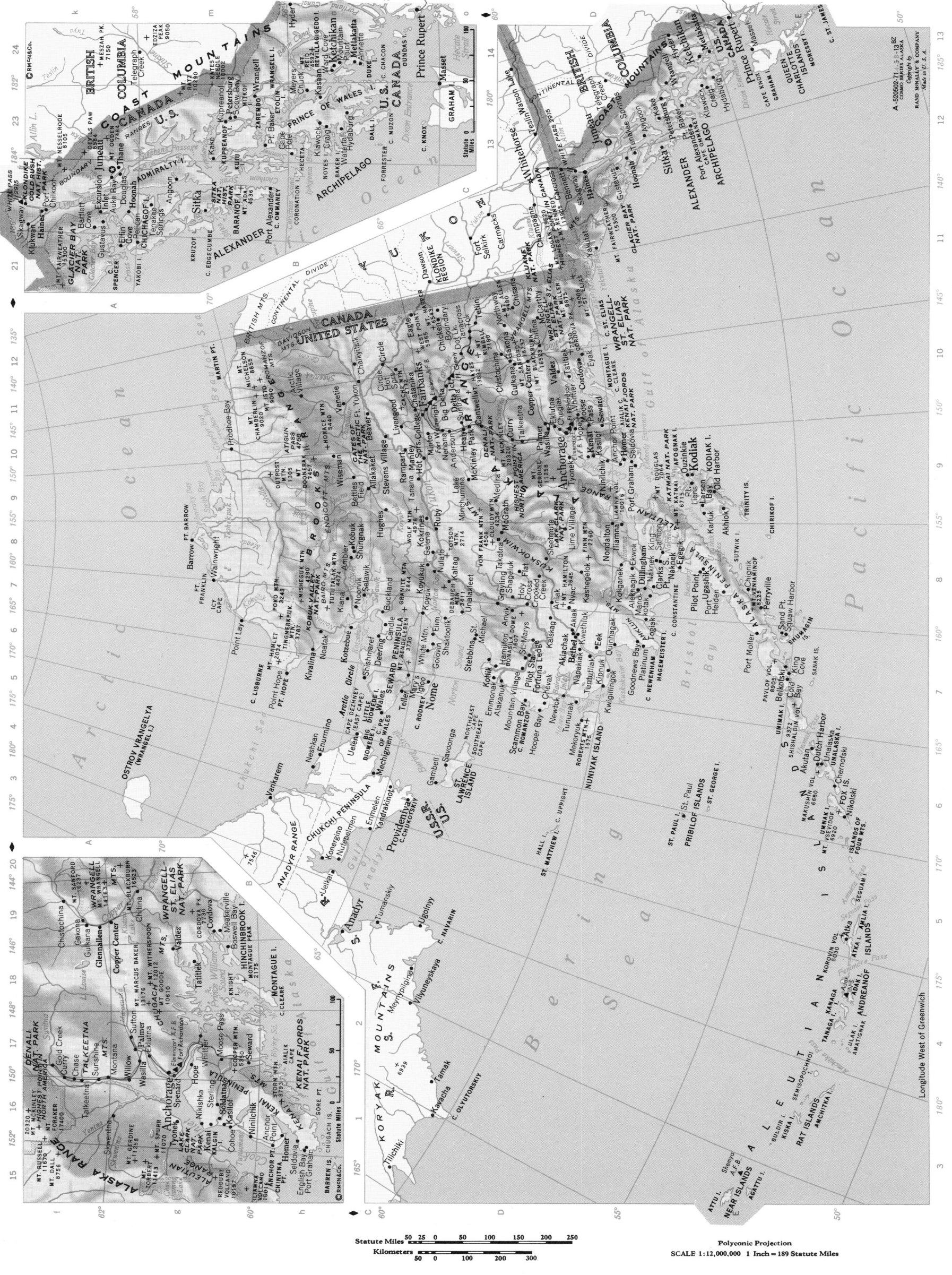

Statute Miles 50 25 0 50 100 150 200 250
Kilometers 50 0 100 200 300

Polyconic Projection
SCALE 1:12,000,000 1 Inch = 189 Statute Miles

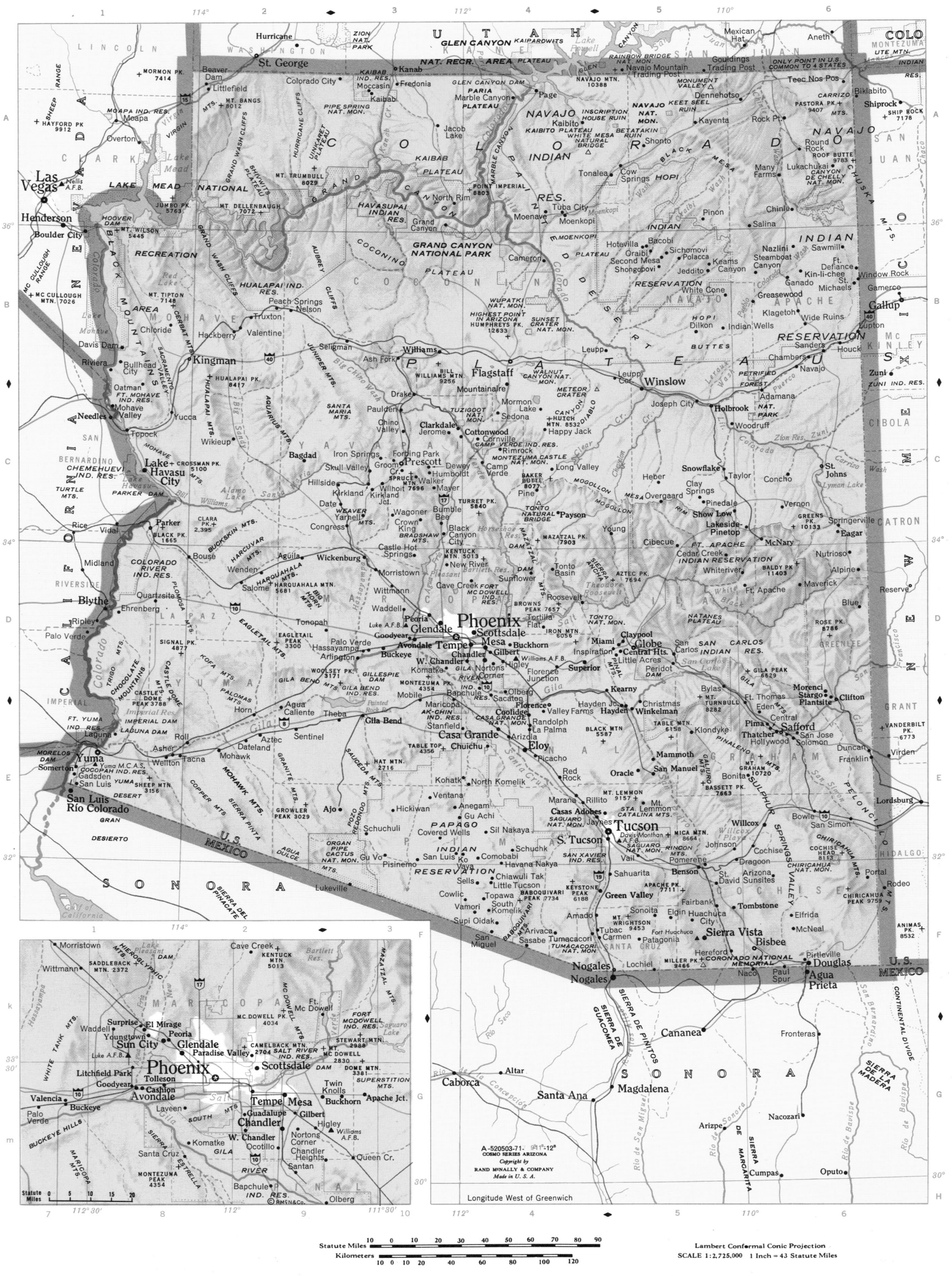

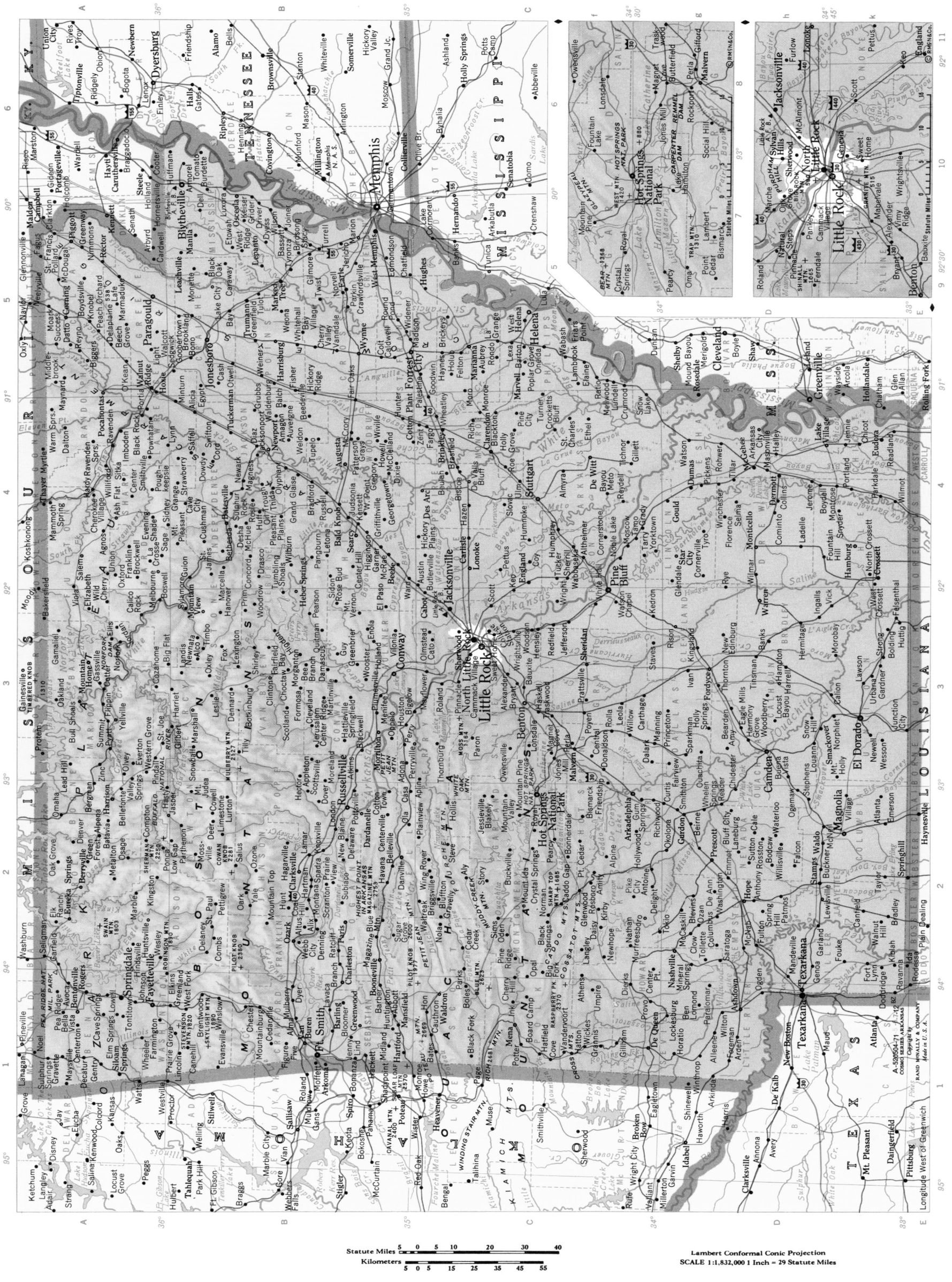

Statute Miles 5 0 5 10 20 30 40
Kilometers 5 0 5 15 25 35 45 55

Lambert Conformal Conic Projection
SCALE 1:1,832,000 1 Inch = 29 Statute Miles

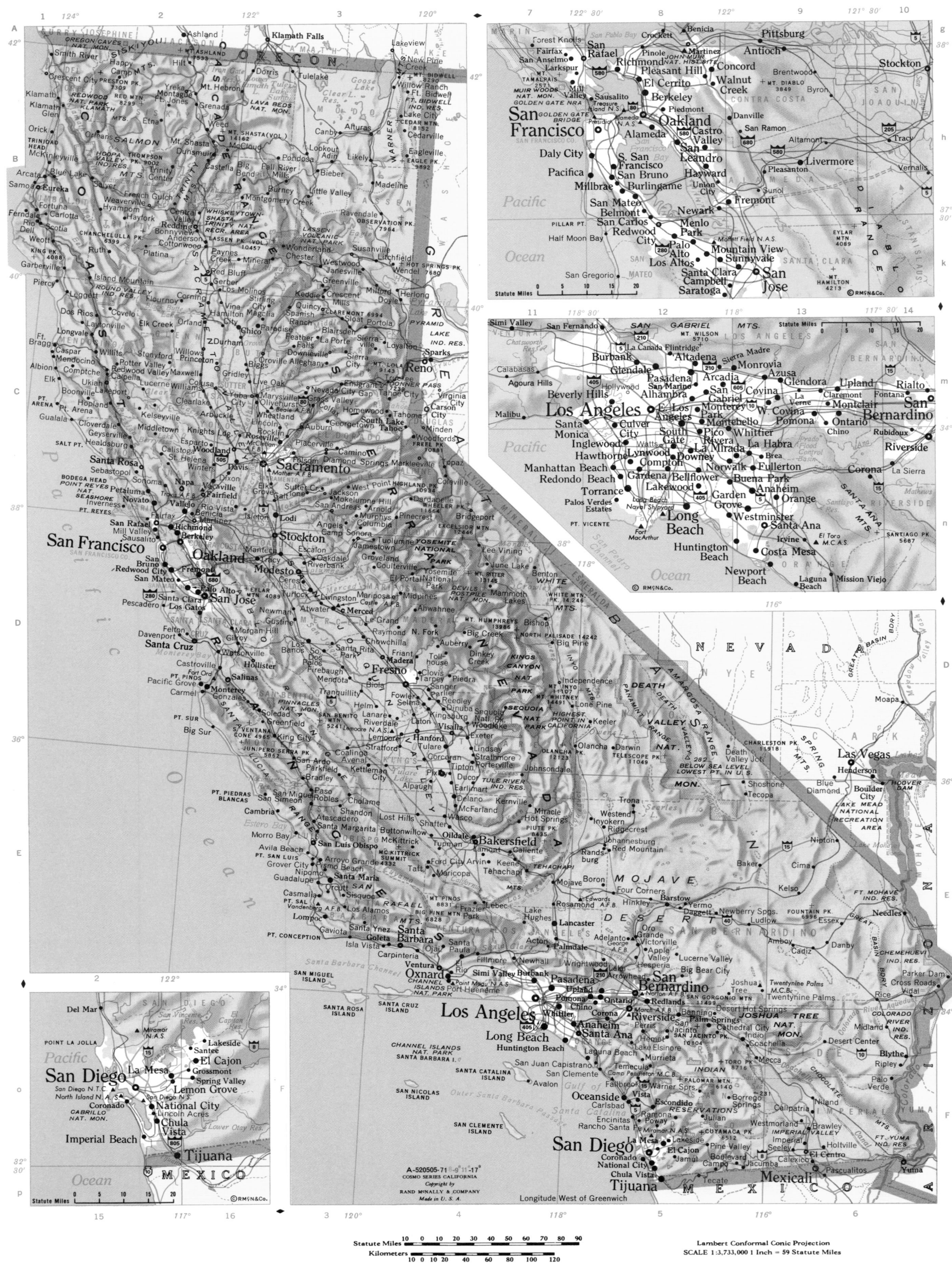

Statute Miles 5 0 5 10 20 30 40 50
Kilometers 5 0 5 15 25 35 45 55 65 75

Lambert Conformal Conic Projection
SCALE 1:2,186,000   1 Inch = 34.5 Statute Miles

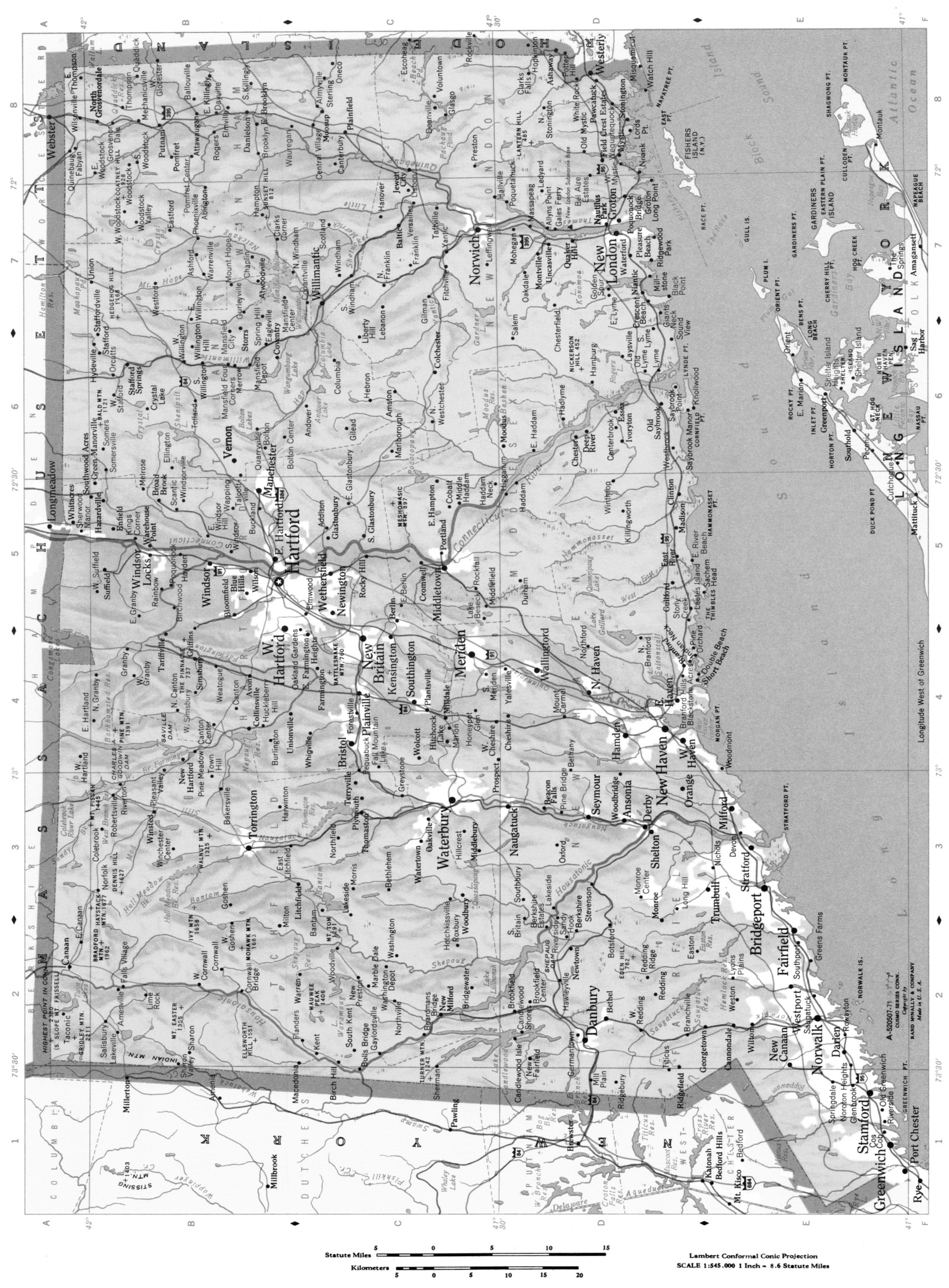

Statute Miles

Kilometers

Lambert Conformal Conic Projection
SCALE 1:545,000 1 Inch = 8.6 Statute Miles

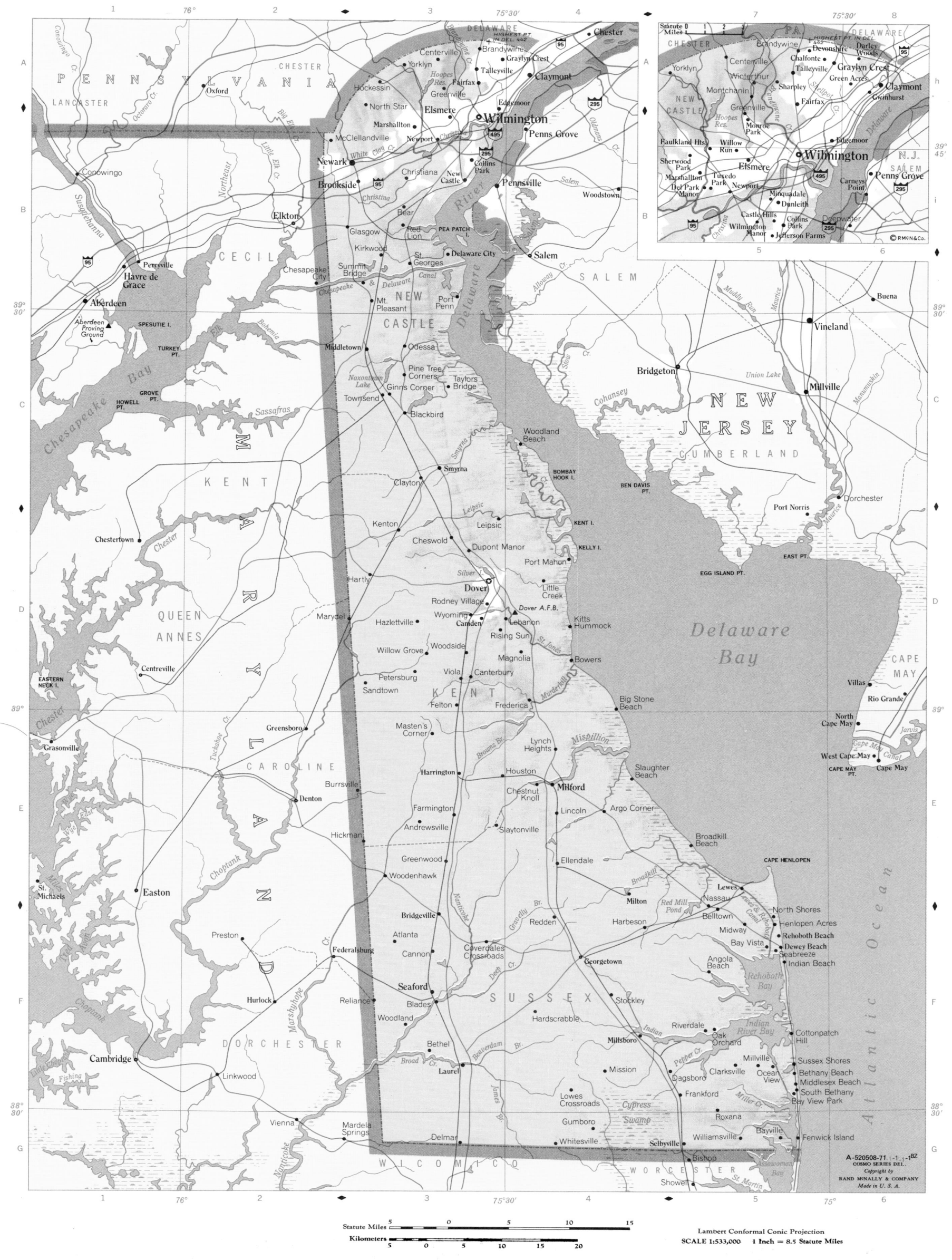

Statute Miles
5   0   5   10   15

Kilometers
5   0   5   10   15   20

Lambert Conformal Conic Projection
SCALE 1:533,000   1 Inch = 8.5 Statute Miles

A-520508-71
COSMO SERIES DEL.
Copyright by
RAND MCNALLY & COMPANY
Made in U.S.A.

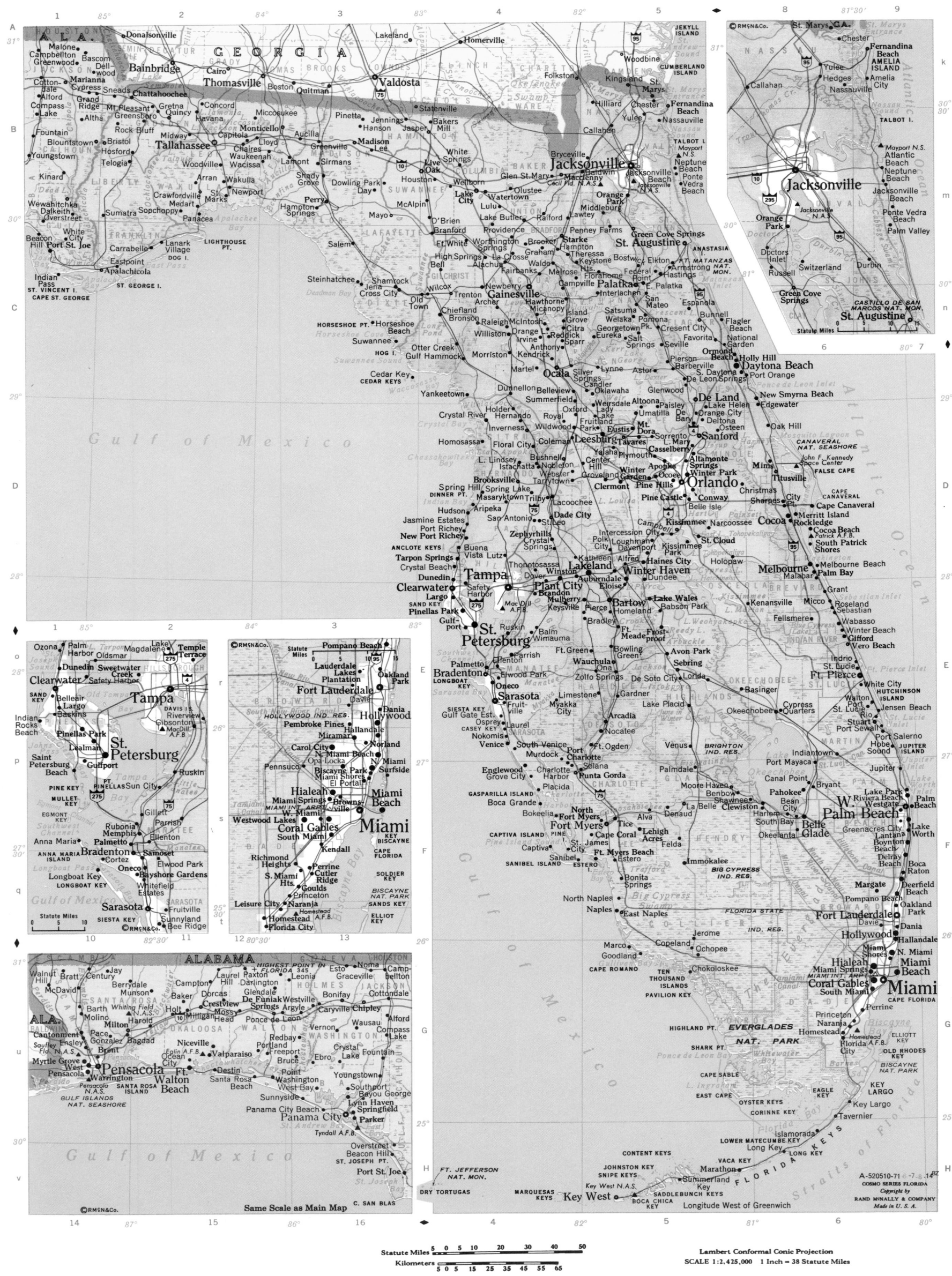

Statute Miles 5 0 5 10 20 30 40 50
Kilometers 5 0 5 15 25 35 45 55 65

Lambert Conformal Conic Projection
SCALE 1:2,425,000   1 Inch = 38 Statute Miles

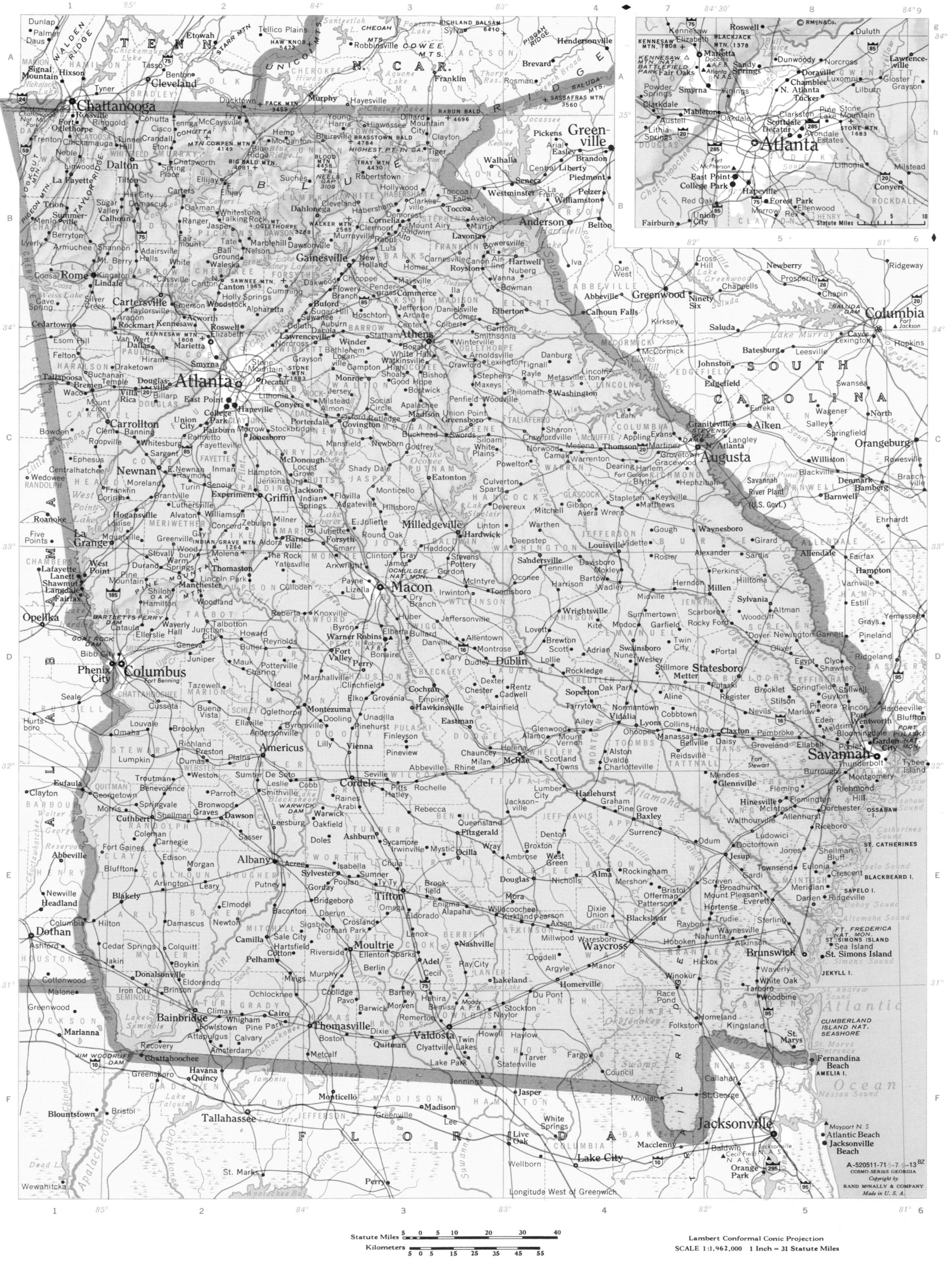

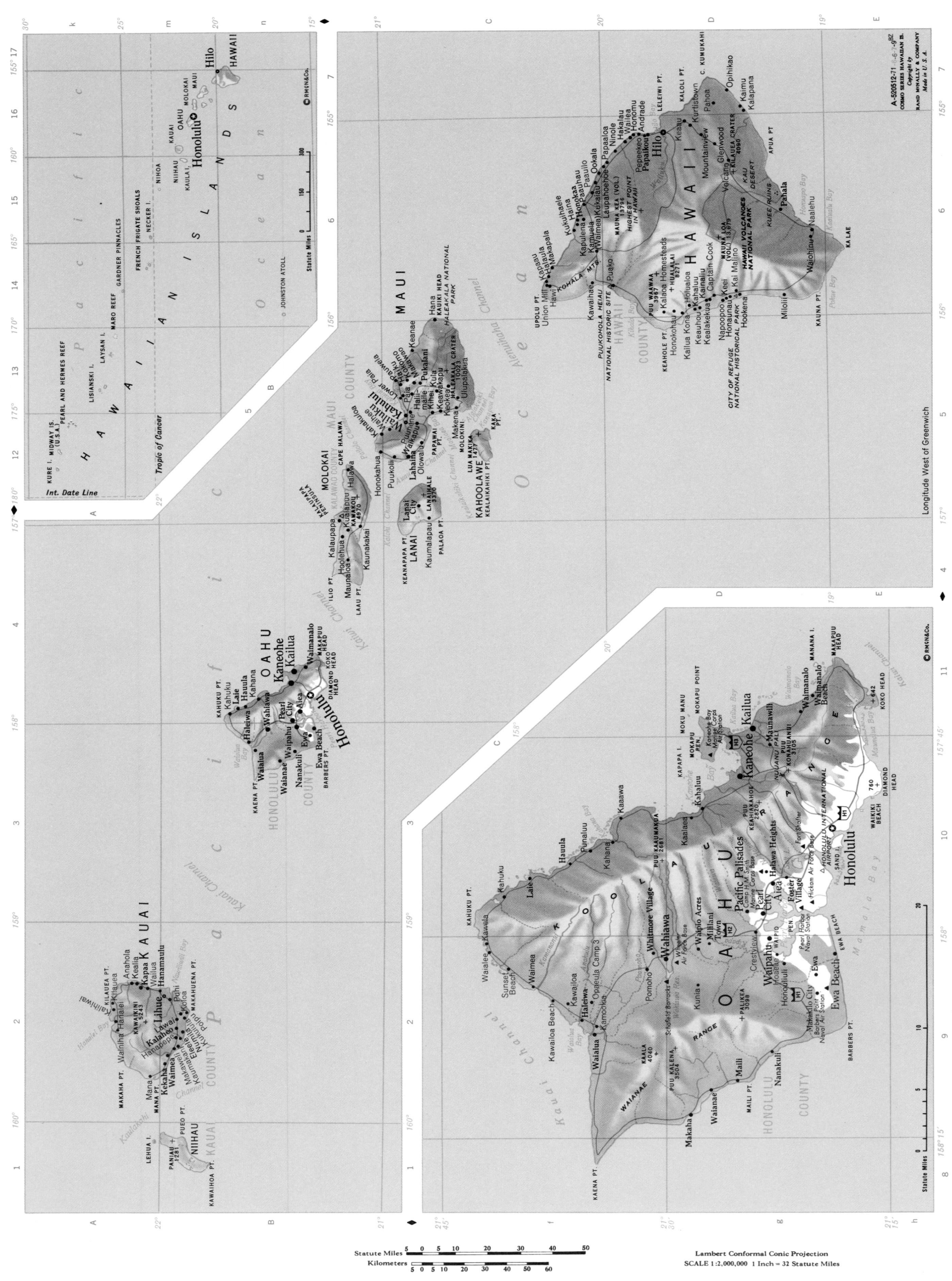

Lambert Conformal Conic Projection
SCALE 1:2,000,000 1 Inch = 32 Statute Miles

Statute Miles
Kilometers

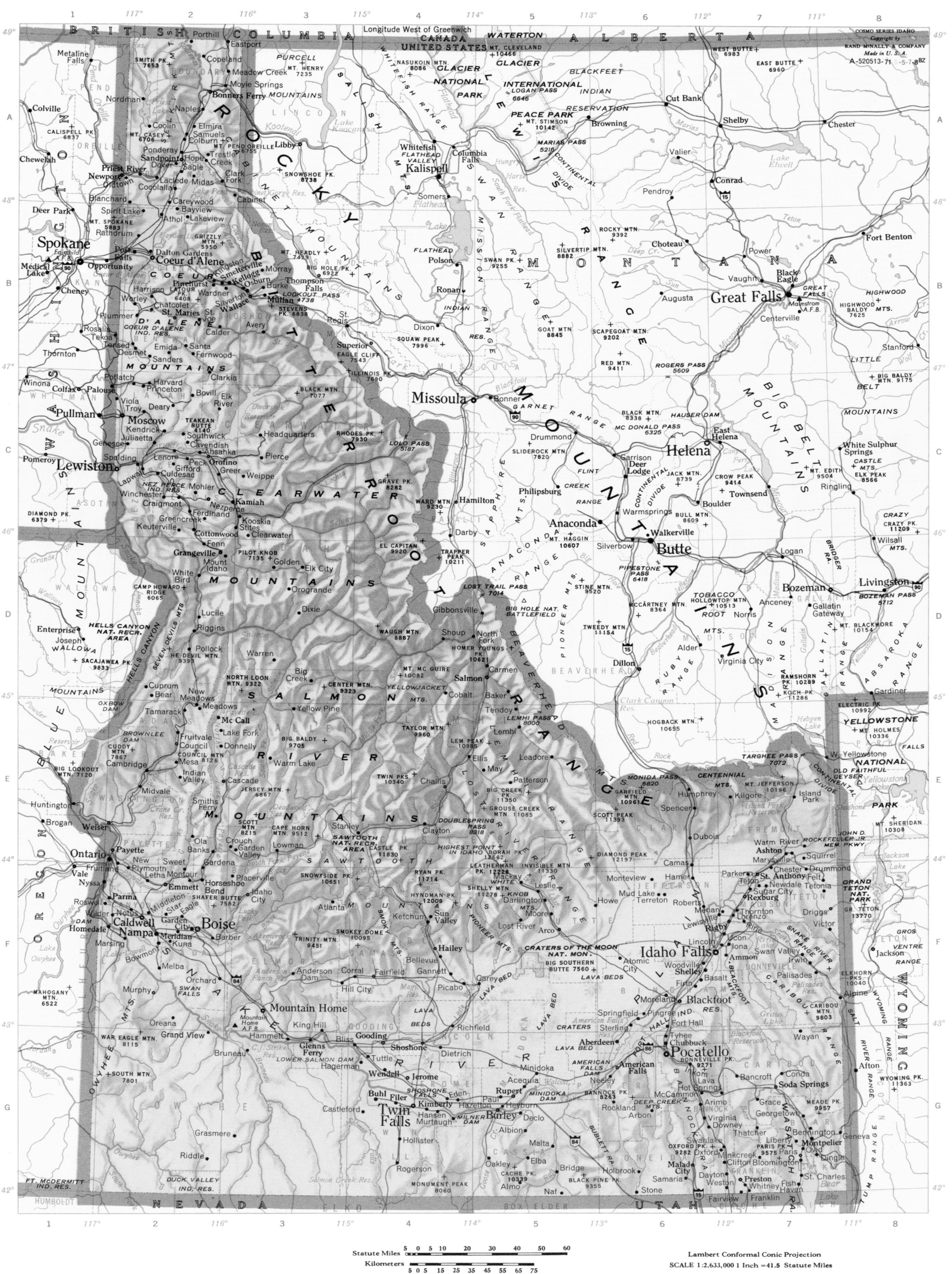

Statute Miles

Kilometers

Lambert Conformal Conic Projection
SCALE 1:2,633,000 1 Inch = 41.5 Statute Miles

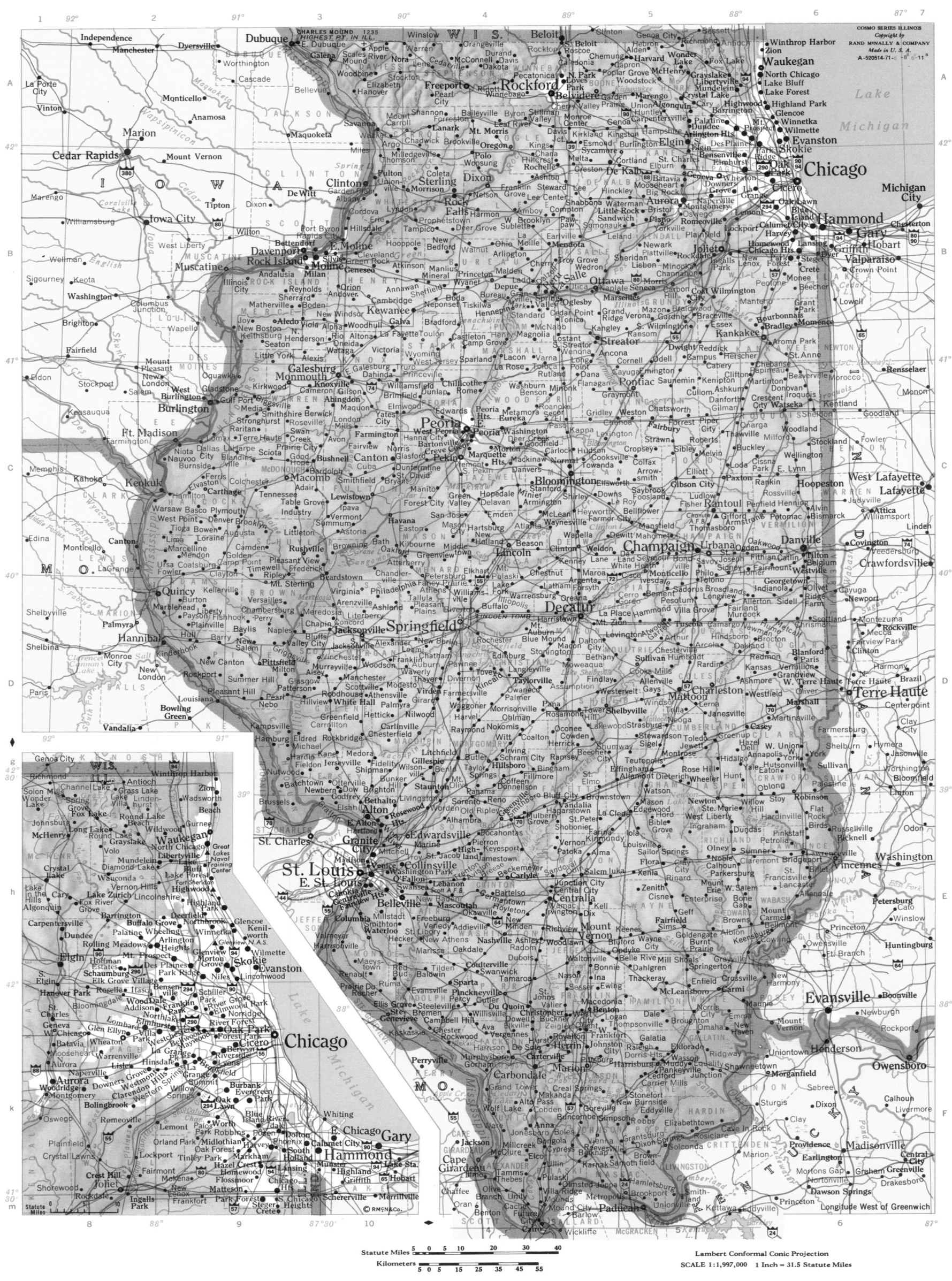

Statute Miles 5 0 5 10 20 30 40
Kilometers 5 0 5 15 25 35 45 55

Lambert Conformal Conic Projection
SCALE 1:1,997,000   1 Inch = 31.5 Statute Miles

Longitude West of Greenwich

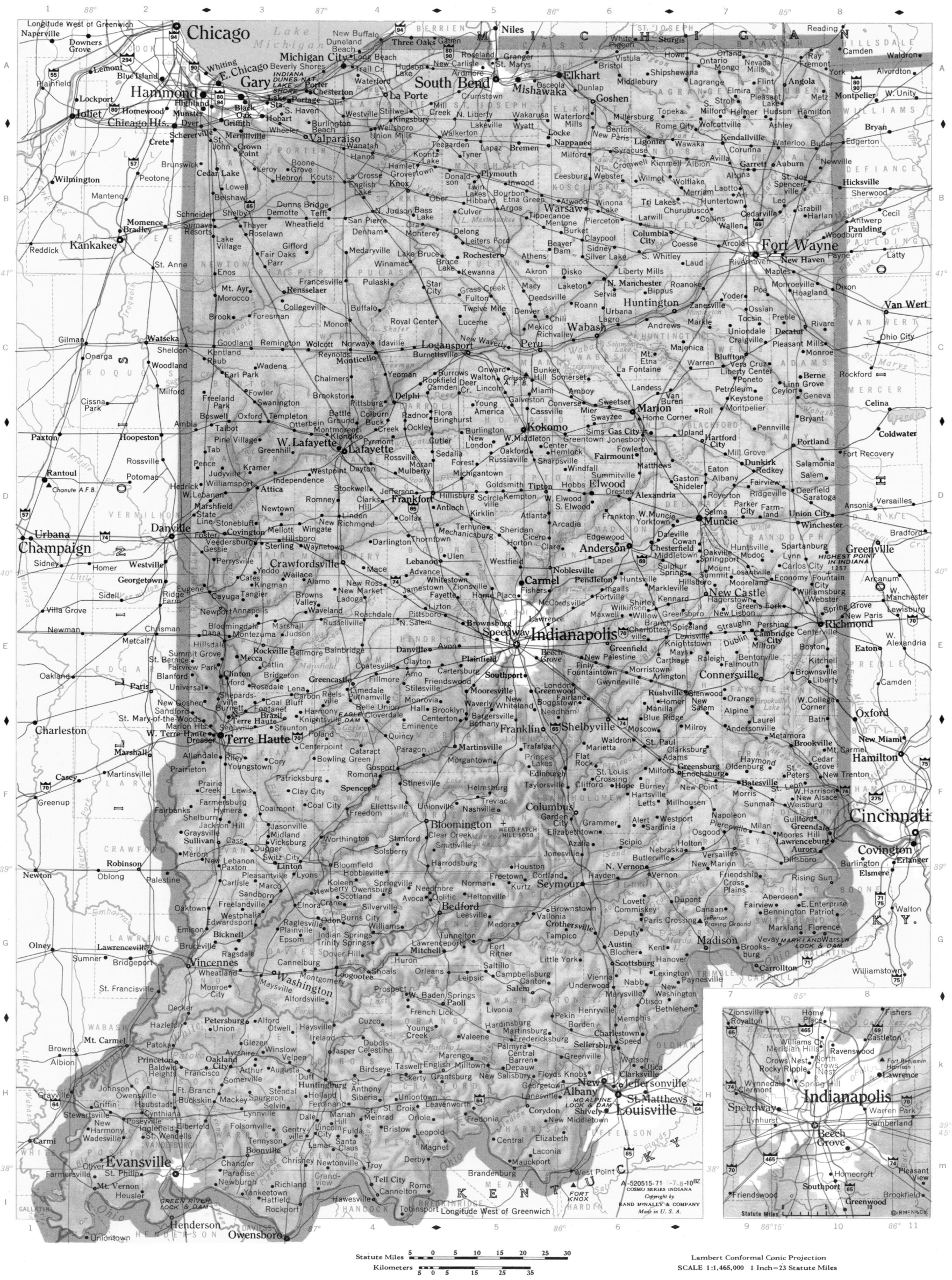

Lambert Conformal Conic Projection
SCALE 1:1,465,000   1 Inch = 23 Statute Miles

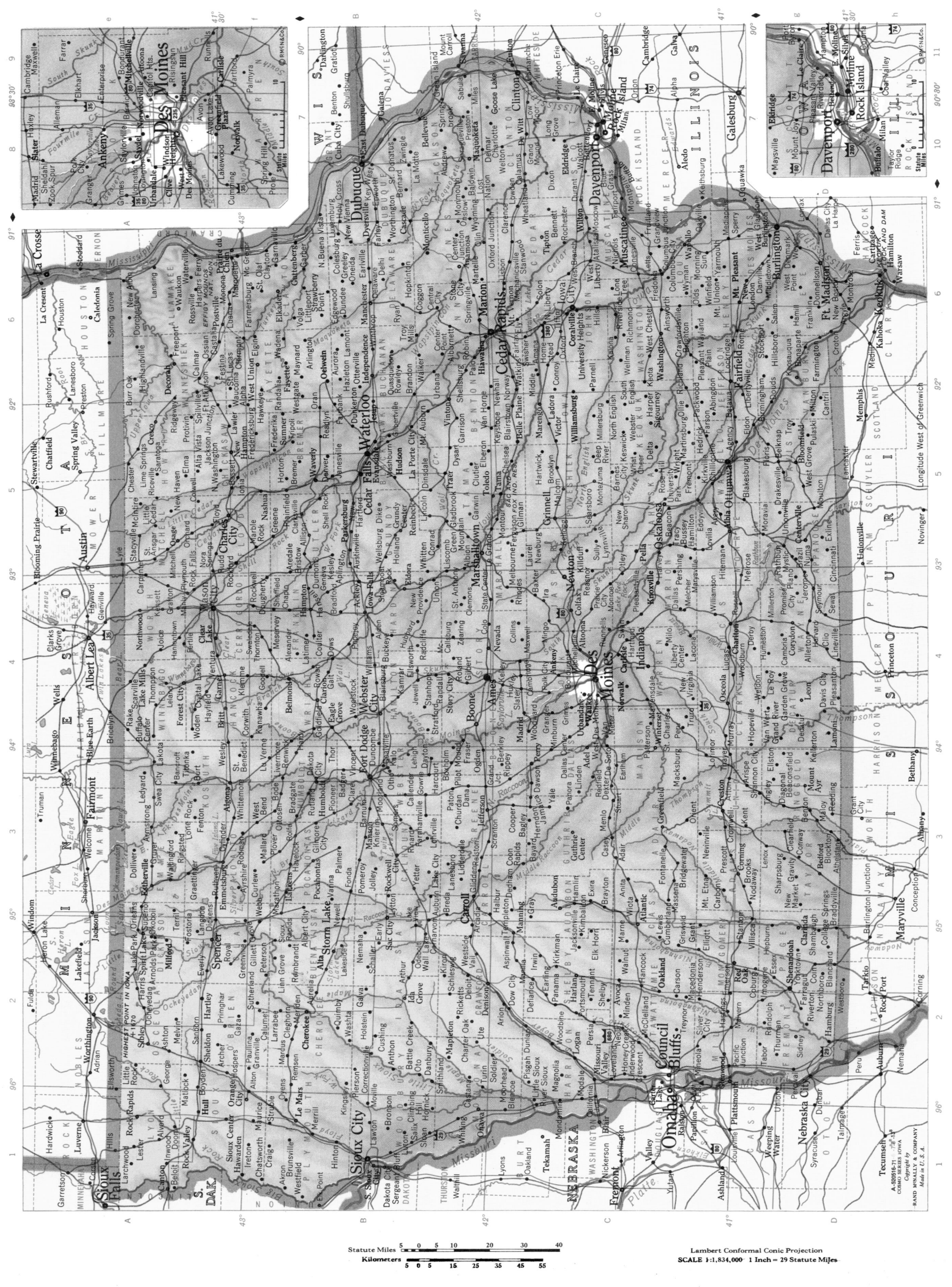

Statute Miles 5 0 5 10 20 30 40
Kilometers 5 0 5 15 25 35 45 55

Lambert Conformal Conic Projection
SCALE 1:1,834,000   1 Inch = 29 Statute Miles

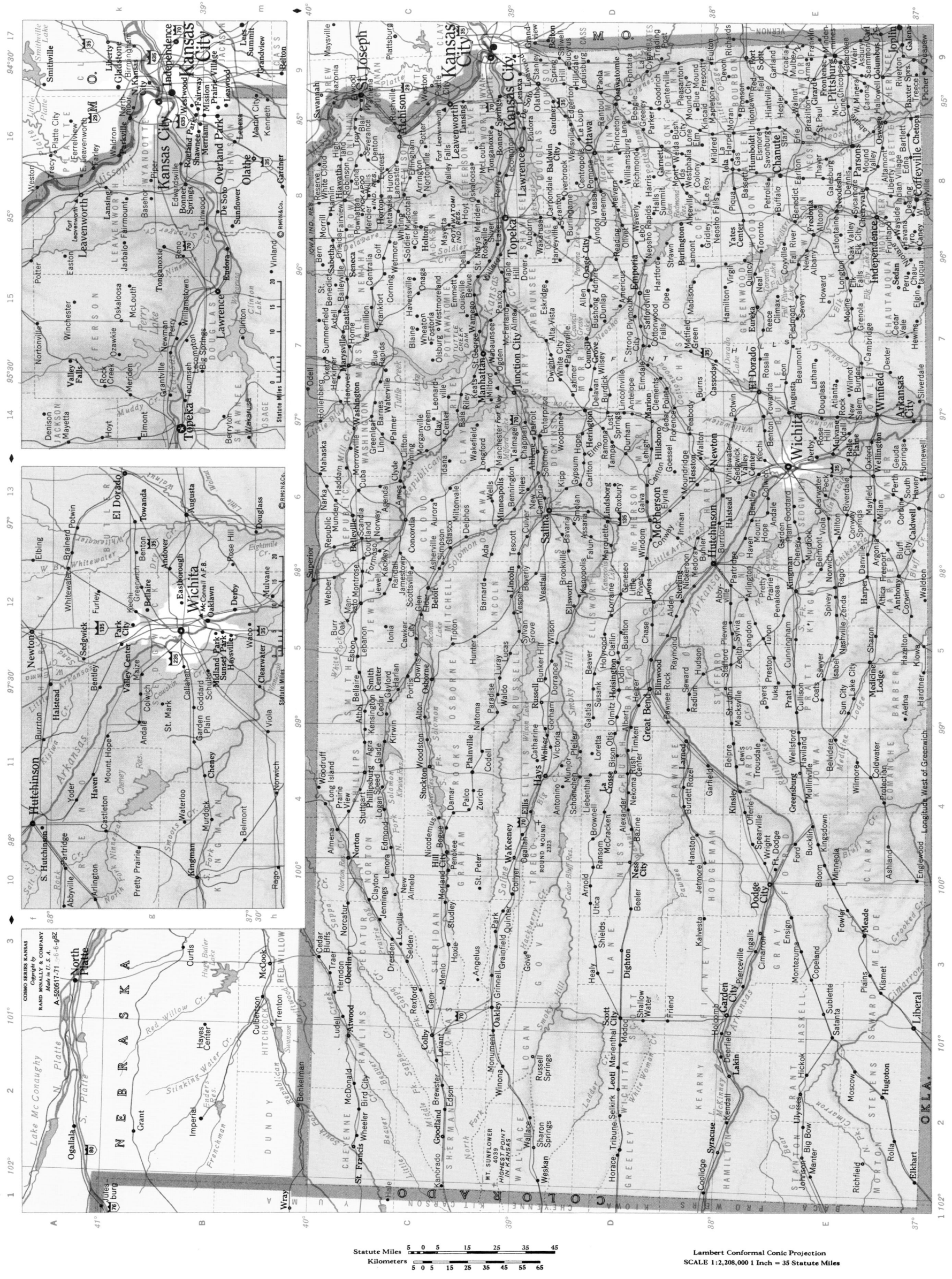

Statute Miles 5 0 5 15 25 35 45
Kilometers 5 0 5 15 25 35 45 55 65

Lambert Conformal Conic Projection
SCALE 1:2,208,000 1 Inch = 35 Statute Miles

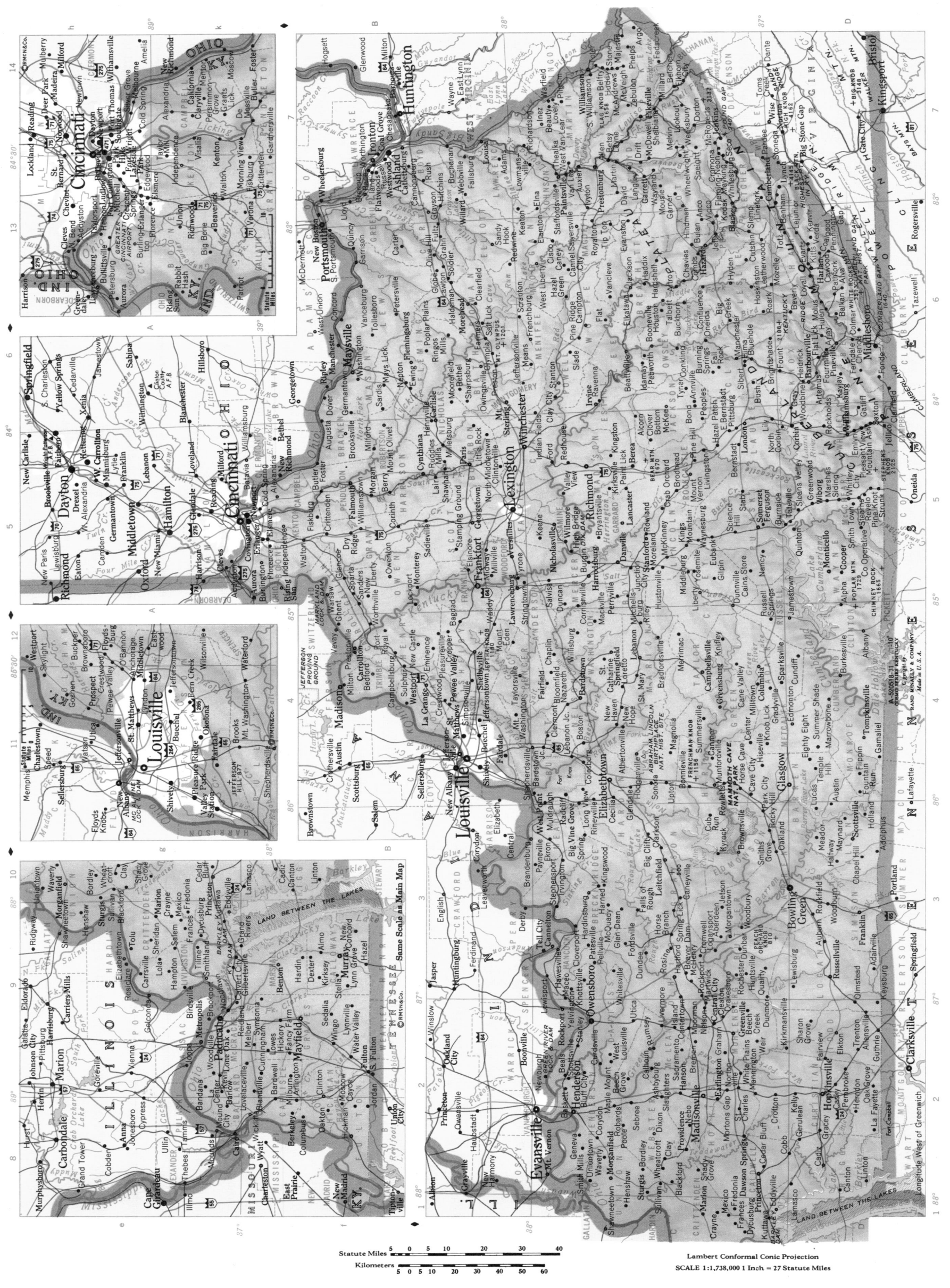

Lambert Conformal Conic Projection
SCALE 1:1,738,000 1 Inch = 27 Statute Miles

Statute Miles 5 0 5 10 20 30 40
Kilometers 5 0 5 10 20 30 40 50 60

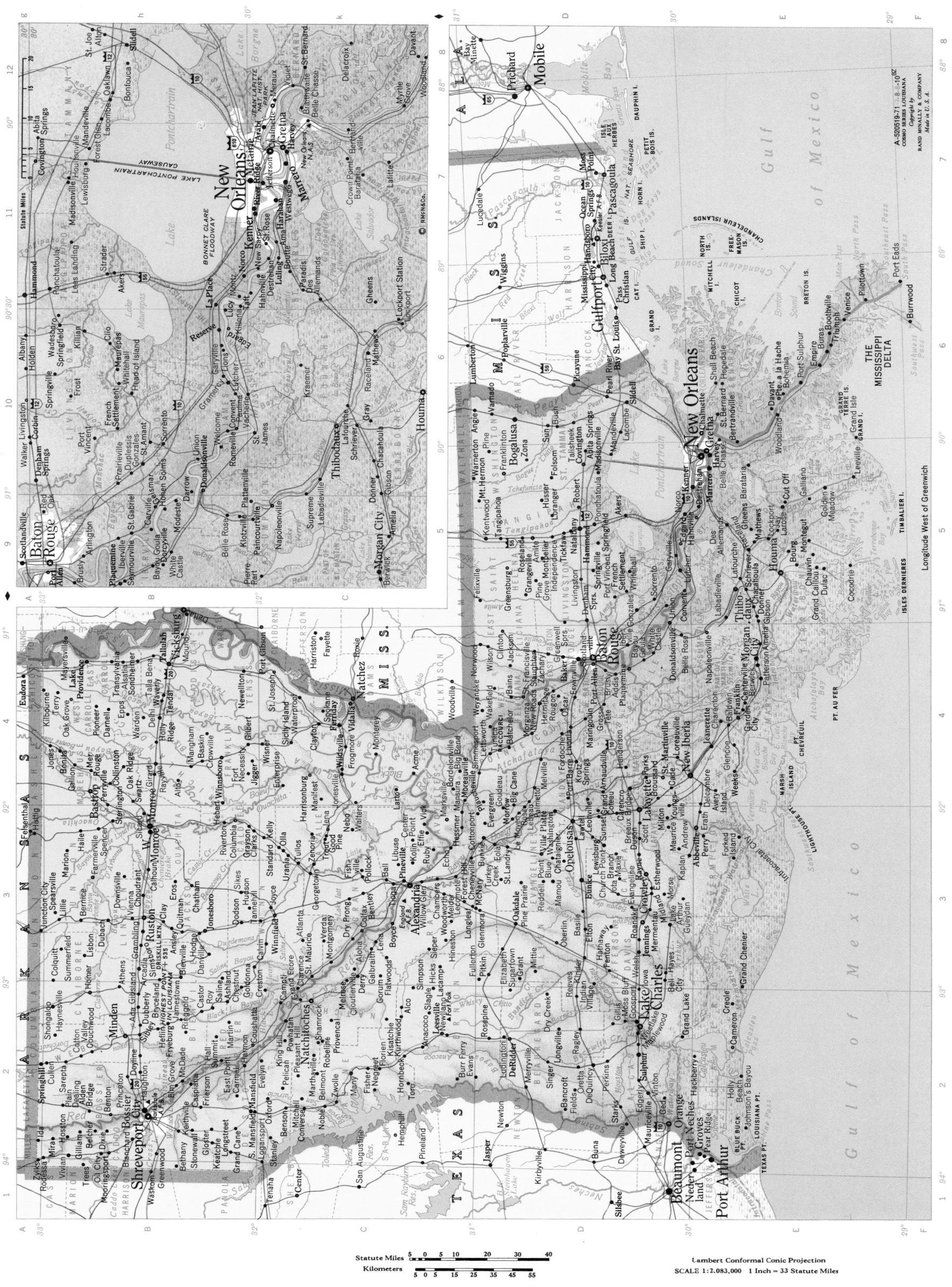

Statute Miles 5 0 5 10 20 30 40
Kilometers 5 0 5 15 25 35 45 55

Lambert Conformal Conic Projection
SCALE 1:2,083,000 1 Inch = 33 Statute Miles

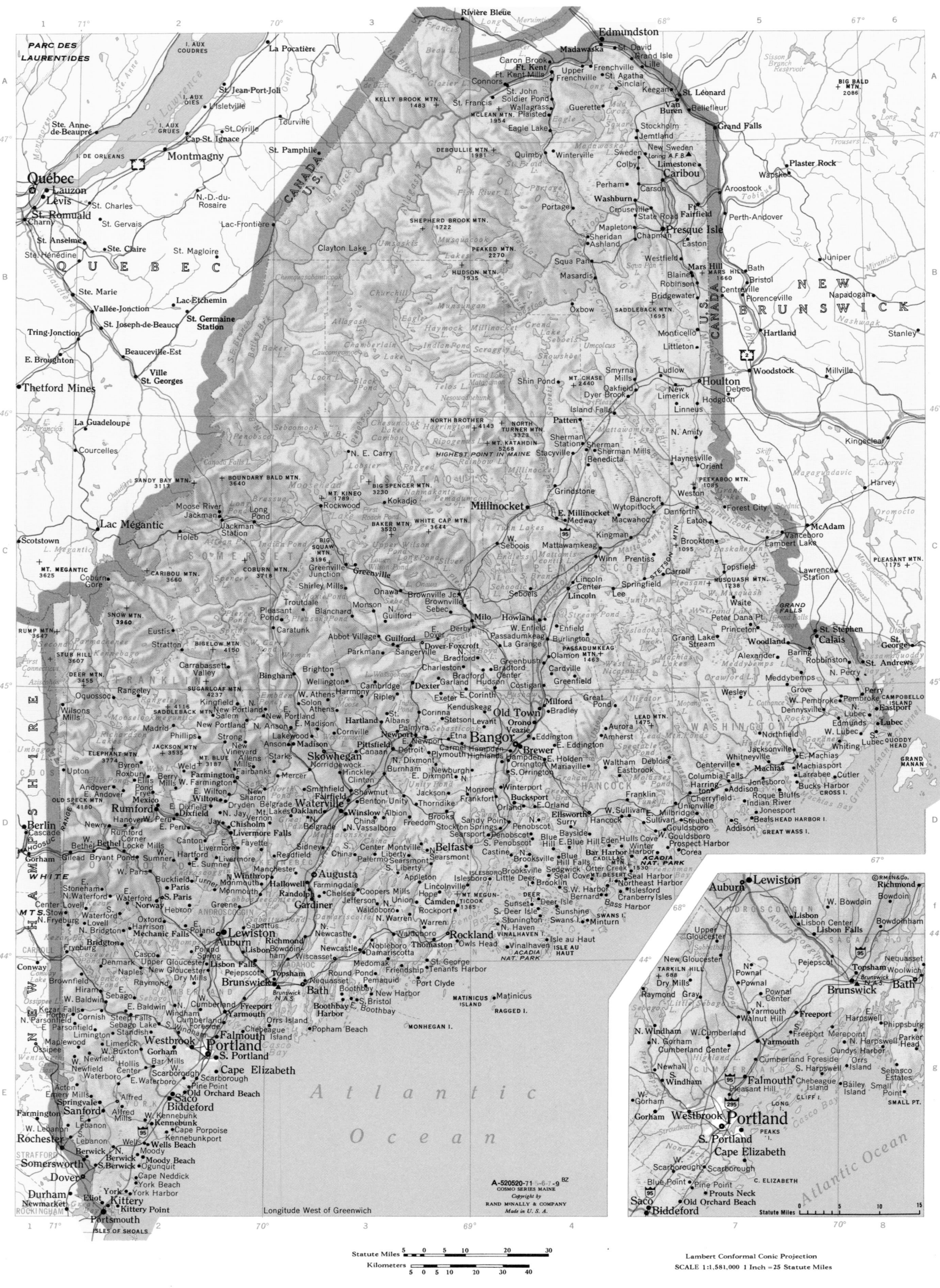

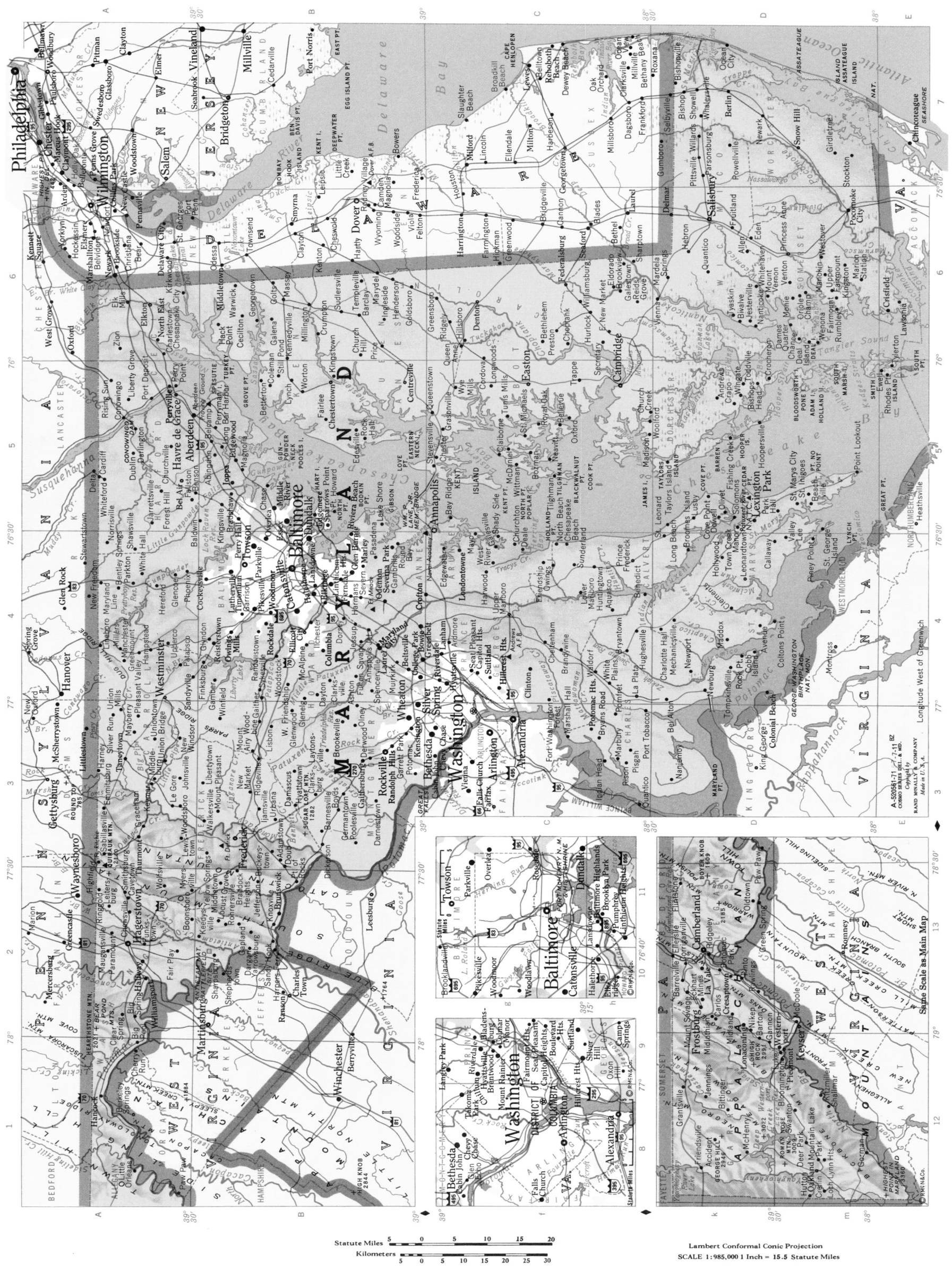

Statute Miles

Kilometers

Lambert Conformal Conic Projection
SCALE 1:985,000 1 Inch = 15.5 Statute Miles

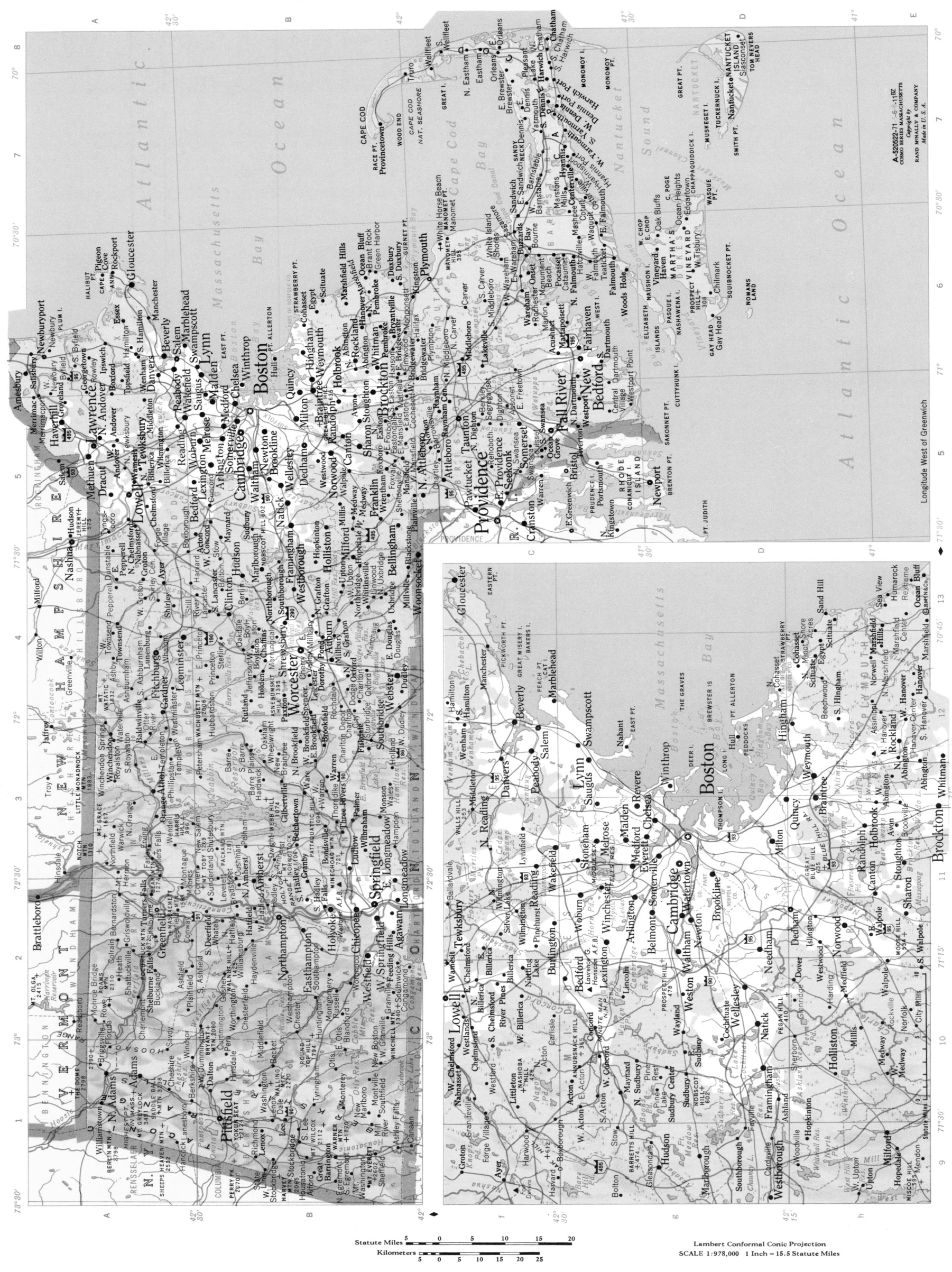

Statute Miles

Kilometers

Lambert Conformal Conic Projection
SCALE 1:978,000 1 Inch = 15.5 Statute Miles

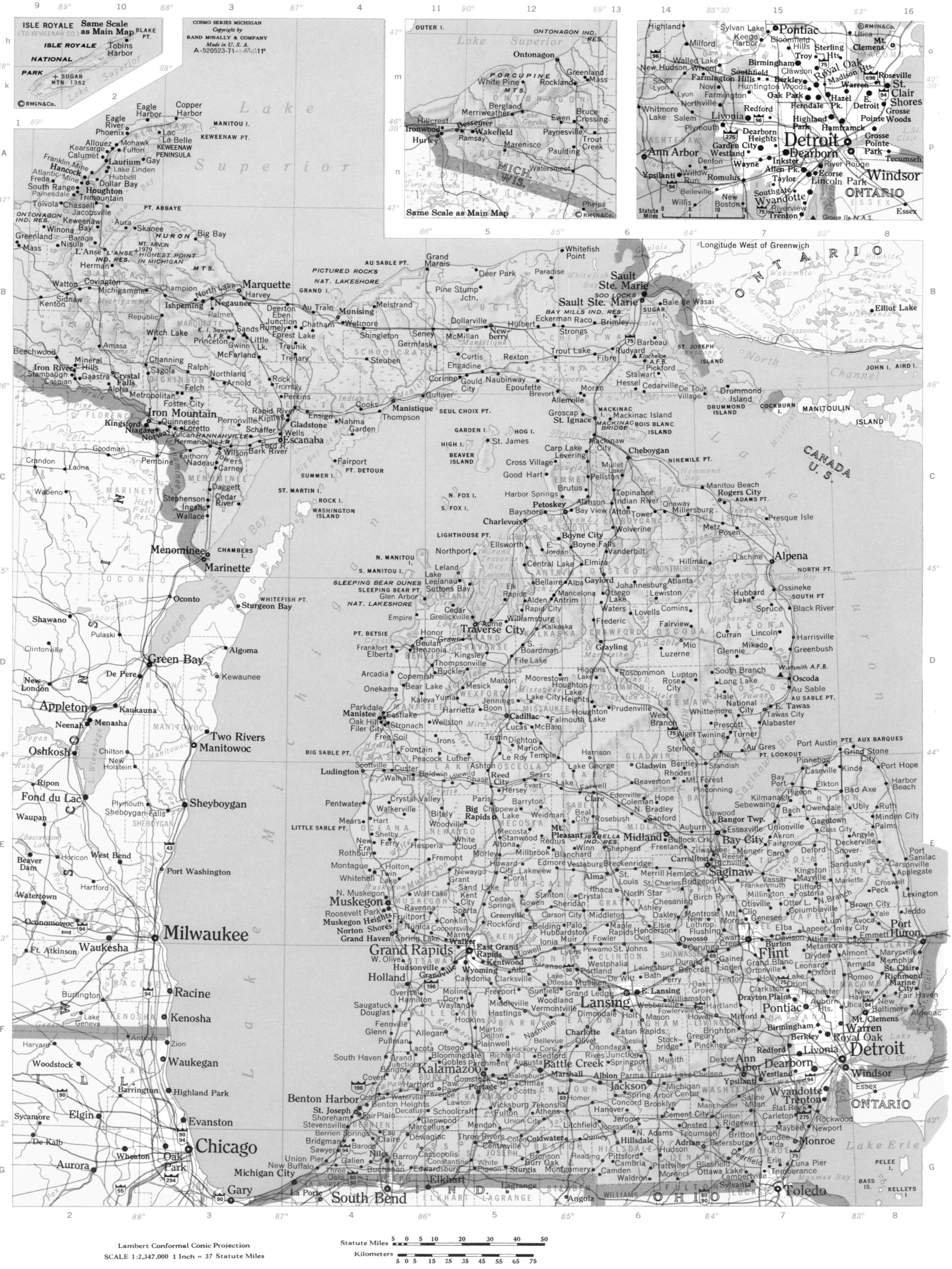

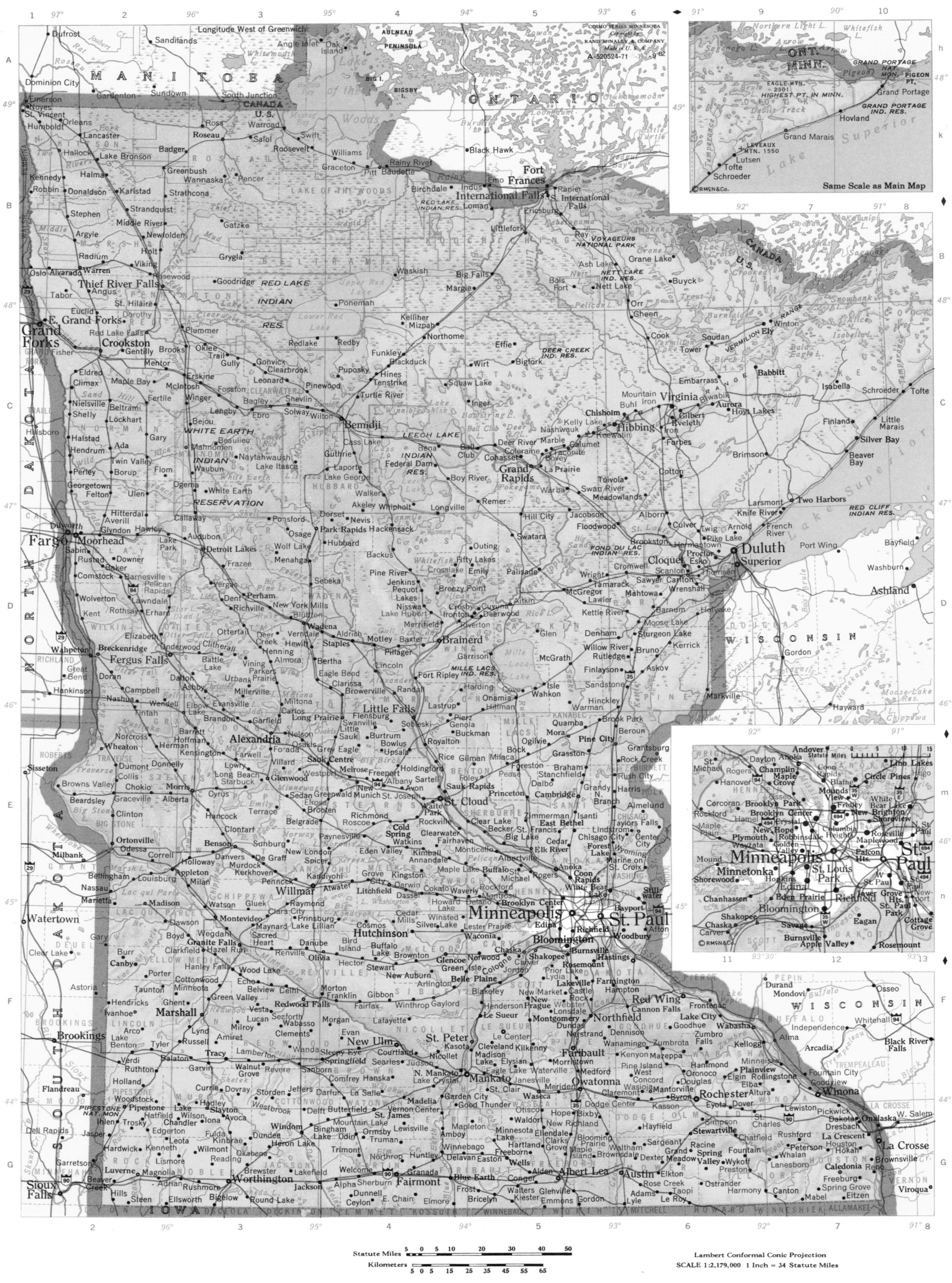

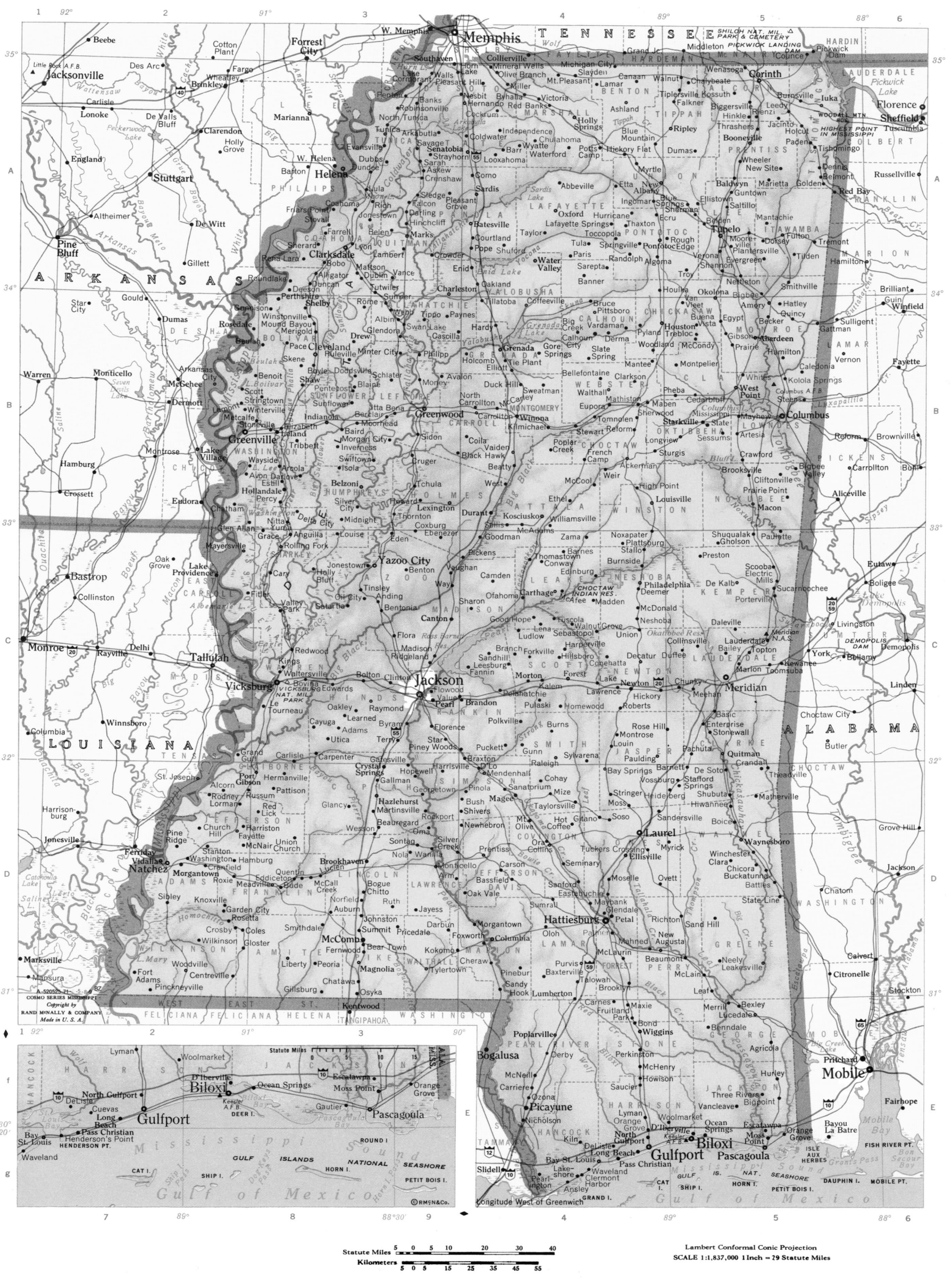

Lambert Conformal Conic Projection
SCALE 1:1,837,000 1 Inch = 29 Statute Miles

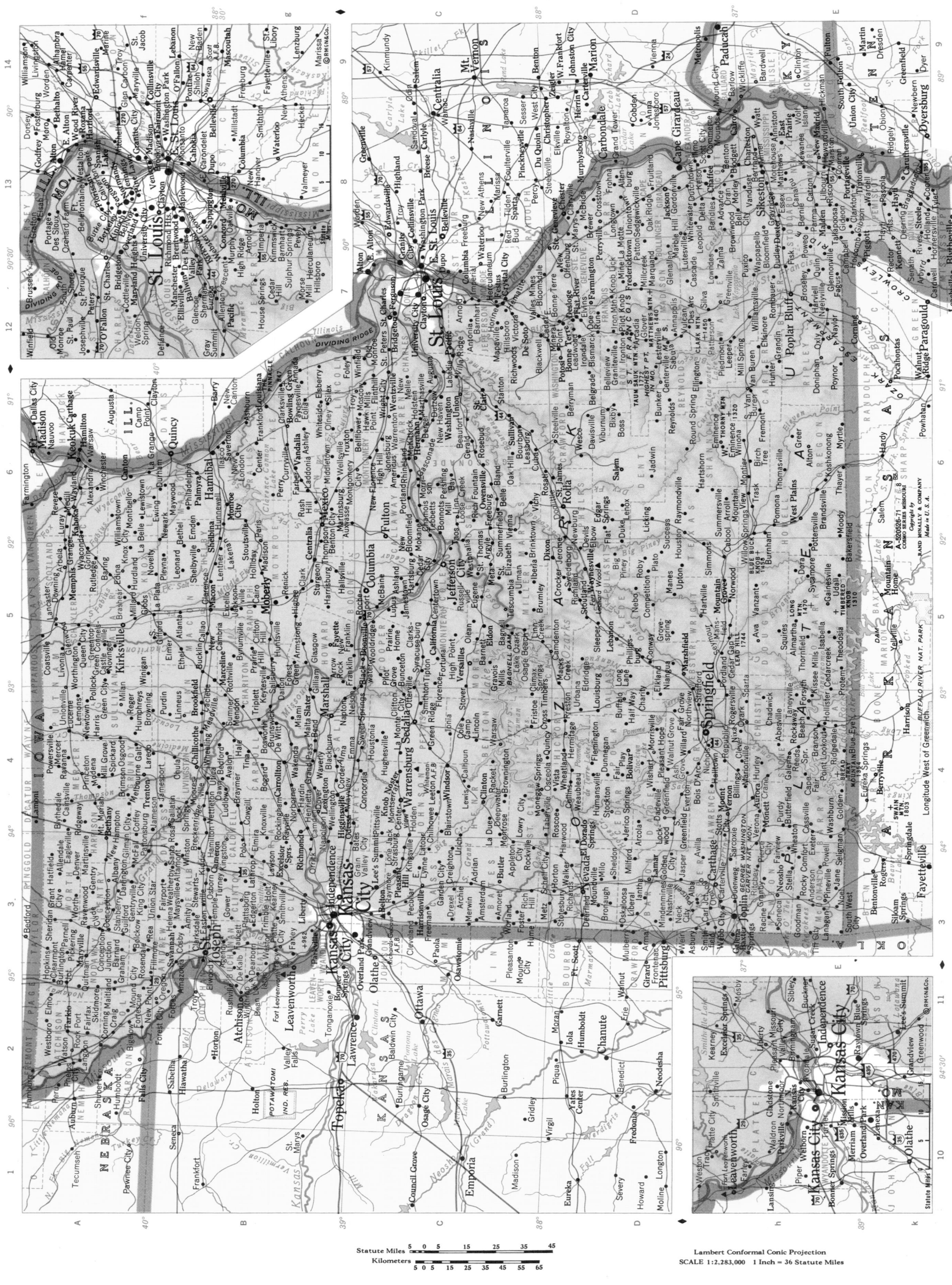

Statute Miles 5 0 5 15 25 35 45
Kilometers 5 0 5 15 25 35 45 55 65

Lambert Conformal Conic Projection
SCALE 1:2,283,000   1 Inch = 36 Statute Miles

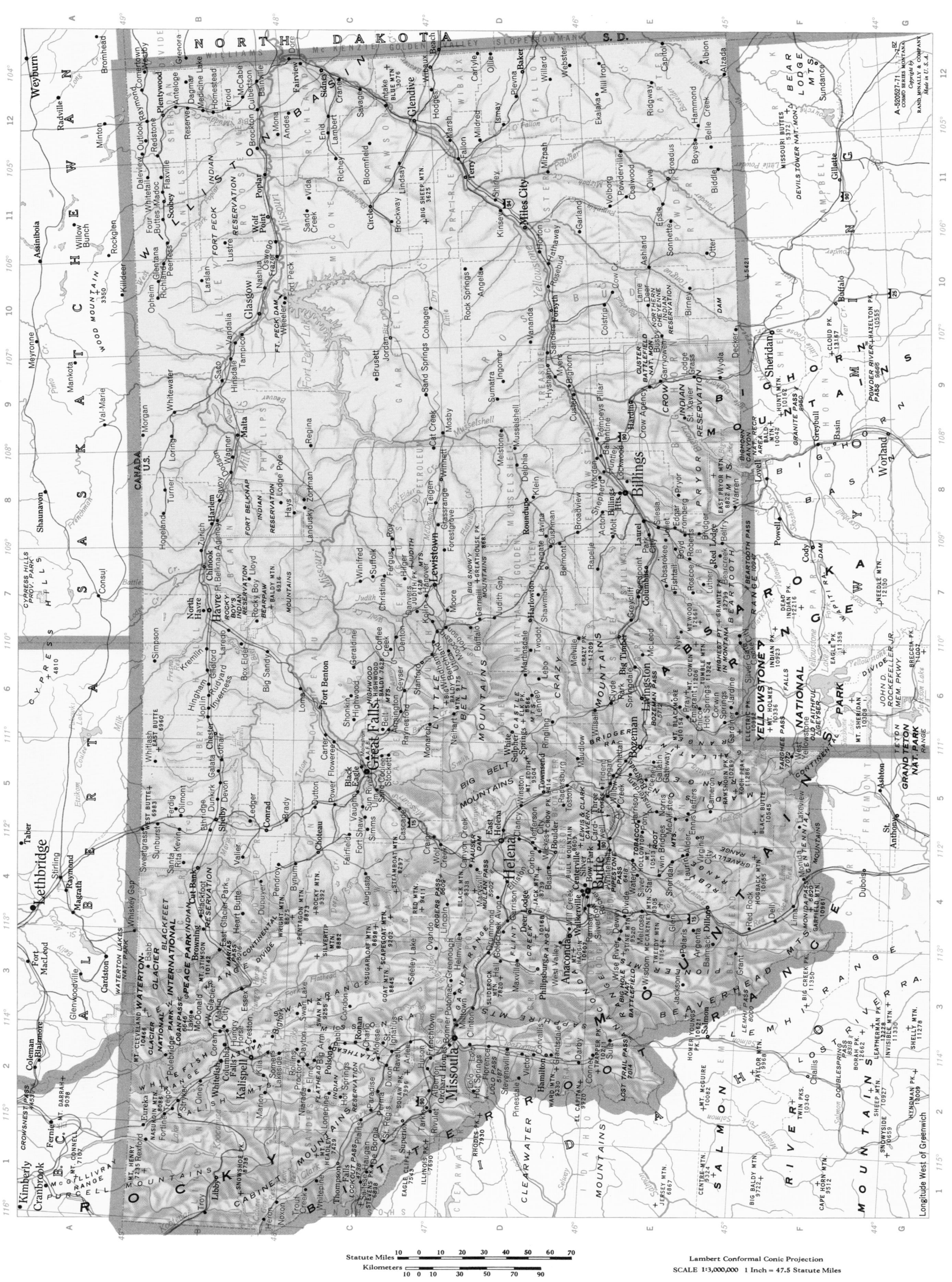

Statute Miles 10 0 10 20 30 40 50 60 70
Kilometers 10 0 10 30 50 70 90

Lambert Conformal Conic Projection
SCALE 1:3,000,000 1 Inch = 47.5 Statute Miles

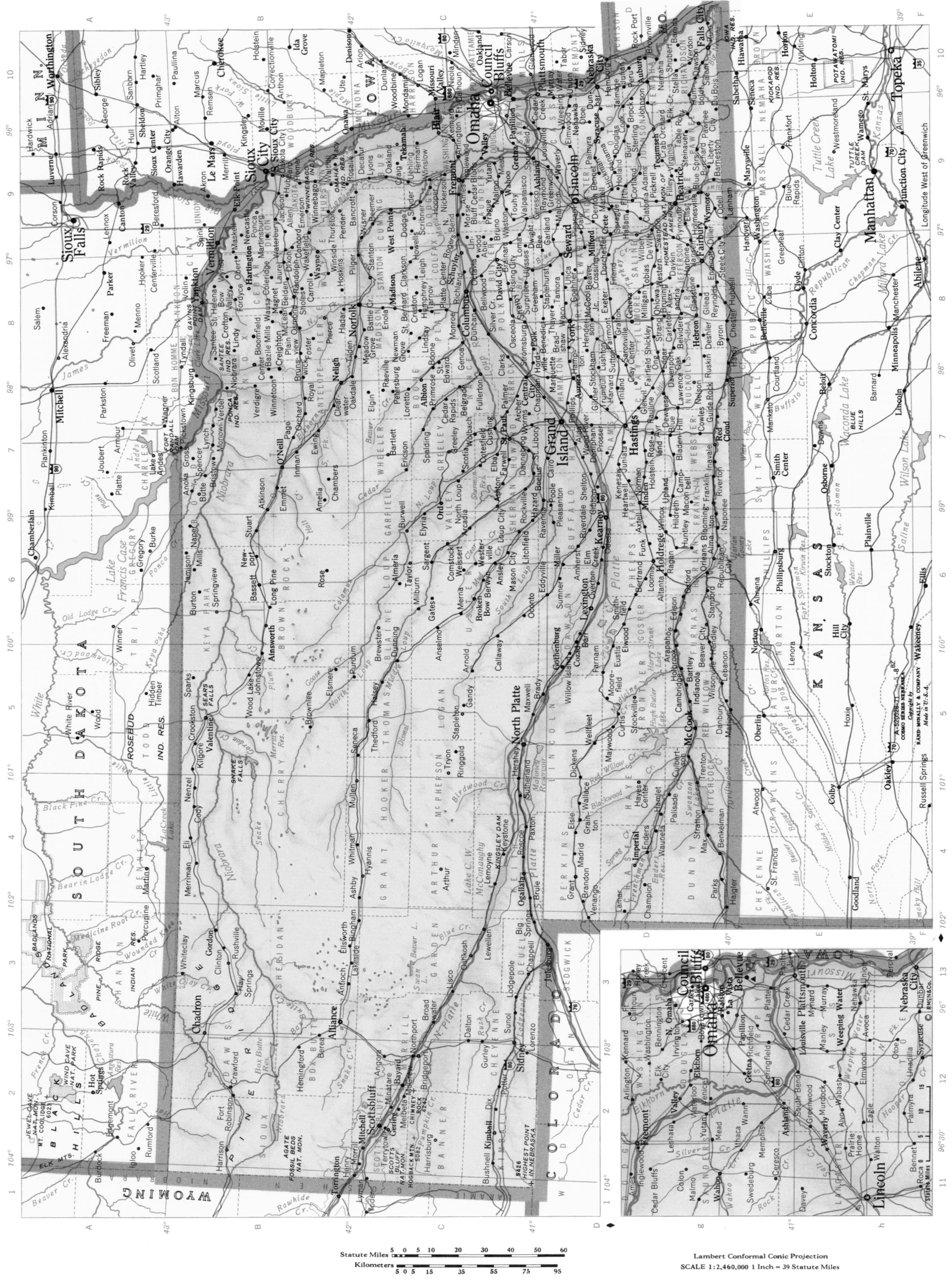

Statute Miles

Kilometers

Lambert Conformal Conic Projection
SCALE 1:2,460,000 1 Inch = 39 Statute Miles

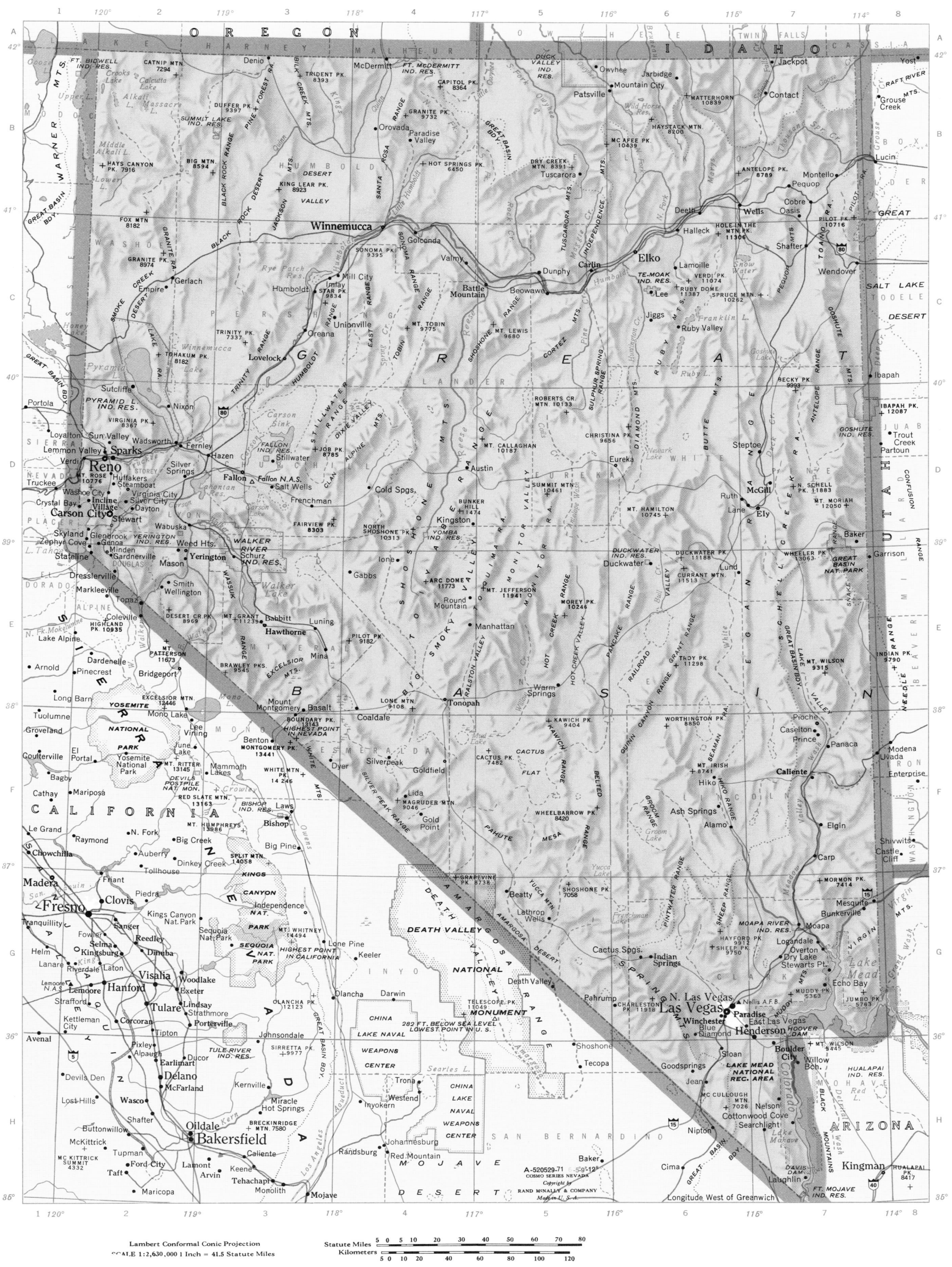

Same Scale as Main Map

QUEBEC
CANADA
U. S.

COMPTON

Ascot

Hereford Mtn. 2760

Salmon Mtn. 3364

Rump Mtn. 3647

Shatney Mtn. 2170 Happy Corner Stub Hill 3607

Pittsburg

Beecher Falls

Stewartstown
W. Stewartstown

Stewartstown Hollow

Colebrook   Dixville Notch

DIXVILLE PK. 3482

Blue Mtn. 3723

Sugarloaf 3701
N. Stratford

VERMONT

ESSEX

CRYSTAL MTN.

WHITCOMB MTN.

Errol

COSMO SERIES NEW HAMP.
Copyright by
RAND McNALLY & COMPANY
Made in U. S. A.
A-520530-71

Lambert Conformal Conic Projection
SCALE 1:792,000   1 Inch = 12.75 Statute Miles

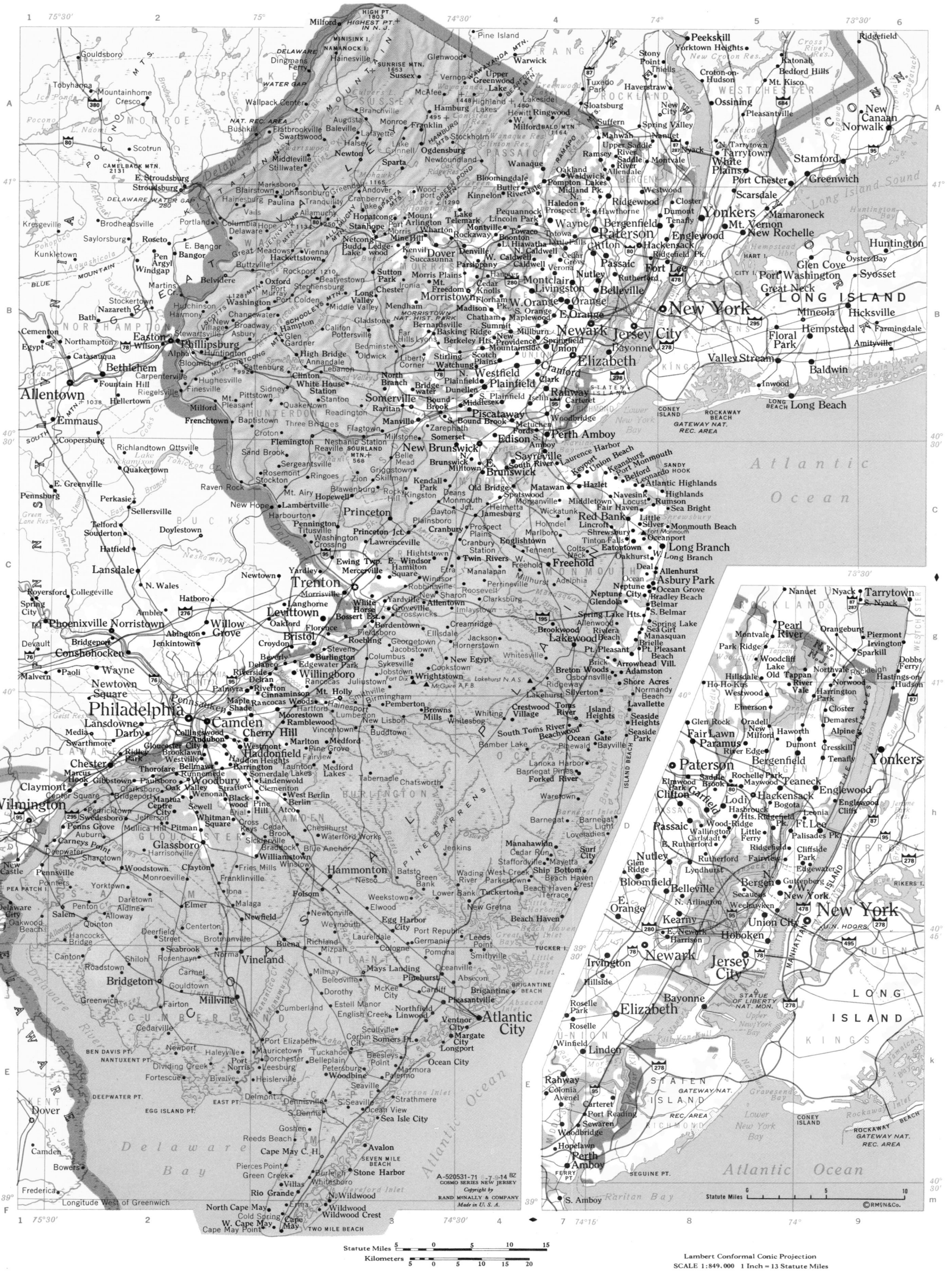

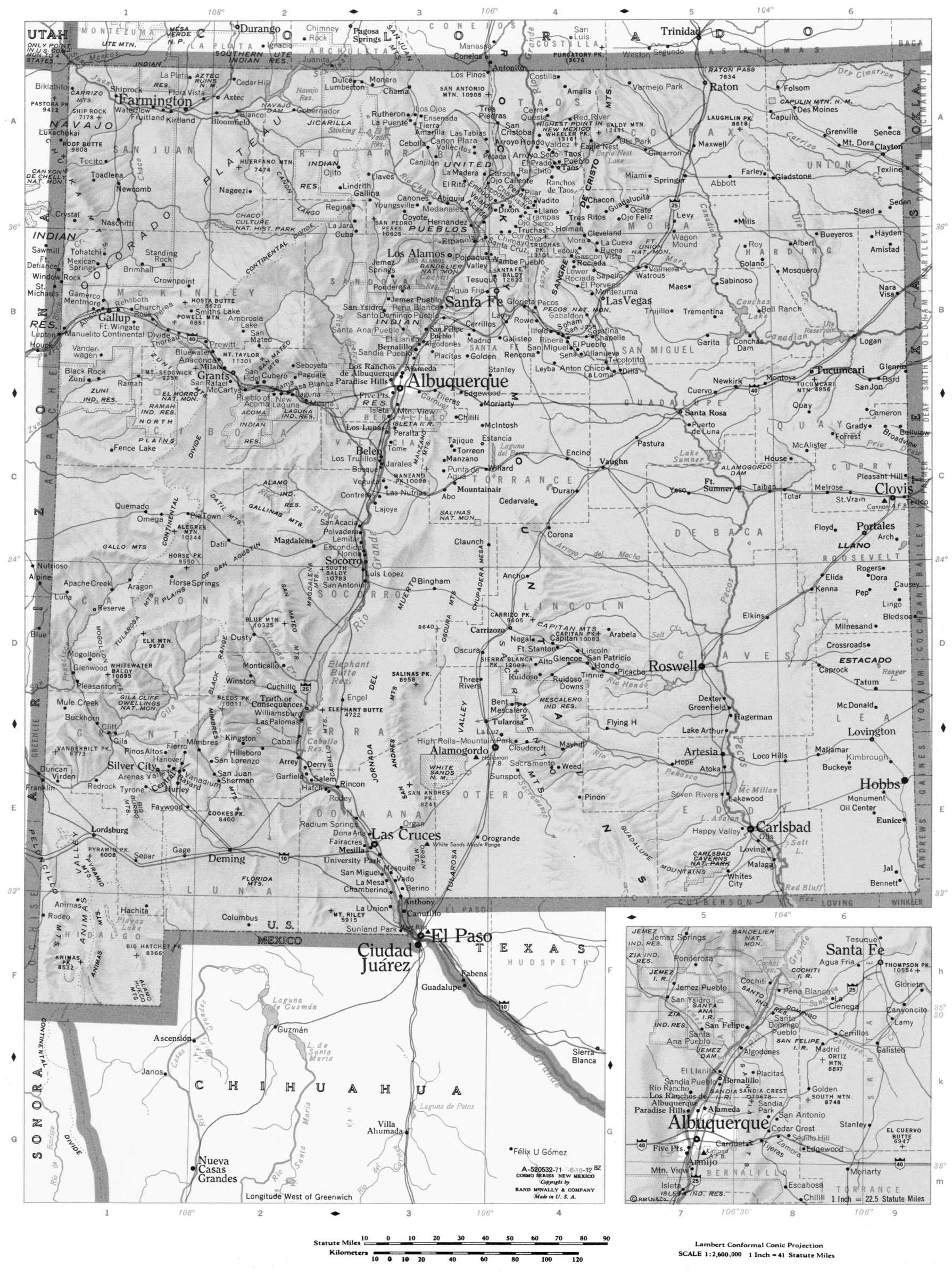

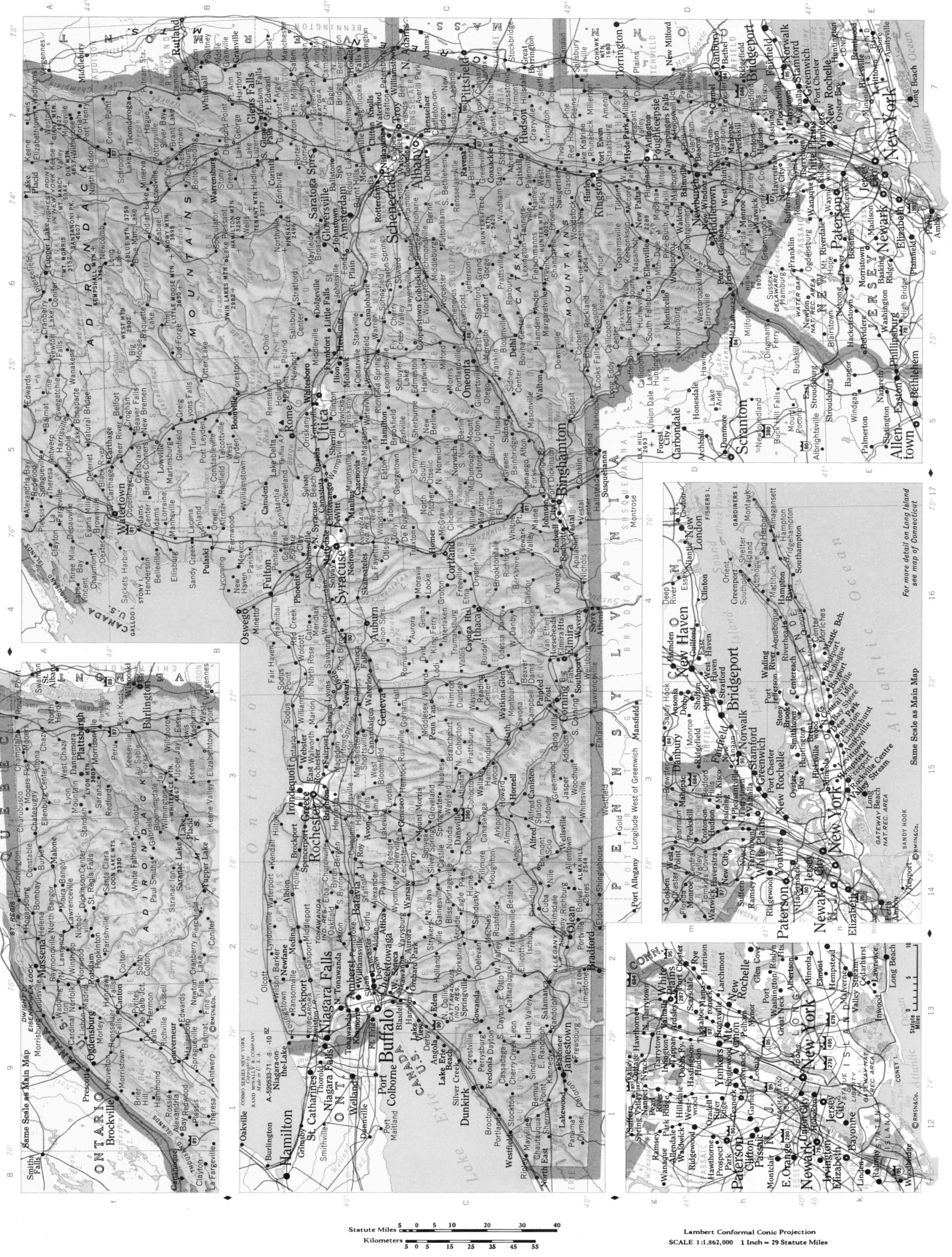

Statute Miles 5 0 5 10 20 30 40
Kilometers 5 0 5 15 25 35 45 55

Lambert Conformal Conic Projection
SCALE 1:1,862,000   1 Inch = 29 Statute Miles

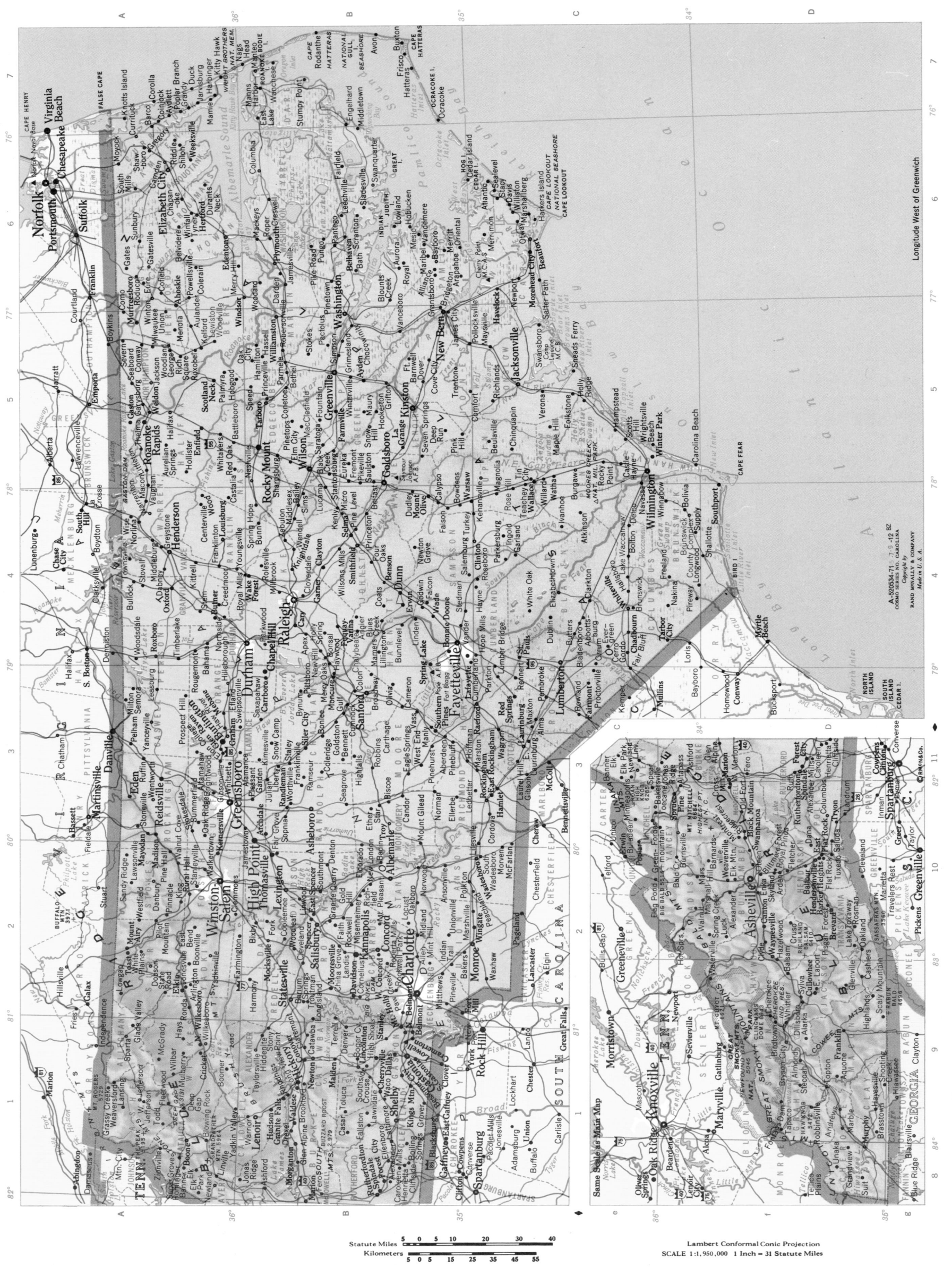

Statute Miles
Kilometers

Lambert Conformal Conic Projection
SCALE 1:1,950,000   1 Inch = 31 Statute Miles

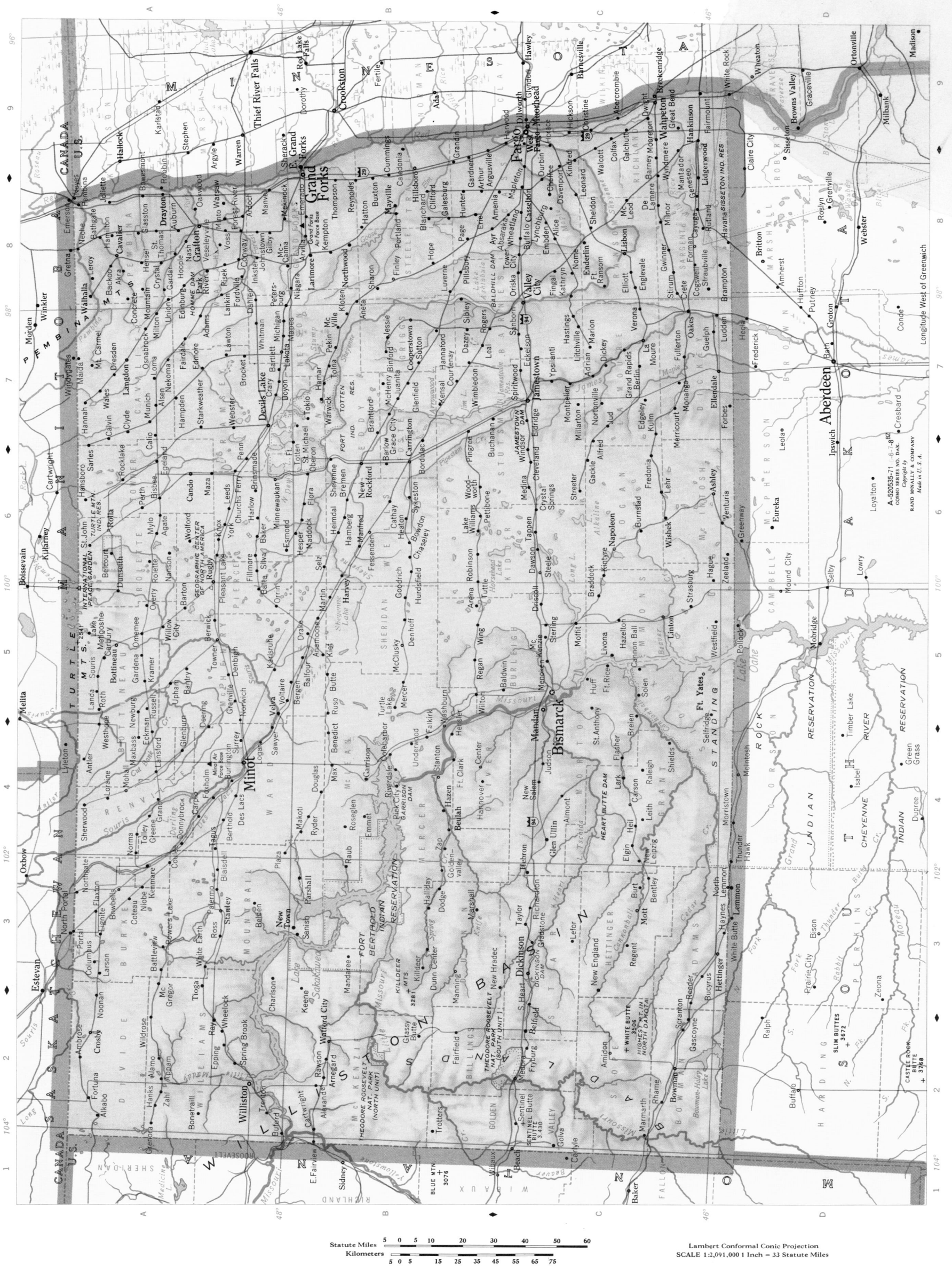

Statute Miles
Kilometers

Lambert Conformal Conic Projection
SCALE 1:2,091,000 1 Inch = 33 Statute Miles

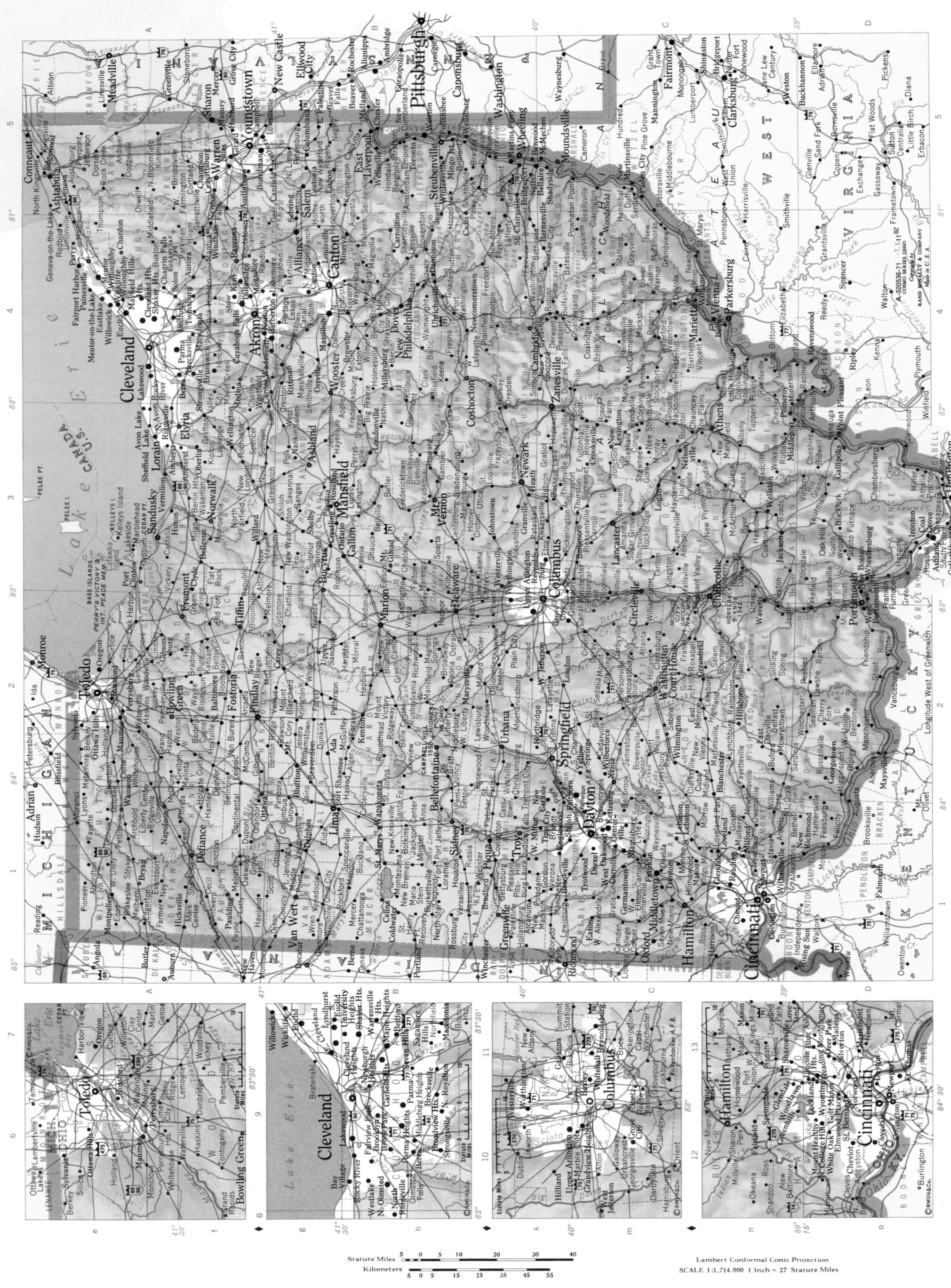

Statute Miles 5 0 5 10 20 30 40
Kilometers 5 0 5 15 25 35 45 55

Lambert Conformal Conic Projection
SCALE 1:1,714,000 1 Inch = 27 Statute Miles

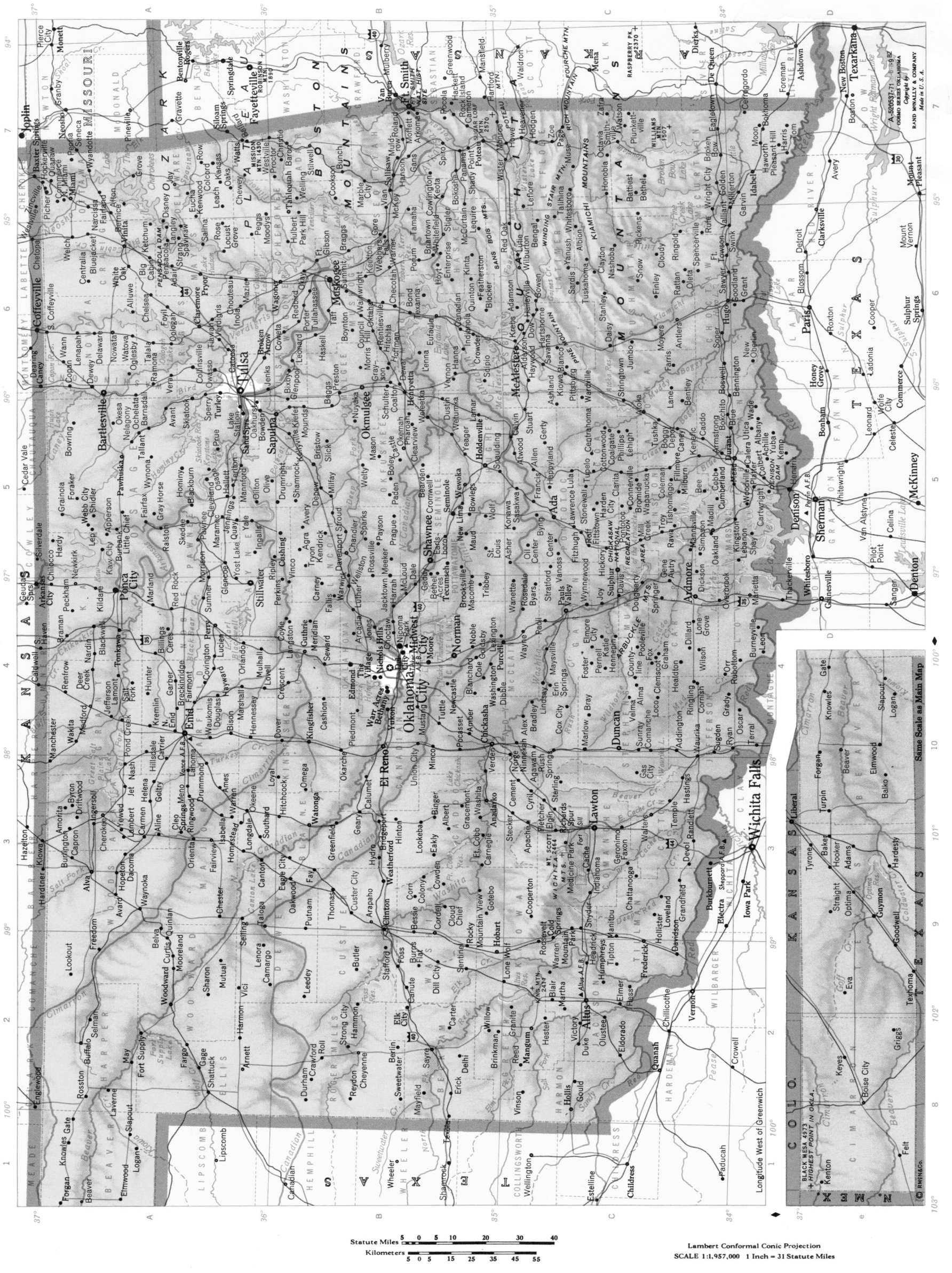

Statute Miles 5 0 5 10   20   30   40
Kilometers 5 0 5 15   25   35   45   55

Lambert Conformal Conic Projection
SCALE 1:1,957,000   1 Inch = 31 Statute Miles

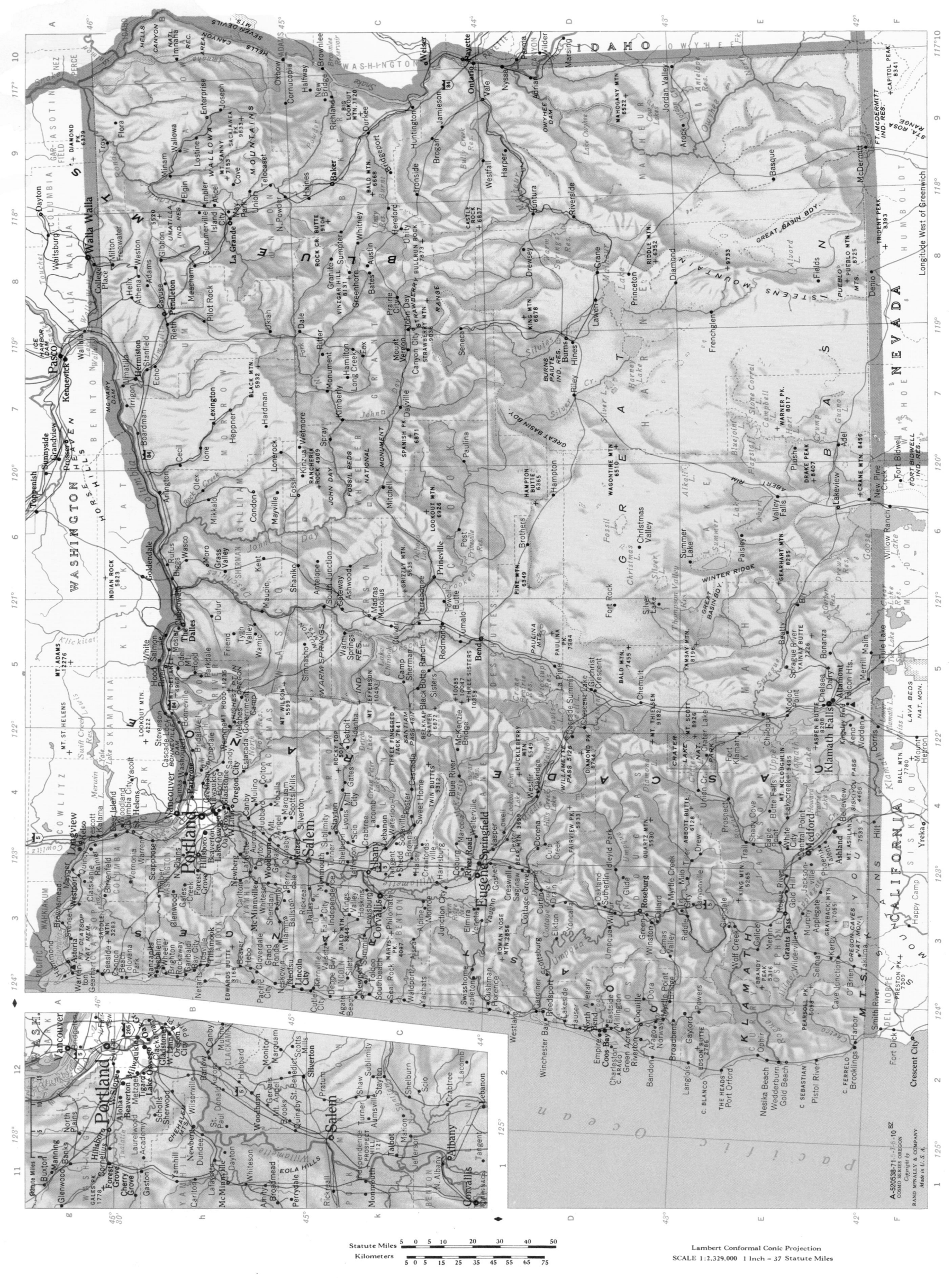

Statute Miles 5 0 5 10 20 30 40 50
Kilometers 5 0 5 15 25 35 45 55 75

Lambert Conformal Conic Projection
SCALE 1:2,329,000 1 Inch = 37 Statute Miles

A-50058-71 -4.5-10 82
COSMO SERIES OREGON
Copyright by
Rand McNally & Company
Made in U.S.A.

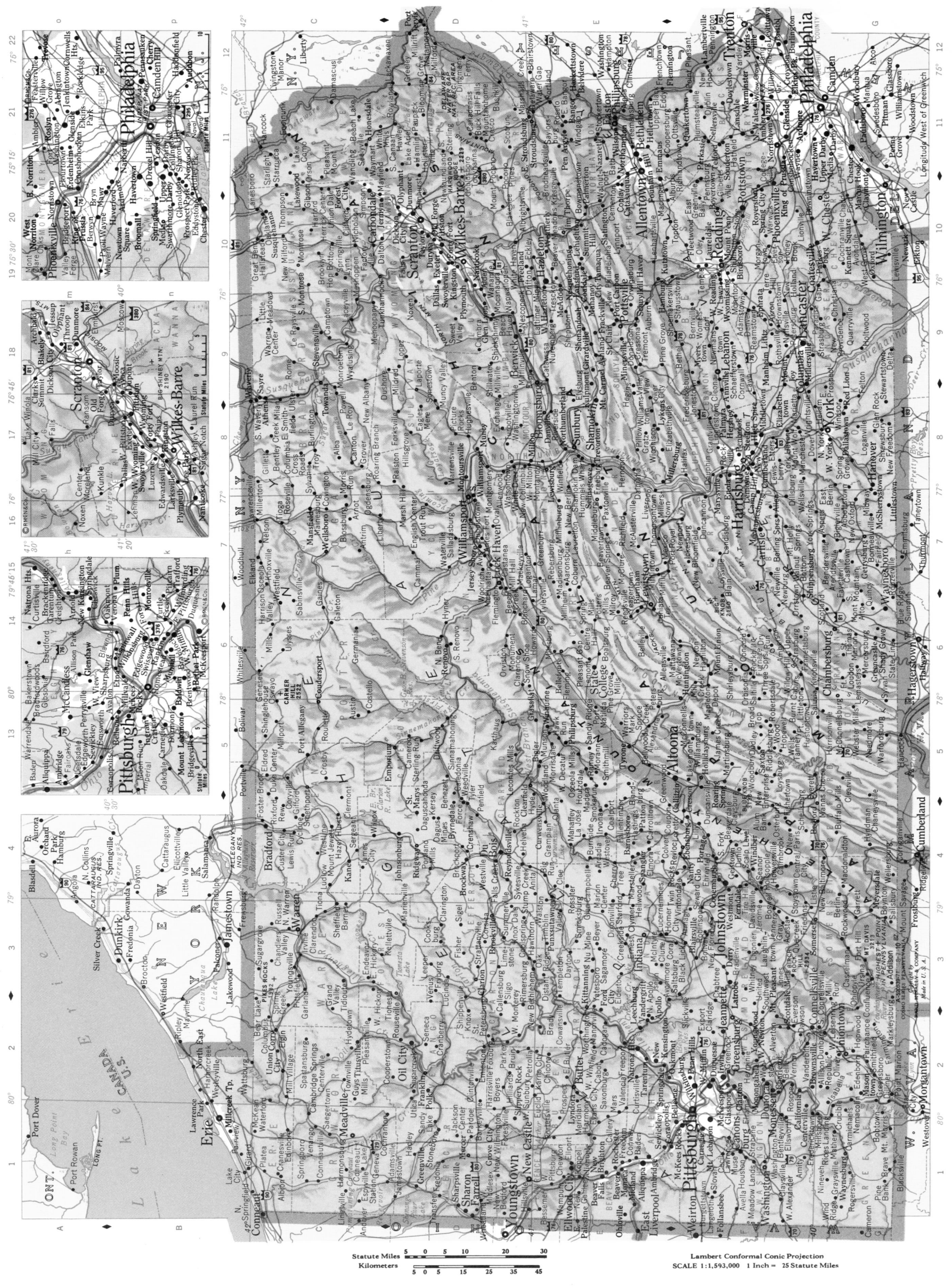

Statute Miles
Kilometers

Lambert Conformal Conic Projection
SCALE 1:1,593,000   1 Inch = 25 Statute Miles

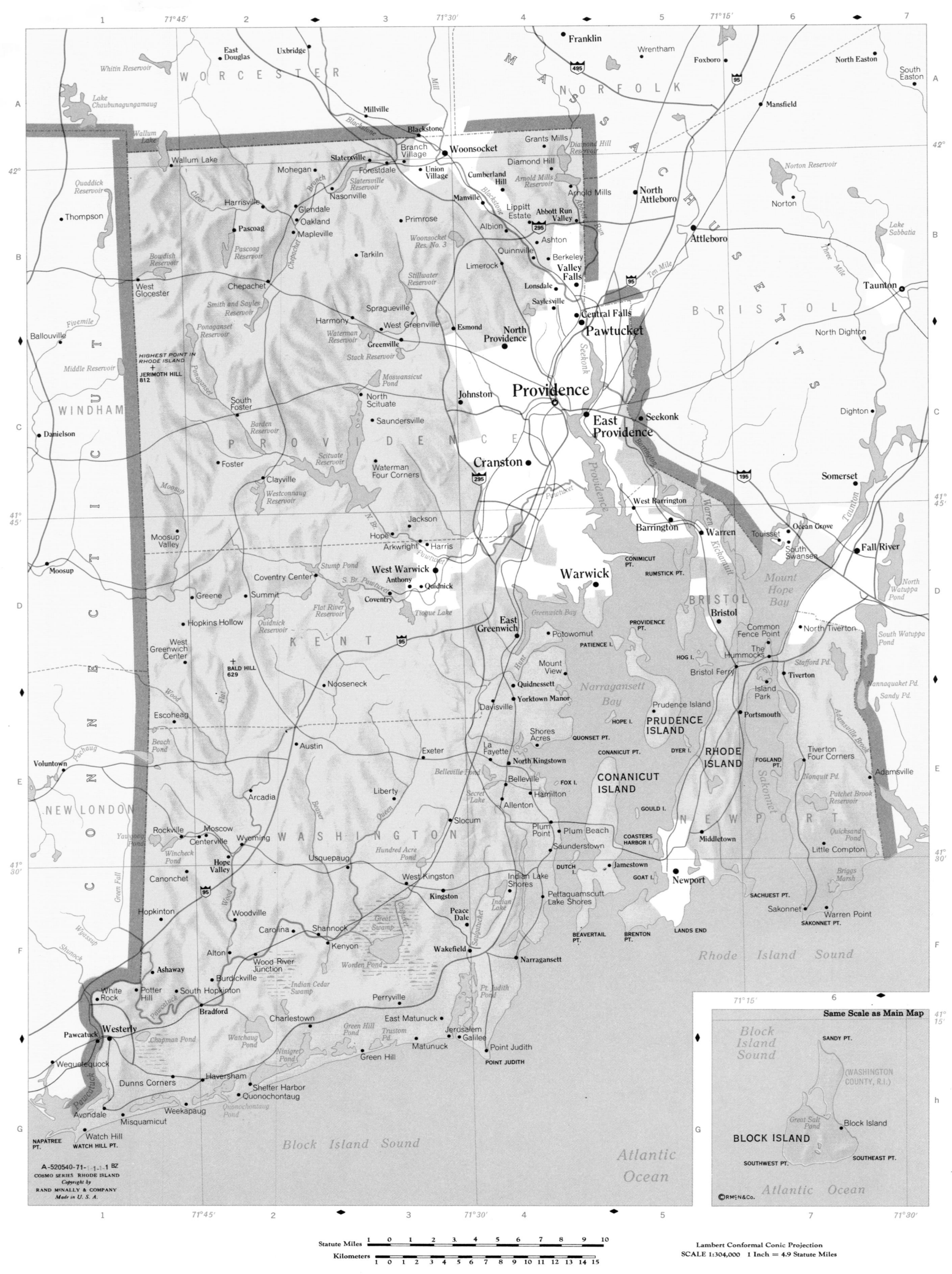

Same Scale as Main Map

BLOCK ISLAND

A-520540-71-1-1-1-1 BZ
COSMO SERIES RHODE ISLAND
Copyright by
RAND McNALLY & COMPANY
Made in U. S. A.

Statute Miles 1 0 1 2 3 4 5 6 7 8 9 10
Kilometers 1 0 1 2 3 4 5 6 7 8 9 10 11 12 13 14 15

Lambert Conformal Conic Projection
SCALE 1:304,000   1 Inch = 4.9 Statute Miles

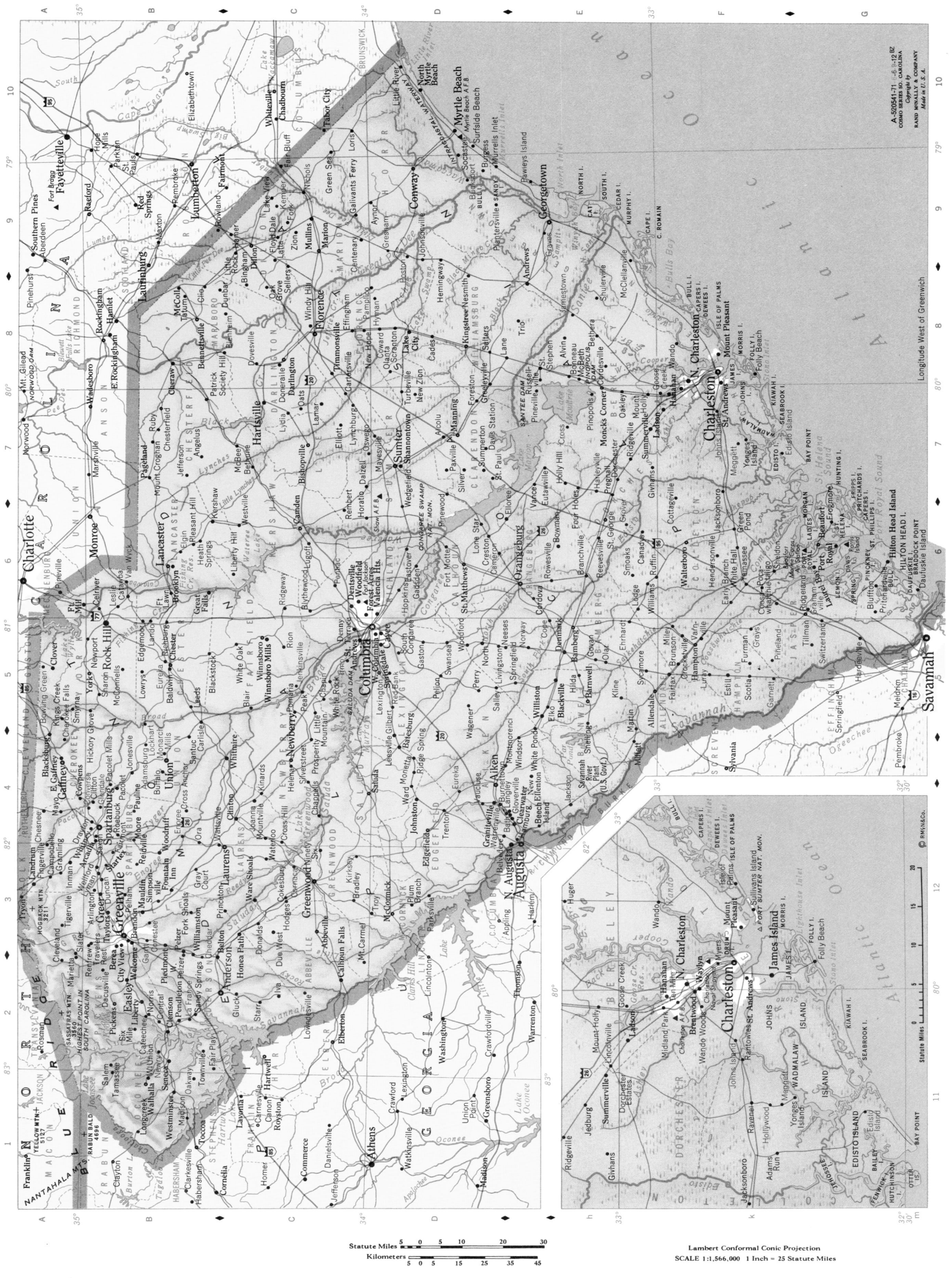

A-500541-71 -6 ‖-12 BZ
COSMO SERIES SO. CAROLINA
Copyright by
RAND M¢NALLY & COMPANY
Made in U. S. A.

Statute Miles 5 0 5 10 20 30
Kilometers 5 0 5 15 25 35 45

Lambert Conformal Conic Projection
SCALE 1:1,566,000 1 Inch = 25 Statute Miles

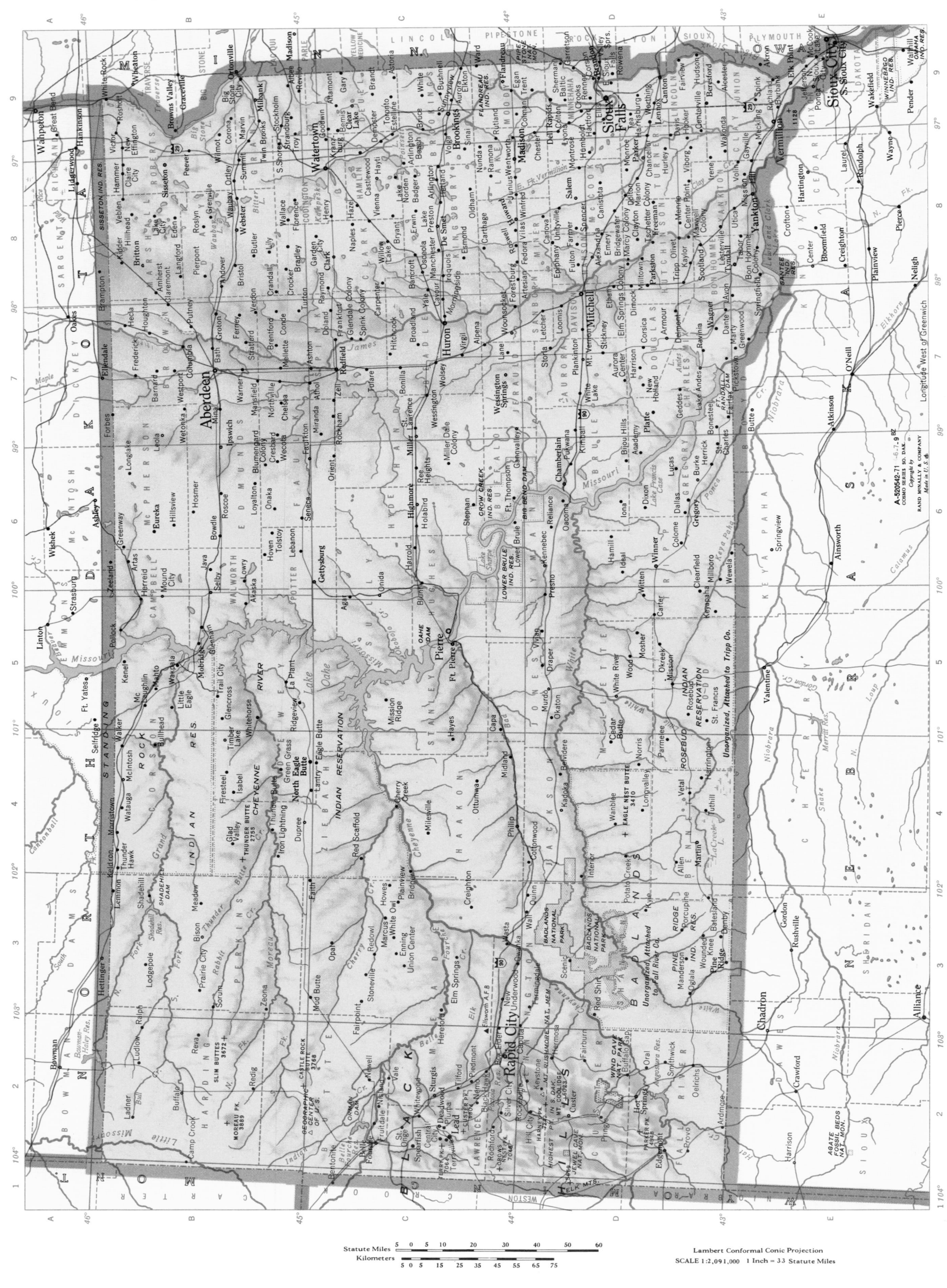

Statute Miles 5 0 5 10 20 30 40 50 60

Kilometers 5 0 5 15 25 35 45 55 65 75

Lambert Conformal Conic Projection
SCALE 1:2,091,000   1 Inch = 33 Statute Miles

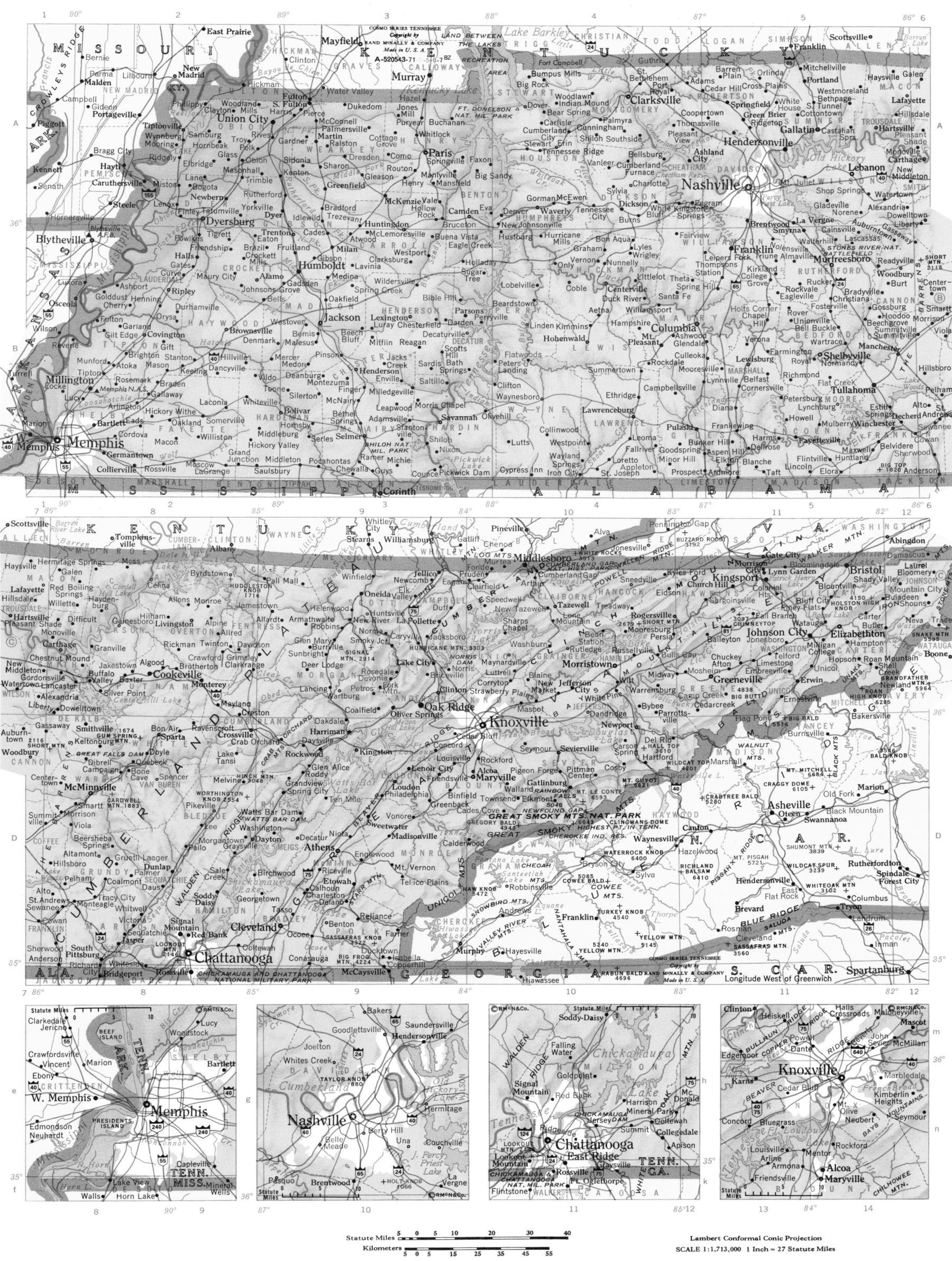

Lambert Conformal Conic Projection
SCALE 1:1,713,000 1 Inch = 27 Statute Miles

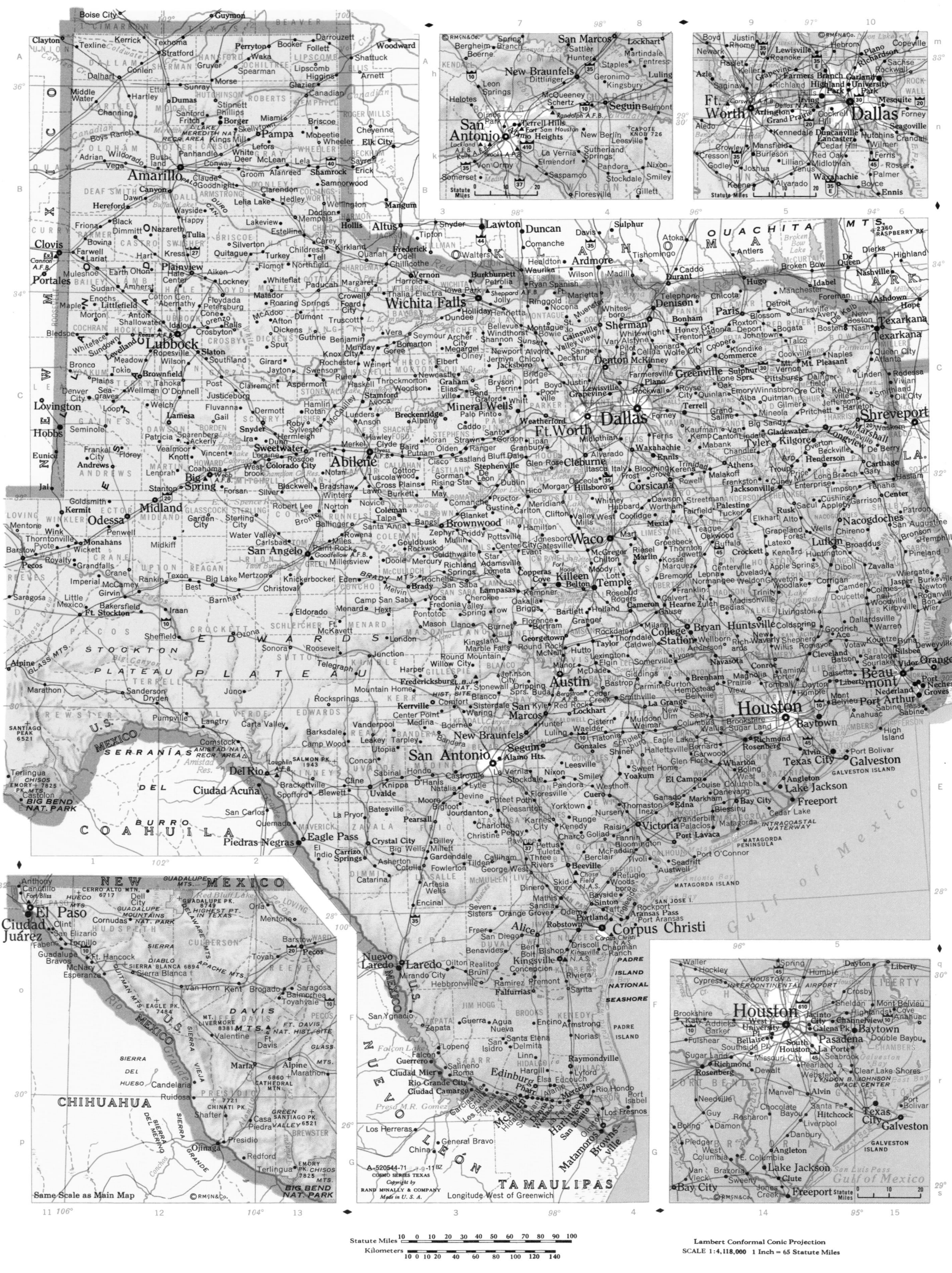

Statute Miles 10 0 10 20 30 40 50 60 70 80 90 100
Kilometers 10 0 10 20 40 60 80 100 120 140

Lambert Conformal Conic Projection
SCALE 1:4,118,000 1 Inch = 65 Statute Miles

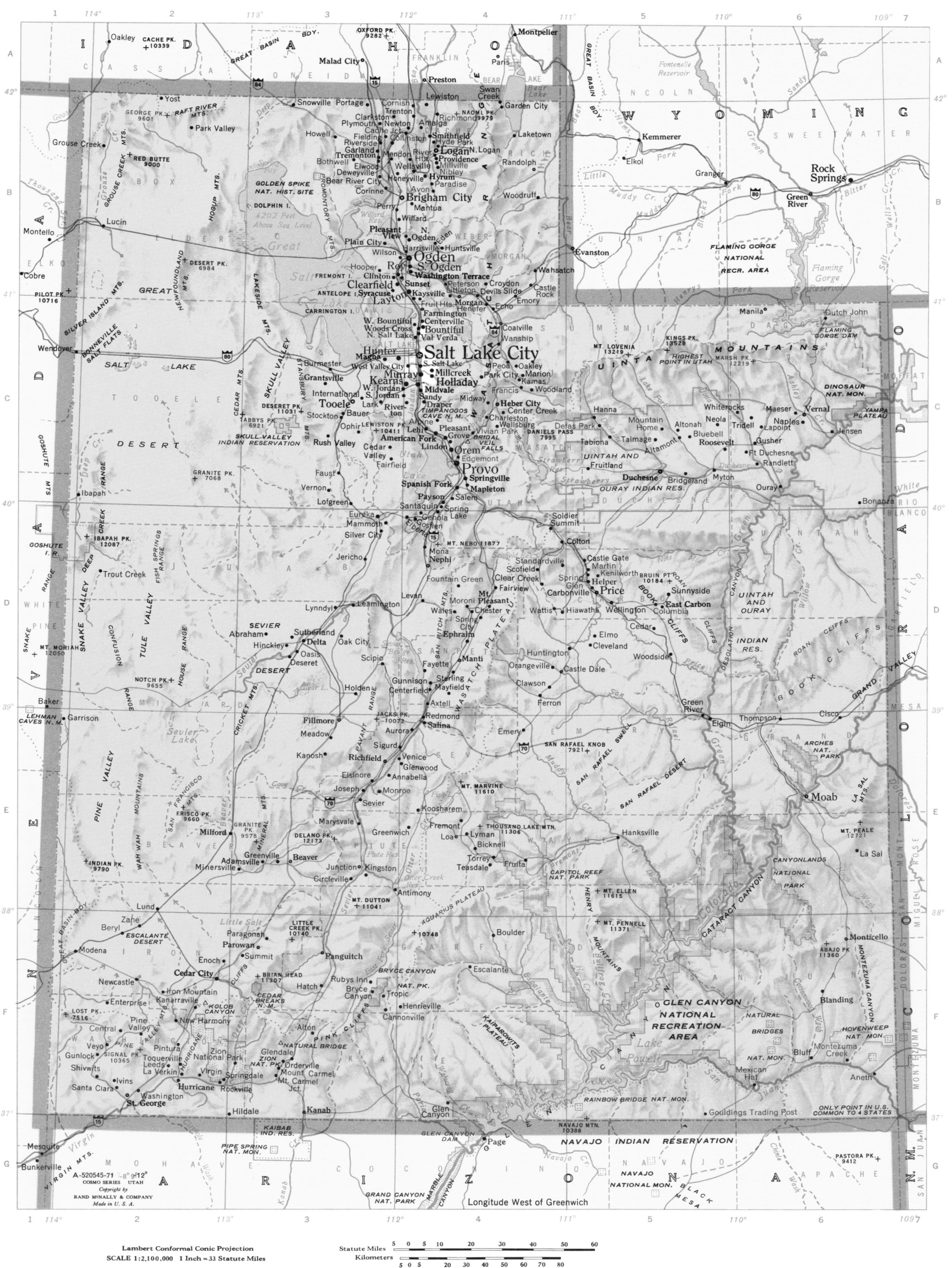

Lambert Conformal Conic Projection
SCALE 1:2,100,000   1 Inch = 33 Statute Miles

Statute Miles
Kilometers

Longitude West of Greenwich

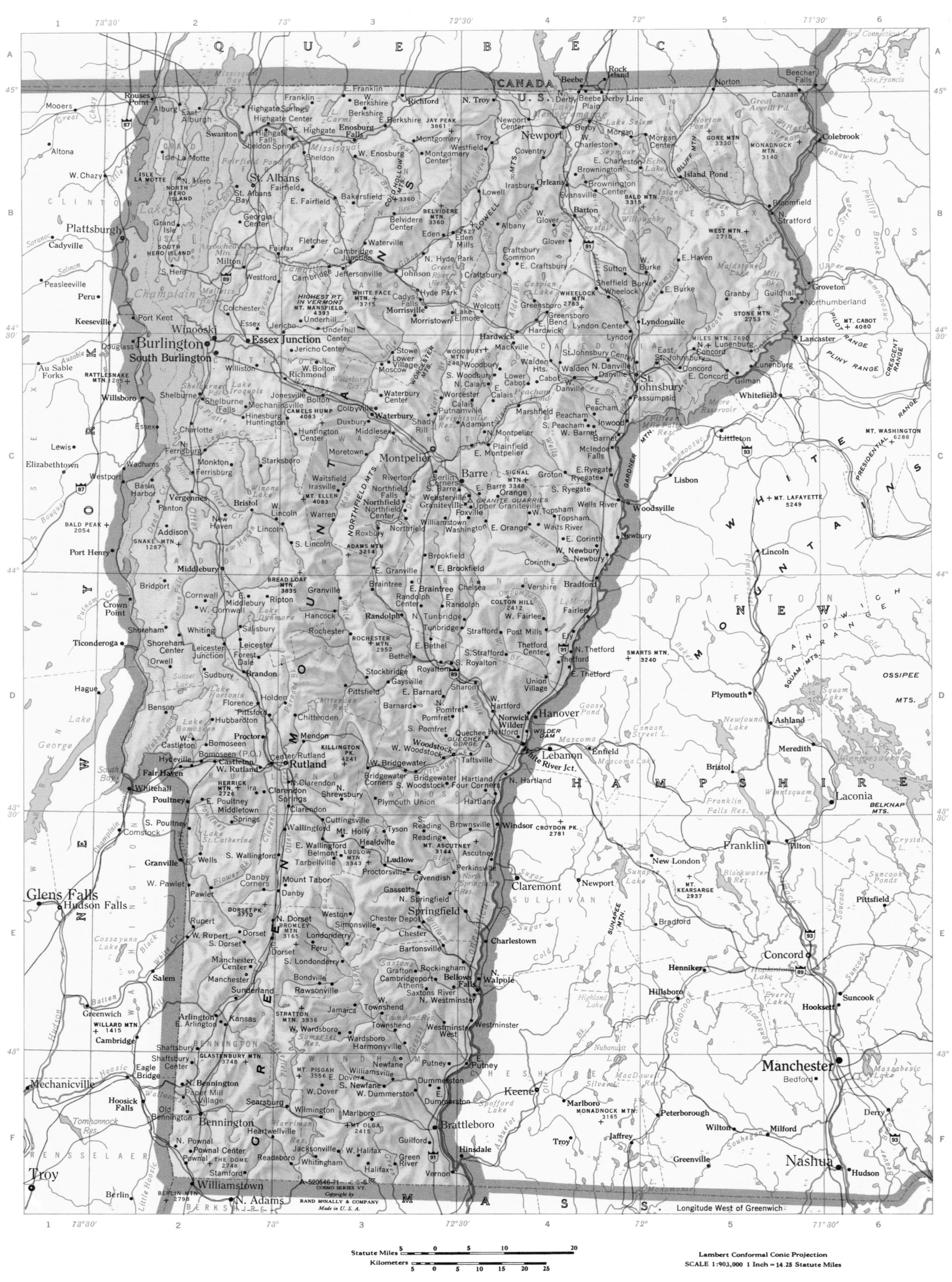

Statute Miles 5   0   5   10   20
Kilometers 5   0   5   10   15   20   25

Lambert Conformal Conic Projection
SCALE 1:903,000 1 Inch = 14.25 Statute Miles

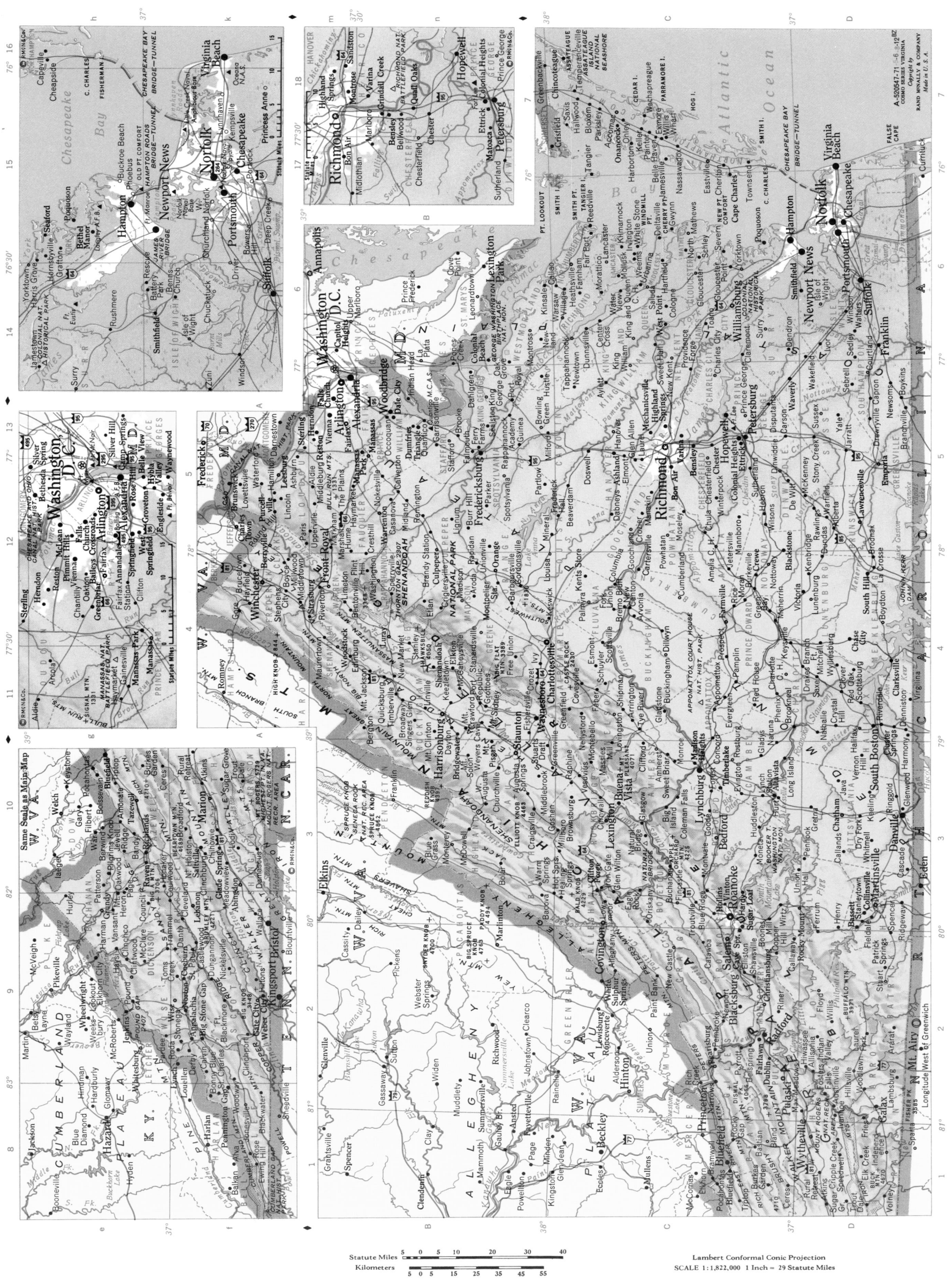

Statute Miles
Kilometers

Lambert Conformal Conic Projection
SCALE 1:1,822,000 1 Inch = 29 Statute Miles

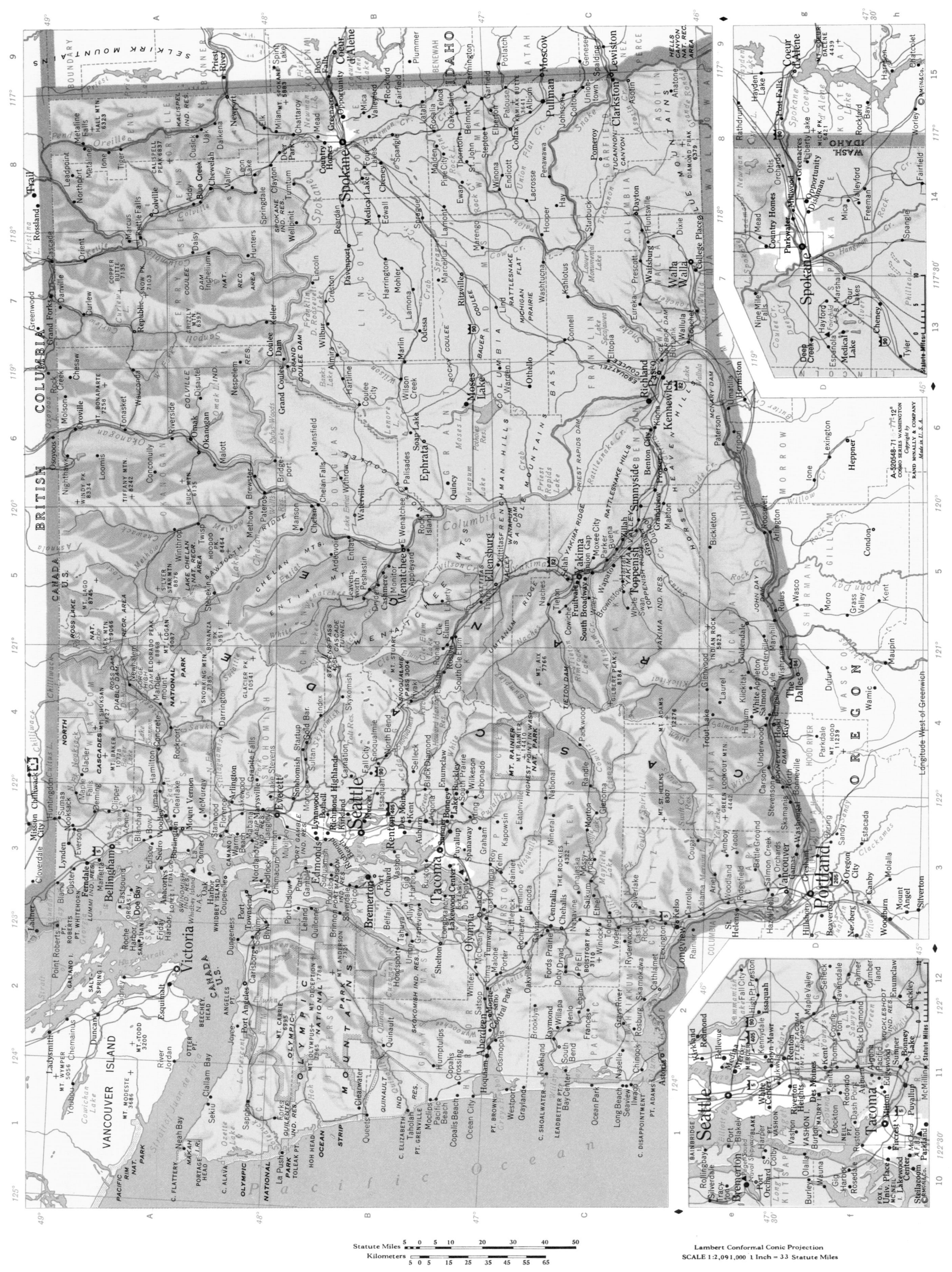

Statute Miles 5 0 5 10 20 30 40 50
Kilometers 5 0 5 15 25 35 45 55 65

Lambert Conformal Conic Projection
SCALE 1:2,091,000 1 Inch = 33 Statute Miles

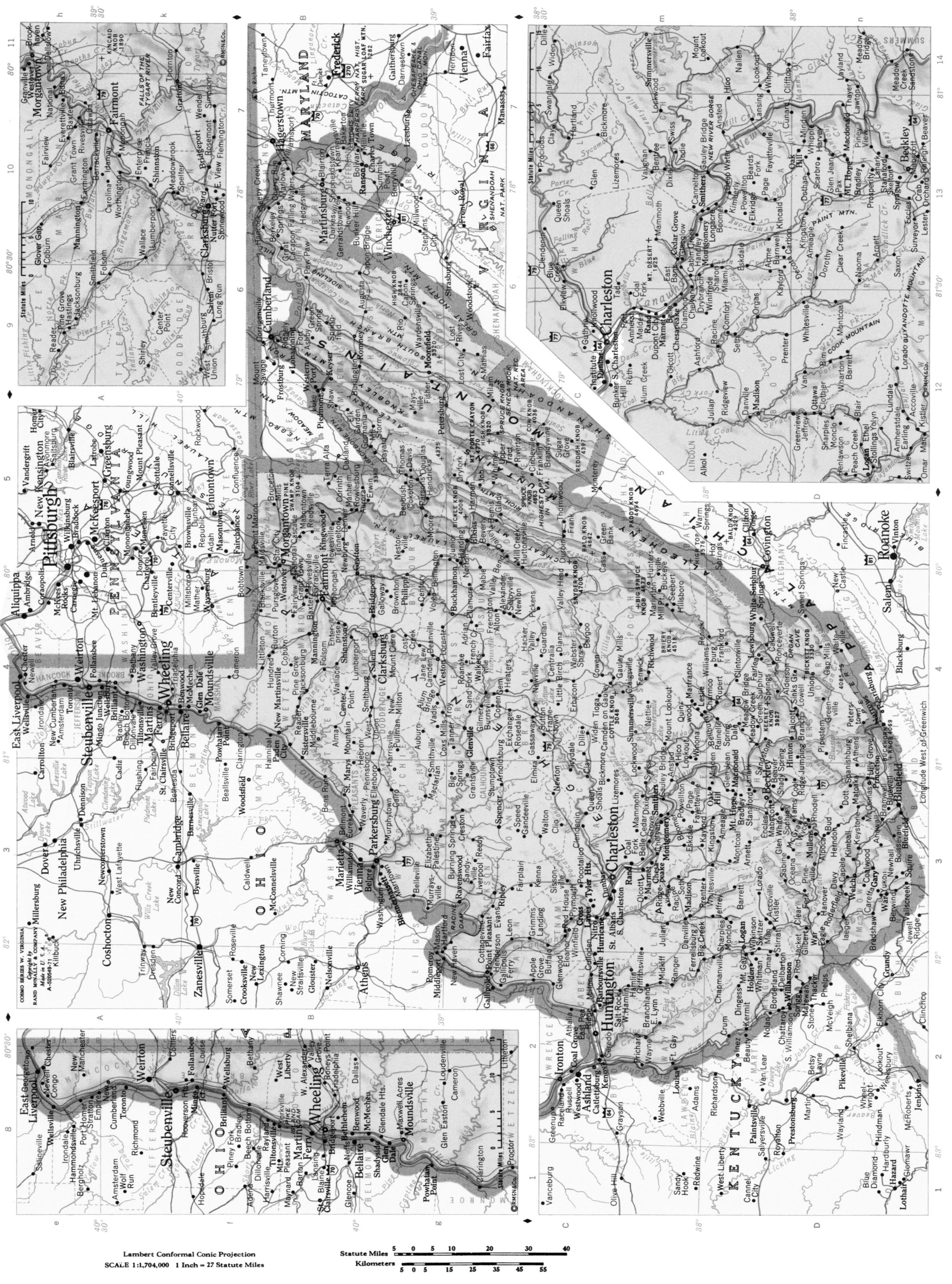

Lambert Conformal Conic Projection
SCALE 1:1,704,000 1 Inch = 27 Statute Miles

Statute Miles
Kilometers

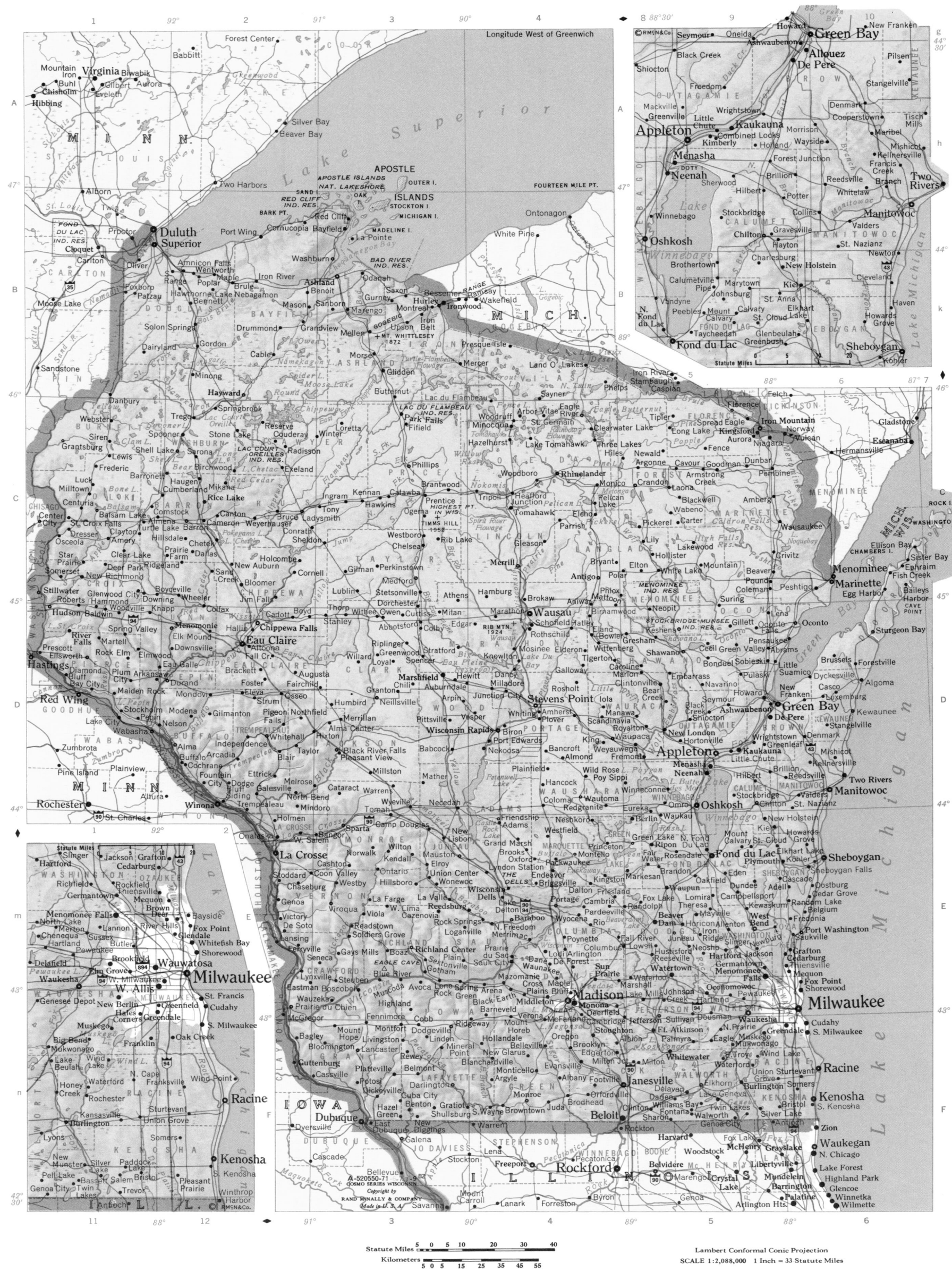

Longitude West of Greenwich

Lambert Conformal Conic Projection
SCALE 1:2,088,000   1 Inch = 33 Statute Miles

Statute Miles

Kilometers

A-520550-71
COSMO SERIES WISCONSIN
Copyright by
RAND McNALLY & COMPANY
Made in U.S.A.
© RMSN&Co.

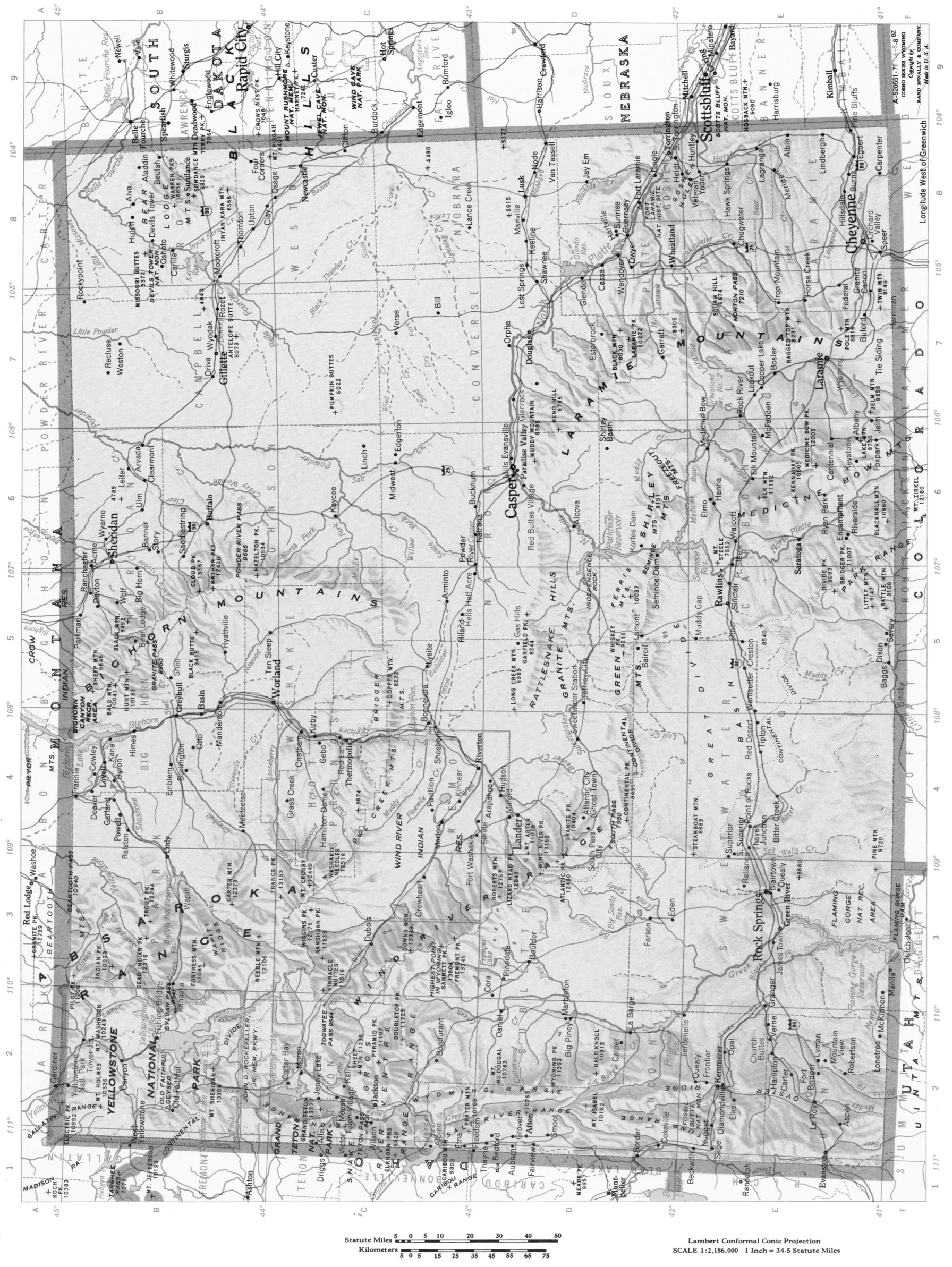

Statute Miles 5 0 5 10 20 30 40 50
Kilometers 5 0 5 15 25 35 45 55 65 75

Lambert Conformal Conic Projection
SCALE 1:2,186,000   1 Inch = 34.5 Statute Miles

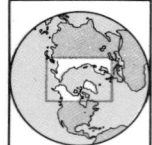

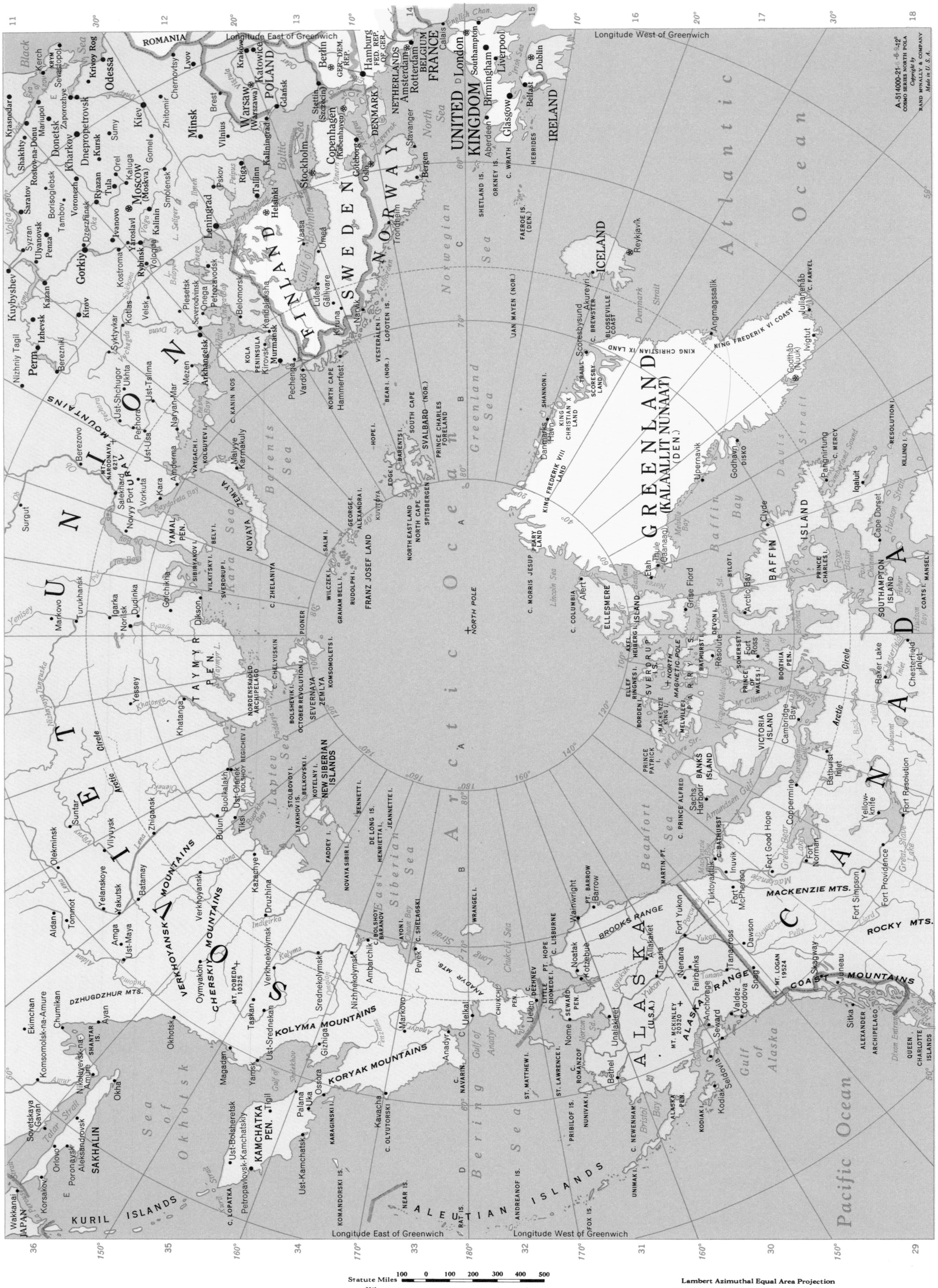

Statute Miles 100 0 100 200 300 400 500

Kilometers 100 0 100 300 500 700

Lambert Azimuthal Equal Area Projection
SCALE 1:28,000,000 1 Inch = 442 Statute Miles

INDEX TO WORLD REFERENCE MAPS

INTRODUCTION TO THE INDEX

This universal index includes in a single alphabetical list approximately 78,000 names of features that appear on the reference maps. Each name is followed by the name of the country or continent in which it is located, a map-reference key and a page reference.

Names The names of cities appear in the index in regular type. The names of all other features appear in *italics*, followed by descriptive terms (hill, mtn., state) to indicate their nature.

Names that appear in shortened versions on the maps due to space limitations are spelled out in full in the index. The portions of these names omitted from the maps are enclosed in brackets — for example, Acapulco [de Juárez].

Abbreviations of names on the maps have been standardized as much as possible. Names that are abbreviated on the maps are generally spelled out in full in the index.

Country names and names of features that extend beyond the boundaries of one country are followed by the name of the continent in which each is located. Country designations follow the names of all other places in the index. The locations of places in the United States, Canada, and the United Kingdom are further defined by abbreviations that indicate the state, province, or political division in which each is located.

All abbreviations used in the index are defined in the List of Abbreviations below.

Alphabetization Names are alphabetized in the order of the letters of the English alphabet. Spanish *ll* and *ch*, for example, are not treated as distinct letters. Furthermore, diacritical marks are disregarded in alphabetization — German or Scandinavian *ä* or *ö* are treated as *a* or *o*.

The names of physical features may appear inverted, since they are always alphabetized under the proper, not the generic, part of the name, thus: 'Gibraltar, Strait of'. Otherwise every entry, whether consisting of one word or more, is alphabetized as a single continuous entity. 'Lakeland', for example, appears after 'La Crosse' and before 'La Salle'. Names beginning with articles (Le Havre, Den Helder, Al Manṣūrah) are not inverted. Names beginning 'St.', 'Ste.' and 'Sainte' are alphabetized as though spelled 'Saint'.

In the case of identical names, towns are listed first, then political divisions, then physical features. Entries that are completely identical are listed alphabetically by country name.

Map-Reference Keys and Page References The map-reference keys and page references are found in the last two columns of each entry.

Each map-reference key consists of a letter and number. The letters appear along the sides of the maps. Lowercase letters indicate reference to inset maps. Numbers appear across the tops and bottoms of the maps.

Map reference keys for point features, such as cities and mountain peaks, indicate the locations of the symbols. For extensive areal features, such as countries or mountain ranges, locations are given for the approximate centers of the features. Those for linear features, such as canals and rivers, are given for the locations of the names.

Names of some important places or features that are omitted from the maps due to space limitations are included in the index. Each of these places is identified by an asterisk (*) preceding the map-reference key.

The page number generally refers to the main map for the country in which the feature is located. Page references to two-page maps always refer to the left-hand page.

LIST OF ABBREVIATIONS

Afg.	Afghanistan	D.C., U.S.	District of Columbia, U.S.	Jord.	Jordan	N.M., U.S.	New Mexico, U.S.	St. C.-N.	St. Christopher-Nevis
Afr.	Africa			Kir.	Kiribati	N. Mar. Is.	Northern Mariana Islands	St. Hel.	St. Helena
Ak., U.S.	Alaska, U.S.	De., U.S.	Delaware, U.S.	Ks., U.S.	Kansas, U.S.			St. Luc.	St. Lucia
Al., U.S.	Alabama, U.S.	Den.	Denmark	Kuw.	Kuwait	Nmb.	Namibia	*stm.*	stream (river, creek)
Alb.	Albania	*dep.*	dependency, colony	Ky., U.S.	Kentucky, U.S.	Nor.	Norway	S. Tom./P.	Sao Tome and Principe
Alg.	Algeria	*depr.*	depression	*l.*	lake, pond	Norf. I.	Norfolk Island		
Alta.	Alberta, Can.	*dept.*	department, district	La., U.S.	Louisiana, U.S.	N.S.	Nova Scotia, Can.	St. P./M.	St. Pierre and Miquelon
Am. Sam.	American Samoa	*des.*	desert	Leb.	Lebanon	Nv., U.S.	Nevada, U.S.		
anch.	anchorage	Dji.	Djibouti	Leso.	Lesotho	N.W. Ter.	Northwest Territories, Can.	*strt.*	strait, channel, sound
And.	Andorra	Dom.	Dominica	Lib.	Liberia				
Ang.	Angola	Dom. Rep.	Dominican Republic	Liech.	Liechtenstein	N.Y., U.S.	New York, U.S.	St. Vin.	St. Vincent and the Grenadines
Ant.	Antarctica	Ec.	Ecuador	Lux.	Luxembourg	N.Z.	New Zealand		
Antig.	Antigua and Barbuda	Eg.	Egypt	Ma., U.S.	Massachusetts, U.S.	Oc.	Oceania	Sud.	Sudan
		El Sal.	El Salvador			Oh., U.S.	Ohio, U.S.	Sur.	Suriname
Ar., U.S.	Arkansas, U.S.	Eng., U.K.	England, U.K.	Madag.	Madagascar	Ok., U.S.	Oklahoma, U.S.	*sw.*	swamp, marsh
Arg.	Argentina	Eq. Gui.	Equatorial Guinea	Malay.	Malaysia	Ont.	Ontario, Can.	Swaz.	Swaziland
Aus.	Austria	*est.*	estuary	Mald.	Maldives	Or., U.S.	Oregon, U.S.	Swe.	Sweden
Austl.	Australia	Eth.	Ethiopia	Man.	Manitoba, Can.	Pa., U.S.	Pennsylvania, U.S.	Switz.	Switzerland
Az., U.S.	Arizona, U.S.	Eur.	Europe	Marsh. Is.	Marshall Islands	Pak.	Pakistan	Tai.	Taiwan
b.	bay, gulf, inlet, lagoon	Faer. Is.	Faeroe Islands	Mart.	Martinique	Pan.	Panama	Tan.	Tanzania
		Falk. Is.	Falkland Islands	Maur.	Mauritania	Pap. N. Gui.	Papua New Guinea	T./C. Is.	Turks and Caicos Islands
Bah.	Bahamas	Fin.	Finland	May.	Mayotte	Para.	Paraguay		
Bahr.	Bahrain	Fl., U.S.	Florida, U.S.	Md., U.S.	Maryland, U.S.	P.E.I.	Prince Edward Island, Can.	*ter.*	territory
Barb.	Barbados	*for.*	forest, moor	Me., U.S.	Maine, U.S.			Thai.	Thailand
B.A.T.	British Antarctic Territory	Fr.	France	Mex.	Mexico	*pen.*	peninsula	Tn., U.S.	Tennessee, U.S.
		Fr. Gu.	French Guiana	Mi., U.S.	Michigan, U.S.	Phil.	Philippines	Tok.	Tokelau
B.C.	British Columbia, Can.	Fr. Poly.	French Polynesia	Micron.	Federated States of Micronesia	Pit.	Pitcairn	Trin.	Trinidad and Tobago
		F.S.A.T.	French Southern and Antarctic Territory			*pl.*	plain, flat		
Bdi.	Burundi			Mid. Is.	Midway Islands	*plat.*	plateau, highland	T.T.P.I.	Trust Territory of the Pacific Islands
Bel.	Belgium			*mil.*	military installation	Pol.	Poland		
Ber.	Bermuda	Ga., U.S.	Georgia, U.S.	Mn., U.S.	Minnesota, U.S.	Port.	Portugal	Tun.	Tunisia
Bhu.	Bhutan	Gam.	Gambia	Mo., U.S.	Missouri, U.S.	P.R.	Puerto Rico	Tur.	Turkey
B.I.O.T.	British Indian Ocean Territory	Ger.	Germany	Mon.	Monaco	*prov.*	province, region	Tx., U.S.	Texas, U.S.
		Gib.	Gibraltar	Mong.	Mongolia	Que.	Quebec, Can.	U.A.E.	United Arab Emirates
Bngl.	Bangladesh	Grc.	Greece	Monts.	Montserrat	*reg.*	physical region		
Bol.	Bolivia	Gren.	Grenada	Mor.	Morocco	*res.*	reservoir	Ug.	Uganda
Boph.	Bophuthatswana	Grnld.	Greenland	Moz.	Mozambique	Reu.	Reunion	U.K.	United Kingdom
Bots.	Botswana	Guad.	Guadeloupe	Mrts.	Mauritius	*rf.*	reef, shoal	Ur.	Uruguay
Braz.	Brazil	Guat.	Guatemala	Ms., U.S.	Mississippi, U.S.	R.I., U.S.	Rhode Island, U.S.	U.S.	United States
Bru.	Brunei	Gui.	Guinea	Mt., U.S.	Montana, U.S.	Rom.	Romania	Ut., U.S.	Utah, U.S.
Bul.	Bulgaria	Gui.-B.	Guinea-Bissau	*mth.*	river mouth or channel	Rw.	Rwanda	Va., U.S.	Virginia, U.S.
Burkina	Burkina Faso	Guy.	Guyana			S.A.	South America	*val.*	valley, watercourse
c.	cape, point	Hi., U.S.	Hawaii, U.S.	*mtn.*	mountain	S. Afr.	South Africa	Vat.	Vatican City
Ca., U.S.	California, U.S.	*hist.*	historic site, ruins	*mts.*	mountains	Sask.	Saskatchewan, Can.	Ven.	Venezuela
Cam.	Cameroon	*hist. reg.*	historic region	Mwi.	Malawi			V.I., Br.	Virgin Islands, British
Camb.	Cambodia	H.K.	Hong Kong	N.A.	North America	Sau. Ar.	Saudi Arabia		
Can.	Canada	Hond.	Honduras	N.B.	New Brunswick, Can.	S.C., U.S.	South Carolina, U.S.	Viet.	Vietnam
Cay. Is.	Cayman Islands	Hung.	Hungary			*sci.*	scientific station	V.I.U.S.	Virgin Islands (U.S.)
Cen. Afr. Rep.	Central African Republic	*i.*	island	N.C., U.S.	North Carolina, U.S.	Scot., U.K.	Scotland, U.K.	*vol.*	volcano
		Ia., U.S.	Iowa, U.S.	N. Cal.	New Caledonia	S.D., U.S.	South Dakota, U.S.	Vt., U.S.	Vermont, U.S.
Christ. I.	Christmas Island	I.C.	Ivory Coast	N. Cyp.	North Cyprus	Sen.	Senegal	Wa., U.S.	Washington, U.S.
clf.	cliff, escarpment	Ice.	Iceland	N.D., U.S.	North Dakota, U.S.	Sey.	Seychelles	Wal./F.	Wallis and Futuna
co.	county, parish	*ice*	ice feature, glacier	Ne., U.S.	Nebraska, U.S.	Sing.	Singapore	Wi., U.S.	Wisconsin, U.S.
Co., U.S.	Colorado, U.S.	Id., U.S.	Idaho, U.S.	Neth.	Netherlands	S. Kor.	South Korea	W. Sah.	Western Sahara
Col.	Colombia	Il., U.S.	Illinois, U.S.	Neth. Ant.	Netherlands Antilles	S.L.	Sierra Leone	W. Sam.	Western Samoa
Com.	Comoros	In., U.S.	Indiana, U.S.	Newf.	Newfoundland, Can.	S. Mar.	San Marino	*wtfl.*	waterfall
cont.	continent	Indon.	Indonesia	N.H., U.S.	New Hampshire, U.S.	Sol. Is.	Solomon Islands	W.V., U.S.	West Virginia, U.S.
C.R.	Costa Rica	I. of Man	Isle of Man			Som.	Somalia	Wy., U.S.	Wyoming, U.S.
crat.	crater	Ire.	Ireland	Nic.	Nicaragua	Sov. Un.	Soviet Union	Yugo.	Yugoslavia
Ct., U.S.	Connecticut, U.S.	*is.*	islands	Nig.	Nigeria	Sp. N. Afr.	Spanish North Africa	Yukon	Yukon Territory, Can.
ctry.	country	Isr.	Israel	N. Ire., U.K.	Northern Ireland, U.K.				
C.V.	Cape Verde	Isr. Occ.	Israeli Occupied Territories			Sri L.	Sri Lanka	Zam.	Zambia
Cyp.	Cyprus			N.J., U.S.	New Jersey, U.S.	*state*	state, republic, canton	Zimb.	Zimbabwe
Czech.	Czechoslovakia	Jam.	Jamaica	N. Kor.	North Korea				

INDEX

A

Name	Map Ref.	Page
Aachen, Ger.	C3	18
Aalen, Ger.	D5	18
A'alī an Nīl (Upper Nile), prov., Sud.	D3	47
Aalsmeer, Neth.	B4	17
Aalst (Alost), Bel.	B6	16
Aalten, Neth.	C6	17
Äänekoski, Fin.	F11	14
Aarau, Switz.	E4	18
Aare, stm., Switz.	E3	18
Aargau, state, Switz.	B4	20
Aaronsburg, Pa., U.S.	E7	115
Aarschot, Bel.	D4	17
Aba, China	E5	31
Aba, Nig.	E6	45
Aba, Zaire	A5	48
Aba, Nig.	E6	45
Abacaxis, stm., Braz.	C3	59
Ābādān, Iran	B4	38
Ābādeh, Iran	F6	39
Abadla, Alg.	C4	44
Abaeté, Braz.	B3	56
Abaetetuba, Braz.	C5	59
Abagnar Qi, China	C7	32
Abag Qi, China	C6	32
Abai, Para.	E4	55
Abajo Peak, mtn., Ut., U.S.	F6	121
Abakaliki, Nig.	E6	45
Abakan, Sov. Un.	D12	29
Abala, Congo	B2	48
Abala, Niger	D5	45
Abancay, Peru	B4	78
Abanda, stm., Braz.	C5	22
Abanilla, Spain	B3	23
Abano Terme, Italy	F6	39
Abar Kūh, Iran	C6	41
'Abasān, Isr. Occ.	C13	31
Abashiri, Japan	D2	47
Abau, Pap. N. Gui.	m12	50
Abaya, Lake, l., Eth.	D4	47
Abbaye, Point, c., Mi., U.S.	B2	99
Abbeville, Fr.	B4	16
Abbeville, Al., U.S.	D4	78
Abbeville, Ga., U.S.	E3	87
Abbeville, La., U.S.	E3	95
Abbeville, Ms., U.S.	A4	101
Abbeville, S.C., U.S.	C3	117
Abbeville, co., S.C., U.S.	C2	117
Abbey, Sask.	G1	75
Abbeydorney, Ire.	E2	11
Abbeyfeale, Ire.	E2	11
Abbey Head, c., Scot., U.K.	F5	13
Abbeyleix, Ire.	E4	11
Abbiategrasso, Italy	B2	23
Abbotsford, B.C.	f13	69
Abbotsford, Wi., U.S.	D3	126
Abbott, Ar., U.S.	B1	81
Abbott Butte, mtn., Or., U.S.	E4	114
Abbott Run, stm., R.I., U.S.	B4	116
Abbottsburg, N.C., U.S.	C4	110
Abbottstown, Pa., U.S.	G7	115
Abbot Village, Me., U.S.	C3	96
Abbyville, Ks., U.S.	E5	93
'Abd al Kūrī, i., Yemen	D5	38
Abdulino, Sov. Un.	E19	8
Abe, Lake, l., Afr.	C5	47
Abéché, Chad	C4	46
Abee, Alta.	B4	68
Abejorral, Col.	E4	60
Abengourou, I.C.	E4	45
Abenrå, Den.	C3	15
Abeokuta, Nig.	E5	45
Aberaeron, Wales, U.K.	B3	12
Aberchirder, Scot., U.K.	D5	13
Abercorn, Que.	D5	74
Abercrombie, N.D., U.S.	C9	111
Aberdare, Wales, U.K.	C5	12
Aberdaron, Wales, U.K.	C4	12
Aberdeen, Sask.	E2	75
Aberdeen, S. Afr.	D3	49
Aberdeen, Scot., U.K.	B5	10
Aberdeen, Id., U.S.	G6	89
Aberdeen, Md., U.S.	A5	97
Aberdeen, Ms., U.S.	B5	101
Aberdeen, N.C., U.S.	B3	110
Aberdeen, Oh., U.S.	D2	112
Aberdeen, S.D., U.S.	B7	118
Aberdeen, Wa., U.S.	C2	124
Aberdeen Lake, l., N.W. Ter.	D13	66
Aberdeen Proving Ground, mil., Md., U.S.	A5	97
Aberdeen Township, N.J., U.S.	*C4	107
Aberdyfi, Wales, U.K.	B3	12
Aberfeldy, Scot., U.K.	B5	10
Aberfoyle, Scot., U.K.	D4	13
Abergavenny, Wales, U.K.	C5	12
Abernant, Al., U.S.	B2	78
Abernethy, Sask.	G3	75
Abernethy, Tx., U.S.	C2	120
Abert, Lake, l., Or., U.S.	E6	114
Abert Rim, clf., Or., U.S.	E6	114
Aberystwyth, Wales, U.K.	D4	12
Abesville, Me., U.S.	D4	96
Abhā, Sau. Ar.	D4	38
Abhar, Iran	B5	38
Abidjan, I.C.	E4	45
Abie, Ne., U.S.	C9	104
Abilene, Ks., U.S.	D6	93
Abilene, Tx., U.S.	C3	120
Abingdon, Eng., U.K.	C6	12
Abingdon, Il., U.S.	C3	90
Abingdon, Va., U.S.	f10	123
Abington, Ct., U.S.	B7	84
Abington, Ma., U.S.	B6	98
Abington [Township], Pa., U.S.	o21	115
Abiquiu, N.M., U.S.	A3	108
Abisko, Swe.	C8	14
Abita Springs, La., U.S.	D5	95
Abitibi, stm., Can.	o19	73
Abitibi, Lake, l., Can.	G16	66
Ablon, Fr.	h10	16
Abloviak Fiord, Que.	f8	72
Aboisso, I.C.	E4	45
Abomey, Benin	E5	45
Abongabong, mtn., Indon.	J2	35
Abony, Hung.	B5	24
Abou Deïa, Chad	C3	46
Aboyne, Scot., U.K.	C6	13
Abraham Lake, res., Alta.	C2	68
Abraham Lincoln Birthplace National Historic Site, hist., Ky., U.S.	C4	94
Abrams, Wi., U.S.	D5	126
Abrantes, Port.	C1	22
Ábrego, Col.	B3	60
Abreojos, Punta, c., Mex.	B2	63
Abruzzi, prov., Italy	C4	23
Absaraka, N.D., U.S.	C8	111
Absaroka Range, mts., U.S.	F7	127
Absarokee, Mt., U.S.	E7	103
Absecon, N.J., U.S.	E4	107
Absecon Inlet, b., N.J., U.S.	E4	107
Abu 'Alī, i., Sau. Ar.	H4	39
Abu Dhabi (Abū Ẓaby), U.A.E.	C5	38
Abū Dīs, Isr. Occ.	h12	41
Abū Ḥadd, Bi'r, well, Eg.	E6	43
Abū Ḥamad, Sud.	D3	47
Abū Ḥammād al Maḥaṭṭah, Eg.	D3	41
Abū Ḥummuṣ, Eg.	C2	41
Abuja, Nig.	E6	45
Abū Kabīr, Eg.	D3	41
Abū Kamāl, Syria	B4	38
Abū Kershola, Sud.	D3	47
Abū Khawf, Mushāsh, well, Eg.	E6	41
Abūksāh, Eg.	E2	41
Abumombazi, Zaire	A3	48
Abū Mūsá, i., U.A.E.	I7	39
Abunã, Braz.	A2	55
Abunã (Abuná), stm., S.A.	A2	55
Abuná (Abunã), stm., S.A.	A2	55
Abū Qīr, Eg.	C2	41
Abū Qīr Bay, b., Eg.	I8	43
Abū Qurqāş, Eg.	C2	41
Abū Road, India	E4	37
Abu Simbel (Abū Sunbul), hist., Eg.	E6	43
Abū Sufyān, 'Idd, well, Sud.	B2	47
Abū Ṭabarī, well, Sud.	B2	47
Abū 'Urūq, well, Sud.	B3	47
Abū Zanīmah, Eg.	D6	43
Åby (part of Norrköping), Swe.	u34	14
Åbybro, Den.	A3	15
Abyei, Sud.	D2	47
Abyssinia see Ethiopia, ctry., Afr.	D4	47
Academia, Oh., U.S.	B3	112
Academy, S.D., U.S.	D6	118
Acadia, co., La., U.S.	D3	95
Acadia National Park, Me., U.S.	D4	96
Acadia Valley, Alta.	D5	68
Acaituba, Braz.	B2	59
Acajutla, El Sal.	D3	62
Acámbaro, Mex.	C4	63
Acaponeta, Mex.	C3	63
Acapulco [de Juárez], Mex.	D4	63
Acaraí Mountains, mts., S.A.	C3	59
Acaraú, Braz.	B2	57
Acaray, stm., Para.	E5	55
Acari, Braz.	h5	57
Acarí, Peru	E3	58
Acarigua, Ven.	B4	60
Acatlán [de Osorio], Mex.	D5	63
Acayucan, Mex.	D6	63
Accident, Md., U.S.	k12	97
Accomac, co., Va., U.S.	C7	123
Accomack, co., Va., U.S.	C7	123
Accord, N.Y., U.S.	D6	109
Accoville, W.V., U.S.	D3	125
Accra, Ghana	E4	45
Accrington, Eng., U.K.	A5	12
Ace, Tx., U.S.	D5	120
Aceguá, Ur.	E2	56
Acequia, Id., U.S.	G5	89
Achacachi, Bol.	C2	55
Achalpur, India	C2	37
Achao, Chile	E1	56
Achar, Ur.	D3	13
Acharacle, Scot., U.K.	D3	13
Acheng, China	B10	31
Achenkirch, Aus.	B7	20
Achern, Ger.	E3	19
Achicourt, Fr.	D5	16
Achille, Ok., U.S.	D5	113
Achill Head, c., Ire.	D1	11
Achill Island, i., Ire.	D1	10
Achill Sound, Ire.	D2	10
Achinsk, Sov. Un.	D12	29
Achiras, Arg.	A4	54
Achisay, Sov. Un.	E7	28
Achtubinsk, Sov. Un.	D3	28
Acıpayam, Tur.	D7	25
Acireale, Italy	F5	23
Ackerly, Tx., U.S.	C2	120
Ackerman, Ms., U.S.	B4	101
Ackley, Ia., U.S.	B4	92
Acklins Island, i., Bah.	C6	64
Acmar, Al., U.S.	B3	78
Acme, Alta.	D4	68
Acme, Mi., U.S.	D5	99
Acme, Wa., U.S.	A3	124
Acme, W.V., U.S.	m13	125
Acme, Wy., U.S.	B6	127
Acobamba, Peru	C2	120
Acoma Indian Reservation, N.M., U.S.	C2	108
Acomayo, Peru	D3	58
Aconcagua, Cerro, mtn., Arg.	A3	54
Acopiara, Braz.	B3	57
Acorizal, Braz.	B1	56
Acosta, Pa., U.S.	F3	115
Acoyapa, Nic.	E5	62
Acquapendente, Italy	D6	23
Acquarossa, Switz.	E4	21
Acqui [Terme], Italy	B2	23
Acre, state, Braz.	C4	58
Acre, stm., S.A.	C4	58
Acree, Ga., U.S.	E2	87
Actinolite, Ont.	C7	73
Acton, Ont.	D4	73
Acton, Ca., U.S.	E4	82
Acton, Me., U.S.	E2	96
Acton, Mt., U.S.	E8	103
Acton Vale, Que.	D5	74
Actopan, Mex.	m14	63
Açu, Braz.	B3	57
Acushnet, Ma., U.S.	C6	98
Acworth, Ga., U.S.	B2	87
Acworth, N.H., U.S.	D2	106
Ada, Ghana	E5	45
Ada, Ks., U.S.	C6	93
Ada, La., U.S.	C2	95
Ada, Mn., U.S.	C2	100
Ada, Oh., U.S.	B2	112
Ada, Ok., U.S.	C5	113
Ada, Yugo.	C5	24
Ada, co., Id., U.S.	F2	89
Ada, Cape, c., Sov. Un.	G19	8
Ada, Mount, mtn., Ak., U.S.	m22	79
Adair, Il., U.S.	C3	90
Adair, Ia., U.S.	C3	92
Adair, Ok., U.S.	A6	113
Adair, co., Ia., U.S.	C3	92
Adair, co., Ky., U.S.	C4	94
Adair, co., Mo., U.S.	A5	102
Adair, co., Ok., U.S.	B7	113
Adairsville, Ga., U.S.	B2	87
Adairville, Ky., U.S.	D3	94
Adak, Ak., U.S.	E4	79
Adak Island, i., Ak., U.S.	E4	79
Adak Naval Station, mil., Ak., U.S.	E4	79
Adamant, Vt., U.S.	C3	122
Adamantina, Braz.	C2	56
Adamaoua, mts., Afr.	D2	46
Adam Island, i., Md., U.S.	D5	97
Adami Tulu, Eth.	F6	91
Adams, In., U.S.	B7	94
Adams, Ky., U.S.	A1	98
Adams, Mn., U.S.	G6	100
Adams, N.Y., U.S.	B4	109
Adams, N.D., U.S.	A7	111
Adams, Ok., U.S.	e9	113
Adams, Or., U.S.	B8	114
Adams, Tn., U.S.	A4	119
Adams, Wi., U.S.	E4	126
Adams, co., Co., U.S.	B6	83
Adams, co., Id., U.S.	E2	89
Adams, co., Il., U.S.	D2	90
Adams, co., In., U.S.	C8	91
Adams, co., Ia., U.S.	C3	92
Adams, co., Ms., U.S.	D2	101
Adams, co., Ne., U.S.	D7	104
Adams, co., N.D., U.S.	C3	111
Adams, co., Oh., U.S.	D2	112
Adams, co., Pa., U.S.	G7	115
Adams, co., Wa., U.S.	B7	124
Adams, co., Wi., U.S.	D4	126
Adams, Mount, mtn., N.H., U.S.	B4	106
Adams, Mount, mtn., Wa., U.S.	C4	124
Adams Bridge, rf., Asia	G6	36
Adams Center, N.Y., U.S.	B5	109
Adams City, Co., U.S.	*B6	83
Adams Lake, l., B.C.	D8	69
Adams Mountain, mtn., Ma., U.S.	A2	98
Adams Mountain, mtn., Vt., U.S.	C3	122
Adamson, Ok., U.S.	C6	113
Adams Point, c., Mi., U.S.	C7	99
Adams Run, S.C., U.S.	k11	117
Adamstown, N.J., U.S.	C4	107
Adamstown, Md., U.S.	B3	97
Adamstown, Pa., U.S.	F9	115
Adamsville, Que.	D5	74
Adamsville, Al., U.S.	f7	78
Adamsville, Pa., U.S.	D1	115
Adamsville, R.I., U.S.	E6	116
Adamsville, Tn., U.S.	B3	119
Adamsville, Tx., U.S.	D3	120
Adamsville, Ut., U.S.	E3	121
Adamsville Brook, stm., R.I., U.S.	E6	116
Adana, Tur.	D10	40
Adanac, Sask.	E1	75
Adapazarı, Tur.	B8	40
Adarama, Sud.	B4	47
Adare, Ire.	I3	11
Adare, Cape, c., Ant.	B30	7
Adavale, Austl.	B5	51
Ad Dab'ah, Eg.	B2	41
Ad Daḥnā', des., Sau. Ar.	C4	38
Ad Dāmir, Sud.	B3	47
Ad Dammām, Sau. Ar.	C5	38
Ad Dibdibah, pl., Sau. Ar.	G3	39
Ad Dilinjāt, Eg.	D2	41
Addington, Ok., U.S.	C4	113
Addis, La., U.S.	D4	95
Addis Ababa (Addis Abeba), Eth.	A2	47
Addison, Al., U.S.	A2	78
Addison, Ct., U.S.	C5	84
Addison, Il., U.S.	k8	90
Addison, Me., U.S.	D5	96
Addison, N.Y., U.S.	C3	109
Addison, Tx., U.S.	*n10	120
Addison, Vt., U.S.	C2	122
Addison, co., Vt., U.S.	C2	122
Addyston, Oh., U.S.	o12	112
Adel, Ga., U.S.	E3	87
Adel, Ia., U.S.	C3	92
Adel, Or., U.S.	E7	114
Adelaide, Austl.	F6	50
Adelaide Island, i., Ant.	B5	7
Adelanto, Ca., U.S.	E5	82
Adelboden, Switz.	D4	21
Adélie Coast, Ant.	C26	7
Adelphi, Md., U.S.	*B4	97
Adelphi, Oh., U.S.	C3	112
Adelphia, N.J., U.S.	C4	107
Aden ('Adan), Yemen	D4	38
Aden, Gulf of, b.	D4	38
Adena, Oh., U.S.	B5	112
Adenau, Ger.	C1	19
Adi, i., Indon.	F8	34
Adieu, Cape, c., Austl.	F5	50
Adige, stm., Italy	A4	23
Adigrat, Eth.	C4	47
Adilābād, India	H7	37
Adin, Ca., U.S.	B3	82
Adirondack Mountains, mts., N.Y., U.S.	A6	109
Adi Ugri, Eth.	C4	47
Adıyaman, Tur.	C12	40
Adjud, Rom.	B8	24
Adjuntas, P.R.	B2	65
Adlavik Islands, is., Newf.	g10	72
Adliswil, Switz.	B6	21
Admaston, Ont.	B8	73
Admiral, Sask.	H1	75
Admirals Beach, Newf.	E5	72
Admiralty Bay, b., Ak., U.S.	A9	79
Admiralty Gulf, b., Austl.	B4	50
Admiralty Inlet, b., N.W. Ter.	B15	66
Admiralty Island, i., Ak., U.S.	m22	79
Admiralty Islands, is., Pap. N. Gui.	h12	50
Admiralty Mountains, mts., Ant.	B29	7
Admire, Ks., U.S.	D7	93
Adobe Acres, N.M., U.S.	B3	108
Adobe Creek, stm., Co., U.S.	C7	83
Adobe Creek Reservoir, res., Co., U.S.	C7	83
Ado-Ekiti, Nig.	*E6	45
Adok, Sud.	D3	47
Adolphus, Ky., U.S.	D3	94
Adona, Ar., U.S.	B3	81
Adoni, India	*E6	36
Adony, Hung.	B4	24
Adour, stm., Fr.	F3	16
Adra, Spain	D4	22
Adrano, Italy	F5	23
Adrar, Alg.	D4	44
Adrar, reg., Maur.	B2	45
Adré, Chad	C4	46
Adria, Italy	B4	23
Adrian, Ga., U.S.	D4	87
Adrian, Mi., U.S.	G6	99
Adrian, Mn., U.S.	G3	100
Adrian, Mo., U.S.	C3	102
Adrian, N.D., U.S.	C7	111
Adrian, Or., U.S.	D9	114
Adrian, Tx., U.S.	B1	120
Adrian, W.V., U.S.	C4	125
Adriatic Sea, Eur.	G12	8
Adrigole, Ire.	F2	11
Advance, In., U.S.	D4	91
Advance, Mo., U.S.	D8	102
Advocate Harbour, N.S.	D5	71
Adwa (Adowa), Eth.	C4	47
Adzopé, I.C.	E4	45
Ǣbelø, i., Den.	C4	15
Ǣrø, i., Den.	C4	15
Aegean Sea	C5	40
Aegeri, Lake, l., Switz.	B4	20
Ǣrøskøbing, Den.	D4	15
Aesch, Switz.	B4	21
Aetna, Alta.	E4	68
Aetna, Tn., U.S.	B4	119
Afars and Issas see Djibouti, ctry., Afr.	C5	47
Affoltern am Albis, Switz.	B3	21
Affton, Mo., U.S.	*f13	102
Afghanistan, ctry., Asia	B3	36
Afgooye, Som.	E6	47
Afikpo, Nig.	E6	45
Afmadow, Som.	E5	47
Afognak Island, i., Ak., U.S.	D9	79
Afono Bay, b., Am. Sam.	G13	52
Afonso Cláudio, Braz.	C4	56
Africa, cont.	F8	42
Afton, De., U.S.	*A4	85
Afton, Ia., U.S.	C3	92
Afton, Mi., U.S.	C6	99
Afton, Mn., U.S.	F6	100
Afton, N.Y., U.S.	C5	109
Afton, Ok., U.S.	A7	113
Afton, Tx., U.S.	C11	119
Afton, Wy., U.S.	D2	127
Aftout, reg., Alg.	D4	44
Afuá, Braz.	C4	59
'Afula, Isr.	B7	41
Afyon, Tur.	C8	40
Agadem, Niger	C7	45
Agadez, Niger	C6	45
Agadir, Mor.	C3	44
Agana, Guam	L9	52
Agana Bay, b., Guam	L9	52
Agana Heights, Guam	*L9	52
Agana Naval Air Station, mil., Guam	L10	52
Agar, India	F5	37
Agar, S.D., U.S.	C5	118
Agartala, India	D9	36
Agassiz, B.C.	E7	69
Agassiz, Cape, c., Ant.	C6	7
Agat, Guam	M9	52
Agatayn Hiid, Mong.	A3	32
Agat Bay, b., Guam	M9	52
Agate, Co., U.S.	B7	83
Agate, N.D., U.S.	A6	111
Agate Beach, Or., U.S.	C2	114
Agate Fossil Beds National Monument, Ne., U.S.	B2	104
Agattu Island, i., Ak., U.S.	E2	79
Agawam, Ma., U.S.	B2	98
Agawam, Ok., U.S.	C4	113
Agawam, stm., Ma., U.S.	E6	45
Agboville, I.C.	E4	45
Agde, Fr.	F5	16
Agege, Nig.	*E5	45
Agematsu, Japan	n16	33
Agen, Fr.	E4	16
Agency, Ia., U.S.	D5	92
Agency, Mo., U.S.	B3	102
Agenda, Ks., U.S.	C6	93
Ageo, Japan	*I9	33
Ageri, Lake, l., Switz.	B4	20
Agersø, i., Den.	C5	15
Agfayan Bay, b., Guam	M10	52
Aghā Jārī, Iran	F4	39
Aghleam, Ire.	C1	11
Agincourt (part of Scarborough), Ont.	k15	73
Agingan, Puntan, c., N. Mar. Is.	D7	52
Aginskoye, Sov. Un.	A7	31
Agno, Italy	F5	23
Agno, stm., Phil.	n12	34
Agno, Phil.	o13	34
Agnone, Italy	D5	23
Agogna, stm., Italy	D4	23
Agogo, Ghana	A4	81
Agordo, Italy	C8	20
Agra, India	m11	36
Agra, Ks., U.S.	C6	93
Agra, Ok., U.S.	B5	113
Ağrı (Karaköse), Tur.	C14	40
Agri Point, c., Phil.	o13	34
Agrigento, Italy	F4	23
Agrínion, Grc.	C3	40
Agripoli, Italy	D5	23
Agryz, Sov. Un.	D19	8
Agua Boa, Braz.	B4	56
Aguachica, Col.	B3	60
Aguadas, Col.	B2	60
Aguada, P.R.	B1	65
Aguadilla, P.R.	B1	65
Aguadilla, Bahía de, b., P.R.	B1	65
Aguadulce, Pan.	F7	62
Agua Dulce Mountains, mts., Az., U.S.	E2	80
Agua Fria, N.M., U.S.	B3	108
Agua Fria, stm., Az., U.S.	D3	80
Aguaí, Braz.	m8	56
Aguán, stm., Hond.	C4	62
Aguanish, Que.	h9	72
Aguanus, stm., Que.	h9	72
Aguapey, stm., Arg.	E4	55
Agua Prieta, Mex.	A3	63
Aguaray, Arg.	A3	55
Aguarico, stm., S.A.	B2	58
Aguascalientes, Mex.	C4	63
Aguascalientes, state, Mex.	C4	63
Agudos, Braz.	C3	56
Águeda, Port.	B1	22
Águeda, stm., Eur.	B2	22
Aguelhok, Mali	C5	45
Aguêraktem, well, Mali	B3	45
Aguila, Az., U.S.	D2	80
Aguilar, Spain	D3	22
Aguilar, Co., U.S.	D6	83
Águilas, Spain	D5	22
Aguja, Cabo de la, c., Col.	A3	60
Aguja, Punta, c., Peru	C1	58
Agulhas, Cape, c., S. Afr.	D3	49
Agulhas Negras, Pico das, mtn., Braz.	h5	56
Agusan, stm., Phil.	D7	34
Ahaggar, mts., Alg.	E6	44
Ahaggar, Tassili ta-n-, plat., Alg.	E6	44
Ahar, Iran	B3	39
Ahascragh, Ire.	D3	11
Ahaus, Ger.	A2	19
Ahırlı, Tur.	C6	25
Ahklun Mountains, mts., Ak., U.S.	D7	79
Ahlen, Ger.	C3	18
Ahlhorn, Ger.	F2	15
Ahmadābād (Ahmedabad), India	D5	36
Ahmadnagar, India	E5	36
Ahmadpur East, Pak.	C5	36
Ahmar, 'Erg el, des., Afr.	D5	47
Ahmar Mountains, mts., Eth.	D5	47
Ahmic Lake, l., Ont.	B5	73
Ahome, Mex.	B3	63
Ahoskie, N.C., U.S.	A6	110
Ahousat, B.C.	E4	69
Ahrensbök, Ger.	D4	15
Ahsahka, Id., U.S.	C2	89
Ahtanum Creek, stm., Wa., U.S.	C5	124
Ahuacatlán, Mex.	m11	63
Ahuachapán, El Sal.	D3	62
Ahualulco de Mercado, Mex.	m11	63
Åhus, Swe.	B4	38
Ahvāz (Nāsiri), Iran	B4	38
Ahvenanmaa (Åland), is., Fin.	G9	14
Ahwahnee, Ca., U.S.	D4	82
Ahwar, Yemen	C6	47
Aialik, Cape, c., Ak., U.S.	D10	79
Aibonito, P.R.	B3	65
Aichach, Ger.	E6	19
Aigen [in Mühlkreis], Aus.	D6	18
Aigle, Switz.	E3	18
Aiguá, Ur.	E2	56
Aigues-Mortes, Fr.	F6	16
Aiguilles, Fr.	E2	20
Aija, Peru	C2	58
Aikawa, Japan	G9	33
Aiken, S.C., U.S.	D4	117
Aiken, Tx., U.S.	B2	120
Aiken, co., S.C., U.S.	D4	117
Aikens Lake, l., Man.	D4	70
Ailey, Ga., U.S.	D4	87
Ailsa Craig, Ont.	D3	73
Ailsa Craig, i., Scot., U.K.	F3	13
Ain, dept., Fr.	C1	20
Ain, stm., Fr.	F7	16
Aïn ben Tili, Maur.	A3	45
Aïn el Beïda, Alg.	B6	44
Aínos, mtn., Grc.	C3	40
Aïn Sefra, Alg.	C4	44
Aïn Témouchent, Alg.	B4	44
Aïn Wessara, Alg.	B5	44
Aipe, Col.	C2	60
Aiquile, Bol.	C2	55
Airaines, Fr.	E1	17
Airdrie, Alta.	D3	68
Airdrie, Scot., U.K.	E5	13
Aire, stm., Eng., U.K.	A6	12
Aire, stm., Fr.	C6	16
Aire-sur-l'Adour, Fr.	F3	16
Aire [-sur-la-Lys], Fr.	B5	16
Air Force Island, i., N.W. Ter.	C18	66
Airline, Ga., U.S.	B3	87
Air Park West, Ne., U.S.	D9	104
Aisén del General Carlos Ibáñez del Campo, prov., Chile	D7	52
Aishihik Lake, l., Yukon	D5	66
Aisne, dept., Fr.	C6	16
Aisne, stm., Fr.	C6	16
Aitkin, Mn., U.S.	D5	100
Aitkin, co., Mn., U.S.	D5	100
Aitolikón, Grc.	C3	40
Aiud, Rom.	B6	24
Aiuruoca, stm., Braz.	g5	56
Aix, Mount, mtn., Wa., U.S.	C4	124
Aix-en-Provence, Fr.	F6	16
Aix-les-Bains, Fr.	E6	16
Aiyáleon, Grc.	g11	25
Aíyina (Aegina), i., Grc.	D4	25
Aíyion, Grc.	C4	25
Aizu-takada, Japan	H9	33
Aizu-wakamatsu, Japan	H9	33
Ajaccio, Fr.	D2	23
Ajaccio, Gulf of, b., Fr.	D2	23
Ajax, Ont.	D6	73
Ajayan Bay, b., Guam	M9	52
Ajdābiyā, Libya	G11	64
Ajjer, Tassili-n-, plat., Alg.	D6	44
'Ajlūn, Jord.	B7	41
Ajmer, India	C5	36
Akaishi-sammyaku, mts., Japan	n17	33
Akaki Beseka, Eth.	*D4	47
Akalkot, India	I6	37
Akaroa, N.Z.	O14	51
'Akasha East, Sud.	A3	47
Akashi, Japan	I7	33
Akaska, S.D., U.S.	B5	118
Akbulak, Sov. Un.	E20	8
Akçaabat, Tur.	B12	40
Akçadağ, Tur.	C11	40
Ak-Chin Indian Reservation, Az., U.S.	E3	80
Akdağmadeni, Tur.	C10	40
Akechi, Japan	n16	33
Akeley, Mn., U.S.	C4	100
Aken, Ger.	B7	19
Akers, La., U.S.	D5	95
Aketi, Zaire	A3	48
Akhaltsikhe, Sov. Un.	B14	40
Akharnaí, Grc.	g11	25
Akhdar, Al Jabal al, mts., Libya	C4	43
Akhdar, Al Jabal al, mts., Oman	C5	38
Akhelóös, stm., Grc.	C3	25
Akhiok, Ak., U.S.	D9	79
Akhisar, Tur.	C6	40
Akhmîm, Eg.	C3	38
Akhtopol, Bul.	D8	24
Akhtyrka, Sov. Un.	F10	27
Aki, Japan	J6	33
Akiachak, Ak., U.S.	C7	79
Akimiski Island, i., N.W. Ter.	F16	66
Akita, Japan	D13	33
Akjoujt, Maur.	C2	45
Akkeshi, Japan	E12	33
'Akko, Isr.	F10	40
Akobo, Sud.	D3	47
Akobo, stm., Afr.	D3	47
Akola, India	D6	36
Akonolinga, Cam.	E2	46
Akordat, Eth.	B4	47
Akosombo Dam, Ghana	*E5	45
Akpatok Island, i., N.W. Ter.	D19	66
Akra, N.D., U.S.	A8	111
Akranes, Ice.	n21	14
Akrítas, Ákra, c., Grc.	D3	40
Akron, Al., U.S.	C2	78
Akron, Co., U.S.	A7	83
Akron, In., U.S.	B5	91
Akron, Ia., U.S.	B1	92
Akron, N.Y., U.S.	B2	109
Akron, Oh., U.S.	A4	112
Akron, Pa., U.S.	F9	115
Aksaray, Tur.	C10	40
Akşehir, Tur.	C8	40
Akseki, Tur.	D8	40
Aksenovo-Zilovskoye, Sov. Un.	D14	29
Aksha, Sov. Un.	A7	31
Akshimrau, Sov. Un.	E4	28
Aksu, China	E11	29
Aksum, Eth.	C4	47
Aktogay, Sov. Un.	D9	28
Aktumsyk, Sov. Un.	D5	28
Aktyubinsk, Sov. Un.	D8	28
Akulivik, Que.	f11	74
Akure, Nig.	E6	45
Akureyri, Ice.	n23	14
Akuseki Island, i., Japan	L4	33
Akutan, Ak., U.S.	D5	79
Akyab see Sittwe, Burma	D9	36
Alabama, state, U.S.	D3	78
Alabama, stm., Al., U.S.	D2	78
Alabama Port, Al., U.S.	E1	78
Alabaster, Al., U.S.	B3	78
Alabaster, Mi., U.S.	D7	99
Alabat, i., Phil.	o14	34
Al Abyaḍ, Libya	D2	43
Al Abyār, Libya	C4	43
Alachua, Fl., U.S.	C4	86
Alachua, co., Fl., U.S.	C4	86
Aladdin, Wy., U.S.	B8	127
Alagna [Valsesia], Italy	C3	23
Alagoa Grande, Braz.	C3	57
Alagoas, state, Braz.	C3	57
Alagoinhas, Braz.	B5	57
Alagón, Spain	B2	22
Alagón, stm., Spain	B2	22
Al 'Ajamīyīn, Eg.	E2	41
Al 'Ajrūd, well, Eg.	D6	43
Alajuela, C.R.	E8	63
Alajuela, Lago, res., Pan.	k11	62
Alakanuk, Ak., U.S.	C7	79
Alakol, Lake, l., Sov. Un.	D10	28
Alalakeiki Channel, strt., Hi., U.S.	C5	88
Al 'Alamayn, Eg.	B2	41
Alalaú, stm., Braz.	C2	59
Alamance, N.C., U.S.	A3	110
Alamance, co., N.C., U.S.	B3	110
'Alam ar Rūm, Ra's, c., Egypt	H4	43
Alameda, Sask.	H4	75
Alameda, Ca., U.S.	h8	82
Alameda, N.M., U.S.	B3	108
Alameda, co., Ca., U.S.	D3	82
Alameda Naval Air Station, mil., Ca., U.S.	h8	82
Al 'Āmirīyah, Eg.	n12	41
Alaminos, Phil.	n12	34
Alamito Creek, stm., Tx., U.S.	p12	120
Alamo, Mex.	m15	63
Alamo, Ga., U.S.	*D2	87
Alamo, Nv., U.S.	E3	105
Alamo, Tn., U.S.	B2	119
Alamo, N.D., U.S.	A2	111
Alamo, Tx., U.S.	F3	120
Alamo, stm., Ca., U.S.	F6	82
Alamogordo, N.M., U.S.	E4	108
Alamogordo Dam, N.M., U.S.	C5	108
Alamo Heights, Tx., U.S.	E3	120
Alamo Hueco Mountains, mts., N.M., U.S.	F1	108

Index

Name	Map Ref.	Page

Alamo Indian Reservation, N.M., U.S. ... C2 108
Alamo Lake, res., Az., U.S. ... C2 80
Alamos, Mex. ... B3 63
Alamosa, Co., U.S. ... D5 83
Alamosa, co., Co., U.S. ... D5 83
Alamosa, stm., Co., U.S. ... D4 83
Alamosa Creek, stm., N.M., U.S. ... D2 108
Alamosa East, Co., U.S. ... D5 83
Åland see Ahvenanmaa, is., Fin. ... G9 14
Alanreed, Tx., U.S. ... B2 120
Alanson, Mi., U.S. ... C6 99
Alanya, Tur. ... D9 40
Alaotra, Lac, l., Madag. ... g9 49
Alapaha, Ga., U.S. ... E3 87
Alapaha, stm., U.S. ... E3 87
Alapayevsk, Sov. Un. ... B6 28
Al 'Aqabah, Jord. ... C3 38
Al Aqsa Mosque, Isr. Occ. ... m14 41
Al 'Arīsh, Eg. ... C6 43
Alasdair, Sgurr, mtn., Scot., U.K. ... C2 13
Alaşehir, Tur. ... C7 40
Alaska, state, U.S. ... C9 79
Alaska, Gulf of, b., Ak., U.S. ... D10 79
Alaska Peninsula, pen., Ak., U.S. ... D8 79
Alaska Range, mts., Ak., U.S. ... C9 79
Alassio, Italy ... C2 23
Alatna, stm., Ak., U.S. ... B9 79
Al 'Aṭrūn, Sud. ... B2 47
Alatyr, Sov. Un. ... D16 27
Alausi, Ec. ... B2 58
Alava, Cape, c., Wa., U.S. ... A1 124
Alaverdi, Sov. Un. ... B15 40
Al 'Ayyāṭ, Eg. ... E3 41
Al 'Ayzarīyah (Bethany), Isr. Occ. ... h12 41
Al 'Azīzīyah, Libya ... C2 43
Alb, stm., Ger. ... A5 21
Alba, Italy ... B2 23
Alba, Mi., U.S. ... D6 99
Alba, Mo., U.S. ... D3 102
Alba, Pa., U.S. ... C8 115
Alba, Tx., U.S. ... E5 120
Albacete, Spain ... C5 22
Al Badārī, Eg. ... D6 43
Alba de Tormes, Spain ... B3 22
Ålbæk, Den. ... A4 15
Ålbæk Bugt, b., Den. ... A4 15
Al Bahnasā, Eg. ... H8 40
Al Bahr al Abyaḍ, prov., Sud. ... C3 47
Al Baḥr al Aḥmar (Red Sea), prov., Sud. ... B4 47
Alba Iulia, Rom. ... B6 24
Al Bājūr, Eg. ... D3 41
Albalate [del Arzobispo], Spain ... B5 22
Al Ballaḥ, Eg. ... D4 41
Albanel, Lac, l., Que. ... F18 66
Albani, Colli, hills, Italy ... h9 23
Albania, ctry., Eur. ... B2 40
Albano, Lake, l., Italy ... h9 23
Albano Laziale, Italy ... D4 23
Albany, Austl. ... F2 50
Albany, N.S. ... E4 71
Albany, P.E.I. ... C6 71
Albany, Ca., U.S. ... *h8 82
Albany, Ga., U.S. ... E2 87
Albany, Il., U.S. ... B3 90
Albany, In., U.S. ... D7 91
Albany, Ky., U.S. ... D4 94
Albany, La., U.S. ... g10 95
Albany, Mn., U.S. ... E4 100
Albany, Mo., U.S. ... A3 102
Albany, N.H., U.S. ... C4 106
Albany, N.Y., U.S. ... C7 109
Albany, Oh., U.S. ... C3 112
Albany, Ok., U.S. ... D5 113
Albany, Or., U.S. ... C3 114
Albany, Tx., U.S. ... C3 120
Albany, Vt., U.S. ... B4 122
Albany, Wi., U.S. ... F4 126
Albany, Wy., U.S. ... E6 127
Albany, co., N.Y., U.S. ... C6 109
Albany, co., Wy., U.S. ... E7 127
Albany, stm., Ont. ... o18 73
Al Barkāt, Libya ... E2 43
Al Baṭanūn, Eg. ... D2 41
Albatross Bay, b., Austl. ... B7 50
Al Baṭrūn, Leb. ... E10 40
Al Bawīṭī, Eg. ... D5 43
Al Bayḍa, Libya ... C4 43
Albee, S.D., U.S. ... B9 118
Albemarle, N.C., U.S. ... B2 110
Albemarle, co., Va., U.S. ... C4 123
Albemarle, Punta, c., Ec. ... f5 58
Albemarle Lake, l., Ms., U.S. ... C2 101
Albemarle Sound, strt., N.C., U.S. ... A6 110
Albenga, Italy ... B2 23
Alberche, stm., Spain ... B3 22
Ålberga (part of Eskilstuna), Swe. ... u34 14
Albergaria-a-Velha, Port. ... B1 22
Albersdorf, Ger. ... D3 15
Albert, Fr. ... B5 16
Albert, Ks., U.S. ... D4 93
Albert, N.M., U.S. ... B6 108
Albert, Ok., U.S. ... B3 113
Albert, co., N.B. ... D5 71
Alberta, Al., U.S. ... C2 78
Alberta, Mn., U.S. ... E2 100
Alberta, Va., U.S. ... D5 123
Alberta, prov., Can. ... C4 68
Alberta, Mount, mtn., Alta. ... C2 68
Albert Canyon, B.C. ... D9 69
Albert City, Ia., U.S. ... B3 92
Albert Edward, Mount, mtn., Pap. N. Gui. ... k12 50
Albert Lea, Mn., U.S. ... G5 100
Albert Markham, Mount, mtn., Ant. ... A28 7
Albert Nile, stm., Ug. ... A5 48
Alberton, P.E.I. ... C5 71
Alberton, Mt., U.S. ... C2 103
Albertson, N.Y., U.S. ... k13 109
Albertville, Sask. ... D3 75
Albertville, Fr. ... E7 16
Albertville, Al., U.S. ... A3 78
Albertville, Mn., U.S. ... E5 100
Albeuve, Switz. ... C3 21
Albi, Fr. ... F5 16
Albia, Ia., U.S. ... C5 92
Albin, Wy., U.S. ... E8 127
Albina, Sur. ... A4 59
Albino, Italy ... E8 21
Albion, Ca., U.S. ... C2 82
Albion, Il., U.S. ... E5 90
Albion, In., U.S. ... B7 91
Albion, Ia., U.S. ... B5 92
Albion, Me., U.S. ... D3 96

Albion, Mi., U.S. ... F6 99
Albion, Ne., U.S. ... C7 104
Albion, N.Y., U.S. ... B2 109
Albion, Ok., U.S. ... C6 113
Albion, Pa., U.S. ... C1 115
Albion, R.I., U.S. ... B4 116
Albion, Wa., U.S. ... C8 124
Albion, Wi., U.S. ... F4 126
Al Bīrah, Isr. Occ. ... h11 41
Alborán, i., Spain ... E4 22
Ålborg, Den. ... I3 14
Ålborg Bugt, b., Den. ... B4 15
Alborn, Mn., U.S. ... D6 100
Albox, Spain ... D4 22
Albreda, B.C. ... C8 69
Albrightsville, Pa., U.S. ... D10 115
Al Bu'ayrāt, Libya ... C3 43
Albufeira, Port. ... D1 22
Al Bunbah, Libya ... F4 40
Albuñol, Spain ... D4 22
Albuquerque, N.M., U.S. ... B3 108
Al Buraymī, Oman ... C5 38
Alburg, Vt., U.S. ... B2 122
Alburnett, Ia., U.S. ... B6 92
Alburquerque, Spain ... C4 22
Alburtis, Pa., U.S. ... F10 115
Albury, Austl. ... G8 50
Al Buṣaylī, Eg. ... C2 41
Alca, Peru ... E4 58
Alcabideche, Port. ... f9 22
Alcácer do Sal, Port. ... C1 22
Alcalá de Chivert, Spain ... B6 22
Alcalá [de Guadaira], Spain ... D3 22
Alcalá de Henares, Spain ... B4 22
Alcalá de los Gazules, Spain ... D3 22
Alcalá la Real, Spain ... D4 22
Alcalde, N.M., U.S. ... A3 108
Alcamo, Italy ... F4 23
Alcanadre, stm., Spain ... B5 22
Alcanar, Spain ... B6 22
Alcañiz, Spain ... B5 22
Alcântara, Braz. ... B2 57
Alcantarilla, Spain ... D5 22
Alcaraz, Spain ... C4 22
Alcaudete, Spain ... D3 22
Alcázar de San Juan, Spain ... C4 22
Alcester, S.D., U.S. ... D9 118
Alcira, Spain ... C5 22
Alco, Ar., U.S. ... B3 81
Alco, La., U.S. ... C2 95
Alcoa, Tn., U.S. ... D10 119
Alcobendas, Spain ... o17 22
Alcochete, Port. ... f10 22
Alcolu, S.C., U.S. ... D7 117
Alcomdale, Alta. ... C4 68
Alcona, co., Mi., U.S. ... D7 99
Alcora, Spain ... B5 22
Alcorcón, Spain ... p17 22
Alcorisa, Spain ... B5 22
Alcorn, Ms., U.S. ... D2 101
Alcorn, co., Ms., U.S. ... A5 101
Alcovy, stm., Ga., U.S. ... C3 87
Alcoy, Spain ... C5 22
Alcoy, Nevado, mtn., Peru ... D2 58
Alda, Ne., U.S. ... D7 104
Aldama, Mex. ... B3 63
Aldan, Sov. Un. ... D15 29
Aldan, stm., Sov. Un. ... C16 29
Aldan Plateau, plat., Sov. Un. ... D15 29
Al Dār al Bayḍā', hist., Eg. ... D3 41
Aldeburgh, Eng., U.K. ... B9 12
Alden, Il., U.S. ... A5 90
Alden, Ia., U.S. ... B4 92
Alden, Ks., U.S. ... D5 93
Alden, Mi., U.S. ... D5 99
Alden, Mn., U.S. ... G5 100
Alden, N.Y., U.S. ... C2 109
Alden, Pa., U.S. ... D9 115
Alder, Mt., U.S. ... E4 103
Alder, Ben, mtn., Scot., U.K. ... C4 13
Alder Brook, stm., Vt., U.S. ... B4 122
Alderney, i., Guernsey ... F5 10
Aldershot, Eng., U.K. ... E6 10
Alderson, Ok., U.S. ... C6 113
Alderson, W.V., U.S. ... D4 125
Aldersyde, Alta. ... D4 68
Alderwood Manor, Wa., U.S. ... *B3 124
Aldie, Va., U.S. ... B5 123
Aldine, N.J., U.S. ... D2 107
Aldora, Ga., U.S. ... C2 87
Aldrich, Al., U.S. ... B3 78
Aldrich, Mn., U.S. ... D4 100
Aledo, Il., U.S. ... B3 90
Aledo, Tx., U.S. ... n9 120
Aleg, Maur. ... C2 45
Alegre, Braz. ... C4 59
Alegrete, Braz. ... D1 56
Alegros Mountain, mtn., N.M., U.S. ... C2 108
Alejandro Selkirk, Isla, i., Chile ... Q2 53
Aleknagik, Ak., U.S. ... D8 79
Aleksandrov, Sov. Un. ... G9 27
Aleksandrov, Sov. Un. ... C12 27
Aleksandrov-Gay, Sov. Un. ... C3 28
Aleksandrovskoye, Sov. Un. ... A9 28
Aleksandrovsk [-Sakhalinskij], Sov. Un. ... D17 29
Aleksandrów [Kujawski], Pol. ... C5 26
Aleksandrów [Łódzki], Pol. ... C5 26
Aleksin, Sov. Un. ... D11 27
Aleksinac, Yugo. ... E4 24
Alemania, Arg. ... E2 55
Além Paraíba, Braz. ... g6 59
Alençon, Fr. ... C4 16
Alenquer, Braz. ... C4 59
Alenquer, Port. ... C1 22
Alentejo, hist. reg., Port. ... C2 22
Alenuihaha Channel, strt., Hi., U.S. ... C5 88
Aleppo (Halab), Syria ... B3 38
Aléria, Fr. ... — 7
Alert, N.W. Ter. ... k39 66
Alert, In., U.S. ... D7 91
Alert Bay, B.C. ... D4 69
Alès, Fr. ... E6 16
Alessandria, Italy ... B2 23
Ålestrup, Den. ... B3 15
Ålesund, Nor. ... F2 14
Aleutian Islands, is., Ak., U.S. ... E3 79
Aleutian Range, mts., Ak., U.S. ... D9 79
Alex, Ok., U.S. ... C4 113
Alexander, Man. ... E1 70
Alexander, Ar., U.S. ... C3 81
Alexander, Ia., U.S. ... B4 92
Alexander, Ks., U.S. ... D4 93
Alexander, Me., U.S. ... C5 96
Alexander, N.Y., U.S. ... C2 109

Alexander, N.C., U.S. ... f10 110
Alexander, N.D., U.S. ... B2 111
Alexander, W.V., U.S. ... C4 125
Alexander, co., Il., U.S. ... F4 90
Alexander, co., N.C., U.S. ... B1 110
Alexander Archipelago, is., Ak., U.S. ... D12 79
Alexander Bay, S. Afr. ... C2 49
Alexander City, Al., U.S. ... C4 78
Alexander Island, i., Ant. ... B5 7
Alexander Mills, N.C., U.S. ... B1 110
Alexandra, B.C. ... C6 69
Alexandra, N.Z. ... P12 51
Alexandra, i., Sov. Un. ... B10 128
Alexandretta, Gulf of, b., Tur. ... D10 40
Alexandretta see Iskenderun, Tur. ... D11 40
Alexandria (Al Iskandarīyah), Eg. ... B3 38
Alexandria, Rom. ... D7 24
Alexandria, B.C. ... C6 69
Alexandria, In., U.S. ... D6 91
Alexandria, Ky., U.S. ... B5 94
Alexandria, La., U.S. ... C3 95
Alexandria, Mn., U.S. ... E3 100
Alexandria, Mo., U.S. ... A6 102
Alexandria, Ne., U.S. ... D8 104
Alexandria, N.H., U.S. ... C3 106
Alexandria, Oh., U.S. ... B3 112
Alexandria, Pa., U.S. ... E5 115
Alexandria, S.D., U.S. ... D8 118
Alexandria, Tn., U.S. ... A5 119
Alexandria, Va., U.S. ... B5 123
Alexandria Bay, N.Y., U.S. ... A5 109
Alexandrina, Lake, l., Austl. ... G2 51
Alexandroúpolis, Grc. ... B5 40
Alexis, Il., U.S. ... B3 90
Alexis, stm., Newf. ... B3 72
Alexis Creek, B.C. ... C6 69
Aley, stm., Sov. Un. ... E25 8
Aleysk, Sov. Un. ... D11 29
Alfalfa, co., Ok., U.S. ... A3 113
Al Fallūjah, Iraq ... F14 40
Al Fandaqūmīyah, Isr. Occ. ... B7 41
Alfaro, Spain ... A5 22
Al Fashn, Eg. ... D6 43
Alfatar, Bul. ... D8 24
Al Fāw, Iraq ... G4 39
Al Fayyūm, Eg. ... C3 38
Alfeld, Ger. ... B4 19
Alfenas, Braz. ... C3 56
Alfiós (Alpheus), stm., Grc. ... E8 20
Alfonsine, Italy ... E8 20
Alford, Eng., U.K. ... A8 12
Alford, Scot., U.K. ... C6 13
Alford, Fl., U.S. ... B1 86
Alford, In., U.S. ... H3 91
Alford, Ma., U.S. ... B1 98
Alfordsville, In., U.S. ... G4 91
Alfortville, Fr. ... g10 16
Alfred, Ont. ... B10 73
Alfred, Me., U.S. ... E2 96
Alfred, N.Y., U.S. ... C3 109
Alfred Mills, Me., U.S. ... E2 96
Alfred Station, N.Y., U.S. ... C3 109
Al Fujayrah, U.A.E. ... C5 38
Al Fuqahā', Libya ... D3 43
Algarrobal, Chile ... E1 55
Algarrobo del Águila, Arg. ... B3 54
Algarve, hist. reg., Port. ... D1 22
Algeciras, Spain ... D3 22
Algemesí, Spain ... C5 22
Alger, Mi., U.S. ... D6 99
Alger, Oh., U.S. ... B2 112
Alger, co., Mi., U.S. ... B4 99
Algeria, ctry., Afr. ... D5 44
Algete, Spain ... o18 22
Al Ghayatah, Eg. ... D2 41
Al Ghaydah, Yemen ... B7 47
Alghero, Italy ... D2 23
Al Ghurdaqah, Eg. ... D6 43
Algiers (El Djazair), Alg. ... B5 44
Algoa, Ar., U.S. ... *B4 81
Algoa Bay, b., S. Afr. ... D4 49
Algodón, stm., Peru ... B3 58
Algodones, N.M., U.S. ... B3 108
Algoma, Ms., U.S. ... A4 101
Algoma, Wi., U.S. ... D6 126
Algoma, dept., Ont. ... A2 73
Algoma Mills, Ont. ... A2 73
Algona, Ia., U.S. ... A3 92
Algona, Wa., U.S. ... f11 124
Algonac, Mi., U.S. ... F8 99
Algonquin, Il., U.S. ... h8 90
Algonquin, Ont. ... C9 73
Algonquin Park, Ont. ... B6 73
Algonquin Provincial Park, Ont. ... B6 73

Aliceville, Ks., U.S. ... D8 93
Alicia, Ar., U.S. ... B4 81
Alicudi, i., Italy ... E5 23
Alida, Sask. ... H5 75
Aligarh, India ... C6 36
Aligūdarz, Iran ... E4 39
Alindao, Cen. Afr. Rep. ... E4 46
Aline, Ga., U.S. ... D4 87
Aline, Ok., U.S. ... A3 113
Alingsås, Swe. ... I5 14
Ālīpur Duār, India ... D12 37
Aliquippa, Pa., U.S. ... E1 115
Al 'Irq, Libya ... D4 43
Ali-Sabieh, Dji. ... C5 47
Alistráti, Grc. ... B4 25
Aliwal North, S. Afr. ... C4 49
Alix, Alta. ... C4 68
Alix, Ar., U.S. ... B2 81
Al Jabalayn, Sud. ... C3 47
Al Jafūrah, des., Sau. Ar. ... I5 39
Al Jaghbūb, Libya ... D4 43
Al Jahrah, Kuw. ... G3 39
Al Jānīyah, Isr. Occ. ... h11 41
Al Jawf, Libya ... E4 43
Al Jawf, Sau. Ar. ... C3 38
Al Jawsh, Libya ... C2 43
Al Jazīrah, prov., Sud. ... C3 47
Aljezur, Port. ... D1 22
Al Jubayl, Sau. Ar. ... H4 39
Al Junaynah, Sud. ... C1 47
Aljustrel, Port. ... D1 22
Al Kāb, Eg. ... D4 41
Alkabo, N.D., U.S. ... A2 111
Al Kahfah, Sau. Ar. ... I14 40
Alkali Lake, l., Nv., U.S. ... B2 105
Alkali Creek, stm., Or., U.S. ... E6 114
Alkaline Lake, l., N.D., U.S. ... C6 111
Al Karak, Jord. ... G10 40
Al Karnak, Eg. ... D6 43
Al Kawm aṭ Ṭawīl, Eg. ... C3 41
Al Khābūrah, Oman ... C5 38
Al Khālis, Iraq ... E15 40
Al Khandaq, Sud. ... C3 47
Al Khārijah, Eg. ... C3 38
Al Khartūm, prov., Sud. ... C3 47
Al Khaṣab, Oman ... C5 38
Al Khums, Libya ... C2 43
Al Khurmah, Sau. Ar. ... C4 38
Al Khushnīyah, Isr. Occ. ... A7 41
Alkionídhes, is., Grc. ... g9 25
Alkionídhes Gulf, b., Grc. ... g10 25
Alkmaar, Neth. ... A4 17
Al Kūbrī, Eg. ... m12 125
Al Kūfah, Iraq ... G15 40
Al Kuntillah, Eg. ... E6 41
Al Kūt, Iraq ... E5 38
Allagash, stm., Me., U.S. ... B3 96
Allagash Lake, l., Me., U.S. ... B3 96
Allahābād, India ... C7 36
Allakaket, Ak., U.S. ... B9 79
Allamakee, co., Ia., U.S. ... A6 92
Allamuchy Mountain, mtn., N.J., U.S. ... B3 107
Allan, Sask. ... F2 75
Allanmyo, Burma ... E10 36
Allardt, Tn., U.S. ... C9 119
Allariz, Spain ... A2 22
Allatoona Lake, res., Ga., U.S. ... B2 87
Alleene, Ar., U.S. ... D1 81
Allegan, Mi., U.S. ... F5 99
Allegan, co., Mi., U.S. ... F5 99
Allegany, N.Y., U.S. ... C2 109
Allegany, Or., U.S. ... D2 114
Allegany, co., Md., U.S. ... k13 97
Allegany, co., N.Y., U.S. ... C2 109
Allegany Indian Reservation, N.Y., U.S. ... C2 109
Alleghany, Ca., U.S. ... C3 82
Alleghany, co., N.C., U.S. ... A1 110
Alleghany, co., Va., U.S. ... C2 123
Alleghany, co., Pa., U.S. ... E1 115
Allegheny, stm., U.S. ... E2 115
Allegheny Front, mtn., W.V., U.S. ... B5 125
Allegheny Mountain, mtn., U.S. ... E1 115
Allegheny Plateau, plat., U.S. ... E1 115
Allegheny Reservoir, res., U.S. ... C2 109
Alleman, Ia., U.S. ... C4 92
Allemands, Bayou Des, stm., La., U.S. ... k11 95
Allemands, Lac Des, l., La., U.S. ... E5 95
Allen, Al., U.S. ... D2 78
Allen, Ks., U.S. ... D7 93
Allen, Ne., U.S. ... B9 104
Allen, Ok., U.S. ... C5 113
Allen, Pa., U.S. ... F7 115
Allen, S.D., U.S. ... D4 118
Allen, Tx., U.S. ... *C4 120
Allen, co., In., U.S. ... B7 91
Allen, co., Ks., U.S. ... E8 93
Allen, co., Ky., U.S. ... D3 94
Allen, co., Oh., U.S. ... B1 112
Allen, Lough, l., Ire. ... C2 10
Allen, Mount, mtn., N.Z. ... Q11 51
Allen, Mount, mtn., Ak., U.S. ... C11 79
Allendale, Il., U.S. ... E6 90
Allendale, N.J., U.S. ... A4 107
Allendale, S.C., U.S. ... F5 117
Allendale, Wy., U.S. ... *D6 127
Allendale, co., S.C., U.S. ... F5 117
Allende, Mex. ... B4 63
Allenhurst, Ga., U.S. ... E5 87
Allenhurst, N.J., U.S. ... C4 107
Allen Park, Mi., U.S. ... p15 99
Allenport, Pa., U.S. ... F2 115
Allensville, Ky., U.S. ... D3 94
Allensville, Oh., U.S. ... C3 112
Allensville, Pa., U.S. ... E6 115
Allenton, Mo., U.S. ... f12 102
Allenton, Wi., U.S. ... E5 126
Allentown, Ga., U.S. ... D3 87
Allentown, N.J., U.S. ... C3 107
Allentown, N.Y., U.S. ... C2 109

Allentown, Pa., U.S. ... E11 115
Allenville, Il., U.S. ... D5 90
Allenwood, N.J., U.S. ... C4 107
Allenwood, Pa., U.S. ... D8 115
Alleppey, India ... G6 36
Aller, stm., Eur. ... B4 18
Allerton, Il., U.S. ... D6 90
Allerton, Ia., U.S. ... D4 92
Allerton, Point, c., Ma., U.S. ... B6 98
Allgäuer Alps, mts., Eur. ... B9 21
Allgood, Al., U.S. ... B3 78
Alliance, Alta. ... C5 68
Alliance, Ne., U.S. ... B3 104
Alliance, N.C., U.S. ... B6 110
Alliance, Oh., U.S. ... B4 112
Al Lidām, Sau. Ar. ... A5 47
Allier, stm., Fr. ... D5 16
Alligator, Ms., U.S. ... A3 101
Alligator, stm., N.C., U.S. ... B6 110
Alligator Lake, l., Me., U.S. ... D4 96
Allihies, Ire. ... F1 11
Allingåbro, Den. ... C8 15
Allinge [-Sandvig], Den. ... C8 15
Allison, Co., U.S. ... D3 83
Allison, Ia., U.S. ... B5 92
Allison, Pa., U.S. ... G2 115
Allison, Tx., U.S. ... B2 120
Allison Park, Pa., U.S. ... h14 115
Alliston, Ont. ... C5 73
Al Līth, Sau. Ar. ... C4 38
Alloa, Scot., U.K. ... B5 10
Allouez, Mi., U.S. ... A2 99
Allouez, Wi., U.S. ... h9 126
Alloway, N.J., U.S. ... D2 107
Alloway Creek, stm., N.J., U.S. ... D2 107
All Pines, Belize ... B3 62
Allred, Tn., U.S. ... C8 119
Allschwil, Switz. ... A4 21
Allston, Ma., U.S. ... g12 98
Allumette Lake, l., Can. ... B7 73
Alluwe, Ok., U.S. ... A6 113
Allyn, Wa., U.S. ... B3 124
Alma, N.B. ... D5 71
Alma, Ont. ... D4 73
Alma, Que. ... A6 74
Alma, Ar., U.S. ... B1 81
Alma, Co., U.S. ... B4 83
Alma, Ga., U.S. ... E4 87
Alma, Il., U.S. ... E5 90
Alma, Ks., U.S. ... C7 93
Alma, Mi., U.S. ... E6 99
Alma, Mo., U.S. ... B4 102
Alma, Ne., U.S. ... D6 104
Alma, N.C., U.S. ... C3 110
Alma, Ok., U.S. ... C4 113
Alma, W.V., U.S. ... B4 125
Alma, Wi., U.S. ... D2 126
Alma-Ata, Sov. Un. ... E10 29
Alma Center, Wi., U.S. ... D3 126
Almada, Port. ... C1 22
Almadén, Spain ... C3 22
Al Mafraq, Jord. ... F11 40
Almagro, Spain ... C4 22
Alma Hill, hill, N.Y., U.S. ... C2 109
Al Maḥallah al Kubrā, Eg. ... D3 41
Al Maḥmūdīyah, Eg. ... D2 41
Al Maḥmūdīyah, Iraq ... F15 40
Al Maḥsamah, Eg. ... D4 41
Al Makīlī, Libya ... F4 40
Almanor, Lake, l., Ca., U.S. ... B3 82
Almansa, Spain ... C5 22
Al Manṣūrah, Eg. ... B3 38
Al Manzilah, Eg. ... C3 41
Almanzora, stm., Spain ... D4 22
Al Marj, Libya ... C4 43
Almartha, Mo., U.S. ... E5 102
Al Maṭarīyah, Eg. ... C4 41
Al Maṭarīyah, Eg. ... D4 41
Almaville, Tn., U.S. ... B5 119
Al Mayādīn, Syria ... B4 38
Almazán, Spain ... B4 22
Al Mazār, Eg. ... C5 41
Al Mazār, Jord. ... C7 41
Al Mazra'ah, Jord. ... D4 41
Almeirim, Braz. ... C4 59
Almeirim, Port. ... C1 22
Almelo, Neth. ... A7 16
Almelund, Mn., U.S. ... E6 100
Almena, Ks., U.S. ... C4 93
Almena, Wi., U.S. ... C1 126
Almenara, Spain ... B5 22
Almendralejo, Spain ... C2 22
Almería, Spain ... D4 22
Almería, stm., Spain ... D4 22
Almería, Gulf of, b., Spain ... D4 22
Almetyevsk, Sov. Un. ... *D8 27
Älmhult, Swe. ... B8 15
Al Minyā, Eg. ... E3 38
Al Miqdādīyah, Iraq ... E4 39
Almira, Wa., U.S. ... B7 124
Almirante, Pan. ... F6 62
Almirante Brown, Arg. ... g7 54
Almirós, Grc. ... C4 40
Almo, Id., U.S. ... G5 89
Almo, Ky., U.S. ... f9 94
Almodóvar [del Campo], Spain ... C3 22
Almogía, Spain ... D3 22
Almon, Ga., U.S. ... C3 87
Almond, N.Y., U.S. ... C3 109
Almond, Wi., U.S. ... D4 126
Almont, Co., U.S. ... C4 83
Almont, Mi., U.S. ... F7 99
Almont, N.D., U.S. ... C4 111
Almonte, Ont. ... B8 73
Almonte, stm., Spain ... C3 22
Almora, India ... C6 36
Al Mudawwarah, Jord. ... E8 41
Al Mughayyir, Isr. Occ. ... g12 47
Al Muglad, Sud. ... C2 47
Al Mukalla, Yemen ... B6 47
Al Mukhā, Yemen ... D4 38
Almuñécar, Spain ... D4 22
Al Musallamīyah, Sud. ... C3 47
Al Musayyib, Iraq ... F15 40
Al Muwaylih, Sau. Ar. ... I10 40
Almyville, Ct., U.S. ... C5 84

Alor, i., Indon. ... G6 34
Álora, Spain ... D3 22
Alor Setar, Malay. ... D2 34
Alosno, Spain ... D2 22
Alost see Aalst, Bel. ... B6 16
Alotau, Pap. N. Gui. ... m13 50
Alpachin, Arg. ... B4 54
Alpaugh, Ca., U.S. ... E4 82
Alpbach, Aus. ... E5 18
Alpena, Ar., U.S. ... A2 81
Alpena, Mi., U.S. ... C7 99
Alpena, S.D., U.S. ... C7 118
Alpena, co., Mi., U.S. ... D7 99
Alpha, Il., U.S. ... B3 90
Alpha, Ia., U.S. ... A5 92
Alpha, Ky., U.S. ... D4 94
Alpha, Mi., U.S. ... B2 99
Alpha, Mn., U.S. ... G4 100
Alpha, N.J., U.S. ... B2 107
Alpharetta, Ga., U.S. ... B2 87
Alphen aan den Rijn, Neth. ... B4 17
Alpheus see Alfiós, stm., Grc. ... D3 25
Alpiarça, Port. ... C1 22
Alpine, Az., U.S. ... D6 80
Alpine, Ca., U.S. ... *F5 82
Alpine, N.J., U.S. ... *h9 107
Alpine, N.Y., U.S. ... E7 91
Alpine, Or., U.S. ... C3 114
Alpine, Tn., U.S. ... C8 119
Alpine, Tx., U.S. ... D1 120
Alpine, Ut., U.S. ... C4 121
Alpine, Wy., U.S. ... C1 127
Alpine, co., Ca., U.S. ... C4 82
Alpine Junction, Wy., U.S. ... *C1 127
Alpoca, W.V., U.S. ... D3 125
Alps, mts., Eur. ... E4 18
Al Qadārif, Sud. ... B3 47
Al Qadīmah, Sau. Ar. ... C3 38
Al Qā'im, Iraq ... E13 40
Al Qāmishlī, Syria ... B4 38
Al Qanāṭir, Eg. ... D2 41
Al Qanṭarah, Eg. ... D4 41
Al Qaryah ash Sharqīyah, Libya ... C2 43
Al Qaryatayn, Syria ... E11 40
Al Qaṣabāt, Libya ... C2 43
Al Qaṣr, Eg. ... C2 38
Al Qaṭīf, Sau. Ar. ... C4 38
Al Qaṭrānah, Jord. ... G11 40
Al Qaṭrūn, Libya ... E2 43
Al Qaṭṭah, Eg. ... D2 41
Al Qunfudhah, Sau. Ar. ... D4 38
Al Qurnah, Iraq ... F3 39
Al Quṣaymah, Eg. ... D6 41
Al Quṣayr, Eg. ... C3 38
Al Qutaynah, Sud. ... C3 47
Alrø, Den. ... B4 15
Als, i., Den. ... D3 15
Alsace, hist. reg., Fr. ... C7 16
Alsask, Sask. ... F1 75
Alsasua, Spain ... A4 22
Alsdorf, Ger. ... D6 17
Alsea, Or., U.S. ... C3 114
Alsek, stm., N.A. ... D5 66
Alsen, N.D., U.S. ... A7 111
Alsenbrück-Langmeil, Ger. ... D2 19
Alsey, Il., U.S. ... D3 90
Alsike (part of Uppsala), Swe. ... *t35 14
Alsip, Il., U.S. ... *k9 90
Alstead, N.H., U.S. ... D2 106
Alstead, stm., Sask. ... B2 75
Alstead Center, N.H., U.S. ... D2 106
Alston, Eng., U.K. ... F6 13
Alston, Ga., U.S. ... D4 87
Alta, Ia., U.S. ... B2 92
Alta, Ut., U.S. ... *C4 121
Alta, Wy., U.S. ... C1 127
Alta Gracia, Arg. ... A4 54
Altagracia de Orituco, Ven. ... B4 60
Altai, Mong. ... m12 82
Altamaha, stm., Ga., U.S. ... E4 87
Altamaha Sound, strt., Ga., U.S. ... E5 87
Altamahaw, N.C., U.S. ... A3 110
Altamira, Braz. ... C4 59
Altamira, Chile ... E2 55
Altamira, Mex. ... C5 63
Altamirano, Arg. ... g7 54
Altamont, Man. ... E2 70
Altamont, Il., U.S. ... D5 90
Altamont, Ks., U.S. ... E8 93
Altamont, Mo., U.S. ... B3 102
Altamont, N.Y., U.S. ... C6 109
Altamont, Or., U.S. ... E5 114
Altamont, S.D., U.S. ... C9 118
Altamont, Tn., U.S. ... D8 119
Altamont, Ut., U.S. ... C5 121
Altamonte Springs, Fl., U.S. ... D5 86
Altamura, Italy ... D6 23
Altapass, N.C., U.S. ... f10 110
Altar, Mex. ... A2 63
Altario, Alta. ... C5 68
Alta Vista, Ia., U.S. ... A5 92
Altavista, Va., U.S. ... C3 123
Altay, China ... B2 31
Altay, Mong. ... B5 31
Altay Shan, mts., Asia ... B2 31
Altdorf, Switz. ... E4 18
Altdorf [bei Nürnberg], Ger. ... D6 19
Altefähr, Ger. ... D7 15
Altenberg, Ger. ... E7 15
Altenbruch, Ger. ... E2 15
Altenburg, Ger. ... E3 15
Altenburg, Mo., U.S. ... D8 102
Altenkirchen, Ger. ... C2 19
Altentreptow, Ger. ... E7 15
Alter do Chão, Port. ... C1 22
Alti, Fl., U.S. ... B1 86
Altheim, Aus. ... A9 18
Altheimer, Ar., U.S. ... C4 81
Altkirch, Fr. ... B3 20
Altmar, N.Y., U.S. ... B5 109
Altmühl, stm., Ger. ... D5 19
Altnaharra, Scot., U.K. ... B4 13
Alto, Ga., U.S. ... B3 87
Alto, La., U.S. ... B4 95
Alto, Mi., U.S. ... F5 99
Alto, N.M., U.S. ... D4 108
Alto, Tn., U.S. ... D5 119
Alto, Tx., U.S. ... D5 120
Alto Araguaia, Braz. ... D5 56
Alto Cedro, Cuba ... D6 64
Alto Garças, Braz. ... C2 57
Alto Longá, Braz. ... C2 57
Alto Molócuè, Moz. ... A6 49

Name	Map Ref.	Page
Altomünster, Ger.	A7	20
Alton, Ont.	D4	73
Alton, Eng., U.K.	C7	12
Alton, Al., U.S.	B3	78
Alton, Il., U.S.	E3	90
Alton, Ia., U.S.	B2	92
Alton, Ks., U.S.	C5	93
Alton, La., U.S.	h12	95
Alton, Mo., U.S.	E6	102
Alton, N.H., U.S.	D4	106
Alton, Oh., U.S.	m10	112
Alton, R.I., U.S.	F2	116
Alton, Ut., U.S.	F3	121
Alton, W.V., U.S.	C4	125
Altona, Man.	E3	70
Altona (part of Hamburg), Ger.	E3	15
Altona, Il., U.S.	B3	90
Altona, N.Y., U.S.	B7	91
Altona, N.Y., U.S.	f11	109
Altonah, Ut., U.S.	C5	121
Alton Bay, N.H., U.S.	D4	106
Altoona, Al., U.S.	A3	78
Altoona, Fl., U.S.	D5	86
Altoona, Ia., U.S.	C4	92
Altoona, Ks., U.S.	E8	93
Altoona, Pa., U.S.	E5	115
Altoona, Wi., U.S.	D2	126
Alto Paraguai, Braz.	A1	56
Alto Paraguay, dept., Para.	D4	55
Alto Paraná, dept., Para.	D5	55
Alto Pass, Il., U.S.	F4	90
Alto Purus, stm., Peru	D3	58
Altötting, Ger.	A8	20
Altrincham, Eng., U.K.	A5	12
Altro, Ky., U.S.	C6	94
Altstätten, Switz.	B5	20
Āltūn Kūprī, Iraq	E15	40
Altun Shan, mts., China	D2	31
Alturas, Ca., U.S.	B3	82
Alturas, Mn., U.S.	B3	82
Altus, Ar., U.S.	B2	81
Altus, Ok., U.S.	C2	113
Altus Air Force Base, mil., Ok., U.S.	C2	113
Altus Reservoir, res., Ok., U.S.	C2	113
Altusried, Ger.	A9	21
Alt Zachun, Ger.	E5	15
Al 'Ubaylah, Sau. Ar.	C5	38
Al Qayyah, Sud.	C2	47
Alum Bank, Pa., U.S.	F4	115
Alum Bridge, W.V., U.S.	B4	125
Alum Creek, W.V., U.S.	m12	125
Alum Creek, stm., Oh., U.S.	k11	112
Aluminé, Arg.	B2	54
Alum Rock, Ca., U.S.	*k9	82
Alupka, Sov. Un.	I10	27
Al 'Uqaylah, Libya	C3	43
Al 'Uqayr, Sau. Ar.	I5	39
Alutom, Mount, hill, Guam	L9	52
Alva, Fl., U.S.	F5	86
Alva, Ky., U.S.	D6	94
Alva, Ok., U.S.	A3	113
Alva, Wy., U.S.	B8	127
Alvarado, Mex.	D5	63
Alvarado, Tx., U.S.	C4	120
Alvaton, Ky., U.S.	C2	87
Älvdalen, Swe.	G6	14
Alvear, Arg.	E4	55
Alvena, Sask.	E2	75
Alverca, Port.	f9	22
Alverton, Pa., U.S.	F2	115
Alvesta, Swe.	B8	15
Alvin, Il., U.S.	C6	90
Alvin, S.C., U.S.	E8	117
Alvin, Tx., U.S.	E5	120
Alvinston, Ont.	E3	73
Alvo, Ne., U.S.	h12	104
Alvord, Ia., U.S.	A1	92
Alvord, Tx., U.S.	C4	120
Alvord Lake, l., Or., U.S.	E8	114
Alvordton, Oh., U.S.	A1	112
Älvsborg, co., Swe.	A6	15
Älvsered, Swe.	A6	15
Älvsjö (part of Stockholm), Swe.	t36	14
Al Wajh, Sau. Ar.	C3	38
Alwar, India	C6	36
Al Wāsitah, Eg.	E3	41
Alxa Zuoqi, China	D6	31
Alyat, Sov. Un.	F3	28
Alyth, Scot., U.K.	D5	13
Alytus, Sov. Un.	A8	26
Alz, stm., Ger.	D6	18
Alzada, Mt., U.S.	E12	103
Alzey, Ger.	D3	19
Ama, La., U.S.	k11	95
Amatsu-kominato, Japan	n19	33
Amazon, Sask.	F3	75
Amazon (Solimões) (Amazonas), stm., S.A.	D5	53
Amazonas, state, Braz.	C2	59
Amazonas, dept., Col.	D3	60
Amazonas, dept., Peru	C2	58
Amazonas, ter., Ven.	C4	60
Amazonia, Mo., U.S.	B3	102
Ambājōgāi, India	H6	37
Ambāla, India	B6	36
Ambalavao, Madag.	h9	49
Ambam, Cam.	E2	46
Ambanja, Madag.	f9	49
Ambarchik, Sov. Un.	C19	29
Ambato, Ec.	B2	58
Ambato Boeny, Madag.	g9	49
Ambatolampy, Madag.	g9	49
Ambatondrazaka, Madag.	g9	49
Ambatosoratra, Madag.	g9	49
Amber, Ok., U.S.	B4	113
Amberg, Ger.	D5	18
Amberg, Wi., U.S.	C6	126
Ambérieu [-en-Bugey], Fr.	E6	16
Amberson, Pa., U.S.	F6	115
Ambert, Fr.	E5	16
Ambia, In., U.S.	D2	91
Ambikāpur, India	D7	36
Ambil Island, i., Phil.	p13	34
Ambilobe, Madag.	f9	49
Amble-by-the-Sea, Eng., U.K.	A6	12
Ambler, Ak., U.S.	B8	79
Ambler, Pa., U.S.	F11	115
Amboca, Peru	D2	58
Ambo Channel, strt., Marsh Is.	S17	52
Ambodifototra, Madag.	g9	49
Amboina see Ambon, Indon.	F7	34
Amboise, Fr.	D6	16
Ambon, Indon.	F7	34
Ambon, i., Indon.	F7	34
Ambositra, Madag.	h9	49
Ambovombe, Madag.	h9	49
Amboy, Ca., U.S.	E6	82
Amboy, Il., U.S.	B4	90
Amboy, In., U.S.	C6	91
Amboy, Mn., U.S.	G4	100
Amboy, Wa., U.S.	D3	124
Ambriz, Ang.	C1	48
Ambrose, Ga., U.S.	E3	87
Ambrose, N.D., U.S.	A2	111
Ambrosia Lake, N.M., U.S.	B1	108
Ambuar, Indon.	F8	34
Amchitka Island, i., Ak., U.S.	E4	79
Amchitka Pass, strt., Ak., U.S.	E4	79
Am Dam, Chad	C4	46
Amden, Switz.	B7	21
Amderma, Sov. Un.	C9	29
Ameagle, W.V., U.S.	D3	125
Ameca, Mex.	C4	63
Ameca, stm., Mex.	m11	63
Amecameca [de Juárez], Mex.	n14	63
Ameland, i., Neth.	A6	16
Amelia, La., U.S.	E4	95
Amelia, Ne., U.S.	B7	104
Amelia, co., Va., U.S.	C4	123
Amelia City, Fl., U.S.	k9	86
Amelia Court House, Va., U.S.	C5	123
Amelia Island, i., Fl., U.S.	k9	86
Amelinghausen, Ger.	E4	15
Amendolara, Italy	E6	23
Amenia, N.Y., U.S.	D7	109
Amenia, N.D., U.S.	B8	111
American, stm., Ca., U.S.	C3	82
American, South Fork, stm., Ca., U.S.	C3	82
Americana, Braz.	m8	56
American Canyon, Ca., U.S.	*C2	82
American Falls, Id., U.S.	G6	89
American Falls Dam, Id., U.S.	G6	89
American Falls Reservoir, res., Id., U.S.	F5	89
American Fork, Ut., U.S.	C4	121
American Highland, plat., Ant.	B20	7
American Samoa, dep., Oc.	G11	6
Americus, Ga., U.S.	D2	87
Americus, Ks., U.S.	D7	93
Americus, Mo., U.S.	C5	102
Amersfoort, Neth.	A6	16
Amery, Man.	A4	70
Amery, Wi., U.S.	C1	126
Amery Ice Shelf, ice, Ant.	C20	7
Ames, Ia., U.S.	B4	92
Ames, Ks., U.S.	C6	93
Ames, Ne., U.S.	C9	104
Ames, Ok., U.S.	A3	113
Amesbury, Ma., U.S.	A6	98
Amesville, Ct., U.S.	B2	84
Amga, Sov. Un.	C16	29
Amgu, Sov. Un.	D8	33
Amguid, Alg.	D6	44
Amgun, stm., Sov. Un.	D16	29
Amherst, N.S.	D5	71
Amherst, Co., U.S.	A8	83
Amherst, Ma., U.S.	B2	98
Amherst, Ne., U.S.	D6	104
Amherst, N.H., U.S.	E3	106
Amherst, N.Y., U.S.	C2	109
Amherst, Oh., U.S.	A3	112
Amherst, S.D., U.S.	B8	118
Amherst, Tx., U.S.	B1	120
Amherst, Va., U.S.	C3	123
Amherst, Wi., U.S.	D4	126
Amherst, co., Va., U.S.	C3	123
Amherstburg, Ont.	E1	73
Amherstdale, W.V., U.S.	n12	125
Amiata, mtn., Italy	C3	23
Amidon, N.D., U.S.	C2	111
Amiens, Fr.	C5	16
Aminuis, Nmb.	B2	49
'Āmir, Ra's, c., Libya	G24	2
Amirante Islands, is., Sey.	G24	2
Amir Kabir Dam, Iran	C5	39
Amisk, Alta.	C5	68
Amisk Lake, l., Sask.	C4	75
Amistad National Recreation Area, Tx., U.S.	E2	120
Amistad Reservoir, res., N.A.	E2	120
Amite, co., Ms., U.S.	D3	101
Amite, stm., La., U.S.	D5	95
Amity, Ar., U.S.	C2	81
Amity, Mo., U.S.	B3	102
Amity, Or., U.S.	B3	114
Amity, Pa., U.S.	F1	115
Amityville, N.Y., U.S.	E7	109
Amlekhganj, Nepal	G11	37
Amlia Island, i., Ak., U.S.	E5	79
Amlwch, Wales, U.K.	A3	12
'Ammān, Jord.	B3	38
Ammanford, Wales, U.K.	C3	12
Ammeloe, Ger.	A1	19
Ammendorf, Ger.	B6	19
Ammer Lake, l., Ger.	D5	18
Ammon, Id., U.S.	F7	89
Ammonoosuc, stm., N.H., U.S.	B3	106
Amnicon Falls, Wi., U.S.	B2	126
Amo, In., U.S.	E4	91
Amonate, Va., U.S.	e10	123
Amoret, Mo., U.S.	C3	102
Amorgós, i., Grc.	D5	40
Amorinópolis, Braz.	B2	56
Amorita, Ok., U.S.	A3	113
Amory, Ms., U.S.	B5	101
Amos, Que.	k11	74
Amoy see Xiamen, China	G8	31
Ampanihy, Madag.	h8	49
Amparo, Braz.	C3	56
Ampelókipoi, Grc.	*B4	25
Amper, stm., Ger.	E6	19
Ampezzo, Italy	C8	20
Amposta, Spain	B6	22
Amrāvati (Amraoti), India	D6	36
Amreli, India	G3	37
Amriswil, Switz.	A7	21
Amritsar, India	B5	36
Amroha, India	C7	37
Amrum, i., Ger.	A4	18
Amsteg, Switz.	C6	21
Amstelveen, Neth.	*B4	17
Amsterdam, Neth.	A6	16
Amsterdam, Ga., U.S.	F2	87
Amsterdam, Mo., U.S.	C3	102
Amsterdam, Mt., U.S.	E5	103
Amsterdam, N.Y., U.S.	C6	109
Amsterdam, Oh., U.S.	B5	112
Amsterdam, Île, i., F.S.A.T.	I2	2
Amstetten, Aus.	B2	124
Am Timan, Chad	C4	46
Amu Darya, stm., Asia	F9	29
Amukta Pass, strt., Ak., U.S.	E5	79
Amulet, Sask.	H3	75
Amund Ringnes Island, i., N.W. Ter.	m32	66
Amundsen Bay, b., Ant.	C17	7
Amundsen Gulf, b., N.W. Ter.	B8	66
Amundsen-Scott, sci., Ant.	A17	7
Amundsen Sea, Ant.	B36	7
Amuntai, Indon.	F5	34
Amur (Heilong Jiang), stm., Asia	E16	29
Amvrakía, Gulf of, b., Grc.	C3	25
Amy, Ar., U.S.	D3	81
Amzi, Oued ti-n-, val., Afr.	E5	44
Anabar, stm., Sov. Un.	B14	29
'Anabtā, Isr. Occ.	f11	41
Anaco, Ven.	B5	60
Anacoco, La., U.S.	C2	95
Anacoco, Bayou, stm., La., U.S.	D2	95
Anaconda, Mt., U.S.	D4	103
Anaconda, N.M., U.S.	B2	108
Anaconda Range, mts., Mt., U.S.	E3	103
Anacortes, Wa., U.S.	A3	124
Anacostia, stm., U.S.	C4	97
Anacostia, Northwest Branch, stm., Md., U.S.	B3	97
Anacuao, Mount, mtn., Phil.	n13	34
Anadarko, Ok., U.S.	B3	113
Anadia, Braz.	C3	57
Anadyr, Sov. Un.	C20	29
Anadyr, stm., Sov. Un.	C20	29
Anadyr, Gulf of, Sov. Un.	C21	29
Anadyr Mountains, mts., Sov. Un.	C20	29
Anae, i., Guam	M9	52
Anáfi (Anaphe), i., Grc.	D5	40
Anagance, N.B.	D4	71
'Ānah, Iraq	E13	40
Anaheim, Ca., U.S.	F5	82
Anahim Lake, B.C.	C5	69
Anahola, Hi., U.S.	A2	88
Anahuac, Tx., U.S.	E5	120
Anahulu, stm., Hi., U.S.	f9	88
Anajás, Braz.	D9	55
Anak, N. Kor.	G2	33
Anakāpalle, India	E7	36
Anakie, Austl.	A6	51
Anaklia, Sov. Un.	A13	40
Analalava, Madag.	f9	49
Anamã, Braz.	C2	59
Anama Bay, Man.	D2	70
Ana María, Golfo de, b., Cuba	C7	64
Anambas Islands, is., Indon.	E3	34
Anamoose, N.D., U.S.	B5	111
Anamosa, Ia., U.S.	B6	92
Anamur, Tur.	*D9	40
Anamur, Cape, c., Tur.	D9	40
Anandale, La., U.S.	*C3	95
Ananea (Poto), Peru	D4	58
Anantapur, India	F6	36
Anantnāg, India	B6	36
Ananyev, Sov. Un.	H8	27
Anao Point, c., Guam	L10	52
Anapa, Sov. Un.	I11	27
Anaphe see Anáfi, i., Grc.	D5	40
Anápolis, Braz.	C4	56
Anapu, stm., Braz.	F7	39
Anār, Iran	C7	39
Anārak, Iran	B6	39
Anār Darreh, Afg.	E10	39
Anastasia Island, i., Fl., U.S.	C5	86
'Anātā, Isr. Occ.	h12	41
Anatone, Wa., U.S.	C8	124
Añatuya, Arg.	E3	55
Anauá, stm., Braz.	B9	31
Anawalt, W.V., U.S.	D3	125
Ancash, dept., Peru	C2	58
Ancasti, Sierra, mts., Arg.	D4	80
Ancha, Sierra, mts., Az., U.S.	D4	80
Anchieta, Braz.	C4	56
Anching see Anqing, China	E8	31
Anchorage, Ky., U.S.	g11	94
Anchorage, Ak., U.S.	C10	79
Anchor Point, Ak., U.S.	D9	79
Anchor Point, c., Ak., U.S.	h15	79
Ancienne-Lorette, Que.	C6	74
Anclote Keys, is., Fl., U.S.	D4	86
Anco, Ky., U.S.	C6	94
Ancón, Peru	D2	58
Ancona, Italy	D5	23
Ancona, Il., U.S.	B5	90
Ancón de Sardinas, Bahía de, b., S.A.	C2	60
Ancud, Chile	D2	54
Ancud, Golfo de, b., Chile	D2	54
Anda, China	B10	31
Andacollo, Arg.	B2	54
Andahuaylas, Peru	D3	58
Andale, Ks., U.S.	E6	93
Andalgalá, Arg.	E2	55
Åndalsnes, Nor.	F2	14
Andalusia, Al., U.S.	D3	78
Andalusia, Il., U.S.	B3	90
Andalusia, hist. reg., Spain	D3	22
Andaman and Nicobar Islands, ter., India	*F9	36
Andaman Islands, is., India	*F9	36
Andaman Sea, Asia	F10	36
Andamarca, Bol.	C2	55
Andamarca, Peru	D3	58
Andapa, Madag.	f9	49
Andavaka, Cap, c., Madag.	i9	49
Andebu, Nor.	p28	14
Andeer, Switz.	C7	21
Andenne, Bel.	D5	17
Anderlecht, Bel.	B6	16
Andermatt, Switz.	C4	20
Andernach, Ger.	C3	18
Andersen Air Force Base, mil., Guam	L10	52
Anderslöv, Swe.	C7	15
Anderson, Ar., U.S.	A2	81
Anderson, Al., U.S.	A2	78
Anderson, Ak., U.S.	C10	79
Anderson, Ca., U.S.	B2	82
Anderson, In., U.S.	D6	91
Anderson, Mo., U.S.	E3	102
Anderson, S.C., U.S.	B2	117
Anderson, Tn., U.S.	D8	119
Anderson, Tx., U.S.	D4	120
Anderson, co., Ks., U.S.	D8	93
Anderson, co., Ky., U.S.	B4	94
Anderson, co., S.C., U.S.	B2	117
Anderson, co., Tn., U.S.	C9	119
Anderson, co., Tx., U.S.	D5	120
Anderson, stm., N.W. Ter.	C7	66
Anderson, stm., In., U.S.	H4	91
Anderson Ranch Reservoir, res., Id., U.S.	F3	89
Andersonville, Ga., U.S.	D2	87
Andersonville, In., U.S.	F7	91
Andes, Col.	B2	60
Andes, N.Y., U.S.	C6	109
Andes, mts., S.A.	E4	53
Andes, Lake, l., S.D., U.S.	D7	118
Andfjorden, strt., Nor.	C7	14
Andhra Pradesh, state, India	E6	36
Andikíthira, i., Grc.	E4	40
Andilamena, Madag.	g9	49
Andīmeshk, Iran	C5	39
Andizhan, Sov. Un.	E10	29
Andkhvoy, Afg.	A4	36
Andoas, Peru	B2	58
Andong, S. Kor.	D10	31
Andorra, And.	A6	22
Andorra, ctry., Eur.	A6	22
Andover, Eng., U.K.	C6	12
Andover, Ct., U.S.	C6	84
Andover, Il., U.S.	B3	90
Andover, Ks., U.S.	g12	93
Andover, Me., U.S.	D2	96
Andover, Ma., U.S.	A5	98
Andover, Mn., U.S.	m12	100
Andover, N.H., U.S.	D3	106
Andover, N.Y., U.S.	C3	109
Andover, Oh., U.S.	A5	112
Andover, S.D., U.S.	B8	118
Andover Lake, res., Ct., U.S.	C6	84
Andøya, i., Nor.	C6	14
Andradina, Braz.	D6	56
Andraitx, Spain	C7	22
Andreanof Islands, is., Ak., U.S.	E4	79
Andréville, Que.	B8	74
Andrew, Alta.	C6	68
Andrew, Ia., U.S.	B7	92
Andrew, co., Mo., U.S.	B3	102
Andrew Island, i., N.S.	D9	71
Andrews, In., U.S.	C6	91
Andrews, N.C., U.S.	f9	110
Andrews, S.C., U.S.	E8	117
Andrews, Tx., U.S.	C1	120
Andrews, co., Tx., U.S.	C1	120
Andrews Air Force Base, mil., Md., U.S.	C4	97
Andreyevka, Sov. Un.	G11	27
Andria, Italy	D6	23
Androka, Madag.	h8	49
Ándros, Grc.	D5	40
Ándros, i., Grc.	D5	40
Androscoggin, stm., Me., U.S.	D2	96
Androscoggin, co., Me., U.S.	D2	96
Androscoggin Lake, l., Me., U.S.	D2	96
Andros Island, i., Bah.	B5	64
Andrychów, Pol.	h10	21
Andújar, Spain	C3	22
Andulo, Ang.	D2	48
Anécho, Togo	E5	45
Anefis i-n-Darane, Mali	C5	45
Anegada, Bahía de, b., Arg.	C4	54
Anegada, i., V.I., Br.	G15	64
Anegada Passage, strt., N.A.	E3	80
Anegam, Az., U.S.	E3	80
Anelo, Arg.	B3	54
Anerley, Sask.	F2	75
Aneroid, Sask.	H2	75
Aneth, Ut., U.S.	F6	121
Aneto, Pico de, mtn., Spain	A6	22
Angamos, Punta, c., Chile	D1	55
Ang'angxi, China	B9	31
Angara, stm., Sov. Un.	D12	29
Angaur, i., Palau	R17	52
Angela, Mt., U.S.	D10	103
Ángel de la Guarda, Isla, i., Mex.	B2	63
Angeles, Phil.	o13	34
Angel Falls, wtfl., Ven.	B5	60
Ängelholm, Swe.	B8	15
Angelica, N.Y., U.S.	C2	109
Angelina, co., Tx., U.S.	D5	120
Angels Camp, Ca., U.S.	C3	82
Angelus, Ks., U.S.	C3	93
Angermünde, Ger.	B7	19
Ångermanälven, stm., Swe.	F7	14
Angers, Fr.	D3	16
Angicos, Braz.	C3	57
Angie, La., U.S.	D6	95
Angier, N.C., U.S.	B4	110
Angikuni Lake, l., N.W. Ter.	D13	66
Angkor, hist., Camb.	C2	34
Angle Inlet, Mn., U.S.	A3	100
Angle Lake, Wa., U.S.	*B3	124
Anglem, Mount, mtn., N.Z.	Q11	51
Anglesey, i., Wales, U.K.	D4	10
Anglet, Fr.	F3	16
Angleton, Tx., U.S.	E5	120
Angliers, Que.	G17	66
Angling Lake, l., Man.	C5	70
Ango, Zaire	A4	48
Angoche, Moz.	A6	49
Angoche, Ilha, i., Moz.	B2	54
Angol, Chile	A8	91
Angola, In., U.S.	C1	109
Angola, N.Y., U.S.	D2	48
Angola, ctry., Afr.	D2	48
Angola Swamp, sw., N.C., U.S.	C5	110
Angora, Ne., U.S.	C2	104
Angora see Ankara, Tur.	C9	40
Angostura Reservoir, res., S.D., U.S.	D2	118
Angoulême, Fr.	E4	16
Angra do Heroísmo, Port.	g9	44
Angra dos Reis, Braz.	C4	56
Angren, Sov. Un.	E7	28
Anguang, China	B10	32
Anguilla, Ms., U.S.	C3	101
Anguilla, ctry., N.A.	G13	64
Anguille, Cape, c., Newf.	E2	72
Angumu, Zaire	B4	48
Angus, Ont.	C5	73
Angusville, Man.	D1	70
Anholt, Den.	B5	15
Anholt, i., Den.	B5	15
Anhua, China	J4	32
Anhui, prov., China	E8	31
Anhwei see Anhui, prov., China	E8	31
Aniak, Ak., U.S.	C8	79
Aniche, Fr.	D3	17
Aniene (Teverone), stm., Italy	h9	23
Animas, N.M., U.S.	F1	108
Animas, stm., U.S.	D3	83
Animas Mountains, mts., N.M., U.S.	F1	108
Animas Peak, mtn., N.M., U.S.	F1	108
Animas Valley, val., N.M., U.S.	F1	108
Anina, Rom.	C5	24
Anita, Ia., U.S.	C3	92
Anita, Pa., U.S.	D4	115
Aniva, Cape, c., Sov. Un.	B13	31
Aniva Bay, b., Sov. Un.	C11	33
Aniwa, Wi., U.S.	C4	126
Anjār, India	D5	36
Anjō, Japan	o15	33
Anjou, Que.	p19	74
Anjou, hist. reg., Fr.	D3	16
Anju, N. Kor.	G2	33
Anjum, Neth.	A6	17
Ankang, China	E7	31
Ankara, Tur.	C9	40
Ankavandra, Madag.	g9	49
Ankazoabo, Madag.	h8	49
Ankazobe, Madag.	g9	49
Ankeny, Ia., U.S.	C4	92
An Khe, Viet.	C4	34
Anklam, Ger.	B6	18
Ankober, Eth.	D4	47
Ankoro, Zaire	C4	48
Anlong, China	F6	31
Anlu, China	I5	32
Ann, Cape, c., Ant.	C18	7
Ann, Cape, c., Ma., U.S.	A6	98
Anna, Sov. Un.	F13	27
Anna, Il., U.S.	F4	90
Anna, Oh., U.S.	B1	112
Anna, Tx., U.S.	C4	120
Anna, Lake, res., Va., U.S.	B5	123
Annaba (Bône), Alg.	B6	44
Annaberg-Buchholz, Ger.	C6	18
An Nabk, Syria	E11	40
Annaburg, Ger.	B8	19
Annalee Heights, Va., U.S.	*B5	123
An Nafūd, des., Sau. Ar.	C4	38
An Najaf, Iraq	H9	40
An Nakhl, Eg.	B5	41
Annam, hist. reg., Viet.	B4	34
An Nāsirīyah, Iraq	H9	40
Annamitique, Chaîne, mts., Asia	B3	34
Annan, Scot., U.K.	C5	10
Annan, stm., Scot., U.K.	C5	13
Annandale, Mn., U.S.	E4	100
Annandale, N.J., U.S.	B3	107
Annandale, Va., U.S.	g12	123
Annapolis, Il., U.S.	D6	90
Annapolis, Md., U.S.	C5	97
Annapolis, co., N.S.	E4	71
Annapolis, stm., N.S.	E4	71
Annapolis Junction, Md., U.S.	B4	97
Annapolis Royal, N.S.	E4	71
Annapūrna, mtn., Nepal	G10	37
Ann Arbor, Mi., U.S.	F7	99
Anna Regina, Guy.	A3	59
Annawan, Il., U.S.	B4	90
Anne Arundel, co., Md., U.S.	B4	97
Annecy, Fr.	E7	16
Annecy, Lake, l., Fr.	D2	20
Annecy-le-Vieux, Fr.	D10	103
Annemasse, Fr.	E7	16
Annette, Ak., U.S.	D13	79
Anniston, Mo., U.S.	E8	102
Anniston, Al., U.S.	B4	78
Annonay, Fr.	E6	16
Annone, Lago di, l., Italy	E7	21
Annot, Fr.	E7	16
Annotto Bay, Jam.	E15	65
An Nuhūd, Sud.	C4	47
An Nu'mānīyah, Iraq	E2	39
Annursnack Hill, hill, Ma., U.S.	g10	98
Annville, Ky., U.S.	C6	94
Annville, Pa., U.S.	F8	115
Anoka, Mn., U.S.	E5	100
Anoka, Ne., U.S.	B7	104
Anoka, co., Mn., U.S.	E5	100
Anori, Braz.	C2	59
Áno Viánnos, Grc.	E5	25
Anóyia, Grc.	E6	25
Anping, China	A5	70
Anqing, China	E8	31
Ansbach, Ger.	D5	18
Anse d'Hainault, Haiti	E6	64
Anselmo, Ne., U.S.	C6	104
Anserma, Col.	B2	60
Anshan, China	C9	31
Anshun, China	F6	31
Ansley, Al., U.S.	D3	78
Ansley, Ms., U.S.	E4	101
Ansley, Ne., U.S.	C6	104
Anson, Me., U.S.	D3	96
Anson, Tx., U.S.	C3	120
Anson, co., N.C., U.S.	B2	110
Anson Bay, b., Austl.	B5	50
Ansonia, Oh., U.S.	B1	112
Ansonville, N.C., U.S.	B2	110
Anstruther, Scot., U.K.	D6	13
Ansudu, Indon.	F9	34
Anta, Peru	D3	58
Antabamba, Peru	D3	58
Antakya (Antioch), Tur.	D11	40
Antalaha, Madag.	f10	49
Antalāt, Libya	C4	43
Antalāt, well, Libya	G3	40
Antalya, Tur.	D8	40
Antalya, Gulf of, b., Tur.	D8	40
Antananarivo, Madag.	g9	49
Antananarivo, prov., Madag.	g9	49
Antarctica, cont.	A19	7
Antarctic Peninsula, pen., Ant.	C6	7
Antelope, Sask.	G1	75
Antelope, Ks., U.S.	D7	93
Antelope, Mt., U.S.	B12	103
Antelope, Or., U.S.	C5	114
Antelope, S.D., U.S.	*D5	118
Antelope, co., Ne., U.S.	B7	104
Antelope Butte, mtn., Wy., U.S.	B7	127
Antelope Creek, stm., Wy., U.S.	C7	127
Antelope Island, i., Ut., U.S.	B3	121
Antelope Lake, l., Sask.	G1	75
Antelope Mine, Zimb.	B4	49
Antelope Peak, mtn., Nv., U.S.	C7	105
Antelope Range, mts., Nv., U.S.	D7	105
Antelope Reservoir, res., Or., U.S.	E9	114
Antelope Wash, val., Nv., U.S.	D5	105
Antequera, Spain	D3	22
Antero, Mount, mtn., Co., U.S.	C4	83
Antero Reservoir, res., Co., U.S.	C5	83
Anthon, Ia., U.S.	B2	92
Anthony, Fl., U.S.	C4	86
Anthony, Ks., U.S.	E5	93
Anthony, N.M., U.S.	F3	108
Anthony, R.I., U.S.	D3	116
Anthony Creek, stm., W.V., U.S.	D4	125
Anti-Atlas, mts., Afr.	C3	44
Antibes, Fr.	F7	16
Anticosti, Île d', i., Que.	k14	74
Antietam Creek, stm., Md., U.S.	B2	97
Antietam National Battlefield Site, hist., Md., U.S.	B2	97
Antigo, Wi., U.S.	C4	126
Antigonish, N.S.	D8	71
Antigonish, co., N.S.	D7	71
Antigua, i., Antig.	H14	64
Antigua and Barbuda, ctry., N.A.	H14	64
Antigua Guatemala, Guat.	E6	63
Antilla, Cuba	D6	64
Antimony, Ut., U.S.	E3	121
Antioch, Ca., U.S.	h9	82
Antioch, Il., U.S.	A5	90
Antioch, In., U.S.	D5	91
Antioch, Ne., U.S.	B3	104
Antioch see Antakya, Tur.	D11	40
Antioquia, Col.	B2	60
Antioquia, dept., Col.	B2	60
Antipodes Islands, is., N.Z.	J8	2
Antler, N.D., U.S.	A4	111
Antler, stm., N.A.	E1	70
Antlers, Ok., U.S.	C6	113
Antofagasta, Chile	D1	55
Antofagasta, prov., Chile	E2	55
Antofagasta de la Sierra, Arg.	E2	55
Antofalla, Volcán, vol., Arg.	E2	55
Antón, Pan.	J8	82
Anton, Tx., U.S.	C1	120
Anton Chico, N.M., U.S.	B4	108
Antongila, Helodrano, b., Madag.	g9	49
Antonia, Mo., U.S.	C7	102
Antonina, Braz.	D3	57
Antônio Carlos, Braz.	g6	56
Antônio de Biedma, Arg.	B4	56
Antônio Dias, Braz.	B4	56
Antony, Fr.	g10	16
Antratsit, Sov. Un.	q22	27
Antrim, Mi., U.S.	D5	99
Antrim, N.H., U.S.	D3	106
Antrim, Pa., U.S.	C7	115
Antrim, co., Mi., U.S.	D5	99
Antsalova, Madag.	g8	49
Antsiranana, Madag.	f9	49
Antsohihy, Madag.	f9	49
Antwerp, N.Y., U.S.	A5	109
Antwerp, Oh., U.S.	A1	112
Antwerp, prov., Bel.	C4	17
Antwerpen see Antwerp, Bel.	C4	17
Anua, Am. Sam.	F13	52
An Uaimh (Navan), Ire.	D3	10
Anuradhapura, Sri L.	G7	36
Anvers Island, i., Ant.	C6	7

Name	Map Ref.	Page
Anvik, Ak., U.S.	C7	79
Anxi, China	F8	31
Anxi, China	C4	31
Anyang, China	D7	31
Anyang, S. Kor.	*H3	33
A'nyêmaqên Shan, mts., China	D4	31
Anyi, China	G4	32
Anykščiai, Sov. Un.	A8	26
Anza, Col.	B2	60
Anza, stm., Italy	E5	21
Anzac, Alta.	A5	68
Anzhero-Sudzhensk, Sov. Un.	D11	29
Anzin, Fr.	D3	17
Anzio, Italy	D4	23
Anzoátegui, state, Ven.	B5	60
Aoji-ri, N. Kor.	E5	33
Aomoen Island, i., Marsh Is.	P18	52
Aomon, i., Marsh Is.	S18	52
Aomori, Japan	C13	31
Aoral, Mount, mtn., Camb.	C2	34
Aosta, Italy	B1	23
Aou Hofrit, well, W. Sah.	E2	44
Aouk, Bahr, stm., Afr.	D3	46
Aoukâr, reg., Maur.	C2	45
Aoyama, Japan	o15	33
Aozou, Chad	A3	46
Apa, stm., S.A.	D4	55
Apache, Ok., U.S.	C3	113
Apache, co., Az., U.S.	B6	80
Apache Creek, N.M., U.S.	D1	108
Apache Junction, Az., U.S.	m9	80
Apache Peak, mtn., Az., U.S.	F5	80
Apalachee, Ga., U.S.	C3	87
Apalachee Bay, b., Fl., U.S.	B2	86
Apalachicola, Fl., U.S.	C1	86
Apalachicola, stm., Fl., U.S.	B1	86
Apalachicola Bay, b., Fl., U.S.	C2	86
Apalachin, N.Y., U.S.	C4	109
Apan, Mex.	n14	63
Apaporis, stm., S.A.	D3	60
Aparri, Phil.	B6	34
Apatin, Yugo.	C4	24
Apatity, Sov. Un.	D15	14
Apatzingán [de la Constitución], Mex.	n12	63
Apeldoorn, Neth.	A6	16
Apennines, mts., Italy	C4	23
Apennine Tunnel, Italy	B3	23
Apérathos, Grc.	D5	25
Apex, N.C., U.S.	B4	110
Apex Mountain, mtn., Yukon	D5	66
Api, mtn., Nepal	C8	37
Apia, W. Sam.	F12	52
Apiacás, Serra dos, plat., Braz.	E3	59
Apia Harbour, b., W. Sam.	F12	52
Apiaí, Braz.	C3	56
Apishapa, stm., Co., U.S.	D6	83
Apison, Tn., U.S.	h11	119
Apizaco, Mex.	n14	63
Aplao, Peru	E3	58
Aplin, Ar., U.S.	C3	81
Aplington, Ia., U.S.	B5	92
Apo, Mount, mtn., Phil.	D7	34
Apodi, Braz.	C3	57
Apohaqui, N.B.	D4	71
Apolda, Ger.	C5	18
Apolima Island, i., W. Sam.	F11	52
Apolima Strait, strt., W. Sam.	F11	52
Apollo, Pa., U.S.	E2	115
Apolo, Bol.	B2	55
Apopka, Fl., U.S.	D5	86
Apopka, Lake, l., Fl., U.S.	D5	86
Aporé, Braz.	B2	56
Aporé, stm., Braz.	B2	56
Apostle Islands, is., Wi., U.S.	A3	126
Apostle Islands National Lakeshore, Wi., U.S.	A3	126
Apóstoles, Arg.	E4	55
Appalachia, Va., U.S.	f9	123
Appalachian Mountains, mts., N.A.	C11	76
Appam, N.D., U.S.	A2	111
Appanoose, co., Ia., U.S.	D5	92
Appenzell, Switz.	E4	18
Appenzell-Ausser Rhoden, state, Switz.	B5	20
Appenzell-Inner Rhoden, state, Switz.	B5	20
Apperson, Ia., U.S.	A5	113
Appingedam, Neth.	A6	17
Apple, stm., Wi., U.S.	C1	126
Appleby, Eng., U.K.	F6	13
Appleby, Tx., U.S.	D5	120
Apple Creek, Oh., U.S.	B4	112
Applecross, Scot., U.K.	C3	13
Applegate, Mi., U.S.	E8	99
Applegate, Or., U.S.	E3	114
Applegate, stm., Or., U.S.	E3	114
Apple Grove, W.V., U.S.	C2	125
Apple Hill, Ont.	B10	73
Apple Orchard Mountain, mtn., Va., U.S.	C3	123
Apple River, N.S.	D5	71
Apple River, Il., U.S.	A3	90
Apple Springs, Tx., U.S.	D5	120
Appleton, Ar., U.S.	B3	81
Appleton, Me., U.S.	D3	96
Appleton, Mn., U.S.	E2	100
Appleton, Tn., U.S.	B4	124
Appleton, Wi., U.S.	D5	126
Appleton City, Mo., U.S.	C3	102
Apple Valley, Ca., U.S.	E5	82
Apple Valley, Mn., U.S.	n12	100
Apple Valley, N.D., U.S.	*C5	111
Applewood, Co., U.S.	B5	83
Appleyard, Wa., U.S.	B5	124
Appling, Ga., U.S.	C4	87
Appling, co., Ga., U.S.	E4	87
Appomattox, Va., U.S.	C4	123
Appomattox, stm., Va., U.S.	C4	123
Appomattox Court House National Historical Park, Va., U.S.	C4	123
Apra Harbor, b., Guam	L9	52
Aprelsk, Sov. Un.	D14	29
Aprilia, Italy	D4	23
Apsheron Peninsula, pen., Sov. Un.	G19	8
Apsley, Ont.	C6	73
Apt, Fr.	F6	16
Aptos, Ca., U.S.	*D3	82
Apua Point, c., Hi., U.S.	D6	88
Apucarana, Braz.	C2	56
Apulia (Puglia), prov., Italy	D6	23
Apure, state, Ven.	B4	60
Apure, stm., Ven.	B4	60
Apurímac, dept., Peru	D3	58
Apurímac, stm., Peru	D4	58
Aqaba, Gulf of, b.	C3	38
'Aqiq, Sud.	B4	47
'Aqrabá, Syria	A8	41
'Aqrabah, Isr. Occ.	B7	41
Aquarius Mountains, mts., Az., U.S.	C2	80
Aquarius Plateau, plat., Ut., U.S.	E4	121
Aquasco, Md., U.S.	C4	97
Aquebogue, N.Y., U.S.	n16	109
Aquidauana, Braz.	C1	56
Aquila see L'Aquila, Italy	C4	23
Aquileia, Italy	D9	20
Aquiles Serdán, Mex.	B3	63
Aquin, Haiti	E7	64
Aquone, N.C., U.S.	f9	110
Ara, India	C7	36
Arab, Al., U.S.	A3	78
'Arab, Bahr al, stm., Sud.	D2	47
Arab, Khalīj al, b., Egypt	G7	40
Arab, Shatt al, stm., Iraq	B4	38
Arabelo, Ven.	C5	60
Arabi, Ga., U.S.	E3	87
Arabi, La., U.S.	k11	95
Arabian Desert, des., Eg.	C3	38
Arabian Sea	H9	30
Araçá, stm., Braz.	B2	59
Aracaju, Braz.	D3	57
Araçatuba, Braz.	C2	56
Aracena, Spain	D2	22
Aracruz, Braz.	B4	56
Araçuaí, Braz.	B4	56
Arad, Rom.	B5	24
Arada, Chad	B4	46
Aragarças, Braz.	B2	56
Arago, U.S.	D2	114
Arago, Cape, c., Or., U.S.	D2	114
Aragon, Ga., U.S.	B1	87
Aragon, N.M., U.S.	D1	108
Aragon, hist. reg., Spain	B5	22
Aragón, stm., Spain	A5	22
Aragua, state, Ven.	A4	60
Araguacema, Braz.	D5	59
Araguaçu, Braz.	E5	59
Aragua de Barcelona, Ven.	B5	60
Araguaia, Braço Menor, stm., Braz.	E5	59
Araguaia National Park, Braz.	E4	59
Araguao, Boca, mth., Ven.	B5	60
Araguari, Braz.	B5	56
Araguari, stm., Braz.	B4	59
Arai, Japan	H9	33
Arai, Japan	o16	33
Ārak, Iran	D5	44
Arāk, Iran	B4	38
Arakan Range, mts., Burma	E6	35
Arakkonam, India	F6	36
Araks, stm., Asia	B3	39
Aral Sea, Sov. Un.	E9	29
Aralsk, Sov. Un.	D6	28
Aramac, Austl.	D8	50
Arambaza, Col.	D3	60
Ārān, Iran	E6	39
Aranda de Duero, Spain	B4	22
Arandas, Mex.	m12	63
Aran Island, i., Ire.	C2	10
Aran Islands, is., Ire.	D2	10
Aranjuez, Spain	B4	22
Aranos, Nmb.	B2	49
Aransas, co., Tx., U.S.	E4	120
Aransas Bay, b., Tx., U.S.	E4	120
Aransas Pass, Tx., U.S.	F4	120
Aranyaprathet, Thai.	C4	34
Araouane, Mali	C4	45
Arapaho, Ok., U.S.	B3	113
Arapahoe, Co., U.S.	C8	83
Arapahoe, Ne., U.S.	D6	104
Arapahoe, N.C., U.S.	B6	110
Arapahoe, Wy., U.S.	D4	127
Arapahoe, co., Co., U.S.	B6	83
Arapey, Ur.	E1	56
Arapey Grande, stm., Ur.	E1	56
Arapkir, Tur.	C12	40
Arapongas, Braz.	C2	56
Araranguá, Braz.	D3	56
Araraquara, Braz.	C3	56
Araras, Braz.	G7	59
Ararat, Austl.	G1	51
Ararat, Mount, mtn., Tur.	D2	123
Ararat, Mount, mtn., Tur.	C15	40
Araripe, Chapada do, plat., Braz.	C3	57
Araruna, Braz.	h6	59
Arauca, Col.	B3	60
Arauca, dept., Col.	B3	60
Arauca, stm., S.A.	B3	60
Arauco, Chile	B2	54
Araújos, Braz.	E7	59
Aravalli Range, mts., India.	D5	36
Araxá, Braz.	E6	59
Araya, Ven.	A5	60
Araya, Punta de, c., Ven.	A5	60
Arba Minch, Eth.	D4	47
Arbela, Sov. Un.	A5	102
Arboga, Swe.	t33	14
Arbois, Fr.	D6	16
Árboles, U.S.	D3	83
Arbon, Switz.	B5	20
Arbon, Id., U.S.	G6	89
Arborea (Mussolinia), Italy	D4	23
Arborfield, Sask.	D4	75
Arborg, Man.	D3	70
Arbor Vitae, Wi., U.S.	C4	126
Arbroath, Scot., U.K.	B5	10
Arbuckle, Ca., U.S.	C2	82
Arbuckle, Lake, l., Fl., U.S.	E5	86
Arbuckle Mountains, mts., Ok., U.S.	C4	113
Arbuckles, Lake of the, res., Ok., U.S.	C5	113
Arbyrd, Mo., U.S.	E7	102
Arc, Bayou des, stm., Ar., U.S.	B4	81
Arcadon, Fr.	c3	82
Arcade, Ca., U.S.	*C3	82
Arcade, Ga., U.S.	B3	87
Arcade, N.Y., U.S.	C2	109
Arcadia, N.S.	F3	71
Arcadia, Ca., U.S.	m12	82
Arcadia, Fl., U.S.	E5	86
Arcadia, In., U.S.	D5	91
Arcadia, Ks., U.S.	E9	93
Arcadia, La., U.S.	B3	95
Arcadia, Mi., U.S.	D4	99
Arcadia, Mo., U.S.	D7	102
Arcadia, Ne., U.S.	C7	104
Arcadia, Ok., U.S.	B4	113
Arcadia, R.I., U.S.	E2	116
Arcadia, S.C., U.S.	B4	117
Arcadia, Wi., U.S.	D2	126
Arcanum, Oh., U.S.	C1	112
Arcata, Ca., U.S.	B1	82
Arc Dome, mtn., Nv., U.S.	E4	105
Arcelia, Mex.	n13	63
Arcey, Fr.	A2	21
Archambault, Lac, l., Que.	C3	74
Archbald, Pa., U.S.	m18	115
Archbold, Oh., U.S.	A1	112
Archdale, N.C., U.S.	B3	110
Archer, Fl., U.S.	C4	86
Archer, Ia., U.S.	A2	92
Archer, Ne., U.S.	C7	104
Archer, co., Tx., U.S.	C3	120
Archer, stm., Austl.	B7	50
Archer City, Tx., U.S.	C3	120
Archer's Post, Kenya	A6	48
Archerwill, Sask.	E4	75
Arches National Park, Ut., U.S.	E6	121
Archidona, Spain	D2	22
Archie, Mo., U.S.	C3	102
Archie, La., U.S.	G3	75
Archive, Sask.	G3	75
Arco, Id., U.S.	F5	89
Arco, Mn., U.S.	F2	100
Arcola, Sask.	H4	75
Arcola, Il., U.S.	D5	90
Arcola, In., U.S.	B7	91
Arcola, Ms., U.S.	B3	101
Arcola, Mo., U.S.	D4	102
Arcola, Va., U.S.	g11	123
Arcos, Mo., U.S.	C1	21
Arcos de la Frontera, Spain	D3	22
Arcoverde, Braz.	C3	57
Arctic Bay, N.W. Ter.	B16	66
Arctic Ocean	A1	128
Arctic Village, Ak., U.S.	B10	79
Arcueil, Fr.	g10	16
Arda, stm., Eur.	E7	24
Ardabīl (Ardebil), Iran	B4	38
Ardagh, Ire.	E2	11
Ardahan, Tur.	B14	40
Ardakān, Iran	B5	38
Ardakān, Iran	E6	39
Ardara, Ire.	C3	11
Ardath, Sask.	F2	75
Ardatov, Sov. Un.	D16	27
Ardbeg, Ont.	B4	73
Ardea, Italy	h9	23
Ardebil see Ardabīl, Iran	B4	38
Arden, Ire.	E2	10
Arden, Man.	D2	70
Arden, Ont.	C8	73
Arden, Den.	B3	15
Arden, Ar., U.S.	D1	81
Arden, Ca., U.S.	*C2	82
Arden, N.C., U.S.	f10	110
Arden Hills, Mn., U.S.	*m12	100
Ardennes, dept., Fr.	E4	17
Ardennes, reg., Eur.	B6	16
Ardenno, Italy	C5	20
Ardenvoir, Wa., U.S.	B5	124
Arden, mtn., Ire.	D4	11
Ardglass, N. Ire., U.K.	C6	11
Ardgroom, Ire.	F2	11
Ardila, stm., Eur.	C2	22
Ardill, Sask.	H3	75
Ardino, Bul.	E7	24
Ardley, Alta.	C4	68
Ardmore, Ire.	F4	11
Ardmore, Al., U.S.	A3	78
Ardmore, In., U.S.	A5	91
Ardmore, Md., U.S.	C4	97
Ardmore, Ok., U.S.	C4	113
Ardmore, Pa., U.S.	F11	115
Ardmore, S.D., U.S.	D2	118
Ardmore, Tn., U.S.	B5	119
Ardnamurchan, Point of, c., Scot., U.K.	D2	13
Ardnaree, Ire.	C2	11
Ardnave Point, c., Scot., U.K.	E2	13
Ardoch, N.D., U.S.	A8	111
Ardpatrick Point, c., Scot., U.K.	E3	13
Ardres, Fr.	D1	17
Ardrossan, Austl.	G1	51
Ardrossan, Alta.	C4	68
Ardrossan, Scot., U.K.	C4	10
Ardsley, N.Y., U.S.	g13	109
Arecibo, P.R.	G11	64
Aredale, Ia., U.S.	B5	92
Areia, Braz.	h6	57
Areia Branca, Braz.	B3	57
Arelee, Sask.	E2	75
Arena, N.D., U.S.	B5	111
Arena, Wi., U.S.	E4	126
Arena, Point, c., Ca., U.S.	C1	82
Arena, Punta, c., Mex.	D7	99
Arenac, co., Mi., U.S.	D7	99
Arenápolis, Braz.	A1	56
Arenas de San Pedro, Spain	B3	22
Arenas Valley, N.M., U.S.	E1	108
Arendonk, Bel.	C5	17
Arendsee, Ger.	F5	15
Arendtsville, Pa., U.S.	G7	115
Arenillas, Ec.	D2	60
Arenzville, Il., U.S.	D3	90
Areópolis, Grc.	D4	25
Arequipa, Peru	E3	58
Arequipa, dept., Peru	E3	58
Arezzo, Italy	C3	23
Arga, stm., Spain	A5	22
Argalasti, Grc.	p18	22
Arganda, Spain	F3	16
Argelès-Gazost, Fr.	A8	21
Argen, stm., Ger.	A8	21
Argenta, Italy	B3	23
Argenta, Il., U.S.	D5	90
Argentan, Fr.	C6	16
Argentat, Fr.	E4	16
Argenthal, Ger.	C3	21
Argentina, co., Que.	D3	74
Argenteuil, Fr.	C5	16
Argenteuil, co., Que.	D3	74
Argentina, ctry., S.A.	G4	53
Argenton-sur-Creuse, Fr.	D4	16
Argentré, Fr.	E3	16
Arghandāb, stm., Afg.	E13	39
Argir, Fr.	E13	39
Argo, Sud.	B3	47
Argo, Il., U.S.	k9	90
Argo, Ky., U.S.	C7	94
Argo Corner, De., U.S.	k7	85
Argolís, Gulf of, b., Grc.	n13	25
Argonia, Ks., U.S.	E6	93
Argonne, Wi., U.S.	C5	126
Argonne, reg., Fr.	C6	16
Argonne, Forêt d', for., Fr.	E4	17
Árgos, Grc.	D4	40
Argos, In., U.S.	B5	91
Argos Orestikón, Grc.	B3	25
Argostólion, Grc.	C3	40
Argun, stm., Asia	D14	29
Argungu, Nig.	D5	45
Argusville, N.D., U.S.	B9	111
Argyle, Fl., U.S.	u15	86
Argyle, Ga., U.S.	E4	87
Argyle, Ia., U.S.	D6	92
Argyle, Mi., U.S.	E8	99
Argyle, Mn., U.S.	B2	100
Argyle, Mo., U.S.	C5	102
Argyle, N.Y., U.S.	B7	109
Argyle, Wi., U.S.	F4	126
Argyle, Lake, res., Austl.	C4	50
Argyll, hist. reg., Scot., U.K.	I4	14
Århus, co., Den.	B4	15
Århus, Den.	B4	15
Ari, In., U.S.	B7	91
Ariake Bay, b., Japan	K5	33
Ariano, Spain	A4	22
Ariano Irpino, Italy	D5	23
Ariano nel Polesine, Italy	E8	20
Ariari, stm., Col.	C3	60
Arica, Chile	C1	55
Arica, Col.	D3	60
Arichat, N.S.	D8	71
Ariège, stm., Fr.	F4	16
Ariel, Wa., U.S.	D3	124
Arikaree, stm., U.S.	B6	24
Arikaree, stm., U.S.	B8	83
Arima, Trin.	K14	64
Arimo, Id., U.S.	G6	89
Arinos, stm., Braz.	B4	55
Arinos, stm., Braz.	D4	63
Ario de Rosales, Mex.	C2	92
Arion, Ia., U.S.	D4	86
Aripeka, Fl., U.S.	K14	64
Aripo, El Cerro del, mtn., Trin.	K14	64
Aripuaná, Braz.	D2	59
Aripuaná, stm., Braz.	D2	59
Arisaig, Scot., U.K.	D3	13
Árīsh, Wādī al, val., Eg.	D6	41
Arispe, Ia., U.S.	D3	92
Aristazabal Island, i., B.C.	C3	69
Ariton, Al., U.S.	D4	78
Arivaca, Az., U.S.	F4	80
Arivonimamo, Madag.	g9	49
Arizaro, Salar de, pl., Arg.	B3	54
Arizona, state, U.S.	C4	80
Arizona Sunsites, Az., U.S.	F6	80
Arjang, Swe.	A2	63
Arjeplog, Swe.	D8	14
Arjona, Col.	A2	60
Arjona, Spain	D3	22
Arkabutla, Ms., U.S.	A3	101
Arkabutla Lake, res., Ms., U.S.	A4	101
Arkadelphia, Al., U.S.	B3	78
Arkadelphia, Ar., U.S.	C2	81
Arkaig, Loch, l., Scot., U.K.	D3	13
Arkalyk, Sov. Un.	D7	28
Arkansas, co., Ar., U.S.	C4	81
Arkansas, state, U.S.	C3	81
Arkansas, Salt Fork, stm., U.S.	A3	113
Arkansas City, Ar., U.S.	D4	81
Arkansas City, Ks., U.S.	E6	93
Arkansaw, Wi., U.S.	D1	126
Arkhangelsk, Sov. Un.	C7	29
Arkhangelskoye, Sov. Un.	F13	27
Arkin, Wa., U.S.	B5	124
Árki, i., Grc.	D6	25
Arkles-la-Bataille, Fr.	D1	81
'Arrābah, Isr. Occ.	B7	41
Ar Rahad, Sud.	B7	113
Arkona, Ont.	D3	73
Arkona, Kap (The Skaw), c., Ger.	D7	15
Arkport, N.Y., U.S.	C3	109
Arkville, N.Y., U.S.	C6	109
Arkwright, R.I., U.S.	D3	87
Arkwright, stm., Austl.	D3	116
Arlanc, Fr.	D5	16
Arlanza, stm., Spain	A4	22
Arlanzón, stm., Spain	A4	22
Arlberg Tunnel, Aus.	A5	18
Arles, Mt., U.S.	C2	103
Arles, Fr.	F6	16
Arley, Al., U.S.	A2	78
Arlington, Az., U.S.	D3	80
Arlington, Co., U.S.	C7	83
Arlington, Ga., U.S.	E2	87
Arlington, Il., U.S.	B4	90
Arlington, In., U.S.	E6	91
Arlington, Ia., U.S.	B6	92
Arlington, Ks., U.S.	E5	93
Arlington, Ky., U.S.	f9	94
Arlington, Mn., U.S.	F4	100
Arlington, Ne., U.S.	C9	104
Arlington, N.Y., U.S.	D7	109
Arlington, N.C., U.S.	A2	112
Arlington, Oh., U.S.	B2	112
Arlington, Or., U.S.	B6	114
Arlington, S.C., U.S.	B3	117
Arlington, S.D., U.S.	C8	118
Arlington, Tn., U.S.	B2	119
Arlington, Tx., U.S.	n9	120
Arlington, Vt., U.S.	E2	122
Arlington, Va., U.S.	B5	123
Arlington, Wa., U.S.	A3	124
Arlington, co., Va., U.S.	g12	123
Arlington, Lake, res., Tx., U.S.	n9	120
Arlington Beach, S.D., U.S.	C8	118
Arlington Heights, Il., U.S.	A5	90
Arma, Ks., U.S.	E9	93
Arm, stm., Sask.	F3	75
Ārma, Grc.	g10	25
Arlon, Bel.	F5	17
Arly, stm., Fr.	D3	21
Armada, Mi., U.S.	F8	99
Armagh, Que.	C7	74
Armagh, N. Ire., U.K.	C5	11
Armathwaite, Tn., U.S.	C9	119
Armavir, Sov. Un.	E2	29
Armenia, Col.	B2	60
Armenia, state, Sov. Un.	n12	63
Armentières, Fr.	B5	16
Armería, stm., Mex.	H9	33
Armijo, N.M., U.S.	k7	108
Armington, Mt., U.S.	C6	103
Armit Lake, l., Can.	C1	70
Armley, Sask.	E4	75
Armona, N.Y., U.S.	*g13	109
Armorel, Ar., U.S.	B6	81
Armour, S.D., U.S.	D7	118
Armour, S.D., U.S.	C8	118
Armstead, Al., U.S.	B3	78
Armstrong, B.C.	D8	69
Armstrong, Fl., U.S.	C5	86
Armstrong, Il., U.S.	C6	90
Armstrong, Ia., U.S.	A3	92
Armstrong, Mo., U.S.	B5	102
Armstrong, Ok., U.S.	C5	113
Armstrong, Tx., U.S.	F4	120
Armstrong, co., Pa., U.S.	E2	115
Armstrong, co., Tx., U.S.	B2	120
Armstrong Creek, Wi., U.S.	C5	126
Armstrong Station, Ont.	F15	66
Armuchee, Ga., U.S.	B1	87
Armyansk, Sov. Un.	H9	27
Arnaud, stm., Que.	E18	66
Arnaudville, La., U.S.	D4	95
Arneburg, Ger.	F5	15
Arnedo, Spain	A4	22
Arnett, Ok., U.S.	A3	113
Arnett, W.V., U.S.	D3	125
Arney, stm., N. Ire., U.K.	C4	11
Arnhem, Neth.	B6	16
Arnhem, Cape, c., Austl.	B6	50
Arnhem Land, reg., Austl.	B5	50
Arnissa, Grc.	B3	25
Arno, stm., Italy	C3	23
Arnold, Ca., U.S.	C3	82
Arnold, Ks., U.S.	D3	93
Arnold, Md., U.S.	*B4	97
Arnold, Mi., U.S.	B3	99
Arnold, Ne., U.S.	C6	104
Arnold, Mo., U.S.	C7	102
Arnold, Pa., U.S.	h14	115
Arnold Mills, R.I., U.S.	B4	116
Arnold Mills Reservoir, res., R.I., U.S.	B4	116
Arnolds Park, Ia., U.S.	A2	92
Arnoldsville, Ga., U.S.	C3	87
Arnot, Pa., U.S.	C7	115
Arnouville, Fr.	g10	16
Arnøya, i., Nor.	B9	14
Arnprior, Ont.	B8	73
Arnsberg, Ger.	C4	18
Arnstadt, Ger.	C5	18
Arnstein, Ont.	B5	73
Arys, Sov. Un.	E7	28
Åre, i., Den.	C3	15
Aroa, Ven.	A4	60
Aroab, Nmb.	C2	49
Arock, Or., U.S.	E9	114
Aroda, Va., U.S.	B4	123
Arolla, Switz.	D3	21
Arolsen, Ger.	B4	19
Aroma, Sud.	B4	47
Aroma Park, Il., U.S.	B6	90
Arona, Italy	E6	21
Aroostook, N.B.	C2	71
Aroostook, co., Me., U.S.	B4	96
Aroostook, stm., N.A.	B4	96
Arop, i., Pap. N. Gui.	k12	50
Åros, Nor.	p28	14
Arouca, Trin.	N23	65
Arpa, Tx., U.S.	C5	120
Arpajon, Fr.	F2	17
Arpin, Wi., U.S.	D3	126
Arques, Fr.	D2	17
Arques-la-Bataille, Fr.	E9	12
Arraias, Braz.	D1	57
Arraias, stm., Braz.	F8	62
Arraiolos, Port.	B4	22
Ar Ramādī, Iraq	B3	38
Ar Ramthā, Jord.	B7	41
Arran, Sask.	F5	75
Arran, Fr., U.S.	B2	83
Arran, Island of i., Scot., U.K.	C4	10
Ar Rank, Sud.	C3	47
Ar Raqqah, Syria	B3	38
Arras, Fr.	B5	16
Ar Rawdah, Eg.	E3	41
Arrecifes, Arg.	g6	54
Arrecifes, stm., Arg.	g6	54
Arrey, N.M., U.S.	E2	108
Arriaga, Mex.	D6	63
Arriba, Co., U.S.	B7	83
Arriikan Island, i., Marsh Is.	P18	52
Arrington, Ks., U.S.	C8	93
Arrington, Va., U.S.	C4	123
Arroio Grande, Braz.	E2	56
Arroll, Mo., U.S.	D6	102
Arrone, stm., Italy	h8	23
Arrow, Lough, l., Ire.	C4	11
Arrow Creek, stm., Mt., U.S.	C6	103
Arrow Head Lodge, Wy., U.S.	*B5	127
Arrowhead Mountain Lake, res., Vt., U.S.	B6	114
Arrowhead Village, N.J., U.S.	C4	107
Arrow Rock, Mo., U.S.	B5	102
Arrowrock Reservoir, res., Id., U.S.	F3	89
Arrowsmith, Il., U.S.	C5	90
Arrowwood, Alta.	D4	68
Arrowwood Lake, res., N.D.	B7	111
Arroyo, P.R.	C3	65
Arroyo de la Luz, Spain	B3	22
Arroyo Grande, Ca., U.S.	E3	82
Arroyo Hondo, N.M., U.S.	f10	110
Arroyo Seco, N.M., U.S.	A4	108
Ar Rumaythah, Iraq	A4	108
Ar Ruşayfah, Jord.	F2	39
Ar Ruşayriş, Sud.	B7	41
Ar Ruţbah, Iraq	C3	47
Ar Ruwayḩī, hist., Jord.	B3	38
Árta, dept., Grc.	D7	41
Árta, Grc.	*C3	25
Artamovsk, Sov. Un.	B3	25
Arter, Mount, mtn., Wy., U.S.	E27	8
Artemovskiy, Sov. Un.	G11	27
Artemus, Ky., U.S.	D6	94
Artena, Italy	h9	23
Arter, Mount, mtn., Wy., U.S.	D4	127
Artesia, Ca., U.S.	*n12	82
Artesia, Ms., U.S.	B5	101
Artesia, N.M., U.S.	E5	108
Artesia, S.D., U.S.	C8	118
Artesia Wells, Tx., U.S.	E3	120
Arth, Switz.	B4	20
Arthabaska, Que.	C6	74
Arthabaska, co., Que.	C5	74
Arthur, Ont.	D4	73
Arthur, Il., U.S.	D5	90
Arthur, In., U.S.	H3	91
Arthur, Ia., U.S.	B2	92
Arthur, Ne., U.S.	C4	104
Arthur, N.D., U.S.	B8	111
Arthur, Tn., U.S.	C10	119
Arthur, co., Ne., U.S.	C4	104
Arthur, Lake, l., La., U.S.	D3	95
Arthur, Lake, res., Pa., U.S.	E1	115
Arthur Kill, stm., N.J., U.S.	k8	107
Artibonite, stm., Haiti	E18	66
Artigas, Ur.	E1	56
Artland, Sask.	E1	75
Artois, hist. reg., Fr.	B5	16
Artois, Collines de l', hills, Fr.	B5	16
Artvin, Tur.	B13	40
Aru, Zaire	A5	48
Aru, Ug.	A5	48
Aruanã, Braz.	A2	56
Aruba, ctry., N.A.	H17	65
Arucas, Spain	m14	21
Aru Islands, is., Indon.	G8	34
Arun, stm., Eng., U.K.	D7	12
Arunachal Pradesh, state, India	C10	36
Arundel, Que.	D3	74
Arundel, Eng., U.K.	D7	12
Arundel Village, Md., U.S.	*h11	97
Arusha, Tan.	B6	48
Arusha, prov., Tan.	B6	48
Aruwimi, stm., Zaire	A4	48
Arvada, Co., U.S.	B5	83
Arvada, Wy., U.S.	B6	127
Aragh, Ire.	D4	11
Arvayheer, Mong.	B5	31
Arve, stm., Eur.	A6	24
Arvida, Que.	A2	92
Arvidsjaur, Swe.	E8	14
Arvigo, Switz.	D7	21
Arvika, Swe.	K5	14
Arvilla, N.D., U.S.	B8	111
Arvin, Ca., U.S.	C4	82
Arvon, Mount, mtn., Mi., U.S.	B2	99
Arvonia, Va., U.S.	C4	123
Arxan, China	B8	31
Arys, Sov. Un.	E7	28
Arzamas, Sov. Un.	D14	27
Arzgir, Sov. Un.	II15	27
Arzúa, Spain	A1	22
Aš, Czech.	B3	23
Aså, Den.	A4	15
Asab, Nmb.	C2	49
Asad, Lake, res., Syria	B12	40
Asahi, Mount, mtn., Japan	E11	33
Asahikawa, Japan	C13	31
Asan Bay, b., S. Kor.	H3	33
Asan Point, c., Guam	L9	52
Asansol, India	D8	36
Asau Bay, b., W. Sam.	F11	52
Asbach, Ger.	C2	18
Asbest, Sov. Un.	D6	29
Asbestos, Que.	D6	74
Asbury, Mo., U.S.	D3	102
Asbury Park, N.J., U.S.	C4	107
Ascensión, co., La., U.S.	D5	95
Ascensión, i., St. Hel.	G4	42
Aschaffenburg, Ger.	D4	18
Aschersleben, Ger.	C5	18
Ascoli Piceno, Italy	D5	23
Ascope, Peru	C2	58
Ascotán, Chile	A3	54
Ascot-Corner, Que.	D6	74
Ascutney, Vt., U.S.	E4	122
Ascutney, Mount, mtn., Vt., U.S.	E4	122
Aseb, Eth.	C5	47
Asela, Eth.	C5	47
Åsele, Swe.	E7	14
Asenovgrad, Bul.	E7	24
Asha, Sov. Un.	D5	29
Ashanti, prov., Ghana	E4	45
Ashaway, R.I., U.S.	F1	116
Ashbourne, Eng., U.K.	A6	12
Ashburn, Ga., U.S.	E3	87
Ashburn, Mo., U.S.	B6	102
Ashburn, Va., U.S.	A5	123
Ashburnham, Ma., U.S.	A4	98
Ashburton, N.Z.	O13	51
Ashburton, Eng., U.K.	D4	11
Ashburton, stm., Austl.	B3	78
Ashby, Al., U.S.	B3	78
Ashby, Mn., U.S.	D3	100
Ashby, Ma., U.S.	A4	98
Ashby, Ne., U.S.	B4	104
Ashbyburg, Ky., U.S.	C2	94
Ashcroft, B.C.	D7	69
Ashdod, Isr.	C6	41
Ashdot Ya'aqov, Isr.	B7	41
Ashdown, Ar., U.S.	D1	81
Ashe, co., N.C., U.S.	A1	110
Asheboro, N.C., U.S.	B3	110
Ashepoo, stm., S.C., U.S.	F6	117
Asher, Ok., U.S.	C5	113
Ashern, Man.	D2	70
Asherton, Tx., U.S.	E3	120
Asheville, N.C., U.S.	f10	110
Ashfield, Ma., U.S.	A2	98
Ashflat, Ar., U.S.	A4	81
Ashford, Eng., U.K.	C8	12
Ashford, Al., U.S.	D4	78
Ashford, Ct., U.S.	B7	84
Ashford, W.V., U.S.	m12	125
Ash Fork, Az., U.S.	B3	80
Ash Grove, Mo., U.S.	D4	102
Ashiaman, Ghana	*E4	45
Ashikaga, Japan	H9	33
Ashington, Eng., U.K.	F10	13
Ashio, Japan	H9	33
Ashizuri, Cape, c., Japan	J6	33
Ashkhabad, Sov. Un.	I10	28
Ashkum, Il., U.S.	C6	90
Ash Lake, Mn., U.S.	B6	100
Ashland, Al., U.S.	B4	78
Ashland, Il., U.S.	D3	90
Ashland, Ks., U.S.	E4	93
Ashland, Ky., U.S.	B7	94
Ashland, La., U.S.	B2	95
Ashland, Me., U.S.	B4	96
Ashland, Ma., U.S.	g10	98
Ashland, Mt., U.S.	A4	101
Ashland, Ne., U.S.	C9	104
Ashland, N.H., U.S.	C3	106
Ashland, Oh., U.S.	*B3	112

Ashl-Babo

Index

Name	Map Ref.	Page
Ashland, Ok., U.S.	C5	113
Ashland, Or., U.S.	E4	114
Ashland, Pa., U.S.	E9	115
Ashland, Va., U.S.	C5	123
Ashland, Wi., U.S.	B3	126
Ashland, co., Oh., U.S.	B3	112
Ashland, co., Wi., U.S.	B3	126
Ashland, Mount, mtn., Or., U.S.	E4	114
Ashland City, Tn., U.S.	A4	119
Ashland Reservoir, res., Ma., U.S.	h10	98
Ashley, Il., U.S.	E4	90
Ashley, In., U.S.	A7	91
Ashley, Mi., U.S.	E6	99
Ashley, Mo., U.S.	B6	102
Ashley, N.D., U.S.	C6	111
Ashley, Oh., U.S.	B3	112
Ashley, Pa., U.S.	n17	115
Ashley, co., Ar., U.S.	D4	81
Ashley, stm., S.C., U.S.	F7	117
Ashley Creek, stm., Ut., U.S.	C6	121
Ashley Falls, Ma., U.S.	B1	98
Ashmont, Alta.	B5	68
Ashmore, Il., U.S.	D5	90
Ashmore Islands, is., Austl.	B3	50
Ashmūn, Eg.	D2	41
Ashnola, stm., N.A.	A5	124
Ashokan, N.Y., U.S.	D6	109
Ashokan Reservoir, res., N.Y., U.S.	D6	109
Ashport, Tn., U.S.	B2	119
Ashqelon, Isr.	B3	38
Ash Shabakah, Iraq	B4	38
Ash Shabb, well, Eg.	E5	43
Ash Shallāl, Eg.	E6	43
Ash Shallūfah, Eg.	D4	41
Ash Shamālīyah (Northern), prov., Sud.	B2	47
Ash Shāriqah, U.A.E.	C5	38
Ash Sharqāṭ, Iraq	B4	38
Ash Shaṭrah, Iraq	F3	39
Ash Shawāshinah, Eg.	E2	41
Ash Shawbak, Jord.	D7	41
Ash Shawmarah, Leb.	A7	41
Ash Shaykh Jarrāh (part of Jerusalem), Isr. Occ.	m14	41
Ash Shaykh Sa'd, Syria	B7	41
Ash Shiḥr, Yemen	D4	38
Ash Shumlul, Sau. Ar.	H3	39
Ash Shurayk, Sud.	B3	47
Ash Springs, Nv., U.S.	F6	105
Ashtabula, Oh., U.S.	A5	112
Ashtabula, co., Oh., U.S.	A5	112
Ashtabula, Lake, res., N.D., U.S.	B8	111
Ashton, Ont.	B8	73
Ashton, Id., U.S.	E7	89
Ashton, Il., U.S.	B4	90
Ashton, Ia., U.S.	A2	92
Ashton, Md., U.S.	B3	97
Ashton, Mi., U.S.	E5	99
Ashton, Ne., U.S.	C7	104
Ashton, R.I., U.S.	B4	116
Ashton, S.D., U.S.	C7	118
Ashuanipi Lake, l., Newf.	h8	72
Ashuelot, N.H., U.S.	E2	106
Ashuelot, stm., N.H., U.S.	E2	106
Ashville, Man.	D1	70
Ashville, Al., U.S.	B3	78
Ashville, Oh., U.S.	C3	112
Ashwaubenon, Wi., U.S.	D5	126
Ashwood, Or., U.S.	C6	114
Ashwood, Tn., U.S.	B4	119
Asia, cont.	E11	30
Asiago, Italy	D7	20
Asia Minor, reg., Tur.	C10	40
Asifābād, India	H7	37
Asiga, Puntan, c., N. Mar. Is.	D7	52
Asiga Point, c., Guam	M10	52
Asinara, Gulf of, b., Italy	D2	23
Asinara Island, i., Italy	D2	23
Asino, Sov. Un.	B11	28
'Asīr, reg., Sau. Ar.	D4	38
'Asīrah ash Shamālīyah, Isr. Occ.	g12	41
Asker, Nor.	p28	14
Askersund, Swe.	H6	14
Askew, Ms., U.S.	A3	101
Askham, S. Afr.	C3	49
Askim, Nor.	p29	14
Askim, Swe.	A5	15
Askival, mtn., Scot., U.K.	D2	13
Askö, i., Swe.	u35	14
Askov, Mn., U.S.	D6	100
Āsmār, Afg.	D15	39
Asmara (Asmera), Eth.	B4	47
Asnæs, Den.	C5	15
Asnebumskit Hill, hill, Ma., U.S.	B4	98
Åsnen, l., Swe.	B8	15
Asnières [-sur-Seine], Fr.	C5	16
Asopós, stm., Grc.	g11	25
Asosa, Eth.	C3	47
Asotin, Wa., U.S.	C8	124
Asotin, co., Wa., U.S.	C8	124
Asotin Creek, stm., Wa., U.S.	C8	124
Aspe, Spain	C5	22
Aspen, Co., U.S.	B4	83
Aspen Butte, mtn., Or., U.S.	E4	114
Aspen Hill, Md., U.S.	*B3	97
Aspen Hill, Tn., U.S.	B4	119
Asperg, Ger.	E4	19
Aspermont, Tx., U.S.	C2	120
Aspers, Pa., U.S.	G7	115
Aspinwall, Ia., U.S.	C2	92
Aspinwall, Pa., U.S.	k14	115
Aspiring, Mount, mtn., N.Z.	P12	51
Aspres [-sur-Buëch], Fr.	E1	20
Asprópirgos, Grc.	g11	25
Aspy Bay, b., N.S.	C9	71
Asquith, Sask.	E2	75
Assabet, stm., Ma., U.S.	g9	98
Aş Şabyā, Sau. Ar.	D4	38
Aş Şaff, Eg.	E3	41
Aş Şaffānīyeh, Sau. Ar.	C4	38
Aş Şāfī, Jord.	C7	41
Assaikwatamo, stm., Man.	A3	70
Aş Şāliḥīyah, Eg.	D4	41
As Sallūm, Eg.	B2	38
As Salmān, Iraq	B4	38
As Salṭ, Jord.	F10	40
Assam, state, India	C9	36
As Samū', Isr. Occ.	C7	41
Aş Şanamayn, Syria	A8	41
Assaria, Ks., U.S.	D6	93
Assateague Island, i., U.S.	D7	97
Assateague Island National Seashore, U.S.	D7	97
Assawoman Bay, b., Md., U.S.	D7	97
Assawompset Pond, l., Ma., U.S.	C6	98
Assen, Neth.	A7	16
Assens, Den.	C3	15
Assens, Den.	B4	15
As Sinbillāwayn, Eg.	D3	41
Assini, I.C.	E4	45
Assiniboia, Sask.	H2	75
Assiniboine, stm., Can.	E2	70
Assiniboine, Mount, mtn., Can.	D3	68
Assinika, stm., Man.	C4	70
Assinippi, Ma., U.S.	h12	98
Assis, Braz.	C2	56
Assis Brasil, Braz.	D4	58
Assisi, Italy	C4	23
Asso, Italy	E7	21
Assonet, Ma., U.S.	C5	98
As Sudd, reg., Sud.	D3	47
Aş Şūfīyah, Eg.	D3	41
As Sulaymānīyah, Iraq	B4	38
As Sulaymānīyah, Sau. Ar.	C4	38
As Sulayyil, Sau. Ar.	A6	47
As Sulṭān, Libya	C3	43
Aş Şummān, plat., Sau. Ar.	H3	39
Assumption, Il., U.S.	D4	90
Assumption, co., La., U.S.	E4	95
As Suwaydā', Syria	F11	40
Astakós, Grc.	C3	25
Āstārā, Iran	B4	39
Asten, Neth.	C5	17
Asterābād see Gorgān, Iran	B5	38
Asti, Italy	B2	23
Astipálaia, i., Grc.	D6	40
Astola, i., Pak.	I11	39
Aston, Pa., U.S.	*p20	115
Aston Jonction, Que.	C5	74
Astor, Fl., U.S.	C5	86
Astorga, Spain	A2	22
Astoria, Il., U.S.	C3	90
Astoria, Or., U.S.	A3	114
Astoria, S.D., U.S.	C9	118
Astorville, Ont.	A5	73
Astrakhan, Sov. Un.	E7	29
Astura, stm., Italy	h9	23
Asturias, hist. reg., Spain	A2	22
Asuisui, Cape, c., W. Sam.	F11	52
Asuke, Japan	n16	33
Asunción, Para.	E4	55
Asunción Mita, Guat.	C3	62
Asunción Nochixtlán, Mex.	o15	63
Åsunden, l., Swe.	A7	15
Aswān, Eg.	C3	38
Aswān High Dam, Eg.	C3	38
Asyūṭ, Eg.	C3	38
Atacama, prov., Chile	E2	55
Atacama, Salar de, pl., Chile	D2	55
Atacama Desert, des., Chile	D2	55
'Aṭā'iṭah, Jabal al, mtn., Jord.	D7	41
Atakpamé, Togo	E5	45
Atalaia, Braz.	k5	57
Atalaia do Norte, Braz.	C3	58
Atalándi, Grc.	C4	25
Atalaya, Peru	D3	58
Atalissa, Ia., U.S.	C6	92
Atami, Japan	n18	33
Atar, Maur.	B2	45
'Aṭārūt, Isr. Occ.	h11	41
Atascadero, Ca., U.S.	E3	82
Atascosa, co., Tx., U.S.	E3	120
Atasu, Sov. Un.	D8	28
Atauro, i., Indon.	G7	34
Atáviros, mtn., Grc.	D6	25
Atbarah, Sud.	B3	47
'Aṭbarah, stm., Afr.	B4	47
Atbasar, Sov. Un.	D9	29
Atchafalaya, stm., La., U.S.	D4	95
Atchafalaya Bay, b., La., U.S.	E4	95
Atchison, Ks., U.S.	C8	93
Atchison, co., Ks., U.S.	C8	93
Atchison, co., Mo., U.S.	A2	102
Atco, N.J., U.S.	D3	107
Atgidon, Puntan, c., N. Mar. Is.	E7	52
Ath, Bel.	D3	17
Athabasca, Alta.	B4	68
Athabasca, stm., Alta.	f8	68
Athabasca, Lake, l., Can.	m7	75
Athalia, Oh., U.S.	D3	112
Athalmer, B.C.	D10	69
Athapapuskow Lake, l., Man.	B1	70
Atha Road (part of Pickering), Ont.	k15	73
Athboy, Ire.	D5	11
Athelstan, Que.	D3	74
Athena, Or., U.S.	B8	114
Athenry, Ire.	D3	11
Athens, Ont.	C9	73
Athens (Athínai), Grc.	D4	40
Athens, Al., U.S.	A3	78
Athens, Ar., U.S.	C3	87
Athens, Ga., U.S.	D4	90
Athens, Il., U.S.	D4	90
Athens, In., U.S.	B5	91
Athens, La., U.S.	B2	95
Athens, Me., U.S.	D3	96
Athens, Mi., U.S.	F5	99
Athens, N.Y., U.S.	C7	109
Athens, Oh., U.S.	C3	112
Athens, Pa., U.S.	C8	115
Athens, Tn., U.S.	D9	119
Athens, Tx., U.S.	C5	120
Athens, Vt., U.S.	E3	122
Athens, W.V., U.S.	D3	125
Athens, Wi., U.S.	C3	126
Athens, co., Oh., U.S.	C3	112
Athensville, Il., U.S.	D3	90
Atherley, Ont.	C5	73
Atherton, Austl.	C8	50
Atherton, Ca., U.S.	*k8	82
Athertonville, Ky., U.S.	C4	94
Athi, stm., Kenya	B6	48
Athiémé, Benin	E5	45
Athleague, Ire.	D3	11
Athlone, Ire.	D4	11
Athok, Burma	E10	36
Athol, Id., U.S.	B2	89
Athol, Ks., U.S.	C5	93
Athol, Ma., U.S.	A3	98
Athol, S.D., U.S.	C7	118
Athol Island, i., Bah.	m18	64
Áthos, mtn., Grc.	B5	40
Ath Thamad, Eg.	D6	43
Athy, Ire.	D3	10
Ati, Chad	C3	46
Atibaia, Braz.	m8	56
Atico, Peru	E3	58
Aticonipi, Lac, l., Que.	C2	72
Atikameg, Alta.	B3	68
Atik Lake, l., Man.	B4	70
Atikokan, Ont.	o17	73
Atikonak Lake, l., Newf.	h8	72
Atimonan, Phil.	p13	34
Atiquizaya, El Sal.	D3	62
Atka, Ak., U.S.	E5	79
Atka Island, i., Ak., U.S.	E5	79
Atkarsk, Sov. Un.	F15	27
Atkins, Ar., U.S.	B3	81
Atkins, Va., U.S.	D1	123
Atkinson, Ga., U.S.	E5	87
Atkinson, Il., U.S.	B3	90
Atkinson, Ne., U.S.	B7	104
Atkinson, N.H., U.S.	E4	106
Atkinson, N.C., U.S.	C4	110
Atkinson, co., Ga., U.S.	E4	87
Atkinson Lake, l., Man.	A4	70
Atlanta, Ar., U.S.	D2	81
Atlanta, Ga., U.S.	C2	87
Atlanta, Id., U.S.	F3	89
Atlanta, Il., U.S.	C4	90
Atlanta, In., U.S.	D5	91
Atlanta, Ks., U.S.	E7	93
Atlanta, La., U.S.	C3	95
Atlanta, Mi., U.S.	C6	99
Atlanta, Mo., U.S.	B5	102
Atlanta, Ne., U.S.	D6	104
Atlanta, N.Y., U.S.	C3	109
Atlanta, Oh., U.S.	C2	112
Atlanta, Tx., U.S.	C5	120
Atlantic, Ia., U.S.	C2	92
Atlantic, N.C., U.S.	C6	110
Atlantic, co., N.J., U.S.	E3	107
Atlantic Beach, Fl., U.S.	m9	86
Atlantic City, N.J., U.S.	E4	107
Atlantic City, Wy., U.S.	D4	127
Atlantic Highlands, N.J., U.S.	C4	107
Atlantic Mine, Mi., U.S.	A2	99
Atlántico, dept., Col.	A2	60
Atlantic Ocean	G8	5
Atlantic Peak, mtn., Wy., U.S.	D3	127
Atlas Mountains, mts., Afr.	C4	44
Atlas Saharien, mts., Alg.	C5	44
Atlee, Alta.	D5	68
Atlin, B.C.	m16	69
Atlin Lake, l., Can.	E6	66
'Atlit, Isr.	B6	41
Atlixco, Mex.	n14	63
Atmore, Al., U.S.	D2	78
Atna Peak, mtn., B.C.	C3	69
Atocha, Bol.	D2	55
Atoka, N.M., U.S.	E5	108
Atoka, Ok., U.S.	C5	113
Atoka, Tn., U.S.	B2	119
Atoka, co., Ok., U.S.	C5	113
Atoka Reservoir, res., Ok., U.S.	C5	113
Atomic City, Id., U.S.	F6	89
Atotonilco el Alto, Mex.	m12	63
Atoyac, Mex.	m12	63
Atoyac, stm., Mex.	n14	63
Atrak, stm., Asia	B5	38
Ätran, stm., Swe.	B6	15
Atrato, stm., Col.	B2	60
Atrek (Atrak), stm., Asia	C7	39
Atsugi, Japan	n18	33
Atsukeshi Bay, b., Japan	E12	33
Atsuma, Japan	E10	33
Atsumi, Japan	o16	33
Atsumi Bay, b., Japan	o16	33
At Tabbīn, Eg.	E3	41
Aṭ Ṭafīlah, Jord.	G10	40
Aṭ Ṭā'if, Sau. Ar.	C4	38
Attala, co., Ms., U.S.	B4	101
Attalla, Al., U.S.	A3	78
Aṭ Ṭallāb, Libya	E4	43
At Tamīmī, Libya	C4	43
Attapu, Laos	C3	34
Attapulgus, Ga., U.S.	F2	87
'Aṭṭārah, Isr. Occ.	h11	41
Attawapiskat, Ont.	n19	73
Attawapiskat, stm., Ont.	n18	73
Attawaugan, Ct., U.S.	B8	84
Aṭ Ṭayrīyah, Eg.	D2	41
Attean Pond, l., Me., U.S.	C2	96
Atterberry, Il., U.S.	C4	90
Attica, In., U.S.	D3	91
Attica, Ks., U.S.	E5	93
Attica, Mi., U.S.	E7	99
Attica, N.Y., U.S.	C2	109
Attica, Oh., U.S.	A3	112
Attica, hist. reg., Grc.	g11	25
Attigny, Fr.	E4	17
Attikamagen Lake, l., Newf.	g8	72
Aṭ Ṭīnah, Eg.	C4	41
Attleboro, Ma., U.S.	C5	98
Attleborough, Eng., U.K.	B9	12
Attock, Pak.	B5	36
Attu Island, i., Ak., U.S.	E2	79
Aṭ Ṭūr, Eg.	D6	43
Aṭ Ṭūr, Isr. Occ.	m14	41
Aṭ Ṭuwayyah, Sau. Ar.	I13	40
Attymon, Ire.	D3	11
Atuel, stm., Arg.	B3	54
Atui, Uad, val., Afr.	B2	45
Atu'u, Am. Sam.	F13	52
Åtvidaberg, Swe.	H6	14
Atwater, Sask.	G4	75
Atwater, Ca., U.S.	D3	82
Atwater, Mn., U.S.	E4	100
Atwood, Ont.	D3	73
Atwood, Co., U.S.	A7	83
Atwood, Il., U.S.	D5	90
Atwood, In., U.S.	B6	91
Atwood, Ks., U.S.	C2	93
Atwood, Ok., U.S.	C5	113
Atwood, Tn., U.S.	B3	119
Atwood Lake, res., Oh., U.S.	B4	112
Atwoodville, Ct., U.S.	B7	84
Aua, Am. Sam.	F13	52
Auau Channel, strt., Hi., U.S.	C5	88
Aubagne, Fr.	F6	16
Aube, dept., Fr.	F4	17
Aube, stm., Fr.	F4	17
Aubenas, Fr.	E6	16
Auberry, Ca., U.S.	D4	82
Aubervilliers, Fr.	g10	16
Aubière, Fr.	E5	16
Aubigny-sur-Nère, Fr.	D5	16
Aubin, Fr.	E5	16
Aubrey, Que.	D4	74
Aubrey, Ar., U.S.	C5	81
Aubrey Cliffs, clf., Az., U.S.	B2	80
Auburn, Ont.	D3	73
Auburn, Al., U.S.	C4	78
Auburn, Ca., U.S.	C3	82
Auburn, Ga., U.S.	B3	87
Auburn, Il., U.S.	D4	90
Auburn, In., U.S.	B7	91
Auburn, Ia., U.S.	B3	92
Auburn, Ks., U.S.	D8	93
Auburn, Ky., U.S.	D3	94
Auburn, Me., U.S.	D2	96
Auburn, Ma., U.S.	B4	98
Auburn, Mi., U.S.	E6	99
Auburn, Ms., U.S.	D3	101
Auburn, Ne., U.S.	D10	104
Auburn, N.H., U.S.	D4	106
Auburn, N.J., U.S.	D2	107
Auburn, N.Y., U.S.	C4	109
Auburn, N.D., U.S.	A8	111
Auburn, Pa., U.S.	E9	115
Auburn, Wa., U.S.	B3	124
Auburn, W.V., U.S.	B4	125
Auburn, Wy., U.S.	D1	127
Auburndale, Fl., U.S.	D5	86
Auburndale, Wi., U.S.	D3	126
Auburn Heights, Mi., U.S.	F7	99
Auburntown, Tn., U.S.	B5	119
Aubusson, Fr.	E5	16
Auch, Fr.	F4	16
Auchel, Fr.	D2	17
Auchterarder, Scot., U.K.	D5	13
Aucilla, Fl., U.S.	B3	86
Aucilla, stm., Fl., U.S.	B3	86
Auckland, N.Z.	L15	51
Auckland Islands, is., N.Z.	J8	2
Aude, stm., Fr.	F5	16
Audet, Que.	D7	74
Audierne, Fr.	C1	16
Audincourt, Fr.	D7	16
Audrain, co., Mo., U.S.	B6	102
Audubon, Ia., U.S.	C3	92
Audubon, Mn., U.S.	D3	100
Audubon, N.J., U.S.	D2	107
Audubon, Pa., U.S.	*F11	115
Audubon, co., Ia., U.S.	C2	92
Audun-le-Roman, Fr.	E5	17
Aue, Ger.	C6	18
Auerbach, Ger.	C7	19
Augathella, Austl.	B6	51
Auggen, Ger.	A4	21
Aughnacloy, N. Ire., U.K.	C5	11
Aughrim, Ire.	E5	11
Auglaize, co., Oh., U.S.	B1	112
Auglaize, stm., Oh., U.S.	A1	112
Au Gres, Mi., U.S.	D7	99
Augsburg, Ger.	D5	18
August, Ca., U.S.	*D3	82
Augusta, Austl.	F2	50
Augusta, Italy	F5	23
Augusta, Ar., U.S.	B4	81
Augusta, Ga., U.S.	C5	87
Augusta, Il., U.S.	C3	90
Augusta, Ks., U.S.	E7	93
Augusta, Ky., U.S.	B6	94
Augusta, Me., U.S.	D3	96
Augusta, Mi., U.S.	F5	99
Augusta, Mo., U.S.	C7	102
Augusta, Mt., U.S.	C4	103
Augusta, Oh., U.S.	B4	112
Augusta, W.V., U.S.	B6	125
Augusta, Wi., U.S.	D2	126
Augusta, co., Va., U.S.	B3	123
Augusta Springs, Va., U.S.	B3	123
Augusta Victoria Hospital, Isr. Occ.	m14	41
Augustenborg, Den.	D3	15
Augustów, Pol.	B7	26
Augustus, Mount, mtn., Austl.	D2	50
Aulander, N.C., U.S.	A5	110
Auld, Lake, l., Austl.	D3	50
Aulendorf, Ger.	B5	20
Aulnay-sous-Bois, Fr.	g11	16
Aulne, stm., Fr.	C2	16
Aulneau Peninsula, pen., Ont.	E4	70
Aulnoye [-Aymeries], Fr.	D3	17
Ault, Co., U.S.	A6	83
Ault, Piz, mtn., Switz.	C7	21
Aumale, Fr.	E9	12
Aumsville, Or., U.S.	k12	114
Auneuil, Fr.	E2	17
Auning, Den.	B4	15
Auno, Nig.	D7	45
Aunu'u Island, i., Am. Sam.	G13	52
Aur, i., Malay.	K6	35
Aura, Mi., U.S.	B2	99
Auraiya, India	D7	37
Aurangābād, India	E6	36
Auray, Fr.	D2	16
Aurelia, Ia., U.S.	B2	92
Aurelian Springs, N.C., U.S.	A5	110
Aurich, Ger.	B3	18
Auriflama, Braz.	C2	56
Aurillac, Fr.	E5	16
Aurora, Ont.	C5	73
Aurora, Guy.	A3	59
Aurora, Co., U.S.	B6	83
Aurora, Il., U.S.	B5	90
Aurora, In., U.S.	F8	91
Aurora, Ia., U.S.	B6	92
Aurora, Ks., U.S.	C6	93
Aurora, Me., U.S.	D4	96
Aurora, Mn., U.S.	C6	100
Aurora, Mo., U.S.	E4	102
Aurora, Ne., U.S.	D7	104
Aurora, N.Y., U.S.	C4	109
Aurora, N.C., U.S.	B6	110
Aurora, Oh., U.S.	A4	112
Aurora, Or., U.S.	B4	114
Aurora, S.D., U.S.	C9	118
Aurora, Ut., U.S.	E4	121
Aurora, W.V., U.S.	B5	125
Aurora, Wi., U.S.	C5	126
Aurora, co., S.D., U.S.	D7	118
Aurora Center, S.D., U.S.	D7	118
Aurskog, Nor.	p29	14
Aus, Nmb.	C2	49
Au Sable, Mi., U.S.	D7	99
Au Sable, stm., Mi., U.S.	D6	99
Ausable, stm., N.Y., U.S.	f11	109
Au Sable, North Branch, stm., Mi., U.S.	D6	99
Au Sable Forks, N.Y., U.S.	f11	109
Au Sable Point, c., Mi., U.S.	B4	99
Au Sable Point, c., Mi., U.S.	D7	99
Auschwitz see Oświęcim, Pol.	C5	26
Aussa, stm., Italy	D9	20
Austell, Ga., U.S.	h7	87
Austin, Man.	E2	70
Austin, Ar., U.S.	C4	81
Austin, In., U.S.	G6	91
Austin, Ky., U.S.	D3	94
Austin, Mn., U.S.	G6	100
Austin, Nv., U.S.	D4	105
Austin, Oh., U.S.	C8	114
Austin, Or., U.S.	C8	114
Austin, Pa., U.S.	C5	115
Austin, R.I., U.S.	E2	116
Austin, Tx., U.S.	D4	120
Austin, co., Tx., U.S.	E4	120
Austin, Lake, l., Austl.	E2	50
Austinburg, Oh., U.S.	A5	112
Austintown, Oh., U.S.	A5	112
Austinville, Ia., U.S.	B5	92
Austinville, Va., U.S.	D2	123
Australia, ctry., Oc.	E6	50
Australian Capital Territory, ter., Austl.	G7	51
Austria, ctry., Eur.	E7	18
Austwell, Tx., U.S.	E4	120
Autauga, co., Al., U.S.	C3	78
Autaugaville, Al., U.S.	C3	78
Authie, stm., Fr.	D2	17
Autlán de Navarro, Mex.	D4	63
Au Train, Mi., U.S.	B4	99
Autun, Fr.	D6	16
Auvergne, Ar., U.S.	B4	81
Auvergne, hist. reg., Fr.	E5	16
Auvergne Mountains, mts., Fr.	E5	16
Auvers [-sur-Oise], Fr.	E2	17
Auxerre, Fr.	D5	16
Auxier, Ky., U.S.	C7	94
Auxi-le-Château, Fr.	D2	17
Auxonne, Fr.	D6	16
Auxvasse, Mo., U.S.	B6	102
Auyán Tepuy, mtn., Ven.	B5	60
Auyuittuq National Park, N.W. Ter.	C19	66
Auzangate, Nevado, mtn., Peru	D3	58
Ava, Il., U.S.	F4	90
Ava, Mo., U.S.	E5	102
Ava, Oh., U.S.	C4	112
Avakubi, Zaire	A4	48
Avallon, Fr.	D5	16
Avalon, Ca., U.S.	F4	82
Avalon, Ga., U.S.	B3	87
Avalon, Ms., U.S.	B3	101
Avalon, Mo., U.S.	B4	102
Avalon, N.J., U.S.	E3	107
Avalon, Pa., U.S.	h13	115
Avalon, Lake, res., N.M., U.S.	E5	108
Avalon Peninsula, pen., Newf.	E5	72
Avanos, Tur.	C10	40
Avant, Ok., U.S.	A5	113
Avard, Ok., U.S.	A3	113
Avaré, Braz.	C3	56
Aveiro, Port.	B1	22
Avella, Pa., U.S.	F1	115
Avellaneda, Arg.	A5	54
Avellino, Italy	D5	23
Avenal, Ca., U.S.	E3	82
Avenches, Switz.	C3	21
Avenel, Md., U.S.	*B4	97
Avenel, N.J., U.S.	k7	107
Avening, Ont.	C4	73
Aventura, Fl., U.S.	*G6	86
Avenue, Md., U.S.	D4	97
Avenwedde, Ger.	B3	19
Avera, Ga., U.S.	C4	87
Averill, Mn., U.S.	D2	100
Averill Park, N.Y., U.S.	C7	109
Aversa, Italy	D5	23
Avery, Id., U.S.	B3	89
Avery, Ia., U.S.	C5	92
Avery, Ok., U.S.	B5	113
Avery, Tx., U.S.	C5	120
Avery, co., N.C., U.S.	e11	110
Avery Island, La., U.S.	E4	95
Aves, Islas de, is., Ven.	A4	60
Avesnes, Fr.	D3	17
Avesta, Swe.	G7	14
Avezzano, Italy	C4	23
Aviá Terai, Arg.	E3	55
Aviemore, Scot., U.K.	C5	13
Avigliano, Italy	D5	23
Avignon, Fr.	F6	16
Ávila, Spain	B3	22
Avila Beach, Ca., U.S.	E3	82
Avilés, Spain	A3	22
Avilla, In., U.S.	B7	91
Avilla, Mo., U.S.	D3	102
Avis, Pa., U.S.	D7	115
Avisio, stm., Italy	C7	20
Aviston, Il., U.S.	E4	90
Avize, Fr.	F4	17
Avlón, Grc.	g11	25
Avlum, Den.	B2	15
Avoca, Al., U.S.	A2	78
Avoca, Ar., U.S.	A1	81
Avoca, In., U.S.	G4	91
Avoca, Ia., U.S.	C2	92
Avoca, Mi., U.S.	E8	99
Avoca, Mn., U.S.	G3	100
Avoca, Ne., U.S.	h12	104
Avoca, N.Y., U.S.	C3	109
Avoca, Pa., U.S.	m18	115
Avoca, Tx., U.S.	C3	120
Avoca, Wi., U.S.	E3	126
Avocado Heights, Ca., U.S.	*m13	82
Avola, B.C.	D8	69
Avola, Italy	F5	23
Avon, Ct., U.S.	E4	73
Avon, Ct., U.S.	B4	84
Avon, Il., U.S.	C3	90
Avon, In., U.S.	E5	91
Avon, Ia., U.S.	e8	92
Avon, Ma., U.S.	B5	98
Avon, Mn., U.S.	E4	100
Avon, Ms., U.S.	B2	101
Avon, Mt., U.S.	D4	103
Avon, N.Y., U.S.	C3	109
Avon, N.C., U.S.	B7	110
Avon, Oh., U.S.	A3	112
Avon, S.D., U.S.	E7	118
Avon, co., Eng., U.K.	C5	12
Avon, stm., Austl.	F2	50
Avon, stm., Eng., U.K.	D6	10
Avon, stm., Eng., U.K.	E6	10
Avon, stm., Eng., U.K.	C5	12
Avon, stm., Scot., U.K.	C5	13
Avon by the Sea, N.J., U.S.	*C4	107
Avondale, Az., U.S.	D3	80
Avondale, Co., U.S.	C6	83
Avondale, La., U.S.	*E5	95
Avondale, Mo., U.S.	h10	102
Avondale, Oh., U.S.	*C1	112
Avondale, Pa., U.S.	G10	115
Avondale, R.I., U.S.	G1	116
Avondale Estates, Ga., U.S.	h8	87
Avon Lake, Ia., U.S.	e8	92
Avon Lake, Oh., U.S.	A3	112
Avonlea, Sask.	G3	75
Avonmore, Pa., U.S.	E3	115
Avon Park, Fl., U.S.	E5	86
Avoyelles, co., La., U.S.	C3	95
Avranches, Fr.	C3	16
Awa, Japan	N5	52
Awa Island, i., Japan	G9	33
Awaji, Japan	o14	33
Awaji Island, i., Japan	I7	33
Awasa, Eth.	D4	47
Awash, Eth.	D5	47
Awash, stm., Eth.	C5	47
Awbārī, Libya	D2	43
Awdheegle, Som.	E5	47
Awe, Loch, l., Scot., U.K.	D3	13
Awjilah, Libya	D4	43
Awka, Nig.	*E6	45
Awlef, Alg.	D5	44
Axel, Neth.	C3	17
Axel Heiberg Island, i., N.W. Ter.	m33	66
Axial Basin, Co., U.S.	A2	83
Axim, Ghana	F4	45
Axiós (Vardar), stm., Eur.	B4	40
Axis, Al., U.S.	E1	78
Ax-les-Thermes, Fr.	F4	16
Axson, Ga., U.S.	E4	87
Axtell, Ks., U.S.	C7	93
Axtell, Ne., U.S.	D6	104
Axtell, Ut., U.S.	D4	121
Ayé, Fr.	C5	16
Ay, stm., Sov. Un.	B5	28
Ayabaca, Peru	B2	58
Ayabe, Japan	n14	33
Ayacucho, Arg.	B5	54
Ayacucho, Peru	D3	58
Ayacucho, dept., Peru	D3	58
Ayaguz, Sov. Un.	E11	29
Ayamonte, Spain	D2	22
Ayan, Sov. Un.	D16	29
Ayapel, Col.	B2	60
Ayaş, Tur.	B9	40
Ayaviri, Peru	D3	58
Aydar, stm., Sov. Un.	G12	27
Ayden, N.C., U.S.	B5	110
Aydın, Tur.	D6	40
Aydlett, N.C., U.S.	A7	110
Ayer, Ma., U.S.	A4	98
Ayers Cliff, Que.	D5	74
Ayers Rock, mtn., Austl.	E5	50
Ayeyarwady, stm., Burma	D10	36
Ayia, Grc.	C4	25
Ayía Paraskeví, Grc.	C6	25
Ayiásos, Grc.	C6	25
Áyioi Theódhoroi, Grc.	h10	25
Áyios Dhimítrios, Grc.	g11	25
Áyios Evstrátios, i., Grc.	C5	25
Áyios Nikólaos, Grc.	E5	25
Aylen Lake, l., Ont.	B7	73
Aylesbury, Sask.	G3	75
Aylesbury, Eng., U.K.	E6	10
Aylesford, N.S.	D5	71
Aylett, Va., U.S.	C5	123
Aylmer, Mount, mtn., Alta.	D3	68
Aylmer East, Que.	D2	74
Aylmer Lake, l., N.W. Ter.	D11	66
Aylmer West, Ont.	E4	73
Aylsham, Sask.	D4	75
Aynor, S.C., U.S.	D9	117
'Ayn Yabrūd, Isr. Occ.	h11	41
Ayon Island, i., Sov. Un.	B9	29
Ayora, Spain	C5	22
Ayorou, Niger	D5	45
'Ayoûn el 'Atroûs, Maur.	C3	45
Ayr, Austl.	C8	50
Ayr, Ont.	D4	73
Ayr, Scot., U.K.	C4	10
Ayr, Ne., U.S.	D7	104
Ayr, N.D., U.S.	B8	111
Ayr, stm., Scot., U.K.	E4	13
Ayre, Point of, c., I. of Man	F4	13
Ayrshire, In., U.S.	H3	91
Ayrshire, Ia., U.S.	A3	92
Aysary, Sov. Un.	C8	28
Aysha, Eth.	C5	47
Ayton, Ont.	C4	73
Aytos, Bul.	D8	24
Aytré, Fr.	D3	16
Ayu Islands, is., Indon.	E8	34
Ayutla [de los Libres], Mex.	D5	63
Ayvacık, Tur.	C6	40
Ayvalık, Tur.	C6	40
Azalea Park, Fl., U.S.	*D5	86
Azalia, In., U.S.	F6	91
Azama, Japan	O5	52
Āzamgarh, India	D9	36
Azángaro, Peru	D3	58
Azaouâd, reg., Mali	C4	45
Azaouak, Vallée de l', val., Afr.	C5	45
Azare, Nig.	D7	45
Āzar Shahr, Iran	B4	38
Azcapotzalco (part of Mexico City), Mex.	h9	63
Azemmour, Mor.	C3	44
Azerbaijan, hist. reg., Iran	B4	38
Azerbaijan S.S.R., state, Sov. Un.	E7	29
Aziscohos Lake, l., Me., U.S.	C1	96
Azle, Tx., U.S.	n9	120
Azogues, Ec.	B2	58
Azores, is., Port.	g10	41
Azores, is., Port.	g9	44
Azov, Sov. Un.	H12	27
Azov, Sea of, Sov. Un.	E6	29
Azrou, Mor.	C3	44
Aztec, Az., U.S.	E2	80
Aztec, N.M., U.S.	A2	108
Aztec Peak, mtn., Az., U.S.	D5	80
Aztec Ruins National Monument, N.M., U.S.	A1	108
Azua, Dom. Rep.	E8	64
Azuaga, Spain	C3	22
Azuay, prov., Ec.	B2	58
Azuero, Peninsula de, pen., Pan.	G7	62
Azul, Arg.	B5	54
Azul, Cordillera, mts., Peru	C2	58
Azul, Serra, plat., Braz.	A2	56
Azurduy, Bol.	C3	55
Azusa, Ca., U.S.	m13	82
Az Zabdānī, Syria	F11	40
Az Ẓāhirīyah, Isr. Occ.	C6	41
Az Ẓahrān (Dhahran), Sau. Ar.	C4	38
Az Zaqāzīq, Eg.	C6	43
Az Zarqā', Jord.	B3	38
Az Zāwiyah, Libya	C2	43
Az Zaydāb, Sud.	B3	47
'Azzāz, Ra's, c., Libya	C4	43
Azzel Matti, Sebkha, pl., Alg.	D5	44
Az Zubayr, Iraq	F3	39
'Azzūn, Isr. Occ.	g11	41

B

Name	Map Ref.	Page
Baal, Ger.	C6	17
Baalbek, Leb.	B3	38
Baar, Switz.	B6	21
Baardheere, Som.	E5	47
Baargaal, Som.	C8	47
Baarle-Hertog, Bel.	C4	17
Baba Burnu, c., Tur.	C6	40
Babadag, Rom.	C9	24
Babaeski, Tur.	B6	25
Babahoyo, Ec.	B2	58
Babana, Nig.	D5	45
Babanūsah, Sud.	C2	47
Babar Islands, is., Indon.	G7	34
Babati, Tan.	B6	48
Babayevo, Sov. Un.	B11	27
Babb, Mt., U.S.	B3	103
Babb Creek, stm., Pa., U.S.	C7	115
Babbie, Al., U.S.	D3	78
Babbitt, Mn., U.S.	C7	100
Babbitt, Nv., U.S.	E3	105
Babcock, Wi., U.S.	D3	126
Babelthuap International Airport, Palau	R17	52
Babelthuap Island, i., Palau	R17	52
Babenhausen, Ger.	A6	20
Babi, i., Indon.	K2	35
Babine, stm., B.C.	B4	69
Babine Lake, l., B.C.	B5	69
Babine Range, mts., B.C.	B4	69
Babo, Indon.	F8	34
Bābol, Iran	B5	38
Bābol Sar, Iran	C6	39
Baboosic Lake, N.H., U.S.	E3	106
Baboquivari Mountains, mts., Az., U.S.	F4	80

Name	Map Ref.	Page
Baboquivari Peak, mtn., Az., U.S.	F4	80
Baboua, Cen. Afr. Rep.	D2	46
Babson Park, Fl., U.S.	E5	86
Babuskin, Sov. Un.	A6	31
Babuyan Islands, is., Phil.	B6	34
Babyak, Bul.	E6	24
Babylon, N.Y., U.S.	n15	109
Baca, co., Co., U.S.	D8	83
Bacabal, Braz.	B2	57
Bacajá, stm., Braz.	C4	59
Bacalar, Mex.	D7	63
Bacan, i., Indon.	F7	34
Bacău, Rom.	B8	24
Baccalieu Island, i., Newf.	D5	72
Bac Can, Viet.	A6	35
Baccarat, Fr.	C7	16
Baccaro Point, c., N.S.	F4	71
Bacerac, Mex.	A3	63
Bach, Mi., U.S.	E7	99
Bacharach, Ger.	C2	19
Bach Long Vi, i., Viet.	B7	35
Back, stm., N.W. Ter.	C12	66
Back, stm., S.C., U.S.	h12	117
Bačka Palanka, Yugo.	C4	24
Bačka Topola, Yugo.	C4	24
Back Bay, N.B.	D3	71
Backbone Mountain, mtn., U.S.	m12	97
Backnang, Ger.	E4	19
Backoo, N.D., U.S.	A8	111
Backus, Mn., U.S.	D4	100
Bac Lieu, Viet.	D3	34
Bac Ninh, Viet.	A3	34
Bacobi, Az., U.S.	B5	80
Bacolod, Phil.	C6	34
Bacon, co., Ga., U.S.	E4	87
Baconton, Ga., U.S.	E2	87
Bacoor, Phil.	o13	34
Bacova, Va., U.S.	B3	123
Bac Quang, Viet.	A6	35
Bacqueville-en-Caux, Fr.	E9	12
Bácsalmás, Hung.	B4	24
Bácum, Mex.	B2	63
Bad, stm., S.D., U.S.	C5	118
Bad, stm., Wi., U.S.	B3	126
Badagara, India	F6	36
Bad Aibling, Ger.	B7	20
Badajoz, Spain	C2	22
Badalona, Spain	B7	22
Badanah, Sau. Ar.	B4	38
Bad Axe, Mi., U.S.	E8	99
Bad Bergzabern, Ger.	D2	19
Bad Berneck, Ger.	C6	19
Bad Bramstedt, Ger.	E3	15
Baddeck, N.S.	C9	71
Bad Doberan, Ger.	A5	18
Bad Düben, Ger.	B7	19
Baden, Ont.	D4	73
Baden, Switz.	E4	18
Baden, Pa., U.S.	E1	115
Baden, hist. reg., Ger.	D4	18
Baden-Baden, Ger.	D4	18
Baden [bei Wien], Aus.	D8	18
Baden-Württemberg, state, Ger.	D4	19
Bad Freienwalde, Ger.	B7	18
Bad Friedrichshall, Ger.	D4	19
Badgastein, Aus.	E6	18
Badger, Newf.	D3	72
Badger, Ia., U.S.	B3	92
Badger, Mn., U.S.	B2	100
Badger, S.D., U.S.	C8	118
Badger Creek, stm., Co., U.S.	B7	83
Bad Godesberg, Ger.	C2	19
Bad Hersfeld, Ger.	C4	18
Bad Homburg [vor der Höhe], Ger.	C4	18
Bad Honnef, Ger.	C2	19
Bad Hönningen, Ger.	C2	19
Badia Polesine, Italy	D7	20
Badīn, Pak.	E2	37
Badin, N.C., U.S.	B2	110
Badin Lake, res., N.C., U.S.	B2	110
Bad Ischl, Aus.	E6	18
Bad Kissingen, Ger.	C5	18
Bad Kreuznach, Ger.	D3	18
Badlands, hills, S.D., U.S.	D3	118
Badlands, reg., U.S.	C2	111
Badlands National Park, S.D., U.S.	D3	118
Bad Langensalza, Ger.	C5	18
Bad Lauterberg, Ger.	B5	19
Bad Leonfelden, Aus.	E9	19
Bad Liebenwerda, Ger.	B8	19
Bad Lippspringe, Ger.	B3	19
Bad Mergentheim, Ger.	D4	19
Bad Münstereifel, Ger.	C1	19
Bad Muskau, Ger.	B9	19
Bad Nauheim, Ger.	C3	19
Bad Neustadt [an der Saale], Ger.	C5	19
Bad Oeynhausen, Ger.	A3	19
Bad Oldesloe, Ger.	B5	18
Badong, China	E7	31
Bad Orb, Ger.	C4	19
Badoumbé, Mali	D2	45
Bad Pyrmont, Ger.	B4	19
Bad Ragaz, Switz.	E4	18
Bad Reichenhall, Ger.	E6	18
Bad River Indian Reservation, Wi., U.S.	B3	126
Bad Salzuflen, Ger.	B4	18
Bad Salzungen, Ger.	C5	19
Bad Schandau, Ger.	C9	19
Bad Segeberg, Ger.	E4	15
Bad Sülze, Ger.	D6	15
Bad Tennstedt, Ger.	B5	19
Bad Tölz, Ger.	E5	18
Badu, i., Austl.	A7	50
Badulla, Sri L.	G7	36
Badwater Creek, stm., Wy., U.S.	C5	127
Bad Wildungen, Ger.	B4	19
Bad Windsheim, Ger.	D5	19
Bad Wörishofen, Ger.	B6	20
Bad Wurzach, Ger.	B5	20
Baena, Spain	D3	22
Baependi, Braz.	C4	56
Baeza, Ec.	B2	58
Baeza, Spain	D4	22
Bafang, Cam.	D2	46
Bafatá, Gui.-B.	D2	45
Baffin Bay, b., N.A.	B14	61
Baffin Bay, b., Tx., U.S.	E4	120
Baffin Island, i., N.W. Ter.	C18	66
Bafia, Cam.	E2	46
Bafoulabé, Mali	D2	45
Bafoussam, Cam.	*D2	46
Bāfq, Iran	B5	38
Bafra, Tur.	B10	40
Bafra, Cape, c., Tur.	B11	40
Bāft, Iran	G8	39
Bafwasende, Zaire	A4	48
Bagabag, Phil.	n13	34
Bagaces, C.R.	E7	63
Bagamoyo, Tan.	C6	48
Bagana, Nig.	E6	45
Bagansiapiapi, Indon.	E2	34
Bagata, Zaire	B2	48
Bagdad, Az., U.S.	C2	80
Bagdad, Fl., U.S.	u14	86
Bagdad, Ky., U.S.	B4	94
Bagé, Braz.	E2	56
Bagenkop, Den.	D4	15
Bāgerhāt, Bngl.	F12	37
Baggs, Wy., U.S.	E5	127
Bāghah, 'Ayn al, well, Eg.	E5	41
Baghdād, Iraq	B4	38
Bagheria, Italy	E4	23
Baghlān, Afg.	A4	36
Bagley, Ia., U.S.	C3	92
Bagley, Mn., U.S.	C3	100
Bagley, Wi., U.S.	F2	126
Bagnacavallo, Italy	E7	20
Bagnara [Calabra], Italy	E5	23
Bagnell, Mo., U.S.	C5	102
Bagnell Dam, Mo., U.S.	C5	102
Bagnères-de-Bigorre, Fr.	F4	16
Bagnères-de-Luchon, Fr.	F4	16
Bagnolet, Fr.	g10	16
Bagnols, Fr.	E6	16
Bago, Burma	E10	36
Bågø, i., Den.	C3	15
Bagoé, stm., Afr.	D3	45
Bagolino, Italy	D6	20
Bagot, co., Que.	D5	74
Bagrationovsk, Sov. Un.	A6	26
Baguio, Phil.	B6	34
Bagzane, Monts, mts., Niger	C6	45
Bahama, N.C., U.S.	A4	110
Bahamas, ctry., N.A.	B5	64
Bahār, Iran	D4	39
Baharampur, India	D8	36
Bahāwalnagar, Pak.	C5	36
Bahāwalpur, Pak.	C5	36
Bahia, state, Braz.	D2	57
Bahía, Islas de la, is., Hond.	D7	63
Bahía Blanca, Arg.	B4	54
Bahía Bustamante, Arg.	D3	54
Bahía de Caráquez, Ec.	B1	58
Bahía Negra, Para.	D4	55
Bahir Dar, Eth.	C4	47
Bahraich, India	D8	37
Bahrain, ctry., Asia	C5	38
Baḥr al Ghazāl, prov., Sud.	D2	47
Baḥr aş Şāfī, des., Asia	D4	38
Baḥrīyah, Al Wāḥāt al, well, Eg.	D5	43
Bāhū Kalāt, Iran	I10	39
Baía dos Tigres, Ang.	E1	48
Baia-Mare, Rom.	B6	24
Baião, Braz.	C5	59
Baïbokoum, Chad	D3	46
Baicheng, China	B9	31
Baie-Comeau, Que.	k13	74
Baie de Wasai, Mi., U.S.	B6	99
Baie-d'Urfé, Que.	q19	74
Baie-Johan-Beetz, Que.	h9	72
Baiersbronn, Ger.	E3	19
Baie-Sainte-Catherine, Que.	A8	74
Baie-Saint-Paul, Que.	B7	74
Baie Verte, N.B.	C5	71
Baie Verte, Newf.	D3	72
Baihe, China	H4	32
Baikal, Lake, l., Sov. Un.	D13	29
Baikal Mountains, mts., Sov. Un.	D13	29
Baikunthpur, India	F9	37
Bailén, Spain	C4	22
Băilești, Rom.	C6	24
Bailey, Co., U.S.	B5	83
Bailey, Ms., U.S.	C5	101
Bailey, N.C., U.S.	B4	110
Bailey, co., Tx., U.S.	B1	120
Bailey Brook, stm., Me., U.S.	B2	96
Bailey Island, Me., U.S.	g8	96
Bailey Island, i., S.C., U.S.	k11	117
Baileys Crossroads, Va., U.S.	g12	123
Baileys Harbor, Wi., U.S.	C6	126
Baileyton, Al., U.S.	A3	78
Baileyton, Tn., U.S.	C11	119
Baileyville, Il., U.S.	A4	90
Baileyville, Ks., U.S.	C7	93
Bailieborough, Ire.	D5	11
Bailundo, Ang.	D2	48
Bainbridge, Ga., U.S.	F2	87
Bainbridge, In., U.S.	E4	91
Bainbridge, N.Y., U.S.	C5	109
Bainbridge, Oh., U.S.	C2	112
Bainbridge Island, i., Wa., U.S.	e10	124
Bain-de-Bretagne, Fr.	D3	16
Bains, La., U.S.	D4	95
Bainville, Mt., U.S.	B12	103
Baiquan, China	B10	31
Baird, Ms., U.S.	B3	101
Baird, Tx., U.S.	C3	120
Bairdford, Pa., U.S.	h14	115
Baird Inlet, b., Ak., U.S.	C7	79
Baird Mountains, mts., Ak., U.S.	B7	79
Bairiki, Kir.	R18	52
Bairiki, i., Kir.	R18	52
Bairin Youqi, China	C8	32
Bairin Zuoqi, China	B8	32
Bairnsdale, Austl.	G8	50
Bairoil, Wy., U.S.	D5	127
Baïse, stm., Fr.	F4	16
Baixo Longa, Ang.	E2	48
Baja, Hung.	B4	24
Baja California Norte, state, Mex.	A1	63
Baja California Sur, state, Mex.	B2	63
Bajestān, Iran	D9	39
Bajimba, Mount, mtn., Austl.	D8	51
Bajmok, Yugo.	C4	24
Bajo Boquete, Pan.	F6	62
Bajram-Ali, Sov. Un.	C11	39
Bakala, Cen. Afr. Rep.	D4	46
Bakar, Yugo.	C2	24
Bakel, Sen.	D2	45
Baker, Ca., U.S.	E5	82
Baker, Fl., U.S.	u15	86
Baker, La., U.S.	D4	95
Baker, Mn., U.S.	D6	100
Baker, Mt., U.S.	D12	103
Baker, Nv., U.S.	D7	105
Baker, N.D., U.S.	A6	111
Baker, Ok., U.S.	e9	113
Baker, Or., U.S.	C9	114
Baker, co., Fl., U.S.	B4	86
Baker, co., Ga., U.S.	E2	87
Baker, co., Or., U.S.	C9	114
Baker, stm., N.H., U.S.	C3	106
Baker, Mount, mtn., Wa., U.S.	A4	124
Baker Butte, mtn., Az., U.S.	C4	80
Baker Hill, Al., U.S.	D4	78
Baker Island, i., Oc.	F11	6
Baker Island, i., Ak., U.S.	n22	79
Baker Lake, N.W. Ter.	D13	66
Baker Lake, l., N.W. Ter.	D13	66
Baker Lake, l., Me., U.S.	B3	96
Baker Lake, res., Wa., U.S.	A4	124
Baker Mountain, mtn., Me., U.S.	C3	96
Bakers, N.C., U.S.	B2	110
Bakers Bayou, stm., Ar., U.S.	k11	81
Bakersfield, Ca., U.S.	E4	82
Bakersfield, Mo., U.S.	E5	102
Bakersfield, Vt., U.S.	B3	122
Bakers Island, i., Ma., U.S.	f12	98
Bakers Mill, Fl., U.S.	B4	86
Bakerstown, Pa., U.S.	h14	115
Bakersville, Ct., U.S.	B3	84
Bakersville, N.C., U.S.	e10	110
Bakerton, W.V., U.S.	B7	125
Bakewell, Eng., U.K.	A6	12
Bakhchisaray, Sov. Un.	I9	27
Bakhmut, stm., Sov. Un.	q21	27
Bākhtarān (Kermānshāh), Iran	B4	38
Bakır, stm., Tur.	C6	25
Bako, Eth.	D4	47
Bako, I.C.	E3	45
Bakony Mountains, mts., Hung.	B3	24
Bakool, prov., Som.	E5	47
Bakouma, Cen. Afr. Rep.	D4	46
Bakoye, stm., Afr.	D3	45
Baku, Sov. Un.	E7	29
Baku, Zaire	A5	48
Bakundi, Nig.	E7	45
Bakungan, Indon.	K2	35
Bala, Ont.	B5	73
Bal'ā, Isr. Occ.	f11	41
Balâ, Tur.	C9	40
Bala, Wales, U.K.	B4	12
Bala, Ks., U.S.	C7	93
Balabac Island, i., Phil.	D5	34
Balabac Strait, strt., Asia	D5	34
Balabalagun Islands, is., Indon.	F5	34
Balad, Iraq	D2	39
Bālāghāt, India	G8	37
Balaguer, Spain	B6	22
Balaka, Mwi.	D6	48
Balakhna, Sov. Un.	D17	8
Balakhta, Sov. Un.	D27	8
Balaklava, Austl.	G2	51
Balakleya, Sov. Un.	G11	27
Balakovo, Sov. Un.	*D7	29
Balallan, Scot., U.K.	B2	13
Bālā Morghāb, Afg.	D11	39
Balancán [de Domínguez], Mex.	D6	63
Balanga, Phil.	o13	34
Balāngīr, India	G9	37
Balashov, Sov. Un.	F14	27
Balassagyarmat, Hung.	A4	24
Balāţ, Eg.	D5	43
Balaton, Mn., U.S.	F3	100
Balaton, Lake, l., Hung.	B3	24
Balayan, Phil.	p13	34
Balayan Bay, b., Phil.	p13	34
Balbi, mtn., Pap. N. Gui.	*G9	6
Balboa, Pan.	m11	62
Balboa Heights, Pan.	m11	62
Balbriggan, Ire.	D5	11
Balcad, Som.	E6	47
Balcarce, Arg.	B5	54
Balcarres, Sask.	G4	75
Balch, Ar., U.S.	B4	81
Balchik, Bul.	D9	24
Balch Springs, Tx., U.S.	*n10	120
Balclutha, N.Z.	Q12	51
Bald Creek, N.C., U.S.	f10	110
Bald Eagle Lake, l., Mn., U.S.	m12	100
Bald Eagle Lake, l., Mn., U.S.	C7	100
Baldegger Lake, l., Switz.	B5	21
Bald Hill, hill, R.I., U.S.	D2	116
Baldhill Dam, N.D., U.S.	B7	111
Bald Knob, Ar., U.S.	B4	81
Bald Knob, mtn., Va., U.S.	c3	123
Bald Knob, mtn., W.V., U.S.	C5	125
Bald Knoll, mtn., Wy., U.S.	D2	127
Bald Mountain, mtn., Ct., U.S.	B6	84
Bald Mountain, mtn., N.J., U.S.	A4	107
Bald Mountain, mtn., Or., U.S.	D5	114
Bald Mountain, mtn., Or., U.S.	C9	114
Bald Mountain, mtn., Vt., U.S.	B5	122
Bald Mountain, mtn., Wy., U.S.	B5	127
Bald Mountains, mts., N.C., U.S.	f10	110
Baldock Lake, l., Man.	A3	70
Baldur, Man.	E2	70
Baldwin, Fl., U.S.	B5	86
Baldwin, Ga., U.S.	B3	87
Baldwin, Il., U.S.	E4	90
Baldwin, Ia., U.S.	B7	92
Baldwin, La., U.S.	E4	95
Baldwin, Md., U.S.	B5	97
Baldwin, Mi., U.S.	E5	99
Baldwin, N.Y., U.S.	*E7	109
Baldwin, N.D., U.S.	B5	111
Baldwin, Pa., U.S.	k13	115
Baldwin, S.C., U.S.	B5	117
Baldwin, Wi., U.S.	D1	126
Baldwin, co., Al., U.S.	E2	78
Baldwin, co., Ga., U.S.	C3	87
Baldwin City, Ks., U.S.	D8	93
Baldwin Heights, In., U.S.	H2	91
Baldwin Park, Ca., U.S.	*E4	82
Baldwinsville, N.Y., U.S.	B4	109
Baldwinton, Sask.	E1	75
Baldwinville, Ma., U.S.	A3	98
Baldwyn, Ms., U.S.	A5	101
Baldy Mountain, mtn., B.C.	D7	69
Baldy Mountain, mtn., Man.	D1	70
Baldy Mountain, mtn., Mt., U.S.	B7	103
Baldy Mountain, mtn., N.M., U.S.	A4	108
Baldy Peak, mtn., Az., U.S.	D6	80
Bale, prov., Eth.	D5	47
Balearic Islands, is., Spain	C7	22
Baleia, Ponta da, c., Braz.	E3	57
Baleine, Rivière à la, stm., Que.	g13	74
Baler, Phil.	o13	34
Baler Bay, b., Phil.	o13	34
Baleshare, i., Scot., U.K.	C1	13
Bāleshwar, India	D8	36
Balesin, i., Phil.	o14	34
Baleville, N.J., U.S.	A3	107
Balfate, Hond.	C4	62
Balfour, N.C., U.S.	f10	110
Balfour, N.D., U.S.	B5	111
Balgonie, Sask.	G3	75
Bāli, India	E4	37
Bali, i., Indon.	G5	34
Balıkesir, Tur.	C6	40
Balikpapan, Indon.	F5	34
Balingen, Ger.	A4	20
Balintang Channel, strt., Phil.	B6	34
Bali Sea, Indon.	G5	34
Baliuag, Phil.	o13	34
Balje, Ger.	B4	18
Baljennie, Sask.	E2	75
Balkan, Ky., U.S.	D6	94
Balkan Mountains, mts., Eur.	D7	24
Balkh, Afg.	A4	36
Balkhash, Sov. Un.	E10	29
Balkhash, Lake, l., Sov. Un.	E10	29
Balki, Sov. Un.	H10	27
Balko, Ok., U.S.	e10	113
Ball, La., U.S.	C3	95
Balla, Ire.	D2	11
Ballachulish, Scot., U.K.	D3	13
Ballagh, Ire.	E4	11
Ballaghaderreen, Ire.	D3	11
Ballantine, Mt., U.S.	E8	103
Ballantrae, Scot., U.K.	C4	10
Ballarat (Ballaarat), Austl.	G7	50
Ballard, Ok., U.S.	A7	113
Ballard, co., Ky., U.S.	e8	94
Ballard, Lake, l., Austl.	E3	50
Ballardvale, Ma., U.S.	f11	98
Ballater, Scot., U.K.	B5	10
Ball Club, Mn., U.S.	C5	100
Ball Club Lake, l., Mn., U.S.	C5	100
Ballé, Mali	C3	45
Ballenas, Bahía de, b., Mex.	B2	63
Ballenstedt, Ger.	B6	19
Balleny Islands, is., Ant.	C29	7
Ballerup [-Målov], Den.	C6	15
Ball Ground, Ga., U.S.	B2	87
Ballia, India	E10	37
Ballina, Austl.	E9	50
Ballina, Ire.	C2	10
Ballina, Ire.	E3	11
Ballinakill, Ire.	E4	11
Ballinalack, Ire.	D4	11
Ballinascarty, Ire.	F3	11
Ballinasloe, Ire.	D2	10
Ballindine, Ire.	D3	11
Ballineen, Ire.	F3	11
Ballingarry, Ire.	E3	11
Ballingeary, Ire.	F2	11
Ballinger, Tx., U.S.	D3	120
Ballinluig, Scot., U.K.	D5	13
Ballinrobe, Ire.	D2	11
Ballinskelligs Bay, b., Ire.	F1	11
Ballintra, Ire.	C3	11
Ballitore, Ire.	D5	11
Ball Mountain Lake, res., Vt., U.S.	E3	122
Ballouville, Ct., U.S.	B8	84
Ballston, Or., U.S.	B3	114
Ballston Spa, N.Y., U.S.	B7	109
Ballwin, Mo., U.S.	f12	102
Bally, Pa., U.S.	F10	115
Ballybofey, Ire.	C4	11
Ballybunnion, Ire.	E2	11
Ballycanew, Ire.	E5	11
Ballycastle, Ire.	C2	11
Ballycastle, N. Ire., U.K.	C3	10
Ballyconneely, Ire.	D1	11
Ballyconnell, Ire.	C4	11
Ballycroy, Ire.	C2	11
Ballyduff, Ire.	E3	11
Ballyduff, Ire.	E2	11
Ballyferriter, Ire.	E1	11
Ballygar, Ire.	D3	11
Ballygorman, Ire.	B4	11
Ballyhaunis, Ire.	D3	11
Ballyheige, Ire.	E2	11
Ballyhoura Mountains, mts., Ire.	E3	11
Ballyjamesduff, Ire.	D4	11
Ballykelly, N. Ire., U.K.	B4	11
Ballylongford, Ire.	E2	11
Ballymahon, Ire.	D4	11
Ballymena, N. Ire., U.K.	C3	10
Ballymoe, Ire.	D3	11
Ballymoney, N. Ire., U.K.	B5	11
Ballymote, Ire.	C3	11
Ballymurray, Ire.	D3	11
Ballynahinch, N. Ire., U.K.	C6	11
Ballyneety, Ire.	E3	11
Ballynoe, Ire.	E3	11
Ballysadare, Ire.	C3	11
Ballyshannon, Ire.	C2	10
Ballyteige Bay, b., Ire.	E5	11
Ballyvaghan, Ire.	D2	11
Ballyvourney, Ire.	F2	11
Balm, Fl., U.S.	E4	86
Balmat, N.Y., U.S.	A5	109
Balmazújváros, Hung.	B5	24
Balmhorn, mtn., Switz.	D4	21
Balmoral, Man.	D3	70
Balmoral, N.B.	B3	71
Balmoral Castle, hist., Scot., U.K.	C5	13
Balmorhea, Tx., U.S.	o13	120
Balmville, N.Y., U.S.	D6	109
Baloda Bāzār, India	G9	37
Balonne, stm., Austl.	E8	50
Bālotra, India	C5	36
Balrāmpur, India	D9	37
Balranald, Austl.	G4	51
Balș, Rom.	C7	24
Balsam, N.C., U.S.	f9	110
Balsam Lake, Wi., U.S.	C1	126
Balsam Lake, l., Ont.	C6	73
Balsam Lake, l., Wi., U.S.	C1	126
Balsas, Braz.	C1	57
Balsas, Mex.	D5	63
Balsas, stm., Braz.	C1	57
Balsas, stm., Mex.	D4	63
Balsas, Rio das, stm., Braz.	D1	57
Balsthal, Switz.	B4	21
Balta, Sov. Un.	H7	27
Balta, N.D., U.S.	A5	111
Baltasar Brum, Ur.	E1	56
Baltic, Ct., U.S.	C7	84
Baltic, Oh., U.S.	B4	112
Baltic, S.D., U.S.	D9	118
Baltic Sea, Eur.	I8	14
Balţīm, Eg.	C3	41
Baltimore, Ont.	C6	73
Baltimore, Ire.	F2	11
Baltimore, Md., U.S.	B4	97
Baltimore, Oh., U.S.	C3	112
Baltimore, co., Md., U.S.	B4	97
Baltimore Highlands, Md., U.S.	h11	97
Baltinglass, Ire.	E5	11
Baltiysk, Sov. Un.	A5	26
Baltra, Isla, i., Ec.	g5	58
Baltrum, Ger.	A7	17
Baltrum, i., Ger.	A7	17
Baluchistan, hist. reg., Asia	C3	36
Balya, Tur.	C6	25
Balzac, Alta.	D3	68
Balzar, Ec.	B2	58
Balzers, Liech.	B8	21
Bam, Iran	C5	38
Bama, Nig.	D7	45
Bamako, Mali	D3	45
Bamba, Mali	C4	45
Bambang, Phil.	n13	34
Bambari, Cen. Afr. Rep.	D4	46
Bamberg, Ger.	D5	18
Bamberg, S.C., U.S.	E5	117
Bamberg, co., S.C., U.S.	E5	117
Bamber Lake, N.J., U.S.	D4	107
Bambesa, Zaire	A4	48
Bambuí, Braz.	C3	56
Bamburgh, Eng., U.K.	E7	13
Bam Co, l., China	B9	36
Bamenda, Cam.	D2	46
Bampūr, Iran	H10	39
Bampūr, stm., Iran	H9	39
Ban, Carn, mtn., Scot., U.K.	C4	13
Banagher, Ire.	D4	11
Banahao, Mount, mtn., Phil.	o13	34
Banalia, Zaire	A4	48
Banamba, Mali	D3	45
Banana, Zaire	C1	48
Bananal, Braz.	h5	56
Bananal, Ilha do, i., Braz.	E4	59
Banana River, b., Fl., U.S.	D6	86
Bananeiras, Braz.	C3	57
Banās, stm., India	E4	37
Banās, Ra's, c., Eg.	C3	38
Banat, hist. reg., Eur.	C5	24
Banbridge, N. Ire., U.K.	C3	10
Banbury, Eng., U.K.	D6	10
Banchory, Scot., U.K.	C6	13
Bancos, Bahía, b., Ec.	g5	58
Bancroft, Ont.	B7	73
Bancroft, Id., U.S.	G7	89
Bancroft, Ia., U.S.	A3	92
Bancroft, Me., U.S.	C4	96
Bancroft, Mi., U.S.	F6	99
Bancroft, Ne., U.S.	B9	104
Bancroft, S.D., U.S.	C8	118
Bancroft, Wi., U.S.	D4	126
Bānda, India	C7	36
Banda Aceh, Indon.	k11	34
Banda Banda, Mount, mtn., Austl.	E9	51
Banda Islands, is., Indon.	F7	34
Bandama, stm., I.C.	E3	45
Bandana, Ky., U.S.	e9	94
Bandar see Machilīpatnam, India	E7	36
Bandar Baharu, Malay.	J4	35
Bandar Beheshtī, Iran	I10	39
Bandar-e 'Abbās, Iran	C5	38
Bandar-e Anzalī (Bandar-e Pahlavī), Iran	B4	38
Bandar-e Būshehr, Iran	G5	39
Bandar-e Deylam, Iran	F5	39
Bandar-e Khomeynī (Bandar-e Shāhpūr), Iran	F4	39
Bandar-e Lengeh, Iran	H7	39
Bandar-e Māhshahr, Iran	*F4	39
Bandar-e Pahlavī see Bandar-e Anzalī, Iran	B4	38
Bandar-e Rīg, Iran	G5	39
Bandar-e Shāh see Bandar-e Torkeman, Iran	B5	38
Bandar-e Shāhpūr see Bandar-e Khomeynī, Iran	F4	39
Bandar-e Torkeman (Bandar-e Shāh), Iran	B5	38
Bandar Maharani see Muar, Malay.	K5	35
Bandar Seri Begawan (Brunei), Bru.	E5	34
Banda Sea, Indon.	G7	34
Bande, Spain	A2	22
Banded Peak, mtn., Co., U.S.	D4	83
Bandeira, Pico da, mtn., Braz.	C4	56
Bandelier National Monument, N.M., U.S.	B3	108
Bandera, Arg.	E3	55
Bandera, Tx., U.S.	E3	120
Bandera, co., Tx., U.S.	E3	120
Banderas, Bahía de, b., Mex.	m11	63
Bandholm, Den.	D5	15
Bandiagara, Mali	D4	45
Bāndīkūi, India	D6	37
Bandırma, Tur.	B7	40
Bandon, Ire.	F3	11
Bandon, Or., U.S.	D2	114
Bandon, stm., Ire.	F3	11
Bandundu, Zaire	B2	48
Bandung, Indon.	G3	34
Bandy, Va., U.S.	e10	123
Bāneh, Iran	D2	39
Banes, Cuba	D6	64
Banff, Alta.	D3	68
Banff, Scot., U.K.	B5	10
Banff National Park, Alta.	D2	68
Banfora, Burkina	D4	45
Bangalore, India	F6	36
Bangassou, Cen. Afr. Rep.	E4	46
Bangeta, Mount, mtn., Pap. N. Gui.	k12	50
Banggai, Indon.	F6	34
Banggi Island, i., Malay.	D5	34
Banggong Co, l., China	B6	36
Bangka, i., Indon.	F3	34
Bangkalan, Indon.	G4	34
Bangkok (Krung Thep), Thai.	C2	34
Bangladesh, ctry., Asia	D9	36
Bangor, Sask.	G4	75
Bangor, Ire.	C2	11
Bangor, N. Ire., U.K.	C4	10
Bangor, Wales, U.K.	D4	10
Bangor, Al., U.S.	B3	78
Bangor, Me., U.S.	D4	96
Bangor, Mi., U.S.	F4	99
Bangor, N.Y., U.S.	f10	109
Bangor, Pa., U.S.	E11	115
Bangor, Wi., U.S.	E3	126
Bangor Township, Mi., U.S.	E7	99
Bangs, Tx., U.S.	D3	120
Bangs, Mount, mtn., Az., U.S.	A2	80
Bang Saphan, Thai.	C1	34
Bangu, Zaire	C3	48
Bangued, Phil.	B6	34
Bangui, Cen. Afr. Rep.	E3	46
Bangweulu, Lake, l., Zam.	D4	48
Banhā, Eg.	B3	38
Ban Hat Yai see Hat Yai, Thai.	D2	34
Baní, Dom. Rep.	E8	64
Bani, Phil.	n12	34
Bani, stm., Mali	D3	45
Baniara, Pap. N. Gui.	k12	50
Banī Na'īm, Isr. Occ.	C7	41
Banister, stm., Va., U.S.	D4	123
Banī Suhaylah, Isr. Occ.	C6	41
Banī Suwayf, Eg.	C3	38
Bāniyās, Isr. Occ.	B3	38
Banja Luka, Yugo.	C3	24
Banjarmasin, Indon.	F4	34
Banjul, Gam.	D1	45
Bankas, Mali	D4	45
Bankeryd, Swe.	A8	15
Bankfoot, Scot., U.K.	D5	13
Bankhead, Al., U.S.	A2	78
Bankhead Lake, res., Al., U.S.	B2	78
Banks, Al., U.S.	D4	78
Banks, Ar., U.S.	D3	81
Banks, Id., U.S.	E2	89
Banks, Ms., U.S.	A3	101
Banks, Or., U.S.	g11	114
Banks, co., Ga., U.S.	B3	87
Banksian, stm., Can.	C4	70
Banks Island, i., B.C.	C2	69
Banks Island, i., N.W. Ter.	B8	66
Banks Lake, res., Ga., U.S.	E3	87
Banks Lake, res., Wa., U.S.	B6	124
Banks Peninsula, pen., N.Z.	O14	51
Bankston, Al., U.S.	B2	78
Bankstown, Austl.	*F9	50
Bānkura, India	D8	36
Bann, stm., N. Ire., U.K.	B5	11
Bannack, Mt., U.S.	E4	103
Banner, Ms., U.S.	A4	101
Banner, Wy., U.S.	B6	127
Banner, co., Ne., U.S.	C2	104
Banner Elk, N.C., U.S.	A1	110
Banning, Ca., U.S.	F5	82
Banning, Ga., U.S.	C2	87
Bannock, co., Id., U.S.	G6	89
Bannockburn, Ont.	C7	73
Bannock Peak, mtn., Id., U.S.	F6	89
Bannock Range, mts., Id., U.S.	G6	89
Bannu, Pak.	B5	36
Bañolas, Spain	A7	22
Baños, Ec.	B2	58
Bansha, Ire.	E3	11
Banská Bystrica, Czech.	D5	26
Banská Štiavnica, Czech.	D5	26
Bansko, Bul.	E6	24
Bānswāra, India	F5	37
Bantam, Ct., U.S.	C3	84
Bantam, stm., Ct., U.S.	B3	84
Bantam Lake, l., Ct., U.S.	C3	84
Banteer, Ire.	E3	11
Bantry, Ire.	E2	10
Bantry, N.D., U.S.	A5	111
Bantry Bay, b., Ire.	E2	10
Banyak Islands, is., Indon.	m11	34
Banyo, Cam.	D2	46
Banyuwangi, Indon.	G4	34
Banzare Coast, Ant.	C25	7
Baocheng, China	E6	31
Baode, China	E4	32
Baodi, China	E7	32
Baoding, China	D8	31
Bao Ha, Viet.	A6	35
Baoji, China	E6	31
Baokang, China	E7	31
Bao Loc, Viet.	C3	34
Baoqing, China	C6	33
Baoshan, China	F4	31
Baoting, China	C8	35
Baotou, China	C6	31
Baoulé, stm., Afr.	D3	45
Baoulé, stm., Mali	D3	45
Baoying, China	H8	32
Bapaume, Fr.	D2	17
Bapchule, Az., U.S.	D4	80
Baptiste, Ont.	B6	73
Baptistown, N.J., U.S.	B2	107
Bāqa el Gharbiyya, Isr.	B7	41
Ba'qūbah, Iraq	B4	38
Baquedano, Chile	D2	55
Bar, Fr.	C6	16
Bar, Sov. Un.	G6	27
Bar, Yugo.	D4	24
Baraawe, Som.	E5	47
Barabinsk, Sov. Un.	D10	29
Baraboo, Wi., U.S.	E4	126
Baraboo, stm., Wi., U.S.	E3	126
Baracaldo, Spain	A4	22
Baracoa, Cuba	D6	64
Barada, Ne., U.S.	D10	104
Baradero, Arg.	f7	54
Baraga, Mi., U.S.	B2	99
Baraga, co., Mi., U.S.	B2	99
Bārah, Sud.	C3	47
Barahona, Dom. Rep.	E8	64
Barajas de Madrid, Spain	p17	22
Bārākpur, India	F12	37
Bāramūla, India	B5	36
Bārān, India	E6	37
Baranagar, India	*D8	36
Baranof Island, i., Ak., U.S.	m22	79
Baranov, Cape, c., Sov. Un.	C34	128
Baranovichi, Sov. Un.	E5	27
Barão de Melgaço, Braz.	B1	56
Barataria, Trin.	N23	65
Barataria, La., U.S.	E5	95
Barataria, Bayou, stm., La., U.S.	k11	95
Barataria Bay, b., La., U.S.	E6	95
Barat Daya Islands, is., Indon.	G7	34
Baraya, Col.	C2	60
Barbacena, Braz.	C4	56
Barbacoas, Col.	C2	60
Barbado, stm., Braz.	C3	55
Barbados, ctry., N.A.	J15	64
Barbalha, Braz.	C3	57
Barbar, Sud.	B3	47
Barbastro, Spain	A6	22
Barbate [de Franco], Spain	D3	22
Barbeau, Mi., U.S.	B6	99
Barbeau Peak, mtn., N.W. Ter.	k37	66
Barber, Ar., U.S.	B1	81
Barber, co., Ks., U.S.	E5	93
Barbers Point, c., Hi., U.S.	B3	88
Barbers Point Naval Air Station, mil., Hi., U.S.	g9	88
Barberton, S. Afr.	C5	49
Barberton, Oh., U.S.	A4	112
Barberville, Fl., U.S.	C5	86
Barbezieux, Fr.	E3	16
Barbil, India	F10	37
Barbour, co., Al., U.S.	D4	78
Barbour, co., W.V., U.S.	B4	125
Barboursville, Va., U.S.	B4	123
Barboursville, W.V., U.S.	C2	125
Barbourville, Ky., U.S.	D6	94
Barbuda, i., Antig.	H14	64
Barby, Ger.	B6	19
Barca de Alva, Port.	B2	22
Barcaldine, Austl.	D8	50
Barcarena, Port.	f9	22
Barcarrota, Spain	C2	22
Barcellona [Pozzo di Gotto], Italy	E5	23
Barcelona, Spain	B7	22
Barcelona, Ven.	A5	60
Barcelonnette, Fr.	E7	16
Barcelos, Braz.	C2	59
Barcelos, Port.	B1	22
Barclay, Md., U.S.	B6	97
Barco, N.C., U.S.	A7	110
Barcoo, stm., Austl.	D7	50
Barcroft, Lake, res., Va., U.S.	g12	123
Bard, N.M., U.S.	B6	108
Barda del Medio, Arg.	B3	54
Bardaï, Chad	A3	46

Name	Map Ref.	Page
Bardawīl, Sabkhat al, sw., Eg.	C5	41
Bardawil Peninsula, spit, Eg.	C4	41
Barddhamān, India	D8	36
Bardejov, Czech.	D6	26
Barden Reservoir, res., R.I., U.S.	C2	116
Bardi, Italy	E5	20
Bardīyah, Libya	C5	43
Bardolph, Il., U.S.	C3	90
Bardonecchia, Italy	D2	20
Bardsey Island, i., Wales, U.K.	B3	12
Bardstown, Ky., U.S.	C4	94
Bardstown Junction, Ky., U.S.	C4	94
Bardswell Group, is., B.C.	C3	69
Bardwell, Ky., U.S.	f9	94
Bardwell Lake, res., Tx., U.S.	C4	120
Bare Hill Pond, l., Ma., U.S.	g9	98
Bareilly, India	C6	36
Barenburg, Ger.	F2	15
Barentin, Fr.	C4	16
Barents, i., Nor.	B12	128
Barents Sea, Eur.	B6	29
Barentu, Eth.	B4	47
Barfleur, Pointe de, c., Fr.	C3	16
Bargarh, India	G9	37
Bargersville, In., U.S.	E5	91
Barguzin, Sov. Un.	D13	29
Bar Harbor, Me., U.S.	D4	96
Bari, Italy	D6	23
Bari, prov., Som.	D6	47
Barillas, Guat.	C2	62
Barinas, Ven.	B3	60
Barinas, state, Ven.	B4	60
Baring, Me., U.S.	C5	96
Baring, Mo., U.S.	A5	102
Bāripada, India	D8	36
Bariri, Braz.	C3	56
Bārīs, Eg.	E6	43
Barisāl, Bngl.	D9	36
Barisan Mountains, mts., Indon.	F2	34
Barito, stm., Indon.	F4	34
Barium Springs, N.C., U.S.	B2	110
Barker, N.Y., U.S.	B2	109
Barker Heights, N.C., U.S.	f10	110
Barkerville, B.C.	C7	69
Barkeyville, Pa., U.S.	D2	115
Barkhamsted Reservoir, res., Ct., U.S.	B3	84
Barkley, Lake, res., U.S.	f10	94
Barkley Dam, Ky., U.S.	e9	94
Barkley Sound, strt., B.C.	E5	69
Barkly East, S. Afr.	D4	49
Barkly Tableland, plat., Austl.	C6	50
Barkmere, Que.	C3	74
Barkol, China	C3	31
Bark Point, c., Wi., U.S.	B2	126
Bark River, Mi., U.S.	C3	99
Barksdale, Tx., U.S.	E2	120
Barksdale Air Force Base, mil., La., U.S.	B2	95
Bar Lake, l., Sask.	B2	75
Bar-le-Duc, Fr.	C6	16
Barlee, Lake, l., Austl.	E2	50
Barletta, Italy	D6	23
Barling, Ar., U.S.	B1	81
Barlow, Ky., U.S.	e8	94
Barlow, N.D., U.S.	B6	111
Barlow, Or., U.S.	h12	114
Bārmer, India	C5	36
Bar Mills, Me., U.S.	E2	96
Barmouth, Wales, U.K.	D4	10
Barna, Ire.	D2	11
Barnaby River, N.B.	C4	71
Barnard, Ks., U.S.	C5	93
Barnard, Mo., U.S.	A3	102
Barnard, S.D., U.S.	B7	118
Barnard, Vt., U.S.	D3	122
Barnard Castle, Eng., U.K.	F7	13
Barnardsville, N.C., U.S.	f10	110
Barnasht, Eg.	E3	41
Barnaul, Sov. Un.	D11	29
Barnegat, N.J., U.S.	D4	107
Barnegat Bay, b., N.J., U.S.	D4	107
Barnegat Inlet, b., N.J., U.S.	D4	107
Barnegat Light, N.J., U.S.	D4	107
Barnegat Pines, N.J., U.S.	D4	107
Barne Inlet, b., Ant.	g40	7
Barnes, Ks., U.S.	C7	93
Barnes, Pa., U.S.	C3	115
Barnes, co., N.D., U.S.	B7	111
Barnesboro, Pa., U.S.	E4	115
Barnes City, Ia., U.S.	C5	92
Barnes Corners, N.Y., U.S.	B5	109
Barnes Creek, stm., La., U.S.	D2	95
Barnes Sound, strt., Fl., U.S.	G6	86
Barneston, Ne., U.S.	D9	104
Barnesville, Ga., U.S.	C2	87
Barnesville, Md., U.S.	B3	97
Barnesville, Mn., U.S.	D2	100
Barnesville, Oh., U.S.	C4	112
Barnet (part of London), Eng., U.K.	k12	10
Barnet, Vt., U.S.	C4	122
Barnett, Mo., U.S.	C5	102
Barneveld, Neth.	B5	17
Barneveld, Wi., U.S.	E4	126
Barneville-Carteret, Fr.	F6	10
Barney, Ga., U.S.	F3	87
Barney, N.D., U.S.	C8	111
Barney, Mount, mtn., Austl.	D9	51
Barnhart, Tx., U.S.	C7	102
Barnhart, Tx., U.S.	D2	120
Barnhill, Oh., U.S.	B4	112
Barnsdall, Ok., U.S.	A5	113
Barnsley, Eng., U.K.	A6	12
Barnstable, Ma., U.S.	C7	98
Barnstable, co., Ma., U.S.	C7	98
Barnstaple, Eng., U.K.	E4	10
Barnstaple Bay, b., Eng., U.K.	C3	12
Barnstead, N.H., U.S.	D4	106
Barnston, Que.	D6	74
Barnum, Ia., U.S.	B3	92
Barnum, Mn., U.S.	D6	100
Barnwell, Alta.	E4	68
Barnwell, S.C., U.S.	E5	117
Barnwell, co., S.C., U.S.	E5	117
Baro, Nig.	E6	45
Baro, stm., Afr.	D3	47
Baroda, Mi., U.S.	G4	99
Baroda see Vadodara, India	D5	36
Baron, Ok., U.S.	B7	113
Barons, Alta.	E4	68
Barques, Pointe aux, c., Mi., U.S.	D8	99
Barquisimeto, Ven.	A4	60
Barr, Fr.	C7	16
Barr, Co., U.S.	B6	83
Barr, Ra's al, c., Eg.	C3	41
Barra, Braz.	h5	57
Barra, Braz.	D2	57
Barra, i., Scot., U.K.	B3	10
Barra, Sound of, strt., Scot., U.K.	C1	13
Barraba, Austl.	E8	51
Barra Bonita, Braz.	m7	56
Barracão, Braz.	D2	56
Barrackville, W.V., U.S.	B4	125
Barra de Río Grande, Nic.	D6	62
Barra do Corda, Braz.	C1	57
Barra do Garças, Braz.	B2	56
Barra do Pirai, Braz.	C4	56
Barra Head, c., Scot., U.K.	B3	10
Barra Mansa, Braz.	C4	56
Barranca, Peru	B2	58
Barranca, N.M., U.S.	*A3	108
Barrancabermeja, Col.	B3	60
Barrancas, Ven.	B5	60
Barrancos, Peru	*D2	58
Barranco, Peru	*D2	58
Barranquilla, Col.	A3	60
Barraza, Chile	A2	54
Barre, Lake, l., La., U.S.	E5	95
Barre, Vt., U.S.	C4	122
Barre des Écrins, mtn., Fr.	E7	16
Barre Falls Reservoir, res., Ma., U.S.	B4	98
Barreiras, Braz.	D2	57
Barreirinha, Braz.	C3	59
Barreirinhas, Braz.	B2	57
Barreiro, Port.	C1	22
Barreiros, Braz.	C3	57
Barrelville, Md., U.S.	k13	97
Barren, co., Ky., U.S.	D4	94
Barren, stm., Ky., U.S.	C3	94
Barren, Nosy, is., Madag.	g8	49
Barren Island, i., Md., U.S.	D5	97
Barren Islands, is., Ak., U.S.	h15	79
Barren Plain, Tn., U.S.	A5	119
Barren River Lake, res., Ky., U.S.	D3	94
Barre Plains, Ma., U.S.	B3	98
Barretos, Braz.	C3	56
Barrett, Mn., U.S.	E3	100
Barrett, W.V., U.S.	D3	125
Barretts Hill, hill, Ma., U.S.	g9	98
Barrhead, Alta.	B3	68
Barrhead, Scot., U.K.	E4	13
Barrhill, Scot., U.K.	E4	13
Barrie, Ont.	C5	73
Barrie Island, i., Ont.	B2	73
Barrière, B.C.	D7	69
Barrier Bay, b., Ant.	C21	7
Barrier Lake, l., Sask.	E4	75
Barrier Range, mts., Austl.	F7	50
Barrigada, Guam	L10	52
Barrington, N.S.	F4	71
Barrington, Il., U.S.	A5	90
Barrington, N.H., U.S.	D4	106
Barrington, N.J., U.S.	D2	107
Barrington, R.I., U.S.	D5	116
Barrington, stm., R.I., U.S.	C5	116
Barrington Lake, l., Man.	A1	70
Barrington Passage, N.S.	F4	71
Barrington Tops, mtn., Austl.	F8	51
Barro Alto, Braz.	B5	56
Barron, Wi., U.S.	C2	126
Barron, co., Wi., U.S.	C2	126
Barronett, Wi., U.S.	C2	126
Barron Lake, Mi., U.S.	G4	99
Barrouaillie, St. Vin.	U26	65
Barrow, Arg.	B4	54
Barrow, Ak., U.S.	A8	79
Barrow, i., Austl.	D2	50
Barrow, stm., Ire.	D3	10
Barrow, Point, c., Ak., U.S.	A8	79
Barrow-in-Furness, Eng., U.K.	F4	13
Barrow Strait, strt., N.W. Ter.	B14	66
Barrowsville, Ma., U.S.	C5	98
Barruelo de Santullán, Spain	A3	22
Barry (Vale of Glamorgan), Wales, U.K.	C4	12
Barry, Il., U.S.	D2	90
Barry, co., Mi., U.S.	F5	99
Barry, co., Mo., U.S.	E4	102
Barryton, Mi., U.S.	E5	99
Barryville, N.Y., U.S.	D6	109
Bārsi, India	C5	36
Barsinghausen, Ger.	A4	19
Barstow, Ca., U.S.	E5	82
Barstow, Tx., U.S.	D1	120
Bar-sur-Aube, Fr.	C6	16
Bartelso, Il., U.S.	E4	90
Barth, Ger.	A6	18
Barth, Fl., U.S.	u14	86
Bartholomew, co., In., U.S.	F6	91
Bartholomew, Bayou, stm., U.S.	D4	81
Bartibog Bridge, N.B.	B4	71
Bartica, Guy.	A3	59
Bartin, Tur.	B9	40
Bartle Frere, Mount, mtn., Austl.	C8	50
Bartlesville, Ok., U.S.	A6	113
Bartlett, Il., U.S.	*k8	90
Bartlett, Ks., U.S.	E8	93
Bartlett, Ne., U.S.	C7	104
Bartlett, N.H., U.S.	B4	106
Bartlett, N.D., U.S.	A7	111
Bartlett, Oh., U.S.	C4	112
Bartlett, Tn., U.S.	B2	119
Bartlett, Tx., U.S.	D4	120
Bartlett Cove, Ak., U.S.	k22	79
Bartlett Reservoir, res., Az., U.S.	D4	80
Bartletts Ferry Dam, U.S.	C4	87
Bartletts Harbour, Newf.	C3	72
Bartley, Ne., U.S.	D5	104
Bartolomeu Dias, Moz.	B6	49
Barton, Vt., U.S.	B4	122
Barton, Ar., U.S.	C5	81
Barton, Md., U.S.	k12	97
Barton, Oh., U.S.	B5	112
Barton, Vt., U.S.	B4	122
Barton, co., Ks., U.S.	D4	93
Barton, co., Mo., U.S.	D3	102
Barton, stm., Vt., U.S.	B4	122
Bartonsville, Vt., U.S.	E3	122
Barton-upon-Humber, Eng., U.K.	A7	12
Bartonville, Il., U.S.	C4	90
Bartoszyce, Pol.	A6	26
Bartow, Ga., U.S.	D4	87
Bartow, Fl., U.S.	E5	86
Barú, Volcán, vol., Pan.	F6	62
Baruun-Urt, Mong.	B7	31
Barvenkovo, Sov. Un.	G11	27
Barview, Or., U.S.	*D2	114
Barwāni, India	F5	37
Barwick, Ga., U.S.	F3	87
Barwon, stm., Austl.	E8	50
Barybino, Sov. Un.	n17	27
Barycz, stm., Pol.	C4	26
Basalt, Co., U.S.	B3	83
Basalt, Id., U.S.	F6	89
Basalt, Nv., U.S.	E3	105
Basankusu, Zaire	A2	48
Basbula, Sov. Un.	E6	28
Basco, Phil.	A6	34
Basco, Il., U.S.	C2	90
Bascom, Fl., U.S.	B1	86
Bascom, Oh., U.S.	A2	112
Bascuñán, Cabo, c., Chile	E1	55
Basehor, Ks., U.S.	k16	93
Basekpio, Zaire	A3	48
Basel, Switz.	E3	18
Basel-Land, state, Switz.	B3	20
Basel-Stadt, state, Switz.	B3	20
Bashan Lake, l., Ct., U.S.	D6	84
Bashaw, Alta.	C4	68
Bashi, Al., U.S.	D2	78
Bashi Channel, strt., Asia	A6	34
Basiad Bay, b., Phil.	o14	34
Basilan Island, i., Phil.	D6	34
Basildon, Eng., U.K.	C8	12
Basile, La., U.S.	D3	95
Basilicata (Lucania), prov., Italy	D6	23
Basílio, Braz.	E2	56
Basin, Mt., U.S.	D4	103
Basin, Wy., U.S.	B4	127
Basinger, Fl., U.S.	E5	86
Basingstoke, Eng., U.K.	E6	10
Basin Harbor, Vt., U.S.	C2	122
Basin Lake, l., Sask.	E3	75
Baška, Yugo.	C2	23
Baskahegan Lake, l., Me., U.S.	C5	96
Baskatong, Réservoir, res., Que.	k11	74
Baskerville, Ky., U.S.	C2	94
Baskin, Fl., U.S.	p10	86
Baskin, La., U.S.	B4	95
Basking Ridge, N.J., U.S.	B3	107
Basoko, Zaire	A3	48
Basongo, Zaire	B4	48
Basora, Punt, c., Neth. Ant.	H17	65
Basque Provinces, hist. reg., Spain	A4	22
Basra (Al Baṣrah), Iraq	B4	38
Bas-Rhin, dept., Fr.	F7	17
Bassano, Alta.	D4	68
Bassano del Grappa, Italy	B3	23
Bassas da India, rf., Reu.	B6	49
Basse-Pointe, Mart.	S10	65
Basse Santa Su, Gam.	D2	45
Basse-Terre, Guad.	I14	64
Basseterre, St. C.-N.	H13	64
Basse-Terre, i., Guad.	Q8	65
Bassett, Ar., U.S.	B5	81
Bassett, Ia., U.S.	A5	92
Bassett, Ks., U.S.	E8	93
Bassett, Ne., U.S.	B6	104
Bassett, Va., U.S.	D3	123
Bassett, Wi., U.S.	n11	126
Bassett Creek, stm., Al., U.S.	D2	78
Bassett Peak, mtn., Az., U.S.	E5	80
Bassfield, Ms., U.S.	D4	101
Bass Harbor, Me., U.S.	D4	96
Bassikounou, Maur.	C3	45
Bass Islands, is., Oh., U.S.	A3	112
Bass Lake, In., U.S.	B4	91
Bass River, N.S.	D6	71
Bass Strait, strt., Austl.	n15	50
Bassum, Ger.	F2	15
Basswood, Man.	D1	70
Basswood Lake, l., Mn., U.S.	B7	100
Båstad, Swe.	B6	15
Bastak, Iran	H7	39
Bastelica, Fr.	D9	23
Basti, India	G9	37
Bastia, Fr.	C2	23
Bastian, Va., U.S.	C1	123
Bastogne, Bel.	B6	16
Bastrop, La., U.S.	B4	95
Bastrop, Tx., U.S.	D4	120
Bastrop, co., Tx., U.S.	D4	120
Basturäsk, Swe.	E9	14
Basyūn, Eg.	D2	41
Bata, Eq. Gui.	E1	46
Bataan Peninsula, pen., Phil.	o13	34
Batabanó, Cuba	C2	64
Batabanó, Golfo de, b., Cuba	C2	64
Bataguaçu, Braz.	C2	56
Batala, India	B6	36
Batamay, Sov. Un.	C15	29
Batang, China	E7	30
Batangafo, Cen. Afr. Rep.	D3	46
Batangas, Phil.	C6	34
Batan Islands, is., Phil.	A6	34
Bátaszék, Hung.	B4	24
Batatais, Braz.	C3	56
Batavia, Arg.	A3	54
Batavia, Ar., U.S.	A2	81
Batavia, Il., U.S.	B5	90
Batavia, Ia., U.S.	D5	92
Batavia, N.Y., U.S.	C2	109
Batavia, Oh., U.S.	C1	112
Batataysk, Sov. Un.	H12	27
Batchelor, La., U.S.	D4	95
Batchelor Bay, b., N.C., U.S.	B6	110
Batchtown, Il., U.S.	D3	90
Batdambang, Camb.	C2	34
Bateman, Sask.	H2	75
Bates, Ar., U.S.	C1	81
Bates, Or., U.S.	C8	114
Bates, co., Mo., U.S.	C3	102
Batesburg, S.C., U.S.	D4	117
Batesland, S.D., U.S.	D3	118
Bates City, Mo., U.S.	C3	102
Batesville, Ar., U.S.	B4	81
Batesville, In., U.S.	F7	91
Batesville, Ms., U.S.	A4	101
Batesville, Oh., U.S.	C4	112
Batesville, Tx., U.S.	E3	120
Bath, N.B.	C2	71
Bath, Ont.	C8	73
Bath, Jam.	F16	65
Bath, Eng., U.K.	E5	10
Bath, Il., U.S.	C3	90
Bath, In., U.S.	E8	91
Bath, Me., U.S.	E3	96
Bath, Mi., U.S.	F6	99
Bath, N.H., U.S.	B3	106
Bath, N.Y., U.S.	C3	109
Bath, N.C., U.S.	B6	110
Bath, Pa., U.S.	E11	115
Bath, S.C., U.S.	D4	117
Bath, S.D., U.S.	B7	118
Bath, co., Ky., U.S.	B6	94
Bath, co., Va., U.S.	B3	123
Baṭḥ al Ghūl, Jord.	C7	41
Bathgate, Scot., U.K.	E5	13
Bathgate, N.D., U.S.	A8	111
Bathinda, India	B5	37
Bathsheba, Barb.	J15	64
Bath Springs, Tn., U.S.	B3	119
Bathurst, Austl.	F8	50
Bathurst, N.B.	B4	71
Bathurst, i., Austl.	B5	50
Bathurst, Cape, c., N.W. Ter.	B7	66
Bathurst Inlet, N.W. Ter.	C11	66
Bathurst Inlet, b., N.W. Ter.	C11	66
Bathurst Island, i., N.W. Ter.	m31	66
Batié, Burkina	E4	45
Batiki, i., Fiji	H15	52
Batiscan, Que.	C5	74
Batiscan, stm., Que.	B5	74
Batkanu, S.L.	E2	45
Batman, Tur.	D13	40
Batna, Alg.	B6	44
Batoche, Sask.	E2	75
Baton Rouge, La., U.S.	D4	95
Batouri, Cam.	E2	46
Batson, Tx., U.S.	D5	120
Batsto, N.J., U.S.	D3	107
Batsto, stm., N.J., U.S.	D3	107
Battambang see Batdambang, Camb.	C2	34
Batten Kill, stm., U.S.	E2	122
Battery Park, Va., U.S.	k14	123
Batticaloa, Sri L.	G7	36
Battiest, Ok., U.S.	C7	113
Battle, stm., Can.	F11	66
Battleboro, N.C., U.S.	A5	110
Battle Creek, Sask.	H1	75
Battle Creek, Ia., U.S.	B2	92
Battle Creek, Mi., U.S.	F5	99
Battle Creek, Ne., U.S.	C8	104
Battle Creek, stm., N.A.	B7	103
Battleford, Sask.	E1	75
Battle Ground, In., U.S.	C4	91
Battle Ground, Wa., U.S.	D3	124
Battle Lake, Mn., U.S.	D3	100
Battlement Mesa, mtn., Co., U.S.	B2	83
Battle Mountain, Nv., U.S.	C5	105
Battle Mountain, mtn., Wy., U.S.	B3	127
Battles, Ms., U.S.	D5	101
Battleview, N.D., U.S.	A3	111
Battonya, Hung.	B5	24
Battrum, Sask.	G1	75
Batu, mtn., Eth.	D4	47
Batuc, Mex.	B2	63
Batu Islands, is., Indon.	F1	34
Batumi, Sov. Un.	E7	29
Baturaja, Indon.	F2	34
Baturino, Sov. Un.	B11	28
Baturité, Braz.	B3	57
Bat Yam, Isr.	g9	41
Baubau, Indon.	G6	34
Bauchi, Nig.	D6	45
Baudette, Mn., U.S.	B4	100
Baudó, Serranía de, mts., Col.	C3	60
Bauer, Ut., U.S.	C3	121
Bauer Coulee, val., Wa., U.S.	B7	124
Baugé, Fr.	D3	16
Bauld, Cape, c., Newf.	C4	72
Bauma, Switz.	B6	21
Baume-les-Dames, Fr.	D7	16
Baunei, Italy	D2	23
Baures, Bol.	B3	55
Baures, stm., Bol.	B3	55
Bauru, Braz.	C3	56
Bautzen, Ger.	C7	18
Bauxite, Ar., U.S.	C3	81
Bavaria, Ks., U.S.	D6	93
Bavaria, hist. reg., Ger.	D5	18
Bavarian Alps, mts., Eur.	B7	20
Bavay, Fr.	A5	16
Bave, Nosy, i., Madag.	f9	49
Bawal, Alta.	C4	68
Baxdo, Som.	D6	47
Baxian, China	E7	32
Baxley, Ga., U.S.	E4	87
Baxter, Ia., U.S.	C4	92
Baxter, Mn., U.S.	D4	100
Baxter, Tn., U.S.	C8	119
Baxter, W.V., U.S.	B4	125
Baxter, co., Ar., U.S.	A3	81
Baxter Springs, Ks., U.S.	E9	93
Baxterville, Ms., U.S.	D4	101
Bay, Ar., U.S.	B5	81
Bay, prov., Som.	D6	47
Bay, co., Fl., U.S.	u16	86
Bay, co., Mi., U.S.	E6	99
Bay, Laguna de, l., Phil.	o13	34
Bay al Kabīr, Wādī, val., Libya	C2	43
Bayambang, Phil.	o13	34
Bayamo, Cuba	D5	64
Bayamón, P.R.	G11	64
Bayan, China	C3	28
Bayanaul, Sov. Un.	C9	28
Bayanga, Cen. Afr. Rep.	E3	46
Bayanhongor, Mong.	B6	31
Bayan Obo, China	C3	32
Bayard, Ia., U.S.	C3	92
Bayard, Ne., U.S.	C2	104
Bayard, N.M., U.S.	E1	108
Bayard, W.V., U.S.	B5	125
Bayberry, N.Y., U.S.	B4	109
Bayboro, N.C., U.S.	B6	110
Bayble, Scot., U.K.	B2	13
Baybay, Phil.	o13	34
Bayburt, Tur.	B13	40
Bay Center, Wa., U.S.	C2	124
Bay City, Mi., U.S.	E7	99
Bay City, Or., U.S.	B3	114
Bay City, Tx., U.S.	E5	120
Bay City, Wi., U.S.	D1	126
Baydarata, Bay, Sov. Un.	B22	3
Bay de Verde, Newf.	D5	72
Baydhabo, Som.	E5	47
Baydrag, stm., Mong.	B6	31
Bayern, state, Ger.	D6	19
Bayeux, Fr.	C3	16
Bayfield, Ont.	D3	73
Bayfield, Co., U.S.	D3	83
Bayfield, Wi., U.S.	B3	126
Bayfield, co., Wi., U.S.	B2	126
Bay Head, N.J., U.S.	*C4	107
Bayındır, Tur.	C6	25
Baykonyr see Leninsk, Sov. Un.	D7	28
Bay L'Argent, Newf.	E4	72
Baylis, Il., U.S.	D2	90
Baylor, co., Tx., U.S.	C3	120
Baymak, Sov. Un.	C5	28
Bay Mills Indian Reservation, Mi., U.S.	B6	99
Bay Minette, Al., U.S.	E2	78
Bayombong, Phil.	n17	34
Bayonet Point, Fl., U.S.	*D4	86
Bayonne, Fr.	F3	16
Bayonne, N.J., U.S.	B4	107
Bayou Bodcau Reservoir, res., La., U.S.	B2	95
Bayou Cane, La., U.S.	*E5	95
Bayou D'Arbonne Lake, res., La., U.S.	B2	95
Bayou George, Fl., U.S.	u16	86
Bayou Goula, La., U.S.	D4	95
Bayou La Batre, Al., U.S.	E1	78
Bayou Pines, Fl., U.S.	*E4	86
Bay Point, c., S.C., U.S.	G7	117
Bayport, N.S.	E5	71
Bay Port, Mi., U.S.	E7	99
Bayport, Mn., U.S.	E6	100
Bayport, N.Y., U.S.	n15	109
Bayramiç, Tur.	C6	25
Bayreuth, Ger.	D5	18
Bay Ridge, Md., U.S.	C5	97
Bayrischzell, Ger.	B7	20
Bay Roberts, Newf.	E5	72
Bays, Lake of, l., Ont.	B5	73
Bay Saint Louis, Ms., U.S.	E4	101
Bayshore, Mi., U.S.	C5	99
Bay Shore, N.Y., U.S.	q10	109
Bayshore Gardens, Fl., U.S.	q10	86
Bayside, Tx., U.S.	E4	120
Bayside, Wi., U.S.	m12	126
Bays Mountains, mtn., Tn., U.S.	n14	119
Bays Mountains, mtn., Tn., U.S.	C10	119
Bay Springs, Ms., U.S.	D4	101
Baysun, Sov. Un.	B13	39
Bayt al Faqīh, Yemen	C5	47
Bayt Dajan, Isr. Occ.	g12	41
Baytīllū, Isr. Occ.	h11	41
Bayt Jālā, Isr. Occ.	C7	41
Baytown, Tx., U.S.	E5	120
Bay Trail, Sask.	E3	75
Bayview, Al., U.S.	f7	78
Bayview, Id., U.S.	B2	89
Bay View, Mi., U.S.	C6	99
Bay View, Oh., U.S.	A3	112
Bays Wharf, Al., U.S.	E2	78
Bayville, N.J., U.S.	D4	107
Bayville, N.Y., U.S.	*E7	109
Bay Village, Oh., U.S.	h9	112
Bayville, De., U.S.	G5	85
Bayville, N.J., U.S.	D4	107
Bazán, Spain	A5	22
Bazaruto, Ilha do, i., Moz.	B6	49
Bazemore, Al., U.S.	B2	78
Bazhong, China	E8	31
Bazile Mills, Ne., U.S.	B8	104
Bazmān, Kūh-e, mtn., Iran	G10	39
Baztán, Spain	A5	22
Beach, N.D., U.S.	C1	111
Beach, Il., U.S.	h9	90
Beachburg, Ont.	B8	73
Beach City, Oh., U.S.	B4	112
Beach Haven, N.J., U.S.	D4	107
Beach Haven, Pa., U.S.	D9	115
Beach Haven Crest, N.J., U.S.	D4	107
Beach Haven Inlet, b., N.J., U.S.	D4	107
Beach Haven Terrace, N.J., U.S.	D4	107
Beach Lake, Pa., U.S.	C11	115
Beach Pond, l., U.S.	C8	84
Beachport, Austl.	H3	51
Beachville, Md., U.S.	D5	97
Beachwood, N.J., U.S.	D4	107
Beachwood, Oh., U.S.	*h10	112
Beachy Head, c., Eng., U.K.	D8	12
Beacon, Ia., U.S.	C5	92
Beacon, N.Y., U.S.	D7	109
Beacon Falls, Ct., U.S.	D3	84
Beacon Hill, Fl., U.S.	C1	86
Beaconsfield, Que.	q19	74
Beaconsfield, Eng., U.K.	e10	113
Beacon Square, Fl., U.S.	*D4	86
Beadle, Sask.	F1	75
Beadle, co., S.D., U.S.	C7	118
Beagle, Ok., U.S.	D9	93
Beagle, Canal, strt., S.A.	h12	54
Beale, Cape, c., B.C.	E5	69
Beale Air Force Base, mil., Ca., U.S.	C3	82
Beallsville, Oh., U.S.	C4	112
Beallsville, Pa., U.S.	F1	115
Bealeton, Va., U.S.	B5	123
Beals, Me., U.S.	D5	96
Bean Lake, Mo., U.S.	B3	102
Bean Station, Tn., U.S.	C10	119
Bear, De., U.S.	B3	85
Bear, i., Nor.	B13	128
Bear, stm., U.S.	B3	121
Bear Creek, Al., U.S.	A2	78
Bear Creek, Wi., U.S.	D5	126
Bear Creek, stm., U.S.	A1	78
Bear Creek, stm., Az., U.S.	E4	114
Bear Creek, stm., Co., U.S.	E8	127
Bear Creek, stm., Or., U.S.	D3	81
Bear Creek, stm., Wy., U.S.	D4	127
Bearpaw Mountains, mts., Mt., U.S.	B7	103
Bear Peninsula, pen., Ant.	B1	7
Bear Pond Mountains, mts., Md., U.S.	A2	97
Bear River, N.S.	E4	71
Bear River City, Ut., U.S.	B3	121
Bear Spring, Tn., U.S.	A4	119
Bear Swamp, sw., Ma., U.S.	h11	98
Bear Tooth Pass, Wy., U.S.	B3	127
Beartooth Range, mts., U.S.	E7	103
Bear Town, Ms., U.S.	D3	101
Beartown Mountain, mtn., Va., U.S.	f10	123
Beas de Segura, Spain	C4	22
Beason, Il., U.S.	C4	90
Beata, Cabo, c., Dom. Rep.	F8	64
Beaton, B.C.	D9	69
Beatrice, Al., U.S.	D2	78
Beatrice, Ne., U.S.	D9	104
Beatrice, Zimb.	A5	49
Beattie, Ks., U.S.	C7	93
Beatty, Nv., U.S.	G5	105
Beatty, Or., U.S.	E5	114
Beattyville, Ky., U.S.	C6	94
Beatyestown, N.J., U.S.	B3	107
Beaucaire, Fr.	F6	16
Beauce, co., Que.	C7	74
Beauceville-Est, Que.	C7	74
Beaucoup Creek, stm., La., U.S.	B3	95
Beaufort, Malay.	D5	34
Beaufort, Mo., U.S.	C6	102
Beaufort, N.C., U.S.	C6	110
Beaufort, S.C., U.S.	G6	117
Beaufort, co., N.C., U.S.	B5	110
Beaufort, co., S.C., U.S.	G6	117
Beaufort Island, i., Ant.	e38	7
Beaufort Marine Corps Air Station, mil., S.C., U.S.	F6	117
Beaufort Sea, N.A.	B7	66
Beaufort West, S. Afr.	D3	49
Beaugency, Fr.	D4	16
Beauharnois, Que.	D4	74
Beauharnois, co., Que.	D3	74
Beau Lake, l., Me., U.S.	A3	96
Beaulieu, Que.	n17	74
Beaulieu, Mn., U.S.	C3	100
Beauly, Scot., U.K.	C4	13
Beauly, stm., Scot., U.K.	C4	13
Beaumaris, Wales, U.K.	A3	12
Beaumont, Bel.	D4	17
Beaumont, Alta.	C4	68
Beaumont, Newf.	D4	72
Beaumont, Que.	C6	74
Beaumont, Fr.	F4	16
Beaumont, Ca., U.S.	*F5	82
Beaumont, Ks., U.S.	E7	93
Beaumont, Ms., U.S.	D5	101
Beaumont, Tx., U.S.	D5	120
Beaumont [-sur-Oise], Fr.	E2	17
Beaune, Fr.	D6	16
Beauport, Que.	n17	74
Beaupré, Que.	B7	74
Beauregard, Ms., U.S.	D4	101
Beauregard, co., La., U.S.	D2	95
Beaurivage, Que.	C6	74
Beausejour, Man.	D3	70
Beauty, Ky., U.S.	C7	94
Beauvais, Fr.	C5	16
Beauval, Sask.	B2	75
Beauvallon, Alta.	C5	68
Beaver, Ak., U.S.	B10	79
Beaver, Ar., U.S.	*A2	81
Beaver, Oh., U.S.	C3	112
Beaver, Ok., U.S.	A1	113
Beaver, Or., U.S.	B3	114
Beaver, Pa., U.S.	E1	115
Beaver, Ut., U.S.	E3	121
Beaver, W.V., U.S.	D3	125
Beaver, Wi., U.S.	D5	126
Beaver, co., Ok., U.S.	e10	113
Beaver, co., Pa., U.S.	E1	115
Beaver, co., Ut., U.S.	E2	121
Beaver, stm., Can.	B2	75
Beaver, stm., N.Y., U.S.	A5	109
Beaver, stm., R.I., U.S.	E2	116
Beaver, stm., U.S.	E2	113
Beaver Brook, stm., N.H., U.S.	E4	106
Beaver City, Ne., U.S.	D6	104
Beaver Creek, B.C.	E5	69
Beavercreek, Oh., U.S.	C1	112
Beaver Creek, stm., Sask.	F2	75
Beaver Creek, stm., U.S.	E4	104
Beaver Creek, stm., Co., U.S.	B7	83
Beaver Creek, stm., Ia., U.S.	e8	92
Beaver Creek, stm., Ky., U.S.	C7	94
Beaver Creek, stm., Md., U.S.	A2	97
Beaver Creek, stm., Mt., U.S.	B9	103
Beaver Creek, stm., Ne., U.S.	B9	104
Beaver Creek, stm., N.D., U.S.	C1	111
Beaver Creek, stm., Oh., U.S.	C1	112
Beaver Creek, stm., Ok., U.S.	C3	113
Beaver Creek, stm., Tn., U.S.	m13	119
Beaver Creek, stm., Wy., U.S.	D4	127
Beaver Creek Mountains, mts., Al., U.S.	B3	78
Beaver Crossing, Ne., U.S.	D8	104
Beaverdale, Pa., U.S.	F4	115
Beaver Dam, Az., U.S.	A2	80
Beaver Dam, Wi., U.S.	E5	126
Beaverdam, Oh., U.S.	B2	112
Beaverdam, Va., U.S.	C5	123
Beaverdam Branch, stm., De., U.S.	F3	85
Beaverdam Lake, res., Wi., U.S.	E5	126
Beaverdell, B.C.	E8	69
Beaver Falls, N.Y., U.S.	B5	109
Beaver Falls, Pa., U.S.	E1	115
Beaverhead, co., Mt., U.S.	E3	103
Beaverhead Mountains, mts., U.S.	E4	103
Beaverhill Lake, l., Alta.	C4	68
Beaver Hill Lake, l., Man.	B4	70
Beaver Island, i., Mi., U.S.	C5	99
Beaver Lake, l., Alta.	B5	68

Name — Map Ref. — Page

Beaver Lake, res., Ar., U.S. — A2 81
Beaverlick, Ky., U.S. — k13 94
Beaverlodge, Alta. — B1 68
Beaver Meadows, Pa., U.S. — E10 115
Beaver Point, Co., U.S. — A5 83
Beaver Ridge, mtn., Tn., U.S. — D9 119
Beaver Run Reservoir, res., Pa., U.S. — F2 115
Beaver Springs, Pa., U.S. — E7 115
Beavertail Point, c., R.I., U.S. — F4 116
Beaverton, Ont. — C5 73
Beaverton, Al., U.S. — B1 78
Beaverton, Mi., U.S. — E6 99
Beaverton, Or., U.S. — B4 114
Beavertown, Pa., U.S. — E7 115
Beaverville, Il., U.S. — C6 90
Beazley, Ar., U.S. — A3 54
Bebedouro, Braz. — C3 56
Bebra, Ger. — C4 19
Bécancour, Que. — C5 74
Bécancour, stm., Que. — C6 74
Beccles, Eng., U.K. — B9 12
Bečej, Yugo. — C5 24
Becerreá, Spain — A2 22
Béchar, Alg. — C4 44
Becharof Lake, l., Ak., U.S. — D8 79
Bechyně, Czech. — D9 19
Beckemeyer, Il., U.S. — E4 90
Becker, Mn., U.S. — E5 100
Becker, Ms., U.S. — B5 101
Becker, co., Mn., U.S. — D3 100
Becket, Ma., U.S. — B1 98
Beckham, co., Ok., U.S. — B2 113
Beckley, W.V., U.S. — D3 125
Beckum, Ger. — B3 19
Beckville, Tx., U.S. — C5 120
Beckwith Creek, stm., La., U.S. — D2 95
Becky Peak, mtn., Nv., U.S. — D7 105
Bedale, Eng., U.K. — F7 13
Bédarieux, Fr. — F5 16
Bedburg, Ger. — C1 19
Bederkesa, Ger. — E2 15
Bedford, N.S. — E6 71
Bedford, Que. — D5 74
Bedford, Eng., U.K. — D6 10
Bedford, In., U.S. — G5 91
Bedford, Ia., U.S. — D3 92
Bedford, Ky., U.S. — B4 94
Bedford, Ma., U.S. — B5 98
Bedford, Mo., U.S. — F5 99
Bedford, Mo., U.S. — B4 102
Bedford, N.H., U.S. — A4 112
Bedford, Oh., U.S. — A4 112
Bedford, Pa., U.S. — F4 115
Bedford, Tx., U.S. — *n9 120
Bedford, Va., U.S. — C3 123
Bedford, Wy., U.S. — D2 127
Bedford, co., Pa., U.S. — G4 115
Bedford, co., Tn., U.S. — B5 119
Bedford, co., Va., U.S. — C3 123
Bedford Heights, Oh., U.S. — *h9 112
Bedford Hills, N.Y., U.S. — D7 109
Bedfordshire, co., Eng., U.K. — B7 12
Bedias, Tx., U.S. — D5 120
Bedlington, Eng., U.K. — C6 10
Bedminster, N.J., U.S. — B3 107
Bedourie, Austl. — B2 51
Bedrock, Co., U.S. — C2 83
Bedzin, Pol. — g10 26
Bee, Ne., U.S. — C8 104
Bee, co., Tx., U.S. — E4 120
Beebe, Ar., U.S. — B4 81
Beebe Plain, Vt., U.S. — A4 122
Bee Branch, Ar., U.S. — B3 81
Beech Bluff, Tn., U.S. — B3 119
Beech Bottom, W.V., U.S. — f8 125
Beech Creek, Ky., U.S. — C2 94
Beech Creek, Pa., U.S. — D6 115
Beecher, Il., U.S. — B6 90
Beecher, Mi., U.S. — E7 99
Beecher City, Il., U.S. — D5 90
Beechey Head, c., B.C. — h12 69
Beech Fork, stm., Ky., U.S. — C4 94
Beech Grove, Ar., U.S. — A5 81
Beech Grove, In., U.S. — E5 91
Beech Grove, Ky., U.S. — C2 94
Beechgrove, Tn., U.S. — B5 119
Beech Island, S.C., U.S. — E4 117
Beechwood, N.B. — C2 71
Beechwood, Mi., U.S. — h12 98
Beechy, Sask. — G2 75
Beecroft Head, c., Austl. — B5 51
Beedeville, Ar., U.S. — B4 81
Beef Island, i., V.I., Br. — e8 119
Beef Island, i., V.I., Br. — B6 65
Beek, Neth. — D5 17
Beeler, Ks., U.S. — D3 93
Beelitz, Ger. — A7 19
Beemer, Ne., U.S. — C9 104
Beenleigh, Austl. — C9 51
Bee Ridge, Fl., U.S. — q11 86
Beersheba (Be'er Sheva'), Isr. — B3 38
Beersheba Springs, Tn., U.S. — D8 119
Beersville, N.B. — C4 71
Beeskow, Ger. — B7 18
Beesleys Point, N.J., U.S. — E3 107
Beethoven Peninsula, pen., Ant. — B5 7
Beeton, Ont. — C5 73
Beetzendorf, Ger. — F5 15
Beeville, Tx., U.S. — E4 120
Befale, Zaire — A3 48
Beg, Lough, l., N. Ire., U.K. — C5 11
Bega, Austl. — G8 50
Beggs, Ok., U.S. — B5 113
Begicheva, i., Sov. Un. — C12 29
Béhague, Pointe, c., Fr. Gu. — B4 59
Behāla (South Suburban), India — *D8 36
Behbahān, Iran — C5 38
Behm Canal, strt., Ak., U.S. — n24 79
Behshahr, Iran — C6 39
Bei'an, China — B10 31
Beigi, Eth. — D3 47
Beihai, China — G6 31
Beijing (Peking), China — C8 31
Beili, China — C8 35
Beingries, Ger. — D6 19
Beinamar, Chad — D3 46
Beipiao, China — *C9 31
Beira, Moz. — A5 49
Beira, hist. reg., Port. — D2 22
Beirne, Ar., U.S. — D2 81
Beirut (Bayrūt), Leb. — B3 38
Beiseker, Alta. — D4 68
Beitbridge, Zimb. — B6 49
Beius, Rom. — B6 24
Béja, Tun. — B6 44
Béja, Port. — B6 44

Bejaïa (Bougie), Alg. — B6 44
Béjar, Spain — B3 22
Bejou, Mn., U.S. — C3 100
Bejuco, Pan. — F8 62
Bekabad, Sov. Un. — G22 8
Bekdash, Sov. Un. — E4 28
Békés, Hung. — B5 24
Békéscsaba, Hung. — B5 24
Bekily, Madag. — h9 49
Bela, India — E8 37
Bela, Pak. — C4 36
Bela Crkva, Yugo. — C5 24
Belaga, Malay. — E4 34
Bel Air, Md., U.S. — A5 97
Bel Aire, Ks., U.S. — g12 93
Bel Air Estates, Ct., U.S. — D7 84
Belalcázar, Spain — C3 22
Bel Alton, Md., U.S. — D4 97
Belampalli, India — E6 36
Bélanger, stm., Man. — C3 70
Bélanger, stm., Sask. — B2 75
Bela, Port. — f9 22
Belaya, stm., Sov. Un. — B4 28
Belaya Glina, Sov. Un. — H13 27
Belaya Tserkov, Sov. Un. — G8 27
Belcamp, Md., U.S. — B5 97
Belcher, Ky., U.S. — C7 94
Belcher, La., U.S. — B2 95
Belcherāgh, Afg. — D12 39
Belcher Islands, is., N.W. Ter. — E17 66
Belchertown, Ma., U.S. — B3 98
Belcourt, N.D., U.S. — A6 111
Belcoville, N.J., U.S. — E3 107
Belden, Ms., U.S. — A5 101
Belden, Ne., U.S. — B8 104
Belden, N.D., U.S. — A3 111
Belding, Mi., U.S. — E5 99
Belecke, Ger. — B3 19
Beled Weyne, Som. — E6 47
Belém (Pará), Braz. — D4 55
Belem, Port. — f9 22
Belén, Para. — D4 55
Belen, Ms., U.S. — A3 101
Belen, N.M., U.S. — C3 108
Belen, Ur. — E1 56
Belén de Escobar, Arg. — g7 54
Belenkoye, Sov. Un. — q20 17
Belev, Sov. Un. — E11 27
Belfair, Wa., U.S. — B3 124
Belfast, N. Ire., U.K. — C4 10
Belfast, Me., U.S. — D3 96
Belfast, N.Y., U.S. — C2 109
Belfast, N.C., U.S. — B5 110
Belfast, Oh., U.S. — C2 112
Belfast, Tn., U.S. — B5 119
Belfast Lough, b., N. Ire., U.K. — C6 11
Belfield, N.D., U.S. — C2 111
Belford, Eng., U.K. — E7 13
Belford, N.J., U.S. — C4 107
Belfort, Fr. — D7 16
Belfort, N.Y., U.S. — B5 109
Belfort, ter., Fr. — B2 20
Belfry, Ky., U.S. — C7 94
Belfry, Mt., U.S. — E8 103
Belgaum, India — C3 36
Belgica Mountains, mts., Ant. — B16 7
Belgium, Il., U.S. — C6 90
Belgium, Wi., U.S. — E6 126
Belgium, ctry., Eur. — B6 16
Belgorod, Sov. Un. — F11 27
Belgorod-Dnestrovskiy, Sov. Un. — H8 27
Belgrade, Mn., U.S. — E3 100
Belgrade, Mo., U.S. — D7 102
Belgrade, Mt., U.S. — E5 103
Belgrade, Ne., U.S. — C7 104
Belgrade (Beograd), Yugo. — C5 24
Belgrade Lakes, Me., U.S. — D3 96
Belgreen, Al., U.S. — A2 78
Belhaven, N.C., U.S. — B6 110
Belice, stm., Italy — F4 23
Beli Lom, stm., Bul. — D8 24
Belington, W.V., U.S. — B5 125
Belitung, i., Indon. — F3 34
Belize, ctry., N.A. — D7 63
Belize City, Belize — B3 62
Belize [City], Belize — D7 63
Bel'kovo, Sov. Un. — B11 33
Belknap, Il., U.S. — F5 90
Belknap, co., N.H., U.S. — C3 106
Belknap Crater, crat., Or., U.S. — C5 114
Belknap Mountain, mtn., N.H., U.S. — C4 106
Belkovski, stm., Sov. Un. — B11 29
Bell, Ca., U.S. — *E4 82
Bell, Fl., U.S. — C4 86
Bell, co., Ky., U.S. — D6 94
Bell, co., Tx., U.S. — D4 120
Bella Bella, B.C. — C3 69
Bellac, Fr. — D4 16
Bella Coola, B.C. — C4 69
Bella Coola, stm., B.C. — C4 69
Bellagio, Italy — D5 20
Bellaire, Fl., U.S. — *m8 86
Bellaire, Ks., U.S. — C5 93
Bellaire, Mi., U.S. — D5 99
Bellaire, Oh., U.S. — B5 112
Bellaire, Tx., U.S. — r14 120
Bellano, Italy — D7 21
Bellary, India — E4 36
Bella Unión, Ur. — E1 56
Bella Vista, Arg. — E4 55
Bella Vista, Arg. — E4 55
Bella Vista, Para. — E1 56
Bella Vista, Ar., U.S. — A1 81
Bella Vista, Braz. — C1 56
Bellbrook, Oh., U.S. — C1 112
Bell Buckle, Tn., U.S. — B5 119
Bell City, La., U.S. — D3 95
Bell City, Mo., U.S. — D8 102
Belle, Mo., U.S. — C6 102
Belle, stm., La., U.S. — k9 95
Belleair, Fl., U.S. — p10 86
Belle Bay, Newf. — E4 72
Belle Center, Oh., U.S. — B2 112
Belle Chasse, La., U.S. — E5 95
Bellechasse, co., Que. — C7 74
Belle Creek, Mt., U.S. — E11 103
Belledune, N.B. — B4 71
Belleek, N. Ire., U.K. — C3 11
Bellefontaine, Ms., U.S. — B4 101
Bellefontaine, Oh., U.S. — B2 112

Bellefontaine Neighbors, Mo., — *f13 102
Bellefonte, Ar., U.S. — A2 81
Bellefonte, De., U.S. — *A3 85
Bellefonte, Pa., U.S. — E6 115
Belle Fourche, S.D., U.S. — C2 118
Belle Fourche, stm., U.S. — C3 118
Belle Fourche Reservoir, res., S.D., U.S. — C2 118
Bellegarde, Fr. — D6 16
Belle Glade, Fl., U.S. — F6 86
Belle Haven, Va., U.S. — C7 123
Belleherbe, Fr. — B2 21
Belle Hôtesse, mtn., Guad. — Q8 65
Belle Isle, Fl., U.S. — D5 86
Belle Isle, i., Newf. — C3 72
Belle Isle, Strait of, strt., Newf. — C3 72
Belle Isle Creek, N.B. — D4 71
Belle Mead, N.J., U.S. — C3 107
Belle Meade, Tn., U.S. — g10 119
Belle Mina, Al., U.S. — A3 78
Belleoram, Newf. — E4 72
Belleplain, N.J., U.S. — E3 107
Belle-Plaine, Sask. — G3 75
Belle Plaine, Ia., U.S. — C5 92
Belle Plaine, Ks., U.S. — E6 93
Belle Plaine, Mn., U.S. — F5 100
Belle Rive, Il., U.S. — E5 90
Belle River, Ont. — E2 73
Belle Rose, La., U.S. — D4 95
Belle Union, In., U.S. — E4 91
Belle Valley, Oh., U.S. — C4 112
Belle Vernon, Pa., U.S. — F2 115
Belleview, Fl., U.S. — C4 86
Belleview, Mo., U.S. — D7 102
Belle View, Va., U.S. — g12 123
Belleville, N.S. — F4 71
Belleville, Ont. — C7 73
Belleville, Fr. — D6 16
Belleville, Il., U.S. — E4 90
Belleville, Ks., U.S. — C6 93
Belleville, Mi., U.S. — p15 99
Belleville, N.J., U.S. — B4 107
Belleville, N.Y., U.S. — B4 109
Belleville, Pa., U.S. — E6 115
Belleville, R.I., U.S. — E4 116
Belleville, W.V., U.S. — B3 125
Belleville, Wi., U.S. — F4 126
Belleville Pond, l., R.I., U.S. — E4 116
Belleville [-sur-Meuse], Fr. — C6 17
Bellevue, Id., U.S. — F4 89
Bellevue, Ia., U.S. — B7 92
Bellevue, Ky., U.S. — h13 94
Bellevue, Mi., U.S. — F5 99
Bellevue, Ne., U.S. — C10 104
Bellevue, Oh., U.S. — A3 112
Bellevue, Pa., U.S. — F1 115
Bellevue, Tx., U.S. — C3 120
Bellevue, Wa., U.S. — e11 124
Bellflower, Ca., U.S. — n12 82
Bellflower, Il., U.S. — C5 90
Bellflower, Mo., U.S. — B6 102
Bell Gardens, Ca., U.S. — *n12 82
Bellingham, Eng., U.K. — F6 13
Bellingham, Ma., U.S. — B5 98
Bellingham, Mn., U.S. — E2 100
Bellingham, Wa., U.S. — A3 124
Bellingshausen Sea, Ant. — B3 7
Bellinzona, Switz. — E4 18
Bell Island, i., Newf. — E5 72
Bell Island, i., Newf. — C4 72
Bellmawr, N.J., U.S. — D2 107
Bellmead, Tx., U.S. — *D4 120
Bellmont, Il., U.S. — E6 90
Bellmore, In., U.S. — E3 91
Bellmore, N.Y., U.S. — *m15 109
Bello, Col. — B2 60
Bellows Falls, Vt., U.S. — E4 122
Bellport, N.Y., U.S. — n16 109
Bell Ranch, N.M., U.S. — B5 108
Bells, Tn., U.S. — B2 119
Bells Corners, Ont. — h12 73
Bellshill, Scot., U.K. — *E4 13
Bells Creek, stm., W.V., U.S. — m13 125
Belluno, Italy — A4 23
Bellview, N.M., U.S. — C6 108
Bell Ville, Arg. — A4 54
Bellville, Ga., U.S. — D5 87
Bellville, Oh., U.S. — B3 112
Bellville, Tx., U.S. — E4 120
Bellwood, Al., U.S. — D4 78
Bellwood, Il., U.S. — k9 90
Bellwood, Pa., U.S. — E5 115
Bellwood, Va., U.S. — n18 123
Belly, stm., N.A. — E4 68
Belmar, N.J., U.S. — C4 107
Bélmez, Spain — C3 22
Belmond, Ia., U.S. — B4 92
Belmont, Man. — E2 70
Belmont, Ca., U.S. — h8 82
Belmont, La., U.S. — C2 95
Belmont, Ma., U.S. — g11 98
Belmont, Ms., U.S. — A5 101
Belmont, N.H., U.S. — D4 106
Belmont, N.Y., U.S. — C2 109
Belmont, N.C., U.S. — B1 110
Belmont, Oh., U.S. — B4 112
Belmont, Tx., U.S. — k8 120
Belmont, Vt., U.S. — E3 122
Belmont, W.V., U.S. — B3 125
Belmont, Wi., U.S. — F3 126
Belmont, co., Oh., U.S. — C4 112
Belmonte, Braz. — C9 57
Belmont Heights, Ut., U.S. — *C4 121
Belmopan, Belize — D7 63
Belmore, Oh., U.S. — A2 112
Belmullet, Ire. — C1 11
Belo, Madag. — e8 49
Beloeil, Que. — D4 74
Belogorsk, Sov. Un. — D15 29
Belo Horizonte, Braz. — E7 57
Beloit, Ks., U.S. — C5 93
Beloit, Oh., U.S. — B5 112
Beloit, Wi., U.S. — F4 126
Beloit North, Wi., U.S. — F4 126
Belokany, Sov. Un. — B16 40

Belomorsk, Sov. Un. — C6 29
Belopolye, Sov. Un. — F10 27
Beloretsk, Sov. Un. — D8 29
Belovo, Sov. Un. — E26 8
Beloye, Lake, l., Sov. Un. — A11 27
Belozersk, Sov. Un. — B11 27
Belp, Switz. — C4 21
Belper, Eng., U.K. — A6 12
Belpre, Ks., U.S. — E4 93
Belpre, Oh., U.S. — C4 112
Belshaw, In., U.S. — B3 91
Belspring, Va., U.S. — C2 123
Belt, Mt., U.S. — C6 103
Belt Creek, stm., Mt., U.S. — C6 103
Belted Range, mts., Nv., U.S. — F5 105
Belterra, Braz. — D7 55
Belton, Mo., U.S. — C3 102
Belton, S.C., U.S. — B3 117
Belton, Tx., U.S. — D4 120
Belton Lake, res., Tx., U.S. — D4 120
Beltra, Ire. — C3 11
Beltrami, co., Mn., U.S. — C2 100
Beltrami, co., Mn., U.S. — B3 100
Beltsville, Md., U.S. — B4 97
Beltsy, Sov. Un. — H6 27
Belukha, Mount, mtn., Sov. Un. — E11 29
Belumut, mtn., Malay. — L5 35
Beluran, Malay. — D5 34
Belvedere, Ga., U.S. — *C2 87
Belvedere, S.C., U.S. — D4 117
Belvedere Marittimo, Italy — E5 23
Belvedere Park, Ga., U.S. — *h8 87
Belvidere, De., U.S. — *B3 85
Belvidere, Il., U.S. — A5 90
Belvidere, Ks., U.S. — E4 93
Belvidere, Ne., U.S. — D8 104
Belvidere, N.J., U.S. — B2 107
Belvidere, N.C., U.S. — A6 110
Belvidere, S.D., U.S. — D4 118
Belvidere, Tn., U.S. — B5 119
Belvidere Center, Vt., U.S. — B3 122
Belvidere Mountain, mtn., Vt., U.S. — B3 122
Belview, Mn., U.S. — F3 100
Belvue, Ks., U.S. — C7 93
Belwood, Ont. — D4 73
Belyando, stm., Austl. — D8 50
Belyy, Sov. Un. — D9 27
Belyy Bom, Sov. Un. — E26 8
Belyy Island, i., Sov. Un. — B9 29
Belyye Berega, Sov. Un. — E10 27
Belyy Yar, Sov. Un. — B11 28
Belzig, Ger. — A7 19
Belzoni, Ms., U.S. — B3 101
Bembézar, stm., Spain — C3 22
Bement, Il., U.S. — D5 90
Bemidji, Mn., U.S. — C4 100
Bemidji, Lake, l., Mn., U.S. — C4 100
Bemis, Tn., U.S. — B3 119
Bemis, W.V., U.S. — C5 125
Bemiss, Ga., U.S. — F3 87
Bemus Point, N.Y., U.S. — C1 109
Bena, Mn., U.S. — C4 100
Benāb, Iran — C3 39
Benabarre, Spain — A6 22
Benalla, Austl. — G8 50
Benalto, Alta. — C3 68
Benares see Vārānasi, India — H9 37
Benátky [nad Jizerou], Czech. — n18 26
Benavente, Spain — A3 22
Benavides, Tx., U.S. — F3 120
Benbane Head, c., N. Ire., U.K. — B5 11
Benbecula, i., Scot., U.K. — C1 13
Ben Bolt, Tx., U.S. — F3 120
Benbow, Fl., U.S. — F5 86
Benbrook Lake, res., Tx., U.S. — *n9 120
Benbush, W.V., U.S. — C5 125
Benchland, Mt., U.S. — C7 103
Ben Davis Point, c., N.J., U.S. — E2 107
Bendeleben, Mount, mtn., Ak., U.S. — B7 79
Bender Beyla, Som. — D7 47
Bendersville, Pa., U.S. — G7 115
Bendigo, Austl. — G7 50
Bendorf, Ger. — C2 19
Bene Beraq, Isr. — g10 41
Benedict, Ks., U.S. — E8 93
Benedict, Md., U.S. — C4 97
Benedict, Ne., U.S. — C8 104
Benedict, Mount, mtn., Newf. — g10 72
Benedicta, Me., U.S. — C4 96
Benenitra, Madag. — h9 49
Beneraird, hill, Scot., U.K. — F3 13
Benešov, Czech. — D3 26
Bénestroff, Fr. — F6 17
Benevento, Italy — D5 23
Benevolence, Ga., U.S. — E2 87
Benewah, co., Id., U.S. — B2 89
Benezett, Pa., U.S. — D5 115
Benfeld, Fr. — A3 20
Bengal, hist. reg., Asia — D8 36
Bengal, Bay of, b., Asia — F8 36
Ben Gardane, Tun. — C7 44
Bengbu, China — C4 31
Benghazi (Banghāzī), Libya — C4 43
Bengkalis, i., Indon. — E2 34
Bengkulu, Indon. — F2 34
Bengo, dept., Ang. — C1 48
Bengough, Sask. — H3 75
Benguela, Ang. — D1 48
Benguela, dept., Ang. — D1 48
Benham, Ky., U.S. — D7 94
Ben Hill, co., Ga., U.S. — E3 87
Beni, Zaire — A4 48
Beni, dept., Bol. — B2 55
Béni Abbès, Alg. — C4 44
Benicarló, Spain — B6 22
Benicia, Ca., U.S. — C2 82
Benicito, stm., Bol. — B2 55
Beni Mellal, Mor. — C3 44
Benin, ctry., Afr. — E6 45
Benin, Bight of, Afr. — E6 45
Benin City, Nig. — E6 45
Benisa, Spain — C6 22
Beni Saf, Alg. — B4 44
Benito, Man. — D1 70
Benito Juárez, Arg. — B5 54
Benjamin, Tx., U.S. — C3 120
Benjamin Constant, Braz. — B3 58
Benkelman, Ne., U.S. — D4 104
Benkovac, Yugo. — C2 25
Benld, Il., U.S. — D4 90

Ben Lomond, Ar., U.S. — D1 81
Ben Lomond, Ca., U.S. — *D2 82
Benmore, Lake, res., N.Z. — P12 51
Bennet, Ne., U.S. — D9 104
Bennett, Co., U.S. — B6 83
Bennett, Ia., U.S. — C7 92
Bennett, N.C., U.S. — B3 110
Bennett, Wi., U.S. — B2 126
Bennett, co., S.D., U.S. — D4 118
Bennett Creek, stm., Md., U.S. — B3 97
Bennett Island, i., Sov. Un. — B18 29
Bennett Lake, l., Man. — C3 70
Bennettsbridge, Ire. — E4 11
Bennettsville, S.C., U.S. — B8 117
Bennington, Id., U.S. — G7 89
Bennington, In., U.S. — G7 91
Bennington, Ks., U.S. — C6 93
Bennington, Ne., U.S. — g12 104
Bennington, N.H., U.S. — D3 106
Bennington, Ok., U.S. — C5 113
Bennington, Vt., U.S. — F2 122
Bennington, co., Vt., U.S. — E2 122
Bennion, Ut., U.S. — *C4 121
Benns Church, Va., U.S. — k14 123
Benoit, Ms., U.S. — B2 101
Benoit, Wi., U.S. — B2 126
Benoits Cove, Newf. — D2 72
Bénoué (Benue), stm., Afr. — E7 45
Benoy, Chad — D3 46
Benque Viejo, Belize — B3 62
Bensalem, Pa., U.S. — *F12 115
Bensberg, Ger. — C2 19
Bensenville, Il., U.S. — B6 90
Bensheim, Ger. — D4 18
Bensley, Va., U.S. — C5 123
Benson, Sask. — H4 75
Benson, Az., U.S. — F5 80
Benson, Il., U.S. — C4 90
Benson, La., U.S. — C2 95
Benson, Md., U.S. — A5 97
Benson, Mn., U.S. — E3 100
Benson, N.C., U.S. — B4 110
Benson, co., N.D., U.S. — A6 111
Bens Run, W.V., U.S. — B3 125
Bent, co., Co., U.S. — D7 83
Bentheim, Ger. — A2 19
Bentinck, i., Burma — G2 34
Bentiu, Sud. — D2 47
Bentley, Alta. — C3 68
Bentley, Ks., U.S. — E6 93
Bentley, La., U.S. — C3 95
Bentley, Mi., U.S. — E6 99
Bentley, N.D., U.S. — C3 111
Bentley, Ok., U.S. — C6 113
Bentley Creek, Pa., U.S. — C8 115
Bentley Springs, Md., U.S. — A4 97
Bentleyville, Pa., U.S. — F1 115
Benton, N.B. — D2 71
Benton, Ar., U.S. — C3 81
Benton, Ca., U.S. — D5 82
Benton, Il., U.S. — E5 90
Benton, Ia., U.S. — D3 92
Benton, Ks., U.S. — E6 93
Benton, Ky., U.S. — f9 94
Benton, La., U.S. — B2 95
Benton, Me., U.S. — D3 96
Benton, Mo., U.S. — D8 102
Benton, Pa., U.S. — D9 115
Benton, Tn., U.S. — D9 119
Benton, Wi., U.S. — F3 126
Benton, co., Ar., U.S. — A1 81
Benton, co., In., U.S. — C3 91
Benton, co., Ia., U.S. — B5 92
Benton, co., Mn., U.S. — E4 100
Benton, co., Ms., U.S. — A4 101
Benton, co., Mo., U.S. — C4 102
Benton, co., Or., U.S. — C3 114
Benton, co., Tn., U.S. — A3 119
Benton, co., Wa., U.S. — C6 124
Benton City, Mo., U.S. — B6 102
Benton City, Wa., U.S. — C6 124
Benton Harbor, Mi., U.S. — F4 99
Benton Heights, Mi., U.S. — F4 99
Bentonia, Ms., U.S. — C3 101
Benton Ridge, Oh., U.S. — A2 112
Bentonville, Ar., U.S. — A1 81
Bentonville, Oh., U.S. — D2 112
Bentonville, Va., U.S. — B4 123
Bentree, W.V., U.S. — m13 125
Bentung, Malay. — L6 35
Benue (Bénoué), stm., Afr. — E7 45
Benwood, W.V., U.S. — f8 125
Benxi, China — C7 31
Benzie, co., Mi., U.S. — D4 99
Benzonia, Mi., U.S. — D4 99
Beo, Indon. — E7 34
Béoumi, I.C. — E4 45
Beowawe, Nv., U.S. — C5 105
Beppu, Japan — J5 33
Beqa, Fiji — I15 52
Beqa Passage, strt., Fiji — I14 52
Bequia, i., St. Vin. — U26 64
Berach, stm., India — G6 37
Berati, Alb. — B2 25
Berau Bay, b., Indon. — F8 34
Berbera, Som. — C4 47
Berbérati, Cen. Afr. Rep. — E3 46
Berbice, stm., Guy. — C6 59
Berceto, Italy — E6 20
Bercher, Switz. — C3 21
Berchtesgaden, Ger. — E6 19
Berck, Fr. — B4 16
Berclair, Tx., U.S. — E4 120
Berdichev, Sov. Un. — G6 27
Berdsk, Sov. Un. — D24 8
Berdyansk, Sov. Un. — H11 27
Berea, Ky., U.S. — C5 94
Berea, Ne., U.S. — B3 104
Berea, Oh., U.S. — A4 112
Berea, S.C., U.S. — B3 117
Berebere, Indon. — E7 34
Beregovo, Sov. Un. — G2 27
Berens, stm., Can. — C3 70
Berens Island, i., Man. — C3 70
Berens River, Man. — C3 70
Beresford, N.B. — B4 71
Beresford, S.D., U.S. — D9 118
Berettyóújfalu, Hung. — B5 24
Berezina, stm., Sov. Un. — E8 27
Berezna, Sov. Un. — F8 27
Berezniki, Sov. Un. — D8 29

Berezovo, Sov. Un. — C9 29
Berg, Nor. — q27 14
Berga, Spain — A6 22
Berga, Swe. — B8 15
Bergama, Tur. — C6 25
Bergamasque Alps, mts., Italy — D5 20
Bergamo, Italy — B2 23
Bergedorf, Ger. — B5 18
Bergen, Ger. — F3 15
Bergen, Nor. — G1 14
Bergen, N.Y., U.S. — B3 109
Bergen, N.D., U.S. — A5 111
Bergen, co., N.J., U.S. — A4 107
Bergen aan Zee, Neth. — B4 17
Bergen [auf Rügen], Ger. — A6 18
Bergenfield, N.J., U.S. — B4 107
Bergen see Mons, Bel. — B5 16
Bergen op Zoom, Neth. — B6 16
Berger, Mo., U.S. — C6 102
Bergerac, Fr. — E4 16
Bergheim, Tx., U.S. — h7 120
Bergholz, Oh., U.S. — B5 112
Bergisch Gladbach, Ger. — C3 18
Bergkamen, Ger. — B2 19
Bergland, Mi., U.S. — m12 99
Bergoo, W.V., U.S. — C4 125
Bergstrom Air Force Base, mil., Tx., U.S. — D4 120
Bergton, Va., U.S. — B4 123
Berguent, Mor. — C4 44
Bergün, Switz. — C8 21
Bering Sea — D32 128
Bering Strait, strt. — C6 79
Berino, N.M., U.S. — E3 108
Berislav, Sov. Un. — H9 27
Berja, Spain — D4 22
Berkane, Mor. — C4 44
Berkeley, Ont. — C4 73
Berkeley, Ca., U.S. — D2 82
Berkeley, Il., U.S. — *k9 90
Berkeley, Mo., U.S. — f13 102
Berkeley, R.I., U.S. — B4 116
Berkeley, co., S.C., U.S. — E8 117
Berkeley, co., W.V., U.S. — B6 125
Berkeley, Cabo, c., Ec. — f5 58
Berkeley Heights, N.J., U.S. — B4 107
Berkeley Springs, W.V., U.S. — B6 125
Berkey, Oh., U.S. — A2 112
Berkley, Ia., U.S. — C3 92
Berkley, Ma., U.S. — C5 98
Berkley, Mi., U.S. — F7 99
Berkner Island, i., Ant. — B7 7
Berkovitsa, Bul. — F9 24
Berks, co., Pa., U.S. — F9 115
Berkshire, Ma., U.S. — A1 98
Berkshire, N.Y., U.S. — C4 109
Berkshire, co., Eng., U.K. — C6 12
Berkshire, co., Ma., U.S. — B1 98
Berkshire Estates, Ct., U.S. — D2 84
Berkshire Hills, hills, Ma., U.S. — B1 98
Berland, stm., Alta. — C1 68
Berleburg, Ger. — B3 19
Berlenga Islands, is., Port. — C1 22
Berlin, Ger. — B6 18
Berlin, Ct., U.S. — C5 84
Berlin, Ga., U.S. — E3 87
Berlin, Md., U.S. — D7 97
Berlin, Ma., U.S. — B4 98
Berlin, N.H., U.S. — B4 106
Berlin, N.J., U.S. — D3 107
Berlin, N.Y., U.S. — C7 109
Berlin, N.D., U.S. — C7 111
Berlin, Pa., U.S. — G4 115
Berlin, Wi., U.S. — E5 126
Berlin, Mount, mtn., Ant. — B35 7
Berlin Corners, Vt., U.S. — C3 122
Berlin Heights, Oh., U.S. — A3 112
Berlin Lake, res., Oh., U.S. — A4 112
Berlin Mountain, mtn., Ma., U.S. — A1 98
Berlin [West], state, Ger. — F7 15
Bermejo, stm., Arg. — A4 54
Bermejo, stm., S.A. — A5 54
Bermeo, Spain — A4 22
Bermuda, dep., N.A. — F14 61
Bermuda, i., N.A. — p20 64
Bern, Switz. — E3 18
Bernalillo, N.M., U.S. — B3 108
Bernalillo, co., N.M., U.S. — C3 108
Bernam, stm., Malay. — L6 35
Bernard, Ia., U.S. — B7 92
Bernard, Mi., U.S. — D5 99
Bernard Lake, l., Ont. — B5 73
Bernardo, N.M., U.S. — C3 108
Bernardsville, N.J., U.S. — B3 107
Bernasconi, Arg. — B4 54
Bernau [am Chiemsee], Ger. — E6 19
Bernau [bei Berlin], Ger. — B6 18
Bernay, Fr. — C4 16
Bernburg, Ger. — C6 18
Berndorf, Aus. — E8 19
Berne, N.Y., U.S. — C6 109
Berneray, i., Scot., U.K. — C1 13
Bernese Alps, mts., Switz. — E3 18
Bernice, La., U.S. — B3 95
Bernice, Ok., U.S. — A7 113
Bernie, Mo., U.S. — E8 102
Bernina, Piz, mtn., Eur. — C5 20
Bernina Pass, Switz. — C5 20
Bernville, Pa., U.S. — F9 115
Beroroha, Madag. — h9 49
Beroun, Czech. — D3 26
Berounka, stm., Czech. — C3 26
Berrechid, Mor. — C4 44
Berre [-l'Étang], Fr. — F6 16
Berri, Austl. — F7 50
Berrien, co., Ga., U.S. — E3 87
Berrien, co., Mi., U.S. — G4 99
Berrien Springs, Mi., U.S. — G4 99
Berry, Al., U.S. — B2 78
Berry, Ky., U.S. — B5 94
Berry, hist. reg., Fr. — D4 16
Berrydale, Fl., U.S. — u14 86
Berryessa, Lake, res., Ca., U.S. — C2 82
Berry Hill, Tn., U.S. — g10 119
Berryton, Ga., U.S. — B1 87
Berryton, Ks., U.S. — m14 93
Berryville, Ar., U.S. — A2 81
Berryville, Va., U.S. — A5 123
Bersenbrück, Ger. — B7 17
Bershad, Sov. Un. — G7 27
Bertha, Mn., U.S. — D3 100
Berthier, co., Que. — C4 74

Index

Name	Map Ref.	Page
Berthierville, Que.	C4	74
Berthold, N.D., U.S.	A4	111
Berthoud, Co., U.S.	A5	83
Berthoud Pass, Co., U.S.	B5	83
Bertie, co., N.C., U.S.	A5	110
Bertoua, Cam.	E2	46
Bertraghboy Bay, b., Ire.	D2	11
Bertram, Tx., U.S.	D4	120
Bertrand, Mi., U.S.	*G5	99
Bertrand, Mo., U.S.	E8	102
Bertrand, Ne., U.S.	D6	104
Bertrandville, La., U.S.	E5	95
Bertrix, Bel.	C6	16
Berwick, N.S.	D5	71
Berwick, Il., U.S.	C3	90
Berwick, Ia., U.S.	e8	92
Berwick, La., U.S.	E4	95
Berwick, Me., U.S.	E2	96
Berwick, N.D., U.S.	A5	111
Berwick, Pa., U.S.	D9	115
Berwick-upon-Tweed, Eng., U.K.	C6	10
Berwind, W.V., U.S.	D3	125
Berwyn, Alta.	A2	68
Berwyn, Il., U.S.	k9	90
Berwyn, Ne., U.S.	C6	104
Berwyn, Pa., U.S.	o20	115
Beryl, Ut., U.S.	F2	121
Besalampy, Madag.	g8	49
Besançon, Fr.	D7	16
Besar Hantu, mtn., Malay.	K4	35
Beskid Mountains, mts., Eur.	C6	44
Beskra, Alg.	B2	75
Besnard Lake, l., Sask.	B2	75
Besni, Tur.	D11	40
Bessèges, Fr.	E6	16
Bessemer, Al., U.S.	B3	78
Bessemer, Mi., U.S.	n11	99
Bessemer, Pa., U.S.	E1	115
Bessemer City, N.C., U.S.	B1	110
Bessie, Ok., U.S.	B3	113
Best, Tx., U.S.	D2	120
Bestfield, De., U.S.	*B3	85
Bestobe, Sov. Un.	C8	28
Betafo, Madag.	g9	49
Betanzos, Spain	A1	22
Bétaré Oya, Cam.	D2	46
Betatakin Ruin, hist., Az., U.S.	A5	80
Bet Guvrin, Isr.	C6	41
Bethalto, Il., U.S.	E3	90
Bethanien, Nmb.	C2	49
Bethany, Ont.	C6	73
Bethany, Ct., U.S.	D4	84
Bethany, Il., U.S.	D5	90
Bethany, In., U.S.	F5	91
Bethany, La., U.S.	B1	95
Bethany, Mo., U.S.	A3	102
Bethany, Oh., U.S.	n13	112
Bethany, Ok., U.S.	B4	113
Bethany, W.V., U.S.	A4	125
Bethany see Al 'Ayzarīyah, Isr. Occ.	h12	41
Bethany Beach, De., U.S.	F5	85
Bethel, Ak., U.S.	C7	79
Bethel, Ct., U.S.	D2	84
Bethel, De., U.S.	F3	85
Bethel, Ky., U.S.	B6	94
Bethel, Me., U.S.	D2	96
Bethel, Mn., U.S.	B5	102
Bethel, N.C., U.S.	B5	110
Bethel, Oh., U.S.	D1	112
Bethel, Ok., U.S.	C7	113
Bethel, Pa., U.S.	F9	115
Bethel, Vt., U.S.	D3	122
Bethel Acres, Ok., U.S.	#C2	113
Bethel Park, Pa., U.S.	k14	115
Bethel Springs, Tn., U.S.	B3	119
Bethera, S.C., U.S.	E8	117
Bethesda, Wales, U.K.	A3	12
Bethesda, Md., U.S.	C3	97
Bethesda, Oh., U.S.	B4	112
Bethlehem (Bayt Laḥm), Isr. Occ.	G10	40
Bethlehem, S. Afr.	C4	49
Bethlehem, Ct., U.S.	C3	84
Bethlehem, Ga., U.S.	C3	87
Bethlehem, In., U.S.	G7	91
Bethlehem, Md., U.S.	C6	97
Bethlehem, N.H., U.S.	B3	106
Bethlehem, Pa., U.S.	E11	115
Bethlehem, W.V., U.S.	f8	125
Bethlehem Junction, N.H., U.S.	B3	106
Bethpage, N.Y., U.S.	*E7	109
Bethpage, Tn., U.S.	A5	119
Bethulie, S. Afr.	G3	49
Bethune, Sask.	B5	16
Bethune, Fr.	B8	83
Bethune, Co., U.S.	C7	117
Bethune, S.C., U.S.		
Betico, i., N.Y., U.S.	R18	52
Betioky, Madag.	h8	49
Bet Nehemya, Isr.	h10	41
Betong, Thai.	D2	34
Betong, Thai.	B3	51
Betoota, Austl.		
Betpak-Dala, des., Sov. Un.	D7	28
Betroka, Madag.	h9	49
Bet She'an, Isr.	B7	41
Bet Shemesh, Isr.	C6	41
Betsiamites, Que.	k13	74
Betsiboka, stm., Madag.	g9	49
Betsie, Point, c., Mi., U.S.	D4	99
Betsy Layne, Ky., U.S.	C7	94
Bette, mtn., Libya	E3	43
Bettendorf, Ia., U.S.	C7	92
Betterton, Md., U.S.	B5	97
Bettiah, India	D10	37
Bettles Field, Ak., U.S.	B9	79
Bettsville, Oh., U.S.	A2	112
Bettyhill, Scot., U.K.	A4	10
Betūl, India	D6	36
Betwa, stm., India	D6	36
Betzdorf, Ger.	C2	19
Beulah, Al., U.S.	C4	78
Beulah, Co., U.S.	C6	83
Beulah, Mi., U.S.	D4	99
Beulah, Ms., U.S.	B3	101
Beulah, N.D., U.S.	B4	111
Beulah, Wy., U.S.	B8	127
Beulah, Lake, l., Ms., U.S.	B3	101
Beulaville, N.C., U.S.	C5	110
Beuthen see Bytom, Pol.	C5	26
B. Everett Jordan Lake, res., N.C., U.S.	B3	110
Beverley, Sask.	G1	75
Beverley, Eng., U.K.	D6	10
Beverley Head, c., Newf.	C6	93
Beverly, Eng., U.K.	D6	94
Beverly, Ky., U.S.	D6	94
Beverly, Ma., U.S.	A6	98
Beverly, N.J., U.S.	C3	107
Beverly, Oh., U.S.	C4	112
Beverly, Tn., U.S.	m14	119
Beverly, W.V., U.S.	C5	125
Beverly Hills, Ca., U.S.	m12	82
Beverly Hills, Mi., U.S.	*o15	99
Beverly Shores, In., U.S.	A4	91
Beverstedt, Ger.	E2	15
Beverwijk, Neth.	A6	16
Bewdley, Ont.	C6	73
Bex, Switz.	D3	21
Bexar, co., Tx., U.S.	E3	120
Bexhill-on-Sea, Eng., U.K.	D8	12
Bexley, Oh., U.S.	m11	112
Beya, Sov. Un.	E27	8
Beykoz, Tur.	H7	25
Beyla, Gui.	G4	45
Beylul, Eth.	C5	47
Beypazarı, Tur.	D8	40
Beyşehir, Tur.	D8	40
Beyşehir, Lake, l., Tur.	D8	40
Bezau, Aus.	C3	57
Bezerros, Braz.	C11	27
Bezhetsk, Sov. Un.	F5	16
Béziers, Fr.	D8	24
Bezons, Fr.	g9	16
Bhadrāchalam, India	I8	37
Bhadrak, India	G11	37
Bhag, Pak.	C4	36
Bhāgalpur, India	C8	36
Bhairab Bazar, Bngl.	E5	37
Bhakkar, Pak.	B5	36
Bhaktapur, Nepal	C8	36
Bhamo, Burma	D10	36
Bhandara, India	G7	37
Bharatpur, India	C6	36
Bharatpur, Nepal	D10	37
Bharūch, India	D5	36
Bhātpāra, India	D8	36
Bhāvnagar, India	D5	36
Bhāwānipatna, India	H9	37
Bheigeir, Beinn, hill, Scot., U.K.	E2	13
Bhilai (Bhilainagar), India	*D7	36
Bhilai, India	G8	37
Bhīlwāra, India	E5	37
Bhīma, stm., India	E6	36
Bhind, India	C6	37
Bhiwāni, India	C6	37
Bhola, Bngl.	F13	37
Bhopāl, India	D6	36
Bhor, India	E5	36
Bhubaneshwar, India	D8	36
Bhuj, India	D4	36
Bhumiphol (Yanhee) Dam, Thai.	D3	35
Bhusāwal, India	G5	37
Bhutan, ctry., Asia	C9	36
Bia, Mount, mtn., Laos	B2	34
Biabou, Zaire	A4	48
Biafort, Bight of, Afr.	E1	46
Biak, i., Indon.	F9	34
Biała Podlaska, Pol.	B7	26
Biała Przemsza, stm., Pol.	g11	26
Białogard (Belgard), Pol.	A4	26
Białystok, Pol.	B7	26
Bian, Bidean nam, mtn., Scot., U.K.	D4	13
Bianco, Italy	E6	23
Biankouma, I.C.	E3	45
Biarritz, Fr.	F3	16
Biasca, Switz.	C4	20
Bibā, Eg.	D6	43
Bibai, Japan	E10	33
Bibala, Ang.	D1	48
Bibb, co., Al., U.S.	C2	78
Bibb, co., Ga., U.S.	D3	87
Bibb City, Ga., U.S.	D2	87
Biberach, Ger.	D4	18
Biberist, Switz.	B4	21
Bibiani, Ghana	E4	45
Bible Grove, Il., U.S.	E5	90
Bible Hill, Tn., U.S.	B3	119
Bic, Que.	A9	74
Bic, Île du, i., Que.	A9	74
Bicaz, Lake, res., Rom.	B8	24
Bicester, Eng., U.K.	C6	12
Biche, Lac la, l., Alta.	B4	68
Bichl, Ger.	B7	20
Bickerton, Cape, c., Ant.	C26	7
Bickett Knob, mtn., W.V., U.S.	C5	125
Bickle Knob, mtn., W.V., U.S.	C5	125
Bickleton, Wa., U.S.	D5	124
Bickmore, W.V., U.S.	C3	125
Bicknell, In., U.S.	G3	91
Bicknell, Ut., U.S.	E4	121
Bicoli, Indon.	E7	34
Bicske, Hung.	B4	24
Bid, India	H5	37
Bīdar, India	E6	36
Biddeford, Me., U.S.	E2	96
Biddiyā, Isr. Occ.	g11	41
Biddle, Mt., U.S.	E11	103
Bideford, Eng., U.K.	E4	10
Bidwell, Oh., U.S.	D3	112
Bidwell, Mount, mtn., Ca., U.S.	B3	82
Bié, dept., Ang.	D2	48
Bieber, Ca., U.S.	B3	82
Biebrza, stm., Pol.	B7	26
Biedenkopf, Ger.	E3	18
Biel, Switz.	E3	21
Biel, Switz.	B3	20
Biel (Bienne), Lake, l., Switz.	B3	20
Bielawa, Pol.	C4	26
Bield, Man.	D1	70
Bielefeld, Ger.	B4	18
Biella, Italy	B2	23
Bielsk Podlaski, Pol.	B7	26
Bielsko-Biała, Pol.	D5	26
Bielstein, Sask.	H4	75
Bien Hoa, Viet.	G7	35
Bienville, Ca., U.S.	B3	95
Bienville, co., La., U.S.	B2	95
Bienville, Lac, l., Que.	g12	74
Bierawka, stm., Pol.	g9	26
Bieruń Nowy, Pol.	g10	26
Bieruń Stary, Pol.	g10	26
Biese, stm., Ger.	F5	15
Bièvre, Fr.	E4	19
Bièvres, Fr.	g9	16
Biferno, stm., Italy	D5	23
Big, stm., Sask.	D2	75
Big, stm., Mo., U.S.	c7	102
Big, Tur.	C7	40
Big A Mountain, mtn., Va., U.S.	e9	123
Big Bald, Mn., U.S.	C2	100
Big Bald, mtn., Ga., U.S.	f10	110
Big Bald Mountain, mtn., N.B.	B3	71
Big Baldy, mtn., Id., U.S.	E3	89
Big Baldy Mountain, mtn., Mt., U.S.	D6	103
Big Bay, Mi., U.S.	B3	99
Big Bay, b., N.Z.	P11	51
Big Bay De Noc, b., Mi., U.S.	C4	99
Big Bayou, stm., Ar., U.S.	D4	81
Big Bear, Ca., U.S.	*E5	82
Big Bear City, Ca., U.S.	*E5	82
Big Beaver, Sask.	H3	75
Bigbee Valley, Ms., U.S.	B5	101
Big Belt Mountains, mts., Mt., U.S.	D5	103
Big Bend, Ca., U.S.	B3	82
Big Bend, La., U.S.	C4	95
Big Bend, Wi., U.S.	n11	126
Big Bend Dam, S.D., U.S.	C6	118
Big Bend National Park, Tx., U.S.	E1	120
Big Bend Reservoir, res., Alta.	C3	68
Big Birch Lake, l., Mn., U.S.	E4	100
Big Black, stm., Me., U.S.	B3	96
Big Black, stm., Ms., U.S.	C3	101
Big Blue, stm., In., U.S.	E6	91
Big Bone, Ky., U.S.	k13	94
Big Bow, Ks., U.S.	E2	93
Big Burro Mountains, mts., N.M., U.S.	E1	108
Big Butt, mtn., Tn., U.S.	C11	119
Big Cabin, Ok., U.S.	A6	113
Big Cabin Creek, stm., Ok., U.S.	A6	113
Big Canyon, val., Tx., U.S.	D1	120
Big Chino Wash, val., Az., U.S.	B3	80
Big Clifty, Ky., U.S.	C3	94
Big Coal, stm., W.V., U.S.	C3	125
Big Corney Bayou, stm., U.S.	D3	81
Big Costilla Peak, mtn., N.M., U.S.	A4	108
Big Creek, B.C.	D6	69
Big Creek, Ca., U.S.	D4	82
Big Creek, Id., U.S.	D3	89
Big Creek, Ky., U.S.	C6	94
Big Creek, Ms., U.S.	B4	101
Big Creek, W.V., U.S.	C2	125
Big Creek, stm., B.C.	D6	69
Big Creek, stm., Ar., U.S.	C5	81
Big Creek, stm., In., U.S.	H2	91
Big Creek, stm., In., U.S.	G7	91
Big Creek, stm., Ks., U.S.	D4	93
Big Creek, stm., La., U.S.	B4	95
Big Creek, stm., Ms., U.S.	D5	101
Big Creek, stm., Mo., U.S.	C3	102
Big Creek, stm., Tn., U.S.	C11	119
Big Creek Lake, res., Al., U.S.	E1	78
Big Creek Peak, mtn., Id., U.S.	E5	89
Big Cypress Indian Reservation, Fl., U.S.	F5	86
Big Cypress Swamp, sw., Fl., U.S.	F5	86
Big Darby Creek, stm., Oh., U.S.	C2	112
Big Delta, Ak., U.S.	C10	79
Big Dry Creek, stm., Mt., U.S.	C10	103
Big Duke Dam, N.C., U.S.	B2	110
Big Eau Pleine, stm., Wi., U.S.	D3	126
Big Eau Pleine Reservoir, res., Wi., U.S.	D3	126
Bigej Island, i., Marsh Is.	S17	52
Big Elk Creek, stm., Md., U.S.	A6	97
Bigelow, Ar., U.S.	B3	81
Bigelow, Mn., U.S.	G3	100
Bigelow, Mo., U.S.	A2	102
Bigelow, Mount, mtn., Me., U.S.	C2	96
Big Escambia Creek, stm., U.S.	D2	78
Big Falls, Mn., U.S.	B5	100
Big Flat, Ar., U.S.	A3	81
Big Flat Mountain, mtn., Va., U.S.	B4	123
Big Flats, N.Y., U.S.	C4	109
Bigfoot, Tx., U.S.	E3	120
Bigfork, Mn., U.S.	C5	100
Bigfork, Mt., U.S.	B2	103
Big Fork, stm., Mn., U.S.	B5	100
Big Frog Mountain, mtn., Tn., U.S.	D9	119
Biggar, Sask.	E1	75
Biggar, Scot., U.K.	F5	13
Bigger Island, i., Marsh Is.	S17	52
Biggers, Ar., U.S.	A5	81
Biggersville, Ms., U.S.	A5	101
Biggleswade, Eng., U.K.	B7	12
Biggs, Ca., U.S.	C3	82
Biggs, Or., U.S.	B6	114
Biggsville, Il., U.S.	C2	90
Big Gull Lake, l., Ont.	C8	73
Big Gully Creek, stm., Sask.	D1	75
Big Hatchet Peak, mtn., N.M., U.S.	F1	108
Big Hole, stm., Mt., U.S.	E4	103
Big Hole National Battlefield, hist., Mt., U.S.	E3	103
Bighorn, Mt., U.S.	D9	103
Big Horn, Wy., U.S.	B5	127
Big Horn, co., Mt., U.S.	E9	103
Big Horn, co., Wy., U.S.	B4	127
Bighorn, stm., U.S.	B6	76
Bighorn Canyon National Recreation Area, U.S.	E8	103
Bighorn Lake, res., U.S.	E8	103
Bighorn Mountains, mts., U.S.	B5	127
Big Horn Mountains, mts., Az., U.S.	D2	80
Bigi Island, i., Marsh Is.	S17	52
Big Island, Va., U.S.	C3	123
Big Island, i., N.W. Ter.	D18	66
Big Island, i., Ont.	C7	33
Big Kandiyohi Lake, l., Mn., U.S.	F4	100
Big Knob, mtn., Pa., U.S.	F6	115
Big Knob, mtn., Pa., U.S.	f9	123
Big Lake, Mn., U.S.	E5	100
Big Lake, Tx., U.S.	D1	120
Big Lake, l., Me., U.S.	C5	96
Bigler, Pa., U.S.	E5	115
Biglerville, Pa., U.S.	G7	115
Big Lookout Mountain, mtn., Or., U.S.	C9	114
Big Lost, stm., Id., U.S.	F5	89
Big Moose, N.Y., U.S.	B6	109
Big Mossy Point, c., Man.	B2	105
Big Mountain, mtn., Nv., U.S.	B3	105
Big Muddy, stm., Il., U.S.	F4	90
Big Muddy Creek, stm., Mt., U.S.	B12	103
Big Muddy Lake, l., Sask.	H3	75
Big Nemaha, stm., Ne., U.S.	D10	104
Bignona, Sen.	D1	45
Big North Mountain, mts., Va., U.S.	A4	123
Bigonville, Lux.	E5	17
Big Otter, stm., Va., U.S.	C3	123
Big Pine, Ca., U.S.	D4	82
Big Pine Creek, stm., In., U.S.	D3	91
Big Pine Lake, l., Mn., U.S.	D3	100
Big Pine Mountain, mtn., Ca., U.S.	E4	82
Big Piney, Wy., U.S.	D2	127
Big Piney, stm., Mo., U.S.	D5	102
Big Piney Creek, stm., Ar., U.S.	B2	81
Big Pipe Creek, stm., Md., U.S.	A3	97
Bigpoint, Ms., U.S.	E5	101
Big Pool, Md., U.S.	A1	97
Big Prairie, Oh., U.S.	B3	112
Big Quill Lake, l., Sask.	F3	75
Big Raccoon Creek, stm., In., U.S.	E4	91
Big Rapids, Mi., U.S.	E5	99
Big Rib, stm., Wi., U.S.	C3	126
Big River, Sask.	D2	75
Big Rock, Tn., U.S.	B5	90
Big Rock, Tn., U.S.	A4	119
Big Rock Mountain, mtn., Ar., U.S.	h10	81
Big Run, Pa., U.S.	D4	115
Big Sable Point, c., Mi., U.S.	D4	99
Big Sandy, Mt., U.S.	B6	103
Big Sandy, Tn., U.S.	A3	119
Big Sandy, Tx., U.S.	C5	120
Big Sandy, stm., U.S.	C2	125
Big Sandy, stm., Az., U.S.	C2	80
Big Sandy, stm., Tn., U.S.	B3	119
Big Sandy, stm., Wy., U.S.	D3	127
Big Sandy Creek, stm., Co., U.S.	C8	83
Big Sandy Creek, stm., Mt., U.S.	B6	103
Big Sandy Creek, stm., W.V., U.S.	C3	125
Big Sandy Lake, l., Ont.	E5	70
Big Sandy Lake, l., Sask.	C3	75
Big Sandy Lake, l., Mn., U.S.	D5	100
Big Sandy Reservoir, res., Wy., U.S.	D3	127
Big Satilla Creek, stm., Ga., U.S.	E4	87
Big Savage Mountain, mtn., U.S.	k12	97
Big Sheep Mountain, mtn., Mt., U.S.	C11	103
Big Shiney Mountain, mtn., Pa., U.S.	n18	115
Big Sioux, stm., U.S.	E9	118
Big Slough, stm., Ga., U.S.	F2	87
Big Smoky Valley, val., Nv., U.S.	E4	105
Big Snowy Mountains, mts., Mt., U.S.	D7	103
Big Southern Butte, mtn., Id., U.S.	F5	89
Big South Fork, stm., Ky., U.S.	k13	94
Big Spencer Mountain, mtn., Me., U.S.	C3	96
Big Spring, Ky., U.S.	C3	94
Big Spring, Md., U.S.	A2	97
Big Spring, Tx., U.S.	C2	120
Big Springs, Ks., U.S.	k15	93
Big Springs, Ne., U.S.	C3	104
Big Spruce Knob, mtn., W.V., U.S.	C3	125
Big Squaw Mountain, mtn., Me., U.S.	C3	96
Bigstick Lake, l., Sask.	G1	75
Big Stone, co., Mn., U.S.	E2	100
Bigstone, stm., Man.	B4	70
Big Stone Beach, De., U.S.	C3	84
Big Stone City, S.D., U.S.	B9	118
Big Stone Gap, Va., U.S.	f9	123
Bigstone Lake, l., Man.	C4	70
Bigstone Lake, l., Sask.	E2	75
Big Stone Lake, l., U.S.	E2	100
Big Sunflower, stm., Ms., U.S.	B3	101
Big Sur, Ca., U.S.	D3	82
Big Thompson, stm., Co., U.S.	A5	83
Big Timber, Mt., U.S.	E7	103
Big Top, mtn., Tn., U.S.	B5	119
Big Trout Lake, Ont.	n17	73
Big Trout Lake, l., Ont.	n17	73
Biguaçu, Braz.	D3	56
Big Valley, Alta.	C4	68
Big Walnut Creek, stm., Oh., U.S.	m11	112
Big Wells, Tx., U.S.	E3	120
Big Wills Creek, stm., Al., U.S.	A3	78
Big Wills Valley, val., Al., U.S.	A4	78
Bigwood, Ont.	A4	73
Big Wood, stm., Id., U.S.	F4	89
Bihać, Yugo.	C2	24
Bihār, India	D8	36
Bihār, state, India	D8	36
Bijzīri, i., Marsh Is.	S18	52
Bijagós, Arquipélago dos, is., Gui.-B.	D1	45
Bijāpur, India	E6	36
Bijār, Iran	D3	39
Bijeljina, Yugo.	C4	24
Bijelo Polje, Yugo.	D4	24
Bijie, China	F6	31
Bijnor, India	C6	37
Bijou Creek, stm., Co., U.S.	B6	83
Bijou Hills, S.D., U.S.	D6	118
Bīkāner, India	C5	36
Bikenibeu, Kir.	R18	52
Bikin, Sov. Un.	B11	31
Bikin, stm., Sov. Un.	C7	33
Bikini, atoll, Marsh Is.	F10	6
Bikini, i., Marsh Is.	f8	72
Bikita, Zimb.		
Bilāspur, India	D7	36
Bilauktaung Range, mts., Asia	C1	34
Bilbao, Spain	A4	22
Bilbays, Eg.	D3	41
Bildudalur, Ice.	n21	14
Bileća, Yugo.	D3	24
Bilecik, Tur.	B7	40
Biłgoraj, Pol.	C7	26
Bili, Zaire	A4	48
Bilibino, Sov. Un.	E10	36
Bilina, Czech.	C8	26
Bilk Creek Mountains, mts., Nv., U.S.	B3	105
Bill, Wy., U.S.	C7	127
Billarp, Ga., U.S.	D3	91
Billerica, Ma., U.S.	A5	98
Billet, Il., U.S.	E6	90
Billings, Mo., U.S.	D4	102
Billings, Mt., U.S.	E8	103
Billings, Ok., U.S.	A4	113
Billings, co., N.D., U.S.	B2	111
Billings Heights, Mt., U.S.	E8	103
Billingsley, Al., U.S.	C3	78
Bill Williams, stm., Az., U.S.	C1	80
Bill Williams Mountain, mtn., Az., U.S.	B3	80
Bilma, Niger	C7	45
Biloela, Austl.	D9	50
Biloxi, Ms., U.S.	E5	101
Biloxi, stm., Ms., U.S.	E4	101
Biloxi Bay, b., Ms., U.S.	f8	101
Bilqās Qism Awwal, Eg.	C3	41
Biltine, Chad	C4	46
Biltmore Forest, N.C., U.S.	f10	110
Bilugyun, i., Burma	D2	35
Bilzen, Bel.	D5	17
Bim, W.V., U.S.	n12	125
Bimbéréké, Benin	D5	45
Bimberi Peak, mtn., Austl.	C4	51
Bimini Islands, is., Bah.	B4	64
Bīna-Etāwa, India	E7	37
Binangonan, Phil.	o13	34
Bindloss, Alta.	D5	68
Bindura, Zimb.	A5	49
Binfield, Tn., U.S.	D9	119
Binford, N.D., U.S.	B7	111
Binga, Zaire	A3	48
Binga, Monte, mtn., Afr.	A5	49
Bingamon Creek, stm., W.V., U.S.	k10	125
Bingen, Ger.	D3	18
Bingen, Wa., U.S.	D4	124
Bingham, Il., U.S.	D4	90
Bingham, Me., U.S.	C3	96
Bingham, Ne., U.S.	B3	104
Bingham, N.M., U.S.	D3	108
Bingham, co., Id., U.S.	F6	89
Bingham Lake, Mn., U.S.	G3	100
Binghamton, N.Y., U.S.	C5	109
Bingley, Eng., U.K.	G7	13
Bingöl, Tur.	C13	40
Binhai, China	E8	31
Binjai, Indon.	m11	34
Binnaway, Austl.	A4	21
Binningen, Switz.	D1	70
Binscarth, Man.	D1	70
Bintan, i., Indon.	L6	35
Bintang, mtn., Malay.	J4	35
Bintang, stm., Malay.	A7	34
Bint Jubayl, Leb.	A7	41
Bintuhan, Indon.	E4	34
Bintulu, Malay.	E4	34
Binxian, China	D6	31
Binxian, China	D3	33
Binyamina, Isr.	B6	41
Bío-Bío, prov., Chile	B2	54
Bío-Bío, stm., Chile	B2	54
Bioko, i., Eq. Gui.	E1	46
Biola, Ca., U.S.	D3	82
Bippus, In., U.S.	C6	91
Bira, Sov. Un.	B6	33
Birak, Sov. Un.	B11	31
Birakan, Sov. Un.	B11	31
Birao, Cen. Afr. Rep.	C4	46
Birch, Can.	A4	75
Birch, stm., W.V., U.S.	C4	125
Birchdale, Mn., U.S.	B4	100
Birch Hill, Ct., U.S.	C2	84
Birch Hills, Sask.	E3	75
Birch Island, B.C.	D8	69
Birch Lake, l., Alta.	C5	68
Birch Lake, l., Sask.	D1	75
Birch Lake, l., N.C., U.S.	D6	79
Birch Lake, l., Mn., U.S.	C7	100
Birch River, Man.	C1	70
Birch Run, Mi., U.S.	E7	99
Birch Tree, Mo., U.S.	E6	102
Birchwood, Ct., U.S.	B5	84
Birchwood, Tn., U.S.	D9	119
Birchwood, Wi., U.S.	C2	126
Birchwood City, Md., U.S.	C5	97
Birchwood Park, De., U.S.	*B3	85
Birchy Bay, Newf.	D4	72
Bird City, Ks., U.S.	C2	93
Bird Creek, stm., Ok., U.S.	A6	113
Bird Island, Mn., U.S.	F4	100
Bird Island, i., N.C., U.S.	D5	110
Birds, Il., U.S.	E6	90
Birdsboro, Pa., U.S.	F10	115
Birds Creek, Ont.	B7	73
Birdseye, In., U.S.	H4	91
Birdsong, Ar., U.S.	B5	81
Birdsville, Austl.	E6	50
Birdsville, Ky., U.S.	e9	94
Birdtown, N.C., U.S.	f9	110
Birdum, Austl.	C5	50
Birecik, Tur.	D11	40
Bireun, Indon.	J2	35
Birganj, Nepal	D10	37
Birigui, Braz.	C2	56
Bīrjand, Iran	B5	38
Birk, Wādī, val., Sau. Ar.	C4	38
Birka, Isr.	D3	41
Birkat as Sab', Eg.	D3	41
Birkenfeld, Ger.	D2	18
Birkenfeld, Or., U.S.	B3	114
Birkenhead, Eng., U.K.	D5	10
Birmingham, Sask.	G4	75
Birmingham, Eng., U.K.	D6	10
Birmingham, Al., U.S.	B3	78
Birmingham, Mi., U.S.	F7	99
Birmingham, Mo., U.S.	h11	102
Birmingham, N.J., U.S.	D3	107
Bir Mogrein (Fort Trinquet), Maur.	A2	45
Birney, Mt., U.S.	E10	103
Birnie, Man.	D2	70
Birni Ngaouré, Niger	D5	45
Birni Kebbi, Nig.	D5	45
Birni Nkonni, Niger	E6	29
Birobidzhan, Sov. Un.	D4	126
Biron, Wi., U.S.	D3	126
Birr, Ire.	B3	51
Birsay, Sask.	F2	75
Birsk, Sov. Un.	D20	31
Birta, Man.	D1	70
Birtle, Man.	A6	32
Biruinta, Mong.	A6	32
Birūr, India	F6	80
Birżai, Lith.	F6	16
Birżebbuġa, Malta	H5	32
Bisbee, Az., U.S.	F6	80
Bisbee, N.D., U.S.	A6	111
Biscay, Bay of, b., Eur.	D4	5
Biscayne, Key, i., Fl., U.S.	s13	86
Biscayne Bay, b., Fl., U.S.	G6	86
Biscayne Gardens, Fl., U.S.	*s13	86
Biscayne National Monument, Fl., U.S.	G6	86
Bischeim, Fr.	F7	17
Bischofshofen, Aus.	B9	20
Bischofswerda, Ger.	B9	19
Bischwiller, Fr.	F7	17
Biscoe, Ar., U.S.	C4	81
Biscoe, N.C., U.S.	B3	110
Biscoe Islands, is., Ant.	C6	7
Biševo, i., Yugo.	D3	24
Bishārah, Ma'ṭan, well, Libya	F11	37
Bishnupur, India	F11	37
Bisho, Ciskei	D4	49
Bishop, Ca., U.S.	D4	82
Bishop, Md., U.S.	D7	97
Bishop, Tx., U.S.	F4	120
Bishop Auckland, Eng., U.K.	F7	13
Bishopric, Sask.	H3	75
Bishop's Castle, Eng., U.K.	B5	12
Bishop's Falls, Newf.	D4	72
Bishops Head, Md., U.S.	D5	97
Bishops Mills, Ont.	C9	73
Bishopton, Que.	D6	74
Bishopville, Md., U.S.	D7	97
Bishopville, S.C., U.S.	C7	117
Bismarck, Ar., U.S.	C2	81
Bismarck, Il., U.S.	C6	90
Bismarck, Mo., U.S.	D7	102
Bismarck, N.D., U.S.	C5	111
Bismarck, Cape, c., Grnld.	A16	128
Bismarck Archipelago, is., Pap. N. Gui.	h12	50
Bismarck Range, mts., Pap. N. Gui.	k11	50
Bismarck Sea, Pap. N. Gui.	h12	50
Bismark, Ger.	F5	15
Bison, Ks., U.S.	D4	93
Bison, Ok., U.S.	A4	113
Bison, S.D., U.S.	B3	118
Bison Lake, l., Alta.	A2	68
Bison Peak, mtn., Co., U.S.	B5	83
Bissau, Gui.-B.	D1	45
Bissett, Man.	D4	70
Bistineau, Lake, res., La., U.S.	B2	95
Bistrița, Rom.	B7	24
Bistrița, stm., Rom.	B7	24
Bitam, Gabon	E2	46
Bitburg, Ger.	E6	17
Bitche, Fr.	E7	17
Bitely, Mi., U.S.	E5	99
Bitlis, Tur.	C14	40
Bitola, Yugo.	C5	24
Bitonto, Italy	D6	23
Bittencourt, Braz.	B4	58
Bitterfeld, Ger.	B7	19
Bitterfontein, S. Afr.	D2	49
Bitter Lake, l., Sask.	G1	75
Bitter Lake, l., S.D., U.S.	B8	118
Bittern Lake, Alta.	C4	68
Bitterroot, stm., Mt., U.S.	D2	103
Bitterroot Range, mts., U.S.	B3	89
Bittinger, Md., U.S.	k12	97
Bitung, Indon.	E7	34
Bityug, stm., Sov. Un.	F13	27
Bivalve, Md., U.S.	D6	97
Bivalve, N.J., U.S.	E2	107
Biwabik, Mn., U.S.	C6	100
Biwa Lake, l., Japan	n15	33
Bixby, Mn., U.S.	G5	100
Bixby, Mo., U.S.	D6	102
Bixby, N.C., U.S.	B2	110
Bixby, Ok., U.S.	B6	113
Biya, stm., Sov. Un.	E26	8
Biyala, Eg.	C3	41
Biyang, China	H5	32
Biysk, Sov. Un.	D11	29
Bjelovar, Yugo.	B3	24
Bjerringbro, Den.	C3	14
Bjørkelangen, Nor.	E4	75
Björk Lake, l., Sask.	D4	78
Black, Al., U.S.	B1	120
Black, Tx., U.S.	B5	35
Black, stm., Asia	D4	70
Black, stm., Man.	E13	65
Black, stm., Jam.	B3	96
Black, stm., N.A.	D5	80
Black, stm., Az., U.S.	B4	81
Black, stm., La., U.S.	C4	95
Black, stm., Mi., U.S.	E8	99
Black, stm., N.Y., U.S.	B4	109
Black, stm., N.C., U.S.	C4	110
Black, stm., S.C., U.S.	D8	117
Black, stm., Vt., U.S.	E3	122
Black, stm., Vt., U.S.	B4	122
Black, stm., Wi., U.S.	D3	126
Black Bayou, stm., La., U.S.	E5	95
Black Bear Bay, b., Newf.	B4	72
Black Bear Creek, stm., Ok., U.S.	A4	113
Blackbeard Island, i., Ga., U.S.	E5	87
Black Bear Island Lake, l., Sask.	B3	75
Blackbird, De., U.S.	C3	85
Blackburn, Eng., U.K.	D5	10
Blackburn, Ok., U.S.	A5	113
Blackburn, Mount, mtn., Ak., U.S.	C11	79
Black Butte, mtn., Mt., U.S.	F5	103
Black Butte, mtn., Wy., U.S.	B5	127
Black Butte Lake, res., Ca., U.S.	C2	82
Black Butte Ranch, Or., U.S.	C5	114
Black Canyon, val., Co., U.S.	C3	83
Black Canyon City, Az., U.S.	C3	80
Black Canyon of the Gunnison National Monument, Co., U.S.	C3	83
Black Creek, B.C.	E5	69
Black Creek, Wi., U.S.	D5	126
Black Creek, stm., Ms., U.S.	D4	101
Black Creek, stm., S.C., U.S.	B7	117
Black Diamond, Alta.	D3	68
Black Diamond, Al., U.S.	b6	124
Black Diamond, Wa., U.S.	B4	124
Black Down Hills, hills, Eng., U.K.	E5	10
Blackduck, Mn., U.S.	C4	100
Black Eagle, Mt., U.S.	C5	103
Black Earth, Wi., U.S.	E4	126
Blackey, Ky., U.S.	C7	94
Blackfeet Indian Reservation, Mt., U.S.	B4	103
Blackfoot, Alta.	C5	68
Blackfoot, Id., U.S.	F6	89
Blackfoot, Mt., U.S.	B4	103
Blackfoot, stm., Mt., U.S.	C3	103

Name	Map Ref.	Page

Blackfoot Mountains, mts., Id., U.S. — F7 89
Blackfoot Reservoir, res., Id., U.S. — G7 89
Blackford, Ky., U.S. — C2 94
Blackford, co., In., U.S. — D7 91
Black Forest, Co., U.S. — C6 83
Black Forest, mts., Ger. — E4 18
Blackfork, Oh., U.S. — D3 112
Blackhall Mountain, mtn., Wy., U.S. — E6 127
Black Hawk, Ms., U.S. — B3 101
Black Hawk, S.D., U.S. — C2 118
Black Hawk, co., Ia., U.S. — B5 92
Black Hills, mts., U.S. — C2 118
Blackie, Alta. — D4 68
Black Island, i., Ant. — f38 7
Black Island, i., Man. — D3 70
Black Jack, Mo., U.S. — *f13 102
Blackjack Mountain, mtn., Ga., U.S. — h7 87
Black Lake, Que. — C6 74
Black Lake, I., Sask. — m7 75
Black Lake, I., Mi., U.S. — C6 99
Black Lake, I., N.Y., U.S. — f9 109
Black Lake Bayou, stm., La., U.S. — B2 95
Blacklick, Oh., U.S. — m11 112
Black Lick, Pa., U.S. — F3 115
Blacklick Estates, Oh., U.S. — m11 112
Black Mesa, mtn., Az., U.S. — A5 80
Black Mesa, mtn., Ok., U.S. — e8 113
Black Mingo Creek, stm., S.C., U.S. — D9 117
Blackmore, Mount, mtn., Mt., U.S. — E6 103
Black Mountain, N.C., U.S. — f10 110
Black Mountain, mtn., Az., U.S. — D7 94
Black Mountain, mtn., Az., U.S. — E4 80
Black Mountain, mtn., Co., U.S. — A5 83
Black Mountain, mtn., Id., U.S. — C3 89
Black Mountain, mtn., Mt., U.S. — D4 103
Black Mountain, mtn., Or., U.S. — B7 114
Black Mountain, mtn., Wy., U.S. — D7 127
Black Mountain, mtn., Wy., U.S. — B5 127
Black Mountains, mts., Wales, U.K. — C4 12
Black Mountains, mts., Az., U.S. — B1 80
Black Oak, Ia., U.S. — B5 81
Black Oak, In., U.S. — A3 91
Black Peak, mtn., Az., U.S. — C1 80
Black Pine, mtn., Id., U.S. — G5 89
Black Point, Ct., U.S. — D7 84
Black Point Beach Club, Ct., U.S. — *D7 84
Black Point, mt., I.e., U.S. — B3 96
Blackpool, Eng., U.K. — D5 10
Black Range, mts., N.M., U.S. — D2 108
Black River, Jam. — E5 64
Black River, Mi., U.S. — D7 99
Black River, N.Y., U.S. — A5 109
Black River, stm., Jam. — F13 65
Black River Falls, Wi., U.S. — D3 126
Black Rock, Ar., U.S. — A4 81
Black Rock, N.M., U.S. — B1 108
Black Rock Desert, des., Nv., U.S. — B3 105
Black Rock Range, mts., Nv., U.S. — B3 105
Blacksburg, S.C., U.S. — A4 117
Blacksburg, Va., U.S. — C2 123
Black Sea — G15 8
Blacks Fork, stm., U.S. — E3 127
Blacks Harbour, N.B. — D3 71
Blackshear, Ga., U.S. — E4 87
Blackshear, Lake, res., Ga., U.S. — E2 87
Blacksod Bay, b., Ire. — C1 10
Black Springs, Ar., U.S. — C2 81
Black Springs, Nv., U.S. — *D2 105
Black Squirrel Creek, stm., Co., U.S. — C6 83
Blackstock, Ont. — C6 73
Blackstock, S.C., U.S. — B5 117
Blackstone, Ma., U.S. — B4 98
Blackstone, Va., U.S. — C5 123
Blackstone, stm., Alta. — C2 68
Blackstone, stm., R.I., U.S. — B4 116
Blackstrap Reservoir, res., Sask. — F2 75
Black Sugarloaf Mountain, mtn., Austl. — E9 51
Blacksville, W.V., U.S. — B4 125
Black Thunder Creek, stm., Wy., U.S. — C8 127
Black Tickle, Newf. — B4 72
Blacktown, Austl. — *F9 50
Blackville, N.B. — C4 71
Blackville, S.C., U.S. — E5 117
Blacknox, Pa., U.S. — k14 115
Blaye, Fr. — E3 16
Błażowa, Pol. — D7 26
Bleckede, Ger. — E4 15
Bleckley, co., Ga., U.S. — D3 87
Bled, Yugo. — C1 20
Błędów, Pol. — g10 26
Bledsoe, co., Tn., U.S. — D8 119
Bledsoe, Al., U.S. — B5 78
Blencoe, Ia., U.S. — C1 92
Blendecques, Fr. — D2 17
Blenheim, Ont. — E3 73
Blenheim, N.Z. — N14 51
Blenheim, S.C., U.S. — B8 117
Blennerhassett, W.V., U.S. — B3 125
Blessing, Tx., U.S. — E4 120
Blessington, Ire. — D5 11
Bletchley, Eng., U.K. — C7 12
Blevins, Ar., U.S. — D2 81
Blija, Neth. — A5 17
Blind River, Ont. — A2 73
Bliss, N.Y., U.S. — C2 109
Bliss, N.Y., U.S. — G7 99
Blissfield, Oh., U.S. — B4 112
Blissville, Al., U.S. — *G4 34
Blita, Indon. — A4 106
Blitta, Togo — G6 45
Blocher, In., U.S. — G6 91
Blocker, Ok., U.S. — B6 113
Block Island, R.I., U.S. — h7 116
Block Island, i., R.I., U.S. — h7 116
Block Island Sound, strt., U.S. — G2 116

Blagoevgrad (Gorna Dzhumaya), Bul. — D6 24
Blagoveshchensk, Sov. Un. — D20 8
Blagoveshchensk, Sov. Un. — D15 29
Blain, Fr. — D3 16
Blain, Pa., U.S. — F7 115
Blaine, Ks., U.S. — C7 93
Blaine, Me., U.S. — B5 96
Blaine, Mn., U.S. — m12 100
Blaine, Ms., U.S. — B3 101
Blaine, Wa., U.S. — A3 124
Blaine, co., Id., U.S. — F4 89
Blaine, co., Mt., U.S. — B7 103
Blaine, co., Ne., U.S. — C6 104
Blaine, co., Ok., U.S. — B3 113
Blaine Creek, stm., Ky., U.S. — B7 94
Black Island, i., Wa., U.S. — E2 75
Blair, Ks., U.S. — C8 93
Blair, Ne., U.S. — C9 104
Blair, Ok., U.S. — C2 113
Blair, S.C., U.S. — C5 117
Blair, W.V., U.S. — n12 125
Blair, Wi., U.S. — D2 126
Blair, co., Pa., U.S. — E5 115
Blair Athol, Austl. — D8 50
Blair Athol, Scot., U.K. — D5 13
Blairgowrie, Scot., U.K. — B5 10
Blairsburg, Ia., U.S. — B4 92
Blairsden, Ca., U.S. — C3 82
Blairstown, Ia., U.S. — C5 92
Blairstown, Mo., U.S. — C4 102
Blairsville, Ga., U.S. — B3 87
Blairsville, Pa., U.S. — F3 115
Blairton, W.V., U.S. — B7 125
Blaisdell, N.D., U.S. — A3 111
Blaj, Rom. — B6 24
Blake Island, i., Wa., U.S. — e11 124
Blakely, Mn., U.S. — F5 100
Blakely, Ar., U.S. — C2 81
Blakely, Ga., U.S. — E2 87
Blakely, Pa., U.S. — m18 115
Blake Point, c., Mi., U.S. — h10 99
Blakeslee, Oh., U.S. — A1 112
Blakeslee, Pa., U.S. — D10 115
Blâmont, Fr. — F6 17
Blanc, Cap, c., Afr. — B1 45
Blanc, Cap, c., Tun. — F2 23
Blanc, Mont, mtn., Eur. — E7 16
Blanca, Co., U.S. — D5 83
Blanca, Bahía, b., Arg. — B4 54
Blanca, Cordillera, mts., Peru — C2 58
Blanca, Sierra, mtn., Tx., U.S. — o12 120
Blanca Peak, mtn., Co., U.S. — D5 83
Blanchard, Ia., U.S. — A2 89
Blanchard, La., U.S. — B2 95
Blanchard, Me., U.S. — C3 96
Blanchard, Mi., U.S. — E5 99
Blanchard, N.D., U.S. — B8 111
Blanchard, Ok., U.S. — B4 113
Blanchard, Pa., U.S. — D6 115
Blanchard, Wa., U.S. — A3 124
Blanchard, stm., Oh., U.S. — A1 112
Blanchardville, Wi., U.S. — F4 126
Blancharville Coast, Grnld. — C17 128
Blanche, Que. — D2 74
Blanche, Tn., U.S. — B5 119
Blanche, Lake, I., Austl. — E6 50
Blanchester, Oh., U.S. — C2 112
Blanco, N.M., U.S. — A2 108
Blanco, Ok., U.S. — C6 113
Blanco, Tx., U.S. — D3 120
Blanco, co., Tx., U.S. — D3 120
Blanco, stm., Arg. — E2 55
Blanco, stm., Mex. — n15 62
Blanco, Cabo, c., C.R. — F5 62
Blanco, Cabo, c., Peru — E2 58
Blanco, Cape, c., Or., U.S. — E2 114
Blanc-Sablon, Que. — C3 72
Bland, Mo., U.S. — C6 102
Bland, Va., U.S. — C1 123
Bland, co., Va., U.S. — C1 123
Blandburg, Pa., U.S. — E5 115
Blandford, Ma., U.S. — B2 98
Blandford Forum, Eng., U.K. — D5 12
Blanding, Ut., U.S. — F6 121
Blandinsville, Il., U.S. — C3 90
Blanford, In., U.S. — E2 91
Blangkejeren, Indon. — K2 33
Blangy-sur-Bresle, Fr. — E9 12
Blankenberge, Bel. — C3 17
Blankenburg, Ger. — C5 18
Blankenfelde, Ger. — A8 19
Blankenheim, Ger. — C1 19
Blanket, Tx., U.S. — D3 120
Blanquilla, Isla, i., Ven. — A5 60
Blantyre, Mwi. — E6 49
Blarney, Ire. — F3 11
Blatná, Czech. — D8 19
Blato, Yugo. — D3 24
Blaubeuren, Ger. — E4 19
Blauvelt, N.Y., U.S. — *g13 109
Blåvands Huk, c., Den. — C2 15
Blawenburg, N.J., U.S. — C3 107
Blawnox, Pa., U.S. — k14 115

Blockton, Ia., U.S. — D3 92
Blodgett, Mo., U.S. — D8 102
Blodgett Landing, N.H., U.S. — D2 106
Bloedel, B.C. — D5 69
Bloemfontein, S. Afr. — C4 49
Blois, Fr. — D4 16
Blokhus, Den. — A3 15
Blomberg, Ger. — B4 19
Blommestein Meer, res., Sur. — B3 59
Blönduós, Ice. — n22 14
Błonie, Pol. — m13 26
Blood Mountain, mtn., Ga., U.S. — B3 87
Bloodsworth Island, i., Md., U.S. — D5 97
Bloodvein, stm., Can. — D7 70
Bloody Foreland, c., Ire. — B3 11
Bloom, Ks., U.S. — E4 93
Bloom, Slieve, mts., Ire. — D4 11
Bloomdale, Oh., U.S. — A2 112
Bloomer, Ar., U.S. — B1 81
Bloomer, Wi., U.S. — C2 126
Bloomfield, N.B. — D4 71
Bloomfield, Ont. — D7 73
Bloomfield, Ct., U.S. — B5 84
Bloomfield, In., U.S. — F4 91
Bloomfield, Ia., U.S. — D5 92
Bloomfield, Ky., U.S. — C4 94
Bloomfield, Mo., U.S. — E8 102
Bloomfield, Mt., U.S. — C12 103
Bloomfield, Ne., U.S. — B8 104
Bloomfield, N.J., U.S. — h8 107
Bloomfield, N.M., U.S. — A2 108
Bloomfield, Township, Mi., U.S. — o15 99
Bloomingburg, Oh., U.S. — C2 112
Bloomingdale, Ga., U.S. — D5 87
Bloomingdale, Il., U.S. — k8 90
Bloomingdale, In., U.S. — E3 91
Bloomingdale, Mi., U.S. — F5 99
Bloomingdale, N.J., U.S. — A4 107
Bloomingdale, N.Y., U.S. — f10 109
Bloomingdale, Tn., U.S. — C11 119
Blooming Grove, Pa., U.S. — D11 115
Blooming Grove, Tx., U.S. — C4 120
Blooming Prairie, Mn., U.S. — G5 100
Bloomington, Ca., U.S. — *m14 82
Bloomington, Id., U.S. — G7 89
Bloomington, Il., U.S. — C4 90
Bloomington, In., U.S. — F4 91
Bloomington, Md., U.S. — m12 97
Bloomington, Mn., U.S. — F5 100
Bloomington, Ne., U.S. — D6 104
Bloomington, Tx., U.S. — E4 120
Bloomington, Ut., U.S. — *F2 121
Bloomington, Wi., U.S. — F3 126
Bloomington, Lake, res., Il., U.S. — C5 90
Bloomsburg, Pa., U.S. — E9 115
Bloomsbury, N.J., U.S. — B2 107
Bloomsdale, Mo., U.S. — C7 102
Bloomville, N.Y., U.S. — C6 109
Bloomville, Oh., U.S. — A2 112
Blossburg, Al., U.S. — f7 78
Blossom, Tx., U.S. — C5 120
Blount, co., Al., U.S. — B3 78
Blount, co., Tn., U.S. — D10 119
Blounts Creek, N.C., U.S. — B6 110
Blountstown, Fl., U.S. — B1 86
Blountsville, Al., U.S. — A3 78
Blountville, Tn., U.S. — C11 119
Blowing Rock, N.C., U.S. — A1 110
Bloxom, Va., U.S. — C7 123
Blucher, Sask. — E2 75
Bludenz, Aus. — E4 18
Blue, Az., U.S. — C5 113
Blue, Ok., U.S. — D6 80
Blue, stm., Co., U.S. — B4 83
Blue, stm., In., U.S. — H5 91
Blue, stm., Mo., U.S. — k10 102
Blue, stm., Ok., U.S. — C5 113
Blue, Bayou, stm., La., U.S. — E5 95
Blue, Mount, mtn., Me., U.S. — D2 96
Blue Anchor, N.J., U.S. — D3 107
Blue Ash, Oh., U.S. — o13 112
Bluebell, Ut., U.S. — C5 121
Bluebell, stm., B.C. — A7 69
Blue Buck Knob, hill, Mo., U.S. — E5 102
Blue Buck Point, c., La., U.S. — E2 95
Blue Creek, Al., U.S. — g6 78
Blue Creek, Wa., U.S. — A8 124
Blue Creek, W.V., U.S. — m13 125
Blue Creek, stm., Ne., U.S. — C3 104
Blue Creek, stm., W.V., U.S. — m13 125
Blue Cypress Lake, I., Fl., U.S. — E6 86
Blue Diamond, Nv., U.S. — G6 105
Blue Earth, Mn., U.S. — G4 100
Blue Earth, co., Mn., U.S. — G4 100
Blue Earth, stm., Mn., U.S. — G4 100
Boca Chica Key, i., Fl., U.S. — H5 86
Blue Glacier, ice, Ant. — e39 7
Blue Grass, Ia., U.S. — C7 92
Blue Grass, Va., U.S. — B3 123
Blue Hill, Me., U.S. — D4 96
Blue Hill, Ne., U.S. — D7 104
Blue Hill Falls, Me., U.S. — D4 96
Blue Hill Range, hills, Ma., U.S. — h11 98
Blue Hills, Ct., U.S. — B5 84
Blue Hills of Couteau, hills, Newf. — E3 72
Bluehole, Ky., U.S. — C6 94
Blue Island, Il., U.S. — B6 90
Bluejacket, Ok., U.S. — A6 113
Bluejoint Lake, I., Or., U.S. — E7 114
Blue Knob, mtn., Pa., U.S. — F4 115
Blue Lake, Ca., U.S. — B2 82
Blue Mesa Reservoir, res., Co., U.S. — C3 83
Blue Mound, Il., U.S. — D5 90
Blue Mound, Ks., U.S. — D8 93
Blue Mountain, Ar., U.S. — B2 81
Blue Mountain, Ms., U.S. — A4 101
Blue Mountain, mtn., N.B. — B3 71
Blue Mountain, mtn., Newf. — C3 72
Bloodine, Mount, mtn., B.C. — C1 81
Blue Mountain, mtn., Mt., U.S. — C12 103
Blue Mountain, mtn., N.H., U.S. — A4 106
Blue Mountain, mtn., N.M., U.S. — D2 108
Blue Mountain, mtn., N.Y., U.S. — B6 109
Blue Mountain, mtn., Pa., U.S. — F6 115

Blue Mountain Lake, N.Y., U.S. — B6 109
Blue Mountain Lake, res., Ar., U.S. — B2 81
Blue Mountain Peak, mtn., Jam. — E5 64
Blue Mountains, mts., Austl. — F8 51
Blue Mountains, mts., Jam. — E15 65
Blue Mountains, mts., Jam. — A4 76
Blue Mud Bay, b., Austl. — B6 50
Blue Nile, stm., Afr. — C3 47
Bluenose Lake, I., N.W. Ter. — C9 66
Blue Point, Me., U.S. — g7 96
Blue Rapids, Ks., U.S. — C7 93
Blue Ridge, Alta. — B3 68
Blue Ridge, Ga., U.S. — B2 87
Blue Ridge, In., U.S. — E6 91
Blue Ridge, Va., U.S. — C3 123
Blue Ridge, mtn., U.S. — C11 76
Blue Ridge Lake, res., Ga., U.S. — B2 87
Blue Ridge Summit, Pa., U.S. — G7 115
Blue River, B.C. — C8 69
Blue River, Or., U.S. — C4 114
Blue River, Wi., U.S. — E3 126
Bluesky, Alta. — A1 68
Blue Springs, Al., U.S. — D4 78
Blue Springs, Mo., U.S. — A5 101
Blue Springs, Mo., U.S. — h11 102
Blue Springs, Ne., U.S. — D9 104
Blue Stack Mountains, mts., Ire. — C3 11
Bluestone, stm., W.V., U.S. — D3 125
Bluestone Lake, res., U.S. — D3 125
Bluevale, Ont. — D3 73
Bluewater, N.M., U.S. — B2 108
Bluewell, W.V., U.S. — D3 125
Bluff, N.Z. — Q12 51
Bluff, Ut., U.S. — F6 121
Bluff City, Ar., U.S. — D2 81
Bluff City, Il., U.S. — E4 90
Bluff City, Ks., U.S. — E6 93
Bluff City, Ky., U.S. — C2 94
Bluff City, Tn., U.S. — C11 119
Bluff Creek, stm., Ks., U.S. — E5 93
Bluff Creek, stm., Ok., U.S. — A4 113
Bluff Dale, Tx., U.S. — C3 120
Bluffdale, Ut., U.S. — *C4 121
Bluff Knoll, mtn., Austl. — F2 50
Bluff Lake, res., Ms., U.S. — B5 101
Bluff Park, Al., U.S. — g7 78
Bluffs, Il., U.S. — D3 90
Bluffton, Ga., U.S. — E2 87
Bluffton, In., U.S. — C7 91
Bluffton, Mn., U.S. — D3 100
Bluffton, Oh., U.S. — B2 112
Bluffton, S.C., U.S. — G6 117
Böhme, stm., Ger. — F3 15
Böhme, stm., Ger. — A3 19
Bohol, i., Phil. — D6 34
Bohol Sea, Phil. — D6 34
Boiano, Italy — H9 23
Boiestown, N.B. — C3 71
Boiling Springs, N.C., U.S. — B1 110
Boiling Springs, Pa., U.S. — F7 115
Bois, Lac des, I., N.W. Ter. — C7 66
Bois, Rio dos, stm., Braz. — C1 57
Bois Blanc Island, i., Mi., U.S. — C6 99
Bois Brule, stm., Wi., U.S. — B2 126
Boischâtel, Que. — C6 74
Bois-Colombes, Fr. — g10 16
Boisdale, N.S. — C9 71
Boisdale, Loch, b., Scot., U.K. — C1 13
Bois D'Arc, Mo., U.S. — D4 102
Bois-des-Filion, Que. — p19 74
Bois de Sioux, stm., Mn., U.S. — E2 100
Boise, Id., U.S. — F3 89
Boise, co., Id., U.S. — F3 89
Boise City, Ok., U.S. — e8 113
Bois Fort, Mn., U.S. — C6 100
Boissevain, Man. — E1 70
Boissevain, Va., U.S. — e10 123
Boistfort Peak, mtn., Wa., U.S. — C2 124
Boisvert, Pointe au, c., Que. — A8 74
Boizenburg, Ger. — B5 18
Bojador, Cabo, c., W. Sah. — D2 44
Bojnürd, Iran — B5 38
Bokchito, Ok., U.S. — C5 113
Boké, Gui. — F2 44
Bokeelia, Fl., U.S. — F4 86
Bokhoma, Ok., U.S. — C7 113
Boko, Zaire — C2 48
Bokokyaadai Island, i., Marsh Is. — P18 52
Bokoro, Chad — C3 46
Bokororyuru Island, i., Marsh Is. — P18 52
Bokoshe, Ok., U.S. — B7 113
Bokungu, Zaire — B4 48
Bol, Chad — C2 46
Bolafa, Zaire — A3 48
Bolama, Gui.-B. — D1 45
Bolan, Va., U.S. — B3 123
Bolaños, stm., Mex. — m12 63
Bolbec, Fr. — C7 16
Bolckow, Mo., U.S. — A3 102
Boldon, Eng. — C5 10
Boleko, Zaire — B3 48
Boles, Ar., U.S. — C1 81
Boles, Il., U.S. — F5 90
Boles, N.M., U.S. — *E4 108
Boley, Ok., U.S. — B5 113
Bolgatanga, Ghana — D4 45
Boli, China — B11 31
Bolia, Zaire — B3 48
Boligee, Al., U.S. — C1 78
Bolinao, Phil. — n12 34
Bolinao, Cape, c., Phil. — n12 34
Boling, Tx., U.S. — E5 120
Bolingbrook, Il., U.S. — k8 90
Bolivar, Al., U.S. — D1 78
Bolívar, Col. — B2 60
Bolivar, Mo., U.S. — D4 102
Bolivar, N.Y., U.S. — C2 109
Bolivar, Tn., U.S. — B3 119
Bolivar, W.V., U.S. — B7 125
Bolívar, state, Ven. — B5 60
Bolívar, prov., Ec. — H3 60
Bolívar, co., Ms., U.S. — B3 101
Bolívar, dept., Col. — B2 60
Bolívar, Cerro, mtn., Ven. — B5 60
Bolívar, Pico, mtn., Ven. — B3 60
Bolivia, N.C., U.S. — C4 110
Bolivia, ctry., S.A. — C2 55
Bolkhov, Sov. Un. — E11 27
Bollebygd, Swe. — A6 15
Bollène, Fr. — E6 16

Boelus, Ne., U.S. — C7 104
Boende, Zaire — B3 48
Boerne, Tx., U.S. — E3 120
Boeuf, stm., La., U.S. — C4 95
Boeuf, Bayou, stm., La., U.S. — D3 95
Boeuf, Lake, I., La., U.S. — k10 95
Bofete, Braz. — m7 56
Boffa, Gui. — D2 45
Bogale, Burma — E10 36
Bogallua, i., Marsh Is. — S18 52
Bogan, i., Marsh Is. — S18 52
Bogan, stm., Austl. — E6 51
Bogandé, Burkina — D4 45
Bogard, Mo., U.S. — B4 102
Bogart, Ga., U.S. — C3 87
Bogata, Tx., U.S. — C5 120
Bogatynia, Pol. — *C4 26
Bogatynia, Pol. — C9 19
Bogbonga, Zaire — A3 48
Bogen, Ger. — E7 19
Bogenfels, Nmb. — E2 49
Bogense, Den. — C4 15
Boger City, N.C., U.S. — B1 110
Boggeragh Mountains, mts., Ire. — E1 11
Boggerik Island, i., Marsh Is. — S17 52
Boggstown, In., U.S. — E6 91
Bogno, Switz. — D7 21
Bognor Regis, Eng., U.K. — D7 12
Bogoduchov, Sov. Un. — F10 27
Bogon, i., Marsh Is. — S18 52
Bogor (Buitenzorg), Indon. — G3 34
Bogor, Indon. — G3 34
Bogoroditsk, Sov. Un. — E12 27
Bogotá, Col. — C3 60
Bogota, N.J., U.S. — h8 107
Bogota, Tn., U.S. — A2 119
Bogotol, Sov. Un. — D26 8
Bogra, Bngl. — D8 36
Boguchany, Sov. Un. — D28 8
Bogué, Maur. — C2 45
Bogue, Ks., U.S. — C4 93
Bogue Chitto, Ms., U.S. — D3 101
Bogue Chitto, stm., U.S. — D5 95
Bogue Inlet, b., N.C., U.S. — C5 110
Bogue Phalia, stm., Ms., U.S. — B3 101
Boguslav, Sov. Un. — G8 27
Boguslavsk, i., Marsh Is. — E14 65
Bo Hai, b., China — D8 31
Bohain[-en-Vermandois], Fr. — C5 16
Boharm, Sask. — G3 75
Bohemia, La., U.S. — E6 95
Bohemia, N.Y., U.S. — *n15 109
Bohemia, hist. reg., Czech. — D6 18
Bohemian Forest, mts., Eur. — D6 18
Bohemian-Moravian Highlands, plat., Czech. — D3 26
Böhme, stm., Ger. — F3 15
Böhmte, Ger. — A3 19
Bohol, i., Phil. — D6 34
Bohol Sea, Phil. — D6 34
Boiano, Italy — H9 23
Boiestown, N.B. — C3 71
Boiling Springs, N.C., U.S. — B1 110
Boiling Springs, Pa., U.S. — F7 115
Bois, Lac des, I., N.W. Ter. — C7 66
Bois, Rio dos, stm., Braz. — C1 57
Bois Blanc Island, i., Mi., U.S. — C6 99
Bois Brule, stm., Wi., U.S. — B2 126
Boischâtel, Que. — C6 74
Bois-Colombes, Fr. — g10 16
Boisdale, N.S. — C9 71
Boisdale, Loch, b., Scot., U.K. — C1 13
Bois D'Arc, Mo., U.S. — D4 102
Bois-des-Filion, Que. — p19 74
Bois de Sioux, stm., Mn., U.S. — E2 100
Boise, Id., U.S. — F3 89
Boise, co., Id., U.S. — F3 89
Boise City, Ok., U.S. — e8 113
Bois Fort, Mn., U.S. — C6 100
Boissevain, Man. — E1 70
Boissevain, Va., U.S. — e10 123
Boistfort Peak, mtn., Wa., U.S. — C2 124
Boisvert, Pointe au, c., Que. — A8 74
Boizenburg, Ger. — B5 18
Bojador, Cabo, c., W. Sah. — D2 44
Bojnürd, Iran — B5 38
Bokchito, Ok., U.S. — C5 113
Boké, Gui. — F2 44

Bolligen, Switz. — C4 21
Bolling, Al., U.S. — D3 78
Bollinger, co., Mo., U.S. — D7 102
Bollnäs, Swe. — G7 14
Bollullos [par del Condado], Spain — D2 22
Bolmen, I., Swe. — B7 15
Bolnisi, Sov. Un. — B15 40
Bolobo, Zaire — B2 48
Bologna, Italy — B3 23
Bolognesi, Peru — C3 58
Bologoye, Sov. Un. — C10 27
Bolomba, Zaire — A2 48
Bolon, Lake, I., Sov. Un. — B8 33
Bolotnoye, Sov. Un. — B10 29
Bolovens, Plateau des, plat., Laos — E7 35
Bolsena, Lake, I., Italy — *C4 26
Bolshaya Kamenka, stm., Sov. Un. — q22 27
Bolshaya Viska, Sov. Un. — G8 27
Bolshevik, i., Sov. Un. — B4 128
Bolshoy Irgiz, stm., Sov. Un. — C3 28
Bolshoy Uzen, stm., Sov. Un. — D3 28
Bolshoy Yugan, stm., Sov. Un. — B8 28
Bolsward, Neth. — A5 17
Bolton, Eng., U.K. — D5 10
Bolton, Ct., U.S. — B6 84
Bolton, Ma., U.S. — B4 98
Bolton, Ms., U.S. — C3 101
Bolton, N.C., U.S. — C4 110
Bolton, Vt., U.S. — C3 122
Bolton, co., Man. — B4 70
Bolton Center, Ct., U.S. — B6 84
Bolton Lake, I., Man. — B4 70
Bolton Lakes, I., Ct., U.S. — B6 84
Bolton Landing, N.Y., U.S. — B7 109
Bolu, Tur. — A2 119
Bolus Head, c., Ire. — F1 11
Bolvadin, Tur. — C8 40
Bolzano, Italy — A3 23
Boma, Zaire — C1 48
Bomarton, Tx., U.S. — C3 120
Bombala, Austl. — G8 50
Bombay, India — E5 36
Bombay Hook Island, i., De., U.S. — C4 85
Bomboma, Zaire — A2 48
Bom Conselho, Braz. — C3 57
Bom Despacho, Braz. — B3 56
Bom Jardim, Braz. — B2 57
Bom Jardim de Goiás, Braz. — B2 57
Bom Jardim de Minas, Braz. — g5 56
Bom Jesus, Braz. — D2 56
Bom Jesus, Braz. — A4 57
Bom Jesus da Lapa, Braz. — A4 57
Bomokandi, stm., Zaire — A4 48
Bomongo, Zaire — A2 48
Bom Retiro, Braz. — D3 56
Bomoseen, Vt., U.S. — D2 122
Bomoseen, Lake, I., Vt., U.S. — D2 122
Bomu, stm., Afr. — E4 46
Bon, Cap, c., Tun. — B7 44
Bon Accord, Alta. — C4 68
Bonaigarh, India — G10 37
Bon Air, Al., U.S. — B3 78
Bon Air, Tn., U.S. — D8 119
Bon Air, Va., U.S. — C5 123
Bonaire, Ga., U.S. — D3 87
Bonaire, i., Neth. Ant. — D5 62
Bonanza, Nic. — D5 62
Bonanza, Ar., U.S. — B1 81
Bonanza, Or., U.S. — E5 114
Bonanza, Ut., U.S. — C6 121
Bonanza City, Co., U.S. — C4 83
Bonanza Peak, mtn., Wa., U.S. — A5 124
Bonaparte, Ia., U.S. — D6 92
Bonaparte, stm., B.C. — D7 69
Bonaparte, Mount, mtn., Wa., U.S. — A6 124
Bonaparte, Lake, I., B.C. — D7 69
Bon Aqua, Tn., U.S. — B4 119
Boñar, Spain — A3 22
Bonar Bridge, Scot., U.K. — C4 13
Bonarlaw, Ont. — C7 73
Bonasila Dome, mtn., Ak., U.S. — C7 79
Bonaventure, Que. — A4 71
Bonaventure, Fl., U.S. — *F6 86
Bonavista, Newf. — D5 72
Bonavista, Cape, c., Newf. — D5 72
Bonavista Bay, b., Newf. — D5 72
Bond, Co., U.S. — B4 83
Bond, Ky., U.S. — C5 94
Bond, Ms., U.S. — B6 101
Bond, Ok., U.S. — B6 113
Bond, co., Il., U.S. — E4 90
Bondeno, Italy — E6 21
Bondo, Zaire — A4 48
Bondoukou, I.C. — E4 45
Bondsville, Ma., U.S. — B3 98
Bonduel, Wi., U.S. — D5 126
Bondurant, Ia., U.S. — C4 92
Bondurant, Wy., U.S. — C2 127
Bondville, Il., U.S. — C5 90
Bondville, Vt., U.S. — E3 122
Bondy, Fr. — g10 16
Bone, Gulf of, b., Indon. — F6 34
Bone, Ghana — E4 45
Bone Cave, Tn., U.S. — D8 119
Bone Gap, Il., U.S. — E6 90
Bone Lake, I., Wi., U.S. — C1 126
Bonesteel, S.D., U.S. — D7 118
Bonetraill, N.D., U.S. — E2 55
Bonete, Cerro, mtn., Arg. — D2 55
Bonfield, Ont. — A5 73
Bonfouca, La., U.S. — h12 95
Bonga, Eth. — D4 47
Bongandanga, Zaire — A3 48
Bongo, Chad — C3 46
Bong Son, Viet. — C3 34
Bonham, Tx., U.S. — C4 120
Bon Homme Colony, S.D., U.S. — E8 118
Bon Homme, co., S.D., U.S. — E8 118
Bonifacio, Fr. — D2 23
Bonifacio, Strait of, strt., Eur. — D2 23
Bonifay, Fl., U.S. — u16 86
Bonilla, S.D., U.S. — C7 118
Bonin Islands, is., Japan — E8 4
Bonita, Ca., U.S. — *F5 82
Bonita, La., U.S. — B4 95
Bonita Springs, Fl., U.S. — F5 86
Bonito, Braz. — C1 56
Bonlee, N.C., U.S. — B3 110
Bonn, Ger. — E2 19
Bonneau, S.C., U.S. — E8 117
Bonneauville, Pa., U.S. — G7 115
Bonne Bay (Woody Point), Newf. — D3 72
Bonne Bay, b., Newf. — D3 72
Bonne Idee, Bayou, stm., La., U.S. — B4 95
Bonner, Mt., U.S. — D3 103

Name	Map Ref.	Page

Bonner, co., Id., U.S. A2 89
Bonnerdale, Ar., U.S. C2 81
Bonners Ferry, Id., U.S. A2 89
Bonner Springs, Ks., U.S. . . . C9 93
Bønnerup Strand, Den. B4 15
Bonne-sur-Ménoge, Fr. D1 21
Bonnet, Lac du, l., Man. D4 70
Bonnétable, Fr. C4 16
Bonnet Clare Floodway, La.,
   U.S. h11 95
Bonne Terre, Mo., U.S. D7 102
Bonneville, Fr. C2 20
Bonneville, Or., U.S. B5 114
Bonneville, co., Id., U.S. . . . F7 89
Bonneville Dam, U.S. B4 114
Bonneville Peak, mtn., Id.,
   U.S. F6 89
Bonneville Salt Flats, pl., Ut.,
   U.S. C2 121
Bonnevoie-Sud, Lux. *E6 17
Bonney Lake, Wa., U.S. B3 124
Bonnie, Il., U.S. E5 90
Bonnie Doone, N.C., U.S. . . . B4 110
Bonnieville, Ky., U.S. C4 94
Bonnots Mill, Mo., U.S. C6 102
Bonny, Nig. F6 45
Bonny Blue, Va., U.S. f8 123
Bonny Reservoir, res., Co.,
   U.S. B8 83
Bonnyville, Alta. B5 68
Bono, Ar., U.S. B5 81
Bono, Oh., U.S. *A2 112
Bonorva, Italy D2 23
Bonriki, Kir. R18 52
Bonriki, i., Kir. R18 52
Bons, Fr. D1 21
Bonsal, N.C., U.S. B4 110
Bon Secour, Al., U.S. E2 78
Bonshaw, P.E.I. C6 71
Bontang, Indon. E5 34
Bonthe, S.L. E2 45
Bon Wier, Tx., U.S. D6 120
Book Cliffs, clf., U.S. D6 121
Booker, Tx., U.S. A2 120
Booker T. Washington
   National Monument, Va.,
   U.S. C3 123
Booligal, Austl. F5 51
Boolylglass, Ire. E4 11
Boomer, N.C., U.S. A1 110
Boomer, W.V., U.S. C3 125
Boone, Mi., U.S. D5 99
Boone, Co., U.S. C6 83
Boone, Ia., U.S. B4 92
Boone, Ne., U.S. C8 104
Boone, N.C., U.S. A1 110
Boone, co., Ar., U.S. A2 81
Boone, co., Il., U.S. A5 90
Boone, co., In., U.S. D4 91
Boone, co., Ia., U.S. B3 92
Boone, co., Ky., U.S. B5 94
Boone, co., Mo., U.S. B5 102
Boone, co., Ne., U.S. C7 104
Boone, co., W.V., U.S. C3 125
Boone, stm., Ia., U.S. B4 92
Boone Grove, In., U.S. B3 91
Boone Lake, res., Tn., U.S. . . C11 119
Boones Mill, Va., U.S. C3 123
Booneville, Ar., U.S. B2 81
Booneville, Ky., U.S. C6 94
Booneville, Ms., U.S. A5 101
Boonsboro, Md., U.S. A2 97
Boons Pond, l., Ma., U.S. . . . g10 98
Boonton, N.J., U.S. B4 107
Boonville, Ca., U.S. C2 82
Boonville, In., U.S. H3 91
Boonville, Mo., U.S. C5 102
Boonville, N.Y., U.S. B5 109
Boonville, N.C., U.S. A2 110
Boorama, Som. C5 47
Boosaaso, Som. C6 47
Booth, Al., U.S. C3 78
Boothbay, Me., U.S. E3 96
Boothbay Harbor, Me., U.S. . . E3 96
Boothby, Cape, c., Ant. C18 7
Boothia, Gulf of, b., N.W. Ter. . B14 66
Boothia Peninsula, pen., N.W.
   Ter. B14 66
Booths Creek, stm., W.V.,
   U.S. h11 125
Boothville, La., U.S. E6 95
Bootle, Eng., U.K. A4 12
Booué, Gabon F2 46
Bophuthatswana, ctry., Afr. . . C4 49
Bopolu, Lib. E2 45
Boppard, Ger. C3 18
Boquerón, dept., Para. D3 55
Boquerón, stm., Pan. k11 62
Boquerón, Bahía de, b., P.R. . . B1 65
Bor, Sud. D3 47
Bor, Yugo. C6 24
Boraha, Nosy, i., Madag. . . . g10 49
Borah Peak, mtn., Id., U.S. . . E5 89
Borås, Swe. I5 14
Borāzjān, Iran G5 39
Borba, Braz. C3 59
Borculo, Neth. B6 17
Bordeaux, Fr. E6 16
Bordelonville, La., U.S. C4 95
Borden, Sask. E2 75
Borden, In., U.S. H6 91
Borden, co., Tx., U.S. C2 120
Borden Island, i., N.W. Ter. . . m29 66
Borden Peninsula, pen., N.W.
   Ter. B16 66
Borden Springs, Al., U.S. . . . B4 78
Bordentown, N.J., U.S. C3 107
Borderland, W.V., U.S. D2 125
Borders, prov., Scot., U.K. . . E5 13
Bordertown, Austl. G7 50
Bordighera, Italy C1 23
Bordj Bou Arreridj, Alg. B5 44
Bordj Omar Idriss, Alg. D6 44
Bordley, Ky., U.S. C2 94
Bordulac, N.D., U.S. B7 111
Boré, Mali C4 45
Boren, l., Swe. u33 14
Borensberg, Swe. u33 14
Borgå, Fin. G11 14
Börger, Ger. B7 17
Borger, Neth. B6 17
Borger, Tx., U.S. B2 120
Borgholm, Swe. I7 14
Borghorst, Ger. A2 19
Borg Mountain, mtn., Ant. . . . B12 7
Borgne, stm., Switz. D3 21
Borgne, Lac, b., La., U.S. . . . D6 95
Borgomanero, Italy B2 23
Borgo Panigale, Italy k9 23
Borgosesia, Italy E5 21
Borgo Val di Taro, Italy B2 23
Borgo Val di Sugana, Italy . . . C7 20
Boring, Or., U.S. B4 114
Borislav, Sov. Un. G4 27
Borisoglebsk, Sov. Un. D7 29

Borisov, Sov. Un. D7 27
Borispol, Sov. Un. F8 27
Borja, Peru B2 58
Borja, Spain B5 22
Borjas Blancas, Spain B6 22
Borken, Ger. B1 19
Borken, Ger. B4 19
Borkop, Den. C3 15
Børkou, hist. reg., Chad B3 46
Borkum, Ger. A6 17
Borkum, i., Ger. B3 18
Borlänge, Swe. G6 14
Bormes, Fr. F7 16
Bormida, stm., Italy E4 20
Bormio, Italy C6 20
Borna, Ger. B7 19
Borne, Neth. B6 17
Borneo (Kalimantan), i., Asia . . E4 34
Bornheim, Ger. C1 19
Bornholm, co., Den. C8 15
Bornholm, i., Den. J6 14
Bornholmsgat, strt., Eur. C8 15
Bornos, Spain D3 22
Borobudur, hist., Indon. G4 34
Boromlya, Sov. Un. F10 27
Boromo, Burkina D4 45
Boron, Ca., U.S. E5 82
Borovan, Bul. D6 24
Borovichi, Sov. Un. D6 29
Borovskoye, Sov. Un. q21 27
Borraan, Som. C6 47
Borrby, Swe. C8 15
Borre, Den. D6 15
Borrego Springs, Ca., U.S. . . F5 82
Borris, Ire. E3 11
Borrisokane, Ire. E3 11
Borrisoleigh, Ire. E4 11
Borroloola, Austl. C6 50
Borşa, Rom. B7 24
Bort-les-Orgues, Fr. E5 16
Borūjen, Iran F5 39
Borūjerd, Iran B4 38
Borup, Mn., U.S. C2 100
Borzhomi, Sov. Un. B14 40
Borzna, Sov. Un. F9 27
Borzonasca, Italy E5 20
Borzya, Sov. Un. A8 31
Bosa, Italy D2 23
Bosanska Dubica, Yugo. C3 24
Bosanska Gradiška, Yugo. . . . C3 24
Bosanska Kostajnica, Yugo. . . C3 24
Bosanski Novi, Yugo. C3 24
Bosanski Petrovac, Yugo. . . . C3 24
Bosanski Šamac, Yugo. C4 24
Bosavi, Mount, mtn., Pap. N.
   Gui. k11 50
Boscawen, N.H., U.S. D3 106
Boscobel, Wi., U.S. E3 126
Boshan, China D8 31
Boshrūyeh, Iran E8 39
Boskovice, Czech. D4 26
Bosler, Wy., U.S. E7 127
Bosna, stm., Yugo. C3 24
Bosnia, hist. reg., Yugo. C3 24
Bosnik, Indon. F9 34
Bosobolo, Zaire A2 48
Bosporus, strt. B7 40
Bosque, N.M., U.S. C3 108
Bosque, co., Tx., U.S. D4 120
Boss, Mo., U.S. D6 102
Bossangoa, Cen. Afr. Rep. . . . D3 46
Bossembélé, Cen. Afr. Rep. . . D3 46
Bossert Estates, N.J., U.S. . . . C3 107
Bossier, co., La., U.S. B2 95
Bossier City, La., U.S. B2 95
Bosso, Niger D7 45
Bosso, Dallol, val., Niger D5 45
Boston, Lake, l., China C2 31
Boston, Eng., U.K. D6 10
Boston, Ga., U.S. F3 87
Boston, In., U.S. E8 91
Boston, Ky., U.S. C4 94
Boston, Ma., U.S. B5 98
Boston Bar, B.C. E7 69
Boston Bay, b., Ma., U.S. . . . B6 98
Boston Heights, Oh., U.S. . . . h9 112
Boston Mountains, mts., Ar.,
   U.S. B2 81
Bostonnais, stm., Que. B5 74
Bostwick, Fl., U.S. C5 86
Bostwick, Ga., U.S. C3 87
Boswarlos, Newf. D2 72
Boswell, B.C. E9 69
Boswell, Al., U.S. D4 78
Boswell, In., U.S. A3 81
Boswell, Ok., U.S. C3 91
Boswell, Ok., U.S. C6 113
Boswell, Pa., U.S. F3 115
Bosworth, Mo., U.S. B4 102
Botany Bay, b., Austl. F9 50
Boteti, stm., Bots. B3 49
Botetourt, co., Va., U.S. C3 123
Botev, mtn., Bul. D7 24
Botevgrad, Bul. D6 24
Botha, Alta. C4 68
Bothell, Wa., U.S. B3 124
Bothnia, Gulf of, b., Eur. F9 14
Bothwell, Ont. E3 73
Bothwell, P.E.I. C7 71
Botkins, Oh., U.S. B1 112
Botkyrka, Swe. t35 14
Botolan, Phil. o13 34
Botoşani, Rom. B8 24
Botsford, Ct., U.S. D2 84
Botswana, ctry., Afr. B3 49
Bottineau, N.D., U.S. A5 111
Bottineau, co., N.D., U.S. . . . A5 111
Bottrop, Ger. B1 19
Botucatu, Braz. A7 56
Botwood, Newf. D4 72
Bouaflé, I.C. E3 45
Bouaké, I.C. E3 45
Bouar, Cen. Afr. Rep. D2 46
Bou Arfa, Mor. C4 44
Boucau, Fr. F3 16
Boucher, Lac, l., Que. C2 74
Boucherville, Que. D4 74
Bouchette, Que. D2 74
Bouctouche, N.B. C5 71
Boudenib, Mor. B4 44
Boú Djébéha, well, Mali C4 45
Boudreaux, Lake, l., La., U.S. . . E5 95
Boudry, Switz. D1 21
Bougainville, i., Pap. N. Gui. . . G9 4
Bougouni, Mali D3 45
Bouillon, Bel. E5 17
Boulder, Co., U.S. A5 83
Boulder, Co., U.S. B2 89
Boulder, Mt., U.S. D4 103
Boulder, Ut., U.S. F4 121
Boulder, Wy., U.S. D3 127
Boulder, co., Co., U.S. A5 83
Boulder City, Nv., U.S. H7 105
Boulder Creek, Ca., U.S. . . . *D2 82
Boulder Hill, Il., U.S. *B5 90

Boulevard, Ca., U.S. F5 82
Boulevard Heights, Md., U.S. . f9 97
Boulevard Park, Wa., U.S. . . *B3 124
Bouligny, Fr. E5 17
Boulogne-Billancourt, Fr. C5 16
Boulogne-sur-Mer, Fr. B4 16
Boulsa, Burkina D4 45
Boumalne, Mor. C3 44
Boumdeït, Maur. C2 45
Bouna, I.C. E4 45
Boundary, Ak., U.S. C11 79
Boundary, co., Id., U.S. A2 89
Boundary Bald Mountain,
   mtn., Me., U.S. C2 96
Boundary Bay, b., Wa., U.S. . . A3 124
Boundary Bend, Austl. G4 51
Boundary Peak, mtn., Nv.,
   U.S. F3 105
Boundary Ranges, mts., N.A. . . k22 79
Bound Brook, N.J., U.S. B3 107
Boundiali, I.C. E3 45
Bountiful, Ut., U.S. C4 121
Bounty, Sask. F2 75
Bounty Islands, is., N.Z. Q17 51
Bourbeuse, stm., Mo., U.S. . . C6 102
Bourbon, In., U.S. B5 91
Bourbon, Mo., U.S. C6 102
Bourbon, co., Ks., U.S. E9 93
Bourbon, co., Ky., U.S. B5 94
Bourbonnais, Il., U.S. B6 90
Bourbonnais, hist. reg., Fr. . . . D5 16
Bourbonne-les-Bains, Fr. C4 45
Bourem, Mali E5 95
Bourg, La., U.S. D6 71
Bourg-de-Péage, Fr. E6 16
Bourg [-en-Bresse], Fr. D6 16
Bourges, Fr. D5 16
Bourget, Ont. B9 73
Bourget, Lake, l., Fr. D1 20
Bourg-la-Reine, Fr. g10 16
Bourgoin [-Jallieu], Fr. F5 39
Bourg-Saint-Andéol, Fr. E6 16
Bourg-Saint-Maurice, Fr. D2 20
Bourke, Austl. F8 50
Bourne, Eng., U.K. B7 12
Bourne, Ma., U.S. C6 98
Bournemouth, Eng., U.K. . . . E6 10
Bourneville, Oh., U.S. C2 112
Bou Saâda, Alg. B5 44
Bouse, Az., U.S. D2 80
Bousso, Chad C3 46
Boutilimit, Maur. C2 45
Boutte, La., U.S. k11 95
Bouvet, i., Ant. D13 7
Bovey, Mn., U.S. C5 100
Bovill, Id., U.S. C2 89
Bovina, Ms., U.S. C3 101
Bovina, Tx., U.S. B1 120
Bovina Center, N.Y., U.S. . . . C6 109
Bow, N.H., U.S. D3 106
Bow, Wa., U.S. A3 124
Bow, stm., Alta. D4 68
Bowbells, N.D., U.S. A3 111
Bowden, Alta. D4 68
Bowden, Ok., U.S. A5 113
Bowdens, N.C., U.S. B4 110
Bowdish Reservoir, res., R.I.,
   U.S. B1 116
Bowdle, S.D., U.S. B6 118
Bowdoin, Me., U.S. E3 96
Bowdoinham, Me., U.S. D3 96
Bowdon, Ga., U.S. C1 87
Bowdon, N.D., U.S. B6 111
Bowen, Austl. C8 50
Bowen, Il., U.S. C2 90
Bowen, De., U.S. D4 85
Bowerston, Oh., U.S. B4 112
Bowersville, Ga., U.S. B3 87
Bowersville, Oh., U.S. C2 112
Bowesmont, N.D., U.S. A8 111
Bowie, Az., U.S. E6 80
Bowie, Co., U.S. C3 83
Bowie, Md., U.S. C4 97
Bowie, Tx., U.S. C4 120
Bowie, co., Tx., U.S. C5 120
Bowie Creek, stm., Ms., U.S. . *B3 101
Bow Island, Alta. E5 68
Bowkerville, N.H., U.S. E2 106
Bow Lake, l., N.H., U.S. D4 106
Bowlegs, Ok., U.S. B5 113
Bowler, Wi., U.S. D5 126
Bowling Green, Fl., U.S. E5 86
Bowling Green, In., U.S. F4 91
Bowling Green, Ky., U.S. D3 94
Bowling Green, Mo., U.S. . . . B6 102
Bowling Green, Oh., U.S. . . . A2 112
Bowling Green, S.C., U.S. . . . A5 117
Bowling Green, Va., U.S. . . . B5 123
Bowlus, Mn., U.S. E4 100
Bowman, Ga., U.S. B3 87
Bowman, N.D., U.S. C2 111
Bowman, S.C., U.S. E6 117
Bowman, co., N.D., U.S. . . . C2 111
Bowman Creek, stm., Pa.,
   U.S. m16 115
Bowman-Haley Lake, res.,
   N.D., U.S. C2 111
Bowman Island, i., Ant. C23 7
Bowmanstown, Pa., U.S. E10 115
Bowmanville (part of
   Newcastle), Ont. D6 73
Bow Mar, Co., U.S. *B5 83
Bowmont, Id., U.S. F2 89
Bowmore, Scot., U.K. F2 13
Bowokan Islands, is., Indon. . . F6 34
Bowral, Austl. F9 51
Bowring, Ok., U.S. A5 113
Bowron, stm., B.C. C7 69
Bowron Lake Provincial Park,
   B.C. C7 69
Bowser Lake, l., B.C. A3 69
Bowstring Lake, l., Mn., U.S. . . C5 100
Bow Valley, Ne., U.S. B8 104
Boxborough, Ma., U.S. A5 98
Box Butte, co., Ne., U.S. . . . B2 104
Box Butte Creek, stm., Ne.,
   U.S. B3 104
Box Butte Reservoir, res., Ne.,
   U.S. B3 104
Box Elder, Mt., U.S. B6 103
Box Elder, S.D., U.S. C2 118
Box Elder, co., Ut., U.S. B2 121
Box Elder Creek, stm., Co.,
   U.S. A6 83
Boxelder Creek, stm., Mt.,
   U.S. E12 103
Box Elder Creek, stm., Mt.,
   U.S. C8 103
Boxford, Ma., U.S. A6 98
Boxholm, Ia., U.S. B3 92
Boxian, China E8 31
Boxmeer, Neth. C5 17
Boxtel, Neth. B6 16

Boyacá, dept., Col. B3 60
Boyang, China J7 32
Boyce, La., U.S. C3 95
Boyce, Tx., U.S. n10 120
Boyce, Va., U.S. A4 123
Boyceville, Wi., U.S. C1 126
Boyd, Mn., U.S. F3 100
Boyd, Mt., U.S. E7 103
Boyd, Tx., U.S. C4 120
Boyd, Wi., U.S. D2 126
Boyd, co., Ky., U.S. B7 94
Boyd, co., Ne., U.S. B7 104
Boydell, Ar., U.S. D4 81
Boyden, Ia., U.S. A2 92
Boyd Glacier, ice, Ant. B34 7
Boyd Lake, l., Me., U.S. C4 96
Boyds, Md., U.S. B3 97
Boyd's Cove, Newf. A5 81
Boydton, Va., U.S. D4 123
Boyer, stm., Ia., U.S. C2 92
Boyera, Zaire k13 97
Boyer Knob, mtn., Md., U.S. . . C7 83
Boyero, Co., U.S. C7 83
Boyers, Pa., U.S. E11 103
Boyertown, Pa., U.S. C2 78
Boykin, Al., U.S. D4 88
Boykin, Ga., U.S. B3 87
Boykins, Va., U.S. D5 123
Boyle, Alta. B4 68
Boyle, Ire. C2 10
Boyle, Ms., U.S. B3 101
Boyle, co., Ky., U.S. C5 94
Boylston, Ma., U.S. B4 98
Boyne, stm., Ire. D5 11
Boyne City, Mi., U.S. C6 99
Boyne Falls, Mi., U.S. C6 99
Boynton, Ok., U.S. B6 113
Boynton, Pa., U.S. G3 115
Boynton Beach, Fl., U.S. F6 86
Boyoma Falls (Stanley Falls),
   wtfl., Zaire A4 48
Boy River, Mn., U.S. C4 100
Boys Ranch, Tx., U.S. B1 120
Boys Town, Ne., U.S. g12 104
Boz, Cape, c., Tur. B7 24
Bozcaada, Tur. C6 24
Bozca Island (Tenedos), i.,
   Tur. D7 25
Bozdoğan, Tur. E5 103
Bozeman, Mt., U.S. E6 103
Bozeman Pass, Mt., U.S. E6 103
Bozoum, Cen. Afr. Rep. D3 46
Bozovici, Rom. C5 24
Bozdüsh, Küh-e, mts., Iran . . . C4 39
Bozüyük, Tur. C8 40
Bra, Italy B1 23
Brabant, prov., Bel. D4 17
Brabant, i., Ant. C6 7
Brabant Lake, l., Sask. m8 75
Brač, i., Yugo. D3 24
Bracadale, Scot., U.K. C2 13
Bracadale, Loch, b., Scot.,
   U.K. C2 13
Bracciano, Italy g8 23
Bracciano, Lake, l., Italy C4 23
Bracebridge, Ont. B5 73
Brackett, Oh., U.S. C9 118
Braceville, Il., U.S. B5 90
Brach, Libya D2 43
Bracken, Sask. H1 75
Bracken, co., Ky., U.S. B5 94
Bracken Lake, l., Man. C2 70
Brackenridge, Pa., U.S. h15 115
Brackett, Wi., U.S. D2 126
Brackettville, Tx., U.S. E2 120
Brackley, Eng., U.K. B6 12
Brackwell, Eng., U.K. C7 12
Brackwede, Ger. B3 19
Brad, Rom. B6 24
Bradano, stm., Italy D6 23
Braddock, N.J., U.S. D3 107
Braddock, N.D., U.S. C5 111
Braddock, Pa., U.S. k14 115
Braddock Point, c., S.C., U.S. . G6 117
Braddock Heights, Md., U.S. . . B2 97
Braddyville, Ia., U.S. D2 92
Braden, Tn., U.S. B2 119
Bradenton, Fl., U.S. E4 86
Bradenton Beach, Fl., U.S. . . . F3 115
Bradford, Ont. C5 73
Bradford, Eng., U.K. D6 10
Bradford, Al., U.S. D3 78
Bradford, Il., U.S. B4 90
Bradford, Me., U.S. C4 96
Bradford, N.H., U.S. D3 106
Bradford, Oh., U.S. B1 112
Bradford, Pa., U.S. C4 115
Bradford, R.I., U.S. F1 116
Bradford, Tn., U.S. A3 119
Bradford, Vt., U.S. D4 122
Bradford, co., Fl., U.S. C4 86
Bradford, co., Pa., U.S. C8 115
Bradford Mountain, mtn., Ct.,
   U.S. B2 84
Bradfordwoods, Pa., U.S. . . . h13 115
Bradgate, Ia., U.S. B3 92
Bradley, Ca., res., Me., U.S. . . C3 96
Bradnell, Oh., U.S. g9 112
Bratislava, Czech. G17 26
Bradley, Al., U.S. D2 78
Bradley, Ar., U.S. D2 81
Bradley, Ca., U.S. E3 82
Bradley, Fl., U.S. E5 86
Bradley, Il., U.S. B6 90
Bradley, Oh., U.S. D4 96
Bradley, Ok., U.S. C4 113
Bradley, S.C., U.S. C3 117
Bradley, S.D., U.S. B8 118
Bradley, W.V., U.S. D3 125
Bradley, co., Ar., U.S. D3 81
Bradley, co., Tn., U.S. D9 119
Bradley Beach, N.J., U.S. . . . C4 107
Bradleyton, Ar., U.S. D4 78
Brador, Baie de, b., Que. C2 72
Bradshaw, Md., U.S. B5 97
Bradshaw, Ne., U.S. D8 104
Bradshaw, W.V., U.S. D3 125
Bradshaw Mountains, mts.,
   Az., U.S. C3 80
Bradstreet, Ma., U.S. A5 98
Brady, Mt., U.S. B5 103
Brady, Ne., U.S. C5 104
Brady, Tx., U.S. D3 120
Bradyville, Tn., U.S. B5 119
Brædstrup, Den. C3 15
Braemar, Scot., U.K. D5 13
Braeside, Ont. B8 73

Braga, Port. B1 22
Bragado, Arg. B4 54
Bragança, Braz. B1 57
Bragança, Port. B2 22
Bragança Paulista, Braz. E8 102
Braggadocio, Mo., U.S. B6 113
Braggs, Ok., U.S. B5 100
Braham, Mn., U.S. D7 36
Brāhmani, stm., India E7 36
Brahmapur, India D2 126
Brahmaputra (Yarlung Zangbo
   Jiang), stm., Asia C9 36
Braidwood, Il., U.S. B5 90
Brăila, Rom. C8 24
Brainard, Ne., U.S. C9 104
Braine-le-Comte, Bel. g12 17
Brainerd, Ks., U.S. D4 100
Braintree, Eng., U.K. C8 12
Braintree, Ma., U.S. B5 98
Brake, Ger. D12 122
Brakel, Ger. k12 95
Brakpan, S. Afr. B4 18
Bralorne, B.C. B4 19
Bramsche, Ger. *C4 49
Bramming, Den. D6 69
Brampton, Eng., U.K. A4 113
Brampton, Ont. C2 15
Bramwell, W.V., U.S. B7 17
Branch, Newf. D3 95
Branch, Ar., U.S. E5 72
Branch, La., U.S. B2 81
Branch, Wi., U.S. D3 95
Branch, co., Mi., U.S. D6 99
Branch, stm., R.I., U.S. G5 99
Branch, stm., Wi., U.S. B3 116
Branch Lake, l., Me., U.S. . . . h10 126
Branchland, W.V., U.S. D4 96
Branchville, N.J., U.S. C2 125
Branchville, Al., U.S. A3 116
Branchville, Ct., U.S. B3 78
Branchville, S.C., U.S. D2 84
Branchville, Va., U.S. E6 117
Branco, stm., Braz. D5 123
Branco, co., Braz. B3 55
Brandberg, mtn., Nmb. D4 55
Brande, Den. B1 49
Brandenburg, Ger. C3 15
Brandenburg, Ky., U.S. B6 18
Brandenburg, hist. reg., Ger. . . B6 18
Brandon, Man. C3 94
Brandon, Fl., U.S. E2 70
Brandon, Ms., U.S. E4 86
Brandon, Mn., U.S. C3 101
Brandon, Ne., U.S. E3 100
Brandon, S.C., U.S. C4 101
Brandon, S.D., U.S. B2 117
Brandon, Vt., U.S. D9 118
Brandon, Wi., U.S. D2 122
Brandon Head, c., Ire. E5 126
Brandon Mountain, mtn., Ire. . . E1 11
Brandsen, Arg. D1 10
Brandsville, Mo., U.S. B5 54
Brandt, Oh., U.S. E6 102
Brandt, S.D., U.S. C1 112
Brandvlei, S. Afr. C9 118
Brandy Peak, mtn., Or., U.S. . . D3 49
Brandys nad Labem, Czech. . . E3 114
Brandýs-Stará Boleslav,
   Czech. n18 26
Brandy Station, Va., U.S. . . . B5 123
Branewo, Pol. C4 97
Branford, Ct., U.S. D4 84
Branford, Fl., U.S. C4 86
Branford Hills, Ct., U.S. D4 84
Braniewo, Pol. A5 26
Bransfield Strait, strt., Ant. . . . C7 7
Brańsk, Pol. B7 26
Branson, Co., U.S. D7 83
Branson, Mo., U.S. E4 102
Brant, Alta. D4 68
Brant, co., Ont. D4 73
Brant, Alta. B2 119
Branford, N.D., U.S. B7 111
Brantford, Ont. D4 73
Brantley, Al., U.S. D3 78
Brantley, co., Ga., U.S. E4 87
Brant Rock, Ma., U.S. B6 98
Brantville, N.B. B5 71
Bras-d'Apic, Que. C7 74
Bras d'Or Lake, l., N.S. D9 71
Brasher, Mo., U.S. A5 102
Brasília, Braz. A3 119
Brasília, Braz. B5 56
Brasília de Minas, Braz. B5 56
Braşov (Oraşul-Stalin), Rom. . . C7 24
Brasstown, Ga., U.S. f9 110
Brasstown Bald, mtn., Ga.,
   U.S. B3 87
Brassua, Lake, res., Me., U.S. . C3 96
Bratenahl, Oh., U.S. g9 112
Bratislava, Czech. G17 26
Bratsk, Sov. Un. D13 29
Bratsk Reservoir, res., Sov.
   Un. D13 29
Brattleboro, Vt., U.S. F3 122
Brattvær, Nor. D6 14
Braunau [am Inn], Aus. G13 26
Braunfels, Tx., U.S. E3 120
Braunschweig, Ger. B5 18
Brava, Austl. g11 115
Brāviken, b., Swe. u34 14
Brawley, Ca., U.S. F6 82
Brawley Peaks, mts., Nv., U.S. . E3 105
Bray, Ire. D5 11
Bray Head, c., Ire. F1 11
Braymer, Mo., U.S. B4 102
Brazeau, stm., Alta. C2 68
Brazeau, Mount, mtn., Alta. . . C2 68
Brazil, ctry., S.A. C5 53
Brazil, In., U.S. E3 91
Brazil, Tn., U.S. B2 119
Brazilian Highlands, plat.,
   Braz. C5 53
Brazilton, Ks., U.S. E9 93

Brazoria, Tx., U.S. r14 120
Brazoria, co., Tx., U.S. E5 120
Brazos, co., Tx., U.S. D4 120
Brazos, stm., Tx., U.S. D4 120
Brazzaville, Congo B2 48
Brčko, Yugo. C4 24
Brda, stm., Pol. B4 26
Brea, Ca., U.S. n13 82
Brea, Punta, c., P.R. C2 65
Bread Loaf Mountain, mtn.,
   Vt., U.S. D3 122
Breakenridge, Mount, mtn.,
   B.C. E7 69
Breakeyville, Que. o17 74
Breakers Point, c., Am. Sam. . . F13 52
Bream Bay, b., N.Z. K15 51
Breared, Swe. B7 15
Breathitt, co., Ky., U.S. C6 94
Breaux Bridge, La., U.S. D4 95
Brechin, Ont. C5 73
Brechin, Scot., U.K. B5 10
Breckenridge, Que. h12 73
Breckenridge, Co., U.S. B4 83
Breckenridge, Mi., U.S. E6 99
Breckenridge, Mn., U.S. D2 100
Breckenridge, Tx., U.S. C3 120
Breckenridge Hills, Mo., U.S. . *f13 102
Breckinridge, co., Ky., U.S. . . C3 94
Brecknock, Peninsula, pen.,
   Chile h11 54
Brecksville, Oh., U.S. A4 112
Břeclav, Czech. D4 26
Brecon (Brecknock), Wales,
   U.K. E5 10
Brecon Beacons, mtn., Wales,
   U.K. E5 10
Breda, Neth. B6 16
Breda, Ia., U.S. B3 92
Bredasdorp, S. Afr. D3 49
Bredebro, Den. D2 15
Bredenbury, Sask. G4 75
Bredstedt, Ger. D2 15
Bredy, Sov. Un. E21 8
Bree, Bel. C5 17
Breese, Il., U.S. E4 90
Breezy Point, Mn., U.S. D4 100
Bregalnica, stm., Yugo. E6 24
Bregenz, Aus. E4 18
Bregenzerach, stm., Aus. B8 21
Breidafjörður, b., Ice. n21 14
Breid Bay, b., Ant. B15 7
Breien, N.D., U.S. C5 111
Breil, Fr. F7 16
Breisach, Ger. A3 20
Brejinho de Nazaré, Braz. . . . E5 59
Brejo, Braz. B2 57
Bremen, Al., U.S. B2 78
Bremen, Ga., U.S. C1 87
Bremen, In., U.S. B5 91
Bremen, Ky., U.S. C2 94
Bremen, N.D., U.S. B6 111
Bremen, Oh., U.S. C3 112
Bremen, state, Ger. E2 15
Bremen, co., Ia., U.S. B5 92
Bremerhaven (Wesermünde),
   Ger. B4 18
Bremerton, Wa., U.S. B3 124
Bremervörde, Ger. E3 15
Bremo Bluff, Va., U.S. C4 123
Bremond, Tx., U.S. D4 120
Breña, Peru *D2 58
Brenham, Tx., U.S. D4 120
Brenner Pass, Eur. A3 23
Brent, Ont. A6 73
Brent, Al., U.S. C2 78
Brent, Fl., U.S. u14 86
Brenta, stm., Italy D7 20
Brentford, S.D., U.S. B7 118
Brentwood, W.V., U.S. *D3 125
Brenton Point, c., R.I., U.S. . . F5 116
Brentwood, Eng., U.K. k13 10
Brentwood, Ca., U.S. h9 82
Brentwood, Md., U.S. f9 97
Brentwood, Mo., U.S. f13 102
Brentwood, N.H., U.S. E4 106
Brentwood, N.Y., U.S. E7 109
Brentwood, Oh., U.S. *o12 112
Brentwood, Pa., U.S. k14 115
Brentwood, S.C., U.S. k11 117
Brentwood, Tn., U.S. A5 119
Breskens, Neth. C3 17
Breslau see Wrocław, Pol. . . . C4 26
Bresle, stm., Fr. C4 16
Bressanone, Italy A3 23
Bressuire, Fr. D3 16
Brest, Fr. C1 16
Brest (Brest-Litovsk), Sov. Un. . D5 29
Brétigny [-Notre-Dame], Fr. . . F2 17
Breton, Alta. C3 68
Breton, Pertuis, strt., Fr. D3 16
Breton Islands, is., La., U.S. . . E6 95
Breton Sound, strt., La., U.S. . E6 95
Breton Woods, N.J., U.S. . . . C4 107
Brett, Cape, c., N.Z. K15 51
Bretton Woods, N.H., U.S. . . . B4 106
Breuil, Italy D3 20
Brevard, N.C., U.S. f10 110
Brevard, co., Fl., U.S. E6 86
Breves, Braz. C4 59
Brevik (part of Porsgrunn),
   Nor. p27 14
Brevoort Lake, l., Mi., U.S. . . . B6 99
Brevort, Mi., U.S. B6 99
Brewarrina, Austl. E8 50
Brewer, Me., U.S. D4 96
Brewer, Mo., U.S. D8 102
Brewster, Lib. E2 45
Brewster, Ks., U.S. C2 93
Brewster, Mn., U.S. G3 100
Brewster, Ne., U.S. C6 104
Brewster, N.Y., U.S. D7 109
Brewster, Oh., U.S. B4 112
Brewster, Wa., U.S. A6 124
Brewster, co., Tx., U.S. D1 120
Brewster, Kap, c., Grnld. . . . B18 61
Brewster Islands, is., Ma.,
   U.S. g12 98
Brewton, Al., U.S. D2 78
Brewton, Ga., U.S. D4 87
Brezhnev see Naberezhnyye
   Chelny, Sov. Un. D8 29
Březnice, Yugo. C2 24
Březnice, Czech. D8 19
Breznik, Bul. D6 24

Name	Map Ref.	Page
Brezno, Czech.	D5	26
Bria, Cen. Afr. Rep.	D4	46
Brian Boru Peak, mtn., B.C.	B4	69
Briançon, Fr.	E7	16
Brian Head, mtn., Ut., U.S.	F3	121
Briarcliff, Pa., U.S.	p20	115
Briarcliff Manor, N.Y., U.S.	*D7	109
Briare, Fr.	D5	16
Briartown, Ok., U.S.	B6	113
Brice, Oh., U.S.	m11	112
Bricelyn, Mn., U.S.	G5	100
Briceville, Tn., U.S.	C9	119
Brickeys, Ar., U.S.	C5	81
Brick [Township], N.J., U.S.	C4	107
Bridal Veil, Or., U.S.	B4	114
Bridal Veil Falls, wtfl., Ut., U.S.	C4	121
Bride, stm., Ire.	E3	11
Bridesville, B.C.	E8	69
Bridge, stm., B.C.	D6	69
Bridgeboro, Ga., U.S.	E3	87
Bridge City, La., U.S.	*E5	95
Bridge City, Tx., U.S.	*D6	120
Bridge Creek, stm., Sask.	H1	75
Bridgeford, Sask.	G2	75
Bridgehampton, N.Y., U.S.	n16	109
Bridge Lake, B.C.	D7	69
Bridgeland, Ut., U.S.	C5	121
Bridgend, Wales, U.K.	C4	12
Bridgeport (part of Kitchener), Ont.	D4	73
Bridgeport, Al., U.S.	A4	78
Bridgeport, Ca., U.S.	C4	82
Bridgeport, Ct., U.S.	E3	84
Bridgeport, Il., U.S.	E6	90
Bridgeport, Mi., U.S.	E7	99
Bridgeport, Ne., U.S.	C2	104
Bridgeport, N.J., U.S.	D2	107
Bridgeport, Oh., U.S.	B5	112
Bridgeport, Ok., U.S.	B3	113
Bridgeport, Or., U.S.	C9	114
Bridgeport, Pa., U.S.	o20	115
Bridgeport, Tx., U.S.	C4	120
Bridgeport, Wa., U.S.	B6	124
Bridgeport, W.V., U.S.	B4	125
Bridger, Mt., U.S.	E8	103
Bridger, S.D., U.S.	C4	118
Bridger Mountains, mts., Wy., U.S.	C5	127
Bridger Peak, mtn., Wy., U.S.	E5	127
Bridger Range, mts., Mt., U.S.	E6	103
Bridgeton, In., U.S.	E3	91
Bridgeton, Mo., U.S.	C7	102
Bridgeton, N.J., U.S.	E2	107
Bridgeton, N.C., U.S.	B5	110
Bridgetown, Barb.	J15	64
Bridgetown, Oh., U.S.	*o12	112
Bridgeview, Il., U.S.	*k9	90
Bridgeville, De., U.S.	F3	85
Bridgeville, Pa., U.S.	k13	115
Bridgewater, N.S.	E5	71
Bridgewater, Ct., U.S.	C2	84
Bridgewater, Ia., U.S.	C3	92
Bridgewater, Me., U.S.	B5	96
Bridgewater, Ma., U.S.	C6	98
Bridgewater, N.H., U.S.	C3	106
Bridgewater, N.J., U.S.	B3	107
Bridgewater, S.D., U.S.	D8	118
Bridgewater, Vt., U.S.	D3	122
Bridgewater, Va., U.S.	B4	123
Bridgewater Corners, Vt., U.S.	D3	122
Bridgman, Mi., U.S.	G4	99
Bridgnorth, Eng., U.K.	B5	12
Bridgton, Me., U.S.	D2	96
Bridgwater, Eng., U.K.	E5	10
Bridgwater Bay, b., Eng., U.K.	C4	12
Bridlington, Eng., U.K.	D5	10
Bridport, Eng., U.K.	D5	12
Bridport, Vt., U.S.	D2	122
Brielle, N.J., U.S.	C4	107
Brienz, Switz.	E4	18
Brienz, Lake, l., Switz.	C3	20
Brier Creek, stm., Ga., U.S.	C5	87
Briercrest, Sask.	G3	75
Briereville, Alta.	B5	68
Brier Hill, N.Y., U.S.	f9	109
Briery Knob, mtn., W.V., U.S.	C4	125
Briey, Fr.	E5	16
Brig, Switz.	E3	18
Brigantine, N.J., U.S.	E4	107
Brigantine Beach, N.J., U.S.	E4	107
Brig Bay, Newf.	C3	72
Brigden, Ont.	E2	73
Brigg, Eng., U.K.	A7	12
Briggs, Ne., U.S.	*C10	104
Briggs, Tx., U.S.	D4	120
Briggsdale, Co., U.S.	A6	83
Briggs Marsh, sw., R.I., U.S.	F6	116
Briggsville, Ar., U.S.	C2	81
Briggsville, Ma., U.S.	A1	98
Briggsville, Wi., U.S.	E4	126
Brigham City, Ut., U.S.	B3	121
Brig Harbour Island, i., Newf.	A3	72
Bright, Ont.	D4	73
Brighton, Ont.	C7	73
Brighton, Eng., U.K.	E6	10
Brighton, Al., U.S.	B3	78
Brighton, Co., U.S.	B6	83
Brighton, Il., U.S.	D3	90
Brighton, Ia., U.S.	C6	92
Brighton, Me., U.S.	C3	96
Brighton, Mi., U.S.	F7	99
Brighton, N.Y., U.S.	B3	109
Brighton, Or., U.S.	B3	114
Brighton, Tn., U.S.	B2	119
Brighton, Ut., U.S.	*C4	121
Brighton Indian Reservation, Fl., U.S.	E5	86
Brightsand Lake, l., Sask.	D1	75
Brightshade, Ky., U.S.	C6	94
Brignoles, Fr.	F5	16
Brihuega, Spain	B4	22
Brilhante, stm., Braz.	C1	56
Brilliant, B.C.	E9	69
Brilliant, Al., U.S.	A2	78
Brilliant, Oh., U.S.	B5	112
Brillion, Wi., U.S.	D5	126
Brilon, Ger.	B3	19
Brimfield, Il., U.S.	C4	90
Brimfield, Ma., U.S.	*B3	98
Brimhall, N.M., U.S.	B1	108
Brimley, Mi., U.S.	B6	99
Brimson, Mn., U.S.	C7	100
Brimson, Mo., U.S.	A4	102
Brindisi, Italy	D6	23
Bringhurst, In., U.S.	C5	91
Brinje, Yugo.	D10	21
Brinkhaven, Oh., U.S.	B3	112
Brinkley, Ar., U.S.	C4	81
Brinkman, Ok., U.S.	B2	113
Brinktown, Mo., U.S.	C5	102
Brinkworth, Austl.	F2	51
Brinnon, Wa., U.S.	B3	124
Brinsmade, N.D., U.S.	A6	111
Brinson, Ga., U.S.	F2	87
Brion, Île, i., Que.	B8	71
Brione (Verzasca), Switz.	D6	21
Brioude, Fr.	E5	16
Brisbane, Austl.	E9	50
Briscoe, Tx., U.S.	B2	120
Briscoe, co., Tx., U.S.	B2	120
Brissago, Switz.	D6	21
Bristol, N.B.	C2	71
Bristol, Eng., U.K.	E5	10
Bristol, Co., U.S.	C8	83
Bristol, Ct., U.S.	C4	84
Bristol, Fl., U.S.	B2	86
Bristol, Ga., U.S.	E4	87
Bristol, Il., U.S.	B5	90
Bristol, In., U.S.	A6	91
Bristol, Me., U.S.	*E3	96
Bristol, N.H., U.S.	C3	106
Bristol, R.I., U.S.	D5	116
Bristol, S.D., U.S.	B8	118
Bristol, Tn., U.S.	C11	119
Bristol, Vt., U.S.	C2	122
Bristol, Va., U.S.	f9	123
Bristol, W.V., U.S.	B4	125
Bristol, Wi., U.S.	F5	126
Bristol, co., Ma., U.S.	C5	98
Bristol, co., R.I., U.S.	D5	116
Bristol Bay, b., Ak., U.S.	D7	79
Bristol Channel, strt., U.K.	E4	10
Bristol Ferry, R.I., U.S.	D5	116
Bristol [Township], Pa., U.S.	F12	115
Bristolville, Oh., U.S.	A5	112
Bristow, In., U.S.	H4	91
Bristow, Ia., U.S.	B5	92
Bristow, Ne., U.S.	B7	104
Bristow, Ok., U.S.	B5	113
Britannia Bay (part of Ottawa), Ont.	h12	73
Britannia Beach, B.C.	E6	69
Britannia Range, mts., Ant.	B28	7
British Antarctic Territory, dep., S.A.	*C7	124
British Columbia, prov., Can.	C6	69
British Indian Ocean Territory, dep., Afr.	*G25	2
British Mountains, mts., N.A.	B12	79
British Virgin Islands, dep., N.A.	G12	64
Britstown, S. Afr.	D3	49
Britt, Ont.	B4	73
Britt, Ia., U.S.	A4	92
Brittany, hist. reg., Fr.	C2	16
Britton, Mi., U.S.	G7	99
Britton, S.D., U.S.	B8	118
Brive [-la-Gaillarde], Fr.	E4	16
Briviesca, Spain	A4	22
Brixham, Eng., U.K.	E5	10
Brno, Czech.	D4	26
Broa, Ensenada de la, b., Cuba	C3	64
Broad, stm., Ga., U.S.	B4	87
Broad, stm., S.C., U.S.	C5	117
Broadacres, Sask.	E1	75
Broadalbin, N.Y., U.S.	B6	109
Broad Bay, b., Scot., U.K.	B2	13
Broadback, stm., Que.	F17	66
Broadbent, Or., U.S.	E2	114
Broad Brook, Ct., U.S.	B5	84
Broad Creek, stm., De., U.S.	F3	85
Broaddus, Tx., U.S.	D5	120
Broadford, Scot., U.K.	C3	13
Broadford, Va., U.S.	f10	123
Broad Haven, b., Ire.	C2	11
Broadhurst, Ga., U.S.	E5	87
Broadkill, stm., De., U.S.	E4	85
Broadkill Beach, De., U.S.	E5	85
Broadland, S.D., U.S.	C7	118
Broadlands, Il., U.S.	D6	90
Broadmeadows, Austl.	*G7	50
Broadmoor, Co., U.S.	C6	83
Broadmoor, La., U.S.	*D3	95
Broad Run, stm., Va., U.S.	g11	123
Broad Sound, strt., Austl.	D8	50
Broad Top, Pa., U.S.	F5	115
Broadus, Mt., U.S.	E11	103
Broadview, Sask.	G4	75
Broadview, Il., U.S.	*k9	90
Broadview, N.M., U.S.	C6	108
Broadview Heights, Oh., U.S.	h9	112
Broadview Park, Fl., U.S.	F6	86
Broadwater, co., Mt., U.S.	D5	103
Broadwater, Ne., U.S.	C3	104
Broadway, N.J., U.S.	B2	107
Broadway, N.C., U.S.	B3	110
Broadway, Oh., U.S.	B2	112
Broadway, Va., U.S.	B4	123
Broager, Den.	D3	15
Brochet, Man.	f7	70
Brock, Sask.	F1	75
Brock, Ne., U.S.	D10	104
Brocken, mtn., Ger.	B5	19
Brocket, Alta.	E4	68
Brocket, N.D., U.S.	A7	111
Brock Island, i., N.W. Ter.	m29	66
Brockport, N.Y., U.S.	B3	109
Brockport, Pa., U.S.	D4	115
Brockton, Ma., U.S.	B5	98
Brockton, Mt., U.S.	B12	103
Brockton Reservoir, res., Ma., U.S.	h11	98
Brockville, Ont.	C9	73
Brockway, Mt., U.S.	C11	103
Brockway, Pa., U.S.	D4	115
Brockwell, Ar., U.S.	A4	81
Brocton, Il., U.S.	D6	90
Brocton, N.Y., U.S.	C1	109
Broderick, Sask.	F2	75
Brodeur Peninsula, pen., N.W. Ter.	B15	66
Brodhead, Ky., U.S.	C5	94
Brodhead, Wi., U.S.	F4	126
Brodheadsville, Pa., U.S.	E11	115
Brodick, Scot., U.K.	E3	13
Brodnax, Va., U.S.	D4	123
Brodnica, Pol.	B5	26
Brody, Sov. Un.	G5	27
Brogan, Or., U.S.	C9	114
Brokaw, Wi., U.S.	C4	126
Broken Arrow, Ok., U.S.	A6	113
Broken Bow, Ne., U.S.	C6	104
Broken Bow, Ok., U.S.	C7	113
Broken Bow Lake, res., Ok., U.S.	C7	113
Broken Hill, Austl.	F7	50
Brokopondo, Sur.	A3	59
Brokopondo, dept., Sur.	C4	59
Brome, Que.	D5	74
Brome, Ger.	B5	19
Brome, co., Que.	D5	74
Brome, Lac, l., Que.	D5	74
Bromhead, Sask.	H4	75
Bromide, Ok., U.S.	C5	113
Bromley (part of London), Eng., U.K.	m13	10
Bromley Mountain, mtn., Vt., U.S.	E3	122
Bromptonville, Que.	D6	74
Bromsgrove, Eng., U.K.	B5	12
Bromyard, Eng., U.K.	B5	12
Bronaugh, Mo., U.S.	D3	102
Bronderslev, Den.	A3	15
Brong-Ahafo, prov., Ghana	E4	45
Bronnitsy, Sov. Un.	n18	27
Brønnøysund, Nor.	E5	14
Bronson, Fl., U.S.	C4	86
Bronson, Ia., U.S.	B1	92
Bronson, Ks., U.S.	E8	93
Bronson, Mi., U.S.	G5	99
Bronson, Tx., U.S.	D6	120
Bronte, Italy	D2	23
Bronte, Tx., U.S.	D2	120
Bronwood, Ga., U.S.	E2	87
Bronx, co., N.Y., U.S.	E7	109
Bronxville, N.Y., U.S.	h13	109
Brook, In., U.S.	C3	91
Brookdale, Man.	D2	70
Brooke, co., W.V., U.S.	A4	125
Brooke, Va., U.S.	B5	123
Brookeville, Md., U.S.	B3	97
Brookfield, N.S.	D6	71
Brookfield, Ct., U.S.	D2	84
Brookfield, Ga., U.S.	E3	87
Brookfield, Il., U.S.	k9	90
Brookfield, In., U.S.	m11	91
Brookfield, Ma., U.S.	B3	98
Brookfield, Mo., U.S.	B4	102
Brookfield, N.H., U.S.	C4	106
Brookfield, N.Y., U.S.	C5	109
Brookfield, Vt., U.S.	C3	122
Brookfield, Va., U.S.	B5	123
Brookfield, Wi., U.S.	m11	126
Brookfield Center, Ct., U.S.	D2	84
Brookford, N.C., U.S.	B1	110
Brookhaven, Ms., U.S.	D3	101
Brookhaven, Pa., U.S.	*p20	115
Brookhaven, W.V., U.S.	h11	125
Brooking, Sask.	H3	75
Brookings, Or., U.S.	E2	114
Brookings, S.D., U.S.	C9	118
Brookings, co., S.D., U.S.	C9	118
Brookland, Ar., U.S.	B5	81
Brooklandville, Md., U.S.	g10	97
Brooklawn, N.J., U.S.	D2	107
Brooklet, Ga., U.S.	D5	87
Brookline, Ma., U.S.	B5	98
Brookline, N.H., U.S.	E3	106
Brooklyn, N.S.	E5	71
Brooklyn, Al., U.S.	D3	78
Brooklyn, Ct., U.S.	B8	84
Brooklyn, Ga., U.S.	D2	87
Brooklyn, Il., U.S.	C3	90
Brooklyn, Ia., U.S.	C5	92
Brooklyn, Mi., U.S.	F6	99
Brooklyn, Ms., U.S.	D4	101
Brooklyn, Oh., U.S.	h9	112
Brooklyn, Pa., U.S.	C10	115
Brooklyn, Wi., U.S.	F4	126
Brooklyn Center, Mn., U.S.	E5	100
Brooklyn Park, Md., U.S.	h11	97
Brooklyn Park, Mn., U.S.	m12	100
Brookmere, B.C.	E7	69
Brookneal, Va., U.S.	C4	123
Brook Park, Mn., U.S.	E5	100
Brook Park, Oh., U.S.	h9	112
Brookport, Il., U.S.	F5	90
Brookridge, Co., U.S.	*B6	83
Brooks, Alta.	D5	68
Brooks, Ia., U.S.	D3	92
Brooks, Ky., U.S.	g11	94
Brooks, Me., U.S.	D3	96
Brooks, Mn., U.S.	C2	100
Brooks, Or., U.S.	h12	114
Brooks, Wi., U.S.	E4	126
Brooks, co., Ga., U.S.	F3	87
Brooks, co., Tx., U.S.	F3	120
Brooks Air Force Base, mil., Tx., U.S.	k7	120
Brooksburg, In., U.S.	G7	91
Brooksby, Sask.	E3	75
Brookshire, Tx., U.S.	E5	120
Brookside, Al., U.S.	f7	78
Brookside, Co., U.S.	C5	83
Brookside, De., U.S.	*B3	85
Brookston, In., U.S.	C4	91
Brookston, Mn., U.S.	D6	100
Brooksville, Fl., U.S.	D4	86
Brooksville, Ky., U.S.	B5	94
Brooksville, Me., U.S.	D4	96
Brooksville, Ms., U.S.	B5	101
Brooksville, Ok., U.S.	B5	113
Brookton, Me., U.S.	C5	96
Brooktondale, N.Y., U.S.	C4	109
Brookview, Md., U.S.	C6	97
Brookville, In., U.S.	F8	91
Brookville, Ma., U.S.	h11	98
Brookville, N.Y., U.S.	*E7	109
Brookville, Oh., U.S.	C1	112
Brookville, Pa., U.S.	D3	115
Brookville Lake, res., In., U.S.	E7	91
Brookwood, Al., U.S.	B2	78
Brookwood, N.J., U.S.	C4	107
Broomall, Pa., U.S.	p20	115
Broome, Austl.	C3	50
Broome, co., N.Y., U.S.	C5	109
Broomes Island, Md., U.S.	D4	97
Broomfield, Co., U.S.	B5	83
Brooten, Mn., U.S.	E3	100
Brora, Scot., U.K.	C5	13
Brora, stm., Scot., U.K.	C5	13
Brösarp, Swe.	E7	15
Broseley, Mo., U.S.	E7	102
Brosna, stm., Ire.	D4	11
Brossard, Que.	q20	74
Brotas de Macaúbas, Braz.	D2	57
Brothers, Or., U.S.	D6	114
Brotherton, Tn., U.S.	C8	119
Brothertown, Wi., U.S.	k9	126
Brotmanville, N.J., U.S.	D2	107
Brou, Fr.	C4	16
Brough, Eng., U.K.	F6	13
Brough Head, c., Scot., U.K.	A5	13
Broughton, Il., U.S.	F5	90
Broussard, La., U.S.	B2	95
Brovst, Den.	A3	15
Browardale, Fl., U.S.	r13	86
Browerville, Mn., U.S.	D4	100
Brown, co., Il., U.S.	D3	90
Brown, co., In., U.S.	F5	91
Brown, co., Ks., U.S.	C8	93
Brown, co., Mn., U.S.	F4	100
Brown, co., Ne., U.S.	B6	104
Brown, co., Oh., U.S.	D2	112
Brown, co., S.D., U.S.	B7	118
Brown, co., Tx., U.S.	D3	120
Brown, co., Wi., U.S.	D6	126
Brown Point, c., Wa., U.S.	C1	124
Brown Deer, Wi., U.S.	m12	126
Brownell, Ks., U.S.	D4	93
Brownfield, Il., U.S.	F5	90
Brownfield, Me., U.S.	E2	96
Brownfield, Tx., U.S.	C1	120
Brownfields, La., U.S.	*D4	95
Browning, Il., U.S.	C3	90
Browning, Mo., U.S.	A4	102
Browning, Mt., U.S.	B3	103
Browning Entrance, strt., B.C.	C2	69
Brownington, Mo., U.S.	C4	102
Brownington Center, Vt., U.S.	B4	122
Brownlee, Sask.	G2	75
Brownlee, Ne., U.S.	B5	104
Brownlee, Or., U.S.	C10	114
Brownlee Dam, U.S.	E2	89
Brownlee Reservoir, res., U.S.	C10	114
Browns, Il., U.S.	E6	90
Browns, stm., Vt., U.S.	B2	122
Brownsboro, Ky., U.S.	g11	94
Browns Branch, stm., De., U.S.	E3	85
Brownsburg, Que.	D3	74
Brownsburg, In., U.S.	E5	91
Brownsburg, Va., U.S.	C3	123
Brownsdale, Mn., U.S.	G6	100
Browns Inlet, b., N.C., U.S.	C5	110
Browns Mills, N.J., U.S.	D3	107
Brownstown, In., U.S.	G5	91
Brownstown, Pa., U.S.	F9	115
Brownstown, Wa., U.S.	C5	124
Brownstown Head, c., Ire.	E4	11
Browns Valley, In., U.S.	E4	91
Browns Valley, Mn., U.S.	E2	100
Brownsville, Fl., U.S.	s13	86
Brownsville, Ky., U.S.	C3	94
Brownsville, La., U.S.	B3	95
Brownsville, Mn., U.S.	G7	100
Brownsville, Or., U.S.	C4	114
Brownsville, Pa., U.S.	F2	115
Brownsville, Tn., U.S.	B2	119
Brownsville, Tx., U.S.	G4	120
Brownsville, Vt., U.S.	E4	122
Brownsville, Wi., U.S.	E5	126
Brownton, Mn., U.S.	F4	100
Brownton, W.V., U.S.	B4	125
Brownvale, Alta.	A2	68
Brownville, Al., U.S.	B2	78
Brownville, Me., U.S.	C3	96
Brownville, N.Y., U.S.	A5	109
Brownville Junction, Me., U.S.	C3	96
Brown Willy, hill, Eng., U.K.	D3	12
Brownwood, Mo., U.S.	D8	102
Brownwood, Tx., U.S.	D3	120
Brownwood, Lake, res., Tx., U.S.	D3	120
Broxton, Ga., U.S.	E4	87
Broyhill Park, Va., U.S.	*B5	123
Brozas, Spain	C2	22
Bruay [-en-Artois], Fr.	B5	16
Bruce, Alta.	C4	68
Bruce, Fl., U.S.	u16	86
Bruce, Ms., U.S.	B4	101
Bruce, S.D., U.S.	C9	118
Bruce, Wi., U.S.	C2	126
Bruce, co., Ont.	C3	73
Bruce, Mount, mtn., Austl.	D2	50
Bruce Crossing, Mi., U.S.	m12	99
Brucefield, Ont.	D3	73
Bruce Lake, l., In., U.S.	B5	91
Bruce National Park, Ont.	B3	73
Bruce Peninsula, pen., Ont.	B3	73
Bruceton, Tn., U.S.	A3	119
Bruceton Mills, W.V., U.S.	B5	125
Bruceville, Va., U.S.	A4	123
Bruceville, In., U.S.	G3	91
Bruchsal, Ger.	D4	18
Bruck, Aus.	A8	20
Bruck [an der Leitha], Aus.	A7	19
Bruck [an der Mur], Aus.	E7	18
Brückenau, Ger.	C4	19
Bruderheim, Alta.	C4	68
Bruff, Ire.	E3	11
Bruges see Brugge, Bel.	B5	16
Brugg, Switz.	B5	21
Brugge (Bruges), Bel.	B5	16
Bruin Point, mtn., Ut., U.S.	D5	121
Bruja, Cerro, mtn., Pan.	k11	62
Brûlé, Alta.	C2	68
Brûlé, Ne., U.S.	C4	104
Brule, Wi., U.S.	B2	126
Brule, co., S.D., U.S.	D6	118
Brûlé Lake, l., Alta.	C2	68
Brule Lake, l., Mn., U.S.	k9	100
Brumath, Fr.	C7	16
Brumley, Mo., U.S.	C5	102
Brumley Mountain, mtn., Va., U.S.	f9	123
Brundidge, Al., U.S.	D4	78
Bruneau, Id., U.S.	G3	89
Bruneau, stm., U.S.	G3	89
Brunei, ctry., Asia	E4	34
Brunei Bay, b., Asia	D5	34
Brunette Island, i., Newf.	E4	72
Bruni, Tx., U.S.	F3	120
Brunico, Italy	C7	20
Brunnen, Switz.	C6	21
Brunner, Lake, l., N.Z.	O13	51
Bruno, Sask.	E3	75
Bruno, Mn., U.S.	D6	100
Bruno, Ne., U.S.	C9	104
Brunsbüttel, Ger.	E15	15
Brunson, S.C., U.S.	F5	117
Brunsville, Ia., U.S.	B1	92
Brunswick see Braunschweig, Ger.	B5	18
Brunswick, Ga., U.S.	E5	87
Brunswick, Md., U.S.	B2	97
Brunswick, Me., U.S.	E3	96
Brunswick, Mo., U.S.	B4	102
Brunswick, Ne., U.S.	B8	104
Brunswick, N.C., U.S.	C4	110
Brunswick, Oh., U.S.	A4	112
Brunswick, co., N.C., U.S.	C4	110
Brunswick, co., Va., U.S.	D5	123
Brunswick, Peninsula, pen., Chile	h11	54
Brunswick Naval Air Station, mil., Me., U.S.	E3	96
Bruree, Ire.	E3	11
Brusett, Mt., U.S.	C9	103
Brush, Co., U.S.	A7	83
Brushy Mountain, mtn., Va., U.S.	C1	123
Brushy Mountains, mts., N.C., U.S.	B1	110
Brus Laguna, Hond.	D8	63
Brusly, La., U.S.	D4	95
Brusque, Braz.	D3	56
Brussels (Bruxelles), Bel.	B6	16
Brussels, Ont.	D3	73
Brussels, Il., U.S.	E3	90
Brussels, Wi., U.S.	D6	126
Brusson, Italy	E4	21
Bruton, Eng., U.K.	C5	12
Brutus, Mi., U.S.	B6	99
Bruyères, Fr.	A20	16
Bryan, Oh., U.S.	A1	112
Bryan, Tx., U.S.	D4	120
Bryan, co., Ga., U.S.	D5	87
Bryan, co., Ok., U.S.	D5	113
Bryans Road, Md., U.S.	C3	97
Bryant, Ar., U.S.	C3	81
Bryant, Fl., U.S.	F6	86
Bryant, In., U.S.	D8	91
Bryant, S.D., U.S.	C8	118
Bryant Creek, stm., Mo., U.S.	E5	102
Bryant Mountain, mtn., Ma., U.S.	B2	98
Bryant Pond, Me., U.S.	D2	96
Bryantown, Md., U.S.	C4	97
Bryant Pond, Me., U.S.	D2	96
Bryantsville, Ky., U.S.	C5	94
Bryantville, Ma., U.S.	B6	98
Bryce Canyon, Ut., U.S.	F3	121
Bryce Canyon National Park, Ut., U.S.	F3	121
Bryceland, La., U.S.	B3	95
Bryceville, Fl., U.S.	B5	86
Brynica, stm., Pol.	g9	26
Bryn Mawr, Pa., U.S.	o20	115
Bryn Mawr, Wa., U.S.	e11	124
Bryson, Tx., U.S.	C3	120
Bryson City, N.C., U.S.	f9	110
Brzeg, Pol.	C4	26
Brzesko, Pol.	D6	26
Brzeziny, Pol.	C5	26
Brzozów, Pol.	D7	26
B-Say-Tah, Sask.	G4	75
Bua, Fiji	H15	52
Bu'aale, Som.	E5	47
Bua Bay, b., Fiji	H15	52
Buariki, Kir.	R18	52
Buba, Gui.-B.	D2	45
Bübiyān, i., Kuw.	C4	38
Bucaramanga, Col.	B3	60
Buccaneer Archipelago, is., Austl.	C3	50
Buchach, Sov. Un.	G5	27
Buchanan, Sask.	F4	75
Buchanan, Lib.	E2	45
Buchanan, Ga., U.S.	C1	87
Buchanan, Mi., U.S.	G4	99
Buchanan, N.D., U.S.	B7	111
Buchanan, Tn., U.S.	A3	119
Buchanan, Va., U.S.	C3	123
Buchanan, co., Ia., U.S.	B6	92
Buchanan, co., Mo., U.S.	B3	102
Buchanan, co., Va., U.S.	e9	123
Buchanan, Lake, l., Austl.	D8	50
Buchan Ness, c., Scot., U.K.	C7	13
Buchans, Newf.	D3	72
Buchardo, Arg.	A4	54
Bucharest (București), Rom.	C8	24
Buchboden, Ger.	D4	19
Buchen, Ger.	A9	21
Buchholz, Ger.	E3	18
Buchloe, Ger.	B5	20
Buchs, Ger.	B5	20
Buchtel, Oh., U.S.	C3	112
Buckatunna, Ms., U.S.	D5	101
Buck Creek, In., U.S.	D4	91
Buck Creek, stm., Ga., U.S.	A7	87
Buck Creek, stm., Ky., U.S.	m11	94
Bückeburg, Ger.	A4	19
Buckeye, Az., U.S.	D3	80
Buckeye, Ia., U.S.	B4	92
Buckeye, W.V., U.S.	C4	125
Buckeye Hills, hills, Az., U.S.	m7	80
Buckeye Lake, Oh., U.S.	C3	112
Buckeystown, Md., U.S.	B3	97
Buckfield, Me., U.S.	D2	96
Buckhannon, W.V., U.S.	C4	125
Buckhaven, Scot., U.K.	B5	10
Buckhead, Ga., U.S.	C3	87
Buck Hill Falls, Pa., U.S.	D11	115
Buckhorn, Az., U.S.	D6	80
Buckhorn, Ky., U.S.	C6	94
Buckhorn, N.M., U.S.	D1	108
Buckhorn Knob, mtn., W.V., U.S.	C5	125
Buckhorn Lake, res., Ky., U.S.	C6	94
Buckie, Scot., U.K.	f9	13
Buckingham, Que.	D2	74
Buckingham, Eng., U.K.	C6	12
Buckingham, co., Va., U.S.	C4	123
Buckinghamshire, co., Eng., U.K.	C7	12
Buck Lake, l., Alta.	C4	68
Buckland, Que.	C7	74
Buckland, Ak., U.S.	B7	79
Buckland, Ma., U.S.	A2	98
Buckland, Oh., U.S.	B1	112
Bucklin, Ks., U.S.	E4	93
Bucklin, Mo., U.S.	B5	102
Buckley, Il., U.S.	C5	90
Buckley, Mn., U.S.	D5	100
Buckley, Wa., U.S.	B3	124
Bucknell Manor, Va., U.S.	*B5	123
Buckner, Ar., U.S.	D2	81
Buckner, Il., U.S.	F4	90
Buckner, Ky., U.S.	g12	94
Buckner, Mo., U.S.	h11	102
Bucks, Al., U.S.	D1	78
Bucks, co., Pa., U.S.	F11	115
Bucks Harbor, Me., U.S.	D5	96
Buckskin, In., U.S.	H3	91
Buckskin Mountains, mts., Az., U.S.	C2	80
Bucksport, Me., U.S.	D4	96
Bucksport, S.C., U.S.	D9	117
Buckville, Ar., U.S.	C2	81
Bucoda, Wa., U.S.	C3	124
Buco Zau, Ang.	B1	48
Bucyrus, Ks., U.S.	D9	93
Bucyrus, N.D., U.S.	C3	111
Bucyrus, Oh., U.S.	B3	112
Bud, Wy., U.S.	D3	125
Buda, Il., U.S.	B4	90
Buda, Tx., U.S.	D4	120
Budapest, Hung.	B4	24
Budaun, India	C7	37
Budd Coast, Ant.	C24	7
Budd Lake, l., N.J., U.S.	B3	107
Buddon Ness, c., Scot., U.K.	D6	13
Buddonovsk, Sov. Un.	G17	8
Buddtown, N.J., U.S.	D3	107
Bude, Eng., U.K.	E4	10
Bude, Ms., U.S.	D3	101
Bude Bay, b., Eng., U.K.	D3	12
Budjala, Zaire	A2	48
Budrio, Italy	E6	21
Budva, Yugo.	D5	23
Budyně [nad Ohří], Czech.	n17	26
Buea, Cam.	E1	46
Buechel, Ky., U.S.	g11	94
Buena, N.J., U.S.	D3	107
Buena, Wa., U.S.	C5	124
Buena Park, Ca., U.S.	n12	82
Buenaventura, Col.	C2	60
Buenaventura, Mex.	B3	63
Buena Vista, Bol.	C5	55
Buena Vista, Al., U.S.	D2	78
Buena Vista, Co., U.S.	C4	83
Buena Vista, Ga., U.S.	D2	87
Buena Vista, Fl., U.S.	D2	87
Buena Vista, Ms., U.S.	B5	101
Buena Vista, N.M., U.S.	B4	108
Buena Vista, Oh., U.S.	C4	112
Buena Vista, Tn., U.S.	B3	119
Buena Vista, Va., U.S.	C3	123
Buena Vista, co., Ia., U.S.	B2	92
Bueno, stm., Chile	D2	54
Buenópolis, Braz.	B4	56
Buenos Aires, Arg.	A5	54
Buenos Aires, C.R.	F6	62
Buenos Aires, Pan.	k11	62
Buenos Aires, prov., Arg.	B4	54
Buenos Aires, Lago l. (Lago General Carrera), l., S.A.	D2	54
Bueyeros, N.M., U.S.	B6	108
Buffalo, Alta.	D5	68
Buffalo, Al., U.S.	C4	78
Buffalo, Il., U.S.	D4	90
Buffalo, Ia., U.S.	C7	92
Buffalo, Ks., U.S.	E8	93
Buffalo, Mn., U.S.	E5	100
Buffalo, Mo., U.S.	D4	102
Buffalo, N.Y., U.S.	C2	109
Buffalo, N.D., U.S.	C8	111
Buffalo, Oh., U.S.	C4	112
Buffalo, Ok., U.S.	A2	113
Buffalo, S.C., U.S.	B4	117
Buffalo, S.D., U.S.	B2	118
Buffalo, Tx., U.S.	D5	120
Buffalo, W.V., U.S.	C3	125
Buffalo, Wi., U.S.	D2	126
Buffalo, Wy., U.S.	B6	127
Buffalo, co., Ne., U.S.	D6	104
Buffalo, co., S.D., U.S.	C6	118
Buffalo, co., Wi., U.S.	D2	126
Buffalo, stm., Ar., U.S.	B3	81
Buffalo, stm., Mn., U.S.	D2	100
Buffalo, stm., Tn., U.S.	B4	119
Buffalo, stm., Wi., U.S.	D2	126
Buffalo Bill Reservoir, res., Wy., U.S.	B3	127
Buffalo Center, Ia., U.S.	A4	92
Buffalo Creek, Co., U.S.	B5	83
Buffalo Creek, stm., W.V., U.S.	f8	125
Buffalo Creek, stm., W.V., U.S.	h10	125
Buffalo Creek, stm., W.V., U.S.	n12	125
Buffalo Gap, Sask.	H3	75
Buffalo Gap, S.D., U.S.	D2	118
Buffalo Grove, Il., U.S.	h9	90
Buffalo Lake, Mn., U.S.	F4	100
Buffalo Lake, l., N.W. Ter.	D9	66
Buffalo Lake, res., Tx., U.S.	B1	120
Buffalo Lake, l., Alta.	C4	68
Buffalo Mills, Pa., U.S.	G4	115
Buffalo Narrows, Sask.	m7	75
Buffalo Pound Lake, l., Sask.	G3	75
Buffalo Valley, Tn., U.S.	C8	119
Buff Bay, Jam.	E15	64
Buffer Lake, l., Sask.	E2	75
Buffumville Lake, res., Ma., U.S.	B4	98
Buford, Co., U.S.	B3	83
Buford, Ga., U.S.	B2	87
Buford, Oh., U.S.	C2	112
Buford, Wy., U.S.	E7	127
Bug, stm., Eur.	B6	24
Buga, Col.	C2	60
Buganga, Ug.	B5	48
Bugene, Tan.	B5	48
Bugio, i., Port.	h12	22
Bugojno, Yugo.	D5	21
Bugsuk Island, i., Phil.	D5	34
Bugt, China	C9	32
Bugul'ma, Sov. Un.	C8	28
Buguruslan, Sov. Un.	C8	28
Buhl, Fr.	D7	16
Bühl, Ger.	B4	20
Buhl, Al., U.S.	B2	78
Buhl, Id., U.S.	G4	89
Buhl, Mn., U.S.	C6	100
Buhler, Ks., U.S.	D6	93
Bühlertal, Ger.	E3	18
Bui Dam, Ghana	E4	45
Buies Creek, N.C., U.S.	B4	110
Builth Wells, Wales, U.K.	B4	12
Buitenpost, Neth.	D3	22
Bujalance, Spain	D3	22
Bujumbura, Bdi.	B4	48
Bukama, Zaire	C4	48
Bukavu, Zaire	B4	48
Bukene, Tan.	B5	48
Bukhara, Sov. Un.	F9	29

Name	Map Ref.	Page
Bukittinggi, Indon.	F2	34
Bukoba, Tan.	B5	48
Bukovina, hist. reg., Eur.	B7	24
Bukuru, Nig.	E6	45
Bula, Indon.	F8	34
Bula, Zaire	A4	48
Bülach, Switz.	A6	21
Buladean, N.C., U.S.	e10	110
Buladeen, Tn., U.S.	C11	119
Bulan, Ky., U.S.	C6	94
Bulan, Phil.	n12	34
Bulawayo, Zimb.	B4	49
Buldir Island, i., Ak., U.S.	E3	79
Bulgan, Mong.	B5	31
Bulgaria, ctry., Eur.	D7	24
Bulgroo, Austl.	B4	51
Buliya, Fiji	I15	52
Bulkley, stm., B.C.	B4	69
Bulkley Ranges, mts., B.C.	B4	69
Bull, stm., B.C.	E3	68
Bullange see Büllingen, Bel.	D6	17
Bullaque, stm., Spain	C3	22
Bullard, Ga., U.S.	D3	87
Bullas, Spain	C5	22
Bullaxaar, Som.	C5	47
Bullay, Ger.	C2	19
Bull Creek, stm., Nv., U.S.	E6	105
Bull Creek, stm., S.D., U.S.	B2	118
Bulle, Switz.	C3	20
Bullen Baai, b., Neth. Ant.	H18	65
Bullfrog Creek, stm., Ut., U.S.	F5	121
Bullhead, S.D., U.S.	B4	118
Bullhead City, Az., U.S.	B1	80
Büllingen (Bullange), Bel.	D6	17
Bull Island, i., S.C., U.S.	G6	117
Bull Island, i., S.C., U.S.	F8	117
Bull Island, i., S.C., U.S.	D9	117
Bullitt, co., Ky., U.S.	C4	94
Bullittsville, Ky., U.S.	h13	94
Bull Mountain, mtn., Mt., U.S.	D4	103
Bulloch, co., Ga., U.S.	D5	87
Bullock, N.C., U.S.	A4	110
Bullock, co., Al., U.S.	C4	78
Bullock Creek, Mi., U.S.	E6	99
Bulloo, stm., Austl.	E7	50
Bulloo Lake, l., Austl.	E7	50
Bull Run, stm., Va., U.S.	g11	123
Bull Run Mountains, mts., Va., U.S.	B5	123
Bullrun Ridge, mtn., Or., U.S.	m13	119
Bullrun Rock, mtn., Or., U.S.	C8	114
Bulls Bay, b., S.C., U.S.	F8	117
Bulls Bridge, Ct., U.S.	C1	84
Bulls Gap, Tn., U.S.	C10	119
Bull Shoals, Ar., U.S.	A3	81
Bull Shoals Lake, res., U.S.	A3	81
Bull Sluice Lake, res., Ga., U.S.	h8	87
Bully Creek Reservoir, res., Or., U.S.	C9	114
Bulnes, Chile	B2	54
Bulolo, Pap. N. Gui.	k12	50
Bulsār, India	G4	37
Bultfontein, S. Afr.	C4	49
Bulun, Sov. Un.	B15	29
Bulungu, Zaire	B2	48
Bulwark, Alta.	C5	68
Bulyea, Sask.	G3	75
Bumba, Zaire	A3	48
Bumping, stm., Wa., U.S.	C4	124
Bumpus Mills, Tn., U.S.	A4	119
Buna, Tx., U.S.	D6	120
Bunbury, Austl.	F2	50
Bunceton, Mo., U.S.	C5	102
Bunch, Ok., U.S.	B7	113
Bunche Park, Fl., U.S.	*s13	86
Buncombe, Il., U.S.	F5	90
Buncombe, co., N.C., U.S.	f10	110
Buncrana, Ire.	B4	11
Bundaberg, Austl.	D9	50
Bünde, Ger.	A3	19
Būndi, India	E5	37
Bundick Creek, stm., La., U.S.	D2	95
Bundoran, Ire.	C3	11
Bunessan, Scot., U.K.	D2	13
Bungay, Eng., U.K.	B9	12
Bunger Hills, hills, Ant.	C23	7
Bungo Strait, strt., Japan	J6	33
Bunia, Zaire	A5	48
Bunker, Mo., U.S.	D6	102
Bunker Hill, Il., U.S.	D4	90
Bunker Hill, In., U.S.	C5	91
Bunker Hill, Ks., U.S.	D5	93
Bunker Hill, Or., U.S.	*D2	114
Bunker Hill, Tn., U.S.	B5	119
Bunker Hill, W.V., U.S.	B6	125
Bunker Hill, W.V., U.S.	m12	105
Bunker Hill, mtn., Nv., U.S.	D5	105
Bunkerville, Nv., U.S.	G7	105
Bunkeya, Zaire	D4	48
Bunkie, La., U.S.	D3	95
Bunn, N.C., U.S.	B4	110
Bunnahowen, Ire.	C2	11
Bunnell, Fl., U.S.	C5	86
Bunnlevel, N.C., U.S.	B4	110
Buolkalakh, Sov. Un.	B12	28
Buon Me Thuot, Viet.	C3	34
Buor-Khaya Bay, b., Sov. Un.	B18	28
Bura, Kenya	B7	48
Buram, Sud.	C2	47
Buras, La., U.S.	E6	95
Buraydah, Sau. Ar.	C4	38
Burayk, Libya	D2	43
Burbank, Ca., U.S.	E4	82
Burbank, Il., U.S.	k9	90
Burbank, Ok., U.S.	A5	113
Burbank, S.D., U.S.	E9	118
Burbank, Wa., U.S.	C7	124
Burchard, Ne., U.S.	D9	104
Burco, Som.	D6	47
Burdekin, stm., Austl.	C8	50
Burden, Ks., U.S.	E7	93
Burdett, Alta.	E5	68
Burdett, Ks., U.S.	D4	93
Burdett, N.Y., U.S.	C4	109
Burdette, Ar., U.S.	B6	81
Burdick, Ks., U.S.	D7	93
Burdickville, R.I., U.S.	F2	116
Burdur, Tur.	D8	40
Bureau, Il., U.S.	B4	90
Bureau, co., Il., U.S.	B4	90
Burein Mountains, mts., Sov. Un.	B6	33
Büren, Ger.	B3	19
Büren [an der Aare], Switz.	B3	21
Bureya, Sov. Un.	B10	31
Bureya, stm., Sov. Un.	A5	33
Burford, Ont.	D4	73
Bür Fu'ad, Eg.	C4	41
Burg, Ger.	A6	19
Burg, Ger.	D5	15
Burgas, Bul.	D8	24
Burgas, Gulf of, b., Bul.	D8	24
Burgaw, N.C., U.S.	C5	110
Burgdorf, Ger.	F3	15
Burgdorf, Switz.	E3	18
Burgeo, Newf.	E3	72
Burgersdorp, S. Afr.	D4	49
Burgess, S.C., U.S.	D9	117
Burgess Hill, Eng., U.K.	D7	12
Burgettstown, Pa., U.S.	F1	115
Burghausen, Ger.	A8	20
Burghead, Scot., U.K.	C5	13
Burgin, Ky., U.S.	C5	94
Burglengenfeld, Ger.	D7	19
Burgoon, Oh., U.S.	A2	112
Burgos, Phil.	n12	34
Burgos, Spain	A4	22
Burgstädt, Ger.	C7	19
Burgsteinfurt, Ger.	A2	19
Burgsvik, Swe.	I8	14
Burgundy, hist. reg., Fr.	D6	16
Burhānpur, India	D6	36
Burhave, Ger.	E2	15
Burhi Gandak, stm., India	E10	37
Buri, Braz.	m7	57
Burica, Punta, c., N.A.	*f11	124
Burin, Newf.	E4	72
Burin, Isr. Occ.	g12	41
Burin Peninsula, pen., Newf.	E4	72
Buriram, Thai.	C2	34
Buritama, Braz.	C2	56
Burj al 'Arab, Eg.	G7	40
Bur Safājah, Eg.	C3	38
Burkburnett, Tx., U.S.	B3	120
Burke, Id., U.S.	B3	89
Burke, N.Y., U.S.	f10	109
Burke, S.D., U.S.	D6	118
Burke, Vt., U.S.	B5	122
Burke, Va., U.S.	*B5	123
Burke, co., Ga., U.S.	C4	87
Burke, co., N.C., U.S.	B1	110
Burke, co., N.D., U.S.	A3	111
Burke Channel, strt., B.C.	C4	69
Burke City, Mo., U.S.	f13	102
Burkehaven, N.H., U.S.	D2	106
Burke Island, i., Ant.	B2	7
Burkes Garden, Va., U.S.	C1	123
Burkesville, Ky., U.S.	D4	94
Burket, In., U.S.	B6	91
Burketon Station (part of Newcastle), Ont.	C6	73
Burketown, Austl.	C6	50
Burkett, Tx., U.S.	C3	120
Burkettsville, Oh., U.S.	B1	112
Burkeville, Tx., U.S.	D6	120
Burkeville, Va., U.S.	C4	123
Burk's Falls, Ont.	B5	73
Burkville, Al., U.S.	C3	78
Burleigh, N.J., U.S.	E3	107
Burleigh, co., N.D., U.S.	C5	111
Burleson, Tx., U.S.	n9	120
Burleson, co., Tx., U.S.	D4	120
Burley, Id., U.S.	G5	89
Burley, Wa., U.S.	f10	124
Burlingame, Ca., U.S.	h8	82
Burlingame, Ks., U.S.	D8	93
Burlington, Newf.	D3	72
Burlington, Ont.	D5	73
Burlington, Co., U.S.	B8	83
Burlington, Ct., U.S.	B4	84
Burlington, Il., U.S.	A5	90
Burlington, In., U.S.	D5	91
Burlington, Ia., U.S.	D6	92
Burlington, Ks., U.S.	D8	93
Burlington, Ky., U.S.	A5	94
Burlington, Me., U.S.	C4	96
Burlington, Ma., U.S.	f11	98
Burlington, N.J., U.S.	C3	107
Burlington, N.C., U.S.	A3	110
Burlington, N.D., U.S.	A4	111
Burlington, Ok., U.S.	A3	113
Burlington, Pa., U.S.	C8	115
Burlington, Vt., U.S.	C2	122
Burlington, Wa., U.S.	A3	124
Burlington, W.V., U.S.	B6	125
Burlington, Wi., U.S.	F5	126
Burlington, Wy., U.S.	B4	127
Burlington, co., N.J., U.S.	D3	107
Burlington Beach, In., U.S.	B3	91
Burlington Junction, Mo., U.S.	A2	102
Burlyu-Tobe, Sov. Un.	D9	28
Burma (Myanmar), ctry., Asia	D10	36
Burnaby, B.C.	E6	69
Burnaby Island, i., B.C.	C2	69
Burnet, Tx., U.S.	D3	120
Burnet, co., Tx., U.S.	D3	120
Burnett, In., U.S.	E3	91
Burnett, Wi., U.S.	C1	126
Burnett, co., Wi., U.S.	C1	126
Burnett, stm., Austl.	B8	51
Burnettown, S.C., U.S.	D4	117
Burnettsville, In., U.S.	C4	91
Burney, Ca., U.S.	B3	82
Burney, In., U.S.	F6	91
Burneyville, Ok., U.S.	D4	113
Burnham, Me., U.S.	D3	96
Burnham, Mo., U.S.	E6	102
Burnham, Pa., U.S.	E6	115
Burnham-on-Sea / Highbridge, Eng., U.K.	C5	12
Burnie, Austl.	o15	50
Burning Springs, Ky., U.S.	C6	94
Burning Springs, W.V., U.S.	C3	125
Burnley, Eng., U.K.	D5	10
Burns, Co., U.S.	B4	83
Burns, Ks., U.S.	D7	93
Burns, Or., U.S.	D7	114
Burns, Tn., U.S.	A4	119
Burns, Wy., U.S.	E8	127
Burns City, In., U.S.	G4	91
Burns Flat, Ok., U.S.	B2	113
Burnside, Il., U.S.	C2	90
Burnside, Ky., U.S.	D5	94
Burns Paiute Indian Reservation, Or., U.S.	D7	114
Burnstad, N.D., U.S.	C6	111
Burnsville, N.B.	B4	71
Burnsville, Al., U.S.	C3	78
Burnsville, Mn., U.S.	F5	100
Burnsville, Ms., U.S.	A5	101
Burnsville, N.C., U.S.	f10	110
Burnsville, W.V., U.S.	C4	125
Burnsville Lake, res., W.V., U.S.	C4	125
Burnt Cabins, Pa., U.S.	F6	115
Burnt Corn, Al., U.S.	D2	78
Burnt Hills, N.Y., U.S.	C7	109
Burnt Island, Newf.	E2	72
Burntisland, Scot., U.K.	D5	13
Burnt Mills, Lake, l., Va., U.S.	k14	123
Burnt Prairie, Il., U.S.	E5	90
Burnt River, Ont.	C6	73
Burntside Lake, l., Mn., U.S.	C6	100
Burntwood, stm., Man.	B2	70
Burntwood Lake, l., Man.	B1	70
Burnwell, Al., U.S.	f6	78
Burqā, Isr. Occ.	b7	41
Burr, Mn., U.S.	F2	100
Burr, Ne., U.S.	D9	104
Burra, Austl.	F2	51
Burragorang, Lake, l., Austl.	F7	51
Burray, i., Scot., U.K.	B6	13
Burrendong Reservoir, res., Austl.	F7	51
Burr Ferry, La., U.S.	C2	95
Burr Hill, Va., U.S.	B5	123
Burriana, Spain	C5	22
Burr Oak, Ia., U.S.	A6	92
Burr Oak, Ks., U.S.	C5	93
Burr Oak, Mi., U.S.	G5	99
Burr Oak Reservoir, res., Oh., U.S.	C3	112
Burroughs, Ga., U.S.	E5	87
Burrow Head, c., Scot., U.K.	E5	13
Burrows, In., U.S.	C5	91
Burr Ridge, Il., U.S.	*B6	90
Burrton, Ks., U.S.	D6	93
Burruyacú, Arg.	E3	55
Burrville, Tn., U.S.	C9	119
Burrwood, La., U.S.	E4	72
Burry Port, Wales, U.K.	C3	12
Bursa, Tur.	B7	40
Būr Safājah, Eg.	C3	38
Bursey, Mount, mtn., Ant.	B35	7
Burstall, Sask.	G1	75
Burt, Ia., U.S.	A3	92
Burt, N.D., U.S.	C3	111
Burt, co., Ne., U.S.	C9	104
Burta, Austl.	F3	51
Būr Tawfiq, Eg.	E4	41
Burt Lake, l., Mi., U.S.	C6	99
Burton, B.C.	D9	69
Burton, Il., U.S.	D2	90
Burton, Mi., U.S.	E7	99
Burton, Ne., U.S.	B6	104
Burton, Oh., U.S.	A4	112
Burton, Tx., U.S.	D4	120
Burton, Wa., U.S.	f11	124
Burton, W.V., U.S.	B4	125
Burton, Lake, res., Ga., U.S.	B3	87
Burtonport, Ire.	B3	11
Burton upon Trent, Eng., U.K.	D6	10
Burträsk, Swe.	E9	14
Burtrum, Mn., U.S.	E4	100
Burtts Corner, N.B.	C3	71
Burțus, Eg.	D3	41
Buru, i., Indon.	F7	34
Burūk, Wādī al, val., Eg.	D5	41
Burullus, Lake, l., Eg.	C2	41
Burūn, Ra's, c., Eg.	C5	41
Burundi, ctry., Afr.	B5	48
Bururi, Bdi.	B4	48
Burwash, Ont.	A4	73
Burwell, Ne., U.S.	C6	104
Bury, Que.	D6	74
Bury, Eng., U.K.	A5	12
Burynshik, Sov. Un.	D4	28
Bury Saint Edmunds, Eng., U.K.	C4	68
Busby, Alta.	C4	68
Busby, Mt., U.S.	E10	103
Büschfeld, Ger.	D1	19
Bush, Ky., U.S.	C6	94
Bush, La., U.S.	D6	95
Bush City, Ks., U.S.	D8	93
Bushenyi, Ug.	B5	48
Bushimaie, stm., Zaire	C3	48
Bushiribana, Aruba	G17	65
Bushkill, Pa., U.S.	D11	115
Bushland, Tx., U.S.	B1	120
Bushmills, N. Ire., U.K.	B6	11
Bushnell, Fl., U.S.	D4	86
Bushnell, Il., U.S.	C3	90
Bushnell, Ne., U.S.	C2	104
Bushong, Ks., U.S.	D7	93
Bushton, Ks., U.S.	D5	93
Busia, Zaire	A3	48
Businga, Zaire	A3	48
Busk, Sov. Un.	G5	27
Busko [Zdrój], Pol.	C6	26
Buşra ash Shām, Syria	F11	40
Bussang, Fr.	A2	21
Busselton, Austl.	F2	50
Busseto, Italy	E6	20
Bussey, Ia., U.S.	C5	92
Bussum, Neth.	A6	16
Busto Arsizio, Italy	B2	23
Busu-Djanoa, Zaire	A3	48
Büsum, Ger.	D2	15
Buta, Zaire	A3	48
Buta Ranquil, Arg.	B3	54
Butare, Rw.	B4	48
Bute, Island of, i., Scot., U.K.	B3	13
Butedale, B.C.	C3	69
Bute Inlet, b., B.C.	D5	69
Butere, Kenya	A5	48
Butha Qi, China	B9	31
Buthier, stm., Italy	D3	20
Butler, Al., U.S.	C1	78
Butler, Ga., U.S.	D2	87
Butler, Il., U.S.	D4	90
Butler, In., U.S.	B8	91
Butler, Ky., U.S.	B5	94
Butler, Mo., U.S.	C3	102
Butler, N.J., U.S.	B4	107
Butler, Oh., U.S.	B3	112
Butler, Ok., U.S.	B2	113
Butler, Pa., U.S.	E2	115
Butler, S.D., U.S.	B8	118
Butler, Tn., U.S.	C11	119
Butler, Wi., U.S.	m11	126
Butler, co., Al., U.S.	D3	78
Butler, co., Ia., U.S.	B5	92
Butler, co., Ks., U.S.	E7	93
Butler, co., Ky., U.S.	C3	94
Butler, co., Mo., U.S.	E7	102
Butler, co., Ne., U.S.	C8	104
Butler, co., Oh., U.S.	C1	112
Butler, co., Pa., U.S.	E2	115
Butlers Bridge, Ire.	C4	11
Butlerville, In., U.S.	F6	91
Butmīyah, Isr. Occ.	B7	41
Buton, N.C., U.S.	A4	110
Butovo, Sov. Un.	n17	27
Buttahatchee, stm., U.S.	B5	101
Butte, Mt., U.S.	E4	103
Butte, Ne., U.S.	B7	104
Butte, co., Ca., U.S.	C3	82
Butte, co., Id., U.S.	F5	89
Butte, co., S.D., U.S.	C2	118
Butte des Morts, Lake, l., Wi., U.S.	D5	126
Butte Falls, Or., U.S.	E4	114
Butte Mountains, mts., Nv., U.S.	D6	105
Butterfield, Ar., U.S.	g8	81
Butterfield, Mn., U.S.	G4	100
Butterfield, Mo., U.S.	E4	102
Butternut, Wi., U.S.	B3	126
Butternut Lake, l., Wi., U.S.	C5	126
Butters, N.C., U.S.	C4	110
Butterworth, Malay.	D2	34
Butterworth, Transkei	E3	49
Buttevant, Ire.	E3	11
Button Islands, is., N.W. Ter.	f8	72
Button Islands, is., N.W. Ter.	f8	72
Buttonwillow, Ca., U.S.	E4	82
Butts, co., Ga., U.S.	C2	87
Butuan, Phil.	D7	34
Buturlinovka, Sov. Un.	F13	27
Butzbach, Ger.	C3	19
Bützow, Ger.	B6	15
Buuhoodle, Som.	D6	47
Buulo Berde, Som.	F5	47
Buur Gaabo, Som.	E5	47
Buur Hakaba, Som.	E5	47
Buxtehude, Ger.	B4	18
Buxton, Guy.	A3	59
Buxton, Eng., U.K.	A6	12
Buxton, N.C., U.S.	B8	111
Buxton, N.D., U.S.	B8	111
Buxton, Or., U.S.	g11	114
Buxton, Mount, mtn., B.C.	D3	69
Buxton Center, Me., U.S.	*E2	96
Buy, Sov. Un.	B2	28
Buyck, Mn., U.S.	B6	100
Buynaksk, Sov. Un.	E3	28
Buyr Lake, l., Asia	B8	31
Büyükliman see Vakfikebir, Tur.		
Büyükmenderes, stm., Tur.	D7	40
Buzachi Peninsula, pen., Sov. Un.	E4	28
Buzancy, Fr.	E4	17
Buzău, Rom.	C8	24
Buzău, stm., Rom.	C8	24
Buzaymah, Libya	E4	43
Buzet, Yugo.	C1	24
Buzuluk, Sov. Un.	C4	28
Buzzard Roost, mtn., N.C., U.S.	B1	110
Buzzards Bay, Ma., U.S.	C6	98
Buzzards Bay, b., Ma., U.S.	C6	98
Byala, Bul.	D7	24
Byala Slatina, Bul.	D6	24
Byam Martin Island, i., N.W. Ter.	m31	66
Byars, Ok., U.S.	C4	113
Bybee, Tn., U.S.	C10	119
Bydgoszcz, Pol.	B5	26
Byelorussia (White Russia), state, Sov. Un.	D5	29
Byemoor, Alta.	D4	68
Byer, Oh., U.S.	C3	112
Byers, Co., U.S.	B6	83
Byers, Ks., U.S.	E5	93
Byers, Tx., U.S.	C4	113
Byesville, Oh., U.S.	C4	112
Byfield, Ma., U.S.	A6	98
Byglandsfjord, Nor.	H2	14
Byhalia, Ms., U.S.	A4	101
Bykovo, Sov. Un.	n18	27
Bykovo, Sov. Un.	G15	27
Bylas, Az., U.S.	D5	80
Bylot Island, i., N.W. Ter.	B17	66
Byng, Ok., U.S.	C5	113
Byng Inlet, Ont.	B4	73
Bynum, Mt., U.S.	C4	103
Bynum, N.C., U.S.	B3	110
Bynumville, Mo., U.S.	B5	102
Byram, Ms., U.S.	C3	101
Byrd, sci., Ant.	A36	7
Byrd Glacier, ice, Ant.	g40	7
Byrdstown, Tn., U.S.	C8	119
Byrnedale, Pa., U.S.	D4	115
Byrock, Austl.	E6	51
Byromville, Ga., U.S.	D3	87
Byron, Ca., U.S.	h9	82
Byron, Il., U.S.	A4	90
Byron, Me., U.S.	D2	96
Byron, Mn., U.S.	F6	100
Byron, Ne., U.S.	D8	104
Byron, N.Y., U.S.	B2	109
Byron, Ok., U.S.	A3	113
Byron, Wy., U.S.	B4	127
Byron, Cape, c., Austl.	E9	50
Byrum, Den.	A5	15
Byšice-Liblice, Czech.	n18	26
Bystrzyca [Kłodzka], Pol.	C5	26
Bytom (Beuthen), Pol.	C5	26
Bytów, Pol.	B5	26
Byzantium see İstanbul, Tur.	B7	40

C

Name	Map Ref.	Page
Ca, stm., Asia	C6	35
Caacupé, Para.	E4	55
Caaguazú, dept., Para.	E4	55
Čaǎk, Yugo.	D5	24
Cáala, Ang.	D2	48
Caamaño Sound, strt., B.C.	C3	69
Caapucú, Para.	E4	55
Caazapá, Para.	E4	55
Caazapá, dept., Para.	E4	55
Cabaceiras, Braz.	h5	57
Cabalete, i., Phil.	o13	34
Caballo, N.M., U.S.	E2	108
Caballo Mountains, mts., N.M., U.S.	E2	108
Caballo Reservoir, res., N.M., U.S.	E2	108
Cabana, Peru	C2	58
Cabanatuan, Phil.	o13	34
Cabano, Que.	B9	74
Cabarita, Jam.	E12	65
Cabarrus, co., N.C., U.S.	B2	110
Cabarruyan Island, i., Phil.	n12	34
Cabbage Swamp, sw., Fl., U.S.	m9	86
Cabeceiras, Braz.	B3	56
Cabedelo, Braz.	B5	57
Cabell, co., W.V., U.S.	C2	125
Cabery, Il., U.S.	C5	90
Cabeza del Buey, Spain	C3	22
Cabezas, Bol.	G6	58
Cabimas, Ven.	A3	60
Cabin Creek, W.V., U.S.	m13	125
Cabin Creek, stm., W.V., U.S.	m13	125
Cabinda, Ang.	C1	48
Cabinda, dept., Ang.	C1	48
Cabinet Gorge Reservoir, res., Mt., U.S.	B1	103
Cabinet Mountains, mts., Mt., U.S.	B1	103
Cabin John, Md., U.S.	C3	97
Cable, Wi., U.S.	B2	126
Cabo, Braz.	k6	57
Cabo Blanco, Arg.	F3	54
Cabo Delgado, dept., Moz.	D6	48
Cabo Frio, Braz.	G7	57
Cabo Gracias a Dios, Nic.	C6	63
Cabonga, Réservoir, res., Que.	k11	74
Cabool, Mo., U.S.	D5	102
Caboolture, Austl.	C9	51
Cabora Bassa Lake, res., Moz.	A5	49
Cabo Raso, Arg.	C3	54
Cabot, Ar., U.S.	C3	81
Cabot, Pa., U.S.	E2	115
Cabot, Vt., U.S.	C4	122
Cabot, Mount, mtn., N.H., U.S.	A4	106
Cabot Head, c., Ont.	B3	73
Cabot Strait, strt., Can.	G20	66
Cabra, Spain	D3	22
Cabras Island, i., Guam	L9	52
Cabrera Baja, Sierra de la, mts., Spain	A2	22
Cabrera Island, i., Spain	C7	22
Cabri, Sask.	G1	75
Cabriel, stm., Spain	C5	22
Cabrillo National Monument, Ca., U.S.	o15	82
Cabrobó, Braz.	C3	57
Caçador, Braz.	D2	56
Caçapava do Sul, Braz.	E2	56
Capacon, stm., W.V., U.S.	B6	125
Cacequi, Braz.	D2	56
Cáceres, Braz.	C4	56
Cáceres, Col.	B2	60
Cáceres, Spain	C2	22
Cáceres, dept., Peru	C2	58
Cachan, Fr.	g10	16
Cache, Ok., U.S.	C3	113
Cache, co., Ut., U.S.	B4	121
Cache, stm., Ar., U.S.	C4	81
Cache, stm., Il., U.S.	F4	90
Cache Bay, Ont.	A5	73
Cache Creek, B.C.	D7	69
Cache Creek, stm., Ca., U.S.	C2	82
Cache Junction, Ut., U.S.	B3	121
Cache la Poudre, stm., Co., U.S.	A5	83
Cache la Poudre, North Fork, stm., Co., U.S.	A5	83
Cache Mountain, mtn., Ak., U.S.	B10	79
Cache Peak, mtn., Id., U.S.	G5	89
Cachí, Arg.	E2	55
Cachimbo, Serra do, mts., Braz.	D3	57
Cachoeira, Braz.	D3	57
Cachoeira do Arari, Braz.	C5	59
Cachoeira do Sul, Braz.	E2	56
Cachoeiro de Itapemirim, Braz.	C4	56
Caçiporé, stm., Braz.	B4	59
Caciporé, Cabo, c., Braz.	B4	59
Cacique, Pan.	h11	62
Cacolo, Ang.	D2	48
Caconda, Ang.	D2	48
Caconde, Braz.	k8	56
Cacouna-Station, Que.	B8	74
Cacula, Ang.	D2	48
Caculé, Braz.	A4	56
Cadca, Czech.	B5	26
Caddo, La., U.S.	C2	95
Caddo, Ok., U.S.	C5	113
Caddo, Tx., U.S.	C3	120
Caddo, co., La., U.S.	B2	95
Caddo, co., Ok., U.S.	B3	113
Caddo, stm., Ar., U.S.	C2	81
Caddo Creek, stm., Ok., U.S.	C4	113
Caddo Gap, Ar., U.S.	C2	81
Caddo Lake, res., U.S.	B2	95
Caddo Mountains, mtn., Ar., U.S.	C1	81
Cade, La., U.S.	D4	95
Cader Idris, mtn., Wales, U.K.	B4	12
Cades, S.C., U.S.	D8	117
Cades, Tn., U.S.	B3	119
Cades Cove, Tn., U.S.	D10	119
Cadet, Mo., U.S.	C7	102
Cadillac, Sask.	H2	75
Cadillac, Fr.	E3	16
Cadillac, Mi., U.S.	D5	99
Cadillac Mountain, mtn., Me., U.S.	D4	96
Cádiz, Spain	D2	22
Cadiz, Ky., U.S.	D2	94
Cadiz, Oh., U.S.	B4	112
Cadiz, Gulf of, b., Eur.	D2	22
Cadogan, Alta.	C5	68
Cadomin, Alta.	C2	68
Cadott, Wi., U.S.	D2	126
Cadotte, stm., Alta.	A2	68
Cadwell, Ga., U.S.	D3	87
Cadyville, N.Y., U.S.	f11	109
Caen, Fr.	C3	16
Caernarfon, Wales, U.K.	A4	10
Caernarfon Bay, b., Wales, U.K.	D4	10
Caerphilly, Wales, U.K.	C4	12
Caesar Creek Lake, res., Oh., U.S.	C2	112
Caetité, Braz.	A4	56
Cafayate, Arg.	E2	55
Cagayan, stm., Phil.	B6	34
Cagayan de Oro, Phil.	D6	34
Cagayan Islands, is., Phil.	D5	34
Cagayan Sulu Island, i., Phil.	D5	34
Cagli, Italy	E2	23
Cagliari, Italy	E2	23
Cagliari, Gulf of, b., Italy	E2	23
Cagnes-sur-Mer, Fr.	F7	16
Caguán, stm., Col.	C3	60
Caguas, P.R.	G11	64
Cahaba, stm., Al., U.S.	C2	78
Cahaba Heights, Al., U.S.	*B3	78
Cahaba Valley, val., Al., U.S.	B3	78
Caha Mountains, mts., Ire.	E2	11
Caher, Ire.	E4	11
Cahersiveen, Ire.	F1	11
Cahokia, Il., U.S.	E3	90
Cahone, Co., U.S.	D2	83
Cahore Point, c., Ire.	E5	11
Cahors, Fr.	E4	16
Caiabis, Serra dos, plat., Braz.	E3	59
Caianda, Braz.	B2	56
Caibarién, Cuba	C4	64
Cai Be, stm., Viet.	k9	34
Caicedonia, Col.	C2	60
Caicó, Braz.	C3	57
Caicos Islands, is., T./C. Is.	D8	64
Caicos Passage, strt., N.A.	C7	64
Caillou Bay, b., La., U.S.	E5	95
Caillou Lake, l., La., U.S.	E5	95
Caimanera, Cuba	E6	64
Caiman Point, c., Phil.	o12	34
Caimito, stm., Pan.	m11	62
Cains, stm., N.B.	C4	71
Cains Store, Ky., U.S.	C5	94
Cainsville, Mo., U.S.	A4	102
Cainsville, Tn., U.S.	B5	119
Caintown, Ont.	C9	73
Cairnbrook, Pa., U.S.	F4	115
Cairngorm Mountains, mts., Scot., U.K.	C5	13
Cairns, Austl.	C8	50
Cairnsmore of Carsphairn, mtn., Scot., U.K.	E4	13
Cairn Table, mtn., Scot., U.K.	E5	13
Cairo (Al Qāhirah), Eg.	B3	38
Cairo, Ga., U.S.	F2	87
Cairo, Il., U.S.	F4	90
Cairo, Mo., U.S.	B5	102
Cairo, Ne., U.S.	D7	104
Cairo, N.Y., U.S.	C6	109
Cairo, Oh., U.S.	B1	112
Cairo, W.V., U.S.	B3	125
Caiundo, Ang.	E2	48
Cajacay, Peru	D2	58
Cajamarca, Peru	C2	58
Cajamarca, dept., Peru	C2	58
Cajatambo, Peru	D2	58
Cajazeiras, Braz.	C3	57
Čajniče, Yugo.	D4	24
Čakovec, Yugo.	B3	24
Čakovice, Czech.	n18	26
Calabar, Nig.	F6	45
Calabasas, Ca., U.S.	m11	82
Calabogie, Ont.	B8	73
Calabogie Lake, l., Ont.	B8	73
Calabozo, Ven.	B4	60
Calabria, prov., Italy	E6	23
Calafat, Rom.	D6	24
Calafate, Arg.	E2	54
Calagua Islands, is., Phil.	o14	34
Calahorra, Spain	A5	22
Calais, Fr.	B4	16
Calais, Me., U.S.	C5	96
Calais, Vt., U.S.	C4	122
Calama, Chile	D2	55
Calamar, Col.	A3	60
Calamar, Col.	C3	60
Calamian Group, is., Phil.	C6	34
Calamocha, Spain	B5	22
Calamus, Ia., U.S.	C7	92
Calamus, stm., Ne., U.S.	B6	104
Calañas, Spain	D2	22
Calanda, Spain	B5	22
Calanscio, Sarīr, des., Afr.	H5	40
Calanscio, Sarīr, des., Libya	D4	43
Calapan, Phil.	C6	34
Calăraşi, Rom.	C8	24
Calarcá, Col.	C2	60
Calasparra, Spain	C5	22
Calatayud, Spain	B5	22
Calau, Ger.	B8	19
Calavo Gardens, Ca., U.S.	*o16	82
Calbe, Ger.	B6	19
Calbuco, Chile	C2	54
Calcasieu, co., La., U.S.	D2	95
Calcasieu, stm., La., U.S.	D2	95
Calcasieu Lake, l., La., U.S.	E2	95
Calcasieu Pass, strt., La., U.S.	E2	95
Calceta, Ec.	B1	58
Calchaquí, Arg.	E2	55
Calçoene, Braz.	B4	59
Calcutta, India	D8	36
Calcutta, Oh., U.S.	B5	112
Calcutta Lake, l., Nv., U.S.	B2	105
Caldaro, Italy	C7	20
Caldas da Rainha, Port.	C1	22
Calder, Sask.	F5	75
Calder, Id., U.S.	B2	89
Calder, stm., Eng., U.K.	A6	12
Calder, Loch, l., Scot., U.K.	B5	13
Caldera, Chile	E1	55
Calderwood, Tn., U.S.	D10	119
Caldron Falls Reservoir, res., Wi., U.S.	C5	126
Caldwell, Ar., U.S.	B5	81
Caldwell, Id., U.S.	F2	89
Caldwell, Ks., U.S.	E6	93
Caldwell, N.J., U.S.	B4	107
Caldwell, Oh., U.S.	C4	112
Caldwell, Tx., U.S.	D4	120
Caldwell, W.V., U.S.	D4	125
Caldwell, co., Ky., U.S.	C2	94
Caldwell, co., Mo., U.S.	B3	102
Caldwell, co., N.C., U.S.	B1	110
Caldwell, co., Tx., U.S.	E4	120
Cale, Ar., U.S.	D2	81
Caledon, Ont.	D5	73
Caledon, N. Ire., U.K.	E4	11
Caledonia, Ont.	D5	73
Caledonia, Mi., U.S.	F5	99
Caledonia, Mn., U.S.	G7	100
Caledonia, Ms., U.S.	B5	101
Caledonia, N.Y., U.S.	C3	109
Caledonia, N.D., U.S.	B3	112
Caledonia, Oh., U.S.	B2	112
Caledonia, Pa., U.S.	D5	115
Caledonia, co., Vt., U.S.	C4	122
Caledonian Canal, Scot., U.K.	B4	10
Calella, Spain	B7	22
Calera, Al., U.S.	B3	78
Calera, Ok., U.S.	D5	113
Caleta Olivia, Arg.	F3	54
Calexico, Ca., U.S.	F6	82
Calf of Man, i., I. of Man	C4	10
Calgary, Alta.	D3	68
Calheta, Port.	h11	22
Calhoun, Al., U.S.	C3	78
Calhoun, Ga., U.S.	B2	87
Calhoun, Il., U.S.	E5	90
Calhoun, Ky., U.S.	C2	94
Calhoun, La., U.S.	B3	95
Calhoun, Mo., U.S.	C4	102
Calhoun, Tn., U.S.	D9	119
Calhoun, co., Al., U.S.	B4	78
Calhoun, co., Ar., U.S.	D3	81
Calhoun, co., Fl., U.S.	B1	86
Calhoun, co., Ga., U.S.	E2	87
Calhoun, co., Il., U.S.	D3	90

Index

Name	Map Ref.	Page

Calhoun, co., Ia., U.S. — B3 92
Calhoun, co., Mi., U.S. — F5 99
Calhoun, co., Ms., U.S. — B4 101
Calhoun, co., S.C., U.S. — D6 117
Calhoun, co., Tx., U.S. — E4 120
Calhoun, co., W.V., U.S. — C3 125
Calhoun City, Ms., U.S. — B4 101
Calhoun Falls, S.C., U.S. — C2 117
Cali, Col. — C2 60
Calico Rock, Ar., U.S. — A3 81
Caliente, Ca., U.S. — E4 82
Caliente, Nv., U.S. — F7 105
Califon, N.J., U.S. — B3 107
California, Ky., U.S. — k14 94
California, Md., U.S. — *D4 97
California, Mo., U.S. — C5 102
California, Pa., U.S. — F2 115
California, state, U.S. — D4 82
California, Golfo de, b., Mex. — C3 60
California Aqueduct, Ca., U.S. — E4 82
California Junction, Ia., U.S. — C1 92
California Oil Camp, Co., U.S. — A2 83
Calingasta, Arg. — A3 54
Calio, N.D., U.S. — A7 111
Calion, Ar., U.S. — D3 81
Calipatria, Ca., U.S. — F6 82
Calispell Peak, mtn., Wa., U.S. — A8 124
Calistoga, Ca., U.S. — C2 82
Callabonna, Austl. — D3 51
Callabonna, Lake, l., Austl. — D3 51
Callaghan, Mount, mtn., Nv., U.S. — D5 105
Callahan, Fl., U.S. — B5 86
Callahan, Ks., U.S. — g12 93
Callahan, co., Tx., U.S. — C3 120
Callan, Ire. — E4 11
Callander, Ont. — A5 73
Callander, Scot., U.K. — B4 10
Callao, Peru — D2 58
Callao, Mo., U.S. — B5 102
Callao, Va., U.S. — C6 123
Callao, dept., Peru — *D2 58
Callaway, Fl., U.S. — *u16 86
Callaway, Md., U.S. — D4 97
Callaway, Mn., U.S. — D3 100
Callaway, Ne., U.S. — C6 104
Callaway, Va., U.S. — C2 123
Callaway, co., Mo., U.S. — C6 102
Callender, Ia., U.S. — B3 92
Callensburg, Pa., U.S. — D2 115
Callery, Pa., U.S. — E1 115
Callicoon, N.Y., U.S. — D5 109
Callicoon Center, N.Y., U.S. — D6 109
Calliham, Tx., U.S. — E3 120
Calling Lake, Alta. — B4 68
Calling Lake, l., Alta. — B4 68
Calloway, co., Ky., U.S. — f9 94
Calmar, Alta. — C4 68
Calmar, Ia., U.S. — A6 92
Calne, Eng., U.K. — C5 12
Caloosahatchee, stm., Fl., U.S. — F5 86
Caloundra, Austl. — E9 50
Calpella, Ca., U.S. — C2 82
Calpet, Wy., U.S. — D2 127
Caltagirone, Italy — F5 23
Caltanissetta, Italy — F5 23
Caltra, Ire. — D3 11
Caluire [-et-Cuire], Fr. — E6 16
Calulo, Ang. — D1 48
Calumet, Que. — D3 74
Calumet, Ia., U.S. — B2 92
Calumet, Mi., U.S. — A2 99
Calumet, Mn., U.S. — C5 100
Calumet, Ok., U.S. — B3 113
Calumet, co., Wi., U.S. — D5 126
Calumet, Lake, l., Il., U.S. — k9 90
Calumet City, Il., U.S. — B6 90
Calumet Park, Il., U.S. — *k9 90
Calumet Sag Channel, Il., U.S. — k9 90
Calumetville, Wi., U.S. — h9 126
Calunda, Ang. — D3 48
Caluula, Som. — C7 47
Calvary, Ga., U.S. — F2 87
Calvary, Wi., U.S. — k9 126
Calvert, Al., U.S. — D1 78
Calvert, Tx., U.S. — D4 120
Calvert, co., Md., U.S. — C4 97
Calvert City, Ky., U.S. — e9 94
Calvert Island, i., B.C. — D3 69
Calverton, Md., U.S. — B4 97
Calverton, Va., U.S. — B5 123
Calverton Park, Mo., U.S. — f13 102
Calvi, Fr. — C2 23
Calvillo, Mex. — m12 63
Calvin, La., U.S. — C3 95
Calvin, N.D., U.S. — A7 111
Calvin, Ok., U.S. — C5 113
Calvinia, S. Afr. — D2 49
Calvörde, Ger. — A6 19
Calw, Ger. — E3 19
Calwa, Ca., U.S. — *D4 82
Calypso, N.C., U.S. — B4 110
Calzada de Calatrava, Spain — C4 22
Cam, stm., Eng., U.K. — D7 10
Camabatela, Ang. — C2 48
Camacho, Mex. — C4 63
Camacupa, Ang. — D2 48
Camagüey, Cuba — D5 64
Camagüey, prov., Cuba — D5 64
Camajuaní, Cuba — C4 64
Camak, Ga., U.S. — C4 87
Camamu, Braz. — D3 57
Camaná, Peru — D3 58
Camanche, Ia., U.S. — C7 92
Camanducaia, Braz. — m8 56
Camano Island, i., Wa., U.S. — A3 124
Camapuã, Braz. — B2 56
Camaquã, Braz. — E2 56
Camaquã, stm., Braz. — E2 56
Camararé, stm., Braz. — E3 59
Camargo, Bol. — D5 55
Camargo, Mex. — D5 63
Camargo, Ok., U.S. — A2 113
Camarillo, Ca., U.S. — *E4 82
Camarón, Cabo, c., Hond. — D7 63
Camarones, Arg. — C3 54
Camarones, Bahía, b., Arg. — C3 54
Camas, Wa., U.S. — D3 124
Camas, co., Id., U.S. — F4 89
Camas Valley, Or., U.S. — D3 114
Ca Mau, Viet. — D2 34
Ca Mau, Cape, c., Viet. — D2 34
Camberwell, Austl. — *G8 50
Cambodia, ctry., Asia — C3 34
Camborne [-Redruth], Eng., U.K. — E4 10
Cambra, Pa., U.S. — D9 115
Cambrai, Fr. — B5 16
Cambria, Ia., U.S. — D4 92
Cambria, Mi., U.S. — G6 99

Cambria, Wi., U.S. — E4 126
Cambria, co., Pa., U.S. — E4 115
Cambrian Mountains, mts., Wales, U.K. — D5 10
Cambrian Park, Ca., U.S. — *D3 82
Cambridge, Ont. — D4 73
Cambridge, Eng., U.K. — D7 10
Cambridge, Il., U.S. — B3 90
Cambridge, Ia., U.S. — C4 92
Cambridge, Ks., U.S. — E7 93
Cambridge, Me., U.S. — C3 96
Cambridge, Md., U.S. — C5 97
Cambridge, Ma., U.S. — B5 98
Cambridge, Mn., U.S. — E5 100
Cambridge, Ne., U.S. — D5 104
Cambridge, N.Y., U.S. — B7 109
Cambridge, Oh., U.S. — B4 112
Cambridge, Vt., U.S. — B3 122
Cambridge, Wi., U.S. — E4 126
Cambridge Bay, N.W. Ter. — C12 66
Cambridge City, In., U.S. — E7 91
Cambridge Junction, Vt., U.S. — B3 122
Cambridge Reservoir, res., Ma., U.S. — g10 98
Cambridge Springs, Pa., U.S. — C1 115
Cambridgeshire, co., Eng., U.K. — B7 12
Cambuí, Braz. — m8 56
Cambundi-Catembo (Nova Gaia), Ang. — D2 48
Camden, Al., U.S. — D2 78
Camden, Ar., U.S. — D3 81
Camden, De., U.S. — D3 85
Camden, Il., U.S. — C3 90
Camden, In., U.S. — C4 91
Camden, Me., U.S. — D3 96
Camden, Mi., U.S. — G6 99
Camden, Ms., U.S. — C4 101
Camden, Mo., U.S. — C3 102
Camden, N.J., U.S. — D2 107
Camden, N.Y., U.S. — B5 109
Camden, N.C., U.S. — A6 110
Camden, Oh., U.S. — C1 112
Camden, S.C., U.S. — C6 117
Camden, Tn., U.S. — A3 119
Camden, Tx., U.S. — D5 120
Camden, W.V., U.S. — B4 125
Camden, co., Ga., U.S. — F5 87
Camden, co., Mo., U.S. — C5 102
Camden, co., N.J., U.S. — D3 107
Camden, co., N.C., U.S. — A6 110
Camden on Gauley, W.V., U.S. — C4 125
Camdenton, Mo., U.S. — D5 102
Camelback Mountain, mtn., Az., U.S. — k9 80
Camelot, Wa., U.S. — *C3 124
Camels Hump, mtn., Vt., U.S. — C3 122
Camerino, Italy — C4 23
Cameron, Az., U.S. — C4 80
Cameron, Il., U.S. — C3 90
Cameron, La., U.S. — E2 95
Cameron, Mo., U.S. — B3 102
Cameron, Mt., U.S. — E5 103
Cameron, N.C., U.S. — B3 110
Cameron, Ok., U.S. — B7 113
Cameron, S.C., U.S. — D6 117
Cameron, Tx., U.S. — D4 120
Cameron, W.V., U.S. — B4 125
Cameron, Wi., U.S. — C2 126
Cameron, co., La., U.S. — E2 95
Cameron, co., Pa., U.S. — D5 115
Cameron, co., Tx., U.S. — F4 120
Cameron Hills, hills, Can. — E9 66
Cameron Island, i., N.W. Ter. — m31 66
Cameron Park, Ca., U.S. — *C3 82
Cameroun, ctry., Afr. — D2 46
Cameroun, Mont, mtn., Cam. — E1 46
Cametá, Braz. — B4 59
Camiling, Phil. — o13 34
Camilla, Ga., U.S. — E2 87
Camiña, Chile — C2 55
Caminha, Port. — B1 22
Camino, Ca., U.S. — C3 82
Camissombo (Verísimo Sarmento), Ang. — C3 48
Camlachie, Ont. — D2 73
Cammack Village, Ar., U.S. — C3 81
Camocim, Braz. — D7 115
Camooweal, Austl. — C2 50
Camopi, stm., Fr. Gu. — C4 59
Camp, co., Tx., U.S. — C5 120
Campagna di Roma, reg., Italy — h9 23
Campaign, Tn., U.S. — D8 119
Campana, Arg. — g7 54
Campana, Isla, i., Chile — D1 54
Campanario, Spain — C3 22
Campania, prov., Italy — D5 23
Campania Island, i., B.C. — C3 69
Campbell, Al., U.S. — D2 78
Campbell, Ca., U.S. — k8 82
Campbell, Fl., U.S. — D5 86
Campbell, Mn., U.S. — E2 100
Campbell, Mo., U.S. — E7 102
Campbell, Ne., U.S. — D7 104
Campbell, N.Y., U.S. — C3 109
Campbell, Oh., U.S. — A5 112
Campbell, co., Ky., U.S. — B5 94
Campbell, co., S.D., U.S. — B5 118
Campbell, co., Tn., U.S. — C9 119
Campbell, co., Va., U.S. — C3 123
Campbell, co., Wy., U.S. — B7 127
Campbell, Cape, c., N.Z. — N15 51
Campbellford, Ont. — C7 73
Campbell Hill, hill, Oh., U.S. — B2 112
Campbell Island, i., B.C. — C3 69
Campbell Island, i., N.Z. — J8 2
Campbell Lake, l., Or., U.S. — E7 114
Campbell River, B.C. — D5 69
Campbells Bay, Que. — B8 73
Campbellsburg, In., U.S. — G5 91
Campbellsburg, Ky., U.S. — B4 94
Campbells Creek, stm., W.V., U.S. — m13 125
Campbellsville, Ky., U.S. — C4 94
Campbellton, N.B. — A3 71
Campbellton, Newf. — D4 72
Campbellton, P.E.I. — C5 71
Campbelltown, Austl. — *F9 50
Campbeltown, Scot., U.K. — F7 10
Camp Creek, Tn., U.S. — C11 119
Camp Crook, S.D., U.S. — B2 118
Camp Douglas, Wi., U.S. — E3 126
Campeche, Mex. — D6 63
Campeche, state, Mex. — D6 63
Campeche, Bahía de, b., Mex. — C6 63

Campechuela, Cuba — D5 64
Camperdown, Austl. — I4 51
Campertogno, Italy — E5 21
Camperville, Man. — D1 70
Camp Grove, Il., U.S. — B4 90
Camp Pha, Viet. — A3 34
Camp Hill, Al., U.S. — C4 78
Camp Hill, Pa., U.S. — F8 115
Camp H. M. Smith Marine Corps Base, mil., Hi., U.S. — g10 88
Camp Howard Ridge, mtn., Id., U.S. — D2 89
Campiglia Marittima, Italy — C3 23
Campina Grande, Braz. — C3 57
Campinas, Braz. — C3 56
Campina Verde, Braz. — B3 56
Campion, Co., U.S. — A5 83
Campo, Cam. — E1 46
Campo, Ca., U.S. — F5 82
Campo, Co., U.S. — D8 83
Campoalegre, Col. — C2 60
Campo Alegre de Goiás, Braz. — B3 56
Campobasso, Italy — D5 23
Campobello, S.C., U.S. — A3 117
Campobello Island, i., N.B. — E3 71
Campo Belo, Braz. — C3 56
Campo de Criptana, Spain — C4 22
Campodolcino, Italy — D7 21
Campo Gallo, Arg. — E3 55
Campo Grande, Braz. — C2 56
Campo Maior, Braz. — B2 57
Campo Maior, Port. — C2 22
Campo Mourão, Braz. — C2 56
Campo Real, Spain — p18 22
Campos, Braz. — C4 56
Campos Altos, Braz. — B3 56
Campos Belos, Braz. — A3 56
Camposampiero, Italy — D7 20
Campos Novos, Braz. — D2 56
Campos Sales, Braz. — C2 57
Campo Tencia, mtn., Switz. — D6 21
Campo Tures, Italy — C7 20
Camp Pendleton Marine Corps Base, mil., Ca., U.S. — F5 82
Camp Point, Il., U.S. — C2 90
Camp San Saba, Tx., U.S. — D3 120
Camp Sherman, Or., U.S. — C5 114
Camp Springs, Md., U.S. — f9 97
Campti, La., U.S. — C2 95
Campton, Fl., U.S. — v15 86
Campton, Ga., U.S. — C3 87
Campton, Ky., U.S. — C6 94
Campton, N.H., U.S. — C3 106
Camptown, Pa., U.S. — C9 115
Campus, Il., U.S. — B5 90
Camp Verde, Az., U.S. — C4 80
Camp Verde Indian Reservation, Az., U.S. — C4 80
Campville, Fl., U.S. — C4 86
Camp Wood, Tx., U.S. — E2 120
Cam Ranh, Viet. — G8 35
Cam Ranh Bay, b., Viet. — G8 35
Camrose, Alta. — C4 68
Camuquém, Ven. — B5 60
Canaan, N.B. — C4 71
Canaan, Ct., U.S. — A2 84
Canaan, In., U.S. — G7 91
Canaan, Me., U.S. — D3 96
Canaan, Ms., U.S. — A4 101
Canaan, N.H., U.S. — C2 106
Canaan, N.Y., U.S. — C7 109
Canaan, Vt., U.S. — A5 122
Canaan, stm., N.B. — C4 71
Canaan Center, N.H., U.S. — C2 106
Canaan Street, N.H., U.S. — C2 106
Canada, ctry., N.A. — E13 66
Canada Bay, b., Newf. — C3 72
Cañada de Gómez, Arg. — A4 54
Canada Falls Lake, res., Me., U.S. — C2 96
Canadensis, Pa., U.S. — D11 115
Canadian, Ok., U.S. — B6 113
Canadian, Tx., U.S. — B2 120
Canadian, co., Ok., U.S. — B3 113
Canadian, stm., U.S. — C7 76
Canadys, S.C., U.S. — E6 117
Canaima National Park, Ven. — B5 60
Canajoharie, N.Y., U.S. — C6 109
Çanakkale, Tur. — B6 40
Canal Flats, B.C. — D10 69
Canal Fulton, Oh., U.S. — B4 112
Canalou, Mo., U.S. — E8 102
Canal Point, Fl., U.S. — F6 86
Canal Winchester, Oh., U.S. — C3 112
Canandaigua, N.Y., U.S. — C3 109
Canandaigua Lake, l., N.Y., U.S. — C3 109
Cananea, Mex. — A2 63
Cananéia, Braz. — D3 56
Canápolis, Braz. — B3 56
Cañar, Ec. — B2 58
Cañar, prov., Ec. — B2 58
Canary Islands, is., Spain — m14 22
Canaseraga, N.Y., U.S. — C3 109
Canastota, N.Y., U.S. — B5 109
Canastra, Serra da, mts., Braz. — D6 56
Canaveral, Cape, c., Fl., U.S. — E3 57
Canaveral National Seashore, Fl., U.S. — D6 86
Canavieiras, Braz. — E3 57
Cañazas, Pan. — F7 62
Cañazas, Pan. — C7 62
Canazei, Italy — C7 20
Canberra, Austl. — G8 50
Canby, Ca., U.S. — B3 82
Canby, Mn., U.S. — F2 100
Canby, Or., U.S. — B4 114
Cancale, Fr. — C3 16
Canche, stm., Fr. — D1 17
Cancún, Mex. — C7 63
Candeias, stm., Braz. — D2 59
Candela, Mex. — D5 63
Candelaria, Cuba — C3 64
Candelaria, Phil. — o12 34
Candelaria, stm., Mex. — A2 63
Candeleda, Spain — B3 22
Candia see Iráklion, Grc. — E5 25
Candia, N.H., U.S. — D4 106
Candiac, Que. — q19 74
Candle, Ak., U.S. — B7 79
Candle Lake, l., Sask. — D3 75
Candler, Fl., U.S. — C5 86
Candler, co., Ga., U.S. — D4 87
Candlewood, Lake, l., Ct., U.S. — D1 84
Candlewood Isle, Ct., U.S. — D2 84
Candlewood Knolls, Ct., U.S. — *D2 84
Candlewood Shores, Ct., U.S. — D2 84
Candlewood Trails, Ct., U.S. — *C2 84

Cando, Sask. — E1 75
Cando, N.D., U.S. — A6 111
Candor, N.Y., U.S. — C4 109
Candor, N.C., U.S. — B3 110
Cane, stm., La., U.S. — C2 95
Canea see Khaniá, Grc. — E5 40
Canehill, Ar., U.S. — B1 81
Canela, Braz. — D2 56
Canelones, Ur. — E1 56
Canelones, dept., Ur. — g8 54
Canendiyu, dept., Para. — D4 55
Cañete, Chile — B2 54
Cane Valley, Ky., U.S. — C4 94
Caney, Ks., U.S. — E8 93
Caney, Ky., U.S. — C6 94
Caney, Ok., U.S. — C5 113
Caney, stm., Ok., U.S. — A5 113
Caney Creek, stm., Tx., U.S. — r14 120
Caney Fork, stm., Tn., U.S. — C8 119
Caneyville, Ky., U.S. — C3 94
Canfield, Ar., U.S. — D2 81
Canfield, Oh., U.S. — A5 112
Cangallo, Peru — D3 58
Cangamba, Ang. — D2 48
Cangas, Spain — A1 22
Cangas de Narcea, Spain — A2 22
Cangas de Onís, Spain — A3 22
Cangombe, Ang. — D3 48
Canguaretama, Braz. — C3 57
Canguçu, Braz. — E2 56
Cangzhou, China — D8 31
Canhotinho, Braz. — k5 57
Caniapiscau, stm., Que. — g13 74
Caniapiscau, Lac, l., Que. — h12 74
Canicanian, Phil. — o14 34
Canicattì, Italy — F4 23
Caniles, Spain — D4 22
Canim Lake, B.C. — D7 69
Canim Lake, l., B.C. — D7 69
Canindé, Braz. — B3 57
Canindé, stm., Braz. — C2 57
Canistear Reservoir, res., N.J., U.S. — A4 107
Canisteo, N.Y., U.S. — C3 109
Canisteo, stm., N.Y., U.S. — C3 109
Canistota, S.D., U.S. — D8 118
Canjilon, N.M., U.S. — A3 108
Canlaon Volcano, vol., Phil. — C6 34
Canmer, Ky., U.S. — C4 94
Canmore, Alta. — D3 68
Canna, i., Scot., U.K. — B3 10
Canna, Sound of, strt., Scot., U.K. — C2 13
Cannelburg, In., U.S. — G5 91
Cannel City, Ky., U.S. — C6 94
Cannelton, In., U.S. — I4 91
Cannelton, W.V., U.S. — m13 125
Cannes, Fr. — F7 16
Cannes, Bayou des, stm., La., U.S. — D3 95
Canneto sull'Oglio, Italy — D6 20
Cannich, Scot., U.K. — C4 13
Canning, Austl. — *F2 50
Canning, N.S. — D5 71
Cannington, Ont. — C5 73
Cannock, Eng., U.K. — B5 12
Cannon, De., U.S. — F3 85
Cannon, co., Tn., U.S. — B5 119
Cannon, stm., Mn., U.S. — F5 100
Cannon Air Force Base, mil., N.M., U.S. — C6 108
Cannonball, N.D., U.S. — C5 111
Cannonball, stm., N.D., U.S. — C5 111
Cannon Beach, Or., U.S. — B3 114
Cannon Falls, Mn., U.S. — F6 100
Cannonsburg, Ky., U.S. — B7 94
Cannonsville Reservoir, res., N.Y., U.S. — C5 109
Cannonville, Ut., U.S. — F3 121
Canoas, stm., Braz. — D2 56
Canoe, B.C. — D8 69
Canoe, Al., U.S. — D2 78
Canoe, stm., B.C. — C8 69
Canoe Lake, Ont. — B6 73
Canoinhas, Braz. — D2 56
Canon, Ga., U.S. — B3 87
Canonchet, R.I., U.S. — F1 116
Canon City, Co., U.S. — C5 83
Canones, N.M., U.S. — A3 108
Canon Plaza, N.M., U.S. — A3 108
Canonsburg, Pa., U.S. — F1 115
Canoochee, stm., Ga., U.S. — D5 87
Canora, Sask. — F4 75
Canosa [di Puglia], Italy — D6 23
Canouan, i., St. Vin. — V26 65
Canova, S.D., U.S. — D8 118
Cañovanas, P.R. — B4 65
Canso, N.S. — D8 71
Cantabrian Mountains, mts., Spain — A3 22
Cantanhede, Port. — B1 22
Cantário, stm., Braz. — E2 59
Cantaura, Ven. — B5 60
Canterbury, Austl. — *F9 50
Canterbury, N.B. — D2 71
Canterbury, Eng., U.K. — E7 10
Canterbury, Ct., U.S. — C8 84
Canterbury, De., U.S. — D3 85
Canterbury, N.H., U.S. — D3 106
Canterbury Bight, N.Z. — P13 51
Can Tho, Viet. — G6 35
Canton, Ct., U.S. — B4 84
Canton, Ga., U.S. — B2 87
Canton, Il., U.S. — C3 90
Canton, Ks., U.S. — D6 93
Canton, Me., U.S. — D2 96
Canton, Ma., U.S. — B5 98
Canton, Mn., U.S. — G7 100
Canton, Ms., U.S. — C3 101
Canton, Mo., U.S. — A6 102
Canton, N.J., U.S. — E2 107
Canton, N.Y., U.S. — f10 109
Canton, N.C., U.S. — f10 110
Canton, Oh., U.S. — B4 112
Canton, Ok., U.S. — A3 113
Canton, Pa., U.S. — C8 115
Canton, S.D., U.S. — D9 118
Canton, Tx., U.S. — C5 120
Canton, Wi., U.S. — C2 126
Canton Center, Ct., U.S. — B4 84
Canton see Guangzhou, China — G7 31
Canton Lake, res., Ok., U.S. — A3 113
Cantonment, Fl., U.S. — u14 86
Cantril, Ia., U.S. — D5 92
Cantù, Italy — D4 20
Cantuar, Sask. — G1 75
Cantwell, Ak., U.S. — C10 79
Canumã, stm., Braz. — C3 59
Canutama, Braz. — D2 59

Canute, Ok., U.S. — B2 113
Canutillo, Tx., U.S. — o11 120
Canwood, Sask. — D2 75
Cany-Barville, Fr. — C7 16
Canyon, Tx., U.S. — B2 120
Canyon, co., Id., U.S. — F2 89
Canyon City, Or., U.S. — C8 114
Canyoncito, N.M., U.S. — h9 108
Canyon Country, Ca., U.S. — *E4 82
Canyon Creek, Mt., U.S. — D4 103
Canyon de Chelly National Monument, Az., U.S. — A6 80
Canyon Ferry Lake, res., Mt., U.S. — D5 103
Canyon Lake, res., Tx., U.S. — E3 120
Canyonlands National Park, Ut., U.S. — E6 121
Canyonville, Or., U.S. — E3 114
Cao Bang, Viet. — A7 35
Caonao, stm., Cuba — D4 64
Caorle, Italy — D8 20
Capac, Mi., U.S. — F8 99
Capanaparo, stm., S.A. — B4 60
Capanema, Braz. — B1 57
Capão Bonito, Braz. — C3 56
Capão Doce, Morro do, mtn., Braz. — D2 56
Caparica, Port. — f9 22
Caparo, stm., Ven. — B3 60
Capasin, Sask. — A3 60
Capatárida, Ven. — A3 60
Cap-aux-Meules, Que. — B8 71
Cap aux Meules, Île du, i., Que. — B8 71
Capbreton, Fr. — F3 16
Cap-Chat, Que. — G19 66
Cap-de-la-Madeleine, Que. — C5 74
Capdenac-Gare, Fr. — E5 16
Cape, prov., S. Afr. — D3 49
Cape Barren, i., Austl. — o15 51
Cape Breton, co., N.S. — C9 71
Cape Breton Highlands National Park, N.S. — C9 71
Cape Breton Island, i., N.S. — C9 71
Cape Broyle, Newf. — E5 72
Cape Canaveral, Fl., U.S. — D6 86
Cape Charles, Newf. — B4 72
Cape Charles, Va., U.S. — C6 123
Cape Coast, Ghana — E4 45
Cape Cod Bay, b., Ma., U.S. — C7 98
Cape Cod Canal, Ma., U.S. — C6 98
Cape Cod National Seashore, Ma., U.S. — C7 98
Cape Coral, Fl., U.S. — F5 86
Cape Dorset, N.W. Ter. — D17 66
Cape Elizabeth, Me., U.S. — E2 96
Cape Fair, Mo., U.S. — E4 102
Cape Fear, stm., N.C., U.S. — C4 110
Cape Girardeau, Mo., U.S. — D8 102
Cape Girardeau, co., Mo., U.S. — D8 102
Cape Hatteras National Seashore, N.C., U.S. — B7 110
Cape Horn Mountain, mtn., Id., U.S. — E3 89
Cape Island, i., S.C., U.S. — E9 117
Cape la Hune, Newf. — E3 72
Cape May, N.J., U.S. — F3 107
Cape May, co., N.J., U.S. — E3 107
Cape May Court House, N.J., U.S. — E3 107
Cape May Point, N.J., U.S. — F3 107
Cape Neddick, Me., U.S. — E2 96
Cape Pole, Ak., U.S. — n23 79
Cape Porpoise, Me., U.S. — E2 96
Cape Ray, Newf. — E2 72
Capers Inlet, b., S.C., U.S. — k12 117
Capers Island, i., S.C., U.S. — G11 117
Capers Island, i., S.C., U.S. — F8 117
Cape Sable Island, i., N.S. — F4 71
Cape Saint Claire, Md., U.S. — *B5 97
Capesterre, Guad. — H14 64
Cape Tormentine, N.B. — C6 71
Cape Town (Kaapstad), S. Afr. — D3 49
Cape Verde, ctry., Afr. — E3 42
Capeville, Va., U.S. — h16 123
Cape Vincent, N.Y., U.S. — A4 109
Cape York Peninsula, pen., Austl. — B7 50
Cap-Haïtien, Haiti — E7 64
Capibaribe, stm., Braz. — k5 57
Capilla del Monte, Arg. — g7 54
Capilla del Señor, Arg. — g7 54
Capim, stm., Braz. — B1 57
Capinota, Bol. — C2 55
Capira, Pan. — H14 64
Capistrano, Braz. — E2 59
Capitan, N.M., U.S. — D4 108
Capitán Bado, Para. — D4 55
Capitan Mountains, mts., N.M., U.S. — D4 108
Capitan Peak, mtn., N.M., U.S. — D4 108
Capitol, Mt., U.S. — E12 103
Capitola, Ca., U.S. — *D3 82
Capitola, Fl., U.S. — *B5 86
Capitol Heights, La., U.S. — *B5 86
Capitol Heights, Md., U.S. — f9 97
Capitol Peak, mtn., Nv., U.S. — B4 105
Capitol Reef National Park, Ut., U.S. — E4 121
Capitol View, S.C., U.S. — *D6 117
Capivari, Braz. — m8 56
Capleville, Tn., U.S. — e9 119
Cap Mountain, mtn., N.W. Ter. — C2 96
Capon Bridge, W.V., U.S. — B6 125
Capon Springs, W.V., U.S. — B6 125
Capote Knob, mtn., Tx., U.S. — k8 120
Cap-Pelé, N.B. — C5 71
Cappoquin, Ire. — I4 11
Capraia, i., Italy — C3 23
Caprara, Point, c., Italy — D7 23
Capreol, Ont. — p19 73
Capri, i., Italy — D5 23
Capricorn Channel, strt., Austl. — D9 51
Capricorn Group, is., Austl. — A8 51
Caprock, N.M., U.S. — C6 108
Capron, Il., U.S. — A5 90
Capron, Va., U.S. — D5 123
Capshaw, Al., U.S. — A3 78
Captain Cook, Hi., U.S. — D6 88
Captiva, Fl., U.S. — F4 86
Captiva Island, i., Fl., U.S. — F4 86
Capua, Italy — D5 23
Capulin, N.M., U.S. — A6 108

Capulin Mountain National Monument, N.M., U.S. — A6 108
Caputa, S.D., U.S. — D3 118
Caquetá, dept., Col. — C3 60
Caquetá (Japurá), stm., S.A. — D3 60
Carabaña, Spain — p18 22
Carabanchel Bajo, Spain — p17 22
Carabinani, stm., Braz. — D5 60
Carabobo, state, Ven. — A4 60
Caracal, Rom. — C7 24
Caracaraí, Braz. — B2 59
Caracas, Ven. — A4 60
Caraguatay, Para. — E4 55
Carai, Braz. — B4 56
Carajás, Braz. — D5 59
Carajás, Serra dos, mts., Braz. — D4 59
Carangola, Braz. — C4 56
Caransebeş, Rom. — C6 24
Carapari, Bol. — D3 55
Carapeguá, Para. — E4 55
Carapó, Braz. — C1 56
Caraquet, N.B. — B5 71
Caratasca, Laguna de, b., Hond. — D8 63
Caratinga, Braz. — C4 56
Caratunk, Me., U.S. — C3 96
Carauari, Braz. — B1 57
Caraúbas, Braz. — h5 57
Caraúbas, Braz. — C3 57
Caravaca, Spain — C5 22
Caravelas, Braz. — E3 57
Caravelí, Peru — E3 58
Caraway, Ar., U.S. — B5 81
Caraz, Peru — C2 58
Carazinho, Braz. — D2 56
Carballino, Spain — A1 22
Carballo, Spain — A1 22
Carberry, Man. — E2 70
Carbet, Pitons du, mts., Mart. — S10 19
Carbó, Mex. — B2 63
Carbon, Ia., U.S. — D3 92
Carbon, In., U.S. — E3 91
Carbon, Tx., U.S. — C3 120
Carbon, W.V., U.S. — m13 125
Carbon, co., Mt., U.S. — E7 103
Carbon, co., Pa., U.S. — E10 115
Carbon, co., Ut., U.S. — D5 121
Carbon, co., Wy., U.S. — E5 127
Carbonado, Wa., U.S. — B3 124
Carbonara, Capo, c., Italy — E2 23
Carbondale, Alta. — C4 68
Carbondale, Co., U.S. — B3 83
Carbondale, Il., U.S. — F4 90
Carbondale, Ks., U.S. — D8 93
Carbondale, Oh., U.S. — C3 112
Carbondale, Pa., U.S. — C10 115
Carbonear, Newf. — E5 72
Carbon Hill, Al., U.S. — B2 78
Carbon Hill, Il., U.S. — B5 90
Carbonia, Italy — E2 23
Carbonne, Fr. — F4 16
Carbonville, Ut., U.S. — D5 121
Carbury, N.D., U.S. — A5 111
Carcagente, Spain — C5 22
Carcans, Étang de, b., Fr. — E3 16
Carcassonne, Fr. — F5 16
Carchi, prov., Ec. — A2 58
Carcross, Yukon — D6 66
Çardak, Tur. — D7 25
Cardale, Man. — D1 70
Cárdenas, Cuba — C3 64
Cárdenas, Mex. — m14 63
Çardi, Tur. — C7 25
Cardiel, Lago, l., Arg. — D2 54
Cardiff, Wales, U.K. — E5 10
Cardiff, Al., U.S. — f7 78
Cardiff, Md., U.S. — A5 97
Cardiff, N.J., U.S. — E3 107
Cardigan, P.E.I. — C7 71
Cardigan, Wales, U.K. — D4 10
Cardigan, Mount, mtn., N.H., U.S. — C3 106
Cardigan Bay, b., P.E.I. — C7 71
Cardigan Bay, b., Wales, U.K. — D4 10
Cardinal, Ont. — C9 73
Cardinal Lake, l., Alta. — A2 68
Cardington, Oh., U.S. — B3 112
Cardona, Spain — C3 22
Cardross, Sask. — H3 75
Cardston, Alta. — E4 68
Cardville, Me., U.S. — C4 96
Cardwell, Mo., U.S. — E7 102
Cardwell, Mt., U.S. — E5 103
Cardwell Mountain, mtn., Tn., U.S. — D8 119
Carega, mtn., Italy — B6 20
Carei, Rom. — B6 24
Carencro, La., U.S. — D3 95
Carenero, Ven. — A4 60
Carentan, Fr. — C3 16
Caretta, W.V., U.S. — D3 125
Carey, Id., U.S. — F5 89
Carey, Oh., U.S. — B2 112
Carey, Tx., U.S. — B2 120
Carey, Lake, l., Austl. — E3 50
Careysburg, Lib. — G2 45
Careywood, Id., U.S. — A2 89
Carhaix, Fr. — C2 16
Carhuás, Peru — C2 58
Cariaco, Ven. — A5 60
Cariamanga, Ec. — B2 58
Cariati, Italy — E6 23
Cariba, Punta, c., Col. — B3 53
Caribbean Sea — H12 61
Caribou, Me., U.S. — A5 96
Caribou, co., Id., U.S. — G7 89
Caribou Island, i., N.S. — D7 71
Caribou Lake, l., Me., U.S. — C3 96
Caribou Mountain, mtn., Id., U.S. — F7 89
Caribou Mountains, mts., Me., U.S. — C2 96
Caribou Mountains, mts., Alta. — f7 68
Caribou Range, mts., Id., U.S. — G7 89
Carichic, Mex. — B3 63
Carievale, Sask. — H5 75
Carignan, Fr. — C6 16
Carinhanha, Braz. — A4 56
Carini, Italy — E4 23
Carinish, Scot., U.K. — C1 13
Caripe, Ven. — A5 60
Carinthia, hist. reg., Aus. — E6 18
Caripito, Ven. — A5 60
Cariús, Braz. — C3 57
Carl Blackwell, Lake, res., Ok., U.S. — A4 113
Carle Place, N.Y., U.S. — *n15 109
Carleton, Mi., U.S. — F7 99
Carleton, Ne., U.S. — D8 104
Carleton, co., N.B. — C2 71
Carleton, Mount, mtn., N.B. — B3 71
Carleton Place, Ont. — B8 73

Name	Map Ref.	Page
Carletonville, S. Afr.	C4	49
Carlile, Wy., U.S.	B8	127
Carlin, Nv., U.S.	C5	105
Carlingford, Ire.	C5	11
Carlingford Lough, b., Eur.	F13	8
Carlinville, Il., U.S.	D4	90
Carlisle, Eng., U.K.	C5	10
Carlisle, Ar., U.S.	C4	81
Carlisle, In., U.S.	G3	91
Carlisle, Ia., U.S.	C4	92
Carlisle, Ky., U.S.	B5	94
Carlisle, Ma., U.S.	f10	98
Carlisle, Oh., U.S.	C3	101
Carlisle, Pa., U.S.	C1	112
Carlisle, S.C., U.S.	F7	115
Carlisle, Tn., U.S.	B5	117
Carlisle, co., Ky., U.S.	A4	119
Carlisle, co., Ky., U.S.	f8	94
Carlit, Pic, mtn., Fr.	F4	16
Carl Junction, Mo., U.S.	D3	102
Carlock, Il., U.S.	C4	90
Carloforte, Italy	E2	23
Carlos, Md., U.S.	k13	97
Carlos, Mn., U.S.	E3	100
Carlos Casares, Arg.	B4	54
Carlos Chagas, Braz.	B4	56
Carlos City, In., U.S.	D7	91
Carlos Tejedor, Arg.	B4	54
Carlota, Ca., U.S.	B1	82
Carlow, Ire.	D3	10
Carlow, co., Ire.	E5	11
Carloway, Scot., U.K.	B2	13
Carlowville, Al., U.S.	C2	78
Carlsbad, Ca., U.S.	F5	82
Carlsbad, N.M., U.S.	E5	108
Carlsbad, Tx., U.S.	D2	120
Carlsbad Caverns National Park, N.M., U.S.	E5	108
Carlsbad Springs, Ont.	h13	73
Carlsborg, Wa., U.S.	A2	124
Carlstadt, N.J., U.S.	h8	107
Carlton, Sask.	E2	75
Carlton, Eng., U.K.	B6	12
Carlton, Al., U.S.	D2	78
Carlton, Ga., U.S.	B3	87
Carlton, Ks., U.S.	D6	93
Carlton, Mn., U.S.	D6	100
Carlton, Or., U.S.	B3	114
Carlton, Tx., U.S.	D3	120
Carlton, co., Mn., U.S.	D6	100
Carluke, Scot., U.K.	E5	13
Carlyle, Sask.	H4	75
Carlyle, Il., U.S.	E4	90
Carlyle, Il., U.S.	D12	103
Carlyle Lake, res., Il., U.S.	E4	90
Carmacks, Yukon	D5	66
Carmagnola, Italy	B1	23
Carman, Man.	E2	70
Carmangay, Alta.	D4	68
Carmanville, Newf.	D4	72
Carmarthen, Wales, U.K.	E4	10
Carmarthen Bay, b., Wales, U.K.	E4	10
Carmaux, Fr.	E5	16
Carmel, Sask.	E3	75
Carmel, Ca., U.S.	D3	82
Carmel, In., U.S.	E5	91
Carmel, La., U.S.	B2	95
Carmel, Me., U.S.	D3	96
Carmel, N.J., U.S.	E2	107
Carmel, N.Y., U.S.	D7	109
Carmel, Mount, mtn., Isr.	B7	41
Carmel Head, c., Wales, U.K.	A3	12
Carmelo, Ur.	E1	56
Carmen, Ar., U.S.	F4	80
Carmen, Id., U.S.	D5	89
Carmen, Ok., U.S.	A3	113
Carmen, Isla, i., Mex.	E4	63
Carmen, Río del, stm., Chile	E1	55
Carmen Alto, Chile	D2	55
Carmen de Areco, Arg.	A5	54
Carmen [del Paraná], Para.	E4	55
Carmen de Patagones, Arg.	C4	54
Carmer Hill, hill, Pa., U.S.	C6	115
Carmi, Il., U.S.	E5	90
Carmi, Lake, l., Vt., U.S.	B3	122
Carmichael, Bah.	m17	64
Carmichael, Sask.	G1	75
Carmichael, Ca., U.S.	*C3	82
Carmichaels, Pa., U.S.	G2	115
Carmona, Spain	D3	22
Carnarvon, Austl.	D1	50
Carnarvon, S. Afr.	D3	49
Carnarvon, Ca., U.S.	B2	92
Carnation, Wa., U.S.	B4	124
Carnaxide, Port.	f9	22
Carndonagh, Ire.	B4	11
Carnduff, Sask.	H5	75
Carnegie, Pa., U.S.	E2	87
Carnegie, Ok., U.S.	B3	113
Carnegie, Pa., U.S.	F1	115
Carnegie, Lake, l., Austl.	E3	50
Carnes, Ms., U.S.	E4	101
Carnesville, Ga., U.S.	B3	87
Carnew, Ire.	E5	11
Carney, Md., U.S.	*B4	97
Carney, Mi., U.S.	C3	99
Carney, Ok., U.S.	B4	113
Carneys Point, N.J., U.S.	D2	107
Carnforth, Eng., U.K.	F6	13
Carnic Alps, mts., Eur.	A4	23
Car Nicobar, i., India	G9	36
Carnlough, N. Ire., U.K.	C6	11
Carnot, Cen. Afr. Rep.	D3	46
Carnot, Pa., U.S.	*F1	115
Carnoustie, Scot., U.K.	D6	13
Carnsore Point, c., Ire.	D3	10
Carnuel, N.M., U.S.	E5	108
Caro, Mi., U.S.	E7	99
Carol City, Fl., U.S.	s13	86
Caroleen, N.C., U.S.	B1	110
Carolina, Braz.	E9	54
Carolina, P.R.	*B4	65
Carolina, R.I., U.S.	F2	116
Carolina, W.V., U.S.	k10	125
Carolina Beach, N.C., U.S.	C5	110
Carolinas, Puntan de, N. Mar.		
Caroline, Alta.	E7	52
Caroline, Wi., U.S.	C3	68
Caroline, co., Md., U.S.	D5	126
Caroline, co., Va., U.S.	C6	97
Caroline, atoll, Kir.	C5	123
Caroline Islands, is., T.T.P.I.	G13	6
Carol Stream, Il., U.S.	F8	6
Caron, Sask.	*k8	90
Carona, Switz.	G3	75
Caroni, stm., Trin.	E9	93
Caroní, stm., Ven.	N23	65
Carora, Ven.	B5	60
Carouge, Switz.	A3	60
Carp, Ont.	E3	18
Carp, Ont.	B8	73
Carpathian Mountains, mts., Eur.	F13	8
Carpentaria, Gulf of, b., Austl.	B6	50
Carpenter, Ia., U.S.	A4	92
Carpenter, S.D., U.S.	C8	118
Carpenter, Wy., U.S.	E8	127
Carpenter Dam, Ar., U.S.	g7	81
Carpentersville, Il., U.S.	A5	90
Carpentras, Fr.	E6	16
Carpi, Italy	B3	23
Carpinteria, Ca., U.S.	E4	82
Carpio, N.D., U.S.	A4	111
Carp Lake, l., B.C.	B6	69
Carr, Co., U.S.	A6	83
Carrabassett Valley, Me., U.S.	C2	96
Carrabelle, Fl., U.S.	C2	86
Carradale, Scot., U.K.	E3	13
Carrantuohill, mtn., Ire.	D2	10
Carrara, Italy	B3	23
Carrauntoohil, mtn., Ire.	D2	10
Carrboro, N.C., U.S.	B3	110
Carrbridge, Scot., U.K.	C5	13
Carrcroft Crest, De., U.S.	*A3	85
Carriacou, i., Gren.	W26	65
Carrickfergus, N. Ire., U.K.	C4	10
Carrickmacross, Ire.	D5	11
Carrick on Shannon, Ire.	D3	11
Carrick on Suir, Ire.	D3	10
Carrick, Mount, mtn., Wa., U.S.	B2	13
Carrier, Que.	o17	74
Carrier, Ok., U.S.	A3	113
Carriere, Ms., U.S.	E4	101
Carrier Mills, Il., U.S.	F5	90
Carrigaholt, Ire.	D3	11
Carrigaline, Ire.	F3	11
Carrigan, Mount, mtn., N.H., U.S.	B4	106
Carrigan Head, c., Ire.	C3	11
Carrington, N.D., U.S.	B6	111
Carrington Island, i., Ut., U.S.	C3	121
Carrión, stm., Spain	A3	22
Carrión de los Condes, Spain	A3	22
Carrizal Bajo, Chile	E1	55
Carrizo Creek, stm., U.S.	A1	120
Carrizo Mountain, mtn., N.M., U.S.	D4	108
Carrizo Mountains, mts., U.S.	A6	80
Carrizo Springs, Tx., U.S.	E3	120
Carrizo Wash, val., U.S.	C6	80
Carrizozo, N.M., U.S.	D4	108
Carr Mountain, mtn., N.H., U.S.	C3	106
Carroll, Ia., U.S.	B3	92
Carroll, Me., U.S.	C4	96
Carroll, Ne., U.S.	B8	104
Carroll, Oh., U.S.	C3	112
Carroll, co., Ar., U.S.	A2	81
Carroll, co., Ga., U.S.	C1	87
Carroll, co., Il., U.S.	A4	90
Carroll, co., In., U.S.	C4	91
Carroll, co., Ia., U.S.	B3	92
Carroll, co., Ky., U.S.	B4	94
Carroll, co., Md., U.S.	A3	97
Carroll, co., Ms., U.S.	B4	101
Carroll, co., Mo., U.S.	B4	102
Carroll, co., N.H., U.S.	C4	106
Carroll, co., Oh., U.S.	B4	112
Carroll, co., Tn., U.S.	B3	119
Carroll, co., Va., U.S.	D2	123
Carrolls, Wa., U.S.	C3	124
Carrollton, Al., U.S.	B1	78
Carrollton, Ga., U.S.	C1	87
Carrollton, Il., U.S.	D3	90
Carrollton, Ky., U.S.	B4	94
Carrollton, Mi., U.S.	E7	99
Carrollton, Ms., U.S.	B4	101
Carrollton, Mo., U.S.	B4	102
Carrollton, Oh., U.S.	B4	112
Carrollton, Tx., U.S.	*n10	120
Carrolltown, Pa., U.S.	E4	115
Carrollwood, Fl., U.S.	*E4	86
Carron, stm., Scot., U.K.	C3	13
Carron, Loch, b., Scot., U.K.	B4	10
Carrot, stm., Can.	D4	75
Carrot River, Sask.	D4	75
Carrowmore Lake, l., Ire.	C2	11
Carrsville, Ky., U.S.	e9	94
Carruthers, Sask.	E1	75
Carrville, Al., U.S.	C4	78
Carry Falls Reservoir, res., N.Y., U.S.	f10	109
Carrying Place, Ont.	C7	73
Çarşamba, Tur.	B11	40
Carseland, Alta.	D4	68
Carson, Ca., U.S.	*E4	82
Carson, Ia., U.S.	C2	92
Carson, Me., U.S.	B4	96
Carson, Ms., U.S.	D4	101
Carson, N.M., U.S.	A4	108
Carson, Va., U.S.	C5	123
Carson, Wa., U.S.	D4	124
Carson, co., Tx., U.S.	B2	120
Carson, stm., Nv., U.S.	D2	105
Carson City, Mi., U.S.	E6	99
Carson City, Nv., U.S.	D2	105
Carson Lake, l., Nv., U.S.	D3	105
Carson Sink, l., Nv., U.S.	D3	105
Carson Spring, Tn., U.S.	D10	119
Carstairs, Alta.	D3	68
Carswell Air Force Base, mil., Tx., U.S.	n9	120
Cartagena, Chile	A2	54
Cartagena, Col.	A2	60
Cartagena, Spain	D5	22
Cartago, Col.	C2	60
Cartago, C.R.	F8	63
Carta Valley, Tx., U.S.	E2	120
Cartaxo, Port.	C1	22
Cartaya, Spain	D2	22
Carter, Ok., U.S.	B6	94
Carter, S.D., U.S.	C6	103
Carter, Tn., U.S.	B2	113
Carter, Wi., U.S.	C11	119
Carter, Wy., U.S.	C5	126
Carter, co., Ky., U.S.	E2	127
Carter, co., Mo., U.S.	B6	94
Carter, co., Mt., U.S.	E7	102
Carter, co., Ok., U.S.	E12	103
Carter, co., Tn., U.S.	C4	113
Carter Dome, mtn., N.H., U.S.	C11	119
Carteret, N.J., U.S.	B4	106
Carteret, co., N.C., U.S.	A4	107
Carter Lake, Ia., U.S.	C6	110
Carter Mountain, mtn., Wy., U.S.	C2	92
Carters, Ga., U.S.	B3	127
Cartersburg, In., U.S.	B2	87
	E5	91
Carters Lake, res., Ga., U.S.	B2	87
Cartersville, Ga., U.S.	B2	87
Cartersville, S.C., U.S.	C7	117
Cartersville, Va., U.S.	C4	123
Carterville, Il., U.S.	F4	90
Carterville, Mo., U.S.	D3	102
Carthage, Ar., U.S.	C3	81
Carthage, Il., U.S.	C2	90
Carthage, In., U.S.	E6	91
Carthage, Ms., U.S.	C4	101
Carthage, Mo., U.S.	D3	102
Carthage, N.Y., U.S.	B5	109
Carthage, N.C., U.S.	B3	110
Carthage, S.D., U.S.	C8	118
Carthage, Tn., U.S.	C8	119
Carthage, Tx., U.S.	C5	120
Carthage, hist., Tun.	B7	44
Cartier, i., Austl.	B3	50
Cartwright, Man.	E2	70
Cartwright, Newf.	B3	72
Cartwright, N.D., U.S.	B2	111
Cartwright, Ok., U.S.	D5	113
Caruaru, Braz.	C3	57
Carúpano, Ven.	A5	60
Caruthersville, Mo., U.S.	E8	102
Carver, Ma., U.S.	C6	98
Carver, Mn., U.S.	F5	100
Carver, co., Mn., U.S.	F5	100
Carver Ranch Estates, Fl., U.S.	*r13	86
Carville, La., U.S.	h9	95
Carvin, Fr.	D2	17
Cary, Ga., U.S.	D3	87
Cary, Il., U.S.	A5	90
Cary, Ms., U.S.	C3	101
Cary, N.C., U.S.	B4	110
Caryville, Fl., U.S.	u16	86
Caryville, Tn., U.S.	C9	119
Casa, Ar., U.S.	B2	81
Casablanca, Mor.	C3	44
Casa Blanca, N.M., U.S.	B2	108
Casa Branca, Braz.	C3	56
Casa de Oro, Ca., U.S.	*F5	82
Casa Grande, Az., U.S.	E4	80
Casa Grande National Monument, Az., U.S.	E4	80
Casale Monferrato, Italy	B2	23
Casalmaggiore, Italy	B3	23
Casanare, dept., Col.	B3	60
Casanare, stm., Col.	B3	60
Casanova, Va., U.S.	B5	123
Casape, Italy	h9	23
Casa Piedra, Tx., U.S.	p12	120
Casar, N.C., U.S.	B1	110
Casarano, Italy	D7	23
Casas Adobes, Az., U.S.	E5	80
Casas Grande, Az., U.S.	A1	120
Cascade, B.C.	E9	69
Cascade, Co., U.S.	C6	83
Cascade, Id., U.S.	E2	89
Cascade, Ia., U.S.	B6	92
Cascade, Mo., U.S.	D7	102
Cascade, Mt., U.S.	C5	103
Cascade, Va., U.S.	D3	123
Cascade, Wi., U.S.	E5	126
Cascade, co., Mt., U.S.	C5	103
Cascade Locks, Or., U.S.	B5	114
Cascade Point, c., N.Z.	O12	51
Cascade Range, mts., N.A.	B3	76
Cascade Reservoir, res., Id., U.S.	E3	89
Cascade Summit, Or., U.S.	D4	114
Cascade Tunnel, Wa., U.S.	B4	124
Cascade Vista, Wa., U.S.	*B3	124
Cascadia, Or., U.S.	C4	114
Cascais, Port.	C1	22
Cascais Bay, b., Port.	f9	22
Cascajal, stm., Pan.	h11	62
Cascavel, Braz.	C2	56
Cascavel, Braz.	B3	57
Cascilla, Ms., U.S.	B3	101
Casco, Me., U.S.	D2	96
Casco, Wi., U.S.	D6	126
Casco Bay, b., Me., U.S.	E3	96
Caselton, N.Y., U.S.	F7	105
Caserta, Italy	D5	23
Caseville, Mi., U.S.	E8	99
Casey, Il., U.S.	D6	90
Casey, Ia., U.S.	C3	92
Casey, co., Ky., U.S.	C5	94
Casey, sci., Ant.	C24	7
Casey, Mount, mtn., Id., U.S.	A2	89
Casey Bay, b., Ant.	C17	7
Casey Key, i., Fl., U.S.	E4	86
Caseyr (Cape Guardafui), c., Som.	C7	47
Cash, Ar., U.S.	B5	81
Cashel, Ire.	C3	10
Cashel, Ire.	D2	11
Cashiers, N.C., U.S.	f9	110
Cashion, Az., U.S.	m8	80
Cashion, Ok., U.S.	B4	113
Cashmere, Wa., U.S.	B5	124
Cashton, Wi., U.S.	E3	126
Casigua, Ven.	C6	60
Casiguran, Phil.	n14	34
Casiguran Sound, strt., Phil.	n13	34
Casilda, Arg.	A4	54
Casilda, Cuba	D4	64
Casino, Austl.	D9	51
Casiquiare, stm., Ven.	C4	60
Casky, Ky., U.S.	D2	94
Čáslav, Czech.	D2	26
Casma, Peru	C2	58
Casmalia, Ca., U.S.	E3	82
Caspar, Ca., U.S.	C2	82
Caspe, Spain	B5	22
Casper, Wy., U.S.	D6	127
Caspian, Mi., U.S.	B2	99
Caspiana, La., U.S.	B2	95
Caspian Depression, pl., Sov. Un.	E8	29
Caspian Lake, l., Vt., U.S.	B4	122
Caspian Sea	F5	16
Cass, In., U.S.	C3	91
Cass, W.V., U.S.	D3	90
Cass, co., Il., U.S.	D3	90
Cass, co., In., U.S.	C5	91
Cass, co., Ia., U.S.	C3	92
Cass, co., Mi., U.S.	G4	99
Cass, co., Mn., U.S.	D4	100
Cass, co., Mo., U.S.	C3	102
Cass, co., Ne., U.S.	D9	104
Cass, co., N.D., U.S.	C8	111
Cass, co., Tx., U.S.	C5	120
Cass, stm., Mi., U.S.	E7	99
Cassadaga, N.Y., U.S.	C1	109
Cassá de la Selva, Spain	A5	22
Cassai (Kasai), stm., Afr.	D3	48
Cass City, Mi., U.S.	E7	99
Cassel, Fr.	B10	17
Cassel see Kassel, Ger.	C4	18
Casselberry, Fl., U.S.	*D5	86
Casselman, Ont.	B9	73
Casselman, Pa., U.S.	G3	115
Casselman, stm., U.S.	k12	97
Casselton, N.D., U.S.	C8	111
Cassia, co., Id., U.S.	G5	89
Cassiar, B.C.	m17	69
Cassiar Mountains, mts., Can.	E6	66
Cassidy, B.C.	f12	69
Cassilândia, Braz.	B2	56
Cassinga, Ang.	E2	48
Cassino, Italy	D4	23
Cass Lake, Mn., U.S.	C4	100
Cass Lake, l., Mn., U.S.	C4	100
Cassoday, Ks., U.S.	D7	93
Cassopolis, Mi., U.S.	G4	99
Casstown, Oh., U.S.	B1	112
Cassville, Ga., U.S.	B2	87
Cassville, Mo., U.S.	E4	102
Cassville, Wi., U.S.	F3	126
Castaia, Ia., U.S.	A6	92
Castalia, N.C., U.S.	A4	110
Castalia, Oh., U.S.	A3	112
Castalian Springs, Tn., U.S.	A5	119
Castana, Ia., U.S.	B2	92
Castanea, Pa., U.S.	D7	115
Castanheira de Pêra, Port.	C1	22
Castaños, Mex.	B4	63
Castel di Guido, Italy	h8	23
Castelfranco Emilia, Italy	E7	20
Castelfranco Veneto, Italy	D7	20
Castel Gandolfo, Italy	h9	23
Castel Giuliano, Italy	g8	23
Casteljaloux, Fr.	E4	16
Castellammare, Italy	D3	20
Castellane, Fr.	E6	16
Castelli, Arg.	B5	54
Castellón de la Plana, Spain	C5	22
Castel Madama, Italy	h9	23
Castelnaudary, Fr.	F4	16
Castelo, Braz.	C4	56
Castelo Branco, Port.	C2	22
Castelo de Vide, Port.	C2	22
Castel San Pietro dell'Emilia, Italy	E7	20
Castelsarrasin, Fr.	F4	16
Castelvetrano, Italy	H3	51
Castile, N.Y., U.S.	C2	109
Castillo, Pampa del, pl., Arg.	D3	54
Castillo de San Marcos National Monument, Fl., U.S.	n9	86
Castillos, Ur.	E2	56
Castine, Me., U.S.	D4	96
Castione [della Presolana], Italy	E9	21
Castle, Ok., U.S.	B5	113
Castle Air Force Base, mil., Ca., U.S.	D3	82
Castlebar, Ire.	D2	10
Castlebay, Scot., U.K.	D1	13
Castlebellingham, Ire.	C5	11
Castleberry, Al., U.S.	D2	78
Castleblayney, Ire.	C5	11
Castlecomer, Ire.	E4	11
Castle Dale, Ut., U.S.	D4	121
Castlederg, N. Ire., U.K.	C4	11
Castle Dome Mountains, mts., Az., U.S.	D1	80
Castle Dome Peak, mtn., Az., U.S.	D1	80
Castle Douglas, Scot., U.K.	C5	10
Castlefinn, Ire.	C4	11
Castleford, Id., U.S.	G4	89
Castlegar, B.C.	E9	69
Castlegregory, Ire.	E1	11
Castle Harbour, b., Ber.	o20	64
Castle Hayne, N.C., U.S.	C5	110
Castle Hills, De., U.S.	i7	85
Castle Hot Springs, Az., U.S.	D3	80
Castleisland, Ire.	E2	11
Castlemaine, Austl.	H5	51
Castlemaine, Ire.	E2	11
Castlemartyr, Ire.	F3	11
Castle Mountain, mtn., Yukon	C6	66
Castle Mountains, mts., U.S.	D6	103
Castle Park, Ca., U.S.	*o15	82
Castle Peak, mtn., Co., U.S.	B4	83
Castle Peak, mtn., Id., U.S.	E4	89
Castle Point, Mo., U.S.	f13	102
Castlepollard, Ire.	D4	11
Castlerea, Ire.	D3	11
Castlereagh, N. Ire., U.K.	*C6	11
Castlereagh, stm., Austl.	F7	51
Castle Rock, Co., U.S.	B6	83
Castle Rock, Mn., U.S.	F5	100
Castle Rock, Wa., U.S.	C3	124
Castle Rock, Or., U.S.	C8	114
Castle Rock Butte, mtn., S.D., U.S.	B2	118
Castle Rock Lake, res., Wi., U.S.	E3	126
Castle Shannon, Pa., U.S.	*k13	115
Castleton, Ont.	C7	73
Castleton, Jam.	E15	65
Castleton, Il., U.S.	B4	90
Castleton, Ks., U.S.	g11	93
Castleton, Vt., U.S.	D2	122
Castleton on Hudson, N.Y., U.S.	C7	109
Castletown, I. of Man	F4	13
Castletown Geoghegan, Ire.	D4	11
Castletownroche, Ire.	E3	11
Castlewellan, N. Ire., U.K.	C6	11
Castlewood, S.D., U.S.	C8	118
Castlewood, Va., U.S.	f9	123
Castor, Alta.	C5	68
Castor, stm., Mo., U.S.	D7	102
Castor Creek, stm., La., U.S.		
Castorland, N.Y., U.S.	B5	109
Castres, Fr.	F5	16
Castries, St. Luc.	J14	64
Castro, Braz.	C3	56
Castro, Chile	E2	56
Castro, co., Tx., U.S.	B1	120
Castro Alves, Braz.	B3	57
Castro Daire, Port.	B2	22
Castro del Río, Spain	D3	22
Castro Marim, Port.	D2	22
Castropol, Spain	A2	22
Castrop-Rauxel, Ger.	*C3	18
Castro Urdiales, Spain	A3	22
Castro Valley, Ca., U.S.	h8	82
Castro Verde, Port.	D2	22
Castroville, Ca., U.S.	D3	82
Castroville, Tx., U.S.	E3	120
Castrovirreina, Peru	C2	58
Castuera, Spain	C3	22
Caswell, co., N.C., U.S.	A3	110
Cat, stm., Can.		
Catacamas, Hond.	A7	63
Catacaos, Peru	C1	58
Catacocha, Ec.	B2	58
Catacombs, hist., Italy	h9	23
Cataguases, Braz.	C4	56
Cataguases, co., La., U.S.	C4	95
Catahoula Lake, l., La., U.S.	C3	95
Catalão, Braz.	B5	56
Catalca, Tur.	B7	40
Catalina, Newf.	D5	72
Catalina, Chile	E2	55
Catalina Foothills, Az., U.S.	*E5	80
Catalonia, hist. reg., Spain	B6	22
Catamarca, Arg.	E2	55
Catamarca, prov., Arg.	E2	55
Catanauan, Phil.	p14	34
Catanduanes, i., Phil.	C6	34
Catanduva, Braz.	C3	56
Catania, Italy	F5	23
Catania, Gulf of, b., Italy	F5	23
Cataño, P.R.	B3	65
Catanzaro, Italy	E6	23
Cataouatche, Lake, l., La., U.S.	k11	95
Cataract, In., U.S.	F4	91
Cataract, Wi., U.S.	D3	126
Cataract Canyon, val., Ut., U.S.	F5	121
Catarroja, Spain	C5	22
Catasauqua, Pa., U.S.	E11	115
Catastrophe, Cape, c., Austl.	F6	50
Catatumbo, stm.	C6	60
Cataumet, Ma., U.S.	C6	98
Catawba, N.C., U.S.	B1	110
Catawba, S.C., U.S.	B6	117
Catawba, Va., U.S.	C2	123
Catawba, W.V., U.S.	h10	125
Catawba, Wi., U.S.	C3	126
Catawba, co., N.C., U.S.	B1	110
Catawba, stm., S.C., U.S.	B6	117
Catawba, South Fork, stm., N.C., U.S.	B1	110
Catawba Island, Oh., U.S.	A3	112
Catawissa, Pa., U.S.	E9	115
Catcreek, Mt., U.S.	C8	103
Cateechee, S.C., U.S.	B2	117
Cates, In., U.S.	E3	91
Cathance, Lake, l., Me., U.S.	D5	96
Catharine, Ks., U.S.	D4	93
Cathay, N.D., U.S.	B6	111
Cathcart, Lake, l., Me., U.S.	n9	86
Cathedral Bluffs, clf., Co., U.S.	B2	83
Cathedral Caverns, Al., U.S.	A3	78
Cathedral City, Ca., U.S.	F5	82
Cathedral Mountain, mtn., Tx., U.S.	o13	120
Cathedral of the Pines, N.H., U.S.	E3	106
Catherine, Al., U.S.	C2	78
Catherine, Lake, res., Ar., U.S.	C3	81
Cathlamet, Wa., U.S.	C2	124
Catirol, Arg.	B5	54
Cat Island, i., Bah.	C10	64
Cat Island, i., Ma., U.S.	f12	98
Cat Island, i., Ms., U.S.	E4	101
Cat Island, i., S.C., U.S.	E9	117
Cativá, Pan.	k11	62
Catlettsburg, Ky., U.S.	B7	94
Catlin, Il., U.S.	C6	90
Catlin, In., U.S.	E3	91
Catnip Mountain, mtn., Nv., U.S.	B2	105
Cato, N.Y., U.S.	B4	109
Catoche, Cabo, c., Mex.	A7	63
Catoctin Mountain, mtn., U.S.	B2	97
Catonsville, Md., U.S.	B4	97
Catoosa, Ok., U.S.	A6	113
Catoosa, co., Ga., U.S.	B1	87
Catriló, Arg.	B4	54
Catrimani, Braz.	B2	59
Catrimani, stm., Braz.	B2	59
Catron, Mo., U.S.	E8	102
Catron, co., N.M., U.S.	D1	108
Catskill, N.Y., U.S.	C7	109
Catskill Mountains, mts., N.Y., U.S.	C6	109
Catt, Mount, mtn., B.C.	D3	69
Cattaraugus, N.Y., U.S.	C2	109
Cattaraugus, co., N.Y., U.S.	C2	109
Cattaraugus Creek, stm., N.Y., U.S.	C2	109
Cattaraugus Indian Reservation, N.Y., U.S.	C2	109
Cattolica, Italy	C4	23
Catumbela, stm., Ang.	D1	48
Catwick, Îles, is., Viet.	G8	35
Caubvick, Mount (Mont d'Iberville), mtn., Can.	f9	72
Cauca, dept., Col.	C2	60
Cauca, stm., Col.	B2	60
Caucasia, Col.	B2	60
Caucasus Mountains, mts., Sov. Un.	E7	29
Caucomgomoc Lake, l., Me., U.S.	B3	70
Caudebec, Fr.	C4	16
Caudete, Spain	C5	22
Caudry, Fr.	B5	16
Caughnawaga, Que.	g12	102
Caulfield, Austl.	*G8	50
Caúngula, Ang.	C2	48
Cauquenes, Chile	B2	54
Caura, stm., Ven.	B5	60
Causey, N.M., U.S.	D6	108
Caussade, Fr.	E4	16
Cauterets, Fr.	C1	81
Caution, Cape, c., B.C.	D4	69
Cauto, stm., Cuba	D5	64
Cauvery, stm., India	F6	36
Cavalcante, Braz.	A3	56
Cavalier, N.D., U.S.	A8	111
Cavalier, co., N.D., U.S.	A7	111
Cavalla (Cavally), stm., Afr.	H3	45
Cavallo, stm., Italy	C3	10
Cavan, Ire.	C4	11
Cavan, co., Ire.	C4	11
Cavarzere, Italy	D7	20
Cave City, Ar., U.S.	B4	81
Cave City, Ky., U.S.	C4	94
Cave Creek, Az., U.S.	D4	80
Cave Creek, stm., Az., U.S.	*k9	80
Cave-in-Rock, Il., U.S.	F5	90
Cave Junction, Or., U.S.	E3	114
Cave Mountain, mtn., Va., U.S.	E1	75
Cave Run Lake, res., Ky., U.S.	B6	94
Cave Spring, Ga., U.S.	B1	87
Cave Spring, Va., U.S.	C2	123
Cave Springs, Ar., U.S.	A1	81
Cavetown, Md., U.S.	A2	97
Caviana, Ilha, i., Braz.	B4	59
Cavite, Phil.	o13	34
Cavour, S.D., U.S.	C7	118
Cavour, Wi., U.S.	C5	126
Cawdor, Scot., U.K.	C5	13
Cawker City, Ks., U.S.	C5	93
Cawood, Ky., U.S.	D6	94
Caxias, Braz.	B2	57
Caxias do Sul, Braz.	D2	56
Caxito, Ang.	C1	48
Cayambe, Ec.	A2	58
Cayambe, vol., Ec.	A2	58
Cayce, Ky., U.S.	f8	94
Cayce, S.C., U.S.	D5	117
Cayenne, Fr. Gu.	B4	59
Cayenne, ter., Fr. Gu.	B4	59
Cayeux-sur-Mer, Fr.	D9	12
Cayey, P.R.	G11	64
Cayey, Sierra de, mts., P.R.	B3	65
Cayley, Alta.	D4	68
Cayman Brac, i., Cay. Is.	E4	64
Cayman Islands, dep., N.A.	D8	63
Caynabo, Som.	D6	47
Cay Point, c., Bah.	n17	64
Cayuga, Ont.	E5	73
Cayuga, In., U.S.	E3	91
Cayuga, Ms., U.S.	C3	101
Cayuga, N.D., U.S.	C8	111
Cayuga, co., N.Y., U.S.	C4	109
Cayuga Heights, N.Y., U.S.	C4	109
Cayuga Lake, l., N.Y., U.S.	C4	109
Cazaux, Étang de, b., Fr.	E3	16
Cazenovia, N.Y., U.S.	C5	109
Cazombo, Ang.	D4	48
Cazorla, Spain	D4	22
Cea, Spain	A3	22
Ceanannus Mór (Kells), Ire.	D5	11
Ceará, state, Braz.	C3	57
Ceará Mirim, Braz.	C3	57
Ceará-Mirim, stm., Braz.	g6	57
Cebolla, N.M., U.S.	A3	108
Cebolla Creek, stm., Co., U.S.	C3	83
Cebollar, Arg.	E2	55
Cebollati, stm., Ur.	E2	56
Cebreros, Spain	B3	22
Cebu, Phil.	C6	34
Cebu, i., Phil.	C6	34
Cecil, Al., U.S.	C3	78
Cecil, Ga., U.S.	E3	87
Cecil, Oh., U.S.	A1	112
Cecil, Pa., U.S.	F1	115
Cecil, co., Md., U.S.	A6	97
Cecilia, Ky., U.S.	C4	94
Cecilton, Md., U.S.	B6	97
Cecil Field Naval Air Station, mil., Fl., U.S.	B5	86
Cecilia, Italy	C3	23
Cedar, Ks., U.S.	C5	93
Cedar, Mi., U.S.	D5	99
Cedar, Mn., U.S.	E5	100
Cedar, co., Ia., U.S.	C6	92
Cedar, co., Mo., U.S.	D4	102
Cedar, co., Ne., U.S.	B8	104
Cedar, stm., Ia., U.S.	C6	92
Cedar, stm., Wa., U.S.	B4	124
Cedar Bluff, Al., U.S.	A4	78
Cedar Bluff, Ky., U.S.	C2	94
Cedar Bluff, Tn., U.S.	D9	119
Cedar Bluff Reservoir, res., Ks., U.S.	D4	93
Cedar Bluffs, Ks., U.S.	C3	93
Cedar Bluffs, Ne., U.S.	C9	104
Cedar Breaks National Monument, Ut., U.S.	F3	121
Cedar Brook, N.J., U.S.	D3	107
Cedarburg, Wi., U.S.	E6	126
Cedarbutte, S.D., U.S.	D4	118
Cedar City, Mo., U.S.	C5	102
Cedar City, Ut., U.S.	F2	121
Cedar Creek, La., U.S.	D5	80
Cedar Creek, Mo., U.S.	E5	102
Cedar Creek, Ne., U.S.	C9	104
Cedar Creek, Tn., U.S.	C11	119
Cedar Creek, Tx., U.S.	D4	120
Cedar Creek, stm., Co., U.S.	A7	83
Cedar Creek, stm., In., U.S.	B7	91
Cedar Creek, stm., N.J., U.S.	D4	107
Cedar Creek, stm., N.D., U.S.	C3	111
Cedar Creek, stm., Oh., U.S.	e7	112
Cedar Creek Lake, res., Tx., U.S.	C4	120
Cedar Crest, N.M., U.S.	k8	108
Cedaredge, Co., U.S.	C3	83
Cedar Falls, l., Man.	B5	92
Cedar Gap, Mo., U.S.	D5	102
Cedar Grove, Fl., U.S.	F8	91
Cedar Grove, N.J., U.S.	B4	107
Cedar Grove, W.V., U.S.	C3	125
Cedar Grove, Wi., U.S.	E6	126
Cedar Hill, Mo., U.S.	g12	102
Cedar Hill, N.M., U.S.	A2	108
Cedar Hill, Tn., U.S.	A5	119
Cedar Hill, Tx., U.S.	n10	120
Cedar Hills, Or., U.S.	*h12	114
Cedarhurst, N.Y., U.S.	k13	109
Cedar Island, i., N.C., U.S.	C6	110
Cedar Island, i., N.C., U.S.	C6	110
Cedar Island, i., S.C., U.S.	E9	117
Cedar Island, i., Va., U.S.	C7	123
Cedar Key, Fl., U.S.	C3	86
Cedar Keys, is., Fl., U.S.	C3	86
Cedar Knolls, N.J., U.S.	B4	107
Cedar Lake, Ont.	B3	91
Cedar Lake, In., U.S.	A6	73
Cedar Lake, res., Ont.	C1	70
Cedar Lake, res., Il., U.S.	F4	90
Cedar Mills, Mn., U.S.	F4	100
Cedar Mountain, mtn., Ca., U.S.	B3	82
Cedar Mountains, mts., Ut., U.S.	C2	121
Cedar Point, Il., U.S.	B4	90
Cedar Point, Ks., U.S.	D7	93
Cedar Point, c., Md., U.S.	D5	97
Cedar Point, c., Oh., U.S.	A3	112
Cedar Point, c., Oh., U.S.	e7	112
Cedar Rapids, Ia., U.S.	C6	92
Cedar Rapids, Ne., U.S.	C7	104
Cedar River, Mi., U.S.	C3	99
Cedar Run, N.J., U.S.	D4	107
Cedar Springs, Ont.	E2	73
Cedar Springs, Ga., U.S.	E1	87
Cedar Springs, Mi., U.S.	E5	99

Name	Map Ref.	Page
Cedar Swamp, sw., Ma., U.S.	f11	98
Cedartown, Ga., U.S.	B1	87
Cedarvale, B.C.	B3	69
Cedar Vale, Ks., U.S.	E7	93
Cedarvale, N.M., U.S.	C4	108
Cedar Valley, Ut., U.S.	C3	121
Cedarville, Ar., U.S.	B1	81
Cedarville, Ca., U.S.	B3	82
Cedarville, Il., U.S.	A4	90
Cedarville, In., U.S.	B7	91
Cedarville, Ma., U.S.	*C6	98
Cedarville, N.J., U.S.	E2	107
Cedarville, N.Y., U.S.	C5	109
Cedarville, Oh., U.S.	C2	112
Cedoux, Sask.	H4	75
Cedros, Hond.	C4	62
Cedros, Isla, i., Mex.	B1	63
Ceduna, Austl.	F5	50
Ceel Buur, Som.	E6	47
Ceel Xamurre, Som.	D6	47
Ceepeecee, B.C.	E4	69
Ceerigaabo, Som.	C6	47
Cefalù, Italy	E5	23
Cega, stm., Spain	B3	22
Cegléd, Hung.	D6	23
Ceglie Messapico, Italy	D6	23
Cehegín, Spain	C5	22
Čelákovice, Czech.	m18	26
Celaya, Mex.	m13	63
Celebes (Sulawesi), i., Indon.	F6	34
Celebes Sea, Asia	E6	34
Celendín, Peru	C2	58
Celestine, In., U.S.	H4	91
Celica, Ec.	B2	58
Celina, Oh., U.S.	B1	112
Celina, Tn., U.S.	C8	119
Celina, Tx., U.S.	C4	120
Celje, Yugo.	B2	24
Celle, Ger.	B5	18
Cellina, stm., Italy	C8	20
Celoron, N.Y., U.S.	C1	109
Celriver, S.C., U.S.	B6	117
Celtic Sea, Eur.	F5	14
Cemaes Head, c., Wales, U.K.	B3	12
Cement, Ok., U.S.	C3	113
Cement City, Mi., U.S.	F6	99
Cementon, Pa., U.S.	E10	115
Çemişgezek, Tur.	C12	40
Cenderawasih Bay, b., Indon.	F9	34
Cenon, Fr.	E3	16
Centenary, S.C., U.S.	C9	117
Centennial, Wy., U.S.	E6	127
Centennial Lake, res., Ont.	B7	73
Centennial Mountains, mts., Id., U.S.	E7	89
Center, Co., U.S.	D4	83
Center, Ga., U.S.	B3	87
Center, In., U.S.	D5	91
Center, Ky., U.S.	C4	94
Center, Mo., U.S.	B6	102
Center, Ne., U.S.	B8	104
Center, N.D., U.S.	B4	111
Center, Ok., U.S.	C5	113
Center, Tx., U.S.	D5	120
Center Barnstead, N.H., U.S.	D4	106
Centerbrook, Ct., U.S.	D6	84
Centerburg, Oh., U.S.	B3	112
Center City, Mn., U.S.	E6	100
Center City, Tx., U.S.	D3	120
Center Conway, N.H., U.S.	C4	106
Center Creek, Ut., U.S.	C4	121
Center Cross, Va., U.S.	C6	123
Centereach, N.Y., U.S.	n15	109
Center Effingham, N.H., U.S.	C4	106
Centerfield, Ut., U.S.	D4	121
Center Harbor, N.H., U.S.	C4	106
Center Hill, Ar., U.S.	B4	81
Center Hill, Fl., U.S.	D5	86
Center Hill Lake, res., Tn., U.S.	C8	119
Center Junction, Ia., U.S.	B6	92
Center Line, Mi., U.S.	*p15	99
Center Lovell, Me., U.S.	D2	96
Center Montville, Me., U.S.	D3	96
Center Moreland, Pa., U.S.	m17	115
Center Moriches, N.Y., U.S.	n16	109
Center Mountain, mtn., Id., U.S.	D3	89
Center Ossipee, N.H., U.S.	C4	106
Center Point, Al., U.S.	f7	78
Center Point, Ar., U.S.	C2	81
Centerpoint, In., U.S.	F3	91
Center Point, Ia., U.S.	B6	92
Center Point, La., U.S.	C3	95
Center Point, S.D., U.S.	D8	118
Center Point, Tx., U.S.	E3	120
Center Point, W.V., U.S.	B4	125
Center Ridge, Ar., U.S.	B3	81
Center Sandwich, N.H., U.S.	C4	106
Center Square, N.J., U.S.	D2	107
Center Star, Al., U.S.	A2	78
Center Strafford, N.H., U.S.	D4	106
Centerton, Ar., U.S.	A1	81
Centerton, In., U.S.	E5	91
Centerton, N.J., U.S.	D2	107
Centertown, Ky., U.S.	C3	94
Centertown, Mo., U.S.	C5	102
Centertown, Tn., U.S.	D8	119
Center Tuftonboro, N.H., U.S.	C4	106
Centerview, Mo., U.S.	C4	102
Centerville, Ar., U.S.	B2	81
Centerville, De., U.S.	A3	85
Centerville, Ia., U.S.	D5	92
Centerville, Ks., U.S.	D8	93
Centerville, La., U.S.	E4	95
Centerville, Me., U.S.	D5	96
Centerville, Mo., U.S.	D7	102
Centerville, Nv., U.S.	*E2	105
Centerville, N.C., U.S.	A4	110
Centerville, Oh., U.S.	C1	112
Centerville, Pa., U.S.	F2	115
Centerville, R.I., U.S.	E2	116
Centerville, S.D., U.S.	D9	118
Centerville, Tn., U.S.	B4	119
Centerville, Tx., U.S.	D5	120
Centerville, Ut., U.S.	C4	121
Centerville, Wa., U.S.	D5	124
Cento, Italy	E7	20
Centrahoma, Ok., U.S.	C5	113
Central, Al., U.S.	C3	78
Central, Az., U.S.	E6	80
Central, In., U.S.	H5	91
Central, N.M., U.S.	E1	108
Central, S.C., U.S.	B2	117
Central, Ut., U.S.	F2	121
Central, prov., Ghana	E4	45
Central, prov., Kenya	B6	48
Central, prov., Mwi.	D5	48
Central, prov., Scot., U.K.	D4	13
Central, prov., Zam.	E4	48
Central, dept., Para.	E5	55
Central, Cordillera, mts., Col.	C2	60
Central, Cordillera, mts., C.R.	E5	62
Central, Cordillera, mts., Dom. Rep.	E8	64
Central, Cordillera, mts., P.R.	B2	65
Central, Massif, mts., Fr.	E5	16
Central African Republic, ctry., Afr.	D4	46
Central Barren, In., U.S.	H5	91
Central Bridge, N.Y., U.S.	C6	109
Central Butte, Sask.	G2	75
Central City, Co., U.S.	B5	83
Central City, Il., U.S.	E4	90
Central City, Ia., U.S.	B6	92
Central City, Ky., U.S.	C2	94
Central City, Ne., U.S.	C7	104
Central City, Pa., U.S.	F4	115
Central City, S.D., U.S.	C2	118
Central Falls, R.I., U.S.	B4	116
Centralhatchee, Ga., U.S.	C1	87
Central Heights, Az., U.S.	D5	80
Centralia, Ont.	D3	73
Centralia, Il., U.S.	E4	90
Centralia, Ks., U.S.	C7	93
Centralia, Mo., U.S.	B5	102
Centralia, Ok., U.S.	A6	113
Centralia, Wa., U.S.	C3	124
Central Islip, N.Y., U.S.	n15	109
Central Lake, Mi., U.S.	C5	99
Central Makrán Range, mts., Pak.	C3	36
Central Park, Wa., U.S.	C2	124
Central Point, Or., U.S.	E4	114
Central Range, mts., Pap. N. Gui.	h11	50
Central Range, hills, Trin.	O23	65
Central Siberian Uplands, plat., Sov. Un.	C13	29
Central Square, N.Y., U.S.	B4	109
Central Valley, Ca., U.S.	B2	82
Central Valley, N.Y., U.S.	D6	109
Central Village, Ct., U.S.	C8	84
Central Village, Ma., U.S.	C5	98
Centre, Al., U.S.	A4	78
Centre, co., Pa., U.S.	E6	115
Centre City, N.J., U.S.	D2	107
Centre Hall, Pa., U.S.	E6	115
Centre Peak, mtn., B.C.	B4	69
Centreville, N.B.	C2	71
Centreville, Al., U.S.	C2	78
Centreville, Il., U.S.	E3	90
Centreville, Md., U.S.	B5	97
Centreville, Mi., U.S.	G5	99
Centreville, Ms., U.S.	D2	101
Centreville, Va., U.S.	*B5	123
Centropolis, Ks., U.S.	D8	93
Centuria, Wi., U.S.	C1	126
Century, Fl., U.S.	u14	86
Century, W.V., U.S.	B4	125
Century Village, Fl., U.S.	*F6	86
Cephalonia see Kefallinía, i., Grc.	C3	40
Cephissus see Kifisós, stm., Grc.	g9	25
Ceram, i., Indon.	F7	34
Ceram Sea, Indon.	F7	34
Cerbat Mountains, mts., Az., U.S.	B1	80
Čerčany, Czech.	o18	26
Cereal, Alta.	D5	68
Cereales, Arg.	B4	54
Ceredo, W.V., U.S.	C2	125
Ceres, Braz.	B5	56
Ceres, Italy	D3	20
Ceres, Ca., U.S.	D3	82
Ceres, N.Y., U.S.	C2	109
Ceres, Ok., U.S.	A4	113
Ceres, S. Afr.	H3	49
Céret, Fr.	F5	16
Cereté, Col.	B2	60
Cerignola, Italy	D5	23
Cerknica, Yugo.	C2	24
Cernavodă, Rom.	C9	24
Cernay, Fr.	D7	16
Cerralvo, Mex.	B5	63
Cerralvo, Isla, i., Mex.	C3	63
Cërriku, Alb.	B2	25
Cerrillos, N.M., U.S.	B3	108
Cerritos, Mex.	C4	63
Cerritos, Ca., U.S.	*E4	82
Cerro, N.M., U.S.	A4	108
Cerro Alto Mountain, mtn., Tx., U.S.	o12	120
Cerro Azul, Peru	D2	58
Cerro Colorado, Ur.	E1	56
Cerro de Pasco, Peru	D2	58
Cerro Gordo, Il., U.S.	D5	90
Cerro Gordo, N.C., U.S.	C4	110
Cerro Gordo, co., Ia., U.S.	A4	92
Cêrro Largo, Braz.	D2	56
Cerulean, Ky., U.S.	D2	94
Cervantes, Phil.	B6	34
Cervera del Río Alhama, Spain	A5	22
Cerveteri, Italy	g8	23
Cervignano del Friuli, Italy	D9	20
Cesar, dept., Col.	B3	60
Cesena, Italy	B4	23
Cesenatico, Italy	B4	23
Česká Kamenice, Czech.	C9	19
Česká Lípa, Czech.	C4	26
Česká Třebová, Czech.	D4	26
České Budějovice, Czech.	D3	26
Český Brod, Czech.	n18	26
Český Krumlov, Czech.	D3	26
Česma, stm., Yugo.	C3	24
Çeşme, Tur.	L10	25
Cessford, Alta.	D5	68
Cessnock, Austl.	F9	50
Cestos, stm., Lib.	E3	45
Cetina, stm., Yugo.	C3	24
Cetinje, Yugo.	D4	24
Cetraro, Italy	E5	23
Cetti Bay, b., Guam	M9	52
Ceuta, Sp. N. Afr.	B3	44
Cévennes, reg., Fr.	E5	16
Cevio, Switz.	E5	21
Ceyhan, Tur.	*D10	40
Ceyhan, stm., Tur.	D11	40
Ceylon, Ont.	C4	73
Ceylon, Sask.	H3	75
Ceylon, In., U.S.	C8	91
Ceylon, Mn., U.S.	G4	100
Ceylon see Sri Lanka, ctry., Asia	G7	36
Chabařovice, Czech.	C8	19
Chacabuco, Arg.	B4	54
Chacachacare, i., Trin.	N22	65
Chachahuila, La., U.S.	E5	95
Chachapoyas, Peru	C2	58
Chachoengsao, Thai.	F4	35
Chāchro, Pak.	E3	37
Chaco, prov., Arg.	E3	55
Chaco, dept., Para.	D3	55
Chaco, stm., N.M., U.S.	A1	108
Chaco Culture National Historic Park, N.M., U.S.	A2	108
Chacon, N.M., U.S.	A4	108
Chacon, Cape, c., Ak., U.S.	n24	79
Chacuaco Creek, stm., Co., U.S.	D7	83
Chad, ctry., Afr.	B3	46
Chad, Lake, l., Afr.	C2	46
Chadbourn, N.C., U.S.	C4	110
Chadds Ford, Pa., U.S.	G10	115
Chadileuvú, stm., Arg.	B3	54
Chadiza, Zam.	D5	48
Chadron, Ne., U.S.	B3	104
Chadwick, Il., U.S.	A4	90
Chadwick, Mo., U.S.	E4	102
Chadwicks, N.Y., U.S.	B5	109
Chaeryŏng, N. Kor.	G2	33
Chaffee, Mo., U.S.	D8	102
Chaffee, N.D., U.S.	C8	111
Chaffee, co., Co., U.S.	C4	83
Chaffin, Ma., U.S.	B4	98
Chagai Hills, mts., Asia	G11	39
Chaghcharan, Afg.	D12	39
Chagny, Fr.	D6	16
Chagodoshcha, stm., Sov. Un.	B10	27
Chagos Archipelago, is., B.I.O.T.	G25	2
Chagres, stm., Pan.	k11	62
Chagrin Falls, Oh., U.S.	A4	112
Chaguanas, Trin.	N23	65
Chagyl, Sov. Un.	E5	28
Chahal, Guat.	C3	62
Chahār Borjak, Afg.	D6	36
Chāībāsa, India	D8	36
Chai Nat, Thai.	E4	35
Chaiyaphum, Thai.	B2	34
Chajari, Arg.	B4	54
Chakachamna Lake, l., Ak., U.S.	g15	79
Chake Chake, Tan.	C6	48
Chakradharpur, India	D8	36
Chakwāl, Pak.	B5	36
Chala, Peru	E3	58
Chalan Kanoa, N. Mar. Is.	L9	52
Chalan Pago, Guam	L10	52
Chalatenango, El Sal.	C3	62
Chalchuapa, El Sal.	D3	62
Chalco, Canal de, Mex.	h9	63
Chaleur Bay, b., Can.	B4	71
Chalfont, De., U.S.	h7	85
Chalhuanca, Peru	D3	58
Chaling, China	K5	32
Chalke see Khálki, i., Grc.	—	—
Chalk River, Ont.	A7	73
Chalkyitsik, Ak., U.S.	B11	79
Challans, Fr.	D3	16
Challapata, Bol.	C2	55
Challis, Id., U.S.	E4	89
Chalmers, In., U.S.	C4	91
Chalmette, La., U.S.	E6	95
Châlons-sur-Marne, Fr.	C6	16
Chalon-sur-Saône, Fr.	D6	16
Chaltel, Cerro see Fitzroy, Monte, mtn., S.A.	D2	54
Chālūs, Iran	A5	38
Chalybeate, Ms., U.S.	A5	101
Chalybeate, N.C., U.S.	B4	110
Cham, Ger.	D7	19
Cham, Switz.	B5	21
Cham, i., Viet.	E8	35
Chama, Co., U.S.	D5	83
Chama, N.M., U.S.	A3	108
Chama, Rio, stm., N.M., U.S.	A3	108
Chamaicó, Arg.	B4	54
Chamalières, Fr.	E5	16
Chaman, Pak.	D6	36
Chamba, Tan.	D6	48
Chamba, India	C6	36
Chambal, stm., India	E3	36
Chamberino, N.M., U.S.	E3	108
Chamberlain, Sask.	G3	75
Chamberlain, S.D., U.S.	D6	118
Chamberlain Lake, l., Me., U.S.	B3	96
Chamberlin, Mount, mtn., Ak., U.S.	B10	79
Chambers, Az., U.S.	B6	80
Chambers, La., U.S.	C3	95
Chambers, Ne., U.S.	B7	104
Chambers, co., Al., U.S.	C4	78
Chambers, co., Tx., U.S.	E5	120
Chambersburg, Il., U.S.	D3	90
Chambersburg, Pa., U.S.	G6	115
Chambers Island, i., Wi., U.S.	C6	126
Chambéry, Fr.	E6	16
Chambeshi, stm., Zam.	D5	48
Chamblee, Ga., U.S.	h8	87
Chambly, Que.	D4	74
Chambly, Fr.	C5	16
Chambly, co., Que.	D4	74
Chambord, Que.	A5	74
Chamcook, N.B.	D2	71
Chamical, Arg.	B3	54
Chamisal, N.M., U.S.	A4	108
Chamois, Mo., U.S.	C6	102
Chamonix [-Mont-Blanc], Fr.	E7	16
Champ, Md., U.S.	D6	97
Champagne, Yukon	D5	66
Champagne, hist. reg., Fr.	C6	16
Champagnole, Fr.	C6	16
Champaign, Il., U.S.	C5	90
Champaign, co., Il., U.S.	C5	90
Champaign, co., Oh., U.S.	B2	112
Champapasak, Laos	D4	35
Champdoré, Lac, l., Que.	g8	72
Champerico, Guat.	D2	62
Champéry, Switz.	D2	21
Champex, Switz.	D2	21
Champigneulles, Fr.	F6	17
Champigny-sur-Marne, Fr.	g11	16
Champion, Alta.	D4	68
Champion, Mi., U.S.	B3	99
Champion, Ne., U.S.	D4	104
Champion, Oh., U.S.	A5	112
Champion Creek Reservoir, res., Tx., U.S.	C5	120
Champions, Tx., U.S.	*E5	120
Champlain, Que.	C5	74
Champlain, N.Y., U.S.	f11	109
Champlain, Lake, l., N.A.	B2	122
Champlin, Mn., U.S.	m12	100
Champlitte [-et-le-Prêlot], Fr.	D6	16
Champneys West, Newf.	D5	72
Champotón, Mex.	D6	63
Chana, Il., U.S.	A4	90
Chañaral, Chile	E1	55
Chança, stm., Eur.	D2	22
Chancay, Peru	D2	58
Chance, Al., U.S.	D2	78
Chance, Md., U.S.	D6	97
Chancellor, Al., U.S.	D4	78
Chancellor, S.D., U.S.	D8	118
Chan Chan, hist., Peru	C2	58
Chanchelulla Peak, mtn., Ca., U.S.	B2	82
Chanco, Chile	B2	54
Chandalar, stm., Ak., U.S.	B10	79
Chandausi, India	C7	37
Chandeleur Islands, is., La., U.S.	E7	95
Chandeleur Sound, strt., La., U.S.	E6	95
Chandigarh, India	*B6	36
Chandigarh, ter., India	*B6	36
Chandler, Que.	k14	74
Chandler, Az., U.S.	D4	80
Chandler, In., U.S.	H3	91
Chandler, Mn., U.S.	G3	100
Chandler, Ok., U.S.	B5	113
Chandler, Tx., U.S.	C5	120
Chandler Heights, Az., U.S.	m9	80
Chandlers Valley, Pa., U.S.	C3	115
Chandlerville, Il., U.S.	C3	90
Chandos Lake, l., Ont.	C6	73
Chandpur, Bngl.	D9	36
Chandrapur, India	E6	36
Chaneysville, Pa., U.S.	G5	115
Chang, i., Thai.	F5	35
Changane, stm., Moz.	B5	49
Changbai Mountains, mts., Asia	E3	33
Changchou see Zhangzhou, China	G8	31
Changchun, China	C10	31
Changde, China	F7	31
Change Islands, Newf.	D4	72
Changewater, N.J., U.S.	B3	107
Chang Jiang see Yangtze, stm., China	E8	31
Changjin-ŭp, N. Kor.	F3	33
Changli, China	E8	31
Changling, China	B10	32
Changping, China	D7	32
Changsha, China	F7	31
Changshu, China	I9	32
Changsŏng, N. Kor.	F2	33
Changting, China	F8	31
Changwu, China	D6	31
Changxing, China	I8	32
Changyŏn, N. Kor.	G2	33
Changzhi, China	D7	31
Changzhou, China	C6	31
Chanhassen, Mn., U.S.	n11	100
Channahon, Il., U.S.	B5	90
Channel Country, reg., Austl.	D6	50
Channel Islands, is., Eur.	C4	16
Channel Islands National Park, Ca., U.S.	F4	82
Channel Lake, Il., U.S.	H8	90
Channel-Port-aux-Basques, Newf.	E2	72
Channelview, Tx., U.S.	r14	120
Channing, Mi., U.S.	B2	99
Channing, Tx., U.S.	B1	120
Chantada, Spain	A2	22
Chanthaburi, Thai.	C2	34
Chantilly, Fr.	C5	16
Chantilly, Va., U.S.	g12	123
Chantrey Inlet, b., N.W. Ter.	C13	66
Chanute, Ks., U.S.	E8	93
Chanute Air Force Base, mil., Il., U.S.	C5	90
Chao'an, China	G8	31
Chao Lake, l., China	I7	32
Chao Phraya, stm., Thai.	C2	34
Chaor He, stm., China	B9	31
Chaoyang, China	C9	31
Chaoyang, China	*G8	31
Chapadinha, Braz.	B7	57
Chapala, Lago de, l., Mex.	m12	63
Chaparral, Col.	C2	60
Chapayevsk, Sov. Un.	C8	28
Chapel Hill, Ky., U.S.	D3	94
Chapel Hill, N.C., U.S.	B3	110
Chapel Hill, Tn., U.S.	B5	119
Chapelle, Jam.	E14	65
Chapin, Il., U.S.	D3	90
Chapin, Ia., U.S.	B4	92
Chapin, S.C., U.S.	C5	117
Chaplain, Ct., U.S.	B7	84
Chaplin, Sask.	G2	75
Chaplin, Ky., U.S.	C4	94
Chaplin Lake, l., Sask.	G2	75
Chaplygin, Sov. Un.	E12	27
Chapman, Al., U.S.	D3	78
Chapman, Ks., U.S.	D7	93
Chapman, Ne., U.S.	C7	104
Chapman, Cape, c., N.W. Ter.	C15	66
Chapman Pond, l., Ct., U.S.	D7	84
Chapman Ranch, Tx., U.S.	F4	120
Chapmanville, W.V., U.S.	D2	125
Chappaquiddick Island, i., Ma., U.S.	D7	98
Chappell, Ne., U.S.	C3	104
Chaptico Creek, stm., Md., U.S.	D4	97
Char, well, Maur.	B2	44
Charadai, Arg.	B4	54
Charagua, Bol.	C3	55
Charalá, Col.	D6	60
Charaña, Bol.	G6	58
Charcas, Mex.	C4	63
Charco, Tx., U.S.	E4	120
Charcot Island, i., Ant.	C5	7
Chard, Eng., U.K.	E5	12
Chardon, Oh., U.S.	A4	112
Chardzhou, Sov. Un.	F9	28
Charente, stm., Fr.	E3	16
Charenton, La., U.S.	E4	95
Charenton-le-Pont, Fr.	g10	17
Charette, Mo., U.S.	C6	102
Chari, stm., Afr.	F3	46
Chārīkār, Afg.	A4	36
Charing, Ga., U.S.	D2	87
Chariton, Ia., U.S.	C4	92
Chariton, co., Mo., U.S.	B4	102
Chariton, stm., U.S.	A5	102
Charity, Guy.	A3	59
Charity, Mo., U.S.	D4	102
Charlemont, Ma., U.S.	A2	98
Charleroi, Bel.	B6	16
Charleroi, Pa., U.S.	F2	115
Charles, co., Md., U.S.	C3	97
Charles, stm., Ma., U.S.	B5	98
Charles, Cape, c., Ak., U.S.	C6	123
Charles, Cape, c., Va., U.S.	C6	123
Charles A. Goodwin Dam, Ct., U.S.	B3	84
Charlesbourg, Que.	n17	74
Charlesburg, Wi., U.S.	k9	126
Charles City, Ia., U.S.	A5	92
Charles City, Va., U.S.	C5	123
Charles City, co., Va., U.S.	C5	123
Charles Mill Lake, res., Oh., U.S.	B3	112
Charles Mix, co., S.D., U.S.	D7	118
Charles Mound, hill, Il., U.S.	A3	90
Charleston, Ar., U.S.	B1	81
Charleston, Il., U.S.	D5	90
Charleston, Me., U.S.	C3	96
Charleston, Ms., U.S.	A3	101
Charleston, Mo., U.S.	E8	102
Charleston, Or., U.S.	D2	114
Charleston, S.C., U.S.	F8	117
Charleston, Ut., U.S.	C4	121
Charleston, W.V., U.S.	C3	125
Charleston, co., S.C., U.S.	F8	117
Charleston Air Force Base, mil., S.C., U.S.	k11	117
Charleston Naval Shipyard, mil., S.C., U.S.	k12	117
Charleston Park, Nv., U.S.	*G6	105
Charleston Peak, mtn., Nv., U.S.	G6	105
Charlestown, St. C-N.	H13	64
Charlestown, In., U.S.	H6	91
Charlestown, Md., U.S.	A6	97
Charlestown, N.H., U.S.	D2	106
Charlestown, R.I., U.S.	F2	116
Charles Town, W.V., U.S.	B7	125
Charleville, Austl.	E8	50
Charleville-Mézières, Fr.	C6	16
Charlevoix, Mi., U.S.	C5	99
Charlevoix, co., Mi., U.S.	C5	99
Charlevoix, Lake, l., Mi., U.S.	C5	99
Charlevoix-Est, co., Que.	B7	74
Charlevoix-Ouest, co., Que.	B7	74
Charlie Lake, B.C.	A7	69
Charlo, N.B.	B3	71
Charlo, Mt., U.S.	C2	103
Charlotte, Mi., U.S.	F6	99
Charlotte, N.C., U.S.	B2	110
Charlotte, Tn., U.S.	A4	119
Charlotte, Tx., U.S.	E3	120
Charlotte, co., N.B.	D2	71
Charlotte, co., Va., U.S.	C4	123
Charlotte Court House, Va., U.S.	C4	123
Charlotte Hall, Md., U.S.	D4	97
Charlotte Harbor, Fl., U.S.	F4	86
Charlotte Harbor, b., Fl., U.S.	F4	86
Charlotte Lake, l., B.C.	C5	69
Charlottenburg, Sur.	B4	59
Charlottesville, In., U.S.	E6	91
Charlottesville, Va., U.S.	B4	123
Charlottetown, Newf.	B3	72
Charlottetown, P.E.I.	C6	71
Charlotte Town (Gouyave), Gren.	W25	65
Charlottetown, Trin.	M24	65
Charlotteville, Ga., U.S.	D4	87
Charlton, co., Ga., U.S.	F4	87
Charlton, Ma., U.S.	B4	98
Charlton City, Ma., U.S.	B4	98
Charlton Depot, Ma., U.S.	B4	98
Charlton Island, i., N.W. Ter.	n20	73
Charly [-sur-Marne], Fr.	F3	17
Charmco, W.V., U.S.	C4	125
Charmes, Fr.	C7	16
Charmey, Switz.	C3	21
Charny, Fr.	C6	74
Charouine, Alg.	D4	44
Charquemont, Fr.	B2	21
Charron Lake, l., Man.	C4	70
Charsk, Sov. Un.	D10	28
Charter Oak, Ca., U.S.	*E5	82
Charter Oak, Ia., U.S.	B2	92
Charters Towers, Austl.	D8	50
Chartier, Que.	D6	74
Chartres, Fr.	C4	16
Charysh, stm., Sov. Un.	C10	28
Chascomús, Arg.	B5	54
Chase, B.C.	D8	69
Chase, Ks., U.S.	D5	93
Chase, Md., U.S.	B5	97
Chase, Mi., U.S.	E5	99
Chase, co., Ks., U.S.	D7	93
Chase, co., Ne., U.S.	D4	104
Chase, Mount, mtn., Me., U.S.	B4	96
Chase City, Va., U.S.	D4	123
Chase River, B.C.	f12	69
Chasicó, Arg.	C3	54
Chaska, Mn., U.S.	F5	100
Chasov Yar, Sov. Un.	q20	27
Chassahowitzka Bay, b., Fl., U.S.	D4	86
Chassell, Mi., U.S.	B2	99
Chasseral, mtn., Switz.	B3	21
Chasseron, Mont, mtn., Switz.	C2	21
Chataignier, La., U.S.	D3	95
Chatanika, Ak., U.S.	C10	79
Château-d'Oex, Switz.	D3	21
Châteaubriant, Fr.	D3	16
Château-du-Loir, Fr.	D4	16
Châteaudun, Fr.	C4	16
Château-Gontier, Fr.	D3	16
Châteauguay, Que.	D4	74
Châteauguay, co., Que.	D4	74
Châteauguay Heights, Que.	q19	74
Châteauneuf, Fr.	D4	16
Château-Renault, Fr.	D5	16
Château-Richer, Que.	n18	74
Châteauroux, Fr.	D4	16
Château-Salins, Fr.	F6	17
Château-Thierry, Fr.	C5	16
Châtel, Fr.	D2	21
Châtellerault, Fr.	D4	16
Châtel-Saint-Denis, Switz.	C2	21
Chatfield, Man.	D3	70
Chatfield, Ar., U.S.	B5	81
Chatfield, Mn., U.S.	G6	100
Chatfield, Oh., U.S.	B3	112
Chatham, N.B.	B4	71
Chatham, Ont.	E2	73
Chatham, Eng., U.K.	E7	12
Chatham, Il., U.S.	D4	90
Chatham, La., U.S.	B3	95
Chatham, Mi., U.S.	B4	99
Chatham, Ms., U.S.	B5	101
Chatham, N.H., U.S.	C4	106
Chatham, N.J., U.S.	B4	107
Chatham, N.Y., U.S.	C7	109
Chatham, Oh., U.S.	A3	112
Chatham, Va., U.S.	D3	123
Chatham, co., Ga., U.S.	E5	87
Chatham, co., N.C., U.S.	B3	110
Chatham Head, N.B.	B4	71
Chatham Islands, is., N.Z.	I11	6
Chatham Sound, strt., B.C.	B2	69
Chatham Strait, strt., Ak., U.S.	m22	79
Châtillon, Italy	D2	20
Châtillon-sur-Seine, Fr.	D6	16
Chatkal Range, mts., Sov. Un.	E8	28
Chatom, Al., U.S.	D1	78
Chatsworth, Ont.	C4	73
Chatsworth, Ga., U.S.	B2	87
Chatsworth, Il., U.S.	C5	90
Chatsworth, N.J., U.S.	D3	107
Chatsworth Reservoir, res., Ca., U.S.	m11	82
Chattahoochee, Fl., U.S.	B2	86
Chattahoochee, co., Ga., U.S.	D2	87
Chattahoochee, stm., U.S.	E1	87
Chattanooga, Ok., U.S.	C3	113
Chattanooga, Tn., U.S.	D8	119
Chattaroy, Wa., U.S.	B8	124
Chattaroy, W.V., U.S.	D2	125
Chatteris, Eng., U.K.	B8	12
Chattooga, co., Ga., U.S.	B1	87
Chattooga, stm., U.S.	B1	117
Chatuge Lake, res., U.S.	g9	110
Chaudière, stm., Que.	C7	74
Chau Doc, Viet.	I8	35
Chauk, Burma	D9	36
Chaumont, Fr.	C6	16
Chaumont, N.Y., U.S.	A4	109
Chaun Bay, b., Sov. Un.	B34	128
Chauncey, Ga., U.S.	D3	87
Chauncey, Oh., U.S.	C3	112
Chauncy Lake, l., Ma., U.S.	g9	98
Chauny, Fr.	C5	16
Chautauqua, Ks., U.S.	E7	93
Chautauqua, co., Ks., U.S.	E7	93
Chautauqua, co., N.Y., U.S.	C1	109
Chautauqua, S.D., U.S.	*D8	118
Chautauqua Lake, l., N.Y., U.S.	C1	109
Chauvigny, Fr.	D4	16
Chauvin, Alta.	C5	68
Chauvin, La., U.S.	E5	95
Chavanga, Sov. Un.	D17	14
Chaves, Braz.	D8	57
Chaves, Port.	C3	22
Chaves, co., N.M., U.S.	D5	108
Chavies, Ky., U.S.	C6	94
Chaviva, Col.	E6	60
Chavuma, Zam.	D4	48
Chazelles, Fr.	G11	16
Chazy, N.Y., U.S.	f11	109
Cheadle, Alta.	D4	68
Cheaha Mountain, mtn., Al., U.S.	B4	78
Cheam (part of London), Eng., U.K.	m12	10
Cheapside, Va., U.S.	h16	123
Cheat, Shavers Fork, stm., W.V., U.S.	B5	125
Cheatham, co., Tn., U.S.	A4	119
Cheatham Reservoir, res., Tn., U.S.	A4	119
Cheat Mountain, mtn., W.V., U.S.	C5	125
Cheb, Czech.	C2	26
Chebacco Lake, l., Ma., U.S.	f12	98
Chebanse, Il., U.S.	C6	90
Cheboksary, Sov. Un.	D7	29
Cheboygan, Mi., U.S.	C6	99
Cheboygan, co., Mi., U.S.	C6	99
Chech, 'Erg, des., Afr.	E4	44
Chechaouene, Mor.	B3	44
Chechŏn, S. Kor.	H4	33
Checotah, Ok., U.S.	B6	113
Chedabucto Bay, b., N.S.	D8	71
Cheddar, Eng., U.K.	C5	12
Cheddar, S.C., U.S.	B3	117
Cheduba Island, i., Burma	E9	36
Cheecham Hills, hills, Alta.	B5	68
Cheektowaga, N.Y., U.S.	C2	109
Cheepie, Austl.	C5	51
Cheeseman Lake, res., Co., U.S.	B5	83
Chegutu, Zimb.	A5	49
Chehalem Mountains, mts., Or., U.S.	h12	114
Chehalis, Wa., U.S.	C3	124
Chehalis, stm., Wa., U.S.	C3	124
Cheju, S. Kor.	J3	33
Cheju Island, i., S. Kor.	D10	31
Cheju Strait, strt., S. Kor.	J3	33
Chekhov, Sov. Un.	C10	33
Chekiang see Zhejiang, prov., China	F9	31
Chekunda, Sov. Un.	A6	33
Chela, Serra da, mtn., Ang.	E1	48
Chelan, Sask.	E4	75
Chelan, Wa., U.S.	B5	124
Chelan, co., Wa., U.S.	B4	124
Chelan, Lake, l., Wa., U.S.	A5	124
Chelan Falls, Wa., U.S.	B5	124
Chelan Mountains, mts., Wa., U.S.	A5	124
Cheleiros, Port.	f9	22
Cheleken, Sov. Un.	B6	39
Cheleken Peninsula, pen., Sov. Un.	B6	39
Chelforó, Arg.	B3	54
Chélia, Djebel, mtn., Alg.	B6	44
Chéliff, Oued, stm., Alg.	A5	44
Chelkar, Sov. Un.	E8	29
Chelles, Fr.	C7	16
Chełm, Pol.	C7	26
Chełmno, Pol.	B5	26
Chelmsford, Eng., U.K.	E7	10
Chelmsford, Ma., U.S.	A5	98

Index

Name	Map Ref.	Page
Chełmża, Pol.	B5	26
Chelsea, Que.	D2	74
Chelsea (part of London), Eng., U.K.	m12	10
Chelsea, Al., U.S.	g7	78
Chelsea, Ia., U.S.	C5	92
Chelsea, Me., U.S.	D3	96
Chelsea, Ma., U.S.	B5	98
Chelsea, Mi., U.S.	F6	99
Chelsea, Ok., U.S.	A6	113
Chelsea, S.D., U.S.	B7	118
Chelsea, Vt., U.S.	D4	122
Chelsea, Wi., U.S.	C3	126
Chelsea Estates, De., U.S.	*B3	85
Cheltenham, Eng., U.K.	E5	10
Cheltenham, Oh., U.S.	C4	97
Cheltenham Township, Pa., U.S.	*o21	115
Chelva, Spain	C5	22
Chelyabinsk, Sov. Un.	D9	29
Chelyan, W.V., U.S.	C3	125
Chelyuskin, Cape, c., Sov. Un.	B13	29
Chelyuskintsy Ice Tongue, ice, Ant.	C21	7
Chemainus, B.C.	E6	69
Chemal, Sov. Un.	E26	8
Chemehuevi Indian Reservation, Ca., U.S.	E6	82
Chemillé, Fr.	D3	16
Chemin Craig, Que.	o17	74
Chemnitz (Karl-Marx-Stadt), Ger.	E12	14
Chemquasabamticook Lake (Ross Lake), l., Me., U.S.	B3	96
Chemult, Or., U.S.	D5	114
Chemung, Ia., U.S.	A5	90
Chemung, co., N.Y., U.S.	C4	109
Chemung, stm., N.Y., U.S.	C8	115
Chemung Lake, l., Ont.	C6	73
Chenāb, stm., Asia	B5	36
Chenachane, Alg.	D4	44
Chenango, co., N.Y., U.S.	C5	109
Chenango, stm., N.Y., U.S.	C5	109
Chenango Bridge, N.Y., U.S.	C5	109
Chenango Forks, N.Y., U.S.	C5	109
Chenārān, Iran	C9	39
Chene, Bayou, stm., La., U.S.	k9	95
Chenequa, Wi., U.S.	m11	126
Chenes, River Aux, b., La., U.S.	k12	95
Chénéville, Que.	D2	74
Cheney, Ks., U.S.	E6	93
Cheney, Wa., U.S.	B8	124
Cheney Reservoir, res., Ks., U.S.	E6	93
Cheneyville, La., U.S.	C3	95
Chengchou see Zhengzhou, China	E7	31
Chengde, China	C8	31
Chengdu (Chengtu), China	E5	31
Chenggu, China	E8	31
Chenghai, China	G8	31
Chengkou, China	I3	32
Chengmai, China	C8	35
Chengshan Point, c., China	D9	31
Chengtu see Chengdu, China	E5	31
Chenoa, Il., U.S.	C5	90
Chenoa, Ky., U.S.	D6	94
Chenôve, Fr.	E12	16
Chenowith, Or., U.S.	B5	114
Chenxi, China	F7	31
Chenzhou, China	F7	31
Chepachet, R.I., U.S.	B2	116
Chepachet, stm., R.I., U.S.	B2	116
Chepén, Peru	C2	58
Chepes, Arg.	A3	54
Chepo, Pan.	F8	62
Chepstow, Wales, U.K.	E5	10
Cheptsa, stm., Sov. Un.	D19	8
Chequamegon Bay, b., Wi., U.S.	B3	126
Cher, stm., Fr.	D4	16
Cheraw, Co., U.S.	C7	83
Cheraw, S.C., U.S.	B8	117
Cherbourg, Fr.	C3	16
Cherchell, Alg.	B5	44
Cherdyn, Sov. Un.	A5	28
Cheremkhovo, Sov. Un.	D13	29
Cherepanovo, Sov. Un.	C10	28
Cherepovets, Sov. Un.	D6	29
Cherhill, Alta.	C3	68
Cheriton, Va., U.S.	C7	123
Cherkassy, Sov. Un.	G9	27
Cherkessk, Sov. Un.	G17	8
Cherlakskiy, Sov. Un.	C8	28
Chernigov, Sov. Un.	D6	29
Chernigovka, Sov. Un.	H11	27
Chernobay, Sov. Un.	D3	33
Chernobyl, Sov. Un.	F9	27
Chernogorsk, Sov. Un.	E27	8
Chernomorskoye, Sov. Un.	I9	27
Chernovtsy, Sov. Un.	E5	29
Chernoye, Sov. Un.	r32	14
Chernyakhovsk (Insterburg), Sov. Un.	D3	27
Cherokee, Al., U.S.	A2	78
Cherokee, Ia., U.S.	B2	92
Cherokee, Ks., U.S.	E9	93
Cherokee, N.C., U.S.	f9	110
Cherokee, Ok., U.S.	A3	113
Cherokee, Tx., U.S.	D3	120
Cherokee, co., Al., U.S.	A4	78
Cherokee, co., Ga., U.S.	B2	87
Cherokee, co., Ia., U.S.	B2	92
Cherokee, co., Ks., U.S.	E9	93
Cherokee, co., N.C., U.S.	f8	110
Cherokee, co., Ok., U.S.	A6	113
Cherokee, co., S.C., U.S.	A4	117
Cherokee, co., Tx., U.S.	C5	120
Cherokee Indian Reservation, N.C., U.S.	f9	110
Cherokee Lake, res., Tn., U.S.	C10	119
Cherokees, Lake O' The, res., Ok., U.S.	A7	113
Cherokee Sound, Bah.	A5	64
Cherokee Village, Ar., U.S.	*A4	81
Cherquenco, Chile	B2	54
Cherrapunji, India	C9	36
Cherry, Il., U.S.	B4	90
Cherry, Tn., U.S.	B3	119
Cherry, co., Ne., U.S.	B4	104
Cherry Creek, N.Y., U.S.	C1	109
Cherry Creek, S.D., U.S.	C4	118
Cherry Creek, stm., Co., U.S.	B6	83
Cherry Creek, stm., S.D., U.S.	C3	118
Cherryfield, Me., U.S.	D5	96
Cherry Fork, Oh., U.S.	D2	112
Cherry Hill, N.J., U.S.	g11	114
Cherry Hills Village, Co., U.S.	*B6	83
Cherryland, Ca., U.S.	*D2	82
Cherry Point, c., Va., U.S.	C6	123
Cherry Point Marine Corps Air Station, mil., N.C., U.S.	C6	110
Cherry Run, W.V., U.S.	B6	125
Cherry Tree, Pa., U.S.	E4	115
Cherryvale, Ks., U.S.	E8	93
Cherry Valley, Ont.	D7	73
Cherry Valley, Ar., U.S.	B5	81
Cherry Valley, Ca., U.S.	*F5	82
Cherry Valley, Il., U.S.	A5	90
Cherry Valley, Ma., U.S.	B4	98
Cherry Valley, N.Y., U.S.	C6	109
Cherryville, N.C., U.S.	B1	110
Cherskiy Mountains, mts., Sov. Un.	C17	29
Chesaning, Mi., U.S.	E6	99
Chesapeake, Oh., U.S.	D3	112
Chesapeake, Va., U.S.	D6	123
Chesapeake, W.V., U.S.	C3	125
Chesapeake and Delaware Canal, U.S.	B3	85
Chesapeake Bay, b., U.S.	C12	76
Chesapeake Bay Bridge-Tunnel, Va., U.S.	D7	123
Chesapeake Beach, Md., U.S.	C4	97
Chesapeake City, Md., U.S.	A6	97
Chesaw, Wa., U.S.	A6	124
Chesdin, Lake, res., Va., U.S.	C5	123
Chesha Bay, b., Sov. Un.	B18	8
Chesham, Eng., U.K.	k11	10
Chesham, N.H., U.S.	E2	106
Cheshire, Ct., U.S.	D4	84
Cheshire, Ma., U.S.	A1	98
Cheshire, Oh., U.S.	D3	112
Cheshire, co., Eng., U.K.	A5	12
Cheshire, co., N.H., U.S.	E2	106
Cheshire Reservoir, res., Ma., U.S.	A1	98
Cheshunt, Eng., U.K.	k12	10
Chesilhurst, N.J., U.S.	D3	107
Chesley, Ont.	C3	73
Chesnee, S.C., U.S.	A4	117
Chester, N.S.	E5	71
Chester, Eng., U.K.	B5	10
Chester, Ar., U.S.	B1	81
Chester, Ca., U.S.	B3	82
Chester, Ct., U.S.	D6	84
Chester, Fl., U.S.	B5	86
Chester, Ga., U.S.	D3	87
Chester, Id., U.S.	F7	89
Chester, Il., U.S.	F4	90
Chester, Ia., U.S.	A5	92
Chester, Md., U.S.	C5	97
Chester, Ma., U.S.	B2	98
Chester, Mt., U.S.	B6	103
Chester, Ne., U.S.	D8	104
Chester, N.H., U.S.	E4	106
Chester, N.J., U.S.	B3	107
Chester, N.Y., U.S.	D6	109
Chester, Oh., U.S.	C4	112
Chester, Ok., U.S.	A3	113
Chester, Pa., U.S.	G11	115
Chester, S.C., U.S.	B5	117
Chester, S.D., U.S.	D9	118
Chester, Ut., U.S.	D4	121
Chester, Vt., U.S.	E3	122
Chester, Va., U.S.	C5	123
Chester, W.V., U.S.	A4	125
Chester, co., Pa., U.S.	G10	115
Chester, co., S.C., U.S.	B3	117
Chester, co., Tn., U.S.	B3	119
Chester, co., Md., U.S.	B5	97
Chester Basin, N.S.	E5	71
Chester Depot, Vt., U.S.	E3	122
Chesterfield, Eng., U.K.	D6	10
Chesterfield, Il., U.S.	D3	90
Chesterfield, In., U.S.	D6	91
Chesterfield, Ma., U.S.	B2	98
Chesterfield, N.H., U.S.	E2	106
Chesterfield, S.C., U.S.	B7	117
Chesterfield, Tn., U.S.	B5	119
Chesterfield, co., S.C., U.S.	B7	117
Chesterfield, co., Va., U.S.	C5	123
Chesterfield, Îles, is., N. Cal.	H9	6
Chesterfield Inlet, N.W. Ter.	D14	66
Chesterfield Inlet, b., N.W. Ter.	D14	66
Chesterhill, Oh., U.S.	C4	112
Chesterton, In., U.S.	A3	91
Chestertown, Md., U.S.	B5	97
Chestertown, N.Y., U.S.	B7	109
Chester Township, Pa., U.S.	*p20	115
Chesterville, Ont.	B9	73
Chesterville, Il., U.S.	D5	90
Chesterville, Oh., U.S.	B3	112
Chestnut, Il., U.S.	C4	90
Chestnut, La., U.S.	B2	95
Chestnut Hill Estates, De., U.S.	*B3	85
Chestnut Knoll, De., U.S.	E4	85
Chestnut Mound, Tn., U.S.	C8	119
Chestnut Ridge, N.Y., U.S.	*D6	109
Chesuncook Lake, l., Me., U.S.	C3	96
Cheswick, Pa., U.S.	h14	115
Cheswold, De., U.S.	D3	85
Chetac, Lake, l., Wi., U.S.	C2	126
Chetco, stm., Or., U.S.	E2	114
Chetek, Wi., U.S.	C2	126
Chetek, Lake, l., Wi., U.S.	C2	126
Chéticamp, N.S.	C9	71
Chetopa, Ks., U.S.	E8	93
Chetumal, Mex.	D7	63
Chetumal Bay, b., N.A.	D7	63
Chetwynd, B.C.	B7	69
Chevak, Ak., U.S.	C6	79
Chevelon Creek, stm., Az., U.S.	C5	80
Cheverie, N.S.	D5	71
Cheverly, Md., U.S.	*C4	97
Cheviot, Oh., U.S.	C1	112
Cheviot, N.Z.	O14	51
Chevreuil, Bayou, stm., La., U.S.	k10	95
Chevreuil, Point, c., La., U.S.	E4	95
Chevy Chase, Md., U.S.	*C4	97
Chewack, stm., Wa., U.S.	A5	124
Chewalla, Tn., U.S.	B3	119
Chewelah, Wa., U.S.	A8	124
Chewsville, Md., U.S.	A2	97
Chewton, Pa., U.S.	E1	115
Cheyenne, Ok., U.S.	B2	113
Cheyenne, Wy., U.S.	E8	127
Cheyenne, co., Co., U.S.	C8	83
Cheyenne, co., Ks., U.S.	C2	93
Cheyenne, co., Ne., U.S.	C2	104
Cheyenne, stm., U.S.	C4	118
Cheyenne, Dry Fork, stm., Wy., U.S.	C7	127
Cheyenne River Indian Reservation, S.D., U.S.	B4	118
Cheyenne Wells, Co., U.S.	C8	83
Chhapra, India	H11	37
Chhatarpur, India	E7	37
Chhatrapur, India	H10	37
Chhindwāra, India	F7	37
Chhukha Dzong, Bhu.	D12	37
Chi, stm., Thai.	E6	35
Chiai, Tai.	*G9	31
Chiang Kham, Thai.	C4	35
Chiang Khong, Thai.	A2	34
Chiang Mai, Thai.	B1	34
Chiang Rai, Thai.	B1	34
Chiapa de Corzo, Mex.	D6	63
Chiapas, state, Mex.	D6	63
Chiari, Italy	B2	23
Chiasso, Switz.	E7	21
Chiautla de Tapia, Mex.	n14	63
Chiavari, Italy	B2	23
Chiavenna, Italy	C5	23
Chiba, Japan	D13	31
Chibemba, Ang.	E1	48
Chibia, Ang.	E1	48
Chiblow Lake, l., Ont.	A1	73
Chibougamau, Que.	k12	74
Chibuto, Moz.	B5	49
Chicacomico, stm., Md., U.S.	D6	97
Chicago, Il., U.S.	B6	90
Chicago Heights, Il., U.S.	B6	90
Chicago Ridge, Il., U.S.	*k9	90
Chicago Sanitary and Ship Canal, Il., U.S.	k8	90
Chicapa, stm., Afr.	C3	48
Chichagof Island, i., Ak., U.S.	m22	79
Chichaoua, Mor.	C3	44
Chicheng, China	D6	32
Chichén Itzá, hist., Mex.	C7	63
Chichester, Eng., U.K.	E6	10
Chichester, N.H., U.S.	D4	106
Chichibu, Japan	n18	33
Chickahominy, stm., Va., U.S.	C5	123
Chickamauga, Ga., U.S.	B1	87
Chickamauga and Chattanooga National Military Park, U.S.	k11	119
Chickamauga Dam, Tn., U.S.	h11	119
Chickamauga Lake, res., Tn., U.S.	D8	119
Chickasaw, Al., U.S.	E1	78
Chickasaw, co., Ia., U.S.	A5	92
Chickasaw, co., Ms., U.S.	B5	101
Chickasawhay, stm., Ms., U.S.	D5	101
Chickasaw National Recreation Area, Ok., U.S.	C5	113
Chickasha, Ok., U.S.	B4	113
Chickasha, Lake, res., Ok., U.S.	B3	113
Chicken, Ak., U.S.	C11	79
Chickwolnepy Stream, stm., N.H., U.S.	A4	106
Chiclana [de la Frontera], Spain	D2	22
Chiclayo, Peru	C2	58
Chico, Ca., U.S.	C3	82
Chico, Tx., U.S.	C4	120
Chico, Wa., U.S.	B3	124
Chico, stm., Arg.	C3	54
Chico, stm., Arg.	D3	54
Chico, stm., Mex.	h9	63
Chicoa, Moz.	A5	49
Chico Creek, stm., Co., U.S.	C6	83
Chico Hot Springs, Mt., U.S.	E6	103
Chicomo, Moz.	B5	49
Chico North, Ca., U.S.	*C3	82
Chicontepec, Mex.	m14	63
Chicopee, Ga., U.S.	B3	87
Chicopee, Ks., U.S.	E9	93
Chicopee, Ma., U.S.	B2	98
Chicora, Pa., U.S.	E2	115
Chicot, co., Ar., U.S.	D4	81
Chicot, Lake, l., Ar., U.S.	D4	81
Chicot Island, i., La., U.S.	E6	95
Chicoutimi, Que.	A6	74
Chicoutimi, co., Que.	A6	74
Chicoutimi, stm., Que.	A5	74
Chico West, Ca., U.S.	*C3	82
Chidester, Ar., U.S.	D2	81
Chidley, Cape, c., Can.	f8	72
Chieeretè Island, i., Marsh Is.	P18	52
Chiefland, Fl., U.S.	C4	86
Chiefs Point, c., Ont.	C3	73
Chiem Lake, l., Ger.	E6	18
Chien, Bayou de, stm., Ky., U.S.	f8	94
Chieri, Italy	B1	23
Chiers, stm., Eur.	C5	16
Chiese, stm., Italy	C5	23
Chieti, Italy	C5	23
Chifeng, China	C8	31
Chigasaki, Japan	*l9	33
Chigirin, Sov. Un.	G9	27
Chignahuapan, Mex.	n14	63
Chignecto, Cape, c., N.S.	D5	71
Chignecto Bay, b., Can.	D5	71
Chignik, Ak., U.S.	D8	79
Chigu, stm., Afr.	A5	49
Chigubo, Moz.	B5	49
Chih-chiang see Zhijiang, China	F3	31
Chihli, Gulf of see Bo Hai, b., China	D9	31
Chihuahua, Mex.	B3	63
Chihuahua, state, Mex.	B3	63
Chii, Mount, mtn., S. Kor.	I3	33
Chikaskia, stm., U.S.	A4	113
Chikura, Japan	o18	33
Chilapa [de Alvarez], Mex.	D5	63
Chilca, Peru	D2	58
Chilcotin, stm., B.C.	D6	69
Childers, Austl.	E10	53
Childersburg, Al., U.S.	B3	78
Childress, Tx., U.S.	B2	120
Childress, co., Tx., U.S.	B2	120
Chile, ctry., S.A.	G3	53
Chilecito, Arg.	A3	54
Chilete, Peru	C2	58
Chili, N.M., U.S.	*A3	108
Chili, Wi., U.S.	D3	126
Chilibre, Pan.	k11	62
Chili Center, N.Y., U.S.	*B3	109
Chilika Lake, l., India	H10	37
Chililabombwe (Bancroft), Zam.	D4	48
Chilili, N.M., U.S.	C3	108
Chilkat Pass, B.C.	E5	66
Chilko, stm., B.C.	D6	69
Chilko Lake, l., B.C.	D5	69
Chillán, Chile	B2	54
Chillicothe, Ia., U.S.	C5	92
Chillicothe, Il., U.S.	C4	90
Chillicothe, Mo., U.S.	B4	102
Chillicothe, Oh., U.S.	C3	112
Chillicothe, Tx., U.S.	B3	120
Chilliwack, B.C.	E7	69
Chilliwack, stm., N.A.	A4	124
Chillum, Md., U.S.	f9	97
Chilmark, Ma., U.S.	D6	98
Chilocco, Ok., U.S.	A4	113
Chiloé, Isla de, i., Chile	C2	54
Chiloquin, Or., U.S.	E5	114
Chilpancingo [de los Bravos], Mex.	D5	63
Chilton, Tx., U.S.	D4	120
Chilton, Wi., U.S.	D5	126
Chilton, co., Al., U.S.	C3	78
Chiluage, Ang.	C3	48
Chilumba, Mwi.	D5	48
Chilung (Keelung), Tai.	F9	31
Chimacum, Wa., U.S.	A3	124
Chimalhuacán, Mex.	h10	63
Chimaltenango, Guat.	F8	62
Chimán, Pan.	D4	17
Chimay, Bel.	A4	108
Chimayo, N.M., U.S.	A5	108
Chimbay, Sov. Un.	E8	29
Chimborazo, prov., Ec.	B2	58
Chimborazo, vol., Ec.	B2	58
Chimbote, Peru	C2	58
Chimkent, Sov. Un.	E9	29
Chimney Rock, Co., U.S.	D3	83
Chimney Rock, mtn., Ky., U.S.	D5	94
Chimney Rock, mtn., Ne., U.S.	C2	104
Chimneytop, mtn., Tn., U.S.	C11	119
Chimoio, Moz.	A5	49
Chixoy, stm., Guat.	C2	62
Chin, Cape, c., Ont.	C3	73
China, Japan	O5	52
China, Mex.	B5	63
China, Me., U.S.	D3	96
China, ctry., Asia	E6	31
China Grove, N.C., U.S.	B2	110
Chinaja, Guat.	D6	63
China Lake, l., Me., U.S.	D3	96
Chinan see Jinan, China	D8	31
Chinandega, Nic.	E7	63
Chinati Peak, mtn., Tx., U.S.	p12	120
Chincha Alta, Peru	D2	58
Chincheros, Peru	D3	58
Chinchilla [de Monte Aragón], Spain	C5	22
Chincoteague, Va., U.S.	C7	123
Chincoteague Bay, b., U.S.	D7	97
Chinde, Moz.	A6	49
Chinde, S. Kor.	I3	33
Chindwin, stm., Burma	C10	36
Chinga, Zam.	D4	48
Chinguar, Ang.	D2	48
Chinguetti, Maur.	B2	45
Chinhae, S. Kor.	I4	33
Chinhoyi, Zimb.	A5	49
Chiniot, Pak.	B4	37
Chinipas, Mex.	B3	63
Chinit, stm., Camb.	F6	35
Chinju, S. Kor.	D10	31
Chinju, S. Kor.	I4	33
Chinko, stm., Cen. Afr. Rep.	D4	46
Chin Lakes, l., Alta.	E4	68
Chinle, Az., U.S.	A6	80
Chinle Wash, val., U.S.	A6	80
Chinmen see Jinmen, China	E6	31
Chinnampo see Nampo, N. Kor.	D10	31
Chino, Ca., U.S.	F5	82
Chinon, Fr.	D4	16
Chinook, Alta.	D5	68
Chinook, Mt., U.S.	B7	103
Chinook, Lake, res., Or., U.S.	C5	114
Chinook Cove, B.C.	D7	69
Chino Valley, Az., U.S.	C3	80
Chinquapin, N.C., U.S.	C5	110
Chinsali, Zam.	D5	48
Chintheche, Mwi.	D5	48
Chinú, Col.	B2	60
Chióggia, Italy	B4	23
Chios see Khíos, i., Grc.	C5	40
Chipata (Fort Jameson), Zam.	D5	48
Chipinge, Zimb.	B5	49
Chipley, Fl., U.S.	u16	86
Chipman, Alta.	C4	71
Chipman, N.B.	C1	71
Chipola, stm., Fl., U.S.	B1	86
Chippenham, Eng., U.K.	C5	12
Chippewa, co., Mi., U.S.	B6	99
Chippewa, co., Mn., U.S.	E3	100
Chippewa, co., Wi., U.S.	C2	126
Chippewa, stm., Mi., U.S.	E6	99
Chippewa, stm., Mn., U.S.	n14	126
Chippewa, East Branch, stm., Mn., U.S.	E3	100
Chippewa, East Fork, stm., Wi., U.S.	C2	126
Chippewa, Lake, l., Wi., U.S.	C2	126
Chippewa Falls, Wi., U.S.	D2	126
Chippewa Lake, Mi., U.S.	E5	99
Chipping Norton, Eng., U.K.	C6	12
Chipuriro, Zimb.	A5	49
Chiputneticook Lakes, l., N.A.	C5	96
Chiquimula, Guat.	E7	63
Chiquimulilla, Guat.	C2	62
Chiquinquirá, Col.	B3	60
Chira, stm., S.A.	B1	58
Chirāla, India	E6	36
Chiradzulu, Mwi.	E6	48
Chirchik, Sov. Un.	E7	28
Chiredzi, Zimb.	B5	49
Chireno, Tx., U.S.	D5	120
Chirfa, Niger	B7	47
Chirikof Island, i., Ak., U.S.	D8	79
Chiriquí, Golfo de, b., Pan.	F6	62
Chiriquí Grande, Pan.	F6	62
Chiripó, Cerro, mtn., C.R.	F6	62
Chirpan, Bul.	F7	24
Chirundu, Zimb.	A4	49
Chisago, co., Mn., U.S.	E6	100
Chisago City, Mn., U.S.	E6	100
Chisamba, Zam.	D4	48
Chisana, Ak., U.S.	C11	79
Chisasibi, Que.	h11	74
Chisholm, Alta.	B3	68
Chisholm, Me., U.S.	D2	96
Chisholm, Mn., U.S.	C6	100
Chișineu-Criș, Rom.	B5	24
Chisos Mountains, mts., Tx., U.S.	E1	120
Chistochina, Ak., U.S.	C11	79
Chistopol, Sov. Un.	B4	28
Chita, Sov. Un.	D14	29
Chitado, Ang.	E1	48
Chitato, Ang.	C3	48
Chitek, Sask.	D2	75
Chitek Lake, l., Man.	C2	70
Chitembo, Ang.	D2	48
Chitina, Ak., U.S.	C11	79
Chitina, stm., Ak., U.S.	g19	79
Chitipa, Mwi.	*E10	33
Chitradurga, India	A5	36
Chitrāl, Pak.	G7	62
Chitré, Pan.	D9	36
Chittagong, Bngl.	B5	109
Chittenango, N.Y., U.S.	B5	109
Chittenden, Vt., U.S.	D2	122
Chittenden, co., Vt., U.S.	C2	122
Chittenden Reservoir, res., Vt., U.S.	D4	17
Chittoor, India	F6	36
Chitungwiza, Zimb.	A5	49
Chiuchiu, Chile	D2	55
Chiume, Ang.	E3	48
Chiúme, Ang.	E3	48
Chivasso, Italy	B1	23
Chivay, Peru	D3	58
Chivhu, Zimb.	A5	49
Chivilcoy, Arg.	A4	54
Chixoy, stm., Guat.	C2	62
Chizhapka, stm., Sov. Un.	B9	28
Chmielnik, Pol.	C6	26
Choapa, stm., Chile	A2	54
Choapan, Mex.	D5	63
Chobe, stm., Afr.	A3	49
Choccolocco, Al., U.S.	B4	78
Choccolocco Creek, stm., Al., U.S.	B3	78
Chochiwon, S. Kor.	H3	33
Chocó, dept., Col.	B2	60
Chocolate Mountains, mts., U.S.	F6	82
Choconta, Col.	B3	60
Chocorua, N.H., U.S.	C4	106
Chocorua, Mount, mtn., N.H., U.S.	C4	106
Chocowinity, N.C., U.S.	B5	110
Choctaw, Ar., U.S.	B3	81
Choctaw, co., Al., U.S.	C1	78
Choctaw, co., Ms., U.S.	B4	101
Choctaw, co., Ok., U.S.	C6	113
Choctawhatchee, stm., Al., U.S.	D4	78
Choctawhatchee, West Fork, stm., Al., U.S.	D4	78
Choctawhatchee Bay, b., Fl., U.S.	u15	86
Choctaw Indian Reservation, Ms., U.S.	C4	101
Chodzież, Pol.	B4	26
Choele Choel, Arg.	B3	54
Chōfu, Japan	*l9	33
Choiceland, Sask.	D3	75
Choiseul, i., Sol.Is.	G9	6
Choisy-le-Roi, Fr.	g10	16
Choix, Mex.	B3	63
Chojna, Pol.	B3	26
Chojnice, Pol.	B4	26
Chojnów, Pol.	C3	26
Chōkai, Mount, mtn., Japan	G10	33
Choke Canyon Reservoir, res., Tx., U.S.	E3	120
Chokio, Mn., U.S.	E2	100
Chokoloskee, Fl., U.S.	G5	86
Chokwé, Moz.	B5	49
Cholame, Ca., U.S.	E3	82
Cholet, Fr.	D3	16
Cholo, Mwi.	D5	48
Cholula [de Rivadabia], Mex.	n14	63
Choluteca, Hond.	E7	63
Choluteca, stm., Hond.	D4	62
Choma, Zam.	E4	48
Chomo Lhāri, mtn., Asia	D12	37
Chomutov, Czech.	C3	26
Chonan, S. Kor.	H3	33
Chon Buri, Thai.	C2	34
Chone, Ec.	B1	58
Chong'an, China	K8	32
Chongju, N. Kor.	C10	31
Chongjin, N. Kor.	B12	31
Chongju, S. Kor.	*I3	33
Chongqing (Chungking), China	F6	31
Chongren, China	K6	32
Chongsŏng, N. Kor.	A13	31
Chŏnju, S. Kor.	D10	31
Chonos, Archipiélago de los, is., Chile	C2	54
Chonzie, Ben, mtn., Scot., U.K.	D5	13
Chopim, stm., Braz.	C2	54
Choptank, Md., U.S.	C6	97
Choptank, stm., Md., U.S.	C5	97
Chorrillos, Peru	D2	58
Chortkov, Sov. Un.	G3	27
Chorwŏn, N. Kor.	D10	31
Chorwŏn, S. Kor.	C5	48
Chorzów, Pol.	C5	26
Chosan, N. Kor.	F2	33
Chōshi, Japan	I10	33
Chosica, Peru	D2	58
Chos Malal, Arg.	B2	54
Choszczno, Pol.	B3	26
Chota, Peru	C2	58
Choteau, Mt., U.S.	C4	103
Chotětov, Czech.	n18	24
Choudrant, La., U.S.	B3	95
Choudrant, Bayou, stm., La., U.S.	B3	95
Choum, Maur.	B2	45
Choushan Islands see Zhoushan Islands, is., China	E9	31
Chouteau, Ok., U.S.	A6	113
Chouteau, co., Mt., U.S.	C6	103
Chowan, co., N.C., U.S.	A6	110
Chowchilla, Ca., U.S.	D3	82
Choybalsan, Mong.	B7	31
Choyr, Mong.	B6	31
Chrisman, Il., U.S.	D6	90
Chrisney, In., U.S.	H3	91
Christchurch, N.Z.	O14	51
Christchurch, Eng., U.K.	E6	12
Christian, co., Il., U.S.	D4	90
Christian, co., Ky., U.S.	D2	94
Christian, co., Mo., U.S.	E4	102
Christiana, Jam.	E14	64
Christiana, De., U.S.	B3	85
Christiana, Pa., U.S.	G9	115
Christiana, Tn., U.S.	B5	119
Christian Hollow, N.H., U.S.	D2	106
Christian Island, i., Ont.	C4	73
Christiansburg, Oh., U.S.	B1	112
Christiansburg, Va., U.S.	C2	123
Christiansfeld, Den.	C3	15
Christian Sound, strt., Ak., U.S.	n22	79
Christiansted, V.I.U.S.	H12	64
Christina, Mt., U.S.	C7	103
Christina, stm., Alta.	A5	68
Christina, stm., De., U.S.	A5	85
Christina, Lake, l., Mn., U.S.	D3	100
Christina Lake, l., Alta.	B5	68
Christina Peak, mtn., Nv., U.S.	D6	105
Christine, N.D., U.S.	C9	111
Christine, Tx., U.S.	E3	120
Christmas, Fl., U.S.	D5	86
Christmas Island, dep., Oc.	G6	6
Christmas Island see Kiritimati Island, i., Kir.	F12	6
Christmas Lake, l., Or., U.S.	D6	114
Christmas Valley, Or., U.S.	D6	114
Christopher, Il., U.S.	F4	90
Christoval, Tx., U.S.	D2	120
Chromo, Co., U.S.	D4	83
Chrudim, Czech.	D3	26
Chrysler, Al., U.S.	D2	78
Chrzanów, Pol.	g10	26
Chu, Sov. Un.	G23	8
Chubbuck, Id., U.S.	G6	89
Chubut, prov., Arg.	C3	54
Chubut, stm., Arg.	C3	54
Chu Chua, B.C.	D7	69
Chuckey, Tn., U.S.	C11	119
Chudovo, Sov. Un.	B8	27
Chugach Islands, is., Ak., U.S.	h16	79
Chugach Mountains, mts., Ak., U.S.	g18	79
Chuguyev, Sov. Un.	G11	27
Chugwater, Wy., U.S.	E8	127
Chugwater Creek, stm., Wy., U.S.	B3	78
Chuichu, Az., U.S.	E4	80
Chuius Mountain, mtn., B.C.	B5	69
Chukai (Kemaman), Malay.	J5	35
Chukchi Sea	C32	128
Chukotsk Peninsula, pen., Sov. Un.	C32	128
Chula, Ga., U.S.	E3	87
Chula, Mo., U.S.	B4	102
Chula, Va., U.S.	C5	123
Chula Vista, Ca., U.S.	F5	82
Chulucanas, Peru	B1	58
Chulumani, Bol.	C2	55
Chulym, Sov. Un.	B10	28
Chulym, stm., Sov. Un.	D11	29
Chumbicha, Arg.	A2	54
Chumikan, Sov. Un.	D16	29
Chumphon, Thai.	D2	35
Chumysh, stm., Sov. Un.	C10	28
Chun'an, China	J8	32
Chunchŏn, S. Kor.	H3	33
Chunchula, Al., U.S.	E1	78
Chungju, S. Kor.	H3	33
Chungking see Chongqing, China	F6	31
Chungmu, S. Kor.	H4	33
Chunky, Ms., U.S.	C5	101
Chunya, Tan.	C5	48
Chuói, i., Viet.	H6	35
Chupaca, Peru	D2	58
Chupadera Mesa, mtn., N.M., U.S.	D3	108
Chupadero, N.M., U.S.	*B4	108
Chupara Point, c., Trin.	N23	57
Chuquibamba, Peru	E3	58
Chuquicamata, Chile	D2	55
Chuquisaca, dept., Bol.	D3	55
Chur, Switz.	E14	18
Churchbridge, Sask.	G5	75
Church Creek, Md., U.S.	C5	97
Church Hill, Md., U.S.	B6	97
Church Hill, Tn., U.S.	C11	119
Churchill, Man.	f9	70
Churchill, co., Nv., U.S.	*A5	110
Churchill, stm., Can.	E13	66
Churchill, stm., Newf.	h9	72
Churchill, Cape, c., Man.	f9	70
Churchill, Mount, mtn., B.C.	m7	75
Churchill Falls, wtfl., Newf.	h7	72
Churchill Lake, l., Me., U.S.	B3	96
Church Mountain, mtn., B.C.	f14	69
Church Point, N.S.	E3	71
Church Point, La., U.S.	D3	95
Church Rock, N.M., U.S.	B1	108
Churchs Ferry, N.D., U.S.	A6	111
Church Stretton, Eng., U.K.	B5	12
Churchton, Md., U.S.	C4	97
Churchville, N.Y., U.S.	B3	109
Churchville, Va., U.S.	B3	123
Churdan, Ia., U.S.	B3	92
Chūru, India	C5	37
Churubusco, In., U.S.	B7	91
Churubusco, N.Y., U.S.	f11	109
Churuguara, Ven.	A4	60
Churumuco, Mex.	n13	63
Chushul, India	B6	36
Chuska Mountains, mts., Az., U.S.	A6	80
Chusovaya, stm., Sov. Un.	D20	8
Chusovoy, Sov. Un.	B5	28
Chust, Sov. Un.	G23	8
Chuxian, China	H8	32
Chuxiong, China	F5	31
Chuy, Ur.	*G3	34
Cianjur, Indon.	*G3	34
Ciano d'Enza, Italy	E6	20
Cianorte, Braz.	C2	54
Cibecue, Az., U.S.	C5	80
Cibola, co., N.M., U.S.	C1	108
Cibolo Creek, stm., Tx., U.S.	h7	120
Cicero, Il., U.S.	B6	90
Cicero, In., U.S.	D5	91
Cicero Dantas, Braz.	B7	57
Ciche, Sgurr na, mtn., Scot., U.K.	D3	13
Cicia, i., Fiji	H16	52
Cidra, Lago de, res., P.R.	B3	65
Ciechanów, Pol.	B6	26
Ciechocinek, Pol.	D4	64
Ciego de Avila, Cuba	C4	64
Ciego de Avila, prov., Cuba	C4	64
Ciempozuelos, Spain	B4	22
Ciénaga, Col.	A3	60
Ciénaga de Oro, Col.	B2	60
Cienfuegos, Cuba	C3	64
Cienfuegos, prov., Cuba	C3	64
Cieszyn, Pol.	D5	26

Name	Map Ref.	Page

Cieza, Spain — C5 22
Ciężkowice, Pol. — g10 26
Cigüela, stm., Spain — C4 22
Cihanbeyli, Tur. — C9 40
Cihuatlán, Mex. — n11 63
Cilacap, Indon. — G3 34
Cili, China — J4 32
Cima, Ca., U.S. — E6 82
Cimarron, Co., U.S. — C3 83
Cimarron, Ks., U.S. — E3 93
Cimarron, N.M., U.S. — A5 108
Cimarron, co., Ok., U.S. — e8 113
Cimarron, stm., U.S. — C8 76
Cimarron, North Fork, stm., U.S. — E2 93
Cimarron Hills, Co., U.S. — *C6 83
Cîmpina, Rom. — C7 24
Cîmpulung, Rom. — C7 24
Cîmpulung Moldovenesc, Rom. — B7 24
Cincinnati, Ia., U.S. — D5 92
Cincinnati, Oh., U.S. — C1 112
Cincinnatus, N.Y., U.S. — C5 109
Cinconsine, Lac, l., Que. — B4 74
Çine, Tur. — D7 25
Cinnaminson, N.J., U.S. — D3 107
Cintalapa [de Figueroa], Mex. — D6 63
Cinto, Monte, mtn., Fr. — m23 16
Cipolletti, Arg. — B3 54
Circle, Ak., U.S. — B11 79
Circle, Mt., U.S. — C11 103
Circle Hot Springs, Ak., U.S. — B11 79
Circle Pines, Mn., U.S. — m12 100
Circleville, Ks., U.S. — C8 93
Circleville, Oh., U.S. — C3 112
Circleville, Ut., U.S. — E3 121
Circleville, W.V., U.S. — C5 125
Cirebon, Indon. — G3 34
Cirencester, Eng., U.K. — E6 10
Cirí, stm., Pan. — m10 62
Cisco, Ga., U.S. — B2 87
Cisco, Il., U.S. — C5 90
Cisco, Tx., U.S. — C3 120
Cisco, Ut., U.S. — E6 121
Ciskei, ctry., Afr. — D4 49
Cisne, Il., U.S. — E5 90
Cisneros, Col. — B2 60
Cisnes, stm., Chile — C2 54
Cispus, stm., Wa., U.S. — C4 124
Cissna Park, Il., U.S. — C6 90
Cistern, Tx., U.S. — E4 120
Cisterna di Latina, Italy — h9 23
Cistierna, Spain — A3 22
Citac, Nevado, mtn., Peru — D2 58
Citra, Fl., U.S. — C4 86
Citronelle, Al., U.S. — D1 78
Citrus, Ca., U.S. — *E5 82
Citrus, co., Fl., U.S. — D4 86
Citrus Heights, Ca., U.S. — *C3 82
Cittadella, Italy — B3 23
Città di Castello, Italy — C4 23
City Mills, Ma., U.S. — h10 98
City of Commerce, Ca., U.S. — n12 82
City of Refuge National Historical Park, Hi., U.S. — D5 88
City Point, Fl., U.S. — D6 86
City View, S.C., U.S. — B3 117
Ciudad Acuña, Mex. — B4 63
Ciudad Altamirano, Mex. — n13 63
Ciudad Bolívar, Ven. — B5 60
Ciudad Bolivia, Ven. — B3 60
Ciudad Camargo, Mex. — B3 63
Ciudad de la Habana, prov., Cuba — C2 64
Ciudad del Carmen, Mex. — D6 63
Ciudad del Maíz, Mex. — C5 63
Ciudad de Naucalpan de Juárez, Mex. — h9 63
Ciudad de Valles, Mex. — C5 63
Ciudad de Villaldama, Mex. — B4 63
Ciudadela, Spain — B7 22
Ciudad Guayana, Ven. — B5 60
Ciudad Guzmán, Mex. — D4 63
Ciudad Hidalgo, Mex. — n13 63
Ciudad Ixtepec, Mex. — D5 63
Ciudad Juárez, Mex. — A3 63
Ciudad Lerdo, Mex. — B4 63
Ciudad López Mateos, Mex. — g9 63
Ciudad Madero, Mex. — C5 63
Ciudad Mante, Mex. — C5 63
Ciudad Melchor Múzquiz, Mex. — B4 63
Ciudad Mendoza, Mex. — n15 63
Ciudad Obregón, Mex. — B3 63
Ciudad Ojeda, Ven. — A3 60
Ciudad Piar, Ven. — B5 60
Ciudad Real, Spain — C4 22
Ciudad Rodrigo, Spain — B2 22
Ciudad Serdán, Mex. — n15 63
Ciudad Tecún Umán, Guat. — C1 62
Ciudad Victoria, Mex. — C5 63
Cividale del Friuli, Italy — A4 23
Civitanova Marche, Italy — C4 23
Civitavecchia, Italy — C3 23
Civray, Fr. — D4 16
Çivril, Tur. — C7 40
Cizre, Tur. — D14 40
C.J. Strike Reservoir, res., Id., U.S. — G3 89
Clackamas, Or., U.S. — h12 114
Clackamas, co., Or., U.S. — B4 114
Clacton-on-Sea, Eng., U.K. — C9 12
Claflin, Ks., U.S. — D5 93
Claiborne, Al., U.S. — D2 78
Claiborne, La., U.S. — *B3 95
Claiborne, Md., U.S. — C5 97
Claiborne, co., La., U.S. — B2 95
Claiborne, co., Ms., U.S. — D3 101
Claiborne, co., Tn., U.S. — C10 119
Claiborne, Lake, res., La., U.S. — B3 95
Clair, N.B. — B1 71
Clair, Sask. — E3 75
Claire, Lake, l., Alta. — f8 68
Claire City, S.D., U.S. — B8 118
Clair Engle Lake, res., Ca., U.S. — B2 82
Clairfield, Tn., U.S. — C10 119
Clair-Mel City, Fl., U.S. — *E4 86
Clairmont, Alta. — B1 68
Clairton, Pa., U.S. — F2 115
Clallam, co., Wa., U.S. — B1 124
Clallam Bay, Wa., U.S. — A1 124
Clamart, Fr. — g10 16
Clamecy, Fr. — D5 16
Clam Lake, l., Sask. — B3 75
Clam Lake, l., Wi., U.S. — C1 126
Clan Alpine Mountains, mts., Nv., U.S. — D4 105
Clancy, Mt., U.S. — D5 103
Clandeboye, Ont. — D3 73
Clandonald, Alta. — C5 68
Clanton, Al., U.S. — C3 78
Clanwilliam, Man. — D2 70

Clanwilliam, S. Afr. — D2 49
Clapperton Island, i., Ont. — A2 73
Clara, Ire. — D4 11
Clara, Ms., U.S. — D5 101
Clara City, Mn., U.S. — F3 100
Clara Peak, mtn., Az., U.S. — C2 80
Clare, Austl. — F6 50
Clare, In., U.S. — D6 91
Clare, Ia., U.S. — B3 92
Clare, Mi., U.S. — E6 99
Clare, co., Ire. — E3 11
Clare, co., Mi., U.S. — E6 99
Clare, stm., Ire. — D3 11
Clarecastle (Clare), Ire. — E3 11
Claregalway, Ire. — D3 11
Clare Island, i., Ire. — D1 10
Claremont, Ca., U.S. — m13 82
Claremont, Il., U.S. — E6 90
Claremont, Mn., U.S. — F6 100
Claremont, N.H., U.S. — D2 106
Claremont, N.C., U.S. — B1 110
Claremont, S.D., U.S. — B7 118
Claremont, Va., U.S. — C6 123
Claremont, mtn., Ca., U.S. — C3 82
Claremore, Ok., U.S. — A6 113
Claremorris, Ire. — D2 10
Clarence, Al., U.S. — A3 78
Clarence, Ia., U.S. — C6 92
Clarence, La., U.S. — C2 95
Clarence, Mo., U.S. — B5 102
Clarence, Pa., U.S. — D6 115
Clarence, N.Y., U.S. — C2 109
Clarence, N.Z. — O14 51
Clarence, Isla, i., Chile — h11 54
Clarence Cannon Lake, res., Mo., U.S. — B6 102
Clarence Island, i., B.A.T. — C7 7
Clarence Strait, strt., Austl. — B5 50
Clarence Strait, strt., Ak., U.S. — n23 79
Clarence Town, Bah. — B9 64
Clarenceville, Que. — D4 74
Clarendon, Ar., U.S. — C4 81
Clarendon, Pa., U.S. — C3 115
Clarendon, Tx., U.S. — B2 120
Clarendon, Vt., U.S. — D3 122
Clarendon, co., S.C., U.S. — D7 117
Clarendon, co., Vt., U.S. — E2 122
Clarendon Hills, Il., U.S. — k9 90
Clarendon Springs, Vt., U.S. — D2 122
Clarendon Station, Ont. — C8 73
Clarenville, Newf. — D4 72
Claresholm, Alta. — D4 68
Claridge, Pa., U.S. — F2 115
Clarie Coast, Ant. — C26 7
Clarinda, Ia., U.S. — D2 92
Clarington, Oh., U.S. — C5 112
Clarington, Pa., U.S. — D3 115
Clarion, Ia., U.S. — B4 92
Clarion, Pa., U.S. — D3 115
Clarion, co., Pa., U.S. — D3 115
Clarion, stm., Pa., U.S. — D3 115
Clarissa, Mn., U.S. — D4 100
Clarita, Ok., U.S. — C5 113
Clark, Co., U.S. — A4 83
Clark, Mo., U.S. — B5 102
Clark, N.J., U.S. — B4 107
Clark, Oh., U.S. — B4 112
Clark, S.D., U.S. — C8 118
Clark, co., Ar., U.S. — C2 81
Clark, co., Id., U.S. — E6 89
Clark, co., Il., U.S. — D6 90
Clark, co., In., U.S. — H6 91
Clark, co., Ks., U.S. — E4 93
Clark, co., Ky., U.S. — C5 94
Clark, co., Mo., U.S. — A6 102
Clark, co., Nv., U.S. — G6 105
Clark, co., Oh., U.S. — C2 112
Clark, co., S.D., U.S. — C8 118
Clark, co., Wa., U.S. — D3 124
Clark, co., Wi., U.S. — D3 126
Clark, Lake, l., Ak., U.S. — C9 79
Clark, Point, c., Ont. — C3 73
Clark Colony, S.D., U.S. — *C8 118
Clarkdale, Az., U.S. — C3 80
Clarkdale, Ga., U.S. — h7 87
Clarke, co., Al., U.S. — D2 78
Clarke, co., Ga., U.S. — C3 87
Clarke, co., Ia., U.S. — C4 92
Clarke, co., Ms., U.S. — C5 101
Clarke, co., Va., U.S. — A4 123
Clarke City, Que. — h8 72
Clarke Lake, l., Sask. — C2 75
Clarkesville, Ga., U.S. — B3 87
Clarkfield, Mn., U.S. — F3 100
Clark Fork, Id., U.S. — A2 89
Clark Fork, stm., U.S. — C1 103
Clarkia, Id., U.S. — B3 89
Clark Mountain, mtn., Mo., U.S. — D7 102
Clarkrange, Tn., U.S. — C8 119
Clarks, La., U.S. — B3 95
Clarks, Ne., U.S. — C8 104
Clarks, stm., Ky., U.S. — f9 94
Clarks, West Fork, stm., Ky., U.S. — f9 94
Clarksboro, N.J., U.S. — D2 107
Clarksburg, Ont. — C4 73
Clarksburg, Md., U.S. — B3 97
Clarksburg, Mo., U.S. — C5 102
Clarksburg, N.J., U.S. — C4 107
Clarksburg, Oh., U.S. — C2 112
Clarksburg, Tn., U.S. — B3 119
Clarksburg, W.V., U.S. — B4 125
Clarksdale, Ms., U.S. — A3 101
Clarksdale, Mo., U.S. — B3 102
Clarks Falls, Ct., U.S. — D8 84
Clarks Grove, Mn., U.S. — G5 100
Clark's Harbour, N.S. — F4 71
Clarks Hill, In., U.S. — D4 91
Clarkson, Ky., U.S. — C3 94
Clarkson, Ne., U.S. — C8 104
Clarks Point, Ak., U.S. — D8 79
Clarks Summit, Pa., U.S. — m18 115
Clarkston, Ga., U.S. — h8 87
Clarkston, Mi., U.S. — F7 99
Clarkston, Ut., U.S. — B3 121
Clarkston, Wa., U.S. — C8 124
Clarksville, N.S. — D6 71
Clarksville, Ar., U.S. — B2 81
Clarksville, De., U.S. — F5 85
Clarksville, Fl., U.S. — B1 86
Clarksville, Ia., U.S. — B5 92
Clarksville, In., U.S. — H6 91
Clarksville, Mi., U.S. — F5 99
Clarksville, Oh., U.S. — C2 112
Clarksville, Tn., U.S. — A4 119
Clarksville, Tx., U.S. — C5 120
Clarksville, Va., U.S. — D4 123
Clarkton, Mo., U.S. — E8 102
Clarkton, N.C., U.S. — C4 110
Claryville, Ky., U.S. — k14 94
Clashmore, Ire. — E4 11
Clatonia, Ne., U.S. — D9 104

Clatskanie, Or., U.S. — A3 114
Clatsop, co., Or., U.S. — A3 114
Claude, Tx., U.S. — B2 120
Claudy, N. Ire., U.K. — C4 11
Claunch, N.M., U.S. — C3 108
Clausthal-Zellerfeld, Ger. — C5 18
Clavet, Sask. — F2 75
Clawson, Mi., U.S. — o15 99
Clawson, Ut., U.S. — D4 121
Claxton, Ga., U.S. — D5 87
Clay, Al., U.S. — f7 78
Clay, Ky., U.S. — C2 94
Clay, La., U.S. — B3 95
Clay, N.Y., U.S. — B4 109
Clay, W.V., U.S. — C3 125
Clay, Wy., U.S. — B8 127
Clay, co., Al., U.S. — B4 78
Clay, co., Ar., U.S. — A5 81
Clay, co., Fl., U.S. — B5 86
Clay, co., Ga., U.S. — E2 87
Clay, co., Il., U.S. — E5 90
Clay, co., In., U.S. — F3 91
Clay, co., Ia., U.S. — A2 92
Clay, co., Ks., U.S. — C6 93
Clay, co., Ky., U.S. — C6 94
Clay, co., Mn., U.S. — D2 100
Clay, co., Ms., U.S. — B5 101
Clay, co., Mo., U.S. — B3 102
Clay, co., Ne., U.S. — D7 104
Clay, co., N.C., U.S. — f9 110
Clay, co., S.D., U.S. — E8 118
Clay, co., Tn., U.S. — C8 119
Clay, co., Tx., U.S. — C3 120
Clay Center, Ks., U.S. — C6 93
Clay Center, Ne., U.S. — D7 104
Clay Center, Oh., U.S. — A2 112
Clay City, Il., U.S. — E5 90
Clay City, In., U.S. — F3 91
Clay City, Ky., U.S. — C6 94
Clay Creek, stm., Co., U.S. — C8 83
Clay Creek, stm., S.D., U.S. — D8 118
Claydon, Sask. — H1 75
Clayhatchee, Al., U.S. — D4 78
Clay Head, c., I. of Man — F4 13
Claymont, De., U.S. — A4 85
Claypool, Az., U.S. — D5 80
Claypool, In., U.S. — B6 91
Claysburg, Pa., U.S. — F5 115
Clay Springs, Az., U.S. — C5 80
Claysville, Pa., U.S. — F1 115
Clayton, Ont. — B8 73
Clayton, Al., U.S. — D4 78
Clayton, De., U.S. — C3 85
Clayton, Ga., U.S. — B3 87
Clayton, Id., U.S. — E4 89
Clayton, Il., U.S. — C3 90
Clayton, In., U.S. — E4 91
Clayton, Ia., U.S. — B6 92
Clayton, Ks., U.S. — C3 93
Clayton, La., U.S. — C4 95
Clayton, Mo., U.S. — C7 102
Clayton, N.J., U.S. — D2 107
Clayton, N.M., U.S. — A6 108
Clayton, N.Y., U.S. — A4 109
Clayton, N.C., U.S. — B4 110
Clayton, Ok., U.S. — C6 113
Clayton, S.D., U.S. — D8 118
Clayton, Tn., U.S. — A2 119
Clayton, Wa., U.S. — B8 124
Clayton, Wi., U.S. — C1 126
Clayton, co., Ga., U.S. — C2 87
Clayton, co., Ia., U.S. — B6 92
Clayton Lake, Me., U.S. — B3 96
Claytor Lake, res., Va., U.S. — C2 123
Clayville, R.I., U.S. — C2 116
Clear, stm., Alta. — A1 68
Clear, stm., R.I., U.S. — B2 116
Clear, Cape, c., Ire. — E2 10
Clear, Lake, l., Ont. — B7 73
Clear Boggy Creek, stm., Ok., U.S. — C5 113
Clearbrook, Mn., U.S. — C3 100
Clear Creek, In., U.S. — F4 91
Clear Creek, Ut., U.S. — D4 121
Clear Creek, W.V., U.S. — n13 125
Clear Creek, stm., Co., U.S. — B5 83
Clear Creek, stm., Az., U.S. — C4 80
Clear Creek, stm., Ne., U.S. — C4 104
Clear Creek, stm., Tn., U.S. — C9 119
Clear Creek, stm., Wy., U.S. — B6 127
Cleare, Cape, c., Ak., U.S. — D10 79
Clearfield, Ia., U.S. — D3 92
Clearfield, Ky., U.S. — B6 94
Clearfield, Pa., U.S. — D5 115
Clearfield, S.D., U.S. — D5 118
Clearfield, Ut., U.S. — B3 121
Clearfield, co., Pa., U.S. — D5 115
Clear Fork, W.V., U.S. — D3 125
Clear Fork, stm., W.V., U.S. — n13 125
Clear Island, i., Ire. — F2 11
Clearlake, Ca., U.S. — C2 82
Clear Lake, Ia., U.S. — A4 92
Clear Lake, Mn., U.S. — E5 100
Clear Lake, S.D., U.S. — C9 118
Clearlake, Wa., U.S. — A3 124
Clear Lake, Wi., U.S. — C1 126
Clear Lake City, U.S. — r14 120
Clear Lake Shores, Tx., U.S. — r15 120
Clearmont, Mo., U.S. — A2 102
Clearmont, Wy., U.S. — B6 127
Clear Spring, Md., U.S. — A2 97
Clear Stream, stm., N.H., U.S. — g7 106
Clearview, Ok., U.S. — B5 113
Clearview City, Ks., U.S. — g12 93
Clearville, Pa., U.S. — G5 115
Clearwater, Man. — D2 70
Clearwater, Fl., U.S. — E4 86
Clearwater, Id., U.S. — C3 89
Clearwater, Ks., U.S. — E6 93
Clearwater, Mn., U.S. — E4 100
Clearwater, Ne., U.S. — B7 104
Clearwater, S.C., U.S. — E4 117
Clearwater, co., Id., U.S. — C3 89
Clearwater, co., Mn., U.S. — C3 100
Clearwater, stm., Alta. — D3 68
Clearwater, stm., Alta. — C1 68
Clearwater, stm., B.C. — C7 69
Clearwater, stm., Can. — A5 68
Clearwater, stm., Id., U.S. — C3 89
Clearwater, stm., Mn., U.S. — C3 100
Clearwater Lake, l., B.C. — C7 69
Clearwater Lake, l., Mo., U.S. — D7 102
Clearwater Lake, res., Mo., U.S. — D7 102

Clearwater Mountains, mts., Id., U.S. — C2 89
Clearwater Provincial Park, Man. — C1 70
Cleator Moor, Eng., U.K. — F5 13
Cleburne, Tx., U.S. — C4 120
Cleburne, co., Al., U.S. — B4 78
Cleburne, co., Ar., U.S. — B3 81
Cle Elum, Wa., U.S. — B4 124
Cle Elum, stm., Wa., U.S. — B4 124
Cle Elum Lake, res., Wa., U.S. — B4 124
Cleethorpes, Eng., U.K. — A7 12
Cleggan, Ire. — D1 11
Cleghorn, Ia., U.S. — B2 92
Clementon, N.J., U.S. — D3 107
Clements, Ks., U.S. — D7 93
Clements, Md., U.S. — D4 97
Clements, Mn., U.S. — F3 100
Clementsport, N.S. — E4 71
Clementsvale, N.S. — E4 71
Clemmons, N.C., U.S. — A2 110
Clemons, Ia., U.S. — B4 92
Clemons, N.Y., U.S. — B7 109
Clemscott, Ok., U.S. — C4 113
Clemson, S.C., U.S. — B2 117
Clendenin, W.V., U.S. — C3 125
Clendening Lake, res., Oh., U.S. — B4 112
Cleona, Pa., U.S. — F9 115
Cleo Springs, Ok., U.S. — A3 113
Clermont, Austl. — D8 50
Clermont, Que. — B7 74
Clermont, Fr. — E2 17
Clermont, Fl., U.S. — D5 86
Clermont, Ga., U.S. — B3 87
Clermont, Ia., U.S. — A6 92
Clermont, Ky., U.S. — C4 94
Clermont, co., Oh., U.S. — C1 112
Clermont Harbor, Ms., U.S. — E4 101
Clermont-Ferrand, Fr. — E5 16
Clermont-l'Hérault, Fr. — F5 16
Clerval, Fr. — B1 21
Clervaux, Lux. — D6 17
Clevedon, Eng., U.K. — C5 12
Cleveland, Al., U.S. — A3 78
Cleveland, Ga., U.S. — B3 87
Cleveland, Il., U.S. — B3 90
Cleveland, Mn., U.S. — F5 100
Cleveland, Ms., U.S. — B3 101
Cleveland, N.M., U.S. — A5 108
Cleveland, N.Y., U.S. — B5 109
Cleveland, N.C., U.S. — B2 110
Cleveland, N.D., U.S. — C6 111
Cleveland, Oh., U.S. — A4 112
Cleveland, Ok., U.S. — A5 113
Cleveland, S.C., U.S. — A2 117
Cleveland, Tn., U.S. — D9 119
Cleveland, Tx., U.S. — D5 120
Cleveland, Ut., U.S. — D5 121
Cleveland, Va., U.S. — f9 123
Cleveland, Wi., U.S. — k10 126
Cleveland, co., Eng., U.K. — F7 13
Cleveland, co., Ar., U.S. — D3 81
Cleveland, co., N.C., U.S. — B1 110
Cleveland, co., Ok., U.S. — B4 113
Cleveland, Mount, mtn., Mt., U.S. — B3 103
Cleveland Heights, Oh., U.S. — A4 112
Cleveland Hills, hills, Eng., U.K. — F7 13
Clevelândia, Braz. — D2 56
Cleves, Oh., U.S. — o12 112
Cleves see Kleve, Ger. — C3 18
Clew Bay, b., Ire. — D2 10
Clewiston, Fl., U.S. — F6 86
Clichy, Fr. — g10 16
Clifden, Ire. — D1 10
Cliff, N.M., U.S. — E1 108
Cliff Island, i., Me., U.S. — g7 96
Clifford, Ont. — D4 73
Clifford, In., U.S. — F6 91
Clifford, Mi., U.S. — E7 99
Clifford, N.D., U.S. — B8 111
Clifford, Va., U.S. — C3 123
Cliffside, N.C., U.S. — B1 110
Cliffside Park, N.J., U.S. — h9 107
Clifftop, W.V., U.S. — m14 125
Clifton, Az., U.S. — D6 80
Clifton, Co., U.S. — B2 83
Clifton, Id., U.S. — G7 89
Clifton, Ks., U.S. — C6 93
Clifton, N.J., U.S. — B4 107
Clifton, S.C., U.S. — B4 117
Clifton, Tn., U.S. — B4 119
Clifton, Tx., U.S. — D4 120
Clifton, Va., U.S. — g12 123
Clifton City, Mo., U.S. — C4 102
Clifton Forge, Va., U.S. — C3 123
Clifton Heights, Pa., U.S. — *p20 115
Clifton Hill, Mo., U.S. — B5 102
Clifton Knolls, N.Y., U.S. — C7 109
Clifton Springs, N.Y., U.S. — C3 109
Cliftonville, Ms., U.S. — B5 101
Climax, Sask. — H1 75
Climax, Co., U.S. — B4 83
Climax, Ga., U.S. — F2 87
Climax, Mi., U.S. — F5 99
Climax, Mn., U.S. — C2 100
Climax, N.C., U.S. — B3 110
Climax Springs, Mo., U.S. — C4 102
Climbing Hill, Ia., U.S. — B1 92
Clinch, co., Ga., U.S. — F4 87
Clinch, stm., U.S. — D9 119
Clinchco, Va., U.S. — e9 123
Clinchfield, Ga., U.S. — D3 87
Clinch Mountain, mtn., U.S. — C10 119
Clinchport, Va., U.S. — f9 123
Clingmans Dome, mtn., U.S. — D10 119
Clint, Tx., U.S. — o11 120
Clinton, B.C. — D7 69
Clinton, Ont. — D3 73
Clinton, Al., U.S. — B1 78
Clinton, Ar., U.S. — B3 81
Clinton, Ct., U.S. — D5 84
Clinton, Ia., U.S. — C7 92
Clinton, Il., U.S. — C5 90
Clinton, In., U.S. — E3 91
Clinton, Ky., U.S. — f9 94
Clinton, La., U.S. — D4 95
Clinton, Me., U.S. — D3 96
Clinton, Md., U.S. — C4 97
Clinton, Ma., U.S. — B4 98

Clinton, Mi., U.S. — F7 99
Clinton, Mn., U.S. — E2 100
Clinton, Ms., U.S. — C3 101
Clinton, Mo., U.S. — C4 102
Clinton, Mt., U.S. — D3 103
Clinton, Ne., U.S. — B3 104
Clinton, N.H., U.S. — D3 106
Clinton, N.J., U.S. — B3 107
Clinton, N.Y., U.S. — B5 109
Clinton, N.C., U.S. — C4 110
Clinton, Ok., U.S. — B3 113
Clinton, S.C., U.S. — C4 117
Clinton, Tn., U.S. — C9 119
Clinton, Ut., U.S. — B3 121
Clinton, Wa., U.S. — B3 124
Clinton, Wi., U.S. — F5 126
Clinton, co., Il., U.S. — E4 90
Clinton, co., In., U.S. — D4 91
Clinton, co., Ia., U.S. — C7 92
Clinton, co., Ky., U.S. — D4 94
Clinton, co., Mi., U.S. — F6 99
Clinton, co., Mo., U.S. — B3 102
Clinton, co., N.Y., U.S. — f11 109
Clinton, co., Oh., U.S. — C2 112
Clinton, co., Pa., U.S. — D6 115
Clinton, Lake, res., Il., U.S. — C5 90
Clinton-Colden Lake, l., N.W. Ter. — D11 66
Clinton Lake, res., Ks., U.S. — m15 93
Clinton Reservoir, res., N.J., U.S. — A4 107
Clinton Township, Mi., U.S. — *F8 99
Clintonville, Ky., U.S. — B5 94
Clintonville, Wi., U.S. — D5 126
Clintwood, Va., U.S. — e9 123
Clio, Al., U.S. — D4 78
Clio, Ia., U.S. — D4 92
Clio, Mi., U.S. — E7 99
Clio, S.C., U.S. — B8 117
Clio, W.V., U.S. — C3 125
Clipperton, atoll, Fr. Poly. — F15 6
Clisham, mtn., Scot., U.K. — C2 13
Clitherall, Mn., U.S. — D3 100
Clitheroe, Eng., U.K. — G6 13
Clive, Alta. — C4 68
Clive, Ia., U.S. — e8 92
Cliza, Bol. — C5 55
Cloan, Sask. — E1 75
Cloghan, Ire. — C4 11
Cloghane, Ire. — E1 11
Clogheen, Ire. — E3 11
Clogher Head, c., Ire. — D5 11
Clonakilty, Ire. — E2 10
Clonakilty Bay, b., Ire. — E2 10
Cloncurry, Austl. — D7 50
Clones, Ire. — C4 11
Clonmany, Ire. — B4 11
Clonmel, Ire. — D3 10
Clonmellon, Ire. — D4 11
Cloone, Ire. — D4 11
Clontarf, Mn., U.S. — E3 100
Clo-oose, B.C. — E5 69
Cloppenburg, Ger. — C4 18
Clopton, Al., U.S. — D4 78
Cloquet, Mn., U.S. — D6 100
Cloquet, stm., Mn., U.S. — C6 100
Clothier, W.V., U.S. — n12 125
Cloud, co., Ks., U.S. — C6 93
Cloud Chief, Ok., U.S. — B3 113
Cloudcroft, N.M., U.S. — E4 108
Cloud Peak, mtn., Wy., U.S. — B5 127
Cloudy Bay, b., N.Z. — N15 51
Cloudy Mountain, mtn., Ak., U.S. — C8 79

Cloutierville, La., U.S. — C3 95
Clover, S.C., U.S. — A5 117
Clover, Va., U.S. — D4 123
Clover Bottom, Ky., U.S. — C5 94
Cloverdale, B.C. — f13 69
Cloverdale, Al., U.S. — A2 78
Cloverdale, Ca., U.S. — C2 82
Cloverdale, In., U.S. — E4 91
Cloverdale, Va., U.S. — *C3 123
Cloverleaf, Tx., U.S. — *r14 120
Cloverport, Ky., U.S. — C3 94
Clovis, Ca., U.S. — D4 82
Clovis, N.M., U.S. — C6 108
Clow, Ar., U.S. — C3 81
Cloyne, Ont. — C7 73
Cluj-Napoca, Rom. — B6 24
Clune, Austl. — E3 50
Clusone, Italy — D5 20
Cluster Springs, Va., U.S. — D4 123
Clute, Tx., U.S. — r14 120
Clutha, stm., N.Z. — P12 51
Clutier, Ia., U.S. — B5 92
Clwyd, co., Wales, U.K. — A4 12
Clyattville, Ga., U.S. — F3 87
Clyde, Alta. — C4 68
Clyde, N.W. Ter. — B19 66
Clyde, Ks., U.S. — C6 93
Clyde, Mo., U.S. — A2 102
Clyde, N.Y., U.S. — B4 109
Clyde, N.C., U.S. — f10 110
Clyde, Oh., U.S. — A3 112
Clyde, Tx., U.S. — C3 120
Clyde, stm., Scot., U.K. — E4 13
Clyde, Firth of, est., Scot., U.K. — C4 10
Clyde Park, Mt., U.S. — E6 103
Clymer, N.Y., U.S. — C1 109
Clymer, Pa., U.S. — E3 115
Cnossus, hist., Grc. — E5 25
Côa, stm., Port. — B2 22
Coachella, Ca., U.S. — F5 82
Coachella Canal, Ca., U.S. — F6 82
Coachford, Ire. — F3 11
Coahoma, Tx., U.S. — C2 120
Coahoma, co., Ms., U.S. — A3 101
Coahuila, state, Mex. — B4 63
Coal, co., Ok., U.S. — C5 113
Coal Bluff, In., U.S. — F3 91
Coal Branch, N.B. — C5 71
Coal City, Il., U.S. — B5 90
Coal City, W.V., U.S. — n13 125
Coalcomán [de Matamoros], Mex. — D4 63

Coal Creek, Co., U.S. — C5 83
Coal Creek, stm., In., U.S. — E3 91
Coal Creek, stm., Ok., U.S. — B6 113
Coaldale, Alta. — E4 68
Coaldale, Co., U.S. — C5 83
Coaldale, Nv., U.S. — E4 105
Coaldale, Pa., U.S. — E10 115
Coalfield, Tn., U.S. — C9 119
Coal Fork, W.V., U.S. — C3 125
Coal Fork, stm., W.V., U.S. — m13 125
Coalgate, Ok., U.S. — C5 113
Coalgood, Ky., U.S. — D6 94
Coal Grove, Oh., U.S. — D3 112
Coal Harbour, B.C. — D4 69
Coal Hill, Ar., U.S. — B2 81
Coalhurst, Alta. — E4 68
Coaling, Al., U.S. — B2 78
Coalinga, Ca., U.S. — D3 82
Coalmont, B.C. — E7 69
Coalmont, Co., U.S. — A4 83
Coalmont, In., U.S. — F3 91
Coalmont, Tn., U.S. — D8 119
Coalport, Pa., U.S. — E4 115
Coalspur, Alta. — C2 68
Coalton, Oh., U.S. — C3 112
Coalville, Eng., U.K. — B6 12
Coalville, Ia., U.S. — B3 92
Coalville, Ut., U.S. — C4 121
Coalwood, W.V., U.S. — D3 125
Coamo, P.R. — B3 65
Coari, Braz. — C2 59
Coari, stm., Braz. — C2 59
Coast, prov., Kenya — B6 48
Coasters Harbor Island, i., R.I., U.S. — E5 116
Coast Mountains, mts., N.A. — E6 66
Coast Ranges, mts., U.S. — D3 76
Coatbridge, Scot., U.K. — C5 10
Coatepec, Mex. — n15 63
Coatepeque, Guat. — C2 62
Coatesville, In., U.S. — E4 91
Coatesville, Pa., U.S. — G10 115
Coatney Hill, mtn., Ct., U.S. — B7 84
Coatopa, Al., U.S. — C1 78
Coats, Ks., U.S. — E5 93
Coats, N.C., U.S. — B4 110
Coatsburg, Il., U.S. — C2 90
Coats Island, i., N.W. Ter. — D16 66
Coats Land, reg., Ant. — B9 7
Coatsville, Mo., U.S. — A5 102
Coatzacoalcos (Puerto México), Mex. — D6 63
Cobalt, Ont. — p19 73
Cobalt, Ct., U.S. — C5 84
Cobalt, Id., U.S. — D4 89
Cobán, Guat. — C2 62
Cobar, Austl. — F8 50
Cobb, Ga., U.S. — E3 87
Cobb, Ky., U.S. — D2 94
Cobb, Ok., U.S. — C5 113
Cobb, Wi., U.S. — F3 126
Cobb, stm., Mn., U.S. — G5 100
Cobb Island, Md., U.S. — D4 97
Cobb Mountain Reservoir, res., Ma., U.S. — B2 98
Cobbosseecontee Lake, l., Me., U.S. — D3 96
Cobbtown, Ga., U.S. — D4 87
Cobden, Ont. — B8 73
Cobden, Il., U.S. — F4 90
Cobequid Mountains, mts., N.S. — D5 71
Cobh, Ire. — E2 10
Cobham, Eng., U.K. — m12 12
Cobija, Chile — D2 55
Coble, Tn., U.S. — B4 119
Coblence see Koblenz, Ger. — C3 18
Cobleskill, N.Y., U.S. — C6 109
Coboconk, Ont. — C6 73
Cobourg, Ont. — D6 73
Cobourg Peninsula, pen., Austl. — B5 50
Cobre, Nv., U.S. — B7 105
Côbuè, Moz. — D5 48
Cobun Creek, stm., W.V., U.S. — h11 125
Coburg, Austl. — *G7 50
Coburg, Ger. — C5 18
Coburg, Ia., U.S. — D2 92
Coburg, Or., U.S. — C3 114
Coburg Island, i., N.W. Ter. — m36 66
Coburn Gore, Me., U.S. — C2 96
Coburn Mountain, mtn., Me., U.S. — C2 96
Cocentaina, Spain — C5 22
Cochabamba, Bol. — C5 55
Cochabamba, dept., Bol. — C5 55
Cochecho, stm., N.H., U.S. — D5 106
Cochem, Ger. — E6 18
Cochetopa Creek, stm., Co., U.S. — C4 83
Cochetopa Hills, mts., Co., U.S. — C4 83
Cochin, India — G6 36
Cochin China, hist. reg., Viet. — H6 35
Cochin Point, c., Phil. — o13 34
Cochise, co., Az., U.S. — F5 80
Cochise Head, mtn., Az., U.S. — E6 80
Cochiti, N.M., U.S. — h8 108
Cochiti Indian Reservation, N.M., U.S. — h8 108
Cochiti Reservoir, res., N.M., U.S. — B3 108
Cochituate, Ma., U.S. — g10 98
Cochituate, Lake, l., Ma., U.S. — g10 98
Cochran, Ga., U.S. — D3 87
Cochran, co., Tx., U.S. — C1 120
Cochrane, Alta. — D3 68
Cochrane, Ont. — o19 73
Cochrane, Wi., U.S. — D2 126
Cochranton, Pa., U.S. — C1 115
Cochranville, Pa., U.S. — G10 115
Cockburn, Austl. — F3 51
Cocke, co., Tn., U.S. — D10 119
Cockermouth, Eng., U.K. — F5 13
Cockeysville, Md., U.S. — B4 97
Cockrell Hill, Tx., U.S. — n10 120
Coco, stm., N.A. — A4 61
Coco, Isla del, i., C.R. — C2 53
Cocoa, Fl., U.S. — D6 86
Cocoa Beach, Fl., U.S. — D6 86

Name	Map Ref.	Page
Cocoa West, Fl., U.S.	*D6	86
Cocobeach, Gabon	E1	46
Cocolalla, Id., U.S.	A2	89
Coconino, co., Az., U.S.	B3	80
Coconino Plateau, plat., Az., U.S.	B3	80
Coconut Creek, Fl., U.S.	*F6	86
Cocopah Indian Reservation, Az., U.S.	E1	80
Cocos Bay, b., Trin.	O23	65
Cocos Island, i., Guam	M9	52
Cocos Islands (Keeling Islands), is., Oc.	G3	2
Cocos Lagoon, b., Guam	M9	52
Coco Solo, Pan.	k11	62
Cocula, Mex.	C4	63
Cod, Cape, c., Ma., U.S.	C7	98
Codajás, Braz.	C2	59
Codell, Ks., U.S.	C4	93
Coden, Al., U.S.	E1	78
Codera, Cabo, c., Ven.	A4	60
Coderre, Sask.	G2	75
Codesa, Alta.	B1	68
Codette, Sask.	D3	75
Codigoro, Italy	E8	20
Codington, co., S.D., U.S.	C8	118
Cod Island, i., Newf.	g9	72
Codó, Braz.	B2	57
Codogno, Italy	B2	23
Codpa, Chile	C2	55
Codroipo, Italy	D8	20
Codroy, Newf.	E2	72
Codroy Pond, Newf.	D2	72
Cody, Ne., U.S.	B4	104
Cody, Wy., U.S.	B3	127
Codys, N.B.	D4	71
Coeburn, Va., U.S.	f9	123
Coe Hill, Ont.	C7	73
Coesfeld, Ger.	C3	18
Coessee, In., U.S.	B7	91
Coeur d'Alene, Id., U.S.	B2	89
Coeur d'Alene, stm., Id., U.S.	B2	89
Coeur d'Alene Indian Reservation, Id., U.S.	B2	89
Coeur d'Alene Lake, res., Id., U.S.	B2	89
Coeur d'Alene Mountains, mts., Id., U.S.	B2	89
Coevorden, Neth.	B6	17
Coffee, co., Al., U.S.	D3	78
Coffee, co., Ga., U.S.	E4	87
Coffee, co., Tn., U.S.	B5	119
Coffee Creek, Mt., U.S.	C6	103
Coffeen, Il., U.S.	D4	90
Coffee Springs, Al., U.S.	D4	78
Coffeeville, Al., U.S.	D1	78
Coffeeville, Ms., U.S.	B4	101
Coffey, Mo., U.S.	A3	102
Coffey, co., Ks., U.S.	D8	93
Coffeyville, Ks., U.S.	E8	93
Coffin, Île, i., Que.	B8	71
Coffs Harbour, Austl.	F9	50
Cofield, N.C., U.S.	A6	110
Cogdell, Ga., U.S.	E4	87
Coggon, Ia., U.S.	B6	92
Coghinas, stm., Italy	D2	23
Cognac, Fr.	E3	16
Cogswell, N.D., U.S.	C8	111
Cohagen, Mt., U.S.	C10	103
Cohansey, stm., N.J., U.S.	E2	107
Cohasset, Ma., U.S.	B6	98
Cohasset, Mn., U.S.	C5	100
Cohocton, N.Y., U.S.	C3	109
Cohocton, stm., N.Y., U.S.	C3	109
Cohoe, Ak., U.S.	g16	79
Cohoes, N.Y., U.S.	C7	109
Cohoon, Lake, res., Va., U.S.	k14	123
Cohutta, Ga., U.S.	B2	87
Cohutta Mountain, mtn., Ga., U.S.	B2	87
Coiba, Isla de, i., Pan.	G7	62
Coig, stm., Arg.	E2	54
Coihaique, Chile	D2	54
Coila, Ms., U.S.	B3	101
Coils Creek, stm., Nv., U.S.	D5	105
Coimbatore, India	H4	37
Coimbra, Port.	D3	22
Coin, Spain	D2	22
Coin, Ia., U.S.	D2	92
Coinjock, N.C., U.S.	A7	110
Coipasa, Laguna, l., Bol.	C2	55
Coipasa, Salar de, pl., S.A.	C2	55
Coire, Loch, l., Scot., U.K.	B4	13
Cojedes, state, Ven.	f9	60
Cojutepeque, El Sal.	D3	62
Cokato, Mn., U.S.	E4	100
Coke, co., Tx., U.S.	D2	120
Coker, Al., U.S.	B2	78
Coketon, W.V., U.S.	B5	125
Cokeville, Wy., U.S.	D2	127
Colac, Austl.	G7	50
Colares, Port.	f9	22
Colatina, Braz.	B4	56
Colbeck, Cape, c., Ant.	B33	7
Colbert, Ga., U.S.	B3	87
Colbert, Ok., U.S.	D5	113
Colbert, co., Al., U.S.	A2	78
Colbert Heights, Al., U.S.	A2	78
Colbio, Som.	F5	47
Colborne, Ont.	C7	73
Colbún, Chile	B2	54
Colburn, In., U.S.	A2	89
Colby, Ks., U.S.	C2	93
Colby, Me., U.S.	B4	96
Colby, Wi., U.S.	D3	126
Colbyville, Vt., U.S.	C3	122
Colchester, Eng., U.K.	C6	84
Colchester, Il., U.S.	C3	90
Colchester, Vt., U.S.	C2	122
Colchester, co., N.S.	D6	71
Colcord, Ok., U.S.	A7	113
Cold, stm., N.H., U.S.	C4	106
Cold, stm., N.H., U.S.	D2	106
Cold Bay, Ak., U.S.	E7	79
Cold Fell, mtn., Eng., U.K.	F6	13
Cold Hollow Mountains, mts., Vt., U.S.	B3	122
Colditz, Ger.	B7	19
Cold Lake, Alta.	B5	68
Cold Lake, l., Can.	B5	68
Cold River, Ky., U.S.	C7	94
Cold Spring, Ky., U.S.	A5	94
Cold Spring, Mn., U.S.	E4	100
Cold Spring, N.J., U.S.	F3	107
Cold Spring, N.Y., U.S.	D7	109
Cold Spring Harbor, N.Y., U.S.	*n15	109
Cold Spring, Nv., U.S.	D4	105
Coldstream, Scot., U.K.	E6	13
Cold Stream Pond, l., Me., U.S.	C4	96
Coldwater, Ont.	C5	73
Coldwater, Ks., U.S.	E4	93
Coldwater, Mi., U.S.	G5	99
Coldwater, Ms., U.S.	A4	101
Coldwater, Oh., U.S.	B1	112
Coldwater, stm., Ms., U.S.	A3	101
Coldwater Creek, stm., U.S.	e9	113
Cole, Ok., U.S.	B4	113
Cole, co., Mo., U.S.	C5	102
Colebrook, Ct., U.S.	B3	84
Colebrook, N.H., U.S.	g7	106
Colebrook River Lake, res., Ct., U.S.	A3	84
Cole Camp, Mo., U.S.	C4	102
Coleen, stm., Ak., U.S.	B11	79
Coleharbor, N.D., U.S.	B4	111
Cole Lake, Ont.	C8	73
Coleman, P.E.I.	C5	71
Coleman, Fl., U.S.	D4	86
Coleman, Ga., U.S.	E2	87
Coleman, Md., U.S.	B5	97
Coleman, Mi., U.S.	E6	99
Coleman, Ok., U.S.	C5	113
Coleman, Tx., U.S.	D3	120
Coleman, Wi., U.S.	C5	126
Coleman, co., Tx., U.S.	D3	120
Coleman Falls, Va., U.S.	C3	123
Colerain, N.C., U.S.	A6	110
Coleraine, Austl.	H3	51
Coleraine, Que.	D6	74
Coleraine, N. Ire., U.K.	C3	10
Coleraine, Mn., U.S.	C5	100
Coleridge, Ne., U.S.	B8	104
Coleridge, N.C., U.S.	B3	110
Coles, Ms., U.S.	D2	101
Coles, co., Il., U.S.	D5	90
Coles, Punta, c., Peru	E3	58
Colesberg, S. Afr.	D4	49
Colesburg, Ia., U.S.	B6	92
Colesburg, Ky., U.S.	C4	94
Coleta, Il., U.S.	B4	90
Coleville, Sask.	F1	75
Coleville, Ca., U.S.	C4	82
Colfax, Sask.	H4	75
Colfax, Ca., U.S.	C3	82
Colfax, Ia., U.S.	C4	92
Colfax, In., U.S.	D4	91
Colfax, La., U.S.	C3	95
Colfax, N.D., U.S.	C9	111
Colfax, Wi., U.S.	D2	126
Colfax, Wa., U.S.	C8	124
Colfax, co., Ne., U.S.	C8	104
Colfax, co., N.M., U.S.	A5	108
Colgate, Sask.	H4	75
Colhué Huapi, Lago, l., Arg.	E3	54
Colibris, Pointe des, c., Guad.	Q9	65
Colico, Italy	C5	20
Colijnsplaat, Neth.	C3	17
Colima, Mex.	D4	63
Colima, state, Mex.	D4	63
Colima, Nevado de, mtn., Mex.	n12	63
Colinas, Braz.	C2	57
Colinet, Newf.	E5	72
Colinton, Alta.	B4	68
Coll, i., Scot., U.K.	B3	10
Collbran, Co., U.S.	B10	79
College, Ak., U.S.	C10	79
College City, Ca., U.S.	C2	82
College Corner, Oh., U.S.	C1	112
Collegedale, Tn., U.S.	h11	119
College Grove, Tn., U.S.	B5	119
College Park, Ga., U.S.	C2	87
College Park, Md., U.S.	C4	97
College Place, Wa., U.S.	C7	124
College Springs, Ia., U.S.	D2	92
College Station, Ar., U.S.	C3	81
College Station, Tx., U.S.	D4	120
Collegeville, Ar., U.S.	*C3	81
Collegeville, In., U.S.	C3	91
Collegeville, Pa., U.S.	F11	115
College Ward, Ut., U.S.	*B4	121
Colleton, co., S.C., U.S.	F6	117
Colleyville, Tx., U.S.	*n9	120
Collie, Austl.	F2	50
Collier, co., Fl., U.S.	F5	86
Collier Bay, b., Austl.	C3	50
Collier City, Fl., U.S.	*F6	86
Colliers, W.V., U.S.	f8	125
Collierville, Tn., U.S.	B2	119
Collin, co., Tx., U.S.	C4	120
Collingdale, Pa., U.S.	p20	115
Collingswood, N.J., U.S.	D2	107
Collingsworth, co., Tx., U.S.	B2	120
Collingwood, Ont.	C4	73
Collins, Ga., U.S.	D4	87
Collins, Ia., U.S.	C4	92
Collins, Ms., U.S.	D4	101
Collins, Mo., U.S.	D4	102
Collins, Wi., U.S.	h10	126
Collins Park, De., U.S.	B3	85
Collinston, La., U.S.	B4	95
Collinston, Ut., U.S.	B3	121
Collinsville, Al., U.S.	A4	78
Collinsville, Ct., U.S.	B4	84
Collinsville, Il., U.S.	E4	90
Collinsville, Ms., U.S.	C5	101
Collinsville, Ok., U.S.	A6	113
Collinsville, Tx., U.S.	C4	120
Collinwood, Tn., U.S.	B4	119
Collipulli, Chile	D2	54
Collooney, Ire.	C3	11
Collyer, Ks., U.S.	C3	93
Colman, S.D., U.S.	D9	118
Colmar, Fr.	D7	16
Colmar, Ky., U.S.	D6	94
Colmar Manor, Md., U.S.	f9	97
Colmenar de Oreja, Spain	B4	22
Colmenar Viejo, Spain	B4	22
Colmesneil, Tx., U.S.	D5	120
Colnett, Cabo, c., Mex.	A1	63
Colo, Ia., U.S.	B4	92
Cologne (Köln), Ger.	C3	18
Cologne, Mn., U.S.	F5	100
Cologne, N.J., U.S.	D3	107
Colômbia, Braz.	F4	57
Colombia, Col.	C3	60
Colombia, ctry., S.A.	C3	60
Colombo, Sri L.	G6	36
Colón, Arg.	A5	54
Colón, Cuba	C6	64
Colón, Pan.	F8	62
Colon, Ne., U.S.	g11	104
Colon, N.C., U.S.	B3	110
Colón, Archipiélago de (Galápagos Islands), is., Ec.	g5	58
Colona, Co., U.S.	C3	83
Colonia, N.J., U.S.	k7	107
Colonia, dept., Ur.	g8	54
Colonia del Sacramento, Ur.	g8	54
Colonia Dora, Arg.	E3	55
Colonia Las Heras, Arg.	D3	54
Colônia Leopoldina, Braz.	k6	57
Colonial Beach, Va., U.S.	B6	123
Colonial Heights, Tn., U.S.	C11	119
Colonial Heights, Va., U.S.	C5	123
Colonial National Historical Park, Va., U.S.	C6	123
Colonial Park, Pa., U.S.	*F8	115
Colonia Mennonita, Para.	D3	55
Colonie, N.Y., U.S.	C7	109
Colonna, Italy	h9	23
Colonne, Cape, c., Italy	E6	23
Colonsay, Sask.	F3	75
Colonsay, i., Scot., U.K.	B3	10
Colony, Ks., U.S.	D8	93
Colony, Ok., U.S.	B3	113
Colorado, C.R.	E8	63
Colorado, co., Tx., U.S.	E4	120
Colorado, state, U.S.	B5	83
Colorado, stm., Arg.	B4	54
Colorado, stm., N.A.	D5	76
Colorado, stm., Tx., U.S.	D3	120
Colorado City, Az., U.S.	A3	80
Colorado City, Co., U.S.	D6	83
Colorado City, Tx., U.S.	C2	120
Colorado City Lake, res., Tx., U.S.	C2	120
Colorado National Monument, Co., U.S.	B2	83
Colorado Plateau, plat., U.S.	B4	80
Colorado River Aqueduct, Ca., U.S.	F6	82
Colorado River Indian Reservation, U.S.	D1	80
Colorados, Archipiélago de los, is., Cuba	C1	64
Colorado Springs, Co., U.S.	C6	83
Colotlán, Mex.	C4	63
Colquechaca, Bol.	C2	55
Colquitt, Ga., U.S.	E2	87
Colquitt, co., Ga., U.S.	E3	87
Colrain, Ma., U.S.	A2	98
Colstrip, Mt., U.S.	E10	103
Colt, Ar., U.S.	B5	81
Coltauco, Chile	C2	54
Colter Bay, Wy., U.S.	C2	127
Colton, Ca., U.S.	*E5	82
Colton, N.Y., U.S.	f10	109
Colton, Or., U.S.	B4	114
Colton, S.D., U.S.	D9	118
Colton, Wa., U.S.	C8	124
Colton Hill, mtn., Vt., U.S.	D4	122
Coltons Point, Md., U.S.	D4	97
Colts Neck, N.J., U.S.	C4	107
Columbia, Al., U.S.	D4	78
Columbia, Ca., U.S.	C3	82
Columbia, Ct., U.S.	C6	84
Columbia, Il., U.S.	E3	90
Columbia, Ky., U.S.	C4	94
Columbia, La., U.S.	B3	95
Columbia, Md., U.S.	B4	97
Columbia, Ms., U.S.	D4	101
Columbia, Mo., U.S.	C5	102
Columbia, N.C., U.S.	B6	110
Columbia, Pa., U.S.	F9	115
Columbia, S.C., U.S.	C5	117
Columbia, S.D., U.S.	B7	118
Columbia, Tn., U.S.	B4	119
Columbia, co., Ar., U.S.	D2	81
Columbia, co., Fl., U.S.	B4	86
Columbia, co., Ga., U.S.	C4	87
Columbia, co., N.Y., U.S.	C7	109
Columbia, co., Or., U.S.	B3	114
Columbia, co., Pa., U.S.	D9	115
Columbia, co., Wa., U.S.	C7	124
Columbia, co., Wi., U.S.	E4	126
Columbia, stm., N.A.	A3	76
Columbia, Cape, c., N.W. Ter.	k37	66
Columbia, Mount, mtn., Can.	C2	68
Columbia Basin, Wa., U.S.	C6	124
Columbia City, In., U.S.	B7	91
Columbia City, Or., U.S.	B4	114
Columbia Cross Roads, Pa., U.S.	C8	115
Columbia Falls, Me., U.S.	D5	96
Columbia Falls, Mt., U.S.	B2	103
Columbia Heights, Mn., U.S.	m12	100
Columbia Lake, l., B.C.	D10	69
Columbia Lake, res., Ct., U.S.	C6	84
Columbia Mountains, mts., B.C.	C7	69
Columbiana, Al., U.S.	B3	78
Columbiana, Oh., U.S.	B5	112
Columbiana, co., Oh., U.S.	B5	112
Columbiaville, Mi., U.S.	E7	99
Columbine, Co., U.S.	*B5	83
Columbus, Ar., U.S.	D2	81
Columbus, Ga., U.S.	D2	87
Columbus, In., U.S.	F6	91
Columbus, Ks., U.S.	E9	93
Columbus, Ky., U.S.	f8	94
Columbus, Ms., U.S.	B5	101
Columbus, Mt., U.S.	E7	103
Columbus, N.C., U.S.	f10	110
Columbus, N.D., U.S.	A3	111
Columbus, Ne., U.S.	C8	104
Columbus, N.M., U.S.	F2	108
Columbus, Oh., U.S.	C2	112
Columbus, Tx., U.S.	E4	120
Columbus, Wi., U.S.	E4	126
Columbus, co., N.C., U.S.	C4	110
Columbus Air Force Base, mil., Ms., U.S.	B5	101
Columbus City, Ia., U.S.	C6	92
Columbus Grove, Oh., U.S.	B1	112
Columbus Junction, Ia., U.S.	C6	92
Columbus Lake, res., Ms., U.S.	B5	101
Colusa, Ca., U.S.	C2	82
Colusa, co., Ca., U.S.	C2	82
Colver, Pa., U.S.	E4	115
Colville, stm., Ak., U.S.	A8	124
Colville, Wa., U.S.	A8	124
Colville Indian Reservation, Wa., U.S.	A6	124
Colville Lake, l., N.W. Ter.	C7	66
Colvin Mountain, mtn., Al., U.S.	A3	78
Colvos Passage, strt., Wa., U.S.	f10	124
Colwell, Ia., U.S.	A5	92
Colwich, Ks., U.S.	E6	93
Colwood, B.C.	h12	69
Colwyn Bay, Wales, U.K.	A4	12
Colyell Creek, stm., La., U.S.	h10	95
Comabbio, Lago di, l., Italy	E6	21
Comacchio, Italy	B4	23
Comacchio, Valli di, b., Italy	E8	20
Comal, co., Tx., U.S.	E3	120
Comalapa, Guat.	E6	63
Comalcalco, Mex.	D6	63
Coman, Mount, mtn., Ant.	B6	7
Comanche, Ok., U.S.	C4	113
Comanche, Tx., U.S.	D3	120
Comanche, co., Ks., U.S.	E4	93
Comanche, co., Ok., U.S.	C3	113
Comanche, co., Tx., U.S.	D3	120
Comarapa, Bol.	C3	55
Comayagua, Hond.	E7	63
Combahee, stm., S.C., U.S.	F6	117
Combeaufontaine, Fr.	B1	20
Comber, Ont.	E2	73
Comber, N. Ire., U.K.	C6	11
Combermere, Ont.	B7	73
Combined Locks, Wi., U.S.	h9	126
Combs, Ar., U.S.	B3	81
Combs, Ky., U.S.	C6	94
Comer, Al., U.S.	B3	78
Comer, Ga., U.S.	B3	87
Comfort, stm., Austl.	B7	51
Comfort, N.C., U.S.	B5	110
Comfort, Tx., U.S.	E3	120
Comfort, W.V., U.S.	m12	125
Comfrey, Mn., U.S.	F4	100
Comilla, Bngl.	D9	36
Comines, Bel.	D2	17
Cominto, Ar., U.S.	D4	81
Comiskey, In., U.S.	G6	91
Comiso, Italy	F5	23
Comitán [de Domínguez], Mex.	D6	63
Commack, N.Y., U.S.	*n15	109
Commentry, Fr.	D5	16
Commerce, Ga., U.S.	B3	87
Commerce, Mo., U.S.	D8	102
Commerce, Ok., U.S.	A7	113
Commerce, Tx., U.S.	C5	120
Commerce City, Co., U.S.	B6	83
Commercial Point, Oh., U.S.	C2	112
Commercy, Fr.	C6	16
Commewijne, dept., Sur.	A4	59
Commissaires, Lac des, l., Que.	A5	74
Committee Bay, b., N.W. Ter.	C15	66
Common Fence Point, R.I., U.S.	D6	116
Commonwealth Bay, b., Ant.	C27	7
Commonwealth Range, mts., Ant.	A30	7
Communism Peak, mtn., Sov. Un.	F10	29
Como, Italy	B2	23
Como, Co., U.S.	B5	83
Como, Ms., U.S.	A4	101
Como, N.C., U.S.	A5	110
Como, Tn., U.S.	A3	119
Como, Lago, l., Italy	C5	20
Comobabi, Az., U.S.	E3	80
Comodoro Rivadavia, Arg.	E3	54
Comorin, Cape, c., India	G6	36
Comoros, ctry., Afr.	H10	42
Compass Lake, Fl., U.S.	B1	86
Competition, Mo., U.S.	D5	102
Compiègne, Fr.	C5	16
Compostela, Mex.	m11	63
Comptche, Ca., U.S.	C2	82
Compton, Que.	D6	74
Compton, Ar., U.S.	A2	81
Compton, Ca., U.S.	n12	82
Compton, Il., U.S.	B4	90
Compton, co., Que.	D6	74
Comstock, Mi., U.S.	F5	99
Comstock, Mn., U.S.	D2	100
Comstock, Ne., U.S.	C6	104
Comstock, Tx., U.S.	C1	120
Comstock, Wi., U.S.	C2	126
Comté, stm., Fr. Gu.	C7	59
Comtois, Que.	A5	74
Conakry, Gui.	E2	45
Conanicut Island, i., R.I., U.S.	E5	116
Conanicut Point, c., R.I., U.S.	E5	116
Conasauga, Tn., U.S.	D9	119
Conasauga, stm., U.S.	B1	119
Concan, Tx., U.S.	E3	120
Concarneau, Fr.	D2	16
Conceição das Alagoas, Braz.	C7	57
Conceição do Araguaia, Braz.	E9	59
Conceição do Norte, Braz.	D1	57
Concepción, Arg.	E2	55
Concepción, Bol.	C3	55
Concepción, Chile	D2	54
Concepción, Guat.	D6	63
Concepción, Para.	A4	55
Concepción, Phil.	o13	34
Concepción, Tx., U.S.	F3	120
Concepción, dept., Para.	D4	55
Concepción, Laguna, l., Bol.	C3	55
Concepción, Punta, c., Mex.	D4	63
Concepción del Oro, Mex.	C4	63
Concepción del Uruguay, Arg.	C5	56
Conception, Mo., U.S.	A3	102
Conception, Point, c., Ca., U.S.	E3	82
Conception Bay, b., Newf.	E5	72
Conception Bay South, Newf.	E5	72
Conception Island, i., Bah.	C6	64
Conception Junction, Mo., U.S.	A3	102
Conchas, Braz.	m7	56
Conchas, N.M., U.S.	B5	108
Conchas Lake, res., N.M.	B5	108
Conche, Newf.	C4	72
Concho, Ok., U.S.	B4	113
Conchillas, Ur.	g7	54
Concho, co., Tx., U.S.	D3	120
Conchos, stm., Mex.	B4	63
Concord, Ar., U.S.	B4	81
Concord, Ca., U.S.	h8	82
Concord, Fl., U.S.	B2	86
Concord, Ga., U.S.	C2	87
Concord, Il., U.S.	D3	90
Concord, Ky., U.S.	B6	94
Concord, Ma., U.S.	B5	98
Concord, Mo., U.S.	g13	102
Concord, N.C., U.S.	B2	110
Concord, Pa., U.S.	F6	115
Concord, N.H., U.S.	D9	119
Concord, Tn., U.S.	D9	119
Concord, Vt., U.S.	C5	122
Concord, stm., Ma., U.S.	A5	98
Concordia, Arg.	A5	54
Concordia, Col.	B2	60
Concordia, Peru	B3	58
Concordia, Ks., U.S.	C6	93
Concordia, Mo., U.S.	C4	102
Concordia, co., La., U.S.	C4	95
Concrete, N.D., U.S.	A8	111
Concrete, Wa., U.S.	A4	124
Condamine, stm., Austl.	E9	50
Conde, Braz.	B7	57
Conde, S.D., U.S.	B7	118
Condé [-sur-l'Escaut], Fr.	E9	50
Condé-sur-Marne, Fr.	E4	17
Condé-sur-Noireau, Fr.	C3	16
Condeúba, Braz.	D6	57
Condino, Italy	F8	50
Condobolin, Austl.	F4	51
Condom, Fr.	E4	16
Condon, Mt., U.S.	C3	103
Condon, Or., U.S.	B6	114
Cóndor, Cordillera del, mts., S.A.	B2	58
Cone, Tx., U.S.	C2	120
Conecuh, co., Al., U.S.	D2	78
Conecuh, stm., U.S.	D3	78
Conegliano [Veneto], Italy	B4	23
Conehatta, Ms., U.S.	C4	101
Conejos, Co., U.S.	D4	83
Conejos, co., Co., U.S.	D4	83
Conejos, stm., Co., U.S.	D4	83
Conejos Peak, mtn., Co., U.S.	D4	83
Conemaugh, Pa., U.S.	F4	115
Conemaugh River Lake, res., Pa., U.S.	F3	115
Conestee, S.C., U.S.	B3	117
Conesus Lake, l., N.Y., U.S.	C3	109
Conesville, Ia., U.S.	C6	92
Conesville, Oh., U.S.	B4	112
Conetoe, N.C., U.S.	B5	110
Coney Island (part of New York), N.Y., U.S.	k13	109
Conflans-en-Jarnisy, Fr.	E5	17
Conflans-Sainte-Honorine, Fr.	g9	16
Confluence, Ky., U.S.	C6	94
Confluence, Pa., U.S.	G3	115
Confolens, Fr.	D4	16
Confusion Bay, b., Newf.	D4	72
Confusion Range, mts., Ut., U.S.	D2	121
Confuso, stm., Para.	D4	55
Cong, Ire.	D2	11
Congamond Lakes, l., U.S.	A4	84
Congaree, stm., S.C., U.S.	D6	117
Congaree Swamp National Monument, S.C., U.S.	D6	117
Conger, Mn., U.S.	G5	100
Congers, N.Y., U.S.	*D7	109
Congleton, Eng., U.K.	A5	12
Congo, Oh., U.S.	e8	125
Congo, W.V., U.S.	e8	125
Congo, ctry., Afr.	B2	48
Congo (Zaïre), stm., Afr.	H2	75
Congress, Sask.	C3	80
Congress, Az., U.S.	C3	80
Conifer, Co., U.S.	*B5	83
Conil [de la Frontera], Spain	D2	22
Coninicut Point, c., R.I., U.S.	D5	116
Coniston Water, l., Eng., U.K.	F5	13
Conklin, Alta.	B5	68
Conklin, N.Y., U.S.	C5	109
Conlen, Tx., U.S.	A1	120
Conley, Ga., U.S.	*C2	87
Conn, Lough, l., Ire.	C2	10
Connacht (Connaught), hist. reg., Ire.	D2	11
Connaught see Connacht, hist. reg., Ire.	D2	11
Conneaut, Oh., U.S.	A5	112
Conneaut Creek, stm., Oh., U.S.	A5	112
Conneaut Lake, Pa., U.S.	C1	115
Conneaut Lake, l., Pa., U.S.	C1	115
Conneautville, Pa., U.S.	C1	115
Connecticut, state, U.S.	C5	84
Connecticut, stm., U.S.	C5	84
Connell, Wa., U.S.	C7	124
Connellsville, Pa., U.S.	F2	115
Connelly Springs, N.C., U.S.	B1	110
Conner, Mt., U.S.	E2	103
Connersville, In., U.S.	E7	91
Connoire Bay, b., Newf.	E3	72
Connors, N.B.	B1	71
Conococheague Creek, stm., Md., U.S.	A2	97
Conover, N.C., U.S.	B1	110
Conowingo, Md., U.S.	A5	97
Conowingo Dam, Md., U.S.	A5	97
Conquest, Sask.	F2	75
Conrad, Ia., U.S.	B5	92
Conrad, Mt., U.S.	B5	103
Conrath, Wi., U.S.	C2	126
Conroe, Tx., U.S.	D5	120
Conroy, La., U.S.	C6	92
Consecon, Ont.	C7	73
Conselheiro Lafaiete, Braz.	F7	57
Consett, Eng., U.K.	F7	13
Conshohocken, Pa., U.S.	F11	115
Consolación del Sur, Cuba	C2	64
Con Son, is., Viet.	J5	34
Consort, Alta.	C5	68
Constable, N.Y., U.S.	f10	109
Constableville, N.Y., U.S.	B5	109
Constance, Ky., U.S.	*A5	94
Constance, Lake, l., Eur.	H9	18
Constance see Konstanz, Ger.		
Constanța, Rom.	C9	24
Constantia, N.Y., U.S.	B4	109
Constantina, Spain	D3	22
Constantine (Qacentina), Alg.	B7	40
Constantine, Cape, c., Ak., U.S.	D8	79
Constantinople see İstanbul, Tur.	B7	40
Constitución, Chile	D2	54
Consuegra, Spain	C4	22
Consul, Sask.	H1	75
Contact, Nv., U.S.	B7	105
Contai, India	G11	37
Contamana, Peru	C3	58
Contas, Rio de, stm., Braz.	C8	57
Contendas do Sincorá, Braz.	A4	56
Content Keys, is., Fl., U.S.	H5	86
Continental, Oh., U.S.	A1	112
Continental Divide, N.M., U.S.	B1	108
Continental Peak, mtn., Wy., U.S.	D4	127
Continental Reservoir, res., Co., U.S.	D3	83
Contoocook, N.H., U.S.	D3	106
Contoocook, stm., N.H., U.S.	D3	106
Contra Costa, co., Ca., U.S.	B3	60
Contratación, Col.	B2	60
Contrecoeur, Que.	D4	74
Contreras, N.M., U.S.	C3	108
Contrexéville, Fr.	A1	20
Contumazá, Peru	C2	58
Contwoyto Lake, l., N.W. Ter.	C10	66
Convent, La., U.S.	D5	95
Converse, In., U.S.	C6	91
Converse, La., U.S.	C2	95
Converse, S.C., U.S.	B4	117
Converse, Tx., U.S.	*E3	120
Converse, co., Wy., U.S.	C7	127
Convoy, Oh., U.S.	B1	112
Conway, P.E.I.	C6	71
Conway, Ar., U.S.	B3	81
Conway, Fl., U.S.	D5	86
Conway, Ia., U.S.	D3	92
Conway, Ks., U.S.	D6	93
Conway, Ma., U.S.	A2	98
Conway, Mo., U.S.	D5	102
Conway, N.H., U.S.	C4	106
Conway, N.C., U.S.	A5	110
Conway, N.D., U.S.	A8	111
Conway, Pa., U.S.	E1	115
Conway, S.C., U.S.	D9	117
Conway, Wales, U.K.	A4	12
Conway, Lake, res., Ar., U.S.	B3	81
Conway, Lake, l., N.H., U.S.	C4	106
Conway Springs, Ks., U.S.	E6	93
Conwy, Wales, U.K.	A4	12
Conyers, Ga., U.S.	C2	87
Cook, Austl.	F5	50
Cook, Mn., U.S.	C6	100
Cook, Ne., U.S.	D9	104
Cook, co., Ga., U.S.	E3	87
Cook, co., Il., U.S.	B6	90
Cook, co., Mn., U.S.	k9	100
Cook, Cape, c., B.C.	D4	69
Cook, Mount, mtn., N.Z.	O13	51
Cooke, co., Tx., U.S.	C4	120
Cooke City, Mt., U.S.	E7	103
Cookes Peak, mtn., N.M., U.S.	E2	108
Cookeville, Tn., U.S.	C8	119
Cook Ice Shelf, ice, Ant.	C28	7
Cook Inlet, b., Ak., U.S.	D9	79
Cook Islands, ctry., Oc.	G12	6
Cook Mountain, mtn., W.V., U.S.	n12	125
Cook Point, c., Md., U.S.	C5	97
Cooks, Mi., U.S.	C4	99
Cooksburg, Pa., U.S.	D3	115
Cooks Falls, N.Y., U.S.	D6	109
Cookshire, Que.	D6	74
Cooks Harbour, Newf.	C4	72
Cooks Mills, Il., U.S.	D5	90
Cookson, Ok., U.S.	B7	113
Cookstown, Ont.	C5	73
Cookstown, N. Ire., U.K.	C5	11
Cook Strait, strt., N.Z.	N15	51
Cooksville, Il., U.S.	C5	90
Cooktown, Austl.	C8	50
Cookville, Tx., U.S.	C5	120
Coolaney, Ire.	C3	11
Cooleemee, N.C., U.S.	B2	110
Coolgardie, Austl.	F3	50
Coolidge, Az., U.S.	E4	80
Coolidge, Ga., U.S.	E3	87
Coolidge, Ks., U.S.	E2	93
Coolidge, Tx., U.S.	D4	120
Coolidge, Mount, mtn., S.D., U.S.	D2	118
Coolin, Id., U.S.	A2	89
Cool Ridge, W.V., U.S.	D3	125
Coolspring, Pa., U.S.	D3	115
Coolville, Oh., U.S.	C4	112
Cooma, Austl.	G8	50
Coonabarabran, Austl.	F8	50
Coonamble, Austl.	F8	50
Coon Rapids, Ia., U.S.	C3	92
Coon Rapids, Mn., U.S.	E5	100
Coon Valley, Wi., U.S.	E2	126
Cooper, Ia., U.S.	C3	92
Cooper, Tx., U.S.	C5	120
Cooper, co., Mo., U.S.	C5	102
Cooper, stm., S.C., U.S.	F8	117
Cooper, East Branch, stm., S.C., U.S.	E8	117
Cooper, West Branch, stm., S.C., U.S.	E8	117
Co Operative, Ky., U.S.	D5	94
Cooper City, Fl., U.S.	*F6	86
Cooper Creek, stm., Austl.	E7	50
Cooper Mountain, mtn., Ak., U.S.	g17	79
Coopers, La., U.S.	*B2	95
Coopersburg, Pa., U.S.	F11	115
Coopers Mills, Me., U.S.	D3	96
Cooperstown, N.Y., U.S.	C6	109
Cooperstown, N.D., U.S.	B7	111
Coopersville, Mi., U.S.	E5	99
Cooperton, Ok., U.S.	C3	113
Coopertown, Tn., U.S.	A5	119
Coos, co., N.H., U.S.	A4	106
Coos, co., Or., U.S.	D2	114
Coos, stm., Or., U.S.	D2	114
Coosa, Ga., U.S.	B1	87
Coosa, co., Al., U.S.	C3	78
Coosa, stm., U.S.	C3	78
Coosada, Al., U.S.	C3	78
Coosawattee, stm., Ga., U.S.	B2	87
Coosawhatchie, S.C., U.S.	F6	117
Coosawhatchie, stm., S.C., U.S.	F5	117
Coos Bay, Or., U.S.	D2	114
Cootehill, Ire.	C4	11
Cooter, Mo., U.S.	E8	102
Copacabana, Bol.	C2	55
Copainalá, Mex.	D6	63
Copake, N.Y., U.S.	C7	109
Copalis Beach, Wa., U.S.	B1	124
Copalis Crossing, Wa., U.S.	C2	124
Copán, Hond.	A6	113
Cope, Co., U.S.	B8	83
Cope, S.C., U.S.	E5	117
Copeland, Fl., U.S.	G5	86
Copeland, Ks., U.S.	E3	93
Copemish, Mi., U.S.	D4	99
Copen, W.V., U.S.	C4	125
Copenhagen (København), Den.	J5	14
Copenhagen, N.Y., U.S.	B5	109

Name	Map Ref.	Page

Copetonas, Arg. — B4 54
Copeville, Tx., U.S. — m10 120
Copiague, N.Y., U.S. — *n15 109
Copiah, co., Ms., U.S. — D3 101
Copiapó, Chile — E1 55
Copiapó, stm., Chile — E1 55
Coplay, Pa., U.S. — E10 115
Copparo, Italy — B3 23
Coppename, stm., Sur. — A3 59
Copper, stm., Ak., U.S. — C11 79
Copperas Cove, Tx., U.S. — D4 120
Copperbelt, prov., Zam. — D4 48
Copper Butte, mtn., Wa., U.S. — A7 124
Copper Center, Ak., U.S. — C10 79
Copper Cliff (part of Sudbury), Ont. — A3 73
Copper Harbor, Mi., U.S. — A3 99
Copperhill, Tn., U.S. — D9 119
Copper Hill, Va., U.S. — C2 123
Coppermine, N.W. Ter. — C9 66
Coppermine, stm., N.W. Ter. — C10 66
Copper Mountain, B.C. — E7 69
Copper Mountain, mtn., Wy., U.S. — C5 127
Copper Mountains, mtn., Az., U.S. — E2 80
Copper Ridge, mtn., Tn., U.S. — m13 119
Copper Ridge, mtn., Va., U.S. — f9 123
Copperton, Ut., U.S. — *C3 121
Coppet, Switz. — D1 21
Copton Creek, stm., Alta. — B1 68
Coqên, China — B10 37
Coquet, stm., Eng., U.K. — E7 13
Coquille, Or., U.S. — D2 114
Coquimbo, Chile — E1 55
Coquimbo, prov., Chile — F1 55
Cora, Wy., U.S. — D3 127
Corabia, Rom. — D7 24
Coração de Jesus, Braz. — B4 56
Coracora, Peru — E3 58
Coral, Ont. — o19 73
Coral, Mi., U.S. — E5 99
Coral, Pa., U.S. — F3 115
Coral Gables, Fl., U.S. — G6 86
Coral Hills, Md., U.S. — *C4 97
Coral Sea, Oc. — G9 6
Coral Springs, Fl., U.S. — *F6 86
Coral Terrace, Fl., U.S. — *G6 86
Coralville, Ia., U.S. — C6 92
Coralville Lake, res., Ia., U.S. — C5 92
Coral Way Village, Fl., U.S. — *G6 86
Coram, Mt., U.S. — B2 103
Coram, N.Y., U.S. — *n15 109
Corangamite, Lake, l., Austl. — I4 51
Coraopolis, Pa., U.S. — E1 115
Corato, Italy — D6 23
Corbeil [-Essonnes], Fr. — C5 16
Corbeny, Fr. — E3 17
Corbett, N.Y., U.S. — C5 109
Corbetton, Ont. — C4 73
Corbie, Fr. — C5 16
Corbin, Ks., U.S. — E6 93
Corbin, Ky., U.S. — D5 94
Corbin, Mt., U.S. — D4 103
Corbin City, N.J., U.S. — E3 107
Corby, Eng., U.K. — B7 12
Corcoran, Ca., U.S. — D4 82
Corcoran, Mn., U.S. — m11 100
Corcovado, Golfo, b., Chile — C2 54
Cord, Ar., U.S. — B4 81
Cordaville, Ma., U.S. — g9 98
Cordele, Ga., U.S. — E3 87
Cordell, Ok., U.S. — B3 113
Cordell Hull Lake, res., Tn., U.S. — C8 119
Corder, Mo., U.S. — B4 102
Cordesville, S.C., U.S. — E8 117
Cordillera, dept., Para. — D4 55
Córdoba, Arg. — A4 54
Córdoba, Mex. — n15 63
Córdoba, Spain — D3 22
Córdoba, prov., Arg. — A4 54
Córdoba, dept., Col. — B2 60
Cordon, Phil. — n13 34
Córdova, Peru — D2 58
Cordova, Al., U.S. — B2 78
Cordova, Ak., U.S. — C10 79
Cordova, Il., U.S. — B3 90
Cordova, Md., U.S. — C6 97
Cordova, Ne., U.S. — *D8 104
Cordova, N.M., U.S. — A4 108
Cordova, N.C., U.S. — C3 110
Cordova, S.C., U.S. — E6 117
Cordova, Tn., U.S. — B2 119
Cordova Mines, Ont. — C7 73
Cordova Peak, mtn., Ak., U.S. — C10 79
Corea, Me., U.S. — D5 96
Coreaú, Braz. — B2 57
Corella, Spain — A5 22
Corfu, N.Y., U.S. — C2 109
Corfu see Kérkira, i., Grc. — C2 40
Cori, Italy — h9 23
Corigliano, Italy — E6 23
Corinna, Me., U.S. — D3 96
Corinne, Mn., U.S. — B5 99
Corinne, Ut., U.S. — B3 121
Corinne, W.V., U.S. — *D3 125
Corinne Key, i., Fl., U.S. — G6 86
Corinth, Ga., U.S. — C2 87
Corinth, Ky., U.S. — B5 94
Corinth, Ms., U.S. — A5 101
Corinth, N.Y., U.S. — B7 109
Corinth, Vt., U.S. — C4 122
Corinth, W.V., U.S. — B5 125
Corinth, Bay of, b., Grc. — h9 25
Corinth, Gulf of, b., Grc. — C4 25
Corinth Canal, Grc. — h10 25
Corinto, Nic. — B4 56
Corinto, Braz. — E7 63
Corisco, Isla de, i., Eq. Gui. — E1 46
Cork, N.B. — D3 71
Cork, Ire. — E2 10
Cork, co., Ire. — F3 11
Cork Harbour, b., Ire. — E2 10
Corleone, Italy — F4 23
Çorlu, Tur. — B6 40
Cormeilles-en-Parisis, Fr. — g9 16
Cormoran Reef, rf., Palau — R17 52
Cormorant, Man. — B1 70
Cormorant Lake, l., Man. — B1 70
Corn, Ok., U.S. — B3 113
Cornaca, S.C., U.S. — C3 117
Cornelia, Ga., U.S. — B3 87
Cornelius, N.C., U.S. — B2 110
Cornelius, Or., U.S. — g11 114
Cornell, Il., U.S. — C5 90
Cornell, Wi., U.S. — C2 126
Cornellà, Spain — B7 22
Corner Brook, Newf. — D3 72
Corner Inlet, b., Austl. — I6 51
Cornerstone, Ar., U.S. — C4 81
Cornersville, Tn., U.S. — B5 119
Cornville, Ar., U.S. — D4 81

Cornfield Point, c., Ct., U.S. — D6 84
Cornhill, N.B. — D4 71
Cornimont, Fr. — B2 20
Corning, Sask. — H4 75
Corning, Ar., U.S. — A5 81
Corning, Ca., U.S. — C2 82
Corning, Ia., U.S. — D3 92
Corning, Ks., U.S. — C7 93
Corning, Mo., U.S. — A2 102
Corning, N.Y., U.S. — C3 109
Corning, Oh., U.S. — C3 112
Cornish, Me., U.S. — E2 96
Cornish, Ok., U.S. — C4 113
Cornish, Ut., U.S. — B4 121
Cornish Flat, N.H., U.S. — D2 106
Cornish Center, N.H., U.S. — D2 106
Cornish Mills, N.H., U.S. — D2 106
Cornishville, Ky., U.S. — C5 94
Corno Grande, mtn., Italy — C4 23
Cornucopia, Wi., U.S. — B2 126
Cornville, Me., U.S. — D3 96
Cornwall, Ont. — B10 73
Cornwall, Ct., U.S. — B2 84
Cornwall, Pa., U.S. — F9 115
Cornwall, Vt., U.S. — D2 122
Cornwall, Va., U.S. — C2 123
Cornwall, co., Eng., U.K. — D3 12
Cornwall Bridge, Ct., U.S. — B2 84
Cornwallis Island, i., N.W. Ter. — m33 66
Cornwall Island, i., N.W. Ter. — m32 66
Cornwall-on-Hudson, N.Y., U.S. — D6 109
Cornwells Heights, Pa., U.S. — o22 115
Coro, Ven. — A4 60
Coroatá, Braz. — B2 57
Corocoro, Bol. — C2 55
Coroico, Bol. — C2 55
Corolla, N.C., U.S. — A7 110
Coromandel Coast, India — F7 36
Coromandel Peninsula, pen., N.Z. — L15 51
Corona, Ca., U.S. — B2 78
Corona, Ca., U.S. — F5 82
Corona, N.M., U.S. — C4 108
Corona, S.D., U.S. — B9 118
Coronach, Sask. — H3 75
Coronado, Ca., U.S. — F5 82
Coronado, Co., U.S. — *B6 83
Coronado, Bahía de, b., C.R. — F6 62
Coronado National Memorial, Az., U.S. — F5 80
Coronation, Alta. — C5 68
Coronation Gulf, b., N.W. Ter. — C10 66
Coronation Island, i., B.A.T. — C2 7
Coronation Island, i., Ak., U.S. — n22 79
Coronda, Arg. — A4 54
Coronel, Chile — B2 54
Coronel Dorrego, Arg. — B4 54
Coronel Murta, Braz. — B4 56
Coronel Oviedo, Para. — E4 55
Coronel Pringles, Arg. — B4 54
Coronel Suárez, Arg. — B4 54
Coronie, dept., Sur. — A3 59
Coropuna, Nevado, mtn., Peru — F3 58
Corowa, Austl. — G6 51
Corozal, Belize — D7 64
Corozal, Col. — B2 60
Corozal, Switz. — C3 21
Corpataux, Switz. — D3 54
Corpen, Arg. — E1 20
Corps, Fr. — E1 20
Corpus Christi, Tx., U.S. — F4 120
Corpus Christi Naval Air Station, mil., Tx., U.S. — F4 120
Corral, Chile — B2 54
Corral, Id., U.S. — F4 89
Corral de Almaguer, Spain — C4 22
Corrales, Col. — B3 60
Corralillo, Cuba — C3 64
Corraun, Ire. — D2 11
Correctionville, Ia., U.S. — B2 92
Corregidor Island, i., Phil. — o13 34
Correll, Mn., U.S. — E2 100
Corrente, Braz. — D1 57
Correntes, Braz. — k5 57
Correntina, Braz. — A4 56
Corrib, Lough, l., Ire. — D2 10
Corrientes, Arg. — E4 55
Corrientes, prov., Arg. — E4 55
Corrientes, stm., Arg. — E4 55
Corrientes, stm., S.A. — A3 59
Corrientes, Cabo, c., Col. — B2 60
Corrientes, Cabo, c., Cuba — D1 64
Corrientes, Cabo, c., Mex. — C3 63
Corrientes, Ensenada de, b., Cuba — D1 64
Corrigan, Tx., U.S. — D5 120
Corriganville, Md., U.S. — k13 97
Corrofin, Ire. — E2 11
Corry, Pa., U.S. — C2 115
Corryton, Tn., U.S. — C10 119
Corse, Cap, c., Fr. — C2 23
Corsica, Pa., U.S. — D3 115
Corsica, S.D., U.S. — D7 118
Corsica, i., Fr. — C2 23
Corsicana, Tx., U.S. — C4 120
Corson, S.D., U.S. — D9 118
Corson, co., S.D., U.S. — B4 118
Cortazar, Mex. — *h7 82
Corte, Fr. — C2 23
Corte Alto, Chile — E2 54
Cortegana, Spain — D2 22
Corte Madera, Ca., U.S. — *h7 82
Cortemilia, Italy — E4 20
Cortes [de la Frontera], Spain — D3 22
Cortez, Co., U.S. — D2 83
Cortez, Fl., U.S. — q10 86
Cortez Mountains, mts., Nv., U.S. — C5 105
Cortina d'Ampezzo, Italy — A4 23
Cortland, Il., U.S. — B5 90
Cortland, Ne., U.S. — D9 104
Cortland, N.Y., U.S. — C4 109
Cortland, Oh., U.S. — A5 112
Cortland, co., N.Y., U.S. — C4 109
Cortona, Italy — C3 23
Coruche, Port. — C1 22
Çorum, stm., Asia — B13 40
Çorum, Tur. — B10 40
Çorumbá, stm., Braz. — B1 56
Corumbá, Braz. — B3 56
Corunna, Ont. — E2 73
Corunna, In., U.S. — B7 91
Corunna, Mi., U.S. — F6 99
Corvallis, Mt., U.S. — D2 103
Corvallis, Or., U.S. — C3 114
Corvo, i., Port. — g8 44
Corwin, Ia., U.S. — A3 92
Corwith, Ia., U.S. — B4 92
Corwin Springs, Mt., U.S. — E6 103
Cory, In., U.S. — F3 91
Corydon, In., U.S. — H5 91

Corydon, Ia., U.S. — D4 92
Corydon, Ky., U.S. — C2 94
Coryell, co., Tx., U.S. — D4 120
Cos see Kos, i., Grc. — D6 40
Cosalá, Mex. — C3 63
Cosamaloapan [de Carpio], Mex. — D5 63
Cosby, Mo., U.S. — A3 102
Cosby, Tn., U.S. — D10 119
Coscomatepec [de Bravo], Mex. — n15 63
Cosegüina, Punta, c., Nic. — D4 62
Cosenza, Italy — E6 23
Coshocton, Oh., U.S. — B4 112
Coshocton, co., Oh., U.S. — B4 112
Cosmopolis, Wa., U.S. — C2 124
Cosmos, Mn., U.S. — F4 100
Cosne, Fr. — D5 16
Cossatot, stm., Ar., U.S. — C1 81
Cossatot Mountains, mtn., Ar., U.S. — C2 81
Cossonay, Switz. — C2 20
Costa Mesa, Ca., U.S. — n13 82
Costa Rica, ctry., N.A. — F6 62
Costello, Pa., U.S. — C5 115
Costelloe, Ire. — D2 11
Costigan, Me., U.S. — C4 96
Costilla, N.M., U.S. — A4 108
Costilla, co., Co., U.S. — D5 83
Coswig, Ger. — B8 19
Coswig, Ger. — B7 19
Cotabato, Phil. — D6 34
Cotagaita, Bol. — D2 55
Cotahuasi, Peru — E3 58
Coteau, N.D., U.S. — A3 111
Coteau-Landing, Que. — D3 74
Coteaux, Haiti — E6 64
Côte d'Or, reg., Fr. — D6 16
Côtes de Fer, Haiti — E7 64
Cotesfield, Ne., U.S. — C7 104
Cotija de la Paz, Mex. — n12 63
Cotingo, stm., Braz. — B2 59
Cotonou, Benin — E5 45
Cotopaxi, Co., U.S. — C5 83
Cotopaxi, prov., Ec. — B2 58
Cotopaxi, vol., Ec. — B2 58
Cotswold Hills, hills, Eng., U.K. — E5 10
Cottage Grove, Mn., U.S. — n13 100
Cottage Grove, Or., U.S. — D3 114
Cottage Grove, Tn., U.S. — A3 119
Cottage Grove Reservoir, res., Or., U.S. — D3 114
Cottageville, S.C., U.S. — F7 117
Cottageville, W.V., U.S. — C3 125
Cottam, Ont. — E2 73
Cottbus, Ger. — C7 18
Cottel Island, i., Newf. — D5 72
Cotter, Ar., U.S. — A3 81
Cottian Alps, mts., Eur. — B7 16
Cottle, co., Tx., U.S. — B2 120
Cottle Knob, mtn., W.V., U.S. — C4 125
Cottleville, Mo., U.S. — f12 102
Cotton, Ga., U.S. — E2 87
Cotton, Mn., U.S. — C6 100
Cotton, co., Ok., U.S. — C3 113
Cotton Center, Tx., U.S. — B1 120
Cottondale, Al., U.S. — B2 78
Cottondale, Fl., U.S. — B1 86
Cottonpatch Hill, De., U.S. — F5 85
Cotton Plant, Ar., U.S. — B4 81
Cottonport, La., U.S. — C3 95
Cottonton, Al., U.S. — C4 78
Cottonwood, Al., U.S. — A5 119
Cottonwood, Az., U.S. — C3 80
Cottonwood, Ca., U.S. — B2 82
Cottonwood, Id., U.S. — C2 89
Cottonwood, Mn., U.S. — F3 100
Cottonwood, Ok., U.S. — C5 113
Cottonwood, S.D., U.S. — D4 118
Cottonwood, Tx., U.S. — C3 120
Cottonwood, Ut., U.S. — *C4 121
Cottonwood, co., Mn., U.S. — F3 100
Cottonwood, stm., Ks., U.S. — D7 93
Cottonwood, stm., Mn., U.S. — F3 100
Cottonwood Cove, Nv., U.S. — H7 105
Cottonwood Creek, stm., Wy., U.S. — D2 127
Cottonwood Creek, stm., Wy., U.S. — C4 127
Cottonwood Heights, Ut., U.S. — *C4 121
Cottonwood Wash, val., Ut., U.S. — F6 121
Cotuit, Ma., U.S. — C7 98
Cotulla, Tx., U.S. — E3 120
Couchiching, Lake, l., Ont. — C5 73
Couchwood, La., U.S. — B2 95
Coudekerque-Branche, Fr. — B5 16
Couderay, Wi., U.S. — C2 126
Coudersport, Pa., U.S. — C5 115
Coudres, Île aux, i., Que. — B7 74
Couëron, Fr. — D3 16
Cougar, Wa., U.S. — C3 124
Cougar Reservoir, res., Or., U.S. — C4 114
Couhé, Fr. — A3 111
Coulee City, Wa., U.S. — B6 124
Coulee Creek, stm., Wa., U.S. — g13 124
Coulee Dam, Wa., U.S. — B7 124
Coulee Dam National Recreation Area, Wa., U.S. — A7 124
Coulman Island, i., Ant. — B29 7
Coulommiers, Fr. — C5 16
Coulsdon (part of London), Eng., U.K. — m12 10
Coulter, Ia., U.S. — B4 92
Coulterville, Ca., U.S. — D3 82
Coulterville, Il., U.S. — E4 90
Coulwood, Va., U.S. — f9 123
Counce, Tn., U.S. — B3 119
Council, Ga., U.S. — F4 87
Council, Id., U.S. — E2 89
Council, N.C., U.S. — C4 110
Council, Ks., U.S. — E8 93
Council Bluffs, Ia., U.S. — C2 92
Council Grove, Ks., U.S. — D7 93
Council Grove Lake, res., Ks., U.S. — D7 93
Council Hill, Ok., U.S. — B6 113
Council Mountain, mtn., Id., U.S. — E2 89
Country Club Hills, Il., U.S. — *k9 90
Country Homes, Wa., U.S. — *B8 124
Countryside, Il., U.S. — *k9 90
Countyline, Ok., U.S. — C4 113
Coupar Angus, Scot., U.K. — B5 10
Coupeville, Wa., U.S. — A3 124
Coupon, Pa., U.S. — F5 115
Courantyne, stm., S.A. — A3 59
Courbevoie, Fr. — g10 16
Courcelles, Que. — D7 74
Courceval, Que. — D4 74
Courland Lagoon, b., Sov. Un. — D2 29
Courmayeur, Italy — D2 20
Coursan, Fr. — F5 16

Courtenay, B.C. — E5 69
Courtenay, N.D., U.S. — B7 111
Courte Oreilles, Lac, l., Wi., U.S. — C2 126
Courtland, Ont. — E4 73
Courtland, Al., U.S. — A2 78
Courtland, Ks., U.S. — C6 93
Courtland, Mn., U.S. — F4 100
Courtland, Ms., U.S. — A4 101
Courtland, Va., U.S. — D5 123
Courtmacsherry, Ire. — F3 11
Courtrai see Kortrijk, Bel. — B5 16
Courtright, Ont. — E2 73
Coushatta, La., U.S. — B2 95
Coutances, Fr. — C3 16
Coutras, Fr. — E3 16
Coutts, Alta. — E5 68
Couvin, Bel. — D4 17
Cove, Ar., U.S. — C1 81
Cove, Mn., U.S. — D5 100
Cove, Or., U.S. — B9 114
Cove City, N.C., U.S. — B5 110
Cove Creek, stm., Ut., U.S. — E3 121
Covedale, Oh., U.S. — o12 112
Covelo, Ca., U.S. — C2 82
Coventry, Ct., U.S. — B6 84
Coventry, De., U.S. — *B3 85
Coventry, R.I., U.S. — D3 116
Coventry, Vt., U.S. — B4 122
Cove Point, Md., U.S. — D5 97
Cove Point, c., Md., U.S. — D5 97
Coverdales Crossroads, De., U.S. — F3 85
Covered Wells, Az., U.S. — E3 80
Covert, Mi., U.S. — F4 99
Covesville, Va., U.S. — C4 123
Coviłhã, Port. — E3 22
Covina, Ca., U.S. — m13 82
Covington, Ga., U.S. — C3 87
Covington, In., U.S. — D3 91
Covington, Ky., U.S. — A5 94
Covington, La., U.S. — D5 95
Covington, Mi., U.S. — B2 99
Covington, Oh., U.S. — B1 112
Covington, Ok., U.S. — A4 113
Covington, Tn., U.S. — B2 119
Covington, Va., U.S. — C2 123
Covington, co., Al., U.S. — D3 78
Covington, co., Ms., U.S. — D4 101
Cowal, Lake, l., Austl. — F6 51
Cowan, In., U.S. — D7 91
Cowan, Tn., U.S. — B5 119
Cowan, stm., Sask. — C2 75
Cowan, Lake, l., Austl. — F3 50
Cowangie, Austl. — G3 51
Cowan Knob, mtn., Ar., U.S. — B2 81
Cowansville, Que. — D5 74
Cowansville, Pa., U.S. — E2 115
Coward, S.C., U.S. — D8 117
Cowarts, Al., U.S. — D4 78
Cow Creek, stm., Ks., U.S. — D5 93
Cow Creek, stm., Wa., U.S. — C7 124
Cowden, Il., U.S. — D5 90
Cowdenbeath, Scot., U.K. — D5 13
Cowee Mountains, mts., N.C., U.S. — f9 110
Cowen, W.V., U.S. — C4 125
Cowen, Mount, mtn., Mt., U.S. — E6 103
Cowes, Eng., U.K. — E6 10
Coweta, Ok., U.S. — B6 113
Coweta, co., Ga., U.S. — C2 87
Cowgill, Mo., U.S. — B4 102
Cow Head, Newf. — D3 72
Cowiche, Wa., U.S. — C5 124
Cowichan, co., N.C., U.S. — C3 110
Cowichan Bay, B.C. — g12 69
Cowichan Lake, l., B.C. — E5 69
Cowiche, Wa., U.S. — C5 124
Cowley, Alta. — E4 68
Cowley, Wy., U.S. — B4 127
Cowley, co., Ks., U.S. — E7 93
Cowley, Az., U.S. — F4 80
Cowling, Il., U.S. — E6 90
Cowlington, Ok., U.S. — B7 113
Cowlitz, co., Wa., U.S. — C3 124
Cowlitz, stm., Wa., U.S. — C3 124
Cowpasture, stm., Va., U.S. — B3 123
Cowpens, S.C., U.S. — A4 117
Cowra, Austl. — F7 51
Cowskin Creek, stm., Ks., U.S. — g11 93
Cow Springs, Az., U.S. — A5 80
Coxburg, Ms., U.S. — B3 101
Coxsackie, N.Y., U.S. — C7 109
Cox's Cove, Newf. — D2 72
Coxs Mills, W.V., U.S. — B4 125
Coy, Al., U.S. — D2 78
Coy, Ar., U.S. — C4 81
Coyame, Mex. — B3 63
Coyanosa Draw, val., Tx., U.S. — D1 120
Coya Sur, Chile — D2 55
Coyoacán (part of Mexico City), Mex. — m12 19
Coyote, N.M., U.S. — A3 108
Coyote Basin, Co., U.S. — A2 83
Coyuca de Catalán, Mex. — n13 63
Coyuca, Ks., U.S. — E8 93
Cozad, Ne., U.S. — D6 104
Cozahome, Ar., U.S. — A3 81
Cozumel, Mex. — C7 63
Cozumel, Isla de, i., Mex. — C7 63
Crab Creek, stm., Wa., U.S. — B7 124
Crab Creek, stm., Wa., U.S. — C6 124
Crab Orchard, Ky., U.S. — C5 94
Crab Orchard, Tn., U.S. — D8 119
Crab Orchard, W.V., U.S. — D3 125
Crab Orchard Lake, res., Il., U.S. — F4 90
Crab Orchard Mountains, mts., Tn., U.S. — D8 119
Crabtree, Or., U.S. — C4 114
Crabtree Mills, Que. — D4 74
Cracking, stm., Sask. — D4 75
Cracow, Austl. — D9 51
Cradock, S. Afr. — H5 48
Craftsbury, Vt., U.S. — B4 122

Craftsbury Common, Vt., U.S. — B4 122
Cragford, Al., U.S. — B4 78
Craig, Ak., U.S. — D13 79
Craig, Co., U.S. — A3 83
Craig, Ia., U.S. — B1 92
Craig, Mo., U.S. — A2 102
Craig, Mt., U.S. — C5 103
Craig, Ne., U.S. — C9 104
Craig, co., Ok., U.S. — A6 113
Craig, co., Va., U.S. — C2 123
Craig Air Force Base, mil., Al., U.S. — C3 78
Craig Creek, stm., Va., U.S. — C2 123
Craighead, co., Ar., U.S. — B5 81
Craigmont, Id., U.S. — C2 89
Craigmyle, Alta. — D4 68
Craigsville, Va., U.S. — B3 123
Craigsville, W.V., U.S. — C4 125
Craigville, In., U.S. — C7 91
Craik, Sask. — F3 75
Crail, Scot., U.K. — D6 13
Crailsheim, Ger. — D5 18
Craiova, Rom. — C6 24
Cramerton, N.C., U.S. — B1 110
Cranberry, Pa., U.S. — D2 115
Cranberry Isles, Me., U.S. — D4 96
Cranberry Lake, N.Y., U.S. — A6 109
Cranberry Lake, l., N.Y., U.S. — A6 109
Cranberry Portage, Man. — B1 70
Cranbrook, B.C. — E10 69
Cranbury, N.J., U.S. — C3 107
Crandall, Sask. — B2 87
Crandall, S.D., U.S. — B8 118
Crandall, Tx., U.S. — n10 120
Crandon, Wi., U.S. — C5 126
Crane, Az., U.S. — E1 80
Crane, In., U.S. — G4 91
Crane, Mo., U.S. — E4 102
Crane, Mt., U.S. — C12 103
Crane, Or., U.S. — D8 114
Crane, Tx., U.S. — D1 120
Crane, co., Tx., U.S. — D1 120
Crane Creek, stm., Oh., U.S. — e7 112
Crane Creek Reservoir, res., Id., U.S. — E2 89
Crane Hill, Al., U.S. — A2 78
Crane Lake, Mn., U.S. — B6 100
Crane Lake, l., Sask. — G1 75
Crane Lake, l., Il., U.S. — C3 90
Crane Lake, l., Mn., U.S. — B6 100
Crane Mountain, mtn., Or., U.S. — E6 114
Crane Prairie Reservoir, res., Or., U.S. — D5 114
Cranesville, Pa., U.S. — C1 115
Crane Valley, Sask. — H3 75
Cranfield, Ms., U.S. — D2 101
Cranford, N.J., U.S. — B4 107
Cransac, Fr. — E5 16
Cranston, R.I., U.S. — C4 116
Cranston, co., N.C., U.S. — B5 110
Crapaud, P.E.I. — C6 71
Crapo, Md., U.S. — D5 97
Crary, N.D., U.S. — A7 111
Crary Mountains, mts., Ant. — B1 7
Crasna, stm., Eur. — B6 24
Crater Lake, Or., U.S. — E4 114
Crater Lake, l., St. Vin. — U26 65
Crater Lake National Park, Or., U.S. — E4 114
Craters of the Moon National Monument, Id., U.S. — F5 89
Cratéus, Braz. — C2 57
Crato, Braz. — C3 57
Craughwell, Ire. — D3 11
Craven, Sask. — G3 75
Craven, co., N.C., U.S. — B5 110
Cravinhos, Braz. — k8 56
Crawford, Co., U.S. — C3 83
Crawford, Ga., U.S. — C3 87
Crawford, Ms., U.S. — B5 101
Crawford, Ne., U.S. — B2 104
Crawford, Tn., U.S. — C8 119
Crawford, co., Ar., U.S. — B1 81
Crawford, co., Ga., U.S. — D3 87
Crawford, co., Il., U.S. — D6 90
Crawford, co., In., U.S. — H4 91
Crawford, co., Ia., U.S. — B2 92
Crawford, co., Ks., U.S. — E9 93
Crawford, co., Mi., U.S. — D6 99
Crawford, co., Mo., U.S. — D6 102
Crawford, co., Oh., U.S. — B3 112
Crawford, co., Pa., U.S. — C1 115
Crawford, co., Wi., U.S. — E3 126
Crawford Bay, B.C. — E9 69
Crawford Notch, N.H., U.S. — B4 106
Crawford Notch State Park, N.H., U.S. — B4 106
Crawfordsville, Ar., U.S. — B5 81
Crawfordsville, In., U.S. — D4 91
Crawfordsville, Or., U.S. — C4 114
Crawfordville, Fl., U.S. — B2 86
Crawfordville, Ga., U.S. — C4 87
Crawley, Eng., U.K. — C7 12
Crayne, Ky., U.S. — e9 94
Crazy Mountains, mts., Mt., U.S. — D6 103
Crazy Peak, mtn., Mt., U.S. — D6 103
Crazy Woman Creek, stm., Wy., U.S. — B6 127
Creal Springs, Il., U.S. — F5 90
Creamridge, N.J., U.S. — C3 107
Crean Lake, l., Sask. — C2 75
Creamery, Ks., U.S. — E8 93
Credit, stm., Ont. — D4 73
Crediton, Eng., U.K. — D4 12
Crediton, Ont. — D3 73
Cree, stm., Sask. — E11 66
Creede, Co., U.S. — D4 83
Creedmoor, N.C., U.S. — A4 110
Creek, co., Ok., U.S. — B5 113
Creek Village, Bah. — m18 64
Creelman, Sask. — H4 75
Creeslough, Ire. — D3 11
Cregganbaun, Ire. — D2 11
Creighton, Mo., U.S. — C3 102
Creighton, Ne., U.S. — B8 104
Creighton, Pa., U.S. — h14 115
Creighton, Sask. — C4 75
Creil, Fr. — C5 16
Crema, Italy — B2 23
Cremona, Alta. — D3 68
Cremona, Italy — B3 23
Crenshaw, Ms., U.S. — A3 101
Crenshaw, Pa., U.S. — D4 115
Crenshaw, co., Al., U.S. — D3 78

Creola, Al., U.S. — E1 78
Creole, La., U.S. — E2 95
Crépy-en-Valois, Fr. — E2 17
Cres, l., Yugo. — C2 24
Cresaptown, Md., U.S. — k13 97
Cresbard, S.D., U.S. — B7 118
Crescent, Ga., U.S. — E5 87
Crescent, Ia., U.S. — C2 92
Crescent, Mo., U.S. — f12 102
Crescent, Ok., U.S. — B4 113
Crescent, Or., U.S. — D5 114
Crescent, Lake, l., Wa., U.S. — A2 124
Crescent City, Ca., U.S. — B1 82
Crescent City, Fl., U.S. — C5 86
Crescent City, Il., U.S. — C6 90
Crescent Lake, l., Fl., U.S. — C5 86
Crescent Lake, l., Or., U.S. — D5 114
Crescent Mills, Ca., U.S. — B3 82
Crescent Range, mtn., N.H., U.S. — B4 106
Crescent Spur, B.C. — C7 69
Cresco, Ia., U.S. — A5 92
Cresco, Pa., U.S. — D11 115
Crespo, Arg. — A4 54
Cresskill, N.J., U.S. — h9 107
Cresson, Pa., U.S. — F4 115
Cresson, Tx., U.S. — n9 120
Cressona, Pa., U.S. — E9 115
Crest, Fr. — E6 16
Cresta, Switz. — D8 21
Crested Butte, Co., U.S. — C4 83
Cresthaven, Fl., U.S. — *F6 86
Crest Hill, Il., U.S. — k8 90
Crestline, Ca., U.S. — *E5 82
Crestline, Oh., U.S. — B3 112
Creston, B.C. — E9 69
Creston, Newf. — E4 72
Creston, Il., U.S. — B5 90
Creston, Ia., U.S. — C3 92
Creston, La., U.S. — C2 95
Creston, Mt., U.S. — B2 103
Creston, Ne., U.S. — C8 104
Creston, Oh., U.S. — B4 112
Creston, S.C., U.S. — D6 117
Creston, Tn., U.S. — C5 119
Creston, Wa., U.S. — B7 124
Creston, W.V., U.S. — C3 125
Creston, Wy., U.S. — E5 127
Crestone, Co., U.S. — D5 83
Crestone Peak, mtn., Co., U.S. — D5 83
Crestview, Fl., U.S. — u15 86
Crestview, Ky., U.S. — g10 88
Crestwood, Il., U.S. — *k9 90
Crestwood, Ky., U.S. — B4 94
Crestwood, Mo., U.S. — *f13 102
Crestwood Village, N.J., U.S. — D4 107
Crestwynd, Sask. — G3 75
Creswell, N.C., U.S. — B6 110
Creswell, Or., U.S. — D3 114
Crete, Il., U.S. — B6 90
Crete, Ne., U.S. — D9 104
Crete, N.D., U.S. — C8 111
Crete, i., Grc. — E5 40
Crete, Sea of, Grc. — D5 40
Créteil, Fr. — g10 16
Cretone, Italy — g9 23
Creus, Cape, c., Spain — A7 22
Creuse, stm., Fr. — D4 16
Creutzwald, Fr. — C7 16
Crevasse Valley Glacier, ice, Ant. — B34 7
Creve Coeur, Il., U.S. — C4 90
Creve Coeur, Mo., U.S. — *f13 102
Crèvecœur-le-Grand, Fr. — E2 17
Crevillente, Spain — C5 22
Crewe, Eng., U.K. — D5 10
Crewe, Va., U.S. — C4 123
Crewkerne, Eng., U.K. — D5 12
Criciúma, Braz. — D3 56
Cricket, N.C., U.S. — A1 110
Cricket Mountains, mts., Ut., U.S. — E3 121
Cridersville, Oh., U.S. — B1 112
Crieff, Scot., U.K. — B5 10
Criffell, mtn., Scot., U.K. — F5 13
Criglersville, Va., U.S. — B4 123
Crikvenica, Yugo. — C6 29
Crimea, pen., Sov. Un. — E6 29
Crimmitschau, Ger. — C7 18
Crimson Lake Provincial Park, Alta. — C3 68
Crinan, Scot., U.K. — D3 13
Cridersville, Oh., U.S. — B1 112
Cripple Creek, Co., U.S. — C5 83
Cripple Creek, Va., U.S. — D1 123
Crişana-Maramureş, hist. reg., Rom. — B6 24
Crisfield, Md., U.S. — E6 97
Crisp, co., Ga., U.S. — E3 87
Criss Creek, B.C. — D7 69
Crissolo, Italy — E3 20
Cristal, Monts de, mts., Gabon — A2 46
Cristalina, Braz. — B3 56
Cristóbal, Pan. — k11 62
Cristóbal Colón, Pico, mtn., Col. — A3 60
Crişu Alb, stm., Eur. — B5 24
Crittenden, Ky., U.S. — B5 94
Crittenden, co., Ar., U.S. — B5 81
Crittenden, co., Ky., U.S. — e9 94
Crivitz, Ger. — B6 18
Crivitz, Wi., U.S. — C6 126
Crixás, Braz. — A3 56
Crna, stm., Yugo. — H4 24
Crna, stm., Yugo. — E5 24
Črnomelj, Yugo. — — 24
Croatia, hist. reg., Yugo. — C2 24
Croche, stm., Que. — A5 74
Crocheron, Md., U.S. — D5 97
Crocker, Mo., U.S. — D5 102
Crocker, S.D., U.S. — B8 118
Crockett, Ca., U.S. — g8 82
Crockett, Tx., U.S. — D5 120
Crockett, co., Tn., U.S. — B2 119
Crockett, co., Tx., U.S. — D2 120
Crockett Mills, Tn., U.S. — B2 119
Crocketts Bluff, Ar., U.S. — C4 81
Crocketville, S.C., U.S. — F5 117
Crofton, Ky., U.S. — C2 94
Crofton, Md., U.S. — B4 97
Crofton, Ne., U.S. — B8 104
Croghan, N.Y., U.S. — B5 109
Croghan Mountain, mtn., Ire. — E5 11
Crohy Head, c., Ire. — D3 11
Croix, stm., U.S. — C3 126
Croix, Lac la, l., Mn., U.S. — B6 100
Croker, i., Austl. — B5 51
Croker, Cape, c., Ont. — B4 73
Cromarty, Scot., U.K. — B4 10
Cromer, Man. — E1 70
Cromer, Eng., U.K. — B9 12
Cromona, Ky., U.S. — C7 94
Cromwell, N.Z. — P12 51
Cromwell, Al., U.S. — C1 78

Name — Map Ref. — Page

Cromwell, Ct., U.S. — C5 84
Cromwell, In., U.S. — B6 91
Cromwell, Ia., U.S. — C3 92
Cromwell, Ky., U.S. — C3 94
Cromwell, Mn., U.S. — D6 100
Cromwell, Ok., U.S. — B5 113
Crook, Eng., U.K. — F7 13
Crook, Co., U.S. — A8 83
Crook, co., Or., U.S. — C6 114
Crook, co., Wy., U.S. — B8 127
Crooked, stm., B.C. — B6 69
Crooked, stm., Or., U.S. — C6 114
Crooked Creek, Ak., U.S. — C8 79
Crooked Creek, stm., Ar., U.S. — A3 81
Crooked Creek, stm., In., U.S. — k10 91
Crooked Creek, stm., Pa., U.S. — C7 115
Crooked Creek Lake, res., Pa., U.S. — E3 115
Crooked Island, i., Bah. — C6 64
Crooked Island Passage, strt., Bah. — C6 64
Crooked Lake, l., Newf. — D7 72
Crooked Lake, l., Sask. — G4 75
Crooked Lake, l., Fl., U.S. — E5 86
Crooked Lake, l., Mn., U.S. — B7 100
Crooked River, Sask. — E4 75
Crooks, S.D., U.S. — D9 118
Crooks Lake, l., Nv., U.S. — B2 105
Crookston, Mn., U.S. — C2 100
Crookston, Ne., U.S. — B5 104
Crookston, Ire. — F3 11
Crooksville, Oh., U.S. — C3 112
Crookwell, Austl. — G7 51
Croom, Ire. — B4 94
Cropper, Ky., U.S. — C5 90
Cropsey, Il., U.S. — E6 99
Croque Harbour, b., Newf. — D5 100
Crosby, Mn., U.S. — D2 101
Crosby, Ms., U.S. — A2 111
Crosby, N.D., U.S. — C5 115
Crosby, Pa., U.S. — r14 120
Crosby, co., Tx., U.S. — C2 120
Crosby, Mount, mtn., Wy., U.S. — C3 127
Crosbyton, Tx., U.S. — C2 120
Crosland, Ga., U.S. — E3 87
Cross, S.C., U.S. — E7 117
Cross, co., Ar., U.S. — B5 81
Cross, stm., Afr. — E6 45
Cross, Cape, c., Nmb. — B1 49
Cross Anchor, S.C., U.S. — B4 117
Cross Bay, b., Man. — C2 70
Crossbost, Scot., U.K. — B2 13
Cross City, Fl., U.S. — C3 86
Cross Creek, N.B. — C3 71
Cross Creek, stm., W.V., U.S. — f8 125
Crossett, Ar., U.S. — D4 81
Cross Fell, mtn., Eng., U.K. — F6 13
Crossfield, Alta. — D3 68
Crosshaven, Ire. — F3 11
Cross Hill, S.C., U.S. — C4 117
Cross Island, i., Me., U.S. — D5 96
Cross Keys, N.J., U.S. — D2 107
Cross Lake, Man. — B3 70
Crosslake, Mn., U.S. — D4 100
Cross Lake, l., Man. — B3 70
Cross Lake, l., Me., U.S. — B2 96
Cross Lake, res., La., U.S. — C3 125
Crossman Peak, mtn., Az., U.S. — C1 80
Cross Mill, N.C., U.S. — f10 110
Crossmolina, Ire. — C2 11
Cross Mountains, mtn., Az., U.S. — C1 80
Cross Plains, In., U.S. — G7 91
Cross Plains, Tn., U.S. — A5 119
Cross Plains, Tx., U.S. — C3 120
Cross Plains, Wi., U.S. — E4 126
Crossroads, N.M., U.S. — D6 108
Cross Roads Ohio, Tn., U.S. — D7 119
Cross Sound, strt., Ak., U.S. — k21 79
Cross Timbers, Mo., U.S. — C4 102
Crosstown, Mo., U.S. — D8 102
Cross Village, Mi., U.S. — C5 99
Crossville, Al., U.S. — A4 78
Crossville, Il., U.S. — E5 90
Crossville, Tn., U.S. — D8 119
Crosswicks, N.J., U.S. — C3 108
Croswell, Mi., U.S. — E8 99
Crothersville, In., U.S. — G6 91
Croton, Ia., U.S. — D6 92
Croton, N.J., U.S. — B3 107
Croton, Oh., U.S. — B3 112
Crotone (Croton), Italy — E6 23
Croton-on-Hudson, N.Y., U.S. — D7 109
Crottendorf, Ger. — C7 19
Crouch, Eng., U.K. — E3 89
Crouse, N.C., U.S. — B1 110
Crouseville, Me., U.S. — B4 96
Crow, Mn., U.S. — F4 100
Crow, North Fork, stm., Mn., U.S. — E4 100
Crow Agency, Mt., U.S. — E9 103
Crow Creek, stm., U.S. — A6 83
Crow Creek Indian Reservation, S.D., U.S. — C6 118
Crowder, Ms., U.S. — A3 101
Crowder, Ok., U.S. — B6 113
Crowduck Lake, l., Man. — E4 70
Crowell, Tx., U.S. — C3 120
Crowheart, Wy., U.S. — C3 127
Crow Indian Reservation, Mt., U.S. — E9 103
Crowley, Co., U.S. — C7 83
Crowley, La., U.S. — D3 95
Crowley, Tx., U.S. — n9 120
Crowley, co., Co., U.S. — C7 83
Crowley, Lake, res., Ca., U.S. — D4 82
Crowleys Ridge, mtn., U.S. — B5 81
Crown City, Oh., U.S. — D3 112
Crown King, Az., U.S. — C3 80
Crown Point, In., U.S. — B3 91
Crown Point, La., U.S. — k11 95
Crownpoint, N.M., U.S. — B1 108
Crown Point, N.Y., U.S. — C7 109
Crow Peak, mtn., Mt., U.S. — D5 103
Crowsnest, B.C. — E10 69
Crowsnest Pass, Alta. — E3 68
Crowsnest Pass, Can. — E3 68
Crows Nest Peak, mtn., S.D., U.S. — C2 118
Crowville, La., U.S. — B4 95
Crow Wing, co., Mn., U.S. — D4 100
Crow Wing, stm., Mn., U.S. — D4 100
Croydon, Austl. — C7 50
Croydon (part of London), Eng., U.K. — E6 10
Croydon, N.H., U.S. — D2 106
Croydon, Pa., U.S. — F12 115
Croydon, Ut., U.S. — B4 121
Croydon Flat, N.H., U.S. — D2 106

Croydon Peak, mtn., N.H., U.S. — D2 106
Crozet, Va., U.S. — B4 123
Crozet, Îles, is., F.S.A.T. — J24 2
Crozier, Va., U.S. — C5 123
Crozon, Fr. — C1 16
Cruachan, Ben, mtn., Scot., U.K. — D3 13
Cruagh Island, i., Ire. — D1 11
Crucero, Peru — D3 58
Cruces, Cuba — C3 64
Cruces, Punta, c., Col. — B2 60
Crucible, Pa., U.S. — G1 115
Cruden Bay, Scot., U.K. — B6 10
Cruger, Ms., U.S. — B3 101
Crum, W.V., U.S. — D2 125
Crumlin, N. Ire., U.K. — C5 11
Crummock Water, l., Eng., U.K. — F5 13
Crump Lake, l., Or., U.S. — E7 114
Crumpton, Md., U.S. — B6 97
Crumrod, Ar., U.S. — C5 81
Crumstown, In., U.S. — A5 91
Cruseilles, Fr. — C2 20
Crusheen, Ire. — E3 11
Cruso, N.C., U.S. — f10 110
Crutwell, Sask. — D2 75
Cruz, Cabo, c., Cuba — E5 64
Cruz Alta, Arg. — A4 54
Cruz Alta, Braz. — D2 56
Cruz Bay, V.I.U.S. — B6 65
Cruz del Eje, Arg. — C4 56
Cruzeiro, Braz. — G6 57
Cruzeiro do Oeste, Braz. — G2 56
Cruzeiro do Sul, Braz. — C3 58
Cruz Grande, Chile — E1 55
Crysler, Ont. — B9 73
Crystal, Mi., U.S. — E6 99
Crystal, Mn., U.S. — m12 100
Crystal, N.D., U.S. — A8 111
Crystal, stm., Co., U.S. — B3 83
Crystal Bay, Nv., U.S. — D1 105
Crystal Bay, b., Fl., U.S. — D4 86
Crystal Beach, Fl., U.S. — D4 86
Crystal City, Man. — E2 70
Crystal City, Mo., U.S. — C7 102
Crystal City, Tx., U.S. — E3 120
Crystal Falls, Mi., U.S. — B2 99
Crystal Hill, Va., U.S. — D4 123
Crystal Lake, Ct., U.S. — B6 84
Crystal Lake, Fl., U.S. — u16 86
Crystal Lake, Il., U.S. — A5 90
Crystal Lake, l., Ct., U.S. — A4 92
Crystal Lake, l., Ct., U.S. — B6 84
Crystal Lake, l., Mi., U.S. — D4 99
Crystal Lake, l., N.H., U.S. — D4 106
Crystal Lake, l., Vt., U.S. — B4 122
Crystal Lawns, Il., U.S. — k8 90
Crystal Manor, Il., U.S. — k8 90
Crystal Mountain, mtn., N.H., U.S. — g7 106
Crystal Pond, res., Ct., U.S. — B7 84
Crystal River, Fl., U.S. — D4 86
Crystal Springs, Sask. — E3 75
Crystal Springs, Ar., U.S. — C2 81
Crystal Springs, Fl., U.S. — D4 86
Crystal Springs, Ms., U.S. — D3 101
Crystal Springs, N.D., U.S. — C6 111
Crystal Valley, Mi., U.S. — E4 99
Csongrád, Hung. — B5 24
Csorna, Hung. — B3 24
Cuajone, Peru — E3 58
Cuamba, Moz. — D6 48
Cuando, stm., Afr. — H8 42
Cuando Cubango, dept., Ang. — E2 48
Cuangar, Ang. — E2 48
Cuango, Ang. — C2 48
Cuango (Kwango), stm., Afr. — C2 48
Cuanza, stm., Ang. — C2 48
Cuanza-Norte, dept., Ang. — C1 48
Cuanza-Sul, dept., Ang. — D1 48
Cuarto, stm., Arg. — A4 54
Cuauhtémoc, Mex. — B3 63
Cuautepec (part of Mexico City), Mex. — g9 63
Cuautla [Morelos], Mex. — n14 63
Cuba, Port. — G2 22
Cuba, Al., U.S. — C1 78
Cuba, Il., U.S. — C3 90
Cuba, Ks., U.S. — C6 93
Cuba, Mo., U.S. — C6 102
Cuba, N.M., U.S. — A3 108
Cuba, N.Y., U.S. — C2 109
Cuba, Oh., U.S. — C2 112
Cuba, ctry., N.A. — C4 64
Cuba City, Wi., U.S. — F3 126
Cubal, Ang. — D1 48
Cubero, N.M., U.S. — B2 108
Cub Run, Ky., U.S. — C3 94
Cucamonga, Ca., U.S. — *m13 82
Cuchara, Co., U.S. — D6 83
Cucharas, stm., Co., U.S. — D6 83
Cuchillo, N.M., U.S. — D2 108
Cuchivero, Ven. — B4 60
Cúcuti, Braz. — F4 60
Cúcuta, Col. — B3 60
Cudahy, Ca., U.S. — *E4 82
Cudahy, Wi., U.S. — F6 126
Cuddalore, India — F6 37
Cuddapah, India — F6 37
Cuddy Mountain, mtn., Id., U.S. — E2 89
Cudgewa, Austl. — H6 51
Cudworth, Sask. — E3 75
Cue, Austl. — E2 50
Cuéllar, Spain — B3 22
Cuenca, Ec. — B2 58
Cuenca, Spain — B4 22
Cuenca, Sierra de, mts., Spain — B4 22
Cuencamé [de Ceniceros], Mex. — C4 63
Cuernavaca, Mex. — D5 63
Cuero, Tx., U.S. — E4 120
Cuervo, N.M., U.S. — B5 108
Cuetzalan, Mex. — m15 63
Cuevas, Ms., U.S. — f7 101
Cuevas [del Almanzora], Spain — D5 22
Cuglieri, Italy — D2 23
Cuiabá, Braz. — B1 56
Cuiabá, stm., Braz. — B1 56
Cuicas, Ven. — B3 60
Cuicatlán, Mex. — o15 63
Cuilapa, Guat. — C2 62
Cuilcagh, mtn., Eur. — C4 11
Cuilco, Guat. — C2 62
Cuillin Hills, hills, Scot., U.K. — C2 13
Cuimba, Ang. — C1 48
Cuipo, Pan. — k10 62
Cuíto, stm., Ang. — E2 48
Cuíto-Cuanavale, Ang. — E2 48
Cuitzeo, Lago de, l., Mex. — n13 63
Cuiuni, stm., Braz. — C2 59
Cuivre, West Fork, stm., Mo., U.S. — B6 102
Culberson, co., Tx., U.S. — o12 120

Culbertson, Mt., U.S. — B12 103
Culbertson, Ne., U.S. — D5 104
Culcairn, Austl. — G6 51
Culdaff Bay, b., Ire. — B4 11
Culdesac, Id., U.S. — C2 89
Culebra, P.R. — B5 65
Culebra, Isla de, i., P.R. — G12 64
Culebra Peak, mtn., Co., U.S. — D5 83
Culgoa, stm., Austl. — E8 50
Culhuacán (part of Mexico City), Mex. — h9 63
Culiacán, Mex. — C3 63
Cúllar de Baza, Spain — D4 22
Cullen, Scot., U.K. — B6 10
Cullen, La., U.S. — B2 95
Cullenoka, Tn., U.S. — B5 119
Cullera, Spain — C5 22
Cullison, Ks., U.S. — E5 93
Cullman, Al., U.S. — A3 78
Cullman, co., Al., U.S. — A3 78
Culloden, Ga., U.S. — D2 87
Culloden, W.V., U.S. — C2 125
Cullom, Il., U.S. — C5 90
Cullomburg, Al., U.S. — D1 78
Cullowhee, N.C., U.S. — f9 110
Culp Creek, Or., U.S. — D4 114
Culpeper, Va., U.S. — B5 123
Culpeper, co., Va., U.S. — B5 123
Cultus Lake, B.C. — f14 69
Culuene, stm., Braz. — A2 56
Culver, In., U.S. — B5 91
Culver, Ks., U.S. — D6 93
Culver, Mn., U.S. — D6 100
Culver, Or., U.S. — C5 114
Culver, Point, c., Austl. — F3 50
Culver City, Ca., U.S. — m12 82
Culvers Lake, l., N.J., U.S. — A3 107
Culzean Bay, b., Scot., U.K. — E4 13
Cumaná, Ven. — A5 60
Cumbal, Nevado de, mtn., Col. — C2 60
Cumberland, B.C. — E5 69
Cumberland, Ont. — g13 73
Cumberland, Ia., U.S. — C3 92
Cumberland, Ky., U.S. — D7 94
Cumberland, Md., U.S. — k13 97
Cumberland, N.J., U.S. — E3 107
Cumberland, N.C., U.S. — B4 110
Cumberland, Oh., U.S. — C4 112
Cumberland, Ok., U.S. — C5 113
Cumberland, Va., U.S. — C4 123
Cumberland, Wa., U.S. — f12 124
Cumberland, Wi., U.S. — C1 126
Cumberland, co., N.S. — D5 71
Cumberland, co., Il., U.S. — D5 90
Cumberland, co., Ky., U.S. — D4 94
Cumberland, co., Me., U.S. — E2 96
Cumberland, co., N.J., U.S. — E2 107
Cumberland, co., N.C., U.S. — B4 110
Cumberland, co., Pa., U.S. — F7 115
Cumberland, co., Tn., U.S. — D8 119
Cumberland, co., Va., U.S. — C5 123
Cumberland, stm., U.S. — C11 76
Cumberland, Lake, res., Ky., U.S. — D5 94
Cumberland, South Fork, stm., U.S. — D5 94
Cumberland Center, Me., U.S. — g7 96
Cumberland City, Tn., U.S. — A4 119
Cumberland Foreside, Me., U.S. — E2 96
Cumberland Furnace, Tn., U.S. — A4 119
Cumberland Gap, Tn., U.S. — C10 119
Cumberland Gap National Historical Park, U.S. — D6 94
Cumberland Hill, R.I., U.S. — B4 116
Cumberland House, Sask. — D4 75
Cumberland Island National Seashore, Ga., U.S. — F5 87
Cumberland Lake, l., Sask. — C4 75
Cumberland Mountain, mtn., Tn., U.S. — C9 119
Cumberland Peninsula, pen., N.W. Ter. — C20 66
Cumberland Plateau, plat., U.S. — D8 119
Cumberland Sound, strt., N.W. Ter. — C19 66
Cumbernauld, Scot., U.K. — *E5 13
Cumbres Pass, Co., U.S. — D4 83
Cumbria, co., Eng., U.K. — F6 13
Cut Throat Island, i., Newf. — A3 72
Cuttingsville, Vt., U.S. — E3 122
Cumberland, Ga., U.S. — B2 87
Cumming, Ga., U.S. — B2 87
Cumming, Ia., U.S. — f8 92
Cummings, N.D., U.S. — B8 111
Cummington, Ma., U.S. — B2 98
Cummins, Austl. — F7 50
Cumnock [and Holmhead], Scot., U.K. — F4 13
Cumpas, Mex. — A3 63
Çumra, Tur. — D9 40
Cuna, stm., Ca., U.S. — E4 82
Cunco, Chile — D2 54
Cundinamarca, dept., Col. — E5 60
Cundiyo, N.M., U.S. — *B4 108
Cundys Harbor, Me., U.S. — g8 96
Cunene, dept., Ang. — E2 48
Cunene, stm., Afr. — E1 48
Cuneo, Italy — B1 23
Cunha, Braz. — A4 54
Cunnamulla, Austl. — E8 50
Cunningham, Ks., U.S. — E5 93
Cunningham, Ky., U.S. — f9 94
Cunningham, Tn., U.S. — A4 119
Cupar, Sask. — G3 75
Cupar, Scot., U.K. — E5 13
Cupertino, Ca., U.S. — *k8 82
Cupica, Col. — B2 60
Cupica, Golfo de, b., Col. — B2 60
Curaçá, Braz. — E11 57
Curaçao, i., Neth. Ant. — H18 65
Curacó, stm., Arg. — D3 54
Curanilahue, Chile — D2 54
Curaray, stm., S.A. — B3 58
Curatabaca, mtn., Rom. — C2 24
Curdsville, Ky., U.S. — C2 94
Curéanti National Recreation Area, Co., U.S. — C3 83
Curepto, Chile — D2 54
Curiapo, Ven. — B5 60
Curicó, Chile — D2 54
Curicuriari, Braz. — D4 60
Curimataú, stm., Braz. — h6 57
Curitiba, Braz. — D3 56
Curitibanos, Braz. — D2 56
Curlew, Wa., U.S. — A7 124
Curlew Creek, stm., Wa., U.S. — A7 124
Curlew Lake, l., Wa., U.S. — A7 124
Curon Venosta, Italy — C6 20
Currais Novos, Braz. — C3 57

Curralinho, Braz. — C5 59
Curran, Ont. — B10 73
Curran, Mi., U.S. — D7 99
Currans, Ire. — E2 11
Currant, Nv., U.S. — *D7 105
Currant Creek, stm., Co., U.S. — C5 83
Currant Mountain, mtn., Nv., U.S. — E6 105
Current, stm., U.S. — A5 81
Current, stm., U.S. — F3 100
Currie, Mn., U.S. — A6 110
Currituck, N.C., U.S. — A6 110
Currituck, co., N.C., U.S. — A6 110
Curryville, Mo., U.S. — C6 108
Curtea-de-Argeş, Rom. — E2 114
Curtice, Oh., U.S. — B6 102
Curtin, Rom. — A2 112
Curtis, Ne., U.S. — D5 104
Curtis, Ar., U.S. — B5 99
Curtis, Mi., U.S. — D3 126
Curtiss, Wi., U.S. — E2 115
Curuá, stm., Braz. — C4 59
Curuá, stm., Braz. — D4 59
Curuá do Sul, stm., Braz. — C4 59
Curupira, Serra de, mts., S.A. — C5 60
Curuzú Cuatiá, Arg. — B5 54
Curvelo, Braz. — E6 57
Curwensville, Pa., U.S. — C8 21
Curwensville Lake, res., Pa., U.S. — E4 115
Cushendall, N. Ire., U.K. — B5 11
Cushing, Ia., U.S. — B2 92
Cushing, Ne., U.S. — C7 104
Cushing, Ok., U.S. — B5 113
Cushing, Tx., U.S. — D5 120
Cushman, Ar., U.S. — B4 81
Cushman, Lake, res., Wa., U.S. — B2 124
Cusick, Wa., U.S. — A8 124
Cusihuiriáchic, Mex. — B3 63
Cusseta, Al., U.S. — C4 78
Cusseta, Ga., U.S. — D2 87
Custar, Oh., U.S. — A2 112
Custer, Mi., U.S. — E4 99
Custer, S.D., U.S. — D2 118
Custer, co., Co., U.S. — C5 83
Custer, co., Id., U.S. — E4 89
Custer, co., Mt., U.S. — D11 103
Custer, co., Ne., U.S. — C6 104
Custer, co., Ok., U.S. — B2 113
Custer, co., S.D., U.S. — D2 118
Custer Battlefield National Monument, Mt., U.S. — E9 103
Custer City, Ok., U.S. — B3 113
Custer City, Pa., U.S. — C4 115
Custer Peak, mtn., S.D., U.S. — C2 118
Cut Bank, Mt., U.S. — B4 103
Cutbank, stm., Alta. — B1 68
Cut Bank Creek, stm., N.D., U.S. — A4 111
Cutchogue, N.Y., U.S. — m16 109
Cutervo, Peru — C2 58
Cuthbert, Ga., U.S. — E2 87
Cutler, Ont. — A2 73
Cutler, Fl., U.S. — *G6 86
Cutler, Il., U.S. — E4 90
Cutler, Me., U.S. — C5 96
Cutler, Mi., U.S. — D5 96
Cutler Ridge, Fl., U.S. — s13 86
Cutlerville, Mi., U.S. — *F5 99
Cutoff, Daisy, Or., U.S. — E5 114
Cut Off, La., U.S. — E5 95
Cutral-Có, Arg. — D3 54
Cuttack, India — D8 36
Cutzamalá, stm., Mex. — n13 63
Cuxhaven, Ger. — B4 18
Cuyahoga, co., Oh., U.S. — A4 112
Cuyahoga, stm., Oh., U.S. — A4 112
Cuyahoga Falls, Oh., U.S. — A4 112
Cuyama, stm., Ca., U.S. — E4 82
Cuyamaca Peak, mtn., Ca., U.S. — m13 125
Cuyamungue, N.M., U.S. — *B4 108
Cuylerville, N.Y., U.S. — C3 109
Cuyo Islands, is., Phil. — C6 34
Cuyuna, N.M., U.S. — *B4 108
Cuyuni, stm., S.A. — A3 59
Cuzco, Peru — D3 58
Cuzco, In., U.S. — H4 91
Cuzco, dept., Peru — D3 58
Cwmbran, Wales, U.K. — C5 12
C.W. McConaughy, Lake, res., Ne., U.S. — C4 104
Cybinka, Pol. — A9 19
Cyclades, is., Grc. — D5 40
Cyclone, Pa., U.S. — C4 115
Cygnet, Oh., U.S. — A2 112
Cynthiana, In., U.S. — H2 91
Cynthiana, Ky., U.S. — B5 94
Cynthiana, Oh., U.S. — C2 112
Cypress, Al., U.S. — D2 78
Cypress, Ca., U.S. — *n12 82
Cypress, Il., U.S. — B3 90
Cypress, Tx., U.S. — r14 120
Cypress Bayou, stm., Ar., U.S. — B3 81
Cypress Creek, stm., Tx., U.S. — G10 66
Cypress Hills, hills, Can. — E5 68
Cypress Hills Provincial Park, Alta. — H1 75
Cypress Hills Provincial Park, Sask. — *F6 86
Cypress Inn, Tn., U.S. — B3 119
Cypress Lake, Fl., U.S. — H1 75
Cypress Lake, l., Fl., U.S. — D5 86
Cypress Quarters, Fl., U.S. — E6 86
Cypress River, Man. — E6 86
Cypress Swamp, sw., U.S. — F4 85
Cypress Creek, stm., Tx., U.S. — D5 120
Cyprus, ctry., Asia — E9 40
Cyprus, North, ctry., Asia — E9 40

Cyrenaica (Barqah), hist. reg., Libya — C5 59
Cyril, Ok., U.S. — B10 73
Cyril, stm., Man. — B4 70
Cyrus, Mn., U.S. — E3 100
Czar, Alta. — C5 68
Czarna, stm., Pol. — k14 26
Czarna Przemsza, stm., Pol. — g10 26
Czarnków, Pol. — B4 26
Czechoslovakia, ctry., Eur. — C5 26
Czechowice-Dziedzice, Pol. — h10 26
Czersk, Pol. — B4 26
Częstochowa, Pol. — C5 26
Człuchów, Pol. — B4 26

D

Da'an, China — B11 32
Daaquam, Que. — C7 74
Dabakala, I.C. — E4 45
Daba Mountains, mts., China — I4 32
Dabdab, Libya — D2 43
Dabeiba, Col. — B2 60
Dabie (part of Szczecin), Pol. — B3 26
Dabie Mountains, mts., China — I5 32
Ďáblice, Czech. — n18 26
Dabneys, Va., U.S. — C5 123
Dabola, Gui. — D2 45
Daborow, Som. — D6 47
Dabou, I.C. — E4 45
Dąbrowa Białostocka, Pol. — B7 26
Dąbrowa Górnicza, Pol. — C5 26
Dąbrowa [Tarnowska], Pol. — C6 26
Dacca see Dhaka, Bngl. — D9 36
Dachau, Ger. — D5 18
Dacoma, Ok., U.S. — A3 113
Dacono, Co., U.S. — A6 83
Dacula, Ga., U.S. — C3 87
Dadanawa, Guy. — B3 59
Daday, Tur. — B9 40
Dade, co., Fl., U.S. — B1 87
Dade, co., Ga., U.S. — B1 87
Dade, co., Mo., U.S. — D4 102
Dade City, Fl., U.S. — D4 86
Dadeville, Al., U.S. — C4 78
Dadeville, Mo., U.S. — D4 102
Dādra and Nagar Haveli, ter., India — *D5 36
Dādu, Pak. — C4 36
Daet, Phil. — o14 34
Dafoe, Sask. — F3 75
Dafoe, stm., Man. — B4 70
Dagana, Sen. — C1 45
Dagenham (part of London), Eng., U.K. — k13 10
Daggett, Ca., U.S. — E5 82
Daggett, Mi., U.S. — C3 99
Daggett, co., Ut., U.S. — C6 121
Dagmar, Mt., U.S. — B12 103
Dagsboro, De., U.S. — F5 85
Dagu, China — E7 32
Dagupan, Phil. — n13 34
Daguscahonda, Pa., U.S. — D4 115
Dagus Mines, Pa., U.S. — D4 115
Dāhānu, India — G4 37
Dahinda, Il., U.S. — C3 90
Da Hinggan Ling (Greater Khingan Range), mts., China — B9 31
Dahlak Archipelago, is., Eth. — B5 47
Dahlen, N.D., U.S. — A8 111
Dahlgren, Il., U.S. — E5 90
Dahlgren, Va., U.S. — B5 123
Dahlonega, Ga., U.S. — B3 87
Dahme, Ger. — B8 19
Dāhod, India — F5 37
Dahomey see Benin, ctry., Afr. — E5 45
Dahra, Libya — D3 43
Dahshūr, Eg. — E3 41
Dahūk, Iraq — D14 40
Daicheng, China — E7 32
Dailey, W.V., U.S. — C5 125
Daimiel, Spain — C4 22
Daingean, Ire. — D4 11
Daingerfield, Tx., U.S. — C5 120
Daiō, Japan — o15 33
Daiō, Cape, c., Japan — I8 33
Dairen see Dalian, China — D9 31
Dairy, Or., U.S. — E5 114
Dairyland, Wi., U.S. — B1 126
Daisetta, Tx., U.S. — D5 120
Daisy, Ar., U.S. — C2 81
Daisy, Ga., U.S. — D5 87
Daixian, China — D7 31
Dajabón, Dom. Rep. — E8 64
Dakar, Sen. — D1 45
Dākhilah, Al Wāḥāt ad, well, Eg. — D5 43
Dakhla, W. Sah. — E1 44
Dakoro, Niger — D6 45
Dakota, Il., U.S. — A4 90
Dakota, co., Mn., U.S. — F5 100
Dakota, co., Ne., U.S. — B9 104
Dakota City, Ia., U.S. — B3 92
Dakota City, Ne., U.S. — B9 104
Dákura, Nic. — C6 62
Dakwa, Zaire — A4 48
Dalaas, Aus. — B9 21
Dalälven, stm., Swe. — D2 45
Dalmaine, dept., Ang. — G6 14
Dalark, Ar., U.S. — C3 81
Dalarö, Swe. — t36 14
Da Lat, Viet. — C3 36
Dālbandin, Pak. — C3 36
Dalbeattie, Scot., U.K. — F5 13
D'Albertis Dome, mtn., Pap. N. Gui. — k11 50
Dalby, Mn., U.S. — E5 100
Dalby, Austl. — E9 50
Dalby, Swe. — C7 15
Dalcahue, Chile — E2 54
Dale, Il., U.S. — F5 90
Dale, In., U.S. — H4 91
Dale, Ok., U.S. — B4 113
Dale, Or., U.S. — C8 114
Dale, co., Al., U.S. — D4 78
Dale City, Va., U.S. — B5 123
Dale Hollow Lake, res., U.S. — C8 119
Daleville, Al., U.S. — D4 78
Daleville, In., U.S. — D6 91
Daleville, Ms., U.S. — C5 101
Dalhart, Tx., U.S. — A1 120
Dalhousie, N.B. — A3 71
Dalhousie, India — A5 37
Dalhousie Junction, N.B. — A3 71
Dali, China — E6 31
Dalian (Lüda), China — D9 31
Dalias, Spain — D4 22

Daliburgh, Scot., U.K. — C1 13
Daliyat et Karmil, Isr. — B7 41
Dalkeith, Scot., U.K. — E5 13
Dalkeith, Fl., U.S. — B1 86
Dalkena, Wa., U.S. — A8 124
Dalkey, Ire. — D5 11
Dall, Mount, mtn., Ak., U.S. — f15 79
Dallam, co., Tx., U.S. — A1 120
Dallardsville, Tx., U.S. — D5 120
Dallas, Al., U.S. — B3 78
Dallas, Ga., U.S. — C2 87
Dallas, Ia., U.S. — C4 92
Dallas, N.C., U.S. — B1 110
Dallas, Or., U.S. — C3 114
Dallas, Pa., U.S. — D10 115
Dallas, S.D., U.S. — D6 118
Dallas, Tx., U.S. — C4 120
Dallas, W.V., U.S. — f8 125
Dallas, Wi., U.S. — C2 126
Dallas, co., Al., U.S. — C2 78
Dallas, co., Ar., U.S. — D3 81
Dallas, co., Ia., U.S. — C3 92
Dallas, co., Mo., U.S. — D4 102
Dallas, co., Tx., U.S. — C4 120
Dallas Center, Ia., U.S. — C4 92
Dallas City, Il., U.S. — C2 90
Dallas Naval Air Station, mil., Tx., U.S. — n9 120
Dallastown, Pa., U.S. — G8 115
Dall Island, i., Ak., U.S. — n23 79
Dalmally, Scot., U.K. — D4 13
Dalmatia, Pa., U.S. — E8 115
Dalmatia, hist. reg., Yugo. — D3 24
Dalmellington, Scot., U.K. — C4 10
Dalmeny, Sask. — E2 75
Dalnerechensk, Sov. Un. — E16 119
Dalnyaya, Sov. Un. — D11 33
Daloa, I.C. — E3 45
Dalou Mountains, mts., China — A3 47
Dalqū, Sud. — A3 47
Dalroy, Alta. — D4 68
Dalry, Scot., U.K. — E4 13
Dalrymple, Mount, mtn., Austl. — D8 50
Dālṭenganj, India — D7 36
Dalton, Ga., U.S. — A4 81
Dalton, Ma., U.S. — B2 87
Dalton, Mn., U.S. — B1 98
Dalton, Mn., U.S. — D3 100
Dalton, Ne., U.S. — C3 104
Dalton, N.H., U.S. — B3 106
Dalton, N.Y., U.S. — C3 109
Dalton, Oh., U.S. — C10 115
Dalton, Wi., U.S. — E4 126
Dalton City, Il., U.S. — D5 90
Dalton Gardens, Id., U.S. — B2 89
Dalton Iceberg Tongue, ice, Ant. — C25 7
Dalwhinnie, Scot., U.K. — B5 10
Daly, stm., Austl. — B5 50
Daly City, Ca., U.S. — h8 82
Dalzell, Il., U.S. — B4 90
Dalzell, S.C., U.S. — C7 117
Damān, India — D5 36
Damān and Diu, ter., India — *D5 36
Damanhūr, Eg. — C6 41
Damaqun Mountains, mts., China — D7 32
Damar, Ks., U.S. — C4 93
Damar, i., Indon. — G7 34
Damara, Cen. Afr. Rep. — D3 46
Damariscotta, Me., U.S. — D3 96
Damariscotta Lake, l., Me., U.S. — D3 96
Damascus (Dimashq), Syria — B3 38
Damascus, Ga., U.S. — E2 87
Damascus, Ga., U.S. — B2 87
Damascus, Md., U.S. — B3 97
Damascus, Oh., U.S. — C11 115
Damascus, Va., U.S. — f10 123
Damascus Gate, hist., Isr. Occ. — m14 41
Damaturu, Nig. — C7 45
Damba, Ang. — C2 48
Dame Marie, Cap, c., Haiti — E6 64
Dames Quarter, Md., U.S. — D6 97
Dam Gamad, Sud. — E4 46
Dāmghān, Iran — B5 38
Damietta Branch, stm., Eg. — D3 41
Damietta see Dumyāṭ, Eg. — B3 41
Daming, China — F6 32
Dāmiyā, Jord. — g13 41
Damme, Ger. — B9 17
Dāmodar, stm., India — F10 37
Damoh, India — F7 37
Damon, Tx., U.S. — r14 120
Damongo, Ghana — E4 45
Dampier, Austl. — D2 50
Dampier Archipelago, is., Austl. — D2 50
Dampier Strait, strt., Indon. — F8 34
Damvant, Switz. — B2 21
Dan, stm., U.S. — E3 123
Dana, Sask. — E3 75
Dana, In., U.S. — B3 91
Dana, Ia., U.S. — B3 92
Dana, N.C., U.S. — f10 110
Danané, I.C. — E3 45
Da Nang, Viet. — B3 34
Dana Point, Ca., U.S. — *F5 82
Dānāpur, India — E10 37
Danbury, Ct., U.S. — D2 84
Danbury, Ia., U.S. — B2 92
Danbury, Ne., U.S. — D5 104
Danbury, N.H., U.S. — C3 106
Danbury, N.C., U.S. — A2 110
Danbury, Tx., U.S. — r14 120
Danbury, Wi., U.S. — B1 126
Danby, N.Y., U.S. — E6 82
Danby, Vt., U.S. — E3 122
Danby Corners, Vt., U.S. — B1 73
Dancy, Al., U.S. — B1 78
Dancyville, Tn., U.S. — B2 119
Dande, stm., Ang. — C1 48
Dandenong, Austl. — *G8 51
Dandong, China — C9 31
Dandridge, Tn., U.S. — C10 119
Dane, Wi., U.S. — E4 126
Dane, co., Wi., U.S. — E4 126
Danevang, Tx., U.S. — E4 120
Danfeng, China — H4 32
Danforth, Il., U.S. — C6 90
Danforth, Me., U.S. — C5 96
Danforth Hills, mts., Co., U.S. — A8 83
Dangila, Eth. — C7 47
Dangshan, China — A7 119
Dangtu, China — I4 32
Dangyang, China — F2 30
Dania, Fl., U.S. — *F6 86
Daniel, Ut., U.S. — *C4 121

Index

Name	Map Ref.	Page
Daniel, Wy., U.S.	D2	127
Daniels, co., Mt., U.S.	B11	103
Daniel's Harbour, Newf.	C3	72
Danielson, Ct., U.S.	B8	84
Daniels Pass, Ut., U.S.	C4	121
Danielsville, Ga., U.S.	B3	87
Danilov, Sov. Un.	B13	27
Danilovgrad, Yugo.	D4	24
Danjo Island, i., Japan	J4	33
Danli, Hond.	E7	63
Dannebrog, Ne., U.S.	C7	104
Dannemarie, Fr.	A3	21
Dannemora, N.Y., U.S.	f11	109
Dannenberg, Ger.	E5	15
Dannevirke, N.Z.	N16	51
Dannike, Swe.	A7	15
Dans Mountain, mtn., Md., U.S.	k13	97
Dansville, N.Y., U.S.	C3	109
Dante, S.D., U.S.	D7	118
Dante, Tn., U.S.	m14	119
Dante, Va., U.S.	f9	123
Dantewāra, India	H8	37
Danube, stm., Eur.	F3	100
Danube, stm., Eur.	G14	18
Danube Delta, Eur.	I7	27
Danubyu, Burma	D1	35
Danvers, Il., U.S.	C4	90
Danvers, Ma., U.S.	A6	98
Danvers, Mn., U.S.	E3	100
Danvers, Mt., U.S.	C7	103
Danville, Que.	D5	74
Danville, Al., U.S.	A2	78
Danville, Ar., U.S.	B2	81
Danville, Ca., U.S.	h9	82
Danville, Ga., U.S.	D3	87
Danville, Il., U.S.	C6	90
Danville, In., U.S.	E4	91
Danville, Ia., U.S.	D6	92
Danville, Ks., U.S.	E6	93
Danville, Ky., U.S.	C5	94
Danville, La., U.S.	B3	95
Danville, N.H., U.S.	E4	106
Danville, Oh., U.S.	B3	112
Danville, Pa., U.S.	E8	115
Danville, Vt., U.S.	C4	122
Danville, Va., U.S.	D3	123
Danville, Wa., U.S.	A7	124
Danville, W.V., U.S.	C3	125
Danxian, China	C8	35
Danzhai, China	K2	32
Danzig, Gulf of, b., Eur.	A5	26
Danzig see Gdańsk, Pol.	A5	26
Daosa, India	D6	37
Daoxian, China	F7	31
Daphne, Al., U.S.	E2	78
Dapp, Alta.	B4	68
Da Qaidam, China	D4	31
Daqing (Anda), China	*B10	31
Darā, Syria	F11	40
Dārāb, Iran	G7	39
Darabani, Rom.	A8	24
Daraj, Libya	C2	43
Darasun, Sov. Un.	D14	29
Darawah, Eg.	D3	41
Darbandi Khan Dam, Iraq	D2	39
Darbhanga, India	C8	36
D'Arbonne, Bayou, stm., La., U.S.	B3	95
Darburruk, Som.	D5	47
Darby, Mt., U.S.	D2	103
Darby, Pa., U.S.	G11	115
Darbydale, Oh., U.S.	m10	112
Darby Township, Pa., U.S.	*G11	115
Darbyville, Oh., U.S.	C2	112
Dar Chebika, Mor.	D2	44
D'Arcy Station, Sask.	F1	75
Dardanelle, Ar., U.S.	B2	81
Dardanelle, Ca., U.S.	C4	82
Dardanelle Lake, res., Ar., U.S.	B2	81
Dardanelles, strt.	B5	40
Darden, N.C., U.S.	B6	110
Darden, Tn., U.S.	B3	119
Dardenne Creek, stm., Mo., U.S.	f12	102
Dare, co., N.C., U.S.	B7	110
Darende, Tur.	C11	40
Dar es Salaam, Tan.	C6	48
Daretown, N.J., U.S.	D2	107
Darfo, Italy	D6	20
Darfur, India	F4	100
Dārfūr al Janūbīyah (Southern Darfur), prov., Sud.	C1	47
Dārfūr ash Shamālīyah (Northern Darfur), prov., Sud.	B2	47
Dargan, Md., U.S.	B2	97
Dargan-Ata, Sov. Un.	A11	39
Dargaville, N.Z.	K14	51
Darhan, Mong.	B6	31
Darhan Muminggan Lianheqi, China	D4	32
Darien, Ct., U.S.	E2	84
Darien, Ga., U.S.	E5	87
Darien, Il., U.S.	*k9	90
Darien, Wi., U.S.	F5	126
Darién, Gulf of, b.	F9	62
Darién, Serranía del, mts.	F9	62
Dariense, Cordillera, mts., Nic.	D5	62
Darjeeling, India	C8	36
Darke, co., Oh., U.S.	B1	112
Darkesville, W.V., U.S.	B6	125
Darley Woods, De., U.S.	h8	85
Darling Woods, De., U.S.	A3	101
Darling, stm., Austl.	F5	50
Darling, Lake, res., N.D., U.S.	A4	111
Darling Downs, reg., Austl.	E9	50
Darlingford, Man.	E2	70
Darling Range, mts., Austl.	F3	50
Darlington, Eng., U.K.	C6	10
Darlington, Al., U.S.	v15	86
Darlington, Fl., U.S.	u15	86
Darlington, Id., U.S.	F5	89
Darlington, In., U.S.	D4	91
Darlington, Md., U.S.	A5	97
Darlington, Mo., U.S.	A3	102
Darlington, S.C., U.S.	C8	117
Darlington, Wi., U.S.	F3	126
Darlington, co., S.C., U.S.	C8	117
Darłowo, Pol.	A4	26
Darmody, Sask.	G2	75
Darmstadt, Ger.	D4	18
Darnah, Libya	C4	43
Darnell, La., U.S.	B4	95
Darnestown, Md., U.S.	B3	97
Darney, Fr.	A2	20
Darnley, Cape, c., Ant.	C19	7
Daro, Malay.	E4	34
Daroca, Spain	B5	22
Darr, Ne., U.S.	D6	104
Darrah, Mount, mtn., Can.	E3	68
Darreh Gaz, Iran	C9	39
Darrington, Wa., U.S.	A4	124
Darrouzett, Tx., U.S.	A2	120
Darrow, La., U.S.	h10	95
Darsser Ort, c., Ger.	D6	15
Dart, stm., Eng., U.K.	D4	12
Dart, Cape, c., Ant.	B36	7
Dartmoor, for., Eng., U.K.	E5	10
Dartmouth, N.S.	E6	71
Dartmouth, Eng., U.K.	E5	10
Dartmouth Woods, De., U.S.	*A3	85
Daru, Pap. N. Gui.	k11	50
Daruvar, Yugo.	C3	24
Darvel Bay, b., Malay.	E5	34
Darwin, Austl.	B5	50
Darwin, Ca., U.S.	D5	82
Darwin, Mn., U.S.	E4	100
Darwin, Isla, i., Ec.	f5	58
Darwin Glacier, ice, Ant.	f41	7
Darwin Island, i., Austl.	B5	50
Datça, Tur.	D6	25
Dateland, Az., U.S.	E2	80
Datia, India	E7	37
Datian, China	L7	32
Datil, N.M., U.S.	C2	108
Datil Mountains, mts., N.M., U.S.	C2	108
Datong, China	C7	31
Datto, Ar., U.S.	A5	81
Datu, Cape, c., Asia	E3	34
Datze, stm., Ger.	E7	15
Daudnagar, India	E10	37
Daufuskie Island, S.C., U.S.	G6	117
Daufuskie Island, i., S.C., U.S.	G6	117
Daugava (Western Dvina), stm., Sov. Un.	C5	27
Daugavpils (Dvinsk), Sov. Un.	D6	27
Daule, Ec.	A2	58
Daule, Ec.	B2	58
Daun, Ger.	C1	19
Daund, India	H5	37
Daung, i., Burma	F3	35
Dauphin, Man.	D1	70
Dauphin, Pa., U.S.	F8	115
Dauphin, co., Pa., U.S.	F8	115
Dauphin, stm., Man.	D2	70
Dauphiné, hist. reg., Fr.	E6	16
Dauphin Island, Al., U.S.	E1	78
Dauphin Island, i., Al., U.S.	E1	78
Dauphin Lake, l., Man.	D2	70
Daus, Tn., U.S.	D8	119
Dāvangere, India	F6	36
Davant, La., U.S.	E6	95
Davao, Phil.	D7	34
Davao Gulf, b., Phil.	D7	34
Dāvar Panāh, Iran	H11	39
Daveluyville, Que.	C5	74
Davenport, Ca., U.S.	D2	82
Davenport, Fl., U.S.	D5	86
Davenport, Ne., U.S.	D8	104
Davenport, N.Y., U.S.	C6	109
Davenport, N.D., U.S.	C8	111
Davenport, Ok., U.S.	B5	113
Davenport, Wa., U.S.	B7	124
Davenport Downs, Austl.	B3	51
Daventry, Eng., U.K.	B6	12
Davey, Ne., U.S.	h11	104
David, Pan.	F6	62
David, Ky., U.S.	C7	94
David City, Ne., U.S.	C8	104
David-Gorodok, Sov. Un.	E6	27
Davidson, Sask.	F3	75
Davidson, N.C., U.S.	B2	110
Davidson, Ok., U.S.	C2	113
Davidson, Tn., U.S.	C8	119
Davidson, co., N.C., U.S.	B2	110
Davidson, co., Tn., U.S.	A5	119
Davidson Mountains, mts., Ak., U.S.	B11	79
Davidsville, Pa., U.S.	F4	115
Davie, Fl., U.S.	F6	86
Davie, co., N.C., U.S.	B2	110
Davies Bay, b., Ant.	C26	7
Daviess, co., In., U.S.	G3	91
Daviess, co., Ky., U.S.	C2	94
Daviess, co., Mo., U.S.	B3	102
Davin, Sask.	G3	75
Davis, Ca., U.S.	C3	82
Davis, Il., U.S.	A4	90
Davis, N.C., U.S.	C6	110
Davis, Ok., U.S.	C4	113
Davis, S.D., U.S.	D9	118
Davis, W.V., U.S.	B5	125
Davis, co., Ia., U.S.	D5	92
Davis, co., Ut., U.S.	C3	121
Davis, Mount, mtn., Pa., U.S.	G3	115
Davisboro, Ga., U.S.	D4	87
Davis City, Ia., U.S.	D4	92
Davis Creek, stm., W.V., U.S.	m12	125
Davis Dam, Az., U.S.	B1	80
Davis Dam, U.S.	H7	105
Davis Inlet, Newf.	g9	72
Davis Islands, is., Fl., U.S.	p11	86
Davis Junction, Il., U.S.	A4	90
Davis Lake, l., Or., U.S.	E5	114
Davis-Monthan Air Force Base, mil., Az., U.S.	E5	80
Davis Mountains, mts., Tx., U.S.	o12	120
Davison, Mi., U.S.	E7	99
Davison, co., S.D., U.S.	D7	118
Davis Sea, Ant.	C22	7
Davis Station, S.C., U.S.	D7	117
Davis Strait, strt., N.A.	C15	61
Daviston, Al., U.S.	B4	78
Davisville, N.H., U.S.	D3	106
Davisville, R.I., U.S.	E4	116
Davle, Czech.	o17	26
Davos, Switz.	E4	18
Davy, W.V., U.S.	D3	125
Dawa, China	*C9	31
Dawa, stm., Afr.	E5	47
Dawasir, Wādī ad, val., Sau. Ar.	C4	38
Dawei, Burma	F10	36
Dawes, co., Ne., U.S.	B2	104
Dawn, Mo., U.S.	B4	102
Dawna Range, mts., Burma	D3	35
Dawros Head, c., Ire.	C3	11
Daws Island, i., S.C., U.S.	G6	117
Dawson, Yukon	E2	67
Dawson, Ga., U.S.	E2	87
Dawson, Ia., U.S.	C3	92
Dawson, Mn., U.S.	F2	100
Dawson, Ne., U.S.	D10	104
Dawson, N.D., U.S.	C6	111
Dawson, Pa., U.S.	F2	115
Dawson, Tx., U.S.	C4	120
Dawson, co., Ga., U.S.	B2	87
Dawson, co., Mt., U.S.	C11	103
Dawson, co., Ne., U.S.	D6	104
Dawson, co., Tx., U.S.	C1	120
Dawson, stm., Austl.	D8	50
Dawson, Mount, mtn., B.C.	D9	69
Dawson Creek, B.C.	B7	69
Dawson-Lambton Glacier, ice, Ant.	B10	7
Dawson Range, mts., Yukon	D5	66
Dawson Springs, Ky., U.S.	C2	94
Dawsonville, Ga., U.S.	B2	87
Dax, Fr.	F3	16
Daxian, China	E6	31
Day, Fl., U.S.	B3	86
Day, co., S.D., U.S.	B8	118
Daykin, Ne., U.S.	D8	104
Daylesford, Austl.	H5	51
Daym Zubayr, Sud.	D2	47
Dayong, China	J4	32
Dayr al Balaḥ, Isr. Occ.	C6	41
Dayr az Zawr, Syria	B4	38
Dayr Dibwān, Isr. Occ.	h12	41
Dayr 'Allā, Jord.	g13	41
Dayr Istiyā, Isr. Occ.	g11	41
Dayrūṭ, Eg.	D6	43
Daysland, Alta.	C4	68
Daysville, Tn., U.S.	D9	119
Dayton, Al., U.S.	C2	78
Dayton, Id., U.S.	G7	89
Dayton, In., U.S.	D4	91
Dayton, Ia., U.S.	B3	92
Dayton, Ky., U.S.	h14	94
Dayton, Md., U.S.	B4	97
Dayton, Mn., U.S.	m12	100
Dayton, Nv., U.S.	D2	105
Dayton, N.J., U.S.	C3	107
Dayton, N.Y., U.S.	C2	109
Dayton, Oh., U.S.	C1	112
Dayton, Or., U.S.	B3	114
Dayton, Pa., U.S.	E3	115
Dayton, Tn., U.S.	D8	119
Dayton, Tx., U.S.	D5	120
Dayton, Va., U.S.	B4	123
Dayton, Wa., U.S.	C8	124
Dayton, Wy., U.S.	B5	127
Daytona Beach, Fl., U.S.	C5	86
Dayu, China	F7	31
Dayville, Ct., U.S.	B8	84
Dayville, Or., U.S.	C7	114
Dazey, N.D., U.S.	B7	111
De Aar, S. Afr.	D3	49
Dead, North Branch, stm., Me., U.S.	C2	96
Dead, South Branch, stm., Me., U.S.	C2	96
Dead Creek, stm., Vt., U.S.	C2	122
Dead Diamond, stm., N.H., U.S.	g7	106
Dead Indian Peak, mtn., Wy., U.S.	B3	127
Dead Lake, l., Mn., U.S.	D3	100
Dead Lake, res., Fl., U.S.	B1	86
Deadman Bay, b., Fl., U.S.	C3	86
Deadman Creek, stm., Wa., U.S.	g14	124
Dead Sea, l., Asia	B3	38
Deadwood, S.D., U.S.	C2	118
Deadwood Reservoir, res., Id., U.S.	E3	89
Deaf Smith, co., Tx., U.S.	B1	120
Deakin Bay, b., Ant.	C28	7
Deal, Eng., U.K.	C9	12
Deal, N.J., U.S.	C4	107
Deal Island, Md., U.S.	D6	97
Deal Island, i., Md., U.S.	D6	97
Dean, stm., B.C.	C4	69
Deanburg, Tn., U.S.	B3	119
Dean Channel, strt., B.C.	C4	69
Deán Funes, Arg.	A4	54
Deans, N.J., U.S.	C3	107
Deanville, W.V., U.S.	B4	125
Dearborn, Mi., U.S.	F7	99
Dearborn, co., In., U.S.	F7	91
Dearborn Heights, Mi., U.S.	p15	99
Dearborn Street, N.J., U.S.	D2	107
Dearing, Ga., U.S.	C4	87
Dearing, Ks., U.S.	E8	93
Deary, Id., U.S.	C2	89
Dease Arm, b., N.W. Ter.	C8	66
Dease Lake, B.C.	m16	69
Dease Strait, strt., N.W. Ter.	C11	66
Death Valley, val., Ca.	D5	82
Death Valley Junction, Ca.	D5	82
Death Valley National Monument, Ca.	D5	82
Deatsville, Al., U.S.	C3	78
Deauville, Fr.	C3	16
Deaver, Wy., U.S.	B4	127
Deba, Nig.	*D6	45
De Baca, co., N.M., U.S.	C5	108
Debaltsevo, Sov. Un.	q21	27
Debao, China	G6	31
Debar, Yugo.	E5	24
De Berry, Tx., U.S.	C5	120
Debica, Pol.	C6	26
Deblin, Pol.	D6	26
Deblois, Me., U.S.	D4	96
Debno, Pol.	B3	26
Debno, Pol.	C6	26
Debo, Lac, l., Mali	C4	45
De Borgia, Mt., U.S.	C1	103
Deboullie Mountain, mtn., Me.	B4	96
Debovo, Bul.	D7	24
Debre Birhan, Eth.	D4	47
Debrecen, Hung.	B5	24
Debre Markos, Eth.	C4	47
Debre Tabor, Eth.	C4	47
Debre Zeyit, Eth.	*D4	47
De Cade, Lake, l., La., U.S.	E5	95
Decatur, Al., U.S.	A3	78
Decatur, Ar., U.S.	A1	81
Decatur, Ga., U.S.	C2	87
Decatur, Il., U.S.	D5	90
Decatur, In., U.S.	C8	91
Decatur, Ia., U.S.	D4	92
Decatur, Mi., U.S.	F5	99
Decatur, Ms., U.S.	C4	101
Decatur, Ne., U.S.	B9	104
Decatur, Tn., U.S.	D9	119
Decatur, Tx., U.S.	C4	120
Decatur, co., Ga., U.S.	F2	87
Decatur, co., In., U.S.	F6	91
Decatur, co., Ia., U.S.	D4	92
Decatur, co., Ks., U.S.	C3	93
Decatur, co., Tn., U.S.	B3	119
Decatur, Lake, res., Il., U.S.	D5	90
Decaturville, Tn., U.S.	B3	119
Decazeville, Fr.	E5	16
Deccan, plat., India	E6	36
Deception, Mount, mtn., Wa., U.S.	B2	124
Deception Lake, l., Sask.	A7	75
Decherd, Tn., U.S.	B5	119
Děčín, Czech.	C3	26
Decize, Fr.	D5	16
Decker, Man.	D1	70
Decker, In., U.S.	G2	91
Decker, Mt., U.S.	E10	103
Decker Lake, B.C.	B5	69
Deckers, Co., U.S.	B5	83
Deckerville, Mi., U.S.	E8	99
Declo, Id., U.S.	G5	89
Decorah, Ia., U.S.	A6	92
Decota, W.V., U.S.	m13	125
Dededo, Guam	L10	52
Deder, Eth.	D5	47
Dedham, Ia., U.S.	C3	92
Dedham, Ma., U.S.	B5	98
Dedinovo, Sov. Un.	n19	27
Dedougou, Burkina	D4	45
Dedu, China	B3	33
Dédza, Mwi.	D5	48
Dee, stm., U.K.	D5	10
Dee, stm., Scot., U.K.	B5	10
Deedsville, In., U.S.	C5	91
Deel, Ire.	E3	11
Deemer, Ms., U.S.	C4	101
Deep, stm., N.C., U.S.	B3	110
Deep Brook, N.S.	E4	71
Deep Creek, stm., De., U.S.	F3	85
Deep Creek, stm., Mt., U.S.	C4	103
Deep Creek, stm., Ut., U.S.	B3	121
Deep Creek, stm., Ut., U.S.	C2	121
Deep Creek, stm., Va., U.S.	F3	121
Deep Creek, stm., Wa., U.S.	g13	124
Deep Creek Lake, res., Md., U.S.	K12	97
Deep Creek Mountains, mts., Id., U.S.	G6	89
Deep Creek Range, mts., Ut., U.S.	D2	121
Deep Fork, stm., Ok., U.S.	B5	113
Deep Gap, N.C., U.S.	A1	110
Deep Inlet, b., Newf.	g10	72
Deep Red Creek, stm., Ok., U.S.	C3	113
Deep River, Ont.	A7	73
Deep River, Ct., U.S.	D6	84
Deep River, Ia., U.S.	C5	92
Deep Run, N.C., U.S.	B5	110
Deepstep, Ga., U.S.	C4	87
Deepwater, Mo., U.S.	C4	102
Deepwater, N.J., U.S.	D1	107
Deep Water, W.V., U.S.	m13	125
Deer, Ar., U.S.	B2	81
Deer Creek, Il., U.S.	C4	90
Deer Creek, In., U.S.	C5	91
Deer Creek, Mn., U.S.	D3	100
Deer Creek, Ok., U.S.	A4	113
Deer Creek, stm., In., U.S.	C5	91
Deer Creek, stm., Ms., U.S.	B3	101
Deer Creek, stm., Oh., U.S.	C2	112
Deer Creek Indian Reservation, Mn., U.S.	C5	100
Deerfield, Il., U.S.	h9	90
Deerfield, Ks., U.S.	E2	93
Deerfield, Ma., U.S.	A2	98
Deerfield, Mi., U.S.	G7	99
Deerfield, Mo., U.S.	D3	102
Deerfield, N.H., U.S.	D4	106
Deerfield, Oh., U.S.	A4	112
Deerfield, Wi., U.S.	E4	126
Deerfield Beach, Fl., U.S.	F6	86
Deerfield Street, N.J., U.S.	D2	107
Deer Grove, Il., U.S.	B4	90
Deering, Ak., U.S.	B7	79
Deering, Mo., U.S.	E8	102
Deering, N.D., U.S.	A4	111
Deer Island, Or., U.S.	B4	114
Deer Island, i., Me., U.S.	D4	96
Deer Island, i., Ms., U.S.	f8	101
Deer Isle, Me., U.S.	D4	96
Deer Isle, i., Me., U.S.	D4	96
Deer Lake, l., Newf.	D3	72
Deer Lake, l., Mn., U.S.	C5	100
Deer Lodge, Mt., U.S.	D4	103
Deer Lodge, co., Mt., U.S.	E3	103
Deer Mountain, mtn., Me., U.S.	C2	96
Deer Park, Al., U.S.	D1	78
Deer Park, Md., U.S.	m12	97
Deer Park, Mi., U.S.	B5	99
Deer Park, N.Y., U.S.	n15	109
Deer Park, Oh., U.S.	*r14	120
Deer Park, Tx., U.S.	*r14	120
Deer Park, Wa., U.S.	B8	124
Deer Park, Wi., U.S.	C1	126
Deer Pond, l., Newf.	D4	72
Deer River, Mn., U.S.	C5	100
Deer River, N.Y., U.S.	B5	109
Deer Trail, Co., U.S.	B6	83
Deerwood, Mn., U.S.	D5	100
Deeson, Ms., U.S.	A3	101
Deex Nugaaleed, stm., Som.	D6	47
Defas, Eth.	A5	47
Deferiet, N.Y., U.S.	A5	109
Defiance, Mo., U.S.	f12	102
Defiance, Oh., U.S.	A1	112
Defiance, co., Oh., U.S.	A1	112
Defiance, Mount, mtn., Or., U.S.	B5	114
Deford, Mi., U.S.	E7	99
De Forest, Wi., U.S.	E4	126
De Funiak Springs, Fl., U.S.	u15	86
Dêgê, China	E4	31
Degeberga, Swe.	C8	15
Degelis, Que.	B9	74
Degerön, Swe.	u33	14
Degersheim, Switz.	B7	21
Deggendorf, Ger.	D6	18
De Graff, Mn., U.S.	E3	100
De Graff, Oh., U.S.	B2	112
De Gray Lake, res., Ar., U.S.	C2	81
De Grey, stm., Austl.	D2	50
Deh Bīd, Iran	B5	38
Dehibat, Tun.	C7	44
Dehiwala-Mount Lavinia, Sri L.	*G6	36
Deh Kord, Iran	E4	39
Dehlorān, Iran	E3	39
Dehpehk, i., Micron.	Q17	52
Dehra Dūn, India	B6	36
Deh Shū, Afg.	F11	39
Deinze, Bel.	D3	17
Dej, Rom.	B6	24
Dejvice (part of Prague), Czech.	n17	26
Dekalb, Il., U.S.	B5	90
De Kalb, Ms., U.S.	C5	101
De Kalb, Mo., U.S.	B3	102
De Kalb, N.Y., U.S.	f9	109
De Kalb, Tx., U.S.	C5	120
De Kalb, co., Al., U.S.	A4	78
De Kalb, co., Ga., U.S.	C2	87
De Kalb, co., Il., U.S.	B5	90
De Kalb, co., In., U.S.	B7	91
De Kalb, co., Mo., U.S.	B3	102
De Kalb, co., Tn., U.S.	D8	119
De Kalb Junction, N.Y., U.S.	f9	109
Dekemhare, Eth.	B4	47
Dekese, Zaire	B3	48
Deke Sokehs, i., Micron.	Q17	52
Dekoa, Cen. Afr. Rep.	D3	46
Delacroix, La., U.S.	k12	95
Delafield, Wi., U.S.	m11	126
De Laire, Ca., U.S.	*n12	82
De Lamere, N.D., U.S.	C8	111
Delanco, N.J., U.S.	C3	107
De Land, Fl., U.S.	C5	86
De Land, Il., U.S.	C5	90
Delaney, Ar., U.S.	B2	81
Delano, Ca., U.S.	E4	82
Delano, Mn., U.S.	E5	100
Delano, Tn., U.S.	D9	119
Delano Peak, mtn., Ut., U.S.	E3	121
Delanson, N.Y., U.S.	C6	109
Delaplaine, Ar., U.S.	A5	81
Delaram, Afg.	E11	39
Delaronde Lake, l., Sask.	C2	75
Delavan, Il., U.S.	C4	90
Delavan, Ks., U.S.	D7	93
Delavan, Mn., U.S.	G4	100
Delavan, Wi., U.S.	F5	126
Delavan Lake, Wi., U.S.	*F5	126
Delaware, Ont.	E3	73
Delaware, Ar., U.S.	B2	81
Delaware, Ia., U.S.	B6	92
Delaware, Oh., U.S.	B2	112
Delaware, Ok., U.S.	A6	113
Delaware, co., In., U.S.	D7	91
Delaware, co., Ia., U.S.	B6	92
Delaware, co., N.Y., U.S.	C5	109
Delaware, co., Oh., U.S.	B2	112
Delaware, co., Ok., U.S.	A7	113
Delaware, co., Pa., U.S.	G11	115
Delaware, state, U.S.	D3	85
Delaware, stm., U.S.	E2	107
Delaware, East Branch, stm., N.Y., U.S.	C5	109
Delaware, West Branch, stm., U.S.	C5	109
Delaware Bay, b., U.S.	C12	76
Delaware City, De., U.S.	B3	85
Delaware Lake, res., Oh., U.S.	B3	112
Delaware Mountains, mts., Tx., U.S.	o12	120
Delaware Water Gap, Pa., U.S.	E11	115
Delaware Water Gap, N.J.	B2	107
Delaware Water Gap National Recreation Area, U.S.	B2	107
Delbarton, W.V., U.S.	D2	125
Delburne, Alta.	C4	68
Delcambre, La., U.S.	E4	95
Del City, Ok., U.S.	B4	113
Delco, N.C., U.S.	C4	110
Deleau, Man.	E1	70
Delémont, Switz.	E3	18
De Leon, Tx., U.S.	C3	120
De Leon Springs, Fl., U.S.	C5	86
Delevan, N.Y., U.S.	C2	109
Delft, Neth.	A5	17
Delft, Mn., U.S.	G3	100
Delfzijl, Neth.	A7	16
Delgada, Punta, c., Arg.	D7	54
Delgado, Cabo, c., Moz.	A2	48
Delgertsogt, Mong.	A2	32
Delhi, Ont.	E4	73
Delhi, India	B6	36
Delhi, Ia., U.S.	B6	92
Delhi, La., U.S.	B4	95
Delhi, N.Y., U.S.	C6	109
Delhi, Ok., U.S.	B2	113
Delhi, ter., India	*C6	36
Delhi Hills, Oh., U.S.	*o12	112
Delia, Alta.	C4	68
Delia, Ks., U.S.	C8	93
Delicias, Mex.	*B3	63
Delight, Ar., U.S.	C2	81
Delingha, China	D1	78
Delisle, Sask.	F2	75
De Lisle, Ms., U.S.	E4	101
Delitzsch, Ger.	C6	18
Dell, Ar., U.S.	B5	81
Dell, Mt., U.S.	F4	103
Dell City, Tx., U.S.	o11	120
Delle, Fr.	B3	20
Dellenbaugh, Mount, mtn., Az., U.S.	A2	80
Dell Rapids, S.D., U.S.	D9	118
Dellroy, Oh., U.S.	B4	112
Dellslow, W.V., U.S.	h11	125
Dellwood, Mn., U.S.	B1	86
Dellwood, Mo., U.S.	*f13	102
Delmar, Al., U.S.	A2	78
Del Mar, Ca., U.S.	o15	82
Delmar, De., U.S.	G3	85
Delmar, Ia., U.S.	B7	92
Delmar, Md., U.S.	D6	97
Delmar, N.Y., U.S.	C7	109
Delmas, Sask.	E1	75
Delmenhorst, Ger.	B4	18
Delmita, Tx., U.S.	F3	120
Delmont, N.J., U.S.	E3	107
Delmont, S.D., U.S.	D7	118
Del Norte, Co., U.S.	D4	83
Del Norte, co., Ca., U.S.	B2	82
Deloit, Ia., U.S.	B2	92
Delong, In., U.S.	B5	91
De Long Islands, is., Sov. Un.	B35	128
Deloraine, Man.	E1	70
Deloro, Ont.	C7	73
Delorme, Lac, l., Que.	F18	66
Delos see Dhílos, i., Grc.	D5	25
Del Park Manor, De., U.S.	i7	85
Delphi, In., U.S.	C4	91
Delphia, Mt., U.S.	D8	103
Delphos, Ks., U.S.	C6	93
Delphos, Oh., U.S.	B1	112
Delray Beach, Fl., U.S.	*D4	86
Del Rio, Tn., U.S.	D10	119
Del Rio, Tx., U.S.	E2	120
Delson, Que.	q19	74
Delta, Ont.	C8	73
Delta, Al., U.S.	B4	78
Delta, Co., U.S.	C2	83
Delta, Ia., U.S.	C5	92
Delta, La., U.S.	B5	95
Delta, Mo., U.S.	D8	102
Delta, Oh., U.S.	A1	112
Delta, Pa., U.S.	G9	115
Delta, Ut., U.S.	D3	121
Delta, co., Co., U.S.	C3	83
Delta, co., Mi., U.S.	C3	99
Delta, co., Tx., U.S.	C5	120
Delta, reg., Ms., U.S.	B3	101
Delta Amacuro, ter., Ven.	B5	60
Delta Barrage, Eg.	D3	41
Delta Beach, Man.	D2	70
Delta City, Ms., U.S.	B3	101
Delta Junction, Ak., U.S.	C10	79
Delta Peak, mtn., B.C.	A3	69
Delta Reservoir, res., N.Y., U.S.	B5	109
Deltaville, Va., U.S.	C6	123
Delton, Mi., U.S.	F5	99
Deltona, Fl., U.S.	D5	86
Delungra, Austl.	D8	51
Delvin, Ire.	D4	11
Delvina, Alb.	C3	25
Delyatin, Sov. Un.	G5	27
Demaine, Sask.	G2	75
Demanda, Sierra de la, mtn., Spain	A4	22
Demarest, N.J., U.S.	h9	107
Demavend, Mount, mtn., Iran	B5	38
Demba, Zaire	C3	48
Dembi Dolo, Eth.	D3	47
Demerara, stm., Guy.	A3	59
Demidov, Sov. Un.	D8	27
Deming, N.M., U.S.	E2	108
Deming, Wa., U.S.	A3	124
Demini, stm., Braz.	B2	59
Demirci, Tur.	C7	40
Demir Kapija, Yugo.	E6	24
Demmin, Ger.	B6	18
Demmitt, Alta.	B1	68
Demnat, Mor.	C3	44
Demopolis, Al., U.S.	C2	78
Demopolis Dam, Al., U.S.	C2	78
Demorest, Ga., U.S.	B3	87
Demorestville, Ont.	C7	73
De Mossville, Ky., U.S.	k14	94
Demotte, In., U.S.	B3	91
Dempo, mtn., Indon.	F2	34
Dempster, S.D., U.S.	C9	118
Demyanka, stm., Sov. Un.	B8	28
Demyansk, Sov. Un.	B5	28
Denain, Fr.	B5	16
Denakil (Danakil), reg., Eth.	C5	47
Denali National Park, Ak., U.S.	C9	79
Denare Beach, Sask.	C4	75
Denau, Sov. Un.	H22	29
Denaud, Fl., U.S.	F5	86
Denbigh, Wales, U.K.	D5	10
Denbigh, N.D., U.S.	A5	111
Den Burg, Neth.	A4	17
Denby, S.D., U.S.	D3	118
Dendermonde, Bel.	C4	17
Dendron, Va., U.S.	C6	123
Denezhkin Kamen, Mount, mtn., Sov. Un.	A5	28
Dengkou, China	D2	32
Denham, In., U.S.	B4	91
Denham, Mn., U.S.	D6	100
Denham, Mount, mtn., Jam.	E13	65
Denham Springs, La., U.S.	D5	95
Den Helder, Neth.	A6	16
Denhoff, N.D., U.S.	B5	111
Denholm, Sask.	E1	75
Den Hoorn, Neth.	A4	17
Denia, Spain	C6	22
Deniau, Que.	B8	74
Deniliquin, Austl.	G7	50
Denio, Nv., U.S.	B3	105
Denison, Ia., U.S.	B2	92
Denison, Ks., U.S.	k14	93
Denison, Tx., U.S.	C4	120
Denison Dam, U.S.	D5	113
Denizli, Tur.	D7	40
Denman Glacier, ice, Ant.	C22	7
Denmark, N.S.	D6	71
Denmark, Me., U.S.	D2	96
Denmark, S.C., U.S.	E5	117
Denmark, Tn., U.S.	B2	119
Denmark, Wi., U.S.	D6	126
Denmark, ctry., Eur.	I3	14
Denmark Strait, strt.	C17	128
Dennard, Ar., U.S.	B3	81
Dennehotso, Az., U.S.	A6	80
Denning, Ar., U.S.	B2	81
Dennis, Ks., U.S.	E8	93
Dennis, Ma., U.S.	C7	98
Dennis, Ms., U.S.	A5	101
Dennis Hill, mtn., Ct., U.S.	B3	84
Dennison, Mn., U.S.	F6	100
Dennison, Oh., U.S.	B4	112
Dennis Port, Ma., U.S.	C7	98
Dennisville, N.J., U.S.	E3	107
Denny, Scot., U.K.	*D5	13
Dennysville, Me., U.S.	D5	96
Denny Terrace, S.C., U.S.	C5	117
Den Oever, Neth.	B5	17
Denpasar, Indon.	G5	34
Dent, Mn., U.S.	D3	100
Dent, co., Mo., U.S.	D6	102
Denton, Ga., U.S.	E4	87
Denton, Ks., U.S.	C8	93
Denton, Md., U.S.	C6	97
Denton, Mt., U.S.	C6	103
Denton, Ne., U.S.	p14	99
Denton, N.C., U.S.	B2	110
Denton, Tx., U.S.	C4	120
Denton, co., Tx., U.S.	C4	120
D'Entrecasteaux, Point, c.	F2	50
D'Entrecasteaux Islands, is., Pap. N. Gui.	k13	50
Dents Du Midi, mts., Switz.	D2	21
Dentsville, S.C., U.S.	C6	117
Denver, Co., U.S.	B6	83
Denver, Ia., U.S.	B5	92
Denver, In., U.S.	C5	91
Denver, Mo., U.S.	A3	102

Name	Map Ref.	Page
Denver, N.C., U.S.	B1	110
Denver, Pa., U.S.	F9	115
Denver, Tn., U.S.	A4	119
Denver, W.V., U.S.	B5	125
Denver, co., Co., U.S.	B6	83
Denver City, Tx., U.S.	C1	120
Denville, N.J., U.S.	B4	107
Denzil, Sask.	E1	75
Deoghar, India	E11	37
De Panne, Bel.	C2	17
Departure Bay, B.C.	f12	69
Depauville, N.Y., U.S.	A4	109
Depauw, In., U.S.	H5	91
De Pere, Wi., U.S.	D5	126
Depew, N.Y., U.S.	C2	109
Depew, Ok., U.S.	B5	113
Depoe Bay, Or., U.S.	C2	114
Depok, Indon.	*G3	34
Deport, Tx., U.S.	C5	120
Deposit, N.Y., U.S.	C5	109
Depósito, Braz.	B2	59
Depot Harbour, Ont.	B4	73
Depue, Il., U.S.	B4	90
Deputy, In., U.S.	G6	91
Dêqên, China	F4	31
De Queen, Ar., U.S.	C1	81
De Queen Lake, res., Ar., U.S.	C1	81
Dequen-Nord, Que.	A5	74
De Quincy, La., U.S.	D2	95
Dera, Lak., stm., Afr.	E5	47
Dera Ghāzi Khān, Pak.	B5	36
Dera Ismāïl Khān, Pak.	B5	36
Derbent, Sov. Un.	I14	27
Derbetovka, Sov. Un.	I14	27
Derby, Austl.	C3	50
Derby, N.B.	C4	71
Derby, Eng., U.K.	D6	10
Derby, Ct., U.S.	D3	84
Derby, Ia., U.S.	H4	91
Derby, Ia., U.S.	D4	92
Derby, Ks., U.S.	E6	93
Derby, Me., U.S.	C4	96
Derby, N.Y., U.S.	E4	101
Derby, N.Y., U.S.	C2	109
Derby, Oh., U.S.	C2	112
Derby, Va., U.S.	f9	123
Derby Junction, N.B.	C4	71
Derby Line, Vt., U.S.	A4	122
Derbyshire, co., Eng., U.K.	A6	12
Derecske, Hung.	B5	24
Derg, Lough, l., Ire.	D2	10
Der Grabow, b., Ger.	D6	15
De Ridder, La., U.S.	D2	95
Derik, Tur.	D13	40
Derma, Ms., U.S.	B4	101
Dermott, Ar., U.S.	D4	81
Dernieres, Isles, is., La., U.S.	E5	95
Derravaragh, Lough, l., Ire.	D3	10
Derrieusseaux Creek, stm., Ar., U.S.	C3	81
Derry, La., U.S.	C3	95
Derry, N.H., U.S.	E4	106
Derry, N.H., U.S.	E2	108
Derry, Pa., U.S.	F3	115
Derrybrien, Ire.	D3	11
Derry see Londonderry, N. Ire., U.K.	C3	10
Derudeb, Sud.	B4	47
De Ruyter, N.Y., U.S.	C5	109
Derventa, Yugo.	C3	24
Derwent, Alta.	C5	68
Derwent, Oh., U.S.	C4	112
Derwent, stm., Eng., U.K.	F8	13
Derwent, stm., Eng., U.K.	F6	13
Derwent, stm., Eng., U.K.	F5	13
Derwood, Md., U.S.	B3	97
Derzhavinsk, Sov. Un.	C7	28
Desaguadero, stm., Arg.	A3	54
Desaguadero, stm., Bol.	C2	55
Desamparados, C.R.	E5	95
Des Allemands, La., U.S.	*F5	62
Des Arc, Ar., U.S.	C4	81
Des Arc, Mo., U.S.	D7	102
Desbiens, Que.	A6	74
Desboro, Ont.	C3	73
Descalvado, Braz.	k8	56
Descartes, Fr.	D4	16
Deschaillons [-sur-Saint-Laurent], Que.	C5	74
Deschambault, Que.	C6	74
Deschambault, Sask.	C4	75
Deschambault Lake, l., Sask.	C4	75
Deschênes, Que.	D2	74
Deschutes, co., Or., U.S.	D5	114
Deschutes, stm., Or., U.S.	B6	114
Dese, Eth.	C4	47
Deseado, stm., Arg.	D3	54
Desengaño, Punta, c., Arg.	D3	54
Desenzano del Garda, Italy	D6	20
Deseret, Ut., U.S.	D3	121
Deseret Peak, mtn., Ut., U.S.	C3	121
Deseronto, Ont.	C7	73
Desert, Mount, mtn., W.V., U.S.	m13	125
Deserta Grande, i., Port.	h12	52
Desert Center, Ca., U.S.	F6	82
Desert Creek Peak, mtn., Nv., U.S.	E2	105
Desert Hot Springs, Ca., U.S.	F5	82
Desert Peak, mtn., Ut., U.S.	B2	121
Desert Valley, val., Nv., U.S.	B3	105
Desha, Ar., U.S.	B4	81
Desha, co., Ar., U.S.	D4	81
Deshler, Ne., U.S.	D8	104
Deshler, Oh., U.S.	A2	112
Desio, Italy	D5	20
Des Lacs, N.D., U.S.	A4	111
Des Lacs, stm., N.D., U.S.	A4	111
Desloge, Mo., U.S.	D7	102
Desmarais, Alta.	B4	68
Desmet, Id., U.S.	B2	89
De Smet, S.D., U.S.	C8	118
Desmochados, Para.	E4	55
Des Moines, Ia., U.S.	C4	92
Des Moines, N.M., U.S.	A6	108
Des Moines, Wa., U.S.	B3	124
Des Moines, co., Ia., U.S.	D6	92
Des Moines, stm., U.S.	D5	92
Des Moines, East Fork, stm., U.S.	A3	92
Desna, stm., Sov. Un.	F8	27
Desolación, Isla, i., Chile	h11	54
Desolation Canyon, val., Ut., U.S.	D5	121
De Soto, Ga., U.S.	E2	87
De Soto, Ia., U.S.	F4	90
De Soto, Ia., U.S.	C3	92
De Soto, Ks., U.S.	D9	93
De Soto, Ks., U.S.	D5	101
De Soto, Mo., U.S.	C7	102
De Soto, Tx., U.S.	*n10	120
De Soto, Wi., U.S.	E2	126
De Soto, co., Fl., U.S.	E5	86
De Soto, co., Ms., U.S.	A3	101
De Soto City, Fl., U.S.	E5	86
Despard, W.V., U.S.	k10	125
Des Peres, Mo., U.S.	f13	102
Día, i., Grc.	E5	25
Des Plaines, Il., U.S.	A6	90
Des Plaines, stm., U.S.	k8	90
Dessau, Ger.	C6	18
Destin, Fl., U.S.	u15	86
Destrehan, La., U.S.	E5	95
Desvres, Fr.	D1	17
Dete, Zimb.	A4	49
Detlor, Ont.	B7	73
Detmold, Ger.	C4	18
Detour, Point, c., Mi., U.S.	C4	99
De Tour Village, Mi., U.S.	C7	99
Detroit, Al., U.S.	A1	78
Detroit, Ks., U.S.	D6	93
Detroit, Me., U.S.	D3	96
Detroit, Mi., U.S.	F7	99
Detroit, Or., U.S.	C4	114
Detroit, Tx., U.S.	C5	120
Detroit, stm., N.A.	F7	99
Detroit Lake, res., Or., U.S.	C4	114
Detroit Lakes, Mn., U.S.	D3	100
Detva, Czech.	D5	26
Deuel, co., Ne., U.S.	C3	104
Deuel, co., S.D., U.S.	C9	118
Deurne (part of Antwerp), Bel.	B6	16
Deux Frères, Les, is., Viet.	H7	35
Deux-Montagnes, Que.	p19	74
Deux-Montagnes, co., Que.	D3	74
Deux Montagnes, Lac des, l., Que.	q19	74
Deux-Rivières, Ont.	A6	73
Deva, Rom.	C6	24
De Valls Bluff, Ar., U.S.	C4	81
Dévaványa, Hung.	B5	24
Deventer, Neth.	A7	16
Devereux, Ga., U.S.	C3	87
Deveron, stm., Scot., U.K.	C6	13
DeView, Bayou, stm., Ar., U.S.	B4	81
Devil River Peak, mtn., N.Z.	N14	51
Devils Elbow, Mo., U.S.	D5	102
Devils Island see Diable, Île du, i., Fr. Gu.	A4	59
Devils Lake, N.D., U.S.	A7	111
Devils Lake, l., N.D., U.S.	A6	111
Devils Paw, mtn., Ak., U.S.	k23	79
Devils Postpile National Monument, Ca., U.S.	D4	82
Devils Slide, Ut., U.S.	B4	121
Devils Tower, Wy., U.S.	B8	127
Devils Tower National Monument, Wy., U.S.	B8	127
Devil Track Lake, l., Mn., U.S.	k9	100
Devin, Bul.	E7	24
Devine, Tx., U.S.	E3	120
Devizes, Eng., U.K.	C6	12
Devol, Ok., U.S.	C3	113
Devola, Oh., U.S.	C4	112
Devoll, stm., Alb.	B3	25
Devon, Alta.	C4	68
Devon, Ks., U.S.	E9	93
Devon, Mt., U.S.	B5	103
Devon, Pa., U.S.	*o20	115
Devon, co., Eng., U.K.	D4	12
Devon Island, i., N.W. Ter.	m34	66
Devonia, Tn., U.S.	C9	119
Devonport, Austl.	o15	50
Devonshire, De., U.S.	h7	85
Dewalt, Tx., U.S.	r14	120
Dewar Lake, Sask.	F1	75
Dewar, Ok., U.S.	B6	113
Dewberry, Alta.	C5	68
Dewdney, B.C.	D7	104
Dewees Inlet, b., S.C., U.S.	k12	117
Dewees Island, i., S.C., U.S.	F8	117
Dewey, Az., U.S.	C3	80
Dewey, Il., U.S.	C5	90
Dewey, Mt., U.S.	E4	103
Dewey, Ok., U.S.	A6	113
Dewey, co., Ok., U.S.	B2	113
Dewey, co., S.D., U.S.	B4	118
Dewey Beach, De., U.S.	F5	85
Dewey Lake, res., Ky., U.S.	C7	94
Deweyville, Tx., U.S.	D6	120
Deweyville, Ut., U.S.	B3	121
De Winton, Alta.	D3	68
Dewitt, Ar., U.S.	C4	81
Dewitt, Il., U.S.	C5	90
De Witt, Ia., U.S.	C7	92
De Witt, Mi., U.S.	F6	99
De Witt, Mo., U.S.	B4	102
De Witt, Ne., U.S.	D9	104
De Witt, N.Y., U.S.	B4	109
De Witt, Va., U.S.	C5	123
De Witt, co., Il., U.S.	C5	90
De Witt, co., Tx., U.S.	E4	120
Dewsbury, Eng., U.K.	A6	12
Dexing, China	J7	32
Dexter, Ga., U.S.	D3	87
Dexter, Ia., U.S.	C3	92
Dexter, Ky., U.S.	f9	94
Dexter, Me., U.S.	C3	96
Dexter, Mi., U.S.	F7	99
Dexter, Mn., U.S.	G6	100
Dexter, Mo., U.S.	E8	102
Dexter, N.M., U.S.	D5	108
Dexter, N.Y., U.S.	A4	109
Dexter, Or., U.S.	D4	114
Dexter, Lake, l., Fl., U.S.	C5	86
Dey-Dey, Lake, l., Austl.	E5	50
Deyhūk, Iran	D7	39
Deyyer, Iran	H6	39
Dez, stm., Iran	B4	38
Dezful, Iran	B4	38
Dezhou, China	D8	31
Dhahab, Egy.	H10	40
Dhahran see Az Zahrān, Sau. Ar.	C4	38
Dhaka (Dacca), Bngl.	D9	36
Dhamār, Yemen	E4	38
Dhamtari, India	G8	37
Dhankuta, Nepal	D11	37
Dhār, India	F5	37
Dharmapuri, India	F6	37
Dharmjaygarh, India	D7	36
Dharmshāla, India	B6	36
Dhaulpur, India	D6	37
Dhawlāgiri, mtn., Nepal	C7	36
Dhekélia, Grc.	g11	25
Dhenoúsa, i., Grc.	D5	25
Dhibān, Jord.	G10	40
Dhidhimótikhon, Grc.	B6	25
Dhilos (Delos), i., Grc.	D5	25
Dhimitsána, Grc.	D4	25
Dhodhekánisos, is., Grc.	D6	25
Dhomhnuill, Sgurr, mtn., Scot., U.K.	D3	13
Dhorāji, India	G3	37
Dhrépanon, Cape, c., Grc.	C4	25
Dhuburi, India	D12	37
Dhule, India	D5	36
Dhuusa Mareeb, Som.	D6	47
Diable, Île du (Devils Island), i., Fr. Gu.	A4	59
Diable, Pointe du, c., Mart.	S11	65
Diablo, Canyon, val., Az., U.S.	C3	20
Diablo, Mount, mtn., Ca., U.S.	h9	82
Diablo Heights, Pan.	m11	62
Diablo Lake, res., Wa., U.S.	A4	124
Diablo Range, mts., Ca., U.S.	D3	82
Diagonal, Ia., U.S.	D3	92
Diamante, Arg.	A4	54
Diamantina, Braz.	B4	56
Diamantina, stm., Austl.	D7	50
Diamond, Oh., U.S.	A4	112
Diamond, W.V., U.S.	m12	125
Diamond Bar, Ca., U.S.	*n13	82
Diamond Bluff, Wi., U.S.	D1	126
Diamond City, Alta.	E4	68
Diamond Harbour, India	F12	37
Diamond Head, crat., Hi., U.S.	B4	88
Diamond Hill, R.I., U.S.	B4	116
Diamond Hill Reservoir, res., R.I., U.S.	A4	116
Diamond Lake, Il., U.S.	h9	90
Diamond Lake, l., Or., U.S.	D4	114
Diamond Mountains, mts., Nv., U.S.	D6	105
Diamond Peak, mtn., Co., U.S.	A2	83
Diamond Peak, mtn., Id., U.S.	E5	89
Diamond Peak, mtn., Or., U.S.	D4	114
Diamond Peak, mtn., Wa., U.S.	C8	124
Diamond Point, N.Y., U.S.	B7	109
Diamond Springs, Ca., U.S.	C3	82
Diamondville, Wy., U.S.	E2	127
Diana, Tn., U.S.	B5	119
Diana, W.V., U.S.	C4	125
Dianalund, Den.	C5	15
Dianbai, China	G7	31
Dianjiang, China	I2	31
Dianópolis, Braz.	D1	57
Diapaga, Burkina	D5	45
Diapitan Bay, b., Phil.	n14	34
Diaz, Ar., U.S.	B4	81
Dibaya, Zaire	C3	48
Dibble, Ok., U.S.	B4	113
Dibble Iceberg Tongue, ice, Ant.	C26	7
Diboll, Tx., U.S.	D5	120
Dibrell, Tn., U.S.	D8	119
Dibrugarh, India	C9	36
Dickens, Ia., U.S.	A2	92
Dickens, Ne., U.S.	D5	104
Dickens, Tx., U.S.	C2	120
Dickens, co., Tx., U.S.	C2	120
Dickenson, co., Va., U.S.	e9	123
Dickerson, Md., U.S.	B3	97
Dickey, N.D., U.S.	C7	111
Dickey, co., N.D., U.S.	C7	111
Dickeyville, Wi., U.S.	F3	126
Dickinson, Al., U.S.	D2	78
Dickinson, N.D., U.S.	C3	111
Dickinson, Tx., U.S.	*r14	120
Dickinson, co., Ia., U.S.	A2	92
Dickinson, co., Ks., U.S.	D6	93
Dickinson, co., Mi., U.S.	B3	99
Dickinson Center, N.Y., U.S.	f10	109
Dickinson Dam, N.D., U.S.	C3	111
Dickson, Ok., U.S.	C5	113
Dickson, Tn., U.S.	A4	119
Dickson, co., Tn., U.S.	A4	119
Dickson City, Pa., U.S.	D10	115
Dicle (Tigris), stm., Asia	D13	40
Didsbury, Alta.	D3	68
Die, Fr.	E6	16
Diébougou, Burkina	D4	45
Dieburg, Ger.	D3	19
Diefenbaker, Lake, res., Sask.	F2	75
Diégo-Suarez see Antsiranana, Madag.	f9	49
Diekirch, Lux.	E6	17
Diemel, stm., Ger.	C4	18
Dien Bien Phu, Viet.	B5	35
Diepholz, Ger.	C4	18
Dieppe, N.B.	C5	71
Dieppe, Fr.	C4	16
Dierks, Ar., U.S.	C1	81
Di'er Songhua, stm., China	B7	32
Diessen, Ger.	B7	20
Diest, Bel.	C4	17
Dieterich, Il., U.S.	D5	90
Dietikon, Switz.	B5	21
Dieuze, Fr.	C7	17
Diever, Neth.	B6	17
Diez, Ger.	C2	19
Diffa, Niger	D7	45
Differdange, Lux.	E5	17
Difficult, Tn., U.S.	C8	119
Digboi, India	C10	36
Digby, N.S.	E4	71
Digby, co., N.S.	E3	71
Dighton, Ks., U.S.	D3	93
Dighton, Ma., U.S.	C5	98
Dighton, Mi., U.S.	E5	99
Digne, Fr.	E7	16
Digoin, Fr.	D5	16
Digul, stm., Indon.	G10	34
Dijon, Fr.	D6	16
Dike, Ia., U.S.	B5	92
Dikhil, Dji.	C5	47
Dikili, Tur.	C6	25
Dikimis, Egy.	H10	40
Diksmuide, Bel.	C2	17
Dikson, Sov. Un.	B11	29
Dikwa, Nig.	D7	45
Dila, Eth.	D5	47
Dili, Indon.	G7	34
Dilia, stm., Niger	D7	45
Dilke, Sask.	G3	75
Dilkon, Az., U.S.	B5	80
Dillard, Ga., U.S.	B3	87
Dillard, Or., U.S.	D3	114
Dill City, Ok., U.S.	B2	113
Dille, W.V., U.S.	C4	125
Dillenburg, Ger.	C3	19
Diller, Ne., U.S.	D9	104
Dilley, Tx., U.S.	E3	120
Dilliner, Pa., U.S.	G2	115
Dilling, Sud.	C2	47
Dillingen, Ger.	D1	19
Dillingen [an der Donau], Ger.	D5	18
Dillingham, Ak., U.S.	D8	79
Dillon, Co., U.S.	B4	83
Dillon, Mt., U.S.	E4	103
Dillon, S.C., U.S.	C9	117
Dillon, co., S.C., U.S.	C9	117
Dillon, stm., Can.	B5	68
Dillon Lake, l., Sask.	B6	68
Dillon Lake, res., Oh., U.S.	B3	112
Dillon Reservoir, res., Co., U.S.	B4	83
Dillonvale, Oh., U.S.	B5	112
Dillsboro, In., U.S.	F7	91
Dillsboro, N.C., U.S.	f9	110
Dillsburg, Pa., U.S.	F7	115
Dillwyn, Va., U.S.	C4	123
Dilman see Salmās, Iran	B2	39
Dilolo, Zaire	D3	48
Dilworth, Mn., U.S.	D2	100
Dimbelenge, Zaire	C3	48
Dimbokro, I.C.	E4	45
Dimboola, Austl.	G8	50
Dimbovita, stm., Rom.	D7	24
Dimitrovgrad, Bul.	D6	24
Dimitrovgrad, Yugo.	D6	24
Dimmit, co., Tx., U.S.	E3	120
Dimmitt, Tx., U.S.	B1	120
Dimock, S.D., U.S.	D8	118
Dimona, Isr.	C7	41
Dimondale, Mi., U.S.	F6	99
Dinagat Island, i., Phil.	C7	34
Dinājpur, Bngl.	E12	37
Dinan, Fr.	C2	16
Dinant, Bel.	B6	16
Dinar, Tur.	C8	25
Dinard, Fr.	C2	16
Dinaric Alps, mts., Yugo.	F6	36
Dindigul, India	G5	37
Dingalan Bay, b., Phil.	o13	34
Dingbian, China	D6	31
Dingelstädt, Ger.	C5	19
Dingess, W.V., U.S.	D2	125
Dinghai, China	E9	31
Dingle, Ire.	D1	10
Dingle, Id., U.S.	D7	89
Dingle Bay, b., Ire.	D1	10
Dingmans Ferry, Pa., U.S.	D12	115
Dingo, Austl.	A7	51
Dingolfing, Ger.	D7	19
Dinguiraye, Gui.	D2	45
Dingwall, N.S.	C9	71
Dingwall, Scot., U.K.	B4	10
Dingxian, China	C4	31
Dingxin, China	C4	31
Dingxing, China	E6	32
Dinh Lap, Viet.	B7	35
Dinkelsbühl, Ger.	D5	19
Dinkey Creek, Ca., U.S.	D4	82
Dinklage, Ger.	F2	15
Dinner Point, c., Fl., U.S.	D4	86
Dinorwic Lake, l., Ont.	E5	70
Dinosaur, Co., U.S.	A1	83
Dinosaur National Monument, U.S.	C6	121
Dinosaur Provincial Park, Alta.	D5	68
Dinsdale, Sask.	B5	92
Dinslaken, Ger.	B1	19
Dinsmore, Sask.	F2	75
Dinuba, Ca., U.S.	D4	82
Dinwiddie, Va., U.S.	C5	123
Dinwiddie, co., Va., U.S.	C5	123
Dioila, Mali	D3	45
Dionísio, Braz.	E7	57
Diourbel, Sen.	D1	45
Diphu Pass, Asia	C10	36
Diplo, Pak.	E2	37
Dipper Harbour West, N.B.	D3	71
Dippoldiswalde, Ger.	C8	19
Diré, Mali	B7	50
Direction, Cape, c., Austl.	B7	50
Dire Dawa, Eth.	D5	47
Diriamba, Nic.	E7	63
Dirico, Ang.	E1	50
Dirk Hartog, i., Austl.	E1	50
Dirkou, Niger	C7	45
Dirmil, Tur.	D7	25
Dirranbandi, Austl.	E8	50
Dirty Devil, stm., Ut., U.S.	E5	121
Disappointment, Cape, c., Falk. Is.	D9	7
Disappointment, Cape, c., Wa., U.S.	C1	124
Disappointment, Lake, l., Austl.	D3	50
Disappointment Creek, stm., Co., U.S.	D2	83
Discovery, Mount, mtn., Ant.	f39	7
Disentis (Mustèr), Switz.	C4	21
Dishman, Wa., U.S.	g14	124
Dishnā, Eg.	D6	43
Disko, In., U.S.	B6	91
Disko, i., Grnld.	C15	61
Disley, Sask.	G3	75
Dismal, stm., Ne., U.S.	C5	104
Dismal Peak, mtn., Va., U.S.	C2	123
Disney, Ok., U.S.	A6	113
Disputanta, Va., U.S.	C5	123
Disraëli, Que.	D6	74
Diss, Eng., U.K.	B9	12
Distant, Pa., U.S.	E3	115
District Heights-Forestville, Md., U.S.	*C4	97
District of Columbia, dept., U.S.	f8	97
Distrito Especial (Bogotá), dept., Col.	C3	60
Distrito Federal (Federal District), state, Mex.	D5	63
Distrito Federal, dept., Arg.	g7	54
Distrito Federal, dept., Braz.	B3	56
Distrito Federal, dept., Ven.	A4	60
Disūq, Eg.	C6	43
Ditzum, Ger.	A7	17
Diu, India	D5	36
Divénié, Congo	B1	48
Divernon, Il., U.S.	D4	90
Dives-sur-Mer, Fr.	C3	16
Divide, co., N.D., U.S.	A2	111
Divide Peak, mtn., Wy., U.S.	E5	127
Dividing Creek, N.J., U.S.	E2	107
Dividing Creek, stm., Md., U.S.	D6	97
Divinópolis, Braz.	E7	57
Divion, Fr.	D5	17
Divisões, Serra das, hills, Braz.	B2	56
Divnoye, Sov. Un.	o18	26
Divo, I.C.	E3	45
Divriği, Tur.	C12	40
Dix, Il., U.S.	E5	90
Dix, Ne., U.S.	C2	104
Dix Dam, Ky., U.S.	C5	94
Dixence, stm., Switz.	D2	21
Dixfield, Me., U.S.	D2	96
Dix Hills, N.Y., U.S.	*n15	109
Dixiana, Al., U.S.	B3	78
Dixie, Al., U.S.	D3	78
Dixie, Ga., U.S.	F3	87
Dixie, Id., U.S.	D3	89
Dixie, La., U.S.	B2	95
Dixie, Wa., U.S.	C7	124
Dixie, W.V., U.S.	C3	125
Dixie, co., Fl., U.S.	C3	86
Dixie Union, Ga., U.S.	E4	87
Dixie Valley, val., Nv., U.S.	D4	105
Dix Mountain, mtn., N.Y., U.S.	A7	109
Dixon, Ca., U.S.	C3	82
Dixon, Il., U.S.	B4	90
Dixon, In., U.S.	C8	91
Dixon, Ky., U.S.	C2	94
Dixon, Mo., U.S.	C5	102
Dixon, Mt., U.S.	C2	103
Dixon, Ne., U.S.	A4	108
Dixon, N.M., U.S.	A4	108
Dixon, Oh., U.S.	B1	112
Dixon, S.D., U.S.	D6	118
Dixon, Wy., U.S.	E5	127
Dixon, co., Ne., U.S.	B9	104
Dixon Entrance, strt., N.A.	C2	78
Dixons Mills, Al., U.S.	C2	78
Dixon Springs, Il., U.S.	F5	90
Dixonville, Alta.	A2	68
Dixville, Que.	D6	74
Dixville Notch, N.H., U.S.	g7	106
Dixville Notch, N.H., U.S.	g7	106
Dixville Peak, mtn., N.H., U.S.	g7	106
Diyarbakır, Tur.	D13	40
Dizy-Magenta, Fr.	E3	17
Dizy-le-Gros, Fr.	E3	17
Dja, stm., Afr.	E2	46
Djado, Niger	B7	45
Djakarta see Jakarta, Indon.	G3	34
Djakovica, Yugo.	C4	24
Djakovo, Yugo.	B1	48
Djambala, Congo	B1	48
Djanet, Alg.	E6	44
Djaravica, mtn., Yugo.	D5	24
Djédaa, Chad	C3	46
Djédeida, Tur.	F23	23
Djelfa, Alg.	D5	46
Djénné, Mali	D4	45
Djerba, Île de, i., Tun.	C7	45
Djerid, Chott, sw., Tun.	C6	44
Djibouti, Dji.	C5	47
Djibouti, ctry., Afr.	C5	47
Djibo, Burkina	E5	16
Djokupunda, Zaire	C3	48
Djolu, Zaire	A3	48
Djoua, stm., Afr.	E2	46
Djougou, Benin	E5	45
Djugu, Zaire	A5	48
Djurdjevac, Yugo.	B3	24
Djursholm, Swe.	t36	14
D'Lo, Ms., U.S.	D4	101
Długa, Pol.	k14	26
Dmitriyev-Lgovskiy, Sov. Un.	E10	27
Dmitrov, Sov. Un.	C11	27
Dmitrovsk-Orlovskiy, Sov. Un.	E10	27
Dneprodzerzhinsk, Sov. Un.	G10	27
Dnepropetrovsk, Sov. Un.	E6	29
Dnestr, stm., Sov. Un.	H7	27
Dnieper see Dnepr, stm., Sov. Un.		
Dno, Sov. Un.	D5	29
Doaktown, N.B.	C3	71
Doany, Madag.	f9	49
Doba, Chad	D3	46
Dobbins Air Force Base, mil., Ga., U.S.	h7	87
Dobbinton, Ont.	C3	73
Dobbs Ferry, N.Y., U.S.	g13	109
Döbeln, Ger.	C7	18
Doberai Peninsula, pen., Indon.	F8	34
Doberlug-Kirchhain, Ger.	B8	19
Doblas, Arg.	B4	54
Doblos, Indon.	G8	34
Dobo, Indon.	G8	34
Doboj, Yugo.	C4	24
Doboy Sound, b., Ga., U.S.	e18	87
Dobřejovice, Czech.	o18	27
Dobříš, Czech.	n18	26
Dobrovice, Czech.	n18	26
Dobruja, reg., Eur.	C9	24
Dobšiná, Czech.	D6	26
Dobson, N.C., U.S.	A2	110
Doce, stm., Braz.	E2	57
Docena, Al., U.S.	f7	78
Dock Junction, Ga., U.S.	E5	87
Dockton, Wa., U.S.	f11	124
Doctor Arroyo, Mex.	C4	63
Doctor Pedro P. Peña, Para.	D3	55
Doctors Inlet, Fl., U.S.	m8	86
Doctors Lake, l., Fl., U.S.	m8	86
Doddridge, Ar., U.S.	D2	81
Doddridge, co., W.V., U.S.	B4	125
Dodds, Alta.	C5	68
Dodge, Ne., U.S.	C9	104
Dodge, N.D., U.S.	B3	111
Dodge, Wi., U.S.	D2	126
Dodge, co., Ga., U.S.	D3	87
Dodge, co., Mn., U.S.	G6	100
Dodge, co., Ne., U.S.	C9	104
Dodge, co., Wi., U.S.	E5	126
Dodge Center, Mn., U.S.	F6	100
Dodge City, Ks., U.S.	E3	93
Dodge Park, Md., U.S.	*C4	97
Dodgeville, Oh., U.S.	A5	112
Dodgeville, Wi., U.S.	F3	126
Dodman Point, c., Eng., U.K.	E4	12
Dodoma, Tan.	C6	48
Dodoma, prov., Tan.	C6	48
Dodsland, Sask.	F1	75
Dodson, Mt., U.S.	B8	103
Dodson, Tx., U.S.	B2	120
Doe River, B.C.	A7	69
Doerun, Ga., U.S.	E2	87
Doe Run, Mo., U.S.	D7	102
Dog, stm., Vt., U.S.	C3	122
Dogai Coring, l., China	B8	36
Dog Creek, B.C.	D6	69
Dog Keys Pass, strt., Ms., U.S.	g8	101
Dog Lake, l., Man.	D2	70
Dol, Fr.	C3	16
Doland, S.D., U.S.	C7	118
Dolavón, Arg.	C3	54
Dolbeau, Que.	k12	74
Dôle, Fr.	D6	16
Dolega, Pan.	D3	47
Doleib Hill, Sud.	D3	47
Doles, U.S.	E3	87
Dolgellau, Wales, U.K.	B4	12
Dolgeville, N.Y., U.S.	B6	109
Dolina, Sov. Un.	C7	92
Dolinsk, Sov. Un.	B13	31
Dolinskoye, Sov. Un.	B9	24
Dollar Bay, Mi., U.S.	A2	99
Dollard, Sask.	H1	75
Dollart, b., Eur.	A7	17
Dolliver, Ia., U.S.	A3	92
Dolní Kubín, Czech.	D5	26
Dolomite, Al., U.S.	g7	78
Dolomites, mts., Italy	A3	23
Dolores, Arg.	B5	54
Dolores, Guat.	D7	63
Dolores, Mex.	B3	63
Dolores, Col.	D2	83
Dolores, Ur.	E1	56
Dolores, co., Co., U.S.	D2	83
Dolores, stm., U.S.	E7	121
Dolores Hidalgo, Mex.	m13	63
Dolphin and Union Strait, strt., N.W. Ter.	C9	66
Dolphin Head, mtn., Jam.	E12	65
Dolphin Island, i., Ut., U.S.	B3	121
Dolton, Il., U.S.	k9	90
Dolton, S.D., U.S.	D8	118
Dom, mtn., Switz.	D4	21
Domadare, Som.	E5	47
Domat-Ems, Switz.	C7	21
Domažlice, Czech.	D2	26
Dombarovskiy, Sov. Un.	C5	28
Dombås, Nor.	F3	14
Dombasle[-sur-Meurthe], Fr.	F6	17
Dombe Grande, Ang.	D1	48
Dombóvár, Hung.	B4	24
Domburg, Neth.	C3	17
Dôme, Puy de, mtn., Fr.	E5	16
Dome Mountain, mtn., Az., U.S.	k9	80
Dome of the Rock, Isr. Occ.	m14	41
Dome Peak, mtn., Co., U.S.	B3	83
Domeyko, Cordillera, mts., Chile	D2	55
Domfront, Fr.	C3	16
Dominica, ctry., N.A.	i14	64
Dominican Republic, ctry., N.A.	E8	64
Dominica Passage, strt., N.A.	I14	64
Dominion, N.S.	C9	71
Dominion, Cape, c., N.W. Ter.	C18	66
Dominion City, Man.	E3	70
Dominion Lake, l., Newf.	h9	72
Dömitz, Ger.	B5	18
Dommel, stm., Eur.	C5	17
Domodedovo, Sov. Un.	n17	27
Domodossola, Italy	A2	23
Dom Pedrito, Braz.	E2	56
Dompierre [-sur-Authie], Fr.	D1	17
Domremy, Sask.	E3	75
Domuyo, Volcán, vol., Arg.	B2	54
Don, stm., Sov. Un.	H13	27
Don, stm., Scot., U.K.	C6	13
Dona Ana, N.M., U.S.	E3	108
Dona Ana, co., N.M., U.S.	E2	108
Donaghadee, N. Ire., U.K.	C4	10
Donald, Ont.	C6	73
Donald, Or., U.S.	h12	114
Donalda, Alta.	C4	68
Donaldson, Ar., U.S.	C3	81
Donaldson, Mn., U.S.	B2	100
Donaldsonville, La., U.S.	D4	95
Donalsonville, Ga., U.S.	E2	87
Donard, Ire.	D5	11
Donard, Slieve, mtn., N. Ire., U.K.	C4	10
Donaueschingen, Ger.	B4	20
Donauwörth, Ger.	E5	19
Doncaster, Sask.	F2	75
Doncaster and Templestowe, Austl.	*G8	50
Dondo, Ang.	C1	48
Dondo, Moz.	A5	49
Donegal, Ire.	C2	10
Donegal, co., Ire.	C4	11
Donegal Bay, b., Ire.	C2	11
Donegal Point, c., Ire.	E2	11
Doneraile, S.C., U.S.	C8	117
Donets Basin, Sov. Un.	q21	27
Donetsk, Sov. Un.	E6	29
Dongara, Austl.	E1	50
Dongchuan, China	B7	36
Dongfang, China	C8	35
Donggala, Indon.	F5	34
Dongguang, China	F7	32
Dong Hoi, Viet.	B3	34
Dongning, China	D5	32
Dongo, Zaire	A2	48
Dongola, China	D8	31
Dongou, Congo	A2	48
Dongsheng, China	D6	31
Dongtan, China	D8	31
Dongting Hu, l., China	F7	31
Dongxiang, China	J7	32
Dongzhi, China	I7	32
Doniphan, Mo., U.S.	E7	102
Doniphan, Ne., U.S.	D7	104
Doniphan, co., Ks., U.S.	C8	93
Donkey Creek, stm., Wy., U.S.	B7	127
Donley, co., Tx., U.S.	B2	120
Donna, Tx., U.S.	F3	120
Donnacona, Que.	C6	74
Donnellson, Il., U.S.	D4	90
Donnellson, Ia., U.S.	D6	92
Donnelly, Alta.	B2	68
Donnelly, Id., U.S.	E2	89
Donnelly, Mn., U.S.	E2	100
Donner Pass, Ca., U.S.	C3	82
Donner, La., U.S.	E5	95
Dois Córregos, Braz.	m7	56
Donnybrook, N.D., U.S.	A4	111
Donora, Pa., U.S.	F2	115
Donovan, Il., U.S.	C6	90

Name	Map Ref.	Page
Don Peninsula, pen., B.C.	C3	69
Donzère, Fr.	E6	16
Dooagh, Ire.	D1	11
Doogort, Ire.	C1	11
Doole, Tx., U.S.	D3	120
Dooling, Ga., U.S.	D3	87
Doolittle, Mo., U.S.	D6	102
Dooly, co., Ga., U.S.	D3	87
Doon, Ia., U.S.	A1	92
Doon, Loch, l., Scot., U.K.	E4	13
Doonbeg, Ire.	E2	11
Doonerak, Mount, mtn., Ak., U.S.	B9	79
Door, co., Wi., U.S.	D6	126
Doornik see Tournai, Bel.	D3	17
Dora, Al., U.S.	B2	78
Dora, Mo., U.S.	E5	102
Dora, N.M., U.S.	D6	108
Dora, Lake, l., Austl.	D3	50
Dora Baltea, stm., Italy	B1	23
Doran, Mn., U.S.	D2	100
Doraville, Ga., U.S.	h8	87
Dorbod, China	A11	32
Dorcas, Fl., U.S.	u15	86
Dorcheat, Bayou, stm., U.S.	B2	95
Dorchester, N.B.	D5	71
Dorchester, Eng., U.K.	E5	10
Dorchester, Ga., U.S.	E5	87
Dorchester, Ia., U.S.	A6	92
Dorchester, Ne., U.S.	D8	104
Dorchester, N.J., U.S.	E3	107
Dorchester, S.C., U.S.	E7	117
Dorchester, Wi., U.S.	C3	126
Dorchester, co., Que.	C7	74
Dorchester, co., Md., U.S.	D5	97
Dorchester, co., S.C., U.S.	E7	117
Dorchester, Cape, c., N.W. Ter.	C17	66
Dorchester Crossing, N.B.	C5	71
Dorchester Estates, S.C., U.S.	k11	117
Dorcyville, La., U.S.	h9	95
Dordogne, stm., Fr.	E4	16
Dordrecht, Neth.	B6	16
Dordrecht, S. Afr.	D4	49
Doré, l., Sask.	C2	75
Doré, Lake, l., Ont.	B7	73
Doré Lake, Sask.	C2	75
Doré Lake, l., Sask.	C2	75
Dorena, Or., U.S.	D4	114
Dorena, Lake, res., Or., U.S.	D3	114
Dorenlee, Alta.	C4	68
Dores, Scot., U.K.	C4	13
Dores do Indaiá, Braz.	B3	56
Dorfen, Ger.	A8	20
Dorgali, Italy	D2	23
Dörgön Nuur, l., Mong.	B3	31
Dori, Burkina	D4	45
Dorion-Vaudreuil, Que.	q18	74
Dorking, Eng., U.K.	m12	10
Dormagen, Ger.	*C3	18
Dormans, Fr.	C5	17
Dormont, Pa., U.S.	k13	115
Dornbirn, Aus.	E4	18
Dornie, Scot., U.K.	C3	13
Dornoch, Scot., U.K.	C4	13
Dornoch Firth, est., Scot., U.K.	B5	10
Dorogobuzh, Sov. Un.	D9	27
Dorohoi, Rom.	B8	24
Dorothy, Alta.	D4	68
Dorothy, Mn., U.S.	C2	100
Dorothy, N.J., U.S.	E3	107
Dorothy, W.V., U.S.	n13	125
Dorothy Pond, Ma., U.S.	B4	98
Dorr, Mi., U.S.	F5	99
Dorrance, Ks., U.S.	D5	93
Dorre, i., Austl.	E1	50
Dorrigo, Austl.	E9	51
Dorris, Ca., U.S.	B3	82
Dorris Heights, Il., U.S.	F5	90
Dorset, Ont.	B6	73
Dorset, Oh., U.S.	A5	112
Dorset, Vt., U.S.	E2	122
Dorset, co., Eng., U.K.	D5	12
Dorset Peak, mtn., Vt., U.S.	E2	122
Dorsey, Md., U.S.	B4	97
Dorsey, Ms., U.S.	A5	101
Dorsten, Ger.	B1	19
Dortmund, Ger.	C3	18
Dortmund Ems Canal, Ger.	B7	17
Dorton, Ky., U.S.	C7	94
Dörtyol, Tur.	D11	40
Do Rūd, Iran	E4	39
Dorum, Ger.	B7	17
Doruma, Zaire	A4	48
Dorval, Que.	q19	74
Dos Bahías, Cabo, c., Arg.	C3	54
Dos Bocas, Lago, res., P.R.	B2	64
Dos Hermanas, Spain	D3	22
Dos Quebradas, Col.	*C2	60
Dosquet, Que.	C6	74
Dos Rios, Ca., U.S.	C2	82
Dosse, stm., Ger.	E6	15
Dosso, Niger	D5	45
Dossor, Sov. Un.	D4	28
Doswell, Va., U.S.	C5	123
Dothan, Al., U.S.	D4	78
Dothan, Al., U.S.	n13	78
Doting Cove, Newf.	D5	72
Dot Lake, Ak., U.S.	C11	79
Dott, W.V., U.S.	D3	125
Doty, Wa., U.S.	C2	124
Douai, Fr.	B5	16
Douala, Cam.	E1	46
Douarnenez, Fr.	C1	16
Double Bayou, Tx., U.S.	r15	120
Double Beach, Ct., U.S.	D4	84
Double Mer, b., Newf.	A2	72
Double Mountain, mtn., Al., U.S.	g7	78
Double Oak Mountain, mtn., Al., U.S.	g7	78
Doublespring Pass, Id., U.S.	E5	89
Double Springs, Al., U.S.	A2	78
Doubletop Peak, mtn., Wy., U.S.	C2	127
Doubs, Md., U.S.	B3	97
Doubs, dept., Fr.	B2	20
Doubs, stm., Eur.	D7	16
Doubtful Sound, strt., N.Z.	P11	51
Doucette, Tx., U.S.	D5	120
Douds, Ia., U.S.	D5	92
Doué, Fr.	D3	16
Douentza, Mali	D4	45
Dougherty, Ia., U.S.	B4	92
Dougherty, Ok., U.S.	C4	113
Dougherty, co., Ga., U.S.	E2	87
Douglas, Ont.	B7	73
Douglas, I. of Man	C4	10
Douglas, S. Afr.	D3	49
Douglas, Scot., U.K.	E5	13
Douglas, Az., U.S.	F6	80
Douglas, Ga., U.S.	E4	87
Douglas, Ma., U.S.	B4	98
Douglas, Mi., U.S.	F4	99

Name	Map Ref.	Page
Douglas, Mn., U.S.	F6	100
Douglas, Ne., U.S.	D9	104
Douglas, N.D., U.S.	B4	111
Douglas, Ok., U.S.	A4	113
Douglas, W.V., U.S.	B5	125
Douglas, Wy., U.S.	D7	127
Douglas, co., Co., U.S.	B6	83
Douglas, co., Ga., U.S.	C2	87
Douglas, co., Il., U.S.	D5	90
Douglas, co., Ks., U.S.	D8	93
Douglas, co., Mn., U.S.	E3	100
Douglas, co., Mo., U.S.	E5	102
Douglas, co., Ne., U.S.	C9	104
Douglas, co., Nv., U.S.	E2	105
Douglas, co., Or., U.S.	D3	114
Douglas, co., S.D., U.S.	D7	118
Douglas, co., Wa., U.S.	B6	124
Douglas, co., Wi., U.S.	B2	126
Douglas, Mount, mtn., Ak., U.S.	D9	79
Douglas Channel, strt., B.C.	C3	69
Douglas Creek, stm., Co., U.S.	B2	83
Douglas Lake, B.C.	D7	69
Douglas Lake, l., Mi., U.S.	C6	99
Douglas Lake, res., Tn., U.S.	D10	119
Douglas Point, c., Ont.	C3	73
Douglass, Ks., U.S.	E7	93
Douglass Station, Man.	E2	70
Douglastown, N.B.	B4	71
Douglasville, Ga., U.S.	C2	87
Doullens, Fr.	B5	16
Doulus Head, c., Ire.	F1	11
Doumé, Cam.	E2	46
Dour, Bel.	D3	17
Doura, Mali	D3	45
Dourado, Braz.	m7	56
Dourados, Braz.	C2	56
Douro (Duero), stm., Eur.	D5	22
Dousman, Wi., U.S.	E5	126
Douz, Tun.	C6	44
Dove Creek, Co., U.S.	D2	83
Dover, Eng., U.K.	E7	10
Dover, Ar., U.S.	B2	81
Dover, De., U.S.	D3	85
Dover, Fl., U.S.	D4	86
Dover, Id., U.S.	D5	87
Dover, Id., U.S.	A2	89
Dover, Ks., U.S.	D8	93
Dover, Ky., U.S.	B6	94
Dover, Ma., U.S.	h10	98
Dover, Mn., U.S.	G6	100
Dover, Mo., U.S.	B4	102
Dover, N.H., U.S.	D5	106
Dover, N.J., U.S.	B3	107
Dover, N.C., U.S.	B5	110
Dover, Oh., U.S.	B4	112
Dover, Ok., U.S.	A4	113
Dover, Tn., U.S.	A4	119
Dover, stm., Alta.	A4	68
Dover, Strait of, strt., Eur.	B5	16
Dover Air Force Base, mil., De., U.S.	D4	85
Dover-Foxcroft, Me., U.S.	C3	96
Dover Hill, In., U.S.	G4	91
Dover Plains, N.Y., U.S.	D7	109
Dovesville, S.C., U.S.	C8	117
Dovray, Mn., U.S.	F3	100
Dovrefjell, mts., Nor.	F3	14
Dow, Il., U.S.	D3	90
Dow, Ok., U.S.	C6	113
Dowa, Mwi.	D5	48
Dowagiac, Mi., U.S.	G4	99
Dow City, Ia., U.S.	C2	92
Dowell, Il., U.S.	F4	90
Dowell, Md., U.S.	D5	97
Dowelltown, Tn., U.S.	C8	119
Dowlatābād, Afg.	C13	39
Dowlat Yar, Afg.	B4	36
Dowling Lake, l., Alta.	D4	68
Dowling Park, Fl., U.S.	B3	86
Downer, Mn., U.S.	D2	100
Downers Grove, Il., U.S.	B5	90
Downey, Ca., U.S.	n12	82
Downey, Id., U.S.	G6	89
Downham Market, Eng., U.K.	B8	12
Downieville, Ca., U.S.	C3	82
Downing, Mo., U.S.	A5	102
Downing, Wi., U.S.	C1	126
Downingtown, Pa., U.S.	F10	115
Downpatrick, N. Ire., U.K.	C4	10
Downpatrick Head, c., Ire.	C2	11
Downs, Il., U.S.	C5	90
Downs, Ks., U.S.	C5	93
Downs Mountain, mtn., Wy., U.S.	C3	127
Downsville, La., U.S.	B3	95
Downsville, N.Y., U.S.	C5	109
Downsville, Wi., U.S.	D2	126
Downton, Mount, mtn., B.C.	C5	69
Dows, Ia., U.S.	B4	92
Dowshī, Afg.	D14	39
Doyle, Ca., U.S.	B3	82
Doyle, Tn., U.S.	D8	119
Doyles, Newf.	E2	72
Doylestown, Oh., U.S.	B4	112
Doylestown, Pa., U.S.	F11	115
Doyline, La., U.S.	B2	95
Doyon, N.D., U.S.	A7	111
Dozier, Al., U.S.	D3	78
Dozois, Réservoir, Que.	F7	77
Dra'a, Hamada du, des., Alg.	D3	44
Drâa, Oued, val., Afr.	C3	44
Drabenderhöhe, Ger.	C2	19
Drachten, Neth.	A6	17
Dracut, Ma., U.S.	A5	98
Drăgănești-Vlașca, Rom.	E8	24
Draganovo, Bul.	D7	24
Drăgășani, Rom.	D7	24
Dragons Mouth, strt.	N22	65
Dragoon, Az., U.S.	E5	80
Dragør, Den.	C6	15
Draguignan, Fr.	F7	16
Dragvograd, Yugo.	B2	24
Drain, Or., U.S.	D3	114
Drake, Sask.	F3	75
Drake, Az., U.S.	C3	80
Drake, Co., U.S.	A5	83
Drake, N.D., U.S.	B5	111
Drakensberg, mts., Afr.	D4	49
Drake Passage, strt.	J16	2
Drake Peak, mtn., Or., U.S.	E6	114
Drakes Branch, Va., U.S.	D4	123
Drakes Creek, stm., Ky., U.S.	D3	94
Drakes Creek, West Fork, stm., Ky., U.S.	D3	94
Drakesville, Ia., U.S.	C5	92
Draketown, Ga., U.S.	C1	87
Dráma, Grc.	B5	40
Drama, prov., Pol.	g9	14
Drammen, Nor.	H4	14
Dramselva, stm., Nor.	p27	14
Drancy, Fr.	g10	16

Name	Map Ref.	Page
Dranse, stm., Fr.	C2	20
Draper, S.D., U.S.	D5	118
Draper, Ut., U.S.	C4	121
Draperstown, N. Ire., U.K.	C5	11
Drasco, Ar., U.S.	B4	81
Drava (Drau), stm., Eur.	C4	24
Draveil, Fr.	F2	17
Dravuni, i., Fiji	I15	52
Drawsko [Pomorskie], Pol.	B3	26
Drayton, Ont.	D4	73
Drayton, N.D., U.S.	A8	111
Drayton, S.C., U.S.	B4	117
Drayton Plains, Mi., U.S.	F7	99
Drayton Valley, Alta.	C3	68
Dreamland Villa, Az., U.S.	*D4	80
Drebkau, Ger.	C7	18
Drelsdorf, Ger.	D5	15
Drenthe, prov., Neth.	B6	17
Dresbach, Mn., U.S.	G7	100
Dresden, Ger.	E2	73
Dresden, Ger.	C6	18
Dresden, Ks., U.S.	C3	93
Dresden, Oh., U.S.	B3	112
Dresden, Tn., U.S.	A3	119
Dresser, Wi., U.S.	C1	126
Dresslerville, Nv., U.S.	E2	105
Dreux, Fr.	C4	16
Drew, Ms., U.S.	B3	101
Drew, co., Ar., U.S.	D4	81
Drewryville, Va., U.S.	D5	123
Drewsey, Or., U.S.	D8	114
Drews Reservoir, res., Or., U.S.	E6	114
Drexel, Mo., U.S.	C3	102
Drexel, N.C., U.S.	B1	110
Drexel, Oh., U.S.	C1	112
Drexel Hill, Pa., U.S.	p20	115
Driffield, Eng., U.K.	C6	12
Driftpile, Alta.	B3	68
Driftwood, Alta.	B3	68
Driftwood, Ok., U.S.	A3	113
Driftwood, Pa., U.S.	D5	115
Driftwood Creek, stm., Ne., U.S.	D4	104
Driggs, Id., U.S.	F7	89
Drimoleague, Ire.	F2	11
Drina, stm., Yugo.	C4	24
Drin Gulf, b., Alb.	B2	25
Drini, stm., Alb.	A3	25
Drinkwater, Sask.	G3	75
Driscoll, N.D., U.S.	C5	111
Driscoll, Tx., U.S.	F4	120
Driskill Mountain, hill, La., U.S.	B3	95
Driver, Ar., U.S.	B5	81
Drøbak, Nor.	H4	14
Drobeta-Turnu-Severin, Rom.	C6	24
Drogheda, Ire.	H6	11
Drogobych, Sov. Un.	G4	27
Droitwich, Eng., U.K.	C3	11
Dromahair, Ire.	C3	11
Dromod, Ire.	D4	11
Drôme, stm., Fr.	E6	16
Dromod, Ire.	D4	11
Dromore, N. Ire., U.K.	C4	11
Dromore West, Ire.	C3	11
Dronero, Italy	E3	20
Dronfield, Eng., U.K.	A6	12
Dronninglund, Den.	A4	15
Dropmore, Man.	D1	70
Druid Hills, Ga., U.S.	*C2	87
Druid, Sask.	F1	75
Drulingen, Fr.	E2	19
Drumbeg, Scot., U.K.	B3	13
Drumbo, Ont.	D4	73
Drumcliff, Ire.	C3	11
Drumheller, Alta.	D4	68
Drumlish, Ire.	D4	11
Drummond, Id., U.S.	F7	89
Drummond, Mt., U.S.	D3	103
Drummond, Ok., U.S.	A3	113
Drummond, Wi., U.S.	B2	126
Drummond, co., Que.	D5	74
Drummond, Lake, l., Va., U.S.	D6	123
Drummond Island, Mi., U.S.	B7	99
Drummond Island, i., Mi., U.S.	C7	99
Drummond Range, mts., Austl.	D8	50
Drummondville, Que.	D5	74
Drummondville-Sud, Que.	C4	73
Drummore, Scot., U.K.	F4	13
Drumquin, N. Ire., U.K.	C4	11
Drumright, Ok., U.S.	B5	113
Drumshanbo, Ire.	C3	11
Drunsina, Sov. Un.	C36	128
Druzhkovka, Sov. Un.	q20	27
Drweca, stm., Pol.	B5	26
Dryad, Wa., U.S.	C2	124
Dryberry Lake, l., Ont.	E5	70
Dry Branch, Ga., U.S.	D3	87
Drybranch, W.V., U.S.	m13	125
Dry Creek, La., U.S.	D2	95
Dry Creek, stm., Ks., U.S.	g12	93
Dry Creek Mountain, mtn., Nv., U.S.	B5	105
Dryden, Ont.	o16	73
Dryden, Ar., U.S.	*B5	81
Dryden, Me., U.S.	D2	96
Dryden, Mi., U.S.	F7	99
Dryden, N.Y., U.S.	C4	109
Dryden, Tx., U.S.	D1	120
Dryden, Wa., U.S.	B5	124
Dry Fork, Va., U.S.	D3	123
Dryfork, W.V., U.S.	C5	125
Dry Fork, stm., Mo., U.S.	D6	102
Dry Fork, stm., W.V., U.S.	B5	125
Dry Fork, stm., W.V., U.S.	B5	125
Drygalski Island, i., Ant.	C22	7
Dry Harbour Mountains, mts., Jam.	E14	65
Dry Mills, Me., U.S.	E2	96
Dry Prong, La., U.S.	C3	95
Dry Ridge, Ky., U.S.	B5	94
Dry Run, Pa., U.S.	F6	115
Drysdale, stm., Austl.	B5	50
Dry Tortugas, is., Fl., U.S.	H5	86
Drywood, Man.	E2	70
Dschang, Cam.	D2	46
Duaiheb, Hasi, well, W. Sah.	A2	44
Duaringa, Austl.	D9	51
Duarte, Pico, mtn., Dom. Rep.	E8	64
Duart Point, c., Scot., U.K.	C3	13
Dubá, Sau. Ar.	A5	37
Dubach, La., U.S.	B3	95
Dubai (Dubayy), U.A.E.	D6	37
Dubawnt, stm., N.W. Ter.	D12	66
Dubawnt Lake, l., N.W. Ter.	D12	66
Du Bay, Lake, res., Wi., U.S.	D4	126
Dubberly, La., U.S.	B2	95

Name	Map Ref.	Page
Dubbo, Austl.	F8	50
Dübendorf, Switz.	B6	21
Dumka, India	E11	37
Dublin (Baile Átha Cliath), Ire.	D3	10
Dublin, Al., U.S.	C3	78
Dublin, Ca., U.S.	*D3	82
Dublin, De., U.S.	D4	87
Dublin, In., U.S.	E7	91
Dublin, Md., U.S.	A5	97
Dublin, Ms., U.S.	A3	101
Dublin, N.H., U.S.	E2	106
Dublin, N.C., U.S.	C4	110
Dublin, Oh., U.S.	k10	112
Dublin, Pa., U.S.	F11	115
Dublin, Tx., U.S.	C3	120
Dublin, Va., U.S.	C2	123
Dublin Bay, b., Ire.	D5	11
Dublin Shore, N.S.	E5	71
Dublón, i., Micron.	Q18	52
Dubnica [nad Váhom], Czech.	E6	89
Dubois, Id., U.S.	E4	90
Dubois, In., U.S.	H4	91
Du Bois, Ne., U.S.	D9	104
Du Bois, Pa., U.S.	D4	115
Dubois, Wy., U.S.	C3	127
Dubois, co., In., U.S.	H4	91
Duboistown, Pa., U.S.	D7	115
Dubossary, Sov. Un.	H7	27
Dubossary Reservoir, res., Sov. Un.	B9	24
Dubovka, Sov. Un.	D2	28
Dubovka, Sov. Un.	s31	14
Dubrovnik, Yugo.	D4	24
Dubuc, Sask.	G4	75
Dubuque, Ia., U.S.	A3	48
Dubuque, co., Ia., U.S.	B7	92
Dubuque, co., Ia., U.S.	B7	92
Duchcov, Czech.	C2	26
Duchesne, Ut., U.S.	C5	121
Duchesne, co., Ut., U.S.	C5	121
Duchesne, stm., Ut., U.S.	C5	121
Duchess, Alta.	D5	68
Ducie, atoll, Pit.	H14	2
Duck, N.C., U.S.	A7	110
Duck, stm., Tn., U.S.	B4	119
Duck Bay, Man.	C1	70
Duck Creek, stm., De., U.S.	C4	85
Duck Creek, stm., Nv., U.S.	D7	105
Duck Creek, stm., Oh., U.S.	C4	112
Duck Creek, stm., Wi., U.S.	h9	126
Duck Hill, Ms., U.S.	B4	101
Duck Lake, Sask.	E2	75
Duck Lake, l., Man.	B2	70
Duck Lake, l., Me., U.S.	C4	96
Duck Lake Post, Man.	f8	70
Duck Mountain, hills, Man.	D1	70
Duck Mountain Provincial Park, Man.	D1	70
Duck Mountain Provincial Park, Sask.	F5	75
Duck Valley Indian Reservation, U.S.	B5	105
Duckwater, Nv., U.S.	E6	105
Duckwater Indian Reservation, Nv., U.S.	E6	105
Duckwater Peak, mtn., Nv., U.S.	E6	105
Ducor, Ca., U.S.	E4	82
Dudelange, Lux.	E6	17
Duderstadt, Ger.	B5	19
Dudinka, Sov. Un.	C11	29
Dudley, Eng., U.K.	D5	10
Dudley, Ga., U.S.	D3	87
Dudley, Ma., U.S.	B4	98
Dudley, Mo., U.S.	E7	102
Dudley, N.C., U.S.	B4	110
Dudley, Pa., U.S.	F5	115
Dudweiler, Ger.	D2	19
Duékoué, I.C.	E3	45
Duenweg, Mo., U.S.	D3	102
Dueré, Braz.	E5	59
Duero (Douro), stm., Eur.	B3	22
Due West, S.C., U.S.	C3	117
Duff, Sask.	G4	75
Duff, Tn., U.S.	H3	91
Duffee, Ms., U.S.	C5	101
Duffer Peak, mtn., Nv., U.S.	B3	105
Duffield, Alta.	C3	68
Duff Reef, rf., Fiji	H16	52
Dufftown, Scot., U.K.	D5	13
Dufour, Or., U.S.	B5	114
Dufrost, Man.	E3	70
Dugdemona, stm., La., U.S.	B3	95
Dug Hill Ridge, mtn., Md., U.S.	A4	97
Dugi, i., Yugo.	C2	24
Duhamel, Que.	C2	74
Duida, Cerro, mtn., Ven.	C4	60
Duisburg, Ger.	C1	19
Duitama, Col.	C5	60
Duiwelskloof, S. Afr.	B5	49
Dujuuma, Som.	E5	47
Dukan Dam, Iraq	C2	39
Duke, Al., U.S.	B4	78
Duke, Mo., U.S.	D5	102
Duke, Ok., U.S.	C2	113
Duke Center, Pa., U.S.	C5	115
Duke Island, i., Ak., U.S.	n24	79
Dukes, co., Ma., U.S.	D6	98
Dukhān, Fadiat, Sud.	D3	47
Duki, Pak.	B4	36
Dukla Pass, Eur.	F6	26
Dukou, China	*F5	31
Dulac, La., U.S.	E5	95
Dulawan, Phil.	D7	33
Dulce, N.M., U.S.	A2	108
Dulce, stm., Arg.	E3	53
Dülken, Ger.	C6	17
Dülmen, Ger.	A6	91
Dulowa, Pol.	g11	6
Duluth, Ga., U.S.	B2	87
Duluth, Mn., U.S.	D6	100
Dûmã, Isr. Occ.	g12	41
Dūmā, Syria	*F11	40
Dumaran Island, i., Phil.	C5	34
Dumas, Ar., U.S.	D4	81
Dumas, Ms., U.S.	A5	101
Dumas, Tx., U.S.	B2	120
Dumbarton, Scot., U.K.	E4	13
Dumbéa, Nig.	D7	45
Dumdum, India	I13	37
Dumfries, Va., U.S.	B5	123

Name	Map Ref.	Page
Dumfries and Galloway, prov., Scot., U.K.	E4	13
Dummer, Sask.	H3	75
Dümmer, l., Ger.	F2	15
Dummerston, Vt., U.S.	F3	122
Dumont, Ia., U.S.	B5	92
Dumont, Mn., U.S.	E2	100
Dumont, N.J., U.S.	B5	107
Dumont, Tx., U.S.	C2	120
Dumont d'Urville, sci., Ant.	C27	7
Dumyât (Damietta), Eg.	B3	38
Dunaff Head, c., Ire.	B4	11
Dunaföldvár, Hung.	B4	24
Dunaire, Ga., U.S.	*h8	87
Dunajec, stm., Eur.	D6	26
Dunajská Streda, Czech.	D4	26
Dunany Point, c., Ire.	D5	11
Dunapataj, Hung.	B4	24
Dunaújváros, Hung.	B4	24
Dunav (Danube), stm., Eur.	D6	26
Dunay, Sov. Un.	E6	33
Dunayevtsy, Sov. Un.	G6	27
Dunbar, Scot., U.K.	B5	10
Dunbar, Ky., U.S.	C3	94
Dunbar, Ne., U.S.	D9	104
Dunbar, Pa., U.S.	G2	115
Dunbar, S.C., U.S.	C3	117
Dunbar, W.V., U.S.	C3	125
Dunbarton, N.H., U.S.	D3	106
Dunbeath, Scot., U.K.	B5	13
Dunblane, Sask.	F2	75
Dunblane, Scot., U.K.	C5	13
Dunboyne, Ire.	H6	11
Dunbridge, Oh., U.S.	f6	112
Duncan, B.C.	E6	69
Duncan, Az., U.S.	E6	80
Duncan, Ky., U.S.	C4	94
Duncan, Ms., U.S.	A3	101
Duncan, Ne., U.S.	C8	104
Duncan, Ok., U.S.	C4	113
Duncan, S.C., U.S.	B3	117
Duncan, stm., B.C.	D9	69
Duncan Falls, Oh., U.S.	C4	112
Duncan Lake, res., B.C.	D9	69
Duncannon, Pa., U.S.	F7	115
Duncansby Head, c., Scot., U.K.	A5	10
Duncansville, Pa., U.S.	F5	115
Duncanville, Al., U.S.	B2	78
Duncanville, Tx., U.S.	n10	120
Duncombe, Ia., U.S.	B4	92
Duncormick, Ire.	E5	11
Dundalk, Ont.	C4	73
Dundalk, Ire.	C3	10
Dundalk, Md., U.S.	B4	97
Dundalk Bay, b., Ire.	D3	11
Dundas, Ont.	D5	73
Dundas, Il., U.S.	E5	90
Dundas, Oh., U.S.	C3	112
Dundas, co., Ont.	B9	73
Dundas Island, i., B.C.	B2	69
Dundas Strait, strt., Austl.	B6	50
Dundee, S. Afr.	D5	49
Dundee, Scot., U.K.	C5	10
Dundee, Fl., U.S.	D5	86
Dundee, Il., U.S.	A5	90
Dundee, Ia., U.S.	B6	92
Dundee, Ky., U.S.	C3	94
Dundee, Mi., U.S.	G7	99
Dundee, Ms., U.S.	A3	101
Dundee, N.Y., U.S.	C4	109
Dundee, Or., U.S.	h11	114
Dundee, Tx., U.S.	C3	120
Dundee, W.V., U.S.	C5	125
Dundrum, Ire.	E3	11
Dundrum Bay, b., N. Ire., U.K.	C4	10
Dundurn, Sask.	F2	75
Dunean, S.C., U.S.	*D3	117
Dunedin, N.Z.	P13	51
Dunedin, Fl., U.S.	D4	86
Duneland Beach, In., U.S.	A4	91
Dunellen, N.J., U.S.	B4	107
Dunfanaghy, Ire.	B4	11
Dunfermline, Il., U.S.	C3	90
Dunfermline, Scot., U.K.	B5	10
Dungannon, Ont.	D3	73
Dungannon, N. Ire., U.K.	C4	11
Dungannon, Va., U.S.	f9	123
Dungarpur, India	F4	37
Dungarvan, Ire.	D3	10
Dungarvan Harbour, b., Ire.	E4	11
Dungarvon, stm., N.B.	B3	71
Dungeness, Wa., U.S.	A2	124
Dungeness, c., Eng., U.K.	E7	10
Dungeness, stm., Wa., U.S.	A2	124
Dungiven, N. Ire., U.K.	C5	11
Dunglow, Ire.	C3	11
Dungu, Zaire	A4	48
Dungun, Malay.	J5	35
Dunham, Que.	D5	74
Dunhua, China	C10	31
Dunhuang, China	C5	31
Dunkard Creek, stm., U.S.	B4	125
Dunkeld, Scot., U.K.	D5	13
Dunkerque, Fr.	B5	16
Dunkerrin, Ire.	E4	11
Dunkery Hill, hill, Eng., U.K.	C4	12
Dunkineely, Ire.	C3	11
Dunkirk, In., U.S.	D7	91
Dunkirk, N.Y., U.S.	C1	109
Dunkirk, Oh., U.S.	B2	112
Dunklin, co., Mo., U.S.	E7	102
Dún Laoghaire, Ire.	D5	11
Dunlap, Il., U.S.	C4	90
Dunlap, Ia., U.S.	C2	92
Dunlap, Ks., U.S.	D7	93
Dunlap, Tn., U.S.	D8	119
Dunlavin, Ire.	D5	11
Dunleer, Ire.	D5	11
Dunleith, De., U.S.	i7	85
Dunloup Creek, stm., W.V., U.S.	n13	125
Dunmanway, Ire.	F2	11
Dunmor, Ky., U.S.	C2	94
Dunmore, Pa., U.S.	D10	115
Dunmore, Lake, l., Vt., U.S.	D2	122
Dunmore East, Ire.	E5	11
Dunmore Town, Bah.	B6	64
Dunn, N.C., U.S.	B4	110
Dunn, Tx., U.S.	C2	120
Dunn, co., N.D., U.S.	B3	111

Name	Map Ref.	Page
Dunn, co., Wi., U.S.	D2	126
Dunnamanagh, N. Ire., U.K.	C4	11
Dunn Center, N.D., U.S.	B3	111
Dunnegan, Mo., U.S.	D4	102
Dunnell, Mn., U.S.	G4	100
Dunnellon, Fl., U.S.	C4	86
Dünnern, stm., Switz.	B4	21
Dunning, Ne., U.S.	C5	104
Dunn Loring Woods, Va., U.S.	*B5	123
Dunnottar, Man.	D3	70
Dunns Bridge, In., U.S.	B4	91
Dunns Corners, R.I., U.S.	G1	116
Dunnsville, Va., U.S.	C6	123
Dunnville, Ont.	E5	73
Dunnville, Ky., U.S.	C5	94
Dunoon, Scot., U.K.	C4	10
Dunphy, Nv., U.S.	C5	105
Dunqulah, Sud.	B3	47
Dunrea, Man.	E2	70
Dunrobin, Ont.	B8	73
Duns, Scot., U.K.	E6	13
Dunseith, N.D., U.S.	A5	111
Dunsmuir, Ca., U.S.	B2	82
Dunstable, Eng., U.K.	C7	12
Dunstable, Ma., U.S.	A5	98
Dun-sur-Auron, Fr.	E5	17
Duntroon, Ont.	C4	73
Dunvegan, Scot., U.K.	C2	13
Dunvegan, Loch, b., Scot., U.K.	C2	13
Dunvegan Head, c., Scot., U.K.	C2	13
Dunville, Newf.	E5	72
Dunwoody, Ga., U.S.	*h8	87
Duolun, China	C8	31
Du Page, co., Il., U.S.	B5	90
Du Page, stm., Il., U.S.	k8	90
Dupax, Phil.	m13	34
Duplessis, La., U.S.	h10	95
Duplin, co., N.C., U.S.	C5	110
Dupont, Co., U.S.	B6	83
Du Pont, Ga., U.S.	F4	87
Dupont, In., U.S.	G6	91
Dupont, La., U.S.	*D4	95
Dupont, Oh., U.S.	A1	112
Du Pont, Wa., U.S.	B3	124
Dupont, Bayou, stm., La., U.S.	k11	95
Dupont City, W.V., U.S.	m12	125
Dupont Manor, De., U.S.	D3	85
Dupree, S.D., U.S.	B4	118
Dupuyer, Mt., U.S.	B4	103
Duquesne, Pa., U.S.	F2	115
Du Quoin, Il., U.S.	E4	90
Dūrā, Isr. Occ.	C7	41
Durance, stm., Fr.	F6	16
Durand, Ga., U.S.	D2	87
Durand, Il., U.S.	A4	90
Durand, Mi., U.S.	F6	99
Durand, Wi., U.S.	D2	126
Durango (Victoria de Durango), Mex.	C4	63
Durango, Co., U.S.	D3	83
Durango, state, Mex.	C7	62
Durant, Ms., U.S.	B4	101
Durant, Ok., U.S.	D5	113
Durants Neck, N.C., U.S.	A6	110
Duraton, stm., Spain	B4	22
Durazno, Ur.	E1	56
Durazno, dept., Ur.	f8	54
Durban, Man.	D1	70
Durban, S. Afr.	D5	49
Durbin, N.D., U.S.	C5	125
Durbin, W.V., U.S.	C5	125
Durbin Creek, stm., Fl., U.S.	m8	86
Düren, Ger.	*D7	36
Durg, India	F11	37
Durgāpur, India	C4	73
Durham, Eng., U.K.	C6	10
Durham, Ca., U.S.	C3	82
Durham, Ct., U.S.	D5	84
Durham, Ks., U.S.	D6	93
Durham, Me., U.S.	E2	96
Durham, Mo., U.S.	B6	102
Durham, N.H., U.S.	D5	106
Durham, N.C., U.S.	B4	110
Durham, Or., U.S.	B2	113
Durham (Regional Municipality), co., Ont.	C6	73
Durham, co., Eng., U.K.	F7	13
Durham, co., N.C., U.S.	A4	110
Durham Bridge, N.B.	C3	71
Durham Downs, Austl.	E3	51
Durham-Sud, Que.	B5	71
Durhamville, Tn., U.S.	B2	119
Durkee, Or., U.S.	C9	114
Durmersheim, Ger.	E3	19
Durmitor, mtn., Yugo.	C3	24
Durness, Scot., U.K.	A4	10
Durness, Kyle of, b., Scot., U.K.	B4	13
Durnford, Punta, c., W. Sah.	E1	44
Dürrboden, Switz.	C8	21
Durrell, Newf.	B2	25
Durrësi, Alb.	B2	25
Durrow, Ire.	E2	11
Durrus, Ire.	F2	11
Dursey Island, i., Ire.	F1	11
Dursunbey, Tur.	C7	25
Durango, state, Mex.	B2	48
Durrūz, Jabal ad, mts., Syria	F11	40
D'Urville, Cape, c., Indon.	F9	34
D'Urville Island, i., N.Z.	N14	51
Duryea, Pa., U.S.	D10	115
Dushan, China	F6	31
Dushanbe, Sov. Un.	F9	29
Dushaymī, Jazā'ir, is., Eg.	C2	41
Dushore, Pa., U.S.	C9	115
Dusky Sound, strt., N.Z.	P11	51
Düsseldorf, Ger.	C3	18
Dustin, Ok., U.S.	B5	113
Dusty, N.M., U.S.	D2	108
Dutch Creek, stm., Co., U.S.	D5	83
Dutchess, co., N.Y., U.S.	D7	109
Dutch Harbor, Ak., U.S.	E5	79
Dutch Island, i., R.I., U.S.	F4	116
Dutchtown, Mo., U.S.	D8	102
Dutton, Ont.	E3	73
Dutton, Al., U.S.	A4	78
Dutton, Mount, mtn., Ut., U.S.	E3	121
Dutton, Mt., U.S.	C7	102
Duval, Sask.	F3	75
Duval, co., Fl., U.S.	B5	86
Duval, co., Tx., U.S.	E3	120
Duvergé, Dom. Rep.	E8	64
Duvno, Yugo.	B3	24
Duxbury, Ma., U.S.	B6	98
Duxbury, Vt., U.S.	C3	122

Name	Map Ref.	Page
Duyun, China	F6	31
Düzce, Tur.	B8	40
Dvina Bay, b., Sov. Un.	C16	8
Dvůr Králové [nad Labem], Czech.	C3	26
Dwārka, India	F2	37
Dwight, Il., U.S.	B5	90
Dwight, Ks., U.S.	D7	93
Dwight, Ma., U.S.	B3	98
Dwight, Ne., U.S.	C8	104
Dwight, N.D., U.S.	C9	111
Dwight D. Eisenhower Lock, N.Y., U.S.	f9	109
Dworshak Reservoir, res., Id., U.S.	C3	89
Dwyer, Wy., U.S.	D8	127
Dyakovo, Sov. Un.	r22	27
Dyatkovo, Sov. Un.	E10	27
Dyaul, i., Pap. N. Gui.	h13	50
Dyce, Scot., U.K.	C6	13
Dyckesville, Wi., U.S.	D6	126
Dycusburg, Ky., U.S.	e9	94
Dyer, Ar., U.S.	B1	81
Dyer, In., U.S.	A2	91
Dyer, Nv., U.S.	F3	105
Dyer, Tn., U.S.	A3	119
Dyer, co., Tn., U.S.	A2	119
Dyer Bay, Ont.	B3	73
Dyer Bay, b., Ont.	B3	73
Dyer Brook, Me., U.S.	B4	96
Dyer Island, i., R.I., U.S.	E5	116
Dyero, Mali	D3	45
Dyersburg, Tn., U.S.	A2	119
Dyersville, Ia., U.S.	B6	92
Dyess, Ar., U.S.	B5	81
Dyess Air Force Base, mil., Tx., U.S.	C3	120
Dyfed, ctry., Wales, U.K.	C3	12
Dyje, stm., Eur.	D3	26
Dykh-Tau, Mount, mtn., Sov. Un.	*E7	29
Dyment, Ont.	E5	70
Dysart, Sask.	G3	75
Dysart, Ia., U.S.	B5	92
Dzalaata, Mong.	B2	32
Dzamīn Üüd, Mong.	B4	32
Dzaoudzi, May.	f9	49
Dzaudzhikau see Ordzhonikidze, Sov. Un.	E7	29
Dzavhan, stm., Mong.	B3	31
Dzerzhinsk, Sov. Un.	q20	27
Dzerzhinsk, Sov. Un.	C14	27
Dzerzhinsk, Sov. Un.	E6	27
Dzhalal-Abad, Sov. Un.	E10	29
Dzhankoy, Sov. Un.	I10	27
Dzhebel, Sov. Un.	B7	39
Dzhetygara, Sov. Un.	C6	28
Dzhezkazgan, Sov. Un.	D7	28
Dzhizak, Sov. Un.	G22	8
Dzhugdzhur Mountains, mts., Sov. Un.	D16	29
Dzhungarian Alatau Mountains, mts., Asia	D9	28
Dzhusaly, Sov. Un.	D6	28
Działdowo, Pol.	B6	26
Działoszyce, Pol.	C6	26
Dzierzoniów, Pol.	C4	26
Dzilam González, Mex.	C7	63
Dzioua, Alg.	C6	44
Dzitbalché, Mex.	C6	63
Dzulfa, Sov. Un.	C15	40
Dzungarian Basin see Junggar Pendi, China	B2	31
Dzuunmod, Mong.	B6	31

E

Eads, Co., U.S.	C8	83
Eads, Tn., U.S.	B2	119
Eagan, Mn., U.S.	n12	100
Eagan, Tn., U.S.	C10	119
Eagar, Az., U.S.	C6	80
Eagle, Ak., U.S.	C11	79
Eagle, Co., U.S.	B4	83
Eagle, Id., U.S.	F2	89
Eagle, Ne., U.S.	h12	104
Eagle, N.Y., U.S.	C2	109
Eagle, Wi., U.S.	F5	126
Eagle, co., Co., U.S.	B4	83
Eagle, stm., Newf.	g9	—
Eagle Bend, Mn., U.S.	D3	100
Eagle Bridge, N.Y., U.S.	C7	109
Eagle Butte, S.D., U.S.	C4	118
Eagle Cave, Wi., U.S.	E3	126
Eagle City, Ok., U.S.	B3	113
Eagle Cliff, Wn., U.S.	B3	89
Eagle Creek, Tn., U.S.	B4	119
Eagle Creek, stm., Sask.	F2	75
Eagle Creek, stm., In., U.S.	D5	91
Eagle Creek, stm., Ky., U.S.	B5	94
Eagle Creek Reservoir, res., In., U.S.	E5	91
Eagle Dam, In., U.S.	E4	91
Eagle Grove, Ia., U.S.	B4	92
Eagle Harbor, Mi., U.S.	A2	99
Eagle Key, Fl., U.S.	G6	86
Eagle Lake, Me., U.S.	A4	96
Eagle Lake, Mn., U.S.	F5	100
Eagle Lake, Tx., U.S.	E4	120
Eagle Lake, Wi., U.S.	*F5	126
Eagle Lake, l., Ont.	E5	70
Eagle Lake, l., Ca., U.S.	B3	82
Eagle Lake, l., Me., U.S.	A4	96
Eagle Lake, l., Me., U.S.	B3	96
Eagle Lake, l., Ms., U.S.	C3	101
Eagle Lake, l., Wi., U.S.	C4	126
Eagle Mills, Ar., U.S.	D3	81
Eagle Mountain, mtn., Mn., U.S.	k9	100
Eagle Mountain Lake, res., Tx., U.S.	m9	120
Eagle Nest, N.M., U.S.	A4	108
Eagle Nest Butte, mtn., S.D., U.S.	D4	118
Eaglenest Lake, l., Can.	A4	66
Eagle Nest Lake, l., N.M., U.S.	A4	108
Eagle Pass, Tx., U.S.	E2	120
Eagle Peak, mtn., Ca., U.S.	B3	82
Eagle Peak, mtn., Tx., U.S.	o12	120
Eagle Point, Or., U.S.	E4	114
Eagle River, Ont.	E5	70
Eagle River, Mi., U.S.	A2	99
Eagle River, Wi., U.S.	C4	126
Eagle Rock, Va., U.S.	C3	123
Eaglesham, Alta.	B2	68
Eagles Mere, Pa., U.S.	D8	115
Eagle Springs, N.C., U.S.	B3	110
Eagletail Mountains, mts., Az., U.S.	D2	80
Eagletail Peak, mtn., Az., U.S.	D2	80
Eagle Village, Tn., U.S.	*D10	119
Eagletown, Ok., U.S.	C7	113
Eagleville, Ca., U.S.	B3	82

Eagleville, Ct., U.S.	B6	84
Eagleville, Mo., U.S.	A4	102
Eagleville, Tn., U.S.	B5	119
Eakly, Ok., U.S.	B3	113
Ealing (part of London), Eng., U.K.	k12	10
Eardley, Que.	g11	73
Eardley Lake, l., Man.	C3	70
Earle, Ar., U.S.	B5	81
Earlham, Ia., U.S.	C3	92
Earl Grey, Sask.	G3	75
Earlimart, Ca., U.S.	E4	82
Earling, Ia., U.S.	C2	92
Earling, W.V., U.S.	n12	125
Earlington, Ky., U.S.	C2	94
Earl Island, i., Newf.	B3	72
Earl Park, In., U.S.	C3	91
Earlsboro, Ok., U.S.	B5	113
Earlton, Ks., U.S.	E8	93
Earlville, Il., U.S.	B5	90
Earlville, Ia., U.S.	B6	92
Earlville, N.Y., U.S.	C5	109
Early, Ia., U.S.	B2	92
Early, co., Ga., U.S.	E2	87
Early Branch, S.C., U.S.	F6	117
Earn, stm., Scot., U.K.	D5	13
Earn, Loch l., Scot., U.K.	D4	13
Earth, Tx., U.S.	B1	120
Easingwold, Eng., U.K.	F7	13
Easky, Ire.	C3	11
Easley, S.C., U.S.	B2	117
East, stm., Ont.	B5	73
East, stm., Ct., U.S.	D5	84
East, stm., N.Y., U.S.	k13	109
East, stm., Wi., U.S.	h9	126
Eastaboga, Al., U.S.	B3	78
East Acton, Ma., U.S.	g10	98
East Alburgh, Vt., U.S.	B2	122
East Alstead, N.H., U.S.	D2	106
East Alton, Il., U.S.	E3	90
East Andover, Me., U.S.	D2	96
East Andover, N.H., U.S.	D3	106
East Angus, Que.	D6	74
East Arlington, Ma., U.S.	E2	122
East Aurora, N.Y., U.S.	C2	109
East Baldwin, Me., U.S.	E2	96
East Bangor, Pa., U.S.	E11	115
East Bank, W.V., U.S.	m13	125
East Barnard, Vt., U.S.	D3	122
East Barre, Vt., U.S.	C4	122
East Baton Rouge, co., La., U.S.	D4	95
East Bay, b., Fl., U.S.	u16	86
East Bay, b., Tx., U.S.	R15	120
East Beckwith Mountain, mtn., Co., U.S.	C3	83
East Berbice-Corentyne, dept., Guy.	B3	59
East Berlin, Ct., U.S.	C5	84
East Berlin, Pa., U.S.	G8	115
East Bernard, Tx., U.S.	E4	120
East Bernstadt, Ky., U.S.	C5	94
East Bethel, Mn., U.S.	E5	100
East Bethel, Vt., U.S.	D3	122
East Billerica, Ma., U.S.	f11	98
East Blue Hill, Me., U.S.	D4	96
East Bonne Terre, Mo., U.S.	D7	102
East Boothbay, Me., U.S.	E3	96
Eastborough, Ks., U.S.	g12	93
East Brady, Pa., U.S.	E2	115
East Braintree, Man.	E4	70
East Braintree, Vt., U.S.	D3	122
East Branch, N.Y., U.S.	D5	109
East Branch Clarion River Lake, res., Pa., U.S.	C4	115
East Brewster, Ma., U.S.	C7	98
East Brewton, Al., U.S.	D2	78
East Bridgewater, Ma., U.S.	B6	98
Eastbrook, Me., U.S.	D4	96
East Brookfield, Ma., U.S.	B3	98
East Brookfield, Vt., U.S.	C3	122
East Brooklyn, Ct., U.S.	B8	84
East Broughton, Que.	C6	74
East Brunswick, N.J., U.S.	C4	107
East Burke, Vt., U.S.	B5	122
East Butler, Pa., U.S.	E2	115
East Butte, mtn., Mt., U.S.	B5	103
East Cache Creek, stm., Ok., U.S.	C3	113
East Calais, Vt., U.S.	C4	122
East Canaan, Ct., U.S.	A3	84
East Candia, N.H., U.S.	D4	106
East Cape, c., N.Z.	L17	51
East Cape, c., Fl., U.S.	G5	86
East Carbon, Ut., U.S.	D5	121
East Carroll, co., La., U.S.	B4	95
East Chain, Mn., U.S.	G3	100
East Channel, strt., Marsh Is.	S18	52
East Charleston, Vt., U.S.	B5	122
East Chelmsford, Ma., U.S.	f10	98
Eastchester, N.Y., U.S.	*n15	109
East Chicago, In., U.S.	A3	91
East Chicago Heights, Il., U.S.	*k9	90
East China Sea, Asia	F10	31
East Chop, c., Ma., U.S.	D6	98
East Cleveland, Oh., U.S.	g9	112
East-Clifton, Que.	D6	74
East Columbia, Tx., U.S.	r14	120
East Compton, Ca., U.S.	*F4	82
East Concord, Vt., U.S.	C5	122
East Conway, N.H., U.S.	B4	106
East Corinth, Me., U.S.	D3	96
East Corinth, Vt., U.S.	C4	122
East Cote Blanche Bay, b., La., U.S.	E4	95
East Coulee, Alta.	D4	68
East Danville, Vt., U.S.	C4	122
East Demerara-West Coast Berbice, dept., Guy.	A3	59
East Dennis, Ma., U.S.	C7	98
East Dereham, Eng., U.K.	B8	12
East Derry, N.H., U.S.	E4	106
East Detroit, Mi., U.S.	p16	99
East Dixfield, Me., U.S.	D2	96
East Dixmont, Me., U.S.	D3	96
East Dorset, Vt., U.S.	E2	122
East Douglas, Ma., U.S.	B4	98
East Dover, Ma., U.S.	h10	98
East Dover, Vt., U.S.	F3	122
East Dubuque, Il., U.S.	A3	90
East Dummerston, Vt., U.S.	F3	122
East Eddington, Me., U.S.	D4	96
East Ellijay, Ga., U.S.	B2	87
Eastend, Sask.	H1	75
East End Point, c., Bah.	m18	64
East Enterprise, In., U.S.	H7	91
Easter, Mount, mtn., Ct., U.S.	B2	84
Easter Island see Pascua, Isla de, i., Chile	H15	6
Eastern, prov., Ghana	E5	45

Eastern, prov., Kenya	B6	48
Eastern, prov., Zam.	D5	48
Eastern Bay, b., Md., U.S.	C5	97
Eastern Channel, strt., Japan	J4	33
Eastern Ghāts, mts., India	E7	36
Eastern Island, i., Newf.	C4	72
Eastern Island, i., Mid. Is.	K4	52
Eastern Neck Island, i., Md., U.S.	B5	97
Eastern Point, c., Ma., U.S.	f13	98
Easterville, Man.	C2	70
East Fairfield, Vt., U.S.	B3	122
East Fairview, N.D., U.S.	B1	111
East Falmouth, Ma., U.S.	C6	98
East Farmingdale, N.Y., U.S.	*E7	109
East Farmington Heights, Ct., U.S.	C4	84
East Feliciana, co., La., U.S.	D4	95
East Flanders, prov., Bel.	C3	17
East Flat Rock, N.C., U.S.	f10	110
East Flevoland, reg., Neth.	B5	17
Eastford, Ct., U.S.	B7	84
East Fork, stm., Wy., U.S.	D3	127
East Fork Lake, res., Oh., U.S.	C1	112
East Foxboro, Ma., U.S.	B5	98
East Franklin, Vt., U.S.	B3	122
East Freetown, Ma., U.S.	C6	98
East Frisian Islands, is., Ger.	B3	18
East Fultonham, Oh., U.S.	C3	112
East Gaffney, S.C., U.S.	A4	117
East Galesburg, Il., U.S.	C3	90
Eastgate, Wa., U.S.	*e11	124
East Glacier Park, Mt., U.S.	B3	103
East Glastonbury, Ct., U.S.	C5	84
East Glenville, N.Y., U.S.	*C7	109
East Grafton, N.H., U.S.	C3	106
East Granby, Ct., U.S.	B5	84
East Grand Forks, Mn., U.S.	C2	100
East Grand Rapids, Mi., U.S.	F5	99
East Granville, Vt., U.S.	C3	122
East Greenville, Pa., U.S.	F10	115
East Greenwich, R.I., U.S.	D4	116
East Grinstead, Eng., U.K.	C8	12
East Gwillimbury, Ont.	C5	73
East Haddam, Ct., U.S.	D6	84
East Half Hollow Hills, N.Y., U.S.	*n15	109
East Hampden, Me., U.S.	*D4	96
East Hampstead, N.H., U.S.	E4	106
East Hampton, Ct., U.S.	C5	84
East Hampton, Ma., U.S.	B2	98
East Hampton, N.Y., U.S.	n16	109
East Hanover, N.J., U.S.	*B4	107
East Hardwick, Vt., U.S.	B4	122
East Harpswell, Me., U.S.	g8	96
East Hartford, Ct., U.S.	B5	84
East Haven, Ct., U.S.	D4	84
East Haven, Vt., U.S.	B5	122
East Haverhill, N.H., U.S.	C3	106
East Hebron, N.H., U.S.	C3	106
East Helena, Mt., U.S.	D5	103
East Hemet, Ca., U.S.	*F5	82
East Hickory, Pa., U.S.	C3	115
East Highgate, Vt., U.S.	B3	122
East Hills, N.Y., U.S.	*E7	109
East Holden, Me., U.S.	D4	96
East Holderness, N.H., U.S.	C3	106
East Islip, N.Y., U.S.	*n15	109
East Jordan, N.S.	F4	71
East Jordan, Mi., U.S.	C5	99
East Juliette, Ga., U.S.	C3	87
East Kelowna, B.C.	E8	69
East Kilbride, Scot., U.K.	E4	13
East Killingly, Ct., U.S.	B8	84
East Kingston, N.H., U.S.	E4	106
Eastlake, Mi., U.S.	D4	99
East Lake, N.C., U.S.	B7	110
Eastlake, Oh., U.S.	A4	112
East Lake, l., Ont.	C5	70
East Lake Tohopekaliga, l., Fl., U.S.	D5	86
East La Mirada, Ca., U.S.	*F5	82
Eastland, Tx., U.S.	C3	120
Eastland, co., Tx., U.S.	C3	120
Eastland Township, Ut., U.S.	*F6	121
East Lansing, Mi., U.S.	f9	99
East Laport, Il., U.S.	B4	90
East Las Vegas, Nv., U.S.	G6	105
East Laurinburg, N.C., U.S.	C3	110
East Lebanon, Me., U.S.	E2	96
Eastleigh, Eng., U.K.	D6	12
East Lempster, N.H., U.S.	D2	106
East Liberty, Oh., U.S.	B2	112
East Litchfield, Ct., U.S.	B3	84
East Livermore, Me., U.S.	D2	96
East Liverpool, Oh., U.S.	B5	112
East Loch Roag, b., Scot., U.K.	B2	13
East Loch Tarbert, b., Scot., U.K.	C2	13
East London (Oos-Londen), S. Afr.	D4	49
East Longmeadow, Ma., U.S.	B2	98
East Los Angeles, Ca., U.S.	*m12	82
East Lyme, Ct., U.S.	D7	84
East Lynn, Il., U.S.	C6	90
East Lynn, W.V., U.S.	C2	125
East Lynne, Mo., U.S.	C3	102
East Lynn Lake, res., W.V., U.S.	C2	125
East Machias, Me., U.S.	D5	96
East Madison, Me., U.S.	D3	96
Eastmain, Que.	h11	74
Eastmain, stm., Que.	F18	66
Eastmain-Opinaca, Réservoir, res., Que.	h11	74
Eastman, Que.	D5	74
Eastman, Ga., U.S.	D3	87
Eastman, Wi., U.S.	E2	126
East Mansfield, Ma., U.S.	B5	98
East Marietta, Ga., U.S.	*C2	87
East Marion, Ma., U.S.	*C6	98
East Marion, N.Y., U.S.	*m16	109
East Matunuck, R.I., U.S.	F3	116
East Meadow, N.Y., U.S.	*n15	109
East Meredith, N.Y., U.S.	C6	109
East Middlebury, Vt., U.S.	D2	122
East Midvale, Ut., U.S.	*C4	121
East Millbury, Ma., U.S.	*B4	98
East Millinocket, Me., U.S.	C4	96
East Moline, Il., U.S.	B3	90
East Monroe, Oh., U.S.	C2	112
East Montpelier, Vt., U.S.	C4	122
East Naples, Fl., U.S.	F5	86
East Newark, N.J., U.S.	k8	107
East New Market, Md., U.S.	C6	97
East Newnan, Ga., U.S.	C2	87
East Newport, Me., U.S.	D3	96
East New Portland, Me., U.S.	D3	96
East Nishnabotna, stm., Ia., U.S.	C2	92
East Norriton, Pa., U.S.	o20	115
East Northport, N.Y., U.S.	*n15	109

East Olympia, Wa., U.S.	C3	124
Easton, Ct., U.S.	D2	84
Easton, Il., U.S.	C4	90
Easton, Ks., U.S.	k15	93
Easton, Md., U.S.	C5	97
Easton, Me., U.S.	B5	96
Easton, Mn., U.S.	G5	100
Easton, Mo., U.S.	B3	102
Easton, N.H., U.S.	C3	106
Easton, Pa., U.S.	E11	115
Easton, Wa., U.S.	B4	124
Eastondale, Ma., U.S.	B5	98
Easton Reservoir, res., Ct., U.S.	E2	84
East Orange, N.J., U.S.	B4	107
East Orange, Vt., U.S.	C4	122
East Orland, Me., U.S.	D4	96
East Orleans, Ma., U.S.	C8	98
East Otis, Ma., U.S.	B1	98
East Otto, N.Y., U.S.	C2	109
East Palatka, Fl., U.S.	C5	86
East Palestine, Oh., U.S.	B5	112
East Palo Alto, Ca., U.S.	*D2	82
East Parsonfield, Me., U.S.	E2	96
East Pass, strt., Fl., U.S.	C2	86
East Patchogue, N.Y., U.S.	*n16	109
East Peacham, Vt., U.S.	C4	122
East Pea Ridge, W.V., U.S.	C2	125
East Peoria, Il., U.S.	C4	90
East Pepperell, Ma., U.S.	A4	98
East Peru, Me., U.S.	D2	96
East Petersburg, Pa., U.S.	F9	115
East Pine, B.C.	B7	69
East Pittsburgh, Pa., U.S.	k14	115
Eastpoint, Fl., U.S.	C2	86
East Point, Ga., U.S.	C2	87
East Point, La., U.S.	B2	95
East Point, c., P.E.I.	C8	71
East Point, c., Ma., U.S.	B6	98
East Point, c., N.J., U.S.	E2	107
East Point, c., V.I.U.S.	C6	65
East Poland, Me., U.S.	D2	96
East Poplar, Sask.	H3	75
Eastport, Newf.	D5	72
Eastport, Id., U.S.	A2	89
Eastport, Me., U.S.	D6	96
Eastport, N.Y., U.S.	n16	109
East Portal, Co., U.S.	B5	83
East Porterville, Ca., U.S.	*D5	82
East Poultney, Vt., U.S.	D2	122
East Prairie, Mo., U.S.	E8	102
East Princeton, Ma., U.S.	A4	98
East Prospect, Pa., U.S.	G8	115
East Providence, R.I., U.S.	C4	116
East Pryor Mountain, mtn., Mt., U.S.	E8	103
East Quogue, N.Y., U.S.	n16	109
East Randolph, N.Y., U.S.	C2	109
East Randolph, Vt., U.S.	D3	122
East Range, mts., Nv., U.S.	C4	105
East Retford, Eng., U.K.	A7	12
East Ridge, Tn., U.S.	h11	119
East Rindge, N.H., U.S.	E2	106
East River, Ct., U.S.	D5	84
East River Mountain, mts., U.S.	C1	123
East River Sheet Harbour, N.S.	E7	71
East Rochester, N.Y., U.S.	B3	109
East Rockaway, N.Y., U.S.	*k13	109
East Rockingham, N.C., U.S.	C3	110
East Rutherford, N.J., U.S.	h8	107
East Ryegate, Vt., U.S.	C4	122
East Saint Johnsbury, Vt., U.S.	C5	122
East Saint Louis, Il., U.S.	E3	90
East Salt Creek, stm., Co., U.S.	B2	83
East Sandwich, Ma., U.S.	C7	98
East Sebago, Me., U.S.	E2	96
East Selkirk, Man.	D3	70
East Siberian Sea, Sov. Un.	B18	29
Eastside, Or., U.S.	D2	114
East Sioux Falls, S.D., U.S.	D9	118
East Smithfield, Pa., U.S.	C8	115
Eastsound, Wa., U.S.	A3	124
East Sparta, Oh., U.S.	B4	112
East Spencer, N.C., U.S.	B2	110
East Springfield, N.Y., U.S.	C6	109
East Stoneham, Me., U.S.	D2	96
East Stroudsburg, Pa., U.S.	D11	115
East Sudbury, Ma., U.S.	g10	98
East Sullivan, Me., U.S.	D4	96
East Sullivan, N.H., U.S.	D2	106
East Sumner, Me., U.S.	D2	96
East Sussex, co., Eng., U.K.	D7	12
East Swanzey, N.H., U.S.	E2	106
East Tawas, Mi., U.S.	D7	99
East Templeton, Ma., U.S.	A3	98
East Thermopolis, Wy., U.S.	*C4	127
East Thetford, Vt., U.S.	D4	122
East Thompson, Ct., U.S.	A8	84
East Trout Lake, l., Sask.	C3	75
East Troy, Wi., U.S.	F5	126
East Tustin, Ca., U.S.	*n13	82
East Unity, N.H., U.S.	D2	106
East Vestal, N.Y., U.S.	C5	109
East View, W.V., U.S.	k10	125
Eastville, Va., U.S.	C7	123
East Wakefield, N.H., U.S.	C4	106
East Walker, stm., U.S.	E2	105
East Wallingford, Vt., U.S.	E3	122
East Walpole, Ma., U.S.	h11	98
East Wareham, Ma., U.S.	C6	98
East Washington, Pa., U.S.	F1	115
East Waterboro, Me., U.S.	E2	96
East Waterford, Me., U.S.	D2	96
East Wenatchee, Wa., U.S.	B5	124
Eden Hill, hill, Ct., U.S.	D6	96
East Wilton, Me., U.S.	D2	96
East Windsor, N.J., U.S.	C3	107
East Windsor Hill, Ct., U.S.	B5	84
Eastwood, Ky., U.S.	g12	94
Eastwood, N.C., U.S.	*F5	99
Eastwood Hills, Ut., U.S.	*C4	121
East Woodstock, Ct., U.S.	B8	84
East Worcester, N.Y., U.S.	C6	109
East York, Ont.	D5	73
Eaton, Co., U.S.	A6	83
Eaton, In., U.S.	D7	91
Eaton, Oh., U.S.	C1	112
Eaton, N.Y., U.S.	C5	109
Eaton, Tn., U.S.	A2	119
Eaton, co., Mi., U.S.	F6	99
Eaton Center, N.H., U.S.	C4	106
Eatonia, Sask.	F1	75
Eaton Rapids, Mi., U.S.	F6	99
Eatonton, Ga., U.S.	C3	87
Eatontown, N.J., U.S.	C4	107
Eatonville, Wa., U.S.	C3	124

Eau Claire, co., Wi., U.S.	D2	126
Eau Claire, stm., Wi., U.S.	D2	126
Eau Claire, Lac à l', l., Que.	g11	74
Eau Galle, Wi., U.S.	D1	126
Eauze, Fr.	F4	16
Ebadon Island, i., Marsh Is.	S17	52
Ebb and Flow Lake, l., Man.	D2	70
Ebbw Vale (Blaenau Gwent), Wales, U.K.	C4	12
Ebeleben, Ger.	B5	19
Ebeltoft, Den.	B4	15
Ebenezer, Sask.	F4	75
Ebenezer, Ms., U.S.	C3	101
Eben Junction, Mi., U.S.	B4	99
Eberbach, Ger.	D3	19
Ebersbach, Ger.	B9	19
Ebermannstadt, Ger.	D6	19
Ebersbach, Ger.	E4	19
Eberswalde [-Finow], Ger.	B7	18
Ebetsu, Japan	E10	33
Ebeye, Marsh Is.	S17	52
Ebingen, Ger.	D4	18
Eboli, Italy	D5	23
Ebolowa, Cam.	E2	46
Ebro, Fl., U.S.	u16	86
Ebro, Mn., U.S.	C3	100
Ebro, stm., Spain	A5	21
Eccles, W.V., U.S.	n13	125
Eceabat, Tur.	I10	40
Echague, Phil.	n13	34
Echallens, Switz.	C2	21
Echeconnee Creek, stm., Ga., U.S.	D3	87
Ếdhessa, Grc.	I5	40
Echigawa, Japan	n15	33
Echo, Al., U.S.	D4	78
Echo, La., U.S.	C3	95
Echo, Mn., U.S.	F3	100
Echo, Or., U.S.	B7	114
Echo, Ut., U.S.	C4	121
Echo Bay, Nv., U.S.	G7	105
Echoing, stm., Can.	B5	70
Echo Lake, l., Ont.	B2	78
Echola, Al., U.S.	D3	96
Echols, co., Ga., U.S.	F4	87
Echt, Neth.	C5	17
Echt, Scot., U.K.	C6	13
Echternach, Lux.	C7	16
Echuca, Austl.	G7	50
Ếcija, Spain	D3	22
Eckelson, N.D., U.S.	C7	111
Eckerman, Mi., U.S.	B5	99
Eckernförde, Ger.	A4	18
Eckernförder Bucht, b., Ger.	D4	15
Eckerty, In., U.S.	H4	91
Eckhart Mines, Md., U.S.	k13	97
Eckley, Co., U.S.	A8	83
Eckley, Pa., U.S.	E10	115
Eckman, N.D., U.S.	A4	111
Eckman, W.V., U.S.	*D3	125
Eckville, Alta.	C3	68
Eclectic, Al., U.S.	C3	78
Eclipse Sound, strt., N.W. Ter.	B17	66
Econfina, stm., Fl., U.S.	B3	86
Economy, N.S.	D6	71
Economy, In., U.S.	E7	91
Economy, Pa., U.S.	h13	115
Ếcorces, Rivière aux, stm., Que.	A6	74
Ecorse, Mi., U.S.	p15	99
Ecru, Ms., U.S.	A4	101
Ector, co., Tx., U.S.	D1	120
Ecuador, ctry., S.A.	B2	58
Edam, Neth.	B5	17
Edam, Sask.	D1	75
Edberg, Alta.	C4	68
Edcouch, Tx., U.S.	F4	120
Eddiceton, Ms., U.S.	D3	101
Eddington, Me., U.S.	D4	96
Eddy, co., N.M., U.S.	E5	108
Eddy, co., N.D., U.S.	B7	111
Eddystone Rocks, Eng., U.K.	p20	115
Eddyville, Ia., U.S.	C5	92
Eddyville, Ky., U.S.	e9	94
Eddyville, Ne., U.S.	C6	104
Ede, Neth.	*E5	45
Ede, Nig.	*E5	45
Edéa, Cam.	H7	51
Eden, Austl.	H7	51
Eden, Man.	D2	70
Eden, Az., U.S.	E6	80
Eden, Id., U.S.	G4	89
Eden, Md., U.S.	D6	97
Eden, N.C., U.S.	A3	110
Eden, N.Y., U.S.	C2	109
Eden, S.D., U.S.	B8	118
Eden, Tx., U.S.	D3	120
Eden, Ut., U.S.	B4	121
Eden, Vt., U.S.	B4	122
Eden, Wi., U.S.	E5	126
Eden, Wy., U.S.	D3	127
Eden, stm., Eng., U.K.	G9	13
Eden, stm., Scot., U.K.	D5	13
Eden Lake, l., Man.	A1	70
Eden Mills, Vt., U.S.	B4	122
Eden Prairie, Mn., U.S.	n12	100
Edenton, N.C., U.S.	A6	110
Eden Valley, Mn., U.S.	E4	100
Edenville, Mi., U.S.	E6	99
Edenwold, Sask.	G3	75
Ederville, Md., U.S.	B5	97
Edersee, Ger.	C4	18
Edgar, Mt., U.S.	E8	103
Edgar, Ne., U.S.	D7	104
Edgar, Wi., U.S.	D3	126
Edgar, co., Il., U.S.	D6	90
Edgard, La., U.S.	E5	95
Edgar Springs, Mo., U.S.	D6	102
Edgartown, Ma., U.S.	D6	98
Edgecombe, co., N.C., U.S.	B5	110
Edgecumbe, Cape, c., Ak., U.S.	m21	79
Edgefield, S.C., U.S.	D4	117
Edgefield, co., S.C., U.S.	D4	117
Edgeley, N.D., U.S.	C7	111
Edgemere, Md., U.S.	B5	97

Edgemont, Ar., U.S.	*B3	81
Edgemont, Ca., U.S.	*F5	82
Edgemont, S.D., U.S.	D2	118
Edgemoor, De., U.S.	A3	85
Edgemoor, S.C., U.S.	B5	117
Edgemoor, Tn., U.S.	m13	119
Edgerly, La., U.S.	D2	95
Edgerton, Alta.	C5	68
Edgerton, Ks., U.S.	D8	93
Edgerton, Mn., U.S.	G2	100
Edgerton, Mo., U.S.	B3	102
Edgerton, Oh., U.S.	A1	112
Edgerton, Wi., U.S.	F4	126
Edgewater, Al., U.S.	f7	78
Edgewater, Co., U.S.	*B5	83
Edgewater, Fl., U.S.	D6	86
Edgewater, Md., U.S.	C4	97
Edgewater, N.J., U.S.	h9	107
Edgewater Park, N.J., U.S.	C3	107
Edgewood, B.C.	E8	69
Edgewood, Il., U.S.	E5	90
Edgewood, In., U.S.	D6	91
Edgewood, Ia., U.S.	B6	92
Edgewood, Ky., U.S.	h13	94
Edgewood, Md., U.S.	B5	97
Edgewood, N.M., U.S.	B3	108
Edgewood, Oh., U.S.	A5	112
Edgewood, Pa., U.S.	k14	115
Edgewood, Wa., U.S.	f11	124
Edgeworth, Pa., U.S.	h13	115
Edgeworthstown see Mostrim, Ire.	D4	11
Edgigen Island, i., Marsh Is.	S17	52
Edina, Mn., U.S.	F5	100
Edina, Mo., U.S.	A5	102
Edinboro, Pa., U.S.	C1	115
Edinburg, Il., U.S.	D4	90
Edinburg, In., U.S.	F6	91
Edinburg, N.D., U.S.	A8	111
Edinburg, Tx., U.S.	F3	120
Edinburg, Va., U.S.	B4	123
Edinburgh, Scot., U.K.	C5	10
Edinburgh, Va., U.S.	F6	91
Edirne, Tur.	B6	40
Edison, Ga., U.S.	E2	87
Edison, Ne., U.S.	D6	104
Edison, N.J., U.S.	B4	107
Edison, Oh., U.S.	B3	112
Edison, Wa., U.S.	A3	124
Edisto, stm., S.C., U.S.	E6	117
Edisto, North Fork, stm., S.C., U.S.	D5	117
Edisto, South Fork, stm., S.C., U.S.	D5	117
Edisto Island, S.C., U.S.	F7	117
Edisto Island, i., S.C., U.S.	F7	117
Edith, Mount, mtn., Mt., U.S.	D5	103
Edithburgh, Austl.	G1	51
Edmeston, N.Y., U.S.	C5	109
Edmond, Ks., U.S.	C4	93
Edmond, Ok., U.S.	B4	113
Edmonds, Wa., U.S.	B3	124
Edmondson, Ar., U.S.	B5	81
Edmondson Heights, Md., U.S.	g10	97
Edmonson, co., Ky., U.S.	C3	94
Edmonton, Alta.	C4	68
Edmonton, Ky., U.S.	D4	94
Edmore, Mi., U.S.	E5	99
Edmore, N.D., U.S.	A7	111
Edmund Lake, l., Man.	B5	70
Ếdouard, Lac, l., Que.	B5	74
Edremit, Tur.	C6	25
Edremit, Gulf of, b., Tur.	C6	25
Edson, Alta.	C2	68
Edson, Ks., U.S.	C2	93
Edson, B., stm., Or., U.S.	E2	114
Eduardo Castex, Arg.	B4	54
Eduni, Mount, mtn., N.W. Ter.	D7	66
Edwall, Wa., U.S.	B8	124
Edward, Lake, l., Afr.	B4	48
Edward, Ont.	h13	73
Edwards, Co., U.S.	B4	83
Edwards, Il., U.S.	C4	90
Edwards, Ms., U.S.	C3	101
Edwards, N.Y., U.S.	A5	109
Edwards, co., Il., U.S.	E5	90
Edwards, co., Ks., U.S.	E4	93
Edwards, co., Tx., U.S.	E2	120
Edwards Air Force Base, mil., Ca., U.S.	E5	82
Edwardsburg, Mi., U.S.	G4	99
Edwards Butte, mtn., Or., U.S.	B3	114
Edwards Plateau, plat., Tx., U.S.	D2	120
Edwardsport, In., U.S.	G3	91
Edwardsville, Al., U.S.	B4	78
Edwardsville, Il., U.S.	E4	90
Edwardsville, Ks., U.S.	k16	93
Edwardsville, Pa., U.S.	n17	115
Edward VIII Bay, b., Ant.	C18	7
Edward VII Peninsula, pen., Ant.	B33	7
Edwin, Al., U.S.	D4	78
Edzell, Scot., U.K.	D6	13
Eek, Ak., U.S.	C7	79
Eekloo, Bel.	C3	17
Eel, stm., Ca., U.S.	B2	82
Eel, stm., In., U.S.	F3	91
Eel, stm., In., U.S.	C6	91
Eferding, Aus.	C3	95
Effie, Co., U.S.	A7	100
Effie, Mn., U.S.	C5	100
Effigy Mounds National Monument, Ia., U.S.	A6	92
Effingham, Il., U.S.	D5	90
Effingham, Ks., U.S.	C8	93
Effingham, N.H., U.S.	C5	106
Effingham, S.C., U.S.	C8	117
Effingham, co., Ga., U.S.	D5	87
Effingham, co., Il., U.S.	D5	90
Effingham Falls, N.H., U.S.	C4	106
Effon-Alaiye, Nig.	*E5	45
Efland, N.C., U.S.	A3	110
Eforie Sud (Vasile Roaită), Rom.	C9	24
Eforie Sud (Vasile Roaită), Rom.	*C5	24
Ega, stm., Spain	A4	22
Egadi Islands, is., Italy	E4	23
Egan, S.D., U.S.	D9	118
Egan Range, mts., Nv., U.S.	E7	105
Eganville, Ont.	B7	73
Egbert, Wy., U.S.	E8	127
Egedesminde, Grnld.	*C15	61
Egegik, Ak., U.S.	D8	79

Name	Map Ref.	Page

Egeland, N.D., U.S. — A6 111
Egeln, Ger. — B6 19
Eger, Hung. — B5 24
Egersund, Nor. — H2 14
Egerton, Mount, mtn., Ant. — A28 7
Eggebek, Ger. — D3 15
Eggenfelden, Ger. — E7 19
Egg Harbor, Wi., U.S. — C6 126
Egg Harbor City, N.J., U.S. — D3 107
Egg Island Point, c., N.J., U.S. — E2 107
Egg Lake, l., Sask. — C3 75
Egilsstadir, Ice. — n25 14
Égletons, Fr. — E5 16
Eglin Air Force Base, mil., Fl., U.S. — u15 86
Eglinton Island, i., N.W. Ter. — m28 66
Eglisau, Switz. — A6 21
Egmond aan Zee, Neth. — B4 17
Egmont, Cape, c., N.Z. — M14 51
Egmont, Mount, mtn., N.Z. — M15 51
Egmont Bay, b., P.E.I. — C5 71
Egmont Channel, strt., Fl., U.S. — p10 86
Egmont Key, i., Fl., U.S. — p10 86
Egnar, Co., U.S. — D2 83
Egremont, Alta. — B4 68
Egremont, Eng., U.K. — F5 13
Egridir, Tur. — D8 40
Egridir, Lake, l., Tur. — C8 40
Egrigoz, mtn., Tur. — C7 25
Egtved, Den. — C3 15
Egypt, Ar., U.S. — B5 81
Egypt, Ga., U.S. — D5 87
Egypt, Ma., U.S. — B6 98
Egypt, Ms., U.S. — C3 101
Egypt, ctry., Afr. — C2 38
Egypt, Lake of, res., Il., U.S. — F5 90
Egypt Lake, Fl., U.S. — *D4 86
Ehrenberg, Ar., U.S. — D1 80
Ehrenfeld, Pa., U.S. — F4 115
Ehrhardt, S.C., U.S. — E5 117
Éibar, Spain — A4 22
Eibau, Ger. — C9 19
Eibenstock, Ger. — C7 19
Eichstätt, Ger. — D5 18
Eider, stm., Ger. — A4 18
Eidsberg, Nor. — H4 14
Eidson, Tn., U.S. — C10 119
Eidsvold, Austl. — E9 50
Eidsvoll, Nor. — G4 14
Eielson Air Force Base, mil., Ak., U.S. — C10 79
Eifel, mts., Ger. — C3 18
Eige, Carn, mtn., Scot., U.K. — C3 13
Eiger, mtn., Switz. — C5 21
Eigg, i., Scot., U.K. — B3 10
Eigg, Sound of, strt., Scot., U.K. — D2 13
Eightmile Creek, stm., Ks., U.S. — h12 93
Eights Coast, Ant. — B3 7
Eighty Eight, Ky., U.S. — D4 94
Eikeren, l., Nor. — p28 14
Eildon, Lake, res., Austl. — H6 51
Eileen Lake, l., N.W. Ter. — D11 66
Eilenburg, Ger. — C6 18
Eiler Rasmussen, Cape, c., Grnld. — A16 128
Eil Malk, i., Palau — R17 52
Einbeck, Ger. — C4 18
Eindhoven, Neth. — B6 16
Einsiedeln, Switz. — B4 20
Eirunepé, Braz. — C5 58
Eisenach, Ger. — C5 18
Eisenberg, Ger. — C6 19
Eisenhower, Mount, mtn., N.H., U.S. — B4 106
Eisenhüttenstadt, Ger. — B7 18
Eisenstadt, Aus. — E8 18
Eiserfeld, Ger. — C2 19
Eisfeld, Ger. — C5 19
Eisleben, Ger. — C5 18
Eita, Kir. — R18 52
Eita, i., Kir. — R18 52
Eitorf, Ger. — C2 19
Eitzen, Mn., U.S. — G7 100
Ejby, Den. — C3 15
Ejea de los Caballeros, Spain — A5 22
Ejeda, Madag. — h8 49
Ejigbo, Nig. — *E5 45
Ejstrup, Den. — C3 15
Ejutla de Crespo, Mex. — D5 63
Ekalaka, Mt., U.S. — E12 103
Ekenäs, Fin. — G10 14
Ekeren (part of Antwerp), Bel. — C4 17
Ekhínos, Grc. — B5 25
Ekhmîn, Grc. — B5 25
Ekimchan, Sov. Un. — D16 29
Ekoln, l., Swe. — t35 14
Ekron, Ky., U.S. — C3 94
Eksjö, Swe. — I6 14
Ekumakoko, Zaire — B3 48
Ekwan, stm., Ont. — F15 66
Ekwok, Ak., U.S. — D8 79
El Aaiún, W. Sah. — D2 44
Elaine, Ar., U.S. — C5 81
Elamanchili, India — I9 37
Elamton, Ky., U.S. — C6 94
Elamville, Al., U.S. — D4 78
Eland, Wi., U.S. — D4 126
El Arahal, Spain — D3 22
Elassón, Grc. — B4 25
Elat, Isr. — E6 41
Elazig, Tur. — C12 40
Elba, Al., U.S. — D3 78
Elba, Id., U.S. — G5 89
Elba, Mi., U.S. — E7 99
Elba, Mn., U.S. — F6 100
Elba, Ne., U.S. — C7 104
Elba, N.Y., U.S. — B2 109
Elba, i., Italy — C3 23
El Banco, Col. — B5 60
Elbasani, Alb. — B3 40
El Baúl, Ven. — B4 60
Elbe (Labe), stm., Eur. — B4 18
Elberfeld, In., U.S. — H3 91
Elberon, Ia., U.S. — B5 92
Elbert, Tx., U.S. — C3 120
Elbert, co., Ga., U.S. — B4 87
Elbert, co., Co., U.S. — B6 83
Elbert, Mount, mtn., Co., U.S. — B4 83
Elberta, Al., U.S. — E2 78
Elberta, Mi., U.S. — D4 99
Elberta, Ut., U.S. — D4 121
Elberton, Ga., U.S. — B4 87
Elbeuf, Fr. — C4 16
El Beyyadh, Alg. — C5 44
Elbigenalp, Aus. — B6 20
Elbing, Ks., U.S. — f12 93
Elbistan, Tur. — C11 40
Elblag, Pol. — A5 26
El Bluff, Nic. — E8 63
El Bolsón, Arg. — C2 54
El Bonillo, Spain — C4 22

El Bordo, Col. — C2 60
El Boulaïda (Blida), Alg. — B5 44
Elbow, Sask. — F2 75
Elbow, stm., Alta. — D3 68
Elbow Lake, Mn., U.S. — E3 100
Elbow Lake, l., Man. — B1 70
Elbridge, Tn., U.S. — A2 119
Elburg, Neth. — B5 17
Elburn, Il., U.S. — B5 90
El Burgo de Osma, Spain — B4 22
Elburz Mountains, mts., Iran — B5 38
El Cajon, Ca., U.S. — F5 82
El Callao, Ven. — B6 60
El Campo, Tx., U.S. — E4 120
El Capitan, mtn., Mt., U.S. — D2 103
El Capitan Reservoir, res., Ca., U.S. — o16 82
El Carmen, Bol. — C4 55
El Carmen de Bolivar, Col. — B2 60
El Carrizo, Mex. — B3 63
El Centro, Ca., U.S. — F6 82
El Cerrito, Ca., U.S. — h8 82
El Cerro, Bol. — C3 55
El Chaparro, Ven. — B4 60
Elche, Spain — C5 22
Elcho, Wi., U.S. — C4 126
Elco, Il., U.S. — F4 90
El Cocuy, Col. — B3 60
El Cuervo Butte, mtn., N.M., U.S. — k9 108
Elda, Spain — C5 22
Elde, stm., Ger. — B5 18
Elderon, Wi., U.S. — D4 126
Eldersley, Sask. — E4 75
Elderton, Pa., U.S. — E3 115
El Diviso, Col. — C2 60
El Djelfa, Alg. — C5 44
El Djouf, des., Afr. — B3 45
El Dorado, Braz. — C3 56
Eldorado, Ont. — C7 73
Eldorado, Sask. — m7 75
Eldorado, Mex. — C3 63
El Dorado, Ar., U.S. — D3 81
Eldorado, Il., U.S. — F5 90
El Dorado, Ks., U.S. — E7 93
Eldorado, Md., U.S. — C6 97
El Dorado, N.C., U.S. — B2 110
Eldorado, Oh., U.S. — C1 112
El Dorado, Ok., U.S. — C2 113
Eldorado, Tx., U.S. — D2 120
El Dorado, co., Ca., U.S. — C3 82
El Dorado Peak, mtn., Wa., U.S. — A4 124
Eldorado Springs, Co., U.S. — B5 83
El Dorado Springs, Mo., U.S. — D3 102
Eldorendo, Ga., U.S. — E2 87
Eldoret, Kenya — A6 48
Eldred, Il., U.S. — D3 90
Eldred, Mn., U.S. — C2 100
Eldred, Pa., U.S. — C5 115
Eldridge, Al., U.S. — B2 78
Eldridge, Ia., U.S. — C7 92
Eldridge, Mo., U.S. — D5 102
Eleanor, W.V., U.S. — C3 125
Electra, Tx., U.S. — B3 120
Electra Lake, res., Co., U.S. — D3 83
Electric Mills, Ms., U.S. — C5 101
Electric Peak, mtn., Co., U.S. — C5 83
Electric Peak, mtn., Mt., U.S. — E6 103
Elektrogorsk, Sov. Un. — n18 27
Elektrostal, Sov. Un. — n18 27
El Encanto Heights, Ca., U.S. — *E4 82
Elephant Butte, mtn., N.M., U.S. — D2 108
Elephant Butte Reservoir, res., N.M., U.S. — D2 108
Elephant Island, i., B.A.T. — C7 7
Elephant Mountain, mtn., Me., U.S. — D2 96
El Escorial, Spain — o16 22
El Eulma, Alg. — B6 44
Eleusis see Elevsís, Grc. — g11 25
Eleuthera, i., Bah. — B5 64
Eleva, Wi., U.S. — D2 126
Eleven Mile Canyon Reservoir, res., Co., U.S. — C5 83
Eleven Point, stm., U.S. — A4 81
Elevsís (Eleusis), Grc. — g11 25
Elevsís, Gulf of, b., Grc. — g11 25
Elfers, Fl., U.S. — D4 86
El Fasher (Al Fāshir), Sud. — C2 47
El Ferrol [del Caudillo], Spain — A1 22
Elfin Cove, Ak., U.S. — k21 79
Elfrida, Az., U.S. — F6 80
Elfros, Sask. — F4 75
El Fud, Eth. — D5 47
El Fuerte, Mex. — B3 63
El Galhak, Sud. — C3 47
El Ghazawet, Alg. — B4 44
Elgin, Man. — E1 70
Elgin, N.B. — D4 71
Elgin, Scot., U.K. — B5 10
Elgin, Al., U.S. — A2 78
Elgin, Az., U.S. — F5 80
Elgin, Il., U.S. — A5 90
Elgin, Ia., U.S. — B6 92
Elgin, Ks., U.S. — E7 93
Elgin, Mn., U.S. — F6 100
Elgin, Ne., U.S. — C7 104
Elgin, N.D., U.S. — C4 111
Elgin, Ok., U.S. — C3 113
Elgin, Or., U.S. — B9 114
Elgin, S.C., U.S. — B5 117
Elgin, Tx., U.S. — D4 120
Elgin, co., Ont. — E3 73
Elgol, Scot., U.K. — D5 10
Elgon, Mount, mtn., Afr. — A5 48
El Grara, Alg. — C5 44
El Grullo, Mex. — n11 63
El Huecú, Arg. — B2 54
Eli, Ne., U.S. — B4 104
Eliasville, Tx., U.S. — C3 120
Elida, N.M., U.S. — D6 108
Elida, Oh., U.S. — B1 112
Elikón Óros (Helicon), mtn., Grc. — g9 25
Elila, stm., Zaire — B4 48
Elim, Ak., U.S. — C7 79
El Indio, Tx., U.S. — E2 120
Eliot, Me., U.S. — E2 96
Élisabethville see Lubumbashi, Zaire — D4 48
Elista, Sov. Un. — H15 27
Elizabeth, Austl. — F6 50
Elizabeth, Co., U.S. — B6 83

Elizabeth, Ga., U.S. — C2 87
Elizabeth, Il., U.S. — A3 90
Elizabeth, In., U.S. — H6 91
Elizabeth, La., U.S. — D3 95
Elizabeth, Mn., U.S. — D2 100
Elizabeth, Ms., U.S. — B3 101
Elizabeth, N.J., U.S. — B4 107
Elizabeth, W.V., U.S. — B3 125
Elizabeth, Cape, c., Wa., U.S. — B1 124
Elizabeth Islands, is., Ma., U.S. — D6 98
Elizabethton, Tn., U.S. — C11 119
Elizabethtown, Il., U.S. — F5 90
Elizabethtown, In., U.S. — F6 91
Elizabethtown, Ky., U.S. — C4 94
Elizabethtown, N.Y., U.S. — A7 109
Elizabethtown, N.C., U.S. — C4 110
Elizabethville, Pa., U.S. — E8 115
El Jadida, Mor. — C3 44
El Jebel, Co., U.S. — B3 83
Elk, Pol. — B7 26
Elk, Ca., U.S. — C2 82
Elk, Wa., U.S. — A8 124
Elk, co., Ks., U.S. — E7 93
Elk, co., Pa., U.S. — D4 115
Elk, stm., B.C. — D10 69
Elk, stm., U.S. — A2 78
Elk, stm., Ks., U.S. — E7 93
Elk, stm., W.V., U.S. — C3 125
Elkader, Ia., U.S. — B6 92
El Kairouan, Tun. — B7 44
El Kala, Alg. — F2 23
El Kasserine, Tun. — B6 44
Elkatawa, Ky., U.S. — C6 94
Elk City, Id., U.S. — D3 89
Elk City, Ks., U.S. — E8 93
Elk City, Ne., U.S. — g12 104
Elk City, Ok., U.S. — B2 113
Elk City Lake, res., Ks., U.S. — E7 93
Elk Creek, Ne., U.S. — D9 104
Elk Creek, Va., U.S. — D1 123
Elk Creek, stm., Ok., U.S. — B2 113
Elk Creek, stm., S.D., U.S. — C3 118
El Kef, Tun. — B6 44
El Kere, Eth. — D5 47
Elk Falls, Ks., U.S. — E7 93
Elkford, B.C. — D10 69
Elk Garden, W.V., U.S. — B5 125
Elk Grove, Ca., U.S. — C3 82
Elk Grove Village, Il., U.S. — h9 90
Elkhart, In., U.S. — A6 91
Elkhart, Ia., U.S. — e8 92
Elkhart, Ks., U.S. — E2 93
Elkhart, Tx., U.S. — D5 120
Elkhart, Mi., U.S. — C5 99
Elkhart, co., In., U.S. — A6 91
Elkhart, stm., In., U.S. — B6 91
Elkhart Lake, Wi., U.S. — E5 126
Elkhorn, Man. — E1 70
Elk Horn, Ia., U.S. — C2 92
Elkhorn, Ne., U.S. — g12 104
Elkhorn, W.V., U.S. — *D3 125
Elkhorn, Wi., U.S. — F5 126
Elkhorn, stm., Ne., U.S. — B7 104
Elkhorn, North Fork, stm., Ne., U.S. — B7 104
Elkhorn, South Fork, stm., Ne., U.S. — B7 104
Elk Horn City, Ky., U.S. — C7 94
Elkhorn Peaks, mts., Id., U.S. — F7 89
Elkhovo, Bul. — D8 24
Elkin, N.C., U.S. — A2 110
Elkins, Ar., U.S. — A1 81
Elkins, N.H., U.S. — D3 106
Elkins, W.V., U.S. — C5 125
Elkins Park, Pa., U.S. — F11 115
Elk Island, l., Man. — D3 70
Elk Island National Park, Alta. — C4 68
Elkland, Mo., U.S. — D4 102
Elkland, Pa., U.S. — C7 115
Elk Mills, Md., U.S. — A6 97
Elkmont, Al., U.S. — A3 78
Elkmont, Tn., U.S. — D10 119
Elk Mound, Wi., U.S. — D2 126
Elk Mountain, Wy., U.S. — E6 127
Elk Mountain, mtn., N.M., U.S. — D1 108
Elk Mountain, mtn., Wy., U.S. — E6 127
Elk Mountains, mts., U.S. — D1 118
Elk Mountains, mts., Co., U.S. — B3 83
Elko, B.C. — E10 69
Elko, Ga., U.S. — D3 87
Elko, Nv., U.S. — C6 105
Elko, co., Nv., U.S. — B6 105
Elk Peak, mtn., Mt., U.S. — D6 103
Elk Point, Alta. — C5 68
Elk Point, S.D., U.S. — E9 118
Elk Ranch, Ar., U.S. — A2 81
Elk Rapids, Mi., U.S. — D5 99
Elkridge, Md., U.S. — B4 97
Elkridge, W.V., U.S. — m13 125
Elk River, Id., U.S. — C2 89
Elk River, Mn., U.S. — E5 100
Elk Springs, Co., U.S. — A2 83
Elkton, Fl., U.S. — C5 86
Elkton, Ky., U.S. — D2 94
Elkton, Md., U.S. — A6 97
Elkton, Mi., U.S. — E7 99
Elkton, Or., U.S. — D3 114
Elkton, S.D., U.S. — C9 118
Elkton, Tn., U.S. — B5 119
Elkton, Va., U.S. — B4 123
Elk Valley, Tn., U.S. — C9 119
Elkville, Il., U.S. — F4 90
Ellaball, Ga., U.S. — D5 87
Ellamore, W.V., U.S. — C4 125
Ellaville, Ga., U.S. — D2 87
Ellef Ringnes Island, i., N.W. Ter. — m31 66
Ellen, Mount, mtn., Ut., U.S. — E5 121
Ellen, Mount, mtn., Vt., U.S. — C3 122
Ellenboro, N.C., U.S. — B1 110
Ellenboro, W.V., U.S. — B3 125
Ellenburg Center, N.Y., U.S. — f11 109
Ellendale, De., U.S. — E4 85
Ellendale, Mn., U.S. — G5 100
Ellendale, N.D., U.S. — C7 111
Ellensburg, Wa., U.S. — C5 124
Ellenton, Fl., U.S. — E4 86
Ellenton, Ga., U.S. — E3 87
Ellenville, N.Y., U.S. — D6 109
Ellenwood, Ga., U.S. — h8 87
Eller Island, i., Marsh Is. — S17 52
Ellershouse, N.S. — E6 71

Ellerslie, Ga., U.S. — D2 87
Ellesmere Island, i., N.W. Ter. — m35 66
Ellesmere Port, Eng., U.K. — A5 12
Ellettsville, In., U.S. — F4 91
Ellice Islands see Tuvalu, ctry., Oc. — G10 6
Ellichpur see Achalpur, India — B4 36
Ellicott City, Md., U.S. — B4 97
Ellicottville, N.Y., U.S. — C2 109
Ellijay, Ga., U.S. — B2 87
Ellington, Ct., U.S. — B6 84
Ellington, Mo., U.S. — D7 102
Ellinwood, Ks., U.S. — D5 93
Elliot, S. Afr. — D4 49
Elliot Lake, Ont. — A2 73
Elliot Lake, l., Man. — C4 70
Elliott, Ia., U.S. — C2 92
Elliott, Ms., U.S. — B4 101
Elliott, N.D., U.S. — C8 111
Elliott, S.C., U.S. — C7 117
Elliott, co., Ky., U.S. — B6 94
Elliott Bay, b., Wa., U.S. — e11 124
Elliott Key, i., Fl., U.S. — G6 86
Elliott Knob, mtn., Va., U.S. — B3 123
Elliston, Newf. — D4 72
Elliston, Mt., U.S. — D4 103
Elliston, Va., U.S. — C2 123
Ellistown, Ms., U.S. — A5 101
Ellisville, Ms., U.S. — D4 101
Ellisville, Mo., U.S. — f12 102
Ellon, Scot., U.K. — B5 10
Ellore see Elūru, India — E7 36
Elloree, S.C., U.S. — D7 117
Ellport, Pa., U.S. — E1 115
Ellrich, Ger. — B5 19
Ells, stm., Alta. — A4 68
Ellsinore, Mo., U.S. — E7 102
Ellston, Ia., U.S. — D3 92
Ellsworth, Il., U.S. — C5 90
Ellsworth, Ia., U.S. — B4 92
Ellsworth, Ks., U.S. — D5 93
Ellsworth, Me., U.S. — D4 96
Ellsworth, Mi., U.S. — C5 99
Ellsworth, Mn., U.S. — G2 100
Ellsworth, Ne., U.S. — B3 104
Ellsworth, Pa., U.S. — F1 115
Ellsworth, Wi., U.S. — D1 126
Ellsworth, co., Ks., U.S. — D5 93
Ellsworth Air Force Base, mil., S.D., U.S. — C2 118
Ellsworth Hill, mtn., Ct., U.S. — B2 84
Ellsworth Land, reg., Ant. — B4 7
Ellsworth Mountains, mts., Ant. — B4 7
Ellwangen, Ger. — D5 18
Ellwood City, Pa., U.S. — E1 115
Elm, stm., N.D., U.S. — B8 111
Elma, Ia., U.S. — A5 92
Elma, Wa., U.S. — C2 124
El Mahdia, Tun. — B7 44
Elmali, Tur. — D7 25
El Manteco, Ven. — B5 60
Elm Creek, Man. — E2 70
Elm Creek, Ne., U.S. — D6 104
Elm Creek, stm., Mn., U.S. — G4 100
Elmdale, Ks., U.S. — D7 93
Elmendorf, Tx., U.S. — k7 120
Elmendorf Air Force Base, mil., Ak., U.S. — C10 79
El Menia, Alg. — C5 44
Elm Mills, Md., U.S. — A6 97
Elmer, Mo., U.S. — B5 102
Elmer, N.J., U.S. — D2 107
Elmer, Ok., U.S. — C2 113
El Metlaoui, Tun. — C6 44
El Mghayyar, Alg. — C6 44
Elm Grove, La., U.S. — B2 95
Elm Grove, Wi., U.S. — m11 126
Elmhurst, Il., U.S. — B6 90
Elmhurst, Pa., U.S. — D10 115
El Milagro, Arg. — A3 54
Elmira, Ont. — D4 73
Elmira, P.E.I. — C7 71
Elmira, In., U.S. — A7 91
Elmira, Mi., U.S. — C6 99
Elmira, Mo., U.S. — B3 102
Elmira, N.Y., U.S. — C4 109
Elmira, Or., U.S. — C3 114
Elmira Heights, N.Y., U.S. — C4 109
Elmo, Ks., U.S. — D6 93
Elmo, Mo., U.S. — A2 102
Elmo, Ut., U.S. — D5 121
El Mokhine, Tun. — B7 44
Elmont, Ks., U.S. — k14 93
Elmont, N.Y., U.S. — k13 109
Elmora, Pa., U.S. — E4 115
Elmore, Al., U.S. — C3 78
Elmore, Mn., U.S. — G4 100
Elmore, Oh., U.S. — A2 112
Elmore, co., Al., U.S. — C3 78
Elmore, co., Id., U.S. — F3 89
Elmore City, Ok., U.S. — C4 113
El Morro National Monument, N.M., U.S. — B1 108
El Mreiti, well, Maur. — B3 45
Elmsdale, N.S. — E6 71
Elmshorn, Ger. — B4 18
Elm Springs, S.D., U.S. — C3 118
Elm Springs Colony, S.D., U.S. — D8 118
Elmvale, Ont. — C5 73
Elmville, Ct., U.S. — C8 84
Elmwood, Ont. — C3 73
Elmwood, Il., U.S. — C3 90
Elmwood, Ne., U.S. — D10 104
Elmwood, Ok., U.S. — A1 113
Elmwood, Wi., U.S. — D1 126
Elmwood Park, Il., U.S. — k9 90
Elmwood Park, N.J., U.S. — h8 107
Elmwood Place, Oh., U.S. — o13 112

Elna, Ky., U.S. — C7 94
Elne, Fr. — F5 16
El Nevado, Cerro, mtn., Arg. — B3 54
El Obeid (Al Ubayyiḍ), Sud. — C3 47
El Oro, prov., Ec. — B2 58
El Oso, Ven. — C4 60
Eloy, Az., U.S. — E4 80
El Palmar, Ven. — B6 60
El Palmito, Mex. — B3 63
El Paraíso, Hond. — D4 62
El Paso, Ar., U.S. — B3 81
El Paso, Il., U.S. — C5 90
El Paso, Tx., U.S. — o11 120
El Paso, co., Co., U.S. — C6 83
El Paso, co., Tx., U.S. — o11 120
El Porvenir, N.M., U.S. — B4 108
El Portal, Ca., U.S. — D4 82
El Portal, Fl., U.S. — s13 86
El Prado, N.M., U.S. — A4 108
El Progreso, Guat. — g6 58
El Progreso, Hond. — C4 62
El Puerto de Santa María, Spain — D2 22
El Qoll, Alg. — B6 44
Elqui, stm., Chile — F1 55
Elrama, Pa., U.S. — F2 115
El Real, Pan. — B4 62
El Reno, Ok., U.S. — B4 113
El Rio, Ca., U.S. — E4 82
El Rito, N.M., U.S. — A3 108
Elrod, Al., U.S. — B2 78
Elrosa, Mn., U.S. — E4 100
Elrose, Sask. — F1 75
Elroy, Wi., U.S. — E3 126
Elsa, Yukon — D6 66
Elsa, Tx., U.S. — F4 120
Elsah, Il., U.S. — D3 90
El Salto, Mex. — C3 63
El Salvador, ctry., N.A. — E7 63
El Samán de Apure, Ven. — B4 60
El Sauce, Nic. — E7 63
El Segundo, Ca., U.S. — *n12 82
El Seibo, Dom. Rep. — E9 64
Elsie, Ne., U.S. — D4 104
Elsie, Mi., U.S. — E6 99
Elsinore, Ky., U.S. — B5 94
Elsinore, Ut., U.S. — E3 121
Elsinore see Helsingør, Den. — I5 14
Elsmere, De., U.S. — B3 85
Elsmere, Ne., U.S. — B5 104
Elsmere, N.Y., U.S. — *n15 109
El Sobrante, Ca., U.S. — *h8 82
El Sombrero, Ven. — B4 60
Elsterwerda, Ger. — C6 18
Elstow, Sask. — F2 75
El Tarf, Alg. — F2 23
El Tigre, Ven. — B5 60
El Tocuyo, Ven. — B4 60
Elton, La., U.S. — D3 95
Elton, Wi., U.S. — C5 126
Eltopia, Wa., U.S. — C7 124
El Toro, Ca., U.S. — *n13 82
El Toro Marine Corps Air Station, mil., Ca., U.S. — n13 82
El Tránsito, Chile — E1 55
El Trapiche, Col. — C2 60
El Triunfo, Hond. — D4 62
El Triunfo, Mex. — C2 63
El Tucuche, mtn., Trin. — N23 65
El Turbio, Arg. — E2 54
Elūru (Ellore), India — E7 36
Elva, Man. — E1 70
El Vado Reservoir, res., N.M., U.S. — A3 108
El Valle, Pan. — F7 62
El Valle, N.M., U.S. — *A4 108
Elvas, Port. — C3 22
Elvaston, Il., U.S. — C2 90
Elverson, Pa., U.S. — F10 115
Elverum, Nor. — G4 14
El Viejo, Nic. — D4 62
El Vigía, Ven. — B3 60
Elvins, Mo., U.S. — D7 102
El Volcán, Chile — C2 54
El Wad, Alg. — C6 44
El Wak, Kenya — A7 48
Elwell, Lake, res., Mt., U.S. — B5 103
Elwha, stm., Wa., U.S. — A2 124
Elwood, In., U.S. — D6 91
Elwood, Ks., U.S. — C9 93
Elwood, Ne., U.S. — D6 104
Elwood, N.J., U.S. — D3 107
Elwood, N.Y., U.S. — *n15 109
Elwood Park, Fl., U.S. — E4 86
Elwood Park, Il., U.S. — k9 90
Elwood Park, N.J., U.S. — h8 107
Ely, Eng., U.K. — I13 13
Ely, Ia., U.S. — C6 92
Ely, Mn., U.S. — C7 100
Ely, Nv., U.S. — D7 105
Ely, Vt., U.S. — D4 122
Elyria, Ne., U.S. — C7 104
Elyria, Oh., U.S. — A3 112
Elysburg, Pa., U.S. — E8 115
Elysian, Mn., U.S. — F5 100
Elzach, Ger. — A3 20
Emämshahr (Shāhrūd), Iran — B5 38
Emanuel, co., Ga., U.S. — D4 87
Emba, Sov. Un. — D5 28
Emba, stm., Sov. Un. — D5 28
Embarcación, Arg. — D3 55
Embarras, stm., Il., U.S. — E6 90
Embarrass, Mn., U.S. — C6 100
Embarrass, Wi., U.S. — D5 126
Embarrass, stm., Wi., U.S. — D5 126
Embira, stm., Braz. — C3 58
Emblem, Wy., U.S. — B4 127
Embreeville, Tn., U.S. — C11 119
Embro, Ont. — D4 73
Embrun, Ont. — B9 73
Embrun, Fr. — F16 16
Embu, Kenya — B6 48
Embudo, N.M., U.S. — A4 108
Emden, Ger. — B3 18
Emden, Il., U.S. — C4 90

Emden, Mo., U.S. — B6 102
Emelle, Al., U.S. — C1 78
Emerado, N.D., U.S. — B8 111
Emerald, Austl. — D9 50
Emerald, Ne., U.S. — *D9 104
Emerald, Wi., U.S. — C1 126
Emerson, Man. — E3 70
Emerson, Ar., U.S. — D2 81
Emerson, Ga., U.S. — B2 87
Emerson, Ia., U.S. — C2 92
Emerson, Ne., U.S. — B9 104
Emerson, N.J., U.S. — h8 107
Emery, S.D., U.S. — D8 118
Emery, Ut., U.S. — E4 121
Emery, co., Ut., U.S. — E5 121
Emery Mills, Me., U.S. — E2 96
Emet, Tur. — C7 25
Emida, Id., U.S. — B2 89
Emigrant, Mt., U.S. — E6 103
Emigrant Gap, Ca., U.S. — C3 82
Emiliano Zapata, Mex. — D6 63
Emilia-Romagna, prov., Italy — B3 23
Emily, Mn., U.S. — D5 100
Emily, Lake, l., Mn., U.S. — E3 100
Emine, Cape, c., Bul. — D8 24
Eminence, In., U.S. — F4 91
Eminence, Ky., U.S. — B4 94
Eminence, Mo., U.S. — D6 102
Emington, Il., U.S. — B5 90
Emirau, i., Pap. N. Gui. — h13 50
Emirdağ, Tur. — C7 25
Emison, In., U.S. — G3 91
Emlenton, Pa., U.S. — D2 115
Emlyn, Ky., U.S. — D5 94
Emma, Il., U.S. — F5 90
Emma, Mo., U.S. — C4 102
Emma Lake, l., Sask. — D3 75
Emmaus, Pa., U.S. — E11 115
Emme, stm., Switz. — B4 21
Emmeline Lake, l., Sask. — C2 75
Emmen, Neth. — A7 16
Emmen, Switz. — B5 21
Emmendingen, Ger. — A3 20
Emmerich, Ger. — C3 18
Emmet, Ar., U.S. — D2 81
Emmet, Ne., U.S. — B7 104
Emmet, N.D., U.S. — B4 111
Emmet, co., Ia., U.S. — A3 92
Emmet, co., Mi., U.S. — C6 99
Emmetsburg, Ia., U.S. — A3 92
Emmett, Id., U.S. — F2 89
Emmett, Ks., U.S. — C7 93
Emmett, Mi., U.S. — E8 99
Emmitsburg, Md., U.S. — A3 97
Emmonak, Ak., U.S. — C7 79
Emmons, Mn., U.S. — G5 100
Emmons, co., N.D., U.S. — C5 111
Emory, Tx., U.S. — C5 120
Emory Peak, mtn., Tx., U.S. — E1 120
Empangeni, S. Afr. — E6 49
Empedrado, Arg. — E4 55
Empire, Al., U.S. — B2 78
Empire, Co., U.S. — B5 83
Empire, Ga., U.S. — D3 87
Empire, La., U.S. — E6 95
Empire, Mi., U.S. — D4 99
Empire, Nv., U.S. — C2 105
Empire, Oh., U.S. — B5 112
Empoli, Italy — C3 23
Emporia, Ks., U.S. — D7 93
Emporia, Va., U.S. — D5 123
Emporium, Pa., U.S. — D5 115
Empress, Alta. — D5 68
Emptinne, Bel. — B5 17
Ems, stm., Eur. — B3 18
Emsdale, Ont. — B5 73
Emsdetten, Ger. — B3 18
Ems Jade Canal, Ger. — A7 17
Emsworth, Pa., U.S. — h13 115
Emyvale, Ire. — C5 11
Ena, Japan — n16 33
Ena, Mount, mtn., Japan — n16 33
Enard Bay, b., Scot., U.K. — B3 13
Encampment, Wy., U.S. — E6 127
Encantado, Cape, c., Phil. — o13 34
Encarnación, Para. — E4 55
Encarnación de Díaz, Mex. — m12 63
Enchant, Alta. — D4 68
Enchi, Ghana — A5 48
Encinal, N.M., U.S. — *B2 108
Encinal, Tx., U.S. — E3 120
Encinitas, Ca., U.S. — F5 82
Encino, N.M., U.S. — *A4 108
Encino, Tx., U.S. — F3 120
Encontrados, Ven. — B3 60
Encounter Bay, b., Austl. — G6 50
Endako, B.C. — B5 69
Endako, stm., B.C. — B5 69
Ende, Indon. — G6 34
Endeavor, Pa., U.S. — C3 115
Endeavor, Wi., U.S. — E4 126
Endeavour, Sask. — E4 75
Endelave, i., Den. — C4 15
Enderby, B.C. — D8 69
Enderby Land, reg., Ant. — C18 7
Enderlin, N.D., U.S. — C8 111
Enders, Ne., U.S. — D4 104
Enders Reservoir, res., Ne., U.S. — D4 104
Endiang, Alta. — C4 68
Endicott, N.Y., U.S. — C4 109
Endicott, Wa., U.S. — C8 124
Endicott Mountains, mts., Ak., U.S. — B9 79
Endless Lake, l., Me., U.S. — C4 96
Endwell, N.Y., U.S. — C4 109
Ene, stm., Peru — D3 58
Enebakk, Nor. — p29 14
Energetik, Sov. Un. — C5 28
Enewetak, atoll, Marsh Is. — S18 52
Enez, Tur. — B6 40
Enfield, Austl. — *F6 50
Enfield, N.S. — E6 71
Enfield (part of London), Eng., U.K. — k12 13
Enfield, Ct., U.S. — B5 84
Enfield, Il., U.S. — E5 90
Enfield, Me., U.S. — C4 96
Enfield, N.H., U.S. — C3 106
Enfield, N.C., U.S. — A5 110
Enfield Center, N.H., U.S. — C3 106
Engadine, Mi., U.S. — B5 99
Engaño, Cape, c., Dom. Rep. — E10 64
Engaru, Japan — D11 33
Engebi, i., Marsh Is. — S18 52
'En Gedi, Isr. — C7 41
Engelberg, Switz. — B5 21
Engelhard, N.C., U.S. — B7 110
Engels, Sov. Un. — F16 27
Engen, Ger. — A6 21
'En Gev, Isr. — B7 41
Enghien, Bel. — D4 17
Enghien, Fr. — g10 16

Index

Name	Map Ref.	Page
England, Ar., U.S.	C4	81
England, ter., U.K.	D6	10
England Air Force Base, mil., La., U.S.	C3	95
Englee, Newf.	C3	72
Englefeld, Sask.	E3	75
Engleside, Va., U.S.	g12	123
Englevale, N.D., U.S.	C8	111
Englewood, Co., U.S.	B6	83
Englewood, Fl., U.S.	F4	86
Englewood, Ks., U.S.	E4	93
Englewood, N.J., U.S.	B5	107
Englewood, Oh., U.S.	C1	112
Englewood, Tn., U.S.	D9	119
Englewood Cliffs, N.J., U.S.	h9	107
English, In., U.S.	H5	91
English Bay, Ak., U.S.	h16	79
English Center, Pa., U.S.	D7	115
English Channel, strt., Eur.	F5	10
English Coast, Ant.	B5	7
English Creek, N.J., U.S.	E3	107
English Harbour West, Newf.	E4	72
English Lake, In., U.S.	B4	91
Englishtown, N.J., U.S.	C4	107
Enguera, Spain	C5	22
'En Harod, Isr.	B7	41
Enid, Ms., U.S.	A4	101
Enid, Mt., U.S.	C12	103
Enid, Ok., U.S.	A4	113
Enid Lake, res., Ms., U.S.	A4	101
Enigma, Ga., U.S.	E3	87
Enilda, Alta.	B2	68
Enirik Island, i., Marsh Is.	P18	52
eNjesuthi, mtn., S. Afr.	C4	49
Enka, N.C., U.S.	f10	110
'En Kerem, Isr.	h11	41
Enkhuizen, Neth.	B5	17
Enköping, Swe.	H7	14
Enmore, Guy.	A3	59
Enna, Italy	F5	23
Ennadai Lake, l., N.W. Ter.	D12	66
Ennedi, plat., Chad	B4	46
Ennell, Lough, l., Ire.	D4	11
Enngonia, Austl.	D5	51
Ennigerloh, Ger.	D3	19
Enning, S.D., U.S.	C3	118
Ennis, Ire.	D2	10
Ennis, Mt., U.S.	E5	103
Ennis, Tx., U.S.	C4	120
Enniscorthy, Ire.	D3	10
Enniskillen, N. Ire., U.K.	C3	10
Ennistimon, Ire.	D2	10
Enns, Aus.	D7	18
Enns, stm., Aus.	D7	18
Ennylabegan Island, i., Marsh Is.	S17	52
Enoch, Ut., U.S.	F3	121
Enochs, Tx., U.S.	C1	120
Enola, Ar., U.S.	B3	81
Enola, Ne., U.S.	C8	104
Enola, Pa., U.S.	F8	115
Enon, Al., U.S.	C4	78
Enon, Oh., U.S.	C2	112
Enoree, S.C., U.S.	B4	117
Enoree, stm., S.C., U.S.	B3	117
Enos, In., U.S.	B3	91
Enosburg Falls, Vt., U.S.	B3	122
Enriquillo, Dom. Rep.	F8	64
Enriquillo, Lago, l., Dom. Rep.	E8	64
Enschede, Neth.	A7	16
Ensenada, Guy.	g8	54
Ensenada, Mex.	A1	63
Ensenada, N.M., U.S.	A3	108
Enshi, China	E6	31
Enshu Bay, b., Japan	I8	33
Ensign, Alta.	D4	68
Ensign, Ks., U.S.	E3	93
Ensign, Mi., U.S.	C4	99
Ensisheim, Fr.	B3	20
Ensley, Fl., U.S.	u14	86
Entebbe, Ug.	A5	48
Enterprise, Ont.	C8	73
Enterprise, Guy.	A3	59
Enterprise, Al., U.S.	D4	78
Enterprise, Ia., U.S.	e8	92
Enterprise, Ks., U.S.	D6	93
Enterprise, La., U.S.	C4	95
Enterprise, Ms., U.S.	C5	101
Enterprise, Ok., U.S.	B6	113
Enterprise, Or., U.S.	B9	114
Enterprise, Ut., U.S.	F2	121
Enterprise, W.V., U.S.	B4	125
Entiat, Wa., U.S.	B5	124
Entiat, stm., Wa., U.S.	B5	124
Entiat, Lake, l., Wa., U.S.	B5	124
Entiat Mountains, mts., Wa., U.S.	B5	124
Entrance, Alta.	C2	68
Entraygues, Fr.	E5	16
Entrée, Île d', i., Que.	B8	71
Entre Minho e Douro, hist. reg., Port.	B1	22
Entre Ríos, prov., Arg.	A5	54
Entwistle, Alta.	C3	68
Enugu, Nig.	E6	45
Enumclaw, Wa., U.S.	B4	124
Envermeu, Fr.	E9	12
Envigado, Col.	*B2	60
Enville, Tn., U.S.	B3	119
Envira, Braz.	C3	58
Enyu Channel, strt., Marsh Is.	P18	52
Enyu Island, i., Marsh Is.	P18	52
Enz, stm., Ger.	D4	18
Enza, stm., Italy	E6	20
Enzan, Japan	n17	33
Eola, La., U.S.	D3	95
Eola Hills, hills, Or., U.S.	h11	114
Eolia, Mo., U.S.	B6	102
Eolie Islands, is., Italy	E5	23
Eoline, Al., U.S.	C2	78
Epe, Neth.	B5	17
Epéna, Congo	A2	48
Épernay, Fr.	C5	16
Epes, Al., U.S.	C1	78
Ephesus, Ga., U.S.	C1	87
Ephesus, hist., Tur.	D6	25
Ephraim, Ut., U.S.	D4	121
Ephraim, Wi., U.S.	C6	126
Ephrata, Pa., U.S.	F9	115
Ephrata, Wa., U.S.	B6	124
Épila, Spain	B5	22
Épinal, Fr.	C7	16
Épinay [-sur-Seine], Fr.	g10	16
Epiphany, S.D., U.S.	D8	118
Epirus, hist. reg., Grc.	C3	25
Epoufette, Mi., U.S.	B5	99
Epping, Eng., U.K.	k13	10
Epping, N.D., U.S.	D4	106
Epping, N.H., U.S.	A2	111
Eppingen, Ger.	D3	19
Epps, La., U.S.	B4	95
Epsom, In., U.S.	G3	91
Epsom, N.H., U.S.	D4	106
Epsom [and Ewell], Eng., U.K.	m12	10
Epukiro, Nmb.	B2	49
Epworth, Ia., U.S.	B7	92
Eqlīd, Iran	F6	39
Equality, Al., U.S.	C3	78
Equality, Il., U.S.	F5	90
Equatorial Guinea, ctry., Afr.	E1	46
Équeurdreville, Fr.	C3	16
Equinunk, Pa., U.S.	C11	115
Erath, La., U.S.	E3	95
Erath, co., Tx., U.S.	C3	120
Erba, Italy	E7	21
Erba, Jabal, mtn., Sud.	A4	47
Erbach, Ger.	D3	19
Erbacon, W.V., U.S.	C4	125
Erbendorf, Ger.	D7	19
Erciyes Mountain, mtn., Tur.	C10	40
Ercsi, Hung.	B4	24
Érd, Hung.	B4	24
Erdek, Tur.	B6	25
Erdene, Mong.	C7	31
Erdene-Dzuu, Mong.	B5	31
Erdenetsagaan, Mong.	B6	32
Erdenheim, Pa., U.S.	o21	115
Erding, Ger.	D5	18
Erebus, Mount, mtn., Ant.	B29	7
Erechim, Braz.	D2	56
Ereğli, Tur.	D10	40
Ereğli, Tur.	B8	40
Erenhot, China	C4	32
Eresós, Grc.	C5	25
Erétria (Néa Psará), Grc.	g11	25
Erft, stm., Ger.	C1	19
Erfurt, Ger.	C5	18
Eria, stm., Spain	A2	22
Eriboll, Loch, b., Scot., U.K.	B4	13
Erice, Italy	E4	23
Erick, Ok., U.S.	B2	113
Erickson, B.C.	E9	69
Erickson, Man.	D2	70
Ericsburg, Mn., U.S.	B5	100
Ericson, Ne., U.S.	C7	104
Erie, Co., U.S.	A5	83
Erie, Il., U.S.	B3	90
Erie, Ks., U.S.	E8	93
Erie, Mi., U.S.	G7	99
Erie, N.D., U.S.	B8	111
Erie, Pa., U.S.	B1	115
Erie, co., N.Y., U.S.	C2	109
Erie, co., Oh., U.S.	A3	112
Erie, co., Pa., U.S.	C1	115
Erie, Lake, l., N.A.	B11	76
Erieau, Ont.	E3	73
Erie Canal, N.Y., U.S.	B5	109
Eriksdale, Man.	D2	70
Erímanthos, mtn., Grc.	D3	25
Erimo, Cape, c., Japan	C13	31
Erin, Ont.	D4	73
Erin, Tn., U.S.	A4	119
Erin Point, c., Trin.	O22	65
Erin Springs, Ok., U.S.	C4	113
Eriskay, i., Scot., U.K.	C1	13
Erisort, Loch, b., Scot., U.K.	B2	13
Erithrai, Grc.	C4	25
Eritrea, prov., Eth.	B4	47
Erkelenz, Ger.	C6	17
Erken, i., Swe.	t36	14
Erlangen, Ger.	D5	18
Erlanger, Ky., U.S.	A5	94
Erling, Lake, res., Ar., U.S.	D2	81
Erma, N.J., U.S.	F3	107
Ermelo, Neth.	B5	17
Ermelo, S. Afr.	C5	49
Ermenek, Tur.	D9	40
Ermont, Fr.	g10	16
Ermoúpolis (Syros), Grc.	D5	40
Erne, Upper Lough, l., Eur.	C3	10
Ernée, Fr.	D5	16
Ernest, Pa., U.S.	E3	115
Ernestina, Arg.	g7	54
Ernestville, Tn., U.S.	C11	119
Ernfold, Sask.	G2	75
Erode, India	*F6	36
Eromanga, Austl.	E2	51
Eros, La., U.S.	B3	95
Errigal Mountain, mtn., Ire.	C2	10
Erris Head, c., Ire.	C1	10
Errol, N.H., U.S.	A4	106
Errol Heights, Or., U.S.	*h12	114
Erskine, Alta.	C4	68
Erskine, Mn., U.S.	C3	100
Erstein, Fr.	C7	16
Erstfeld, Switz.	C4	20
Erving, Ma., U.S.	A3	98
Erwin, N.C., U.S.	B4	110
Erwin, S.D., U.S.	C8	118
Erwin, Tn., U.S.	C11	119
Erwin, W.V., U.S.	B5	125
Erwinville, La., U.S.	D4	95
Erwood, Sask.	E4	75
Erzincan, Tur.	C12	40
Erzurum, Tur.	C13	40
Esan, Cape, c., Japan	F10	33
Esashi, Japan	C13	31
Esashi, Japan	D11	33
Esbjerg, Den.	J3	14
Esbon, Ks., U.S.	C5	93
Escabosa, N.M., U.S.	m8	108
Escada, Braz.	k6	57
Escalante, Ut., U.S.	F4	121
Escalante, stm., Ut., U.S.	F4	121
Escalante Creek, stm., Co., U.S.	C2	83
Escalante Desert, des., Ut., U.S.	F2	121
Escalón, Mex.	B4	63
Escalon, Ca., U.S.	D3	82
Escambia, co., Al., U.S.	D2	78
Escambia, co., Fl., U.S.	u14	86
Escambia, stm., Fl., U.S.	u14	86
Escanaba, Mi., U.S.	C3	99
Escanaba, stm., Mi., U.S.	B3	99
Escárcega, Mex.	D6	63
Escatawpa, Ms., U.S.	E5	101
Escatawpa, stm., U.S.	D5	101
Eschede, Ger.	C5	18
Escholzmatt, Switz.	C4	21
Esch-sur-Alzette, Lux.	C7	16
Eschwege, Ger.	C5	18
Eschweiler, Ger.	C6	18
Escobal, Pan.	k11	62
Escocesa, Bahía, b., Dom. Rep.	E9	64
Escoheag, R.I., U.S.	E1	116
Escondida, N.M., U.S.	C3	108
Escondido, stm., Nic.	D6	62
Escondido, Ca., U.S.	F5	82
Escoumins, Rivière des, stm., Que.	A8	74
Escuinapa [de Hidalgo], Mex.	C3	63
Escuintla, Guat.	C2	62
Escuminac, Que.	A3	71
Escuminac, Point, c., N.B.	B5	71
Eséka, Cam.	E2	46
Esens, Ger.	A7	17
Esfahān (Isfahan), Iran	B5	38
Esgueva, stm., Spain	B3	22
Esher (part of London), Eng., U.K.	m12	10
Eshimba, Zaire	C3	48
Eshkāshem, Afg.	C15	39
Eshowe, S. Afr.	C5	49
Esigodini, Zimb.	B4	49
Esk, stm., U.K.	E6	13
Esk, stm., Eng., U.K.	F5	13
Eskbank, Sask.	G2	75
Eskdale, W.V., U.S.	C3	125
Eskilstuna, Swe.	H7	14
Eskimo Lakes, l., N.W. Ter.	C6	66
Eskimo Point, N.W. Ter.	D14	66
Eskişehir, Tur.	C8	40
Esko, Mn., U.S.	D6	100
Eskridge, Ks., U.S.	D7	93
Eslāmābād, Iran	*D3	39
Eslarn, Ger.	D7	19
Eslava, stm., Mex.	h9	63
Eslöv, Swe.	C7	15
Esmeralda, co., Nv., U.S.	F4	105
Esmeraldas, Ec.	A2	58
Esmeraldas, prov., Ec.	A2	58
Esmond, Il., U.S.	A5	90
Esmond, N.D., U.S.	A6	111
Esmond, R.I., U.S.	B4	116
Esmont, Va., U.S.	C4	123
Esom Hill, Ga., U.S.	C1	87
Espada, Punta, c., Col.	A6	60
Espanola, Ont.	A3	73
Espanola, Fl., U.S.	C5	86
Espanola, N.M., U.S.	B3	108
Española, Isla (Hood), i., Ec.	g6	58
Esparto, Ca., U.S.	C2	82
Esperance, Austl.	F3	50
Esperance, Wa., U.S.	*B3	124
Esperanza, Arg.	A4	54
Esperanza, Peru	C3	58
Esperanza, Tx., U.S.	o12	120
Esperanza, stm., Pan.	k12	62
Esperanza, sci., Ant.	C7	7
Espichel, Cape, c., Port.	C1	22
Espinal, Col.	C3	60
Espinhaço, Serra do, mts., Braz.	E6	53
Espírito Santo, state, Braz.	E8	53
Espíritu Santo, i., Vanuatu	H10	6
Espita, Mex.	C6	63
Espoo, Fin.	*G11	14
Esposende, Port.	B1	22
Espungabera, Moz.	B5	49
Espy, Pa., U.S.	D9	115
Espyville Station, Pa., U.S.	C1	115
Esquatzel Coulee, val., Wa., U.S.	C6	124
Esquel, Arg.	C2	54
Esquimalt, B.C.	E6	69
Esquina, Arg.	F4	55
Essaouira (Mogador), Mor.	C3	44
Essen, Bel.	C4	17
Essen, Ger.	C3	18
Essendon, Austl.	*G7	50
Essendon, Mount, mtn., Austl.	E5	68
Essequibo, stm., Guy.	B3	59
Essex, Ont.	E2	73
Essex, Ca., U.S.	E6	82
Essex, Ct., U.S.	D6	84
Essex, Il., U.S.	B5	90
Essex, Ia., U.S.	D2	92
Essex, Md., U.S.	B5	97
Essex, Ma., U.S.	A6	98
Essex, Mo., U.S.	E8	102
Essex, Mt., U.S.	B3	103
Essex, N.Y., U.S.	f11	109
Essex, Vt., U.S.	C2	122
Essex, co., Ont.	E2	73
Essex, co., Eng., U.K.	*B5	12
Essex, co., Ma., U.S.	A5	98
Essex, co., N.J., U.S.	B4	107
Essex, co., N.Y., U.S.	B7	109
Essex, co., Vt., U.S.	B5	122
Essex, co., Va., U.S.	C6	123
Essex, Punta, c., Ec.	g5	58
Essex Fells, N.J., U.S.	*B4	107
Essex Junction, Vt., U.S.	C2	122
Essexville, Mi., U.S.	E7	99
Es' Sider, Libya	C3	47
Esslingen, Ger.	D4	18
Essonne, dept., Fr.	C5	16
Es Suki, Sud.	C3	47
Est, Île de l', i., Que.	B8	71
Est, Pointe de l', c., Que.	B8	71
Estacada, Or., U.S.	B4	114
Estacado, Llano, pl., U.S.	C1	120
Estados, Isla de los, i., Arg.	h13	54
Eşţahbān, Iran	G7	39
Estaire, Ont.	A4	73
Estância, Braz.	D3	57
Estancia, N.M., U.S.	C3	108
Estarreja, Port.	B1	22
Estcourt, S. Afr.	C4	49
Este, Italy	B5	23
Este, Punta, c., P.R.	B5	65
Esteli, Nic.	A4	62
Estella, Spain	A4	22
Estelle, La., U.S.	*E5	95
Estelline, S.D., U.S.	C9	118
Estelline, Tx., U.S.	B2	120
Estell Manor, N.J., U.S.	E3	107
Estepa, Spain	D3	22
Estepona, Spain	D3	22
Esterhazy, Sask.	G4	75
Esternay, Fr.	C5	16
Esternberg, Aus.	E8	19
Estero Bay, b., Ca., U.S.	E3	82
Estero Bay, b., Fl., U.S.	F5	86
Estero Island, i., Fl., U.S.	F5	86
Estes Park, Co., U.S.	A5	83
Estevan, Sask.	H4	75
Estevan Group, is., B.C.	C2	69
Estevan Point, B.C.	E4	69
Esther, Alta.	D5	68
Estherville, Ia., U.S.	A3	92
Estherwood, La., U.S.	D3	95
Estill, Ms., U.S.	B3	101
Estill, S.C., U.S.	F5	117
Estill, co., Ky., U.S.	C6	94
Estillfork, Al., U.S.	A3	78
Estill Springs, Tn., U.S.	B5	119
Estlin, Sask.	G3	75
Esto, Fl., U.S.	u16	86
Eston, Sask.	F1	75
Estonia, state, Sov. Un.	D5	29
Estrées-Saint-Denis, Fr.	E2	17
Estrela, Braz.	D2	56
Estrela, mtn., Port.	*B2	22
Estrela, Serra da, mts., Port.	B2	22
Estrela do Norte, Braz.	A5	56
Estrela do Sul, Braz.	B3	56
Estremadura, hist. reg., Port.	C1	22
Estremadura, hist. reg., Spain	C2	22
Estremoz, Port.	C2	22
Estuary, Sask.	G1	75
Esztergom, Hung.	B4	24
Etah, Grnld.	B13	61
Etain, Fr.	E5	17
Étalans, Fr.	B1	21
Étampes, Fr.	C5	16
Étang-du-Nord, Que.	B8	71
Étaples, Fr.	B4	16
Etāwah, India	C6	36
Eternity Range, mts., Ant.	C6	7
Ethan, S.D., U.S.	D8	118
Ethel, Ont.	D3	73
Ethel, Ar., U.S.	C4	81
Ethel, Ms., U.S.	B4	101
Ethel, Mo., U.S.	B5	102
Ethel, Wa., U.S.	C3	124
Ethel, W.V., U.S.	n12	125
Ethelbert, Man.	D1	70
Ethelsville, Al., U.S.	B1	78
Ethelton, Sask.	E3	75
Ether, N.C., U.S.	B3	110
Ethete, Wy., U.S.	D4	127
Ethiopia, ctry., Afr.	D4	47
Ethiopian Plateau, plat., Eth.	D4	47
Ethridge, Mt., U.S.	B5	103
Ethridge, Tn., U.S.	B4	119
Etive, Loch, l., Scot., U.K.	D3	13
Etlan, Va., U.S.	B4	123
Etna, Ca., U.S.	B2	82
Etna, Me., U.S.	D3	96
Etna, N.H., U.S.	C2	106
Etna, N.Y., U.S.	C4	109
Etna, Pa., U.S.	k14	115
Etna, Wy., U.S.	C1	127
Etna, Mount, mtn., Italy	F5	23
Etna Green, In., U.S.	B5	91
Etobicoke, Ont.	D5	73
Etolin Island, i., Ak., U.S.	m23	79
Etolin Strait, strt., Ak., U.S.	C6	79
Eton, Ga., U.S.	B2	87
Etoshapan, pl., Nmb.	A2	49
Etowah, Ar., U.S.	B5	81
Etowah, Tn., U.S.	D9	119
Etowah, co., Al., U.S.	A3	78
Etowah, stm., Ga., U.S.	B2	87
Etra, N.J., U.S.	C3	107
Étréat, Fr.	C4	16
Etroubles, Italy	E3	21
Etta, Ms., U.S.	A4	101
Ettelbruck, Lux.	E6	17
Etten, i., Micron.	Q18	52
Etter, Tx., U.S.	B2	120
Etterbeek, Bel.	*D4	17
Etters, Pa., U.S.	F8	115
Ettington, Sask.	H2	75
Et Tini, hill, N. Mar. Is.	D7	52
Ettlingen, Ger.	E3	19
Ettrick, Va., U.S.	C5	123
Ettrick, Wi., U.S.	D2	126
Etzatlán, Mex.	m11	63
Etzikom, Alta.	E5	68
Etzikom Coulee, stm., Alta.	B4	16
Eu, Fr.	C4	16
Euboea see Évvoia, i., Grc.		
Eucha, Ok., U.S.	A7	113
Euclid, Mn., U.S.	C2	100
Euclid, Oh., U.S.	A4	112
Euclid, Pa., U.S.	E2	115
Eucumbene, Lake, l., Austl.	H7	51
Eudora, Ar., U.S.	D4	81
Eudora, Ks., U.S.	D8	93
Eudunda, Austl.	G2	51
Eufaula, Al., U.S.	D4	78
Eufaula, Ok., U.S.	B6	113
Eufaula Lake, res., Ok., U.S.	B6	113
Eugene, Mo., U.S.	C5	102
Eugene, Or., U.S.	C3	114
Eugenia, Punta, c., Mex.	B1	63
Eulaton, Al., U.S.	B4	78
Euless, Tx., U.S.	*n9	120
Eulonia, Ga., U.S.	E5	87
Eunice, La., U.S.	D3	95
Eunice, N.M., U.S.	E6	108
Eupen, Bel.	B7	16
Euphrates, stm., Asia	B3	38
Eupora, Ms., U.S.	B4	101
Eure, N.C., U.S.	A6	110
Eure, stm., Fr.	C4	16
Eureka, N.W. Ter.	m34	66
Eureka, Ca., U.S.	B1	82
Eureka, Il., U.S.	C4	90
Eureka, Ks., U.S.	E7	93
Eureka, Mo., U.S.	f12	102
Eureka, Mt., U.S.	B1	103
Eureka, Nv., U.S.	D6	105
Eureka, S.D., U.S.	B6	118
Eureka, Ut., U.S.	D3	121
Eureka, Wa., U.S.	C7	124
Eureka, W.V., U.S.	B3	125
Eureka, co., Nv., U.S.	D5	105
Eureka Sound, strt., N.W. Ter.	m34	66
Eureka Springs, Ar., U.S.	A2	81
Euroa, Austl.	H5	51
Europa, Île, i., Reu.	B7	49
Europa Point, c., Gib.	D3	22
Europe, cont.	E13	8
Euskirchen, Ger.	C6	18
Eustis, Fl., U.S.	D5	86
Eustis, Me., U.S.	C2	96
Eutaw, Al., U.S.	C2	78
Eutawville, S.C., U.S.	E7	117
Eutin, Ger.	A5	18
Eutsuk Lake, l., B.C.	C4	69
Eva, Al., U.S.	A3	78
Eva, Tn., U.S.	A4	119
Evale, Ang.	E2	48
Evançon, stm., Italy	E4	21
Evangeline, co., La., U.S.	D3	95
Evans, Co., U.S.	A6	83
Evans, Ga., U.S.	C4	87
Evans, W.V., U.S.	C3	125
Evans, Lac, l., Que.	o20	73
Evans, Mount, mtn., Co., U.S.	B5	83
Evans City, Pa., U.S.	E1	115
Evansdale, Ia., U.S.	B5	92
Evans Mills, N.Y., U.S.	A5	109
Evansport, Oh., U.S.	A1	112
Evans Strait, strt., N.W. Ter.	D16	66
Evanston, Co., U.S.	A6	83
Evanston, Il., U.S.	A6	90
Evanston, Ky., U.S.	C6	94
Evanston, Wy., U.S.	E2	127
Evansville, Ar., U.S.	B1	81
Evansville, In., U.S.	I2	91
Evansville, Mn., U.S.	D3	100
Evansville, Ms., U.S.	A3	101
Evansville, Vt., U.S.	B4	122
Evansville, Wi., U.S.	F4	126
Evant, Tx., U.S.	D3	120
Evanton, Scot., U.K.	C4	13
Evart, Mi., U.S.	E5	99
Evarts, Ky., U.S.	D6	94
Eveleth, Mn., U.S.	C6	100
Even Yehuda, Isr.	f10	41
Everard, Lake, l., Austl.	F5	50
Everest, Ks., U.S.	C8	93
Everest, Mount, mtn., Asia	C8	36
Everett, Ont.	C5	73
Everett, Ga., U.S.	E5	87
Everett, Ma., U.S.	g11	98
Everett, Pa., U.S.	F5	115
Everett, Wa., U.S.	B3	124
Everett, Mount, mtn., Ma., U.S.	B1	98
Everett Lake, res., N.H., U.S.	D3	106
Everettville, W.V., U.S.	h10	125
Evergem, Bel.	C3	17
Everglades National Park, Fl., U.S.	G5	86
Evergreen, Al., U.S.	D3	78
Evergreen, Co., U.S.	B5	83
Evergreen, La., U.S.	D3	95
Evergreen, Ms., U.S.	A5	101
Evergreen, N.C., U.S.	C4	110
Evergreen, Va., U.S.	C4	123
Evergreen Park, Il., U.S.	k9	90
Everly, Ia., U.S.	A2	92
Everman, Tx., U.S.	*n9	120
Everson, Pa., U.S.	F2	115
Everson, Wa., U.S.	A3	124
Everton, Ar., U.S.	A3	81
Everton, Mo., U.S.	D4	102
Evesham, Eng., U.K.	I11	12
Evesham, Sask.	B6	12
Évian-les-Bains, Fr.	C2	20
Evinayong, Eq. Gui.	E2	46
Evington, Va., U.S.	C3	123
Evolène, Switz.	D3	21
Évora, Port.	C2	22
Évora, dist., Port.	C2	22
Évreux, Fr.	C4	16
Évron, Fr.	C3	16
Évros (Maritsa) (Meriç), stm., Eur.	B6	25
Evrótas, stm., Grc.	D4	25
Evstratios, i., Grc.	C5	40
Évvoia (Euboea), i., Grc.	C4	40
Ewa, Hi., U.S.	B3	88
Ewa Beach, Hi., U.S.	B3	88
Ewa Beach, Hi., U.S.	g9	88
Ewan, Wa., U.S.	B8	124
Ewarton, Jam.	E14	65
Ewe, Loch, b., Scot., U.K.	C3	13
Ewell, Md., U.S.	D5	97
Ewen, Mi., U.S.	m12	99
Ewing, Il., U.S.	E5	90
Ewing, Ky., U.S.	B6	94
Ewing, Mo., U.S.	A6	102
Ewing, Ne., U.S.	B7	104
Ewing Township, N.J., U.S.	C3	107
Excel, Al., U.S.	D2	78
Excello, Mo., U.S.	B5	102
Excelsior Mountain, mtn., Ca., U.S.	C4	82
Excelsior Mountains, mts., Nv., U.S.	E3	105
Excelsior Springs, Mo., U.S.	B3	102
Exchange, Pa., U.S.	D8	115
Exchange, W.V., U.S.	C4	125
Exe, stm., Eng., U.K.	D4	12
Executive Committee Range, mts., Ant.	B36	7
Exeland, Wi., U.S.	C2	126
Exeter, Ont.	D3	73
Exeter, Eng., U.K.	E5	10
Exeter, Ca., U.S.	D4	82
Exeter, Mo., U.S.	E4	102
Exeter, Ne., U.S.	D8	104
Exeter, N.H., U.S.	E5	106
Exeter, Pa., U.S.	D10	115
Exeter, R.I., U.S.	E3	116
Exeter, stm., N.H., U.S.	E5	106
Exira, Ia., U.S.	C3	92
Exline, Ia., U.S.	D5	92
Exmoor, for., Eng., U.K.	E5	10
Exmore, Va., U.S.	C7	123
Exmouth, Austl.	D1	50
Exmouth, Eng., U.K.	E5	10
Exmouth Gulf, b., Austl.	D1	50
Expanse, Sask.	H3	75
Experiment, Ga., U.S.	C2	87
Exploits, stm., Newf.	D3	72
Exploits, Bay of, b., Newf.	D4	72
Export, Pa., U.S.	F2	115
Exshaw, Alta.	D3	68
Extension, B.C.	f12	69
Exuma Sound, strt., Bah.	B5	64
Eyasi, Lake, l., Tan.	B6	48
Eyebrow, Sask.	G2	75
Eyehill Creek, stm., Can.	D7	75
Eyl, Som.	D6	47
Eylar Mountain, mtn., Ca., U.S.	D3	82
Eynort, Loch, b., Scot., U.K.	C1	13
Eyota, Mn., U.S.	G6	100
Eyre, Lake, l., Austl.	E6	50
Eyrecourt, Ire.	D3	11
Eyre North, Lake, l., Austl.	E6	50
Eyre Peninsula, pen., Austl.	F6	50
Eyre South, Lake, l., Austl.	h7	87
Ezeiza, Arg.	g7	54
Ezine, Tur.	C6	40

F

Name	Map Ref.	Page
Fabens, Tx., U.S.	o11	120
Faber, Va., U.S.	C4	123
Faber Lake, l., N.W. Ter.	D9	66
Fabius, N.Y., U.S.	C5	109
Fabius, stm., Mo., U.S.	A6	102
Fåborg, Den.	C4	15
Fabriano, Italy	C4	23
Fabyan, Ct., U.S.	A8	84
Facatativá, Col.	C3	60
Fachi, Niger	C7	45
Facpi Point, c., Guam	M9	52
Factoryville, Pa., U.S.	C10	115
Fada, Chad	B4	46
Fada Ngourma, Burkina	D5	45
Faddeya Gulf, b., Sov. Un.	B13	28
Faddey Island, i., Sov. Un.	B17	29
Fadian Point, c., Guam	L10	52
Faenza, Italy	B3	23
Faeroe Islands, ctry., Eur.	C7	8
Fafa, Mali	C5	45
Fafe, Port.	B1	22
Fafen, stm., Eth.	D5	47
Faga'alu, Am. Sam.	F13	52
Fagaitua Bay, b., Am. Sam.	G13	52
Fagaloa Bay, b., W. Sam.	F12	52
Fagamalo, W. Sam.	F11	52
Fágăraş, Rom.	C7	24
Fagatogo, Am. Sam.	F13	52
Fågelsjö, Swe.	t36	14
Fagernes, Nor.	G3	14
Fagersta, Swe.	G6	14
Faggo, Nig.	D6	45
Fagnano, Lago, l., S.A.	h12	54
Faguibine, Lac, l., Mali	C4	45
Fagus, Mo., U.S.	E7	102
Fahan, Ire.	B4	11
Faial, i., Port.	g8	44
Faichuk, is., Micron.	Q18	52
Fã'id, Eg.	D4	41
Faido, Switz.	D6	21
Fairbairn Reservoir, res., Austl.	A7	51
Fairbank, Az., U.S.	F5	80
Fairbank, Ia., U.S.	B5	92
Fairbanks, Ak., U.S.	C10	79
Fairbanks, Fl., U.S.	C4	86
Fairbanks, La., U.S.	F2	91
Fairbanks, Me., U.S.	D2	96
Fair Bluff, N.C., U.S.	C3	110
Fairborn, Oh., U.S.	C1	112
Fairburn, Ga., U.S.	C2	87
Fairburn, S.D., U.S.	D2	118
Fairbury, Il., U.S.	C5	90
Fairbury, Ne., U.S.	D8	104
Fairchild, Wi., U.S.	D3	126
Fairchild Air Force Base, mil., Wa., U.S.	g13	124
Fairdale, Ky., U.S.	B4	94
Fairdale, N.D., U.S.	A7	111
Fairfax, Ca., U.S.	C2	82
Fairfax, De., U.S.	A3	85
Fairfax, Ia., U.S.	C6	92
Fairfax, Mn., U.S.	F4	100
Fairfax, Mo., U.S.	A2	102
Fairfax, Ok., U.S.	A5	113
Fairfax, S.C., U.S.	F5	117
Fairfax, S.D., U.S.	D7	118
Fairfax, Vt., U.S.	B2	122
Fairfax, Va., U.S.	B5	123
Fairfax, co., Va., U.S.	B5	123
Fairfax Station, Va., U.S.	g12	123
Fairfield, Austl.	*F9	51
Fairfield, Al., U.S.	*B3	78
Fairfield, Ca., U.S.	C2	82
Fairfield, Ct., U.S.	E2	84
Fairfield, Il., U.S.	E5	90
Fairfield, Ia., U.S.	C6	92
Fairfield, Ky., U.S.	C4	94
Fairfield, Me., U.S.	D3	96
Fairfield, Mt., U.S.	C5	103
Fairfield, N.J., U.S.	*B4	107
Fairfield, N.C., U.S.	B6	110
Fairfield, Oh., U.S.	B2	111
Fairfield, Pa., U.S.	G7	115
Fairfield, Tx., U.S.	D4	120
Fairfield, Ut., U.S.	C3	121
Fairfield, Vt., U.S.	B2	122
Fairfield, Wa., U.S.	B8	124
Fairfield, co., Ct., U.S.	D2	84
Fairfield, co., Oh., U.S.	C3	112
Fairfield, co., S.C., U.S.	C5	117
Fairfield Bay, Ar., U.S.	B3	81
Fairfield Pond, l., Vt., U.S.	B3	122
Fairgrove, Mi., U.S.	E7	99
Fair Grove, Mo., U.S.	D4	102
Fair Grove, N.C., U.S.	B1	110
Fairhaven, Ma., U.S.	C6	98
Fair Haven, Mi., U.S.	F8	99
Fair Haven, Mn., U.S.	E4	100
Fair Haven, N.J., U.S.	C4	107
Fair Haven, N.Y., U.S.	B4	109
Fair Haven, Vt., U.S.	D2	122
Fair Head, c., N. Ire., U.K.	B5	11
Fairholme, Sask.	D1	75
Fairland, Al., U.S.	E2	78
Fairland, In., U.S.	E6	91
Fairland, Ok., U.S.	A7	113
Fair Lawn, N.J., U.S.	h8	107
Fairlawn, Oh., U.S.	*A4	112
Fairlea, W.V., U.S.	D4	125
Fairlee, Md., U.S.	B5	97
Fairlee, Vt., U.S.	D3	122
Fairlight, Sask.	H5	75
Fairmont, Il., U.S.	C6	90
Fairmont, Mn., U.S.	G4	100
Fairmont, N.C., U.S.	C3	110
Fairmont, Ne., U.S.	D8	104
Fairmont, Ok., U.S.	A4	113
Fairmont, W.V., U.S.	B4	125
Fairmount, Ga., U.S.	B2	87
Fairmount, Il., U.S.	C6	90
Fairmount, In., U.S.	D6	91
Fairmount, Md., U.S.	D6	97
Fairmount, N.Y., U.S.	*B4	109
Fairmount, N.D., U.S.	C9	111
Fairmount Heights, Md., U.S.	f9	97
Fair Oaks, Ca., U.S.	*C3	82
Fair Oaks, Ga., U.S.	h7	87
Fair Oaks, In., U.S.	B3	91

Name	Map Ref.	Page

Fairoaks, Pa., U.S. — h13 115
Fair Plain, Mi., U.S. — F4 99
Fairplain, W.V., U.S. — C3 125
Fairplay, Co., U.S. — B5 83
Fair Play, Md., U.S. — A2 97
Fair Play, Mo., U.S. — D4 102
Fair Play, S.C., U.S. — B2 117
Fairpoint, Oh., U.S. — B5 112
Fairpoint, S.D., U.S. — C3 118
Fairport, Ia., U.S. — C7 92
Fairport, Mi., U.S. — C4 99
Fairport, Mo., U.S. — B3 102
Fairport, N.Y., U.S. — B3 109
Fair Port, Va., U.S. — C6 123
Fairport Harbor, Oh., U.S. — A4 112
Fairton, N.J., U.S. — E2 107
Fairvale, N.B. — D4 71
Fairview, Ar., U.S. — A1 68
Fairview, Al., U.S. — *D4 81
Fairview, Il., U.S. — C3 90
Fairview, In., U.S. — D7 91
Fairview, Ks., U.S. — C8 93
Fairview, Ky., U.S. — D2 94
Fairview, Mi., U.S. — D6 99
Fairview, Mo., U.S. — E3 102
Fairview, Mt., U.S. — C12 103
Fairview, N.J., U.S. — D3 107
Fairview, N.J., U.S. — h8 107
Fairview, N.Y., U.S. — *D7 109
Fairview, Oh., U.S. — B4 112
Fairview, Ok., U.S. — A3 113
Fairview, Or., U.S. — *B4 114
Fairview, Pa., U.S. — B1 115
Fairview, S.D., U.S. — D9 118
Fairview, Tn., U.S. — B4 119
Fairview, Ut., U.S. — D4 121
Fairview, W.V., U.S. — B4 125
Fairview, Wy., U.S. — D2 127
Fairview Heights, Il., U.S. — E3 90
Fairview Park, Oh., U.S. — g9 112
Fairview Peak, mtn., Nv., U.S. — D3 105
Fairview Peak, mtn., Or., U.S. — D4 114
Fairview Shores, Fl., U.S. — *D5 86
Fair Water, Wi., U.S. — E5 126
Fairway, Ks., U.S. — k16 93
Fairweather, Mount, mtn., N.A. — D12 79
Fairwood, Wa., U.S. — *B8 124
Fairwood, Wa., U.S. — *B3 124
Fairy Glen, Sask. — D3 75
Faisalabad (Lyallpur), Pak. — B5 36
Faison, N.C., U.S. — B4 110
Faith, N.C., U.S. — B2 110
Faith, S.D., U.S. — B3 118
Faithorn, Mi., U.S. — C3 99
Faizābād (Fyzabad), India — C7 36
Fajardo, P.R. — G12 64
Fakenham, Eng., U.K. — B8 12
Fakfak, Indon. — F8 34
Fakse, Den. — C6 15
Fakse Bugt, b., Den. — C6 15
Fakse Ladeplads, Den. — C6 15
Faku, China — C10 32
Fal, stm., Eng., U.K. — D3 12
Falaba, S.L. — E2 45
Falaise, Fr. — C3 16
Falalu, i., Micron. — Q18 52
Falciu, Rom. — B9 24
Falcon, Ar., U.S. — D2 81
Falcon, Co., U.S. — C6 83
Falcon, Ms., U.S. — A3 101
Falcon, N.C., U.S. — B4 110
Falcón, state, Ven. — A4 60
Falconer, N.Y., U.S. — C1 109
Falcon Heights, Mn., U.S. — n12 100
Falcon Heights, Or., U.S. — E5 114
Falcon Lake, res., N.A — F3 120
Faléa, Mali — D2 45
Falefa Harbour, b., W. Sam. — F12 52
Falelima, W. Sam. — F11 52
Falémé, stm., Afr. — D2 45
Faleolo International Airport, W. Sam. — F12 52
Faleshty, Sov. Un. — B8 24
Falfurrias, Tx., U.S. — F3 120
Falher, Alta. — B2 68
Falkenberg, Ger. — B8 19
Falkenberg, Swe. — B6 15
Falkenstein, Ger. — C7 19
Falkirk, Scot., U.K. — C5 10
Falkirk, N.D., U.S. — B4 111
Falkland, B.C. — D8 69
Falkland Islands (Islas Malvinas), dep., S.A. — I5 53
Falkner, Ms., U.S. — A5 101
Falköping, Swe. — H5 14
Falkville, Al., U.S. — A3 78
Fall, Ger. — B7 20
Fall, stm., Ks., U.S. — E7 93
Fall Branch, Tn., U.S. — C11 119
Fallbrook, Ca., U.S. — F5 82
Fall City, Wa., U.S. — B4 124
Fall Creek, Wi., U.S. — D2 126
Fall Creek, stm., In., U.S. — k10 91
Fallentimber, Pa., U.S. — E4 115
Falling Creek, stm., Va., U.S. — n17 123
Falling Rock Creek, stm., W.V., U.S. — m13 125
Falling Water, Tn., U.S. — h11 119
Falling Waters, W.V., U.S. — B6 125
Fallis, Ok., U.S. — B4 113
Fall Mountain Lake, Ct. U.S. — C4 84
Fållnäs, Swe. — u35 14
Fallon, Mt., U.S. — D11 103
Fallon, Nv., U.S. — D3 105
Fallon, co., Mt., U.S. — D12 103
Fallon Indian Reservation, Nv., U.S. — D3 105
Fallon Naval Air Station, mil., Nv., U.S. — D3 105
Fall River, Ks., U.S. — E7 93
Fall River, Ma., U.S. — C5 98
Fallriver, Tn., U.S. — B4 119
Fall River, Wi., U.S. — E4 126
Fall River, co., S.D., U.S. — D2 118
Fall River Lake, res., Ks., U.S. — E7 93
Fall River Mills, Ca., U.S. — B3 82
Fall Rock, Ky., U.S. — C6 94
Falls, co., Tx., U.S. — D4 120
Fallsburg, N.Y., U.S. — *D9 119
Falls Church, Va., U.S. — g12 123
Falls City, Ne., U.S. — D10 104
Falls City, Or., U.S. — C3 114
Falls of Rough, Ky., U.S. — C3 94
Fallston, Md., U.S. — A5 97
Fallston, N.C., U.S. — B1 110
Falls Township, Pa., U.S. — *F12 115
Falls Village, Ct., U.S. — B2 84
Falmouth, N.S. — E5 71
Falmouth, Jam. — E5 64
Falmouth, Eng., U.K. — E3 12
Falmouth, In., U.S. — E7 91
Falmouth, Ky., U.S. — B5 94

Falmouth, Me., U.S. — E2 96
Falmouth, Ma., U.S. — C6 98
Falmouth, Mi., U.S. — D5 99
Falmouth, Va., U.S. — B5 123
Falmouth Bay, b., Eng., U.K. — D2 12
Falsa Chipana, Punta, c., Chile — D1 55
False Cape, c., Fl., U.S. — D6 86
False Cape, c., Va., U.S. — D7 123
False Bay, b., S. Afr. — D2 49
Falso, Cabo, c., Hond. — C6 62
Falster, i., Den. — D5 15
Falsterbo, Swe. — C6 15
Fălticeni, Rom. — B8 24
Falun, Swe. — G6 14
Falun, Ks., U.S. — D6 93
Famagusta see Gazimağusa, N. Cyp. — E9 40
Famatina, Sierra de, mts., Arg. — E2 55
Family Lake, l., Man. — D4 70
Fanan, i., Micron. — Q18 52
Fanapanges, i., Micron. — Q18 52
Fancy Farm, Ky., U.S. — f9 94
Fancy Prairie, Il., U.S. — D4 90
Fang, Thai. — H5 32
Fangcheng, China — H5 32
Fangxian, China — E7 31
Fannettsburg, Pa., U.S. — F6 115
Fannin, Tx., U.S. — E4 120
Fannin, co., Ga., U.S. — B2 87
Fannin, co., Tx., U.S. — C4 120
Fanning Island see Tabuaeran Island, atoll, Kir. — F12 6
Fanny, Mount, mtn., Or., U.S. — B9 114
Fanny Bay, B.C. — E5 69
Fannystelle, Man. — E3 70
Fano, Italy — C4 23
Fanø, i., Den. — C2 15
Fanø Bugt, b., Den. — C2 15
Fanonchuluyan, Bahia, b., N. Mar. Is. — D8 52
Fan Si Pan, mtn., Viet. — A5 35
Fanwood, N.J., U.S. — *B4 107
Fāqūs, Eg. — D3 41
Faradje, Zaire — A4 48
Faradofay, Madag. — h9 49
Farafangana, Madag. — h9 49
Farāfirah, Al Wāḥat al, well, Eg. — C2 38
Farāh, Afg. — B3 36
Farah, stm., Afg. — B3 36
Faramana, Burkina — D4 45
Faranah, Gui. — D4 45
Farasan Islands, is., Sau. Ar. — D4 38
Farber, Mo., U.S. — B6 102
Fareham, Eng., U.K. — D6 12
Farewell, Cape, c., N.Z. — N14 51
Fargo, Ga., U.S. — F4 87
Fargo, N.D., U.S. — C9 111
Fargo, Ok., U.S. — A2 113
Far Hills, N.J., U.S. — B3 107
Fār'ah, Wādī al, val., Isr. Occ. — g12 41
Faribault, Mn., U.S. — F5 100
Faribault, co., Mn., U.S. — G4 100
Farīdpur, Bngl. — I13 37
Farīdpur, India — C7 36
Fārīghah, Wādī al, val., Libya — G3 40
Farilhões Islands, is., Port. — C1 22
Fārīmān, Iran — D9 39
Farina, Austl. — E6 51
Farina, Il., U.S. — E5 90
Farisita, Co., U.S. — D5 83
Farīskūr, Eg. — C3 41
Farley, Ia., U.S. — B6 92
Farley, Ma., U.S. — A3 98
Farley, Mo., U.S. — B3 102
Farley, N.M., U.S. — A5 108
Farmer, Oh., U.S. — A1 112
Farmer City, Il., U.S. — C5 90
Farmers, Ky., U.S. — B6 94
Farmers Branch, Tx., U.S. — n10 120
Farmersburg, Ia., U.S. — B6 92
Farmersburg, In., U.S. — F3 91
Farmersville, Al., U.S. — C3 78
Farmersville, Ca., U.S. — *D4 82
Farmersville, Oh., U.S. — C1 112
Farmersville, Tx., U.S. — C4 120
Farmerville, La., U.S. — B3 95
Farmingdale, Me., U.S. — D3 96
Farmingdale, N.J., U.S. — *C4 107
Farmingdale, N.Y., U.S. — *n15 109
Farmington, Ar., U.S. — A1 81
Farmington, Ct., U.S. — C4 84
Farmington, De., U.S. — E3 85
Farmington, Il., U.S. — C3 90
Farmington, Ia., U.S. — D6 92
Farmington, Me., U.S. — D2 96
Farmington, Mi., U.S. — p15 99
Farmington, Mn., U.S. — F5 100
Farmington, Mo., U.S. — D7 102
Farmington, N.H., U.S. — D4 106
Farmington, N.M., U.S. — A1 108
Farmington, Pa., U.S. — G2 115
Farmington, Ut., U.S. — B4 121
Farmington, Wa., U.S. — B8 124
Farmington, W.V., U.S. — h10 125
Farmington, stm., Ct., U.S. — B4 84
Farmington, West Branch, stm., Ct., U.S. — A4 84
Farmington Hills, Mi., U.S. — o15 99
Farmland, In., U.S. — D7 91
Farm Pond, l., Ma., U.S. — g10 98
Farmville, N.C., U.S. — B5 110
Farmville, Va., U.S. — C4 123
Farnam, Ne., U.S. — D5 104
Farnborough, Eng., U.K. — C7 12
Farner, Tn., U.S. — D9 119
Farnham, Que. — D5 74
Farnham, Va., U.S. — C6 123
Farnham, Mount, mtn., B.C. — D9 69
Farnhamville, Ia., U.S. — B3 92
Färnigen, Switz. — C6 21
Faro, Braz. — D7 59
Faro, Port. — D2 22
Farragut, Ia., U.S. — D2 92
Farragut, Tn., U.S. — *D9 119
Farrar, stm., Scot., U.K. — C4 13
Farrāshband, Iran — G6 39
Farrell, Ms., U.S. — A3 101
Farrellton, Que. — D2 74
Farrerdale, Sask. — F3 75
Farris, Ok., U.S. — C6 113
Farris, i., Nor. — n27 14
Farrukhābād, India — C6 36
Fars, hist. reg., Iran — C5 38
Fársala (Pharsalus), Grc. — C4 25
Fārsī, i., Sau. Ar. — H4 39
Farsø, Den. — B3 15

Farson, Ia., U.S. — C5 92
Farson, Wy., U.S. — D3 127
Farsund, Nor. — H2 14
Fartak, Ra's, c., Yemen — D5 38
Fårup, Den. — B3 15
Farvel, Kap, c., Grnld. — D16 61
Farwell, Mi., U.S. — E6 99
Farwell, Mn., U.S. — E3 100
Farwell, Ne., U.S. — C7 104
Farwell, Tx., U.S. — B1 120
Fasā, Iran — G6 39
Fasano, Italy — D6 23
Fashoda see Kodok, Sudan — D3 47
Fassett, Que. — D3 74
Fastnet Rock, rock, Ire. — J2 11
Fastov, Sov. Un. — F7 27
Fatehpur, India — C7 36
Fatsa, Tur. — B11 40
Fatumafuti, Am. Sam. — F13 52
Fatuosofia, Cape, c., W. Sam. — F13 52
Faucett, Mo., U.S. — B3 102
Faulenfürst, Ger. — A5 21
Faulk, co., S.D., U.S. — B6 118
Faulkland Heights, De., U.S. — i7 85
Faulkner, co., Ar., U.S. — B3 81
Faulkton, S.D., U.S. — B6 118
Faunsdale, Al., U.S. — C2 78
Fauquembergues, Fr. — D10 12
Fauquier, B.C. — E8 69
Fauquier, co., Va., U.S. — B5 123
Faust, Alta. — B3 68
Favara, Italy — F4 23
Faverges, Fr. — D2 20
Faverney, Fr. — A1 21
Faversham, Eng., U.K. — C8 12
Favorita, Fl., U.S. — C5 86
Fawcett Lake, l., Alta. — B4 68
Fawnie Nose, mtn., B.C. — C5 69
Fawnie Range, mts., B.C. — C5 69
Faxaflói, b., Ice. — n21 14
Faxälven, stm., Swe. — F6 14
Faxon, Ok., U.S. — C3 113
Faxon, Tn., U.S. — A3 119
Fay, Ok., U.S. — B3 113
Fayd, Sau. Ar. — I14 40
Fayette, Al., U.S. — B2 78
Fayette, Ia., U.S. — B6 92
Fayette, Me., U.S. — D2 96
Fayette, Ms., U.S. — D2 101
Fayette, Mo., U.S. — B5 102
Fayette, Oh., U.S. — A1 112
Fayette, Ut., U.S. — D4 121
Fayette, co., Al., U.S. — B2 78
Fayette, co., Ga., U.S. — C2 87
Fayette, co., Il., U.S. — D5 90
Fayette, co., In., U.S. — E7 91
Fayette, co., Ia., U.S. — B6 92
Fayette, co., Ky., U.S. — B5 94
Fayette, co., Oh., U.S. — C2 112
Fayette, co., Pa., U.S. — G2 115
Fayette, co., Tn., U.S. — B2 119
Fayette, co., Tx., U.S. — E4 120
Fayette, co., W.V., U.S. — C3 125
Fayetteville, Al., U.S. — B3 78
Fayetteville, Ar., U.S. — A1 81
Fayetteville, Ga., U.S. — C2 87
Fayetteville, N.C., U.S. — B4 110
Fayetteville, Oh., U.S. — C2 112
Fayetteville, Pa., U.S. — G6 115
Fayetteville, Tn., U.S. — B5 119
Fayetteville, W.V., U.S. — C3 125
Faylakah, i., Kuw. — G4 39
Fays-Billot, Fr. — B1 20
Fayville, Ma., U.S. — g9 98
Faywood, N.M., U.S. — E1 108
Fazenda Nova, Braz. — B2 56
Fdérik, Maur. — B2 45
Fear, Cape, c., N.C., U.S. — D5 110
Feasterville, Pa., U.S. — o21 115
Feather, stm., Ca., U.S. — C3 82
Feather, Middle Fork, stm., Ca., U.S. — C3 82
Feather, Mount, mtn., Ant. — e40 7
Feather Falls, Ca., U.S. — C3 82
Featherston, Ok., U.S. — B6 113
Fécamp, Fr. — C4 16
Federal, Arg. — A5 54
Federal Dam, Mn., U.S. — C4 100
Federal Heights, Co., U.S. — *B6 83
Federal Point, Fl., U.S. — C5 86
Federalsburg, Md., U.S. — C6 97
Federal Way, Wa., U.S. — *f11 124
Fedora, S.D., U.S. — C8 118
Fedscreek, Ky., U.S. — C7 94
Feeding Hills, Ma., U.S. — B2 98
Feesburg, Oh., U.S. — D2 112
Fefan, i., Micron. — Q18 52
Fehmarn, i., Ger. — A5 18
Fehmarn Strait, strt., Eur. — D5 15
Feia, Lagoa, b., Braz. — C3 56
Feijó, Braz. — C3 58
Feilding, N.Z. — N15 51
Feira, Port. — E3 22
Feira (Luangwa), Zam. — E5 48
Feira de Santana, Braz. — D5 57
Fejø, i., Den. — D5 15
Felanitx, Spain — C7 22
Felch, Mi., U.S. — C3 99
Felda, Fl., U.S. — F5 86
Feldbach, Aus. — E7 18
Feldberg, Ger. — B4 20
Feldberg, mtn., Ger. — B4 20
Feldkirch, Aus. — E4 19
Felicity, Oh., U.S. — D1 112
Felida, Wa., U.S. — D7 124
Felipe Carrillo Puerto, Mex. — C13 66
Felix, Cape, c., N.W. Ter. — C9 12
Felixstowe, Eng., U.K. — C9 12
Fellbach, Ger. — E4 19
Fellingsbro, Swe. — t33 14
Fellowship, N.J., U.S. — *D3 107
Fellsmere, Fl., U.S. — E6 86
Felsberg, Ger. — E6 19
Felsenthal, Ar., U.S. — D3 81
Felt, Id., U.S. — F7 89
Felton, Ca., U.S. — D2 82
Felton, De., U.S. — D3 85
Felton, Mn., U.S. — C2 100
Felton, Pa., U.S. — G8 115
Feltre, Italy — A3 23
Femunden, l., Nor. — F4 14
Fena Valley Reservoir, res., Guam — M9 52
Fence, Wi., U.S. — C5 126
Fence, stm., Mi., U.S. — B2 99
Fence Lake, N.M., U.S. — C1 108
Fence Lake, l., Wi., U.S. — C4 126
Fenelon Falls, Ont. — C6 73
Fengcheng, China — F8 31
Fengcheng, China — D11 32

Fengdu, China — E6 31
Fengjie, China — E6 31
Fengning, China — D7 32
Fengqing, China — G4 31
Fengxian, China — H2 32
Fengxiang, China — G2 32
Fengzhen, China — D5 32
Fenimore Pass, strt., Ak., U.S. — E6 99
Fenn, Id., U.S. — D2 89
Fennimore, Wi., U.S. — F3 126
Fennville, Mi., U.S. — F4 99
Fenoarivo Atsinanana, Madag. — g9 49
Fenton, Sask. — D3 75
Fenton, Ia., U.S. — A3 92
Fenton, La., U.S. — D3 95
Fenton, Mi., U.S. — F7 99
Fentress, Tx., U.S. — h8 120
Fentress, co., Tn., U.S. — C9 119
Fenwick, W.V., U.S. — C4 125
Fenwick Island, De., U.S. — G5 85
Fenwick Island, i., S.C., U.S. — k11 117
Fenyang, China — G4 75
Feodosiya, Sov. Un. — I10 27
Fer, Point au, c., La., U.S. — E4 95
Ferbane, Ire. — D4 11
Ferdig, Mt., U.S. — B5 103
Ferdinand, Id., U.S. — C2 89
Ferdinand, In., U.S. — H4 91
Ferdinandshof, Ger. — E7 15
Ferdows, Iran — B5 38
Fère-Champenoise, Fr. — F3 17
Ferentino, Italy — D4 23
Fergana, Sov. Un. — E8 28
Fergana Mountains, mts., Sov. Un. — E8 28
Fergus, Ont. — D4 73
Fergus, Mt., U.S. — C7 103
Fergus, co., Mt., U.S. — C7 103
Fergus, B.C. — D9 69
Fergus Falls, Mn., U.S. — D2 100
Ferguson, B.C. — D9 69
Ferguson, Ia., U.S. — C5 92
Ferguson, Ky., U.S. — C5 94
Ferguson, Mo., U.S. — C7 102
Ferintosh, Alta. — C4 68
Ferké see Ferkéssédougou, I.C. — E3 45
Ferkéssédougou, I.C. — E3 45
Ferme-Neuve, Que. — C2 74
Fermeuse, Newf. — E5 72
Fermo, Italy — C7 23
Fermont, Que. — h13 74
Fermoselle, Spain — B2 22
Fermoy, Ire. — D2 10
Fernandina, Isla (Narborough), i., Ec. — g5 58
Fernando de Noronha, Ilha, i., Braz. — B4 57
Fernandópolis, Braz. — C2 56
Fernando Póo see Bioko, i., Eq. Gui. — E1 46
Fernán-Núñez, Spain — D3 22
Fernbank, Al., U.S. — B1 78
Ferndale, Ont. — g11 94
Ferndale, Ar., U.S. — g11 81
Ferndale, Ca., U.S. — B1 82
Ferndale, Ky., U.S. — D6 94
Ferndale, Md., U.S. — B4 97
Ferndale, Mi., U.S. — P15 99
Ferndale, Oh., U.S. — F4 115
Ferndale, Pa., U.S. — F4 115
Ferndale, S.C., U.S. — A3 117
Ferndale, Wa., U.S. — A3 124
Ferney, S.D., U.S. — B7 118
Fernie, B.C. — E10 69
Fernley, Nv., U.S. — D2 105
Fern Park, Fl., U.S. — *D5 86
Fern Ridge Lake, res., Or., U.S. — C3 114
Ferns, Ire. — E5 11
Fernwood, Id., U.S. — B2 89
Fernwood, Ms., U.S. — D3 101
Fernwood, N.Y., U.S. — B4 109
Ferrara, Italy — B3 23
Ferreira do Alentejo, Port. — C1 22
Ferreira do Zêzere, Port. — C2 22
Ferrellsburg, W.V., U.S. — C2 125
Ferrelo, Cape, c., Or., U.S. — E2 114
Ferreñafe, Peru — C2 58
Ferrette, Fr. — A3 21
Ferriday, La., U.S. — C4 95
Ferrières, Italy — E5 20
Ferris, Il., U.S. — C2 90
Ferris, Tx., U.S. — C4 120
Ferrisburg, Vt., U.S. — C2 122
Ferris Mountains, mts., Wy., U.S. — D5 127
Ferron, Ut., U.S. — D4 121
Ferros, Braz. — B4 56
Ferry, Mi., U.S. — E4 99
Ferry, co., Wa., U.S. — A7 124
Ferry Farms, Va., U.S. — B5 123
Ferry Point, c., N.J., U.S. — k7 107
Ferrysburg, Mi., U.S. — E4 99
Fertile, Ia., U.S. — A4 92
Fertile, Mn., U.S. — C2 100
Fès, Mor. — B4 44
Feshi, Zaire — C3 48
Fessenden, N.D., U.S. — B6 111
Festina, Ia., U.S. — A6 92
Festus, Mo., U.S. — C7 102
Fetești, Rom. — C8 24
Fethard, Ire. — E4 11
Fethiye, Tur. — D6 40
Fetisovo, Sov. Un. — I6 28
Feucht, Ger. — D6 19
Feuchtwangen, Ger. — D5 19
Feudal, Sask. — F2 75
Feuilles, Rivière aux, stm., Que. — g12 74
Feurs, Fr. — E6 16
Feversham, Ont. — C4 73
Feyzābād, Afg. — A5 36
Fezzan (Fazzān), hist. reg., Libya — D2 40
Ffestiniog, Wales, U.K. — D5 10
Fhada, Beinn, mtn., Scot., U.K. — B4 10
Fiambalá, Arg. — B2 54
Fianarantsoa, Madag. — h9 49
Fianarantsoa, prov., Madag. — h9 49
Fianga, Chad — D3 46
Ficarolo, Italy — B6 20
Fichtelgebirge, mts., Ger. — C6 19
Fidalgo Island, i., Wa., U.S. — A3 124
Fidelity, Il., U.S. — D3 90
Fidenza, Italy — B3 23
Fidler Lake, l., Man. — A3 70
Fieldale, Va., U.S. — D3 123

Field Crest Estates, Ct., U.S. — D8 84
Fielding, Sask. — E2 75
Fielding, Ut., U.S. — B3 121
Fieldon, Il., U.S. — D3 90
Fields, La., U.S. — D2 95
Fields, Or., U.S. — E8 114
Fields, Lake, l., La., U.S. — k10 95
Fields, Lake, stm., Fl., U.S. — B3 86
Fieldsboro, N.J., U.S. — C3 107
Fieri, Alb. — B1 22
Fierro Urco, mtn., Ec. — B2 58
Fiesch, Switz. — D5 21
Fiesole, Italy — C3 23
Fife, prov., Scot., U.K. — D5 13
Fife, Lake, l., Sask. — H3 75
Fife Lake, Mi., U.S. — D5 99
Fife Lake, l., Sask. — H3 75
Fife Ness, c., Scot., U.K. — B5 10
Fifield, Wi., U.S. — C3 126
Fifteenmile Creek, stm., Wy., U.S. — B4 127
Fifteen Mile Falls Reservoir, res., U.S. — C5 122
Fifty Lakes, Mn., U.S. — D4 100
Figeac, Fr. — E5 16
Fig Garden, Ca., U.S. — *D4 82
Figtree, Zimb. — B4 49
Figueira da Foz, Port. — B1 22
Figueras, Spain — A7 22
Figuig, Mor. — C4 44
Fiji, ctry., Oc. — H10 6
Fik, Eth. — D5 47
Filchner Ice Shelf, ice, Ant. — B8 7
File Lake, l., Man. — B1 70
Filer, Id., U.S. — G4 89
Filey, Eng., U.K. — F8 13
Filiatrá, Grc. — D3 25
Filicudi, i., Italy — E5 23
Filingué, Niger — D5 45
Filisur, Switz. — C8 21
Filley, Ne., U.S. — D9 104
Fillmore, Sask. — H4 75
Fillmore, Ca., U.S. — E4 82
Fillmore, In., U.S. — E4 91
Fillmore, Mo., U.S. — A3 102
Fillmore, N.Y., U.S. — C2 109
Fillmore, Ok., U.S. — C5 113
Fillmore, Ut., U.S. — E3 121
Fillmore, co., Mn., U.S. — G6 100
Fillmore, co., Ne., U.S. — D8 104
Fimi, stm., Zaire — B2 48
Finale Emilia, Italy — E7 20
Fincastle, Va., U.S. — C3 123
Finch, Ont. — B9 73
Findhorn, stm., Scot., U.K. — C5 13
Findlater, Sask. — G3 75
Findlay, Il., U.S. — D5 90
Findlay, Oh., U.S. — A2 112
Findlay, Mount, mtn., B.C. — D9 69
Fingal, N.D., U.S. — C8 111
Finger, Tn., U.S. — B3 119
Finger Lake, l., Ont. — C5 70
Fingoè, Moz. — A5 49
Finike, Tur. — D7 40
Finisterre, Cape, c., Spain — A1 22
Finjasjön, l., Swe. — B7 15
Finke, stm., Austl. — E5 51
Finland, Mn., U.S. — C7 100
Finland, ctry., Eur. — E12 14
Finland, Gulf of, b., Eur. — H12 14
Finlay, stm., B.C. — m17 69
Finlayson, Mn., U.S. — D6 100
Finley, N.D., U.S. — B8 111
Finley, Ok., U.S. — C6 113
Finley, Tn., U.S. — A2 119
Finleyson, Ga., U.S. — D3 87
Finly, In., U.S. — E6 91
Finmoore, B.C. — C6 69
Finnegan, Alta. — D4 68
Finney, co., Ks., U.S. — D3 93
Finn Mountain, mtn., Ak., U.S. — C8 79
Finschhafen, Pap. N. Gui. — k12 50
Finspång, Swe. — u33 14
Finsteraarhorn, mtn., Switz. — C4 20
Finsterwalde, Ger. — C6 18
Fintona, N. Ire., U.K. — C4 11
Fintown, Ire. — B3 11
Fionn Loch, l., Scot., U.K. — C3 13
Fiq, Isr. Occ. — F10 40
Fir, stm., Sask. — D4 75
Fircrest, Wa., U.S. — f10 124
Firebaugh, Ca., U.S. — D3 82
Firenzuola, Italy — B3 23
Firesteel, S.D., U.S. — B4 118
Firestone, Co., U.S. — A6 83
Firmat, Arg. — A4 54
Firminy, Fr. — E6 16
Fir Mountain, Sask. — H2 75
Firozābād, India — C6 36
Firozpur, India — B5 36
Firsby, Eng., U.K. — A8 13
Firth, Id., U.S. — F6 89
Firth, Ne., U.S. — D9 104
Firūzābād, Iran — G6 39
Firūzkūh, Iran — B5 38
Fischot Island, i., Newf. — C4 72
Fish, stm., Nmb. — E2 49
Fish, stm., Al., U.S. — E2 78
Fish, stm., Me., U.S. — A4 96
Fish Cove Point, c., Newf. — A3 72
Fish Creek, Wi., U.S. — C6 126
Fish Creek, stm., W.V., U.S. — g8 125
Fisheating Creek, stm., Fl., U.S. — F5 86
Fisher, Ar., U.S. — B5 81
Fisher, Il., U.S. — C5 90
Fisher, La., U.S. — C2 95
Fisher, Mn., U.S. — C2 100
Fisher, Pa., U.S. — D3 115
Fisher, W.V., U.S. — B5 125
Fisher, co., Tx., U.S. — C2 120
Fisher, stm., Man. — D3 70
Fisher Bay, b., Man. — D3 70
Fisher Branch, Man. — D3 70
Fisher Glacier, ice, Ant. — B19 7
Fisher Lake, l., In., U.S. — A5 91
Fishermans Island, i., Va., U.S. — h15 91
Fishers, In., U.S. — E5 91
Fishers Island, i., N.Y., U.S. — m16 109
Fishers Peak, mtn., Co., U.S. — D6 83
Fisher Strait, strt., N.W. Ter. — D16 66

Fishersville, Va., U.S. — B4 123
Fishertown, Pa., U.S. — F4 115
Fisherville, Ont. — E5 73
Fishguard [and Goodwick], Wales, U.K. — E4 10
Fish Haven, Id., U.S. — G7 89
Fishhook, Il., U.S. — D3 90
Fishing Bay, b., Md., U.S. — D5 97
Fishing Creek, Md., U.S. — D5 97
Fishing Creek, stm., N.C., U.S. — A5 110
Fishing Creek, stm., S.C., U.S. — B5 117
Fishing Creek, stm., W.V., U.S. — B4 125
Fishing Creek, North Fork, stm., W.V., U.S. — h9 125
Fishing Creek, South Fork, stm., W.V., U.S. — h9 125
Fishing Creek Reservoir, res., S.C., U.S. — B6 117
Fishing Lake, l., Sask. — C4 70
Fishing Lake, l., Sask. — F4 75
Fishkill, N.Y., U.S. — D7 109
Fish Lake, l., Ut., U.S. — E4 121
Fish River Lake, l., Me., U.S. — B4 96
Fish Springs Range, mts., Ut., U.S. — D2 121
Fishtail, Mt., U.S. — E7 103
Fishtail Point, c., Mrshl. Is. — f39 7
Fishtrap Lake, res., Ky., U.S. — C7 94
Fishville, La., U.S. — C3 95
Fisk, Mo., U.S. — E7 102
Fiskburg, Ky., U.S. — B5 94
Fiskdale, Ma., U.S. — B3 98
Fismes, Fr. — F3 17
Fitch-Bay, Que. — D5 74
Fitchburg, Ma., U.S. — A4 98
Fitchburg, Wi., U.S. — *F4 126
Fitchville, Ct., U.S. — C7 84
Fithian, Il., U.S. — C6 90
Fitler, Ms., U.S. — C2 101
Fittstown, Ok., U.S. — C5 113
Fitzgerald, Ga., U.S. — E3 87
Fitzhugh, Ok., U.S. — C5 113
Fitz Hugh Sound, strt., B.C. — C4 69
Fitzpatrick, Que. — B5 74
Fitz Roy, Arg. — B3 54
Fitzroy, stm., Austl. — C3 51
Fitzroy, stm., Austl. — D9 50
Fitzroy, Monte (Cerro Chaltel), mtn., S.A. — D2 54
Fitzroy Harbour, Ont. — B8 73
Fitzwilliam, N.H., U.S. — E2 106
Fitzwilliam Depot, N.H., U.S. — E2 106
Fitzwilliam Island, i., Ont. — B3 73
Fiume see Rijeka, Yugo. — C2 23
Fiumicino, Italy — h8 23
Five Island Lake, l., Ia., U.S. — A3 92
Five Islands, N.S. — D5 71
Fivemile Creek, stm., Wy., U.S. — C4 127
Fivemiletown, N. Ire., U.K. — C4 11
Five Points, Al., U.S. — B4 78
Five Points, N.M., U.S. — B3 108
Fizi, Zaire — B4 48
Fjärås Kyrkby, Swe. — A6 15
Fjärdhundra, Swe. — t34 14
Fjerritslev, Den. — A3 15
Flagg Mountain, hill, Al., U.S. — C3 78
Flag Knob, mtn., Ky., U.S. — C7 94
Flagler, Co., U.S. — B7 83
Flagler, co., Fl., U.S. — C5 86
Flagler Beach, Fl., U.S. — C5 86
Flag Pond, Tn., U.S. — C11 119
Flagstaff, Az., U.S. — B4 80
Flagstaff Lake, l., Or., U.S. — E7 114
Flagtown, N.J., U.S. — B3 107
Flamanda, Lac, l., Que. — B4 74
Flambeau, stm., Wi., U.S. — C3 126
Flambeau, South Fork, stm., Wi., U.S. — C3 126
Flamborough Head, c., Eng., U.K. — C6 13
Flaming Gorge Dam, Ut., U.S. — C6 121
Flaming Gorge National Recreation Area, U.S. — E3 127
Flaming Gorge Reservoir, res., U.S. — E3 127
Flanagan, Il., U.S. — C5 90
Flanders, Ont. — E5 70
Flanders, Ct., U.S. — C2 84
Flanders, N.J., U.S. — *B3 107
Flanders, hist. reg., Eur. — C9 16
Flandreau, S.D., U.S. — C9 118
Flandreau Indian Reservation, S.D., U.S. — C9 118
Flannan Islands, is., Scot., U.K. — A8 15
Flåren, l., Swe. — A8 15
Flasher, N.D., U.S. — C4 111
Flat, Ak., U.S. — C8 79
Flat, Mo., U.S. — D6 102
Flat, stm., Mi., U.S. — E5 99
Flat, stm., N.C., U.S. — A4 110
Flat, stm., R.I., U.S. — C2 116
Flat Bay, Newf. — D2 72
Flat Brook, stm., N.J., U.S. — A3 107
Flatbush, Alta. — B3 68
Flat Creek, Al., U.S. — D2 78
Flat Creek, Tn., U.S. — B5 119
Flathead, co., Mt., U.S. — B2 103
Flathead, stm., N.A. — E10 69
Flathead, North Fork, stm., N.A. — B2 103
Flathead, South Fork, stm., Mt., U.S. — C3 103
Flathead Indian Reservation, Mt., U.S. — C2 103
Flathead Valley, val., Mt., U.S. — C2 103
Flat Lake, l., Alta. — B4 68
Flat Lake, l., La., U.S. — k9 95
Flatlands, N.B. — B3 71
Flat Lick, Ky., U.S. — D6 94
Flat Mountain, mtn., N.Z. — P11 51
Flatonia, Tx., U.S. — E4 120
Flat River, P.E.I. — C7 71
Flat River Reservoir, res., R.I., U.S. — D3 116
Flat Rock, Al., U.S. — A4 78
Flat Rock, Il., U.S. — F6 90
Flat Rock, Mi., U.S. — p15 99
Flat Rock, N.C., U.S. — f10 110
Flat Rock, Oh., U.S. — A3 112
Flatrock, stm., In., U.S. — F6 91
Flatrock Lake, l., Man. — B1 70
Flattery, Cape, c., Wa., U.S. — A1 124
Flatts, Ber. — p20 64
Flatwoods, Ky., U.S. — B7 94

Name | Map Ref. | Page

Flatwoods, La., U.S. — C3 95
Flatwoods, Tn., U.S. — B4 119
Flatwoods, W.V., U.S. — *C4 125
Flawil, Switz. — B5 20
Flaxcombe, Sask. — F1 75
Flaxton, N.D., U.S. — A3 111
Flaxville, Mt., U.S. — B11 103
Fleet, Alta. — C5 68
Fleet, Eng., U.K. — C7 12
Fleetwood, Eng., U.K. — G5 13
Fleetwood, N.C., U.S. — A1 110
Fleetwood, Pa., U.S. — F10 115
Fleischmanns, N.Y., U.S. — C6 109
Flekkefjord, Nor. — H2 14
Fleming, Sask. — G5 75
Fleming, Co., U.S. — A8 83
Fleming, Ga., U.S. — E5 87
Fleming, Pa., U.S. — E6 115
Fleming, co., Ky., U.S. — B6 94
Fleming-Neon, Ky., U.S. — C7 94
Flemingsburg, Ky., U.S. — B6 94
Flemington, Ga., U.S. — E5 87
Flemington, Mo., U.S. — D4 102
Flemington, N.J., U.S. — B3 107
Flemington, Pa., U.S. — D7 115
Flemington, W.V., U.S. — k10 125
Flen, Swe. — t34 14
Flensburg, Ger. — A4 18
Flensburg, Mn., U.S. — E4 100
Flensburg Fjord, b., Eur. — D3 15
Flers, Fr. — C3 16
Flesherton, Ont. — C4 73
Fletcher, Ont. — E2 73
Fletcher, N.C., U.S. — f10 110
Fletcher, Ok., U.S. — B1 112
Fletcher, Ok., U.S. — C3 113
Fletcher, Vt., U.S. — B3 122
Fletcher Islands, is., Ant. — B3 7
Fleur-de-Lys, Newf. — C3 72
Fleurier, Switz. — C2 20
Flieden, Ger. — C4 19
Flims, Switz. — C7 21
Flinders, stm., Austl. — C7 50
Flinders Island, i., Austl. — F5 50
Flinders Range, mts., Austl. — F6 50
Flin Flon, Man. — B1 70
Flint, Wales, U.K. — A4 12
Flint, In., U.S. — A7 91
Flint, Mi., U.S. — E7 99
Flint, stm., Ga., U.S. — E2 87
Flint City, Al., U.S. — A3 78
Flint Creek, stm., Al., U.S. — A3 78
Flint Creek Range, mts., Mt., U.S. — D3 103
Flinthill, Mo., U.S. — C7 102
Flint Hill, Va., U.S. — B4 123
Flint Hills, hills, Ks., U.S. — D7 93
Flint Island, i., Kir. — G12 6
Flintoft, Sask. — H2 75
Flinton, Ont. — C7 73
Flint Run, stm., W.V., U.S. — k9 125
Flintville, Tn., U.S. — B5 119
Flintstone, Md., U.S. — k13 97
Flipper Point, c., Wake I. — A2 52
Flippin, Ar., U.S. — A3 81
Flippin, Ky., U.S. — D4 94
Flixecourt, Fr. — D2 17
Flöha, Ger. — C8 19
Flom, Mn., U.S. — C2 100
Flomaton, Al., U.S. — D2 78
Flomot, Tx., U.S. — B2 120
Flood Range, mts., Ant. — B35 7
Floodwood, Mn., U.S. — D6 100
Flora, Il., U.S. — E5 90
Flora, In., U.S. — C4 91
Flora, Ms., U.S. — C3 101
Flora, N.D., U.S. — B6 111
Florahome, Fl., U.S. — C5 86
Florala, Al., U.S. — D3 78
Floral City, Fl., U.S. — D4 86
Floral Park, N.Y., U.S. — *k13 109
Flora Vista, N.M., U.S. — A1 108
Florence (Firenze), Italy — C3 23
Florence, Al., U.S. — A2 78
Florence, Az., U.S. — D4 80
Florence, Ca., U.S. — *n12 82
Florence, Co., U.S. — C5 83
Florence, In., U.S. — G8 91
Florence, Ky., U.S. — D7 93
Florence, Ky., U.S. — A5 94
Florence, Ms., U.S. — C3 101
Florence, Mo., U.S. — C5 102
Florence, N.J., U.S. — D2 103
Florence, N.J., U.S. — C3 107
Florence, Or., U.S. — D2 114
Florence, S.C., U.S. — C8 117
Florence, S.D., U.S. — B8 118
Florence, Tx., U.S. — D4 120
Florence, Vt., U.S. — D2 122
Florence, Wa., U.S. — A3 124
Florence, Wi., U.S. — C5 126
Florence, co., S.C., U.S. — C8 117
Florence, co., Wi., U.S. — C5 126
Florence Junction, Az., U.S. — D4 80
Florenceville, N.B. — C2 71
Florencia, Col. — C2 60
Florenville, Bel. — E5 17
Flores, Guat. — D7 63
Flores, dept., Ur. — f8 54
Flores, i., Indon. — G6 34
Flores, i., Port. — g8 44
Flores Island, i., B.C. — E4 69
Flores Sea, Indon. — G5 34
Floresta, Braz. — C3 57
Floresville, Tx., U.S. — E3 120
Florham Park, N.J., U.S. — B4 107
Floriano, Braz. — C2 57
Floriano Peixoto, Braz. — C4 58
Florianópolis, Braz. — D3 56
Florida, Cuba — D4 64
Florida, Ma., U.S. — A1 98
Florida, N.M., U.S. — C3 108
Florida, N.Y., U.S. — D6 109
Florida, Oh., U.S. — A1 112
Florida, Ur. — E1 54
Florida, dept., Ur. — f8 54
Florida, state, U.S. — E5 86
Florida, Cape, c., Fl., U.S. — G6 86
Florida, Straits of, strt., N.A. — F11 76
Florida Bay, b., Fl., U.S. — H6 86
Floridablanca, Col. — *B3 60
Florida City, Fl., U.S. — G6 86
Florida Keys, is., Fl., U.S. — H6 86
Florida Mountains, mts., N.M., U.S. — E2 108
Florida State Indian Reservation, Fl., U.S. — F5 86
Florien, La., U.S. — C2 95
Florin, Ca., U.S. — *C3 82
Flórina (Phlórina), Grc. — B3 25
Floris, Ia., U.S. — D5 92
Florissant, Co., U.S. — C5 83
Florissant, Mo., U.S. — f13 102
Florissant Fossil Beds National Monument, Co., U.S. — C5 83

Flossmoor, Il., U.S. — k9 90
Flournoy, Ca., U.S. — C2 82
Flourtown, Pa., U.S. — o21 115
Flovilla, Ga., U.S. — C3 87
Flower Brook, stm., Vt., U.S. — E2 122
Floweree, Mt., U.S. — *C5 103
Flower Hill, N.Y., U.S. — *E7 109
Flower's Cove, Newf. — C3 72
Flower Station, Ont. — B8 73
Flowery Branch, Ga., U.S. — B3 87
Flowood, Ms., U.S. — C3 101
Floyd, Ia., U.S. — A5 92
Floyd, N.M., U.S. — C6 108
Floyd, Va., U.S. — D2 123
Floyd, co., Ga., U.S. — B1 87
Floyd, co., In., U.S. — H6 91
Floyd, co., Ia., U.S. — A5 92
Floyd, co., Ky., U.S. — C7 94
Floyd, co., Tx., U.S. — B2 120
Floyd, stm., Ia., U.S. — B1 92
Floydada, Tx., U.S. — C2 120
Floyd Dale, S.C., U.S. — C9 117
Floyds Fork, stm., Ky., U.S. — B4 94
Floydsburg, Ky., U.S. — g12 94
Floyds Knobs, In., U.S. — H6 91
Fluchthorn, mtn., Eur. — C9 21
Fluessen, l., Neth. — B5 17
Flumendosa, stm., Italy — E2 23
Flums, Switz. — B7 21
Flushing, Mi., U.S. — E7 99
Flushing, Oh., U.S. — B4 112
Fluvanna, Tx., U.S. — C2 120
Fluvanna, co., Va., U.S. — C4 123
Fly, stm. — k11 50
Fly Creek, N.Y., U.S. — C6 109
Flyinge, Swe. — C7 15
Flynn, N.M., U.S. — D4 108
Foam Lake, Sask. — F4 75
Foam Lake, l., Sask. — F4 75
Foard, co., Tx., U.S. — B3 120
Foard City, N.M., U.S. — B3 95
Foça, Tur. — C6 25
Foča, Yugo. — D4 24
Fochabers, Scot., U.K. — C5 13
Focşani, Rom. — C8 24
Foggia, Italy — D5 23
Fogland Point, c., R.I., U.S. — E6 116
Fogliano, Italy — k9 23
Fogo, Newf. — D4 72
Fogo, Cape, c., Newf. — D5 72
Fogo Island, i., Newf. — D4 72
Fohnsdorf, Aus. — E7 18
Föhr, i., Ger. — A4 18
Foix, Fr. — F4 16
Folcroft, Pa., U.S. — *p20 115
Foley, Al., U.S. — E2 78
Foley, Mn., U.S. — E5 100
Foley, Mo., U.S. — B7 102
Foley Island, i., N.W. Ter. — C17 66
Foligno, Italy — C4 23
Folkestone, Eng., U.K. — E7 10
Folkston, Ga., U.S. — F4 87
Follansbee, W.V., U.S. — A4 125
Follett, Tx., U.S. — A2 120
Follonica, Italy — C3 23
Folly Beach, S.C., U.S. — F8 117
Folly Island, i., S.C., U.S. — F8 117
Folly Lake, N.S. — D6 71
Folsom, Ca., U.S. — C3 82
Folsom, La., U.S. — D5 95
Folsom, N.J., U.S. — D3 107
Folsom, N.M., U.S. — A6 108
Folsom, W.V., U.S. — B4 125
Folsomville, In., U.S. — H3 91
Fomento, Cuba — D5 64
Fonda, Ia., U.S. — B3 92
Fonda, N.Y., U.S. — C6 109
Fond-du-Lac, Sask. — m7 75
Fond du Lac, Wi., U.S. — E5 126
Fond du Lac, co., Wi., U.S. — E5 126
Fond du Lac Indian Reservation, Mn., U.S. — D6 100
Fonde, Ky., U.S. — D6 94
Fondi, Italy — D4 23
Fonsagrada, Spain — A2 22
Fonseca, Golfo de, b., N.A. — E7 63
Fontainebleau, Fr. — C5 16
Fontana, Ca., U.S. — m14 82
Fontana, Ks., U.S. — D9 93
Fontana, Wi., U.S. — F5 126
Fontana Dam, N.C., U.S. — f9 110
Fontana Lake, res., N.C., U.S. — f9 110
Fontanelle, Ia., U.S. — C3 92
Fontanet, In., U.S. — E3 91
Fonte Boa, Braz. — D4 60
Fontenay-le-Comte, Fr. — D3 16
Fontenay [-sous-Bois], Fr. — g10 16
Fontenelle, Wy., U.S. — E2 127
Fontenelle Reservoir, res., Wy., U.S. — D2 127
Foosland, Il., U.S. — C5 90
Foothill Farms, Ca., U.S. — *C3 82
Foothills, Alta. — C2 68
Footville, Wi., U.S. — F4 126
Foping, China — H2 32
Forada, Mn., U.S. — E3 100
Foraker, Oh., U.S. — B2 112
Foraker, Ok., U.S. — A5 113
Foraker, Mount, mtn., Ak., U.S. — f16 79
Forbach, Fr. — C7 16
Forbes, Austl. — C8 50
Forbes, Austl. — C6 100
Forbes, Mn., U.S. — B6 100
Forbes, N.D., U.S. — B2 120
Forbes, N.D., U.S. — D7 111
Forbes, Lac, l., Que. — C3 74
Forbes, Mount, mtn., Alta. — D2 68
Forcados, Nig. — E6 45
Forcalquier, Fr. — F6 16
Force, Pa., U.S. — D5 115
Forchheim, Ger. — D5 18
Ford, Scot., U.K. — E4 13
Ford, Ks., U.S. — E4 93
Ford, co., Il., U.S. — C5 90
Ford, co., Ks., U.S. — E3 93
Ford, stm., Mi., U.S. — C3 99
Ford City, Ca., U.S. — E4 82
Ford City, Pa., U.S. — E2 115
Fordland, Mo., U.S. — D5 102
Fordoche, La., U.S. — D4 95
Ford Ranges, mts., Ant. — B34 7
Ford River, Mi., U.S. — C3 99
Fords, N.J., U.S. — B4 107
Fords Prairie, Wa., U.S. — C2 124
Fordsville, Ky., U.S. — C3 94
Fordville, N.D., U.S. — A8 111
Fordwich, Ont. — D3 73
Fordyce, Ar., U.S. — D3 81
Fordyce, Ne., U.S. — B8 104
Forécariah, Gui. — E2 45
Foreman, Ar., U.S. — D1 81
Foremost, Alta. — E5 68
Foreman, In., U.S. — C3 91

Forest, Bel. — B6 16
Forest, Ont. — D2 73
Forest, In., U.S. — D5 91
Forest, Ms., U.S. — C4 101
Forest, Oh., U.S. — B2 112
Forest, Tx., U.S. — D5 120
Forest, Va., U.S. — C3 123
Forest, co., Pa., U.S. — C3 115
Forest, co., Wi., U.S. — C5 126
Forest, stm., N.D., U.S. — A8 111
Forest Acres, S.C., U.S. — C6 117
Forestburg, Alta. — C4 68
Forestburg, S.D., U.S. — C7 118
Forest City, Il., U.S. — C4 90
Forest City, Ia., U.S. — A4 92
Forest City, Mo., U.S. — C5 96
Forest City, N.C., U.S. — B1 110
Forest City, Pa., U.S. — C11 115
Forestdale, R.I., U.S. — B3 116
Forest Dale, Vt., U.S. — D2 122
Forest Glen, i., U.S. — h12 95
Forest Green, Mo., U.S. — B5 102
Forest Grove, Mt., U.S. — D7 103
Forest Grove, Or., U.S. — B3 114
Forest Hill, La., U.S. — C3 95
Forest Hill, Md., U.S. — A5 97
Forest Hills, Pa., U.S. — *n9 120
Forest Hills, Pa., U.S. — k14 115
Forest Home, Al., U.S. — D3 78
Forest Junction, Wi., U.S. — h9 126
Forest Knolls, Ca., U.S. — g7 82
Forest Lake, Mi., U.S. — B4 99
Forest Lake, Mn., U.S. — E6 100
Forest Lake, N.H., U.S. — B4 106
Foreston, Mn., U.S. — E5 100
Foreston, S.C., U.S. — D7 117
Forest Park, Ga., U.S. — h8 87
Forest Park, Il., U.S. — k9 90
Forest Park, La., U.S. — B3 95
Forest Park, Oh., U.S. — n12 112
Forestport, N.Y., U.S. — B5 109
Forest River, N.D., U.S. — A8 111
Forestville, Md., U.S. — *C4 97
Forestville, N.Y., U.S. — C1 109
Forestville, Pa., U.S. — D1 115
Forestville, Wi., U.S. — D6 126
Forfar, Scot., U.K. — E5 13
Forgan, Sask. — F2 75
Forgan, Ok., U.S. — A1 113
Forges-les-Eaux, Fr. — C4 16
Forget, Sask. — H4 75
Forge Village, Ma., U.S. — A5 98
Forillon, Parc National de, Que. — k14 74
Fork, N.C., U.S. — B2 110
Fork, S.C., U.S. — C9 117
Fork Creek, stm., W.V., U.S. — m12 125
Forked Deer, stm., Tn., U.S. — B2 119
Forked Deer, Middle Fork, stm., Tn., U.S. — D3 119
Forked Deer, North Fork, stm., Tn., U.S. — B3 119
Forked Deer, South Fork, stm., Tn., U.S. — B3 119
Forked Island, La., U.S. — E3 95
Forked River, N.J., U.S. — D4 107
Forkland, Al., U.S. — C2 78
Fork Mountain, Tn., U.S. — C9 119
Fork River, Man. — D1 70
Forks, Wa., U.S. — B1 124
Fork Shoals, S.C., U.S. — B3 117
Forksville, Pa., U.S. — D8 115
Fork Union, Va., U.S. — C4 123
Forkville, Ms., U.S. — C4 101
Forlì, Italy — B4 23
Forman, N.D., U.S. — C8 111
Formazza, Italy — C4 20
Formby, Eng., U.K. — A4 12
Formello, Italy — g8 23
Formentera, i., Spain — C6 22
Formiga, Braz. — C3 56
Formosa, Arg. — E4 55
Formosa, Braz. — B3 56
Formosa, Ont. — C3 73
Formosa, prov., Arg. — B3 55
Formosa, Serra, plat., Braz. — E4 59
Formosa Bay, b., Kenya — B7 48
Formosa see Taiwan, ctry., Asia — G9 31
Formoso, Ks., U.S. — C6 93
Formoso, stm., Braz. — A4 56
Formoso, stm., Braz. — E5 59
Forney, Tx., U.S. — C4 120
Fornovo di Taro, Italy — E6 20
Forres, Scot., U.K. — B5 13
Forrest, Austl. — F4 50
Forrest, Il., U.S. — C5 90
Forrest, N.M., U.S. — C6 108
Forrest, co., Ms., U.S. — D4 101
Forrest, co., Ar., U.S. — B5 81
Forrest City, Ar., U.S. — B5 81
Forrester Island, i., Ak., U.S. — n23 79
Forrest Lakes, l., Austl. — E4 50
Forreston, Il., U.S. — A4 90
Forsan, Tx., U.S. — C2 120
Forsayth, Austl. — C7 50
Forserum, Swe. — A8 15
Förslövsholm, Swe. — B6 15
Forster, Austl. — F9 51
Forster, N.M., U.S. — C7 16
Forst [Lausitz], Ger. — C7 18
Forsyth, Ga., U.S. — C3 87
Forsyth, Il., U.S. — D5 90
Forsyth, Mo., U.S. — E4 102
Forsyth, Mt., U.S. — D10 103
Forsyth, co., Ga., U.S. — B2 87
Forsyth, co., N.C., U.S. — A2 110
Fort Adams, Ms., U.S. — D2 101
Fort Albany, Ont. — n19 73
Fortaleza, Braz. — B3 57
Fortaleza de Ituxi, Braz. — C4 58
Fort Ann, N.Y., U.S. — B7 109
Fort Apache, Az., U.S. — D6 80
Fort Apache Indian Reservation, Az., U.S. — D5 80
Fort-Archambault see Sarh, Chad — D3 46
Fort Ashby, W.V., U.S. — B6 125
Fort Assiniboine, Alta. — B3 68
Fort Atkinson, Ia., U.S. — A6 92
Fort Atkinson, Wi., U.S. — F5 126
Fort Augustus, Scot., U.K. — D4 13
Fort Barnwell, N.C., U.S. — B5 110
Fort Beaufort, S. Afr. — H5 48
Fort Belknap Agency, Mt., U.S. — B8 103
Fort Belknap Indian Reservation, Mt., U.S. — B8 103
Fort Belvoir, mil., Va., U.S. — g12 123
Fort Bend, co., Tx., U.S. — E5 120
Fort Benjamin Harrison, mil., In., U.S. — k10 91
Fort Benning, mil., Ga., U.S. — D2 87
Fort Benton, Mt., U.S. — C6 103

Fort Berthold Indian Reservation, N.D., U.S. — B3 111
Fort Bidwell, Ca., U.S. — B3 82
Fort Bidwell Indian Reservation, Ca., U.S. — B3 82
Fort Blackmore, Va., U.S. — f9 123
Fort Bliss, mil., Tx., U.S. — o11 120
Fort Bragg, Ca., U.S. — C2 82
Fort Bragg, mil., N.C., U.S. — B3 110
Fort Branch, In., U.S. — H2 91
Fort Bridger, Wy., U.S. — E2 127
Fort Calhoun, Ne., U.S. — C9 104
Fort Campbell, mil., U.S. — A4 119
Fort Carson, mil., Co., U.S. — C6 83
Fort Chipewyan, Alta. — f8 68
Fort Clark, N.D., U.S. — B4 111
Fort Clatsop National Memorial, hist., Or., U.S. — A3 114
Fort Cobb, Ok., U.S. — B3 113
Fort Cobb Reservoir, res., Ok., U.S. — B3 113
Fort Collins, Co., U.S. — A5 83
Fort Coulonge, Que. — B8 73
Fort Covington, N.Y., U.S. — f10 109
Fort Crampel, Cen. Afr. Rep. — D4 46
Fort Davis, Al., U.S. — C4 78
Fort Davis, Tx., U.S. — o13 120
Fort Davis National Historic Site, hist., Tx., U.S. — o13 120
Fort Defiance, Az., U.S. — B6 80
Fort-de-France, Mart. — I14 64
Fort-de-France, Baie de, b., Mart. — S10 65
Fort Deposit, Al., U.S. — D3 78
Fort Detrick, mil., Md., U.S. — B3 97
Fort Devens, mil., Ma., U.S. — f9 98
Fort Dix, mil., N.J., U.S. — C3 107
Fort Dodge, Ia., U.S. — B3 92
Fort Dodge, Ks., U.S. — E4 93
Fort Donelson National Military Park, Tn., U.S. — A4 119
Fort Duchesne, Ut., U.S. — C6 121
Forteau, Newf. — C3 72
Fort Edward, N.Y., U.S. — B7 109
Fort Erie, Ont. — E6 73
Fortescue, Mo., U.S. — A2 102
Fortescue, stm., Austl. — D2 50
Fort Eustis, mil., Va., U.S. — h14 123
Fort Fairfield, Me., U.S. — B5 96
Fort Fitzgerald, Alta. — f8 68
Fort Foureau, Cam. — C3 46
Fort-Foureau, Chad — C3 46
Fort Frances, Ont. — o16 73
Fort Fraser, B.C. — B5 69
Fort Frederica National Monument, Ga., U.S. — E1 87
Fort Gaines, Ga., U.S. — E1 87
Fort Garland, Co., U.S. — D5 83
Fort Gay, W.V., U.S. — C2 125
Fort Gibson, Ok., U.S. — B6 113
Fort Gibson Lake, res., Ok., U.S. — A6 113
Fort Good Hope, N.W. Ter. — C7 66
Fort Gordon, mil., Ga., U.S. — C4 87
Fort Grahame, B.C. — E8 66
Fort Greely, mil., Ak., U.S. — C10 79
Fort Green, Fl., U.S. — E5 86
Forth, stm., Scot., U.K. — D4 13
Forth, Firth of, est., Scot., U.K. — B5 10
Fort Hall, Kenya — B6 48
Fort Hall, Id., U.S. — F6 89
Fort Hall Indian Reservation, Id., U.S. — F6 89
Fort Hancock, Tx., U.S. — o12 120
Fort Hill, Pa., U.S. — G3 115
Fort Hood, mil., Tx., U.S. — D4 120
Fort Howard, Md., U.S. — B5 97
Fort Huachuca, mil., Az., U.S. — F5 80
Fortierville, Que. — C5 74
Fortine, Mt., U.S. — B2 103
Fortín Uno, Arg. — B3 54
Fort Jackson, mil., S.C., U.S. — C6 117
Fort Jefferson National Monument, Fl., U.S. — H4 86
Fort Jennings, Oh., U.S. — B1 112
Fort Jones, Ca., U.S. — B2 82
Fort Kent, Alta. — B5 68
Fort Kent, Me., U.S. — A4 96
Fort Kent Mills, Me., U.S. — A4 96
Fort Klamath, Or., U.S. — E5 114
Fort Knox, mil., Ky., U.S. — B4 94
Fort-Lamy see N'Djamena, Chad — C3 46
Fort Langley, B.C. — f13 69
Fort Laramie, Wy., U.S. — D8 127
Fort Laramie National Historic Site, hist., Wy., U.S. — D8 127
Fort Lauderdale, Fl., U.S. — F6 86
Fort Lawn, S.C., U.S. — B6 117
Fort Leavenworth, mil., Ks., U.S. — C9 93
Fort Lee, N.J., U.S. — B5 107
Fort Lee, mil., Va., U.S. — C5 123
Fort Leonard Wood, mil., Mo., U.S. — D5 102
Fort Lewis, mil., Wa., U.S. — B3 124
Fort Liard, N.W. Ter. — D8 66
Fort-Liberté, Haiti — E8 64
Fort Littleton, Pa., U.S. — F5 115
Fort Loramie, Oh., U.S. — B1 112
Fort Loudon, Pa., U.S. — G6 115
Fort Loudoun Lake, res., Tn., U.S. — D9 119
Fort Lupton, Co., U.S. — A6 83
Fort MacArthur, mil., Ca., U.S. — n12 82
Fort MacKay, Alta. — f8 68
Fort Macleod, Alta. — E4 68
Fort Madison, Ia., U.S. — D6 92
Fort Matanzas National Monument, Fl., U.S. — C5 86
Fort McClellan, mil., Al., U.S. — B4 78
Fort McDermitt Indian Reservation, U.S. — B4 105
Fort McDowell, Az., U.S. — k9 80
Fort McDowell Indian Reservation, Az., U.S. — D5 80
Fort McHenry National Monument And Historic Shrine, Md., U.S. — g11 97
Fort McKavett, Tx., U.S. — D2 120
Fort McKinley, Oh., U.S. — *C1 112
Fort McMurray, Alta. — A5 68
Fort McPherson, N.W. Ter. — C6 66
Fort Meade, Fl., U.S. — E5 86
Fort Meade, mil., Md., U.S. — B4 97
Fort Meadow Reservoir, res., Ma., U.S. — g9 98
Fort Mill, S.C., U.S. — A6 117
Fort Miller, N.Y., U.S. — B7 109
Fort Mitchell, Al., U.S. — C4 78
Fort Mitchell, Ky., U.S. — h13 94
Fort Mitchell, Va., U.S. — D4 123

Fort Mojave Indian Reservation, U.S. — C1 80
Fort Monmouth, mil., N.J., U.S. — C4 107
Fort Monroe, mil., Va., U.S. — h15 123
Fort Morgan, Al., U.S. — E1 78
Fort Morgan, Al., U.S. — A7 83
Fort Morgan, Co., U.S. — D6 117
Fort Motte, S.C., U.S. — F5 86
Fort Myer, mil., Va., U.S. — g12 123
Fort Myers, Fl., U.S. — F5 86
Fort Myers Beach, Fl., U.S. — B4 95
Fort Necessity, La., U.S. — m18 69
Fort Nelson, B.C. — D7 66
Fort Norman, N.W. Ter. — E5 86
Fort Ogden, Fl., U.S. — B1 87
Fort Oglethorpe, Ga., U.S. — D3 82
Fort Ord, mil., Ca., U.S. — A4 78
Fort Payne, Al., U.S. — D6 94
Fort Peck, Mt., U.S. — B10 103
Fort Peck Dam, Mt., U.S. — B10 103
Fort Peck Indian Reservation, Mt., U.S. — B11 103
Fort Peck Lake, res., Mt., U.S. — C9 103
Fort Pierce, Fl., U.S. — E6 86
Fort Pierce Inlet, b., Fl., U.S. — E6 86
Fort Pierre, S.D., U.S. — C5 118
Fort Plain, N.Y., U.S. — C6 109
Fort Portal, Ug. — A5 48
Fort Providence, N.W. Ter. — D9 66
Fort Qu'Appelle, Sask. — G4 75
Fort Randall Dam, S.D., U.S. — D7 118
Fort Ransom, N.D., U.S. — C8 111
Fort Recovery, Oh., U.S. — B1 112
Fort Reliance, N.W. Ter. — D11 66
Fort Resolution, N.W. Ter. — D10 66
Fortress Mountain, mtn., Wy., U.S. — B3 127
Fort Rice, N.D., U.S. — C5 111
Fort Richardson, mil., Ak., U.S. — *C10 79
Fort Riley, mil., Ks., U.S. — C7 93
Fort Ripley, Mn., U.S. — D4 100
Fort Ritchie, mil., Md., U.S. — A3 97
Fort Ritner, In., U.S. — G5 91
Fort Robinson, Ne., U.S. — B2 104
Fort Rock, Or., U.S. — D6 114
Fortrose, N.Z. — Q12 51
Fortrose, Scot., U.K. — C4 13
Fort Ross, N.W. Ter. — B14 66
Fort Rucker, mil., Al., U.S. — D4 78
Fort Saint James, B.C. — B5 69
Fort Saint John, B.C. — A7 69
Fort Sam Houston, mil., Tx., U.S. — k7 120
Fort Saskatchewan, Alta. — C4 68
Fort Scott, Ks., U.S. — E9 93
Fort Severn, Ont. — n18 73
Fort Shafter, mil., Hi., U.S. — g10 88
Fort Shaw, Mt., U.S. — C5 103
Fort Shawnee, Oh., U.S. — B1 112
Fort Sheridan, mil., Il., U.S. — A6 90
Fort-Shevchenko, Sov. Un. — E4 28
Fort Sibut, Cen. Afr. Rep. — D3 46
Fort Sill, mil., Ok., U.S. — C3 113
Fort Simpson, N.W. Ter. — D8 66
Fort Smith, Alta. — f8 68
Fort Smith, N.W. Ter. — D10 66
Fort Smith, Ar., U.S. — B1 81
Fort Stanton, N.M., U.S. — D4 108
Fort Steele, B.C. — E10 69
Fort Steele, Wy., U.S. — E6 127
Fort Stewart, mil., Ga., U.S. — D5 87
Fort Stockton, Tx., U.S. — D1 120
Fort Sumner, N.M., U.S. — C5 108
Fort Sumner National Monument, S.C., U.S. — k12 117
Fort Supply, Ok., U.S. — A2 113
Fort Supply Lake, res., Ok., U.S. — A2 113
Fort Thomas, Az., U.S. — D6 80
Fort Thomas, Ky., U.S. — h14 94
Fort Thompson, S.D., U.S. — C6 118
Fort Totten, N.D., U.S. — B7 111
Fort Totten Indian Reservation, N.D., U.S. — B7 111
Fort Towson, Ok., U.S. — C6 113
Fortuna, Ca., U.S. — B1 82
Fortuna, Mo., U.S. — C5 102
Fortuna, N.D., U.S. — A2 111
Fortuna Ledge (Marshall), Ak., U.S. — C7 79
Fortune, Newf. — E4 72
Fortune Bay, b., Newf. — E4 72
Fortune Harbour, Newf. — D4 72
Fort Union National Monument, N.M., U.S. — B5 108
Fort Valley, Ga., U.S. — D3 87
Fort Vermilion, Alta. — f7 68
Fortville, In., U.S. — E6 91
Fort Wainwright, mil., Ak., U.S. — *C10 79
Fort Walton Beach, Fl., U.S. — u15 86
Fort Washakie, Wy., U.S. — C4 127
Fort Washington, Pa., U.S. — o21 115
Fort Washington Forest, Md., U.S. — *C4 97
Fort Wayne, In., U.S. — B7 91
Fort Wellington, Guy. — A3 59
Fort White, Fl., U.S. — B4 86
Fort William, Scot., U.K. — D3 13
Fort Wingate, N.M., U.S. — B1 108
Fort Worth, Tx., U.S. — C4 120
Fort Wright, Ky., U.S. — h13 94
Fort Yates, N.D., U.S. — C5 111
Fort Yukon, Ak., U.S. — B10 79
Fort Yuma Indian Reservation, Ca., U.S. — F6 82
Foryle, Lough, b., Eur. — C3 10
Forūr, i., Iran — H7 39
Foshan, China — *G7 31
Foss, Ok., U.S. — B2 113
Fossano, Italy — E2 23
Fossato, Nor. — p29 14
Foss Reservoir, res., Ok., U.S. — B2 113
Fossil Butte National Monument, Wy., U.S. — D6 114
Fossil Lake, l., Or., U.S. — D6 114
Fossombrone, Italy — C4 23
Foss Reservoir, res., Ok., U.S. — B2 113
Fosston, Mn., U.S. — C3 100
Fosston, Sask. — E4 75
Foster, Ky., U.S. — B5 94
Foster, Ne., U.S. — B8 104
Foster, Or., U.S. — C4 114
Foster, R.I., U.S. — C1 116
Foster, Wi., U.S. — D2 126
Foster, co., N.D., U.S. — B7 111
Foster Brook, Pa., U.S. — C4 115
Foster City, Ca., U.S. — *h8 82
Foster City, Mi., U.S. — C3 99

Fosters, Al., U.S. — B2 78
Fosters Falls, Va., U.S. — D2 123
Fosters Pond, l., Ma., U.S. — f11 98
Fosterville, Tn., U.S. — B5 119
Foster Village, Hi., U.S. — g10 88
Fostoria, Al., U.S. — C3 78
Fostoria, Ia., U.S. — A2 92
Fostoria, Ks., U.S. — C7 93
Fostoria, Mi., U.S. — E7 99
Fostoria, Oh., U.S. — A2 112
Fougamou, Gabon — F2 46
Fougères, Fr. — C3 16
Foul, i., Scot., U.K. — g9 10
Foula, i., Scot., U.K. — g9 10
Foulness Island, i., Eng., U.K. — C8 12
Foulwind, Cape, c., N.Z. — N13 51
Foumban, Cam. — D2 46
Foum el Hassane, Mor. — D3 44
Fount, Ky., U.S. — D6 94
Fountain, Al., U.S. — D2 78
Fountain, Co., U.S. — C6 83
Fountain, Fl., U.S. — B1 86
Fountain, Mi., U.S. — D4 99
Fountain, Mn., U.S. — G6 100
Fountain, N.C., U.S. — B5 110
Fountain, co., In., U.S. — D3 91
Fountain City, In., U.S. — E8 91
Fountain City, Wi., U.S. — D2 126
Fountain Creek, stm., Co., U.S. — C6 83
Fountain Green, Ut., U.S. — D4 121
Fountain Hill, Ar., U.S. — D4 81
Fountain Hill, Pa., U.S. — E11 115
Fountain Inn, S.C., U.S. — B3 117
Fountain Lake, Ar., U.S. — f8 81
Fountain Place, La., U.S. — D4 95
Fountain Run, Ky., U.S. — D4 94
Fountaintown, In., U.S. — C5 111
Fountain Valley, Ca., U.S. — *n13 82
Four Buttes, Mt., U.S. — B11 103
Fourchambault, Fr. — D5 16
Fourche, co., Ar., U.S. — *C3 81
Fourche Creek, stm., Ar., U.S. — k10 81
Fourche LaFave, stm., Ar., U.S. — C2 81
Fourche Maline, stm., Ok., U.S. — C6 113
Fourche Mountain, mtn., Ar., U.S. — C2 81
Fourchu, N.S. — D9 71
Four Corners, Ca., U.S. — E5 82
Four Corners, Or., U.S. — *C4 114
Four Corners, Wy., U.S. — B8 127
Four Lakes, Wa., U.S. — B8 124
Fourmies, Fr. — B6 16
Fourmile, Ky., U.S. — D6 94
Fourmile Creek, stm., Ia., U.S. — e8 92
Four Mountains, Islands of the, is., Ak., U.S. — E6 79
Fournier, Ont. — B10 73
Four Oaks, N.C., U.S. — B4 110
Fouta Djalon, reg., Gui. — D2 45
Feveaux Strait, strt., N.Z. — Q11 51
Fowey, Eng., U.K. — D3 12
Fowey, Newf. — D3 12
Fowler, Ca., U.S. — D4 82
Fowler, Co., U.S. — C6 83
Fowler, Il., U.S. — C2 90
Fowler, In., U.S. — C3 91
Fowler, Ks., U.S. — E3 93
Fowler, Mi., U.S. — E6 99
Fowler, In., U.S. — D6 91
Fowlerton, Tx., U.S. — E3 120
Fowlerville, Mi., U.S. — F6 99
Fowlkes, Tn., U.S. — B2 119
Fowlstown, Ga., U.S. — F2 87
Fox, Ar., U.S. — B3 81
Fox, Ok., U.S. — C4 113
Fox, Or., U.S. — C7 114
Fox, stm., Man. — B4 70
Fox, stm., Mi., U.S. — B5 90
Fox, stm., Wi., U.S. — B4 99
Fox, stm., Wi., U.S. — D5 126
Fox, stm., Wi., U.S. — C7 73
Foxboro, Ont. — B5 98
Foxboro, Ma., U.S. — B1 126
Foxboro, Wi., U.S. — *h14 115
Fox Chapel, Pa., U.S. — E2 68
Fox Creek, Alta. — F4 13
Foxdale, I. of Man — C17 66
Foxe Basin, b., N.W. Ter. — D16 66
Foxe Channel, strt., N.W. Ter. — C17 66
Foxe Peninsula, pen., N.W. Ter. — D3 72
Foxford, Sask. — D2 11
Fox Harbour, Newf. — E5 72
Fox Harbour, Newf. — E4 72
Foxholm, N.D., U.S. — A4 111
Fox Island, i., R.I., U.S. — f10 124
Fox Island, i., Wa., U.S. — E6 79
Fox Islands, is., Ak., U.S. — E6 79
Fox Lake, Il., U.S. — A5 90
Fox Lake, Wi., U.S. — E5 126
Fox Lake, l., Wi., U.S. — h8 90
Fox Mountain, mtn., Yukon — D6 66
Fox Mountain, mtn., Nv., U.S. — B2 105
Foxpark, Wy., U.S. — E6 127
Fox Point, Wi., U.S. — E6 126
Fox River Grove, Il., U.S. — h8 90
Foxton, N.Z. — N15 51
Foxvale, N.D., U.S. — B5 98
Fox Valley, Sask. — G1 75
Foxville, Vt., U.S. — C4 122
Foxworth, Ms., U.S. — D4 101
Foyil, Ok., U.S. — A6 113
Foyle, stm., Eur. — C4 11
Foyle, Lough, b., Eur. — C3 10
Foynes, Ire. — D2 11
Foz do Cunene, Ang. — E1 48
Foz do Iguaçu, Braz. — D2 56
Foz do Jordão, Braz. — C3 58
Foz do Pauini, Braz. — C4 58
Frackville, Pa., U.S. — E9 115
Fraga, Spain — B6 22
Fraile Muerto, Ur. — C4 54
Framellville, W.V., U.S. — C4 125
Framnes Mountains, mts., Ant. — C19 7
Framingham, Ma., U.S. — C5 98
França, Braz. — D2 56
Franca, Braz. — D2 57
Francavilla Fontana, Italy — D6 23
Frances, ctry., Eur. — D5 16
Frances, Ky., U.S. — e9 94
Francés, Cabo, c., Cuba — D2 64
Francestown, N.H., U.S. — E3 106
Franceville, In., U.S. — C4 91
Franceville, Gabon — F2 46
Franche-Comté, hist. reg., Fr. — D6 16
Francis, Sask. — G4 75
Francis, Ut., U.S. — C4 121
Francis, W.V., U.S. — k10 125

Name	Map Ref.	Page

Francis, Lake, l., N.H., U.S. — f7 106
Francis Case, Lake, res., S.D., U.S. — D6 118
Francisco, In., U.S. — H3 91
Francisco Sá, Braz. — B4 56
Francis Creek, Wi., U.S. — h10 126
Francistown, Bots. — B4 49
François, Newf. — E3 72
François Lake, l., B.C. — C5 69
Franconia, N.H., U.S. — B3 106
Franconia, Va., U.S. — *B5 123
Franconia Notch, N.H., U.S. — B3 106
Franconville, Fr. — g9 16
Francs Peak, mtn., Wy., U.S. — C3 127
Franeker, Neth. — A5 17
Frank, W.V., U.S. — C5 125
Frankel City, Tx., U.S. — C1 120
Frankenberg, Ger. — C8 19
Frankenberg [-Eder], Ger. — C4 19
Frankenmuth, Mi., U.S. — E7 99
Frankenthal, Ger. — D4 18
Frankewing, Tn., U.S. — B5 119
Frankfield, Jam. — E14 65
Frankford, Ont. — C7 73
Frankford, De., U.S. — F5 85
Frankford, Mo., U.S. — B6 102
Frankford, W.V., U.S. — D4 125
Frankfort see Kilcormac, Ire. — D4 11
Frankfort, S. Afr. — C4 49
Frankfort, Il., U.S. — m9 90
Frankfort, In., U.S. — D4 91
Frankfort, Ks., U.S. — C7 93
Frankfort, Ky., U.S. — B5 94
Frankfort, Me., U.S. — D4 96
Frankfort, Mi., U.S. — D4 99
Frankfort, N.Y., U.S. — B5 109
Frankfort, Oh., U.S. — C2 112
Frankfort, S.D., U.S. — C7 118
Frankfurt [am Main], Ger. — D4 18
Fränkische Saale, stm., Ger. — C5 19
Frank Lake, l., Alta. — D4 68
Franklin, Man. — D2 70
Franklin, Al., U.S. — D2 78
Franklin, Az., U.S. — E6 80
Franklin, Ar., U.S. — A4 81
Franklin, Ct., U.S. — C7 84
Franklin, Ga., U.S. — C1 87
Franklin, Id., U.S. — G7 89
Franklin, Il., U.S. — D3 90
Franklin, In., U.S. — F5 91
Franklin, Ia., U.S. — D6 92
Franklin, Ks., U.S. — E9 93
Franklin, Ky., U.S. — D3 94
Franklin, La., U.S. — E4 95
Franklin, Me., U.S. — D4 96
Franklin, Ma., U.S. — B5 98
Franklin, Mn., U.S. — F4 100
Franklin, Ne., U.S. — D7 104
Franklin, N.H., U.S. — D3 106
Franklin, N.J., U.S. — A3 107
Franklin, N.Y., U.S. — C5 109
Franklin, N.C., U.S. — f9 110
Franklin, Oh., U.S. — C1 112
Franklin, Pa., U.S. — D2 115
Franklin, Tn., U.S. — B5 119
Franklin, Tx., U.S. — D4 120
Franklin, Va., U.S. — D6 123
Franklin, W.V., U.S. — C5 125
Franklin, Wi., U.S. — n11 126
Franklin, dept., N.W. Ter. — B15 66
Franklin, co., Ar., U.S. — A2 78
Franklin, co., Ar., U.S. — B2 81
Franklin, co., Fl., U.S. — C2 86
Franklin, co., Ga., U.S. — B3 87
Franklin, co., Id., U.S. — G7 89
Franklin, co., Il., U.S. — F5 90
Franklin, co., In., U.S. — F7 91
Franklin, co., Ia., U.S. — B4 92
Franklin, co., Ks., U.S. — D8 93
Franklin, co., Ky., U.S. — B5 94
Franklin, co., La., U.S. — B4 95
Franklin, co., Me., U.S. — C2 96
Franklin, co., Ma., U.S. — A2 98
Franklin, co., Ms., U.S. — D3 101
Franklin, co., Mo., U.S. — C6 102
Franklin, co., Ne., U.S. — D7 104
Franklin, co., N.Y., U.S. — f10 109
Franklin, co., N.C., U.S. — A4 110
Franklin, co., Oh., U.S. — B2 112
Franklin, co., Pa., U.S. — G6 115
Franklin, co., Tn., U.S. — B5 119
Franklin, co., Tx., U.S. — C5 120
Franklin, co., Vt., U.S. — B2 122
Franklin, co., Va., U.S. — D3 123
Franklin, co., Wa., U.S. — C6 124
Franklin, Point, c., Ak., U.S. — A8 79
Franklin D. Roosevelt Lake, res., Wa., U.S. — B7 124
Franklin Falls Reservoir, res., N.H., U.S. — C3 106
Franklin Grove, Il., U.S. — B4 90
Franklin Island, i., Ont. — B4 73
Franklin Lake, l., N.W. Ter. — C13 66
Franklin Lake, l., Nv., U.S. — C6 105
Franklin Lakes, N.J., U.S. — *B4 107
Franklin Mine, Mi., U.S. — A2 99
Franklin Mountains, mts., N.W. Ter. — C8 66
Franklin Park, Il., U.S. — k9 90
Franklin Park, Pa., U.S. — h13 115
Franklin Square, N.Y., U.S. — *E7 109
Franklin Strait, strt., N.W. Ter. — B13 66
Franklinton, La., U.S. — D5 95
Franklinton, N.C., U.S. — A4 110
Franklinville, N.J., U.S. — D2 107
Franklinville, N.Y., U.S. — C2 109
Frankston, Austl. — *G8 50
Frankston, Tx., U.S. — C5 120
Franksville, Wi., U.S. — n12 126
Franktown, Co., U.S. — B6 83
Franktown, Co., U.S. — D8 71
Frankville, Al., U.S. — D1 78
Frannie, Wy., U.S. — B4 127
Franz Josef Land, is., Sov. Un. — B8 29
Frascati, Italy — D4 23
Fraser, Co., U.S. — B5 83
Fraser, Ia., U.S. — B4 92
Fraser, i., Austl. — *o16 50
Fraser, i., Austl. — E9 50
Fraser, stm., B.C. — E7 69
Fraser, stm., Newf. — g9 72
Fraser, Mount, mtn., Can. — D3 49
Fraserburg, S. Afr. — D3 49
Fraserburgh, Scot., U.K. — B6 10
Fraserdale, Ont. — o19 73
Fraser Lake, B.C. — B5 69
Fraser Lake, l., B.C. — B5 69
Fraser Plateau, plat., B.C. — C5 69
Fraserwood, Man. — D3 70
Frasne, Fr. — *C2 20

Frauenfeld, Switz. — E4 18
Fray Bentos, Ur. — E1 56
Fray Marcos, Ur. — E1 56
Frazee, Mn., U.S. — D3 100
Frazer, Mt., U.S. — B10 103
Frazeysburg, Oh., U.S. — B3 112
Frazier Park, Ca., U.S. — E4 82
Freda, Mi., U.S. — A2 99
Frederic, Mi., U.S. — D6 99
Frederic, Wi., U.S. — C1 126
Frederica, De., U.S. — D4 85
Fredericia, Den. — J3 14
Frederick, Co., U.S. — A6 83
Frederick, Il., U.S. — C3 90
Frederick, Md., U.S. — B3 97
Frederick, Ok., U.S. — C2 113
Frederick, S.D., U.S. — B7 118
Frederick, co., Md., U.S. — B3 97
Frederick, co., Va., U.S. — A4 123
Frederick Hall, Jam. — C5 123
Fredericksburg, In., U.S. — H5 91
Fredericksburg, Ia., U.S. — B5 92
Fredericksburg, Oh., U.S. — B4 112
Fredericksburg, Pa., U.S. — F9 115
Fredericksburg, Tx., U.S. — D3 120
Fredericksburg, Va., U.S. — B5 123
Fredericktown, Mo., U.S. — D7 102
Fredericktown, Oh., U.S. — B3 112
Fredericktown, Pa., U.S. — F1 115
Frederickton, N.B. — D3 71
Fredericton Junction, N.B. — D3 71
Frederika, Ia., U.S. — B5 92
Frederiksberg, Den. — *J5 14
Frederiksborg, co., Den. — C6 15
Frederikshavn, Den. — I4 14
Frederikssund, Den. — C6 15
Frederiksted, V.I.U.S. — H12 64
Frederiksværk, Den. — C6 15
Frederik Willem IV Vallen, wtfl., Sur. — B3 59
Fredonia, Al., U.S. — C4 78
Fredonia, Az., U.S. — A3 80
Fredonia, In., U.S. — H5 91
Fredonia, Ks., U.S. — E8 93
Fredonia, Ky., U.S. — C1 94
Fredonia, N.Y., U.S. — C1 109
Fredonia, N.D., U.S. — C6 111
Fredonia, Pa., U.S. — D1 115
Fredonia, Tx., U.S. — D3 120
Fredonia, Wi., U.S. — E6 126
Fredrikstad, Nor. — H4 14
Freeborn, co., Mn., U.S. — G5 100
Freeburg, Il., U.S. — E4 90
Freeburg, Mn., U.S. — G7 100
Freeburg, Mo., U.S. — C6 102
Freeburg, Pa., U.S. — E8 115
Freedom, Ca., U.S. — *D3 82
Freedom, In., U.S. — F4 91
Freedom, Me., U.S. — D3 96
Freedom, N.H., U.S. — C4 106
Freedom, Ok., U.S. — A2 113
Freedom, Pa., U.S. — E1 115
Freedom, Wi., U.S. — h9 126
Freedom, Wy., U.S. — D2 127
Freehold, N.J., U.S. — C4 107
Freeland, Mi., U.S. — E6 99
Freeland, N.C., U.S. — C4 110
Freeland, Pa., U.S. — D10 115
Freeland Park, In., U.S. — C3 91
Freelandville, In., U.S. — G3 91
Freel Peak, mtn., Ca., U.S. — C4 82
Freels, Cape, c., Newf. — E5 72
Freels, Cape, c., Newf. — D5 72
Freeman, Mo., U.S. — C3 102
Freeman, S.D., U.S. — D8 118
Freeman, Wa., U.S. — g14 124
Freeman, stm., Alta. — B3 68
Freeman, Lake, l., In., U.S. — C4 91
Freemansburg, Pa., U.S. — E11 115
Freemanville, Al., U.S. — D2 78
Freemason Islands, is., La., U.S. — E7 95
Freemount, Ire. — E3 11
Freeport, Bah. — *A4 64
Freeport, Fl., U.S. — u15 86
Freeport, Il., U.S. — A4 90
Freeport, Ks., U.S. — E6 93
Freeport, Me., U.S. — E3 96
Freeport, Mi., U.S. — F5 99
Freeport, Mn., U.S. — E4 100
Freeport, N.Y., U.S. — n15 109
Freeport, Oh., U.S. — B4 112
Freeport, Pa., U.S. — E2 115
Freeport, Tx., U.S. — E5 120
Freer, Tx., U.S. — F3 120
Free Soil, Mi., U.S. — D4 99
Freestone, co., Tx., U.S. — D4 120
Freetown, P.E.I. — C6 71
Freetown, S.L. — E2 45
Freetown, In., U.S. — G5 91
Free Union, Va., U.S. — B4 123
Freeville, N.Y., U.S. — C4 109
Freezeout Mountains, mts., Wy., U.S. — D6 127
Fregenal de la Sierra, Spain — C2 22
Fregene, Italy — h8 23
Freiberg, Ger. — C8 18
Freiberger Mulde, stm., Eur. — B8 19
Freiburg, Ger. — E3 15
Freiburg [im Breisgau], Ger. — D3 18
Freienbach, Switz. — B6 21
Freirina, Chile — E1 55
Freising, Ger. — D5 18
Freistadt, Aus. — D7 18
Freital, Ger. — B8 19
Fréjus, Fr. — F7 16
Fréjus Tunnel, Eur. — D1 20
Frelighsburg, Que. — D5 74
Fremantle, Austl. — F2 50
Fremont, Ca., U.S. — h8 82
Fremont, Ia., U.S. — C5 92
Fremont, In., U.S. — A7 91
Fremont, Mi., U.S. — E5 99
Fremont, N.H., U.S. — E4 106
Fremont, N.C., U.S. — B5 110
Fremont, Oh., U.S. — A2 112
Fremont, Wi., U.S. — D5 126
Fremont, co., Co., U.S. — C5 83
Fremont, co., Id., U.S. — E7 89
Fremont, co., Ia., U.S. — D2 92
Fremont, co., Wy., U.S. — C3 127
Fremont, stm., Ut., U.S. — E5 121
Fremont Island, i., Ut., U.S. — B3 121
Fremont Lake, l., Wy., U.S. — D3 127
Fremont Peak, mtn., Wy., U.S. — C3 127
French, stm., Ont. — A4 73

French Broad, stm., U.S. — D10 119
Frenchburg, Ky., U.S. — C6 94
French Camp, Ms., U.S. — B4 101
French Creek, W.V., U.S. — C4 125
French Creek, stm., Man. — A5 70
French Creek, stm., Pa., U.S. — C2 115
French Frigate Shoals, rf., Hi., U.S. — m14 88
Frenchglen, Or., U.S. — E8 114
French Guiana, dep., S.A. — B4 59
French Gulch, Ca., U.S. — B2 82
French Island, Wi., U.S. — *E2 126
French Lick, In., U.S. — G4 91
Frenchman, stm., N.A. — A8 103
Frenchman Bay, b., Me., U.S. — D4 96
Frenchman Butte, Sask. — D1 75
Frenchman Creek, stm., U.S. — D4 104
Frenchman Hills, hills, Wa., U.S. — C6 124
Frenchman Knob, mtn., Ky., U.S. — C4 94
Frenchman Lake, l., Nv., U.S. — G6 105
Frenchman's Cove, Newf. — D2 72
Frenchman's Cove, Newf. — E4 72
Frenchmans Island, Newf. — B4 72
Frenchpark, Ire. — D3 11
French Polynesia, dep., Oc. — H13 6
French River, Mn., U.S. — D7 100
French Settlement, La., U.S. — D5 95
French Southern and Antarctic Territories, dep., Afr. — *J1 2
Frenchton, W.V., U.S. — C4 125
Frenchtown, Mt., U.S. — C2 103
Frenchtown, N.J., U.S. — B2 107
French Village, N.S. — E6 71
Frenchville, Me., U.S. — A4 96
Frenda, Alg. — B5 44
Freshfield, Mount, mtn., Can. — D2 68
Freshwater, Eng., U.K. — D6 12
Freshford, Ire. — E4 11
Fresnes, Fr. — B5 16
Fresnillo [de González Echeverría], Mex. — C4 63
Fresno, Ca., U.S. — D4 82
Fresno, co., Ca., U.S. — D4 82
Fresno Reservoir, res., Mt., U.S. — B6 103
Freudenstadt, Ger. — D4 18
Frévent, Fr. — B5 16
Frewsburg, N.Y., U.S. — C1 109
Freyburg, Ger. — B6 19
Freycinet Peninsula, pen., Austl. — o15 50
Freyenstein, Ger. — E6 15
Freyming-Merlebach, Fr. — E6 17
Freyung, Ger. — E8 19
Fria, Gui. — D2 45
Fria, Cape, c., Nmb. — A1 49
Friant, Ca., U.S. — D4 82
Friars Point, Ms., U.S. — A3 101
Frías, Arg. — E2 55
Fribourg, Switz. — E3 18
Fribourg, state, Switz. — C3 20
Friday Harbor, Wa., U.S. — A2 124
Fridley, Mn., U.S. — m12 100
Fridtjof Nansen, Mount, mtn., Ant. — A32 7
Friedberg, Ger. — C4 18
Friedens, Pa., U.S. — F3 115
Friedland, Ger. — B6 18
Friedrichroda, Ger. — C5 19
Friedrichshafen, Ger. — E4 18
Friedrichskoog, Ger. — D2 15
Friedrichstadt, Ger. — D2 19
Friedrichsthal, Ger. — D2 19
Friend, Ks., U.S. — D3 93
Friend, Ne., U.S. — D8 104
Friendship, Ar., U.S. — C3 81
Friendship, In., U.S. — G7 91
Friendship, Md., U.S. — C4 97
Friendship, N.Y., U.S. — C2 109
Friendship, Oh., U.S. — D2 112
Friendship, Tn., U.S. — B2 119
Friendship, Wi., U.S. — E4 126
Friendsville, Md., U.S. — k12 97
Friendsville, Tn., U.S. — D9 119
Friendswood, In., U.S. — n13 82
Friendswood, Tx., U.S. — *r14 120
Friesen, La., U.S. — B2 95
Fripps Island, i., S.C., U.S. — G7 117
Fries, Va., U.S. — D2 123
Friesach, Aus. — E7 18
Friesack, Ger. — F6 15
Friesland, prov., Neth. — A5 17
Fries Mills, N.J., U.S. — D2 107
Friesoythe, Ger. — A7 17
Frigate Point, c., Mid. Is. — K3 52
Frío, co., Tx., U.S. — E3 120
Frío, stm., Tx., U.S. — E3 120
Frio Draw, val., U.S. — C6 108
Frisco, Ca., U.S. — A5 101
Frisco, N.C., U.S. — B7 110
Frisco City, Al., U.S. — D2 78
Frisco Peak, mtn., Ut., U.S. — E2 121
Frissell, Mount, mtn., U.S. — A2 84
Fristoe, Mo., U.S. — C4 102
Fritch, Tx., U.S. — B2 120
Fritsla, Swe. — A6 15
Fritzlar, Ger. — C4 18
Friuli-Venezia Giulia, prov., Italy — C8 20
Frobisher, Sask. — H4 75
Frobisher Bay, b., N.W. Ter. — D19 66
Frobisher Lake, l., Sask. — m7 75
Frog Lake, l., Alta. — C5 68
Frogmore, La., U.S. — C4 95
Frogmore, S.C., U.S. — G6 117
Frohna, Mo., U.S. — D8 102
Froid, Mt., U.S. — B12 103
Frolovo, Sov. Un. — G14 27
Fromberg, Mt., U.S. — E8 103
Frome, Jam. — E14 65
Frome, Eng., U.K. — C5 12
Frome, stm., Eng., U.K. — D5 12
Frome, Lake, l., Austl. — F6 50
Fronteira, Port. — C3 22
Frontenac, Mn., U.S. — F6 100
Frontenac, co., Ont. — C8 73
Frontenac, co., Que. — D7 74
Frontera, Mex. — D6 63
Frontier, Sask. — H1 75
Frontier, Wy., U.S. — E2 127
Frontier, co., Ne., U.S. — D5 104
Frontignan, Fr. — F5 16
Frontino, Páramo, mtn., Col. — B2 60
Front Range, mts., Co., U.S. — A5 83
Front Royal, Va., U.S. — B4 123
Frosinone, Italy — D4 23

Frost, Mn., U.S. — G5 100
Frost, Tx., U.S. — C4 120
Frostburg, Md., U.S. — k13 97
Frostproof, Fl., U.S. — E5 86
Frouard, Fr. — F6 17
Froude, Sask. — H4 75
Frøya, i., Nor. — F3 14
Fruges, Fr. — D2 17
Fruita, Co., U.S. — B2 83
Fruita, Ut., U.S. — E4 121
Fruitdale, Al., U.S. — D1 78
Fruitdale, S.D., U.S. — C2 118
Fruit Heights, Ut., U.S. — B4 121
Fruithurst, Al., U.S. — B4 78
Fruitland, Id., U.S. — F2 89
Fruitland, Ks., U.S. — E8 93
Fruitland, Md., U.S. — D6 97
Fruitland, Mo., U.S. — D8 102
Fruitland, N.M., U.S. — A1 108
Fruitland, Tn., U.S. — B3 119
Fruitland, Ut., U.S. — C5 121
Fruitland Park, Fl., U.S. — D5 86
Fruitland Park, Ms., U.S. — E4 101
Fruitport, Mi., U.S. — E4 99
Fruitvale, B.C. — E9 69
Fruitvale, Co., U.S. — B2 83
Fruitvale, Id., U.S. — E2 89
Fruitvale, Tn., U.S. — B3 119
Fruitvale, Wa., U.S. — C5 124
Fruitville, Fl., U.S. — E4 86
Frunze, Sov. Un. — H10 27
Frutal, Braz. — C3 56
Frutigen, Switz. — C4 21
Fry, Ga., U.S. — B2 87
Fryazevo, Sov. Un. — n18 27
Frýburg, Pa., U.S. — D2 115
Frýdek-Místek, Czech. — D5 26
Frýdlant, Czech. — C5 26
Frye, Me., U.S. — D2 96
Fryeburg, La., U.S. — B2 95
Fryeburg, Me., U.S. — D2 96
Frys, Sask. — H5 75
Fú'an, China — K8 32
Fuchou see Fuzhou, China — F8 31
Fuchū, Japan — *I9 33
Fuding, China — K9 32
Fuencarral, Spain — p17 22
Fuente-Álamo [de Murcia], Spain — D5 22
Fuente de Cantos, Spain — C2 22
Fuente el Saz, Spain — o17 22
Fuente Obejuna, Spain — C3 22
Fuentesaúco, Spain — B3 22
Fuentes [de Andalucía], Spain — D3 22
Fuerte, stm., Mex. — B3 63
Fuerte Olimpo, Para. — D4 55
Fuerteventura, i., Spain — m14 22
Fuglebjerg, Den. — C5 15
Fugou, China — D2 31
Fugu, China — D9 32
Fuhai, China — B2 31
Fuji, Japan — n17 33
Fuji, Mount, vol., Japan — I9 33
Fujian, prov., China — F8 31
Fujieda, Japan — o17 33
Fujimi, Japan — n17 33
Fujin, China — B11 31
Fujinomiya, Japan — n17 33
Fujioka, Japan — *I9 33
Fujisawa, Japan — *I9 33
Fuji-yoshida, Japan — n17 33
Fukagawa, Japan — E10 33
Fukien see Fujian, prov., China — F8 31
Fukuchiyama, Japan — I7 33
Fukue Island, i., Japan — J4 33
Fukui, Japan — D12 31
Fukuoka, Japan — E11 31
Fukuoka, Japan — I4 33
Fukushima, Japan — I8 33
Fukushima, Japan — H10 33
Fukuyama, Japan — I6 33
Fūlādī, Kūh-e, mtn., Afg. — D13 39
Fulaga, i., Fiji — I16 52
Fulaga Passage, strt., Fiji — I16 52
Fulda, Ger. — C4 18
Fulda, In., U.S. — H4 91
Fulda, Mn., U.S. — G3 100
Fulda, stm., Ger. — B4 19
Fuling, China — J2 32
Fullarton, Ont. — D3 73
Fullerton, Ca., U.S. — n13 82
Fullerton, La., U.S. — D3 95
Fullerton, Ne., U.S. — C8 104
Fullerton, N.D., U.S. — C7 111
Fulshear, Tx., U.S. — r14 120
Fulton, Al., U.S. — D2 78
Fulton, Ar., U.S. — D2 81
Fulton, Il., U.S. — B3 90
Fulton, In., U.S. — C5 91
Fulton, Ks., U.S. — D9 93
Fulton, Ky., U.S. — f9 94
Fulton, Md., U.S. — B4 97
Fulton, Ms., U.S. — A5 101
Fulton, Mo., U.S. — C6 102
Fulton, N.Y., U.S. — B4 109
Fulton, Oh., U.S. — B3 112
Fulton, S.D., U.S. — D8 118
Fulton, Tn., U.S. — C8 119
Fulton, co., Ar., U.S. — A4 81
Fulton, co., Ga., U.S. — C2 87
Fulton, co., Il., U.S. — C3 90
Fulton, co., In., U.S. — B5 91
Fulton, co., Ky., U.S. — f9 94
Fulton, co., N.Y., U.S. — B6 109
Fulton, co., Oh., U.S. — A1 112
Fulton, co., Pa., U.S. — G5 115
Fultondale, Al., U.S. — f7 78
Fultonham, N.Y., U.S. — C6 109
Fumay, Fr. — C6 16
Funabashi, Japan — n19 33
Funafuti, Tuvalu — G10 6
Funchal, Port. — h12 22
Fundación, Col. — A3 60
Fundão, Braz. — E8 56
Fundão, Port. — B2 22
Fundy, Bay of, b., Can. — D4 71
Fundy National Park, N.B. — D4 71
Funhalouro, Moz. — B5 49
Funing, China — G6 31
Funing, China — H8 32
Funing Bay, b., China — K9 32
Funk, Ne., U.S. — D6 104
Funkley, Mn., U.S. — C4 100
Funkstown, Md., U.S. — A2 97
Funtua, Nig. — D6 45
Fuping, China — E6 32
Fuping, China — F8 31
Fuqing, China — K8 32
Fuquay-Varina, N.C., U.S. — B4 110
Fur, i., Den. — B3 15
Furancungo, Moz. — D5 48
Furano, Japan — E11 33

Fürg, Iran — C5 38
Furka Pass, Switz. — C5 21
Furley, Ks., U.S. — g12 93
Furman, Al., U.S. — C3 78
Furman, S.C., U.S. — F5 117
Furmanov, Sov. Un. — C13 27
Furmanovka, Sov. Un. — E8 28
Furnace Brook, stm., Vt., U.S. — D2 122
Furnas, co., Ne., U.S. — D6 104
Furnas, Represa de, res., Braz. — C3 56
Furneaux Group, is., Austl. — o15 50
Furness, Sask. — D1 75
Furqlus, Syria — E11 40
Fürstenau, Ger. — B7 17
Fürstenfeld, Aus. — B9 20
Fürstenfeldbruck, Ger. — A7 20
Fürstenwalde [Spree], Ger. — D5 18
Fürth, Ger. — D5 18
Furth im Wald, Ger. — D7 19
Furukawa, Japan — H8 33
Furu Mountain, hill, Japan — P17 52
Fusagasugá, Col. — C3 60
Fuschl [am See], Aus. — B9 20
Fushun, China — C9 31
Fusilier, Sask. — F1 75
Fusong, China — E3 33
Füssen, Ger. — E5 18
Fusui, China — A7 35
Futatsune, rock, Japan — P17 52
Future City, Il., U.S. — F4 90
Fuwah, Egy. — C2 41
Fuxian, China — E9 32
Fuxian, China — F3 32
Fuxian Hu, l., China — G5 31
Fuxin, China — C9 31
Fuyang, China — E8 31
Fuyang, China — E8 31
Fuyu, China — B2 33
Fuyu, China — C2 33
Fuyuan, China — A12 31
Fuyun, China — B3 31
Fuzhou (Fuchou), China — F8 31
Fuzhou, China — J7 32
Fyffe, Al., U.S. — A4 78
Fyn, co., Den. — C4 15
Fyn, i., Den. — J4 14
Fyne, Loch, b., Scot., U.K. — B4 10

G

Gaalkacyo, Som. — D6 47
Gaastra, Mi., U.S. — B2 99
Gabaldón, N.M., U.S. — B4 108
Gabarus, N.S. — D9 71
Gabbs, Nv., U.S. — E4 105
Gabela, Ang. — D1 48
Gabès, Tun. — C7 44
Gabès, Golfe de, b., Tun. — C7 44
Gabin, Pol. — B5 26
Gabon, ctry., Afr. — F2 46
Gaborone, Bots. — B4 49
Gabriel, Mount, hill, Ire. — F2 11
Gabriels, N.Y., U.S. — f10 109
Gabriola, B.C. — f12 69
Gabrovo, Bul. — D7 24
Gachsārān, Iran — F5 39
Gackle, N.D., U.S. — C6 111
Gacko, Yugo. — D4 24
Gadag, India — E6 36
Gadmen, Switz. — C5 21
Gadsby, Alta. — C4 68
Gadsden, Al., U.S. — A3 78
Gadsden, Az., U.S. — E1 80
Gadsden, S.C., U.S. — D6 117
Gadsden, Tn., U.S. — B3 119
Gadsden, co., Fl., U.S. — B2 86
Gadych, Sov. Un. — F10 27
Gaeta, Italy — C7 23
Gaeta, Gulf of, b., Italy — D4 23
Gaffney, S.C., U.S. — A4 117
Gafour, Tun. — B6 44
Gafsa, Tun. — C6 44
Gagan Island, i., Marsh Is. — S17 52
Gagarin, Sov. Un. — D10 27
Gage, Ok., U.S. — A2 113
Gage, co., Ne., U.S. — D9 104
Gage, Cape, c., P.E.I. — C5 71
Gagetown, N.B. — D3 71
Gagetown, Mi., U.S. — E7 99
Gaggenau, Ger. — D4 19
Gagliano del Capo, Italy — E7 23
Gagnoa, I.C. — E4 45
Gagnon, Que. — h13 74
Gagny, Fr. — g11 16
Gahanna, Oh., U.S. — k11 112
Gaibandha, Bngl. — E12 37
Gail, Tx., U.S. — C2 120
Gail, stm., Aus. — C9 20
Gaildorf, Ger. — E4 19
Gaillac, Fr. — F4 16
Gaillard, Lake, l., Ct., U.S. — D5 84
Gaines, Mi., U.S. — F7 99
Gaines, co., Tx., U.S. — C5 120
Gainesboro, Tn., U.S. — C8 119
Gaines Creek, stm., Ok., U.S. — C6 113
Gainesville, Al., U.S. — C1 78
Gainesville, Fl., U.S. — C4 86
Gainesville, Ga., U.S. — B3 87
Gainesville, Mo., U.S. — E5 102
Gainesville, N.Y., U.S. — C2 109
Gainesville, Tx., U.S. — C4 120
Gainesville, Va., U.S. — g11 123
Gainsborough, Sask. — H5 75
Gainsborough, Eng., U.K. — H12 12
Gairdner, Lake, l., Austl. — F6 50
Gairloch, Loch, b., Scot., U.K. — C3 13
Gaixian, China — C11 31
Gakona, Ak., U.S. — C10 79
Galahad, Alta. — C5 68
Galapagar, Spain — o16 22
Galapagos Islands see Colón, Archipiélago de, is., Ec. — g5 58
Galashiels, Scot., U.K. — F10 13
Galați (Galacz), Rom. — C9 24
Galatia, Il., U.S. — F5 90
Galatia, Ks., U.S. — D5 93
Galatina, Italy — E7 23
Galátsion, Grc. — *C4 25
Galawinta, Austl. — B6 50
Galax, Va., U.S. — D2 123
Galaxídhion, Grc. — K6 25
Galchutt, N.D., U.S. — C9 111
Gáldar, Spain — m14 22
Galeana, Mex. — A3 63
Galena, Ak., U.S. — C8 79
Galena, Il., U.S. — A3 90

Galena, Ks., U.S. — E9 93
Galena, Md., U.S. — B6 97
Galena, Mo., U.S. — E4 102
Galena, Oh., U.S. — B3 112
Galena Park, Tx., U.S. — r14 120
Galeota Point, c., Trin. — K14 64
Galera, Punta, c., Chile — B2 54
Galera, Punta, c., Ec. — A1 58
Galera Point, c., Trin. — K14 64
Galesburg, Ks., U.S. — E8 93
Galesburg, Mi., U.S. — F5 99
Galesburg, N.D., U.S. — B8 111
Gales Creek, Or., U.S. — B3 114
Gales Ferry, Ct., U.S. — D7 84
Galesville, Md., U.S. — C4 97
Galesville, Wi., U.S. — D2 126
Galeton, Co., U.S. — A6 83
Galeton, Pa., U.S. — C6 115
Galetta, Ont. — B8 73
Galeville, N.Y., U.S. — *B4 109
Galgaduud, prov., Som. — D6 47
Galiano Island, i., B.C. — E6 69
Galich, Sov. Un. — B22 28
Galicia, hist. reg., Eur. — D6 26
Galicia, hist. reg., Spain — A1 22
Galien, Mi., U.S. — G4 99
Galilee, R.I., U.S. — F3 116
Galilee, hist. reg., Isr. — B7 41
Galilee, Lake, l., Austl. — D8 50
Galilee, Sea of see Kinneret, Yam, l., Isr. — B7 41
Galina Point, c., Jam. — E15 65
Galion, Oh., U.S. — B3 112
Galisteo Creek, stm., N.M., U.S. — k8 108
Galite Channel, strt., Tun. — F2 23
Galiuro Mountains, mts., Az., U.S. — E5 80
Galivants Ferry, S.C., U.S. — C9 117
Gallan Head, c., Scot., U.K. — B1 13
Gallant, Al., U.S. — B3 78
Gallarate, Italy — B2 23
Gällared, Swe. — A8 15
Gallatin, Mo., U.S. — B4 102
Gallatin, Tn., U.S. — A5 119
Gallatin, co., Il., U.S. — F5 90
Gallatin, co., Ky., U.S. — B5 94
Gallatin, co., Mt., U.S. — E5 103
Gallatin, stm., Mt., U.S. — E5 103
Gallatin Gateway, Mt., U.S. — E5 103
Gallatin Range, mts., Mt., U.S. — E5 103
Gallaway, Tn., U.S. — B2 119
Galle, Sri L. — G7 36
Gállego, stm., Spain — A5 22
Gallegos, stm., Arg. — E2 54
Galley Head, c., Ire. — F3 11
Gallia, co., Oh., U.S. — D3 112
Galliano, La., U.S. — E5 95
Galliate, Italy — D4 23
Gallicano nel Lazio, Italy — h9 23
Gallina, N.M., U.S. — A3 108
Gallinas, Punta, c., Col. — A3 60
Gallinas Mountains, mts., N.M., U.S. — C2 108
Gallion, Al., U.S. — C2 78
Gallipoli, Italy — D6 23
Gallipoli see Gelibolu, Tur. — B6 40
Gallipoli Peninsula, pen., Tur. — B6 40
Gallipolis, Oh., U.S. — D3 112
Gallipolis Ferry, W.V., U.S. — C2 125
Gallitzin, Pa., U.S. — F4 115
Gällivare, Swe. — D9 14
Gallneukirchen, Aus. — E9 19
Gallo, stm., Spain — B5 22
Gallo Mountains, mts., N.M., U.S. — C1 108
Galloway, Oh., U.S. — m10 112
Galloway, W.V., U.S. — B4 125
Galloway, Wi., U.S. — D4 126
Galloway, Mull of, c., Scot., U.K. — F4 13
Gällstad, Swe. — A7 15
Gallup, N.M., U.S. — B1 108
Galoa Bay, b., Fiji — H15 52
Galoa Harbour, b., Fiji — I15 52
Galt, Ca., U.S. — C3 82
Galt, Ia., U.S. — B4 92
Galt, Mo., U.S. — A4 102
Galten, b., Swe. — t34 14
Galtür, Aus. — C6 20
Galtymore Mountain, mtn., Ire. — E3 11
Galva, Il., U.S. — B3 90
Galva, Ia., U.S. — B2 92
Galva, Ks., U.S. — D6 93
Galveston, In., U.S. — C5 91
Galveston, Tx., U.S. — E5 120
Galveston, co., Tx., U.S. — E5 120
Galveston Bay, b., Tx., U.S. — E5 120
Galveston Island, i., Tx., U.S. — E5 120
Gálvez, Arg. — A4 54
Galway, Ire. — D2 10
Galway, co., Ire. — D2 10
Galway Bay, b., Ire. — D2 10
Gamaches, Fr. — E9 12
Gamagōri, Japan — o16 33
Gamaliel, Ar., U.S. — A3 81
Gamaliel, Ky., U.S. — D4 94
Gamba, China — C12 37
Gamba, Zaire — B3 48
Gambaga, Ghana — D5 45
Gambela, Eth. — D3 47
Gambell, Ak., U.S. — C5 79
Gamber, Md., U.S. — B4 97
Gambia, ctry., Afr. — D1 45
Gambia, stm., Afr. — D2 45
Gambier, Oh., U.S. — B3 112
Gambier, is., Fr. Poly. — m17 64
Gamboa, Pan. — k11 62
Gamboma, Congo — B3 48
Gamboula, Cen. Afr. Rep. — E3 47
Gameleira, Braz. — C3 57
Gamerco, N.M., U.S. — B1 108
Gammertingen, Ger. — A5 20
Gammon, stm., Can. — D4 70
Gamo Gofa, prov., Eth. — D4 47
Gamph, Slieve, mts., Ire. — C3 11
Ganado, Az., U.S. — B6 80
Ganado, Tx., U.S. — E4 120
Gananoque, Ont. — C8 73
Gancheng, China — D1 35
Ganda, Ang. — D2 48
Gandajika, Zaire — C4 48
Gandak, stm., Asia — D10 37
Gandeeville, W.V., U.S. — C3 125
Gander, Newf. — D4 72
Gander, stm., Newf. — D4 72
Gander Bay, Newf. — D4 72
Gander Lake, l., Newf. — D4 72

Name	Map Ref.	Page

Gāndhinagar, India — D5 36
Gandhi Reservoir, res., India — E5 37
Gandia, Spain — C5 22
Gandy, Ne., U.S. — C5 104
Gangānagar, India — C5 36
Gangāpur, India — D6 37
Gangaw, Burma — D9 36
Gangdise Mountains, mts., China — B9 37
Ganges, B.C. — g12 69
Ganges, Fr. — F5 16
Ganges, Oh., U.S. — B3 112
Ganges, stm., Asia — D8 36
Ganges, Mouths of the, mth., Asia — D8 36
Gang Mills, N.Y., U.S. — C3 109
Gangtok, India — C8 36
Gangu, China — E6 31
Gani, Indon. — F7 34
Gan Jiang, stm., China — K6 32
Gannan, China — C1 33
Gannat, Fr. — D5 16
Gannet Islands, is., Newf. — B3 72
Gannett Peak, mtn., Wy., U.S. — C3 127
Gannon, Md., U.S. — k12 97
Gannvalley, S.D., U.S. — C7 118
Gano, Oh., U.S. — n13 112
Gans, Ok., U.S. — B7 113
Gansevoort, N.Y., U.S. — B7 109
Gansu, prov., China — D5 31
Ganta, Lib. — E3 45
Gantt, Al., U.S. — D3 78
Gantt, S.C., U.S. — B3 117
Gantt Lake, res., Al., U.S. — D3 78
Gantts Quarry, Al., U.S. — B3 78
Ganyu, China — E8 31
Ganzhou, China — F7 31
Gao, Mali — C5 45
Gao'an, China — J6 13
Gaoil, Sliabh, mtn., Scot., U.K. — E3 13
Gaoua, Burkina — D4 45
Gaoual, Gui. — D2 45
Gaoyou, China — H8 32
Gaoyou Lake, l., China — H8 32
Gap, Fr. — E7 16
Gap, Pa., U.S. — G9 115
Gapan, Phil. — o13 34
Gapland, Md., U.S. — B2 97
Gap Mills, W.V., U.S. — D4 125
Gar, China — B7 36
Gara, Lough, l., Ire. — D2 10
Garacad, Som. — D6 47
Garachiné, Pan. — F8 62
Garachiné, Punta, c., Pan. — F8 62
Garanhuns, Braz. — C3 57
Garapan, N. Mar. Is. — D7 52
Garapan, Lagunan, b., N. Mar. Is. — D7 52
Garau, Canal de, Mex. — h9 63
Garbahaarrey, Som. — E5 47
Garber, Ia., U.S. — B6 92
Garber, Ok., U.S. — A4 113
Garberville, Ca., U.S. — B2 82
Garbsen, Ger. — *B4 18
Garça, Braz. — C3 56
Garching [an der Alz], Ger. — A8 20
Garcia, Co., U.S. — D5 83
Garciasville, Tx., U.S. — F3 120
Gard, stm., Fr. — E6 16
Garda, Lake, l., Italy — B3 23
Gardanne, Fr. — F6 16
Gardar, N.D., U.S. — A8 111
Gardelegen, Ger. — B5 18
Garden, co., Ne., U.S. — C3 104
Gardena, Ca., U.S. — n12 82
Gardena, N.D., U.S. — A5 111
Garden City, Al., U.S. — A3 78
Garden City, Co., U.S. — *A6 83
Garden City, Id., U.S. — F2 89
Garden City, In., U.S. — F6 91
Garden City, Ks., U.S. — E3 93
Garden City, La., U.S. — E4 95
Garden City, Mi., U.S. — p15 99
Garden City, Mn., U.S. — F4 100
Garden City, Mo., U.S. — C3 102
Garden City, N.Y., U.S. — *E7 109
Garden City, S.D., U.S. — C8 118
Garden City, Tx., U.S. — D2 120
Garden City, Ut., U.S. — B4 121
Garden City Park, N.Y., U.S. — *n15 109
Gardendale, Al., U.S. — B3 78
Gardendale, Tx., U.S. — E3 120
Garden Grove, Ca., U.S. — n13 82
Garden Grove, Ia., U.S. — D4 92
Garden Home, Or., U.S. — *B4 114
Garden Island, i., Mi., U.S. — C5 99
Garden of Gethsemane, Isr. Occ. — m14 41
Garden Plain, Il., U.S. — B3 90
Garden Plain, Ks., U.S. — E6 93
Garden Prairie, Il., U.S. — A5 90
Garden Reach, India — *D8 36
Gardenton, Man. — E3 70
Garden Valley, Id., U.S. — E3 89
Gardi, Ga., U.S. — E4 83
Gardeyz, Afg. — E5 37
Gardiner, Me., U.S. — D3 96
Gardiner, Mt., U.S. — E6 103
Gardiner, Or., U.S. — D2 114
Gardiners Island, i., N.Y., U.S. — m16 109
Gardner, Co., U.S. — D6 83
Gardner, Fl., U.S. — E5 86
Gardner, Il., U.S. — B5 90
Gardner, Ks., U.S. — D9 93
Gardner, Ma., U.S. — A4 98
Gardner, N.D., U.S. — B9 111
Gardner, Tn., U.S. — A3 119
Gardner Canal, strt., B.C. — C3 69
Gardner Lake, l., Me., U.S. — D5 96
Gardner Mountain, mtn., N.H., U.S. — B3 106
Gardner Pinnacles, Hi., U.S. — k14 88
Gardnersville, Ky., U.S. — k14 94
Gardnerville, Nv., U.S. — E2 105
Gardone Riviera, Italy — D6 20
Gardone Val Trompia, Italy — D6 20
Garešnica, Yugo. — C3 24
Garfield, Al., U.S. — A2 81
Garfield, Co., U.S. — C4 83
Garfield, Ga., U.S. — D4 83
Garfield, Ks., U.S. — D4 93
Garfield, Mn., U.S. — E3 100
Garfield, N.J., U.S. — h8 107
Garfield, N.M., U.S. — E2 108
Garfield, Wa., U.S. — B8 124
Garfield, co., Co., U.S. — B2 83
Garfield, co., Mt., U.S. — C9 103
Garfield, co., Ne., U.S. — C6 104
Garfield, co., Ok., U.S. — A4 113
Garfield, co., Ut., U.S. — F4 121

Garfield, co., Wa., U.S. — C8 124
Garfield Heights, Oh., U.S. — h9 112
Garfield Mountain, mtn., Mt., U.S. — F4 103
Garfield Park, De., U.S. — *B3 85
Garfield Peak, mtn., Wy., U.S. — D5 127
Gargaliánoi, Grc. — D3 25
Gargano Peninsula, pen., Italy — D5 23
Gargnano, Italy — D6 20
Garibaldi, Braz. — D2 56
Garibaldi, Or., U.S. — B3 114
Garibaldi, Mount, mtn., B.C. — D6 69
Garibaldi Provincial Park, B.C. — D6 69
Garissa, Kenya — B6 48
Garita, N.M., U.S. — B5 108
Garland, Al., U.S. — D3 78
Garland, Ks., U.S. — E9 93
Garland, Me., U.S. — C3 96
Garland, Ne., U.S. — D9 104
Garland, N.C., U.S. — C4 110
Garland, Pa., U.S. — C3 115
Garland, Tn., U.S. — B2 119
Garland, Tx., U.S. — n10 120
Garland, Ut., U.S. — B3 121
Garland, Wy., U.S. — B4 127
Garland, co., Ar., U.S. — C2 81
Garm, Sov. Un. — H23 8
Garmisch-Partenkirchen, Ger. — E5 18
Garmouth, Scot., U.K. — D5 8
Garnavillo, Ia., U.S. — B6 92
Garnell, Mt., U.S. — D7 103
Garner, Ar., U.S. — B4 81
Garner, Ia., U.S. — A4 92
Garner, Ky., U.S. — C7 94
Garner, N.C., U.S. — B4 110
Garnet Range, mts., Mt., U.S. — D3 103
Garnett, Ks., U.S. — D8 93
Garnett, S.C., U.S. — F5 117
Garnish, Newf. — E4 72
Garnpung, Lake, l., Austl. — F4 51
Garonne, stm., Eur. — E3 16
Garoowe, Som. — D6 47
Garou, Lac, l., Mali — C4 45
Garoua, Cam. — D2 46
Garretson, S.D., U.S. — D9 118
Garrett, Il., U.S. — D5 90
Garrett, In., U.S. — B7 91
Garrett, Ky., U.S. — C7 94
Garrett, Pa., U.S. — G3 115
Garrett, Wy., U.S. — D7 127
Garrett, co., Md., U.S. — k12 97
Garrett Park, Md., U.S. — *B3 97
Garrettsville, Oh., U.S. — A4 112
Garrick, Sask. — D5 75
Garrison, Ia., U.S. — B5 92
Garrison, Ky., U.S. — B6 94
Garrison, Md., U.S. — B4 97
Garrison, Mn., U.S. — D5 100
Garrison, Mt., U.S. — D4 103
Garrison, N.D., U.S. — B4 111
Garrison, Tx., U.S. — D5 120
Garrison, Ut., U.S. — E1 121
Garrison Dam, N.D., U.S. — B4 111
Garrisonville, Va., U.S. — B5 123
Garristown, Ire. — H5 11
Garron Point, c., N. Ire., U.K. — B6 11
Garrote, Pan. — h11 62
Garrovillas, Spain — C2 22
Garry, stm., Scot., U.K. — D5 13
Garry Lake, l., N.W. Ter. — C13 66
Garryowen, Mt., U.S. — E9 103
Garsen, Kenya — B7 48
Garson Lake, l., Can. — A5 68
Garson Quarry, Man. — A5 70
Garstang, Eng., U.K. — G6 13
Garth, Al., U.S. — A3 78
Garthby Station (Beaulac), Que. — D6 74
Gartz, Ger. — E8 15
Garut, Indon. — G3 34
Garvagh, N. Ire., U.K. — C5 11
Garve, Scot., U.K. — C4 13
Garvin, Mn., U.S. — F3 100
Garvin, Ok., U.S. — D7 113
Garvin, co., Ok., U.S. — C4 113
Garwin, Ia., U.S. — B5 92
Garwolin, Pol. — C6 26
Garwood, N.J., U.S. — *B4 107
Garwood, Tx., U.S. — E4 120
Gary, In., U.S. — A3 91
Gary, Mn., U.S. — C2 100
Gary, S.D., U.S. — C9 118
Gary, Tx., U.S. — C5 120
Gary, W.V., U.S. — D3 125
Garyarsa, China — B8 37
Garysburg, N.C., U.S. — A5 110
Garyville, La., U.S. — D5 95
Garza, co., Tx., U.S. — C2 120
Garza García, Mex. — *B4 63
Garza-Little Elm Reservoir, res., Tx., U.S. — C4 120
Garzón, Col. — C2 60
Gas, Ks., U.S. — E8 93
Gasconade, co., Mo., U.S. — C6 102
Gasconade, stm., Mo., U.S. — C6 102
Gasconade, Osage Fork, stm., Mo., U.S. — D5 102
Gascony, hist. reg., Fr. — E3 16
Gascoyne, N.D., U.S. — C2 111
Gascoyne, stm., Austl. — E2 50
Gashaka, Nig. — G8 45
Gasherbrum, mtn., Asia — *A6 36
Gas Hills, Wy., U.S. — D5 127
Gashua, Nig. — D7 45
Gasparilla Island, i., Fl., U.S. — F4 86
Gaspé, Que. — k14 74
Gaspé, Cap, c., Que. — G20 66
Gaspésie, Péninsule de la, pen., Que. — k13 74
Gasport, N.Y., U.S. — B2 109
Gasque, Al., U.S. — E1 78
Gassaway, Tn., U.S. — D8 119
Gassaway, W.V., U.S. — C4 125
Gassetts, Vt., U.S. — E3 122
Gassol, Nig. — G7 45
Gassville, Ar., U.S. — A3 81
Gaston, In., U.S. — D7 91
Gaston, N.C., U.S. — A5 110
Gaston, S.C., U.S. — D5 117
Gaston, co., N.C., U.S. — B1 110
Gaston, Lake, res., U.S. — A5 110
Gaston Dam, N.C., U.S. — A5 110
Gastonia, N.C., U.S. — B1 110
Gastre, Arg. — C3 54
Gata, Cape, c., Spain — D4 22
Gata, Sierra de, mts., Spain — D4 22
Gatas, Cape, c., Cyp. — E9 40
Gatchina, Sov. Un. — B8 27

Gate, Ok., U.S. — A1 113
Gate City, Va., U.S. — f9 123
Gatehouse of Fleet, Scot., U.K. — F4 13
Gates, Ne., U.S. — C6 104
Gates, N.Y., U.S. — B3 109
Gates, N.C., U.S. — A6 110
Gates, Or., U.S. — C4 114
Gates, Tn., U.S. — B2 119
Gates, co., N.C., U.S. — A6 110
Gateshead, Eng., U.K. — C6 10
Gatesville, Ms., U.S. — D3 101
Gatesville, N.C., U.S. — A6 110
Gatesville, Tx., U.S. — D4 120
Gateway, Ar., U.S. — *A2 81
Gateway, Co., U.S. — C2 83
Gateway, Or., U.S. — C5 114
Gatineau, Que. — D2 74
Gatineau, co., Que. — C2 74
Gatineau, stm., Que. — D2 74
Gatineau, Parc de la, Que. — D2 74
Gatliff, Ky., U.S. — D5 94
Gatlinburg, Tn., U.S. — D10 119
Gato, Co., U.S. — D3 83
Gattman, Ms., U.S. — B5 101
Gatton, Austl. — C9 51
Gatún, Pan. — k11 62
Gatún, Lago, res., Pan. — k11 62
Gatun Locks, Pan. — k11 62
Gatzke, Mn., U.S. — B3 100
Gau, i., Fiji — I15 52
Gauer Lake, l., Man. — A3 70
Gauja, stm., Sov. Un. — D5 7
Gaula, stm., Nor. — F4 14
Gauley, stm., W.V., U.S. — C3 125
Gauley Bridge, W.V., U.S. — C3 125
Gauley Mills, W.V., U.S. — C4 125
Gause, Tx., U.S. — D4 120
Gautier, Ms., U.S. — f8 101
Gavá, Spain — B7 22
Gávdhos, i., Grc. — E5 40
Gavião, stm., Braz. — E3 16
Gavins Point Dam, U.S. — B8 104
Gäv Khūnī, Bāțlāq-e, sw., Iran — C6 39
Gävle, Swe. — G7 14
Gävlebukten, b., Swe. — G7 14
Gavrilovka, Sov. Un. — G11 27
Gavrilov Posad, Sov. Un. — C13 27
Gawler, Austl. — G2 51
Gawler Ranges, mts., Austl. — F6 50
Gay, Ga., U.S. — C2 87
Gay, Mi., U.S. — A2 99
Gaya, India — D7 36
Gaya, Niger — D5 45
Gaya, Nig. — D6 45
Gay Head, Ma., U.S. — D6 98
Gay Head, c., Ma., U.S. — D6 98
Gaylesville, Al., U.S. — A4 78
Gaylord, Ks., U.S. — C5 93
Gaylord, Mi., U.S. — C6 99
Gaylord, Mn., U.S. — F4 100
Gaylord, Or., U.S. — E2 114
Gaylordsville, Ct., U.S. — C2 84
Gays, Il., U.S. — D5 90
Gaysin, Sov. Un. — G7 27
Gays Mills, Wi., U.S. — E3 126
Gayville, S.D., U.S. — D8 118
Gaza (Ghazzah), Isr. Occ. — D5 41
Gaza, Ia., U.S. — B2 92
Gaza, dept., Moz. — B5 49
Gaza Strip, ter., Isr. Occ. — C6 41
Gaziantep, Tur. — D11 40
Gazimağusa, N. Cyp. — D9 40
Gboko, Nig. — E6 45
Gdańsk (Danzig), Pol. — A5 26
Gdov, Sov. Un. — B6 27
Gdynia, Pol. — A5 26
Gearhart, Or., U.S. — A3 114
Gearhart Mountain, mtn., Or., U.S. — E6 114
Geary, N.B. — D3 71
Geary, Ok., U.S. — B3 113
Geary, co., Ks., U.S. — C7 93
Geauga, co., Oh., U.S. — A4 112
Gebeit Mine, Sud. — A4 47
Gebze, Tur. — B7 25
Ged, La., U.S. — E2 95
Geddes, S.D., U.S. — D7 118
Gedera, Isr. — C4 41
Gedinne, Bel. — E4 17
Gediz, Tur. — C7 40
Gediz, stm., Tur. — C3 25
Gedo, prov., Som. — E5 47
Gedser, Den. — C4 15
Geel, Bel. — C4 17
Geelong, Austl. — G7 50
Geetbets, Bel. — D5 17
Gefell, Ger. — E5 19
Geiger, Al., U.S. — C1 78
Geisenfeld, Ger. — E6 19
Geislingen, Ger. — C5 19
Geismar, La., U.S. — h9 95
Geistown, Pa., U.S. — F4 115
Geist Reservoir, res., In., U.S. — E6 91
Geita, Tan. — B5 48
Gejiu, China — G5 31
Gela, Italy — F5 23
Gelderland, prov., Neth. — C5 17
Geldermalsen, Neth. — C5 17
Geldern, Ger. — D2 19
Geldrop, Neth. — D5 17
Geleen, Neth. — D5 17
Gelendzhik, Sov. Un. — I11 27
Gelfingen, Switz. — B5 21
Gelibolu (Gallipoli), Tur. — I11 25
Gelligaer, Wales, U.K. — J9 13
Gellinam Island, i., Marsh Is. — S17 52
Gelnhausen, Ger. — E5 19
Gelsenkirchen, Ger. — D3 19
Gelting, Ger. — A5 18
Gem, Alta. — D4 68
Gem, Id., U.S. — *B3 89
Gem, Ks., U.S. — C3 93
Gem, W.V., U.S. — E2 125
Gem, co., Id., U.S. — E2 89
Gemas, Malay. — K5 35
Gembloux, Bel. — D4 17
Gemena, Zaire — A2 48
Gemert, Neth. — C5 17
Gemla, Swe. — H6 15
Gemlik, Tur. — B7 40
Gemona del Friuli, Italy — C7 20
Gemünden, Ger. — E5 19
Gem Village, Co., U.S. — D3 83
Genale (Jubba), stm., Afr. — C5 47
Genarp, Swe. — I6 15
Gene Autry, Ok., U.S. — C4 113
General Acha, Arg. — B4 54
General Alvear, Arg. — B5 54

General Alvear, Arg. — A3 54
General Belgrano, Arg. — B5 54
General Carrera, Lago (Lago Buenos Aires), l., S.A. — F2 54
General Conesa, Arg. — C4 54
General Enrique Martínez, Ur. — E2 56
General Eugenio A. Garay, Para. — D3 55
General José de San Martín Zapallar, Arg. — E4 55
General Juan Madariaga, Arg. — B5 54
General Lavalle, Arg. — B5 54
General La Madrid, Arg. — B4 54
General Martín Miguel de Güemes, Arg. — D2 55
General Paz, Arg. — E4 55
General Pico, Arg. — B4 54
General Pinedo, Arg. — B3 54
General Roca, Arg. — g7 54
General San Martín, Arg. — g7 54
General Sarmiento, Arg. — D1 56
General Tinio, Phil. — o13 34
General Toshevo, Bul. — D9 24
General Viamonte, Arg. — B4 54
General Villegas, Arg. — B4 54
Genesee, Id., U.S. — C2 89
Genesee, Mi., U.S. — E7 99
Genesee, Pa., U.S. — C6 115
Genesee, co., Mi., U.S. — E7 99
Genesee, co., N.Y., U.S. — B2 109
Genesee, stm., N.Y., U.S. — C2 109
Genesee Depot, Wi., U.S. — n11 126
Geneseo, Il., U.S. — B3 90
Geneseo, Ks., U.S. — D5 93
Geneseo, N.Y., U.S. — C3 109
Geneseo, N.D., U.S. — C8 111
Geneva (Genève), Switz. — E3 18
Geneva, Al., U.S. — D4 78
Geneva, Ga., U.S. — D2 83
Geneva, Id., U.S. — G7 89
Geneva, Il., U.S. — B5 90
Geneva, In., U.S. — C8 91
Geneva, Ia., U.S. — B4 92
Geneva, Ky., U.S. — C2 94
Geneva, Ne., U.S. — D8 104
Geneva, N.Y., U.S. — C4 109
Geneva, Oh., U.S. — A5 112
Geneva, Pa., U.S. — C1 115
Geneva, co., Al., U.S. — D4 78
Geneva, Lake, l., Eur. — E3 18
Geneva, Lake, l., Wi., U.S. — F5 126
Geneva-on-the-Lake, Oh., U.S. — A5 112
Genève, state, Switz. — C2 20
Genichesk, Sov. Un. — H10 27
Genil, stm., Spain — D3 22
Génissiat, Fr. — C1 20
Genk, Bel. — B6 16
Gennep, Neth. — C5 17
Gennes, Fr. — D3 16
Gennevilliers, Fr. — g10 16
Genoa (Genova), Italy — B2 23
Genoa, Ar., U.S. — D2 81
Genoa, Co., U.S. — B7 83
Genoa, Il., U.S. — A5 90
Genoa, Ne., U.S. — C8 104
Genoa, N.Y., U.S. — C4 109
Genoa, Oh., U.S. — A2 112
Genoa, Wi., U.S. — E2 126
Genoa City, Wi., U.S. — F5 126
Genoa, Gulf of, b., Italy — B2 23
Genola, Mn., U.S. — E4 100
Genola, Ut., U.S. — D4 121
Genolier, Switz. — D1 21
Genovesa, Isla, i., Ec. — f6 58
Gent (Ghent), Bel. — B5 16
Gentbrugge (part of Gent), Bel. — C3 17
Genthin, Ger. — D3 91
Gentilly, Fr. — g10 16
Gentilly, La., U.S. — k11 95
Gentofte, Den. — *C6 15
Gentry, Ar., U.S. — A1 81
Gentry, Mo., U.S. — A3 102
Gentry, co., Mo., U.S. — A3 102
Gentryville, In., U.S. — H3 91
Genzano di Roma, Italy — h9 23
Geographe Bay, b., Austl. — F2 50
Geographe Channel, strt., Austl. — D1 50
Geographical Society Island, i., Grnld. — B16 128
Geokchay, Sov. Un. — G18 8
George, S. Afr. — D3 49
George, Ia., U.S. — A2 92
George, N.C., U.S. — A5 110
George, co., Ms., U.S. — E5 101
George, i., Sov. Un. — B10 128
George, stm., Que. — g13 74
George, Cape, c., N.S. — D8 71
George, Lake, l., Austl. — E3 51
George, Lake, l., N.S. — E3 71
George, Lake, l., Fl., U.S. — C5 86
George, Lake, l., N.Y., U.S. — B7 109
George Air Force Base, mil., Ca., U.S. — E5 82
George B. Stevenson Reservoir, res., Pa., U.S. — D6 115
George Hill, mtn., Md., U.S. — k12 97
George Island, i., Newf. — A3 72
George Peak, mtn., Ut., U.S. — B2 121
Georgesville, Oh., U.S. — m10 112
George Town, Austl. — o15 50
George Town, Bah. — C6 64
Georgetown, P.E.I. — C7 71
Georgetown, Cay. Is. — D8 63
Georgetown, Gam. — D2 45
Georgetown, Guy. — A3 59
Georgetown, Ar., U.S. — B4 81
Georgetown, Ca., U.S. — C3 82
Georgetown, Co., U.S. — B5 83
Georgetown, Ct., U.S. — D2 84
Georgetown, De., U.S. — F4 85
Georgetown, Fl., U.S. — C5 86
Georgetown, Ga., U.S. — E1 83
Georgetown, Id., U.S. — G7 89
Georgetown, Il., U.S. — D6 90
Georgetown, In., U.S. — H6 91
Georgetown, Ky., U.S. — B5 94
Georgetown, La., U.S. — C3 95
Georgetown, Md., U.S. — B6 97
Georgetown, Ma., U.S. — A6 98
Georgetown, Mn., U.S. — C2 100
Georgetown, Ms., U.S. — D3 101
Georgetown, N.Y., U.S. — C5 109
Georgetown, Oh., U.S. — D2 112
Georgetown, S.C., U.S. — E9 117
Georgetown, Tn., U.S. — D8 119
Georgetown, Tx., U.S. — D4 120
Georgetown, co., S.C., U.S. — E9 117
George Town (Pinang), Malay. — L6 34
George V Coast, Ant. — C28 7
Georgeville, Que. — D5 74

George VI Sound, strt., Ant. — B6 7
George Washington Birthplace National Monument, Va., U.S. — B6 123
George Washington Carver National Monument, Mo., U.S. — E3 102
George West, Tx., U.S. — E3 120
Georgia, state, Sov. Un. — E7 29
Georgia, state, U.S. — D3 87
Georgia, Strait of, strt., N.A. — E5 69
Georgia Center, Vt., U.S. — B2 122
Georgian Bay, b., Ont. — B3 73
Georgina, stm., Austl. — D6 50
Georgiu-Dez, Sov. Un. — F12 27
Georgiyevsk, Sov. Un. — G17 8
Gera, Ger. — C6 18
Geraardsbergen, Bel. — D3 17
Geral, Serra, clf., Braz. — D2 56
Geral de Goiás, Serra, clf., Braz. — D1 57
Geraldine, Al., U.S. — A4 78
Geraldine, Mt., U.S. — C6 103
Geraldton, Austl. — E1 50
Geraldton, Ont. — o18 73
Gérardmer, Fr. — A2 20
Gerber, Ca., U.S. — B2 82
Gerber Reservoir, res., Or., U.S. — E5 114
Gerbstedt, Ger. — D6 19
Gerçüş, Tur. — D13 40
Gerdau, stm., Ger. — F4 15
Gerdine, Mount, mtn., Ak., U.S. — C9 79
Gerede, Tur. — B9 40
Gereshk, Afg. — B3 36
Gérgal, Spain — D4 22
Gérin, Que. — C4 74
Gering, Ne., U.S. — C2 104
Gerlachovka, mtn., Czech. — D6 26
Germania, N.J., U.S. — D3 107
Germania, Pa., U.S. — C6 115
Germania, Col. — C2 60
Germansen Landing, B.C. — B5 69
Germantown, Il., U.S. — E4 90
Germantown, Ky., U.S. — B6 94
Germantown, Md., U.S. — B3 97
Germantown, Oh., U.S. — C1 112
Germantown, Tn., U.S. — B2 119
Germantown, Wi., U.S. — E5 126
Germany, ctry., Eur. — C4 18
Germersheim, Ger. — D3 19
Germfask, Mi., U.S. — B5 99
Germiston, S. Afr. — C4 49
Gernsbach, Ger. — B6 19
Gernsheim, Ger. — D3 19
Gero, Japan — n16 33
Gerolzhofen, Ger. — D5 19
Geronimo, Ok., U.S. — C4 109
Geronimo, Tx., U.S. — h8 120
Gerrardstown, W.V., U.S. — B6 125
Gersfeld, Ger. — C4 19
Gersthofen, Ger. — E5 19
Gertrudis Sánchez (part of Mexico City), Mex. — h9 63
Gerty, Ok., U.S. — C5 113
Gervais, Or., U.S. — B4 114
Gerze, Tur. — B10 40
Geseke, Ger. — B3 19
Gesher HaZiw, Isr. — A7 41
Gessie, In., U.S. — D3 91
Getafe, Spain — B4 22
Gethsémani, Que. — h9 72
Gettysburg, Oh., U.S. — B1 112
Gettysburg, Pa., U.S. — G7 115
Gettysburg, S.D., U.S. — C6 118
Getúlio Vargas, Braz. — D2 56
Getz Ice Shelf, ice, Ant. — B36 7
Geuda Springs, Ks., U.S. — E6 93
Gevelsberg, Ger. — B2 19
Geyser, Mt., U.S. — C6 103
Geyserville, Ca., U.S. — C2 82
Geyve, Tur. — B8 40
Ghabīyah, Wādī al, val., Eg. — E5 41
Ghaggar, stm., India — C5 37
Ghāghara, stm., India — C7 36
Ghaghar Reservoir, res., India — E9 37
Ghana, ctry., Afr. — E4 45
Ghanzi, Bots. — B3 49
Ghardaïa, Alg. — C5 44
Ghāt, Libya — D2 43
Ghawr ash Sharqīyah, Qanāt al, Jord. — C4 41
Ghazal, Bahr al, stm., Sud. — D3 47
Ghazal, Bahr al, stm., Chad — D2 46
Ghāziābād, India — *C6 36
Ghāzīpur, India — E9 37
Ghaznī, Afg. — B4 36
Gheens, La., U.S. — E5 95
Ghent, Ky., U.S. — B5 94
Ghent see Gent, Bel. — B5 16
Gheorghe Gheorghiu-Dej, Rom. — B8 24
Gheorgheni, Rom. — B7 24
Gherla, Rom. — B6 24
Ghilizane, Alg. — B5 44
Ghlò, Beinn a', mtn., Scot., U.K. — D5 13
Ghudāmis, Libya — C1 43
Ghūrīān, Afg. — D10 39
Giannutri, i., Italy — C3 23
Giant Mountain, mtn., N.Y., U.S. — A7 109
Giants Neck, Ct., U.S. — D7 84
Giaveno, Italy — D2 23
Gibbon, Mn., U.S. — F4 100
Gibbon, Ne., U.S. — D7 104
Gibbons, Alta. — C4 68
Gibbonsville, Id., U.S. — D5 89
Gibbs, Mo., U.S. — A5 102
Gibbstown, N.J., U.S. — D2 107
Gibeon, Nmb. — C2 49
Gibland, La., U.S. — B3 95
Gibraléon, Spain — D2 22
Gibraltar, dep., Eur. — D3 22
Gibraltar, Strait of, strt. — E2 22
Gibraltar Point, c., Eng., U.K. — A8 12
Gibsland, La., U.S. — B2 95
Gibson, Ga., U.S. — C4 87
Gibson, La., U.S. — E5 95
Gibson, Ms., U.S. — B5 101
Gibson, Mo., U.S. — E7 102

Gibson, N.C., U.S. — C3 110
Gibson, Pa., U.S. — C10 115
Gibson, Tn., U.S. — B3 119
Gibson, co., In., U.S. — H2 91
Gibson, co., Tn., U.S. — A3 119
Gibsonburg, Oh., U.S. — A2 112
Gibson City, Il., U.S. — C5 90
Gibson Desert, des., Austl. — D3 50
Gibsonia, Pa., U.S. — h14 115
Gibson Island, i., Md., U.S. — B5 97
Gibsons, B.C. — E6 69
Gibsonton, Fl., U.S. — p11 86
Giddings, Tx., U.S. — D4 120
Gideon, Mo., U.S. — E8 102
Gidole, Eth. — D4 47
Gien, Fr. — D5 16
Giessen, Ger. — C4 18
Gifford, Ar., U.S. — g8 81
Gifford, Fl., U.S. — E6 86
Gifford, Id., U.S. — C2 89
Gifford, Il., U.S. — C5 90
Gifford, In., U.S. — B3 91
Gifford, Pa., U.S. — C4 115
Giffre, stm., Fr. — D2 21
Gifhorn, Ger. — F4 15
Gift, Tn., U.S. — B2 119
Gifu, Japan — D12 31
Giganta, Sierra de la, mts., Mex. — B2 63
Gigante, Col. — C2 60
Gigha Island, i., Scot., U.K. — E3 13
Gig Harbor, Wa., U.S. — B3 124
Giglio, i., Italy — C3 23
Gihon, stm., Vt., U.S. — B3 122
Gijón, Spain — A3 22
Gila, N.M., U.S. — E1 108
Gila, co., Az., U.S. — D5 80
Gila, stm., U.S. — D5 76
Gila Bend, Az., U.S. — E3 80
Gila Bend Indian Reservation, Az., U.S. — D3 80
Gila Bend Mountains, mts., Az., U.S. — D2 80
Gila Cliff Dwellings National Monument, N.M., U.S. — D1 108
Gila Mountains, mts., Az., U.S. — D6 80
Gila Peak, mtn., Az., U.S. — D6 80
Gila River Indian Reservation, Az., U.S. — D4 80
Gilbert, Az., U.S. — D4 80
Gilbert, Ar., U.S. — B3 81
Gilbert, Ia., U.S. — B4 92
Gilbert, La., U.S. — B4 95
Gilbert, Mn., U.S. — C6 100
Gilbert, Or., U.S. — *B4 114
Gilbert, S.C., U.S. — D5 117
Gilbert, W.V., U.S. — D3 125
Gilbert, stm., Austl. — C7 50
Gilbert Islands see Kiribati, ctry., Oc. — G11 6
Gilbert Islands, is., Kir. — G10 6
Gilbertown, Al., U.S. — D1 78
Gilbert Peak, mtn., Wa., U.S. — C4 124
Gilbert Plains, Man. — D1 70
Gilbertsville, Ky., U.S. — f9 94
Gilbertsville, N.Y., U.S. — C5 109
Gilbertsville, Pa., U.S. — F10 115
Gilbertville, Ia., U.S. — B5 92
Gilbertville, Ma., U.S. — B3 98
Gilboa, Oh., U.S. — A2 112
Gilchrist, Or., U.S. — D5 114
Gilchrist, co., Fl., U.S. — C4 86
Gilcrest, Co., U.S. — A6 83
Gildford, Mt., U.S. — B6 103
Gilead, Ct., U.S. — C6 84
Gilead, Me., U.S. — D2 96
Gilead, Ne., U.S. — D8 104
Giles, co., Tn., U.S. — B4 119
Giles, co., Va., U.S. — C2 123
Gilford, I., N. Ire., U.K. — C5 11
Gilford, N.H., U.S. — C4 106
Gilford Island, i., B.C. — D4 69
Gilford Park, N.J., U.S. — *D4 107
Gilgandra, Austl. — E7 51
Gilgit, Pak. — A5 36
Gil Island, i., B.C. — C3 69
Gill, Co., U.S. — A6 83
Gill, Lough, l., Ire. — C3 11
Gillam, Man. — A4 70
Gilleleje, Den. — B6 15
Gillen, Lake, l., Austl. — E3 50
Gillespie, Il., U.S. — D4 90
Gillespie, co., Tx., U.S. — D3 120
Gillespie Dam, Az., U.S. — D3 80
Gillett, Ar., U.S. — C4 81
Gillett, Pa., U.S. — C8 115
Gillett, Tx., U.S. — k8 120
Gillett, Wi., U.S. — D5 126
Gillett Grove, Ia., U.S. — A2 92
Gillette, Wy., U.S. — B7 127
Gilliam, La., U.S. — B2 95
Gilliam, Mo., U.S. — B4 102
Gilliam, co., Or., U.S. — B6 114
Gillingham, Eng., U.K. — C8 12
Gillis Point, N.S. — C9 71
Gilly (part of Charleroi), Bel. — B6 16
Gilman, Ct., U.S. — C7 84
Gilman, Il., U.S. — C5 90
Gilman, Ia., U.S. — B5 92
Gilman, Vt., U.S. — C5 122
Gilman, Wi., U.S. — C3 126
Gilman City, Mo., U.S. — A4 102
Gilmanton, N.H., U.S. — D4 106
Gilmanton, Wi., U.S. — D2 126
Gilmore Iron Works, N.H., U.S. — D4 106
Gilmer, Tx., U.S. — C5 120
Gilmer, W.V., U.S. — C4 125
Gilmer, co., Ga., U.S. — B2 83
Gilmer, co., W.V., U.S. — C4 125
Gilmore, Ar., U.S. — B5 81
Gilmore City, Ia., U.S. — B3 92
Gilo, stm., Eth. — D3 47
Gilpin, Ky., U.S. — C5 94
Gilpin, co., Co., U.S. — B5 83
Gilroy, Sask. — G2 75
Gilroy, Ca., U.S. — D3 82
Gilson, Il., U.S. — B3 90
Gilsum, N.H., U.S. — D2 106
Giltedge, Mt., U.S. — D7 103
Giltner, Ne., U.S. — D7 104
Giluwe, Mount, mtn., Pap. N. Gui. — k11 50
Gimli, Man. — D3 70

Name	Map Ref.	Page

Ginir, Eth. D5 47
Ginns Corner, De., U.S. . . . C3 85
Ginosa, Italy D6 23
Ginowan, Japan O5 52
Ginzo [de Limia], Spain A2 22
Gioia del Colle, Italy D6 23
Gioiosa Ionica, Italy E6 23
Girard, Ga., U.S. C5 87
Girard, Il., U.S. D4 90
Girard, Ks., U.S. E9 93
Girard, La., U.S. B4 95
Girard, Oh., U.S. A5 112
Girard, Pa., U.S. B1 115
Girard, Tx., U.S. C2 120
Girardot, Col. C3 60
Girardville, Pa., U.S. E9 115
Girdletree, Md., U.S. D7 97
Giresun, Tur. B12 40
Giri, stm., Zaire A2 48
Giridih, India D8 36
Girna, stm., India G5 37
Girne, N. Cyp. E9 40
Giromagny, Fr. D7 16
Girón, Ec. B2 58
Gironde, est., Fr. E3 16
Giroux, Fr. E3 70
Girouxville, Alta. B2 68
Girvan, Scot., U.K. C4 10
Girvin, Sask. F3 75
Girvin, Tx., U.S. D1 120
Gisborne, N.Z. M17 51
Gisborne Lake, l., Newf. . . . E4 72
Giscome, B.C. B6 69
Gisenyi, Rw. B4 48
Gislaved, Swe. A7 15
Gisors, Fr. C4 16
Gitega, Bdi. B4 48
Giulianova, Italy C4 23
Giurgiu, Rom. D7 24
Giv'atayim, Isr. g10 41
Give, Den. C3 15
Givet, Fr. B6 16
Givhans, S.C., U.S. E7 117
Givors, Fr. E6 16
Givry, l., Micron. Q18 52
Giza (Al Jīzah), Eg. B3 38
Giza, Pyramids of, hist., Egypt E3 41
Gizāb, Afg. E13 39
Gizhiga, Sov. Un. C19 29
Giżycko, Pol. A6 26
Gjirokastra, Alb. B3 40
Gjoa Haven, N.W. Ter. C13 66
Gjøvik, Nor. G4 14
Glace Bay, N.S. C10 71
Glacier, B.C. D9 69
Glacier, Wa., U.S. A4 124
Glacier, co., Mt., U.S. B3 103
Glacier Bay, b., Ak., U.S. . . . k21 79
Glacier Bay National Park, Ak.,
    U.S. D12 79
Glacier National Park, B.C. . . D9 69
Glacier National Park, Mt.,
    U.S. B2 103
Glacier Peak, mtn., Wa., U.S. A4 124
Gladbeck, Ger. B1 19
Gladbrook, Ia., U.S. B5 92
Glade, Ks., U.S. C4 93
Glade Creek, stm., W.V., U.S. C6 124
Glade Creek, stm., W.V., U.S. n14 125
Glade Creek, stm., W.V., U.S. n13 125
Glade Park, Co., U.S. B2 83
Glades, co., Fl., U.S. F5 86
Glade Spring, Va., U.S. f10 123
Glade Valley, N.C., U.S. . . . A1 110
Gladeview, Fl., U.S. *G6 86
Gladeville, Tn., U.S. A5 119
Gladewater, Tx., U.S. C5 120
Gladmar, Sask. H3 75
Gladstone, Austl. D9 50
Gladstone, Man. D2 70
Gladstone, Il., U.S. C3 90
Gladstone, Mi., U.S. C4 99
Gladstone, Mo., U.S. h10 102
Gladstone, Ne., U.S. D8 104
Gladstone, N.J., U.S. B3 107
Gladstone, N.M., U.S. A6 108
Gladstone, N.D., U.S. C3 111
Gladstone, Or., U.S. B4 114
Gladstone, Va., U.S. C4 123
Glad Valley, S.D., U.S. B4 118
Gladwin, Mi., U.S. E6 99
Gladwin, co., Mi., U.S. D6 99
Glady, W.V., U.S. C5 125
Gladys, Va., U.S. C3 123
Glåma, stm., Nor. G5 14
Glamis, Calif. F2 75
Glamoč, Yugo. C3 24
Glan, i., Nor. u33 14
Glan, stm., Ger. D2 19
Glana, Switz. D1 21
Glandorf, Oh., U.S. A1 112
Glanshammar (part of Örebro),
    Swe. t33 14
Glärnisch, mts., Switz. C4 20
Glarus, Switz. C4 20
Glarus, state, Switz. B5 20
Glarus Alps, mts., Switz. . . . C6 21
Glasco, Ks., U.S. C6 93
Glasco, N.Y., U.S. C7 109
Glascock, co., Ga., U.S. . . . C4 87
Glasford, Il., U.S. C4 90
Glasgo, Ct., U.S. C8 84
Glasgow, Scot., U.K. C4 10
Glasgow, Il., U.S. D3 90
Glasgow, Ky., U.S. C4 94
Glasgow, Mo., U.S. B5 102
Glasgow, Mt., U.S. B10 103
Glasgow, Va., U.S. C3 123
Glasgow, W.V., U.S. m13 125
Glasgow Village, Mo., U.S. . . *f13 102
Glaslyn, Sask. D1 75
Glasnevin, Sask. H3 75
Glass, Tn., U.S. A2 119
Glassboro, N.J., U.S. D2 107
Glasscock, co., Tx., U.S. . . . D2 120
Glassmanor, Md., U.S. *C4 97
Glass Mountains, mts., Tx.,
    U.S. D1 120
Glassport, Pa., U.S. F2 115
Glasston, N.D., U.S. A8 111
Glastenbury Mountain, mtn.,
    Vt., U.S. F2 122
Glastonbury, Eng., U.K. C5 84
Glastonbury, Ct., U.S. C5 84
Glauchau, Ger. C6 18
Glazier, Tx., U.S. A2 120
Glazier Lake, l., Me., U.S. . . A3 96
Glazov, Sov. Un. B4 28
Glazypeau Mountain, mtn.,
    Ar., U.S. f7 81
Gleason, Tn., U.S. A3 119
Gleason, Wi., U.S. C4 126
Gleasondale, Ma., U.S. g9 98
Gleichen, Alta. D4 68
Gleiwitz see Gliwice, Pol. . . . C5 26

Glen, Mn., U.S. D5 100
Glen, Mt., U.S. E4 103
Glen, N.H., U.S. B4 106
Glen, W.V., U.S. m13 125
Glenade, Ire. C3 11
Glen Alice, Tn., U.S. D9 119
Glen Allan, Ms., U.S. B2 101
Glen Allen, Al., U.S. B2 78
Glen Allen, Mo., U.S. D7 102
Glen Allen, Va., U.S. C5 123
Glen Alpine, N.C., U.S. B1 110
Glenamaddy, Ire. D3 11
Glenamoy, Ire. C2 11
Glénan, Îles de, is., Fr. D1 16
Glenarm, N. Ire., U.K. C6 11
Glenavon, Sask. G4 75
Glen Avon, Ca., U.S. m14 82
Glenbain, Sask. H2 75
Glenbarr, Scot., U.K. E3 13
Glenbeigh, Ire. E2 11
Glenbeulah, Wi., U.S. k9 126
Glenboro, Man. E2 70
Glenbrook, Nv., U.S. D2 105
Glenburn, N.D., U.S. A4 111
Glen Burnie, Md., U.S. B4 97
Glen Burnie Park, Md., U.S. . *B4 97
Glenbush, Sask. D2 75
Glen Campbell, Pa., U.S. . . . E4 115
Glen Canyon, val., U.S. G4 121
Glen Canyon, Ut., U.S. F4 121
Glen Canyon Dam, Az., U.S. . A4 80
Glen Canyon National
    Recreation Area, U.S. . . . F5 121
Glencar, Ire. E2 11
Glen Carbon, Il., U.S. *E4 90
Glencliff, N.H., U.S. C3 106
Glencoe, Ont. E3 73
Glencoe, Al., U.S. B4 78
Glencoe, Il., U.S. A6 90
Glencoe, Ky., U.S. B5 94
Glencoe, La., U.S. E4 95
Glencoe, Md., U.S. A4 97
Glencoe, Mn., U.S. F4 100
Glencoe, Mo., U.S. f12 102
Glencoe, N.M., U.S. D4 108
Glencolumbkille, Ire. C3 11
Glen Cove, N.Y., U.S. h13 109
Glencross, S.D., U.S. B5 118
Glendale, Ar., U.S. D4 81
Glendale, Ca., U.S. m12 82
Glendale, Co., U.S. *B6 83
Glendale, Fl., U.S. v15 86
Glendale, Ky., U.S. C4 94
Glendale, Ms., U.S. D4 101
Glendale, N.H., U.S. *f13 102
Glendale, Oh., U.S. C1 112
Glendale, Or., U.S. E3 114
Glendale, R.I., U.S. B2 116
Glendale, S.C., U.S. B4 117
Glendale, Tn., U.S. B5 119
Glendale, Ut., U.S. F3 121
Glendale, W.V., U.S. B4 125
Glendale, Wi., U.S. m12 126
Glendale Colony, S.D., U.S. . C7 118
Glendale Heights, Il., U.S. . . *k8 90
Glendale Heights, W.V., U.S. . g8 125
Glen Dean, Ky., U.S. C3 94
Glendevey, Co., U.S. A5 83
Glendive, Mt., U.S. C12 103
Glendo, Wy., U.S. D7 127
Glendola, N.J., U.S. C4 107
Glendora, Ca., U.S. m13 82
Glendora, Ms., U.S. B3 101
Glendora, N.J., U.S. *D2 107
Glendo Reservoir, res., Wy.,
    U.S. D8 127
Glendowan, Ire. C4 11
Glen Easton, W.V., U.S. g8 125
Glen Echo, Md., U.S. f8 97
Glen Elder, Ks., U.S. C5 93
Glen Flora, Tx., U.S. E4 120
Glen Flora, Wi., U.S. B4 11
Glen Gardner, N.J., U.S. . . . B3 107
Glengarriff, Ire. F2 11
Glengarry, co., Ont. B10 73
Glenham, N.Y., U.S. D7 109
Glenham, S.D., U.S. B5 118
Glen Haven, Co., U.S. A5 83
Glen Head, N.Y., U.S. *h13 109
Glen Innes, Austl. E9 50
Glen Jean, W.V., U.S. D3 125
Glen Kerr, Sask. G2 75
Glen Lake, l., Mi., U.S. D5 99
Glenluce, Scot., U.K. F4 13
Glen Lyon, Pa., U.S. D9 115
Glenmont, Oh., U.S. B3 112
Glenmora, La., U.S. D3 95
Glenmorgan, Austl. C7 51
Glenn, Mi., U.S. F4 99
Glenn, co., Ca., U.S. C2 82
Glen Dale, Md., U.S. *C4 97
Glennie, Mi., U.S. D7 99
Glennville, Mo., U.S. E7 102
Glenns Ferry, Id., U.S. G3 89
Glenrothes, Scot., U.K. D5 13
Glen Saint Mary, Fl., U.S. . . B4 86
Glens Falls, N.Y., U.S. B7 109
Glenshaw, Pa., U.S. h14 115
Glenside, Pa., U.S. F2 75
Glenside, Pa., U.S. F11 115
Glentana, Mt., U.S. B10 103

Glenties, Ire. C3 11
Glentworth, Sask. H2 75
Glen Ullin, N.D., U.S. C4 111
Glenview, Il., U.S. h9 90
Glenview Naval Air Station,
    mil., Il., U.S. h9 90
Glenvil, Ne., U.S. D7 104
Glenville, Ire. E3 11
Glenville, Mn., U.S. G5 100
Glenville, N.C., U.S. f9 110
Glenville, W.V., U.S. C4 125
Glen White, W.V., U.S. D3 125
Glen Wilton, Va., U.S. C3 123
Glenwood, Newf. D4 72
Glenwood, Al., U.S. D3 78
Glenwood, Ar., U.S. C2 81
Glenwood, Fl., U.S. C5 86
Glenwood, Ga., U.S. D4 87
Glenwood, Il., U.S. *k9 90
Glenwood, In., U.S. E7 91
Glenwood, Ia., U.S. C2 92
Glenwood, Md., U.S. B3 97
Glenwood, Mn., U.S. E3 100
Glenwood, Mo., U.S. A5 102
Glenwood, N.M., U.S. D1 108
Glenwood, Or., U.S. B3 114
Glenwood, Ut., U.S. E4 121
Glenwood, Va., U.S. D3 123
Glenwood, Wa., U.S. C4 124
Glenwood, W.V., U.S. C2 125
Glenwood City, Wi., U.S. . . . C1 126
Glenwood Farms, Va., U.S. . . *C5 123
Glenwood Hills, Va., U.S. . . . *C2 87
Glenwood Springs, Co., U.S. . B3 83
Glenwoodville, Alta. E4 68
Gletsch, Switz. C5 21
Glezen, In., U.S. H3 91
Glidden, Sask. F1 75
Glidden, Ia., U.S. B3 92
Glidden, Wi., U.S. B3 126
Glide, Or., U.S. D3 114
Glifádha, Grc. h11 25
Glin, Ire. E2 11
Glittertinden, mtn., Nor. G3 14
Gliwice (Gleiwitz), Pol. C5 26
Globe, Az., U.S. D5 80
Globe, Ky., U.S. B6 94
Globino, Sov. Un. G9 27
Głogów, Pol. C4 26
Glorenza, Italy A3 23
Glória, Braz. C5 57
Glória de Goitá, Braz. k6 57
Glorieta, N.M., U.S. B4 108
Glorieuses, Îles, is., Reu. . . . f9 49
Glossop, Eng., U.K. A6 12
Gloster, Ga., U.S. h8 87
Gloster, La., U.S. B2 95
Gloster, Ms., U.S. D2 101
Gloucester, Ont. h12 73
Gloucester, Eng., U.K. E5 10
Gloucester, Ma., U.S. A6 98
Gloucester, Tn., U.S. C6 123
Gloucester, co., N.B. B4 71
Gloucester, co., N.J., U.S. . . D2 107
Gloucester, co., Va., U.S. . . . C6 123
Gloucester City, N.J., U.S. . . D2 107
Gloucester Point, Va., U.S. . . C6 123
Gloucestershire, co., Eng.,
    U.K. C7 12
Glouster, Oh., U.S. C3 112
Glover, Mo., U.S. D7 102
Glover, Vt., U.S. B4 122
Glover Gap, W.V., U.S. h10 125
Glover Island, i., Newf. D3 72
Gloversville, N.Y., U.S. B6 109
Glovertown, Newf. D4 72
Gloverville, S.C., U.S. E4 117
Głubczyce, Pol. C4 26
Głubokoye, Sov. Un. D6 27
Głuchołazy, Pol. C4 26
Gluck, S.C., U.S. C2 117
Glücksburg, Ger. D3 15
Glückstadt, Ger. E3 15
Gluek, Mn., U.S. E3 100
Glukhov, Sov. Un. F9 27
Glussk, Sov. Un. E7 27
Glyndon, Md., U.S. B4 97
Glyndon, Mn., U.S. D2 100
Glyngøre, Den. B2 15
Glynn, co., Ga., U.S. E5 87
Gmünden, Aus. E6 18
Gnadenhutten, Oh., U.S. . . . B4 112
Gnarp, Swe. t35 14
Gniezno, Pol. B4 26
Gnjilane, Yugo. D5 24
Gnoien, Ger. E5 15
Goa, state, India E5 36
Goālpāra, India D13 37
Goat Fell, mtn., Scot., U.K. . . E3 13
Goat Island, i., R.I., U.S. . . . F5 116
Goat Island Point, c., Am.
    Sam. F13 52
Goat Mountain, mtn., Mt., U.S. C3 103
Goat Rock Dam, U.S. C4 78
Goba, Eth. D5 47
Gobabis, Nmb. B2 49
Gobernador, N.M., U.S. A2 108
Gobernador Gregores, Arg. . . D2 54
Gobernador Udaondo, Arg. . . g7 54
Gobi Desert, des., Asia C5 31
Gobles, Mi., U.S. F5 99
Gobō, Japan J7 33
Goch, Ger. C3 18
Gochas, Nmb. B2 49
Godāvari, stm., India E6 36
Godāvari, Mouths of the, mth.,
    India E7 36
Goddard, Ks., U.S. E6 93
Goderich, Ont. D3 73
Godfrey, Ont. C8 73
Godfrey, Il., U.S. E3 90
Godhavn, Grnld. C15 61
Godhra, India F4 37
Godley, Tx., U.S. n9 120
Gods, stm., Man. B4 70
Gods Lake, Man. B4 70
Gods Lake, l., Man. B4 70
Godthåb (Nuuk), Grnld. C15 61
Godwin Austen, see K2, mtn.,
    Asia A6 36
Goehner, Ne., U.S. D8 104
Goélands, Lac aux, l., Que. . g8 72
Goes, Neth. C3 17
Goff, Ks., U.S. C8 93
Goffstown, N.H., U.S. D3 106
Gogama, Ont. A3 73
Gogebic, co., Mi., U.S. n12 99
Gogebic, Lake, l., Mi., U.S. . . m12 99
Gogebic Range, hills, U.S. . . B3 126

Goglio, Italy D5 21
Gohfeld, Ger. A3 19
Göhren, Ger. D7 15
Goiana, Braz. C4 57
Goiandira, Braz. B3 56
Goianésia, Braz. B3 56
Goiânia, Braz. B3 56
Goianinha, Braz. h6 57
Goiás, Braz. B2 56
Goiás, state, Braz. B3 56
Goiatuba, Braz. B3 56
Goil, Loch, b., Scot., U.K. . . . D4 13
Goito, Italy D6 20
Gojam, prov., Eth. C4 47
Gojō, Japan o14 33
Gökçeada, i., Tur. B5 25
Göksun, Tur. C11 40
Gokwe, Zimb. A4 49
Gol, Nor. G3 14
Gola Island, i., Ire. B3 11
Golam Head, c., Ire. D2 11
Golbāf, Iran C5 38
Golchikha, Sov. Un. B11 29
Golconda, Il., U.S. F5 90
Golconda, Nv., U.S. C4 105
Goldach, Switz. B7 21
Gotdap, Pol. A7 26
Gold Bar, Wa., U.S. B4 124
Gold Beach, Or., U.S. E2 114
Goldberg, Ger. E6 15
Goldboro, N.S. D8 71
Gold Bridge, B.C. D6 69
Gold Coast see Southport,
    Austl. E9 50
Gold Creek, Ak., U.S. f17 79
Goldcreek, Mt., U.S. D4 103
Golddust, Tn., U.S. B2 119
Golden, B.C. D9 69
Golden, Ire. E4 11
Golden, Co., U.S. B5 83
Golden, Il., U.S. C2 90
Golden, Ms., U.S. A5 101
Golden, Mo., U.S. E3 102
Golden, N.M., U.S. B3 108
Golden, Ok., U.S. C7 113
Golden Bay, b., N.Z. N14 51
Golden Beach, Fl., U.S. *G6 86
Golden City, Mo., U.S. D3 102
Goldendale, Wa., U.S. D5 124
Golden Ears Provincial Park,
    B.C. E6 69
Goldengate, Il., U.S. E5 90
Golden Gate Bridge, Ca., U.S. h7 82
Golden Gate National
    Recreation Area, Ca., U.S. . *G6 86
Golden Glades, Fl., U.S. *G6 86
Golden Meadow, La., U.S. . . E5 95
Golden Lake, Ont. B7 73
Golden Lake, l., Ont. B7 73
Golden Prairie, Sask. G1 75
Golden Spike National Historic
    Site, hist., Ut., U.S. B3 121
Golden Spur, Ct., U.S. D7 84
Golden Valley, Mn., U.S. . . . n12 100
Golden Valley, N.D., U.S. . . . B3 111
Golden Valley, co., Mt., U.S. . D7 103
Golden Valley, co., N.D., U.S. B2 111
Goldenville, N.S. D7 71
Gopālganj, India D10 37
Gopto Lake, l., Pol. B5 26
Göppingen, Ger. D4 18
Góra, Pol. C4 26
Góra Kalwaria, Pol. C6 26
Gorakhpur, India C7 36
Gorday, Sask. E3 75
Gördes, Tur. C7 25
Gordil, Cen. Afr. Rep. D4 46
Gordo, Al., U.S. B2 78
Gordon, Al., U.S. D4 78
Gordon, Ga., U.S. D3 87
Gordon, Ne., U.S. B3 104
Gordon, Oh., U.S. C1 112
Gordon, Tx., U.S. C3 120
Gordon, Wi., U.S. B2 126
Gordon, co., Ga., U.S. B2 87
Gordon Creek, stm., Ne., U.S. B5 104
Gordon Horne Peak, mtn.,
    B.C. D8 69
Gordon Lake, l., Alta. A5 68
Gordon Lake, l., Sask. D4 75
Gordon's Corner, N.J., U.S. . . *C4 107
Gordonsville, Tn., U.S. C8 119
Gordonsville, Va., U.S. B4 123
Gordonville, Mo., U.S. D8 102
Gore, N.S. D6 71
Gore, Eth. D4 47
Gore, N.Z. Q12 51
Gore, Oh., U.S. C3 112
Gore, Ok., U.S. B6 113
Gore, Va., U.S. A4 123
Gore Bay, Ont. A2 73
Goree, Tx., U.S. C3 120
Gore Mountain, mtn., Vt., U.S. B6 97
Gore Point, c., Ak., U.S. . . . h16 79
Gore Range, mts., Co., U.S. . B4 83
Gore Springs, Ms., U.S. B4 101
Goreville, Il., U.S. F5 90
Gorey, Ire. E5 11
Gorgān (Asterābād), Iran . . . C7 39
Gorgān, stm., Iran C7 39
Gorgan Bay, b., Iran B7 38
Gorgas, Al., U.S. B2 78
Gorge High Dam, Wa., U.S. . . A4 124
Gorgona, Isla, i., Col. B3 60
Gorham, Ks., U.S. D4 93
Gorham, Me., U.S. E2 96
Gorham, N.H., U.S. B4 106
Gorham, N.Y., U.S. C3 109
Gori, Sov. Un. E2 29
Gorin, Mo., U.S. A5 102
Gorinchem, Neth. C5 17
Goris, Sov. Un. F7 29
Gorizia, Italy B4 23
Gorkha, Nepal C10 37
Gorki, Sov. Un. D8 27
Gorki see Nizhniy Novgorod,
    Sov. Un. D7 29
Gorki Reservoir, res., Sov.
    Un. D7 29
Gorlev, Den. C5 15
Gorlice, Pol. D6 26
Görlitz, Ger. C7 18
Gorlovka, Sov. Un. G12 27
Gorm, Loch, l., Scot., U.K. . . E1 13
Gorman, Md., U.S. m12 97
Gorman, Tx., U.S. C3 120
Gormania, W.V., U.S. B5 125
Gormley (part of Whitchurch-
    Stouffville), Ont. k15 73

Gorna Oryakhovitsa, Bul. . . . D7 24
Gornji Milanovac, Yugo. C5 24
Gorno-Altaysk, Sov. Un. D11 29
Gornozavodsk, Sov. Un. C10 33
Gorodenka, Sov. Un. G5 27
Gorodets, Sov. Un. D17 8
Gorodnya, Sov. Un. F8 27
Gorodok, Mong. A5 31
Gorodok, Sov. Un. G4 27
Gorodok, Sov. Un. D7 27
Goroka, Pap. N. Gui. k12 50
Goroke, Austl. H3 51
Gorontalo, Indon. E6 34
Gorore, Ire. q21 27
Gort, Ire. D3 11
Gortahork, Ire. B3 11
Gorumna, i., Ire. D2 11
Goryn, stm., Sov. Un. F6 27
Gorzów [Wielkopolski], Pol. . . B3 26
Gosford, Austl. F8 51
Goshen, Ca., U.S. D4 82
Goshen, Al., U.S. D3 78
Goshen, Ct., U.S. B3 84
Goshen, In., U.S. A6 91
Goshen, Ky., U.S. g11 94
Goshen, Ma., U.S. B2 98
Goshen, N.H., U.S. D2 106
Goshen, N.J., U.S. E3 107
Goshen, N.Y., U.S. D6 109
Goshen, Oh., U.S. C1 112
Goshen, Or., U.S. D3 114
Goshen, Ut., U.S. D4 121
Goshen, Va., U.S. C3 123
Goshen, co., Wy., U.S. D8 127
Goshen Hole, Wy., U.S. D8 127
Goshogawara, Japan F10 33
Goshute Indian Reservation,
    U.S. D7 105
Goshute Lake, l., Nv., U.S. . . C7 105
Goshute Mountains, mts., Nv.,
    U.S. C7 105
Goslar, Ger. C5 18
Gosnell, Ar., U.S. *B6 81
Gosnells, Austl. *F2 50
Gosper, co., Ne., U.S. D6 104
Gospić, Yugo. C2 24
Gosport, Eng., U.K. D6 12
Gosport, Al., U.S. D2 78
Gosport, In., U.S. F4 91
Gossau, Switz. B7 21
Gossville, Tn., U.S. B5 119
Gossville, N.H., U.S. D4 106
Gostivar, Yugo. E5 24
Gostyń, Pol. C4 26
Gostynin, Pol. B5 26
Gostynka, stm., Pol. g9 26
Gotebo, Ok., U.S. B3 113
Göteborg (Gothenburg), Swe. . I4 14
Göteborg och Bohus, co.,
    Swe. A5 15
Gotel Mountains, mts., Afr. . . D2 46
Gotemba, Japan n18 33
Gotha, Ger. C5 18
Gotham, Wi., U.S. E3 126
Gothenburg, Ne., U.S. D5 104
Gotland, i., Swe. I8 14
Gotō Islands, is., Japan J4 33
Gotse Delchev (Nevrokop),
    Bul. E6 24
Göttingen, Ger. C4 18
Gottwaldov (Zlín), Czech. . . . D4 26
Götzis, Aus. B8 21
Goubangzi, China D9 32
Gouda, Neth. A6 16
Goudeau, La., U.S. D3 95
Goudry, Sen. D2 45
Goudoumaria, Niger D7 45
Goudswaard, Neth. C4 17
Gough, Ga., U.S. C4 87
Gough Island, i., St. Hel. . . . I9 5
Gough Lake, l., Alta. C4 68
Gouin, Réservoir, res., Que. . k12 74
Goulburn, Austl. F8 50
Gould, Que. D6 74
Gould, Ar., U.S. A4 83
Gould, Ok., U.S. C2 113
Gouldbusk, Tx., U.S. D3 120
Gould City, Mi., U.S. B5 99
Goulding, Fl., U.S. u14 86
Goulding Cay, i., Bah. m16 64
Gouldings Trading Post, Ut.,
    U.S. F5 121
Gould Island, i., R.I., U.S. . . E5 116
Goulds, Fl., U.S. s13 86
Gouldsboro, Me., U.S. D4 96
Gouldsboro, Pa., U.S. D11 115
Gouldtown, N.J., U.S. E2 107
Gouménissa, Grc. I6 25
Goundam, Mali C4 45
Gounou Gaya, Chad D3 46
Gourdon, Fr. E4 16
Goure, Niger D7 45
Gourma Rharous, Mali C4 45
Gournay-en-Bray, Fr. C4 16
Gouro, Chad B3 46
Gouverneur, N.Y., U.S. f9 109
Govan, Sask. F3 75
Gove, S.C., U.S. E5 117
Gove, co., Ks., U.S. D3 93
Govenlock, Sask. H1 75
Governador Valadares, Braz. . B4 56
Government Camp, Or., U.S. . B5 114
Governors Harbour, Bah. . . . B5 64
Govind Ballabh Pant
    Reservoir, res., India . . . F9 37
Govind Reservoir, res., India . B6 37
Gowan, stm., Man. C2 70
Gowanda, N.Y., U.S. C1 109
Gowen, Mi., U.S. E5 99
Gowen, Ok., U.S. C6 113
Gower, Mo., U.S. B3 102
Gowna, Lough, l., Ire. D4 11
Gowrie, Ia., U.S. B3 92
Goya, Arg. E4 54
Goz Beïda, Chad C4 46
Graaff-Reinet, S. Afr. D3 49
Grabill, In., U.S. B8 91
Grabow, Ger. E5 15
Gračanica, Yugo. C4 24
Grace, Id., U.S. G7 89
Grace, Ms., U.S. C3 101
Grace, Mount, mtn., Ma., U.S. A3 98
Gracefield, Que. D2 74
Gracemont, Ok., U.S. B3 113
Graceton, Mn., U.S. B3 100
Graceville, Fl., U.S. u16 86
Graceville, Mn., U.S. E2 100

Name	Map Ref.	Page
Gracewood, Ga., U.S.	C4	87
Gracey, Ky., U.S.	D2	94
Gracias, Hond.	E7	63
Graciosa, i., Port.	g9	44
Gradačac, Yugo.	C4	24
Gradizhsk, Sov. Un.	G9	27
Grado, Italy	D9	20
Grado, Spain	A2	22
Grady, Ar., U.S.	C4	81
Grady, N.M., U.S.	C6	108
Grady, Ok., U.S.	C4	113
Grady, co., Ga., U.S.	F2	87
Grady, co., Ok., U.S.	C4	113
Gradyville, Ky., U.S.	C4	94
Graettinger, Ia., U.S.	A3	92
Grafenau, Ger.	E9	19
Graford, Tx., U.S.	C3	120
Grafton, Austl.	E9	50
Grafton, Ont.	D6	73
Grafton, Il., U.S.	E3	90
Grafton, Ia., U.S.	A4	92
Grafton, Ma., U.S.	B4	98
Grafton, Ne., U.S.	D8	104
Grafton, N.H., U.S.	C3	106
Grafton, N.Y., U.S.	C7	109
Grafton, N.D., U.S.	A8	111
Grafton, Oh., U.S.	A3	112
Grafton, Va., U.S.	h15	123
Grafton, W.V., U.S.	B4	125
Grafton, Wi., U.S.	E6	126
Grafton, co., N.H., U.S.	C3	106
Grafton Center, N.H., U.S.	C3	106
Graham, Ca., U.S.	*n12	82
Graham, Fl., U.S.	C4	86
Graham, Ga., U.S.	E4	87
Graham, Ky., U.S.	C2	94
Graham, Mo., U.S.	A2	102
Graham, N.C., U.S.	A3	110
Graham, Ok., U.S.	C4	113
Graham, Tn., U.S.	B4	119
Graham, Tx., U.S.	C3	120
Graham, Wa., U.S.	B3	124
Graham, co., Az., U.S.	E5	80
Graham, co., Ks., U.S.	C4	93
Graham, co., N.C., U.S.	f9	110
Graham, stm., B.C.	A6	69
Graham, Lake, res., Tx., U.S.	C3	120
Graham, Mount, mtn., Az., U.S.	E6	80
Graham Bell, i., Sov. Un.	A7	128
Graham Creek, stm., In., U.S.	G6	91
Graham Island, i., B.C.	C1	69
Graham Island, i., N.W. Ter.	m33	66
Graham Lake, i., Alta.	A3	68
Graham Lake, i., Me., U.S.	D4	96
Graham Land, reg., Ant.	C6	7
Grahamstown, S. Afr.	D4	49
Grahamsville, N.Y., U.S.	D6	109
Grahamville, S.C., U.S.	G6	117
Grahn, Ky., U.S.	B6	94
Graian Alps, mts., Eur.	E7	16
Grainfield, Ks., U.S.	C3	93
Grainger, Alta.	D4	68
Grainger, co., Tn., U.S.	C10	119
Grainland, Sask.	F2	75
Grainola, Ok., U.S.	A5	113
Grainton, Ne., U.S.	D4	104
Grain Valley, Mo., U.S.	B3	102
Grajaú, Braz.	C1	57
Grajaú, stm., Braz.	B1	57
Grajewo, Pol.	B7	26
Gram, Den.	C3	15
Gramada, Bul.	D6	24
Gramalote, Col.	B3	60
Gramastetten, Aus.	E9	19
Grambling, La., U.S.	B3	95
Gramercy, La., U.S.	h10	95
Gramling, S.C., U.S.	A3	117
Grammer, In., U.S.	F6	91
Grammichele, Italy	F5	23
Grampian, Pa., U.S.	E4	115
Grampian, prov., Scot., U.K.	C6	13
Grampian Mountains, mts., Scot., U.K.	B4	10
Gramshi, Alb.	B3	25
Gramzow, Ger.	E8	15
Gran, Mount, mtn., Ant.	B29	7
Granada, Nic.	E7	63
Granada, Spain	D4	22
Granada, Co., U.S.	C8	83
Granada, Mn., U.S.	G4	100
Granard, Ire.	C4	11
Granbury, Tx., U.S.	C4	120
Granby, Que.	D5	74
Granby, Co., U.S.	A5	83
Granby, Ct., U.S.	B4	84
Granby, Ma., U.S.	B2	98
Granby, Mo., U.S.	E3	102
Granby, Vt., U.S.	B5	122
Granby, Lake, res., Co., U.S.	A5	83
Granby, Island, i., Newf.	E4	72
Gran Canal del Desagüe, Mex.	g9	63
Gran Canaria, i., Spain	n14	22
Gran Chaco, pl., S.A.	D3	55
Grand, co., Co., U.S.	A4	83
Grand, co., Ut., U.S.	E6	121
Grand, stm., Ont.	D4	73
Grand, stm., Mi., U.S.	E5	99
Grand, stm., Mo., U.S.	A3	102
Grand, stm., Oh., U.S.	A4	112
Grand, stm., S.D., U.S.	B4	118
Grand, North Fork, stm., U.S.	B2	118
Grand, South Fork, stm., S.D., U.S.	B3	118
Grand Bahama, i., Bah.	A4	64
Grand Bank, Newf.	E4	72
Grand-Bassam, I.C.	E4	45
Grand Bay, N.B.	D3	71
Grand Bay, Al., U.S.	E1	78
Grand Bayou, stm., La., U.S.	k10	95
Grand Bayou, stm., La., U.S.	h9	95
Grand Bend, Ont.	D3	73
Grand Blanc, Mi., U.S.	F7	99
Grand Bonhomme, mtn., St. Vin.	U26	65
Grand-Bourg, Guad.	I14	64
Grand Bruit, Newf.	E2	72
Grand Caillou, La., U.S.	E5	95
Grand Canal (Da Yunhe), China	E8	31
Grand Canal, Ire.	D4	11
Grand Cane, La., U.S.	B2	95
Grand Canyon, Az., U.S.	A3	80
Grand Canyon, Az., U.S.	A3	80
Grand Canyon National Park, Az., U.S.	B3	80
Grand Cayman, i., Cay. Is.	D8	63
Grand Centre, Alta.	B5	68
Grand Cess, Lib.	F3	45
Grand Chenier, La., U.S.	E3	95
Grand Codroy, stm., Newf.	E2	72
Grand Combin, mtn., Switz.	D3	20
Grand Coteau, La., U.S.	D3	95
Grand Coulee, Wa., U.S.	B6	124
Grand Coulee Dam, Wa., U.S.	B6	124
Grande, stm., Arg.	B3	54
Grande, stm., Arg.	D2	55
Grande, stm., Bol.	C3	55
Grande, stm., Braz.	B2	56
Grande, stm., Braz.	D2	57
Grande, Bahía, b., Arg.	E3	54
Grande, Boca, mth., Ven.	B5	60
Grande, Ilha, i., Braz.	h5	56
Grande, Rio, stm., N.A.	E7	76
Grande, Serra, mts., Braz.	C2	57
Grande-Anse, N.B.	B4	71
Grand Cache, Alta.	C1	68
Grand Ecore, La., U.S.	C2	95
Grande de Arecibo, stm., P.R.	B2	65
Grande [de Matagalpa], stm., Nic.	E8	63
Grande de Santiago, stm., Mex.	C3	63
Grande de Tarija, stm., S.A.	D5	55
Grande-Digue, N.B.	D4	74
Grande-Ligne, Que.	D4	74
Grande-Entrée, Que.	B8	71
Grande Prairie, Alta.	B1	68
Grand Erg de Bilma, des., Niger	C7	45
Grand Erg Occidental, des., Alg.	C5	44
Grand Erg Oriental, des., Alg.	C6	44
Grande rivière de la Baleine, stm., Que.	g11	74
Grande Ronde, stm., U.S.	C8	124
Grandes, Salinas, pl., Arg.	F2	55
Grandes-Bergeronnes, Que.	A8	74
Grandes-Piles, Que.	C5	74
Grande-Étang, N.S.	C8	71
Grande-Terre, i., Guad.	Q9	65
Grande Vigie, Pointe de la, c., Guad.	P9	65
Grand Falls (Grand-Sault), N.B.	B2	71
Grand Falls, Newf.	D4	72
Grandfalls, Tx., U.S.	D1	120
Grand Falls, wtfl., Me., U.S.	C5	96
Grand Falls Lake, i., N.A.	C5	96
Grandfather Mountain, mtn., N.C., U.S.	A1	110
Grandfield, Ok., U.S.	C3	113
Grand Forks, B.C.	E8	69
Grand Forks, N.D., U.S.	B8	111
Grand Forks, co., N.D., U.S.	B8	111
Grand Forks Air Force Base, mil., N.D., U.S.	B8	111
Grand Glaise, Ar., U.S.	B4	81
Grand Gorge, N.Y., U.S.	C6	109
Grand Gulf, Ms., U.S.	C2	101
Grand Harbour, N.B.	E3	71
Grand Haven, Mi., U.S.	E4	99
Grand Hogback, mtn., Co., U.S.	B3	83
Grand Island, Ne., U.S.	D7	104
Grand Island, i., La., U.S.	D6	95
Grand Island, i., Mi., U.S.	B4	99
Grand Isle, La., U.S.	E6	95
Grand Isle, Me., U.S.	A4	96
Grand Isle, Vt., U.S.	B2	122
Grand Isle, co., Vt., U.S.	B2	122
Grand Isle, i., La., U.S.	E6	95
Grand Junction, Co., U.S.	B2	83
Grand Junction, Ia., U.S.	B3	92
Grand Junction, Mi., U.S.	F4	99
Grand Junction, Tn., U.S.	B3	119
Grand lac Bostonnais, l., Que.	B5	74
Grand-Lahou, I.C.	E3	45
Grand Lake, Co., U.S.	A5	83
Grand Lake, La., U.S.	D2	95
Grand Lake, l., N.B.	D3	71
Grand Lake, l., Newf.	B1	72
Grand Lake, l., Newf.	D3	72
Grand Lake, l., N.A.	C5	96
Grand Lake, l., La., U.S.	E6	95
Grand Lake, l., La., U.S.	E3	95
Grand Lake, l., Mi., U.S.	C7	99
Grand Lake, l., Oh., U.S.	B1	112
Grand Lake Matagamon, l., Me., U.S.	B4	96
Grand Lake Seboeis, l., Me., U.S.	B4	96
Grand Lake Stream, Me., U.S.	C5	96
Grand Ledge, Mi., U.S.	F6	99
Grand Lieu, Lac de, l., Fr.	D3	16
Grand Manan Channel, strt., N.A.	D6	96
Grand Manan Island, i., N.B.	E3	71
Grand Marais, Mi., U.S.	B5	99
Grand Marais, Mn., U.S.	k9	100
Grand Marsh, Wi., U.S.	E4	126
Grand Meadow, Mn., U.S.	G6	100
Grand-Mère, Que.	C5	74
Grand Mesa, mtn., Co., U.S.	C2	83
Grand Mound, Ia., U.S.	C7	92
Grand Pass, Mo., U.S.	B4	102
Grand Portage, Mn., U.S.	k10	100
Grand Portage Indian Reservation, Mn., U.S.	k10	100
Grand Portage National Monument, Mn., U.S.	h10	100
Grand Prairie, Tx., U.S.	n10	120
Grand Pré, N.S.	D5	71
Grand Rapids, Man.	C2	70
Grand Rapids, Mi., U.S.	F5	99
Grand Rapids, Mn., U.S.	C5	100
Grand Rapids, N.D., U.S.	C7	111
Grand Rapids, Oh., U.S.	f6	112
Grand Ridge, Fl., U.S.	B1	86
Grand Ridge, Il., U.S.	B5	90
Grand River, N.S.	D9	71
Grand River, Ia., U.S.	D4	92
Grand River, Ky., U.S.	f9	94
Grand' Rivière, Mart.	S10	65
Grand Ronde, Or., U.S.	B3	114
Grand Saline, Tx., U.S.	C5	120
Grand Santi, Fr. Gu.	B4	59
Grandson, Switz.	E6	20
Grand Terrace, Ca., U.S.	*E5	82
Grand Teton, mtn., Wy., U.S.	C2	127
Grand Teton National Park, Wy., U.S.	C2	127
Grand Tower, Il., U.S.	F4	90
Grand Traverse, co., Mi., U.S.	D5	99
Grand Traverse Bay, b., Mi., U.S.	C5	99
Grand Traverse Bay, East Arm, b., Mi., U.S.	D5	99
Grand Traverse Bay, West Arm, b., Mi., U.S.	D5	99
Grand Valley, Ont.	D4	73
Grand Valley, Co., U.S.	C2	115
Grand Valley, val., U.S.	B2	83
Grandview, Man.	D1	70
Grand View, Id., U.S.	G2	89
Grandview, Il., U.S.	D6	90
Grandview, In., U.S.	i4	91
Grandview, Ia., U.S.	C6	92
Grandview, Mo., U.S.	C3	102
Grandview, Oh., U.S.	C4	112
Grandview, Tn., U.S.	D9	119
Grandview, Wa., U.S.	C6	124
Grand View, Wi., U.S.	B2	126
Grandview Heights, Oh., U.S.	m10	112
Grandville, Mi., U.S.	F5	99
Grandvilliers, Fr.	E1	17
Grand Wash Cliffs, clf., Az., U.S.	B2	80
Grandy, Mn., U.S.	E5	100
Grandy, N.C., U.S.	A7	110
Grangärde (part of Ludvika), Swe.	G6	14
Grangeburg, Al., U.S.	D4	78
Grangemouth, Scot., U.K.	D5	13
Grange-over-Sands, Eng., U.K.	A5	91
Granger, Ia., U.S.	C4	92
Granger, In., U.S.	A5	91
Granger, Mo., U.S.	A6	102
Granger, Tx., U.S.	D4	120
Granger, Wa., U.S.	C5	124
Granger, Wy., U.S.	E3	127
Granges [-sur-Vologne], Fr.	A2	20
Grangeville, Id., U.S.	D2	89
Grangeville, La., U.S.	D5	95
Granisle, B.C.	B4	69
Granite, Co., U.S.	B4	83
Granite, Ok., U.S.	C2	113
Granite, Or., U.S.	C8	114
Granite, Ut., U.S.	*C4	121
Granite, co., Mt., U.S.	D3	103
Granite Canon, Wy., U.S.	E7	127
Granite City, Il., U.S.	E3	90
Granite Falls, Mn., U.S.	F3	100
Granite Falls, N.C., U.S.	B1	110
Granite Falls, Wa., U.S.	A4	124
Granite Harbor, b., Ant.	e39	7
Granite Lake, res., Newf.	D3	72
Granite Mountain, mtn., Ak., U.S.	B7	79
Granite Mountain, mtn., Ar., U.S.	C3	81
Granite Mountains, mts., Az., U.S.	E2	80
Granite Mountains, mts., Wy., U.S.	D5	127
Granite Park, Ut., U.S.	*C4	121
Granite Pass, Wy., U.S.	B5	127
Granite Peak, mtn., Mt., U.S.	E7	103
Granite Peak, mtn., Nv., U.S.	C2	105
Granite Peak, mtn., Nv., U.S.	B4	105
Granite Peak, mtn., Ut., U.S.	B2	121
Granite Peak, mtn., Ut., U.S.	C2	121
Granite Peak, mtn., Wy., U.S.	C3	127
Granite Point, c., Newf.	C3	72
Granite Quarry, N.C., U.S.	B2	110
Granite Range, mts., Nv., U.S.	C2	105
Graniteville, Ma., U.S.	f10	98
Graniteville, Mo., U.S.	D7	102
Graniteville, S.C., U.S.	D4	117
Graniteville, Vt., U.S.	C4	122
Granja, Braz.	D3	57
Granja de Torrehermosa, Spain	C3	22
Granma, prov., Cuba	D5	64
Grannis, Ar., U.S.	C1	81
Grano, N.D., U.S.	A4	111
Granollers, Spain	B7	22
Gran Paradiso, mtn., Italy	D3	20
Gransee, Ger.	E7	15
Grant, Al., U.S.	A3	78
Grant, Co., U.S.	C5	83
Grant, Fl., U.S.	E6	86
Grant, Ia., U.S.	C2	92
Grant, La., U.S.	D3	95
Grant, Mi., U.S.	E5	99
Grant, Mt., U.S.	E3	103
Grant, Ne., U.S.	D4	104
Grant, Ok., U.S.	D6	113
Grant, co., Ar., U.S.	C3	81
Grant, co., In., U.S.	D6	91
Grant, co., Ks., U.S.	E2	93
Grant, co., Ky., U.S.	B5	94
Grant, co., La., U.S.	C3	95
Grant, co., Mn., U.S.	E2	100
Grant, co., Ne., U.S.	C4	104
Grant, co., N.M., U.S.	E1	108
Grant, co., N.D., U.S.	C4	111
Grant, co., Ok., U.S.	A4	113
Grant, co., Or., U.S.	C7	114
Grant, co., S.D., U.S.	B9	118
Grant, co., Wa., U.S.	B6	124
Grant, co., W.V., U.S.	B5	125
Grant, co., Wi., U.S.	F3	126
Grant, Mount, mtn., Nv., U.S.	E3	105
Grant City, Mo., U.S.	A3	102
Grantham, Eng., U.K.	D6	10
Grantham, N.H., U.S.	D2	106
Granton, Ont.	D3	73
Granton, Wi., U.S.	D3	126
Grantown-on-Spey, Scot., U.K.	D5	13
Grant Park, Il., U.S.	B6	90
Grant Range, mts., Nv., U.S.	E6	105
Grants, N.M., U.S.	B2	108
Grantsboro, N.C., U.S.	B6	110
Grantsburg, Il., U.S.	F5	90
Grantsburg, Wi., U.S.	C1	126
Grantsdale, Mt., U.S.	D2	103
Grants Lick, Ky., U.S.	k14	94
Grants Pass, Or., U.S.	E3	114
Grantsville, Md., U.S.	k12	97
Grantsville, Ut., U.S.	C3	121
Grantsville, W.V., U.S.	C3	125
Grant Town, W.V., U.S.	B4	125
Grantville, Ga., U.S.	C2	87
Grantville, Ks., U.S.	C8	93
Grantville, Pa., U.S.	F8	115
Granum, Alta.	E4	68
Granville, Fr.	C5	16
Granville, Il., U.S.	B4	90
Granville, Ia., U.S.	B2	92
Granville, N.Y., U.S.	B7	109
Granville, N.D., U.S.	A5	111
Granville, Oh., U.S.	B3	112
Granville, Tn., U.S.	C8	119
Granville, Vt., U.S.	C3	122
Granville, W.V., U.S.	h11	125
Granville, co., N.C., U.S.	A4	110
Granville Centre, N.S.	E4	71
Granville Ferry, N.S.	E4	71
Granville Lake, l., Man.	A1	70
Grão Mogol, Braz.	D7	57
Grapeland, Tx., U.S.	D5	120
Grapeview, Wa., U.S.	C4	124
Grapevine, Ca., U.S.	E4	82
Grapevine Lake, res., Tx., U.S.	n9	120
Grapevine Peak, mtn., Nv., U.S.	G4	105
Gras, Lac de, l., N.W. Ter.	D10	66
Grasonville, Md., U.S.	C5	97
Grass, stm., Man.	B7	70
Grass, stm., N.Y., U.S.	f9	109
Grass Creek, In., U.S.	C5	91
Grass Creek, Wy., U.S.	C4	127
Grasse, Fr.	F7	16
Grasselli, Al., U.S.	B3	78
Grassflat, Pa., U.S.	D5	115
Grassington, Eng., U.K.	F7	13
Grass Lake, Il., U.S.	h8	90
Grass Lake, Mi., U.S.	F6	99
Grass Lake, l., Il., U.S.	h8	90
Grassrange, Mt., U.S.	C8	103
Grass River Provincial Park, Man.	B1	70
Grasston, Mn., U.S.	E5	100
Grass Valley, Ca., U.S.	C3	82
Grass Valley, Or., U.S.	B5	114
Grassy Brook, stm., Vt., U.S.	E3	122
Grassy Butte, N.D., U.S.	B2	111
Grassy Creek, N.C., U.S.	A1	110
Grassy Lake, Alta.	E5	68
Grassy Lake, l., La., U.S.	k9	95
Gråsten, Den.	D3	15
Grates Cove, Newf.	D5	72
Grates Point, c., Newf.	D5	72
Gratiot, Oh., U.S.	C3	112
Gratiot, Wi., U.S.	F3	126
Gratiot, co., Mi., U.S.	E6	99
Gratis, Oh., U.S.	C1	112
Gratz, Pa., U.S.	E8	115
Graubünden, state, Switz.	C5	20
Graulhet, Fr.	F4	16
Gravatá, Braz.	C3	57
Grave Creek, stm., W.V., U.S.	g8	125
Gravedona, Italy	D7	21
Gravelbourg, Sask.	H2	75
Gravelines, Fr.	D2	17
Gravelly, Ar., U.S.	C2	81
Gravelly Branch, stm., De., U.S.	F4	85
Gravelly Range, mts., Mt., U.S.	E4	103
Gravenhurst, Ont.	C5	73
Grave Peak, mtn., Id., U.S.	C4	89
Graves, Ga., U.S.	E2	87
Graves, S.C., U.S.	E9	117
Graves, co., Ky., U.S.	f9	94
Gravesend, Eng., U.K.	h9	126
Gravette, Ar., U.S.	A1	81
Gravina [in Puglia], Italy	D6	23
Gravity, Ia., U.S.	D3	92
Gravois, Pointe à, c., Haiti	E7	64
Gravois Mills, Mo., U.S.	C5	102
Grawn, Mi., U.S.	D5	99
Gray, Sask.	G3	75
Gray, Fr.	D6	16
Gray, Ga., U.S.	C3	87
Gray, Ia., U.S.	C3	92
Gray, Ky., U.S.	D5	94
Gray, La., U.S.	E5	95
Gray, Me., U.S.	E2	96
Gray, co., Ks., U.S.	E3	93
Gray, co., Tx., U.S.	B2	120
Grayback Mountain, mtn., Or., U.S.	E3	114
Gray Court, S.C., U.S.	B3	117
Gray Gables, Ma., U.S.	*C6	98
Gray Horse, Ok., U.S.	A5	113
Grayland, Wa., U.S.	C1	124
Grayling, Ak., U.S.	C7	79
Grayling, Mi., U.S.	D6	99
Graylyn Crest, De., U.S.	A3	85
Graymont, Il., U.S.	C5	90
Grays, Eng., U.K.	m13	10
Grays, Ar., U.S.	B4	81
Grays Harbor, co., Wa., U.S.	B2	124
Grays Harbor, b., Wa., U.S.	C1	124
Grayslake, Il., U.S.	A5	90
Grays Lake, sw., Id., U.S.	F7	89
Grayson, Sask.	G4	75
Grayson, Al., U.S.	A3	78
Grayson, Ga., U.S.	C3	87
Grayson, Ky., U.S.	B7	94
Grayson, co., Ky., U.S.	C3	94
Grayson, co., Tx., U.S.	C4	120
Grayson, co., Va., U.S.	D1	123
Grayson, Lake, res., Ky., U.S.	B7	94
Grays Peak, mtn., Co., U.S.	B5	83
Grays River, Wa., U.S.	C2	124
Gray Summit, Mo., U.S.	g12	102
Graysville, Al., U.S.	f7	78
Graysville, In., U.S.	F2	91
Graysville, Pa., U.S.	G1	115
Graysville, Tn., U.S.	D8	119
Grayville, Il., U.S.	E5	90
Graz, Aus.	B2	24
Greasewood, Az., U.S.	B6	80
Great, stm., Jam.	E13	65
Great Abaco, i., Bah.	A5	64
Great Alföld, pl., Hung.	B5	24
Great Artesian Basin, Austl.	E7	50
Great Australian Bight, Austl.	F4	50
Great Averill Pond, l., Vt., U.S.	B5	122
Great Barrier Island, i., N.Z.	L15	51
Great Barrier Reef, rf., Austl.	C8	50
Great Barrington, Ma., U.S.	B1	98
Great Basin, U.S.	C4	76
Great Basin National Park, Nv., U.S.	E7	105
Great Bay, b., N.H., U.S.	D5	106
Great Bay, b., N.J., U.S.	D4	107
Great Bear Lake, l., N.W. Ter.	C8	66
Great Bend, Ks., U.S.	D5	93
Great Bend, N.D., U.S.	C9	111
Great Bend, Pa., U.S.	C10	115
Great Bitter Lake, l., Eg.	D4	41
Great Blasket Island, i., Ire.	E1	11
Great Blue Hill, hill, Ma., U.S.	B5	98
Great Burnt Lake, l., Newf.	D3	72
Great Cacapon, W.V., U.S.	B6	125
Great Camanoe, i., V.I. Br.	B6	65
Great Captain Island, i., Ct., U.S.	F1	84
Great Channel, strt., Asia	G9	36
Great Deer, Sask.	E2	75
Great Dismal Swamp, sw., U.S.	D6	123
Great Divide Basin, Wy., U.S.	E4	127
Great Dividing Range, mts., Austl.	F9	50
Great Driffield, Eng., U.K.	G7	13
Great Duck Island, i., Ont.	B2	73
Great East Lake, l., U.S.	C5	106
Great Egg Harbor, stm., N.J., U.S.	D3	107
Greater Antilles, is., N.A.	H13	61
Greater Cincinnati Airport, Ky., U.S.	h13	94
Greater Khingan Range see Da Hinggan Ling, mts., China	B9	31
Greater London, co., Eng., U.K.	C7	12
Greater Manchester, co., Eng., U.K.	*A5	12
Great Exuma, i., Bah.	C6	64
Great Fall, wtfl., Guy.	A2	59
Great Falls, mtn., U.S.	D3	70
Great Falls, Mt., U.S.	C5	103
Great Falls, S.C., U.S.	B6	117
Great Falls Dam, Tn., U.S.	D6	119
Great Guana Cay, i., Bah.	B5	64
Great Harbour Deep, b., Newf.	C3	72
Greathouse Peak, mtn., Mt., U.S.	D7	103
Great Inagua, i., Bah.	D7	64
Great Indian Desert (Thar Desert), des., Asia	C5	36
Great Island, spit, Ma., U.S.	C7	98
Great Island, i., N.C., U.S.	B6	110
Great Karroo, plat., S. Afr.	D3	49
Great Lake, l., Austl.	o15	50
Great Lakes Naval Training Center, mil., Il., U.S.	h9	90
Great Malvern, Eng., U.K.	B5	12
Great Miami, stm., U.S.	C1	112
Great Misery Island, i., Ma., U.S.	f12	98
Great Moose Lake, l., Me., U.S.	D3	96
Great Neck, N.Y., U.S.	h13	109
Great Neck Estates, N.Y., U.S.	*E7	109
Great Nicobar, i., India	G9	36
Great North Mountain, mtn., U.S.	C6	125
Great Ouse, stm., Eng., U.K.	D7	10
Great Pedro Bluff, c., Jam.	F13	65
Great Pee Dee, stm., U.S.	D9	117
Great Point, c., Ma., U.S.	D4	98
Great Pond, Me., U.S.	D3	96
Great Pond, l., Ma., U.S.	h12	98
Great Pond, l., Ma., U.S.	h11	98
Great Quittacas Pond, l., Ma., U.S.	C6	98
Great Ruaha, stm., Tan.	C6	48
Great Sacandaga Lake, l., N.Y., U.S.	C6	109
Great Saint Bernard Pass, Eur.	B1	23
Great Salt Lake, l., Ut., U.S.	B3	121
Great Salt Lake Desert, des., Ut., U.S.	C2	121
Great Salt Plains Lake, res., Ok., U.S.	A3	113
Great Salt Pond, l., Jam.	F15	65
Great Sand Dunes National Monument, Co., U.S.	D5	83
Great Sand Hills, hills, Sask.	G1	75
Great Sandy Desert, des., Austl.	D4	50
Great Sea Reef, rf., Fiji	H15	52
Great Seneca Creek, stm., Md., U.S.	B3	97
Great Skellig Island, i., Ire.	F11	11
Great Slave Lake, l., N.W. Ter.	D10	66
Great Smoky Mountains, mts., U.S.	B8	119
Great Smoky Mountains National Park, U.S.	B8	119
Great Sound, strt., Ber.	p19	64
Great Swamp, sw., R.I., U.S.	F3	116
Great Tenasserim, stm., Burma	F3	35
Great Torrington, Eng., U.K.	D12	12
Great Valley, val., U.S.	C2	123
Great Victoria Desert, des., Austl.	E4	50
Great Village, N.S.	D6	71
Great Wall, hist., China	C8	31
Great Wass Island, i., Me., U.S.	D5	96
Great Yarmouth, Eng., U.K.	D7	10
Great Zab, stm., Asia	D14	40
Gredos, Sierra de, mts., Spain	B3	22
Greece, N.Y., U.S.	B3	109
Greece, ctry., Eur.	C4	40
Greeley, Co., U.S.	A6	83
Greeley, Ia., U.S.	B6	92
Greeley, Ks., U.S.	C8	93
Greeley, Ne., U.S.	C7	104
Greeley, Pa., U.S.	D12	115
Greeley, co., Ks., U.S.	D2	93
Greeley, co., Ne., U.S.	C7	104
Greeleyville, S.C., U.S.	D8	117
Greely Fiord, N.W. Ter.	k35	66
Green, Ks., U.S.	C6	93
Green, Or., U.S.	D3	114
Green, co., Ky., U.S.	C4	94
Green, co., Wi., U.S.	F4	126
Green, stm., N.B.	B1	71
Green, stm., U.S.	C6	76
Green, stm., Il., U.S.	B4	90
Green, stm., Ky., U.S.	C2	94
Green, stm., Wa., U.S.	B3	124
Greenacres, Ca., U.S.	*E4	82
Greenacres, Wa., U.S.	B8	124
Greenacres City, Fl., U.S.	F6	86
Greenback, Tn., U.S.	D9	119
Greenbackville, Va., U.S.	D7	123
Green Bank, N.J., U.S.	D3	107
Green Bank, W.V., U.S.	C4	125
Green Bay, Wi., U.S.	D6	126
Green Bay, b., U.S.	D3	126
Greenbelt, Md., U.S.	C4	97
Greenbriar, Al., U.S.	g12	123
Greenbrier, Ar., U.S.	B3	81
Greenbrier, Tn., U.S.	A5	119
Greenbrier, co., W.V., U.S.	D4	125
Greenbrier, stm., W.V., U.S.	D4	125
Green Brook, N.J., U.S.	*B4	107
Greenbush, Mn., U.S.	B2	100
Greenbush, Mi., U.S.	D7	99
Greenbush, Wi., U.S.	k9	126
Green Camp, Oh., U.S.	B2	112
Greencastle, In., U.S.	E4	91
Greencastle, Pa., U.S.	G6	115
Green City, Mo., U.S.	A5	102
Green Court, Alta.	B3	68
Green Cove Springs, Fl., U.S.	C5	86
Green Creek, N.J., U.S.	E3	107
Greendale, In., U.S.	F8	91
Greendale, Ut., U.S.	*C6	121
Greendale, Wi., U.S.	F6	126
Greendell, N.J., U.S.	B3	107
Greene, Ia., U.S.	B5	92
Greene, Me., U.S.	D2	96
Greene, N.Y., U.S.	C5	109
Greene, N.D., U.S.	A4	111
Greene, co., Al., U.S.	C1	78
Greene, co., Ar., U.S.	A5	81
Greene, co., Ga., U.S.	C3	87
Greene, co., Il., U.S.	D3	90
Greene, co., In., U.S.	F4	91
Greene, co., Ia., U.S.	B3	92
Greene, co., Ms., U.S.	D5	101
Greene, co., Mo., U.S.	D4	102
Greene, co., N.Y., U.S.	C6	109
Greene, co., N.C., U.S.	B5	110
Greene, co., Oh., U.S.	C2	112
Greene, co., Pa., U.S.	G1	115
Greene, co., Tn., U.S.	C11	119
Greene, co., Va., U.S.	B4	123
Greeneville, Tn., U.S.	C11	119
Greenfield, Ar., U.S.	B5	81
Greenfield, Ca., U.S.	D3	82
Greenfield, Il., U.S.	D3	90
Greenfield, In., U.S.	E6	91
Greenfield, Ia., U.S.	C3	92
Greenfield, Ma., U.S.	A2	98
Greenfield, Me., U.S.	C4	96
Greenfield, Mo., U.S.	D4	102
Greenfield, N.H., U.S.	E3	106
Greenfield, N.M., U.S.	D5	108
Greenfield, Oh., U.S.	C2	112
Greenfield, Ok., U.S.	A3	113
Greenfield, Tn., U.S.	A3	119
Greenfield, Va., U.S.	C4	123
Greenfield, Wi., U.S.	n11	126
Greenfield Plaza, Ia., U.S.	e8	92
Green Forest, Ar., U.S.	A2	81
Green Grass, S.D., U.S.	B4	118
Green Harbor, Ma., U.S.	B6	98
Greenhill, Al., U.S.	A2	78
Greenhill, N.S.	D3	71
Green Hill, R.I., U.S.	G3	116
Green Hill Pond, l., R.I., U.S.	G3	116
Greenhills, Oh., U.S.	n12	112
Greenhorn Creek, stm., Co., U.S.	D6	83
Green Island, Ia., U.S.	B7	92
Green Island, N.Y., U.S.	*C7	109
Green Isle, Mn., U.S.	F4	100
Green Lake, Sask.	C2	75
Green Lake, Ut., U.S.	*C6	121
Green Lake, Wi., U.S.	E5	126
Green Lake, co., Wi., U.S.	E4	126
Green Lake, l., B.C.	D7	69
Green Lake, l., Sask.	C2	75
Green Lake, l., Me., U.S.	D4	96
Green Lake, l., Wi., U.S.	E5	126
Greenland, Ar., U.S.	B1	81
Greenland, Mi., U.S.	B1	99
Greenland (Kalaallit Nunaat), ctry., N.A.	B16	61
Greenland Sea	B15	128
Greenlawn, N.Y., U.S.	*h13	109
Greenleaf, Ks., U.S.	C7	93
Greenleaf, Wi., U.S.	D5	126
Green Lookout Mountain, mtn., Wa., U.S.	D3	124
Green Lowther, mtn., Scot., U.K.	E5	13
Green Manorville, Ct., U.S.	B5	84
Greenmount, Md., U.S.	A4	97
Green Mountain, Ia., U.S.	B5	92
Green Mountain Falls, Co., U.S.	f10	110
Green Mountain Reservoir, res., Co., U.S.	*C6	83
Green Mountains, mts., Vt., U.S.	B4	83
Green Mountains, mts., Wy., U.S.	F2	122
Green Mountains, mts., Wy., U.S.	D5	127
Greenock, Pa., U.S.	F2	115
Greenock, Scot., U.K.	C4	10
Greenore Point, c., Ire.	E5	11
Greenough, Mt., U.S.	D3	103
Greenough, Point, c., Ont.	C3	73
Green Peter Lake, res., Or., U.S.	C4	114
Green Pond, Al., U.S.	B2	78
Green Pond, S.C., U.S.	F6	117
Green Pond, N.J., U.S.	A4	107
Green Pond Mountain, mtn., N.J., U.S.	B3	107
Greenport, N.Y., U.S.	m16	109
Green Ridge, Mo., U.S.	C4	102
Green River, Ut., U.S.	E5	121
Green River, Wy., U.S.	E3	127
Green River Lake, res., Ky., U.S.	C4	94
Green River Lock and Dam, U.S.	I2	91
Green River Reservoir, res., Vt., U.S.	B3	122
Green Rock, Il., U.S.	B3	90
Greensboro, Al., U.S.	C2	78
Greensboro, Fl., U.S.	B2	86
Greensboro, Ga., U.S.	C3	87
Greensboro, In., U.S.	E7	91
Greensboro, Md., U.S.	C6	97
Greensboro, N.C., U.S.	A3	110
Greensboro, Pa., U.S.	G2	115
Greensboro, Vt., U.S.	B4	122
Greensboro Bend, Vt., U.S.	B4	122
Greensburg, In., U.S.	F7	91
Greensburg, Ks., U.S.	E4	93
Greensburg, Ky., U.S.	C4	94
Greensburg, La., U.S.	D5	95
Greensburg, Pa., U.S.	F2	115
Green Sea, S.C., U.S.	C10	117
Greens Fork, In., U.S.	E7	91
Greenspond, Newf.	D5	72
Green Spring, W.V., U.S.	B6	125
Green Springs, Oh., U.S.	A2	112
Green Sulphur Springs, W.V., U.S.	D4	125
Green Swamp, sw., N.C., U.S.	C4	110
Greentown, In., U.S.	D6	91
Greentown, Oh., U.S.	B4	112
Greentree, Pa., U.S.	*k13	115
Greenup, Il., U.S.	D5	90

Name	Map Ref.	Page
Greenup, Ky., U.S.	B7	94
Greenup, co., Ky., U.S.	B7	94
Green Valley, Az., U.S.	F5	80
Green Valley, Il., U.S.	C4	90
Green Valley, Mn., U.S.	F3	100
Green Valley, Wi., U.S.	D5	126
Green Valley, val., Tx., U.S.	p13	120
Greenview, Il., U.S.	C4	90
Greenview, W.V., U.S.	n12	125
Greenville, Lib.	E3	45
Greenville, Al., U.S.	D3	78
Greenville, Ca., U.S.	B3	82
Greenville, De., U.S.	A3	85
Greenville, Fl., U.S.	B3	86
Greenville, Ga., U.S.	C2	87
Greenville, Il., U.S.	E4	90
Greenville, In., U.S.	H6	91
Greenville, Ia., U.S.	A2	92
Greenville, Ky., U.S.	C2	94
Greenville, Me., U.S.	C3	96
Greenville, Mi., U.S.	E5	99
Greenville, Ms., U.S.	B2	101
Greenville, Mo., U.S.	D7	102
Greenville, N.H., U.S.	E3	106
Greenville, N.Y., U.S.	*n15	109
Greenville, N.C., U.S.	B5	110
Greenville, Oh., U.S.	B1	112
Greenville, Pa., U.S.	D1	115
Greenville, R.I., U.S.	C3	116
Greenville, S.C., U.S.	B3	117
Greenville, Tx., U.S.	C4	120
Greenville, Ut., U.S.	E3	121
Greenville, Va., U.S.	C3	123
Greenville, W.V., U.S.	D4	125
Greenville, Wi., U.S.	h8	126
Greenville, co., S.C., U.S.	B3	117
Greenville Creek, stm., Oh., U.S.	B1	112
Greenville Junction, Me., U.S.	C3	96
Greenwald, Mn., U.S.	E4	100
Greenwater Lake Provincial Park, Sask.	E4	75
Greenway, Man.	E2	70
Greenway, Ar., U.S.	A5	81
Greenwell Springs, La., U.S.	D5	95
Greenwich (part of London), Eng., U.K.	m13	10
Greenwich, Ct., U.S.	E1	84
Greenwich, Ks., U.S.	g12	93
Greenwich, N.J., U.S.	E2	107
Greenwich, N.Y., U.S.	B7	109
Greenwich, Oh., U.S.	A3	112
Greenwich, Ut., U.S.	E4	121
Greenwich, Va., U.S.	*B5	123
Greenwich Bay, b., R.I., U.S.	D4	116
Greenwich Hill, N.B.	D3	71
Greenwich Point, c., Ct., U.S.	E1	84
Greenwood, B.C.	E8	69
Greenwood, De., U.S.	E3	85
Greenwood, Fl., U.S.	B1	86
Greenwood, In., U.S.	E5	91
Greenwood, Ky., U.S.	D5	94
Greenwood, La., U.S.	B2	95
Greenwood, Ms., U.S.	B3	101
Greenwood, Mo., U.S.	k11	102
Greenwood, Ne., U.S.	D9	104
Greenwood, N.Y., U.S.	C3	109
Greenwood, Pa., U.S.	E5	115
Greenwood, S.C., U.S.	C3	117
Greenwood, S.D., U.S.	E7	118
Greenwood, Wi., U.S.	D6	126
Greenwood, co., Ks., U.S.	E7	93
Greenwood, co., S.C., U.S.	C3	117
Greenwood, Lake, res., In., U.S.	G4	91
Greenwood, Lake, res., S.C., U.S.	C4	117
Greenwood Lake, N.Y., U.S.	D6	109
Greenwood Lake, l., U.S.	A4	107
Greenwood Lake, l., Mn., U.S.	C7	100
Greenwood Village, Co., U.S.	*B6	83
Greer, Id., U.S.	C2	89
Greer, Mo., U.S.	E6	102
Greer, S.C., U.S.	B3	117
Greer, co., Ok., U.S.	C2	113
Greers Ferry Lake, res., Ar., U.S.	B3	81
Greeson, Lake, res., Ar., U.S.	C2	81
Greetsiel, Ger.	A7	19
Gregg, co., Tx., U.S.	C5	120
Gregoire Lake, l., Alta.	A5	68
Gregory, Ar., U.S.	B4	81
Gregory, Mi., U.S.	F6	99
Gregory, N.C., U.S.	A6	110
Gregory, S.D., U.S.	D6	118
Gregory, co., S.D., U.S.	D6	118
Gregory, stm., Austl.	C6	50
Gregory, Lake, l., Austl.	E6	50
Gregory Bald, mtn., Tn., U.S.	D10	119
Gregory Range, mts., Austl.	C7	50
Greifswald, Ger.	A6	18
Greifswalder Bodden, b., Ger.	D7	15
Greig, N.Y., U.S.	B5	109
Greilickville, Mi., U.S.	D5	99
Grein, Aus.	D7	18
Greiz, Ger.	C6	18
Grelton, Oh., U.S.	A1	112
Gremyachinsk, Sov. Un.	D20	8
Grená, Den.	B4	15
Grenada, Ca., U.S.	B2	82
Grenada, Ms., U.S.	B4	101
Grenada, co., Ms., U.S.	B4	101
Grenada, ctry., N.A.	J14	64
Grenada Lake, res., Ms., U.S.	B4	101
Grenade, Fr.	F4	16
Grenadine Islands, is., N.A.	V26	65
Grenagh, Ire.	E3	11
Grenay, Fr.	D2	17
Grenchen, Switz.	B3	20
Grenen (The Skaw), spit, Den.	A4	15
Grenfell, Sask.	G4	75
Grenoble, Fr.	E6	16
Grenola, Ks., U.S.	E7	93
Grenora, N.D., U.S.	A2	111
Grenville, Que.	D3	74
Grenville, Gren.	W25	65
Grenville, N.M., U.S.	A6	108
Grenville, S.D., U.S.	B8	118
Grenville, co., Ont.	C9	73
Grenville, Cape, c., Austl.	B7	50
Grenville, Point, c., Wa., U.S.	B1	124
Grenville Channel, strt., B.C.	C3	69
Gresham, Or., U.S.	B4	114
Gresham, S.C., U.S.	D9	117
Gresham, Wi., U.S.	D5	126
Gresham Park, Ga., U.S.	*h8	87
Gretna, Man.	E3	70
Gretna, Scot., U.K.	F5	10
Gretna, Fl., U.S.	B2	86
Gretna, La., U.S.	E5	95
Gretna, Ne., U.S.	D9	104
Gretna, Va., U.S.	D3	123
Greven, Ger.	A2	19
Grevená, Grc.	B3	25
Grevenbroich, Ger.	B1	19
Grevesmühlen, Ger.	E5	15
Grey, co., Ont.	C4	73
Grey, stm., Newf.	E3	72
Grey, Wi., N.Z.	O13	51
Greybull, Wy., U.S.	B4	127
Greybull, stm., Wy., U.S.	B4	127
Greycliff, Mt., U.S.	E7	103
Grey Islands, is., Newf.	C4	72
Greylock, Mount, mtn., Ma., U.S.	A1	98
Grey Range, mts., Austl.	E7	50
Greys, stm., Wy., U.S.	C2	127
Greystone, Ct., U.S.	C3	84
Greystone, N.C., U.S.	A4	110
Greytown, S. Afr.	C5	49
Greytown, N.Z.	O13	51
Gribbell Island, i., B.C.	C3	69
Gridley, Ca., U.S.	C3	82
Gridley, Il., U.S.	C5	90
Gridley, Ks., U.S.	D8	93
Gridley Mountain, mtn., Ct., U.S.	A2	84
Griekwastad, S. Afr.	C3	49
Griesheim, Ger.	D3	19
Grieskirchen, Aus.	D6	18
Griffin, Sask.	H4	75
Griffin, Ga., U.S.	C2	87
Griffin, In., U.S.	H2	91
Griffiss Air Force Base, mil., N.Y., U.S.	B5	109
Griffith, Austl.	F8	50
Griffith, In., U.S.	A3	91
Griffith Island, i., Ont.	C4	73
Griffithsville, W.V., U.S.	C3	125
Grifton, N.C., U.S.	B5	110
Griggs, Ok., U.S.	e8	113
Griggs, co., N.D., U.S.	B7	111
Griggstown, N.J., U.S.	C3	107
Griggsville, Il., U.S.	D3	90
Grijalva, stm., Mex.	B9	24
Grim, Cape, c., Austl.	o14	50
Grimari, Cen. Afr. Rep.	D4	46
Grimes, Al., U.S.	D4	78
Grimes, Ia., U.S.	C4	92
Grimes, co., Tx., U.S.	D4	120
Grimesland, N.C., U.S.	B5	110
Grimma, Ger.	C6	18
Grimmen, Ger.	D7	15
Grimmialp, Switz.	C4	21
Grimms Landing, W.V., U.S.	C3	125
Grimsby, Ont.	D5	73
Grimsby, Eng., U.K.	D6	10
Grímsey, i., Ice.	m23	14
Grimshaw, Alta.	A2	68
Grimstad, Nor.	H3	14
Grimsthorpe, Ont.	B2	73
Grindall Creek, Va., U.S.	n18	123
Grindelwald, Switz.	C5	21
Grindsted, Den.	C2	15
Grindstone, Me., U.S.	C4	96
Grind Stone City, Mi., U.S.	D8	99
Grinem, i., Marsh Is.	S18	52
Grinnell, Ia., U.S.	C5	92
Grinnell, Ks., U.S.	C3	93
Grinnell Peninsula, pen., N.W. Ter.	m32	66
Grise Fiord, N.W. Ter.	m35	66
Gris-Nez, Cap, c., Fr.	D9	12
Grissom Air Force Base, mil., In., U.S.	C5	91
Griswold, Man.	E1	70
Griswold, Ia., U.S.	C2	92
Griswoldville, Ma., U.S.	A2	98
Grizzly Mountain, mtn., Id., U.S.	B2	89
Grizzly Mountain, mtn., Or., U.S.	C6	114
Grizzly Mountain, mtn., Wa., U.S.	A7	124
Groais Island, i., Newf.	C4	72
Grodków, Pol.	C4	26
Grodno, Sov. Un.	E4	27
Grodzisk Mazowiecki, Pol.	m13	26
Grodzisk [Wielkopolski], Pol.	B4	26
Groenlo, Neth.	B6	17
Groesbeck, Oh., U.S.	*o12	112
Groesbeck, Tx., U.S.	D4	120
Groix, Île de, i., Fr.	D2	16
Grójec, Pol.	C6	26
Grombalia, Tun.	F3	23
Gronau, Ger.	B6	18
Gronau, Ger.	A4	19
Groningen, Neth.	A7	16
Groningen, Sur.	A6	17
Groningen, prov., Neth.	D5	15
Groom, Tx., U.S.	B2	120
Groom Lake, l., Nv., U.S.	F6	105
Groom Range, mts., Nv., U.S.	F6	105
Grootfontein, Nmb.	A2	49
Grootvloer, pl., S. Afr.	C3	49
Groscap, Mi., U.S.	C6	99
Grosio, Italy	D9	21
Groslay, Fr.	g10	16
Gros-Mécatina, Île du, i., Que.	C2	72
Gros Morne, mtn., Newf.	D3	72
Gros Morne National Park, Newf.	D3	72
Gross, Ne., U.S.	B7	104
Grossbreitenbach, Ger.	C6	19
Grosse Ile, Mi., U.S.	*F7	99
Grosse Île, i., Que.	B8	71
Grosse Isle Naval Air Station, mil., Mi., U.S.	p15	99
Grosse Laaber, stm., Ger.	E7	19
Grossenhain, Ger.	C6	18
Grosse Pointe, Mi., U.S.	p16	99
Grosse Pointe Farms, Mi., U.S.	*F8	99
Grosse Pointe Park, Mi., U.S.	p16	99
Grosse Pointe Woods, Mi., U.S.	p16	99
Grosser Arber, mtn., Ger.	D8	19
Grosser Röder, stm., Ger.	B8	19
Grosser Plön, l., Ger.	E7	19
Grosser Priel, mtn., Aus.	E7	18
Grosse Tete, La., U.S.	D4	95
Grosseto, Italy	C3	23
Gross-Gerau, Ger.	D3	19
Grossglockner, mtn., Aus.	C6	18
Grossmont, Ca., U.S.	o16	82
Grossostheim, Ger.	D4	19
Grossräschen, Ger.	B9	19
Grossröhrsdorf, Ger.	B8	19
Grosvenor Dale, Ct., U.S.	B8	84
Gros Ventre, stm., Wy., U.S.	C2	127
Gros Ventre Range, mts., Wy., U.S.	C2	127
Groswater Bay, b., Newf.	A3	72
Groton, Ct., U.S.	D7	84
Groton, Ma., U.S.	A4	98
Groton, N.H., U.S.	C3	106
Groton, N.Y., U.S.	C4	109
Groton, S.D., U.S.	B7	118
Groton, Vt., U.S.	C4	122
Grottaferrata, Italy	h9	23
Grottaglie, Italy	D6	23
Grottoes, Va., U.S.	B4	123
Grouard Mission, Alta.	B2	68
Grouse Creek, Ut., U.S.	B2	121
Grouse Creek, stm., Ks., U.S.	E7	93
Grouse Creek, stm., Ut., U.S.	B2	121
Grouse Creek Mountain, mtn., Id., U.S.	E5	89
Grouse Creek Mountains, mts., Ut., U.S.	B2	121
Grovania, Ga., U.S.	D3	87
Grove, Me., U.S.	C5	96
Grove, Ok., U.S.	A7	113
Grove City, Fl., U.S.	F4	86
Grove City, Mn., U.S.	E4	100
Grove City, Oh., U.S.	C2	112
Grove City, Pa., U.S.	D1	115
Grove Hill, Al., U.S.	D2	78
Groveland, Ca., U.S.	D3	82
Groveland, Fl., U.S.	D5	86
Groveland, Ma., U.S.	A5	98
Groveland, N.Y., U.S.	C3	109
Grove Mountains, mts., Ant.	B21	7
Grove Point, c., Md., U.S.	B5	97
Groveport, Oh., U.S.	C3	112
Grover, Co., U.S.	A6	83
Grover, N.C., U.S.	B1	110
Grover, Pa., U.S.	C8	115
Grover, S.C., U.S.	E6	117
Grover, Wy., U.S.	D2	127
Grover City, Ca., U.S.	E3	82
Grover Hill, Oh., U.S.	A1	112
Grovertown, In., U.S.	B4	91
Groves, Tx., U.S.	E6	120
Grovespring, Mo., U.S.	D5	102
Groveton, N.H., U.S.	A3	106
Groveton, Tx., U.S.	D5	120
Groveton, Va., U.S.	g12	123
Groveton Gardens, Va., U.S.	*B5	123
Groveville, N.J., U.S.	C3	107
Growler Peak, mtn., Az., U.S.	E2	80
Groznyy, Sov. Un.	E7	29
Grubbs, Ar., U.S.	B4	81
Grudovo, Bul.	D8	24
Grudziądz, Pol.	B5	26
Grues, Île aux, i., Que.	B7	74
Gruetli-Laager, Tn., U.S.	D8	119
Gruinard Bay, b., Scot., U.K.	C3	13
Grulla, Tx., U.S.	F3	120
Grünberg, Ger.	C4	19
Grundy, Va., U.S.	e9	123
Grundy, co., Il., U.S.	B5	90
Grundy, co., Ia., U.S.	B5	92
Grundy, co., Mo., U.S.	A4	102
Grundy, co., Tn., U.S.	D8	119
Grundy Center, Ia., U.S.	B5	92
Grünstadt, Ger.	D3	19
Grunthal, Man.	E3	70
Grüsch, Switz.	C8	21
Gruver, Ia., U.S.	A3	92
Gruver, Tx., U.S.	A2	120
Gruyères, Switz.	C3	21
Gruž (part of Dubrovnik), Yugo.	D4	24
Gryazi, Sov. Un.	E13	27
Gryazovets, Sov. Un.	B13	27
Gryfice, Pol.	B3	26
Gryfino, Pol.	B3	26
Gúdar, Sierra de, mts., Spain	B5	22
Gudauta, Sov. Un.	A13	40
Gudena, stm., Den.	B3	15
Gudermes, Sov. Un.	E3	28
Gudhjem, Den.	C8	15
Guabito, Pan.	F6	62
Guacanayabo, Golfo de, b., Cuba	D5	64
Gu Achi, Az., U.S.	E3	80
Guadalajara, Mex.	C4	63
Guadalajara, Spain	C3	22
Guadalcanal, i., Sol.Is.	G9	6
Guadalcanal, Spain	D2	22
Guadalentín, stm., Spain	D3	22
Guadalhorce, stm., Spain	D3	22
Guadalmena, stm., Spain	C4	22
Guadalope, stm., Spain	B5	22
Guadalquivir, stm., Spain	D2	22
Guadalupe, Mex.	*B4	63
Guadalupe, Az., U.S.	m9	80
Guadalupe, Ca., U.S.	E3	82
Guadalupe, co., N.M., U.S.	C5	108
Guadalupe, co., Tx., U.S.	E4	120
Guadalupe, Isla de, i., Mex.	E15	6
Guadalupe, Sierra de, mts., Spain	C2	22
Guadalupe Mountains, mts., U.S.	E5	108
Guadalupe Mountains National Park, Tx., U.S.	o12	120
Guadalupe Peak, mtn., Tx., U.S.	o12	120
Guadalupita, N.M., U.S.	A4	108
Guadarrama, stm., Spain	m17	22
Guadarrama, Sierra de, mts., Spain	B4	22
Guadeloupe, dep., N.A.	H14	64
Guadeloupe Passage, strt., N.A.	H14	64
Guadiana, stm., Eur.	D2	22
Guadiana Menor, stm., Spain	D4	22
Guadiela, stm., Spain	C4	22
Guadix, Spain	D4	22
Guafo, Isla, i., Chile	F8	55
Guagua, Phil.	o13	34
Guaíba, Braz.	C6	56
Guainía, dept., Col.	C4	60
Guainía, stm., S.A.	C4	60
Guaíra, Braz.	E4	56
Guajará Mirim, Braz.	F6	56
Gualaceo, Ec.	I3	60
Gualán, Guat.	C3	63
Gualaquiza, Ec.	D2	60
Gualeguay, Arg.	A5	54
Gualeguaychú, Arg.	A5	54
Guam, dep., Oc.	F8	6
Guamá, stm., Braz.	B1	57
Guaminí, Arg.	B4	54
Guamúchil, Mex.	B3	63
Guanacaste, Cordillera de, mts., C.R.	E5	62
Guanahacabibes, Golfo de, b., Cuba	C1	64
Guana Island, i., V.I., Br.	B6	65
Guanajay, Cuba	C2	64
Guanajuato, Mex.	C4	63
Guanajuato, state, Mex.	C4	63
Guanambi, Braz.	A4	56
Guanare, Ven.	B4	60
Guandacol, Arg.	E2	55
Guandi, China	E4	33
Guane, Cuba	C1	64
Guang'an, China	I2	32
Guangchang, China	K7	32
Guangde, China	I8	32
Guangdong, prov., China	G7	31
Guangxi Zhuangzu, prov., China	G6	31
Guangyuan, China	E6	31
Guangzhou (Canton), China	G7	31
Guánica, P.R.	C2	65
Guánica, Laguna de, l., P.R.	B2	65
Guano Lake, l., Or., U.S.	E7	114
Guantánamo, Cuba	D6	64
Guantánamo, prov., Cuba	D6	64
Guanxian, China	F6	32
Guanyun, China	G8	32
Guapí, Col.	C2	60
Guapiara, Braz.	C3	56
Guápiles, C.R.	E6	62
Guaporé (Iténez), stm., S.A.	B3	55
Guaqui, Bol.	F1	57
Guará, Braz.	A5	56
Guara, Sierra de, mts., Spain	C5	57
Guarabira, Braz.	C3	57
Guaranda, Ec.	B2	58
Guaranésia, Braz.	k8	56
Guarapari, Braz.	D2	56
Guarapuava, Braz.	B2	56
Guararapes, Braz.	C2	56
Guaratinguetá, Braz.	C3	56
Guaratuba, Braz.	D3	56
Guarda, Port.	B2	22
Guardafui, Cape see Caseyr, c., Som.	C7	47
Guardia Mitre, Arg.	C4	54
Guardo, W.V., U.S.	C4	125
Guareí, Braz.	m7	56
Guareña, Spain	C2	22
Guárico, state, Ven.	B4	60
Guárico, stm., Ven.	B4	60
Guarujá, Braz.	n8	56
Guarulhos, Braz.	m8	56
Guasave, Mex.	B3	63
Guasdualito, Ven.	B3	60
Guaspati, Ven.	B5	60
Guastalla, Italy	B3	23
Guatemala, Guat.	E6	63
Guatemala, ctry., N.A.	D6	63
Guateque, Col.	C3	60
Guatimozín, Arg.	A4	54
Guatopo National Park, Ven.	A4	60
Guatrache, Arg.	C4	54
Guaviare, dept., Col.	C3	60
Guaviare, stm., Col.	C3	60
Guayabal, Cuba	D5	64
Guayaguayare, Trin.	O23	65
Guayama, P.R.	H11	64
Guayaquil, Ec.	B1	58
Guayaquil, Golfo de, b., S.A.	B1	58
Guayaramerín, Bol.	B1	58
Guayas, prov., Ec.	B1	58
Guaymas, Mex.	B2	63
Guaynabo, P.R.	A2	120
Guazacapán, Guat.	C2	62
Gubakha, Sov. Un.	B5	28
Gubbio, Italy	C4	23
Guben, Ger.	C7	18
Gubin, Pol.	B9	19
Gucheng, China	H4	32
Gudalur, India	G4	36
Gudivada, India	D6	36
Gudur, India	F5	36
Guebwiller, Fr.	D7	16
Guéckédou, Gui.	E2	45
Guelma, Alg.	B6	44
Guelph, Ont.	D4	73
Guelph, N.D., U.S.	C7	111
Guénette, Que.	C2	74
Güera, W. Sah.	E1	44
Guercif, Mor.	C4	44
Guéréda, Chad	C4	46
Guerette, Me., U.S.	A4	96
Guernica y Luno, Spain	F3	75
Guernsey, Sask.	F3	75
Guernsey, Wy., U.S.	D8	127
Guernsey, co., Oh., U.S.	B4	112
Guernsey, i., Guernsey	F5	10
Guernsey, dep., Eur.	F5	10
Guerra, Tx., U.S.	F3	120
Guerrero, state, Mex.	D4	63
Guest Peninsula, pen., Ant.	B34	7
Gueugnon, Fr.	D6	16
Gueydan, La., U.S.	D3	95
Guffey, Co., U.S.	C5	83
Gugegwe Island, i., Marsh Is.	S17	52
Guia Lopes da Laguna, Braz.	C1	56
Guibes, Nmb.	C2	49
Guichi, China	I7	32
Guide, China	D5	31
Guider, Cam.	D2	46
Guide Rock, Ne., U.S.	D7	104
Guidonia [Montecelio], Italy	D4	23
Guiglo, I.C.	E3	45
Guilarte, Monte, mtn., P.R.	B2	65
Guild, N.H., U.S.	D2	106
Guildford, Eng., U.K.	E6	10
Guildhall, Vt., U.S.	B5	122
Guilford, Ct., U.S.	D5	84
Guilford, Me., U.S.	C3	96
Guilford, N.Y., U.S.	C5	109
Guilford, co., N.C., U.S.	A3	110
Guilin, China	F7	31
Guillaume-Delisle, Lac, l., Que.	E17	66
Guillestre, Fr.	D7	16
Guimarães, Braz.	B2	57
Guimarães, Port.	o1	64
Guin, Al., U.S.	B2	78
Guin, Al., U.S.	B5	123
Guinea, ctry., Afr.	D2	45
Guinea, Gulf of, b., Afr.	F4	42
Guinea-Bissau, ctry., Afr.	D1	45
Guiné, Cuba	C2	64
Güines, Cuba	C1	64
Guingamp, Fr.	C2	16
Guion, Ar., U.S.	B4	81
Güira de Melena, Cuba	C2	64
Güiratinga, Braz.	B2	56
Güiria, Ven.	A5	60
Guisanbourg, Fr. Gu.	B4	59
Guisborough, Eng., U.K.	F7	13
Guise, Fr.	C5	16
Guist Creek, stm., Ky., U.S.	B4	94
Guitiriz, Spain	A2	22
Guixi, China	J7	32
Guixian, China	G6	31
Guiyang, China	F6	31
Guizhou, prov., China	F6	31
Gujan, China	E3	16
Gujarat, state, India	D5	36
Gujranwala, Pak.	B5	36
Gujrat, Pak.	*B5	36
Gulbarga, India	E6	36
Guldborg, Den.	D5	15
Gulf, co., Fl., U.S.	C1	86
Gulf Breeze, Fl., U.S.	*u14	86
Gulf Gate Estates, Fl., U.S.	*E4	86
Gulf Hammock, Fl., U.S.	C4	86
Gulf Islands National Seashore, U.S.	E5	101
Gulfport, Fl., U.S.	E4	86
Gulfport, Ms., U.S.	E4	101
Gulf Shores, Al., U.S.	E2	78
Gulgong, Austl.	F7	51
Gulkana, Ak., U.S.	C10	79
Gullion, Slieve, mtn., N. Ire.	C5	11
Gull Island, i., N.C., U.S.	B7	110
Gull Lake, Sask.	G1	75
Gull Lake, l., Alta.	C4	68
Gull Lake, l., Mn., U.S.	D4	100
Güllük, Tur.	D6	40
Gully, Mn., U.S.	C3	100
Gulu, Ug.	A5	48
Gulyantsi, Bul.	D7	24
Gulyaypole, Sov. Un.	H11	27
Gumaca, Phil.	p14	34
Gumba, Zaire	A3	48
Gumbo, De., U.S.	G4	85
Gumefens, Switz.	C3	21
Gumel, Nig.	D6	45
Gummersbach, Ger.	B2	19
Gum Spring Mountain, mtn., Tn., U.S.	D8	119
Gum Springs, Ar., U.S.	C2	81
Gum Swamp Creek, stm., Ga., U.S.	D3	87
Gümüshane, Tur.	B12	40
Guna, India	D6	36
Guna, India	E6	37
Guna, mtn., Eth.	C4	47
Gundelfingen, Ger.	E5	19
Gungu, Zaire	C2	48
Gunisao, stm., Man.	C3	70
Gunisao Lake, l., Man.	C3	70
Gunlock, Ut., U.S.	F2	121
Gunn, Ms., U.S.	C4	101
Gunnar, Sask.	m7	75
Gunnbjørn Fjeld, mtn., Grnld.	*C17	128
Gunnedah, Austl.	F9	50
Gunnison, Co., U.S.	C4	83
Gunnison, Ms., U.S.	B3	101
Gunnison, Ut., U.S.	D4	121
Gunnison, co., Co., U.S.	C3	83
Gunnison, stm., Co., U.S.	C2	83
Gunnison, Mount, mtn., Co., U.S.	C3	83
Gunnworth, Sask.	F1	75
Gunpowder Creek, stm., Ky., U.S.	k13	94
Gunpowder Neck, c., Md., U.S.	B5	97
Gunpowder River, b., Md., U.S.	B5	97
Gunter Air Force Base, mil., Al., U.S.	C3	78
Guntersville, Al., U.S.	A3	78
Guntersville Dam, Al., U.S.	A3	78
Guntersville Lake, res., Al., U.S.	A3	78
Gunton, Man.	D3	70
Guntown, Ms., U.S.	A5	101
Guntur, India	E7	36
Gunungsitoli, Indon.	L2	35
Günzburg, Ger.	E5	19
Gunzenhausen, Ger.	D5	19
Guoyang, China	H7	32
Gura Humorului, Rom.	A5	37
Gurdaspur, India	A5	37
Gurdon, Ar., U.S.	D2	81
Gurgueia, stm., Braz.	C2	57
Guri, Embalse de, Ven.	B5	60
Gurjevsk, Sov. Un.	E26	8
Gurk, stm., Aus.	E7	18
Gurley, Al., U.S.	A3	78
Gurley, Ne., U.S.	C3	104
Gurley, Tn., U.S.	A5	119
Gurnee, Il., U.S.	h9	90
Gurnet Point, c., Ma., U.S.	B6	98
Gurney, Wi., U.S.	B3	126
Gurué, Moz.	A6	49
Gurupá, Braz.	C4	59
Gurupi, stm., Braz.	B1	57
Gurupi, Cabo, c., Braz.	E8	59
Guryev, Sov. Un.	E8	29
Gusau, Nig.	D5	45
Gusev, Sov. Un.	A7	26
Gushi, China	H5	32
Gushikawa, Japan	O5	52
Gus-Khrustalnyy, Sov. Un.	D13	27
Gustavo A. Madero (part of Mexico City), Mex.	h9	63
Gustavus, Ak., U.S.	D12	79
Güsten, Ger.	B6	19
Gustine, Ca., U.S.	D3	82
Gustine, Tx., U.S.	D3	120
Güstrow, Ger.	B6	18
Gütersloh, Ger.	E9	19
Gutau, Aus.	B9	19
Guthrie, Ky., U.S.	D2	94
Guthrie, Ok., U.S.	B4	113
Guthrie, Tx., U.S.	C2	120
Guthrie, W.V., U.S.	m12	125
Guthrie, co., Ia., U.S.	C3	92
Guthrie Center, Ia., U.S.	C3	92
Guttenberg, Ia., U.S.	B7	92
Guttenberg, N.J., U.S.	h8	107
Gu Vo, Az., U.S.	E3	80
Guwāhāti, India	C9	36
Guy, Ar., U.S.	B3	81
Guy, Tx., U.S.	r14	120
Guyana, ctry., S.A.	A3	59
Guyandotte, stm., W.V., U.S.	C2	125
Guyandotte Mountain, mtn., W.V., U.S.	n12	125
Guyang, China	D4	32
Guyenne, hist. reg., Fr.	E4	16
Guymon, Ok., U.S.	e9	113
Guyot, Mount, mtn., U.S.	D10	119
Guyra, Austl.	E8	51
Guys, Tn., U.S.	B3	119
Guysborough, N.S.	D8	71
Guysborough, co., N.S.	D7	71
Guys Mills, Pa., U.S.	C2	115
Guyton, Ga., U.S.	D5	87
Guyuan, China	G2	32
Guyuan, China	D6	32
Guzar, Sov. Un.	B13	39
Güzelyurt, N. Cyp.	E9	40
Guzhen, China	H7	32
Gvardeysk, Sov. Un.	A6	26
Gwabegar, Austl.	E7	51
Gwädar, Pak.	B5	36
Gwai, Zimb.	A4	49
Gwalior, India	C6	36
Gwanda, Zimb.	B4	49
Gwane, Zaire	A4	48
Gwda, stm., Pol.	B4	26
Gweebarra Bay, b., Ire.	C3	11
Gweesalia, Ire.	C2	11
Gwembe, Zam.	C10	79
Gwent, co., Wales, U.K.	A5	12
Gweru, Zimb.	A4	49
Gwinhurst, De., U.S.	h8	85
Gwinn, Mi., U.S.	B3	99
Gwinner, N.D., U.S.	C8	111
Gwinnett, co., Ga., U.S.	C2	87
Gwydyr Bay, b., Ak., U.S.	A10	79
Gwynedd, co., Wales, U.K.	A3	12
Gwynn, Va., U.S.	C6	123
Gwynneville, In., U.S.	E6	91
Gwynns Falls, stm., Md., U.S.	g10	97
Gyandzha, Sov. Un.	E7	29
Gyangzê, China	C8	36
Gyaring Co, l., China	B8	36
Gyaring Hu, l., China	E4	31
Gyirong, China	C10	37
Gympie, Austl.	E9	50
Gyöngyös, Hung.	B4	24
Győr (Raab), Hung.	B3	24
Gypsera, Switz.	C3	21
Gypsum, Co., U.S.	B4	83
Gypsum, Ks., U.S.	D6	93
Gypsum, Oh., U.S.	A3	112
Gypsumville, Man.	D2	70
Gyula, Hung.	B5	24

H

Name	Map Ref.	Page
Haag [in Oberbayern], Ger.	A8	20
Haakon, co., S.D., U.S.	C4	118
Haaksbergen, Neth.	B6	17
Haamstede, Neth.	C3	17
Haapamäki, Fin.	F11	14
Haapsalu, Sov. Un.	B4	27
Ha Arava (Wādī al Jayb), val., Asia	D7	41
Haarlem, Neth.	A6	16
Haarlemmermeer, Neth.	A6	16
Hab, stm., Pak.	I13	39
Habermehl Peak, mtn., Ant.	B13	7
Habersham, Ga., U.S.	B3	87
Habersham, co., Ga., U.S.	B3	87
Haboru, Japan	D10	33
Hachiman, Japan	n15	33
Hachinohe, Japan	F10	33
Hachiōji, Japan	I9	33
Hachita, N.M., U.S.	F1	108
Hack, Mount, mtn., Austl.	E2	51
Hackberry, Az., U.S.	B2	80
Hackberry, La., U.S.	E2	95
Hackberry Creek, stm., Ks., U.S.	D3	93
Hackensack, Mn., U.S.	D4	100
Hackensack, N.J., U.S.	B4	107
Hackensack, stm., N.J., U.S.	h8	107
Hacker Valley, W.V., U.S.	C4	125
Hacketstown, Ire.	E5	11
Hackett, Ar., U.S.	B1	81
Hackettstown, N.J., U.S.	B3	107
Hackleburg, Al., U.S.	A2	78
Hackney (part of London), Eng., U.K.	k12	10
Hack Point, Md., U.S.	B6	97
Hacoda, Al., U.S.	D3	78
Hacq, i., Micron.	Q18	52
Hadāribah, Ra's al, c., Sud.	A4	47
Hadassah Alef Hospital, Isr.	m14	41
Hadd, Ra's al, c., Oman	D6	38
Haddam, Ct., U.S.	D5	84
Haddam, Ks., U.S.	C6	93
Haddington, Scot., U.K.	E6	13
Haddix, Ky., U.S.	C6	94
Haddock, Ga., U.S.	C3	87
Haddon Heights, N.J., U.S.	D2	107
Haddonfield, N.J., U.S.	D2	107
Haddon Heights, N.J., U.S.	D2	107
Hadejia, Nig.	D7	45
Hadejia, stm., Nig.	D6	45
Hadera, Isr.	F10	41
Haderslev, Den.	C2	15
Hadim, Tur.	D9	40
Hadleigh, Eng., U.K.	B8	12
Hadley, Ma., U.S.	F3	100
Hadley, N.Y., U.S.	B7	109
Hadley, Pa., U.S.	D1	115
Hadley Bay, b., N.W. Ter.	B11	66
Hadley Lake, l., Me., U.S.	D5	96
Hadlock, Wa., U.S.	A3	124
Hadlyme, Ct., U.S.	D6	84
Ha Dong, Viet.	D4	35
Hadramawt, reg., Yemen	D4	38
Hadsten, Den.	B3	15
Hadsund, Den.	B3	15
Haeju, N. Kor.	C10	33
Haenam, S. Kor.	I3	33
Haerhpin see Harbin, China	B10	33
Hafford, Sask.	E2	75
Hafnarfjördur, Ice.	n22	14
Hafun, Ras, c., Som.	C7	47
Hagan, Ga., U.S.	D4	87
Hagari, stm., India	F4	36
Hagaribommanahalli, India	F6	36
Hagerman, Id., U.S.	G4	89
Hagerman, N.M., U.S.	D5	108
Hagerstown, In., U.S.	E7	91
Hagerstown, Md., U.S.	A2	97
Hagemeister Island, i., Ak., U.S.	D7	79
Hagen, Sask.	E3	75

Name	Map Ref.	Page
Hagen, Ger.	C3	18
Hagenow, Ger.	E5	15
Hagensborg, B.C.	C4	69
Hagere Hiywet, Eth.	G4	89
Hagerman, Id., U.S.	D5	108
Hagerman, N.M., U.S.	k15	73
Hagerman Corners, Ont.	E7	91
Hagerstown, Ind., U.S.	A2	97
Hagerstown, Md., U.S.	E4	73
Hagersville, Ont.	D4	70
Haggart Lake, l., Ont.	D3	103
Haggin, Mount, mtn., Mt., U.S.	A6	35
Ha Giang, Viet.	E2	11
Hags Head, c., Ire.	E2	75
Hague, Sask.	B7	109
Hague, N.Y., U.S.	C6	111
Hague, N.D., U.S.	C6	111
Hague, Cape de la, c., Fr.	C3	16
Haguenau, Fr.	C7	16
Hagues Peak, mtn., Co., U.S.	A5	83
Ha! Ha!, Baie des, b., Que.	C2	72
Ha! Ha!, Lac, l., Que.	A7	74
Hahira, Ga., U.S.	F3	87
Hahnville, La., U.S.	E5	95
Haicheng, China	G8	31
Haicheng, China	D10	32
Haichow Bay see Haizhou Bay, b., China	G8	32
Hai Duong, Viet.	B7	35
Haifa (Hefa), Isr.	B3	38
Haifa, Bay of see Hefa, Mifraz, b., Isr.	B6	41
Haigerloch, Ger.	A4	20
Haigler, Ne., U.S.	D4	104
Haikang, China	G6	31
Haikou, China	B4	34
Haiku, Hi., U.S.	C5	88
Hā'il, Sau. Ar.	C4	38
Hailar, China	B8	31
Haile, La., U.S.	B3	95
Hailesboro, N.Y., U.S.	f9	109
Hailey, Id., U.S.	F4	89
Haileybury, Ont.	p20	73
Haileyville, Ok., U.S.	C6	113
Hailong, China	C10	31
Hailun, China	B10	31
Haimen, China	F9	32
Haimen, China	I9	32
Hainan Island, i., China	B3	34
Hainaut, prov., Bel.	D3	17
Haines, Ak., U.S.	D12	79
Haines, Or., U.S.	C9	114
Haines City, Fl., U.S.	D5	86
Haines Falls, N.Y., U.S.	C6	109
Hainesport, N.J., U.S.	D3	107
Hainesville, N.J., U.S.	A3	107
Hainichen, Ger.	C8	19
Haining, China	I9	32
Hai Phong, Viet.	A3	34
Hairy Hill, Alta.	C5	68
Haiti, ctry., N.A.	E7	64
Haiyang, China	F9	32
Haiyuan, China	F1	32
Haizhou, China	E8	31
Haizhou Bay, b., China	G8	32
Hajdúböszörmény, Hung.	B5	24
Hajdúhadház, Hung.	B5	24
Hajdúnánás, Hung.	B5	24
Hajdúszoboszló, Hung.	B5	24
Hajiki, Cape, c., Japan	G9	33
Hajnówka, Pol.	B7	26
Hakalau, Hi., U.S.	D6	88
Hakkâri, Tur.	D14	40
Hakken, Mount, mtn., Japan	I7	33
Hakodate, Japan	C13	31
Hākra Branch, stm., Pak.	C4	37
Haku, Mount, mtn., Japan	m15	33
Halabjah, Iraq	D2	39
Halā'ib, Eg.	E7	43
Halaula, Hi., U.S.	C6	88
Halawa, Cape, c., Hi., U.S.	B5	88
Halawa Heights, Hi., U.S.	g10	88
Halberstadt, Ger.	H4	75
Halbrite, Sask.	C3	92
Halbur, Ia., U.S.	C6	34
Halcon, Mount, mtn., Phil.	B6	94
Haldeman, Ky., U.S.	H4	14
Halden, Nor.	B5	18
Haldensleben, Ger.	E5	73
Haldimand, Ont.	E5	73
Haldimand, co., Ont.	B8	83
Hale, Co., U.S.	D7	99
Hale, Mi., U.S.	B4	102
Hale, Mo., U.S.	C2	78
Hale, co., Al., U.S.	B2	120
Hale, co., Tx., U.S.		
Haleakala Crater, crat., Hi., U.S.	C5	88
Haleakala National Park, Hi., U.S.	C6	88
Haleburg, Al., U.S.	D4	78
Hale Center, Tx., U.S.	B2	120
Haledon, N.J., U.S.	*B4	107
Haleiwa, Hi., U.S.	B3	88
Hales Corners, Wi., U.S.	n11	126
Halesowen, Eng., U.K.	B5	12
Halesworth, Eng., U.K.	B9	12
Halethorpe, Md., U.S.	B4	97
Haleyville, Al., U.S.	A2	78
Haleyville, N.J., U.S.	E2	107
Half Assini, Ghana	E4	45
Half Hollow Hills, N.Y., U.S.	*h13	109
Half-Moon Bay, N.Z.	Q12	51
Half Moon Bay, Ca., U.S.	k8	82
Halfway, Ky., U.S.	D3	94
Halfway, Md., U.S.	A2	97
Halfway, Or., U.S.	D4	102
Half Way, Mo., U.S.	C9	114
Halfway, stm., B.C.	A6	69
Halfway Numatak, mtn., Ant.	f40	7
Halhūl, Isr. Occ.	C7	41
Haliburton, Ont.	B6	73
Haliburton, co., Ont.	B6	73
Halibut Point, c., Ma., U.S.	A6	98
Halifax, Eng., U.K.	E6	71
Halifax, Eng., U.K.	D6	10
Halifax, N.S.	E6	71
Halifax, Ma., U.S.	C6	98
Halifax, N.C., U.S.	A5	110
Halifax, Pa., U.S.	F8	115
Halifax, Vt., U.S.	F3	122
Halifax, Va., U.S.	D4	123
Halifax, co., N.C., U.S.	A5	110
Halifax, co., Va., U.S.	D4	123
Halifax Bay, b., Austl.	C8	50
Haliimaile, Hi., U.S.	C5	88
Halīl, stm., Iran	C5	38
Halkirk, Alta.	C4	68
Hall, In., U.S.	E4	91
Hall, Mt., U.S.	D3	103
Hall, N.Y., U.S.	C3	109
Hall, co., Ga., U.S.	B3	87
Hall, co., Ne., U.S.	D7	104
Hall, co., Tx., U.S.	B2	120
Halla, Mount, mtn., S. Kor.	J3	33
Halladale, stm., Scot., U.K.	B5	13
Hallam, Ne., U.S.	D9	104
Hallam Peak, mtn., B.C.	C8	69
Halland, co., Swe.	B6	15
Hallandale, Fl., U.S.	G6	86
Hallands Väderö, i., Swe.	B6	15
Hall Basin, b., N.A.	k39	66
Hallboro, Man.	D2	70
Halle, Bel.	D4	17
Halle, Ger.	C5	18
Halle, Ger.	A3	19
Halle, Aus.	E6	18
Halleck, Nv., U.S.	C6	105
Hallein, Aus.		
Halle-Neustadt, Ger.	*C6	18
Hällestad, Swe.	u33	14
Hallett, Ok., U.S.	A5	113
Hallettsville, Tx., U.S.	E4	120
Halley, Ar., U.S.	D4	81
Halley Bay, sci., Ant.	B10	7
Halliday, N.D., U.S.	B3	111
Hallie, Wi., U.S.	D2	126
Hallim, S. Kor.	J3	33
Hall Island, i., Ak., U.S.	C5	79
Hall Meadow Brook, stm., Ct., U.S.	B3	84
Hall Meadow Brook Reservoir, res., Ct., U.S.	B3	84
Hall Mountain, mtn., Wa., U.S.	A8	124
Hallock, Mn., U.S.	B2	100
Hallowell, Ks., U.S.	E9	93
Hallowell, Me., U.S.	D3	96
Hall Peninsula, pen., N.W. Ter.	D19	66
Halls, Ga., U.S.	B2	87
Halls, Tn., U.S.	B2	119
Halls, Tn., U.S.	*C10	119
Hallsberg, Swe.	t33	14
Hallsboro, N.C., U.S.	C4	110
Halls Creek, Austl.	C4	50
Halls Creek, stm., Ut., U.S.	F5	121
Halls Crossroads, Tn., U.S.	m14	119
Halls Harbour, N.S.	D5	71
Halls Stream, stm., N.H., U.S.	f7	106
Halls Summit, Ks., U.S.	D8	93
Hallstead, Pa., U.S.	C10	115
Hall Summit, La., U.S.	B2	95
Hallsville, Mo., U.S.	B5	102
Hallsville, Oh., U.S.	C3	112
Hallsville, Tx., U.S.	C5	120
Hall Top, mtn., Tn., U.S.	D10	119
Halltown, Mo., U.S.	D4	102
Hallville, Ct., U.S.	C7	84
Hallwil Lake, l., Switz.	B4	20
Hallwood, Va., U.S.	C7	123
Halma, Mn., U.S.	B2	100
Halmahera, i., Indon.	E7	34
Halmahera Sea, Indon.	F7	34
Halmstad, Swe.	I5	14
Hals, Den.	B4	15
Halsell, Al., U.S.	C1	78
Halsey, Ne., U.S.	C5	104
Halsey, N.J., U.S.	A3	107
Halsey, Or., U.S.	C3	114
Hälsö, i., Swe.	A5	15
Halstad, Mn., U.S.	C2	100
Halstead, Eng., U.K.	C8	12
Halstead, Ks., U.S.	E6	93
Haltern, Ger.	B2	19
Haltia, mtn., Eur.	C9	14
Haltom City, Tx., U.S.	*n9	120
Halton, co., Ont.	D5	73
Halton Hills, Ont.	D5	73
Haltwhistle, Eng., U.K.	F6	13
Ham, Fr.	E3	17
Hamada, Japan	I6	33
Hamadān, Iran	B4	38
Hamāh, Syria	B5	38
Hamahika Island, i., Japan	o5	52
Hamamatsu, Japan	H10	33
Hamar, Nor.	C4	14
Hamar, N.D., U.S.	B7	111
Hamath see Hamah, Syria		
Hambantota, Sri L.		
Hamberg, N.D., U.S.	B6	111
Hamber Provincial Park, B.C.	C8	69
Hamblen, co., Tn., U.S.	C10	119
Hamburg, Ger.	B6	94
Hamburg, Ar., U.S.	D4	81
Hamburg, Ct., U.S.	D6	84
Hamburg, Ia., U.S.	D2	92
Hamburg, Ms., U.S.	D2	101
Hamburg, N.J., U.S.	A3	107
Hamburg, N.Y., U.S.	C2	109
Hamburg, Pa., U.S.	E10	115
Hamburg, Wi., U.S.	C4	126
Hamburg, state, Ger.	B5	18
Hamburg Mountains, mts., N.J., U.S.	A3	107
Hamd, Wādī al, val., Sau. Ar.	C3	38
Hamden, Ct., U.S.	D4	84
Hamden, N.Y., U.S.	C6	109
Hamden, Oh., U.S.	C3	112
Hämeenlinna, Fin.	G11	14
Hamel, Mn., U.S.	m11	100
Hameln, Ger.	B4	18
Hamer, Id., U.S.	F6	89
Hamer, S.C., U.S.	C9	117
Hamersley Range, mts., Austl.	D2	50
Hamersville, Oh., U.S.	D2	112
Hamhŭng, N. Kor.	D12	31
Hami, China	D6	92
Hamill, La., U.S.	D6	92
Hamilton, S.D., U.S.	G7	50
Hamilton, Austl.	p20	64
Hamilton, Ber.	D5	73
Hamilton, Ont.	L15	51
Hamilton, N.Z.	C4	10
Hamilton, Scot., U.K.	A2	78
Hamilton, Al., U.S.	A7	79
Hamilton, Co., U.S.	D2	87
Hamilton, Ga., U.S.	D5	73
Hamilton, Il., U.S.	C2	90
Hamilton, In., U.S.	A8	91
Hamilton, co., Fl., U.S.	B3	86
Hamilton, co., Il., U.S.	E5	90
Hamilton, co., In., U.S.	D5	91
Hamilton, co., Ia., U.S.	B4	92
Hamilton, co., Ks., U.S.	E2	93
Hamilton, co., Ne., U.S.	D7	104
Hamilton, co., N.Y., U.S.	B6	109
Hamilton, co., Oh., U.S.	C1	112
Hamilton, co., Tn., U.S.	D8	119
Hamilton, co., Tx., U.S.	D3	120
Hamilton, Lake, res., Ar., U.S.	C2	81
Hamilton, Mount, mtn., Ak., U.S.	C8	79
Hamilton, Mount, mtn., Ca., U.S.	k9	82
Hamilton, Mount, mtn., Nv., U.S.	D6	105
Hamilton City, Ca., U.S.	C2	82
Hamilton Dome, Wy., U.S.	C4	127
Hamilton Inlet, b., Newf.	A2	72
Hamilton Mountain, mtn., N.Y., U.S.	B6	109
Hamilton Reservoir, res., Ma., U.S.	B3	98
Hamilton Sound, strt., Newf.	D4	72
Hamilton Square, N.J., U.S.	C3	107
Hamina, Fin.	G12	14
Hamiota, Man.	D1	70
Hamīrpur, India	C7	36
Hamjong-ni, N. Kor.	G2	33
Ham Lake, Mn., U.S.	*m12	100
Hamler, Oh., U.S.	A1	112
Hamlet, In., U.S.	B4	91
Hamlet, Ne., U.S.	D4	104
Hamlet, N.C., U.S.	C3	110
Hamlet, Mount, mtn., Ak., U.S.	B6	79
Hamletsburg, Il., U.S.	F5	90
Hamlin, Ks., U.S.	C8	93
Hamlin, Pa., U.S.	D11	115
Hamlin, Tx., U.S.	C2	120
Hamlin, W.V., U.S.	C2	125
Hamlin, co., S.D., U.S.	C8	118
Hamlin Lake, l., Mi., U.S.	E4	99
Hammam Lif, Tun.	F3	44
Hammām, Hawr al, l., Iraq	t35	14
Hammārby, Swe.	t35	14
Hammarsjön, l., Swe.	C8	15
Hamme, Bel.	C4	17
Hammel, Den.	B3	15
Hammelburg, Ger.	C4	19
Hammer, S.D., U.S.	B8	118
Hammerfest, Nor.	B10	14
Hammett, Id., U.S.	G3	89
Hamm [in Westfalen], Ger.	C3	18
Hammon, Ok., U.S.	B2	113
Hammonasset, stm., Ct., U.S.	D5	84
Hammonasset Point, c., Ct., U.S.	E5	84
Hammond, Il., U.S.	D5	90
Hammond, In., U.S.	A2	91
Hammond, La., U.S.	D5	95
Hammond, Mn., U.S.	F6	100
Hammond, Mt., U.S.	E12	103
Hammond, N.Y., U.S.	A5	109
Hammond, Or., U.S.	A3	114
Hammond, Wi., U.S.	D1	126
Hammond Bay, b., Mi., U.S.	C6	99
Hammondsport, N.Y., U.S.	C3	109
Hammonton, N.J., U.S.	D3	107
Hamneda, Swe.	B7	15
Ham-Nord, Que.	D6	74
Hamoyet, Jabal, mtn., Afr.	B4	47
Hampden, Newf.	D3	72
Hampden, N.Z.	P13	51
Hampden, Me., U.S.	D4	96
Hampden, Ma., U.S.	B3	98
Hampden, N.D., U.S.	A7	111
Hampden, co., Ma., U.S.	B2	98
Hampden Highlands, Me., U.S.	D4	96
Hampshire, Tn., U.S.	B4	119
Hampshire, co., Eng., U.K.	C6	12
Hampshire, co., Ma., U.S.	B2	98
Hampshire, co., W.V., U.S.	B6	125
Hampstead, N.B.	D3	71
Hampstead (part of London), Eng., U.K.	k12	10
Hampstead, Md., U.S.	A4	97
Hampstead, N.H., U.S.	E4	106
Hampstead, N.C., U.S.	C5	110
Hampton, N.B.	D4	71
Hampton, Ar., U.S.	D3	81
Hampton, Ct., U.S.	B7	84
Hampton, Fl., U.S.	C4	86
Hampton, Ga., U.S.	C2	87
Hampton, Ia., U.S.	B4	92
Hampton, Ky., U.S.	e9	94
Hampton, Md., U.S.	*B4	97
Hampton, Ne., U.S.	D8	104
Hampton, N.H., U.S.	E5	106
Hampton, N.J., U.S.	B3	107
Hampton, N.Y., U.S.	B7	109
Hampton, Or., U.S.	D6	114
Hampton, S.C., U.S.	F5	117
Hampton, Tn., U.S.	C11	119
Hampton, Va., U.S.	C6	123
Hampton, co., S.C., U.S.	F5	117
Hampton Bays, N.Y., U.S.	n16	109
Hampton Beach, N.H., U.S.	E5	106
Hampton Butte, mtn., Or., U.S.	D6	114
Hampton Falls, N.H., U.S.	E5	106
Hampton Roads, anch., Va., U.S.	k15	123
Hampton Roads Bridge-Tunnel, Va., U.S.	k15	123
Hamrā', Al Hammādah al, pl., Afr.	D2	43
Hams Fork, stm., Wy., U.S.	E2	127
Ham-Sud, Que.	D6	74
Ham Tan, Viet.	G7	35
Hamtramck, Mi., U.S.	p15	99
Hamyang, S. Kor.	I3	33
Han, stm., Asia	H4	31
Hana, Hi., U.S.	C6	88
Hanahan, S.C., U.S.	F7	117
Hanalei, Hi., U.S.	A2	88
Hanalei Bay, b., Hi., U.S.	A2	88
Hanamaki, Japan	G10	33
Hanamaulu, Hi., U.S.	B2	88
Hanapepe, Hi., U.S.	B2	88
Hanau, Ger.	C4	18
Hanceville, Al., U.S.	A3	78
Hancheng, China	G4	31
Hancock, Ia., U.S.	C2	92
Hancock, Me., U.S.	D4	96
Hancock, Md., U.S.	A1	97
Hancock, Mi., U.S.	A2	99
Hancock, Mn., U.S.	E3	100
Hancock, N.H., U.S.	E3	106
Hancock, N.Y., U.S.	C5	109
Hancock, Vt., U.S.	D3	122
Hancock, W.V., U.S.	B6	125
Hancock, Wi., U.S.	D4	126
Hancock, co., Ga., U.S.	C3	87
Hancock, co., Il., U.S.	C2	90
Hancock, co., In., U.S.	E6	91
Hancock, co., Ia., U.S.	A4	92
Hancock, co., Ky., U.S.	C3	94
Hancock, co., Me., U.S.	D4	96
Hancock, co., Ms., U.S.	E4	101
Hancock, co., Oh., U.S.	A2	112
Hancock, co., Tn., U.S.	C10	119
Hancock, co., W.V., U.S.	A4	125
Hancock Pond, l., Me., U.S.	E2	96
Hancocks Bridge, N.J., U.S.	D2	107
Hand, co., S.D., U.S.	C6	118
Handa, Japan	o15	33
Handa, Tan.	C7	47
Handa, i., Scot., U.K.	B3	13
Handan, China	D9	31
Handaqi, China	A3	33
Handel, Sask.	E1	75
Handeni, Tan.	C6	48
Handley, W.V., U.S.	m13	125
Handsworth, Sask.	H4	75
Hanford, Ca., U.S.	D4	82
Hangchou see Hangzhou, China	E9	31
Hangchow Bay see Hangzhou Bay, b., China	I9	32
Hangelsberg, Ger.	F7	15
Hanging Rock, Oh., U.S.	D3	112
Hangingstone, stm., Alta.	A5	68
Hangman Creek, stm., Wa., U.S.	B8	124
Hangö, Fin.	H10	14
Hangu, China	*D8	31
Hangzhou (Hangchou), China	E9	31
Hangzhou Bay, b., China	I9	32
HaNiqra, Rosh, c., Asia	A7	41
Hanita, Isr.	A7	41
Hankinson, N.D., U.S.	C9	111
Hanks, N.D., U.S.	A2	111
Hanksville, Ut., U.S.	E5	121
Hanley, Sask.	F3	75
Hanley Falls, Mn., U.S.	F3	100
Hanlontown, Ia., U.S.	A4	92
Hann, Mount, mtn., Austl.	C5	50
Hanna, Alta.	D5	68
Hanna, In., U.S.	B4	91
Hanna, Ok., U.S.	B6	113
Hanna, Ut., U.S.	C5	121
Hanna, Wy., U.S.	E6	127
Hanna City, Il., U.S.	C4	90
Hannaford, N.D., U.S.	B7	111
Hannah, N.D., U.S.	A7	111
Hannahville Indian Reservation, Mi., U.S.	C3	99
Hannawa Falls, N.Y., U.S.	f10	109
Hannibal, Mo., U.S.	B6	102
Hannibal, N.Y., U.S.	B4	109
Hannibal, Oh., U.S.	C5	112
Hannover, Ger.	B4	18
Hannover, N.D., U.S.	B4	111
Hanöbukten, b., Swe.	J6	14
Hanoi (Ha Noi), Viet.	A3	34
Hanover, Ont.	C3	73
Hanover, Ar., U.S.	B3	81
Hanover, Ct., U.S.	C7	84
Hanover, Il., U.S.	A3	90
Hanover, In., U.S.	G7	91
Hanover, Ks., U.S.	C7	93
Hanover, Ma., U.S.	B6	98
Hanover, Mn., U.S.	m11	100
Hanover, N.H., U.S.	C2	106
Hanover, N.M., U.S.	E1	108
Hanover, Oh., U.S.	B3	112
Hanover, Pa., U.S.	G8	115
Hanover, Va., U.S.	C5	123
Hanover, W.V., U.S.	D3	125
Hanover, co., Va., U.S.	C5	123
Hanover, hist. reg., Ger.	B4	18
Hanover, Isla, i., Chile	G1	69
Hanover Center, Ma., U.S.	h12	98
Hanover Center, N.H., U.S.	C2	106
Hanover Park, Il., U.S.	k8	90
Hanoverton, Oh., U.S.	B5	112
Hanover Township, N.J., U.S.	B4	107
Hansard, B.C.	B7	69
Hansboro, N.D., U.S.	A6	111
Hansell, Ia., U.S.	B4	92
Hansen, Id., U.S.	G4	89
Hansford, co., Tx., U.S.	A2	120
Han Shui, stm., China	E7	31
Hanska, Mn., U.S.	F4	100
Hanson, Ky., U.S.	C2	94
Hanson, Ma., U.S.	B6	98
Hanson, co., S.D., U.S.	D8	118
Hanson Lake, l., Sask.	C4	75
Hanstholm (Hansted), Den.	A2	15
Hanston, Ks., U.S.	D4	93
Hants, co., N.S.	D5	71
Hant's Harbour, Newf.	D5	72
Hantsport, N.S.	D5	71
Hanumangarh, India	F5	37
Hanyin, China	E8	31
Hanzhong, China	E8	31
Hāora, India	I13	36
Haparanda, Swe.	D14	14
Hapeville, Ga., U.S.	C2	87
Happy, Tx., U.S.	B2	120
Happy Camp, Ca., U.S.	B2	82
Happy Corner, N.H., U.S.	f7	106
Happy Jack, Az., U.S.	C4	80
Happy Valley, N.M., U.S.	E5	108
Happy Valley-Goose Bay, Newf.	B1	72
Hapsu, N. Kor.	F4	33
Haql, Sau. Ar.	C3	38
Harad, Sau. Ar.	C4	38
Harahan, La., U.S.	k11	95
Haralson, co., Ga., U.S.	C1	87
Harare, Zimb.	A5	49
Harash, Bi'r al, well, Libya	D4	43
Haraze, Chad	C4	46
Harbin (Haerhpin), China	B10	31
Harborcreek, Pa., U.S.	B2	115
Harbor, Or., U.S.	E2	114
Harbor Beach, Mi., U.S.	E8	99
Harbor Springs, Mi., U.S.	C6	99
Harborton, Va., U.S.	C7	123
Harbor View, Oh., U.S.	e7	112
Harbour Breton, Newf.	E4	72
Harbour Buffett, Newf.	E4	72
Harbour Deep, Newf.	C3	72
Harbour Grace, Newf.	E5	72
Harbour Mille, Newf.	E4	72
Harbourton, N.J., U.S.	C3	107
Harbourville, N.S.	D5	71
Harburg (part of Hamburg), Ger.	E3	15
Hårby, Den.	C4	15
Harcourt, N.B.	C4	71
Harcourt, Ia., U.S.	B3	92
Harcuvar Mountains, mts., Az., U.S.	D2	80
Harda, India	F6	37
Hardangerfjorden, Nor.	H1	14
Hardangerjøkulen, ice, Nor.	G2	14
Hardangervidda, plat., Nor.	G2	14
Hardaway, Al., U.S.	C4	78
Hardee, co., Fl., U.S.	E5	86
Hardeeville, S.C., U.S.	G5	117
Hardeman, co., Tn., U.S.	B2	119
Hardeman, co., Tx., U.S.	B3	120
Hardenberg, Neth.	C6	17
Harderwijk, Neth.	C5	113
Hardesty, Ok., U.S.	e9	113
Hardey, W.V., U.S.	m13	75
Hardin, Il., U.S.	D3	90
Hardin, Ky., U.S.	f9	94
Hardin, Mo., U.S.	B4	102
Hardin, Mt., U.S.	E9	103
Hardin, co., Il., U.S.	F5	90
Hardin, co., Ia., U.S.	B4	92
Hardin, co., Ky., U.S.	C4	94
Hardin, co., Oh., U.S.	B2	112
Hardin, co., Tn., U.S.	B3	119
Hardin, co., Tx., U.S.	D5	120
Harding, Ma., U.S.	h10	98
Harding, Mn., U.S.	D10	100
Harding, W.V., U.S.	C5	125
Harding, co., N.M., U.S.	B5	108
Harding, co., S.D., U.S.	B2	118
Harding, Lake, res., U.S.	C4	78
Harding Lake, l., Man.	A2	70
Hardinsburg, In., U.S.	H5	91
Hardinsburg, Ky., U.S.	C3	94
Hardinville, Il., U.S.	E6	90
Hardisty, Alta.	C5	68
Hardisty Lake, l., N.W. Ter.	D9	66
Hardoi, India	D8	37
Hardshell, Ky., U.S.	C6	94
Hardtner, Ks., U.S.	E5	93
Hardwick, Ga., U.S.	C3	87
Hardwick, Ma., U.S.	B3	98
Hardwick, Mn., U.S.	G2	100
Hardwick, Vt., U.S.	B4	122
Hardwicke, N.B.	B5	71
Hardwood Ridge, mtn., Pa., U.S.	D11	115
Hardy, Sask.	H3	75
Hardy, Ar., U.S.	A4	81
Hardy, Ia., U.S.	B3	92
Hardy, Ms., U.S.	B4	101
Hardy, Ne., U.S.	D8	104
Hardy, Va., U.S.	A5	123
Hardy, co., W.V., U.S.	B6	125
Hardy Lake, res., In., U.S.	G6	91
Hare Bay, Newf.	D4	72
Hare Bay, b., Newf.	C3	72
Harer (Harar), Eth.	D6	47
Haren, Neth.	D5	47
Harerge, prov., Eth.	C4	16
Harfleur, Fr.	C10	115
Harford, co., Md., U.S.	A5	97
Harford, Pa., U.S.	C10	115
Hargeysa, Som.	D5	47
Harghita, mtn., Rom.	B7	24
Hargill, Tx., U.S.	F3	120
Hargrave, Man.	E1	70
Hargrave, stm., Man.	B2	70
Hargrave Lake, l., Man.	B2	70
Hari, stm., Indon.	F2	34
Harīd, Wādī al, val., Syria	C6	36
Harīr, Wādī al, val., Syria	B8	41
Harīrūd, stm., Asia	B1	36
Harker Heights, Tx., U.S.	*D4	120
Harkers Island, N.C., U.S.	C6	110
Harlan, Ia., U.S.	C2	92
Harlan, In., U.S.	B8	91
Harlan, Ks., U.S.	C5	93
Harlan, Ky., U.S.	D6	94
Harlan, co., Ky., U.S.	D6	94
Harlan, co., Ne., U.S.	D6	104
Harlan County Lake, res., Ne., U.S.	E6	104
Harlech, Wales, U.K.	B3	12
Harlem, Ga., U.S.	C4	87
Harlem, Mt., U.S.	B8	103
Harleton, Tx., U.S.	C5	120
Harleyville, S.C., U.S.	E7	117
Harlingen, Neth.	A6	16
Harlingen, Tx., U.S.	F4	120
Harlow, Eng., U.K.	C8	12
Harlowton, Mt., U.S.	D7	103
Harman, Va., U.S.	A2	123
Harman, W.V., U.S.	C5	125
Harmans, Md., U.S.	B4	97
Harmon, Il., U.S.	B4	90
Harmon, La., U.S.	A2	95
Harmon, Ok., U.S.	A2	113
Harmon, co., Ok., U.S.	C2	113
Harmon Creek, stm., W.V., U.S.	f8	125
Harmonsburg, Pa., U.S.	C1	115
Harmony, In., U.S.	E3	91
Harmony, Me., U.S.	D3	96
Harmony, Mn., U.S.	G6	100
Harmony, N.C., U.S.	B2	110
Harmony, Pa., U.S.	E1	115
Harmony, R.I., U.S.	B3	116
Harmony Grove, Ar., U.S.	D3	123
Harmony Hills, De., U.S.	*B3	85
Harmonyville, Vt., U.S.	E3	81
Harms, Tn., U.S.	B5	119
Harpers Ferry, W.V., U.S.	B7	125
Harpers Ferry National Historical Park, W.V., U.S.	B7	125
Harpersville, Al., U.S.	B3	78
Harperville, Ms., U.S.	C4	101
Harper Woods, Mi., U.S.	*p16	99
Harpeth, stm., Tn., U.S.	A5	119
Harpster, Oh., U.S.	B2	112
Harpswell Center, Me., U.S.	*E3	96
Harptree, Sask.	H3	75
Harquahala Mountain, mtn., Az., U.S.	D2	80
Harquahala Mountains, mts., Az., U.S.	D2	80
Harrah, Ok., U.S.	B4	113
Harrah, Wa., U.S.	C5	124
Harray, Loch of, l., Scot., U.K.	A5	13
Harrells, N.C., U.S.	C4	110
Harricana, stm., Can.	F17	66
Harriet, Ar., U.S.	B3	81
Harrietta, Mi., U.S.	D5	99
Harriettsville, Oh., U.S.	C4	112
Harriman, Tn., U.S.	D9	119
Harriman, Wy., U.S.	E7	127
Harriman Reservoir, res., Vt., U.S.	F3	122
Harrington, Me., U.S.	D5	96
Harrington, Wa., U.S.	B7	124
Harrington Park, N.J., U.S.	h9	107
Harrington Pond, l., Me., U.S.	C3	96
Harrington Sound, strt., Ber.	o20	64
Harriott Lake, l., Sask.	A4	75
Harris, Sask.	F2	75
Harris, Scot., U.K.	B3	10
Harris, Ia., U.S.	A2	92
Harris, Mn., U.S.	E6	100
Harris, Mo., U.S.	A4	102
Harris, Ok., U.S.	D7	113
Harris, R.I., U.S.	D3	116
Harris, Tn., U.S.	A3	119
Harris, co., Ga., U.S.	D2	87
Harris, co., Tx., U.S.	E5	120
Harris, Lake, l., Fl., U.S.	D5	86
Harris, Sound of, strt., Scot., U.K.	C1	13
Harrisburg, Ar., U.S.	B5	81
Harrisburg, Il., U.S.	F5	90
Harrisburg, Mo., U.S.	B5	102
Harrisburg, Ne., U.S.	C2	104
Harrisburg, Or., U.S.	C3	114
Harrisburg, Pa., U.S.	F8	115
Harrisburg, S.D., U.S.	D9	118
Harris Grove, Ia., U.S.	h15	123
Harris Hill, N.Y., U.S.	*C2	109
Harris Hill, hill, Ma., U.S.	A3	98
Harrismith, S. Afr.	A2	81
Harrison, Ar., U.S.	D4	87
Harrison, Ga., U.S.	B2	89
Harrison, Id., U.S.	F4	90
Harrison, Il., U.S.	D2	96
Harrison, Me., U.S.	D6	99
Harrison, Mi., U.S.	E5	103
Harrison, Mt., U.S.	B2	104
Harrison, Ne., U.S.	k8	107
Harrison, N.J., U.S.	h13	109
Harrison, N.Y., U.S.	C1	112
Harrison, Oh., U.S.	D7	118
Harrison, S.D., U.S.	h11	119
Harrison, Tn., U.S.	C2	92
Harrison, co., Ia., U.S.	B5	94
Harrison, co., Ky., U.S.	E4	101
Harrison, co., Ms., U.S.	A3	102
Harrison, co., Mo., U.S.	B4	112
Harrison, co., Oh., U.S.	C5	120
Harrison, co., Tx., U.S.	B4	125
Harrison, co., W.V., U.S.	g10	72
Harrison, Cape, c., Newf.	A9	79
Harrison Bay, b., Ak., U.S.	C4	95
Harrisonburg, La., U.S.	B4	123
Harrisonburg, Va., U.S.	f14	69
Harrison Hot Springs, B.C.	E7	69
Harrison Lake, l., B.C.	*F8	99
Harrison Township, Mi., U.S.	C6	115
Harrison Valley, Pa., U.S.	E3	90
Harrisonville, Mo., U.S.	C3	102
Harrisonville, Pa., U.S.	G5	115
Harriston, Ont.	D4	73
Harriston, Ms., U.S.	D2	101
Harristown, Il., U.S.	D4	90
Harrisville, Mi., U.S.	D7	99
Harrisville, Ms., U.S.	D3	101
Harrisville, N.H., U.S.	E2	106
Harrisville, N.Y., U.S.	A5	109
Harrisville, Pa., U.S.	D1	115
Harrisville, R.I., U.S.	B2	116
Harrisville, Ut., U.S.	B4	121
Harrisville, W.V., U.S.	B3	125
Harrod, Oh., U.S.	B2	112
Harrodsburg, In., U.S.	F4	91
Harrodsburg, Ky., U.S.	C5	94
Harrods Creek, stm., Ky., U.S.	g11	94
Harrogate, Eng., U.K.	C6	10
Harrold, S.D., U.S.	C6	118
Harrow, Ont.	E2	73
Harrowby, Man.	D1	70
Harrowsmith, Ont.	C8	73
Harrys, stm., Newf.	D2	72
Harry S. Truman Reservoir, res., Mo., U.S.	C4	102
Harry Strunk Lake, res., Ne., U.S.	D5	104
Harsin, Iran	D3	39
Harstad, Nor.	C7	14
Hart, Mi., U.S.	E4	99
Hart, Tx., U.S.	B1	120
Hart, co., Ga., U.S.	B4	87
Hart, co., Ky., U.S.	C4	94
Hart, Lake, l., Fl., U.S.	D5	86
Hartell, Alta.	D3	68
Hartfield, Va., U.S.	*C6	123
Hartford, Al., U.S.	D4	78
Hartford, Ar., U.S.	B1	81
Hartford, Ct., U.S.	B5	84
Hartford, Il., U.S.	*G8	91
Hartford, Ia., U.S.	C4	92
Hartford, Ky., U.S.	C3	94
Hartford, Me., U.S.	D2	96
Hartford, Mi., U.S.	F4	99
Hartford, N.Y., U.S.	B7	109
Hartford, S.D., U.S.	D10	118
Hartford, Tn., U.S.	D11	119
Hartford, Vt., U.S.	D4	122
Hartford, W.V., U.S.	C2	125
Hartford, Wi., U.S.	E5	126
Hartford, co., Ct., U.S.	B4	84

Name	Map Ref.	Page
Hartford City, In., U.S.	D7	91
Hartha, Ger.	B7	19
Hartington, Ne., U.S.	B8	104
Hart Island, i., Md., U.S.	B5	97
Hart Lake, l., Or., U.S.	E7	114
Hartland, N.B.	C2	71
Hartland, Me., U.S.	D3	96
Hartland, Mi., U.S.	F7	99
Hartland, Mn., U.S.	G5	100
Hartland, Wi., U.S.	D4	122
Hartland, W.V., U.S.	m13	125
Hartland, Wi., U.S.	E5	126
Hartland Four Corners, Vt., U.S.	D4	122
Hartland Point, c., Eng., U.K.	E4	12
Hartlepool, Eng., U.K.	C6	10
Hartley, Ia., U.S.	A2	92
Hartley, Tx., U.S.	B1	120
Hartley, co., Tx., U.S.	B1	120
Hartline, Wa., U.S.	B6	124
Hartly, De., U.S.	D3	85
Hartman, Ar., U.S.	B2	81
Hartman, Co., U.S.	C8	83
Hart Mountain, mtn., Man.	C1	70
Hartney, Man.	E1	70
Hartsburg, Il., U.S.	C4	90
Hartsburg, Mo., U.S.	C5	102
Hartsdale, N.Y., U.S.	*n15	109
Hartsel, Co., U.S.	B5	83
Hartselle, Al., U.S.	A3	78
Hartsfield, Ga., U.S.	E3	87
Hartshorn, Mo., U.S.	D6	102
Hartshorne, Ok., U.S.	C6	113
Hartsville, In., U.S.	F6	91
Hartsville, S.C., U.S.	C7	117
Hartsville, Tn., U.S.	A5	119
Hartuv, Isr.	h11	41
Hartville, Mo., U.S.	D5	102
Hartville, Oh., U.S.	B4	112
Hartville, Wy., U.S.	D8	127
Hartwell, Ga., U.S.	B4	87
Hartwell Lake, res., U.S.	B1	117
Hartwick, Ia., U.S.	C5	92
Hartwick, N.Y., U.S.	C5	109
Har Us Lake, l., Mong.	B3	31
Harvard, Id., U.S.	C2	89
Harvard, Il., U.S.	A5	90
Harvard, Ia., U.S.	D4	92
Harvard, Ma., U.S.	B4	98
Harvard, Ne., U.S.	D7	104
Harvard, Mount, mtn., Co., U.S.	C4	83
Harvel, Il., U.S.	D4	90
Harvest, Al., U.S.	A3	78
Harvey, N.B.	D3	71
Harvey, N.B.	D5	71
Harvey, Il., U.S.	B6	90
Harvey, Il., U.S.	C5	92
Harvey, La., U.S.	E5	95
Harvey, Mi., U.S.	B3	99
Harvey, N.D., U.S.	B6	111
Harvey, W.V., U.S.	n13	125
Harvey, co., Ks., U.S.	D6	93
Harvey Lake, res., Pa., U.S.	m16	115
Harvey Mountain, mtn., U.S.	B1	96
Harveysburg, Oh., U.S.	C1	112
Harveys Creek, stm., Pa., U.S.	n16	115
Harveyville, Ks., U.S.	D8	93
Harviell, Mo., U.S.	E7	102
Harwich, Eng., U.K.	E7	10
Harwich, Ma., U.S.	C7	98
Harwich Port, Ma., U.S.	C7	98
Harwinton, Ct., U.S.	B3	84
Harwood, Ont.	C6	73
Harwood, Md., U.S.	C4	97
Harwood, Ma., U.S.	f9	98
Harwood, Mo., U.S.	D3	102
Harwood, N.D., U.S.	C9	111
Harwood Heights, Il., U.S.	*k9	90
Haryāna, state, India	C6	36
Harzgerode, Ger.	B6	19
Harz Mountains, mts., Eur.	C5	18
Ḥasā, Wādī al, val., Jord.	D7	41
Ḥasanah, Bi'r, well, Egy.	D5	41
Hasan Daği, mtn., Tur.	C10	40
Ḥasan Kīādeh, Iran	C4	39
Hasbrouck Heights, N.J., U.S.	h8	107
Hasdo, stm., India	F9	37
Hase, stm., Ger.	B3	18
Haselünne, Ger.	B3	18
Hashimoto, Japan	o14	33
Haskell, Ar., U.S.	C3	81
Haskell, Ok., U.S.	B6	113
Haskell, Tx., U.S.	C3	120
Haskell, co., Ks., U.S.	E3	93
Haskell, co., Ok., U.S.	B6	113
Haskell, co., Tx., U.S.	C3	120
Haskins, Oh., U.S.	A2	112
Haslach, Aus.	G14	19
Hasle, Den.	C8	15
Haslemere, Eng., U.K.	C7	12
Haslet, Tx., U.S.	n9	120
Haslett, Mi., U.S.	*F6	99
Haslev, Den.	C6	15
Hassan, India	F6	36
Hassayampa, stm., Az., U.S.	D3	80
Hassell, N.C., U.S.	B5	110
Hasselt, Bel.	B6	16
Hasselt, Neth.	B6	17
Hassfurt, Ger.	C5	19
Hassi Messaoud, Alg.	C6	44
Hassleben, Ger.	E7	15
Hässleholm, Swe.	I5	14
Hassloch, Ger.	D3	19
Hastings, Barb.	K20	65
Hastings, Ont.	C7	73
Hastings, N.Z.	M16	51
Hastings, Eng., U.K.	E7	10
Hastings, Fl., U.S.	C5	86
Hastings, Ia., U.S.	C2	92
Hastings, Mi., U.S.	F5	99
Hastings, Mn., U.S.	F6	100
Hastings, Ne., U.S.	D7	104
Hastings, N.D., U.S.	C7	111
Hastings, Ok., U.S.	C3	113
Hastings, Pa., U.S.	E4	115
Hastings, W.V., U.S.	h9	125
Hastings, co., Ont.	C7	73
Hastings-on-Hudson, N.Y., U.S.	h13	109
Hästveda, Swe.	B7	15
Hasty, Ar., U.S.	A2	81
Hasty, Co., U.S.	C8	83
Haswell, Co., U.S.	C7	83
Hatboro, Pa., U.S.	*F11	115
Hatch, N.M., U.S.	E2	108
Hatch, Ut., U.S.	F3	121
Hatchechubbee, Al., U.S.	C4	78
Hatchet Creek, stm., Al., U.S.	B3	78
Hatchet Lake, N.S.	E6	71
Hatchie, stm., Tn., U.S.	B2	119
Hatchineha, Lake, l., Fl., U.S.	D5	86
Hatchville, Ma., U.S.	C6	98
Hatch Wash, val., Ut., U.S.	E6	121
Hat Creek, stm., S.D., U.S.	E2	118
Hateg, Rom.	C6	24
Hatfield, Sask.	F3	75
Hatfield, Ar., U.S.	C1	81
Hatfield, In., U.S.	I3	91
Hatfield, Ma., U.S.	B2	98
Hatfield, Mn., U.S.	G2	100
Hatfield, Mo., U.S.	A3	102
Hatfield, Pa., U.S.	F11	115
Hathaway, Mt., U.S.	D10	103
Häthras, India	D7	37
Ha Tien, Viet.	G6	35
Ha Tinh, Viet.	C6	35
Hatley, Ga., U.S.	E3	87
Hatley, Ms., U.S.	B5	101
Hatley, Wi., U.S.	D4	126
Hat Mountain, mtn., Az., U.S.	E3	80
Hato, Neth. Ant.	H19	65
Hato, Bocht van b., Neth. Ant.	H19	65
Hato Mayor [del Rey], Dom. Rep.	E9	64
Hatta, India	E7	37
Hattem, Neth.	B6	17
Hatteras, N.C., U.S.	B7	110
Hatteras, Cape, c., N.C., U.S.	B7	110
Hatteras Inlet, b., N.C., U.S.	B7	110
Hattfjelldal, Nor.	E6	14
Hattiesburg, Ms., U.S.	D4	101
Hattieville, Ar., U.S.	B3	81
Hattingen, Ger.	*C3	18
Hatton, Sask.	G1	75
Hatton, Al., U.S.	A2	78
Hatton, Ar., U.S.	C1	81
Hatton, N.D., U.S.	B8	111
Hatvan, Hung.	B4	24
Hat Yai (Ban Hat Yai), Thai.	D2	34
Hatzic, B.C.	f13	69
Haubourdin, Fr.	D3	17
Haubstadt, In., U.S.	H2	91
Haugan, Mt., U.S.	C1	103
Haugen, Wi., U.S.	C2	126
Haughton, La., U.S.	B2	95
Haugesund, Nor.	H1	14
Haultain, stm., Sask.	A2	75
Hauppauge, N.Y., U.S.	*n15	109
Hauraki Gulf, b., N.Z.	L15	51
Hausach, Ger.	A4	20
Hauser, Or., U.S.	D2	114
Hauser Dam, Mt., U.S.	D5	103
Haus Stock, mtn., Switz.	C7	21
Haut, Isle au, i., Me., U.S.	D4	96
Haut Atlas, mts., Mor.	C3	44
Haute-Marne, dept., Fr.	A1	20
Hauterive (part of Baie-Comeau), Que.	k13	74
Hautes-Alpes, dept., Fr.	E2	20
Haute-Saône, dept., Fr.	B2	20
Haute-Savoie, dept., Fr.	C2	20
Hautes Fagnes, mts., Eur.	D6	17
Hautmont, Fr.	B5	16
Haut-Rhin, dept., Fr.	B3	20
Hauula, Hi., U.S.	B4	88
Hauzenberg, Ger.	E8	19
Havana (La Habana), Cuba	C2	64
Havana, Al., U.S.	C2	78
Havana, Ar., U.S.	B2	81
Havana, Fl., U.S.	B2	86
Havana, Il., U.S.	C3	90
Havana, Ks., U.S.	E8	93
Havana, N.D., U.S.	D8	111
Havana Nakya, Az., U.S.	E4	80
Havasu, Lake, res., U.S.	C1	80
Havasupai Indian Reservation, Az., U.S.	A3	80
Havel, stm., Eur.	F6	15
Havelberg, Ger.	F6	15
Havelock, N.B.	D4	71
Havelock, Ont.	C7	73
Havelock, Ia., U.S.	B3	92
Havelock, N.C., U.S.	C6	110
Haven, Ks., U.S.	E6	93
Haven, Wi., U.S.	k10	126
Havensville, Ks., U.S.	C7	93
Haverford [Township], Pa., U.S.	o20	115
Haverfordwest, Wales, U.K.	C3	12
Haverhill, Eng., U.K.	B8	12
Haverhill, Ma., U.S.	A5	98
Haverhill, N.H., U.S.	B2	106
Haversham, R.I., U.S.	G2	116
Haverstraw, N.Y., U.S.	D7	109
Havertown, Pa., U.S.	G11	115
Haviland, Ks., U.S.	E4	93
Haviland, Oh., U.S.	A1	112
Havířov, Czech.	*D5	26
Havlíčkův Brod, Czech.	D3	26
Havre, Mt., U.S.	B7	103
Havre-Aubert, Île du, i., Que.	B8	71
Havre aux Maisons, Île du, i., Que.	B8	71
Havre Boucher, N.S.	D8	71
Havre de Grace, Md., U.S.	A5	97
Havre North, Mt., U.S.	B7	103
Havre Saint Pierre, Que.	h9	72
Havza, Tur.	B10	40
Haw, stm., N.C., U.S.	B3	110
Hawaii, co., Hi., U.S.	D6	88
Hawaii, state, U.S.	C5	88
Hawaii, i., U.S.	D6	88
Hawaiian Gardens, Ca., U.S.	*n12	82
Hawaiian Islands, is., Hi., U.S.	m14	88
Hawaii Volcanoes National Park, Hi., U.S.	D6	88
Hawarden, Sask.	F2	75
Hawarden, Ia., U.S.	A1	92
Hawea, Lake, l., N.Z.	P12	51
Hawera, N.Z.	M15	51
Hawes, Eng., U.K.	F6	13
Hawesville, Ky., U.S.	C3	94
Hawi, Hi., U.S.	C6	88
Hawick, Scot., U.K.	C5	10
Hawk, stm., Newf.	B3	72
Hawke Bay, b., N.Z.	M16	51
Hawke Island, i., Newf.	B4	72
Hawker, Austl.	F7	50
Hawkes, Mount, mtn., Ant.	A7	7
Hawkesbury, Ont.	B10	73
Hawkesbury Island, i., B.C.	C3	69
Hawkestone, Ont.	C5	73
Hawkeye, Ia., U.S.	B6	92
Hawkins, Wi., U.S.	C3	126
Hawkins, co., Tn., U.S.	C11	119
Hawkinsville, Ga., U.S.	D3	87
Hawkinsville, De., U.S.	D3	85
Hazor Ashdod, Isr.	h9	41
Hazor HaGelilit, Isr.	B7	41
Head Harbour Island, i., Me., U.S.	D5	96
Headland, Al., U.S.	D4	78
Hawley, Tx., U.S.	C3	120
Hawleyville, Ct., U.S.	D2	84
Haworth, N.J., U.S.	h9	107
Haworth, Ok., U.S.	D7	113
Haw River, N.C., U.S.	A3	110
Hawshī 'Īsá, Eg.	D2	41
Hawthorn, Pa., U.S.	D3	115
Hawthorne, Ca., U.S.	n12	82
Hawthorne, Fl., U.S.	C4	86
Hawthorne, Nv., U.S.	E3	105
Hawthorne, N.J., U.S.	B4	107
Hawthorne, N.Y., U.S.	g13	109
Hawthorne, Wi., U.S.	B2	126
Haxtun, Co., U.S.	A8	83
Hay, Austl.	F7	50
Hay, Wa., U.S.	C8	124
Hay, stm., Austl.	D6	50
Hay, stm., Can.	E9	66
Hay, stm., Can.	E3	66
Hayange, Fr.	C7	16
Hayden, Al., U.S.	B3	78
Hayden, Az., U.S.	E5	80
Hayden, Co., U.S.	A3	83
Hayden, Ct., U.S.	B5	84
Hayden, Id., U.S.	*B2	89
Hayden, In., U.S.	G6	91
Haydenburg, Tn., U.S.	C8	119
Hayden Lake, l., Id., U.S.	*B2	89
Haydenville, Ma., U.S.	B2	98
Haydenville, Oh., U.S.	C3	112
Hayes, La., U.S.	D3	95
Hayes, S.D., U.S.	C4	118
Hayes, co., Ne., U.S.	D4	104
Hayes, stm., Man.	B5	70
Hayes, Mount, mtn., Ak., U.S.	C10	79
Hayes Center, Ne., U.S.	D4	104
Hayesville, N.C., U.S.	f9	110
Hayesville, Oh., U.S.	B3	112
Hayesville, Or., U.S.	*C4	114
Hayfield, Man.	E1	70
Hayfield, Mn., U.S.	G6	100
Hayfork, Ca., U.S.	B2	82
Hayford Peak, mtn., Nv., U.S.	G6	105
Hay Island, i., Ont.	C4	73
Hay Lakes, Alta.	C4	68
Haylow, Ga., U.S.	F4	87
Hayma, Tur.	C9	40
Haymarket, Va., U.S.	B5	123
Haymock Lake, l., Me., U.S.	B3	96
Haymond, Fr.	F7	91
Haynes, Alta.	C4	68
Haynes, Ar., U.S.	C5	81
Haynes, N.D., U.S.	D3	111
Haynesville, La., U.S.	B2	95
Haynesville, Me., U.S.	C5	96
Hayneville, Al., U.S.	C3	78
Hay-on-Wye, Wales, U.K.	B4	12
Hay River, N.W. Ter.	D9	66
Hays, Ks., U.S.	D4	93
Hays, Mt., U.S.	C8	103
Hays, N.C., U.S.	A1	110
Hays, Yemen	C5	47
Hays, co., Tx., U.S.	D4	120
Hays Canyon Peak, mtn., Nv., U.S.	B2	105
Hayti, Mo., U.S.	E8	102
Hayti, S.D., U.S.	C8	118
Hayti Heights, Mo., U.S.	E8	102
Hayward, Ca., U.S.	h8	82
Hayward, Wi., U.S.	B2	126
Hayward Addition, S.D., U.S.	*D8	118
Haywards Heath, Eng., U.K.	E7	12
Haywood, Man.	E2	70
Haywood, N.C., U.S.	B3	110
Haywood, Ok., U.S.	C6	113
Haywood, co., N.C., U.S.	f9	110
Haywood, co., Tn., U.S.	B2	119
Hazar, Küh-e, mtn., Iran	G8	39
Hazard, Ky., U.S.	C6	94
Hazard, Ne., U.S.	C6	104
Hazardville, Ct., U.S.	B5	84
Hazārībāg, India	E10	37
Hazebrouck, Fr.	B4	16
Hazel, Ky., U.S.	f9	94
Hazel, S.D., U.S.	C8	118
Hazel Crest, Il., U.S.	k9	90
Hazel Dell, Il., U.S.	D5	90
Hazel Dell, Wa., U.S.	D3	124
Hazel Green, Al., U.S.	A3	78
Hazel Green, Ky., U.S.	C6	94
Hazel Green, Wi., U.S.	F3	126
Hazelhurst, Wi., U.S.	C4	126
Hazel Hurst, Pa., U.S.	C4	115
Hazel Park, Mi., U.S.	p15	99
Hazel Patch, Ky., U.S.	C5	94
Hazel Run, Mn., U.S.	F3	100
Hazelton, B.C.	B4	69
Hazelton, Ks., U.S.	E5	93
Hazelton, N.D., U.S.	C5	111
Hazelton, Pa., U.S.	E10	115
Hazlett, Lake, l., Austl.	D4	50
Hazlettville, De., U.S.	D3	85
Headley, Mount, mtn., Mt., U.S.	C1	103
Head of Island, La., U.S.	h10	95
Headquarters, Id., U.S.	C3	89
Headrick, Ok., U.S.	C2	113
Heafford Junction, Wi., U.S.	C4	126
Healdsburg, Ca., U.S.	C2	82
Healdton, Ok., U.S.	C4	113
Healdville, Vt., U.S.	E3	122
Healing Springs, Va., U.S.	C3	123
Healy, Ak., U.S.	C10	79
Healy, Ks., U.S.	D3	93
Heanna, Japan	O5	52
Heard, co., Ga., U.S.	C1	87
Heard Island, i., Austl.	J1	2
Hearne, Tx., U.S.	D4	120
Hearne, Sask.	G3	75
Hearst, Ont.	o19	73
Hearst Island, i., Ant.	C6	7
Heart, stm., N.D., U.S.	C3	111
Heart, stm., Alta.	B2	68
Heart Butte, Mt., U.S.	B4	103
Heart Butte Dam, N.D., U.S.	C4	111
Hearthstone Mountain, mtn., Md., U.S.	A2	97
Heart Lake, l., Alta.	B5	68
Heart Lake, l., Wy., U.S.	B2	127
Heart's Content, Newf.	E5	72
Heartwell, Ne., U.S.	D7	104
Heaters, W.V., U.S.	C4	125
Heath, Al., U.S.	D3	78
Heath, Ma., U.S.	A2	98
Heath, Oh., U.S.	B3	112
Heatherton, N.S.	D8	71
Heath Springs, S.C., U.S.	B6	117
Heathsville, Va., U.S.	C6	123
Heavener, Ok., U.S.	C7	113
Heaundā, Nepal	D10	37
Hebbronville, Tx., U.S.	F3	120
Hebei, prov., China	D8	31
Hebel, Austl.	D6	51
Heber, Az., U.S.	C5	80
Heber City, Ut., U.S.	C4	121
Heber Springs, Ar., U.S.	B3	81
Hebert, La., U.S.	B4	95
Hébertville, Que.	A6	74
Hebgen Lake, res., Mt., U.S.	F5	103
Hebi, China	*D7	31
Hebo, Or., U.S.	B3	114
Hebrides, Sea of the, Scot., U.K.	B3	10
Hebron, Newf.	f9	72
Hebron, Ct., U.S.	C6	84
Hebron, Il., U.S.	A5	90
Hebron, In., U.S.	B3	91
Hebron, Ky., U.S.	h13	94
Hebron, Me., U.S.	D2	96
Hebron, Md., U.S.	D6	97
Hebron, N.H., U.S.	C3	106
Hebron, N.D., U.S.	C3	111
Hebron, Oh., U.S.	C3	112
Hebron, Tx., U.S.	m10	120
Hebron, W.V., U.S.	B3	125
Heby, Swe.	t34	14
Hecate Strait, strt., B.C.	C2	69
Hecelchakán, Mex.	C6	63
Hechingen, Ger.	G4	19
Hechtel, Bel.	C5	17
Hechuan, China	E6	31
Hecker, Il., U.S.	E4	90
Hecklingen, Ger.	B6	19
Hecla, Man.	D3	70
Hecla, S.D., U.S.	B7	118
Hecla Island, i., Man.	D3	70
Hectanooga, N.S.	E3	71
Hector, Ar., U.S.	B3	81
Hector, Mn., U.S.	F4	100
Hede, Swe.	F5	14
Hedemora, Swe.	G6	14
Hedensted, Den.	C3	15
Hedgehog Hill, hill, Ct., U.S.	B7	84
Hedges, Fl., U.S.	k8	86
Hedgesville, W.V., U.S.	B7	125
Hedley, B.C.	E7	69
Hedley, Tx., U.S.	B2	120
Hedo, Cape, c., Japan	N6	52
Hedon, Eng., U.K.	A7	12
Hedrick, In., U.S.	D2	91
Hedrick, Ia., U.S.	C5	92
Heeia, Hi., U.S.	*B4	88
Heel Point, c., Wake I.	A2	52
Heeney, Co., U.S.	A4	83
Heerde, Neth.	B6	17
Heerenveen, Neth.	A6	16
Heerlen, Neth.	B6	16
Heessen, Ger.	B2	19
Hefa, Mifraz (Bay of Haifa), b., Isr.	B6	41
Hefei, China	E8	31
Heflin, Al., U.S.	B4	78
Heflin, La., U.S.	B2	95
Hefner, Lake, res., Ok., U.S.	B4	113
Hegang, China	B11	31
Hegins, Pa., U.S.	E9	115
Heidelberg, Austl.	*G8	50
Heidelberg, Ger.	D4	18
Heidelberg, S. Afr.	D3	49
Heidelberg, Ms., U.S.	D5	101
Heidelberg, Switz.	B8	21
Heidenau, Ger.	C8	19
Heidenheim, Ger.	C5	18
Heidenreichstein, Ger.	C5	18
Heihe (Aihui), China	A10	31
Heilbron, S. Afr.	C4	49
Heilbronn, Ger.	D4	18
Heiligenblut, Aus.	D8	20
Heiligenhafen, Ger.	C5	15
Heiligenstadt, Ger.	C5	18
Heilongjiang, prov., China	B10	31
Heilong Jiang (Amur), stm., Asia	B10	31
Heilungkiang see Heilongjiang, prov., China	B10	31
Heilwood, Pa., U.S.	E4	115
Heimdal, N.D., U.S.	B6	111
Heinola, Fin.	G12	14
Heinsburg, Alta.	C5	68
Heiskell, Tn., U.S.	m13	119
Hejaz, reg., Sau. Ar.	C3	38
Hejian, China	E7	32
Hekla, Mount, vol., Ice.	n23	14
Hekou, China	A5	35
Hel, Pol.	A5	26
Helagsfjället, mtn., Swe.	F5	14
Helan Shan, mts., China	D6	31
Helbra, Ger.	B6	19
Helena, Ar., U.S.	C5	81
Helena, Ca., U.S.	B2	82
Helena, Ga., U.S.	D4	87
Helena, Mo., U.S.	B3	102
Helena, Mt., U.S.	D4	103
Helena, N.Y., U.S.	f10	109
Helena, Oh., U.S.	A2	112
Helena, S.C., U.S.	C4	117
Helensburgh, Scot., U.K.	B4	10
Helenwood, Tn., U.S.	C9	119
Helga å, stm., Swe.	B8	15
Helgasjön, l., Swe.	B8	15
Helgeröd, Nor.	p28	14
Helgoland, i., Ger.	A3	18
Helgoland Bay, b., Ger.	D2	15
Heli, China	C5	33
Helicon see Elikón Óros, mtn., Grc.	g9	25
Helix, Or., U.S.	B8	114
Hellam, Pa., U.S.	G8	115
Hellenthal, Ger.	D6	17
Hellertown, Pa., U.S.	E11	115
Hellín, Spain	C5	22
Hells Canyon, val., U.S.	B10	114
Hells Canyon National Recreation Area, U.S.	B10	114
Hell-Ville, Madag.	f9	49
Helm, Ca., U.S.	D3	82
Helmand, stm., Asia	B3	36
Helmbrechts, Ger.	C6	19
Helmer, Id., U.S.	*C2	89
Helmer, In., U.S.	A7	91
Helmeringhausen, Nmb.	C2	49
Helmetta, N.J., U.S.	C4	107
Helmond, Neth.	B6	16
Helmsburg, In., U.S.	F5	91
Helmsdale, Scot., U.K.	B5	13
Helmsdale, stm., Scot., U.K.	B5	13
Helmsley, Eng., U.K.	F7	13
Helmstedt, Ger.	B5	18
Helong, China	D4	103
Helotes, Tx., U.S.	h7	120
Helper, Ut., U.S.	D5	121
Helsingborg, Swe.	I5	14
Helsingør, Den.	I5	14
Helsinki, Fin.	G11	14
Helston, Eng., U.K.	D2	12
Heltonville, In., U.S.	G5	91
Hepu, China	G6	31
Heqing, China	F5	31
Herāt, Afg.	B3	36
Herbert, Sask.	G2	75
Herbertingen, Ger.	A5	20
Herbert Peak, mtn., N.Z.	O14	51
Herbes, Isle aux, i., Al., U.S.	E1	78
Herblay, Fr.	g9	17
Herblet Lake, l., Man.	B2	70
Herborn, Ger.	C3	19
Herceg-Novi, Yugo.	D2	24
Hercegovina, hist. reg., Yugo.	D4	24
Herculaneum, Mo., U.S.	C7	102
Hercules, Ca., U.S.	*g8	82
Herdecke, Ger.	B2	19
Heredia, C.R.	E8	63
Hereford, Eng., U.K.	D5	10
Hereford, Az., U.S.	F5	80
Hereford, Md., U.S.	A6	83
Hereford, Or., U.S.	C8	114
Hereford, S.D., U.S.	C3	118
Hereford, Tx., U.S.	B1	120
Hereford and Worcester, co., Eng., U.K.	B5	12
Hereford Inlet, b., N.J., U.S.	E3	107
Hérémence, Switz.	D3	21
Herencia, Spain	C4	22
Herentals, Bel.	C4	17
Herford, Ger.	B4	18
Héricourt, Fr.	B2	21
Herington, Ks., U.S.	D7	93
Herisau, Switz.	E4	18
Heritage Range, mts., Ant.	B3	7
Heritage Village, Ct., U.S.	*D3	84
Herkimer, Ks., U.S.	C7	93
Herkimer, N.Y., U.S.	B6	109
Herkimer, co., N.Y., U.S.	B5	109
Herman, Mi., U.S.	B2	99
Herman, Mn., U.S.	E2	100
Herman, Ne., U.S.	C9	104
Hermano Peak, mtn., Co., U.S.	D2	83
Hermansville, Mi., U.S.	C3	99
Hermantown, Mn., U.S.	D6	100
Hermanville, Ms., U.S.	D3	101
Hermeskeil, Ger.	D1	19
Herminie, Pa., U.S.	F2	115
Hermiston, Or., U.S.	B7	114
Hermitage, Newf.	E4	72
Hermitage, Ar., U.S.	D3	81
Hermitage, Mo., U.S.	D4	102
Hermitage, Pa., U.S.	*D1	115
Hermitage Bay, b., Newf.	E3	72
Hermitage Springs, Tn., U.S.	C5	120
Hermleigh, Tx., U.S.	C2	120
Hermon, Me., U.S.	*D4	96
Hermon, N.Y., U.S.	f9	109
Hermon, Mount, mtn., Asia	F11	40
Hermosa, S.D., U.S.	D2	118
Hermosa Beach, Ca., U.S.	*n12	82
Hermosillo, Mex.	B2	63
Hernád, stm., Eur.	A5	24
Hernandarias, Para.	E5	55
Hernandez, N.M., U.S.	A3	108
Hernando, Fl., U.S.	D4	86
Hernando, co., Fl., U.S.	D4	86
Herndon, Ga., U.S.	C3	92
Herndon, Ks., U.S.	C3	93
Herndon, Ky., U.S.	D2	94
Herndon, Pa., U.S.	E8	115
Herndon, Va., U.S.	B5	123
Herndon, W.V., U.S.	D3	125
Herne, Ger.	B2	19
Herne Bay, Eng., U.K.	I3	13
Herod's Gate, hist., Isr. Occ.	m14	41
Heroica Caborca, Mex.	A2	63
Heroica Nogales, Mex.	A2	63
Heron, Mt., U.S.	B1	103
Heron Bay, Al., U.S.	E1	78
Heron Lake, Mn., U.S.	G3	100
Henniker, N.H., U.S.	D3	106
Henning, Il., U.S.	C6	90
Henning, Mn., U.S.	D3	100
Henning, Tn., U.S.	B2	119
Henribourg, Sask.	D3	75
Henrico, co., Va., U.S.	C5	123
Henrietta, Mo., U.S.	B4	102
Henrietta, N.Y., U.S.	B3	109
Henrietta, N.C., U.S.	B1	110
Henrietta, Tx., U.S.	C3	120
Henrietta Island, i., Sov. Un.	B35	128
Henrietta Maria, Cape, c., Ont.	n19	73
Henrieville, Ut., U.S.	F4	121
Henry, Il., U.S.	B4	90
Henry, Ne., U.S.	C1	104
Henry, S.D., U.S.	C8	118
Henry, Tn., U.S.	A3	119
Henry, Va., U.S.	D3	123
Henry, co., Al., U.S.	D4	78
Henry, co., Ga., U.S.	C2	87
Henry, co., Il., U.S.	B3	90
Henry, co., In., U.S.	E7	91
Henry, co., Ia., U.S.	C6	92
Henry, co., Ky., U.S.	B4	94
Henry, co., Mo., U.S.	C4	102
Henry, co., Oh., U.S.	A1	112
Henry, co., Tn., U.S.	A3	119
Henry, co., Va., U.S.	D3	123
Henry, Mount, mtn., Mt., U.S.	B1	103
Henryetta, Ok., U.S.	B6	113
Henry Kater, Cape, c., N.W. Ter.	C19	66
Henry Mountains, mts., Ut., U.S.	E5	121
Henry Pittier National Park, Ven.	A4	60
Henrys Fork, stm., U.S.	E2	127
Henryville, Que.	D4	74
Henryville, In., U.S.	G6	91
Henryville, Ky., U.S.	B5	94
Hensall, Ont.	D3	73
Hensel, N.D., U.S.	A8	111
Henshaw, Ky., U.S.	e9	94
Hensler, N.D., U.S.	B4	111
Hensley, Ar., U.S.	C3	81
Henson Creek, stm., Md., U.S.	f9	97
Hentiyn Nuruu, mts., Mong.	B6	31
Henzada, Burma	E10	36
Hepburn, Sask.	E2	75
Hepburn, Ia., U.S.	D2	92
Hepburn, Oh., U.S.	B2	112
Hephzibah, Ga., U.S.	C4	87
Hepler, Ks., U.S.	E9	93
Heppenheim, Ger.	D3	19
Heppner, Or., U.S.	B7	114
Hepworth, Ont.	C3	73

Name	Map Ref.	Page

Hérouxville, Que. — C5 74
Herreid, S.D., U.S. — B5 118
Herrenberg, Ger. — E3 19
Herrick, Il., U.S. — D5 90
Herrick, S.D., U.S. — D6 118
Herrick Center, Pa., U.S. — C11 115
Herrick Creek, stm., B.C. — B7 69
Herrick Mountain, mtn., Vt., U.S. — D2 122
Herriman, Ut., U.S. — *C3 121
Herrin, Il., U.S. — F4 90
Herring Bay, b., Md., U.S. — C4 97
Herring Cove, N.S. — E6 71
Herring Run, stm., Md., U.S. — g11 97
Herrington Lake, res., Ky., U.S. — C5 94
Hersbruck, Ger. — D6 19
Herschel, Sask. — F1 75
Herscher, Il., U.S. — B5 90
Hersey, Mi., U.S. — E5 99
Hershey, Ne., U.S. — C5 104
Hershey, Pa., U.S. — F8 115
Herstal, Bel. — B6 16
Herten, Ger. — *C3 19
Hertford, Eng., U.K. — E6 10
Hertford, N.C., U.S. — A6 110
Hertford, co., N.C., U.S. — A5 110
Hertfordshire, co., Eng., U.K. — C7 12
Hervás, Spain — B3 22
Hervey Bay, b., Austl. — D9 50
Hervey-Jonction, Que. — C5 74
Herxheim, Ger. — D3 19
Herzberg, Ger. — F7 15
Herzberg, Ger. — B8 19
Herzberg [am Harz], Ger. — B5 19
Herzliyya, Isr. — F10 40
Herzogenaurach, Ger. — D5 19
Herzogenbuchsee, Switz. — B4 21
Hesdin, Fr. — A7 17
Hesel, Ger. — B6 11
Hesper, N.D., U.S. — B6 111
Hesperia, Ca., U.S. — E5 82
Hesperia, Mi., U.S. — E4 99
Hesperus, Co., U.S. — D2 83
Hesperus Mountain, mtn., Co., U.S. — D2 83
Hess, Ok., U.S. — C2 113
Hesse, hist. reg., Ger. — C4 18
Hessel, Mi., U.S. — B6 99
Hesselager, Den. — C4 15
Hesselø, i., Den. — B5 15
Hessen, state, Ger. — C3 19
Hessmer, La., U.S. — C3 95
Hesston, Ks., U.S. — D6 93
Hetland, S.D., U.S. — C8 118
Hettick, Il., U.S. — D3 90
Hettinger, N.D., U.S. — D3 111
Hettinger, co., N.D., U.S. — C3 111
Hettstedt, Ger. — B6 19
Heusler, In., U.S. — I2 91
Heuvelton, N.Y., U.S. — f9 109
Heves, Hung. — B5 24
Heward, Sask. — H4 75
Hewins, Ks., U.S. — E7 93
Hewitt, Mn., U.S. — D3 100
Hewitt, N.J., U.S. — A4 107
Hewitt, Tx., U.S. — *D4 120
Hewitt, Wi., U.S. — D3 126
Hewlett, N.Y., U.S. — *n14 109
Hexham, Eng., U.K. — F6 13
Hexian, China — G7 31
Hexigten Qi, China — C7 32
Hext, Tx., U.S. — D3 120
Heyang, China — G4 32
Heyburn, Id., U.S. — G5 89
Heyworth, Il., U.S. — C5 90
Heze (Caozhou), China — *D8 31
Heze, China — G6 32
Hialeah, Fl., U.S. — G6 86
Hiattville, Ks., U.S. — E9 93
Hiawassee, Ga., U.S. — B3 87
Hiawatha, Ks., U.S. — C8 93
Hiawatha, Ut., U.S. — D5 121
Hiawatha Camp, Co., U.S. — A2 83
Hibbard, In., U.S. — B5 91
Hibbing, Mn., U.S. — C6 100
Hickam Air Force Base, mil., Hi. — g10 88
Hickiwan, Az., U.S. — E3 80
Hickman, De., U.S. — E3 85
Hickman, Ky., U.S. — f8 94
Hickman, Ne., U.S. — D9 104
Hickman, co., Ky., U.S. — f8 94
Hickman, co., Tn., U.S. — B4 119
Hickman's Harbour, Newf. — D5 72
Hickok, Ks., U.S. — E2 93
Hickory, Ky., U.S. — f9 94
Hickory, Ms., U.S. — C4 101
Hickory, N.C., U.S. — B1 110
Hickory, Ok., U.S. — C5 113
Hickory, co., Mo., U.S. — D4 102
Hickory Corners, Mi., U.S. — F5 99
Hickory Flat, Ms., U.S. — A4 101
Hickory Grove, S.C., U.S. — B5 117
Hickory Hills, Il., U.S. — *k9 90
Hickory Plains, Ar., U.S. — C4 81
Hickory Ridge, Ar., U.S. — B5 81
Hickory Valley, Tn., U.S. — B2 119
Hickory Withe, Tn., U.S. — B2 119
Hicks, La., U.S. — C2 95
Hicks, Pt., c., Austl. — H7 51
Hickson, Ont. — D4 73
Hickson Lake, l., Sask. — A3 75
Hicksville, N.Y., U.S. — E7 109
Hicksville, Oh., U.S. — A1 112
Hico, Tx., U.S. — D3 120
Hico, W.V., U.S. — C3 125
Hida, stm., Japan — n16 33
Hidalgo, Il., U.S. — D5 90
Hidalgo, Tx., U.S. — F3 120
Hidalgo, state, Mex. — C5 63
Hidalgo, co., N.M., U.S. — F1 108
Hidalgo, co., Tx., U.S. — F3 120
Hidalgo del Parral, Mex. — B3 63
Hiddenite, N.C., U.S. — B1 110
Hideaway Park, Co., U.S. — B5 83
Hidrolina, Braz. — A3 56
Hieroglyphic Mountains, mts., Az., U.S. — k8 80
Hierro, i., Spain — n13 22
Higashi, Japan — N6 52
Higashiizu, Japan — o18 33
Higbee, Mo., U.S. — B5 102
Higden, Ar., U.S. — B3 81
Higdon, Al., U.S. — A4 78
Higganum, Ct., U.S. — D5 84
Higgins, Tx., U.S. — A2 120
Higgins Lake, Mi., U.S. — D6 99
Higgins Lake, l., Mi., U.S. — D6 99
Higgins Millpond, res., Md., U.S. — C6 97

Higginson, Ar., U.S. — B4 81
Higginsport, Oh., U.S. — D2 112
Higginsville, Mo., U.S. — B4 102
High Bluff, Man. — D2 70
High Bridge, Ky., U.S. — C5 94
High Bridge, N.H., U.S. — E3 106
High Bridge, N.J., U.S. — B3 107
Highfalls, N.C., U.S. — B3 110
High Falls Reservoir, res., Wi., U.S. — C5 126
Highfield, Md., U.S. — A3 97
Highgate, Ont. — E3 73
Highgate Falls, Vt., U.S. — B2 122
High Hill, Mo., U.S. — C6 102
High Hill Lake, l., Man. — B4 70
High Island, Tx., U.S. — E5 120
High Island, i., Mi., U.S. — C5 99
High Knob, mtn., Va., U.S. — A4 123
High Knob, mtn., W.V., U.S. — C5 125
Highland, Ca., U.S. — *E5 82
Highland, Il., U.S. — E4 90
Highland, In., U.S. — A3 91
Highland, Ks., U.S. — C8 93
Highland, Mi., U.S. — o14 99
Highland, N.Y., U.S. — D7 109
Highland, Oh., U.S. — C2 112
Highland, Wi., U.S. — E3 126
Highland, prov., Scot., U.K. — B4 13
Highland, co., Oh., U.S. — C2 112
Highland, co., Va., U.S. — B3 123
Highland Falls, N.Y., U.S. — *D6 109
Highland Grove, Ont. — B6 73
Highland Heights, Oh., U.S. — *g10 112
Highland Home, Al., U.S. — D3 78
Highland Lake, l., Me., U.S. — g7 96
Highland Lakes, N.J., U.S. — A4 107
Highland Park, Il., U.S. — A6 90
Highland Park, Mi., U.S. — p15 99
Highland Park, N.J., U.S. — *C4 107
Highland Park, Tx., U.S. — n10 120
Highland Peak, mtn., Ca., U.S. — C4 82
Highland Point, c., Fl., U.S. — G5 86
Highlands, N.J., U.S. — C5 107
Highlands, N.C., U.S. — f9 110
Highlands, Tx., U.S. — r14 120
Highlands, co., Fl., U.S. — E5 86
Highland Springs, Va., U.S. — C5 123
Highlandville, Ia., U.S. — A6 92
High Level, Alta. — f7 68
Highmore, S.D., U.S. — C6 118
High Point, Ms., U.S. — B4 101
High Point, Mo., U.S. — C5 102
High Point, N.C., U.S. — B2 110
High Point, Wa., U.S. — e12 124
High Prairie, Alta. — B2 68
High Ridge, Mo., U.S. — g12 102
High River, Alta. — D4 68
High Rock, mtn., Md., U.S. — k12 97
Highrock Lake, l., Man. — B1 70
High Rock Lake, res., N.C., U.S. — B2 110
High Rolls Mountain Park, N.M., U.S. — E4 108
High Shoals, Ga., U.S. — C3 87
High Shoals, N.C., U.S. — B1 110
High Spire, Pa., U.S. — F8 115
High Springs, Fl., U.S. — C4 86
High Tatra Mountains, mts., Eur. — D5 26
High Top, mtn., W.V., U.S. — C5 125
Hightstown, N.J., U.S. — C3 107
Highview, Ky., U.S. — *g11 94
High Willhays, mtn., Eng., U.K. — D3 12
Highwood, Il., U.S. — A6 90
Highwood, Mt., U.S. — C6 103
Highwood Baldy, mtn., Mt., U.S. — C6 103
High Wycombe, Eng., U.K. — E6 10
Higley, Az., U.S. — D4 80
Higüero, Punta, c., P.R. — B1 65
Higüey, Dom. Rep. — E9 64
Higura Island, i., Japan — H8 33
Hiiraan, prov., Som. — E6 47
Hiiumaa, i., Sov. Un. — B4 27
Hiko, Nv., U.S. — F6 105
Hikone, Japan — n15 33
Hiko Range, mts., Nv., U.S. — F6 105
Hikurangi, mtn., N.Z. — L17 51
Hilāl, Jabal, mts., Eg. — D5 41
Hilbert, Wi., U.S. — D5 126
Hilda, Alta. — D5 68
Hilda, S.C., U.S. — E5 117
Hildale, Ut., U.S. — F3 121
Hildburghausen, Ger. — C5 18
Hilden, N.S. — D6 71
Hilden, Ger. — B1 19
Hildesheim, Ger. — B4 18
Hildreth, Ne., U.S. — D6 104
Hiles, Wi., U.S. — C5 126
Hilger, Mt., U.S. — C7 103
Hilham, Tn., U.S. — C8 119
Hill, N.H., U.S. — C3 106
Hill, co., Mt., U.S. — B6 103
Hill, co., Tx., U.S. — D4 120
Hilla see Al Ḥillah, Iraq — B4 38
Hillaby, Mount, mtn., Barb. — K20 65
Hillared, Swe. — A7 15
Hill City, Ga., U.S. — B2 87
Hill City, Id., U.S. — F3 89
Hill City, Ks., U.S. — C4 93
Hill City, Mn., U.S. — D5 100
Hill City, S.D., U.S. — D2 118
Hillcrest, Mi., U.S. — n11 99
Hillcrest, N.Y., U.S. — *n15 109
Hillcrest Center, Ca., U.S. — *E4 82
Hillcrest Heights, Md., U.S. — C4 97
Hillegom, Neth. — B4 17
Hillerød, Den. — *C2 104
Hillhead, S.D., U.S. — B8 118
Hilliard, Alta. — B5 68
Hilliard, Fl., U.S. — B5 86
Hilliard, Oh., U.S. — k10 112
Hilliards, Pa., U.S. — D2 115
Hillier, Ont. — C7 73
Hillisburg, In., U.S. — D5 91
Hillister, Tx., U.S. — D5 120
Hillman, Mi., U.S. — C7 99
Hillman, Mn., U.S. — D5 100
Hillmond, Sask. — D1 75
Hillrose, Co., U.S. — A7 83
Hills, Ia., U.S. — C6 92
Hills, Mn., U.S. — G2 100
Hillsboro, Al., U.S. — A2 78
Hillsboro, Ga., U.S. — C3 87
Hillsboro, Il., U.S. — D4 90
Hillsboro, In., U.S. — D3 91
Hillsboro, Ia., U.S. — D6 92
Hillsboro, Ks., U.S. — D6 93

Hillsboro, Md., U.S. — C6 97
Hillsboro, Ms., U.S. — C4 101
Hillsboro, Mo., U.S. — C7 102
Hillsboro, N.H., U.S. — D3 106
Hillsboro, N.M., U.S. — E2 108
Hillsboro, N.D., U.S. — B8 111
Hillsboro, Oh., U.S. — C2 112
Hillsboro, Or., U.S. — B4 114
Hillsboro, Tn., U.S. — D8 119
Hillsboro, Tx., U.S. — C4 120
Hillsboro, W.V., U.S. — C4 125
Hillsboro, Wi., U.S. — E3 126
Hillsburgh, Ont. — D4 73
Hillsborough, Gren. — W25 65
Hillsborough, St. Vin. — W26 65
Hillsborough, Ca., U.S. — *h8 82
Hillsborough, co., Fl., U.S. — E4 86
Hillsborough, co., N.H., U.S. — E3 106
Hillsborough Bay, b., P.E.I. — C6 71
Hillsborough Lower Village, N.H., U.S. — D3 106
Hillsborough Upper Village, N.H., U.S. — D3 106
Hillsdale, Ont. — C5 73
Hillsdale, Il., U.S. — B3 90
Hillsdale, In., U.S. — E3 91
Hillsdale, Ks., U.S. — D9 93
Hillsdale, Mi., U.S. — G6 99
Hillsdale, N.J., U.S. — g8 107
Hillsdale, N.Y., U.S. — C7 109
Hillsdale, Ok., U.S. — A4 113
Hillsdale, Tn., U.S. — A5 119
Hillsdale, Wi., U.S. — C2 126
Hillsdale, Wy., U.S. — E8 127
Hillsdale, co., Mi., U.S. — G6 99
Hillsgrove, Pa., U.S. — D8 115
Hillside, Az., U.S. — C3 80
Hillside, Co., U.S. — C5 83
Hillside, Il., U.S. — *k9 90
Hillside, N.J., U.S. — k8 107
Hillside Heights, De., U.S. — *B3 85
Hillspring, Alta. — E4 68
Hillston, Austl. — F5 51
Hillsview, S.D., U.S. — B6 118
Hillsville, Pa., U.S. — D1 115
Hillsville, Va., U.S. — D2 123
Hilltonia, Ga., U.S. — D5 87
Hilltown, N. Ire., U.K. — C5 11
Hillview, Il., U.S. — D3 90
Hillview, Ky., U.S. — *g11 94
Hillville, Tn., U.S. — B2 119
Hilo, Hi., U.S. — D6 88
Hilo Bay, b., Hi., U.S. — D6 88
Hilpoltstein, Ger. — D6 19
Hilton, Ga., U.S. — E1 87
Hilton, N.Y., U.S. — B3 109
Hilton Head Island, S.C., U.S. — G6 117
Hilton Head Island, i., S.C., U.S. — G6 117
Hiltons, Va., U.S. — f9 123
Hilversum, Neth. — A6 16
Hima, Ky., U.S. — C6 94
Himachal Pradesh, state, India — B6 37
Himalayas, mts., Asia — C8 36
Himeji, Japan — I7 33
Himi, Japan — H8 33
Himrod, N.Y., U.S. — C4 109
Hinche, Haiti — E7 64
Hinchinbrook, i., Austl. — C8 50
Hinchinbrook Island, i., Ak., U.S. — g18 79
Hinchliffe, Sask. — E4 75
Hinch Mountain, mtn., Tn., U.S. — D9 119
Hinckley, Eng., U.K. — B12 12
Hinckley, Il., U.S. — B5 90
Hinckley, Me., U.S. — D3 96
Hinckley, Mn., U.S. — D6 100
Hinckley, Oh., U.S. — A4 112
Hinckley, Ut., U.S. — D3 121
Hinckley Reservoir, res., N.Y., U.S. — B5 109
Hindindí Barrage, Iraq — F15 40
Hindman, Ky., U.S. — C7 94
Hindmarsh, Lake, l., Austl. — G3 51
Hinds, co., Ms., U.S. — C3 101
Hindsboro, Il., U.S. — D5 90
Hinds Lake, l., Newf. — D3 72
Hindsville, Ar., U.S. — A2 81
Hindu Kush, mts., Asia — A5 36
Hines, Mn., U.S. — C4 100
Hines, Or., U.S. — D7 114
Hinesburg, Vt., U.S. — C2 122
Hines Creek, Alta. — A1 68
Hines Creek, stm., Alta. — A1 68
Hineston, La., U.S. — C3 95
Hinesville, Ga., U.S. — E5 87
Hingham, Ma., U.S. — B6 98
Hingham, Mt., U.S. — B6 103
Hingham Bay, b., Ma., U.S. — g12 98
Hingoli, India — C13 40
Hinnøya, i., Nor. — C6 14
Hinojosa [del Duque], Spain — C3 22
Hinsdale, Il., U.S. — k9 90
Hinsdale, Ma., U.S. — B1 98
Hinsdale, Mt., U.S. — B9 103
Hinsdale, N.H., U.S. — E2 106
Hinsdale, N.Y., U.S. — C2 109
Hinsdale, co., Co., U.S. — D3 83
Hinterrhein, Switz. — C7 21
Hinterrhein, stm., Switz. — C7 21
Hinton, Alta. — C2 68
Hinton, Ia., U.S. — B1 92
Hinton, Ok., U.S. — B3 113
Hinton, W.V., U.S. — D4 125
Hirado Island, i., Japan — J4 33
Hiraiwa Cape, c., Japan — P17 52
Hirakata, Japan — *I7 33
Hirakud Reservoir, res., India — G9 37
Hiram, Ga., U.S. — C2 87
Hiram, Me., U.S. — E2 96
Hiram, Oh., U.S. — A4 112
Hiratsuka, Japan — n17 33
Hîrlău, Rom. — B8 24
Hiroo, Japan — E11 33
Hirosaki, Japan — C13 31
Hiroshima, Japan — E11 31
Hirschberg see Jelenia Góra, Pol. — C3 26
Hirson, Fr. — C6 17
Hîrşova, Rom. — D11 24
Hirtshals, Den. — A3 15
Hîsâr, India — D6 37
Hisarönü, Tur. — B9 40
Hiseville, Ky., U.S. — C4 94

Hispaniola, i., N.A. — E8 64
Ḥīt, Iraq — F14 40
Hitachi, Japan — D13 31
Hitchcock, Sask. — H4 75
Hitchcock, Ok., U.S. — B3 113
Hitchcock, S.D., U.S. — C7 118
Hitchcock, Tx., U.S. — r14 120
Hitchcock, co., Ne., U.S. — D4 104
Hitchcock Lake, Ct., U.S. — C4 84
Hitchin, Eng., U.K. — C7 12
Hitchins, Ky., U.S. — B7 94
Hitchita, Ok., U.S. — B6 113
Hiteman, Ia., U.S. — C5 92
Hitoyoshi, Japan — J5 33
Hitra, i., Nor. — F3 14
Hitterdal, Mn., U.S. — D2 100
Hittisau, Aus. — B8 21
Hitzacker, Ger. — E5 15
Hiwannee, Ms., U.S. — D5 101
Hiwasee, Va., U.S. — D2 123
Hiwassee, stm., Tn., U.S. — D9 119
Hiwassee Lake, res., N.C., U.S. — f8 110
Hixon, B.C. — C6 69
Hixton, Wi., U.S. — D2 126
Hjallerup, Den. — A4 15
Hjälmaren, l., Swe. — H7 14
Hjälmseryd, Swe. — A8 15
Hjo, Swe. — H6 14
Hjørring, Den. — I3 14
Hkakabo Razi, mtn., Burma — C10 36
Hlohovec, Czech. — D4 26
Ho, Ghana — E5 45
Hoa Binh, Viet. — B6 35
Hoaeae, Hi., U.S. — g9 88
Hoagland, In., U.S. — C8 91
Hoback, stm., Wy., U.S. — C2 127
Hobart, Austl. — o15 50
Hobart, In., U.S. — A3 91
Hobart, N.Y., U.S. — C6 109
Hobart, Ok., U.S. — B2 113
Hobbema, Alta. — C4 68
Hobbieville, In., U.S. — G4 91
Hobbs, N.M., U.S. — D6 108
Hobbs Island, Al., U.S. — A3 78
Hobe Sound, Fl., U.S. — E6 86
Hoboken (part of Antwerp), Bel. — A5 16
Hoboken, Ga., U.S. — E4 87
Hoboken, N.J., U.S. — k8 107
Hobro, Den. — B3 15
Hobson, Mt., U.S. — D7 103
Hobson Lake, l., B.C. — C7 69
Hobucken, N.C., U.S. — B6 110
Hobyo, Som. — D6 47
Hochfeld, Nmb. — B2 49
Hochheim, Tx., U.S. — E4 120
Höchst (part of Frankfurt am Main), Ger. — C3 19
Höchstadt [an der Aisch], Ger. — D5 19
Hockenheim, Ger. — D3 19
Hockerville, Ok., U.S. — A7 113
Hockessin, De., U.S. — A3 85
Hocking, co., Oh., U.S. — C3 112
Hocking, stm., Oh., U.S. — C3 112
Hockingport, Oh., U.S. — C4 112
Hockley, Tx., U.S. — q14 120
Hockley, co., Tx., U.S. — C1 120
Hoddesdon, Eng., U.K. — k13 10
Hodeida (Al Ḥudaydah), Yemen — D4 38
Hodge, La., U.S. — B3 95
Hodgdon, Me., U.S. — B5 96
Hodgeman, co., Ks., U.S. — D4 93
Hodgen, Ok., U.S. — C7 113
Hodgenville, Ky., U.S. — C4 94
Hodges, Al., U.S. — A2 78
Hodges, S.C., U.S. — C3 117
Hodges Hill, hill, Newf. — D4 72
Hodges Village Reservoir, res., Ma., U.S. — B4 98
Hodgson, Man. — D3 70
Hódmezővásárhely, Hung. — B5 24
Hodonín, Czech. — D4 26
Hoehne, Co., U.S. — D6 83
Hoek van Holland (part of Rotterdam), Neth. — C4 17
Hoensbroek, Neth. — D5 17
Hoeryŏng, N. Kor. — E4 33
Hoey, Sask. — E3 75
Hof, Ger. — C6 18
Hof, Nor. — p28 14
Hoffman, Mn., U.S. — E3 100
Hoffman, N.C., U.S. — B3 110
Hoffman Estates, Il., U.S. — h8 90
Hofgeismar, Ger. — B4 19
Höfn, Ice. — n25 14
Hofsjökull, ice, Ice. — n23 14
Höfu, Japan — I5 33
Höganäs, Swe. — B6 15
Hogansville, Ga., U.S. — C2 87
Hogback Mountain, mtn., Mt., U.S. — F4 103
Hogback Mountain, mtn., Ne., U.S. — C2 104
Hogback Mountain, mtn., S.C., U.S. — A3 117
Hogeland, Mt., U.S. — B8 103
Hog Island, i., Fl., U.S. — C3 86
Hog Island, i., Mi., U.S. — C5 99
Hog Island, i., N.C., U.S. — B6 110
Hog Island, i., R.I., U.S. — D5 116
Hog Island, i., Va., U.S. — C7 123
Hogup Mountains, mts., Ut., U.S. — B2 121
Hoh, stm., Wa., U.S. — B1 124
Hohen Solms, La., U.S. — h9 95
Hohenwald, Tn., U.S. — B4 119
Hohe Tauern, mts., Aus. — E6 18
Hoh Head, c., Wa., U.S. — B1 124
Hohhot, China — C7 31
Hohoe, Ghana — E5 45
Hohokus, N.J., U.S. — h8 107
Hohwachter Bucht, b., Ger. — D4 15
Hoima, Ug. — A5 48
Hoisington, Ks., U.S. — D5 93
Hoi Xuan, Viet. — B6 35
Hokah, Mn., U.S. — G7 100
Hoke, co., N.C., U.S. — B3 110
Hokes Bluff, Al., U.S. — B4 78
Hokitika, N.Z. — O13 51
Hokkaidō, i., Japan — C13 31
Holabird, S.D., U.S. — C6 118
Holbæk, Den. — C5 15
Holbeach, Eng., U.K. — B8 12
Holbrook, Az., U.S. — C5 80
Holbrook, Id., U.S. — G6 89

Holbrook, Ma., U.S. — B5 98
Holbrook, Ne., U.S. — D5 104
Holbrook, N.Y., U.S. — *n15 109
Holcomb, Ks., U.S. — E3 93
Holcomb, Ms., U.S. — B4 101
Holcomb, Mo., U.S. — E7 102
Holcombe, Wi., U.S. — C2 126
Holden, Alta. — C4 68
Holden, La., U.S. — g10 95
Holden, Ma., U.S. — B4 98
Holden, Mo., U.S. — C4 102
Holden, W.V., U.S. — D2 125
Holdenville, Ok., U.S. — B5 113
Holderness, N.H., U.S. — C3 106
Holdfast, Sask. — G3 75
Holdingford, Mn., U.S. — E4 100
Holdrege, Ne., U.S. — D6 104
Hole in the Mountain Peak, Nv., U.S. — C6 105
Holetown, Barb. — K20 65
Holgate, Oh., U.S. — A1 112
Holguín, Cuba — D5 64
Holguín, prov., Cuba — D6 64
Holiday, Fl., U.S. — D4 86
Holiday City at Berkeley, N.J., U.S. — *D4 107
Holladay, Tn., U.S. — B3 119
Holladay, Ut., U.S. — C4 121
Holland, Man. — E2 70
Holland, Ar., U.S. — B3 81
Holland, In., U.S. — H3 91
Holland, Ia., U.S. — B5 92
Holland, Ky., U.S. — D3 94
Holland, Ma., U.S. — B3 98
Holland, Mi., U.S. — F4 99
Holland, Mn., U.S. — F2 100
Holland, Mo., U.S. — E8 102
Holland, Ne., U.S. — D9 104
Holland, N.Y., U.S. — C2 109
Holland, Oh., U.S. — A2 112
Holland, Pa., U.S. — *F12 115
Holland, Tx., U.S. — D4 120
Holland, Wi., U.S. — h9 126
Holland Centre, Ont. — C4 73
Holland Island, i., Md., U.S. — D5 97
Holland see Netherlands, ctry., Eur. — A6 16
Holland Patent, N.Y., U.S. — B5 109
Holland Point, c., Md., U.S. — C4 97
Holland Straits, strt., Md., U.S. — D5 97
Hollandsburg, Oh., U.S. — C1 112
Hollenberg, Ks., U.S. — C7 93
Holley, N.Y., U.S. — B2 109
Hollick-Kenyon Plateau, plat., Ant. — B2 7
Holliday, Mo., U.S. — B5 102
Holliday, Tx., U.S. — C3 120
Hollidaysburg, Pa., U.S. — F5 115
Hollins, Al., U.S. — B3 78
Hollins, Va., U.S. — C3 123
Hollis, N.H., U.S. — E3 106
Hollis, Ok., U.S. — C2 113
Hollis Center, Me., U.S. — E2 96
Hollis Reservoir, res., Trin. — N23 65
Hollister, Ca., U.S. — D3 82
Hollister, Id., U.S. — G4 89
Hollister, Mo., U.S. — E4 102
Hollister, N.C., U.S. — A5 110
Hollister, Ok., U.S. — C3 113
Hollister, Wi., U.S. — C5 126
Hollisterville, Pa., U.S. — D11 115
Holloman Air Force Base, mil., N.M., U.S. — E3 108
Holloway, Mn., U.S. — E3 100
Holloway Terrace, De., U.S. — *B3 85
Hollow Rock, Tn., U.S. — A3 119
Hollowtop Mountain, mtn., Mt., U.S. — E4 103
Hollsopple, Pa., U.S. — F4 115
Holly, Co., U.S. — C8 83
Holly, Mi., U.S. — F7 99
Holly Beach, La., U.S. — E2 95
Holly Bluff, Ms., U.S. — C3 101
Holly Grove, Ar., U.S. — C4 81
Holly Hill, Fl., U.S. — C5 86
Holly Hill, S.C., U.S. — E7 117
Holly Pond, Al., U.S. — A3 78
Holly Ridge, La., U.S. — B4 95
Holly Ridge, N.C., U.S. — C5 110
Holly Shelter Swamp, sw., N.C., U.S. — C5 110
Holly Springs, Ar., U.S. — D3 81
Holly Springs, Ga., U.S. — B2 87
Holly Springs, Ms., U.S. — A4 101
Holly Springs, N.C., U.S. — B4 110
Hollywood, Al., U.S. — A4 78
Hollywood, Az., U.S. — E6 80
Hollywood, Ar., U.S. — C2 81
Hollywood (part of Los Angeles), Ca., U.S. — m12 82
Hollywood, Fl., U.S. — F6 86
Hollywood, Md., U.S. — D4 97
Hollywood, S.C., U.S. — k11 117
Hollywood Indian Reservation, Fl., U.S. — r13 86
Holman, N.W. Ter. — B9 66
Holmdel, N.J., U.S. — A4 108
Holmen, Wi., U.S. — E2 126
Holmes, co., Fl., U.S. — u16 86
Holmes, co., Ms., U.S. — B3 101
Holmes, co., Oh., U.S. — B4 112
Holmes, Mount, mtn., Wy., U.S. — B2 127
Holmes Lake, l., Man. — A3 70
Holmesville, Oh., U.S. — B4 112
Holmsbu, Nor. — p28 14
Holmsund, Swe. — F9 14
Ḥolon, Isr. — B6 41
Holopaw, Fl., U.S. — D5 86
Holroyd, Austl. — *F9 50
Holstebro, Den. — I3 14
Holstein, Ont. — C4 73
Holstein, Ia., U.S. — B2 92
Holstein, Mo., U.S. — C6 102
Holsteinsborg, Grnld. — *C15 61
Holston, Middle Fork, stm., Va., U.S. — f10 123

Holston High Knob, mtn., Tn., U.S. — C11 119
Holsworthy, Eng., U.K. — D3 12
Holt, Al., U.S. — B2 78
Holt, Fl., U.S. — u15 86
Holt, Mi., U.S. — F6 99
Holt, Mn., U.S. — B2 100
Holt, Mo., U.S. — B3 102
Holt, co., Mo., U.S. — A2 102
Holt, co., Ne., U.S. — B7 104
Holt Creek, stm., Ne., U.S. — B6 104
Holt Knob, mtn., Tn., U.S. — g10 119
Holton, In., U.S. — F7 91
Holton, Ks., U.S. — C8 93
Holton, Mi., U.S. — E4 99
Holt Reservoir, res., Al., U.S. — B2 78
Holts Corner, Tn., U.S. — B5 119
Holtsville, N.Y., U.S. — *n15 109
Holtville, Al., U.S. — C3 78
Holtville, Ca., U.S. — F6 82
Holtwood, Pa., U.S. — G9 115
Holualoa, Hi., U.S. — D6 88
Holy Cross, Ak., U.S. — C8 79
Holy Cross, Ia., U.S. — B7 92
Holy Cross, Mountain of the, mtn., Co., U.S. — B4 83
Holyhead, Wales, U.K. — D4 10
Holy Island, i., Eng., U.K. — C6 10
Holy Island, i., Wales, U.K. — D4 10
Holyoke, Co., U.S. — A8 83
Holyoke, Ma., U.S. — B2 98
Holyoke, Mn., U.S. — D6 100
Holyoke Range, hills, Ma., U.S. — B2 98
Holyrood, Ks., U.S. — D5 93
Holy Sepulchre, The Church of the, Isr. Occ. — m14 41
Holzgau, Aus. — B9 21
Holzkirchen, Ger. — B7 20
Holzminden, Ger. — C4 18
Homalin, Burma — D9 36
Homathko, stm., B.C. — D5 69
Homberg, Ger. — B4 19
Homberg, Ger. — B1 19
Hombetsu, Japan — E11 33
Hombori, Mali — C4 45
Hombourg-Haut, Fr. — E6 17
Homburg, Ger. — D2 19
Homburg see Bad Homburg, Ger. — C4 18
Home, Ks., U.S. — C7 93
Home Bay, b., N.W. Ter. — C19 66
Home Corner, In., U.S. — C6 91
Homécourt, Fr. — C6 16
Homecroft, In., U.S. — m10 91
Homedale, Id., U.S. — F2 89
Home Gardens, Ca., U.S. — *n13 82
Home Hill, Austl. — C8 50
Homeland, Ca., U.S. — D4 83
Homeland, Fl., U.S. — E5 86
Homeland, Ga., U.S. — F4 87
Homeland Park, S.C., U.S. — *B2 117
Home Place, In., U.S. — E5 91
Homer, Ak., U.S. — D9 79
Homer, Ga., U.S. — B3 87
Homer, Il., U.S. — C6 90
Homer, In., U.S. — E6 91
Homer, La., U.S. — B2 95
Homer, Mi., U.S. — F6 99
Homer, Ne., U.S. — B9 104
Homer, N.Y., U.S. — C4 109
Homer City, Pa., U.S. — E3 115
Homerville, Ga., U.S. — E4 87
Homer Youngs Peak, mtn., Mt., U.S. — E3 103
Homestead, Fl., U.S. — G6 86
Homestead, Ia., U.S. — C6 92
Homestead, Mt., U.S. — B12 103
Homestead, Ok., U.S. — A3 113
Homestead Air Force Base, mil., Fl., U.S. — G6 86
Homestead National Monument of America, Ne., U.S. — D9 104
Hometown, Il., U.S. — *k9 90
Homewood, Al., U.S. — g7 78
Homewood, Ca., U.S. — C3 82
Homewood, Il., U.S. — B6 90
Homewood, Ms., U.S. — C4 101
Homewood, Oh., U.S. — B4 112
Hominy, Ok., U.S. — A5 113
Hominy Creek, stm., Ok., U.S. — A5 113
Homme Dam, N.D., U.S. — A8 111
Hommura, Japan — o18 33
Homochitto, stm., Ms., U.S. — D2 101
Homosassa, Fl., U.S. — D4 86
Homs (Hims), Syria — B3 38
Hon, Ar., U.S. — C1 81
Honaker, Va., U.S. — e10 123
Honan see Henan, prov., China — E7 31
Honaunau, Hi., U.S. — D6 88
Honaz, mtn., Tur. — B3 40
Honda, Col. — B3 60
Hondo, Alta. — B3 68
Hondo, N.M., U.S. — D4 108
Hondo, Tx., U.S. — E3 120
Hondo, stm., Mex. — h9 63
Hondo, Rio, stm., N.M., U.S. — D4 108
Honduras, ctry., N.A. — D7 63
Honduras, Cabo de, c., Hond. — D7 63
Honduras, Gulf of, b., N.A. — C3 117
Honea Path, S.C., U.S. — C3 117
Hønefoss, Nor. — G4 14
Honey Brook, Pa., U.S. — F10 115
Honey Creek, Ia., U.S. — C2 92
Honey Creek, Wi., U.S. — n11 126
Honey Grove, Tx., U.S. — C5 120
Honey Lake, l., Ca., U.S. — B3 82
Honeypot Glen, Ct., U.S. — C4 84
Honeyville, Ut., U.S. — B3 121
Honfleur, Fr. — C4 16
Hon Gai, Viet. — B7 35
Hong'an, China — I6 32
Honga River, b., Md., U.S. — D5 97
Honghu, China — F2 31
Hongshui He, stm., China — G8 31
Hongwŏn, N. Kor. — E8 33
Hongze, Hu, l., China — G9 6
Honiara, Sol.Is. — H7 6 (?)
Honiton, Eng., U.K. — A5 10 (?)
Honobia, Ok., U.S. — C7 113
Honokaa, Hi., U.S. — C6 88

Name	Map Ref.	Page
Honokahua, Hi., U.S.	B5	88
Honokohau, Hi., U.S.	D6	88
Honolulu, Hi., U.S.	B4	88
Honolulu, co., Hi., U.S.	B3	88
Honolulu International Airport, Hi., U.S.	g10	88
Honomu, Hi., U.S.	D6	88
Honor, Mi., U.S.	D4	99
Honoraville, Al., U.S.	D3	78
Honouliuli, Hi., U.S.	g9	88
Hon Quan, Viet.	G7	35
Honshū, i., Japan	D12	31
Honuapo Bay, b., Hi., U.S.	D6	88
Hood, Co., Tx., U.S.	C4	120
Hood, Mount, mtn., Or., U.S.	B5	114
Hood Canal, b., Wa., U.S.	B2	124
Hoodoo, Tn., U.S.	B5	119
Hoodoo Peak, mtn., Wa., U.S.	A5	124
Hood Point, c., Austl.	F2	50
Hood River, Or., U.S.	B5	114
Hood River, co., Or., U.S.	B5	114
Hoodsport, Wa., U.S.	B2	124
Hoogeveen, Neth.	B6	17
Hoogezand, Neth.	A6	17
Hookena, Hi., U.S.	D6	88
Hooker, Ok., U.S.	e9	113
Hooker, S.D., U.S.	D8	118
Hooker, co., Ne., U.S.	C4	104
Hooker, Bi'r, well, Eg.	D2	41
Hooker, Mount, mtn., Can.	C8	69
Hookerton, N.C., U.S.	B5	110
Hook Head, c., Ire.	E5	11
Hooksett, N.H., U.S.	D4	106
Hoolehua, Hi., U.S.	B4	88
Hoonah, Ak., U.S.	D12	79
Hoopa Valley Indian Reservation, Ca., U.S.	B2	82
Hooper, Co., U.S.	D5	83
Hooper, Ne., U.S.	C9	104
Hooper, Ut., U.S.	B3	121
Hooper, Wa., U.S.	C7	124
Hooper Bay, Ak., U.S.	C6	79
Hooper Creek, stm., Ne., U.S.	h12	104
Hooper Islands, is., Md., U.S.	D5	97
Hooper Strait, strt., Md., U.S.	D5	97
Hoopersville, Md., U.S.	D5	97
Hoopes Reservoir, res., De., U.S.	A3	85
Hoopeston, Il., U.S.	C6	90
Hopedale Harbour, Newf.	C3	72
Hoople, N.D., U.S.	A8	111
Hooppole, Il., U.S.	B4	90
Hoorn, Neth.	A6	16
Hoosac Range, mts., U.S.	A1	98
Hoosic, stm., U.S.	C7	109
Hoosick Falls, N.Y., U.S.	C7	109
Hoosier, Sask.	F1	75
Hoosuc Range, mts., U.S.	D1	96
Hoover, Al., U.S.	*g7	78
Hoover Dam, U.S.	G7	105
Hoover Reservoir, res., Oh., U.S.	B3	112
Hooversville, Pa., U.S.	F4	115
Hopa, Tur.	B13	40
Hopatcong, N.J., U.S.	B3	107
Hopatcong, Lake, l., N.J., U.S.	A3	107
Hop Bottom, Pa., U.S.	C10	115
Hope, B.C.	E7	69
Hope, Ak., U.S.	C10	79
Hope, Ar., U.S.	D2	81
Hope, Id., U.S.	A2	89
Hope, In., U.S.	F6	91
Hope, Ks., U.S.	D6	93
Hope, Me., U.S.	D3	96
Hope, Mi., U.S.	E6	99
Hope, Mn., U.S.	G5	100
Hope, N.M., U.S.	E5	108
Hope, N.D., U.S.	B8	111
Hope, R.I., U.S.	D3	116
Hope, i., Nor.	B12	128
Hope, Ben, mtn., Scot., U.K.	A4	10
Hope, Loch, l., Scot., U.K.	B4	13
Hope, Point, c., Ak., U.S.	B3	79
Hopedale, Newf.	g9	72
Hopedale, Il., U.S.	C4	90
Hopedale, Ma., U.S.	E6	95
Hopedale, La., U.S.	B4	98
Hopedale, Oh., U.S.	B5	112
Hope see Hebei, prov., China	D8	31
Hope Hull, Al., U.S.	C3	78
Hope Island, i., B.C.	D4	69
Hope Island, i., R.I., U.S.	E5	116
Hopelawn, N.J., U.S.	k7	107
Hopelchén, Mex.	D7	63
Hope Mills, N.C., U.S.	C4	110
Hopes Advance, Cap, c., Que.	f13	74
Hopeton, Ok., U.S.	A3	113
Hopetoun, Austl.	G4	51
Hopetown, S. Afr.	C3	49
Hope Valley, R.I., U.S.	E2	116
Hopeville, In., U.S.	D4	92
Hopewell, N.S.	D7	71
Hopewell, Ms., U.S.	D3	101
Hopewell, N.J., U.S.	C3	107
Hopewell, Oh., U.S.	C3	112
Hopewell, Va., U.S.	C5	123
Hopewell Cape, N.B.	D5	71
Hopewell Junction, N.Y., U.S.	D7	109
Hopi Buttes, mtn., Az., U.S.	B5	80
Hopi Indian Reservation, Az., U.S.	A5	80
Hopkins, Mi., U.S.	F5	99
Hopkins, Mn., U.S.	n12	100
Hopkins, Mo., U.S.	A3	102
Hopkins, S.C., U.S.	D6	117
Hopkins, co., Ky., U.S.	C2	94
Hopkins, co., Tx., U.S.	C5	120
Hopkinsville, Ky., U.S.	D2	94
Hopkinton, Ia., U.S.	B6	92
Hopkinton, Ma., U.S.	B4	98
Hopkinton, N.H., U.S.	D3	106
Hopkinton, N.Y., U.S.	f10	109
Hopkinton, R.I., U.S.	F1	116
Hopkinton Lake, res., N.H., U.S.	D3	106
Hopland, Ca., U.S.	C2	82
Hopson, Tn., U.S.	C11	119
Hopwood, Pa., U.S.	G2	115
Hoquiam, Wa., U.S.	C2	124
Horace, Ks., U.S.	D2	93
Horace, N.D., U.S.	C9	111
Horace Mountain, mtn., Ak., U.S.	B10	79
Horatio, Ar., U.S.	D1	81
Horatio, S.C., U.S.	C6	117
Horaž d'ovice, Czech.	D8	19
Horb, Ger.	E3	19
Hørby, Den.	A4	15
Hörby, Swe.	C7	15
Horconcitos, Pan.	F6	62
Hord, Il., U.S.	E5	90
Hordville, Ne., U.S.	C8	104
Horgen, Switz.	E4	18
Horicon, Wi., U.S.	E5	126
Horine, Mo., U.S.	C7	102
Horizon, Sask.	H3	75
Horlick Mountains, mts., Ant.	A36	7
Hormoz, i., Iran	H8	39
Hormuz, Strait of, strt., Asia	C5	38
Horn, Aus.	D7	18
Horn, c., Ice.	m21	14
Horn, Cape, c., Chile	k12	54
Hornavan, l., Swe.	D7	14
Hornbeak, Tn., U.S.	A2	119
Hornbeck, La., U.S.	C2	95
Hornburg, Ger.	A5	19
Horncastle, Eng., U.K.	A7	12
Hornell, N.Y., U.S.	C3	109
Hornerstown, N.J., U.S.	C3	107
Hornersville, Mo., U.S.	E7	102
Horn Head, c., Ire.	B4	11
Hornick, Ia., U.S.	B1	92
Horning's Mills, Ont.	C4	73
Horní Počernice, Czech.	n18	26
Horn Island, i., Ms., U.S.	E5	101
Horn Island Pass, strt., Ms., U.S.	g8	101
Horn Lake, Ms., U.S.	A3	101
Horn Mountain, mtn., Al., U.S.	B3	78
Horn Plateau, plat., N.W. Ter.	D9	66
Horn Pond, l., Ma., U.S.	g11	98
Hornsby, Tn., U.S.	B3	119
Hornsbyville, Va., U.S.	h15	123
Hornsea, Eng., U.K.	D6	10
Hornslet, Den.	B4	15
Hörnum, Ger.	A4	18
Hořovice, Czech.	D8	19
Horqin Youyi Qianqi, China	A10	32
Horqin Youyi Zhongqi, China	B9	32
Horqueta, Para.	D4	55
Horred, Swe.	A6	15
Horry, co., S.C., U.S.	D10	117
Horse, stm., Alta.	A5	68
Horse, stm., Ct., U.S.	C6	84
Horse Branch, Ky., U.S.	C3	94
Horse Cave, Ky., U.S.	C4	94
Horse Creek, Wy., U.S.	E7	127
Horse Creek, stm., U.S.	E8	127
Horse Creek, stm., Co., U.S.	C7	83
Horse Creek, stm., Mo., U.S.	D4	102
Horse Creek Reservoir, res., Co., U.S.	C7	83
Horsefly, B.C.	C7	69
Horsefly Lake, l., B.C.	C7	69
Horsehead Lake, l., N.D., U.S.	B6	111
Horseheads, N.Y., U.S.	C4	109
Horse Heaven Hills, hills, Wa., U.S.	C6	124
Horse Islands, Newf.	C4	72
Horse Mountain, mtn., N.M., U.S.	D1	108
Horsens, Den.	J3	14
Horseshoe Beach, Fl., U.S.	C3	86
Horseshoe Bend, Id., U.S.	F2	89
Horseshoe Bend National Military Park, U.S.	C4	78
Horseshoe Cove, b., Fl., U.S.	C3	86
Horseshoe Lake, l., Man.	C4	70
Horseshoe Point, c., Fl., U.S.	C5	86
Horseshoe Reservoir, res., Az., U.S.	C4	80
Horse Springs, N.M., U.S.	D1	108
Horsham, Austl.	G7	50
Horsham, Eng., U.K.	C7	12
Horšovský Týn, Czech.	D7	19
Horta, Port.	g8	44
Horten, Nor.	H4	14
Hortense, Ga., U.S.	E5	87
Horton, Al., U.S.	A3	78
Horton, In., U.S.	D5	91
Horton, Ks., U.S.	B8	93
Horton, Mo., U.S.	D3	102
Horton, stm., N.W. Ter.	C8	66
Hortonia, Lake, l., Vt., U.S.	D2	122
Hortonville, Wi., U.S.	D5	126
Hørve, Den.	C5	15
Hörvik, Swe.	B8	15
Horw, Switz.	B5	21
Hoschton, Ga., U.S.	B3	87
Hosford, Fl., U.S.	B2	86
Hoshāb, Pak.	H11	39
Hoshiārpur, India	B6	36
Hoskins, Ne., U.S.	B8	104
Hoskins, Or., U.S.	C3	114
Hoskinston, Ky., U.S.	C6	94
Hosmer, B.C.	E10	69
Hosmer, S.D., U.S.	B6	118
Hospers, Ia., U.S.	A2	92
Hospital, Ire.	E3	11
Hospitalet, Spain	B7	22
Hosston, La., U.S.	B2	95
Hosta Butte, mtn., N.M., U.S.	B1	108
Hoste, Isla, i., Chile	k12	54
Hot, Thai.	C3	35
Hotaka, Mount, mtn., Japan	H8	33
Hotan, China	A6	36
Hotan He, stm., China	A7	36
Hotchkiss, Co., U.S.	C3	83
Hotchkissville, Ct., U.S.	C3	84
Hot Coffee, Ms., U.S.	D4	101
Hot Creek Range, mts., Nv., U.S.	E5	105
Hot Creek Valley, val., Nv., U.S.	E5	105
Hotevilla, Az., U.S.	A6	19
Hoting, Swe.	E7	14
Hot Spring, co., Ar., U.S.	C2	81
Hot Springs, Mt., U.S.	C2	103
Hot Springs see Truth or Consequences, N.M., U.S.	D2	108
Hot Springs, N.C., U.S.	f10	110
Hot Springs, S.D., U.S.	D2	118
Hot Springs, Va., U.S.	C3	123
Hot Springs, co., Wy., U.S.	C4	127
Hot Springs National Park, Ar., U.S.	C2	81
Hot Springs National Park, Ar., U.S.	C2	81
Hot Springs Peak, mtn., Ca., U.S.	B3	82
Hot Springs Peak, mtn., Nv., U.S.	B4	105
Hot Sulphur Springs, Co., U.S.	A4	83
Hottah Lake, l., N.W. Ter.	C9	66
Hotte, Massif de la, mts., Haiti	B2	80
Houck, Az., U.S.	B6	80
Houffalize, Bel.	D5	17
Houghton, Mi., U.S.	A2	99
Houghton, N.Y., U.S.	C2	109
Houghton, S.D., U.S.	B7	118
Houghton, co., Mi., U.S.	B2	99
Houghton Lake, Mi., U.S.	D6	99
Houghton Lake, l., Mi., U.S.	D6	99
Houghton Lake Heights, Mi., U.S.	D6	99
Houilles, Fr.	g9	16
Houlka, Ms., U.S.	A4	101
Houlton, Me., U.S.	B5	96
Houltonville, La., U.S.	h11	95
Houma, La., U.S.	E5	95
Houmt Essouk, Tun.	C7	44
Houndé, Burkina	D4	45
Hourn, Loch, b., Scot., U.K.	C3	13
Housatonic, Ma., U.S.	B1	98
Housatonic, stm., U.S.	D3	84
House, N.M., U.S.	C6	108
House, stm., Alta.	B4	68
House Range, mts., Ut., U.S.	D2	121
House Springs, Mo., U.S.	g12	102
Houston, B.C.	B4	69
Houston, Al., U.S.	A2	78
Houston, Ar., U.S.	B3	81
Houston, De., U.S.	E3	85
Houston, In., U.S.	F5	91
Houston, Mn., U.S.	G7	100
Houston, Mo., U.S.	D6	102
Houston, Oh., U.S.	B1	112
Houston, Pa., U.S.	F1	115
Houston, Tx., U.S.	E5	120
Houston, co., Al., U.S.	D4	78
Houston, co., Ga., U.S.	D3	87
Houston, co., Mn., U.S.	G7	100
Houston, co., Tn., U.S.	A4	119
Houston, co., Tx., U.S.	D5	120
Houston, stm., La., U.S.	D2	95
Houston, Lake, res., Tx., U.S.	r14	120
Houstonia, Mo., U.S.	C4	102
Houston Intercontinental Airport, Tx., U.S.	r14	120
Houtzdale, Pa., U.S.	E5	115
Hovd, Mong.	B3	31
Hovd, stm., Mong.	B3	31
Hove, Eng., U.K.	E6	10
Hövelhof, Ger.	B3	19
Hoven, S.D., U.S.	B6	118
Hovenweep National Monument, Ut., U.S.	F6	121
Hovland, Mn., U.S.	k10	100
Hövsgöl Lake, l., Mong.	A5	31
Howar, Wādī, val., Afr.	B2	47
Howard, Al., U.S.	B2	78
Howard, Co., U.S.	C5	83
Howard, Ks., U.S.	E7	93
Howard, Ms., U.S.	B3	101
Howard, N.Y., U.S.	C3	109
Howard, Oh., U.S.	B3	112
Howard, Pa., U.S.	D6	115
Howard, S.D., U.S.	D8	118
Howard, Wi., U.S.	D5	126
Howard, co., Ar., U.S.	C2	81
Howard, co., In., U.S.	C5	91
Howard, co., Ia., U.S.	A5	92
Howard, co., Md., U.S.	B4	97
Howard, co., Mo., U.S.	B5	102
Howard, co., Ne., U.S.	C7	104
Howard, co., Tx., U.S.	C2	120
Howard City, Mi., U.S.	E5	99
Howard Hanson Reservoir, res., Wa., U.S.	B4	124
Howard Lake, Mn., U.S.	E4	100
Howard Prairie Lake, res., Or., U.S.	E4	114
Howards Grove-Millersville, Wi., U.S.	E6	126
Howardville, Mo., U.S.	E8	102
Howe, Id., U.S.	F6	89
Howe, In., U.S.	A7	91
Howe, Ok., U.S.	C7	113
Howe, Cape, c., Austl.	G9	50
Howell, Mi., U.S.	F7	99
Howell, co., Mo., U.S.	E6	102
Howells, Ne., U.S.	C8	104
Howes, S.D., U.S.	C3	118
Howe Sound, strt., B.C.	E6	69
Howick, Que.	D4	74
Howison, Ms., U.S.	E4	101
Howland, Me., U.S.	C4	96
Howland, Oh., U.S.	*A5	112
Howland Island, i., Oc.	F11	6
Howley, Newf.	D3	72
Howley, Mount, mtn., Newf.	D2	72
Howser, B.C.	D9	69
Howson Peak, mtn., B.C.	B4	69
Howth (part of Dublin), Ire.	D5	11
Hoxie, Ar., U.S.	A5	81
Hoxie, Ks., U.S.	C3	93
Höxter, Ger.	B4	19
Hoy, i., Scot., U.K.	A5	10
Hoya, Ger.	B4	18
Hoyerswerda, Ger.	C7	18
Hoylake, Eng., U.K.	A4	12
Hoyleton, Il., U.S.	E4	90
Hoyo, Sierra del, mts., Spain	o17	22
Hoyt, N.B.	D3	71
Hoyt, Co., U.S.	A6	83
Hoyt, Ks., U.S.	C8	93
Hoyt, Ok., U.S.	B6	113
Hoyt Lakes, Mn., U.S.	C6	100
Hoytville, Oh., U.S.	A2	112
Hradec Králové, Czech.	C3	26
Hranice, Czech.	D6	26
Hřínová, Czech.	C7	26
Hsinchu, Tai.	G9	31
Hsipaw, Burma	B3	34
Huacho, Peru	D2	58
Huachuca City, Az., U.S.	F5	80
Huacrachuco, Peru	C2	58
Huade, China	D5	32
Huadian, China	C10	31
Huai'an (Huaicheng), China	H8	32
Huaibei, China	C9	31
Huaide, China	C9	31
Huailai, China	D5	32
Huainan, China	E8	31
Huairou, China	D7	32
Huaiyin, China	E8	31
Huajuapan de León, Mex.	D5	63
Hualalai, vol., Hi., U.S.	D6	88
Hualapai Indian Reservation, Az., U.S.	B2	80
Hualapai Mountains, mts., Az., U.S.	C2	80
Hualapai Peak, mtn., Az., U.S.	B2	80
Hualgayoc, Peru	C2	58
Hualien, Tai.	G9	31
Huallaga, stm., Peru	C2	58
Huallanca, Peru	C2	58
Huamachuco, Peru	C2	58
Huamantla, Mex.	n15	63
Huambo, Ang.	D2	48
Huambo, dept., Ang.	D2	48
Huancabamba, Peru	C2	58
Huancané, Peru	E4	58
Huancavelica, Peru	D2	58
Huancavelica, dept., Peru	D2	58
Huancayo, Peru	D2	58
Huanchaca, Bol.	D2	55
Huangchuan, China	H6	32
Huanggang, China	E8	31
Huang He (Yellow), stm., China	D8	31
Huangling, China	D6	31
Huangmei, China	I6	32
Huangpo, China	K2	32
Huangshi, China	E8	31
Huangyan, China	J9	32
Huanguyan, China	D5	31
Huanjiang, China	G6	31
Huanta, Peru	D3	58
Huánuco, Peru	C2	58
Huánuco, dept., Peru	C2	58
Huanuni, Bol.	C2	55
Huara, Chile	C2	55
Huaral, Peru	D2	58
Huaraz, Peru	C2	58
Huari, Bol.	C2	55
Huariaca, Peru	C2	58
Huarina, Bol.	C2	58
Huarmey, Peru	D2	58
Huascarán, Nevado, mtn., Peru	C2	58
Huasco, Chile	E1	55
Huasco, stm., Chile	E1	55
Huatabampo, Mex.	B3	63
Huatusco [de Chicuellar], Mex.	n15	63
Huauchinango, Mex.	m14	63
Huaxian, China	G6	32
Huayllay, Peru	D2	58
Huaytará, Peru	D2	58
Huayuan, China	J3	32
Hubbard, Sask.	F4	75
Hubbard, Ia., U.S.	B4	92
Hubbard, Mn., U.S.	D4	100
Hubbard, Ne., U.S.	B9	104
Hubbard, Oh., U.S.	A5	112
Hubbard, Or., U.S.	B4	114
Hubbard, Tx., U.S.	D4	120
Hubbard, co., Mn., U.S.	C4	100
Hubbard Creek Lake, res., Tx., U.S.	C3	120
Hubbard Lake, Mi., U.S.	D7	99
Hubbard Lake, l., Mi., U.S.	D7	99
Hubbards, N.S.	E5	71
Hubbardston, Ma., U.S.	B3	98
Hubbardston, Mi., U.S.	E6	99
Hubbardton, stm., Vt., U.S.	D2	122
Hubbell, Mi., U.S.	A2	99
Hubbell, Ne., U.S.	D8	104
Hubei, prov., China	E7	31
Huben, Aus.	C8	20
Huber, Ga., U.S.	D3	87
Huberdeau, Que.	D3	74
Huber Heights, Oh., U.S.	*C1	112
Huber Ridge, Oh., U.S.	*B3	112
Huber South, Oh., U.S.	*C1	112
Hubli-Dhārwār, India	E6	36
Huckleberry Hill, Ct., U.S.	B4	84
Huckleberry Mountain, mtn., Or., U.S.	D4	114
Huddersfield, Eng., U.K.	D6	10
Huddinge, Swe.	*H7	14
Huddleston, Va., U.S.	C3	123
Huddleston Knob, mtn., Tn., U.S.	C8	119
Hude, Ger.	E2	15
Hudiksvall, Swe.	G7	14
Hudson, Que.	D3	74
Hudson, Co., U.S.	A6	83
Hudson, Fl., U.S.	D4	86
Hudson, Il., U.S.	C5	90
Hudson, Ia., U.S.	B5	92
Hudson, Ks., U.S.	D5	93
Hudson, Ma., U.S.	B4	98
Hudson, Mi., U.S.	G6	99
Hudson, N.H., U.S.	E4	106
Hudson, N.Y., U.S.	C7	109
Hudson, N.C., U.S.	B1	110
Hudson, Oh., U.S.	A4	112
Hudson, S.D., U.S.	D9	118
Hudson, Wi., U.S.	D1	126
Hudson, Wy., U.S.	D4	127
Hudson, co., N.J., U.S.	B4	107
Hudson, stm., Ga., U.S.	B3	87
Hudson, Lake, res., Ok., U.S.	A6	113
Hudson Bay, Sask.	E4	75
Hudson Bay, b., Can.	D15	66
Hudson Falls, N.Y., U.S.	B7	109
Hudson Hope, B.C.	A6	69
Hudson Mountain, mtn., Me., U.S.	B3	96
Hudson Mountains, mts., Ant.	B3	7
Hudson Strait, strt., Can.	D18	66
Hudsonville, Mi., U.S.	F5	99
Hudspeth, co., Tx., U.S.	o12	120
Hudwin Lake, l., Man.	C4	70
Hue, Viet.	B3	34
Huedin, Rom.	B6	24
Huehuetenango, Guat.	D6	63
Huejotzingo, Mex.	n14	63
Huejutla [de Reyes], Mex.	m14	63
Huelma, Spain	D3	22
Huelva, Spain	D2	22
Huentelauquén, Chile	D2	54
Huércal-Overa, Spain	D5	22
Huerfano, stm., Co., U.S.	D6	83
Huerfano, co., Co., U.S.	D6	83
Huerfano Mountain, mtn., N.M., U.S.	A2	108
Huerva, stm., Spain	D5	22
Huesca, Spain	A5	22
Huéscar, Spain	D4	22
Huetamo de Núñez, Mex.	D4	63
Huete, Spain	B4	22
Huetter, Id., U.S.	*B2	89
Hueytown, Al., U.S.	g6	78
Huff, N.D., U.S.	C5	111
Huffakers, Nv., U.S.	D2	105
Huger, S.C., U.S.	h12	117
Huggins, Mo., U.S.	D5	104
Hugh Butler Lake, res., Ne., U.S.	D5	104
Hughenden, Austl.	D7	50
Hughenden, Alta.	C5	68
Hughes, Ak., U.S.	B9	79
Hughes, Ar., U.S.	C5	81
Hughes, co., Ok., U.S.	B5	113
Hughes, co., S.D., U.S.	C5	118
Hughes, stm., Man.	A1	70
Hughes, North Fork, stm., W.V., U.S.	B3	125
Hughes, South Fork, stm., W.V., U.S.	B3	125
Hughesville, Md., U.S.	C4	97
Hughesville, N.J., U.S.	B2	107
Hughesville, Pa., U.S.	D8	115
Hughson, Ca., U.S.	D3	82
Hugli, stm., India	D8	36
Hugo, Co., U.S.	B7	83
Hugo, Mn., U.S.	m13	100
Hugo, Ok., U.S.	C6	113
Hugo Lake, res., Ok., U.S.	C6	113
Huguley, Al., U.S.	*C4	78
Huichang, China	F8	31
Huichapan, Mex.	m14	63
Huichón, N. Kor.	F3	33
Huíla, dept., Ang.	D2	48
Huila, dept., Col.	C2	60
Huila, Nevado del, mtn., Col.	C2	60
Huili, China	F5	31
Huimanguillo, Mex.	B1	62
Huimin, China	D8	31
Huiñaimarca, Lago de, l., S.A.	E4	58
Huinan, China	E3	33
Huitzuco [de los Figueroa], Mex.	n14	63
Huixtla, Mex.	D6	63
Huizen, Neth.	B5	17
Huizhou, China	G7	31
Hukuntsi, Bots.	B3	49
Hulan, China	B10	31
Hulbert, Mi., U.S.	B5	99
Hulbert, Ok., U.S.	B6	113
Hulen, Ky., U.S.	D6	94
Hulett, Wy., U.S.	B8	127
Hulin, China	B6	33
Hull, Que.	D2	74
Hull, Ia., U.S.	A1	92
Hull, Il., U.S.	D2	90
Hull, Ma., U.S.	B6	98
Hull, co., Que.	D2	74
Hull Glacier, ice, Ant.	B35	7
Hull see Kingston upon Hull, Eng., U.K.	D6	10
Hulls Cove, Me., U.S.	D4	96
Hulst, Neth.	C4	17
Hulun Hu, l., China	B8	31
Hulwān, Eg.	E3	41
Huma, China	A10	31
Humacao, P.R.	B4	65
Humaitá, Braz.	D2	55
Humaita, Arg.	D2	55
Humansdorp, S. Afr.	D3	49
Humansville, Mo., U.S.	D4	102
Humarock, Ma., U.S.	h13	98
Humber, stm., Eng., U.K.	D6	10
Humberside, co., Eng., U.K.	G8	13
Humbird, Wi., U.S.	D3	126
Humble, Tx., U.S.	E5	120
Humble City, N.M., U.S.	E5	108
Humboldt, Sask.	E3	75
Humboldt, Az., U.S.	C3	80
Humboldt, Il., U.S.	D5	90
Humboldt, Ks., U.S.	E8	93
Humboldt, Ne., U.S.	D10	104
Humboldt, Nv., U.S.	C3	105
Humboldt, S.D., U.S.	D8	118
Humboldt, Tn., U.S.	B3	119
Humboldt, co., Ca., U.S.	B2	82
Humboldt, co., Ia., U.S.	B3	92
Humboldt, co., Nv., U.S.	B3	105
Humboldt, stm., Nv., U.S.	C3	105
Humboldt, North Fork, stm., Nv., U.S.	B6	105
Humboldt Mountains, mts., Ant.	B14	7
Humboldt Range, mts., Nv., U.S.	C3	105
Hume, Mo., U.S.	C3	102
Hume, N.Y., U.S.	C2	109
Hume, Va., U.S.	B5	123
Hume, Lake, l., Austl.	G6	51
Humenné, Czech.	B6	26
Humeston, Ia., U.S.	D4	92
Hummels Wharf, Pa., U.S.	E8	115
Humpata, Ang.	E1	48
Humphrey, Ne., U.S.	C8	104
Humphreys, co., Ms., U.S.	B3	101
Humphreys, co., Tn., U.S.	A4	119
Humphreys, Mount, mtn., Ca., U.S.	D4	82
Humphreys Peak, mtn., Az., U.S.	B4	80
Humpolec, Czech.	D3	26
Humptulips, Wa., U.S.	B2	124
Hūn, Libya	D3	43
Hunáflói, b., Ice.	n22	14
Hunan, prv., China	F7	31
Hunchun, China	C11	31
Hundested, Den.	C5	15
Hundred, W.V., U.S.	B4	125
Hundred Acre Pond, l., R.I., U.S.	E3	116
Hunedoara, Rom.	C6	24
Hünfeld, Ger.	C4	19
Hungary, ctry., Eur.	B4	24
Hungerford, Austl.	D5	51
Hungnam, N. Kor.	D10	31
Hungry Hill, mtn., Ire.	F2	11
Hungry Horse, Mt., U.S.	B3	103
Hungry Horse Reservoir, res., Mt., U.S.	B3	103
Huningue, Fr.	B3	20
Hunish, Rubha, c., Scot., U.K.	C6	13
Hunjiang, China	C10	31
Hunn, I., Swe.	u33	14
Hunnewell, Mo., U.S.	B6	102
Hunsrück, mts., Ger.	D2	18
Hunt, China	B9	32
Hunt, co., Tx., U.S.	C4	120
Hunt, stm., R.I., U.S.	D4	116
Hunte, stm., Ger.	F2	15
Hunter, Ar., U.S.	B4	81
Hunter, Ks., U.S.	C5	93
Hunter, N.D., U.S.	B8	111
Hunter, Ok., U.S.	A4	113
Hunter, i., Austl.	o14	50
Hunter, Cape, c., N.W. Ter.	B18	66
Hunterdon, co., N.J., U.S.	B3	107
Hunter Island, i., B.C.	D3	69
Hunter Mountain, mtn., N.Y., U.S.	C6	109
Hunter River, P.E.I.	C6	71
Hunters, Wa., U.S.	A7	124
Huntersfield Mountain, mtn., N.Y., U.S.	C6	109
Huntersville, W.V., U.S.	C4	125
Huntertown, In., U.S.	B7	91
Hunting Creek, stm., Md., U.S.	C4	97
Huntingburg, In., U.S.	H4	91
Huntingdon, B.C.	f13	69
Huntingdon, Que.	D3	74
Huntingdon, Eng., U.K.	B7	12
Huntingdon, Pa., U.S.	F6	115
Huntingdon, Tn., U.S.	A3	119
Huntingdon, co., Que.	D3	74
Huntingdon, co., Pa., U.S.	F5	115
Huntington, Ar., U.S.	B1	81
Huntington, In., U.S.	C7	91
Huntington, Ma., U.S.	B2	98
Huntington, N.J., U.S.	B2	107
Huntington, N.Y., U.S.	E7	109
Huntington, Or., U.S.	C9	114
Huntington, Tx., U.S.	D5	120
Huntington, Ut., U.S.	D5	121
Huntington, Vt., U.S.	C2	122
Huntington, Va., U.S.	*B5	123
Huntington, W.V., U.S.	C2	125
Huntington, co., In., U.S.	C6	91
Huntington Bay, N.Y., U.S.	*E7	109
Huntington Beach, Ca., U.S.	F4	82
Huntington Center, Vt., U.S.	C3	122
Huntington Creek, stm., Nv., U.S.	C6	105
Huntington Lake, res., In., U.S.	C7	91
Huntington Park, Ca., U.S.	*E4	82
Huntington Station, N.Y., U.S.	*E7	109
Huntington Woods, Mi., U.S.	p15	99
Huntingtown, Md., U.S.	C4	97
Huntland, Tn., U.S.	B5	119
Huntley, Il., U.S.	A5	90
Huntley, Mn., U.S.	G4	100
Huntley, Mt., U.S.	E8	103
Huntley, Ne., U.S.	D6	104
Huntley, Wy., U.S.	E8	127
Huntly, Scot., U.K.	B5	13
Hunt Mountain, mtn., Wy., U.S.	B5	127
Hunts Point, N.S.	F5	71
Huntsville, Ont.	B5	73
Huntsville, Al., U.S.	A3	78
Huntsville, Ar., U.S.	A2	81
Huntsville, In., U.S.	E6	91
Huntsville, Ky., U.S.	C3	94
Huntsville, Mo., U.S.	B5	102
Huntsville, Tn., U.S.	C9	119
Huntsville, Tx., U.S.	D5	120
Huntsville, Ut., U.S.	B4	121
Hunucmá, Mex.	C7	63
Hunyuan, China	D7	32
Huon Gulf, b., Pap. N. Gui.	k12	50
Huoshan, China	I7	32
Huoxian, China	F4	32
Hurayḍīn, Wādī, val., Eg.	D6	41
Hurd, Cape, c., Ont.	B3	73
Hurdland, Mo., U.S.	A5	102
Hurdsfield, N.D., U.S.	B6	111
Hure Qi, China	C9	32
Hurley, Ms., U.S.	E5	101
Hurley, Mo., U.S.	E4	102
Hurley, N.M., U.S.	E1	108
Hurley, N.Y., U.S.	D6	109
Hurley, S.D., U.S.	D8	118
Hurley, Va., U.S.	e9	123
Hurley, Wi., U.S.	B3	126
Hurleyville, N.Y., U.S.	D6	109
Hurlford, Scot., U.K.	B5	13
Hurmāgai, Pak.	G12	39
Huron, In., U.S.	G4	91
Huron, Ks., U.S.	C8	93
Huron, Oh., U.S.	A3	112
Huron, S.D., U.S.	C7	118
Huron, co., Ont.	D3	73
Huron, co., Mi., U.S.	E7	99
Huron, co., Oh., U.S.	A3	112
Huron, stm., Mi., U.S.	p14	99
Huron, Lake, l., N.A.	B11	73
Huron Mountains, hills, Mi., U.S.	B3	99
Hurricane, Al., U.S.	E2	78
Hurricane, Ms., U.S.	A4	101
Hurricane, Ut., U.S.	F2	121
Hurricane, W.V., U.S.	C2	125
Hurricane Cliffs, clf., Az., U.S.	A2	80
Hurricane Creek, stm., Ar., U.S.	C3	81
Hurricane Creek, stm., Ga., U.S.	E4	87
Hurricane Mills, Tn., U.S.	A4	119
Hurricane Mountain, mtn., Tn., U.S.	C9	119
Hurst, Il., U.S.	F4	90
Hurst, Tx., U.S.	*n9	120
Hurstville, Austl.	*F9	51
Hurt, Va., U.S.	C3	123
Hurtsboro, Al., U.S.	C4	78
Hurup, Den.	B2	15
Huşi, Rom.	B9	24
Huskvarna (part of Jönköping), Swe.	I6	14
Huson, Mt., U.S.	C3	103
Hussar, Alta.	D4	68
Hussar, Wa., U.S.	D5	95
Hustburg, Tn., U.S.	A4	119
Hustisford, Wi., U.S.	E5	126
Hustle, Va., U.S.	C5	123
Hustontown, Pa., U.S.	F5	115
Hustonville, Ky., U.S.	C5	94
Husum, Ger.	A4	18
Husum, Wa., U.S.	D4	124
Hutchins, Tx., U.S.	n10	120
Hutchinson, Ks., U.S.	D6	93
Hutchinson, Mn., U.S.	F4	100
Hutchinson, N.J., U.S.	B2	107
Hutchinson, co., S.D., U.S.	D8	118
Hutchinson, co., Tx., U.S.	B2	120
Hutchinson Island, i., Fl., U.S.	E6	86
Hutchinson Island, i., S.C., U.S.	k11	117
Hutch Mountain, mtn., Az., U.S.	C4	80
Hutsonville, Il., U.S.	D6	90
Hüttental, Ger.	C3	19

Index

Name	Map Ref.	Page
Huttig, Ar., U.S.	D3	81
Hutto, Tx., U.S.	D4	120
Hutton, Md., U.S.	m12	97
Huttonsville, W.V., U.S.	C5	125
Huttwil, Switz.	B4	21
Hutuo He, stm., China	E5	32
Huu, Indon.	G5	34
Ḥuwwārah, Isr. Occ.	g12	41
Ḥuwwārah, Isr. Occ.	B7	41
Huxford, Al., U.S.	D2	78
Huxley, Alta.	D4	68
Huxley, Ia., U.S.	C4	92
Huy, Bel.	B6	16
Hūzgān, Iran	F4	39
Huzhou, China	*E9	32
Hvalpsund, Den.	B3	15
Hvannadalshnúkur, mtn., Ice.	n24	14
Hvar, i., Yugo.	D3	24
Hvidbjerg, Den.	B2	15
Hvide Sande, Den.	C2	15
Hvidovre, Den.	*C6	15
Hvitstein, Nor.	p28	14
Hvittingfoss (part of Kongsberg), Nor.	p28	14
Hwange, Zimb.	A4	49
Hwang Ho see Huang He, stm., China	D8	31
Hyak, Wa., U.S.	B4	124
Hyampom, Ca., U.S.	B2	82
Hyannis, Ma., U.S.	C7	98
Hyannis, Ne., U.S.	C4	104
Hyannis Port, Ma., U.S.	C7	98
Hyargas Lake, l., Mong.	B3	31
Hyas, Sask.	F4	75
Hyatts, Oh., U.S.	B2	112
Hyattsville, Md., U.S.	B3	97
Hyattsville, Md., U.S.	C4	97
Hyattville, Wy., U.S.	B5	127
Hybart, Al., U.S.	D2	78
Hybla Valley, Va., U.S.	g12	123
Hyco, stm., N.c., U.S.	A3	110
Hyco Lake, res., N.C., U.S.	D13	79
Hydaburg, Pa., U.S.	D5	115
Hyde, Pa., U.S.	D5	115
Hyde, co., N.C., U.S.	B6	110
Hyde, co., S.D., U.S.	C6	118
Hyden, Austl.	F2	50
Hyden, Ky., U.S.	C6	94
Hyde Park, Guy.	A3	59
Hyde Park, N.Y., U.S.	D7	109
Hyde Park, Ut., U.S.	B4	121
Hyde Park, Vt., U.S.	B3	122
Hyder, Ak., U.S.	D13	79
Hyderābād, India	E6	36
Hyderābād, Pak.	C4	36
Hydetown, Pa., U.S.	C2	115
Hydeville, Ct., U.S.	B6	84
Hydeville, Vt., U.S.	D2	122
Hydra see Ídhra, i., Grc.	D4	25
Hydraulic, B.C.	C7	69
Hydro, Ok., U.S.	B3	113
Hyères, Fr.	F7	16
Hyères, Îles d', is., Fr.	F7	16
Hyesan, N. Kor.	C10	31
Hygiene, Co., U.S.	A5	83
Hylo, Alta.	B4	68
Hyman, S.C., U.S.	D8	117
Hymera, In., U.S.	F3	91
Hyndman, Pa., U.S.	G4	115
Hyndman Peak, mtn., Id., U.S.	F4	89
Hyner, Pa., U.S.	D6	115
Hyŏpchŏn, S. Kor.	I4	33
Hyrum, Ut., U.S.	B4	121
Hyrynsalmi, Fin.	E13	14
Hysham, Mt., U.S.	D9	103
Hythe, Alta.	B1	68
Hythe, Eng., U.K.	C9	12
Hyvinkää, Fin.	*G11	14

I

Name	Map Ref.	Page
Iaco (Yaco), stm., S.A.	D4	58
Iaeger, W.V., U.S.	D3	125
Ialomița, stm., Rom.	C8	24
Iamonia, Lake, l., Fl., U.S.	B2	86
Iantha, Mo., U.S.	D3	102
Iapu, Braz.	B4	56
Iași, Rom.	B8	24
Iatan, Mo., U.S.	B3	102
Iates Point, c., Guam	L10	52
Iatt, Lake, res., La., U.S.	C3	95
Iauaretê, Braz.	C4	60
Iba, Phil.	o12	34
Ibadan, Nig.	A6	45
Ibagué, Col.	C2	60
Ibanda, Ug.	B5	48
Ibapah, Ut., U.S.	C2	121
Ibapah Peak, mtn., Ut., U.S.	D2	121
Ibar, stm., Yugo.	D5	24
Ibaraki, Japan	*I7	33
Ibarra, Ec.	A2	58
Ibb, Yemen	C5	41
Ibbenbüren, Ger.	A2	19
Iberá, Laguna, l., Arg.	E4	55
Iberia, Mo., U.S.	C5	102
Iberia, Oh., U.S.	B3	112
Iberia, co., La., U.S.	E4	95
Iberville, Que.	D4	74
Iberville, La., U.S.	D4	95
Iberville, co., La., U.S.	D4	95
Iberville, Mont d' (Mount Caubvick), mtn., Can.	g14	66
Ibi, Nig.	E6	45
Ibi, Japan	n15	33
Ibiá, Braz.	B5	56
Ibiapaba, Serra da, mts., Braz.	B3	56
Ibicuí, stm., Braz.	D1	56
Ibicuy, Braz.	E1	56
Ibirapuitã, stm., Braz.	E1	56
Ibitinga, Braz.	B3	56
Ibiza (Iviza), Spain	C6	22
Ibiza, i., Spain	C6	22
Ibo, Moz.	D7	48
'Ibri, Oman	C5	38
Ibu, Japan	N6	52
Iburg, Ger.	A3	19
Ica, Peru	D2	58
Ica, dept., Peru	D2	58
Içá (Putumayo), stm., S.A.	D4	60
Icacos Point, c., Trin.	O22	65
Içana, Braz.	A4	58
Içana (Isana), stm., S.A.	C4	60
Ice Harbor Dam, Wa., U.S.	C7	124
İçel (Mersin), Tur.	D10	40
Iceland, ctry., Eur.	n23	14
Icém, Braz.	B3	56
Ice Mountain, mtn., B.C.	B7	69
Ichikawa, Japan	n18	33
Ichinomiya, Japan	n15	33
Ichinoseki, Japan	G10	33
Ichnya, Sov. Un.	F9	27
Icicle Creek, stm., Wa., U.S.	B5	124
Ickesburg, Pa., U.S.	F7	115
Icó, Braz.	C3	57
Icy Cape, c., Ak., U.S.	A7	79
Icy Strait, strt., Ak., U.S.	k22	79
Ida, Mi., U.S.	G7	99
Ida, co., Ia., U.S.	B2	92
Ida, Lake, l., Mn., U.S.	D3	100
Idabel, Ok., U.S.	D7	113
Ida Grove, Ia., U.S.	B2	92
Idah, Nig.	E6	45
Idaho, co., Id., U.S.	D3	89
Idaho, state, U.S.		89
Idaho City, Id., U.S.	F3	89
Idaho Falls, Id., U.S.	F6	89
Idaho Springs, Co., U.S.	B5	83
Idalia, Co., U.S.	B8	83
Idalou, Tx., U.S.	C2	120
Idamay, W.V., U.S.	k10	125
Idana, Ks., U.S.	C6	93
Idanha, Or., U.S.	C4	114
Idanha-a-Nova, Port.	C2	22
Idar-Oberstein, Ger.	D2	19
Idaville, In., U.S.	C4	91
Idaville, Pa., U.S.	B3	114
'Idd al Ghanam, Sud.	C1	47
Iddesleigh, Alta.	D5	68
Ideal, Ga., U.S.	D2	87
Ideal, S.D., U.S.	D6	118
Idehan, des., Libya	D2	43
Ider, Al., U.S.	A4	78
Ider, stm., Mong.	B4	31
Idfinā, Eg.	C2	41
Idfū, Eg.	C3	38
Idhra, Grc.	D4	25
Ídhra (Hydra), i., Grc.	D4	25
Idi, Indon.	D1	34
Idiofa, Zaire	C2	41
Idku, Eg.	C2	41
Idkū Lake, l., Eg.		
Idlewild, Mi., U.S.	E5	99
Idlewild Park, Or., U.S.	D3	114
Idlib, Syria	E11	40
Idnah, Isr. Occ.	C6	41
Idrigill Point, c., Scot., U.K.	C2	13
Idrija, Yugo.	B2	24
Idritsa, Sov. Un.	C7	21
Idro, Lake, l., Italy	D6	20
Idutywa, Transkei	D4	49
Ie, Japan	N5	52
Ie Island, i., Japan	N5	52
Iepê, Braz.	C2	56
Ieper (Ypres), Bel.	B5	16
Ierápetra, Grc.	E5	40
Ierissós, Grc.		
Iesi (Jesi), Italy	C4	23
Ifakara, Tan.	C6	48
Ife, Nig.	E5	45
Iferouâne, Niger	A5	45
Ifôghas, Adrar des, mts., Afr.	B5	45
Ifon-Oshogbo, Nig.	*E5	45
Iganga, Ug.	A5	48
Igaraçu, Braz.	C4	57
Igara Paraná, stm., Col.	D3	60
Igarapava, Braz.	C3	56
Igarapé Açu, Braz.	B1	57
Igarapé-Miri, Braz.	C5	59
Igarka, Sov. Un.	C11	29
Igbo-Ora, Nig.	*E5	45
Iğdır, Tur.	C15	40
Iglesia, Arg.	F2	55
Iglesias, Italy	E2	23
Ignacio, Co., U.S.	D3	83
Iğneada, Tur.	B6	40
Igny, Fr.	h9	16
Igornitsa, Grc.	C3	25
Igra, Sov. Un.	B4	28
Igreja, Morro da, mtn., Braz.	D3	56
Iguaçu, stm., S.A.	D2	56
Iguala, Mex.	D5	63
Igualada, Spain	B6	22
Iguape, Braz.	D2	56
Iguassu Falls, wtfl., S.A.	D2	56
Iguatemi, stm., Braz.	C2	56
Iguatu, Braz.	C3	57
Iguéla, Gabon	F1	46
Iguîdi, 'Erg, dunes, Afr.	D3	44
Igurin, i., Marsh Is.	S18	52
Ih Bogd Mountain, mtn., Mong.	C5	31
Iheya Island, i., Japan	N5	52
Ihiala, Nig.	E6	45
Ihlen, Mn., U.S.	G2	100
Ihosy, Madag.	h9	49
Iida, Japan	I8	33
Iidaan, Som.	D4	47
Iide, Mount, mtn., Japan	H9	33
Iijima, Japan	n16	33
Iisalmi, Fin.	F12	14
Iizuka, Japan	J5	33
Ijamsville, Md., U.S.	B3	97
Ijebu Igbo, Nig.	E5	45
Ijebu Ode, Nig.	E5	45
Ijero-Ekiti, Nig.	*E6	45
IJmuiden, Neth.	B2	17
IJssel, stm., Neth.	B4	17
IJsselmeer (Zuider Zee), l., Neth.	A6	16
Ijuí, Braz.	D2	56
Ijuí, stm., Braz.	D2	56
Ikaalinen, Fin.	G10	14
Ikare, Nig.	*E6	45
Ikaría, i., Grc.	D6	40
Ikast, Den.	C2	15
Ike, i., Japan	O6	52
Ikeda, Japan	o14	33
Ikela, Zaire	B3	48
Ikerre, Nig.	*E6	45
Ikhtiman, Bul.	D6	24
Iki Island, i., Japan	J4	33
Ikire, Nig.	*E5	45
Ikirun, Nig.	*E5	45
Ikole, Nig.	*E6	45
Ikorodu, Nig.	*E6	45
Ikot Ekpene, Nig.	E6	45
Ila, Nig.	E5	45
Ila, Ga., U.S.	B3	87
Ilagan, Phil.	o7	34
Ĭlām, Iran	E3	39
Ilanz, Switz.	D3	21
Ilasco, Mo., U.S.	B6	102
Iława, Pol.	B4	26
Ilawe-Ekiti, Nig.	*E6	45
Ilchester, Md., U.S.	B4	97
Ilderton, Ont.	D3	73
Île-à-la-Crosse, Sask.	B2	75
Île-à-la-Crosse, Lac, l., Sask.	B2	75
Ilebo (Port-Francqui), Zaire	C4	48
Île-de-France, hist. reg., Fr.	C5	16
Ilek, stm., Sov. Un.	E20	8
Île-Perrot, Que.	q19	74
Ileret, Kenya	A6	48
Îles, Lac des, l., Sask.	B6	68
Ilesha, Nig.	E5	45
Ilfeld, N.M., U.S.	B4	108
Ilford, Man.	A4	70
Ilfracombe, Eng., U.K.	E4	10
Ilgın, Tur.	C8	40
Ilhavo, Port.	B1	22
Ilhéus, Braz.	D3	57
Ili, stm., Asia	E10	29
Iliamna, Ak., U.S.	D8	79
Iliamna Lake, l., Ak., U.S.	D8	79
Iliamna Volcano, vol., Ak., U.S.	C9	79
Iliff, Co., U.S.	A7	83
Iliki, Lake, l., Grc.	g10	25
Ilinskaya, Sov. Un.	I13	27
Iliodhrómia, i., Grc.	C4	25
Ilion, N.Y., U.S.	B5	109
Iliopolis, Il., U.S.	D4	90
Ilizi, Alg.	D6	44
Ilkeston, Eng., U.K.	B6	12
Ilkley, Eng., U.K.	G7	13
Ill, stm., Asia	E4	18
Illampu, Nevado, mtn., Bol.	C2	55
Illana Bay, b., Phil.	D6	34
Illapel, Chile	A2	54
Ille, Fr.	F5	
Illéla, Niger	D6	45
Iller, stm., Ger.	D5	18
Illfurth, Fr.	A3	21
Illiers, Fr.	C4	16
Illinois, state, U.S.		90
Illinois, stm., U.S.	A7	113
Illinois, stm., Il., U.S.	B5	90
Illinois, stm., Or., U.S.	E3	114
Illinois City, Il., U.S.	B3	90
Illinois Peak, mtn., Id., U.S.	B3	89
Illiopolis, Il., U.S.	D4	90
Illizi, Alg.	D6	44
Illkirch-Graffenstaden, Fr.	F7	17
Illmo, Mo., U.S.	D8	102
Illnau [-Effretikon], Switz.	B6	21
Illo, Nig.	D5	45
Illora, Spain	D4	22
Ilmen, Lake, l., Sov. Un.	B8	27
Ilmenau, Ger.	C5	18
Ilmenau, stm., Ger.	B5	18
Ilo, Peru	D3	58
Ilobu, Nig.	*E5	45
Iloilo, Phil.	C6	34
Ilorin, Nig.	E5	45
Ilovaysk, Sov. Un.	r21	27
Ilovlya, Sov. Un.	D2	28
Ilsenburg, Ger.	B5	19
Ilubabor, prov., Eth.	D3	47
Ilwaco, Wa., U.S.	C1	124
Iwaki, Indon.	G7	34
Iłża, Pol.	C6	26
Imabari, Japan	I6	33
Imabetsu, Japan	F10	33
Imambaba, Braz.	C11	39
Iman, stm., Sov. Un.	B11	31
Imandra, Lake, l., Sov. Un.	B15	8
Imatra, Fin.	*G13	14
Imazu, Japan	n14	33
Imbābah (part of Giza), Eg.	D1	41
Imbabura, prov., Ec.	A2	58
Imbituba, Braz.	D3	56
Imbituva, Braz.	B9	114
Imboden, Ar., U.S.	A4	81
Ime, Beinn, mtn., Scot., U.K.	D4	13
Imgyt Marsh, sw., Sov. Un.	B8	28
Imi, Eth.	D5	47
Imilac, Chile	D2	55
Imlay, Nv., U.S.	C3	105
Imlay City, Mi., U.S.	E7	99
Imlaystown, N.J., U.S.	C3	107
Immeln, l., Swe.	B8	15
Immenstadt, Ger.	E5	18
Immokalee, Fl., U.S.	F5	86
Imnaha, Or., U.S.	B10	114
Imnaha, stm., Or., U.S.	B10	114
Imogene, Ia., U.S.	D2	92
Imola, Italy	B3	23
Imotski, Yugo.	D3	24
Imperatriz, Braz.	C1	57
Imperia, Italy	C2	23
Imperial, Sask.	F3	75
Imperial, Ca., U.S.	F6	82
Imperial, Mo., U.S.	C7	102
Imperial, Ne., U.S.	D4	104
Imperial, Pa., U.S.	k13	115
Imperial, Tx., U.S.	D1	120
Imperial, co., Ca., U.S.	F6	82
Imperial Beach, Ca., U.S.	o15	82
Imperial Dam, U.S.	E1	80
Imperial Mills, Alta.	B5	68
Imperial Reservoir, res., U.S.	E1	80
Imperial Valley, val., Ca., U.S.	F6	82
Impfondo, Congo	A2	48
Imphāl, India	D9	36
Imst, Aus.	h11	41
'Imwās, Isr. Occ.	n16	41
Ina, Japan	I9	33
Ina, stm., Pol.	B3	26
Ina, Japan	n14	33
Inabu, Braz.	*B9	40
Inajá, Braz.	C3	57
In-Alei, well, Mali	C4	45
I-n-Amguel, Alg.	E6	44
Inanwatan, Indon.	F8	34
Iñapari, Peru	D4	58
Inarajan Bay, b., Guam	M9	52
Inari, Fin.	C12	14
Inari, l., Fin.	C12	14
Inawashiro, l., Japan	H10	33
In Azaoua, well, Niger	B6	45
Inca, Spain	C7	22
Incastro, stm., Italy	h9	23
Ince, Cape, c., Tur.	A10	40
Incesu, Tur.	C10	40
Inchard, Loch, b., Scot., U.K.	B7	13
Inchelium, Wa., U.S.	A7	124
Inch'ŏn, S. Kor.	D12	31
Incline Village, Nv., U.S.	D2	105
Indaiatuba, Braz.	m8	56
Indalsälven, stm., Swe.	F7	14
Indaw, Burma	D10	36
Independence, Ca., U.S.	D4	82
Independence, Ia., U.S.	B6	92
Independence, Ks., U.S.	E8	93
Independence, Ky., U.S.	B5	94
Independence, La., U.S.	D5	95
Independence, Mo., U.S.	B3	102
Independence, Oh., U.S.	h9	112
Independence, Or., U.S.	C3	114
Independence, Va., U.S.	D1	123
Independence, Wi., U.S.	D2	126
Independence, co., Ar., U.S.	B4	81
Independence, stm., N.Y., U.S.	B5	109
Independence Mountains, mts., Nv., U.S.	C5	105
Independence National Historical Park, Pa., U.S.	p21	115
Independence Rock, mtn., Wy., U.S.	D5	127
Independencia, Bol.	C2	55
Inderborskiy, Sov. Un.	D4	28
Index, Wa., U.S.	B4	124
India, ctry., Asia	D6	36
Indiahoma, Ok., U.S.	C3	113
Indian, stm., Ont.	B7	73
Indian, stm., Mi., U.S.	F4	85
Indiana, Pa., U.S.	E3	115
Indiana, co., Pa., U.S.	E3	115
Indiana, state, U.S.	E5	91
Indiana Dunes National Lakeshore, In., U.S.	A3	91
Indian Agency, Co., U.S.	D3	83
Indian Bay, b., Fl., U.S.	E5	91
Indian Beach, De., U.S.	D4	86
Indian Brook, N.S.	C9	71
Indian Cedar Swamp, sw., R.I., U.S.	F2	116
Indian Cove, Ct., U.S.	*D4	84
Indian Creek, stm., In., U.S.	H5	91
Indian Creek, stm., Md., U.S.	C4	97
Indian Creek, stm., Oh., U.S.	C1	112
Indian Creek, stm., S.D., U.S.	B2	118
Indian Creek, stm., Tn., U.S.	B3	119
Indian Creek, stm., W.V., U.S.	k9	125
Indian Creek, stm., W.V., U.S.	D4	125
Indian Grave Mountain, hill, Ga., U.S.	C2	87
Indian Harbour Beach, Fl., U.S.	*D6	86
Indian Head, Sask.	G4	75
Indian Head, Md., U.S.	C3	97
Indian Heights, In., U.S.	*D5	91
Indian Hills, Co., U.S.	*B5	83
Indian Island, i., N.C., U.S.	B6	110
Indian Lake, N.Y., U.S.	B6	109
Indian Lake, l., Mi., U.S.	C4	99
Indian Lake, l., N.Y., U.S.	B6	109
Indian Lake, l., Oh., U.S.	B2	112
Indian Lake, l., R.I., U.S.	F4	116
Indian Lake Shores, R.I., U.S.	F4	116
Indian Mound, Tn., U.S.	A4	119
Indian Mound Beach, Ma., U.S.	C6	98
Indian Mountain, mtn., Ct., U.S.	B2	84
Indian Neck, Ct., U.S.	D4	84
Indian Ocean	G2	2
Indianola, Il., U.S.	D6	90
Indianola, Ia., U.S.	C4	92
Indianola, Ms., U.S.	B3	101
Indianola, Ne., U.S.	D5	104
Indianola, Ok., U.S.	B6	113
Indianópolis, Braz.	B5	56
Indian Peak, mtn., Ut., U.S.	E2	121
Indian Peak, mtn., Wy., U.S.	B3	127
Indian Pond, l., Me., U.S.	B3	96
Indian Pond, l., Me., U.S.	D3	96
Indian Pond, l., Me., U.S.	C3	96
Indian Prairie Canal, Fl., U.S.	E5	86
Indian Ridge Estates, Az., U.S.	E5	80
Indian River, Oh., U.S.	C6	73
Indian River, De., U.S.	D5	96
Indian River, Me., U.S.	C6	99
Indian River, Mi., U.S.	E6	86
Indian River, co., Fl., U.S.	F5	85
Indian River Bay, b., De., U.S.	F5	85
Indian Rock, mtn., Wa., U.S.	D5	124
Indian Rocks Beach, Fl., U.S.	p10	86
Indian Springs, In., U.S.	G4	91
Indian Springs, Nv., U.S.	G6	105
Indiantown, Fl., U.S.	E6	86
Indian Trail, N.C., U.S.	B2	110
Indian Valley, Id., U.S.	E2	89
Indian Valley, Va., U.S.	D2	123
Indian Village, Ks., U.S.	E8	93
Indian Village, La., U.S.	D3	95
Indian Wells, Az., U.S.	B5	80
Indiaporã, Braz.	B2	56
Indigirka, stm., Sov. Un.	C17	29
Indio, Ca., U.S.	F5	82
Indio, stm., Pan.	k10	62
Indochina, reg., Asia	B3	34
Indonesia, ctry., Asia	F5	36
Indore, India	D6	36
Indragiri, stm., Indon.	E3	34
Indramayu, Indon.	G3	34
Indrāvati, stm., India	E7	36
Indre, Fl., U.S.	E6	86
Indus, Fl., U.S.	B5	100
Indus, Ms., U.S.	B5	100
Indus, stm., Asia	C4	36
Industry, Il., U.S.	C3	90
Ine, Japan	n14	33
Inebolu, Tur.	B9	40
Inegöl, Tur.	*B7	40
Inez, Ky., U.S.	C7	94
Inez, Tx., U.S.	E4	120
Infanta, Phil.	o13	34
Infanta, Phil.	o12	34
Infantes, Col.	M9	52
Infiernillo, Presa del, res., Mex.	D4	63
Infiesto, Spain	A3	22
Ingá, Braz.	h6	57
Inga Dam, Zaire	C1	48
Ingalls, Ar., U.S.	D3	81
Ingalls, In., U.S.	E6	91
Ingalls, Ks., U.S.	E3	93
Ingalls, Mi., U.S.	C3	99
Ingalls, Ok., U.S.	A5	113
Ingalls Park, Il., U.S.	B5	90
Ingende, Zaire	B3	48
Ingeniero Jacobacci, Arg.	E3	54
Ingeniero Luiggi, Arg.	B4	54
Ingersheim, Ger.	h9	19
Ingersoll, Ont.	D4	73
Ingham, Austl.	C8	50
Ingham, co., Mi., U.S.	F6	99
Ingleside, Md., U.S.	B6	97
Ingleside, Tx., U.S.	F4	120
Inglewood, Austl.	D8	51
Inglewood, Ont.	m12	73
Inglewood, N.Z.	M15	51
Inglewood, Ca., U.S.	*n12	82
Inglewood, Ne., U.S.	C9	104
Inglewood, Tn., U.S.	*B3	126
Inglis, Man.	D1	70
Ingoda, stm., Sov. Un.	B7	31
Ingold, N.C., U.S.	C4	110
Ingoldsby, Ont.	C6	73
Ingolf, Ont.	E4	70
Ingolstadt, Ger.	D5	18
Ingomar, Ms., U.S.	A4	101
Ingomar, Pa., U.S.	h13	115
Ingonish, N.S.	C9	71
Ingonish Beach, N.S.	C9	71
Ingornachoix Bay, b., Newf.	C3	72
Ingraham, Lake, l., Fl., U.S.	G5	86
Ingrāj Bāzār (English Bāzār), India	E12	37
Ingram, Pa., U.S.	k13	115
Ingram, Tx., U.S.	E3	120
Ingram, Wi., U.S.	C3	126
Ingrid Christensen Coast, Ant.	C20	7
In Guezzam, Alg.	F6	44
Inguri, stm., Sov. Un.	H9	27
Ingulets, stm., Sov. Un.	H9	27
Inhambane, Moz.	B6	49
Inhambane, dept., Moz.	B6	49
Inhambane, Baía de, b., Moz.	B6	49
Inhambupe, Braz.	D3	57
Inhaminga, Moz.	A5	49
Inharrime, Moz.	B6	49
Inhuçu, Braz.	B2	57
Inhumas, Braz.	B3	56
Iniesta, Spain	C5	22
Inírida, stm., Col.	*C4	60
Inisa, Nig.	*E5	45
Inishark, i., Ire.	D1	11
Inishbofin, i., Ire.	D1	11
Inishcrone, Ire.	D2	11
Inisheer, i., Ire.	D2	11
Inishkea Islands, is., Ire.	D1	11
Inishmaan, i., Ire.	D2	11
Inishmore, i., Ire.	D2	11
Inishmurray, i., Ire.	C3	11
Inishowen Head, c., Ire.	E1	11
Inishtooskert, i., Ire.	D1	10
Inishtrahull, rock, Ire.	C3	10
Inishturk, i., Ire.	D1	10
Inishvickillane, i., Ire.	E1	11
Inistioge, Ire.	E4	11
Injune, Austl.	B7	51
Inkerman, N.B.	B5	71
Inkom, Id., U.S.	G6	89
Inkster, Mi., U.S.	p15	99
Inkster, N.D., U.S.	A8	111
Inland, Ne., U.S.	D7	104
Inle Lake, l., Burma	B2	35
Inlet, N.Y., U.S.	B6	109
Inman, Ks., U.S.	D6	93
Inman, Ne., U.S.	B7	104
Inman, S.C., U.S.	A3	117
Inn, stm., Eur.	B5	18
Inner Hebrides, is., Scot., U.K.	B3	10
Innerleithen, Scot., U.K.	F10	13
Inner Mongolia (Nei Mongol), prov., China	C7	31
Inner Sound, strt., Scot., U.K.	C8	10
Innisfail, Austl.	C8	50
Innisfail, Alta.	C4	68
Innisfree, Alta.	C5	68
Inniswold, La., U.S.	*D4	95
Innokentyevskiy, Sov. Un.	B10	31
Innsbruck, Aus.	C6	18
Inny, stm., Ire.	D4	11
Ino, Japan	J6	33
Inocência, Braz.	B2	56
Inola, Ok., U.S.	A6	113
Inongo, Zaire	B2	48
Inowrocław, Pol.	B3	21
Ins, Switz.	B3	21
In Salah, Alg.	D5	44
Insch, Scot., U.K.	C6	13
Inscription House Ruin, hist., Az., U.S.	A5	80
Insein, Burma	E10	36
Insinger, Sask.	F4	75
Inspiration, Az., U.S.	D5	80
Institute, W.V., U.S.	C3	125
Instow, Sask.	H1	75
Inta, Sov. Un.	B21	8
Intercession City, Fl., U.S.	D5	86
Interior, S.D., U.S.	D4	118
Interlachen, Fl., U.S.	C5	86
Interlaken, Switz.	E3	18
Interlaken, Ma., U.S.	*B1	98
Interlaken, N.Y., U.S.	C4	109
International Peace Garden, N.A.	A5	111
International Falls, Mn., U.S.	B5	100
Intersection Mountain, mtn., Can.	C8	69
Intervale, N.H., U.S.	B4	106
Inthanon, mount, mtn., Thai.	B1	34
Intiyaco, Arg.	B4	54
Intracoastal City, La., U.S.	E3	55
Intracoastal Waterway, U.S.	E7	36
Introbio, Italy	E7	21
Intuto, Peru	B3	58
Inubō, Cape, c., Japan	I10	33
Inukjuak, Que.	g11	74
Inútil, Bahía, b., Chile	h12	54
Inuvik, N.W. Ter.	C6	66
Inveraray, Scot., U.K.	B4	66
Inver Bay, b., Ire.	C3	11
Inverbervie, Scot., U.K.	D6	13
Invercargill, N.Z.	Q12	51
Inverell, Austl.	E9	50
Invergarry, Scot., U.K.	C4	13
Invergordon, Scot., U.K.	C4	13
Inver Grove Heights, Mn., U.S.	n12	100
Invermay, Sask.	F4	75
Invermere, B.C.	D9	69
Inverness, N.S.	C8	71
Inverness, Que.	C6	74
Inverness, Scot., U.K.	C4	13
Inverness, Ca., U.S.	C2	82
Inverness, Fl., U.S.	D4	86
Inverness, Il., U.S.	*A5	90
Inverness, Ms., U.S.	B3	101
Inverness, Mt., U.S.	B6	103
Inverness, co., N.S.	C8	71
Inverurie, Scot., U.K.	C6	13
Invisible Mountain, mtn., U.S.	F5	89
Inyo, co., Ca., U.S.	D5	82
Inyo, Mount, mtn., Ca., U.S.	D5	82
Inyokern, Ca., U.S.	E5	82
Inyo Mountains, mts., Ca., U.S.	D4	82
Inyonga, Tan.	C5	48
Inza, Sov. Un.	E16	27
Inzana Lake, l., B.C.	B6	69
Ioánnina, Grc.	C3	40
Ioanga, Sov. Un.	D18	14
Iola, Il., U.S.	E5	90
Iola, Ks., U.S.	E8	93
Iola, Wi., U.S.	D4	126
Iona, N.S.	D9	71
Iona, Id., U.S.	F7	89
Iona, Mn., U.S.	G3	100
Iona, N.J., U.S.	D2	107
Iona, S.D., U.S.	D6	118
Iona, i., Scot., U.K.	D2	13
Ione, Ca., U.S.	C3	82
Ione, Co., U.S.	A6	83
Ione, Nv., U.S.	E4	105
Ione, Or., U.S.	B7	114
Ione, Wa., U.S.	A8	124
Ionia, Ia., U.S.	A5	92
Ionia, Ks., U.S.	C5	93
Ionia, Mi., U.S.	F5	99
Ionia, Mo., U.S.	C4	102
Ionia, co., Mi., U.S.	F5	99
Ionian Islands, is., Grc.	C3	25
Ionian Sea, Eur.	H12	8
Íos, i., Grc.	D5	40
Iosco, co., Mi., U.S.	D7	99
Iosegun, stm., Alta.	B2	68
Iowa, Ia., U.S.	C5	92
Iowa, co., Ia., U.S.	C5	92
Iowa, co., Wi., U.S.	E3	126
Iowa, state, U.S.	C4	92
Iowa, stm., Ia., U.S.	C6	92
Iowa, West Branch, stm., Ia., U.S.	B4	92
Iowa City, Ia., U.S.	C6	92
Iowa Falls, Ia., U.S.	B4	92
Iowa Indian Reservation, U.S.	C8	93
Iowa Park, Tx., U.S.	C3	120
Ipameri, Braz.	B5	56
Ipava, Il., U.S.	C3	90
Ipel' (Ipoly), stm., Eur.	D5	26
Iphigenia Bay, b., Ak., U.S.	n22	79
Ipiales, Col.	C2	60
Ipirá, Braz.	D3	57
Ipiranga, Braz.	E2	34
Ipoh, Malay.	*B9	40
Ipoly (Ipel'), stm., Eur.	D5	26
Iporá, Braz.	B2	56
Ippy, Cen. Afr. Rep.	B4	46
Ipsala, Tur.	B6	40
Ipswich, Austl.	E9	50
Ipswich, Eng., U.K.	D7	10
Ipswich, Ma., U.S.	A6	98
Ipswich, S.D., U.S.	B6	118
Ipswich, stm., Ma., U.S.	A6	98
Ipu, Braz.	B2	57
Ipueiras, Braz.	B2	57
Iqaluit, N.W. Ter.	D19	66
Iquique, Chile	D1	55
Iquitos, Peru	B3	58
Ira, Ia., U.S.	C4	92
Ira, Tx., U.S.	C2	120
Iraan, Tx., U.S.	D2	120
Iracoubo, Fr. Gu.	A4	59
Iraí, Braz.	D2	56
Iráklion (Candia), Grc.	E5	40
Irala, Para.	E5	55
Iran, Plateau of, plat., Asia	B5	36
Iran, ctry., Asia	B5	38
Īrānshahr, Iran	H10	39
Irapa, Ven.	A5	60
Irapuato, Mex.	C4	63
Iraq, ctry., Asia	B4	38
Irasburg, Vt., U.S.	B4	122
Irazú, Volcán, vol., C.R.	F6	62
Irbid, Jord.	B3	38
Irbil, Iraq	B4	38
Irbit, Sov. Un.	D21	8
Irebu, Zaire	B2	48
Iredell, co., N.C., U.S.	B2	110
Ireland, In., U.S.	H3	91
Ireland, ctry., Eur.	D3	10
Ireland Island, i., Ber.	p19	64
Irene, S.D., U.S.	D8	118
Ireton, Ia., U.S.	B1	92
Irgiz, stm., Sov. Un.	D6	28
Iri, S. Kor.	I3	33
Irian Jaya, prov., Indon.	F9	34
Iriba, Chad	B4	46
Iriklinskoye Reservoir, res., Sov. Un.	C5	28
Iringa, Tan.	C6	48
Iringa, prov., Tan.	C6	48
Iriomote Island, i., Japan	G9	31
Irion, co., Tx., U.S.	D2	120
Iriri, stm., Braz.	C4	59
Irish, stm., Mn., U.S.	F6	105
Irish Sea, Eur.	D4	10
Irō, Cape, c., Japan	I9	33
Iron, co., Mi., U.S.	B2	99
Iron, co., Mo., U.S.	D7	102
Iron, co., Ut., U.S.	F2	121
Iron, co., Wi., U.S.	B3	126
Iron Belt, Wi., U.S.	B3	126
Iron City, Ga., U.S.	E2	87
Iron City, Tn., U.S.	B4	119
Irondale, Al., U.S.	f7	78
Irondale, Mo., U.S.	D7	102
Irondale, Oh., U.S.	B5	112
Irondequoit, N.Y., U.S.	B3	109
Iron Gate, val., Eur.	C5	24
Iron Gate Reservoir, res., Ca., U.S.	B2	82
Iron Gate Reservoir, res., Eur.	C5	24
Ironia, N.J., U.S.	B3	107
Iron Lightning, S.D., U.S.	B4	118
Iron Mountain, Mi., U.S.	C2	99
Iron Mountain, mtn., Az., U.S.	D7	102
Iron Mountain, mtn., N.M., U.S.	A1	92
Iron Mountain, mtn., Wy., U.S.	E7	127
Iron Mountains, mts., Az., U.S.	D1	123
Iron Mountains, mts., U.S.	D1	123
Iron Ridge, Wi., U.S.	E5	126
Iron River, Mi., U.S.	B2	99
Iron River, Wi., U.S.	B2	126
Irons, Mi., U.S.	E5	99
Ironside, Que.	h12	74
Ironside, Or., U.S.	C9	114

Index

Name	Map Ref.	Page

Ironspot, Oh., U.S. — C3 112
Iron Springs, Az., U.S. — C3 80
Ironton, Mn., U.S. — D5 100
Ironton, Mo., U.S. — D7 102
Ironton, Oh., U.S. — D3 112
Ironwood, Mi., U.S. — n11 99
Iroquois, Ont. — C9 73
Iroquois, Il., U.S. — C6 90
Iroquois, S.D., U.S. — C8 118
Iroquois, co., Il., U.S. — C6 90
Iroquois, stm., U.S. — C6 90
Iroquois, Lake, l., Vt., U.S. — B2 122
Iroquois Falls, Ont. — o19 73
Irrawaddy see Ayeyarwady, stm., Burma — D10 36
Irricana, Alta. — D4 68
Irrigon, Or., U.S. — B7 114
Irt, stm., Eng., U.K. — F5 13
Irthing, stm., Eng., U.K. — F6 13
Irtysh, Sov. Un. — C8 28
Irtysh, stm., Sov. Un. — D9 29
Irumu, Zaire — A4 48
Irún, Spain — A5 22
Irvine, Alta. — E5 68
Irvine, Scot., U.K. — C4 10
Irvine, Ca., U.S. — n13 82
Irvine, Fl., U.S. — C4 86
Irvine, Ky., U.S. — C6 94
Irvine, Pa., U.S. — C3 115
Irvine, stm., Scot., U.K. — E4 13
Irvines Landing, B.C. — E5 69
Irving, Il., U.S. — D4 90
Irving, Tx., U.S. — n10 120
Irvington, Al., U.S. — E1 78
Irvington, Il., U.S. — E4 90
Irvington, Ky., U.S. — C3 94
Irvington, Ne., U.S. — g12 104
Irvington, N.J., U.S. — k8 107
Irvington, N.Y., U.S. — g13 109
Irvington, Va., U.S. — C6 123
Irvona, Pa., U.S. — E4 115
Irwin, Id., U.S. — F7 89
Irwin, Ia., U.S. — C2 92
Irwin, Pa., U.S. — F2 115
Irwin, co., Ga., U.S. — E3 87
Irwinton, Ga., U.S. — D3 87
Irwinville, Ga., U.S. — E3 87
Isa, Nig. — D6 45
Isaac Lake, l., B.C. — D7 69
Isaacs Harbour, N.S. — D8 71
Isabel, Ks., U.S. — E5 93
Isabel, S.D., U.S. — B4 118
Isabel, Bahía, b., Ec. — g5 58
Isabel, Mount, mtn., Wy., U.S. — D2 127
Isabela, Phil. — D6 34
Isabela, P.R. — A1 65
Isabela, Isla (Albemarle Island), i., Ec. — g5 58
Isabelia, Cordillera, mts., Nic. — D5 62
Isabella, Ga., U.S. — E3 87
Isabella, Mn., U.S. — C7 100
Isabella, Mo., U.S. — E5 102
Isabella, Ok., U.S. — A3 113
Isabella, Pa., U.S. — G2 115
Isabella, Tn., U.S. — D9 119
Isabella, co., Mi., U.S. — E6 99
Isabella Indian Reservation, Mi., U.S. — E6 99
Isabella Lake, l., Mn., U.S. — C7 100
Isaccea, Rom. — C9 24
Isachsen, N.W. Ter. — m31 66
Ísafjardardjúp, Ice. — m21 14
Ísafjördur, Ice. — m21 14
Isahaya, Japan — J5 33
Isaka, Zaire — B2 48
Isana (Içana), stm., S.A. — C4 60
Isanga, Zaire — B3 48
Isanti, Mn., U.S. — E5 100
Isanti, co., Mn., U.S. — E5 100
Isar, stm., Eur. — D6 18
Isarco, stm., Eur. — A3 23
Ìsáwíyah, Isr. Occ. — m14 41
Ìsáwíyah, Sau. Ar. — G12 40
Isbergues, Fr. — D2 17
Isbister, stm., Man. — C4 70
Ischgl, Aus. — B9 21
Ischia, i., Italy — D4 23
Ischua, N.Y., U.S. — C2 109
Ise (Uji-yamada), Japan — I8 33
Ise, stm., Ger. — F4 15
Ise Bay, b., Japan — o15 33
Isefjord, b., Den. — C5 15
Isel, stm., Aus. — E6 18
Iselin, N.J., U.S. — B4 107
Iselin, Pa., U.S. — E3 115
Isen, stm., Ger. — A8 20
Isenthal, Switz. — C6 21
Iseo, Lake, l., Italy — B3 23
Isère, dept., Fr. — D1 20
Isère, stm., Fr. — E6 16
Iserlohn, Ger. — B2 19
Isernia, Italy — D5 23
Isesaki, Japan — H9 33
Iseyin, Nig. — E5 45
Isfahan see Esfahán, Iran — B5 38
Ishikari Bay, b., Japan — E10 33
Ishim, Sov. Un. — D9 29
Ishim, stm., Sov. Un. — D9 29
Ishimbay, Sov. Un. — C8 28
Ishinomaki, Japan — D13 31
Ishioka, Japan — m19 33
Ishpeming, Mi., U.S. — B3 99
Isigny-sur-Mer, Fr. — C3 16
Isil-Kul, Sov. Un. — C8 28
Isinglass, stm., N.H., U.S. — D4 106
Isiolo, Kenya — A6 48
Isiro, Madag. — A4 48
Isisford, Austl. — B5 51
Iskenderun (Alexandretta), Tur. — D11 40
Iskilip, Tur. — B10 40
Iskitim, Sov. Un. — E25 8
Ìskûr, stm., Bul. — D6 24
Iskushuban, Som. — B3 73
Iskwatikan Lake, l., Sask. — D2 75
Isla Cristina, Spain — H4 22
Islāmābād, Pak. — B5 36
Islamorada, Fl., U.S. — H6 86
Island, Ky., U.S. — C2 94
Island, co., Wa., U.S. — A3 124
Island Beach, N.J., U.S. — D4 107
Island-Brook, Que. — D6 74
Island City, Or., U.S. — B8 114
Island Creek, Ma., U.S. — *B6 98
Island Falls, Sask. — B4 75
Island Falls, Me., U.S. — B4 96
Island Grove, Fl., U.S. — C4 86
Island Heights, N.J., U.S. — D4 107
Island Lake, Man. — C4 70
Island Lake, l., Man. — C4 70
Island Lake, l., Mn., U.S. — C4 100
Island Lake, stm., Man. — B4 70
Island Park, Id., U.S. — E7 89
Island Park, N.Y., U.S. — *E7 109

Island Park, R.I., U.S. — E6 116
Island Park Reservoir, res., Id., U.S. — E7 89
Island Pond, Vt., U.S. — B5 122
Island Pond, l., N.H., U.S. — E4 106
Islands, Bay of, b., Newf. — D2 72
Islands, Bay of, b., N.Z. — K15 51
Isla Vista, Ca., U.S. — E4 82
Islay, Alta. — C5 68
Islay, i., Scot., U.K. — C3 10
Islay, Sound of, strt., Scot., U.K. — E3 13
Isle, Mn., U.S. — D5 100
Isle, stm., Fr. — E4 16
Isle au Haut, Me., U.S. — D4 96
Isle-aux-Morts, Newf. — E2 72
Isle La Motte, Vt., U.S. — B2 122
Isle of Man, ctry., Eur. — C4 10
Isle of Palms, S.C., U.S. — k12 117
Isle of Wight, Va., U.S. — D6 123
Isle of Wight, co., Eng., U.K. — D6 12
Isle of Wight, co., Va., U.S. — D6 123
Isle of Wight Bay, b., Md., U.S. — D7 97
Isle Pierre, B.C. — C6 69
Isle Royale National Park, Mi., U.S. — h9 99
Islesboro, Me., U.S. — D4 96
Islesboro Island, i., Me., U.S. — D4 96
Islesford, Me., U.S. — D4 96
Isleta, N.M., U.S. — C3 108
Isleta Indian Reservation, N.M., U.S. — C3 108
Isleton, Ca., U.S. — C3 82
Islington, Ma., U.S. — h11 98
Islip, N.Y., U.S. — *n15 109
Islip Terrace, N.Y., U.S. — *n15 109
Ismael Cortinas, Ur. — f5 54
Ismailia, Eg. — B3 38
Ismâ'îlîyah Canal, Eg. — D3 41
Ismay, Mt., U.S. — D12 103
Isnã, Eg. — C3 38
Isny, Ger. — A9 21
Isoka, Zam. — D5 48
Isola, Ms., U.S. — B3 101
Isola della Scala, Italy — D7 20
Isola di Capo Rizzuto, Italy — E6 23
Isonzo, stm., Eur. — A4 23
Isparta, Tur. — D8 40
İspir, Tur. — B13 40
Israel, ctry., Asia — B3 38
Israel, stm., N.H., U.S. — B3 106
Israeli Occupied Areas, dep., Asia — B7 41
Issano, Guy. — A3 59
Issaquah, Wa., U.S. — B3 124
Issaquena, co., Ms., U.S. — C2 101
Issia, I.C. — E3 45
Issoire, Fr. — E3 16
Issoudun, Fr. — D4 16
Issuna, Tan. — C5 48
Issy, Fr. — g10 16
Issyk-Kul, Lake, l., Sov. Un. — E10 29
Istachatta, Fl., U.S. — D4 86
Ìstâdeh-ye Moqor, Âb-e, l., Afg. — B4 36
İstanbul (Constantinople) (Byzantium), Tur. — B7 40
Istiaia, Grc. — C4 25
Istmina, Col. — B2 60
Isto, Mount, mtn., Ak., U.S. — B11 79
Istokpoga, Lake, l., Fl., U.S. — E5 86
Istranca Mountains, mts., Tur. — B7 40
Istres, Fr. — F6 16
Istrian Peninsula, pen., Yugo. — C1 24
Itá, Braz. — D2 56
Itá, Para. — E4 55
Itabaiana, Braz. — C3 57
Itabaiana, Braz. — D3 57
Itabaianinha, Braz. — D3 57
Itabapoana, stm., Braz. — C4 57
Itaberaba, Braz. — D2 57
Itaberaí, Braz. — B3 56
Itabira, Braz. — B4 56
Itabirito, Braz. — C4 56
Itabuna, Braz. — D3 57
Itacajá, Braz. — C4 59
Itacaiúnas, stm., Braz. — C3 59
Itacoatiara, Braz. — C3 59
Itaeté, Braz. — C3 58
Itaguaçu, Braz. — B4 56
Itaguara, Braz. — C4 56
Itaguí, Col. — *B2 60
Itaí, Braz. — G4 56
Itaituba, Braz. — C3 59
Itajá, Braz. — B2 56
Itajaí, Braz. — D3 56
Itajubá, Braz. — D1 56
Italy, Tx., U.S. — C4 120
Italy, ctry., Eur. — C4 23
Italy Cross, N.S. — E5 71
Itamaracá, Ilha de, i., Braz. — h6 57
Itamarandiba, Braz. — B4 56
Itambacuri, Braz. — B4 56
Itambé, Braz. — B4 56
Itami, Japan — o14 33
Itanhaém, Braz. — n8 56
Itapaci, Braz. — A3 56
Itapagipe, Braz. — B3 56
Itapecuru, stm., Braz. — B2 57
Itapecuru-Mirim, Braz. — C4 56
Itapemirim, Braz. — C4 56
Itaperuna, Braz. — C4 56
Itapetinga, Braz. — m7 56
Itapetininga, stm., Braz. — m7 56
Itapeva, Braz. — C3 56
Itapicuru, stm., Braz. — D3 57
Itapipoca, Braz. — m8 56
Itapira, Braz. — G5 56
Itapirapuã, Braz. — k7 56
Itápolis, Braz. — C2 56
Itaporã, Braz. — C3 56
Itapúa, dept., Para. — D3 56
Itaqui, Braz. — B2 56
Itararé, Braz. — A6 56
Itararé, stm., Braz. — A6 56
Itārsi, India — F6 37
Itasca, Il., U.S. — k8 90
Itasca, Tx., U.S. — C4 120
Itasca, co., Mn., U.S. — C5 100
Itasca, Lake, l., Mn., U.S. — C3 100
Itatiaia National Park, Braz. — h5 56
Itatiba, Braz. — m8 56
Itatinga, Braz. — m7 56
Itaúna, Braz. — C4 56
Itawamba, co., Ms., U.S. — A5 101
Itéa, Grc. — K7 25
Iténez (Guaporé), stm., S.A. — B3 55
Itenhém, Braz. — B4 56
Ithaca, Mi., U.S. — E6 99

Ithaca, Ne., U.S. — g11 104
Ithaca, N.Y., U.S. — C4 109
Ithaca see Itháki, i., Grc. — C3 25
Itháki, Grc. — C3 25
Itháki (Ithaca), i., Grc. — C3 25
Itigi, Tan. — C5 48
Itimbiri, stm., Zaire — A3 48
Itinga, Braz. — B4 56
Itiquira, Braz. — B2 56
Itiquira, stm., Braz. — *B1 56
Itiquira, stm., Braz. — B1 56
Itirapina, Braz. — m8 56
Itō, Japan — o18 33
Itoigawa, Japan — H8 33
Itoko, Zaire — B3 48
Itoman, Japan — O5 52
Itta Bena, Ms., U.S. — B3 101
Itu, Braz. — G5 56
Ituango, Col. — B2 60
Ituí, stm., Braz. — B3 58
Ituiutaba, Braz. — B3 56
Itumbiara, Braz. — B3 56
Ituna, Sask. — F4 75
Ituporanga, Braz. — D3 56
Iturama, Braz. — B2 56
Ituverava, Braz. — C3 56
Ituxi, stm., Braz. — C4 58
Ityåy al Bárúd, Eg. — D2 41
Itzehoe, Ger. — B4 18
Iuka, Il., U.S. — E5 90
Iuka, Ks., U.S. — E5 93
Iuka, Ms., U.S. — A5 101
Iva, S.C., U.S. — C2 117
Iva, W. Sam. — F11 52
Ivaí, stm., Braz. — C2 56
Ivalo, Fin. — C12 14
Ivan, Ar., U.S. — D3 81
Ivangrad, Yugo. — G5 27
Ivanhoe, Austl. — F5 51
Ivanhoe, Mn., U.S. — F2 100
Ivanhoe, N.C., U.S. — C4 110
Ivanhoe, Va., U.S. — D2 123
Ivanić Grad, Yugo. — C3 24
Ivano-Frankovsk, Sov. Un. — G5 27
Ivanovichi, Sov. Un. — D7 27
Ivanovka, Sov. Un. — q21 27
Ivanovo, Sov. Un. — D7 29
Ivanovo, Sov. Un. — A4 33
Ivanteyevka, Sov. Un. — n17 33
Ivdel, Sov. Un. — D7 29
Ivesdale, Il., U.S. — D5 90
Ives Estates, Fl., U.S. — *G6 86
Ivigtut, Grnld. — C19 128
Ivinheima, stm., Braz. — C2 56
Ivins, Ut., U.S. — F2 121
Ivohibe, Madag. — h9 49
Ivor, Va., U.S. — D6 123
Ivory Coast, ctry., Afr. — E3 45
Ivoryton, Ct., U.S. — D6 84
Ivösjön, l., Swe. — B8 15
Ivrea, Italy — B1 23
Ivry-Nord, Que. — C3 74
Ivry-sur-Seine, Fr. — g10 16
Ivujivik, Que. — f11 74
Ivy, Va., U.S. — B4 123
Ivydale, W.V., U.S. — C3 125
Ivy Mountain, mtn., Ct., U.S. — B3 84
Ivyton, Ky., U.S. — C7 94
Ivywild, Co., U.S. — C6 83
Iwaki (Taira), Japan — H10 33
Iwaki, Mount, mtn., Japan — F10 33
Iwakuni, Japan — I6 33
Iwamizawa, Japan — E10 33
Iwanai, Japan — E10 33
Iwate, Mount, mtn., Japan — G10 33
Iwo, Nig. — E5 45
Iwo Jima, i., Japan — E8 6
Iwón, N. Kor. — F4 33
Ixelles (Elsene), Bel. — *D4 17
Ixiamas, Bol. — B2 55
Ixmiquilpan, Mex. — m14 63
Ixtacalco (part of Mexico City), Mex. — h9 63
Ixtapa, Punta, c., Mex. — D4 63
Ixtapalapa (part of Mexico City), Mex. — h9 63
Ixtlán de Juárez, Mex. — o15 63
Ixtlán del Río, Mex. — G7 63
Izabal, Lago de, l., Guat. — D7 63
Ìzad Khvāst, Iran — F6 39
Izamal, Mex. — C7 63
Izard, co., Ar., U.S. — A4 81
Izberbash, Sov. Un. — E3 28
Izegem, Bel. — D3 17
Izena Island, i., Japan — N5 52
Izhevsk (Ustinov), Sov. Un. — D7 29
Izhma, stm., Sov. Un. — C19 8
Izmail, Sov. Un. — I7 27
Izmir (Smyrna), Tur. — C6 40
Izmit (Kocaeli) (Nicomedia), Tur. — B7 40
İznik (Nicaea), Tur. — B7 40
Izozog, Bañados de, sw., Bol. — C3 55
Iztaccíhuatl, vol., Mex. — n14 63
Izúcar de Matamoros, Mex. — n14 63
Izuhara, Japan — I4 33
Izu Islands, is., Japan — D8 6
Izumo, Japan — I6 33
Izyum, Sov. Un. — G11 27

J

Jabal al Awlíyá', Sud. — B3 47
Jabalón, stm., Spain — C4 22
Jabalpur, India — D6 36
Jabályah, Isr. Occ. — C4 41
Jablonec [nad Nisou], Czech. — B5 26
Jablonná, Czech. — o17 26
Jablunkov Pass, Czech. — D5 26
Jaboatão, Braz. — C4 57
Jaboticabal, Braz. — B5 56
Jabrin, i., Iran — C5 38
Jaca, Spain — B5 22
Jacala de Ledesma, Mex. — m14 63
Jacaraci, Braz. — B6 56
Jacaré, stm., Braz. — D2 57
Jacareí, Braz. — m9 56
Jacarezinho, Braz. — C2 56
Jáchymov, Czech. — E11 26
Jaciara, Ms., U.S. — A5 101
Jacinto City, Tx., U.S. — r14 120
Jack, Al., U.S. — D4 78
Jack, co., Tx., U.S. — C3 120
Jackfish Lake, l., Sask. — D1 75
Jackhead Harbour, Man. — D3 70
Jackman, Me., U.S. — C2 96
Jackman Station, Me., U.S. — C2 96

Jack Mountain, mtn., Mt., U.S. — D4 103
Jack Mountain, mtn., Va., U.S. — B3 123
Jack Mountain, mtn., Wa., U.S. — A5 124
Jackpot, Nv., U.S. — B7 105
Jacksboro, Tn., U.S. — C9 119
Jacksboro, Tx., U.S. — C3 120
Jacks Creek, Tn., U.S. — B3 119
Jacks Mountain, mtn., Pa., U.S. — E6 115
Jackson, Al., U.S. — D2 78
Jackson, Ca., U.S. — C3 82
Jackson, Ga., U.S. — C3 87
Jackson, Ky., U.S. — C6 94
Jackson, La., U.S. — D4 95
Jackson, Me., U.S. — D3 96
Jackson, Mi., U.S. — F6 99
Jackson, Mn., U.S. — G4 100
Jackson, Ms., U.S. — C3 101
Jackson, Mo., U.S. — D8 102
Jackson, Mt., U.S. — E3 103
Jackson, Ne., U.S. — B9 104
Jackson, N.H., U.S. — B4 106
Jackson, N.J., U.S. — C4 107
Jackson, N.C., U.S. — A5 110
Jackson, Oh., U.S. — C3 112
Jackson, R.I., U.S. — D3 116
Jackson, S.C., U.S. — E4 117
Jackson, Tn., U.S. — B3 119
Jackson, Wi., U.S. — E5 126
Jackson, Wy., U.S. — C2 127
Jackson, co., Al., U.S. — A3 78
Jackson, co., Ar., U.S. — B4 81
Jackson, co., Co., U.S. — A4 83
Jackson, co., Fl., U.S. — B1 86
Jackson, co., Ga., U.S. — B3 87
Jackson, co., Il., U.S. — F4 90
Jackson, co., In., U.S. — G5 91
Jackson, co., Ia., U.S. — B7 92
Jackson, co., Ks., U.S. — C8 93
Jackson, co., Ky., U.S. — C5 94
Jackson, co., Mi., U.S. — F6 99
Jackson, co., Mn., U.S. — G3 100
Jackson, co., Ms., U.S. — E5 101
Jackson, co., Mo., U.S. — B3 102
Jackson, co., N.C., U.S. — f9 110
Jackson, co., Oh., U.S. — C3 112
Jackson, co., Ok., U.S. — C2 113
Jackson, co., Or., U.S. — E4 114
Jackson, co., S.D., U.S. — D4 118
Jackson, co., Tn., U.S. — C8 119
Jackson, co., Tx., U.S. — E4 120
Jackson, co., W.V., U.S. — C3 125
Jackson, co., Wi., U.S. — D3 126
Jackson, stm., Va., U.S. — C3 123
Jackson, Lake, l., Fl., U.S. — E5 86
Jackson, Lake, l., Fl., U.S. — B2 86
Jackson, Mount, mtn., Ant. — B6 7
Jackson, Mount, mtn., N.H., U.S. — B4 106
Jackson, Port, b., Austl. — F8 51
Jacksonboro, S.C., U.S. — F7 117
Jacksonburg, W.V., U.S. — B4 125
Jackson Center, Oh., U.S. — B1 112
Jackson Center, Pa., U.S. — D1 115
Jackson Dam, Al., U.S. — D2 78
Jackson Hill, In., U.S. — F3 91
Jackson Junction, Ia., U.S. — A5 92
Jackson Lake, res., Ga., U.S. — C3 87
Jackson Lake, res., Wy., U.S. — C2 127
Jackson Mountain, mtn., Me., U.S. — D2 96
Jackson Mountains, mts., Nv., U.S. — B3 105
Jacksonport, Ar., U.S. — B4 81
Jackson's Arm, Newf. — D3 72
Jacksons Gap, Al., U.S. — C4 78
Jacksonville, Al., U.S. — B4 78
Jacksonville, Ar., U.S. — C3 81
Jacksonville, Fl., U.S. — B5 86
Jacksonville, Ga., U.S. — E4 87
Jacksonville, Il., U.S. — D3 90
Jacksonville, Me., U.S. — D5 96
Jacksonville, N.C., U.S. — C5 110
Jacksonville, Oh., U.S. — C3 112
Jacksonville, Or., U.S. — E4 114
Jacksonville, Tx., U.S. — D5 120
Jacksonville, Vt., U.S. — F3 122
Jacksonville Beach, Fl., U.S. — B5 86
Jacksonville Naval Air Station, mil., Fl., U.S. — B5 86
Jacks Peak, mtn., Ut., U.S. — E3 121
Jacktown, Ok., U.S. — B4 113
Jacmel, Haiti — E11 64
Jacob, Congo — B1 48
Jacobābād, Pak. — C4 36
Jacobina, Braz. — D2 57
Jacob Lake, Az., U.S. — A3 80
Jacobson, Mn., U.S. — D5 100
Jacobstown, N.J., U.S. — C3 107
Jacobsville, Mi., U.S. — B2 99
Jacques-Cartier, Détroit de, strt., Que. — h8 72
Jacques-Cartier, Mont, mtn., Que. — G19 66

Jacques-Cartier, stm., Que. — B6 74
Jacquet River, N.B. — B4 71
Jacquinot Bay, b., Pap. N. Gui. — k13 50
Jacuí, stm., Braz. — D2 56
Jacuípe, stm., Braz. — D3 57
Jacumba, Ca., U.S. — F5 82
Jacundá, stm., Braz. — C3 59
Jadadpur, India — *D8 36
Jaddi, Rãs, c., Pak. — I11 39
Jade, Ger. — A8 17
Jade Bay, b., Ger. — B4 18
Jãdú, Libya — C2 43
Jadwin, Mo., U.S. — D6 102
Jaén, Peru — B2 58
Jaén, Spain — C3 22
Jaffa, Cape, c., Austl. — G6 50
Jaffa Gate, hist., Isr. Occ. — m14 41
Jaffna, Sri L. — G7 36
Jaffrey, N.H., U.S. — E2 106
Jaffrey Center, N.H., U.S. — E2 106
Jagādhri, India — E7 36
Jagdalpur, India — B6 37
Jaggayyapeta, India — D6 37
Jagin, stm., Iran — H9 39
Jagst, stm., Ger. — A4 19
Jaguaquara, Braz. — D2 57
Jaguarão, Braz. — E2 56
Jaguari, stm., Braz. — m13 56
Jaguaribe, stm., Braz. — D3 57
Jagüey Grande, Cuba — C3 64
Jahānah, Syria — *F11 40
Jahrom, Iran — C5 39
Jaicós, Braz. — D2 57
Jailolo, Indon. — E8 34
Jaipur, India — G9 36
Jaisalmer, India — D8 36
Jājapur, India — J7 36
Jajce, Yugo. — C3 24

Jakarta (Djakarta), Indon. — G3 34
Jakin, Ga., U.S. — E2 87
Jakobstad, Fin. — F10 14
Jal, N.M., U.S. — E6 108
Jalálábád, Afg. — B5 36
Jalálah al Baḥrīyah, Jabal, plat., Eg. — E4 41
Jalandhar, India — B6 36
Jalapa, Guat. — E6 63
Jalapa Enríquez, Mex. — D5 63
Jālaun, India — C6 36
Jālgaon, India — D6 36
Jalisco, Mex. — m11 63
Jalisco, state, Mex. — C3 63
Jālna, India — E6 36
Jalón, stm., Spain — B5 22
Jālor, India — E4 37
Jalpa, Mex. — C4 63
Jalpan, Mex. — C5 63
Jālū, Wāḥat, well, Libya — D4 43
Jālūlā, Iraq — D2 39
Jamaame, Som. — E5 47
Jamaica, Ia., U.S. — C3 92
Jamaica, Vt., U.S. — E3 122
Jamaica, ctry., N.A. — E5 64
Jamaica Bay, b., N.Y., U.S. — k13 109
Jamaica Channel, strt., N.A. — E6 64
Jamálpur, Bngl. — E12 37
Jamanxim, stm., Braz. — D3 59
Jamari, stm., Braz. — D2 59
Jambi, Indon. — F2 34
Jambuair, Cape, c., Indon. — D1 34
James, Ga., U.S. — D3 87
James, stm., Alta. — D3 68
James, stm., Mo., U.S. — E4 102
James, stm., Va., U.S. — C5 123
James, Lake, l., In., U.S. — A7 91
James, Lake, res., N.C., U.S. — B1 110
James Bay, b., Can. — F16 66
James Branch, stm., De., U.S. — F3 85
Jamesburg, N.J., U.S. — C4 107
James City, N.C., U.S. — B5 110
James City, Pa., U.S. — C4 115
James City, co., Va., U.S. — C6 123
James Craik, Arg. — A4 54
James Creek, Pa., U.S. — F5 115
James Island, B.C. — g12 69
James Island, S.C., U.S. — k12 117
James Island, i., Md., U.S. — C5 97
James Island, i., S.C., U.S. — F8 117
Jameson, Mo., U.S. — A4 102
Jamesport, Mo., U.S. — B4 102
James River Bridge, Va., U.S. — k15 123
James Ross Island, i., Ant. — C7 7
James Ross Strait, strt., N.W. Ter. — C13 66
Jamestown, Austl. — F2 51
Jamestown, Ire. — D3 11
Jamestown, Al., U.S. — A4 78
Jamestown, Ca., U.S. — D3 82
Jamestown, Co., U.S. — A5 83
Jamestown, Il., U.S. — E4 90
Jamestown, In., U.S. — E4 91
Jamestown, Ks., U.S. — C6 93
Jamestown, Ky., U.S. — D4 94
Jamestown, La., U.S. — B2 95
Jamestown, Mo., U.S. — C5 102
Jamestown, N.Y., U.S. — C1 109
Jamestown, N.C., U.S. — B3 110
Jamestown, N.D., U.S. — C7 111
Jamestown, Oh., U.S. — C2 112
Jamestown, Pa., U.S. — D1 115
Jamestown, R.I., U.S. — F5 116
Jamestown, S.C., U.S. — E8 117
Jamestown, Tn., U.S. — C9 119
Jamestown, Town, Wy., U.S. — E3 127
Jamestown Dam, N.D., U.S. — C7 111
Jamestown Reservoir, res., N.D., U.S. — C7 111
Jamesville, N.C., U.S. — B6 110
Jamesville, Va., U.S. — C7 123
Jamiltepec, Mex. — D5 63
Jamison, Pa., U.S. — B6 104
Jammā'īn, Isr. Occ. — g11 41
Jammerbugten, b., Den. — A3 15
Jammu, India — A6 36
Jammu and Kashmir, dep., Asia — A6 36
Jamnagar (Navanagar), India — D5 36
Jāmpur, Pak. — C3 36
Jamsah, Eg. — D6 43
Jamshedpur, India — D8 36
Jämshög, Swe. — B8 15
Jamul, Ca., U.S. — F5 82
Jamuna, stm., Bngl. — E12 37
Jandaia, Braz. — B4 56
Jandaq, Iran — D7 39
Jandiatuba, stm., Braz. — B4 58
Jándula, stm., Spain — C4 22
Jane, Mo., U.S. — E3 102
Jane Lew, W.V., U.S. — B4 125
Janesville, Ca., U.S. — B3 82
Janesville, Il., U.S. — D5 90
Janesville, Ia., U.S. — B5 92
Janesville, Mn., U.S. — F5 100
Janesville, Wi., U.S. — F4 126
Janeville, N.B. — B5 71
Jangipur, India — E12 37
Janin, Isr. Occ. — B7 41
Janos, Mex. — A3 63
Jánoshalma, Hung. — B4 24
Janow, Man. — C2 70
Janów Lubelski, Pol. — F3 26
Jansen, Sask. — F3 75
Jansen, Co., U.S. — D6 83
Jansen, Ne., U.S. — D8 104
Januária, Braz. — B5 56
Jaora, India — D2 57

Jardine, Mt., U.S. — E6 103
Jardines de la Reina, Archipiélago de los, is., Cuba — D4 64
Jardinópolis, Braz. — k8 56
Järfälla, Swe. — *H7 14
Jargalang, China — C10 32
Jargalant, Mong. — B7 31
Jari, stm., Braz. — A4 59
Jārlåsa (part of Uppsala), Swe. — t35 14
Järna (part of Södertälje), Swe. — t35 14
Jarnac, Fr. — E3 16
Jarny, Fr. — E5 17
Jarocin, Pol. — C4 26
Jaroměř, Czech. — C7 26
Jarosław, Pol. — D5 26
Jaroso, Co., U.S. — D5 83
Jarratt, Va., U.S. — D5 123
Jarrettsville, Md., U.S. — A5 97
Jarrow, Alta. — C5 68
Jaru, Braz. — B3 55
Jarud Qi, China — C9 31
Jarvenpää, Fin. — E4 73
Jarvie, Alta. — B4 68
Jarvis, Ont. — E4 73
Jarvisburg, N.C., U.S. — A7 110
Jasień, Pol. — B10 19
Jãsk, Iran — I8 39
Jasło, Pol. — D6 26
Jasmin, Sask. — F4 75
Jasmine Estates, Fl., U.S. — D4 86
Jason Peninsula, pen., Ant. — C6 7
Jasonville, In., U.S. — F3 91
Jasper, Alta. — C1 68
Jasper, Ont. — C9 73
Jasper, Al., U.S. — B2 78
Jasper, Ar., U.S. — B2 81
Jasper, Fl., U.S. — B4 86
Jasper, Ga., U.S. — B2 87
Jasper, In., U.S. — H4 91
Jasper, Mn., U.S. — G2 100
Jasper, Mo., U.S. — D3 102
Jasper, N.Y., U.S. — C3 109
Jasper, Oh., U.S. — C2 112
Jasper, Or., U.S. — D4 114
Jasper, Tn., U.S. — D8 119
Jasper, Tx., U.S. — D6 120
Jasper, co., Ga., U.S. — C3 87
Jasper, co., Il., U.S. — D5 90
Jasper, co., In., U.S. — C3 91
Jasper, co., Ia., U.S. — C4 92
Jasper, co., Ms., U.S. — C4 101
Jasper, co., Mo., U.S. — D3 102
Jasper, co., S.C., U.S. — G5 117
Jasper, co., Tx., U.S. — D5 120
Jasper Lake, l., Alta. — C1 68
Jasper National Park, Alta. — C1 68
Jastarnia, Pol. — A5 26
Jastrzebia Góra, Pol. — A5 26
Jastrzebie-Zdrój, Pol. — h9 26
Jászapáti, Hung. — B5 24
Jászberény, Hung. — B4 24
Jataí, Braz. — B2 56
Jāti, Pak. — E2 37
Jatibonico, Cuba — D4 64
Játiva, Spain — C5 22
Jatni, India — G10 37
Jaú, Braz. — C3 56
Jaú, stm., Braz. — C2 59
Jauaperi, stm., Braz. — B2 59
Jauja, Mex. — C5 63
Jaunpur, India — C7 36
Java, S.D., U.S. — B6 118
Java (Jawa), i., Indon. — G3 34
Java Sea, Indon. — G4 34
Javari see Yavarí, stm., S.A. — B3 58
Jávea, Spain — C6 22
Jawhār, India — H4 37
Jawor, Pol. — g10 26
Jaworzno, Pol. — g10 26
Jay, Fl., U.S. — u14 86
Jay, Me., U.S. — D2 96
Jay, N.Y., U.S. — f11 109
Jay, Ok., U.S. — A7 113
Jay, co., In., U.S. — D7 91
Jayanca, Peru — B2 58
Jaya Peak, mtn., Indon. — F9 34
Jayapura, Indon. — F10 34
Jay Em, Wy., U.S. — D8 127
Jayton, Tx., U.S. — C2 120
Jay Peak, mtn., Vt., U.S. — B3 122
Jaypur, India — C7 36
Jaz Mūrīān, Hāmūn-e, l., Iran — H9 39
J. B. Thomas, Lake, res., Tx., U.S. — C2 120
Jean, Nv., U.S. — H6 105
Jeanerette, La., U.S. — E4 95
Jean Lafitte National Historical Park, La., U.S. — k12 95
Jeannette, Pa., U.S. — F2 115
Jeannette Island, i., Sov. Un. — B35 128
Jebba, Nig. — E5 45
Jeberos, Peru — B2 58
Jedburg, S.C., U.S. — h11 117
Jedburgh, Sask. — F4 75
Jedburgh, Scot., U.K. — C5 10
Jeddito, Az., U.S. — B5 80
Jeddo, Mi., U.S. — E8 99
Jeddore Lake, res., Newf. — D3 72
Jedrzejów, Pol. — C6 26
Jeetze, stm., Eur. — B5 18
Jeff, Ky., U.S. — C6 94
Jeff Davis, co., Ga., U.S. — E4 87
Jeff Davis, co., Tx., U.S. — o12 120
Jefferies, Mt., U.S. — F3 100
Jeffers, Mn., U.S. — G3 100
Jefferson, Co., U.S. — B5 83
Jefferson, Ga., U.S. — B3 87
Jefferson, Ia., U.S. — B3 92
Jefferson, La., U.S. — k11 95
Jefferson, Md., U.S. — B2 97
Jefferson, N.H., U.S. — B4 106
Jefferson, N.Y., U.S. — C6 109
Jefferson, N.C., U.S. — A1 110
Jefferson, Oh., U.S. — A5 112
Jefferson, Ok., U.S. — A4 113
Jefferson, Or., U.S. — C3 114
Jefferson, S.C., U.S. — B7 117
Jefferson, Tx., U.S. — C5 120
Jefferson, Wi., U.S. — E5 126
Jefferson, co., Al., U.S. — B3 78
Jefferson, co., Ar., U.S. — C3 81

Name	Map Ref.	Page
Jefferson, co., Co., U.S.	B5	83
Jefferson, co., Fl., U.S.	B3	86
Jefferson, co., Ga., U.S.	C4	87
Jefferson, co., Id., U.S.	F6	89
Jefferson, co., Il., U.S.	E5	90
Jefferson, co., In., U.S.	G6	91
Jefferson, co., Ks., U.S.	C5	92
Jefferson, co., Ky., U.S.	C8	93
Jefferson, co., Ky., U.S.	B4	94
Jefferson, co., La., U.S.	E5	95
Jefferson, co., Ms., U.S.	D2	101
Jefferson, co., Mo., U.S.	C7	102
Jefferson, co., Mt., U.S.	D4	103
Jefferson, co., Ne., U.S.	D8	104
Jefferson, co., N.Y., U.S.	A5	109
Jefferson, co., Oh., U.S.	B5	112
Jefferson, co., Ok., U.S.	C4	113
Jefferson, co., Or., U.S.	C5	114
Jefferson, co., Pa., U.S.	D3	115
Jefferson, co., Tn., U.S.	C10	119
Jefferson, co., Tx., U.S.	E5	120
Jefferson, co., Wa., U.S.	B7	125
Jefferson, co., W.V., U.S.	B7	125
Jefferson, co., Wi., U.S.	E5	126
Jefferson, Mount, mtn., Id., U.S.	E7	89
Jefferson, Mount, mtn., Nv., U.S.	E5	105
Jefferson, Mount, mtn., Or., U.S.	C5	114
Jefferson City, Mo., U.S.	C5	102
Jefferson City, Mt., U.S.	D5	103
Jefferson City, Tn., U.S.	C10	119
Jefferson Davis, co., La., U.S.	D3	95
Jefferson Davis, co., Ms., U.S.	D4	101
Jefferson Farms, De., U.S.	i7	85
Jefferson Hill, Ky., U.S.	g11	94
Jefferson Manor, Va., U.S.	*B5	123
Jefferson Proving Ground, mil., In., U.S.	G7	91
Jeffersontown, Ky., U.S.	B4	94
Jefferson Valley, N.Y., U.S.	*D7	109
Jefferson Village, Va., U.S.	*B5	123
Jeffersonville, Ga., U.S.	D3	87
Jeffersonville, In., U.S.	H6	91
Jeffersonville, Ky., U.S.	C6	94
Jeffersonville, N.Y., U.S.	D6	109
Jeffersonville, Oh., U.S.	C2	112
Jeffersonville, Vt., U.S.	B3	122
Jeffrey, W.V., U.S.	D3	125
Jeffrey City, Wy., U.S.	E5	127
Jeffries Creek, stm., S.C., U.S.	C8	117
Jega, Nig.	D5	45
Jehossee Island, i., S.C., U.S.	k11	117
Jejui-Guazú, stm., Para.	D4	55
Jēkabpils, Sov. Un.	C5	27
Jekyll Island, i., Ga., U.S.	E5	87
Jelenia Góra (Hirschberg), Pol.	C3	26
Jelgava (Yelgava), Sov. Un.	C4	27
Jellico, Tn., U.S.	C3	119
Jelling, Den.	C3	15
Jelm, Wy., U.S.	E6	127
Jelm Mountain, mtn., Wy., U.S.	E7	127
Jelöya, i., Nor.	p28	14
Jemaja, i., Indon.	K6	35
Jember, Indon.	G4	34
Jemez, stm., N.M., U.S.	k7	108
Jemez Dam, N.M., U.S.	k7	108
Jemez Indian Reservation, N.M., U.S.	h7	108
Jemez Pueblo, N.M., U.S.	B3	108
Jemez Springs, N.M., U.S.	B3	108
Jemison, Al., U.S.	C3	78
Jemseg, N.B.	D3	71
Jemtland, Me., U.S.	A4	96
Jena, Ger.	C5	18
Jena, La., U.S.	C3	95
Jena, La., U.S.	C3	95
Jenaz, Switz.	C8	21
Jenbach, Aus.	B7	20
Jendouba, Tun.	F2	23
Jenera, Oh., U.S.	B2	112
Jenison, Mi., U.S.	*F5	99
Jenkins, Ky., U.S.	C7	94
Jenkins, co., Ga., U.S.	D4	100
Jenkins, co., Ga., U.S.	D3	107
Jenkins, co., Ga., U.S.	D5	87
Jenkinsburg, Ga., U.S.	C2	87
Jenkinsville, S.C., U.S.	C5	117
Jenkintown, Pa., U.S.	o21	115
Jenks, Ok., U.S.	A6	113
Jenner, Alta.	D5	68
Jenners, Pa., U.S.	F3	115
Jennie, Ar., U.S.	D4	81
Jennings, Fl., U.S.	B3	86
Jennings, Ks., U.S.	C3	93
Jennings, La., U.S.	D3	95
Jennings, Md., U.S.	k12	97
Jennings, Mi., U.S.	D5	99
Jennings, Ok., U.S.	f13	102
Jennings, Ok., U.S.	A5	113
Jennings, co., In., U.S.	G6	91
Jennings Lodge, Or., U.S.	*B4	114
Jenny Jump Mountain, mtn., N.J., U.S.	B3	107
Jenny Lind, Ar., U.S.	B1	81
Jensen, Ut., U.S.	C6	121
Jensen Beach, Fl., U.S.	E6	86
Jeptha Knob, hill, Ky., U.S.	B4	94
Jequié, Braz.	B4	56
Jequitinhonha, Braz.	E2	57
Jequitinhonha, stm., Braz.	E2	57
Jerada, Mor.	C4	44
Jerauld, co., S.D., U.S.	C7	118
Jérémie, Haiti	E6	64
Jeremoabo, Braz.	D3	57
Jerez de García Salinas, Mex.	C4	63
Jerez de la Frontera, Spain	D2	22
Jerez de los Caballeros, Spain	C4	22
Jericho, Austl.	A6	51
Jericho (Arīḥā), Isr. Occ.	C7	41
Jericho, N.Y., U.S.	*E7	109
Jericho, Vt., U.S.	B3	122
Jericho Center, Vt., U.S.	C3	122
Jerico Springs, Mo., U.S.	D3	102
Jerimoth Hill, hill, R.I., U.S.	C1	116
Jermyn, Pa., U.S.	C10	115
Jermyn, Tx., U.S.	C3	120
Jerome, Az., U.S.	C3	80
Jerome, Id., U.S.	D4	81
Jerome, Id., U.S.	G4	89
Jerome, Mi., U.S.	F6	99
Jerome, Mo., U.S.	D5	102
Jerome, Pa., U.S.	F4	115
Jerome, co., Id., U.S.	G4	89
Jeromesville, Oh., U.S.	B3	112
Jersey, co., Il., U.S.	D3	90
Jersey, dep., Eur.	F5	10
Jersey City, N.J., U.S.	B4	107
Jersey Mountain, mtn., Id., U.S.	E3	89
Jersey Shore, Pa., U.S.	D7	115
Jerseyville, Il., U.S.	D3	90
Jerumenha, Braz.	C2	57
Jerusalem (Yerushalayim), Isr.	B3	81
Jerusalem, Ar., U.S.	B3	81
Jerusalem, Oh., U.S.	C4	112
Jervis Bay, b., Austl.	G9	50
Jervis Inlet, b., B.C.	D6	69
Jesenice Reservoir, res., Czech.	C7	19
Jesenik, Czech.	C4	26
Jessamine, co., Ky., U.S.	C5	94
Jessen, Ger.	B7	19
Jessie, N.D., U.S.	B7	111
Jessieville, Ar., U.S.	C2	81
Jessnitz, Ger.	B7	19
Jessore, Bngl.	F12	37
Jessup, Md., U.S.	B4	97
Jessup, Md., U.S.	m18	115
Jesup, Ga., U.S.	E5	87
Jesup, Ia., U.S.	B5	92
Jesup, Lake, l., Fl., U.S.	D5	86
Jésus, Île, i., Que.	p19	74
Jesús Câmara, Mex.	g6	57
Jesús María, Arg.	A4	54
Jesús María, Peru	*D2	58
Jet, Ok., U.S.	A3	113
Jetersville, Va., U.S.	C4	123
Jetmore, Ks., U.S.	D4	93
Jetson, Ky., U.S.	C3	94
Jette, Bel.	D4	17
Jeumont, Fr.	D4	17
Jever, Ger.	B3	18
Jewel Cave National Monument, S.D., U.S.	D2	118
Jewell, Ia., U.S.	B4	92
Jewell, Ks., U.S.	C5	93
Jewell, Oh., U.S.	A1	112
Jewell, co., Ks., U.S.	C5	93
Jewell Ridge, Va., U.S.	e10	123
Jewett, Il., U.S.	D5	90
Jewett, Oh., U.S.	B4	112
Jewett, Tx., U.S.	D4	120
Jewett City, Ct., U.S.	C8	84
Jewett Lake, l., Sask.	A3	75
Jeziorka, stm., Pol.	m14	26
Jhal, Pak.	C1	37
Jhālāwār, India	E6	37
Jhal Jhao, Pak.	C4	36
Jhang Sadar, Pak.	B4	37
Jhānsi, India	C6	36
Jhawāni, Nepal	D10	37
Jhelum, Pak.	B5	36
Jhelum, stm., Asia	C5	36
Jhunjhunūn, India	E6	37
Jialing Jiang, stm., China	E6	31
Jiamusi, China	B11	31
Ji'an, China	F7	31
Ji'an, China	D12	32
Jianchang, China	D11	32
Jiande, China	J8	32
Jiangling, China	E7	31
Jiangmen, China	G7	31
Jiangsu, prov., China	E9	31
Jiangxi, prov., China	F8	31
Jiangyin (Chengjiang), China	I9	32
Jiangyou, China	E5	31
Jianli, China	J5	32
Jianning, China	K7	32
Jian'ou, China	F8	31
Jianping, China	C8	31
Jianshi, China	I3	32
Jianshui, China	G5	31
Jianyang, China	K8	32
Jiaohe, China	E3	33
Jiaoxian, China	D9	31
Jiaozuo, China	D7	31
Jiashan, China	H8	32
Jiaxian, China	E4	32
Jiaxing, China	E9	31
Jiayu, China	I5	32
Jicarilla Indian Reservation, N.M., U.S.	A2	108
Jičín, Czech.	C3	26
Jiddah, Sau. Ar.	C3	38
Jiddī, Jabal al, mtn., Eg.	D5	41
Jidy, Bi'r al, well, Eg.	D5	41
Jiekkevarri, mtn., Nor.	F4	32
Jiexiu, China	D6	31
Jieyang, China	G8	31
Jifnā, Isr. Occ.	h11	41
Jigger, La., U.S.	B4	95
Jiggs, Nv., U.S.	C6	105
Jihlava, Czech.	D3	26
Jihočeský, prov., Czech.	D9	19
Jijel, Alg.	B6	44
Jijia, stm., Rom.	B8	24
Jijiga, Eth.	D5	47
Jijona, Spain	C5	22
Jilbānah, Bi'r al, well, Eg.	D4	41
Jilib, Som.	E5	47
Jilin, China	C10	31
Jilin, prov., China	C10	31
Jiloca, stm., Spain	B5	22
Jílové u Prahy, Czech.	o18	26
Jima, Eth.	D4	47
Jimbolia, Rom.	C5	24
Jimena [de los Frontera], Spain	*D3	22
Jim Falls, Wi., U.S.	C2	126
Jim Hogg, co., Tx., U.S.	F3	120
Jim Lake, res., N.D., U.S.	B7	111
Jimo, China	F9	32
Jim Thorpe, Pa., U.S.	E10	115
Jim Wells, co., Tx., U.S.	F3	120
Jināh, China	D6	43
Jincheng, China	G5	32
Jindřichův Hradec, Czech.	D3	26
Jingbian, China	F2	32
Jingchuan, China	G2	32
Jingde, China	I8	32
Jingdezhen, China	F8	31
Jing He, stm., China	G3	32
Jinghong, China	I5	32
Jingmen, China	I5	32
Jingning, China	G1	32
Jingshan, China	I5	32
Jingxi, China	D9	32
Jingxian, China	K3	32
Jingxing, China	A10	32
Jingziguan, China	H4	32
Jinhua, China	F8	31
Jining, China	D8	31
Jining, China	C7	31
Jinja, Ug.	A5	48
Jinniu, China	I6	32
Jinotega, Nic.	E7	63
Jinotepe, Nic.	E7	63
Jinsha Jiang, stm., China	F4	31
Jinshi, China	J4	32
Jinta, China	*C9	31
Jinxi, China	*C9	31
Jinxian, China	J9	32
Jinyun, China	C9	31
Jinzhou, China	B3	55
Ji-Paraná, Braz.	D2	59
Jiparaná, stm., Braz.	B1	58
Jipijapa, Ec.	D3	62
Jiquilisco, El Sal.	n12	63
Jiquilpan de Juárez, Mex.	val.	
Jīrāft, Wādī al (Naḥal Paran), Eg.	E6	41
Jirjā, Eg.	C3	38
Jirkov, Czech.	C8	19
Jisr ash Shughūr, Syria	E11	41
Jiu, stm., Rom.	C6	24
Jiujiang, China	F8	31
Jiuquan, China	D4	31
Jiurongcheng, China	F10	32
Jixi, China	B11	31
Jixian, China	G6	32
Jizera, stm., Czech.	C9	19
Joaçaba, Braz.	D2	56
Joaíma, Braz.	B4	56
Joanna, S.C., U.S.	C4	117
João Belo see Xai-Xai, Moz.	C5	49
João Câmara, Braz.	g6	57
João Pessoa (Paraíba), Braz.	C4	57
João Pinheiro, Braz.	B3	56
Joaquín V. González, Arg.	E3	55
Job, W.V., U.S.	C5	125
Job Peak, mtn., Nv., U.S.	D3	105
Jobstown, N.J., U.S.	C3	107
Jocassee, Lake, res., B1	117
Jocotepec, Mex.	m12	63
Jódar, Spain	D4	22
Jo Daviess, co., Il., U.S.	A3	90
Jodhpur, India	C5	36
Jodie, W.V., U.S.	m13	125
Jodoigne, Bel.	D4	17
Joe Batt's Arm [-Barr'd Islands-Shoal Bay], Newf.	D4	72
Joensuu, Fin.	F13	14
Joes, Co., U.S.	B8	83
Joes Brook, stm., Vt., U.S.	C4	122
Joes Creek, stm., W.V., U.S.	m12	125
Joetsu, Japan	H9	33
Jœuf, Fr.	C6	16
Joffre, Mount, mtn., Can.	D5	71
Joggins, N.S.	D5	71
Jogjakarta see Yogyakarta, Indon.	G4	34
Johannesburg, S. Afr.	C4	49
Johannesburg, Ca., U.S.	E5	82
Johannesburg, Mi., U.S.	D6	99
John, Cape, c., N.S.	D6	71
John Crow Mountains, mts., Jam.	E16	65
John Day, Or., U.S.	C8	114
John Day, stm., Or., U.S.	B6	114
John Day, North Fork, stm., Or., U.S.	C7	114
John Day Dam, U.S.	D5	124
John Day Fossil Beds National Monument, Or., U.S.	C6	114
John F. Kennedy Space Center, sci., Fl., U.S.	D6	86
John H. Kerr Dam, Va., U.S.	D4	123
John H. Kerr Reservoir, res., U.S.	D4	123
John Martin Reservoir, res., Co., U.S.	C7	83
John Muir National Historical Site, hist., Ca., U.S.	h8	82
John o'Groats, Scot., U.K.	B5	13
John Redmond Reservoir, res., Ks., U.S.	D8	93
Johnsburg, Il., U.S.	h8	90
Johnsburg, N.Y., U.S.	B7	109
Johnsburg, Wi., U.S.	k9	126
John Sevier, Tn., U.S.	m14	119
Johns Island, S.C., U.S.	F7	117
Johns Island, i., S.C., U.S.	F7	117
Johnson, Ar., U.S.	A1	81
Johnson, In., U.S.	H2	91
Johnson, Ks., U.S.	E2	93
Johnson, Ne., U.S.	D10	104
Johnson, Vt., U.S.	B3	122
Johnson, Wa., U.S.	C8	124
Johnson, co., Ar., U.S.	B2	81
Johnson, co., Ga., U.S.	D4	87
Johnson, co., Il., U.S.	F5	90
Johnson, co., In., U.S.	F5	91
Johnson, co., Ia., U.S.	C6	92
Johnson, co., Ks., U.S.	D9	93
Johnson, co., Ky., U.S.	C7	94
Johnson, co., Mo., U.S.	C4	102
Johnson, co., Ne., U.S.	D9	104
Johnson, co., Tn., U.S.	C12	119
Johnson, co., Tx., U.S.	C4	120
Johnson, co., Wy., U.S.	B6	127
Johnsonburg, Pa., U.S.	C4	115
Johnson City, N.Y., U.S.	C5	109
Johnson City, Tn., U.S.	C11	119
Johnson City, Tx., U.S.	D3	120
Johnson Creek, Wi., U.S.	E5	126
Johnsondale, Ca., U.S.	E4	82
Johnson's Bayou, La., U.S.	E2	95
Johnsons Grove, Tn., U.S.	B2	119
Johnsonville, S.C., U.S.	D9	117
Johnston, Ia., U.S.	e8	92
Johnston, R.I., U.S.	C4	116
Johnston, S.C., U.S.	D4	117
Johnston, co., N.C., U.S.	B4	110
Johnston, co., Ok., U.S.	C5	113
Johnston, i., Oc.	E11	6
Johnston, Lake, l., Austl.	F3	50
Johnston City, Il., U.S.	F5	90
Johnstone, Scot., U.K.	*E4	13
Johnstone Strait, strt., B.C.	D4	69
Johnstone Bay, i., Fl., U.S.	H5	86
Johnston's Point, c., Scot., U.K.		
Johnstown, Co., U.S.	A6	83
Johnstown, Ne., U.S.	B5	104
Johnstown, N.Y., U.S.	B6	109
Johnstown, N.D., U.S.	B3	111
Johnstown, Oh., U.S.	B3	112
Johnstown, Pa., U.S.	F4	115
Johnsville, Md., U.S.	A3	97
Johntown, Tx., U.S.	C5	120
Johnville, Que.	D6	74
John W. Flannagan Reservoir, res., Va., U.S.	e9	123
Johor, state, Malay.	*E2	34
Johor Baharu, Malay.	*E2	34
Joice, Ia., U.S.	A4	92
Joigny, Fr.	D5	16
Joiner, Ar., U.S.	B5	81
Joinville, Braz.	D3	56
Joinville, Fr.	C6	16
Joinville Island, i., Ant.	C7	9
Jojutla, Mex.	n14	63
Jokkmokk, Swe.	D8	14
Jolfā, Iran	B2	39
Joliet, Il., U.S.	B5	90
Joliet, Mt., U.S.	E8	103
Joliette, Que.	C4	74
Joliette, N.D., U.S.	A8	111
Joliette, co., Que.	C3	74
Jolo, Phil.	D6	34
Jolo, W.V., U.S.	D3	125
Jomalig Island, i., Phil.	o14	34
Jomda, China	E4	31
Jonava, Sov. Un.	A8	26
Jonava, Phil.	n13	34
Jones, Al., U.S.	C3	78
Jones, Ga., U.S.	E5	87
Jones, La., U.S.	B4	95
Jones, Ok., U.S.	B4	113
Jones, co., Ga., U.S.	C3	87
Jones, co., Ia., U.S.	B6	92
Jones, co., Ms., U.S.	D4	101
Jones, co., N.C., U.S.	B5	110
Jones, co., S.D., U.S.	D5	118
Jones, co., Tx., U.S.	C3	120
Jonesboro, Ar., U.S.	B5	81
Jonesboro, Ga., U.S.	C2	87
Jonesboro, Il., U.S.	F4	90
Jonesboro, In., U.S.	D6	91
Jonesboro, La., U.S.	B3	95
Jonesboro, Me., U.S.	D5	96
Jonesburg, Mo., U.S.	C6	102
Jones Creek, Tx., U.S.	s14	120
Jonesmill, Ar., U.S.	C3	81
Jones Mills, Pa., U.S.	F3	115
Jones Mountains, mts., Ant.	B7	7
Jonesport, Me., U.S.	D5	96
Jones Sound, strt., N.W. Ter.	m34	66
Jonestown, Ms., U.S.	A3	101
Jonestown, Ms., U.S.	C3	101
Jonestown, Pa., U.S.	F9	115
Jonesville, In., U.S.	F6	91
Jonesville, La., U.S.	C4	95
Jonesville, Mi., U.S.	F6	99
Jonesville, N.C., U.S.	A2	110
Jonesville, S.C., U.S.	B4	117
Jonesville, Va., U.S.	C3	122
Jonesville, Vt., U.S.	f8	123
Jönköping, Swe.	I6	14
Jönköping, co., Swe.	A8	15
Jonquière, Que.	A6	74
Jonuta, Mex.	D6	63
Jonzac, Fr.	E3	16
Joplin, Mo., U.S.	D3	102
Joplin, Mt., U.S.	B6	103
Joppa, Al., U.S.	A3	78
Joppa, Il., U.S.	F5	90
Joppa, Md., U.S.	B5	97
Jordan, Ar., U.S.	A1	81
Jordan, Mn., U.S.	F5	100
Jordan, Mt., U.S.	C10	103
Jordan, N.Y., U.S.	B4	109
Jordan, ctry., Asia	B3	38
Jordan, stm., Asia	B7	41
Jordan, stm., Ut., U.S.	C4	121
Jordan Creek, stm., U.S.	E9	114
Jordan Lake, l., N.C.	E4	71
Jordan Lake, res., Al., U.S.	C3	78
Jordan Valley, Or., U.S.	D9	114
Jorhāt, India	C9	36
Jörn, Swe.	E9	14
Jornado del Muerto, des., N.M., U.S.	D3	108
Jos, Nig.	E6	45
José Batlle y Ordóñez, Ur.	E1	56
José de San Martín, Arg.	C2	54
José María Blanco, Arg.	B4	54
Joseph, Or., U.S.	B9	114
Joseph, Ut., U.S.	E3	121
Joseph, Lac, l., Newf.	h8	72
Joseph, Lake, l., Ont.	B5	73
Joseph Bonaparte Gulf, b., Austl.	B4	50
Joseph City, Az., U.S.	C5	80
Josephine, co., Or., U.S.	E3	114
Josephville, Mo., U.S.	f12	102
Joshua, Tx., U.S.	n9	120
Joshua Tree, Ca., U.S.	E5	82
Joshua Tree National Monument, Ca., U.S.	F6	82
Josselin, Fr.	C2	16
Jostedalsbreen, ice, Nor.	G2	14
Jost Van Dyke, i., V.I., Br.	B6	65
Jotunheimen, mts., Nor.	G3	14
Jourdanton, Tx., U.S.	E3	120
Joure, Neth.	B6	17
Joutsa, Fin.	F11	14
Joutseno, Fin.	F12	14
Jovellanos, Cuba	C3	64
Joveyn, Afg.	B3	36
Joviânia, Braz.	B3	56
Jowai, India	E4	47
Joy, Il., U.S.	B3	90
Joy, Ok., U.S.	C4	113
Joyce, La., U.S.	C3	95
Joyce, Wa., U.S.	A2	124
Józefów, Pol.	m14	26
J. Percy Priest Lake, res., Tn., U.S.	A5	119
Juab, co., Ut., U.S.	D2	121
Juaja, Peru	D2	58
Juan Aldama, Mex.	C4	63
Juan B. Arruabarrena, Arg.	A5	54
Juan de Fuca, Strait of, strt., N.A.	A1	124
Juan Díaz (part of Panamá), Pan.	k12	62
Juan E. Barra, Arg.	D4	54
Juan Fernández, Archipiélago, is., Chile	G2	53
Juanita, N.D., U.S.	C2	111
Juanita, Wa., U.S.	*B3	124
Juan José Castelli, Arg.	B3	55
Juanjui, Peru	C2	58
Juan L. Lacaze, Ur.	g8	54
Juárez, Mex.	B4	63
Juaso, Ghana	E4	45
Juazeiro, Braz.	C3	57
Juazeiro do Norte, Braz.	E3	57
Jûbâ, Sud.	E3	47
Juba (Genale), stm., Afr.	E5	47
Jubbada Dhexe, prov., Som.	E5	47
Jubbada Hoose, prov., Som.	E5	47
Jubbah, Sau. Ar.	I13	40
Jubbah, Sau. Ar.	B2	38
Jubilee Lake, l., Newf.	E8	72
Juby, Cap, c., Mor.	D2	44
Juçara, Braz.	B2	56
Júcaro, Cuba	D4	64
Juchipila, Mex.	m12	63
Juchipila, stm., Mex.	m12	63
Juchitán [de Zaragoza], Mex.	D5	63
Jucuapa, El Sal.	D3	62
Jud, N.D., U.S.	C7	111
Juda, Wi., U.S.	F4	126
Judean Hills, hills, Asia	C7	41
Judenburg, Aus.	E7	18
Judique, N.S.	D8	71
Judith, stm., Mt., U.S.	C7	103
Judith Basin, co., Mt., U.S.	C6	103
Judith Gap, Mt., U.S.	D7	103
Judith Island, i., N.C., U.S.	B6	110
Judith Mountains, mts., Mt., U.S.	C7	103
Judith Peak, mtn., Mt., U.S.	C7	103
Judson, In., U.S.	E3	91
Judson, Mn., U.S.	F4	100
Judson, N.D., U.S.	C4	111
Judsonia, Ar., U.S.	B4	81
Judyville, In., U.S.	D3	91
Juelsminde, Den.	C4	15
Jufayr, Bi'r al, well, Eg.	D4	41
Juigalpa, Nic.	D5	62
Juiz de Fora, Braz.	C4	56
Jujuy, prov., Arg.	D2	55
Jujuy, stm., Zam.	D2	55
Jukkasjärvi (part of Kiruna), Swe.	D9	14
Julesburg, Co., U.S.	A8	83
Juliaca, Peru	E3	58
Juliaetta, Id., U.S.	C2	89
Julian, Ca., U.S.	F5	82
Julian, Ne., U.S.	D10	104
Julian, N.C., U.S.	B3	110
Julian, W.V., U.S.	C3	125
Julian Alps, mts., Eur.	C2	24
Juliana Top, mtn., Sur.	B3	59
Julianehåb, Grnld.	C16	61
Jülich, Ger.	D6	17
Juliette, Ga., U.S.	C3	87
Julimes, Mex.	B3	63
Júlio de Castilhos, Braz.	D2	56
Julita, Swe.	t34	14
Juliustown, N.J., U.S.	C3	107
Julu, China	F6	32
Jumayl, Bi'r, well, Eg.	D5	41
Jumboo, Som.	F5	47
Jumbo Peak, mtn., Nv., U.S.	I6	14
Jumet (part of Charleroi), Bel.	B6	16
Jumilla, Spain	C5	22
Jump, stm., Wi., U.S.	C3	126
Jump, North Fork, stm., Wi., U.S.	C3	126
Jump, South Fork, stm., Wi., U.S.	C3	126
Jumping Branch, W.V., U.S.	D4	125
Jumping Lake, l., Sask.	E3	75
Jūnāgadh, India	D5	36
Juncos, P.R.	B4	65
Junction, Il., U.S.	F5	90
Junction, Oh., U.S.	A1	112
Junction, Tx., U.S.	D3	120
Junction, Ut., U.S.	E3	121
Junction, ctry., Asia	B3	38
Junction City, Ga., U.S.	D2	87
Junction City, Ks., U.S.	C7	93
Junction City, Ky., U.S.	C5	94
Junction City, La., U.S.	A3	95
Junction City, Oh., U.S.	C3	112
Junction City, Or., U.S.	C3	114
Junction City, Wi., U.S.	D4	126
Jundiaí, Braz.	C3	56
Juneau, Ak., U.S.	D13	79
Juneau, Wi., U.S.	E5	126
Juneau, co., Wi., U.S.	E3	126
Junee, Austl.	F8	50
June in Winter, Lake, l., Fl., U.S.	E5	86
June Lake, Ca., U.S.	D4	82
Jungfrau, mtn., Switz.	E3	18
Junggar Pendi (Dzungarian Basin), China	B2	31
Junglinster, Lux.	E6	17
Juniata, Ne., U.S.	D7	104
Juniata, co., Pa., U.S.	F7	115
Juniata, Pa., U.S.	F7	115
Juniata, Raystown Branch, stm., Pa., U.S.	F5	115
Juniata Terrace, Pa., U.S.	E6	115
Junín, Arg.	A4	54
Junín, Peru	D2	58
Junín, dept., Peru	D2	58
Junín, Lago, l., Peru	D2	58
Junín de los Andes, Arg.	C2	54
Junior, W.V., U.S.	C5	125
Junior, Lake, l., Me., U.S.	C4	96
Juniper, N.B.	C2	71
Juniper Mountains, mts., Az., U.S.	B2	80
Junipero Serra Peak, mtn., Ca., U.S.	D3	82
Junius, S.D., U.S.	D8	118
Juno, Tx., U.S.	D2	120
Junqalī, prov., Sud.	D3	47
Juntura, Or., U.S.	D8	114
Jupiter, Fl., U.S.	F6	86
Jupiter Inlet, b., Fl., U.S.	F6	86
Jupiter Island, i., Fl., U.S.	F6	86
Juquiá, Braz.	C3	56
Juquitiba, Braz.	m8	56
Jura, state, Switz.	B3	20
Jura, dept., Fr.	E6	16
Jura, i., Scot., U.K.	C4	13
Jura, Sound of, strt., Scot., U.K.	C4	10
Jura Mountains, mts., Eur.	E3	18
Jurbarkas, Sov. Un.	A7	26
Jurf ad Darāwīsh, Jord.	G10	40
Juruá, Braz.	B2	59
Juruá, stm., S.A.	D3	59
Juruena, stm., Braz.	D3	59
Juskatla, B.C.	C1	69
Jussey, Fr.	D6	16
Justice, Il., U.S.	*k9	90
Justice, Tx., U.S.	C4	120
Justin, Tx., U.S.	C4	120
Jutaí, Braz.	B2	59
Jutaí, stm., Braz.	B2	59
Jüterbog, Ger.	B6	18
Juticalpa, Guat.	E7	63
Juticalpa, Hond.	D3	62
Juventud, Isla de la (Isle of Pines), i., Cuba	D2	64
Juxian, China	G8	32
Juyongguan Pass, China	D7	32
Južna Morava, stm., Yugo.	D5	24
Jyderup, Den.	C5	15
Jyväskylä, Fin.	F11	14

K

K2 (Godwin Austen), mtn., Asia	A6	36
Kaawaa, Hi., U.S.	f10	88
Kaala, mtn., Hi., U.S.	f9	88
Kaalualu Bay, b., Hi., U.S.	E6	88
Kaaumakua, Puu, mtn., Hi., U.S.	f10	88
Kabala, S.L.	E2	45
Kabale, Ug.	B4	48
Kabalega Falls (Murchison Falls), wtfl., Ug.	A5	48
Kabalo, Zaire	C4	48
Kabambare, Zaire	B4	48
Kabara, i., Fiji	I16	52
Kabarnet, Kenya	A6	48
Kabba, Nig.	E6	45
Kabenga, Zaire	C4	48
Kabetogama Lake, l., Mn., U.S.	B5	100
Kabinda, Zaire	C3	48
Kabīr Kūh, mts., Iran	E3	39
Kabompo, Zam.	D3	48
Kabompo, stm., Zam.	D2	48
Kabong, Malay.	E4	34
Kabongo, Zaire	C4	48
Kabul (Kābol), Afg.	B4	36
Kabul, stm., Asia	D14	39
Kabwe (Broken Hill), Zam.	D4	48
Kachchh, Gulf of (Kutch), b., India	D4	36
Kachess Lake, res., Wa., U.S.	B4	124
Kachug, Sov. Un.	D13	29
Kackley, Ks., U.S.	C6	93
Kadan, i., Burma	I5	35
Kadavu, i., Fiji	I15	52
Kade, Ghana	E4	45
Kadena, Japan	O5	52
Kadet Channel, strt., Eur.	A6	18
Kading, stm., Laos	C9	35
Kadınhanı, Tur.	C9	40
Kadiolo, Mali	D3	45
Kadiri, India	F6	36
Kadirli, Tur.	*D11	40
Kadoka, S.D., U.S.	D4	118
Kadoma, Zimb.	A4	49
Kaduna, Nig.	D6	45
Kaduna, stm., Nig.	D6	45
Kādugli, Sud.	C2	47
Kaédi, Maur.	C2	44
Kaélé, Cam.	C2	46
Kaena Point, c., Hi., U.S.	B3	88
Kaeryŏng, S. Kor.	H4	33
Kaesŏng, N. Kor.	B3	38
Käf, Sau. Ar.	B3	38
Kafanchan, Nig.	D1	45
Kaffrine, Sen.	D1	45
Kafia Kingi, Sud.	D1	47
Kafr ad Dawwār, Eg.	C2	41
Kafr ash Shaykh, Eg.	C2	41
Kafr az Zayyāt, Eg.	D2	41
Kafr Mālik, Isr. Occ.	h12	41
Kafr Qaddūm, Isr. Occ.	g11	41
Kafr Qāsim, Isr.	g10	41
Kafr Salīm, Isr.	C2	41
Kafr Saqr, Eg.	D3	41
Kafr Ṭarkhān al Gharbī, Eg.	E3	41
Kafr Zībād, Isr. Occ.	g11	41
Kafue, Zam.	E4	48
Kafue, stm., Zam.	E4	48
Kagan, Sov. Un.	B12	39
Kagawong, Ont.	B2	73
Kagera, stm., Afr.	B4	48
Kağızman, Tur.	B14	40
Kagoshima, Japan	E11	31
Kagoshima Bay, b., Japan	K5	33
Kagul, Sov. Un.	I7	27
Kahakuloa, Hi., U.S.	C5	88
Kahaluu, Hi., U.S.	g10	88
Kahaluu, Hi., U.S.	f10	88
Kahama, Tan.	B5	48
Kahana, Hi., U.S.	B4	88
Kahana Bay, b., Hi., U.S.	f10	88
Kahayan, stm., Indon.	F4	34
Kahemba, Zaire	C2	48
Kahla, Ger.	C6	19
Kahlotus, Wa., U.S.	C7	124
Kahnūj, Iran	C5	39
Kahoka, Mo., U.S.	A6	102
Kahoolawe, i., Hi., U.S.	C5	88
Kahramanmaraş, Tur.	D11	40
Kahuku, Hi., U.S.	B4	88
Kahuku Point, c., Hi., U.S.	B4	88
Kahului, Hi., U.S.	C5	88
Kahului Bay, b., Hi., U.S.	C5	88
Kaiama, Nig.	E5	45
Kaiapoi, N.Z.	O14	51
Kaibab, Az., U.S.	A3	80
Kaibab Indian Reservation, Az., U.S.	A3	80
Kaibab Plateau, plat., Az., U.S.	A3	80
Kaibito, Az., U.S.	A4	80
Kaibito Plateau, plat., Az., U.S.	A4	80
Kaieteur Fall, wtfl., Guy.	A3	59
Kaifeng, China	E7	31
Kaihua, China	J8	32
Kai Islands, is., Indon.	G8	34
Kaikoura, N.Z.	O14	51
Kaikoura Peninsula, pen., N.Z.	E2	45
Kailahun, S.L.	E2	45
Kailas Range see Gangdise Mountains, mts., China	B9	37
Kailu, China	A8	32
Kailua, Hi., U.S.	B4	88
Kailua Bay, b., Hi., U.S.	g11	88
Kailua Kona, Hi., U.S.	D6	88
Kai Malino, Hi., U.S.	D6	88
Kaimana, Indon.	F8	34
Kaimu, Hi., U.S.	D6	88
Kainalu, Hi., U.S.	B4	88
Kainan, Japan	I7	33
Kainji Dam, Nig.	E5	45
Kainji Lake, res., Nig.	D5	45
Kaipara Harbour, b., N.Z.	L15	51
Kaiparowits Plateau, plat., Ut., U.S.	F4	121
Kaipokok Bay, b., Newf.	g10	72
Kaiserslautern, Ger.	A5	21
Kaiserstuhl, Switz.	A5	21
Kaitaia, N.Z.	K14	51
Kaitangata, N.Z.	Q12	51
Kaithal, India	C6	37
Kaiwi Channel, strt., Hi., U.S.	B4	88
Kaixian, China	C11	32
Kaiyuan, China	C12	32
Kaizuka, Japan	o14	33
Kajaani, Fin.	E12	14
Kajakī, Band-e, res., Afg.	E12	39
Kajiado, Kenya	B6	48

Name	Map Ref.	Page
Kajikazawa, Japan	n17	33
Kākā, Sud.	C3	47
Kakagi Lake, l., Ont.	E5	70
Kakamas, S. Afr.	C3	49
Kakamega, Kenya	A5	48
Kaka Point, c., Hi., U.S.	C5	88
Kake, Ak., U.S.	D13	79
Kakegawa, Japan	o17	33
Kakhovka, Sov. Un.	H9	27
Kakhovka Reservoir, res., Sov. Un.	E6	29
Kākināda (Cocanada), India	E7	36
Kakisa Lake, l., N.W. Ter.	D9	66
Kakogawa, Japan	*I7	33
Kakuma, Kenya	A5	48
Kakwa, stm., Can.	B1	68
Kālābagh, Pak.	B5	36
Kalabáka, Grc.	C3	25
Kalabakan, Malay.	E5	34
Kalābishah, Eg.	E6	43
Kalabo, Zam.	D3	48
Kalach, Sov. Un.	F13	27
Kalach-na-Donu, Sov. Un.	G14	27
Kaladar, Ont.	C7	73
Ka Lae, c., Hi., U.S.	E6	88
Kalahari Desert, des., Afr.	B3	49
Kalahari Gemsbok National Park, S. Afr.	C3	49
Kalaheo, Hi., U.S.	A2	88
Kalaho, Pidos, hill, N. Mar. Is.	C8	52
Kalai-Mor, Sov. Un.	D11	39
Kalama, Wa., U.S.	C3	124
Kálámai, Grc.	D4	40
Kalamaki, Tur.	D7	25
Kalamariá, Grc.	*B4	25
Kalamazoo, Mi., U.S.	F5	99
Kalamazoo, co., Mi., U.S.	F5	99
Kalamazoo, stm., Mi., U.S.	F5	99
Kalambo Falls, wtfl., Afr.	C2	48
Kalandula, Ang.	C2	48
Kalaoa Homesteads, Hi., U.S.	D6	88
Kalaotoa, i., Indon.	G6	34
Kalapana, Hi., U.S.	D7	88
Kalasin, Thai.	D5	35
Kalāt, Pak.	C4	36
Kalaupapa, Hi., U.S.	B5	88
Kalaupapa Peninsula, pen., Hi., U.S.	B5	88
Kalávrita, Grc.	C4	25
Kalawao, co., Hi., U.S.	B5	88
Kalb, Ra's al, c., Yemen	D4	38
Kalbā', U.A.E.	C5	38
Kalecik, Tur.	B9	40
Kaleden, B.C.	E8	69
Kalegauk, i., Burma	E2	35
Kalehe, Zaire	B4	48
Kaleköy, Tur.	B5	25
Kalemie (Albertville), Zaire	C4	48
Kalena, Puu, mtn., Hi., U.S.	g9	88
Kaleva, Mi., U.S.	D4	99
Kalevala, Sov. Un.	E14	14
Kalewa, Burma	D9	36
Kalgalaksha, Sov. Un.	E16	14
Kalgin Island, i., Ak., U.S.	g16	79
Kalgoorlie, Austl.	F3	50
Kalibo, Phil.	C6	34
Kalihiwai, Hi., U.S.	A2	88
Kalima, Zaire	B4	48
Kálimnos, Grc.	D6	25
Kálimnos, i., Grc.	D6	40
Kaliningrad, Sov. Un.	n17	27
Kaliningrad (Königsberg), Sov. Un.	D5	27
Kalininsk, Sov. Un.	F15	27
Kalinkovichi, Sov. Un.	E7	27
Kalis, Som.	D6	47
Kāli Sindh, stm., India	E6	37
Kalispel Indian Reservation, Wa., U.S.	A8	124
Kalispell, Mt., U.S.	B2	103
Kalisz, Pol.	C5	26
Kaliua, Tan.	C5	48
Kalixälven, stm., Swe.	D10	14
Kalkaska, Mi., U.S.	D5	99
Kalkaska, co., Mi., U.S.	D5	99
Kalkfeld, Nmb.	B2	49
Kalkrand, Nmb.	B2	49
Kallithéa, Grc.	h11	25
Kallsjön, l., Swe.	F5	14
Kalmalo, Nig.	D6	45
Kalmar, Swe.	I5	14
Kalmar, co., Swe.	I7	14
Kalmarsund, strt., Swe.	I7	14
Kalmykovo, Sov. Un.	D4	28
Kalo, Ia., U.S.	B3	92
Kalocsa, Hung.	B4	24
Kalohi Channel, strt., Hi., U.S.	C4	88
Kaloli Point, c., Hi., U.S.	D7	88
Kalomo, Zam.	D4	48
Kalona, Ia., U.S.	C6	92
Kalone Peak, mtn., B.C.	C4	69
Kālpi, India	D7	37
Kalskag, Ak., U.S.	C7	79
Kaltag, Ak., U.S.	C8	79
Kaluga, Sov. Un.	D6	29
Kalulushi, Zam.	D4	48
Kalundborg, Den.	C5	15
Kalush, Sov. Un.	G5	27
Kałuszyn, Pol.	B6	26
Kalvarija, Sov. Un.	A7	26
Kalvehave, Den.	D6	15
Kalvesta, Ks., U.S.	D3	93
Kalvsjön, l., Swe.	A7	15
Kalyān, India	H4	37
Kama, Zaire	B4	48
Kamaing, Burma	C10	36
Kama, stm., Sov. Un.	D8	29
Kamaishi, Japan	D13	31
Kamakou, mtn., Hi., U.S.	B5	88
Kamakura, Japan	n18	33
Kamakwie, S.L.	E2	45
Kamananui Stream, stm., Hi., U.S.	f9	88
Kamaniskeg Lake, l., Ont.	B7	73
Kamanjab, Nmb.	A1	49
Kamanyola, Zaire	B4	48
Kamarān, i., Yemen	E3	38
Kama Reservoir, res., Sov. Un.	D8	29
Kāmārhāti, India	*D8	36
Kamaria Fall, wtfl., Guy.	A3	59
Kama Rock, i., Japan	P17	52
Kamas, Ut., U.S.	C4	121
Kamatsi Lake, l., Sask.	A4	75
Kambalda, Austl.	F3	50
Kambove, Zaire	D4	48
Kamchatka Peninsula, pen., Sov. Un.	D18	29
Kamenets-Podolskiy, Sov. Un.	G6	27
Kamenjak, Cape, c., Yugo.	C1	24
Kamenka, Sov. Un.	G7	27
Kamenka, Sov. Un.	C5	29
Kamen-na-Obi, Sov. Un.	D11	29
Kamensk-Shakhtinskiy, Sov. Un.	G13	27
Kamensk-Uralskiy, Sov. Un.	D9	29
Kamenz, Ger.	C7	18
Kameoka, Japan	o14	33
Kämet, mtn., Asia	B7	37
Kamiah, Id., U.S.	C2	89
Kamiak Butte, mtn., Wa., U.S.	C8	124
Kamień Pomorski, Pol.	B3	26
Kamina, Zaire	C4	48
Kamioka, Japan	m16	33
Kammuri, Mount, mtn., Japan	I6	33
Kamo, Sov. Un.	B15	40
Kamoa Mountains, mts., Guy.	B3	59
Kamooloa, Hi., U.S.	f9	88
Kamouraska, Que.	B8	74
Kamouraska, co., Que.	B8	74
Kampala, Ug.	A5	48
Kampar, Malay.	J4	35
Kampar, stm., Indon.	E2	34
Kampen, Neth.	A6	16
Kampeska, Lake, l., S.D., U.S.	C8	118
Kamphaeng Phet, Thai.	D3	35
Kampong Cham, Camb.	C3	34
Kampong Chhnang, Camb.	C2	34
Kampong Khleang, Camb.	F6	35
Kampong Saom, Camb.	C2	34
Kampong Saom Bay, b., Camb.	C2	34
Kampong Spoe, Camb.	G6	35
Kampong Thum, Camb.	C2	34
Kampot, Camb.	C2	34
Kampsville, Il., U.S.	D3	90
Kampuchea see Cambodia, ctry., Asia	F6	34
Kamrar, Ia., U.S.	B4	92
Kamsack, Sask.	F5	75
Kamuchawie Lake, l., Can.	A4	75
Kamuela (Waimea), Hi., U.S.	C6	88
Kamuli, Ug.	A5	48
Kamyshevakha, Sov. Un.	q21	27
Kamyshin, Sov. Un.	F15	27
Kamyshlov, Sov. Un.	B6	28
Kanab, Ut., U.S.	F3	121
Kanab Creek, stm., U.S.	A3	80
Kanabec, co., Mn., U.S.	E5	100
Kanacea, i., Fiji	H16	52
Kanaga Island, i., Ak., U.S.	E4	79
Kanairiktok, stm., Newf.	g9	72
Kananaskis, Alta.	D3	68
Kananga (Luluabourg), Zaire	C3	48
Kanapou Bay, b., Hi., U.S.	C5	88
Kanarraville, Ut., U.S.	F2	121
Kanata, Ont.	D9	73
Kanauga, Oh., U.S.	D3	112
Kanawha, Ia., U.S.	B4	92
Kanawha, co., W.V., U.S.	C3	125
Kanawha, stm., W.V., U.S.	C3	125
Kanayama, Japan	n16	33
Kanazawa, Japan	D12	31
Kanbe, Burma	*E10	36
Kanchanaburi, Thai.	E3	35
Kānchenjunga, mtn., Asia	C8	36
Kānchipuram (Conjeeveram), India	F7	36
Kānchrāpāra, India	*D8	36
Kandahar (Qandahār), Afg.	B4	36
Kandahar, Sask.	F3	75
Kandalaksha, Sov. Un.	C6	29
Kandalaksha Bay, b., Sov. Un.	B15	8
Kandangan, Indon.	F5	34
Kandel, Ger.	D3	19
Kandern, Ger.	A4	21
Kandersteg, Switz.	C3	20
Kandi, Benin	D5	45
Kandıra, Tur.	B8	40
Kandiyohi, Mn., U.S.	E4	100
Kandiyohi, co., Mn., U.S.	E3	100
Kandla, India	F3	37
Kandrāch, Pak.	C4	36
Kandreho, Madag.	g9	49
Kandy, Sri L.	G7	36
Kane, Il., U.S.	D3	90
Kane, Pa., U.S.	C4	115
Kane, co., Il., U.S.	B5	90
Kane, co., Ut., U.S.	F3	121
Kane Basin, strt., N.A.	m38	66
Kaneohe, Hi., U.S.	g10	88
Kaneohe Bay, b., Hi., U.S.	g10	88
Kaneohe Bay Marine Corps Air Station, mil., Hi., U.S.	g10	88
Kanevskaya, Sov. Un.	H12	27
Kang, Bots.	B3	49
Kangaba, Mali	D3	45
Kangal, Tur.	C11	40
Kangar, Malay.	I4	35
Kangaroo, i., Austl.	G6	50
Kangbao, China	C7	31
Kangding, China	E5	31
Kangdong, N. Kor.	G3	33
Kangean Islands, is., Indon.	G5	34
Kanggye, N. Kor.	C10	31
Kangiqsualujjuaq, Que.	f8	72
Kangiqsujuaq, Que.	f12	74
Kangirsuk, Que.	f12	74
Kangley, Il., U.S.	B5	90
Kangnŭng, S. Kor.	D10	31
Kango, Gabon	E2	46
Kangrinboqê Mountain, mtn., China	C6	37
Kani, Burma	A1	35
Kani, I.C.	E3	45
Kaniama, Zaire	C3	48
Kanimekh, Sov. Un.	A12	39
Kanin Nos, Cape, c., Sov. Un.	C7	29
Kanin Peninsula, pen., Sov. Un.	B5	29
Kankakee, Il., U.S.	B6	90
Kankakee, co., Il., U.S.	B5	90
Kankakee, stm., U.S.	B5	90
Kankan, Gui.	D3	45
Kankossa, Maur.	C2	45
Kannapolis, N.C., U.S.	B2	110
Kannauj, India	D7	37
Kannus, Fin.	E11	14
Kano, Nig.	D6	45
Kanopolis Lake, res., Ks., U.S.	D5	93
Kanorado, Ks., U.S.	*D8	93
Kanosh, Ut., U.S.	E3	121
Kanoya, Japan	K5	33
Kānpur, India	C7	36
Kansas, Il., U.S.	D6	90
Kansas, Oh., U.S.	A2	112
Kansas, Ok., U.S.	A7	113
Kansas, state, U.S.	D5	93
Kansas, stm., Ks., U.S.	C7	93
Kansas City, Ks., U.S.	C9	93
Kansas City, Mo., U.S.	B3	102
Kansasville, Wi., U.S.	n11	126
Kansk, Sov. Un.	D12	29
Kansu see Gansu, prov., China	D5	31
Kantang, Thai.	D1	34
Kanton Island, i., Kir.	G11	6
Kantunilkín, Mex.	C7	63
Kanturk, Ire.	D3	11
Kanuku Mountains, mts., Guy.	B3	59
Kanuma, Japan	H9	33
Kanye, Bots.	B4	49
Kaohsiung, Tai.	G9	31
Kaoko Veld, plat., Nmb.	A1	49
Kaolack, Sen.	D1	45
Kaouar, reg., Niger	C7	45
Kapaa, Hi., U.S.	A2	88
Kapaau, Hi., U.S.	C6	88
Kapal, Sov. Un.	F24	8
Kapandríton, Grc.	g11	25
Kapanga, Zaire	C3	48
Kapapa Island, i., Hi., U.S.	g10	88
Kapchagay, Sov. Un.	E9	28
Kapchagay Reservoir, res., Sov. Un.	E9	28
Kapenguria, Kenya	A6	48
Kapfenberg, Aus.	E7	18
Kapiri Mposhi, Zam.	D4	48
Kapit, Malay.	E4	34
Kaplan, La., U.S.	D3	95
Kaplice, Czech.	E9	19
Kapoeta, Sud.	E3	47
Kaposvár, Hung.	B3	24
Kaposvar Creek, stm., Sask.	G4	75
Kapowsin, Wa., U.S.	C3	124
Kappa, Il., U.S.	C4	90
Kapšān, Iran	F4	38
Kapuas, stm., Indon.	F4	34
Kapubawe, Hi., U.S.	C6	88
Kapuskasing, Ont.	o19	73
Kapustin Yar, Sov. Un.	D3	28
Kaputar, mtn., Austl.	E8	51
Kapuvár, Hung.	B3	24
Kara, Sov. Un.	C9	29
Kara-Bogaz-Gol, Sov. Un.	E4	28
Kara-Bogaz-Gol Gulf, b., Sov. Un.	E4	28
Karabük, Tur.	*B9	40
Karachev, Sov. Un.	E10	27
Karāchi, Pak.	D4	36
Karāchi Cantonment, Pak.	*D4	36
Karaganda, Sov. Un.	D19	29
Karaginski Island, i., Sov. Un.	D10	29
Karaj, Iran	D5	39
Karakax, Sov. Un.	D10	28
Karakelong, i., Indon.	E7	34
Karakoram Pass, Asia	A6	36
Karakoram Range, mts., Asia	A6	36
Karaköse see Ağrı, Tur.	C14	40
Kara-Kum, des., Sov. Un.	E8	29
Kara-Kum Canal, Sov. Un.	H21	8
Karaman, Tur.	D9	40
Karamay, China	B1	31
Karamea, N.Z.	N14	51
Karamea Bight, N.Z.	N13	51
Karamürsel, Tur.	B7	40
Karanpur, Tur.	D9	40
Karasburg, Nmb.	C2	49
Kara Sea, Sov. Un.	B9	29
Karasjok, Nor.	C6	29
Karasu, Sov. Un.	C6	29
Karasuk, Sov. Un.	C9	29
Karatas, Cape, c., Tur.	D10	40
Karatau Range, mts., Sov. Un.	E7	28
Karatobe, Sov. Un.	D4	28
Karatsu, Japan	J4	33
Karauli, India	D6	37
Karaulkeldy, Sov. Un.	D5	28
Karawanken, mts., Eur.	E7	18
Karbalā', Iraq	F15	40
Kárcag, Hung.	B5	24
Karczew, Pol.	m14	26
Kardhítsa, Grc.	C3	40
Karema, Tan.	C5	48
Karesuando (part of Kiruna), Swe.	C10	14
Kargasok, Sov. Un.	D11	29
Kargat, Sov. Un.	D25	8
Kargil, India	B6	36
Kargopol, Sov. Un.	A12	27
Kariai, Grc.	B5	25
Kariba, Zimb.	A4	49
Kariba, Lake, res., Afr.	A4	49
Karibib, Nmb.	C2	49
Karikari, Cape, c., N.Z.	K14	51
Karimata Islands, is., Indon.	F3	34
Karimata Strait, strt., Indon.	F3	34
Karīmnagar, India	H7	37
Karimunjawa Islands, is., Indon.	G4	34
Karin, Som.	C6	47
Karisimbi, Volcán, vol., Afr.	B4	48
Káristos, Grc.	C5	40
Karkaralinsk, Sov. Un.	E10	29
Karkheh, stm., Iran	E3	39
Karkinit Gulf, b., Sov. Un.	I9	27
Karl-Marx-Stadt see Chemnitz, Ger.	C6	18
Karlobag, Yugo.	C2	24
Karloske, stm., Man.	B4	70
Karlovac, Yugo.	C2	24
Karlovo, Bul.	D7	24
Karlovy Vary, Czech.	C2	26
Karlshamn, Swe.	I6	14
Karlskoga, Swe.	H6	14
Karlskrona, Swe.	I6	14
Karlsruhe, Ger.	D3	19
Karlsruhe, N.D., U.S.	A5	111
Karlstad, Mn., U.S.	B2	100
Karlstad, Swe.	H5	14
Karlstadt, Ger.	D4	19
Karluk, Ak., U.S.	D9	79
Karnak, Il., U.S.	F5	90
Karnāl, India	*C6	37
Karnāli, stm., Nepal	C8	37
Karnataka, state, India	E4	36
Karnes, co., Tx., U.S.	E4	120
Karnes City, Tx., U.S.	E4	120
Karnobat, Bul.	D8	24
Karns City, Pa., U.S.	E2	115
Karoi, Zimb.	A4	49
Karonga, Mwi.	C5	48
Karora, Sud.	B4	47
Kárpathos, i., Grc.	E6	40
Karpenísion, Grc.	C3	25
Karratha, Austl.	D2	50
Kars, Tur.	B14	40
Karsakpay, Sov. Un.	E9	29
Karsha, Sov. Un.	D4	28
Karshi, Sov. Un.	F9	29
Karstädt, Ger.	B6	18
Kartal, Tur.	B6	25
Kartaly, Sov. Un.	D9	29
Karthaus, Pa., U.S.	D5	115
Kartuzy, Pol.	A5	26
Kārūn, stm., Iran	F4	39
Karup, Den.	B3	15
Karup, Å, stm., Den.	B3	15
Karval, Co., U.S.	C7	83
Karvia, Fin.	F10	14
Karviná, Czech.	D5	26
Kārwār, India	F5	36
Kas, Den.	A3	15
Kaş, Tur.	D7	40
Kasaan, Ak., U.S.	n23	79
Kasai (Cassai), stm., Afr.	B2	48
Kasaji, Zaire	D3	48
Kasama, Zam.	D5	48
Kasane, Bots.	A4	49
Kasanga, Tan.	C5	48
Kasaragod, India	F5	36
Kasba, India	E11	37
Kasba Lake, l., N.W. Ter.	D12	66
Kasba Tadla, Mor.	C3	44
Kasempa, Zam.	D4	48
Kasenga, Zaire	D4	48
Kasese, Ug.	A5	48
Kāshān, Iran	B5	38
Kashi, China	F10	29
Kashihara, Japan	o14	33
Kashima, Japan	n19	33
Kashira, Sov. Un.	D12	27
Kashiwa, stm., Sov. Un.	n18	27
Kashiwazaki, Japan	H9	33
Kāshmar (Turshīz), Iran	B5	38
Kashmor, Pak.	C2	37
Kasilof, Ak., U.S.	C9	79
Kasimov, Sov. Un.	D13	27
Kaskaskia, Il., U.S.	F4	90
Kaskaskia, stm., Il., U.S.	D5	90
Kaskö, Fin.	F9	14
Kaslo, B.C.	E9	69
Kasongo, Zaire	B4	48
Kasongo-Lunda, Zaire	C2	48
Kásos, i., Grc.	E6	40
Kasota, Mn., U.S.	F5	100
Kassalá, Sud.	B4	47
Kassalá, prov., Sud.	B4	47
Kassandra, Gulf of, b., Grc.	C4	25
Kassel (Cassel), Ger.	C4	18
Kasson, Mn., U.S.	F6	100
Kastamonu, Tur.	A9	40
Kastiyu, Puntan, c., N. Mar. Is.	E7	52
Kastoria, Grc.	B3	40
Kástron, Grc.	g10	25
Kasukabe, Japan	n18	33
Kasulu, Tan.	B5	48
Kasumiga-Ura, l., Japan	H10	33
Kasungu, Mwi.	D5	48
Kasūr, Pak.	B5	36
Katako-Kombe, Zaire	B3	48
Katanga, hist. reg., Zaire	C4	48
Katanning, Austl.	F2	50
Katano Point, c., Japan	P17	52
Katata, Japan	n14	33
Katepwa Beach, Sask.	G4	75
Katerini, Grc.	B4	40
Katherine, Austl.	B5	50
Kāthiāwār Peninsula, pen., India	D4	36
Kathleen, Fl., U.S.	D4	86
Kathmandu (Kāthmāndaū), Nepal	C8	37
Kathryn, Alta.	D4	68
Kathryn, N.D., U.S.	C8	111
Kathua, India	A6	36
Katie, Ok., U.S.	C4	113
Katihār, India	E11	37
Katiola, I.C.	E3	45
Katire, Sud.	E3	47
Katlehong, S. Afr.	*C4	49
Katmai, Mount, mtn., Ak., U.S.	D9	79
Katmai National Park, Ak., U.S.	D9	79
Kato Alepokhórion, Grc.	g10	25
Katokhí, Grc.	C3	25
Katombe, Zaire	C3	48
Katoomba, Austl.	F9	50
Katowice (Stalinogród), Pol.	C5	26
Kātrīnā, Jabal, mtn., Eg.	D6	43
Katrineholm, Swe.	H7	14
Katsina, Nig.	D6	45
Katsina Ala, stm., Afr.	E6	45
Katsuta, Japan	*H10	33
Katsuyama, Japan	m15	33
Kattakurgan, Sov. Un.	H22	8
Kattegat, strt., Eur.	I4	14
Katun, stm., Sov. Un.	E26	8
Katwijk aan Zee, Neth.	B4	17
Katy, Tx., U.S.	r14	120
Kau, Indon.	E7	34
Kauai, co., Hi., U.S.	B1	88
Kauai, i., Hi., U.S.	A2	88
Kauai Channel, strt., Hi., U.S.	B3	88
Kau Desert, des., Hi., U.S.	D6	88
Kaufbeuren, Ger.	E5	18
Kaufman, Tx., U.S.	C4	120
Kaufman, co., Tx., U.S.	C4	120
Kauhajoki, Fin.	F10	14
Kauhava, Fin.	F10	14
Kauiki Head, c., Hi., U.S.	C6	88
Kaukauna, Wi., U.S.	D5	126
Kaukau Veld, plat., Afr.	B3	49
Kaula Island, i., Hi., U.S.	m15	88
Kaulakahi Channel, strt., Hi., U.S.	A2	88
Kaumalapau, Hi., U.S.	C5	88
Kauna Point, c., Hi., U.S.	D6	88
Kaunakakai, Hi., U.S.	B5	88
Kaunas, Sov. Un.	C5	27
Kaura Namoda, Nig.	D6	45
Kautokeino, Nor.	C10	14
Kavacha, Sov. Un.	C19	29
Kavaja, Alb.	E5	25
Kavála, Grc.	B5	40
Kavála, Gulf of, b., Grc.	B5	40
Kávali, India	F5	36
Kavarna, Bul.	D9	24
Kavieng, Pap. N. Gui.	h13	50
Kavīr, Dasht-e, des., Iran	B5	38
Kävlinge, Swe.	C7	15
Kaw, Fr. Gu.	B4	59
Kawagama Lake, l., Ont.	B6	73
Kawagoe, Japan	n18	33
Kawaguchi, Japan	n18	33
Kawaihae, Hi., U.S.	C6	88
Kawaihoa Point, c., Hi., U.S.	B1	88
Kawaikini, mtn., Hi., U.S.	A2	88
Kawailoa, Hi., U.S.	f9	88
Kawailoa Beach, Hi., U.S.	f9	88
Kawakawa, N.Z.	K15	51
Kawambwa, Zam.	C4	48
Kawardha, India	F8	37
Kawasaki, Japan	D12	31
Kawbar, Isr. Occ.	h11	41
Kaw City, Ok., U.S.	A5	113
Kaweenakumik Lake, l., Man.	C2	70
Kawela, Hi., U.S.	C5	88
Kawhia Harbour, b., N.Z.	M15	51
Kawich Peak, mtn., Nv., U.S.	F5	105
Kawich Range, mts., Nv., U.S.	F5	105
Kawkareik, Burma	D3	35
Kaw Lake, res., Ok., U.S.	A5	113
Kawm Hamādah, Eg.	D2	41
Kawm Umbū, Eg.	C3	38
Kawthaung, Burma	F10	36
Kay, co., Ok., U.S.	A4	113
Kaya, Burkina	D4	45
Kayan, stm., Indon.	E5	34
Kayangel Islands, is., Palau	R17	52
Kaycee, Wy., U.S.	C6	127
Kayenta, Az., U.S.	A5	80
Kayes, Congo	B1	48
Kayes, Mali	D2	45
Kayford, W.V., U.S.	C3	125
Kayjay, Ky., U.S.	D6	94
Kaylor, S.D., U.S.	D8	118
Kayō, Japan	N6	52
Kayser Gebergte, mts., Sur.	B3	59
Kayseri, Tur.	C10	40
Kaysville, Ut., U.S.	B4	121
Kayuagung, Indon.	F2	34
Kayville, Sask.	H3	75
Kazachye, Sov. Un.	B16	29
Kazakh Hills, hills, Sov. Un.	D7	28
Kazakh S.S.R., state, Sov. Un.	E9	29
Kazalinsk, Sov. Un.	D6	28
Kazan, Sov. Un.	D7	29
Kazan, stm., N.W. Ter.	D12	66
Kazanlŭk, Bul.	D7	24
Kazbek, mtn., Sov. Un.	B4	40
Kazerūn, Iran	C5	39
Kazhim, Sov. Un.	A4	28
Kazi-Magomed, Sov. Un.	E3	28
Kazimierz [Dolny], Pol.	C6	26
Kazincbarcika, Hung.	A5	24
Kazumba, Zaire	C3	48
Kazym, stm., Sov. Un.	C22	8
Kdyně, Czech.	D8	19
Kéa, Grc.	D5	40
Kéa, i., Grc.	D5	40
Keaau, Hi., U.S.	D6	88
Keady, N. Ire., U.K.	C5	11
Keahiakahoe, Puu, mtn., Hi., U.S.	g10	88
Keahole Point, c., Hi., U.S.	D5	88
Kealaikahiki Channel, strt., Hi., U.S.	C4	88
Kealaikahiki Point, c., Hi., U.S.	C5	88
Kealakekua, Hi., U.S.	D6	88
Kealia, Hi., U.S.	A2	88
Keams Canyon, Az., U.S.	B5	80
Keanae, Hi., U.S.	C5	88
Keanapapa Point, c., Hi., U.S.	C4	88
Keansburg, N.J., U.S.	C4	107
Kearney, Mo., U.S.	B3	102
Kearney, Ne., U.S.	D7	104
Kearney, co., Ne., U.S.	D7	104
Kearneysville, W.V., U.S.	B7	125
Kearns, Ut., U.S.	C4	121
Kearny, Az., U.S.	D5	80
Kearny, N.J., U.S.	h8	107
Kearny, co., Ks., U.S.	E2	93
Kearsarge, Mi., U.S.	A2	99
Kearsarge, Mount, mtn., N.H., U.S.	D3	106
Kearsarge North, mtn., N.H., U.S.	B4	106
Keatchie, La., U.S.	B2	95
Keatley, Sask.	E2	75
Keaton, Ky., U.S.	C7	94
Keats, Ks., U.S.	C7	93
Keauhou, Hi., U.S.	D6	88
Keban Reservoir, res., Tur.	C12	40
Kébémer, Sen.	C1	45
Kebnekaise, mtn., Swe.	C11	14
Kebock Head, c., Scot., U.K.	B2	13
Kebri Dehar, Eth.	D6	45
Kecskemét, Hung.	B4	24
Kedah, state, Malay.	J4	35
Kedainiai, Sov. Un.	A8	26
Keddie, Ca., U.S.	B3	82
Kedges Straits, strt., Md., U.S.	D5	97
Kedgwick, N.B.	B2	71
Kedong, China	B3	31
Kédougou, Sen.	D1	45
Kędzierzyn-Koźle, Pol.	*C5	26
Keedysville, Md., U.S.	B2	97
Keefers, B.C.	D7	69
Keego Harbor, Mi., U.S.	o15	99
Keei, Hi., U.S.	D6	88
Keeler, Ca., U.S.	D5	82
Keeling, Tn., U.S.	B2	119
Keene, Ont.	C6	73
Keene, Ky., U.S.	B5	94
Keene, N.H., U.S.	E2	106
Keene, N.Y., U.S.	A7	109
Keene, Oh., U.S.	B4	112
Keene, Tx., U.S.	n9	120
Keene Valley, N.Y., U.S.	f11	109
Keeney Knob, mtn., W.V., U.S.	D4	125
Keensburg, Il., U.S.	E6	90
Keeseville, N.Y., U.S.	f11	109
Keesler Air Force Base, mil., Ms., U.S.	E5	101
Keetmanshoop, Nmb.	C2	49
Keet Seel Ruin, hist., Az., U.S.	A5	80
Keewatin, Ont.	E4	70
Keewatin, Mn., U.S.	C5	100
Keewatin, dept., N.W. Ter.	D13	66
Keewatin, co., Man.	A1	70
Keezletown, Va., U.S.	B4	123
Kefa, prov., Eth.	D4	47
Kefallinía (Cephalonia), i., Grc.	C3	40
Kefar Blum, Isr.	A7	41
Kefar 'Eqron, Isr.	h10	41
Kefar Monash, Isr.	f10	41
Kefar Sava, Isr.	B6	41
Kefar Yona, Isr.	f10	41
Keffi, Nig.	*E6	45
Keflavík, Ice.	o21	14
Ke Ga, Cape, c., Viet.	F8	35
Kegaska, Que.	h9	72
Kegonsa, Lake, l., Wi., U.S.	F4	126
Kehl, Ger.	E1	21
Keho Lake, l., Alta.	A4	68
Kehsi Mansam, Burma	B2	35
Keighley, Eng., U.K.	D6	10
Keilor, Austl.	*G7	50
Keimoes, S. Afr.	C3	49
Keiser, Ar., U.S.	B5	81
Keitele, l., Fin.	F11	14
Keith, Austl.	H3	51
Keith, Scot., U.K.	D5	10
Keith, co., Ne., U.S.	C4	104
Keithley Creek, B.C.	C7	69
Keithsburg, Il., U.S.	B3	90
Keithville, La., U.S.	B2	95
Keitum, Ger.	D2	15
Keizer, Or., U.S.	C3	114
Kejimkujik Lake, l., N.S.	E4	71
Kejimkujik National Park, N.S.	E4	71
Kekaha, Hi., U.S.	B2	88
Kékes, mtn., Hung.	*B5	24
Kelafo, Eth.	D5	47
Kelan, China	E4	32
Kelang, Malay.	J5	35
Keldron, S.D., U.S.	B4	118
Kelfield, Sask.	F1	75
Kelford, N.C., U.S.	A5	110
Kelheim, Ger.	E6	19
Kelibia, Tun.	F3	23
Kelkit, stm., Tur.	B11	40
Kell, Il., U.S.	E5	90
Kellé, Congo	B1	48
Kellenhusen, Ger.	D5	15
Keller, Tx., U.S.	n9	120
Keller, Va., U.S.	C7	123
Keller, Wa., U.S.	A7	124
Keller Lake, l., Sask.	A2	75
Kellerman, Al., U.S.	B2	78
Kellerton, Ia., U.S.	D3	92
Kellerville, Il., U.S.	D3	90
Kellett, Cape, c., N.W. Ter.	B7	66
Kellettville, Pa., U.S.	D3	115
Kelley, Ia., U.S.	C4	92
Kelleys Island, Oh., U.S.	A3	112
Kelleys Island, i., Oh., U.S.	A3	112
Kelliher, Sask.	F4	75
Kelliher, Mn., U.S.	C4	100
Kellnersville, Wi., U.S.	D6	126
Kelloe, Man.	D1	70
Kellogg, Id., U.S.	B2	89
Kellogg, Ia., U.S.	C5	92
Kellogg, Mn., U.S.	F6	100
Kells see Ceanannus Mór, Ire.	D5	11
Kelly, Ky., U.S.	D2	94
Kelly, La., U.S.	C3	95
Kelly, Wy., U.S.	C2	127
Kelly Air Force Base, mil., Tx., U.S.	k7	120
Kelly Brook Mountain, mtn., Me., U.S.	A3	96
Kelly Island, i., De., U.S.	B7	85
Kelly Lake, B.C.	C5	100
Kellyton, Al., U.S.	B3	78
Kellyville, Ok., U.S.	B5	113
Kelmé, Sov. Un.	A7	26
Kélo, Chad	D3	46
Kelowna, B.C.	E8	69
Kelsey, Alta.	C4	68
Kelsey Lake, l., Man.	C1	70
Kelseyville, Ca., U.S.	C2	82
Kelso, Scot., U.K.	H5	75
Kelso, Ca., U.S.	E6	82
Kelso, Mo., U.S.	D8	102
Kelso, Wa., U.S.	C3	124
Keluang, Malay.	E2	34
Kelvington, Sask.	E4	75
Kelwood, Man.	D2	70
Kem, stm., Sov. Un.	E16	14
Kemano, B.C.	C4	69
Kembé, Cen. Afr. Rep.	E4	46
Kemerovo, Sov. Un.	D11	29
Kemi, Fin.	E11	14
Kemijärvi, Fin.	D12	14
Kemijärvi, l., Fin.	D12	14
Kemijoki, stm., Fin.	D11	14
Kemmerer, Wy., U.S.	E2	127
Kemmuna, well, Libya		
Kemnath, Ger.	D6	19
Kemnay, Man.	E1	70
Kemp, Lake, res., Tx., U.S.	C3	120
Kemp Coast, Ant.	C18	7
Kempele, Fin.	E11	14
Kempen, Ger.	D2	15
Kemp Peninsula, pen., Ant.	B6	7
Kempsey, Austl.	F9	50
Kempshall Mountain, mtn., N.Y., U.S.	A6	109
Kempten [in Allgäu], Ger.	E5	18
Kempton, Il., U.S.	B5	90
Kempton, Pa., U.S.	E10	115
Kemptville, Ont.	B9	73
Kenai, Ak., U.S.	C9	79
Kenai Fjords National Park, Ak., U.S.	D10	79
Kenai Mountains, mts., Ak., U.S.	h16	79
Kenai Peninsula, pen., Ak., U.S.	h16	79
Kenamu, stm., Newf.	B1	72
Kenansville, Fl., U.S.	E5	86
Kenansville, N.C., U.S.	C5	110
Kenaston, Sask.	E3	75
Kenbridge, Va., U.S.	D4	123

Name	Map Ref.	Page
Ken Caryl, Co., U.S.	*B5	83
Kendal, Sask.	G4	75
Kendal, Eng., U.K.	C5	10
Kendall, Fl., U.S.	s13	86
Kendall, Ks., U.S.	E2	93
Kendall, N.Y., U.S.	B2	109
Kendall, Wi., U.S.	E3	126
Kendall, co., Il., U.S.	B5	90
Kendall, co., Tx., U.S.	E3	120
Kendall Green, Fl., U.S.	*F6	86
Kendall Park, N.J., U.S.	C3	107
Kendallville, In., U.S.	B7	91
Kendari, Indon.	F6	34
Kendrāparha, India	D8	36
Kendrick, Id., U.S.	C2	89
Kendrick, Ok., U.S.	B5	113
Kendujhargarh, India	G10	37
Kenduskeag, Me., U.S.	D4	96
Kenedy, Tx., U.S.	E4	120
Kenedy, co., Tx., U.S.	F4	120
Kenefic, Ok., U.S.	C5	113
Kenel, S.D., U.S.	B5	118
Kenema, S.L.	E2	45
Kenesaw, Ne., U.S.	D7	104
Kenge, Zaire	B2	48
Kēng Tung, Burma	D10	36
Kenhardt, S. Afr.	D2	45
Kéniéba, Mali	C2	45
Kenilworth, Il., U.S.	h9	90
Kenilworth, N.J., U.S.	*B4	107
Kenilworth, Ut., U.S.	D5	121
Kenitra, Mor.	C3	44
Kenly, N.C., U.S.	B4	110
Kenmare, Ire.	E2	11
Kenmare, N.D., U.S.	A3	111
Kenmare, stm., Ire.	E1	11
Kenmore, N.Y., U.S.	C1	109
Kenmore, Wa., U.S.	*B3	124
Kenna, N.M., U.S.	D6	108
Kenna, W.V., U.S.	C3	125
Kennaday Peak, mtn., Wy., U.S.	E6	127
Kennan, Wi., U.S.	C3	126
Kennard, In., U.S.	E6	91
Kennard, Ne., U.S.	C9	104
Kennard, Tx., U.S.	D5	120
Kennebago Lake, l., Me., U.S.	C2	96
Kennebec, S.D., U.S.	D5	118
Kennebec, co., Me., U.S.	D3	96
Kennebec, stm., Me., U.S.	D3	96
Kennebunk, Me., U.S.	E2	96
Kennebunkport, Me., U.S.	E2	96
Kennedale, Tx., U.S.	n9	120
Kennedy, Sask.	G4	75
Kennedy, Al., U.S.	B2	78
Kennedy, Mn., U.S.	B2	100
Kennedy, N.Y., U.S.	C1	109
Kennedy, Mount, mtn., Yukon	D5	66
Kennedy Channel, strt., N.A.	k38	66
Kennedy Entrance, strt., Ak., U.S.	D9	79
Kennedy Heights, La., U.S.	*E5	95
Kennedy Lake, l., Sask.	D4	75
Kennedy Township, Pa., U.S.	*F1	115
Kennedyville, Md., U.S.	B6	97
Kenner, La., U.S.	E5	95
Kennesaw, Ga., U.S.	B2	87
Kennesaw Mountain, mtn., Ga., U.S.	C2	87
Kennesaw Mountain National Battlefield Park, Ga., U.S.	h7	87
Kennet, stm., Eng., U.K.	C6	12
Kennetcook, N.S.	D6	71
Kenneth, Ks., U.S.	m16	93
Kenneth, Mn., U.S.	G2	100
Kennett, Mo., U.S.	E7	102
Kennett Square, Pa., U.S.	G10	115
Kennewick, Wa., U.S.	C6	124
Kenney, Il., U.S.	C4	90
Kenney Dam, B.C.	C5	69
Kennisis Lake, l., Ont.	B6	73
Kennydale, Wa., U.S.	e11	124
Keno, Or., U.S.	E5	114
Kénogami, Que.	A6	74
Kénogami, Lac, l., Que.	A6	74
Kenora, Ont.	o16	73
Kenora, dept., Ont.	o17	73
Kenosha, Wi., U.S.	F6	126
Kenosha, co., Wi., U.S.	F5	126
Kenova, W.V., U.S.	C2	125
Ken Rock, Il., U.S.	*A4	90
Kensal, N.D., U.S.	B7	111
Kensett, Ar., U.S.	B4	81
Kensett, Ia., U.S.	A4	92
Kensico Reservoir, res., N.Y., U.S.	g13	109
Kensington, P.E.I.	C6	71
Kensington (part of London), Eng., U.K.	k12	10
Kensington, Ca., U.S.	*h8	82
Kensington, Ct., U.S.	C4	84
Kensington, Ks., U.S.	C4	93
Kensington, Md., U.S.	B3	97
Kensington, Mn., U.S.	E3	100
Kensington, N.H., U.S.	E5	106
Kensington, Oh., U.S.	B5	112
Kent, Al., U.S.	C4	78
Kent, Ct., U.S.	C2	84
Kent, In., U.S.	G6	91
Kent, Ia., U.S.	D3	92
Kent, Mn., U.S.	D2	100
Kent, Oh., U.S.	A4	112
Kent, Or., U.S.	B6	114
Kent, Tx., U.S.	o12	120
Kent, Wa., U.S.	B3	124
Kent, co., N.B.	C4	71
Kent, co., Ont.	E2	73
Kent, co., Eng., U.K.	C8	12
Kent, co., De., U.S.	D3	85
Kent, co., Md., U.S.	B5	97
Kent, co., Mi., U.S.	E5	99
Kent, co., R.I., U.S.	D2	116
Kent, co., Tx., U.S.	C2	120
Kent Bridge, Ont.	E2	73
Kent City, Mi., U.S.	E5	99
Kent Island, i., De., U.S.	D4	85
Kent Island, i., Md., U.S.	C5	97
Kent Junction, N.B.	C4	71
Kentland, In., U.S.	C3	91
Kenton, Man.	E1	70
Kenton, De., U.S.	D3	85
Kenton, Ky., U.S.	k14	94
Kenton, Oh., U.S.	B2	112
Kenton, Tn., U.S.	A2	119
Kenton, co., Ky., U.S.	B5	94
Kent Point, c., Md., U.S.	C5	97
Kents Store, Va., U.S.	C4	123
Kentucky, state, U.S.	C4	94
Kentucky, stm., Ky., U.S.	B5	94
Kentucky, Middle Fork, stm., Ky., U.S.	C6	94
Kentucky, North Fork, stm., Ky., U.S.	C6	94
Kentucky, South Fork, stm., Ky., U.S.	C6	94
Kentucky Dam, Ky., U.S.	e9	94
Kentucky Lake, res., U.S.	C10	76
Kentucky Ridge, mtn., Ky., U.S.	D6	94
Kentville, N.S.	D5	71
Kentwood, La., U.S.	D5	95
Kentwood, Mi., U.S.	F5	99
Kenvil, N.J., U.S.	B3	107
Kenvir, Ky., U.S.	D6	94
Kenwood, Oh., U.S.	*A4	112
Kenya, ctry., Afr.	A6	48
Kenya, Mount see Kirinyaga, mtn., Kenya	B6	48
Kenyon, Mn., U.S.	F6	100
Kenyon, R.I., U.S.	F2	116
Keo, Ar., U.S.	C3	81
Keokea, Hi., U.S.	C5	88
Keokuk, Ia., U.S.	D6	92
Keokuk, co., Ia., U.S.	C5	92
Keokuk Lock and Dam, U.S.	D6	92
Keoma, Alta.	D4	68
Keosauqua, Ia., U.S.	D6	92
Keota, Co., U.S.	A6	83
Keota, Ia., U.S.	C6	92
Keota, Ok., U.S.	B7	113
Keowee, Lake, res., S.C., U.S.	B2	117
Kepno, Pol.	C5	26
Keppel, Sask.	E2	75
Kepsut, Tur.	B5	25
Kerala, state, India	F6	36
Kerang, Austl.	G7	50
Keratsinion, Grc.	*D4	25
Kerby, Or., U.S.	E3	114
Kerch, Sov. Un.	E6	29
Kerchemya, Sov. Un.	C19	8
Kerch Strait, strt., Sov. Un.	I11	27
Kerema, Pap. N. Gui.	k12	50
Keremeos, B.C.	E8	69
Kerempe, Cape, c., Tur.	A9	40
Keren, Eth.	B4	47
Kerend, Iran	D3	39
Kerens, Tx., U.S.	C4	120
Kerguélen, Îles, is., F.S.A.T.	J1	2
Kerhonkson, N.Y., U.S.	D6	109
Kerkebet, Eth.	B4	47
Kerkhoven, Mn., U.S.	E3	100
Kerki, Sov. Un.	H22	8
Kérkira (Corfu), i., Grc.	C2	40
Kérkira, Grc.	C2	40
Kerkrade, Neth.	B7	16
Kermadec Islands, is., N.Z.	I11	6
Kermān, Iran	B5	38
Kermānshāh see Bakhtarān, Iran	B4	38
Kerme, Gulf of, b., Tur.	H4	25
Kermit, Tx., U.S.	D1	120
Kermit, W.V., U.S.	D2	125
Kermode, Mount, mtn., B.C.	C2	69
Kern, co., Ca., U.S.	E4	82
Kern, stm., Ca., U.S.	E4	82
Kernersville, N.C., U.S.	A2	110
Kernville, Ca., U.S.	E4	82
Kéros, i., Grc.	C5	20
Kérouané, Gui.	E3	45
Kerpen, Ger.	C1	19
Kerr, co., Tx., U.S.	D3	120
Kerr, Lake, l., Fl., U.S.	C5	86
Kerrick, Mn., U.S.	D6	100
Kerrick, Tx., U.S.	A1	120
Kerrobert, Sask.	F1	75
Kerrville, Tx., U.S.	E2	120
Kerry, co., Ire.	E2	11
Kerry Head, c., Ire.	E2	11
Kersey, Co., U.S.	A6	83
Kersey, Pa., U.S.	D4	115
Kershaw, S.C., U.S.	B6	117
Kershaw, co., S.C., U.S.	C6	117
Kersley, B.C.	C6	69
Kerteminde, Den.	C4	15
Kerulen, stm., Asia	B7	31
Kerzaz, Alg.	D4	44
Kerzers, Switz.	C3	21
Kesan, Tur.	B6	40
Kesch, Piz, mtn., Switz.	C5	20
Kesennuma, Japan	G10	33
Kesh, N. Ire., U.K.	C4	11
Keshan, China	B10	31
Keshena, Wi., U.S.	D5	126
Keshendeh, Afg.	C13	39
Kesley, Ia., U.S.	B5	92
Kestenga, Sov. Un.	E14	14
Keswick, Ont.	C5	73
Keswick, Eng., U.K.	F5	13
Keswick, Ia., U.S.	C5	92
Keswick, Va., U.S.	B4	123
Keszthely, Hung.	B3	24
Ket, stm., Sov. Un.	B10	28
Keta, Ghana	E5	45
Ketapang, Indon.	F3	34
Ketchikan, Ak., U.S.	D13	79
Ketchum, Id., U.S.	F4	89
Kete Krachi, Ghana	E4	45
Ketmen Range, mts., Asia	E10	28
Ketona, Al., U.S.	f7	78
Kétou, Benin	E5	45
Kętrzyn, Pol.	A6	26
Kettering, Eng., U.K.	D6	10
Kettering, Md., U.S.	*C4	97
Kettle, stm., N.A.	E8	69
Kettle, stm., Mn., U.S.	D6	100
Kettle Creek, stm., Pa., U.S.	D6	115
Kettle Creek Lake, res., Pa., U.S.	D6	115
Kettle Falls, Wa., U.S.	A7	124
Kettleman City, Ca., U.S.	E4	82
Kettle River, Mn., U.S.	D6	100
Kettwig, Ger.	B1	19
Kęty, Pol.	D5	26
Ketzin, Ger.	A7	19
Keuka Lake, l., N.Y., U.S.	C3	109
Keuterville, Id., U.S.	C2	89
Kevil, Ky., U.S.	e9	94
Kevin, Mt., U.S.	B5	103
Kewanee, Il., U.S.	B4	90
Kewanee, Ms., U.S.	B5	101
Kewanee, Mo., U.S.	E8	102
Kewanna, In., U.S.	B5	91
Kewaskum, Wi., U.S.	E5	126
Kewaunee, Wi., U.S.	D6	126
Kewaunee, co., Wi., U.S.	D6	126
Keweenaw, co., Mi., U.S.	A2	99
Keweenaw Bay, Mi., U.S.	B2	99
Keweenaw Bay, b., Mi., U.S.	B2	99
Keweenaw Peninsula, pen., Mi., U.S.	A3	99
Keweenaw Point, c., Mi., U.S.	A3	99
Key, Lough, l., Ire.	C3	11
Keya Paha, co., Ne., U.S.	B6	104
Keya Paha, stm., Ne., U.S.	A5	104
Key Biscayne, Fl., U.S.	*G6	86
Keyes, Man.	D2	70
Keyes, Ok., U.S.	e8	113
Keyesport, Il., U.S.	E4	90
Keyhole Reservoir, res., Wy., U.S.	B8	127
Key Junction, Ont.	B4	73
Key Largo, Fl., U.S.	G6	86
Keymar, Md., U.S.	A3	97
Keynsham, Eng., U.K.	C5	12
Keyport, N.J., U.S.	C4	107
Keyser, W.V., U.S.	B6	125
Keystone, Ia., U.S.	C5	92
Keystone, Ne., U.S.	C4	104
Keystone, S.D., U.S.	D2	118
Keystone, W.V., U.S.	D3	125
Keystone, Wy., U.S.	E6	127
Keystone Heights, Fl., U.S.	C4	86
Keystone Lake, res., Ok., U.S.	A5	113
Keystone Peak, mtn., Az., U.S.	F4	80
Keysville, Ga., U.S.	C4	87
Keysville, Va., U.S.	C4	123
Keytesville, Mo., U.S.	B5	102
Key West, Fl., U.S.	H5	86
Key West, La., U.S.	B7	92
Key West Naval Air Station, mil., Fl., U.S.	H5	86
Kezar Falls, Me., U.S.	E2	96
Kezar Lake, l., Me., U.S.	D2	96
Kezar Pond, l., Me., U.S.	D2	96
Kezhma, Sov. Un.	D13	28
Kežmarok, Czech.	D6	26
Khabab, Syria	A8	41
Khabarovsk, Sov. Un.	E16	29
Khabīs see Shahdād, Iran	F8	39
Khachmas, Sov. Un.	E3	28
Khaïdhárion, Grc.	*C4	25
Khairpur, Pak.	C4	36
Khakhea, Bots.	B3	49
Khalandrion, Grc.	*C4	25
Khalia, Grc.	g11	25
Khálki (Chalke), i., Grc.	D6	25
Khalkís, Grc.	C4	40
Khalūf, Oman	E5	39
Khambhāliya, India	H4	37
Khambhāt, India	F4	37
Khambhāt, Gulf of b., India	D5	36
Khāmgaon, India	D6	36
Khāmgaon, India	I8	37
Khammam, India	A4	36
Khānābād, Afg.	B4	38
Khānaqīn, Iraq	B4	38
Khānदेश, India	H4	37
Khandwa, India	D6	36
Khaniá (Canea), Grc.	E14	25
Khaniá, Gulf of, b., Grc.	E4	25
Khanka, Lake see Xingkai Hu, l., Asia	B11	31
Khānpur, Pak.	C5	36
Khanty-Mansiysk, Sov. Un.	A7	28
Kharagpur, India	D8	36
Khārān, Pak.	G12	39
Kharānaq, Iran	E7	39
Kharg Island, i., Iran	C4	38
Khargon, India	G5	37
Khārijah, Al Wāḥāt al, well, Eg.	C3	38
Kharkov, Sov. Un.	E5	29
Kharmān, Kūh-e, mtn., Iran	G6	39
Kharmanli, Bul.	A8	24
Kharovsk, Sov. Un.	B13	27
Khartoum (Al Kharṭūm), Sud.	B3	47
Khartoum North (Al Kharṭūm Baḥrī), Sud.	B3	47
Khartsyzsk, Sov. Un.	q21	30
Khasavyurt, Sov. Un.	G18	8
Khāsh, Afg.	B3	36
Khāsh, Iran	G10	39
Khāsh, stm., Afg.	B3	36
Khashm al Qirbah, Khazzān, res., Sud.	C4	47
Khashuri, Sov. Un.	B14	40
Khasi Hills, mts., India	C9	36
Khaskovo, Bul.	E7	24
Khatanga, stm., Sov. Un.	B13	29
Khavast, Sov. Un.	E7	29
Khemisset, Mor.	*C3	44
Khemmarat, Thai.	D6	35
Khenchla, Alg.	B6	44
Khenifra, Mor.	C3	44
Kherson, Sov. Un.	H9	27
Kheta, stm., Sov. Un.	B12	29
Khieo Peak, mtn., Thai.	E4	35
Khilok, Sov. Un.	D14	29
Khimki, Sov. Un.	n17	30
Khios, Grc.	C5	40
Khíos (Chios), i., Grc.	C5	40
Khirbat al Ghazālah, Syria	B7	41
Khisfin, Isr. Occ.	B7	41
Khiva, Sov. Un.	E6	28
Khlebarovo (Tsar Kaloyan), Bul.	D8	24
Khmelnik, Sov. Un.	G7	27
Khmelnitskiy, Sov. Un.	H6	27
Khoai, i., Viet.	H6	35
Khodzhent, Sov. Un.	E5	28
Khodzheyli, Sov. Un.	E5	28
Kholm, Afg.	B4	36
Kholm, Sov. Un.	C8	27
Kholmsk, Sov. Un.	E17	29
Khomeyn, Iran	E5	39
Khomeynīshahr, Iran	E5	39
Khon Kaen, Thai.	B2	35
Khoper, stm., Sov. Un.	F14	27
Khor, stm., Sov. Un.	B12	31
Khóra Sfakíon, Grc.	E5	25
Khordha, India	G10	37
Khorinsk, Sov. Un.	B6	31
Khorog, Sov. Un.	F10	29
Khorol, Sov. Un.	H4	31
Khorramābād, Iran	B4	39
Khorramshahr, Iran	B4	39
Khotin, Sov. Un.	G6	27
Khouribga, Mor.	D3	44
Khowst, Afg.	B4	36
Khram Yai, i., Thai.	F4	35
Khrisoúpolis, Grc.	B5	28
Khromtau, Sov. Un.	E6	28
Khu Khan, Thai.	E6	35
Khulna, Bngl.	D8	36
Khunzakh, Sov. Un.	A16	40
Khurja, India	C6	36
Khurr, Wādī al, val., Asia	G14	40
Khushāb, Pak.	A4	37
Khust, Sov. Un.	G4	27
Khuzdār, Pak.	C4	36
Khvāf, Iran	B6	38
Khvor, Iran	E7	39
Khvormūj, Iran	G5	39
Khvoy, Iran	B4	38
Khwae Noi, stm., Thai.	B5	36
Khyber Pass, Asia	H15	52
Kia, i., Fiji	C6	113
Kiamichi, stm., Ok., U.S.	C7	74
Kiamika, Que.	C2	74
Kiamika, stm., Que.	B7	79
Kiana, Ak., U.S.	B7	79
Kibangou, Congo	B1	48
Kibau, Tan.	C6	48
Kibiereqe, Tan.	C6	48
Kibombo, Zaire	B4	48
Kibondo, Tan.	B5	48
Kibwezi, Kenya	B6	48
Kičevo, Yugo.	E5	24
Kickamuit, stm., R.I., U.S.	D5	116
Kickapoo, stm., Wi., U.S.	E3	126
Kickapoo, Lake, res., Tx., U.S.	C3	120
Kickapoo Creek, stm., Il., U.S.	C4	90
Kickapoo Indian Reservation, Ks., U.S.	C8	93
Kicking Horse Pass, Can.	D2	68
Kidal, Mali	C5	45
Kidder, Mo., U.S.	B3	102
Kidder, S.D., U.S.	B8	118
Kidder, co., N.D., U.S.	C6	111
Kidderminster, Eng., U.K.	D5	10
Kidira, Sen.	D2	45
Kidnappers, Cape, c., N.Z.	M16	51
Kidron, Valley of, val., Isr. Occ.	m14	41
Kidsgrove, Eng., U.K.	A5	12
Kidugallo, Tan.	C6	48
Kidwelly, Wales, U.K.	C3	12
Kief, N.D., U.S.	B5	111
Kiefer, Ok., U.S.	B5	113
Kiel, Ger.	A5	18
Kiel, Wi., U.S.	E5	126
Kiel Bay, b., Ger.	A5	18
Kiel Canal, Ger.	A4	18
Kielce, Pol.	C6	26
Kiental, Switz.	C4	21
Kiester, Mn., U.S.	G5	100
Kiev, Sov. Un.	D6	29
Kiev Reservoir, res., Sov. Un.	C2	45
Kiffa, Maur.	C2	45
Kifisiá, Grc.	g11	25
Kifisós (Cephisus), stm., Grc.	g9	25
Kifisós, stm., Grc.	g11	25
Kifrī, Iraq	E15	40
Kigali, Rw.	B5	48
Kiği, Tur.	C13	40
Kigoma, Tan.	B4	48
Kigoma, prov., Tan.	B5	48
Kihei, Hi., U.S.	C5	88
Kiholo Bay, b., Hi., U.S.	D6	88
Kii Strait, strt., Japan	J7	33
Kikinda, Yugo.	C5	24
Kikongo, Zaire	B2	48
Kikori, Pap. N. Gui.	k11	50
Kikori, stm., Pap. N. Gui.	k11	50
Kikwit, Zaire	C2	48
Kila, Mt., U.S.	B2	103
Kilauea, Hi., U.S.	A2	88
Kilauea Crater, crat., Hi., U.S.	D6	88
Kilauea Point, c., Hi., U.S.	A2	88
Kilbaha, Ire.	E2	11
Kilbeggan, Ire.	C4	11
Kilbourne, Il., U.S.	C3	90
Kilbourne, Oh., U.S.	B3	112
Kilbrannan Sound, strt., Scot., U.K.	E3	13
Kilburn, N.B.	C2	71
Kilburn, Eng., U.K.	D7	11
Kilcar, Eng., U.K.	D7	11
Kilchoan, Scot., U.K.	D1	13
Kilchreest, Ire.	D3	11
Kilchu, N. Kor.	F4	33
Kilcock, Ire.	D5	11
Kilcolgan, Ire.	D3	11
Kilconnell, Ire.	D3	11
Kilcoole, Ire.	D5	11
Kilcormac (Frankford), Ire.	D4	11
Kilcullen, Ire.	D5	11
Kildare (Saint-Ambroise-de-Kildare), Que.	C4	74
Kildare, Ok., U.S.	A4	113
Kildare, co., Ire.	D5	11
Kildare, Cape, c., P.E.I.	C6	71
Kildorrery, Ire.	D4	11
Kilembe, Ug.	A5	48
Kilembe, Zaire	C2	48
Kilfenora, Ire.	D3	11
Kilfinnane, Ire.	E3	11
Kilgarvan, Ire.	F2	11
Kilgore, Ne., U.S.	A4	113
Kilgore, Tx., U.S.	C5	120
Kilifi, Kenya	B6	48
Kilimanjaro, prov., Tan.	B6	48
Kilimanjaro, mtn., Tan.	B6	48
Kilimatinde, Tan.	C5	48
Kilindoni, Tan.	C6	48
Kilis, Tur.	D11	40
Kiliya, Sov. Un.	I7	27
Kilkee, Ire.	D2	11
Kilkeel, N. Ire., U.K.	D6	11
Kilkenny, Ire.	D5	11
Kilkenny, Mn., U.S.	F5	100
Kilkenny, co., Ire.	D4	11
Kilkieran, Ire.	D2	11
Kilkieran Bay, b., Ire.	D2	11
Kilkis, Grc.	B4	25
Killadoon, Ire.	C2	11
Killadysert, Ire.	D2	11
Killala, Ire.	C2	11
Killala Bay, b., Ire.	C2	11
Killaloe, Ire.	D3	11
Killaloe Station, Ont.	B7	73
Killaly, Sask.	G4	75
Killam, Alta.	C5	68
Killarney, Man.	E2	70
Killarney, Ire.	E2	11
Killarney, Lake, l., Bah.	m17	64
Killarney Provincial Park, Ont.	A3	73
Killashandra, Ire.	C4	11
Killavally, Ire.	C2	11
Killbuck, Oh., U.S.	B4	112
Killbuck Creek, stm., Oh., U.S.	B3	112
Killdeer, N.D., U.S.	B3	111
Killdeer Mountains, mts., N.D., U.S.	B3	111
Killduff, Ia., U.S.	C5	92
Killearn, Fl., U.S.	*B2	86
Killeen, Tx., U.S.	D4	120
Killen, Al., U.S.	A2	78
Killenaule, Ire.	E4	11
Killeter, N. Ire., U.K.	C4	11
Killian, La., U.S.	h10	95
Killiecrankie, Pass of, Scot., U.K.	D5	13
Killik, stm., Ak., U.S.	B9	79
Killilan, Scot., U.K.	D3	13
Killimor, Ire.	D3	11
Killin, Scot., U.K.	E4	13
Killingly Center, Ct., U.S.	*B8	84
Killington Peak, mtn., Vt., U.S.	D3	122
Killingworth, Ct., U.S.	D5	84
Killíni, Grc.	D3	25
Killini Island, i., Can.	f8	72
Killona, La., U.S.	h11	95
Killorglin, Ire.	E2	11
Killucan, Ire.	D4	11
Killybegs, Ire.	C3	11
Killyleagh, N. Ire., U.K.	C6	11
Kilmacthomas, Ire.	E4	11
Kilmaine, Ire.	D2	11
Kilmallock, Ire.	E3	11
Kilmanagh, Mi., U.S.	E7	99
Kilmarnock, Scot., U.K.	C4	10
Kilmarnock, Va., U.S.	C6	123
Kilmelford, Scot., U.K.	D3	13
Kilmez, Sov. Un.	B24	28
Kilmichael, Ms., U.S.	B4	101
Kiln, Ms., U.S.	E4	101
Kilosa, Tan.	C6	48
Kilrea, N. Ire., U.K.	C5	11
Kilronan, Ire.	D2	11
Kilrush, Ire.	D2	10
Kilsyth, Scot., U.K.	C4	13
Kiltamagh, Ire.	C3	11
Kiltimagh, Ire.	D3	11
Kiltoom, Ire.	D3	11
Kilwa, Zaire	C4	48
Kilwa Kisiwani, Tan.	C6	48
Kilwa Kivinje, Tan.	C6	48
Kilwa Masoko, Tan.	C6	48
Kimamba, Tan.	C6	48
Kimball, Mn., U.S.	E4	100
Kimball, Ne., U.S.	C2	104
Kimball, S.D., U.S.	D7	118
Kimball, W.V., U.S.	D3	125
Kimball, co., Ne., U.S.	C2	104
Kimball, Mount, mtn., Ak., U.S.	C11	79
Kimballton, Ia., U.S.	C2	92
Kimberley, B.C.	E9	69
Kimberley, S. Afr.	C3	49
Kimberley Plateau, plat., Austl.	C4	50
Kimberlin Heights, Tn., U.S.	n14	119
Kimberly, Al., U.S.	B3	78
Kimberly, Id., U.S.	G4	89
Kimberly, Or., U.S.	C7	114
Kimberly, W.V., U.S.	m13	125
Kimberly, Wi., U.S.	h9	126
Kimble, co., Tx., U.S.	D2	120
Kimbolton, Oh., U.S.	B4	112
Kimbrough, Al., U.S.	C2	78
Kimch'aek (Sŏngjin), N. Kor.	C10	31
Kimch'ŏn, S. Kor.	H4	33
Kimesville, N.C., U.S.	B3	110
Kimiwan Lake, l., Alta.	B2	68
Kimmell, In., U.S.	B6	91
Kimmins, Tn., U.S.	B4	119
Kimmswick, Mo., U.S.	g13	102
Kimowan, stm., Sask.	A6	68
Kimry, Sov. Un.	C11	27
Kin, Japan	O5	52
Kinabalu, Mount, mtn., Malay.	D5	34
Kinard, Fl., U.S.	B1	86
Kinards, S.C., U.S.	C4	117
Kinbasket Lake, res., B.C.	D8	69
Kinbrace, Scot., U.K.	B5	13
Kinbrae, Mn., U.S.	G3	100
Kincaid, Sask.	H2	75
Kincaid, Il., U.S.	D4	90
Kincaid, Ks., U.S.	D8	93
Kincaid, W.V., U.S.	m13	125
Kincaid, Lake, res., Il., U.S.	D4	90
Kincardine, Ont.	C3	73
Kinchafoonee Creek, stm., Ga., U.S.	E2	87
Kincheloe Air Force Base, mil., Mi., U.S.	B6	99
Kinde, Mi., U.S.	E8	99
Kinder, La., U.S.	D3	95
Kinderhook, Il., U.S.	D2	90
Kinderhook, N.Y., U.S.	C7	109
Kindersley, Sask.	F1	75
Kindia, Gui.	D2	45
Kindu, Zaire	B4	48
Kinešma, Sov. Un.	C14	27
Kineo, Mount, mtn., Me., U.S.	C3	96
King, N.C., U.S.	A2	110
King, Wi., U.S.	D4	126
King, co., Tx., U.S.	C2	120
King, co., Wa., U.S.	B3	124
King, i., Austl.	G7	50
King and Queen, co., Va., U.S.	C6	123
King and Queen Court House, Va., U.S.	C6	123
Kingaroy, Austl.	E10	51
King Christian IX Land, reg., Grnld.	C18	128
King Christian X Land, reg., Grnld.	B17	128
King City, Ont.	k14	73
King City, Ca., U.S.	D3	82
King City, Mo., U.S.	A3	102
King Cove, Ak., U.S.	E7	79
King David Hotel, Isr.	m14	41
King Ferry, N.Y., U.S.	C4	109
Kingfield, Me., U.S.	D2	96
Kingfisher, Ok., U.S.	B3	113
Kingfisher, co., Ok., U.S.	B3	113
King Frederik VIII Land, reg., Grnld.	B17	128
King Frederik VI Coast, Grnld.	C19	128
King George, Va., U.S.	B5	123
King George, co., Va., U.S.	B5	123
King George, Mount, mtn., B.C.	D10	69
King George Island, i., B.A.T.	B1	7
King George Sound, strt., Austl.	G2	50
King Hill, Id., U.S.	F3	89
King Island, i., B.C.	C3	69
King Lake, res., Il., U.S.	*C9	104
King Lear Peak, mtn., Nv., U.S.	B3	105
King Leopold Ranges, mts., Austl.	C4	50
Kingman, Alta.	C4	68
Kingman, Az., U.S.	B1	80
Kingman, In., U.S.	E3	91
Kingman, Ks., U.S.	E5	93
Kingman, Me., U.S.	C4	96
Kingman, co., Ks., U.S.	E5	93
King Mountain, mtn., Ok., U.S.	C2	113
King Mountain, mtn., Or., U.S.	E3	114
King Mountain, mtn., Or., U.S.	D8	114
King of Prussia, Pa., U.S.	F11	115
King Peak, mtn., Ca., U.S.	B1	82
Kings, Il., U.S.	A4	90
Kings, Ms., U.S.	C3	101
Kings, co., N.B.	D4	71
Kings, co., N.S.	E5	71
Kings, co., P.E.I.	C7	71
Kings, co., Ca., U.S.	D4	82
Kings, co., N.Y., U.S.	E7	109
Kings, stm., Ire.	E4	11
Kings, stm., Ar., U.S.	A2	81
Kings, stm., Ca., U.S.	D4	82
Kings, stm., Nv., U.S.	B3	105
King Salmon, Ak., U.S.	D8	79
Kingsbridge, Eng., U.K.	D4	12
Kingsburg, Ca., U.S.	D4	82
Kingsbury, In., U.S.	A4	91
Kingsbury, co., S.D., U.S.	C8	118
Kings Canyon National Park, Ca., U.S.	D4	82
Kingsclear, N.B.	D3	71
Kings Corner, Ct., U.S.	B5	84
Kingscote, Austl.	G6	50
Kings Creek, S.C., U.S.	A5	117
Kingsdown, Ks., U.S.	E4	93
Kingsey-Falls, Que.	D5	74
Kingsford, Mi., U.S.	C2	99
Kingsgate, B.C.	E9	69
Kingsgate, Wa., U.S.	*B3	124
Kings Grant, N.C., U.S.	*C5	110
Kingsland, Ar., U.S.	D3	81
Kingsland, Ga., U.S.	F5	87
Kingsland, Tx., U.S.	D3	120
Kingsley, Ia., U.S.	B2	92
Kingsley, Mi., U.S.	D5	99
Kingsley Dam, Ne., U.S.	C4	104
King's Lynn, Eng., U.K.	D7	10
Kingsmere Lake, l., Sask.	C2	75
Kings Mill, Tx., U.S.	B2	120
Kings Mills, Oh., U.S.	C1	112
Kings Mountain, Ky., U.S.	C5	94
Kings Mountain, N.C., U.S.	B1	110
King Sound, strt., Austl.	C3	50
Kings Park, N.Y., U.S.	*E7	109
Kings Park West, Va., U.S.	*B5	123
Kings Peak, mtn., Ut., U.S.	C5	121
King's Point, Newf.	D3	72
Kings Point, Fl., U.S.	*F6	86
Kings Point, N.Y., U.S.	*E7	109
Kingsport, Tn., U.S.	C11	119
Kingston, Ont.	C8	73
Kingston, Jam.	E6	64
Kingston, N.Z.	P12	51
Kingston, Ga., U.S.	B2	87
Kingston, Id., U.S.	B2	89
Kingston, Il., U.S.	A5	90
Kingston, Ma., U.S.	C6	98
Kingston, Mi., U.S.	E7	99
Kingston, Mo., U.S.	B3	102
Kingston, N.H., U.S.	E4	106
Kingston, N.Y., U.S.	D6	109
Kingston, Oh., U.S.	C3	112
Kingston, Ok., U.S.	D5	113
Kingston, Pa., U.S.	D10	115
Kingston, R.I., U.S.	F3	116
Kingston, Tn., U.S.	D9	119
Kingston, Ut., U.S.	E3	121
Kingston, Wa., U.S.	B3	124
Kingston, W.V., U.S.	D3	125
Kingston, Wi., U.S.	E4	126
Kingston Southeast, Austl.	G6	50
Kingston Springs, Tn., U.S.	A4	119
Kingston upon Hull, Eng., U.K.	D6	10
Kingston upon Thames (part of London), Eng., U.K.	m12	10
Kingstown, St. Vin.	J14	64
Kingstree, S.C., U.S.	D8	117
Kings Valley, Or., U.S.	C3	114
Kingsville, Ont.	E2	73
Kingsville, Md., U.S.	B5	97
Kingsville, Mo., U.S.	C3	102
Kingsville, Tx., U.S.	F4	120
Kingsville Naval Air Station, mil., Tx., U.S.	F4	120
Kingswood, Ky., U.S.	C3	94
Kingua, Eg.	B4	12
Kingurutik Lake, l., Newf.	g9	72
Kingussie, Scot., U.K.	B6	10
King William, Va., U.S.	C5	123
King William, co., Va., U.S.	C5	123
King William Island, i., N.W. Ter.	C13	66
King William's Town, S. Afr.	D4	49
Kingwood, Tx., U.S.	*E5	120
Kingwood, W.V., U.S.	B5	125
Kinistino, Sask.	E3	75
Kinkaid Lake, res., Il., U.S.	F4	90
Kinkora, P.E.I.	C6	71
Kinley, Sask.	E2	75
Kin-Li-Chee, Az., U.S.	B6	80
Kinlochewe, Scot., U.K.	D3	13
Kinloch Hourn, Scot., U.K.	C3	13
Kinmount, Ont.	C6	73
Kinmundy, Il., U.S.	E5	90
Kinnairds Head, c., Scot., U.K.	B6	10
Kinnear, Wy., U.S.	C4	127
Kinnelon, N.J., U.S.	B4	107
Kinneret, Yam (Sea of Galilee), l., Isr.	B7	41
Kinomoto, Japan	n15	33
Kinosaki, Japan	I7	33
Kinross, P.E.I.	C7	71
Kinross, Scot., U.K.	D5	13
Kinsale, Ire.	E3	11
Kinsale, Va., U.S.	B6	123
Kinsealy, Alta.	C5	68
Kinsey, Al., U.S.	D4	78
Kinsey, Mt., U.S.	D11	103
Kinshasa (Léopoldville), Zaire	B2	48
Kinsley, Ks., U.S.	E4	93
Kinsman, Oh., U.S.	A5	112
Kinston, Al., U.S.	D3	78

Name	Map Ref.	Page
Kinston, N.C., U.S.	B5	110
Kinta, Ok., U.S.	B6	113
Kintampo, Ghana	E4	45
Kintinku, Tan.	C6	48
Kintore, Scot., U.K.	C6	13
Kintyre, Mull of, c., Scot., U.K.	E3	13
Kinuso, Alta.	B3	68
Kinvarra, Ire.	D3	11
Kinyangiri, Tan.	B5	48
Kinyeti, mtn., Sud.	E3	47
Kinzig, stm., Ger.	C4	19
Kinzig, stm., Ger.	E2	19
Kinzua, Or., U.S.	C6	114
Kioa, i., Fiji	H15	52
Kiona, Wa., U.S.	C6	124
Kioshkokwi Lake, l., Ont.	A6	73
Kiosk, Ont.	A6	73
Kiowa, Ont.	B6	83
Kiowa, Ks., U.S.	E5	93
Kiowa, Ok., U.S.	C6	113
Kiowa, co., U.S.	C8	83
Kiowa, co., Ks., U.S.	E4	93
Kiowa, co., Ok., U.S.	C2	113
Kiowa Creek, stm., Co., U.S.	B6	83
Kiowa Creek, stm., Co., U.S.	A1	113
Kipahigan Lake, l., Can.	B5	75
Kipahulu, Hi., U.S.	*C5	88
Kipapa Stream, stm., Hi., U.S.	g9	88
Kiparissía, Grc.	D3	25
Kiparissía, Gulf of, b., Grc.	D3	25
Kipembawe, Tan.	C5	48
Kipili, Tan.	C5	48
Kipini, Kenya	B7	48
Kipling, Sask.	G4	75
Kipling, Mi., U.S.	C3	99
Kipnuk, Ak., U.S.	C7	79
Kipp, Alta.	E4	68
Kipp, Ks., U.S.	D6	93
Kipton, Oh., U.S.	A3	112
Kipushi, Zaire	D4	48
Kirby, Ar., U.S.	C2	81
Kirby, Tx., U.S.	*E3	120
Kirby, Wy., U.S.	C4	127
Kirbyville, Tx., U.S.	D6	120
Kirchberg, Switz.	*B7	21
Kirchdorf, Ger.	E5	15
Kirchhain, Ger.	C3	19
Kirchheimbolanden, Ger.	D2	19
Kirchheim [unter Teck], Ger.	E4	19
Kirchhundem, Ger.	B3	19
Kirdāsah, Eg.	D3	41
Kirensk, Sov. Un.	D13	29
Kirghiz S.S.R., state, Sov. Un.	E10	29
Kirgiz Range, mts., Sov. Un.	E8	28
Kiri, Zaire	B2	48
Kiribati, ctry., Oc.	G11	6
Kınıkhan, Tur.	*D11	40
Kırıkkale, Tur.	C9	40
Kirin see Jilin, prov., China	C10	31
Kirinian, i., Marsh Is.	S18	52
Kirinyaga (Mount Kenya), mtn., Kenya	B6	48
Kiritimati Island (Christmas Island), i., Kir.	F12	6
Kirk, Co., U.S.	B8	83
Kirkby Lonsdale, Eng., U.K.	F6	13
Kirkby Stephen, Eng., U.K.	F6	13
Kirkcaldy, Alta.	D4	68
Kirkcaldy, Scot., U.K.	F3	13
Kirkcolm, Scot., U.K.	C5	10
Kirkcudbright, Scot., U.K.	C5	10
Kirkcudbright Bay, b., Scot., U.K.	F4	13
Kirkenes, Nor.	C13	14
Kirkersville, Oh., U.S.	C5	112
Kirkfield, Ont.	C5	73
Kirkintilloch, Scot., U.K.	E4	13
Kirkland, Al., U.S.	D2	78
Kirkland, Az., U.S.	C3	80
Kirkland, Ga., U.S.	E4	87
Kirkland, Il., U.S.	A5	90
Kirkland, Tn., U.S.	B5	119
Kirkland, Tx., U.S.	B3	120
Kirkland, Wa., U.S.	B3	124
Kirkland Lake, Ont.	o19	73
Kirklareli, Tur.	B6	40
Kirklin, In., U.S.	D5	91
Kirkman, Ia., U.S.	C2	92
Kirkmansville, Ky., U.S.	D2	94
Kirkoswald, Eng., U.K.	F6	13
Kirkpatrick, Mount, mtn., Ant.	A29	7
Kirkpatrick Lake, l., Alta.	D5	68
Kirksey, Ky., U.S.	f9	94
Kirksey, S.C., U.S.	C3	117
Kirksville, Ky., U.S.	C5	94
Kirksville, Mo., U.S.	A5	102
Kirkton, Ont.	D3	73
Kirkton of Glenisla, Scot., U.K.	D5	13
Kirkūk, Iraq	B4	38
Kirkville, Ia., U.S.	C5	92
Kirkwall, Scot., U.K.	A5	10
Kirkwood, S. Afr.	D4	49
Kirkwood, De., U.S.	B3	85
Kirkwood, Il., U.S.	C3	90
Kirkwood, Mo., U.S.	f13	102
Kirn, Ger.	D3	18
Kiron, Ia., U.S.	B2	92
Kirov, Sov. Un.	D7	29
Kirovakan, Sov. Un.	B15	40
Kirov Bay, b., Sov. Un.	B4	39
Kirovgrad, Sov. Un.	B6	28
Kirovograd, Sov. Un.	G9	27
Kirovsk, Sov. Un.	C6	29
Kirriemuir, Alta.	D5	68
Kirriemuir, Scot., U.K.	D5	13
Kirsanov, Sov. Un.	E14	27
Kırşehir, Tur.	C10	40
Kırthar Range, mts., Pak.	C4	36
Kirtland, N.M., U.S.	A1	108
Kirtland, Oh., U.S.	*C1	112
Kirtland Air Force Base, mil., N.M., U.S.	k7	108
Kiruna, Swe.	D9	14
Kirundu, Zaire	B4	48
Kirwin, Ks., U.S.	C4	93
Kirwin Reservoir, res., Ks., U.S.	C4	93
Kiryū, Japan	H9	33
Kisaki, Tan.	C6	48
Kisanga, Zaire	C4	48
Kisangani (Stanleyville), Zaire	A4	48
Kisarazu, Japan	n18	33
Kisatchie, La., U.S.	C2	95
K.I. Sawyer Air Force Base, mil., Mi., U.S.	B3	99
Kisbey, Sask.	H4	75
Kiselevsk, Sov. Un.	C11	28
Kisengwa, Zaire	C4	48
Kīsh, i., Iran	H6	39
Kishanganj, India	D11	37
Kishangarh, India	C5	36
Kishi, Nig.	E5	45
Kishinev, Sov. Un.	E6	29
Kishiwada, Japan	o14	33
Kishorganj, Bngl.	D9	36
Kishwaukee, stm., Il., U.S.	A5	90
Kisii, Kenya	B5	48
Kisiju, Tan.	C6	48
Kisiwa Creek, stm., Ks., U.S.	g11	93
Kisiwani, Tan.	B6	48
Kiska Island, i., Ak., U.S.	E3	79
Kiskatinaw, stm., B.C.	B7	69
Kiskittogisu Lake, l., Man.	B2	70
Kiskitto Lake, l., Man.	B2	70
Kiskőrös, Hung.	B4	24
Kiskundorozsma (part of Szeged), Hung.	B5	24
Kiskunfélegyháza, Hung.	B4	24
Kiskunhalas, Hung.	B4	24
Kiskunmajsa, Hung.	B4	24
Kislovodsk, Sov. Un.	E2	28
Kismaayo, Som.	F5	47
Kismet, Ks., U.S.	E3	93
Kiso-sammyaku, mts., Japan	n16	33
Kissamos, Grc.	E4	25
Kissee Mills, Mo., U.S.	E4	102
Kisseynew Lake, l., Can.	B1	70
Kissidougou, Gui.	E2	45
Kissimmee, Fl., U.S.	D5	86
Kissimmee, stm., Fl., U.S.	E5	86
Kissimmee, Lake, l., Fl., U.S.	E5	86
Kissimmee, Lake, Fl., U.S.	D5	86
Kississing, Man.	B1	70
Kississing, stm., Man.	B1	70
Kississing Lake, l., Man.	B1	70
Kisslegg, Ger.	A8	21
Kistefjellet, mtn., Nor.	C8	14
Kistigan Lake, l., Man.	B5	70
Kistler, W.V., U.S.	D3	125
Kistrand, Nor.	B11	14
Kisújszállás, Hung.	B5	24
Kisumu, Kenya	A5	48
Kisvárda, Hung.	A6	24
Kita, Mali	D3	45
Kita, Mount, mtn., Japan	I9	33
Kita-ibaraki, Japan	H10	33
Kita-iwo, i., Japan	E8	6
Kitakyūshū, Japan	E11	31
Kitale, Kenya	A5	48
Kitami, Japan	E11	33
Kitangari, Tan.	D6	48
Kit Carson, Co., U.S.	C8	83
Kit Carson, co., Co., U.S.	B8	83
Kitchell, In., U.S.	E8	91
Kitchener, Ont.	D4	73
Kite, Ga., U.S.	D4	87
Kitgum, Ug.	A5	48
Kithira, Grc.	D4	25
Kithira (Cythera), i., Grc.	D4	25
Kithnos, i., Grc.	D5	40
Kitimat, B.C.	B3	69
Kitridge Point, c., Barb.	K21	65
Kitsap, co., Wa., U.S.	B3	124
Kitscoty, Alta.	C5	68
Kittanning, Pa., U.S.	E2	115
Kittatinny Mountain, mtn., U.S.	B2	107
Kittery, Me., U.S.	E2	96
Kittery Point, Me., U.S.	E2	96
Kittilä, Fin.	D11	14
Kittitas, Wa., U.S.	C5	124
Kittitas, co., Wa., U.S.	B5	124
Kittitas Valley, val., Wa., U.S.	B5	124
Kittrell, N.C., U.S.	A4	110
Kitts, Ky., U.S.	D6	94
Kitts Hummock, De., U.S.	D4	85
Kittson, co., Mn., U.S.	B2	100
Kitty Hawk, N.C., U.S.	A7	110
Kitty Hawk Bay, b., N.C., U.S.	A7	110
Kitui, Kenya	B4	48
Kitwanga, B.C.	B3	69
Kitwe, Zam.	D4	48
Kitzbühel, Aus.	E6	18
Kitzingen, Ger.	D5	18
Kitzmiller, Md., U.S.	m12	97
Kivalina, Ak., U.S.	B7	79
Kivu, hist. reg., Zaire	B4	48
Kivu, Lac, l., Afr.	B4	48
Kiya, stm., Sov. Un.	D26	8
Kiyan, Japan	O5	52
Kiyan Point, c., Japan	O5	52
Kıyıköy, Tur.	B7	40
Kiyiu Lake, l., Sask.	F1	75
Kizel, Sov. Un.	B5	28
Kizil, stm., Tur.	B10	40
Kizlyar, Sov. Un.	A8	39
Kizyl-Arvat, Sov. Un.	F8	29
Kjaekan, Nor.	C10	14
Kjellerup, Den.	B3	15
Kjelvik, Nor.	B12	14
Kladno, Czech.	C3	26
Klagenfurt, Aus.	E7	18
Klagetoh, Az., U.S.	B6	80
Klaipėda (Memel), Sov. Un.	B1	82
Klamath, Ca., U.S.	B1	82
Klamath, co., Or., U.S.	E5	114
Klamath, stm., U.S.	B2	76
Klamath Falls, Or., U.S.	E5	114
Klamath Glen, Ca., U.S.	B1	82
Klamath Mountains, mts., U.S.	E2	114
Klanxbüll, Ger.	A5	19
Klarälven, stm., Eur.	G5	14
Klatovy, Czech.	D2	26
Klawer, S. Afr.	D2	49
Klawock, Ak., U.S.	D13	79
Kleberg, co., Tx., U.S.	F4	120
Kleena Kleene, B.C.	C5	69
Klein, Tx., U.S.	*D5	120
Kleinburg, Ont.	k14	73
Klemme, Ia., U.S.	A4	92
Klerksdorp, S. Afr.	C4	49
Kletnya, Sov. Un.	E9	27
Kletsk, Sov. Un.	E7	27
Kleve (Cleves), Ger.	C3	18
Klibreck, Ben, mtn., Scot., U.K.	B4	13
Kličany, Czech.	n17	26
Klickitat, Wa., U.S.	D4	124
Klickitat, co., Wa., U.S.	D4	124
Klickitat, stm., Wa., U.S.	C4	124
Klimovsk, Sov. Un.	n17	27
Klimovsk, Sov. Un.	C11	27
Klin, Sov. Un.	D5	69
Klinaklini, stm., B.C.	D5	69
Kline, S.C., U.S.	E5	117
Klingenthal, Ger.	C7	19
Klínovec, mtn., Czech.	C7	19
Klintsy, Sov. Un.	E9	27
Klippan, Swe.	B7	15
Klitmøller, Den.	A2	15
Ključ, Yugo.	C3	24
Klobuck, Pol.	C5	26
Kloch Lake, l., B.C.	B5	69
Klock, Ont.	A6	73
Klodnica, stm., Pol.	g9	26
Kłodzko, Pol.	C4	26
Klondike, Tx., U.S.	C5	120
Klondike Gold Rush National Historical Park, Ak., U.S.	k22	79
Klondike Region, hist. reg., Yukon	D5	66
Klondyke, Az., U.S.	E5	80
Klos, Alb.	B3	25
Klostermansfeld, Ger.	B6	19
Klosterneuburg, Aus.	D8	18
Kloten, Switz.	B6	21
Kloten, N.D., U.S.	B7	111
Klotzsche, Ger.	B8	19
Klotzville, La., U.S.	h9	95
Kluane Lake, l., Yukon	D5	66
Kluane National Park, Yukon	D5	66
Kluczbork, Pol.	C5	26
Klukwan, Ak., U.S.	k22	79
Klutina Lake, l., Ak., U.S.	g19	79
Klütz, Ger.	E5	15
Klyazma, stm., Sov. Un.	C13	27
Klyuchevskaya Sopka, vol., Sov. Un.	D18	29
Knapp, Wi., U.S.	D1	126
Knapp Creek, stm., W.V., U.S.	C5	125
Knaresborough, Eng., U.K.	F7	13
Knee Lake, l., Man.	B4	70
Knee Lake, l., Sask.	B2	75
Kneebeck, Ger.	F4	15
Knesset, Isr.	m14	41
Knezha, Bul.	D7	24
Knickerbocker, Tx., U.S.	D2	120
Knierim, Ia., U.S.	B3	92
Knife, stm., N.D., U.S.	B3	111
Knife River, Mn., U.S.	D7	100
Knifley, Ky., U.S.	C4	94
Knightdale, N.C., U.S.	B4	110
Knight Inlet, b., B.C.	D5	69
Knight Island, i., Ak., U.S.	g18	79
Knighton, Wales, U.K.	I9	13
Knights Landing, Ca., U.S.	C3	82
Knights Town, Ire.	F1	11
Knightstown, In., U.S.	E6	91
Knightsville, In., U.S.	E3	91
Knightville Reservoir, res., Ma., U.S.	B2	98
Knin, Yugo.	C3	24
Knippa, Tx., U.S.	E3	120
Knislinge, Swe.	B8	15
Knittelfeld, Aus.	E7	18
Knob Creek, stm., Ky., U.S.	g11	94
Knobel, Ar., U.S.	A5	81
Knob Lick, Ky., U.S.	C4	94
Knob Lick, Mo., U.S.	D7	102
Knobly Mountain, mtn., W.V., U.S.	B5	125
Knob Noster, Mo., U.S.	C4	102
Knobsville, Pa., U.S.	F6	115
Knockadoon Head, c., Ire.	F4	11
Knockalong, mtn., Ire.	C3	11
Knockanefune, hill, Ire.	E2	11
Knockboy, mtn., Ire.	F2	11
Knocklong, Ire.	E3	11
Knockmealdown Mountains, mts., Ire.	D2	10
Knokke [-Heist], Bel.	C3	17
Knollwood, Ct., U.S.	D6	84
Knollwood, W.V., U.S.	m12	125
Knops Pond, l., Ma., U.S.	f9	98
Knott, Tx., U.S.	C2	120
Knott, co., Ky., U.S.	C6	94
Knotts Island, N.C., U.S.	A7	110
Knottsville, Ky., U.S.	C3	94
Knowles, Ok., U.S.	A1	113
Knowlton, Wi., U.S.	D4	126
Knox, Austl.	*G8	50
Knox, In., U.S.	B4	91
Knox, N.D., U.S.	A6	111
Knox, Pa., U.S.	D2	115
Knox, co., Il., U.S.	s31	14
Knox, co., In., U.S.	G3	91
Knox, co., Ky., U.S.	D6	94
Knox, co., Me., U.S.	D4	96
Knox, co., Mo., U.S.	A5	102
Knox, co., Ne., U.S.	B8	104
Knox, co., Oh., U.S.	B3	112
Knox, co., Tn., U.S.	C10	119
Knox, co., Tx., U.S.	C3	120
Knox, Cape, c., B.C.	B1	69
Knox City, Mo., U.S.	A5	102
Knox City, Tx., U.S.	C3	120
Knox Coast, Ant.	C23	7
Knox Dale, Pa., U.S.	D3	115
Knoxville, Al., U.S.	C2	78
Knoxville, Ga., U.S.	D3	87
Knoxville, Ia., U.S.	C4	92
Knoxville, Il., U.S.	C3	90
Knoxville, Md., U.S.	B2	97
Knoxville, Pa., U.S.	C7	115
Knoxville, Tn., U.S.	D10	119
Knurów, Pol.	g9	26
Knysna, S. Afr.	D3	49
Knyszyn, Pol.	B7	26
Ko, Mount, mtn., Sov. Un.	C8	33
Kobayashi, Japan	K5	33
Kōbe, Japan	E11	31
Kobelyaki, Sov. Un.	G10	27
København, co., Den.	C6	15
Koblenz (Coblence), Ger.	C3	18
Koboko, Ug.	A5	48
Kobroor, i., Indon.	G8	34
Kobuk, Ak., U.S.	B8	79
Kobuk, stm., Ak., U.S.	B8	79
Kobuk Valley National Park, Ak., U.S.	B8	79
Koca, stm., Czech.	o17	26
Kočani, Yugo.	B6	24
Kocaeli see İzmit, Tur.	B7	40
Kočevje, Yugo.	C2	24
Koch Bihār, India	C8	36
Kōchi, Japan	E11	31
Koch Peak, mtn., Mt., U.S.	E5	103
Kock, Pol.	C7	26
Kodaira, Japan	*D5	33
Kodak, Ky., U.S.	C10	119
Kodari, Nepal	D10	37
Kodiak, Ak., U.S.	D9	79
Kodiak Island, i., Ak., U.S.	D9	79
Kodok (Fashoda), Sud.	E6	47
Koek Joeri, Neth. Ant.	H18	65
Koes, Nmb.	D3	49
Koettlitz Glacier, ice, Ant.	f39	7
Kofa Mountains, mts., Az., U.S.	D2	80
Koffiefontein, S. Afr.	C4	49
Koforidua, Ghana	E4	45
Kōfu, Japan	I9	33
Koga, Japan	m18	33
Kogaluk, stm., Newf.	g9	72
Køge, Den.	C6	15
Køge Bugt, b., Den.	C6	15
Kohala Mountains, mts., Hi., U.S.	C6	88
Kohāt, Pak.	B5	36
Kohler, Az., U.S.	E3	80
Kohīma, India	C9	36
Kohler, Wi., U.S.	E6	126
Kohtla-Järve, Sov. Un.	B6	27
Koidu, S.L.	E2	45
Koindu, Japan	E10	29
Koje Island, i., S. Kor.	I4	33
Kokand, Sov. Un.	E10	29
Kokanee Glacier Provincial Park, B.C.	E9	69
Kokchetav, Sov. Un.	D9	29
Kokkola, Fin.	F10	14
Koko, Nig.	D5	45
Koko Head, c., Hi., U.S.	B4	88
Kokolik, stm., Ak., U.S.	B7	79
Kokomo, In., U.S.	C5	88
Kokomo, In., U.S.	D5	91
Kokomo, Ms., U.S.	D3	101
Koko Nor see Qinghai Hu, l., China	D4	31
Kokopo, Pap. N. Gui.	h13	50
Kokosing, stm., Oh., U.S.	B3	112
Kokrines, Ak., U.S.	C9	79
Koksan, N. Kor.	G3	33
Koksilah, B.C.	g12	69
Koksoak, stm., Que.	E19	66
Kokstad, S. Afr.	D4	49
Kola, Sov. Un.	C15	14
Ko Lanta, i., Thai.	I3	35
Kola Peninsula, pen., Sov. Un.	C6	29
Kord Kūy, Iran	C7	39
Kolār, India	F5	36
Kolār Gold Fields, India	*F6	36
Kolari, Fin.	D10	14
Kolárovo, Czech.	E4	26
Kolāyat, India	D4	37
Kolbäck, Swe.	t34	14
Kolaka, Indon.	G6	34
Kolbio, Kenya	B7	48
Kolbuszowa, Pol.	C6	26
Kolchugino, Sov. Un.	C12	27
Kolczewo, Pol.	E8	15
Kolda, Sen.	D2	45
Koldewey, i., Grnld.	B16	128
Kolding, Den.	C3	15
Koleč, Czech.	n17	26
Koléen, In., U.S.	G4	91
Kolezhma, Sov. Un.	E16	14
Kolguyev Island, i., Sov. Un.	C7	29
Kolhapur, India	E5	36
Koliganek, Ak., U.S.	D8	79
Kolimbine, stm., Afr.	D2	45
Kolín, Czech.	C3	26
Kolin, La., U.S.	C3	95
Kolki, Sov. Un.	h11	25
Kolleda, Ger.	B6	19
Kolno, Pol.	B6	26
Kolo, Pol.	B5	26
Kołobrzeg, Pol.	B2	26
Koloa, Hi., U.S.	B2	88
Kolob Canyon, val., Ut., U.S.	F2	121
Kolobrzeg, Pol.	A3	26
Kolokani, Mali	D3	45
Kolomna, Sov. Un.	D6	29
Kolomyya, Sov. Un.	G5	27
Kolondiéba, Mali	D3	45
Kolonia, Micron.	Q17	52
Kolonodale, Indon.	F6	34
Kolp, stm., Sov. Un.	B10	27
Kolpashevo, Sov. Un.	B10	28
Kolpino, Sov. Un.	s31	14
Kolsva, Swe.	*G5	14
Kolwezi, Zaire	D4	48
Kolyberovo, Sov. Un.	n18	27
Kolyma, stm., Sov. Un.	C18	29
Kolyma Mountains, mts., Sov. Un.	C18	29
Komandorski Islands, is., Sov. Un.	B5	29
Komárno, Man.	D3	70
Komárno, Czech.	E5	26
Komárom, Hung.	B4	24
Komatipoort, S. Afr.	C5	49
Komatke, Az., U.S.	D3	80
Komatsu, Japan	H8	33
Komatsushima, Japan	I7	33
Komló, Hung.	B4	24
Kommunizma, Pik, mtn., Afr.	G12	29
Komodo, i., Indon.	G5	34
Komoé, stm., Afr.	E4	45
Komono, Congo	B1	48
Komoran, i., Indon.	G9	34
Komotini, Grc.	B5	40
Komsberg, mts., S. Afr.	D3	49
Komsomolets, i., Sov. Un.	A4	128
Komsomolsk [-na-Amure], Sov. Un.	D16	29
Kontagora, Nig.	D6	45
Kontcha, Cam.	D2	46
Kontich, Bel.	C4	17
Kontiomäki, Fin.	E13	14
Kon Tum, Viet.	C3	34
Konya, Tur.	D9	40
Konyang, S. Kor.	I3	33
Konzhakovskiy Kamen, mtn., Sov. Un.	B5	28
Koocanusa, Lake, res., N.A.	B1	103
Koochiching, co., Mn., U.S.	B4	100
Koolau Range, mts., Hi., U.S.	f10	88
Kooloonong, Austl.	G4	51
Koontz Lake, In., U.S.	B5	91
Koosharem, Ut., U.S.	E4	121
Kooskia, Id., U.S.	C3	89
Kootenai, co., Id., U.S.	*A2	89
Kootenai, Id., U.S.	B2	89
Kootenai, stm., N.A.	E10	69
Kootenay Lake, l., B.C.	D9	69
Kootenay National Park, B.C.	D9	69
Kopervik, Nor.	H1	14
Kopet Mountains, mts., Asia	B8	39
Kopeysk, Sov. Un.	B6	28
Köping, Swe.	H6	14
Koppány, stm., Hung.	B4	24
Kopparberg, Swe.	G6	14
Koppel, Pa., U.S.	E1	115
Koprivnica, Yugo.	B3	24
Kopychintsy, Sov. Un.	G6	27
Korab, mtn., Eur.	E5	24
Korahe, Eth.	D5	47
Korarou, Lac, l., Mali	C4	45
Korba, India	D5	37
Korba, Tun.	F3	23
Korbach, Ger.	B3	19
Korbu, mtn., Malay.	J4	35
Korçë, Alb.	B3	40
Korčula, i., Yugo.	D3	24
Korea, North, ctry., Asia	D10	31
Korea, South, ctry., Asia	D10	31
Korea Bay, b., Asia	D9	31
Korea Strait, strt., Asia	E10	31
Korec, Sov. Un.	F6	27
Korets, Sov. Un.	o17	26
Kori Creek, stm., India	F2	37
Korídhallos, Grc.	*D4	25
Korínthos (Corinth), Grc.	D4	25
Kōriyama, Japan	H10	33
Korkuteli, Tur.	D8	40
Korla, China	C2	31
Körmend, Hung.	B3	24
Kornat, i., Yugo.	D2	24
Korneuburg, Aus.	D8	18
Kornwestheim, Ger.	E4	19
Koro, Mali	D4	45
Koro, i., Fiji	H15	52
Korogwe, Tan.	C6	48
Koronis, Lake, l., Mn., U.S.	E4	100
Koropion, Grc.	h11	25
Koror, Palau	R17	52
Koror, i., Palau	R17	52
Korosten, Sov. Un.	F7	27
Koro Toro, Chad	B3	46
Korotoyak, Sov. Un.	F12	27
Korovin Volcano, vol., Ak., U.S.	E5	79
Korsakov, Sov. Un.	E17	29
Korsnäs, Fin.	A5	28
Korsør, Den.	C5	15
Kortrijk (Courtrai), Bel.	C3	17
Korucam, Cape, c., N. Cyp.	E9	40
Korumburra, Austl.	I5	51
Koryak Mountains, mts., Sov. Un.	C19	29
Kos, Grc.	D6	40
Kos (Cos), i., Grc.	D6	40
Koschagyl, Sov. Un.	D4	28
Kościerzyna, Pol.	A4	26
Kosciusko, Ms., U.S.	B4	101
Kosciusko, co., In., U.S.	B6	91
Kosciusko, Mount, mtn., Austl.	G9	51
Kösdaği, mtn., Tur.	C14	40
Koshigaya, Japan	*I9	33
Koshiki Islands, is., Japan	K4	33
Koshkonong, Lake, l., Wi., U.S.	F5	126
Košice, Czech.	D6	26
Košiře (part of Prague), Czech.	n17	26
Koskaecodde Lake, l., Newf.	D4	72
Koslan, Sov. Un.	C18	8
Kosŏng, N. Kor.	G4	33
Kosovska Mitrovica, Yugo.	D5	24
Kosrae, i., Micron.	Q19	6
Kossae, Tx., U.S.	*D4	120
Kösslarn, Ger.	A9	20
Kossol Passage, strt., Palau	R17	52
Kossol Reef, rf., Palau	R17	52
Kossuth, Ms., U.S.	A5	101
Kossuth, co., Ia., U.S.	A3	92
Kostelec, Czech.	o18	26
Kostroma, Sov. Un.	D7	29
Kostrzyn, Pol.	B3	26
Koszalin (Köslin), Pol.	A3	26
Köszeg, Hung.	B3	24
Kota, India	D5	36
Kota Baharu, Malay.	D2	34
Kotaagung, Indon.	B4	34
Kotabumi, Indon.	L4	35
Kota Kinabalu, Malay.	D5	34
Kotamobagu, Indon.	E6	34
Kotel, Bul.	D8	24
Kotelnich, Sov. Un.	H14	29
Kotel'nyy Island, i., Sov. Un.	B16	29
Köthen, Ger.	C5	18
Kotka, Fin.	G12	14
Kotlas, Sov. Un.	C7	29
Kotlik, Ak., U.S.	C7	79
Kotonkoro, Nig.	D6	45
Kotor, Yugo.	D4	24
Kotor Bay, b., Yugo.	C3	24
Kotor Varoš, Yugo.	C3	24
Kotovsk, Sov. Un.	E13	27
Kotovsk, Sov. Un.	H7	27
Kotri, Pak.	E2	37
Kottagūdem, India	C5	36
Kotte, Sri L.	*G6	36
Kotto, stm., Cen. Afr. Rep.	D4	47
Kotuy, stm., Sov. Un.	C13	29
Kotzebue, Ak., U.S.	B7	79
Kotzebue Sound, strt., Ak., U.S.	B7	79
Kouandé, Benin	D5	45
Kouango, Cen. Afr. Rep.	D4	46
Kouchibouguac, stm., N.B.	C4	71
Kouchibouguac National Park, N.B.	C5	71
Koula-Moutou, Gabon	F2	46
Koulikoro, Mali	D3	45
Koumra, Chad	D3	46
Koungheul, Sen.	D2	45
Kounradskiy, Sov. Un.	D9	28
Kountze, Tx., U.S.	D5	120
Koupéla, Burkina	D4	45
Kouri Island, i., Japan	N6	52
Kourou, Fr. Gu.	A4	59
Kouroussa, Gui.	D3	45
Koussi, Emi, mtn., Chad	B3	46
Koutiala, Mali	D3	45
Kouts, In., U.S.	B3	91
Kouvola, Fin.	G12	14
Ko Vaya, Az., U.S.	E4	80
Kovel, Sov. Un.	F5	27
Kovrov, Sov. Un.	C13	27
Kowloon, H.K.	G7	31
Köyceğiz, Tur.	D7	25
Koyuk, Ak., U.S.	C7	79
Koyuk, stm., Ak., U.S.	C8	79
Koyukuk, Ak., U.S.	B8	79
Koyukuk, stm., Ak., U.S.	B8	79
Kozan, Tur.	D10	40
Kozáni, Grc.	B3	25
Kozelsk, Sov. Un.	D10	27
Kozienice, Pol.	C6	26
Koźle, Pol.	C5	26
Kozloduy, Bul.	D6	24
Kozu-shima, i., Japan	I9	33
Kozuchów, Pol.	B2	26
Kpandu, Ghana	E4	45
Kra, Isthmus of, Asia	C1	34
Krabi, Thai.	H3	35
Kracheh, Camb.	C3	34
Kraemer, La., U.S.	k10	95
Kragerø, Nor.	H3	14
Kragujevac, Yugo.	C5	24
Kraków, Pol.	C5	26
Krakower, l., Ger.	E5	15
Kraljevo, Yugo.	D5	24
Královské Vinohrady (part of Prague), Czech.	n17	26
Kralupy [nad Vltavou], Czech.	n17	26
Králův Dvůr, Czech.	o17	26
Kramatorsk, Sov. Un.	G11	27
Kramer, In., U.S.	D3	91
Kramer, N.D., U.S.	A5	111
Kranidhion, Grc.	D4	25
Kranj, Yugo.	B2	24
Kranzburg, S.D., U.S.	C9	118
Kraslice, Czech.	C2	26
Krasnaya Polyana, Sov. Un.	q22	27
Krásník, Pol.	C7	26
Krasnoarmeysk, Sov. Un.	F15	27
Krasnoarmeysk, Sov. Un.	G15	27
Krasnoarmeysk, Sov. Un.	C7	28
Krasnodar, Sov. Un.	E6	29
Krasnodon, Sov. Un.	q22	27
Krasnogorsk, Sov. Un.	B11	33
Krasnograd, Sov. Un.	G10	27
Krasnogvardeyskoye, Sov. Un.	H13	27
Krasnokamsk, Sov. Un.	B5	28
Krasnoselkup, Sov. Un.	B25	8
Krasnoselye, Sov. Un.	G9	27
Krasnoslobodsk, Sov. Un.	D14	27
Krasnoslobodsk, Sov. Un.	D2	28
Krasnoturinsk, Sov. Un.	B6	28
Krasnoufimsk, Sov. Un.	D21	8
Krasnouralsk, Sov. Un.	B6	28
Krasnovishersk, Sov. Un.	A5	28
Krasnovodsk, Sov. Un.	D12	29
Krasnoyarsk, Sov. Un.	s31	14
Krasnoznamenskiy, Sov. Un.	C7	28
Krasnystaw, Pol.	C7	26
Krasnyy Kholm, Sov. Un.	B11	27
Krasnyy Kut, Sov. Un.	q21	27
Krasnyy Liman, Sov. Un.	q20	27
Krasnyy Luch, Sov. Un.	q21	27
Krasnyy Sulin, Sov. Un.	H13	27
Krasnyy Yar, Sov. Un.	F15	27
Kratovo, Yugo.	D6	24
Kraul Mountains, mts., Ant.	B11	7
Krawang, Indon.	*G3	34
Krebs, Ok., U.S.	C6	113
Krefeld, Ger.	C3	18
Kremenchug Reservoir, res., Sov. Un.	E5	29
Kremenets, Sov. Un.	F5	27
Kremennaya, Sov. Un.	p21	27
Kremikovtsi, Bul.	D6	24
Kremlin, Mt., U.S.	B6	103
Kremlin, Ok., U.S.	A4	113
Kremmling, Co., U.S.	A4	83
Krems [am der Donau], Aus.	E10	115
Kresgeville, Pa., U.S.	E10	115
Kress, Tx., U.S.	B2	120
Kreuzlingen, Switz.	A5	21
Krichev, Sov. Un.	E9	27
Kriens, Switz.	B4	21
Krilon, Cape, c., Sov. Un.	D11	33
Krilon Peninsula, pen., Sov. Un.	C10	33
Krishna, stm., India	E6	36
Krishnagiri, India	F6	36
Krishnanagar, India	F12	37
Kristiansand, Nor.	I6	14
Kristiansand, co., Swe.	F2	14
Kristianstad, Swe.	F9	14
Kristiinankaupunki, Fin.	F9	14
Kriva Palanka, Yugo.	D6	24
Krivoy Rog, Sov. Un.	H9	27
Kiževci, Yugo.	B3	24
Krk, i., Yugo.	D3	24
Krka, stm., Yugo.	C3	24
Krnov, Czech.	D4	26
Krokeaí, Grc.	D4	25
Krokstadelva, Nor.	p28	14
Krolevets, Sov. Un.	F9	27
Kroměříž, Czech.	D4	26
Kromy, Sov. Un.	E10	27
Kronach, Ger.	C6	18
Kronau, Sask.	G3	75
Kronoberg, co., Swe.	B7	15
Kronprins Olav Kyst, Ant.	B13	7
Kronshtadt, Sov. Un.	D5	15
Kröpelin, Ger.	D5	15
Kröslin, Ger.	I13	27
Krosno, Pol.	D6	26
Krosno Odrzańskie, Pol.	B2	26
Krotoszyn, Pol.	C4	26
Krotz Springs, La., U.S.	D4	95
Krško, Yugo.	C2	24
Kruger National Park, S. Afr.	C5	49
Krugersdorp, S. Afr.	C4	49
Kruibeke, Bel.	C4	17
Kruja, Alb.	B3	25
Krui, Indon.	A2	34
Krumovgrad, Bul.	E8	24
Kruševac, Yugo.	D5	24
Kruševo, Yugo.	B5	24
Kruszwica, Pol.	B5	26
Kruzof Island, i., Ak., U.S.	m21	79

Name — Map Ref. — Page

Krydor, Sask. — E2 75
Krymsk, Sov. Un. — I11 27
Krynica, Pol. — D6 26
Krynki, Pol. — B7 26
Ksar el Kebir, Mor. — B3 44
Ksar es Souk, Mor. — C4 44
Kuala Kangsar, Malay. — J4 35
Kualakurun, Indon. — F4 34
Kuala Lipis, Malay. — E2 34
Kuala Lumpur, Malay. — E2 34
Kualapuu, Hi., U.S. — B4 88
Kuala Terengganu, Malay. — D2 34
Kuandang, Indon. — E6 34
Kuandian, China — D11 31
Kuantan, Malay. — E2 34
Kuba, Sov. Un. — E3 28
Kuban, stm., Sov. Un. — I13 27
Kubitzer Bodden, b., Ger. — D7 15
Kubokawa, Japan — J6 33
Kuching, Malay. — E4 34
Kuchinoerabu Island, i., Japan — K5 33
Kuchino Island, i., Japan — L4 33
Kuçovë see Stalin, Alb. — B2 25
Küçükmenderes, stm., Tur. — C6 25
Kudaka Island, i., Japan — O5 52
Kudat, Malay. — D5 34
Kudirkos Naumiestis, Sov. Un. — A7 26
Kudus, Indon. — G4 34
Kudymkar, Sov. Un. — B4 28
Kuee Ruins, hist., Hi., U.S. — D6 88
Kufstein, Aus. — E6 18
Kuhayli, Sud. — B3 47
Kuhēsi, Alb. — A3 25
Kūh Lab, Ra's-e, c., Iran — I10 39
Kūhpāyeh, Iran — D2 48
Kuito, Ang. — D2 48
Kuiu Island, i., Ak., U.S. — m23 79
Kuji, Japan — F10 33
Kujū, Mount, mtn., Japan — J5 33
Kukaiau, Hi., U.S. — C6 88
Kukawa, Nig. — D7 45
Kuki, Japan — m18 33
Kukuihaele, Hi., U.S. — C6 88
Kukuiula, Hi., U.S. — B2 88
Kuku Point, c., Wake I. — A1 52
Kula, Bul. — D6 24
Kula, Tur. — C7 25
Kula, Hi., U.S. — C5 88
Kula, Yugo. — C4 24
Kula Kangri, mtn., Bhu. — C9 36
Kulebaki, Sov. Un. — D14 29
Kulim, Malay. — J4 35
Kulltorp, Swe. — A7 15
Kulm, N.D., U.S. — C7 111
Kulmbach, Ger. — C5 18
Kulpmont, Pa., U.S. — E9 115
Kulunda, Sov. Un. — C9 28
Kulunda, Lake, l., Sov. Un. — C9 28
Kulwin, Austl. — G4 51
Kulyab, Sov. Un. — H22 8
Küm, stm., S. Kor. — H3 33
Kuma, stm., Sov. Un. — F18 8
Kumagaya, Japan — m18 33
Kumai, Indon. — F4 34
Kumamoto, Japan — E11 31
Kumano Bay, b., Japan — J8 33
Kumanovo, Yugo. — D5 24
Kumasi, Ghana — E4 45
Kumba, Cam. — E1 46
Kumba-konam, India — F6 36
Kumbo, Cam. — D2 46
Kümhwa, S. Kor. — G3 33
Kumi, Ug. — A5 48
Kumihama, Japan — n14 33
Kumla, Swe. — H6 14
Kummerower Lake, l., Ger. — E6 15
Kumo, Nig. — E7 45
Kumukahi, Cape, c., Hi., U.S. — D7 88
Kuna, Id., U.S. — F2 89
Kundar, stm., Asia — B2 37
Kundiawa, Pap. N. Gui. — k11 50
Kuneitra (Al Qunaytirah), Isr. Occ. — A7 41
Kunggyü Lake, l., China — B9 37
Kunghit Island, i., B.C. — C2 69
Kungrad, Sov. Un. — E5 28
Kungsbacka, Swe. — A6 15
Kungsör, Swe. — t34 14
Kungu, Zaire — A2 48
Kungur, Sov. Un. — B5 28
Kunia, Hi., U.S. — g9 88
Kunigami, Japan — N6 52
Kunimi, Mount, mtn., Japan — J5 33
Kunkle, Pa., U.S. — m17 115
Kunlun Shan, mts., China — F11 30
Kunming, China — F5 31
Kunsan, S. Kor. — D10 31
Kunszentmárton, Hung. — B5 24
Künzelsau, Ger. — D4 19
Kuolayarvi, Sov. Un. — D13 14
Kuop, atoll, Micron. — Q18 52
Kuopio, Fin. — F12 14
Kupa, stm., Yugo. — C2 24
Kupang, Indon. — G6 34
Kupino, Sov. Un. — C9 28
Kupreanof, Ak., U.S. — m23 79
Kupreanof Island, i., Ak., U.S. — m23 79
Kupyansk, Sov. Un. — G11 27
Kur, stm., Sov. Un. — B7 33
Kura, stm., Asia — E3 28
Kurakhovo, Sov. Un. — r20 27
Kurashiki, Japan — I6 33
Kuray, Sov. Un. — E26 8
Kuraymah, Sud. — B3 47
Kurayyimah, Jord. — f13 41
Kurdistan, hist. reg., Asia — B4 38
Kurdufān al Janūbīyah (Southern Kurdufan), prov., Sud. — C2 47
Kurdufān ash Shamālīyah (Northern Kurdufan), prov., Sud. — C2 47
Kürdzhali, Bul. — E7 24
Kure, Japan — E11 31
Kure Island, i., Hi., U.S. — k12 88
Kuressaare, Sov. Un. — B4 27
Kureyka, Sov. Un. — C12 29
Kurgaldzhinskiy, Sov. Un. — C8 28
Kurgan, Sov. Un. — D9 29
Kurganinsk, Sov. Un. — G17 28
Kurgan-Tyube, Sov. Un. — H22 8
Kuria Muria Islands (Khūryān Mūryān), is., Oman — E5 38
Kurīgrām, Bngl. — E12 37
Kuril Islands, is., Sov. Un. — E17 29
Kuril Strait, strt., Sov. Un. — D18 29
Kurinskaya, Cape, c., Sov. Un. — H18 8
Kurmuk, Sud. — C3 47
Kurnool, India — E6 36
Kuro Island, i., Japan — K4 33
Kuroki, Sask. — F4 75
Kurovskoye, Sov. Un. — n18 27
Kurow, N.Z. — P13 51
Kurri Kurri, Austl. — F9 50
Kursk, Sov. Un. — D6 29

Kuršumlija, Yugo. — D5 24
Kurthwood, La., U.S. — C2 95
Kurtistown, Hi., U.S. — D6 88
Kurtz, In., U.S. — G5 91
Kurume, Japan — E11 31
Kurunegala, Sri L. — G7 36
Kuşadası, Tur. — D6 25
Kusakaki Island, i., Japan — K4 33
Kusatsu, Japan — n14 33
Kusel, Ger. — D2 19
Kushchevskaya, Sov. Un. — H12 27
Kushimoto, Japan — J7 33
Kushiro, Japan — C13 31
Kushka, Sov. Un. — F9 29
Kushmurun, Sov. Un. — C6 28
Kushmurun, Lake, l., Sov. Un. — C6 28
Kuskokwim, stm., Ak., U.S. — C8 79
Kuskokwim Bay, b., Ak., U.S. — D7 79
Kuskokwim Mountains, mts., Ak., U.S. — C8 79
Kuş Lake, l., Tur. — B6 25
Küsnacht, Switz. — B6 21
Küssnacht [am Rigi], Switz. — B5 21
Küsten, Sov. Un. — D9 29
Küsten Canal, Ger. — B7 17
Küstī, Sud. — C3 47
Kut, i., Thai. — G5 35
Kuta, Alb. — B2 25
Kutacane, Indon. — C7 40
Kutch, Gulf of see Kachchh, Gulf of, b., India — D4 36
Kutch, Rann of, pl., Asia — D4 36
Kutina, Yugo. — C3 24
Kutná Hora, Czech. — D3 26
Kutno, Pol. — B5 26
Kuttawa, Ky., U.S. — e9 94
Kutu, Zaire — B2 48
Kutum, Sud. — C1 47
Kuturaja see Banda Aceh, Indon. — k11 34
Kuty, Sov. Un. — A7 24
Kutztown, Pa., U.S. — E10 115
Kuujjuaq, Que. — g13 74
Kuum-ni, N. Kor. — G2 33
Kuusamo, Fin. — E13 14
Kuvandyk, Sov. Un. — E20 8
Kuwait (Al Kuwayt), Kuw. — C4 38
Kuwait, ctry., Asia — C4 38
Kuwait Bay, b., Kuw. — G4 39
Kuwana, Japan — m17 33
Kuybyshev, Sov. Un. — B9 28
Kuybyshev see Samara, Sov. Un. — D8 29
Kuybyshevo, Sov. Un. — H12 27
Kuybyshev Reservoir, res., Sov. Un. — D7 29
Küysanjaq, Iraq — D15 40
Kuyto, l., Sov. Un. — E14 14
Kuznetsk, Sov. Un. — E16 27
Kuznetsk Basin, Sov. Un. — D25 8
Kuznetsovo, Sov. Un. — C10 33
Kuzomen, Sov. Un. — D17 14
Kvarner, b., Yugo. — C2 24
Kvismare Kanal, Swe. — t33 14
Kvitøya, i., Nor. — A11 128
Kwajalein, atoll, Marsh Is. — F10 6
Kwajalein Island, i., Marsh Is. — S17 52
Kwakoegron, Sur. — A3 59
Kwale, Kenya — B6 48
Kwa Mashu, S. Afr. — *C5 49
Kwamouth, Zaire — B2 48
Kwa Mtoro, Tan. — C6 48
Kwangju, S. Kor. — D10 31
Kwango (Cuango), stm., Afr. — C2 48
Kwangsi Chuang see Guangxi Zhuangzu, prov., China — G6 31
Kwangtung see Guangdong, prov., China — G7 31
Kwatisore, Indon. — F8 34
Kweichow see Guizhou, prov., China — F6 31
Kwekwe, Zimb. — A4 49
Kwenge, stm., Afr. — C2 48
Kwethluk, Ak., U.S. — C7 79
Kwidzyn, Pol. — B5 26
Kwigillingok, Ak., U.S. — D7 79
Kwilu, stm., Afr. — B2 48
Kwinana, Austl. — F2 50
Kwoka, Mount, mtn., Indon. — F9 34
Kyabé, Chad — D3 46
Kyaikto, Burma — D2 35
Kyakhta, Sov. Un. — D13 29
Kyaukpadaung, Burma — B1 35
Kyaukpyu, Burma — E9 36
Kyaukse, Burma — D10 36
Kybartai, Sov. Un. — A7 26
Kyle, Czech. — n18 26
Kyle, Sask. — G1 75
Kyle, Tx., U.S. — E4 120
Kyle Ford, Tn., U.S. — C10 119
Kylestrome, Scot., U.K. — B7 13
Kyll, stm., Ger. — E6 17
Kyllburg, Ger. — D6 17
Kyōga, Cape, c., Japan — I7 33
Kyoga, Lake, l., Ug. — A5 48
Kyōmipo see Songnim, N. Kor. — G2 33
Kyonggi Bay, b., Asia — F2 33
Kyongju, S. Kor. — D10 31
Kyongsong, N. Kor. — F4 33
Kyōto, Japan — D12 31
Kyritz, Ger. — B6 18
Kyrkjebö, Nor. — G1 14
Kyrock, Ky., U.S. — C3 94
Kyshtovka, Sov. Un. — D24 8
Kyshtym, Sov. Un. — C4 28
Kyuquot Sound, strt., B.C. — E4 69
Kyūroku Island, i., Japan — F9 33
Kyūshū, i., Japan — E11 31
Kyustendil, Bul. — D6 24
Kyzyl, Sov. Un. — D12 29
Kyzyl-Kiya, Sov. Un. — E8 28
Kyzyl-Kum, des., Sov. Un. — E9 28
Kyzyltas Mountains, mts., Sov. Un. — D9 28
Kzyl-Orda, Sov. Un. — E9 28

L

Laa [an der Thaya], Aus. — D8 18
Laage, Ger. — E6 15
La Almunia de Doña Godina, Spain — B5 22
Laas Caanood, Som. — D6 47
La Asunción, Ven. — A5 60

Laau Point, c., Hi., U.S. — B4 88
Labadie, Mo., U.S. — C7 102
Labadieville, La., U.S. — E5 95
La Banda, Arg. — E3 55
La Barca, Mex. — C4 63
La Barge, Wy., U.S. — D2 127
La Barge Creek, stm., Wy., U.S. — D2 127
Labasa, Fiji — H15 52
La Baule-Escoublac, Fr. — D2 16
Labe, Gui. — D2 45
Labe (Elbe), stm., Eur. — C7 18
Labelle, Que. — C3 74
La Belle, Fl., U.S. — F5 86
La Belle, Mo., U.S. — A6 102
Labelle, co., Que. — C2 74
La Belle-Île, i., Fr. — D2 16
Laberge, Lake, l., Yukon — D5 66
Labette, Ks., U.S. — E8 93
Labette, co., Ks., U.S. — E8 93
Labette Creek, stm., Ks., U.S. — E8 93
Labin, Yugo. — C2 24
La Bisbal, Spain — B7 22
Labo, Phil. — o14 34
Labo, Mount, mtn., Phil. — p14 34
La Boca, Pan. — m11 62
Laboe, Ger. — D4 15
La Bolt, S.D., U.S. — *B9 118
Laboulaye, Arg. — A4 54
Labouheyre, Fr. — E3 16
Labrador, reg., Newf. — g9 72
Labrador City, Newf. — h8 72
Labrador Sea, N.A. — g10 72
Lábrea, Braz. — D2 59
La Brea, Trin. — O22 65
La Broquerie, Man. — E3 70
Labuan Island, i., Malay. — D4 34
Labuha, Indon. — F7 34
Labuhanbilik, Indon. — K4 35
Labuk Bay, b., Malay. — D5 34
Lac-à-Beauce, Que. — B5 74
Lacadena, Sask. — G1 75
La Calera, Chile — B2 54
Lacamp, La., U.S. — C3 95
La Canada Flintridge, Ca., U.S. — m12 82
La Capelle [-en-Thiérache], Fr. — C5 16
La Carlota, Arg. — A4 54
La Carolina, Spain — C4 22
Lac-aux-Brochets, Que. — B5 74
Lac-aux-Sables, Que. — C5 74
Lac-Baker, N.B. — B1 71
Lac-Beauport, Que. — n17 74
Lac-Bouchette, Que. — A5 74
Lac-Brome, Que. — D5 74
Lac Courte Oreilles Indian Reservation, Wi., U.S. — C2 126
Lac-des-Écorces, Que. — C2 74
Lac-des-Seize-Îles, Que. — D3 74
Lac du Bonnet, Man. — D3 70
Lac du Flambeau, Wi., U.S. — C4 126
Lac du Flambeau Indian Reservation, Wi., U.S. — C3 126
Lac-Édouard, Que. — B5 74
La Ceiba, Hond. — D7 63
La Ceiba, Ven. — B3 60
La Center, Ky., U.S. — e9 94
Lac-Etchemin, Que. — C7 74
Lacey, Wa., U.S. — B3 124
Laceys Spring, Al., U.S. — A3 78
Laceyville, Pa., U.S. — C9 115
Lac-Frontière, Que. — C7 74
La Charité, Fr. — D5 16
La Chartre, Fr. — C4 16
La Chaux-de-Fonds, Switz. — E3 18
Lachay, Punta, c., Peru — D2 58
Lachen, Switz. — B6 21
Lachine, Que. — D4 74
Lachine, Mi., U.S. — C7 99
Lachlan, stm., Austl. — F8 50
La Chorrera, Col. — D3 60
La Chorrera, Pan. — F2 62
Lachute, Que. — D3 74
Laçi, Alb. — B2 25
La Cienega, N.M., U.S. — h8 108
La Ciotat, Fr. — F6 16
Lackawanna, N.Y., U.S. — C2 109
Lackawanna, co., Pa., U.S. — D10 115
Lackawaxen, Pa., U.S. — D12 115
Lackland Air Force Base, mil., Tx., U.S. — k7 120
Lac La Belle, Mi., U.S. — A2 99
Lac La Hache, B.C. — D7 69
Lac la Ronge Provincial Park, Sask. — B3 75
Laclede, Id., U.S. — A2 89
La Clede, Il., U.S. — E5 90
Laclede, Mo., U.S. — B4 102
Laclede, co., Mo., U.S. — D5 102
Lac-Mégantic, Que. — D7 74
La Cocha, Arg. — E2 55
Lacolle, Que. — D4 74
La Colorada, Mex. — C3 63
Lacomb, Or., U.S. — C4 114
Lacombe, Alta. — C4 68
Lacombe, La., U.S. — D6 95
Lacombe Bayou, stm., La., U.S. — h12 95
Lacon, Il., U.S. — B4 90
Lacona, Ia., U.S. — C4 92
Lacona, N.Y., U.S. — B4 109
La Concepción, Pan. — F6 62
La Conception, Que. — C3 74
Laconia, In., U.S. — H5 91
Laconia, N.H., U.S. — C4 106
Laconia, Tn., U.S. — B2 119
Laconia, Gulf of, b., Grc. — M6 25
La Conner, Wa., U.S. — A3 124
Lacoochee, Fl., U.S. — D4 86
La Coruña, Spain — A1 22
Lacota, Mi., U.S. — F4 99
La Courneuve, Fr. — g10 16
Lacq, Fr. — I5 16
Lac qui Parle, co., Mn., U.S. — F2 100
Lac qui Parle, stm., Mn., U.S. — F2 100
Lac qui Parle, West Branch, stm., Mn., U.S. — F2 100
La Creek Lake, l., S.D., U.S. — D4 118
La Crescent, Mn., U.S. — G7 100
La Crescenta, Ca., U.S. — *m12 82
La Crete, Alta. — f7 68
La Crosse, Ar., U.S. — A4 81
La Crosse, Fl., U.S. — C4 86

La Crosse, In., U.S. — B4 91
La Crosse, Ks., U.S. — D4 93
La Crosse, Va., U.S. — D4 123
Lacrosse, Wa., U.S. — C8 124
La Crosse, Wi., U.S. — E2 126
La Crosse, co., Wi., U.S. — E2 126
La Crosse, stm., Wi., U.S. — E3 126
La Cruz, Col. — C2 60
La Cruz, C.R. — E5 62
La Cruz, Mex. — C5 63
La Cruz [de Río Grande], Nic. — D5 62
Lac-Saguay, Que. — C2 74
Lac-Saint-Jean-Est, co., Que. — A6 74
Lac-Saint-Jean-Ouest, co., Que. — A5 74
Lac-Vert, Sask. — E3 75
La Cygne, Ks., U.S. — D9 93
Ladário, Braz. — B1 56
Ladd, Il., U.S. — B4 90
Ladder Creek, stm., Ks., U.S. — D2 93
Laddonia, Mo., U.S. — B6 102
Ladelle, Ar., U.S. — D4 81
Ladera Heights, Ca., U.S. — *m12 82
La Désirade, i., Guad. — Q9 65
Ladies Island, i., S.C., U.S. — G6 117
Ladispoli, Italy — h8 23
Ladner, B.C. — f13 69
Lādnūn, India — E4 36
Ladoga, In., U.S. — E4 91
Ladoga, Lake, l., Sov. Un. — C6 29
Ladonia, Tx., U.S. — C5 120
Ladora, Ia., U.S. — C5 92
La Dorada, Col. — B3 60
Ladson, S.C., U.S. — F7 117
Ladue, Mo., U.S. — *C7 102
Ladue, Mo., U.S. — C7 102
Ladybank, Scot., U.K. — D5 13
Ladybrand, S. Afr. — C4 49
Lady Lake, Fl., U.S. — D5 86
Lady Laurier, Mount, mtn., B.C. — A6 69
Ladysmith, B.C. — E6 69
Ladysmith, S. Afr. — C4 49
Ladysmith, Wi., U.S. — C2 126
Lae, Pap. N. Gui. — k12 50
Læsø, i., Den. — A4 15
La Esmeralda, Ven. — C4 60
La Esperanza, Cuba — C2 64
La Esperanza, Hond. — C3 62
La Estrada, Spain — A1 22
La Estrella, Bol. — C5 55
La Farge, Wi., U.S. — E3 126
Lafayette, Al., U.S. — C4 78
Lafayette, Ca., U.S. — *h8 82
Lafayette, Co., U.S. — B5 83
Lafayette, Ga., U.S. — B1 87
La Fayette, Il., U.S. — B4 90
Lafayette, In., U.S. — D4 91
Lafayette, Ky., U.S. — D2 94
Lafayette, La., U.S. — D3 95
Lafayette, Mn., U.S. — F4 100
Lafayette, N.J., U.S. — A3 107
La Fayette, N.Y., U.S. — C4 109
Lafayette, Oh., U.S. — B1 112
Lafayette, Or., U.S. — B3 114
Lafayette, R.I., U.S. — E4 116
Lafayette, Tn., U.S. — A5 119
Lafayette, co., Ar., U.S. — D2 81
Lafayette, co., Fl., U.S. — C3 86
Lafayette, co., La., U.S. — D3 95
Lafayette, co., Ms., U.S. — A4 101
Lafayette, co., Mo., U.S. — B4 102
Lafayette, co., Wi., U.S. — F3 126
Lafayette, Mount, mtn., N.H., U.S. — B3 106
Lafayette Southwest, La., U.S. — *D3 95
Lafe, Ar., U.S. — A5 81
La Fère, Fr. — C5 16
La Feria, Tx., U.S. — F4 120
La Ferté-Bernard, Fr. — C4 16
La Ferté-Macé, Fr. — C5 16
La Ferté-sous-Jouarre, Fr. — C5 16
Lafferty, Oh., U.S. — B4 112
Lafia, Nig. — E6 45
Lafiagi, Nig. — E6 45
Lafitte, La., U.S. — k11 95
Laflèche, Sask. — H2 75
La Flèche, Fr. — D3 16
La Follette, Tn., U.S. — C9 119
La Fontaine, In., U.S. — C6 91
Lafontaine, Ks., U.S. — E8 93
Lafourche, La., U.S. — E5 95
Lafourche, co., La., U.S. — E5 95
Lafourche, Bayou, stm., La., U.S. — E5 95
La France, S.C., U.S. — B2 117
La Galeria, stm., Italy — h8 23
La Galite, i., Tun. — G4 44
Lagan, Swe. — I5 14
Lage, Ger. — B8 19
Lågen, stm., Nor. — G3 14
Lagg, Scot., U.K. — E3 13
Laggan, Loch, res., Scot., U.K. — D4 13
Laggan Bay, b., Scot., U.K. — E2 13
Laghouat, Alg. — C5 44
La Gloria, Col. — B3 60
Lagny, Fr. — C5 16
Lago, Mount, mtn., Wa., U.S. — A5 124
Lagoa, Port. — D1 22
Lagonda, La., U.S. — *E4 95
Lago Posadas, Arg. — D2 54
Lago Ranco, Chile — E2 55
Lagos, Nig. — E5 45
Lagos, Port. — D1 22
Lagos de Moreno, Mex. — C4 63
La Goulette, Tun. — *B7 44
Lago Viedma, Arg. — D2 54
La Grand'Combe, Fr. — E6 16
La Grande, Or., U.S. — B8 114
La Grande, stm., Que. — h11 74
La Grande Deux, Réservoir, res., Que. — h11 74
La Grande Quatre, Réservoir, res., Que. — F18 6
La Grange, Ar., U.S. — C5 81
La Grange, Ga., U.S. — *D6 86
Lagrange, Il., U.S. — B6 90
La Grange, In., U.S. — A7 91
Lagrange, In., U.S. — A7 91
La Grange, Ky., U.S. — B4 94
La Grange, Mo., U.S. — A6 102
La Grange, N.C., U.S. — B5 110
Lagrange, Oh., U.S. — A3 112
La Grange, Tn., U.S. — B2 119
La Grange, Tx., U.S. — E4 120
La Grange, Wy., U.S. — E8 127
Lagrange, co., In., U.S. — A7 91
La Grange Highlands, Il., U.S. — *k9 90
La Gran Sabana, pl., Ven. — B5 60
Lagro, In., U.S. — C6 91

La Grue Bayou, stm., Ar., U.S. — C4 81
La Guadeloupe (Saint-Evariste), Que. — D7 74
La Guaira, Ven. — A4 60
La Guardia, Spain — B1 22
La Guata, Hond. — C4 62
Laguna, Braz. — D3 56
Laguna, N.M., U.S. — B2 108
Laguna Beach, Ca., U.S. — F5 82
Laguna Dam, U.S. — E1 80
Laguna Hills, Ca., U.S. — *n13 82
Laguna Indian Reservation, N.M., U.S. — C2 108
Laguna Niguel, Ca., U.S. — *F5 82
Lagunas, Peru — C2 58
Lagunillas, Bol. — C5 55
La Habana, prov., Cuba — C6 64
La Habra, Ca., U.S. — *n13 82
Lahad Datu, Malay. — E5 34
Lahaina, Hi., U.S. — C5 88
La Harpe, Il., U.S. — C3 90
La Harpe, Ks., U.S. — E8 93
Lahat, Indon. — F2 34
La Have, N.S. — E5 71
La Have, stm., N.S. — E5 71
La Have Island, i., N.S. — E5 71
Lahfān, Bi'r, well, Eg. — D5 41
Lāhījān, Iran — C5 39
Lahn, stm., Ger. — C4 18
Laholm, Swe. — B7 15
Laholmsbukten, b., Swe. — B6 15
Lahore, Pak. — B5 36
Lahore Cantonment, Pak. — *B5 36
Lahr, Ger. — D3 18
Lahri, Pak. — E4 36
Lahti, Fin. — G11 14
La Huaca, Peru — B1 58
Laï, Chad — D3 46
Lai Chau, Viet. — A5 35
Laichow Bay see Laizhou Wan, b., China — D8 31
Laide, Scot., U.K. — C3 13
Laidon, Loch, l., Scot., U.K. — D4 13
Laie, Hi., U.S. — B4 88
Laifeng, China — J3 32
L'Aigle, Fr. — C4 16
L'Aigle Creek, stm., Ar., U.S. — D3 81
Laihka, Burma — B2 35
Laingsburg, S. Afr. — D3 49
Laingsburg, Mi., U.S. — F6 99
Laird, Ky., U.S. — C5 94
Laird, Sask. — E2 75
Laird, Co., U.S. — A8 83
Lairg, Scot., U.K. — C4 13
Lairi, Batha de, stm., Chad — C3 46
Laiwui, Indon. — F7 34
Laiyang, China — D9 31
Laiyuan, China — E6 32
Laizhou Wan, b., China — D8 31
La Jalca, Peru — B2 58
La Jara, Co., U.S. — D5 83
La Jara, N.M., U.S. — A3 108
Laje Point, c., Port. — f9 22
La Jolla, Point, c., Ca., U.S. — o15 82
La Jose, Pa., U.S. — E5 115
Lajosmizse, Hung. — B4 24
La Joya (part of Mexico City), Mex. — h9 63
La Joya, Peru — E3 58
La Junta, Co., U.S. — D7 83
Lajes, Braz. — C3 57
Lake, Ms., U.S. — C4 101
Lake, co., Ca., U.S. — C2 82
Lake, co., Co., U.S. — B4 83
Lake, co., Fl., U.S. — D5 86
Lake, co., Il., U.S. — A6 90
Lake, co., In., U.S. — B3 91
Lake, co., Mi., U.S. — E5 99
Lake, co., Mn., U.S. — C7 100
Lake, co., Mt., U.S. — C2 103
Lake, co., Oh., U.S. — A4 112
Lake, co., Or., U.S. — E6 114
Lake, co., S.D., U.S. — C8 118
Lake, co., Tn., U.S. — A2 119
Lake Alfred, Fl., U.S. — D5 86
Lake Andes, S.D., U.S. — D7 118
Lake Ariel, Pa., U.S. — D11 115
Lake Arrowhead, Ca., U.S. — E5 82
Lake Arthur, La., U.S. — D3 95
Lake Arthur, N.M., U.S. — E5 108
Lakeba Passage, strt., Fiji — H16 52
Lake Barcroft, Va., U.S. — *B5 123
Lake Benton, Mn., U.S. — F2 100
Lake Beseck, Ct., U.S. — D5 84
Lake Beulah, Wi., U.S. — n11 126
Lake Bluff, Il., U.S. — A6 90
Lake Bonaparte, N.Y., U.S. — A5 109
Lake Bronson, Mn., U.S. — B2 100
Lake Bruce, In., U.S. — B4 91
Lake Butler, Fl., U.S. — B4 86
Lake Cargelligo, Austl. — F8 50
Lake Carmel, N.Y., U.S. — *E7 109
Lake Carroll, Il., U.S. — *A4 90
Lake Charles, La., U.S. — D2 95
Lake Chelan National Recreation Area, Wa., U.S. — A5 124
Lake City, Ar., U.S. — B5 81
Lake City, Co., U.S. — D3 83
Lake City, Fl., U.S. — B4 86
Lake City, Ia., U.S. — B3 92
Lake City, Ks., U.S. — E5 93
Lake City, Mi., U.S. — D5 99
Lake City, Mn., U.S. — F6 100
Lake City, Pa., U.S. — B1 115
Lake City, S.C., U.S. — D8 117
Lake City, S.D., U.S. — B8 118
Lake City, Tn., U.S. — C9 119
Lake Clark National Park, U.S. — C9 79
Lake Cormorant, Ms., U.S. — A3 101
Lake Cowichan, B.C. — g11 69
Lakecreek, Or., U.S. — E4 114
Lake Crystal, Mn., U.S. — F4 100
Lake Delton, Wi., U.S. — E4 126
Lake District, reg., Eng., U.K. — G10 13
Lake Elmo, Mn., U.S. — *n13 100
Lake Elsinore, Ca., U.S. — F5 82
Lake Erie Beach, N.Y., U.S. — C1 109
Lakefield, Mn., U.S. — G3 100

Lake Forest, Fl., U.S. — *s13 86
Lake Forest, Il., U.S. — A6 90
Lake Fork, Id., U.S. — E2 89
Lake Fork, stm., Co., U.S. — C3 83
Lake Fork, stm., Ut., U.S. — C5 121
Lake Geneva, Wi., U.S. — F5 126
Lake George, Co., U.S. — C5 83
Lake George, Mi., U.S. — E6 99
Lake George, N.Y., U.S. — B7 109
Lake Grinnell, N.J., U.S. — A3 107
Lake Grove, N.Y., U.S. — *E7 109
Lake Harbour, N.W. Ter. — D19 66
Lake Havasu City, Az., U.S. — C1 80
Lake Helen, Fl., U.S. — D5 86
Lake Hiawatha, N.J., U.S. — B4 107
Lake Hubert, Mn., U.S. — D4 100
Lake Hughes, Ca., U.S. — E4 82
Lake Huntington, N.Y., U.S. — D5 109
Lakehurst, N.J., U.S. — C4 107
Lakehurst Naval Air Station, mil., N.J., U.S. — C4 107
Lake in the Hills, Il., U.S. — h8 90
Lake Itasca, Mn., U.S. — C3 100
Lake Jackson, Tx., U.S. — E5 120
Lake Katrine, N.Y., U.S. — D7 109
Lakeland, Fl., U.S. — D5 86
Lakeland, Ga., U.S. — E3 87
Lakeland Highlands, Fl., U.S. — *E5 86
Lake Leelanau, Mi., U.S. — D5 99
Lake Lenore, Sask. — E3 75
Lake Lillian, Mn., U.S. — F4 100
Lake Linden, Mi., U.S. — A2 99
Lake Lindsey, Fl., U.S. — D4 86
Lake Lorraine, Fl., U.S. — *u15 86
Lake Louise, Alta. — D2 68
Lake Luzerne, N.Y., U.S. — B7 109
Lake Magdalene, Fl., U.S. — o11 86
Lake Mary, Fl., U.S. — D5 86
Lake McDonald, Mt., U.S. — B3 103
Lake Mead National Recreation Area, U.S. — H7 105
Lake Meredith National Recreation Area, Tx., U.S. — B2 120
Lake Metigoshe, N.D., U.S. — A5 111
Lake Mills, Ia., U.S. — A4 92
Lake Mills, Wi., U.S. — E5 126
Lake Minchumina, Ak., U.S. — C9 79
Lakemont, Pa., U.S. — F5 115
Lake Mountain, mtn., Wy., U.S. — E6 127
Lakemore, Oh., U.S. — A4 112
Lakenan, Mo., U.S. — B5 102
Lake Nebagamon, Wi., U.S. — B2 126
Lake Norden, S.D., U.S. — C8 118
Lake Odessa, Mi., U.S. — F5 99
Lake Of The Woods, co., Mn., U.S. — B4 100
Lake Orion, Mi., U.S. — F7 99
Lake Oswego, Or., U.S. — B4 114
Lake Ozark, Mo., U.S. — C5 102
Lake Park, Fl., U.S. — F6 86
Lake Park, Ga., U.S. — F3 87
Lake Park, Ia., U.S. — A2 92
Lake Park, Mn., U.S. — D2 100
Lake Placid, Fl., U.S. — E5 86
Lake Placid, N.Y., U.S. — A7 109
Lake Pleasant, N.Y., U.S. — B6 109
Lake Pontchartrain Causeway, La., U.S. — h11 95
Lakeport, Ca., U.S. — C2 82
Lake Preston, S.D., U.S. — C8 118
Lake Providence, La., U.S. — B4 95
Lake Range, mts., Nv., U.S. — C2 105
Lakeridge, Va., U.S. — *B5 123
Lake Ridge, Va., U.S. — B5 123
Lake River, Ont. — n19 73
Lake Ronkonkoma, N.Y., U.S. — *n15 109
Lake Shore, Md., U.S. — B5 97
Lakeshore, Ms., U.S. — *E4 101
Lake Shore, Ut., U.S. — *C4 121
Lakeside, N.S. — E6 71
Lakeside, Ca., U.S. — F5 82
Lakeside, Ct., U.S. — C3 84
Lakeside, Mt., U.S. — B2 103
Lakeside, Oh., U.S. — A3 112
Lakeside, Or., U.S. — D2 114
Lakeside, Tx., U.S. — n9 120
Lakeside, Va., U.S. — *B5 123
Lakeside Mountains, mts., Ut., U.S. — B3 121
Lakeside Park, Ky., U.S. — h13 94
Lakeside-Pinetop, Az., U.S. — C6 80
Lake Station, In., U.S. — A3 91
Lake Station, Ok., U.S. — B5 113
Lake Stevens, Wa., U.S. — A3 124
Lake Superior Provincial Park, Ont. — p18 73
Lake Swamp, stm., S.C., U.S. — D8 117
Lake Tansi, Tn., U.S. — D8 119
Lake Telemark, N.J., U.S. — B4 107
Lake Tomahawk, Wi., U.S. — C4 126
Laketon, Tx., U.S. — B2 120
Laketown, Ut., U.S. — B4 121
Lake Toxaway, N.C., U.S. — f10 110
Lake Traverse, Ont. — B6 73
Lake Valley, Sask. — G2 75
Lake Valley, val., Nv., U.S. — *B1 87
Lakeview, Ar., U.S. — A3 81
Lakeview, Ca., U.S. — B2 82
Lakeview, Ga., U.S. — B2 87
Lakeview, Id., U.S. — A2 89
Lakeview, Mi., U.S. — E5 99
Lakeview, Mt., U.S. — F5 103
Lake View, N.Y., U.S. — C2 109
Lakeview, Oh., U.S. — B2 112
Lakeview, Or., U.S. — E6 114
Lake View, S.C., U.S. — C9 117
Lakeview, Tx., U.S. — B2 120
Lake Village, Ar., U.S. — D4 81
Lake Village, In., U.S. — B3 91
Lakeville, Ct., U.S. — B2 84
Lakeville, Ma., U.S. — C6 98
Lakeville, Mn., U.S. — F5 100
Lakeville, N.Y., U.S. — C3 109
Lake Waccamaw, N.C., U.S. — C4 110
Lake Wales, Fl., U.S. — E5 86
Lake Williams, N.D., U.S. — B6 111
Lake Wilson, Mn., U.S. — G3 100
Lake Winola, Pa., U.S. — m17 115
Lake Wissota, Wi., U.S. — *D2 126
Lakewood, Ca., U.S. — n12 82
Lakewood, Co., U.S. — B5 83
Lakewood, Il., U.S. — D5 90
Lakewood, Ia., U.S. — f8 92
Lakewood, Me., U.S. — D3 96

Name	Map Ref.	Page

Lakewood, N.J., U.S. C4 107
Lakewood, N.M., U.S. E5 108
Lakewood, N.Y., U.S. C1 109
Lakewood, Oh., U.S. A4 112
Lakewood, Pa., U.S. C10 115
Lakewood, Wa., U.S. A3 124
Lakewood Center, Wa., U.S. . . B3 124
Lake Worth, Fl., U.S. F6 86
Lake Worth Inlet, b., Fl., U.S. . F7 86
Lake Zurich, Il., U.S. h8 90
Lakhī, Afg. B3 36
Lakhīmpur, India C7 36
Lakhta (part of Leningrad),
  Sov. Un. r31 14
Lakin, Ks., U.S. E2 93
Lakota, I.C. E3 45
Lakota, Ia., U.S. A3 92
Lakota, N.D., U.S. A7 111
Laksefjorden, Nor. B12 14
Lakshadweep (Laccadive,
  Minicoy and Amīndīvi
  Islands), ter., India *F5 36
Lakshadweep (Laccadive
  Islands), is., India F5 36
La Laguna, Spain m13 22
La Libertad, El Sal. D3 62
La Libertad, Guat. B2 62
La Libertad, dept., Peru C2 58
La Ligua, Chile A2 54
Lalín, Spain A1 22
La Línea, Spain D3 22
La Loche, Sask. m7 75
La Loche, Lac, l., Sask. A6 68
La Loma, N.M., U.S. B4 108
La Luz, N.M., U.S. D4 108
La Macarena, Serranía de,
  mts., Col. C3 60
La Machine, Fr. D5 16
La Maddalena, Italy D2 23
La Madera, N.M., U.S. A3 108
Lama-Kara, Togo E5 45
La Malbaie, Que. B7 74
Lamaline, Newf. E4 72
La Mancha, reg., Spain C4 22
Lamanibot Sanhilo, Puntan, c.,
  N. Mar. Is. D7 52
Lamar, Ar., U.S. B2 81
Lamar, Co., U.S. C8 83
Lamar, In., U.S. H4 91
Lamar, Ms., U.S. A4 101
Lamar, Mo., U.S. D3 102
Lamar, Ne., U.S. D4 104
Lamar, Ok., U.S. B5 113
Lamar, Pa., U.S. D7 115
Lamar, S.C., U.S. C7 117
Lamar, co., Al., U.S. B1 78
Lamar, co., Ga., U.S. C2 87
Lamar, co., Ms., U.S. D4 101
Lamar, co., Tx., U.S. C5 120
Lamar, stm., Wy., U.S. B2 127
Lamarche, Fr. A1 20
La Marmora, Punta, mtn., Italy D2 23
La Marque, Tx., U.S. *r15 120
Lamas, Peru C2 58
Lamasco, Ky., U.S. f10 94
La Mauricie, Parc National de,
  Que. C5 74
Lamb, co., Tx., U.S. B1 120
Lamballe, Fr. C2 16
Lambaréné, Gabon F2 46
Lambayeque, Peru C2 58
Lambayeque, dept., Peru . . . C2 58
Lambay Island, i., Ire. D5 11
Lambert, Ms., U.S. A3 101
Lambert, Mt., U.S. C12 103
Lambert, Ok., U.S. A3 113
Lambert Glacier, ice, Ant. . . . B19 7
Lambert Lake, Me., U.S. C5 96
Lamberton, Mn., U.S. F3 100
Lambert's Bay, S. Afr. D2 49
Lambertville, Mi., U.S. G7 99
Lambertville, N.J., U.S. C3 107
Lambeth, Ont. E3 73
Lambeth (part of London),
  Eng., U.K. m12 10
Lambourn, Eng., U.K. C6 12
Lambrecht (Pfalz), Ger. D3 19
Lambro, stm., Italy D5 20
Lambrook, Ar., U.S. C5 81
Lambsburg, Va., U.S. D2 123
Lamb's Head, c., Ire. F1 11
Lambton, Que. D6 74
Lambton, co., Ont. E2 73
Lambton, Cape, c., N.W. Ter. . B8 66
Lamdessar, Indon. G8 34
Lame Deer, Mt., U.S. E10 103
Lamego, Port. B2 22
Lamèque, N.B. B5 71
Lamèque, Île, i., N.B. B5 71
La Merced (Superi), Arg. . . . E2 55
La Mesa, Ca., U.S. F5 82
La Mesa, N.M., U.S. E3 108
Lamesa, Tx., U.S. C2 120
Lamia, Grc. C4 40
La Minerve, Que. C3 74
Lamington, Mount, mtn., Pap.
  N. Gui. k12 50
La Mirada, Ca., U.S. *E4 82
Lamlam, Mount, mtn., Guam . M9 52
Lamlash, Scot., U.K. E3 13
Lammermuir Hills, hills, Scot.,
  U.K. E6 13
Lammhult, Swe. A8 15
Lamoil, i., Micron. Q18 52
La Moille, Il., U.S. B4 90
Lamoille, Nv., U.S. C6 105
Lamoille, co., Vt., U.S. B3 122
Lamoille, stm., Vt., U.S. B3 122
Lamoille, North Branch, stm.,
  Vt., U.S. B3 122
La Moine, stm., Il., U.S. C3 90
Lamona, Wa., U.S. B7 124
Lamon Bay, b., Phil. C6 34
Lamoni, Ia., U.S. D4 92
Lamont, Alta. C4 68
Lamont, Ca., U.S. E4 82
Lamont, Fl., U.S. B3 86
Lamont, Ia., U.S. B6 92
Lamont, Ks., U.S. D7 93
Lamont, Ms., U.S. B2 101
Lamont, Ok., U.S. A4 113
Lamont, Wa., U.S. B8 124
Lamont, Wy., U.S. D5 127
La Monte, Mo., U.S. C4 102
La Motte, Il., U.S. B7 92
La Motte, Isle, i., Vt., U.S. . . . B2 122
La Moure, N.D., U.S. C7 111
La Moure, co., N.D., U.S. . . . C7 111
Lampa, Peru E3 58
Lampang, Thai. B1 34
Lampasas, Tx., U.S. D3 120
Lampasas, co., Tx., U.S. D3 120
Lampertheim, Ger. D3 19

Lampeter, Wales, U.K. B3 12
Lamphun, Thai. C3 35
Lampman, Sask. H4 75
Lamprey, stm., N.H., U.S. . . . D4 106
Lamu, Kenya B7 48
La Mure, Fr. E6 16
Lamy, N.M., U.S. B4 108
Lanagan, Mo., U.S. E3 102
Lanai, i., Hi., U.S. C4 88
Lanai City, Hi., U.S. C5 88
Lanaihale, mtn., Hi., U.S. . . . C5 88
Lanak La, Asia B7 36
Lanao, Lake, l., Phil. D6 34
Lanare, Ca., U.S. D4 82
Lanark, Ont. C8 73
Lanark, Scot., U.K. C5 10
Lanark, Il., U.S. A4 90
Lanark, W.V., U.S. D3 125
Lanark, co., Ont. B8 73
Lanark Village, Fl., U.S. C2 86
Lanbi, i., Burma G3 35
Lancang, China *A4 85
Lancaster, De., U.S. G4 31
Lancaster, Eng., U.K. C5 10
Lancaster, Ca., U.S. E4 82
Lancaster, Il., U.S. E6 90
Lancaster, Ks., U.S. C8 93
Lancaster, Ky., U.S. C5 94
Lancaster, Ma., U.S. B4 98
Lancaster, Mn., U.S. B2 100
Lancaster, Mo., U.S. A5 102
Lancaster, N.H., U.S. B3 106
Lancaster, N.Y., U.S. C2 109
Lancaster, Oh., U.S. C3 112
Lancaster, Pa., U.S. F9 115
Lancaster, S.C., U.S. B6 117
Lancaster, Tn., U.S. C8 119
Lancaster, Tx., U.S. n10 120
Lancaster, Va., U.S. C6 123
Lancaster, Wi., U.S. F3 126
Lancaster, co., Ne., U.S. D9 104
Lancaster, co., Pa., U.S. G9 115
Lancaster, co., S.C., U.S. . . . B6 117
Lancaster, co., Va., U.S. C6 123
Lancaster Sound, strt., N.W.
  Ter. B15 66
Lancaster Village, De., U.S. . . *A3 85
Lance, Point, c., Newf. E4 72
Lance Creek, Wy., U.S. C8 127
Lance Creek, stm., Wy., U.S. . C8 127
Lancer, Sask. G1 75
Lanchou see Lanzhou, China . D5 31
Lanciano, Italy C5 23
Lancing, Tn., U.S. C8 119
Łańcut, Pol. C7 26
Lancy, Switz. D1 21
Landa, N.D., U.S. A5 111
Landaff Center, N.H., U.S. . . . B3 106
Landau [an der Isar], Ger. . . . D6 18
Landau [in der Pfalz], Ger. . . . D4 18
Land Between the Lakes, U.S. . f9 94
Landeck, Aus. E5 18
Landen, Bel. D5 17
Lander, Wy., U.S. D4 127
Lander, co., Nv., U.S. C4 105
Landerneau, Fr. C1 16
Landess, In., U.S. C6 91
Landing Lake, l., Man. B4 70
Landis, Sask. E1 75
Landis, N.C., U.S. B2 110
Landisburg, Pa., U.S. F7 115
Landivisiau, Fr. C1 16
Landø, S.C., U.S. B5 117
Land O' Lakes, Wi., U.S. B4 126
Landover, Md., U.S. *C4 97
Landquart, Switz. C8 21
Landquart, stm., Switz. C8 21
Landrum, S.C., U.S. A3 117
Landsberg, Ger. D5 18
Land's End, Eng., U.K. E4 10
Lands End, c., R.I., U.S. F5 116
Landshut, Ger. D6 18
Landskrona, Swe. J5 14
Landsman Creek, stm., Co.,
  U.S. B8 83
Landsort, Swe. u35 14
Landusky, Mt., U.S. C8 103
Lane, Il., U.S. C5 90
Lane, Ks., U.S. D8 93
Lane, Nv., U.S. D7 105
Lane, Ok., U.S. C6 113
Lane, S.C., U.S. D8 117
Lane, S.D., U.S. C7 118
Lane, Tn., U.S. A2 119
Lane, co., Ks., U.S. D3 93
Lane, co., Or., U.S. C4 114
Laneburg, Ar., U.S. D2 81
La Negra, Chile D1 55
Lanesboro, Ma., U.S. A1 98
Lanesboro, Mn., U.S. G7 100
Lanesboro, Pa., U.S. C10 115
Lanesville, In., U.S. H6 91
Lanett, Al., U.S. C4 78
Lanfine, Alta. D5 68
Lang, Sask. H3 75
Langå, Den. B3 15
Langa Langa, Zaire C4 48
Langãdhás, Grc. B4 25
Langanes, i., Ice. m25 14
Langarūd, Iran C5 39
Långås, Swe. B6 15
Lang Bay, B.C. E5 69
Langdale, Al., U.S. D4 68
Langdale, Alta. D4 68
Langeac, Fr. E5 16
L'Ange-Gardien, Que. n17 74
Langeland, i., Den. D4 15
Langelandsbælt, strt., Den. . . D4 15
Langeloth, Pa., U.S. F1 115
Langen, Ger. D3 19
Langenau, Ger. E5 19
Langenburg, Sask. G5 75
Langenfeld, Ger. C4 19
Langenhagen, Ger. C4 19
Langenthal, Switz. E3 18
Langenzenn, Ger. D5 19
Langeoog, i., Ger. B3 18
Langerak, strt., Den. A4 15
Langesund, Nor. H3 14
Langeten, stm., Switz. B4 21
Langford, B.C. h12 69
Langford, S.D., U.S. B8 118
Långhalsen, Swe. u34 14
Langham, Sask. E2 75
Langham, Swe. A7 15
Langham, Scot., U.K. E5 13

Langhorne, Pa., U.S. F12 115
Langjökull, ice, Ice. n22 14
Langkawi, i., Malay. I3 35
Langlade, co., Wi., U.S. C4 126
Langlade, i., St. P./M. E3 72
La Porte, Co., In., U.S. A4 91
Langley, B.C. f13 69
Langley, Ar., U.S. C2 81
Langley, Ky., U.S. C7 94
Langley, Ok., U.S. A6 113
Langley, S.C., U.S. E4 117
Langley, U.S. A3 124
Langley Air Force Base, mil.,
  Va., U.S. h15 123
Langley Park, Md., U.S. f9 97
Langleyville, Il., U.S. D4 90
Langlois, Or., U.S. E2 114
Langnau [in Emmental], Switz. E3 18
Langogne, Fr. E5 16
Langon, Fr. E3 16
Langøya, i., Nor. C6 14
Langres, Fr. D6 16
Langres, Plateau de, plat., Fr. . D6 16
Langruth, Man. D2 70
Langsa, Indon. E1 34
Lang Son, Viet. B7 35
Langstaff, Ont. k15 73
Langston, Al., U.S. A3 78
Langston, Ok., U.S. B4 113
Langston, Ont. E4 73
Langtry, Tx., U.S. E2 120
Languedoc, hist. reg., Fr. . . . F5 16
L'Anguille, stm., Ar., U.S. . . . B5 81
Langzhong, China E8 31
Lanham, Md., U.S. C4 97
Lanier, co., Ga., U.S. E3 87
Lanigan, Sask. F3 75
Lanigan Creek, stm., Sask. . . F3 75
Lanín, Volcán, vol., S.A. B2 54
Lankin, N.D., U.S. A8 111
Lanklaar, Bel. C5 17
Lannion, Fr. C2 16
Lannon, Wi., U.S. m11 126
L'Annonciation, Que. C3 74
Lanoka Harbor, N.J., U.S. . . . D4 107
Lanoraie, Que. D4 74
Lansdale, Pa., U.S. F11 115
Lansdowne, Ont. C8 73
Lansdowne, Md., U.S. B4 97
Lansdowne, Pa., U.S. *p20 115
Lansdowne House, Ont. n18 73
L'Anse, Mi., U.S. B2 99
L'Anse-au-Clair, Newf. C3 72
L'Anse-au-Loup, Newf. C3 72
L'Anse-aux-Meadows, Newf. . C4 72
L'Anse Indian Reservation,
  Mi., U.S. B2 99
L'Anse-Saint-Jean, Que. A7 74
Lansford, N.D., U.S. A4 111
Lansford, Pa., U.S. E10 115
Lansing, Il., U.S. B6 90
Lansing, Ia., U.S. A6 92
Lansing, Ks., U.S. C9 93
Lansing, Mi., U.S. F6 99
Lansing, N.C., U.S. A1 110
Lansing, W.V., U.S. m13 125
Lanslebourg, Fr. D2 20
Lantana, Fl., U.S. F6 86
Lantern Hill, hill, Ct., U.S. . . . D8 84
Lantry, S.D., U.S. B4 118
Lanusei, Italy E2 23
Lanuvio, Italy h9 23
Lanxi, China F8 31
Lanxi, China A12 32
Lanzada, Italy D8 21
Lanzarote, i., Spain m15 22
Lanzhou (Lanchou), China . . . D5 31
Laoag, Phil. B6 34
Lao Cai, Viet. A7 35
Laohekou, China E7 31
Laoighis see Laois, co., Ire. . . I4 11
Laois, co., Ire. D4 11
Laolao, Bahía, b., N. Mar. Is. . D8 52
Laolao Kattan, Puntan, c., N.
  Mar. Is. D8 52
Laon, Fr. C5 16
Laona, Wi., U.S. C5 126
La Oroya, Peru D2 58
Laos, ctry., Asia B2 34
Laotto, In., U.S. B7 91
Lapa, Braz. D3 56
La Palma, Pan. F8 62
La Palma, Az., U.S. E4 80
La Palma, Ca., U.S. *n12 82
La Palma, i., Spain m13 22
La Palma [del Condado],
  Spain D2 22
La Paloma, Ur. C6 56
La Pampa, prov., Arg. B3 54
La Paragua, Ven. B5 60
La Passe, Ont. B8 73
La Patrie, Que. D6 74
La Paz, Arg. A5 54
La Paz, Arg. A3 54
La Paz, Bol. A3 60
La Paz, Col. A3 60
La Paz, Hond. E7 63
La Paz, Mex. C4 63
La Paz, dept., Bol. q19 74
La Paz, co., Az., U.S. D2 80
La Paz, Bahía de, b., Mex. . . C4 63
La Pedrera, Col. D4 60
Lapeer, Mi., U.S. E7 99
Lapeer, co., Mi., U.S. E7 99
La Perouse Strait, strt., Asia . D10 33
La Piedad [Cavadas], Mex. . . m12 63
Lapine, Al., U.S. D3 78
La Pine, Or., U.S. D5 114
La Place, Il., U.S. D5 90
La Place, La., U.S. h11 95
Lapland, reg., Eur. C11 14
La Plant, S.D., U.S. B5 118
La Plata, Arg. A5 54
La Plata, Col. F4 60
La Plata, Md., U.S. C4 97
La Plata, Mo., U.S. A5 102
La Plata, N.M., U.S. A1 108
La Plata, co., Co., U.S. D3 83
La Plata Mountains, mts., Co.,
  U.S. D2 83
La Plata Peak, mtn., Co., U.S. B4 83
La Platte, stm., Vt., U.S. C2 122
La Pobla de Lillet, Spain A4 15
La Pocatière, Que. B7 74
La Poile Bay, b., Newf. E2 72
Lapoint, Ut., U.S. C6 121
La Pointe [-Station], Que. . . . B8 74
La Pola [de Gordón], Spain . . A3 22
Laporte, Sask. F1 75
La Porte, Co., U.S. C3 82

Laporte, Co., U.S. A5 83
La Porte, In., U.S. A4 91
Laporte, Mn., U.S. C4 100
Laporte, Pa., U.S. D9 115
Las Piedras, Arg. E1 56
La Porte, Tx., U.S. r14 120
La Porte, co., In., U.S. A4 91
Lappeenranta, Fin. G13 14
Lappfjärd, Swe. t33 14
La Prairie, Que. D4 74
La Prairie, Mn., U.S. C5 100
Laprairie, co., Que. D4 74
Laprida, Arg. B4 54
La Pryor, Tx., U.S. E3 120
Lâpseki, Tur. B6 40
Laptev Sea, Sov. Un. B15 29
La Puebla, Spain C7 22
La Puebla de Montalbán,
  Spain C3 22
La Puente, Ca., U.S. *m13 82
La Puente, N.M., U.S. A3 108
La Purísima, Mex. B2 63
La Push, Wa., U.S. B1 124
La Quiaca, Arg. A3 54
L'Aquila (Aquila), Italy C4 23
Lara, state, Ven. A3 60
Larache, Mor. B3 44
Lārak, i., Iran H8 39
Laramie, Wy., U.S. E7 127
Laramie, co., Wy., U.S. E8 127
Laramie, stm., U.S. E7 127
Laramie Mountains, mts., Wy.,
  U.S. D7 127
Laramie Peak, mtn., Wy., U.S. D7 127
Laranjeiras, Braz. D3 57
Laranjeiras do Sul, Braz. . . . D2 56
Larantuka, Indon. G6 34
Larche Pass, Eur. E2 20
Larder Lake, Ont. k11 73
Laredo, Spain A4 22
Laredo, Mo., U.S. A4 102
Laredo, Tx., U.S. F3 120
Laredo Sound, strt., B.C. . . . C3 69
La Réole, Fr. E4 16
Lares, P.R. B2 65
Largeau, Chad B3 46
Largentière, Fr. E6 16
Largo, Fl., U.S. E4 86
Largo, Cañon, val., N.M., U.S. A2 108
Largo, Cayo, i., Cuba D3 64
Largo, Key, i., Fl., U.S. G6 86
Largs, Scot., U.K. E4 13
Lariat, S., Fr. B1 120
La Ricamarie, Fr. E6 16
Larimer, co., Co., U.S. A5 83
Larimore, N.D., U.S. B8 111
Larino, Italy D5 23
La Rioja, Arg. A3 54
La Rioja, Cuba D5 64
La Rioja, prov., Arg. A2 55
Lárisa, Grc. C4 40
Laristan, hist. reg., Iran C5 38
La Riviera, Man. E2 70
La Rivière, Man. E2 70
Lark, N.D., U.S. C4 111
Lark, Ut., U.S. C3 121
Lark Harbour, Newf. D2 72
Larkinsville, Al., U.S. A3 78
Larkspur, Ca., U.S. h7 82
Larkspur, Co., U.S. B6 83
Larksville, Pa., U.S. n17 115
Larnaca see Lárnax, Cyp. . . . E9 40
Lárnax (Larnaca), Cyp. E9 40
Larne, N. Ire., U.K. C4 10
Larned, Ks., U.S. D4 93
La Robla, Spain A3 22
La Rochelle, Fr. D3 16
La-Roche-sur-Foron, Fr. D7 16
La Roche-sur-Yon, Fr. D3 16
La Roda, Spain C4 22
La Romana, Dom. Rep. E9 64
La Ronge, Sask. B3 75
La Rose, Il., U.S. C4 90
Larose, La., U.S. E5 95
Larrabee, Ia., U.S. B2 92
Larrys River, N.S. D8 71
Larsen Bay, Ak., U.S. D9 79
Larsen Ice Shelf, ice, Ant. . . . C6 7
Larslan, Mt., U.S. B10 103
Larsmont, Mn., U.S. D7 100
Larson, N.D., U.S. A3 111
Larto, La., U.S. C3 95
La Rubia, Arg. F3 55
La Rue, Oh., U.S. B2 112
Larue, co., Ky., U.S. C4 94
Laruns, Fr. F3 16
Larvik, Nor. H3 14
Larwill, In., U.S. B6 91
Laryak, Sov. Un. C25 8
La Sagra, mtn., Spain D4 22
La Sal, Ut., U.S. E6 121
LaSalle, Co., U.S. A6 83
La Salle, Il., U.S. B4 90
La Salle, co., Il., U.S. B4 90
La Salle, co., La., U.S. C3 95
La Salle, co., Tx., U.S. E3 120
Lārāk, co., Il., U.S. B4 90
La Salle, co., Tx., U.S. E3 120
La Sarre, Que. k11 74
Lasborg, Aus. E9 19
Lascahobas, Haiti E8 64
Lascano, Ur. C6 56
Lascar, Volcán, vol., Chile . . . D2 55
Lascassas, Tn., U.S. B5 119
L'Ascension, Que. A6 74
La Scie, Newf. D4 72
Las Coloradas, Arg. B2 54
Las Cruces, N.M., U.S. E3 108
La Serena, Chile E1 55
La Seyne [-sur-Mer], Fr. B5 54
Las Flores, Arg. B5 54
Lashburn, Sask. D1 75
Lashio, Burma D10 36
Lask, Pol. B5 26
Las Lajas, Arg. F2 62
Las Lajas, Arg. F7 62
Las Lomitas, Arg. D3 55
Las Marismas, sw., Spain . . . D2 22
La Solana, Spain C4 22
Las Palmas, Pan. F7 62

Las Palmas [de Gran Canaria],
  Spain m14 22
La Spezia, Italy B2 23
Las Piedras, Arg. E1 56
Las Piedras, Río de, stm.,
  Peru D3 58
Las Plumas, Arg. C3 54
Las Rosas, Arg. A4 54
Las Rozas de Madrid, Spain . p17 22
Lassance, Braz. B4 56
Lassen, co., Ca., U.S. B3 82
Lassen, co., Ca., U.S. B3 82
Lassen Peak, vol., Ca., U.S. . . B3 82
Lassen Volcanic National Park,
  Ca., U.S. B3 82
Last Chance, Co., U.S. B7 83
Last Mountain Lake, l., Sask. . F3 75
Las Termas, Arg. E3 55
Las Truchas, Mex. D4 63
Lastrup, Mn., U.S. D4 100
Las Tunas, prov., Cuba D5 64
Las Varillas, Arg. A4 54
Las Vegas, Nv., U.S. G6 105
Las Vegas, N.M., U.S. B4 108
Las Vegas, Mex. n15 63
La Tabatière, Que. C2 72
Latacunga, Ec. B2 58
La Tagua, Col. D3 60
Latah, co., Id., U.S. C2 89
Latakia (Al Lādhiqīyah), Syria B3 38
Latchford, Ont. A6 74
La Teste-de-Buch, Fr. E3 16
Latexo, Tx., U.S. D5 120
Latham, Il., U.S. D4 90
Latham, Ks., U.S. E7 93
Latham, N.Y., U.S. *n15 109
Lathrop, Mo., U.S. B3 102
Lathrop Wells, Nv., U.S. G5 105
L'Ardoise, N.S. D9 71
Latimer, Ia., U.S. B4 92
Latimer, co., Ok., U.S. C6 113
Latina, Italy D4 23
Latium (Lazio), prov., Italy . . . C4 23
Latoritsa (Latorica), stm., Sov.
  Un. D7 26
La Torrecilla, mtn., P.R. B3 65
La Tortuga, Isla, i., Ven. A4 60
Latour, Mo., U.S. C3 102
La Tour-du-Pin, Fr. E6 16
Latour Peak, mtn., Id., U.S. . . B2 89
La Tremblade, Fr. E4 16
La Trinité, Mart. I14 64
La Vega, Dom. Rep. E8 64
La Vela de Coro, Ven. A4 60
Latrobe, Pa., U.S. F3 115
Latrün, Isr. Occ. C6 41
Latta, S.C., U.S. C9 117
Lattimer Mines, Pa., U.S. . . . E10 115
Lattimore, N.C., U.S. B1 110
Latty, Oh., U.S. A1 112
La Tuque, Que. B5 74
Lātūr, India H6 37
Latvia, state, Sov. Un. D5 29
Latvia, state, Sov. Un. D5 29
Lauca, stm., Bol. C2 55
Laucala, i., Fiji H16 52
Lauchhammer, Ger. B8 19
Laud, In., U.S. B7 91
Lauda, Ger. D4 19
Lauder, Man. E1 70
Lauder, Scot., U.K. E6 13
Lauderdale, Ms., U.S. C5 101
Lauderdale, co., Al., U.S. . . . A2 78
Lauderdale, co., Ms., U.S. . . . C5 101
Lauderdale, co., Tn., U.S. . . . B2 119
Lauderdale Lakes, Fl., U.S. . . *r13 86
Lauderhill, Fl., U.S. *r13 86
Lauenburg, Ger. E4 15
Lauf [an der Pegnitz], Ger. . . D6 19
Laufen, Ger. B8 20
Laufen, Switz. B4 21
Laughery Creek, stm., In.,
  U.S. F7 91
Laughlin, Nv., U.S. H7 105
Laughlin Air Force Base, mil.,
  Tx., U.S. E2 120
Laughlin Peak, mtn., N.M.,
  U.S. A5 108
Lau Group, is., Fiji I16 52
Laujar, Ger. E5 19
Lauli'ifou, Am. Sam. F13 52
Launceston, Austl. o15 50
Launceston, Eng., U.K. E4 10
Launching Point, c., P.E.I. . . . C7 71
La Unión, Chile C2 54
La Unión, Col. C3 60
La Unión, El Sal. D3 62
La Unión, Mex. H9 63
La Unión, Peru C2 58
Laupahoehoe, Hi., U.S. C6 88
Laupheim, Ger. E5 19
Laura, Sask. E2 75
Laura, Marsh. Is. C8 52
Laurel, De., U.S. G3 85
Laurel, Fl., U.S. E4 86
Laurel, In., U.S. E7 91
Laurel, Md., U.S. B4 97
Laurel, Ms., U.S. D4 101
Laurel, Mt., U.S. E8 103
Laurel, Ne., U.S. B8 104
Laurel, Ont. F3 73
Laurel, co., Ky., U.S. C5 94
Laurel Bay, S.C., U.S. G6 117
Laurel Bloomery, Tn., U.S. . . C12 119
Laurel Creek, stm., W.V., U.S. n14 125
Laurel Creek, stm., W.V., U.S. m12 125
Laureldale, N.J., U.S. D3 107
Laureldale, Pa., U.S. F10 115
Laureles, Ur. E1 56
Laurel Fork, stm., W.V., U.S. . C5 125
Laurel Hill, Fl., U.S. u15 86
Laurel Hill, N.C., U.S. C3 110
Laurel Mountain, mtn., W.V.,
  U.S. B5 125
Laurel Run, Pa., U.S. n17 115

Laurelton, Pa., U.S. E7 115
Laurelville, Oh., U.S. C3 112
Laurelwood Academy, Or.,
  U.S. h11 114
Laurence G. Hanscom Air
  Force Base, mil., Ma., U.S. . g10 98
Laurence Harbor, N.J., U.S. . . C4 107
Laurencekirk, Scot., U.K. . . . D6 13
Laurens, Ia., U.S. B3 92
Laurens, S.C., U.S. C3 117
Laurens, co., Ga., U.S. D4 87
Laurens, co., S.C., U.S. C4 117
Laurentides, Que. D4 74
Laurentides, Parc Provincial
  des, Que. B6 74
Laurentum, hist., Italy h8 23
Lauria Inferiore, Italy D5 23
Laurie, Sask. G7 62
Laurier, Man. A1 70
Laurier, Que. C6 74
Laurier, Que. C6 74
Laurierville, Que. C6 74
Laurin, Mt., U.S. E4 103
Laurinburg, N.C., U.S. C3 110
Lauritzen Bay, b., Ant. C28 7
Laurium, Mi., U.S. A2 99
Laurium see Lávrion, Grc. . . . D5 25
Lausanne, Switz. E3 18
Lauscha, Ger. C6 19
Laut, i., Indon. F5 34
Laut, i., Indon. J8 35
Lautaro, Chile B2 54
Lauterbach, Ger. C4 19
Lauterbrunnen, Switz. C4 21
Lauterecken, Ger. D2 19
Laut Kecil Islands, is., Indon. . F5 34
Lautoka, Fiji H14 52
Lautoka, Fiji C6 74
Lava Beds National
  Monument, Ca., U.S. B3 82
Lavaca, Al., U.S. C1 78
Lavaca, Ar., U.S. B1 81
Lavaca, co., Tx., U.S. E4 120
Lava Hot Springs, Id., U.S. . . G6 89
Laval, Que. D4 74
Laval, Fr. C3 16
La Vale, Md., U.S. k13 97
Lavalle, Arg. A3 54
La Valle, Wi., U.S. E3 126
Lavallette, N.J., U.S. D4 107
La Valley, Co., U.S. D5 83
Lavaltrie, Que. D4 74
La Vega, Dom. Rep. E8 64
La Vela de Coro, Ven. A4 60
Lavelanet, Fr. F4 16
Lavello, Italy D5 23
L'Avenir, Que. D5 74
La Vergne, Tn., U.S. A5 119
La Verkin, Ut., U.S. F2 121
La Verne, Ca., U.S. m13 82
La Verne, Ca., U.S. A2 113
La Vernia, Tx., U.S. E3 120
Laverton, Austl. E4 50
La Veta, Co., U.S. D5 83
Laviana, Spain A3 22
La Victoria, Peru *D2 58
La Victoria, Ven. A4 60
Lavieille, Lake, l., Ont. B6 73
Lavillette, N.B. B4 71
Lavina, Mt., U.S. D8 103
Lavinia, Braz. C2 56
Lavinia, Tn., U.S. B3 119
La Vista, Ga., U.S. h8 87
La Vista, Ne., U.S. g12 104
La Viuda, mtn., Peru C2 58
Lavonia, Ga., U.S. B3 87
Lavon Lake, res., Tx., U.S. . . m10 120
Lavoy, Alta. C5 68
Lavras, Braz. C4 56
Lavras da Mangabeira, Braz. . C3 57
Lavras do Sul, Braz. E2 56
Lávrion (Laurium), Grc. D5 25
Lavumisa, Swaz. C5 49
Lawa, Hi., U.S. B2 88
Lawen, Or., U.S. D8 114
Lawford Lake, l., Man. B3 70
Lawit, mtn., Malay. J5 35
Lawley, Al., U.S. C3 78
Lawn, Newf. E4 72
Lawn, Pa., U.S. F8 115
Lawn, Tx., U.S. C3 120
Lawndale, Ca., U.S. *E4 82
Lawndale, N.C., U.S. B1 110
Lawnside, N.J., U.S. *D2 107
Lawra, Ghana D4 45
Lawrence, N.Z. P12 51
Lawrence, In., U.S. E5 91
Lawrence, Ks., U.S. D8 93
Lawrence, Ma., U.S. A5 98
Lawrence, Mi., U.S. F4 99
Lawrence, Ne., U.S. D7 104
Lawrence, N.Y., U.S. k13 109
Lawrence, Pa., U.S. F1 115
Lawrence, co., Al., U.S. A2 78
Lawrence, co., Ar., U.S. A4 81
Lawrence, co., Il., U.S. E6 90
Lawrence, co., In., U.S. G4 91
Lawrence, co., Ky., U.S. B7 94
Lawrence, co., Ms., U.S. D3 101
Lawrence, co., Mo., U.S. D4 102
Lawrence, co., Oh., U.S. D3 112
Lawrence, co., Pa., U.S. E1 115
Lawrence, co., S.D., U.S. . . . C2 118
Lawrence, co., Tn., U.S. B4 119
Lawrenceburg, In., U.S. F8 91
Lawrenceburg, Ky., U.S. B5 94
Lawrenceburg, Tn., U.S. B4 119
Lawrenceport, In., U.S. G5 91
Lawrenceton, N.B. E4 71
Lawrencetown, N.S. D5 74
Lawrenceville, Ga., U.S. C3 87
Lawrenceville, Il., U.S. E6 90
Lawrenceville, N.J., U.S. C3 107
Lawrenceville, N.Y., U.S. . . . f10 109
Lawrenceville, Pa., U.S. C7 115
Lawrenceville, Va., U.S. D5 123
Lawshe, Pa., U.S. D2 112
Lawson, Sask. D3 81
Lawson, Ar., U.S. D3 81
Lawson, Mo., U.S. B3 102
Lawsonia, Md., U.S. E6 97
Lawsonville, N.C., U.S. A2 110

Name	Map Ref.	Page

Lawtell, La., U.S. — D3 95
Lawtey, Fl., U.S. — B4 86
Lawton, Ky., U.S. — B6 94
Lawton, Mi., U.S. — F5 99
Lawton, N.D., U.S. — A7 111
Lawton, Ok., U.S. — C3 113
Lawyersville, N.Y., U.S. — C6 109
Lawz, Jabal al, mtn., Sau. Ar. — H10 40
Lax Kw'alaams, B.C. — B2 69
Laxou, Fr. — C7 16
Lay, Point, c., Viet. — D7 84
Lay Dam, Al., U.S. — C3 78
Lay Lake, res., Al., U.S. — B3 78
Layland, W.V., U.S. — n14 125
Layou, St. Vin. — U26 65
Laysan Island, i., Hi., U.S. — k13 88
Laysville, Ct., U.S. — D6 84
Layton, Ut., U.S. — B4 121
Laytonsville, Md., U.S. — B3 97
Laytonville, Ca., U.S. — C2 82
Lazdijai, Sov. Un. — A7 26
Lazear, Co., U.S. — C3 83
Łaziska Górne, Pol. — g9 26
Lea, co., N.M., U.S. — D6 108
Lea, stm., Eng., U.K. — k12 10
Leach, Ok., U.S. — A7 113
Leachville, Ar., U.S. — B5 81
Leacross, Sask. — D3 75
Lead, S.D., U.S. — C2 118
Leadbetter Point, c., Wa., U.S. — C1 124
Leader, Sask. — G1 75
Lead Hill, Ar., U.S. — A3 81
Lead Mountain, mtn., Me., U.S. — D5 102
Lead Mountain, mtn., Me., U.S. — D4 96
Lead Mountain Ponds, l., Me., U.S. — D4 96
Leadore, Id., U.S. — E5 89
Leadville, Co., U.S. — B4 83
Leadwood, Mo., U.S. — D7 102
Leaf, Ms., U.S. — D5 101
Leaf, stm., Ms., U.S. — D5 101
Leaf Lake, l., Sask. — E4 75
Leaf Rapids, Man. — A1 70
Leaf River, Il., U.S. — A4 90
League City, Tx., U.S. — *r14 120
Leah, Ga., U.S. — C4 87
Leake, co., Ms., U.S. — C4 101
Leakesville, Ms., U.S. — D5 101
Leakey, Tx., U.S. — E3 120
Leal, N.D., U.S. — B7 111
Lealman, Fl., U.S. — p10 86
Leamington, Ont. — E2 73
Leamington, Ut., U.S. — D3 121
Leamington see Royal Leamington Spa, Eng., U.K. — D6 10
Leane, Lough, l., Ire. — E2 11
Leapwood, Tn., U.S. — B3 119
Learned, Ms., U.S. — C3 101
Leary, Ga., U.S. — E2 87
Leasburg, Mo., U.S. — C6 102
Leasburg, N.C., U.S. — A3 110
Leaside (part of East York), Ont. — m15 73
Leask, Sask. — E2 75
Leatherhead, Eng., U.K. — m12 10
Leatherman Peak, mtn., Id., U.S. — E5 89
Leatherwood, Ky., U.S. — C6 94
L'Eau Frais Creek, stm., Ar., U.S. — C3 81
Leavenworth, In., U.S. — H5 91
Leavenworth, Ks., U.S. — C9 93
Leavenworth, Wa., U.S. — B5 124
Leavenworth, co., Ks., U.S. — C8 93
Leavittsburg, Oh., U.S. — A5 112
Leawood, Ks., U.S. — D9 93
Łeba, Pol. — A4 26
Lebam, Wa., U.S. — C2 124
Lebanon, Ct., U.S. — C7 84
Lebanon, De., U.S. — D4 85
Lebanon, Il., U.S. — E4 90
Lebanon, In., U.S. — D5 91
Lebanon, Ks., U.S. — C5 93
Lebanon, Ky., U.S. — C4 94
Lebanon, Mo., U.S. — D5 102
Lebanon, Ne., U.S. — D5 104
Lebanon, N.H., U.S. — C2 106
Lebanon, N.J., U.S. — B3 107
Lebanon, Oh., U.S. — C1 112
Lebanon, Or., U.S. — C4 114
Lebanon, Pa., U.S. — F9 115
Lebanon, S.D., U.S. — B6 118
Lebanon, Tn., U.S. — A5 119
Lebanon, Va., U.S. — f9 123
Lebanon, co., Pa., U.S. — F8 115
Lebanon, ctry., Asia — B3 38
Lebanon Junction, Ky., U.S. — C4 94
Le Bardo, Tun. — *B7 44
Lebeau, La., U.S. — D4 95
Lebec, Ca., U.S. — E4 82
Lebedin, Sov. Un. — F10 29
Lebedyan, Sov. Un. — E12 27
Le Biot, Fr. — D2 21
Le Blanc, Fr. — D4 16
Le Blanc-Mesnil, Fr. — g10 16
Lebo, Ks., U.S. — D8 93
Lebo, Zaire — A3 48
Lebork, Pol. — A4 26
Le Bourg-d'Oisans, Fr. — D2 20
Le Bourget, Fr. — g10 16
Le Bouscat, Fr. — E3 16
Le Brassus, Switz. — C1 21
Lebret, Sask. — G4 75
Lebrija, Spain — D2 22
Lebu, Chile — B2 54
Lebyazhye, Sov. Un. — B7 28
Le Cateau, Fr. — B5 16
Lecce, Italy — D7 23
Lecco, Italy — B2 23
Lecco, Lake, l., Italy — E7 23
Le Center, Mn., U.S. — F5 100
Lech, stm., Eur. — D5 18
Le Chambon-Feugerolles, Fr. — E6 16
Le Château, Fr. — E3 16
Lechbruck, Ger. — B6 16
Le Chesnay, Fr. — g9 16
Le Chesne, Fr. — E4 17
Leck, Ger. — D2 15
Le Claire, Ia., U.S. — C7 92
Leclercville, Que. — C6 74
Lecompte, La., U.S. — C3 95
Lecompton, Ks., U.S. — C8 93
Léconi, Gabon — F2 46
Leconte, Mount, mtn., Tn., U.S. — D10 119
Lecontes Mills, Pa., U.S. — D6 115
Le Creusot, Fr. — D6 16
Le Croisic, Fr. — D2 16
Le Crotoy, Fr. — D9 12
Lectoure, Fr. — F4 16
Łęczyca, Pol. — B5 26

Ledbetter, N.C., U.S. — C3 110
Ledbury, Eng., U.K. — B5 12
Ledčice, Czech. — n17 26
Ledeberg (part of Gent), Bel. — C3 17
Ledesma, Spain — B2 22
Ledford, Il., U.S. — F5 90
Ledger, Mt., U.S. — B5 103
Ledgewood, N.J., U.S. — B3 107
Ledo, India — C10 36
Ledoux, N.M., U.S. — B4 108
Leduc, Alta. — C4 68
Ledyard, Ct., U.S. — D7 84
Ledyard, Ia., U.S. — A3 92
Lee, Fl., U.S. — B3 86
Lee, Il., U.S. — B5 90
Lee, Me., U.S. — C4 96
Lee, Ma., U.S. — B1 98
Lee, Nv., U.S. — C6 105
Lee, N.H., U.S. — D4 106
Lee, co., Al., U.S. — C4 78
Lee, co., Ar., U.S. — C5 81
Lee, co., Fl., U.S. — F5 86
Lee, co., Ga., U.S. — E2 87
Lee, co., Il., U.S. — B4 90
Lee, co., Ia., U.S. — D6 92
Lee, co., Ky., U.S. — C6 94
Lee, co., Ms., U.S. — A5 101
Lee, co., N.C., U.S. — B3 110
Lee, co., S.C., U.S. — C7 117
Lee, co., Tx., U.S. — D4 120
Lee, co., Va., U.S. — f8 123
Lee, stm., Ire. — E2 11
Lee Center, Il., U.S. — B4 90
Leechburg, Pa., U.S. — E2 115
Leech Lake, l., Sask. — F4 75
Leech Lake, l., Mn., U.S. — C4 100
Leech Lake Indian Reservation, Mn., U.S. — C4 100
Leechville, N.C., U.S. — B6 110
Leedey, Ok., U.S. — B2 113
Leedom Estates, De., U.S. — *B3 85
Leeds, Eng., U.K. — D6 10
Leeds, Al., U.S. — B3 78
Leeds, N.D., U.S. — A6 111
Leeds, S.C., U.S. — B5 117
Leeds [and Grenville], co., Ont. — C7 73
Leeds Point, N.J., U.S. — E4 107
Leeds-Village, Que. — C6 74
Leek, Eng., U.K. — A5 12
Leelanau, co., Mi., U.S. — D5 99
Leelanau, Lake, l., Mi., U.S. — C5 99
Leenaun, Ire. — D2 11
Lee Park, Pa., U.S. — n17 115
Leeper, Mo., U.S. — D7 102
Leeper, Pa., U.S. — D2 115
Leer, Ger. — B7 16
Leesburg, Al., U.S. — A4 78
Leesburg, Fl., U.S. — D5 86
Leesburg, Ga., U.S. — E2 87
Leesburg, In., U.S. — B6 91
Leesburg, N.J., U.S. — E3 107
Leesburg, Oh., U.S. — C2 112
Leesburg, Va., U.S. — A5 123
Lees Landing, La., U.S. — h11 95
Lees Summit, Mo., U.S. — C3 102
Leesville, Ct., U.S. — *C6 84
Leesville, In., U.S. — G5 91
Leesville, La., U.S. — C2 95
Leesville, Oh., U.S. — B4 112
Leesville, S.C., U.S. — D4 117
Leesville, Tx., U.S. — E4 120
Leesville Lake, res., Va., U.S. — C3 123
Leetes Island, Ct., U.S. — D5 84
Leeton, Austl. — G6 51
Leeton, Mo., U.S. — C4 102
Leetonia, Oh., U.S. — B5 112
Leetsdale, Pa., U.S. — h13 115
Leeuwarden, Neth. — A6 16
Leeuwin, Cape, c., Austl. — F2 50
Leeville, La., U.S. — E5 95
Lee Vining, Ca., U.S. — D4 82
Leeward Islands, is., N.A. — H13 64
Le Ferriere, Italy — h9 23
Leffingwell, Ct., U.S. — C7 84
Leflore, Ok., U.S. — C7 113
Leflore, co., Ms., U.S. — B3 101
Le Flore, co., Ok., U.S. — C7 113
Lefor, N.D., U.S. — C3 111
Lefors, Tx., U.S. — B2 120
Le François, Mart. — I14 64
Lefroy, Ont. — C5 73
Lefroy, Lake, l., Austl. — F3 50
Leftrook Lake, l., Man. — A2 70
Legal, Alta. — C4 68
Leganés, Spain — p17 22
Legaspi, Phil. — C6 34
Legau, Ger. — E5 18
Leggett, Ca., U.S. — C2 82
Leghorn see Livorno, Italy — C3 23
Legionowo, Pol. — k13 29
Legnago, Italy — D7 20
Legnano, Italy — B2 23
Legnica (Liegnitz), Pol. — C4 26
Le Gore, Md., U.S. — A3 97
Le Grand, Ca., U.S. — D3 82
Le Grand, Ia., U.S. — B5 92
Le Grand-Quevilly, Fr. — C4 16
Le Gros Cap, c., Que. — B7 71
Leh, India — B6 36
Le Havre, Fr. — C4 16
Lehi, Ut., U.S. — C4 121
Lehigh, Ia., U.S. — B3 92
Lehigh, Ks., U.S. — D6 93
Lehigh, Ok., U.S. — C5 113
Lehigh, co., Pa., U.S. — E10 115
Lehigh, stm., Pa., U.S. — E10 115
Lehigh Acres, Fl., U.S. — F5 86
Lehighton, Pa., U.S. — E10 115
Lehinch, Ire. — E2 11
Lehman, Pa., U.S. — n16 115
Lehr, N.D., U.S. — C6 111
Lehrte, Ger. — C5 16
Lehua Island, i., Hi., U.S. — A1 88
Leiah, Pak. — E4 36
Leibnitz, Aus. — E7 18
Leicester, Eng., U.K. — D6 10
Leicester, Ma., U.S. — B4 98
Leicester, N.Y., U.S. — C2 109
Leicester, Vt., U.S. — D2 122
Leicester Junction, Vt., U.S. — D2 122
Leicestershire, co., Eng., U.K. — B6 12
Leichhardt, Austl. — *F9 50
Leichhardt, stm., Austl. — C7 50
Leiden, Neth. — A6 16
Leigh, Ne., U.S. — C8 104
Leigh Creek, Austl. — F7 51
Leighlinbridge, Ire. — E5 11
Leighton, Al., U.S. — A2 78
Leighton, Ia., U.S. — C5 92
Leinan, Sask. — G2 75
Leine, stm., Eur. — B4 18

Leinster, hist. reg., Ire. — D4 11
Leinster, Mount, mtn., Ire. — E5 11
Leipalingis, Sov. Un. — A7 26
Leipers Fork, Tn., U.S. — B5 119
Leipsic, De., U.S. — D3 85
Leipsic, In., U.S. — G5 91
Leipsic, Oh., U.S. — A2 112
Leipsic, stm., De., U.S. — C3 85
Leipzig, Sask. — E1 75
Leipzig, Ger. — C6 18
Leiria, Port. — C1 22
Leiston, Eng., U.K. — B9 12
Leitchfield, Ky., U.S. — C3 94
Leitches Creek, N.S. — C9 71
Leiter, Wy., U.S. — B6 127
Leiters Ford, In., U.S. — B5 91
Leith, N.D., U.S. — C4 111
Leitha, stm., Eur. — B3 24
Leitrim, co., Ire. — C3 11
Leiva, Cerro, mtn., Col. — C3 60
Leixlip, Ire. — D5 11
Leizhou Bandao, pen., China — G7 31
Leizhou Bay, b., China — B9 35
Lejunior, Ky., U.S. — D6 94
Lek, stm., Neth. — C4 17
Leka, i., Nor. — A1 15
Lekeba, i., Fiji — I16 52
Lekoa, i., S. Afr. — *C4 44
Leksand, Swe. — C5 15
Leksula, Indon. — F7 34
Lela, Tx., U.S. — B2 120
Le Lamentin, Mart. — S10 65
Leland, Il., U.S. — B5 90
Leland, Ia., U.S. — A4 92
Leland, Mi., U.S. — C5 99
Leland, Ms., U.S. — B3 101
Leland, Wa., U.S. — B3 124
Leleiwi Point, c., Hi., U.S. — D7 88
Lelequé, Arg. — C2 54
Lelia Lake, Tx., U.S. — B2 120
Leloaloa, Am. Sam. — F13 52
Le Locle, Switz. — E3 18
Le Lorrain, Mart. — S10 65
Leloup, Ks., U.S. — D8 93
Lelystad, Neth. — B5 16
Le Maire, Estrecho de, strt., Arg. — h12 54
Le Mans, Fr. — C4 16
Le Marin, Mart. — I14 64
Le Mars, Ia., U.S. — B1 92
Lemasters, Pa., U.S. — G6 115
Lemay, Mo., U.S. — *g13 102
Lembach, Fr. — F7 17
Lemberg, Sask. — G4 75
Lemdiyya, Alg. — m8 56
Leme, Braz. — m8 57
Lemelerveld, Neth. — B6 17
Lemery, Phil. — p13 34
Lemesós (Limassol), Cyp. — E9 40
Lemgo, Ger. — B4 18
Lemhi, Id., U.S. — E5 89
Lemhi, co., Id., U.S. — E4 89
Lemhi, stm., Id., U.S. — E5 89
Lemhi Pass, Id., U.S. — E5 89
Lemhi Range, mts., Id., U.S. — E5 89
Lemieux, Que. — C5 74
Lemitar, N.M., U.S. — C3 108
Lemmer, Neth. — B5 17
Lemmon, S.D., U.S. — B3 118
Lemmon, Mount, mtn., Az., U.S. — E5 80
Lemmon Valley, Nv., U.S. — D2 105
Lemnos see Limnos, i., Grc. — C5 40
Lemon, Lake, l., In., U.S. — F5 91
Lemon Fair, stm., Vt., U.S. — C2 122
Lemon Grove, Ca., U.S. — o15 82
Lemon Island, i., S.C., U.S. — G6 117
Lemons, Mo., U.S. — A4 102
Lemont, Il., U.S. — B5 90
Lemont, Pa., U.S. — E6 115
Lemonweir, stm., Wi., U.S. — D3 126
Lemoore, Ca., U.S. — D4 82
Lemoore Naval Air Station, mil., Ca., U.S. — D4 82
Lemoore Station, Ca., U.S. — *D4 82
Le Moyen, La., U.S. — D3 95
Lemoyne, Ne., U.S. — C4 104
Lemoyne, Oh., U.S. — f7 112
Lempa, stm., N.A. — D3 62
Lempster, N.H., U.S. — E2 106
Lemvig, Den. — C1 15
Lena, Il., U.S. — A3 90
Lena, In., U.S. — E3 91
Lena, La., U.S. — C3 95
Lena, Ms., U.S. — C4 101
Lena, Wi., U.S. — D5 126
Lena, stm., Sov. Un. — C15 29
Lenapah, Ok., U.S. — A6 113
Lenawee, co., Mi., U.S. — G6 99
Lençóis, Braz. — D2 57
Lengby, Mn., U.S. — C3 100
Lengede, Ger. — A5 18
Lenger, Sov. Un. — E7 28
Lengerich, Ger. — A2 18
Lenghu, China — D3 31
Lengshuijiang, China — *C4 31
Lenhartsville, Pa., U.S. — E10 115
Lenham, Eng., U.K. — E2 28
Lenin, Sov. Un. — C6 29
Leningrad, Sov. Un. — n17 27
Leningradskaya, sci., Ant. — C28 7
Leninogorsk, Sov. Un. — D11 29
Leninskoye, Sov. Un. — C7 28
Lenk, Switz. — C3 20
Lenkoran, Sov. Un. — B7 38
Lenna, stm., Ger. — B6 113
Lenne, stm., Ger. — B2 18?

Lenore Lake, l., Sask. — E3 75
Lenore Lake, l., Wa., U.S. — B6 124
Lenox, Al., U.S. — D2 78
Lenox, Ga., U.S. — E3 87
Lenox, Ia., U.S. — D3 92
Lenox, Ma., U.S. — B1 98
Lenox, Mo., U.S. — D6 102
Lenox, Tn., U.S. — A2 119
Lenox Dale, Ma., U.S. — B1 98
Lens, Fr. — B5 16
Lensk, Sov. Un. — B11 33
Lentner, Mo., U.S. — B5 102
Lenzburg, Il., U.S. — E4 90
Lenzen, Ger. — B5 16
Lenzerheide, Switz. — C8 21
Léo, Burkina — D4 45
Leo, In., U.S. — B7 91
Léogâne, Haiti — E7 64
Leola, Ar., U.S. — C3 81
Leola, S.D., U.S. — B7 118
Leoma, Tn., U.S. — B4 119
Leominster, Eng., U.K. — B5 12
Leominster, Ma., U.S. — A4 98
León, Nic. — E7 63
León, Spain — A3 22
Leon, Ia., U.S. — D4 92
Leon, Ks., U.S. — E7 93
Leon, N.Y., U.S. — C1 109
Leon, Ok., U.S. — D4 113
Leon, W.V., U.S. — C3 125
Leon, co., Fl., U.S. — B2 86
Leon, co., Tx., U.S. — D4 120
Leon, hist. reg., Spain — B3 22
Leona, Tx., U.S. — C8 93
Leonard, Ont. — h13 73
Leonard, Mi., U.S. — F7 99
Leonard, Mo., U.S. — C3 100
Leonard, N.D., U.S. — C8 111
Leonard, Ok., U.S. — B6 113
Leonard, Tx., U.S. — C4 120
Leonardtown, Md., U.S. — D4 97
Leonardsville, N.Y., U.S. — C5 109
Leonardville, N.B. — E3 71
Leonardville, Ks., U.S. — C7 93
Leonberg, Ger. — C4 63
León [de los Aldamas], Mex. — C4 63
Leone, Am. Sam. — G13 52
Leone Bay, Am. Sam. — G13 52
Leonforte, Italy — F5 23
Leongatha, Austl. — I5 51
Leonia, Fl., U.S. — u15 86
Leonia, N.J., U.S. — h9 107
Leonidion, Grc. — C4 40
Leonora, Austl. — *E3 50
Leon Valley, Tx., U.S. — *E3 120
Leopold, In., U.S. — H4 91
Leopold and Astrid Coast, Ant. — C21 7
Leopoldina, Braz. — C4 56
Leopoldsburg, Bel. — C5 17
Léopoldville see Kinshasa, Zaire — B2 48
Leota, Mn., U.S. — G2 100
Leoti, Ks., U.S. — D2 93
Leoville, Sask. — D2 75
Leoville, Ks., U.S. — C3 93
Leovo, Sov. Un. — H7 27
Lepanto, Ar., U.S. — B5 81
Lepe, Spain — D2 22
Lepel, Sov. Un. — D7 27
Le Petit-Quevilly, Fr. — C4 16
Lepihué, Chile — C2 54
Leping, China — J7 32
Le-Plain-de-Coravillers, Fr. — A2 21
Le Plessis-Belleville, Fr. — E2 17
Le Plessis-Robinson, Fr. — G10 16
Lepreau, N.B. — D3 71
Lepreau, Point, c., N.B. — D3 71
Lepsinsk, Sov. Un. — F25 8
Lepsy, Sov. Un. — D9 28
Le Puy [-en-Velay], Fr. — E5 16
Le Quesnoy, Fr. — D3 17
Lequire, Ok., U.S. — B6 113
Le Raincy, Fr. — g11 16
Le Raysville, Pa., U.S. — C9 115
Lercara Friddi, Italy — *F4 23
Lerdo, Mex. — D2 62
Léré, Chad — G8 42
Lérida, Col. — B6 60
Lérida, Spain — A4 22
Lerma, Spain — B3 22
Lerma, stm., Mex. — m13 63
Lermoos, Aus. — B6 20
Lerna, Il., U.S. — D5 90
Le Robert, Mart. — S11 65
Léros, i., Grc. — D6 40
Leross, Sask. — F4 75
Leroux Wash, val., Az., U.S. — B5 80
Leroy, Sask. — F3 75
Leroy, Al., U.S. — D2 78
Leroy, Il., U.S. — C5 90
Le Roy, Il., U.S. — C5 90
Leroy, Ia., U.S. — D9 93
Le Roy, Ia., U.S. — A5 92
Leroy, Ks., U.S. — D8 93
Le Roy, Mi., U.S. — D5 99
Le Roy, Mn., U.S. — G6 100
Le Roy, N.Y., U.S. — C3 109
Leroy, N.D., U.S. — A8 111
Le Roy, Pa., U.S. — C8 115
Lerum, Swe. — A6 15
Le Russey, Fr. — B2 21
Lerwick, Scot., U.K. — g10 10
Léry, Que. — q19 74
Léry, Lake, l., La., U.S. — k12 95
Les Abymes, Guad. — Q8 65
Le Saint-Esprit, Mart. — S11 65
Lesbos see Lésvos, i., Grc. — C5 40
Les Cayes, Haiti — E7 64
Les Diablerets, Switz. — C3 20
Les Éboulements, Que. — B7 74
Les Echelles, Fr. — D1 20
Le Sentier, Switz. — C1 21
Le Sépey, Switz. — D3 20
Les Escoumins, Que. — A8 74
Les Étroits, Que. — A9 74
Les Fonds, Que. — o16 74
Leshan, China — F5 31
Leshara, Ne., U.S. — g12 104
Les Haudères, Switz. — D5 20
Lesina, Lake, b., Italy — h9 23
Lesko, Pol. — h7 26
Leslie, Sask. — F4 75
Leslie, Ar., U.S. — B3 81
Leslie, Ga., U.S. — E2 87
Leslie, Id., U.S. — F5 89

Leslie, Mi., U.S. — F6 99
Leslie, S.C., U.S. — B6 117
Leslie, W.V., U.S. — C4 125
Leslie, co., Ky., U.S. — C6 94
Leslieville, Alta. — C3 68
Les Lilas, Fr. — g10 16
Lesneven, Fr. — C1 16
Lesnoy, Sov. Un. — B4 28
Lesogorsk, Sov. Un. — B11 33
Lesozavodsk, Sov. Un. — E16 29
Lesotho, ctry., Afr. — C4 49
Lesparre, Fr. — E3 16
Les Ponts-de-Cé, Fr. — D3 16
Les Rousses, Fr. — D1 21
Les Sables-d'Olonne, Fr. — D3 16
Lesser Antilles, is. — B4 53
Lesser Khing Range see Xiao Hinggan Ling), mts., China — B10 31
Lesser Slave Lake, l., Alta. — B3 68
Lesser Sunda Islands (Nusa Tenggara), is., Indon. — G5 34
Lessines, Bel. — D3 17
Lester, Ia., U.S. — A2 92
Lester, W.V., U.S. — n13 125
Lester Prairie, Mn., U.S. — F4 100
Lesterville, Mo., U.S. — D7 102
Lesterville, S.D., U.S. — D8 118
Lestock, Sask. — F3 75
Le Sueur, Mn., U.S. — F5 100
Le Sueur, co., Mn., U.S. — F5 100
Les Verrières, Switz. — C1 21
Lésvos (Lesbos), i., Grc. — C5 40
Lexa, Ar., U.S. — C5 81
Letart Falls, Oh., U.S. — D4 112
Letcher, S.D., U.S. — D7 118
Letcher, co., Ky., U.S. — C7 94
Le Teil, Fr. — E6 16
Letellier, Man. — E3 70
Lethbridge, Alta. — E4 68
Lethbridge, Newf. — D5 72
Lethem, Guy. — B3 59
Le Thillot, Fr. — B2 21
Leti Islands, is., Indon. — G7 34
Leticia, Col. — D4 60
Letohatchee, Al., U.S. — C3 78
Letona, Ar., U.S. — B4 81
Le Touquet-Paris-Plage, Fr. — D9 17
Le Tourneau, Ms., U.S. — C3 101
Letpadan, Burma — E10 36
Le Tréport, Fr. — B4 16
Letsok-Aw-i., Burma — u15 36
Letterfrack, Ire. — D2 11
Letterkenny, Ire. — C3 10
Lettermullan, Ire. — D2 11
Letts, In., U.S. — F6 91
Letts, Ia., U.S. — C6 92
Lettsworth, La., U.S. — D4 95
Leucas see Levkás, i., Grc. — C3 40
Leuctra see Lévktra, Grc. — g10 25
Leuk, Switz. — D4 21
Leukerbad, Switz. — D4 21
Leulumoega, W. Sam. — F12 52
Leupp, Az., U.S. — B5 80
Leupp Corner, Az., U.S. — B5 80
Leuser, mtn., Indon. — m11 34
Leushinskiy Tuman, Lake, l., Sov. Un. — B6 28
Leutkirch, Ger. — B6 16
Leuven (Louvain), Bel. — D3 17
Leuze, Bel. — D3 17
Levádhia, Grc. — C4 40
Levallois-Perret, Fr. — g10 16
Levan, Ut., U.S. — D4 121
Levanna, mtn., Eur. — E7 16
Levant, Me., U.S. — D4 96
Levant, Ks., U.S. — C2 93
Levanger, Nor. — E7 16
Levelland, Tx., U.S. — C1 120
Leven, Scot., U.K. — B5 16
Leveque, Cape, c., Austl. — C3 50
Le Portel, Fr. — B2 98
Leverett, Ma., U.S. — B2 98
Leverett Glacier, ice, Ant. — A32 7
Levering, Mi., U.S. — C6 99
Leverkusen, Ger. — B1 19
Levice, Czech. — B29 7
Levick, Mount, mtn., Ant. — B29 7
Levie, Fr. — C1 21
Levier, Fr. — C1 21
Le Vigan, Fr. — E5 16
Levin, N.Z. — N15 51
Lévis, Que. — C6 74
Lévis, co., Que. — C6 74
Levisa Fork, stm., Ky., U.S. — C7 94
Levítha, i., Grc. — D6 25
Levittown, N.Y., U.S. — *E7 109
Levittown, Pa., U.S. — F12 115
Levkás (Leucas), i., Grc. — C3 40
Lévktra (Leuctra), Grc. — g10 25
Levoča, Czech. — D6 26
Levuka, Fiji — H15 52
Levy, co., Fl., U.S. — C4 86
Levy, Lake, l., Fl., U.S. — C4 86
Lewellen, Ne., U.S. — C3 104
Lewes, Eng., U.K. — E8 10
Lewes, De., U.S. — E5 85
Lewes and Rehoboth Canal, De., U.S. — F5 85
Lewis, Ia., U.S. — C2 92
Lewis, In., U.S. — F3 91
Lewis, Ks., U.S. — E4 93
Lewis, Mo., U.S. — C6 74
Lewis, Wi., U.S. — C1 126
Lewis, co., Ky., U.S. — B6 94
Lewis, co., Mo., U.S. — A6 102
Lewis, co., N.Y., U.S. — B5 109
Lewis, co., Tn., U.S. — B4 119
Lewis, co., Wa., U.S. — C3 124
Lewis, co., W.V., U.S. — C4 125
Lewis, stm., Wa., U.S. — C4 124
Lewis, Butt of, c., Scot., U.K. — A3 16
Lewis, Isle of, i., Scot., U.K. — D6 8
Lewis, Mount, mtn., Nv., U.S. — C5 105
Lewis and Clark Cavern, Mt., U.S. — D5 103
Lewis and Clark Lake, res., ... — E8 118

Lewis Creek, stm., Sask. — F3 75
Lewis Creek, stm., Vt., U.S. — C2 122
Lewis Hills, hills, Newf. — D2 72
Lewis Lake, l., Wy., U.S. — B2 127
Lewisport, Ky., U.S. — C3 94
Lewisporte, Newf. — D4 72
Lewis Range, mts., N.A. — A5 76
Lewis Run, Pa., U.S. — C4 115
Lewis Smith Lake, res., Al., U.S. — B2 78
Lewiston, Id., U.S. — C1 89
Lewiston, Me., U.S. — D2 96
Lewiston, Mi., U.S. — D6 99
Lewiston, Mn., U.S. — G7 100
Lewiston, N.Y., U.S. — B1 109
Lewiston, Ut., U.S. — B4 121
Lewiston Peak, mtn., Ut., U.S. — C3 121
Lewiston Woodville, N.C., U.S. — A5 110
Lewistown, Il., U.S. — C3 90
Lewistown, Md., U.S. — A3 97
Lewistown, Mo., U.S. — A6 102
Lewistown, Mt., U.S. — C7 103
Lewistown, Pa., U.S. — E6 115
Lewisville, N.B. — C5 71
Lewisville, Ar., U.S. — D2 81
Lewisville, Id., U.S. — F6 89
Lewisville, In., U.S. — E7 91
Lewisville, Mn., U.S. — G4 100
Lewisville, Oh., U.S. — C4 112
Lewisville, Tx., U.S. — C4 120
Lewisville Lake, res., Tx., U.S. — C4 120
Lexington, Al., U.S. — A2 78
Lexington, Ga., U.S. — C3 87
Lexington, Il., U.S. — C5 90
Lexington, In., U.S. — G6 91
Lexington, Ky., U.S. — B5 94
Lexington, Ma., U.S. — B5 98
Lexington, Mi., U.S. — E8 99
Lexington, Mo., U.S. — B4 102
Lexington, Ne., U.S. — D6 104
Lexington, N.Y., U.S. — C6 109
Lexington, N.C., U.S. — B2 110
Lexington, Oh., U.S. — B3 112
Lexington, Ok., U.S. — B4 113
Lexington, Or., U.S. — B7 114
Lexington, S.C., U.S. — D5 117
Lexington, Tn., U.S. — B3 119
Lexington, Tx., U.S. — D4 120
Lexington, Va., U.S. — C3 123
Lexington, co., S.C., U.S. — D5 117
Lexington Park, Md., U.S. — D5 97
Leyba, N.M., U.S. — B4 108
Leyburn, Eng., U.K. — F7 13
Leyond, stm., Man. — D2 21
Leysin, Switz. — D2 21
Leyte, i., Phil. — C7 34
Leżajsk, Pol. — C7 26
Lezha, Alb. — B2 40
Lézignan, Fr. — F5 16
Lgov, Sov. Un. — F10 27
Lhasa, China — F3 31
L'Haÿ-les-Roses, Fr. — g10 16
Lhazê, China — C11 31
Lhokseumawe, Indon. — k11 34
Lhoksukon, Indon. — J2 36
Liangcheng, China — D5 32
Liangping, China — I2 32
Lianhua, China — K5 32
Lianjiang, China — B9 35
Lianyungang, China — E8 31
Lianyungang, China — G8 31
Liaocheng, China — F6 32
Liaodong Bay, b., China — E9 31
Liao He, stm., China — C9 31
Liaoning, prov., China — C9 31
Liaotung Bay see Liaodong Bay, b., China — E9 32
Liaotung Peninsula, pen., China see Liaodong Peninsula, pen., China — D9 31
Liaoyang, China — C9 31
Liaoyuan, China — C10 31
Liard, stm., Can. — E7 66
Liart, Fr. — E4 17
Liathach, mtn., Scot., U.K. — C2 60
Líbano, Col. — B3 70
Libau, Ger. — D3 70
Libby, Mt., U.S. — B1 103
Libčice, Czech. — n17 26
Libenge, Zaire — A2 48
Liberal, Ks., U.S. — E3 93
Liberal, Mo., U.S. — D3 102
Liberec, Czech. — E7 26
Liberia, C.R. — E7 63
Liberia, ctry., Afr. — B4 45
Libertad, Ven. — C2 60
Libertador General Bernardo O'Higgins, prov., Chile — A2 54
Libertador General San Martín, Arg. — D3 55
Liberty, Sask. — F3 75
Liberty, Il., U.S. — G7 89
Liberty, In., U.S. — E8 91
Liberty, Ky., U.S. — C5 94
Liberty, Me., U.S. — D3 96
Liberty, Ms., U.S. — D3 101
Liberty, Mo., U.S. — B3 102
Liberty, N.Y., U.S. — D6 109
Liberty, N.C., U.S. — B3 110
Liberty, Pa., U.S. — C7 115
Liberty, S.C., U.S. — B2 117
Liberty, Tn., U.S. — B5 119
Liberty, Tx., U.S. — D5 120
Liberty, co., Fl., U.S. — B2 86
Liberty, co., Ga., U.S. — E5 87
Liberty, co., Mt., U.S. — B5 103
Liberty, co., Tx., U.S. — D5 120
Liberty Acres, Ca., U.S. — *n12 82
Liberty Center, Ia., U.S. — C4 92
Liberty Center, Oh., U.S. — A1 112
Liberty Corner, N.J., U.S. — B3 107
Liberty Grove, Md., U.S. — A6 97
Liberty Hill, Ct., U.S. — C6 84
Liberty Hill, S.C., U.S. — C6 117
Liberty Lake, Wa., U.S. — g14 124
Liberty Lake, res., Md., U.S. — B4 97
Liberty Mills, In., U.S. — B6 91
Libertytown, Md., U.S. — B3 97
Libertyville, Il., U.S. — A6 90
Libertyville, Ia., U.S. — D5 92
Libiąż, Pol. — C1 19
Libourne, Fr. — E3 16
Libramont, Bel. — E5 17
Libreville, Gabon — E1 46
Libuse, La., U.S. — C3 95

Name	Map Ref.	Page
Libušin, Czech.	n17	26
Libya, ctry., Afr.	D3	43
Libyan Desert, des., Afr.	D4	43
Libyan Plateau, plat., Afr.	C4	43
Licantén, Chile	B2	54
Licata, Italy	F4	23
Lice, Tur.	C13	40
Licenza, Italy	g9	23
Lichfield, Eng., U.K.	B6	12
Lichinga, Moz.	D6	48
Lichtenburg, S. Afr.	C4	48
Lichtenfels, Ger.	C6	19
Lichtenstein, Ger.	C7	19
Lick Creek, stm., Tn., U.S.	C11	119
Licking, Mo., U.S.	D6	102
Licking, co., Oh., U.S.	B3	112
Licking, stm., Ky., U.S.	B5	94
Licking, North Fork, stm., Ky., U.S.	B5	94
Licking, South Fork, stm., Ky., U.S.	B5	94
Licosa, Point, c., Italy	D5	23
Licungó, stm., Moz.	A6	49
Lida, Sov. Un.	E5	27
Lida, Lake, l., Mn., U.S.	D3	100
Liddel Water, stm., U.K.	E6	13
Lidderdale, Ia., U.S.	B3	92
Lidgerwood, N.D., U.S.	C8	111
Lidhult, Swe.	B7	15
Lidice, Czech.	C3	26
Lidingö, Swe.	H8	14
Lidköping, Swe.	H5	14
Lido di Roma, Italy	h8	23
Lidzbark Warmiński, Pol.	A6	26
Liebenthal, Sask.	G1	75
Liebenthal, Ks., U.S.	D4	93
Lieberose, Ger.	B9	19
Liechtenstein, ctry., Eur.	E4	18
Liège, Bel.	B6	16
Liège, prov., Bel.	D5	17
Liege, stm., Man.	A4	68
Liegnitz see Legnica, Pol.	C4	26
Lieksa, Fin.	F14	14
Lienen, Ger.	A2	19
Lienz, Aus.	E6	18
Liepāja, Sov. Un.	C3	27
Lier (Lierre), Bel.	B6	16
Lierneux, Bel.	D5	17
Lierre see Lier, Bel.	B6	16
Liestal, Switz.	D2	17
Liévin, Fr.	B9	16
Lièvre, Rivière du, stm., Que.	D2	74
Lièvres, Île aux, i., Que.	B8	74
Liffey, stm., Ire.	C3	10
Lifford, Ire.	C3	10
Liftwood, De., U.S.	*A3	85
Light, Ar., U.S.	A5	81
Lighthouse Inlet, b., S.C., U.S.	k12	117
Lighthouse Point, Fl., U.S.	*F6	86
Lighthouse Point, c., Fl., U.S.	C2	86
Lighthouse Point, c., La., U.S.	E3	95
Lighthouse Point, c., Mi., U.S.	C5	99
Lightning Creek, stm., Wy., U.S.	C8	127
Lightning Ridge, Austl.	D6	51
Lignite, N.D., U.S.	A3	111
Lignum, Va., U.S.	B5	123
Ligny-en-Barrois, Fr.	F5	17
Ligonha, stm., Moz.	E6	48
Ligonier, In., U.S.	B6	91
Ligonier, Pa., U.S.	F3	115
Ligovo (part of Leningrad), Sov. Un.	s31	14
Liguria, prov., Italy	E4	20
Liguria, prov., Italy	B2	20
Ligurian Apennines, mts., Italy	E4	20
Ligurian Sea, Eur.	C2	20
Lihue, Hi., U.S.	B2	88
Lijiang, China	F5	31
Lijin, China	F8	32
Likasi, Zaire	D4	48
Likely, B.C.	C7	69
Likely, Ca., U.S.	B3	82
Likhoslavl, Sov. Un.	C10	27
Likino-Dulevo, Sov. Un.	n18	27
Lilbourn, Mo., U.S.	E8	102
Lilburn, Ga., U.S.	h8	87
L'Ile-Rousse, Fr.	C2	23
Lilesville, N.C., U.S.	C3	110
Liling, China	K5	32
Lille, Fr.	B5	16
Lille, Me., U.S.	A4	96
Lille Baelt, strt., Den.	B4	83
Lillehammer, Nor.	G4	14
Lillers, Fr.	D2	17
Lillesand, Nor.	H3	14
Lillestrøm, Nor.	H4	14
Lillian, Al., U.S.	E2	78
Lillian, Tx., U.S.	n9	120
Lillie, La., U.S.	B3	95
Lillington, N.C., U.S.	B4	110
Lillinonah, Lake, l., Ct., U.S.	C2	84
Lilloet, B.C.	D7	69
Lilloet, stm., B.C.	D6	69
Lilloet Lake, l., B.C.	D6	69
Lilloet Range, mts., B.C.	E7	69
Lilly, Ga., U.S.	D3	87
Lilly, Pa., U.S.	F4	115
Lilly Fork, stm., W.V., U.S.	m13	125
Lilly Grove, W.V., U.S.	D3	125
Lilongwe, Mwi.	D5	48
Lily, Ky., U.S.	C5	94
Lily, S.D., U.S.	B8	118
Lily, Wi., U.S.	C5	126
Lim, stm., Yugo.	D4	24
Lima, Para.	D4	55
Lima, Peru	D2	58
Lima, Il., U.S.	C2	90
Lima, Mt., U.S.	F4	103
Lima, N.Y., U.S.	C3	109
Lima, Oh., U.S.	B1	112
Lima, dept., Peru	D2	58
Lima, stm., Eur.	B1	22
Lima Duarte, Braz.	C4	56
Limanowa, Pol.	D6	26
Lima Reservoir, res., Mt., U.S.	F4	103
Limassol see Lemesós, Cyp.	B5	11
Limay, stm., Arg.	B3	54
Limay Mahuida, Arg.	D3	54
Limbach [-Oberfrohna], Ger.	C7	19
Limbe, Cam.	I1	46
Limbé, Haiti	E7	64
Limburg, Ger.	E2	18
Limburg, prov., Bel.	D5	17
Limburg, prov., Neth.	e6	17
Lime City, Oh., U.S.	e6	112
Limedale, In., U.S.	E4	91
Limeil-Brévannes, Fr.	h10	16
Limeira, Braz.	G5	57
Limerick, Sask.	H2	75
Limerick, Ire.	I4	10
Limerick, Me., U.S.	E2	96
Limerick, co., Ire.	I3	10
Lime Rock, Ct., U.S.	B2	84
Limerock, R.I., U.S.	B4	116
Lime Springs, Ia., U.S.	A5	92
Limestone, Ar., U.S.	B2	81
Limestone, Fl., U.S.	E5	86
Limestone, Me., U.S.	B5	96
Limestone, N.Y., U.S.	C2	109
Limestone, Pa., U.S.	D3	115
Limestone, Tn., U.S.	C11	119
Limestone, co., Al., U.S.	A2	78
Limestone, co., Tx., U.S.	D4	120
Limestone, stm., Man.	A4	70
Limestone Bay, b., Man.	C2	70
Limestone Point, pen., Man.	C2	70
Limeton, Va., U.S.	B4	123
Limmen Bight, Austl.	B6	50
Limni, Grc.	C4	25
Límnos (Lemnos), i., Grc.	C5	40
Limoeiro, Braz.	C3	57
Limoeiro do Norte, Braz.	C3	57
Limoges, Ont.	B9	73
Limoges, Fr.	E4	16
Limón, C.R.	E8	63
Limón, Hond.	D7	63
Limon, Co., U.S.	B7	83
Limón, Bahía, b., Pan.	k11	62
Limousin, hist. reg., Fr.	E4	16
Limousin Plateau, plat., Fr.	E4	16
Limoux, Fr.	F5	16
Limpopo, stm., Afr.	B5	49
Lîñah, Sau. Ar.	H14	40
Linard, mtn., Switz.	C9	21
Linares, Chile	B2	54
Linares, Col.	C2	60
Linares, Mex.	C5	63
Linares, Spain	C4	22
Linaro, Cape, c., Italy	C3	23
Lince, Peru	*D2	58
Linch, Wy., U.S.	C6	127
Linchuan, China	F8	31
Lincoln, Arg.	A4	54
Lincoln, Ont.	D5	73
Lincoln, Eng., U.K.	D6	10
Lincoln, Al., U.S.	B3	78
Lincoln, Ar., U.S.	B1	81
Lincoln, Ca., U.S.	C3	82
Lincoln, De., U.S.	E4	85
Lincoln, Id., U.S.	F7	89
Lincoln, Il., U.S.	C4	90
Lincoln, Ks., U.S.	C5	93
Lincoln, Ia., U.S.	B5	92
Lincoln, Me., U.S.	C4	96
Lincoln, Ma., U.S.	g10	98
Lincoln, Mi., U.S.	D7	99
Lincoln, Mo., U.S.	C4	102
Lincoln, Mt., U.S.	D4	103
Lincoln, Ne., U.S.	D9	104
Lincoln, N.M., U.S.	D4	108
Lincoln, Tn., U.S.	B5	119
Lincoln, Vt., U.S.	C3	122
Lincoln, Va., U.S.	A5	123
Lincoln, co., Ar., U.S.	D4	81
Lincoln, co., Co., U.S.	C7	83
Lincoln, co., Ga., U.S.	C4	87
Lincoln, co., Id., U.S.	G4	89
Lincoln, co., Ks., U.S.	C5	93
Lincoln, co., Ky., U.S.	C5	94
Lincoln, co., La., U.S.	B3	95
Lincoln, co., Me., U.S.	D3	96
Lincoln, co., Mn., U.S.	F2	100
Lincoln, co., Ms., U.S.	D3	101
Lincoln, co., Mo., U.S.	B7	102
Lincoln, co., Mt., U.S.	B1	103
Lincoln, co., Ne., U.S.	D5	104
Lincoln, co., Nv., U.S.	F6	105
Lincoln, co., N.M., U.S.	D4	108
Lincoln, co., N.C., U.S.	B1	110
Lincoln, co., Ok., U.S.	B5	113
Lincoln, co., Or., U.S.	C3	114
Lincoln, co., S.D., U.S.	D9	118
Lincoln, co., Tn., U.S.	B5	119
Lincoln, co., Wa., U.S.	B7	124
Lincoln, co., W.V., U.S.	C2	125
Lincoln, co., Wi., U.S.	C4	126
Lincoln, co., Wy., U.S.	D2	127
Lincoln, Mount, mtn., Co., U.S.	B4	83
Lincoln Acres, Ca., U.S.	o15	82
Lincoln Center, Me., U.S.	C4	96
Lincoln City, In., U.S.	H4	91
Lincoln City, Or., U.S.	C3	114
Lincoln Heights, Oh., U.S.	o13	112
Lincoln Park, Co., U.S.	C5	83
Lincoln Park, Ga., U.S.	D2	87
Lincoln Park, Mi., U.S.	p15	99
Lincoln Park, N.J., U.S.	B4	107
Lincoln Sea, N.A.	A15	61
Lincolnshire, Il., U.S.	h9	90
Lincolnshire, co., Eng., U.K.	A7	12
Lincoln Tomb State Memorial, hist., Il., U.S.	D4	90
Lincolnton, Ga., U.S.	C4	87
Lincolnton, N.C., U.S.	B1	110
Lincoln Village, Ca., U.S.	*g10	82
Lincoln Village, Oh., U.S.	*m10	112
Lincolnville, Ks., U.S.	D7	93
Lincolnville, Me., U.S.	D3	96
Lincolnville, S.C., U.S.	h11	117
Lincolnwood, Il., U.S.	h9	90
Lind, Wa., U.S.	B7	124
Linda, Ca., U.S.	C3	82
Lindale, Ga., U.S.	B1	87
Lindale, Tx., U.S.	C5	120
Lindau, Ger.	E4	18
Lindbergh, Alta.	C5	68
Linden, Alta.	D4	68
Linden, Al., U.S.	C2	78
Linden, Ca., U.S.	C3	82
Linden, In., U.S.	D4	91
Linden, Ia., U.S.	C3	92
Linden, Mi., U.S.	F7	99
Linden, N.J., U.S.	k8	107
Linden, N.C., U.S.	B4	110
Linden, Tn., U.S.	B4	119
Linden, Tx., U.S.	C5	120
Linden, Wi., U.S.	F3	126
Lindenhurst, Il., U.S.	h8	90
Lindenhurst, N.Y., U.S.	n15	109
Lindenwold, N.J., U.S.	D3	107
Linderöd, Swe.	I7	15
Lindesberg, Swe.	H6	14
Lindgren Acres, Fl., U.S.	*G6	86
Líndhos, Grc.	D7	25
Lindi, Tan.	C7	48
Lindi, prov., Tan.	C6	48
Lindi, stm., Zaire	A4	48
Lindian, China	A11	32
Lindlar, Ger.	B2	19
Lindome, Swe.	A6	15
Lindon, Co., U.S.	B7	83
Lindon, Ut., U.S.	C4	121
Lindow, Ger.	F6	15
Lindrith, N.M., U.S.	A2	108
Lindsay, Ont.	C6	73
Lindsay, Ca., U.S.	D4	82
Lindsay, Mt., U.S.	C11	103
Lindsay, Ne., U.S.	C8	104
Lindsay, Ok., U.S.	C4	113
Lindsborg, Ks., U.S.	D6	93
Lindside, Oh., U.S.	A2	112
Lindstrom, Mn., U.S.	E6	100
Lindy, Ne., U.S.	B8	104
Lineboro, Md., U.S.	A4	97
Linefork, Ky., U.S.	C7	94
Linesville, Pa., U.S.	C1	115
Lineville, Al., U.S.	B4	78
Lineville, Ia., U.S.	D4	92
Linfen, China	D7	31
Linganore Creek, stm., Md., U.S.	B3	97
Lingao, China	B3	35
Lingayen, Phil.	B6	34
Lingayen Gulf, b., Phil.	n13	34
Lingen, Ger.	B3	18
Lingga Islands, is., Indon.	F2	34
Lingle, Wy., U.S.	D8	127
Linglestown, Pa., U.S.	F8	115
Lingling, China	F7	31
Lingshan, China	D6	108
Linguère, Sen.	C1	45
Lingwu, China	E2	32
Lingyuan, China	C8	31
Linhai, China	F9	31
Linhares, Braz.	E5	57
Linhe, China	D2	32
Linh Peak, mtn., Viet.	B3	34
Linjiang, China	F3	33
Linkou, China	B11	31
Linköping, Swe.	H6	14
Linière, Que.	C7	74
Linn, Ks., U.S.	C6	93
Linn, Mo., U.S.	C6	102
Linn, Tx., U.S.	F3	120
Linn, co., Ia., U.S.	B6	92
Linn, co., Ks., U.S.	D9	93
Linn, co., Mo., U.S.	B4	102
Linn, co., Or., U.S.	C4	114
Linn Creek, Mo., U.S.	C5	102
Linneus, Me., U.S.	B5	96
Linneus, Mo., U.S.	B4	102
Linnhe, Loch, b., Scot., U.K.	B4	11
Lino Lakes, Mn., U.S.	m12	100
Linqing, China	D8	31
Linru, China	G5	32
Lins, Braz.	C3	56
Linstead, Jam.	E14	65
Lintan, China	E5	31
Lintao, China	D5	31
Linth, stm., Switz.	B5	20
Linthal, Switz.	C7	21
Linthicum Heights, Md., U.S.	B4	97
Lintlaw, Sask.	E4	75
Linton, Que.	B5	74
Linton, Ga., U.S.	C3	87
Linton, In., U.S.	F3	91
Linton, Ky., U.S.	D2	94
Linton, N.D., U.S.	C5	111
Linville, N.C., U.S.	A1	110
Linville, Va., U.S.	B4	123
Linwood, Ont.	D4	73
Linwood, In., U.S.	D6	91
Linwood, Ks., U.S.	m15	93
Linwood, Ma., U.S.	B4	98
Linwood, Mi., U.S.	E7	99
Linwood, Ne., U.S.	C9	104
Linwood, N.J., U.S.	E3	107
Linwood, N.C., U.S.	B2	110
Linworth, Oh., U.S.	k10	112
Linxi, China	C8	32
Linxia, China	D5	31
Linyi, China	D8	31
Linz, Aus.	D7	18
Lions, La., U.S.	h10	95
Lions, Gulf of, b., Fr.	F6	16
Lion's Head, Ont.	C3	73
Lionville, Pa., U.S.	F10	115
Lipa, Phil.	C6	34
Lipan, Tx., U.S.	C4	120
Lipari, Italy	E5	23
Lipari, i., Italy	E5	23
Lipetsk, Sov. Un.	D6	29
Lipez, Cerro, mtn., Bol.	D2	55
Lipik, Yugo.	C2	24
Liping, China	F6	31
Lipljan, Sov. Un.	A8	24
Lipno, Pol.	B5	26
Lipno Reservoir, res., Czech.	E9	19
Lipova, Rom.	B5	24
Lippe, stm., Ger.	C4	18
Lippitt Estate, R.I., U.S.	B4	116
Lippstadt, Ger.	C4	18
Lipscomb, Al., U.S.	B3	78
Lipscomb, co., Tx., U.S.	A2	120
Lipsoí, i., Grc.	D6	25
Lipton, Sask.	G4	75
Lipu, China	G7	31
Lira, Ug.	A5	48
Li Rangu, Sud.	E2	47
Lircay, Peru	D4	23
Liria, Spain	D7	21
Lisala, Zaire	A3	48
Lisbon (Lisboa), Port.	C1	22
Lisbon, Al., U.S.	C2	78
Lisbon, Il., U.S.	B5	90
Lisbon, Ia., U.S.	C6	92
Lisbon, Me., U.S.	D2	96
Lisbon, Md., U.S.	B3	97
Lisbon, N.H., U.S.	B3	106
Lisbon, N.Y., U.S.	f9	109
Lisbon, N.D., U.S.	C8	111
Lisbon, Oh., U.S.	B5	112
Lisbon Center, Me., U.S.	f7	96
Lisbon Falls, Me., U.S.	E2	96
Lisburn, N. Ire., U.K.	C6	10
Lisburne, Cape, c., Ak., U.S.	A6	79
Liscannor Bay, b., Ire.	E2	11
Liscarney, Ire.	D1	11
Lisco, Ne., U.S.	C3	104
Liscomb, N.S.	D7	71
Liscomb, Ia., U.S.	B5	92
Lisdoonvarna, Ire.	D2	11
Lishi, China	F4	32
Lishu, China	C11	32
Lishui, China	F8	31
Lisianski Island, i., Hi., U.S.	k13	88
Lisichansk, Sov. Un.	q21	27
Lisieux, Fr.	C4	16
Liskeard, Eng., U.K.	D3	12
Lisle, Switz.	C1	21
Lisle, Ont.	C5	73
Lisle, Il., U.S.	k8	90
L'Isle [-sur-le-Doubs], Fr.	B2	20
L'Islet, co., Que.	B7	74
L'Islet-sur-Mer, Que.	B7	74
L'Isle-Verte, Que.	A8	74
Lisman, Al., U.S.	C1	78
Lismore, Austl.	E9	50
Lismore, N.S.	D7	71
Lismore, Ire.	E4	11
Lismore, Mn., U.S.	G3	100
Lismore Island, i., Scot., U.K.	D3	13
Lisnaskea, N. Ire., U.K.	C4	11
List, Ger.	C2	15
Listafjorden, b., Nor.	H2	14
Lister, B.C.	E9	69
Listie, Pa., U.S.	F3	115
Listowel, Ont.	D4	73
Listowel, Ire.	D2	10
Litang, China	F5	31
Litava, stm., Czech.	o16	26
Litchfield, Ca., U.S.	B3	82
Litchfield, Ct., U.S.	C3	84
Litchfield, Il., U.S.	D4	90
Litchfield, Mi., U.S.	F6	99
Litchfield, Mn., U.S.	E4	100
Litchfield, Ne., U.S.	C6	104
Litchfield, N.H., U.S.	E4	106
Litchfield, co., Ct., U.S.	B2	84
Litchfield Park, Az., U.S.	m8	80
Litchville, N.D., U.S.	C7	111
Liteň, Czech.	o17	26
Literberry, Il., U.S.	D3	90
Lithgow, Austl.	F8	51
Lithia Springs, Ga., U.S.	h7	87
Lithinon, Cape, c., Grc.	E5	25
Lithonia, Ga., U.S.	C2	87
Lithuania, state, Sov. Un.	D5	29
Lititz, Pa., U.S.	F9	115
Litókhoron, Grc.	B4	25
Litoměřice, Czech.	C3	26
Litomyšl, Czech.	D4	26
Litsitele, Swe.	t35	14
Littau, Switz.	B5	21
Little, stm., U.S.	B5	81
Little, stm., U.S.	D7	113
Little, stm., Ct., U.S.	C7	84
Little, stm., Ga., U.S.	C3	87
Little, stm., Ga., U.S.	E3	87
Little, stm., Ky., U.S.	D2	94
Little, stm., La., U.S.	C3	95
Little, stm., N.C., U.S.	B3	110
Little, stm., Ok., U.S.	B5	113
Little, stm., S.C., U.S.	C2	117
Little, stm., Tn., U.S.	n14	119
Little, stm., Vt., U.S.	C3	122
Little, stm., Va., U.S.	D2	123
Little Alföld, pl., Hung.	C7	21
Little America, Wy., U.S.	*E3	127
Little Andaman, i., India	F9	36
Little Arkansas, stm., Ks., U.S.	D6	93
Little Bay Islands, Newf.	D4	72
Little Bear Lake, l., Sask.	C3	75
Little Beaver Creek, stm., Ks., U.S.	C2	93
Little Belt Mountains, mts., Mt., U.S.	D6	103
Little Bighorn, stm., U.S.	E9	103
Little Birch, W.V., U.S.	C4	125
Little Bitter Lake, l., Eg.	D1	41
Little Black, stm., Me., U.S.	A3	96
Little Blue, stm., U.S.	C6	93
Little Blue, stm., In., U.S.	H5	91
Little Boars Head, N.H., U.S.	E5	106
Little Bow, stm., Alta.	D4	68
Little Britain, Ont.	C6	73
Little Bullhead, Man.	D3	70
Little Cacapon, stm., W.V., U.S.	B6	125
Little Cadotte, stm., Alta.	A2	68
Little Canada, Mn., U.S.	*m12	100
Little Carpathians, mts., Czech.	D4	26
Little Catalina, Newf.	D5	72
Little Cayman, i., Cay. Is.	E3	64
Little Cedar, stm., Ia., U.S.	A5	92
Little Chief, Ok., U.S.	A5	113
Little Choptank River, b., Md., U.S.	C5	97
Little Churchill, stm., Man.	A4	70
Little Chute, Wi., U.S.	D5	126
Little Coal, stm., W.V., U.S.	C3	125
Little Colorado, stm., Az., U.S.	B4	80
Little Compton, R.I., U.S.	E6	116
Little Creek, De., U.S.	C4	85
Little Creek Naval Amphibious Base, mil., Va., U.S.	k15	123
Little Creek Peak, mtn., Ut., U.S.	F3	121
Little Current, Ont.	B3	73
Little Deer Isle, Me., U.S.	D4	96
Little Diomede Island, i., Ak., U.S.	B6	79
Little Dry Creek, stm., Mt., U.S.	C10	103
Little Eagle, S.D., U.S.	B5	118
Little Egg Harbor, b., N.J., U.S.	D4	107
Little Egg Inlet, b., N.J., U.S.	E4	107
Little Falls, Mn., U.S.	E4	100
Little Falls, N.J., U.S.	B4	107
Little Falls, N.Y., U.S.	B6	109
Little Ferry, N.J., U.S.	h8	107
Littlefield, Az., U.S.	A2	80
Littlefield, Tx., U.S.	C1	120
Little Fishing Creek, stm., W.V., U.S.	h9	125
Little Fork, stm., Mn., U.S.	B5	100
Little Frog Mountain, mtn., Tn., U.S.	D9	119
Little Goose Creek, stm., Wy., U.S.	B6	127
Little Grand Rapids, Newf.	D4	72
Little Gunpowder Falls, stm., Md., U.S.	A4	97
Littlehampton, Eng., U.K.	D7	12
Little Harbour Deep, Newf.	C4	72
Little Hocking, Oh., U.S.	C4	112
Little Humboldt, stm., Nv., U.S.	B4	105
Little Humboldt, North Fork, stm., Nv., U.S.	B4	105
Little Humboldt, South Fork, stm., Nv., U.S.	B5	105
Little Inagua, i., Bah.	D7	64
Little Kanawha, stm., W.V., U.S.	C4	125
Little Kanawha, West Fork, stm., W.V., U.S.	C4	125
Little Lake, Mi., U.S.	B3	99
Little Lake, l., La., U.S.	E5	95
Littlelot, Tn., U.S.	B4	119
Little Lynches, stm., S.C., U.S.	C8	117
Little Manatee, stm., Fl., U.S.	p11	86
Little Manitou Lake, l., Sask.	F3	75
Little Marais, Mn., U.S.	C7	100
Little Mazarn Creek, stm., Ar., U.S.	g7	81
Little Meadows, Pa., U.S.	C9	115
Little Mecatina, stm., Can.	h9	72
Little Mexico, Tx., U.S.	D1	120
Little Miami, stm., Oh., U.S.	C1	112
Little Miami, East Fork, stm., Oh., U.S.	C1	112
Little Miami, Todd Fork, stm., Oh., U.S.	C1	112
Little Missouri, stm., Ar., U.S.	D2	81
Little Moose Mountain, mtn., N.Y., U.S.	B6	109
Little Mountain, S.C., U.S.	C5	117
Little Mountain, mtn., Wy., U.S.	D5	127
Little Muddy, stm., Il., U.S.	E4	90
Little Muddy, stm., N.D., U.S.	A2	111
Little Orleans, Md., U.S.	A1	97
Little Osage, stm., U.S.	E9	93
Little Otter Creek, stm., Vt., U.S.	C2	122
Little Owyhee, stm., U.S.	B5	105
Little Pee Dee, stm., S.C.	C9	117
Little Pigeon Creek, stm., In., U.S.	I3	91
Little Pipe Creek, stm., Md., U.S.	A3	97
Little Playgreen Lake, l., Man.	C3	70
Little Powder, stm., U.S.	F11	103
Little Quill Lake, l., Sask.	F3	75
Little Rann of Kachchh, pl., India	J4	37
Little Red, stm., U.S.	B4	81
Little Red, Middle Fork, stm., Ar., U.S.	B3	81
Little River, Al., U.S.	D2	78
Little River, Ks., U.S.	D5	93
Little River, S.C., U.S.	D10	117
Little River, co., Ar., U.S.	D1	81
Little River Inlet, b., S.C., U.S.	D10	117
Little Rock, Ar., U.S.	C3	81
Little Rock, Il., U.S.	B5	90
Little Rock, Ia., U.S.	A2	92
Little Rock, Ky., U.S.	B5	94
Little Rock Air Force Base, mil., Ar., U.S.	C3	81
Little Sable Point, c., Mi., U.S.	E4	99
Little Sachigo Lake, l., Ont.	A7	76
Little Saint Bernard Pass, Eur.	E7	16
Little Salt Lake, l., Ut., U.S.	F3	121
Little Sand Creek, stm., Mn., U.S.	D6	100
Little Sandy, stm., Ky., U.S.	B6	94
Little Sandy Creek, stm., Wy., U.S.	D3	127
Little Sauk, Mn., U.S.	E4	100
Little Sebago Lake, l., Me., U.S.	g7	96
Little Silver, N.J., U.S.	C4	107
Little Sioux, Ia., U.S.	B2	92
Little Sioux, stm., U.S.	B2	92
Little Sioux, West Fork, stm., Ia., U.S.	B2	92
Little Smoky, stm., Alta.	B2	68
Little Snake, stm., U.S.	A2	83
Little Southwest Miramichi, stm., N.B.	C3	71
Little Spokane, stm., Wa., U.S.	B8	124
Littlestown, Pa., U.S.	G7	115
Little Suamico, Wi., U.S.	D6	126
Little Tallapoosa, stm., U.S.	B4	78
Little Tenmile Creek, stm., W.V., U.S.	k10	125
Little Tennessee, stm., U.S.	D9	119
Littleton, Al., U.S.	f7	78
Littleton, Co., U.S.	B6	83
Littleton, Il., U.S.	C3	90
Littleton, Ma., U.S.	f10	98
Littleton, N.C., U.S.	A5	110
Littleton, N.H., U.S.	B3	106
Littleton, W.V., U.S.	B4	125
Little Tucson, Az., U.S.	F4	80
Little Valley, Ca., U.S.	B3	82
Little Valley, N.Y., U.S.	C2	109
Little Wabash, stm., Il., U.S.	E5	90
Little Walnut, stm., Ks., U.S.	g13	93
Little West Fork, stm., Tn., U.S.	A4	119
Little White, stm., S.D., U.S.	D5	118
Little Wolf, stm., Wi., U.S.	D4	126
Little Wood, stm., Id., U.S.	F4	89
Little York, In., U.S.	G6	91
Little York, Il., U.S.	B3	90
Little Zab, stm., Asia	E15	40
Littoria see Latina, Italy	D4	23
Litvínov, Czech.	C8	19
Liuba, China	E8	31
Liucheng, China	G6	31
Liucura, Chile	B2	54
Liuhe, China	C11	32
Liupan Mountains, mts., China	J5	31
Liuyang, China	G6	31
Liuzhou, China	G6	31
Livelong, Sask.	D1	75
Lively, Ont.	A3	73
Livengood, Ak., U.S.	B10	79
Livenza, stm., Italy	C3	82
Live Oak, Ca., U.S.	C3	82
Live Oak, Fl., U.S.	B4	86
Live Oak, co., Tx., U.S.	E3	120
Live Oak Manor, La., U.S.	*E5	95
Livermore, Ca., U.S.	h9	82
Livermore, Ia., U.S.	B3	92
Livermore, Ky., U.S.	C2	94
Livermore, Me., U.S.	D2	96
Livermore, Mount, mtn., Tx., U.S.	o12	120
Livermore Falls, Me., U.S.	D2	96
Livermore Falls, N.H., U.S.	C3	106
Liverpool, Austl.	*F9	50
Liverpool, N.S.	E5	71
Liverpool, Eng., U.K.	D5	10
Liverpool, Pa., U.S.	E7	115
Liverpool, Tx., U.S.	r14	120
Liverpool, W.V., U.S.	C3	125
Liverpool Bay, b., N.W. Ter.	B7	66
Livigno, Italy	C9	21
Livingston, Guat.	D7	63
Livingston, Al., U.S.	C1	78
Livingston, Ca., U.S.	D3	82
Livingston, Il., U.S.	E4	90
Livingston, Ky., U.S.	C5	94
Livingston, La., U.S.	D5	95
Livingston, Mt., U.S.	E6	103
Livingston, N.J., U.S.	B4	107
Livingston, N.Y., U.S.	C7	109
Livingston, S.C., U.S.	D5	117
Livingston, Tn., U.S.	C8	119
Livingston, Tx., U.S.	D5	120
Livingston, Wi., U.S.	F3	126
Livingston, co., Il., U.S.	C5	90
Livingston, co., Ky., U.S.	e9	94
Livingston, co., La., U.S.	D5	95
Livingston, co., Mi., U.S.	F7	99
Livingston, co., Mo., U.S.	B4	102
Livingston, co., N.Y., U.S.	C3	109
Livingston, Lake, res., Tx., U.S.	D5	120
Livingstone, Zam.	E4	48
Livingstone Falls, wtfl., Afr.	*C1	48
Livingston Island, i., B.A.T.	C6	7
Livingston Manor, N.Y., U.S.	D6	109
Livno, Yugo.	D3	24
Livny, Sov. Un.	E11	27
Livona, N.D., U.S.	C5	111
Livonia, In., U.S.	G5	91
Livonia, La., U.S.	D4	95
Livonia, Mi., U.S.	F7	99
Livonia, Mo., U.S.	A5	102
Livonia, N.Y., U.S.	C3	109
Livorno (Leghorn), Italy	C3	23
Livramento do Brumado, Braz.	g11	57
Livry-Gargan, Fr.	C6	16
Liwale, Tan.	C7	48
Lixian, China	J4	32
Liyang, China	I8	32
Lizard Creek, stm., Ia., U.S.	B3	92
Lizard Head Pass, Co., U.S.	D3	83
Lizard Head Peak, mtn., Wy., U.S.	D3	127
Lizard Point, c., Eng., U.K.	F4	10
Lizella, Ga., U.S.	D3	87
Lizemores, W.V., U.S.	C3	125
Lizton, In., U.S.	E4	91
Ljubljana, Yugo.	B2	24
Ljubuški, Yugo.	D3	24
Ljungby, Swe.	I5	14
Ljusdal, Swe.	G7	14
Ljusnan, stm., Swe.	G7	14
Ljusterö, Swe.	t36	14
Llandeilo, Wales, U.K.	C4	12
Llandovery, Wales, U.K.	C4	12
Llandrindod Wells, Wales, U.K.	D5	10
Llandudno, Wales, U.K.	B4	12
Llanelli, Wales, U.K.	E4	10
Llanes, Spain	A3	22
Llanfyllin, Wales, U.K.	B4	12
Llangefni, Wales, U.K.	A3	12
Llangollen, Wales, U.K.	B4	12
Llangollen Estates, De., U.S.	*B3	85
Llangynog, Wales, U.K.	B4	12
Llanidloes, Wales, U.K.	B4	12
Llano, N.M., U.S.	A4	108
Llano, Tx., U.S.	D3	120
Llano, co., Tx., U.S.	D3	120
Llanos, pl., S.A.	B3	60
Llanquihue, Lago, l., Chile	C2	54
Llanrwst, Wales, U.K.	A4	12
Llata, Peru	C2	58
Llaves, N.M., U.S.	A3	108
Llerena, Spain	C2	22
Lleyn Peninsula, pen., Wales, U.K.	D4	12
Llico, Chile	A2	55
Llobregat, stm., Spain	B6	22
Lloyd, Ky., U.S.	B7	94
Lloyd, Fl., U.S.	B2	86
Lloyd Harbor, N.Y., U.S.	*E7	109
Lloydminster, Alta.	C5	68
Lloydminster (Alta. and Sask.), Sask.	D1	75
Lloyds, stm., Newf.	D3	72
Lluchmayor, Spain	C7	22
Llullaillaco, Volcán, vol., S.A.	A3	54
Lo, stm., Viet.	B6	35
Loa, Ut., U.S.	E4	121
Loa, stm., Chile	A3	54
Loachapoka, Al., U.S.	C4	78
Loami, Il., U.S.	D4	90
Loange, stm., Afr.	C2	49
Lobatse, Bots.	C4	49
Löbau, Ger.	D7	18
Lobaye, stm., Cen. Afr. Rep.	H9	46
Lobelville, Tn., U.S.	B4	119
Lobería, Arg.	B5	54
Lobito, Ang.	D1	48
Lobnya, Sov. Un.	m17	27
Lobos, Phil.	p13	34
Lobos, Arg.	B5	54
Lobos, Cabo, c., Mex.	B2	63
Lobos, Punta, c., Mex.	G6	63
Lobos de Tierra, Isla, i., Peru	B1	58
Lobster Lake, l., Me., U.S.	C3	96
Loburg, Ger.	A7	19
Locarno, Switz.	F4	21
Lochaber, Scot., U.K.	D4	13
Lochalsh, Scot., U.K.	C3	13
Lochcarron, Scot., U.K.	D3	13
Lochearnhead, Scot., U.K.	D4	13
Lochem, Neth.	D6	17
Loches, Fr.	D4	16
Lochgilphead, Scot., U.K.	D3	13
Lochinver, Scot., U.K.	B3	13
Loch Lynn Heights, Md., U.S.	m12	97
Lochmaben, Scot., U.K.	E5	13
Lochmere, N.H., U.S.	D3	106
Lochnagar, mtn., Scot., U.K.	E5	13
Lochranza, Scot., U.K.	E3	13
Loch Raven Reservoir, res., Md., U.S.	B4	97
Lochsa, stm., Id., U.S.	C3	89
Lochy, Loch, l., Scot., U.K.	D4	13
Lockbourne, Oh., U.S.	m11	112
Locke, N.Y., U.S.	C4	109
Locke, Tn., U.S.	B1	119

Name	Map Ref.	Page
Locke Mills, Me., U.S.	D2	96
Lockeport, N.S.	F4	71
Lockerbie, Scot., U.K.	E5	13
Lockesburg, Ar., U.S.	D1	81
Lockhart, Al., U.S.	D3	78
Lockhart, Fl., U.S.	*D5	86
Lockhart, Mn., U.S.	C2	100
Lockhart, S.C., U.S.	B5	117
Lockhart, Tx., U.S.	E4	120
Lock Haven, Pa., U.S.	D7	115
Lockland, Oh., U.S.	o13	112
Lockney, Tx., U.S.	B2	120
Lockport, Man.	D3	70
Lockport, Il., U.S.	B5	90
Lockport, Ky., U.S.	B5	94
Lockport, La., U.S.	E5	95
Lockport, N.Y., U.S.	B2	109
Lockridge, Ia., U.S.	C6	92
Lock Springs, Mo., U.S.	B4	102
Lockwood, Sask.	F3	75
Lockwood, Mo., U.S.	D4	102
Lockwood, Mt., U.S.	E8	103
Lockwood, W.V., U.S.	C3	125
Loc Ninh, Viet.	G7	35
Loco, Ok., U.S.	C4	113
Loco Hills, N.M., U.S.	E6	108
Locumba, Peru	E3	58
Locust, N.J., U.S.	C4	107
Locust, N.C., U.S.	B2	110
Locust Bayou, Ar., U.S.	D3	81
Locust Creek, stm., Mo., U.S.	B4	102
Locust Fork, stm., Al., U.S.	B3	78
Locust Grove, Ga., U.S.	C2	87
Locust Grove, Md., U.S.	B2	97
Locust Grove, N.Y., U.S.	*C7	109
Locust Grove, Ok., U.S.	A6	113
Locust Hill (part of Markham), Ont.	k15	73
Lod, Isr.	G10	40
Loda, Il., U.S.	C5	90
Loděnice, stm., Czech.	n17	26
Löderup, Swe.	C8	15
Lodève, Fr.	F5	16
Lodge, Newf.	B4	72
Lodge, S.C., U.S.	E6	117
Lodge Creek, stm., N.A.	B7	103
Lodge Grass, Mt., U.S.	E9	103
Lodgepole, Alta.	C3	68
Lodgepole, Ne., U.S.	C3	104
Lodgepole, S.D., U.S.	B3	118
Lodgepole Creek, stm., U.S.	C3	104
Lodi, Italy	B2	23
Lodi, Ca., U.S.	C3	82
Lodi, N.J., U.S.	h8	107
Lodi, N.Y., U.S.	C4	109
Lodi, Oh., U.S.	A3	112
Lodi, Wi., U.S.	E4	126
Lodi, Zaire	B3	48
Lodja, Zaire	B3	48
Lodore, Canyon of, val., Co., U.S.	A2	83
Lods, Fr.	B2	20
Lodwar, Kenya	A6	48
Łódź, Pol.	C5	26
Loeches, Spain	p18	22
Loei, Thai.	D4	35
Loelli, I., Sud.	D3	47
Loeriesfontein, S. Afr.	D2	49
Lofer, Aus.	B8	20
Lofoten, is., Nor.	C5	14
Loftus, Eng., U.K.	F8	13
Loga, Niger	D5	45
Logan, Il., U.S.	F5	90
Logan, Ia., U.S.	C2	92
Logan, Ks., U.S.	C4	93
Logan, Mt., U.S.	E5	103
Logan, N.M., U.S.	B6	108
Logan, N.D., U.S.	A4	111
Logan, Oh., U.S.	C3	112
Logan, Ok., U.S.	A1	113
Logan, Ut., U.S.	B4	121
Logan, W.V., U.S.	D3	125
Logan, co., Ar., U.S.	B2	81
Logan, co., Co., U.S.	A7	83
Logan, co., Il., U.S.	C4	90
Logan, co., Ks., U.S.	D2	93
Logan, co., Ky., U.S.	D3	94
Logan, co., Ne., U.S.	C5	104
Logan, co., N.D., U.S.	B2	112
Logan, co., Oh., U.S.	B4	113
Logan, co., W.V., U.S.	D3	125
Logan, Mount, mtn., Yukon	D4	66
Logan, Mount, mtn., Wa., U.S.	A5	124
Logan Creek, stm., Ne., U.S.	B9	104
Logandale, Nv., U.S.	G7	105
Logan Lake, B.C.	D7	69
Logan Martin Lake, res., Al., U.S.	B3	78
Logan Mountains, mts., Yukon	D7	66
Logan Pass, U.S.	B2	103
Logansport, In., U.S.	C5	91
Logansport, Ky., U.S.	C3	94
Logansport, La., U.S.	C2	95
Loganton, Pa., U.S.	D7	115
Loganville, Ga., U.S.	C3	87
Loganville, Pa., U.S.	G8	115
Loganville, Wi., U.S.	E3	126
Loge, stm., Ang.	C1	48
Loggieville, N.B.	B4	71
Log Lane Village, Co., U.S.	A7	83
Logone, stm., Afr.	C3	46
Logroño, Spain	A4	22
Logrosán, Spain	C3	22
Løgstør, Den.	B3	15
Løgumkloster, Den.	C2	15
Lohals, Den.	C4	15
Lohārdaga, India	D7	36
Lohr, Ger.	D4	19
Lohrville, Ia., U.S.	B3	92
Loi, mtn., Laos	B5	35
Loikaw, Burma	D4	16
Loir, stm., Fr.	D3	16
Loire, stm., Fr.	D3	16
Loíza, Lago, res., P.R.	B3	65
Loja, Ec.	D3	58
Loja, Spain	D3	22
Loja, prov., Ec.	B2	58
Lokandu, Zaire	B4	48
Lokan Reservoir, res., Fin.	C13	14
Lokeren, Bel.	C3	17
Lokhvitsa, Sov. Un.	F9	27
Lokichar, Kenya	A6	48
Lokichokio, Kenya	A5	48
Lokitaung, Kenya	A6	48
Løkken, Den.	A3	15
Lokoja, Nig.	E6	45
Lokolama, Zaire	B3	48
Lokoro, stm., Zaire	B3	48
Lokossa, Benin	E5	45
Lol, stm., Sud.	D2	47
Lola, Ky., U.S.	e9	94
Lola, Mount, mtn., Ca., U.S.	C3	82
Loliondo, Tan.	B6	48
Lolland, i., Den.	J4	14
Lollar, Ger.	C3	19
Lollie, Ga., U.S.	D4	87
Lolo, Mt., U.S.	D2	103
Lolo Hot Springs, Mt., U.S.	C4	89
Lolo Pass, U.S.	D6	24
Lom, Bul.	D6	24
Loma, Co., U.S.	B2	83
Loma, Mt., U.S.	C6	103
Loma, Ne., U.S.	C9	104
Loma, N.D., U.S.	A7	111
Loma Linda, Ca., U.S.	*E5	82
Loma Mountains, mts., S.L.	E2	45
Loman, Mn., U.S.	B5	100
Lomas, Peru	E3	58
Lomas de Zamora, Arg.	A5	54
Lomax, Al., U.S.	C3	78
Lomax, Il., U.S.	C2	90
Lombard, Il., U.S.	k8	90
Lombardia, Serra, plat., Braz.	B4	59
Lombardia (Lombardy), prov., Italy	D5	20
Lombardy (Lombardia), prov., Italy	B2	23
Lombez, Fr.	G6	34
Lombok, i., Indon.	G5	34
Lombok Strait, strt., Indon.	G5	34
Lomé, Togo	E5	45
Lomela, Zaire	B3	48
Lomela, stm., Zaire	B3	48
Lometa, Tx., U.S.	D3	120
Lomié, Cam.	E2	46
Lomira, Wi., U.S.	E5	126
Lomita, Ca., U.S.	*E4	82
Lommel, Bel.	C5	17
Lomond, Alta.	D4	68
Lomond, Newf.	D3	72
Lomond, Loch, l., Scot., U.K.	B4	10
Lomonosov, Sov. Un.	s30	14
Lomonosovka, Sov. Un.	C7	28
Lompoc, Ca., U.S.	E3	82
Lom Sak, Thai.	D4	35
Łomża, Pol.	B7	26
Lonaconing, Md., U.S.	k13	97
Londesborough, Ont.	D3	73
London, Ont.	E3	73
London, Eng., U.K.	E6	10
London, Ar., U.S.	B2	81
London, In., U.S.	E6	91
London, Ky., U.S.	C5	94
London, Oh., U.S.	C2	112
London, Tx., U.S.	D3	120
London (Heathrow) Airport, Eng., U.K.	m12	10
Londonderry (Derry), N. Ire., U.K.	C3	10
Londonderry, N.H., U.S.	E4	106
Londonderry, Oh., U.S.	C3	112
Londonderry, Vt., U.S.	E3	122
Londonderry, Cape, c., Austl.	B4	50
Londonderry, Isla, i., Chile	k11	54
London Mills, Il., U.S.	C3	90
Londontowne, Md., U.S.	C4	97
Londrina, Braz.	C2	56
Lone Elm, Ks., U.S.	D8	93
Lone Grove, Ok., U.S.	C4	113
Lone Jack, Mo., U.S.	C3	102
Lonely Island, i., Ont.	B3	73
Lone Mountain, Tn., U.S.	C10	119
Lone Mountain, mtn., Nv., U.S.	E4	105
Lone Oak, Ky., U.S.	e9	94
Lone Oak, Tx., U.S.	C5	120
Lone Pine, Ca., U.S.	D4	82
Lonepine, Mt., U.S.	C2	103
Lone Rock, Sask.	D1	75
Lone Rock, Ia., U.S.	A3	92
Lonerock, Or., U.S.	B7	114
Lone Rock, Wi., U.S.	E3	126
Lone Star, S.C., U.S.	D6	117
Lone Tree, Ia., U.S.	C6	92
Lonetree, Wy., U.S.	E2	127
Lone Tree Creek, stm., Co., U.S.	A6	83
Lone Wolf, Ok., U.S.	C2	113
Long, co., Ga., U.S.	E5	87
Longa, stm., Ang.	D3	48
Longá, stm., Braz.	B2	57
Longacre, W.V., U.S.	m13	125
Longarone, Italy	C8	20
Long Bar Harbor, Md., U.S.	B5	97
Long Bay, b., Jam.	E12	65
Long Bay, b., Jam.	F14	65
Long Beach, Ca., U.S.	F4	82
Long Beach, In., U.S.	A4	91
Long Beach, Md., U.S.	D5	97
Long Beach, Ms., U.S.	E3	100
Long Beach, Ms., U.S.	g7	101
Long Beach, N.Y., U.S.	E7	109
Long Beach, Wa., U.S.	C1	124
Long Beach Naval Shipyard, mil., Ca., U.S.	n12	82
Longboat Key, Fl., U.S.	q10	86
Longboat Key, i., Fl., U.S.	E4	86
Longboat Pass, strt., Fl., U.S.	q10	86
Long Bottom, Oh., U.S.	C4	112
Long Branch (part of Etobicoke), Ont.	m14	73
Long Branch, N.J., U.S.	C5	107
Long Branch, Tx., U.S.	C5	120
Longbranch, Wa., U.S.	B3	124
Long Cay, i., Bah.	m17	64
Long Creek, Or., U.S.	C7	114
Longcreek, S.C., U.S.	B1	117
Long Creek, stm., N.A.	H3	75
Long Creek Mountain, mtn., Wy., U.S.	D5	127
Longdale, Ok., U.S.	A3	113
Long Eaton, Eng., U.K.	B6	12
Long Eddy, N.Y., U.S.	D5	109
Longford, Ont.	C5	73
Longford, Ire.	D3	10
Longford, Eng., U.K.	C5	12
Longford, co., Ire.	D4	11
Long Grove, Ia., U.S.	C7	92
Long Harbour [-Mount Arlington Heights], Newf.	*D7	84
Long Hill, Ct., U.S.	F5	109
Longiram, Indon.	F5	34
Long Island, N.S.	C4	93
Longisland, N.C., U.S.	B3	110
Long Island, Va., U.S.	C3	123
Long Island, i., Bah.	C8	64
Long Island, i., Me., U.S.	E3	71
Long Island, i., Me., U.S.	g7	96
Long Island, i., Ma., U.S.	g12	98
Long Island, i., N.Y., U.S.	E7	109
Long Island, i., N.D., U.S.	A4	111
Long Island Sound, strt., U.S.	E7	109
Long Key, Fl., U.S.	H6	86
Long Key, i., Fl., U.S.	H6	86
Longkou, China	F9	32
Longlac, Ont.	G15	66
Long Lake, Il., U.S.	h8	90
Long Lake, Mi., U.S.	D7	99
Long Lake, N.Y., U.S.	B6	109
Longlake, S.D., U.S.	B6	118
Long Lake, Wi., U.S.	C5	126
Long Lake, l., N.B.	B3	71
Long Lake, l., Me., U.S.	A4	96
Long Lake, l., Me., U.S.	D2	96
Long Lake, l., Mi., U.S.	D5	99
Long Lake, l., Mi., U.S.	C7	99
Long Lake, l., Mn., U.S.	D2	100
Long Lake, l., N.Y., U.S.	B6	109
Long Lake, l., N.D., U.S.	C6	111
Long Lake, l., Wa., U.S.	C2	125
Long Lake Colony, S.D., U.S.	*B7	118
Long Lane, Mo., U.S.	D5	102
Longleaf, La., U.S.	C3	95
Longlin, China	G6	31
Longmeadow, Ma., U.S.	B2	98
Longmont, Co., U.S.	A5	83
Long Mountain, mtn., Mo., U.S.	E5	102
Long Mountain, mtn., N.H., U.S.	A4	106
Long Pine, Ne., U.S.	B6	104
Long Point, N.S.	D8	71
Long Point, Ont.	E4	73
Long Point, Il., U.S.	B5	90
Long Point, c., Man.	C2	70
Long Point, c., Newf.	D2	72
Long Point, pen., Ont.	E4	73
Long Pond, l., Me., U.S.	C3	96
Long Pond, l., Me., U.S.	C2	96
Long Pond, l., Me., U.S.	C6	98
Long Pond, l., Me., U.S.	C6	98
Long Pond, res., Fl., U.S.	C4	86
Longport, N.J., U.S.	E3	107
Long Prairie, Mn., U.S.	E4	100
Longquan, China	F8	31
Long Range Mountains, mts., Newf.	D3	72
Longreach, Austl.	D7	50
Longridge, Eng., U.K.	G6	13
Long Run, W.V., U.S.	k9	125
Long Strait, strt., Sov. Un.	B20	29
Longstreet, La., U.S.	B2	95
Longton, Ks., U.S.	E7	93
Longtown, Eng., U.K.	E6	13
Longtown, Mo., U.S.	D8	102
Longueau, Fr.	E2	17
Longueuil, Que.	D4	74
Longuyon, Fr.	C6	16
Longvale, Ca., U.S.	C2	82
Long Valley, Az., U.S.	C4	80
Long Valley, N.J., U.S.	B3	107
Longvalley, S.D., U.S.	D4	118
Longview, Alta.	D3	68
Longview, Il., U.S.	D5	90
Long View, Ky., U.S.	C4	94
Longview, Ms., U.S.	B5	101
Long View, N.C., U.S.	B1	110
Los Angeles Aqueduct, Ca., U.S.	E4	82
Longview, Tx., U.S.	C5	120
Longview, Wa., U.S.	C3	124
Longville, La., U.S.	D2	95
Longville, Mn., U.S.	C4	100
Longwood, Fl., U.S.	*D5	86
Longwood, Ca., U.S.	C4	110
Longwoods, Md., U.S.	C5	97
Longwy, Fr.	C6	16
Longxian, China	G2	32
Long Xuyen, Viet.	G6	35
Longyan, China	F6	32
Longyao, China	B3	33
Longzhen, China	B13	31
Longzhou, China	G6	31
Lonkin, Burma	C10	36
Lonoke, Ar., U.S.	C4	81
Lonoke, co., Ar., U.S.	C4	81
Lönsdal, Nor.	D6	14
Lonsdale, Ont.	C7	73
Lonsdale, Mn., U.S.	F5	100
Lonsdale, R.I., U.S.	B4	116
Lons-le-Saunier, Fr.	D6	16
Lontzen, Bel.	D5	17
Looe, Eng., U.K.	D3	12
Loogootee, In., U.S.	G4	91
Lookeba, Ok., U.S.	B3	113
Lookout, Ca., U.S.	B3	82
Lookout, W.V., U.S.	C7	94
Lookout, W.V., U.S.	C3	125
Lookout, Cape, c., N.C., U.S.	C6	110
Lookout, Point, c., Mi., U.S.	d7	99
Lookout Mountain, Tn., U.S.	h11	119
Lookout Mountain, mtn., U.S.	D8	119
Lookout Mountain, mtn., Or., U.S.	C6	114
Lookout Pass, U.S.	B3	89
Lookout Point Lake, res., Or., U.S.	D4	114
Loomis, Sask.	H1	75
Loomis, Ne., U.S.	D6	104
Loomis, S.D., U.S.	D7	118
Loomis, Wa., U.S.	A6	124
Loon, stm., Alta.	A3	68
Loon, stm., Man.	A1	70
Loon Bay, Newf.	D4	72
Loon Lake, Wa., U.S.	A8	124
Loon Lake, l., Alta.	A3	68
Loon Lake, l., Can.	B1	70
Loon Lake, l., Me., U.S.	B3	96
Loon Lake Mountains, mtn., N.Y., U.S.	f10	109
Loon Straits, Man.	D3	70
Loop, Tx., U.S.	C1	120
Loop Creek, stm., W.V., U.S.	m13	125
Loop Head, c., Ire.	D1	10
Loos, Fr.	D3	17
Loosahatchie, stm., Tn., U.S.	B2	119
Loose Creek, Mo., U.S.	C6	102
Lopatka, Cape, c., Sov. Un.	D18	29
Lop Buri, Thai.	D2	34
Lopeno, Tx., U.S.	F3	120
Lopez, Pa., U.S.	D9	115
Lopez, Cap, c., Gabon	F1	46
Lopez Bay, b., Phil.	p14	34
Lopez Island, i., Wa., U.S.	A3	124
Lop Nur, l., China	D3	31
Lopori, stm., Zaire	A3	48
Lopphavet, b., Nor.	B9	14
Lora, Hāmūn-i, l., Asia	G12	39
Lorado, W.V., U.S.	D3	125
Lorain, Oh., U.S.	A3	112
Lorain, co., Oh., U.S.	A3	112
Loraine, Il., U.S.	C2	90
Loraine, N.D., U.S.	A4	111
Loraine, Tx., U.S.	C2	120
Loralai, Pak.	E2	38
Loramie, Lake, res., Oh., U.S.	B1	112
Loranger, La., U.S.	D5	95
Lorca, Spain	D5	22
Lord Howe Island, i., Austl.	I9	6
Lordsburg, N.M., U.S.	E1	108
Lords Point, Ct., U.S.	D8	84
Loreauville, La., U.S.	D4	95
Loreburn, Sask.	F2	75
Lore City, Oh., U.S.	C4	112
Lorena, Braz.	C3	56
Lorengau, Pap. N. Gui.	k8	50a
Lorentz, W.V., U.S.	h12	50
Lorenzo, Id., U.S.	B4	125
Lorenzo, Ne., U.S.	F7	89
Lorenzo, Tx., U.S.	C2	104
Lorenzo Geyres, Ur.	C2	120
Loreto, Braz.	E1	54
Loreto, Col.	C1	57
Loreto, Italy	D3	60
Loreto, Mex.	C7	23
Loreto, Para.	D2	63
Loreto, dept., Peru	D5	55
Loretta, Ks., U.S.	D3	58
Loretta, Wi., U.S.	D4	93
Lorette, Man.	C3	126
Loretteville, Que.	E3	70
Loretto, Ky., U.S.	C6	74
Loretto, Mi., U.S.	C4	94
Loretto, Pa., U.S.	C3	99
Loretto, Tn., U.S.	C7	104
Lorica, Col.	F4	115
Lorida, Fl., U.S.	B2	60
Lorient, Fr.	E5	86
L'Original, Ont.	D3	16
Lorimor, Ia., U.S.	B10	73
Loring, Mt., U.S.	C3	92
Loring Air Force Base, mil., Me., U.S.	B9	103
Loris, S.C., U.S.	B5	96
Lorlie, Sask.	C10	117
Lorman, Ms., U.S.	G4	75
Lorne, Scot., i., B.C.	D2	101
Lorne, N.B.	C2	69
Lorn, Firth of, est., Scot., U.K.	B3	71
Lorneville, Ont.	B4	10
Lorquin, Fr.	C5	73
Lörrach, Ger.	F6	17
Lorraine, N.Y., U.S.	E3	18
Lorraine, hist. reg., Fr.	B5	109
Lorraine Plateau, plat., Fr.	C7	16
Lorsch, Ger.	D3	19
Lorton, Va., U.S.	D4	19
Lorup, Ger.	*B5	123
Los Alamitos, Ca., U.S.	B7	17
Los Alamos, Ca., U.S.	*F5	82
Los Alamos, N.M., U.S.	E3	82
Los Alamos, co., N.M., U.S.	B3	108
Los Altos, Ca., U.S.	B3	108
Los Altos Hills, Ca., U.S.	k8	82
Los Amates, Guat.	*k8	82
Los Andes, Chile	D7	63
Los Ángeles, Chile	A2	54
Los Angeles, Ca., U.S.	B2	54
Los Angeles, co., Ca., U.S.	E4	82
Los Angeles Aqueduct, Ca., U.S.	E4	82
Losantville, In., U.S.	D7	91
Los Banos, Ca., U.S.	D3	82
Los Blancos, Arg.	D3	55
Los Cerrillos, Arg.	A3	54
Los Ebanos, Tx., U.S.	F3	120
Los Fresnos, Tx., U.S.	F4	120
Los Gatos, Ca., U.S.	D2	82
Los Hermanos, Islas, is., Ven.	A5	60
Los Lagos, Chile	B2	54
Los Lagos, prov., Chile	C2	54
Los Lunas, N.M., U.S.	C3	108
Los Mochis, Mex.	D3	63
Los Molinos, Ca., U.S.	B2	82
Los Monjes, Islas, is., Ven.	A3	60
Los Nietos, Ca., U.S.	*n12	82
Los Ojos, N.M., U.S.	A3	108
Losombo, Zaire	A2	48
Los Osos, Ca., U.S.	*E3	82
Los Padillas, N.M., U.S.	*B3	108
Los Palacios, Cuba	C2	64
Los Palacios [y Villafranca], Spain	D3	22
Los Peares, Spain	A2	22
Los Pinos, N.M., U.S.	A3	108
Los Pinos, stm., Co., U.S.	D3	83
Los Ranchos de Albuquerque, N.M., U.S.	B3	108
Los Remedios, stm., Mex.	g9	63
Los Reyes [de Salgado], Mex.	D4	63
Los Reyes la Paz, Mex.	h10	63
Los Ríos, prov., Ec.	H2	58
Los Roques, Islas, is., Ven.	A4	60
Los Santos, Pan.	G7	62
Los Santos [de Maimona], Spain	C2	22
Los Sarmientos, Arg.	E2	55
Los Sauces, Chile	B2	54
Lossiemouth, Scot., U.K.	C5	13
Lössnitz, Ger.	C7	19
Lost, In., U.S.	G4	91
Lost, stm., Wa., U.S.	A5	124
Lost, stm., W.V., U.S.	B6	125
Lost City, W.V., U.S.	B6	125
Lost Creek, stm., Ar., U.S.	C3	81
Lost Creek, stm., Wy., U.S.	D4	127
Los Taques, Ven.	A3	60
Los Teques, Ven.	A4	60
Los Testigos, Islas, is., Ven.	A5	60
Lost Hills, Ca., U.S.	E4	82
Lostine, Or., U.S.	B9	114
Lost Nation, Ia., U.S.	C7	92
Lost Peak, mtn., Ut., U.S.	D1	121
Lost Ranger Peak, mtn., Co., U.S.	A4	83
Lost River, Id., U.S.	F5	89
Lost River, W.V., U.S.	B6	125
Lost River Glacial Caverns, N.H., U.S.	B3	106
Lost River Range, mts., Id., U.S.	E5	89
Los Trujillos, N.M., U.S.	C3	108
Lost Springs, Ks., U.S.	D7	93
Lost Springs, Wy., U.S.	D8	127
Lost Trail Pass, U.S.	D5	89
Los Vigiles, N.M., U.S.	*B4	108
Los Vilos, Chile	A2	54
Lota, Chile	B2	54
Lotawana, Lake, res., Mo., U.S.	k11	102
Lotbinière, co., Que.	C6	74
Lothair, Mt., U.S.	B5	103
Lothian, prov., Scot., U.K.	E5	13
Loto, Zaire	B4	48
Lotofaga, W. Sam.	F12	52
Lötschberg Tunnel, Switz.	E3	18
Lott, Tx., U.S.	D4	120
Lotung, Tai.	G9	31
Louang Namtha, Laos	B4	35
Louangphrabang, Laos	B3	34
Louann, Ar., U.S.	D3	81
Loubomo, Congo	B1	48
Loudenville, W.V., U.S.	g8	125
Loudon, N.H., U.S.	D4	106
Loudon, Tn., U.S.	D9	119
Loudon, co., Tn., U.S.	D9	119
Loudonville, N.Y., U.S.	*C7	109
Loudoun, co., Va., U.S.	A5	123
Loudun, Fr.	D4	16
Louga, Sen.	C1	45
Loughborough, Eng., U.K.	D6	10
Loughman, Fl., U.S.	D5	86
Loughrea, Ire.	D2	10
Loughros More Bay, b., Ire.	C3	11
Louin, Ms., U.S.	C4	101
Louisa, Ky., U.S.	B7	94
Louisa, Va., U.S.	B4	123
Louisa, co., Ia., U.S.	C6	92
Louisa, co., Va., U.S.	C5	123
Louisa, Lake, l., Fl., U.S.	D5	86
Louisbourg, N.S.	D10	71
Louisburg, Ks., U.S.	D9	93
Louisburg, Mn., U.S.	E2	100
Louisburg, Mo., U.S.	D4	102
Louisburg, N.C., U.S.	A4	110
Louisburgh, Ire.	D2	11
Louisdale, N.S.	D8	71
Louise, Ga., U.S.	C2	87
Louise, Ms., U.S.	C3	101
Louise, Tx., U.S.	E4	120
Louise, W.V., U.S.	f8	125
Louise, Lake, l., Ak., U.S.	f18	79
Louise, Lake, l., B.C.	C2	69
Louiseville, Que.	C5	74
Louisiade Archipelago, is., Pap. N. Gui.	G9	6
Louisiana, Mo., U.S.	B6	102
Louisiana, state, U.S.	C3	95
Louisiana Point, c., La., U.S.	E2	95
Louis Trichardt, S. Afr.	B4	49
Louisville, Al., U.S.	D4	78
Louisville, Co., U.S.	B5	83
Louisville, Ga., U.S.	C4	87
Louisville, Il., U.S.	E5	90
Louisville, Ky., U.S.	C7	93
Louisville, Ms., U.S.	B4	101
Louisville, Ne., U.S.	D9	104
Louisville, N.Y., U.S.	f9	109
Louisville, Oh., U.S.	B4	112
Louisville, Tn., U.S.	D9	119
Louis-XIV, Pointe, c., Que.	h11	74
Loukhi, Sov. Un.	D15	14
Loulé, Port.	D2	22
Louny, Czech.	C2	26
Loup, co., Ne., U.S.	C6	104
Loup, stm., Ne., U.S.	C8	104
Loup, Rivière du, stm., Que.	B7	74
Loup, Rivière du, stm., Que.	B8	74
Loup City, Ne., U.S.	C7	104
Lourdes, Newf.	D2	72
Lourdes, La., U.S.	C6	74
Lourdes, Fr.	F3	16
Lourenço Marques see Maputo, Moz.	C5	49
Loures, Port.	f9	22
Lousã, Port.	B1	22
Lousã, Port.	A2	22
Louth, Ire.	D5	11
Louth, Eng., U.K.	D7	10
Louth, co., Ire.	D5	11
Loutrá Aidhipsoú, Grc.	C4	25
Loutrákion, Grc.	h9	25
Loutre, Bayou de, stm., La., U.S.	B3	95
Louvain see Leuven, Bel.	B6	16
Louvale, Ga., U.S.	D2	87
Louviers, Fr.	C4	16
Louviers, Co., U.S.	B6	83
Lovat, stm., Sov. Un.	C8	27
Lovelaceville, Ky., U.S.	f9	94
Loveladies, N.J., U.S.	D4	107
Lovelady, Tx., U.S.	D5	120
Loveland, Ia., U.S.	A5	83
Loveland, Oh., U.S.	C2	92
Lovell, Me., U.S.	D2	96
Lovell, Ok., U.S.	A4	113
Lovell, Wy., U.S.	B4	127
Lovells, Mi., U.S.	D6	99
Lovelock, Nv., U.S.	C3	105
Lovely, Ky., U.S.	C7	94
Lovenia, Mount, mtn., Ut., U.S.	C5	121
Love Point, c., Md., U.S.	B5	97
Loverna, Sask.	F1	75
Loves Park, Il., U.S.	A4	90
Lovett, Ga., U.S.	D4	87
Lovettsville, Va., U.S.	A5	123
Lovewell Pond, l., Me., U.S.	D2	96
Lovick, Al., U.S.	f7	78
Lovilia, Ia., U.S.	C5	92
Loving, N.M., U.S.	E5	108
Loving, co., Tx., U.S.	D1	120
Lovington, Il., U.S.	D5	90
Lovington, Ia., U.S.	e8	92
Lovington, N.M., U.S.	E6	108
Lovosice, Czech.	C9	19
Low, Que.	D2	74
Low, Cape, c., N.W. Ter.	D15	66
Lowa, Zaire	B5	48
Lowa, stm., Zaire	B5	48
Lowden, Ia., U.S.	C7	92
Low Farm, Man.	E3	70
Lowell, Ar., U.S.	A1	81
Lowell, In., U.S.	B3	91
Lowell, Ma., U.S.	A5	98
Lowell, Mi., U.S.	F5	99
Lowell, N.C., U.S.	B1	110
Lowell, Oh., U.S.	C4	112
Lowell, Or., U.S.	D4	114
Lowell, Vt., U.S.	B3	122
Lowell, W.V., U.S.	C3	125
Lowellville, Oh., U.S.	A5	112
Lower Arrow Lake, res., B.C.	E8	69
Lower Bank, N.J., U.S.	D3	107
Lower Brule, S.D., U.S.	C6	118
Lower Brule Indian Reservation, S.D., U.S.	C6	118
Lower Burrell, Pa., U.S.	*h15	115
Lower Cabot, Vt., U.S.	C4	122
Lower California, pen., Mex.	B2	63
Lower East Pubnico, N.S.	F4	71
Lower Hutt, N.Z.	N15	51
Lower Island Cove, Newf.	D5	72
Lower Klamath Lake, l., Ca., U.S.	B3	82
Lower Loch Erne, l., N. Ire., U.K.	C3	10
Lower Manitou Lake, l., Ont.	E5	70
Lower Marlboro, Md., U.S.	C4	97
Lower Matecumbe Key, i., Fl., U.S.	H6	86
Lower Merion Township, Pa., U.S.	*F11	115
Lower Monumental Lake, res., Wa., U.S.	C7	124
Lower Moreland Township, Pa., U.S.	*F11	115
Lower New York Bay, b., N.J., U.S.	B4	107
Lower Otay Reservoir, res., Ca., U.S.	o16	82
Lower Paia, Hi., U.S.	C5	88
Lower Peach Tree, Al., U.S.	D2	78
Lower Red Lake, l., Mn., U.S.	C3	100
Lower Rice Lake, l., Mn., U.S.	C3	100
Lower Salem, Oh., U.S.	C4	112
Lower Salmon Dam, Id., U.S.	G4	89
Lower Southampton Township, Pa., U.S.	*G11	115
Lower Village, Vt., U.S.	C3	122
Lower West Pubnico, N.S.	F4	71
Lower Wilson Pond, l., Me., U.S.	C3	96
Lower Woods Harbour, N.S.	F4	71
Lowes, Ky., U.S.	D7	10
Lowestoft, Eng., U.K.	B6	102
Lowgap, N.C., U.S.	A2	110
Lowicz, Pol.	B5	26
Lowland, N.C., U.S.	B6	110
Lowman, Id., U.S.	E3	89
Lowmansville, Ky., U.S.	C7	94
Lowmoor, Va., U.S.	C3	123
Low Moor, Ia., U.S.	C7	92
Lowndes, Mo., U.S.	D7	102
Lowndes, co., Al., U.S.	C3	78
Lowndes, co., Ga., U.S.	F3	87
Lowndes, co., Ms., U.S.	B5	101
Lowndesboro, Al., U.S.	C3	78
Lowndesville, S.C., U.S.	C2	117
Lowry, Mn., U.S.	E3	100
Lowry, S.D., U.S.	B6	118
Lowry Air Force Base, mil., Co., U.S.	B6	83
Lowry City, Mo., U.S.	C4	102
Lowrys, S.C., U.S.	B5	117
Low Tatra Mountains, mts., Czech.	D5	26
Lowville, N.Y., U.S.	B5	109
Loxahatchee, Fl., U.S.	F6	86
Loxley, Al., U.S.	E2	78
Loxton, Austl.	G3	51
Loyal, Ok., U.S.	B3	113
Loyal, Wi., U.S.	D3	126
Loyalist, Alta.	D5	68
Loyalton, Ca., U.S.	C3	82
Loyalton, S.D., U.S.	B6	118
Loyalty Islands, is., N. Cal.	H10	2
Loysburg, Pa., U.S.	F5	115
Loysville, Pa., U.S.	F7	115
Loznica, Yugo.	B3	24
Loze, Fr.	B3	18
Lozova, Sov. Un.	G11	27
Lozovatka, Sov. Un.	h9	25
Lozoya, Canal of, Spain	o17	22
Lualaba, stm., Zaire	B4	48
Luama, stm., Zaire	B5	48
Lua Makika, crat., Hi., U.S.	C5	88
Luampa, Zam.	E3	48
Lu'an, China	I7	32
Luana, Ia., U.S.	A6	92
Luanda, Ang.	C1	48
Luanda, Braz.	C2	56
Luanda, dept., Ang.	C1	48
Luang, mtn., Thai.	D1	34
Luang Chiang Dao, mtn., Thai.	D3	34
Luanguinga, stm., Afr.	A3	53
Luangwa, stm., Afr.	C8	31
Luanhe, stm., China	D4	48
Luanshya, Zam.	D4	48
Luanxian, China	E8	32
Luapula, prov., Zam.	D4	48
Luarca, Spain	A2	22
Luashi, Zaire	D3	48
Luau, Ang.	E1	46
Lubaczów, Pol.	C7	26
Lubang, Phil.	p13	34
Lubang, i., Phil.	p14	34
Lubang Islands, is., Phil.	C6	34
Lubango, Ang.	D1	48
Lubartów, Pol.	C7	26
Lubawa, Pol.	B5	26
Lübbecke, Ger.	A3	19
Lübben, Ger.	G6	91
Lübbenau, Ger.	B8	19
Lubbock, Tx., U.S.	C2	120
Lubbock, co., Tx., U.S.	C2	120
Lübeck, Ger.	D6	96
Lübeck Bay, b., Eur.	A5	19
Lubefu, Zaire	B4	48
Lubero, Zaire	B5	48
Lubicon Lake, l., Alta.	A3	68
Lubilash, stm., Zaire	C4	48
Lubin, Pol.	C3	26
Lublin, Pol.	C7	26
Lublin, Wi., U.S.	D3	126
Lubliniec, Pol.	C5	26
Lubny, Sov. Un.	F9	27
Luboń, Pol.	B4	26
Lubsko, Pol.	C3	26
Lübtheen, Ger.	E5	15
Lubudi, stm., Zaire	C4	48
Lubumbashi (Élisabethville), Zaire	D4	48
Lubutu, Zaire	B4	48
Lucama, N.C., U.S.	*B4	110
Lucan, Ont.	D3	73
Lucan, Ire.	D5	11
Lucan, Mn., U.S.	F3	100
Lucania, Mount, mtn., Yukon	D4	66
Lucas, Ia., U.S.	C4	92
Lucas, Ks., U.S.	C5	93
Lucas, Ky., U.S.	D3	94

Name	Map Ref.	Page

Lucas, Mi., U.S. D5 99
Lucas, Oh., U.S. B3 112
Lucas, S.D., U.S. D6 118
Lucas, co., Oh., U.S. C4 92
Lucas, co., Oh., U.S. A2 112
Lucasville, Oh., U.S. D3 112
Lucca, Italy C3 23
Lucé, Fr. C4 16
Luce, co., Mi., U.S. B5 99
Lucea, Jam. E4 64
Luce Bay, b., Scot., U.K. C4 10
Lucedale, Ms., U.S. E5 101
Lucena, Phil. C6 34
Lucena, Spain D3 22
Lucena del Cid, Spain B5 22
Lučenec, Czech. D5 26
Lucera, Italy D5 23
Lucerne, Ca., U.S. C2 82
Lucerne, Co., U.S. A6 83
Lucerne, In., U.S. C5 91
Lucerne, Mo., U.S. A4 102
Lucerne, Lake of l., Switz. E4 18
Lucernemines, Pa., U.S. E3 115
Lucerne Valley, Ca., U.S. E5 82
Luceville, Que. A9 74
Luchou see Luzhou, China F6 31
Lüchow, Ger. F5 15
Luchuan, China A9 35
Lucien, Ok., U.S. D3 101
Lucien, Ok., U.S. A4 113
Lucile, Id., U.S. D2 89
Lucille, Al., U.S. B2 78
Lucinda, Pa., U.S. D2 115
Lucipara Islands, is., Indon. G7 34
Lucira, Ang. D1 48
Luck, Wi., U.S. C1 126
Luckau, Ger. C6 18
Luckenwalde, Ger. B6 18
Luckey, Oh., U.S. A2 112
Luck Lake, l., Sask. G2 75
Lucknow, Ont. D3 73
Lucknow, India C7 36
Lucky Lake, Sask. G2 75
Lucky MacCamp, Wy., U.S. *D5 127
Lucky Peak Lake, res., Id., U.S. F3 89
Luçon, Fr. D3 16
Lucrecia, Cabo, c., Cuba D6 64
Lucy, La., U.S. h10 95
Lucy, Tn., U.S. B2 119
Lüda see Dalian, China D9 31
Ludden, N.D., U.S. C7 111
Ludell, Ks., U.S. C3 93
Lüdenscheid, Ger. C3 18
Lüderitz, Nmb. C2 49
Ludgate, Ont. B4 73
Ludhiāna, India B6 36
Luding, China F5 31
Lüdinghausen, Ger. B2 19
Ludington, Mi., U.S. E4 99
Ludlow, N.B. C3 71
Ludlow, Eng., U.K. D5 10
Ludlow, Il., U.S. C5 90
Ludlow, Ky., U.S. h13 94
Ludlow, Me., U.S. B4 96
Ludlow, Ma., U.S. B3 98
Ludlow, Mo., U.S. C4 101
Ludlow, Mo., U.S. B4 102
Ludlow, Pa., U.S. C4 115
Ludlow, S.D., U.S. B2 118
Ludlow, Vt., U.S. E3 122
Ludlow Falls, Oh., U.S. B1 112
Ludlow Mountain, mtn., Vt., U.S. E3 122
Ludowici, Ga., U.S. E5 87
Ludvika, Swe. G6 14
Ludwigsburg, Ger. D4 18
Ludwigshafen [am Rhein], Ger. D4 18
Ludwigslust, Ger. B5 18
Luebo, Zaire C3 48
Lueders, Tx., U.S. C3 120
Luena, Ang. D2 48
Luepa, Ven. B5 60
Lüeyang, China H2 32
Lufkin, Tx., U.S. D5 120
Lufuna, Zaire C2 48
Luga, Sov. Un. B7 27
Luga, stm., Sov. Un. B7 27
Lugagnano Val d'Arda, Italy E5 20
Lugan, stm., Sov. Un. q22 27
Luganchik, stm., Sov. Un. q22 27
Lugansk, Sov. Un. E6 29
Lugano, Switz. E4 18
Lugano, Lake, l., Eur. E7 21
Lugau, Ger. C7 19
Lugenda, stm., Moz. D6 48
Lugnaquillia Mountain, mtn., Ire. D3 10
Lugo, Italy B3 23
Lugo, Spain A2 22
Lugoff, S.C., U.S. C6 117
Lugoj, Rom. C5 24
Lugovoy, Sov. Un. E8 28
Luhuo, China E5 31
Luiana, Ang. E3 48
Luidhorn, Neth. A6 17
Luik see Liège, Bel. B6 16
Luing, i., Scot., U.K. D3 13
Luís Correia, Braz. B2 57
Luís Gomes, Braz. C3 57
Luis Lopez, N.M., U.S. D3 108
Luiza, Zaire C3 48
Lujuna Point, c., Guam L10 52
Lukachukai, Az., U.S. A6 80
Luke, Md., U.S. m12 97
Luke Air Force Base, mil., Az., U.S. D3 80
Lukenie, stm., Zaire B2 48
Lukeville, Az., U.S. F3 80
Lukolela, Zaire B2 48
Lukovit, Bul. D7 24
Łuków, Pol. C7 26
Lukoyanov, Sov. Un. D15 29
Lukuga, stm., Zaire C4 48
Lukulu, Zam. D3 48
Lula, Ga., U.S. B3 87
Lula, Ms., U.S. A3 101
Lula, Ok., U.S. C5 113
Luleå, Swe. E10 14
Luleälven, stm., Swe. D9 14
Lüleburgaz, Tur. B6 40
Luling, La., U.S. k11 95
Luling, Tx., U.S. E4 120
Lulong, China D8 31
Lulu, Fl., U.S. B4 86
Lulua, stm., Zaïre C3 48
Luluabourg see Kananga, Zaire C3 48
Lum, Mi., U.S. E7 99
Lumba, Zaire A2 48
Lumbala N'guimbo, Ang. D3 48
Lumber, stm., U.S. C9 117
Lumber Bridge, N.C., U.S. C3 110

Lumber City, Ga., U.S. E4 87
Lumberport, W.V., U.S. B4 125
Lumberton, Ms., U.S. D4 101
Lumberton, N.J., U.S. D3 107
Lumberton, N.M., U.S. A3 108
Lumberton, N.C., U.S. C3 110
Lumbo, Moz. E7 48
Lumby, B.C. D8 69
Luminao Reef, rf., Guam L9 52
Lummi Indian Reservation, Wa., U.S. A3 124
Lumpkin, Ga., U.S. D2 87
Lumpkin, co., Ga., U.S. B2 87
Lumsden, Newf. D5 72
Lumsden, Sask. G3 75
Lumsden, N.Z. P12 51
Lumsden, Scot., U.K. C6 13
Lumsden Beach, Sask. G3 75
Luna, N.M., U.S. D1 108
Luna, co., N.M., U.S. E2 108
Luna Pier, Mi., U.S. G7 99
Lund, B.C. D5 69
Lund, Swe. J5 14
Lund, Nv., U.S. E6 105
Lundale, W.V., U.S. n12 125
Lunda Norte, dept., Ang. C2 48
Lundar, Man. D2 70
Lundazi, Zam. D5 48
Lundbreck, Alta. E3 68
Lundby, Den. C5 15
Lundby, Swe. t34 14
Lunderskov, Den. C3 15
Lundu, Malay. E3 34
Lundy, i., Eng., U.K. E4 10
Lune, stm., Eng., U.K. F6 13
Lüneburg, Ger. B5 15
Lunel, Fr. F6 16
Lünen, Ger. B2 19
Lunenburg, N.S. E5 71
Lunenburg, Ma., U.S. A4 98
Lunenburg, Vt., U.S. C5 122
Lunenburg, Va., U.S. D4 123
Lunenburg, co., N.S. E5 71
Lunenburg, co., Va., U.S. D4 123
Lunéville, Fr. C7 16
Lungi, S.L. E2 45
Lungué-Bungo, stm., Afr. D3 48
Lüni, stm., India C5 36
Lunino, Sov. Un. E15 27
Lunsar, S.L. E2 45
Lunyama, Zaire C4 48
Luochuan, China D6 31
Luoding, China A9 35
Luohe, China E7 31
Luoning, China G4 32
Luoshan, China H6 32
Luoyang, China E7 31
Luozi, Zaire B1 48
Lupeni, Zimb. A4 49
Lupeni, Rom. C6 24
Lupton, Mi., U.S. D6 99
Lupton, Mi., U.S. D6 99
Lupus, Mo., U.S. C5 102
Luque, Para. E4 55
Luquillo, Sierra de, mts., P.R. B4 65
Lürah, stm., Afg. B4 36
Luray, Ks., U.S. C5 93
Luray, Mo., U.S. A6 102
Luray, S.C., U.S. F5 117
Luray, Tn., U.S. B3 119
Luray, Va., U.S. B4 123
Lure, Fr. D7 16
Lure, Lake, res., N.C., U.S. f10 110
Lurgan, N. Ire., U.K. C3 10
Luribay, Bol. C2 55
Lúrio, stm., Moz. D7 48
Lurton, Ar., U.S. B2 81
Lusaka, Zam. E4 48
Lusaka, prov., Zam. E4 48
Lusako, Zaire B4 48
Lusambo, Zaire B3 48
Lusby, Md., U.S. D5 97
Luscar, Alta. C2 68
Luseland, Sask. E1 75
Lushan, China H5 32
Lushan, China F8 34
Lushnja, Alb. B2 25
Lushoto, Tan. B6 48
Lushton, Ne., U.S. D8 104
Lüshun, China D9 31
Lusignan, Fr. D4 16
Lusk, Wy., U.S. D8 127
Lüt, Dasht-e, des., Iran B5 38
Lutcher, La., U.S. D5 95
Lutesville, Mo., U.S. D8 102
Luther, Mi., U.S. D5 99
Luther, Mt., U.S. E7 103
Luther, Ok., U.S. B4 113
Luthersville, Ga., U.S. C2 87
Lutherville-Timonium, Md., U.S. B4 97
Lutie, Ok., U.S. C6 113
Lütjenburg, Ger. A5 18
Luton, Eng., U.K. E6 10
Luton, Ia., U.S. B1 92
Lutong, Malay. E4 34
Lutsen, Mn., U.S. k9 100
Lutsk, Sov. Un. F5 27
Luttrell, Tn., U.S. C10 119
Lutts, Tn., U.S. B4 119
Lutugino, Sov. Un. q22 27
Lutz, Fl., U.S. D4 86
Lützelburg, Fr. D4 86
Lützow-Holm Bay, b., Ant. C16 7
Luuq, Som. E5 47
Luverne, Al., U.S. D3 78
Luverne, Ia., U.S. B3 92
Luverne, Mn., U.S. G2 100
Luverne, N.D., U.S. B8 111
Luvua, stm., Zaire C4 48
Luwingu, Zam. D4 48
Luxapallila Creek, stm., U.S. B5 101
Luxembourg, prov., Bel. E5 17
Luxembourg, ctry., Eur. E5 17
Luxembourg, Lux. E5 17
Luxemburg, Ia., U.S. B6 92
Luxemburg, Wi., U.S. D6 126
Luxeuil-les-Bains, Fr. D7 16
Luxi, China F7 31
Luxomni, Ga., U.S. h8 87
Luxor (Al Uqşur), Eg. C3 43
Luxor, hist., Egypt D6 43
Luxora, Ar., U.S. B6 81
Luz, Braz. E6 57
Luza, Sov. Un. A3 28
Luza, stm., Sov. Un. A3 28
Luzern, Switz. E4 18
Luzern, state, Switz. E4 18
Luzerne, Mi., U.S. D6 99
Luzerne, Pa., U.S. n17 115
Luzerne, co., Pa., U.S. D9 115

Luzhou (Luchou), China F6 31
Luziânia, Braz. B5 56
Lužnice, stm., Eur. D3 26
Luzon, i., Phil. B6 34
Luzon Strait, strt., Asia A6 34
Lvov, Sov. Un. E5 29
Lyakhov Islands, is., Sov. Un. B1 128
Lyall, Mount, mtn., N.Z. P11 51
Lyall Island, i., B.C. C2 69
Lyerly, Ga., U.S. B1 87
Lyford, In., U.S. E3 91
Lyford, Tx., U.S. F4 120
Lygnern, i., Swe. A6 15
Lykens, Pa., U.S. E8 115
Lyle, Mn., U.S. G6 100
Lyle, Wa., U.S. D4 124
Lyleton, Man. E1 70
Lyles, Tn., U.S. B4 119
Lyman, Ne., U.S. C1 104
Lyman, S.C., U.S. B3 117
Lyman, Ut., U.S. E4 121
Lyman, Wy., U.S. E2 127
Lyman, co., S.D., U.S. D6 118
Lyman Lake, res., Az., U.S. C6 80
Lyme, Ct., U.S. D6 84
Lyme, N.H., U.S. C2 106
Lyme Bay, b., Eng., U.K. D5 12
Lyme Center, N.H., U.S. C2 106
Lymington, Eng., U.K. D6 12
Lynbrook, N.Y., U.S. *E7 109
Lynch, Ky., U.S. D7 94
Lynch, Md., U.S. B5 97
Lynch, Ne., U.S. B7 104
Lynchburg, N.D., U.S. C8 111
Lynchburg, Oh., U.S. C2 112
Lynchburg, S.C., U.S. C7 117
Lynchburg, Tn., U.S. B5 119
Lynchburg, Va., U.S. C3 123
Lynches, stm., S.C., U.S. D8 117
Lynch Heights, De., U.S. E4 85
Lynch Station, Va., U.S. *C3 123
Lyncourt, N.Y., U.S. *B4 109
Lynd, Mn., U.S. F3 100
Lyndborough, N.H., U.S. E3 106
Lyndeborough, N.H., U.S. A3 124
Lynde Point, c., Ct., U.S. D6 84
Lyndhurst, Ont. C8 73
Lyndhurst, N.J., U.S. h8 107
Lyndhurst, Oh., U.S. g10 112
Lyndon, Il., U.S. B4 90
Lyndon, Ks., U.S. D8 93
Lyndon, Ky., U.S. g11 94
Lyndon, Vt., U.S. B4 122
Lyndon B. Johnson National Historical Site, hist., Tx., U.S. D3 120
Lyndon B. Johnson Space Center, sci., Tx., U.S. r14 120
Lyndon Center, Vt., U.S. B4 122
Lyndon Station, Wi., U.S. E4 126
Lyndonville, N.Y., U.S. B2 109
Lyndonville, Vt., U.S. B4 122
Lyndora, Pa., U.S. E2 115
Lyngby [-Tårbæk], Den. C6 15
Lynn, Al., U.S. A2 78
Lynn, Ar., U.S. A4 81
Lynn, In., U.S. D8 91
Lynn, Ma., U.S. B6 98
Lynn, Pa., U.S. C10 115
Lynn, co., Tx., U.S. C2 120
Lynn, Lake, res., W.V., U.S. B5 125
Lynn Canal, b., Ak., U.S. k22 79
Lynndyl, Ut., U.S. D3 121
Lynne, Fl., U.S. C5 86
Lynne Acres, Md., U.S. B4 97
Lynnfield, Ma., U.S. f11 98
Lynn Garden, Tn., U.S. C11 119
Lynn Grove, Ky., U.S. f9 94
Lynn Haven, Fl., U.S. u16 86
Lynnhaven Roads, b., Va., U.S. k15 123
Lynn Lake, Man. A1 70
Lynnport, Pa., U.S. E10 115
Lynnville, In., U.S. H3 91
Lynnville, Ia., U.S. C5 92
Lynnville, Ky., U.S. f9 94
Lynnville, Tn., U.S. B4 119
Lynnwood, Wa., U.S. B3 124
Lynton, Eng., U.K. E4 10
Lynwood, Ca., U.S. n12 82
Lyoffans, Fr. E2 16
Lyon, Fr. E6 16
Lyon, co., Ia., U.S. A1 92
Lyon, co., Ks., U.S. D7 93
Lyon, co., Ky., U.S. C1 94
Lyon, co., Mn., U.S. F3 100
Lyon, co., Nv., U.S. D2 105
Lyon, co., Nv., U.S. D2 105
Lyon, stm., Scot., U.K. D4 13
Lyon Creek, stm., Ks., U.S. D7 93
Lyon Mountain, N.Y., U.S. f11 109
Lyon Mountain, mtn., N.Y., U.S. f11 109
Lyonnais, hist. reg., Fr. E6 16
Lyons, Co., U.S. A5 83
Lyons, Ga., U.S. D4 87
Lyons, In., U.S. G3 91
Lyons, Ks., U.S. D5 93
Lyons, Mi., U.S. F6 99
Lyons, Ne., U.S. C9 104
Lyons, N.Y., U.S. B3 109
Lyons, Oh., U.S. A1 112
Lyons, Or., U.S. C4 114
Lyons, S.D., U.S. D9 118
Lyons, Tx., U.S. D4 120
Lyons Falls, N.Y., U.S. B5 109
Lyons Plains, Ct., U.S. E2 84
Lyracrumpane, Ire. E2 11
Lys, stm., Fr. D3 17
Lysá [nad Labem], Czech. n18 26
Lysaya Gora, Sov. Un. G8 27
Lysekil, Swe. H4 14
Lysite, Wy., U.S. C5 127
Lyss, Switz. B3 21
Lyster Station, Que. C6 74

Lysva, Sov. Un. D8 29
Lytham Saint Anne's, Eng., U.K. A5 12
Lytle, Oh., U.S. C1 112
Lytle, Tx., U.S. E3 120
Lytton, B.C. D7 69
Lytton, Ia., U.S. B3 92
Lytton, Sov. Un. G6 27
Lyubertsy, Sov. Un. n17 27
Lyuboml, Sov. Un. D7 24
Lyudinovo, Sov. Un. E10 27

M

Ma, stm., Asia A2 34
Ma'ād, Jord. B7 41
Maalaea, Hi., U.S. *C5 88
Maalaea Bay, b., Hi., U.S. C5 88
Ma'alot-Tarshiha, Isr. B7 41
Maam Cross, Ire. D2 11
Ma'anshan, China *E8 31
Ma'arrat an Nu'mān, Syria *E11 40
Maas, Ire. C3 11
Maas (Meuse), stm., Eur. B6 16
Maaseik, Bel. C5 17
Maastricht, Neth. o13 34
Mabalacat, Phil. B6 16
Mabana, Wa., U.S. A3 124
Mabank, Tx., U.S. C4 120
Mabaruma, Guy. A3 59
Mabber, Ras, c., Som. D7 47
Mabel, Mn., U.S. G7 100
Mabel Lake, l., B.C. D8 69
Mabelvale, Ar., U.S. k10 81
Mabens, Mb., U.S. B4 101
Maberly, Ont. C8 73
Mableton, Ga., U.S. h7 87
Mablethorpe, Eng., U.K. A8 12
Mabote, Moz. B5 49
Mabscott, W.V., U.S. D3 125
Mabton, Wa., U.S. C5 124
Mabuela, Japan O5 52
Macachín, Arg. B4 54
Macaé, Braz. C4 56
Macaíba, Braz. g6 57
Macalelon, Phil. p14 34
Macalister, B.C. C6 69
MacAlpine Lake, l., N.W. Ter. C12 66
Macan Islands, is., Indon. G6 34
Macao, dep., Asia G7 31
Macapá, Braz. B4 59
Macará, Ec. B2 58
Macas, Ec. B2 58
Macau, Braz. C3 57
Macaúbas, Braz. A4 56
Maccagno [Superiore], Italy D6 21
Maccan, N.S. D5 71
Maccarese, Italy h8 23
MacClenny, Fl., U.S. B4 86
Macclesfield, Eng., U.K. D5 10
Macclesfield, N.C., U.S. B5 110
Macculloch, Cape, c., N.W. Ter. B18 66
Madaba, Tan. E4 48
Madaba, Jord. D5 41
Madagascar, ctry., Afr. g9 49
Madā'in Şāliḥ, Sau. Ar. D7 43
Madalena, Braz. A4 56
Madame, Isle, i., N.S. D9 71
Madang, Pap. N. Gui. k12 50
Madaoua, Niger D6 45
Mādārīpur, Bngl. F13 37
Madawaska, Me., U.S. A4 96
Madawaska, co., N.B. B1 71
Madawaska, stm., Can. B9 74
Madawaska Lake, l., Me., U.S. A4 96
Madeira, Oh., U.S. o13 112
Madeira, i., Port. h11 42
Madeira, stm., S.A. D2 59
Madeira Islands, is., Port. B4 25
Madeira, hist. reg., Eur. B4 25
Madeleine, Gui. E3 45
Madeline, Ca., U.S. B3 82
Madeline Island, i., Wi., U.S. B3 126
Madera, Mex. B3 63
Madera, Ca., U.S. D3 82
Madera, Pa., U.S. E5 115
Madera, co., Ca., U.S. D4 82
Madgaon, India E2 36
Madge Lake, l., Sask. D1 70
Madhupur, India E11 37
Madhya Pradesh, state, India D6 36
Madill, Ok., U.S. C5 113
Madimba, Zaire C2 48
Madīnat ash Sha'b, Yemen H4 38
Madingou, Congo B1 48
Madison, Al., U.S. A3 78
Madison, Ar., U.S. B5 81
Madison, Ct., U.S. D5 84
Madison, Fl., U.S. B3 86
Madison, Ga., U.S. C3 87
Madison, Il., U.S. E3 90
Madison, In., U.S. G7 91
Madison, Ks., U.S. D7 93
Madison, Me., U.S. D3 96
Madison, Mn., U.S. E2 100
Madison, Mo., U.S. B5 102
Madison, Ne., U.S. C8 104
Madison, N.J., U.S. B4 107
Madison, N.C., U.S. A3 110
Madison, Oh., U.S. A4 112
Madison, S.D., U.S. D9 118
Madison, W.V., U.S. C3 125
Madison, Wi., U.S. E4 126
Madison, co., Al., U.S. A3 78
Madison, co., Ar., U.S. B2 81
Madison, co., Fl., U.S. B3 86
Madison, co., Ga., U.S. B3 87
Madison, co., Id., U.S. F7 89
Madison, co., Il., U.S. E4 90
Madison, co., In., U.S. D6 91
Madison, co., Ia., U.S. C3 92
Madison, co., Ky., U.S. C5 94
Madison, co., Ms., U.S. C4 101
Madison, co., Mo., U.S. D7 102
Madison, co., Mt., U.S. E5 103
Madison, co., Ne., U.S. C8 104
Madison, co., N.Y., U.S. C5 109
Madison, co., N.C., U.S. f10 110
Madison, co., Oh., U.S. C2 112
Madison, co., Tn., U.S. B3 119
Madison, co., Tx., U.S. D5 120
Madison, co., Va., U.S. B4 123
Madison, stm., Mt., U.S. E5 103
Madisonburg, Pa., U.S. E7 115
Madison Heights, Mi., U.S. o15 99
Madison Heights, Va., U.S. C3 123
Madison Lake, Mn., U.S. F5 100
Madison Range, mts., Mt., U.S. E5 103
Madisonville, Ky., U.S. C2 94
Madisonville, La., U.S. D5 95
Madisonville, Tn., U.S. D9 119
Madisonville, Tx., U.S. D5 120
Madiun, Indon. G4 34
Madoc, Ont. C7 73
Madoc, Mt., U.S. B11 103
Mado Gashi, Kenya A6 48
Madon, stm., Fr. A2 20
Madona, Sov. Un. C6 27
Madonna di Campiglio, Italy C6 20
Madrakah, Ra's al, c., Oman D5 38
Madras, India F7 36
Madras, Or., U.S. C5 114
Madras see Tamil Nadu, state, India
Madre, Laguna, b., Mex. C5 63
Madre, Laguna, b., Tx., U.S. F4 120
Madre, Sierra, mts., N.A. D6 63
Madre de Dios, dept., Peru D3 58
Madre de Dios, stm., S.A. C2 58
Madre de Dios, Isla, i., Chile E1 54
Madre del Sur, Sierra, mts., Mex. D4 63
Madre Occidental, Sierra, mts., Mex. B3 63
Madre Oriental, Sierra, mts., Mex. C5 63
Madrid, Spain B4 22
Madrid, Al., U.S. D4 78
Madrid, Ia., U.S. C4 92
Madrid, Ne., U.S. D4 104
Madrid, N.Y., U.S. f9 109
Madridejos, Spain C4 22
Madrūsah, Libya E2 43
Madura, i., Indon. G4 34
Madurai, India G6 36
Maebashi, Japan D12 31
Mae Hong Son, Thai. A4 35
Maella, Spain B6 22
Maengsan, N. Kor. G3 33
Maeser, Ut., U.S. C6 121
Maesteg, Wales, U.K. A4 10
Maestra, Sierra, mts., Cuba D5 64
Maevatanana, Madag. g9 49
Maeystown, Il., U.S. E3 90
Ma'fan, Libya D2 43
Mafeking, Man. C1 70
Mafeking see Mafikeng, S. Afr. C4 49
Maffra, Austl. H6 51
Mafia, i., Tan. C6 48
Mafikeng, S. Afr. C4 49
Mafra, Braz. C4 49
Mafra, Port. C1 22
Magadan, Sov. Un. D18 29
Magadi, Kenya B6 48
Magadi, Lake, l., Kenya B6 48
Magaguadavic Lake, l., N.B. D2 71
Magalia, Ca., U.S. C3 82
Magallanes y Antártica Chilena, prov., Chile h11 54
Maganey, Ire. E5 11
Maganga, Zaire A4 48
Magangué, Col. B3 60
Magaria, Niger D6 45
Magat, stm., Phil. n13 34
Magazine, Ar., U.S. B2 81
Magazine Mountain, mtn., Ar., U.S. B2 81
Magdalena, Arg. B5 54
Magdalena, Bol. B3 55
Magdalena, N.M., U.S. C2 108
Magdalena, dept., Col. A3 60
Magdalena, stm., Col. B3 60
Magdalena, stm., Mex. h9 63
Magdalena, Isla, i., Chile C2 54
Magdalena [de Kino], Mex. A2 63
Magdalena del Mar, Peru *D2 58
Magdalena Mountains, mts., N.M., U.S. D2 108
Magdeburg, Ger. B5 18
Magdel'el, Isr. g10 41
Magé, Braz. g10 57
Magee, Ms., U.S. D4 101
Magelang, Indon. G4 34
Magellan, Strait of (Estrecho de Magallanes), strt., S.A. h11 54
Magenta, Italy B2 23
Maggia, stm., Switz. C4 20
Maggie Creek, stm., Nv., U.S. C5 105
Maggiore, Lake, l., Eur. A2 23
Maghāghah, Eg. D6 43
Maghama, Maur. C2 45
Maghera, N. Ire., U.K. C5 11
Magherafelt, N. Ire., U.K. C5 11
Magic Reservoir, res., Id., U.S. F4 89
Magilligan Point, c., N. Ire., U.K. B5 11
Maglaj, Yugo. C4 24
Maglić, Yugo. D5 24
Maglie, Italy D7 23
Magna, Ut., U.S. C3 121
Magness, Ar., U.S. B4 81
Magnet, Man. D2 70
Magnet, Ne., U.S. H5 91
Magnet, Ne., U.S. B8 104
Magnetawan, Ont. B5 73
Magnetawan, stm., Ont. A4 73
Magnet Cove, Ar., U.S. C3 81
Magnetic Springs, Oh., U.S. B2 112
Magnitogorsk, Sov. Un. D8 29
Magnolia, De., U.S. D4 85
Magnolia, Ia., U.S. C2 92
Magnolia, Ky., U.S. C4 94
Magnolia, Md., U.S. B5 97
Magnolia, Ms., U.S. D3 101
Magnolia, N.C., U.S. C4 110
Magnolia, Oh., U.S. B4 112
Magnolia, Tx., U.S. D5 120
Magnolia Springs, Al., U.S. H16 52
Mago, i., Fiji C6 94
Magoffin, co., Ky., U.S. B2 112
Magog, Que. D5 74
Magothy River, b., Md., U.S. B4 97
Magoúla, Grc. g11 25
Magpie, Que. h8 72

Name	Map Ref.	Page
Magpie, stm., Que.	h8	72
Magrath, Alta.	E4	68
Magruder Mountain, mtn., Nv., U.S.	F4	105
Maguari, Cabo, c., Braz.	B1	57
Magude, Moz.	B5	49
Magway, Burma	D9	36
Mahābād, Iran	B4	38
Mahabo, Madag.	h8	49
Mahaffey, Pa., U.S.	E4	115
Mahagi, Zaire	A5	48
Mahaicony Village, Guy.	A3	59
Mahajanga, Madag.	g9	49
Mahajanga, prov., Madag.	g9	49
Mahakam, stm., Indon.	F5	34
Mahalatswe, Bots.	B4	49
Maḥallāt, Iran	E5	39
Mahānadi, stm., India	D7	36
Mahanoro, Madag.	g9	49
Mahanoy City, Pa., U.S.	E9	115
Mahārāshtra, state, India	D6	36
Maha Sarakham, Thai.	B2	34
Mahaska, Ks., U.S.	C6	93
Mahaska, co., Ia., U.S.	C5	92
Maḥattat Dab'ah, Jord.	C8	41
Mahbūbnagar, India	E6	36
Mahenge, Tan.	C6	48
Mahesāna, India	F4	37
Mahi, stm., India	D5	36
Mahia Peninsula, pen., N.Z.	M16	51
Mahned, Ms., U.S.	D4	101
Mahnomen, Mn., U.S.	C3	100
Mahnomen, co., Mn., U.S.	C3	100
Mahoba, India	E7	37
Mahogany Mountain, mtn., Or., U.S.	D9	114
Mahomet, Il., U.S.	C5	90
Mahón, Spain	C8	22
Mahone Bay, N.S.	E5	71
Mahoning, co., Oh., U.S.	B5	112
Mahoning, stm., U.S.	A5	112
Mahoosuc Range, mts., N.H., U.S.	B4	106
Mahopac, N.Y., U.S.	D7	109
Mahto, S.D., U.S.	B5	118
Mahtowa, Mn., U.S.	D6	100
Mahuta, Tan.	D6	48
Mahuva, India	G3	37
Mahwah, N.J., U.S.	A4	107
Maîche, Fr.	B2	20
Maicurú, stm., Braz.	C4	59
Maida, N.D., U.S.	A7	111
Maiden, N.C., U.S.	B1	110
Maidenhead, Eng., U.K.	C7	12
Maiden Rock, Wi., U.S.	D1	126
Maidens, rock, N. Ire., U.K.	C6	11
Maidstone, Sask.	D1	75
Maidstone, Eng., U.K.	E7	10
Maidstone Lake, l., Vt., U.S.	B5	122
Maidsville, W.V., U.S.	B5	125
Maiduguri, Nig.	D7	45
Maihar, India	E8	37
Maikala Range, mts., India	F8	37
Maiko, stm., Zaire	B4	48
Maikoor, i., Indon.	g9	34
Maili, Hi., U.S.	g9	88
Maili Point, c., Hi., U.S.	g9	88
Maillard, Que.	B7	74
Mailley-et-Chazelot, Fr.	D4	18
Main, stm., Ger.	A1	21
Main, stm., N. Ire., U.K.	C5	11
Main-à-Dieu, N.S.	C10	71
Mainburg, Ger.	E6	19
Main Centre, Sask.	G2	75
Main Channel, strt., Ont.	B3	73
Mai-Ndombe, Lac, l., Zaire	B2	48
Maine, N.Y., U.S.	C4	109
Maine, hist. reg., Fr.	C4	16
Maine, state, U.S.	C3	96
Mainesburg, Pa., U.S.	C7	115
Maïné-Soroa, Niger	D7	45
Mainland, i., Scot., U.K.	g10	10
Mainland, i., Scot., U.K.	A5	10
Mainland, stm., Man.	C4	70
Main Pass, strt., La., U.S.	E6	95
Maintirano, Madag.	g8	49
Main Topsail, mtn., Newf.	D3	72
Mainz (Mayence), Ger.	D4	18
Maipo, Volcán, vol., S.A.	A3	54
Maipú, Arg.	B5	54
Maiquetía, Ven.	A4	60
Maira, stm., Italy	E3	20
Mairiporã, Braz.	m8	56
Maisí, Punta de, c., Cuba	D6	64
Maisonnette, N.B.	B4	71
Maisons-Laffitte, Fr.	g11	16
Maitland, Austl.	F9	50
Maitland, N.S.	D6	71
Maitland, Ont.	C9	73
Maitland, Fl., U.S.	*D5	86
Maitland, Mo., U.S.	A2	102
Maiz, Islas del, is., Nic.	E8	63
Maize, Ks., U.S.	g12	93
Maizières-lès-Vic, Fr.	E1	19
Maizuru, Japan	I7	33
Majagual, Col.	B3	60
Majene, Indon.	F5	34
Majenica, In., U.S.	C7	91
Majestic, Ky., U.S.	C7	94
Maji, Eth.	D4	47
Major, Sask.	F1	75
Major, co., Ok., U.S.	A3	113
Majuro, atoll, Marsh Is.	F10	6
Makaha, Hi., U.S.	g9	88
Makaha Point, c., Hi., U.S.	A2	88
Makah Indian Reservation, Wa., U.S.	A1	124
Makahuena Point, c., Hi., U.S.	B2	88
Makakilo City, Hi., U.S.	g9	88
Makalado, Zaire	A4	48
Makallé, Arg.	B5	54
Makālu, mtn., Asia	*C8	36
Makanda, Il., U.S.	F4	90
Makanza, Zaire	A2	48
Makapala, Hi., U.S.	C6	88
Makapuu Head, c., Hi., U.S.	B4	88
Makarov, Sov. Un.	B13	31
Makarska, Yugo.	D3	24
Makasar see Ujungpandang, Indon.	G5	34
Makat, Sov. Un.	E8	29
Makawao, Hi., U.S.	C5	88
Makaweli, Hi., U.S.	B2	88
Makeni, S.L.	E2	45
Makeyevka, Sov. Un.	E6	29
Makgadikgadi Pans, pl., Bots.	B4	49
Makhachkala, Sov. Un.	B7	38
Makharadze, Sov. Un.	B14	40
Makhfar al Quwayrah, Jord.	E7	41
Makinak, Man.	D2	70
Makindu, Kenya	B6	48
Makinsk, Sov. Un.	C8	28
Makkinga, Neth.	B6	17
Makkovik, Newf.	g10	72
Makkum, Neth.	A5	17
Maknassy, Tun.	C6	44
Makó, Hung.	B5	24
Makogai, i., Fiji	H15	52
Makokou, Gabon	E2	46
Makoti, N.D., U.S.	B4	111
Makoua, Congo	A2	48
Maków [Mazowiecki], Pol.	B6	26
Makrana, Kenya	B6	48
Makteïr, reg., Maur.	B2	45
Makū, Iran	B2	39
Makumbi, Zaire	C3	48
Makurazaki, Japan	K5	33
Makurdi, Nig.	E6	45
Makushin Volcano, vol., Ak., U.S.	E6	79
Mala, Punta, c., Pan.	G8	62
Malabar, Fl., U.S.	D6	86
Malabar Coast, India	F6	36
Malabo, Eq. Gui.	E1	46
Mal Abrigo, Ur.	E1	56
Malacca, Strait of, strt., Asia	E2	34
Malacca see Melaka, Malay.	E2	34
Malad City, Id., U.S.	G6	89
Malafede, stm., Italy	h8	23
Málaga, Col.	D3	22
Málaga, Spain	D3	22
Málaga, N.J., U.S.	D2	107
Málaga, N.M., U.S.	E5	108
Málaga Bay, b., Spain	D3	22
Malagash, N.S.	D6	71
Malagón, Spain	C4	22
Malaimbandy, Madag.	h9	49
Malaita, i., Sol.Is.	G9	6
Malakal, Sud.	D3	47
Malakof, Fr.	g10	16
Malakoff, Tx., U.S.	C4	120
Malalbergo, Italy	E7	20
Malambo, Col.	*A3	60
Malang, Indon.	G4	34
Malange see Malanje, Ang.	C2	48
Malange, Ang.	C2	48
Malanje, dept., Ang.	C2	48
Malanje, Ang.	C2	48
Malanville, Benin	D5	45
Malanzán, Arg.	A3	54
Mata Panew, stm., Pol.	f9	26
Mälaren, l., Swe.	t34	14
Malargüe, Arg.	B3	54
Malartic, Que.	k11	74
Malaspina, Arg.	C4	54
Malaspina Glacier, ice, Ak., U.S.	D11	79
Malatya, Tur.	C12	40
Malawi, ctry., Afr.	D5	48
Malaya Vishera, Sov. Un.	B9	27
Malaybalay, Phil.	D7	34
Malāyer, Iran	D4	39
Malay Peninsula, pen., Asia	D2	34
Malaysia, ctry., Asia	E4	34
Malazgirt, Tur.	C14	40
Malbaie, stm., Que.	B7	74
Mal Bay, b., Ire.	D2	10
Malbork, Pol.	A5	26
Malchin, Ger.	B6	18
Malchow, Ger.	B6	18
Malcolm, Ne., U.S.	D9	104
Malcom, Ia., U.S.	C5	92
Malden, Il., U.S.	B4	90
Malden, Ma., U.S.	B5	98
Malden, Mo., U.S.	E8	102
Malden, Wa., U.S.	B8	124
Malden, W.V., U.S.	m12	125
Malden Island, i., Kir.	G12	6
Maldives, ctry., Asia	G5	36
Maldon, Eng., U.K.	C8	12
Maldonado, Ur.	E2	56
Malè, Italy	C6	20
Maléa, Ákra, c., Grc.	D4	40
Mālegaon, India	G5	37
Malema, Moz.	D6	48
Malemba-Nkulu, Zaire	C4	48
Māler Kotla, India	B6	36
Malesherbes, Fr.	C5	16
Malesus, Tn., U.S.	B3	119
Malha Wells, Sud.	B2	47
Malheur, co., Or., U.S.	D9	114
Malheur, stm., Or., U.S.	D9	114
Malheur Lake, l., Or., U.S.	D8	114
Mali, Gui.	D2	45
Mali, ctry., Afr.	C4	45
Mali, i., Burma	F3	35
Mali, i., Fiji	H15	52
Malibu, Ca., U.S.	m11	82
Maligne Lake, l., Alta.	C2	68
Mālihah, Bi'r, well, Eg.	E5	41
Malik, Wādī al, val., Sud.	B4	47
Malin, Ire.	F7	27
Malin, Or., U.S.	E5	114
Malinau, Indon.	E6	34
Malin Beg, Ire.	C3	11
Malindi, Kenya	B7	48
Malines see Mechelen, Bel.	D5	26
Malin Head, c., Ire.	C3	10
Malino, Sov. Un.	n18	27
Malinta, Oh., U.S.	A1	112
Maliwun, Burma	F10	36
Malkara, Tur.	B6	40
Malko Tŭrnovo, Bul.	E8	24
Mallaig, Alta.	B5	68
Mallaig, Scot., U.K.	B4	10
Mallard, Ia., U.S.	B3	92
Mallawī, Eg.	C6	41
Mallersdorf, Ger.	E7	19
Malles Venosta, Italy	C6	20
Mallet Creek, Oh., U.S.	A4	112
Malletts Bay, b., Vt., U.S.	B2	122
Mallorca, i., Spain	C7	22
Mallorytown, Ont.	C9	73
Mallow, Ire.	D2	10
Malmbäck, Swe.	A8	15
Malmberget, Swe.	D9	14
Malmédy, Bel.	E7	16
Malmköping, Swe.	t34	14
Malmö, Swe.	J5	14
Malmö, Ne., U.S.	C9	104
Malmöhus, co., Swe.	H8	14
Malmyzh, Sov. Un.	B12	31
Maloarkhangelsk, Sov. Un.	E11	27
Maloggia (Maloja), Switz.	C5	20
Malolo, i., Fiji	H14	52
Malolos, Phil.	o13	34
Malone, Ont.	B5	73
Malone, Fl., U.S.	B1	86
Malone, N.Y., U.S.	f10	109
Malone, Wa., U.S.	C2	124
Maloney Reservoir, res., Ne., U.S.	C5	104
Malonga, Zaire	D4	48
Malonno, Italy	D9	21
Malonton, Man.	D3	70
Malott, Wa., U.S.	A6	124
Maloy, Ia., U.S.	D3	92
Maloyaroslavets, Sov. Un.	D11	27
Malpelo, Isla de, i., Col.	C2	53
Malpeque Bay, b., P.E.I.	C6	71
Mālpura, India	D5	37
Malsch, Ger.	E3	19
Malta, Id., U.S.	G5	89
Malta, Il., U.S.	B5	90
Malta, Mt., U.S.	B9	103
Malta, Oh., U.S.	C4	112
Malta, ctry., Eur.	H11	8
Malta Bend, Mo., U.S.	B4	102
Malthöhe, Nmb.	B2	49
Malton (part of Mississauga), Ont.	m14	73
Malton, Eng., U.K.	C6	10
Malung, Swe.	D4	78
Malvern, Al., U.S.	D4	78
Malvern, Ar., U.S.	C3	81
Malvern, Ia., U.S.	D2	92
Malvern, Oh., U.S.	B4	112
Malvern, Pa., U.S.	o19	115
Malvérnia, Moz.	B5	49
Malye Karmakuly, Sov. Un.	D3	28
Malyy Uzen, stm., Sov. Un.	D3	28
Mamala Bay, b., Hi., U.S.	g10	88
Mamanguape, Braz.	C3	57
Mamantel, Mex.	A2	62
Mamaroneck, N.Y., U.S.	h13	109
Mamba, Japan	m17	33
Mambasa, Zaire	A4	48
Mamberamo, stm., Indon.	F9	34
Mamelodi, S. Afr.	*C4	49
Ma-Me-O Beach, Alta.	C4	68
Mamers, Fr.	C4	16
Mamers, N.C., U.S.	B4	110
Mamfe, Cam.	D1	46
Mamie, N.C., U.S.	A7	110
Mamiña, Chile	D2	55
Mammern, Switz.	A6	21
Mammoth, Az., U.S.	E5	80
Mammoth, Ut., U.S.	D3	121
Mammoth, W.V., U.S.	C3	125
Mammoth Cave National Park, Ky., U.S.	C4	94
Mammoth Lakes, Ca., U.S.	D4	82
Mammoth Spring, Ar., U.S.	A4	81
Mamonovo, Sov. Un.	A5	26
Mamoré, stm., S.A.	B2	55
Mamou, Gui.	D2	45
Mamou, La., U.S.	D3	95
Mampong, Ghana	E4	45
Mamry, Lake, l., Pol.	A6	26
Mamuju, Indon.	F5	34
Man, I.C.	E3	45
Man, W.V., U.S.	D3	125
Man, stm., Sask.	C4	10
Man, Isle of, i., I. of Man	C6	10
Man, Fr. Gu.	A2	59
Mana, Hi., U.S.	A2	88
Mana, stm., Fr. Gu.	B8	59
Manabí, prov., Ec.	B1	58
Manacacias, stm., Col.	C3	60
Manacapuru, Braz.	D5	59
Manacor, Spain	C7	22
Manado, Indon.	E6	34
Mañagaha, Isleta, i., N. Mar. Is.	D7	52
Managua, Nic.	D4	63
Managua, Lago de, l., Nic.	D4	63
Manahawkin, N.J., U.S.	D4	107
Manakara, Madag.	h9	49
Manakin, Va., U.S.	C5	123
Manalapan, N.J., U.S.	C4	107
Manam, i., Pap. N. Gui.	h12	50
Manama, Bahr.	C5	38
Manana Island, i., Hi., U.S.	g11	88
Mananara, Madag.	g9	49
Mananara, stm., Madag.	h9	49
Manangatang, Austl.	F7	50
Mananjary, Madag.	h9	49
Manantenina, Madag.	h9	49
Manantico Creek, stm., N.J., U.S.	E3	107
Manapire, stm., Ven.	B4	60
Mana Point, c., Hi., U.S.	A2	88
Manas He, stm., China	B2	31
Manas Hu, l., China	B2	31
Manasquan, N.J., U.S.	C4	107
Manasquan, stm., N.J., U.S.	C4	107
Manassa, Co., U.S.	D5	83
Manassas, Ga., U.S.	D4	87
Manassas, Va., U.S.	B5	123
Manassas National Battlefield Park, Va., U.S.	g11	123
Manassas Park, Va., U.S.	B5	123
Manatee, co., Fl., U.S.	E4	86
Manatee, stm., Fl., U.S.	E4	86
Manatí, P.R.	B3	65
Manaus, Braz.	C2	59
Manavgat, Tur.	D8	40
Manawa, Wi., U.S.	D5	126
Manawan Lake, l., Sask.	B4	75
Mancelona, Mi., U.S.	D5	99
Manchac, Bayou, stm., La., U.S.	h10	95
Mancha Real, Spain	D4	22
Manchaug, Ma., U.S.	B4	98
Manchester, Eng., U.K.	D5	10
Manchester, Ct., U.S.	B5	84
Manchester, Ga., U.S.	D2	87
Manchester, Il., U.S.	D3	90
Manchester, Ia., U.S.	B6	92
Manchester, Ks., U.S.	C6	93
Manchester, Ky., U.S.	C6	94
Manchester, Me., U.S.	D3	96
Manchester, Md., U.S.	A4	97
Manchester, Ma., U.S.	A6	98
Manchester, Mi., U.S.	F6	99
Manchester, Mo., U.S.	f12	102
Manchester, N.H., U.S.	E4	106
Manchester, N.Y., U.S.	C3	109
Manchester, Oh., U.S.	D2	112
Manchester, Pa., U.S.	A3	113
Manchester, S.D., U.S.	C8	118
Manchester, Tn., U.S.	B5	119
Manchester, Vt., U.S.	E2	122
Manchester Center, Vt., U.S.	E2	122
Manchuria, hist. reg., China	B10	31
Mancos, Co., U.S.	D2	83
Mancos, stm., U.S.	D2	83
Mand, stm., Iran	G6	39
Manda, Tan.	D5	48
Mandabe, Madag.	h8	49
Mandaguari, Braz.	C2	56
Mandal, Nor.	H2	14
Mandalay, Burma	D10	36
Mandalgovi, Mong.	B6	31
Mandali, Iraq	E2	39
Mandalya, Gulf of, b., Tur.	D6	25
Mandan, N.D., U.S.	C5	111
Mandara Mountains, mts., Afr.	C2	46
Mandar Bay, b., Indon.	F5	34
Mandaree, N.D., U.S.	B3	111
Mandeb, Bab el, strt.	D4	38
Mandel, Afg.	E10	39
Mandera, Kenya	A7	48
Manderfeld, Bel.	D3	118
Manderson, S.D., U.S.	D3	118
Manderson, Wy., U.S.	B5	127
Mandeure, Fr.	B2	21
Mandeville, Jam.	E5	64
Mandeville, Que.	C4	74
Mandeville, Ar., U.S.	D2	81
Mandeville, La., U.S.	D5	95
Mandidzudzure, Zimb.	A5	49
Mandimba, Moz.	D6	48
Mandla, India	C2	15
Māndra (Cutch Māndvi), India	C2	15
Mandra, Grc.	g9	49
Mandritsara, Madag.	g9	49
Mandsaur, India	D6	36
Mandurah, Austl.	F2	50
Manduria, Italy	D6	23
Māndvi, India	C2	36
Mandya, India	F4	36
Mane, Fr.	A4	56
Manfred, N.D., U.S.	B6	111
Manfredonia, Italy	D5	23
Manfredonia, Gulf of, b., Italy	D6	23
Manga, Braz.	A4	56
Mangaldan, Phil.	B6	34
Mangalia, Rom.	D9	24
Mangalore, India	F5	36
Mangaratiba, Braz.	h5	56
Mangatarem, Phil.	o13	34
Mangerton Mountain, mtn., Ire.	F2	11
Mangham, La., U.S.	B4	95
Mangkalihat, Cape, c., Indon.	E6	34
Mangoche, Mwi.	D6	48
Mangoky, stm., Madag.	h8	49
Mangole, i., Indon.	F7	34
Mangualde, Port.	B2	22
Mangueni, Plateau de, plat., Niger	B7	45
Mangum, Ok., U.S.	C2	113
Manhasset, N.Y., U.S.	*h13	109
Manhattan, Ks., U.S.	C7	93
Manhattan, Mt., U.S.	E5	103
Manhattan, Nv., U.S.	E4	105
Manhattan Beach, Ca., U.S.	n12	82
Manhattan Island, i., N.Y., U.S.	h13	109
Manheim, Pa., U.S.	F9	115
Manhica, Moz.	C5	49
Manhuaçu, Braz.	C4	56
Maniago, Italy	C8	20
Maniamba, Moz.	D6	48
Manic, I.C.	D6	48
Manica, dept., Moz.	A5	49
Manicoré, Braz.	D2	59
Manicoré, stm., Braz.	D2	59
Manicouagan, stm., Que.	G19	66
Manicouagan, Réservoir, res., Que.	h13	74
Manifest, La., U.S.	C4	95
Manteno, Il., U.S.	C4	95
Manigotagan, Man.	D3	70
Manigotagan Lake, l., Man.	D4	70
Manila, Phil.	C6	34
Manila, Ar., U.S.	B6	81
Manila, Ut., U.S.	C6	121
Manila Bay, b., Phil.	o13	34
Manilla, Austl.	E8	51
Manilla, In., U.S.	E6	91
Manilla, Ia., U.S.	C2	92
Manipur, state, India	D9	36
Manisa, Tur.	C6	40
Manistee, Mi., U.S.	D4	99
Manistee, co., Mi., U.S.	D5	99
Manistee, stm., Mi., U.S.	D5	99
Manistique, Mi., U.S.	B4	99
Manistique Lake, l., Mi., U.S.	B5	99
Manito, Il., U.S.	C4	90
Manitoba, prov., Can.	C3	70
Manitoba, Lake, l., Man.	D2	70
Manitou, Man.	E2	70
Manitou, Ok., U.S.	C3	113
Manitou, stm., Ont.	E5	73
Manitou, Lake, l., Ont.	B3	73
Manitou Beach, Sask.	F3	75
Manitou Island, i., Mi., U.S.	C7	99
Manitou Island, i., Mi., U.S.	A3	99
Manitou Lake, l., Ont.	A6	73
Manitou Lake, l., Sask.	E1	75
Manitoulin, dept., Ont.	B2	73
Manitoulin Island, i., Ont.	B2	73
Manitou Springs, Co., U.S.	C6	83
Manitowaning, Ont.	B3	73
Manitowoc, Wi., U.S.	D6	126
Manitowoc, co., Wi., U.S.	D5	126
Manitowoc, stm., Wi., U.S.	h10	126
Manitowoc, North Branch, stm., Wi., U.S.	h9	126
Manitowoc, South Branch, stm., Wi., U.S.	k9	126
Maniwaki, Que.	D2	11
Manizales, Col.	B2	60
Manja, Madag.	h8	49
Manjacaze, Moz.	B5	49
Manjimup, Austl.	F2	50
Mānjra, stm., India	E6	36
Mankato, Ks., U.S.	C5	93
Mankato, Mn., U.S.	F5	100
Mankota, Sask.	H2	75
Manley, Ne., U.S.	h12	104
Manley Hot Springs, Ak., U.S.	B9	79
Manlius, Il., U.S.	B4	90
Manlius, N.Y., U.S.	C5	109
Manlléu, Spain	A7	22
Manly, Ia., U.S.	A4	92
Manly, Tn., U.S.	C3	119
Manmād, India	J7	37
Mannar, Sri L.	H5	36
Mannar, Gulf of, b., Asia	H5	36
Mannford, Ok., U.S.	A5	113
Mannheim, Ger.	D4	18
Mannington, W.V., U.S.	B4	125
Manns Choice, Pa., U.S.	G4	115
Manns Harbor, N.C., U.S.	B7	110
Mannsville, N.Y., U.S.	B5	109
Mannsville, Ok., U.S.	C5	113
Mannu, stm., Italy	E2	23
Mannville, Alta.	C5	68
Manoa, Bol.	A2	55
Man of War Bay, b., Trin.	M24	65
Manokin, Md., U.S.	D6	97
Manokotak, Ak., U.S.	D8	79
Manokwari, Indon.	F8	34
Manombo, Madag.	h8	49
Manomet, Ma., U.S.	C6	98
Manomet Hill, hill, Ma., U.S.	C6	98
Manomet Point, c., Ma., U.S.	C6	98
Manono, Fr.	C4	74
Manono, i., W. Sam.	F11	52
Manor, Sask.	H4	75
Manor, Ga., U.S.	E4	87
Manor, Tx., U.S.	D4	120
Manorhamilton, Ire.	C3	11
Manorhaven, N.Y., U.S.	*h13	109
Manorville, Pa., U.S.	E2	115
Manorville, R.I., U.S.	B2	116
Manosque, Fr.	F6	16
Manotick, Ont.	B9	73
Manouane, Lac, l., Que.	h12	74
Manp'o, N. Kor.	F3	33
Manresa, Spain	B6	22
Mansa (Fort Roseberry), Zam.	D4	48
Mānsa, India	A4	56
Mansa Konko, Gam.	C5	49
Manseau, Que.	C5	74
Mansel Island, i., N.W. Ter.	D17	66
Mansfield, Eng., U.K.	D6	10
Mansfield, Austl.	B1	81
Mansfield, Ar., U.S.	B1	81
Mansfield, Ga., U.S.	C3	87
Mansfield, Il., U.S.	C5	90
Mansfield, La., U.S.	B2	95
Mansfield, Ma., U.S.	B5	98
Mansfield, Mo., U.S.	D5	102
Mansfield, Oh., U.S.	B3	112
Mansfield, Pa., U.S.	C7	115
Mansfield, S.D., U.S.	B7	118
Mansfield, Tn., U.S.	A3	119
Mansfield, Tx., U.S.	n9	120
Mansfield, Wa., U.S.	B6	124
Mansfield, Mount, mtn., Vt., U.S.	B3	122
Mansfield Center, Ct., U.S.	B7	84
Mansfield Depot, Ct., U.S.	B6	84
Mansfield Four Corners, Ct., U.S.	B7	84
Mansfield Hollow Lake, res., Ct., U.S.	B7	84
Manson, Ia., U.S.	B3	92
Manson, Wa., U.S.	B5	124
Manson, B.C.	B5	69
Manson Creek, B.C.	B5	69
Mansonville, Que.	D5	74
Mansura, La., U.S.	C3	95
Manta, Ec.	B1	58
Mantachie, Ms., U.S.	A5	101
Mantador, N.D., U.S.	C9	111
Mantagao, stm., Man.	D3	70
Mantario, Sask.	F1	75
Manteca, Ca., U.S.	D3	82
Mantee, Ms., U.S.	B4	101
Manteno, Il., U.S.	B6	90
Manteo, N.C., U.S.	B7	110
Mantes [-la-Jolie], Fr.	C4	16
Manti, Ut., U.S.	D4	121
Mantiqueira, Serra da, mts., Braz.	C4	56
Manton, Mi., U.S.	D5	99
Mantorville, Mn., U.S.	F6	100
Mantova (Mantua), Italy	B3	23
Mantua, N.J., U.S.	D2	107
Mantua, Oh., U.S.	A4	112
Mantua Hills, Va., U.S.	*B5	123
Manú, Peru	D3	58
Manuel Benavides, Mex.	B4	63
Manuel Urbano, Braz.	C2	58
Manui, i., Indon.	F6	34
Manukau Harbour, b., N.Z.	L15	51
Manulla, Ire.	D2	11
Manumuskin, stm., N.J., U.S.	E3	107
Manus, i., Pap. N. Gui.	A8	11
Manvel, N.D., U.S.	A8	111
Manvel, Tx., U.S.	r14	120
Manville, N.J., U.S.	B3	107
Manville, R.I., U.S.	B4	116
Manville, Wy., U.S.	D8	127
Many, La., U.S.	C2	95
Manyara, Lake, l., Tan.	B6	48
Manyberries, Alta.	E5	68
Manych, stm., Sov. Un.	H13	27
Manych, stm., Sov. Un.	H14	27
Many Farms, Az., U.S.	A6	80
Many Island Lake, l., Can.	D5	68
Manyoni, Tan.	C5	48
Manzanares, Spain	C4	22
Manzanares, stm., Spain	o17	22
Manzanares Canal, Spain	p17	22
Manzanillo, Cuba	D5	64
Manzanillo, Mex.	D4	63
Manzanillo, Punta, c., Pan.	F8	62
Manzano, N.M., U.S.	C3	108
Manzanola, Co., U.S.	C7	83
Manzano Mountains, mts., N.M., U.S.	C3	108
Manzano Peak, mtn., N.M., U.S.	C3	108
Manzhouli, China	B9	31
Manzilah, Lake, l., Eg.	C3	41
Manzini, Swaz.	C5	49
Mao, Chad	D9	46
Mao, Dom. Rep.	E8	64
Maoke Mountains, mts., Indon.	F9	34
Maoming, China	G7	31
Mapam Yumco, l., China	A4	36
Mapastepec, Mex.	B7	62
Mapaville, Mo., U.S.	C7	102
Mapes, N.D., U.S.	A7	111
Mapia Islands, is., Indon.	B5	60
Mapire, Ven.	B5	60
Mapiri, Bol.	A2	55
Maple (part of Vaughan), Ont.	k14	73
Maple, Tx., U.S.	C1	120
Maple, Wi., U.S.	B2	126
Maple, stm., N.D., U.S.	g11	111
Maple, stm., Ia., U.S.	B2	92
Maple Island, Mn., U.S.	G5	100
Maple Lake, Mn., U.S.	E5	100
Maple Mount, Ky., U.S.	C5	94
Maple Rapids, Mi., U.S.	E6	99
Maple Plain, Mn., U.S.	m11	100
Maple Ridge, B.C.	E6	69
Maple Shade, N.J., U.S.	D2	107
Maplesville, Al., U.S.	C3	78
Mapleton, Ks., U.S.	D9	93
Mapleton, Me., U.S.	B4	96
Mapleton, Mn., U.S.	G5	100
Mapleton, N.D., U.S.	C8	111
Mapleton, Or., U.S.	C3	114
Mapleton, Ut., U.S.	C4	121
Mapleton Depot, Pa., U.S.	F6	115
Maple Valley, Wa., U.S.	f11	124
Mapleville, R.I., U.S.	B2	116
Maplewood, Me., U.S.	E2	96
Maplewood, Mn., U.S.	n12	100
Maplewood, Mo., U.S.	f13	102
Maplewood, N.J., U.S.	B4	107
Mapuera, stm., Braz.	C3	59
Maputo (Lourenço Marques), Moz.	C5	49
Maputo, dept., Moz.	C5	49
Maqāriyūs, Dayr, hist., Eg.	D2	41
Maqellarë, Alb.	B3	25
Maqna, Sau., Ar.	C3	38
Maquela do Zombo, Ang.	C2	48
Maquinchao, Arg.	C3	54
Maquoketa, Ia., U.S.	B7	92
Maquoketa, stm., Ia., U.S.	B6	92
Maquoketa, North Fork, stm., Ia., U.S.	B7	92
Maquon, Il., U.S.	C3	90
Mar, Serra do, clf., Braz.	D3	56
Mara, prov., Tan.	B5	48
Maraã, Braz.	D5	59
Marabá, Braz.	B4	59
Maracá, Ilha de, i., Braz.	A3	60
Maracaibo, Ven.	A3	60
Maracaibo, Lago de, l., Ven.	C1	56
Maracaju, Braz.	C1	56
Maracaju, Serra de, hills, S.A.	C2	56
Maracay, Ven.	A4	60
Marādah, Libya	D6	45
Maradi, Niger	D6	45
Marāgheh, Iran	B4	38
Maragogi, Braz.	k6	57
Maragogipe, Braz.	B9	57
Marais des Cygnes, stm., U.S.	D8	93
Marajó, Baia de, b., Braz.	C5	59
Marajó, Ilha de, i., Braz.	C5	59
Maramec, Ok., U.S.	A5	113
Marana, Az., U.S.	E4	80
Marand, Iran	B4	38
Maranguape, Braz.	B3	57
Maranhão, state, Braz.	B1	57
Marano, Laguna di, b., Italy	D9	21
Maranoa, stm., Austl.	E8	50
Marañón, stm., Peru	D3	16
Marans, Fr.	D3	16
Mărăşeşti, Rom.	C8	24
Marathon, Fl., U.S.	H5	86
Marathon, Ont.	o18	73
Marathón, Grc.	g11	25
Marathon, N.Y., U.S.	C4	109
Marathon, Tx., U.S.	D1	120
Marathon, Wi., U.S.	D4	126
Marathon, co., Wi., U.S.	D4	126
Maratua, i., Indon.	E5	34
Marau, Braz.	D2	56
Marāwah, Libya	C4	43
Marawī, Sud.	B3	47
Maravatío de Ocampo, Mex.	n13	63
Marbach [am Neckar], Ger.	E4	19
Marbella, Spain	D3	22
Marble, Co., U.S.	B3	83
Marble, Mn., U.S.	C5	100
Marble, N.C., U.S.	f9	110
Marble Bar, Austl.	D2	50
Marble Canyon, val., Az., U.S.	A4	80
Marble City, Ok., U.S.	B7	113
Marble Cliff, Oh., U.S.	m10	112
Marble Dale, Ct., U.S.	C2	84
Marble Falls, Tx., U.S.	D3	120
Marble Hall, S. Afr.	B4	49
Marble Hall, Il., U.S.	B2	90
Marblehead, Ma., U.S.	B6	98
Marblehead, Oh., U.S.	A3	112
Marblehill, Ga., U.S.	B2	87
Marble Hill, Mo., U.S.	D8	102
Marblemount, Wa., U.S.	A4	124
Marble Mountain, N.S.	D8	71
Marble Rock, Ia., U.S.	B5	92
Marbleton, Que.	D6	74
Marbleton, Wy., U.S.	D2	127
Marburg, Ger.	C4	18
Marbury, Al., U.S.	C3	78
Marbury, Md., U.S.	C3	97
Marcala, Hond.	C3	62
Marcali, Italy	E2	75
Marcelin, Sask.	E2	75
Marcella, Ar., U.S.	B4	81
Marcelline, Il., U.S.	C2	90
Marcellus, Mi., U.S.	F5	99
Marcellus, N.Y., U.S.	C4	109
Marcellus, Wa., U.S.	B8	124
March Air Force Base, mil., Ca., U.S.	F5	82
Marchand, Man.	E3	70
Marche, hist. reg., Fr.	F8	16
Marche-en-Famenne, Bel.	D5	17
Marchena, Spain	D3	22
Marchena, Isla, i., Ec.	C4	53
Marches (Marche), prov., Italy	C4	23
Mar Chiquita, Laguna, l., Arg.	A4	54
Marco, Fl., U.S.	G5	86
Marcola, Or., U.S.	C3	114
Marcos Juárez, Arg.	A4	54
Marcus, Ia., U.S.	B2	92
Marcus, S.D., U.S.	C3	118
Marcus, Wa., U.S.	A7	124
Marcus Baker, Mount, mtn., Ak., U.S.	g18	79
Marcus Hook, Pa., U.S.	G11	115
Marcy, Mount, mtn., N.Y., U.S.	A7	109
Marcy Colony, S.D., U.S.	B5	36
Mardān, Pak.	B5	36
Mar del Plata, Arg.	g6	56
Mardela Springs, Md., U.S.	D6	97
Mardin, Tur.	D13	40
Marechal Deodoro, Braz.	C3	57
Maree, Loch, l., Scot., U.K.	C3	13

Name	Map Ref.	Page
Mareeba, Austl.	C8	50
Marenanuka, Kir.	R18	52
Marengo, Sask.	F1	75
Marengo, Il., U.S.	A5	90
Marengo, In., U.S.	H5	91
Marengo, Ia., U.S.	C5	92
Marengo, Oh., U.S.	B3	112
Marengo, Wa., U.S.	B7	124
Marengo, Wi., U.S.	B3	126
Marengo, co., Al., U.S.	C2	78
Marenisco, Mi., U.S.	n12	99
Marennes, Fr.	E3	16
Maretz, Fr.	D3	17
Mareuil-sur-Ourcq, Fr.	E3	17
Marfa, Tx., U.S.	o12	120
Marfrance, W.V., U.S.	C4	125
Margai Co, l., China	A8	36
Marganets, Sov. Un.	H10	27
Margaree, N.S.	C8	71
Margaree Harbour, N.S.	C8	71
Margaret, Man.	E2	70
Margaret, Al., U.S.	B3	78
Margaret, Tx., U.S.	B3	120
Margaret, co., Ca., U.S.	D4	71
Margaretsville, N.Y., U.S.	C6	109
Margarita, Isla de, i., Ven.	A5	60
Margate, Eng., U.K.	E7	10
Margate, Fla., U.S.	F6	86
Margate, Md., U.S.	*B4	97
Margate City, N.J., U.S.	E3	107
Margerum, Al., U.S.	A1	78
Margherita Peak, mtn., Afr.	A4	48
Marghī, Afg.	D13	39
Marghūb, Kūh-e, mtn., Iran	E8	39
Margie, Mn., U.S.	B5	100
Margilan, Sov. Un.	E10	29
Margny-lès-Compiègne, Fr.	E2	17
Margo, Sask.	F4	75
Mărgow, Dasht-e, des., Afg.	F11	39
Margrethe, Lake, l., Mi., U.S.	D6	99
Marguerite Bay, b., Ant.	C6	7
Mariah Hill, In., U.S.	H4	91
María la Baja, Col.	A2	60
Marian, Austl.	o15	50
Mariana Islands, is., Oc.	E5	6
Marianna, Ar., U.S.	C5	81
Marianna, Fl., U.S.	B1	86
Mariánské Lázně, Czech.	D2	26
Mariapolis, Man.	E2	70
Marias, stm., Mt., U.S.	B4	103
Marías, Islas, is., Mex.	C3	63
Marias Pass, Mt., U.S.	B3	103
Maria Stein, Oh., U.S.	B1	112
Maria van Diemen, Cape, c., N.Z.	K14	51
Mariaville, Me., U.S.	D4	96
Maribel, N.C., U.S.	B6	110
Maribel, Wi., U.S.	h10	126
Maribo, Den.	D5	15
Maribor, Yugo.	B2	24
Maricá, Braz.	h6	56
Maricaban Island, i., Phil.	p13	34
Maricopa, Az., U.S.	E3	80
Maricopa, co., Az., U.S.	E4	82
Maricopa, co., Az., U.S.	D3	80
Maricopa Mountains, mts., Az., U.S.	m7	80
Marīdī, Sud.	A5	47
Marié, stm., Braz.	D4	60
Mariedamm, Swe.	u33	14
Mariefred, Swe.	t35	14
Marie-Galante, i., Guad.	l14	64
Mariehamn, Fin.	G8	14
Marie Lake, l., Alta.	B5	68
Mariembourg, Bel.	D4	17
Mariemont, Oh., U.S.	o13	112
Marienberg, Ger.	C8	19
Mariental, Nmb.	B2	49
Marienthal, Ks., U.S.	D2	93
Marienville, Pa., U.S.	D3	115
Marie-Reine, Alta.	A2	68
Maries, co., Mo., U.S.	C6	102
Mariestad, Swe.	H5	14
Marietta, Ga., U.S.	C2	87
Marietta, In., U.S.	F6	91
Marietta, Mn., U.S.	E2	100
Marietta, Ms., U.S.	A5	101
Marietta, Oh., U.S.	C4	112
Marietta, Ok., U.S.	D4	113
Marietta, S.C., U.S.	A2	117
Marietta, Wa., U.S.	A3	124
Marieville, Que.	D4	74
Mariinsk, Sov. Un.	B11	28
Marijampolė, Sov. Un.	A7	26
Mari Lake, l., Sask.	B4	75
Marília, Braz.	C2	56
Marimba, Ang.	C2	48
Marín, Spain	A1	22
Marin, co., Ca., U.S.	C2	82
Marina, Ca., U.S.	*D3	82
Marina del Rey, Ca., U.S.	*n12	82
Marina di Ravenna, Italy	E7	20
Marine, Il., U.S.	E4	90
Marine City, Mi., U.S.	F8	99
Marine On St. Croix, Mn., U.S.	E6	100
Marinette, Wi., U.S.	C6	126
Marinette, co., Wi., U.S.	C5	126
Maringá, Braz.	C2	56
Maringa, stm., Zaire	A4	48
Maringouin, La., U.S.	D4	95
Marinha Grande, Port.	C1	22
Marino, Italy	h9	23
Marion, Austl.	*G6	50
Marion, Al., U.S.	C2	78
Marion, Ar., U.S.	B5	81
Marion, Ct., U.S.	C4	84
Marion, Il., U.S.	F5	90
Marion, In., U.S.	C6	91
Marion, Ia., U.S.	B6	92
Marion, Ks., U.S.	D6	93
Marion, Ky., U.S.	e9	94
Marion, La., U.S.	B3	95
Marion, Ma., U.S.	C6	98
Marion, Mi., U.S.	D5	99
Marion, Mt., U.S.	B2	103
Marion, Ne., U.S.	D5	104
Marion, N.Y., U.S.	B3	109
Marion, N.C., U.S.	B1	110
Marion, N.D., U.S.	C7	111
Marion, Oh., U.S.	B3	112
Marion, Or., U.S.	k12	114
Marion, Pa., U.S.	G6	115
Marion, S.C., U.S.	C9	117
Marion, S.D., U.S.	D8	118
Marion, Ut., U.S.	C4	121
Marion, Va., U.S.	f10	123
Marion, Wi., U.S.	D5	126
Marion, co., Al., U.S.	A2	78
Marion, co., Ar., U.S.	A3	81
Marion, co., Fl., U.S.	C4	86
Marion, co., Ga., U.S.	D2	87
Marion, co., Il., U.S.	E4	90
Marion, co., In., U.S.	E5	91
Marion, co., Ia., U.S.	C4	92
Marion, co., Ks., U.S.	D6	93
Marion, co., Ky., U.S.	C4	94
Marion, co., Ms., U.S.	D4	101
Marion, co., Mo., U.S.	B6	102
Marion, co., Oh., U.S.	B2	112
Marion, co., Or., U.S.	C4	114
Marion, co., S.C., U.S.	C9	117
Marion, co., Tn., U.S.	D8	119
Marion, co., Tx., U.S.	C5	120
Marion, co., W.V., U.S.	B4	125
Marion, Lake, res., S.C., U.S.	E7	117
Marion Center, Pa., U.S.	E3	115
Marion Heights, Pa., U.S.	F3	91
Marion Junction, Al., U.S.	C2	78
Marion Station, Md., U.S.	D6	97
Marionville, Mo., U.S.	D4	102
Mariposa, Ca., U.S.	D4	82
Mariposa, co., Ca., U.S.	D3	82
Mariscal Estigarribia, Para.	D3	55
Marissa, Il., U.S.	E4	90
Maritime Alps, mts., Eur.	E7	16
Maritsa (Évros) (Meriç), stm., Eur.	A5	25
Mariupol, Sov. Un.	E6	29
Marīvān, Iran	D3	39
Marj 'Uyūn, Leb.	F10	40
Marka, Som.	E4	47
Marka Kul, l., Sov. Un.	B2	31
Markala, Mali	D3	45
Markam, China	F4	31
Markaryd, Swe.	I5	14
Mark Center, Oh., U.S.	A1	112
Markdale, Ont.	C4	73
Marked Tree, Ar., U.S.	B5	81
Markerwaard, reg., Neth.	B5	17
Market Drayton, Eng., U.K.	B5	12
Market Harborough, Eng., U.K.	B7	12
Markethill, N. Ire., U.K.	C5	11
Market Rasen, Eng., U.K.	A7	12
Market Weighton, Eng., U.K.	G8	13
Markham, Ont.	D5	73
Markham, Il., U.S.	k9	90
Markham, Tx., U.S.	E4	120
Markham, Va., U.S.	B5	123
Markham, Mount, mtn., Ant.	A29	7
Marki, Pol.	k14	26
Markinch, Sask.	G3	75
Markkleeberg, Ger.	B7	19
Markland, In., U.S.	G7	91
Markland Lock and Dam, U.S.	B5	94
Markle, In., U.S.	C7	91
Markleeville, Ca., U.S.	C4	82
Markleville, In., U.S.	E6	91
Markleysburg, Pa., U.S.	G3	115
Markneukirchen, Ger.	C7	19
Markovka, Sov. Un.	G12	27
Markovo, Sov. Un.	C11	29
Markranstädt, Ger.	B7	19
Marks, Ms., U.S.	A3	101
Marksboro, N.J., U.S.	B3	107
Marksville, La., U.S.	C3	95
Marktheidenfeld, Ger.	D4	19
Marktredwitz, Ger.	C6	18
Markville, Mn., U.S.	D6	100
Marl, Ger.	*C3	18
Marland, Ok., U.S.	A4	113
Marlboro, Alta.	C2	68
Marlboro, N.J., U.S.	C4	107
Marlboro, N.Y., U.S.	D6	109
Marlboro, Vt., U.S.	F3	122
Marlboro, Va., U.S.	n17	123
Marlboro, co., S.C., U.S.	B8	117
Marlborough, Guy.	A3	59
Marlborough, Eng., U.K.	C6	12
Marlborough, Ct., U.S.	C6	84
Marlborough, Ma., U.S.	B4	98
Marlborough, N.H., U.S.	E2	106
Marle, Fr.	E3	17
Marlene Village, Or., U.S.	*B4	114
Marlette, Mi., U.S.	E7	99
Marley, Md., U.S.	B4	97
Marlin, Tx., U.S.	D4	120
Marlin, Wa., U.S.	B7	124
Marlinton, W.V., U.S.	C4	125
Marlow, Ger.	D6	15
Marlow, Al., U.S.	E2	78
Marlow, Ga., U.S.	D5	87
Marlow, N.H., U.S.	D2	106
Marlow, Ok., U.S.	C4	113
Marlow, W.V., U.S.	B7	125
Marlow Heights, Md., U.S.	*C4	97
Marlton, N.J., U.S.	D3	107
Marly-le-Roi, Fr.	g9	16
Marmaduke, Ar., U.S.	A5	81
Marmara, Sea of	B7	40
Marmara Island, i., Tur.	B6	25
Marmaris, Tur.	D2	41
Marmarth, N.D., U.S.	C2	111
Marmelos, Rio dos, stm., Braz.	D2	59
Marmet, W.V., U.S.	C3	125
Marmolada, mtn., Italy	C7	20
Marmora, Ont.	C7	73
Marmora, N.J., U.S.	E3	107
Marmore, stm., Italy	E4	21
Marnay, Fr.	B1	20
Marnaz, Fr.	D2	21
Marne, Ger.	E3	15
Marne, Mi., U.S.	E5	99
Marne, dept., Fr.	C5	16
Marne au Rhin, Canal de la, Fr.	F4	17
Maroa, Il., U.S.	D4	90
Maroa, Ven.	C4	60
Maroantsetra, Madag.	g9	49
Marondera, Zimb.	A5	49
Marone, Italy	E9	21
Maroni, stm., S.A.	B8	59
Maroochydore-Mooloolaba, Austl.		
Maro Reef, rf., Hi., U.S.	k13	88
Maroua, Cam.	C2	46
Marovoay, Madag.	g9	49
Marowijne, dept., Sur.	B8	59
Marquam, Or., U.S.	B4	114
Marquart, Ont.	D7	102
Marquesas Islands, is., Fr. Poly.	G13	6
Marquesas Keys, is., Fl., U.S.	H4	86
Marquette, Man.	D3	70
Marquette, Ia., U.S.	A6	92
Marquette, Ks., U.S.	D6	93
Marquette, Mi., U.S.	B3	99
Marquette, Ne., U.S.	D8	104
Marquette, co., Mi., U.S.	B3	99
Marquette, co., Wi., U.S.	E4	126
Marquette Heights, Il., U.S.	C4	90
Marquez, Tx., U.S.	D4	120
Marquis, Sask.	G3	75
Marquise, Fr.	D9	12
Marrah, Jabal, mts., Sud.	C1	47
Marrakech, Mor.	C3	44
Marree, Austl.	E6	50
Marrero, La., U.S.	E5	95
Marrickville, Austl.	*F9	50
Marriott, Ut., U.S.	*B3	121
Marromeu, Moz.	A6	49
Marrowbone, Ky., U.S.	D4	94
Mars, Pa., U.S.	E1	115
Mars, Rivière à, stm., Que.	A7	74
Marsabit, Kenya	A6	48
Marsala, Italy	F4	23
Marsā Buraygah, Libya	C3	43
Marsā Maṭrūḥ, Eg.	B2	38
Marsā Sūsah, Libya	C4	43
Marsden, Sask.	E1	75
Marseillan, Fr.	F5	16
Marseille, Fr.	F6	16
Marseilles, Il., U.S.	B5	90
Marshall, Sask.	D1	75
Marshall, Lib.	B4	90
Marshall, Ar., U.S.	B3	81
Marshall, Il., U.S.	D6	90
Marshall, In., U.S.	E3	91
Marshall, Mi., U.S.	F6	99
Marshall, Mn., U.S.	F3	100
Marshall, Mo., U.S.	B4	102
Marshall, N.C., U.S.	f10	110
Marshall, N.D., U.S.	B3	111
Marshall, Ok., U.S.	A4	113
Marshall, Tx., U.S.	C5	120
Marshall, Va., U.S.	B5	123
Marshall, Wa., U.S.	g13	124
Marshall, Wi., U.S.	E4	126
Marshall, co., Al., U.S.	A3	78
Marshall, co., Il., U.S.	B4	90
Marshall, co., In., U.S.	B5	91
Marshall, co., Ia., U.S.	C4	92
Marshall, co., Ks., U.S.	C7	93
Marshall, co., Ky., U.S.	f9	94
Marshall, co., Mn., U.S.	B2	100
Marshall, co., Ms., U.S.	A4	101
Marshall, co., Ok., U.S.	C5	113
Marshall, co., S.D., U.S.	B8	118
Marshall, co., Tn., U.S.	B5	119
Marshall, co., W.V., U.S.	B4	125
Marshall Corner, N.H., U.S.	E4	106
Marshall Islands, ter., T.T.P.I.	F10	6
Marshalls Creek, Pa., U.S.	D11	115
Marshallton, De., U.S.	B3	85
Marshalltown, Ia., U.S.	B5	92
Marshallville, Ga., U.S.	D3	87
Marshallville, Oh., U.S.	B4	112
Marshes Siding, Ky., U.S.	D5	94
Marshfield, In., U.S.	D3	91
Marshfield, Ma., U.S.	B6	98
Marshfield, Mo., U.S.	D5	102
Marshfield, Vt., U.S.	C4	122
Marshfield, Wi., U.S.	D3	126
Marshfield Hills, Ma., U.S.	B6	98
Marsh Fork, stm., W.V., U.S.	n13	125
Marsh Harbour, Bah.	A5	64
Marsh Hill, Pa., U.S.	D8	115
Marsh Hill, Me., U.S.	B5	96
Marsh Hill, N.C., U.S.	f10	110
Marsh Hill, mtn., Me., U.S.	B5	96
Marsh Island, i., La., U.S.	E4	95
Marsh Lake, res., Mn., U.S.	E2	100
Marsh Peak, mtn., Ut., U.S.	C6	121
Marshyhope Creek, stm., Md., U.S.	C6	97
Marsing, Id., U.S.	F2	89
Marstal, Den.	D4	15
Marsteller, Pa., U.S.	E4	115
Marston, Mo., U.S.	E8	102
Marston, N.C., U.S.	B3	110
Marstons Mills, Ma., U.S.	C7	98
Mart, Tx., U.S.	D4	120
Martaban, Burma	E4	36
Martaban, Gulf of, b., Burma	E10	36
Martapura, Indon.	F4	34
Martel, Fl., U.S.	C4	86
Martelange, Bel.	E5	17
Martell, Ne., U.S.	D9	104
Martell, Wi., U.S.	D1	126
Martha, Ok., U.S.	C2	113
Marthasville, Mo., U.S.	C6	102
Martha's Vineyard, i., Ma., U.S.	D6	98
Marthaville, La., U.S.	C2	95
Martí, Cuba	D5	64
Martigano, Lake, l., Italy	g8	23
Martigny[-Ville], Switz.	E3	18
Martigues, Fr.	F6	16
Martin, Czech.	D5	26
Martin, Ga., U.S.	B3	87
Martin, Ky., U.S.	C7	94
Martin, La., U.S.	B2	95
Martin, Mi., U.S.	F5	99
Martin, N.D., U.S.	B5	111
Martin, Oh., U.S.	e7	112
Martin, S.C., U.S.	E5	117
Martin, S.D., U.S.	D4	118
Martin, Tn., U.S.	A3	119
Martin, co., Fl., U.S.	E6	86
Martin, co., In., U.S.	G4	91
Martin, co., Ky., U.S.	C7	94
Martin, co., Mn., U.S.	G4	100
Martin, co., N.C., U.S.	B5	110
Martin, co., Tx., U.S.	C2	120
Martina [Franca], Italy	D6	23
Martin City, Mt., U.S.	B3	103
Martindale, Ca., U.S.	C2	82
Martinez, Ca., U.S.	C2	82
Martinique, dep., N.A.	I14	64
Martin Lake, res., Al., U.S.	C4	78
Martin Peninsula, pen., Ant.	B1	7
Martin Point, c., Ak., U.S.	A11	79
Martinsburg, Mo., U.S.	B6	102
Martinsburg, Oh., U.S.	B3	112
Martinsburg, Pa., U.S.	F5	115
Martinsburg, W.V., U.S.	B7	125
Martinsdale, Mt., U.S.	D6	103
Martins Ferry, Oh., U.S.	B5	112
Martins Pond, l., Ma., U.S.	f11	98
Martinsville, Il., U.S.	D6	90
Martinsville, In., U.S.	F5	91
Martinsville, Ms., U.S.	D3	101
Martinsville, Mo., U.S.	A3	102
Martinsville, Va., U.S.	D3	123
Martinton, Il., U.S.	C5	90
Martinville, Que.	D6	74
Martofte, Den.	C4	15
Martos, Spain	D4	22
Martre, Lac la, l., N.W. Ter.	D9	66
Martwick, Ky., U.S.	C2	94
Marty, S.D., U.S.	E7	118
Marudi, Malay.	E4	34
Ma'rūf, Afg.	B4	36
Marugame, Japan	I6	33
Marum, Neth.	A6	17
Marumsco Creek, stm., Md., U.S.	D6	97
Marvejols, Fr.	E5	16
Marvel, Al., U.S.	B2	78
Marvel, Co., U.S.	D2	83
Marvin, S.D., U.S.	C9	118
Marvine, Mount, mtn., Ut., U.S.	E4	121
Marvyn, Al., U.S.	C4	78
Marwayne, Alta.	C5	68
Mary, Sov. Un.	F9	29
Mary, Lake, l., Mn., U.S.	E3	100
Mary, Lake, l., Ms., U.S.	D2	101
Maryborough, Austl.	G7	50
Maryborough, Austl.	G7	50
Marydel, De., U.S.	D3	85
Marydel, Md., U.S.	B6	97
Maryfield, Sask.	H5	75
Maryland, state, U.S.	B4	97
Maryland City, Md., U.S.	B4	97
Maryland Heights, Mo., U.S.	f13	102
Maryland Line, Md., U.S.	A4	97
Maryland Point, c., Md., U.S.	D3	97
Maryport, Eng., U.K.	C5	10
Mary's Harbour, Newf.	B4	72
Mary's Igloo, Ak., U.S.	B6	79
Marys Peak, mtn., Or., U.S.	C3	114
Marystown, Newf.	E4	72
Marysvale, Ut., U.S.	E3	121
Marysville, N.B.	D3	71
Marysville, Ca., U.S.	C3	82
Marysville, Id., U.S.	E7	89
Marysville, Ks., U.S.	C7	93
Marysville, Mi., U.S.	F8	99
Marysville, Oh., U.S.	B2	112
Marysville, Pa., U.S.	F8	115
Marysville, Wa., U.S.	A3	124
Maryville, Il., U.S.	k9	126
Maryville, Mo., U.S.	A3	102
Maryville, Tn., U.S.	D10	119
Marzagão, Braz.	B3	56
Marzūq, Libya	D2	43
Marzūq, Idehan, dunes, Libya	D2	43
Mas'adah, Isr. Occ.	A7	41
Masai Steppe, pl., Tan.	B6	48
Masaka, Ug.	B5	48
Masalembu Besar, i., Indon.	G4	34
Masalok, Puntan, c., N. Mar. Is.	D7	52
Masan, S. Kor.	D10	31
Masardis, Me., U.S.	B4	96
Masaryktown, Fl., U.S.	D4	86
Masasi, Tan.	D6	48
Masatepe, Nic.	E4	62
Masaua, Eth.	A6	47
Masbate, Phil.	C6	34
Masbate, i., Phil.	C6	34
Mascarene Islands, is., Afr.	H24	2
Mascoma, stm., N.H., U.S.	C2	106
Mascoma Lake, l., N.H., U.S.	C2	106
Mascot, Tn., U.S.	C10	119
Mascota, Mex.	m11	63
Mascotte, Fl., U.S.	D5	86
Mascouche, Que.	D4	74
Mascoutah, Il., U.S.	E4	90
Mascuspana, Mex.	B1	62
Masefield, Sask.	H2	75
Mashābah, Sau. Ar.	C3	38
Mash'abbe Sade, Isr.	D6	41
Masham, Eng., U.K.	F7	13
Mashapaug Pond, l., Ct., U.S.	A7	84
Mashhad, Iran	B5	38
Mashīz, Iran	F5	39
Mashkel, Hāmūn-i, reg., Pak.	G11	39
Māshkīd, stm., Asia	H11	39
Mashpee, Ma., U.S.	C7	98
Mashra' ar Raqq, Sud.	D2	47
Masi-Manimba, Zaire	B2	48
Masindi, Ug.	A5	48
Masīrah, i., Oman	C6	38
Masisea, Peru	C3	58
Masisi, Zaire	B4	48
Masjed-e Soleymān, Iran	B4	38
Mask, Lough, l., Ire.	C2	11
Maskanah, Syria	D12	40
Maskell, Ne., U.S.	B9	104
Maskinongé, Que.	C4	74
Maskinongé, co., Que.	C4	74
Masnières, Fr.	D3	17
Masoala, Cap, c., Madag.	g10	49
Mason, Il., U.S.	E5	90
Mason, Mi., U.S.	F6	99
Mason, Nv., U.S.	E2	105
Mason, Oh., U.S.	C1	112
Mason, Tn., U.S.	B2	119
Mason, Tx., U.S.	D3	120
Mason, W.V., U.S.	B2	125
Mason, co., Il., U.S.	C4	90
Mason, co., Ky., U.S.	B6	94
Mason, co., Mi., U.S.	D4	99
Mason, co., Tx., U.S.	D3	120
Mason, co., Wa., U.S.	B2	124
Mason, co., W.V., U.S.	C3	125
Mason City, Il., U.S.	C4	90
Mason City, Ia., U.S.	A4	92
Mason City, Ne., U.S.	C6	104
Masontown, Pa., U.S.	G2	115
Masontown, W.V., U.S.	B5	125
Masonville, Ar., U.S.	D4	81
Masonville, Co., U.S.	A5	83
Masonville, N.Y., U.S.	C5	109
Masqaṭ, Oman	C6	38
Massa, Italy	B3	23
Massabesic Lake, l., N.H., U.S.	E4	106
Massac, co., Il., U.S.	F5	90
Massachusetts, state, U.S.	B4	98
Massachusetts Bay, b., Ma., U.S.	B6	98
Massacre Lake, l., Nv., U.S.	B2	105
Massaemett Mountain, mtn., Ma., U.S.	A2	98
Massafra, Italy	D6	23
Massakory, Chad	C3	46
Massa Marittima, Italy	C3	23
Massangena, Moz.	B5	49
Massanutten Mountain, mts., Va., U.S.	B4	123
Massapê, Braz.	B2	57
Massapequa, N.Y., U.S.	*E7	109
Massapequa Park, N.Y., U.S.	*E7	109
Massapoag Lake, l., Ma., U.S.	h11	98
Massasecum, Lake, l., N.H., U.S.	D3	106
Massawa (Mitsiwa), Eth.	B4	47
Massena, Ia., U.S.	C3	92
Massena, N.Y., U.S.	f10	109
Massenya, Chad	C3	46
Masset, B.C.	C1	69
Masset Inlet, b., B.C.	C1	69
Massey, Ont.	A2	73
Massey, Md., U.S.	B6	97
Massies Mill, Va., U.S.	C3	123
Massillon, Oh., U.S.	B4	112
Massinga, Moz.	B6	49
Massive, Mount, mtn., Co., U.S.	B4	83
Masson Island, i., Ant.	C22	7
Masten's Corner, De., U.S.	E3	85
Mastergeehy, Ire.	F1	11
Masterton, N.Z.	N15	51
Mastic, N.Y., U.S.	*n16	109
Mastic Beach, N.Y., U.S.	*n16	109
Mastigouche, Réserve, Que.	C4	74
Mastung, Pak.	C3	38
Mastūrah, Sau. Ar.	C2	38
Masuda, Japan	I5	33
Masuria, reg., Pol.	B6	26
Masury, Oh., U.S.	A5	112
Masvingo (Nyanda), Zimb.	B5	49
Mata, Zaire	C3	48
Mata Amarilla, Arg.	D2	54
Matachewan, Ont.	p19	73
Mata de São João, Braz.	D3	57
Matadi, Zaire	C1	48
Matador, Sask.	G2	75
Matador, Tx., U.S.	B2	120
Matagalpa, Nic.	E7	63
Matagorda, co., Tx., U.S.	E5	120
Matagorda Bay, b., Tx., U.S.	E4	120
Matagorda Island, i., Tx., U.S.	E4	120
Matagorda Peninsula, pen., Tx., U.S.	E5	120
Matak, i., Indon.	K7	35
Matam, Sen.	C2	45
Matamoros, Mex.	B5	63
Matamoros [de la Laguna], Mex.	B4	63
Matane, Que.	k13	74
Matanuska, stm., Ak., U.S.	g18	79
Matanzas, Cuba	C3	64
Matanzas, prov., Cuba	C3	64
Matanzas Inlet, b., Fl., U.S.	C5	86
Matão, Braz.	k7	56
Matapédia, Que.	B3	71
Matará, Sri L.	G7	36
Mataram, Indon.	G5	34
Matarani, Peru	E3	58
Matarca, Col.	D3	60
Mataró, Spain	B7	22
Matatiele, S. Afr.	H5	49
Matátula, Cape, c., Am. Sam.	G13	52
Matáutu, W. Sam.	F12	52
Matawan, N.J., U.S.	C4	107
Matawin, stm., Que.	C4	74
Matehuala, Mex.	C4	63
Mateko, Zaire	B2	48
Matera, Italy	D6	23
Mátészalka, Hung.	B6	24
Mateur, Tun.	F2	23
Matewan, W.V., U.S.	D2	125
Matfield Green, Ks., U.S.	D7	93
Mather, Man.	E2	70
Mather, Pa., U.S.	G1	115
Mather, Wi., U.S.	D3	126
Mather Air Force Base, mil., Ca., U.S.	C3	82
Mather Peaks, mts., Wy., U.S.	B5	127
Matherville, Il., U.S.	B3	90
Matheson, Co., U.S.	B6	83
Matheson, Ont.	p20	73
Mathews, Al., U.S.	C3	78
Mathews, Va., U.S.	C6	123
Mathews, co., Va., U.S.	C6	123
Mathews, Lake, l., Ca., U.S.	n14	82
Mathias, W.V., U.S.	B5	125
Mathis, Tx., U.S.	E4	120
Mathiston, Ms., U.S.	B4	101
Mathura (Muttra), India	C6	36
Mati, stm., Alb.	B2	25
Matiakoali, Burkina	D5	45
Matinenda Lake, l., Ont.	A2	73
Matinicus, Me., U.S.	E3	96
Matinicus Island, i., Me., U.S.	E3	96
Matlock, Eng., U.K.	A6	12
Matlock, Il., U.S.	A2	92
Matoaca, W.V., U.S.	C5	123
Matoaka, W.V., U.S.	D3	125
Mato Grosso, state, Braz.	B2	55
Mato Grosso, Planalto do, plat., Braz.	B6	55
Mato Grosso do Sul, state, Braz.	B1	55
Matosinhos, Port.	B1	22
Maṭraḥ, Oman	C6	38
Matraville, Sov. Un.	B11	31
Matsqui, B.C.	f13	69
Matsu, China	*I9	31
Matsue, Japan	D11	31
Matsumae, Japan	F10	33
Matsumoto, Japan	A4	32
Matsusaka, Japan	E11	31
Matsuyama, Japan	I5	33
Matsuzaki, Japan	o17	33
Mattamiscontis Lake, l., Me., U.S.	C4	96
Mattaponi, stm., Va., U.S.	C5	123
Mattawa, Ont.	A6	73
Mattawamkeag, Me., U.S.	C4	96
Mattawamkeag, stm., Me., U.S.	C4	96
Mattawamkeag, East Branch, stm., Me., U.S.	C4	96
Mattawamkeag, West Branch, stm., Me., U.S.	C4	96
Mattawamkeag Lake, l., Me., U.S.	C4	96
Mattawana, Pa., U.S.	F6	115
Mattawoman Creek, stm., Md., U.S.	C3	97
Matterhorn, mtn., Eur.	B1	23
Matterhorn, mtn., Nv., U.S.	B6	105
Matterson Inlet, b., Ant.	g40	7
Matter Vispa, stm., Switz.	D4	21
Matteson, Il., U.S.	k9	90
Matthews, Ga., U.S.	C4	87
Matthews, In., U.S.	D7	91
Matthews, Mo., U.S.	E8	102
Matthews, N.C., U.S.	B2	110
Matthews Mountain, mtn., Mo., U.S.	D6	102
Matthews Ridge, Guy.	A2	59
Matthew Town, Bah.	D7	64
Mattituck, N.Y., U.S.	n16	109
Mattoon, Il., U.S.	D5	90
Mattoon, Wi., U.S.	C4	126
Mattoon, Lake, res., Il., U.S.	D5	90
Mattson, Ms., U.S.	A3	101
Mattydale, N.Y., U.S.	B4	109
Matucana, Peru	D2	58
Matuku Island, i., Fiji	I15	52
Matundu, Zaire	A3	48
Matunuck, R.I., U.S.	G3	116
Matura Bay, b., Trin.	N23	65
Maturín, Ven.	B5	60
Maúa, Moz.	D6	48
Mauban, Phil.	o13	34
Maubeuge, Fr.	B5	16
Ma-Ubin, Burma	D1	35
Mauchline, Scot., U.K.	E4	13
Mauckport, In., U.S.	H5	91
Maud, Scot., U.K.	B5	10
Maud, Oh., U.S.	n13	112
Maud, Ok., U.S.	B5	113
Maudlow, Mt., U.S.	D5	103
Maués, Braz.	C3	59
Maués-Açu, stm., Braz.	C3	59
Mauganj, India	E8	37
Maugansville, Md., U.S.	A2	97
Maugerville, N.B.	D3	71
Maughold Head, c., I. of Man	F4	13
Maui, co., Hi., U.S.	C5	88
Maui, i., Hi., U.S.	C5	88
Mauk, Ga., U.S.	D2	87
Mauldin, S.C., U.S.	B3	117
Maule, prov., Chile	B2	54
Mauléon [-Licharre], Fr.	F3	16
Maumakeogh, hill, Ire.	C2	11
Maumee, In., U.S.	A2	112
Maumee, stm., U.S.	A2	112
Maumee Bay, b., U.S.	G7	99
Maumelle, Lake, res., Ar., U.S.	C3	81
Maun, Bots.	A3	49
Mauna Kea, vol., Hi., U.S.	D6	88
Maunaloa, Hi., U.S.	B4	88
Mauna Loa, vol., Hi., U.S.	D6	88
Maunalua Bay, b., Hi., U.S.	g10	88
Maunath Bhanjan, India	E9	37
Maunawili, Hi., U.S.	g10	88
Maungdaw, Burma	D9	36
Maunie, Il., U.S.	E5	90
Maunoir, Lac, l., N.W. Ter.	B5	114
Maupin, Or., U.S.	B5	114
Maurepas, La., U.S.	h10	95
Maurepas, Lake, l., La., U.S.	D5	95
Maurertown, Va., U.S.	B4	123
Maurice, La., U.S.	B1	92
Maurice, stm., N.J., U.S.	E2	107
Maurice, Lake, l., Austl.	E5	50
Mauricetown, N.J., U.S.	E3	107
Mauritania, ctry., Afr.	C2	45
Mauritius, ctry., Afr.	H24	2
Maury, co., Tn., U.S.	B4	119
Maury City, Tn., U.S.	B2	119
Maury Island, pen., Wa., U.S.	f11	124
Mauston, Wi., U.S.	E3	126
Mauterndorf, Aus.	E6	18
Mauwee Peak, mtn., Ct., U.S.	B2	84
Maverick, co., Tx., U.S.	E2	120
Mavinga, Ang.	E3	48
Mawdesley Lake, l., Man.	B1	70
Mawer, Sask.	G2	75
Mawjib, Wādī al, val., Jord.	C7	41
Mawlaik, Burma	D9	36
Mawlamyine, Burma	E10	36
Mawson, sci., Ant.	C19	7
Mawson Coast, Ant.	C19	7
Mawson Escarpment, clf., Ant.	B19	7
Mawson Glacier, ice, Ant.	e40	7
Mawson Peninsula, pen., Ant.	C28	7
Max, N.D., U.S.	C4	104
Max, N.D., U.S.	B4	111
Maxbass, N.D., U.S.	A5	111
Maxcanú, Mex.	C6	63
Maxeys, Ga., U.S.	C3	87
Maxie, La., U.S.	D3	95
Maxinkuckee, Lake, l., In., U.S.	B5	91
Maxixe, Moz.	B6	49
Max Meadows, Va., U.S.	D2	123
Maxstone, Sask.	H2	75
Maxton, N.C., U.S.	C3	110
Maxville, Mt., U.S.	D3	103
Maxville, Oh., U.S.	B10	13
Maxwell, Ca., U.S.	C2	82
Maxwell, Ia., U.S.	C4	92
Maxwell, Ne., U.S.	C5	104
Maxwell, N.M., U.S.	A5	108
Maxwell, Ne., U.S.	C5	104
Maxwell Air Force Base, mil., Al., U.S.	C3	78
Maxwell Colony, S.D., U.S.	D8	118
May, Id., U.S.	E5	89
May, Ok., U.S.	A2	113
May, Isle of, i., Scot., U.K.	D6	13
May, Mount, mtn., Can.	m17	39
Maya, Mesa de, mtn., Co., U.S.	D7	83
Mayaguana, i., Bah.	H9	33
Mayaguana Passage, strt., Bah.	C7	64
Mayagüez, P.R.	G11	64
Mayagüez, Bahía de, b., P.R.	E1	65
Mayama, Congo	B2	48
Maya Mountains, mts., N.A.	B3	62
Mayarí, Cuba	D6	64

Name	Map Ref.	Page
Mayaro Bay, b., Trin.	O24	65
Maybank, Ms., U.S.	D4	101
Maybee, Mi., U.S.	F7	99
Maybell, Co., U.S.	A2	83
Maybeury, W.V., U.S.	A3	97
Mayberry, Md., U.S.	*D3	125
Maybole, Scot., U.K.	C4	10
Maybole, Som.	C6	47
Maydi, Yemen	D4	38
Maydūm Pyramid, hist., Egypt	E3	41
Mayen, Ger.	C3	18
Mayence see Mainz, Ger.	D4	18
Mayenne, Fr.	C3	16
Mayenne, stm., Fr.	D3	16
Mayer, Az., U.S.	C3	80
Mayersville, Ms., U.S.	C2	101
Mayerthorpe, Alta.	C3	68
Mayes, co., Ok., U.S.	A6	113
Mayesville, S.C., U.S.	D7	117
Mayetta, Ks., U.S.	C8	93
Mayetta, N.J., U.S.	D4	107
Mayfair, Sask.	E2	75
Mayfield, Ks., U.S.	E6	93
Mayfield, Ky., U.S.	f9	94
Mayfield, N.Y., U.S.	B4	109
Mayfield, Ok., U.S.	B2	113
Mayfield, Pa., U.S.	C10	115
Mayfield, Ut., U.S.	D4	121
Mayfield Heights, Oh., U.S.	A4	112
Mayfield Lake, res., Wa., U.S.	C3	124
Mayflower, Ar., U.S.	C3	81
Mayflower Village, Ca., U.S.	*E4	82
Mayger, Or., U.S.	A3	114
Mayhew, Ms., U.S.	B5	101
Mayhill, N.M., U.S.	E4	108
Maykain, Sov. Un.	C9	28
Mayking, Ky., U.S.	C7	94
Maykop, Sov. Un.	G17	13
Mayland, Tn., U.S.	C8	119
Maymont, Sask.	E2	75
Maymyo, Burma	D10	36
Maynard, Ar., U.S.	A5	81
Maynard, Ia., U.S.	B6	92
Maynard, Ma., U.S.	B5	98
Maynard, Mn., U.S.	F3	100
Maynardville, Tn., U.S.	C10	119
Mayne, B.C.	g12	69
Mayne Island, i., B.C.	g12	69
Maynooth, Ont.	B7	73
Maynooth, Ire.	D5	11
Mayo, Yukon	D5	66
Mayo, Fl., U.S.	B3	86
Mayo, Md., U.S.	C4	97
Mayo, S.C., U.S.	A4	117
Mayo, co., Ire.	D2	11
Mayo, stm., Mex.	D2	54
Mayodan, N.C., U.S.	A3	110
Mayo Lake, l., Yukon	D6	66
Mayon Volcano, vol., Phil.	C6	34
Mayor Pablo Lagerenza, Para.	f9	49
Mayotte, dep., Afr.	f9	49
May Park, Or., U.S.	B8	114
May Pen, Jam.	F5	64
Mayport Naval Station, mil., Fl., U.S.	B5	86
Mayreau, i., St. Vin.	V26	65
Mayrhofen, Aus.	B7	20
Mays, In., U.S.	E7	91
Mays Landing, N.J., U.S.	E3	107
Mays Lick, Ky., U.S.	B6	94
Maysville, Al., U.S.	A3	78
Maysville, Ar., U.S.	A1	81
Maysville, Ga., U.S.	B3	87
Maysville, In., U.S.	G3	91
Maysville, Ky., U.S.	B6	94
Maysville, Mo., U.S.	B3	102
Maysville, N.C., U.S.	C5	110
Maysville, Ok., U.S.	C4	113
Maysville, W.V., U.S.	B5	125
Mayumba, Gabon	F2	46
Māyūram, India	F6	36
Mayview, Mo., U.S.	B4	102
Mayville, Mi., U.S.	E7	99
Mayville, N.Y., U.S.	C1	109
Mayville, N.D., U.S.	B8	111
Mayville, Or., U.S.	B6	114
Mayville, Wi., U.S.	E5	126
Maywood, Ca., U.S.	*n12	82
Maywood, Il., U.S.	k9	90
Maywood, Mo., U.S.	B6	102
Maywood, Ne., U.S.	D5	104
Maywood, N.J., U.S.	h8	107
Maywood Park, Or., U.S.	B4	114
Maza, Arg.	B4	54
Maza, N.D., U.S.	A6	111
Mazabuka, Zam.	E4	48
Mazagão, Braz.	C4	59
Mazamet, Fr.	F5	16
Mazapil, Mex.	C4	63
Mazara del Vallo, Italy	F4	23
Mazār-e Sharīf, Afg.	A4	36
Mazār'i an Nūbānī, Isr. Occ.	g11	41
Mazarn Creek, stm., Ar., U.S.	g7	81
Mazarredo, Arg.	D3	54
Mazarrón, Spain	D5	22
Mazaruni, stm., Guy.	A2	59
Mazaruni-Potaro, dept., Guy.	E4	59
Mazatenango, Guat.	E6	63
Mazatlán, Mex.	C3	63
Mazatzal Mountains, mts., Az., U.S.	C4	80
Mazatzal Peak, mtn., Az., U.S.	C4	80
Mažeikiai, Sov. Un.		
Mazenod, Sask.	H2	75
Mazeppa, Mn., U.S.	F6	100
Mazie, Ok., U.S.	A6	113
Mazomanie, Wi., U.S.	E4	126
Mazon, Il., U.S.	B5	90
Mazzarino, Italy	F5	23
Mbabane, Swaz.	C5	49
Mbaïki, Cen. Afr. Rep.	E3	46
Mbala (Abercorn), Zam.	C5	48
Mbale, Ug.	A5	48
Mbalmayo, Cam.	E2	46
Mbamba Bay, Tan.	D5	48
Mbandaka, Zaire	A2	48
M'banza Congo, Ang.	C1	48
Mbanza-Ngungu, Zaire	C1	48
Mbarara, Ug.	B5	48
Mbari, stm., Cen. Afr. Rep.	D4	46
Mberengwa, Zimb.	B4	49
Mbeya, Tan.	C5	48
Mbeya, prov., Tan.	C5	48
Mbinda, Congo	B1	48
Mbour, Sen.	D1	45
Mbout, Maur.	C2	45
Mbuji-Mayi, Zaire	C3	48
Mburucuyá, Arg.	E4	55
McAdam, N.B.	D2	71
McAdams, Ms., U.S.	B4	101
McAdoo, Pa., U.S.	E9	115
McAdoo, Tx., U.S.	C2	120
McAfee, Ms., U.S.	C4	101
McAfee Peak, mtn., Nv., U.S.	B6	105
McAlester, Ok., U.S.	C6	113
McAlester, Lake, res., Ok., U.S.	B6	113
McAlister, N.M., U.S.	C6	108
McAlisterville, Pa., U.S.	E7	115
McAllen, Tx., U.S.	F3	120
McAllister, Mt., U.S.	E5	103
McAlmont, Ar., U.S.	h10	81
McAlpin, Fl., U.S.	B4	86
McAlpine, Md., U.S.	B4	97
McAlpine Lock and Dam, U.S.	H6	91
McAndrews, Ky., U.S.	C7	94
McArthur, Oh., U.S.	C3	112
McAuley, Man.	D1	70
McBain, Mi., U.S.	D5	99
McBaine, Mo., U.S.	C5	102
McBee, S.C., U.S.	C7	117
McBride, B.C.	C7	69
Mcbride, Mo., U.S.	D8	102
McCabe, Mt., U.S.	B12	103
McCall, Id., U.S.	E2	89
McCalla, Al., U.S.	g6	78
McCall Creek, Ms., U.S.	D3	101
McCallsburg, Ia., U.S.	B4	92
McCamey, Tx., U.S.	D1	120
McCammon, Id., U.S.	G6	89
McCandless, Pa., U.S.	h13	115
McCanna, N.D., U.S.	A8	111
McCarley, Ms., U.S.	B4	101
McCarthy, Ak., U.S.	C11	79
McCartney Mountain, mtn., Mt., U.S.	E4	103
McCartys, N.M., U.S.	B2	108
McCaskill, Ar., U.S.	D2	81
McCauley Island, i., B.C.	C2	69
McCauley, Wa., U.S.	B2	124
McCaysville, Ga., U.S.	B2	87
McChord Air Force Base, mil., Wa., U.S.	f11	124
McClain, co., Ok., U.S.	C4	113
McCleave, Ks., U.S.	C8	83
McCleary, Wa., U.S.	B2	124
McClellan Air Force Base, mil., Ca., U.S.	C4	82
McClelland, Ar., U.S.	B4	81
McClelland, Ia., U.S.	C2	92
McClellandville, De., U.S.	B2	85
McClellanville, S.C., U.S.	E9	117
McCleod, N.D., U.S.	E6	103
McClintock, Mount, mtn., Ant.	A28	7
McCloud, Ca., U.S.	B2	82
McClure, Il., U.S.	F4	90
McClure, Oh., U.S.	A2	112
McClure, Pa., U.S.	E7	115
McClure, Va., U.S.	e9	123
McClusky, N.D., U.S.	B5	111
McComas, W.V., U.S.	D3	125
McComb, Ms., U.S.	D3	101
McComb, Oh., U.S.	A2	112
McCondy, Ms., U.S.	B5	101
McCone, co., Mt., U.S.	C11	103
McConnell, Il., U.S.	A4	90
McConnell, co., Tn., U.S.	A3	119
McConnell Air Force Base, mil., Ks., U.S.	g12	93
McConnells, S.C., U.S.	B5	117
McConnellsburg, Pa., U.S.	G6	115
McConnellstown, Pa., U.S.	F5	115
McConnelsville, Oh., U.S.	C4	112
McCook, Ne., U.S.	D5	104
McCook, co., S.D., U.S.	D8	118
McCook Lake, S.D., U.S.	E9	118
McCool, Ms., U.S.	B4	101
McCoole, Md., U.S.	m13	97
McCool Junction, Ne., U.S.	D8	104
McCord, Sask.	H3	75
McCordsville, In., U.S.	E6	91
McCormick, S.C., U.S.	D3	117
McCormick, co., S.C., U.S.	D3	117
McCoy, Co., U.S.	B4	83
McCracken, Ks., U.S.	D4	93
McCracken, co., Ky., U.S.	e9	94
McCreary, Man.	D2	70
McCreary, co., Ky., U.S.	D5	94
McCrory, Ar., U.S.	B4	81
McCulloch, co., Tx., U.S.	D3	120
McCullough, Al., U.S.	D2	78
McCullough Mountain, mtn., Nv., U.S.	H6	105
McCullum, Al., U.S.	B4	102
McCune, Ks., U.S.	E8	93
McCurtain, Ok., U.S.	B7	113
McCurtain, co., Ok., U.S.	C7	113
McCutchenville, Oh., U.S.	B2	112
McDade, Tx., U.S.	D4	120
McDaniel, Md., U.S.	C5	97
McDavid, Fl., U.S.	u14	86
McDermitt, Nv., U.S.	B4	105
McDermott, Oh., U.S.	D2	112
McDonald, Ks., U.S.	C2	93
McDonald, Ms., U.S.	C4	101
McDonald, Pa., U.S.	F1	115
McDonald, Tn., U.S.	h12	119
McDonald, co., Mo., U.S.	E3	102
McDonald Creek, stm., Mt., U.S.	C8	103
McDonald Islands, is., Austl.	J1	2
McDonough, Ga., U.S.	C2	87
McDonough, N.Y., U.S.	C5	109
McDonough, co., Il., U.S.	C3	90
McDougal, Ar., U.S.	A5	81
McDougall, Mount, mtn., Wy., U.S.	D2	127
McDowell, Ky., U.S.	C7	94
McDowell, Va., U.S.	B3	123
McDowell, co., N.C., U.S.	f10	110
McDowell, co., W.V., U.S.	D3	125
McDowell Mountains, mts., Az., U.S.	k9	80
McDowell Peak, mtn., Az., U.S.	k9	80
McDuffie, co., Ga., U.S.	C4	87
McElhattan, Pa., U.S.	D7	115
McElroy Creek, stm., W.V., U.S.	k9	125
McEwen, Tn., U.S.	A4	119
McFaddin, Wy., U.S.	E4	120
McFall, Mo., U.S.	A3	102
McFarlan, N.C., U.S.	C3	110
McFarland, Ca., U.S.	E4	82
McFarland, Ks., U.S.	C7	93
McFarland, Wi., U.S.	E4	126
McGaheysville, Va., U.S.	B4	123
McGee, Sask.	F1	75
McGehee, Ar., U.S.	D4	81
McGill, Nv., U.S.	D7	105
McGillivray, Lac, l., Que.	A7	73
McGivney, N.B.	C3	71
McGrady, N.C., U.S.	A1	110
McGrath, Ak., U.S.	C8	79
McGrath, Mn., U.S.	D5	100
McGraw, N.Y., U.S.	C4	109
McGraws, W.V., U.S.	D3	125
McGregor, Ia., U.S.	A6	92
McGregor, Mn., U.S.	D5	100
McGregor, N.D., U.S.	A3	111
McGregor, Tx., U.S.	D4	120
McGregor, stm., B.C.	B7	69
McGregor Lake, l., Alta.	D4	68
McGrew, Ne., U.S.	C2	104
McGuffey, Oh., U.S.	B2	112
McGuire, Mount, mtn., Id., U.S.	D4	89
McGuire Air Force Base, mil., N.J., U.S.	C3	107
McHenry, Il., U.S.	A5	90
McHenry, Ky., U.S.	C3	94
McHenry, Md., U.S.	k12	97
McHenry, Ms., U.S.	E4	101
McHenry, N.D., U.S.	B7	111
McHenry, co., Il., U.S.	A5	90
McHenry, co., N.D., U.S.	A5	111
Mchinga, Tan.	C6	48
Mchinji, Mwi.	D5	48
McHue, Ar., U.S.	B4	81
McIndoe Falls, Vt., U.S.	C4	122
McIntire, Ia., U.S.	A5	92
McIntosh, Mn., U.S.	C2	100
McIntosh, N.M., U.S.	C3	108
McIntosh, S.D., U.S.	B4	118
McIntosh, co., Ga., U.S.	E5	87
McIntosh, co., N.D., U.S.	C6	111
McIntosh, co., Ok., U.S.	B6	113
McIntosh Lake, l., Sask.	B3	75
McIntosh Run, stm., Md., U.S.	D4	97
McIntyre, Ga., U.S.	D3	87
McIntyre, Pa., U.S.	E3	115
McKague, Sask.	E4	75
McKean, Pa., U.S.	C1	115
McKean, co., Pa., U.S.	C4	115
McKee, Ky., U.S.	C6	94
McKee City, N.J., U.S.	E3	107
McKeesport, Pa., U.S.	F2	115
McKees Rocks, Pa., U.S.	F1	115
McKenney, Va., U.S.	D5	123
McKenzie, Al., U.S.	D3	78
McKenzie, N.D., U.S.	C5	111
McKenzie, Tn., U.S.	A3	119
McKenzie, co., N.D., U.S.	B2	111
McKenzie, stm., Or., U.S.	C4	114
McKenzie Bridge, Or., U.S.	C4	114
McKerrow, Ont.	A3	73
McKinley, co., N.M., U.S.	B1	108
McKinley, Mount, mtn., Ak., U.S.	C9	79
McKinley Park, Ak., U.S.	C10	79
McKinleyville, Ca., U.S.	B1	82
McKinney, Ky., U.S.	C5	94
McKinney, Tx., U.S.	C4	120
McKinney, Lake, l., Ks., U.S.	E3	127
McKinnon, Wy., U.S.	E3	127
McKittrick, Ca., U.S.	E4	82
McKittrick, Mo., U.S.	C6	102
McKittrick Summit, mtn., Ca., U.S.	E4	82
McKnight Lake, l., Man.	A1	70
McLain, Ms., U.S.	D5	101
McLaughlin, Alta.	C5	68
McLaughlin, S.D., U.S.	B5	118
McLaughlin, Man.	D4	70
McLaurin, Ms., U.S.	D4	101
McLean, Sask.	G3	75
McLean, Il., U.S.	C4	90
McLean, Ne., U.S.	B8	104
McLean, Tx., U.S.	B2	120
McLean, Va., U.S.	g12	123
McLean, co., Il., U.S.	C4	90
McLean, co., Ky., U.S.	C2	94
McLean, co., N.D., U.S.	B4	111
McLean Lake, l., Sask.	A6	68
McLean Mountain, mtn., Me., U.S.	A4	96
McLeansboro, Il., U.S.	E5	90
McLemoresville, Tn., U.S.	B3	119
McLennan, Alta.	B2	68
McLennan, co., Tx., U.S.	D4	120
McLennan Lake, l., Sask.	B3	75
McLeod, N.D., U.S.	C8	111
McLeod, co., Mn., U.S.	F4	100
McLeod, stm., Alta.	C2	68
McLeod Bay, b., N.W. Ter.	D10	66
McLeod Lake, B.C.	B6	69
McLeod Lake, l., B.C.	B6	69
M'Clintock Channel, strt., N.W. Ter.	B12	66
McLoud, Ok., U.S.	B4	113
McLoughlin, Mount, mtn., Or., U.S.	E4	114
McLouth, Ks., U.S.	C8	93
M'Clure, Cape, c., N.W. Ter.	B8	66
M'Clure Strait, strt., N.W. Ter.	B9	66
McMahon, Sask.	G2	75
McMechen, W.V., U.S.	B4	125
McMillan, Mi., U.S.	B5	99
McMillan, Lake, res., N.M., U.S.	E5	108
McMillin, Wa., U.S.	f11	124
McMinn, co., Tn., U.S.	D9	119
McMinnville, Or., U.S.	B3	114
McMinnville, Tn., U.S.	D8	119
McMorran, Sask.	F1	75
McMullen, co., Tx., U.S.	E3	120
McMurdo, sci., Ant.	C9	7
McMurdo Sound, strt., Ant.	B29	7
McNab, Ar., U.S.	D2	81
McNabb, Il., U.S.	B4	90
McNair, Ms., U.S.	D2	101
McNairy, Tn., U.S.	B3	119
McNairy, co., Tn., U.S.	B3	119
McNary, Az., U.S.	C6	80
McNary, Tx., U.S.	o11	120
McNary Dam, U.S.	B7	114
McNaughton Lake, res., B.C.		
McNeal, Az., U.S.	F6	80
McNeil, Ar., U.S.	D2	81
McNeil, Tx., U.S.	D4	120
McNeil, Mount, mtn., B.C.	*B4	114
McNeil Island, i., Wa., U.S.	f10	124
McNeill, Ms., U.S.	E4	101
McNutts Island, i., N.S.	F4	71
McPhail, Mount, mtn., Man.	D5	70
McPherson, Ks., U.S.	D6	93
McPherson, co., Ks., U.S.	D6	93
McPherson, co., Ne., U.S.	C4	104
McPherson, co., S.D., U.S.	B6	118
McQuady, Ky., U.S.	C3	94
McQueeney, Tx., U.S.	h7	120
McRae, Ar., U.S.	B4	81
McRae, Ga., U.S.	D4	87
McRoberts, Ky., U.S.	C7	94
McSherrystown, Pa., U.S.	G7	115
McTaggart, Sask.	H3	75
McTavish, Man.	E3	70
McVeigh, Ky., U.S.	C7	94
McVeytown, Pa., U.S.	F6	115
McVille, N.D., U.S.	B7	111
McWilliams, Al., U.S.	D2	78
Me, i., Viet.	C6	35
Meacham, Sask.	E3	75
Meacham, Or., U.S.	B8	114
Mead, Co., U.S.	A6	83
Mead, Ne., U.S.	C9	104
Mead, Ok., U.S.	D5	113
Mead, Wa., U.S.	B8	124
Mead, Lake, res., U.S.	A1	80
Meade, Ks., U.S.	E3	93
Meade, co., Ks., U.S.	E3	93
Meade, co., Ky., U.S.	C3	94
Meade, co., S.D., U.S.	C3	118
Meade, stm., Ak., U.S.	B8	79
Meaden Peak, mtn., Co., U.S.	A3	83
Meade Peak, mtn., Id., U.S.	G7	89
Meador, S.D., U.S.	D3	94
Meadow, S.D., U.S.	B3	118
Meadow, Tx., U.S.	C1	120
Meadow, Ut., U.S.	E3	121
Meadow, stm., W.V., U.S.	C4	125
Meadow Bridge, W.V., U.S.	D4	125
Meadowbrook, De., U.S.	*D5	86
Meadowbrook, W.V., U.S.	k10	125
Meadow Creek, W.V., U.S.	D4	125
Meadow Creek, stm., W.V., U.S.	n14	125
Meadow Grove, Ne., U.S.	B8	104
Meadow Lake, Sask.	n7	75
Meadow Lands, Pa., U.S.	F1	115
Meadow Mountain, mtn., U.S.	k12	97
Meadowood, De., U.S.	*B3	85
Meadows, Id., U.S.	E2	89
Meadows, Mn., U.S.	B4	106
Meadowview, Va., U.S.	f10	123
Meadville, Mo., U.S.	B4	102
Meadville, Ms., U.S.	D3	101
Meadville, Pa., U.S.	C1	115
Meaford, Ont.	C4	73
Meagher, co., Mt., U.S.	D6	103
Meaghers Grant, N.S.	E6	71
Mealy Mountains, mts., Newf.	h9	72
Meandarra, Austl.	C7	51
Meander Creek Reservoir, res., Oh., U.S.	A5	112
Means, Ky., U.S.	C6	94
Mearim, stm., Braz.	C1	57
Mearns, Mi., U.S.	E2	21
Meaux, Fr.	C5	16
Mebane, N.C., U.S.	A3	110
Mecca (Makkah), Sau. Ar.	C3	38
Mecca, Ca., U.S.	F5	82
Mecca, In., U.S.	E3	91
Mecca, Oh., U.S.	D2	96
Mechanic Falls, Me., U.S.	D5	91
Mechanicsburg, In., U.S.	D4	90
Mechanicsburg, Oh., U.S.	B2	112
Mechanicsburg, Pa., U.S.	F7	115
Mechanicsville, Ct., U.S.	B8	84
Mechanicsville, Ia., U.S.	C6	92
Mechanicsville, Md., U.S.	D4	97
Mechanicsville, Vt., U.S.	C2	122
Mechanicville, N.Y., U.S.	C7	109
Mechant, Lake, l., La., U.S.	E4	95
Mechelen (Malines), Bel.	B6	16
Mechriyya, Alg.	B4	44
Meck Island, i., Marsh Is.	S17	52
Mecklenburg, co., N.C., U.S.	B2	110
Mecklenburg, co., Va., U.S.	D4	123
Mecklenburg, hist. reg., Ger.	B5	18
Mecklenburg Bay, b., Eur.	D5	15
Meckling, S.D., U.S.	E8	118
Meconta, Moz.	E6	48
Mecosta, Mi., U.S.	E5	99
Mecosta, co., Mi., U.S.	E5	99
Mecúfi, Moz.	D7	48
Medak, India	H7	37
Medan, Indon.	E1	34
Medanos, N.M., U.S.	A3	108
Médanos, Arg.	f7	54
Medanosa, Punta, c., Arg.	D3	54
Medart, Fl., U.S.	B2	86
Medaryville, In., U.S.	B4	91
Meddybemps, Me., U.S.	C5	96
Meddybumps Lake, l., Me., U.S.	C5	96
Medeglia, Switz.	D6	21
Medellín, Col.	B2	60
Medemblik, Neth.	B5	17
Médenine, Tun.	C7	44
Médéa, Maur.	C1	45
Medfield, Ma., U.S.	h10	98
Medford, Ma., U.S.	B5	98
Medford, Mn., U.S.	F5	100
Medford, N.J., U.S.	D3	107
Medford, N.Y., U.S.	*n15	109
Medford, Ok., U.S.	A4	113
Medford, Or., U.S.	E4	114
Medford, Wi., U.S.	C3	126
Medford Lakes, N.J., U.S.	D3	107
Medgidia, Rom.	C9	24
Media, Il., U.S.	C3	90
Media, Pa., U.S.	G11	115
Mediapolis, Ia., U.S.	C6	92
Mediaş, Rom.	B7	24
Medical Lake, Wa., U.S.	B8	124
Medicina, Italy	E7	21
Medicine Bow, stm., Wy., U.S.	E6	127
Medicine Bow Mountains, mts., U.S.	E6	127
Medicine Bow Peak, mtn., Wy., U.S.	E6	127
Medicine Creek, stm., Mo., U.S.	B4	102
Medicine Creek, stm., Ne., U.S.	D5	104
Medicine Lake, Mt., U.S.	B12	103
Medicine Lodge, Ks., U.S.	E5	93
Medicine Lodge, stm., U.S.	E4	93
Medicine Park, Ok., U.S.	C3	113
Medill, Mo., U.S.	A6	102
Medina (Al Madīnah), Sau. Ar.	C3	38
Medina, N.Y., U.S.	B2	109
Medina, N.D., U.S.	C6	111
Medina, Oh., U.S.	A4	112
Medina, Tn., U.S.	B3	119
Medina, Tx., U.S.	E3	120
Medina, Wa., U.S.	e11	124
Medina, co., Oh., U.S.	A4	112
Medina, co., Tx., U.S.	E3	120
Medina, stm., Tx., U.S.	k7	120
Medina del Campo, Spain	B3	22
Medina de Ríoseco, Spain	B3	22
Medina-Sidonia, Spain	D3	22
Meductic, N.B.	D2	71
Medjerda, stm., Tun.	F2	23
Medjerda, Monts de la, mts., Afr.	F2	23
Medjez el Bab, Tun.	F2	23
Medomak, Me., U.S.	D3	96
Medon, Tn., U.S.	B3	119
Medora, Man.	E1	70
Medora, Il., U.S.	D3	90
Medora, In., U.S.	G5	91
Medora, Ks., U.S.	D6	93
Medora, N.D., U.S.	C2	111
Medouneu, Gabon	A2	46
Medstead, Sask.	D1	75
Medveditsa, stm., Sov. Un.	F15	27
Medvedovskaya, Sov. Un.	I12	27
Medvezh'i Islands, is., Sov. Un.	B19	29
Medvezhyegorsk, Sov. Un.	C6	29
Medway, Me., U.S.	C4	96
Medway, Ma., U.S.	B5	98
Medway, stm., N.S.	E5	71
Medzhibozh, Sov. Un.	G6	27
Meekatharra, Austl.	E2	50
Meeker, Co., U.S.	A3	83
Meeker, Ok., U.S.	B5	113
Meeker, co., Mn., U.S.	E4	100
Meelpaeg Lake, res., Newf.	D3	72
Meerane, Ger.	C6	18
Meerbusch, Ger.	*C3	18
Meerle, Bel.	C4	17
Meersburg, Ger.	A7	21
Meerut, India	*C6	36
Meeteetse, Wy., U.S.	B4	127
Megali Canal, Grc.	g10	25
Megalópolis, Grc.	D5	25
Mégantic, co., Que.	D6	74
Mégantic, Lac, l., Que.	D7	74
Mégantic, Mont, mtn., Que.	D6	74
Mégara, Grc.	C4	40
Megargel, Al., U.S.	D2	78
Megargel, Tx., U.S.	C3	120
Megève, Fr.	E2	21
Meggett, S.C., U.S.	F7	117
Meghalaya, state, India	C9	36
Megunticook, Mount, mtn., Me., U.S.	D3	96
Mehadia, Rom.	C6	24
Mehar, Pak.	C4	36
Mehekar, India	G6	37
Meherrin, Va., U.S.	C4	123
Meherrin, stm., U.S.	A4	110
Mehlville, Mo., U.S.	f13	102
Mehoopany, Pa., U.S.	C9	115
Mehrān, Iran	C3	39
Mehun-sur-Yèvre, Fr.	D5	16
Meia Ponte, stm., Braz.	B3	56
Meiganga, Cam.	C2	46
Meighen Island, i., N.W. Ter.	K32	66
Meigs, Ga., U.S.	E2	87
Meigs, co., Oh., U.S.	C3	112
Meigs, co., Tn., U.S.	D9	119
Meiktila, Burma	D10	36
Meiners Oaks, Ca., U.S.	*E4	82
Meiningen, Ger.	C5	18
Meiringen, Switz.	E4	18
Meissen, Ger.	C6	18
Meizhou, China	G8	31
Mejillones, Chile	D1	55
Mékambo, Gabon	A2	46
Mekele, Eth.	C7	45
Mékhé, Sen.	C1	45
Meknès, Mor.	B3	44
Mekong, stm., Asia	H13	30
Mekoryuk, Ak., U.S.	C6	79
Melaka (Malacca), Malay.	K5	35
Melaka, state, Malay.	K5	35
Melba, Id., U.S.	F2	89
Melber, Ky., U.S.	f9	94
Melbern, Oh., U.S.	A1	112
Melbeta, Ne., U.S.	C2	104
Melbourne, Austl.	G8	50
Melbourne, Ont.	E3	73
Melbourne, Ar., U.S.	A4	81
Melbourne, Fl., U.S.	D6	86
Melbourne, Ia., U.S.	C4	92
Melbourne, Ky., U.S.	h14	94
Melbourne, Mo., U.S.	A4	102
Melbourne Beach, Fl., U.S.	D6	86
Melcher, Ia., U.S.	C4	92
Melchor, La., U.S.	D3	95
Meldorf, Ger.	D3	15
Meldrum Bay, Ont.	B1	73
Melekeok, Palau	R17	52
Melenki, Sov. Un.	D13	27
Mélèzes, Rivière aux, stm., Que.	g12	74
Melfa, Va., U.S.	C7	123
Melfi, Chad	C3	46
Melfi, Italy	D5	23
Melfort, Sask.	E3	75
Melghir, Chott, l., Alg.	C6	44
Melilla, Sp. N. Afr.	A4	44
Melipilla, Chile	A2	54
Mélisey, Fr.	A2	21
Melita, Man.	E1	70
Melitopol, Sov. Un.	H10	27
Melito di Porto Salvo, Italy	F5	23
Melle, Fr.	D3	16
Melle, Ger.	A3	19
Mellen, Wi., U.S.	B3	126
Mellette, S.D., U.S.	B7	118
Mellette, co., S.D., U.S.	D5	118
Mellott, In., U.S.	D3	91
Mellrichstadt, Ger.	C5	18
Mellum, i., Ger.	E2	15
Mellwood, Ar., U.S.	C5	81
Melmore, Oh., U.S.	A2	112
Mělník, Czech.	n18	26
Melo, Ur.	E2	56
Melocheville, Que.	q19	74
Melrose, N.B.	C6	71
Melrose, Ct., U.S.	B5	84
Melrose, Fl., U.S.	C4	86
Melrose, Ia., U.S.	D4	92
Melrose, La., U.S.	C3	95
Melrose, Ma., U.S.	B5	98
Melrose, Mn., U.S.	E4	100
Melrose, N.M., U.S.	C6	108
Melrose, Oh., U.S.	A1	112
Melrose, Wi., U.S.	D3	126
Melrose Park, Fl., U.S.	r13	86
Melrose Park, Il., U.S.	*k9	90
Mels, Switz.	B7	21
Melstone, Mt., U.S.	D9	103
Melstrand, Mi., U.S.	B4	99
Melsungen, Ger.	B4	19
Melton Hill Lake, res., Tn., U.S.	D9	119
Melton Mowbray, Eng., U.K.	B7	12
Melun, Fr.	C5	16
Melvaig, Scot., U.K.	C3	13
Melvern Lake, res., Ks., U.S.	D8	93
Melville, Sask.	G4	75
Melville, La., U.S.	D4	95
Melville, Mt., U.S.	D7	103
Melville, N.Y., U.S.	*n15	109
Melville, i., Austl.	B5	50
Melville, Cape, c., Austl.	B7	50
Melville, Lake, l., Newf.	B2	72
Melville, Bugt, b., Grnld.	B14	61
Melville Hills, hills, N.W. Ter.	C8	66
Melville Island, i., N.W. Ter.	m30	66
Melville Island, i., Austl.	B5	50
Melville Peninsula, pen., N.W. Ter.	C16	66
Melvin, Al., U.S.	D1	78
Melvin, Il., U.S.	C5	90
Melvin, Ia., U.S.	A2	92
Melvin, Ky., U.S.	C7	94
Melvin, Tx., U.S.	D3	120
Melvin, Lough, l., Eur.	C3	11
Melvindale, Mi., U.S.	*p7	99
Melvin Village, N.H., U.S.	C4	106
Melyana, Alg.	B5	44
Mélykút, Hung.	B4	24
Memba, Moz.	D7	48
Memboro, Indon.	E5	34
Memmingen, Ger.	E5	18
Mempawah, Indon.	E5	34
Memphis, Fl., U.S.	p10	86
Memphis, Mi., U.S.	F8	99
Memphis, Mo., U.S.	A6	102
Memphis, Ne., U.S.	C9	104
Memphis, Tn., U.S.	B1	119
Memphis, Tx., U.S.	B2	120
Memphis, hist., Eg.	C3	38
Memphis Naval Air Station, mil., Tn., U.S.	B2	119
Memphremagog, Lake, l., N.A.	D5	74
Memramcook, N.B.	C5	71
Mena, Ar., U.S.	C1	81
Menagha, Mn., U.S.	D3	100
Menai Strait, strt., Wales, U.K.	C4	12
Ménaka, Mali	F5	45
Menan, Id., U.S.	F7	89
Menands, N.Y., U.S.	*C7	109
Menard, Tx., U.S.	D3	120
Menard, co., Il., U.S.	C4	90
Menard, co., Tx., U.S.	D3	120
Menasha, Wi., U.S.	D5	126
Mendawai, stm., Indon.	F4	34
Mende, Fr.	E5	16
Menden, Ger.	B2	19
Mendenhall, Ms., U.S.	D4	101
Mendes, Ga., U.S.	E5	87
Mendham, N.J., U.S.	B3	107
Mendham, Sask.	G1	75
Mendi, Eth.	D4	47
Mendip Hills, hills, Eng., U.K.	C5	12
Mendocino, Ca., U.S.	C2	82
Mendocino, co., Ca., U.S.	C2	82
Mendon, Il., U.S.	C2	90
Mendon, Mi., U.S.	F5	99
Mendon, Mo., U.S.	B4	102
Mendon, Oh., U.S.	B1	112
Mendon, Ut., U.S.	B3	121
Mendon, Vt., U.S.	D3	122
Mendota, Ca., U.S.	D3	82
Mendota, Il., U.S.	B4	90
Mendota, Lake, l., Wi., U.S.	E4	126
Mendota Heights, Mn., U.S.	*m13	100
Mendoza, Arg.	A3	54
Mendoza, Pan.	k11	62
Mendoza, prov., Arg.	A3	54
Mendrisio, Switz.	E6	21
Mene de Mauroa, Ven.	A3	60
Mene Grande, Ven.	B3	60
Menemen, Tur.	C6	25
Menen, Bel.	D3	17
Menfi, Italy	F4	23
Mengcheng, China	E8	31
Menggala, Indon.	F3	34
Menghai, China	B5	35
Mengla, China	G4	31
Mengzi, China	G5	31
Menifee, Ar., U.S.	B3	81
Menifee, co., Ky., U.S.	C6	94
Menihek Lakes, l., Newf.	g8	72
Menindee, Austl.	F7	50
Menindee Lake, l., Austl.	F4	51
Menlo, Ga., U.S.	B1	87
Menlo, Ia., U.S.	C3	92
Menlo, Wa., U.S.	C2	124
Menlo Park, Ca., U.S.	k8	82
Menno, S.D., U.S.	D8	118
Meno, Ok., U.S.	A3	113
Menoken, N.D., U.S.	C5	111
Menominee, Mi., U.S.	C3	99
Menominee, co., Mi., U.S.	C3	99
Menominee, co., Wi., U.S.	C5	126
Menominee, stm., U.S.	C6	126
Menominee Indian Reservation, Wi., U.S.	C5	126
Menomonee, stm., Wi., U.S.	m11	126
Menomonee Falls, Wi., U.S.	E5	126
Menomonie, Wi., U.S.	D2	126
Menongue, Ang.	D2	48
Menor, Mar, b., Spain	D5	22
Menorca, i., Spain	K5	23
Mentana, Italy	g9	23
Mentawai, Islands, is., Indon.	F1	34
Mentmore, N.M., U.S.	B1	108
Menton, Fr.	F7	16
Mentone, Al., U.S.	A4	78
Mentone, In., U.S.	B5	91

Name	Map Ref.	Page
Mentone, Tx., U.S.	D1	120
Mentor, Ky., U.S.	k14	94
Mentor, Mn., U.S.	C2	100
Mentor, Oh., U.S.	A4	112
Mentor, Tn., U.S.	n13	119
Mentor-on-the-Lake, Oh., U.S.	A4	112
Menzel Bourguiba, Tun.	B6	44
Menzies, Mount, mtn., Ant.	B19	7
Menziken, Switz.	B5	21
Meoqui, Mex.	B3	63
Meota, Sask.	D1	75
Meppel, Neth.	A7	16
Meppen, Ger.	B4	18
Meqerghane, Sebkha, pl., Alg.	D5	44
Mequon, Wi., U.S.	E6	126
Merabolo, Gulf of, b., Grc.	E5	25
Meramec, stm., Mo., U.S.	C7	102
Merano, Italy	A3	23
Merasheen, Newf.	E4	72
Merasheen Island, i., Newf.	E4	72
Merate, Italy	E7	21
Merauke, Indon.	G10	34
Meraux, La., U.S.	k12	95
Mercâra, India	F6	36
Merced, Ca., U.S.	D3	82
Merced, co., Ca., U.S.	D3	82
Merced, stm., Ca., U.S.	D3	82
Mercedes, Arg.	A3	54
Mercedes, Arg.	A5	54
Mercedes, Arg.	E4	55
Mercedes, Tx., U.S.	F4	120
Mercedes, Ur.	E1	56
Mercer, Me., U.S.	D3	96
Mercer, Mo., U.S.	A4	102
Mercer, N.D., U.S.	B5	111
Mercer, Oh., U.S.	B1	112
Mercer, Pa., U.S.	D1	115
Mercer, Tn., U.S.	B2	119
Mercer, Wi., U.S.	B3	126
Mercer, co., Il., U.S.	B3	90
Mercer, co., Ky., U.S.	C5	94
Mercer, co., Mo., U.S.	A4	102
Mercer, co., N.J., U.S.	C3	107
Mercer, co., N.D., U.S.	B4	111
Mercer, co., Oh., U.S.	B1	112
Mercer, co., Pa., U.S.	D1	115
Mercer, co., W.V., U.S.	D3	125
Mercer Island, N.M., U.S.	B3	124
Mercer Island, i., Wa., U.S.	e11	124
Mercersburg, Pa., U.S.	G6	115
Mercerville, N.J., U.S.	C3	107
Mercês, Braz.	g6	56
Merchantville, N.J., U.S.	*D2	107
Mercier, Que.	D4	74
Mercier, Ks., U.S.	C8	93
Mercoal, Alta.	C2	68
Mercury Bay, b., N.Z.	L15	51
Mercury Islands, is., N.Z.	L15	51
Mercy, Cape, c., N.W. Ter.	D20	66
Meredith, Co., U.S.	B4	83
Meredith, N.H., U.S.	C3	106
Meredith, Lake, l., Co., U.S.	C7	83
Meredith, Lake, res., Tx., U.S.	B2	120
Meredith Center, N.H., U.S.	C3	106
Meredosia, Il., U.S.	D3	90
Meredosia Lake, l., Il., U.S.	D3	90
Mereeg, Som.	E6	47
Merefa, Sov. Un.	G11	27
Merepoint, Me., U.S.	g7	96
Mergui, Burma	F10	36
Mergui Archipelago, is., Burma	F10	36
Meriç (Maritsa) (Évros), stm., Eur.	B6	25
Merid, Sask.	F1	75
Mérida, Mex.	C7	63
Mérida, Spain	C2	22
Mérida, Ven.	B3	60
Mérida, state, Ven.	B3	60
Meriden, Ct., U.S.	C4	84
Meriden, Ia., U.S.	B2	92
Meriden, Ks., U.S.	C8	93
Meriden, Mn., U.S.	F5	100
Meriden, N.H., U.S.	E2	106
Meriden, Wy., U.S.	E8	127
Meridian, Ga., U.S.	E5	87
Meridian, Id., U.S.	F2	89
Meridian, Ms., U.S.	C5	101
Meridian, N.Y., U.S.	B4	109
Meridian, Ok., U.S.	B4	113
Meridian, Pa., U.S.	E2	115
Meridian, Tx., U.S.	D4	120
Meridian Hills, In., U.S.	k10	91
Meridian Naval Air Station, mil., Ms., U.S.	C5	101
Meridianville, Al., U.S.	A3	78
Mérignac, Fr.	E3	16
Merigold, Ms., U.S.	B3	101
Merigomish, N.S.	D7	71
Merikarvia, Fin.	G9	14
Meringur, Austl.	G3	51
Merino, Co., U.S.	A7	83
Meriwether, co., Ga., U.S.	C2	87
Merizo, Guam	M9	52
Merkel, Tx., U.S.	C2	120
Merkinė, Sov. Un.	A8	26
Merksem (part of Antwerp), Bel.	B6	16
Merksplas, Bel.	B6	16
Merkys, stm., Sov. Un.	D5	27
Merlin, Ont.	E2	73
Merlin, Or., U.S.	E3	114
Merlo, Arg.	g7	54
Mermentau, La., U.S.	D3	95
Mermentau, stm., La., U.S.	D3	95
Mern, Den.	C6	15
Merna, Ne., U.S.	C6	104
Merom, In., U.S.	F2	91
Meron, Mount, mtn., Isr.	A7	41
Merredin, Austl.	F2	50
Merriam, In., U.S.	B7	91
Merriam, Ks., U.S.	k16	93
Merrick, N.Y., U.S.	*n15	109
Merrick, co., Ne., U.S.	C7	104
Merrick, mtn., Scot., U.K.	E4	13
Merrick Brook, stm., Ct., U.S.	C7	84
Merrickville, Ont.	C9	73
Merricourt, N.D., U.S.	C7	111
Merrifield, Mn., U.S.	D4	100
Merrifield, Va., U.S.	*B5	123
Merrill, Ia., U.S.	B1	92
Merrill, Mi., U.S.	E6	99
Merrill, Ms., U.S.	E5	101
Merrill, Or., U.S.	E5	114
Merrillan, Wi., U.S.	D3	126
Merrillville, In., U.S.	B3	91
Merrimac, Ky., U.S.	C4	94
Merrimac, Ma., U.S.	A5	98
Merrimac, Wi., U.S.	E4	126
Merrimack, N.H., U.S.	E4	106
Merrimack, co., N.H., U.S.	D3	106
Merrimack, stm., U.S.	A5	98
Merrimacport, Ma., U.S.	A5	98
Merriman, Ne., U.S.	B4	104
Merrimon, N.C., U.S.	C6	110
Merritt, B.C.	D7	69
Merritt, N.C., U.S.	B6	110
Merritt Island, Fl., U.S.	D6	86
Merritt Reservoir, res., Ne., U.S.	B5	104
Merriwa, Austl.	F8	51
Merriweather, Mi., U.S.	m12	99
Mer Rouge, La., U.S.	B4	95
Merrow, Ct., U.S.	B6	84
Merry Hill, N.C., U.S.	A6	110
Merrymeeting Lake, l., N.H., U.S.	D4	106
Merry Oaks, N.C., U.S.	B3	110
Merryville, La., U.S.	D2	95
Mersa Fatma, Eth.	B5	47
Merseburg, Ger.	C5	18
Mersey, stm., Eng., U.K.	D5	10
Merseyside, co., Eng., U.K.	A4	12
Mershon, Ga., U.S.	E4	87
Mersing, Malay.	E2	34
Merti, Kenya	A6	48
Mértola, Port.	D2	22
Merton, Wi., U.S.	m11	126
Mertzon, Tx., U.S.	D2	120
Meru, Kenya	A6	48
Meru, Mount, mtn., Tan.	B6	48
Mervelier, Switz.	B4	21
Merville, Fr.	D2	17
Merwin, Sask.	D1	75
Merwin, Mo., U.S.	C3	102
Merwin Lake, res., Wa., U.S.	C3	124
Méry [-sur-Seine], Fr.	F3	17
Merzifon, Tur.	B10	40
Merzig, Ger.	E6	17
Mesa, Az., U.S.	D4	80
Mesa, Co., U.S.	B2	83
Mesa, Id., U.S.	E2	89
Mesa, co., Co., U.S.	C2	83
Mesa, co., Mn., U.S.	C6	100
Mesabi Range, hills, Mn., U.S.	C6	100
Mesagne, Italy	D6	23
Mesa Mountain, mtn., Co., U.S.	D4	83
Mesa Verde National Park, Co., U.S.	D2	83
Mescalero, N.M., U.S.	D4	108
Mescalero Indian Reservation, N.M., U.S.	D4	108
Meschede, Ger.	B3	19
Mesegon, i., Micron.	Q18	52
Mesena, Ga., U.S.	C4	87
Meshcherskoye, Sov. Un.	n17	27
Meshchovsk, Sov. Un.	D10	27
Meshkovskaya, Sov. Un.	G13	27
Meshomasic Mountain, mtn., Ct., U.S.	C5	84
Meshoppen, Pa., U.S.	C9	115
Mesic, N.C., U.S.	B6	110
Mesilinka, stm., B.C.	A5	69
Mesick, Mi., U.S.	D5	99
Mesilla, N.M., U.S.	E3	108
Mesita, Co., U.S.	D5	83
Mesita, N.M., U.S.	C2	108
Mesocco, Switz.	C5	21
Mesolóngion, Grc.	C3	40
Mesquita, Braz.	B4	56
Mesquite, Nv., U.S.	G7	105
Mesquite, N.M., U.S.	E3	108
Mesquite, Tx., U.S.	n10	120
Messalonskee Lake, l., Me., U.S.	D3	96
Messápion Óros, mtn., Grc.	g10	25
Messen, Switz.	B3	21
Messina, S. Afr.	B5	49
Messina, Strait of, strt., Italy	E5	23
Messíni, Grc.	D3	25
Messíni, Gulf of, b., Grc.	D4	25
Messkirch, Ger.	B5	20
Mesta (Néstos), stm., Eur.	B4	25
Mestghanem (Mostaganem), Alg.	B5	44
Mestre, Italy	B4	23
Mesudiye, Tur.	B11	40
Meta, Mo., U.S.	C5	102
Meta, dept., Col.	C3	60
Meta, stm., S.A.	B4	60
Métabetchouan, Que.	A6	74
Métabetchouane, stm., Que.	A5	74
Meta Incognita Peninsula, pen., N.W. Ter.	D19	66
Metairie, La., U.S.	k11	95
Metaline, Wa., U.S.	A8	124
Metaline Falls, Wa., U.S.	A8	124
Metamora, Il., U.S.	C4	90
Metamora, In., U.S.	F7	91
Metamora, Mi., U.S.	F7	99
Metamora, Oh., U.S.	A2	112
Metán, Arg.	E3	55
Metangula, Moz.	D5	48
Metapán, El Sal.	C3	62
Meta Pond, l., Newf.	D4	72
Metaponto, Italy	D6	23
Metarica, Moz.	D6	48
Métascouac, Lac, l., Que.	B6	74
Metasville, Ga., U.S.	C4	87
Metcalf, Il., U.S.	D6	90
Metcalfe, Ont.	B9	73
Metcalfe, Ms., U.S.	B2	101
Metcalfe, co., Ky., U.S.	C4	94
Metchosin, B.C.	h12	69
Metedeconk, North Branch, stm., N.J., U.S.	C4	107
Metedeconk, South Branch, stm., N.J., U.S.	C3	107
Meteghan River, N.S.	E3	71
Meteghan Station, N.S.	E3	71
Metema, Eth.	C4	47
Meteor Crater, crat., Az., U.S.	C4	80
Methow, Wa., U.S.	A5	124
Methow, stm., Wa., U.S.	A5	124
Methuen, Ma., U.S.	A5	98
Metiskow, Alta.	C5	68
Metlakatla, Ak., U.S.	D13	79
Metolius, Or., U.S.	C5	114
Metonga, Lake, l., Wi., U.S.	C5	126
Metropolis, Il., U.S.	F5	90
Metropolitana, prov., Chile	A2	54
Métsovon, Grc.	C3	25
Mettawee, stm., U.S.	E2	122
Metter, Ga., U.S.	D4	87
Mettet, Bel.	D4	17
Mettingen, Ger.	A2	19
Mettlach, Ger.	B1	19
Mettmann, Ger.	B1	19
Metuchen, N.J., U.S.	B4	107
Metula, Isr.	A7	41
Metz, Fr.	C7	16
Metz, In., U.S.	A8	91
Metz, Mi., U.S.	C7	99
Metz, Mo., U.S.	D3	102
Metzeral, Fr.	B3	20
Metzger, Or., U.S.	h12	114
Meudon, Fr.	g9	16
Meulaboh, Indon.	m11	34
Meung, Fr.	D4	16
Meureudu, Indon.	J2	35
Meurthe, stm., Fr.	F6	17
Meurthe-et-Moselle, dept., Fr.	F6	17
Meuse (Maas), stm., Eur.	C6	16
Meuse, dept., Fr.	E5	17
Meuse, Côtes de, mtn., Fr.	C6	16
Mexia, Tx., U.S.	D4	120
Mexia, Lake, res., Tx., U.S.	D4	120
Mexican Hat, Ut., U.S.	F6	121
Mexican Springs, N.M., U.S.	B1	108
Mexico, In., U.S.	C5	91
Mexico, Ky., U.S.	e9	94
Mexico, Me., U.S.	D2	96
Mexico, Mo., U.S.	B6	102
Mexico, N.Y., U.S.	B4	109
Mexico, Pa., U.S.	E7	115
México, state, Mex.	D5	63
Mexico, ctry., N.A.	D5	63
Mexico, Gulf of, b., N.A.	G11	61
Mexico City, Mex.	D5	63
Meycauayan, Phil.	o13	34
Meydān-e Gel, pl., Iran	G7	39
Meydani, Ra's-e, c., Iran	C5	38
Meyers Chuck, Ak., U.S.	n23	79
Meyersdale, Pa., U.S.	G3	115
Meyísti, i., Grc.	D7	25
Meymaneh, Afg.	A4	36
Meyrin, Switz.	D1	21
Meyronne, Sask.	H2	75
Mèze, Fr.	F5	16
Mezen, Sov. Un.	C7	29
Mezen, stm., Sov. Un.	C7	29
Mezen Bay, b., Sov. Un.	B17	8
Mezhdurechenskiy, Sov. Un.	B7	28
Meziadin Lake, l., B.C.	A3	69
Mézières, Switz.	C2	21
Mézin, Fr.	E3	16
Mezőkövesd, Hung.	B5	24
Mezőtúr, Hung.	B5	24
Mezzolombardo, Italy	C7	20
Mga, Sov. Un.	s32	14
Mga, stm., Sov. Un.	s32	14
Mhor, Beinn, mtn., Scot., U.K.	C1	13
Mhor, Loch, l., Scot., U.K.	C4	13
Mhow, India	F5	37
Miahuatlán de Porfirio Díaz, Mex.	D5	63
Miajadas, Spain	C3	22
Miami, Az., U.S.	D5	80
Miami, Fl., U.S.	G6	86
Miami, In., U.S.	C5	91
Miami, Mo., U.S.	B4	102
Miami, N.M., U.S.	A5	108
Miami, Ok., U.S.	A7	113
Miami, Tx., U.S.	B2	120
Miami, W.V., U.S.	m13	125
Miami, co., In., U.S.	C5	91
Miami, co., Ks., U.S.	D9	93
Miami, co., Oh., U.S.	B1	112
Miami Beach, Fl., U.S.	G6	86
Miami Canal, Fl., U.S.	F6	86
Miami International Airport, Fl., U.S.	G6	86
Miami Lakes, Fl., U.S.	*G6	86
Miamisburg, Oh., U.S.	C1	112
Miami Shores, Fl., U.S.	G6	86
Miami Springs, Fl., U.S.	G6	86
Miamitown, Oh., U.S.	o12	112
Miändoāb, Iran	C3	39
Miandrivazo, Madag.	g9	49
Miāneh, Iran	C3	39
Miangas Island, i., Indon.	D7	34
Mianning, China	F5	31
Mianus Reservoir, res., U.S.	E1	84
Miānwāli, Pak.	B5	36
Mianyang, China	E5	31
Mianyang, China	I5	32
Miarinarivo, Madag.	g9	49
Miass, Sov. Un.	C6	28
Miass, stm., Sov. Un.	C6	28
Miasteczko Śląskie, Pol.	f9	26
Miastko, Pol.	A4	26
Mica Creek, B.C.	C8	69
Mica Mountain, mtn., Az., U.S.	E5	80
Micanopy, Fl., U.S.	C4	86
Micco, Fl., U.S.	E6	86
Miccosukee, Fl., U.S.	B2	86
Miccosukee, Lake, res., Fl., U.S.	B2	86
Michael, Lake, l., Newf.	A2	72
Michalovce, Czech.	B6	24
Michałów-Reginów, Pol.	k13	26
Michaud, Point, c., N.S.	D9	71
Michelson, Mount, mtn., Ak., U.S.	B11	79
Michendorf, Ger.	A8	19
Michichi, Alta.	D4	68
Michie, Tn., U.S.	B3	119
Michigamme, Lake, l., Mi., U.S.	B2	99
Michigamme Reservoir, res., Mi., U.S.	B2	99
Michigan, N.D., U.S.	A7	111
Michigan, state, U.S.	E6	99
Michigan, Lake, l., U.S.	B10	76
Michigan Center, Mi., U.S.	F6	99
Michigan City, In., U.S.	A4	91
Michigan City, Ms., U.S.	A4	101
Michigan Island, i., Wi., U.S.	B3	126
Michigan Prairie, reg., Wa., U.S.		
Michigantown, In., U.S.	D5	91
Michoacán, state, Mex.	D4	63
Michurin (Tsarevo), Bul.	E13	27
Micoud, St. Luc.	J14	64
Micro, N.C., U.S.	B4	110
Micronesia, Federated States of, ter., T.T.P.I.	F9	6
Midai, i., Indon.	K7	35
Midale, Sask.	H4	75
Midas, Nv., U.S.	A2	89
Middelburg, Neth.	B5	16
Middelburg, S. Afr.	D4	49
Middelfart, Den.	C3	15
Middelharnis, Neth.	C4	17
Middelkerke, Bel.	C2	17
Middle, Ia., U.S.	C6	92
Middle, stm., B.C.	B5	69
Middle, stm., Ia., U.S.	C3	92
Middle, stm., Mn., U.S.	B2	100
Middle Andaman, i., India	F9	36
Middleboro, Ma., U.S.	C6	98
Middlebourne, W.V., U.S.	B4	125
Middlebranch, Oh., U.S.	B4	112
Middlebro, Man.	E4	70
Middlebrook, Va., U.S.	B3	123
Middleburg, Fl., U.S.	B5	86
Middleburg, Ky., U.S.	C5	94
Middleburg, Md., U.S.	A3	97
Middleburg, N.C., U.S.	A4	110
Middleburg, Pa., U.S.	E7	115
Middleburg, Tn., U.S.	B3	119
Middleburg, Va., U.S.	B5	123
Middleburgh, N.Y., U.S.	C6	109
Middlebury, Ct., U.S.	C3	84
Middlebury, In., U.S.	A6	91
Middlebury, Vt., U.S.	C2	122
Middlefield, Ct., U.S.	C5	84
Middlefield, Oh., U.S.	A4	112
Middle Granville, N.Y., U.S.	B7	109
Middle Ground, rf., Mid. Is.	J3	52
Middle Haddam, Ct., U.S.	C5	84
Middle Island, N.Y., U.S.	*n16	109
Middle Island Creek, stm., W.V., U.S.	B3	125
Middle Lake, Sask.	E3	75
Middle Loup, stm., Ne., U.S.	C5	104
Middle Musquodoboit, N.S.	D6	71
Middle Nodaway, stm., Ia., U.S.	C3	92
Middle Patuxent, stm., Md., U.S.	B4	97
Middle Point, Oh., U.S.	B1	112
Middleport, N.Y., U.S.	B2	109
Middleport, Oh., U.S.	C3	112
Middle Raccoon, stm., Ia., U.S.	C3	92
Middle River, Md., U.S.	B5	97
Middle River, Mn., U.S.	B2	100
Middlesboro, Ky., U.S.	D6	94
Middlesbrough (Teesside), Eng., U.K.	C6	10
Middlesex, Belize	D7	63
Middlesex, N.J., U.S.	B4	107
Middlesex, N.Y., U.S.	C3	109
Middlesex, Vt., U.S.	C3	122
Middlesex, co., Ct., U.S.	D5	84
Middlesex, co., Ma., U.S.	A5	98
Middlesex, co., N.J., U.S.	C4	107
Middlesex Fells Reservation, Ma., U.S.	g11	98
Middle Stewiacke, N.S.	D6	71
Middleton, N.S.	E4	71
Middleton, Id., U.S.	F2	89
Middleton, Ma., U.S.	A5	98
Middleton, Mi., U.S.	E6	99
Middleton, N.H., U.S.	D4	106
Middleton, Tn., U.S.	B3	119
Middleton, Wi., U.S.	E4	126
Middletown, Ca., U.S.	C2	82
Middletown, Ct., U.S.	C5	84
Middletown, De., U.S.	C3	85
Middletown, In., U.S.	D6	91
Middletown, Ia., U.S.	D6	92
Middletown, Md., U.S.	B2	97
Middletown, Mo., U.S.	B6	102
Middletown, N.J., U.S.	C4	107
Middletown, N.Y., U.S.	D6	109
Middletown, N.C., U.S.	B6	110
Middletown, Oh., U.S.	C1	112
Middletown, Pa., U.S.	F8	115
Middletown, R.I., U.S.	E5	116
Middletown, Va., U.S.	A4	123
Middletown Springs, Vt., U.S.	E2	122
Middletown Township, Pa., U.S.	*G11	115
Middle Valley, N.J., U.S.	B3	107
Middleville, Mi., U.S.	F5	99
Middleville, N.Y., U.S.	B6	109
Midfield, Al., U.S.	g7	78
Mid Glamorgan, co., Wales, U.K.	C4	12
Midhurst, Ont.	C5	73
Midi d'Ossau, Pic du, mtn., Fr.	F5	16
Midkiff, Tx., U.S.	D2	120
Midkiff, W.V., U.S.	C2	125
Midland, Ont.	C5	73
Midland, Ar., U.S.	B1	81
Midland, In., U.S.	F3	91
Midland, La., U.S.	D3	95
Midland, Md., U.S.	k13	97
Midland, Mi., U.S.	E6	99
Midland, N.C., U.S.	B2	110
Midland, Oh., U.S.	C1	112
Midland, Pa., U.S.	E1	115
Midland, S.D., U.S.	C4	118
Midland, Tx., U.S.	D1	120
Midland, Va., U.S.	B5	123
Midland, co., Mi., U.S.	E6	99
Midland, co., Tx., U.S.	D1	120
Midland City, Al., U.S.	D4	78
Midland Park, Ks., U.S.	g12	93
Midland Park, N.J., U.S.	h8	107
Midland Park, S.C., U.S.	k11	117
Midleton, Ire.	E2	10
Midlothian, Il., U.S.	k9	90
Midlothian, Md., U.S.	k13	97
Midlothian, Tx., U.S.	C4	120
Midlothian, Va., U.S.	m17	123
Midnapore, Alta.	D3	68
Midnight, Ms., U.S.	B3	101
Midongy Sud, Madag.	h9	49
Midpines, Ca., U.S.	D3	82
Midreshet Ben Gurion, Isr.	D6	41
Midvale, Id., U.S.	E2	89
Midvale, Ut., U.S.	C4	121
Midville, Ga., U.S.	D4	87
Midway, B.C.	E8	69
Midway, De., U.S.	F5	85
Midway, Ga., U.S.	E5	87
Midway, Ky., U.S.	B5	94
Midway, Or., U.S.	*B4	114
Midway, Tn., U.S.	C11	119
Midway, Ut., U.S.	C4	121
Midway Islands, dep., Oc.	E11	6
Midway Naval Station, mil., Mid. Is.	K3	52
Midway Range, mts., B.C.	E8	69
Midwest, Wy., U.S.	C6	127
Midwest City, Ok., U.S.	B4	113
Midyat, Tur.	D13	40
Miechów, Pol.		
Międzychód, Pol.	B3	26
Międzyrzec [Podlaski], Pol.	C7	26
Międzyrzecz, Pol.	B3	26
Międzyzdroje, Pol.	g10	26
Mielec, Pol.	C6	26
Mien, l., Swe.	B8	15
Mienia, stm., Pol.	m14	26
Mier, In., U.S.	C6	91
Miercurea Ciuc, Rom.		
Mieres, Spain	A3	22
Miesbach, Ger.	D5	20
Mieso, Eth.	D5	47
Mifflin, Pa., U.S.	E7	115
Mifflin, Tn., U.S.	B3	119
Mifflin, co., Pa., U.S.	E6	115
Mifflinburg, Pa., U.S.	E7	115
Mifflintown, Pa., U.S.	E7	115
Mifflinville, Pa., U.S.	D9	115
Migdal, Isr.	B7	41
Migennes, Fr.	D5	16
Migliarino, Italy	E7	20
Miguel Alemán, Presa, res., Mex.	n15	63
Miguel Alves, Braz.	B2	57
Miguel Auza, Mex.	E7	63
Mihai Viteazu, Rom.		
Mihama, Japan	o15	33
Mijares, stm., Spain	B5	22
Mijdahah, Yemen	C6	47
Mikado, Sask.	F4	75
Mikado, Mi., U.S.	D7	99
Mikana, Wi., U.S.	C2	126
Mikha Tskhakaya, Sov. Un.	A14	40
Mikhaylov, Sov. Un.	D12	27
Mikhaylov, Cape, c., Ant.	C24	7
Mikhaylovgrad, Bul.	D6	24
Mikhaylovka, Sov. Un.	F14	27
Mikhaylovka, Sov. Un.	H10	27
Mikhaylovskiy, Sov. Un.	C9	28
Mikindani, Tan.	D7	48
Mikkalo, Or., U.S.	B6	114
Mikkeli, Fin.	G12	14
Mikołów, Pol.	g9	26
Mikonos, i., Grc.	D5	25
Mikope, Zaire	C4	48
Mikulov, Czech.	D4	24
Mikumi, Tan.	C6	48
Mikura Island, i., Japan	J9	33
Milaca, Mn., U.S.	E5	100
Milagro, Ec.	B2	58
Milam, W.V., U.S.	C5	125
Milam, co., Tx., U.S.	D4	120
Milan, Ont.	D6	74
Milan (Milano), Italy	B2	23
Milan, Ga., U.S.	D3	87
Milan, Il., U.S.	B3	90
Milan, In., U.S.	F7	91
Milan, Ks., U.S.	E6	93
Milan, Mi., U.S.	F7	99
Milan, Mo., U.S.	A4	102
Milan, N.H., U.S.	B4	106
Milan, N.M., U.S.	B2	108
Milan, Oh., U.S.	A3	112
Milan, Tn., U.S.	B3	119
Milan, Wa., U.S.	B8	124
Milano, Tx., U.S.	D4	120
Milâs, Tur.	D2	25
Milazzo, Italy	E6	23
Milbank, S.D., U.S.	B9	118
Milbanke Sound, strt., B.C.	C3	69
Milbridge, Me., U.S.	D5	96
Milburn, Ky., U.S.	f9	94
Milburn, Ok., U.S.	C5	113
Milden, Sask.	F2	75
Mildenhall, Eng., U.K.	B8	12
Mildmay, Ont.	C3	73
Mildred, Sask.	D2	75
Mildred, Mt., U.S.	D12	103
Mildura, Austl.	F5	50
Miléai, Grc.		
Miles, Austl.	E9	51
Miles, Ia., U.S.	B7	92
Miles, Tx., U.S.	D2	120
Miles City, Mt., U.S.	D11	103
Miles Mountain, mtn., Vt., U.S.	C5	122
Milestone, Sask.	G3	75
Milesville, S.D., U.S.	C4	118
Mileto, Italy	E6	23
Milevsko, Czech.		
Miley, S.C., U.S.	E6	117
Milfay, Ok., U.S.	B5	113
Milford, Ct., U.S.	E3	84
Milford, De., U.S.	F4	85
Milford, Il., U.S.	C6	90
Milford, In., U.S.	B6	91
Milford, Ia., U.S.	A2	92
Milford, Ks., U.S.	C7	93
Milford, Me., U.S.	D4	96
Milford, Ma., U.S.	B4	98
Milford, Mi., U.S.	F7	99
Milford, Ne., U.S.	D8	104
Milford, N.H., U.S.	E3	106
Milford, N.J., U.S.	B2	107
Milford, N.Y., U.S.	C6	109
Milford, Oh., U.S.	C1	112
Milford, Pa., U.S.	D12	115
Milford, Tx., U.S.	C4	120
Milford, Ut., U.S.	E2	121
Milford, Va., U.S.	B5	123
Milford Center, Oh., U.S.	B2	112
Milford Lake, res., Ks., U.S.	C6	93
Milford Sound, strt., N.Z.	P11	51
Milh, Ra's al, c., Libya		
Milicz, Pol.		
Miling, Austl.		
Milk, stm., N.A.		
Milk Creek, stm., Co., U.S.	A3	83
Milk River, Alta.	E4	68
Milk River Ridge Reservoir, res., Alta.		
Mill, stm., Ma., U.S.	h9	98
Milladore, Wi., U.S.	D4	126
Millard, Ky., U.S.	C7	94
Millard, Mo., U.S.	A5	102
Millard, co., Ut., U.S.	D2	121
Millarton, N.D., U.S.	C7	111
Millau, Fr.	E5	16
Millbank, Ont.	D4	73
Millboro, S.D., U.S.	D6	118
Millbrae, Ca., U.S.	h8	82
Millbridge, Ont.	C7	73
Millbrook, Ont.	C6	73
Millbrook, Ont.	C3	78
Millbrook, Mi., U.S.	E5	99
Millbrook, N.Y., U.S.	D7	109
Mill Brook, stm., Vt., U.S.	B5	122
Millbury, Ma., U.S.	B4	98
Millbury, Oh., U.S.	e7	112
Mill City, Nv., U.S.	C3	105
Mill City, Or., U.S.	C4	114
Mill City, Pa., U.S.	m17	115
Millcreek, Il., U.S.	F4	90
Mill Creek, In., U.S.	A4	91
Mill Creek, Ok., U.S.	C5	113
Mill Creek, Pa., U.S.	F6	115
Millcreek, Ut., U.S.	C4	121
Mill Creek, W.V., U.S.	C5	125
Mill Creek, stm., In., U.S.	F4	91
Mill Creek, stm., Ks., U.S.	C7	93
Mill Creek, stm., N.J., U.S.	D1	107
Mill Creek, stm., Oh., U.S.	B2	112
Mill Creek, stm., Tn., U.S.	G10	119
Mill Creek, stm., W.V., U.S.	C3	125
Mill Creek, stm., W.V., U.S.	m13	125
Millcreek Township, Pa., U.S.	B1	115
Milledgeville, Ga., U.S.	C3	87
Milledgeville, Il., U.S.	B4	90
Milledgeville, Tn., U.S.	B3	119
Mille Îles, Rivière des, stm., Que.	p19	74
Mille Lacs, co., Mn., U.S.	E5	100
Mille Lacs Indian Reservation, Mn., U.S.	D5	100
Mille Lacs Lake, l., Mn., U.S.	D5	100
Millen, Ga., U.S.	D5	87
Miller, Mo., U.S.	D4	102
Miller, Ne., U.S.	D6	104
Miller, S.D., U.S.	C6	118
Miller, co., Ar., U.S.	D2	81
Miller, co., Ga., U.S.	E2	87
Miller, co., Mo., U.S.	C5	102
Miller, Mount, mtn., Ak., U.S.	C11	79
Miller Creek, stm., B.C.	F5	69
Miller Dale Colony, S.D., U.S.	C6	118
Miller Peak, mtn., Az., U.S.	F5	80
Miller Place, N.Y., U.S.	*n16	109
Miller Run, stm., Vt., U.S.	B4	122
Millers, stm., Ma., U.S.	A3	98
Millers Falls, Ma., U.S.	A3	98
Millers Ferry, Al., U.S.	C2	78
Millers Ferry Dam, Al., U.S.	C2	78
Millersport, Oh., U.S.	C3	112
Millerstown, Pa., U.S.	E7	115
Millersview, Tx., U.S.	D3	120
Millersville, Oh., U.S.	*n12	112
Millersville, Pa., U.S.	F9	115
Millerton, N.B.	B4	71
Millerton, Ia., U.S.	D4	92
Millerton, N.Y., U.S.	D7	109
Millerton, Ok., U.S.	D6	113
Millerton, Pa., U.S.	C8	115
Millerton Lake, res., Ca., U.S.	D4	82
Milltown, Newf.	D3	72
Millerville, Al., U.S.	B4	78
Millerville, Mn., U.S.	D3	100
Millet, Alta.	C4	68
Millett, S.C., U.S.	E4	117
Millett, Tx., U.S.	E3	120
Mill Grove, Mo., U.S.	A4	102
Mill Hall, Pa., U.S.	D7	115
Millhousen, In., U.S.	F7	91
Millhurst, N.J., U.S.	C4	107
Milligan, Fl., U.S.	u15	86
Milligan, Ne., U.S.	D8	104
Milligan College, Tn., U.S.	C11	119
Milliken, Co., U.S.	A6	83
Millington, Md., U.S.	B6	97
Millington, Mi., U.S.	E7	99
Millington, N.J., U.S.	B3	107
Millington, Tn., U.S.	B2	119
Millinocket, Me., U.S.	B4	96
Millinocket Lake, l., Me., U.S.	B4	96
Millinocket Lake, l., Me., U.S.	B3	96
Mill Iron, Mt., U.S.	E12	103
Millis, Ma., U.S.	B5	98
Mills, N.M., U.S.	A5	108
Mills, Wy., U.S.	D6	127
Mills, co., Ia., U.S.	D2	92
Mills, co., Tx., U.S.	D3	120
Millsboro, De., U.S.	F4	85
Millsboro, Pa., U.S.	G1	115
Mill Shoals, Il., U.S.	E5	90
Millstadt, Il., U.S.	E3	90
Millston, Wi., U.S.	D3	126
Millstone, stm., N.J., U.S.	C4	107
Milltown, N.B.	D2	71
Milltown, In., U.S.	H5	91
Milltown, Mt., U.S.	D3	103
Milltown, N.J., U.S.	C4	107
Milltown, S.D., U.S.	D8	118

Name | Map Ref. | Page

Milltown, Wi., U.S. C1 126
Milltown [-Head of Bay d'Espoir], Newf. E4 72
Milltown Malbay, Ire. E2 11
Millvale, Pa., U.S. k14 115
Mill Valley, Ca., U.S. D2 82
Mill Village, N.S. E5 71
Mill Village, Pa., U.S. C2 115
Millville, N.B. C2 71
Millville, De., U.S. F5 85
Millville, Ky., U.S. B5 94
Millville, Ma., U.S. B4 98
Millville, N.J., U.S. E2 107
Millville, Oh., U.S. n12 112
Millville, Pa., U.S. D9 115
Millville, Ut., U.S. B4 121
Millville, W.V., U.S. B7 125
Millville Lake, N.H., U.S. E4 106
Millwood, Ga., U.S. E4 87
Millwood, Oh., U.S. B3 112
Millwood, Va., U.S. A4 123
Millwood, Wa., U.S. g14 124
Millwood Lake, res., Ar., U.S. D1 81
Milmay, N.J., U.S. E3 107
Milner, B.C. f13 69
Milner, Co., U.S. A3 83
Milner, Ga., U.S. C2 87
Milner Dam, Id., U.S. G5 89
Milnesand, N.M., U.S. D6 108
Milnor, N.D., U.S. C8 111
Milo, Alta. D4 68
Milo, Ia., U.S. C4 92
Milo, Me., U.S. C4 96
Milo, Mo., U.S. D3 102
Milo, Or., U.S. E3 114
Mililolii, Hi., U.S. D6 88
Mílos, i., Grc. D5 40
Milparinka, Austl. D3 51
Milpitas, Ca., U.S. *k9 82
Milroy, In., U.S. F7 91
Milroy, Mn., U.S. F3 100
Milroy, Pa., U.S. E6 115
Milstead, Al., U.S. C4 78
Milstead, Ga., U.S. C3 87
Miltenberg, Ger. D4 19
Milton, N.S. E5 71
Milton, Ont. D5 73
Milton, N.Z. Q12 51
Milton, Ct., U.S. B2 84
Milton, De., U.S. E4 85
Milton, Fl., U.S. u14 86
Milton, Il., U.S. D3 90
Milton, Ia., U.S. E7 91
Milton, Ia., U.S. D5 92
Milton, Ks., U.S. E6 93
Milton, Ky., U.S. B4 94
Milton, La., U.S. D3 95
Milton, Ma., U.S. B5 98
Milton, N.H., U.S. D5 106
Milton, N.Y., U.S. D7 109
Milton, N.C., U.S. A3 110
Milton, N.D., U.S. A7 111
Milton, Pa., U.S. D8 115
Milton, Vt., U.S. B2 122
Milton, Wa., U.S. f11 124
Milton, W.V., U.S. C2 125
Milton, Wi., U.S. F5 126
Milton Lake, I., Oh., U.S. A4 112
Miltona, Mn., U.S. D3 100
Miltona, Lake, I., Mn., U.S. D3 100
Milton-Freewater, Or., U.S. B8 114
Milton Keynes, Eng., U.K. B7 12
Milton Mills, N.H., U.S. C5 106
Milton Reservoir, res., Co., U.S. A6 83
Miltonvale, Ks., U.S. C6 93
Milverton, Ont. D4 73
Milwaukee, N.C., U.S. A5 110
Milwaukee, Wi., U.S. E6 126
Milwaukee, co., Wi., U.S. E6 126
Milwaukee, stm., Wi., U.S. m12 126
Milwaukie, Or., U.S. B4 114
Mimbres, N.M., U.S. E2 108
Mimbres Mountains, mts., N.M., U.S. E2 108
Mimico (part of Etobicoke), Ont. m15 73
Mimizan, Fr. E3 16
Mimoň, Czech. C9 19
Mimongo, Gabon F2 46
Mimosa Park, La., U.S. *E5 95
Mims, Fl., U.S. D6 86
Mina, Nv., U.S. E3 105
Mina, S.D., U.S. B7 118
Minā' al Aḥmadī, Kuw. D5 39
Mināb, Iran H8 39
Minago, stm., Man. B2 70
Minaki, Ont. J5 73
Minamata, Japan E9 6
Minami-iwo, i., Japan E8 6
Minami-Tori Island, i., Japan E9 6
Minas, Cuba D5 64
Minas, Ur. E1 56
Minas Basin, b., N.S. D5 71
Minas Channel, strt., N.S. D5 71
Minas de Corrales, Ur. E1 56
Minas de Oro, Hond. C4 62
Minas de Ríotinto, Spain D2 22
Minas Gerais, state, Braz. B4 56
Minas Novas, Braz. B4 56
Minatare, Ne., U.S. C2 104
Minatitlán, Mex. D6 63
Minbu, Burma D9 36
Minburn, Alta. C5 68
Minburn, Ia., U.S. C3 92
Mincio, stm., Italy D6 20
Minco, Ok., U.S. B4 113
Mindanao, i., Phil. D6 34
Mindel, stm., Ger. A6 20
Mindelheim, Ger. A6 20
Mindemoya, Ont. B2 73
Minden, Ont. C6 73
Minden, Ger. B4 18
Minden, Ia., U.S. C2 92
Minden, La., U.S. B2 95
Minden, Ne., U.S. D7 104
Minden, Nv., U.S. E2 105
Minden City, Mi., U.S. E8 99
Mindenmines, Mo., U.S. D2 102
Mindi, Pan. k11 62
Mindoro, Wi., U.S. E2 126
Mindoro, i., Phil. C6 34
Mindoro Strait, strt., Phil. C6 34
Mine Centre, Ont. E5 70
Minechoag Mountain, hill, Ma., U.S. B3 98
Minehead, Eng., U.K. E4 12
Mine Head, c., Ire. F4 11
Mine Hill, N.J., U.S. B3 107
Mine La Motte, Mo., U.S. D7 102
Mineola, Ia., U.S. C2 92
Mineola, N.Y., U.S. E7 109

Mineola, Tx., U.S. C5 120
Miner, Mo., U.S. E8 102
Miner, co., S.D., U.S. D8 118
Mineral, Ca., U.S. B3 82
Mineral, Il., U.S. B4 90
Mineral, Va., U.S. B5 123
Mineral, Wa., U.S. C3 124
Mineral, co., Co., U.S. D4 83
Mineral, co., Mt., U.S. C1 103
Mineral, co., Nv., U.S. E3 105
Mineral, co., W.V., U.S. B4 125
Mineral City, Oh., U.S. B4 112
Mineral del Monte, Mex. m14 63
Mineral del Oro, Mex. n13 63
Mineral Hills, Mi., U.S. B2 99
Mineral Mountains, mts., Ut., U.S. E3 121
Mineral Park, Tn., U.S. h11 119
Mineral Point, Mo., U.S. D7 102
Mineral Point, Wi., U.S. F3 126
Mineral, Alta. C4 68
Mineral Springs, Ar., U.S. D2 81
Mineral Wells, Tx., U.S. A4 101
Mineral Wells, Tx., U.S. C4 120
Minersville, Oh., U.S. C4 112
Minersville, Pa., U.S. E9 115
Minersville, Ut., U.S. E3 121
Minerva, N.Y., U.S. B7 109
Minerva, Oh., U.S. B4 112
Minervino Murge, Italy D6 23
Miscou Centre, N.B. B5 71
Miscouche, P.E.I. C6 71
Miscou Island, i., N.B. B5 71
Miscou Point, c., N.B. A5 71
Misenheimer, N.C., U.S. B2 110
Mishan, China D6 33
Mishawaka, In., U.S. A5 91
Mishegewut Mountain, mtn., Ak., U.S. B7 79
Mishicot, Wi., U.S. D6 126
Mishima, Japan I9 33
Mishmar, Sud. B4 47
Misiones, prov., Arg. E5 55
Misiones, dept., Para. E4 55
Miskitos, Cayos, is., Nic. E8 63
Miskolc, Hung. A5 24
Mismār, Sud. B4 47
Misool, i., Indon. F7 34
Misquamicut, R.I., U.S. G1 116
Miṣr al Jadīdah (Heliopolis) (part of Cairo), Eg. D3 41
Mișrātah, Libya C3 43
Missaukee, co., Mi., U.S. D5 99
Missaukee, Lake, l., Mi., U.S. D5 99
Missinaibi, stm., Ont. G16 66
Mission, Ks., U.S. m16 93
Mission, S.D., U.S. D5 118
Mission, Tx., U.S. F3 120
Mission City, B.C. E6 69
Mission Hill, S.D., U.S. E8 118
Mission Hills, Ks., U.S. *k16 93
Mission Mountain, mtn., Ok., U.S. A7 113
Mission Range, mts., Mt., U.S. C3 103
Mission Ridge, S.D., U.S. C5 118
Mission Viejo, Ca., U.S. n13 82
Missisquoi, stm., Sask. D4 75
Missisquoi, stm., Que. D4 74
Missisquoi Lake, Mn., U.S. G5 100
Missisquoi Bay, b., Vt., U.S. A2 122
Mississauga, Ont. D5 73
Mississinewa, stm., In., U.S. D7 91
Mississinewa Lake, res., In., U.S. C6 91
Mississippi, co., Ar., U.S. B5 81
Mississippi, co., Mo., U.S. E8 102
Mississippi, state, U.S. C4 101
Mississippi, stm., U.S. D9 76
Mississippi Delta, La., U.S. E6 95
Mississippi Lake, I., Ont. B8 73
Mississippi Sound, strt., U.S. E5 101
Mississippi State, Ms., U.S. B5 101
Missoula, Mt., U.S. D2 103
Missoula, co., Mt., U.S. D2 103
Missouri, Mor. C4 44
Missouri, state, U.S. C5 102
Missouri, stm., U.S. B8 76
Missouri Buttes, mtn., Wy., U.S. B8 127
Missouri City, Mo., U.S. h11 102
Missouri City, Tx., U.S. r14 120
Missouri Valley, Ia., U.S. C2 92
Mistassini, Que. h12 74
Mistassini, Lac, l., Que. h12 74
Mistastin Lake, l., Newf. g9 72
Mistatim, Sask. E4 75
Mistelbach [an der Zaya], Aus. G16 18
Misti, Volcán, vol., Peru E3 58
Mistissini, Que. h12 74
Mistretta, Italy F5 23
Misurata, Punta, c., Mex. C3 63
Mitaka, Japan *I9 33
Mitchell, Austl. I8 33
Mitcham, Austl. *F6 50
Mitchell, Austl. E8 50
Mitchell, Ont. D3 73
Mitchell, Ga., U.S. C4 87
Mitchell, Il., U.S. E3 90
Mitchell, In., U.S. G5 91
Mitchell, Ia., U.S. A5 92
Mitchell, Ne., U.S. C2 104
Mitchell, S.D., U.S. D7 118
Mitchell, co., Ga., U.S. E2 87
Mitchell, co., Ia., U.S. A5 92
Mitchell, co., Ks., U.S. C5 93
Mitchell, co., N.C., U.S. e10 110
Mitchell, co., Tx., U.S. C2 120
Mitchell, stm., Austl. C7 50
Mitchell, Lake, l., Mi., U.S. D5 99
Mitchell, Lake, res., Al., U.S. C3 78
Mitchell, Mount, mtn., N.C., U.S. f10 110
Mitchell Island, i., La., U.S. E6 95
Mitchellsburg, Ky., U.S. C5 94
Mitchellville, In., U.S. C4 92
Mitchellville, Tn., U.S. A5 119
Mitchelstown, Ire. D2 11
Mît Fâris, Eg. D3 41
Mît Ghamr, Eg. D3 41
Mithapur, India *m13 36
Mitilíni, Grc. C6 40
Mitishto, stm., Man. B2 70
Mitkof Island, i., Ak., U.S. m23 79
Mitla Pass, Eg. C10 36
Mito, Japan H10 33
Mitra do Bispo, mtn., Braz. h5 56
Mitre, mtn., N.Z. N15 51
Mitry-Mory, Fr. E2 17
Mitsinjo, Madag. g9 49
Mittellband Canal, Eur. B5 18
Mogi-Mirim, Braz. C3 56
Mittersill, Aus. B8 20
Mitterteich, Ger. D6 19
Mittie, La., U.S. D3 95

Mittlerer Isar Kanal, Ger. A7 20
Mittweida, Ger. C6 18
Mitú, Col. C3 60
Mitumba, Monts, mts., Zaire C4 48
Mitwaba, Zaire E2 46
Mitzic, Gabon n18 33
Miura, Japan m14 33
Mixquiahuala, Mex. o14 63
Mixteco, stm., Mex. G9 27
Miyagi Island, i., Japan O5 52
Miyake, Island, i., Japan I9 33
Miyako, Japan G10 33
Miyakonojō, Japan K5 33
Miyazaki, Japan K5 33
Miyazu, Japan n14 33
Mizdah, Libya C2 43
Mize, Ms., U.S. D4 101
Mizen Head, c., Ire. F2 11
Mizil, Rom. C8 24
Mizoram, state, India D9 36
Mizpah, Mn., U.S. C4 100
Mizpah, N.H., U.S. *g7 106
Mizpah, N.J., U.S. E3 107
Mizpah Creek, stm., Mt., U.S. E11 103
Mizpé Ramon, Isr. G10 40
Mizque, Bol. C2 55
Mjölby, Swe. H6 14
Mjøsa, l., Nor. G4 14
Mkalama, Tan. B5 48
Mladá Boleslav, Czech. C3 26
Mlanje, Mts., Mlw. B6 26
Mljet, i., Yugo. D3 24
Mnichovo Hradiště, Czech. C9 19
Mnyusi, Tan. C6 48
Mo, Nor. D6 14
Moa, i., Austl. B7 50
Moab, Ut., U.S. E6 121
Moala Island, i., Fiji I15 52
Moamba, Moz. C5 49
Moanda, Gabon F2 46
Moande, Zaire G7 105
Moark, Ar., U.S. A5 81
Moar Lake, l., Can. D4 70
Moate, Ire. D4 11
Moba, Zaire C4 48
Mobara, Japan n19 33
Mobaye, Cen. Afr. Rep. E4 46
Mobayi-Mbongo, Zaire A3 48
Mobeetie, Tx., U.S. B2 120
Moberly, Mo., U.S. B5 102
Moberly Lake, B.C. B7 69
Moberly Lake, B.C. B7 69
Mobile, Newf. E5 72
Mobile, Al., U.S. E1 78
Mobile, Az., U.S. D3 80
Mobile, co., Al., U.S. E1 78
Mobile, stm., Al., U.S. E1 78
Mobile Bay, b., Al., U.S. E1 78
Mobridge, S.D., U.S. B5 118
Mobula, Zaire A4 48
Moca, Dom. Rep. E8 64
Mocajuba, Braz. D9 54
Moçambique, Moz. D7 48
Moçâmedes see Namibe, Ang. D1 49
Mocanaqua, Pa., U.S. D9 115
Moccasin, Az., U.S. A3 80
Moccasin, Mt., U.S. C7 103
Moce, i., Fiji I16 52
Mocha, Isla, i., Chile B2 54
Moc Hoa, Viet. G6 35
Mocho Mountains, mts., Jam. E14 65
Mochudi, Bots. B4 49
Mocímboa da Praia, Moz. D7 48
Möckeln, l., Swe. B8 15
Mocksville, N.C., U.S. B2 110
Moclips, Wa., U.S. B1 124
Môco, Serra, mtn., Ang. D2 48
Mocoa, Col. C2 60
Mococa, Braz. C2 55
Mocomoco, Bol. B3 63
Mocorito, Mex. B3 63
Moctezuma, Mex. m14 63
Moctezuma, stm., Mex. G7 76
Mocuba, Moz. D6 49
Mocubúri, Moz. C2 92
Modale, Ia., U.S. D2 20
Modane, Fr. D6 83
Model, Co., U.S. D6 83
Model Reservoir, res., Co., U.S. D6 83
Modena, Italy B3 23
Modena, Mo., U.S. A4 102
Modena, N.Y., U.S. D6 109
Modena, Ut., U.S. F2 121
Modena, Wi., U.S. D2 126
Modeste, La., U.S. h9 95
Modesto, Ca., U.S. D3 82
Modesto, Il., U.S. D4 90
Modica, Italy F5 23
Modin, Pol. k13 26
Mödling, Aus. G16 18
Modoc, Ga., U.S. D4 87
Modoc, In., U.S. D7 91
Modoc, Ks., U.S. D2 93
Modoc, co., Ca., U.S. B3 82
Modoc Point, Or., U.S. E5 114
Modřany, Czech. o17 26
Moe, Austl. G8 50
Moehau, mtn., N.Z. L15 51
Moeliro, Zaire A4 80
Moen, i., Micron. Q18 52
Moenave, Az., U.S. A4 80
Moengo, Sur. A4 59
Moenkopi, Az., U.S. A4 80
Moenkopi Plateau, plat., Az., U.S. A4 80
Moenkopi Wash, val., Az., U.S. A5 80
Moerbeke, Bel. C3 17
Moers, Ger. B1 19
Moesa, stm., Switz. D7 21
Moeskroen see Mouscron, Bel. B5 16
Moffat, Scot., U.K. E5 13
Moffat, Co., U.S. D5 83
Moffat, co., Co., U.S. A2 83
Moffat Tunnel, Co., U.S. B5 83
Moffett, co., Co., U.S. B7 113
Moffett Field Naval Air Station, mil., Ca., U.S. k8 82
Moffit, N.D., U.S. C5 111
Moga, India E6 36
Mogadishu (Muqdisho), Som. H4 47
Mogadore, Oh., U.S. A4 112
Mogi das Cruzes, Braz. C3 56
Mogilev, Sov. Un. D6 29
Mogilev-Podolskiy, Sov. Un. G2 27
Mogi-Guaçu, Braz. G6 29
Mogi-Guaçu, Braz. k8 56
Mogi das Cruzes, Braz. C3 56
Mogilev, Pol. B4 26
Mogincual, Moz. A7 49
Mogi-Mirim, Braz. C3 56
Mogochin, Sov. Un. D14 29
Mogocha, Sov. Un. B10 31
Mogok, Burma D10 36

Møn, i., Den. C6 15
Mona, i., U.S. D4 121
Mona, Isla de, i., P.R. G11 64
Mona, Punta, c., C.R. F6 62
Monaca, Pa., U.S. E1 115
Monaco, ctry., Eur. F7 16
Monadhliath Mountains, mts., Scot., U.K. C4 13
Monadnock, Mount, mtn., N.H., U.S. E2 106
Monadnock Mountain, mtn., Vt., U.S. B5 122
Monagas, state, Ven. B5 60
Monaghan, Ire. C4 11
Monaghan, co., Ire. C4 11
Monahans, Tx., U.S. D1 120
Monamolin, Ire. E5 11
Monango, N.D., U.S. C7 111
Mona Passage, strt., N.A. E10 64
Monarch, Alta. E4 68
Monarch, Mt., U.S. C6 103
Monarch Mills, S.C., U.S. B4 117
Monarch Mountain, mtn., B.C. D5 69
Monarch Pass, Co., U.S. C4 83
Monashee Mountains, mts., B.C. D8 69
Monastir, Tun. B7 44
Monastyrshchina, Sov. Un. D8 27
Monavatu, mtn., Fiji H14 52
Moncalieri, Italy B1 23
Monção, Braz. B1 57
Moncey, Fr. B1 21
Monchegorsk, Sov. Un. D15 14
Mönchengladbach, Ger. C3 18
Monchique, Port. D1 22
Monchique, Serra de, mts., Port. D1 22
Moncks Corner, S.C., U.S. E7 117
Monclo, W.V., U.S. D3 125
Monclova, Mex. B4 63
Monclova, Oh., U.S. e6 112
Moncton, N.B. B3 110
Moncure, N.C., U.S. B3 110
Moncton, N.B. C1 92
Mondamin, Ia., U.S. B1 22
Mondego, stm., Port. B1 22
Mondego, Cabo, c., Port. B1 22
Mond Lake, l., Aus. B9 20
Mondoñedo, Spain A2 22
Mondorf-les-Bains, Lux. E6 17
Mondovi, Italy B1 23
Mondovi, Wi., U.S. D2 126
Monee, Il., U.S. B6 90
Monegaw Springs, Mo., U.S. C4 102
Monemvasía, Grc. D4 25
Moneron Island, i., Sov. Un. C10 33
Monessen, Pa., U.S. F2 115
Moneta, Va., U.S. C3 123
Monett, Mo., U.S. E4 102
Monetta, S.C., U.S. D4 117
Monette, Ar., U.S. B5 81
Money, Ms., U.S. B3 101
Moneymore, N. Ire., U.K. C5 11
Monfalcone, Italy A4 23
Monforte de Lemos, Spain A2 22
Monfort Heights, Oh., U.S. o12 112
Monga, Zaire A3 48
Mongaguá, Braz. n8 56
Mongala, Sud. D3 47
Mongala, stm., Zaire A3 48
Mộng Hsat, Burma B3 35
Mộng Mit, Burma D10 36
Mongo, Chad C3 46
Mongo, i., Indon. A3 48
Mongo, In., U.S. A7 91
Mongolia (part of Markham), Ont. k15 73
Mongolia, ctry., Asia B5 31
Mongolia, Plateau of, plat., Mong. B6 31
Mộng Pan, Burma C3 35
Mongu, Zaire E3 48
Mộng Yai, Burma A2 35
Monhegan Island, i., Me., U.S. E3 96
Mönh Hayrhan Mountain, mtn., Mong. B3 31
Moniac, Ga., U.S. F4 87
Moniaive, Scot., U.K. E5 13
Monico, Wi., U.S. C5 126
Monida Pass, U.S. E6 89
Monie, Md., U.S. D6 97
Moninabad see Ambājogāi, India H6 37
Moniquirá, Col. C5 60
Moniteau, co., Mo., U.S. C5 102
Monitor, Alta. D5 68
Monitor, Or., U.S. h12 114
Monitor Range, mts., Nv., U.S. C5 105
Monitor Valley, val., Nv., U.S. D5 105
Monivea, Ire. D3 11
Monkey Point, c., Nic. E6 62
Monkey River, Belize B3 62
Monkira, Austl. D3 51
Monkoto, Zaire B3 48
Monkton, Ont. D3 73
Monkton, Vt., U.S. C2 122
Mon Louis, Al., U.S. E1 78
Monmouth, Wales, U.K. C5 12
Monmouth, Il., U.S. C3 90
Monmouth, Me., U.S. D3 96
Monmouth, Or., U.S. C3 114
Monmouth, co., N.J., U.S. C4 107
Monmouth Beach, N.J., U.S. C5 107
Monmouth Junction, N.J., U.S. C4 107
Monmouth Mountain, mtn., B.C. D6 69
Monnow, stm., U.K. C5 12
Mono, co., Ca., U.S. D4 82
Mono, Lake, l., Ca., U.S. D4 82
Monocacy, stm., Md., U.S. B3 97
Mono Lake, l., Ca., U.S. D4 82
Monomac, Lake, l., U.S. E3 106
Monomoy Point, c., Ma., U.S. C7 98
Monon, In., U.S. C4 91
Monona, Ia., U.S. A6 92
Monona, Wi., U.S. E4 126
Monona, co., Ia., U.S. B1 92
Monona, Lake, l., Wi., U.S. E4 126
Monongah, W.V., U.S. B4 125
Monongahela, Pa., U.S. F2 115
Monongahela, stm., U.S. G2 115
Monongalia, co., W.V., U.S. B5 125
Monopoli, Italy D6 23
Monor, Hung. B4 24
Monos Island, i., Trin. N22 65
Monóvar, Spain C5 22
Monoville, Tn., U.S. C8 119
Monowi, Ne., U.S. B7 104
Monowice, Pol. g10 26
Monponsett, Ma., U.S. B6 98
Monreale, Italy E4 23
Monroe, Ct., U.S. C4 81
Monroe, Ar., U.S. D3 84
Monroe, Ga., U.S. C3 87

Index

Name	Map Ref.	Page
Monroe, In., U.S.	C8	91
Monroe, Ia., U.S.	C4	92
Monroe, La., U.S.	B3	95
Monroe, Me., U.S.	D3	96
Monroe, Mi., U.S.	G7	99
Monroe, Ne., U.S.	C8	104
Monroe, N.H., U.S.	B2	106
Monroe, N.J., U.S.	A3	107
Monroe, N.Y., U.S.	D6	109
Monroe, N.C., U.S.	C2	110
Monroe, Oh., U.S.	C1	112
Monroe, Oh., U.S.	C7	113
Monroe, Or., U.S.	C3	114
Monroe, S.D., U.S.	D8	118
Monroe, Tn., U.S.	C8	119
Monroe, Ut., U.S.	E3	121
Monroe, Va., U.S.	C3	123
Monroe, Wi., U.S.	F4	126
Monroe, co., Al., U.S.	D2	78
Monroe, co., Ar., U.S.	C4	81
Monroe, co., Fl., U.S.	G5	86
Monroe, co., Ga., U.S.	D3	87
Monroe, co., Il., U.S.	E3	90
Monroe, co., In., U.S.	F4	91
Monroe, co., Ia., U.S.	D5	92
Monroe, co., Ky., U.S.	D4	94
Monroe, co., Mi., U.S.	G7	99
Monroe, co., Ms., U.S.	B5	101
Monroe, co., Mo., U.S.	B5	102
Monroe, co., N.Y., U.S.	B3	109
Monroe, co., Oh., U.S.	C4	112
Monroe, co., Pa., U.S.	D11	115
Monroe, co., Tn., U.S.	D9	119
Monroe, co., W.V., U.S.	D4	125
Monroe, co., Wi., U.S.	E3	126
Monroe Bridge, Ma., U.S.	A2	98
Monroe Center, Ct., U.S.	D3	84
Monroe Center, Il., U.S.	A5	90
Monroe City, In., U.S.	G3	91
Monroe City, Mo., U.S.	B6	102
Monroe Lake, res., In., U.S.	F5	91
Monroe Park, De., U.S.	h7	85
Monroeton, Pa., U.S.	C9	115
Monroeville, Al., U.S.	D2	78
Monroeville, In., U.S.	C8	91
Monroeville, N.J., U.S.	D2	107
Monroeville, Oh., U.S.	A3	112
Monroeville, Pa., U.S.	k14	115
Monrovia, Lib.	E2	45
Monrovia, Ca., U.S.	m13	82
Monrovia, In., U.S.	E5	91
Mons (Bergen), Bel.	B5	16
Monsarás, Ponta do, c., Braz.	E3	57
Monschau, Ger.	D6	17
Monselice, Italy	D6	20
Monsey, N.Y., U.S.	*m14	109
Møns Klint, clf., Den.	D6	15
Monson, Me., U.S.	C3	96
Monson, Ma., U.S.	B3	98
Montabaur, Ger.	C2	19
Montagnais Point, c., Newf.	B1	72
Montague, P.E.I.	C7	71
Montague, Ca., U.S.	B2	82
Montague, Ma., U.S.	A2	98
Montague, Mi., U.S.	E4	99
Montague, Tx., U.S.	C4	120
Montague, co., Tx., U.S.	C4	120
Montague Island, i., Ak., U.S.	D10	79
Montague Lake, l., Sask.	H3	75
Montague Peak, mtn., Ak., U.S.	g18	79
Montague Strait, strt., Ak., U.S.	h18	79
Montalbán, Spain	B5	22
Montalegre, Port.	B2	22
Mont Alto, Pa., U.S.	G6	115
Montalto, mtn., Italy	E5	23
Montana, Ak., U.S.	g17	79
Montana, state, U.S.	D7	103
Montana-Vermala, Switz.	D3	21
Montánchez, Spain	C2	22
Montandon, Pa., U.S.	E8	115
Montargis, Fr.	D5	16
Montataire, Fr.	E2	17
Montauban, Fr.	E4	16
Montauban-les-Mines, Que.	C5	74
Montauk, N.Y., U.S.	m17	109
Montbard, Fr.	D6	16
Montbéliard, Fr.	D7	16
Mont Belvieu, Tx., U.S.	E5	120
Montblanch, Spain	B6	22
Mont Blanc Tunnel, Eur.	E7	16
Montbozon, Fr.	B1	21
Montbrison, Fr.	E6	16
Montcalm, co., Que.	C3	74
Montcalm, co., Mi., U.S.	E5	99
Montcalm, Pic de, mtn., Fr.	F4	16
Mont-Carmel, Que.	B8	74
Montceau-les-Mines, Fr.	D6	16
Mont Cenis Pass, Fr.	E7	16
Montcerf, Que.	C1	74
Montchanin, Fr.	D6	16
Montclair, De., U.S.	h7	85
Montclair, Ca., U.S.	m13	82
Montclair, N.J., U.S.	B4	107
Mont Clare, Pa., U.S.	o19	115
Montcoal, W.V., U.S.	D3	125
Montcornet, Fr.	E3	17
Mont-de-Marsan, Fr.	F3	16
Montdidier, Fr.	C5	16
Monteagle, Tn., U.S.	D8	119
Monte Alegre, Braz.	C2	56
Monte Alegre de Goiás, Braz.	A3	56
Monte Azul, Braz.	B4	56
Montebello, Que.	D3	74
Montebello, Ca., U.S.	m12	82
Montebello, Va., U.S.	C3	123
Montebello Islands, is., Austl.	D2	50
Montebelluna, Italy	D8	20
Monte Carmelo, Braz.	B3	56
Monte Caseros, Arg.	A5	54
Montecatini Terme, Italy	C3	23
Montecelio, Italy	g9	23
Montecito, Ca., U.S.	*E4	82
Monte Comán, Arg.	A3	54
Monte Cristi, Dom. Rep.	E8	64
Monte Cristo, Bol.	B1	58
Montecristo, i., Italy	C3	23
Montefrío, Spain	D3	22
Montego Bay, Jam.	E5	64
Montego Bay, b., Jam.	E13	65
Montegut, La., U.S.	E5	95
Monteiro, Braz.	C3	57
Monteith, Mount, mtn., B.C.	B6	69
Montelavar, Port.	f9	22
Montélimar, Fr.	E6	16
Montelindo, stm., Para.	D4	55
Montellano, Spain	D3	22
Montello, Nv., U.S.	B7	105
Montello, Wi., U.S.	E4	126
Montemayor, Meseta de, plat., Arg.	C3	54
Montemorelos, Mex.	B5	63
Montemor-o-Novo, Port.	C1	22
Montenegro, Braz.	B5	56
Montenegro, hist. reg., Yugo.	D4	24
Monte Patria, Chile	A2	54
Monte Plata, Dom. Rep.	E9	64
Monte Porzio Catone, Italy	h9	23
Montepuez, Moz.	D6	48
Montepulciano, Italy	C3	23
Monte Quemado, Arg.	E3	55
Montereau [-faut-Yonne], Fr.	C5	16
Monterey, Al., U.S.	D3	78
Monterey, Ca., U.S.	D3	82
Monterey, In., U.S.	B4	91
Monterey, Ky., U.S.	B5	94
Monterey, La., U.S.	C4	95
Monterey, Ma., U.S.	B1	98
Monterey, Tn., U.S.	C8	119
Monterey, Va., U.S.	B3	123
Monterey, co., Ca., U.S.	D3	82
Monterey Bay, b., Ca., U.S.	D2	82
Monterey Park, Ca., U.S.	m12	82
Montería, Col.	B2	60
Monteros, Arg.	E2	55
Monterotondo, Italy	g9	23
Monterrey, Mex.	B4	63
Montesano, Wa., U.S.	C2	124
Monte Sano Mountain, mtn., Al., U.S.	A3	78
Monte Sant'Angelo, Italy	D5	23
Monte Santo, Braz.	D3	57
Monte Santu, Capo di, c., Italy	D2	23
Montes Claros, Braz.	B4	56
Montevallo, Al., U.S.	B3	78
Montevarchi, Italy	C3	23
Montevideo, Mn., U.S.	F3	100
Montevideo, Ur.	E1	56
Monteview, Id., U.S.	F6	89
Monte Vista, Co., U.S.	D4	83
Montezuma, In., U.S.	E3	91
Montezuma, Ga., U.S.	D2	87
Montezuma, In., U.S.	E3	91
Montezuma, Ks., U.S.	E3	93
Montezuma, N.M., U.S.	B4	108
Montezuma, Oh., U.S.	B1	112
Montezuma, co., Co., U.S.	D2	83
Montezuma Canyon, val., Ut., U.S.	F6	121
Montezuma Castle National Monument, Az., U.S.	C4	80
Montezuma Creek, Ut., U.S.	F6	121
Montezuma Peak, mtn., Az., U.S.	D3	80
Montfaucon, Switz.	B3	21
Montfort, Que.	D3	74
Montfort, Wi., U.S.	F3	126
Montfort-sur-Meu, Fr.	D4	16
Mont-Tremblant, Que.	C3	74
Mont-Tremblant, Parc Provincial du, Que.	C3	74
Montgomery, Wales, U.K.	I8	12
Montgomery, Al., U.S.	C3	78
Montgomery, Ga., U.S.	E5	87
Montgomery, Il., U.S.	B5	90
Montgomery, In., U.S.	G3	91
Montgomery, La., U.S.	C3	95
Montgomery, Ma., U.S.	B2	98
Montgomery, Mi., U.S.	G6	99
Montgomery, N.Y., U.S.	D6	109
Montgomery, Oh., U.S.	o13	112
Montgomery, Pa., U.S.	D8	115
Montgomery, Vt., U.S.	B3	122
Montgomery, W.V., U.S.	C3	125
Montgomery, co., Al., U.S.	C3	78
Montgomery, co., Ar., U.S.	C2	81
Montgomery, co., Ga., U.S.	D4	87
Montgomery, co., Il., U.S.	D4	90
Montgomery, co., In., U.S.	D4	91
Montgomery, co., Ia., U.S.	C2	92
Montgomery, co., Ks., U.S.	E8	93
Montgomery, co., Ky., U.S.	B6	94
Montgomery, co., Md., U.S.	B3	97
Montgomery, co., Ms., U.S.	B4	101
Montgomery, co., Mo., U.S.	C6	102
Montgomery, co., N.Y., U.S.	C6	109
Montgomery, co., N.C., U.S.	B3	110
Montgomery, co., Oh., U.S.	C1	112
Montgomery, co., Pa., U.S.	F11	115
Montgomery, co., Tn., U.S.	A4	119
Montgomery, co., Tx., U.S.	D5	120
Montgomery, co., Va., U.S.	C2	123
Montgomery Center, Vt., U.S.	B3	122
Montgomery City, Mo., U.S.	C6	102
Montgomery Creek, Ca., U.S.	B3	82
Montgomery see Sāhīwāl, Pak.	B5	36
Montgomery Village, Md., U.S.	*B3	97
Monthermé, Fr.	E4	17
Monthey, Switz.	C2	21
Monticello, P.E.I.	C7	71
Monticello, Ar., U.S.	D4	81
Monticello, Fl., U.S.	B3	86
Monticello, Ga., U.S.	C3	87
Monticello, Il., U.S.	C5	90
Monticello, In., U.S.	C4	91
Monticello, Ia., U.S.	B6	92
Monticello, Ky., U.S.	D5	94
Monticello, Me., U.S.	B5	96
Monticello, Mn., U.S.	E5	100
Monticello, Ms., U.S.	D3	101
Monticello, Mo., U.S.	A6	102
Monticello, N.M., U.S.	D2	108
Monticello, N.Y., U.S.	D6	109
Monticello, Ut., U.S.	F6	121
Monticello, Wi., U.S.	F4	126
Mont Ida, Ks., U.S.	D8	93
Montier, Mo., U.S.	D6	102
Montier-en-Der, Fr.	F4	17
Montiers-sur-Saulx, Fr.	D7	16
Montignac, Fr.	E4	16
Montigny [-lés-Metz], Fr.	C7	16
Montijo, Port.	C1	22
Montijo, Spain	C4	22
Montilla, Spain	D3	22
Monti Verdi, Ut., U.S.	*B4	121
Montivilliers, Fr.	C7	16
Mont-Joli, Que.	A9	74
Mont-Laurier, Que.	C3	74
Montmagny, Que.	C7	74
Montmartre, Sask.	G4	75
Montmédy, Fr.	E5	17
Montmirail, Fr.	F3	17
Montmorenci, In., U.S.	D3	91
Montmorenci, S.C., U.S.	D4	117
Montmorency, co., Mi., U.S.	C6	99
Montmorency, stm., Que.	B6	74
Montmorency Number One, co., Que.	B6	74
Montmorency Number Two, co., Que.	C7	74
Montmorillon, Fr.	D4	16
Montney, B.C.	A7	69
Monto, Austl.	B8	51
Montone, stm., Italy	B3	23
Montoro, Spain	C3	22
Montour, co., Pa., U.S.	D8	115
Montour Falls, N.Y., U.S.	C4	109
Montoursville, Pa., U.S.	D8	115
Montoya, N.M., U.S.	B5	108
Montpelier, Id., U.S.	G7	89
Montpelier, In., U.S.	C7	91
Montpelier, La., U.S.	D5	95
Montpelier, Ms., U.S.	B5	101
Montpelier, N.D., U.S.	C7	111
Montpelier, Oh., U.S.	A1	112
Montpelier, Vt., U.S.	C3	122
Montpelier Station, Va., U.S.	B4	123
Montpellier, Que.	D2	74
Montpellier, Fr.	F5	16
Montréal, Wi., U.S.	B3	126
Montréal, stm., Sask.	C3	75
Montréal, Île de, i., Que.	q19	74
Montreal Lake, Sask.	C3	75
Montreal Lake, l., Sask.	C3	75
Montréal-Nord, Que.	p19	74
Montreat, N.C., U.S.	f10	110
Montreuil, Fr.	C5	16
Montreuil [-sous-Bois], Fr.	C5	16
Montreuil-sur-Mer, Fr.	B4	16
Montreux, Switz.	E3	18
Montricher, Switz.	C1	21
Montrond, B.C.	E9	69
Montrose, Scot., U.K.	B5	10
Montrose, Al., U.S.	E2	78
Montrose, Ar., U.S.	D4	81
Montrose, Co., U.S.	C3	83
Montrose, Ga., U.S.	D3	87
Montrose, Il., U.S.	D5	90
Montrose, Ia., U.S.	D6	92
Montrose, Ks., U.S.	E7	93
Montrose, Mi., U.S.	E7	99
Montrose, Mo., U.S.	C4	102
Montrose, Pa., U.S.	C10	115
Montrose, S.D., U.S.	D8	118
Montrose, Va., U.S.	m18	123
Montrose, co., Co., U.S.	C2	83
Montross, Va., U.S.	B6	123
Montrouge, Fr.	g10	16
Mont-Royal, Que.	p19	74
Mont-Saint-Martin, Fr.	C6	16
Mont-Saint-Michel, Fr.	C3	16
Montserrat, Mo., U.S.	C4	102
Montserrat, dep., N.A.	H13	64
Montserrat, mtn., Spain	B6	22
Mont-Tremblant, Que.	C3	74
Montvale, N.J., U.S.	A4	107
Montvale, Va., U.S.	C3	123
Mont Vernon, N.H., U.S.	E3	106
Montville, Ct., U.S.	D7	84
Montville, Ma., U.S.	B1	98
Montville, N.J., U.S.	B4	107
Montz, La., U.S.	h11	95
Montzen, Bel.	D5	17
Monument, Co., U.S.	B6	83
Monument, Ks., U.S.	C2	93
Monument, N.M., U.S.	E6	108
Monument, Or., U.S.	C7	114
Monument, Pa., U.S.	D6	115
Monument Beach, Ma., U.S.	C6	98
Monument Heights, Va., U.S.	*C5	123
Monument Peak, mtn., Co., U.S.	B3	83
Monument Peak, mtn., Id., U.S.	G4	89
Monument Valley, Ut., U.S.	*F5	121
Monument Valley, val., Az., U.S.	A5	80
Monywa, Burma	D10	36
Monza, Italy	B2	23
Monze, Zam.	E4	48
Monzón, Peru	C2	58
Monzón, Spain	B6	22
Moodus, Ct., U.S.	D6	84
Moodus Reservoir, res., Ct., U.S.	C6	84
Moody, Me., U.S.	E2	96
Moody, Mo., U.S.	E6	102
Moody, Tx., U.S.	D4	120
Moody, co., S.D., U.S.	C9	118
Moody Air Force Base, mil., Ga., U.S.	F3	87
Moody Beach, Me., U.S.	E2	96
Moodys, Ok., U.S.	A7	113
Mooers Forks, N.Y., U.S.	f11	109
Moon, Ok., U.S.	D7	113
Moonachie, N.J., U.S.	*B4	107
Moon Lake, l., Austl.	C7	51
Moon Run, Pa., U.S.	k13	115
Moonta, Austl.	F6	50
Moora, Austl.	F2	50
Moorabbin, Austl.	*G8	50
Moorcroft, Wy., U.S.	B8	127
Moore, Id., U.S.	F5	89
Moore, Mt., U.S.	D7	103
Moore, Ok., U.S.	B4	113
Moore, S.C., U.S.	B3	117
Moore, Tx., U.S.	E3	120
Moore, W.V., U.S.	D5	125
Moore, co., N.C., U.S.	B3	110
Moore, co., Tn., U.S.	B5	119
Moore, co., Tx., U.S.	B2	120
Moore, Lake, l., Austl.	E3	50
Moore Dam, U.S.	B3	106
Moorefield, Ky., U.S.	B6	94
Moorefield, Ne., U.S.	C5	104
Moorefield, W.V., U.S.	B6	125
Moore Haven, Fl., U.S.	F5	86
Mooreland, Ok., U.S.	A2	113
Moore Park, Man.	D1	70
Moore Reservoir, res., U.S.	B3	106
Mooresburg, Tn., U.S.	C10	119
Moores Corner, Ma., U.S.	A3	98
Moores Creek National Military Park, N.C., U.S.	C4	110
Moores Hill, In., U.S.	F7	91
Mooresville, In., U.S.	E5	91
Mooresville, Mi., U.S.	D5	99
Mooresville, N.C., U.S.	B2	110
Mooreton, N.D., U.S.	C9	111
Mooreville, Ms., U.S.	A5	101
Moorhead, Ia., U.S.	C2	92
Moorhead, Mn., U.S.	D2	100
Moorhead, Ms., U.S.	B3	101
Mooring, Tn., U.S.	A2	119
Mooringsport, La., U.S.	B2	95
Moor Lake, Ont.	A7	73
Moorland, Ia., U.S.	B3	92
Moorpark, Ca., U.S.	*E4	82
Moosburg, Ger.	E6	19
Moose, Wy., U.S.	C2	127
Moose, stm., N.H., U.S.	B4	106
Moose, stm., N.Y., U.S.	B5	109
Moose Creek, Ont.	B10	73
Moose Factory, Ont.	o19	73
Moosehead Lake, l., Me., U.S.	C3	96
Mooseheart, Il., U.S.	B5	90
Moose Heights, B.C.	C6	69
Moose Hill, hill, Ma., U.S.	h11	98
Moosehorn, Man.	D2	70
Moose Island, i., Man.	D3	70
Moose Jaw, Sask.	G3	75
Moose Jaw, stm., Sask.	G3	75
Moose Lake, Man.	C1	70
Moose Lake, Mn., U.S.	D6	100
Moose Lake, l., B.C.	C1	68
Moose Lake, l., Wi., U.S.	B2	126
Mooseleuk Stream, stm., Me., U.S.	B4	96
Mooselookmeguntic Lake, l., Me., U.S.	D2	96
Moose Mountain, mtn., Sask.	H4	75
Moose Mountain, mtn., N.H., U.S.	C2	106
Moose Mountain Creek, stm., Sask.	H4	75
Moose Mountain Provincial Park, Sask.	H4	75
Moose Pass, Ak., U.S.	C10	79
Moose River, Me., U.S.	C2	96
Moosic, Pa., U.S.	m18	115
Moosilauke, Mount, mtn., N.H., U.S.	B3	106
Moosomin, Sask.	G5	75
Moosonee, Ont.	o19	73
Moosup, Ct., U.S.	C8	84
Moosup, stm., U.S.	C1	116
Mopang Lake, l., Me., U.S.	D5	96
Mopeia Velha, Moz.	A6	49
Mopti, Mali	D4	45
Moquegua, Peru	E3	58
Moquegua, dept., Peru	E3	58
Mór, Hung.	H18	21
Mor, i., Micron.	Q18	52
Mór, Glen, val., Scot., U.K.	D8	10
Mor, Sgurr, mtn., Scot., U.K.	C3	13
Mora, Cam.	C2	46
Mora, Spain	C4	22
Mora, Swe.	G6	14
Mora, Ga., U.S.	E4	87
Mora, Mn., U.S.	E5	100
Mora, N.M., U.S.	A5	108
Mora, co., N.M., U.S.	A5	108
Mora, stm., N.M., U.S.	B5	108
Morača, stm., Yugo.	D4	24
Moradābād, India	C6	36
Morada Nova, Braz.	C3	57
Mora de Ebro, Spain	B6	22
Morafenobe, Madag.	g8	49
Moraga, Pol.	B6	26
Moraga, Ca., U.S.	*D2	82
Moraine, Oh., U.S.	*C1	112
Morales, Guat.	G3	62
Morales, Mex.	k13	63
Moramanga, Madag.	g9	49
Moran, In., U.S.	D4	91
Moran, Ks., U.S.	E8	93
Moran, Mi., U.S.	B6	99
Moran, Tx., U.S.	C3	120
Moran, Wy., U.S.	C2	127
Morann, Pa., U.S.	F5	115
Morant Bay, Jam.	F5	64
Morant, Loch, l., Scot., U.K.	D3	13
Morant Point, c., Jam.	F5	64
Morar, Loch, l., Scot., U.K.	D3	13
Morarano, Peru	C2	58
Morat (Murten), Switz.	B2	21
Morat, Lake, l., Switz.	C3	20
Morata de Tajuña, Spain	p18	22
Moratalla, Spain	C5	22
Morava, stm., Eur.	B6	22
Moravia, Ia., U.S.	D5	92
Moravia, N.Y., U.S.	C4	109
Moravia, hist. reg., Czech.	D4	26
Morava, stm., Eur.	D4	26
Morawa, Austl.	E3	50
Morawhanna, Guy.	A3	59
Moray, Bol.	D2	55
Moray Firth, est., Scot., U.K.	B5	10
Morbach, Ger.	D2	19
Morbegno, Italy	D8	21
Morcenx, Fr.	F3	16
Morden, Man.	E2	70
Morden, N.S.	D5	71
Mordialloc, Austl.	F8	50
Mordovo, Sov. Un.	I23	27
More, Ben, mtn., Scot., U.K.	B3	10
More, Ben, mtn., Scot., U.K.	E7	13
More Assynt, Ben, mtn., Scot., U.K.	A4	10
Moreau, stm., S.D., U.S.	B3	118
Moreau, North Fork, stm., S.D., U.S.	B2	118
Moreau, South Fork, stm., S.D., U.S.	B2	118
Moreauville, La., U.S.	C4	95
Morecambe, Eng., U.K.	F6	13
Morecambe Bay, b., Eng., U.K.	D5	125
Moree, Austl.	E8	50
Morehead, Ky., U.S.	B6	94
Morehead City, N.C., U.S.	C6	110
Morehouse, Mo., U.S.	E8	102
Morehouse, co., La., U.S.	B4	95
Morel, P.E.I.	C7	71
Morell, P.E.I.	C7	71
Morella, Spain	E11	22
Morelia, Mex.	D4	63
Morelos, state, Mex.	D5	63
Morena, Sierra, mts., Spain	C3	22
Morenci, Az., U.S.	D6	80
Morenci, Mi., U.S.	G6	99
Moreno, Arg.	h35	54
Moreno Valley, Ca., U.S.	*F5	82
Moreton Bay, b., Austl.	D9	51
Moreton-in-Marsh, Eng., U.K.	J11	13
Moreton Island, i., Austl.	E5	51
Moreuil, Fr.	C5	16
Morewood, Ont.	B9	73
Morey, Lake, l., Vt., U.S.	D4	122
Morey Peak, mtn., Nv., U.S.	E5	105
Morez, Fr.	D7	16
Morgan, Austl.	G2	51
Morgan, Ga., U.S.	E2	87
Morgan, Ky., U.S.	B5	94
Morgan, Mn., U.S.	F4	100
Morgan, Tx., U.S.	C4	120
Morgan, Ut., U.S.	B4	121
Morgan, Vt., U.S.	B4	122
Morgan, co., Al., U.S.	A3	78
Morgan, co., Co., U.S.	A7	83
Morgan, co., Ga., U.S.	C3	87
Morgan, co., Il., U.S.	D3	90
Morgan, co., In., U.S.	F5	91
Morgan, co., Ky., U.S.	C6	94
Morgan, co., Mo., U.S.	C5	102
Morgan, co., Oh., U.S.	C4	112
Morgan, co., Tn., U.S.	C9	119
Morgan, co., Ut., U.S.	B4	121
Morgan, co., W.V., U.S.	B6	125
Morgan Center, Vt., U.S.	B5	122
Morgan City, La., U.S.	E4	95
Morgan City, Ms., U.S.	B3	101
Morganfield, Ky., U.S.	C2	94
Morgan Hill, Ca., U.S.	D3	82
Morgan Island, i., S.C., U.S.	G6	117
Morgan Point, c., Ct., U.S.	E4	84
Morganton, Ar., U.S.	B3	81
Morganton, Ga., U.S.	B2	87
Morganton, N.C., U.S.	B1	110
Morgantown, Ky., U.S.	C3	94
Morgantown, Ms., U.S.	D4	101
Morgantown, Pa., U.S.	F10	115
Morgantown, Tn., U.S.	D8	119
Morgantown, W.V., U.S.	B5	125
Morganville, Ks., U.S.	C6	93
Morganville, N.J., U.S.	C4	107
Morganza, La., U.S.	D4	95
Morges, Switz.	C2	20
Morgex, Italy	D3	20
Morghāb, stm., Asia	A3	36
Morhange, Fr.	F6	17
Moriah, Trin.	M24	65
Moriah, N.Y., U.S.	A7	109
Moriah, Mount, mtn., Nv., U.S.	D7	105
Moriah, Mount, mtn., N.H., U.S.	B4	106
Moriarty, N.M., U.S.	C3	108
Morice, stm., B.C.	B4	69
Morice Lake, l., B.C.	B4	69
Moriguchi, Japan	*17	33
Morin-Heights, Que.	D3	74
Morinville, Alta.	C4	68
Morioka, Japan	D13	31
Morisset-Station, Que.	C7	74
Morkill, stm., B.C.	C7	69
Morlaix, Fr.	C2	16
Morland, Ks., U.S.	C3	93
Morley, Alta.	D3	68
Morley, Mi., U.S.	E5	99
Morley, Mo., U.S.	D8	102
Morley, N.Y., U.S.	f9	109
Mormon Lake, Az., U.S.	C4	80
Mormon Peak, mtn., Nv., U.S.	G7	105
Morne-à-l'Eau, Guad.	Q9	65
Morningdale, Ma., U.S.	B4	98
Morningside, S.D., U.S.	C7	118
Morning Sun, Ia., U.S.	C6	92
Mornington, Isla, i., Chile	D1	54
Mornington Island, i., Austl.	B6	50
Moro, Ar., U.S.	C5	81
Moro, Or., U.S.	B6	114
Morobay, Ar., U.S.	D3	81
Morobe, Pap. N. Gui.	k12	50
Morocco, In., U.S.	C3	91
Morocco, ctry., Afr.	C3	44
Morococha, Peru	D2	58
Morogoro, Tan.	C6	48
Morogoro, prov., Tan.	C6	48
Moroleón, Mex.	m13	63
Morombe, Madag.	h8	49
Morón, Arg.	g7	54
Morón, Cuba	C4	64
Mörön, Mong.	B5	31
Morona, stm., Peru	B2	58
Morona-Santiago, prov., Ec.	G5	58
Morondava, Madag.	h8	49
Morón de la Frontera, Spain	D3	22
Moroni, Ut., U.S.	D4	121
Morotai, i., Indon.	E7	34
Moroto, Ug.	A6	48
Morozovsk, Sov. Un.	G13	27
Morpeth, Ont.	E3	73
Morpeth, Eng., U.K.	E7	13
Morrin, Alta.	D4	68
Morrinhos, Braz.	D3	57
Morrinsville, N.Z.	L15	51
Morris, Man.	E3	70
Morris, Al., U.S.	B3	78
Morris, Ct., U.S.	C3	84
Morris, Ga., U.S.	E2	87
Morris, Il., U.S.	B5	90
Morris, In., U.S.	F7	91
Morris, Mn., U.S.	E3	100
Morris, N.Y., U.S.	C5	109
Morris, Ok., U.S.	B6	113
Morris, Pa., U.S.	B6	115
Morris, co., Ks., U.S.	D7	93
Morris, co., N.J., U.S.	B3	107
Morris, co., Tx., U.S.	C5	120
Morris, Mount, mtn., N.Y., U.S.	A6	109
Morrisburg, Ont.	C9	73
Morris Chapel, Tn., U.S.	B3	119
Morris Island, i., S.C., U.S.	F8	117
Morris Jesup, Kap, c., Grnld.	A17	66
Morrison, Il., U.S.	B4	90
Morrison, Ok., U.S.	A4	113
Morrison, Tn., U.S.	B5	119
Morrison, co., Mn., U.S.	D4	100
Morrison City, Tn., U.S.	C11	119
Morrisonville, Il., U.S.	D4	90
Morrisonville, N.Y., U.S.	f11	109
Morris Plains, N.J., U.S.	B4	107
Morris Run, Pa., U.S.	C7	115
Morriston, Fl., U.S.	C4	86
Morristown, Az., U.S.	D3	80
Morristown, In., U.S.	E6	91
Morristown, Mn., U.S.	F5	100
Morristown, N.J., U.S.	B4	107
Morristown, N.Y., U.S.	f9	109
Morristown, Tn., U.S.	C10	119
Morristown, Vt., U.S.	B3	122
Morristown National Historical Park, N.J., U.S.	B3	107
Morrisville, Mo., U.S.	D4	102
Morrisville, N.Y., U.S.	C5	109
Morrisville, Pa., U.S.	F12	115
Morrisville, Vt., U.S.	B3	122
Morrito, Nic.	E7	63
Morro, Ec.	B1	58
Morro, Punta, c., Chile	E1	55
Morro, Punta, c., Mex.	D6	63
Morro Bay, Ca., U.S.	E3	82
Morro do Chapéu, Braz.	D2	57
Morropón, Peru	C2	58
Morrosquillo, Golfo de, b., Col.	B2	60
Morrow, Ga., U.S.	C2	87
Morrow, La., U.S.	D3	95
Morrow, co., Oh., U.S.	B3	112
Morrow, co., Or., U.S.	B7	114
Morrowville, Ks., U.S.	C6	93
Mors, i., Den.	B2	15
Morse, Sask.	G3	75
Morse, La., U.S.	D3	95
Morse, Tx., U.S.	A2	120
Morse, Wi., U.S.	B3	126
Morse Bluff, Ne., U.S.	C9	104
Morse Mill, Mo., U.S.	g12	102
Morse Reservoir, res., In., U.S.	D5	91
Morses Creek, stm., N.J., U.S.	k8	107
Morshansk, Sov. Un.	E13	27
Mortagne, Fr.	C4	16
Mortara, Italy	B2	23
Morteau, Fr.	D7	16
Morteros, Arg.	A4	54
Mortes, Rio das, stm., Braz.	E4	59
Mortlach, Sask.	G2	75
Morton, Il., U.S.	C4	90
Morton, Mn., U.S.	F4	100
Morton, Ms., U.S.	C4	101
Morton, Tx., U.S.	C1	120
Morton, Wa., U.S.	C3	124
Morton, co., Ks., U.S.	E2	93
Morton, co., N.D., U.S.	C4	111
Morton Grove, Il., U.S.	h9	90
Morton Pass, Wy., U.S.	E7	127
Mortons Gap, Ky., U.S.	C2	94
Moruga, Trin.	O23	65
Moruya, Austl.	G8	51
Morvan Mountains, mts., Fr.	D6	16
Morven, Ga., U.S.	F3	87
Morven, N.C., U.S.	C2	110
Morven, mtn., Scot., U.K.	B5	13
Morwell, Austl.	G8	50
Moryakovskiy Zaton, Sov. Un.	r32	14
Morye, Fr.	D10	27
Mosalsk, Sov. Un.	D10	27
Mosbach, Ger.	D4	19
Mosby, Mo., U.S.	h11	102
Mosby, Mt., U.S.	D9	103
Mosca, Co., U.S.	D5	83
Moscarello, Italy	k9	23
Moscos Islands, is., Burma	F10	36
Moscow (Moskva), Sov. Un.	D6	29
Moscow, Id., U.S.	C2	89
Moscow, In., U.S.	F6	91
Moscow, Ks., U.S.	E2	93
Moscow, Oh., U.S.	D1	112
Moscow, Pa., U.S.	m18	115
Moscow, R.I., U.S.	E2	116
Moscow, Tn., U.S.	B2	119
Moscow, Vt., U.S.	C3	122
Moscow Mills, Mo., U.S.	C7	102
Mosel (Moselle), stm., Eur.	D3	18
Moseley, Va., U.S.	C5	123
Moselle, Ms., U.S.	D4	101
Moselle, dept., Fr.	E6	17
Moselle (Mosel), stm., Eur.	C7	16
Mosers River, N.S.	E7	71
Moses Coulee, val., Wa., U.S.	B6	124
Moses Lake, Wa., U.S.	B6	124
Moses Lake, l., Wa., U.S.	B6	124
Mosgiel, N.Z.	P13	51
Mosheim, Tn., U.S.	C11	119
Mosherville, Mi., U.S.	D5	118
Moshi, Tan.	B6	48
Moshupa, Bots.	B4	49
Mosier, Or., U.S.	B5	114
Mosinee, Wi., U.S.	D4	126
Mosjøen, Nor.	E5	14
Moskva, Sov. Un.	n18	27
Mosley Creek, stm., B.C.	D5	69
Mosomane (Artesia), Bots.	B4	49
Mosonmagyaróvár, Hung.	B3	24
Mosquera, Col.	C2	60
Mosquero, N.M., U.S.	B6	108
Mosquito, Newf.	D6	72
Mosquito Creek, stm., Ia., U.S.	C2	92
Mosquito Creek Lake, res., Oh., U.S.	A5	112
Mosquito Lagoon, b., Fl., U.S.	D6	86
Mosquitos, Golfo de los, b., Pan.	F7	62
Moss, Nor.	H4	14
Moss, Ms., U.S.	D4	101
Moss, Tn., U.S.	C8	119
Mossaka, Congo	B2	48
Mossbank, Sask.	H3	75
Moss Bluff, La., U.S.	D2	95
Mosselbaai (Mossel Bay), S. Afr.	D3	49
Mossendjo, Congo	B1	48
Mossleigh, Alta.	D4	68
Mossman, Austl.	C8	50
Moss Mountain, mtn., Ar., U.S.	C3	81
Mossoró, Braz.	C3	57
Moss Point, Ms., U.S.	E5	101
Mossville, Il., U.S.	C4	90
Mossy, stm., Man.	D2	70
Mossy, stm., Sask.	D2	75
Mossy Head, Fl., U.S.	u15	86
Mossyrock, Wa., U.S.	C3	124
Most, Czech.	C2	26
Mostar, Yugo.	D3	24
Mostefa, Cap, c., Tun.	F3	23
Móstoles, Spain	p17	22
Mostrim (Edgeworthstown), Ire.	D4	11
Mosul (Al Mawsil), Iraq	B4	38
Moswansicut Pond, l., R.I., U.S.	C3	116
Motagua, stm., N.A.	E6	63
Motala, Swe.	H6	14
Motátán, Ven.	B3	60
Motherwell, Scot., U.K.	C5	10
Motihāri, India	D10	37

Name	Map Ref.	Page
Motilla del Palancar, Spain	C5	22
Motley, Mn., U.S.	D4	100
Motley, co., Tx., U.S.	B2	120
Motobu, Japan	N5	52
Motomachi, Japan	o18	33
Moto Mountain, hill, Japan	P17	52
Motril, Spain	D4	22
Motru, stm., Rom.	C6	24
Mott, N.D., U.S.	C3	111
Motta di Livenza, Italy	D8	20
Motueka, N.Z.	N14	51
Motul [de Felipe Carrillo Puerto], Mex.	C7	63
Motupe, Peru	C2	58
Moturiki, i., Fiji	H15	52
Mou, Den.	B4	15
Mouaskar, Alg.	B5	44
Moúdhros (Mudros), Grc.	C5	25
Moudjéria, Maur.	C2	45
Moudon, Switz.	C2	20
Mouila, Gabon	F2	46
Moulamein Billabong Creek, stm., Austl.	G5	51
Mould Bay, N.W. Ter.	m28	66
Moule, Guad.	H14	64
Moulins, Fr.	D5	16
Moulouya, Oued, stm., Mor.	C4	44
Moulton, Al., U.S.	A2	78
Moulton, Ia., U.S.	D5	92
Moultonboro, N.H., U.S.	C4	106
Moultrie, Ga., U.S.	E3	87
Moultrie, co., Il., U.S.	D5	90
Moultrie, Lake, res., S.C., U.S.	E7	117
Mound, La., U.S.	B4	95
Mound, Mn., U.S.	n11	100
Mound Bayou, Ms., U.S.	B3	101
Mound City, Il., U.S.	F4	90
Mound City, Ks., U.S.	D9	93
Mound City, Mo., U.S.	A2	102
Mound City, S.D., U.S.	B5	118
Mound City Group National Monument, mon., U.S.	C2	112
Moundou, Chad	D3	46
Moundridge, Ks., U.S.	D6	93
Mounds, Il., U.S.	F4	90
Mounds, Ok., U.S.	B5	113
Mounds View, Mn., U.S.	m12	100
Moundsville, W.V., U.S.	B4	125
Mound Valley, Ks., U.S.	E8	93
Moundville, Al., U.S.	C2	78
Moundville, Mo., U.S.	D3	102
Mounier, Mont, mtn., Fr.	E7	16
Mountain, N.D., U.S.	A8	111
Mountain, W.V., U.S.	B4	125
Mountain, Wi., U.S.	C5	126
Mountainair, N.M., U.S.	C3	108
Mountainaire, Az., U.S.	B4	80
Mountain Ash, Ky., U.S.	D5	94
Mountainboro, Al., U.S.	A3	78
Mountain Brook, Al., U.S.	g7	78
Mountainburg, Ar., U.S.	B1	81
Mountain City, Ga., U.S.	B3	87
Mountain City, Nv., U.S.	B6	105
Mountain City, Tn., U.S.	C12	119
Mountain Dale, N.Y., U.S.	D6	109
Mountain Fork, stm., U.S.	C7	113
Mountain Grove, Ont.	C8	73
Mountain Grove, Mo., U.S.	D5	102
Mountain Home, Ar., U.S.	A3	81
Mountain Home, Id., U.S.	F3	89
Mountainhome, Pa., U.S.	D11	115
Mountain Home, Tx., U.S.	D3	120
Mountain Home, Ut., U.S.	C5	121
Mountain Home Air Force Base, mil., Id., U.S.	F3	89
Mountain Iron, Mn., U.S.	C6	100
Mountain Lake, Mn., U.S.	G4	100
Mountain Lake, l., Sask.	B3	75
Mountain Lake Park, Md., U.S.	m12	97
Mountain Lakes, N.J., U.S.	*B4	107
Mountain Nile (Al Baḥr al Jabal), stm., Sud.	D3	47
Mountain Park, Alta.	C2	68
Mountain Park, Fl., U.S.	*C2	87
Mountain Park, Ok., U.S.	C3	113
Mountain Pine, Ar., U.S.	C2	81
Mountain Point, Ak., U.S.	n24	79
Mountainside, N.J., U.S.	B4	107
Mountain Springs, Nv., U.S.	*G6	105
Mountain Valley, Alta.	E4	68
Mountain View, Alta.	B3	81
Mountain View, Ar., U.S.	B3	81
Mountain View, Ca., U.S.	k8	82
Mountain View, Co., U.S.	*B5	83
Mountain View, Co., U.S.	*A5	83
Mountainview, Hi., U.S.	D6	88
Mountain View, Mo., U.S.	D6	102
Mountain View, N.M., U.S.	C3	108
Mountain View, Ok., U.S.	B3	113
Mountain View, Wy., U.S.	E2	127
Mountain View, Wy., U.S.	*D6	127
Mountain Village, Ak., U.S.	C7	79
Mount Airy, Ga., U.S.	B3	87
Mount Airy, Md., U.S.	B3	97
Mount Airy, N.J., U.S.	C3	107
Mount Airy, N.C., U.S.	A2	110
Mount Albert, Ont.	C5	73
Mount Angel, Or., U.S.	B4	114
Mount Arlington, N.J., U.S.	B3	107
Mount Assiniboine Provincial Park, B.C.	D10	69
Mount Athos, ter., Grc.	B5	25
Mount Auburn, Il., U.S.	D4	90
Mount Auburn, Ia., U.S.	B5	92
Mount Ayr, In., U.S.	C3	91
Mount Ayr, Ia., U.S.	D3	92
Mount Barker, Austl.	G2	51
Mount Bellew Bridge, Ire.	D3	11
Mount Berry, Ga., U.S.	B1	87
Mount Blanchard, Oh., U.S.	B2	112
Mount Brydges, Ont.	E3	73
Mount Calvary, Wi., U.S.	E5	126
Mount Carleton Provincial Park, N.B.	B3	71
Mount Carmel, Al., U.S.	C3	78
Mount Carmel, Il., U.S.	E6	90
Mount Carmel, In., U.S.	F8	91
Mount Carmel, N.D., U.S.	A7	111
Mount Carmel, Oh., U.S.	o13	112
Mount Carmel, Pa., U.S.	E9	115
Mount Carmel, S.C., U.S.	C2	117
Mount Carmel, Ut., U.S.	F3	121
Mount Carmel Junction, Ut., U.S.	F3	121
Mount Carmel [-Mitchell's Brook-Saint Catherine's], Newf.	E5	72
Mount Carroll, Il., U.S.	A4	90
Mount Clare, W.V., U.S.	B4	125
Mount Clemens, Mi., U.S.	F8	99
Mount Clinton, Va., U.S.	B4	123
Mount Cory, Oh., U.S.	B2	112
Mount Crawford, Va., U.S.	B4	123
Mount Croghan, S.C., U.S.	B7	117
Mount Darwin, Zimb.	A5	49
Mount Desert, Me., U.S.	*D4	96
Mount Desert Island, i., Me., U.S.	D4	96
Mount Dora, Fl., U.S.	D5	86
Mount Dora, N.M., U.S.	A6	108
Mount Eaton, Oh., U.S.	B4	112
Mount Eden, Ky., U.S.	B4	94
Mount Elgin, Ont.	E4	73
Mount Emmons, Ut., U.S.	*C5	121
Mount Enterprise, Tx., U.S.	D5	120
Mount Ephraim, N.J., U.S.	*D2	107
Mount Erie, Il., U.S.	E5	90
Mount Etna, In., U.S.	C6	91
Mount Etna, Ia., U.S.	C3	92
Mount Forest, Ont.	D4	73
Mount Forest, Mi., U.S.	E6	99
Mount Freedom, N.J., U.S.	B3	107
Mount Gambier, Austl.	G7	50
Mount Gay, W.V., U.S.	D2	125
Mount Gilead, N.C., U.S.	B3	110
Mount Gilead, Oh., U.S.	B3	112
Mount Hagen, Pap. N. Gui.	k11	50
Mount Healthy, Oh., U.S.	o12	112
Mount Hebron, Ca., U.S.	B2	82
Mount Hermon, La., U.S.	D5	95
Mount Hermon, Ma., U.S.	A3	98
Mount Heron, Va., U.S.	e9	123
Mount Holly, Ar., U.S.	D3	81
Mount Holly, N.J., U.S.	D3	107
Mount Holly, N.C., U.S.	B1	110
Mount Holly, S.C., U.S.	E7	117
Mount Holly, Vt., U.S.	E3	122
Mount Holly Springs, Pa., U.S.	F7	115
Mount Hood, Or., U.S.	B5	114
Mount Hope, Ont.	D5	73
Mount Hope, Al., U.S.	A2	78
Mount Hope, Ks., U.S.	E6	93
Mount Hope, W.V., U.S.	D3	125
Mount Hope, Wi., U.S.	F3	126
Mount Hope, stm., Ct., U.S.	B7	84
Mount Hope Bay, b., U.S.	D6	116
Mount Horeb, Wi., U.S.	E4	126
Mount Ida, Ar., U.S.	C2	81
Mount Idaho, Id., U.S.	D2	89
Mount Isa, Austl.	D6	50
Mount Jackson, Va., U.S.	B4	123
Mount Jewett, Pa., U.S.	C4	115
Mount Joy, Ia., U.S.	h10	92
Mount Joy, Pa., U.S.	F9	115
Mount Judea, Ar., U.S.	B2	81
Mount Juliet, Tn., U.S.	A5	119
Mount Kisco, N.Y., U.S.	D7	109
Mountlake Terrace, Wa., U.S.	*B3	124
Mount Lebanon, Pa., U.S.	F1	115
Mount Lemmon, Az., U.S.	E5	80
Mount Lookout, W.V., U.S.	C4	125
Mount Magnet, Austl.	E2	50
Mount Meigs, Al., U.S.	C3	78
Mountmellick, Ire.	D4	11
Mount Montgomery, Nv., U.S.	F3	105
Mount Morgan, Austl.	D9	50
Mount Moriah, Mo., U.S.	A4	102
Mount Morris, Il., U.S.	A4	90
Mount Morris, Mi., U.S.	E7	99
Mount Morris, N.Y., U.S.	C3	109
Mount Olive, Al., U.S.	f7	78
Mount Olive, Il., U.S.	D4	90
Mount Olive, Ms., U.S.	D4	101
Mount Olive, N.C., U.S.	B4	110
Mount Olive, Tn., U.S.	n14	119
Mount Olivet, Ky., U.S.	B5	94
Mount Olympus, Ut., U.S.	*C4	121
Mount Orab, Oh., U.S.	C2	112
Mount Pearl, Newf.	E5	72
Mount Penn, Pa., U.S.	F10	115
Mount Pleasant, Ar., U.S.	B4	81
Mount Pleasant, Fl., U.S.	B2	86
Mount Pleasant, Ia., U.S.	D6	92
Mount Pleasant, Mi., U.S.	E6	99
Mount Pleasant, Ms., U.S.	A4	101
Mount Pleasant, N.J., U.S.	B2	107
Mount Pleasant, N.C., U.S.	B2	110
Mount Pleasant, Pa., U.S.	F2	115
Mount Pleasant, S.C., U.S.	F8	117
Mount Pleasant, Tn., U.S.	B4	119
Mount Pleasant, Tx., U.S.	C5	120
Mount Pleasant, Ut., U.S.	D4	121
Mount Pocono, Pa., U.S.	D11	115
Mount Prospect, Il., U.S.	A6	90
Mount Pulaski, Il., U.S.	C4	90
Mountrail, co., N.D., U.S.	A3	111
Mount Rainier, Md., U.S.	f9	97
Mount Rainier National Park, Wa., U.S.	C4	124
Mount Revelstoke National Park, B.C.	D8	69
Mount Robson Provincial Park, B.C.	C8	69
Mount Rogers National Recreation Area, Va., U.S.	D1	123
Mount Rushmore National Memorial, hist., S.D., U.S.	D2	118
Mount Savage, Md., U.S.	k13	97
Mount's Bay, b., Eng., U.K.	D2	12
Mount Shasta, Ca., U.S.	B2	82
Mount Sidney, Va., U.S.	B4	123
Mount Sinai, N.Y., U.S.	*n15	109
Mount Solon, Va., U.S.	B3	123
Mount Sterling, Al., U.S.	C1	78
Mount Sterling, Il., U.S.	D3	90
Mount Sterling, Ky., U.S.	B6	94
Mount Sterling, Oh., U.S.	C2	112
Mount Stewart, P.E.I.	C7	71
Mount Storm, W.V., U.S.	B5	125
Mount Summit, In., U.S.	D7	91
Mount Sunapee, N.H., U.S.	D2	106
Mount Tabor, Vt., U.S.	E3	122
Mount Uniacke, N.S.	E6	71
Mount Union, Ia., U.S.	C6	92
Mount Union, Pa., U.S.	F6	115
Mount Upton, N.Y., U.S.	C5	109
Mount Vernon, Al., U.S.	D1	78
Mount Vernon, Ga., U.S.	D4	87
Mount Vernon, Il., U.S.	E5	90
Mount Vernon, In., U.S.	I2	91
Mount Vernon, Ia., U.S.	C6	92
Mount Vernon, Ky., U.S.	C5	94
Mount Vernon, Me., U.S.	D3	96
Mount Vernon, Mo., U.S.	D4	102
Mount Vernon, N.Y., U.S.	h13	109
Mount Vernon, Oh., U.S.	*B3	112
Mount Vernon, Or., U.S.	C7	114
Mount Vernon, S.D., U.S.	D7	118
Mount Vernon, Tn., U.S.	C9	119
Mount Vernon, Tx., U.S.	C5	120
Mount Vernon, Va., U.S.	B5	123
Mount Vernon, Wa., U.S.	A3	124
Mount Victory, Oh., U.S.	B2	112
Mount View, R.I., U.S.	D4	116
Mountville, Ga., U.S.	C2	87
Mountville, S.C., U.S.	C4	117
Mount Washington, Ky., U.S.	B4	94
Mount Washington, Ma., U.S.	B1	98
Mount Wolf, Pa., U.S.	F8	115
Mount Zion, Ga., U.S.	C1	87
Mount Zion, Il., U.S.	D5	90
Moura, Austl.	D8	50
Moura, Braz.	C2	59
Moura, Port.	C2	22
Mourdi, Dépression du, depr., Chad	B4	46
Mourmelon-le-Grand, Fr.	E4	17
Mourne Mountains, mts., N. Ire., U.K.	C3	10
Mouscron (Moeskroen), Bel.	B5	16
Mousie, Ky., U.S.	C7	94
Moussoro, Chad	C3	46
Mouthe, Fr.	C1	21
Moutier, Switz.	B3	21
Moûtiers[-Tarentaise], Fr.	E7	16
Mouy, Fr.	E2	17
Moville, Ire.	B4	11
Moville, Ia., U.S.	B1	92
Moweaqua, Il., U.S.	D4	90
Mower, co., Mn., U.S.	G6	100
Mowrystown, Oh., U.S.	C2	112
Moxahala, Oh., U.S.	C3	112
Moxee City, Wa., U.S.	C5	124
Moxico, dept., Ang.	D3	48
Moxie Pond, l., Me., U.S.	C3	96
Moxley, Ga., U.S.	D4	87
Moy, stm., Ire.	C2	11
Moy, Cnoc, hill, Scot., U.K.	C3	13
Moyale, Eth.	E4	47
Moyale, Kenya	A6	48
Moyamba, S.L.	E2	45
Moyculen, Ire.	D2	11
Moyers, Ok., U.S.	C6	113
Moyie, B.C.	E10	69
Moyie Springs, Id., U.S.	A2	89
Moynalty, Ire.	D5	11
Moyo, Ug.	A6	48
Moyobamba, Peru	C2	58
Moyock, N.C., U.S.	A6	110
Moyuta, Guat.	C2	62
Moza, Isr.	h11	41
Mozambique, ctry., Afr.	H9	42
Mozambique Channel, strt., Afr.	H10	42
Mozart, Sask.	F3	75
Mozdok, Sov. Un.	E2	28
Mozelle, Ky., U.S.	D6	94
Mozhaysk, Sov. Un.	D11	27
Mozhga, Sov. Un.	D19	8
Mozyr, Sov. Un.	E7	27
Mpanda, Tan.	C5	48
Mpika, Zam.	D5	48
Mporokoso, Zam.	C5	48
Mpouya, Congo	B2	48
Mpraeso, Ghana	E4	45
Mpulungu, Zam.	C5	48
Mpwapwa, Tan.	C6	48
Mrągowo, Pol.	B8	18
Mšec, Czech.	n16	26
Mšeneláznĕ, Czech.	n17	26
M'Sila, Alg.	B5	44
Msta, stm., Sov. Un.	B5	28
Mstislavl', Sov. Un.	D8	27
Mtakuja, Tan.	C5	48
Mtsensk, Sov. Un.	E11	27
Mtubatuba, S. Afr.	C5	49
Mtwara, Tan.	D7	48
Mtwara, prov., Tan.	D6	48
Mu, stm., Burma	A1	35
Muaná, Braz.	D9	59
Muang Khammouan, Laos	D6	35
Muang Khong, Laos	C3	34
Muang Khongxedon, Laos	E6	35
Muang Lan, Laos	C6	35
Muang Ou Nua, Laos	A4	35
Muang Ou Tai, Laos	A4	35
Muang Pakxan, Laos	C5	35
Muang Sing, Laos	A4	35
Muang Souy, Laos	C5	35
Muang Xaignabouri, Laos	C4	35
Muang Xepon, Laos	D7	35
Muar (Bandar Maharani), Malay.	*E2	34
Muar, Malay.	K5	34
Muaratewe, Indon.	F5	34
Mubārak, Jabal, mtn., Asia	I13	39
Mubende, Ug.	A5	48
Mubi, Nig.	D7	45
Mucajaí, stm., Braz.	B5	59
Mücheln, Ger.	B6	19
Muchkapskiy, Sov. Un.	F14	27
Muchot, Puntan, c., N. Mar. Is.	D7	52
Much Wenlock (Wenlock), Eng., U.K.	B5	12
Muck, i., Scot., U.K.	B3	10
Muckalee Creek, stm., Ga., U.S.	D2	87
Muckleshoot Indian Reservation, Wa., U.S.	f11	124
Muconda, Ang.	D3	48
Mucuri, Braz.	E3	57
Mucuri, stm., Braz.	E3	57
Mucusso, Ang.	E3	48
Mud, stm., Mn., U.S.	B3	100
Mud, stm., W.V., U.S.	C2	125
Muda, stm., Malay.	I4	35
Mudanjiang, China	C10	31
Mudan Jiang, stm., China	D4	33
Mudanya, Tur.	B7	25
Mud Butte, S.D., U.S.	C3	118
Mud Creek, stm., Al., U.S.	g6	78
Mud Creek, stm., Co., U.S.	D8	83
Mud Creek, stm., Ne., U.S.	C6	104
Mud Creek, stm., Ok., U.S.	C4	113
Muddy, Il., U.S.	F5	90
Muddy Boggy Creek, stm., Ok., U.S.	C6	113
Muddy Creek, stm., Co., U.S.	A4	83
Muddy Creek, stm., Ut., U.S.	E4	121
Muddy Creek, stm., Wy., U.S.	D6	127
Muddy Creek, stm., Wy., U.S.	E2	127
Muddy Creek Mountain, mtn., Ar., U.S.	C2	81
Muddy Gap, l., Sask.	E1	75
Muddy Mountain, mtn., Wy., U.S.	D6	127
Muddy Mountains, mts., Nv., U.S.	G7	105
Muddy Peak, mtn., Nv., U.S.	G7	105
Müden, Ger.	F4	15
Mudgee, Austl.	F7	51
Mudjatik, stm., Sask.	A2	75
Mud Lake, Id., U.S.	F6	89
Mud Lake, l., Me., U.S.	A4	96
Mud Lake, l., Nv., U.S.	F4	105
Mud Lick Creek, stm., Ky., U.S.	k13	94
Mudon, Burma	E10	36
Mudros see Moúdhros, Grc.	C5	25
Mudug, prov., Som.	D6	47
Mueda, Moz.	D6	48
Muenster, Sask.	E3	75
Muenster, Tx., U.S.	C4	120
Muff, Ire.	B4	11
Mufulira, Zam.	D4	48
Mugarripup, China	A11	37
Mugia, Spain	A1	22
Muğla, Tur.	D7	40
Mugodzhary Mountains, hills, Sov. Un.	D5	28
Muhammad Qawl, Sud.	A4	47
Mühlacker, Ger.	E3	19
Mühldorf, Ger.	D6	18
Muhlenberg, co., Ky., U.S.	C2	94
Mühlhausen [in Thüringen], Ger.	C5	18
Mühlig-Hofmann Mountains, mts., Ant.	B13	7
Muhulu, Zaire	B4	48
Muhutwe, Tan.	B5	48
Mui, i., Marsh Is.	S18	52
Muine Bheag, Ire.	E5	11
Muir, Mi., U.S.	E6	99
Muirkirk, Scot., U.K.	E4	13
Muirkirk, Md., U.S.	B4	97
Muir Woods National Monument, Ca., U.S.	h7	82
Mukachevo, Sov. Un.	G4	27
Mukah, Malay.	E4	34
Mukdahan, Thai.	D6	35
Mukden see Shenyang, China	C9	31
Mukilteo, Wa., U.S.	B3	124
Mukutawa, stm., Man.	C3	70
Mukwonago, Wi., U.S.	F5	126
Mula, Spain	C5	22
Mulanje, Mwi.	D6	48
Mulberry, Ar., U.S.	B1	81
Mulberry, Fl., U.S.	E5	86
Mulberry, In., U.S.	D4	91
Mulberry, Ks., U.S.	E9	93
Mulberry, N.C., U.S.	A1	110
Mulberry, Oh., U.S.	C1	112
Mulberry, Tn., U.S.	B5	119
Mulberry, stm., Ar., U.S.	B1	81
Mulberry Fork, stm., Al., U.S.	B3	78
Mulberry Grove, Il., U.S.	E4	90
Mulberry Mountain, mtn., Ar., U.S.	B3	81
Mulchén, Chile	B2	54
Mulde, stm., Ger.	C6	18
Muldoon, Tx., U.S.	E4	120
Muldraugh, Ky., U.S.	C4	94
Muldrow, Ok., U.S.	B7	113
Mule Creek, N.M., U.S.	D1	108
Mulegé, Mex.	B2	63
Muleshoe, Tx., U.S.	B1	120
Mulga, Al., U.S.	B3	78
Mulgrave, N.S.	D8	71
Mulhacén, mtn., Spain	D4	22
Mulhall, Ok., U.S.	A4	113
Mülheim [an der Ruhr], Ger.	C3	18
Mulhouse, Fr.	D7	16
Muling, China	D5	33
Muling He, stm., China	D6	33
Mulino, Or., U.S.	B4	114
Mulinu'u, Cape, c., W. Sam.	F11	52
Mulitapu'ili, Cape, c., W. Sam.	F12	52
Mull, Island of, i., Scot., U.K.	B4	10
Mull, Sound of, strt., Scot., U.K.	D3	13
Mullaghcleevaun, mtn., Ire.	D5	11
Mullan, Id., U.S.	B3	89
Mullan Pass, Mt., U.S.	D4	103
Mullen, Ne., U.S.	B4	104
Mullens, W.V., U.S.	D3	125
Muller Mountains, mts., Indon.	E4	34
Mullet Key, i., Fl., U.S.	p10	86
Mullet Lake, Mi., U.S.	C6	99
Mullet Peninsula, pen., Ire.	C1	10
Mullett Lake, l., Mi., U.S.	C6	99
Mullewa, Austl.	E2	50
Mull Head, c., Scot., U.K.	B6	13
Mullheim, Ger.	E3	18
Mullica, stm., N.J., U.S.	D3	107
Mullica Hill, N.J., U.S.	D2	107
Mulliken, Mi., U.S.	F6	99
Mullin, Tx., U.S.	D3	120
Mullinavat, Ire.	E4	11
Mullingar, Ire.	D3	10
Mullins, S.C., U.S.	C9	117
Mullinville, Ks., U.S.	E4	93
Müllrose, Ger.	C7	18
Mulobezi, Zam.	E4	48
Mulroy Bay, b., Ire.	B4	11
Multān, Pak.	B5	36
Multnomah, co., Or., U.S.	B4	114
Mulurulu, Lake, l., Austl.	F4	51
Mulvane, Ks., U.S.	E6	93
Mulvihill, Man.	D2	70
Mumbwa, Zam.	D4	48
Mummy Range, mts., Co., U.S.	A5	83
Mun, stm., Thai.	C6	35
Muna, Mex.	C7	63
Münchberg, Ger.	C6	19
München see Munich, Ger.	D5	18
Munchŏn, N. Kor.	G3	33
Muncie, In., U.S.	D7	91
Muncy, Pa., U.S.	D8	115
Mundare, Alta.	C4	68
Munday, Tx., U.S.	C3	120
Mundelein, Il., U.S.	A5	90
Münden, Ger.	C4	19
Mundford, Ky., U.S.	C4	94
Mungallala Creek, stm., Austl.	E8	51
Mungári, Moz.	A6	49
Mungbere, Zaire	A5	48
Munger, Mi., U.S.	E7	99
Munger, India	C8	36
Mungindi, Austl.	E8	51
Munhall, Pa., U.S.	k14	115
Munich (München), Ger.	D5	18
Munising, Mi., U.S.	B4	99
Munith, Mi., U.S.	F6	99
Munjor, Ks., U.S.	D4	93
Munnsville, N.Y., U.S.	C5	109
Muñoz, Phil.	o19	34
Muñoz Gamero, Península, pen., Chile	h11	54
Munro Lake, l., Man.	C3	70
Münsingen, Switz.	C4	21
Munson, Alta.	D4	68
Munson, Fl., U.S.	u15	86
Munson, Pa., U.S.	E5	115
Munsonville, N.H., U.S.	D2	106
Munster, Fr.	C7	16
Munster, Ger.	B5	18
Munster, In., U.S.	A2	91
Münster [in Westfalen], Ger.	C3	18
Münster, hist. reg., Ire.	E3	11
Munsungan Lake, l., Me., U.S.	B3	96
Muntenia, hist. reg., Rom.	F3	24
Muntok, Indon.	B6	34
Munuscong Lake, l., Mi., U.S.	B6	99
Muonio, Fin.	D10	14
Muonio, stm., Eur.	C6	21
Muotathal, Switz.	B2	24
Muotathal, Switz.	B3	24
Mura (Mura), stm., Eur.	G9	33
Murakami, Japan	E6	41
Muräkh, Bi'r, well, Eg.	D8	20
Murano, Italy	B3	28
Murashi, Sov. Un.	E5	16
Murat, Fr.	C7	25
Murat, stm., Tur.	C13	40
Murat, Tur.	E7	18
Muravera, Italy	E2	23
Mürcheh Khvort, Iran	E5	39
Murchison, N.Z.	N14	51
Murchison, stm., Austl.	E2	50
Murchison Falls see Kabalega Falls, wtfl., Ug.	A5	48
Murcia, Spain	C5	22
Murcia, hist. reg., Spain	C5	22
Murcki, Pol.	g10	26
Murdo, S.D., U.S.	D5	118
Murdock, Fl., U.S.	E4	86
Murdock, Ks., U.S.	E6	93
Murdock, Mn., U.S.	E3	100
Murdock, Ne., U.S.	h12	104
Mureş, stm., Eur.	C6	24
Muret, Fr.	F4	16
Murewa, Zimb.	A5	49
Murfreesboro, Ar., U.S.	C2	81
Murfreesboro, N.C., U.S.	A5	110
Murfreesboro, Tn., U.S.	B5	119
Murgha Kibzai, Pak.	B4	36
Murgon, Austl.	E9	50
Muriaé, Braz.	E3	57
Muriel Lake, l., Alta.	B5	68
Müritz Lake, l., Ger.	B6	18
Murici, Braz.	k6	57
Murici, Braz.	B5	48
Mürmansk, Sov. Un.	C6	29
Murnau, Ger.	B7	20
Murom, Sov. Un.	D13	27
Muroran, Japan	C13	31
Muros, Spain	A1	22
Muroto, Japan	J7	33
Muroto, Cape, c., Japan	J7	33
Murphy, Id., U.S.	E3	87
Murphy, Id., U.S.	F2	89
Murphy, Mo., U.S.	g13	102
Murphy, N.C., U.S.	f8	110
Murphy, Or., U.S.	E3	114
Murphy Island, i., S.C., U.S.	E9	117
Murphys, Ca., U.S.	C3	82
Murphysboro, Il., U.S.	F4	90
Murphytown, W.V., U.S.	B3	125
Murray, Id., U.S.	B3	89
Murray, Ia., U.S.	C4	92
Murray, Ky., U.S.	f9	94
Murray, Ne., U.S.	D10	104
Murray, Ut., U.S.	C4	121
Murray, co., Ga., U.S.	B2	87
Murray, co., Mn., U.S.	F3	100
Murray, co., Ok., U.S.	C4	113
Murray, co., Austl.	F7	50
Murray, stm., B.C.	B7	69
Murray, Cape, c., Ant.	f40	7
Murray, Lake, res., Ok., U.S.	C4	113
Murray, Lake, res., S.C., U.S.	C5	117
Murray Bridge, Austl.	E2	50
Murray City, Oh., U.S.	D7	71
Murray Harbour, P.E.I.	C7	71
Murray Head, c., P.E.I.	C7	71
Murray Lake, l., Alta.	E5	68
Murray River, P.E.I.	C7	71
Murraysburg, S. Afr.	D3	49
Murrayville, B.C.	f13	69
Murrayville, Il., U.S.	D3	90
Murrayville, Il., U.S.	B3	125
Murrells Inlet, S.C., U.S.	D9	117
Murrells Inlet, S.C., U.S.	D10	117
Murren, Switz.	C4	21
Murrhardt, Ger.	E4	19
Murrumbidgee, stm., Austl.	F8	50
Murrupula, Moz.	E6	49
Mursala, i., Indon.	K3	35
Murska Sobota, Yugo.	B3	24
Murtaugh, Id., U.S.	G4	89
Murten, Switz.	C3	21
Murud, India	E5	36
Murwāra, India	D7	36
Murwillumbah, Austl.	E9	50
Murzuq, Libya	D7	91
Muş, Tur.	C13	40
Musaid, Libya	C4	43
Muşaiyib, hist., Bul.	D6	24
Musan, N. Kor.	C10	31
Mūsá Qal'eh, Afg.	E12	39
Musashino, Japan	*l9	33
Muscat see Masqaţ, Oman	C5	38
Muscle Shoals, Al., U.S.	A2	78
Musclow, Mount, mtn., B.C.	C4	69
Muscoda, Wi., U.S.	E3	126
Muscogee, co., Ga., U.S.	D2	87
Musconetcong, stm., N.J.	B4	107
Musconetcong Mountain, mtn., N.J., U.S.	B3	107
Muscooten Bay, l., Il., U.S.	C8	93
Muscotah, Ks., U.S.	C8	93
Muscoy, Ca., U.S.	*E5	82
Muse, Pa., U.S.	F1	115
Muse, Pa., U.S.	F1	115
Museum, Oh., U.S.	C7	113
Mushie, Zaire	B2	48
Mushin, Nig.	E5	45
Mushketovo, Sov. Un.	r20	27
Musi, stm., Indon.	F2	34
Muskeg Bay, b., Mn., U.S.	B3	100
Muskeget Channel, strt., Ma., U.S.	D7	98
Muskeget Island, i., Ma., U.S.	D7	98
Muskego, Wi., U.S.	F5	126
Muskego Lake, l., Wi., U.S.	n11	126
Muskegon, Mi., U.S.	E4	99
Muskegon, co., Mi., U.S.	E4	99
Muskegon, stm., Mi., U.S.	E4	99
Muskegon Heights, Mi., U.S.	E4	99
Muskegon Lake, l., Mi., U.S.	E4	99
Muskingum, co., Oh., U.S.	B4	112
Muskingum, stm., Oh., U.S.	B4	112
Muskö, Swe.	u36	14
Muskogee, Ok., U.S.	B6	113
Muskogee, co., Ok., U.S.	B6	113
Muskoka, Lake, l., Ont.	C5	73
Muskrat Dam Lake, res., Ont.	C6	70
Muskwa, stm., Alta.	A3	68
Muslimbāgh, Pak.	B4	36
Musoma, Tan.	B5	48
Musquacook Lakes, l., Me., U.S.	B3	96
Musquaro, Lac, l., Que.	h14	74
Musquash, N.B.	D3	71
Musquodoboit Harbour, N.S.	E6	71
Musselburgh, Scot., U.K.	C5	10
Musselshell, Mt., U.S.	D9	103
Musselshell, co., Mt., U.S.	D8	103
Musselshell, stm., Mt., U.S.	D9	103
Mussende, Ang.	D2	48
Mussidan, Fr.	E4	16
Mussolinia see Arborea, Italy	E2	23
Mussuma, Ang.	D3	48
Mustafakemalpaşa, Tur.	B7	40
Mustang, Ok., U.S.	B4	113
Mustinka, stm., Mn., U.S.	E2	100
Mustique, i., St. Vin.	V26	65
Mustvee, Sov. Un.	B6	27
Muswellbrook, Austl.	F9	50
Mût, Eg.	D9	40
Mut, Tur.	E7	40
Mutá, Ponta do, c., Braz.	D5	57
Mutare, Zimb.	A5	49
Mutayin, Yemen	B5	47
Mutena, Zaire	C3	48
Muti, i., Marsh Is.	S18	52
Mutoko, Zimb.	A5	49
Mutombo-Mukulu, Zaire	C3	48
Mutorashanga, Zimb.	A5	49
Mutsu, Japan	F10	33
Mutsu Bay, b., Japan	F10	33
Mutton Bay, Que.	C2	72
Mutton Mountains, mts., Or., U.S.	C5	114
Mutual, Ok., U.S.	A2	113
Muţūbis, Eg.	G2	41
Mutzig, Fr.	F7	17
Mu Us Shamo (Ordos Desert), des., China	D6	31
Muxima, Ang.	C1	48
Muyinga, Bdi.	B5	48
Muynak, Sov. Un.	E5	28
Muyula, i., Pap. N. Gui.	k13	50
Muzaffargarh, Pak.	B3	36
Muzaffarnagar, India	C6	36
Muzaffarpur, India	C8	36
Muzambinho, Braz.	k8	56
Muzi, Sov. Un.	B21	8
Muzon, Cape, c., Ak., U.S.	n23	79
Muztag, mtn., China	A8	36
Muztag, mtn., China	A7	36
Muztagata, mtn., China	F10	29
Mwadui, Tan.	B5	48
Mwami, Zimb.	A4	49
Mwanza, Tan.	B5	48
Mwanza, prov., Tan.	B5	48
Mwaya, Tan.	C5	48
Mweelrea, mtn., Ire.	D2	11
Mweka, Zaire	C3	48
Mwene-Ditu, Zaire	C3	48
Mwenezi, Zimb.	B5	49
Mwenga, Zaire	B4	48
Mweru, Lake, l., Afr.	C5	48
Mwimba, Zaire	C3	48
Mwinilunga, Zam.	D3	48
Myājlār, India	D3	37
Myakka, stm., Fl., U.S.	E4	86
Myakka City, Fl., U.S.	E4	86
Myanaung, Burma	C1	35
Myaungmya, Burma	D1	35
Mycenae, hist., Grc.	F5	25
Myers Corner, N.Y., U.S.	*D7	109
Myerstown, Pa., U.S.	F9	115
Myersville, Md., U.S.	A2	97
Myingyan, Burma	D10	36
Myitkyina, Burma	C10	36
Myitnge, stm., Burma	B2	35
Myjava, Czech.	D4	26
Mylo, N.D., U.S.	A6	111
Mymensingh, Bngl.	D9	37
Mynaral, Sov. Un.	D7	29
Mynard, Ne., U.S.	h13	104
Myrick, Ms., U.S.	D5	101
Myrnam, Alta.	C5	68
Myrtle, Ms., U.S.	A4	101
Myrtle, Mo., U.S.	E6	102
Myrtle Beach, S.C., U.S.	D10	117
Myrtle Beach Air Force Base, mil., S.C., U.S.	D10	117
Myrtle Creek, Or., U.S.	D3	114
Myrtle Grove, Fl., U.S.	u14	86
Myrtle Grove, La., U.S.	k12	95
Myrtle Point, Or., U.S.	D2	114
Myrtlewood, Al., U.S.	C2	78
Mysen, Nor.	p29	14
Myślenice, Pol.	D5	26
Myślibórz, Pol.	g10	26
Mysłowice, Pol.	F6	36
Mysore see Karnataka, state, India	F6	36
Mystic, Ct., U.S.	D8	84
Mystic, Ia., U.S.	D5	92
Mystic Lakes, l., Ma., U.S.	g11	98
Myszków, Pol.	f10	26
My Tho, Viet.	C3	34
Mytilene see Mitilíni, Grc.	C6	40
Mytishchi, Sov. Un.	n17	27
Myton, Ut., U.S.	C5	121
Mže, stm., Czech.	D8	19

Name	Map Ref.	Page
Mzimba, Mwi.	D5	48
Mzuzu, Mwi.	D5	48

N

Name	Map Ref.	Page
Naab, stm., Ger.	D7	19
Naalehu, Hi., U.S.	D6	88
Naamans Garden, De., U.S.	*A3	85
Na'an, Isr.	h10	41
Naantali, Fin.	G10	14
Naas, Ire.	D3	10
Nabā, Jabal (Mount Nebo), mtn., Jord.	C7	41
Nabadwīp, India	*D8	36
Nabb, In., U.S.	G6	91
Nabberu, Lake, l., Austl.	E3	50
Nabburg, Ger.	D7	19
Nabeina, Kir.	R18	52
Nabekavu, Fiji	H15	52
Nabeul, Tun.	B7	44
Nabi Shuayb, Mount, mtn., Yemen	*D4	38
Nabnasset, Ma., U.S.	A5	98
Naboomspruit, S. Afr.	B4	49
Nabouwalu, Fiji	H15	52
Nabq, Eg.	H10	40
Nābulus, Isr. Occ.	B3	38
Nacala, Moz.	D7	48
Nacaome, Hond.	D4	62
Naches, Wa., U.S.	C5	124
Naches, stm., Wa., U.S.	C5	124
Nachingwea, Tan.	D6	48
Náchod, Czech.	C4	26
Nacilau Point, c., Fiji	H14	52
Nacimiento, Chile	B2	54
Nacimiento Reservoir, res., Ca., U.S.	E3	82
Nacka, Swe.	*H8	14
Nacmine, Alta.	D4	68
Naco, Az., U.S.	F6	80
Nacogdoches, Tx., U.S.	D5	120
Nacogdoches, co., Tx., U.S.	D5	120
Nacozari [de García], Mex.	A3	63
Nacula, i., Fiji	H14	52
Nadarzyn, Pol.	m13	26
Nadeau, Mi., U.S.	C3	99
Naden Harbour, b., B.C.	B1	69
Nadi, Fiji	H14	52
Nadiād, India	F4	37
Nădlac, Rom.	B5	24
Nador, Mor.	B4	44
Naduri, Fiji	H15	52
Nadvornaya, Sov. Un.	G5	27
Nadym, stm., Sov. Un.	B23	8
Næstved, Den.	J4	14
Nafada, Nig.	D7	45
Nafishah, Eg.	D4	41
Naga, Phil.	C6	34
Naga Hills, mts., Asia	C10	36
Nāgāland, state, India	*C9	36
Nagano, Japan	D12	31
Nagaoka, Japan	D12	31
Nāgappattinam, India	F6	36
Nagarote, Nic.	D4	62
Nagar Pārkar, Pak.	D5	36
Nāgaur, India	D4	37
Nageezi, N.M., U.S.	A2	108
Nāgercoil, India	G6	36
Nagiba, Phil.	p13	34
Nagles Mountains, mts., Ire.	E3	11
Nago, Japan	N5	52
Nago Bay, b., Japan	N5	52
Nagog Pond, l., Ma., U.S.	f10	98
Nagold, Ger.	E3	19
Nagoya, Japan	D12	31
Nāgpur, India	D6	36
Nagqu, China	E3	31
Nags Head, N.C., U.S.	B7	110
Nagua, Dom. Rep.	E9	64
Naguabo, P.R.	B4	65
Nagykanizsa, Hung.	B3	24
Nagykőrös, Hung.	B4	24
Naha, Japan	F10	31
Nahalat Yehuda, Isr.	h10	41
Nahanni National Park, N.W. Ter.	D7	66
Nahant, Ma., U.S.	g12	98
Nahariyya, Isr.	B7	41
Nahāvand, Iran	D4	39
Nahe, stm., Ger.	D3	18
Nahma, Mi., U.S.	C4	99
Nahmakanta Lake, l., Me., U.S.	C3	96
Nahuel Huapi, Arg.	C2	54
Nahuel Huapi, Lago, l., Arg.	C2	54
Nahuel Niyeu, Arg.	C3	54
Nakunta, Ga., U.S.	E5	87
Naic, Phil.	o13	34
Naicam, Sask.	E3	75
Naiguatá, Pico, mtn., Ven.	A4	60
Naihāti, India	*D8	36
Naila, Ger.	C6	19
Nailaga, Fiji	H14	52
Nain, Newf.	g9	72
Nā'īn, Iran	C5	39
Naini Tāl, India	C7	37
Nairai, i., Fiji	H15	52
Nairn, Scot., U.K.	B5	10
Nairn, stm., Scot., U.K.	C4	10
Nairobi, Kenya	B6	48
Naitonitoni, Fiji	l15	52
Naivasha, Kenya	B6	48
Najafābād, Iran	C5	39
Naj' Ḩammādī, Eg.	D6	43
Najībābād, India	C7	37
Najin, N. Kor.	C11	31
Najran, well, Sau. Ar.	D4	38
Naju, S. Kor.	I3	33
Nakadōri Island, i., Japan	J4	33
Nakagusuku Bay, b., Japan	O5	33
Nakaminato, Japan	m19	33
Nakamura, Japan	J6	33
Nakaoso, Japan	N6	52
Nakatsu, Japan	J5	33
Nakfa, Eth.	B4	47
Nakhichevan, Sov. Un.	F3	28
Nakhodka, Sov. Un.	D6	31
Nakhon Chai Si, stm., Thai.	E4	35
Nakhon Pathom, Thai.	B2	34
Nakhon Phanom, Thai.	B2	34
Nakhon Ratchasima, Thai.	B2	34
Nakhon Sawan, Thai.	B1	34
Nakhon Si Thammarat, Thai.	C2	34
Nakina, Ont.	o18	73
Nakło [nad Notecia], Pol.	B4	26
Naknek, Ak., U.S.	D8	79
Naknek Lake, l., Ak., U.S.	D8	79
Nakskov, Den.	J4	14
Nakuru, Kenya	B6	48

Name	Map Ref.	Page
Nakusp, B.C.	D9	69
Nāl, stm., Pak.	C4	36
Nalchik, Sov. Un.	E2	28
Nallen, W.V., U.S.	m14	125
Nalón, stm., Spain	A2	22
Nālūt, Libya	C2	43
Nam, stm., Asia	B3	35
Nam, stm., S. Kor.	I4	33
Namacurra, Moz.	A6	49
Namak, Daryācheh-ye, l., Iran	D5	39
Namak, Kavīr-e, des., Iran	D8	39
Namaka, Man.	D4	68
Namakan Lake, l., N.A.	B6	100
Namangan, Sov. Un.	E10	29
Namanock Island, i., N.J., U.S.	A3	107
Namanyere, Tan.	C5	48
Namapa, Moz.	D6	48
Namasagali, Ug.	A6	48
Namatanai, Pap. N. Gui.	h13	50
Nambe Pueblo, N.M., U.S.	B4	108
Nambour, Austl.	E9	50
Nam Co, l., China	E3	31
Nam Dinh, Viet.	A3	34
Nāmdö, i., Swe.	t36	14
Nam Du Islands, is., Viet.	D2	34
Namekagon, stm., Wi., U.S.	B2	126
Namekagon Lake, l., Wi., U.S.	B2	126
Namen see Namur, Bel.	B6	16
Nametil, Moz.	A6	49
Namew Lake, l., Can.	C5	75
Namib Desert, des., Afr.	B1	49
Namibe (Moçâmedes), Ang.	E1	48
Namibe, dept., Ang.	E1	48
Namibia (South West Africa), ctry., Afr.	B2	49
Namiquipa, Mex.	B3	63
Namjagbarwa Feng, mtn., China	F4	31
Namlea, Indon.	F7	34
Nam Ngum Reservoir, res., Laos	C5	35
Namoi, stm., Austl.	F8	50
Namoruputh, Kenya	A6	48
Nampa, Alta.	A2	68
Nampa, Id., U.S.	F2	89
Nampala, Mali	C3	45
Nampo (Chinnampo), N. Kor.	D10	31
Nampula, Moz.	A6	49
Nampula, dept., Moz.	D6	48
Namsen, stm., Nor.	E4	14
Namsos, Nor.	E4	14
Namu, B.C.	D4	69
Namu Island, i., Marsh Is.	P18	52
Namur (Namen), Bel.	B6	16
Namur, Que.	D3	74
Namur, prov., Bel.	D4	17
Namur Island, i., Marsh Is.	S17	52
Namutoni, Nmb.	A2	49
Namwala, Zam.	E4	48
Namwŏn, S. Kor.	I3	33
Namysłów, Pol.	C4	26
Nan, Thai.	C4	35
Nan, stm., Thai.	B2	34
Nana, stm., Cen. Afr. Rep.	D3	46
Nanaimo, B.C.	E6	78
Nanakuli, Hi., U.S.	B3	88
Nanao, Japan	H8	33
Nanatsu Island, i., Japan	H8	33
Nance, co., Ne., U.S.	C7	104
Nanchang, China	F8	31
Nancheng, China	F8	31
Nanchong, China	E6	31
Nanchuan, China	J2	32
Nancy, Fr.	C7	16
Nancy Creek, stm., Ga., U.S.	h8	87
Nanda Devi, mtn., India	B7	36
Nānded, India	H6	37
Nandurbār, India	D4	37
Nanfeng, China	K7	32
Nanga Eboko, Cam.	E2	46
Nanga Parbat, mtn., Pak.	A5	36
Nangis, Fr.	F2	17
Nangong, China	F6	32
Nang Rong, Thai.	E6	35
Nanhua, China	F5	31
Nanjemoy, Md., U.S.	D3	97
Nanjing (Nanking) China	E8	31
Nankin, Oh., U.S.	B3	112
Nanking see Nanjing, China	E8	31
Nanning, China	G6	31
Nanoose Bay, B.C.	f11	69
Nanowin, stm., Man.	C3	70
Nanping, China	F8	31
Nansemond, stm., Va., U.S.	k14	123
Nanson, N.D., U.S.	A6	111
Nantel, Que.	C3	74
Nanterre, Fr.	g9	16
Nanteuil-le-Haudouin, Fr.	E2	17
Nantian, China	J9	32
Nanticoke, Ont.	E4	73
Nanticoke, Pa., U.S.	D10	115
Nanticoke, stm., U.S.	D6	97
Nanton, Alta.	D4	68
Nantong, China	E9	31
Nantua, Fr.	D6	16
Nantucket, co., Ma., U.S.	D7	98
Nantucket Island, i., Ma., U.S.	D7	98
Nantucket Sound, strt., Ma., U.S.	C7	98
Nantuxent Point, c., N.J., U.S.	E2	107
Nantwich, Eng., U.K.	A5	12
Nanty Glo, Pa., U.S.	F4	115
Nanuet, N.Y., U.S.	g12	109
Nanukuloa, Fiji	H15	52
Nanuku Passage, strt., Fiji	H16	52
Nanuku Reef, rf., Fiji	H16	52
Nanuque, Braz.	E8	57
Nanyang, China	E7	31
Nanyuki, Kenya	I4	32
Nanzhang, China	I4	32
Nao, Cabo, c., Spain	C6	23
Naoli He, stm., China	C6	33
Náoussa, Grc.	I5	25
Napa, Ca., U.S.	C2	82
Napa, co., Ca., U.S.	C2	82
Napadogan, N.B.	C3	71
Napakiak, Ak., U.S.	C7	79
Napaktak Bay, b., Newf.	f9	72
Napanee, Ont.	C8	73
Napanoch, N.Y., U.S.	D6	109
Napatree Point, c., R.I., U.S.	G1	116
Napavine, Wa., U.S.	C3	124
Nape, Laos	C6	35

Name	Map Ref.	Page
Naper, Ne., U.S.	B6	104
Naperville, Il., U.S.	B5	90
Napetipi, stm., Can.	C2	72
Napf, mtn., Switz.	C4	21
Napier, N.Z.	M16	51
Napier Mountains, mts., Ant.	C18	7
Napierville, Que.	D4	74
Napierville, co., Que.	D4	74
Napinka, Man.	E1	70
Naples, Il., U.S.	B5	90
Naples, Fl., U.S.	F5	86
Naples, Id., U.S.	A2	89
Naples, Il., U.S.	D3	90
Naples, Me., U.S.	E2	96
Naples, N.Y., U.S.	C3	109
Naples, S.D., U.S.	C8	118
Naples, Tx., U.S.	C5	120
Naples, Ut., U.S.	C6	121
Naples (Napoli), Italy	D5	23
Naples, Gulf of, b., Italy	D5	23
Naples Park, Fl., U.S.	*F5	86
Napo, prov., Ec.	B2	58
Napo, stm., S.A.	B3	58
Napoleon, In., U.S.	F7	91
Napoleon, Mo., U.S.	B3	102
Napoleon, N.D., U.S.	C6	111
Napoleon, Oh., U.S.	A1	112
Napoleonville, La., U.S.	E4	95
Naponee, Ne., U.S.	D6	104
Nappanee, In., U.S.	B5	91
Napton, Mo., U.S.	B4	102
Naqadeh, Iran	C2	39
Nara, Japan	o14	31
Nara, Mali	C3	45
Nara Canal, Pak.	D2	37
Naracoorte, Austl.	G7	50
Naramata, B.C.	E8	69
Na'rān, Isr. Occ.	A7	41
Naranja, Fl., U.S.	G6	86
Narathiwat, Thai.	D2	34
Nara Visa, N.M., U.S.	B6	108
Nārāyanganj, Bngl.	D9	36
Nārāyanpet, India	I6	37
Narbonne, Fr.	F5	16
Narberth, Pa., U.S.	p20	115
Narcisse, Ok., U.S.	A7	113
Narcisse, Man.	D3	70
Narcoossee, Fl., U.S.	D5	86
Nardin, Ok., U.S.	A4	113
Nardò, Italy	D7	23
Nares Strait, strt., N.A.	m37	66
Narew, stm., Eur.	B6	26
Narita, Japan	n19	33
Narka, Ks., U.S.	C6	93
Narmada, stm., India	D6	36
Narodnaya, Mount, mtn., Sov. Un.	C9	29
Naro-Fominsk, Sov. Un.	D11	27
Narok, Kenya	B6	48
Narol, Man.	D3	70
Narrabri, Austl.	F8	50
Narragansett, R.I., U.S.	F4	116
Narragansett Bay, b., R.I., U.S.	E5	116
Narraguagus, stm., Me., U.S.	D5	96
Narran, stm., Austl.	D6	51
Narrandera, Austl.	F8	50
Narran Lake, l., Austl.	D6	51
Narraway, stm., Can.	B7	69
Narrogin, Austl.	F2	50
Narromine, Austl.	F7	51
Narrows, Va., U.S.	C2	123
Narrowsburg, N.Y., U.S.	D5	109
Narsimhapur, India	F7	37
Narsīpatnam, India	I9	37
Naruna, Va., U.S.	C3	123
Narva, Sov. Un.	B7	27
Narvik, Nor.	C7	14
Narwar, Mar. Sov. Un.	C8	29
Naryilco, Austl.	D3	51
Narym, Sov. Un.	D25	8
Naryn, Sov. Un.	E9	28
Naryn, stm., Sov. Un.	E10	28
Narynkol, Sov. Un.	E10	28
Na Sam, Viet.	A7	35
Na San, Thai.	D1	34
Nase, Japan	F10	31
Naseby, N.Z.	P13	51
Naseby, Wa., U.S.	C2	124
Nash, N.D., U.S.	A8	111
Nash, Ok., U.S.	A3	113
Nash, co., N.C., U.S.	A4	110
Nashawena Island, i., Ma., U.S.	k33	66
Nash Creek, N.B.	B3	71
Nāshik, India	E5	36
Nashoba, Ok., U.S.	C6	113
Nashoba Hill, hill, Ma., U.S.	f10	98
Nashua, Ia., U.S.	A5	92
Nashua, Mn., U.S.	D2	100
Nashua, Mt., U.S.	B10	103
Nashua, N.H., U.S.	E4	106
Nashua, stm., N.H., U.S.	A4	106
Nashville, Ar., U.S.	D2	81
Nashville, Ga., U.S.	E3	87
Nashville, Il., U.S.	E4	90
Nashville, In., U.S.	F5	91
Nashville, Ks., U.S.	E5	93
Nashville, Mi., U.S.	F5	99
Nashville, Mo., U.S.	D3	102
Nashville, N.C., U.S.	B5	110
Nashville, Oh., U.S.	B3	112
Nashville, Tn., U.S.	A5	119
Nashwauk, stm., N.B.	C3	71
Nashwaaksis, N.B.	D3	71
Nashwauk, Mn., U.S.	C5	100
Našice, Yugo.	C2	24
Nasielsk, Pol.	B6	26
Nasīrābād, India	E10	37
Naṣīr, Bi'r, well, Eg.	E13	39
Nāsijärvi, l., Fin.	G10	14
Nāsik see Ahvāz, Iran	B4	38
Nāsiri see Ahvāz, Iran	C5	58
Nasik, i., Grc.	I4	32
Nason, Il., U.S.	E5	90
Nasonville, R.I., U.S.	B3	116
Nassau, Bah.	B5	64
Nassau, N.Y., U.S.	C7	109
Nassau, co., Fl., U.S.	B5	86
Nassau, co., N.Y., U.S.	E7	109
Nassau, stm., Fl., U.S.	B5	86
Nassau, Bahia, b., Chile	k12	54
Nassau International Airport, Bah.	m17	64
Nassau Shores, N.Y., U.S.	*n15	109
Nassau Sound, b., Fl., U.S.	B5	86
Nassauville, Fl., U.S.	B5	86

Name	Map Ref.	Page
Nassawadox, Va., U.S.	C7	123
Nassawango Creek, stm., Md., U.S.	D7	97
Nasser, Lake, res., Afr.	E6	43
Nassjö, Swe.	I6	14
Nasugbu, Phil.	o13	34
Nasukoin Mountain, mtn., Mt., U.S.	B2	103
Nata, Bots.	B4	49
Natá, Pan.	F7	62
Natagaima, Col.	C2	60
Natal, Braz.	C3	57
Natal, prov., S. Afr.	C5	49
Natalbany, La., U.S.	D5	95
Natalia, Tx., U.S.	E3	120
Natanes Plateau, plat., Az., U.S.	D5	80
Natashquan, Que.	h9	72
Natashquan, stm., Can.	h9	72
Natawa Bay, b., Fiji	H15	52
Natchaug, stm., Ct., U.S.	B7	84
Natchez, Ms., U.S.	D2	101
Natchitoches, La., U.S.	C2	95
Natchitoches, co., La., U.S.	C2	95
Natewa Bay, b., Fiji	H15	52
Nathalie, Va., U.S.	D4	123
Nathrop, Co., U.S.	C4	83
Natick, Ma., U.S.	B5	98
Natimuk, Austl.	H3	51
Nation, stm., B.C.	B6	69
National, Wa., U.S.	C4	124
National City, Ca., U.S.	F5	82
National City, Mi., U.S.	D7	99
National Gardens, Fl., U.S.	C5	86
National Park, N.J., U.S.	*D2	107
Natitingou, Benin	D5	45
Natividade, Braz.	D1	57
Natoma, Ks., U.S.	C4	93
Natrona, co., Wy., U.S.	C6	127
Natrona, Wy., U.S.	D5	127
Natrona Heights, Pa., U.S.	E2	115
Natrūn, Isr. Occ.	A7	41
Natuna Besar, i., Indon.	E3	34
Natuna, is., Indon.	E3	34
Natural Bridge, Al., U.S.	A2	78
Natural Bridge, N.Y., U.S.	A5	109
Natural Bridge, Va., U.S.	C3	123
Natural Bridge, Ut., U.S.	F3	121
Natural Bridge, Va., U.S.	C3	123
Natural Bridges National Monument, Ut., U.S.	F6	121
Naturaliste, co., Austl.	F1	50
Natural Steps, Ar., U.S.	h10	81
Naturita, Co., U.S.	C2	83
Naubinway, Mi., U.S.	B5	99
Nauders, Aus.	E5	18
Nauen, Ger.	B6	18
Naugatuck, Ct., U.S.	D3	84
Naugatuck, stm., Ct., U.S.	D3	84
Naumburg, Ger.	C5	19
Naumburg [an der Saale], Ger.	C5	18
Naupa, Ger.	B7	19
Naupactus see Návpaktos, Grc.	C3	25
Ñaupe, Peru	C2	58
Nauru, ctry., Oc.	G10	6
Naushon Island, i., Ma., U.S.	D6	98
Nauta, Peru	B3	58
Nautilus Park, Ct., U.S.	D7	84
Nautla, Mex.	C5	63
Nauvoo, Al., U.S.	B2	78
Nauvoo, Il., U.S.	C2	90
Nauwigewauk, N.B.	D4	71
Nava, Lake, l., Spain	A3	22
Nava del Rey, Spain	B3	22
Navahermosa, Spain	C3	22
Navajo, Az., U.S.	B6	80
Navajo, co., Az., U.S.	B5	80
Navajo Dam, N.M., U.S.	A2	108
Navajo Indian Reservation, U.S.	A4	80
Navajo Mountain, mtn., Ut., U.S.	F5	121
Navajo National Monument, Az., U.S.	A5	80
Navajo Reservoir, res., U.S.	A2	108
Navalcarnero, Spain	B3	22
Navalmoral de la Mata, Spain	C3	22
Navan, Ont.	B9	73
Navan see An Uaimh, Ire.	D3	10
Navarino, Wi., U.S.	D5	126
Navarino, Isla, i., Chile	k12	54
Navarre, Oh., U.S.	B4	112
Navarre, hist. reg., Spain	A5	22
Navarro, co., Tx., U.S.	C4	120
Navas de Tolosa, Spain	C4	22
Navasota, Tx., U.S.	D4	120
Navassa, N.C., U.S.	C4	110
Navassa Island, i., N.A.	E6	64
Navatu, rf., Fiji	l16	52
Nāvekvarn, Swe.	u34	14
Navesink, N.J., U.S.	C4	107
Navet Reservoir, res., Trin.	O23	65
Navia, Arg.	A3	54
Navia, stm., Spain	A2	22
Navidad, Chile	A2	54
Naviti, i., Fiji	H14	52
Navolato, Mex.	C3	63
Návplion, Grc.	D4	25
Návpaktos (Naupactus), Grc.	D4	25
Navsāri, India	G4	37
Nawābshāh, Pak.	C4	36
Nawāda, India	E10	37
Nawah, Afg.	E13	39
Nawiliwili Bay, b., Hi., U.S.	B2	88
Nāxos, Grc.	D5	40
Náxos, i., Grc.	L8	25
Nay, Fr.	F3	16
Nāy Band, Iran	E8	39
Nāy Band, Iran	H6	39
Nāy Band, Ra'se, c., Iran	H6	39
Naylor, Mo., U.S.	E7	102
Nayoro, Japan	D11	33
Naytahwaush, Mn., U.S.	C3	100
Nazaré, Port.	C1	22
Nazareth (Nazerat), Isr.	B3	38
Nazareth, Ky., U.S.	B4	94
Nazareth, Tx., U.S.	B1	120

Name	Map Ref.	Page
Nazário, Braz.	B3	56
Nazas, Mex.	B4	63
Nazas, stm., Mex.	B4	63
Nazca, Peru	D3	58
Nazilli, Tur.	D7	40
Nazimovo, Sov. Un.	D27	8
Naziya, Sov. Un.	s32	14
Nazko, stm., B.C.	C6	69
Nazlini, Az., U.S.	B6	80
Nazret, Eth.	B4	47
Nazyvayevsk, Sov. Un.	B8	29
Ncheu, Mwi.	B5	48
Ndala, Tan.	B5	48
Ndalatando, Ang.	C1	48
N'dalatando, Ang.	B4	102
Ndélé, Cen. Afr. Rep.	D4	46
N'Djamena (Fort-Lamy), Chad	C3	46
Ndjolé, Gabon	F2	46
Ndola, Zam.	D4	48
Neagh, Lough, l., N. Ire., U.K.	C3	10
Neah Bay, Wa., U.S.	A1	124
Néa Ionía, Grc.	*C4	25
Neal, Ks., U.S.	E7	93
Neales, stm., Austl.	E6	50
Néa Liósia, Grc.	*C4	25
Néa Páfos, Cyp.	E9	40
Néa Palátia, Grc.	g11	25
Neápolis, Grc.	D4	25
Neápolis, Grc.	E5	25
Néa Psará see Erétria, Grc.	g11	25
Néa Smírni, Grc.	*D4	25
Neath, Wales, U.K.	E5	10
Neavitt, Md., U.S.	C5	97
Neba, Japan	n16	33
Nebel, stm., Ger.	B5	18
Nebine Creek, stm., Austl.	D6	51
Nebit-Dag, Sov. Un.	B7	39
Neblina, Pico da, mtn., S.A.	C4	60
Nebo, Il., U.S.	D3	90
Nebo, Ky., U.S.	C2	94
Nebo, La., U.S.	C3	95
Nebo, Mo., U.S.	D5	102
Nebo, Mount, mtn., Ar., U.S.	B2	81
Nebo, Mount see Nabā, Jabal, mtn., Jord.	C7	41
Nebraska, In., U.S.	G4	91
Nebraska, state, U.S.	C6	104
Nebraska City, Ne., U.S.	D10	104
Nebužely, Czech.	n18	26
Necedah, Wi., U.S.	D3	126
Nechako, stm., B.C.	C5	69
Nechako Range, mts., B.C.	C5	69
Neche, N.D., U.S.	A8	111
Neches, stm., Tx., U.S.	D5	120
Nechí, Col.	B3	60
Nechí, stm., Col.	B3	60
Nechranice Reservoir, res., Czech.	C8	19
Neckar, stm., Ger.	D4	18
Neckarsulm, Ger.	D3	84
Neck City, Mo., U.S.	D3	102
Necker Island, i., Hi., U.S.	m15	88
Nececohea, Arg.	B5	54
Nederland, Co., U.S.	B5	83
Nederland, Tx., U.S.	E6	120
Neder Rijn, mth., Neth.	C4	109
Nedrow, N.Y., U.S.	C4	109
Needham, In., U.S.	E5	91
Needham, Ma., U.S.	g11	98
Needle Mountain, mtn., Wy., U.S.	B3	127
Needles, Ca., U.S.	E6	82
Needmore, In., U.S.	G4	91
Needmore, Pa., U.S.	G5	115
Needville, Tx., U.S.	r14	120
Neelin, Man.	E2	70
Neels Gap, Ga., U.S.	B3	87
Neely, Ms., U.S.	D5	101
Neelyville, Mo., U.S.	E7	102
Neemuch see Nimach, India	H6	37
Neenah, Wi., U.S.	D5	126
Neepawa, Man.	D2	70
Neepelt, Bel.	C5	17
Neeses, S.C., U.S.	E5	117
Neffs, Oh., U.S.	B5	112
Neffsville, Pa., U.S.	F9	115
Neftah, Tun.	C6	44
Neftegorsk, Sov. Un.	G16	8
Nefyn, Wales, U.K.	B3	12
Negage, Ang.	B3	48
Neganuee, Mi., U.S.	B3	99
Negaunee, Eth.	B3	99
Negeri Sembilan, state, Malay.	K5	35
Negev Desert, des., Isr.	D6	41
Negley, Oh., U.S.	B5	112
Negomano, Moz.	E6	48
Negombo, Sri L.	G6	36
Negotin, Yugo.	C6	24
Negra, Cordillera, mts., Peru	C2	58
Negra, Punta, c., Peru	C1	58
Negreet, La., U.S.	C2	95
Negreira, Spain	A1	22
Negro, stm., Bol.	B3	56
Negro, stm., Braz.	B1	56
Negro, stm., Braz.	D2	56
Negro, stm., S.A.	E1	56
Negro Mountain, mtn., Md., U.S.	k12	97
Negros, i., Phil.	D6	34
Negru-Vodă, Rom.	D9	24
Neguac, N.B.	B4	71
Nehalem, Or., U.S.	B3	114
Nehalem, stm., Or., U.S.	B3	114
Nehawka, Ne., U.S.	D10	104
Nehbandān, Iran	F10	39
Nehe, China	B2	33
Neheim-Hüsten, Ger.	C3	18
Nehíba, Dom. Rep.	E8	64
Neidpath, Sask.	G2	75
Neihart, Mt., U.S.	D6	103
Neihuang, China	G6	32
Neijiang, China	F5	31
Neilburg, Sask.	E1	75
Neillsville, Wi., U.S.	D3	126
Neilton, Wa., U.S.	B2	124
Nei Monggol see Inner Mongolia, prov., China	C7	31
Neisse, stm., Eur.	B7	19
Neiva, Col.	C2	60
Neixiang, China	I3	32
Nejd, reg., Sau. Ar.	C4	38
Nejdek, Czech.	E11	19
Nekemte, Eth.	B4	47
Nekoma, Ks., U.S.	D4	93
Nekoma, N.D., U.S.	A7	111
Nek's Ziyyona, Isr.	B4	41
Nekso, Den.	A5	15
Nelidovo, Sov. Un.	C9	27
Neligh, Ne., U.S.	B7	104

Name	Map Ref.	Page
Nellis Air Force Base, mil., Nv., U.S.	G6	105
Nellore, India	F7	36
Nellysford, Va., U.S.	C4	123
Nelma, Sov. Un.	C9	33
Nelson, B.C.	E9	69
Nelson, N.Z.	N14	51
Nelson, Az., U.S.	B2	80
Nelson, Ga., U.S.	B2	87
Nelson, Il., U.S.	B4	90
Nelson, Ky., U.S.	C2	94
Nelson, Mn., U.S.	E3	100
Nelson, Mo., U.S.	B4	102
Nelson, Ne., U.S.	D7	104
Nelson, Nv., U.S.	H7	105
Nelson, N.H., U.S.	E2	106
Nelson, Pa., U.S.	C7	115
Nelson, Wi., U.S.	D1	126
Nelson, co., Ky., U.S.	C4	94
Nelson, co., N.D., U.S.	B7	111
Nelson, co., Va., U.S.	C5	123
Nelson, Cape, c., Austl.	I3	51
Nelson Forks, B.C.	m18	69
Nelson House, Man.	B2	70
Nelson Lake, l., Man.	B2	70
Nelsonville, Oh., U.S.	C3	112
Nelspruit, S. Afr.	C5	49
Néma, Maur.	C3	45
Nemacolin, Pa., U.S.	G2	115
Nemadji, stm., U.S.	B1	126
Nemaha, Ia., U.S.	B2	92
Nemaha, Ne., U.S.	D10	104
Nemaha, co., Ks., U.S.	C7	93
Nemaha, co., Ne., U.S.	D10	104
Nemakščiai, Sov. Un.	A7	26
Neman, Sov. Un.	A7	26
Neman (Nemunas), stm., Sov. Un.	E5	27
Nembe, Nig.	F6	45
Nemeiben Lake, l., Sask.	B3	75
Nemi, Lake, l., Italy	h9	23
Nemiscau, Que.	h11	74
Nemo, S.D., U.S.	C2	118
Nemours, Fr.	C5	16
Nemunas (Neman) stm., Sov. Un.	D4	27
Nemuro, Japan	C14	31
Nemuro Strait, strt., Asia	D12	33
Nenagh, Ire.	D2	10
Nenana, Ak., U.S.	C10	79
Nendeln, Liech.	B8	21
Nene, stm., Eng., U.K.	B8	12
Nenjiang, China	B10	31
Nen Jiang, stm., China	B9	31
Nenzel, Ne., U.S.	B4	104
Nenzing, Aus.	B8	21
Neodesha, Ks., U.S.	E8	93
Neoga, Il., U.S.	D5	90
Neola, Ia., U.S.	C2	92
Neola, Ut., U.S.	C5	121
Néon Karlovásion, Grc.	D6	25
Neopit, Wi., U.S.	D5	126
Neosho, Mo., U.S.	E3	102
Neosho, Wi., U.S.	E5	126
Neosho, co., Ks., U.S.	E8	93
Neosho, stm., Ok., U.S.	A6	113
Neosho Falls, Ks., U.S.	D8	93
Neosho Rapids, Ks., U.S.	D8	93
Neotsu, Or., U.S.	B3	114
Nepal, ctry., Asia	C7	36
Nepālganj, Nepal	*C8	36
Nepaug, Ct., U.S.	*B4	84
Nepaug Reservoir, res., Ct., U.S.	B3	84
Nepean, Ont.	B9	73
Nepewassi Lake, l., Ont.	A4	73
Nephi, Ut., U.S.	D4	121
Nephton, Ont.	C7	73
Nepisiguit, stm., N.B.	B3	71
Nepisiguit Bay, b., N.B.	B4	71
Nepomuk, Czech.	D1	19
Neponset, Il., U.S.	B4	90
Neponset, stm., Ma., U.S.	h11	98
Nepton, Ky., U.S.	B6	94
Neptune, Sask.	H3	75
Neptune, N.J., U.S.	C4	107
Neptune Beach, Fl., U.S.	B5	86
Neptune City, N.J., U.S.	C4	107
Nera, stm., Italy	E4	23
Nérac, Fr.	E4	16
Nerchinsk, Sov. Un.	D14	29
Nerchinskiy Zavod, Sov. Un.	A8	31
Nerekhta, Sov. Un.	C13	27
Neretva, stm., Yugo.	D3	24
Neriquinha, Ang.	E3	48
Neris, stm., Sov. Un.	D6	27
Nerja, Spain	D4	22
Nerpichye, Sov. Un.	B12	33
Nerstrand, Mn., U.S.	F5	100
Nerva, Spain	D2	22
Nes, Neth.	A5	17
Nesbit, Ms., U.S.	A3	101
Nesbitt, Man.	E2	70
Nesco, N.J., U.S.	D3	107
Nesconset, N.Y., U.S.	*n15	109
Nescopeck, Pa., U.S.	D9	115
Nesebŭr, Bul.	D8	24
Neshanic Station, N.J., U.S.	B3	107
Nesher, Isr.	F7	41
Neshkoro, Wi., U.S.	E4	126
Neshoba, Ms., U.S.	C4	101
Neshoba, co., Ms., U.S.	C4	101
Nesika Beach, Or., U.S.	E2	114
Neskaupstadur, Ice.	n26	14
Neskowin, Or., U.S.	B3	114
Nesle, Fr.	E2	17
Nesmith, S.C., U.S.	D8	117
Nesodden, Nor.	p28	14
Nesowadnehunk, l., Me., U.S.	B3	96
Nespelem, Wa., U.S.	A7	124
Nesquehoning, Pa., U.S.	E10	115
Ness, co., Ks., U.S.	D4	93
Ness, Loch, l., Scot., U.K.	D4	93
Ness City, Ks., U.S.	D4	93
Nesselrode, Mount, mtn., U.S.	B6	69
Nesselwang, Ger.	E5	18
Nesslau, Switz.	B6	21
Nessmersiel, Ger.	A7	19
Nesterov, Sov. Un.	A7	26
Nesterov, Sov. Un.	A7	26
Nestoria, China	I3	32
Nestorville, W.V., U.S.	B5	125
Néstos (Mesta), stm., Eur.	I6	27
Nesvizh, Sov. Un.	E6	27
Netarts, Or., U.S.	B3	114
Netcong, N.J., U.S.	B3	107
Netherhill, Sask.	F1	75
Netherlands, ctry., Eur.	A6	16

Name	Map Ref.	Page
Netherlands Antilles, ctry., N.A.	A4	60
Nether Providence Township, Pa., U.S.	*G11	115
Nethy Bridge, Scot., U.K.	C5	13
Netolice, Czech.	D9	19
Netrakona, Bngl.	E13	37
Nettie, W.V., U.S.	C4	125
Nettilling Lake, l., N.W. Ter.	C18	66
Nett Lake, Mn., U.S.	B5	100
Nett Lake, l., Mn., U.S.	B5	100
Nett Lake Indian Reservation, Mn., U.S.	B6	100
Nettleton, Ms., U.S.	A5	101
Nettleton, Mo., U.S.	B4	102
Nettuno, Italy	k9	23
Netvořice, Czech.	o18	26
Netzahualcóyotl, Mex.	h9	63
Neubeckum, Ger.	B3	19
Neubrandenburg, Ger.	B6	18
Neuburg [an der Donau], Ger.	D5	18
Neuchâtel, Switz.	E3	18
Neuchâtel, state, Switz.	C2	20
Neuchâtel, Lake, l., Switz.	E3	18
Neudorf, Sask.	G4	75
Neuenegg, Switz.	C3	21
Neuenkirchen, Ger.	E3	15
Neuenrade, Ger.	B2	19
Neuerburg, Ger.	E6	17
Neufchâteau, Bel.	E5	17
Neufchâteau, Fr.	C6	16
Neufchâtel-en-Bray, Fr.	C4	16
Neufchâtel-sur-Aisne, Fr.	E4	17
Neufelden, Aus.	D6	18
Neugersdorf, Ger.	C9	19
Neuharlingersiel, Ger.	A7	17
Neuhaus, Ger.	E4	15
Neuhaus, Ger.	C6	19
Neuilly [-sur-Seine], Fr.	g11	16
Neu-Isenburg, Ger.	C3	19
Neukirchen am Grossvenediger, Aus.	B8	20
Neumarkt, Ger.	D5	18
Neumarkt-Sankt Veit, Ger.	A8	20
Neumünster, Ger.	A4	18
Neunburg vorm Wald, Ger.	D7	19
Neunkirch, Switz.	A6	21
Neunkirchen, Aus.	D2	19
Neuquén, Arg.	B3	54
Neuquén, prov., Arg.	B3	54
Neuquén, stm., Arg.	B3	54
Neurara, Chile	D2	55
Neuruppin, Ger.	B6	18
Neuse, stm., N.C., U.S.	B6	110
Neusiedler Lake, l., Eur.	E8	18
Neuss, Ger.	B1	19
Neustadt, Ont.	C4	73
Neustadt, Ger.	B9	19
Neustadt, Ger.	C6	19
Neustadt, Ger.	E4	18
Neustadt, Ger.	C4	19
Neustadt am Rübenberge, Ger.	F3	15
Neustadt [an der Aisch], Ger.	D5	18
Neustadt [an der Dosse], Ger.	B6	18
Neustadt an der Waldnaab, Ger.	D7	19
Neustadt [an der Weinstrasse], Ger.	D4	18
Neustadt [bei Coburg], Ger.	C5	18
Neustadt-Glewe, Ger.	E5	15
Neustadt [in Holstein], Ger.	A5	18
Neustrelitz, Ger.	B6	18
Neu-Ulm, Ger.	D5	18
Neuville, Que.	C6	74
Neuville-lès-Dieppe, Fr.	E9	12
Neuwerk, i., Ger.	E2	15
Neuwied, Ger.	C3	18
Neva, Tn., U.S.	C12	119
Neva, stm., Sov. Un.	s31	14
Nevada, Ia., U.S.	B4	92
Nevada, Mo., U.S.	D3	102
Nevada, Oh., U.S.	B2	112
Nevada, co., Ar., U.S.	D2	81
Nevada, co., Ca., U.S.	C3	82
Nevada, state, U.S.	D5	105
Nevada, Sierra, mts., Spain	D4	22
Nevada, Sierra, mts., Ca., U.S.	D4	82
Nevada City, Ca., U.S.	C3	82
Nevada Mills, In., U.S.	A7	91
Nevado, Cerro, mtn., Col.	C3	60
Nevel, Sov. Un.	C7	27
Nevelsk, Sov. Un.	B13	31
Nevelski, Mount, mtn., Sov. Un.	A11	33
Nevers, Fr.	D5	16
Neversink, stm., N.Y., U.S.	D6	109
Neversink Reservoir, res., N.Y., U.S.	D6	109
Nevesinje, Yugo.	D4	24
Neville, Sask.	H2	75
Neville, Fr.	E8	12
Nevils, Ga., U.S.	D5	87
Nevinnomyssk, Sov. Un.	G17	8
Nevinville, Ia., U.S.	C3	92
Nevis, Mn., U.S.	D4	100
Nevis, i., St. C.-N.	H13	64
Nevis, Ben, mtn., Scot., U.K.	B4	10
Nevis, Loch, b., Scot., U.K.	C3	13
Nevşehir, Tur.	C10	40
New, stm., U.S.	C3	125
New, stm., Az., U.S.	k8	80
New, stm., N.C., U.S.	C5	110
Newala, Tan.	D6	48
New Albany, In., U.S.	H6	91
New Albany, Ks., U.S.	E8	93
New Albany, Ms., U.S.	A4	101
New Albany, Oh., U.S.	k11	112
New Albany, Pa., U.S.	C9	115
New Albin, Ia., U.S.	A6	92
Newald, Wi., U.S.	C5	126
New Alsace, In., U.S.	F8	91
New Amsterdam, Guy.	A3	59
Newark, Ar., U.S.	B4	81
Newark, Ca., U.S.	h8	82
Newark, De., U.S.	B3	85
Newark, Il., U.S.	B5	90
Newark, Md., U.S.	D7	97
Newark, Mo., U.S.	B6	102
Newark, N.J., U.S.	B4	107
Newark, N.Y., U.S.	B3	109
Newark, Oh., U.S.	B3	112
Newark, Tx., U.S.	m9	120
Newark Bay, b., N.J., U.S.	k8	107
Newark Lake, l., Nv., U.S.	D6	105
Newark Valley, N.Y., U.S.	C4	109
New Athens, Il., U.S.	E4	90
New Athens, Oh., U.S.	B4	112
New Auburn, Mn., U.S.	F4	100
New Auburn, Wi., U.S.	C2	126
New Augusta, Ms., U.S.	D4	101
Newaygo, Mi., U.S.	E5	99
Newaygo, co., Mi., U.S.	E5	99
New Baden, Il., U.S.	E4	90
New Baltimore, Mi., U.S.	F8	99
New Baltimore, N.Y., U.S.	C7	109
New Baltimore, Oh., U.S.	n12	112
New Baltimore, Pa., U.S.	G4	115
New Bedford, Il., U.S.	B4	90
New Bedford, Ma., U.S.	C6	98
New Bedford, Pa., U.S.	D1	115
Newberg, Or., U.S.	B4	114
New Berlin, Il., U.S.	D4	90
New Berlin, N.Y., U.S.	C5	109
New Berlin, Pa., U.S.	E7	115
New Berlin, Tx., U.S.	k7	120
New Berlin, Wi., U.S.	n11	126
Newbern, Al., U.S.	C2	78
Newbern, Il., U.S.	D3	90
New Bern, N.C., U.S.	B5	110
Newbern, Tn., U.S.	A2	119
Newberry, Fl., U.S.	C4	86
Newberry, In., U.S.	G3	91
Newberry, Mi., U.S.	B5	99
Newberry, S.C., U.S.	C4	117
Newberry Springs, Ca., U.S.	E5	82
Newberry, co., S.C., U.S.	C4	117
New Bethlehem, Pa., U.S.	D3	115
New Bloomfield, Mo., U.S.	C5	102
New Bloomfield, Pa., U.S.	F7	115
New Bloomington, Oh., U.S.	B2	112
Newboro, Ont.	C8	73
New Boston, Il., U.S.	B3	90
New Boston, Ia., U.S.	D6	92
New Boston, Ma., U.S.	B1	98
New Boston, Mi., U.S.	p15	99
New Boston, N.H., U.S.	E3	106
New Boston, Oh., U.S.	D3	112
New Boston, Tx., U.S.	C5	120
New Braintree, Ma., U.S.	B3	98
New Braunfels, Tx., U.S.	E3	120
New Bremen, N.Y., U.S.	B5	109
New Bremen, Oh., U.S.	B1	112
New Bridge, Or., U.S.	C9	114
New Brigden, Alta.	D5	68
New Brighton, Mn., U.S.	m12	100
New Brighton, Pa., U.S.	E1	115
New Britain, Ct., U.S.	C4	84
New Britain, i., Pap. N. Gui.	k13	50
New Brockton, Al., U.S.	D4	78
Newbrook, Alta.	B4	68
New Brunswick, N.J., U.S.	C4	107
New Brunswick, prov., Can.	C3	71
New Buffalo, Mi., U.S.	G4	99
Newburg, Ia., U.S.	C5	92
Newburg, Ky., U.S.	*B4	94
Newburg, Mo., U.S.	D6	102
Newburg, N.D., U.S.	A5	111
Newburg, Pa., U.S.	F6	115
Newburg, W.V., U.S.	B5	125
Newburg, Wi., U.S.	E5	126
Newburgh, Ont.	C8	73
Newburgh, Scot., U.K.	C7	13
Newburgh, In., U.S.	I3	91
Newburgh, Me., U.S.	D4	96
Newburgh, N.Y., U.S.	D6	109
Newburgh Heights, Oh., U.S.	h9	112
New Burnside, Il., U.S.	F5	90
Newbury, Ont.	E3	73
Newbury, Eng., U.K.	E6	10
Newbury, Ma., U.S.	A6	98
Newbury, N.H., U.S.	D2	106
Newbury, Vt., U.S.	C4	122
Newburyport, Ma., U.S.	A6	98
New Caledonia, dep., Oc.	H10	6
New Cambria, Ks., U.S.	D6	93
New Cambria, Mo., U.S.	B5	102
New Canaan, Ct., U.S.	E2	84
New Canton, Il., U.S.	D2	90
New Canton, Va., U.S.	C4	123
New Carlisle, Que.	A4	71
New Carlisle, In., U.S.	A4	91
New Carlisle, Oh., U.S.	C1	112
New Carrollton, Md., U.S.	*C4	97
New Cassel, N.Y., U.S.	*n15	109
New Castle, hist. reg., Spain	C4	22
Newcastle, Austl.	F8	50
Newcastle, N.B.	C4	71
Newcastle, Ont.	D6	73
Newcastle, Ire.	E4	11
Newcastle, S. Afr.	C4	49
Newcastle, N. Ire., U.K.	C6	11
New Castle, Al., U.S.	B3	78
New Castle, Co., U.S.	B3	83
New Castle, De., U.S.	B3	85
New Castle, In., U.S.	E7	91
New Castle, Ky., U.S.	B4	94
Newcastle, Me., U.S.	D3	96
New Castle, N.H., U.S.	D5	106
Newcastle, Ok., U.S.	B4	113
New Castle, Pa., U.S.	D1	115
Newcastle, Tx., U.S.	C3	120
New Castle, Ut., U.S.	F2	121
New Castle, Va., U.S.	C2	123
Newcastle, Wy., U.S.	C8	127
New Castle, co., De., U.S.	B3	85
Newcastle Creek, N.B.	C3	71
Newcastle Emlyn, Wales, U.K.	B3	12
Newcastle Mine, Alta.	D4	68
Newcastle-under-Lyme, Eng., U.K.	A5	12
Newcastle upon Tyne, Eng., U.K.	C6	10
Newcastle West, Ire.	E2	11
Newcestown, Ire.	E3	11
New City, N.Y., U.S.	D6	109
New Columbia, Pa., U.S.	D8	115
Newcomb, N.M., U.S.	A1	108
Newcomb, N.Y., U.S.	A6	92
Newcomb, Tn., U.S.	A7	119
Newcomerstown, Oh., U.S.	B4	112
New Concord, Ky., U.S.	f9	94
New Concord, Oh., U.S.	C4	112
New Cumberland, Pa., U.S.	F8	115
New Cumberland, W.V., U.S.	A4	125
New Cumnock, Scot., U.K.	C4	10
Newdale, Man.	D1	70
Newdale, Id., U.S.	F7	89
New Dayton, Alta.	E4	68
New Delhi, India	C6	36
New Denmark, N.B.	C2	71
New Denver, B.C.	D9	69
New Diggings, Wi., U.S.	F3	126
New Durham, N.H., U.S.	D4	106
New Edinburg, Ar., U.S.	D3	81
New Effington, S.D., U.S.	B9	118
New Egypt, N.J., U.S.	C3	107
Newell, Ar., U.S.	B3	81
Newell, Ia., U.S.	B2	92
Newell, S.D., U.S.	C2	118
Newell, W.V., U.S.	A4	125
Newell, Lake, l., Alta.	D5	68
New Ellenton, S.C., U.S.	E4	117
Newellton, La., U.S.	B4	95
New England, N.D., U.S.	C3	111
Newenham, Cape, c., Ak., U.S.	D7	79
New Enterprise, Pa., U.S.	F5	115
New Era, Mi., U.S.	E4	99
New Sha'anan, Isr.	m14	41
New Fairfield, Ct., U.S.	D2	84
Newfane, N.Y., U.S.	B2	109
Newfane, Vt., U.S.	F3	122
Newfield, Me., U.S.	E2	96
Newfield, N.J., U.S.	D2	107
Newfields, N.H., U.S.	D5	106
New Florence, Mo., U.S.	C6	102
New Florence, Pa., U.S.	F3	115
Newfolden, Mn., U.S.	B2	100
Newfound Gap, U.S.	f9	110
Newfound Lake, l., N.H., U.S.	C3	106
Newfoundland, N.J., U.S.	A4	107
Newfoundland, Pa., U.S.	D11	115
Newfoundland, prov., Can.	D4	72
Newfoundland, i., Newf.	D3	72
Newfoundland Mountains, mts., Ut., U.S.	B2	121
New Franken, Wi., U.S.	D6	126
New Franklin, Mo., U.S.	B5	102
New Freedom, Pa., U.S.	G8	115
New Galilee, Pa., U.S.	E1	115
New Galloway, Scot., U.K.	C4	10
New Gate, hist., Isr.	m14	41
New Germany, N.S.	E5	71
New Glarus, Wi., U.S.	F4	126
New Glasgow, N.S.	D7	71
New Gloucester, Me., U.S.	E2	96
New Goshen, In., U.S.	E3	91
New Gretna, N.J., U.S.	D4	107
New Guinea, i.	G8	6
Newhalem, Wa., U.S.	A4	124
Newhalen, Ak., U.S.	D8	79
Newhall, Ca., U.S.	E4	82
Newhall, Ia., U.S.	C6	92
Newhall, W.V., U.S.	D3	125
New Hamburg, Ont.	D4	73
New Hampshire, state, U.S.	C3	106
New Hampton, Ia., U.S.	A5	92
New Hampton, Mo., U.S.	A3	102
New Hampton, N.H., U.S.	C3	106
New Hanover, co., N.C., U.S.	C5	110
New Hanover, i., Pap. N. Gui.	h12	50
New Harbor, Me., U.S.	E3	96
New Harbour, Newf.	E5	72
New Harmony, In., U.S.	H2	91
New Harmony, Ut., U.S.	F2	121
New Hartford, Ct., U.S.	B4	84
New Hartford, Ia., U.S.	B5	92
New Haven, Ct., U.S.	D4	84
New Haven, Il., U.S.	F5	90
New Haven, In., U.S.	B7	91
New Haven, Ky., U.S.	C4	94
New Haven, Mi., U.S.	F8	99
New Haven, Mo., U.S.	C6	102
New Haven, N.Y., U.S.	B4	109
New Haven, Oh., U.S.	A3	112
New Haven, Vt., U.S.	C2	122
New Haven, W.V., U.S.	C3	125
New Haven, co., Ct., U.S.	D4	84
New Haven, stm., Vt., U.S.	C2	122
New Haven Harbor, b., Ct., U.S.	E4	84
New Hazelton, B.C.	B4	69
New Hebrides see Vanuatu, ctry., Oc.	H10	6
Newhebron, Ms., U.S.	D4	101
New Hill, N.C., U.S.	B4	110
New Holland, Ga., U.S.	B3	87
New Holland, Il., U.S.	C4	90
New Holland, Oh., U.S.	C2	112
New Holland, Pa., U.S.	F9	115
New Holland, S.D., U.S.	D7	118
New Holstein, Wi., U.S.	E5	126
New Hope, Al., U.S.	A3	78
New Hope, Ky., U.S.	C4	94
New Hope, Mn., U.S.	m12	100
New Hope, N.C., U.S.	*B4	110
New Hope, Pa., U.S.	F12	115
New Hope Mountain, mtn., Al., U.S.	g7	78
New Hradec, N.D., U.S.	B3	111
New Hudson, Mi., U.S.	o14	99
New Hyde Park, N.Y., U.S.	*E7	109
New Iberia, La., U.S.	D4	95
Newington, Ct., U.S.	C5	84
Newington, Ga., U.S.	D5	87
Newington, Va., U.S.	*B5	123
New Inlet, b., N.C., U.S.	D5	110
New Inn, Ire.	E4	11
New Ipswich, N.H., U.S.	E3	106
New Ireland, i., Pap. N. Gui.	h13	50
New Jersey, state, U.S.	C4	107
New Johnsonville, Tn., U.S.	A4	119
New Kensington, Pa., U.S.	E2	115
New Kent, Va., U.S.	C5	123
New Kent, co., Va., U.S.	C5	123
Newkirk, N.M., U.S.	B5	108
Newkirk, Ok., U.S.	A4	113
New Knoxville, Oh., U.S.	B1	112
New Kowloon, H.K.	*G7	31
New Laguna, N.M., U.S.	B2	108
New Lake, l., N.C., U.S.	B6	110
Newland, N.C., U.S.	A1	110
New Lebanon, In., U.S.	E2	91
New Lebanon, N.Y., U.S.	C7	109
New Leipzig, N.D., U.S.	C4	111
New Lenox, Il., U.S.	B6	90
New Lexington, Oh., U.S.	C3	112
New Liberty, Ky., U.S.	B5	94
New Lima, Ok., U.S.	B5	113
New Limerick, Me., U.S.	B5	96
New Lisbon, In., U.S.	E7	91
New Lisbon, N.J., U.S.	D3	107
New Lisbon, Wi., U.S.	E3	126
New Liskeard, Ont.	p20	73
New Llano, La., U.S.	C2	95
Newllano, W.V., U.S.	C4	125
New London, Ct., U.S.	D7	84
New London, Ia., U.S.	D6	92
New London, Mn., U.S.	E4	100
New London, Mo., U.S.	B6	102
New London, N.H., U.S.	D3	106
New London, N.C., U.S.	B2	110
New London, Oh., U.S.	A3	112
New London, Wi., U.S.	D5	126
New London, co., Ct., U.S.	C7	84
New London Submarine Base, mil., U.S.	D7	84
New Lothrop, Mi., U.S.	E7	99
New Lowell, Ont.	C5	73
New Madison, Oh., U.S.	C1	112
New Madrid, Mo., U.S.	E8	102
New Madrid, co., Mo., U.S.	E8	102
New Market, Austl.	D2	50
Newman, Ca., U.S.	D3	82
Newman, Il., U.S.	D6	90
Newman, Ks., U.S.	k15	93
Newman Lake, l., Wa., U.S.	B8	124
Newman Grove, Ne., U.S.	C8	104
Newman Lake, l., Wa., U.S.	B8	124
Newmanstown, Pa., U.S.	F9	115
Newmarket, Ont.	C5	73
Newmarket, Ire.	E2	11
Newmarket, Eng., U.K.	B8	12
New Market, Al., U.S.	A3	78
New Market, Ia., U.S.	D3	92
New Market, In., U.S.	E4	91
New Market, Md., U.S.	B3	97
New Market, Mn., U.S.	F5	100
New Market, N.H., U.S.	D5	106
New Market, Tn., U.S.	C10	119
New Market, Va., U.S.	B4	123
Newmarket on Fergus, Ire.	E3	11
New Marlboro, Ma., U.S.	B1	98
New Marshfield, Oh., U.S.	C3	112
New Martinsville, W.V., U.S.	B4	125
New Matamoras, Oh., U.S.	C4	112
New Meadows, Id., U.S.	D2	89
New Melle, Mo., U.S.	C7	102
New Mexico, state, U.S.	C3	108
New Miami, Oh., U.S.	C1	112
New Middletown, In., U.S.	H5	91
New Milford, Ct., U.S.	C2	84
New Milford, N.J., U.S.	h8	107
New Milford, Pa., U.S.	C10	115
New Mills, N.B.	B3	71
New Milton, W.V., U.S.	B4	125
New Minden, Il., U.S.	E4	90
New Munich, Mn., U.S.	E4	100
New Munster, Wi., U.S.	n11	126
Newnan, Ga., U.S.	C2	87
Newnans Lake, l., Fl., U.S.	C4	86
Newnata, Ar., U.S.	B3	81
New Norfolk, Austl.	o15	50
New Norway, Alta.	C4	68
New Offenburg, Mo., U.S.	D7	102
New Orleans, La., U.S.	E5	95
New Orleans Naval Air Station, mil., La., U.S.	k11	95
New Osgoode, Sask.	E4	75
New Oxford, Pa., U.S.	G7	115
New Palestine, In., U.S.	E6	91
New Paltz, N.Y., U.S.	D6	109
New Paris, In., U.S.	B6	91
New Paris, Oh., U.S.	C1	112
New Paris, Pa., U.S.	F4	115
New Perlican, Newf.	E5	72
New Philadelphia, Oh., U.S.	B4	112
New Philadelphia, Pa., U.S.	E9	115
New Pine Creek, Ca., U.S.	B3	82
New Pine Creek, Or., U.S.	E6	114
New Plymouth, N.Z.	M15	51
New Plymouth, Id., U.S.	F2	89
New Plymouth, Oh., U.S.	C3	112
New Point, In., U.S.	F7	91
New Point, Mo., U.S.	A2	102
New Point Comfort, c., Va., U.S.	C6	123
New Port, Neth. Ant.	H19	65
Newport, Ire.	D2	11
Newport, Eng., U.K.	E6	10
Newport, Eng., U.K.	B5	12
Newport, Wales, U.K.	E5	10
Newport, Ar., U.S.	B4	81
Newport, De., U.S.	B3	85
Newport, Fl., U.S.	B2	86
Newport, In., U.S.	E3	91
Newport, Ky., U.S.	A5	94
Newport, Me., U.S.	D3	96
Newport, Mi., U.S.	G7	99
Newport, Mn., U.S.	n13	100
Newport, N.H., U.S.	D2	106
Newport, N.J., U.S.	E2	107
Newport, N.Y., U.S.	B5	109
Newport, N.C., U.S.	C6	110
Newport, Oh., U.S.	C4	112
Newport, Or., U.S.	C2	114
Newport, Pa., U.S.	F7	115
Newport, R.I., U.S.	F5	116
Newport, S.C., U.S.	B5	117
Newport, Tn., U.S.	D10	119
Newport, Tx., U.S.	C3	120
Newport, Vt., U.S.	B4	122
Newport, Va., U.S.	C2	123
Newport, Wa., U.S.	A8	124
Newport, co., R.I., U.S.	E5	116
Newport Beach, Ca., U.S.	n13	82
Newport Hills, Wa., U.S.	*e11	124
New Portland, Me., U.S.	D2	96
Newport News, Va., U.S.	D6	123
New Port Richey, Fl., U.S.	D4	86
Newport Station, N.S.	E5	71
New Prague, Mn., U.S.	F5	100
New Preston, Ct., U.S.	C2	84
New Providence, Ia., U.S.	B4	92
New Providence, N.J., U.S.	B4	107
New Providence, i., Bah.	B5	64
Newquay, Eng., U.K.	E4	10
New Quay, Wales, U.K.	B3	12
New Raymer, Co., U.S.	A7	83
New Richland, Mn., U.S.	G5	100
New Richmond, Que.	A4	71
New Richmond, In., U.S.	D4	91
New Richmond, Oh., U.S.	D1	112
New Richmond, Wi., U.S.	C1	126
New Riegel, Oh., U.S.	A2	112
New River, Az., U.S.	D3	80
New River, Tn., U.S.	C9	119
New River Gorge, val., W.V., U.S.	m13	125
New River Inlet, b., N.C., U.S.	C5	110
New River Station, N.C., U.S.	*C5	110
New Road, N.S.	D6	71
New Roads, La., U.S.	D4	95
New Rochelle, N.Y., U.S.	E7	109
New Rockford, N.D., U.S.	B6	111
New Ross, N.S.	E5	71
New Ross, Ire.	E3	11
Newry, N. Ire., U.K.	C6	11
Newry, Me., U.S.	D2	96
Newry, S.C., U.S.	B2	117
New Salem, N.D., U.S.	C4	111
New Salem, Ks., U.S.	E7	93
New Salem, Ma., U.S.	A3	98
New Salem, Pa., U.S.	G2	115
New Sarepta, Alta.	C4	68
New Sarpy, La., U.S.	k11	95
New Sharon, Ia., U.S.	C5	92
New Sharon, Me., U.S.	D2	96
New Sharon, N.J., U.S.	C3	107
New Siberian Islands, is., Sov. Un.	B18	29
New Site, Al., U.S.	B4	78
New Site, Ms., U.S.	A5	101
New Smyrna Beach, Fl., U.S.	C6	86
New South Wales, state, Austl.	F8	50
New Straitsville, Oh., U.S.	C3	112
New Sweden, Me., U.S.	B4	96
New Tazwell, Tn., U.S.	C10	119
New Toronto (part of Etobicoke), Ont.	m14	73
Newtok, Ak., U.S.	C7	79
New Town, N.D., U.S.	B3	111
Newtown, Newf.	D5	72
Newtown, Wales, U.K.	D5	10
Newtown, Ct., U.S.	D2	84
Newtown, In., U.S.	D3	91
Newtown, Mo., U.S.	A4	102
Newtown, Oh., U.S.	C1	112
Newtown, Pa., U.S.	F12	115
Newtown, Va., U.S.	C5	123
Newtownabbey, N. Ire., U.K.	C6	11
Newtownards, N. Ire., U.K.	C4	10
Newtown Crommelin, N. Ire., U.K.	C5	11
Newtownhamilton, N. Ire., U.K.	C5	11
Newtown Mount Kennedy, Ire.	D5	11
Newtown Square, Pa., U.S.	p20	115
Newtownstewart, N. Ire., U.K.	C4	11
New Trenton, In., U.S.	F8	91
New Ulm, Mn., U.S.	F4	100
New Ulm, Tx., U.S.	E4	120
New Underwood, S.D., U.S.	C3	118
New Vienna, Ia., U.S.	B6	92
New Vienna, Oh., U.S.	C2	112
New Village, N.J., U.S.	B3	107
Newville, Al., U.S.	D4	78
Newville, Pa., U.S.	F7	115
Newville, W.V., U.S.	C4	125
New Vineyard, Me., U.S.	D2	96
New Virginia, Ia., U.S.	C4	92
New Washington, In., U.S.	G6	91
New Washington, Oh., U.S.	B3	112
New Washoe City, Nv., U.S.	*D2	105
New Waterford, N.S.	C9	71
New Waterford, Oh., U.S.	B5	112
New Waverly, In., U.S.	C5	91
New Waverly, Tx., U.S.	D5	120
New Westminster, B.C.	E6	69
New Whiteland, In., U.S.	D5	91
New Wilmington, Pa., U.S.	D1	115
New Windsor, Il., U.S.	B3	90
New Windsor, Md., U.S.	A3	97
New Windsor, N.Y., U.S.	D6	109
New Woodstock, N.Y., U.S.	C5	109
New World Island, i., Newf.	D4	72
New York, N.Y., U.S.	k13	109
New York, co., N.Y., U.S.	k13	109
New York Mills, Mn., U.S.	D3	100
New York Mills, N.Y., U.S.		
New Zealand, ctry., Oc.	N14	51
New Zion, S.C., U.S.	D7	117
Ney, Oh., U.S.	A1	112
Neya, Sov. Un.	B2	28
Neye Island, i., Guam	M9	52
Ney Lake, l., Can.	C5	70
Neyrīz, Iran	C5	38
Neyshābūr, Iran	A6	38
Nezhin, Sov. Un.	F5	8
Nezperce, Id., U.S.	*C2	89
Nez Perce, co., Id., U.S.	*C2	89
Nez Perce Indian Reservation, Id., U.S.	C2	89
Nezpique, Bayou, stm., La., U.S.	D3	95
Ngabang, Indon.	E3	34
Ngabé, Congo	B2	48
Ngala, Nig.	F7	45
Ngami, Lake, l., Bots.	B3	49
Nganglong Ringco, l., China	D7	36
Ngangzê Lake, l., China	B11	37
Ngaoundéré, Cam.	G8	45
Ngara, Tan.	B5	48
Ngaruangl Reef, rf., Palau	R17	52
Ngaruawahia, N.Z.	M16	51
Ngatapa, N.Z.	M16	51
Ngatik Islands, is., ...	R17	52
Ngemelis Islands, is., Palau	R17	52
Ngeregekabou, i., Palau	R17	52
Ngeremlengui, Palau	R17	52
Ngermechau, Palau	R17	52
Ngeruktabel, i., Palau	R17	52
Ngetbong, Palau	R17	52
Ngetkib, Palau	R17	52
Ngong, Kenya	B6	48
Ngoring Hu, l., China	E6	30
Ngounié, stm., Gabon	F2	46
Nguigmi, Niger	F7	45
Nguru, Nig.	F7	45
Nhamundá, Braz.	C7	59
Nhamundá, stm., Braz.	C7	59
Nha Trang, Viet.	C3	34
Nhill, Austl.	H3	51
Nhulunbuy, Austl.	B6	50
Niafounké, Mali	D4	45
Niagara, N.D., U.S.	A8	111
Niagara, Wi., U.S.	C6	126
Niagara, co., Ont.	D5	73
Niagara, co., N.Y., U.S.	B2	109
Niagara, stm., N.A.	B1	109
Niagara Falls, Ont.	D5	73
Niagara Falls, N.Y., U.S.	B1	109
Niagara-on-the-Lake, Ont.	D5	73
Niagara Town, N.Y., U.S.	*B2	109
Niamey, Niger	D5	45
Niamtougou, Togo	E5	45
Niangara, Zaire	A4	48
Niangua, Mo., U.S.	D5	102
Niangua, stm., Mo., U.S.	D5	102
Niantic, Ct., U.S.	D7	84
Niarada, Mt., U.S.	C2	103
Nias, i., Indon.	E1	34
Niassa, dept., Moz.	D6	48
Nibe, Den.	B3	15
Nibley, Ut., U.S.	B4	121
Nicaragua, ctry., N.A.	E7	63
Nicaragua, Lago de, l., Nic.	E7	63
Nicastro (Lamezia Terme), Italy	E6	23
Nicatous Lake, l., Me., U.S.	C4	96
Nice, Fr.	F7	16
Niceville, Fl., U.S.	u15	86
Nichicun, Lac, l., Que.	h12	74
Nichinan, Japan	K5	33
Nicholas, co., Ky., U.S.	B6	94
Nicholas, co., W.V., U.S.	C4	125
Nicholas Channel, strt., N.A.	C3	64
Nicholasville, Ky., U.S.	C5	94
Nichols, Ia., U.S.	C6	92
Nichols, Mo., U.S.	D4	102
Nichols, N.Y., U.S.	C4	109
Nichols, S.C., U.S.	C9	117
Nichols Hills, Ok., U.S.	B4	113
Nicholson, Ms., U.S.	E4	101
Nicholson, Pa., U.S.	C10	115
Nicholson, stm., Austl.	C6	50
Nicholville, N.Y., U.S.	f10	109
Nickajack Lake, res., Tn., U.S.	D8	119
Nickel Centre, Ont.	p19	73
Nickelsville, Va., U.S.	f9	123
Nickerie, dept., Sur.	B3	59
Nickerie, stm., Sur.	A3	59
Nickerson, Ks., U.S.	D5	93
Nickerson, Ne., U.S.	C9	104
Nickerson Hill, hill, Ct., U.S.	D6	84
Nicobar Islands, is., India	G9	36
Nicodemus, Ks., U.S.	C4	93
Nicola, B.C.	D7	69
Nicola, stm., B.C.	D7	69
Nicolet, Que.	C5	74
Nicolet, co., Que.	C5	74
Nicolet, stm., Que.	C5	74
Nicollet, Lake, l., Mi., U.S.	B6	99
Nicollet, Mn., U.S.	F4	100
Nicollet, co., Mn., U.S.	F4	100
Nicolls Town, Bah.	B4	64
Nicosia (Levkosía / Lefkoşa), Cyp.	E9	40
Nicosia [Sicilia], Italy	F5	23
Nicotera, Italy	E5	23
Nicoya, C.R.	E7	63
Nicoya, Golfo de, b., C.R.	F5	62
Nicoya, Península de, pen., C.R.	F7	63
Nictaux Falls, N.S.	E4	71
Nida, stm., Pol.	C6	26
Nid à l'Aigle, Cap du, c., St. P./M.	E3	72
Nidau Rock, hill, Japan	P17	52
Nidd, stm., Eng., U.K.	F7	13
Nidda, Ger.	C3	19
Nidda, stm., Ger.	C4	19
Nidwalden, state, Switz.	C4	20
Nidzica, Pol.	B6	26
Niebüll, Ger.	D2	15
Niederbronn-les-Bains, Fr.	F7	17
Niedermarsberg, Ger.	B3	19
Niedersachsen, state, Ger.	F3	15
Nielsville, Mn., U.S.	C2	100
Nienburg, Ger.	B4	18
Niemodlin, Pol.	C4	26
Niers, stm., Eur.	C6	17
Niesky, Ger.	B9	19
Niesse, Pol.	B5	26
Nietleben, Ger.	B6	19
Nieuw Amsterdam, Sur.	A3	59
Nieuwegein, Neth.	*B5	17
Nieuweroord, Neth.	B6	17
Nieuw Nickerie, Sur.	A3	59
Nieuwpoort, Bel.	C2	17
Nigadoo, N.B.	B4	71
Nigel, ctry., Afr.	C4	69
Niger, ctry., Afr.	E6	45
Niger, stm., Afr.	E6	45
Niger Delta, Nig.	F6	45
Nigeria, ctry., Afr.	E6	45
Nighthawk, Wa., U.S.	A6	124
Nihing, stm., Asia	H11	39
Nihoa, i., Hi., U.S.	m15	88
Nihoa, i., Hi., U.S.	D12	31
Niigata, Japan	J6	33
Niihau, i., Hi., U.S.	B1	88
Nii Island, i., Japan	I9	33
Niimi, Japan	I6	33
Nijar, Spain	D4	22
Nijkerk, Neth.	B5	17
Nijmegen, Neth.	B6	16
Nikaia, Grc.	*D4	25
Nikep, Md., U.S.	k13	97
Nikikis, Ak., U.S.	g16	79
Nikitinka, Sov. Un.	D9	27
Nikitovka, Sov. Un.	q21	27
Nikki, Benin	E5	45
Nikkō, Japan	D12	31
Nikolayev, Sov. Un.	E6	8
Nikolayevsk [-na-Amure], Sov. Un.	D17	29
Nikolsk, Sov. Un.	B3	28
Nikolsk, Sov. Un.	A5	28
Nikonovskoye, Sov. Un.	n18	27
Nikopol, Bul.	H10	24
Nikopol', Sov. Un.	B11	40
Nikshahr, Iran	H10	39
Nikšić, Yugo.	D4	24
Niland, Ca., U.S.	F6	82
Nile, stm., Afr.	C12	45
Niles, Ca., U.S.	h9	82
Niles, Il., U.S.	h9	90
Niles, Mi., U.S.	G4	99
Niles, Oh., U.S.	A5	112
Nilwood, Il., U.S.	D4	90
Nīmach, India	E5	37

Name	Map Ref.	Page
Nimba, Mont, mtn., Afr.	E3	45
Nimba Mountains, mts., Afr.	E3	45
Nîmes, Fr.	F6	16
Nimmons, Ar., U.S.	A5	81
Nimpkish, stm., B.C.	D4	69
Nimrod Glacier, ice, Ant.	A29	7
Nimrod Lake, res., Ar., U.S.	C2	81
Nimule, Sud.	E3	47
Ninemile Creek, stm., Ks., U.S.	k15	93
Nine Mile Creek, stm., Ut., U.S.	D5	121
Nine Mile Falls, Wa., U.S.	g13	124
Ninemile Point, c., Mi., U.S.	C6	99
Ninette, Man.	E2	70
Ninety Mile Beach, Austl.	G8	50
Ninety Six, S.C., U.S.	C3	117
Nineveh, Pa., U.S.	G1	115
Nineveh, hist., Iraq	B4	38
Ninga, Man.	E2	70
Ning'an, China	C10	31
Ningbo, China	F9	31
Ningde, China	F8	31
Ningdu, China	K6	32
Ninghai, China	J9	32
Ninghua, China	K7	32
Ningjin, China	F6	32
Ningming, China	A7	35
Ningqiang, China	H2	32
Ningsia Hui see Ningxia Huizu, prov., China	D6	31
Ningwu, China	D7	31
Ningxia Huizu, prov., China	D6	31
Ningxian, China	D6	31
Ninh Binh, Viet.	A3	34
Niniget Pond, l., R.I., U.S.	G2	116
Ninilchik, Ak., U.S.	C9	79
Ninnekah, Ok., U.S.	C4	113
Ninnescah, stm., Ks., U.S.	E6	93
Ninnescah, North Fork, stm., Ks., U.S.	E5	93
Ninnescah, South Fork, stm., Ks., U.S.	E5	93
Ninnis Glacier, ice, Ant.	C27	7
Ninole, Hi., U.S.	D6	88
Ninove, Bel.	D4	17
Nioaque, Braz.	C1	56
Niobe, N.D., U.S.	A3	111
Niobrara, co., Wy., U.S.	C8	127
Niobrara, stm., U.S.	B7	104
Nioki, Zaire	B2	48
Nioro, Mali	A3	45
Nioro du Rip, Sen.	D1	45
Nioro du Sahel, Mali	C3	45
Niort, Fr.	D3	16
Niota, Tn., U.S.	D9	119
Niotaze, Ks., U.S.	E7	93
Nipawin, Sask.	D4	75
Nipawin Provincial Park, Sask.	C3	75
Nipekamew Lake, l., Sask.	C3	75
Nipew Lake, l., Sask.	B3	75
Nipigon, Ont.	o17	73
Nipigon, Lake, l., Ont.	o17	73
Nipishish Lake, l., Newf.	g9	72
Nipissing, dept., Ont.	A6	73
Nipissing, Lake, l., Ont.	A5	73
Nipomo, Ca., U.S.	E3	82
Nippers Harbour, Newf.	D4	72
Nipple Mountain, mtn., Co., U.S.	D2	83
Nipton, Ca., U.S.	E6	82
Niquelândia, Braz.	A3	56
Niquero, Cuba	D5	64
Nirasaki, Japan	n17	33
Nirmal, India	H7	37
Nirmāli, India	D11	37
Niš, Yugo.	D5	24
Nisa, Port.	C2	22
Nišava, stm., Eur.	D6	24
Nishinomiya, Japan	*I7	33
Nishio, Japan	o16	33
Niskayuna, N.Y., U.S.	C7	109
Nisland, S.D., U.S.	C2	118
Nisqually, stm., Wa., U.S.	C3	124
Nissan, Swe.	H8	15
Nissum Bredning, b., Den.	B2	15
Nissum Fjord, Den.	B2	15
Nisswa, Mn., U.S.	D4	100
Nistowiak Lake, l., Sask.	B3	75
Nisula, Mi., U.S.	B2	99
Niterói, Braz.	C4	56
Nith, stm., Scot., U.K.	E5	13
Nitra, Czech.	D5	26
Nitra, stm., Czech.	D5	26
Nitro, W.V., U.S.	C3	125
Nitta Yuma, Ms., U.S.	B3	101
Nittenau, Ger.	D7	19
Niue, ctry., Oc.	H11	6
Nivelles, Bel.	B6	16
Nivernais, hist. reg., Fr.	D5	16
Nivernais, Côtes du, hills, Fr.	D5	16
Niverville, Man.	E3	70
Nivskiy, Sov. Un.	D15	14
Niwot, Co., U.S.	A5	83
Nixa, Mo., U.S.	D4	102
Nixburg, Al., U.S.	C3	78
Nixon, Nv., U.S.	D2	105
Nixon, Tx., U.S.	B3	119
Nixon, Tx., U.S.	E4	120
Nizāmābād, India	H7	37
Nizām Sāgar, res., India	H7	37
Nīzgān, Afg.	E11	39
Nizhnozero, Sov. Un.	E18	14
Nizhnekamsk, Sov. Un.	*D8	27
Nizhnekolymsk, Sov. Un.	C19	29
Nizhne-Leninskoye, Sov. Un.	C6	33
Nizhneudinsk, Sov. Un.	D12	29
Nizhneye, Sov. Un.	q21	27
Nizhniy Chir, Sov. Un.	G14	27
Nizhniy Lomov, Sov. Un.	E14	27
Nizhniy Novgorod	D7	29
Nizhniy Pyandzh, Sov. Un.	H22	8
Nizhniy Tagil, Sov. Un.	D9	29
Nizhnyaya Tunguska, stm., Sov. Un.	C12	29
Nizhnyaya Tura, Sov. Un.	D21	8
Nizip, Tur.	*D11	40
Nizmennyy, Cape, c., Sov. Un.	E7	33
Nizza Monferrato, Italy	E3	20
Njazidja, i., Com.	D6	41
Njazidja, Nabal, mtn.,	D6	41
Njombe, Tan.	C6	48
Njurunda, Swe.	F7	14
Nkambe, Cam.	D2	46
Nkayi, Zimb.	A4	49
Nkhata Bay, Mwi.	D5	48
Nkhota Kota, Mwi.	D5	48
Nkongsamba, Cam.	E1	46
Nnewi, Nig.	E6	45
Noākhāli, Bngl.	F13	37
Noank, Ct., U.S.	D8	84
Noasca, Italy	D3	20
Noatak, Ak., U.S.	B7	79
Noatak, stm., Ak., U.S.	B7	79
Nobel, Ont.	B4	73
Nobeoka, Japan	J5	33
Noble, Ga., U.S.	B1	87
Noble, Il., U.S.	E5	90
Noble, La., U.S.	C2	95
Noble, Ok., U.S.	B4	113
Noble, co., In., U.S.	B7	91
Noble, co., Ok., U.S.	C4	112
Noble, co., Oh., U.S.	A4	113
Nobleboro, Me., U.S.	D3	96
Nobles, co., Mn., U.S.	G3	100
Noblesville, In., U.S.	D6	91
Nobleton, Fl., U.S.	D4	86
Noboribetsu, Japan	E10	33
Nobscot Hill, hill, Ma., U.S.	B5	98
Nocatee, Fl., U.S.	E5	86
Nocona, Tx., U.S.	C4	120
Nodaway, Ia., U.S.	D3	92
Nodaway, co., Mo., U.S.	A3	102
Nodaway, stm., U.S.	A2	102
Node, Wy., U.S.	D8	127
Noel, Mo., U.S.	E3	102
Noel Paul's Brook, stm., Newf.	D3	72
Noelville, Ont.	A4	73
Nogal, N.M., U.S.	D4	108
Nogales, Mex.	n15	63
Nogales, Az., U.S.	F5	80
Nogara, Italy	D7	20
Nōgata, Japan	J5	33
Nogent-en-Bassigny, Fr.	C6	16
Nogent-le-Rotrou, Fr.	C4	16
Nogent [-sur-Marne], Fr.	g10	16
Nogent-sur-Seine, Fr.	C5	16
Noginsk, Sov. Un.	D12	27
Nogoa, stm., Austl.	B6	51
Nogoyá, Arg.	A5	54
Nohar, India	C5	36
Noheji, Japan	F10	33
Noirmoutier, Île de, i., Fr.	D2	16
Noisy-le-Sec, Fr.	g10	16
Nojima, Cape, c., Japan	I9	33
Nokesville, Va., U.S.	B5	123
Nok Kundi, Pak.	G11	39
Nokomis, Sask.	F3	75
Nokomis, Fl., U.S.	E4	86
Nokomis, Il., U.S.	D4	90
Nokomis, Lake, res., Wi., U.S.	C4	126
Nokou, Chad	B2	48
Nola, Cen. Afr. Rep.	E3	46
Nola, Italy	D5	23
Nola, Ms., U.S.	D3	101
Nolan, Tx., U.S.	C2	120
Nolan, W.V., U.S.	D2	125
Nolan, co., Tx., U.S.	C2	120
Nolensville, Tn., U.S.	B5	119
Nolichucky, stm., Tn., U.S.	C10	119
Nolin, stm., Ky., U.S.	C3	94
Nolin Lake, res., Ky., U.S.	C3	94
Nolin Point, Newf.	D3	72
Nolinsk, Sov. Un.	B3	28
Noma, Fl., U.S.	u16	86
Noma, Cape, c., Japan	K5	33
Nomans Land, i., Ma., U.S.	D6	98
Nombre de Dios, Pan.	h12	62
Nome, Ak., U.S.	C6	79
Nome, N.D., U.S.	C8	111
Noménny, Fr.	F6	17
Nomgon, Mong.	C1	32
Nominingue, Que.	C2	74
Nomoneas, is., Micron.	Q18	52
Nonacho Lake, l., N.W. Ter.	D11	66
Nondalton, Ak., U.S.	C8	79
Nonesuch, stm., Me., U.S.	g7	96
Nong'an, China	C10	31
Nong Khai, Thai.	B2	34
Nongoma, S. Afr.	C5	49
Nonoava, Mex.	B3	63
Nonquit Pond, l., R.I., U.S.	E6	116
Nooksack, Wa., U.S.	A3	124
Nooksack, North Fork, stm., Wa., U.S.	A4	124
Nooksack, South Fork, stm., Wa., U.S.	A3	124
Noonan, N.D., U.S.	A2	111
Noone, N.H., U.S.	E3	106
Noordpunt, c., Neth. Ant.	H18	65
Noordwijk-Binnen, Neth.	B4	17
Noorvik, Ak., U.S.	B7	79
Nootka Island, i., B.C.	E4	69
Nootka Sound, strt., B.C.	E4	69
Nopiming Provincial Park, Man.	D4	70
No Point, Point, c., Md., U.S.	D5	97
Noquebay, Lake, l., Wi., U.S.	C6	126
Nóqui, Ang.	C1	48
Nora, Sask.	E4	75
Nora, Swe.	H6	14
Nora, Il., U.S.	A4	90
Noranda, Que.	k11	74
Nora Springs, Ia., U.S.	A5	92
Norbertville, Que.	C6	74
Norborne, Mo., U.S.	B4	102
Norcatur, Ks., U.S.	C3	93
Norco, Ca., U.S.	*n13	82
Norco, La., U.S.	D5	95
Norcross, Ga., U.S.	C2	87
Norcross, Mn., U.S.	E2	100
Nord, dept., Fr.	D2	17
Nord, Canal du, Fr.	D3	17
Nordborg, Den.	C3	15
Nordby, Den.	C4	15
Nordby, Den.	C2	68
Nordegg, stm., Alta.	C3	68
Norden, Ger.	B4	18
Nordenham, Ger.	B4	18
Nordenskjöld Archipelago, is., Sov. Un.	B4	128
Nordenskjöld Ice Tongue, ice, Ant.	e39	7
Norderney, Ger.	A7	17
Norderney, i., Ger.	B3	18
Norderstedt, Ger.	*B5	18
Nordfjord, Nor.	G1	14
Nordhausen, Ger.	C5	18
Nordhorn, Ger.	B3	15
Nordjylland, co., Den.	B3	15
Nordland, Wa., U.S.	B3	124
Nordland, co., Nor.	D5	18
Nordmaling, Swe.	E5	14
Nordman, Id., U.S.	A2	89
Nordostrundingen, c., Grnld.	A19	61
Nordreisa, Nor.	C9	14
Nordrhein-Westfalen, state, Ger.	B7	19
Nordstrand, i., Ger.	A4	18
Nore, stm., Ire.	D3	10
Norene, Tn., U.S.	A5	119
Norfolk, Ct., U.S.	B3	84
Norfolk, Ma., U.S.	h10	98
Norfolk, Ne., U.S.	B8	104
Norfolk, N.Y., U.S.	f9	109
Norfolk, Va., U.S.	D6	123
Norfolk, co., Ont.	E4	73
Norfolk, co., Eng., U.K.	B8	12
Norfolk, co., Ma., U.S.	B5	98
Norfolk Island, dep., Oc.	H10	6
Norfolk Island, dep., Oc., U.S.		
Norfolk Naval Base, mil., Va., U.S.	k15	123
Norfolk Naval Shipyard, mil., Va., U.S.	k15	123
Norfolk, Ar., U.S.	A3	81
Norfork Dam, Ar., U.S.	A3	81
Norfork Lake, res., U.S.	A3	81
Norge, Ok., U.S.	C4	113
Norias, Tx., U.S.	F4	120
Norilsk, Sov. Un.	C11	29
Norland, Fl., U.S.	s13	86
Norlina, N.C., U.S.	A4	110
Norma, N.J., U.S.	E2	107
Norma, N.D., U.S.	A4	111
Norma, Tn., U.S.	C9	119
Normal, Al., U.S.	A3	78
Normal, Il., U.S.	C5	90
Norman, Ar., U.S.	C2	81
Norman, Ne., U.S.	D7	104
Norman, N.C., U.S.	B3	110
Norman, Ok., U.S.	B4	113
Norman, co., Mn., U.S.	C2	100
Norman, Lake, res., N.C., U.S.	B2	110
Normanby, stm., Austl.	B7	50
Normandy, Mo., U.S.	f13	102
Normandy, Tn., U.S.	B5	119
Normandy, Hills of, hills, Fr.	C3	16
Normandy Beach, N.J., U.S.	C4	107
Normangee, Tx., U.S.	D4	120
Norman Island, i., V.I., Br.	B6	65
Norman Park, Ga., U.S.	E3	87
Normanton, Austl.	C7	50
Normantown, Ga., U.S.	D4	87
Norman Wells, N.W. Ter.	C7	66
Norphlet, Ar., U.S.	D3	81
Norquay, Sask.	F4	75
Norquincó, Arg.	C2	54
Norrahammar, Swe.	A8	15
Norridge, Il., U.S.	k9	90
Norridgewock, Me., U.S.	D3	96
Norris, Il., U.S.	B4	90
Norris, Mt., U.S.	E5	103
Norris, S.C., U.S.	B2	117
Norris, S.D., U.S.	D4	118
Norris, Tn., U.S.	C9	119
Norris Arm, Newf.	D4	72
Norris City, Il., U.S.	F5	90
Norris Dam, Tn., U.S.	C9	119
Norris Lake, res., Tn., U.S.	C10	119
Norris Point, Newf.	D3	72
Norristown, Pa., U.S.	F11	115
Norrisville, Md., U.S.	A4	97
Norrköping, Swe.	H7	14
Norrtälje, Swe.	H8	14
Norseman, Austl.	F3	50
Norte, Cabo, c., Braz.	B5	59
Norte, Canal do, strt., Braz.	B4	59
Norte, Punta, c., Arg.	C4	54
Norte, Serra do, plat., Braz.	E3	59
Norte de Santander, dept., Col.	B3	60
Nortelândia, Braz.	A1	56
North, S.C., U.S.	D5	117
North, Va., U.S.	C6	123
North, stm., Newf.	B3	72
North, stm., Al., U.S.	B2	78
North, stm., Ia., U.S.	f8	92
North, stm., Ma., U.S.	h12	98
North, stm., W.V., U.S.	B6	125
North, Cape, c., N.S.	B9	71
North Abington, Ma., U.S.	B6	98
North Acton, Ma., U.S.	f10	98
North Adams, Ma., U.S.	A1	98
North Adams, Mi., U.S.	G6	99
North Albany, Or., U.S.	k11	114
North Amherst, Ma., U.S.	B2	98
North Amity, Me., U.S.	C5	96
North Amityville, N.Y., U.S.	*n15	109
Northampton, Austl.	E1	50
Northampton, Eng., U.K.	D6	10
Northampton, Ma., U.S.	B2	98
Northampton, Pa., U.S.	E11	115
Northampton, co., N.C., U.S.	A5	110
Northampton, co., Pa., U.S.	E11	115
Northamptonshire, co., Eng., U.K.	B7	12
North Andaman, i., India	F9	36
North and Bent Pyramids, hist., Egypt	E3	41
North Andover Gardens, Fl., U.S.	r13	86
North Andover, Ma., U.S.	A5	98
North Anna, stm., Va., U.S.	B5	123
North Anson, Me., U.S.	D3	96
North Apollo, Pa., U.S.	E2	115
North Arapaho Peak, mtn., Co., U.S.	A5	83
North Arlington, N.J., U.S.	h8	107
North Atlanta, Ga., U.S.	h8	87
North Attleboro, Ma., U.S.	C5	98
North Auburn, Ca., U.S.	*C3	82
North Augusta, Ont.	C9	73
North Augusta, S.C., U.S.	D4	117
North Aulatsivik Island, i., Newf.	f9	72
North Aurora, Il., U.S.	k8	90
North Avondale, Co., U.S.	C6	83
North Babylon, N.Y., U.S.	*n15	109
North Baltimore, Oh., U.S.	A2	112
North Bangor, N.Y., U.S.	f10	109
North Battleford, Sask.	E1	75
North Bay, Ont.	A5	73
North Bay Shore, N.Y., U.S.	*n15	109
North Belgrade, Me., U.S.	D3	96
North Bellmore, N.Y., U.S.	*n15	109
North Bellport, N.Y., U.S.	*n16	109
North Belmont, N.C., U.S.	B1	110
North Bend, B.C.	E7	69
North Bend, Ne., U.S.	C9	104
North Bend, Oh., U.S.	o12	112
North Bend, Or., U.S.	D2	114
North Bend, Pa., U.S.	D6	115
North Bend, Wa., U.S.	B4	124
North Bend, Wi., U.S.	H10	6
North Bennington, Vt., U.S.	F2	122
North Bergen, N.J., U.S.	h8	107
North Berwick, Scot., U.K.	D6	13
North Berwick, Me., U.S.	E2	96
North Billerica, Ma., U.S.	A5	98
North Bloomfield, Oh., U.S.	A5	112
North Bonneville, Wa., U.S.	D4	124
North Borough, Ma., U.S.	B4	98
North Braddock, Pa., U.S.	*k14	115
North Bradford, Me., U.S.	C4	96
North Bradley, Mi., U.S.	E6	99
North Branch, Mn., U.S.	E7	99
North Branch, Mn., U.S.	E6	100
North Branch, N.H., U.S.	B3	107
North Branford, Ct., U.S.	D4	84
North Breakers, rf., Mid. Is.	J3	52
Northbridge, Ma., U.S.	B4	98
North Bridgton, Me., U.S.	D2	96
Northbrook, Ont.	C7	73
Northbrook, Il., U.S.	h9	90
Northbrook, Oh., U.S.	*n12	112
North Brookfield, Ma., U.S.	B3	98
North Brother, mtn., Me., U.S.	C4	96
North Brunswick, N.J., U.S.	C4	107
North Buena Vista, Ia., U.S.	B7	92
North Calais, Vt., U.S.	C4	122
North Caldwell, N.J., U.S.	B4	107
North Canadian, stm., Ok., U.S.	A5	113
North Canton, Ct., U.S.	B4	84
North Canton, Ga., U.S.	B2	87
North Canton, Oh., U.S.	B4	112
North Cape, Wi., U.S.	n11	126
North Cape, c., P.E.I.	B6	71
North Cape, c., N.Z.	K14	51
North Cape, c., Nor.	B11	14
North Cape May, N.J., U.S.	F3	107
North Carolina, state, U.S.	B3	110
North Carrollton, Ms., U.S.	B4	101
North Carver, Ma., U.S.	C6	98
North Cascades National Park, Wa., U.S.	A4	124
North Cay, i., Bah.	m17	64
North Channel, strt., Ont.	A2	73
North Channel, strt., U.K.	C3	10
North Charleston, S.C., U.S.	F8	117
North Charlestown, N.H., U.S.	D2	106
North Chatham, N.H., U.S.	B4	106
North Chicago, Il., U.S.	A6	90
North Chichester, N.H., U.S.	D4	106
North City, U.S.	*B3	124
North Clarendon, Vt., U.S.	D3	96
North Cohasset, Ma., U.S.	*h12	98
North Cohocton, N.Y., U.S.	C3	109
North College Hill, Oh., U.S.	o12	112
North Collins, N.Y., U.S.	C2	109
North Concord, Vt., U.S.	C5	122
North Conway, N.H., U.S.	B4	106
North Corbin, Ky., U.S.	D5	94
Northcote, Austl.	*G8	50
North Creek, N.Y., U.S.	B7	109
North Crossett, Ar., U.S.	D4	81
North Crows Nest, In., U.S.	k10	91
North Dakota, state, U.S.	B5	111
North Danville, N.H., U.S.	C4	122
North Dartmouth, Ma., U.S.	C6	98
North Decatur, Ga., U.S.	*h8	87
North Derby, Vt., U.S.	A4	122
North Dighton, Ma., U.S.	C5	98
North Dixmont, Me., U.S.	D3	96
North Downs, plat., Eng., U.K.	E7	10
North Druid Hills, Ga., U.S.	h8	87
North Eagle Butte, S.D., U.S.	B4	118
North East, Md., U.S.	A6	97
North East, Pa., U.S.	B2	115
Northeast, stm., Md., U.S.	A6	97
Northeast Cape, c., Ak., U.S.	C6	79
Northeast Cape Fear, stm., N.C., U.S.	C5	110
North Eastern, prov., Kenya	A6	48
North Eastham, Ma., U.S.	C8	98
Northeast Harbor, Me., U.S.	D4	96
Northeast Henrietta, N.Y., U.S.	B3	109
Northeast Islands, is., Micron.	q18	52
North East Land, i., Nor.	A13	128
North Easton, Ma., U.S.	B5	98
Northeast Point, c., Newf.	B4	72
Northeast Polder, reg., Neth.	B5	17
Northeast Pond, l., N.H., U.S.	D5	106
Northeast Providence Channel, strt., Bah.	B5	64
North Edisto, stm., S.C., U.S.	k11	117
North Egremont, Ma., U.S.	B1	98
North English, Ia., U.S.	C5	92
North English, stm., Ia., U.S.	C5	92
North Enid, Ok., U.S.	A4	113
North Fair Oaks, Ca., U.S.	*k8	82
North Falmouth, Ma., U.S.	C6	98
North Ferrisburg, Vt., U.S.	C2	122
Northfield, B.C.	f12	69
Northfield, Ct., U.S.	C3	84
Northfield, Il., U.S.	*h9	90
Northfield, Ma., U.S.	A3	98
Northfield, Mn., U.S.	F5	100
Northfield, N.H., U.S.	D3	106
Northfield, N.J., U.S.	E3	107
Northfield, Oh., U.S.	h9	112
Northfield, Vt., U.S.	C3	122
Northfield Center, Vt., U.S.	C3	122
Northfield Mountains, mts., Vt., U.S.	C3	122
North Fond du Lac, Wi., U.S.	E5	126
North Foreland, c., Eng. U.K.	E8	12
North Fork, Id., U.S.	D5	89
North Fork Reservoir, res., Or., U.S.	B4	114
North Berwick, Scot., U.K.	D6	13
North Fort Myers, Fl., U.S.	F5	86
North Fox Island, i., Mi., U.S.	C5	99
North Franklin, Ct., U.S.	C7	84
North Freedom, Wi., U.S.	E4	126
North Fryeburg, Me., U.S.	D2	96
Northgate, Sask.	H4	75
Northgate, N.D., U.S.	A3	111
Northglenn, Co., U.S.	B6	83
North Gorham, Me., U.S.	g7	96
North Gower, Ont.	B9	73
North Grafton, Ma., U.S.	B4	98
North Granby, Ct., U.S.	B4	84
North Great River, N.Y., U.S.	*n18	109
North Grosvenordale, Ct., U.S.	B8	84
North Gulf of Évvoia, b., Grc.	C4	25
North Gulfport, Ms., U.S.	E4	101
North Halawa Stream, stm., Hi., U.S.	g10	88
North Haledon, N.J., U.S.	B4	107
North Hampton, N.H., U.S.	E5	106
North Hanover, Ma., U.S.	h12	98
North Harpswell, Me., U.S.	g8	96
North Hartland, Vt., U.S.	D4	122
North Hartland Reservoir, res., Vt., U.S.	D4	122
North Hatfield, Ma., U.S.	B2	98
North Hatley, Que.	D6	74
North Haven, Ct., U.S.	D4	84
North Haven, Me., U.S.	D3	96
North Haverhill, N.H., U.S.	B2	106
North Head, N.B.	E3	71
North Henderson, Il., U.S.	B3	90
North Hero, Vt., U.S.	B2	122
North Hero Island, i., Vt., U.S.	B2	122
North Highlands, Ca., U.S.	*C3	82
North Hill, Wa., U.S.	*B3	124
North Holland (Noord-Holland), prov., Neth.	B4	17
North Holston, stm., U.S.	f10	123
North Hook Lake, l., Tn., U.S.	e8	119
North Horr, Kenya	A6	48
North Houston, Tx., U.S.	*E5	120
North Hudson, N.Y., U.S.	B7	109
North Hudson, Wi., U.S.	*C1	126
North Hyde Park, Vt., U.S.	B3	122
North Industry, Oh., U.S.	B4	112
North Inlet, b., S.C., U.S.	E9	117
North Island, i., N.Z.	M15	51
North Island, i., S.C., U.S.	E9	117
North Island Naval Air Station, mil., Ca., U.S.	o15	82
North Islands, is., La., U.S.	E7	95
North Java, N.Y., U.S.	C2	109
North Jay, Me., U.S.	D2	96
North Judson, In., U.S.	B4	91
North Kansas City, Mo., U.S.	h10	102
North Kingstown, R.I., U.S.	E4	116
North Kingsville, Oh., U.S.	A5	112
North Komelik, Az., U.S.	E4	80
North La Junta, Co., U.S.	C7	83
North Lake, Il., U.S.	k9	90
North Lake, Wi., U.S.	m11	126
North Laramie, stm., Wy., U.S.	D7	127
North Las Vegas, Nv., U.S.	G6	105
North Lauderdale, Fl., U.S.	*r13	86
North La Veta Pass, Co., U.S.	D5	83
North Lawrence, N.Y., U.S.	f10	109
North Lemmon, N.D., U.S.	D3	111
North Lewisburg, Oh., U.S.	B2	112
North Liberty, Ia., U.S.	A5	91
North Liberty, In., U.S.	C6	92
North Lima, Oh., U.S.	B5	112
North Lindenhurst, N.Y., U.S.	*n15	109
North Little Rock, Ar., U.S.	C3	81
North Logan, Ut., U.S.	B4	121
North Loon Mountain, mtn., Id., U.S.	D3	89
North Loup, Ne., U.S.	C7	104
North Loup, stm., Ne., U.S.	B5	104
North Lubec, Me., U.S.	D5	96
North Madison, Oh., U.S.	*A4	112
North Mamm Peak, mtn., Co., U.S.	B3	83
North Manchester, In., U.S.	C6	91
North Manitou Island, i., Mi., U.S.	C4	99
North Mankato, Mn., U.S.	F4	100
North Marshfield, Ma., U.S.	h12	98
North Massapequa, N.Y., U.S.	*E7	109
North Merrick, N.Y., U.S.	*n15	109
North Merrydale, La., U.S.	*D4	95
North Miami, Fl., U.S.	G6	86
North Miami, Ok., U.S.	A7	113
North Miami Beach, Fl., U.S.	s13	86
North Middleboro, Ma., U.S.	C6	98
North Middletown, Ky., U.S.	B5	94
North Monmouth, Me., U.S.	D2	96
North Montpelier, Vt., U.S.	C4	122
North Moose Lake, l., Man.	B1	70
North Mountain, mtn., U.S.	D9	115
North Muskegon, Mi., U.S.	E4	99
North Myrtle Beach, S.C., U.S.	D10	117
North Naples, Fl., U.S.	F5	86
North Negril Point, c., Jam.	E12	65
North Newcastle, Me., U.S.	D3	96
North Newport, N.H., U.S.	D2	106
North New Portland, Me., U.S.	D2	96
North New River Canal, Fl., U.S.	F6	86
North Norwich, N.Y., U.S.	C5	109
North Ogden, Ut., U.S.	B4	121
North Olmsted, Oh., U.S.	h9	112
North Omaha, Ne., U.S.	g13	104
Northome, Mn., U.S.	C4	100
North Orange, Ma., U.S.	A3	98
North Palisade, mtn., Ca., U.S.	D4	82
North Palm Beach, Fl., U.S.	*F6	86
North Park, Il., U.S.	A4	90
North Park, val., Co., U.S.	A4	83
North Parsonfield, Me., U.S.	E2	96
North Pass, strt., La., U.S.	E7	95
North Patchogue, N.Y., U.S.	*n15	109
North Pembroke, Ma., U.S.	B6	98
North Pitcher, N.Y., U.S.	C5	109
North Plainfield, N.J., U.S.	B4	107
North Plains, Or., U.S.	B4	114
North Plains, pl., N.M., U.S.	C1	108
North Platte, Ne., U.S.	C5	104
North Platte, stm., U.S.	B7	76
North Point, c., Barb.	K20	65
North Point, c., Md., U.S.	B5	97
North Point, c., Md., U.S.	C5	97
North Point, c., Mi., U.S.	C7	99
North Pole	A1	128
North Pomfret, Vt., U.S.	D4	122
North Pond, l., Me., U.S.	D3	96
North Pond, l., Me., U.S.	h9	98
North Portal, Sask.	H4	75
North Port, Fl., U.S.	*D4	86
Northport, Mi., U.S.	C5	99
Northport, Ne., U.S.	C2	104
Northport, N.Y., U.S.	*n15	109
Northport, Wa., U.S.	A8	124
North Portal, Sask.	H4	75
North Powder, Or., U.S.	B9	114
North Pownal, Me., U.S.	g7	96
North Pownal, Vt., U.S.	F2	122
North Prairie, Wi., U.S.	F5	126
North Providence, R.I., U.S.	C4	116
North Raccoon, stm., Ia., U.S.	C3	92
North Reading, Ma., U.S.	f11	98
North Richland Hills, Tx., U.S.	n9	120
Northridge, Oh., U.S.	C2	112
Northridge, Oh., U.S.	*C1	112
North Ridgeville, Oh., U.S.	A3	112
North Rim, Az., U.S.	A3	80
North River Bridge, N.S.	C9	71
North Riverside, Il., U.S.	*k9	90
North Robinson, Oh., U.S.	B3	112
North Ronaldsay, i., Scot., U.K.	A5	10
Northrop, Mn., U.S.	G4	100
North Rose, N.Y., U.S.	B4	109
North Royalton, Oh., U.S.	h9	112
North Rustico, P.E.I.	C6	71
North Salem, In., U.S.	E4	91
North Salem, N.H., U.S.	E4	106
North Salt Lake, Ut., U.S.	C4	121
North Sanbornton, N.H., U.S.	C3	106
North Sandwich, N.H., U.S.	C4	106
North Santee, stm., S.C., U.S.	E9	117
North Saskatchewan, stm., Can.	F10	66
North Schell Peak, mtn., Nv., U.S.	D7	105
North Scituate, Ma., U.S.	h12	98
North Scituate, R.I., U.S.	C3	116
North Sea, Eur.	D9	8
Norths Highland, plat., Ant.	C25	7
North Shores, De., U.S.	F5	85
North Shoshone Peak, mtn., Nv., U.S.	D4	105
North Shrewsbury, Vt., U.S.	D3	122
Northside, N.C., U.S.	A4	110
North Sioux City, S.D., U.S.	E9	118
North Skunk, stm., Ia., U.S.	C5	92
North Sound, strt., Ire.	D2	11
North Sound, strt., Scot., U.K.	A6	13
North Spicer Island, i., N.W. Ter.	C17	66
North Springfield, Or., U.S.	*C3	114
North Springfield, Pa., U.S.	B1	115
North Springfield, Vt., U.S.	E3	122
North Springfield, Va., U.S.	*B5	123
North Springfield Reservoir, res., Vt., U.S.	E4	122
North Star, De., U.S.	A3	85
North Star, Mi., U.S.	E6	99
North Star, Oh., U.S.	B1	112
North Stonington, Ct., U.S.	D8	84
North St. Paul, Mn., U.S.	m13	100
North Stradbroke, i., Austl.	E9	50
North Stratford, N.H., U.S.	A3	106
North Sudbury, Ma., U.S.	g10	98
North Sutton, N.H., U.S.	D3	106
North Swansea, Ma., U.S.	C5	98
North Swanzey, N.H., U.S.	E2	106
North Sydney, Austl.	*F9	50
North Sydney, N.S.	C9	71
North Syracuse, N.Y., U.S.	B4	109
North Taranaki Bight, N.Z.	M15	51
North Tarrytown, N.Y., U.S.	D7	109
North Tea Lake, l., Ont.	B5	73
North Terre Haute, In., U.S.	E3	91
North Tewksbury, Ma., U.S.	A5	98
North Thetford, Vt., U.S.	D4	122
North Thompson, stm., B.C.	D8	69
North Tolsta, Scot., U.K.	B2	13
North Tonawanda, N.Y., U.S.	B2	109
North Trenholm, S.C., U.S.	*C6	117
North Troy, Vt., U.S.	A4	122
North Truro, Ma., U.S.	*B7	98
North Tunbridge, Vt., U.S.	D4	122
North Tunica, Ms., U.S.	A3	101
North Turner Mountain, mtn., Me., U.S.	C4	96
North Twin Lake, l., Newf.	D4	72
North Twin Lake, l., Wi., U.S.	B4	126
North Tyne, stm., Eng., U.K.	E6	13
North Uist, i., Scot., U.K.	B3	10
Northumberland, N.H., U.S.	A3	106
Northumberland, co., N.B.	B3	71
Northumberland, co., Eng., U.K.	C6	13
Northumberland, co., Pa., U.S.	D8	115
Northumberland, co., Va., U.S.	C6	123
Northumberland, co., Eng., U.K.		
Northumberland Isles, is., Austl.	D9	50
Northumberland Strait, strt., Can.	C7	71
North Umpqua, stm., Or., U.S.	D3	114
North Uxbridge, Ma., U.S.	B4	98
Northvale, N.J., U.S.	g9	107
North Valley Stream, N.Y., U.S.	*n15	109
North Vancouver, B.C.	f13	69
North Vassalboro, Me., U.S.	D3	96
North Vernon, In., U.S.	F6	91
North Versailles, Pa., U.S.	*k14	115
Northview, Mi., U.S.	*E5	99
Northville, Mo., U.S.	A4	102
Northville, Ct., U.S.	*C1	112
Northville, N.H., U.S.	E3	106
Northville, Ct., U.S.	C3	84
Northville, Mi., U.S.	p15	99
Northville, N.Y., U.S.	B6	109
North Wabasca Lake, l., Alta.	A4	68
North Wales, Pa., U.S.	F11	115
North Walpole, N.H., U.S.	D2	106
North Walsham, Eng., U.K.	D7	10
North Wantagh, N.Y., U.S.	*n15	109
North Warren, Ct., U.S.	C3	115
North Waterford, Me., U.S.	C11	79
North Webster, In., U.S.	B6	91
North Westchester, Ct., U.S.	C6	84
North West, dept., Guy.	A3	59
North West Cape, c., Austl.	D2	50
North Westchester, Ct., U.S.	C6	84
North-Western, prov., Zam.	D4	48
North West Highlands, plat., Scot., U.K.	B4	10
North Westminster, Vt., U.S.	E4	122

Name	Map Ref.	Page
Northwest Miramichi, stm., N.B.	B3	71
Northwest Polder, reg., Neth.	B5	17
Northwest Providence Channel, strt., Bah.	A4	64
North West River, Newf.	B1	72
Northwest Territories, prov., Can.	C13	66
Northwest Upsalquitch, stm., N.B.	B2	71
Northwich, Eng., U.K.	A5	12
North Wildwood, N.J., U.S.	E3	107
North Wilkesboro, N.C., U.S.	A1	110
North Wilmington, Ma., U.S.	f11	98
North Windham, Ct., U.S.	C7	84
North Windham, Me., U.S.	E2	96
Northwood, Ia., U.S.	A4	92
Northwood, N.H., U.S.	D4	106
Northwood, N.D., U.S.	B8	111
Northwood, Oh., U.S.	*c7	112
Northwood Center, N.H., U.S.	D4	106
Northwood Ridge, N.H., U.S.	D4	106
Northwoods, Mo., U.S.	*13	102
North Woodstock, N.H., U.S.	B3	106
North Yarmouth, Me., U.S.	g7	96
North York, Ont.	D5	73
North York, Pa., U.S.	G8	115
North York Moors, hills, Eng., U.K.	C6	10
North Yorkshire, co., Eng., U.K.	F7	13
North Zulch, Tx., U.S.	D4	120
Norton, N.B.	D4	71
Norton, Eng., U.K.	F8	13
Norton, Ks., U.S.	C4	93
Norton, Ma., U.S.	C5	98
Norton, Oh., U.S.	A4	112
Norton, Tx., U.S.	D2	120
Norton, Va., U.S.	f9	123
Norton, W.V., U.S.	C5	125
Norton, co., Ks., U.S.	C4	93
Norton Air Force Base, mil., Ca., U.S.	E5	82
Norton Bay, b., Ak., U.S.	C7	79
Norton Creek, stm., Al., U.S.	B1	78
Norton Pond, l., Vt., U.S.	B5	122
Norton Reservoir, res., Ks., U.S.	C3	93
Nortons Corner, Az., U.S.	D4	80
Norton Shores, Mi., U.S.	E4	99
Norton Sound, strt., Ak., U.S.	C6	79
Nortonville, Ks., U.S.	C8	93
Nortonville, Ky., U.S.	C2	94
Nortonville, N.D., U.S.	C7	111
Nortorf, Ger.	D3	15
Norvegia, Cape, c., Ant.	B11	7
Norwalk, Ca., U.S.	n12	82
Norwalk, Ct., U.S.	E2	84
Norwalk, Ia., U.S.	C4	92
Norwalk, Oh., U.S.	A3	112
Norwalk, Wi., U.S.	E3	126
Norwalk, stm., Ct., U.S.	E2	84
Norwalk Islands, is., Ct., U.S.	E2	84
Norway, In., U.S.	C4	91
Norway, Ia., U.S.	C6	92
Norway, Ks., U.S.	C6	93
Norway, Me., U.S.	D2	96
Norway, Mi., U.S.	C3	99
Norway, S.C., U.S.	D2	114
Norway, S.C., U.S.	E5	117
Norway, ctry., Eur.	F4	14
Norway House, Man.	C3	70
Norway Lake, l., Mn., U.S.	E3	100
Norwegian Bay, b., N.W. Ter.	m33	66
Norwegian Sea, Eur.	C14	128
Norwell, Ma., U.S.	h12	98
Norwich, Ont.	E4	73
Norwich, Eng., U.K.	D7	10
Norwich, Ct., U.S.	C7	84
Norwich, Ks., U.S.	E6	93
Norwich, N.Y., U.S.	C5	109
Norwich, N.D., U.S.	A5	111
Norwich, Vt., U.S.	D4	122
Norwood, Ont.	C7	73
Norwood, Co., U.S.	C2	83
Norwood, Ga., U.S.	C4	87
Norwood, La., U.S.	D4	95
Norwood, Ma., U.S.	B5	98
Norwood, Mn., U.S.	F5	100
Norwood, Mo., U.S.	D5	102
Norwood, N.J., U.S.	h9	107
Norwood, N.Y., U.S.	f10	109
Norwood, N.C., U.S.	B2	110
Norwood, Oh., U.S.	o13	112
Norwood, Pa., U.S.	p20	115
Norwoodville, Ia., U.S.	e8	92
Norwottock, Mount, mtn., Ma., U.S.	B3	98
Nosbonsing, Lake, l., Ont.	A5	73
Noshiro, Japan	F9	33
Nösjön, l., Swe.	A6	15
Nossa Senhora das Dores, Braz.	D3	57
Nossen, Ger.	B8	19
Noss Head, c., Scot., U.K.	B5	13
Nossob, stm., Afr.	C3	49
Nosy Varika, Madag.	h9	49
Notasulga, Al., U.S.	C4	78
Notch Hill, B.C.	D8	69
Notch Mountain, mtn., Ma., U.S.	A3	98
Notch Peak, mtn., Ut., U.S.	D2	121
Noteć, stm., Pol.	B3	26
Notikewin, Alta.	A2	68
Notikewin, stm., Alta.	A1	68
Noto, Italy	F5	23
Noto, Gulf of, b., Italy	F5	23
Notodden, Nor.	H3	14
Noto Island, i., Japan	H8	33
Noto Peninsula, pen., Japan	D12	31
Notoue, Kir.	R18	52
Notre-Dame, N.B.	C5	71
Notre Dame, Monts, mts., Que.	k13	74
Notre Dame de Bois, Newf.	D4	72
Notre Dame de Lourdes, Que.	E2	70
Notre-Dame-de-Montauban, Que.	C5	74
Notre-Dame-des-Bois, Que.	D6	74
Notre-Dame-du-Lac, Que.	B9	74
Notre-Dame-du-Laus, Que.	C2	74
Nottawa, Ont.	C4	73
Nottawasaga Bay, b., Ont.	C4	73
Nottaway, stm., Que.	h11	74
Nottely Lake, res., Ga., U.S.	B2	87
Nottingham, Eng., U.K.	D6	10
Nottingham, N.H., U.S.	D4	106
Nottingham Island, i., N.W. Ter.	D17	66
Nottinghamshire, co., Eng., U.K.	A7	12
Nottoway, Va., U.S.	C4	123
Nottoway, co., Va., U.S.	C4	123
Nottoway, stm., Va., U.S.	D5	123
Notukeu Creek, stm., Sask.	H2	75

Notus, Id., U.S.	F2	89
Nouadhibou, Maur.	B1	45
Nouakchott, Maur.	C1	45
Nouamrhar, Maur.	C1	45
Nouméa, N. Cal.	H10	6
Nouna, Burkina	D4	45
Noupoort, S. Afr.	D3	49
Noutonice, Czech.	n17	26
Nouvelle-France, Cap de, c., Can.	D18	66
Nouzonville, Fr.	C6	16
Nova, Oh., U.S.	A3	112
Nova Caipemba, Ang.	C1	48
Nova Cruz, Braz.	C3	57
Nova Friburgo, Braz.	C4	56
Nova Iguaçu, Braz.	h6	56
Nova Lima, Braz.	C4	56
Nova Londrina, Braz.	C2	56
Nova Lusitânia, Moz.	A5	49
Nova Mambone, Moz.	B6	49
Nova Olinda do Norte, Braz.	C3	59
Nova Ponte, Braz.	B3	56
Nova Prata, Braz.	D2	56
Novar, Ont.	B5	73
Novara, Italy	B2	23
Nova Roma, Braz.	A3	56
Nova Russas, Braz.	B2	57
Nova Scotia, prov., Can.	D6	71
Nova Sofala, Moz.	B5	49
Nova Soure, Braz.	D3	57
Novate Mezzola, Italy	D7	21
Novato, Ca., U.S.	C2	82
Nova Varoš, Yugo.	D4	24
Nova Venécia, Braz.	B4	56
Nova Vida, Braz.	B3	55
Novaya Astrakhan, Sov. Un.	p21	27
Novaya Kazanka, Sov. Un.	F18	8
Novaya Ladoga, Sov. Un.	A9	27
Novaya Lyalya, Sov. Un.	D9	29
Novaya Odessa, Sov. Un.	H8	27
Novaya Sibir Island, i., Sov. Un.	B17	29
Novaya Zemlya, is., Sov. Un.	B8	29
Nova Zagora, Bul.	D8	24
Novelda, Spain	C5	22
Novelty, Mo., U.S.	A5	102
Nové Město [nad Váhom], Czech.	D4	26
Nové Strašecí, Czech.	C8	19
Nové Zámky, Czech.	E5	26
Novgorod, Sov. Un.	D6	29
Novgorod-Severskiy, Sov. Un.	E9	27
Novi, Mi., U.S.	p15	99
Novice, Tx., U.S.	D3	120
Novigrad, Yugo.	C2	24
Novi Ligure, Italy	B2	23
Novinger, Mo., U.S.	A5	102
Novi Pazar, Bul.	D8	24
Novi Pazar, Yugo.	D4	24
Novi Sad, Yugo.	C4	24
Novo, stm., Braz.	g6	56
Novo Airão, Braz.	C2	59
Novoaltaysk, Sov. Un.	E25	8
Novoaminskiy, Sov. Un.	C2	28
Novo Aripuanã, Braz.	D2	59
Novovoronezh, Braz.	G12	27
Novocherkassk, Sov. Un.	H13	27
Nôvo Cruzeiro, Braz.	B4	56
Novoekonomicheskoye, Sov. Un.	q20	27
Novograd-Volynskiy, Sov. Un.	F6	27
Novogrudok, Sov. Un.	E5	27
Novokazalinsk, Sov. Un.	E9	29
Novokurovka, Sov. Un.	B7	33
Novokuybyshevsk, Sov. Un.	*D7	29
Novokuznetsk, Sov. Un.	D11	29
Novomirgorod, Sov. Un.	G8	27
Novomoskovsk, Sov. Un.	G10	27
Novomoskovsk, Sov. Un.	D6	29
Novopokrovskaya, Sov. Un.	I13	27
Novorossiysk, Sov. Un.	E6	29
Novo-Selo, Bul.	C6	24
Novoshakhtinsk, Sov. Un.	H12	27
Novosibirsk, Sov. Un.	D11	29
Novosibirsk Reservoir, res., Sov. Un.	C10	28
Novosil, Sov. Un.	E11	27
Novotroitsk, Sov. Un.	C5	28
Novoukrainka, Sov. Un.	G8	27
Novouzensk, Sov. Un.	C3	28
Novoyeniseyskaya, Sov. Un.	B11	33
Novozybkov, Sov. Un.	E9	27
Nový Bohumín, Czech.	D5	26
Nový Bydžov, Czech.	C5	26
Nový Jičín, Czech.	D5	26
Novyy Oskol, Sov. Un.	F11	27
Novyy Port, Sov. Un.	C10	29
Novyy Urengoy, Sov. Un.	C10	29
Novyy Uzen', Sov. Un.	G19	8
Novyy Vasyugan, Sov. Un.	B9	28
Nowagród, Pol.	B10	19
Nowa Ruda, Pol.	C4	26
Nowa Sól, Pol.	C3	26
Nowata, Ok., U.S.	A6	113
Nowata, co., Ok., U.S.	A6	113
Nowe Warpno, Pol.	B3	26
Nowogard, Pol.	B3	26
Nowogard, stm., Wy., U.S.	B5	127
Nowra-Bomaderry, Austl.	G8	51
Nowshak, mtn., Asia	k17	39
Nowy Dwór [Mazowiecki], Pol.	k13	26
Nowy Sącz, Pol.	D6	26
Nowy Targ, Pol.	D6	26
Nowy Tomyśl, Pol.	B4	26
Noxapater, Ms., U.S.	C4	101
Noxen, Pa., U.S.	D9	115
Noxon, Mt., U.S.	C1	103
Noxon Reservoir, res., Mt., U.S.	C1	103
Noxontown Lake, res., De., U.S.	C3	85
Noxubee, co., Ms., U.S.	B5	101
Noxubee, stm., U.S.	B5	101
Noya, Spain	A1	22
Noyes, Mn., U.S.	B1	100
Noyes Island, i., Ak., U.S.	n22	79
Noyon, Fr.	C5	16
Nozeroy, Fr.	E6	16
Nsanje, Mwi.	E6	48
Nsawam, Ghana	E4	45
Ntem, stm., Afr.	E6	45
Nsukka, Nig.	E2	46
Ntuatabu, Kir.	R18	52
Nūbāriyah, Tur'at an, Eg.	D2	41
Nuberg, Ga., U.S.	B1	41
Nubian Desert, des., Sud.	A3	47
Nuckolls, co., Ne., U.S.	D7	104
Nucla, Co., U.S.	C2	83
Nueces, co., Tx., U.S.	F4	120
Nueces, stm., Tx., U.S.	E3	120
Nueltin Lake, l., Can.	D13	66
Nueva, Isla, i., Chile	k12	54

Nueva Antioquia, Col.	B4	60
Nueva Asunción, dept., Para.	D3	55
Nueva Casas Grandes, Mex.	A3	63
Nueva Esparta, state, Ven.	A5	60
Nueva Gerona, Cuba	D2	64
Nueva Imperial, Chile	B2	54
Nueva Lubecka, Arg.	C2	54
Nueva Ocotepeque, Hond.	C3	62
Nueva Palmira, Ur.	E1	56
Nueva Providencia, Pan.	k11	62
Nueva Rosita, Mex.	B4	63
Nueva San Salvador, El Sal.	D3	62
Nueve de Julio, Arg.	D4	54
Nuevitas, Cuba	D5	64
Nuevo, Golfo, b., Arg.	C4	54
Nuevo Emperador, Pan.	m11	62
Nuevo Laredo, Mex.	B5	63
Nuevo León, state, Mex.	B5	63
Nuevo San Juan, Pan.	k11	62
Nugaal, prov., Som.	D6	47
NuH, Rās, c., Pak.	I1	39
Nuits, Fr.	D6	16
Nuits, Fr.	G14	40
Nukhayb, Iraq	B2	47
Nukhaylah, well, Sud.	H11	6
Nuku'alofa, Tonga	E5	28
Nukus, Sov. Un.	C8	79
Nulato, Ak., U.S.	C5	22
Nules, Spain	B5	122
Nulhegan, stm., Vt., U.S.	D3	50
Nullagine, Austl.	F4	50
Nullarbor Plain, pl., Austl.	D5	92
Numa, Ia., U.S.	E7	45
Numan, Nig.	I9	33
Numazu, Japan	F8	34
Numfoor, i., Indon.	B2	88
Numila, Hi., U.S.	E3	115
Nu Mine, Pa., U.S.	C3	109
Nunawading, Austl.	*G8	50
Nunda, N.Y., U.S.	C8	118
Nunda, S.D., U.S.	B6	12
Nuneaton, Eng., U.K.	D4	87
Nunez, Ga., U.S.	E4	99
Nunica, Mi., U.S.	D6	79
Nunivak Island, i., Ak., U.S.	A6	83
Nunn, Co., U.S.	B4	119
Nunnelly, Tn., U.S.	D2	23
Nuoro, Italy	B2	60
Nuqui, Col.	C3	94
Nura, stm., Sov. Un.	E23	8
Nuremberg, Pa., U.S.	E9	115
Nuremberg see Nürnberg, Ger.	D5	18
Nuri, Mex.	B3	63
Nürnberg (Nuremberg), Ger.	D5	18
Nursery, Tx., U.S.	E4	120
Nürtingen, Ger.	E3	21
Nus, Italy	D13	40
Nusaybin, Tur.	C4	43
Nushki, Pak.	C4	36
Nusle (part of Prague), Czech.	n17	26
Nuthe, stm., Ger.	A8	19
Nut Lake, l., Sask.	F4	75
Nutley, N.J., U.S.	B4	107
Nut Mountain, Sask.	F4	75
Nutrioso, Az., U.S.	D6	80
Nutter Fort, W.V., U.S.	k10	125
Nutting Lake, Ma., U.S.	f10	98
Nutwood, Il., U.S.	D3	90
Nuuanu Pali, Hi., U.S.	g10	88
Nu'utele Island, i., W. Sam.	G12	52
Nuutoi, Cape, c., W. Sam.	G12	52
Nuwara-Eliya, Sri L.	G7	36
Nuwaybi' al Muzayyinah, Eg.	H10	40
Nuyaka, Ok., U.S.	B5	113
Nüzvīd, India	I8	37
Nyac, Ak., U.S.	C8	79
Nyack, N.Y., U.S.	D7	109
Nyala, Sud.	C1	47
Nyamandhlovu, Zimb.	A4	49
Nyamtumbo, Tan.	C7	29
Nyandoma, Sov. Un.	C7	29
Nyanza, Rw.	B5	48
Nyanza, prov., Kenya	B5	48
Nyasa, Lake, l., Afr.	D5	48
Nyborg, Den.	C4	15
Nybro, Swe.	I6	14
Nyda, Sov. Un.	B23	8
Nye, co., Nv., U.S.	E7	103
Nye, mt., Nv., U.S.	E5	105
Nyeri, Kenya	B6	48
Nyilumba, Tan.	D7	48
Nyimba, Zam.	D5	48
Nyíregyháza, Hung.	B11	26
Nykøbing, Den.	I3	14
Nykøbing, Den.	C5	15
Nykøbing Falster, Den.	C5	15
Nykøbing, Den.	D7	15
Nyköping, Swe.	H7	14
Nylstroom, S. Afr.	A7	15
Nymagee, Austl.	F6	51
Nymburk, Czech.	C5	26
Nymindegab, Den.	C2	15
Nynäshamn, Swe.	H7	14
Nyngan, Austl.	F8	50
Nyon, Switz.	C8	18
Nyong, stm., Cam.	E2	46
Nýřany, Czech.	D8	19
Nyrsko, Czech.	D8	19
Nysa, Pol.	C4	26
Nyssa, Or., U.S.	D9	114
Nysted, Den.	D5	15
Nyunzu, Zaire	C5	48
Nzega, Tan.	B5	48
Nzérékoré, Gui.	E3	45
N'zeto, Ang.	B1	48
Nzwani, i., Com.	f8	49

O

Oacoma, S.D., U.S.	D6	118
Oahe, Lake, res., U.S.	A7	76
Oahe Dam, S.D., U.S.	C5	118
Oahu, i., Hi., U.S.	B4	88
Oak, Ne., U.S.	D8	104
Oak Bay, B.C.	h12	69
Oak Bay, N.B.	D2	71
Oak Bluffs, Ma., U.S.	D6	98
Oakboro, N.C., U.S.	B2	110
Oak Brook, Il., U.S.	*k9	90
Oakburn, Man.	D1	70
Oak City, N.C., U.S.	B5	110
Oak City, Ut., U.S.	D3	121
Oak Creek, Co., U.S.	A4	83
Oak Creek, Wi., U.S.	n12	126
Oakdale, Ct., U.S.	D3	82
Oakdale, Ct., U.S.	h8	87
Oakdale, Il., U.S.	E4	90
Oakdale, La., U.S.	D3	95
Oakdale, Mn., U.S.	*n13	100

Oakdale, Ne., U.S.	B8	104
Oakdale, N.Y., U.S.	*n15	109
Oakdale, Pa., U.S.	k13	115
Oakdale, Tn., U.S.	D9	119
Oakdale Manor, Ct., U.S.	*D2	84
Oakengates, Eng., U.K.	B5	12
Oakes, N.D., U.S.	C7	111
Oakesdale, Wa., U.S.	B8	124
Oakey, Austl.	C8	51
Oakfield, Ga., U.S.	E3	87
Oakfield, Me., U.S.	B4	96
Oakfield, N.Y., U.S.	B2	109
Oakfield, Tn., U.S.	B3	119
Oakfield, Wi., U.S.	E5	126
Oakford, Il., U.S.	C4	90
Oak Forest, Il., U.S.	k9	90
Oak Grove, Ky., U.S.	A2	81
Oak Grove, Ky., U.S.	D2	94
Oak Grove, La., U.S.	F7	99
Oak Grove, Mi., U.S.	B4	95
Oak Grove, Or., U.S.	B4	114
Oak Grove, S.C., U.S.	C8	117
Oak Grove, S.C., U.S.	*D5	117
Oak Grove, Va., U.S.	B6	123
Oakham, Eng., U.K.	B7	12
Oakham, Ma., U.S.	B3	98
Oak Harbor, Oh., U.S.	A2	112
Oak Harbor, Wa., U.S.	A3	124
Oak Hill, De., U.S.	*B3	85
Oak Hill, Fl., U.S.	D6	86
Oakhill, Ks., U.S.	*C6	93
Oak Hill, Mi., U.S.	D8	99
Oak Hill, Oh., U.S.	D3	112
Oak Hill, mtn., Ma., U.S.	f9	98
Oakhurst, Ok., U.S.	A5	113
Oak Island, i., Wi., U.S.	B3	126
Oak Lake, Man.	E1	70
Oak Lake, l., Man.	E1	70
Oakland, Ont.	D4	73
Oakland, Al., U.S.	A2	78
Oakland, Ar., U.S.	A3	81
Oakland, Ca., U.S.	D2	82
Oakland, Fl., U.S.	*F6	86
Oakland, Il., U.S.	D5	90
Oakland, Ia., U.S.	C2	92
Oakland, Ky., U.S.	C3	94
Oakland, Me., U.S.	D3	96
Oakland, Md., U.S.	m12	97
Oakland, Ne., U.S.	C9	104
Oakland, N.J., U.S.	A4	107
Oakland, Ok., U.S.	C5	113
Oakland, Pa., U.S.	C10	115
Oakland, R.I., U.S.	B2	116
Oakland, Tn., U.S.	B2	119
Oakland, co., Mi., U.S.	F7	99
Oakland City, In., U.S.	H3	91
Oakland Gardens, Ct., U.S.	C4	84
Oakland Park, Fl., U.S.	r13	86
Oak Lawn, Il., U.S.	B6	90
Oak Lawn, La., U.S.	h12	95
Oaklawn, Ks., U.S.	*G8	93
Oakley, Id., U.S.	G5	89
Oakley, Ks., U.S.	C3	93
Oakley, Mi., U.S.	E6	99
Oakley, Ms., U.S.	C3	101
Oakley, S.C., U.S.	E7	117
Oakley, Ut., U.S.	C4	121
Oaklyn, N.J., U.S.	*D4	107
Oakman, Al., U.S.	B2	78
Oakman, Ga., U.S.	B2	87
Oakmont, Pa., U.S.	E2	115
Oak Mountain, mtn., Ga., U.S.	B2	87
Oak Mountain, mtn., Tn., U.S.	h11	119
Oakner, Man.	D1	70
Oak Orchard, De., U.S.	F5	85
Oak Park, Ca., U.S.	*E5	82
Oak Park, Ga., U.S.	A2	92
Oak Park, Il., U.S.	B6	90
Oak Park, Mi., U.S.	p15	99
Oak Point, Man.	D2	70
Oak Ridge, Fl., U.S.	*D5	86
Oak Ridge, La., U.S.	B4	95
Oak Ridge, Mo., U.S.	D8	102
Oak Ridge, N.C., U.S.	A3	110
Oakridge, Or., U.S.	D4	114
Oak Ridge, Tn., U.S.	C9	119
Oak Ridge Reservoir, res., N.J., U.S.	A3	107
Oak Ridges (part of Richmond Hill), Ont.	k15	73
Oak River, Man.	D1	70
Oaks, Ok., U.S.	A7	113
Oaks, Pa., U.S.	o20	115
Oakton, Ky., U.S.	f8	94
Oakton, Va., U.S.	g12	123
Oaktown, In., U.S.	G3	91
Oak Vale, Ms., U.S.	D3	101
Oakvale, W.V., U.S.	*D4	125
Oak Valley, N.J., U.S.	D2	107
Oakville, Man.	E3	70
Oakville, Ont.	D5	73
Oakville, Ct., U.S.	C3	84
Oakville, In., U.S.	D7	91
Oakville, Mo., U.S.	g13	102
Oakway, S.C., U.S.	B1	117
Oakwood, Ga., U.S.	B3	87
Oakwood, Il., U.S.	C6	90
Oakwood, N.D., U.S.	A8	111
Oakwood, Oh., U.S.	A1	112
Oakwood, Oh., U.S.	C1	112
Oakwood, Ok., U.S.	B3	113
Oakwood, Tx., U.S.	D5	120
Oakwood Beach, N.J., U.S.	e9	123
Oakwood Beach, N.J., U.S.	D1	107
Oamaru, N.Z.	P13	51
Oāmishirasato, Japan	n19	33
Oark, Ar., U.S.	B2	81
Oasis, Ut., U.S.	D3	121
Oaths, S.C., U.S.	C7	117
Oaxaca, state, Mex.	D5	63
Oaxaca [de Juárez], Mex.	D5	63
Ob, stm., Sov. Un.	C9	29
Oba, Ont.	o17	73
Obama, Japan	n14	33
Oban, Sask.	E1	75
Oban, Scot., U.K.	g11	94
O'Bannon, Ky., U.S.	C10	29
Ob Bay, b., Sov. Un.	C9	29
Obed, Alta.	h8	87
Obed, stm., Tn., U.S.	C9	119
Ober, Ar., U.S.	B4	55
Oberá, Arg.	E4	55
Oberammergau, Ger.	B7	24
Oberdrauburg, Aus.	C8	20

Oberhausen, Ger.	C3	18
Oberkirch, Ger.	E3	19
Oberlin, Ks., U.S.	C3	93
Oberlin, La., U.S.	D3	95
Oberlin, Oh., U.S.	A3	112
Obernburg [am Main], Ger.	B6	111
Oberndorf, Ger.	D4	19
Oberösterreich, state, Aus.	E9	19
Oberstaufen, Ger.	B6	20
Oberstdorf, Ger.	E5	18
Obert, Ne., U.S.	B8	104
Oberursel, Ger.	C3	19
Oberwald, Switz.	C4	20
Obetz, Oh., U.S.	C3	112
Óbidos, Braz.	C3	59
Obihiro, Japan	C13	31
Obi Islands, is., Indon.	F7	34
Obion, Tn., U.S.	A2	119
Obion, co., Tn., U.S.	A2	119
Obion, Middle Fork, stm., Tn., U.S.	A3	119
Obion, Rutherford Fork, stm., Tn., U.S.	A3	119
Obion, South Fork, stm., Tn., U.S.	A3	119
Obion Creek, stm., Ky., U.S.	f9	94
Oblachnaya, Mount, mtn., Sov. Un.	E7	33
Oblong, Il., U.S.	D6	90
Obluchye, Sov. Un.	E16	29
Obo, Cen. Afr. Rep.	D5	46
Obock, Dji.	C5	47
Oborniki, Pol.	B4	26
Oboyan, Sov. Un.	F11	27
O'Brien, Fl., U.S.	B4	86
O'Brien, Or., U.S.	E3	114
O'Brien, co., Ia., U.S.	A2	92
Observation Peak, mtn., Ca., U.S.	B3	82
Obuasi, Ghana	E4	45
Obwalden, state, Switz.	C4	20
Ocala, Fl., U.S.	C4	86
Ocampo, Mex.	B3	63
Ocaña, Col.	B3	60
Ocaña, Spain	C3	22
Ocate, N.M., U.S.	A5	108
Occidental, Cordillera, mts., Col.	C2	60
Occidental, Cordillera, mts., Peru	D3	58
Occidental, Cordillera, mts., S.A.	C2	55
Occoquan, Va., U.S.	B5	123
Ocean, co., N.J., U.S.	D4	107
Oceana, W.V., U.S.	D3	125
Oceana, co., Mi., U.S.	E4	99
Oceana Naval Air Station, mil., Va., U.S.	k15	123
Ocean Bluff, Ma., U.S.	B6	98
Ocean City, Fl., U.S.	u15	86
Ocean City, Md., U.S.	D7	97
Ocean City, N.J., U.S.	E3	107
Ocean City, N.J., U.S.	B1	124
Ocean Falls, B.C.	C4	69
Ocean Gate, N.J., U.S.	D4	107
Ocean Grove, Ma., U.S.	C5	98
Ocean Grove, N.J., U.S.	C4	107
Ocean Heights, Ma., U.S.	D6	98
Ocean Park, Wa., U.S.	C1	124
Ocean Port, N.J., U.S.	C4	107
Oceanside, Ca., U.S.	F5	82
Ocean Springs, Ms., U.S.	E5	101
Ocean View, De., U.S.	F5	85
Ocean View, N.J., U.S.	E3	107
Oceanville, N.J., U.S.	E4	107
Ochakov, Sov. Un.	H8	27
Ocheda Lake, l., Mn., U.S.	G3	100
Ochelata, Ok., U.S.	A6	113
Ocheyedan, Ia., U.S.	A2	92
Ocheyedan, stm., Ia., U.S.	A2	92
Ochil Hills, hills, Scot., U.K.	D5	13
Ochiltree, co., Tx., U.S.	A2	120
Ochlocknee, Ga., U.S.	F2	87
Ochlockonee, stm., Fl., U.S.	B2	86
Ochoco Lake, res., Or., U.S.	C6	114
Ochopee, Fl., U.S.	G5	86
Ochre River, Man.	D2	70
Ochsenfurt, Ger.	C5	19
Ochtrup, Ger.	A2	19
Ocilla, Ga., U.S.	E3	87
Ockelbo, Swe.	G7	14
Öckerö, i., Swe.	A5	15
Ockley, In., U.S.	D4	91
Ocmulgee, stm., Ga., U.S.	D3	87
Ocmulgee National Monument, Ga., U.S.	D3	87
Ocna-Sibiului, Rom.	C7	24
Ocnele Mari, Rom.	D7	24
Ocoee, Fl., U.S.	D5	86
Ocoee, Tn., U.S.	D9	119
Ocoee, co., Tn., U.S.	D9	119
Oconee, Peru	C4	63
Oconee, Il., U.S.	D4	90
Oconee, co., Ga., U.S.	C3	87
Oconee, co., S.C., U.S.	B1	117
Oconee, stm., Ga., U.S.	C3	87
Oconee, Lake, res., Ga., U.S.	C3	87
Oconomowoc, Wi., U.S.	E5	126
Oconto, Ne., U.S.	C6	104
Oconto, Wi., U.S.	D6	126
Oconto, co., Wi., U.S.	D5	126
Oconto Falls, Wi., U.S.	D5	126
Ocós, Guat.	C1	62
Ocotal, Nic.	E7	63
Ocotillo, Ca., U.S.	m9	80
Ocotlán, Mex.	C4	63
Ocros, Peru	C8	104
Octavia, Az., U.S.	C8	104
Octavia, Ok., U.S.	C7	113
Octeville, Fr.	C3	16
October Revolution Island, i., Sov. Un.	B4	128
Octoraro Creek, stm., U.S.	A5	97
Ocumare del Tuy, Ven.	A4	60
Oda, Ghana	E4	45
Odanah, Wi., U.S.	B3	126
Odawara, Japan	n18	33
Odda, Nor.	F3	14
Odden, Den.	C4	15
Odebolt, Ia., U.S.	B2	92
Odei, stm., Man.	A3	70
Odell, Il., U.S.	B5	90

Odell, Ne., U.S.	D9	104
Odell, Or., U.S.	B5	114
Odell, Tx., U.S.	B3	120
Odell Lake, l., Or., U.S.	E5	114
Odem, Tx., U.S.	F4	120
Odemira, Port.	D1	22
Ödemiş, Tur.	C7	40
Oden, Ar., U.S.	C2	81
Odendaalsrus, S. Afr.	E9	19
Odense, Den.	C4	15
Odensala, Swe.	t35	14
Odensbacken (part of Örebro), Swe.	t33	14
Odense, Den.	J4	14
Odense Å, stm., Den.	C4	15
Odenton, Md., U.S.	B4	97
Odenville, Al., U.S.	B3	78
Odenwald, mts., Ger.	D3	19
Oder (Odra), stm., Eur.	B3	26
Oder Spree Canal, Ger.	A9	19
Odessa, Ont.	C8	73
Odessa, Sask.	G4	75
Odessa, Sov. Un.	E6	29
Odessa, De., U.S.	C3	85
Odessa, Fl., U.S.	*D4	86
Odessa, Mn., U.S.	E2	100
Odessa, Mo., U.S.	C4	102
Odessa, Ne., U.S.	D6	104
Odessa, N.Y., U.S.	C4	109
Odessa, Tx., U.S.	D1	120
Odessa, Wa., U.S.	B7	124
Odiel, stm., Spain	D2	22
Odienné, I.C.	E3	45
Odin, Ks., U.S.	D5	93
Odin, Ks., U.S.	D5	93
Odin, Mount, mtn., B.C.	D8	69
Odivelas, Port.	f9	22
Odon, In., U.S.	G4	91
O'Donnell, Tx., U.S.	C2	120
Odorheiu Secuiesc, Rom.	B7	24
Odra (Oder), stm., Eur.	B3	26
Odzi, Zimb.	A5	49
Oebisfelde, Ger.	A5	19
Oeiras, Braz.	C2	57
Oeiras, Port.	f9	22
Oelde, Ger.	B3	19
Oelrichs, S.D., U.S.	D2	118
Oelsnitz [im Erzgebirge], Ger.	C6	18
Oelsnitz [im Vogtland], Ger.	C7	19
Oelwein, Ia., U.S.	B6	92
Oensingen, Switz.	B4	21
Oesede, Ger.	A3	19
Oettingen [in Bayern], Ger.	E5	19
Oeyón Island, i., S. Kor.	H2	33
Ofahoma, Ms., U.S.	C4	101
O'Fallon, Il., U.S.	E4	90
O'Fallon, Mo., U.S.	f12	102
O'Fallon Creek, stm., Mt., U.S.	D12	103
Ofanto, stm., Italy	D5	23
Ofaqim, Isr.	*E6	41
Offa, Nig.	*E5	45
Offaly, co., Ire.	D4	11
Offenbach [am Main], Ger.	C4	18
Offenburg, Ger.	D3	18
Offence, Mount of, hist., Isr. Occ.	m14	41
Offerle, Ks., U.S.	E4	93
Offerman, Ga., U.S.	E4	87
Offutt Air Force Base, mil., Ne., U.S.	g3	104
Oficina Pedro de Valdivia, Chile	D2	55
Oftringen, Switz.	B4	21
Ofunato, Japan	G10	33
Oga, Japan	G9	33
Ōgaki, Japan	I8	33
Ogallah, Ks., U.S.	D4	93
Ogallala, Ne., U.S.	C4	104
Oga Peninsula, pen., Japan	G10	33
Ogbomosho, Nig.	E5	45
Ogden, Ar., U.S.	D1	81
Ogden, Il., U.S.	C6	90
Ogden, Ia., U.S.	B3	92
Ogden, Ks., U.S.	C7	93
Ogden, Ut., U.S.	B4	121
Ogden, Mount, mtn., Ak., U.S.	k23	79
Ogdensburg, N.J., U.S.	A3	107
Ogdensburg, N.Y., U.S.	f9	109
Ogdensburg, Wi., U.S.	C8	115
Ogeechee, stm., Ga., U.S.	D5	87
Ogema, Sask.	H3	75
Ogema, Mn., U.S.	C3	100
Ogema, Wi., U.S.	C3	126
Ogemaw, co., Mi., U.S.	D2	81
Ogilvie, Mn., U.S.	E5	100
Ogilvie Mountains, mts., Yukon	D5	66
Oglala, S.D., U.S.	D3	118
Ogle, co., Il., U.S.	A4	90
Oglesby, Il., U.S.	B4	90
Oglesby, Tx., U.S.	A6	113
Oglethorpe, Ga., U.S.	D2	87
Oglethorpe, co., Ga., U.S.	C3	87
Oglethorpe, Mount, mtn., Ga., U.S.	B2	87
Oglio, stm., Italy	B3	23
Ognon, stm., Fr.	B1	20
Ogoamas, mtn., Indon.	E6	34
Ogoja, Nig.	E6	45
Ogooué, stm., Afr.	F2	46
Ogou, stm., Afr., Bul.	g11	26
Ogodzha, Yugo.	C2	24
Ogunquit, Me., U.S.	E2	96
Ogurchinskiy Island, i., Sov. Un.	B6	39
Ohakune, N.Z.	M15	51
O'Hanly, Man.	D4	70
Ōhara, Japan	n19	33
Ohatchee, Al., U.S.	B3	78
Ohaton, Alta.	C4	68
O'Higgins, Lago (Lago San Martín), l., S.A.	D2	54
Ohio, Co., U.S.	C4	83
Ohio, Il., U.S.	B4	90
Ohio, N.Y., U.S.	B6	109
Ohio, co., In., U.S.	G7	91
Ohio, co., Ky., U.S.	C3	94
Ohio, co., W.V., U.S.	A4	125
Ohio, state, U.S.	B3	112
Ohio, stm., U.S.	C11	76
Ohio Brush Creek, stm., Oh., U.S.	D2	112
Ohio City, Oh., U.S.	B1	112
Ohio Peak, mtn., Co., U.S.	C3	83
Ohiopyle, Pa., U.S.	G3	115
Ohiowa, Ne., U.S.	D8	104
Ohlman, Il., U.S.	D4	90
Ohoopee, Ga., U.S.	D4	87

Name	Map Ref.	Page
Ohoopee, stm., Ga., U.S.	D4	87
Ohopoho, Nmb.	A1	49
Ohrdruf, Ger.	C5	19
Ohře, stm., Eur.	C2	26
Ohrid, Yugo.	E5	24
Ohrid, Lake, l., Eur.	E5	24
Ohrigstad, S. Afr.	B5	49
Öhringen, Ger.	D4	19
Oiapoque, Braz.	B4	59
Oiapoque (Oyapock), stm., S.A.	B4	59
Oies, Île aux, i., Que.	B7	74
Oikull, Palau	R17	52
Oil Center, N.M., U.S.	E6	108
Oil City, La., U.S.	B2	95
Oil City, Ms., U.S.	C3	101
Oil City, Pa., U.S.	D2	115
Oil Creek, stm., Pa., U.S.	C2	115
Oildale, Ca., U.S.	E4	82
Oilmont, Mt., U.S.	B5	103
Oil Springs, Ont.	E2	73
Oilton, Ok., U.S.	A5	113
Oilton, Tx., U.S.	F3	120
Oil Trough, Ar., U.S.	B4	81
Oir, Beinn an, mtn., Scot., U.K.	E3	13
Oise, dept., Fr.	E2	17
Oise, stm., Eur.	C5	16
Oiseau, stm., Can.	D4	70
Oisemont, Fr.	E9	12
Ō Island, i., Japan	F9	33
Ō Island, i., Japan	I9	33
Oita, Japan	J5	33
Oiticica, Braz.	C2	57
Ojai, Ca., U.S.	E4	82
Ojinaga, Mex.	B4	63
Ojocaliente, Mex.	C4	63
Ojo Caliente, N.M., U.S.	A3	108
Ojo Feliz, N.M., U.S.	A4	108
Ojo Sarco, N.M., U.S.	A4	108
Ojos del Salado, Nevado, mtn., S.A.	E2	55
Oka, Que.	D3	74
Oka, Nig.	E6	45
Oka, stm., Sov. Un.	C14	27
Okaba, Indon.	G9	34
Okabena, Mn., U.S.	G3	100
Okahandja, Nmb.	B2	49
Okak Islands, is., Newf.	g9	72
Okaloosa, co., Fl., U.S.	u15	86
Okamanpeedan Lake, l., U.S.	A3	92
Okanagan Centre, B.C.	D8	69
Okanagan Falls, B.C.	D8	69
Okanagan Lake, l., B.C.	D8	69
Okanagan Landing, B.C.	D8	69
Okanagan Range, mts., N.A.	E4	69
Okanogan, Wa., U.S.	A6	124
Okanogan, co., Wa., U.S.	A5	124
Okanogan, stm., N.A.	A6	124
Okapilco Creek, stm., Ga., U.S.	E3	87
Okāra, Pak.	B4	37
Okarche, Ok., U.S.	B4	113
Okatibee Reservoir, res., Ms., U.S.	C5	101
Okatoma Creek, stm., Ms., U.S.	D4	101
Okaton, S.D., U.S.	D5	118
Okauchee, Wi., U.S.	*E5	126
Okauchee Lake, Wi., U.S.	E5	126
Okaukuejo, Nmb.	A2	49
Okavango, stm., Afr.	H7	42
Okavango Swamps, sw., Bots.	A3	49
Okawville, Il., U.S.	E4	90
Okay, Ok., U.S.	B6	113
Okaya, Japan	H8	33
Okayama, Japan	E11	31
Okazaki, Japan	o16	33
O'Kean, Ar., U.S.	A5	81
Okeana, Oh., U.S.	n12	112
Okęcie (part of Warsaw), Pol.	m13	26
Okeechobee, Fl., U.S.	E6	86
Okeechobee, co., Fl., U.S.	E6	86
Okeechobee, Lake, l., Fl., U.S.	F6	86
Okeene, Ok., U.S.	A3	113
Okefenokee Swamp, sw., U.S.	F4	87
Okehampton, Eng., U.K.	E4	10
Okemah, Ok., U.S.	B5	113
Okemos, Mi., U.S.	*F6	99
Oker, stm., Ger.	F4	15
Okesa, Ok., U.S.	A5	113
Oketo, Ks., U.S.	C7	93
Okfuskee, co., Ok., U.S.	B5	113
Okha, Sov. Un.	D17	29
Okhotsk, Sov. Un.	D17	29
Okhotsk, Sea of, Asia	D17	29
Okiep, S. Afr.	C2	49
Oki Islands, is., Japan	D11	31
Okinawa Island, i., Japan	F10	31
Oklahoma, co., Ok., U.S.	B4	113
Oklahoma, state, U.S.	B4	113
Oklahoma City, Ok., U.S.	B4	113
Oklawaha, Fl., U.S.	C5	86
Oklawaha, stm., Fl., U.S.	C5	86
Oklawaha, Lake, res., Fl., U.S.	C5	86
Oklee, Mn., U.S.	C2	100
Okmulgee, Ok., U.S.	B6	113
Okmulgee, co., Ok., U.S.	B5	113
Okoboji, Ia., U.S.	A2	92
Okobojo Creek, stm., S.D., U.S.	C5	118
Okolona, Ar., U.S.	D2	81
Okolona, Ky., U.S.	g11	94
Okolona, Ms., U.S.	B5	101
Okondja, Gabon	F2	46
Okotoks, Alta.	D4	68
Okreek, S.D., U.S.	D5	118
Oktaha, Ok., U.S.	B6	113
Oktibbeha, co., Ms., U.S.	B5	101
Oktyabrsk, Sov. Un.	D5	28
Oktyabrskiy, Sov. Un.	C4	28
Okulovka, Sov. Un.	B9	27
Okuma Bay, b., Ant.	B32	7
Okuniew, Pol.	k14	26
Okushiri, Japan	E9	33
Okushiri Island, i., Japan	E9	33
Ola, Ar., U.S.	B2	81
Ola, Id., U.S.	E2	89
Ólafsfjördur, Ice.	m23	14
Ólafsvík, Ice.	n21	14
Olalla, Wa., U.S.	f10	124
Olamon, Me., U.S.	C4	96
Olancha, Ca., U.S.	D5	82
Olancha Peak, mtn., Ca., U.S.	D4	82
Olanchito, Hond.	C4	62
Öland, i., Swe.	I7	14
Olanta, Pa., U.S.	E4	115
Olanta, S.C., U.S.	D8	117
Olar, S.C., U.S.	E5	117
Olascoaga, Arg.	B4	54
Olathe, Co., U.S.	C3	83
Olathe, Ks., U.S.	D9	93
Olavarría, Arg.	C4	54
Oława, Pol.	C4	26

Name	Map Ref.	Page
Olazagutía, Spain	A4	22
Olberg, Az., U.S.	D4	80
Olbernhau, Ger.	C8	19
Olbia, Italy	D2	23
Olcott, N.Y., U.S.	B2	109
Olcott, W.V., U.S.	C3	125
Old Bahama Channel, strt., N.A.	C4	64
Old Bennington, Vt., U.S.	F2	122
Old Bethpage, N.Y., U.S.	*n15	109
Old Bight, Bah.	B6	64
Old Bridge, N.J., U.S.	C4	107
Old Castile, hist. reg., Spain	B4	22
Oldcastle, Ire.	D4	11
Old Crow, Yukon	C5	66
Oldeani, Tan.	B6	48
Olden, Tx., U.S.	C3	120
Oldenburg, Ger.	B4	18
Oldenburg, In., U.S.	F7	91
Oldenburg [in Holstein], Ger.	A5	18
Oldenzaal, Neth.	B6	17
Old Faithful Geyser, Wy., U.S.	B2	127
Old Forge, N.Y., U.S.	B6	109
Old Forge, Pa., U.S.	D10	115
Old Fort, Ak., U.S.	f10	110
Old Fort, Oh., U.S.	A2	112
Old Fort Bay, Que.	C3	72
Oldham, Eng., U.K.	D5	10
Oldham, co., Ky., U.S.	B4	94
Oldham, co., Tx., U.S.	B1	120
Old Harbor, Ak., U.S.	D9	79
Old Harbour Bay, Jam.	F14	65
Old Head of Kinsale, c., Ire.	E2	10
Old Hickory Lake, res., Tn., U.S.	A5	119
Old Lyme, Ct., U.S.	D6	84
Oldman, stm., Alta.	E4	68
Old Man Mountain, mtn., Newf.	D3	72
Old Man of the Mountain, N.H., U.S.	B3	106
Oldmans Creek, stm., N.J., U.S.	D2	107
Oldmeldrum, Scot., U.K.	C6	13
Old Mkushi, Zam.	D4	48
Old Monroe, Mo., U.S.	C7	102
Old Mystic, Ct., U.S.	D8	84
Old Northwood, N.H., U.S.	D4	106
Old Orchard Beach, Me., U.S.	E2	96
Old Perlican, Newf.	D5	72
Old Point Comfort, c., Va., U.S.	h15	123
Old Rhodes Key, i., Fl., U.S.	G6	86
Old Ripley, Il., U.S.	E4	90
Old River Lake, l., Ar., U.S.	k10	81
Olds, Alta.	D3	68
Olds, Ia., U.S.	C6	92
Old Saybrook, Ct., U.S.	D6	84
Oldsmar, Fl., U.S.	o10	86
Old Speck Mountain, mtn., Me., U.S.	D2	96
Old Tampa Bay, b., Fl., U.S.	p10	86
Old Tappan, N.J., U.S.	g9	107
Old Tate, Bots.	B4	49
Old Town, Fl., U.S.	C4	86
Old Town, Id., U.S.	A1	89
Old Town, Me., U.S.	D4	96
Oldtown, Md., U.S.	k13	97
Old Village, N.Y., U.S.	*E7	109
Old Washington, Oh., U.S.	B4	112
Oldwick, N.J., U.S.	B3	107
Old Wives, Sask.	G2	75
Old Wives Lake, l., Sask.	G2	75
Olean, N.Y., U.S.	C2	109
O'Leary, P.E.I.	C5	71
Olecko, Pol.	A7	26
Oleiros, Spain	A1	22
Olekma, stm., Sov. Un.	D15	29
Olekminsk, Sov. Un.	C15	29
Olenek, stm., Sov. Un.	C14	29
Olentangy, stm., Oh., U.S.	B3	112
Oléron, Île d', i., Fr.	E3	16
Oleśnica (Oels), Pol.	C4	26
Olesno, Pol.	C5	26
Oleta, Ok., U.S.	C6	113
Oley, Pa., U.S.	F10	115
Olga, Sov. Un.	F7	29
Olga, Mount, mtn., Vt., U.S.	F3	122
Ölgiy, Mong.	B5	30
Ølgod, Den.	C2	15
Olgopol, Sov. Un.	C11	27
Olhão, Port.	D2	22
Olifants, stm., Afr.	B5	49
Ólimbos, mtn., Cyp.	E9	40
Olímpia, Braz.	C3	56
Olin, Ia., U.S.	B6	92
Olinda, Braz.	E12	57
Olionono, Cape, c., W. Sam.	F12	52
Olite, Spain	A5	22
Oliva, Spain	C5	22
Oliva de la Frontera, Spain	C3	22
Olivais, Port.	f9	22
Olive, Mt., U.S.	E11	103
Olive, Ok., U.S.	A5	113
Olive Branch, Il., U.S.	F4	90
Olive Branch, Ms., U.S.	A4	101
Olivehill, Tn., U.S.	B3	119
Olivehurst, Ca., U.S.	C3	82
Oliveira, Braz.	C4	56
Olivenza, Spain	C2	22
Oliver, B.C.	E8	69
Oliver, Al., U.S.	C1	78
Oliver, Ga., U.S.	D5	87
Oliver, Pa., U.S.	G2	115
Oliver, co., N.D., U.S.	B4	111
Oliver Dam, U.S.	C1	78
Oliver Springs, Tn., U.S.	C9	119
Olivet, Fr.	D8	16
Olivet, Il., U.S.	D6	90
Olivet, Ks., U.S.	D8	93
Olivet, Mi., U.S.	F5	99
Olivet, Mi., U.S.	D6	99
Olivet, S.D., U.S.	D8	118
Olivette, Mo., U.S.	*f13	102
Olivia, Mn., U.S.	F4	100
Olivia, N.C., U.S.	B3	110
Olivone, Switz.	C4	20
Öljaren, i., Swe.	t34	14
Olkusz, Pol.	g11	26
Olla, La., U.S.	C3	95
Ollagüe, Chile	D2	55
Ollei, Palau	R17	52
Ollie, Ia., U.S.	C5	92
Olmito, Tx., U.S.	F4	120
Olmitz, Ks., U.S.	D5	93
Olmos, Peru	C2	58
Olmos Park, Tx., U.S.	k7	120
Olmstead, Ky., U.S.	D2	94
Olmstead, Ut., U.S.	*C4	121

Name	Map Ref.	Page
Olmsted, Il., U.S.	F4	90
Olmsted, co., Mn., U.S.	G6	100
Olmsted Falls, Oh., U.S.	h9	112
Olmstedville, N.Y., U.S.	B7	109
Olney, Il., U.S.	E5	90
Olney, Md., U.S.	B3	97
Olney, Mo., U.S.	B6	102
Olney, Mt., U.S.	B2	103
Olney, Tx., U.S.	C3	120
Olney Springs, Co., U.S.	C7	83
Oloh, Ms., U.S.	D4	101
Olomouc, Czech.	D4	26
Olongapo, Phil.	o13	34
Oloron, Gave d', stm., Fr.	F3	16
Oloron-Sainte-Marie, Fr.	F3	16
Olot, Spain	A7	22
Olowalu, Hi., U.S.	C5	88
Olpe, Ger.	B2	19
Olpe, Ks., U.S.	D7	93
Olsburg, Ks., U.S.	C7	93
Olše, stm., Eur.	h9	26
Olshany, Sov. Un.	F10	27
Olst, Neth.	B6	17
Olsztyn (Allenstein), Pol.	B6	26
Olt, stm., Rom.	C7	24
Olten, Switz.	E3	18
Oltenia, hist. reg., Rom.	C6	24
Oltenița, Rom.	C8	24
Olteț, stm., Rom.	C6	24
Olton, Tx., U.S.	B1	120
Oltu, Tur.	B13	40
Olupona, Nig.	*E5	45
Olustee, Fl., U.S.	B4	86
Olustee, Ok., U.S.	C2	113
Olvenstedt, Ger.	A6	19
Olvera, Spain	D3	22
Olvey, Ar., U.S.	A3	81
Olympia, Ky., U.S.	B6	94
Olympia, Wa., U.S.	B3	124
Olympia, hist., Grc.	C3	25
Olympia Heights, Fl., U.S.	*s13	86
Olympic Mountains, mts., Wa., U.S.	B2	124
Olympic National Park, Wa., U.S.	B2	124
Olympus, Mount, mtn., Grc.	B4	40
Olympus, Mount, mtn., Ky., U.S.	B6	94
Olympus, Mount, mtn., Indon.	D7	88
Olyphant, Pa., U.S.	D10	115
Olyutorski, Cape, c., Sov. Un.	D20	29
Om, stm., Sov. Un.	B9	28
Oma, Ar., U.S.	g7	81
Oma, Ms., U.S.	D3	101
Omae, Cape, c., Japan	o17	33
Omagh, N. Ire., U.K.	C3	10
Omaguas, Peru	B3	58
Omaha, Ga., U.S.	A2	81
Omaha, Ga., U.S.	D1	87
Omaha, Il., U.S.	F5	90
Omaha, Ne., U.S.	C10	104
Omaha Indian Reservation, Ne., U.S.	B9	104
Omak, Wa., U.S.	A6	124
Omak Lake, l., Wa., U.S.	A6	124
Oman, ctry., Asia	C5	38
Oman, Gulf of, b., Asia	C6	38
Omar, W.V., U.S.	D3	125
Omarama, N.Z.	P12	51
Omaruru, Nmb.	B2	49
Omboué, Gabon	F1	46
Ombrone, stm., Italy	C3	23
Omdurman (Umm Durmān), Sud.	H19	65
Omega, Ga., U.S.	E3	87
Omega, N.M., U.S.	C1	108
Omega, Ok., U.S.	B3	113
Omegna, Italy	E5	21
Omemee, Ont.	C6	73
Omemee, N.D., U.S.	A5	111
Omeo, Austl.	H6	51
Omer, Mi., U.S.	D7	99
Om-Hadjer, Chad	B5	74
Ometepe, Isla de, i., Nic.	E5	62
Ometepec, Mex.	D5	63
Om Hajer, Eth.	C4	44
Omigawa, Japan	n19	33
Omineca, stm., B.C.	B5	69
Omineca Mountains, mts., B.C.	A4	69
Ōmiya, Japan	I9	33
Ōmiya, Japan	o15	33
Ommaney, Cape, c., Ak., U.S.	D12	79
Ommen, Neth.	B6	17
Omø, i., Den.	C5	15
Omo, stm., Eth.	D4	47
Omolon, stm., Sov. Un.	C18	29
Ompompanoosuc, stm., Vt., U.S.	D4	122
Ompompanoosuc, West Branch, stm., Vt., U.S.	D4	122
Omro, Wi., U.S.	D5	126
Omsk, Sov. Un.	D10	28
Ōmuta, Japan	J5	33
Omutninsk, Sov. Un.	D19	28
Ona, Fl., U.S.	E5	86
Onaga, Ks., U.S.	C7	93
Onaka, S.D., U.S.	B7	118
Onalaska, Wa., U.S.	C3	124
Onalaska, Wi., U.S.	D5	100
Onamia, Mn., U.S.	D5	100
Onancock, Va., U.S.	C7	123
Onanole, Man.	D2	70
Onao, i., Micron.	Q18	52
Onarga, Il., U.S.	C6	90
Onawa, Ia., U.S.	B1	92
Onawa, Lake, l., Me., U.S.	C3	96
Onaway, Id., U.S.	*C2	89
Onaway, Mi., U.S.	C6	99
Onchan, I. of Man	B4	101
Onchiota, N.Y., U.S.	f10	109
Ondangua, Nmb.	A2	49
Ondava, stm., Czech.	D6	26
Ondjiva (Ngiva), Ang.	A2	49
Ondo, Nig.	E5	45
Öndörhaan, Mong.	B7	31
Oneata, i., Fiji	I16	52
Oneco, Ct., U.S.	C8	84
Oneco, Fl., U.S.	E4	86
Onega, Sov. Un.	C16	8
Onega, stm., Sov. Un.	C16	8
Onega, Lake, l., Sov. Un.	C6	29
One Hundred Fifty Mile House, B.C.	C7	69
One Hundred Mile House, B.C.	D7	69
Oneida, Ar., U.S.	B5	81
Oneida, Ct., U.S.	E7	91
Oneida, Ia., U.S.	B6	92

Name	Map Ref.	Page
Oneida, Ks., U.S.	C8	93
Oneida, Ky., U.S.	C6	94
Oneida, N.Y., U.S.	B5	109
Oneida, Oh., U.S.	C1	112
Oneida, Tn., U.S.	C9	119
Oneida, Wi., U.S.	g9	126
Oneida, co., Id., U.S.	G6	89
Oneida, co., N.Y., U.S.	B5	109
Oneida, co., Wi., U.S.	C4	126
Oneida Lake, l., N.Y., U.S.	B5	109
O'Neill, Ne., U.S.	B7	104
Onekama, Mi., U.S.	D4	99
Onemak Island, i., Marsh Is.	S17	52
Onemak Island, i., Marsh Is.	S17	52
Oneonta, Al., U.S.	B3	78
Oneonta, N.Y., U.S.	C5	109
Ong, Ne., U.S.	D8	104
Ongea Levu, i., Fiji	I16	52
Ongin Hiid, Mong.	B5	31
Ongiyn, stm., Mong.	B5	31
Ongjin, N. Kor.	H2	33
Ongtüstik, Kor.	C5	118
Onida, S.D., U.S.	B6	118
Onilahy, stm., Madag.	h8	49
Oniotto Island, i., Marsh Is.	S17	52
Onitsha, Nig.	E6	45
Only, Va., U.S.	C7	123
Only, Tn., U.S.	B4	119
Onna, Japan	O5	52
Ōno, Japan	n15	33
Ono, i., Fiji	I15	52
Ono Channel, strt., Fiji	I15	52
Onomichi, Japan	I6	33
Onondaga, Mi., U.S.	F6	99
Onondaga, co., N.Y., U.S.	C4	109
Onondaga Indian Reservation, N.Y., U.S.	C4	109
Onoway, Alta.	C3	68
Onset, Ma., U.S.	C6	98
Onslow, Austl.	D2	50
Onslow, co., N.C., U.S.	C5	110
Onslow Bay, b., N.C., U.S.	C5	110
Onsong, N. Kor.	E3	33
Onsted, Mi., U.S.	F6	99
Ontake, Mount, mtn., Japan	n16	33
Ontario, Ca., U.S.	E5	82
Ontario, In., U.S.	A7	91
Ontario, N.Y., U.S.	B3	109
Ontario, Oh., U.S.	B3	112
Ontario, Or., U.S.	C10	114
Ontario, Wi., U.S.	E3	126
Ontario, co., Ont.	C5	73
Ontario, co., N.Y., U.S.	C3	109
Ontario, prov., Can.	C6	73
Ontario, Lake, l., N.A.	B12	76
Onteniente, Spain	C5	22
Ontonagon, Mi., U.S.	m12	99
Ontonagon, co., Mi., U.S.	m12	99
Ontonagon Indian Reservation, Mi., U.S.	B1	99
Onward, In., U.S.	C5	91
Oodnadatta, Austl.	E6	50
Ood Weyne, Som.	D6	47
Ookala, Hi., U.S.	C6	88
Oolitic, In., U.S.	G4	91
Oologah, Ok., U.S.	A6	113
Oologah Lake, res., Ok., U.S.	A6	113
Ooltewah, Tn., U.S.	D8	119
Ooltgensplaat, Neth.	C4	17
Oostburg, Neth.	C3	17
Oostburg, Wi., U.S.	E6	126
Oostende (Ostende), Bel.	B5	16
Oosterend, Neth.	A5	17
Oosterhout, Neth.	C4	17
Oosterschelde, b., Bel.	B5	16
Oostmahorn, Neth.	A6	17
Oost-Vlieland, Neth.	A5	17
Oostvoorne, Neth.	C4	17
Ootmarsum, Neth.	B6	17
Ootsa Lake, B.C.	C4	69
Ootsa Lake, l., B.C.	C4	69
Opal, Alta.	C4	68
Opal, S.D., U.S.	C3	118
Opal, Wy., U.S.	E2	127
Opala, Zaire	B4	48
Opa-Locka, Fl., U.S.	*s13	86
Opaton, Austl.	A4	51
Opatow, Pol.	C6	26
Opava, Czech.	D4	26
Opdyke, Il., U.S.	E5	90
Opelika, Al., U.S.	C4	78
Opelousas, La., U.S.	D3	95
Opeongo Lake, l., Ont.	B6	73
Opequon Creek, stm., W.V., U.S.	B6	125
Opheim, Mt., U.S.	B10	103
Ophir, Or., U.S.	E2	114
Ophir, Ut., U.S.	C3	121
Ophir, Mount, mtn., Indon.	E1	34
Opihikao, Hi., U.S.	D7	88
Opiscotéo, Lac, l., Que.	F19	66
Opobo, Nig.	F6	45
Opochka, Sov. Un.	C7	27
Opoczno, Pol.	C6	26
Opole Lubelskie, Pol.	C7	26
Opore see Porto, Port.	B1	22
Opotiki, N.Z.	M16	51
Oppdal, Nor.	F3	14
Oppelo, Ar., U.S.	B3	81
Opportunity, Wa., U.S.	B8	124
Optic Lake, Man.	B1	70
Optima, Ok., U.S.	e9	113
Optima Reservoir, res., Ok., U.S.	e9	113
Oquawka, Il., U.S.	C3	90
Oquossoc, Me., U.S.	D2	96
Ora, Italy	C7	20
Ora, Ms., U.S.	D4	101
Ora, S.C., U.S.	B3	117
Oracle, Az., U.S.	E5	80
Oradea, Rom.	B5	24
Oradell, N.J., U.S.	h8	107
Oradell Reservoir, res., N.J., U.S.	h9	107
Orai, India	E7	37
Oraibi, Az., U.S.	A5	80
Oraibi Wash, val., Az., U.S.	A5	80
Oran (Wahran), Alg.	A4	42
Oran, Mo., U.S.	D8	102
Oran, Austl.	F8	50
Orange, Fr.	E6	16
Orange, Austl.	n13	84
Orange, Ct., U.S.	D3	84
Orange, In., U.S.	E7	91
Orange, Ma., U.S.	A3	98

Name	Map Ref.	Page
Orange, N.H., U.S.	C3	106
Orange, N.J., U.S.	B4	107
Orange, Tx., U.S.	D6	120
Orange, Vt., U.S.	C4	122
Orange, Va., U.S.	B4	123
Orange, co., Ca., U.S.	F5	82
Orange, co., Fl., U.S.	D5	86
Orange, co., In., U.S.	G5	91
Orange, co., N.Y., U.S.	D6	109
Orange, co., N.C., U.S.	A3	110
Orange, co., Tx., U.S.	D6	120
Orange, co., Vt., U.S.	D3	122
Orange, co., Va., U.S.	B4	123
Orange, Cabo, c., Braz.	B4	59
Orange Beach, Al., U.S.	E2	78
Orangeburg, S.C., U.S.	E6	117
Orangeburg, co., S.C., U.S.	E6	117
Orange City, Fl., U.S.	D5	86
Orange City, Ia., U.S.	B1	92
Orangedale, N.S.	D8	71
Orange Free State, prov., S. Afr.	C4	49
Orange Grove, Ms., U.S.	E5	101
Orange Grove, Tx., U.S.	F4	120
Orange Lake, Fl., U.S.	C4	86
Orange Lake, l., Fl., U.S.	C4	86
Orange Park, Fl., U.S.	B5	86
Orangevale, Ca., U.S.	*C3	82
Orangeville, Il., U.S.	A4	90
Orangeville, Ont.	D4	73
Orangeville, Ut., U.S.	D4	121
Orange Walk, Belize	D7	63
Orani, Phil.	o13	34
Oranienbaum, Ger.	B7	19
Oranienburg, Ger.	B6	18
Oranje Gebergte, mts., Sur.	B4	59
Oranjemund, Nmb.	C2	49
Oranjestad, Aruba	G17	65
Oranmore, Ire.	D3	11
Or 'Aqiva, Isr.	B4	41
Orăștie, Rom.	C6	24
Oravita, Rom.	C5	24
Orba, stm., Italy	E4	20
Orbe, Switz.	C2	21
Orbetello, Italy	C3	23
Orbey, Fr.	A3	20
Orbigo, stm., Spain	A3	22
Orbisonia, Pa., U.S.	F6	115
Orbost, Austl.	H7	51
Örby, Swe.	H6	14
Orcas Island, i., Wa., U.S.	A3	124
Orchard, Co., U.S.	A6	83
Orchard, Id., U.S.	F2	89
Orchard, Ne., U.S.	A5	92
Orchard, Ne., U.S.	B7	104
Orchard, co., I.N.A.	C5	22
Orchard City, Co., U.S.	C3	83
Orchard Farm, Mo., U.S.	f13	102
Orchard Homes, Mt., U.S.	D2	103
Orchard Mesa, Co., U.S.	*B2	83
Orchard Park, N.Y., U.S.	C2	109
Orchards, Wa., U.S.	D3	124
Orchard Valley, Wy., U.S.	E8	127
Orchies, Fr.	D7	17
Orchila, Isla, i., Ven.	A4	60
Orcotuna, Peru	D2	58
Orcutt, Ca., U.S.	E3	82
Orcutts, Ct., U.S.	B6	84
Ord, Ne., U.S.	C7	104
Ord, stm., Austl.	C4	50
Ordale, Sask.	D2	75
Ordenes, Spain	A1	22
Orderville, Ut., U.S.	F3	121
Ording, Ger.	D2	15
Ordoqui, Arg.	B4	54
Ordos Desert see Mu Us Shamo, des., China	D6	31
Ordot, Guam	L10	52
Ordu, Tur.	B11	40
Orduña, Spain	A4	22
Ordway, Co., U.S.	C7	83
Oreana, Il., U.S.	D5	90
Oreana, Nv., U.S.	C3	105
Oreba Island, i., Marsh Is.	S17	52
Örebro, Swe.	H6	14
Ore City, Tx., U.S.	C5	120
Oregon, Il., U.S.	A4	90
Oregon, Mo., U.S.	B2	102
Oregon, Oh., U.S.	A2	112
Oregon, Wi., U.S.	F4	126
Oregon, co., Mo., U.S.	E6	102
Oregon, state, U.S.	C6	114
Oregon Caves National Monument, Or., U.S.	E2	114
Oregon City, Or., U.S.	B4	114
Oregon Inlet, b., N.C., U.S.	B7	110
Orehoved, Den.	D5	15
Orekhov, Sov. Un.	H10	27
Orekhovo-Bul.	D6	24
Orekhovo-Zuyevo, Sov. Un.	D12	27
Orel, Sov. Un.	D6	29
Orem, Ut., U.S.	C4	121
Ore Mountains, mts., Eur.	C6	18
Orenburg, Sov. Un.	D8	29
Orense, Spain	A2	22
Orestes, In., U.S.	D6	91
Orestiás, Grc.	B6	40
Øresund (The Sound), strt., Eur.	J5	14
Oreti, stm., N.Z.	P12	51
Oretta, La., U.S.	D2	95
Orford, N.H., U.S.	C2	106
Orford Ness, c., Eng., U.K.	B9	12
Orfordville, N.H., U.S.	C2	106
Orfordville, Wi., U.S.	F4	126
Organ Cave, W.V., U.S.	D4	125
Organ Mountains, mts., N.M., U.S.	E3	108
Organ Pipe Cactus National Monument, Az., U.S.	E3	80
Orgas, W.V., U.S.	m12	125
Orgaz, Spain	C4	22
Orgeyev, Sov. Un.	C11	27
Orgūn, Afg.	B4	36
Orhon, stm., Mong.	B5	31
Orick, Ca., U.S.	B1	82
Orient, Il., U.S.	F5	90
Orient, Me., U.S.	C5	96
Orient, Oh., U.S.	C2	112
Orient, S.D., U.S.	C6	118
Orient, Wa., U.S.	A8	124
Oriental, N.C., U.S.	B6	110
Oriental, Cordillera, mts., Col.	C3	60
Orihuela, Spain	C5	22
Orillia, Ont.	C5	73
Orinda, Ca., U.S.	*h8	82
Orinoco, stm., S.A.	B5	60

Name	Map Ref.	Page
Oriole, Md., U.S.	D6	97
Orion, Alta.	E5	68
Orion, Phil.	o13	34
Orion, Il., U.S.	B3	90
Oriska, N.D., U.S.	C8	111
Oriskany, N.Y., U.S.	B5	109
Oriskany, Va., U.S.	C3	123
Oriskany Falls, N.Y., U.S.	C5	109
Orissa, state, India	E7	36
Oristano, Italy	D2	23
Oristano, Gulf of, b., Italy	E2	23
Orivesi, l., Fin.	F13	14
Oriximiná, Braz.	C3	59
Orizaba, Mex.	D5	63
Orizaba, Pico de (Citlaltépetl), vol., Mex.	n15	63
Orizona, Braz.	B3	56
Orkanger, Nor.	F3	14
Örkelljunga, Swe.	B7	15
Orkla, stm., Nor.	F4	14
Orkney, Sask.	H2	75
Orkney, prov., Scot., U.K.	A5	10
Orkney Islands, is., Scot., U.K.	A5	10
Orland, Ca., U.S.	o13	120
Orland, Ca., U.S.	C2	82
Orland, In., U.S.	A7	91
Orland, Me., U.S.	D4	96
Orlando, Fl., U.S.	D5	86
Orlando, Ok., U.S.	A4	113
Orland Park, Il., U.S.	k9	90
Orleães, Braz.	D3	56
Orléanais, hist. reg., Fr.	D8	16
Orleans, Ont.	h12	73
Orleans, Ont.	A4	16
Orleans, Ca., U.S.	B2	82
Orleans, In., U.S.	G5	91
Orleans, Ia., U.S.	A2	92
Orleans, Ma., U.S.	C7	98
Orleans, Mn., U.S.	B2	100
Orleans, Ne., U.S.	D6	104
Orleans, Vt., U.S.	B4	122
Orleans, co., La., U.S.	E6	95
Orleans, co., N.Y., U.S.	B2	109
Orleans, co., Vt., U.S.	B4	122
Orléans, Île d', i., Que.	C6	74
Orlík Reservoir, res., Czech.	D9	19
Orlinda, Tn., U.S.	A5	119
Orlová, Czech.	*D5	26
Orlovista, Fl., U.S.	*D5	86
Orlyak, Bul.	D8	24
Orman Dam, S.D., U.S.	C2	118
Ormāra, Pak.	C3	36
Ormāra, Rās, c., Pak.	I12	39
Ormiston, Sask.	H3	75
Ormond Beach, Fl., U.S.	C5	86
Ormond By The Sea, Fl., U.S.	*C5	86
Ormsby, Ont.	C7	73
Ormsby, Mn., U.S.	G4	100
Ormskirk, Eng., U.K.	A5	12
Ormstown, Que.	D3	74
Ornans, Fr.	B2	20
Orne, stm., Fr.	C3	16
Orneta, Pol.	A6	26
Ornö, Swe.	t36	14
Ornö, i., Swe.	t36	14
Örnsköldsvik, Swe.	F8	14
Orø, i., Den.	C5	15
Orocué, Col.	C3	60
Orodara, Burkina	D4	45
Orofino, Id., U.S.	C2	89
Oro Grande, Ca., U.S.	E5	82
Orograndе, N.M., U.S.	E3	108
Orohena, mtn., Fr. Poly.	*H13	6
Oromocto, N.B.	D3	71
Oromocto Lake, l., N.B.	D2	71
Oron, Nig.	F6	45
Oron-la-Ville, Switz.	C2	21
Orono, Ont.	D6	73
Orono, Me., U.S.	D4	96
Orono, Mn., U.S.	*n11	100
Oronoco, Mn., U.S.	F6	100
Oronogo, Mo., U.S.	D3	102
Oronsay, i., Scot., U.K.	D2	13
Oropuche, stm., Trin.	O23	65
Oroquieta, Phil.	D6	34
Orós, Braz.	C3	57
Orosei, Gulf of, b., Italy	B5	23
Orosháza, Hung.	B5	24
Orote Peninsula, pen., Guam	L9	52
Orovada, Nv., U.S.	B4	105
Oroville, Ca., U.S.	C3	82
Oroville, Wa., U.S.	A6	124
Oroville, Lake, res., Ca., U.S.	C3	82
Orpington (part of London), Eng., U.K.	m13	12
Orr, Mn., U.S.	B6	100
Orrick, Mo., U.S.	B3	102
Orrin, N.D., U.S.	A5	111
Orrington, Me., U.S.	D4	96
Orr Lake, l., Man.	A3	70
Orrs Island, Me., U.S.	E3	96
Orrstown, Pa., U.S.	F6	115
Orrum, N.C., U.S.	C3	110
Orrville, Ont.	B5	73
Orrville, Al., U.S.	C2	78
Orrville, Oh., U.S.	B4	112
Orsa, Swe.	G6	14
Orsay, Fr.	F2	17
Orsha, Sov. Un.	D8	27
Orsières, Switz.	C3	20
Orsk, Sov. Un.	D8	29
Orson, Pa., U.S.	C11	115
Orșova, Rom.	C5	24
Ørsted, Den.	B4	15
Ørsundsbro, Swe.	t34	14
Orta, Lake, l., Italy	D4	20
Orta [San Giulio], Italy	E5	21
Ortegal, Cape, c., Spain	A2	22
Orthez, Fr.	F3	16
Ortigueira, Spain	A2	22
Orting, Wa., U.S.	B3	124
Ortisei, Italy	C6	20
Ortiz, Mex.	B3	63
Ortiz, Ven.	B4	60
Ortiz Mountain, mtn., N.M., U.S.	k8	108
Ortley, S.D., U.S.	B8	118
Ortoire, stm., Trin.	O23	65
Ortona, Italy	C5	23
Ortonville, Mi., U.S.	F7	99
Ortonville, Mn., U.S.	E2	100
Oruro, Bol.	C2	55
Oruro, dept., Bol.	C2	55
Orvieto, Italy	C4	23
Orviston, Pa., U.S.	D6	115
Orwell, Oh., U.S.	A5	112
Orwell, Vt., U.S.	D2	122
Orwigsburg, Pa., U.S.	E9	115
Or Yehuda, Isr.	g10	41
Orysa, Tn., U.S.	B2	119

Index

Name	Map Ref.	Page
Orzesze, Pol.	g9	26
Osa, Peninsula de, pen., C.R.	F6	62
Osage, Sask.	H4	75
Osage, Ia., U.S.	A5	92
Osage, Mn., U.S.	D3	100
Osage, Ok., U.S.	A5	113
Osage, Wy., U.S.	C8	127
Osage, co., Ks., U.S.	D8	93
Osage, co., Mo., U.S.	C6	102
Osage, co., Ok., U.S.	A5	113
Osage, stm., Mo., U.S.	C3	102
Osage Beach, Mo., U.S.	C5	102
Osage City, Ks., U.S.	D8	93
Osage Creek, stm., Ar., U.S.	A2	81
Ōsaka, Japan	E12	31
Osaka, Japan	n16	33
Ōsaka Bay, b., Japan	o14	33
Osaka Mountain, hill, Japan	P17	52
Osakis, Mn., U.S.	E3	100
Osakis, Lake, l., Mn., U.S.	E3	100
Osawatomie, Ks., U.S.	D9	93
Osborn, Mo., U.S.	B3	102
Osborne, Ks., U.S.	C5	93
Osborne, co., Ks., U.S.	C5	93
Osbornsville, N.J., U.S.	C4	107
Osburn, Id., U.S.	B3	89
Osby, Swe.	B8	15
Oscar, La., U.S.	D4	95
Oscar, Ok., U.S.	D4	113
Osceola, Ar., U.S.	B6	81
Osceola, In., U.S.	A5	91
Osceola, Ia., U.S.	C4	92
Osceola, Mo., U.S.	C4	102
Osceola, Ne., U.S.	C8	104
Osceola, Pa., U.S.	C7	115
Osceola, S.D., U.S.	C8	118
Osceola, Tx., U.S.	C4	120
Osceola, Wi., U.S.	C1	126
Osceola, co., Fl., U.S.	E5	86
Osceola, co., Ia., U.S.	A2	92
Osceola, co., Mi., U.S.	E5	99
Osceola, co., Mi., U.S.	E5	99
Osceola Mills, Pa., U.S.	E5	115
Oschatz, Ger.	C6	18
Oschersleben, Ger.	B5	18
Oscoda, Mi., U.S.	D7	99
Oscoda, co., Mi., U.S.	D6	99
Oscura Mountains, mts., N.M., U.S.	D3	108
Osek, Czech.	C8	19
Oselki, Sov. Un.	r31	14
Osgood, In., U.S.	F7	91
Osgood, Mo., U.S.	A4	102
Osgood, Oh., U.S.	B1	112
Osgoode, Ont.	B9	73
Osh, Sov. Un.	E10	29
Oshamambe, Japan	E10	33
Oshawa, Ont.	D6	73
Ō-shima, i., Japan	J7	33
Oshkosh, Ne., U.S.	C3	104
Oshkosh, Wi., U.S.	D5	126
Oshnovīyeh, Iran	C2	39
Oshogbo, Nig.	E5	45
Oshoto, Wy., U.S.	B8	127
Oshtorān Kūh, mtn., Iran	E4	39
Oshwe, Zaire	B2	48
Osijek, Yugo.	C4	24
Osilinka, stm., B.C.	A5	69
Osinniki, Sov. Un.	E26	8
Osipovichi, Sov. Un.	E7	27
Oskaloosa, Ia., U.S.	C5	92
Oskaloosa, Ks., U.S.	C8	93
Oskaloosa, Mo., U.S.	D3	102
Oskarshamn, Swe.	I7	14
Oskol, stm., Sov. Un.	G11	27
Oskū, Iran	C2	39
Osler, Sask.	E2	75
Oslo, Nor.	H4	14
Oslo, Mn., U.S.	B1	100
Oslofjorden, Nor.	H4	14
Osma, Spain	B4	22
Osmānābād, India	H6	37
Osmancık, Tur.	B10	40
Osmaneli, Tur.	B7	25
Osmaniye, Tur.	D11	40
Osmond, Ne., U.S.	B8	104
Osnabrock, N.D., U.S.	A7	111
Osnabrück, Ger.	B4	18
Osório, Braz.	D2	56
Osorno, Chile	C2	54
Osov, Czech.	o17	26
Osoyoos, B.C.	E8	69
Osoyoos Lake, l., Wa., U.S.	A6	124
Ospika, stm., B.C.	A6	69
Osprey, Fl., U.S.	E4	86
Oss, Neth.	B6	16
Ossa, Mount, mtn., Austl.	o15	50
Ossabaw Island, i., Ga., U.S.	E5	87
Ossabaw Sound, strt., Ga., U.S.	E6	87
Osseo, Mn., U.S.	m12	100
Osseo, Wi., U.S.	D2	126
Ossian, In., U.S.	C7	91
Ossian, Ia., U.S.	A6	92
Ossineke, Mi., U.S.	D7	99
Ossining, N.Y., U.S.	D7	109
Ossipee, N.H., U.S.	C4	106
Ossipee Lake, l., N.H., U.S.	C4	106
Ossipee Mountains, mts., N.H., U.S.	C4	106
Ossokmanuan Lake, l., Newf.	h8	72
Ossora, Sov. Un.	D34	128
Östanå, Swe.	t36	14
Ostashkov, Sov. Un.	C9	27
Osteen, Fl., U.S.	D5	86
Ostende see Oostende, Bel.	B5	16
Osterburg, Ger.	F5	15
Osterburg, Pa., U.S.	F4	115
Osterode, Ger.	B5	19
Östersund, Swe.	F6	14
Osterville, Ma., U.S.	C7	98
Osterwieck, Ger.	B5	19
Ostia Antica, Italy	h8	23
Ostiglia, Italy	D7	20
Ostrach, Ger.	B5	20
Ostrander, Mn., U.S.	G6	100
Ostrava, Czech.	B2	112
Ostróda, Pol.	B5	26
Ostrog, Sov. Un.	F6	27
Ostrogozhsk, Sov. Un.	F12	27
Ostrołęka, Pol.	B6	26
Ostrov, Czech.	C2	26
Ostrov, Rom.	C8	24
Ostrov, Sov. Un.	C7	27
Ostrowiec 95Świętokrzyski], Pol.	C6	26
Ostrów Lubelski, Pol.	C7	26
Ostrów Mazowiecka, Pol.	B6	26
Ostrów Wielkopolski, Pol.	C4	26
Ostrzeszów, Pol.	C4	26
Ostseebad Graal-Müritz, Ger.	D6	15
Ostseebad Rerik, Ger.	D5	15
Ostuni, Italy	D6	23
Ōsuka, Japan	o16	33
Osŭm, stm., Bul.	D7	24
Osumi Islands, is., Japan	E11	31
Osumi Strait, strt., Japan	K5	33
Osuna, Spain	D3	22
Osvaldo Cruz, Braz.	C2	56
Oswayo, Pa., U.S.	C5	115
Oswegatchie, Ct., U.S.	*D7	84
Oswegatchie, N.Y., U.S.	A5	109
Oswegatchie, stm., N.Y., U.S.	f9	109
Oswego, Il., U.S.	B5	90
Oswego, Ks., U.S.	E8	93
Oswego, Mt., U.S.	B11	103
Oswego, N.Y., U.S.	B4	109
Oswego, S.C., U.S.	C7	117
Oswego, co., N.Y., U.S.	B4	109
Oswego, stm., N.J., U.S.	D4	107
Oswego, stm., N.Y., U.S.	B4	109
Oswestry, Eng., U.K.	D5	10
Oświęcim (Auschwitz), Pol.	D3	101
Osyka, Ms., U.S.	*H9	33
Ōta, Japan	C3	84
Otago Peninsula, pen., N.Z.	P13	51
Otaki, Japan	n19	33
Otar, Sov. Un.	E9	28
Otaru, Japan	C13	31
Otava, stm., Czech.	D8	15
Otavalo, Ec.	A2	58
Otavi, Nmb.	A2	49
Otay, Ca., U.S.	*o15	82
Otchinjau, Ang.	E1	48
Oteen, N.C., U.S.	f10	110
Otego, N.Y., U.S.	C5	109
Otero, Co., U.S.	D7	83
Otero, co., N.M., U.S.	E3	108
Othello, Wa., U.S.	C6	124
Otho, Ia., U.S.	B3	92
Othonoí, i., Grc.	C2	25
Óthris Mountains, mts., Grc.	C4	25
Oti, stm., Afr.	E5	45
Otis, Co., U.S.	A8	83
Otis, In., U.S.	A4	91
Otis, Ks., U.S.	D4	93
Otis, Ma., U.S.	B1	98
Otisco, Mn., U.S.	G5	100
Otisco Lake, l., N.Y., U.S.	C4	109
Otis Orchards, Wa., U.S.	g14	124
Otis Reservoir, res., Ma., U.S.	E7	99
Otisville, Mi., U.S.	E7	99
Otjiwarongo, Nmb.	B2	49
Otley, Ia., U.S.	C4	92
Otočac, Yugo.	D9	104
Otoe, Ne., U.S.	H2	14
Otoe, co., Ne., U.S.	s31	14
Otradnoye, Sov. Un.	D7	23
Otranto, Italy	D2	40
Otranto, Strait of, strt., Eur.	F5	99
Otsego, Mi., U.S.	C5	99
Otsego, co., Mi., U.S.	C5	109
Otsego, co., N.Y., U.S.	D6	99
Otsego Lake, l., Mi., U.S.	C6	109
Otsego Lake, l., N.Y., U.S.	n17	33
Ōtsuki, Japan	C3	104
Ottauquechee, stm., Vt., U.S.	B9	73
Ottawa, Ont.	B5	90
Ottawa, Il., U.S.	D8	93
Ottawa, Ks., U.S.	A1	112
Ottawa, Oh., U.S.	n12	125
Ottawa, W.V., U.S.	C5	93
Ottawa, co., Ks., U.S.	F4	99
Ottawa, co., Mi., U.S.	A2	112
Ottawa, co., Oh., U.S.	A7	113
Ottawa, co., Ok., U.S.	G17	66
Ottawa, stm., Can.	e6	112
Ottawa, stm., Oh., U.S.	B9	73
Ottawa-Carleton, co., Ont.	e6	112
Ottawa Hills, Oh., U.S.	E16	66
Ottawa Islands, is., N.W. Ter.	G7	99
Ottawa Lake, Mi., U.S.	E10	103
Otter, Mt., U.S.	A2	68
Otter, stm., Alta.	D4	12
Otter, stm., Eng., U.K.	D3	91
Otterbein, In., U.S.	D2	19
Otterberg, Ger.	E2	106
Otter Brook, stm., N.H., U.S.	E6	13
Otter Brook Lake, res., N.H., U.S.	E7	99
Otterburn, Que.	E6	13
Otterburne, Man.	E3	70
Otter Creek, Fl., U.S.	C4	86
Otter Creek, Me., U.S.	D4	96
Otter Creek, stm., Ut., U.S.	E4	121
Otter Creek, stm., Vt., U.S.	C2	122
Otter Creek Reservoir, res., Ut., U.S.	E4	121
Otter Islands, is., S.C., U.S.	m11	117
Otter Lake, Mi., U.S.	E7	99
Otter Lake, N.Y., U.S.	B5	109
Otter Lake, l., Sask.	B3	75
Otterndorf, Ger.	E2	15
Otter River, Ma., U.S.	A3	98
Ottersberg, Ger.	E3	15
Ottersleben, Ger.	A6	19
Ottertail, Mn., U.S.	D3	100
Otter Tail, co., Mn., U.S.	D2	100
Otter Tail, stm., Mn., U.S.	D3	100
Otter Tail Lake, l., Mn., U.S.	D3	100
Otterup, Den.	C4	15
Otterville, Ont.	E4	73
Otterville, Il., U.S.	D3	90
Otterville, Ia., U.S.	B6	92
Otterville, Mo., U.S.	C4	102
Otthon, Sask.	F4	75
Ottignies, Bel.	D4	17
Otto, N.Y., U.S.	C2	109
Ottokee, Oh., U.S.	A1	112
Ottone, Italy	E3	20
Ottosen, Ia., U.S.	B3	92
Ottoville, Oh., U.S.	B1	112
Ottsville, Pa., U.S.	F11	115
Ottumwa, Ia., U.S.	C5	92
Ottumwa, S.D., U.S.	C4	118
Otuzco, Peru	B2	58
Otway, N.C., U.S.	C6	110
Otway, Cape, c., Austl.	G7	50
Otway, Seno, b., Chile	h11	54
Otwell, In., U.S.	H3	91
Otwock, Pol.	m14	26
Ötztal Alps, mts., Eur.	B6	20
Ötztaler Ach, stm., Aus.	B6	20
Ou, stm., Laos	D3	34
Ouachita, Ar., U.S.	D3	81
Ouachita, co., Ar., U.S.	D3	81
Ouachita, co., La., U.S.	B3	95
Ouachita, stm., U.S.	D9	76
Ouachita, Lake, res., Ar., U.S.	C2	81
Ouachita Mountains, mts., U.S.	D9	76
Ouadane, Maur.	C2	45
Ouaddai, hist. reg., Chad	C4	46
Ouagadougou, Burkina	D4	45
Ouahigouya, Burkina	D4	45
Ouaka, stm., Cen. Afr. Rep.	D4	46
Oualâta, Maur.	C3	45
Ouallam, Niger	D5	45
Ouallene, Alg.	E5	44
Ouanary, Fr. Gu.	D4	59
Ouanda Djallé, Cen. Afr. Rep.	B3	46
Ouarane, reg., Maur.	C3	44
Ouarzazate, Mor.	A2	44
Oubangui (Ubangi), stm., Afr.	A2	48
Ouddorp, Neth.	D3	17
Oudenaarde, Bel.	D3	17
Oude-Pekela, Neth.	A7	17
Oudtshoorn, S. Afr.	D3	49
Oued Zem, Mor.	*C3	44
Ouellé, I.C.	E4	45
Ouelmé, stm., Que.	D6	71
Ouémé, stm., Benin	E5	45
Ouesso, Congo	A2	48
Ouest, Pointe de l', c., Que.	k8	72
Ouest, Pointe du, c., St. P./M.	E3	72
Ouezzane, Mor.	C3	44
Oughter, Lough, l., Ire.	G6	10
Oughterard, Ire.	D2	11
Ouham, stm., Afr.	D3	46
Ouidah, Benin	E5	45
Oujda, Mor.	C4	44
Oullins, Fr.	E6	16
Oulu, Fin.	E11	14
Oulujärvi, l., Fin.	E12	14
Oum Chalouba, Chad	B4	46
Oum Hadjer, Chad	C3	46
Ounâne, Bîr, well, Mali	B4	45
Ounasjoki, stm., Fin.	D11	14
Ounianga Kébir, Chad	B4	46
Ouray, Co., U.S.	C3	83
Ouray, Ut., U.S.	C6	121
Ouray, co., Co., U.S.	C3	83
Ouray, Mount, mtn., Co., U.S.	C4	83
Ouri, Chad	B2	46
Ouricuri, Braz.	C2	57
Ourinhos, Braz.	C3	56
Ourique, Port.	D1	22
Ouro Fino, Braz.	C3	56
Ouro Prêto, Braz.	C4	56
Ourthe, stm., Bel.	D5	17
Ourukaen Island, i., Marsh Is.	P18	52
Ouse, stm., Eng., U.K.	D6	10
Outagamie, co., Wi., U.S.	D5	126
Outardes Quatre, Réservoir, res., Que.	h13	74
Outer Hebrides, is., Scot., U.K.		
Outer Island, i., Wi., U.S.	A3	126
Outer Santa Barbara Passage, strt., Ca., U.S.	F4	82
Outes, Spain	A1	22
Outing, Mn., U.S.	D5	100
Outlook, Sask.	F2	75
Outlook, Mt., U.S.	B12	103
Outlook, Wa., U.S.	C5	124
Outpost Mountain, mtn., Ak., U.S.	B9	79
Outreau, Fr.	B4	16
Outremont, Que.	p19	74
Ouville-la-Rivière, Fr.	E8	12
Ouzinkie, Ak., U.S.	D9	79
Ovada, Italy	B2	23
Oval, Pa., U.S.	D7	115
Ovalau, i., Fiji	H15	52
Ovalle, Chile	A2	54
Ovana, Cerro, mtn., Ven.	C4	60
Ovando, Mt., U.S.	C3	103
Ovar, Port.	B1	22
Overath, Ger.	C2	19
Overbrook, Ks., U.S.	D8	93
Overbrook, Ok., U.S.	C4	113
Overflowing, stm., Can.	D5	75
Overgaard, Az., U.S.	C5	80
Overijse, Bel.	D4	17
Overijssel, prov., Neth.	B6	17
Overisel, Mi., U.S.	F4	99
Overland, Mo., U.S.	f13	102
Overland Park, Ks., U.S.	m16	93
Overlea, Md., U.S.	B5	97
Overlook, Oh., U.S.	*C1	112
Overly, N.D., U.S.	A5	111
Overstreet, Fl., U.S.	B1	86
Overton, Ne., U.S.	D6	104
Overton, Nv., U.S.	G7	105
Overton, Tx., U.S.	C5	120
Overton, co., Tn., U.S.	C8	119
Övertorneå, Swe.	D10	14
Ovett, Ms., U.S.	D4	101
Ovid, Co., U.S.	A8	83
Ovid, Id., U.S.	G7	89
Ovid, Mi., U.S.	E6	99
Ovid, N.Y., U.S.	C4	109
Oviedo, Spain	A3	22
Ovruch, Sov. Un.	F7	27
Owando, Congo	B2	48
Owaneco, Il., U.S.	D4	90
Owanka, S.D., U.S.	C3	118
Owasco Lake, l., N.Y., U.S.	C4	109
Owasso, Ok., U.S.	A6	113
Owatonna, Mn., U.S.	F5	100
Owbeh, Afg.	D11	39
Owego, N.Y., U.S.	C4	109
Owen, Wi., U.S.	D3	126
Owen, co., In., U.S.	F4	91
Owen, co., Ky., U.S.	B5	94
Owen, Lake, l., Wi., U.S.	B2	126
Owen, Mount, mtn., N.Z.	N14	51
Owen, Mount, mtn., Co., U.S.	C3	83
Owendale, Mi., U.S.	E7	99
Owens, stm., Ca., U.S.	D4	82
Owensboro, Ky., U.S.	C2	94
Owensburg, In., U.S.	G4	91
Owens Creek, stm., Md., U.S.	A3	97
Owens Cross Roads, Al., U.S.	A3	78
Owens Lake, l., Ca., U.S.	D5	82
Owen Sound, Ont.	C4	73
Owen Stanley Range, mts., Pap. N. Gui.	k12	50
Owensville, In., U.S.	H2	91
Owensville, Mo., U.S.	C6	102
Owensville, Oh., U.S.	C1	112
Owenton, Ky., U.S.	B5	94
Owerri, Nig.	E6	45
Owey Island, i., Ire.	B3	11
Owikeno Lake, l., B.C.	D4	69
Owings, Md., U.S.	B4	97
Owings Mills, Md., U.S.	B4	97
Owingsville, Ky., U.S.	B6	94
Owl Creek, stm., Wy., U.S.	C4	127
Owl Creek Mountains, mts., Wy., U.S.	C4	127
Owls Head, Me., U.S.	D3	96
Owo, Nig.	E6	45
Owosso, Mi., U.S.	E6	99
Owsley, co., Ky., U.S.	C6	94
Owyhee, Nv., U.S.	B5	105
Owyhee, co., Id., U.S.	G2	89
Owyhee, stm., U.S.	E9	114
Owyhee, Lake, res., Or., U.S.	D9	114
Owyhee, North Fork, stm., U.S.	E9	114
Owyhee, South Fork, stm., U.S.	G2	89
Owyhee Dam, Or., U.S.	D9	114
Owyhee Mountains, mts., U.S.	G2	89
Öxabäck, Swe.	H4	75
Oxbow, Sask.	H4	75
Oxbow, Me., U.S.	B4	96
Oxbow, Or., U.S.	B10	114
Oxbow Dam, U.S.	E2	89
Oxelösund, Swe.	u35	14
Oxford, N.S.	D6	71
Oxford, Eng., U.K.	E6	10
Oxford, Al., U.S.	B4	78
Oxford, Ar., U.S.	A4	81
Oxford, Ct., U.S.	D3	84
Oxford, Fl., U.S.	D4	86
Oxford, Ga., U.S.	C3	87
Oxford, Id., U.S.	G6	89
Oxford, In., U.S.	C3	91
Oxford, Ia., U.S.	C6	92
Oxford, Ks., U.S.	E6	93
Oxford, La., U.S.	C2	95
Oxford, Me., U.S.	D2	96
Oxford, Md., U.S.	C5	97
Oxford, Ma., U.S.	B4	98
Oxford, Mi., U.S.	F7	99
Oxford, Ms., U.S.	A4	101
Oxford, Ne., U.S.	D6	104
Oxford, N.J., U.S.	B3	107
Oxford, N.Y., U.S.	C5	109
Oxford, N.C., U.S.	A4	110
Oxford, Oh., U.S.	C1	112
Oxford, Pa., U.S.	G10	115
Oxford, Wi., U.S.	E4	126
Oxford, co., Me., U.S.	D2	96
Oxford, co., Ont.	D4	73
Oxford House, Man.	B4	70
Oxford Junction, Ia., U.S.	C7	92
Oxford Lake, l., Man.	B4	70
Oxfordshire, co., Eng., U.K.	C6	12
Oxly, Mo., U.S.	E7	102
Oxnard, Ca., U.S.	E4	82
Oxon Hill, Md., U.S.	f9	97
Oyace, Italy	E3	21
Oyama, B.C.	D8	69
Oyama, Japan	m18	33
Oyapock (Oiapoque), stm., S.A.		
Oyat, stm., Sov. Un.	A10	27
Oyem, Gabon	E2	46
Oyen, Alta.	D5	68
Oyen, Ia., U.S.	B1	92
Öyeren, l., Nor.	p29	14
Oykel, stm., Scot., U.K.	C4	13
Oykel Bridge, Scot., U.K.	C4	13
Oymyakon, Sov. Un.	D7	92
Oyo, Nig.	E5	45
Oyonnax, Fr.	D6	16
Oyster Bay, N.Y., U.S.	E7	109
Oyster Keys, is., Fl., U.S.	G6	86
Oyster Ridge, mtn., Wy., U.S.	E2	127
Ozamiz, Phil.	D6	34
Ozan, Ar., U.S.	C2	81
Ozark, Al., U.S.	D4	78
Ozark, Ar., U.S.	B2	81
Ozark, Mo., U.S.	D4	102
Ozark, co., Mo., U.S.	E5	102
Ozark Escarpment, clf., U.S.	B4	81
Ozark Plateau, plat., U.S.	C9	76
Ozark Reservoir, res., Ar., U.S.	B1	81
Ozarks, Lake of the, res., Mo., U.S.	C5	102
Ozarowice, Pol.	g10	26
Ozaukee, co., Wi., U.S.	E6	126
Ozawkie, Ks., U.S.	k15	93
Ōzd, Hung.	A5	24
Ozernyy, Sov. Un.	C6	28
Ozette Lake, l., Wa., U.S.	A1	124
Ozieri, Italy	D2	23
Ozona, Fl., U.S.	o10	86
Ozona, Ms., U.S.	E4	101
Ozona, Tx., U.S.	D2	120
Ozone, Ar., U.S.	B2	81
Ozone, Tx., U.S.	C5	120
Ozorków, Pol.	C5	26
Ōzu, Japan	J6	33
Ozuluama, Mex.	C5	62

P

Name	Map Ref.	Page
Paar, stm., Ger.	E6	19
Paarl, S. Afr.	D2	49
Paauhau, Hi., U.S.	C6	88
Paauilo, Hi., U.S.	C6	88
Pabbay, i., Scot., U.K.	C1	13
Pabellón, Punta, c., Chile	C2	54
Pabianice, Pol.	C5	26
Pablo, Mt., U.S.	C2	103
Pābna, Bngl.	D8	36
Pacaás Novos, Serra dos, mts., Braz.	E2	59
Pacajá, stm., Braz.	C4	59
Pacasmayo, Peru	C2	58
Pace, Ms., U.S.	B3	101
Pachaug Pond, l., Ct., U.S.	C8	84
Pachmarhi, India	F7	37
Pachuca [de Soto], Mex.	C5	62
Pachuta, Ms., U.S.	C5	101
Pacific, B.C.	B3	69
Pacific, Mo., U.S.	f13	102
Pacific, Wa., U.S.	f11	124
Pacific, co., Wa., U.S.	C2	124
Pacific Beach, Wa., U.S.	B1	124
Pacific City, Or., U.S.	B3	114
Pacific Creek, stm., Wy., U.S.	D3	127
Pacific Grove, Ca., U.S.	D3	82
Pacific Islands, Trust Territory of the, dep., Oc.	F9	6
Pacific Junction, Ia., U.S.	D2	92
Pacific Ocean	E11	6
Pacific Palisades, Hi., U.S.	g10	88
Pacific Ranges, mts., B.C.	D4	69
Pacific Rim National Park, B.C.	E5	69
Packard Mountain, hill, Ma., U.S.	B3	98
Pack Monadnock Mountain, mtn., N.H., U.S.	E3	106
Packwaukee, Wi., U.S.	E4	126
Packwood, Ia., U.S.	C5	92
Pacolet, S.C., U.S.	B4	117
Pacolet, stm., S.C., U.S.	A4	117
Pacolet Mills, S.C., U.S.	A4	117
Pacora, Pan.	k12	62
Pacora, stm., Pan.	k12	62
Pacov, Czech.	D9	19
Pacquet, Newf.	D4	72
Pactola Reservoir, res., S.D., U.S.	C2	118
Pactolus, N.C., U.S.	B5	110
Padang, Indon.	F2	34
Padang, i., Indon.	L5	35
Padang Endau, Malay.	K5	35
Padangpanjang, Indon.	F2	34
Padangsidempuan, Indon.	E1	34
Padauiri, stm., Braz.	B2	59
Paddle Prairie, Alta.	f7	68
Paddock Lake, Wi., U.S.	n11	126
Paddockwood, Sask.	D3	75
Paden, Ms., U.S.	A5	101
Paden, Ok., U.S.	B5	113
Paden City, W.V., U.S.	B4	125
Paderborn, Ger.	C4	18
Padilla, Bol.	C3	55
Padova (Padua), Italy	B3	23
Padra, India		
Padre Island, i., Tx., U.S.	F4	120
Padre Island National Seashore, Tx., U.S.	F4	120
Padroni, Co., U.S.	A7	83
Padstow, Eng., U.K.	D3	12
Padua see Padova, Italy	B3	23
Paducah, Ky., U.S.	e9	94
Paducah, Tx., U.S.	B2	120
Paektu, Mount, mtn., Asia	F4	33
Paepaeolei'a, Cape, c., W. Sam.	F11	52
Paeroa, N.Z.	L15	51
Paestum, hist., Italy	D5	23
Pafúri, Moz.	B5	49
Pagai Selatan, i., Indon.	F2	34
Pagai Utara, i., Indon.	F2	34
Pagan, i., N. Mar. Is.	B5	69
Pagasitikós Kólpos (Gulf of Vólos), b., Grc.	C4	40
Pagat Point, c., Guam	F4	34
Pagato, stm., Sask.	A4	75
Pagau Point, c., Guam	L10	52
Page, N.D., U.S.	B8	111
Page, Ok., U.S.	C7	113
Page, W.V., U.S.	C3	125
Page, co., Ia., U.S.	D2	92
Page, co., Va., U.S.	B4	123
Page Manor, Oh., U.S.	*C1	112
Pagny [-sur-Moselle], Fr.	F5	17
Pago Bay, b., Guam	M10	52
Pagoda Peak, mtn., Co., U.S.	A3	83
Pagoda Point, c., Burma	E9	36
Pago Pago, Am. Sam.	G13	52
Pago Pago Harbor, b., Am. Sam.	F13	52
Pago Point, c., Guam	M10	52
Pagosa Springs, Co., U.S.	D3	83
Pahala, Hi., U.S.	D6	88
Pahang, state, Malay.	K5	35
Pahang, stm., Malay.	E2	34
Pahaska, Wy., U.S.	B3	127
Pahoa, Hi., U.S.	D7	88
Pahokee, Fl., U.S.	F6	86
Pahrump, Nv., U.S.	G6	105
Pahute Mesa, mtn., Nv., U.S.	F5	105
Paia, Hi., U.S.	C5	88
Paignton, Eng., U.K.	K9	12
Päijänne, l., Fin.	G11	14
Pailolo Channel, strt., Hi., U.S.	B5	88
Paincourt, Ont.	E2	73
Paincourtville, La., U.S.	k9	95
Painesdale, Mi., U.S.	A2	99
Painesville, Oh., U.S.	A4	112
Paint Bank, Va., U.S.	C2	123
Paint Creek, stm., Oh., U.S.	C2	112
Paint Creek, North Fork, stm., Oh., U.S.	o10	86
Paint Creek Lake, res., Oh., U.S.	C2	112
Painted Desert, des., Az., U.S.	B4	80
Painted Post, N.Y., U.S.	C3	109
Painted Rock Reservoir, res., Az., U.S.	D3	80
Painter, Va., U.S.	C7	123
Paint Lake, l., Man.	B3	70
Paint Lick, Ky., U.S.	C5	94
Paint Mountain, mtn., W.V., U.S.	n13	125
Paint Rock, Al., U.S.	A3	78
Paint Rock, Tx., U.S.	D3	120
Paintsville, Ky., U.S.	C7	94
Paisley, Ont.	C3	73
Paisley, Fl., U.S.	D5	86
Paisley, Scot., U.K.	E6	114
Paita, Peru	C1	58
Pajarito, N.M., U.S.	*B3	108
Pajaros Point, c., V.I., Br.	A7	65
Pajon Point, c., Guam	L10	52
Pakenham, Ont.	B8	73
Pakhra, stm., Sov. Un.	n17	27
Pakistan, ctry., Asia	C4	36
Pakokku, Burma	D9	36
Pakowki Lake, l., Alta.	E5	68
Pakra, stm., Yugo.	B4	24
Pakwa Lake, l., Man.	B2	70
Pakwe, stm., Bots.	B4	49
Pakxe, Laos	D2	46
Palacios, Tx., U.S.	E4	120
Palafrugell, Spain	B7	22
Palagruža, i., Yugo.	D3	24
Palaiió Fáliron, Grc.	h11	25
Palaiokhóra, Grc.	C3	47
Palamós, Spain	B7	22
Palana, Sov. Un.	D18	29
Palanga, Sov. Un.	D3	27
Palangkaraya, Indon.	F4	34
Pālanpur, India	D5	36
Palapag, Phil.	C7	34
Palas del Rey, Spain	A2	22
Palatine, Il., U.S.	A5	90
Palatka, Fl., U.S.	C5	86
Palau (Belau), ter., T.T.P.I.	F8	6
Palauig, Phil.	o12	34
Palazzolo Acreide, Italy	F5	23
Palco, Ks., U.S.	C4	93
Palembang, Indon.	F2	34
Palena, stm., S.A.	C2	54
Palencia, Spain	A3	22
Palenque, hist., Mex.	B2	62
Palenville, N.Y., U.S.	C6	109
Palermo, Italy	E4	23
Palermo, Me., U.S.	D3	96
Palermo, N.J., U.S.	E3	107
Palermo, N.D., U.S.	A3	111
Palestine, Ar., U.S.	C5	81
Palestine, Ct., U.S.	*D2	84
Palestine, Il., U.S.	D6	90
Palestine, Oh., U.S.	B1	112
Palestine, Tx., U.S.	D5	120
Palestine, hist. reg., Asia	G10	40
Palestine, Lake, res., Tx., U.S.	C5	120
Palestrina, Italy	h9	23
Paletwa, Burma	D9	36
Palghāt, India	F6	36
Palhoça, Braz.	D3	56
Pāli, India	E4	37
Palidoro (Baebiana), Italy	h8	23
Palikea, mtn., Hi., U.S.	g9	88
Paliker Point, c., Micron.	Q17	52
Palimé, Togo	E5	45
Palisade, Mn., U.S.	D5	100
Palisade, Ne., U.S.	D4	104
Palisades, Id., U.S.	F7	89
Palisades, Wa., U.S.	B6	124
Palisades Park, N.J., U.S.	h8	107
Palisades Reservoir, res., U.S.	F7	89
Palisadoes, spit, Jam.	F15	65
Paliseul, Bel.	E5	17
Pālitāna, India	G3	37
Palk Strait, strt., Asia	E3	11
Pallaskenry, Ire.	D3	28
Pallasovka, Sov. Un.	F2	34
Palling, B.C.	B5	69
Palliser, Cape, c., N.Z.	N15	51
Pall Mall, Tn., U.S.	C9	119
Palma, Moz.	D7	48
Palma, stm., Braz.	D1	57
Palma del Río, Spain	D3	22
Palma [de Mallorca], Spain	C7	22
Palmares, Braz.	C3	57
Palmar Sur, C.R.	F6	62
Palmas, Braz.	D2	56
Palmas, Cape, c., Afr.	F3	45
Palmas de Monte Alto, Braz.	A4	56
Palma Sola, Fl., U.S.	*E4	86
Palma Soriano, Cuba	D5	64
Palm Bay, Fl., U.S.	D6	86
Palm Beach, co., Fl., U.S.	F6	86
Palm Beach Gardens, Fl., U.S.	F6	86
Palmdale, Ca., U.S.	E4	82
Palmdale, Fl., U.S.	F5	86
Palm Desert, Ca., U.S.	*F5	82
Palmeira, Braz.	D2	56
Palmeira d'Oeste, Braz.	C2	56
Palmeira dos Indios, Braz.	C3	57
Palmeirinhas, Ponta das, c., Ang.	C1	48
Palmer, Sask.	H2	75
Palmer, Ak., U.S.	C10	79
Palmer, Il., U.S.	D4	90
Palmer, Ia., U.S.	B3	92
Palmer, Ks., U.S.	C6	93
Palmer, Ma., U.S.	B3	98
Palmer, Mi., U.S.	B3	99
Palmer, Ms., U.S.	D4	101
Palmer, Ne., U.S.	C7	104
Palmer, Tn., U.S.	D8	119
Palmer, Tx., U.S.	n10	120
Palmer, Wa., U.S.	f12	124
Palmer, stm., Austl.	B6	7
Palmer Lake, Co., U.S.	B6	83
Palmer Land, reg., Ant.	A11	9
Palmer Park, Md., U.S.	*C4	97
Palmerston, Ont.	D4	73
Palmerston, N.Z.	P13	51
Palmerston North, N.Z.	N15	51
Palmerstown, Tn., U.S.	A3	119
Palmerton, Pa., U.S.	E10	115
Palmetto, Fl., U.S.	E4	86
Palmetto, Ga., U.S.	C2	87
Palmetto, La., U.S.	D4	95
Palmetto Estates, Fl., U.S.	*G6	86
Palm Harbor, Fl., U.S.	o10	86
Palmi, Italy	E5	23
Palmira, Col.	C2	60
Palmira, Cuba	C3	64
Palmitas, Ur.	f8	54
Palmitos, Braz.	D2	56
Palms, Mi., U.S.	E8	99
Palms, Isle of, i., S.C., U.S.	F8	117
Palm Springs, Ca., U.S.	F5	82
Palm Springs, Fl., U.S.	F6	86
Palm Valley, Fl., U.S.	m9	86
Palmyra, In., U.S.	H5	91
Palmyra, Ia., U.S.	f9	92
Palmyra, Me., U.S.	D3	96
Palmyra, Mo., U.S.	B6	102
Palmyra, N.J., U.S.	C2	107
Palmyra, N.Y., U.S.	B3	109
Palmyra, Pa., U.S.	F8	115
Palmyra, Tn., U.S.	A4	119
Palmyra, Va., U.S.	C4	123
Palmyra, atoll, Oc.	F12	6
Palmyras Point, c., India	h8	23
Palo (Alsium), Italy	h8	23
Palo, Ia., U.S.	B6	92
Palo Alto, Ca., U.S.	D2	82
Palo Alto, co., Ia., U.S.	A3	92
Palo Duro Canyon, val., Tx., U.S.	B2	120
Paloich, Sud.	C3	47
Palomar Mountain, mtn., Ca., U.S.	F5	82
Palomas Mountains, mts., Az., U.S.	D2	80
Palombara Sabina, Italy	g9	23
Palo Negro, Ven.	C3	60
Palo Pinto, Tx., U.S.	C3	120
Palo Pinto, co., Tx., U.S.	C3	120
Palopo, Indon.	F6	34
Palos, Cape, c., Spain	D5	22
Palos Heights, Il., U.S.	*k9	90
Palos Hills, Il., U.S.	*k9	90
Palos Park, Il., U.S.	k9	90
Palos Verdes Estates, Ca., U.S.	n12	82
Palourde, Lake, l., La., U.S.	k9	95
Palouse, Wa., U.S.	C8	124
Palouse, stm., Wa., U.S.	C7	124

Index

Name	Map Ref.	Page
Palo Verde, Az., U.S.	D3	80
Palo Verde, Ca., U.S.	F6	82
Palpa, Peru	D3	58
Pålsboda, Swe.	†33	14
Palu, Indon.	*F5	34
Palvār, Küh-e, mtn., Iran	F8	39
Pama, Burkina	D5	45
Pamamaroo Lake, l., Austl.	F4	51
Pambrun, Sask.	H2	75
Pamekasan, Indon.	G4	34
Pamiers, Fr.	F4	16
Pamir, mts., Asia	F10	29
Pamlico, co., N.C., U.S.	B6	110
Pamlico, stm., N.C., U.S.	B6	110
Pamlico Sound, strt., N.C., U.S.	B6	110
Pampa, Tx., U.S.	B2	120
Pampa, reg., Arg.	G4	53
Pampa Grande, Bol.	C3	55
Pampanga, stm., Phil.	o13	34
Pampas, Peru	D3	58
Pampilhosa do Botão, Port.	B1	22
Pamplico, S.C., U.S.	D8	117
Pamplin, Va., U.S.	C4	123
Pamplona, Col.	B3	60
Pamplona, Spain	A5	22
Pamunkey, stm., Va., U.S.	C5	123
Pana, Il., U.S.	D4	90
Panaca, Nv., U.S.	F7	105
Panacea, Fl., U.S.	B2	86
Panache, l., Ont.	A3	73
Panagyurishte, Bul.	D7	24
Panaitan, i., Indon.	G3	34
Panaji, India	E5	36
Panamá, Braz.	B3	56
Panamá, Pan.	F8	62
Panama, Il., U.S.	D4	90
Panama, Ia., U.S.	C2	92
Panama, Ne., U.S.	D9	104
Panama, N.Y., U.S.	C1	109
Panama, Ok., U.S.	B7	113
Panama, ctry., N.A.	F8	62
Panamá, Bahía de, b., Pan.	F8	62
Panamá, Golfo de, b., Pan.	F8	62
Panama Canal, Pan.	k11	62
Panama City, Fl., U.S.	u16	86
Panama City Beach, Fl., U.S.	u16	86
Panamint Range, mts., Ca., U.S.	D5	82
Panao, Peru	C2	58
Panarea, i., Italy	E5	23
Panaro, stm., Italy	B3	23
Panay, i., Phil.	C6	34
Pancake Range, mts., Nv., U.S.	E6	105
Pančevo, Yugo.	C5	24
Panch'iao (T'aipeihsien), Tai.	*F9	31
Pancoastburg, Oh., U.S.	C2	112
Panda, Moz.	B5	49
Pandharpur, India	E6	36
Pāndhurnā, India	G7	37
Pando, Ur.	E1	56
Pando, dept., Bol.	B2	55
Pandora, Oh., U.S.	B2	112
Pandora, Tx., U.S.	E4	120
Pandu, Zaire	A2	48
Panelas, Braz.	k5	57
Panet, Que.	C7	74
Panevėžys, Sov. Un.	D5	27
Panfilov, Sov. Un.	E10	29
Pangala, Congo	B1	48
Pangani, Tan.	C6	48
Pangburn, Ar., U.S.	B4	81
Pangi, Zaire	B4	48
Pangkalanbuun, Indon.	F4	34
Pangkalpinang, Indon.	F3	34
Pangman, Sask.	H3	75
Pangnirtung, N.W. Ter.	C19	66
Pangsau Pass, Asia	C10	36
Panguipulli, Chile	B2	54
Panguitch, Ut., U.S.	F3	121
Panhandle, Tx., U.S.	B2	120
Paniau, mtn., Hi., U.S.	B1	88
Panié, Mont, mtn., N. Cal.	*H10	6
Pānihāti, India	*D8	37
Panīpat, India	C6	37
Paniqui, Phil.	o13	34
Panj, stm., Asia	k17	39
Panjāb, Afg.	D13	39
Panjim see Panaji, India		
Panjgūr, Pak.	C3	36
Panki, India	G13	39
Pankey, Ar., U.S.	h10	81
Pankeyville, Il., U.S.	F5	90
Pankshin, Nig.	E6	45
Panmunjom, N. Kor.	H3	33
Panna, India	D7	36
Panola, Al., U.S.	C1	78
Panola, co., Ms., U.S.	A3	101
Panola, co., Tx., U.S.	C5	120
Panora, Ia., U.S.	C3	92
Panorama, Braz.	C2	56
Pansey, Al., U.S.	D4	78
Panshan, China	D9	32
Panshi, China	C11	32
Pantar, i., Indon.	G6	34
Pantego, N.C., U.S.	B6	110
Pantelleria, Italy	F3	23
Pantelleria, i., Italy	F4	23
Panthersville, Ga., U.S.	*h8	87
Pantin, Fr.	g10	16
Panton, Vt., U.S.	C2	122
Pánuco, Mex.	C5	63
Pánuco, stm., Mex.	k14	63
Panulcillo, Chile	F1	55
Panzi, Zaire	C2	48
Panzós, Guat.	D7	63
Pão de Açúcar, Braz.	C3	57
Paola, Italy	E6	23
Paola, Ks., U.S.	D8	93
Paoli, Co., U.S.	A8	83
Paoli, In., U.S.	G5	91
Paoli, Ok., U.S.	C4	113
Paoli, Pa., U.S.	o20	115
Paonia, Co., U.S.	C3	83
Paoua, Cen. Afr. Rep.	D3	46
Paoy Pet, Camb.	C3	34
Pápa, Hung.	B3	24
Papaaloa, Hi., U.S.	D6	88
Papagayo, Golfo de, b., C.R.	E7	63
Papago Indian Reservation, Az., U.S.	E3	80
Papaikou, Hi., U.S.	D6	88
Papantla [de Olarte], Mex.	C5	63
Papawai Point, c., Hi., U.S.	C5	88
Papeete, Fr. Poly.	H13	6
Papenburg, Ger.	B7	18
Paper Mill Village, Vt., U.S.	F2	122
Papillion, Ne., U.S.	C9	104
Papineau, Il., U.S.	C6	90
Papineau, co., Que.	D2	74
Papineau Lake, l., Ont.	B7	73
Papineauville, Que.	D2	74
Paposo, Chile	E1	55
Papua, Gulf of, b., Pap. N. Gui.	k11	50
Papua New Guinea, ctry., Oc.	G8	6
Papudo, Chile	A2	54
Papun, Burma	E10	36
Paquette, Que.	D6	74
Paquetville, N.B.	B4	71
Pará, stm., Braz.	C4	59
Pará, dept., Sur.	A3	59
Pará, stm., Braz.	C5	59
Pará see Belém, Braz.		
Paracatu, Braz.	B1	57
Parachute, Co., U.S.	B2	83
Paracel Islands, is., Asia	B4	34
Paraćin, Yugo.	D5	24
Paracuru, Braz.	B3	57
Paradis, La., U.S.	k11	95
Paradise, Ca., U.S.	C3	82
Paradise, Ks., U.S.	C5	93
Paradise, Mi., U.S.	B5	99
Paradise, Mt., U.S.	C2	103
Paradise, Nv., U.S.	G6	105
Paradise, Pa., U.S.	G9	115
Paradise, Ut., U.S.	B4	121
Paradise, stm., Newf.	B3	72
Paradise Hill, Sask.	D1	75
Paradise Hills, N.M., U.S.	B3	108
Paradise Island, i., Bah.	m18	64
Paradise River, Newf.	B3	72
Paradise Valley, Alta.	C5	68
Paradise Valley, Az., U.S.	k9	80
Paradise Valley, Nv., U.S.	B4	105
Paradise Valley, Wy., U.S.	D6	127
Paradox, Co., U.S.	C2	83
Paragonah, Ut., U.S.	F3	121
Paragould, Ar., U.S.	A5	81
Paragua, stm., Ven.	B5	60
Paraguaçu, stm., Braz.	D3	57
Paraguaçu Paulista, Braz.	C2	56
Paraguay (Paraguai), stm., S.A.	C4	55
Paraguaná, Península de, pen., Ven.	A4	60
Paraguarí, Para.	E4	55
Paraguarí, dept., Para.	E4	55
Paraguay, ctry., S.A.	D4	55
Paraguay (Paraguai), stm., S.A.	D4	55
Paraíba, state, Braz.	C3	57
Paraíba, stm., Braz.	h6	57
Paraíba do Sul, Braz.	h6	56
Paraíba do Sul, stm., Braz.	g6	56
Paraíso, Mex.	g6	63
Paraíso, Pan.	k11	62
Paraisópolis, Braz.	C3	56
Parakou, Benin	E5	45
Paralomar, Ar., U.S.	D1	81
Paramaribo, Sur.	A3	59
Paramirim, Braz.	A4	56
Paramithiá, Grc.	C3	25
Paramonga, Peru	D2	57
Paramount, Ca., U.S.	*n12	82
Paramount, Md., U.S.	A2	97
Paramus, N.J., U.S.	h8	107
Paran, Nahal, val.	D6	41
Paraná, Arg.	A4	54
Paraná, Braz.	D1	57
Paraná, state, Braz.	C2	56
Paraná, stm., Braz.	D1	57
Paraná, stm., S.A.	G5	53
Paranaíba, Braz.	D3	56
Paranaíba, Braz.	B2	56
Paranaíba, stm., Braz.	B2	56
Paranaiguara, Braz.	B2	56
Paranam, Sur.	A3	59
Paranapanema, Braz.	m7	56
Paranapanema, stm., Braz.	C2	56
Paranapiacaba, Serra do, mts., Braz.	m8	56
Paranavaí, Braz.	C2	56
Paraopeba, Braz.	E2	57
Parapeti, stm., Bol.	C3	55
Paratinga, Braz.	D2	57
Parauaquara, Serra, hill, Braz.	C4	59
Paraúna, Braz.	B4	56
Paray-le-Monial, Fr.	D6	16
Pārbati, stm., India	H6	37
Parbhani, India	C5	36
Parchim, Ger.	B5	18
Parchman, Ms., U.S.	A3	101
Parczew, Pol.	C7	26
Pardee, Va., U.S.	e9	123
Pardeeville, Wi., U.S.	E4	126
Pardes Hanna-Karkur, Isr.	B6	41
Pardo, stm., Braz.	C2	56
Pardo, stm., Braz.	C3	56
Pardo, stm., Braz.	E2	57
Pardubice, Czech.	C3	26
Parecis, Chapada dos, mts., Braz.	B4	55
Paredes de Nava, Spain	C3	22
Parem, i., Micron.	Q18	52
Parempei, i., Micron.	Q17	52
Parent, Que.	k12	74
Parepare, Indon.	F5	34
Párga, Grc.	C3	40
Pargi, Indon.	A3	59
Pargolovo, Sov. Un.	r31	14
Paria, stm., U.S.	A4	80
Paria, Gulf of, b.	A5	60
Paria, Península de, pen., Ven.	A5	60
Pariaguán, Ven.	B5	60
Pariaman, Indon.	F6	34
Paria Plateau, plat., Az., U.S.	A4	80
Paricutín, vol., Mex.	n12	63
Parigi, Indon.	F6	34
Parika, Guy.	A3	59
Parima, Serra, mts., S.A.	B2	59
Parima, Sierra (Serra Parima), mts., S.A.	C5	60
Pariñas, Punta, c., Peru	B1	58
Parintins, Braz.	C3	59
Paris, Ont.	D4	73
Paris, Fr.	C5	16
Paris, Id., U.S.	G7	89
Paris, Il., U.S.	D6	90
Paris, Ky., U.S.	B5	94
Paris, Me., U.S.	D2	96
Paris, Mi., U.S.	E5	99
Paris, Mo., U.S.	B5	102
Paris, Tn., U.S.	A3	119
Paris, Tx., U.S.	C5	120
Paris Crossing, In., U.S.	G6	91
Paris Peak, mtn., Id., U.S.	G7	89
Parisville, Que.	C5	74
Park, Ks., U.S.	C3	93
Park, co., Co., U.S.	B5	83
Park, co., Mt., U.S.	E6	103
Park, co., Wy., U.S.	B3	127
Parkbeg, Sask.	G2	75
Park City, Ks., U.S.	g12	93
Park City, Ky., U.S.	C3	94
Park City, Mt., U.S.	E8	103
Park City, Ut., U.S.	C4	121
Parkdale, P.E.I.	C6	71
Parkdale, Ar., U.S.	D4	81
Parkdale, Mi., U.S.	D4	99
Parkdale, Or., U.S.	B5	114
Parke, co., In., U.S.	E3	91
Parker, Az., U.S.	C1	80
Parker, Co., U.S.	B6	83
Parker, Fl., U.S.	u16	86
Parker, Id., U.S.	F7	89
Parker, Ks., U.S.	E5	101
Parker, Pa., U.S.	D2	115
Parker, S.D., U.S.	D8	118
Parker, Wa., U.S.	C5	124
Parker, co., Tx., U.S.	C4	120
Parker City, In., U.S.	D7	91
Parker Dam, Ca., U.S.	E6	82
Parker Dam, U.S.	C1	80
Parker Peak, mtn., S.D., U.S.	D2	118
Parkers Prairie, Mn., U.S.	D3	100
Parkersburg, Il., U.S.	E5	90
Parkersburg, Ia., U.S.	B5	92
Parkersburg, N.C., U.S.	C4	110
Parkersburg, W.V., U.S.	B3	125
Parkerstown, N.J., U.S.	D4	107
Parkerview, Sask.	F4	75
Parkerville, Ks., U.S.	D7	93
Parkes, Austl.	F8	50
Parkesburg, Pa., U.S.	G10	115
Park Falls, Wi., U.S.	C3	126
Park Forest, Il., U.S.	B6	90
Park Forest South, Il., U.S.	*B6	90
Park Hall, Md., U.S.	D5	97
Park Head, Ont.	C3	73
Parkhill, Ont.	D3	73
Park Hill, Ok., U.S.	B7	113
Park Hills, Ky., U.S.	h13	94
Park Layne, Oh., U.S.	C1	112
Parkland, Alta.	D4	68
Parkland, Wa., U.S.	f11	124
Park Plateau, plat., Co., U.S.	A4	83
Park Range, mts., Co., U.S.	A4	83
Park Rapids, Mn., U.S.	D3	100
Park Ridge, Il., U.S.	B6	90
Park Ridge, N.J., U.S.	g8	107
Park River, N.D., U.S.	A8	111
Parkrose, Or., U.S.	B4	114
Parks, Az., U.S.	C2	81
Parks, Ne., U.S.	D4	104
Parksley, Va., U.S.	C7	123
Parkston, S.D., U.S.	D8	118
Parksville, B.C.	E5	69
Parksville, N.Y., U.S.	D6	109
Parksville, S.C., U.S.	D3	117
Parkton, Md., U.S.	A4	97
Parkton, N.C., U.S.	C3	110
Park Valley, Ut., U.S.	B2	121
Parkville, Md., U.S.	B4	97
Parkville, Mo., U.S.	B3	102
Parkwater, Wa., U.S.	g14	124
Parkway, Ca., U.S.	*C3	82
Parkwood, N.C., U.S.	A4	110
Parla, Spain	p17	22
Parlākimidi, India	H10	37
Parle, Lac qui, l., Mn., U.S.	E10	100
Parlier, Ca., U.S.	D4	82
Parlin, Co., U.S.	C3	83
Parma, Italy	B3	23
Parma, Id., U.S.	F2	89
Parma, Mi., U.S.	F6	99
Parma, Mo., U.S.	E8	102
Parma, Oh., U.S.	A4	112
Parma, stm., Italy	E6	20
Parmachenee Lake, l., Me., U.S.	C2	96
Parma Heights, Oh., U.S.	h9	112
Parmele, N.C., U.S.	B5	110
Parmelee, S.D., U.S.	D4	118
Parmer, co., Tx., U.S.	B1	120
Parnaguá, Braz.	D2	57
Parnaíba, Braz.	B2	57
Parnaíba, stm., Braz.	B2	57
Parnassós, mtn., Grc.	C4	25
Parnell, Ia., U.S.	C6	92
Parnell, Mo., U.S.	A3	102
Párnis Óros, mts., Grc.	g11	25
Pärnu, Sov. Un.	C8	36
Paron, Ar., U.S.	C3	81
Páros, Grc.	D5	25
Páros, i., Grc.	D5	25
Parowan, Ut., U.S.	F3	121
Par Pond, res., S.C., U.S.	D5	117
Parr, In., U.S.	B3	91
Parral, Chile	D2	54
Parramatta, Austl.	*F9	50
Parramore Island, i., Va., U.S.	C7	123
Parras de la Fuente, Mex.	B4	63
Parrett, stm., Eng., U.K.	J10	12
Parrish, Al., U.S.	B2	78
Parrish, Fl., U.S.	E4	86
Parrott, Ga., U.S.	E2	87
Parrott, Va., U.S.	C2	123
Parrottsville, Tn., U.S.	C10	119
Parry, Sask.	H3	75
Parry, Cape, c., N.W. Ter.	B6	66
Parry, Mount, mtn., B.C.	C3	69
Parry Island, i., Marsh Is.	S18	52
Parry Islands, is., N.W. Ter.	m29	66
Parry Sound, Ont.	B4	73
Parry Sound, dept., Ont.	B5	73
Parsberg, Ger.	D5	18
Parshall, Co., U.S.	A4	83
Parshall, N.D., U.S.	B3	111
Parsippany, N.J., U.S.	B4	107
Parsnip, stm., B.C.	B6	69
Parsons, Ks., U.S.	E8	93
Parsons, Tn., U.S.	B3	119
Parsons, W.V., U.S.	B5	125
Parsons Springs, Va., U.S.	D2	123
Parsonsburg, Md., U.S.	D7	97
Parson's Pond, Newf.	C3	72
Partenen, Aus.	C6	20
Parthenay, Fr.	D3	16
Parthenon, Ar., U.S.	B2	81
Partinico, Italy	E4	23
Partlow, Va., U.S.	B5	123
Partridge, Ks., U.S.	E5	93
Partridge Point, c., Newf.	C3	72
Partry, Ire.	D2	11
Paru, stm., Braz.	C4	59
Paru de Oeste, stm., Braz.	C3	59
Parys, S. Afr.	C4	49
Pasadena, Newf.	D3	72
Pasadena, Ca., U.S.	E4	82
Pasadena, Md., U.S.	B4	97
Pasadena, Tx., U.S.	r14	120
Pasaje, Ec.	B1	58
Pa Sak, stm., Thai.	D5	35
Pasay, Phil.	o13	34
Pascagoula, Ms., U.S.	E5	101
Pascagoula, stm., Ms., U.S.	E5	101
Pascagoula Bay, b., Ms., U.S.	f8	101
Pascani, Rom.	B8	24
Pasco, Wa., U.S.	C6	124
Pasco, dept., Peru	D2	58
Pasco, co., Fl., U.S.	D4	86
Pascoag, R.I., U.S.	B2	116
Pascoag Reservoir, res., R.I., U.S.	B2	116
Pascola, Mo., U.S.	E8	102
Pascua, Isla de (Easter Island), i., Chile	H15	6
Pas-de-Calais, dept., Fr.	D2	17
Pasewalk, Ger.	B7	18
Pashkovo, Sov. Un.	B11	31
Pasig, Phil.	o13	34
Pasłęk, Pol.	A5	26
Pasni, Pak.	C3	36
Paso de Indios, Arg.	C3	54
Paso de los Libres, Arg.	E4	55
Paso de los Toros, Ur.	E1	56
Paso Limay, Arg.	C2	54
Paso Robles, Ca., U.S.	E3	82
Pasqua, Sask.	G3	75
Pasquia, stm., Can.	D5	75
Pasquia Hills, hills, Sask.	D4	75
Pasquotank, co., N.C., U.S.	A6	110
Passaconaway, Mount, mtn., N.H., U.S.	C4	106
Passadumkeag, Me., U.S.	C4	96
Passadumkeag Mountain, mtn., Me., U.S.	C4	96
Passage West, Ire.	F3	11
Passaic, N.J., U.S.	B4	107
Passaic, co., N.J., U.S.	A4	107
Passaic, stm., N.J., U.S.	h8	107
Passamaquoddy Bay, b., Me., U.S.	C6	96
Passau, Ger.	D6	18
Pass Christian, Ms., U.S.	E4	101
Passekeag, N.B.	D4	71
Passero, Cape, c., Italy	F5	23
Passo Fundo, Braz.	D2	56
Passos, Braz.	C3	56
Passumpsic, Vt., U.S.	C4	122
Passumpsic, stm., Vt., U.S.	C4	122
Pastaza, prov., Ec.	B2	58
Pastaza, stm., S.A.	B2	58
Pasto, Col.	C2	60
Pastora Peak, mtn., Az., U.S.	A6	80
Pastura, N.M., U.S.	C5	108
Pasuruan, Indon.	G4	34
Paswegin, Sask.	F3	75
Patagonia, Az., U.S.	F5	80
Patagonia, reg., Arg.	D3	54
Patan see Lalitpur, Nepal	C8	36
Patapedia, stm., Can.	B2	71
Patapsco, Md., U.S.	A4	97
Patapsco, stm., Md., U.S.	B4	97
Patapsco, North Branch, stm., Md., U.S.	A4	97
Patargān, Daqq-e, sw., Asia	E10	39
Pataskala, Oh., U.S.	C3	112
Pataz, Peru	C2	58
Patchet Brook Reservoir, res., R.I., U.S.	E6	116
Patchogue, N.Y., U.S.	n15	109
Pat Cleburne, Lake, res., Tx., U.S.	C4	120
Patea, N.Z.	M15	51
Pateley Bridge, Eng., U.K.	F7	13
Pateras Óros, mtn., Grc.	g10	25
Paternò, Italy	F5	23
Paterson, N.J., U.S.	B4	107
Paterson, Wa., U.S.	D6	124
Paterson, stm., Ky., U.S.	C3	94
Pathānkot, India	B6	36
Pathein, mth., Burma	D1	35
Pathein, Burma	C8	36
Pathfinder Reservoir, res., Wy., U.S.	D6	127
Pathfork, Ky., U.S.	D6	94
Pathlow, Sask.	E3	75
Patía, stm., Col.	C2	60
Patiāla, India	B6	36
Patience Island, i., R.I., U.S.	D5	116
Pati Point, c., Guam	L10	52
Patman, Lake, res., Tx., U.S.	C5	120
Patmos, Ar., U.S.	D2	81
Pátmos, i., Grc.	D6	40
Patna, India	H11	37
Patnanongan Island, i., Phil.	o14	34
Patoka, Il., U.S.	E4	90
Patoka, In., U.S.	H2	91
Patoka, stm., In., U.S.	H3	91
Patoka Lake, res., In., U.S.	H4	91
Paton, Ia., U.S.	B3	92
Patos, Braz.	C3	57
Patos, Lagoa dos, b., Braz.	C6	56
Patos de Minas, Braz.	B3	56
Patquía, Arg.	F2	55
Pátrai (Patras), Grc.	C3	40
Pátrai, Gulf of see Patraïkós Kólpos, Grc.		
Patras see Pátrai, Grc.		
Patraïkós Kólpos (Gulf of Pátrai), b., Grc.	C3	40
Patria, Alta.	D5	68
Patricia, Tx., U.S.	C1	120
Patrick, S.C., U.S.	B7	117
Patrick, co., Va., U.S.	D2	123
Patrick Air Force Base, mil., Fl., U.S.	D6	86
Patricksburg, In., U.S.	F4	91
Patrick Springs, Va., U.S.	D2	123
Patriot, In., U.S.	G8	91
Patrocínio, Braz.	B3	56
Patroon, Tx., U.S.	D6	120
Patsaliga Creek, stm., Al., U.S.	D3	78
Patsville, Nv., U.S.	B6	105
Pattani, Thai.	D2	34
Pattani, stm., Thai.	I4	35
Pattaquattic Hill, hill, Ma., U.S.	B3	98
Patten, Me., U.S.	C4	96
Pattenburg, N.J., U.S.	B2	107
Patterson, Ar., U.S.	B4	81
Patterson, Ga., U.S.	E4	87
Patterson, Id., U.S.	E5	89
Patterson, Il., U.S.	D3	90
Patterson, La., U.S.	E4	95
Patterson, Mo., U.S.	D7	102
Patterson, N.Y., U.S.	D7	109
Patterson, Oh., U.S.	B2	112
Patterson, Va., U.S.	e10	123
Patterson Creek, stm., W.V., U.S.	B5	125
Pattison, Ms., U.S.	D3	101
Patton, Mo., U.S.	D7	102
Patton, Pa., U.S.	E4	115
Pattonsburg, Mo., U.S.	A3	102
Pattullo, Mount, mtn., B.C.	A3	69
Patu, Braz.	B3	57
Patuākhāli, Bngl.	F13	37
Patuca, stm., Hond.	D8	63
Patuca, Punta, c., Hond.	D8	63
Patuxent, stm., Md., U.S.	D4	97
Patuxent River Naval Air Test Center, mil., Md., U.S.	D5	97
Patzau, Wi., U.S.	B1	126
Pátzcuaro, Mex.	H9	63
Pátzcuaro, Lago de, l., Mex.	n13	63
Patzicía, Guat.	G2	64
Patzún, Guat.	C2	62
Pau, Fr.	F3	16
Pau, Gave de, stm., Fr.	F3	16
Paucarbamba, Peru	D3	58
Paudalho, Braz.	C3	57
Pau dos Ferros, Braz.	C3	57
Paugh Lake, Ont.	B7	73
Pauillac, Fr.	D3	16
Pauini, Braz.	C4	58
Pauini, stm., Braz.	C4	58
Pauk, Burma	D9	36
Paul, Id., U.S.	G5	89
Paul Island, i., Newf.	g9	72
Paulatuk, N.W. Ter.	C6	66
Paulden, Az., U.S.	C3	80
Paulding, Mi., U.S.	n12	99
Paulding, Ms., U.S.	C4	101
Paulding, Oh., U.S.	A1	112
Paulding, co., Ga., U.S.	C2	87
Paulding, co., Oh., U.S.	A1	112
Paulding Bay, b., Ant.	C25	7
Paulette, Ms., U.S.	B5	101
Paulina, La., U.S.	h10	95
Paulina, N.J., U.S.	B3	107
Paulina, Or., U.S.	C7	114
Paulina Mountains, mts., Or., U.S.	D5	114
Paulina Peak, mtn., Or., U.S.	D5	114
Pauline, Ne., U.S.	D7	104
Pauline, S.C., U.S.	B4	117
Pauline, Mount, mtn., Can.	C1	68
Paulins Kill, stm., N.J., U.S.	A3	107
Paullina, Ia., U.S.	B2	92
Paull Lake, l., Sask.	A3	75
Paulo Afonso, Cachoeira de, wtfl., Braz.	C3	57
Paulsboro, N.J., U.S.	D2	107
Paul Smiths, N.Y., U.S.	f10	109
Paul Stream, stm., Vt., U.S.	B5	122
Pauls Valley, Ok., U.S.	C4	113
Paungde, Burma	E10	36
Paupack, Pa., U.S.	D11	115
Pauto, stm., Col.	B3	60
Pauwela, Hi., U.S.	C5	88
Pavant Range, mts., Ut., U.S.	D3	121
Pavia, Italy	B2	23
Pavilion, N.Y., U.S.	C2	109
Pavilion, Wy., U.S.	C4	127
Pavlodar, Sov. Un.	D10	29
Pavlof Volcano, vol., Ak., U.S.	D7	79
Pavlograd, Sov. Un.	G10	27
Pavlovo, Sov. Un.	D14	27
Pavlovsk, Sov. Un.	s31	14
Pavlovsk, Sov. Un.	F13	27
Pavlovskaya, Sov. Un.	H13	27
Pavlovskiy Posad, Sov. Un.	n18	27
Pavo, Ga., U.S.	F3	87
Pavón, Col.	C3	60
Pawcatuck, Ct., U.S.	D8	84
Pawcatuck, stm., R.I., U.S.	G1	116
Paw Creek, N.C., U.S.	B2	110
Pawhuska, Ok., U.S.	A5	113
Pawlet, Vt., U.S.	E2	122
Pawleys Island, S.C., U.S.	E9	117
Pawling, Ky., U.S.	C3	94
Pawling, N.Y., U.S.	D7	109
Pawnee, Il., U.S.	D4	90
Pawnee, Ok., U.S.	A5	113
Pawnee, co., Ks., U.S.	D4	93
Pawnee, co., Ne., U.S.	D9	104
Pawnee, co., Ok., U.S.	A5	113
Pawnee City, Ne., U.S.	D9	104
Pawnee, stm., Ks., U.S.	D4	93
Pawnee Rock, Ks., U.S.	D4	93
Pawpaw, Il., U.S.	B5	90
Paw Paw, Mi., U.S.	F5	99
Paw Paw, stm., Mi., U.S.	F4	99
Pawpaw Creek, stm., W.V., U.S.	h10	125
Pawtuckaway Pond, l., N.H., U.S.	D4	106
Pawtucket, R.I., U.S.	C4	116
Pawtuxet, stm., R.I., U.S.	C4	116
Pawtuxet, North Branch, stm., R.I., U.S.	D3	116
Pawtuxet, South Branch, stm., R.I., U.S.	D3	116
Paxico, Ks., U.S.	C7	93
Paxoí, i., Grc.	C3	40
Paxton, Fl., U.S.	u15	86
Paxton, Il., U.S.	C5	90
Paxton, Ma., U.S.	B4	98
Paxton, Ne., U.S.	C4	104
Paxtonville, Pa., U.S.	E7	115
Paxville, S.C., U.S.	D7	117
Payakumbuh, Indon.	*F2	34
Payerne, Switz.	C2	21
Payette, Id., U.S.	E2	89
Payette, co., Id., U.S.	E2	89
Payette, North Fork, stm., Id., U.S.	E2	89
Payette, South Fork, stm., Id., U.S.	E3	89
Payette Lake, res., Id., U.S.	E3	89
Payne, Oh., U.S.	A1	112
Payne, co., Ok., U.S.	A4	113
Payne, Lac, l., Que.	g12	74
Paynes, Ms., U.S.	B3	101
Paynes Creek, Ca., U.S.	B3	82
Paynesville, Mn., U.S.	E4	100
Paynesville, Mo., U.S.	B7	102
Payneville, Ky., U.S.	C3	94
Paynton, Sask.	D1	75
Paysandú, Ur.	E1	56
Payson, Az., U.S.	C4	80
Payson, Il., U.S.	D2	90
Payson, Ok., U.S.	B5	113
Payson, Ut., U.S.	C4	121
Pazarbaşı, Cape, c., Tur.	B8	40
Pazardzhik, Bul.	D7	24
Pazin, Yugo.	C1	24
Peabody, Ks., U.S.	D6	93
Peabody, Ma., U.S.	A6	98
Peabody, stm., N.H., U.S.	B4	106
Peace, stm., Ga., U.S.	E9	66
Peace, stm., Fl., U.S.	E4	86
Peace Dale, R.I., U.S.	F3	116
Peace River, Alta.	D4	97
Peach, co., Ga., U.S.	D3	87
Peacham, Vt., U.S.	C4	122
Peacham Pond, res., Vt., U.S.	C4	122
Peach Creek, W.V., U.S.	D3	125
Peachland, B.C.	E8	69
Peachland, N.C., U.S.	C2	110
Peach Orchard, Ar., U.S.	A5	81
Peach Orchard Knob, mtn., Ky., U.S.	C3	94
Peach Point, c., Ma., U.S.	f12	98
Peach Springs, Az., U.S.	B2	80
Peachtree City, Ga., U.S.	*C2	87
Peacock, Mi., U.S.	D5	99
Peacock Hills, hills, N.W. Ter.	C10	66
Peacock Point, c., Wake I.	B2	52
Peacock Sound, strt., Ant.	B2	7
Peaima Fall, wtfl., Guy.	A2	59
Peak, S.C., U.S.	C5	117
Peaked Mountain, mtn., Me., U.S.	B4	96
Peaks Island, i., Me., U.S.	g7	96
Peale, Mount, mtn., Ut., U.S.	E6	121
Peale Island, i., Wake I.	A2	52
Pea Patch Island, i., De., U.S.	B3	85
Pearce, Az., U.S.	F6	80
Pearcy, Ar., U.S.	C2	81
Pea Ridge, Ar., U.S.	A1	81
Pea Ridge National Military Park, Ar., U.S.	A1	81
Pearisburg, Va., U.S.	C2	123
Pearl, Il., U.S.	D3	90
Pearl, Ms., U.S.	C3	101
Pearl, stm., U.S.	D3	101
Pearland, Tx., U.S.	r14	120
Pearl and Hermes Reef, rf., Hi., U.S.	k12	88
Pearl City, Hi., U.S.	B4	88
Pearl City, Il., U.S.	A4	90
Pearl Harbor, b., Hi., U.S.	B3	88
Pearl Harbor Naval Station, mil., Hi., U.S.	g10	88
Pearlington, Ms., U.S.	E4	101
Pearl River, La., U.S.	D6	95
Pearl River, N.Y., U.S.	g12	109
Pearl River, co., Ms., U.S.	E4	101
Pearsall, Tx., U.S.	E3	120
Pearsoll Peak, mtn., Or., U.S.	E3	114
Pearson, Ar., U.S.	B3	81
Pearson, Ga., U.S.	E4	87
Pearson Lake, l., Man.	B3	60
Peary Channel, strt., N.W. Ter.	m30	66
Peary Land, reg., Grnld.	A18	128
Pease, Mn., U.S.	E5	100
Pease, stm., Tx., U.S.	B2	120
Pease Air Force Base, mil., N.H., U.S.	D5	106
Pebane, Moz.	A6	49
Pebas, Peru	B3	58
Pebworth, Ky., U.S.	C6	94
Peć, Yugo.	D5	24
Peçanha, Braz.	B20	8
Pechora, stm., Sov. Un.	C28	29
Pechora Bay, b., Sov. Un.	B19	8
Peck, Id., U.S.	C2	89
Peck, Ks., U.S.	E6	93
Peck, Mi., U.S.	E8	99
Peckerwood Lake, res., Ar., U.S.	C4	81
Peckham, Ok., U.S.	A4	113
Pecos, N.M., U.S.	B4	108
Pecos, Tx., U.S.	D1	120
Pecos, co., Tx., U.S.	D1	120
Pecos, stm., U.S.	D7	76
Pecos National Monument, N.M., U.S.	B4	108
Pécs, Hung.	B4	24
Peculiar, Mo., U.S.	C3	102
Pedasí, Pan.	G7	62
Peddocks Island, i., Ma., U.S.	g12	98
Pedernales, Ven.	B5	60
Pedra Azul, Braz.	D4	57
Pedregal (part of Panamá), Pan.	k12	62
Pedregal, Pan.	F6	62
Pedregal, Ven.	A3	60
Pedreiras, Braz.	B3	57
Pedricktown, N.J., U.S.	D2	107
Pedro Antonio Santos, Mex.	A3	62
Pedro Juan Caballero, Para.	D4	55
Pedro Luro, Arg.	C3	54
Pedro Miguel, Pan.	k11	62
Pedro R. Fernández (Manuel F. Mantilla), Arg.	E4	55
Pedro Velho, Braz.	h6	57
Peebinga, Austl.	G3	51
Peebles, Sask.	G4	75
Peebles, Scot., U.K.	C5	12
Peebles, Oh., U.S.	D2	112
Peebles, Wi., U.S.	k9	126
Peekamoose Mountain, mtn., Me., U.S.	C5	96
Peekskill, N.Y., U.S.	D7	109
Peel, N.B.	C2	71
Peel, I. of Man	G8	13
Peel, co., Ont.	D5	73

Name | Map Ref. | Page

Peel, stm., Can. C5 66
Peel Fell, mtn., U.K. E6 13
Pe Ell, Wa., U.S. C2 124
Peel Sound, strt., N.W. Ter. B13 66
Peene, stm., Ger. B6 18
Peer, Bel. C5 17
Peerless, Mt., U.S. B11 103
Peerless Lake, l., Alta. A3 68
Peers, Alta. C3 68
Peesane, Sask. E4 75
Peetz, Co., U.S. A7 83
Peever, S.D., U.S. B9 118
Pefferlaw, Ont. C5 73
Pegan Hill, hill, Ma., U.S. g10 98
Pegasus Bay, b., N.Z. O14 51
Pegau, Ger. B7 19
Peggs, Ok., U.S. A6 113
Peggy, Tx., U.S. E3 120
Pegnitz, Ger. D6 19
Pegnitz, stm., Ger. D5 18
Pego, Spain C5 22
Pegram, Tn., U.S. A4 119
Pegu Yoma, mts., Burma C1 35
Pehčevo, Yugo. E6 24
Pehuajó, Arg. B4 54
Peine, Ger. B5 18
Peiping see Beijing, China D8 31
Peipus, Lake, l., Sov. Un. D6 29
Peixe, Braz. D1 57
Peixian, China G7 32
Peixian, China G7 32
Pejepscot, Me., U.S. E2 96
Pekalongan, Indon. G3 34
Pekan, Malay. E2 34
Pekanbaru, Indon. E2 34
Pekin, Il., U.S. C4 90
Pekin, In., U.S. G5 91
Pekin, N.D., U.S. B7 111
Peking see Beijing, China D8 31
Pelabuhan Kelang, Malay. K4 35
Pélagos, i., Grc. C5 25
Pelahatchie, Ms., U.S. C4 101
Pelaihari, Indon. F4 34
Pelat, Mont, mtn., Fr. E7 16
Pelée, Montagne, mtn., Mart. I14 64
Pelee Island, i., Ont. F2 73
Peleliu, i., Palau R17 52
Pelham, Ont. D5 73
Pelham, Al., U.S. B3 78
Pelham, Ga., U.S. E2 87
Pelham, Ma., U.S. B3 98
Pelham, N.H., U.S. E4 106
Pelham, N.Y., U.S. *h13 109
Pelham, N.C., U.S. A3 110
Pelham, S.C., U.S. B3 117
Pelham, Tn., U.S. D8 119
Pelham Manor, N.Y., U.S. h13 109
Pelhřimov, Czech. D3 26
Pelican, Ak., U.S. m21 79
Pelican, La., U.S. C2 95
Pelican Bay, b., Man. C1 70
Pelican Lake, Wi., U.S. C4 126
Pelican Lake, l., Alta. B4 68
Pelican Lake, l., Man. C1 70
Pelican Lake, l., Sask. B4 75
Pelican Lake, l., Mn., U.S. D4 100
Pelican Lake, l., Mn., U.S. E5 100
Pelican Lake, l., Mn., U.S. B6 100
Pelican Lake, l., Mn., U.S. D3 100
Pelican Lake, l., Wi., U.S. C4 126
Pelican Mountain, mtn., Alta. B4 68
Pelican Narrows, Sask. B4 75
Pelican Rapids, Man. C1 70
Pelican Rapids, Mn., U.S. D2 100
Péligre, Lac de, res., Haiti E8 64
Pelion, S.C., U.S. D5 117
Pella, Ia., U.S. C5 92
Pell City, Al., U.S. B3 78
Pellice, stm., Italy E3 20
Pell Lake, Wi., U.S. n11 126
Pellston, Mi., U.S. C6 99
Pellville, Ky., U.S. C3 94
Pellworm, i., Ger. A4 18
Pelly, Sask. F5 75
Pelly, stm., Yukon D6 66
Pelly Crossing, Yukon D5 66
Pelly Lake, l., N.W. Ter. C12 66
Pelly Mountains, mts., Yukon D6 66
Peloncillo Mountains, mts., U.S. E1 108
Peloponnesos, hist. reg., Grc. D4 25
Pelotas, Braz. E2 56
Pelotas, stm., Braz. D2 56
Pel'ovo, Bul. D7 24
Pelton, Lake, l., La., U.S. E5 95
Pelusium, hist., Eg. C4 41
Pelusium Bay, b., Eg. C4 41
Pelzer, S.C., U.S. B3 117
Pemadumcook Lake, l., Me., U.S. C3 96
Pemalang, Indon. *G3 34
Pemanggil, i., Malay. K6 35
Pemaquid, Me., U.S. E3 96
Pematangsiantar, Indon. m11 34
Pemba, Moz. D7 48
Pemba, Zam. E4 48
Pemba, prov., Tan. C6 48
Pemba, i., Tan. C6 48
Pemberton, B.C. D6 69
Pemberton, N.J., U.S. D3 107
Pemberton, Oh., U.S. B1 112
Pemberville, Oh., U.S. A2 112
Pembina, N.D., U.S. A8 111
Pembina, co., N.D., U.S. A8 111
Pembina, stm., Alta. C3 68
Pembina, stm., N.A. E2 70
Pembina Mountains, mts., N.A. A7 111
Pembine, Wi., U.S. C6 126
Pembroke, Ont. B7 73
Pembroke, Wales, U.K. E4 10
Pembroke, Ga., U.S. D5 87
Pembroke, Ky., U.S. D2 94
Pembroke, Me., U.S. D5 96
Pembroke, Ma., U.S. B6 98
Pembroke, N.Y., U.S. B2 109
Pembroke, N.C., U.S. C3 110
Pembroke, Va., U.S. C2 123
Pembroke Park, Fl., U.S. *G6 86
Pembroke Pines, Fl., U.S. r13 86
Pembuang, stm., Indon. F4 34
Pemigewasset, stm., N.H., U.S. C3 106
Pemigewasset, East Branch, stm., N.H., U.S. B3 106
Pemiscot, co., Mo., U.S. E8 102
Pemmican Portage, Sask. D4 75
Pemuco, Chile B2 54
Pena Blanca, N.M., U.S. B3 108
Penafiel, Port. B1 22
Peñafiel, Spain B3 22
Peñalara, mtn., Spain B4 22
Penalosa, Ks., U.S. E5 93
Penamacor, Port. B2 22
Penápolis, Braz. C2 56
Peñaranda de Bracamonte, Spain B3 22
Pen Argyl, Pa., U.S. E11 115
Peñarroya-Pueblonuevo, Spain C3 22
Peñas, Cape, c., Spain A3 22
Penas, Golfo de, b., Chile D2 54
Penasco, N.M., U.S. A4 108
Peñasco, Rio, stm., N.M., U.S. E4 108
Penbrook, Pa., U.S. F8 115
Pence, In., U.S. D2 91
Pencer, Mn., U.S. B3 100
Penck Trough, val., Ant. B12 7
Pendéli (Pentelicus), mtn., Grc. g11 25
Pendembu, S.L. E2 45
Pender, Ne., U.S. B9 104
Pender, co., N.C., U.S. C4 110
Pendergrass, Ga., U.S. B3 87
Pender Island, B.C. g12 69
Pendleton, In., U.S. E6 91
Pendleton, Or., U.S. B8 114
Pendleton, S.C., U.S. B2 117
Pendleton, co., Ky., U.S. B5 94
Pendleton, co., W.V., U.S. C5 125
Pendley Hills, Ga., U.S. h8 87
Pend Oreille, co., Wa., U.S. A8 124
Pend Oreille, stm., N.A. A8 124
Pend Oreille, Lake, l., Id., U.S. A2 89
Pend Oreille, Mount, mtn., Id., U.S. A2 89
Pendroy, Mt., U.S. B4 103
Penedo, Braz. D3 57
Penetanguishene, Ont. C5 73
Peneus see Piniós, stm., Grc. C4 40
Penfield, Ga., U.S. C3 87
Penfield, Il., U.S. C6 90
Penfield, N.Y., U.S. *B3 109
Penfield, Pa., U.S. D4 115
Peng'an, China I2 32
Penganga, stm., India H6 37
Penge, Zaire C3 48
Pengibu, i., Indon. L7 35
Penglai, China F9 32
Pengshui, China J3 32
Penguin Islands, is., Newf. E3 72
Penha, Braz. D3 56
Penhold, Alta. C4 68
Penhook, Va., U.S. D3 123
Peniche, Port. C1 22
Penicuik, Scot., U.K. E5 13
Peninsula, Oh., U.S. A4 112
Peninsular Malaysia, hist. reg., Malay. E2 34
Penitas, Tx., U.S. F3 120
Penitente, Serra do, hills, Braz. C1 57
Penitentiary Mountain, hill, Al., U.S. A2 78
Pénjamo, Mex. m13 63
Penn, Sask. D2 75
Penn, N.D., U.S. A6 111
Penn Acres, De., U.S. *B3 85
Pennant Point, c., N.S. E6 71
Pennant Station, Sask. G1 75
Pennask Mountain, mtn., B.C. E7 69
Penne, Italy C4 23
Pennell, Mount, mtn., Ut., U.S. F5 121
Pennellville, N.Y., U.S. B4 109
Penner, stm., India F6 36
Penneshaw, Austl. G1 51
Penney Farms, Fl., U.S. C5 86
Pennfield, N.B. D3 71
Penn Hills, Pa., U.S. k14 115
Penniac, N.B. C3 71
Pennine Alps, mts., Eur. E3 18
Pennines, mts., Eng., U.K. C5 10
Pennington, Al., U.S. C1 78
Pennington, N.J., U.S. C3 107
Pennington, co., Mn., U.S. B2 100
Pennington, co., S.D., U.S. D2 118
Pennington Gap, Va., U.S. f8 123
Pennock, Mn., U.S. E3 100
Pennsauken, N.J., U.S. D2 107
Pennsboro, W.V., U.S. B4 125
Pennsburg, Pa., U.S. F11 115
Penns Grove, N.J., U.S. D2 107
Pennsuco, Fl., U.S. s13 86
Pennsville, N.J., U.S. D1 107
Pennsville, Oh., U.S. C4 112
Pennsylvania, state, U.S. E7 115
Penn Valley, Pa., U.S. o20 115
Pennville, In., U.S. D7 91
Penny, B.C. C7 69
Penn Yan, N.Y., U.S. C3 109
Pennycutaway, stm., Man. A5 70
Penobscot, Me., U.S. D4 96
Penobscot, co., Me., U.S. C4 96
Penobscot, stm., Me., U.S. C4 96
Penobscot, East Branch, stm., Me., U.S. C4 96
Penobscot, North Branch, stm., Me., U.S. B2 96
Penobscot, West Branch, stm., Me., U.S. C3 96
Penobscot Bay, b., Me., U.S. D3 96
Penobscot Lake, l., Me., U.S. C2 96
Penobsquis, N.B. D4 71
Penokee, Ks., U.S. C4 93
Penong, Austl. F5 50
Penonomé, Pan. F7 62
Penrhyn, Cape, c., N.W. Ter. C16 66
Penrith, Austl. *F9 50
Penrith, Eng., U.K. F6 13
Pensacola, Fl., U.S. u14 86
Pensacola, Ok., U.S. A6 113
Pensacola Bay, b., Fl., U.S. u14 86
Pensacola Dam, Ok., U.S. A6 113
Pensacola Mountains, mts., Ant. A6 7
Pensacola Naval Air Station, mil., Fl., U.S. u14 86
Pensaukee, Wi., U.S. D6 126
Pense, Sask. G3 75
Pentagon Mountain, mtn., Mt., U.S. C3 103
Pentecostes, Braz. B3 57
Pentelicus see Pendéli, mtn., Grc. g11 25
Penticton, B.C. E8 69
Pentland Firth, strt., Scot., U.K. A5 10
Pentland Hills, hills, Scot., U.K. E5 13
Penton, N.J., U.S. D2 107
Pentwater, Mi., U.S. E4 99
Penwell, Tx., U.S. D1 120
Penza, Sov. Un. D7 29
Penzance, Sask. F3 75
Penzance, Eng., U.K. E4 10
Penzberg, Ger. E5 18
Penzhina, stm., Sov. Un. C19 29
Penzlin, Ger. E7 15
Peoa, Ut., U.S. C4 121
Peonan Point, c., Man. D2 70
Peoples, Ky., U.S. C5 94
Peoria, Az., U.S. D3 80
Peoria, Il., U.S. C4 90
Peoria, Oh., U.S. B2 112
Peoria, Ok., U.S. A7 113
Peoria, co., Il., U.S. C4 90
Peoria Heights, Il., U.S. C4 90
Peotone, Il., U.S. B6 90
Pep, N.M., U.S. D6 108
Pepacton Reservoir, res., N.Y., U.S. C6 109
Pepeekeo, Hi., U.S. D6 88
Pepin, Wi., U.S. D1 126
Pepin, co., Wi., U.S. D2 126
Pepin, Lake, l., U.S. D1 126
Pepper Creek, stm., De., U.S. F5 85
Pepperell, Ma., U.S. A4 98
Pepper Pike, Oh., U.S. *h10 112
Peqini, Alb. B2 25
Pequabuck, Ct., U.S. C4 84
Pequannock, N.J., U.S. B4 107
Pequeni, stm., Pan. k12 62
Pequest, stm., N.J., U.S. B2 107
Pequop Mountains, mts., Nv., U.S. C7 105
Pequot Lakes, Mn., U.S. D4 100
Perabumulih, Indon. F2 34
Perak, state, Malay. J4 35
Perak, stm., Malay. J4 35
Perakhóra, Grc. g9 25
Perales, stm., Spain p16 22
Perales de Tajuña, Spain p18 22
Peralta, N.M., U.S. C3 108
Pérama, Grc. h11 25
Percival, Ia., U.S. D2 92
Percy, Il., U.S. E4 90
Percy, N.H., U.S. A4 106
Perdido, Al., U.S. D2 78
Perdido, mtn., Spain A6 22
Perdido, stm., U.S. E2 78
Perdido Bay, b., Al., U.S. E2 78
Perdizes, Braz. B3 56
Perdue, Sask. E2 75
Perea, N.M., U.S. B1 108
Pereira, Col. C2 60
Pereira Barreto, Braz. C2 56
Perekop, Sov. Un. H9 27
Pere Marquette, stm., Mi., U.S. E4 99
Peremennyy, Cape, c., Ant. C23 7
Perené, stm., Peru D3 58
Pereslavl-Zalesskiy, Sov. Un. C12 27
Pereyaslav-Khmelnitskiy, Sov. Un. F8 27
Pergamino, Arg. A4 54
Pergine Valsugana, Italy A3 23
Perham, Me., U.S. B4 96
Perham, Mn., U.S. D3 100
Péribonca, Que. A5 74
Peridot, Az., U.S. D5 80
Périgueux, Fr. E4 16
Perijá, Sierra de, mts., S.A. B3 60
Perim, i., Yemen D4 38
Peristérion, Grc. g11 25
Perito Moreno, Arg. D2 54
Perkasie, Pa., U.S. F11 115
Perkins, Que. D2 74
Perkins, Ga., U.S. D5 87
Perkins, Mi., U.S. C3 99
Perkins, Ok., U.S. B4 113
Perkins, co., Ne., U.S. D4 104
Perkins, co., S.D., U.S. B3 118
Perkinston, Ms., U.S. E4 101
Perkinstown, Wi., U.S. C3 126
Perkinsville, Vt., U.S. E3 122
Perla, Ar., U.S. C3 81
Perlas, Archipiélago de las, is., Pan. F8 62
Perlas, Laguna de, b., Nic. E8 63
Perleberg, Ger. B5 18
Perley, Mn., U.S. C2 100
Perlis, state, Malay. I4 35
Perl-Mack, Co., U.S. *B6 83
Perm, Sov. Un. D8 29
Perma, Mt., U.S. C2 103
Përmeti, Alb. B3 25
Pernambuco, state, Braz. C3 57
Pernell, Ok., U.S. C4 113
Pernik, Bul. D6 24
Péronne, Fr. C5 16
Perot, Bayou, stm., La., U.S. k11 95
Perote, Al., U.S. D4 78
Perpignan, Fr. F5 16
Perquimans, co., N.C., U.S. A6 110
Perrin, Tx., U.S. C3 120
Perrine, Fl., U.S. G6 86
Perrineville, N.J., U.S. C4 107
Perris, Ca., U.S. F5 82
Perro, Laguna del, l., N.M., U.S. C4 108
Perronville, Mi., U.S. C3 99
Perros-Guirec, Fr. C2 16
Perrot, Île, i., Que. q19 74
Perry, Ar., U.S. B3 81
Perry, Fl., U.S. B3 86
Perry, Ga., U.S. D3 87
Perry, Il., U.S. D3 90
Perry, Ia., U.S. C3 92
Perry, Ks., U.S. C8 93
Perry, La., U.S. E3 95
Perry, Me., U.S. D5 96
Perry, Mi., U.S. F6 99
Perry, Mo., U.S. B6 102
Perry, N.Y., U.S. C2 109
Perry, Oh., U.S. A4 112
Perry, Ok., U.S. A4 113
Perry, S.C., U.S. D5 117
Perry, Ut., U.S. B3 121
Perry, co., Al., U.S. C2 78
Perry, co., Ar., U.S. C3 81
Perry, co., Il., U.S. E4 90
Perry, co., In., U.S. H4 91
Perry, co., Ky., U.S. C6 94
Perry, co., Ms., U.S. D4 101
Perry, co., Mo., U.S. D8 102
Perry, co., Oh., U.S. C3 112
Perry, co., Pa., U.S. F7 115
Perry, co., Tn., U.S. B4 119
Perrydale, Or., U.S. B3 114
Perry Hall, Md., U.S. B5 97
Perry Heights, Oh., U.S. *B4 112
Perry Lake, res., Ks., U.S. C8 93
Perryman, Md., U.S. B5 97
Perry Peak, mtn., Ma., U.S. B1 98
Perry Point, Md., U.S. A5 97
Perrysburg, N.Y., U.S. C1 109
Perrysburg, Oh., U.S. A2 112
Perrysburg Heights, Oh., U.S. e6 112
Perry Stream, stm., N.H., U.S. f7 106
Perry's Victory and International Peace Memorial, hist., Oh., U.S. A2 112
Perrysville, In., U.S. D3 91
Perrysville, Oh., U.S. B3 112
Perrysville, Pa., U.S. h13 115
Perryton, Tx., U.S. A2 120
Perryvale, Alta. B4 68
Perryville, Ak., U.S. D8 79
Perryville, Ar., U.S. B3 81
Perryville, Ky., U.S. C5 94
Perryville, La., U.S. B4 95
Perryville, Md., U.S. A5 97
Perryville, Mo., U.S. D8 102
Perryville, R.I., U.S. F3 116
Perryville, Tn., U.S. B3 119
Persan, Fr. E2 17
Persepolis, hist., Iran G6 39
Perseverancia, Bol. B3 55
Pershing, In., U.S. E7 91
Pershing, Ia., U.S. C5 92
Pershing, Mo., U.S. C6 102
Pershing, co., Nv., U.S. C3 105
Persia, Ia., U.S. C2 92
Persia, Tn., U.S. C10 119
Persian Gulf, b., Asia C5 38
Persimmon Grove, Ky., U.S. k14 94
Person, co., N.C., U.S. A3 110
Perstorp, Swe. B7 15
Pertek, Tur. C12 40
Perth, Austl. F2 50
Perth, Ont. C8 73
Perth, Scot., U.K. B5 10
Perth, Ks., U.S. E6 93
Perth, N.D., U.S. A6 111
Perth, co., Ont. D3 73
Perth Amboy, N.J., U.S. B4 107
Perth-Andover, N.B. D10 71
Perthshire, Ms., U.S. B3 101
Pertuis, Fr. F6 16
Peru, Il., U.S. B4 90
Peru, In., U.S. C5 91
Peru, Ia., U.S. C4 92
Peru, Ks., U.S. E7 93
Peru, Me., U.S. *D2 96
Peru, Ma., U.S. B1 98
Peru, Ne., U.S. D10 104
Peru, N.Y., U.S. f11 109
Peru, Vt., U.S. E3 122
Peru, ctry., S.A. C2 58
Perugia, Italy C4 23
Peruíbe, Braz. C3 56
Peruque, Mo., U.S. f12 102
Péruwelz, Bel. D3 17
Pervomaysk, Sov. Un. q21 27
Pervomaysk, Sov. Un. G8 27
Pervouralsk, Sov. Un. D8 29
Pesaro, Italy C4 23
Pescadero, Ca., U.S. D2 82
Pescara, Italy C5 23
Pescara, stm., Italy C4 23
Peschanyy, Cape, c., Sov. Un. G19 8
Peschanyy, Cape, c., Sov. Un. B10 33
Pesé, Pan. G7 62
Peshastin, Wa., U.S. B5 124
Peshāwar, Pak. B5 36
Peshkopija, Alb. B3 25
Peshtera, Bul. D7 24
Peshtigo, Wi., U.S. C6 126
Peshtigo, stm., Wi., U.S. C5 126
Peski, Sov. Un. F14 27
Peski, Sov. Un. n18 27
Peski, Sov. Un. C7 28
Peso da Régua, Port. B2 22
Pesotum, Il., U.S. D5 90
Pesqueira, Braz. C3 57
Pessac, Fr. E3 16
Petaca, N.M., U.S. A3 108
Petacas, Cerro, mtn., Col. C2 60
Petaḥ Tiqwa, Isr. B6 41
Petal, Ms., U.S. D4 101
Petaling Jaya, Malay. K4 35
Petaluma, Ca., U.S. C2 82
Pétange, Lux. E5 17
Petatlán, Mex. D4 63
Petauke, Zam. D5 48
Petawawa, Ont. B7 73
Petawawa, stm., Ont. A6 73
Petén Itzá, Lago, l., Guat. B3 62
Petenwell Lake, res., Wi., U.S. D4 126
Peterborough, Austl. F6 50
Peterborough, Ont. C6 73
Peterborough, Eng., U.K. D6 10
Peterborough, N.H., U.S. E3 106
Peterborough, co., Ont. C6 73
Peter Dana Point, Me., U.S. C5 96
Peterhead, Scot., U.K. B6 10
Peter I Island, i., Ant. C3 7
Peter Island, i., V.I., Br. B6 65
Peterlee, Eng., U.K. F7 13
Peter Lougheed Provincial Park, Alta. D3 68
Peterman, Al., U.S. D2 78
Petermann Ranges, mts., Austl. E4 50
Peter Pond Lake, l., Sask. m7 75
Petersburg, Ak., U.S. D13 79
Petersburg, De., U.S. D3 85
Petersburg, Il., U.S. C4 90
Petersburg, In., U.S. H3 91
Petersburg, Ky., U.S. h13 94
Petersburg, Mi., U.S. G7 99
Petersburg, Ne., U.S. C7 104
Petersburg, N.J., U.S. E3 107
Petersburg, N.Y., U.S. C7 109
Petersburg, N.D., U.S. A8 111
Petersburg, Oh., U.S. B5 112
Petersburg, Pa., U.S. E5 115
Petersburg, Tn., U.S. B5 119
Petersburg, Tx., U.S. C2 120
Petersburg, Va., U.S. C5 123
Petersburg, W.V., U.S. B5 125
Peters Creek, stm., W.V., U.S. m14 125
Petersdorf, Ger. D5 15
Petersfield, Man. D3 70
Petersfield, Eng., U.K. C7 12
Petersham, Ma., U.S. B3 98
Peters Landing, Tn., U.S. B4 119
Peters Mountain, mtn., U.S. D4 125
Peterson, Al., U.S. B2 78
Peterson, Ia., U.S. B2 92
Peterson, Mn., U.S. G7 100
Peterson, Ut., U.S. B4 121
Peterson Field, mil., Co., U.S. C6 83
Peterstown, W.V., U.S. D4 125
Petersville, Al., U.S. A2 78
Petersville, Ky., U.S. B6 94
Peter the Great Bay, b., Sov. Un. C11 31
Petilia Policastro, Italy E6 23
Pétionville, Haiti E7 64
Petit Bois Island, i., Ms., U.S. E5 101
Petitcodiac, N.B. D4 71
Petitcodiac, stm., N.B. C5 71
Petit-de-Grat, N.S. D9 71
Petite Amite, stm., La., U.S. h10 95
Petite Rivière, N.S. E5 71
Petite-Rivière-de-l'Artibonite, Haiti E7 64
Petite-Rivière-de-l'Île, N.B. B5 71
Petit-Étang, N.S. C9 71
Petit-Goâve, Haiti E7 64
Petit Jean, stm., Ar., U.S. B2 81
Petit Jean Mountain, mtn., Ar., U.S. C2 81
Petit Lac Des Allemands, l., La., U.S. k11 95
Petit Lake, l., La., U.S. k12 95
Petit-Mécatina, Île du, i., Que. C2 72
Petit-Rocher, N.B. B4 71
Petitsikapau Lake, l., Newf. g8 72
Peto, Mex. C7 63
Petorca, Chile A2 54
Petoskey, Mi., U.S. C6 99
Petra, hist., Jord. D7 41
Petras, Mount, mtn., Ant. B36 7
Petrey, Al., U.S. D3 78
Petrich, Bul. E6 24
Petrified Forest National Park, Az., U.S. B6 80
Petrikov, Sov. Un. E7 27
Petrila, Rom. C6 24
Petrinja, Yugo. C3 24
Petrodvorets, Sov. Un. s30 14
Petrohué, Chile C2 54
Petrokrepost, Sov. Un. B8 27
Petrolândia, Braz. C3 57
Petroleum, In., U.S. C7 91
Petroleum, co., Mt., U.S. C8 103
Petrolia, Ont. E2 73
Petrolia, Il., U.S. E6 90
Petrolia, Ks., U.S. E8 93
Petrolia, Pa., U.S. D2 115
Petrolia, Tx., U.S. B3 120
Petrolina, Braz. C2 57
Petropavlovsk, Sov. Un. D9 29
Petropavlovsk [-Kamchatskiy], Sov. Un. D18 29
Petrópolis, Braz. C4 56
Petros, Tn., U.S. C9 119
Petroșani, Rom. C6 24
Petrovgrad see Zrenjanin, Yugo. C5 24
Petrovsk, Sov. Un. E15 27
Petrovsk-Zabaykalskiy, Sov. Un. D13 29
Petrozavodsk, Sov. Un. C6 29
Pettaquamscutt Lake Shores, R.I., U.S. F4 116
Pettibone, N.D., U.S. B6 111
Pettigo, Ire. C4 11
Pettigrew, Ar., U.S. B2 81
Pettingell Peak, mtn., Co., U.S. B5 83
Pettis, co., Mo., U.S. C4 102
Pettisville, Oh., U.S. A1 112
Pettneu, Aus. B9 21
Pettus, Tx., U.S. E4 120
Petukhovo, Sov. Un. B7 28
Pevek, Sov. Un. C33 128
Pevely, Mo., U.S. g13 102
Pewamo, Mi., U.S. E6 99
Pewaukee, Wi., U.S. E5 126
Pewaukee Lake, l., Wi., U.S. m11 126
Pewee Valley, Ky., U.S. B4 94
Peyton, Co., U.S. B6 83
Pézenas, Fr. F5 16
Pfaffenhofen [an der Ilm], Ger. E6 19
Pfäffikon, Switz. B6 21
Pfarrkirchen, Ger. D6 18
Pfeifer, Ks., U.S. D4 93
Pforzheim, Ger. D4 18
Pfunds, Aus. C6 20
Pfungstadt, Ger. D3 19
Phalodi, India C5 36
Phaltan, India I5 37
Phangan, i., Thai. H4 35
Phangnga, Thai. H3 35
Phanom Dongrak Range, mts., Asia E5 35
Phan Rang, Viet. C3 34
Phan Thiet, Viet. C3 34
Pharr, Tx., U.S. F3 120
Pharsalus see Fársala, Grc. C4 25
Phatthalung, Thai. D2 34
Phayao, Thai. C3 35
Pheba, Ms., U.S. B5 101
Phelps, Ky., U.S. C7 94
Phelps, N.Y., U.S. C3 109
Phelps, Wi., U.S. B4 126
Phelps, co., Mo., U.S. D6 102
Phelps, co., Ne., U.S. D6 104
Phelps City, Mo., U.S. A2 102
Phelps Lake, l., N.C., U.S. B6 110
Phenix, Va., U.S. C4 123
Phenix City, Al., U.S. C4 78
Phetchabun, Thai. B2 34
Phetchabun Range, mts., Thai. E4 35
Phetchaburi, Thai. C1 34
Phichit, Thai. D4 35
Philadelphia, Il., U.S. D3 90
Philadelphia, Ms., U.S. C4 101
Philadelphia, Mo., U.S. B6 102
Philadelphia, N.Y., U.S. A5 109
Philadelphia, Pa., U.S. G11 115
Philadelphia, Tn., U.S. D9 119
Philadelphia, co., Pa., U.S. G12 115
Philadelphia Naval Shipyard, mil., Pa., U.S. P21 115
Phil Campbell, Al., U.S. A2 78
Philip, S.D., U.S. C4 118
Philip, Ms., U.S. B3 101
Philippeville see Skikda, Alg. B6 44
Philippeville, Bel. D4 17
Philippi, W.V., U.S. B4 125
Philippi Glacier, ice, Ant. C21 7
Philippines, ctry., Asia C6 34
Philippine Sea E7 6
Philipsburg, Que. D4 74
Philipsburg, Mt., U.S. D3 103
Philipsburg, Pa., U.S. E5 115
Philipsville, Ont. C8 73
Philleo Lake, l., Wa., U.S. h14 124
Phillip Island, i., Austl. I5 51
Phillippy, Tn., U.S. A2 119
Phillips, Me., U.S. D2 96
Phillips, Ne., U.S. D7 104
Phillips, Ok., U.S. C5 113
Phillips, Tx., U.S. B2 120
Phillips, Wi., U.S. C3 126
Phillips, co., Ar., U.S. C5 81
Phillips, co., Co., U.S. A8 83
Phillips, co., Ks., U.S. C4 93
Phillips, co., Mt., U.S. B8 103
Phillips Brook, stm., N.H., U.S. A4 106
Phillipsburg, Ks., U.S. C4 93
Phillipsburg, Mo., U.S. D5 102
Phillipsburg, N.J., U.S. B2 107
Phillipston, Ma., U.S. A3 98
Philmont, N.Y., U.S. C7 109
Philo, Il., U.S. C5 90
Philo, Oh., U.S. C4 112
Philomath, Ga., U.S. C4 87
Philomath, Or., U.S. C3 114
Philpott Reservoir, res., Va., U.S. D2 123
Phippen, Sask. E1 75
Phippsburg, Co., U.S. A4 83
Phippsburg, Me., U.S. g8 96
Phitsanulok, Thai. B2 34
Phlorina see Flórina, Grc. B3 25
Phlox, Wi., U.S. C4 126
Phnum Penh (Phnom Penh), Camb. C2 34
Phoenicia, N.Y., U.S. C6 109
Phoenix, Az., U.S. D3 80
Phoenix, Il., U.S. k9 90
Phoenix, Md., U.S. A4 97
Phoenix, Mi., U.S. A2 99
Phoenix, N.Y., U.S. B4 109
Phoenix, Or., U.S. E4 114
Phoenix Islands, is., Kir. G11 6
Phoenixville, Pa., U.S. F10 115
Phong, stm., Thai. D5 35
Phongsali, Laos B5 35
Phrae, Thai. B2 34
Phra Nakhon Si Ayutthaya, Thai. E4 35
Phuket, Thai. D1 34
Phuket, i., Thai. I3 35
Phumi Samraong, Camb. E5 35
Phu Quoc, Viet. G5 35
Phu Quoc, i., Viet. G6 35
Phu Tho, Viet. B6 35
Phutthaisong, Thai. E5 35
Piaanu Pass, strt., Micron. Q18 52
Piacenza, Italy B2 23
Pialba, Austl. B9 51
Pianguan, China E4 32
Pianosa, i., Italy C3 23
Pianosa Island, i., Italy C5 23
Piapot, Sask. H1 75
Piaseczno, Pol. m14 26
Piastów, Pol. m13 26
Piatra-Neamț, Rom. B8 24
Piatt, co., Il., U.S. D5 90
Piauí, state, Braz. C2 57
Piauí, stm., Braz. C2 57
Piave, stm., Italy A4 23
Piazza Armerina, Italy F5 23
Pibor, stm., Afr. D3 47
Pibor Post, Sud. D3 47
Pibroch, Alta. B4 68
Picabo, Id., U.S. F4 89
Picacho, Az., U.S. E4 80
Picacho, N.M., U.S. D4 108
Picard, Que. B8 74
Picardy, hist. reg., Fr. C5 16
Picayune, Ms., U.S. E4 101
Piccadilly, Newf. D2 72
Piceance Creek, stm., Co., U.S. B2 83
Pichanal, Arg. D3 55
Picher, Ok., U.S. A7 113
Pichilemu, Chile A2 54
Pichincha, prov., Ec. B2 58
Pickardville, Alta. B4 68
Pickaway, co., Oh., U.S. C2 112
Pick City, N.D., U.S. B4 111
Pickens, Ar., U.S. D4 81
Pickens, Ms., U.S. C4 101
Pickens, Ok., U.S. C6 113
Pickens, S.C., U.S. B2 117
Pickens, W.V., U.S. C4 125
Pickens, co., Al., U.S. B1 78
Pickens, co., Ga., U.S. B2 87
Pickens, co., S.C., U.S. B2 117
Pickensville, Al., U.S. B1 78
Pickerel, Ont. B4 73
Pickerel, Wi., U.S. C5 126
Pickerel, stm., Ont. B4 73
Pickerel Lake, l., Wi., U.S. C5 126
Pickering, Ont. D5 73
Pickering, Eng., U.K. F8 13
Pickering, Mo., U.S. A3 102
Pickerington, Oh., U.S. C3 112
Pickett, co., Tn., U.S. C8 119
Pickford, Mi., U.S. B6 99
Pickrell, Ne., U.S. D9 104
Pickstown, S.D., U.S. D7 118
Pickwick, Mn., U.S. G7 100
Pickwick Dam, Tn., U.S. B3 119
Pickwick Lake, res., U.S. A6 101
Pickworth Point, c., Ma., U.S. f12 98
Pico, i., Port. g8 44
Pico, Ponta do, mtn., Port. *g8 44
Pico Rivera, Ca., U.S. n12 82
Picos, Braz. C2 57
Picton, Ont. D7 73
Picton, N.Z. N14 51
Pictou, N.S. D7 71
Pictou, co., N.S. D7 71
Pictou Island, i., N.S. D7 71
Pictou Landing, N.S. D7 71
Picture Butte, Alta. E4 68
Pictured Rocks National Lakeshore, Mi., U.S. B4 99
Picture Rocks, Pa., U.S. D8 115
Picuí, Braz. h5 57
Picún Leufú, Arg. B3 54
Pidálion, Akrotírion, c., Cyp. E10 40
Pidurutalagala, mtn., Sri L. G7 36
Piedade, Braz. m8 56
Piedad, stm., Mex. h9 63
Piedmont, Que. D3 74
Piedmont, Al., U.S. B4 78
Piedmont, Ca., U.S. h8 82
Piedmont, Ks., U.S. E7 93
Piedmont, Mo., U.S. D7 102
Piedmont, Ok., U.S. B4 113
Piedmont, S.C., U.S. B3 117
Piedmont, S.D., U.S. C2 118
Piedmont, W.V., U.S. B5 125
Piedmont (Piemonte), prov., Italy B1 23
Piedmont Lake, res., Oh., U.S. B4 112
Piedra, Ca., U.S. D4 82
Piedra, stm., Co., U.S. D3 83
Piedrabuena, Spain C3 22
Piedras, stm., Pan. k12 62
Piedras, stm., Pan. k11 62
Piedras, Punta, c., Arg. B5 54
Piedras, Punta, c., Ven. A5 60
Piedras Blancas, Point, c., Ca., U.S. E3 82
Piedras Negras, Guat. D6 63
Piedras Negras, Mex. B4 63
Piedra Sola, Ur. E1 56
Piekary Śląskie, Pol. g9 26
Pieksämäki, Fin. F12 14
Pielinen, l., Fin. F13 14
Piemonte, prov., Italy D3 20
Piendamó, Col. C2 60
Pierce, Co., U.S. A6 83
Pierce, Fl., U.S. E5 86
Pierce, Id., U.S. C3 89
Pierce, Ne., U.S. B8 104
Pierce, Tn., U.S. A3 119
Pierce, co., Ga., U.S. E4 87
Pierce, co., Ne., U.S. B8 104
Pierce, co., N.D., U.S. A5 111
Pierce, co., Wa., U.S. C3 124

Name	Map Ref.	Page
Pierce, co., Wi., U.S.	D1	126
Pierce, Lake, l., Fl., U.S.	E5	86
Pierce City, Mo., U.S.	E3	102
Piercefield, N.Y., U.S.	A6	109
Pierce Lake, l., Can.	B5	70
Pierce Pond, l., Me., U.S.	C2	96
Pierces Point, N.J., U.S.	E3	107
Pierceton, In., U.S.	B6	91
Pierceville, In., U.S.	F7	91
Pierceville, Ks., U.S.	E3	93
Piercy, Ca., U.S.	C2	82
Piermont, N.H., U.S.	C2	106
Pierowall, Scot., U.K.	A6	13
Pierpont, Oh., U.S.	A5	112
Pierpont, S.D., U.S.	B8	118
Pierre, S.D., U.S.	C5	118
Pierre, Bayou, stm., Ms., U.S.	D3	101
Pierrefitte, Fr.	g10	16
Pierrefitte-sur-Aire, Fr.	F5	17
Pierrefonds, Que.	q19	74
Pierre Part, La., U.S.	k9	95
Pierreville, Que.	C5	74
Pierron, Il., U.S.	E4	90
Pierson, Man.	E1	70
Pierson, Fl., U.S.	C5	86
Pierson, Ia., U.S.	B2	92
Pierz, Mn., U.S.	E4	100
Piešťany, Czech.	D4	26
Pietermaritzburg, S. Afr.	C5	49
Pietersburg, S. Afr.	B4	49
Pie Town, N.M., U.S.	C1	108
Pietrasanta, Italy	C3	23
Piet Retief, S. Afr.	C5	49
Pietrosu, mtn., Rom.	B7	24
Pietrosul, mtn., Rom.	B7	24
Pieve di Cadore, Italy	A4	23
Pigeon, Mi., U.S.	E7	99
Pigeon, stm., Man.	C3	70
Pigeon, stm., U.S.	I9	119
Pigeon, stm., In., U.S.	A6	91
Pigeon, stm., Mn., U.S.	h10	100
Pigeon, stm., Wi., U.S.	k10	126
Pigeon Bay, b., Man.	C3	70
Pigeon Cove, Ma., U.S.	A6	98
Pigeon Creek, stm., Al., U.S.	D3	78
Pigeon Creek, stm., In., U.S.	H3	91
Pigeon Falls, Wi., U.S.	D2	126
Pigeon Forge, Tn., U.S.	D10	119
Pigeon Lake, l., Alta.	C3	68
Pigeon Mountain, mtn., U.S.	B1	87
Pigeon Point, c., Mn., U.S.	h10	100
Pigg, stm., Va., U.S.	D3	123
Piggott, Ar., U.S.	A5	81
Pigüé, Arg.	B4	54
Piirai, i., Marsh Is.	S18	52
Pijijiapan, Mex.	D6	63
Pike, N.H., U.S.	B2	106
Pike, N.Y., U.S.	C2	109
Pike, co., Al., U.S.	D4	78
Pike, co., Ar., U.S.	C2	81
Pike, co., Ga., U.S.	C2	87
Pike, co., Il., U.S.	D2	90
Pike, co., In., U.S.	H3	91
Pike, co., Ky., U.S.	C7	94
Pike, co., Ms., U.S.	D3	101
Pike, co., Mo., U.S.	B6	102
Pike, co., Oh., U.S.	C2	112
Pike, co., Pa., U.S.	D11	115
Pike, stm., Wi., U.S.	C6	126
Pike City, Ar., U.S.	C2	81
Pike Island Dam, U.S.	f8	125
Pike Lake, Wi., U.S.	D6	100
Pike Road, N.C., U.S.	B6	110
Pikes Peak, mtn., Co., U.S.	C5	83
Pikes Rocks, mtn., Pa., U.S.	C3	115
Pikesville, Md., U.S.	B4	97
Piketberg, S. Afr.		
Piketon, Oh., U.S.	C2	112
Pikeville, Ky., U.S.	C7	94
Pikeville, N.C., U.S.	B5	110
Pikeville, Tn., U.S.	D8	119
Pikou, China	E10	32
Pikwitonei, Man.	B3	70
Piła, Pol.	B4	26
Pilar, Braz.	C3	57
Pilar, Para.	E4	55
Pilar, N.M., U.S.	A4	108
Pilar de Goiás, Braz.	A3	56
Pilar do Sul, Braz.	m8	56
Pilatus, mtn., Switz.	C4	20
Pilcomayo, stm., S.A.	D4	55
Pilger, Sask.	E3	75
Pilger, Ne., U.S.	B8	104
Pilgrims Knob, Va., U.S.	e10	123
Pilgrim, Ky., U.S.	C7	94
Pilibhit, India	C7	37
Pilica, stm., Pol.	C5	26
Pillager, Mn., U.S.	D4	100
Pillaro, Ec.	B2	58
Pillar Point, c., Ca., U.S.	k7	82
Pilley's Island, Newf.	D4	72
Pillow, Pa., U.S.	E6	115
Pillsbury, N.D., U.S.	B8	111
Pílos, Grc.	D3	25
Pilot Butte, Sask.	G3	75
Pilot Grove, Mo., U.S.	D7	102
Pilot Knob, Mo., U.S.	D7	102
Pilot Knob, mtn., Ar., U.S.	D2	81
Pilot Knob, mtn., Ar., U.S.	C1	81
Pilot Knob, mtn., Id., U.S.	D3	89
Pilot Mound, Man.	E2	70
Pilot Mound, Ia., U.S.	B3	92
Pilot Mountain, N.C., U.S.	A2	110
Pilot Peak, mtn., Nv., U.S.	B7	105
Pilot Peak, mtn., Nv., U.S.	E4	105
Pilot Peak, mtn., Wy., U.S.	B3	127
Pilot Point, Ak., U.S.	D8	79
Pilot Point, Tx., U.S.	C4	120
Pilot Range, mts., Nv., U.S.	B7	105
Pilot Range, mts., N.H., U.S.	A4	106
Pilot Rock, Or., U.S.	B8	114
Pilot Station, Ak., U.S.	C7	79
Pilottown, La., U.S.	E6	95
Pilsen see Plzeň, Czech.		
Pilsen, Ks., U.S.	D6	93
Pilvo, Sov. Un.	A11	33
Pima, Az., U.S.	E6	80
Pima, co., Az., U.S.	E3	80
Pimmit Hills, Va., U.S.	g12	123
Pimpri-Chinchwad, India	*E5	37
Piña, Pan.	k10	62
Pinal, co., Az., U.S.	E4	80
Pinaleno Mountains, mts., Az., U.S.	E5	80
Pinal Mountains, mts., Az., U.S.	D5	80
Pinang see George Town, Malay.	D2	34
Pinang, state, Malay.	J4	33
Pinang, i., Malay.	D2	34
Pınarbaşı, Tur.	C11	40
Pinar del Río, Cuba	C2	64
Pinar del Río, prov., Cuba	C2	64
Pinardville, N.H., U.S.	E3	106
Pinás, Arg.	A3	54
Pinatubo, Mount, mtn., Phil.	o13	34
Pinawa, Man.	D4	70
Pincher Creek, Alta.	E4	68
Pincher Station, Alta.	E4	68
Pinckard, Al., U.S.	D4	78
Pinckney, Mi., U.S.	F7	99
Pinckney Island, i., S.C., U.S.	G6	117
Pinckneyville, Il., U.S.	E4	90
Pinconning, Mi., U.S.	E7	99
Pińczów, Pol.	C6	26
Pindall, Ar., U.S.	A3	81
Pindamonhangaba, Braz.	C3	56
Pindaré, stm., Braz.	B1	57
Pindiga, Nig.	*E7	45
Pindus Mountains, mts., Grc.	C3	40
Pine, Az., U.S.	C4	80
Pine, Co., U.S.	B5	83
Pine, co., Mn., U.S.	D6	100
Pine, stm., B.C.	B6	69
Pine, stm., Man.	D1	70
Pine, stm., Mi., U.S.	D7	99
Pine, stm., Mi., U.S.	D5	99
Pine, stm., N.H., U.S.	C4	106
Pine, stm., Wi., U.S.	C5	126
Pine, stm., Wi., U.S.	C4	126
Pine Apple, Al., U.S.	D3	78
Pine Bank, Pa., U.S.	G1	115
Pine Bluff, Ar., U.S.	C3	81
Pinebluff, N.C., U.S.	B3	110
Pine Bluffs, Wy., U.S.	E8	127
Pine Bridge, Ct., U.S.	D3	84
Pinebur, Ms., U.S.	D4	101
Pine Bush, N.Y., U.S.	D6	109
Pine Castle, Fl., U.S.	D5	86
Pine City, Ar., U.S.	C4	81
Pine City, Mn., U.S.	E6	100
Pine City, Wa., U.S.	B8	124
Pine Creek, Austl.	B5	50
Pine Creek, stm., Alta.	B4	68
Pine Creek, stm., Nv., U.S.	C5	105
Pine Creek, stm., Pa., U.S.	C6	115
Pine Creek, stm., Wa., U.S.	B8	124
Pine Creek Lake, res., Ok., U.S.	C6	113
Pinecrest, Ca., U.S.	C4	82
Pinedale, Al., U.S.	C3	78
Pinedale, Az., U.S.	C5	80
Pinedale, Wy., U.S.	D3	127
Pine Falls, Man.	D3	70
Pine Forest Range, mts., Nv., U.S.	B3	105
Pine Grove, Ga., U.S.	E4	87
Pine Grove, La., U.S.	D5	95
Pine Grove, N.J., U.S.	D3	107
Pine Grove, Pa., U.S.	E9	115
Pine Grove, W.V., U.S.	B4	125
Pine Grove Mills, Pa., U.S.	E6	115
Pine Hall, N.C., U.S.	A2	110
Pine Hill, Austl.	A6	51
Pine Hill, Al., U.S.	D2	78
Pine Hill, Ky., U.S.	C5	94
Pine Hill, N.J., U.S.	D3	107
Pine Hills, Fl., U.S.	D5	86
Pinehouse Lake, Sask.	B2	75
Pinehurst, Ga., U.S.	D3	87
Pinehurst, Id., U.S.	B2	89
Pinehurst, Ma., U.S.	f11	98
Pinehurst, N.J., U.S.	E3	107
Pinehurst, N.C., U.S.	B3	110
Pinehurst Lake, l., Alta.	B5	68
Pine Island, Mn., U.S.	F6	100
Pine Island, N.Y., U.S.	D6	109
Pine Island, i., Fl., U.S.	F4	86
Pine Island Bay, b., Ant.	B2	7
Pine Island Sound, strt., Fl., U.S.	F4	86
Pine Key, i., Fl., U.S.	p10	86
Pine Knot, Ky., U.S.	D5	94
Pine Lake, Ga., U.S.	h8	87
Pine Lake, In., U.S.	A4	91
Pine Lake, l., In., U.S.	g10	98
Pine Lake, l., Wi., U.S.	C5	126
Pineland, S.C., U.S.	F5	117
Pine Lawn, Mo., U.S.	f13	102
Pine Level, Al., U.S.	C3	78
Pine Level, N.C., U.S.	B4	110
Pinellas, co., Fl., U.S.	E4	86
Pinellas, Point, c., Fl., U.S.	p10	86
Pinellas Park, Fl., U.S.	E4	86
Pine Meadow, Ct., U.S.	B4	84
Pine Mountain, Ga., U.S.	D2	87
Pine Mountain, mtn., U.S.	D6	94
Pine Mountain, mtn., Ct., U.S.	B4	84
Pine Mountain, mtn., Or., U.S.	D6	114
Pine Mountain, mtn., Tn., U.S.	C9	119
Pine Mountain, mtn., Wy., U.S.	E3	127
Pine Mountain, hills, U.S.	C6	113
Pineora, Ga., U.S.	D5	87
Pine Orchard, Ct., U.S.	D4	84
Pine Park, Ga., U.S.	F2	87
Pine Plains, N.Y., U.S.	D7	109
Pine Point, N.W. Ter.	D10	66
Pine Point, Me., U.S.	E2	96
Pine Prairie, La., U.S.	D3	95
Pine Rest, Me., U.S.	g10	98
Pine Ridge, Ar., U.S.	C2	81
Pine Ridge, Ky., U.S.	C6	94
Pine Ridge, Ms., U.S.	D2	101
Pine Ridge, S.D., U.S.	D3	118
Pine Ridge, Ne., U.S.	B2	104
Pine Ridge Indian Reservation, S.D., U.S.	D3	118
Pine River, Man.	D1	70
Pine River, Mn., U.S.	D4	100
Pinerolo, Italy	B1	23
Pines, Isle of see Juventud, Isla de la, i., Cuba	D2	64
Pines, Lake o' the, res., Tx., U.S.	C5	120
Pinesdale, Mi., U.S.	D2	103
Pine Stump Junction, Mi., U.S.	B5	99
Pine Swamp Knob, mtn., W.V., U.S.	B5	125
Pinetops, N.C., U.S.	B5	110
Pinetown, N.C., U.S.	B6	110
Pine Tree Corners, De., U.S.	C3	85
Pinetta, Fl., U.S.	B3	86
Pine Valley, Ca., U.S.	F5	82
Pine Valley, N.H., U.S.	E3	106
Pine Valley, Ut., U.S.	F2	121
Pine Valley, val., Ut., U.S.	F2	121
Pine Valley Mountains, mts., Ut., U.S.	F2	121
Pineview, Ga., U.S.	D3	87
Pine Village, In., U.S.	D3	91
Pineville, Ky., U.S.	D6	94
Pineville, La., U.S.	C3	95
Pineville, Mo., U.S.	E3	102
Pineville, N.C., U.S.	B2	110
Pineville, S.C., U.S.	E7	117
Pineville, W.V., U.S.	D3	125
Pinewald, N.J., U.S.	D4	107
Pinewood, Fl., U.S.	s13	86
Pinewood, Mn., U.S.	C3	100
Pinewood, S.C., U.S.	D7	117
Pinewood Park, Fl., U.S.	*G6	86
Piney, Man.	E4	70
Piney Creek, stm., W.V., U.S.	n13	125
Piney Fork, Oh., U.S.	B5	112
Piney Fork, stm., W.V., U.S.	h9	125
Piney Point, Md., U.S.	D4	97
Piney View, W.V., U.S.	n13	125
Piney Woods, Ms., U.S.	C3	101
Ping, stm., Thai.	B1	34
Pingding, China	F5	32
Pingdingshan, China	H5	32
Pingdu, China	D8	31
Pingjiang, China	J5	32
Pingliang, China	D6	31
Pingluo, China	E2	32
Pingnan, China	G7	31
Pingquan, China	D8	32
Pingree, Id., U.S.	F6	89
Pingree, N.D., U.S.	B7	111
Pingwu, China	E5	31
Pingxiang, China	F7	31
Pingxiang, China	G6	31
Pinhal, Braz.	*G6	57
Pinhal Novo, Port.	f10	22
Pinheiro, Braz.	B1	57
Pinhel, Port.	B2	22
Pini, i., Indon.	E1	34
Piniós (Peneus), stm., Grc.	C4	40
Pink Cliffs, clf., Ut., U.S.	F3	121
Pinkham Notch, N.H., U.S.	B4	106
Pink Hill, N.C., U.S.	B5	110
Pinkstaff, Il., U.S.	E6	90
Pinnacle, Ar., U.S.	C3	81
Pinnacle, mtn., N.Y., U.S.	A2	110
Pinnacle, mtn., N.Y., U.S.	B6	109
Pinnacle Buttes, mtn., Wy., U.S.	C3	127
Pinnacles National Monument, U.S.	D3	82
Pinnaroo, Austl.	G3	51
Pinneberg, Ger.	E3	15
Pinnebog, Mi., U.S.	E7	99
Pinola, Ms., U.S.	D4	101
Pinole, Ca., U.S.	h8	82
Piñon, Az., U.S.	A5	80
Piñon, N.M., U.S.	E4	108
Pinopolis, S.C., U.S.	E7	117
Pinopolis Dam, S.C., U.S.	E8	117
Pinos, Mex.	C4	63
Pinos, Mount, mtn., Ca., U.S.	E4	82
Pinos, Point, c., Ca., U.S.	D2	82
Pinos Altos, N.M., U.S.	E1	108
Pinoso, Spain	C5	22
Pinos-Puente, Spain	D4	22
Pins, Pointe aux, c., Ont.	E3	73
Pinsk, Sov. Un.	E6	27
Pinsk Marshes, sw., Sov. Un.	E6	27
Pinson, Al., U.S.	f7	78
Pinson, Tn., U.S.	B3	119
Pinta, Isla, i., Ec.	f5	58
Pinta, Sierra, mts., Az., U.S.	E2	80
Pintados, Chile	A3	55
Pinto, Spain	p17	22
Pinto Butte, mtn., Sask.	H2	75
Pinto Creek, stm., Sask.	H2	75
Pintura, Ut., U.S.	F2	121
Pintwater Range, mts., Nv., U.S.	G6	105
Pinware, stm., Newf.	C3	72
Pinzolo, Italy	C6	20
Pinzón, Isla, i., Ec.	g5	58
Pioche, Nv., U.S.	F7	105
Piombino, Italy	C3	23
Pioneer, Ia., U.S.	B3	92
Pioneer, La., U.S.	B4	95
Pioneer, Oh., U.S.	A1	112
Pioneer Mine, B.C.	D6	69
Pioneer Mountains, mts., Id., U.S.	F5	89
Pioneer Mountains, mts., Mt., U.S.	E3	103
Pioner, i., Sov. Un.	B6	128
Pionki, Pol.	C6	26
Piopolis, Que.	D7	74
Piotrków [Trybunalski], Pol.	C5	26
Piove di Sacco, Italy	D7	20
Pipe, Wi., U.S.	k9	126
Pipe Creek, stm., In., U.S.	D6	91
Piper, Ks., U.S.	k16	93
Piper City, Il., U.S.	C5	90
Pipéri, i., Grc.	C5	25
Piperton, Ont.	h12	73
Pipe Spring National Monument, Az., U.S.	A3	80
Pipestem, W.V., U.S.	D4	125
Pipestem Creek, stm., N.D., U.S.	B6	111
Pipestone, Man.	E1	70
Pipestone, Mn., U.S.	G2	100
Pipestone, co., Mn., U.S.	F2	100
Pipestone Creek, stm., Can.	E1	70
Pipestone National Monument, Mn., U.S.	G2	100
Pipestone Pass, Mt., U.S.	E4	103
Pipinas, Arg.	B5	54
Pipmuacan, Réservoir, res., Que.	k12	74
Piqua, Ks., U.S.	E8	93
Piqua, Oh., U.S.	B1	112
Piquiri, stm., Braz.	B6	56
Piracaia, Braz.	C3	56
Piracicaba, Braz.	C3	56
Piracicaba, stm., Braz.	m8	56
Piracuruca, Braz.	B3	57
Piraju, Braz.	C3	56
Pirajuba, Braz.	B3	56
Pirajuí, Braz.	C3	56
Piramida, Mount, mtn., Sov. Un.	D12	29
Piran, Yugo.	C1	23
Pirané, Arg.	A5	54
Piranga, Braz.	C4	56
Piranga, stm., Braz.	B3	56
Piranhas, Braz.	C2	56
Pīrān Shahr, Iran	C2	39
Pirapora, Braz.	A4	56
Pirassununga, Braz.	C3	56
Pirenópolis, Braz.	B3	56
Pires do Rio, Braz.	B4	56
Pirgos, Grc.	D3	40
Piriápolis, Ur.	E1	55
Pirin Mountains, mts., Bul.	E6	24
Piripiri, Braz.	B3	57
Pirmasens, Ger.	D3	18
Pirna, Ger.	C6	18
Pirot, Yugo.	D6	24
Pirovskoye, Sov. Un.	D27	29
Pirtleville, Az., U.S.	F6	80
Piru, Indon.	F7	34
Piryatin, Sov. Un.	F9	27
Pisa, Italy	C3	23
Pisac, hist., Peru	D3	58
Pisagua, Chile	C1	55
Piscataqua, stm., N.H., U.S.	D5	106
Piscataquis, co., Me., U.S.	C3	96
Piscataquis, stm., Me., U.S.	C3	96
Piscataquog, stm., N.H., U.S.	D3	106
Piscataway, N.J., U.S.	B4	107
Piscataway Creek, stm., Md., U.S.	C4	97
Pisciotta, Italy	D5	23
Pisco, Peru	D2	58
Piseco Lake, l., N.Y., U.S.	B6	109
Písek, Czech.	D3	26
Pisek, N.D., U.S.	A8	111
Pisgah, Al., U.S.	A4	78
Pisgah, Ia., U.S.	C2	92
Pisgah, Md., U.S.	C3	97
Pisgah, Oh., U.S.	n13	112
Pisgah, Mount, mtn., Ct., U.S.	B3	84
Pisgah, Mount, mtn., Vt., U.S.	F3	122
Pisgah Forest, N.C., U.S.	f10	110
Pishan, China	B8	127
Pishin, Pak.	B4	36
Pishin Lora, stm., Asia	C4	36
Pisinemo, Az., U.S.	E3	80
Pisticci, Italy	D6	23
Pistoia, Italy	C3	23
Pistol River, Or., U.S.	E2	114
Pisuerga, stm., Spain	A3	22
Pisz, Pol.	B6	26
Pita, Gui.	D2	45
Pital, Cerro el, mtn., N.A.	*C3	62
Pitanga, Braz.	C6	56
Pitangui, Braz.	B4	56
Pitcairn, Pa., U.S.	k14	115
Pitcairn, dep., Oc.	H14	6
Pitcher Hill, N.Y., U.S.	*B4	109
Piteå, Swe.	E9	14
Piteälven, stm., Swe.	E9	14
Pitești, Rom.	C7	24
Piti, Guam	L9	52
Pitkin, Co., U.S.	C4	83
Pitkin, La., U.S.	D3	95
Pitkin, co., Co., U.S.	B4	83
Pitlochry, Scot., U.K.	B5	10
Pitman, N.J., U.S.	D2	107
Pitomača, Yugo.	C3	24
Pitt, Mn., U.S.	B4	100
Pitt, co., N.C., U.S.	B5	110
Pitt Island, i., B.C.	C3	69
Pittman Center, Tn., U.S.	D10	119
Pitts, Ga., U.S.	D3	87
Pittsboro, In., U.S.	E5	91
Pittsboro, Ms., U.S.	B4	101
Pittsboro, N.C., U.S.	B3	110
Pittsburg, Ca., U.S.	g9	82
Pittsburg, Il., U.S.	F5	90
Pittsburg, Ks., U.S.	E9	93
Pittsburg, Ky., U.S.	C5	94
Pittsburg, Ok., U.S.	C6	113
Pittsburg, co., Ok., U.S.	C6	113
Pittsburg, Pa., U.S.	F11	115
Pittsburgh, Pa., U.S.	F1	115
Pittsfield, Il., U.S.	D3	90
Pittsfield, Me., U.S.	D3	96
Pittsfield, Ma., U.S.	B1	98
Pittsfield, N.H., U.S.	D4	106
Pittsfield, Vt., U.S.	D3	122
Pittsford, Mi., U.S.	G6	99
Pittsford, Vt., U.S.	D2	122
Pittston, Pa., U.S.	D10	115
Pittstown, N.J., U.S.	B3	107
Pittsview, Al., U.S.	C4	78
Pittsville, Md., U.S.	D7	97
Pittsville, Wi., U.S.	D3	126
Pittsylvania, co., Va., U.S.	D3	123
Piumhi, Braz.	C3	56
Piura, Peru	C1	58
Piura, dept., Peru	C1	58
Piute, co., Ut., U.S.	E3	121
Piute Reservoir, res., Ut., U.S.	E3	121
Piuthān, Nepal	C9	37
Piva, stm., Yugo.	D4	24
Pixley, Ca., U.S.	E4	82
Pizzo, Italy	E6	23
P. K. le Roux Dam, res., S. Afr.	D3	49
Placentia, Newf.	E5	72
Placentia, Ca., U.S.	n13	82
Placentia Bay, b., Newf.	E4	72
Placer, co., Ca., U.S.	C3	82
Placerville, Ca., U.S.	C3	82
Placerville, Co., U.S.	C3	83
Placetas, Cuba	C4	64
Placid, Lake, l., Fl., U.S.	E5	86
Placid, Lake, l., N.Y., U.S.	f11	109
Placida, Fl., U.S.	F4	86
Plácido de Castro, Braz.	B3	58
Plácidos, N.M., U.S.	B3	108
Plaffeien, Switz.	C3	21
Plain, Wi., U.S.	E3	126
Plain City, Oh., U.S.	B2	112
Plain City, Ut., U.S.	B3	121
Plain Dealing, La., U.S.	B2	95
Plainfield, Ct., U.S.	C8	84
Plainfield, Il., U.S.	B5	90
Plainfield, Ia., U.S.	B5	92
Plainfield, In., U.S.	E5	91
Plainfield, N.H., U.S.	C2	106
Plainfield, N.J., U.S.	B4	107
Plainfield, Oh., U.S.	B4	112
Plainfield, Vt., U.S.	C4	122
Plainfield, Wi., U.S.	D4	126
Plainfield Heights, Mi., U.S.	E5	99
Plains, Ga., U.S.	D2	87
Plains, Ks., U.S.	E3	93
Plains, Mt., U.S.	C2	103
Plains, Tx., U.S.	C1	120
Plains, Pa., U.S.	n17	115
Plainsboro, N.J., U.S.	C3	107
Plainview, Ar., U.S.	C2	81
Plainview, Mn., U.S.	F6	100
Plainview, Ne., U.S.	B8	104
Plainview, N.Y., U.S.	*E7	109
Plainview, S.D., U.S.	C3	118
Plainview, Tx., U.S.	B2	120
Plainville, Ct., U.S.	C4	84
Plainville, Ga., U.S.	D3	87
Plainville, Il., U.S.	D2	90
Plainville, In., U.S.	G3	91
Plainville, Ks., U.S.	C4	93
Plainville, Ma., U.S.	B5	98
Plainwell, Mi., U.S.	F5	99
Plaisance, Que.	D2	74
Plaisance, Haiti	E7	64
Plaisance, Baie de, b., Que.	B8	71
Plaisance-du-Gers, Fr.	F4	16
Plaisted, Me., U.S.	A4	96
Plaistow, N.H., U.S.	E4	106
Plamondon, Alta.	B4	68
Plaňá, Czech.	D7	19
Planaltina, Braz.	B3	56
Plane, stm., Ger.	A7	19
Plankinton, S.D., U.S.	D7	118
Plano, Il., U.S.	B5	90
Plano, Ia., U.S.	D4	92
Plano, Tx., U.S.	C4	120
Plantagenet, Ont.	B9	73
Plantation, Fl., U.S.	r13	86
Plant City, Fl., U.S.	D4	86
Plantersville, Al., U.S.	C3	78
Plantersville, Ms., U.S.	A5	101
Plantersville, S.C., U.S.	D9	117
Plantsite, Az., U.S.	D6	80
Plantsville, Ct., U.S.	C4	84
Plaquemine, La., U.S.	D4	95
Plaquemines, co., La., U.S.	E6	95
Plasencia, Spain	B2	22
Plast, Sov. Un.	E2	8
Plaster Rock, N.B.	C2	71
Plastun, Sov. Un.	D8	33
Plasy, Czech.	D8	19
Plata, mtn., Switz.	D8	21
Plata, Río de la, est., S.A.	B5	54
Plata, stm., U.S.	B3	82
Platea, Pa., U.S.	C1	115
Plateau, Pa., U.S.	C8	71
Plateau City, Co., U.S.	B3	83
Plateau Creek, stm., Co., U.S.	B2	83
Plate Cove West, Newf.	D5	72
Platina, Ca., U.S.	B2	82
Platinum, Ak., U.S.	D7	79
Platner, Co., U.S.	A7	83
Plato, Sask.	F1	75
Plato, Col.	B3	60
Plato, Mo., U.S.	D5	102
Platón Sánchez, Mex.	m14	63
Platte, S.D., U.S.	D7	118
Platte, co., Mo., U.S.	B3	102
Platte, co., Ne., U.S.	C8	104
Platte, co., Wy., U.S.	D7	127
Platte, stm., Mn., U.S.	E4	100
Platte, stm., Ne., U.S.	D6	104
Platte Center, Ne., U.S.	C8	104
Platte City, Mo., U.S.	B3	102
Plattenville, La., U.S.	k9	95
Platter, Ok., U.S.	D5	113
Platteville, Co., U.S.	A6	83
Platteville, Wi., U.S.	F3	126
Plattling, Ger.	E7	19
Plattsburg, Mo., U.S.	B3	102
Plattsburgh, N.Y., U.S.	f11	109
Plattsburgh Air Force Base, mil., U.S.	f11	109
Plattsmouth, Ne., U.S.	D10	104
Plattville, Il., U.S.	B5	90
Plaucheville, La., U.S.	C4	95
Plauen, Ger.	C6	18
Plauer, Lake, l., Ger.	E6	15
Play Cu, Viet.	F9	35
Playgreen Lake, l., Man.	B2	70
Plaza, N.D., U.S.	A4	111
Pleasant, stm., Me., U.S.	C3	96
Pleasant, Lake, res., Az., U.S.	D3	80
Pleasant, Mount, mtn., Va., U.S.	C3	123
Pleasant Bay, N.S.	C9	71
Pleasant City, Oh., U.S.	C4	112
Pleasantdale, Sask.	D9	
Pleasant Dale, Ne., U.S.	D9	104
Pleasant Gap, Pa., U.S.	E6	115
Pleasant Garden, N.C., U.S.	B3	110
Pleasant Grove, Al., U.S.	g7	78
Pleasant Grove, Ms., U.S.	A3	101
Pleasant Grove, Ut., U.S.	C4	121
Pleasant Hill, Al., U.S.	C3	78
Pleasant Hill, Il., U.S.	D3	90
Pleasant Hill, Ia., U.S.	e8	92
Pleasant Hill, La., U.S.	C2	95
Pleasant Hill, Mo., U.S.	C3	102
Pleasant Hill, N.C., U.S.	A5	110
Pleasant Hill, Oh., U.S.	B1	112
Pleasant Hill, S.C., U.S.	B6	117
Pleasant Hills, Pa., U.S.	*k14	115
Pleasant Hope, Mo., U.S.	D4	102
Pleasant Lake, In., U.S.	A7	91
Pleasant Lake, Ma., U.S.	C7	98
Pleasant Lake, l., N.D., U.S.	A6	111
Pleasant Lake, l., N.H., U.S.	D4	106
Pleasant Mount, Pa., U.S.	C11	115
Pleasanton, Ca., U.S.	h9	82
Pleasanton, Ia., U.S.	D4	92
Pleasanton, Ks., U.S.	D9	93
Pleasanton, Tx., U.S.	E3	120
Pleasant Plains, Ar., U.S.	B4	81
Pleasant Plains, Il., U.S.	D4	90
Pleasant Prairie, Wi., U.S.	n12	126
Pleasants, co., W.V., U.S.	B3	125
Pleasant Shade, Tn., U.S.	C8	119
Pleasant Valley, Ct., U.S.	B4	84
Pleasant Valley, Ia., U.S.	g11	92
Pleasant Valley, Mo., U.S.	h11	102
Pleasant Valley, Nv., U.S.	*D2	105
Pleasant Valley, N.Y., U.S.	D7	109
Pleasant View, Co., U.S.	*B5	83
Pleasant View, Il., U.S.	C3	90
Pleasant View, Ky., U.S.	D5	94
Pleasant View, Tn., U.S.	A4	119
Pleasant View, Ut., U.S.	B3	121
Pleasant View, Wi., U.S.	D3	126
Pleasantville, In., U.S.	G3	91
Pleasantville, Ia., U.S.	C4	92
Pleasantville, N.J., U.S.	E3	107
Pleasantville, N.Y., U.S.	D7	109
Pleasantville, Oh., U.S.	C3	112
Pleasantville, Pa., U.S.	C2	115
Pleasure Beach, Ct., U.S.	D7	84
Pleasure Ridge Park, Ky., U.S.	g11	94
Pleasureville, Ky., U.S.	B4	94
Pledger, Tx., U.S.	r14	120
Pleebo, Lib.	F3	45
Plenița, Rom.	C6	24
Plenty, Sask.	D2	74
Plenty, Bay of, b., N.Z.	L16	51
Plentywood, Mt., U.S.	B12	103
Plérin, Fr.	C2	16
Plesetsk, Sov. Un.	C7	29
Plessis, N.Y., U.S.	A4	96
Plessisville, Que.	C6	74
Pleszew, Pol.	C4	26
Plétipi, Lac, l., Que.	h12	74
Plettenberg, Ger.	B2	19
Pleven, Bul.	D7	24
Plevna, Ks., U.S.	E5	93
Plevna, Mo., U.S.	B5	102
Plevna, Mt., U.S.	D12	103
Pliny Range, mts., N.H., U.S.	B4	106
Pljevlja, Yugo.	D4	24
Plochingen, Ger.	B5	19
Płock, Pol.	B5	26
Ploërmel, Fr.	D2	16
Ploiești, Rom.	C8	24
Plomárion, Grc.	C6	25
Plomb du Cantal, mtn., Fr.	E5	16
Plombières-les-Bains, Fr.	B2	20
Plomosa Mountains, mts., Az., U.S.	D1	80
Plön, Ger.	D4	15
Plonge, Lac la, l., Sask.	B2	75
Płońsk, Pol.	B6	26
Plougastel, Fr.	C1	16
Plovdiv, Bul.	D7	24
Plover, Ia., U.S.	B3	92
Plover, Wi., U.S.	D4	126
Plover, stm., Wi., U.S.	D4	126
Plum, Pa., U.S.	k14	115
Plum, stm., Il., U.S.	C2	118
Plumas, Man.	D2	70
Plumas, co., Ca., U.S.	B3	82
Plum Bayou, stm., Ar., U.S.	k10	81
Plum Beach, Fl., U.S.	E4	116
Plum Branch, S.C., U.S.	D3	117
Plum City, Wi., U.S.	D1	126
Plum Coulee, Man.	E3	70
Plum Creek, stm., Ne., U.S.	D6	104
Plumerville, Ar., U.S.	B3	81
Plum Island, i., Ma., U.S.	A6	98
Plummer, Id., U.S.	B2	89
Plummer, Mn., U.S.	C2	100
Plum Point, R.I., U.S.	E4	116
Plumsteadville, Pa., U.S.	F11	115
Plumtree, Zimb.	B4	49
Plumwood, Oh., U.S.	B2	112
Plunkett, Sask.	F3	75
Plunkettville, Ok., U.S.	C7	113
Plush, Or., U.S.	E7	114
Plymouth, Monts.	H13	64
Plymouth, Eng., U.K.	E4	10
Plymouth, Ct., U.S.	C3	84
Plymouth, Fl., U.S.	D5	86
Plymouth, Il., U.S.	C3	90
Plymouth, In., U.S.	B5	91
Plymouth, Ia., U.S.	A4	92
Plymouth, Ks., U.S.	D7	93
Plymouth, Me., U.S.	D3	96
Plymouth, Ma., U.S.	C6	98
Plymouth, Mn., U.S.	m12	100
Plymouth, Ne., U.S.	D9	104
Plymouth, N.H., U.S.	C3	106
Plymouth, N.C., U.S.	B6	110
Plymouth, Oh., U.S.	A3	112
Plymouth, Pa., U.S.	D10	115
Plymouth, Ut., U.S.	B3	121
Plymouth, Vt., U.S.	E3	122
Plymouth, Wi., U.S.	E6	126
Plymouth, co., Ia., U.S.	B1	92
Plymouth, co., Ma., U.S.	C6	98
Plymouth Bay, b., Ma., U.S.	C6	98
Plymouth Township, Pa., U.S.	*F11	115
Plympton, Ma., U.S.	C6	98
Plzeň (Pilsen), Czech.	D2	26
Pô, Burkina	B3	45
Po, stm., Italy	B3	23
Po, Mouths of the, mth., Italy	B4	23
Poamoho Stream, stm., Hi., U.S.	f9	88
Pobé, Benin	*G7	45
Pobeda, Mount, mtn., Sov. Un.	C36	128
Pobedino, Sov. Un.	B11	33
Pobedy, Peak, mtn., Asia	E11	29
Poca, W.V., U.S.	*C3	125
Pocahontas, Ar., U.S.	A5	81
Pocahontas, Il., U.S.	E4	90
Pocahontas, Ia., U.S.	B3	92
Pocahontas, Tn., U.S.	B3	119
Pocahontas, Va., U.S.	e10	123
Pocahontas, co., Ia., U.S.	B3	92
Pocahontas, co., W.V., U.S.	C4	125
Pocasset, Ma., U.S.	C6	98
Pocasset, Ok., U.S.	B4	113
Pocatalico, stm., W.V., U.S.	C3	125
Pocatello, Id., U.S.	G6	89
Pochep, Sov. Un.	E9	27
Pochutla, Mex.	D5	63
Pocola, Ok., U.S.	B7	113
Pocomoke City, Md., U.S.	D6	97
Pocomoke Sound, strt., Md., U.S.	E6	97
Poconé, Braz.	B1	56
Pocono Mountains, hills, Pa., U.S.	D11	115
Pocono Pines, Pa., U.S.	D11	115
Poços de Caldas, Braz.	C3	56
Pocotopaug Lake, res., Ct., U.S.	C6	84
Pocrí, Pan.	G7	62
Pocumtuck Mountain, mtn., Ma., U.S.	A2	98
Podbořany, Czech.	C8	19
Podgornoye, Sov. Un.	D25	8
Podkamennaya Tunguska, Sov. Un.	C27	8
Podkamennaya Tunguska, stm., Sov. Un.	C12	29
Podolsk, Sov. Un.	D11	27
Podor, Sen.	C2	45
Podporozhye, Sov. Un.	G16	14

Name	Map Ref.	Page
Poe, In., U.S.	C7	91
Poel, i., Ger.	E5	15
Pofadder, S. Afr.	C2	49
Poge, Cape, c., Ma., U.S.	D7	98
Poggibonsi, Italy	C3	23
Pöggstall, Aus.	D7	18
Pogradeci, Alb.	B3	25
Pogranichnoye, Sov. Un.	A11	33
Pogranichnyy, Sov. Un.	D5	33
Pohang, S. Kor.	D10	31
Pohénégamook, Que.	B8	74
Pohnpei, i., Micron.	F9	6
Pohue Bay, b., Hi., U.S.	E6	88
Poinsett, co., Ar., U.S.	B5	81
Poinsett, Cape, c., Ant.	C24	7
Poinsett, Lake, l., Fl., U.S.	D6	86
Poinsett, Lake, l., S.D., U.S.	C8	118
Point Arena, Ca., U.S.	C2	82
Point Baker, Ak., U.S.	D13	79
Point Blue, La., U.S.	D3	95
Point Cedar, Ar., U.S.	C2	81
Point Clear, Al., U.S.	E2	78
Pointe a la Hache, La., U.S.	E6	95
Pointe-à-Pierre, Trin.	O23	65
Pointe-à-Pitre, Guad.	H14	64
Pointe au Baril Station, Ont.	B4	73
Pointe-au-Pic, Que.	B7	74
Pointe-aux-Trembles (part of Montréal), Que.	p20	74
Pointe-Bleue, Que.	A5	74
Pointe-Calumet, Que.	p19	74
Pointe-Claire, Que.	D4	74
Pointe Coupee, co., La., U.S.	C3	95
Pointe-des-Cascades, Que.	q19	74
Pointe du Bois, Man.	D4	70
Pointe-du-Chêne, N.B.	C5	71
Pointe-du-Lac, Que.	C5	74
Point Edward, Ont.	D2	73
Pointe-Noire, Congo	B1	48
Pointe-Noire, Guad.	Q8	65
Pointers, N.J., U.S.	D2	107
Pointe-Verte, N.B.	B4	71
Point Fortin, Trin.	O22	65
Point Hope, Ak., U.S.	B6	79
Point Imperial, mtn., Az., U.S.	A4	80
Point Independence, Ma., U.S.	*C6	98
Point Judith, R.I., U.S.	G4	116
Point Judith Pond, l., R.I., U.S.	F4	116
Point Lake, l., N.W. Ter.	C10	66
Point Leamington, Newf.	D4	72
Point Lookout, Md., U.S.	D5	97
Point Lookout, Mo., U.S.	E4	102
Point Marion, Pa., U.S.	G2	115
Point Mugu Naval Air Station, mil., Ca., U.S.	E4	82
Point of Rocks, Md., U.S.	B2	97
Point of Rocks, Wy., U.S.	E4	127
Point Pelee National Park, Ont.	F2	73
Point Pleasant, N.J., U.S.	C4	107
Point Pleasant, W.V., U.S.	C2	125
Point Pleasant Beach, N.J., U.S.	C4	107
Point Reyes National Seashore, Ca., U.S.	C2	82
Point Roberts, Wa., U.S.	A2	124
Point Sapin, N.B.	C5	71
Point Washington, Fl., U.S.	u15	86
Poipu, Hi., U.S.	B2	88
Poirino, Italy	E3	20
Poison Creek, stm., Wy., U.S.	C5	127
Poisson Blanc, Lac du, res., Que.	C2	74
Poissy, Fr.	C5	16
Poitiers, Fr.	D4	16
Poitou, hist. reg., Fr.	D3	16
Poix, Fr.	E1	17
Pojo, Bol.	C3	55
Pojoaque Valley, N.M., U.S.	B3	108
Pokaran, India	C5	36
Pokataroo, Austl.	D7	51
Pokegama Lake, l., Mn., U.S.	C5	100
Pokegama Lake, l., Wi., U.S.	C2	126
Pokharā, Nepal	C9	36
Pokkye-ri, N. Kor.	G3	33
Poko, Zaire	A4	48
Poko Mountain, mtn., Ak., U.S.	B7	79
Pokrov, Sov. Un.	n19	27
Pokrovskoye, Sov. Un.	H12	27
Polacca, Az., U.S.	B5	80
Polän, Iran	C6	38
Poland, In., U.S.	F4	91
Poland, Me., U.S.	*D2	96
Poland, N.Y., U.S.	A5	109
Poland, ctry., Eur.	C5	26
Poland Spring, Me., U.S.	D2	96
Polar, Wi., U.S.	C5	126
Polar Bear Provincial Park, Ont.	n18	73
Polaris, Mt., U.S.	E3	103
Polar Record Glacier, ice, Ant.	C20	7
Polar Times Glacier, ice, Ant.	C20	7
Polathane see Akçaabat, Tur.	*C9	40
Polatli, Tur.	*B3	13
Polbain, Scot., U.K.	B3	13
Polch, Ger.	C2	19
Polcura, Chile	B2	54
Polebridge, Mt., U.S.	B2	103
Polecat Creek, stm., Ok., U.S.	B5	113
Pol-e Khomrī, Afg.	A4	36
Pole Mountain, mtn., Wy., U.S.	E7	127
Polesella, Italy	E7	20
Polessk, Sov. Un.	A6	26
Polevskoy, Sov. Un.	D21	8
Polgár, Hung.	B5	24
Poli, Cam.	D2	46
Policastro, Gulf of, b., Italy	E5	23
Police, Pol.	B3	26
Poligny, Fr.	D6	16
Polikhnitos, Grc.	o13	34
Polillo, Phil.	o13	34
Polillo Islands, is., Phil.	B6	34
Polillo Strait, strt., Phil.	o13	34
Pólis, Cyp.	E9	40
Polish Mountain, mtn., U.S.	k13	97
Políyiros, Grc.	B4	25
Polk, Ne., U.S.	C8	104
Polk, Oh., U.S.	B3	112
Polk, Pa., U.S.	D2	115
Polk, Tn., U.S.	A2	119
Polk, co., Ar., U.S.	C1	81
Polk, co., Fl., U.S.	E5	86
Polk, co., Ga., U.S.	C1	87
Polk, co., Ia., U.S.	C4	92
Polk, co., Mn., U.S.	C2	100
Polk, co., Mo., U.S.	D4	102
Polk, co., N.C., U.S.	f10	110
Polk, co., Or., U.S.	C3	114
Polk, co., Tn., U.S.	D9	119
Polk, co., Tx., U.S.	D5	120
Polk, co., Wi., U.S.	C1	126
Polk City, Fl., U.S.	D5	86
Polk City, Ia., U.S.	C4	92
Polkton, N.C., U.S.	B2	110
Polkville, Ms., U.S.	C4	101
Pollard, Al., U.S.	D2	78
Pollard, Ar., U.S.	A5	81
Pollensa, Spain	C7	22
Pollock, Id., U.S.	D2	89
Pollock, La., U.S.	C3	95
Pollock, Mo., U.S.	A4	102
Pollock, S.D., U.S.	B5	118
Pollocksville, N.C., U.S.	B5	110
Pollockville, Alta.	D5	68
Polo, Il., U.S.	B4	90
Polo, Mo., U.S.	B3	102
Polochic, stm., Guat.	C3	62
Pologi, Sov. Un.	H11	27
Polonnoye, Sov. Un.	F6	27
Polotsk, Sov. Un.	D7	27
Polson, Mt., U.S.	C2	103
Poltava, Sov. Un.	E6	29
Poltimore, Que.	D2	74
Polunochnoye, Sov. Un.	A6	28
Polvadera, N.M., U.S.	C3	108
Polwarth, Sask.	D2	75
Polyarnyy, Sov. Un.	C15	14
Pomabamba, Peru	C2	58
Pomarão, Port.	D2	22
Pomaria, S.C., U.S.	C5	117
Pomba, stm., Braz.	g6	56
Pomba, stm., Braz.	C3	57
Pombal, Braz.	C1	22
Pombal, Port.	B4	26
Pomerania, hist. reg., Pol.	B4	26
Pomeranian Bay, b., Eur.	D8	15
Pomerene, Az., U.S.	E5	80
Pomeroy, N. Ire., U.K.	C5	11
Pomeroy, Ia., U.S.	B3	92
Pomeroy, Oh., U.S.	C3	112
Pomeroy, Wa., U.S.	C8	124
Pomezia, Italy	h9	23
Pomfret, Ct., U.S.	B8	84
Pomfret, Md., U.S.	C3	97
Pomfret, Vt., U.S.	D3	122
Pomfret Center, Ct., U.S.	B8	84
Pomme de Terre, stm., Mn., U.S.	E3	100
Pomme de Terre, stm., Mo., U.S.	D4	102
Pomme de Terre Lake, res., Mo., U.S.	D4	102
Pomoho, Hi., U.S.	f9	88
Pomona, Ca., U.S.	E5	82
Pomona, Ks., U.S.	D8	93
Pomona, Mo., U.S.	E6	102
Pomona, N.J., U.S.	E3	107
Pomona Lake, res., Ks., U.S.	D7	93
Pomona Park, Fl., U.S.	C5	86
Pomorie, Bul.	D8	24
Pompano Beach, Fl., U.S.	F6	86
Pompano Beach Highlands, Fl., U.S.	*F6	86
Pompeii, hist., Italy	D5	23
Pompeys Pillar, Mt., U.S.	E9	103
Pompton Lakes, N.J., U.S.	A4	107
Pomquet, N.S.	D8	71
Ponaganset, stm., R.I., U.S.	C2	116
Ponaganset Reservoir, res., R.I., U.S.	B2	116
Ponask, stm., Ont.	B5	70
Ponask Lake, l., Ont.	B5	70
Ponass Lakes, l., Sask.	E3	75
Ponca, Ar., U.S.	A2	81
Ponca, Ne., U.S.	B9	104
Ponca City, Ok., U.S.	A4	113
Ponca Creek, stm., U.S.	A6	104
Ponca Indian Reservation, Ne., U.S.	B7	104
Ponce, P.R.	H11	64
Ponce de Leon, Fl., U.S.	u16	86
Ponce de Leon Bay, b., Fl., U.S.	G5	86
Ponce de Leon Inlet, b., Fl., U.S.	C6	86
Poncha Pass, Co., U.S.	C4	83
Poncha Springs, Co., U.S.	C4	83
Ponchatoula, La., U.S.	D5	95
Pond, Ky., U.S.	C2	94
Pond, West Fork, stm., Ky., U.S.	C2	94
Pond Creek, Ok., U.S.	A3	113
Pond Creek, stm., Co., U.S.	C7	83
Pond Creek, stm., Ky., U.S.	g11	94
Pondera, co., Mt., U.S.	B4	103
Ponderay, Id., U.S.	A2	89
Ponderosa, N.M., U.S.	B3	108
Pond Fork, stm., W.V., U.S.	D3	125
Pond Fork, West Fork, stm., W.V., U.S.	n12	125
Pondicherry, ter., India	*F6	36
Pondicherry, ter., India	F6	36
Pond Inlet, N.W. Ter.	B17	66
Pone Island, i., Md., U.S.	D5	97
Poneloya, Nic.	D4	62
Ponemah, Mn., U.S.	B4	100
Poneto, In., U.S.	C7	91
Ponferrada, Spain	A2	22
Pongoma, Sov. Un.	E16	14
Ponhook Lake, l., N.S.	E5	71
Ponkapog Pond, l., Ma., U.S.	h11	98
Ponoka, Alta.	C4	68
Ponoy, Sov. Un.	D19	14
Ponoy, stm., Sov. Un.	B16	8
Pons, Fr.	E3	16
Ponsford, Mn., U.S.	D3	100
Ponta Delgada, Port.	h9	44
Ponta de Pedras, Braz.	C5	59
Ponta Grossa, Braz.	D2	56
Pontal, Braz.	k7	56
Pontalina, Braz.	B3	56
Ponta-à-Mousson, Fr.	C6	16
Ponta Porã, Braz.	C1	56
Pontarlier, Fr.	D7	16
Pontchartrain, Lake, l., La., U.S.	D5	95
Pont-de-Roide, Fr.	B2	20
Pontedera, Italy	C3	23
Ponte de Sor, Port.	C1	22
Pontefract, Eng., U.K.	A6	12
Ponteix, Sask.	H2	75
Ponte Nova, Braz.	C4	56
Pontevedra, Spain	A1	22
Ponte Vedra Beach, Fl., U.S.	B5	86
Pontfaverger-Moronvilliers, Fr.	C5	90
Pontiac, Il., U.S.	C5	90
Pontiac, Mi., U.S.	F7	99
Pontiac, S.C., U.S.	C6	117
Pontianak, Indon.	F3	34
Pontic Mountains, mts., Tur.	B11	40
Pontivy, Fr.	C2	16
Pont-l'Abbé, Fr.	D1	16
Pontoise, Fr.	C5	16
Pontoosuc Lake, l., Ma., U.S.	B1	98
Pontotoc, Ms., U.S.	A4	101
Pontotoc, Tx., U.S.	D3	120
Pontotoc, co., Ms., U.S.	A4	101
Pontotoc, co., Ok., U.S.	C5	113
Pontremoli, Italy	B2	23
Pontresina, Switz.	C5	20
Pontrilas, Sask.	D5	75
Pont-Rouge, Que.	C6	74
Pont-Sainte-Maxence, Fr.	E2	17
Pontypool, Ont.	C6	73
Pontypool, Wales, U.K.	C4	12
Pontypridd (Taff-Ely), Wales, U.K.	C4	12
Pony, Mt., U.S.	E5	103
Ponza, i., Italy	D4	23
Ponziane Islands, is., Italy	D4	23
Poole, Eng., U.K.	E10	10
Poole, Ky., U.S.	C2	94
Poole, Ne., U.S.	D7	104
Pooler, Ga., U.S.	D5	87
Pooles Island, i., Md., U.S.	B5	97
Poolesville, Md., U.S.	B3	97
Poolville, Ok., U.S.	C3	113
Poolewe, Scot., U.K.	C3	13
Pooley Island, i., B.C.	C3	69
Poolowanna Lake, l., Austl.	E6	50
Poolville, Tx., U.S.	C4	120
Poona Beach see Pune, India	E5	36
Poopó, Bol.	C5	55
Poopó, Lago, l., Bol.	C2	55
Poor Knights Islands, is., N.Z.	K15	51
Pootatuck Park, Ct., U.S.	*D2	84
Poopasnaya, Sov. Un.	q21	27
Popayán, Col.	C2	60
Pope, Man.	D1	70
Pope, Ms., U.S.	A4	101
Pope, co., Ar., U.S.	B2	81
Pope, co., Il., U.S.	F5	90
Pope, co., Mn., U.S.	E3	100
Pope Air Force Base, mil., N.C., U.S.	B3	110
Popejoy, Ia., U.S.	B4	92
Poperinge, Bel.	D2	17
Popham Beach, Me., U.S.	E3	96
Popham Point, c., Ont.	B3	73
Poplar, Mt., U.S.	B11	103
Poplar, N.C., U.S.	e10	110
Poplar, Wi., U.S.	B2	126
Poplar, stm., Can.	C3	70
Poplar, stm., N.A.	B11	103
Poplar, stm., Mn., U.S.	C2	100
Poplar, West Fork, stm., U.S.	B11	103
Poplar Bluff, Mo., U.S.	E7	102
Poplar Branch, N.C., U.S.	A7	110
Poplar Creek, Ms., U.S.	B4	101
Poplarfield, Man.	D3	70
Poplar Grove, Ar., U.S.	C5	81
Poplar Grove, Il., U.S.	A5	90
Poplar Island, i., Md., U.S.	C5	97
Poplar Mountain, mtn., Ky., U.S.	D5	94
Poplar Plains, Ky., U.S.	B6	94
Poplar Point, Man.	D3	70
Poplarville, Ms., U.S.	E4	101
Popocatépetl, Volcán, vol., Mex.	n14	63
Popokabaka, Zaire	C2	48
Popondetta, Pap. N. Gui.	k12	50a
Popovo, Bul.	D8	24
Poppel, Bel.	C5	17
Popple, stm., Wi., U.S.	C5	126
Poprad, Czech.	*D6	26
Poquetanuck, Ct., U.S.	D7	84
Poquonock, Ct., U.S.	B5	84
Poquonock Bridge, Ct., U.S.	D7	84
Poquoson, Va., U.S.	C6	123
Porali, stm., Pak.	H13	39
Porangatu, Braz.	A3	56
Porbandar, India	D4	36
Porcher Island, i., B.C.	C2	69
Porcuna, Spain	D3	22
Porcupine, S.D., U.S.	D3	118
Porcupine, stm., N.A.	B11	79
Porcupine, Cape, c., Newf.	B7	72
Porcupine Hills, hills, Can.	E5	75
Porcupine Mountains, mts., Mi., U.S.	m12	99
Porcupine Plain, Sask.	E4	75
Pordenone, Italy	B4	23
Poreč, Yugo.	C1	24
Pori, Fin.	G9	14
Porirua, N.Z.	N15	51
Porjus, Swe.	D8	14
Porkhov, Sov. Un.	C7	27
Porkkala, Fin.	G11	14
Porlamar, Ven.	A5	60
Porlezza, Italy	C2	20
Pornic, Fr.	D2	16
Poroma, Bol.	C2	55
Poronaysk, Sov. Un.	H21	29
Poroshiri, Mount, mtn., Japan	E11	33
Porpoise Bay, b., Ant.	C25	7
Porrentruy, Switz.	E3	18
Porsanger, Nor.	B12	14
Porsgrunn, Nor.	p27	14
Portachuelo, Bol.	C5	55
Portacloy, Ire.	C2	11
Portadown, N. Ire., U.K.	C6	11
Portaferry, N. Ire., U.K.	C6	11
Portage, P.E.I.	C7	71
Portage, Me., U.S.	A4	96
Portage, Mi., U.S.	F5	99
Portage, Pa., U.S.	F4	115
Portage, Ut., U.S.	B3	121
Portage, Wi., U.S.	E4	126
Portage, co., Oh., U.S.	A4	112
Portage, co., Wi., U.S.	D4	126
Portage, stm., Oh., U.S.	B2	112
Portage, North Branch, stm., Oh., U.S.	f7	112
Portage Bay, b., Man.	D2	70
Portage Des Sioux, Mo., U.S.	f13	102
Portage Head, c., Wa., U.S.	A1	124
Portage Island, i., N.B.	B4	71
Portage Lake, l., Me., U.S.	B4	96
Portage Lakes, Oh., U.S.	B4	112
Portage la Prairie, Man.	E2	70
Portageville, Mo., U.S.	E8	102
Portageville, N.Y., U.S.	C2	109
Portal, Az., U.S.	F6	80
Portal, N.D., U.S.	A3	111
Portal, Ga., U.S.	D5	87
Portalegre, Port.	C2	22
Portales, N.M., U.S.	C6	108
Port Alexander, Ak., U.S.	D13	79
Port-Alfred, Que.	A7	74
Port Alfred (Kowie), S. Afr.	D4	49
Port Alice, B.C.	D4	69
Port Allegany, Pa., U.S.	C5	115
Port Allen, La., U.S.	D4	95
Port Angeles, Wa., U.S.	A2	124
Port Anson, Newf.	D4	72
Port Antonio, Jam.	E5	64
Port Aransas, Tx., U.S.	F4	120
Portarlington, Ire.	D5	11
Port Arthur, Tx., U.S.	E6	120
Port Arthur see Lüshun, China	D9	31
Port Askaig, Scot., U.K.	E2	13
Port Augusta, Austl.	F6	50
Port-au-Persil, Que.	B8	74
Port au Port Bay, b., Newf.	D2	72
Port au Port [West-Aguathuna-Felix Cove], Newf.	D2	72
Port-au-Prince, Haiti	E7	64
Port Austin, Mi., U.S.	D7	99
Port Barre, La., U.S.	D4	95
Port-Bergé, Madag.	E8	49
Port Birmingham, Al., U.S.	f9	78
Port Blair, India	H6	37
Port Blakely, Wa., U.S.	e10	124
Port Blandford, Newf.	D4	72
Port Bolivar, Tx., U.S.	E5	120
Port Borden, P.E.I.	C6	71
Port Burwell, Ont.	E4	73
Port Byron, Il., U.S.	B3	90
Port Byron, N.Y., U.S.	B4	109
Port Canning, India	I13	37
Port Carbon, Pa., U.S.	E9	115
Port Carling, Ont.	B5	73
Port-Cartier-Ouest, Que.	k13	74
Port Chalmers, N.Z.	P13	51
Port Charlotte, Fl., U.S.	F4	86
Port Chester, N.Y., U.S.	E1	109
Port Clements, B.C.	C1	69
Port Clinton, Oh., U.S.	A3	112
Port Clyde, Me., U.S.	E3	96
Port Clyde, N.S.	F4	71
Port Colborne, Ont.	E5	73
Port Colden, N.J., U.S.	B3	107
Port Coquitlam, B.C.	E6	69
Port Credit, Ont.	D5	73
Port-Daniel, Que.	A5	71
Port-de-Bouc, Fr.	F6	16
Port-de-Paix, Haiti	E7	64
Port Deposit, Md., U.S.	A5	97
Port Dickinson, N.Y., U.S.	C5	109
Port Dickson, Malay.	M6	34
Port Dover, Ont.	E4	73
Port Edward, B.C.	C2	69
Port Edwards, Wi., U.S.	D4	126
Porteirinha, Braz.	B4	56
Portel, Braz.	C4	59
Port Elgin, N.B.	C5	71
Port Elgin, Ont.	C3	73
Port Elizabeth, S. Afr.	D4	49
Port Elizabeth, N.J., U.S.	E3	107
Port Ellen, Scot., U.K.	E2	13
Porteña, Arg.	A4	54
Porter, Al., U.S.	B2	78
Porter, In., U.S.	A3	91
Porter, Me., U.S.	E2	96
Porter, Mn., U.S.	F2	100
Porter, Ok., U.S.	B6	113
Porter, Tx., U.S.	D5	120
Porter, Wa., U.S.	C2	124
Porter, co., In., U.S.	B3	91
Porter Corners, N.Y., U.S.	B7	109
Porter Creek, stm., W.V., U.S.	m13	125
Porterdale, Ga., U.S.	C3	87
Port Erin, I. of Man	F4	13
Porter Lake, l., Sask.	A2	75
Portersville, Pa., U.S.	E1	115
Porterville, Ca., U.S.	D4	82
Porterville, Ms., U.S.	C5	101
Port Essington, B.C.	B3	69
Port Ewen, N.Y., U.S.	D7	109
Port Fairy, Austl.	I4	51
Port Gamble, Wa., U.S.	B3	124
Port Gamble Indian Reservation, Wa., U.S.	B3	124
Port-Gentil, Gabon	F1	46
Port George, N.S.	D4	71
Port Gibson, Ms., U.S.	D3	101
Port Glasgow, Scot., U.K.	E4	13
Port Graham, Ak., U.S.	D9	79
Port Greville, N.S.	D5	71
Port Harcourt, Nig.	F6	45
Port Hardy, B.C.	D4	69
Port Hastings, N.S.	D8	71
Port Hawkesbury, N.S.	D8	71
Porthcawl, Wales, U.K.	C4	12
Port Hedland, Austl.	D2	50
Port Heiden, Ak., U.S.	D8	79
Port Henry, N.Y., U.S.	A7	109
Port Hill, P.E.I.	C6	71
Porthill, Id., U.S.	A2	89
Porthmadog, Wales, U.K.	B3	12
Port Hood, N.S.	C8	71
Port Hope, Ont.	D6	73
Port Hope, Mi., U.S.	E8	99
Port Hope Simpson, Newf.	B3	72
Port Hueneme, Ca., U.S.	E4	82
Port Huron, Mi., U.S.	F8	99
Portia, Ar., U.S.	A4	81
Portimão, Port.	D1	22
Portis, Ks., U.S.	C5	93
Port Isabel, Tx., U.S.	F4	120
Port Jefferson, N.Y., U.S.	n15	109
Port Jefferson, Oh., U.S.	B1	112
Port Jefferson Station, N.Y., U.S.	*n15	109
Port Jervis, N.Y., U.S.	D6	109
Port Keats, Austl.	B5	50
Port Kent, N.Y., U.S.	f11	109
Portland, Austl.	G7	50
Portland, Ont.	C8	73
Portland, Ar., U.S.	D4	81
Portland, Co., U.S.	C5	83
Portland, In., U.S.	D8	91
Portland, Me., U.S.	E2	96
Portland, Mi., U.S.	F6	99
Portland, N.D., U.S.	C8	111
Portland, Oh., U.S.	C4	112
Portland, Or., U.S.	B4	114
Portland, Pa., U.S.	E11	115
Portland, Tn., U.S.	A5	119
Portland, Tx., U.S.	F4	120
Portland, Bill of, c., Eng., U.K.	E5	10
Portland Bight, Jam.	E6	64
Portland Canal, b., N.A.	B2	69
Portland Creek Pond, l., Newf.	C3	72
Portland Inlet, b., B.C.	B2	69
Portland Mills, Pa., U.S.	D4	115
Portland Point, c., Jam.	F14	65
Portlandville, N.Y., U.S.	C6	109
Port Laoise, Ire.	D5	11
Port Lavaca, Tx., U.S.	E4	120
Portlaw, Ire.	E4	11
Port Leyden, N.Y., U.S.	B5	109
Port Lincoln, Austl.	F6	50
Port Lions, Ak., U.S.	D9	79
Port Loko, S.L.	E2	45
Port Loring, Ont.	B4	73
Port-Louis, Fr.	D2	16
Port-Louis, Guad.	Q8	65
Port Louis, Mrts.	H24	2
Port Ludlow, Wa., U.S.	B3	124
Port Macquarie, Austl.	F9	50
Port Madison Indian Reservation, Wa., U.S.	B3	124
Portmagee, Ire.	F1	11
Portmahomack, Scot., U.K.	C5	13
Port Maitland, N.S.	F3	71
Port Maitland (part of Dunnville), Ont.	E5	73
Port Maria, Jam.	E5	64
Port Matilda, Pa., U.S.	E5	115
Port Mayaca, Fl., U.S.	F6	86
Port McNeil, B.C.	D4	69
Port McNicoll, Ont.	C5	73
Port Medway, N.S.	E5	71
Port Mellon, B.C.	E6	69
Port-Menier, Que.	k8	72
Port Moller, Ak., U.S.	D7	79
Port Monmouth, N.J., U.S.	C4	107
Port Morant, Jam.	F16	65
Port Moresby, Pap. N. Gui.	k12	50a
Port Morien, N.S.	C10	71
Port Morris, N.J., U.S.	B3	107
Port Mouton, N.S.	F5	71
Port Mouton Island, i., N.S.	F5	71
Port Murray, N.J., U.S.	B3	107
Portnahaven, Scot., U.K.	E2	13
Port Neches, Tx., U.S.	E6	120
Portneuf, Que.	C6	74
Portneuf, co., Que.	C5	74
Portneuf-sur-Mer, Que.	A7	74
Port Nolloth, S. Afr.	C2	49
Port Norris, N.J., U.S.	E2	107
Porto (Oporto), Port.	B1	22
Porto Acre, Braz.	C4	58
Porto Alegre, Braz.	E2	56
Porto Alexandre see Tombua, Ang.	E1	48
Porto Amboim, Ang.	D2	48
Porto Belo, Braz.	D3	56
Portobelo, Pan.	F8	62
Porto Calvo, Braz.	C3	57
Port O'Connor, Tx., U.S.	E4	120
Porto de Mós, Port.	C1	22
Porto de Moz, Braz.	C4	59
Portoferraio, Italy	C2	23
Portofino, Italy	E3	20
Port of Ness, Scot., U.K.	B2	13
Port of Spain, Trin.	K14	64
Porto Garibaldi, Italy	E8	20
Porto Grande, Braz.	C4	59
Portogruaro, Italy	B4	23
Portola, Ca., U.S.	C3	82
Porto Lucena, Braz.	D1	56
Portomaggiore, Italy	D5	20
Porto Mendes, Braz.	C2	56
Porto Murtinho, Braz.	D4	55
Porto Nacional, Braz.	D1	57
Porto-Novo, Benin	E5	45
Porto Orange, Fl., U.S.	C6	86
Port Orchard, Wa., U.S.	B3	124
Port Orford, Or., U.S.	E2	114
Porto Santana, Braz.	C4	59
Porto Santo, i., Port.	g12	44
Portoscuso, Italy	E2	23
Porto Seguro, Braz.	E3	57
Porto Torres, Italy	D2	23
Porto-Vecchio, Fr.	D2	23
Porto Velho, Braz.	B5	56
Portoviejo, Ec.	B1	58
Portpatrick, Scot., U.K.	F4	13
Port Penn, De., U.S.	B3	85
Port Perry, Ont.	C6	73
Port Phillip Bay, b., Austl.	G7	50
Port Pirie, Austl.	F6	50
Port Radium, N.W. Ter.	C9	66
Port Reading, N.J., U.S.	k8	107
Port Renfrew, B.C.	E5	69
Port Republic, N.J., U.S.	D4	107
Port Republic, Va., U.S.	B4	123
Port Rexton, Newf.	D5	72
Port Richey, Fl., U.S.	D4	86
Port Rowan, Ont.	E4	73
Port Royal, Ky., U.S.	B4	94
Port Royal, Pa., U.S.	E7	115
Port Royal, S.C., U.S.	G6	117
Port Royal, Tn., U.S.	A4	119
Port Royal, Va., U.S.	B5	123
Port Royal Island, i., S.C., U.S.	G6	117
Port Royal Sound, strt., S.C., U.S.	G6	117
Port Said (Būr Sa'īd), Eg.	B3	38
Port Saint Joe, Fl., U.S.	C1	86
Port Saint Johns, Transkei	D4	49
Port-Saint-Louis [-du-Rhône], Fr.	F6	16
Port Saint Lucie, Fl., U.S.	E6	86
Port Salerno, Fl., U.S.	E6	86
Port Sewall, Fl., U.S.	E6	86
Port Shepstone, S. Afr.	D5	49
Portsmouth, Dom.	I14	64
Portsmouth, Eng., U.K.	E6	10
Portsmouth, N.H., U.S.	D5	106
Portsmouth, Oh., U.S.	D3	112
Portsmouth, R.I., U.S.	E6	116
Portsmouth, Va., U.S.	D6	123
Portsmouth Naval Shipyard, mil., Me., U.S.	D5	106
Portsoy, Scot., U.K.	C6	13
Port Stanley, Ont.	E3	73
Port Sudan (Būr Sūdān), Sud.	M16	45
Port Sulphur, La., U.S.	E6	95
Port Talbot (Afan), Wales, U.K.	C4	12
Port Tobacco Village, Md., U.S.	C3	97
Port Townsend, Wa., U.S.	A3	124
Portugal, ctry., Eur.	C2	22
Portugalete, Spain	A4	22
Portuguesa, state, Ven.	B4	60
Portuguesa, stm., Ven.	B4	60
Portumna, Ire.	D3	11
Port Union, Newf.	D5	72
Port Union, Oh., U.S.	C1	112
Port-Vendres, Fr.	F5	16
Port-Vila, Vanuatu	H10	6
Portville, N.Y., U.S.	C2	109
Port Vincent, La., U.S.	D5	95
Port Vue, Pa., U.S.	*k14	115
Port Wakefield, Austl.	G2	51
Port Washington, N.Y., U.S.	h13	109
Port Washington, Oh., U.S.	B4	112
Port Washington, Wi., U.S.	E6	126
Port Wentworth, Ga., U.S.	D5	87
Port William, Scot., U.K.	F4	13
Port William, Oh., U.S.	C2	112
Port Wing, Wi., U.S.	B2	126
Porum, Ok., U.S.	B6	113
Porvenir, Chile	h11	54
Porz, Ger.	C2	19
Posadas, Arg.	E4	55
Posadas, Spain	D3	22
Poschiavo, Switz.	D9	21
Posen, Il., U.S.	k9	90
Posen, Mi., U.S.	C7	99
Posey, co., In., U.S.	H2	91
Poseyville, In., U.S.	H2	91
Poshekhonye-Volodarsk, Sov. Un.	B12	27
Poso, Indon.	F6	34
Poso, Lake, l., Indon.	F6	34
Posŏng, S. Kor.	I3	33
Possa, Braz.	A3	56
Pössneck, Ger.	C6	19
Post, Or., U.S.	C6	114
Post, Tx., U.S.	C2	120
Poste-de-la-Baleine, Que.	g11	74
Po.st Falls, Id., U.S.	B2	89
Postmasburg, S. Afr.	C3	49
Post Mills, Vt., U.S.	D4	122
Postojna, Yugo.	C2	24
Poston, S.C., U.S.	D9	117
Postville, Newf.	g10	72
Postville, Ia., U.S.	A6	92
Potaro Landing, Guy.	A3	59
Potato Creek, S.D., U.S.	D4	118
Potawatomi Indian Reservation, Ks., U.S.	C8	93
Potchefstroom, S. Afr.	C4	49
Poteau, Ok., U.S.	B7	113
Poteau, stm., U.S.	C1	81
Poteet, Tx., U.S.	E3	120
Potenza, Italy	D5	23
Poteriteri, Lake, l., N.Z.	Q15	51
Potgietersrus, S. Afr.	B4	49
Potholes Reservoir, res., Wa., U.S.	B6	124
Poti, Sov. Un.	G17	8
Poti, stm., Braz.	C2	57
Potiskum, Nig.	D7	45
Potlatch, Id., U.S.	C2	89
Potlatch, stm., Id., U.S.	C6	90
Potomac, Il., U.S.	C6	90
Potomac, Mt., U.S.	D3	103
Potomac, North Branch, stm., U.S.	m12	97
Potomac, South Branch, stm., U.S.	B6	125
Potomac, South Branch, North Fork, stm., W.V., U.S.	C5	125
Potomac, South Branch, South Fork, stm., U.S.	B6	125
Potomac Heights, Md., U.S.	C3	97
Potosí, Bol.	C2	55
Potosi, Mo., U.S.	D7	102
Potosi, Wi., U.S.	F3	126
Potosí, dept., Bol.	D2	55
Potrerillos, Chile	E2	54
Potrerillos, Hond.	C4	62
Potro, Cerro del, mtn., S.A.	B2	54
Potsdam, Ger.	B6	19
Potsdam, N.Y., U.S.	f10	109
Pottawatomie, co., Ks., U.S.	C7	93
Pottawatomie, co., Ok., U.S.	B4	113
Pottawatomie Creek, stm., U.S.	D8	93
Pottawattamie, co., Ia., U.S.	C2	92
Potter, Ne., U.S.	C1	104
Potter, co., Pa., U.S.	C6	115
Potter, co., S.D., U.S.	B6	118
Potter, co., Tx., U.S.	B2	120
Potter Hill, R.I., U.S.	F1	116
Potter Place, N.H., U.S.	D3	106
Potters Mills, Pa., U.S.	E6	115
Pottersville, Mo., U.S.	E5	102
Pottersville, N.J., U.S.	B3	107
Pottersville, N.Y., U.S.	B7	109
Potter Valley, Ca., U.S.	C2	82
Potts Camp, Ms., U.S.	A4	101
Potts Creek, stm., U.S.	C2	123
Pottstown, Pa., U.S.	F10	115
Pottsville, Ar., U.S.	B2	81
Pottsville, Pa., U.S.	E9	115
Pottsville, Tx., U.S.	D3	120
Potwin, Ks., U.S.	E6	93
Pouce Coupe, B.C.	B7	69
Pouch Cove, Newf.	E5	72
Poughkeepsie, Ar., U.S.	A4	81
Poughkeepsie, N.Y., U.S.	D7	109
Poulan, Ga., U.S.	E3	87
Poulsbo, Wa., U.S.	B3	124
Poultney, Vt., U.S.	D2	122
Poultney, stm., Vt., U.S.	e9	123
Pound, Va., U.S.	e9	123
Pound Gap, U.S.	C7	94
Pouso Alegre, Braz.	D2	56
Poutasi, W. Sam.	G12	52
Pouthisat, Camb.	C3	34
Pouxeux, Fr.	A2	20
Považská Bystrica, Czech.	*C16	8
Povenets, Sov. Un.	E16	14
Poverty Bay, b., N.Z.	C6	127
Póvoa de Varzim, Port.	B1	22
Povorotnyy, Cape, c., Sov. Un.	E6	33
Povungnituk, Que.	f11	74
Powassan, Ont.	A5	73
Powder, stm., Or., U.S.	*C9	114
Powder, Middle Fork, stm., Wy., U.S.	C6	127

Name	Map Ref.	Page

Name	Map Ref.	Page
Powder, North Fork, stm., Wy., U.S.	C6	127
Powder, South Fork, stm., Wy., U.S.	C6	127
Powderhorn, Co., U.S.	C3	83
Powder River, Wy., U.S.	C6	127
Powder River, co., Mt., U.S.	E11	103
Powder River Pass, Wy., U.S.	B5	127
Powder Springs, Ga., U.S.	h8	87
Powderville, Mt., U.S.	E11	103
Powder Wash, Co., U.S.	A2	83
Powe, Mo., U.S.	E7	102
Powell, Mo., U.S.	E3	102
Powell, Oh., U.S.	B2	112
Powell, Pa., U.S.	C9	115
Powell, Tn., U.S.	m13	119
Powell, Tx., U.S.	C4	120
Powell, Wy., U.S.	B4	127
Powell, co., Ky., U.S.	C6	94
Powell, co., Mt., U.S.	D4	103
Powell, stm., U.S.	C10	119
Powell, Lake, res., U.S.	F5	121
Powell, Mount, mtn., Co., U.S.	B4	83
Powell Butte, Or., U.S.	C5	114
Powellhurst, Or., U.S.	*B4	114
Powell Mountain, mtn., U.S.	C10	119
Powell Mountain, mtn., N.M., U.S.	B1	108
Powell Park, reg., Co., U.S.	A2	83
Powell River, B.C.	E5	69
Powellsville, N.C., U.S.	A6	110
Powellville, W.V., U.S.	C3	125
Powellville, Md., U.S.	D7	97
Powelton, Ga., U.S.	C4	87
Power, Mt., U.S.	C5	103
Power, co., Id., U.S.	G5	89
Power Head, c., Ire.	F3	11
Powers, Mi., U.S.	C3	99
Powers, Or., U.S.	E2	114
Powers Lake, N.D., U.S.	A3	111
Powersville, Mo., U.S.	A4	102
Powerview, Man.	D3	70
Poweshiek, co., Ia., U.S.	C5	92
Powhatan, Al., U.S.	B2	78
Powhatan, Ar., U.S.	A4	81
Powhatan, La., U.S.	C2	95
Powhatan, Va., U.S.	C5	123
Powhatan, co., Va., U.S.	C5	123
Powhatan Point, Oh., U.S.	C5	112
Powhattan, Ks., U.S.	C8	93
Pownal, Me., U.S.	g7	96
Pownal, Vt., U.S.	F2	122
Pownal Center, Me., U.S.	g7	96
Pownal Center, Vt., U.S.	F2	122
Powys, co., Wales, U.K.	A4	12
Poxoréo, Braz.	B2	56
Poyang Hu, l., China	F8	31
Poyarkovo, Sov. Un.	B4	33
Poydras, La., U.S.	*E6	95
Poyen, Ar., U.S.	C3	81
Poygan, Lake, l., Wi., U.S.	D5	126
Poynette, Wi., U.S.	E4	126
Poynor, Mo., U.S.	E7	102
Poyntzpass, N. Ire., U.K.	C5	11
Poy Sippi, Wi., U.S.	D4	126
Požarevac, Yugo.	C5	24
Poza Rica de Hidalgo, Mex.	m15	63
Poznań, Pol.	B4	26
Pozo Almonte, Chile	D2	55
Pozoblanco, Spain	C3	22
Pozo Colorado, Para.	D4	55
Pozo Redondo Mountains, mts., Az., U.S.	E3	80
Pozos, Mex.	m13	63
Pozuelo de Alarcón, Spain	p17	22
Pozuelos, Ven.	A5	60
Pozuzo, Peru	D2	58
Pozzallo, Italy	F5	23
Pozzuoli, Italy	D5	23
Prachatice, Czech.	E9	19
Prachin Buri, Thai.	C2	34
Prachuap Khiri Khan, Thai.	C1	34
Praco, Al., U.S.	f6	78
Prácticos, Punta de, c., Cuba	D5	64
Prades, Fr.	F5	16
Prado Flood Control Basin, Ca., U.S.	n13	82
Præstø, Den.	C6	15
Praga (part of Warsaw), Pol.	k14	26
Prague (Praha), Czech.	C3	26
Prague, Ne., U.S.	C9	104
Prague, Ok., U.S.	B5	113
Prainha, Braz.	C4	59
Prairie, Ms., U.S.	B5	101
Prairie, co., Ar., U.S.	C4	81
Prairie, co., Mt., U.S.	D11	103
Prairie, co., Mn., U.S.	C5	100
Prairie, co., Wi., U.S.	C4	126
Prairie Bayou, stm., Ar., U.S.	g7	81
Prairie City, Il., U.S.	C3	90
Prairie City, Ia., U.S.	C4	92
Prairie City, Or., U.S.	C8	114
Prairie City, S.D., U.S.	B3	118
Prairie Creek, In., U.S.	F3	91
Prairie Creek Reservoir, res., In., U.S.	D7	91
Prairie Dog Creek, stm., U.S.	C3	93
Prairie Du Chien, Wi., U.S.	E2	126
Prairie Du Rocher, Il., U.S.	E4	90
Prairie du Sac, Wi., U.S.	E4	126
Prairie Farm, Wi., U.S.	C2	126
Prairie Grove, Ar., U.S.	B1	81
Prairie Hill, Mo., U.S.	B5	102
Prairie Home, Mo., U.S.	C5	102
Prairie Home, Ne., U.S.	h11	104
Prairie Point, Ms., U.S.	B5	101
Prairie River, Sask.	E4	75
Prairies, Lake of the, res., Can.	F5	75
Prairies, Rivière des, stm., Que.	p19	74
Prairieton, In., U.S.	F3	91
Prairie View, Ar., U.S.	B2	81
Prairie View, Ks., U.S.	C4	93
Prairie View, Tx., U.S.	D5	120
Prairie Village, Ks., U.S.	m16	93
Prairieville, La., U.S.	h10	95
Pralognan-la-Vanoise, Fr.	C2	20
Pran Buri, Thai.	C2	34
Praszka, Pol.	C5	26
Prata, Braz.	B3	56
Pratāpgarh, India	E5	37
Prater Mountain, mtn., Wy., U.S.	C2	127
Prato, Italy	C3	23
Prats-de-Mollo, Fr.	F5	16
Pratt, Ks., U.S.	E5	93
Pratt, W.V., U.S.	*C3	125
Pratt, co., Ks., U.S.	E5	93
Pratteln, Switz.	A4	21
Prattsburg, N.Y., U.S.	C3	109
Prattsville, Ar., U.S.	C3	81
Prattsville, N.Y., U.S.	C6	109
Prattville, Al., U.S.	C3	78

Name	Map Ref.	Page
Prattville, Mi., U.S.	G6	99
Pravdinsk, Sov. Un.	A6	26
Pravia, Spain	A2	22
Pray, Mt., U.S.	E6	103
Preble, In., U.S.	C7	91
Preble, co., Oh., U.S.	C1	112
Predazzo, Italy	C7	20
Preeceville, Sask.	F4	75
Pregel, stm., Sov. Un.	D3	27
Pregolya, stm., Sov. Un.	A6	26
Pregnall, S.C., U.S.	E7	117
Prelate, Sask.	G1	75
Premana, Italy	D7	21
Premont, Tx., U.S.	F3	120
Prémontré, Fr.	E3	17
Premosello, Italy	D5	21
Prenjasi, Alb.	B3	25
Prenter, W.V., U.S.	C3	125
Prentice, Wi., U.S.	C3	126
Prentiss, Me., U.S.	C4	96
Prentiss, Ms., U.S.	D4	101
Prentiss, co., Ms., U.S.	A5	101
Prenzlau, Ger.	B6	18
Přerov, Czech.	D4	26
Prescott, Ont.	C9	73
Prescott, Az., U.S.	C3	80
Prescott, Ia., U.S.	D2	81
Prescott, Ia., U.S.	C3	92
Prescott, Ks., U.S.	D9	93
Prescott, Mi., U.S.	D7	99
Prescott, Or., U.S.	A4	114
Prescott, Wi., U.S.	D1	126
Prescott, co., Ont.	B10	73
Presho, S.D., U.S.	D5	118
Presidencia Roque Sáenz Peña, Arg.	E3	55
Presidente Epitácio, Braz.	C2	56
Presidente Hayes, dept., Para.	D4	55
Presidente Olegário, Braz.	B3	56
Presidente Prudente, Braz.	C2	56
Presidential Range, mts., N.H., U.S.	B4	106
Presidents Island, i., Tn., U.S.	e8	119
Presidio, Tx., U.S.	p12	120
Presidio, co., Tx., U.S.	o12	120
Presidio of San Francisco, mil., Ca., U.S.	h8	82
Preslav, Bul.	D8	24
Prespa, Lake, l., Eur.	E5	24
Presque Isle, Me., U.S.	B5	96
Presque Isle, Mi., U.S.	C7	99
Presque Isle, Wi., U.S.	B4	126
Presque Isle, co., Mi., U.S.	C6	99
Pressath, Ger.	D6	19
Prestatyn, Wales, U.K.	A4	12
Presteigne, Wales, U.K.	B4	12
Přeštice, Czech.	D8	19
Preston, Austl.	*G8	50
Preston, Eng., U.K.	D5	10
Preston, Ct., U.S.	C8	84
Preston, Ga., U.S.	D2	87
Preston, Id., U.S.	G7	89
Preston, Ia., U.S.	B7	92
Preston, Ks., U.S.	E5	93
Preston, Ky., U.S.	B6	94
Preston, Md., U.S.	C6	97
Preston, Mn., U.S.	G6	100
Preston, Ms., U.S.	C5	101
Preston, Mo., U.S.	D4	102
Preston, Ok., U.S.	B6	113
Preston, Wa., U.S.	e12	124
Preston, co., W.V., U.S.	B5	125
Preston Peak, mtn., Ca., U.S.	B2	82
Prestonsburg, Ky., U.S.	C7	94
Prestrud Inlet, b., Ant.	B33	7
Prestwick, Scot., U.K.	C4	10
Prestwick, Al., U.S.	D2	78
Presumpscot, stm., Me., U.S.	g7	96
Preti, mtn., Italy	C8	20
Pretoria, S. Afr.	C4	49
Pretty Prairie, Ks., U.S.	E5	93
Préveza, Grc.	E5	24
Prewitt, N.M., U.S.	B1	108
Prewitt Reservoir, res., Co., U.S.	A7	83
Prey Veng, Camb.	G6	35
Pribilof Islands, is., Ak., U.S.	D4	24
Priboj, Yugo.	D3	26
Přibram, Czech.	B6	97
Price, Md., U.S.	C5	120
Price, Tx., U.S.	D5	121
Price, Ut., U.S.	C3	126
Price, co., Wi., U.S.	D5	101
Price, stm., Ut., U.S.	k12	117
Price Inlet, b., S.C., U.S.	C3	69
Price Island, i., B.C.	C4	73
Priceville, Ont.	E1	78
Prichard, Al., U.S.	C2	125
Prichard, W.V., U.S.	D3	120
Priddy, Tx., U.S.	D3	22
Priego [de Córdoba], Spain	*D2	89
Priest Lake, l., Id., U.S.	A7	26
Priestley, Mount, mtn., B.C.	B3	69
Priest Rapids Dam, Wa., U.S.	C6	124
Priest Rapids Lake, res., Wa., U.S.	C6	124
Priest River, Id., U.S.	A2	89
Prievidza, Czech.	*D5	26
Prijedor, Yugo.	C3	24
Prijepolje, Yugo.	D4	24
Prikumsk, Sov. Un.	E2	28
Prilep, Yugo.	E5	24
Priluki, Sov. Un.	F9	27
Prim, Point, c., P.E.I.	C6	71
Primate, Sask.	E1	75
Primghar, Ia., U.S.	A2	92
Primolano, Italy	D7	20
Primorsk, Sov. Un.	A6	26
Primorsko-Akhtarsk, Sov. Un.	H12	27
Primrose, Ne., U.S.	C7	104
Primrose, R.I., U.S.	B3	116
Primrose Lake, l., Can.	B6	68
Prince, Sask.	E1	75
Prince, co., P.E.I.	C5	71
Prince, Lake, res., Va., U.S.	k14	123
Prince Albert, Sask.	D3	75
Prince Albert Mountains, mts., Ant.	B29	7

Name	Map Ref.	Page
Prince Albert National Park, Sask.	C2	75
Prince Albert Sound, strt., N.W. Ter.	B9	66
Prince Alfred, Cape, c., N.W. Ter.	B8	66
Prince Charles Foreland, i., Nor.	B14	128
Prince Charles Island, i., N.W. Ter.	C17	66
Prince Charles Mountains, mts., Ant.	B19	7
Prince Edward, co., Ont.	C7	73
Prince Edward, co., Va., U.S.	C4	123
Prince Edward Island, prov., Can.	C6	71
Prince Edward Island National Park, P.E.I.	C6	71
Prince Edward Islands, is., S. Afr.	J23	2
Prince Frederick, Md., U.S.	C4	97
Prince George, B.C.	C6	69
Prince George, Va., U.S.	C5	123
Prince George, co., Va., U.S.	C5	123
Prince Georges, co., Md., U.S.	C4	97
Prince of Wales, i., Austl.	B7	50
Prince of Wales, Cape, c., Ak., U.S.	B6	79
Prince of Wales Island, i., N.W. Ter.	B13	66
Prince of Wales Island, i., Ak., U.S.	n23	79
Prince of Wales Strait, strt., N.W. Ter.	B9	66
Prince Olav Coast, Ant.	C17	7
Prince Patrick Island, i., N.W. Ter.	m27	66
Prince Regent Inlet, b., N.W. Ter.	B14	66
Prince Rupert, B.C.	B2	69
Princes Lakes, In., U.S.	F5	91
Princes Risborough, Eng., U.K.	C7	12
Princess Anne, Md., U.S.	D6	97
Princess Astrid Coast, Ant.	B14	7
Princess Charlotte Bay, b., Austl.	B7	50
Princess Martha Coast, Ant.	B11	7
Princess Ragnhild Coast, Ant.	B15	7
Princess Royal Channel, strt., B.C.	C3	69
Princess Royal Island, i., B.C.	C3	69
Princes Town, Trin.	O23	65
Princeton, Newf.	D5	72
Princeton, Ont.	D4	73
Princeton, Al., U.S.	A3	78
Princeton, Ca., U.S.	C2	82
Princeton, Fl., U.S.	G6	86
Princeton, Id., U.S.	C2	89
Princeton, Il., U.S.	B4	90
Princeton, In., U.S.	H2	91
Princeton, Ia., U.S.	C7	92
Princeton, Ks., U.S.	D8	93
Princeton, Ky., U.S.	C2	94
Princeton, La., U.S.	B2	95
Princeton, Me., U.S.	C5	96
Princeton, Ma., U.S.	B4	98
Princeton, Mn., U.S.	E5	100
Princeton, Mo., U.S.	A4	102
Princeton, N.J., U.S.	C3	107
Princeton, N.C., U.S.	B4	110
Princeton, Or., U.S.	D8	114
Princeton, S.C., U.S.	C3	117
Princeton, W.V., U.S.	D3	125
Princeton, Wi., U.S.	E4	126
Princeton, Mount, mtn., Co., U.S.	C4	83
Princeton Junction, N.J., U.S.	C3	107
Princeville, Que.	C6	74
Princeville, Il., U.S.	C4	90
Princeville, N.C., U.S.	B5	110
Prince William, N.B.	D2	71
Prince William, co., Va., U.S.	B5	123
Prince William Sound, strt., Ak., U.S.	g18	79
Príncipe, i., S. Tom./Pr.	E1	46
Principe Channel, strt., B.C.	C3	69
Prinzapolka, stm., Nic.	C6	114
Prineville, Or., U.S.	C6	114
Prineville Reservoir, res., Or., U.S.	D6	114
Pringle, S.D., U.S.	D2	118
Prinsburg, Mn., U.S.	F3	100
Prinzapolka, Nic.	E8	63
Prinzapolka, stm., Nic.	D6	62
Prior Lake, Mn., U.S.	F5	100
Priozersk, Sov. Un.	A8	27
Pripyat (Pripet), stm., Sov. Un.	E7	27
Prishib, Sov. Un.	B4	39
Priština, Yugo.	D5	24
Pritchett, Co., U.S.	D8	83
Pritchett, Tx., U.S.	C5	120
Pritzerbe, Ger.	F6	15
Pritzwalk, Ger.	B6	18
Privas, Fr.	E6	16
Privert, Lac, l., Que.	g8	72
Privolnoye, Sov. Un.	H9	27
Prizren, Yugo.	D5	24
Prizzi, Italy	F4	23
Probolinggo, Indon.	m13	125
Procious, W.V., U.S.	m13	125
Procter, B.C.	E9	69
Procter, Mn., U.S.	D6	100
Procter, Mt., U.S.	C2	103
Procter, Ok., U.S.	B7	113
Procter, Tx., U.S.	D3	120
Procter, Vt., U.S.	D2	122
Procter, W.V., U.S.	g8	125
Proctor Lake, res., Tx., U.S.	C3	120
Proctorville, Vt., U.S.	E3	122
Proctorville, N.C., U.S.	C3	110
Proctorville, Oh., U.S.	D3	112
Proença-a-Nova, Port.	C2	22
Progreso, Mex.	C7	63
Progreso, Mex.	E2	63
Prokhladnyy, Sov. Un.	D11	29
Prokopyevsk, Sov. Un.	D5	24
Prokuplje, Yugo.	D5	24
Proletars'k, Sov. Un.	H13	27
Proletarsk, Sov. Un.	q21	27
Prome (Pye), Burma	E10	36
Promise City, Ia., U.S.	D5	92
Promissão, Braz.	C3	56
Promontory Mountains, mts., Ut., U.S.	B3	121
Pronsfeld, Ger.	D6	17
Propriá, Braz.	D3	57
Prophetstown, Il., U.S.	B4	90
Proriv, stm., Braz.	D3	57
Prorer Wiek, b., Ger.	D7	15
Prorva, Sov. Un.	D4	28

Name	Map Ref.	Page
Proserpine, Austl.	D8	50
Prosna, stm., Pol.	C5	26
Prosotsáni, Grc.	B4	25
Prospect, N.S.	E6	71
Prospect, Ct., U.S.	C4	84
Prospect, In., U.S.	g11	94
Prospect, Ky., U.S.	g11	94
Prospect, Oh., U.S.	B2	112
Prospect, Or., U.S.	E4	114
Prospect, Pa., U.S.	E1	115
Prospect, Tn., U.S.	B4	119
Prospect, Va., U.S.	C4	123
Prospect Harbor, Me., U.S.	D4	96
Prospect Heights, Co., U.S.	*C5	83
Prospect Heights, Il., U.S.	*h9	90
Prospect Hill, N.C., U.S.	A3	110
Prospect Hill, hill, Ma., U.S.	k11	114
Prospect Hill, hill, Ma., U.S.	D6	98
Prospect Hill, hill, Ma., U.S.	g10	98
Prospect Park, N.J., U.S.	B4	107
Prospect Park, Pa., U.S.	p20	115
Prospect Plains, N.J., U.S.	C4	107
Prosperity, S.C., U.S.	C4	117
Prosperity, W.V., U.S.	n13	125
Prosser, Ne., U.S.	D7	104
Prosser, Wa., U.S.	C6	124
Prostějov, Czech.	D4	26
Prostki, Pol.	B7	26
Protection, Ks., U.S.	E4	93
Protem, Mo., U.S.	E5	102
Protivin, Ia., U.S.	A5	92
Proton Station, Ont.	C4	73
Prouts Neck, Me., U.S.	g7	96
Provadiya, Bul.	D8	24
Provadiyska, stm., Bul.	D8	24
Provencal, La., U.S.	C2	95
Provence, hist. reg., Fr.	F7	16
Providence, Fl., U.S.	G4	86
Providence, Ky., U.S.	C2	94
Providence, R.I., U.S.	C4	116
Providence, Ut., U.S.	B4	121
Providence, co., R.I., U.S.	C2	116
Providence, stm., R.I., U.S.	C5	116
Providence Bay, Ont.	B2	73
Providence Forge, Va., U.S.	C5	123
Providence Point, c., R.I., U.S.	D5	116
Providencia, Isla de, i., Col.	D7	62
Province Lake, l., N.H., U.S.	C5	106
Provincetown, Ma., U.S.	B7	98
Provins, Fr.	C5	16
Provo, Ar., U.S.	C1	81
Provo, S.D., U.S.	D2	118
Provo, Ut., U.S.	C4	121
Provo, stm., Ut., U.S.	C4	121
Provost, Alta.	C5	68
Prozor, Yugo.	D3	24
Pruden, Tn., U.S.	C10	119
Prudence Island, i., R.I., U.S.	E5	116
Prudence Island, i., R.I., U.S.	E5	116
Prudentópolis, Braz.	D2	56
Prudenville, Mi., U.S.	D6	99
Prudhoe Bay, Ak., U.S.	A10	79
Prudhoe Bay, b., Ak., U.S.	A10	79
Prud'homme, Sask.	E3	75
Prudnik, Braz.	C4	26
Prue, Ok., U.S.	A5	113
Prüm, Ger.	C3	18
Pruszków, Pol.	B6	26
Prut, stm., Eur.	B9	24
Pruzhany, Sov. Un.	E5	27
Prydz Bay, b., Ant.	C20	7
Pryor, Mt., U.S.	D6	83
Pryor, Mt., U.S.	E8	103
Pryor, Ok., U.S.	A6	113
Pryor Mountains, mts., Mt., U.S.	E8	103
Przasnysz, Pol.	B6	26
Przedbórz, Pol.	C5	26
Przeworsk, Pol.	C7	26
Przewóz, Pol.	B9	19
Przhevalsk, Sov. Un.	E9	28
Psakhná, Grc.	C4	25
Psará, i., Grc.	C5	40
Psary, Pol.	g10	25
Psel, stm., Sov. Un.	G9	27
Pskov, Sov. Un.	D5	29
Pskov, Lake, l., Sov. Un.	B7	27
Pszczyna, Pol.	D5	26
Pszczynka, stm., Pol.	h10	26
Ptich, stm., Sov. Un.	E7	27
Ptolemaís, Grc.	B3	25
Ptuj, Yugo.	D2	55
Puako, Hi., U.S.	D6	88
Puán, Arg.	B4	54
Pu'apu'a, W. Sam.	F11	52
Pucallpa, Peru	C3	58
Pucheng, China	K8	32
Pucheng, China	G6	32
Puchŏn, S. Kor.	*H3	33
Puck, Pol.	A5	26
Puckaway Lake, l., Wi., U.S.	E4	126
Puckett, Ms., U.S.	C4	101
Pudasjärvi, Fin.	E12	14
Pudozh, Sov. Un.	A11	27
Puebla, state, Mex.	D5	63
Puebla de Don Fadrique, Spain	D4	22
Puebla de Zaragoza, Mex.	A1	22
Pueblo, Co., U.S.	D5	63
Pueblo, co., Co., U.S.	C6	83
Pueblo Colorado Wash, val., Az., U.S.	B6	80
Pueblo Hundido, Chile	C15	14
Pueblo Libre, Peru	*D2	58
Pueblo Mountain, mtn., Or., U.S.	E8	114
Pueblo Mountains, mts., Or., U.S.	E8	114
Pueblo Nuevo (part of Panamá), Pan.	k11	62
Pueblo Nuevo, Ven.	A4	60
Pueblo Reservoir, res., Co., U.S.	C6	83
Puebloviejo, Ec.	B2	58
Puenteareas, Spain	A1	22
Puente-Ceso, Spain	A1	22
Puente-Genil, Spain	D3	22
Puerto, La., U.S.	F8	92
Pu'er, China	G5	31
Puerco, Punta, c., P.R.	B4	60
Puerco, stm., U.S.	B5	80
Puerco, Rio, stm., N.M., U.S.	B2	108
Puerto Acosta, Bol.	D2	54
Puerto Aisén, Chile	D2	54
Puerto Alegre, Bol.	E6	54
Puerto Armuelles, Pan.	F6	62
Puerto Asís, Col.	B3	58
Puerto Ayacucho, Ven.	B4	60
Puerto Baquerizo Moreno, Ec.	g6	58
Puerto Barrios, Guat.	D7	63
Punta de Díaz, Chile	E1	55

Name	Map Ref.	Page
Puerto Belgrano, Arg.	B4	54
Puerto Bermúdez, Peru	D3	58
Puerto Berrío, Col.	B3	60
Puerto Bolívar, Ec.	B1	58
Puerto Cabello, Ven.	A4	60
Puerto Cabezas, Nic.	E8	63
Puerto Carreño, Col.	B4	60
Puerto Casado, Para.	D4	55
Puerto Chicama, Peru	C2	58
Puerto Colombia, Col.	A3	60
Puerto Constanza, Arg.	f7	54
Puerto Cortés, Hond.	D7	63
Puerto Cumarebo, Ven.	A4	60
Puerto de la Cruz, Spain	m13	22
Puerto del Rosario, Spain	m15	22
Puerto del Son, Spain	A1	22
Puerto de Luna, N.M., U.S.	C5	108
Puerto Deseado, Arg.	D3	54
Puerto Eten, Peru	C2	58
Puerto Francisco de Orellana, Ec.	B2	58
Puerto Guaraní, Para.	B2	55
Puerto Heath, Bol.	B2	55
Puerto Inírida, Col.	C4	60
Puerto Jiménez, C.R.	F6	62
Puerto la Cruz, Ven.	A5	60
Puerto Leguízamo, Col.	D3	60
Puerto Limón, Col.	C3	60
Puertollano, Spain	C3	22
Puerto Lobos, Arg.	C3	54
Puerto López, Col.	C3	60
Puerto Madryn, Arg.	C3	54
Puerto Maldonado, Peru	D4	58
Puerto México see Coatzacoalcos, Mex.	D6	63
Puerto Mineral, Arg.	E4	55
Puerto Montt, Chile	D2	54
Puerto Morazán, Nic.	D4	62
Puerto Nariño, Col.	C4	60
Puerto Natales, Chile	E2	54
Puerto Padre, Cuba	D5	64
Puerto Páez, Ven.	B4	60
Puerto Peñasco, Pan.	A2	63
Puerto Pilón, Pan.	k11	62
Puerto Pinasco, Para.	C4	55
Puerto Pirámides, Arg.	C4	54
Puerto Plata, Dom. Rep.	E8	64
Puerto Portillo, Peru	C3	58
Puerto Presidente Stroessner, Para.	E5	55
Puerto Princesa, Phil.	D5	34
Puerto Real, Spain	D2	22
Puerto Rico, ctry., N.A.	G11	64
Puerto Saavedra, Chile	B2	55
Puerto Sastre, Para.	B2	55
Puerto Siles, Bol.	B2	55
Puerto Suárez, Bol.	C2	55
Puerto Supe, Peru	D2	58
Puerto Tejada, Col.	C2	60
Puerto Toledo, Col.	D3	60
Puerto Vallarta, Mex.	C3	63
Puerto Varas, Chile	C2	54
Puerto Victoria, Peru	C3	58
Puerto Viejo, C.R.	F6	62
Puerto Villamizar, Col.	B3	60
Puerto Visser, Arg.	D3	54
Puerto Wiches, Col.	B3	60
Pugachev, Sov. Un.	C8	28
Puget Sound, strt., Wa., U.S.	B3	124
Puget Sound Naval Shipyard, mil., Wa., U.S.	e10	124
Puget-Théniers, Fr.	D7	71
Pugwash, N.S.	D7	71
Puhi, Hi., U.S.	B2	88
Puhsi, China	B2	33
Puigcerdá, Spain	A6	22
Pujehun, S.L.	E2	45
Pujili, Ec.	B2	58
Pukalani, Hi., U.S.	C5	88
Pukaskwa National Park, Ont.	o18	73
Pukch'ŏng, N. Kor.	F4	33
Pukeashun Mountain, mtn., B.C.	D8	69
Pukekohe, N.Z.	L15	51
Pukou, China	H8	32
Puksoozero, Sov. Un.	*C3	19
Puk'u, Hi., U.S.	F4	99
Pula, Italy	E2	23
Pula, Yugo.	C1	24
Pulacayo, Bol.	D2	55
Pulaski, Ga., U.S.	D5	87
Pulaski, Il., U.S.	F4	90
Pulaski, In., U.S.	C4	91
Pulaski, Ms., U.S.	C4	101
Pulaski, N.Y., U.S.	B4	109
Pulaski, Tn., U.S.	B4	119
Pulaski, Va., U.S.	C2	123
Pulaski, Wi., U.S.	D5	126
Pulaski, co., Ar., U.S.	C3	81
Pulaski, co., Ga., U.S.	D3	87
Pulaski, co., Il., U.S.	F4	90
Pulaski, co., In., U.S.	B4	91
Pulaski, co., Ky., U.S.	C5	94
Pulaski, co., Mo., U.S.	D5	102
Pulaski, co., Va., U.S.	C2	123
Puławy, Pol.	C6	26
Pulheim, Ger.	*C3	18
Pullman, Mi., U.S.	F4	99
Pullman, Wa., U.S.	C8	124
Pullman, W.V., U.S.	B4	125
Puloig, Mount, mtn., Phil.	C15	14
Pulozero, Sov. Un.	C15	14
Puttusk, Pol.	B6	26
Puma Lake, l., China	C13	37
Pumphrey, Md., U.S.	h11	97
Pumpkin Buttes, mtn., Wy., U.S.	C7	127
Pumpkin Creek, stm., Mt., U.S.	E11	103
Pumpkin Creek, stm., Ne., U.S.	C2	104
Pumpville, Tx., U.S.	E2	120
Puná, Isla, i., Ec.	B1	58
Punakha, Bhu.	C2	36
Punat, Yugo.	C1	24
Punata, Bol.	C2	55
Punchaw, B.C.	C6	69
Pune, India	C1	36
Pungo Lake, l., N.C., U.S.	B6	110
Pungsan, N. Kor.	F4	33
Punia, Zaire	A5	48
Punjab, state, India	B5	36
Punjab, prov., Pak.	C5	36
Punnichy, Sask.	F3	75
Puno, Peru	D3	58
Puno, dept., Peru	E3	58
Punta Alta, Arg.	B4	54
Punta Arenas, Chile	h11	54

Name	Map Ref.	Page
Punta del Este, Ur.	E2	56
Punta de Piedras, Ven.	A5	60
Punta de Vacas, Arg.	A3	54
Punta Gorda, Belize	D7	63
Punta Gorda, Fl., U.S.	F4	86
Punta Gorda, Bahía de b., Nic.	E8	63
Punta Moreno, Peru	C2	58
Puntarenas, C.R.	E5	62
Punto Fijo, Ven.	A3	60
Puntzi Lake, l., B.C.	C5	69
Punxsutawney, Pa., U.S.	E4	115
Puposky, Mn., U.S.	C4	100
Puquio, Peru	D3	58
Pur, stm., Sov. Un.	C10	29
Pūranpur, India	C8	37
Purcell, Mo., U.S.	D3	102
Purcell, Ok., U.S.	B4	113
Purcell Mountains, mts., N.A.	D9	69
Purcellville, Va., U.S.	A5	123
Purdham Hill, mtn., Ar., U.S.	h10	81
Purdin, Mo., U.S.	B4	102
Purdum, Ne., U.S.	B5	104
Purdy, Mo., U.S.	E4	102
Purépero, Mex.	n12	63
Purgatoire, stm., Co., U.S.	D7	83
Purgatoire Peak, mtn., Co., U.S.	D5	83
Puri, India	E8	36
Purmerend, Neth.	H6	37
Purnea, India	C8	36
Pürnia, India	C8	36
Purple Springs, Alta.	E5	68
Pursglove, W.V., U.S.	B4	125
Puruándiro, Mex.	m13	63
Puruliya, India	D8	36
Purus, stm., S.A.	B4	53
Purvis, Ms., U.S.	D4	101
Purwakarta, Indon.	*G3	34
Purwokerto, Indon.	*G3	34
Puryear, Tn., U.S.	A3	119
Puryŏng-dong, N. Kor.	F4	33
Pusan, S. Kor.	D10	31
Pushaw Lake, l., Me., U.S.	D4	96
Pushkin, Sov. Un.	D6	29
Pushkino, Sov. Un.	C11	27
Pushmataha, Al., U.S.	C1	78
Pushmataha, co., Ok., U.S.	C6	113
Pushthrough, Newf.	E3	72
Pusiano, Lago di, l., Italy	C7	21
Püspökladány, Hung.	B5	24
Pustelnik, Pol.	k14	26
Pustynnaya, Sov. Un.	B8	33
Putao, Burma	C10	36
Puteaux, Fr.	g9	16
Putian, China	F8	31
Putilovo, Sov. Un.	s32	14
Puting, Cape, c., Indon.	F4	34
Putivl, Sov. Un.	F9	27
Putlitz, Ger.	E6	15
Putnam, Al., U.S.	C1	78
Putnam, Ct., U.S.	B8	84
Putnam, Ok., U.S.	B3	113
Putnam, Tx., U.S.	C3	120
Putnam, co., Fl., U.S.	C5	86
Putnam, co., Ga., U.S.	C3	87
Putnam, co., Il., U.S.	B4	90
Putnam, co., In., U.S.	E4	91
Putnam, co., Mo., U.S.	A4	102
Putnam, co., N.Y., U.S.	D7	109
Putnam, co., Oh., U.S.	B1	112
Putnam, co., Tn., U.S.	C8	119
Putnam, co., W.V., U.S.	C3	125
Putnam Station, N.Y., U.S.	B7	109
Putnamville, In., U.S.	E4	91
Putnamville, Vt., U.S.	C3	122
Putney, Ga., U.S.	E2	87
Putney, S.D., U.S.	B7	118
Putney, Vt., U.S.	F3	122
Putre, Chile	C2	55
Puttalam, Sri L.	G6	36
Putte, Neth.	C4	17
Püttlingen, Ger.	D1	19
Putumayo, dept., Col.	C2	60
Putumayo (Içá), stm., S.A.	D3	60
Pütürge, Tur.	C12	40
Puukohola Heiau National Historic Site, hist., Hi., U.S.	D6	88
Puukolii, Hi., U.S.	C5	88
Puulavesi, l., Fin.	G12	14
Puunene, Hi., U.S.	C5	88
Puurs, Bel.	C4	17
Puxico, Mo., U.S.	E7	102
Puyallup, Wa., U.S.	B3	124
Puyallup, stm., Wa., U.S.	C3	124
Puyang, China	G6	32
Puyehue, Chile	C2	54
Puyo, Ec.	B2	58
Pūzak, Hāmūn-e, l., Afg.	F10	39
Pwani, prov., Tan.	C6	48
Pweto, Zaire	B5	48
Pwllheli, Wales, U.K.	A4	10
Pyaozero, l., Sov. Un.	D14	14
Pyapon, Burma	E10	36
Pyasina, stm., Sov. Un.	B12	29
Pyatigorsk, Sov. Un.	E2	28
Pyatt, Ar., U.S.	A3	81
Pyhäjärvi, l., Fin.	G10	14
Pyinmana, Burma	E10	36
Pyland, Ms., U.S.	A5	101
Pyles Fork, stm., W.V., U.S.	h10	125
Pymatuning Reservoir, res., U.S.	C1	115
Pyŏngchang, S. Kor.	H4	33
Pyŏngt'aek, S. Kor.	H3	33
Pyŏngyang, N. Kor.	D10	31
Pyote, Tx., U.S.	D1	120
Pyramid Lake, l., Nv., U.S.	C2	105
Pyramid Lake Indian Reservation, Nv., U.S.	D2	105
Pyramid Mountains, mts., N.M., U.S.	E1	108
Pyramid Peak, mtn., N.M., U.S.	E1	108
Pyramid Peak, mtn., Wy., U.S.	C2	127
Pyramids, hist., Eg.	C3	38
Pyrenees, mts., Eur.	A6	22
Pyrites, N.Y., U.S.	f9	109
Pyrmont, In., U.S.	D4	91
Pyrzyce, Pol.	B1	26
Pyskowice, Pol.	g9	26
Pytalovo, Sov. Un.	B8	27
Pyu, Burma	E10	36

Q

Name	Map Ref.	Page
Qabātiyah, Isr. Occ.	B7	41
Qā'emshahr, Iran	E9	39
Qā'en, Iran	E9	39
Qahar Youyi Zhongqi, China	D5	32
Qaidam Pendi (Tsaidam Basin), China	D3	31
Qalamshāh, Eg.	D4	40

Name	Map Ref.	Page

Qalāt, Afg. — B4 36
Qal' at Bīshah, Sau. Ar. — C4 38
Qal' at Şāliḥ, Iraq — F3 39
Qal' aş Şukkar, Iraq — F3 39
Qal'eh-ye Now, Afg. — D11 39
Qallābāt, Sud. — C4 47
Qalqīliya, Isr. Occ. — B6 41
Qalyūb, Eg. — D3 41
Qamdo, China — E4 31
Qamea, i., Fiji — H16 52
Qamīnīs, Libya — C4 43
Qānā, Leb. — A7 41
Qandahar see Kandahar, Afg. — B4 36
Qandala, Som. — C6 47
Qārah, Egypt — H6 40
Qardho, Som. — D6 47
Qareh, stm., Iran — D5 39
Qārūn, Birkat, l., Eg. — D6 43
Qaryat Abu Nujaym, Libya — C3 43
Qaşr al Farāfirah, Eg. — C2 38
Qaşr Banī Walīd, Libya — C2 43
Qasr el Boukhari, Alg. — B5 44
Qaşr-e Shīrīn, Iran — D2 39
Qa'ṭabah, Yemen — D4 38
Qatar, ctry., Asia — C5 38
Qattara Depression, depr., Eg. — C2 38
Qawz Rajab, Sud. — B4 47
Qazvīn, Iran — B4 38
Qeshm, Iran — H8 39
Qeshm, i., Iran — C5 38
Qezel Owzan, stm., Iran — C4 39
Qian'an, China — D8 31
Qianjiang, China — J3 32
Qianshan, China — I7 32
Qiantang Jiang, stm., China — J8 32
Qianxian, China — G3 32
Qianyang, China — F7 31
Qiaojia, China — F5 31
Qichun, China — I6 32
Qiemo, China — A8 36
Qijiang, China — J2 32
Qila Lādgasht, Pak. — C3 36
Qila Saifullāh, Pak. — B2 37
Qilian Shan, mts., China — D4 31
Qimen, China — J7 32
Qinā, Eg. — C3 38
Qing'an, China — C3 33
Qingdao (Tsingtao), China — D9 31
Qinghai Hu, l., China — D4 31
Qingjian, China — D7 31
Qingjiang, China — J6 32
Qingliu, China — F8 31
Qingpu, China — E9 31
Qingyang, China — D6 31
Qingyuan, China — C11 32
Qingyuan, China — F7 32
Qing Zang Gaoyuan (Plateau of Tibet), plat., China — G11 30
Qin He, stm., China — G5 32
Qinhuangdao, China — D8 31
Qin Ling (Tsinling Shan), mts., China — E6 31
Qinxian, China — F5 32
Qinyang, China — G5 32
Qinzhou, China — B8 35
Qiongshan, China — B8 34
Qiongzhou Haixia, strt., China — A9 31
Qiqian, China — B9 31
Qiqihar (Tsitsihar), China — B7 31
Qiryat Ata, Isr. — C6 41
Qiryat Gat, Isr. — C6 41
Qiryat Mal'akhi, Isr. — g10 41
Qiryat Ono, Isr. — A7 41
Qiryat Shemona, Isr. — B7 41
Qiryat Yam, Isr. — B7 41
Qishn, Yemen — B7 41
Qishon, stm., Isr. — C2 51
Qitai, China — *B11 31
Qitaihe, China — *B11 31
Qiyang, China — F7 31
Qīzān, Sau. Ar. — D4 38
Qnadsa, Alg. — C4 44
Qom, Iran — B5 38
Qom, stm., Iran — E5 39
Qomemiyyut (Talbiya) (part of Jerusalem), Isr. — m14 41
Qomsheh, Iran — E5 39
Quabbin Reservoir, res., Ma., U.S. — B3 98
Quaco Head, c., N.B. — D4 71
Quaddick, Ct., U.S. — B8 84
Quaddick Reservoir, res., Ct., U.S. — B8 84
Quail Oaks, Va., U.S. — n18 123
Quakenbrück, Ger. — B3 18
Quaker City, Oh., U.S. — C4 112
Quaker Hill, Ct., U.S. — D7 84
Quakertown, N.J., U.S. — B3 107
Quakertown, Pa., U.S. — F11 115
Qualicum Beach, B.C. — E5 69
Quality, Ky., U.S. — C3 94
Quamba, Mn., U.S. — E5 100
Quanah, Tx., U.S. — B3 120
Quang Ngai, Viet. — B3 34
Quang Trach, Viet. — D7 35
Quang Tri, Viet. — B3 34
Quannapowitt, Lake, l., Ma., U.S. — f11 98
Quantico, Md., U.S. — D6 97
Quantico, Va., U.S. — B5 123
Quantico Marine Corps Air Station, mil., Va., U.S. — B5 123
Quantico Station, Va., U.S. — *B5 123
Quanzhou, China — F7 31
Quanzhou, China — G8 31
Quapaw, Ok., U.S. — A7 113
Qu'Appelle, Sask. — G4 75
Qu'Appelle, stm., Can. — G4 75
Quarai, Braz. — E1 56
Quaraí, stm., S.A. — E1 56
Quarles Mountains, mts., Indon. — F5 34
Quarryville, N.B. — C4 71
Quarryville, Ct., U.S. — B6 84
Quarryville, Pa., U.S. — G9 115
Quartu Sant' Elena, Italy — E2 23
Quartz Hill, Ca., U.S. — *E4 82
Quartz Mountain, mtn., Or., U.S. — D4 114
Quartzsite, Az., U.S. — D1 80
Quasqueton, Ia., U.S. — B6 92
Quassapaug, Lake, l., Ct., U.S. — C3 84
Quatre, Isle, i., St. Vin. — V26 65
Quatsino Sound, strt., B.C. — D3 69
Quay, N.M., U.S. — C6 108
Quay, co., N.M., U.S. — C6 108
Qūchān, Iran — E3 127
Quealy, Wy., U.S. — E3 127
Quebec, Que. — C6 74
Quebec, prov., Can. — B5 74
Quebeck, Tn., U.S. — D8 119
Quechee, Vt., U.S. — D4 122

Quechee Gorge, val., Vt., U.S. — D4 122
Quecreek, Pa., U.S. — F3 115
Quedlinburg, Ger. — C5 18
Queen, stm., R.I., U.S. — E3 116
Queen, Cape, c., N.W. Ter. — D17 66
Queen Alexandra Range, mts., Ant. — A29 7
Queen Anne, Md., U.S. — C6 97
Queen Annes, co., Md., U.S. — B5 97
Queen Bess, Mount, mtn., B.C. — D5 69
Queenborough [-in-Sheppey], Eng., U.K. — E7 10
Queen Charlotte, B.C. — C1 69
Queen Charlotte Islands, is., B.C. — C1 69
Queen Charlotte Mountains, mts., B.C. — C1 69
Queen Charlotte Sound, strt., B.C. — n17 69
Queen Charlotte Strait, strt., B.C. — D4 69
Queen City, Mo., U.S. — A5 102
Queen City, Tx., U.S. — C5 120
Queen Creek, Az., U.S. — m9 80
Queen Elizabeth Islands, is., N.W. Ter. — k30 66
Queen Fabiola Mountains, mts., Ant. — B16 7
Queen Mary Coast, Ant. — C22 7
Queen Maud Gulf, b., N.W. Ter. — C12 66
Queen Maud Land, reg., Ant. — B15 7
Queen Maud Mountains, mts., Ant. — A31 7
Queens, co., N.B. — D4 71
Queens, co., N.S. — E4 71
Queens, co., P.E.I. — C6 71
Queens, co., N.Y., U.S. — E7 109
Queensborough, Ont. — C7 73
Queensborough, Wa., U.S. — *B3 124
Queensferry, Scot., U.K. — E5 13
Queensferry see South Queensferry, Scot., U.K. — E5 13
Queen Shoals, W.V., U.S. — C3 125
Queensland, Ga., U.S. — E3 87
Queensland, state, Austl. — D7 50
Queensport, N.S. — D8 71
Queens Sound, strt., B.C. — D3 69
Queenstown, Austl. — o15 50
Queenstown, Alta. — D4 68
Queenstown, N.B. — D3 71
Queenstown, N.Z. — P12 51
Queenstown, S. Afr. — H4 49
Queenstown, Md., U.S. — C5 97
Queets, Wa., U.S. — B1 124
Queguay Grande, stm., Ur. — E1 56
Queimadas, Braz. — D3 57
Queimadinhas, Braz. — A4 56
Queixada, Braz. — B4 56
Quela, Ang. — C2 48
Quelelevu, i., Fiji — H16 52
Quelimane, Moz. — A6 49
Quemado, N.M., U.S. — C1 108
Quemado, Tx., U.S. — E2 120
Quemado de Güines, Cuba — C6 64
Quemú Quemú, Arg. — D8 93
Quentin, Ms., U.S. — D3 101
Quepos, C.R. — F5 62
Quequén, Arg. — B5 54
Querétaro, Mex. — C4 63
Querétaro, state, Mex. — C5 63
Querfurt, Ger. — B6 19
Quers, Fr. — A1 21
Quesada, Spain — D4 22
Queshan, China — H6 32
Quesnel, B.C. — C6 69
Quesnel Lake, l., B.C. — C7 69
Questa, N.M., U.S. — A4 108
Quetena, Bol. — D2 55
Quetico Provincial Park, Ont. — o17 73
Quetta, Pak. — B4 36
Quevedo, Ec. — B2 58
Quezaltenango, Guat. — E6 63
Quezaltepeque, El Sal. — D3 62
Quezon City, Phil. — C6 34
Quibala, Ang. — D1 48
Quibdó, Col. — B2 60
Quiberon, Fr. — E5 16
Quiberon Peninsula, pen., Fr. — E6 16
Quicksand Pond, l., R.I., U.S. — E6 116
Quicksburg, Va., U.S. — B4 123
Quidnessett, R.I., U.S. — E4 116
Quidnick, R.I., U.S. — D2 116
Quidnick Reservoir, res., R.I., U.S. — D2 116
Quiindy, Para. — C5 56
Quila, Mex. — E5 63
Quilcene, Wa., U.S. — B3 124
Quilengues, Ang. — D1 48
Quileute Indian Reservation, Wa., U.S. — B1 124
Quilino, Arg. — F3 55
Quillan, Fr. — F5 16
Quill Lake, Sask. — E3 75
Quillota, Chile — A2 54
Quilmes, Arg. — g7 54
Quilon, India — H3 37
Quilpie, Austl. — E7 50
Quilpué, Chile — A2 54
Quilty, Ire. — E2 11
Quimbele, Ang. — C2 48
Quimby, Ia., U.S. — B2 92
Quimby, Me., U.S. — B4 96
Quimilí, Arg. — E3 55
Quimper, Fr. — C1 16
Quimperlé, Fr. — D2 16
Quinby, Or., U.S. — B4 114
Quinault, Wa., U.S. — B2 124
Quinault, Lake, l., Wa., U.S. — B2 124
Quinault Indian Reservation, Wa., U.S. — B1 124
Quince Orchard, Md., U.S. — *B3 97
Quincy, Ca., U.S. — C3 82
Quincy, Fl., U.S. — B2 86
Quincy, Il., U.S. — D2 90
Quincy, In., U.S. — F4 91
Quincy, Ks., U.S. — E8 93
Quincy, Ky., U.S. — B6 94
Quincy, Ma., U.S. — B5 98
Quincy, Mi., U.S. — G5 99
Quincy, Mo., U.S. — B5 101
Quincy, Oh., U.S. — B2 112
Quincy, Pa., U.S. — G6 115
Quincy, Wa., U.S. — B6 124
Quincy Bay, b., Ma., U.S. — g12 98
Quindío, dept., Col. — C2 60

Quinebaug, Ct., U.S. — A8 84
Quinebaug, stm., Ct., U.S. — C8 84
Quines, Arg. — A3 54
Quinga, Moz. — A7 49
Quinhagak, Ak., U.S. — D7 79
Qui Nhon, Viet. — C3 34
Quinlan, Ok., U.S. — A2 113
Quinlan, Tx., U.S. — C4 120
Quinn, S.D., U.S. — D3 118
Quinn, stm., Nv., U.S. — B3 105
Quinn Canyon Range, mts., Nv., U.S. — F6 105
Quinnesec, Mi., U.S. — C3 99
Quinnipiac, stm., Ct., U.S. — D4 84
Quinnville, R.I., U.S. — B4 116
Quintana de la Serena, Spain — C3 22
Quintanar [de la Orden], Spain — C4 22
Quintana Roo, state, Mex. — D7 63
Quinter, Ks., U.S. — C3 93
Quintero, Chile — A2 54
Quinton, Sask. — F3 75
Quinton, Ky., U.S. — D5 94
Quinton, N.J., U.S. — D2 107
Quinton, Ok., U.S. — B6 113
Quinwood, W.V., U.S. — C4 125
Quipapá, Braz. — C5 57
Quipungo, Ang. — D1 48
Quirauk Mountain, mtn., Md., U.S. — A2 97
Quirindi, Austl. — E8 51
Quirinópolis, Braz. — B2 56
Quiriquire, Ven. — B5 60
Quiroga, Spain — A2 22
Quirpon Island, i., Newf. — C4 72
Quissanga, Moz. — D7 48
Quitaque, Tx., U.S. — B2 120
Quita Sueño Bank, Col. — C7 62
Quitman, Ar., U.S. — B3 81
Quitman, Ga., U.S. — F3 87
Quitman, La., U.S. — B3 95
Quitman, Ms., U.S. — C5 101
Quitman, Mo., U.S. — A2 102
Quitman, Tx., U.S. — C5 120
Quitman, co., Ga., U.S. — E1 87
Quitman, co., Ms., U.S. — A3 101
Quitman Mountains, mts., Tx., U.S. — o12 120
Quito, Ec. — B2 58
Quixadá, Braz. — B3 57
Quixeramobim, Braz. — C3 57
Qulin, Mo., U.S. — E7 102
Quonnipaug Lake, l., Ct., U.S. — D5 84
Quonochontaug, R.I., U.S. — G2 116
Quonochontaug Pond, l., R.I., U.S. — G2 116
Quonset Point, c., R.I., U.S. — E4 116
Quorn, Austl. — F2 51
Qurayyah, Wādī, val., Eg. — D6 41
Qūş, Eg. — C3 38
Quşrah, Isr. Occ. — g12 41
Quthing, Leso. — D4 49
Quxian, China — E6 31
Quxian, China — F8 31
Quzhou, China — *F8 31

R

Raab (Rába), stm., Eur. — B2 24
Raabs [an der Thaya], Aus. — D7 18
Raahe, Fin. — E11 14
Raalte, Neth. — B6 17
Ra'ananna, Isr. — g10 41
Raasay, i., Scot., U.K. — C2 13
Rab, i., Yugo. — C2 24
Raba, Indon. — G5 34
Rába (Raab), stm., Eur. — H6 32
Rabastens, Fr. — F4 16
Rabat, Mor. — C3 44
Rabaul, Pap. N. Gui. — h13 50
Rabbit Creek, stm., S.D., U.S. — B3 118
Rabbit Ears Pass, Co., U.S. — A4 83
Rabbit Hash, Ky., U.S. — k13 94
Rabbit Lake, Sask. — D2 75
Rabī, i., Fiji — H16 52
Rābigh, Sau. Ar. — C3 38
Rabun, Al., U.S. — E3 50
Rabun, co., Ga., U.S. — B3 87
Rabun Bald, mtn., Ga., U.S. — B3 87
Rača, Yugo. — C5 24
Raccoon Creek, stm., Oh., U.S. — D3 112
Raccourci Island, i., La., U.S. — D4 95
Race, Cape, c., Newf. — E5 72
Raceland, Ky., U.S. — B7 94
Raceland, La., U.S. — E5 95
Race Pond, Ga., U.S. — F4 87
Rach Gia, Viet. — C2 34
Racibórz, Pol. — E5 26
Racine, Mn., U.S. — G6 100
Racine, Mo., U.S. — E3 102
Racine, Oh., U.S. — D4 112
Racine, W.V., U.S. — A3 119
Racine, Wi., U.S. — F6 126
Racine, co., Wi., U.S. — F5 126
Racine Dam, Oh., U.S. — C3 125
Račiněves, Czech. — n17 26
Racket, N.Y., U.S. — C4 102
Rădăuţi, Rom. — B7 24
Radbuza, stm., Czech. — D7 26
Radcliff, Ky., U.S. — C4 94
Radcliffe, Ia., U.S. — B4 92
Råde, Nor. — p28 14
Radeberg, Ger. — C6 18
Radebeul, Ger. — B8 19
Radford, Va., U.S. — C2 123
Rādhanpur, India — F3 37
Radisson, Sask. — C2 75
Radisson, Wi., U.S. — C2 126
Radium, Ks., U.S. — D5 93
Radium, Mn., U.S. — B2 100
Radium Hot Springs, B.C. — D9 69
Radium Springs, N.M., U.S. — E3 108
Radix, Point, c., Trin. — O24 65
Radley, W.V., U.S. — *E9 93
Radnice, Czech. — D8 26
Radnor, In., U.S. — C4 91
Radnor, Tn., U.S. — B5 119
Radnor Township, Pa., U.S. — *F11 115
Radom, Pol. — D8 26
Radom, Il., U.S. — E4 90
Radomir, Bul. — D6 24
Radomsko, Pol. — D5 26
Radoviš, Yugo. — F7 27
Radstadt, Aus. — E6 18
Radville, Sask. — G3 75
Radway, Alta. — B4 68
Radzionków, Pol. — g9 26
Radzymin, Pol. — k14 26

Radzyń [Podlaski], Pol. — C7 26
Rae, N.W. Ter. — D9 66
Rae Bareli, India — C7 36
Raeford, N.C., U.S. — C3 110
Raesfeld, Ger. — B1 19
Raeside, Lake, l., Austl. — E3 50
Rae Strait, strt., N.W. Ter. — C14 66
Raeville, Ne., U.S. — C7 104
Rafaela, Arg. — A4 54
Rafaḥ, Isr. Occ. — G10 40
Rafaï, Cen. Afr. Rep. — D4 46
Rafḥā', Sau. Ar. — C4 38
Rafsanjān, Iran — F8 39
Raft, stm., Id., U.S. — G5 89
Raft River Mountains, mts., Ut., U.S. — B2 121
Raga, Sud. — D2 47
Ragan, Ne., U.S. — D6 104
Ragay, Phil. — p14 34
Ragay Gulf, b., Phil. — p14 34
Ragged Island, i., Me., U.S. — E4 96
Ragged Island Range, is., Bah. — C6 64
Ragged Lake, l., Me., U.S. — C3 96
Ragged Top Mountain, mtn., Wy., U.S. — E7 127
Raghza, Pak. — B4 36
Ragland, Al., U.S. — B3 78
Raglesville, In., U.S. — G4 91
Ragley, La., U.S. — D2 95
Rago, Ks., U.S. — E5 93
Ragsdale, In., U.S. — G3 91
Ragunda, Swe. — A2 22
Ragusa, Italy — F5 23
Rahad al Bardī, Sud. — C1 47
Rahden, Ger. — F2 15
Rahīmyār Khān, Pak. — C5 36
Rahway, N.J., U.S. — B4 107
Rahway, stm., N.J., U.S. — k7 107
Rāichūr, India — E6 36
Raiford, Fl., U.S. — B4 86
Raigarh, India — D7 36
Railroad Valley, val., Nv., U.S. — E6 105
Raimbault, stm., Que. — A5 74
Raipur, India — D7 36
Ra'īs, Sau. Ar. — C3 38
Raismes, Fr. — D3 17
Raja, Cape, c., Indon. — K2 35
Rājahmundry, India — E7 36
Rajang, stm., Malay. — E4 34
Rājapālaiyam, India — *G6 36
Rājasthān, state, India — C5 36
Rājkot, India — D5 36
Rājpīpla, India — G4 37
Rājshāhi, Bngl. — D8 36
Rakaia, stm., N.Z. — O13 51
Raka Zangbo, stm., China — C11 37
Rake, Ia., U.S. — A4 92
Rakhov, Sov. Un. — A7 24
Rakkestad, Nor. — p29 14
Rakovník, Czech. — C2 26
Rakvere, Sov. Un. — B5 26
Raleigh, Newf. — C4 72
Raleigh, Fl., U.S. — C4 86
Raleigh, Il., U.S. — F5 90
Raleigh, Ms., U.S. — C4 101
Raleigh, N.C., U.S. — B4 110
Raleigh, N.D., U.S. — C4 111
Raleigh, W.V., U.S. — n13 125
Raleigh, co., W.V., U.S. — D3 125
Raleigh Bay, b., N.C., U.S. — C6 110
Raleigh Hills, Or., U.S. — *B4 114
Ralls, Tx., U.S. — C2 120
Ralls, co., Mo., U.S. — B6 102
Ralph, Al., U.S. — B2 78
Ralph, Mi., U.S. — B3 99
Ralph, S.D., U.S. — B2 118
Ralston, Ia., U.S. — B3 92
Ralston, Ne., U.S. — g12 104
Ralston, Ok., U.S. — A5 113
Ralston, Pa., U.S. — D8 115
Ralston, Tn., U.S. — A3 119
Ralston, Wy., U.S. — B4 127
Ralston Valley, val., Nv., U.S. — E4 105
Ram, stm., Alta. — D3 68
Rama, Sask. — E4 75
Rama, Isr. — B7 41
Rama, Nic. — E8 63
Ramaḍi Barrage, Iraq — F14 40
Ramah, Co., U.S. — B6 83
Ramah, N.M., U.S. — B1 108
Ramah Indian Reservation, N.M., U.S. — C1 108
Rām Allāh, Isr. Occ. — C4 41
Ramapo, stm., N.J., U.S. — A4 107
Ramapo Mountains, mts., N.J., U.S. — A4 107
Ramat Gan, Isr. — B6 41
Ramat HaKovesh, Isr. — g10 41
Ramat HaSharon, Isr. — g10 41
Rambervillers, Fr. — C7 16
Ramblewood Acres, De., U.S. — *B3 85
Ramblewood, N.J., U.S. — D3 107
Rambouillet, Fr. — C4 16
Ramea, Newf. — E3 72
Ramea Islands, is., Newf. — E3 72
Ramenskoye, Sov. Un. — D12 27
Ramer, Al., U.S. — C3 78
Ramer, Tn., U.S. — B3 119
Ramey, Pa., U.S. — E5 115
Rāmganga, stm., India — D7 37
Rāmhormoz, Iran — F4 39
Ramirez, Tx., U.S. — F3 120
Ramla, Isr. — H10 40
Rāmnagar, India — D6 41
Ramnäs, Swe. — t34 14
Ramon, Har, mtn., Isr. — D6 41
Ramon, Naḥal, val., Isr. — D6 41
Ramona, Ca., U.S. — F5 82
Ramona, Ks., U.S. — D6 93
Ramona, Ok., U.S. — A6 113

Ramona, S.D., U.S. — C8 118
Ramor, Lough, l., Ire. — D4 11
Rãe... Rampart, Ak., U.S. — B9 79
Rampart Range, mts., Co., U.S. — B5 83
Rāmpur, India — C6 36
Rāpti, stm., Asia — D9 37
Ramsay, Mi., U.S. — n12 99
Ramsayville, Ont. — h12 73
Ramseur, N.C., U.S. — B3 110
Ramsey, I. of Man — C4 10
Ramsey, Eng., U.K. — B7 12
Ramsey, Il., U.S. — E4 90
Ramsey, N.J., U.S. — A4 107
Ramsey, co., Mn., U.S. — E5 100
Ramsey, co., N.D., U.S. — A7 111
Ramsgate, Eng., U.K. — E7 10
Rāmshīr, Iran — F4 39
Ramshorn Peak, mtn., Mt., U.S. — E5 103
Ramshorn Peak, mtn., Wy., U.S. — C3 127
Ramu, stm., Pap. N. Gui. — k11 50
Rānāghāt, India — F12 37
Ranau, Lake, l., Indon. — F2 34
Ranburne, Al., U.S. — B4 78
Rancagua, Chile — A2 54
Rancharia, Braz. — C2 56
Rancheria Rock, mtn., Or., U.S. — C6 114
Ranchester, Wy., U.S. — B5 127
Rānchi, India — D8 36
Rancho Cordova, Ca., U.S. — *C3 82
Rancho Mirage, Ca., U.S. — *F5 82
Rancho Palos Verdes, Ca., U.S. — n12 82
Rancho Rinconado, Ca., U.S. — *k8 82
Ranchos de Taos, N.M., U.S. — A4 108
Ranco, Lago, l., Chile — C2 54
Rancocas, N.J., U.S. — C3 107
Rancocas Creek, stm., N.J., U.S. — C3 107
Rancocas Creek, South Branch, stm., N.J., U.S. — D3 107
Rancocas Woods, N.J., U.S. — D3 107
Rand, Co., U.S. — A4 83
Rand, W.V., U.S. — C3 125
Randalia, Ia., U.S. — B6 92
Randall, Ks., U.S. — C5 93
Randall, Mn., U.S. — D4 100
Randall, co., Tx., U.S. — B2 120
Randallstown, Md., U.S. — B4 97
Randen, Ger. — A6 21
Randle, Wa., U.S. — C4 124
Randleman, N.C., U.S. — B3 110
Randles, Mo., U.S. — D8 102
Randlett, Ok., U.S. — C3 113
Randlett, Ut., U.S. — C6 121
Randolph, Al., U.S. — C3 78
Randolph, Az., U.S. — E4 80
Randolph, Me., U.S. — D3 96
Randolph, Ma., U.S. — B5 98
Randolph, Mn., U.S. — F6 100
Randolph, Ne., U.S. — B8 104
Randolph, N.H., U.S. — B4 106
Randolph, N.Y., U.S. — C2 109
Randolph, Oh., U.S. — A4 112
Randolph, Ut., U.S. — B4 121
Randolph, Vt., U.S. — D3 122
Randolph, Wi., U.S. — E4 126
Randolph, co., Al., U.S. — B4 78
Randolph, co., Ar., U.S. — A4 81
Randolph, co., Ga., U.S. — E2 87
Randolph, co., Il., U.S. — E4 90
Randolph, co., In., U.S. — D7 91
Randolph, co., Mo., U.S. — B5 102
Randolph, co., N.C., U.S. — B3 110
Randolph, co., W.V., U.S. — C5 125
Randolph Air Force Base, mil., Tx., U.S. — h7 120
Randolph Center, Vt., U.S. — D3 122
Randolph Hills, Md., U.S. — B3 97
Random Island, i., Newf. — D5 72
Random Lake, Wi., U.S. — E6 126
Randow, Ger. — B7 18
Randsburg, Ca., U.S. — E5 82
Randwick, Austl. — *F9 50
Ranfurly, Alta. — C5 68
Ranfurly, N.Z. — O13 51
Rangauni Bay, b., N.Z. — K14 51
Rangeley, Me., U.S. — D2 96
Rangeley Lake, l., Me., U.S. — D2 96
Rangely, Co., U.S. — A2 83
Ranger, Ga., U.S. — B2 87
Ranger, Tx., U.S. — C3 120
Ranger, W.V., U.S. — C2 125
Rangia, India — G6 37
Rangiora, N.Z. — O14 51
Rangitata, stm., N.Z. — O13 51
Rangoon (Yangon), Burma — E10 31
Rangpur, Bngl. — C8 36
Ranier, Mn., U.S. — B5 100
Rānīganj, India — D8 36
Rankin, Il., U.S. — C6 90
Rankin, Pa., U.S. — k14 115
Rankin, Tx., U.S. — D2 120
Rankin, co., Ms., U.S. — C4 101
Rannoch, Loch, res., Scot., U.K. — E4 13
Ranong, Thai. — H3 34
Ransom, Il., U.S. — B5 90
Ransom, Ks., U.S. — D4 93
Ransom, Pa., U.S. — m17 115
Ransom, co., N.D., U.S. — C8 111
Ransomville, N.Y., U.S. — B2 109
Ranson, W.V., U.S. — B7 125
Ranum, Den. — B3 18
Raon-l'Étape, Fr. — D14 16
Rapallo, Italy — E3 23
Raper, Cape, c., N.W. Ter. — B11 31
Rāpch, stm., Iran — I9 39
Raphine, Va., U.S. — C3 123
Rapid, stm., Mn., U.S. — B4 100
Rapid, North Branch, stm., Mn., U.S. — B4 100
Rapid City, Man. — D1 70
Rapid City, S.D., U.S. — C2 118
Rapid River, Mi., U.S. — C4 99
Rapids City, Il., U.S. — B3 90

Rappahannock, co., Va., U.S. — B4 123
Rappahannock, stm., Va., U.S. — B5 123
Rappahannock Academy, Va., U.S. — B5 123
Rapperswil, Switz. — B6 21
Rāpti, stm., Asia — D9 37
Raquette, stm., N.Y., U.S. — f10 109
Raquette Lake, N.Y., U.S. — B6 109
Raquette Lake, l., N.Y., U.S. — B6 109
Rardin, Il., U.S. — D5 90
Raritan, Il., U.S. — C3 90
Raritan, N.J., U.S. — B3 107
Raritan, stm., N.J., U.S. — C4 107
Raritan, South Branch, stm., N.J., U.S. — B3 107
Raritan Bay, b., N.J., U.S. — C4 107
Rasa, Punta, c., Arg. — C4 54
Ra's al 'Ayn, Syria — D13 40
Ra's al Khaymah, U.A.E. — C5 38
Ra's al Unūf, Libya — C3 43
Ra's an Naqb, Jord. — C4 41
Ra's a Gharib, Eg. — D6 43
Rashād, Sud. — F10 40
Rashayyā, Leb. — A7 41
Rāshīdah, Ma'ṭan, well, Libya — H3 40
Rashīd (Rosetta), Eg. — B3 38
Rashkov, Sov. Un. — B9 24
Rasht, Iran — B4 38
Raška, Yugo. — D5 24
Raška, stm., Yugo. — D5 24
Raso, Cabo, c., Arg. — C3 54
Raspberry Peak, mtn., Ar., U.S. — C1 81
Rasskazovo, Sov. Un. — E13 27
Ra's Tannūrah, Sau. Ar. — C5 38
Rastatt, Ger. — D4 18
Rastede, Ger. — A8 17
Rastibonne Monastery, Isr. — m14 41
Raszyn, Pol. — m13 26
Rat, stm., Man. — A2 70
Rat, stm., Man. — E3 70
Ratchaburi, Thai. — C1 34
Ratcliff, Ar., U.S. — B2 81
Ratekau, Ger. — C5 18
Rathbun, Ia., U.S. — D5 92
Rathbun Lake, res., Ia., U.S. — D5 92
Rathdrum, Id., U.S. — B2 89
Rathenow, Ger. — B6 18
Rathfriland, N. Ire., U.K. — B5 11
Rathkeale, Ire. — E3 11
Rathlin Island, i., N. Ire., U.K. — C4 11
Rathlin Sound, strt., N. Ire., U.K. — B5 11
Ráth Luirc, Ire. — E3 11
Rathmelton, Ire. — B4 11
Rathmore, Ire. — E2 11
Rathmullen, Ire. — B4 11
Rathnew, Ire. — D5 11
Rathowen, Ire. — D4 11
Rathwell, Man. — E2 70
Ratingen, Ger. — B1 19
Ratio, Ks., U.S. — C5 81
Rat Islands, is., Ak., U.S. — E3 79
Rat Lake, l., Man. — A2 70
Rat Lake, l., Man. — B4 70
Ratlām, India — F5 36
Ratnāgiri, India — E5 36
Ratner, Sask. — D3 75
Raton, N.M., U.S. — A5 108
Raton Pass, N.M., U.S. — A5 108
Rattan, Ok., U.S. — C6 113
Rattenburg, Aus. — E5 18
Rattlesnake Creek, stm., Ks., U.S. — E4 93
Rattlesnake Creek, stm., Oh., U.S. — C2 112
Rattlesnake Creek, stm., Wa., U.S. — C6 124
Rattlesnake Flat, pl., Wa., U.S. — C7 124
Rattlesnake Hills, hills, Wa., U.S. — C6 124
Rattlesnake Hills, hills, Wy., U.S. — D5 127
Rattlesnake Mountain, mtn., Ct., U.S. — C4 84
Rattling Brook, Newf. — D3 72
Rattray Head, c., Scot., U.K. — C7 13
Rättvik, Swe. — G6 14
Ratzeburg, Ger. — E4 15
Ratzeburger, l., Eur. — E4 15
Raub, Malay. — K4 35
Raub, N.D., U.S. — C3 91
Rauch, Arg. — B5 54
Raufarhöfn, Ice. — m25 14
Raukumara, mtn., N.Z. — L17 51
Rauland, Nor. — H2 14
Rauma, Fin. — G9 14
Raurkela, India — F10 37
Rausu, Mount, mtn., Japan — D12 33
Rautalampi, Fin. — F12 14
Ravalli, Mt., U.S. — D2 103
Ravalli, co., Mt., U.S. — D2 103
Ravanna, Mo., U.S. — A4 102
Rāvar, Iran — B5 38
Rava-Russkaya, Sov. Un. — F4 27
Raven, Va., U.S. — e10 123
Ravena, N.Y., U.S. — C7 109
Ravendale, Ca., U.S. — B3 82
Ravenden, Ar., U.S. — A4 81
Ravenden Springs, Ar., U.S. — A4 81
Ravenel, S.C., U.S. — k11 117
Ravenglass, Eng., U.K. — F5 13
Ravenna, Italy — E6 23
Ravenna, Ky., U.S. — C6 94
Ravenna, Mi., U.S. — E5 99
Ravenna, Ne., U.S. — C7 104
Ravenna, Oh., U.S. — A4 112
Raven Park, reg., Co., U.S. — A2 83
Raven Rock, N.J., U.S. — C2 107
Ravenscrag, Sask. — H1 75
Ravenscroft, Tn., U.S. — D8 119
Ravensdale, Wa., U.S. — f12 124
Ravensthorpe, Austl. — k10 51
Ravenswood, W.V., U.S. — C3 125
Ravensworth, Ont. — A3 102
Ravia, Ok., U.S. — C5 113
Rāwalpindi, Pak. — B5 36
Rāwalpindi Cantonment, Pak. — *B5 36
Rawa Mazowiecka, Pol. — B3 90
Rawāndūz, Iraq — D15 40
Rawdon, Que. — C4 74

Rawd Sālim, Bi'r, well, Eg. — D5 41
Rawhide Creek, stm., Wy., U.S. — D8 127
Rawicz, Pol. — C4 26
Rawlings, Md., U.S. — k13 97
Rawlings, Va., U.S. — D5 123
Rawlinna, Austl. — F4 50
Rawlins, Wy., U.S. — E5 127
Rawlins, co., Ks., U.S. — C2 93
Rawson, Arg. — C3 54
Rawson, Arg. — g6 54
Rawson, N.D., U.S. — B2 111
Rawson, Oh., U.S. — B2 112
Rawsonville, Vt., U.S. — E3 122
Ray, In., U.S. — A8 91
Ray, Mn., U.S. — B5 100
Ray, N.D., U.S. — A2 111
Ray, co., Mo., U.S. — B3 102
Ray, Cape, c., Newf. — E2 72
Raya, mtn., Indon. — F4 34
Raya, i., Indon. — J1 35
Rāyagarha, India — H9 37
Raychikhinsk, Sov. Un. — B4 33
Ray City, Ga., U.S. — E3 87
Raygorodka, Sov. Un. — q22 27
Rayle, Ga., U.S. — C4 87
Raymond, Alta. — E4 68
Raymond, Ca., U.S. — D4 82
Raymond, Ga., U.S. — C2 87
Raymond, Il., U.S. — D4 90
Raymond, In., U.S. — F7 91
Raymond, Ks., U.S. — D5 93
Raymond, Me., U.S. — E2 96
Raymond, Ms., U.S. — E3 100
Raymond, Mn., U.S. — C3 101
Raymond, Mt., U.S. — B12 103
Raymond, Ne., U.S. — D9 104
Raymond, N.H., U.S. — D4 106
Raymond, S.D., U.S. — C8 118
Raymond, Wa., U.S. — C2 124
Raymond Terrace, Austl. — F8 51
Raymondville, Mo., U.S. — D6 102
Raymondville, N.Y., U.S. — f10 109
Raymondville, Tx., U.S. — F4 120
Raymore, Sask. — F3 75
Raymore, Mo., U.S. — C3 102
Rayne, La., U.S. — D3 95
Rayner Glacier, ice, Ant. — C17 7
Raynesford, Mt., U.S. — C6 103
Raynham, Ma., U.S. — C5 98
Raynham Center, Ma., U.S. — C5 98
Rayón, Mex. — B2 63
Rayong, Thai. — F4 35
Rayside-Balfour, Ont. — *p19 73
Raytown, Mo., U.S. — h11 102
Rayville, La., U.S. — B4 95
Rayville, Mo., U.S. — B3 102
Razan, Iran — D4 39
Razgrad, Bul. — D8 24
Razlog, Bul. — E6 24
Razorback Mountain, mtn., B.C. — D5 69
Re, i., Viet. — E8 35
Ré, Île de, i., Fr. — D3 16
Rea, Mo., U.S. — A3 102
Rea, Lough, l., Ire. — D3 11
Reader, Ar., U.S. — D2 81
Reader, W.V., U.S. — B4 125
Reader Lake, l., Man. — C1 70
Readfield, Me., U.S. — D3 96
Reading, Eng., U.K. — E6 10
Reading, Ks., U.S. — D8 93
Reading, Ma., U.S. — A5 98
Reading, Mi., U.S. — G6 99
Reading, Oh., U.S. — C1 112
Reading, Pa., U.S. — F10 115
Reading, Vt., U.S. — E3 122
Reading Center, N.Y., U.S. — C4 109
Readland, Ar., U.S. — D4 81
Readlyn, Sask. — H3 75
Readlyn, Ia., U.S. — B5 92
Readsboro, Vt., U.S. — F3 122
Readstown, Wi., U.S. — E3 126
Readyville, Tn., U.S. — B5 119
Reagan, Tn., U.S. — B3 119
Reagan, co., Tx., U.S. — D2 120
Real, co., Tx., U.S. — E3 120
Real, Cordillera, mts., S.A. — C2 55
Realicó, Arg. — B4 54
Realitos, Tx., U.S. — F3 120
Reamstown, Pa., U.S. — F9 115
Reardan, Wa., U.S. — B8 124
Reasnor, Ia., U.S. — C4 92
Reata, Mex. — B4 63
Reaville, N.J., U.S. — C3 107
Reay, Scot., U.K. — B5 13
Rebecca, Ga., U.S. — E3 87
Rebersburg, Pa., U.S. — E7 115
Rebiana, well, Libya — D4 43
Rebiana Sand Sea, des., Libya — E3 43
Reboly, Sov. Un. — F14 14
Rebun Island, i., Japan — D10 33
Recalde, Arg. — B4 54
Recanati, Italy — C4 23
Recherche, Archipelago of the, is., Austl. — F3 50
Rechitsa, Sov. Un. — E8 27
Recife, Braz. — E8 57
Recinto, Chile — B2 54
Recklinghausen, Ger. — C3 18
Recluse, Wy., U.S. — B7 127
Recogne, Bel. — E5 17
Reconquista, Arg. — E4 55
Recovery, Ga., U.S. — F2 87
Recreo, Arg. — E2 55
Rector, Ar., U.S. — A5 81
Red, stm., N.A. — A8 76
Red, stm., U.S. — D9 76
Red, stm., Ky., U.S. — C6 94
Red, Elm Fork, stm., U.S. — A2 119
Red, North Fork, stm., U.S. — B1 113
Red, Salt Fork, stm., U.S. — C2 113
Red, South Fork, stm., U.S. — A5 119
Red, West Fork, stm., U.S. — A4 119
Redang, i., Malay. — J5 35
Redange, Lux. — E5 17
Red Bank, N.J., U.S. — C4 107
Red Bank, S.C., U.S. — D5 117
Red Bank, Tn., U.S. — h11 119
Red Banks, Ms., U.S. — A4 101
Red Bay, Al., U.S. — A1 78
Redbay, Fl., U.S. — u16 86
Red Bay, b., N. Ire., U.K. — B6 11
Redberry Lake, l., Sask. — E2 75
Redbird, Oh., U.S. — A4 112
Redbird, Ok., U.S. — B6 113
Red Bird, stm., Ky., U.S. — C6 94
Red Bluff, Ca., U.S. — B2 82
Red Bluff Lake, res., U.S. — o12 120
Red Boiling Springs, Tn., U.S. — C8 119
Red Bud, Il., U.S. — E4 90
Red Butte, mtn., Ut., U.S. — B2 121

Red Buttes Village, Wy., U.S. — D6 127
Redby, Mn., U.S. — C4 100
Redcar, Eng., U.K. — F7 13
Red Cedar, stm., Wi., U.S. — C2 126
Red Cedar Lake, l., Wi., U.S. — C2 126
Redcliff, Alta. — D5 68
Redcliff, Co., U.S. — B4 83
Red Cliff, Wi., U.S. — B3 126
Redcliffe, Austl. — E9 50
Red Cliff Indian Reservation, Wi., U.S. — B2 126
Red Cloud, Ne., U.S. — D7 104
Redcloud Peak, mtn., Co., U.S. — D3 83
Red Creek, N.Y., U.S. — B4 109
Red Creek, stm., Ms., U.S. — E4 101
Red Cross Lake, l., Man. — B5 70
Red Deer, Alta. — C4 68
Red Deer, stm., Can. — D4 68
Red Deer, stm., Can. — E4 75
Red Deer Lake, l., Man. — C1 70
Reddell, La., U.S. — D3 95
Red Desert, Wy., U.S. — E4 127
Reddick, Fl., U.S. — C4 86
Reddick, Il., U.S. — B5 90
Redding, Ca., U.S. — B2 82
Redding, Ct., U.S. — D2 84
Redding, Ia., U.S. — D3 92
Redding Ridge, Ct., U.S. — D2 84
Reddish Knob, mtn., U.S. — C5 125
Redditch, Eng., U.K. — B6 12
Redditt, Ont. — E4 70
Rede, stm., Eng., U.K. — E6 13
Red Earth Lake, l., Sask. — D4 75
Redenção, Braz. — B3 57
Redeye, stm., Mn., U.S. — D3 100
Red Feather Lakes, Co., U.S. — A5 83
Redfield, Ar., U.S. — C3 81
Redfield, Ia., U.S. — C3 92
Redfield, Ks., U.S. — E9 93
Redfield, N.Y., U.S. — B5 109
Redfield, S.D., U.S. — C7 118
Redford, Mi., U.S. — F7 99
Redford, N.Y., U.S. — f11 109
Redford, Tx., U.S. — p12 120
Redgranite, Wi., U.S. — D4 126
Redhill, Eng., U.K. — m12 11
Red Hook, N.Y., U.S. — C7 109
Redhouse, Ky., U.S. — C5 94
Red House, Va., U.S. — C4 123
Red House, W.V., U.S. — C3 125
Redig, S.D., U.S. — B2 118
Red Indian Lake, l., Newf. — D3 72
Red Island, i., Newf. — E4 72
Red Jacket, W.V., U.S. — D2 125
Redkey, In., U.S. — D7 91
Red Lake, Ont. — o16 73
Red Lake, Mn., U.S. — C3 100
Red Lake, co., Mn., U.S. — C2 100
Red Lake, l., Az., U.S. — B1 80
Red Lake, stm., Mn., U.S. — C2 100
Red Lake Falls, Mn., U.S. — C2 100
Red Lake Indian Reservation, Mn., U.S. — B3 100
Redlands, Ca., U.S. — E5 82
Red Level, Al., U.S. — D3 78
Red Lick, Ms., U.S. — D3 101
Red Lion, Pa., U.S. — G8 115
Red Lodge, Mt., U.S. — E7 103
Red Mill Pond, l., De., U.S. — E5 85
Redmon, Il., U.S. — D6 90
Redmond, Or., U.S. — C5 114
Redmond, Ut., U.S. — E4 121
Redmond, Wa., U.S. — e11 124
Red Mountain, Ca., U.S. — E5 82
Red Mountain, mtn., Al., U.S. — B3 78
Red Mountain, mtn., Ca., U.S. — B2 82
Red Mountain, mtn., Mt., U.S. — C4 103
Red Mountain Pass, Co., U.S. — D3 83
Rednitz, stm., Ger. — D5 18
Red Oak, Ga., U.S. — h7 87
Red Oak, Ia., U.S. — D2 92
Red Oak, N.C., U.S. — A5 110
Red Oak, Ok., U.S. — C6 113
Red Oak, Tx., U.S. — n10 120
Red Oak Mill, N.Y., U.S. — *D7 109
Red Oaks, La., U.S. — h9 95
Redon, Fr. — D2 16
Redonda Islands, is., B.C. — D5 69
Redondela, Spain — A1 22
Redondo, Port. — C2 22
Redondo, Wa., U.S. — f11 124
Redondo Beach, Ca., U.S. — n12 82
Redoubt Volcano, vol., Ak., U.S. — g15 79
Redowl, S.D., U.S. — C3 118
Red Pass, B.C. — C8 69
Red Peak, mtn., Co., U.S. — B4 83
Red Pheasant, Sask. — E1 75
Red Rapids, N.B. — B2 71
Red River, N.M., U.S. — A4 108
Red River, co., La., U.S. — B2 95
Red River, co., Tx., U.S. — C5 120
Red Rock, B.C. — C6 69
Red Rock, Az., U.S. — E4 80
Redrock, N.M., U.S. — E1 108
Red Rock, Ok., U.S. — A4 113
Red Rock, stm., Mt., U.S. — F4 103
Red Rock, Lake, res., Ia., U.S. — C4 92
Redruth, Eng., U.K. — E2 12
Red Scaffold, S.D., U.S. — C4 118
Red Sea — C3 38
Red Shirt, S.D., U.S. — D3 118
Red Springs, N.C., U.S. — C3 110
Redstone, B.C. — C6 69
Redstone, Mt., U.S. — B12 103
Redstone, N.H., U.S. — B4 106
Red Sucker, stm., Man. — B5 70
Red Sucker Lake, l., Man. — B5 70
Red Table Mountain, mts., Co., U.S. — B4 83
Redvale, Co., U.S. — C2 83
Redvers, Sask. — H5 75
Redwater, Alta. — C4 68
Redwater, Mt., U.S. — C11 103
Red Willow, Alta. — C4 68
Red Willow, co., Ne., U.S. — D5 104
Red Willow, stm., Can. — B7 69
Red Willow Creek, stm., Ne., U.S. — D5 104
Redwine, Ky., U.S. — B6 94
Red Wing, Co., U.S. — D5 83
Red Wing, Mn., U.S. — F6 100
Redwood, Ms., U.S. — C3 101
Redwood, N.Y., U.S. — A5 109
Redwood, co., Mn., U.S. — F3 100
Redwood City, Ca., U.S. — D2 82
Redwood Falls, Mn., U.S. — F3 100
Redwood National Park, Ca., U.S. — B2 82

Redwood Valley, Ca., U.S. — C2 82
Red see Yuan Jiang, stm., Asia — G5 36
Ree, Lough, l., Ire. — D2 10
Reece, Ks., U.S. — E7 93
Reece City, Al., U.S. — A3 78
Reed, Ok., U.S. — C2 113
Reed City, Mi., U.S. — E5 99
Reeder, N.D., U.S. — C3 111
Reed Lake, l., Man. — B1 70
Reed Lake, l., Sask. — G2 75
Reedley, Ca., U.S. — D4 82
Reedpoint, Mt., U.S. — E7 103
Reeds Beach, N.J., U.S. — E3 107
Reedsburg, Wi., U.S. — E3 126
Reeds Peak, mtn., N.M., U.S. — D2 108
Reedsport, Or., U.S. — D2 114
Reeds Spring, Mo., U.S. — E4 102
Reedsville, Oh., U.S. — C4 112
Reedsville, Pa., U.S. — E6 115
Reedsville, W.V., U.S. — B5 125
Reedsville, Wi., U.S. — D6 126
Reedurban, Oh., U.S. — *B4 112
Reedville, Va., U.S. — C6 123
Reedy, W.V., U.S. — C3 125
Reedy, stm., S.C., U.S. — C3 117
Reedy Lake, l., Fl., U.S. — E5 86
Reefton, N.Z. — O13 51
Ree Heights, S.D., U.S. — C6 118
Reelfoot Lake, l., Tn., U.S. — A2 119
Reelsville, In., U.S. — E4 91
Reere Island, i., Marsh Is. — P18 52
Reese, Mi., U.S. — E7 99
Reese, stm., Nv., U.S. — C4 105
Reese Air Force Base, mil., Tx., U.S. — C1 120
Reese Station, Oh., U.S. — m11 112
Reeseville, Wi., U.S. — E5 126
Reesville, Oh., U.S. — C2 112
Reeth, Eng., U.K. — F7 13
Reeves, La., U.S. — D2 95
Reeves, co., Tx., U.S. — o13 120
Reeveston, Il., U.S. — F5 90
Reevesville, S.C., U.S. — E6 117
Refresco, Chile — E2 55
Reftele, Swe. — A7 15
Refuge Cove, B.C. — D5 69
Refugio, Tx., U.S. — E4 120
Refugio, co., Tx., U.S. — E4 120
Rega, stm., Pol. — B3 26
Regan, N.D., U.S. — B5 111
Regen, Ger. — E8 19
Regen, stm., Ger. — D6 18
Regensburg, Ger. — D6 18
Regent, Man. — E1 70
Regent, N.D., U.S. — C3 111
Regente, Mo., U.S. — A4 102
Reggane, Alg. — D5 44
Reggio di Calabria, Italy — E5 23
Reggio nell'Emilia, Italy — E3 23
Regina, Sask. — G3 75
Régina, Fr. Gu. — B4 59
Regina, Mt., U.S. — C9 103
Regina, N.M., U.S. — A2 108
Regina Beach, Sask. — G3 75
Register, Ga., U.S. — D5 87
Regna, Swe. — u33 14
Regnitz, stm., Ger. — D5 19
Reguengos de Monsaraz, Port. — C2 22
Rehawa (part of Jerusalem), Isr. — m14 41
Rehna, Ger. — E5 15
Rehoboth, Nmb. — B2 49
Rehoboth, Ma., U.S. — C5 98
Rehoboth, N.M., U.S. — B1 108
Rehoboth Beach, De., U.S. — F5 85
Rehoboth Bay, b., De., U.S. — F5 85
Rehovot, Isr. — C6 41
Reichenbach, Ger. — C6 18
Reichenbach, Ger. — A4 20
Reid, Mount, mtn., Ak., U.S. — n24 79
Reid Lake, res., Sask. — G1 75
Reidland, Ky., U.S. — e9 94
Reids Grove, Md., U.S. — C6 97
Reidsville, Ga., U.S. — D4 87
Reidsville, N.C., U.S. — A3 110
Reidville, S.C., U.S. — B3 117
Reigate, Eng., U.K. — E6 10
Reinbeck, Ia., U.S. — B5 92
Reindeer, stm., Sask. — C3 75
Reindeer Island, i., Man. — C3 70
Reindeer Lake, l., Can. — m8 75
Reinersville, Oh., U.S. — C4 112
Reinfeld, Ger. — E4 15
Reinosa, Spain — A3 22
Reinosa see Reynosa, Mex. — B5 63
Reisterstown, Md., U.S. — B4 97
Reit im Winkl, Ger. — B8 20
Reitz, S. Afr. — C4 49
Reivaara, Swe. — t34 14
Reliance, De., U.S. — F3 85
Reliance, S.D., U.S. — D6 118
Reliance, Tn., U.S. — D9 119
Reliance, Wy., U.S. — E3 127
Remada, Tun. — C7 44
Remanso, Braz. — B2 57
Remanso, Braz. — C2 57
Rembertów (part of Warsaw), Pol. — k14 26
Rembrandt, Ia., U.S. — B2 92
Remecó, Arg. — B4 54
Remedios, Cuba — C4 64
Remedios, Pan. — F7 62
Remer, Mn., U.S. — C5 100
Remington, In., U.S. — C3 91
Remington, Va., U.S. — B5 123
Rémire, Fr. Gu. — B4 59
Remiremont, Fr. — C7 16
Remlap, Al., U.S. — B3 78
Remmel Dam, Ar., U.S. — g8 81
Remscheid, Ger. — C3 18
Remsen, Ia., U.S. — B2 92
Remsen, N.Y., U.S. — B5 109
Remus, Mi., U.S. — E5 99
Rena Lara, Ms., U.S. — A3 101
Renault, Il., U.S. — E4 90
Renco, Ks., U.S. — k15 93
Rencontre East, Newf. — E4 72
Rend Lake, res., Il., U.S. — E5 90
Rendsburg, Ger. — A4 18
Rendville, Oh., U.S. — C3 112
Renedo, Spain — A4 22

Renens, Switz. — C2 21
Renews [-Cappahayden], Newf. — E5 72
Renforth, N.B. — D4 71
Renfrew, Ont. — B8 73
Renfrew, S.C., U.S. — B3 117
Renfrew, co., Ont. — B7 73
Renfrow, Ok., U.S. — A4 113
Rengo, Chile — A2 54
Reni, Sov. Un. — C9 24
Renick, Mo., U.S. — B5 102
Renick, W.V., U.S. — D4 125
Renish Point, c., Scot., U.K. — C2 13
Renmark, Austl. — F7 50
Renner, S.D., U.S. — D9 118
Rennerod, Ger. — C3 19
Rennert, N.C., U.S. — C3 110
Rennes, Fr. — C3 16
Rennick Bay, b., Ant. — C29 7
Rennick Glacier, ice, Ant. — B29 7
Rennie, Man. — E4 70
Reno, Nv., U.S. — D2 105
Reno, co., Ks., U.S. — E5 93
Reno, stm., Italy — E5 23
Reno, Lake, l., Mn., U.S. — E3 100
Reno, Mt., mtn., Wy., U.S. — D6 127
Renous, N.B. — C4 71
Renovo, Pa., U.S. — D6 115
Renown, Sask. — F3 75
Renshou, China — E5 31
Rensselaer, In., U.S. — C3 91
Rensselaer, N.Y., U.S. — C7 109
Rensselaer, co., N.Y., U.S. — C7 109
Rensselaer Falls, N.Y., U.S. — f9 109
Rensselaerville, N.Y., U.S. — C6 109
Rentiesville, Ok., U.S. — B6 113
Renton, Wa., U.S. — B3 124
Rentz, Ga., U.S. — D4 87
Renville, Mn., U.S. — F4 100
Renville, co., Mn., U.S. — F4 100
Renville, co., N.D., U.S. — A4 111
Renwick, Ia., U.S. — B4 92
Repentigny, Que. — D4 74
Repton, Al., U.S. — D2 78
Republic, Ks., U.S. — C6 93
Republic, Mi., U.S. — B3 99
Republic, Mo., U.S. — D4 102
Republic, Oh., U.S. — A2 112
Republic, Pa., U.S. — G2 115
Republic, Wa., U.S. — A7 124
Republic, co., Ks., U.S. — C6 93
Republican, stm., U.S. — C6 93
Republican, North Fork, stm., U.S. — A8 83
Republican, South Fork, stm., U.S. — E4 104
Republican City, Ne., U.S. — D6 104
Repulse Bay, N.W. Ter. — C15 66
Repulse Bay, b., Austl. — D8 50
Requena, Spain — C5 22
Reşadiye, Tur. — B11 40
Resang, Cape, c., Malay. — E2 34
Rescue, Va., U.S. — k14 123
Reserve, Sask. — E4 75
Reserve, Ks., U.S. — C8 93
Reserve, La., U.S. — h10 95
Reserve, Mt., U.S. — B12 103
Reserve, N.M., U.S. — D1 108
Reservoir Pond, l., Ma., U.S. — h11 98
Reshel, Isr. — g10 41
Resistencia, Arg. — E5 55
Reşiţa, Rom. — C5 24
Resko, Pol. — B3 26
Resolute, N.W. Ter. — n32 66
Resolution Island, i., N.W. Ter. — D20 66
Resplendor, Braz. — B4 56
Resthaven Mountain, mtn., Alta. — C1 68
Restigouche, co., N.B. — B2 71
Restigouche, stm., Can. — B2 71
Restinga, Punta, c., Pan. — G7 62
Reston, Man. — E1 70
Reston, Va., U.S. — B5 123
Resülhınzır, c., Tur. — D10 40
Reszel, Pol. — a6 26
Retalhuleu, Guat. — E6 63
Retamito, Arg. — A3 54
Rethel, Fr. — C6 16
Réthimnon, Grc. — E5 40
Retie, Bel. — C5 17
Retlaw, Alta. — D4 68
Retsof, N.Y., U.S. — C3 109
Reubens, Id., U.S. — *C2 89
Reuland, Bel. — D6 17
Réunion, dep., Afr. — H24 2
Reus, Spain — B6 22
Reuss, stm., Switz. — B5 21
Reuterstadt Stavenhagen, Ger. — E6 15
Reutlingen, Ger. — D4 18
Reutte, Aus. — E5 18
Reva, S.D., U.S. — B2 118
Revda, Sov. Un. — B5 28
Revel, Fr. — F5 16
Revelo, Ky., U.S. — D5 94
Revelstoke, B.C. — D8 69
Revelstoke, Lake, res., B.C. — D8 69
Reventazón, Peru — E1 58
Revere, Ma., U.S. — g11 98
Revere, Mo., U.S. — A6 102
Reverie, Tn., U.S. — B2 119
Revigny [-sur-Ornain], Fr. — D2 63
Revillagigedo, Islas, is., Mex. — B9 118
Revillagigedo Island, i., Ak., U.S. — n24 79
Revin, Fr. — B5 16
Revillo, S.D., U.S. — B9 118
Revloc, Pa., U.S. — C6 16
Rew, India — o17 26
Rewa, India — D7 37
Rewári, India — F6 36
Rewey, Wi., U.S. — F3 126
Rex, Ga., U.S. — h8 87
Rex, Mount, mtn., Ant. — B5 7
Rexburg, Id., U.S. — F7 89
Rexford, Ks., U.S. — C3 93
Rexford, Mt., U.S. — B1 103
Rexham, Mt., U.S. — h13 94
Rexton, N.B. — C5 71
Rey, Ga., U.S. — D2 87
Rey Bouba, Cam. — D2 96
Reydell, Ar., U.S. — C4 81
Reydon, Ok., U.S. — B2 113
Reyes, Point, c., Ca., U.S. — C2 82
Reykjavík, Ice. — n22 14
Reyno, Ar., U.S. — A5 81
Reynolds, Ga., U.S. — D2 87

Reynolds, Il., U.S. — B3 90
Reynolds, In., U.S. — C4 91
Reynolds, Mo., U.S. — D6 102
Reynolds, Ne., U.S. — D8 104
Reynolds, N.D., U.S. — B8 111
Reynolds, co., Mo., U.S. — D6 102
Reynoldsburg, Oh., U.S. — C3 112
Reynoldsville, Pa., U.S. — D4 115
Reynosa (Reinosa), Mex. — B5 63
Rezā'īyeh see Orūmīyeh, Iran — B4 38
Rezé, Fr. — D3 16
Rēzekne, Sov. Un. — C6 27
Rezezny, Sov. Un. — B9 24
Rhaetian Alps, mts., Eur. — A3 23
Rhame, N.D., U.S. — C2 111
Rhea, co., Tn., U.S. — D9 119
Rhea, stm., U.S. — D9 119
Rheda-Wiedenbrück, Ger. — B3 19
Rheden, Neth. — A7 16
Rhein, Sask. — F4 75
Rheine, Ger. — B3 19
Rheinfelden, Switz. — A4 21
Rheinhausen, Ger. — C3 18
Rheinland, hist. reg., Ger. — C3 18
Rheinland-Pfalz, state, Ger. — C2 18
Rheinsberg, Ger. — E6 15
Rheinwaldhorn, mtn., Switz. — C5 20
Rhenen, Neth. — C5 17
Rheydt, Ger. — C6 17
Rhinau, Fr. — A3 20
Rhin Canal, Ger. — F6 15
Rhine, Ga., U.S. — E3 87
Rhine, stm., Eur. — C3 18
Rhinebeck, N.Y., U.S. — D7 109
Rhineland, Mo., U.S. — C6 102
Rhinelander, Wi., U.S. — C4 126
Rhinow, Ger. — F6 15
Rhir, Cap, c., Mor. — C3 44
Rhode Island, state, U.S. — D3 116
Rhode Island, i., R.I., U.S. — E5 116
Rhode Island Sound, strt., U.S. — F5 116
Rhodell, W.V., U.S. — D3 125
Rhodes, Ia., U.S. — C4 92
Rhodes, Mi., U.S. — E6 99
Rhodes see Ródhos, i., Grc. — D7 40
Rhodesia see Zimbabwe, ctry., Afr. — A5 49
Rhodes Peak, mtn., Id., U.S. — C4 89
Rhodes Point, Md., U.S. — E5 97
Rhodhiss, N.C., U.S. — B1 110
Rhodope Mountains, mts., Eur. — E7 24
Rhome, Tx., U.S. — m9 120
Rhondda, Wales, U.K. — E5 10
Rhône, stm., Eur. — B1 20
Rhône au Rhin, Canal du, Fr. — A3 20
Rhum, i., Scot., U.K. — B3 10
Rhum, Sound of, strt., Scot., U.K. — B3 10
Rhyl, Wales, U.K. — D5 10
Rhymney, Wales, U.K. — C4 12
Riachão de Santana, Braz. — A4 56
Rialma, Braz. — C5 57
Rialto, Ca., U.S. — m14 82
Rianjo, Spain — A1 22
Riau Islands, is., Indon. — E2 34
Riaza, Spain — A1 22
Ribadavia, Spain — A1 22
Ribadeo, Spain — A2 22
Ribadesella, Spain — A3 22
Ribas do Rio Pardo, Braz. — D6 48
Ribauê, Moz. — D6 48
Ribble, stm., Eng., U.K. — G6 13
Ribe, Den. — C2 15
Ribe, co., Den. — C2 15
Ribeauvillé, Fr. — C7 16
Ribeira, stm., Braz. — C3 56
Ribeira, Italy — F4 23
Ribeira do Pombal, Braz. — D3 57
Ribeirão Bonito, Braz. — m7 56
Ribeirão Branco, Braz. — C3 56
Ribeirão Preto, Braz. — C3 56
Ribera, Italy — F4 23
Ribera, N.M., U.S. — B4 108
Ribérac, Fr. — E4 16
Riberalta, Bol. — B2 55
Rib Lake, Wi., U.S. — C3 126
Ribnitz-Damgarten, Ger. — D6 15
Ribstone, Alta. — C5 68
Ribstone Creek, stm., Alta. — C5 68
Říčany, Czech. — o18 26
Riccione, Italy — B4 23
Rice, Tx., U.S. — C4 120
Rice, Va., U.S. — C4 123
Rice, co., Ks., U.S. — D5 93
Rice, co., Mn., U.S. — F5 100
Riceboro, Ga., U.S. — E5 87
Rice Creek, stm., Mn., U.S. — m12 100
Rice Lake, Wi., U.S. — C2 126
Rice Lake, l., Ont. — C6 73
Rice Lake, l., Mn., U.S. — D5 100
Rices Landing, Pa., U.S. — G1 115
Riceton, Sask. — G3 75
Riceville, Ia., U.S. — A5 92
Riceville, Tn., U.S. — D9 119
Rich, Mor. — B5 44
Rich, co., Ut., U.S. — B4 121
Rich, Cape, c., Ont. — C4 73
Richard, Sask. — E2 75
Richard City, Tn., U.S. — D8 119
Richards, Mo., U.S. — D3 102
Richards, Tx., U.S. — D5 120
Richards-Gebaur Air Force Base, mil., Mo., U.S. — C3 102
Richard's Harbour, Newf. — E3 72
Richardson, Sask. — G3 75
Richardson, Tx., U.S. — n10 120
Richardson, co., Ne., U.S. — D10 104
Richardson Lakes, l., Me. — D2 96
Richardson Mountains, mts., Can. — C5 66
Richardson Park, De., U.S. — *B3 85
Richardson Spur, Ok., U.S. — C3 113
Richardton, N.D., U.S. — C3 111
Richboro, Pa., U.S. — *F11 115
Richburg, N.Y., U.S. — C2 109
Richburg, S.C., U.S. — B5 117
Richdale, Alta. — D5 68
Riche, Pointe, c., Newf. — C3 72
Richelieu, co., Que. — D4 74
Richer, Man. — E3 70
Richey, Mt., U.S. — C11 103
Richfield, Id., U.S. — F4 89
Richfield, Ks., U.S. — E2 93
Richfield, Mn., U.S. — n12 100
Richfield, N.C., U.S. — B2 110
Richfield, Oh., U.S. — A4 112
Richfield, Pa., U.S. — E7 115
Richfield, Ut., U.S. — E3 121
Richfield, Wi., U.S. — m11 126
Richfield Springs, N.Y., U.S. — C5 109

Richford, N.Y., U.S. — C4 109
Richford, Vt., U.S. — B3 122
Rich Fountain, Mo., U.S. — C6 102
Rich Hill, Mo., U.S. — C3 102
Richibucto, N.B. — C5 71
Rich Lake, Alta. — B5 68
Richland, Ga., U.S. — D2 87
Richland, Ia., U.S. — C6 92
Richland, In., U.S. — I3 91
Richland, Mi., U.S. — F5 99
Richland, Mo., U.S. — D5 102
Richland, Mt., U.S. — B10 103
Richland, Ne., U.S. — C8 104
Richland, N.J., U.S. — E3 107
Richland, N.Y., U.S. — B4 109
Richland, Or., U.S. — C9 114
Richland, Wa., U.S. — C6 124
Richland, co., Il., U.S. — E5 90
Richland, co., La., U.S. — B4 95
Richland, co., Mt., U.S. — C12 103
Richland, co., N.D., U.S. — C8 111
Richland, co., Oh., U.S. — B3 112
Richland, co., S.C., U.S. — D6 117
Richland, co., Wi., U.S. — E3 126
Richland Balsam, mtn., N.C., U.S. — f10 110
Richland Center, Wi., U.S. — E3 126
Richland Creek, stm., Tn., U.S. — B5 119
Richland Hills, Tx., U.S. — *C4 120
Richlands, N.C., U.S. — C5 110
Richlands, Va., U.S. — e10 123
Richland Springs, Tx., U.S. — D3 120
Richlandtown, Pa., U.S. — F11 115
Richlea, Sask. — F1 75
Richmond, Austl. — D7 50
Richmond, B.C. — E6 69
Richmond, Ont. — B9 73
Richmond, P.E.I. — C6 71
Richmond, Que. — D5 74
Richmond, N.Z. — N14 51
Richmond, S. Afr. — C5 49
Richmond, S. Afr. — D3 49
Richmond (part of London), Eng., U.K. — C7 12
Richmond, Ca., U.S. — D2 82
Richmond, Il., U.S. — A5 90
Richmond, In., U.S. — E8 91
Richmond, Ks., U.S. — D8 93
Richmond, Ky., U.S. — C5 94
Richmond, Me., U.S. — D3 96
Richmond, Mi., U.S. — F8 99
Richmond, Mo., U.S. — B4 102
Richmond, N.H., U.S. — E2 106
Richmond, Tn., U.S. — B5 119
Richmond, Tx., U.S. — E5 120
Richmond, Ut., U.S. — B4 121
Richmond, Va., U.S. — C5 123
Richmond, co., N.S. — D9 71
Richmond, co., Ga., U.S. — C4 87
Richmond, co., N.Y., U.S. — E6 109
Richmond, co., N.C., U.S. — B3 110
Richmond, co., Va., U.S. — C6 123
Richmond Beach, Wa., U.S. — B3 124
Richmond Dale, Oh., U.S. — C3 112
Richmond Heights, Fl., U.S. — s13 86
Richmond Heights, Mo., U.S. — f13 102
Richmond Heights, Oh., U.S. — *g9 112
Richmond Highlands, Wa., U.S. — B3 124
Richmond Hill, Ont. — D5 73
Richmond Hill, Ga., U.S. — E5 87
Richmond National Battlefield Park, Va., U.S. — n18 123
Richmond Park, Eng., U.K. — m12 10
Richmondville, N.Y., U.S. — C6 109
Richmound, Sask. — G1 75
Rich Mountain, mtn., U.S. — C1 81
Rich Mountain, mtn., U.S. — C1 113
Rich Mountain, mtn., W.V., U.S. — C5 125
Rich Square, N.C., U.S. — A5 110
Richthofen, Mount, mtn., Co., U.S. — A5 83
Richton, Ms., U.S. — D5 101
Richton Park, Il., U.S. — *m9 90
Richvalley, In., U.S. — C6 91
Richview, Il., U.S. — E4 90
Richville, Mn., U.S. — D3 100
Richville, N.Y., U.S. — f9 109
Richwood, Ky., U.S. — k13 94
Richwood, Oh., U.S. — B2 112
Richwood, W.V., U.S. — C4 125
Richwoods, Mo., U.S. — C7 102
Rickenbacker Air Force Base, mil., Oh., U.S. — m11 112
Ricketts, Ia., U.S. — B2 92
Rickman, Tn., U.S. — C8 119
Rickmansworth, Eng., U.K. — k12 10
Rickreall, Or., U.S. — C3 114
Rico, Co., U.S. — D2 83
Riddle, Id., U.S. — G3 89
Riddle, N.C., U.S. — A6 110
Riddle, Or., U.S. — E3 114
Riddle Mountain, mtn., Or., U.S. — D8 114
Riddlesburg, Pa., U.S. — F5 115
Rideau, stm., Ont. — B9 73
Riderwood, Al., U.S. — C1 78
Ridge, N.Y., U.S. — *n16 109
Ridgecrest, Ca., U.S. — E5 82
Ridgecrest, N.C., U.S. — f10 110
Ridgecrest, Wa., U.S. — *B3 124
Ridgedale, Sask. — E3 75
Ridgedale, Mo., U.S. — E4 102
Ridge Farm, Il., U.S. — D6 90
Ridgefield, Ct., U.S. — D2 84
Ridgefield, N.J., U.S. — h8 107
Ridgefield, Wa., U.S. — D3 124
Ridgefield Park, N.J., U.S. — h8 107
Ridgeland, Ms., U.S. — C3 101
Ridgeland, S.C., U.S. — G6 117
Ridgeland, Wi., U.S. — C2 126
Ridgely, Md., U.S. — C6 97
Ridgely, Tn., U.S. — A2 119
Ridgeside, Tn., U.S. — h11 119
Ridge Spring, S.C., U.S. — D4 117
Ridgetop, Tn., U.S. — A5 119
Ridgetown, Ont. — E3 73
Ridgeview, S.D., U.S. — B5 118
Ridgeville, Ont. — D5 73
Ridgeville, In., U.S. — D7 91
Ridgeville, S.C., U.S. — E7 117

Name	Map Ref.	Page
Ridgeville Corners, Oh., U.S.	A1	112
Ridgeway, Ia., U.S.	A6	92
Ridgeway, Mi., U.S.	F7	99
Ridgeway, Mo., U.S.	A4	102
Ridgeway, N.J., U.S.	C4	107
Ridgeway, Oh., U.S.	B2	112
Ridgeway, S.C., U.S.	C6	117
Ridgeway, Va., U.S.	D3	123
Ridgeway, Wi., U.S.	E4	126
Ridgewood, N.J., U.S.	A4	107
Ridgewood Park, Ct., U.S.	D7	84
Ridgway, Co., U.S.	C3	83
Ridgway, Il., U.S.	F5	90
Ridgway, Pa., U.S.	C3	115
Riding Mountain, hills, Man.	D1	70
Riding Mountain National Park, Man.	D1	70
Ridley Park, Pa., U.S.	p20	115
Ridley Township, Pa., U.S.	*G11	115
Ridott, Il., U.S.	A4	90
Ried [im Innkreis], Aus.	D6	18
Riehen, Switz.	A4	21
Rienza, stm., Italy	C7	20
Rienzi, Ms., U.S.	A5	101
Riesa, Ger.	C6	18
Riesco, Isla, i., Chile	h11	54
Riesel, Tx., U.S.	D4	120
Rieth, Or., U.S.	B8	114
Rieti, Italy	C4	23
Riffe Lake, res., Wa., U.S.	C3	124
Rifle, Co., U.S.	B3	83
Rifle, stm., Mi., U.S.	D6	99
Rift Valley, prov., Kenya	A6	48
Rift Valley, val., Afr.	*F9	42
Riga, Sov. Un.	D5	29
Riga, Gulf of b., Sov. Un.	C4	27
Rīgān, Iran	C5	38
Rīgān, Iran	G9	39
Rigaud, Que.	D3	74
Rigby, Id., U.S.	F7	89
Rigestān, reg., Afg.	B4	36
Riggins, Id., U.S.	D2	89
Riggisberg, Switz.	C3	21
Rigi, mtn., Switz.	B4	20
Rigili, i., Marsh Is.	S18	52
Rigney, Fr.	B1	21
Rigo, Pap. N. Gui.	k12	50
Rigolet, Newf.	A2	72
Riihimäki, Fin.	G11	14
Riiser-Larsen Peninsula, pen., Ant.	C16	7
Rijeka (Fiume), Yugo.	C2	24
Rijssen, Neth.	B6	17
Riley, In., U.S.	F3	91
Riley, Ks., U.S.	C7	93
Riley, Ky., U.S.	C4	94
Riley, Or., U.S.	D7	114
Riley, co., Ks., U.S.	C7	93
Riley, Mount, mtn., N.M., U.S.	F2	108
Rillito, Az., U.S.	E4	80
Rilly-la-Montagne, Fr.	E4	17
Rímac, Peru	*D2	58
Rimavská Sobota, Czech.	D6	26
Rimbey, Alta.	C3	68
Rimbo, Swe.	t36	14
Rimella, Italy	E5	21
Rimersburg, Pa., U.S.	D3	115
Rimini, Italy	B4	23
Rîmnicu-Sărat, Rom.	C8	24
Rîmnicu-Vîlcea, Rom.	C7	24
Rimouski, Que.	A9	74
Rimouski, co., Que.	A9	74
Rimouski, stm., Que.	A9	74
Rimouski-Est, Que.	A9	74
Rimrock, Az., U.S.	C4	80
Rimrock Lake, res., Wa., U.S.	C4	124
Rinard, Il., U.S.	E5	90
Rinard, Ia., U.S.	B3	92
Rincon, Ga., U.S.	D5	87
Rincon, N.M., U.S.	E2	108
Rincón, Bahía de, b., P.R.	C3	65
Rinconada, Arg.	D2	55
Rincon del Bonete, Lago Artificial de, res., Ur.	E8	102
Rincón de Romos, Mex.	k12	63
Rincon Mountains, mts., Az., U.S.	E5	80
Rindge, N.H., U.S.	E2	106
Riner, Va., U.S.	C2	123
Rineyville, Ky., U.S.	C4	94
Rīngas, India	D5	37
Ringe, Den.	C4	15
Ringelheim, Ger.	A5	19
Ringel Spitze, mtn., Switz.	C7	21
Ringerike, Nor.	*G4	14
Ringgold, Ga., U.S.	B1	87
Ringgold, La., U.S.	B2	95
Ringgold, Md., U.S.	A2	97
Ringgold, Ne., U.S.	C5	104
Ringgold, Tx., U.S.	C4	120
Ringgold, Va., U.S.	D3	123
Ringgold, co., Ia., U.S.	D3	92
Ringgold Isles, is., Fiji	H16	52
Ringim, Nig.	D6	45
Ringkøbing, Den.	I3	14
Ringkøbing, co., Den.	B2	15
Ringkøbing Fjord, Den.	B2	15
Ringling, Mt., U.S.	D6	103
Ringling, Ok., U.S.	C4	113
Ringoes, N.J., U.S.	C3	107
Ringold, Ok., U.S.	C6	113
Ringos Mills, Ky., U.S.	B6	94
Ringsaker, Nor.	G4	14
Ringsjön, l., Swe.	C7	15
Ringsön, i., Swe.	u35	14
Ringsted, Den.	A3	92
Ringsted, Ia., U.S.	C8	14
Ringvassøya, i., Nor.	B11	14
Ringville, Me.	E4	11
Ringwood, N.J., U.S.	A4	107
Ringwood, Ok., U.S.	A3	113
Riñihue, Chile	B2	54
Rinjani, mtn., Indon.	G5	34
Rinnes, Ben, mtn., Scot., U.K.	C5	13
Rinns Point, c., Scot., U.K.	E2	13
Rinteln, Ger.	A4	19
Rio, Fl., U.S.	E6	86
Rio, Il., U.S.	B3	90
Rio, W.V., U.S.	B6	125
Rio, Wi., U.S.	E4	126
Rio Arriba, co., N.M., U.S.	A2	108
Riobamba, Ec.	B2	58
Río Benito, Eq. Gui.	E1	46
Rio Blanco, co., Co., U.S.	B2	83
Rio Branco, Braz.	E2	56
Rio Branco do Sul, Braz.	D3	56
Rio Brilhante, Braz.	C2	54
Rio Bueno, Chile	D2	54
Rio Caribe, Ven.	A5	60
Rio Chico, Ven.	A4	60
Rio Claro, Braz.	A4	56
Rio Claro, Trin.	O23	65
Rio Colorado, Arg.	B4	54
Rio Cuarto, Arg.	A4	54
Rio de Janeiro, Braz.	C4	56
Rio de Janeiro, state, Braz.	C4	56
Rio de Jesús, Pan.	G7	62
Rio Dell, Ca., U.S.	B1	82
Rio Del Mar, Ca., U.S.	*D3	82
Rio de Oro, Col.	B3	60
Rio do Prado, Braz.	B4	56
Rio do Sul, Braz.	D3	56
Rio Gallegos, Arg.	E3	54
Rio Grande, Arg.	h12	54
Rio Grande, Braz.	E2	56
Rio Grande, Mex.	C4	63
Rio Grande, N.J., U.S.	E3	107
Rio Grande, Oh., U.S.	D3	112
Rio Grande, co., Co., U.S.	D4	83
Rio Grande City, Tx., U.S.	F3	120
Rio Grande do Norte, state, Braz.	C3	57
Rio Grande do Sul, state, Braz.	D2	56
Rio Grande Reservoir, res., Co., U.S.	D3	83
Ríohacha, Col.	A3	60
Rio Hato, Pan.	F7	62
Rio Hondo, Mex.	h9	63
Rio Hondo, Tx., U.S.	F4	120
Rioja, Peru	C2	58
Riolândia, Braz.	B3	56
Rio Linda, Ca., U.S.	*C3	82
Rio Maior, Port.	C1	22
Rio Mayo, Arg.	D2	54
Rio Mulatos, Bol.	C2	55
Rio Muni, prov., Eq. Gui.	C5	117
Rio Negro, Braz.	D3	56
Río Negro, prov., Arg.	C3	54
Rionero in Vulture, Italy	D5	23
Rio Pardo, Braz.	D2	56
Rio Pardo de Minas, Braz.	B4	56
Rio Pomba, Braz.	g6	56
Rio Preto da Eva, Braz.	C3	59
Rio Primero, Arg.	A4	54
Rio Rancho, N.M., U.S.	B3	108
Riosucio, Col.	B2	60
Riosucio, Col.	B2	60
Rio Tercero, Arg.	A4	54
Rio Tinto, Sierra, mtn., Hond.	C5	62
Rio Verde, Braz.	B2	56
Rioverde, Mex.	m13	63
Rio Verde de Mato Grosso, Braz.	B2	56
Rio Vermelho, Braz.	B4	56
Rio Vista, Ca., U.S.	C3	82
Rioz, Fr.	B1	21
Ripley, Ont.	C3	73
Ripley, Eng., U.K.	A6	12
Ripley, Ca., U.S.	F6	82
Ripley, Il., U.S.	C3	90
Ripley, Me., U.S.	D3	96
Ripley, Ms., U.S.	A5	101
Ripley, N.Y., U.S.	C1	109
Ripley, Oh., U.S.	D2	112
Ripley, Ok., U.S.	A5	113
Ripley, Tn., U.S.	B2	119
Ripley, W.V., U.S.	C3	125
Ripley, co., In., U.S.	F7	91
Ripley, co., Mo., U.S.	E7	102
Riplinger, Wi., U.S.	D3	126
Ripogenus Pond, l., Me., U.S.	C3	96
Ripoll, Spain	A7	22
Ripon, Que.	D2	74
Ripon, Eng., U.K.	C6	10
Ripon, Wi., U.S.	E5	126
Rippey, Ia., U.S.	C3	92
Ripples, N.B.	D3	71
Rippowam, stm., Ct., U.S.	E1	84
Ripton, Vt., U.S.	D2	122
Risco, Mo., U.S.	E8	102
Rishiri Island, i., Japan	D10	33
Rishon LeẔiyyon, Isr.	D6	41
Rising City, Ne., U.S.	C8	104
Rising Star, Tx., U.S.	C3	120
Rising Sun, De., U.S.	D3	85
Rising Sun, In., U.S.	G8	91
Risingsun, Ia., U.S.	e9	92
Risingsun, Md., U.S.	A5	97
Risingsun, Oh., U.S.	A2	112
Risle, stm., Fr.	C4	16
Rison, Ar., U.S.	D3	81
Rison, Md., U.S.	C3	97
Risör, Nor.	H3	14
Ritchey, Mo., U.S.	E3	102
Ritchie, co., W.V., U.S.	B3	125
Ritidian Point, c., Guam	L10	52
Ritscher Upland, plat., Ant.	B12	7
Ritter, Or., U.S.	C7	114
Ritter, Mount, mtn., Ca., U.S.	D4	82
Rittman, Oh., U.S.	B4	112
Ritzville, Wa., U.S.	B7	124
Riva [del Garda], Italy	B3	23
Rivanna, stm., Va., U.S.	C4	123
Rivas, In., U.S.	C8	91
Rivas, Nic.	E7	63
Rive-de-Gier, Fr.	E6	16
Rivera, Arg.	B4	54
Rivera, Ur.	E1	56
Riverbank, Ca., U.S.	D3	82
River Bourgeois, N.S.	D9	71
River Cess, Lib.	E3	45
Riverdale, Ca., U.S.	D4	82
Riverdale, Il., U.S.	*C2	87
Riverdale, Ia., U.S.	g11	92
Riverdale, Ks., U.S.	E6	93
Riverdale, Md., U.S.	C4	97
Riverdale, N.D., U.S.	B4	104
Riverdale, N.J., U.S.	A4	107
Riverdale, Ut., U.S.	*B3	121
Riverdale, Ut., U.S.	D4	123
River Edge, N.J., U.S.	h8	107
River Falls, Il., U.S.	k9	90
River Falls, Wi., U.S.	D1	126
River Forest, Il., U.S.	k9	90
Rivergaro, Italy	E5	20
River Grove, Il., U.S.	k9	90
Riverhaven, In., U.S.	B7	91
Riverhead, N.Y., U.S.	n16	109
River Hebert, N.S.	D5	71
River Heights, Ut., U.S.	B4	121
River Hills, Wi., U.S.	m12	126
Riverhurst, Sask.	G2	75
River John, N.S.	D6	71
River Jordan, B.C.	h11	69
River Oaks, Tx., U.S.	*n9	120
River of Ponds, Newf.	C3	72
River Pines, Ma., U.S.	f10	98
Riverport, N.S.	E5	71
River Ridge, La., U.S.	k11	95
River Road, Or., U.S.	C3	114
River Rouge, Mi., U.S.	p15	99
Rivers, Man.	D1	70
Rivers, Lake of the, l., Sask.	H3	75
Riversdale, N.S.	D6	71
Riverside, Al., U.S.	B3	78
Riverside, Ca., U.S.	F5	82
Riverside, Ct., U.S.	D3	84
Riverside, Ga., U.S.	E3	87
Riverside, Il., U.S.	k9	90
Riverside, Ia., U.S.	C6	92
Riverside, Mo., U.S.	h10	102
Riverside, N.J., U.S.	C3	107
Riverside, Or., U.S.	D8	114
Riverside, Pa., U.S.	E8	115
Riverside, Ut., U.S.	B3	121
Riverside, Wa., U.S.	A6	124
Riverside, Wy., U.S.	E6	127
Riverside, co., Ca., U.S.	F5	82
Riverside-Albert, N.B.	D5	71
Riverside Reservoir, res., Co., U.S.	A6	83
River Sioux, Ia., U.S.	C1	92
Riverton, Man.	D3	70
Riverton, N.Z.	Q12	51
Riverton, Ct., U.S.	B3	84
Riverton, Il., U.S.	D4	90
Riverton, Ia., U.S.	D2	92
Riverton, Ks., U.S.	E9	93
Riverton, La., U.S.	B3	95
Riverton, Mn., U.S.	D4	100
Riverton, Ne., U.S.	D7	104
Riverton, N.J., U.S.	C3	107
Riverton, Or., U.S.	C2	121
Riverton, Ut., U.S.	C3	122
Riverton, Vt., U.S.	C2	123
Riverton, Va., U.S.	B4	123
Riverton, W.V., U.S.	C5	125
Riverton, Wy., U.S.	C4	127
Riverton Heights, Wa., U.S.	f11	124
River Vale, N.J., U.S.	h8	107
River View, Al., U.S.	C4	78
Riverview, Fl., U.S.	p11	86
Riverview, Mi., U.S.	p15	99
Rives, Mo., U.S.	E7	102
Rivesaltes, Fr.	A2	119
Rives Junction, Mi., U.S.	F5	16
Rivesville, W.V., U.S.	F6	99
Riviera, Az., U.S.	B4	125
Riviera, Tx., U.S.	B1	80
Riviera Beach, Fl., U.S.	F4	120
Riviera Beach, Md., U.S.	F6	86
Riviera Beach, Md., U.S.	B4	97
Rivière-à-Pierre, Que.	C4	107
Rivière-Bleue, Que.	B5	74
Rivière-du-Loup, Que.	B8	74
Rivière-du-Loup, co., Que.	B8	74
Rivière-Ouelle, Que.	B7	74
Rivière-Trois-Pistoles, Que.	A8	74
Rivière-Verte, N.B.	B1	71
Rivière-Verte, Que.	B8	74
Rivulet, Mt., U.S.	D2	103
Rixford, Pa., U.S.	C5	115
Rixie's, Nv., U.S.	*C5	105
Riyadh (Ar Riyāḍ), Sau. Ar.	C4	38
Rize, Tur.	B13	40
Rizhao, China	D8	31
Rizzuto, Cape, c., Italy	E6	23
Rjukan, Nor.	H3	14
Roachdale, In., U.S.	E4	91
Roads, Oh., U.S.	C3	112
Roadstown, N.J., U.S.	E2	107
Road Town, V.I., Br.	G12	64
Roan Cliffs, clf., U.S.	B1	83
Roan Creek, stm., Co., U.S.	B2	83
Roane, co., Tn., U.S.	D9	119
Roane, co., W.V., U.S.	C3	125
Roan High Knob, mtn., U.S.	C11	119
Roan Mountain, Tn., U.S.	C11	119
Roann, In., U.S.	C6	91
Roanne, Fr.	D6	16
Roanoke, Al., U.S.	B4	78
Roanoke, Il., U.S.	C4	90
Roanoke, In., U.S.	C7	91
Roanoke, La., U.S.	D3	95
Roanoke, Tx., U.S.	m9	120
Roanoke, Va., U.S.	C3	123
Roanoke, W.V., U.S.	C4	125
Roanoke, co., Va., U.S.	C2	123
Roanoke, stm., U.S.	A5	110
Roanoke Rapids, N.C., U.S.	A5	110
Roanoke Rapids Lake, res., U.S.	A5	110
Roan Plateau, plat., U.S.	B2	83
Roaring Branch, Pa., U.S.	C8	115
Roaring Fork, stm., Co., U.S.	C4	83
Roaring Spring, Pa., U.S.	F5	115
Roaring Springs, Tx., U.S.	C2	120
Roaringwater Bay, b., Ire.	F2	11
Roark, Ky., U.S.	C6	94
Roatán, Hond.	D7	63
Roba, Al., U.S.	C4	78
Robards, Ky., U.S.	C2	94
Robb, Alta.	C2	68
Robbin, Mn., U.S.	B1	100
Robbins, Il., U.S.	k9	90
Robbins, N.C., U.S.	B3	110
Robbins, Tn., U.S.	C9	119
Robbinsdale, Mn., U.S.	m12	100
Robbinston, Me., U.S.	C5	96
Robbinsville, N.C., U.S.	f9	110
Robe, stm., Ire.	D2	11
Robeline, La., U.S.	C2	95
Robersonville, N.C., U.S.	B5	110
Robert, La., U.S.	D5	95
Roberta, Ga., U.S.	D2	87
Roberta Mills, N.C., U.S.	B2	110
Robert Lee, Tx., U.S.	D2	120
Roberts, Id., U.S.	F6	89
Roberts, Il., U.S.	C5	90
Roberts, Wi., U.S.	C1	126
Roberts, co., S.D., U.S.	B8	118
Roberts, co., Tx., U.S.	B2	120
Roberts, Cape, c., Ant.	A2	7
Roberts, Point, c., Wa., U.S.	A2	124
Roberts Arm, Newf.	D4	72
Roberts Creek Mountain, mtn., Nv., U.S.	D5	105
Robertsdale, Al., U.S.	E2	78
Robertsdale, Pa., U.S.	F5	115
Robertsfield, reg., Austl.	F7	50
Robert S. Kerr Reservoir, res., Ok., U.S.	B6	113
Roberts Mountain, mtn., Ak., U.S.	C6	79
Roberts Mountain, mtn., Wy., U.S.	D3	127
Robertson, S. Afr.	D3	49
Robertson, Wy., U.S.	E2	127
Robertson, co., Ky., U.S.	B5	94
Robertson, co., Tn., U.S.	A5	119
Robertson, co., Tx., U.S.	D4	120
Robertson, Lac, l., Que.	C2	72
Robertsonville, Que.	C6	74
Roberts Peak, mtn., B.C.	F8	66
Robertsport, Lib.	E2	45
Robertstown, Ga., U.S.	B3	87
Robertsville, Ct., U.S.	B3	84
Robertsville, N.J., U.S.	*C4	107
Robertville, N.B.	B4	71
Roberval, Que.	A5	74
Robeson, co., N.C., U.S.	C3	110
Robin Hood's Bay, Eng., U.K.	F8	13
Robins, Ia., U.S.	B6	92
Robins, Oh., U.S.	C4	112
Robins Air Force Base, mil., Ga., U.S.	D3	87
Robinson, Il., U.S.	D6	90
Robinson, Ks., U.S.	C8	93
Robinson, Me., U.S.	B5	96
Robinson, N.D., U.S.	B6	111
Robinson, Pa., U.S.	F3	115
Robinson, Tx., U.S.	*n10	120
Róbinson Crusoe, Isla, i., Chile	G3	53
Robinson Fork, stm., W.V., U.S.	k9	125
Robinson Fork, stm., W.V., U.S.	m14	125
Robinson Mountain, mtn., Ar., U.S.	A1	81
Robinsons, Newf.	D2	72
Robinsonville, Ms., U.S.	A3	101
Robinvale, Austl.	F7	50
Roblin, Man.	D1	70
Roblin, stm., Man.	A5	70
Roboré, Bol.	C4	55
Robsart, Sask.	H1	75
Robson, B.C.	E9	69
Robson, Mount, mtn., B.C.	C8	69
Robstown, Tx., U.S.	F4	120
Roby, Mo., U.S.	D5	102
Roby, Tx., U.S.	C2	120
Roca, Ne., U.S.	h11	104
Roca, Cape, c., Port.	f9	22
Rocafuerte, Ec.	B1	58
Rocafuerte, Peru	B2	58
Rocca Massima, Italy	h9	23
Roccastrada, Italy	C3	23
Rocha, Ur.	E2	56
Rochdale, Eng., U.K.	D5	10
Rochdale, Ma., U.S.	B4	98
Rochechouart, Fr.	E4	16
Rochedo, Braz.	B2	56
Rochefort, Bel.	B6	16
Rochefort, Fr.	E3	16
Roche Harbor, Wa., U.S.	A2	124
Rochelle, Ga., U.S.	E3	87
Rochelle, Il., U.S.	B4	90
Rochelle, Tx., U.S.	D3	120
Rochelle Park, N.J., U.S.	h8	107
Roche-Percée, Sask.	H4	75
Rocheport, Mo., U.S.	C5	102
Rochester, Alta.	B4	68
Rochester, Eng., U.K.	E7	10
Rochester, Il., U.S.	D4	90
Rochester, In., U.S.	B5	91
Rochester, Ia., U.S.	C6	92
Rochester, Ky., U.S.	C3	94
Rochester, Ma., U.S.	C6	98
Rochester, Mi., U.S.	F7	99
Rochester, Mn., U.S.	F6	100
Rochester, N.H., U.S.	D5	106
Rochester, N.Y., U.S.	B3	109
Rochester, Oh., U.S.	A3	112
Rochester, Pa., U.S.	E1	115
Rochester, Tx., U.S.	C3	120
Rochester, Vt., U.S.	D3	122
Rochester, Wa., U.S.	C2	124
Rochester, Wi., U.S.	n11	126
Rochester Hills, Mi., U.S.	*F7	99
Rochester Mountain, mtn., Vt., U.S.	D3	122
Rochford, S.D., U.S.	C2	118
Rochfort Bridge, Alta.	C3	68
Rochfortbridge, Ire.	D4	11
Rochikarai Island, i., Marsh Is.	P18	52
Rochlitz, Ger.	B7	19
Rociada, N.M., U.S.	B4	108
Rock, Ks., U.S.	E7	93
Rock, Mi., U.S.	B3	99
Rock, co., Mn., U.S.	G2	100
Rock, co., Ne., U.S.	B6	104
Rock, co., Wi., U.S.	F4	126
Rock, stm., U.S.	A1	92
Rock, stm., Wi., U.S.	E5	126
Rockaway, N.J., U.S.	B3	107
Rockaway, Or., U.S.	B3	114
Rockaway Beach, Mo., U.S.	E4	102
Rock Bay, B.C.	D5	69
Rock Bluff, Fl., U.S.	B2	86
Rockbridge, Il., U.S.	D3	90
Rockbridge, co., Va., U.S.	C3	123
Rockcastle, co., Ky., U.S.	C5	94
Rockcastle, stm., Ky., U.S.	C5	94
Rockcliffe, Ont.	h12	73
Rock Creek, B.C.	E8	69
Rock Creek, Ks., U.S.	k14	93
Rock Creek, Mn., U.S.	E6	100
Rock Creek, Oh., U.S.	A5	112
Rock Creek, stm., N.A.	H2	75
Rock Creek, stm., Ks., U.S.	g10	93
Rock Creek, stm., Ne., U.S.	g11	104
Rock Creek, stm., Nv., U.S.	C5	105
Rock Creek, stm., Wa., U.S.	B8	124
Rock Creek, stm., Wy., U.S.	E6	127
Rock Creek Butte, mtn., Or., U.S.	C8	114
Rockdale, Austl.	*F9	50
Rockdale, Ia., U.S.	B7	92
Rockdale, Md., U.S.	B4	97
Rockdale, Tx., U.S.	D4	120
Rockdale, co., Ga., U.S.	C3	87
Rockefeller Plateau, plat., Ant.	A35	7
Rock Elm, Wi., U.S.	D1	126
Rockfall, Ct., U.S.	C5	84
Rock Falls, Il., U.S.	B4	90
Rock Falls, Ia., U.S.	A4	92
Rockfield, In., U.S.	C4	91
Rockfield, Ky., U.S.	D3	94
Rockfield, Wi., U.S.	m11	126
Rockford, Al., U.S.	C3	78
Rockford, Il., U.S.	A4	90
Rockford, Ia., U.S.	A5	92
Rockford, Mi., U.S.	E5	99
Rockford, Mn., U.S.	E5	100
Rockford, Oh., U.S.	B1	112
Rockford, Tn., U.S.	D10	119
Rockford, Wa., U.S.	B8	124
Rockglen, Sask.	H3	75
Rock Hall, Md., U.S.	B5	97
Rockham, S.D., U.S.	C7	118
Rockhampton, Austl.	D9	50
Rockhaven, Sask.	E1	75
Rock Hill, Mo., U.S.	*f13	102
Rock Hill, S.C., U.S.	B5	117
Rockhill Furnace, Pa., U.S.	F6	115
Rockholds, Ky., U.S.	D5	94
Rockingham, Ga., U.S.	E4	87
Rockingham, N.C., U.S.	C3	110
Rockingham, Vt., U.S.	E4	122
Rockingham, co., N.H., U.S.	D4	106
Rockingham, co., N.C., U.S.	A3	110
Rockingham, co., Va., U.S.	B4	123
Rock Island, Que.	D5	74
Rock Island, Il., U.S.	B3	90
Rock Island, Ok., U.S.	B7	113
Rock Island, Wa., U.S.	B5	124
Rock Island, co., Il., U.S.	B3	90
Rock Island, i., Fl., U.S.	C3	86
Rock Island, i., Wi., U.S.	C7	126
Rocklake, N.D., U.S.	A6	111
Rock Lake, l., Man.	E2	70
Rock Lake, l., Wa., U.S.	B8	124
Rockland, Ont.	B9	73
Rockland, Id., U.S.	G6	89
Rockland, Me., U.S.	D3	96
Rockland, Ma., U.S.	B6	98
Rockland, Mi., U.S.	m12	99
Rockland, N.Y., U.S.	D6	109
Rockland, co., N.Y., U.S.	D6	109
Rocklands Reservoir, res., Austl.	H3	51
Rockledge, Fl., U.S.	D6	86
Rockledge, Pa., U.S.	o20	115
Rockleigh, N.J., U.S.	g9	107
Rocklin, Ca., U.S.	C3	82
Rockmart, Ga., U.S.	B1	87
Rock Mountain, mtn., Al., U.S.	B2	78
Rock Point, Az., U.S.	A6	80
Rock Point, Md., U.S.	D4	97
Rockport, Il., U.S.	D2	90
Rockport, In., U.S.	I3	91
Rockport, Ky., U.S.	C3	94
Rockport, Me., U.S.	D3	96
Rockport, Ma., U.S.	A6	98
Rock Port, Mo., U.S.	A2	102
Rockport, N.J., U.S.	B3	107
Rockport, Tx., U.S.	E4	120
Rockport, Wa., U.S.	A4	124
Rock Rapids, Ia., U.S.	A1	92
Rock River, Wy., U.S.	E7	127
Rock Run, Al., U.S.	A4	78
Rock Springs, Mt., U.S.	D10	103
Rocksprings, Tx., U.S.	C2	120
Rock Springs, Wi., U.S.	E4	126
Rock Springs, Wy., U.S.	E3	127
Rockstone, Guy.	A3	59
Rockton, Il., U.S.	A4	90
Rockton, Pa., U.S.	D4	115
Rockvale, Co., U.S.	C5	83
Rockvale, Tn., U.S.	B5	119
Rock Valley, Ia., U.S.	A1	92
Rockville, Ct., U.S.	B6	84
Rockville, In., U.S.	E3	91
Rockville, Md., U.S.	B3	97
Rockville, Mn., U.S.	E4	100
Rockville, Ne., U.S.	C7	104
Rockville, R.I., U.S.	F1	116
Rockville, Ut., U.S.	F2	121
Rockville Centre, N.Y., U.S.	n15	109
Rockwall, Tx., U.S.	C4	120
Rockwall, co., Tx., U.S.	C4	120
Rockwell, Ia., U.S.	B4	92
Rockwell, N.C., U.S.	B2	110
Rockwell City, Ia., U.S.	B3	92
Rockwell Park, N.C., U.S.	B2	110
Rockwood, Ont.	D4	73
Rockwood, Me., U.S.	C3	96
Rockwood, Mi., U.S.	F7	99
Rockwood, Pa., U.S.	G3	115
Rockwood, Tn., U.S.	D9	119
Rocky, Ok., U.S.	B2	113
Rocky, stm., Alta.	C2	68
Rocky, stm., N.C., U.S.	B2	110
Rocky, stm., S.C., U.S.	C2	117
Rocky, East Branch, stm., Oh., U.S.	h9	112
Rocky, West Branch, stm., Oh., U.S.	h9	112
Rocky Bay, b., Newf.	A4	72
Rocky Boy, Mt., U.S.	B7	103
Rocky Boys Indian Reservation, Mt., U.S.	B7	103
Rocky Comfort, Mo., U.S.	E3	102
Rocky Coulee, val., Wa., U.S.	B6	124
Rocky Creek, Fl., U.S.	*o10	86
Rockyford, Alta.	D4	68
Rocky Ford, Co., U.S.	C7	83
Rocky Ford, Ga., U.S.	D5	87
Rocky Fork Lake, l., Oh., U.S.	C2	112
Rocky Gap, Va., U.S.	e10	123
Rocky Harbour, Newf.	D3	72
Rocky Hill, Ct., U.S.	C5	84
Rocky Hill, N.J., U.S.	C3	107
Rocky Hill, S.C., U.S.	C3	117
Rocky Lake, l., Man.	B1	70
Rocky Mount, N.C., U.S.	B5	110
Rocky Mount, Va., U.S.	C3	123
Rocky Mountain, mtn., Mt., U.S.	C4	103
Rocky Mountain House, Alta.	C3	68
Rocky Mountain National Park, Co., U.S.	A5	83
Rocky Mountains, N.A.	E9	61
Rocky Point, N.Y., U.S.	*n16	109
Rocky Point, N.C., U.S.	C5	110
Rocky Ripple, In., U.S.	k10	91
Rocky River, Oh., U.S.	A4	112
Rocky Top, mtn., Or., U.S.	C4	114
Rocroi, Fr.	E4	17
Roda, Va., U.S.	f9	123
Rodach, Ger.	C5	19
Rodanthe, N.C., U.S.	B7	110
Rodarte, N.M., U.S.	*A4	108
Rødby, Den.	D5	15
Rødbyhavn, Den.	D5	15
Roddickton, Newf.	C3	72
Rødding, Den.	C3	15
Roddy, Tn., U.S.	D9	119
Rødekro, Den.	C3	15
Rodeo, Ca., U.S.	*g8	82
Rodeo, N.M., U.S.	F1	108
Roderfield, W.V., U.S.	D3	125
Roderick Island, i., B.C.	C3	69
Rodessa, La., U.S.	B2	95
Rodewisch, Ger.	C7	19
Rodey, N.M., U.S.	E2	108
Rodez, Fr.	E5	16
Ródhos, Grc.	D7	19
Ródhos (Rhodes), i., Grc.	D7	19
Roding, Ger.	A3	92
Rodman, Ia., U.S.	E3	73
Rodney, Ont.	D2	101
Rodney, Ms., U.S.	C6	79
Rodney, Cape, c., Ak., U.S.	D4	72
Rodney Pond, l., Newf.	D3	85
Rodney Village, De., U.S.	A6	110
Roduco, N.C., U.S.	C4	81
Roe, Ar., U.S.	C3	107
Roebling, N.J., U.S.	D2	50
Roebourne, Austl.	B4	117
Roebuck, S.C., U.S.	C3	69
Roebuck Bay, b., Austl.	B5	16
Roeland Park, Ks., U.S.	k16	93
Roermond, Neth.	B6	16
Roeselare (Roulers), Bel.	B5	16
Roessleville, N.Y., U.S.	*C7	109
Roes Welcome Sound, strt., N.W. Ter.	D15	66
Roetgen, Ger.	D6	17
Roff, Ok., U.S.	C5	113
Rogachev, Sov. Un.	E8	27
Rogagua, Laguna, l., Bol.	B2	55
Rogáguado, Laguna, l., Bol.	B2	55
Roganville, Tx., U.S.	D6	120
Rogatica, Yugo.	D4	24
Roger Mills, co., Ok., U.S.	B2	113
Rogers, Ar., U.S.	A1	81
Rogers, Ct., U.S.	B8	84
Rogers, Mn., U.S.	E5	100
Rogers, Ne., U.S.	C9	104
Rogers, N.M., U.S.	D6	108
Rogers, N.D., U.S.	B7	111
Rogers, Oh., U.S.	B5	112
Rogers, co., Ok., U.S.	A6	113
Rogers, Mount, mtn., Va., U.S.	f10	123
Rogers City, Mi., U.S.	C7	99
Rogers Lake, res., Ct., U.S.	D6	84
Rogerson, Id., U.S.	G4	89
Rogers Pass, Mt., U.S.	C4	103
Rogersville, N.B.	C4	71
Rogersville, Al., U.S.	A2	78
Rogersville, Mo., U.S.	D4	102
Rogersville, Pa., U.S.	G1	115
Rogersville, Tn., U.S.	C10	119
Roggen, Co., U.S.	A6	83
Rogozhina, Alb.	B2	25
Rogozno, Pol.	B4	26
Rogue, stm., Or., U.S.	E3	114
Rogue River, Or., U.S.	E3	114
Rohnert Park, Ca., U.S.	*C2	82
Rohrersville, Md., U.S.	B2	97
Rohri Canal, Pak.	D2	37
Rohtak, India	C6	37
Rohwer, Ar., U.S.	D4	81
Roi Et, Thai.	B2	34
Roi Island, i., Marsh Is.	S17	52
Roissy-en-France, Fr.	g11	16
Rojas, Arg.	A4	54
Rojo, Cabo, c., Mex.	m15	63
Rojo, Cabo, c., P.R.	H11	64
Rokan, stm., Indon.	L4	35
Rokeby, Sask.	F4	75
Rokel, stm., S.L.	E2	45
Rokitno, Sov. Un.	F6	27
Rokycany, Czech.	D2	26
Roland, Man.	E3	70
Roland, Ia., U.S.	B4	92
Roland, Ok., U.S.	B7	113
Roland, Lake, res., Md., U.S.	g11	97
Rolesville, N.C., U.S.	B4	110
Rolette, N.D., U.S.	A6	111
Rolette, co., N.D., U.S.	A6	111
Rolfe, Ia., U.S.	B3	92
Roll, In., U.S.	C7	91
Roll, Ok., U.S.	B7	113
Rolla, B.C.	B7	69
Rolla, Ks., U.S.	E2	93
Rolla, Mo., U.S.	D6	102
Rolla, N.D., U.S.	A6	111
Rolle, Switz.	B3	18
Rolleville, Bah.	B9	64
Rollingbay, Wa., U.S.	e10	124
Rolling Fork, Ms., U.S.	C3	101
Rolling Fork, stm., Ar., U.S.	C1	81
Rolling Fork, stm., Ky., U.S.	C4	94
Rolling Hills Estates, Ca., U.S.	*n12	82
Rolling Meadows, Il., U.S.	h8	90
Rollingstone, Mn., U.S.	F7	100
Rollins, Mt., U.S.	B2	103
Rollinsford, N.H., U.S.	D5	106
Rolvsøya, i., Nor.	B10	14
Roma, Austl.	E8	50
Roma, Tx., U.S.	F3	120
Romain, Cape, c., S.C., U.S.	F9	117
Romaine, stm., Can.	h9	72
Roman, Rom.	B8	24
Romania, ctry., Eur.	C7	24
Roman Nose Mountain, mtn., Md., U.S.	m12	97
Roman Nose Mountain, mtn., Or., U.S.	D3	114
Romano, Cape, c., Fl., U.S.	G5	86
Romano, Cayo, i., Cuba	A7	64
Romanshorn, Switz.	A7	21
Romans [-sur-Isère], Fr.	E6	16
Romanzof, Cape, c., Ak., U.S.	B11	79
Romanzof Mountains, mts., Ak., U.S.	B11	79
Romayor, Tx., U.S.	D5	120
Rombauer, Mo., U.S.	E7	102
Rome (Roma), Italy	B1	87
Rome, Ga., U.S.	B1	87
Rome, Il., U.S.	C4	90
Rome, In., U.S.	I4	91
Rome, Ia., U.S.	D6	92
Rome, Ms., U.S.	B3	101
Rome, N.Y., U.S.	B5	109
Rome, Oh., U.S.	D3	112
Rome, Pa., U.S.	C9	115
Rome City, In., U.S.	B7	91

Name	Map Ref.	Page
Romema (part of Jerusalem), Isr.	m14	41
Romeo, Co., U.S.	D4	83
Romeo, Mi., U.S.	F7	99
Romeoville, Il., U.S.	k8	90
Romeville, La., U.S.	h10	95
Romford (part of London), Eng., U.K.	k13	12
Romilly, Fr.	C5	16
Romita, Mex.	m13	63
Romney, In., U.S.	D4	91
Romney, W.V., U.S.	B6	125
Romny, Sov. Un.	F9	27
Rømø, i., Den.	C2	15
Romona, Ind.	F4	91
Romont, Switz.	C2	21
Romorantin, Fr.	D4	16
Rompin, stm., Malay.	K5	32
Romsey, Eng., U.K.	D6	12
Romulus, Mi., U.S.	p15	99
Romulus, N.Y., U.S.	C4	109
Romunum, i., Micron.	Q18	52
Romurikku Island, i., Marsh Is.	P18	52
Ron, Viet.	D7	35
Ron, Cape, c., Viet.	C7	35
Rona, i., Scot., U.K.	C3	13
Rona, i., Scot., U.K.	A3	13
Ronald, Wa., U.S.	B4	124
Ronan, Mt., U.S.	C2	103
Roncador, Serra do, plat., Braz.	E4	59
Roncador Bank, Col.	D7	62
Ronceverte, W.V., U.S.	D4	125
Ronciglione, Italy	C4	23
Ronda, Spain	D3	22
Ronda, N.C., U.S.	A2	110
Rønde, Den.	B4	15
Ronde Island, i., Gren.	W25	65
Rondo, i., Indon.	C5	82
Rondônia, state, Braz.	E2	59
Rondonópolis, Braz.	B2	56
Roneys Point, W.V., U.S.	f8	125
Ronge, Lac la, l., Sask.	B3	75
Rongjiang, China	L3	32
Rongxian, China	G7	31
Ronkiti Harbor, b., Micron.	Q17	52
Ronkonkoma, N.Y., U.S.	*n15	109
Rønne, Den.	J6	14
Rönne, stm., Swe.	B6	15
Ronneburg, Ger.	C7	19
Ronne Entrance, b., Ant.	B5	7
Ronne Ice Shelf, ice, Ant.	B6	7
Ronse, Bel.	B5	16
Ronuro, stm., Braz.	E4	59
Roodepoort-Maraisburg, S. Afr.	*C4	49
Roodeschool, Neth.	A6	16
Roodhouse, Il., U.S.	D3	90
Roof Butte, mtn., Az., U.S.	A6	80
Rooks, co., Ks., U.S.	C4	93
Roopville, Ga., U.S.	C1	87
Roosendaal, Neth.	B6	16
Roosevelt, Az., U.S.	D4	80
Roosevelt, Mn., U.S.	B3	100
Roosevelt, N.Y., U.S.	*n15	109
Roosevelt, Ok., U.S.	C2	113
Roosevelt, Tx., U.S.	D2	120
Roosevelt, Ut., U.S.	C5	121
Roosevelt, Wa., U.S.	D5	124
Roosevelt, co., Mt., U.S.	B11	103
Roosevelt, co., N.M., U.S.	C6	108
Roosevelt, stm., Braz.	D2	59
Roosevelt Campobello International Park, N.A.	E3	71
Roosevelt Island, i., Ant.	B32	7
Roosevelt Park, Mi., U.S.	E4	99
Root, stm., Mn., U.S.	G7	100
Root, stm., Wi., U.S.	n12	126
Rootstown, Oh., U.S.	A4	112
Ropczyce, Pol.	C6	26
Roper, N.C., U.S.	B6	110
Roper, stm., Austl.	B5	50
Ropesville, Tx., U.S.	C1	120
Roque Bluffs, Me., U.S.	D5	96
Roquefort, Fr.	E3	16
Roquetas, Spain	B6	22
Rora Head, c., Scot., U.K.	B5	13
Roraima, ter., Braz.	A2	59
Roraima, Mount, mtn., S.A.	A2	59
Rorke Lake, l., Can.	B5	70
Rorketon, Man.	D2	70
Røros, Nor.	F4	14
Rorschach, Switz.	E4	18
Rosa, La., U.S.	D3	95
Rosa, Monte, mtn., Eur.	B1	23
Rosa, Punta, c., Mex.	B3	63
Rosales, Phil.	o13	34
Rosalia, Ks., U.S.	E7	93
Rosalia, Wa., U.S.	B8	124
Rosalie, Ne., U.S.	B9	104
Rosalind, Alta.	C4	68
Rosamond, Ca., U.S.	E4	82
Rosamond, Il., U.S.	D4	90
Rosamorada, Mex.	k11	63
Rosario, Arg.	A4	54
Rosário, Braz.	B2	57
Rosario, Mex.	C3	63
Rosario, Para.	D4	55
Rosario, Phil.	p13	34
Rosario, Ur.	E1	56
Rosario, [Villa del], Ven.	A3	60
Rosario de la Frontera, Arg.	A3	56
Rosario del Tala, Arg.	A5	54
Rosário do Sul, Braz.	E2	56
Rosário Oeste, Braz.	A1	56
Rosati, Mo., U.S.	C6	102
Rosburg, Wa., U.S.	C2	124
Roscoe, Il., U.S.	A5	90
Roscoe, Mn., U.S.	E4	100
Roscoe, Mo., U.S.	C4	102
Roscoe, Mt., U.S.	E7	103
Roscoe, Ne., U.S.	C4	104
Roscoe, N.Y., U.S.	D6	109
Roscoe, Pa., U.S.	F2	115
Roscoe, S.D., U.S.	B6	118
Roscoe, Tx., U.S.	C2	120
Roscoe Glacier, ice, Ant.	C22	7
Roscommon, Ire.	D2	10
Roscommon, Mi., U.S.	D6	99
Roscommon, co., Ire.	D3	11
Roscommon, co., Mi., U.S.	D6	99
Roscrea, Ire.	D3	10
Rose, Ne., U.S.	B6	104
Rose, Ok., U.S.	A6	113
Rose, Mount, mtn., Nv., U.S.	D2	105
Roseau, Dom.	I14	64
Roseau, Mn., U.S.	B3	100
Roseau, co., Mn., U.S.	B3	100
Roseau, stm., N.A.	E3	70
Roseau, South Fork, stm., Mn., U.S.	B3	100
Rosebery, B.C.	D9	69
Rose-Blanche [-Harbour le Cou], Newf.	E2	72
Roseboro, N.C., U.S.	C4	110
Rosebud, Alta.	D4	68
Rose Bud, Ar., U.S.	B3	81
Rosebud, Mo., U.S.	C6	102
Rosebud, Mt., U.S.	D10	103
Rosebud, S.D., U.S.	D5	118
Rosebud, Tx., U.S.	D4	120
Rosebud, co., Mt., U.S.	D10	103
Rosebud, stm., Alta.	D4	68
Rosebud Creek, stm., Mt., U.S.	E10	103
Rosebud Indian Reservation, S.D., U.S.	D5	118
Roseburg, Or., U.S.	D3	114
Rosebush, Mi., U.S.	E6	99
Rose City, Mi., U.S.	D6	99
Rose Creek, Mn., U.S.	G6	100
Rosedale, Alta.	D4	68
Rosedale, B.C.	f14	69
Rosedale, In., U.S.	E3	91
Rosedale, Md., U.S.	g11	97
Rosedale, Ms., U.S.	B2	101
Rosedale, Ok., U.S.	C4	113
Rosedale, Tn., U.S.	C9	119
Rosedale, Wa., U.S.	f10	124
Rosedale, W.V., U.S.	C4	125
Rosedale Colony, S.D., U.S.	*D8	118
Rose Farm, Oh., U.S.	C3	112
Roseglen, N.D., U.S.	B4	111
Rosehearty, Scot., U.K.	C6	13
Rose Hill, Il., U.S.	D5	90
Rose Hill, Ia., U.S.	C5	92
Rose Hill, Ks., U.S.	E6	93
Rose Hill, Ms., U.S.	C4	101
Rose Hill, N.C., U.S.	C4	110
Rose Hill, Va., U.S.	*B5	123
Rose Hill, Va., U.S.	f8	123
Roseisle, Man.	E2	70
Roseland, Ca., U.S.	*C2	82
Roseland, Fl., U.S.	E6	86
Roseland, In., U.S.	A5	91
Roseland, La., U.S.	D5	95
Roseland, Ne., U.S.	D7	104
Roseland, N.J., U.S.	*B4	107
Roseland, Oh., U.S.	B3	112
Roselawn, In., U.S.	B3	91
Roselle, Il., U.S.	k8	90
Roselle, N.J., U.S.	k7	107
Roselle Park, N.J., U.S.	k7	107
Rose Lynn, Alta.	D5	68
Rosemary, Alta.	B2	119
Rosemary, Alta.	D4	68
Rosemead, Ca., U.S.	*m15	82
Rosemère, Que.	p19	74
Rosemont, Ca., U.S.	*C3	82
Rosemont, N.J., U.S.	C3	107
Rosemont, W.V., U.S.	k10	125
Rosenberg, Tx., U.S.	E5	120
Rosendale, Mo., U.S.	A3	102
Rosendale, Wi., U.S.	E5	126
Roseneath, Ont.	C6	73
Rosenfeld, Man.	E3	70
Rosenhayn, N.J., U.S.	E2	107
Rosenheim, Ger.	E6	18
Rose Peak, mtn., Az., U.S.	D6	80
Rosepine, La., U.S.	D2	95
Rose Point, c., B.C.	C3	69
Rose Prairie, B.C.	A7	69
Roseray, Sask.	G1	75
Roseto, Pa., U.S.	E11	115
Rosetown, Sask.	F1	75
Rosetta, Ms., U.S.	D2	101
Rosetta Branch, stm., Ms., U.S.	C3	101
Rosetta Mouth, mth., Eg.	C2	41
Rosetta, see Rashīd, Eg.	B4	38
Rose Valley, Sask.	E4	75
Rosevear, Alta.	C2	68
Roseville, Ca., U.S.	C3	82
Roseville, Il., U.S.	C3	90
Roseville, Mi., U.S.	o16	99
Roseville, Mn., U.S.	m12	100
Roseville, Oh., U.S.	C3	112
Rosewood, Mn., U.S.	B2	100
Rosewood, Oh., U.S.	B2	112
Rosewood Heights, Il., U.S.	E3	90
Rosharon, Tx., U.S.	r14	120
Rosheim, Fr.	F7	17
Rosh Ha' Ayin, Isr.	B6	41
Rosholt, S.D., U.S.	B9	118
Rosholt, Wi., U.S.	D4	126
Rosh Pinna, Isr.	B7	41
Rosiclare, Il., U.S.	F5	90
Rosie, Ar., U.S.	B4	81
Rosier, Ga., U.S.	D4	87
Rosières-en-Santerre, Fr.	C3	23
Rosignano Marittimo, Italy	C3	23
Rosignol, Guy.	A3	59
Rosiori de Vede, Rom.	C7	24
Roskilde, Den.	C6	15
Roskilde, co., Den.	C6	15
Roslavl, Sov. Un.	E9	27
Roslyn, Pa., U.S.	o21	115
Roslyn, S.D., U.S.	B8	118
Roslyn, Wa., U.S.	B4	124
Roslyn Heights, N.Y., U.S.	h13	109
Rosman, N.C., U.S.	f10	110
Ross, N.Z.	O13	51
Ross, Mn., U.S.	B3	100
Ross, Oh., U.S.	C1	112
Ross, co., Oh., U.S.	C2	112
Ross, Mount, mtn., N.Z.	N15	51
Rossa, Switz.	D7	21
Rossano, Italy	E6	23
Ross Barnett Reservoir, res., Ms., U.S.	C3	101
Rossburg, Oh., U.S.	B1	112
Rossburn, Man.	D1	70
Ross Carbery, Ire.	F2	11
Ross Dam, Wa., U.S.	A4	124
Rosseau, Ont.	B5	73
Rossendale, Man.	E2	70
Rosser, Tx., U.S.	n10	120
Rosses Bay, b., Ire.	B3	11
Rosses Point, Ire.	C3	11
Rossford, Oh., U.S.	A2	112
Ross Ice Shelf, ice, Ant.	A31	7
Rossie, N.Y., U.S.	f9	109
Rossignol, Lake, l., N.S.	E4	71
Rossinière, Switz.	D3	21
Ross Island, i., Ant.	B29	7
Ross Island, i., Man.	B3	70
Rossiter, Pa., U.S.	E4	115
Ross Lake, res., N.A.	A4	124
Ross Lake National Recreation Area, Wa., U.S.	A5	124
Rossland, B.C.	E9	69
Rosslare, Ire.	E5	11
Rosslau, Ger.	B7	19
Rosslea, N. Ire., U.K.	C4	11
Rossmoor, Ca., U.S.	*n12	82
Rosso, Maur.	C1	45
Ross-on-Wye, Eng., U.K.	C5	12
Rossosh, Sov. Un.	F12	27
Ross River, Yukon	D2	81
Ross Sea, Ant.	B31	7
Rosston, Ar., U.S.	D2	81
Rosston, Ok., U.S.	A2	113
Ross Township, Pa., U.S.	*E1	115
Rossville, Ga., U.S.	B1	87
Rossville, Il., U.S.	C6	90
Rossville, In., U.S.	D4	91
Rossville, Ia., U.S.	A6	92
Rossville, Ks., U.S.	C8	93
Rossville, Oh., U.S.	B5	113
Rossville, Tn., U.S.	B2	119
Rossway, N.S.	E4	71
Rosthern, Sask.	E2	75
Rostock, Ger.	A6	18
Rostov, Sov. Un.	C12	27
Rostov-na-Donu, Sov. Un.	E6	29
Roșul Pass, Rom.	C7	24
Roswell, Ga., U.S.	B2	87
Roswell, Id., U.S.	F2	89
Roswell, N.M., U.S.	D5	108
Roswell, S.D., U.S.	C8	118
Rota, Spain	D2	22
Rotan, Tx., U.S.	C2	120
Rotenburg [an der Fulda], Ger.	B4	19
Roth, Ger.	D6	19
Roth, N.D., U.S.	A5	111
Rothaar Mountains, mts., Ger.	C4	18
Rothbury, Eng., U.K.	E7	13
Rothbury, Mi., U.S.	E4	99
Röthenbach [bei Sankt Wolfgang], Ger.	D6	19
Rothenbach im Emmental, Switz.	C4	21
Rothenburg [ob der Tauber], Ger.	D5	18
Rothenthurm, Switz.	B6	21
Rother, stm., Eng., U.K.	D12	12
Rothera, sci., Ant.	C6	7
Rotherham, Eng., U.K.	A6	12
Rothes, Scot., U.K.	C5	13
Rothesay, N.B.	D4	71
Rothesay, Scot., U.K.	C4	10
Rothschild, Wi., U.S.	D4	126
Rothville, Mo., U.S.	B4	102
Roto, Austl.	F5	51
Rotondella, Italy	D6	23
Rotondo, Monte, mtn., Fr.	C2	23
Rotorua, N.Z.	M16	51
Rott, stm., Ger.	E8	19
Rottenburg, Ger.	E3	19
Rottenmann, Aus.	E7	18
Rotterdam, Neth.	B6	16
Rotterdam, N.Y., U.S.	C6	109
Rottumeroog, i., Neth.	A6	17
Rottweil, Ger.	D4	18
Roubaix, Fr.	B5	16
Roubideau Creek, stm., Co., U.S.	C2	83
Roudnice [nad Labem], Czech.	n17	26
Rouen, Fr.	C4	16
Rouge, stm., Que.	D3	74
Rougemont, Fr.	B2	20
Rougemont, N.C., U.S.	A4	110
Rouleau, Sask.	G3	75
Roulers see Roeselare, Bel.	B5	16
Roulette, Pa., U.S.	C5	115
Round Harbour, Newf.	D4	72
Roundhead, Oh., U.S.	B2	112
Round Hill, Alta.	C4	68
Round Hill, Va., U.S.	A5	123
Round Island, i., Ms., U.S.	g8	101
Round Island Passage, strt., Fiji	H14	52
Round Lake, Il., U.S.	h8	90
Round Lake, Mn., U.S.	G3	100
Roundlake, Ms., U.S.	A3	101
Round Lake, N.Y., U.S.	C7	109
Round Lake, l., Ont.	B7	73
Round Lake, l., Ont.	G4	75
Round Lake Beach, Il., U.S.	h8	90
Round Mound, hill, Ks., U.S.	D4	93
Round Mountain, Tx., U.S.	D3	120
Round Mountain, mtn., Austl.	D2	120
Round Oak, Ga., U.S.	C3	87
Round Pond, Ar., U.S.	B5	81
Round Pond, Me., U.S.	E3	96
Round Pond, l., Newf.	D4	72
Round Rock, Az., U.S.	A6	80
Round Rock, Tx., U.S.	D4	120
Round Spring, Mo., U.S.	D6	102
Round Top Hill, mtn., Ma., U.S.	B2	98
Roundup, Mt., U.S.	D8	103
Round Valley Indian Reservation, Ca., U.S.	C2	82
Round Valley Reservoir, res., N.J., U.S.	B3	107
Roura, Fr. Gu.	B5	59
Rousay, i., Scot., U.K.	A5	10
Rouses Point, N.Y., U.S.	f11	109
Rouseville, Pa., U.S.	D2	115
Routon, Tn., U.S.	A3	119
Routt, co., Co., U.S.	A3	83
Rouville, co., Que.	D4	74
Rouyn, Que.	k11	74
Rouzerville, Pa., U.S.	G6	115
Rovaniemi, Fin.	D11	14
Rovato, Italy	B3	23
Rovenki, Sov. Un.	G12	27
Rovenki, Sov. Un.	G12	27
Rover, Ar., U.S.	C2	81
Rover, Tn., U.S.	B5	119
Roveredo, Switz.	D7	21
Rovereto, Italy	B3	23
Rovigo, Italy	B3	23
Rovinj, Yugo.	B3	23
Rovno, Sov. Un.	D5	29
Rovnoye, Sov. Un.	F16	27
Row, Ok., U.S.	A7	113
Rowan, Ia., U.S.	B4	92
Rowan, co., Ky., U.S.	B6	94
Rowan, co., N.C., U.S.	B2	110
Rowan Lake, l., Ont.	E5	70
Rowan's Ravine Provincial Park, Sask.	G3	75
Rowe, Ma., U.S.	A2	98
Rowe, N.M., U.S.	B4	108
Rowena, S.D., U.S.	D9	118
Rowena, Tx., U.S.	D2	120
Rowesville, S.C., U.S.	E6	117
Rowland, Ky., U.S.	C5	94
Rowland, N.C., U.S.	C3	110
Rowland, Pa., U.S.	D11	115
Rowland Heights, Ca., U.S.	*n13	82
Rowlesburg, W.V., U.S.	B5	125
Rowlett, Tx., U.S.	*n9	120
Rowletts, Ky., U.S.	C4	94
Rowley, Ia., U.S.	B6	92
Rowley, Ma., U.S.	A6	98
Rowley Shoals, rf., Austl.	C2	50
Roxana, De., U.S.	G5	85
Roxboro, N.C., U.S.	A4	110
Roxburgh, N.Z.	P12	51
Roxbury, Ct., U.S.	C2	84
Roxbury, Ks., U.S.	D6	93
Roxbury, Me., U.S.	D2	96
Roxbury, N.Y., U.S.	C6	109
Roxbury, Vt., U.S.	C3	122
Roxie, Ms., U.S.	D2	101
Roxobel, N.C., U.S.	A5	110
Roxton, Tx., U.S.	C5	120
Roxton Falls, Que.	D5	74
Roxton Pond, Que.	D5	74
Roy, La., U.S.	B2	95
Roy, Mt., U.S.	C8	103
Roy, N.M., U.S.	B5	108
Roy, Ut., U.S.	B3	121
Roy, Wa., U.S.	C3	124
Roya, Peña, mtn., Spain	B5	22
Royal, Ar., U.S.	C2	81
Royal, Ia., U.S.	A2	92
Royal, Ne., U.S.	B7	104
Royal, N.C., U.S.	B6	110
Royal, stm., Me., U.S.	g7	96
Royal Canal, Ire.	D4	11
Royal Center, In., U.S.	C4	91
Royale, Isle, i., Mi., U.S.	h9	99
Royal Gorge, val., Co., U.S.	C5	83
Royal Leamington Spa, Eng., U.K.	D6	10
Royal Oak, B.C.	h12	69
Royal Oak, Md., U.S.	C5	97
Royal Oak, Mi., U.S.	F7	99
Royal Oak, Mi., U.S.	*F7	99
Royalston, Ma., U.S.	A3	98
Royalton, Il., U.S.	F4	90
Royalton, Ky., U.S.	C6	94
Royalton, Mn., U.S.	E4	100
Royalton, Vt., U.S.	D3	122
Royalty, Tx., U.S.	D1	120
Royan, Fr.	E3	16
Roye, Fr.	C5	16
Royersford, Pa., U.S.	F10	115
Royerton, In., U.S.	D7	91
Royse City, Tx., U.S.	C4	120
Royston, B.C.	E5	69
Royston, Ga., U.S.	B3	87
Rozay-en-Brie, Fr.	F2	17
Rozel, Ks., U.S.	D4	93
Rozet, Wy., U.S.	B7	127
Rožňava, Czech.	D6	26
Rtishchevo, Sov. Un.	E14	27
Ruapehu, Mount, mtn., N.Z.	M15	51
Rub' al Khali, des., Sau. Ar.	C5	38
Rubiataba, Braz.	B3	56
Rubidoux, Ca., U.S.	n14	82
Rubim, Braz.	A4	56
Rubottom, Ok., U.S.	D4	113
Rubtsovsk, Sov. Un.	C10	28
Ruby, Ak., U.S.	C8	79
Ruby, La., U.S.	C3	95
Ruby, S.C., U.S.	B7	117
Ruby Dome, mtn., Nv., U.S.	C6	105
Ruby Lake, l., Nv., U.S.	C6	105
Ruby Mountains, mts., Nv., U.S.	C6	105
Ruby Range, mts., Co., U.S.	C3	83
Ruby Range, mts., Mt., U.S.	E4	103
Ruby Valley, Nv., U.S.	C6	105
Ruchi, i., Marsh Is.	S18	52
Ruda, stm., Ger.	g9	26
Ruda, stm., Pol.	g9	26
Ruda Śląska, Pol.	g9	26
Rudd, Ia., U.S.	A4	92
Ruddell, Sask.	E2	75
Ruddels Mills, Ky., U.S.	B5	94
Rüdesheim, Ger.	D3	18
Rudnichnyy, Sov. Un.	*D9	29
Rudnyy, Sov. Un.	D1	70
Rudolf, Lake, l., Afr.	B4	48
Rudolph, i., Sov. Un.	A8	128
Rudolstadt, Ger.	C5	18
Rüdsar, Iran	*B1	38
Rue, Fr.	B6	99
Rueil-Malmaison, Fr.	g9	16
Ruelle, Fr.	E4	16
Rueun, Switz.	C7	21
Rufa'ah, Sud.	C3	47
Ruffec, Fr.	A3	110
Ruffin, S.C., U.S.	E6	117
Rufiji, stm., Tan.	C6	48
Rufino, Arg.	A4	54
Rufisque, Sen.	D1	45
Rufus, Or., U.S.	B6	114
Rufus Woods Lake, res., Wa., U.S.	A6	124
Rugao, China	H9	32
Rugby, Eng., U.K.	C6	12
Rugby, N.D., U.S.	A6	111
Rugeley, Eng., U.K.	A6	12
Rugged Mountain, mtn., B.C.	D4	69
Ruhengeri, Rw.	B5	48
Ruhla, Ger.	C5	19
Ruhr, stm., Ger.	C3	18
Ruidosa, Tx., U.S.	p12	120
Ruidoso, N.M., U.S.	D4	108
Ruidoso Downs, N.M., U.S.	D4	108
Rujiyoru, i., Marsh Is.	S18	52
Rukoji Island, i., Marsh Is.	P18	52
Rukoji Pass, strt., Marsh Is.	P18	52
Rukuruku Bay, b., Fiji	H15	52
Rukwa, prov., Tan.	C5	48
Rukwa, Lake, l., Tan.	C5	48
Rule, Tx., U.S.	C3	120
Rule Creek, stm., Co., U.S.	D7	83
Ruleville, Ms., U.S.	B3	101
Rulo, Ne., U.S.	D10	104
Rum, stm., Mn., U.S.	D5	100
Ruma, Il., U.S.	E3	90
Ruma, Yugo.	C4	24
Rumbek, Sud.	D2	47
Rumbley, Md., U.S.	D6	97
Rumburk, Czech.	C9	19
Rum Cay, i., Bah.	C6	64
Rum Creek, stm., W.V., U.S.	n12	125
Rumely, Mi., U.S.	B3	99
Rumford, Me., U.S.	D2	96
Rumilly, Fr.	D1	20
Rummah, Wādī ar, val., Sau. Ar.	C4	38
Rummānah, Eg.	C4	41
Rumney, N.H., U.S.	C3	106
Rumney Depot, N.H., U.S.	C3	106
Rumoi, Japan	E10	33
Rumphi, Mwi.	D5	48
Rump Mountain, mtn., Me., U.S.	C1	96
Rumsey, Alta.	D4	68
Rumsey, Ky., U.S.	C2	94
Rumson, N.J., U.S.	C4	107
Rumstick Point, c., R.I., U.S.	D5	116
Runan, China	H6	32
Runcorn, Eng., U.K.	A5	12
Rundu, Nmb.	A2	49
Rung, i., Camb.	G5	35
Runge, Tx., U.S.	E4	120
Rungwa, Tan.	C5	48
Runit Island, i., Marsh Is.	S18	52
Runnells, Ia., U.S.	C4	92
Runnels, co., Tx., U.S.	D3	120
Runnemede, N.J., U.S.	D2	107
Runnymede, Sask.	F5	75
Runtu, Nmb.	A2	49
Ruoqiang, China	D2	31
Ruo Shui, stm., China	C5	31
Rupanco, Chile	C2	54
Rupat, i., Indon.	L4	35
Rupert, Id., U.S.	G5	89
Rupert, Vt., U.S.	E2	122
Rupert, W.V., U.S.	f10	110
Rupert, Rivière de, stm., Que.	h11	74
Rupununi, dept., Guy.	B3	59
Rupununi, stm., Guy.	B3	59
Rur, stm., Eur.	D6	17
Rural Hall, N.C., U.S.	A2	110
Rural Retreat, Va., U.S.	D1	123
Rurrenabaque, Bol.	B2	55
Rurutu, i., Fr. Poly.	D3	71
Rusape, Zimb.	A5	49
Ruşayriş, Khazzān ar, res., Afr.	C3	47
Ruse, Bul.	D7	24
Rush, Ky., U.S.	B7	94
Rush, co., In., U.S.	E6	91
Rush, co., Ks., U.S.	D4	93
Rush, stm., Mn., U.S.	F4	100
Rush, stm., Wi., U.S.	D1	126
Rush Center, Ks., U.S.	D4	93
Rush City, Mn., U.S.	E6	100
Rush Creek, stm., Co., U.S.	C7	83
Rush Creek, stm., Ne., U.S.	C3	104
Rush Creek, stm., Oh., U.S.	B2	112
Rush Creek, stm., Ok., U.S.	C4	113
Rushden, Eng., U.K.	B7	12
Rushford, Mn., U.S.	G7	100
Rushford, N.Y., U.S.	C2	109
Rush Hill, Mo., U.S.	B6	102
Rush Lake, Sask.	G2	75
Rush Lake, l., Mn., U.S.	D3	100
Rush Lake, l., Ne., U.S.	E5	126
Rush Lake, l., Wi., U.S.	E5	126
Rushmore, Mn., U.S.	G3	100
Rushmore, Va., U.S.	h14	123
Rushsylvania, Oh., U.S.	B2	112
Rush Valley, Ut., U.S.	C3	121
Rushville, Il., U.S.	C3	90
Rushville, In., U.S.	E7	91
Rushville, Mo., U.S.	B2	102
Rushville, Ne., U.S.	B3	104
Rushville, N.Y., U.S.	C3	109
Rusk, Tx., U.S.	D5	120
Rusk, co., Tx., U.S.	C5	120
Rusk, co., Wi., U.S.	C2	126
Ruskin, Fl., U.S.	E4	86
Ruskin, Ne., U.S.	D8	104
Rusłan, Afg.	B3	36
Ruso, N.D., U.S.	B5	111
Russas, Braz.	B3	57
Russell, Man.	D1	70
Russell, Ont.	B9	73
Russell, Ar., U.S.	B4	81
Russell, Fl., U.S.	m8	86
Russell, Ia., U.S.	D4	92
Russell, Ks., U.S.	D5	93
Russell, Ky., U.S.	B7	94
Russell, Ma., U.S.	B2	98
Russell, Mn., U.S.	F3	100
Russell, N.Y., U.S.	f9	109
Russell, Pa., U.S.	C3	115
Russell, co., Al., U.S.	C4	78
Russell, co., Ks., U.S.	D5	93
Russell, co., Ky., U.S.	D4	94
Russell, co., Va., U.S.	f9	123
Russell, Mount, mtn., Ak., U.S.	f16	79
Russell Cave National Monument, U.S.	A4	78
Russell Fork, stm., U.S.	C7	94
Russell Island, India	H10	37
Russell Lake, l., Alta.	A3	68
Russell Lake, l., Man.	A1	70
Russell Springs, Ks., U.S.	D2	93
Russell Springs, Ky., U.S.	C4	94
Russellville, Al., U.S.	A2	78
Russellville, Ar., U.S.	B2	81
Russellville, Il., U.S.	E6	90
Russellville, In., U.S.	E4	91
Russellville, Ky., U.S.	D3	94
Russellville, Mo., U.S.	C5	102
Russellville, Oh., U.S.	D2	112
Russellville, S.C., U.S.	E8	117
Russellville, Tn., U.S.	C10	119
Russelsheim, Ger.	D4	18
Russia, Oh., U.S.	B1	112
Russian, stm., Ca., U.S.	C2	82
Russian Soviet Federative Socialist Republic, state, Sov. Un.	C12	29
Russiaville, In., U.S.	D5	91
Russum, Ms., U.S.	D2	101
Rustad, Mn., U.S.	D2	100
Rustavi, Sov. Un.	B15	40
Rustburg, Va., U.S.	C3	123
Rustenburg, S. Afr.	C4	49
Ruston, La., U.S.	B3	95
Ruston, Wa., U.S.	B3	124
Ruswil, Switz.	B5	21
Ruszów, Pol.	B10	19
Rutana, Bdi.	B4	48
Rute, Spain	D3	22
Ruteng, Indon.	G6	34
Ruth, Mi., U.S.	E8	99
Ruth, Ms., U.S.	D3	101
Ruth, Nv., U.S.	D6	105
Ruth, N.C., U.S.	f11	110
Ruth, W.V., U.S.	m12	125
Rutherford, N.J., U.S.	B4	107
Rutherford, Tn., U.S.	A3	119
Rutherford, co., N.C., U.S.	B1	110
Rutherford, co., Tn., U.S.	B5	119
Rutherfordton, N.C., U.S.	B1	110
Rutherglen, Ont.	A5	73
Rutherglen, Scot., U.K.	E4	13
Rutherton, N.M., U.S.	A3	108
Ruthilda, Sask.	F1	75
Ruthin, Wales, U.K.	A4	12
Ruthton, Mn., U.S.	F2	100
Ruthven, Ia., U.S.	A3	92
Rüti, Switz.	B4	20
Rutland, B.C.	E8	69
Rutland, Il., U.S.	C4	90
Rutland, Ia., U.S.	B3	92
Rutland, Ma., U.S.	B4	98
Rutland, N.D., U.S.	C8	111
Rutland, Oh., U.S.	C3	112
Rutland, Vt., U.S.	D2	122
Rutland, co., Vt., U.S.	D2	122
Rutland Station, Sask.	E1	75
Rutledge, Al., U.S.	D3	78
Rutledge, Ga., U.S.	C3	87
Rutledge, Mn., U.S.	D6	100
Rutledge, Mo., U.S.	A5	102
Rutledge, Tn., U.S.	C10	119
Rutog, China	B6	36
Rutshuru, Zaire	B4	48
Rutter, Ont.	A4	73
Ruvo [di Puglia], Italy	D6	23
Ruvu, Tan.	C6	48
Ruvuma, prov., Tan.	D6	48
Ruvuma, stm., Afr.	D6	48
Ruwenzori, mts., Afr.	A4	48
Ruza, Sov. Un.	D11	27
Ruzayevka, Sov. Un.	D15	27
Ružomberok, Czech.	D5	26
Rwanda, ctry., Afr.	B5	48
Ry, Den.	B3	15
Ryan, Ia., U.S.	B6	92
Ryan, Ok., U.S.	C4	113
Ryan Creek, stm., Al., U.S.	A3	78
Ryan Park, Wy., U.S.	E6	127
Ryan Peak, mtn., Id., U.S.	F4	89
Ryazan, Sov. Un.	D6	29
Ryazhsk, Sov. Un.	E13	27
Ryabachye, Sov. Un.	E9	28
Rybachye (part of Leningrad), Sov. Un.	s31	14
Rybinsk, Sov. Un.	D6	29
Rybinsk see Andropov, Sov. Un.		
Rybinsk Reservoir, res., Sov. Un.	D6	29
Rybnik, Pol.	C5	26
Rybnitsa, Sov. Un.	B9	24
Rychnov [nad Kněžnou], Czech.	C4	26
Rycroft, Alta.	B1	68
Ryde, Austl.	*F9	51
Ryde, Eng., U.K.	E6	10
Ryder, N.D., U.S.	B4	111
Ryderwood, Wa., U.S.	C2	124
Rye, Co., U.S.	D6	83
Rye, Eng., U.K.	D8	12
Rye, N.H., U.S.	D5	106
Rye, N.Y., U.S.	h13	109
Rye Beach, N.H., U.S.	E5	106
Rye Brook, N.Y., U.S.	*D7	109
Ryegate, Mt., U.S.	D7	103
Ryegate, Vt., U.S.	C4	122
Rye Patch Dam, Nv., U.S.	C3	105
Rye Patch Reservoir, res., Nv., U.S.	C3	105
Ryerson, Sask.	H5	75
Rygge, Nor.	p28	14
Ryley, Alta.	C4	68
Rylsk, Sov. Un.	F10	27
Rynda, Sov. Un.	C17	14
Ryomgård, Den.	B4	15
Ryōtsu, Japan	*D6	33
Rypin, Pol.	B5	26
Rysy, mtn., Eur.	*D6	26
Ryukyu Islands, is., Japan	F10	31
Rzadza, stm., Pol.	k14	26
Rzeszów, Pol.	C6	26
Rzhev, Sov. Un.	C10	27

S

Name	Map Ref.	Page
Saale, stm., Eur.	C5	18
Saaler Bodden, b., Ger.	D6	15
Saalfeld, Ger.	C5	18
Saalfelden, Aus.	B8	20
Saanen, Switz.	D3	21
Saar, hist. reg., Ger.	D6	17
Saar, stm., Eur.	E6	17
Saarbrücken, Ger.	E6	17
Saarburg, Ger.	E6	17
Saaremaa, Sov. Un.	E6	17
Saarland, state, Ger.	E6	17
Saas-Almagell, Switz.	D4	21
Saas-Fee, Switz.	A1	70
Saavedra, Arg.	B4	54
Saba, i., Neth. Ant.	H13	64
Šabac, Yugo.	C4	24
Sabadell, Spain	B7	22
Sabae, Japan	n15	33
Sabah (North Borneo), state, Malay.	D5	34
Sa'bah, Qārat as, mtn., Libya	D3	43
Sabana, Archipiélago de, is., Cuba	C8	64
Sabana de la Mar, Dom. Rep.	E9	64
Sabanagrande, Hond.	A3	60
Sabanalarga, Col.	A3	60
Sabaneta, Puntan, c., N. Mar. Is.	C8	52
Sabang, Indon.	k11	34
Sabará, Braz.	B4	56
Sābarmati, Isr. Occ.	f11	41
Sabastīyah, Isr. Occ.	f11	41
Sabattus, Me., U.S.	D2	96
Sabattus Pond, l., Me., U.S.	D2	96

Name	Map Ref.	Page
Sabaudia, Italy	D4	23
Sabbathday Pond, l., Me., U.S.	g7	96
Sabetha, Ks., U.S.	C8	93
Sabhah, Libya	D2	43
Sabillasville, Md., U.S.	A3	97
Sabin, Mn., U.S.	D2	100
Sabina, Oh., U.S.	C2	112
Sabinal, Tx., U.S.	E3	120
Sabinas, Mex.	B4	63
Sabinas Hidalgo, Mex.	B4	63
Sabine, Tx., U.S.	E6	120
Sabine, W.V., U.S.	D3	125
Sabine, co., La., U.S.	C2	95
Sabine, co., Tx., U.S.	D6	120
Sabine, stm., U.S.	D6	120
Sabine, Mount, mtn., Ant.	B29	7
Sabine Lake, l., U.S.	E2	95
Sabine Pass, Tx., U.S.	E6	120
Sabine Pass, strt., U.S.	E2	95
Sabinópolis, Braz.	B4	56
Sabinsville, Pa., U.S.	C7	115
Sablé, Fr.	D3	16
Sable, Cape, c., N.S.	H19	66
Sable, Cape, c., Fl., U.S.	G5	86
Sable Island, i., N.S.	F10	71
Sable River, N.S.	F4	71
Sabon Birni, Nig.	D6	45
Sabor, stm., Port.	B2	22
Şabrātah, Libya	*C2	43
Sabrina Coast, Ant.	C25	7
Sabula, la., U.S.	B7	92
Sabula, Mo., U.S.	D7	102
Sabzevār, Iran	B5	38
Sac, co., la., U.S.	B2	92
Sac, stm., Mo., U.S.	D4	102
Sacaba, Bol.	C2	55
Sacajawea, Lake, res., Wa., U.S.	C7	124
Sacajawea Peak, mtn., Or., U.S.	B9	114
Sacandaga Lake, l., N.Y., U.S.	B6	109
Sac and Fox Indian Reservation, la., U.S.	C5	92
Sacaton, Az., U.S.	D4	80
Sacavém, Port.	f9	22
Sac City, la., U.S.	B2	92
Săcele, Rom.	C7	24
Sachem Head, Ct., U.S.	E5	84
Sachigo Lake, l., Ont.	C5	70
Sachse, Tx., U.S.	n10	120
Sachs Harbour, N.W. Ter.	B8	66
Sachsen, state, Ger.	B8	19
Sachsen-Anhalt, state, Ger.	B6	19
Sachuest Point, c., R.I., U.S.	F6	116
Sacile, Italy	D8	20
Sackets Harbor, N.Y., U.S.	B4	109
Säckingen, Ger.	A4	21
Sackville, N.B.	D5	71
Saclay, Fr.	h9	16
Saco, Al., U.S.	D4	78
Saco, Me., U.S.	E2	96
Saco, Mt., U.S.	B9	103
Saco, stm., U.S.	E2	96
Saco, East Branch, stm., N.H., U.S.	B4	106
Sacramento, Ca., U.S.	C3	82
Sacramento, Ky., U.S.	C2	94
Sacramento, N.M., U.S.	E4	108
Sacramento, co., Ca., U.S.	C3	82
Sacramento, stm., Ca., U.S.	C3	82
Sacramento, stm., N.M., U.S.	E4	108
Sacramento Mountains, mts., N.M., U.S.	D4	108
Sacramento Valley, val., Az., U.S.	B1	80
Sacramento Valley, val., Ca., U.S.	C2	82
Sacré-Coeur-Saguenay, Que.	A8	74
Sacred Heart, Mn., U.S.	F3	100
Sacrofano, Italy	g8	23
Sacul, Tx., U.S.	D5	120
Şa'dah, Yemen	D4	38
Sadani, Tan.	C6	48
Saddle (Burnt), stm., Alta.	B1	68
Saddle, stm., N.J., U.S.	h8	107
Saddleback Mountain, mtn., Az., U.S.	k8	80
Saddleback Mountain, mtn., Me., U.S.	D2	96
Saddleback Mountain, mtn., Me., U.S.	B4	96
Saddle Ball Mountain, mtn., Ma., U.S.	A1	98
Saddle Brook, N.J., U.S.	h8	107
Saddlebunch Keys, is., Fl., U.S.	H5	86
Saddle Mountain, mtn., Or., U.S.	B3	114
Saddle Mountains, mts., Wa., U.S.	C5	124
Saddle River, N.J., U.S.	A4	107
Saddlestring, Wy., U.S.	B6	127
Sadieville, Ky., U.S.	B5	94
Sadiya, India	C10	36
Sado, stm., Port.	C1	22
Sado Island, i., Japan	D12	31
Sadorus, Il., U.S.	D5	90
Sadská, Czech.	n18	26
Saeby, Den.	A4	15
Saegertown, Pa., U.S.	C1	115
Safājah, Bür, well, Egypt	H9	40
Safety Harbor, Fl., U.S.	E4	86
Saffell, Ar., U.S.	B4	81
Safford, Al., U.S.	C2	78
Safford, Az., U.S.	E6	80
Saffron Walden, Eng., U.K.	B8	12
Safi, Mor.	C3	44
Safīd Küh, Selseleh-ye, mts., Afg.	D12	39
Safonovo, Sov. Un.	D9	27
Safranbolu, Tur.	B9	40
Safune, W. Sam.	F11	52
Safune Bay, b., W. Sam.	F11	52
Saga, China	C8	36
Saga, Japan	J5	33
Sagadahoc, co., Me., U.S.	E3	96
Sagaing, Burma	D10	36
Sagamihara, Japan	*l9	33
Sagami Sea, b., Japan	n18	33
Sagamore, Ma., U.S.	C6	98
Sagamore, Pa., U.S.	E3	115
Sagamore Beach, Ma., U.S.	*C6	98
Sagamore Hills, Oh., U.S.	h9	112
Sagån, stm., Swe.	t34	14
Sāgar, India	D6	36
Sagara, Japan	o17	33
Sage, Ar., U.S.	A4	81
Sag Harbor, N.Y., U.S.	m16	109
Saginaw, Al., U.S.	B3	78
Saginaw, Mi., U.S.	E7	99
Saginaw, Or., U.S.	D3	114
Saginaw, Tx., U.S.	n9	120
Saginaw, co., Mi., U.S.	E6	99
Saginaw Bay, b., Mi., U.S.	E7	99
Sagiz, Sov. Un.	D4	28
Sagiz, stm., Sov. Un.	D5	28
Sagle, Id., U.S.	A2	89
Saglek Bay, b., Newf.	f9	72
Sagola, Mi., U.S.	B2	99
Saguache, Co., U.S.	C4	83
Saguache, co., Co., U.S.	C4	83
Saguache Creek, stm., Co., U.S.	C4	83
Sagua de Tánamo, Cuba	D6	64
Sagua la Grande, Cuba	C3	64
Saguaro Lake, res., Az., U.S.	k10	80
Saguaro National Monument, Az., U.S.	E5	80
Saguaro National Monument (Tucson Mountain Section), Az., U.S.	E4	80
Saguenay, co., Que.	A8	74
Saguenay, stm., Que.	A7	74
Sagunto, Spain	C5	22
Sahagún, Col.	B2	60
Sahand, Küh-e, mtn., Iran	C3	39
Sahara, des., Afr.	D6	42
Saharanpur, India	C6	36
Saḩrā' at Kubrā, Eg.	D3	41
Sahāranpur, India	B3	63
Sahuaripa, Mex.	B3	63
Sahuayo [de Diaz], Mex.	m12	63
Sahuarita, Az., U.S.	F5	80
Saïda, Sov. Un.	E6	28
Saïda, Alg.	C5	44
Saïdpur, Bngl.	C8	36
Saigō, Japan	H6	33
Saigon see Ho Chi Minh City, Viet.	C3	34
Saiki, Japan	J5	33
Sailor Springs, Il., U.S.	E5	90
Saimaa, l., Fin.	G13	14
Saint Abb's Head, c., Scot., U.K.	E6	13
Saint-Adelphe, Que.	C5	74
Saint-Adolphe, Man.	E3	70
Saint-Affrique, Fr.	F5	16
Saint-Agapit, Que.	C6	74
Sainte Agathe, Me., U.S.	A4	96
Sainte Agathe, Man.	E3	70
Sainte-Agathe, Que.	C6	74
Sainte-Agathe-des-Monts, Que.	C3	74
Sainte-Agnès-du-Dundee, Que.	D3	74
Saint-Aimé (Massueville), Que.	C5	74
Saint-Alban's, Newf.	E4	72
Saint Albans, Eng., U.K.	E6	10
Saint Albans, Me., U.S.	D3	96
Saint Albans, Vt., U.S.	B2	122
Saint Albans, W.V., U.S.	C3	125
Saint Albans Bay, Vt., U.S.	B2	122
Saint Albans Bay, b., Vt., U.S.	B2	122
Saint Albert, Alta.	C4	68
Saint Aldhelm's Head, c., Eng., U.K.	E6	10
Saint-Alexandre, Que.	D4	74
Saint-Alexandre [de-Kamouraska], Que.	B8	74
Saint-Alexis-des-Monts, Que.	C4	74
Saint-Alphonse [-de-Granby], Que.	D5	74
Saint-Amand-les-Eaux, Fr.	D3	17
Saint-Amand-Mont-Rond, Fr.	D5	16
Saint Amant, La., U.S.	h10	95
Saint-Amarin, Fr.	B3	20
Saint-Ambroise, Que.	A6	74
Saint-Anaclet, Que.	A9	74
Saint-André, Cap., c., Madag.	g8	49
Saint-André-Avellin, Que.	D2	74
Saint-André-Est, Que.	D3	74
Saint Andrews, N.B.	D2	71
Saint Andrews, Newf.	E2	72
Saint Andrew's, Scot., U.K.	B5	10
Saint Andrews, S.C., U.S.	F7	117
Saint Andrews, S.C., U.S.	C5	117
Saint Andrews, Tn., U.S.	D8	119
Saint Andrews Bay, b., Scot., U.K.	D6	13
Saint Andrew Sound, strt., Ga., U.S.	F5	87
Sainte-Angèle [-de-Monnoir], Que.	D4	74
Saint-Anicet, Que.	D3	74
Saint Ann, Mo., U.S.	*f13	102
Saint Anna, Wi., U.S.	k9	126
Sainte-Anne, Guad.	H14	64
Sainte Anne, Il., U.S.	B6	90
Sainte-Anne, stm., Que.	B6	74
Sainte-Anne, Lac, l., Alta.	C3	68
Sainte-Anne-de-Beaupré, Que.	B7	74
Sainte-Anne [-de-Bellevue], Que.	q19	74
Sainte-Anne-de-la-Pérade, Que.	C5	74
Sainte Anne-de-Madawaska, N.B.	B1	71
Sainte Anne-des-Chênes, Man.	E3	70
Sainte-Anne [-des-Plaines], Que.	D4	74
Sainte-Anne du Lac, Que.	k11	74
Saint Anns, N.S.	C9	71
Saint Ann's Bay, Jam.	E5	64
Saint Anns Peak, mtn., Trin.	N23	65
Saint-Anselme, Que.	C7	74
Saint Ansgar, la., U.S.	A5	92
Saint Anthony, Newf.	C4	72
Saint Anthony, Id., U.S.	F7	89
Saint Anthony, In., U.S.	H4	91
Saint Anthony, N.D., U.S.	C5	111
Saint Anthony, Mn., U.S.	*E5	100
Saint Antoine, N.B.	C5	71
Saint-Antoine [-de-Tilly], Que.	C6	74
Saint-Antoine [-sur-Richelieu], Que.	D4	74
Saint-Apollinaire, Que.	C6	74
Saint Arnaud, Austl.	H4	51
Saint Arthur, N.B.	B3	71
Saint-Athanase, Que.	B8	74
Saint-Aubert, Que.	B7	74
Saint-Augustin, Que.	D5	80
Saint David, Az., U.S.	F5	80
Saint David, Il., U.S.	C3	90
Saint David, Me., U.S.	A4	96
Saint Augustin, stm., Can.	C2	72
Saint-Augustin-Deux-Montagnes, Que.	p19	74
Saint-Augustin-Nord-Quest, stm., Que.	C2	72
Saint Augustin-Saguenay, Que.	C2	72
Saint Austell, Eng., U.K.	D3	12
Saint-Avold, Fr.	C7	16
Saint-Barbe, Que.	D3	74
Saint-Barnabé-Nord, Que.	C5	74
Saint-Barnabé-Sud, Que.	D5	74
Saint-Barthélemy, Que.	C4	74
Saint-Barthélemy, i., Guad.	H13	64
Saint-Basile, N.B.	B1	71
Saint-Basile [-Sud], Que.	C6	74
Saint-Béatrix, Que.	C4	74
Saint Bees Head, c., Eng., U.K.	C5	10
Saint Benedict, Sask.	E3	75
Saint Benedict, la., U.S.	A3	92
Saint Benedict, Ks., U.S.	C7	93
Saint Benedict, Or., U.S.	h12	114
Saint-Benoît-Labre, Que.	C7	74
Saint Bernard, Que.	C6	74
Saint Bernard, Al., U.S.	A3	78
Saint Bernard, La., U.S.	E6	95
Saint Bernard, Ne., U.S.	C8	104
Saint Bernard, co., La., U.S.	E6	95
Saint Bernice, In., U.S.	E2	91
Saint Bethlehem, Tn., U.S.	A4	119
Sainte-Blandine, Que.	A9	74
Saint Boswells, Sask.	G2	75
Saint Brendan's, Newf.	D5	72
Saint Bride, Mount, mtn., Alta.	D2	68
Saint Bride's, Newf.	E4	72
Saint Brides Bay, b., Wales, U.K.	E4	10
Saint-Brieuc, Fr.	C2	16
Saint Brieux, Sask.	E3	75
Sainte-Brigide [-d'Iberville], Que.	D4	74
Sainte-Brigitte [-des-Saults], Que.	C5	74
Saint-Bruno, Que.	A6	74
Saint-Calais, Fr.	D6	16
Saint-Calixte, Que.	D4	74
Saint-Camille, Que.	D6	74
Saint-Camille [-de-Bellechasse], Que.	C7	74
Saint-Casimir, Que.	C5	74
Saint Catharine, Ky., U.S.	C4	94
Saint Catharines, Ont.	D5	73
Sainte-Catherine, Que.	C4	74
Saint Catherine, Lake, l., Vt., U.S.	E2	122
Saint Catherine, Mount, mtn., Gren.	W25	65
Saint Catherines Island, i., Ga., U.S.	E5	87
Saint Catherine's Point, c., Eng., U.K.	D6	12
Saint Catherines Sound, strt., Ga., U.S.	E5	87
Sainte-Cécile [-de-Frontenac], Que.	D7	74
Saint-Célestin (Annaville), Que.	C5	74
Saint-Césaire, Que.	D4	74
Saint-Chamond, Fr.	E6	16
Saint-Charles, Que.	C7	74
Saint Charles, Ar., U.S.	C4	81
Saint Charles, Id., U.S.	G7	89
Saint Charles, Il., U.S.	B5	90
Saint Charles, Ky., U.S.	C2	94
Saint Charles, Md., U.S.	*C4	97
Saint Charles, Mi., U.S.	E6	99
Saint Charles, Mn., U.S.	G6	100
Saint Charles, Mo., U.S.	C7	102
Saint Charles, S.D., U.S.	D6	118
Saint Charles, Va., U.S.	f8	123
Saint Charles, co., La., U.S.	E5	95
Saint Charles, co., Mo., U.S.	C7	102
Saint Charles Cape, c., Newf.	B4	72
Saint Charles Mesa, Co., U.S.	*D6	83
Saint Chély-d'Apcher, Fr.	E5	16
Saint Christopher (Saint Kitts)-Nevis, ctry., N.A.	H13	64
Saint-Chrysostome, Que.	D4	74
Saint Clair, Mi., U.S.	F8	99
Saint Clair, Mn., U.S.	F5	100
Saint Clair, Mo., U.S.	C6	102
Saint Clair, Pa., U.S.	E9	115
Saint Clair, co., Al., U.S.	B3	78
Saint Clair, co., Il., U.S.	E3	90
Saint Clair, co., Mi., U.S.	F8	99
Saint Clair, co., Mo., U.S.	C4	102
Saint Clair, stm., N.A.	E2	73
Saint Clair, Lake, l., N.A.	E2	73
Sainte-Claire, Que.	C7	74
Saint Clair Shores, Mi., U.S.	p16	99
Saint Clairsville, Oh., U.S.	B5	112
Saint-Claude, Man.	E2	70
Saint-Claude, Fr.	E6	16
Saint-Clément, Que.	B8	74
Saint Clements Creek, stm., Md., U.S.	*C4	97
Sainte-Clothilde, Que.	D5	74
Saint-Cloud, Fr.	g9	16
Saint Cloud, Fl., U.S.	D5	86
Saint Cloud, Mn., U.S.	E4	100
Saint Cloud, Wi., U.S.	E5	126
Saint-Coeur-de-Marie, Que.	A6	74
Saint-Côme, Que.	C4	74
Saint-Constant, Que.	q19	74
Saint Croix, N.B.	D2	71
Sainte-Croix, Que.	C6	74
Sainte-Croix, Switz.	E6	21
Saint Croix, In., U.S.	H4	91
Saint Croix, i., V.I.U.S.	H12	64
Saint Croix, co., Wi., U.S.	C1	126
Saint Croix, stm., N.A.	C5	96
Saint Croix, Lake, l., U.S.	D1	126
Saint Croix, Wi., U.S.	C1	126
Saint Croix Stream, stm., Me., U.S.	B4	96
Saint-Cuthbert, Que.	C4	74
Saint-Cyrille [-de-L'Islet], Que.	B7	74
Saint-Cyrille [-de-Wendover], Que.	D5	74
Saint-Cyr [-sur-Loire], Fr.	D6	16
Saint-Damase, Que.	D4	74
Saint-Damase-des-Aulnaies, Que.	B7	74
Saint-Damien [-de-Buckland], Que.	C7	74
Saint-Damien-de-Brandon, Que.	C4	74
Saint David, Az., U.S.	F5	80
Saint David, Il., U.S.	C3	90
Saint David, Me., U.S.	A4	96
Saint-David-de-l'Auberivière, Que.	n17	74
Saint-David [-d'Yamaska], Que.	D5	74
Saint David's, Newf.	D2	72
Saint David's, Wales, U.K.	C2	12
Saint David's Head, c., Wales, U.K.	E4	10
Saint David's Island, i., Ber.	o21	64
Saint-Denis, Que.	D4	74
Saint-Denis, Fr.	C5	16
Saint-Denis, Reu.	H24	2
Saint-Denis [-de-la-Bouteillerie], Que.	B8	74
Saint-Didace, Que.	B1	71
Saint-Dié, Fr.	C7	16
Saint-Dizier, Fr.	C6	16
Saint-Dominique, Que.	D5	74
Saint-Dominique, Que.	q18	74
Saint-Donat-de-Montcalm, Que.	C3	74
Saint Donatus, la., U.S.	B7	92
Saint-Édouard [-de-Napierville], Que.	q19	74
Saint Edward, Ne., U.S.	C8	104
Sainte-Edwidge, Que.	D6	74
Saint Eleanor's, P.E.I.	C6	71
Saint Elias, Cape, c., Ak., U.S.	D11	79
Saint Elias Mountains, mts., N.A.	C11	79
Saint-Élie, Fr. Gu.	B4	59
Sainte-Élisabeth, Que.	C4	74
Saint Elizabeth, Mo., U.S.	C5	102
Saint Elmo, Al., U.S.	E1	78
Saint Elmo, Il., U.S.	D5	90
Saint-Éloi, Que.	A8	74
Sainte-Émélie-de-l'Énergie, Que.	C4	74
Saint-Émile [-de-Suffolk], Que.	D3	74
Saint-Éphrem [-de-Tring], Que.	C7	74
Saint-Esprit, Que.	D4	74
Saint-Étienne, Fr.	E6	16
Saint-Étienne [-de-Beauharnois], Que.	q19	74
Sainte-Eulalie, Que.	C5	74
Sainte-Euphémie, Que.	D5	74
Sainte-Eusèbe, Que.	B9	74
Saint-Eustache, Que.	D4	74
Saint-Fabien, Que.	A9	74
Sainte-Famille, Que.	C7	74
Sainte-Famille-d'Aumond, Que.	C2	74
Saint-Faustin, Que.	C3	74
Saint-Félicien, Que.	A5	74
Saint-Félix-de-Valois, Que.	C4	74
Saint-Ferdinand (Bernierville), Que.	C6	74
Saint-Ferréol [-les-Neiges], Que.	B7	74
Saint-Fidèle, Que.	B7	74
Saint Fintan's, Newf.	D2	72
Saint-Flavien, Que.	C6	74
Saint-Florent, Fr.	D5	16
Saint Florian, Al., U.S.	A2	78
Saint-Flour, Fr.	F5	16
Saint-Fortunat, Que.	D6	74
Sainte-Foy, Que.	n17	74
Sainte-Foy-la-Grande, Fr.	E4	16
Saint Francis, Ar., U.S.	A5	81
Saint Francis, Ks., U.S.	C2	93
Saint Francis, Me., U.S.	A4	96
Saint Francis, Mn., U.S.	E5	100
Saint Francis, S.D., U.S.	D5	118
Saint Francis, Wi., U.S.	n12	126
Saint Francis, co., Ar., U.S.	B5	81
Saint Francis, stm., N.A.	B8	74
Saint Francis, stm., U.S.	A5	81
Saint Francis, Cape, c., Newf.	E5	72
Saint Francis, Cape, c., S. Afr.	I6	48
Saint Francisville, Il., U.S.	E6	90
Saint Francisville, La., U.S.	D4	95
Saint François, co., Mo., U.S.	D7	102
Saint François, stm., Que.	D5	74
Saint-François, Lac, l., Que.	D6	74
Sainte-Françoise, Que.	A8	74
Saint François Mountains, hills, Mo., U.S.	D7	102
Saint-François-Xavier [-de-Brompton], Que.	D5	74
Saint-Frédéric, Que.	C7	74
Saint Froid Lake, l., Me., U.S.	B4	96
Saint-Fulgence, Que.	A7	74
Saint-Gabriel, Que.	C4	74
Saint-Gabriel, La., U.S.	h9	95
Saint-Gaudens, Fr.	F4	16
Saint-Gédéon, Que.	D7	74
Sainte Genevieve, Mo., U.S.	D7	102
Sainte Genevieve, co., Mo., U.S.	D7	102
Sainte-Geneviève-de-Batiscan, Que.	C5	74
Saint George, Austl.	E8	50
Saint George, Ber.	o20	64
Saint George, N.B.	D3	71
Saint George, Ont.	D4	73
Saint George, Ga., U.S.	F4	87
Saint George, S.C., U.S.	E6	117
Saint George, Ut., U.S.	F2	121
Saint George, Cape, c., Newf.	D2	72
Saint George Island, i., Ak., U.S.	D6	79
Saint George Island, i., Fl., U.S.	C1	86
Saint George Island, i., Md., U.S.	D5	97
Saint Georges, Bel.	D5	17
Saint George's, Newf.	D2	72
Saint-Georges, Fr. Gu.	B4	59
Saint George's, Gren.	J14	64
Saint George's, De., U.S.	B3	85
Saint George's Bay, b., Newf.	D2	72
Saint George's Bay, b., N.S.	D8	71
Saint George's Cathedral, Isr. Occ.	m14	41
Saint George's Channel, strt., Eur.	E3	10
Saint-Georges [-de-Windsor], Que.	D6	74
Saint George's Island, i., Ber.	o20	64
Saint-Georges-Ouest, Que.	C7	74
Saint-Gérard, Que.	D6	74
Saint Germain, Mi., U.S.	F4	99
Saint-Germain, Forêt de, Fr.	g9	16
Saint-Germain-en-Laye, Fr.	g9	16
Sainte-Germaine-Station, Que.	C7	74
Saint-Germain-de-Kamouraska, Que.	B8	74
Saint-Gervais, Que.	C7	74
Saint-Gervais-les-Bains, Fr.	D7	16
Saint-Gilles (Sint-Gillis), Bel.	*D4	17
Saint-Gilles, Que.	C6	74
Saint-Gilles-Croix-de-Vie, Fr.	D5	16
Saint-Gilles-du-Gard, Fr.	F6	16
Saint-Gingolph, Switz.	F6	21
Saint-Girons, Fr.	F4	16
Saint-Gobain, Fr.	C5	16
Saint Gotthard Tunnel, Switz.	E4	18
Saint Govan's Head, c., Wales, U.K.	C3	12
Saint-Grégoire (Larochelle), Que.	C5	74
Saint Gregor, Sask.	E3	75
Saint-Guillaume-d'Upton, Que.	D5	74
Saint Helen, Lake, l., Mi., U.S.	D6	99
Saint Helena, Ca., U.S.	C2	82
Saint Helena, Ne., U.S.	B8	104
Saint Helena, co., La., U.S.	D5	95
Saint Helena, dep., Afr.	H5	42
Saint Helena Island, i., S.C., U.S.	G6	117
Saint Helena Sound, strt., S.C., U.S.	G7	117
Sainte-Hélène [-de-Kamouraska], Que.	B8	74
Saint Helens, Eng., U.K.	A5	12
Saint Helens, Or., U.S.	B4	114
Saint Helens, Mount, vol., Wa., U.S.	C3	124
Saint Helier, Jersey	F5	10
Sainte-Hénédine, Que.	C7	74
Saint-Henri [-de-Lévis], Que.	C6	74
Saint Henry, Oh., U.S.	B1	112
Saint-Herménégilde, Que.	D6	74
Saint-Hilaire, Mn., U.S.	B2	100
Saint-Hilaire-de-Dorset, Que.	D7	74
Saint-Hilarion, Que.	B7	74
Saint-Hippolyte, Fr.	B2	21
Saint-Honoré, Que.	D7	74
Saint-Honoré-de-Témiscouata, Que.	B8	74
Saint-Hubert, Bel.	D5	17
Saint-Hubert, Que.	q20	74
Saint-Hubert-de-Témiscouata, Que.	B8	74
Saint-Hugues, Que.	D5	74
Saint-Hyacinthe, Que.	D5	74
Saint-Hyacinthe, co., Que.	D4	74
Saint Ignace, N.B.	C4	71
Saint Ignace, Mi., U.S.	C6	99
Saint Ignatius, Guy.	B3	59
Saint Ignatius, Mt., U.S.	C2	103
Saint Igntoe, Md., U.S.	D6	74
Saint Inigoes, Md., U.S.	D5	97
Saint-Irénée, Que.	B7	74
Saint Isidore, N.B.	B4	71
Saint-Isidore, Que.	q19	74
Saint-Isidore-d'Auckland, Que.	D6	74
Saint Isidore de Prescott, Ont.	B10	73
Saint Ives, Eng., U.K.	B7	12
Saint Ives, Eng., U.K.	D2	12
Saint Jacob, Il., U.S.	E4	90
Saint Jacobs, Ont.	D4	73
Saint Jacques, N.B.	B1	71
Saint-Jacques, Que.	D4	74
Saint James, Ar., U.S.	B4	81
Saint James, La., U.S.	h10	95
Saint James, Mi., U.S.	C5	99
Saint James, Mn., U.S.	G4	100
Saint James, Mo., U.S.	C6	102
Saint James, N.Y., U.S.	*n15	109
Saint James, co., La., U.S.	D5	95
Saint James, Cape, c., B.C.	D2	69
Saint James City, Fl., U.S.	F4	86
Saint-Jean, co., Que.	D4	74
Saint Jean Baptiste, Man.	E3	70
Saint-Jean-Chrysostome, Que.	o17	74
Saint-Jean-d'Angély, Fr.	E3	16
Saint-Jean-de-Dieu, Que.	A8	74
Saint-Jean-de-Luz, Fr.	F3	16
Saint-Jean-de-Matha, Que.	C4	74
Saint-Jean-de-Maurienne, Fr.	D2	20
Saint-Jean-Port-Joli, Que.	B7	74
Saint-Jean-sur-Richelieu, Que.	D4	74
Saint-Jérôme, Que.	D3	74
Saint Jo, Tx., U.S.	C4	120
Saint-Joachim, Que.	B7	74
Saint-Joachim [-de-Courval], Que.	D5	74
Saint Joe, Ar., U.S.	A3	81
Saint Joe, In., U.S.	B8	91
Saint Joe, stm., Id., U.S.	B3	89
Saint John, In., U.S.	B3	91
Saint John, Ks., U.S.	E5	93
Saint John, Me., U.S.	A4	96
Saint John, N.D., U.S.	A6	111
Saint John, Wa., U.S.	B8	124
Saint John, co., N.B.	D3	71
Saint John, i., V.I.U.S.	G12	64
Saint John, Lake, l., Newf.	C3	72
Saint John, Southeast Branch, stm., N.A.	B2	96
Saint John Bay, b., Newf.	C3	72
Saint John Island, i., Newf.	C3	72
Saint John's, Antig.	H14	64
Saint John's, Newf.	E5	72
Saint Johns, Az., U.S.	C6	80
Saint Johns, Il., U.S.	E4	90
Saint Johns, Mi., U.S.	F6	99
Saint Johns, Mo., U.S.	*f13	102
Saint Johns, Oh., U.S.	B1	112
Saint Johns, co., Fl., U.S.	C5	86
Saint Johns, stm., Fl., U.S.	B5	86
Saint Johnsbury, Vt., U.S.	C4	122
Saint Johnsbury Center, Vt., U.S.	C4	122
Saint John's Point, c., Ire.	G3	11
Saint John's Point, c., N. Ire.	C7	74
Saint Johnsville, N.Y., U.S.	B6	109
Saint John the Baptist, co., La., U.S.	D5	95
Saint Jones, stm., De., U.S.	D4	85
Saint Joseph, N.B.	D5	71
Saint-Joseph, Il., U.S.	C5	90
Saint Joseph, Dom.	I14	64
Saint Joseph, La., U.S.	C4	95
Saint Joseph, Mi., U.S.	F4	99
Saint Joseph, Mn., U.S.	E4	100
Saint Joseph, Mo., U.S.	B3	102
Saint Joseph, Tn., U.S.	B4	119
Saint Joseph, co., In., U.S.	A5	91
Saint Joseph, co., Mi., U.S.	G5	99
Saint Joseph, Lac, l., Que.	C6	74
Saint Joseph, Lake, l., Ont.	o17	73
Saint Joseph Bay, b., Fl., U.S.	C1	86
Saint-Joseph-de-Beauce, Que.	C7	74
Saint-Joseph-de-la-Rive, Que.	B7	74
Saint-Joseph-du-Lac, Que.	p18	74
Saint Joseph Point, c., Fl., U.S.	v16	86
Saint Joseph's, Newf.	E5	72
Saint Joseph Sound, strt., Fl., U.S.	o10	86
Saint-Jovite, Que.	C3	74
Saint-Jude, Que.	D5	74
Saint-Julien [-en-Genevois], Fr.	D1	21
Sainte-Julienne, Que.	C4	74
Sainte-Julie-Station, Que.	C6	74
Saint-Junien, Fr.	E4	16
Saint Just, Eng., U.K.	D2	12
Saint-Just-en-Chaussée, Fr.	E2	17
Sainte-Justine, Que.	C7	74
Sainte-Justine [-de-Newton], Que.	D3	74
Saint-Lambert [-de-Lévis], Que.	C6	74
Saint Landry, La., U.S.	D3	95
Saint Landry, co., La., U.S.	D3	95
Saint-Laurent, Man.	D3	70
Saint-Laurent, Que.	p19	74
Saint-Laurent-Blangy, Fr.	D2	17
Saint-Laurent-de-la-Salanque, Fr.	F5	16
Saint-Laurent [-du-Maroni], Fr. Gu.	A4	59
Saint-Laurent [du Maroni], ter., Fr. Gu.	B4	59
Saint-Laurent-en-Grandvaux, Fr.	C1	20
Saint Lawrence, Austl.	D8	50
Saint Lawrence, Newf.	E4	72
Saint Lawrence, S.D., U.S.	C7	118
Saint Lawrence, co., N.Y., U.S.	A5	109
Saint Lawrence, stm., N.A.	g19	66
Saint Lawrence, Cape, c., N.S.	B9	71
Saint Lawrence, Gulf of, b., Can.	G20	66
Saint Lawrence Island, i., Ak., U.S.	C5	79
Saint Lawrence Islands National Park, Ont.	C9	73
Saint Lazare, Man.	D1	70
Saint-Lazare, Que.	q18	74
Saint Leo, Fl., U.S.	D4	86
Saint-Léon, Que.	C5	74
Saint Leon, In., U.S.	F8	91
Saint-Léonard, N.B.	B2	71
Saint Leonard, Md., U.S.	D4	97
Saint-Léonard-[d'Aston], Que.	C5	74
Saint-Léonard-de-Portneuf, Que.	C6	74
Saint Lewis, stm., Newf.	B3	72
Saint Lewis Sound, strt., Newf.	B4	72
Saint-Lô, Fr.	C5	16
Saint Libory, Il., U.S.	E4	90
Saint Libory, Ne., U.S.	C7	104
Saint-Lin, Fr.	C3	16
Saint Louis, P.E.I.	C5	71
Saint Louis, Sask.	E3	75
Saint Louis, Guad.	R9	65
Saint-Louis, Sen.	C1	45
Saint Louis, Mi., U.S.	E6	99
Saint Louis, Mo., U.S.	C7	102
Saint Louis, Ok., U.S.	B5	113
Saint Louis, co., Mn., U.S.	C6	100
Saint Louis, co., Mo., U.S.	C7	102
Saint Louis, stm., U.S.	D6	100
Saint Louis Bay, b., Ms., U.S.	f7	101
Saint Louis Crossing, In., U.S.	F6	91
Saint-Louis-de-Bonsecours, Que.	D5	74
Saint-Louis-de-Gonzague, Que.	D3	74
Saint Louis-de-Kent, N.B.	C5	71
Saint-Louis-du-Ha! Ha!, Que.	B8	74
Sainte-Louise, Que.	B7	74
Saint Louis Park, Mn., U.S.	n12	100
Saint Louisville, Oh., U.S.	B3	112
Saint-Loup-sur-Semouse, Fr.	B2	20
Saint-Luc, Que.	D4	74
Saint-Luc, Switz.	D4	21
Saint Lucas, la., U.S.	A6	92
Saint Lucia, ctry., N.A.	J14	64
Saint Lucia, Cape, c., S. Afr.	C5	49
Saint Lucia, Lake, l., S. Afr.	C5	49
Saint Lucia Channel, strt., N.A.	I14	64
Saint Lucie, Fl., U.S.	E6	86
Saint Lucie, co., Fl., U.S.	E6	86
Saint Lucie Canal, Fl., U.S.	F6	86
Sainte-Lucie-de-Beauregard, Que.	C7	86
Saint Lucie Inlet, b., Fl., U.S.	E6	86
Saint-Ludger, Que.	D7	74
Sainte-Madeleine, Que.	D4	74
Saint-Magloire, Que.	C7	74
Saint Magnus Bay, b., Scot., U.K.	g10	10
Saint-Maixent-l'École, Fr.	D3	16
Saint-Malachie, Que.	C7	74
Saint-Malo, Man.	E3	70
Saint-Malo, Fr.	C2	16
Saint Malo, Gulf of, b., Fr.	C2	16
Saint-Mandé, Fr.	g10	16
Saint-Marc, Que.	D4	74
Saint-Marc, Haiti	E7	64
Saint-Marc [-des-Carrières], Que.	C5	74
Saint-Marcel-de-L'Islet, Que.	C7	74
Saint Margaret Bay, b., Newf.	C3	72
Saint Margaret's Hope, Scot., U.K.	B6	13
Sainte-Marguerite, stm., Que.	h8	74
Sainte-Marguerite Nord-Est, stm., Que.	A7	74
Sainte-Marguerite-de-Dorchester, Que.	C7	74
Sainte-Marie, Que.	C6	74
Sainte-Marie, Mart.	S11	65
Sainte-Marie, Il., U.S.	E5	90
Sainte-Marie, Cap, c., Madag.	i8	49
Sainte-Marie-aux-Mines, Fr.	A3	20
Sainte Maries, Id., U.S.	B2	89
Saint Mark, Ks., U.S.	g11	93
Saint Marks, Fl., U.S.	B2	86
Sainte-Marthe, Que.	D3	74
Saint Martin, co., In., U.S.	A5	91
Saint Martin, co., N.A.	G13	64
Saint Martin, La., U.S.	D7	95
Saint Martin, Mn., U.S.	E4	100
Saint Martin, Lake, l., Man.	D2	70
Saint-Martin-Boulogne, Fr.	D9	12
Saint Martin Island, i., Fl.	C4	99
Saint Martins, N.B.	D4	71
Saint Martins Station, Man.	D2	70
Saint Martinville, La., U.S.	D4	95

Name	Map Ref.	Page
Saint-Martory, Fr.	F4	16
Saint Mary, Ky., U.S.	C4	94
Saint Mary, Mo., U.S.	D8	102
Saint Mary, co., La., U.S.	E4	95
Saint Mary, stm., B.C.	E2	68
Saint Mary, stm., N.A.	E4	68
Saint Mary-of-the-Woods, In., U.S.	E3	91
Saint Mary Peak, mtn., Austl.	F6	50
Saint Mary Reservoir, res., Alta.	E4	68
Saint Mary's, Newf.	E5	72
Saint Mary's, Ont.	D3	73
Saint Marys, Ak., U.S.	C7	79
Saint Marys, Ga., U.S.	F5	87
Saint Marys, In., U.S.	A5	91
Saint Marys, Ks., U.S.	C7	93
Saint Marys, Oh., U.S.	B1	112
Saint Marys, Pa., U.S.	D4	115
Saint Marys, W.V., U.S.	B3	125
Saint Marys, co., Md., U.S.	D4	97
Saint Marys, stm., N.S.	D8	71
Saint Marys, stm., U.S.	F5	87
Saint Marys, stm., Md., U.S.	D5	97
Saint Mary's, Cape, c., Newf.	E3	71
Saint Mary's Bay, b., N.S.	E3	71
Saint Marys City, Md., U.S.	D5	97
Saint Marys Entrance, strt., Ga., U.S.	F5	87
Saint-Mathieu, Que.	q19	74
Saint-Mathieu, Que.	A9	74
Saint Matthew Island, i., Ak., U.S.	C5	79
Saint Matthews, Ky., U.S.	B4	94
Saint Matthews, S.C., U.S.	D6	117
Saint-Maur-des-Fossés, Fr.	g10	16
Saint-Maurice, Que.	C5	74
Saint-Maurice, Switz.	C3	20
Saint Maurice, La., U.S.	C3	95
Saint-Maurice, co., Que.	C5	74
Saint-Maurice, stm., Que.	C5	74
Saint Meinrad, In., U.S.	H4	91
Sainte-Mélanie, Que.	C4	74
Saint-Memmie, Fr.	F4	17
Sainte-Menehould, Fr.	C6	16
Saint-Méthode [-de-Frontenac], Que.	C6	74
Saint Michael, Alta.	C4	68
Saint Michael, Ak., U.S.	C7	79
Saint Michael, Mn., U.S.	E5	100
Saint Michael, N.D., U.S.	B7	111
Saint Michaels, Az., U.S.	B6	80
Saint Michaels, Md., U.S.	C5	97
Saint Michaels Bay, b., Newf.	B4	72
Saint-Michel, Fr.	E4	17
Saint Michel, Fr.	D2	20
Saint-Michel [-de-Bellechasse], Que.	C7	74
Saint-Michel-de-Napierville, Que.	q19	74
Saint-Michel-des-Saints, Que.	C4	74
Saint-Mihiel, Fr.	C6	16
Saint-Modeste, Que.	B8	74
Sainte-Monique [-de-Nicolet], Que.	C5	74
Saint-Nazaire, Que.	D5	74
Saint-Nazaire, Fr.	D2	16
Saint-Nazaire [-de-Buckland], Que.	C7	74
Saint-Nazaire-de-Chicoutimi, Que.	A6	74
Saint Nazianz, Wi., U.S.	D6	126
Saint Neots, Eng., U.K.	B7	12
Saint-Nérée, Que.	C7	74
Saint-Nicolas, Que.	o17	74
Saint-Nicolas-de-Port, Fr.	F6	17
Saint-Nicolas see Sint-Niklaas, Bel.	B6	16
Saint-Odilon, Que.	C7	74
Saint Olaf, Ia., U.S.	B6	92
Saint-Omer, Fr.	B5	16
Saint Onge, S.D., U.S.	C2	118
Saintonge, hist. reg., Fr.	E3	16
Saint-Ouen, Fr.	g10	16
Saint-Ours, Que.	D4	74
Saint-Pacôme, Que.	B8	74
Saint-Pamphile, Que.	C8	74
Saint Paris, Oh., U.S.	B2	112
Saint Pascal, Que.	B8	74
Saint Patrice, Lac, l., Que.	A7	73
Saint Paul, Alta.	B5	68
Saint Paul, Ar., U.S.	B2	81
Saint Paul, In., U.S.	F6	91
Saint Paul, Ks., U.S.	E8	93
Saint Paul, Mn., U.S.	F5	100
Saint Paul, Ne., U.S.	f12	102
Saint Paul, Ne., U.S.	C7	104
Saint Paul, Or., U.S.	h12	114
Saint Paul, S.C., U.S.	D7	117
Saint Paul, Va., U.S.	f9	123
Saint Paul, stm., Can.	C3	72
Saint Paul, stm., Lib.	E2	45
Saint-Paul, Île, i., F.S.A.T.	I2	2
Saint-Paul-de-Chester, Que.	D6	74
Saint-Paul-de-la-Croix, Que.	B8	74
Saint-Paul-de-Montminy, Que.	C7	74
Saint-Paul-du-Nord, Que.	A8	74
Saint-Paulin, Que.	C4	74
Saint Paul Island, i., B.C.	D9	71
Saint Paul Island, i., Ak., U.S.	D5	79
Saint Pauls, Mn., U.S.	n12	100
Saint Pauls, N.C., U.S.	C4	110
Sainte-Perpétue-de-L'Islet, Que.	B8	74
Saint Peter, Ks., U.S.	C3	93
Saint Peter, Mn., U.S.	F5	100
Saint Peter Port, Guernsey	F5	10
Saint Peters, N.S.	D9	71
Saint Peters, In., U.S.	F7	91
Saint Peters, Mo., U.S.	C7	102
Saint Peters Bay, P.E.I.	C7	71
Saint Petersburg, Fl., U.S.	E4	86
Saint Petersburg, Ru., U.S.	D2	115
Saint Petersburg Beach, Fl., U.S.	p10	86
Saint Philémon, Que.	C7	74
Saint Philip, In., U.S.	I2	91
Saint Philippe [-de-Laprairie], Que.	D4	74
Saint-Philippe-de-Néri, Que.	B8	74
Saint Phillips Island, i., S.C., U.S.	G6	117
Saint-Pie, Que.	D5	74
Saint-Pierre, Mart.	I14	64
Saint-Pierre, St. P./M.	E3	72
Saint-Pierre, St. P./M.	E3	72
Saint-Pierre, Lac, l., Que.	C5	74
Saint-Pierre and Miquelon, dep., N.A.	E3	72
Saint-Pierre-d'Albigny, Fr.	D2	20
Saint-Pierre-en-Port, Fr.	E8	12
Saint-Pierre-Jolys, Man.	E3	70
Saint-Pierre-Montmagny, Que.	C7	74
Saint-Placide, Que.	p18	74
Saint-Pol-de-Léon, Fr.	C2	16
Saint-Pol-sur-Mer, Fr.	C2	16
Saint-Pol [-sur-Ternoise], Fr.	B5	16
Saint-Pourçain, Fr.	D5	16
Saint-Prime, Que.	A5	74
Saint-Prosper, Que.	C5	74
Saint-Prosper-de-Dorchester, Que.	C7	74
Saint Quentin, N.B.	B2	71
Saint-Quentin, Fr.	C5	16
Saint-Raphaël, Que.	C7	74
Saint-Raphaël, Fr.	F7	16
Saint Raphaël-sur-Mer, N.B.	B5	71
Saint-Raymond, Que.	C6	74
Saint-Rédempteur, Que.	o17	74
Saint Regis, Mt., U.S.	C1	103
Saint Regis, stm., N.A.	f10	109
Saint Regis, West Branch, stm., N.Y., U.S.	f10	109
Saint Regis Falls, N.Y., U.S.	f10	109
Saint-Rémi, Que.	D4	74
Saint-Rémi-d'Amherst, Que.	C3	74
Saint-Rémi [-de-Tingwick], Que.	D6	74
Saint-Roch [-de-Richelieu], Que.	D4	74
Saint-Roch-des-Aulnaies, Que.	B7	74
Saint-Romuald, Que.	C6	74
Sainte-Rose, Guad.	H14	64
Sainte Rose, La., U.S.	k11	95
Sainte Rose du Lac, Man.	D2	70
Saintes, Fr.	E3	16
Saintes, Île des, is., Guad.	R8	65
Sainte-Sabine-de-Bellechasse, Que.	C7	74
Saint Samuel, Que.	D7	74
Saint Sanford, Man.	E3	70
Saint Sauveur, N.B.	B4	71
Saint-Sauveur-des-Monts, Que.	D3	74
Saint-Savine, Fr.	D7	74
Saint-Sébastien, Que.	D7	74
Saint-Sébastien, Cap, c., Madag.	f9	49
Saint-Sébastien [-sur-Loire], Fr.	D4	16
Saint-Sever, Fr.	F3	16
Saint-Séverin-de-Beauce, Que.	C6	74
Saint-Siméon, Que.	B8	74
Saint-Siméon, Fr.	F3	17
Saint Simons Island, Ga., U.S.	E5	87
Saint Simons Island, i., Ga., U.S.	E5	87
Saint Simons Sound, strt., Ga., U.S.	E5	87
Sainte-Sixte, Que.	D2	74
Sainte-Sophie [-de-Lévrard], Que.	C5	74
Sainte-Sophie [-de-Mégantic], Que.	C6	74
Saint Stephen, N.B.	D2	71
Saint Stephen, S.C., U.S.	E8	117
Saint Stephens, Al., U.S.	D1	78
Saint Stephens, N.C., U.S.	*B1	110
Saint Stephen's Church, Isr. Occ.	m14	41
Saint Stephen's Gate, hist., Isr. Occ.	m14	41
Saint-Sylvère, Que.	C5	74
Saint-Sylvestre, Que.	C6	74
Saint Tammany, co., La., U.S.	D5	95
Sainte-Thècle, Que.	C5	74
Saint-Théodore, Que.	D7	74
Saint-Théophile, Que.	D7	74
Sainte-Thérèse, Que.	D4	74
Saint Thomas, Ont.	E3	73
Saint Thomas, Mo., U.S.	C5	102
Saint Thomas, N.D., U.S.	A8	111
Saint Thomas, Pa., U.S.	G6	115
Saint Thomas, i., V.I.U.S.	G12	64
Saint-Thomas [-de-Joliette], Que.	C4	74
Saint Timothée, Que.	q18	74
Saint-Tite, Que.	C5	74
Saint-Tite-des-Caps, Que.	B7	74
Saint-Tropez, Fr.	F7	16
Saint-Ubalde, Que.	C5	74
Saint-Urbain-de-Charlevoix, Que.	B7	74
Saint-Urbain [-de-Châteauguay], Que.	q19	74
Saint-Valérien, Que.	C5	74
Saint-Valéry-en-Caux, Fr.	E8	12
Saint-Valéry-sur-Somme, Fr.	B4	16
Saint-Vallier, Que.	C7	74
Saint-Vallier, Fr.	E6	16
Sainte-Véronique, Que.	C3	74
Saint-Victor, Que.	C7	74
Saint-Vincent, Mn., U.S.	B1	100
Saint-Vincent, I., St. Vin.	U26	65
Saint-Vincent, Cap, c., Madag.	h8	49
Saint-Vincent, Cape, c., Port.	D1	22
Saint Vincent, Gulf, b., Austl.	G6	50
Saint Vincent and the Grenadines, ctry., N.A.	J14	64
Saint Vincent Island, i., Fl., U.S.	C1	86
Saint Vincent Passage, strt., N.A.	J14	64
Saint Vincent's [-Saint Stephens-Peter's River], Newf.	E5	72
Saint-Vith, Bel.	D6	17
Saint Walburg, Sask.	D1	75
Saint Wendells, In., U.S.	H2	91
Saint Williams, Ont.	E4	73
Saint Xavier, Mt., U.S.	E9	103
Saint-Yrieix-la-Perche, Fr.	C7	74
Saint-Zacharie, Que.	C7	74
Saint-Zéphirin, Que.	C5	74
Saipan, N. Mar. Is.	E8	6
Saipan Channel, strt., N. Mar. Is.	D7	52
Saipan International Airport, N. Mar. Is.	D7	52
Sairecábur, Cerro, mtn., S.A.	E3	55
Sai Yok, Thai.	E3	35
Sajama, Nevado, mtn., Bol.	C2	58
Saka, Kenya	B6	48
Sa Kaeo, Thai.	F5	35
Sakai, Japan	o14	33
Sakākah, Sau. Ar.	C4	38
Sakakawea, Lake, res., N.D., U.S.	B3	111
Sakami, Lac, l., Que.	F17	66
Sakania, Zaire	D4	48
Sakaraha, Madag.	h8	49
Sakarya, stm., Tur.	B8	40
Sakashita, Japan	n16	33
Sakata, Japan	D12	31
Sakchu, N. Kor.	F2	33
Sakhalin, i., Sov. Un.	D17	29
Sakishima Islands, is., Japan	G9	31
Sakmara, stm., Sov. Un.	C5	28
Sakon Nakhon, Thai.	B2	34
Sakonnet, R.I., U.S.	F6	116
Sakonnet, stm., R.I., U.S.	E6	116
Sakonnet Point, c., R.I., U.S.	F6	116
Sakskøbing, Den.	D5	15
Sakti, India	D7	36
Sala, Swe.	H7	14
Salaberry-de-Valleyfield, Que.	D3	74
Sala Consilina, Italy	D5	23
Saladas, Arg.	E4	55
Saladillo, Arg.	B5	54
Salado, stm., Arg.	B5	54
Salado, stm., Arg.	F3	55
Salado, stm., Arg.	B3	54
Salado, stm., Mex.	B4	63
Salado, Arroyo, stm., Arg.	C3	54
Salado, Rio, stm., N.M., U.S.	C2	108
Salaga, Ghana	E4	45
Sala'ilua, W. Sam.	F11	52
Sala'ilua Bay, b., W. Sam.	F11	52
Salālah, Oman	D5	38
Salamá, Guat.	C2	62
Salamá, Hond.	E7	63
Salamanca, Chile	A2	54
Salamanca, Mex.	m13	63
Salamanca, Spain	B3	22
Salamanca, N.Y., U.S.	C2	109
Salamat, Bahr, stm., Chad	C3	46
Salamaua, Pap. N. Gui.	k12	50
Salamina, Col.	B2	60
Salamis, Grc.	D4	25
Salamís, i., Grc.	h10	25
Salamonia, In., U.S.	D8	91
Salamonie, stm., In., U.S.	C6	91
Salamonie Lake, res., In., U.S.	C6	91
Salar de Pocitos, Arg.	D2	55
Salas, Spain	A2	22
Salatiga, Indon.	*G4	34
Salavat, Sov. Un.	C5	28
Salaverry, Peru	C2	58
Salavina, Arg.	E3	55
Salawati, i., Indon.	F8	34
Sala y Gómez, Isla, i., Chile	H15	6
Salbris, Fr.	D5	16
Salcantay, Nevado, mtn., Peru	D3	58
Salcedo, Ec.	B2	58
Saldanha, S. Afr.	D2	49
Saldus, Sov. Un.	C4	27
Sale, Austl.	I6	51
Sale City, Ga., U.S.	E2	87
Sale Creek, Tn., U.S.	D8	119
Salée, Rivière, strt., Guad.	Q8	65
Salekhard, Sov. Un.	C9	29
Salem, India	F6	36
Salem, Al., U.S.	C4	78
Salem, Ar., U.S.	A4	81
Salem, Ct., U.S.	D6	84
Salem, Il., U.S.	E5	90
Salem, In., U.S.	G5	91
Salem, In., U.S.	D8	91
Salem, Ia., U.S.	D6	92
Salem, Ky., U.S.	e9	94
Salem, Ma., U.S.	A6	98
Salem, Mi., U.S.	p14	99
Salem, Mo., U.S.	D6	102
Salem, Ne., U.S.	D10	104
Salem, N.H., U.S.	E4	106
Salem, N.J., U.S.	D2	107
Salem, N.M., U.S.	E2	108
Salem, N.Y., U.S.	B7	109
Salem, Oh., U.S.	B5	112
Salem, Or., U.S.	C4	114
Salem, S.C., U.S.	B2	117
Salem, S.D., U.S.	D8	118
Salem, Ut., U.S.	C4	121
Salem, Va., U.S.	C2	123
Salem, W.V., U.S.	B4	125
Salem, Wi., U.S.	n11	126
Salem, co., N.J., U.S.	D2	107
Salem, stm., N.J., U.S.	D2	107
Salem, Lake, l., Vt., U.S.	B4	122
Salemburg, N.C., U.S.	B4	110
Salemi, Italy	L7	23
Salen, Scot., U.K.	D3	13
Salen, Scot., U.K.	E4	13
Salerno, Italy	D5	23
Salerno, Gulf of, b., Italy	D5	23
Salfit, Isr. Occ.	B7	41
Salford, Eng., U.K.	D5	10
Salgótarján, Hung.	A4	24
Salgueiro, Braz.	C7	57
Salida, Co., U.S.	C5	83
Salies-de-Béarn, Fr.	F3	16
Salihli, Tur.	C7	25
Salima, Mwi.	D5	48
Salin, Burma	B1	35
Salina, Mex.	A6	80
Salina, Ks., U.S.	D6	93
Salina, Ok., U.S.	A6	113
Salina, Ut., U.S.	E4	121
Salina, i., Italy	E5	23
Salina Cruz, Mex.	D5	63
Salinas, Braz.	A5	56
Salinas, Ec.	B1	58
Salinas, Ca., U.S.	D3	82
Salinas, stm., N.A.	B2	62
Salinas, stm., Ca., U.S.	D3	82
Salinas, Cape, c., Spain	C7	22
Salinas, Pampa de las, pl., Arg.	A3	54
Salinas de Garci Mendoza, Bol.	C2	55
Salinas National Monument, N.M., U.S.	C3	108
Salinas Peak, mtn., N.M., U.S.	D3	108
Saline, La., U.S.	B3	95
Saline, Mi., U.S.	F7	99
Saline, co., Ar., U.S.	C3	81
Saline, co., Il., U.S.	F5	90
Saline, co., Ks., U.S.	D6	93
Saline, co., Mo., U.S.	B4	102
Saline, co., Ne., U.S.	D8	104
Saline, stm., Ar., U.S.	C1	81
Saline, stm., Ar., U.S.	D4	81
Saline, stm., Ks., U.S.	C3	93
Saline, North Fork, stm., Il., U.S.	F5	90
Saline, South Fork, stm., Ar., U.S.	f8	81
Saline Bayou, stm., La., U.S.	B3	95
Saline Lake, res., La., U.S.	C3	95
Salineno, Tx., U.S.	F3	120
Salines, Point, c., Gren.	W25	65
Salines, Pointe des, c., Mart.	T11	65
Salineville, Oh., U.S.	B5	112
Salinópolis, Braz.	B1	57
Salins-les-Bains, Fr.	D6	16
Salisbury, Austl.	*F6	50
Salisbury, N.B.	C4	71
Salisbury, Eng., U.K.	E6	10
Salisbury, Ct., U.S.	B2	84
Salisbury, Md., U.S.	D6	97
Salisbury, Ma., U.S.	A6	98
Salisbury, Mo., U.S.	B5	102
Salisbury, N.H., U.S.	D3	106
Salisbury, N.C., U.S.	B2	110
Salisbury, Pa., U.S.	G3	115
Salisbury, Vt., U.S.	D2	122
Salisbury Center, N.Y., U.S.	B6	109
Salisbury see Harare, Zimb.	A5	49
Salisbury Heights, N.H., U.S.	D3	106
Salisbury Island, i., N.W. Ter.	C16	66
Salisbury Plain, pl., Eng., U.K.	E6	12
Salish Mountains, mts., Mt., U.S.	B2	103
Salitpa, Al., U.S.	D1	78
Salix, Ia., U.S.	B1	92
Salkehatchie, stm., S.C., U.S.	E5	117
Salkum, Wa., U.S.	C3	124
Sallanches, Fr.	D2	20
Salley, S.C., U.S.	D5	117
Saliqueló, Arg.	B4	54
Sallis, Ms., U.S.	B4	101
Sallisaw, Ok., U.S.	B7	113
Salluit, Que.	f11	74
Sallūm, Khalīj as, b., Afr.	G5	40
Salm, i., Sov. Un.	B9	128
Salmás, Iran	B2	39
Salmo, B.C.	E9	69
Salmon, Id., U.S.	D5	89
Salmon, stm., B.C.	B6	69
Salmon, stm., N.B.	C4	71
Salmon, stm., N.B.	B2	71
Salmon, stm., Id., U.S.	f10	109
Salmon, stm., Id., U.S.	D3	89
Salmon, Middle Fork, stm., Id., U.S.	E4	89
Salmon, South Fork, stm., Id., U.S.	E3	89
Salmon Arm, B.C.	D8	69
Salmon-Bay, c.	C3	72
Salmon Creek, Wa., U.S.	D3	124
Salmon Creek Reservoir, res., Id., U.S.	G4	89
Salmon Falls, stm., U.S.	D5	106
Salmon Falls Creek, stm., U.S.	G4	89
Salmon Mountain, mtn., N.H., U.S.	f7	106
Salmon Mountains, mts., Ca., U.S.	B2	82
Salmon Peak, mtn., Tx., U.S.	E2	120
Salmon Point, c., Ont.	D7	73
Salmon River Mountains, mts., U.S.	E3	89
Salmon River Reservoir, res., N.Y., U.S.	B5	109
Salmon Valley, B.C.	B6	69
Salo, Fin.	G10	14
Salò, Italy	D6	20
Salol, Mn., U.S.	B3	100
Salome, Az., U.S.	D2	80
Salon-de-Provence, Fr.	F6	16
Salonika see Thessaloníki, Grc.	B4	40
Salonika, Gulf of see Thermaïkós Kólpos, b., Grc.	B4	40
Salonta, Rom.	B5	24
Salsacate, Arg.	A3	54
Salsette, i., India	H4	37
Salsk, Sov. Un.	H13	27
Salsomaggiore Terme, Italy	B2	23
Salt, stm., Az., U.S.	D4	80
Salt, stm., Ky., U.S.	C4	94
Salt, stm., Mo., U.S.	B6	102
Salt, Middle Fork, stm., Mo., U.S.	B5	102
Salt, North Fork, stm., Mo., U.S.	B5	102
Salt, South Fork, stm., Mo., U.S.	B5	102
Salta, Arg.	D2	55
Salta, prov., Arg.	D3	55
Saltair, Ut., U.S.	C3	121
Saltburn-by-the-Sea, Eng., U.K.	F8	13
Salt Cay, i., Bah.	m18	64
Saltcoats, Sask.	G5	75
Saltcoats, Scot., U.K.	F4	13
Salt Creek, stm., Il., U.S.	C4	90
Salt Creek, stm., Ne., U.S.	h11	104
Salt Creek, stm., N.M., U.S.	D5	108
Salt Creek, stm., Oh., U.S.	C3	112
Salt Creek, stm., Wy., U.S.	C6	127
Salt Fork, Ok., U.S.	A4	113
Salt Fork Lake, res., Oh., U.S.	B4	112
Saltholm, i., Den.	C6	15
Saltillo, Mex.	B4	63
Saltillo, In., U.S.	G5	91
Saltillo, Ms., U.S.	A5	101
Saltillo, Pa., U.S.	F6	115
Salt Lake, co., Ut., U.S.	C3	121
Salt Lake, l., Hi., U.S.	g10	88
Salt Lake City, Ut., U.S.	C4	121
Salt Lick, Ky., U.S.	B6	94
Salto, Braz.	m8	56
Salto, Ur.	C5	55
Salto Grande, Braz.	C3	55
Salton Sea, l., Ca., U.S.	F5	82
Salt Point, c., Ca., U.S.	C2	82
Salt River Indian Reservation, Az., U.S.	k9	80
Salt River Range, mts., Wy., U.S.	D2	127
Salt Rock, W.V., U.S.	C2	125
Saltsjöbaden (part of Nacka), Swe.	t36	14
Saltspring Island, i., B.C.	E6	69
Salt Springs, Fl., U.S.	C5	86
Saltville, Va., U.S.	f10	123
Saltwater, Ky., U.S.	*B3	124
Salt Wells Creek, stm., Wy., U.S.	E4	127
Salud, Pan.	k10	62
Saluda, N.C., U.S.	f10	110
Saluda, S.C., U.S.	C4	117
Saluda, Va., U.S.	C6	123
Saluda, co., S.C., U.S.	C4	117
Saluda, stm., S.C., U.S.	C4	117
Saluda Dam, S.C., U.S.	C5	117
Sālūr, India	E7	36
Salus, Ar., U.S.	B2	81
Saluvia, Pa., U.S.	F5	115
Saluzzo, Italy	B1	23
Salvador, Braz.	D3	57
Salvador, Sask.	E1	75
Salvador, Lake, l., La., U.S.	E5	95
Salvage, Newf.	D5	72
Salvatierra, Mex.	m13	63
Salvisa, Ky., U.S.	C5	94
Salwa Bay, b., Asia	I5	39
Salween (Thanlwin), stm., Asia	D10	36
Salyān, Nepal	C9	37
Salyer, Ca., U.S.	B2	82
Salyersville, Ky., U.S.	C6	94
Salzach, stm., Eur.	E6	18
Salzburg, Aus.	D7	21
Salzburg, state, Aus.	B8	20
Salzgitter, Ger.	B5	18
Salzwedel, Ger.	B5	18
Sama [de Langreo], Spain	A3	22
Samaipata, Bol.	C3	55
Samálá, stm., Guat.	C2	62
Samaná, Dom. Rep.	E9	64
Samaná, Bahía de b., Dom. Rep.	E9	64
Samana Cay, i., Bah.	C7	64
Samandaği, Tur.	D10	40
Samani, Japan	E11	33
Samar, i., Phil.	C7	34
Samar, Isr.	E6	41
Samara, Sov. Un.	D8	29
Samara, stm., Sov. Un.	C4	28
Samarai, Pap. N. Gui.	m13	50
Samarga, Sov. Un.	C9	33
Samaria, Id., U.S.	G6	89
Samariapo, Ven.	B4	60
Samarinda, Indon.	F5	34
Samarkand, Sov. Un.	F9	29
Sāmarrā', Iraq	B4	38
Sāmarrā Barrage, Iraq	E14	40
Samataiuta, W. Sam.	*F11	52
Samatan, Fr.	F4	16
Samawāri, Pak.	C1	37
Sambalpur, India	J11	37
Sambar, Cape, c., Indon.	F4	34
Sambas, Indon.	E3	34
Sambava, Madag.	f10	49
Sambhal, India	C7	37
Sambhar, India	D5	37
Sambor, Sov. Un.	A4	27
Samborombón, Bahia, b., Arg.	B5	54
Sambre, stm., Eur.	D4	17
Samburg, Tn., U.S.	A2	119
Samchŏk, S. Kor.	H4	33
Samchŏnpo, S. Kor.	I4	33
Same, Tan.	B6	48
Samedan, Switz.	C5	20
Sammamish Lake, l., Wa., U.S.	e11	124
Samnorwood, Tx., U.S.	B2	120
Samnū, Libya	B3	46
Samoa, Is.	D6	2
Samokov, Bul.	D6	24
Sámos, Grc.	D6	40
Sámos, i., Grc.	D6	40
Samoset, Fl., U.S.	q10	86
Samosir, i., Indon.	E1	34
Samoth, Il., U.S.	F5	90
Samothrace see Samothráki, i., Grc.	B5	40
Samothráki (Samothrace), i., Grc.	B5	40
Sampacho, Arg.	A4	54
Sampaloc Point, c., Phil.	o13	34
Sampit, Indon.	F4	34
Sampit, stm., S.C., U.S.	E9	117
Sampson, co., N.C., U.S.	C4	110
Sampwe, Zaire	C4	48
Sam Rayburn Reservoir, res., Tx., U.S.	D5	120
Samsang, China	B9	37
Samsø, i., Den.	C4	15
Samsø Bælt, strt., Den.	C4	15
Samson, Al., U.S.	D3	78
Samsun, Tur.	B11	40
Samtown, La., U.S.	*C3	95
Samtredia, Sov. Un.	A14	40
Samuels, Id., U.S.	A2	89
Samur, stm., Sov. Un.	D25	8
Samut Sakhon, Thai.	C2	34
Samut Songkhram, Thai.	C2	34
San, Mali	F4	45
San, stm., Asia	F7	35
San, stm., Eur.	B3	24
Şan'ā', Yemen	D4	38
Sanaag, prov., Som.	C6	47
Sanaga, stm., Cam.	E2	46
San Agustin, Cape, c., Phil.	D7	34
San Agustin, Plains of, pl., N.M., U.S.	C2	108
San Agustin de Valle Fértil, Arg.	A3	54
Sanak Islands, is., Ak., U.S.	E7	79
San Ambrosio, Isla, i., Chile	F3	53
Sanana, i., Indon.	F7	34
Sanandaj, Iran	B4	38
San Andreas, Ca., U.S.	C3	82
San Andrés, Col.	D7	62
San Andres Mountains, mts., N.M., U.S.	E3	108
San Andrés Tetepilco (part of Mexico City), Mex.	h9	63
San Andrés y Providencia, dept., Col.	*D7	62
San Ángelo, Tx., U.S.	D2	120
San Antonio, Arg.	A4	54
San Antonio, Chile	A2	54
San Antonio, N. Mar. Is.	D7	52
San Antonio, Tx., U.S.	E3	120
San Antonio, Cabo, c., Arg.	B5	54
San Antonio, Cabo, c., Cuba	D1	64
San Antonio Abad, Spain	C6	22
San Antonio Bay, b., Tx., U.S.	E4	120
San Antonio de Areco, Arg.	g7	54
San Antonio de los Baños, Cuba	C2	64
San Antonio de los Cobres, Arg.	D2	55
San Antonio Mountain, mtn., N.M., U.S.	A3	108
San Antonio Oeste, Arg.	C4	54
Sanarate, Guat.	C2	62
San Ardo, Ca., U.S.	D3	82
Sanatorium, Ms., U.S.	D4	101
San Augustine, co., Tx., U.S.	D5	120
San Bartolomeo [in Galdo], Italy	D5	23
San Benedetto del Tronto, Italy	C4	23
San Benito, Tx., U.S.	F4	120
San Benito, co., Ca., U.S.	D3	82
San Benito Mountain, mtn., Ca., U.S.	D3	82
San Bernardino, Switz.	D7	21
San Bernardino, Ca., U.S.	E5	82
San Bernardino, co., Ca., U.S.	E5	82
San Bernardo, Chile	A2	54
San Blas, Mex.	m11	63
San Blas, Cape, c., Fl., U.S.	v16	86
San Blas, Cordillera de, mts., Pan.	F8	62
San Blas, Punta, c., Pan.	F8	62
San Bonifacio, Italy	D7	20
San Borja, Bol.	B2	55
San Borja, stm., Mex.	h9	63
Sanborn, Ia., U.S.	A2	92
Sanborn, Mn., U.S.	F3	100
Sanborn, N.D., U.S.	C7	111
Sanborn, Wi., U.S.	B3	126
Sanborn, co., S.D., U.S.	D7	118
Sanbornton, N.H., U.S.	D3	106
Sanbornville, N.H., U.S.	C4	106
San Bruno, Ca., U.S.	D2	82
San Candido, Italy	C8	20
San Carlos, Arg.	A3	54
San Carlos, Chile	B2	54
San Carlos, Mex.	B4	63
San Carlos, Nic.	E8	63
San Carlos, Phil.	o13	34
San Carlos, Az., U.S.	D5	80
San Carlos, Ca., U.S.	k8	82
San Carlos, Ur.	E2	56
San Carlos, Ven.	B4	60
San Carlos de Bariloche, Arg.	C2	54
San Carlos de Río Negro, Ven.	C4	60
San Carlos Indian Reservation, Az., U.S.	D5	80
San Carlos Lake, res., Az., U.S.	D5	80
San Cataldo, Italy	F4	23
Sancerre, Fr.	D4	16
Sánchez, Dom. Rep.	E9	64
Sanch'ung, Tai.	*F9	31
San Ciro de Acosta, Mex.	m14	63
San Clemente, Spain	C4	22
San Clemente, Ca., U.S.	F5	82
San Clemente Island, i., Ca., U.S.	F4	82
San Cristóbal, Arg.	A4	54
San Cristóbal, Dom. Rep.	E8	64
San Cristóbal, Ven.	B3	60
San Cristóbal, i., Sol. Is.	A4	6
San Cristóbal, Isla (Chatham), i., Ec.	g6	58
San Cristóbal, Volcán, vol., Nic.	D4	62
San Cristóbal de las Casas, Mex.	D6	63
Sancti-Spiritus, Cuba	D4	64
Sancti-Spíritus, prov., Cuba	D4	64
Sanctuary, Sask.	G1	75
Sancy, Puy de, mtn., Fr.	E5	16
Sand, stm., Alta.	B5	68
Sanda, Japan	o14	33
Sanda Island, i., Scot., U.K.	E3	13
Sandakan, Malay.	D5	34
Sandalfoot Cove, Fl., U.S.	*F6	86
San Daniele del Friuli, Italy	C8	20
Sandaré, Mali	E3	45
Sanday, i., Scot., U.K.	A5	10
Sanday Sound, strt., Scot., U.K.	A6	13
Sandborn, In., U.S.	G3	91
Sand Brook, N.J., U.S.	C3	107
Sand Coulee, Mt., U.S.	C5	103
Sand Creek, Wi., U.S.	C2	126
Sand Creek, stm., Ks., U.S.	g12	93
Sand Creek, stm., Wy., U.S.	C7	127
Sand Draw, Wy., U.S.	*D4	127
Sande, Nor.	p28	14
Sandefjord, Nor.	p28	14
Sanders, Az., U.S.	B6	80
Sanders, Ky., U.S.	B5	94
Sanders, Mt., U.S.	D9	103
Sanders, co., Mt., U.S.	C1	103
Sanderson, Tx., U.S.	D1	120
Sandersville, Ga., U.S.	D4	87
Sandersville, Ms., U.S.	D4	101
Sandfly Lake, l., Sask.	B2	75
Sand Fork, W.V., U.S.	C4	125
Sandhammaren, c., Swe.	C8	15
Sand Hill, Ms., U.S.	D5	101
Sand Hill, stm., Mn., U.S.	C2	100
Sandhill, stm., Newf.	B3	72
Sandi, India	C7	36
Sandia, Peru	F6	58
Sandia Crest, mtn., N.M., U.S.	k8	108
Sandia Indian Reservation, N.M., U.S.	k7	108
Sandia Mountains, mts., N.M., U.S.	k8	108
Sandia Park, N.M., U.S.	k8	108
San Diego, Ca., U.S.	F5	82
San Diego, co., Ca., U.S.	F5	82
San Diego, Cabo, c., Arg.	h12	54
San Diego Naval Station, mil., Ca., U.S.	o15	82
San Diego Naval Training Center, mil., Ca., U.S.	o15	82
Sandıklı, Tur.	C4	40
Sandilands, Man.	E3	70
San Dimas, Mex.	C3	63
San Dimas, Ca., U.S.	*m13	82
Sand Island, i., Mid. Is.	K3	52

Name	Map Ref.	Page

Sand Island, i., Hi., U.S. — g10 88
Sand Island, i., Wi., U.S. — B3 126
Sand Islet, i., Mid. Is. — J3 52
Sand Key, i., Fl., U.S. — E4 86
Sandlick Creek, stm., W.V., U.S. — n13 125
Sand Mountain, mtn., U.S. — A3 78
Sandnes, Nor. — C3 48
Sandoa, Zaire — C6 26
Sandomierz, Pol. — D9 69
Sandon, B.C. — C2 60
Sandoná, Col. — C2 60
San Donà di Piave, Italy — B4 23
Sandoval, Il., U.S. — E4 90
Sandoval, co., N.M., U.S. — B2 108
Sandover, stm., Austl. — D6 50
Sandoway, Burma — E9 36
Sandown, Eng., U.K. — D6 12
Sandown, N.H., U.S. — E4 106
Sand Point, Ont. — B8 73
Sand Point, Ak., U.S. — D7 79
Sandpoint, Id., U.S. — A2 89
Sands, Mi., U.S. — B3 99
Sands Key, i., Fl., U.S. — s3 86
Sandspit, B.C. — C2 69
Sand Springs, Mt., U.S. — C9 103
Sand Springs, Ok., U.S. — A5 113
Sandston, Va., U.S. — m18 123
Sandstone, Austl. — E2 50
Sandstone, Mn., U.S. — D6 100
Sandstone, W.V., U.S. — D4 125
Sandtown, De., U.S. — D3 85
Sandusky, Mi., U.S. — E8 99
Sandusky, N.Y., U.S. — C2 109
Sandusky, Oh., U.S. — A3 112
Sandusky, co., Oh., U.S. — A2 112
Sandusky, stm., Oh., U.S. — B2 112
Sandusky Bay, b., Oh., U.S. — A3 112
Sandvig (part of Allinge-Sandvig), Den. — C8 15
Sandviken, Swe. — G7 14
Sandwich, Il., U.S. — B5 90
Sandwich, Ma., U.S. — C7 98
Sandwich, N.H., U.S. — C4 106
Sandwich Bay, b., Newf. — B3 72
Sandwich Range, mts., N.H., U.S. — C3 106
Sandwick, B.C. — E5 69
Sandwith, Sask. — D1 75
Sandy, Or., U.S. — B4 114
Sandy, Ut., U.S. — C4 121
Sandy, stm., Me., U.S. — D2 96
Sandy Bay Mountain, mtn., Me., U.S. — C2 96
Sandy Brook, stm., Ct., U.S. — A3 84
Sandy Cape, c., Austl. — D9 50
Sandy Creek, N.Y., U.S. — B4 109
Sandy Creek, stm., Oh., U.S. — B4 112
Sandy Creek, stm., Ok., U.S. — C2 113
Sandy Hook, Ct., U.S. — D2 84
Sandy Hook, Ky., U.S. — B6 94
Sandy Hook, Md., U.S. — B2 97
Sandy Hook, Ms., U.S. — D4 101
Sandy Hook, spit, N.J., U.S. — C5 107
Sandy Island, i., S.C., U.S. — D9 117
Sandy Lake, Man. — D1 70
Sandy Lake, Pa., U.S. — D1 115
Sandy Lake, l., Newf. — D3 72
Sandy Lake, l., Ont. — n16 73
Sandy Lake, l., Sask. — B2 75
Sandy Neck, pen., Ma., U.S. — C7 98
Sandy Point, Me., U.S. — D4 96
Sandy Point, c., Trin. — M24 65
Sandy Point, i., R.I., U.S. — h7 116
Sandy Point, c., V.I.U.S. — C6 65
Sandy Pond, l., Ma., U.S. — g10 98
Sandy Ridge, Al., U.S. — C3 78
Sandy Ridge, N.C., U.S. — A2 110
Sandy Ridge, Pa., U.S. — E5 115
Sandy Ridge, mtn., Va., U.S. — e9 123
Sandy Springs, Ga., U.S. — h8 87
Sandy Springs, S.C., U.S. — B2 117
Sandyville, Md., U.S. — A4 97
Sandyville, W.V., U.S. — C3 125
San Elizario, Tx., U.S. — o11 120
San Enrique, Arg. — B4 54
San Estanislao, Para. — D4 55
San Esteban, Hond. — D7 63
San Felice sul Panaro, Italy — E7 22
San Felipe, Chile — A2 54
San Felipe, Col. — C4 60
San Felipe, Mex. — m13 63
San Felipe, Ven. — A4 60
San Felipe, Punta, c., Mex. — A2 63
San Felipe Indian Reservation, N.M., U.S. — k8 108
San Felipe Pueblo, N.M., U.S. — B3 108
San Feliu de Guixols, Spain — B7 22
San Félix, Isla, i., Chile — F2 53
San Fernando, Arg. — A5 54
San Fernando, Chile — A2 54
San Fernando, Mex. — C5 63
San Fernando, Phil. — o13 34
San Fernando, Spain — D2 22
San Fernando, Trin. — K14 64
San Fernando, Ca., U.S. — m12 82
San Fernando de Apure, Ven. — B4 60
San Fernando de Atabapo, Ven. — C4 60
San Fernando de Henares, Spain — p17 22
San Fidel, N.M., U.S. — B2 108
Sånfjället, mtn., Swe. — F5 14
Sånfjället National Park, Swe. — F5 14
Sanford, Fl., U.S. — D5 86
Sanford, Me., U.S. — E2 96
Sanford, Mi., U.S. — E6 99
Sanford, N.C., U.S. — B3 110
Sanford, Tx., U.S. — B2 120
Sanford, Mount, mtn., Ak., U.S. — C11 79
San Francisco, Arg. — A4 54
San Francisco, Col. — C2 60
San Francisco, Ca., U.S. — D2 82
San Francisco, co., Ca., U.S. — D2 82
San Francisco, stm., U.S. — D6 80
San Francisco, Paso de, S.A. — B2 54
San Francisco Bay, b., Ca., U.S. — h8 82
San Francisco de Borja, Mex. — B3 63
San Francisco del Oro, Mex. — B3 63
San Francisco del Rincón, Mex. — m13 63
San Francisco de Macorís, Dom. Rep. — E9 64
San Francisco Mountains, mts., Ut., U.S. — E2 121
San Francisco Solano, Punta, c., Col. — B2 60

San Gabriel, Ca., U.S. — m12 82
San Gabriel, Punta, c., Mex. — B2 63
San Gabriel Chilac, Mex. — D5 63
San Gabriel Mountains, mts., Ca., U.S. — m12 82
San Gallan, Isla, i., Peru — D2 58
Sangamner, India — H5 37
Sangamon, co., Il., U.S. — D4 90
Sangamon, stm., Il., U.S. — C3 90
Sangatte, Fr. — D9 12
Sangay, Volcán, vol., Ec. — B2 58
Sang-e Māsheh, Afg. — E13 39
Sanger, Ca., U.S. — D4 82
Sanger, Tx., U.S. — C4 120
Sangerhausen, Ger. — C5 18
San Germán, P.R. — B1 65
Sangerville, Me., U.S. — C3 96
Sanggau, Indon. — E4 34
Sangha, stm., Afr. — E3 46
San Giacomo Pass, Eur. — D5 21
Sanghie, i., Indon. — E7 34
San Gil, Col. — B3 60
San Gimignano, Italy — C3 23
San Giovanni in Fiore, Italy — E6 23
San Giovanni in Persiceto, Italy — E7 20
Sangju, S. Kor. — H4 33
Sāngli, India — *E5 36
Sangmélima, Cam. — E2 46
San Gorgonio Mountain, mtn., Ca., U.S. — E5 82
Sangre de Cristo Mountains, mts., U.S. — C6 76
San Gregorio, Ca., U.S. — k8 82
San Gregorio, Ur. — E1 56
Sangre Grande, Trin. — N23 65
Sangro, stm., Italy — D5 23
Sangrur, India — B5 37
Sangudo, Alta. — C3 68
Sangüesa, Spain — A5 22
Sanguinara, stm., Italy — h8 23
Sanhedriyya (part of Jerusalem), Isr. — m14 41
Sanibel, Fl., U.S. — F4 86
Sanibel Island, i., Fl., U.S. — F4 86
San Ignacio, Belize — B3 62
San Ignacio, Bol. — B2 55
San Ignacio, Mex. — B2 63
San Ignacio, Para. — A4 55
San Ildefonso, Cape, c., Phil. — B6 34
San Ildefonso [o la Granja], Spain — B3 22
San Ildefonso Peninsula, pen., Phil. — n14 34
Sanish, N.D., U.S. — B3 111
San Isidro, Arg. — g7 54
San Isidro, Peru — *D2 58
San Isidro, Tx., U.S. — F3 120
San Isidro [del General], C.R. — F6 62
Sanitz, Ger. — D6 15
San Jacinto, Ca., U.S. — F5 82
San Jacinto, co., Tx., U.S. — D5 120
San Jacinto, stm., Tx., U.S. — r14 120
San Jacinto Peak, mtn., Ca., U.S. — F5 82
San Javier, Arg. — A4 54
San Javier, Bol. — C3 55
San Javier, stm., Arg. — F3 55
San Javier [de Loncomilla], Chile — B2 54
San Jerónimo, Serranía de, mts., Col. — B2 60
San Jerónimo Lídice (part of Mexico City), Mex. — h9 63
Sanjiang, China — L3 32
Sanjō, Japan — H9 33
San Joaquin, Para. — D4 55
San Joaquin, co., Ca., U.S. — D3 82
San Joaquin, stm., Ca., U.S. — D3 82
San Joaquin Valley, val., Ca., U.S. — D3 82
San Jon, N.M., U.S. — B6 108
San Jorge, Golfo, b., Arg. — D3 54
San Jose, Belize — B3 62
San José, C.R. — F5 62
San José, Guat. — F8 63
San Jose, i., N. Mar. Is. — E7 52
San Jose, N. Mar. Is. — E7 52
San Jose, Phil. — C6 34
San Jose, Az., U.S. — E6 80
San Jose, Ca., U.S. — D3 82
San Jose, Il., U.S. — C4 90
San Jose, N.M., U.S. — B4 108
San Jose, dept., Ur. — g8 54
San José, stm., B.C. — D7 69
San José, Isla, i., Mex. — B2 63
San José [de Chiquitos, Bol.] — C3 55
San José de Feliciano, Arg. — A5 54
San José de Guanipa (El Tigrito), Ven. — B5 60
San José de Jachal, Arg. — F2 55
San José del Boquerón, Arg. — E3 55
San José del Cabo, Mex. — C3 63
San José del Guaviare, Col. — D5 60
San José de los Molinos, Peru — D2 58
San José de Mayo, Ur. — E1 56
San José de Ocuné, Col. — E5 60
San Jose Island, i., Tx., U.S. — E4 120
San Juan, Arg. — A3 54
San Juan, Phil. — p13 34
San Juan, Phil. — n13 34
San Juan, P.R. — G11 64
San Juan, co., U.S. — D6 83
San Juan, Tx., U.S. — F3 120
San Juan, prov., Arg. — A3 54
San Juan, co., Co., U.S. — D3 83
San Juan, co., N.M., U.S. — A1 108
San Juan, co., Ut., U.S. — F5 121
San Juan, co., Wa., U.S. — A2 124
San Juan, stm., Arg. — A3 54
San Juan, stm., B.C. — g11 69
San Juan, stm., N.A. — E8 63
San Juan, Cabezas de, c., P.R. — E4 55
San Juan Bautista, Para. — E4 55
San Juan Capistrano, Ca., U.S. — F5 82
San Juan de Aragón (part of Mexico City), Mex. — h9 63
San Juan de Colón, Ven. — B2 60
San Juan [de la Maguana], Dom. Rep. — E8 64
San Juan de Lima, Punta, c., Mex. — D4 63
San Juan del Norte, Nic. — E8 63
San Juan de los Cayos, Ven. — A4 60
San Juan de los Lagos, Mex. — m12 63
San Juan de los Morros, Ven. — B4 60

San Juan del Río, Mex. — m13 63
San Juan del Sur, Nic. — E7 63
San Juan Island, i., Wa., U.S. — A2 124
San Juan Mountains, mts., Co., U.S. — D3 83
San Juan Nepomuceno, Col. — B2 60
San Juan Pueblo, N.M., U.S. — *A3 108
San Juan y Martínez, Cuba — C2 64
San Julián, Arg. — D3 54
San Justo, Arg. — A4 54
Sankarani, stm., Afr. — D3 45
Sankt Anton [am Arlberg], Aus. — B6 20
Sankt Blasien, Ger. — B4 20
Sankt Gallen, Switz. — E4 18
Sankt Gallen, state, Switz. — B5 20
Sankt Gallenkirch, Aus. — B8 21
Sankt Georgen [im Attergau], Aus. — B9 20
Sankt Goarshausen, Ger. — C2 19
Sankt Johann [in Tirol], Aus. — B8 20
Sankt Margrethen, Switz. — B8 21
Sankt Michaelisdonn, Ger. — E3 15
Sankt Moritz, Switz. — E4 18
Sankt Olof, Swe. — C8 15
Sankt Pölten, Aus. — E7 18
Sankt Veit [an der Glan], Aus. — E7 18
Sankt Wendel, Ger. — D2 19
Sankuru, stm., Zaire — B3 48
San Leandro, Ca., U.S. — h8 82
San Lorenzo, Arg. — A4 54
San Lorenzo, Ec. — A2 58
San Lorenzo, Hond. — D4 62
San Lorenzo, P.R. — B4 65
San Lorenzo, co., N.M., U.S. — E2 108
San Lorenzo, Cerro, mtn., S.A. — D2 54
San Lorenzo de El Escorial, Spain — B3 22
Sanlúcar [de Barrameda], Spain — D2 22
San Lucas, Bol. — C2 55
San Lucas, Mex. — C2 63
San Lucas, Serranía de, mts., Col. — B3 60
San Luis, Arg. — A3 54
San Luis, Cuba — D7 63
San Luis, Guat. — D7 63
San Luis, Az., U.S. — E3 80
San Luis, Co., U.S. — D5 83
San Luis, prov., Arg. — A3 54
San Luis, stm., Mex. — h9 63
San Luis, Point, c., Ca., U.S. — E3 82
San Luis Creek, stm., Co., U.S. — C5 83
San Luis de la Paz, Mex. — m13 63
San Luis Jilotepeque, Guat. — C3 62
San Luis Obispo, Ca., U.S. — E3 82
San Luis Obispo, co., Ca., U.S. — E3 82
San Luis Pass, strt., Tx., U.S. — r14 120
San Luis Peak, mtn., Co., U.S. — D4 83
San Luis Potosí, Mex. — C4 63
San Luis Potosí, state, Mex. — C4 63
San Luis Río Colorado, Mex. — A2 63
San Luis Valley, val., Co., U.S. — D4 83
San Manuel, Az., U.S. — E5 80
San Marco [in Lamis], Italy — D9 23
San Marcos, Col. — B2 60
San Marcos, Guat. — C2 62
San Marcos, Ca., U.S. — F5 82
San Marcos, Tx., U.S. — E4 120
San Marcos, stm., Tx., U.S. — h8 120
San Marcos de Colón, Hond. — D4 62
San Marino, Ca., U.S. — m12 82
San Marino, ctry., Eur. — C4 23
San Martín, Arg. — A3 54
San Martín, Col. — C4 60
San Martín, dept., Peru — C2 58
San Martín, stm., Bol. — B5 55
San Martín, Lago (Lago O'Higgins), l., S.A. — D2 54
San Martín de la Vega, Spain — p17 22
San Martín de los Andes, Arg. — C2 54
San Martino di Castrozza, Italy — C7 20
San Mateo, Spain — B6 22
San Mateo, Ca., U.S. — D2 82
San Mateo, Fl., U.S. — C5 86
San Mateo, N.M., U.S. — B2 108
San Mateo, co., Ca., U.S. — D2 82
San Mateo, Cabo, c., Ec. — B1 58
San Mateo Mountains, mts., N.M., U.S. — D2 108
San Mateo Mountains, mts., N.M., U.S. — B2 108
San Matías, Bol. — C4 55
San Matías, Golfo, b., Arg. — C4 54
Sanmen Bay, b., China — J9 32
Sanmenxia, China — E7 32
San Miguel, El Sal. — D4 62
San Miguel, Pan. — F8 62
San Miguel, Ca., U.S. — E3 82
San Miguel, N.M., U.S. — E3 108
San Miguel, co., Co., U.S. — D2 83
San Miguel, co., N.M., U.S. — B5 108
San Miguel, stm., Bol. — C3 55
San Miguel, stm., S.A. — C3 55
San Miguel, Golfo de, b., Pan. — F8 63
San Miguel de Allende, Mex. — m13 63
San Miguel de Tucumán, Arg. — E2 55
San Miguel Island, i., Ca., U.S. — *E3 82
San Miguelito, Pan. — *F8 62
San Miguel Mountains, mts., Co., U.S. — D2 83
Sanming, China — K7 32
Sannär, Sud. — C3 47
San Narciso, Phil. — o13 34
San Narciso, Phil. — p14 34
Sannar Dam, Sud. — C3 47
San Nicolás [de los Arroyos], Arg. — A4 54
San Nicolás de los Garzas, Mex. — *B4 63
San Nicolas Island, i., Ca., U.S. — F4 82
Sanniquellie, Lib. — E3 45
Sannois, Fr. — g10 16
Sano, Japan — m18 33
Sanok, Pol. — D7 26
San Onofre, Col. — B2 60
San Pablo, Phil. — o13 34
San Pablo, Col. — B2 60
San Pablo, Ca., U.S. — *h8 82
San Pablo, stm., Bol. — C3 55
San Pablo, Cabo, c., Mex. — C2 63
San Pablo Bay, b., Ca., U.S. — g8 82
San Patricio, N.M., U.S. — D4 108
San Patricio, co., Tx., U.S. — E4 120
San Patricio, Bayou, stm., La., U.S. — C2 95
San Pedrillo, Punta, c., C.R. — F6 62

San Pedro, Arg. — A5 54
San Pedro, Bol. — C3 55
San Pedro, Bol. — C3 57
San Pedro, Chile — D2 55
San Pedro, Para. — D4 55
San Pedro, N.M., U.S. — *B3 108
San Pedro, dept., Para. — D4 55
San Pedro, stm., Mex. — k11 63
San Pedro, stm., N.A. — B2 62
San Pedro, stm., Az., U.S. — E5 80
San Pedro, Punta, c., Chile — E1 55
San Pedro Bay, b., Ca., U.S. — n12 82
San Pedro de Atacama, Chile — D2 55
San Pedro [de Buena Vista], Bol. — C2 55
San Pedro de las Colonias, Mex. — B4 63
San Pedro de Lloc, Peru — C2 58
San Pedro de Macorís, Dom. Rep. — E9 64
San Pedro Mártir, Sierra, mts., Mex. — A1 63
San Pedro Peaks, mts., N.M., U.S. — A3 108
San Pedro Sula, Hond. — D7 63
San Pedro Tlaquepaque see Tlaquepaque, Mex. — m12 63
Sanpete, co., Ut., U.S. — D4 121
San Pierre, In., U.S. — B4 91
San Pietro, i., Italy — J3 23
San Pitch Mountains, mts., Ut., U.S. — D4 121
Sanpoil, stm., Wa., U.S. — A7 124
Sanquhar, Scot., U.K. — E5 13
San Quintín, Phil. — o13 34
San Quintín, Cabo, c., Mex. — A1 63
San Rafael, Arg. — A3 54
San Rafael, Ca., U.S. — D2 82
San Rafael, N.M., U.S. — B2 108
San Rafael, Ven. — A3 60
San Rafael, stm., Ut., U.S. — D5 121
San Rafael del Norte, Nic. — E7 63
San Rafael Desert, des., Ut., U.S. — E5 121
San Rafael Knob, mtn., Ut., U.S. — E5 121
San Rafael Mountains, mts., Ca., U.S. — E4 82
San Rafael Swell, plat., Ut., U.S. — E5 121
San Ramón, Peru — D2 58
San Ramon, Ca., U.S. — h9 82
San Ramón, Ur. — g9 54
San Ramón de la Nueva Orán, Arg. — D3 55
San Remo, Italy — C1 23
San Remo, N.Y., U.S. — *n15 109
San Román, Spain — A12 22
San Roque, N. Mar. Is. — D8 52
San Roque, Spain — D3 22
San Rosendo, Chile — B2 54
San Saba, Tx., U.S. — D3 120
San Saba, co., Tx., U.S. — D3 120
San Salvador, Arg. — A5 54
San Salvador, El Sal. — E7 63
San Salvador (Watling Island), i., Bah. — B6 64
San Salvador, Isla (James), i., Ec. — g5 58
San Salvador de Jujuy, Arg. — D2 55
Sansanné-Mango, Togo — D5 45
Sans Bois Mountains, mts., Ok., U.S. — B6 113
San Sebastián (part of San José), C.R. — F5 62
San Sebastián, Spain — A4 22
San Sebastián, Cabo, c., Arg. — h12 54
San Sebastián de los Reyes, Spain — o17 22
Sansepolcro, Italy — C4 23
San Severo, Italy — D5 23
San Simeon, Ca., U.S. — E3 82
San Simon, Az., U.S. — E6 80
San Simon, stm., Az., U.S. — E6 80
Sans Souci, S.C., U.S. — *B3 117
Santa, Peru — C2 58
Santa, Id., U.S. — B2 89
Santa, stm., Peru — C2 58
Santa Ana, Bol. — B2 55
Santa Ana, Bol. — B1 58
Santa Ana, Ec. — B1 58
Santa Ana, El Sal. — A2 63
Santa Ana, Mex. — A2 63
Santa Ana, Peru — D3 58
Santa Ana, Ca., U.S. — F5 82
Santa Ana, Ven. — C5 60
Santa Ana Indian Reservation, N.M., U.S. — h7 108
Santa Ana Mountains, mts., Ca., U.S. — n13 82
Santa Ana Pueblo, N.M., U.S. — B3 108
Santa Anita (part of Mexico City), Mex. — h9 63
Santa Anna, Tx., U.S. — D3 120
Santa Bárbara, Braz. — E7 57
Santa Bárbara, Chile — B2 54
Santa Bárbara, Hond. — C3 62
Santa Bárbara, Mex. — B3 63
Santa Barbara, Ca., U.S. — E4 82
Santa Barbara, co., Ca., U.S. — E3 82
Santa Barbara Channel, strt., Ca., U.S. — E3 82
Santa Bárbara d'Oeste, Braz. — m8 56
Santa Barbara Island, i., Ca., U.S. — F4 82
Santa Catalina, Arg. — D2 55
Santa Catalina, Gulf of, b., Ca., U.S. — F5 82
Santa Catalina Island, i., Ca., U.S. — F4 82
Santa Catalina Mountains, mts., Az., U.S. — E5 80
Santa Catarina, Mex. — *B4 63
Santa Catarina, state, Braz. — D2 56
Santa Catarina, Ilha de, i., Braz. — D2 56
Santa Clara, Cuba — C4 64
Santa Clara, N.Y., U.S. — f10 109
Santa Clara, Or., U.S. — *C3 114
Santa Clara, Ca., U.S. — D3 82
Santa Clara, Ut., U.S. — F2 121
Santa Clara, co., Ca., U.S. — D3 82
Santa Clara, stm., Ca., U.S. — E4 82
Santa Clara Pueblo, N.M., U.S. — *B3 108
Santa Claus, In., U.S. — H4 91
Santa Clotilde, Peru — B3 58
Santa Coloma de Farnés, Spain — B7 22
Santa Coloma [de Gramanet], Spain — B7 22
Santa Croce, Cape, c., Italy — F5 23

Santa Cruz, Arg. — E3 54
Santa Cruz, Bol. — C3 55
Santa Cruz, Braz. — C3 57
Santa Cruz, Chile — A2 54
Santa Cruz, C.R. — E7 63
Santa Cruz, Phil. — p13 34
Santa Cruz, Phil. — o13 34
Santa Cruz, Phil. — o12 34
Santa Cruz, Ca., U.S. — D2 82
Santa Cruz, N.M., U.S. — B3 108
Santa Cruz, prov., Arg. — D3 54
Santa Cruz, dept., Bol. — C3 55
Santa Cruz, co., Az., U.S. — F5 80
Santa Cruz, co., Ca., U.S. — D2 82
Santa Cruz, stm., Arg. — E3 54
Santa Cruz, stm., Az., U.S. — E4 80
Santa Cruz, Isla (Indefatigable Island), i., Ec. — g5 58
Santa Cruz de la Palma, Spain — m13 22
Santa Cruz del Quiché, Guat. — C2 62
Santa Cruz del Sur, Cuba — D5 64
Santa Cruz de Tenerife, Spain — m13 22
Santa Cruz do Rio Pardo, Braz. — D2 56
Santa Cruz Island, i., Ca., U.S. — F4 82
Santa Cruz Islands, is., Sol.Is. — G10 6
Santa Cruz Mountains, mts., Jam. — F13 65
Santa Elena, Ec. — B1 58
Santa Elena, Tx., U.S. — F3 120
Santa Elena, Bahía de, b., Ec. — B1 58
Santa Elena, Cabo, c., C.R. — E7 63
Santa Elena, Punta, c., Ec. — B1 58
Santa Elena de Uairén, Ven. — C5 60
Santa Eugenia, Spain — A1 22
Santa Eulalia del Río, Spain — C6 22
Santa Fé, Cuba — C2 64
Santa Fe (part of Mexico City), Mex. — h9 63
Santa Fe, N.M., U.S. — B3 108
Santa Fe, Spain — D4 22
Santa Fe, Oh., U.S. — B1 112
Santa Fe, Tn., U.S. — B4 119
Santa Fe, Tx., U.S. — r14 120
Santa Fe, prov., Arg. — A4 54
Santa Fe, co., N.M., U.S. — B3 108
Santa Fe, Isla, i., Ec. — g5 58
Santa Fe Baldy, mtn., N.M., U.S. — B4 108
Santa Fe Springs, Ca., U.S. — *n12 82
Santa Filomena, Braz. — C1 57
Santai, China — E6 31
Santa Inés, Isla, i., Chile — h11 54
Santa Inés Ahuatempan, Mex. — n14 63
Santa Isabel, Arg. — B3 54
Santa Isabel, P.R. — B3 65
Santa Isabel, Pico de, mtn., Eq. Gui. — *E1 46
Santa Isabel de Sihuas, Peru — E3 58
Santa Isabel do Rio Negro, Braz. — C2 59
Santa Lucía, Cuba — D6 64
Santa Lucía, Ur. — E1 56
Santa Lucia, stm., Ur. — g8 54
Santa Lucia Range, mts., Ca., U.S. — E3 82
Santa Magdalena, Isla, i., Mex. — C2 63
Santa Margarita, Ca., U.S. — E3 82
Santa Margarita, Isla de, i., Mex. — C2 63
Santa Maria, Arg. — E2 55
Santa Maria, Braz. — E5 56
Santa Maria, i., Port. — h9 44
Santa Maria, stm., Arg. — E2 55
Santa María, stm., Mex. — m14 63
Santa María, Cabo de, c., Port. — h9 44
Santa Maria [Capua Vetere], Italy — D5 23
Santa María Colotepec, Mex. — D5 63
Santa Maria da Vitória, Braz. — A4 56
Santa María del Oro, Mex. — B3 63
Santa María di Leuca, Cape, c., Italy — E7 23
Santa Maria Maggiore, Italy — E7 23
Santa Maria Mountains, mts., Az., U.S. — C3 80
Santa Marta, Col. — A3 60
Santa Marta, stm., Ven. — C2 60
Santa Marta Grande, Cabo de, c., Braz. — D3 56
Santa Monica, Ca., U.S. — m12 82
Santan, Az., U.S. — m9 80
Santana, Braz. — n13 82
Santana, Port. — h12 44
Santana do Cariri, Braz. — E2 57
Santana do Ipanema, Braz. — D3 120
Santana do Livramento, Braz. — E1 56
Santander, Col. — C2 60
Santander, Spain — A4 22
Santander, dept., Col. — B3 60
Santander Jiménez, Mex. — C5 63
Sant'Angelo Romano, Italy — g9 23
Santanilla, Islas, is., Hond. — B6 62
Santanoni Peak, mtn., N.Y., U.S. — A6 109
Sant'Antioco, i., Italy — E2 23
Santañy, Spain — C7 22
Santaquin, Ut., U.S. — D4 121
Santa Quitéria, Braz. — C4 59
Santarém, Braz. — C4 59
Santaren Channel, strt., Bah. — B4 64
Santa Rita, Braz. — C3 56
Santa Rita, Guam — M9 52
Santa Rita, Mt., U.S. — E4 103
Santa Rita, Ven. — A3 60
Santa Rita Park, Ca., U.S. — D3 82
Santa Rita do Weil, Braz. — D3 82
Santa Rosa, Arg. — A4 54
Santa Rosa, Bol. — B2 55
Santa Rosa, Braz. — D2 56
Santa Rosa, Ec. — B1 58
Santa Rosa, N.M., U.S. — B6 108
Santa Rosa, Ca., U.S. — C2 82
Santa Rosa, co., Fl., U.S. — u14 86
Santa Rosa, Mount, hill, Guam — L10 52
Santa Rosa Beach, Fl., U.S. — u15 86

Santa Rosa de Osos, Col. — B2 60
Santa Rosa [de Río Primero], Arg. — A4 54
Santa Rosa Island, i., Ca., U.S. — F3 82
Santa Rosa Island, i., Fl., U.S. — u14 86
Santa Rosalía, Mex. — B2 63
Santa Rosa Range, mts., Nv., U.S. — B4 105
Santa Teresa Gallura, Italy — D3 23
Santa Úrsula Coapa (part of Mexico City), Mex. — h9 63
Santa Venetia, Ca., U.S. — *D2 82
Santa Vitória do Palmar, Braz. — E2 56
Santa Ynez, Ca., U.S. — E3 82
Santee, Ca., U.S. — o16 82
Santee, stm., S.C., U.S. — E8 117
Santee Dam, S.C., U.S. — E7 117
Santee Indian Reservation, Ne., U.S. — B8 104
Santiago, Braz. — D2 56
Santiago, Chile — A2 54
Santiago, Mex. — C3 63
Santiago, Pan. — F7 62
Santiago, Para. — D2 56
Santiago, Phil. — n13 34
Santiago, stm., S.A. — A2 58
Santiago, Cape, c., Phil. — p13 34
Santiago de Cao, Peru — C2 58
Santiago [de Compostela], Spain — A1 22
Santiago de Cuba, Cuba — E6 64
Santiago de Cuba, prov., Cuba — D6 64
Santiago del Estero, Arg. — E3 55
Santiago del Estero, prov., Arg. — D2 64
Santiago [de los Caballeros], Dom. Rep. — E8 64
Santiago de Machaca, Bol. — C2 55
Santiago Ixcuintla, Mex. — C3 63
Santiago Papasquiaro, Mex. — B4 63
Santiago Peak, mtn., Ca., U.S. — n13 82
Santiago Reservoir, res., Ca., U.S. — n13 82
Santiam Pass, Or., U.S. — C4 114
Säntis, mtn., Switz. — B7 21
Santisteban del Puerto, Spain — C4 22
Santo, Tx., U.S. — B3 120
Santo Amaro, Braz. — D3 57
Santo Amaro, Ilha de, i., Braz. — m8 56
Santo Anastácio, Braz. — D2 56
Santo Ângelo, Braz. — D2 56
Santo Antônio, Braz. — C3 57
Santo Antônio, Ponta de, c., Braz. — E3 57
Santo Antônio de Jesus, Braz. — D3 57
Santo Antônio do Içá, Braz. — D4 60
Santo Corazón, Bol. — C4 55
Santo Domingo, Dom. Rep. — E9 64
Santo Domingo, Nic. — E8 63
Santo Domingo, stm., Mex. — n15 63
Santo Domingo de la Calzada, Spain — A4 22
Santo Domingo de los Colorados, Ec. — B2 58
Santo Domingo Indian Reservation, N.M., U.S. — h8 108
Santo Domingo Pueblo, N.M., U.S. — B3 108
Santoña, Spain — A4 22
Santorini see Thíra, i., Grc. — D5 25
Santos, Braz. — C3 56
Santos Dumont, Braz. — C4 56
Santo Tomás, Nic. — E8 63
Santo Tomás, Peru — D3 58
Santo Tomás, Ven. — B5 60
Santo Tomé, Arg. — E4 55
Santuit, Ma., U.S. — *C7 98
San Valentín, Cerro, mtn., Chile — D2 54
San Vicente, El Sal. — E7 63
San Vicente, N. Mar. Is. — D7 52
San Vicente de Alcántara, Spain — C2 22
San Vicente de Cañete, Peru — D2 58
San Vicente de la Barquera, Spain — A3 22
San Vicente del Caguán, Col. — C3 60
San Vicente Reservoir, res., Ca., U.S. — o16 82
San Vito al Tagliamento, Italy — B4 23
San Xavier Indian Reservation, Az., U.S. — E4 80
San Ygnacio, Tx., U.S. — F3 120
San Ysidro, N.M., U.S. — B3 108
Sanza Pombo, Ang. — C2 48
Sanzhan, China — B3 33
São Bento do Sul, Braz. — D3 56
São Bento do Una, Braz. — k5 57
São Bernardo do Campo, Braz. — C3 56
São Borja, Braz. — D1 56
São Carlos, Braz. — C3 57
São Cristóvão, Braz. — D3 57
São Domingos, Braz. — A3 56
São Félix de Araguaia, Braz. — E4 59
São Félix do Xingu, Braz. — D4 59
São Fidélis, Braz. — C4 56
São Francisco, stm., Braz. — C3 57
São Francisco do Sul, Braz. — D3 56
São Gabriel, Braz. — E2 56
São Gabriel da Cachoeira, Braz. — D4 60
São Gotardo, Braz. — B3 56
Sao Hill, Tan. — C6 48
São Jerônimo, Serra de, plat., Braz. — B2 56
São João da Barra, Braz. — C4 56
São João da Boa Vista, Braz. — C4 56
São João da Ponte, Braz. — B4 56
São João das Lampas, Port. — f2 44
São João del Rei, Braz. — C4 56
São João do Piauí, Braz. — h5 57
São João Nepomuceno, Braz. — C2 57
São Joaquim, Braz. — D3 56
São Joaquim National Park, Braz. — D2 56

São Jorge, i., Port. — g8 44
São José de Mipibu, Braz. — h6 57
São José do Rio Pardo, Braz. — k8 56
São José do Rio Preto, Braz. — D3 56
São José dos Campos, Braz. — D3 56
São José dos Pinhais, Braz. — D3 56
São Leopoldo, Braz. — C3 56
São Lourenço, Braz. — C3 56
São Lourenço, stm., Braz. — B1 56
São Lourenço do Sul, Braz. — E2 56

Name	Map Ref.	Page
São Luís, Braz.	B2	57
São Luís do Quitunde, Braz.	k6	57
São Luís Gonzaga, Braz.	D2	56
São Manuel, Braz.	C3	56
São Manuel, stm., Braz.	C3	56
São Mateus, Braz.	E3	57
São Miguel, i., Port.	h9	44
São Miguel Arcanjo, Braz.	m7	56
São Miguel dos Campos, Braz.	k5	57
Saona, Isla, i., Dom. Rep.	E9	64
Saône, stm., Fr.	D6	16
São Paulo, Braz.	C3	56
São Paulo, state, Braz.	C3	56
São Paulo de Olivença, Braz.	D4	56
São Pedro, Braz.	m8	56
São Pedro do Piauí, Braz.	C2	57
São Raimundo Nonato, Braz.	C2	57
São Romão, Braz.	B3	56
São Roque, Braz.	m8	56
São Roque, Cabo de, c., Braz.	C3	57
Saorre, Mount, mtn., N.W. Ter.	D16	66
São Sebastião, Ilha de, i., Braz.	C3	56
São Sebastião, Ponta, c., Moz.	B6	49
São Sebastião do Caí, Braz.	D2	56
São Sebastião do Paraíso, Braz.	C3	56
São Sepé, Braz.	E2	56
São Simão, Braz.	C3	56
São Tomé, i., S. Tom./P.	E1	46
São Tomé, Braz.	E1	46
São Tomé, Cabo de, c., Braz.	C4	56
São Tomé, Pico de, mtn., S. Tom./P.	*E1	46
Sao Tome and Principe, ctry., Afr.	E1	46
Saoura, Oued, val., Alg.	D4	44
São Vicente, Braz.	C3	56
São Vicente, Port.	h11	22
São Vicente do Sul, Braz.	D2	56
Sápai, Grc.	B5	25
Sapele, Nig.	E6	45
Sapello, N.M., U.S.	B4	108
Sapelo Island, i., Ga., U.S.	E5	87
Sapelo Sound, strt., Ga., U.S.	E5	87
Sapinero, Co., U.S.	C3	83
Sapitwa, mtn., Mwi.	E6	48
Saposoa, Peru	C2	58
Sapozhok, Sov. Un.	E13	27
Sappa Creek, stm., U.S.	E5	104
Sappa Creek, Middle Fork, stm., Ks., U.S.	C2	93
Sappa Creek, South Fork, stm., Ks., U.S.	C3	93
Sappemeer (part of Hoogezand), Neth.	A6	17
Sapphire Mountains, mts., Mt., U.S.	D3	103
Sappington, Mo., U.S.	f13	102
Sapporo, Japan	C13	31
Sapri, Italy	D5	23
Sapulpa, Ok., U.S.	B5	113
Şaqqārah, Eg.	E3	41
Saqqez, Iran	C3	39
Saquarema, Braz.	C4	56
Saquena, Peru	B3	58
Sarāb, Iran	C3	39
Sarābiyūm, Eg.	D4	41
Saraburi, Thai.	E4	35
Saragosa, Tx., U.S.	D1	120
Saragossa, Al., U.S.	B2	78
Saraguro, Ec.	B2	58
Sarah, Ms., U.S.	A3	101
Sarajevo, Yugo.	C4	24
Sarakhs, Sov. Un.	C10	39
Saraktash, Sov. Un.	E20	8
Saraland, Al., U.S.	E1	78
Saramacca, dept., Sur.	B3	59
Saranac, Mi., U.S.	F5	99
Saranac, N.Y., U.S.	f11	109
Saranac, stm., N.Y., U.S.	F11	109
Saranac Inn, N.Y., U.S.	f10	109
Saranac Lake, N.Y., U.S.	f10	109
Saranac Lakes, l., N.Y., U.S.	f10	109
Saranda, Alb.	C3	40
Sarandi, Braz.	D2	56
Sarandi del Yi, Ur.	E1	56
Sarandi Grande, Ur.	E1	56
Sarangani Bay, b., Phil.	D6	34
Sārangpur, India	F6	37
Saranley, Som.	E5	47
Saransk, Sov. Un.	D7	29
Sarapuí, Braz.	m8	56
Sarapul, Sov. Un.	B4	28
Sarasota, Fl., U.S.	E4	86
Sarasota, co., Fl., U.S.	E4	86
Sarasota Bay, b., Fl., U.S.	E4	86
Sarata, Sov. Un.	B9	24
Saratoga, Ar., U.S.	D2	81
Saratoga, Ca., U.S.	k8	82
Saratoga, In., U.S.	D8	91
Saratoga, Ia., U.S.	A5	92
Saratoga, N.C., U.S.	B5	110
Saratoga, Tx., U.S.	D5	120
Saratoga, Wy., U.S.	E6	127
Saratoga, co., N.Y., U.S.	C7	109
Saratoga Lake, l., N.Y., U.S.	C7	109
Saratoga National Historical Park, N.Y., U.S.	B7	109
Saratoga Springs, Fl., U.S.	*E4	86
Saratoga Springs, N.Y., U.S.	D7	29
Saratov, Sov. Un.	D7	29
Sarāvān, Iran	H11	39
Saravan, Laos	E4	35
Sarawak, state, Malay.	E5	34
Saray, Tur.	D7	40
Sarayköy, Tur.	D7	40
Sarbāz, Iran	C6	38
Sárbogárd, Hung.	B4	24
Sarca, stm., Italy	D6	20
Sarcelles, Fr.	g10	16
Sarcoxie, Mo., U.S.	D3	102
Sárda, stm., Asia	C8	37
Sárdalas, Libya	D2	43
Sardinal, Col.	C4	60
Sardinia, In., U.S.	F6	91
Sardinia, Oh., U.S.	C2	112
Sardinia, i., Italy	D2	23
Sardis, Al., U.S.	C2	78
Sardis, Ga., U.S.	D5	87
Sardis, Ky., U.S.	B6	94
Sardis, Ms., U.S.	A4	101
Sardis, Oh., U.S.	C5	112
Sardis, Ok., U.S.	C6	113
Sardis, Tn., U.S.	B3	119
Sardis Lake, res., Ms., U.S.	A4	101
Sarektjåkkå, mtn., Swe.	D7	14
Sar-e Pol, Afg.	C12	39
Sarepta, La., U.S.	B2	95
Sarepta, Ms., U.S.	A4	101
Sargans, Switz.	B5	20
Sargeant, Mn., U.S.	G6	100
Sargent, Ga., U.S.	C2	87
Sargent, Ne., U.S.	C6	104
Sargent, co., N.D., U.S.	C8	111
Sargents, Co., U.S.	C4	83
Sargodha, Pak.	*B5	36
Sarh (Fort-Archambault), Chad	D3	46
Sarhadd, Afg.	k17	39
Sārī, Iran	C6	39
Saría, i., Grc.	E6	25
Sarikamış, Tur.	B14	40
Sarina, Austl.	D8	50
Sarine, stm., Switz.	C3	20
Sariñena, Spain	B5	22
Sarita, Tx., U.S.	F4	120
Sariwŏn, N. Kor.	G2	33
Sark, i., Guernsey	F5	10
Sarkand, Sov. Un.	F24	8
Şarkışla, Tur.	C11	40
Şarköy, Tur.	B6	40
Sarlat, Fr.	E4	16
Sarles, N.D., U.S.	A6	111
Sarmiento, Arg.	D3	54
Sarmiento, Cerro, mtn., Chile	h11	54
Särna, Swe.	G5	14
Sarnen, Switz.	C4	20
Sarnen, Lake, l., Switz.	C4	20
Sarnia, Ont.	E2	73
Sarny, Sov. Un.	F6	27
Särö, Swe.	A5	15
Sarona, Wi., U.S.	C2	126
Saronic Gulf, b., Grc.	D4	25
Saronno, Italy	B2	23
Saronville, Ne., U.S.	D8	104
Saros, Gulf of, b., Tur.	B6	25
Sárospatak, Hung.	A5	24
Sarova, Sov. Un.	D14	27
Šar Planina, mts., Yugo.	E5	24
Sarpsborg, Nor.	p29	14
Sarpy, co., Ne., U.S.	C9	104
Sarrebourg, Fr.	F7	17
Sarreguemines, Fr.	C7	16
Sarre-Union, Fr.	F7	17
Sarria, Spain	A2	22
Sarsfield, Ont.	h13	73
Sarstedt, Ger.	A4	19
Sarstún, stm., N.A.	C3	62
Sartell, Mn., U.S.	E4	100
Sartène, Fr.	D2	23
Sarthe, stm., Fr.	D3	16
Sartrouville, Fr.	g9	16
Sarufutsu, Japan	D11	33
Sárvár, Hung.	B3	24
Sarvestān, Iran	G6	39
Sary-Ishikotrau Desert, des., Sov. Un.	D9	28
Sary-Ozek, Sov. Un.	E9	28
Sarysu, stm., Sov. Un.	D7	28
Sarzana, Italy	B2	23
Sasabe, Az., U.S.	F4	80
Sasaginnigak Lake, l., Man.	D4	70
Sasakwa, Ok., U.S.	C5	113
Sāsarām, India	D7	36
Sasebo, Japan	E10	31
Saskatchewan, prov., Can.	E3	75
Saskatchewan, stm., Can.	F12	66
Saskatoon, Sask.	E2	75
Sasovo, Sov. Un.	D13	27
Saspamco, Tx., U.S.	k7	120
Sasykkol, Lake, l., Sov. Un.	D10	28
Satah Mountain, mtn., B.C.	C5	69
Satanta, Ks., U.S.	E3	93
Sātāra, India	I4	37
Satartia, Ms., U.S.	C3	101
Satauua, W. Sam.	F11	52
Satellite Beach, Fl., U.S.	*D6	86
Säter, Swe.	G6	14
Satilla, stm., Ga., U.S.	E5	87
Satipo, Peru	D3	58
Satırlar, Tur.	D7	25
Satka, Sov. Un.	D8	29
Sätmäla Range, mts., India	H7	37
Satna, India	E8	37
Sátoraljaújhely, Hung.	A5	24
Sātpura Range, mts., India	D6	36
Sätrabrunn, Swe.	t34	14
Satrup, Ger.	D13	15
Satsop, Wa., U.S.	B2	124
Satsuma, Al., U.S.	E1	78
Satsuma, Fl., U.S.	C5	86
Sattahip, Thai.	F4	35
Sattler, Tx., U.S.	h7	120
Satu Mare, Rom.	B6	24
Satun, Thai.	I4	35
Satupa'itea, W. Sam.	F11	52
Saturna Island, i., B.C.	E6	69
Satus Creek, stm., Wa., U.S.	C5	124
Sauce, Arg.	A5	54
Sauceda Mountains, mts., Az., U.S.	E3	80
Saucier, Ms., U.S.	E4	101
Saucillo, Mex.	B3	63
Sauda, Nor.	H2	14
Saudi Arabia, ctry., Asia	C4	38
Saueruiná, stm., Braz.	B4	55
Saufley Field Naval Air Station, mil., Fl., U.S.	u14	86
Saugatuck, Mi., U.S.	F4	99
Saugatuck, stm., Ct., U.S.	E2	84
Saugatucket, stm., R.I., U.S.	F4	116
Saugatuck Reservoir, res., Ct., U.S.	D2	84
Saugerties, N.Y., U.S.	C7	109
Saugus, Ca., U.S.	*E4	82
Saugus, Ma., U.S.	B5	98
Saugus, stm., Ma., U.S.	g11	98
Sauk, co., Wi., U.S.	E4	126
Sauk, stm., Mn., U.S.	E4	100
Sauk, stm., Wa., U.S.	A4	124
Sauk Centre, Mn., U.S.	E4	100
Sauk City, Wi., U.S.	E4	126
Sauk Rapids, Mn., U.S.	E4	100
Sauk Village, Il., U.S.	*m9	90
Saukville, Wi., U.S.	E6	126
Saül, Fr. Gu.	*B7	59
Saulgrub, Ger.	H11	19
Saulnierville, N.S.	E3	71
Saulsbury, Tn., U.S.	B2	119
Saulston, N.C., U.S.	B5	110
Sault-au-Mouton, Que.	A8	74
Sault Sainte Marie, Ont.	p18	73
Sault Sainte Marie, Mi., U.S.	B6	99
Saulx [-de-Vesoul], Fr.	A1	21
Saumâtre, Étang, l., Haiti	E7	64
Saumlaki, Indon.	G8	34
Saumur, Fr.	D3	16
Saunders, co., Ne., U.S.	C9	104
Saunderstown, R.I., U.S.	E4	116
Saundersville, Tn., U.S.	g10	119
Saunemin, Il., U.S.	C5	90
Saurimo, Ang.	C3	48
Sausalito, Ca., U.S.	D2	82
Sauveterre, Fr.	E5	16
Savá, Hond.	C4	62
Sava, stm., Yugo.	C4	24
Savage, Md., U.S.	B4	97
Savage, Mn., U.S.	*F5	100
Savage, Ms., U.S.	A3	101
Savage, Mt., U.S.	C12	103
Savage, stm., Md., U.S.	k12	97
Savalou, Benin	E5	45
Savanna, Il., U.S.	A3	90
Savanna, Ok., U.S.	C6	113
Savannah, Ga., U.S.	D5	87
Savannah, Mo., U.S.	B3	102
Savannah, N.Y., U.S.	B4	109
Savannah, Oh., U.S.	B3	112
Savannah, Tn., U.S.	B3	119
Savannah, stm., U.S.	F5	117
Savannah River Plant, sci., U.S.	E4	117
Savannakhet, Laos	D6	35
Savanna Lake, l., Md., U.S.	D6	97
Savanna-la-Mar, Jam.	E4	64
Savanna, reg., Afr.	B5	49
Sāveh, Iran	D5	39
Săveni, Rom.	B8	24
Saverne, Fr.	C7	16
Savery, Wy., U.S.	E5	127
Savigliano, Italy	B1	23
Savigny [-sur-Orge], Fr.	F2	17
Saville Dam, Ct., U.S.	B4	84
Savoie, dept., Fr.	D2	20
Savona, B.C.	D7	69
Savona, Italy	B2	23
Savona, N.Y., U.S.	C3	109
Savonlinna, Fin.	G13	14
Savoonga, Ak., U.S.	C5	79
Savoy, Il., U.S.	C5	90
Savoy, Ma., U.S.	B6	98
Savran, Sov. Un.	G8	27
Sävsjö, Swe.	A8	15
Savur, Tur.	D13	40
Savusavu Bay, b., Fiji	H15	52
Savu Sea, Indon.	G6	34
Sawahlunto, Indon.	F2	34
Sawâkin (part of Port Sudan), Sud.	B4	47
Sawankhalok, Thai.	D3	35
Sawatch Range, mts., Co., U.S.	B4	83
Sawda', Jabal as, hills, Libya	D3	43
Sawdirī, Sud.	C2	47
Sawel Mountain, mtn., N. Ire., U.K.	C4	11
Sawhāj, Eg.	D6	43
Sawknah, Libya	D3	43
Sawl, Eg.	E3	41
Sawmill, Az., U.S.	B6	80
Sawnee Mountain, mtn., Ga., U.S.	B2	87
Sawn Lake, l., Alta.	A3	68
Sawpit, Co., U.S.	D3	83
Sawtooth Mountains, mts., Id., U.S.	F4	89
Sawtooth National Recreation Area, Id., U.S.	E3	89
Sawtooth Ridge, mtn., Wa., U.S.	A5	124
Sawyer, Ks., U.S.	E5	93
Sawyer, Mi., U.S.	G4	99
Sawyer, Mn., U.S.	D6	100
Sawyer, N.D., U.S.	A4	111
Sawyer, Ok., U.S.	C6	113
Sawyer, co., Wi., U.S.	C2	126
Sawyers Hill, hill, Newf.	E5	72
Sawyerville, Que.	D6	74
Saxapahaw, N.C., U.S.	B3	110
Saxe, Va., U.S.	D4	123
Saxis, Va., U.S.	C7	123
Saxmundham, Eng., U.K.	B9	12
Saxon, W.V., U.S.	n13	125
Saxon, Wi., U.S.	B2	126
Saxonburg, Pa., U.S.	E2	115
Saxony, hist. reg., Ger.	C6	18
Saxton, Pa., U.S.	F5	115
Saxtons, stm., Vt., U.S.	E3	122
Saxtons River, Vt., U.S.	E3	122
Say, Niger	D5	45
Sayán, Peru	D2	58
Sayan Mountains, mts., Asia	D12	29
Saybrook, Il., U.S.	C5	90
Saybrook Manor, Ct., U.S.	D6	84
Saybrook Point, Ct., U.S.	D6	84
Saydā (Sidon), Leb.	B3	38
Şaydel, Ia., U.S.	e8	92
Sayhūt, Yemen	D5	38
Saylorsburg, Pa., U.S.	E11	115
Saylorville, Ia., U.S.	e8	92
Saylorville Lake, res., Ia., U.S.	C4	92
Sayner, Wi., U.S.	C4	126
Saynshand, Mong.	C7	31
Sayre, Al., U.S.	B3	78
Sayre, Ok., U.S.	B2	113
Sayre, Pa., U.S.	C8	115
Sayreton, Al., U.S.	B3	78
Sayr Usa, Mong.	C6	31
Sayreville, N.J., U.S.	C4	107
Sayula, Mex.	H7	63
Sayula, Laguna de, l., Mex.	m12	63
Say'ūn, Yemen	D4	38
Sayville, N.Y., U.S.	n15	109
Sázava, Czech.	o18	21
Sázava, stm., Czech.	D5	18
Sazlıyka, stm., Bul.	D7	24
Scafell Pikes, mtn., Eng., U.K.	F5	13
Scales Mound, Il., U.S.	A3	90
Scalp Level, Pa., U.S.	F4	115
Scaly Mountain, N.C., U.S.	f9	110
Scammon, Ks., U.S.	E9	93
Scammon Bay, Ak., U.S.	C6	79
Scandia, Alta.	D4	68
Scandia, Ks., U.S.	C6	93
Scandia, Mn., U.S.	E6	100
Scandinavia, Wi., U.S.	D4	126
Scanlon, Mn., U.S.	D6	100
Scansano, Italy	C3	23
Scanterbury, Man.	D3	70
Scantic, Ct., U.S.	B5	84
Scanzano, Italy	D6	23
Scapa, Alta.	D5	68
Scapa Flow, b., Scot., U.K.	A5	10
Scapegoat Mountain, mtn., Mt., U.S.	C3	103
Scappoose, Or., U.S.	B4	114
Scarba, i., Scot., U.K.	D3	13
Scarboro, Ga., U.S.	D5	87
Scarborough, Ont.	m15	73
Scarborough, Trin.	K14	64
Scarborough, Eng., U.K.	C6	10
Scarborough, Me., U.S.	E2	96
Scarbro, W.V., U.S.	n13	125
Scariff, Ire.	E3	11
Scariff Island, i., Ire.	F1	11
Scarsdale, N.Y., U.S.	h13	109
Scartaglin, Ire.	E2	11
Scarth, Man.	E1	70
Scarville, Ia., U.S.	A4	92
Scauri, Italy	F4	23
Sceaux, Fr.	g10	16
Scenic, S.D., U.S.	D3	118
Schaal, l., Eur.	E4	15
Schaefferstown, Pa., U.S.	F9	115
Schaerbeek (Schaarbeek), Bel.	*D4	17
Schaffer, Mi., U.S.	C3	99
Schaffhausen, Switz.	E4	20
Schaffhausen, state, Switz.	B4	20
Schagen, Neth.	B4	17
Schaghticoke, N.Y., U.S.	C7	109
Schaller, Ia., U.S.	B2	92
Schärding, Aus.	E8	21
Scharnhörn, i., Ger.	E5	15
Schaumburg, Il., U.S.	h8	90
Schefferville, Que.	h13	74
Schell City, Mo., U.S.	C3	102
Schell Creek Range, mts., Nv., U.S.	D7	105
Schellsburg, Pa., U.S.	F4	115
Schenectady, N.Y., U.S.	C7	109
Schenectady, co., N.Y., U.S.	C6	109
Schenefeld, Ger.	D15	15
Schenevus, N.Y., U.S.	C6	109
Scherer, Lake, res., Ga., U.S.	C3	87
Schererville, In., U.S.	B3	91
Schertz, Tx., U.S.	h7	120
Scheveningen (part of The Hague), Neth.	B4	17
Schiedam, Neth.	B4	17
Schiermonnikoog, i., Neth.	A6	17
Schifferstadt, Ger.	D3	19
Schiller Park, Il., U.S.	k9	90
Schilpario, Italy	C6	20
Schiltigheim, Fr.	C7	16
Schio, Italy	B3	23
Schkeuditz, Ger.	B7	19
Schladming, Aus.	E6	18
Schlater, Ms., U.S.	B3	101
Schlei, b., Ger.	D15	15
Schleicher, co., Tx., U.S.	D2	120
Schleiz, Ger.	C6	19
Schleswig, Ger.	A4	18
Schleswig, Ia., U.S.	B2	92
Schleswig-Holstein, state, Ger.	D3	15
Schleswig-Holstein, hist. reg., Ger.	A4	18
Schley, co., Ga., U.S.	D2	87
Schley, Va., U.S.	C6	123
Schlitz, Ger.	D4	19
Schloss Neuhaus, Ger.	C4	18
Schlüchtern, Ger.	C5	18
Schmalkalden, Ger.	C5	18
Schmölln, Ger.	C7	19
Schnackenburg, Ger.	E5	15
Schneeberg, mtn., Ger.	C6	19
Schneeberg, Ger.	C7	19
Schneider, In., U.S.	B3	91
Schoenchen, Ks., U.S.	D4	93
Schofield, Wi., U.S.	D4	126
Schofield Barracks, mil., Hi., U.S.	g9	88
Schoharie, N.Y., U.S.	C6	109
Schoharie, co., N.Y., U.S.	C5	109
Schoharie Creek, stm., N.Y., U.S.	C6	109
Scholls, Or., U.S.	h12	114
Schönebeck, Aus.	D7	18
Schönebeck, Ger.	B6	19
Schöneck, Ger.	E5	15
Schongau, Ger.	A5	19
Schoodic Lake, l., Me., U.S.	C4	96
Schoolcraft, Mi., U.S.	F5	99
Schoolcraft, co., Mi., U.S.	B4	99
Schooleys Mountain, mtn., N.J., U.S.	B3	107
Schoonhoven, Neth.	C4	17
Schopfheim, Ger.	E4	19
Schorndorf, Ger.	A4	19
Schoten, Bel.	A4	17
Schotten, Ger.	C4	19
Schouten Islands, is., Indon.	F9	34
Schouwen, i., Neth.	D4	18
Schram City, Il., U.S.	D4	90
Schramberg, Ger.	D4	19
Schriever, La., U.S.	E5	95
Schriesheim, Ger.	D5	19
Schroeder, Mn., U.S.	C8	100
Schroon Lake, N.Y., U.S.	B7	109
Schroon Lake, l., N.Y., U.S.	C7	109
Schuchk, Az., U.S.	E3	80
Schuchuli, Az., U.S.	E3	80
Schulenburg, Tx., U.S.	E4	120
Schulte, Ks., U.S.	g12	93
Schulter, Ok., U.S.	B6	113
Schüpfheim, Switz.	C4	20
Schurz, Nv., U.S.	E3	105
Schussen, stm., Ger.	A8	21
Schuyler, Ne., U.S.	C8	104
Schuyler, Va., U.S.	C4	123
Schuyler, co., Il., U.S.	C3	90
Schuyler, co., Mo., U.S.	A5	102
Schuyler, co., N.Y., U.S.	C4	109
Schuyler Lake, N.Y., U.S.	C5	109
Schuylerville, N.Y., U.S.	B7	109
Schuylkill, co., Pa., U.S.	E9	115
Schuylkill, stm., Pa., U.S.	F10	115
Schuylkill Haven, Pa., U.S.	E9	115
Schwabach, Ger.	D6	18
Schwäbische Alb, mts., Ger.	D5	18
Schwäbisch Gmünd, Ger.	D5	18
Schwäbisch Hall, Ger.	D5	18
Schwabmünchen, Ger.	A6	20
Schwandorf, Ger.	D7	18
Schwaner Mountains, mts., Indon.	F4	34
Schwarmstedt, Ger.	F5	15
Schwarza, stm., Ger.	A5	21
Schwarze Elster, stm., Ger.	B8	19
Schwarzenbach [an der Saale], Ger.	C6	19
Schwarzenbek, Ger.	E4	15
Schwarzenberg, Ger.	C7	19
Schwarzenfeld, Ger.	D7	19
Schwarzheide, Ger.	B8	19
Schwaz, Aus.	E5	18
Schwedt, Ger.	B7	18
Schweinfurt, Ger.	C5	18
Schwerin, Ger.	B5	18
Schwerin, Lake, l., Ger.	B5	18
Schwetzingen, Ger.	D3	19
Schwyz, Switz.	E4	18
Schwyz, state, Switz.	B4	20
Science Hill, Ky., U.S.	C5	94
Scilly, Isles of, is., Eng., U.K.	F3	10
Scio, Oh., U.S.	B4	112
Scio, Or., U.S.	C4	114
Scioto, co., Oh., U.S.	D3	112
Scioto, stm., Oh., U.S.	B2	112
Scioto Furnace, Oh., U.S.	D3	112
Scipio, In., U.S.	F6	91
Scipio, Ok., U.S.	B6	113
Scipio, Ut., U.S.	D3	121
Scircleville, In., U.S.	D5	91
Scituate, Ma., U.S.	B6	98
Scituate Reservoir, res., R.I., U.S.	C3	116
Sciuerêf, Libya	D2	43
Scobey, Mt., U.S.	B11	103
Scofield, Ut., U.S.	D4	121
Scofield Reservoir, res., Ut., U.S.	D4	121
Scollard, Alta.	D4	68
Scone, Austl.	F8	51
Scooba, Ms., U.S.	C5	101
Scopus, Mount, mtn., Isr.	m14	41
Scoresbysund, Grnld.	B17	128
Scotch Plains, N.J., U.S.	B4	107
Scotchtown, N.Y., U.S.	*D6	109
Scotia, Ca., U.S.	B1	82
Scotia, Ne., U.S.	C7	104
Scotia, N.Y., U.S.	C7	109
Scotia, S.C., U.S.	F5	117
Scotland, Ont.	D4	73
Scotland, Ar., U.S.	B3	81
Scotland, Ct., U.S.	C7	84
Scotland, Ga., U.S.	D4	87
Scotland, Il., U.S.	D6	90
Scotland, In., U.S.	G4	91
Scotland, N.H., U.S.	E2	106
Scotland, Pa., U.S.	G6	115
Scotland, S.D., U.S.	D8	118
Scotland, co., Mo., U.S.	A5	102
Scotland, co., N.C., U.S.	C3	110
Scotland, ter., U.K.	B4	10
Scotland Neck, N.C., U.S.	A5	110
Scotlandville, La., U.S.	D4	95
Scotrun, Pa., U.S.	D11	115
Scotsburn, N.S.	D7	71
Scotsguard, Sask.	H1	75
Scotstown, Que.	D6	74
Scott, Sask.	E1	75
Scott, Ar., U.S.	C3	81
Scott, Ga., U.S.	D4	87
Scott, La., U.S.	D3	95
Scott, Ms., U.S.	B2	101
Scott, co., Ar., U.S.	C1	81
Scott, co., Il., U.S.	D3	90
Scott, co., In., U.S.	G6	91
Scott, co., Ia., U.S.	C7	92
Scott, co., Ks., U.S.	D3	93
Scott, co., Ky., U.S.	B5	94
Scott, co., Mn., U.S.	F5	100
Scott, co., Mo., U.S.	D8	102
Scott, co., Tn., U.S.	C9	119
Scott, co., Va., U.S.	f9	123
Scott, i., Ant.	C31	7
Scott, sci., Ant.	B29	7
Scott, Cape, c., B.C.	D3	69
Scott, Mount, mtn., Ok., U.S.	C3	113
Scott, Mount, mtn., Or., U.S.	E4	114
Scott Air Force Base, mil., Il., U.S.	E4	90
Scott City, Ks., U.S.	D3	93
Scott City, Mo., U.S.	D8	102
Scottdale, Ga., U.S.	h8	87
Scottdale, Pa., U.S.	F2	115
Scott Glacier, ice, Ant.	C23	7
Scott Islands, is., B.C.	D2	69
Scott Lake, Fl., U.S.	*G6	86
Scott Mountain, mtn., Id., U.S.	E3	89
Scott Peak, mtn., Id., U.S.	E6	89
Scott Reef, rf., Austl.	B5	50
Scott Reservoir, res., N.C., U.S.	A1	110
Scotts, Mi., U.S.	F5	99
Scottsbluff, Ne., U.S.	C2	104
Scotts Bluff, co., Ne., U.S.	C2	104
Scotts Bluff National Monument, Ne., U.S.	C2	104
Scottsboro, Al., U.S.	A3	78
Scottsburg, In., U.S.	G6	91
Scottsburg, Or., U.S.	D3	114
Scottsdale, Az., U.S.	D4	80
Scotts Hill, N.C., U.S.	C5	110
Scotts Hill, Tn., U.S.	B3	119
Scotts Mills, Or., U.S.	B4	114
Scotts Mountain, mtn., N.J., U.S.	B2	107
Scottsville, Ks., U.S.	C6	93
Scottsville, Ky., U.S.	D3	94
Scottsville, N.Y., U.S.	B3	109
Scottsville, Va., U.S.	C4	123
Scott Township, Pa., U.S.	*k13	115
Scottville, Il., U.S.	D3	90
Scottville, Mi., U.S.	E4	99
Scourie, Scot., U.K.	B3	13
Scout Lake, Sask.	H3	75
Scraggly Lake, l., Me., U.S.	B4	96
Scranton, Ia., U.S.	B3	92
Scranton, Ks., U.S.	D8	93
Scranton, N.D., U.S.	C2	111
Scranton, Pa., U.S.	D10	115
Scranton, S.C., U.S.	D8	117
Screven, Ga., U.S.	D4	87
Screven, co., Ga., U.S.	D5	87
Scribner, Ne., U.S.	C9	104
Scridain, Loch, b., Scot., U.K.	D2	13
Scrivia, stm., Italy	E4	20
Scugog, Lake, l., Ont.	C6	73
Scullville, N.J., U.S.	E3	107
Scunthorpe, Eng., U.K.	D6	10
Scuol (Schuls), Switz.	E5	18
Scurry, co., Tx., U.S.	C2	120
Scutari, Lake, l., Eur.	D4	24
Scutari see Shkodra, Alb.	A2	40
Scyrene, Il., U.S.	D3	90
Scyros see Skíros, i., Grc.	C5	40
Seaboard, N.C., U.S.	A5	110
Seabreeze, De., U.S.	F5	85
Sea Bright, N.J., U.S.	C5	107
Seabrook, Md., U.S.	*C4	97
Seabrook, N.H., U.S.	E5	106
Seabrook, N.J., U.S.	E2	107
Seabrook, Tx., U.S.	r14	120
Seabrook Beach, N.H., U.S.	E5	106
Seabrook Island, i., S.C., U.S.	F7	117
Sea Cliff, N.Y., U.S.	*E7	109
Seadrift, Tx., U.S.	E4	120
Seaford, De., U.S.	F3	85
Seaford, N.Y., U.S.	*E7	109
Seaford, Va., U.S.	h15	123
Seaforth, Ont.	D3	73
Seaforth, Mn., U.S.	F3	100
Sea Girt, N.J., U.S.	C4	107
Seagoville, Tx., U.S.	n10	120
Seagram Lakes, l., Sask.	E1	75
Seagrave, Ont.	C6	73
Seagraves, Tx., U.S.	C1	120
Seagrove, N.C., U.S.	B3	110
Seaham, Eng., U.K.	F7	13
Seahouses, Eng., U.K.	E7	13
Sea Isle City, N.J., U.S.	E3	107
Seal, stm., Man.	f8	70
Seal Bay, b., Ant.	B11	7
Seal Beach, Ca., U.S.	*n12	82
Seal Cove, N.B.	E3	71
Seal Cove, Newf.	D3	72
Seale, Al., U.S.	C4	78
Sealevel, N.C., U.S.	C6	110
Seal Harbor, Me., U.S.	D4	96
Seal Lake, l., Newf.	g9	72
Seal Point, c., P.E.I.	C5	71
Seal Rock, Or., U.S.	C2	114
Sealston, Va., U.S.	B5	123
Sealy, Tx., U.S.	E4	120
Seama, N.M., U.S.	B2	108
Seaman, Oh., U.S.	D2	112
Seaman Range, mts., Nv., U.S.	F6	105
Seanor, Pa., U.S.	F4	115
Searchlight, Nv., U.S.	H7	105
Searcy, Ar., U.S.	B4	81
Searcy, co., Ar., U.S.	B3	81
Searight, Al., U.S.	D3	78
Searles, Al., U.S.	B2	78
Searles Lake, l., Ca., U.S.	E5	82
Sears, Mi., U.S.	E5	99
Searsboro, Ia., U.S.	C5	92
Searsmont, Me., U.S.	D3	96
Searsport, Me., U.S.	D4	96
Seaside, Ca., U.S.	*D3	82
Seaside, Or., U.S.	B3	114
Seaside Heights, N.J., U.S.	D4	107
Seaside Park, N.J., U.S.	D4	107
Seaton, Il., U.S.	B3	90
Seat Pleasant, Md., U.S.	C4	97
Seattle, Wa., U.S.	B3	124
Seattle-Tacoma International Airport, Wa., U.S.	f11	124
Sea View, Wa., U.S.	*H13	124
Seaview, N.J., U.S.	E3	107
Seaville, N.J., U.S.	E3	107
Seaward Roads, strt., Mid. Is.	J3	52
Seba Beach, Alta.	D4	68
Sébaco, Nic.	D4	62
Sebago Lake, Me., U.S.	E2	96
Sebago Lake, l., Me., U.S.	E2	96
Sebasco Estates, Me., U.S.	g8	96
Sebastian, Fl., U.S.	E6	86
Sebastian, co., Ar., U.S.	B1	81
Sebastian, Cape, c., Or., U.S.	E2	114
Sebastian Inlet, b., Fl., U.S.	E6	86
Sebastián Vizcaíno, Bahía, b., Mex.	B2	63
Sebasticook Lake, l., Me., U.S.	D3	96
Sebastopol, Ca., U.S.	C2	82
Sebastopol, Ms., U.S.	C4	101
Sebatik Island, i., Asia	E5	34
Sebderat, Eth.	B4	47
Sebec, Me., U.S.	C3	96
Sebec Lake, l., Me., U.S.	C3	96
Sebeka, Mn., U.S.	D3	100
Sebeş, Rom.	C6	24
Sebewaing, Mi., U.S.	E7	99
Sebinkarahisar, Tur.	B12	40
Şebnitz, Ger.	C7	18
Seboeis, Me., U.S.	C4	96
Seboeis, stm., Me., U.S.	B4	96
Seboeis Lake, l., Me., U.S.	C4	96
Sebomook Lake, l., Me., U.S.	C3	96
Seboyeta, N.M., U.S.	B2	108
Sebree, Ky., U.S.	C2	94
Sebrell, Va., U.S.	D5	123
Sebring, Fl., U.S.	E5	86
Sebring, Oh., U.S.	B4	112
Sebringville, Ont.	D3	73
Secaucus, N.J., U.S.	h8	107
Secchia, stm., Italy	B3	23
Sechelt, B.C.	E6	69
Sechura, Peru	C1	58
Sechura, Bahía de, b., Peru	C1	58
Sechura, Desierto de, des., Peru	C1	58
Seclin, Fr.	D3	17
Seco, Ky., U.S.	C7	94
Second Lake, l., N.H., U.S.	f7	106
Second Mesa, Az., U.S.	B5	80
Secor, Il., U.S.	C4	90
Secretan, Sask.	G2	75
Secretary, Md., U.S.	C6	97
Secretary Island, i., N.Z.	P11	51
Secret Lake, l., R.I., U.S.	E4	116
Section, Al., U.S.	A4	78
Sector Popular (part of Mexico City), Mex.	h9	63
Security, Co., U.S.	C6	83
Sedalia, Alta.	D5	68
Sedalia, Co., U.S.	B6	83
Sedalia, In., U.S.	C4	91
Sedalia, Ky., U.S.	f9	94
Sedalia, Mo., U.S.	C4	102
Sedan, Ks., U.S.	E7	93
Sedan, N.M., U.S.	A6	108

Name	Map Ref.	Page
Sedbergh, Eng., U.K.	F6	13
Sederot, Isr.	C6	41
Sedgewick, Alta.	C5	68
Sedgewick, Mount, mtn., N.M., U.S.	B1	108
Sedgewickville, Mo., U.S.	D8	102
Sedgwick, Ar., U.S.	B5	81
Sedgwick, Co., U.S.	A8	83
Sedgwick, Ks., U.S.	E6	93
Sedgwick, Me., U.S.	D4	96
Sedgwick, co., Co., U.S.	A8	83
Sedgwick, co., Ks., U.S.	E6	93
Sédhiou, Sen.	D1	45
Sedillo Hill, N.M., U.S.	k8	108
Sedlčany, Czech.	D9	19
Sedley, Sask.	G3	75
Sedley, Va., U.S.	D6	123
Sedom, Isr.	C7	41
Sedona, Az., U.S.	C4	80
Sedot Yam, Isr.	B6	41
Sedro Woolley, Wa., U.S.	A3	124
Sedrun, Switz.	C6	21
Seebe, Alta.	D3	68
Seeber, stm., Can.	C5	70
Seebert, W.V., U.S.	C4	125
Seehausen, Ger.	F5	15
Seeheim, Nmb.	C2	49
Seeis, Nmb.	B2	49
Seekonk, Ma., U.S.	C5	98
Seekonk, stm., R.I., U.S.	C4	116
Seeley, Ca., U.S.	F6	82
Seeley Lake, Mt., U.S.	C3	103
Seeleys Bay, Ont.	C8	73
Seelow, Ger.	F8	15
Seelyville, In., U.S.	F3	91
Seelyville, Pa., U.S.	C11	115
Sées, Fr.	C4	16
Seesen, Ger.	B5	19
Seez, stm., Switz.	C7	21
Sefadu, S.L.	E2	45
Seferihisar, Tur.	C6	25
Sefid, stm., Iran	C4	39
Sefid Ābeh, Iran	F10	39
Segamat, Malay.	K5	35
Segbwema, S.L.	E2	45
Segesta, hist., Italy	F4	23
Segezha, Sov. Un.	F16	14
Segorbe, Spain	C5	22
Ségou, Mali	D3	45
Segovia, Spain	B3	22
Segozero, l., Sov. Un.	F15	14
Segré, Fr.	D3	16
Segré, stm., Eur.	B6	22
Segregansett, Ma., U.S.	C5	98
Seguam Island, i., Ak., U.S.	E5	79
Seguam Pass, strt., Ak., U.S.	E5	79
Séguédine, Niger	B7	45
Séguéla, I.C.	E3	45
Seguin, Tx., U.S.	E4	120
Seguin Falls, Ont.	B5	73
Segundo, Co., U.S.	D6	83
Segundo, stm., Spain	C5	22
Segura, stm., Spain	C5	22
Sehnkwehn, Lib.	E3	45
Sehore, India	F6	37
Sehwān, Pak.	D1	37
Seibert, Co., U.S.	B8	83
Seiling, Ok., U.S.	A3	113
Seille, stm., Fr.	F6	17
Seinäjoki, Fin.	F10	14
Seine, stm., Fr.	C4	16
Seine, Bay of the, est., Fr.	C3	16
Seine-et-Marne, dept., Fr.	F3	17
Seixal, Port.	f9	22
Sejerby, Den.	C5	15
Sejerø, i., Den.	C5	15
Sejerø Bugt, b., Den.	C5	15
Sekenke, Tan.	B5	48
Seki, Japan	o15	33
Sekiu, Wa., U.S.	A1	124
Sekondi-Takoradi, Ghana	F4	45
Sekota, Eth.	C4	47
Selah, Wa., U.S.	C5	124
Selangor, state, Malay.	K4	35
Selanovtsi, Bul.	D7	24
Selaru, i., Indon.	G8	34
Selatan, Cape, c., Indon.	F4	34
Selatpanjang, Indon.	L5	35
Selawik, Ak., U.S.	B7	79
Selawik Lake, l., Ak., U.S.	B7	79
Selayar, i., Indon.	G6	34
Selb, Ger.	C6	18
Selbourne, Cape, c., Ant.	g40	7
Selbu, Nor.	F4	14
Selby, Eng., U.K.	A6	12
Selby, S.D., U.S.	B5	118
Selbyville, De., U.S.	G5	85
Selbyville, W.V., U.S.	C4	125
Selde, Den.	B3	15
Selden, Ks., U.S.	C3	93
Selden, N.Y., U.S.	*n15	109
Seldovia, Ak., U.S.	D9	79
Selenge, stm., Asia	B5	31
Selenica, Alb.	B2	25
Seienter, I., Ger.	D4	15
Sélestat, Fr.	C7	16
Seietyleniz, Lake, l., Sov. Un.	C8	28
Selfridge, N.D., U.S.	C5	111
Sélibaby, Maur.	C2	45
Selidovo, Sov. Un.	q20	27
Seligenstadt, Ger.	C3	19
Seliger, Lake, l., Sov. Un.	C9	27
Seligman, Az., U.S.	B3	80
Seligman, Mo., U.S.	E4	102
Selinsgrove, Pa., U.S.	E8	115
Selinunte, hist., Italy	F4	23
Selizharovo, Sov. Un.	C9	27
Selkirk, Man.	D3	70
Selkirk, Ont.	E5	73
Selkirk, Scot., U.K.	C5	10
Selkirk, Ks., U.S.	D2	93
Selkirk, Ont.	C5	10
Selkirk Mountains, mts., N.A.	D9	69
Selle, Pic la, mtn., Haiti	E8	64
Selleck, Wa., U.S.	B4	124
Seller Lake, l., Man.	B4	70
Sellers, Al., U.S.	C3	78
Sellers, S.C., U.S.	C9	117
Sellersburg, In., U.S.	H6	91
Sellersville, Pa., U.S.	F11	115
Sells, Az., U.S.	F4	80
Selm, Ger.	B2	19
Selma, Al., U.S.	D6	71
Selma, Al., U.S.	C3	78
Selma, Al., U.S.	D4	81
Selma, Ca., U.S.	D4	82
Selma, In., U.S.	D7	91
Selma, N.C., U.S.	B4	110
Selma, Or., U.S.	E3	114
Selman, Ok., U.S.	A2	113
Selmer, Tn., U.S.	B3	119
Selsey, Eng., U.K.	D7	12
Selsey Bill, c., Eng., U.K.	D7	12
Selva, Arg.	B4	54
Selvagens, Ilhas, is., Port.	m14	22
Selvas, for., Braz.	D4	53
Selvin, In., U.S.	H3	91

Selway, stm., Id., U.S.	C3	89
Selway, Mount, mtn., B.C.	A6	69
Selwyn Lake, l., Can.	k8	108
Selwyn Lake, l., Can.	D6	66
Selwyn Mountains, mts., Can.		
Selz, N.D., U.S.	B6	111
Seman, stm., Alb.	C3	78
Semani, stm., Alb.	B2	25
Semans, Sask.	F3	75
Semara, W. Sah.	D2	44
Semarang, Indon.	G4	34
Semenovka, Sov. Un.	E9	27
Semeru, mtn., Indon.	G4	34
Semikarakorsk, Sov. Un.	D4	101
Seminary, Ms., U.S.	D4	101
Seminoe Dam, Wy., U.S.	D6	127
Seminoe Mountains, mts., Wy., U.S.	D6	127
Seminoe Reservoir, res., Wy., U.S.	D6	127
Seminole, Al., U.S.	E2	78
Seminole, Ok., U.S.	B5	113
Seminole, Tx., U.S.	C1	120
Seminole, co., Fl., U.S.	D5	86
Seminole, co., Ga., U.S.	F2	87
Seminole, co., Ok., U.S.	B5	113
Seminole, Lake, res., U.S.	F2	87
Seminole Park, Fl., U.S.	*p10	86
Semipalatinsk, Sov. Un.	D11	29
Semisopochnoi Island, i., Ak., U.S.	E3	79
Semitau, Indon.	E4	34
Semiyarskoye, Sov. Un.	C9	28
Semliki, stm., Afr.	A5	48
Semmens Lake, l., Man.	B4	70
Semmering Pass, Aus.	E7	18
Semmes, Al., U.S.	E1	78
Semnān, Iran	B5	38
Semois, stm., Eur.	E5	17
Semonov, Sov. Un.	D17	8
Semora, N.C., U.S.	A3	110
Sempach, Switz.	B5	21
Sempacher Lake, l., Switz.	B4	20
Semur-en-Auxois, Fr.	D6	16
Sen, stm., Camb.	F6	35
Sena, N.M., U.S.	B4	90
Senachwine Lake, l., Il., U.S.	B4	90
Senador Pompeu, Braz.	C3	57
Sena Madureira, Braz.	C4	58
Senanga, Zam.	E3	48
Senatobia, Ms., U.S.	H1	75
Senath, Mo., U.S.	E7	102
Senatobia, Ms., U.S.	A4	101
Sendai, Japan	K5	33
Sendai, Japan	D3	16
Sendai, Japan	B6	22
Sendai, Japan	D13	31
Sendai Bay, b., Japan	G10	33
Seneca, Il., U.S.	B5	90
Seneca, Ks., U.S.	C7	93
Seneca, Mo., U.S.	E3	102
Seneca, Ne., U.S.	B5	104
Seneca, N.M., U.S.	A6	108
Seneca, Or., U.S.	C8	114
Seneca, Pa., U.S.	D2	115
Seneca, S.C., U.S.	B2	117
Seneca, S.D., U.S.	B6	118
Seneca, Wi., U.S.	E3	126
Seneca, co., N.Y., U.S.	C4	109
Seneca, co., Oh., U.S.	A2	112
Seneca Falls, N.Y., U.S.	C4	109
Seneca Lake, l., N.Y., U.S.	C4	109
Senecaville, Oh., U.S.	C4	112
Senecaville Lake, res., Oh., U.S.	C4	112
Seneffe, Bel.	D4	17
Senega, i., Afr.	D2	45
Sénégal, ctry., Afr.	C2	45
Senetosa, Point, c., Italy	D2	23
Seney, Mi., U.S.	B5	99
Senftenberg, Ger.	C6	18
Senga Hill, Zam.	A6	48
Sênggê Zangbo, stm., China	B7	36
Senguerr, stm., Arg.	D3	54
Senhor do Bonfim, Braz.	D2	57
Senigallia, Italy	C4	23
Senj, Yugo.	C2	23
Senja, i., Nor.	F7	14
Senlac, Sask.	F4	34
Senlis, Fr.	C5	16
Senneterre, Que.	k11	74
Senoia, Ga., U.S.	C2	87
Sens, Fr.	C5	16
Sense, stm., Switz.	C3	21
Senta, Yugo.	C4	24
Sentani, Indon.	C4	48
Sentinel, Ok., U.S.	B2	113
Sentinel Butte, N.D., U.S.	C2	111
Sentinel Butte, mtn., N.D., U.S.	C2	111
Sentinel Peak, mtn., B.C.	B6	69
Sentinel Range, mts., Ant.	B4	7
Senzu, Japan	n17	33
Seo de Urgel, Spain	A6	22
Seongnam, S. Kor.	*H3	32
Seoni, India	F7	37
Seoul (Sŏul), S. Kor.	D10	31
Sepik, stm., Pap. N. Gui.	h11	50
Sept-Îles (Seven Islands), Que.	h13	74
Sepulga, stm., Al., U.S.	D3	78
Sequatchie, Tn., U.S.	D8	119
Sequatchie, co., Tn., U.S.	D8	119
Sequim, Wa., U.S.	A2	124
Sequoia National Park, Ca., U.S.	D4	82
Sequoia National Park, Ca., U.S.	D4	82
Sequoyah, co., Ok., U.S.	B7	113
Serafimovich, Sov. Un.	G14	27
Serafina, N.M., U.S.	B4	108
Seraing, Bel.	B6	16
Serang, Indon.	k8	35
Serasan, i., Indon.	E4	34
Serbia, hist. reg., Yugo.	C5	24
Serdo, Eth.	C5	47
Serdobsk, Sov. Un.	D4	26
Sered', Czech.	D4	26
Şereflikoçhisar, Tur.	C6	40
Seremban, Malay.	E2	34
Serenje, Zam.	D5	48
Sergeant, In., U.S.	B1	92
Sergeant Bluff, Ia., U.S.	B1	92
Sergeant Bluff, Ia., U.S.	C3	117
Sergino, Sov. Un.	C22	8
Sergipe, state, Braz.	D4	57
Seria, Bru.	E4	34
Séria, Grc.	D5	25
Sérifos, i., Grc.	D5	40
Serina, Italy	C3	21
Seringapatam Reef, rf., Austl.	B3	50
Serinhaém, Braz.	k6	57
Serio, stm., Italy	E8	21
Serles, Tn., U.S.	D7	120
Sernglac, Som.	D4	47
Sernyy Zavod, Sov. Un.	B9	39
Serón, Spain	D4	22

Serov, Sov. Un.	D9	29
Serowe, Bots.	B4	49
Serpa, Port.	D2	22
Serpentine Lakes, l., Austl.	E4	50
Serpents Mouth, strt.	K14	64
Serpukhov, Sov. Un.	D6	29
Serra dos Órgãos National Park, Braz.	h6	56
Sérrai, Grc.	B4	40
Serrana Bank, Col.	C7	62
Serra Negra, Braz.	m8	56
Serranilla Bank, Col.	C8	62
Serranópolis, Braz.	B2	56
Serra Talhada, Braz.	C3	57
Serres, Fr.	E1	20
Serrezuela, Arg.	A3	54
Serrinha, Braz.	D3	57
Sêrro, Braz.	B4	56
Sertã, Port.	C1	22
Sertânia, Braz.	C3	57
Sertãozinho, Braz.	k8	56
Serua, i., Indon.	G8	34
Serui, Indon.	F9	34
Serule, Bots.	B4	49
Sérvia, Grc.	B4	25
Servia, In., U.S.	C6	91
Sêrxü, China	E4	31
Sese Islands, is., Ug.	B5	48
Sesfontein, Nmb.	A1	49
Sesheke, Zam.	E3	48
Sesia, stm., Italy	B2	23
Sesser, Il., U.S.	E4	90
Sessums, Ms., U.S.	B5	101
Sesto [Fiorentino], Italy	C3	23
Šeštokai, Sov. Un.	A7	26
Sesto San Giovanni, Italy	D5	21
Sestriere, Italy	E2	20
Sestri Levante, Italy	B2	23
Sestroretsk, Sov. Un.	A8	27
Setana, Japan	E9	33
Sète, Fr.	F5	16
Sete Guedas National Park, Braz.	C2	56
Sete Lagoas, Braz.	B4	56
Seth, W.V., U.S.	C3	125
Seto, Japan	I8	33
Seton Portage, B.C.	D6	69
Seto Sea, Japan	I6	33
Settat, Mor.	C3	44
Sette Cama, Gabon	F1	46
Settee Lake, l., Sask.	B3	75
Setting Lake, l., Man.	B2	70
Settle, Eng., U.K.	F6	13
Setúbal, Port.	C1	22
Setúbal, Bay of, b., Port.	C1	22
Seul, Lac, l., Ont.	o16	73
Seul Choix Point, c., Mi., U.S.	C5	99
Sevan, Lake, l., Sov. Un.	F2	38
Sevastopol, Sov. Un.	E6	29
Seven Devils Lake, res., Ar., U.S.	D4	81
Seven Devils Mountains, mts., Id., U.S.	D2	89
Seven Heads, c., Ire.	F3	11
Seven Hills, Oh., U.S.	h9	112
Seven Islands Bay, b., Newf.	f9	72
Seven Mile, Oh., U.S.	C1	112
Seven Mile Beach, N.J., U.S.	E3	107
Sevenoaks, Eng., U.K.	m13	10
Seven Oaks, Pa., U.S.	*C5	117
Seven Persons, Alta.	E5	68
Seven Springs, N.C., U.S.	B5	110
Seventy Mile House, B.C.	D7	69
Severance, Co., U.S.	A6	83
Severance, Ks., U.S.	C8	93
Severance, N.H., U.S.	D4	106
Severka, stm., Sov. Un.	n18	27
Severn, Md., U.S.	B4	97
Severn, N.C., U.S.	A5	110
Severn, stm., Ont.	C6	123
Severn, stm., Ont.	n17	73
Severn, Mouth of the, mth., U.K.	D5	10
Severn, Mouth of the, mth., U.K.	C5	12
Severna Park, Md., U.S.	B4	97
Severnaya Zemlya, is., Sov. Un.	B11	29
Severočeský, prov., Czech.	B9	57
Severodonetsk, Sov. Un.	q21	27
Severodvinsk, Sov. Un.	C16	8
Severomorsk, Sov. Un.	C15	14
Severouralsk, Sov. Un.	C21	8
Severy, Ks., U.S.	E7	93
Sevier, Ut., U.S.	E3	121
Sevier, co., Ar., U.S.	D1	81
Sevier, co., Tn., U.S.	D10	119
Sevier, co., Ut., U.S.	E4	121
Sevier, stm., Ut., U.S.	D3	121
Sevier, East Fork, stm., Ut., U.S.	F3	121
Sevier Bridge Reservoir, res., Ut., U.S.	D3	121
Sevier Desert, des., Ut., U.S.	D3	121
Sevier Lake, l., Ut., U.S.	E2	121
Sevierville, Tn., U.S.	D10	119
Sevilla, Col.	C2	60
Sevilla, Spain	D3	22
Seville, Fl., U.S.	C5	86
Seville, Ga., U.S.	E3	87
Seville, Oh., U.S.	A4	112
Sevlievo, Bul.	D7	24
Sevran, Fr.	g11	16
Sèvre, stm., Fr.	D3	16
Sèvre Niortaise, stm., Fr.	g9	16
Sèvres, Fr.	g10	16
Sewal, Ia., U.S.	D4	92
Sewanee, Tn., U.S.	D8	119
Seward, Ak., U.S.	C10	79
Seward, Ne., U.S.	D8	104
Seward, Pa., U.S.	F3	115
Seward, co., Ks., U.S.	E3	93
Seward, co., Ne., U.S.	D8	104
Seward Peninsula, pen., Ak., U.S.	B7	79
Sewaren, N.J., U.S.	k7	107
Sewell, Chile	A2	54
Sewell, N.J., U.S.	D2	107
Sewen, Fr.	A2	21
Sewickley, Pa., U.S.	E1	115
Sexsmith, Alta.	B1	68
Sextonville, Wi., U.S.	E3	126
Seychelles, ctry., Afr.	G24	2
Seydişehir, Tur.	D8	40
Seydisfjördur, Ice.	n26	14
Seyhan (Sarus), stm., Tur.	C10	40
Seylac, Som.	B7	47
Seym, stm., Sov. Un.	F9	27
Seymchan, Sov. Un.	C18	29
Seymour, Austl.	H5	51

Seymour, Ct., U.S.	D3	84
Serowe, Bots.	C5	90
Seymour, In., U.S.	G6	91
Seymour, Ia., U.S.	D4	92
Seymour, Mo., U.S.	D5	102
Seymour, Tn., U.S.	D10	119
Seymour, Tx., U.S.	C3	120
Seymour, Wi., U.S.	D5	126
Seymour Inlet, b., B.C.	D4	69
Seymour Johnson Air Force Base, mil., N.C., U.S.	B5	110
Seymour Lake, l., Vt., U.S.	B4	122
Seymourville, La., U.S.	h9	95
Sézanne, Fr.	C5	16
Sezimbra, Port.	C1	22
Sezze, Italy	D4	23
Sfax, Tun.	C7	44
Shaanxi, prov., China	D6	31
Shabbona, Il., U.S.	B5	90
Shabeellaha Dhexe, prov., Som.	E6	47
Shabeellaha Hoose, prov., Som.	E5	47
Shabeelle (Shebele), stm., Afr.	E5	47
Shabogamo Lake, l., Newf.	h8	72
Shabunda, Zaire	B4	48
Shabwah, Yemen	B6	47
Shache, China	F10	29
Shackelford, co., Tx., U.S.	C3	120
Shackleton, Sask.	G1	75
Shackleton Glacier, ice, Ant.	A31	7
Shackleton Ice Shelf, ice, Ant.	C23	7
Shackleton Range, mts., Ant.	A10	7
Shadehill, S.D., U.S.	B3	118
Shadehill Dam, S.D., U.S.	B3	118
Shadehill Reservoir, res., S.D., U.S.	B3	118
Shades Creek, stm., Al., U.S.	g7	78
Shades Mountain, mtn., Al., U.S.	g7	78
Shadeville, Oh., U.S.	m10	112
Shadow Mountain National Recreation Area, Co., U.S.	A4	83
Shadrinsk, Sov. Un.	B6	28
Shady Cove, Or., U.S.	E4	114
Shady Dale, Ga., U.S.	C3	87
Shady Grove, Al., U.S.	D3	78
Shady Grove, Fl., U.S.	B3	86
Shady Grove, Ky., U.S.	e10	94
Shady Grove, Pa., U.S.	G6	115
Shady Point, Ok., U.S.	B7	113
Shady Rest, Ct., U.S.	*D2	84
Shady Side, Md., U.S.	C4	97
Shadyside, Oh., U.S.	C5	112
Shady Spring, W.V., U.S.	D3	125
Shady Valley, Tn., U.S.	C12	119
Shafer, Lake, l., In., U.S.	C4	91
Shafer Butte, mtn., Id., U.S.	F2	89
Shafter, Ca., U.S.	E4	82
Shafter, Nv., U.S.	C7	105
Shafter, Tx., U.S.	p12	120
Shaftesbury, Eng., U.K.	C5	12
Shaftsbury, Vt., U.S.	E2	122
Shaftsbury Center, Vt., U.S.	E2	122
Shagamu, Nig.	*E5	45
Shageluk, Ak., U.S.	C8	79
Shag Harbour, N.S.	F4	71
Shaguotun, China	D9	32
Shah Alam, Malay.	*K4	35
Shahbanou Farah Dam, Iran	C4	39
Shāhdādkot, Pak.	D1	37
Shahdol, India	F8	37
Shāhgarh, India	C4	36
Shahhāt, Libya	C4	43
Shāhī, i., Iran	C2	39
Shāhjahānpur, India	C7	36
Shāhpur, India	E13	39
Shāhpur, Pak.	C4	36
Shahrak, Afg.	E5	37
Shahrak, Iran	D12	39
Shahr-e Bābak, Iran	B5	38
Shahr-e Kord, Iran	E5	39
Shāhrūd, stm., Iran	C4	39
Shāhrūd see Emāmshahr, Iran	B5	38
Shakawe, Bots.	A3	49
Shaker Heights, Oh., U.S.	A4	112
Shakhrisyabz, Sov. Un.	B13	39
Shakhty, Sov. Un.	E7	29
Shakhunya, Sov. Un.	D8	28
Shaki, Nig.	E5	45
Shakopee, Mn., U.S.	F5	100
Shakotan, Cape, c., Japan	E10	33
Shaktoolik, Ak., U.S.	C7	79
Shala, Lake, l., Eth.	D4	47
Shalath, B.C.	D6	69
Shaler Mountains, mts., N.W. Ter.	B10	66
Shaler Township, Pa., U.S.	*E2	115
Shalkar, Lake, l., Sov. Un.	C5	28
Shallmar, Md., U.S.	m12	97
Shallotte, N.C., U.S.	D4	110
Shallotte Inlet, b., N.C., U.S.	D4	110
Shallowater, Tx., U.S.	C2	120
Shallow Lake, Ont.	C3	73
Shallow Water, Ks., U.S.	D3	93
Sham, Mount, mtn., Oman	C2	39
Shamattawa, Man.	B5	70
Shambat, Sud.	B3	47
Shambaugh, Ia., U.S.	D2	92
Shambe, Sud.	D3	47
Shamli, Iran	H8	39
Shamokin, Pa., U.S.	E8	115
Shamokin Dam, Pa., U.S.	E8	115
Shamrock, Sask.	G2	75
Shamrock, Fl., U.S.	C3	86
Shamrock, Tx., U.S.	B5	113
Shamrock Hills, Oh., U.S.	B2	112
Shamva, Zimb.	A5	49
Shandaken, N.Y., U.S.	C6	109
Shandī, Sud.	B3	47
Shandon, Oh., U.S.	n12	112
Shandong, prov., China	D8	31
Shandong Bandao, pen., China	D9	31
Shangdu, China	D5	31
Shanghai, China	E9	31
Shangnan, China	H4	32
Shangrao, China	F8	31
Shangshui, China	C2	31
Shangsi, China	A7	35
Shangxian, China	H4	32
Shanhaiguan, China	D8	31
Shaniko, Or., U.S.	B6	114
Shannock, R.I., U.S.	F2	116
Shannon, Il., U.S.	B4	90
Shannon, Ms., U.S.	A5	101
Shannon, co., Mo., U.S.	D6	102
Shannon, co., S.D., U.S.	D3	118
Shannon, i., Grnld.	B16	128
Shannon, stm., Ire.	D2	10

Shannon, Lake, l., Wa., U.S.	A4	124
Shannon Airport, Ire.	E3	11
Shannon City, Ia., U.S.	D3	92
Shannontown, S.C., U.S.	D7	117
Shanshan, China	C3	31
Shantou (Swatow), China	G8	31
Shantung see Shandong, prov., China	D8	31
Shantung Peninsula see Shandong Bandao, pen., China	D9	31
Shanwa, Tan.	B5	48
Shanxi, prov., China	D7	31
Shaobo, China	H8	32
Shaoguan, China	G7	31
Shaowu, China	C3	31
Shaoxing, China	F9	31
Shaoyang, China	F7	31
Shap, Eng., U.K.	F6	13
Shapinsay, i., Scot., U.K.	A6	13
Shapio Lake, l., Newf.	g9	72
Shapki, Sov. Un.	s32	14
Shapleigh, Me., U.S.	*E2	96
Shaqqah, Bi'r ash, well, Egypt	G5	40
Sharafkhāneh, Iran	B2	39
Sharangad, Mong.	B2	32
Sharbatāt, Ra's ash-, c., Oman	D5	38
Sharbot Lake, Ont.	C8	73
Sharbot Lake, Ont.	C8	73
Shari, Japan	E12	33
Sharka Bay, b., Austl.	E1	50
Sharkey, co., Ms., U.S.	C3	101
Shark Point, c., Fl., U.S.	H5	86
Sharktooth Mountain, mtn., B.C.	E7	66
Sharm ash Shaykh, Eg.	D6	43
Sharon, Ct., U.S.	B2	84
Sharon, Ga., U.S.	C4	87
Sharon, Ks., U.S.	E5	93
Sharon, Ma., U.S.	B5	98
Sharon, N.H., U.S.	E3	106
Sharon, N.D., U.S.	B8	111
Sharon, Ok., U.S.	A2	113
Sharon, Pa., U.S.	D1	115
Sharon, S.C., U.S.	B5	117
Sharon, Tn., U.S.	A3	119
Sharon, Vt., U.S.	D4	122
Sharon, W.V., U.S.	m13	125
Sharon, Wi., U.S.	F5	126
Sharon Grove, Ky., U.S.	C2	94
Sharon Hill, Pa., U.S.	p20	115
Sharon Park, Oh., U.S.	n12	112
Sharon Springs, Ks., U.S.	D2	93
Sharon Springs, N.Y., U.S.	C6	109
Sharon Valley, Ct., U.S.	B2	84
Sharonville, Oh., U.S.	n13	112
Sharp, co., Ar., U.S.	A4	81
Sharpe, Lake, res., S.D., U.S.	C6	118
Sharpe Lake, l., Man.	B5	70
Sharpes, Fl., U.S.	D6	86
Sharpley, W.V., U.S.	D3	125
Sharples, W.V., U.S.	n7	85
Sharp Top Mountain, mtn., Va., U.S.	C2	81
Sharpsburg, Ia., U.S.	D3	92
Sharpsburg, Ky., U.S.	B6	94
Sharpsburg, Md., U.S.	B2	97
Sharpsburg, N.C., U.S.	B5	110
Sharpsburg, Pa., U.S.	k14	115
Sharps Chapel, Tn., U.S.	C10	119
Sharpsville, In., U.S.	D5	91
Sharpsville, Pa., U.S.	D1	115
Sharptown, Md., U.S.	C6	97
Sharptown, N.J., U.S.	D2	107
Sharya, Sov. Un.	B3	28
Shashi, China	E7	31
Shashi, stm., Afr.	B4	49
Shashke, Sov. Un.	C7	28
Shasta, co., Ca., U.S.	B2	82
Shasta, Mount, vol., Ca., U.S.	B2	82
Shasta Lake, res., Ca., U.S.	B2	82
Shasta Springs, Vt., U.S.	B3	122
Shatney Mountain, mtn., N.H., U.S.	f7	106
Shatsk, Sov. Un.	D13	27
Shattuck, Ok., U.S.	A2	113
Shattuckville, Ma., U.S.	A2	98
Shatura, Sov. Un.	D12	27
Shauck, Oh., U.S.	B3	112
Shaunavon, Sask.	H1	75
Shaw, Ms., U.S.	B3	101
Shaw, Or., U.S.	k12	114
Shaw Air Force Base, mil., S.C., U.S.	D7	117
Shawanaga, Ont.	B4	73
Shawangunk Mountains, mts., N.Y., U.S.	D6	109
Shawano, Wi., U.S.	D5	126
Shawano, co., Wi., U.S.	D5	126
Shawano Lake, l., Wi., U.S.	D5	126
Shawboro, N.C., U.S.	A6	110
Shawbridge, Que.	D3	74
Shawhan, Ky., U.S.	B5	94
Shawinigan, Que.	C5	74
Shawinigan-Sud, Que.	C5	74
Shawmut, Mt., U.S.	D7	103
Shawnee, Ks., U.S.	k16	93
Shawnee, Oh., U.S.	C3	112
Shawnee, Ok., U.S.	B5	113
Shawnee, Wy., U.S.	D7	127
Shawnee, co., Ks., U.S.	D8	93
Shawnee Hills, Oh., U.S.	k10	112
Shawneetown, Il., U.S.	F5	90
Shawsheen, stm., Ma., U.S.	f11	98
Shawsville, Md., U.S.	A4	97
Shawsville, Va., U.S.	C2	123
Shawville, Que.	D1	70
Shay Gap, Austl.	D3	50
Shaykh Miskīn, Syria	B8	41
Shchekino, Sov. Un.	D11	27
Shchetovo, Sov. Un.	n22	27
Shchigry, Sov. Un.	F11	27
Shchors, Sov. Un.	F9	27
Shchuchinsk, Sov. Un.	C8	28
Shchurovo, Sov. Un.	n18	27
Shebergán, Afg.	A4	36
Shebele (Shabeelle), stm., Afr.	E5	47
Sheboygan, Wi., U.S.	E6	126
Sheboygan, co., Wi., U.S.	E6	126
Sheboygan Falls, Wi., U.S.	E6	126
Shedd, Or., U.S.	C3	114
Shedden, Ont.	E3	73
Shediac, N.B.	C5	71
Sheek, Som.	D6	47
Sheelin, Lough, l., Ire.	D3	10
Sheenjek, stm., Ak., U.S.	B11	79

Sheep Creek, stm., Alta.	C1	68
Sheep Haven, b., Ire.	B4	11
Sheep Mountain, mtn., Az., U.S.	E1	80
Sheep Mountain, mtn., Wy., U.S.	C2	127
Sheep Mountain, mtn., Wy., U.S.	B5	127
Sheep Peak, mtn., Nv., U.S.	G6	105
Sheep Range, mts., Nv., U.S.	G6	105
Sheep's Head, c., Ire.	F2	11
Sheeps Heaven Mountain, mtn., Ma., U.S.	A1	98
Sheerness, Alta.	D5	68
Sheerness, Eng., U.K.	C8	12
Sheet Harbour, N.S.	E7	71
Shefar'am, Isr.	B7	41
Shefayim, Isr.	g10	41
Sheffield, Eng., U.K.	D6	10
Sheffield, N.Z.	O14	51
Sheffield, Al., U.S.	A2	78
Sheffield, Il., U.S.	B4	90
Sheffield, Ia., U.S.	B4	92
Sheffield, Ma., U.S.	B1	98
Sheffield, Pa., U.S.	C3	115
Sheffield, Tx., U.S.	D2	120
Sheffield, Vt., U.S.	B4	122
Sheffield Lake, Oh., U.S.	A3	112
Sheffield Lake, l., Newf.	D3	72
Shefford, co., Que.	D5	74
Sheguiandah, Ont.	B3	73
Sheho, Sask.	F4	75
Sheho, stm., Arg.	D2	54
Shekhūpura, Pak.	B4	37
Shelagyaki, Cape, c., Sov. Un.	B33	128
Shelagyote Peak, mtn., B.C.	B4	69
Shelbiana, Ky., U.S.	C7	94
Shelbina, Mo., U.S.	B5	102
Shelburn, In., U.S.	F3	91
Shelburn, Or., U.S.	C4	114
Shelburne, N.S.	F4	71
Shelburne, Ont.	C4	73
Shelburne, Ma., U.S.	A2	98
Shelburne, Vt., U.S.	C2	122
Shelburne Falls, Ma., U.S.	A2	98
Shelburne Pond, l., Vt., U.S.	C2	122
Shelby, Al., U.S.	B3	78
Shelby, In., U.S.	B3	91
Shelby, Ia., U.S.	C2	92
Shelby, Mi., U.S.	E4	99
Shelby, Ms., U.S.	B3	101
Shelby, Mt., U.S.	B5	103
Shelby, Ne., U.S.	C8	104
Shelby, N.C., U.S.	B1	110
Shelby, Oh., U.S.	B3	112
Shelby, co., Al., U.S.	B3	78
Shelby, co., Il., U.S.	D5	90
Shelby, co., In., U.S.	E6	91
Shelby, co., Ia., U.S.	C2	92
Shelby, co., Ky., U.S.	B4	94
Shelby, co., Mo., U.S.	B5	102
Shelby, co., Oh., U.S.	B1	112
Shelby, co., Tn., U.S.	B2	119
Shelby, co., Tx., U.S.	D5	120
Shelbyville, Il., U.S.	D5	90
Shelbyville, In., U.S.	F6	91
Shelbyville, Ky., U.S.	B4	94
Shelbyville, Mo., U.S.	B5	102
Shelbyville, Tn., U.S.	B5	119
Shelbyville, Lake, res., Il., U.S.	D5	90
Shelbyville, Lake, res., Il., U.S.	e8	92
Sheldon, Il., U.S.	C6	90
Sheldon, Ia., U.S.	A2	92
Sheldon, Mo., U.S.	D3	102
Sheldon, N.D., U.S.	C8	111
Sheldon, S.C., U.S.	F6	117
Sheldon, Tx., U.S.	r14	120
Sheldon, Vt., U.S.	B3	122
Sheldon, Wi., U.S.	C3	126
Sheldon Springs, Vt., U.S.	B3	122
Sheldonville, Ma., U.S.	B5	98
Shelekhov, Gulf of, b., Sov. Un.	C18	29
Shelikof Strait, strt., Ak., U.S.	D9	79
Shell, Wy., U.S.	B5	127
Shell, stm., Man.	D1	70
Shell, Loch, b., Scot., U.K.	C2	13
Shellbrook, Sask.	C11	119
Shell Creek, Tn., U.S.	A3	83
Shell Creek, stm., Wy., U.S.	B5	127
Shelley, B.C.	C6	69
Shelley, Id., U.S.	F6	89
Shellharbour, Austl.	G8	51
Shell Lake, Sask.	D2	75
Shell Lake, l., Mn., U.S.	D3	100
Shell Lake, l., Wi., U.S.	C2	126
Shellman, Ga., U.S.	E2	87
Shell Bluff, Ga., U.S.	C5	87
Shellmouth, Man.	D1	70
Shellpot Creek, stm., De., U.S.	h7	85
Shell Rock, Ia., U.S.	B5	92
Shell Rock, stm., Ia., U.S.	B5	92
Shell Rock, West Fork, stm., Ia., U.S.	B5	92
Shellsburg, Ia., U.S.	B6	92
Shelly, Mn., U.S.	C2	100
Shelly Mountain, mtn., Id., U.S.	F5	89
Shelter Harbor, R.I., U.S.	G2	116
Shelter Island, N.Y., U.S.	m16	109
Shelton, Ct., U.S.	D3	84
Shelton, Ne., U.S.	D7	104
Shelton, Wa., U.S.	B2	124
Shemogue, N.B.	C5	71
Shemya Air Force Base, mil., Ak., U.S.	E2	79
Shenandoah, Ia., U.S.	D2	92
Shenandoah, Pa., U.S.	E9	115
Shenandoah, Va., U.S.	B4	123
Shenandoah, co., Va., U.S.	B4	123
Shenandoah, North Fork, stm., Va., U.S.	B4	123
Shenandoah, South Fork, stm., Va., U.S.	B4	123
Shenandoah Mountain, mtn., U.S.	B3	123
Shenandoah National Park, Va., U.S.	B4	123
Shenandoah Valley, val., U.S.	B4	123
Shenango River Lake, res., U.S.	D1	115
Shengjin, China	J9	32
Shenipsit Lake, l., Ct., U.S.	B6	84
Shenqiu, China	D7	31
Shensi see Shaanxi, prov., China	D6	31
Shenyang, China	C9	31
Sheopur, India	E6	37

Name	Map Ref.	Page

Shepard, Alta. — D4 68
Shepard Island, i., Ant. — B35 7
Shepardsville, In., U.S. — E3 91
Shepaug, stm., Ct., U.S. — C2 84
Shepaug Dam, Ct., U.S. — D2 84
Shepaug Reservoir, res., Ct., U.S. — C2 84
Shepetovka, Sov. Un. — F6 27
Shepherd, Mi., U.S. — E6 99
Shepherd, Mt., U.S. — E8 103
Shepherd, Tx., U.S. — D5 120
Shepherdstown, W.V., U.S. — B7 125
Shepherdsville, Ky., U.S. — C4 94
Sheppard Air Force Base, mil., Tx., U.S. — C3 120
Shepparton, Austl. — G8 50
Sheppey, Isle of, i., Eng., U.K. — C8 12
Sheppton, Pa., U.S. — E9 115
Shepton Mallet, Eng., U.K. — C5 12
Sheqi, China — H5 32
Sherab, Sov. Un. — C13 29
Sherard, Ms., U.S. — A3 101
Sherborn, Ma., U.S. — h10 98
Sherborne, Eng., U.K. — D5 12
Sherbro Island, i., S.L. — E2 45
Sherbrooke, Que. — D8 71
Sherbrooke, co., Que. — D6 74
Sherbrooke Lake, l., N.S. — E5 71
Sherburn, Mn., U.S. — G4 100
Sherburne, N.Y., U.S. — C5 109
Sherburne, co., Mn., U.S. — E5 100
Shercock, Ire. — C5 11
Shereshevo, Sov. Un. — B8 26
Sheridan, Ar., U.S. — C3 81
Sheridan, Co., U.S. — *B6 83
Sheridan, Il., U.S. — B5 90
Sheridan, In., U.S. — D5 91
Sheridan, Ky., U.S. — e9 94
Sheridan, Me., U.S. — B4 96
Sheridan, Mi., U.S. — E5 99
Sheridan, Mo., U.S. — A3 102
Sheridan, Mt., U.S. — E4 103
Sheridan, Or., U.S. — B3 114
Sheridan, Wy., U.S. — B6 127
Sheridan, co., Ks., U.S. — C3 93
Sheridan, co., Mt., U.S. — B12 103
Sheridan, co., Ne., U.S. — B3 104
Sheridan, co., N.D., U.S. — B5 111
Sheridan, co., Wy., U.S. — B5 127
Sheridan, Mount, mtn., Wy., U.S. — B2 127
Sheridan Beach, Wa., U.S. — *B3 124
Sheridan Gardens, Wy., U.S. — *B6 127
Sheridan Lake, Co., U.S. — C8 83
Sheringham, Eng., U.K. — D7 10
Sherman, Ct., U.S. — C2 84
Sherman, Me., U.S. — C4 96
Sherman, Ms., U.S. — A5 101
Sherman, Mo., U.S. — f12 102
Sherman, N.Y., U.S. — C1 109
Sherman, S.D., U.S. — D9 118
Sherman, Tx., U.S. — C4 120
Sherman, co., Ks., U.S. — C2 93
Sherman, co., Ne., U.S. — C6 104
Sherman, co., Or., U.S. — B6 114
Sherman, co., Tx., U.S. — A2 120
Sherman Mills, Me., U.S. — C4 96
Sherman Mountain, mtn., Ar., U.S. — A2 81
Sherman Reservoir, res., Ne., U.S. — C7 104
Sherman Station, Me., U.S. — C4 96
Sherpur, Bngl. — E12 37
Sherrard, Il., U.S. — B3 90
Sherrelwood, Co., U.S. — B6 83
Sherridon, Man. — B1 70
Sherrill, Ar., U.S. — C4 81
Sherrill, N.Y., U.S. — B5 109
Sherrodsville, Oh., U.S. — B4 112
's Hertogenbosch, Neth. — B6 16
Sherwood, P.E.I. — C6 71
Sherwood, Ar., U.S. — C3 81
Sherwood, Ms., U.S. — B4 101
Sherwood, N.D., U.S. — A4 111
Sherwood, Oh., U.S. — A1 112
Sherwood, Or., U.S. — h12 114
Sherwood, Tn., U.S. — D9 119
Sherwood, Wi., U.S. — D5 126
Sherwood Manor, Ct., U.S. — A5 84
Sherwood Park, Alta. — C4 68
Sherwood Park, De., U.S. — i7 99
Shetek, Lake, l., Mn., U.S. — G3 100
Shetland Islands, is., Scot., U.K. — g10 10
Shetucket, stm., Ct., U.S. — C7 84
Shevchenko, Sov. Un. — E8 29
Shevlin, Mn., U.S. — C3 100
Shevut 'Am, Isr. — f10 41
Shewa, prov., Eth. — D4 47
Shewa Gimira, Eth. — D4 47
Shexian, China — J8 32
Sheyenne, N.D., U.S. — B6 111
Sheyenne, stm., N.D., U.S. — C8 111
Sheyenne Lake, res., N.D., U.S. — B5 111
Sheykhābād, Afg. — D14 39
Shiant Islands, is., Scot., U.K. — C2 13
Shiawassee, co., Mi., U.S. — F6 99
Shibām, Yemen — D4 38
Shibata, Japan — H9 33
Shibecha, Japan — E12 33
Shibetsu, Japan — D11 33
Shibetsu, Japan — E12 33
Shibīn al Qanāṭir, Eg. — D3 41
Shibin al Kawm, Eg. — K7 32
Shicheng, China — K7 32
Shickley, Ne., U.S. — D8 104
Shickshinny, Pa., U.S. — D9 115
Shidao, China — F10 32
Shideler, In., U.S. — D7 91
Shiderty, stm., Sov. Un. — C8 28
Shidler, Ok., U.S. — A5 113
Shiel, Loch, l., Scot., U.K. — C3 13
Shieldaig, Scot., U.K. — C3 13
Shields, Ks., U.S. — D3 93
Shields, N.D., U.S. — C4 111
Shihezi, China — C2 31
Shijiazhuang, China — D7 31
Shikārpur, Pak. — C4 36
Shikōhābād, India — D7 37
Shikoku, i., Japan — E11 31
Shiliguri, India — C8 36
Shilka, Sov. Un. — D14 29
Shilka, Sov. Un. — A8 31
Shilka, stm., Sov. Un. — D14 29
Shillington, Pa., U.S. — F10 115
Shillong, India — C9 36
Shiloh, Ga., U.S. — D2 87
Shiloh, N.J., U.S. — E2 107
Shiloh, N.C., U.S. — A6 110
Shiloh, Oh., U.S. — B3 112
Shiloh, Pa., U.S. — *G8 115
Shiloh, Tn., U.S. — B3 119
Shiloh, Tn., U.S. — A4 119

Shiloh National Military Park, Tn., U.S. — B3 119
Shimabara, Japan — J5 33
Shimada, Japan — o17 33
Shimanovsk, Sov. Un. — D15 29
Shimber Berris, mtn., Som. — C6 47
Shimen, China — F7 31
Shimizu, Japan — I9 33
Shimla, India — B6 36
Shimodate, Japan — o17 33
Shimoda, Japan — m19 33
Shimoga, India — F6 36
Shimonoseki, Japan — E11 31
Shimotsuma, Japan — m18 33
Shinano, stm., Japan — H9 33
Shindand, Afg. — B3 36
Shiner, Tx., U.S. — E4 120
Shingbwiyang, Burma — C10 36
Shinglehouse, Pa., U.S. — C5 115
Shingleton, Mi., U.S. — B4 99
Shingū, Japan — J8 33
Shinjō, Japan — G10 33
Shinkolobwe, Zaire — D4 48
Shinnston, W.V., U.S. — B4 125
Shin Pond, Me., U.S. — B4 96
Shinshiro, Japan — o16 33
Shinyanga, Tan. — B5 48
Shinyanga, prov., Tan. — B5 48
Shiocton, Wi., U.S. — D5 126
Shiogama, Japan — G10 33
Shiojiri, Japan — m16 33
Shioya, Cape, c., Japan — H10 33
Ship Bottom, N.J., U.S. — D4 107
Ship Cove, Newf. — e9 72
Ship Harbour, N.S. — E7 71
Ship Island, i., Ms., U.S. — E5 101
Ship Island Pass, strt., Ms., U.S. — g7 101
Shipka Pass, Bul. — D7 24
Shipki Pass, India — B7 37
Shipley, Eng., U.K. — G7 13
Shipman, Sask. — D3 75
Shipman, Il., U.S. — D4 90
Shipman, Va., U.S. — C4 123
Shippagan, N.B. — B5 71
Shippensburg, Pa., U.S. — F6 115
Shippenville, Pa., U.S. — D2 115
Shiprock, N.M., U.S. — A1 108
Ship Rock, mtn., N.M., U.S. — A1 108
Shipshewana, In., U.S. — A6 91
Shipyard, Belize — D7 63
Shiquan, China — E6 31
Shirane, Mount, mtn., Japan — H9 33
Shirase Glacier, ice, Ant. — B16 7
Shīrāz, Iran — C5 38
Shirbīn, Eg. — C3 41
Shire, stm., Afr. — E5 48
Shiretoko, Cape, c., Japan — D12 33
Shiribetsu, Mount, mtn., Japan — E10 33
Shiriya, Cape, c., Japan — F10 33
Shīr Kūh, mtn., Iran — F7 39
Shirley, Ar., U.S. — B3 81
Shirley, In., U.S. — E6 91
Shirley, Ma., U.S. — A4 98
Shirley, N.Y., U.S. — *n16 109
Shirley, W.V., U.S. — k9 125
Shirley Basin, Wy., U.S. — D6 127
Shirley Center, Ma., U.S. — A4 98
Shirley Mills, Me., U.S. — C3 96
Shirley Mountains, mts., Wy., U.S. — D6 127
Shirleysburg, Pa., U.S. — F6 115
Shiroishi, Japan — H10 33
Shirotori, Japan — n15 33
Shīrvān, Iran — C8 39
Shishaldin Volcano, vol., Ak., U.S. — E7 79
Shishmaref, Ak., U.S. — B6 79
Shishou, China — J5 32
Shitara, Japan — n16 33
Shively, Ky., U.S. — B4 94
Shivpuri, India — E6 37
Shivwits, Ut., U.S. — F2 121
Shivwits Plateau, plat., Az., U.S. — A2 80
Shiyan, China — *E7 31
Shizuishan, China — D6 31
Shizuoka, Japan — E12 31
Shkhara, Mount, mtn., Sov. Un. — *E7 29
Shkodra (Scutari), Alb. — A2 40
Shkotovo, Sov. Un. — E6 33
Shoal, stm., Man. — C1 70
Shoal Creek, stm., U.S. — B4 119
Shoal Harbour, Newf. — D4 72
Shoal Lake, Man. — D1 70
Shoal Lake, l., Can. — E4 70
Shoals, In., U.S. — G4 91
Shoals, Isles of, is., Me., U.S. — E2 96
Shoalwater, Cape, c., Wa., U.S. — C1 124
Shobonier, Il., U.S. — E4 90
Shoe Cove, Newf. — D4 72
Shoemakersville, Pa., U.S. — F10 115
Sholes, Ne., U.S. — B8 104
Sholomu, Nig. — *E5 45
Shongaloo, La., U.S. — B2 95
Shongopovi, Az., U.S. — B5 80
Shonkin, Mt., U.S. — C6 103
Shonto, Az., U.S. — A5 80
Shooting Creek, N.C., U.S. — f9 110
Shop Springs, Tn., U.S. — A5 119
Shoreacres, B.C. — E9 69
Shore Acres, Ca., U.S. — h13 98
Shore Acres, N.J., U.S. — C4 107
Shore Acres, R.I., U.S. — E4 116
Shoreham, Mi., U.S. — G4 99
Shoreham, Vt., U.S. — D2 122
Shoreview, Mn., U.S. — m12 100
Shorewood, Il., U.S. — k8 90
Shorewood, Mn., U.S. — n11 100
Shorewood, Wi., U.S. — E6 126
Shorewood Hills, Wi., U.S. — *E4 126
Short Beach, Ct., U.S. — D4 84
Shorter, Al., U.S. — C4 78
Shorterville, Al., U.S. — D4 78
Short Falls, N.H., U.S. — D4 106
Short Mountain, mtn., Tn., U.S. — D1 119
Shortsville, N.Y., U.S. — C3 109
Shoshone, Ca., U.S. — E5 82
Shoshone, Id., U.S. — G4 89
Shoshone, co., Id., U.S. — B3 89
Shoshone, stm., Wy., U.S. — B4 127
Shoshone, North Fork, stm., Wy., U.S. — B3 127
Shoshone, South Fork, stm., Wy., U.S. — B3 127
Shoshone Falls, wtfl., Id., U.S. — G4 89
Shoshone Lake, l., Wy., U.S. — B2 127

Shoshone Mountains, mts., Nv., U.S. — E4 105
Shoshone Peak, mtn., Nv., U.S. — G5 105
Shoshone Range, mts., Nv., U.S. — C5 105
Shoshong, Bots. — B4 49
Shoshoni, Wy., U.S. — C4 127
Shostka, Sov. Un. — F9 27
Shouldice, Alta. — D4 68
Shouns, Tn., U.S. — C12 119
Shoup, Id., U.S. — D4 89
Showell, Md., U.S. — D7 97
Show Low, Az., U.S. — C5 80
Shpola, Sov. Un. — G8 27
Shreve, Oh., U.S. — B3 112
Shreveport, La., U.S. — B2 95
Shrewsbury, Eng., U.K. — D5 10
Shrewsbury, Ma., U.S. — B4 98
Shrewsbury, Mo., U.S. — *f13 102
Shrewsbury, N.J., U.S. — C4 107
Shrewsbury, Pa., U.S. — G8 115
Shrīrangapattana, India — F6 36
Shropshire (Salop), co., Eng., U.K. — B5 12
Shrule, Ire. — D2 11
Shuangcheng, China — B10 31
Shuangjiang, China — G4 31
Shuangliao, China — C9 31
Shuangshan, China — C10 32
Shuangyang, China — C11 32
Shuangyashan, China — B11 31
Shubenacadie, N.S. — D6 71
Shubenacadie Lake, l., N.S. — E6 71
Shubert, Ne., U.S. — D10 104
Shubrā al Khaymah, Eg. — C6 43
Shubrā Khīt, Eg. — C2 41
Shubuta, Ms., U.S. — D5 101
Shucheng, China — I7 32
Shu'fāṭ, Isr. Occ. — h11 41
Shujāābād, Pak. — C3 37
Shuksan, Mount, mtn., Wa., U.S. — A4 124
Shulan, China — D3 33
Shulaps Peak, mtn., B.C. — D6 69
Shule He, stm., China — C4 31
Shulerville, S.C., U.S. — E8 117
Shullsburg, Wi., U.S. — F3 126
Shumagin Islands, is., Ak., U.S. — E7 79
Shumaykh, Libya — C2 43
Shumen, Bul. — D8 24
Shumerlya, Sov. Un. — D16 27
Shumikha, Sov. Un. — B6 28
Shumway, Il., U.S. — D5 90
Shūnat Nimrīn, Jord. — h13 41
Shunchang, China — K7 32
Shungnak, Ak., U.S. — B8 79
Shuoxian, China — H5 32
Shuqrah, Yemen — D4 38
Shuqualak, Ms., U.S. — C5 101
Shūr, stm., Iran — D5 39
Shūr, stm., Iran — F7 39
Shūr, stm., Iran — O5 52
Shūshtar, Iran — E4 39
Shuswap, stm., B.C. — D8 69
Shuswap Lake, l., B.C. — D8 69
Shutesbury, Ma., U.S. — B3 98
Shuwak, Sud. — C4 47
Shuwaykah, Isr. Occ. — f11 41
Shuya, Japan — N6 52
Shuya, Sov. Un. — C13 27
Shuzenji, Japan — o17 33
Shwebo, Burma — D10 36
Shwegyin, Burma — D2 35
Siālkot, Pak. — B5 36
Siam, Gulf of see Thailand, Gulf of, b., Asia — C2 34
Siam see Thailand, ctry., Asia — B2 34
Sian see Xi'an, China — E6 31
Siantan, i., Indon. — K7 35
Siasconset, Ma., U.S. — D8 98
Siátista, Grc. — B3 25
Siau, i., Indon. — E7 34
Siauliai, Sov. Un. — D4 27
Sibay, Sov. Un. — C5 28
Sibbald, Alta. — D5 68
Šibenik, Yugo. — D2 24
Siberia, In., U.S. — H4 91
Siberia, reg., Sov. Un. — C13 29
Sibert, Ky., U.S. — C6 94
Siberut, i., Indon. — F1 34
Sibi, Pak. — C4 36
Sibiryakov, i., Sov. Un. — B7 128
Sibiti, Congo — B1 48
Sibiu, Rom. — C7 24
Sibley, Ia., U.S. — A2 92
Sibley, La., U.S. — B2 95
Sibley, Ms., U.S. — D2 101
Sibley, Mo., U.S. — h11 102
Sibley, N.D., U.S. — B8 111
Sibley, co., Mn., U.S. — F4 100
Sibolga, Indon. — E1 34
Sibsāgar, India — C9 36
Sibu, Malay. — E4 34
Sibuatan, mtn., Indon. — K3 35
Sibutu Island, i., Phil. — E5 34
Sibutu Passage, strt., Asia — E5 34
Sibuyan Sea, Phil. — C6 34
Sicamous, B.C. — D8 69
Si Chang, i., Thai. — F4 35
Sichomovi, Az., U.S. — B5 80
Sichuan, prov., China — E5 31
Sicily, i., Italy — F4 23
Sicily Island, La., U.S. — C4 95
Sicklerville, N.J., U.S. — D3 107
Sicuani, Peru — F4 58
Sidamo, prov., Eth. — E4 47
Sideling Hill, mtn., U.S. — A1 97
Sideling Hill Creek, stm., Md., U.S. — A1 97
Sidell, Il., U.S. — D6 90
Siderno Marina, Italy — F6 23
Sídheros, Ákra, c., Grc. — E6 40
Sidhirókastron, Grc. — B4 40
Sīdī Barrānī, Eg. — C5 43
Sidi bel Abbès, Alg. — B4 44
Sidi Bennour, Mor. — B3 44
Sidi Ifni, Mor. — C2 44
Sidi Kacem, Mor. — *C3 44
Sīdī Muḥammad, 'Ayn, well, Libya — H3 40
Sīdī Sālim, Eg. — C2 41
Sidi Slimane, Mor. — *C3 44
Sidlaw Hills, hills, Scot., U.K. — D5 13
Sidley, Mount, mtn., Ant. — B36 7
Sidmouth, Eng., U.K. — D4 12

Sidnaw, Mi., U.S. — B2 99
Sidney, B.C. — E6 69
Sidney, Man. — E2 70
Sidney, Ar., U.S. — A4 81
Sidney, Il., U.S. — C5 90
Sidney, Ia., U.S. — D2 92
Sidney, Mt., U.S. — C12 103
Sidney, Ne., U.S. — C3 104
Sidney, N.J., U.S. — B3 107
Sidney, N.Y., U.S. — C5 109
Sidney, Oh., U.S. — B1 112
Sidney Center, N.Y., U.S. — C5 109
Sidney Lanier, Lake, res., Ga., U.S. — B2 87
Sidon, Ms., U.S. — B3 101
Sidon see Ṣaydā, Leb. — B3 38
Sidra, Gulf of (Khalīj Surt), b., Libya — C3 43
Sidrolândia, Braz. — C2 56
Siebert, Co., U.S. — B7 83
Siedlce, Pol. — B7 26
Sieg, stm., Ger. — C3 18
Siegburg, Ger. — C3 18
Siegen, Ger. — C4 18
Sieglar, Ger. — C2 19
Siemianowice Śląskie, Pol. — g10 26
Siemiatycze, Pol. — B7 26
Siemreab, Camb. — C2 34
Siena, Italy — C3 23
Siena, co., Italy — C3 23
Sieper, La., U.S. — C3 95
Sieradz, Pol. — B5 26
Sierpc, Pol. — B5 26
Sierra, co., Ca., U.S. — C3 82
Sierra, co., N.M., U.S. — D2 108
Sierra Blanca, Tx., U.S. — o12 120
Sierra Blanca Peak, mtn., N.M., U.S. — D4 108
Sierra City, Ca., U.S. — C3 82
Sierra Colorada, Arg. — E3 56
Sierra Estrella, mts., Az., U.S. — m8 80
Sierra Gorda, Chile — D2 55
Sierra Leone, ctry., Afr. — E2 45
Sierra Madre, Ca., U.S. — m12 82
Sierra Mojada, Mex. — B4 63
Sierra Nevada (Simón Bolívar) National Park, Ven. — B3 60
Sierra Vista, Az., U.S. — F5 80
Sierre, Switz. — F3 18
Siesta Key, Fl., U.S. — *E4 86
Siesta Key, i., Fl., U.S. — E4 86
Siewierz, Pol. — g10 26
Sifnos, i., Grc. — D5 40
Sifton, Man. — D1 70
Sigatoka, Fiji — I14 52
Sigel, Il., U.S. — D5 90
Sigel, Pa., U.S. — D3 115
Sigean, Fr. — F5 16
Sighetu Marmației, Rom. — B6 24
Sighișoara, Rom. — C7 24
Sighty Crag, mtn., Eng., U.K. — E6 13
Sigli, Indon. — k11 34
Siglufjörður, Ice. — m23 14
Sigmaringen, Ger. — A5 20
Signachi, Sov. Un. — B15 40
Signal Hill, Ca., U.S. — *n12 82
Signal Mountain, Tn., U.S. — D8 119
Signal Mountain, mtn., Tn., U.S. — C9 119
Signal Mountain, mtn., Vt., U.S. — C4 122
Signal Mountain, mtn., Va., U.S. — g11 123
Signal Peak, mtn., Az., U.S. — D1 80
Signal Peak, mtn., Ut., U.S. — F2 121
Signau, Switz. — C4 21
Signy-l'Abbaye, Fr. — E4 17
Sigourney, Ia., U.S. — C5 92
Sigsbee, Ga., U.S. — E3 87
Sigsig, Ec. — B2 58
Sigtuna, Swe. — t35 14
Siguatepeque, Hond. — C4 62
Sigüenza, Spain — B4 22
Siguiri, Gui. — D3 45
Sigulda, Sov. Un. — E4 27
Sigurd, Ut., U.S. — E4 121
Sihabuhabu, mtn., Indon. — K3 35
Sihanoukville see Kampong Saom, Camb. — C2 34
Sihuas, Peru — C2 58
Si'ir, Isr. Occ. — h13 41
Sijan, i., Micron. — Q18 52
Sikar, India — G6 36
Sikasso, Mali — D3 45
Sikes, La., U.S. — B3 95
Sikeston, Mo., U.S. — E8 102
Sikhote-Alin Mountains, mts., Sov. Un. — E16 29
Sikiá, Grc. — C5 40
Sikinos, i., Grc. — D5 40
Sikkim, state, India — C8 36
Siklós, Hung. — C4 24
Sil, stm., Spain — A2 22
Silandro, Italy — A3 23
Silang, Phil. — o13 34
Silao, Mex. — m13 63
Silas, Al., U.S. — D1 78
Sīlat aẓ Ẓahr, Isr. Occ. — f11 41
Silchar, India — D9 36
Sile, Tur. — B7 40
Siler City, N.C., U.S. — B3 110
Silerton, Tn., U.S. — B3 119
Silesia, Mt., U.S. — E8 103
Silesia, hist. reg., Pol. — C4 26
Siletz, Or., U.S. — C3 114
Silgarhi-Doti, Nepal — C8 37
Silica, Oh., U.S. — e6 112
Silifke, Tur. — D9 40
Siling Co, l., China — B8 36
Silisili, Mount, mtn., W. Sam. — F11 52
Silistra, Bul. — C8 24
Silivri, Tur. — B7 40
Siljan, Nor. — p27 14
Siljan, l., Swe. — G6 14
Silkeborg, Den. — B3 15
Sillery, Que. — n17 74
Silloth, Eng., U.K. — F5 13
Sil Nakaja, N.J., U.S. — E4 80
Siloam, Ga., U.S. — C3 87
Siloam Springs, Ar., U.S. — A1 81
Silsbee, Tx., U.S. — D5 120
Silsby, stm., N.H., U.S. — B4 70
Sils im Domleschg, Switz. — D8 21
Silton, Sask. — G3 75
Siluko, Nig. — H7 45
Silute, Sov. Un. — A6 26
Silva, Mo., U.S. — D7 102

Silva, N.D., U.S. — A6 111
Silva Jardim, Braz. — h6 56
Silvânia, Braz. — B3 56
Silver, S.C., U.S. — C8 117
Silver Bay, Mn., U.S. — C7 100
Silver Bay, N.Y., U.S. — B6 91
Silver City, Ia., U.S. — C2 92
Silver City, Ms., U.S. — B3 101
Silver City, Nv., U.S. — D2 105
Silver City, N.M., U.S. — E1 108
Silver City, Ut., U.S. — C2 118
Silver Cliff, Co., U.S. — C5 83
Silver Creek, Ga., U.S. — B1 87
Silver Creek, Ne., U.S. — C8 104
Silver Creek, N.Y., U.S. — C1 109
Silver Creek, stm., Ne., U.S. — H6 91
Silver Creek, stm., Or., U.S. — D7 114
Silverdale, Ks., U.S. — E7 93
Silverdale, Wa., U.S. — B3 124
Silver Fork, Ut., U.S. — *C4 121
Silver Gate, Mt., U.S. — E7 103
Silver Grove, Ky., U.S. — h14 94
Silverhill, Al., U.S. — E2 78
Silver Hill, Md., U.S. — f9 97
Silver Island Mountains, mts., Ut., U.S. — C2 121
Silver Lake, In., U.S. — B6 91
Silver Lake, Ks., U.S. — C8 93
Silver Lake, Ma., U.S. — f11 98
Silver Lake, Mn., U.S. — F4 100
Silver Lake, N.H., U.S. — C4 106
Silver Lake, Or., U.S. — D5 114
Silver Lake, Wi., U.S. — F5 126
Silver Lake, l., Ont. — E4 70
Silver Lake, l., De., U.S. — A3 92
Silver Lake, l., Ia., U.S. — A3 92
Silver Lake, l., Me., U.S. — C3 96
Silver Lake, l., N.H., U.S. — E2 106
Silver Lake, l., N.H., U.S. — C4 106
Silver Lake, l., Or., U.S. — D7 114
Silver Lake, l., Wa., U.S. — g13 124
Silverlake, Wa., U.S. — E3 11
Silverpeak, Nv., U.S. — F4 105
Silver Peak Range, mts., Nv., U.S. — F4 105
Silver Plume, Co., U.S. — *B5 83
Silver Point, Tn., U.S. — C8 119
Silver Run, Md., U.S. — A3 97
Silver Spring, Md., U.S. — C3 97
Silver Springs, Fl., U.S. — C4 86
Silver Springs, Nv., U.S. — D2 105
Silver Springs, N.Y., U.S. — C2 109
Silver Star Mountain, mtn., Wa., U.S. — A5 124
Silverstreet, S.C., U.S. — C4 117
Silverthrone Mountain, mtn., B.C. — D4 69
Silvertip Mountain, mtn., Mt., U.S. — C3 103
Silverton, B.C. — E9 69
Silverton, Co., U.S. — D3 83
Silverton, Id., U.S. — B3 89
Silverton, N.J., U.S. — C4 107
Silverton, Oh., U.S. — o13 112
Silverton, Or., U.S. — C4 114
Silverton, Tx., U.S. — B2 120
Silverville, In., U.S. — G4 91
Silves, Port. — D1 22
Silvia, Col. — C2 60
Silvies, stm., Or., U.S. — D7 114
Silvis, Il., U.S. — B3 90
Silwān (part of Jerusalem), Isr. Occ. — h11 41
Simanggang, Malay. — E4 34
Simao, China — G5 31
Simav, Tur. — C7 40
Simav, stm., Tur. — B7 25
Simcoe, Ont. — E4 73
Simcoe, co., Ont. — C4 73
Simcoe, Lake, l., Ont. — C5 73
Simdega, India — F10 37
Simeulue, i., Indon. — m11 34
Simferopol, Sov. Un. — E6 29
Simi, i., Grc. — H2 35
Similan Islands, is., Thai. — H2 35
Simikameen, stm., N.A. — K3 35
Simití, Col. — B7 69
Simi Valley, Ca., U.S. — E4 82
Simla, Co., U.S. — B6 83
Simleu Silvaniei, Rom. — B6 24
Simme, stm., Switz. — C3 21
Simmern, Ger. — D2 19
Simmesport, La., U.S. — D4 95
Simmie, Sask. — H1 75
Simmons, Mo., U.S. — D5 102
Simms, Mt., U.S. — C5 103
Simms Point, c., Bah. — m16 64
Simms Stream, stm., N.H. — g7 106
Simonette, stm., Alta. — B1 68
Simonhouse Lake, l., Man. — B1 70
Simonstorp (part of Norrköping), Swe. — u34 14
Simonsville, Vt., U.S. — E3 122
Simoom Sound, B.C. — D4 69
Simpang-kiri, stm., Indon. — K2 35
Simpang Mendes, Braz. — C2 57
Simplon Pass, Switz. — C4 20
Simplon Tunnel, Eur. — A2 23
Simpson, Sask. — F3 75
Simpson, Il., U.S. — F5 90
Simpson, Pa., U.S. — C6 93
Simpson, co., Ky., U.S. — D3 94
Simpson, co., Ms., U.S. — D4 101
Simpson, N.C., U.S. — C5 110
Simpson, W.V., U.S. — k10 125
Simpson Creek, stm., W.V., U.S. — k10 125
Simpson Desert, des., Austl. — E6 50
Simpson Peninsula, pen., N.W. Ter. — C15 66
Simpsonville, S.C., U.S. — B3 117
Sims, Ar., U.S. — C2 81
Sims, Il., U.S. — E5 90
Sims, N.C., U.S. — B4 110
Simsboro, La., U.S. — B3 95
Sims Chapel, Al., U.S. — D1 78

Sinai, S.D., U.S. — C8 118
Sinaia, Rom. — C7 24
Sinai Peninsula, pen., Eg. — C3 38
Sinajana, Guam — L10 52
Sinaloa, state, Mex. — B3 63
Sinaloa [de Leyva], Mex. — B3 63
Sinan, China — F6 31
Sinanju, N. Kor. — G2 33
Sinarū, Eg. — E2 41
Sincan, Tur. — *C9 40
Sinçe, Col. — B2 60
Sincelejo, Col. — B2 60
Sinclair, Man. — E1 70
Sinclair, Me., U.S. — A4 96
Sinclair, Wy., U.S. — E5 127
Sinclair, Lake, res., Ga., U.S. — C3 87
Sinclair's Bay, b., Scot., U.K. — B5 13
Sinclairville, N.Y., U.S. — C1 109
Sind, prov., Pak. — D7 37
Sind, stm., India — D7 37
Sindal, Den. — A4 15
Sindara, Gabon — F2 46
Sindelfingen, Ger. — B3 19
Sindirgi, Tur. — C7 40
Sinelnikovo, Sov. Un. — G10 27
Sines, Port. — D1 22
Sinfra, I.C. — E2 34
Singapore, Sing. — E3 34
Singapore, ctry., Asia — E3 34
Singapore Strait, strt., Asia — L5 35
Singaraja, Indon. — G5 34
Singen (Hohentwiel), Ger. — B4 20
Singer, La., U.S. — D2 95
Singhampton, Ont. — C4 73
Singida, Tan. — B5 48
Singida, prov., Tan. — C5 48
Singitic Gulf, b., Grc. — B4 25
Singkawang, Indon. — E3 34
Singkep, i., Indon. — F2 34
Singkil, Indon. — E1 34
Singleton, Austl. — F8 51
Sinhung, N. Kor. — F3 33
Siniscola, Italy — D2 23
Sinj, Yugo. — C3 47
Sinjah, Sud. — C3 47
Sinjil, Isr. Occ. — g12 41
Sinkāt, Sud. — B4 47
Sinkiang see Xinjiang Uygur, prov., China — C2 31
Sinking Creek, stm., Ky., U.S. — C3 94
Sinking Spring, Oh., U.S. — C2 112
Sinks Grove, W.V., U.S. — D5 125
Sinnamahoning, Pa., U.S. — D5 115
Sinnamary, Fr. Gu. — A4 59
Sinnamahoning Creek, stm., Pa., U.S. — D5 115
Sinnamahoning Creek, First Fork, stm., Pa., U.S. — D5 115
Sinnicolau Mare, Rom. — B5 24
Sinnūris, Eg. — E2 41
Sinop, Tur. — A10 40
Sinpo, N. Kor. — F4 33
Sintaluta, Sask. — G4 75
Sint-Amandsberg (part of Gent), Bel. — C3 17
Sintang, Indon. — E4 34
Sint Christoffelberg, hill, Neth. Ant. — H8 65
Sint Eustatius, i., Neth. Ant. — H13 64
Sint Helenabaai, b., S. Afr. — D2 49
Sint Jacobiparochie, Neth. — A5 17
Sint Kruis, Neth. Ant. — H18 65
Sint-Lenaarts, Bel. — C4 17
Sint Marie, Kaap, c., Neth. Ant. — H18 65
Sint Nicolaas, Aruba — H17 65
Sint-Niklaas (Saint-Nicolas), Bel. — B6 16
Sinton, Tx., U.S. — E4 120
Sintra, Port. — f9 22
Sinú, stm., Col. — B2 60
Sinújiu, N. Kor. — D9 31
Sinyavino, Sov. Un. — s32 14
Sinzig, Ger. — C2 19
Sion, Switz. — E3 18
Sioux, co., Ia., U.S. — A1 92
Sioux, co., Ne., U.S. — B2 104
Sioux, co., N.D., U.S. — C4 111
Sioux Center, Ia., U.S. — A1 92
Sioux City, Ia., U.S. — B1 92
Sioux Falls, S.D., U.S. — D9 118
Sioux Lookout, Ont. — o17 73
Sioux Rapids, Ia., U.S. — B2 92
Sipanok Channel, mth., Sask. — D4 75
Siparia, Trin. — O22 65
Siping, China — C9 31
Sipiwesk Lake, l., Man. — B4 70
Siple, Mount, mtn., Ant. — B36 7
Siple, sci., Ant. — B4 7
Siple Coast, Ant. — A33 7
Sipsey, Al., U.S. — B2 78
Sipsey, stm., Al., U.S. — B2 78
Sipsey Fork, stm., Al., U.S. — A2 78
Sipura, i., Indon. — F1 34
Siquia, stm., Nic. — E6 62
Siquirres, C.R. — I6 62
Siquisique, Ven. — A4 60
Sir Abū Nu'Ayr, i., U.A.E. — I7 39
Siracusa (Syracuse), Italy — F5 23
Sīrājganj, Bngl. — D8 36
Sir Alexander, Mount, mtn., B.C. — C7 69
Sirdar, B.C. — E9 69
Sir Douglas, Mount, mtn., Can. — D3 68
Sir Edward Pellew Group, is., Austl. — C6 50
Siret, Wi., U.S. — C1 126
Siret, Rom. — B8 24
Siret, stm., Eur. — B8 24
Sirhān, Wādī as, val., Asia — C7 43
Sirína, i., Grc. — H7 25
Sirik, Cape, c., Malay. — E4 34
Sirína, i., Grc. — D6 25
Sir James MacBrien, Mount, mtn., N.W. Ter. — D7 66
Sirjān, Iran — D7 39
Sirmans, Fl., U.S. — B3 86
Sirmione, Italy — D5 23
Sironj, India — E6 37
Sirohi, India — H5 37
Sirr, Mushāsh as, well, Eg. — D5 41
Sirrí, i., Iran — C6 36
Sirsa, India — F6 36
Sir Sandford, Mount, mtn., B.C. — D9 69
Sirsi, India — A8 31
Sir-Wilfrid, Mont, mtn., Que. — C2 74
Sir Wilfrid Laurier, Mount, mtn., B.C. — C8 69
Sisak, Yugo. — C3 24
Si Sa Ket, Thai. — B2 34
Sishui, China — G7 32
Sisib Lake, l., Man. — C2 70

Name	Map Ref.	Page

Sisipuk Lake, l., Can. · B1 70
Siskiyou, co., U.S. · B2 82
Siskiyou Mountains, mts., U.S. · F3 114
Siskiyou Pass, Or., U.S. · E4 114
Sisquoc, Ca., U.S. · E3 82
Sissach, Switz. · B4 21
Sisseton, S.D., U.S. · B8 118
Sisseton Indian Reservation, U.S. · B8 118
Sissiboo, stm., N.S. · E4 71
Sisson Branch Reservoir, res., N.B. · B2 71
Sissonville, W.V., U.S. · C3 125
Sīstān, reg., Asia · B6 38
Sister Bay, Wi., U.S. · C6 126
Sisterdale, Tx., U.S. · E3 120
Sisteron, Fr. · E6 16
Sisters, Or., U.S. · C5 114
Sistersville, W.V., U.S. · B4 125
Sītāpur, India · C7 36
Sitia, Grc. · E6 40
Sítio da Abadia, Braz. · A3 56
Sitionuevo, Col. · A3 60
Sitka, Ak., U.S. · D12 79
Sitka National Historical Park, Ak., U.S. · m22 79
Sitka Sound, strt., Ak., U.S. · m22 79
Sittard, Neth. · D5 17
Sittoung, stm., Burma · E10 36
Sittwe (Akyab), Burma · D9 36
Siuna, Nic. · D5 62
Siuri, India · C8 36
Sivas, Tur. · C11 40
Siverek, Tur. · D12 40
Siwah, Eg. · C2 38
Siwalik Range, mts., India · B6 36
Six-Fours-la-Plage, Fr. · F6 16
Sixian, China · H7 32
Si see Xi Jiang, stm., China · G7 31
Six Mile, S.C., U.S. · B2 117
Sixmile Creek, stm., Fl., U.S. · n8 86
Sixmilecross, N. Ire., U.K. · C4 11
Sixt, Fr. · D2 21
Sizhan, China · B2 33
Sjælland, i., Den. · J4 14
Sjællands Odde, pen., Den. · B5 15
Sjenica, Yugo. · D5 24
Sjöbo, Swe. · C7 15
Skælskør, Den. · C5 15
Skærbæk, Den. · C2 15
Skagen, Den. · A4 15
Skagerrak, strt., Eur. · I3 14
Skagit, co., Wa., U.S. · A4 124
Skagit, stm., N.A. · A3 69
Skagway, Ak., U.S. · D12 79
Skälderviken, b., Swe. · B6 15
Skalka Reservoir, res., Czech. · C7 19
Skamania, Wa., U.S. · D3 124
Skamania, co., Wa., U.S. · D3 124
Skamokawa, Wa., U.S. · C2 124
Skanderborg, Den. · B3 15
Skaneateles, N.Y., U.S. · C4 109
Skaneateles Lake, l., N.Y., U.S. · C4 109
Skanee, Mi., U.S. · B2 99
Skånes-Fagerhult, Swe. · B7 15
Skanör, Swe. · C6 15
Skántzoura, i., Grc. · C5 25
Skara, Swe. · H5 14
Skarven, i., Swe. · t35 14
Skarżysko-Kamienna, Pol. · C6 26
Skawa, stm., Pol. · h11 26
Skawina, Pol. · D5 26
Skedee, Ok., U.S. · A5 113
Skeena, stm., B.C. · F7 66
Skeena Mountains, mts., B.C. · D7 10
Skegness, Eng., U.K. · A3 59
Skeldon, Guy. · B5 73
Skeleton Lake, l., Ont. · E9 14
Skellefteå, Swe. · E8 14
Skellefteälven, stm., Swe. · B2 120
Skellytown, Tx., U.S. · n13 125
Skelton, W.V., U.S. · f40 7
Skelton Glacier, ice, Ant. · B3 101
Skene, Ms., U.S. · D5 14
Skerries, Ire. · A4 13
Skhímatárion, Grc. · g11 25
Skiathos, Grc. · C4 25
Skiathos, i., Grc. · C4 25
Skiatook, Ok., U.S. · A5 113
Skiatook Reservoir, res., Ok., U.S. · A5 113
Skibbereen, Ire. · E2 10
Skibby, Den. · C5 15
Skiddaw, mtn., Eng., U.K. · F5 13
Skidegate, B.C. · C2 69
Skidegate Inlet, b., B.C. · C2 69
Skidmore, Mo., U.S. · A2 102
Skidmore, Tx., U.S. · E4 120
Skien, Nor. · H3 14
Skierniewice, Pol. · C6 26
Skiff, Alta. · E5 68
Skihist Mountain, mtn., B.C. · D7 69
Skikda (Philippeville), Alg. · B6 44
Skillet Fork, stm., Il., U.S. · E5 90
Skillman, N.J., U.S. · C3 107
Skipperville, Al., U.S. · D4 78
Skipton, Eng., U.K. · G7 13
Skíros, Grc. · C5 40
Skíros (Scyros), i., Grc. · C5 40
Skive, Den. · B3 15
Skjern, Den. · C2 15
Skjern Å, stm., Den. · h9 26
Škofja Loka, Yugo. · B2 24
Skokie, Il., U.S. · A6 90
Skokomish Indian Reservation, Wa., U.S. · B2 124
Skole, Sov. Un. · D7 26
Skópelos, i., Grc. · C4 40
Skopin, Sov. Un. · E12 27
Skopje, Yugo. · D5 24
Skørping, Den. · B3 15
Skotovataya, Sov. Un. · q20 27
Skotsel, Nor. · p27 14
Skövde, Swe. · H5 14
Skovorodino, Sov. Un. · D15 29
Skowhegan, Me., U.S. · D3 96
Skownan, Man. · D2 70
Skradin, Yugo. · D2 24
Skreen, Ire. · F2 11
Skull, Ire. · F2 11
Skull Valley, val., Ut., U.S. · C3 121
Skull Valley Indian Reservation, Ut., U.S. · C3 121
Skuna, stm., Ms., U.S. · B4 101
Skunk, stm., Ia., U.S. · D6 92
Skurup, Swe. · C7 15
Skvira, Sov. Un. · G7 27
Skwentna, Ak., U.S. · g16 79
Skwentna, stm., Ak., U.S. · g15 79
Skwierzyna (Schwerin), Pol. · B3 26

Skye, Island of, i., Scot., U.K. · B3 10
Skykomish, Wa., U.S. · B4 124
Skykomish, stm., Wa., U.S. · B4 124
Sky Lake, Fl., U.S. · *D5 86
Skyland, Nv., U.S. · D2 105
Skyland, N.C., U.S. · f10 110
Skylight, Ky., U.S. · g11 94
Skylight Mountain, mtn., Ar., U.S. · B1 81
Skyline, Al., U.S. · A3 78
Skyring, Seno, strt., Chile · h11 54
Skyway, Co., U.S. · C5 83
Skyway, Wa., U.S. · *f11 124
Slackwood, N.J., U.S. · *C3 107
Slade, Ky., U.S. · C6 94
Slagelse, Den. · C5 15
Slagle, La., U.S. · C2 95
Slamet, mtn., Indon. · G3 34
Slane, Ire. · D5 11
Slaney, stm., Ire. · E5 11
Slangerup, Den. · C6 15
Slānic, Rom. · C7 24
Slaný, Czech. · n17 26
Slapout, Ok., U.S. · A1 113
Slapy, Czech. · o17 26
Slapy Reservoir, res., Czech. · D9 19
Slater, Co., U.S. · A3 83
Slater, Ia., U.S. · C4 92
Slater, Mo., U.S. · B4 102
Slater, S.C., U.S. · A3 117
Slatersville, R.I., U.S. · A3 116
Slatersville Reservoir, res., R.I., U.S. · B3 116
Slate Spring, Ms., U.S. · B4 101
Slatina, Rom. · C7 24
Slatington, Pa., U.S. · E10 115
Slaton, Tx., U.S. · C2 120
Slaughter, La., U.S. · D4 95
Slaughter Beach, De., U.S. · E4 85
Slaughters, Ky., U.S. · C2 94
Slave, stm., Can. · D10 66
Slave Lake, Alta. · B3 68
Slavgorod, Sov. Un. · D10 29
Slavonia, hist. reg., Yugo. · C3 24
Slavonska Požega, Yugo. · C3 24
Slavonski Brod, Yugo. · C4 24
Slavsk, Sov. Un. · A6 26
Slavyanoserbsk, Sov. Un. · q21 27
Slavyansk, Sov. Un. · G11 27
Slavyansk-na-Kubani, Sov. Un. · I12 27
Sławków, Pol. · g10 26
Sławno, Pol. · A4 26
Slayden, Ms., U.S. · A4 101
Slayton, Mn., U.S. · G3 100
Slaytonville, De., U.S. · E3 85
Sleaford, Eng., U.K. · A7 12
Slea Head, c., Ire. · E1 11
Sleat, Point of, c., Scot., U.K. · C3 13
Sleat, Sound of, strt., Scot., U.K. · C3 13
Sledge, Ms., U.S. · A3 101
Sled Lake, l., Sask. · C2 75
Sleeper, Mo., U.S. · D5 102
Sleeping Bear Dunes National Lakeshore, Mi., U.S. · D4 99
Sleeping Bear Point, c., Mi., U.S. · D4 99
Sleepy Creek, W.V., U.S. · B6 125
Sleepy Eye, Mn., U.S. · F4 100
Sleepy Point, c., Fiji · H15 52
Sleetmute, Ak., U.S. · C8 79
Slemp, Ky., U.S. · C6 94
Slick, Ok., U.S. · B5 113
Slick Rock, Co., U.S. · C2 83
Slickville, Pa., U.S. · F2 115
Slidell, La., U.S. · D6 95
Slide Mountain, mtn., N.Y., U.S. · D6 109
Sliderock Mountain, mtn., Mt., U.S. · D3 103
Slieve Aughty Mountains, mts., Ire. · D3 11
Slievecallan, hill, Ire. · E2 11
Slievekimalta, hill, Ire. · E3 11
Slieve Mish Mountains, mts., Ire. · E2 11
Slievenamon, mtn., Ire. · E4 11
Sligo, Ire. · C2 10
Sligo, Pa., U.S. · D3 115
Sligo, co., Ire. · C3 11
Sligo Bay, b., Ire. · C2 10
Slim Buttes, mtn., S.D., U.S. · B2 118
Slinger, Wi., U.S. · E5 126
Slippery Rock, Pa., U.S. · D1 115
Sliven, Bul. · D8 24
Slivenec, Czech. · n17 26
Sloan, Ia., U.S. · B1 92
Sloan, Nv., U.S. · H6 105
Sloans Valley, Ky., U.S. · D5 94
Sloat, Ca., U.S. · C3 82
Sloatsburg, N.Y., U.S. · *D6 109
Slobodskoy, Sov. Un. · B4 28
Slobozia, Rom. · C8 24
Slocan, B.C. · E9 69
Slocan Lake, l., B.C. · E9 69
Slocomb, Al., U.S. · D4 78
Slocum, R.I., U.S. · E3 116
Slonim, Sov. Un. · E5 27
Slope, co., N.D., U.S. · C2 111
Slough, Eng., U.K. · k11 10
Slovak, Ar., U.S. · C4 81
Slovakia, hist. reg., Czech. · D5 26
Slovan, Pa., U.S. · F1 115
Slovenia, hist. reg., Yugo. · C2 24
Słubice, Pol. · A9 19
Sluch, stm., Sov. Un. · F6 27
Slunj, Yugo. · B4 24
Słupca, Pol. · B4 26
Słupia, stm., Pol. · A4 26
Słupsk, Pol. · A4 26
Slutsk, Sov. Un. · E6 27
Slyne Head, c., Ire. · D1 10
Slyudyanka, Sov. Un. · D13 29
Smackover, Ar., U.S. · D3 81
Smackover Creek, stm., Ar., U.S. · D3 81
Smålandsfarvandet, strt., Den. · C2 15
Small Point, Me., U.S. · g8 96
Small Point, c., Me., U.S. · g8 96
Smallwood Reservoir, res., Newf. · g8 72
Smarr, Ga., U.S. · D3 87
Smarts Mountain, mtn., N.H., U.S. · C2 106
Smartt, Tn., U.S. · D8 119
Smeaton, Sask. · D3 75
Smečno, Czech. · n17 26
Smederevo, Yugo. · C5 24
Smela, Sov. Un. · G8 27
Smelterville, Id., U.S. · B2 89
Smethport, Pa., U.S. · C5 115
Smethwick (Warley), Eng., U.K. · D5 10

Smichov (part of Prague), Czech. · n17 26
Smicksburg, Pa., U.S. · E3 115
Smidovich, Sov. Un. · B6 33
Smiley, Sask. · F1 75
Smiley, Tx., U.S. · E4 120
Smirnovo, Sov. Un. · H11 27
Smith, Alta. · B3 68
Smith, Nv., U.S. · E2 105
Smith, co., Ks., U.S. · C5 93
Smith, co., Ms., U.S. · C4 101
Smith, co., Tn., U.S. · A5 119
Smith, co., Tx., U.S. · C5 120
Smith, stm., Mt., U.S. · D5 103
Smith, stm., Va., U.S. · B3 73
Smith and Sayles Reservoir, res., R.I., U.S. · B2 116
Smith Bay, b., Ak., U.S. · A9 79
Smithboro, Il., U.S. · E4 90
Smithburg, W.V., U.S. · B4 125
Smith Canyon, val., Co., U.S. · D7 83
Smith Center, Ks., U.S. · C5 93
Smithdale, Ms., U.S. · D3 101
Smithers, B.C. · B4 69
Smithers, W.V., U.S. · C3 125
Smithfield, Il., U.S. · C3 90
Smithfield, Me., U.S. · D3 96
Smithfield, Mo., U.S. · D3 102
Smithfield, Ne., U.S. · D6 104
Smithfield, N.C., U.S. · B4 110
Smithfield, Oh., U.S. · B5 112
Smithfield, Pa., U.S. · G2 115
Smithfield, Ut., U.S. · B4 121
Smithfield, Va., U.S. · D6 123
Smithfield, W.V., U.S. · k9 125
Smith Island, i., B.A.T. · C6 7
Smith Island, i., Va., U.S. · C7 123
Smithland, Ia., U.S. · B2 92
Smithland, Ky., U.S. · e9 94
Smithmill, Pa., U.S. · E5 115
Smith Mills, Ky., U.S. · C2 94
Smith Mountain Lake, res., Va., U.S. · C3 123
Smith Peak, mtn., Id., U.S. · A2 89
Smith Peninsula, pen., Ant. · C7 7
Smith Point, c., Ma., U.S. · D7 98
Smith Point, c., Va., U.S. · C6 123
Smith River, Ca., U.S. · B1 82
Smiths, Al., U.S. · C4 78
Smithsburg, Md., U.S. · A2 97
Smiths Cove, N.S. · E4 71
Smiths Falls, Ont. · C8 73
Smiths Ferry, Id., U.S. · E2 89
Smiths Grove, Ky., U.S. · C3 94
Smithshire, Il., U.S. · C3 90
Smithsonia, Ga., U.S. · C2 87
Smith Sound, strt., B.C. · D4 69
Smithton, Austl. · o15 50
Smithton, Il., U.S. · E4 90
Smithton, Mo., U.S. · C4 102
Smith Town, Ky., U.S. · D5 94
Smithtown, N.Y., U.S. · n15 109
Smithville, Ar., U.S. · A4 81
Smithville, Ga., U.S. · E2 87
Smithville, In., U.S. · F4 91
Smithville, Ms., U.S. · A5 101
Smithville, Mo., U.S. · B3 102
Smithville, N.H., U.S. · E3 106
Smithville, N.J., U.S. · D3 107
Smithville, Oh., U.S. · B4 112
Smithville, Ok., U.S. · C7 113
Smithville, Tn., U.S. · D8 119
Smithville, Tx., U.S. · D4 120
Smithville, W.V., U.S. · B3 125
Smithville Flats, N.Y., U.S. · C5 109
Smithville Lake, res., Mo., U.S. · B3 102
Smithwick, S.D., U.S. · D2 118
Smoaks, S.C., U.S. · E6 117
Smoke Creek Desert, des., Nv., U.S. · C2 105
Smokerun, Pa., U.S. · E5 115
Smokey, Cape, c., N.S. · C9 71
Smokey Dome, mtn., Id., U.S. · F4 89
Smoky, stm., Alta. · B1 68
Smoky Cape, c., Austl. · E9 51
Smoky Hill, stm., U.S. · D5 93
Smoky Hill, North Fork, stm., U.S. · C2 93
Smoky Junction, Tn., U.S. · C9 119
Smoky Lake, Alta. · B4 68
Smoky Mountains, mts., Id., U.S. · F4 89
Smøla, i., Nor. · F2 14
Smolan, Ks., U.S. · D6 93
Smolensk, Sov. Un. · E7 27
Smolyan, Bul. · E7 24
Smoot, Wy., U.S. · D2 127
Smooth Rock Falls, Ont. · o19 73
Smoothstone, stm., Sask. · B2 75
Smoothstone Lake, l., Sask. · B2 75
Smoots Creek, stm., Ks., U.S. · g11 93
Smyadovo, Bul. · D8 24
Smygehamn, Swe. · C7 15
Smyrna, Ga., U.S. · C2 87
Smyrna, stm., De., U.S. · C3 85
Smyrna, Mi., U.S. · F5 99
Smyrna, N.Y., U.S. · C5 109
Smyrna, S.C., U.S. · A5 117
Smyrna, Tn., U.S. · B5 119
Smyrna, stm., De., U.S. · C3 85
Smyrna Mills, Me., U.S. · B4 96
Smyth, co., Va., U.S. · f10 123
Smythe, Mount, mtn., B.C. · E8 66
Snaefell, mtn., I. of Man · F4 13
Snake, stm., U.S. · A4 76
Snake, stm., Mn., U.S. · D5 100
Snake, stm., Mn., U.S. · B1 100
Snake, stm., Ne., U.S. · B4 104
Snake Creek, stm., Ne., U.S. · B2 104
Snake Falls, wtfl., Ne., U.S. · B4 104
Snake Indian, stm., Alta. · C1 68
Snake Mountain, mtn., Vt., U.S. · C2 122
Snake Range, mts., Nv., U.S. · E7 105
Snake River Plain, pl., Id., U.S. · G5 89
Snake River Range, mts., U.S. · C2 127
Snake Valley, val., U.S. · E7 105
Snares Islands, is., N.Z. · R11 51
Sneads, Fl., U.S. · B2 86
Sneads Ferry, N.C., U.S. · C5 110
Snedsted, Den. · B2 15
Sneedville, Tn., U.S. · C10 119
Sneek, Neth. · A6 16
Sneem, Ire. · F2 11
Snelling, S.C., U.S. · E5 117
Snellville, Ga., U.S. · *h8 87
Sno, Rio do, stm., Braz. · C1 57
Snežnoye, Sov. Un. · q21 27
Śniardwy Lake, l., Pol. · B6 26
Snipe Keys, is., Fl., U.S. · H5 86
Snipe Lake, l., Alta. · B2 68
Snizort, Loch, b., Scot., U.K. · C2 13

Snøhetta, mtn., Nor. · F3 14
Snohomish, Wa., U.S. · B3 124
Snohomish, co., Wa., U.S. · A4 124
Snoqualmie, Wa., U.S. · B4 124
Snoqualmie, stm., Wa., U.S. · B4 124
Snoqualmie Pass, Wa., U.S. · B4 124
Snøtinden, mtn., Nor. · D5 14
Snov, stm., Sov. Un. · F8 27
Snover, Mi., U.S. · E8 99
Snow, Ok., U.S. · C6 113
Snowbank Lake, l., Mn., U.S. · B7 100
Snow Camp, N.C., U.S. · B3 110
Snowden, Sask. · D3 75
Snowdon, mtn., Wales, U.K. · D4 10
Snowdoun, Al., U.S. · C3 78
Snowflake, Man. · E2 70
Snowflake, Az., U.S. · C5 80
Snow Hill, Ar., U.S. · C2 78
Snow Hill, Md., U.S. · D7 97
Snow Hill, N.C., U.S. · B5 110
Snowking Mountain, mtn., Wa., U.S. · A4 124
Snow Lake, Man. · B1 70
Snow Lake, Ar., U.S. · C4 81
Snowmass, Co., U.S. · B4 83
Snowmass Mountain, mtn., Co., U.S. · B3 83
Snow Peak, mtn., Wa., U.S. · A7 124
Snow Road Station, Ont. · C8 73
Snowshoe Lake, l., Me., U.S. · B4 96
Snowshoe Peak, mtn., Mt., U.S. · B1 103
Snowville, N.H., U.S. · C4 106
Snowville, Ut., U.S. · B3 121
Snowville, Va., U.S. · *C2 123
Snow Water Lake, l., Nv., U.S. · C7 105
Snowy, stm., Austl. · H7 51
Snowy Mountain, mtn., N.Y., U.S. · B6 109
Snowy Mountains, mts., Austl. · G8 50
Snowyside Peak, mtn., Id., U.S. · F4 89
Snyatyn, Sov. Un. · A7 24
Snyder, Ar., U.S. · D4 81
Snyder, Co., U.S. · A7 83
Snyder, Ne., U.S. · C9 104
Snyder, Ok., U.S. · C3 113
Snyder, co., Pa., U.S. · E7 115
Snyder Knob, mtn., W.V., U.S. · C5 125
Soacha, Col. · *C3 60
Soalala, Madag. · g9 49
Soap Lake, Wa., U.S. · B6 124
Soar, stm., Eng., U.K. · B6 12
Soatá, Col. · B3 60
Soay, i., Scot., U.K. · C2 13
Sobat, stm., Sud. · D9 47
Soběslav, Czech. · D9 19
Sobieski, Mn., U.S. · E4 100
Sobieski, Wi., U.S. · D5 126
Sobinka, Sov. Un. · D13 27
Sobral, Braz. · B2 57
Sobti, well, Mali · B4 45
Socastee, S.C., U.S. · D9 117
Sochaczew, Pol. · B6 26
Sochaux, Fr. · A2 21
Sochi, Sov. Un. · I6 29
Social Circle, Ga., U.S. · C3 87
Society Hill, S.C., U.S. · B8 117
Society Islands, is., Fr. Poly. · H12 6
Socompa, Paso de, S.A. · D2 55
Socorro, Braz. · m8 56
Socorro, Col. · B3 60
Socorro, N.M., U.S. · C3 108
Socorro, co., N.M., U.S. · D2 108
Socotra (Suquţrā), i., Yemen · D5 38
Soc Trang, Viet. · D3 34
Socuéllamos, Spain · C4 22
Soda Creek, B.C. · C6 69
Soda Springs, Id., U.S. · G7 89
Sodankylä, Fin. · D12 14
Soddy-Daisy, Tn., U.S. · D8 119
Söderala, Swe. · G7 14
Söderhamn, Swe. · G7 14
Söderköping, Swe. · H7 14
Södertälje, Swe. · t35 14
Sodo, Eth. · D4 47
Sodus, N.Y., U.S. · B3 109
Sodus Point, N.Y., U.S. · B3 109
Soest, Ger. · C4 18
Sofádhes, Grc. · C4 25
Sofala, dept., Moz. · A5 49
Sofia (Sofiya), Bul. · D6 24
Sofia, stm., Madag. · g9 49
Sofiyevka, Sov. Un. · H9 27
Sogamoso, Col. · B3 60
Sögel, Ger. · B7 17
Sognafjorden, Nor. · F1 14
Soğut, Tur. · C8 25
Soham, W.V., U.S. · D4 17
Soignies, Bel. · D4 69
Soissons, Fr. · C5 16
Sokcho, S. Kor. · G4 33
Söke, Tur. · D6 25
Sokehs Passage, strt., Micron. · Q17 52
Sokhondo, mtn., Sov. Un. · E14 29
Sokodé, Togo · E5 45
Sokółka, Pol. · B7 26
Sokolo, Mali · D3 45
Sokolov, Czech. · C7 19
Sokołów [Podlaski], Pol. · B7 26
Sokoto, Nig. · D6 45
Sol, Pico do, mtn., Braz. · C4 56
Soła, Pol. · h10 26
Solana, Fl., U.S. · F5 86
Solander Island, i., N.Z. · Q11 51
Solano, Phil. · n13 34
Solano, N.M., U.S. · B5 108
Solano, co., Ca., U.S. · C2 82
Solapur see Sholapur, India · E5 36
Solbad Hall [in Tirol], Aus. · E5 18
Soldatovo, Sov. Un. · F26 27
Soldier, Ia., U.S. · C2 92
Soldier, Ks., U.S. · C8 93
Soldier, Ky., U.S. · B6 94
Soldier Creek, stm., U.S. · *D5 118
Soldier Creek, stm., Ks., U.S. · C8 93
Soldier Key, i., Fl., U.S. · s13 86
Soldier Pond, Me., U.S. · A4 96
Soldiers Grove, Wi., U.S. · E3 126
Soldier Summit, Ut., U.S. · D4 121
Soldotna, Ak., U.S. · g16 79
Soledad, Col. · A3 60
Soledad, Ca., U.S. · D3 82

Soledad, Ven. · B5 60
Soledad Diez Gutiérrez, Mex. · *C4 63
Soleduck, stm., Wa., U.S. · B1 124
Solesmes, Fr. · D3 17
Solihull, Eng., U.K. · B6 12
Solikamsk, Sov. Un. · D8 29
Sol-Iletsk, Sov. Un. · C5 28
Soliman, Tun. · F3 23
Solingen, Ger. · C3 18
Sollas, Scot., U.K. · C1 13
Sollefteå, Swe. · F7 14
Sóller, Spain · C3 22
Sollentuna, Swe. · *H8 14
Sollihögda, Nor. · p28 14
Solna, Swe. · H7 14
Solo, stm., Indon. · G3 34
Solomon, Az., U.S. · E6 80
Solomon, Ks., U.S. · D6 93
Solomon, stm., Ks., U.S. · C6 93
Solomon, North Fork, stm., Ks., U.S. · C4 93
Solomon, South Fork, stm., Ks., U.S. · C4 93
Solomon Islands, ctry., Oc. · *D3 82
Solomons, Md., U.S. · D5 97
Solomon Sea, Oc. · k12 50
Solon, China · B9 31
Solon, Ia., U.S. · C6 92
Solon, Me., U.S. · D3 96
Solon Mills, Il., U.S. · h8 90
Solon Springs, Wi., U.S. · B2 126
Solothurn, Switz. · E3 18
Solothurn, state, Switz. · E3 18
Solovyevsk, Sov. Un. · D15 29
Šolta, i., Yugo. · D3 24
Soltau, Ger. · B4 18
Solvay, N.Y., U.S. · B4 109
Sölvesborg, Swe. · H10 14
Solvychegodsk, Sov. Un. · C4 28
Solway, Mn., U.S. · C3 100
Solway Firth, est., U.K. · C5 10
Solwezi, Zam. · D4 48
Soma, Tur. · C6 25
Somalia, ctry., Afr. · D6 47
Sombor, Yugo. · C4 24
Sombra, Ont. · E2 73
Sombrerete, Mex. · C4 63
Sombrero Channel, strt., India · G9 36
Sombrio, Braz. · D3 56
Somerdale, N.J., U.S. · D2 107
Somers, Ct., U.S. · B6 84
Somers, Ia., U.S. · B3 92
Somers, Mt., U.S. · B2 103
Somers, Wi., U.S. · F6 126
Somerset, Ber. · p19 64
Somerset, Man. · E2 70
Somerset, Co., U.S. · C3 83
Somerset, In., U.S. · C6 91
Somerset, Ky., U.S. · C5 94
Somerset, Ma., U.S. · C5 98
Somerset, N.J., U.S. · B3 107
Somerset, Oh., U.S. · C3 112
Somerset, Pa., U.S. · F3 115
Somerset, Tx., U.S. · k7 120
Somerset, Wi., U.S. · C1 126
Somerset, co., Eng., U.K. · C5 12
Somerset, co., Md., U.S. · D6 97
Somerset, co., Me., U.S. · C2 96
Somerset, co., N.J., U.S. · B3 107
Somerset, co., Pa., U.S. · G3 115
Somerset East, S. Afr. · D4 49
Somerset Island, i., N.W. Ter. · B14 66
Somers Point, N.J., U.S. · E3 107
Somersville, Ct., U.S. · B6 84
Somersworth, N.H., U.S. · D5 106
Somervell, co., Tx., U.S. · C4 120
Somerville, Al., U.S. · A3 78
Somerville, In., U.S. · H3 91
Somerville, Ma., U.S. · B5 98
Somerville, N.J., U.S. · B3 107
Somerville, Oh., U.S. · C1 112
Somerville, Tn., U.S. · B2 119
Somerville, Tx., U.S. · D4 120
Somerville Lake, res., Tx., U.S. · D4 120
Someş (Szamos), stm., Eur. · B6 24
Somme, dept., Fr. · E2 17
Somme, stm., Fr. · B4 16
Sommepy-[Tahure], Fr. · E4 17
Sömmerda, Ger. · B6 19
Somonauk, Il., U.S. · B5 90
Somosomo, Fiji · H16 52
Somosomo Strait, strt., Fiji · H15 52
Somoto, Nic. · H10 37
Somuncurá, Meseta de, plat., Arg. · E3 54
Somvix, Switz. · C6 21
Son, stm., India · D7 36
Soná, Pan. · J7 62
Soncino, Italy · D5 20
Sønderborg, Den. · D3 15
Sønderjylland, co., Den. · D3 15
Sondershausen, Ger. · C5 18
Sondheimer, La., U.S. · B4 95
Sondrio, Italy · A3 23
Sonepur, India · D7 36
Sonestown, Pa., U.S. · D8 115
Song Cau, Viet. · F8 35
Songea, Tan. · D6 48
Songhua Jiang, stm., China · B10 31
Songjiang, China · E9 31
Songkhla, Thai. · Q11 34
Songnim (Kyŏmipo), N. Kor. · G2 33
Songtao, China · J3 32
Son La, Viet. · B5 34
Sonmiāni, Pak. · I13 39
Sonmiāni Bay, b., Pak. · I13 39
Sonneberg, Ger. · C5 18
Sonningdale, Sask. · E2 75
Sonobe, Japan · n14 35
Sonoita, Az., U.S. · A2 63
Sonoma, Ca., U.S. · F5 80
Sonoma, co., Ca., U.S. · C2 82
Sonoma Peak, mtn., Nv., U.S. · C4 105

Sonoma Range, mts., Nv., U.S. · C4 105
Sonora, Ca., U.S. · D3 82
Sonora, Ky., U.S. · C4 94
Sonora, Oh., U.S. · C4 112
Sonora, Tx., U.S. · D2 120
Sonora, state, Mex. · B2 63
Sonqor, Iran · D3 39
Sonsón, Col. · B2 60
Sonsonate, El Sal. · E7 63
Sontag, Ms., U.S. · D3 101
Son Tay, Viet. · A3 34
Sonthofen, Ger. · A9 21
Sonyea, N.Y., U.S. · C3 109
Sooke, B.C. · E6 69
Soo Locks, N.A. · B6 99
Sopchoppy, Fl., U.S. · B2 86
Soperton, Ga., U.S. · D4 87
Sophia, W.V., U.S. · D3 125
Sopot, Pol. · A5 26
Sopron, Hung. · B3 24
Soquel, Ca., U.S. · *D3 82
Sora, Italy · D4 23
Sorata, Bol. · C2 55
Sorbas, Spain · D4 22
Sorel, Que. · C4 74
Sorell, Cape, c., Austl. · o15 50
Sorento, Il., U.S. · E4 90
Soresina, Italy · D5 20
Soria, Spain · B4 22
Soriano, Ur. · f7 54
Soriano, dept., Ur. · f8 54
Sorø, Den. · C5 15
Sorocaba, Braz. · C3 56
Sorochinsk, Sov. Un. · C4 28
Soroki, Sov. Un. · G7 27
Sorong, Indon. · F8 34
Soroti, Ug. · A5 48
Sørøya, i., Nor. · B10 14
Sorraia, stm., Port. · C1 22
Sorrento, Italy · D5 23
Sorrento, Fl., U.S. · D5 86
Sorrento, La., U.S. · D5 95
Sorsele, Swe. · D6 14
Sorris Sorris, Nmb. · B1 49
Sør Rondane Mountains, mts., Ant. · B15 7
Sorsogon, Phil. · C6 34
Sortavala, Sov. Un. · A8 27
Sorum, S.D., U.S. · B3 118
Sörumsand, Nor. · p29 14
Sŏsan, S. Kor. · H3 33
Sosnogorsk, Sov. Un. · C19 8
Sosnovka, Sov. Un. · E13 27
Sosnowiec, Pol. · C5 26
Soso, Ms., U.S. · D4 101
Sosva, Sov. Un. · C21 8
Sottern, l., Swe. · t33 14
Sotteville-lès-Rouen, Fr. · C4 16
Souanké, Congo · A1 48
Soucook, stm., N.H., U.S. · D4 106
Souderton, Pa., U.S. · F11 115
Soudan, Mn., U.S. · C6 100
Souflion, Grc. · B6 25
Soufrière, St. Luc. · J14 64
Soufrière, mtn., Guad. · Q8 65
Soufrière, mtn., St. Vin. · U26 65
Souhegan, stm., N.H., U.S. · E3 106
Soulac, Fr. · D3 16
Soulanges, co., Que. · D3 74
Sound Beach, N.Y., U.S. · *n16 109
Sounding Creek, stm., Alta. · C5 68
Sound Lake, l., Alta. · C5 68
Sound View, Ct., U.S. · D6 84
Sources, Mount aux, mtn., Afr. · C4 49
Soure, Braz. · C5 59
Soure, Port. · B1 22
Souris, Man. · E1 70
Souris, P.E.I. · C7 71
Souris, N.D., U.S. · A5 111
Souris, stm., N.A. · A7 76
Sourland Mountain, hill, N.J., U.S. · C3 107
Sous, Oued, val., Mor. · C3 44
Sousa, Braz. · B3 57
Sousse, Tun. · B7 44
Soustons, Fr. · F3 16
South, stm., Ont. · B5 73
South, stm., Ga., U.S. · h8 87
South, stm., N.C., U.S. · C4 110
South Acton, Ma., U.S. · g10 98
South Acworth, N.H., U.S. · D5 96
South Addison, Me., U.S. · D5 96
South Africa, ctry., Afr. · C4 49
South Amboy, N.J., U.S. · C4 107
South America, cont. · E5 53
South Amherst, Ma., U.S. · B2 98
South Amherst, Oh., U.S. · A3 112
Southampton, N.B. · D2 71
Southampton, Ont. · C3 73
Southampton, Eng., U.K. · E6 10
Southampton, Ma., U.S. · B2 98
Southampton, N.Y., U.S. · n16 109
Southampton, co., Va., U.S. · D5 123
Southampton, Cape, c., N.W. Ter. · D16 66
Southampton Island, i., N.W. Ter. · D16 66
South Andaman, i., India · F9 36
South Anna, stm., Va., U.S. · C5 123
South Ashburnham, Ma., U.S. · A4 98
South Aulatsivik Island, i., Newf. · g9 72
South Australia, state, Austl. · E5 50
Southaven, Ms., U.S. · A3 101
South Bald Mountain, mtn., Co., U.S. · A5 83
South Baldy, mtn., N.M., U.S. · D2 108
South Barnstead, N.H., U.S. · D4 106
South Barre, Ma., U.S. · B3 98
South Barre, Vt., U.S. · C3 122
South Barrule, hill, I. of Man · F4 13
South Bay, Fl., U.S. · F6 86
Southbeach, Or., U.S. · C2 114
South Belmar, N.J., U.S. · C4 107
South Beloit, Il., U.S. · A4 90
South Bend, In., U.S. · A5 91
South Bend, Ne., U.S. · h12 104
South Bend, Wa., U.S. · C2 124
South Bentinck Arm, b., B.C. · C4 69

Name	Map Ref.	Page
South Berwick, Me., U.S.	E2	96
South Bethany, De., U.S.	F5	85
South Bethlehem, N.Y., U.S.	C7	109
South Bloomfield, Oh., U.S.	C3	112
South Boardman, Mi., U.S.	D5	99
South Bolton, Que.	D5	74
Southborough, Ma., U.S.	B4	98
South Boston, Va., U.S.	D4	123
South Bound Brook, N.J., U.S.	B3	107
South Bradenton, Fl., U.S.	*E4	86
South Branch, Newf.	E2	72
South Branch, Mi., U.S.	D7	99
South Branch Lake, l., Me., U.S.	C4	96
South Branch Mountain, mtn., W.V., U.S.	B6	125
Southbridge, Ma., U.S.	B3	98
South Bristol, Me., U.S.	E3	96
South Britain, Ct., U.S.	D3	84
South Broadway, Wa., U.S.	C5	124
South Brookfield, N.S.	E5	71
South Bruny, i., Austl.	o15	50
South Burlington, Vt., U.S.	C2	122
Southbury, Ct., U.S.	D3	84
South Byfield, Ma., U.S.	A6	98
South Byron, N.Y., U.S.	B2	109
South Cape, c., Nor.	B13	128
South Carolina, state, U.S.	D6	117
South Carver, Ma., U.S.	C6	98
South Channel, strt., Marsh Is.	S18	52
South Charleston, Oh., U.S.	C2	112
South Charleston, W.V., U.S.	C3	125
South Charlestown, N.H., U.S.	D2	106
South Chatham, Ma., U.S.	C7	98
South Chatham, N.H., U.S.	B4	106
South Chicago Heights, Il., U.S.	m9	90
South China, Me., U.S.	D3	96
South China Sea, Asia	H14	30
South Cle Elum, Wa., U.S.	B5	124
South Coffeyville, Ok., U.S.	A6	113
South Colby, Wa., U.S.	e10	124
South Colton, N.Y., U.S.	f10	109
South Congaree, S.C., U.S.	D5	117
South Connellsville, Pa., U.S.	G2	115
South Corning, N.Y., U.S.	C3	109
South Cottonwood, Ut., U.S.	*C4	121
South Dakota, state, U.S.	C5	118
South Danville, N.H., U.S.	E4	106
South Dartmouth, Ma., U.S.	C6	98
South Dayton, N.Y., U.S.	C1	109
South Daytona, Fl., U.S.	C5	86
South Decatur, Ga., U.S.	*h8	87
South Deerfield, Ma., U.S.	B2	98
South Deerfield, N.H., U.S.	D4	106
South Deer Isle, Me., U.S.	D4	96
South Dennis, Ma., U.S.	C7	98
South Dennis, N.J., U.S.	E3	107
South Dorset, Vt., U.S.	E2	122
South Dos Palos, Ca., U.S.	D3	82
South Downs, plat., Eng., U.K.	E6	10
South Dum Dum, India	F12	37
South Duxbury, Ma., U.S.	B6	98
Southeast Cape, c., Ak., U.S.	C6	79
South Easton, Ma., U.S.	B5	98
Southeast Pass, strt., La., U.S.	E7	95
Southeast Point, c., R.I., U.S.	h7	116
South Effingham, N.H., U.S.	C5	106
South Egremont, Ma., U.S.	B1	98
South Elgin, Il., U.S.	B5	90
South El Monte, Ca., U.S.	*m12	82
Southend-on-Sea, Eng., U.K.	E7	10
*South Farmingdale, N.Y., U.S.	*n15	109
Southfield, Ma., U.S.	B1	98
Southfield, Mi., U.S.	o15	99
South Flevoland, reg., Neth.	B5	17
South Fork, Sask.	H1	75
South Fork, Co., U.S.	D4	83
South Fork, Pa., U.S.	F4	115
South Fort George, B.C.	C6	69
South Foster, R.I., U.S.	C2	116
South Fox Island, i., Mi., U.S.	C5	99
South Freeport, Me., U.S.	g7	96
South Fulton, Tn., U.S.	A3	119
South Gastonia, N.C., U.S.	B1	110
South Gate, Ca., U.S.	n12	82
Southgate, Fl., U.S.	*E4	86
Southgate, Ky., U.S.	h14	94
South Gate, Md., U.S.	*B4	97
Southgate, Mi., U.S.	p15	99
South Georgia, i., S.A.	l7	53
South Gifford, Mo., U.S.	A5	102
South Glamorgan, co., Wales, U.K.	C4	12
South Glastonbury, Ct., U.S.	C5	84
Southglenn, Co., U.S.	*B6	83
South Glens Falls, N.Y., U.S.	B7	109
South Grafton, Ma., U.S.	B4	98
South Grand, stm., Mo., U.S.	C3	102
South Greenfield, Mo., U.S.	D4	102
South Gulf of Évvoia, b., Grc.	g11	25
South Hackensack, N.J., U.S.	*B4	107
South Hadley, Ma., U.S.	B2	98
South Hadley Falls, Ma., U.S.	B2	98
South Hamilton, Ma., U.S.	A6	98
South Hampton, N.H., U.S.	E5	106
South Hanover, Ma., U.S.	h12	98
South Harpswell, Me., U.S.	g7	96
South Harwich, Ma., U.S.	C7	98
South Haven, In., U.S.	A3	91
South Haven, Ks., U.S.	E6	93
South Haven, Mi., U.S.	F4	99
South Heart, N.D., U.S.	C3	111
South Heart, stm., Alta.	A2	68
South Hero, Vt., U.S.	B2	122
South Hero Island, i., Vt., U.S.	B2	122
South Hill, N.Y., U.S.	*C4	109
South Hill, Va., U.S.	F5	123
South Hingham, Ma., U.S.	h12	98
South Holland, Il., U.S.	k9	90
South Holland (Zuid-Holland), prov., Neth.	B4	17
South Holston Lake, res., U.S.	A9	119
South Hooksett, N.H., U.S.	D4	106
South Hopkinton, R.I., U.S.	F1	116
South Houston, Tx., U.S.	r14	120
South Huntington, N.Y., U.S.	*n15	109
South Hutchinson, Ks., U.S.	f11	93
South Indian Lake, Man.	A2	70
Southington, Ct., U.S.	C4	84
South International Falls, Mn., U.S.	B5	100
South Island, i., Micron.	Q18	52
South Island, i., N.Z.	O13	51
South Island, i., S.C., U.S.	E9	117
South Jacksonville, Il., U.S.	D3	90
South Jordan, Ut., U.S.	C3	121
South Junction, Man.	E4	70
South Kenosha, Wi., U.S.	F6	126
South Kensington, Md., U.S.	*B3	97
South Kent, Ct., U.S.	C2	84
South Killingly, Ct., U.S.	B8	84
South Komelik, Az., U.S.	F4	80
South Laguna, Ca., U.S.	*F5	82
South Lake Tahoe, Ca., U.S.	C4	82
South Lancaster, Ma., U.S.	B4	98
South Laramie, Wy., U.S.	*E7	127
South Laurel, Md., U.S.	B4	97
South Lebanon, Me., U.S.	E2	96
South Lebanon, Oh., U.S.	C1	112
South Lee, Ma., U.S.	B1	98
South Lincoln, Vt., U.S.	C3	122
South Londonderry, Vt., U.S.	E3	122
South Loup, stm., Ne., U.S.	C6	104
South Lunenburg, Vt., U.S.	C5	122
South Lyme, Ct., U.S.	D6	84
South Lyndeborough, N.H., U.S.	E3	106
South Lyon, Mi., U.S.	F7	99
South Magnetawan, Ont.	B4	73
South Magnetic Pole, Ant.	C26	7
South Manitou Island, i., Mi., U.S.	C4	99
South Mansfield, La., U.S.	B2	95
South Marsh Island, i., Md., U.S.	D5	97
South Medford, Or., U.S.	E4	114
South Merrimack, N.H., U.S.	E3	106
South Miami, Fl., U.S.	G6	86
South Miami Heights, Fl., U.S.	s13	86
South Middleboro, Ma., U.S.	C6	98
South Milford, In., U.S.	A7	91
South Mills, N.C., U.S.	A6	110
South Milwaukee, Wi., U.S.	F6	126
Southminster, Eng., U.K.	C8	12
South Modesto, Ca., U.S.	*D3	82
South Molton, Eng., U.K.	C4	12
Southmont, N.C., U.S.	B2	110
South Montrose, Pa., U.S.	C10	115
South Moose Lake, l., Man.	C1	70
South Mountain, Pa., U.S.	G7	115
South Mountain, mtn., B.C.	B2	97
South Mountain, mtn., Id., U.S.	G2	89
South Mountain, mtn., N.M., U.S.	k8	108
South Mountains, mts., Az., U.S.	m8	80
South Mountains, mts., N.C., U.S.	B1	110
South Naknek, Ak., U.S.	D8	79
South Negril Point, c., Jam.	E4	64
South New Berlin, N.Y., U.S.	C5	109
South Newbury, N.H., U.S.	D2	106
South Newbury, Vt., U.S.	C4	122
South Newfane, Vt., U.S.	F3	122
South New River Canal, Fl., U.S.	r13	86
North Northfield, Vt., U.S.	C3	122
South Nyack, N.Y., U.S.	*D7	109
South Ogden, Ut., U.S.	B4	121
Southold, N.Y., U.S.	m16	109
South Orange, N.J., U.S.	B4	107
South Orkney Islands, is., B.A.T.	C7	7
South Orrington, Me., U.S.	D4	96
South Otselic, N.Y., U.S.	C5	109
South Paris, Me., U.S.	D2	96
South Park, val., Co., U.S.	B5	83
South Pass, Wy., U.S.	D4	127
South Pass, strt., Marsh Is.	S17	52
South Pass, strt., La., U.S.	F6	95
South Pass City, Wy., U.S.	D4	127
South Patrick Shores, Fl., U.S.	D6	86
South Peacham, Vt., U.S.	C4	122
South Pekin, Il., U.S.	C4	90
South Pittsburg, Tn., U.S.	D8	119
South Plainfield, N.J., U.S.	B4	107
South Platte, stm., U.S.	B7	76
South Point, c., Austl.	I6	51
South Point, c., Barb.	K20	65
South Point, c., Newf.	C4	72
South Point, c., Mi., U.S.	D7	99
South Pole, Ant.	A7	7
South Pomfret, Vt., U.S.	D3	122
Southport (Gold Coast), Austl.	E9	50
Southport, Eng., U.K.	D5	10
Southport, Fl., U.S.	u16	86
Southport, In., U.S.	E5	91
Southport, N.Y., U.S.	C4	109
Southport, N.C., U.S.	D4	110
South Portland, Me., U.S.	E2	96
South Portsmouth, Ky., U.S.	B6	94
South Poultney, Vt., U.S.	E2	122
South Prairie, Wa., U.S.	B3	124
South Range, Mi., U.S.	A2	99
South Range, Wi., U.S.	B2	126
South Reading, Vt., U.S.	E3	122
South Renovo, Pa., U.S.	D6	115
South River, Ont.	B5	73
South River, N.J., U.S.	C4	107
South River, b., Md., U.S.	C4	97
South Ronaldsay, i., Scot., U.K.	A5	10
South Royalston, Ma., U.S.	A3	98
South Royalton, Vt., U.S.	D3	122
South Rustico, P.E.I.	C6	71
South Ryegate, Vt., U.S.	C4	122
South Salem, Oh., U.S.	C2	112
South Salt Lake, Ut., U.S.	*C4	121
South Sandwich Islands, is., S.A.	D10	7
South San Francisco, Ca., U.S.	h8	82
South San Gabriel, Ca., U.S.	*m12	82
South San Jose Hills, Ca., U.S.	*m13	82
South Saskatchewan, stm., Can.	F11	69
South Seaville, N.J., U.S.	E3	107
South Setauket, N.Y., U.S.	*n15	109
South Shetland Islands, is., B.A.T.	C7	7
South Shields, Eng., U.K.	C6	10
South Shore, Mo., U.S.	f12	102
South Shore, S.D., U.S.	B9	118
Sparta see Spárti, Grc.	—	—
Sparta, Ky., U.S.	B5	94
Southside, Al., U.S.	B3	78
Southside, N.C., U.S.	B1	110
Southside, Tn., U.S.	A4	119
Southside Place, Tx., U.S.	r14	120
South Sioux City, Ne., U.S.	B9	104
South Skunk, stm., Ia., U.S.	C4	92
South Slocan, B.C.	E9	69
South Solon, Oh., U.S.	C2	112
South Spencer, strt., Ire.	D2	11
South Spicer Island, i., N.W. Ter.	C17	66
South Sterling, Pa., U.S.	D11	115
South Stony Brook, N.Y., U.S.	n15	109
South Strafford, Vt., U.S.	D4	122
South Streator, Il., U.S.	B5	90
South Sumter, S.C., U.S.	*D7	117
South Superior, Wy., U.S.	E4	127
South Sutton, N.H., U.S.	D3	106
South Swansea, Ma., U.S.	C5	98
South Tamworth, N.H., U.S.	C4	106
South Taranaki Bight, N.Z.	M15	51
South Toms River, N.J., U.S.	D4	107
South Torrington, Wy., U.S.	D8	127
South Tucson, Az., U.S.	E5	80
South Tunnel, Tn., U.S.	A5	119
South Twin Lake, l., Newf.	D4	72
South Twin Mountain, mtn., N.H., U.S.	B3	106
South Tyne, stm., Eng., U.K.	F6	13
South Uist, i., Scot., U.K.	B3	10
South Valley Stream, N.Y., U.S.	n15	109
South Van Buren, Mo., U.S.	E6	102
South Venice, Fl., U.S.	E4	86
South Ventana Cone, vol., Ca., U.S.	D3	82
South Vienna, Oh., U.S.	C2	112
South Wabasca Lake, l., Alta.	B4	68
South Wadesboro, N.C., U.S.	C2	110
South Wallingford, Vt., U.S.	E3	122
South Walpole, Ma., U.S.	h10	98
South Waterford, Me., U.S.	D2	96
South Waverly, Pa., U.S.	C8	115
South Wayne, Wi., U.S.	F4	126
South Weare, N.H., U.S.	D3	106
South Webster, Oh., U.S.	D3	112
South Wellfleet, Ma., U.S.	C8	98
South Wellington, B.C.	f12	69
Southwest, Pa., U.S.	F3	115
South West Africa see Namibia, dep., Afr.	B2	49
South West Bay, b., Bah.	n16	64
South Westbury, N.Y., U.S.	n15	109
South West Cape, c., Austl.	o15	50
Southwest Cape, c., N.Z.	Q11	51
Southwest Channel, strt., Fl., U.S.	E4	86
South West City, Mo., U.S.	E3	102
Southwest Harbor, Me., U.S.	D4	96
Southwest Head, c., N.B.	E3	71
Southwest Miramichi, stm., N.B.	C3	71
Southwest Mountains, mts., Va., U.S.	B4	123
Southwest Pass, strt., La., U.S.	E3	95
Southwest Pass, strt., La., U.S.	F6	95
Southwest Passage, strt., Marsh Is.	S18	52
Southwest Point, c., R.I., U.S.	h7	116
South Whitley, In., U.S.	B6	91
South Whittier, Ca., U.S.	*n13	82
Southwick, Id., U.S.	C2	89
Southwick, Ma., U.S.	B2	98
South Williamson, Ky., U.S.	C7	94
South Williamsport, Pa., U.S.	D7	115
South Willington, Ct., U.S.	B6	84
South Willington, Il., U.S.	B5	90
South Windham, Ct., U.S.	C7	84
South Windham, Me., U.S.	E2	96
South Windsor, Ct., U.S.	B5	84
Southwold, Eng., U.K.	B9	12
South Wolfeboro, N.H., U.S.	C4	106
South Wolf Island, i., Newf.	B4	72
Southwood, Co., U.S.	B6	83
Southwood Acres, Ct., U.S.	A5	84
Southwood, Vt., U.S.	C4	122
South Woodstock, Ct., U.S.	B8	84
South Woodstock, Vt., U.S.	D3	122
South Yarmouth, Ma., U.S.	C7	98
South Yorkshire, co., Eng., U.K.	A6	12
South Yuba City, Ca., U.S.	*C3	82
South Zanesville, Oh., U.S.	C3	112
Soverato, Italy	E6	23
Sovereign, Sask.	F2	75
Sovetsk (Tilsit), Sov. Un.	D3	27
Sovetskaya Gavan, Sov. Un.	E16	29
Sovetskaya Gavan, Sov. Un.	B10	33
Soviet Union, ctry., Asia	D11	29
Soweto, S. Afr.	C4	49
Soyo, Ang.	C1	48
Sozh, stm., Sov. Un.	E8	27
Sozopol, Bul.	D8	24
Spa, Bel.	B6	16
Spadra, Ar., U.S.	B2	81
Spain, ctry., Eur.	B4	21
Spalding, Austl.	F2	51
Spalding, Sask.	E3	75
Spalding, Eng., U.K.	D6	10
Spalding, Id., U.S.	C2	89
Spalding, Ne., U.S.	C7	104
Spalding, co., Ga., U.S.	C2	87
Spanaway, Wa., U.S.	B3	124
Spangle, Wa., U.S.	B8	124
Spangler, Pa., U.S.	E4	115
Spaniard's Bay, Newf.	E5	72
Spanish, Ont.	A2	73
Spanish, stm., Ont.	A2	73
Spanishburg, W.V., U.S.	D3	125
Spanish Fork, Ut., U.S.	C4	121
Spanish Fort, Al., U.S.	E2	78
Spanish Lake, Mo., U.S.	f13	102
Spanish North Africa, dep., Afr.	*B4	44
Spanish Peak, mtn., Or., U.S.	C7	114
Spanish Ranch, Ca., U.S.	C3	82
Spanish Town, Jam.	E5	64
Sparkman, Ar., U.S.	D3	81
Sparks, Ga., U.S.	E3	87
Sparks, Ne., U.S.	B5	104
Sparks, Ok., U.S.	B5	113
Sparland, Il., U.S.	B4	90
Sparr, Fl., U.S.	C4	86
Sparreholm, Swe.	t34	14
Sparrows Point, Md., U.S.	B5	97
Sparta see Spárti, Grc.	—	—
Sparta, Il., U.S.	E4	90
Sparta, Ky., U.S.	B5	94
Sparta, Mi., U.S.	E5	99
Sparta, Mo., U.S.	D4	102
Sparta, N.J., U.S.	A3	107
Sparta, N.C., U.S.	A1	110
Sparta, Oh., U.S.	B3	112
Sparta, Tn., U.S.	D8	119
Sparta, Wi., U.S.	E3	126
Sparta Mountains, mts., N.J., U.S.	B3	107
Spartanburg, In., U.S.	D8	91
Spartanburg, S.C., U.S.	B4	117
Spartanburg, co., S.C., U.S.	B3	117
Spartansburg, Pa., U.S.	C2	115
Spárti (Sparta), Grc.	D4	40
Spartivento, Cape, c., Italy	F6	23
Spartivento, Cape, c., Italy	E2	23
Sparwood, B.C.	E10	69
Spas-Demensk, Sov. Un.	D10	27
Spassk-Dalniy, Sov. Un.	E16	29
Spassk-Ryazanskiy, Sov. Un.	D13	27
Spáta, Grc.	h11	25
Spátha, Ákra, c., Grc.	E4	40
Spaulding, Ok., U.S.	B5	113
Spavinaw, Ok., U.S.	A6	113
Spavinaw Creek, stm., Ok., U.S.	A7	113
Spear, Cape, c., Newf.	E5	72
Spearfish, S.D., U.S.	C2	118
Spearhill, Man.	D2	70
Spearman, Tx., U.S.	A2	120
Spearsville, La., U.S.	B3	95
Spearville, Ks., U.S.	E4	93
Speculator, N.Y., U.S.	B6	109
Spedden, Alta.	B5	68
Spednic Lake, l., N.A.	C5	96
Speed, In., U.S.	H6	91
Speed, Ks., U.S.	C4	93
Speed, N.C., U.S.	B5	110
Speed, W.V., U.S.	C3	125
Speedway, In., U.S.	E5	91
Speedwell, Tn., U.S.	C10	119
Speedwell, Va., U.S.	D1	123
Speers, Sask.	E2	75
Speigner, Al., U.S.	C3	78
Speight, Ky., U.S.	C7	94
Spelter, W.V., U.S.	k10	125
Spenard (part of Anchorage), Ak., U.S.	g17	79
Spencer, Id., U.S.	E6	89
Spencer, In., U.S.	F4	91
Spencer, Ia., U.S.	A2	92
Spencer, Ma., U.S.	B4	98
Spencer, Ne., U.S.	B7	104
Spencer, N.Y., U.S.	C4	109
Spencer, N.C., U.S.	B2	110
Spencer, Oh., U.S.	A3	112
Spencer, S.D., U.S.	D8	118
Spencer, Tn., U.S.	D8	119
Spencer, Va., U.S.	D2	123
Spencer, W.V., U.S.	C3	125
Spencer, co., In., U.S.	H4	91
Spencer, co., Ky., U.S.	B4	94
Spencer, Cape, c., Ak., U.S.	k21	79
Spencer Gulf, b., Austl.	F6	50
Spencer Lake, l., Me., U.S.	C2	96
Spencerport, N.Y., U.S.	B3	109
Spencers Island, N.S.	D5	71
Spencerville, In., U.S.	B8	91
Spencerville, Md., U.S.	B4	97
Spencerville, Oh., U.S.	B1	112
Spencerville, Ok., U.S.	C6	113
Spences Bridge, B.C.	D7	69
Spennymoor, Eng., U.K.	F7	13
Sperkhiós, stm., Grc.	C4	25
Sperling, Man.	E3	70
Sperrin Mountains, mts., N. Ire., U.K.	C3	10
Sperry, Ia., U.S.	D6	92
Sperry, Ok., U.S.	A6	113
Sperryville, Va., U.S.	B4	123
Spesutie Island, i., Md., U.S.	B5	97
Spey, stm., Scot., U.K.	B5	10
Speyer, Ger.	D4	18
Sphinx, hist., Eg.	E3	41
Spiceland, In., U.S.	E7	91
Spicer, Mn., U.S.	E4	100
Spickard, Mo., U.S.	A4	102
Spider Lake, l., Wi., U.S.	B2	126
Spiekeroog, i., Ger.	A7	17
Spiekeroog, i., Ger.	B3	18
Spigno Monferrato, Italy	E4	20
Spijkenisse, Neth.	*C4	17
Spillville, Ia., U.S.	A6	92
Spilsby, Eng., U.K.	D7	10
Spinazzola, Italy	D6	23
Spindale, N.C., U.S.	B1	110
Spink, S.D., U.S.	E9	118
Spink, co., S.D., U.S.	C7	118
Spink Colony, S.D., U.S.	C7	118
Spirit Lake, l., Ia., U.S.	A2	92
Spirit Lake, l., Wa., U.S.	C3	124
Spirit River, Alta.	B1	68
Spirit River Flowage, res., Wi., U.S.	C4	126
Spiritwood, Sask.	D2	75
Spiritwood, N.D., U.S.	C7	111
Spišská Nová Ves, Czech.	D6	26
Spit Island, i., Mid. Is.	K3	52
Spitsbergen, i., Nor.	B13	128
Spittal, Aus.	E6	18
Spivey, Ks., U.S.	E5	93
Split, Yugo.	D3	24
Split, Cape, c., N.S.	D5	71
Split Lake, l., Man.	A4	70
Split Rock Creek, stm., U.S.	G2	100
Splügen, Switz.	C5	20
Splügen Pass, Eur.	C5	20
Spofford, N.H., U.S.	E2	106
Spofford, Tx., U.S.	E2	120
Spofford Lake, l., N.H., U.S.	E2	106
Spokane, La., U.S.	C4	95
Spokane, Wa., U.S.	B8	124
Spokane, co., Wa., U.S.	B8	124
Spokane, Mount, mtn., Wa., U.S.	B8	124
Spokane Indian Reservation, Wa., U.S.	B8	124
Spoleto, Italy	C4	23
Spoleto, Italy	C4	23
Spondin, Alta.	D5	68
Spoon, stm., Il., U.S.	C3	90
Spooner, Wi., U.S.	C2	126
Spooner Lake, l., Wi., U.S.	C2	126
Spotswood, N.J., U.S.	C4	107
Spotsylvania, Va., U.S.	B5	123
Spotsylvania, co., Va., U.S.	B5	123
Spotted Island, i., Newf.	B4	72
Spottsville, Ky., U.S.	C2	94
Sprague, Ont.	A2	73
Sprague, Man.	E4	70
Sprague, Al., U.S.	C3	78
Sprague, Ne., U.S.	D9	104
Sprague, Wa., U.S.	B8	124
Sprague, W.V., U.S.	n13	125
Sprague, co., U.S.	E5	114
Sprague Lake, l., Wa., U.S.	B7	124
Sprague River, Or., U.S.	E5	114
Spragueville, Ia., U.S.	B7	92
Spragueville, R.I., U.S.	B3	116
Sprakensehl, Ger.	F4	15
Spratly Island, i., Asia	D4	34
Spray, Or., U.S.	C7	114
Spread Eagle, Wi., U.S.	C5	126
Spreckelsville, Hi., U.S.	*C5	88
Spree, stm., Eur.	B7	18
Spremberg, Ger.	C7	18
Sprigg, W.V., U.S.	D2	125
Spring, Tx., U.S.	q141	120
Spring, stm., Ar., U.S.	A4	81
Spring, stm., Ar., U.S.	A4	81
Spring, South Fork, stm., U.S.	E6	102
Spring Arbor, Mi., U.S.	F6	99
Spring Bay, b., Ut., U.S.	B3	121
Springbok, S. Afr.	C2	49
Springboro, Oh., U.S.	C1	112
Springboro, Pa., U.S.	C1	115
Springbrook, Ia., U.S.	E4	93
Spring Brook, N.D., U.S.	A2	111
Springbrook, Wi., U.S.	C2	126
Spring Brook, stm., Pa., U.S.	n18	115
Springdale, Newf.	D3	72
Springdale, Ar., U.S.	A1	81
Springdale, Mt., U.S.	E6	103
Springdale, Oh., U.S.	n13	112
Springdale, Or., U.S.	B4	114
Springdale, Pa., U.S.	E2	115
Springdale, S.C., U.S.	D5	117
Springdale, Ut., U.S.	F3	121
Springdale, Wa., U.S.	A8	124
Spring Dale, W.V., U.S.	D4	125
Springer, N.M., U.S.	A5	108
Springer, Ok., U.S.	C4	113
Springerton, Il., U.S.	E5	90
Springerville, Az., U.S.	C6	80
Springfield, N.B.	D4	71
Springfield, Ont.	E4	73
Springfield, Co., U.S.	D8	83
Springfield, Fl., U.S.	u16	86
Springfield, Ga., U.S.	D5	87
Springfield, Id., U.S.	F6	89
Springfield, Il., U.S.	D4	90
Springfield, Ky., U.S.	C4	94
Springfield, La., U.S.	D5	95
Springfield, Me., U.S.	C4	96
Springfield, Ma., U.S.	B2	98
Springfield, Mn., U.S.	F4	100
Springfield, Mo., U.S.	D4	102
Springfield, Ne., U.S.	C9	104
Springfield, N.H., U.S.	D2	106
Springfield, N.J., U.S.	B4	107
Springfield, Oh., U.S.	C2	112
Springfield, Or., U.S.	C4	114
Springfield, Pa., U.S.	p20	115
Springfield, S.C., U.S.	E5	117
Springfield, S.D., U.S.	E8	118
Springfield, Tn., U.S.	A5	119
Springfield, Vt., U.S.	E4	122
Springfield, Va., U.S.	g12	123
Springfield, W.V., U.S.	B6	125
Springfield, Lake, res., Il., U.S.	D4	90
Springfield Township, Pa., U.S.	*F11	115
Springfontein, S. Afr.	D4	49
Spring Garden, Al., U.S.	B4	78
Spring Garden, Pa., U.S.	*G8	115
Spring Glen, Ut., U.S.	D5	121
Spring Green, Wi., U.S.	E3	126
Spring Grove, Il., U.S.	h8	90
Spring Grove, Mn., U.S.	G7	100
Spring Grove, Pa., U.S.	G8	115
Spring Hill, Al., U.S.	D4	78
Spring Hill, Ct., U.S.	B7	84
Spring Hill, Fl., U.S.	D4	86
Spring Hill, In., U.S.	k10	91
Spring Hill, Ia., U.S.	f8	92
Spring Hill, Ks., U.S.	D9	93
Spring Hill, La., U.S.	B2	95
Spring Hill, Tn., U.S.	B5	119
Springhill Junction, N.S.	D5	71
Spring Hope, N.C., U.S.	B4	110
Springhouse, B.C.	D6	69
Spring Island, i., S.C., U.S.	G6	117
Spring Lake, Fl., U.S.	D4	86
Spring Lake, Mi., U.S.	E4	99
Spring Lake, N.J., U.S.	C4	107
Spring Lake, N.C., U.S.	B4	110
Spring Lake, l., Me., U.S.	C2	96
Spring Lake Heights, N.J., U.S.	C4	107
Spring Lake Park, Mn., U.S.	*E5	100
Spring Lick, Ky., U.S.	C3	94
Spring Mills, Pa., U.S.	E6	115
Spring Mountains, mts., Nv., U.S.	G6	105
Spring Place, Ga., U.S.	B2	87
Springport, In., U.S.	D7	91
Springs, S. Afr.	C4	49
Springside, Sask.	F4	75
Springsure, Austl.	D9	50
Springvale, Austl.	A3	51
Springvale, Ga., U.S.	B4	87
Springvale, Me., U.S.	E2	96
Spring Valley, Sask.	G3	75
Spring Valley, Ca., U.S.	o16	82
Spring Valley, Il., U.S.	B4	90
Spring Valley, Mn., U.S.	G6	100
Spring Valley, N.Y., U.S.	g12	109
Spring Valley, Oh., U.S.	C1	112
Spring Valley, Wi., U.S.	D1	126
Springview, Ne., U.S.	B6	104
Springville, Al., U.S.	B3	78
Springville, In., U.S.	G4	91
Springville, Ia., U.S.	B6	92
Springville, Ms., U.S.	A4	101
Springville, N.Y., U.S.	C2	109
Springville, Pa., U.S.	C10	115
Springville, Tn., U.S.	A3	119
Springville, Ut., U.S.	C4	121
Springwater, Sask.	F1	75
Springwater, N.Y., U.S.	C3	109
Spruce, Mi., U.S.	D7	99
Spruce Brook, Newf.	D2	72
Spruce Creek, Pa., U.S.	E5	115
Sprucedale, Ont.	B5	73
Spruce Fork, stm., W.V., U.S.	m12	125
Spruce Grove, Alta.	—	—
Spruce Knob, mtn., W.V., U.S.	C6	125
Spruce Knob-Seneca Rocks National Recreation Area, W.V., U.S.	C5	125
Spruce Lake, Sask.	D1	75
Spruce Mountain, mtn., Az., U.S.	C3	80
Spruce Mountain, mtn., Nv., U.S.	C7	105
Spruce Pine, Al., U.S.	A2	78
Spruce Pine, N.C., U.S.	f10	110
Spruce Run Reservoir, res., N.J., U.S.	B3	107
Spruga, Switz.	D6	21
Spur, Tx., U.S.	C2	120
Spurfield, Alta.	B3	68
Spurgeon, In., U.S.	H3	91
Spurn Head, c., Eng., U.K.	A8	12
Spurr, Mount, mtn., Ak., U.S.	g15	79
Spy Hill, Sask.	G6	75
Squamish, B.C.	E6	69
Squam Lake, l., N.H., U.S.	C4	106
Squam Mountains, mts., N.H., U.S.	C3	106
Squantum, N.H., U.S.	C4	106
Squa Pan, Me., U.S.	B4	96
Squapan Lake, l., Me., U.S.	B4	96
Square Islands, Newf.	B4	72
Square Lake, l., Me., U.S.	A4	96
Squatec, Que.	B9	74
Squaw Cap Mountain, mtn., N.B.	B3	71
Squaw Harbor, Ak., U.S.	D7	79
Squaw Hill, mtn., Wy., U.S.	E7	127
Squaw Lake, Mn., U.S.	C4	100
Squaw Peak, mtn., Mt., U.S.	C2	103
Squaw Rapids, Sask.	D4	75
Squibnocket Point, c., Ma., U.S.	D6	98
Squillace, Gulf of, b., Italy	E6	23
Squire, W.V., U.S.	D3	125
Squires, Mo., U.S.	E5	102
Squirrel, Id., U.S.	E7	89
Srbobran, Yugo.	C4	24
Srednekolymsk, Sov. Un.	C18	29
Sredniy Vasyugan, Sov. Un.	D24	8
Šrem, Pol.	B4	26
Sremska Mitrovica, Yugo.	C4	24
Sremski Karlovci, Yugo.	C4	24
Srepok, stm., Asia	C3	34
Sretensk, Sov. Un.	D14	29
Sri Lanka, ctry., Asia	B6	36
Srinagar, India	B5	36
Środa Śląska, Pol.	B4	26
Środa [Wielkopolska], Pol.	B4	26
Staatsburg, N.Y., U.S.	*F5	109
Stab, Ky., U.S.	C5	94
Stack Reservoir, res., R.I., U.S.	C3	116
Stack's Mountains, mts., Ire.	E2	11
Stacy, Mn., U.S.	E5	100
Stacy, N.C., U.S.	C6	110
Stacyville, Ia., U.S.	A5	92
Stacyville, Me., U.S.	B4	96
Stade, Ger.	B4	18
Stadskanaal, Neth.	B7	17
Stadthagen, Ger.	A4	19
Stadtkyll, Ger.	C6	16
Stadtlohn, Ger.	B1	19
Stadtroda, Ger.	C6	19
Stäfa, Switz.	B6	21
Staffa, i., Scot., U.K.	B2	13
Stafford, Eng., U.K.	D6	10
Stafford, Ct., U.S.	B6	84
Stafford, Ks., U.S.	E5	93
Stafford, N.Y., U.S.	C2	109
Stafford, Oh., U.S.	C4	112
Stafford, Va., U.S.	B2	113
Stafford, co., Ks., U.S.	D5	93
Stafford, co., Va., U.S.	B5	123
Stafford Pond, l., R.I., U.S.	D6	116
Staffordshire, co., Eng., U.K.	B5	12
Stafford Springs, Ct., U.S.	B6	84
Staffordville, Ky., U.S.	C7	94
Staffordville, Ct., U.S.	B6	84
Staffordville, N.J., U.S.	D4	107
Staines, Eng., U.K.	m11	12
Stains, Fr.	g10	16
Stairs Mountain, mtn., N.H., U.S.	B4	106
Stakhanov, Sov. Un.	G12	27
Stålboga, Swe.	t34	14
Stalden, Switz.	D4	21
Staley, N.C., U.S.	B3	110
Stalin (Kuçovë), Alb.	B2	25
Stalin, see Volgograd, Sov. Un.	E7	29
Stalingrad see Volgograd, Sov. Un.	E7	29
Stalinogród see Katowice, Pol.	C5	26
Stall Lake, Man.	F13	66
Stallworthy, Cape, c., N.W. Ter.	k33	66
Stalowa Wola, Pol.	C7	26
Stalwart, Sask.	F3	75
Stalwart, N.B.	B6	99
Stambaugh, Mi., U.S.	B2	99
Stamford, Eng., U.K.	B1	12
Stamford, Ct., U.S.	D6	104
Stamford, N.Y., U.S.	C6	109
Stamford, Tx., U.S.	C3	120
Stamford, Vt., U.S.	F2	122
Stamford, Lake, res., Tx., U.S.	C3	120
Stamping Ground, Ky., U.S.	B5	94
Stampriet, Nmb.	B2	49
Stamps, Ar., U.S.	D2	81
Stanaford, W.V., U.S.	D3	125
Stanardsville, Va., U.S.	B4	123
Stanberry, Mo., U.S.	A3	102
Stanchfield, Mn., U.S.	E5	100
Standard, Alta.	D4	68
Standard, Il., U.S.	B4	90
Standard, La., U.S.	C3	95

Name — Map Ref. — Page

Standerton, S. Afr. — C4 49
Standing Rock, Al., U.S. — B4 78
Standing Rock, N.M., U.S. — B1 108
Standing Rock Indian Reservation, U.S. — B4 118
Standish, Me., U.S. — E2 96
Standish, Mi., U.S. — E7 99
Standish, N.Y., U.S. — f11 109
Stanfield, Az., U.S. — E3 80
Stanfield, Or., U.S. — B7 114
Stanford, Ca., U.S. — *k8 82
Stanford, Il., U.S. — C4 90
Stanford, In., U.S. — F4 91
Stanford, Ky., U.S. — C5 94
Stanford, Mt., U.S. — C6 103
Stangelville, Wi., U.S. — D6 126
Stanhope, Que. — C5 49
Stanhope, Eng., U.K. — F6 13
Stanhope, Ia., U.S. — B4 92
Stanhope, N.J., U.S. — B3 107
Staniard Creek, Bah. — B5 64
Stanislaus, co., Ca., U.S. — D3 82
Stanisławów, Pol. — k15 26
Stanke Dimitrov (Dupnitsa), Bul. — D6 24
Stanley, N.B. — C3 71
Stanley, Falk. Is. — I5 53
Stanley, Id., U.S. — E4 89
Stanley, Ks., U.S. — D9 93
Stanley, Ky., U.S. — C2 94
Stanley, La., U.S. — C2 95
Stanley, N.M., U.S. — B4 108
Stanley, N.C., U.S. — B1 110
Stanley, N.D., U.S. — A3 111
Stanley, Va., U.S. — B4 123
Stanley, Wi., U.S. — D3 126
Stanley, co., S.D., U.S. — C5 118
Stanley Falls see Boyoma Falls, wtfl., Zaire — A4 48
Stanleytown, Va., U.S. — D3 123
Stanleyville, N.C., U.S. — A2 110
Stanleyville see Kisangani, Zaire — A4 48
Stanly, co., N.C., U.S. — B2 110
Stanmore, Alta. — D5 68
Stann Creek, Belize — D7 63
Stans, Switz. — C4 20
Stansbury Mountains, mts., Ut., U.S. — C3 121
Stansbury Park, Ut., U.S. — *C3 121
Stanstead, Que. — D5 74
Stanstead, co., Que. — D5 74
Stanthorpe, Austl. — E9 50
Stanton, Al., U.S. — C3 78
Stanton, Ca., U.S. — *n13 82
Stanton, Ia., U.S. — D2 92
Stanton, Ky., U.S. — C6 94
Stanton, Mi., U.S. — E5 99
Stanton, Mo., U.S. — C6 102
Stanton, Ne., U.S. — C8 104
Stanton, N.J., U.S. — B3 107
Stanton, N.D., U.S. — B4 111
Stanton, Tn., U.S. — B2 119
Stanton, Tx., U.S. — C2 120
Stanton, co., Ks., U.S. — E2 93
Stanton, co., Ne., U.S. — C8 104
Stantonsburg, N.C., U.S. — B3 110
Stantonville, Tn., U.S. — B3 119
Stanwood, Ia., U.S. — C6 92
Stanwood, Mi., U.S. — E5 99
Stanwood, Wa., U.S. — A3 124
Staplehurst, Ne., U.S. — D8 104
Staples, Mn., U.S. — D4 100
Staples, Tx., U.S. — H8 120
Stapleton, Al., U.S. — E2 78
Stapleton, Ga., U.S. — C4 87
Stapleton, Ne., U.S. — C5 104
Star, Id., U.S. — F2 89
Star, Ms., U.S. — C3 101
Star, N.C., U.S. — B3 110
Star, Tx., U.S. — D3 120
Starachowice, Pol. — C6 26
Staraya Russa, Sov. Un. — C8 27
Stara Zagora, Bul. — D7 24
Starbuck, Man. — E3 70
Starbuck, Mn., U.S. — E3 100
Starbuck, Wa., U.S. — C7 124
Starbuck Island, i., Kir. — G12 6
Star City, Sask. — E3 75
Star City, Ar., U.S. — D4 81
Star City, In., U.S. — C4 91
Star City, W.V., U.S. — E4 115
Starford, Pa., U.S. — E4 115
Stargard [Szczeciński], Pol. — B3 26
Stargo, Az., U.S. — D6 80
Staritsa, Sov. Un. — C10 27
Stark, Ks., U.S. — E8 93
Stark, N.H., U.S. — A4 106
Stark, co., Il., U.S. — B4 90
Stark, co., N.D., U.S. — C3 111
Stark, co., Oh., U.S. — B4 112
Starke, Fl., U.S. — C4 86
Starke, co., In., U.S. — B4 91
Starkey, Va., U.S. — C3 123
Starks, La., U.S. — D2 95
Starks, Me., U.S. — D3 96
Starksboro, Vt., U.S. — C2 122
Starkville, Co., U.S. — D6 83
Starkville, Ms., U.S. — B5 101
Starkville, N.Y., U.S. — C6 109
Starkweather, N.D., U.S. — A7 111
Star Lake, l., Mn., U.S. — D3 100
Starlight, Pa., U.S. — C11 115
Starnberg, Ger. — B7 20
Starnberg Lake, l., Ger. — E5 18
Starobelsk, Sov. Un. — G12 27
Starodub, Sov. Un. — E9 27
Starogard [Gdański], Pol. — B5 26
Starokonstantinov, Sov. Un. — G6 27
Starominskaya, Sov. Un. — H12 27
Star Peak, mtn., Nv., U.S. — C3 105
Star Prairie, Wi., U.S. — C1 126
Starr, S.C., U.S. — C2 117
Starr, co., Tx., U.S. — F3 120
Starr Mountain, mtn., Tn., U.S. — D9 119
Starrucca, Pa., U.S. — C11 115
Start Bay, b., Eng., U.K. — D4 12
Startex, S.C., U.S. — B3 117
Start Point, c., Eng., U.K. — E5 10
Startup, Wa., U.S. — B4 124
Starý Plzenec, Czech. — D8 19
Staryy Oskol, Sov. Un. — F11 27
Stassfurt, Ger. — C5 18
Staszów, Pol. — C6 26
State Center, Ia., U.S. — B4 92
State College, Pa., U.S. — E6 115
State Line, In., U.S. — C3 91
State Line, Ma., U.S. — B1 98
State Line, Ms., U.S. — D5 101
Stateline, Nv., U.S. — E2 105
State Line, Pa., U.S. — G6 115
Staten Island, i., N.Y., U.S. — k12 109
Statenville, Ga., U.S. — F4 87
State Road, N.C., U.S. — A2 110

Statesboro, Ga., U.S. — D5 87
Statesville, N.C., U.S. — B2 110
Statham, Ga., U.S. — C3 87
Stathelle, Nor. — p27 14
Statue of Liberty National Monument, N.J., U.S. — k8 107
Staufen, Ger. — B3 20
Staunton, Il., U.S. — D4 90
Staunton, In., U.S. — F3 91
Staunton, Va., U.S. — B3 123
Stavanger, Nor. — H1 14
Stave Lake, l., B.C. — f13 69
Staveley, Eng., U.K. — A6 12
Stavelot, Bel. — D5 17
Stavely, Alta. — D4 68
Stavenisse, Neth. — C4 17
Staveren, Neth. — B5 17
Stavropol, Sov. Un. — E7 29
Stawell, Austl. — H4 51
Stayner, Ont. — C4 73
Stayton, Or., U.S. — C4 114
Stead, N.M., U.S. — A6 108
Steamboat Canyon, Az., U.S. — B6 80
Steamboat Mountain, mtn., Mt., U.S. — C4 103
Steamboat Mountain, mtn., Wy., U.S. — E4 127
Steamboat Rock, Ia., U.S. — B4 92
Steamboat Springs, Co., U.S. — A4 83
Stearns, Ky., U.S. — D5 94
Stearns, co., Mn., U.S. — E4 100
Stearns Brook, stm., N.H., U.S. — A4 106
Stebbins, Ak., U.S. — C7 79
Steblev, Sov. Un. — G8 27
Štěchovice, Czech. — o17 26
Štěchovice, Czech. — o17 26
Stecker, Ok., U.S. — C3 113
Stecoah, N.C., U.S. — f9 110
Steele, Al., U.S. — B3 78
Steele, Mo., U.S. — E8 102
Steele, N.D., U.S. — C6 111
Steele, co., Mn., U.S. — F5 100
Steele, co., N.D., U.S. — B8 111
Steele, Mount, mtn., Wy., U.S. — E6 127
Steele City, Ne., U.S. — D8 104
Steelton, Pa., U.S. — F8 115
Steeleville, Il., U.S. — E4 90
Steelville, Mo., U.S. — D6 102
Steen, Mn., U.S. — G2 100
Steenbergen, Neth. — C4 17
Steens, Mn., U.S. — B5 101
Steens Mountain, mts., Or., U.S. — E8 114
Steenwijk, Neth. — B6 17
Steep Falls, Me., U.S. — E2 96
Steephill Lake, l., Sask. — B4 75
Steep Point, c., Austl. — E1 50
Steep Rock, Man. — D2 70
Steep Rock Lake, Ont. — o17 73
Stefănești, Rom. — B8 24
Ştefănie, Lake, l., Afr. — E4 47
Stefansson Island, i., N.W. Ter. — B11 66
Steffisburg, Switz. — C4 21
Stege, Den. — D6 15
Steger, Il., U.S. — B6 90
Stehekin, Wa., U.S. — A5 124
Steilacoom, Wa., U.S. — f10 124
Stein, Ger. — D5 19
Steinach, Aus. — B7 20
Stein [am Rhein], Switz. — E4 18
Steinauer, Ne., U.S. — D9 104
Steinbach, Man. — E3 70
Steinbach-Hallenberg, Ger. — C5 19
Steinfort, Lux. — E5 17
Steinhatchee, Fl., U.S. — C3 86
Steinhatchee, stm., Fl., U.S. — C3 86
Steinhausen, Nmb. — B2 49
Steinhuder, l., Ger. — F3 15
Steinkjer, Nor. — E4 14
Stella, Ont. — C8 73
Stella, Ky., U.S. — f9 94
Stella, Mo., U.S. — E3 102
Stella, Ne., U.S. — D10 104
Stella, mtn., Italy — C5 20
Stellarton, N.S. — D7 71
Stem, N.C., U.S. — A4 110
Stenay, Fr. — E5 17
Stendal, Ger. — B5 18
Stendal, In., U.S. — H3 91
Stenen, Sask. — F4 75
Stenness, Loch of, l., Scot., U.K. — A5 13
Stepanakert, Sov. Un. — F3 28
Stepenitz, stm., Ger. — E6 15
Stephan, S.D., U.S. — C6 118
Stephen, Mn., U.S. — B2 100
Stephens, Ar., U.S. — D2 81
Stephens, Ga., U.S. — C3 87
Stephens, co., Ga., U.S. — B3 87
Stephens, co., Ok., U.S. — C4 113
Stephens, co., Tx., U.S. — C3 120
Stephens, Port, b., Austl. — F9 51
Stephens City, Va., U.S. — A4 123
Stephensburg, N.J., U.S. — B3 107
Stephens City, Va., U.S. — A4 123
Stephens Knob, hill, Ky., U.S. — D5 94
Stephens Lake, res., Man. — A4 70
Stephenson, Mi., U.S. — C3 99
Stephenson, co., Il., U.S. — A4 90
Stephenson, Mount, mtn., Ant. — C6 7
Stephens Passage, strt., Ak., U.S. — m23 79
Stephensport, Ky., U.S. — C3 94
Stephenville, Newf. — D2 72
Stephenville, Tx., U.S. — C3 120
Stephenville Crossing, Newf. — D2 72
Stepnica, Pol. — E8 15
Stepnyak, Sov. Un. — C8 28
Steppes, plat., Sov. Un. — C8 28
Step Pyramid, hist., Egypt — E3 41
Steptoe, Nv., U.S. — D7 105
Steptoe, Wa., U.S. — B8 124
Sterkstroom, S. Afr. — D4 49
Sterling, Ak., U.S. — g16 79
Sterling, Co., U.S. — A7 83
Sterling, Ct., U.S. — C8 84
Sterling, Ga., U.S. — E5 87
Sterling, Il., U.S. — B4 90
Sterling, Ks., U.S. — D5 93
Sterling, Ma., U.S. — B4 98
Sterling, Mi., U.S. — D6 99
Sterling, Ne., U.S. — D9 104
Sterling, N.D., U.S. — C5 111
Sterling, Oh., U.S. — B4 112
Sterling, Ok., U.S. — C4 113
Sterling, co., Tx., U.S. — D2 120
Sterling City, Tx., U.S. — D2 120
Sterling Heights, Mi., U.S. — o15 99
Sterling Reservoir, res., Co., U.S. — A6 83
Sterling Run, Pa., U.S. — D5 115

Sterlington, La., U.S. — B3 95
Sterlitamak, Sov. Un. — D8 29
Sternberg, Ger. — E5 15
Šternberk, Czech. — D4 26
Sterrett, Al., U.S. — B3 78
Štěti, Czech. — C9 19
Stetson, Me., U.S. — D3 96
Stetson Mountain, mtn., Me., U.S. — C4 96
Stettin, Man. — C3 126
Stettin see Szczecin, Pol. — B3 26
Stettin Lagoon, b., Eur. — B3 26
Stettler, Alta. — D5 96
Steuben, Me., U.S. — D5 96
Steuben, Mi., U.S. — B4 99
Steuben, Wi., U.S. — E3 126
Steuben, co., In., U.S. — A7 91
Steuben, co., N.Y., U.S. — C3 109
Steubenville, Oh., U.S. — B5 112
Stevenage, Eng., U.K. — C7 12
Stevens, N.J., U.S. — C3 107
Stevens, co., Ks., U.S. — E2 93
Stevens, co., Mn., U.S. — E3 100
Stevens, co., Wa., U.S. — A7 124
Stevens Creek Dam, U.S. — C4 87
Stevenson, Al., U.S. — A4 78
Stevenson, Ct., U.S. — D3 84
Stevenson, Wa., U.S. — D4 124
Stevenson, stm., Man. — C4 70
Stevenson Lake, l., Man. — C4 70
Stevenson Mountain, mtn., Ar., U.S. — B1 81
Stevens Pass, Wa., U.S. — B4 124
Stevens Peak, mtn., Id., U.S. — B3 89
Stevens Point, Wi., U.S. — D4 126
Stevens Pottery, Ga., U.S. — D3 87
Stevens Village, Ak., U.S. — B10 79
Stevensville, Md., U.S. — C5 97
Stevensville, Mi., U.S. — F4 99
Stevensville, Mt., U.S. — D2 103
Stevensville, Pa., U.S. — C9 115
Steward, Il., U.S. — B4 90
Stewardson, Il., U.S. — D5 90
Stewart, B.C. — B3 69
Stewart, Mn., U.S. — F4 100
Stewart, Ms., U.S. — B4 101
Stewart, Oh., U.S. — C4 112
Stewart, Tn., U.S. — A4 119
Stewart, co., Ga., U.S. — D2 87
Stewart, co., Tn., U.S. — A4 119
Stewart, stm., Yukon — D5 66
Stewart Island, i., N.Z. — Q11 51
Stewart Mountain, mtn., Az., U.S. — k9 80
Stewarton, Scot., U.K. — E4 13
Stewarts Point, Nv., U.S. — G7 105
Stewartstown, N. Ire., U.K. — C5 11
Stewartstown, N.H., U.S. — f6 106
Stewartstown, Pa., U.S. — G8 115
Stewartstown Hollow, N.H., U.S. — g7 106
Stewartsville, Al., U.S. — B3 78
Stewartsville, In., U.S. — H2 91
Stewartsville, Mo., U.S. — B3 102
Stewartsville, N.B. — B4 71
Stewart Valley, Sask. — G2 75
Stewiacke, N.S. — D6 71
Steynsburg, S. Afr. — D4 49
Steyr, Aus. — D7 18
Stickney, Il., U.S. — *k9 90
Stickney, S.D., U.S. — D7 118
Stif (Sétif), Alg. — B6 44
Stigler, Ok., U.S. — B6 113
Stikine, stm., N.A. — E6 66
Stikine, stm., Ak., U.S. — D13 79
Stilesville, In., U.S. — E4 91
Stilis, Grc. — C4 25
Still, stm., Ct., U.S. — B3 84
Stillaguamish, North Fork, stm., Wa., U.S. — A4 124
Stillaguamish, South Fork, stm., Wa., U.S. — A4 124
Stillhouse Hollow Lake, res., Tx., U.S. — D4 120
Stillman Valley, Il., U.S. — A4 90
Stillmore, Ga., U.S. — D4 87
Still Pond, Md., U.S. — B5 97
Still River, Ma., U.S. — E5 69
Stilwater, B.C. —
Stillwater, Mn., U.S. — E6 100
Stillwater, N.Y., U.S. — C7 109
Stillwater, Ok., U.S. — A4 113
Stillwater, Pa., U.S. — D9 115
Stillwater, co., Mt., U.S. — E7 103
Stillwater Range, mts., Nv., U.S. — D3 105
Stillwater Reservoir, res., N.Y., U.S. — B5 109
Stillwater Reservoir, res., R.I., U.S. — B3 116
Stillwell, Ga., U.S. — D5 87
Stilwell, In., U.S. — A4 91
Stilson, Ga., U.S. — D5 87
Stilwell, Ks., U.S. — D9 93
Stilwell, Ok., U.S. — B7 113
Stimson, Mount, mtn., Mt., U.S. — B3 103
Stinear Nunataks, mtn., Ant. — C19 7
Stine Mountain, mtn., Mt., U.S. — E3 103
Stinesville, In., U.S. — F4 91
Stinking Lake, l., N.M., U.S. — A3 108
Stinnett, Tx., U.S. — B2 120
Stinson Lake, N.H., U.S. — C3 106
Ştip, Yugo. — E6 24
Stira, Yugo. —
Stirling, Austl. — F2 50
Stirling, Alta. — E4 68
Stirling, Ont. — C7 73
Stirling, Scot., U.K. — B5 10
Stirling City, Ca., U.S. — C3 82
Stirling City, r., Am. Sam. — G13 52
Stirnat, W.V., U.S. —
Stirum, N.D., U.S. — C8 111
Stites, Id., U.S. — C3 89
Stittsville, Ont. — B9 73
Stjördalshalsen, Nor. — F4 14
Stockach, Ger. — A7 21
Stockbridge, Ga., U.S. — C2 87
Stockbridge, Ma., U.S. — B1 98
Stockbridge, Mi., U.S. — F6 99
Stockbridge, Vt., U.S. — D3 122
Stockbridge-Munsee Indian Reservation, Wi., U.S. — D5 126
Stockdale, Oh., U.S. — D3 112
Stockdale, Tx., U.S. — E4 120
Stockerau, Aus. — G16 18
Stockertown, Pa., U.S. — E11 115
Stockett, Mt., U.S. — C5 103
Stockham, Ne., U.S. — D8 104
Stockholm, Sask. — G4 75
Stockholm, Swe. — H8 14
Stockholm, Me., U.S. — A4 96

Stockholm, N.J., U.S. — A3 107
Stockholm, Wi., U.S. — D1 126
Stockhorn, mtn., Switz. — C3 20
Stockland, Il., U.S. — C6 90
Stockley, De., U.S. — F4 85
Stockport, Eng., U.K. — D5 10
Stockport, Ia., U.S. — D6 92
Stockton, Man. — E2 70
Stockton, Al., U.S. — E2 78
Stockton, Ca., U.S. — D3 82
Stockton, Ga., U.S. — F4 87
Stockton, Il., U.S. — A3 90
Stockton, Ks., U.S. — C4 93
Stockton, Md., U.S. — D7 97
Stockton, Mo., U.S. — D4 102
Stockton, N.J., U.S. — C3 107
Stockton, N.Y., U.S. — C1 109
Stockton, Ut., U.S. — C3 121
Stockton Island, i., Wi., U.S. — B3 126
Stockton Lake, res., Mo., U.S. — D4 102
Stockton-on-Tees, Eng., U.K. — F7 13
Stockton Plateau, plat., Tx., U.S. — D1 120
Stockton Springs, Me., U.S. — D4 96
Stockville, Ne., U.S. — D5 104
Stockwell, In., U.S. — D4 91
Stod, Czech. — D8 19
Stoddard, Wi., U.S. — E2 126
Stoddard, co., Mo., U.S. — E8 102
Stoeckl, Mount, mtn., N.A. — A2 69
Stœng Treng, Camb. — C3 34
Stoer, Point of, c., Scot., U.K. — B3 13
Stoke-Centre, Que. — D6 74
Stoke-on-Trent, Eng., U.K. — D5 10
Stokes, N.C., U.S. — B5 110
Stokes, co., N.C., U.S. — A2 110
Stokes, Mount, mtn., N.Z. — N15 51
Stokesdale, N.C., U.S. — A3 110
Stokesley, Eng., U.K. — F7 13
Stokke, Nor. — p28 14
Stolac, Yugo. — D3 24
Stolberg, Ger. — C3 18
Stolbovaya, Sov. Un. — n17 27
Stolbovoy, i., Sov. Un. — B1 128
Stollberg, Ger. — C7 19
Stollings, W.V., U.S. — n12 125
Stolzenau, Ger. — F3 15
Stone, Eng., U.K. — B5 12
Stone, Id., U.S. — G6 89
Stone, Ky., U.S. — C7 94
Stone, co., Ar., U.S. — B3 81
Stone, co., Ms., U.S. — E4 101
Stone, co., Mo., U.S. — E4 102
Stoneboro, Pa., U.S. — D1 115
Stone City, Ia., U.S. — B6 92
Stone Corral Lake, l., Or., U.S. — E7 114
Stonefort, Il., U.S. — F5 90
Stonega, Va., U.S. — f9 123
Stoneham, Co., U.S. — A7 83
Stoneham, Ma., U.S. — g11 98
Stone Harbor, N.J., U.S. — E3 107
Stonehaven, N.B. — B4 71
Stonehaven, Scot., U.K. — B5 10
Stonehenge, Austl. — B4 51
Stone Lake, Wi., U.S. — C2 126
Stone Mountain, mtn., Ga., U.S. — C2 87
Stone Mountain, mtn., Vt., U.S. — B5 122
Stone Mountains, mts., U.S. — A1 110
Stoner, B.C. — C6 69
Stoner, Co., U.S. — D2 83
Stoneville, Ms., U.S. — B3 101
Stoneville, N.C., U.S. — A3 110
Stoneville, S.D., U.S. — C3 118
Stonewall, Man. — D3 70
Stonewall, La., U.S. — B2 95
Stonewall, Ms., U.S. — C5 101
Stonewall, Ok., U.S. — C5 113
Stonewall, Tx., U.S. — D3 120
Stonewall, co., Tx., U.S. — C2 120
Stonewood, W.V., U.S. — B5 97
Stoney Creek, Ont. — D5 73
Stonington, Co., U.S. — D8 83
Stonington, Ct., U.S. — D8 84
Stonington, Il., U.S. — D4 90
Stonington, Me., U.S. — D4 96
Stono, stm., S.C., U.S. — k11 117
Stono Inlet, b., S.C., U.S. — F8 117
Stony Beach, Sask. — G3 75
Stony Brook, N.Y., U.S. — n15 109
Stony Brook, stm., N.J., U.S. — C3 107
Stony Creek, Ct., U.S. — D5 84
Stony Creek, N.Y., U.S. — B7 109
Stony Creek, Va., U.S. — C5 123
Stony Creek, stm., Va., U.S. — C5 123
Stonyford, Ca., U.S. — C2 82
Stony Island, i., Newf. — B4 72
Stony Island, i., N.Y., U.S. — B4 109
Stony Lake, l., Ont. — C6 73
Stony Mountain, Man. — D3 70
Stony Plain, Alta. — C3 68
Stony Point, N.Y., U.S. — *D7 109
Stony Point, N.C., U.S. — B1 110
Stony Rapids, Sask. — m7 75
Stony Ridge, Oh., U.S. — e6 112
Stör, stm., Ger. — B4 18
Storå, stm., Den. — C2 15
Stora Lulevatten, l., Swe. — D8 14
Stora Sundby, Swe. — t34 14
Storavan, l., Swe. — D8 14
Storden, Mn., U.S. — F3 100
Store Bælt, strt., Den. — C4 15
Store Heddinge, Den. — J5 14
Storey, co., Nv., U.S. — D2 105
Storkow, Ger. — A8 19
Storla, S.D., U.S. — D7 118
Storm Lake, Ia., U.S. — B2 92
Storm Lake, l., Ia., U.S. — B2 92
Storm Mountain, mtn., Ak., U.S. — h16 79
Stormont, co., Ont. — B10 73
Stornoway, Sask. — F4 75
Stornoway, Scot., U.K. — A3 10
Storozhinets, Sov. Un. — G5 27
Storrs, Ct., U.S. — B7 84
Storsjö, l., Swe. — F5 14
Storsjön, l., Swe. — F6 14
Storthoaks, Sask. — H5 75
Storuman, Swe. — E7 14
Storuman, l., Swe. — E7 14
Story, Ar., U.S. — C2 81
Story, Wy., U.S. — B6 127
Story City, Ia., U.S. — B4 92
Stotesbury, Mo., U.S. — D3 102
Stotts City, Mo., U.S. — D4 102

Stottville, N.Y., U.S. — C7 109
Stoughton, Sask. — H4 75
Stoughton, Ma., U.S. — B5 98
Stoughton, Wi., U.S. — F4 126
Stour, stm., Eng., U.K. — E7 10
Stour, stm., Eng., U.K. — E6 10
Stourbridge, Eng., U.K. — B5 12
Stourport-on-Severn, Eng., U.K. — B5 12
Stout, Oh., U.S. — D2 112
Stoutland, Mo., U.S. — D5 102
Stoutsville, Mo., U.S. — B6 102
Stoutsville, Oh., U.S. — C3 112
Stovall, Ga., U.S. — D2 87
Stovall, Ms., U.S. — A3 101
Stovall, N.C., U.S. — A4 110
Stove Creek, Sask. — E4 75
Stover, Mo., U.S. — C5 102
Støvring, Den. — B3 15
Stow, Me., U.S. — D2 96
Stow, Ma., U.S. — B4 98
Stow, Oh., U.S. — A4 112
Stowe, Pa., U.S. — F10 115
Stowe, Vt., U.S. — C3 122
Stowe Township, Pa., U.S. — *k13 115
Stowmarket, Eng., U.K. — D5 10
Stoy, Il., U.S. — E6 90
Stoyoma Mountain, mtn., B.C. — E7 69
Stoystown, Pa., U.S. — F4 115
Strabane, N. Ire., U.K. — C3 10
Strabane, Pa., U.S. — F1 115
Strachur, Scot., U.K. — D3 13
Stradbally, Ire. — D4 11
Stradone, Ire. — D4 11
Strafford, Mo., U.S. — D4 102
Strafford, N.H., U.S. — D4 106
Strafford, Vt., U.S. — D4 122
Strafford, co., N.H., U.S. — D4 106
Straffordville, Ont. — E4 73
Straight, Ok., U.S. — e9 113
Strakonice, Czech. — D2 26
Straldzha, Bul. — D8 24
Stralsund, Ger. — A6 18
Strand, S. Afr. — D2 49
Strandburg, S.D., U.S. — B9 118
Strandby, Den. — A4 15
Strandhill, Ire. — C3 11
Strandquist, Mn., U.S. — B2 100
Strang, Ne., U.S. — D8 104
Strang, Ok., U.S. — A6 113
Stranger Creek, stm., Ks., U.S. — k15 93
Strangford, N. Ire., U.K. — C6 11
Strangford Lough, l., N. Ire., U.K. — C4 10
Strängnäs, Swe. — t35 14
Strängnäs, Swe. — u34 14
Stranraer, Sask. — F1 75
Stranraer, Scot., U.K. — C4 10
Strasbourg, Sask. — F3 75
Strasbourg, Fr. — C7 16
Strasburg, Co., U.S. — B6 83
Strasburg, Il., U.S. — D5 90
Strasburg, Mo., U.S. — C3 102
Strasburg, N.D., U.S. — C5 111
Strasburg, Oh., U.S. — B4 112
Strasburg, Pa., U.S. — G9 115
Strasburg, Va., U.S. — B4 123
Strasswalchen, Aus. — D3 73
Stratford, N.Z. — M15 51
Stratford, Ont. — D4 73
Stratford, Ca., U.S. — D4 82
Stratford, Ct., U.S. — E3 84
Stratford, De., U.S. — *B3 85
Stratford, Ia., U.S. — B4 92
Stratford, N.H., U.S. — A3 106
Stratford, N.J., U.S. — D2 107
Stratford, N.Y., U.S. — B6 109
Stratford, Ok., U.S. — C5 113
Stratford, S.D., U.S. — B7 118
Stratford, Tx., U.S. — A1 120
Stratford, Wi., U.S. — D3 126
Stratford, co., Que. — D6 74
Stratford Landing, Va., U.S. — *B5 123
Stratford Point, c., Ct., U.S. — E3 84
Stratford-upon-Avon, Eng., U.K. — D6 10
Stratham, N.H., U.S. — D5 106
Strathaven, Scot., U.K. — E4 13
Strathclair, Man. — D1 70
Strathclyde, prov., Scot., U.K. — E4 13
Strathcona, Mn., U.S. — B2 100
Strathcona Provincial Park, B.C. — E5 69
Strathlorne, N.S. — C8 71
Strathmere, N.J., U.S. — E3 107
Strathmore, Alta. — D4 68
Strathmore, Ca., U.S. — D4 82
Strathmore, val., Scot., U.K. — C4 107
Strathroy, Ont. — E3 73
Strathy Point, c., Scot., U.K. — B4 13
Strattanville, Pa., U.S. — D3 115
Stratton, Co., U.S. — B8 83
Stratton, Me., U.S. — C2 96
Stratton, Ne., U.S. — D4 104
Stratton, Oh., U.S. — B5 112
Stratton Meadows, Co., U.S. — C6 83
Stratton Mountain, mtn., Vt., U.S. — E3 122
Straubing, Ger. — D6 18
Straubville, N.D., U.S. — C8 111
Straughn, In., U.S. — E7 91
Strausberg, Ger. — F9 15
Strausstown, Pa., U.S. — F9 115
Strawberry, Ar., U.S. — B4 81
Strawberry, stm., Ar., U.S. — A4 81
Strawberry, stm., Ut., U.S. — C5 121
Strawberry Mountain, mtn., Or., U.S. — C8 114
Strawberry Plains, Tn., U.S. — C10 119
Strawberry Point, Ia., U.S. — B6 92
Strawberry Point, c., Ma., U.S. — B6 98
Strawberry Range, mts., Or., U.S. — C8 114

Stříbro, Czech. — D8 19
Strichen, Scot., U.K. — C6 13
Strimón (Struma), stm., Eur. — B4 25
Strimón, Gulf of, b., Grc. — B4 25
Stringer, Ms., U.S. — D4 101
Stringtown, Co., U.S. — B4 83
Stringtown, Ky., U.S. — B5 94
Stringtown, Ms., U.S. — B3 101
Stringtown, Ok., U.S. — C5 113
Strofádhes, is., Grc. — D3 25
Stroh, In., U.S. — A7 91
Strokestown, Ire. — D3 11
Stromboli, i., Italy — E5 23
Strome, Alta. — C4 68
Stromeferry, Scot., U.K. — C3 13
Stromness, Scot., U.K. — B5 13
Stromsburg, Ne., U.S. — C8 104
Stronach, Mi., U.S. — D4 99
Strong, Ar., U.S. — D3 81
Strong, Me., U.S. — D2 96
Strong, stm., Ms., U.S. — C4 101
Strong City, Ks., U.S. — D7 93
Strong City, Ok., U.S. — B2 113
Strongfield, Sask. — F2 75
Stronghurst, Il., U.S. — C3 90
Strongs, Mi., U.S. — B6 99
Strongsville, Oh., U.S. — A4 112
Stronsay, i., Scot., U.K. — A5 10
Strontian, Scot., U.K. — A6 13
Stroud, Eng., U.K. — C5 12
Stroud, Ok., U.S. — B5 113
Stroudsburg, Pa., U.S. — E11 115
Stroudwater, stm., Me., U.S. — g7 96
Struble, Ia., U.S. — B1 92
Struer, Den. — I3 14
Struga, Yugo. — E5 24
Strule, stm., N. Ire., U.K. — C3 11
Strum, Wi., U.S. — D2 126
Struma (Strimón), stm., Eur. — B4 25
Strumble Head, c., Wales, U.K. — B2 12
Strumica, Yugo. — E6 24
Strunk, Ky., U.S. — D5 94
Struthers, Oh., U.S. — A5 112
Stryama, stm., Bul. — D7 24
Stryker, Mt., U.S. — B2 103
Stryker, Oh., U.S. — A1 112
Strykersville, N.Y., U.S. — C2 109
Stryy, Sov. Un. — G4 27
Stryy, stm., Sov. Un. — D7 26
Strzegom, Pol. — C4 26
Strzelce Krajeńskie, Pol. — C5 26
Strzelce [Opolskie], Pol. — C5 26
Strzelecki Creek, stm., Austl. — E7 50
Strzelin, Pol. — C4 26
Strzelno, Pol. — B5 26
Strzemieszyce, Pol. — g10 26
Stuart, Fl., U.S. — E6 86
Stuart, Ia., U.S. — C3 92
Stuart, Ne., U.S. — B6 104
Stuart, Ok., U.S. — C5 113
Stuart, Va., U.S. — D2 123
Stuart, stm., B.C. — B5 69
Stuart, Mount, mtn., Wa., U.S. — B5 124
Stuart Lake, l., B.C. — B5 69
Stuarts Draft, Va., U.S. — B3 123
Stubbekøbing, Den. — D6 15
Stub Hill, mtn., N.H., U.S. — f7 106
Studley, Ks., U.S. — C3 93
Stühlingen, Ger. — A5 21
Stull, stm., Can. — B5 70
Stull Lake, l., Can. — B5 70
Stump Creek, Pa., U.S. — D4 115
Stump Lake, l., N.D., U.S. — B7 111
Stump Pond, res., R.I., U.S. — D2 116
Stumptown, W.V., U.S. — C4 125
Stupart, stm., Man. — B4 70
Stupino, Sov. Un. — D11 27
Sturbridge, Ma., U.S. — B3 98
Sturgeon, Mo., U.S. — B5 102
Sturgeon, stm., Sask. — D2 75
Sturgeon, stm., Mi., U.S. — B4 99
Sturgeon, stm., Mi., U.S. — B6 126
Sturgeon Bay, Wi., U.S. — D6 126
Sturgeon Bay, b., Man. — C3 70
Sturgeon Falls, Ont. — A5 73
Sturgeon Lake, Mn., U.S. — D6 100
Sturgeon Lake, l., Alta. — B2 68
Sturgeon Lake, l., Ont. — C6 73
Sturgeon Lake, l., Ont. — D2 75
Sturgeon Landing, Sask. — C5 75
Sturgeon-weir, stm., Sask. — C4 75
Sturgis, Sask. — F4 75
Sturgis, Ky., U.S. — e10 94
Sturgis, Mi., U.S. — G5 99
Sturgis, Ms., U.S. — B4 101
Sturgis, S.D., U.S. — C2 118
Sturt, Creek, stm., Austl. — C4 50
Sturt Desert, des., Austl. — D3 51
Sturtevant, Wi., U.S. — F6 126
Stutsman, co., N.D., U.S. — B6 111
Stutterheim, S. Afr. — D4 49
Stuttgart, Ger. — D4 18
Stuttgart, Ar., U.S. — C4 81
Stuttgart, Ks., U.S. — C4 93
Styr, stm., Sov. Un. — F5 27
Styria, hist. reg., Aus. — E7 18
Subansiri, stm., India — F11 37
Subarnarekha, stm., India — F11 37
Subi, i., Indon. — K8 35
Subiaco, Ar., U.S. — B2 81

Subic, Phil. — o13 34
Subic Bay, b., Phil. — o13 34
Subotica, Yugo. — B4 24
Sucarnoochee, stm., Al., U.S. — C1 78
Succasunna, N.J., U.S. — B3 107
Success, Sask. — G1 75
Success, Ar., U.S. — A5 81
Success, Mo., U.S. — D5 102
Success, Mount, mtn., N.H., U.S. — B4 106
Suceava, Rom. — B8 24
Suceava, stm., Rom. — B8 24
Suchdol, Czech. — B2 26
Sucha [Beskidzka], Pol. — n17 26
Suchedniów, Pol. — C6 26
Suches, Ga., U.S. — B2 87
Suchitoto, El Sal. — E8 31
Süchow see Xuzhou, China — D2 10
Suck, stm., Ire. — D3 11
Sucre, Bol. — C2 55
Sucre, state, Ven. — A5 60
Sucre, dept., Col. — B2 60
Sucurió, stm., Braz. — C2 56
Sucy-en-Brie, Fr. — g11 16
Sudan, Tx., U.S. — B1 120
Sudan, hist. reg., Afr. — C2 47
Sudan, reg., Afr. — E7 42
Sudbury, Ont. — A4 73

Name	Map Ref.	Page
Sudbury, Eng., U.K.	B8	12
Sudbury, Ma., U.S.	B5	98
Sudbury, Vt., U.S.	D2	122
Sudbury, dept., Ont.	p19	73
Sudbury, stm., Ma., U.S.	B5	98
Sudbury Center, Ma., U.S.	g10	98
Sudbury Reservoir, res., Ma., U.S.	g10	98
Suddie, Guy.	A3	59
Süderbrarup, Ger.	D3	15
Suderburg, Ger.	B5	18
Sudetes, mts., Eur.	C4	26
Sudlersville, Md., U.S.	B6	97
Süd-Nord Canal, Ger.	B7	17
Sudogda, Sov. Un.	D13	27
Sudr, 'Ayn, well, Eg.	E5	41
Sudzha, Sov. Un.	F10	27
Sue, stm., Sud.	D2	47
Sueca, Spain	C5	22
Suez (As Suways), Eg.	C3	38
Suez, Gulf of, b., Eg.	C3	38
Suez Canal, Eg.	B3	38
Suffern, N.Y., U.S.	D6	109
Suffield, Alta.	D5	68
Suffield, Ct., U.S.	B5	84
Suffolk, Va., U.S.	C7	103
Suffolk, Va., U.S.	D6	123
Suffolk, co., Eng., U.K.	B8	12
Suffolk, co., Ma., U.S.	B5	98
Suffolk, co., N.Y., U.S.	n15	109
Sugar, stm., U.S.	F4	126
Sugar, stm., N.H., U.S.	D2	106
Sugar, North Branch, stm., N.H., U.S.	D2	106
Sugar City, Co., U.S.	C7	83
Sugar City, Id., U.S.	F7	89
Sugar Creek, Mo., U.S.	h11	102
Sugarcreek, Pa., U.S.	D2	115
Sugar Creek, stm., In., U.S.	F6	91
Sugar Creek, stm., In., U.S.	E3	91
Sugar Creek, stm., Oh., U.S.	C2	112
Sugar Creek, stm., Pa., U.S.	C8	115
Sugar Grove, N.C., U.S.	A1	110
Sugar Grove, Oh., U.S.	C3	112
Sugar Grove, Va., U.S.	D1	123
Sugar Grove, W.V., U.S.	C5	125
Sugar Hill, Ga., U.S.	B2	87
Sugar Hill, N.H., U.S.	B3	106
Sugar Island, i., Mi., U.S.	B6	99
Sugar Land, Tx., U.S.	E5	120
Sugarland Run, Va., U.S.	A5	123
Sugar Loaf, mtn., Braz.	h6	56
Sugarloaf, mtn., N.H., U.S.	C3	123
Sugarloaf, Oh., U.S.	A4	112
Sugarloaf Mountain, mtn., Me., U.S.	C2	96
Sugar Loaf Mountain, mtn., Md., U.S.	B3	97
Sugarloaf Mountain, mtn., Mt., U.S.	C4	103
Sugar Loaf Mountain, mtn., Ok., U.S.	C7	113
Sugarloaf Point, c., Austl.	F9	51
Sugar Mountain, mtn., Mi., U.S.	k9	99
Sugar Notch, Pa., U.S.	n17	115
Sugartown, La., U.S.	D2	95
Sugar Valley, Ga., U.S.	B1	87
Sugden, Ok., U.S.	C4	113
Suggi Lake, l., Sask.	C4	75
Suggsville, Al., U.S.	D2	78
Şuḩār, Oman	C5	38
Sühbaatar, Mong.	A6	31
Suhl, Ger.	C5	18
Suiattle, stm., Wa., U.S.	A4	124
Suibin, China	C5	33
Suichuan, China	F7	31
Suide, China	D7	31
Suifenhe, China	C11	31
Suihua, China	B10	31
Suijiang, China	F5	31
Suileng, China	C3	33
Suining, China	E6	31
Suipacha, Arg.	g7	54
Suipacha, Bol.	D2	55
Suippes, Fr.	E4	17
Suir, stm., Ire.	D3	10
Suisun City, Ca., U.S.	*C2	82
Suit, N.C., U.S.	f8	110
Suita, Japan	*I7	33
Suitland, Md., U.S.	C4	97
Suixian, China	E7	31
Suixian, China	E4	31
Suizhong, China	D9	32
Sukabumi, Indon.	G3	34
Sukadana, Indon.	F3	34
Sukaraja, Indon.	F4	34
Sukarnapura see Jayapura, Indon.	F10	34
Sukhaya Tunguska, Sov. Un.	B26	8
Sukhobuzimskoye, Sov. Un.	D27	8
Sukhona, stm., Sov. Un.	C7	29
Sukhothai, Thai.	B1	34
Sukhumi, Sov. Un.	G17	8
Sukkur, Pak.	C4	36
Sukumo, Japan	J6	33
Sukunka, stm., B.C.	B7	69
Sul, Canal do, strt., Braz.	C5	59
Sula, Nor.	E3	103
Sula, stm., Sov. Un.	F9	27
Sulaco, stm., Hond.	C4	62
Sulaimān Range, mts., Pak.	C4	36
Sula Islands, is., Indon.	F7	34
Sula Sgeir, i., Scot., U.K.	A2	13
Sulecin, Pol.	B3	26
Sulejówek, Pol.	m14	26
Sule Skerry, rock, Scot., U.K.	A4	13
Sulina, Rom.	C9	24
Sulingen, Ger.	F2	15
Suitelma, mtn., Eur.	D7	14
Sullana, Peru	B1	58
Sulligent, Al., U.S.	D5	90
Sullivan, Il., U.S.	F3	91
Sullivan, In., U.S.	C2	94
Sullivan, Mo., U.S.	C6	102
Sullivan, N.H., U.S.	D2	106
Sullivan, Oh., U.S.	A3	112
Sullivan, Wi., U.S.	E5	126
Sullivan, co., In., U.S.	F3	91
Sullivan, co., Mo., U.S.	A4	102
Sullivan, co., N.H., U.S.	D2	106
Sullivan, co., N.Y., U.S.	D6	109
Sullivan, co., Pa., U.S.	D8	115
Sullivan, co., Tn., U.S.	C11	119
Sullivan Lake, l., Alta.	D5	68
Sullivans Island, S.C., U.S.	k12	117
Sully, co., S.D., U.S.	C5	118
Sulmona, Italy	C5	92
Sulphide, Ont.	C7	73
Sulphur, Ky., U.S.	B4	94
Sulphur, La., U.S.	D2	95
Sulphur, Ok., U.S.	C5	113
Sulphur, stm., Alta.	C1	68
Sulphur, stm., U.S.	D2	81
Sulphur Rock, Ar., U.S.	B4	81
Sulphur Spring Range, mts., Nv., U.S.	C5	105
Sulphur Springs, Ar., U.S.	A1	81
Sulphur Springs, In., U.S.	D7	91
Sulphur Springs, Mo., U.S.	g13	102
Sulphur Springs, Oh., U.S.	B3	112
Sulphur Springs, Tx., U.S.	C5	120
Sulphur Springs Valley, val., Az., U.S.	E6	80
Sultan, Wa., U.S.	B4	124
Sultānpur, India	D9	37
Sulu Archipelago, is., Phil.	D6	34
Sulūq, Libya	C4	43
Sulu Sea, Asia	D5	34
Sulzbach, Ger.	D2	19
Sulzbach-Rosenberg, Ger.	D6	19
Sulzberger Bay, b., Ant.	B33	7
Sumas, Wa., U.S.	A3	124
Sumatra, Fl., U.S.	B2	86
Sumatra, Mt., U.S.	D9	103
Sumatra (Sumatera), i., Indon.	F2	34
Sumava Resorts, In., U.S.	B3	91
Sumba, i., Indon.	G6	34
Sumbar, stm., Sov. Un.	B7	39
Sumbawa, i., Indon.	G5	34
Sumbawa Besar, Indon.	G5	34
Sumbawanga, Tan.	C5	48
Sumbe (Ngunza), Ang.	D1	48
Sumburgh Head, c., Scot., U.K.	h10	10
Sümeg, Hung.	B3	24
Sumenep, Indon.	G4	34
Sumgait, Sov. Un.	A4	39
Sumiswald, Switz.	B4	21
Sumiton, Al., U.S.	B2	78
Summerberry, Sask.	G4	75
Summerdale, Al., U.S.	E2	78
Summerfield, Fl., U.S.	C4	86
Summerfield, Ks., U.S.	C7	93
Summerfield, La., U.S.	B3	95
Summerfield, Mo., U.S.	C6	102
Summerfield, N.C., U.S.	A3	110
Summerfield, Oh., U.S.	C4	112
Summerford, Newf.	D4	72
Summerhill, Ire.	D5	11
Summer Hill, Il., U.S.	D3	90
Summer Island, i., Mi., U.S.	C4	99
Summerland, B.C.	E8	69
Summerland Key, Fl., U.S.	H5	86
Summers, co., W.V., U.S.	D4	125
Summer Shade, Ky., U.S.	D4	94
Summerside, P.E.I.	C6	71
Summersville, Ky., U.S.	C4	94
Summersville, Mo., U.S.	D6	102
Summersville, W.V., U.S.	C4	125
Summersville Lake, res., W.V., U.S.	C4	125
Summerton, S.C., U.S.	D7	117
Summertown, Ga., U.S.	D4	87
Summertown, Tn., U.S.	B4	119
Summerville, Ga., U.S.	B1	87
Summerville, Or., U.S.	B8	114
Summerville, Pa., U.S.	D3	115
Summerville, S.C., U.S.	E7	117
Summit, Ar., U.S.	A3	81
Summit, Il., U.S.	k9	90
Summit, Ms., U.S.	D3	101
Summit, N.J., U.S.	B4	107
Summit, Ok., U.S.	B6	113
Summit, R.I., U.S.	D2	116
Summit, S.D., U.S.	B9	118
Summit, Tn., U.S.	h11	119
Summit, Ut., U.S.	F3	121
Summit, co., Co., U.S.	B4	83
Summit, co., Oh., U.S.	A4	112
Summit, co., Ut., U.S.	C5	121
Summit, mtn., N.Z.	N16	51
Summit Grove, Il., U.S.	E3	91
Summit Hill, Pa., U.S.	E10	115
Summit Lake, B.C.	B6	69
Summit Lake, l., Ca., U.S.	C3	92
Summit Lake Indian Reservation, Nv., U.S.	B2	105
Summit Mountain, mtn., Nv., U.S.	D5	105
Summit Peak, mtn., Co., U.S.	D4	83
Summit Point, W.V., U.S.	B7	125
Summit Station, Pa., U.S.	k11	112
Summitville, Co., U.S.	D4	83
Summitville, In., U.S.	D6	91
Summitville, Tn., U.S.	D8	119
Summum, Il., U.S.	C3	90
Sumner, Ga., U.S.	E3	87
Sumner, Il., U.S.	E6	90
Sumner, Ia., U.S.	B5	92
Sumner, Ms., U.S.	B3	101
Sumner, Mo., U.S.	B4	102
Sumner, Ne., U.S.	D6	104
Sumner, Ok., U.S.	A4	113
Sumner, Wa., U.S.	B3	124
Sumner, co., Ks., U.S.	E6	93
Sumner, co., Tn., U.S.	A5	119
Sumner Lake, res., N.M., U.S.	C5	108
Sumner Strait, strt., Ak., U.S.	m23	79
Sumoto, Japan	I7	33
Šumperk, Czech.	D4	26
Sumpter, Or., U.S.	C8	114
Sumrall, Ms., U.S.	D4	101
Sumter, Ga., U.S.	E2	87
Sumter, S.C., U.S.	D7	117
Sumter, co., Al., U.S.	C1	78
Sumter, co., Fl., U.S.	D4	86
Sumter, co., Ga., U.S.	D2	87
Sumter, co., S.C., U.S.	D7	117
Sumterville, Al., U.S.	C1	78
Sun, stm., U.S.	C5	103
Sun, La., U.S.	D6	95
Sun, stm., Mt., U.S.	C4	103
Sunagawa, Japan	o19	33
Sunapee, N.H., U.S.	D2	106
Sunapee Lake, l., N.H., U.S.	D2	106
Sunapee Mountain, mtn., N.H., U.S.	D2	106
Sunart, Loch, i., Scot., U.K.	D3	13
Sunbright, Tn., U.S.	C9	119
Sunburg, Mn., U.S.	E3	100
Sunburst, Mt., U.S.	B5	103
Sunbury, Oh., U.S.	B3	112
Sunbury, Pa., U.S.	E8	115
Sunbury, co., N.B.	D3	71
Sunchales, Arg.	A4	54
Suncho Corral, Arg.	E3	55
Sunchón, N. Kor.	G2	33
Sunch'ŏn, S. Kor.	I3	33
Sun City, Ca., U.S.	*F5	82
Sun City, Fl., U.S.	p10	86
Sun City, Ks., U.S.	E5	93
Sun City Center, Fl., U.S.	*E4	86
Suncook, N.H., U.S.	D4	106
Suncook, stm., N.H., U.S.	D4	106
Suncook Lakes, l., N.H., U.S.	D4	106
Sundance, Wy., U.S.	B8	127
Sundance Mountain, mtn., Wy., U.S.	B8	127
Sundarbans, reg., Asia	D8	36
Sunda Strait, strt., Indon.	G3	34
Sunday Strait, strt., Austl.	C3	50
Sundbyberg, Swe.	t35	14
Sunderland, Ont.	C5	73
Sunderland, Eng., U.K.	C6	10
Sunderland, Md., U.S.	C4	97
Sunderland, Ma., U.S.	B2	98
Sunderland, Vt., U.S.	E2	122
Sundown, Man.	E3	70
Sundown, Tx., U.S.	C1	120
Sundre, Alta.	D3	68
Sundridge, Ont.	B5	73
Sunds, Den.	B3	15
Sundsvall, Swe.	F7	14
Sunfield, Mi., U.S.	F5	99
Sunflower, Ms., U.S.	B3	101
Sunflower, co., Ms., U.S.	B3	101
Sunflower, Mount, mtn., Ks., U.S.	C2	93
Sungaiguntung, Indon.	E2	34
Sungaipenuh, Indon.	F2	34
Sungai Petani, Malay.	J4	35
Sungari Reservoir, res., China	E3	33
Sungari see Songhua Jiang, stm., Asia	B10	31
Sungurlu, Tur.	B10	40
Sunland Park, N.M., U.S.	F3	108
Sunlight Creek, stm., Wy., U.S.	B3	127
Sunman, In., U.S.	F7	91
Sunne, Swe.	H5	14
Sunnybrae, N.S.	D7	71
Sunnybrook, Alta.	C4	68
Sunny Isles, Fl., U.S.	*G6	86
Sunnyland, Ar., U.S.	q11	86
Sunnymead, Ca., U.S.	*F5	82
Sunnynook, Alta.	D5	68
Sunnyside, Newf.	E5	72
Sunnyside, Ca., U.S.	*D4	82
Sunnyside, Ut., U.S.	u16	86
Sunnyside, Ut., U.S.	D5	121
Sunnyside, Wa., U.S.	C5	124
Sunny South, Al., U.S.	D2	78
Sunnyvale, Ca., U.S.	k8	82
Sunnyview, S.D., U.S.	C9	118
Sunol, Ca., U.S.	h9	82
Sun Prairie, Wi., U.S.	E4	126
Sunray, Ok., U.S.	C4	113
Sunray, Tx., U.S.	A2	120
Sunrise, Fl., U.S.	*r13	86
Sunrise, Wy., U.S.	D8	127
Sunrise Manor, Nv., U.S.	G6	105
Sunrise Mountain, mtn., N.J., U.S.	A3	107
Sun River, Mt., U.S.	C4	103
Sunset, Fl., U.S.	*G6	86
Sunset, La., U.S.	D3	95
Sunset, Me., U.S.	D4	96
Sunset, Tx., U.S.	C4	120
Sunset, Ut., U.S.	B4	121
Sunset Beach, Hi., U.S.	f9	88
Sunset Crater National Monument, Az., U.S.	B4	80
Sunset Hill, hill, Ct., U.S.	B7	84
Sunset Lake, l., Vt., U.S.	D2	122
Sunset Park, Ks., U.S.	g12	93
Sunshine, Austl.	*G7	50
Sunshine, Me., U.S.	D4	96
Sunspot, N.M., U.S.	E4	108
Suntaug Lake, l., Ma., U.S.	f11	98
Suntrana, Ak., U.S.	C10	79
Sun Valley, Id., U.S.	F4	89
Sun Valley, Nv., U.S.	D2	105
Sunyani, Ghana	E4	45
Suo Sea, Japan	J5	33
Suoyarvi, Sov. Un.	F15	14
Supai, Sask.	F1	75
Superior, Az., U.S.	D4	80
Superior, Co., U.S.	B5	83
Superior, Ia., U.S.	A3	92
Superior, Mt., U.S.	C2	103
Superior, Ne., U.S.	D7	104
Superior, Wi., U.S.	B1	126
Superior, Lake, l., N.A.	A10	76
Superstition Mountains, mts., Az., U.S.	m10	80
Suphan Buri, Thai.	E4	35
Supi Oidak, Az., U.S.	F4	80
Supply, N.C., U.S.	C4	110
Supreme, La., U.S.	k9	95
Supung Reservoir, res., Asia	F2	33
Suoyarvi, Sov. Un.	J5	33
Sur, Point, c., Ca., U.S.	D3	82
Sur, stm., Ca., U.S.	D3	82
Surabaya, Indon.	G4	34
Surakarta, Indon.	G4	34
Surakhany, Sov. Un.	I14	27
Surány, Czech.	D5	26
Surat, Austl.	C7	51
Surat, India	D5	36
Sūratgarh, India	C4	37
Surat Thani, Thai.	D1	34
Surazh, Sov. Un.	E9	27
Şūr Bāhir, Isr. Occ.	k11	41
Surco, Peru	*D2	58
Surendranagar, India	F3	37
Suresnes, Fr.	g9	16
Suretka, C.R.	F4	71
Surette Island, N.S.	E4	71
Surf City, N.J., U.S.	D4	107
Surfside, Fl., U.S.	s13	86
Surfside Beach, S.C., U.S.	D10	117
Surgères, Fr.	D3	16
Surgoinsville, Tn., U.S.	C11	119
Surgut, Sov. Un.	C4	28
Surgut, Sov. Un.	C10	29
Suriápet, India	I7	37
Suribachi, Mount, hill, Japan	P17	52
Surigao, Phil.	D7	34
Suriname, dept., Sur.	A3	59
Suriname, ctry., S.A.	C3	59
Surkhan Darya, stm., Sov. Un.	C13	39
Surprise, Ne., U.S.	k8	80
Surprise, Ne., U.S.	C8	104
Surquillo, Peru	*D2	58
Surrency, Ga., U.S.	E4	87
Surrey, N.D., U.S.	A4	111
Surrey, co., Eng., U.K.	C7	12
Surry, Me., U.S.	D4	96
Surry, N.H., U.S.	D2	106
Surry, Va., U.S.	C6	123
Surry, co., N.C., U.S.	A2	110
Surry, co., Va., U.S.	C6	123
Surry Mountain Lake, res., N.H., U.S.	D2	106
Sursee, Switz.	B5	21
Surt, Libya	C3	43
Sürüç, Tur.	D12	40
Suruga Bay, b., Japan	o17	33
Surveyor, W.V., U.S.	n13	125
Sūryāni, Dayr as, hist., Eg.	D2	41
Susa, Italy	B1	23
Sušac, i., Yugo.	D3	24
Sušak (part of Rijeka), Yugo.	C2	24
Susak, i., Yugo.	C2	24
Susanino, Sov. Un.	s31	14
Susank, Ks., U.S.	D5	93
Susanville, Ca., U.S.	B3	82
Sušice, Czech.	D2	26
Susitna, stm., Ak., U.S.	C10	79
Susoh, Indon.	K2	35
Susong, China	I7	32
Susquehanna, Pa., U.S.	C10	115
Susquehanna, co., Pa., U.S.	C10	115
Susquehanna, stm., U.S.	A5	97
Susquehanna, West Branch, stm., Pa., U.S.	D5	115
Susques, Arg.	D2	55
Sussex, N.B.	D4	71
Sussex, N.J., U.S.	A3	107
Sussex, Wi., U.S.	m11	126
Sussex, co., De., U.S.	F4	85
Sussex, co., N.J., U.S.	A3	107
Sussex, co., Va., U.S.	D5	123
Sussex, Shores, De., U.S.	F5	85
Sussex Shores, De., U.S.	F5	85
Sustut, stm., B.C.	A4	69
Susurluk, Tur.	C7	40
Sutcliffe, Nv., U.S.	D2	105
Sutherland, S. Afr.	D3	49
Sutherland, Ia., U.S.	B2	92
Sutherland, Ne., U.S.	C4	104
Sutherland, Ut., U.S.	D3	121
Sutherland, co., Scot.	C5	123
Sutherland Springs, Tx., U.S.	k7	120
Sutlej (Langqên Zangbo), stm., Asia	D3	114
Sutter, co., Ca., U.S.	B6	30
Sutter Creek, Ca., U.S.	C3	82
Suttle, Al., U.S.	C3	82
Sutton, Que.	C2	78
Sutton, Ak., U.S.	D5	74
Sutton, Ma., U.S.	g17	79
Sutton, Ne., U.S.	*B4	98
Sutton, N.H., U.S.	D8	104
Sutton, N.D., U.S.	D3	106
Sutton, Vt., U.S.	B7	111
Sutton, co., Tx., U.S.	B4	122
Sutton Coldfield, Eng., U.K.	D2	120
Sutton in Ashfield, Eng., U.K.	B6	12
Sutton Lake, res., W.V., U.S.	D6	10
Sutton Park, N.J., U.S.	C4	125
Suttons Bay, Mi., U.S.	B3	107
Sutton West, Ont.	D5	99
Suttsu, Japan	C5	73
Sutwik Island, i., Ak., U.S.	E10	33
Suunset, Fl., U.S.	D8	79
Suva, Fiji	I15	52
Suva Harbour, b., Fiji	I15	52
Suwa, Japan	m17	33
Suwałki, Pol.	A7	26
Suwanee, Ga., U.S.	B2	87
Suwannee, Fl., U.S.	C3	86
Suwannee, co., Fl., U.S.	B3	86
Suwannee, stm., U.S.	C4	86
Suwannee Sound, strt., Fl., U.S.	A1	70
Suwanose Island, i., Japan	L4	33
Suwaylih, Jord.	B7	41
Suwaymah, Jord.	h13	41
Suwŏn, S. Kor.	H3	33
Suxian, China	H7	32
Suyo, Peru	B1	58
Suzhou, China	E9	31
Suzu, Cape, c., Japan	H8	33
Suzuka, Japan	o15	33
Suzzara, Italy	E6	20
Svalbard, ter., Nor.	B13	128
Svaneke, Den.	C8	15
Svärtagård, Swe.	D7	104
Svärtan, stm., Swe.	B1	126
Svatovo, Sov. Un.	G12	27
Svay Rieng, Camb.	C3	34
Svealand, Swe.	C7	15
Sveg, Swe.	F6	14
Svendborg, Den.	C4	15
Svene, Nor.	p27	14
Svenljunga, Swe.	A7	15
Svensen, Or., U.S.	A3	114
Sverdlovsk, Sov. Un.	B3	39
Sverdlovsk, Sov. Un.	D9	29
Sverdrup Islands, is., N.W. Ter.	m32	66
Svetlaya, Sov. Un.	C9	33
Svetlograd, Sov. Un.	I14	27
Svicha, stm., Sov. Un.	D8	26
Svilajnac, Yugo.	C5	24
Svilengrad, Bul.	E8	24
Svindal, Nor.	p29	14
Svinninge, Den.	C5	15
Svir, stm., Sov. Un.	A10	27
Svirstroy, Sov. Un.	A9	27
Svishtov, Bul.	D7	24
Svitavy, Czech.	D4	26
Svobodnyy, Sov. Un.	D15	29
Svobodnyy, Cape, c., Sov. Un.	I33	33
Svyatoy Nos, Cape, c., Sov. Un.	B16	29
Swadlincote, Eng., U.K.	B6	12
Swaffham, Eng., U.K.	B8	12
Swain, co., N.C., U.S.	f9	110
Swain Mountain, mtn., Ar., U.S.	A2	81
Swain Reefs, rf., Austl.	D9	50
Swainsboro, Ga., U.S.	D4	87
Swakopmund, Nmb.	B1	49
Swale, stm., Eng., U.K.	C6	10
Swaledale, Ia., U.S.	B4	92
Swalwell, Alta.	D4	68
Swampscott, Ma., U.S.	B6	98
Swampton, N.C., U.S.	D4	87
Swan, Ia., U.S.	C4	92
Swan, stm., Alta.	B3	68
Swan, stm., Man.	C1	70
Swanage, Eng., U.K.	D6	12
Swan Creek, Il., U.S.	C3	90
Swan Creek, Ut., U.S.	B4	121
Swandale, W.V., U.S.	m14	125
Swan Falls, wtfl., Id., U.S.	F2	89
Swan Hill, Austl.	G7	50
Swan Hills, Alta.	B3	68
Swan Hills, hills, Alta.	B3	68
Swanington, In., U.S.	C3	91
Swan Lake, Man.	E2	70
Swanlake, Id., U.S.	G6	89
Swan Lake, Ms., U.S.	B3	101
Swan Lake, Mt., U.S.	C3	103
Swan Lake, l., Man.	C1	70
Swan Lake, l., Me., U.S.	D4	96
Swan Lake, l., Ne., U.S.	C2	104
Swannanoa, N.C., U.S.	f10	110
Swan Peak, mtn., Mt., U.S.	C3	103
Swanquarter, N.C., U.S.	B6	110
Swan Range, mts., Mt., U.S.	C3	103
Swan River, Man.	C1	70
Swan River, Mn., U.S.	C6	100
Swansboro, N.C., U.S.	C5	110
Swansea, Wales, U.K.	E4	10
Swansea, Il., U.S.	E4	90
Swansea, Ma., U.S.	C5	98
Swansea, S.C., U.S.	D5	117
Swansea Bay, b., Wales, U.K.	C4	12
Swansea Center, Ma., U.S.	C5	98
Swans Island, Me., U.S.	D4	96
Swanson, Sask.	F2	75
Swanson Lake, res., Ne., U.S.	D4	104
Swanton, Md., U.S.	m12	97
Swanton, Ne., U.S.	D8	104
Swanton, Oh., U.S.	A2	112
Swanton, Vt., U.S.	B2	122
Swan Valley, Id., U.S.	F7	89
Swanville, Me., U.S.	D4	96
Swanville, Mn., U.S.	E4	100
Swanwick, Il., U.S.	E4	90
Swanwyck Estates, De., U.S.	*B3	85
Swanzey Center, N.H., U.S.	E2	106
Swarthmore, Pa., U.S.	p20	115
Swartmore, Pa., U.S.	C7	40
Swartswood, N.J., U.S.	A3	107
Swartswood Lake, l., N.J., U.S.	A3	107
Swartz, La., U.S.	B4	95
Swartz Creek, Mi., U.S.	F7	99
Swatara, Mn., U.S.	C5	100
Swatara Township, Pa., U.S.	*F8	115
Swatow see Shantou, China	L8	31
Swayzee, In., U.S.	C6	91
Swaziland, ctry., Afr.	D5	49
Swea City, Ia., U.S.	A3	92
Swea City, Ia., U.S.	A3	92
Sweatman, Ms., U.S.	B4	101
Swedeborg, Mo., U.S.	D5	102
Sweden, ctry., Eur.	C5	14
Swedesboro, N.J., U.S.	D2	107
Sweeny, Tx., U.S.	r14	120
Sweet, Id., U.S.	F2	89
Sweet Briar, Va., U.S.	C3	123
Sweetgrass, Mt., U.S.	B5	103
Sweet Grass, co., Mt., U.S.	E7	103
Sweet Home, Or., U.S.	C4	114
Sweet Home, Tx., U.S.	E4	120
Sweetser, In., U.S.	C6	91
Sweet Springs, Mo., U.S.	C4	102
Sweet Valley, Pa., U.S.	D9	115
Sweetwater, Fl., U.S.	*G6	86
Sweetwater, Tn., U.S.	D9	119
Sweetwater, Ok., U.S.	B2	113
Sweetwater, Tx., U.S.	C2	120
Sweetwater, co., Wy., U.S.	E3	127
Sweetwater, stm., Wy., U.S.	D4	127
Sweetwater Creek, Fl., U.S.	p10	86
Sweetwater Creek, stm., Ok., U.S.	B1	113
Sweetwater Station, Wy., U.S.	D4	127
Swellendam, S. Afr.	D3	49
Swenson, Tx., U.S.	C2	120
Swepsonville, N.C., U.S.	A3	110
Świder, stm., Pol.	m14	26
Świdnica, Pol.	C3	26
Świdwin, Pol.	B3	26
Świebodzice, Pol.	C4	26
Świebodzin, Pol.	B3	26
Świecie, Pol.	B5	26
Świętochłowice, Pol.	g9	26
Świętokrzyskie, Góry, mts., Pol.	C6	26
Swift, Mn., U.S.	C3	100
Swift, co., Mn., U.S.	E3	100
Swift, stm., N.H., U.S.	B4	106
Swift Creek, stm., N.C., U.S.	B5	110
Swift Creek, stm., Va., U.S.	n17	123
Swift Creek Reservoir, res., Wa., U.S.	C3	124
Swift Current, Sask.	G2	75
Swiftcurrent Creek, stm., Sask.	H1	75
Swift Diamond, stm., N.H., U.S.	g7	106
Swifton, Ar., U.S.	B4	81
Swiftown, Ms., U.S.	B3	101
Swiftwater, N.H., U.S.	B3	106
Swilly, Lough, b., Ire.	A4	11
Swinburne, Cape, c., N.W. Ter.	B13	66
Swindle Island, i., B.C.	C3	69
Swindon, Eng., U.K.	E6	11
Swinford, Ire.	D3	11
Swink, Co., U.S.	C7	83
Swink, Ok., U.S.	C6	113
Swinomish Indian Reservation, Wa., U.S.	A3	124
Świnoujście, Pol.	B2	26
Swisher, Ia., U.S.	C6	92
Swisher, co., Tx., U.S.	B2	120
Swiss, W.V., U.S.	C3	125
Swisshome, Or., U.S.	C3	114
Swissvale, Pa., U.S.	k14	115
Switz City, In., U.S.	F3	91
Switzer, Mount, mtn., Isr.	B7	41
Switzerland, Fl., U.S.	m8	86
Switzerland, S.C., U.S.	C6	117
Switzerland, co., In., U.S.	G7	91
Switzerland, ctry., Eur.	C4	21
Swords, Ire.	D5	11
Swords, Ga., U.S.	C4	87
Swoyerville, Pa., U.S.	D10	115
Sycamore, Ga., U.S.	E3	87
Sycamore, Il., U.S.	B5	90
Sycamore, Ks., U.S.	E8	93
Sycamore, Oh., U.S.	B2	112
Sycamore, S.C., U.S.	E5	117
Sycamore Creek, stm., Tn., U.S.	A4	119
Sycamore Creek, stm., W.V., U.S.	m13	125
Sychevka, Sov. Un.	D10	27
Syców, Pol.	C4	26
Sydenham, Ont.	C8	73
Sydney, Austl.	F9	50
Sydney, N.S.	C9	71
Sydney Mines, N.S.	C9	71
Sykeston, N.D., U.S.	B6	111
Sykesville, Md., U.S.	B4	97
Sykesville, Pa., U.S.	C3	107
Sykesville, Pa., U.S.	D4	115
Syktyvkar, Sov. Un.	C8	29
Sylacauga, Al., U.S.	B3	78
Sylamore, Ar., U.S.	B3	81
Sylhet, Bngl.	D9	36
Sylling, Nor.	p28	14
Sylt, i., Ger.	A4	18
Sylva, N.C., U.S.	f9	110
Sylvan, Pa., U.S.	G5	115
Sylvan Beach, N.Y., U.S.	B5	109
Sylvan Grove, Ks., U.S.	C5	93
Sylvan Hills, Ar., U.S.	h10	81
Sylvania, Sask.	E3	75
Sylvania, Ga., U.S.	D5	87
Sylvania, Oh., U.S.	A2	112
Sylvania, Pa., U.S.	C8	115
Sylvan Lake, Alta.	C3	68
Sylvan Lake, Mi., U.S.	o15	99
Sylvan Lake, l., In., U.S.	B7	91
Sylvan Pass, Wy., U.S.	B2	127
Sylvarena, Ms., U.S.	C4	101
Sylvester, Ga., U.S.	E3	87
Sylvester, Tx., U.S.	C2	120
Sylvester, Mount, hill, Newf.	D4	72
Sylvia, Ks., U.S.	E5	93
Sylvia, Tn., U.S.	A4	119
Sym, stm., Sov. Un.	C26	8
Symmes Creek, stm., Oh., U.S.	D3	112
Symsonia, Ky., U.S.	f9	94
Syosset, N.Y., U.S.	*E7	109
Syracuse, In., U.S.	B6	91
Syracuse, Ks., U.S.	E2	93
Syracuse, Mo., U.S.	C5	102
Syracuse, Ne., U.S.	D9	104
Syracuse, N.Y., U.S.	B4	109
Syracuse, Oh., U.S.	D4	112
Syracuse, Ut., U.S.	B3	121
Syracuse see Siracusa, Italy	F5	23
Syr Darya, stm., Sov. Un.	E9	29
Syria, ctry., Asia	B3	38
Syriam, Burma	D2	35
Syrian Desert, des., Asia	B3	38
Syros see Ermoúpolis, Grc.	D5	40
Sysladobsis Lake, l., Me., U.S.	C4	96
Sysola, stm., Sov. Un.	C19	8
Syurkum, Cape, c., Sov. Un.	A10	33
Syzran, Sov. Un.	D7	29
Szabadszállás, Hung.	B4	24
Szamos (Someș), stm., Eur.	B6	24
Szamotuły, Pol.	B4	26
Szarvas, Hung.	B5	24
Szczakowa (part of Jaworzno), Pol.	g10	26
Szczebrzeszyn, Pol.	C7	26
Szczecin (Stettin), Pol.	B3	26
Szczecinek, Pol.	B4	26
Szczuczyn, Pol.	B7	26
Szczytno, Pol.	B6	26
Szechwan see Sichuan, prov., China	E5	31
Szeged, Hung.	B5	24
Székesfehérvár, Hung.	B4	24
Szekszárd, Hung.	B4	24
Szentendre, Hung.	B4	24
Szentes, Hung.	B5	24
Szigetvár, Hung.	B3	24
Szolnok, Hung.	B5	24
Szombathely, Hung.	B3	24
Szprotawa, Pol.	C3	26
Sztum, Pol.	B5	26
Szubin, Pol.	B4	26
Szydłowiec, Pol.	C6	26
Szymanów, Pol.	m12	26

T

Taal, Phil.	p13	34
Taal, Lake, l., Phil.	p13	34
Tab, In., U.S.	D3	91
Tabar Islands, is., Pap. N. Gui.	h13	50
Tabas, Iran	E8	39
Tabasco, state, Mex.	D6	63
Tabas Masīnā, Iran	E10	39
Tabatinga, Braz.	k7	56
Tabayin, Burma	A1	35
Tabbys Peak, mtn., Ut., U.S.	C3	121
Tabelbala, Alg.	E4	44
Taber, Alta.	E4	68
Tabernacle, N.J., U.S.	D3	107
Tabernas, Spain	D4	22
Tabernash, Co., U.S.	B5	83
Taberville, Mo., U.S.	C4	102
Tabik Island, i., Marsh Is.	S17	52
Tabiona, Ut., U.S.	C5	121
Tabiteuea, Kir.	R18	52
Tabla, Cerro de la, mtn., P.R.	B3	65
Tablas, Cabo, c., Chile	A2	54
Tablas Island, i., Phil.	C6	34
Table Bay, b., Newf.	B3	72
Table Bay, b., S. Afr.	D2	49
Table Grove, Il., U.S.	C3	90
Table Head, c., Newf.	B4	72
Table Mountain, mtn., Az., U.S.	E2	80
Table Rock, Ne., U.S.	D9	104
Table Rock Lake, res., U.S.	E4	102
Table Top, mtn., Az., U.S.	E3	80
Taboada, Spain	B2	22
Tábor, Czech.	D2	26
Tabor, Ia., U.S.	D2	92
Tabor, Mn., U.S.	B2	100
Tabor, S.D., U.S.	E8	118
Tabor, Mount, mtn., Isr.	B7	41
Tabora, Tan.	C5	48
Tabora, prov., Tan.	C5	48
Tabor City, N.C., U.S.	C4	110
Tabou, I.C.	F3	45
Tabrīz, Iran	B4	38
Tabuaeran (Fanning Island), atoll, Kir.	F12	6
Tabūk, Sau. Ar.	B2	38
Tabusintac, stm., N.B.	*H8	41
Täby, Swe.	t35	14
Tacámbaro de Codallos, Mex.	n13	63
Tacheng, China	B1	31
Tachie, stm., B.C.	B5	69
Tachikawa Point, c., Japan	P17	52
Tachikawa, Japan	n18	33
Táchira, state, Ven.	B3	60
Tachov, Czech.	D1	26
Tacloban, Phil.	C7	34
Tacna, Peru	E4	58
Tacna, Az., U.S.	E1	80
Tacna, dept., Peru	G4	58
Tacoma, Co., U.S.	F9	50
Tacoma, Wa., U.S.	B3	124

Taconic, Ct., U.S. — A2 84
Taconic Range, mts., U.S. — A1 98
Taconite, Mn., U.S. — C5 100
Tacoronte, Spain — m13 22
Tacuarembó, Ur. — E1 56
Tacuatí, Para. — D4 55
Tad, W.V., U.S. — m13 125
Tademaït, Plateau du, plat., Alg. — D5 44
Tadjoura, Dji. — C5 47
Tadoule Lake, l., Man. — f8 70
Tadoussac, Que. — A8 74
T'aebaek-Sanmaek, mts., Asia — H4 33
Taegu, S. Kor. — D10 31
Taejŏn, S. Kor. — D10 31
Taeyu-dong, N. Kor. — F2 33
Tafalla, Spain — A5 22
Tafí Viejo, Arg. — E2 55
Tafo, Ghana — *E4 45
Taft, Ca., U.S. — E4 82
Taft, La., U.S. — k11 95
Taft, Ok., U.S. — B6 113
Taft, Tn., U.S. — B5 119
Taft, Tx., U.S. — F4 120
Taftān, Kūh-e, mtn., Iran — G10 39
Taftsville, Vt., U.S. — D4 122
Tafuna International Airport, Am. Sam. — G13 52
Taganrog, Sov. Un. — H12 27
Taganrog, Gulf of, b., Sov. Un. — H12 27
Tagaytay, Phil. — o13 34
Tagbilaran, Phil. — D6 34
Taghmon, Ire. — E5 11
Taghrīfat, Libya — D3 43
Tagliamento, stm., Italy — C8 20
Tagolo Point, c., Phil. — D6 34
Taguan Point, c., Guam — L10 52
Taguatinga, Braz. — D1 57
Tagus, N.D., U.S. — A4 111
Tagus (Tejo) (Tajo), stm., Eur. — C1 22
Tahan, mtn., Malay. — E2 34
Tahat, mtn., Alg. — E6 44
Tahgong, Puntan, c., N. Mar. Is. — D7 52
Tahiti, i., Fr. Poly. — H13 6
Tahlequah, Ok., U.S. — B7 113
Ṭaḥmā wa Minshāt 'Abd as Sayyid, Eg. — E3 41
Tahoe, Lake, l., U.S. — E1 105
Tahoe City, Ca., U.S. — C3 82
Tahoka, Tx., U.S. — C2 120
Taholah, Wa., U.S. — B1 124
Tahoma, Ca., U.S. — C3 82
Tahoua, Niger — D6 45
Tahquamenon, stm., Mi., U.S. — B5 99
Tahsis, B.C. — E4 69
Ṭahṭā, Eg. — C3 38
Tahtsa Lake, l., B.C. — C4 69
Tahtsa Peak, mtn., B.C. — C4 69
Tahuya, Wa., U.S. — B2 124
Tai, I.C. — E3 45
Tai'an, China — D10 32
Tai'an, China — F7 32
Taiban, N.M., U.S. — C5 108
Taibus Qi, China — D6 32
T'aichung, Tai. — G9 31
Taigu, China — F5 32
Taihape, N.Z. — M15 51
Taiho, Japan — N6 52
Tai Hu, l., China — E8 31
Tailai, China — A10 32
Tailem Bend, Austl. — G6 50
Tailevu Point, c., Fiji — H15 52
Tain, Scot., U.K. — B4 10
T'ainan, Tai. — G9 31
Tainaron, Ákra, c., Grc. — D4 40
Taining, China — K7 32
Taiobeiras, Braz. — B4 56
Taipei, Tai. — G9 31
Taiping, Malay. — E2 34
Taipu, Braz. — g6 52
Taira see Iwaki, Japan — H10 33
Taishun, China — K8 32
Taitao, Península de, pen., Chile — D2 54
T'aitung, Tai. — G9 31
Taivalkoski, Fin. — E13 14
Taiwan, ctry., Asia — G9 31
Taiwan Strait, strt., Asia — G8 31
Taiyiba, Isr. — B7 41
Taiyuan, China — D7 31
Taizhao, China — E3 31
Taizhou, China — H8 32
Ta'izz, Yemen — D4 38
Tajarhī, Libya — E2 43
Tajik S.S.R., state, Sov. Un. — F9 29
Tajimi, Japan — I8 33
Tajique, N.M., U.S. — C3 108
Tajmulco, Volcán, vol., Guat. — C2 62
Tajuña, stm., Spain — B4 22
Tājūrā', Libya — C2 43
Tak, Thai. — B1 34
Takabanare Island, i., Japan — O6 52
Takahe, Mount, mtn., Ant. — B1 7
Takaka, N.Z. — N14 51
Takamatsu, Japan — E11 31
Takaoka, Japan — H8 33
Takapuna, N.Z. — L15 51
Takasaki, Japan — H9 33
Takashippu, Japan — O5 52
Takatō, Japan — n17 33
Takatsuki, Japan — o14 33
Takaw, Burma — B3 35
Takayama, Japan — H8 33
Takefu, Japan — n15 33
Take Islands see Tok Islands, is., Asia — H5 33
Takengon, Indon. — J2 35
Tākestān, Iran — J2 35
Takev, Camb. — G6 35
Takhta-Bazar, Sov. Un. — D11 39
Takhtakupyr, Sov. Un. — E6 28
Takijuq Lake, l., N.W. Ter. — C10 66
Takikawa, Japan — o13 33
Takilma, Or., U.S. — E3 114
Takishiri Island, i., Japan — D10 33
Takla Lake, l., B.C. — B5 69
Taklamakan Shamo, des., China — F11 29
Takoma Park, Md., U.S. — f8 97
Takotna, Ak., U.S. — C8 79
Takpocha, Okso, mtn., N. Mar. Is. — D7 52
Taku, I.C. — k23 79
Takua Pa, Thai. — H3 35
Taku Glacier, ice, Ak., U.S. — k22 79
Takut, Burma — A3 35
Talā, Eg. — D2 41
Tala, Mex. — m12 63
Tala, Ur. — E1 56
Talagante, Chile — A2 54
Talakan, Sov. Un. — B6 33
Talala, Ok., U.S. — A6 113

Talanga, Hond. — C4 62
Talara, Peru — B1 58
Talas, Sov. Un. — E8 28
Talasea, Pap. N. Gui. — k13 50
Talata Mafara, Nig. — D6 45
Talaud Islands, is., Indon. — E7 34
Talavera de la Reina, Spain — C3 22
Talawdī, Sud. — C3 47
Talbert, Ky., U.S. — C6 94
Talbot, In., U.S. — D3 91
Talbot, co., Ga., U.S. — D2 87
Talbot, co., Md., U.S. — C5 97
Talbot Lake, l., Man. — B2 70
Talbotton, Ga., U.S. — D2 87
Talca, Chile — B2 54
Talcahuano, Chile — D8 36
Tālcher, India — C5 120
Talco, Tx., U.S. — C5 120
Talcott, W.V., U.S. — D4 125
Talcottville, N.Y., U.S. — B5 109
Taldy-Kurgan, Sov. Un. — D9 28
Talent, Or., U.S. — E4 114
Tāleshī, Iran — C4 39
Taliabu, i., Indon. — F6 34
Taliaferro, co., Ga., U.S. — C4 87
Talica, Sov. Un. — B6 28
Talihina, Ok., U.S. — C6 113
Talim Island, i., Phil. — o13 34
Tali Post, Sud. — D3 47
Talisay, Phil. — o14 34
Talisheek, La., U.S. — D6 95
Talish Mountains, mts., Asia — B4 39
Talitsa, Sov. Un. — B9 79
Talkeetna, Ak., U.S. — C10 79
Talkeetna Mountains, mts., Ak., U.S. — f17 79
Ṭalkhā, Eg. — C3 41
Talking Rock, Ga., U.S. — B2 87
Talkotna, Ok., U.S. — g11 41
Talladega, Al., U.S. — B4 95
Talladega, co., Al., U.S. — B3 78
Talladega Mountain, mtn., Al., U.S. — B3 78
Talladega Springs, Al., U.S. — D14 40
Tallahala Creek, stm., Ms., U.S. — D4 101
Tallahassee, Fl., U.S. — B2 86
Tallahatchie, co., Ms., U.S. — B3 101
Tallahatchie, stm., Ms., U.S. — B3 101
Tall al Abyaḍ, Syria — B3 38
Tallangatta, Austl. — H6 51
Tallant, Ok., U.S. — A5 113
Tallapoosa, Ga., U.S. — C1 87
Tallapoosa, Mo., U.S. — E8 102
Tallapoosa, co., Al., U.S. — C4 78
Tallapoosa, stm., Al., U.S. — C3 78
Tallard, Fr. — E12 20
Tallassee, Al., U.S. — DzA3 85
Talleyville, De., U.S. — D5 29
Tallmadge, Oh., U.S. — A4 112
Tallow, Ire. — E3 11
Tallula, Il., U.S. — D4 90
Tallulah, La., U.S. — B4 95
Ṭallūzā, Isr. Occ. — f12 41
Talmage, Sask. — H4 75
Talmage, Ks., U.S. — C6 93
Talmage, Ne., U.S. — D9 104
Talmage, Ne., U.S. — C5 121
Talnoye, Sov. Un. — G8 27
Talo, mtn., Eth. — C4 27
Talofofo, Guam — M10 52
Talofofo Bay, b., Guam — M10 52
Taloga, Ok., U.S. — A3 113
Talon, Lake, l., Ont. — A5 73
Talowah, Ms., U.S. — D4 101
Talpa, Tx., U.S. — D3 120
Talpa de Allende, Mex. — m11 63
Talquin, Lake, res., Fl., U.S. — B2 86
Talsi, Sov. Un. — C4 27
Taltal, Chile — E1 55
Taltson, stm., N.W. Ter. — C5 92
Talugtug He, stm., China — B10 31
Taluyuan, China — C4 33
Talwood, Austl. — G8 34
Tama, Ia., U.S. — B5 92
Tamacuarí, Pico, mtn., S.A. — C5 60
Tamaha, Ok., U.S. — B7 113
Tamalameque, Col. — B3 60
Tamale, Ghana — E4 45
Tamalpais, Mount, mtn., Ca., U.S. — h7 82
Tamalpais Valley, Ca., U.S. — *D2 82
Taman, Sov. Un. — I11 27
Tamana, Mount, hill, Trin. — O23 43
Tamanar, Mor. — I6 33
Tamano, Japan — E10 115
Tamaqua, Pa., U.S. — A3 15
Tamar, stm., Eng., U.K. — E2 43
Tamarac, Fl., U.S. — *r13 86
Tamaroa, Il., U.S. — D5 100
Tamarite [de Literal], Spain — B6 22
Tamaroa, Il., U.S. — E4 90
Tamassee, S.C., U.S. — B1 117
Tamaulipas, state, Mex. — C5 63
Tamazula de Gordiano, Mex. — n12 63
Tamazulapan [del Progreso], Mex. — o15 63
Tamazunchale, Mex. — C5 63
Tambach, Kenya — A6 48
Tambacounda, Sen. — D2 45
Tambaú, Braz. — k8 56
També, Braz. — C3 57
Tambelan Besar, i., Indon. — L7 35
Tambelan Islands, is., Indon. — E3 34
Tambo, Austl. — B6 51
Tambo, stm., Peru — E3 58
Tambo, stm., Peru — D3 58
Tambo Grande, Peru — B1 58
Tambohorano, Madag. — g8 49
Tambov, Sov. Un. — D7 26
Tambre, stm., Spain — A2 22
Tamchakett, Maur. — C2 45
Tamdybulak, Sov. Un. — E6 28
Tame, Col. — B3 60
Tâmega, stm., Port. — B2 22
Tamel Aike, Arg. — D2 54
Tamenghest, Alg. — E6 44
Tamenghest, Oued, val., Alg. — D2 45
Tamgué, Massif du, mts., Gui. — D2 45
Tamiahua, Mex. — C5 63
Tamiahua, Laguna de, b., Mex. — D7 52
Tamiami, Fl., U.S. — *G6 86
Tamiami Canal, Fl., U.S. — G6 86
Tamil Nadu (Madras), state, India — G6 36
Tamina, Tx., U.S. — D5 120
Tamiš, Switz. — C7 21
Tamiš, stm., Eur. — C5 24
Tam Ky, Viet. — E8 35
Tamms, Il., U.S. — F4 90
Tamo, Ar., U.S. — C4 81
Tamora, Ne., U.S. — D8 104

Tampa, Fl., U.S. — E4 86
Tampa Bay, b., Fl., U.S. — E4 86
Tampere, Fin. — G10 14
Tampico, Mex. — C5 63
Tampico, Il., U.S. — B4 90
Tampico, In., U.S. — G6 91
Tampico, Mt., U.S. — B10 103
Tams, W.V., U.S. — D3 125
Tamsagbulag, Mong. — B8 31
Tamshiyacu, Peru — D4 60
Tamuning, Guam — L10 52
Tamworth, Austl. — F9 50
Tamworth, Ont. — C8 73
Tamworth, Eng., U.K. — B6 12
Tamworth, N.H., U.S. — C4 106
Tana, Chile — B12 14
Tana, stm., Kenya — B7 48
Tana, Lake, l., Eth. — C4 47
Tanabe, Japan — J7 33
Tanabi, Braz. — C3 56
Tanacross, Ak., U.S. — C11 79
Tanafjorden, Nor. — B13 14
Tanaga Island, i., Ak., U.S. — E4 79
Tanahbala, i., Indon. — F1 34
Tanahgrogot, Indon. — F5 34
Tanahmasa, i., Indon. — F1 34
Tanakpur, India — C8 37
Tanami, Austl. — C4 50
Tan An, Viet. — G7 35
Tanana, Ak., U.S. — B9 79
Tanana, stm., Ak., U.S. — C10 79
Tananarive see Antananarivo, Madag. — g9 49
Tanapag, N. Mar. Is. — D8 52
Tanapag, Lagunan, b., N. Mar. Is. — D7 52
Tanaro, stm., Italy — B2 23
Tanaunella, Italy — D2 23
Tanavuso Point, c., Fiji — H15 52
Tancheng, China — G8 32
Tanchŏn, N. Kor. — F4 33
Tancook Island, i., N.S. — E5 71
Tända, India — D9 37
Tāndalfī, Sud. — C3 47
Tāndārei, Rom. — C8 24
Tandil, Arg. — B5 54
Tando Ādam, Pak. — E2 37
Tandou Lake, l., Austl. — F3 51
Tanega Island, i., Japan — E11 31
Tanegashima Strait, strt., Japan — K5 33
Taney, co., Mo., U.S. — E4 102
Taneycomo, Lake, res., Mo., U.S. — E4 102
Taneytown, Md., U.S. — A3 97
Taneyville, Mo., U.S. — E4 102
Tanezrouft, des., Afr. — E4 44
Tanga, Tan. — C6 48
Tanga, prov., Tan. — B6 48
Tanganyika, Lake, l., Afr. — C4 48
Tangent, Or., U.S. — C3 114
Tangerhütte, Ger. — A6 19
Tangermünde, Ger. — B5 18
Tanggula Shan, mts., China — E3 31
Tanghe, China — E7 31
Tangier (Tanger), Mor. — B3 44
Tangier, In., U.S. — E3 91
Tangier, Va., U.S. — C7 123
Tangier Island, i., Va., U.S. — C6 123
Tangier Sound, strt., Md., U.S. — D6 97
Tangipahoa, La., U.S. — D5 95
Tangipahoa, co., La., U.S. — D5 95
Tangipahoa, stm., La., U.S. — D5 95
Tanglewood, Fl., U.S. — *F5 86
Tangra Yumco, l., China — B8 36
Tangshan, China — D8 31
Tanguiéta, Benin — D5 45
Tanguisson Point, c., Guam — L10 52
Tangwang He, stm., China — B10 31
Tangyuan, China — C4 33
Tanimbar Islands, is., Indon. — G8 34
Taninges, Fr. — F6 36
Tanjore see Thanjāvūr, India — F5 36
Tanjung, Indon. — F5 34
Tanjungbalai, Indon. — E1 34
Tanjungpandan, Indon. — F3 34
Tanjungpinang, Indon. — E5 34
Tānk, Pak. — B5 36
Tännäs, Swe. — F5 14
Tanner, Al., U.S. — A3 78
Tanner, W.V., U.S. — C4 125
Tanner, Mount, mtn., B.C. — E8 69
Tannersville, N.Y., U.S. — C6 109
Tannis Bugt, b., Den. — A4 15
Tannu-Ola Mountains, mts., Asia — A3 31
Tânout, Niger — C6 45
Tanpok, stm., Fr. Gu. — B4 59
Tanque Verde, Az., U.S. — E5 80
Ṭanṭā, Eg. — B3 38
Tantallon, Sask. — G5 75
Tantani, stm., Peru — m11 34
Tantoyuca, Mex. — m14 63
Tanum (Tanumshede), Swe. — H4 14
Tanzania, ctry., Afr. — C5 48
Tao, i., Thai. — G3 35
Tao'an, China — B9 31
Tao'er He, stm., China — B9 31
Taopi, Mn., U.S. — G6 100
Taormina, Italy — F5 23
Taos, Mo., U.S. — C5 102
Taos, N.M., U.S. — A4 108
Taos, co., N.M., U.S. — A4 108
Taos Pueblo, N.M., U.S. — A4 108
Taoudenni, Mali — B4 45
Taoyuan, China — J4 32
Tapachula, Mex. — C2 45
Tapajós, stm., Braz. — D6 59
Tapaktuan, Indon. — E6 34
Tapalquén, Arg. — B5 54
Tapanui, N.Z. — P12 51
Tapauá, Braz. — C4 58
Tapauá, stm., Braz. — C4 58
Tapejara, Braz. — B2 57
Tapeoca, N.C., U.S. — f9 110
Tappahannock, Va., U.S. — C5 123
Tappan, N.Y., U.S. — g13 109
Tappan Lake, res., N.J., U.S. — g9 107
Tappan Lake, res., Oh., U.S. — B4 112
Tappen, N.D., U.S. — C6 111
Tapuaenuku, mtn., N.Z. — N14 51

Taputapu, Cape, c., Am. Sam. — G13 52
Taqāṭu' Ḥayyā, Sud. — B4 47
Taquara, Braz. — D2 56
Taquari, stm., Braz. — B1 56
Taquari, stm., Braz. — D2 56
Taquaritinga, Braz. — k7 56
Taquaritinga do Norte, Braz. — h5 57
Tar, stm., N.C., U.S. — B5 110
Tara, Ont. — C3 73
Tara, Sov. Un. — D10 29
Tara, stm., Sov. Un. — B9 28
Tara, Yugo. — D4 24
Tara, Hill of, hist., Ire. — D5 11
Tarabai, Braz. — C2 56
Tara Hills, Ca., U.S. — *h8 82
Tarakan, Indon. — E5 34
Taraklya, Sov. Un. — D5 34
Tarancón, Spain — B4 22
Taransay, i., Scot., U.K. — C1 13
Taranto, Italy — D6 23
Taranto, Gulf of, b., Italy — D6 23
Tarapacá, Col. — D4 60
Tarapacá, prov., Chile — C2 54
Tarapoto, Peru — C2 58
Tarare, Fr. — F4 16
Tarascon-sur-Ariège, Fr. — F4 16
Tarascon-sur-Rhône, Fr. — F6 16
Tarasp, Switz. — C9 21
Tarata, Bol. — C2 54
Tarata, Peru — E3 58
Tarauacá, Braz. — C3 58
Tarauacá, stm., Braz. — C3 58
Tarawa, atoll, Kir. — F10 6
Tarawera, N.Z. — M16 51
Tarazit, Massif de, mts., Niger — g9 49
Tarazona, Spain — B5 22
Tarazona [de la Mancha], Spain — C5 22
Tarbagatay Range, mts., Asia — B10 30
Tarbat Ness, c., Scot., U.K. — B5 10
Tarbellville, Vt., U.S. — E3 122
Tarbert, Ire. — E2 11
Tarbert, Scot., U.K. — C3 13
Tarbert, Scot., U.K. — E3 13
Tarbes, Fr. — F4 16
Tarbet, Scot., U.K. — D4 13
Tarboro, Ga., U.S. — E5 87
Tarboro, N.C., U.S. — B5 110
Tarbū, Libya — D3 43
Tarcenay, Fr. — B1 21
Tarcento, Italy — C9 20
Tarcoola, Austl. — F5 50
Tardoki-Yani, Mount, mtn., Sov. Un. — B9 33
Taree, Austl. — F9 50
Tarentum, Pa., U.S. — E2 115
Tarfawi, Bi'r, well, Sud. — A3 47
Tarfaya, Mor. — C2 44
Tarfside, Scot., U.K. — D6 13
Targhee Pass, U.S. — E7 89
Tarhūnah, Libya — C2 43
Tarifa, Spain — D3 22
Tarifa, Point, c., Spain — D3 22
Tariffville, Ct., U.S. — B5 84
Tarigtig Point, c., Phil. — n14 34
Tarija, Bol. — D3 55
Tarija, dept., Bol. — D3 55
Tarim, stm., China — E11 29
Tarim Pendi, des., China — E11 29
Tarkastad, S. Afr. — D4 49
Tarkiln, R.I., U.S. — B3 116
Tarkio, Mo., U.S. — A2 102
Tarko-Sale, Sov. Un. — C24 8
Tarkwa, Ghana — E4 45
Tarlac, Phil. — B6 34
Tarland, Scot., U.K. — C6 13
Tarlton, Oh., U.S. — C3 112
Tarm, Den. — C2 15
Tarma, Peru — D2 58
Tarn, stm., Fr. — F4 16
Tarna, stm., Hung. — B4 24
Tarnobrzeg, Pol. — B6 26
Tarnopol, Sask. — E3 75
Tarnov, Ne., U.S. — C6 104
Tarnów, Pol. — B6 26
Tarnowskie Góry, Pol. — B5 22
Taro, stm., Italy — D2 23
Tarom, Austl. — B7 51
Taroudant, Mor. — D4 44
Tarp, Ger. — D4 82
Tarpey, S.J., U.S. — E2 120
Tarpley, Tx., U.S. — E3 120
Tarpon, Lake, l., Fl., U.S. — o10 86
Tarpon Springs, Fl., U.S. — D4 86
Tarqui, Peru — B1 58
Tarquinia, Italy — B2 23
Tarragona, Spain — B6 22
Tarrant, Al., U.S. — f7 78
Tarrant, co., Tx., U.S. — C4 120
Tarrant City, Al., U.S. — B3 78
Tarrasa, Spain — B7 22
Tarry, Ar., U.S. — C4 81
Tarryall Creek, stm., Co., U.S. — B5 83
Tarryall Mountains, mts., Co., U.S. — B5 83
Tarrytown, Ga., U.S. — D4 87
Tarrytown, N.Y., U.S. — D7 109
Tars, Den. — A4 15
Tarsus, Tur. — D10 40
Tartagal, Arg. — D3 55
Tartu, Sov. Un. — B7 26
Tartuguan Point, c., Guam — M10 52
Ţarţūs, Syria — E10 40
Tarutung, Indon. — L3 35
Tarver, Ga., U.S. — F4 87
Tarvin, Sov. Un. — D2 43
Tasajera, Sov. Un. — C6 45
Tasawāh, Libya — D2 43
Taseko, stm., B.C. — D6 69
Taseko Lakes, l., B.C. — D6 69
Taseko Mountain, mtn., B.C. — D6 69
Tashauz, Sov. Un. — E5 28
Tashkent, Sov. Un. — E8 28
Tash-Kumyr, Sov. Un. — E9 28
Tashmalaya, Indon. — m11 34
Tasman Bay, b., N.Z. — N14 51
Tasmania, state, Austl. — o15 50
Tasman Peninsula, pen., Austl. — o15 50
Tasman Sea, Oc. — I9 6
Tasso, Sov. Un. — D9 29
Taswell, In., U.S. — H4 91
Tata, Hung. — B4 24
Tatabánya, Hung. — B4 24
Tatamagouche, N.S. — D6 71
Tatarbunary, Sov. Un. — C9 24
Tatarsk, Sov. Un. — D9 29
Tatar Strait, strt., Sov. Un. — D17 29
Tate, Sask. — B3 75
Tate, Ga., U.S. — B2 87

Tate, co., Ms., U.S. — A4 101
Tateville, Ky., U.S. — D5 94
Tateyama, Japan — I9 33
Tathlina Lake, l., N.W. Ter. — D9 66
Tatitlek, Ak., U.S. — C10 79
Tatla Lake, l., B.C. — C4 110
Tatlayoko Lake, B.C. — C5 69
Tatnam, Cape, c., Man. — f9 77
Tatta, Pak. — D2 36
Tattersall, Eng., U.K. — A7 12
Tattnall, co., Ga., U.S. — D4 87
Tatui, Braz. — C3 56
Tatum, N.M., U.S. — D6 108
Tatum, S.C., U.S. — B8 117
Tatumville, Tn., U.S. — A2 119
Tatvan, Tur. — C14 40
Tauá, Braz. — C2 57
Taubaté, Braz. — C3 56
Tauber, stm., Ger. — D4 19
Tauberbischofsheim, Ger. — D4 19
Taucha, Ger. — D7 19
Tauern Tunnel, Aus. — C9 20
Taughmaconnell, Ire. — D3 11
Taumarunui, N.Z. — L15 51
Taum Sauk Mountain, mtn., Mo., U.S. — D6 102
Taung, Boph. — C3 49
Taungdwingyi, Burma — D10 36
Taunggyi, Burma — D10 36
Taunton, Eng., U.K. — E5 10
Taunton, Ma., U.S. — C5 98
Taunton, Mn., U.S. — F2 100
Taunton, stm., Ma., U.S. — C5 98
Taunton Lakes, N.J., U.S. — D3 107
Taunus, stm., Ger. — C5 19
Taupo, Lake, l., N.Z. — M15 51
Tauragé, Sov. Un. — D4 27
Tauranga, N.Z. — L16 51
Taureau, Réservoir, res., Que. — C4 74
Taurianova, Italy — E6 23
Tauro Point, c., N.Z. — K14 51
Taurus Mountains, mts., Tur. — D8 40
Tauste, Spain — B5 22
Tavannes, Switz. — B3 21
Tavares, Fl., U.S. — D5 86
Tavas, Tur. — D7 25
Tavda, Sov. Un. — D9 29
Tavda, stm., Sov. Un. — D9 29
Tavernier, N.J., U.S. — G6 86
Tavernier, Fl., U.S. — H16 52
Tavernes, Sov. Un. — C5 73
Tavira, Port. — D3 22
Tavistock, Ont. — D4 73
Tavistock, Eng., U.K. — E2 10
Tavolzhan, Sov. Un. — D9 29
Tavoy Point, c., Burma — F2 35
Tavşanlı, Tur. — C7 40
Taw, stm., Eng., U.K. — D4 12
Tawakoni, Lake, res., Tx., U.S. — C4 120
Tawas City, Mi., U.S. — D7 99
Tawas Lake, l., Mi., U.S. — D7 99
Tawatinaw, Alta. — B4 68
Tawau, Malay. — E5 34
Tawe, stm., Wales, U.K. — C4 12
Tawitawi Group, is., Phil. — D6 34
Tawi-Tawi Island, i., Phil. — D5 34
Ţawkar, Sud. — B4 47
Tawny, Ire. — B4 11
Ţawurghā', Libya — C3 43
Taxco de Alarcón, Mex. — n14 63
Tay, stm., Scot., U.K. — B5 10
Tay, Firth of, est., Scot., U.K. — B5 10
Tay, Loch, l., Scot., U.K. — B4 10
Tayabamba, Peru — C2 58
Tayasir, Isr. Occ. — f12 41
Taycheedah, Wi., U.S. — k9 126
Tayga, Sov. Un. — B11 28
Taylor, B.C. — A7 69
Taylor, Az., U.S. — C5 80
Taylor, Mi., U.S. — p15 99
Taylor, Ne., U.S. — C6 104
Taylor, N.D., U.S. — C3 111
Taylor, Pa., U.S. — D10 115
Taylor, Tx., U.S. — D4 120
Taylor, Wi., U.S. — D2 126
Taylor, co., Fl., U.S. — B3 86
Taylor, co., Ga., U.S. — D2 87
Taylor, co., Ia., U.S. — D2 92
Taylor, co., Ky., U.S. — C4 94
Taylor, co., Tx., U.S. — C3 120
Taylor, co., W.V., U.S. — B4 125
Taylor, co., Wi., U.S. — C3 126
Taylor, stm., Man. — C2 70
Taylor, Mount, mtn., N.M., U.S. — B2 108
Taylor Knob, hill, Tn., U.S. — G10 119
Taylor Mill, Ky., U.S. — k14 94
Taylor Mountain, mtn., Id., U.S. — E4 89
Taylor Park Reservoir, res., Co., U.S. — C4 83
Taylor Ridge, mtn., Ga., U.S. — B1 87
Taylors, S.C., U.S. — B3 117
Taylors Bridge, De., U.S. — C3 85
Taylors Falls, Mn., U.S. — E6 100
Taylors Island, Md., U.S. — D5 97
Taylors Island, i., Md., U.S. — D5 97
Taylorsport, Ky., U.S. — h13 94
Taylor Springs, Il., U.S. — D4 90
Taylorsville, Ga., U.S. — B2 87
Taylorsville, In., U.S. — F6 91
Taylorsville, Ky., U.S. — B4 94
Taylorsville, Ms., U.S. — D4 101
Taylorsville, N.C., U.S. — B1 110
Taylorsville, Ut., U.S. — *C4 121
Taylorville, Il., U.S. — D4 90
Taymā, Sau. Ar. — D7 43
Taymouth, N.B. — C3 71
Taymyr Lake, l., Sov. Un. — B13 29
Taymyr Peninsula, pen., Sov. Un. — B12 29
Tay Ninh, Viet. — G7 35
Tayport, Scot., U.K. — B6 13
Tayshet, Sov. Un. — D12 29
Tayside, prov., Scot., U.K. — D5 13
Taytay, Phil. — B6 34
Taytsy, Sov. Un. — s31 14
Taz, stm., Sov. Un. — C11 29
Taza, Mor. — B5 44
Taz Bay, b., Sov. Un. — C7 28
Tazerbo, well, Libya — D4 43
Tazewell, Tn., U.S. — C10 119
Tazewell, Va., U.S. — e10 123
Tazewell, co., Il., U.S. — C4 90
Tazewell, co., Va., U.S. — e10 123
Tazrouk, Alg. — E6 44
Tazin Lake, l., Sask. — l13 75
Tbessa, Alg. — B7 44
Tbilisi, Sov. Un. — E7 26
Tchibanga, Gabon — F2 46

Tchien, Lib. — E3 45
Tchula, Ms., U.S. — B3 101
Tczew, Pol. — A5 26
Tea, S.D., U.S. — D9 118
Tea, stm., Braz. — D4 60
Teachey, N.C., U.S. — C4 110
Tea Creek, stm., Sask. — C2 75
Teague, Tx., U.S. — D4 120
Teakean Butte, mtn., Id., U.S. — C2 89
Te Anau, Lake, l., N.Z. — P11 51
Teaneck, N.J., U.S. — h8 107
Teapa, Mex. — D6 63
Tearaght, i., Ire. — E1 11
Tearinibai, Kir. — R18 52
Teasdale, Ut., U.S. — E4 121
Teaticket, Ma., U.S. — C6 98
Tea Tree Gully, Austl. — *F6 50
Te Awamutu, N.Z. — M15 51
Tebbetts, Mo., U.S. — C6 102
Tebicuary, stm., Para. — D4 55
Tebingtinggi, Indon. — E1 34
Tecalitlán, Mex. — n12 63
Teche, Bayou, stm., La., U.S. — D4 95
Techirghiol, Rom. — C9 24
Tecka, Arg. — C2 54
Tecolotito, N.M., U.S. — B4 108
Tecolutla, stm., Mex. — m15 63
Tecomán, Mex. — D4 63
Tecopa, Ca., U.S. — E5 82
Tecpan de Galeana, Mex. — D4 63
Tecuala, Mex. — C3 63
Tecuci, Rom. — C8 24
Tecumseh, Ont. — E2 73
Tecumseh, Ks., U.S. — k14 93
Tecumseh, Mi., U.S. — G7 99
Tecumseh, Ne., U.S. — D9 104
Tecumseh, Ok., U.S. — B5 113
Tecumseh, Mount, mtn., N.H., U.S. — C3 106
Ted Ceidaar Dabole, Som. — E5 47
Tedrow, Oh., U.S. — A1 112
Tedzhen, Sov. Un. — C10 39
Teec Nos Pos, Az., U.S. — A6 80
Teegarden, In., U.S. — B5 91
Tees, Alta. — C4 68
Teegarden, In., U.S. — B5 91
Tees, stm., Eng., U.K. — C6 10
Teesside see Middlesbrough, Eng., U.K. — C6 10
Teeswater, Ont. — C3 73
Tefé, stm., Braz. — C4 59
Tefé, Braz. — B4 58
Tefé, Lago de, l., Braz. — C2 59
Tefenni, Tur. — D7 25
Tefft, In., U.S. — B4 91
Tegal, Indon. — G3 34
Tegelen, Neth. — C6 17
Tegern Lake, l., Ger. — B7 20
Teglio, Italy — D9 21
Tegucigalpa, Hond. — C3 62
Teguise, Spain — m15 22
Tehachapi, Ca., U.S. — E4 82
Tehachapi Mountains, mts., Ca., U.S. — E4 82
Tehama, co., Ca., U.S. — B2 82
Tehama, Ca., U.S. — B2 82
Tehek Lake, l., N.W. Ter. — C13 66
Tehran, Iran — B5 38
Tehri, India — B7 37
Tehuacán, Mex. — D5 63
Tehuantepec, Mex. — D5 63
Tehuantepec, Golfo de, b., Mex. — D6 63
Tehuitzingo, Mex. — n14 63
Teide, Pico de, mtn., Spain — m13 22
Teifi, stm., Wales, U.K. — B3 12
Teignmouth, Eng., U.K. — E4 12
Teiteiripucchi, i., Marsh Is. — S18 52
Tekamah, Ne., U.S. — C9 104
Tekapo, Lake, l., N.Z. — O13 51
Tekax de Álvaro Obregón, Mex. — C7 63
Tekeli, Sov. Un. — E9 28
Tekeze, stm., Afr. — C6 47
Tekirdağ, Tur. — B1 40
Tekkali, India — H10 37
Tekoa, Wa., U.S. — B8 124
Tekoa, Mi., U.S. — F5 99
Tekro, well, Chad — D3 47
Te Kuiti, N.Z. — M15 51
Tel, stm., India — D7 36
Tela, Hond. — D7 63
Telavi, Sov. Un. — E3 28
Tel Aviv-Yafo (Tel Aviv-Jaffa), Isr. — B3 38
Telde, Spain — m14 22
Telegraph Creek, B.C. — m16 69
Telén, Arg. — C2 54
Teleneshty, Sov. Un. — B9 24
Teleorman, stm., Rom. — C7 24
Telephone, Tx., U.S. — C5 120
Télérthéba, Djebel, mtn., Alg. — E6 44
Telescope Peak, mtn., Ca., U.S. — D5 82
Telfair, co., Ga., U.S. — E4 87
Telford, Eng., U.K. — B5 12
Telford, Pa., U.S. — F11 115
Telford, Tn., U.S. — C11 119
Telfs, Aus. — B2 45
Télimélé, Gui. — D2 45
Telkwa, B.C. — B4 69
Tell, Tx., U.S. — B2 120
Tell City, In., U.S. — I4 91
Teller, Ak., U.S. — B6 79
Teller, co., Co., U.S. — C5 83
Tellico Plains, Tn., U.S. — D9 119
Tellin, Bel. — D3 83
Tel Mond, Isr. — B6 41
Telogia, Fl., U.S. — B2 86
Telok Anson (Teluk Intan), Malay. — E2 34
Teloloapan, Mex. — D5 63
Telos Lake, l., Me., U.S. — B3 96
Telsen, Arg. — C3 54
Tema, Ghana — E5 45
Temax, Mex. — C7 63
Tembo, Zaire — C2 48
Temecula, Ca., U.S. — F5 82
Temelli, Tur. — C8 40
Temirtau, Sov. Un. — D10 29
Témiscaming, Que. — G17 8
Temora, Austl. — G6 51
Temósachic, Mex. — B3 63
Tempe, Az., U.S. — D4 80
Tempe Downs, Austl. — D5 50
Temperance, Mi., U.S. — G7 99
Temperance, stm., Mn., U.S. — C8 100
Temperanceville, Va., U.S. — C7 123
Tempio Pausania, Italy — D2 23
Temple, Ga., U.S. — C1 87

Name	Map Ref.	Page
Temple, Mi., U.S.	D5	99
Temple, N.H., U.S.	E3	106
Temple, Ok., U.S.	C3	113
Temple, Pa., U.S.	F10	115
Temple, Tx., U.S.	D4	120
Temple City, Ca., U.S.	*m12	82
Temple Hill, Ky., U.S.	D4	94
Templemore, Ire.	E4	11
Temple Terrace, Fl., U.S.	o11	86
Templeton, In., U.S.	C3	91
Templeton, Ia., U.S.	C3	92
Templeton, Ma., U.S.	A3	98
Templeton, Pa., U.S.	E3	115
Templeville, Md., U.S.	B6	97
Templin, Ger.	B6	18
Tempoal, stm., Mex.	m14	63
Temryuk, Sov. Un.	I11	27
Temuco, Chile	B2	54
Temuka, N.Z.	P13	51
Temwen, i., Micron.	Q17	52
Tena, Ec.	B2	58
Tenafly, N.J., U.S.	B5	107
Tenaha, Tx., U.S.	D5	120
Tenakee Springs, Ak., U.S.	D12	79
Tenāli, India	*E7	36
Tenancingo [de Degollado], Mex.	D5	63
Tenango del Valle, Mex.	n14	63
Tenant Mountain, mtn., N.Y., U.S.	B6	109
Tenants Harbor, Me., U.S.	E3	96
Tenasserim, Burma	F10	36
Tenay, Fr.	E6	16
Tenby, Wales, U.K.	C3	12
Tendaho, Eth.	C5	47
Tende, Fr.	E7	16
Ten Degree Channel, strt., India	G9	36
Tendoy, Id., U.S.	E5	89
Tendre, Mont, mtn., Switz.	C2	20
Ténéré, des., Niger	C7	45
Tenerife, i., Spain	m13	22
Tênès, Alg.	B5	44
Teng, stm., Burma	B2	35
Tengah Islands, is., Indon.	G5	34
Tengchong, China	F4	31
Tengiz, i., Sov. Un.	D9	29
Tengxian, China	G7	32
Tenino, Wa., U.S.	C3	124
Tenke, Zaire	D4	48
Tenkiller Ferry Lake, res., Ok., U.S.	B6	113
Tenkodogo, Burkina	D4	45
Ten Mile, Tn., U.S.	D9	119
Tenmile, stm., U.S.	B5	116
Tenmile Creek, stm., W.V., U.S.	k10	125
Ten Mile Lake, l., Newf.	C3	72
Tenmile Lake, l., Mn., U.S.	D4	100
Tennant, Ia., U.S.	C2	92
Tennant Creek, Austl.	C5	50
Tennent, N.J., U.S.	C4	107
Tennessee, Il., U.S.	C3	90
Tennessee, state, U.S.	B5	119
Tennessee, stm., U.S.	D10	76
Tennessee City, Tn., U.S.	A4	119
Tennessee Pass, Co., U.S.	B4	83
Tennessee Ridge, Tn., U.S.	A4	119
Tennga, Ga., U.S.	B1	87
Tennille, Ga., U.S.	D4	87
Tennyson, In., U.S.	H3	91
Tenosique [de Pino Suárez], Mex.	D6	63
Tenryū, stm., Japan	n16	33
Tensas, co., La., U.S.	B4	95
Tensas, stm., La., U.S.	B4	95
Tensaw, stm., Al., U.S.	E2	78
Tensed, Id., U.S.	B2	89
Ten Sleep, Wy., U.S.	B5	127
Tenstrike, Mn., U.S.	C4	100
Tenterfield, Austl.	E9	50
Ten Thousand Islands, is., Fl., U.S.	G5	86
Teoccaltiche, Mex.	C4	63
Teófilo Otoni, Braz.	B4	56
Tepa, Indon.	G7	34
Tepalcatepec, Mex.	n12	63
Tepalcatepec, stm., Mex.	n12	63
Tepatitlán [de Morelos], Mex.	C4	63
Tepeji del Río, Mex.	n14	63
Tepelena, Alb.	B2	25
Tepepan (part of Mexico City), Mex.	h9	63
Tepic, Mex.	C4	63
Teplice, Czech.	C2	26
Tepoca, Cabo, c., Mex.	A2	63
Tequila, Mex.	m12	63
Ter, stm., Spain	A7	22
Téra, Niger	D5	45
Teraina Island (Washington Island), i., Kir.	F12	6
Teramo, Italy	C4	23
Ter Apel, Neth.	B7	17
Tercan, Tur.	C13	40
Terceira, i., Port.	g9	44
Tercero, stm., Arg.	A4	54
Terebovlya, Sov. Un.	G5	27
Terek, stm., Sov. Un.	G18	7
Terek Pass, Sov. Un.	G23	8
Terekty, Sov. Un.	D7	28
Terence Bay, N.S.	E6	71
Terengganu, state, Malay.	J5	35
Terenos, Braz.	C2	56
Teresina, Braz.	C2	56
Teresinha, Braz.	B4	59
Teresópolis, Braz.	E3	17
Tergnier, Fr.	E3	17
Terhune, In., U.S.	D5	91
Teriberka, Sov. Un.	C16	14
Terlingua, Tx., U.S.	D1	120
Terlton, Ok., U.S.	A5	113
Termez, Sov. Un.	F9	29
Termini Imerese, Italy	F4	23
Términos, Laguna de, b., Mex.	D6	63
Termoli, Italy	C5	23
Ternate, Indon.	E7	34
Ternate, i., Indon.	E7	34
Terneuzen, Neth.	B5	16
Terney, Sov. Un.	D8	33
Terni, Italy	C4	23
Ternopol, Sov. Un.	G5	27
Terpeniya Bay, b., Sov. Un.	B11	33
Terpeniye, Cape, c., Sov. Un.	B12	33
Terra, W.V., U.S.	B5	125
Terrace, B.C.	B3	69
Terrace, N.H., U.S.	E3	106
Terrace Bay, Ont.	G15	66
Terracina, Italy	D4	23
Terral, Ok., U.S.	D4	113
Terra Nova, Newf.	D4	72
Terra Nova National Park, Newf.	D4	72
Terra Rica, Braz.	C2	56
Terrasson, Fr.	E4	16
Terrebone, Bayou, stm., La., U.S.	k10	95
Terrebonne, Que.	D4	74
Terrebonne, Or., U.S.	C5	114
Terrebonne, co., Que.	C3	74
Terrebonne, co., La., U.S.	E5	95
Terrebonne Bay, b., La., U.S.	E5	95
Terre Haute, Il., U.S.	C3	90
Terre Haute, In., U.S.	F3	91
Terre Hill, Pa., U.S.	F9	115
Terrell, N.C., U.S.	B2	110
Terrell, Tx., U.S.	C4	120
Terrell, co., Ga., U.S.	E2	87
Terrell, co., Tx., U.S.	D1	120
Terrell Hills, Tx., U.S.	k7	120
Terrenceville, Newf.	E4	72
Terreton, Id., U.S.	F6	89
Terril, Ia., U.S.	A3	92
Terror, Mount, mtn., Ant.	e38	7
Terry, La., U.S.	B4	95
Terry, Ms., U.S.	C3	101
Terry, Mt., U.S.	D11	103
Terry, co., Tx., U.S.	C1	120
Terry Peak, mtn., S.D., U.S.	C2	118
Terrytown, La., U.S.	*E5	95
Terrytown, Ne., U.S.	C2	104
Terryville, Ct., U.S.	C3	84
Terryville, N.Y., U.S.	*n15	109
Tersakkan, stm., Sov. Un.	C7	28
Terschelling, i., Neth.	A6	16
Terskey-Alatau Range, mts., Sov. Un.	E9	28
Teruel, Col.	C2	60
Teruel, Spain	B5	22
Terutao, i., Thai.	I3	35
Terwagne, Bel.	D5	17
Tešanj, Yugo.	C3	24
Teshekpuk Lake, l., Ak., U.S.	B4	79
Teshie, Ghana	*E5	45
Teshio, Japan	D10	33
Tesiyn, stm., Asia	B4	31
Teslin, Yukon	D6	66
Teslin Lake, l., Can.	D6	66
Tessalit, Mali	B5	45
Tessaoua, Niger	D6	45
Tessier, Sask.	F2	75
Tessin, Ger.	D6	15
Tesuque, N.M., U.S.	B4	108
Tesuque Pueblo, N.M., U.S.	B4	108
Tetachuck Lake, l., B.C.	C5	69
Tetagouche, stm., N.B.	B3	71
Tetas, Punta, c., Chile	F3	53
Tetbury, Eng., U.K.	C5	12
Tete, Moz.	A5	49
Tete, dept., Moz.	E5	48
Tête-à-la-Baleine, Que.	C2	72
Tête Jaune Cache, B.C.	C8	69
Teterow, Ger.	B6	18
Teteven, Bul.	D7	24
Tetlin, Ak., U.S.	C11	79
Teton, co., Id., U.S.	F7	89
Teton, co., Mt., U.S.	C4	103
Teton, co., Wy., U.S.	C2	127
Teton, stm., Mt., U.S.	C5	103
Tetonia, Id., U.S.	F7	89
Teton Pass, Wy., U.S.	C2	127
Teton Range, mts., Wy., U.S.	C2	127
Teton Village, Wy., U.S.	C2	127
Tétouan, Mor.	B3	44
Tetovo, Yugo.	E5	24
Tettnang, Ger.	A8	21
Teulada, Italy	E2	23
Teúl de González Ortega, Mex.	m12	63
Teulon, Man.	D3	70
Teuri Island, i., Japan	D10	33
Teutopolis, Il., U.S.	D5	90
Teviot, stm., Scot., U.K.	E6	13
Tevriz, Sov. Un.	C8	28
Te Waewae Bay, b., N.Z.	Q11	51
Tewantin-Noosa, Austl.	E9	50
Tewksbury, Ma., U.S.	A5	98
Texada Island, i., B.C.	E5	69
Texarkana, Ar., U.S.	D1	81
Texarkana, Tx., U.S.	C5	120
Texas, co., Mo., U.S.	D5	102
Texas, co., Ok., U.S.	e9	113
Texas, state, U.S.	D3	120
Texas City, Tx., U.S.	E5	120
Texcaltitlán, Mex.	n14	63
Texcoco, Lago de, l., Mex.	g10	63
Texcoco (de Mora), Mex.	n14	63
Texel, i., Neth.	A6	16
Texhoma, Ok., U.S.	e9	113
Texhoma, Tx., U.S.	A2	120
Texico, N.M., U.S.	C6	108
Texline, Tx., U.S.	A1	120
Texoma, Ok., U.S.	D5	113
Texoma, Lake, res., U.S.	D5	113
Teywarah, Afg.	E12	39
Teziutlán, Mex.	D5	63
Tezpur, India	C9	36
Tezzeron Lake, l., B.C.	B5	69
Thabana Ntlenyana, mtn., Leso.	C4	49
Thacker, W.V., U.S.	D2	125
Thackeray, Il., U.S.	E5	90
Thackerville, Ok., U.S.	D4	113
Thai Binh, Viet.	B7	35
Thailand, ctry., Asia	B3	34
Thailand, Gulf of, b., Asia	C2	34
Thai Nguyen, Viet.	B7	35
Thal, Pak.	B5	36
Thale, Ger.	B6	19
Thale Luang, b., Thai.	I4	35
Thalia, Tx., U.S.	C3	120
Thames, N.Z.	L15	51
Thames, stm., Ont.	E2	73
Thames, stm., Eng., U.K.	E6	10
Thames, stm., Ct., U.S.	D7	84
Thames, Firth of, b., N.Z.	L15	51
Thamesville, Ont.	E3	73
Thanesar, India	D7	36
Thanh Hoa, Viet.	C6	35
Thanjāvūr, India	F6	36
Thann, Fr.	D7	16
Thannhausen, Ger.	A6	20
Thāno Bula Khān, Pak.	E1	37
Thaon[-les-Vosges], Fr.	C7	16
Tharād, India	I4	37
Thar Desert (Great Indian Desert), des., Asia	D2	37
Tharrawaddy, Burma	E10	36
Thásos, Grc.	B5	25
Thásos, i., Grc.	B5	40
Thatcher, Az., U.S.	E6	80
Thatcher, Id., U.S.	G7	89
Thaton, Burma	E10	36
Thawville, Il., U.S.	C5	90
Thaxton, Ms., U.S.	A4	101
Thayer, Il., U.S.	D4	90
Thayer, In., U.S.	B3	91
Thayer, Ia., U.S.	C3	92
Thayer, Ks., U.S.	E8	93
Thayer, Mo., U.S.	E6	102
Thayer, Ne., U.S.	D8	104
Thayer, W.V., U.S.	n13	125
Thayer, co., Ne., U.S.	D8	104
Thayetmyo, Burma	C1	35
Thayne, Wy., U.S.	D1	127
Thazi, Burma	B2	35
Thealka, Ky., U.S.	C7	94
Theba, Az., U.S.	E3	80
Thebes, Il., U.S.	F4	90
Thebes, hist., Eg.	C3	38
Thebes see Thívai, Grc.	C4	25
The Bight, Bah.	B6	64
The Cheviot, mtn., Eng., U.K.	E6	13
The Cheviot Hills, hills, U.K.	C5	10
The Colony, Tx., U.S.	C4	120
The Coteau, hills, Sask.	F2	75
The Dalles, Or., U.S.	B5	114
The Dells, val., Wi., U.S.	E4	126
Thedford, Ont.	D3	73
Thedford, Ne., U.S.	C5	104
The Dome, mtn., Vt., U.S.	F2	122
The Entrance, Austl.	F8	51
The Everglades, sw., Fl., U.S.	G6	86
The Father, mtn., Pap. N. Gui.	k13	50
The Fens, sw., Eng., U.K.	B8	12
The Fishing Lake, l., Sask.	G3	75
The Flat Tops, mts., Co., U.S.	B3	83
The Flume, wtfl., N.H., U.S.	B3	106
The Graves, is., Ma., U.S.	g12	98
The Hague ('s Gravenhage), Neth.	A6	16
The Heads, c., Or., U.S.	E2	114
The Hummocks, R.I., U.S.	D6	116
The Landes, reg., Fr.	E3	16
The Little Minch, strt., Scot., U.K.	B3	10
Thelma, N.C., U.S.	A5	110
Thelon, stm., N.W. Ter.	D12	66
The Minch, strt., Scot., U.K.	A4	10
The Narrows, strt., Wa., U.S.	f10	124
Thenay, Eng., U.K.	C5	12
The Naze, c., Nor.	I2	14
The Naze, c., Eng., U.K.	C9	12
The Oa, pen., Scot., U.K.	E2	13
Theodore, Austl.	D9	50
Theodore, Sask.	F4	75
Theodore, Al., U.S.	E1	78
Theodore Roosevelt Lake, res., Az., U.S.	D4	80
Theodore Roosevelt National Park (South Unit), N.D., U.S.	C2	111
Theodore Roosevelt National Park (North Unit), N.D., U.S.	B2	111
Theodosia, Mo., U.S.	E5	102
Theológos, Grc.	B5	25
The Palisades, clf., N.J., U.S.	h9	107
The Pas, Man.	C1	70
The Peak, mtn., N.C., U.S.	A1	110
The Pinnacle, hill, Ct., U.S.	B4	84
The Pinnacle, hill, Mo., U.S.	B7	102
The Plains, Oh., U.S.	C3	112
The Plains, Va., U.S.	B5	123
Thérain, stm., Fr.	E2	17
Theresa, N.Y., U.S.	A5	109
Theresa, Wi., U.S.	E5	126
The Range, N.B.	C4	71
The Raven Point, c., Ire.	E5	11
Thermaïkós Kólpos (Gulf of Salonika), b., Grc.	B4	40
Thérmon, Grc.	C3	25
Thermopolis, Wy., U.S.	C4	127
The Rock, Austl.	D2	87
The Rockies, mts., Wa., U.S.	C3	124
Theron Mountains, mts., Ant.	B10	7
The Solent, strt., Eng., U.K.	D6	12
The Sound see Øresund, strt., Eur.	J5	14
Thessalon, Ont.	p19	73
Thessaloniki (Salonika), Grc.	B4	40
Thessaly, hist. reg., Grc.	C4	25
The Storr, mtn., Scot., U.K.	C2	13
Theta, Tn., U.S.	B4	119
Thetford, Eng., U.K.	D7	10
Thetford, Vt., U.S.	D4	122
Thetford Center, Vt., U.S.	D4	122
Thetford Mines, Que.	C6	74
The Thimbles, is., Ct., U.S.	E5	84
The Village, Ok., U.S.	B4	113
The Village of India, Oh., U.S.	*C1	112
The Wash, b., Eng., U.K.	D7	10
The Wolds, hills, Eng., U.K.	D6	10
The Woodlands, Tx., U.S.	*E5	120
Thibar, Tun.	F2	23
Thibaudeau, Man.	A4	70
Thibodaux, La., U.S.	E5	95
Thicket Portage, Man.	B3	70
Thickwood Hills, hills, Sask.	C1	75
Thida, Ar., U.S.	B4	81
Thief, stm., Mn., U.S.	B2	100
Thief Lake, l., Mn., U.S.	B3	100
Thief River Falls, Mn., U.S.	B2	100
Thiel Mountains, mts., Ant.	A2	7
Thielsen, Mount, mtn., Or., U.S.	D4	114
Thiene, Italy	D7	20
Thiensville, Wi., U.S.	E6	126
Thiers, Fr.	E5	16
Thiès, Sen.	D1	45
Thika, Kenya	B6	48
Thimbu see Thimphu, Bhu.	C8	36
Thimphu (Thimbu), Bhu.	C8	36
Thingangyun, Burma	*E10	36
Thionville, Fr.	C7	16
Thíra, Grc.	D5	40
Thíra, i., Grc.	D5	40
Third Lake, l., N.H., U.S.	f7	106
Thirsk, Eng., U.K.	F7	13
Thisted, Den.	B2	15
Thívai (Thebes), Grc.	C4	25
Tho Chu, is., Viet.	H5	35
Tholen, Neth.	C4	17
Thomas, Ok., U.S.	B3	113
Thomas, Wa., U.S.	f11	124
Thomas, W.V., U.S.	B5	125
Thomas, co., Ga., U.S.	F3	87
Thomas, co., Ks., U.S.	C2	93
Thomas, co., Ne., U.S.	C5	104
Thomasboro, Il., U.S.	C5	90
Thomas Creek, stm., Fl., U.S.	k8	86
Thomas Mountains, mts., Ant.	B5	7
Thomaston, Al., U.S.	C2	78
Thomaston, Ct., U.S.	C3	84
Thomaston, Ga., U.S.	D2	87
Thomaston, Me., U.S.	D3	96
Thomaston, Tx., U.S.	E4	120
Thomaston Reservoir, res., Ct., U.S.	C3	84
Thomastown, Ire.	E4	11
Thomastown, Ms., U.S.	C4	101
Thomasville, Al., U.S.	D2	78
Thomasville, Ga., U.S.	F3	87
Thomasville, Mo., U.S.	E6	102
Thomasville, N.C., U.S.	B2	110
Thomasville, Tn., U.S.	A4	119
Thomlinson, Mount, mtn., B.C.	B3	70
Thompson, Man.	B3	70
Thompson, Ct., U.S.	B8	84
Thompson, Ia., U.S.	A4	92
Thompson, Mi., U.S.	C4	99
Thompson, Mo., U.S.	B6	102
Thompson, N.D., U.S.	B8	111
Thompson, Oh., U.S.	A4	112
Thompson, Pa., U.S.	C10	115
Thompson, stm., B.C.	D7	69
Thompson, stm., U.S.	A4	102
Thompson Creek, stm., Ms., U.S.	D5	101
Thompson Falls, Mt., U.S.	C1	103
Thompson Island, i., Ma., U.S.	g11	98
Thompson Lake, l., U.S.	D2	96
Thompson Peak, mtn., Ca., U.S.	B2	82
Thompson Peak, mtn., N.M., U.S.	h9	108
Thompson Reservoir, res., Or., U.S.	E5	114
Thompsons Station, Tn., U.S.	B5	119
Thompsontown, Pa., U.S.	E7	115
Thompsonville, Il., U.S.	F5	90
Thompsonville, Mi., U.S.	D5	99
Thomson, Ga., U.S.	C4	87
Thomson, Il., U.S.	B3	90
Thomson, Mn., U.S.	D6	100
Thomson, stm., Austl.	D7	50
Thomson's Falls, Kenya	A6	48
Thônes, Fr.	E1	21
Thonon-les-Bains, Fr.	C2	20
Thonotosassa, Fl., U.S.	D4	86
Thor, Ia., U.S.	B3	92
Thorburn, N.S.	D7	71
Thoreau, N.M., U.S.	B1	108
Thorhild, Alta.	B4	68
Thornburg, Ar., U.S.	C3	81
Thornbury, Ont.	C4	73
Thorndale, Ont.	D3	73
Thorndale, Tx., U.S.	D4	120
Thorndike, Me., U.S.	D3	96
Thorndike, Ma., U.S.	B3	98
Thornfield, Mo., U.S.	E5	102
Thornhill, Man.	E2	70
Thornhill, Ont.	k15	73
Thornhill, Scot., U.K.	E5	13
Thornton, Ont.	C5	73
Thornton, Ar., U.S.	D3	81
Thornton, Co., U.S.	*B6	83
Thornton, Ia., U.S.	B4	92
Thornton, Ms., U.S.	B3	101
Thornton, N.H., U.S.	C3	106
Thornton, Tx., U.S.	D4	120
Thornton, Wa., U.S.	B8	124
Thornton, W.V., U.S.	k11	125
Thornton Gap, Va., U.S.	B4	123
Thorntonville, Tx., U.S.	D1	120
Thorntown, In., U.S.	D4	91
Thornville, Oh., U.S.	C3	112
Thornwood, N.Y., U.S.	*m15	109
Thornwood, W.V., U.S.	C5	125
Thorny Mountain, mtn., Mo., U.S.	D6	102
Thorofare, N.J., U.S.	D2	107
Thorold, Ont.	D5	73
Thorp, Wa., U.S.	B5	124
Thorp, Wi., U.S.	D3	126
Thorsby, Alta.	C3	68
Thorsby, Al., U.S.	C3	78
Thouars, Fr.	D3	16
Thousand Islands, is., N.Y., U.S.	A4	109
Thousand Lake Mountain, mtn., Ut., U.S.	E4	121
Thousand Oaks, Ca., U.S.	*E4	82
Thousand Springs Creek, stm., U.S.	B7	105
Thrace, hist. reg., Eur.	B6	25
Thrapston, Eng., U.K.	B7	12
Thrashers, Ms., U.S.	A5	101
Three Bridges, N.J., U.S.	B3	107
Three Fingered Jack, mtn., Or., U.S.	C5	114
Three Forks, Mt., U.S.	E5	103
Three Hills, Alta.	D4	68
Three Kings Islands, is., N.Z.	K14	51
Three Lakes, Wi., U.S.	C4	126
Three Mile Bay, N.Y., U.S.	A4	109
Three Mile Plains, N.S.	E5	71
Three Nunataks, mtn., Ant.	g41	7
Three Oaks, Mi., U.S.	G4	99
Threepoint Lake, l., Man.	B2	70
Three Points, Cape, c., Ghana	F4	45
Three Rivers, Ma., U.S.	B3	98
Three Rivers, Mi., U.S.	G5	99
Three Rivers, Ms., U.S.	E3	101
Three Rivers, Tx., U.S.	E3	120
Three Rock Cove, Newf.	D2	72
Three Sisters, mtn., Or., U.S.	C5	114
Three Springs, Pa., U.S.	F6	115
Throckmorton, Tx., U.S.	C3	120
Throckmorton, co., Tx., U.S.	C3	120
Throop, Pa., U.S.	m18	115
Thu, i., Viet.	G8	35
Thu Dau Mot, Viet.	I5	35
Thuir, Fr.	F5	16
Thule (Qaanaaq), Grnld.	B14	61
Thun, Switz.	E3	18
Thun, Lake, l., Switz.	E3	18
Thunder Bay, dept., Ont.	o17	73
Thunder Bay, Ont.	G14	66
Thunder Bay, b., Mi., U.S.	D7	99
Thunder Bay, stm., Mi., U.S.	D6	99
Thunder Bay, North Branch, stm., Mi., U.S.	C6	99
Thunderbird, Lake, l., Ok., U.S.	B4	113
Thunderbolt, Ga., U.S.	D5	87
Thunder Butte, S.D., U.S.	B3	118
Thunder Butte, mtn., S.D., U.S.	B3	118
Thunder Butte Creek, stm., S.D., U.S.	B4	118
Thunder Hawk, S.D., U.S.	B4	118
Thunder Hills, hills, Sask.	C2	75
Thung Song, Thai.	H3	35
Thur, stm., Switz.	A6	21
Thurgau, state, Switz.	B5	20
Thüringen, state, Ger.	C6	19
Thüringer Wald, mts., Ger.	C5	19
Thuringia, hist. reg., Ger.	C5	18
Thurles, Ire.	E4	11
Thurlow Dam, Al., U.S.	C4	78
Thurman, Ia., U.S.	D2	92
Thurman, Oh., U.S.	D3	112
Thurmont, Md., U.S.	A3	97
Thurø, i., Den.	C4	15
Thursday Island, Austl.	B7	50
Thurso, Que.	D2	74
Thurso, Scot., U.K.	A5	10
Thurso, stm., Scot., U.K.	B5	13
Thurston, Ne., U.S.	B9	104
Thurston, Oh., U.S.	C3	112
Thurston, co., Ne., U.S.	B9	104
Thurston, co., Wa., U.S.	C2	124
Thurston Island, i., Ant.	B3	7
Thusis, Switz.	E4	18
Thuvu, Fiji	I14	52
Thwaites Iceburg Tongue, ice, Ant.	B2	7
Thyborøn, Den.	B2	15
Thyborøn Kanal, strt., Den.	B2	15
Tiahuanaco, Bol.	C2	55
Tiancang, China	C5	31
Tianjin (Tientsin), China	D8	31
Tianjin, China	D4	31
Tianmen, China	I5	32
Tianshui, China	E6	31
Tianzhen, China	D2	32
Tiawah, Ok., U.S.	A6	113
Tibagi, Braz.	C2	56
Tibaji, stm., Braz.	C2	56
Tibasti, Sarīr, des., Libya	D3	46
Tibati, Cam.	D2	46
Tibba, Al., U.S.	D1	78
Tibbie, Al., U.S.	D1	78
Tibé, Pic de, mtn., Gui.	F3	45
Tiber (Tevere), stm., Italy	C4	23
Tiberias (Teverya), Isr.	F10	40
Tibesti, mts., Chad	A3	46
Tibet (Xizang), prov., China	E3	31
Tibiri, Niger	D6	45
Tibooburra, Austl.	E7	50
Tiburón, Ca., U.S.	*h8	82
Tiburón, Isla, i., Mex.	B3	63
Tice, Fl., U.S.	F5	86
Tichborne, Ont.	C8	73
Tichfield, Sask.	F2	75
Tichît, Maur.	C3	45
Tichnor, Ar., U.S.	C4	81
Ticino, state, Switz.	C4	20
Ticino, stm., Eur.	B2	23
Tickfaw, La., U.S.	D5	95
Tickfaw, stm., La., U.S.	C5	95
Ticomán (part of Mexico City), Mex.	h9	63
Ticonderoga, N.Y., U.S.	B7	109
Ticul, Mex.	C7	63
Tide Head, N.B.	B3	71
Tidikelt, pl., Alg.	C5	44
Tidioute, Pa., U.S.	C3	115
Tidjikdja, Maur.	C2	45
Tidore, i., Indon.	E7	34
Tieli, China	*B10	31
Tieling, China	C9	31
Tielmes de Tajuña, Spain	p18	22
Tielt, Bel.	C3	17
Tienen, Bel.	B6	16
Tien Shan, mts., Asia	E10	30
Tientsin see Tianjin, China	D8	31
Tien Yen, Viet.	B7	35
Tierp, Swe.	G7	14
Tierra Amarilla, Chile	E1	55
Tierra Amarilla, N.M., U.S.	A3	108
Tierra Blanca, Mex.	D5	63
Tierra del Fuego, Antártida e Islas del Atlántico Sur, ter., Arg.	h12	54
Tierra del Fuego, Isla Grande de, i., S.A.	h12	54
Tie Siding, Wy., U.S.	E7	127
Tieté, Braz.	C3	56
Tietê, stm., Braz.	C2	56
Tieton, Wa., U.S.	C5	124
Tieton, stm., Wa., U.S.	C4	124
Tieton Dam, Wa., U.S.	C4	124
Tiffany Mountain, mtn., Wa., U.S.	A6	124
Tiffin, Ia., U.S.	C6	92
Tiffin, Oh., U.S.	A2	112
Tiffin, stm., Oh., U.S.	A1	112
Tiflis see Tbilisi, Sov. Un.	F7	27
Tift, co., Ga., U.S.	E3	87
Tifton, Ga., U.S.	E3	87
Tigard, Or., U.S.	h12	114
Tiger, Ga., U.S.	B3	87
Tigerton, Wi., U.S.	D5	126
Tigerville, S.C., U.S.	A3	117
Tighnabruaich, Scot., U.K.	E3	13
Tigil, Sov. Un.	D18	29
Tignall, Ga., U.S.	C4	87
Tignère, Cam.	D2	46
Tignish, P.E.I.	C5	71
Tigray (Tigre), prov., Eth.	C4	47
Tigre, Braz.	g7	54
Tigre, stm., Peru	D2	58
Tigre, stm., Ven.	B2	58
Tigrett, Tn., U.S.	B2	119
Tigris (Dicle), stm., Asia	B3	40
Tiguabos, Cuba	D6	64
Tiguentourine, Alg.	C6	44
Tih, Jabal at, plat., Eg.	E5	41
Tihert, Alg.	A5	44
Tihuatlán, Mex.	m15	63
Tiji, Libya	D3	46
Tijuana, Mex.	A1	63
Tijucas, Braz.	C3	56
Tikal, hist., Guat.	F7	63
Tikamgarh, India	I13	37
Tikhoretsk, Sov. Un.	I13	27
Tikhvin, Sov. Un.	E11	26
Tiko, Cam.	E1	46
Tikrīt, Iraq	E14	40
Tiksi, Sov. Un.	B15	29
Tilamuta, Indon.	E6	34
Tilarán, C.R.	I5	64
Tilburg, Neth.	B6	16
Tilbury, Ont.	E2	73
Tilbury, Eng., U.K.	C7	12
Tilcara, Arg.	D3	55
Tilden, Il., U.S.	E4	90
Tilden, Ne., U.S.	B8	104
Tilden, Tx., U.S.	E3	120
Tilemsès, Niger	C5	45
Tilemsi, Vallée du, val., Mali	C5	45
Tilghman, Md., U.S.	C5	97
Tilghman Island, i., Md., U.S.	C5	97
Tilimsen (Tlemcen), Alg.	C4	44
Tiline, Ky., U.S.	e9	94
Till, stm., Eng., U.K.	E6	13
Tillabéry, Niger	D5	45
Tillamook, Or., U.S.	B3	114
Tillamook, co., Or., U.S.	B3	114
Tillar, Ar., U.S.	D4	81
Tillatoba, Ms., U.S.	B4	101
Tillberga (part of Västerås), Swe.	t34	14
Tiller, Or., U.S.	E4	114
Tillery, Lake, res., N.C., U.S.	B2	110
Tilley, Alta.	D5	68
Tillman, S.C., U.S.	G5	117
Tillman, co., Ok., U.S.	C2	113
Tillmans Corner, Al., U.S.	E1	78
Tillsonburg, Ont.	E4	73
Tillson, N.Y., U.S.	D6	109
Tillsonburg, Ont.	E4	73
Tilly, Ar., U.S.	B3	81
Tilpa, Austl.	E5	51
Tilrhemt, Alg.	C5	44
Tilston, Man.	E1	70
Tilting, Newf.	D4	72
Tilton, Ga., U.S.	B2	87
Tilton, Il., U.S.	C6	90
Tilton, N.H., U.S.	D3	106
Tiltonsville, Oh., U.S.	B5	112
Tim, Sov. Un.	F11	27
Timaná, Col.	C2	60
Timaru, N.Z.	P13	51
Timashevsk, Sov. Un.	I12	27
Timbalier Bay, b., La., U.S.	E5	95
Timbalier Island, i., La., U.S.	E5	95
Timbaúba, Braz.	h6	57
Timbédra, Maur.	C3	45
Timber, Or., U.S.	B3	114
Timbered Knob, mtn., Mo., U.S.	E5	102
Timberlake, N.C., U.S.	A4	110
Timber Lake, S.D., U.S.	B4	118
Timberlake, Va., U.S.	C3	123
Timberville, Va., U.S.	B4	123
Timblin, Pa., U.S.	D3	115
Timbo, Ar., U.S.	B3	81
Timbuktu see Tombouctou, Mali	C4	45
Timerzit, Mor.	C4	44
Timewell, Il., U.S.	C3	90
Timimoun, Alg.	C4	44
Timiris, Cap, c., Maur.	C1	45
Timiskaming, dept., Ont.	o19	73
Timișoara, Rom.	C5	24
Timken, Ks., U.S.	D4	93
Timmendorfer Strand, Ger.	E4	15
Timmins, Ont.	o19	73
Timmonsville, S.C., U.S.	C8	117
Timms Hill, hill, Wi., U.S.	C3	126
Timnath, Co., U.S.	A5	83
Timok, stm., Eur.	D6	24
Timor, i., Indon.	G6	34
Timor Sea	C2	50
Timpanogos Cave National Monument, U.S.	C4	121
Timpas Creek, stm., Co., U.S.	D7	83
Timpson, Tx., U.S.	D5	120
Timrå, Swe.	F7	14
Timsāh, Lake, l., Eg.	D4	41
Tims Ford Lake, res., Tn., U.S.	B5	119
Tin, Ra's at, c., Libya	C4	43
Tina, Mo., U.S.	B4	102
Tinaca Point, c., Phil.	D8	34
Tinahely, Ire.	E5	11
Tinaquillo, Ven.	B4	60
Tindouf, Alg.	D3	44
Tineo, Spain	A2	22
Tinghert, Ḥammādat, plat., Afr.	D2	43
Tinghert, Plateau du (Ḥammādat Tinghert), plat., Afr.	D6	44
Tinglev, Den.	D3	15
Tingley, Ia., U.S.	D3	92
Tingmerkpuk Mountain, mtn., Ak., U.S.	B7	79
Tingo Maria, Peru	C2	58
Tingréla, I.C.	D3	45
Tingri, China	C11	37
Tingsryd, Swe.	B9	15
Tinguipaya, Bol.	C2	55
Tingwick, Que.	D6	74
Tinian, i., N. Mar. Is.	F8	6
Tinian Harbor, b., N. Mar. Is.	E7	52
Tinizong, Switz.	C8	21
Tinker Air Force Base, mil., Ok., U.S.	B4	113
Tinkerville, N.H., U.S.	B3	106
Tinkisso, stm., Gui.	D2	45
Tinley Park, Il., U.S.	k9	90
Tinnie, N.M., U.S.	D4	108
Tinniswood, Mount, mtn., B.C.	D6	69
Tinogasta, Arg.	E2	55
Tinos, Grc.	C5	25
Tinos, i., Grc.	D5	40
Tinqueux, Fr.	C5	17
Tinsley, Ms., U.S.	C3	101
Tinsman, Ar., U.S.	D3	81
Tinsukia, India	C10	36
Tintah, Mn., U.S.	E2	100
Tintigny, Bel.	E7	17
Tintina, Arg.	E3	55
Tintinara, Austl.	G3	51
Tinton Falls, N.J., U.S.	C4	107
Ti-n-Zaouatene, Alg.	E5	44
Tio, Eth.	C5	47
Tioga, Il., U.S.	C2	90
Tioga, La., U.S.	C3	95
Tioga, N.D., U.S.	A3	111
Tioga, Pa., U.S.	C7	115
Tioga, Tx., U.S.	C4	120
Tioga, W.V., U.S.	C4	125
Tioga, co., N.Y., U.S.	C4	109
Tioga, co., Pa., U.S.	C7	115
Tioga, stm., U.S.	C7	115
Tiogue Lake, res., R.I., U.S.	D3	116
Tioman, i., Malay.	K6	35
Tiona, Pa., U.S.	C3	115
Tione di Trento, Italy	C5	20
Tionesta, Pa., U.S.	C3	115
Tionesta Creek, stm., Pa., U.S.	C4	109
Tionesta Lake, res., Pa., U.S.	D3	115
Tioughnioga, stm., N.Y., U.S.	C4	109
Tipler, Wi., U.S.	C5	126
Tiplersville, Ms., U.S.	A5	101
Tippah, co., Ms., U.S.	A4	101
Tippah, stm., Ms., U.S.	A4	101
Tipp City, Oh., U.S.	C1	112
Tippecanoe, Oh., U.S.	B5	112
Tippecanoe, co., In., U.S.	C4	91
Tippecanoe, stm., In., U.S.	D2	91
Tipperary, Ire.	D2	10

Name	Map Ref.	Page
Tipperary, co., Ire.	E4	11
Tippo, Ms., U.S.	B3	101
Tipton, Ca., U.S.	D4	82
Tipton, In., U.S.	D5	91
Tipton, Ia., U.S.	C6	92
Tipton, Ks., U.S.	C5	93
Tipton, Mo., U.S.	C5	102
Tipton, Ok., U.S.	C2	113
Tipton, co., In., U.S.	B2	119
Tipton, co., Tn., U.S.	B2	119
Tipton, Mount, mtn., Az., U.S.	B1	80
Tiptonville, Tn., U.S.	A2	119
Tip Top, Ky., U.S.	C6	94
Tiptop, Va., U.S.	C1	123
Tip Top Mountain, mtn., Ont.	o18	73
Tiquisate, Guat.	C2	62
Ţira, Isr.	B6	41
Tīrān, Jazīrat, i., Sau. Ar.	I10	40
Tirana (Tiranë), Alb.	B2	40
Tiranë see Tirana, Alb.	B2	40
Tirano, Italy	A3	23
Tiraque, Bol.	C2	55
Tiraspol, Sov. Un.	H7	27
Tirat Karmel, Isr.	B6	41
Tirat Ẕevi, Isr.	B7	41
Tire, Tur.	C6	40
Tirebolu, Tur.	B12	40
Tiree, i., Scot., U.K.	B3	10
Tire Hill, Pa., U.S.	F4	115
Tîrgovişte, Rom.	C7	24
Tîrgu-Frumos, Rom.	B8	24
Tîrgu-Jiu, Rom.	C6	24
Tîrgu-Neamţ, Rom.	B8	24
Tîrgu-Ocna, Rom.	B8	24
Tîrgu-Secuiesc, Rom.	B8	24
Tirich Mīr, mtn., Pak.	A5	36
Tiriro, Gui.	D3	45
Tîrlyanskiy, Sov. Un.	E20	8
Tîrnava Mică, stm., Rom.	B7	24
Tîrnăveni, Rom.	C4	25
Tirnavos, Gro.	B3	112
Tiro, Oh., U.S.	B3	112
Tirol (Tyrol), state, Aus.	B7	20
Tirol, hist. reg., Aus.	E5	18
Tiros, Braz.	B5	56
Tirschenreuth, Ger.	D7	19
Tirso, stm., Italy	D2	23
Tirstrup, Den.	B4	15
Tiruchchirāppalli (Trichinopoly), India	F6	36
Tirunelveli (Tinnevelly), India	G6	36
Tiruppur, India	*F6	36
Tisa (Tisza), stm., Eur.	C5	24
Tisaren, l., Swe.	t33	14
Tisch Mills, Wi., U.S.	h10	126
Tisdale, Sask.	E3	75
Tishomingo, Ms., U.S.	A5	101
Tishomingo, Ok., U.S.	C5	113
Tishomingo, co., Ms., U.S.	A5	101
Tiskilwa, Il., U.S.	B4	90
Tisnaren, l., Swe.	u33	14
Tissemsilt, Alg.	B5	44
Tista, stm., Asia	D12	37
Tisvildeleje, Den.	B6	15
Tisza (Tisza), stm., Eur.	B5	24
Tiszaföred, Hung.	B5	24
Tiszakécske, Hung.	B5	24
Titicaca, Lago, l., S.A.	E4	58
Titograd, Yugo.	D4	24
Titonka, Ia., U.S.	A3	92
Titov Veles, Yugo.	D4	24
Titovo Užice, Yugo.	E5	24
Titule, Zaire	A4	48
Titus, co., Tx., U.S.	C5	120
Titusville, Fl., U.S.	D6	86
Titusville, N.J., U.S.	C3	107
Titusville, Pa., U.S.	C2	115
Tivaouane, Sen.	C1	45
Tiverton, N.S.	E3	71
Tiverton, Ont.	C3	73
Tiverton, Eng., U.K.	E5	10
Tiverton, R.I., U.S.	D6	116
Tiverton Four Corners, R.I., U.S.	E6	116
Tivoli, Italy	D4	23
Tivoli, N.Y., U.S.	C7	109
Tivoli, Tx., U.S.	E4	120
Tixtla [de Guerrero], Mex.	o14	63
Tizapán (part of Mexico City), Mex.	h9	63
Tizard Bank, atoll, Asia	C4	34
Tizimín, Mex.	C7	63
Tizi-Ouzou, Alg.	B5	44
Tiznit, Mor.	D3	44
Tjeukemeer, l., Neth.	B5	17
Tlacolula [de Matamoros], Mex.	D5	63
Tlacotalpan, Mex.	D5	63
Tlacotepec, Mex.	o13	63
Tláhuac (part of Mexico City), Mex.	h9	63
Tlahualilo de Zaragoza, Mex.	B4	63
Tlalnepantla, stm., Mex.	g9	63
Tlalnepantla [de Comonfort], Mex.	g9	63
Tlalpan (part of Mexico City), Mex.	h9	63
Tlalpujahua, Mex.	n13	63
Tlaltenango [de Sánchez Román], Mex.	C4	63
Tlaltenco (part of Mexico City), Mex.	h9	63
Tlapa, Mex.	o14	63
Tlapacoyan, Mex.	n15	63
Tlapaneco, stm., Mex.	o14	63
Tlaquepaque (San Pedro Tlaquepaque), Mex.	m12	63
Tlaxcala, state, Mex.	D5	63
Tlaxcala [de Xicohténcatl], Mex.	n14	63
Tlaxco [de Morelos], Mex.	n14	63
Tlaxiaco, Mex.	D5	63
Tłuszcz, Pol.	k14	26
Tmassah, Libya	C4	43
Toadlena, N.M., U.S.	A1	108
Toamasina, Madag.	g9	49
Toamasina, prov., Madag.	g9	49
Toano, Va., U.S.	C6	123
Toano Range, mts., Nv., U.S.	C7	105
Toast, N.C., U.S.	A2	110
Toay, Arg.	B4	54
Toba, Japan	o15	33
Toba, stm., B.C.	D5	69
Toba, Lake, l., Indon.	E1	34
Tobacco Root Mountains, mts., Mt., U.S.	E5	103
Tobago, i., Trin.	K14	64
Tobago Cays, is., St. Vin.	V26	65
Toba Inlet, b., B.C.	D5	69
Tobarra, Spain	C5	22
Tobaru, Japan	O5	52
Tobelo, Indon.	E8	34
Tobercurry, Ire.	C3	11
Tobermory, Ont.	B3	73
Tobermory, Scot., U.K.	D2	13
Tobias, Ne., U.S.	D8	104
Tobiishi Point, c., Japan	P17	52
Tobi Island, i., Japan	G9	33
Tobin, Mount, mtn., Nv., U.S.	C4	105
Tobin Lake, l., Austl.	D4	50
Tobin Lake, l., Sask.	D4	75
Tobins Harbor, Mi., U.S.	h10	99
Tobique, stm., N.B.	B2	71
Tobol, Sov. Un.	C6	28
Tobol, stm., Sov. Un.	D9	29
Tobolsk, Sov. Un.	D9	29
Tobruk see Ţubruq, Libya	C4	43
Toby, Mount, mtn., Ma., U.S.	B2	98
Tobyhanna, Pa., U.S.	D11	115
Tocantinópolis, Braz.	C1	57
Tocantins, stm., Braz.	D6	53
Tocantins National Park, Braz.	A3	56
Toccoa, Ga., U.S.	B3	87
Toccoa, stm., Ga., U.S.	B2	87
Toccoa Falls, Ga., U.S.	B3	87
Toccopola, Ms., U.S.	A4	101
Toce, stm., Italy	C4	23
Tochcha Lake, l., B.C.	B5	69
Tochigi, Japan	H9	33
Toco, Chile	D1	55
Toco, Trin.	N24	65
Tocoa, Hond.	C4	62
Tocopilla, Chile	D1	55
Tocúmen, Pan.	F8	62
Tocumwal, Austl.	G5	51
Tocuyo, stm., Ven.	A4	60
Todd, N.C., U.S.	A1	110
Todd, co., Ky., U.S.	D2	94
Todd, co., Mn., U.S.	D4	100
Todd, co., S.D., U.S.	D5	118
Todd Estates, De., U.S.	*B3	85
Toddville, Md., U.S.	D5	97
Toddy Pond, l., Me., U.S.	D4	96
Todi, Italy	C4	23
Tödi, mtn., Switz.	C4	20
Todos os Santos, Baía de, b., Braz.	D3	57
Todos Santos, Bol.	C2	55
Todos Santos, Mex.	C2	63
Todtnau, Ger.	B3	20
Toe Head, c., Ire.	F2	11
Toe Head, c., Scot., U.K.	C1	13
Tofield, Alta.	C4	68
Tofino, B.C.	E5	69
Tofte, Mn., U.S.	C8	100
Toftlund, Den.	C3	15
Togdheer, prov., Som.	D6	47
Togiak, Ak., U.S.	D7	79
Togian Islands, is., Indon.	F6	34
Togo, Sask.	F5	75
Togo, ctry., Afr.	E5	45
Togtoh, China	D4	32
Togwottee Pass, Wy., U.S.	C2	127
Tohakum Peak, mtn., Nv., U.S.	C2	105
Tohatchi, N.M., U.S.	B1	108
Tohopekaliga, Lake, l., Fl., U.S.	D5	86
Toi, Cape, c., Japan	K5	33
Toivola, Mi., U.S.	B2	99
Toivola, Mn., U.S.	C6	100
Toiyabe Range, mts., Nv., U.S.	D4	105
Tok, Ak., U.S.	C11	79
Tokachi, Mount, mtn., Japan	E11	33
Tokaj, Hung.	A5	24
Tokara Islands, is., Japan	F10	31
Tokara Strait, strt., Japan	K5	33
Tokat, Tur.	B11	40
Tŏkchŏn, N. Kor.	G3	33
Tokeland, Wa., U.S.	C2	124
Tokelau, dep., Oc.	G11	6
Tokio, Ar., U.S.	C2	81
Tokio, N.D., U.S.	B7	111
Tokio, Tx., U.S.	C1	120
Toki Point, c., Wake I.	A1	52
Tok Islands (Take Islands), is., Asia	H5	33
Tokmak, Sov. Un.	H10	27
Tokmak, Sov. Un.	E9	28
Tokoroa, N.Z.	M15	51
Tokuno Island, i., Japan	F10	31
Tokushima, Japan	E11	31
Tokuyama, Japan	J5	33
Tōkyō, Japan	D12	31
Tōkyō Bay, b., Japan	n18	33
Tokzār, Afg.	D13	39
Tol, i., Micron.	Q18	52
Tolar, N.M., U.S.	C6	108
Tolbukhin (Dobrich), Bul.	D8	24
Toleak Point, c., Wa., U.S.	B1	124
Toledo, Braz.	C2	56
Toledo, Ont.	C8	73
Toledo, Spain	C3	22
Toledo, Il., U.S.	D5	90
Toledo, Ia., U.S.	B5	92
Toledo, Oh., U.S.	A2	112
Toledo, Or., U.S.	C3	114
Toledo, Wa., U.S.	C3	124
Toledo, Montes de, mts., Spain	C3	22
Toledo Bend Reservoir, res., U.S.	C2	95
Toler, Ky., U.S.	C7	94
Tolga, Alg.	C6	44
Toliara, Madag.	h8	49
Toliara, prov., Madag.	h8	49
Tolima, dept., Col.	C2	60
Tolima, Nevado del, mtn., Col.	C2	60
Tolimán, Mex.	m14	63
Tolitoli, Indon.	E6	34
Tolken, l., Swe.	A6	15
Tolland, Ct., U.S.	B6	84
Tolland, co., Ct., U.S.	B6	84
Tollense, l., Ger.	E7	15
Tollense, stm., Ger.	E7	15
Tollesboro, Ky., U.S.	B6	94
Tolleson, Az., U.S.	m8	80
Tollette, Ar., U.S.	D2	81
Tolley, N.D., U.S.	A4	111
Tollhouse, Ca., U.S.	D4	82
Tolmachevo, Sov. Un.	E3	55
Tolmezzo, Italy	A4	23
Tolna, Hung.	B4	24
Tolna, N.D., U.S.	B7	111
Tolo, Gulf of, b., Indon.	F6	34
Tolono, Il., U.S.	D5	90
Tolosa, Spain	A4	22
Tolovana Park, Or., U.S.	B3	114
Tolsta Head, c., Scot., U.K.	B2	13
Tolstoi, Man.	E3	70
Tolstoy, S.D., U.S.	B6	118
Toltén, Chile	B2	54
Tolt Reservoir, res., Wa., U.S.	B4	124
Tolú, Col.	B2	60
Tolu, Ky., U.S.	e9	94
Toluca, Il., U.S.	C4	90
Toluca, Nevado de, vol., Mex.	n14	63
Toluca [de Lerdo], Mex.	D5	63
Tolyatti, Sov. Un.	C3	28
Tom, Ok., U.S.	D7	113
Tom, Mount, hill, Ct., U.S.	C2	84
Tomah, Wi., U.S.	E3	126
Tomahawk, Wi., U.S.	C4	126
Tomahawk Lake, l., Wi., U.S.	C4	126
Tomakomai, Japan	E10	33
Tomakovka, Sov. Un.	H10	27
Tomanivi, mtn., Fiji	H15	52
Tomar, Port.	C1	22
Tomari, Sov. Un.	E17	29
Tomaszów Lubelski, Pol.	C7	26
Tomaszów Mazowiecki, Pol.	C6	26
Tomatlán, Mex.	D3	63
Tomato, Ar., U.S.	B6	81
Tomave, Bol.	C2	55
Tombador, Serra do, plat., Braz.	B4	55
Tomball, Tx., U.S.	D5	120
Tombigbee, stm., U.S.	D1	78
Tomboco, Ang.	C1	48
Tombouctou (Timbuktu), Mali	D4	45
Tombstone, Az., U.S.	F5	80
Tombstone Mountain, mtn., Yukon	D5	66
Tombua (Porto Alexandre), Ang.	E1	48
Tomé, Chile	B2	54
Tome, N.M., U.S.	C3	108
Tomelilla, Swe.	C7	15
Tomelloso, Spain	C4	22
Tom Green, co., Tx., U.S.	D2	120
Tomichi Creek, stm., Co., U.S.	C4	83
Tomini, Gulf of, b., Indon.	E6	34
Tominian, Mali	D4	45
Tomintoul, Scot., U.K.	C5	13
Tomkins Cove, N.Y., U.S.	D6	109
Tommot, Sov. Un.	D15	29
Tom Nevers Head, c., Ma., U.S.	D8	98
Tomnolen, Ms., U.S.	B4	101
Tomo, stm., Col.	B4	60
Tomobe, Japan	m19	33
Tomori, Japan	O5	52
Tompkins, Newf.	E2	72
Tompkins, Sask.	G1	75
Tompkins, co., N.Y., U.S.	C4	109
Tompkinsville, Ky., U.S.	D4	94
Tompkinsville, Md., U.S.	D4	97
Tom Price, Austl.	D2	50
Toms, stm., N.J., U.S.	C4	107
Toms, Ridgeway Branch, stm., N.J., U.S.	C4	107
Toms Creek, Va., U.S.	f9	123
Tomsk, Sov. Un.	D11	29
Toms River, N.J., U.S.	D4	107
Tonalá, Mex.	D6	63
Tonalea, Az., U.S.	A5	80
Tonantins, Braz.	D4	60
Tonasket, Wa., U.S.	A6	124
Tonate, Fr. Gu.	B4	59
Tonawanda, N.Y., U.S.	B2	109
Tonawanda Indian Reservation, N.Y., U.S.	B2	109
Tonbridge, Eng., U.K.	C8	12
Tondano, Indon.	E6	34
Tønder, Den.	D2	15
Tone, stm., Japan	n19	33
Tonekābon, Iran	B5	38
Toney, Al., U.S.	A3	78
Tonga, ctry., Oc.	H11	6
Tonganoxie, Ks., U.S.	C8	93
Tongbei, China	B3	33
Tongcheng, China	I7	32
Tongchuan, China	G3	32
Tongeren, Bel.	D5	17
Tongguan, China	A7	50
Tonghe, China	C4	33
Tonghua, China	C10	31
Tongjiang, China	I2	32
Tongjiang, China	C6	33
Tongliao, China	C9	31
Tongling, China	E8	31
Tongoy, Chile	F1	55
Tongren, China	K3	32
Tongue, Scot., U.K.	B4	13
Tongue, stm., Mt., U.S.	E10	103
Tongue, stm., Tx., U.S.	p13	120
Tongue, Kyle of, b., Scot., U.K.	B4	13
Tongyu, China	B10	32
Tongzi, China	J2	32
Tonichi, Mex.	B4	90
Tonichi, Mex.	B3	63
Tonj, Sud.	D2	47
Tōnjum, Nor.	G2	14
Tonk, India	C6	36
Tonkawa, Ok., U.S.	A4	113
Tonkin, hist. reg., Viet.	B6	35
Tonkin, Gulf of, b., Asia	B3	34
Tonle Sap, l., Camb.	C2	34
Tonneins, Fr.	E4	16
Tonnerre, Fr.	D5	16
Tönning, Ger.	D2	15
Tonoloway Ridge, mtn., Md., U.S.	A1	97
Tonopah, Az., U.S.	D3	80
Tonopah, Nv., U.S.	E4	105
Tonosí, Pan.	G7	62
Tönsberg, Nor.	H4	14
Tontitown, Ar., U.S.	A1	81
Tonto, stm., Mex.	n15	63
Tonto Basin, Az., U.S.	D4	80
Tontogany, Oh., U.S.	f6	112
Tonto National Monument, Az., U.S.	D4	80
Tonto Natural Bridge, Az., U.S.	C4	80
Tony, Wi., U.S.	C3	126
Tooele, Ut., U.S.	C3	121
Tooele, co., Ut., U.S.	C2	121
Toole, co., Mt., U.S.	B5	103
Toombs, co., Ga., U.S.	D4	87
Toomsboro, Ga., U.S.	D3	87
Toomsuba, Ms., U.S.	C5	101
Toomyvara, Ire.	D4	11
Toone, Tn., U.S.	B3	119
Toormakeady, Ire.	C2	11
Toowoomba, Austl.	E9	50
Topaz, Ca., U.S.	E7	82
Topeka, In., U.S.	A6	91
Topeka, Ks., U.S.	C8	93
Topinabee, Mi., U.S.	C6	99
Topki, Sov. Un.	B11	28
Topley, B.C.	B4	69
Toplica, stm., Yugo.	D5	24
Topock, Az., U.S.	C1	80
Topol'čany, Czech.	D5	26
Topolnitsa, stm., Bul.	D7	24
Topolobampo, Mex.	B3	63
Topolovgrad, Bul.	D8	24
Toponas, Co., U.S.	A4	83
Topozero, l., Sov. Un.	E14	14
Toppenish, Wa., U.S.	C5	124
Toppenish Ridge, mtn., Wa., U.S.	C5	124
Top Pond, l., Newf.	E3	72
Topsfield, Me., U.S.	C5	96
Topsfield, Ma., U.S.	A6	98
Topsham, Me., U.S.	E3	96
Topsham, Vt., U.S.	C4	122
Topton, N.C., U.S.	f9	110
Topton, Pa., U.S.	F10	115
Toquima Range, mts., Nv., U.S.	E5	105
Torbalı, Tur.	C6	25
Torbat-e Ḩeydarīyeh, Iran	D9	39
Torbat-e Jām, Iran	D10	39
Torbay, Newf.	E5	72
Tor Bay, b., Eng., U.K.	D4	12
Torbert, Mount, mtn., Ak., U.S.	g15	79
Torcello, Italy	D8	20
Torch, stm., Sask.	D4	75
Torch Lake, l., Mi., U.S.	B5	15
Torekov, Swe.	B6	15
Torez, Sov. Un.	q21	27
Torgau, Ger.	C6	18
Torhout, Bel.	B5	16
Toride, Japan	n19	33
Tori Island, i., Japan	J4	33
Torit, Sud.	E3	47
Tormes, stm., Spain	B2	22
Tornado Mountain, mtn., Can.	E3	68
Tornälven, stm., Eur.	D10	14
Torneträsk, l., Swe.	C9	14
Torngat Mountains, mts., Can.	E8	76
Tornillo, Tx., U.S.	o11	120
Tornio, Fin.	E11	14
Tornquist, Arg.	B4	54
Toro, Spain	B3	22
Torö, Swe.	u35	14
Törökszentmiklós, Hung.	D5	73
Toronto, Ont.	D5	73
Toronto, Ks., U.S.	E8	93
Toronto, Oh., U.S.	B5	112
Toronto, S.D., U.S.	C9	118
Toronto Lake, res., Ks., U.S.	E7	93
Toro Peak, mtn., Ca., U.S.	F5	82
Tororo, Ug.	A5	48
Toro Rumi, mtn., Peru	D3	58
Torote, stm., Spain	o18	22
Torpshammar, Swe.	A8	15
Torquay, Sask.	H4	75
Torquay, Eng., U.K.	E5	10
Torrance, Ont.	n12	82
Torrance, Ca., U.S.	n12	82
Torrance, co., N.M., U.S.	C3	108
Torre Annunziata, Italy	D5	22
Torre de Cerredo, mtn., Spain	A3	22
Torre del Greco, Italy	D5	23
Torredonjimeno, Spain	D4	22
Torrejoncillo, Spain	C2	22
Torrejón de Ardoz, Spain	p18	22
Torrelavega, Spain	A3	22
Torremaggiore, Italy	D5	22
Torrens, Lake, l., Austl.	F6	50
Torrente, Spain	C5	22
Torreón, Mex.	C4	63
Torreón, N.M., U.S.	C3	108
Torre-Pacheco, Spain	D5	22
Torres, Braz.	D3	56
Torres Novas, Port.	C1	22
Torres Strait, strt., Austl.	A7	50
Torres Vedras, Port.	C1	22
Torrevieja, Spain	D5	22
Torrey, Ut., U.S.	E4	121
Torridge, stm., Eng., U.K.	D3	12
Torridon, Loch, b., Scot., U.K.	C3	13
Torriglia, Italy	E5	20
Tørring, Den.	C3	15
Torrington, Alta.	D4	68
Torrington, Ct., U.S.	B3	84
Torrington, Wy., U.S.	D8	127
Torrinha, Braz.	m7	56
Torrox, Spain	D4	22
Tors Cove, Newf.	E5	72
Torshälla (part of Eskilstuna), Swe.	t34	14
Tórshavn, Faer. Is.	C7	8
Tortilla Flat, Az., U.S.	G12	64
Tortola, i., V.I., Br.	B4	80
Tortona, Italy	B2	54
Tortosa, Spain	B6	22
Tortosa, Cape, c., Spain	B6	22
Tortue, Île de la, i., Haiti	D7	64
Tortugas, Golfo, b., Col.	C2	60
Torugart Pass, Asia	E9	28
Toruń, Pol.	B5	26
Torup, Swe.	B9	92
Tory Hill, Ont.	C6	73
Tory Island, i., Ire.	A3	11
Torysa, stm., Czech.	D6	26
Tory Sound, strt., Ire.	B3	11
Torzhok, Sov. Un.	C10	27
Torzym, Pol.	A10	19
Tosa-shimizu, Japan	J6	33
Tosno, Sov. Un.	B8	27
Tostado, Arg.	E3	55
Toston, Mt., U.S.	D5	103
Tosya, Tur.	B10	40
Toszek, Pol.	g9	26
Totagatic, stm., Wi., U.S.	B2	126
Totana, Spain	D5	22
Toteng, Bots.	B3	49
Tótkomlós, Hung.	B5	24
Totma, Sov. Un.	C4	28
Totnes, Eng., U.K.	D4	12
Totness, Sur.	A3	59
Toto, Guam	L10	52
Totolapan (part of Mexico City), Mex.	h9	63
Totonicapán, Guat.	E6	63
Totora Palca, Bol.	C2	55
Totoya Island, i., Fiji	I16	52
Totson Mountain, mtn., Ak., U.S.	C8	79
Totten Glacier, ice, Ant.	C24	7
Tottenham, Austl.	F6	51
Tottenham (part of London), Eng., U.K.	k12	10
Tottori, Japan	D11	31
Totz, Ky., U.S.	D6	94
Touba, I.C.	D3	45
Touba, Sen.	D1	45
Toubkal, Jbel, mtn., Mor.	C3	44
Touchet, Wa., U.S.	C7	124
Touchet, stm., Wa., U.S.	C7	124
Touchwood Lake, l., Man.	B4	70
Tougan, Burkina	D4	45
Touggourt, Alg.	C6	44
Tougué, Gui.	D2	45
Touhy, Ne., U.S.	C9	104
Touisset, Ma., U.S.	C5	98
Toul, Fr.	C6	16
Toulépleu, I.C.	E3	45
Toulon, Fr.	F6	16
Toulon, Il., U.S.	B4	90
Toulouse, Fr.	F4	16
Toungo, Nig.	E7	45
Toungoo, Burma	E10	36
Touraine, hist. reg., Fr.	D4	16
Tourcoing, Fr.	B5	16
Tourlaville, Fr.	C3	16
Tournai (Doornik), Bel.	B5	17
Tournon, Fr.	E6	16
Tournus, Fr.	C6	16
Touros, Braz.	C3	57
Tours, Fr.	D4	16
Tourville, Que.	B8	74
Touside, Pic, mtn., Chad	A3	46
Toussaint Creek, stm., Oh., U.S.	f7	112
Toutle, North Fork, stm., Wa., U.S.	C3	124
Tovar, Ven.	B3	60
Tovarkovskiy, Sov. Un.	E12	27
Tovey, Il., U.S.	D4	90
Tow, Tx., U.S.	D3	120
Towaco, N.J., U.S.	B4	107
Towada, l., Japan	F10	33
Towanda, Il., U.S.	C5	90
Towanda, Ks., U.S.	E7	93
Towanda, Pa., U.S.	C9	115
Towanda Creek, stm., Pa., U.S.	C8	115
Towaoc, Co., U.S.	D2	83
Tower, Mi., U.S.	C6	99
Tower, Mn., U.S.	C6	100
Tower City, N.D., U.S.	C8	111
Tower City, Pa., U.S.	E8	115
Tower Hill, Il., U.S.	D5	90
Town and Country, Wa., U.S.	*B8	124
Town Creek, Al., U.S.	A2	78
Town Creek Manor, Md., U.S.	D5	97
Towner, Co., U.S.	C8	83
Towner, N.D., U.S.	A5	111
Towner, co., N.D., U.S.	A6	111
Town Hill, Ct., U.S.	B3	84
Town Hill, hill, Ber.	p20	64
Townley, Al., U.S.	B2	78
Town 'n Country, Fl., U.S.	*E4	86
Town of Tonawanda, N.Y., U.S.	C2	109
Towns, co., Ga., U.S.	B3	87
Townsend, De., U.S.	C3	85
Townsend, Ma., U.S.	A4	98
Townsend, Mt., U.S.	D5	103
Townsend, Tn., U.S.	D10	119
Townsend, Va., U.S.	C7	123
Townshend, Vt., U.S.	E3	122
Townshend Reservoir, res., Vt., U.S.	E3	122
Townsville, Austl.	C8	50
Townsville, N.C., U.S.	A4	110
Townville, Pa., U.S.	C2	115
Townville, S.C., U.S.	B2	117
Towson, Md., U.S.	B4	97
Towuti, Lake, l., Indon.	F6	34
Toxey, Al., U.S.	D1	78
Toyah, Tx., U.S.	o13	120
Toyahvale, Tx., U.S.	o13	120
Toyama, Japan	D12	31
Toyama Bay, b., Japan	H8	33
Toyohashi, Japan	I8	33
Toyokawa, Japan	*I8	33
Toyonaka, Japan	o14	33
Toyota, Japan	n16	33
Tozeur, Tun.	C6	44
Trabancos, stm., Spain	B3	22
Traben-Trarbach, Ger.	D2	19
Trabzon, Tur.	B12	40
Tracadie, N.B.	B5	71
Tracadie, N.S.	D8	71
Tracy, N.B.	D3	71
Tracy, Que.	C4	74
Tracy, Ca., U.S.	D3	82
Tracy, Mn., U.S.	F3	100
Tracy, Mn., U.S.	B3	102
Tracy City, Tn., U.S.	D8	119
Tracys Creek, stm., Md., U.S.	C4	97
Tracyton, Wa., U.S.	e10	124
Tradate, Italy	E6	21
Trade, Tn., U.S.	C12	119
Trade Lake, l., Sask.	B4	75
Tradewater, stm., Ky., U.S.	C2	94
Trading Post, Ks., U.S.	D9	93
Traer, Ia., U.S.	B5	92
Traer, Ks., U.S.	C3	93
Trafalgar, In., U.S.	F5	91
Trafalgar, Cape, c., Spain	D2	22
Trafford, Pa., U.S.	k14	115
Trafford, Lake, l., Fl., U.S.	F5	86
Traiguén, Chile	B2	54
Trail, B.C.	E9	69
Trail, Mn., U.S.	C3	100
Trail, Or., U.S.	E4	114
Trail City, S.D., U.S.	B5	118
Trail Creek, In., U.S.	A4	91
Traill, co., N.D., U.S.	B8	111
Traill, i., Greenld.	B18	128
Trail Ridge, mtn., U.S.	F4	87
Traipu, Braz.	C4	57
Trairi, stm., Braz.	h6	57
Tralee, Ire.	D2	11
Tralee Bay, b., Ire.	E2	11
Tramelan [-Dessus], Switz.	B3	21
Trammel, Va., U.S.	e9	123
Tramore, Ire.	E4	11
Trampas, N.M., U.S.	A4	108
Tramping Lake, Sask.	E1	75
Tramping Lake, l., Sask.	E2	75
Tranås, Swe.	B6	15
Trancão, stm., Port.	I9	22
Trancoso, Port.	B2	22
Tranemo, Swe.	A7	15
Trang, Thai.	D1	34
Trangan, i., Indon.	G8	34
Trani, Italy	D6	23
Tranninh, Plateau du, plat., Laos	C5	35
Tranquility, N.J., U.S.	B3	107
Tranquility, Ca., U.S.	D3	82
Transfer, Pa., U.S.	D1	115
Transkei, ctry., Afr.	D4	49
Transvaal, prov., S. Afr.	B4	49
Transylvania, La., U.S.	B4	95
Transylvania, co., N.C., U.S.	f10	110
Transylvania, hist. reg., Rom.	B6	24
Transylvanian Alps, mts., Rom.	C7	24
Trapani, Italy	E4	23
Trap Mountain, mtn., Ar., U.S.	g7	81
Trappe, Md., U.S.	C5	97
Trappe Creek, stm., Md., U.S.	D7	97
Trapper Peak, mtn., Mt., U.S.	E2	103
Traralgon, Austl.	G8	50
Traryd, Swe.	B7	15
Trasimeno, Lake, l., Italy	C4	23
Trask, Mo., U.S.	E6	102
Traskwood, Ar., U.S.	C3	81
Tras-os-Montes, hist. reg., Port.	B2	22
Trat, Thai.	C2	34
Traun, stm., Aus.	D7	18
Traunik, Mi., U.S.	B4	99
Traun Lake, l., Aus.	E6	18
Traunstein, Ger.	E6	18
Trave, stm., Eur.	E4	15
Travelers Rest, S.C., U.S.	B3	117
Travers, Alta.	D4	68
Travers, Switz.	C2	21
Traverse, co., Mn., U.S.	E2	100
Traverse, Lake, l., U.S.	B9	118
Traverse City, Mi., U.S.	D5	99
Traverspine, stm., Newf.	B1	72
Travers Reservoir, res., Alta.	D4	68
Tra Vinh, Viet.	H7	35
Travis, co., Tx., U.S.	D4	120
Travis Air Force Base, mil., Ca., U.S.	C2	82
Travnik, Yugo.	C3	24
Tray Mountain, mtn., Ga., U.S.	B3	87
Treadway, Tn., U.S.	C10	119
Treasure, co., Mt., U.S.	D9	103
Treasure Island, Fl., U.S.	*p10	86
Treasure Island Naval Station, mil., Ca., U.S.	h8	82
Trebbia, stm., Italy	E5	20
Trebel, stm., Ger.	E6	15
Třebíč, Czech.	D3	26
Trebinje, Yugo.	D4	24
Trebišov, Czech.	D6	26
Treble Mountain, mtn., B.C.	B3	69
Trebloc, Ms., U.S.	B5	101
Třeboň, Czech.	D3	26
Trece Martires, Phil.	o13	34
Treece, Ks., U.S.	E9	93
Trees, La., U.S.	B1	95
Tregaron, Wales, U.K.	G3	75
Trego, Mt., U.S.	B2	103
Trego, Wi., U.S.	C2	126
Trego, co., Ks., U.S.	C4	93
Tréguier, Fr.	C2	16
Treherne, Man.	E2	70
Treig, Loch, res., Scot., U.K.	D4	13
Treinta y Tres, Ur.	E2	56
Treis, Ger.	C2	19
Trélazé, Fr.	D3	16
Trelew, Arg.	C3	54
Trelleborg, Swe.	J5	14
Tremadog Bay, b., Wales, U.K.	D4	10
Tremblant, Mont, mtn., Que.	C3	74
Tremblay, Fr.	g11	16
Trembleur Lake, l., B.C.	B5	69
Trementina, N.M., U.S.	B5	108
Tremiti Islands, is., Italy	C5	23
Tremont, Il., U.S.	C4	90
Tremont, Ms., U.S.	A5	101
Tremont, Pa., U.S.	E9	115
Tremont City, Oh., U.S.	B2	112
Tremonton, Ut., U.S.	B3	121
Tremošná, Czech.	D2	26
Tremp, Spain	A6	22
Trempealeau, Wi., U.S.	D2	126
Trempealeau, co., Wi., U.S.	D2	126
Trenary, Mi., U.S.	B4	99
Trenche, stm., Que.	B5	74
Trenčín, Czech.	D4	26
Trenque Lauquen, Arg.	B4	54
Trent, Ger.	D7	15
Trent, S.D., U.S.	D9	118
Trent, Tx., U.S.	C2	120
Trent, stm., Eng., U.K.	D6	10
Trent, stm., N.C., U.S.	B5	110
Trente et un Milles, Lac des, l., Que.	C2	74
Trentino-Alto Adige, prov., Italy	C7	20
Trento (Trent), Italy	A3	23
Trenton, N.S.	D7	71
Trenton, Ont.	C7	73
Trenton, Al., U.S.	A3	78
Trenton, Fl., U.S.	C4	86
Trenton, Ga., U.S.	B1	87
Trenton, Il., U.S.	E4	90
Trenton, Ky., U.S.	D2	94
Trenton, Mi., U.S.	F7	99
Trenton, Mo., U.S.	A4	102
Trenton, Ne., U.S.	D4	104
Trenton, N.J., U.S.	C3	107
Trenton, N.C., U.S.	B5	110
Trenton, Oh., U.S.	C1	112
Trenton, S.C., U.S.	D4	117
Trenton, Tn., U.S.	B3	119
Trenton, Tx., U.S.	C4	120
Trenton, Ut., U.S.	B4	121
Trepassey, Newf.	E5	72
Trepassey Bay, b., Newf.	E5	72
Tres Algarrobos, Arg.	E1	54
Tres Arroyos, Arg.	B4	54
Tres Árboles, Ur.	E1	56
Tres Cerros, Arg.	D3	54
Tresckow, Pa., U.S.	E10	115
Três Corações, Braz.	C3	56
Tres Esquinas, Col.	C2	60
Três Lagoas, Braz.	C2	56
Tres Marías, Represas, res., Braz.	B3	56
Tres Piedras, N.M., U.S.	A4	108
Tres Puntas, Cabo, c., Arg.	D3	54
Três Rios, Braz.	h6	56
Três Ritos, N.M., U.S.	A4	108
Trestle Creek, Id., U.S.	A2	89
Treuchtlingen, Ger.	E5	19
Treuenbrietzen, Ger.	A7	19
Treutlen, co., Ga., U.S.	D4	87
Treviglio, Italy	A4	23
Trévillers, Fr.	B4	21
Treviño, Spain	A4	22
Treviso, Italy	B4	23
Trevlac, In., U.S.	F5	91

Name	Map Ref.	Page
Trevor, Wi., U.S.	n11	126
Trevorton, Pa., U.S.	E8	115
Trevose, Pa., U.S.	o22	115
Trevose Head, c., Eng., U.K.	D2	12
Treynor, Ia., U.S.	C2	92
Treysa, Ger.	C4	19
Trezevant, Tn., U.S.	A3	119
Trhové Sviny, Czech.	E9	19
Triadelphia, W.V., U.S.	A4	125
Triadelphia Reservoir, res., Md., U.S.	B3	97
Triánda, Grc.	D7	25
Triangle, Va., U.S.	B5	123
Triaucourt [-en-Argonne], Fr.	F5	17
Tribbett, Ms., U.S.	B3	101
Tribbey, Ok., U.S.	B4	113
Tribune, Sask.	H4	75
Tribune, Ks., U.S.	D2	93
Trichinopoly see Tiruchchirāppalli, India	F6	36
Trichūr, India	F6	36
Tri City, Or., U.S.	E3	114
Tridell, Ut., U.S.	C6	121
Trident, Mt., U.S.	E5	103
Trident Peak, mtn., Nv., U.S.	B3	105
Trier, Ger.	D3	18
Trieste, Italy	B4	23
Trieste, Gulf of, b., Eur.	B4	23
Trigg, co., Ky., U.S.	D2	94
Triglav, mtn., Yugo.	B1	24
Trigo Mountains, mts., Az., U.S.	D1	80
Trigueros, Spain	D2	22
Trikala, Grc.	C3	40
Trikhonis, Lake, l., Grc.	C3	25
Trikora, Peak, mtn., Indon.	F9	34
Tri Lakes, In., U.S.	B7	91
Trilby, Fl., U.S.	D4	86
Trilla, Il., U.S.	D5	90
Trillick, N. Ire., U.K.	C4	11
Trim, Ire.	D5	11
Trimble, Mo., U.S.	B3	102
Trimble, Tn., U.S.	A2	119
Trimble, co., Ky., U.S.	B4	94
Trimont, Mn., U.S.	G4	100
Trimonium, Mi., U.S.	A2	99
Trinchera, Co., U.S.	D6	83
Trinchera Creek, stm., Co., U.S.	D5	83
Trincomalee, Sri L.	G7	36
Trindade, i., Braz.	H8	5
Třinec, Czech.	*D5	26
Tring Jonction, Que.	C6	74
Trinidad, Bol.	B3	55
Trinidad, Col.	B3	60
Trinidad, Cuba	D4	64
Trinidad, Co., U.S.	D6	83
Trinidad, Tx., U.S.	C4	120
Trinidad, Ur.	E1	56
Trinidad, i., Trin.	K14	64
Trinidad, Bahía, b., Par.	k11	62
Trinidad, Isla, i., Arg.	B4	54
Trinidad and Tobago, ctry., N.A.	K14	64
Trinity Head, c., Ca., U.S.	B1	82
Trinity, Newf.	D5	72
Trinity, Newf.	D5	72
Trinity, Al., U.S.	A2	78
Trinity, N.C., U.S.	*B3	110
Trinity, Tx., U.S.	D5	120
Trinity, co., Ca., U.S.	B2	82
Trinity, co., Tx., U.S.	D5	120
Trinity, stm., Tx., U.S.	D5	120
Trinity, East Fork, stm., Tx., U.S.	n10	120
Trinity, Elm Fork, stm., Tx., U.S.	m10	120
Trinity, South Fork, stm., Ca., U.S.	B2	82
Trinity, West Fork, stm., Tx., U.S.	n9	120
Trinity Bay, b., Newf.	D5	72
Trinity Center, Ca., U.S.	B2	82
Trinity Islands, is., Ak., U.S.	D9	79
Trinity Mountain, mtn., Id., U.S.	F3	89
Trinity Mountains, mts., Ca., U.S.	B2	82
Trinity Peak, mtn., Nv., U.S.	C3	105
Trinity Range, mts., Nv., U.S.	C3	105
Trinity Springs, In., U.S.	G4	91
Trino, Italy	B2	23
Trinway, Oh., U.S.	B3	112
Trio, S.C., U.S.	E8	117
Trion, Ga., U.S.	B1	87
Triplett, Mo., U.S.	B4	102
Tripoli (Ṭarābulus), Libya	B3	38
Tripoli (Ṭarābulus), Libya	C2	43
Tripoli, Ia., U.S.	B5	92
Tripoli, Wi., U.S.	C4	126
Tripolis, Grc.	D4	40
Tripolitania (Ṭarābulus), hist. reg., Libya	C3	43
Tripp, S.D., U.S.	D8	118
Tripp, co., S.D., U.S.	D6	118
Tripura, state, India	D9	36
Trisanna, stm., Aus.	B9	21
Trischen, i., Ger.	A4	18
Tristan da Cunha, is., St. Hel.	I9	5
Triste, Golfo, b., Ven.	A4	60
Triumph, La., U.S.	E6	95
Triune, Tn., U.S.	B5	119
Triunfo, Braz.	C3	57
Trivandrum, India	G6	36
Trnava, Czech.	D4	26
Trobriand Islands, is., Pap. N. Gui.	k13	50
Trochu, Alta.	D4	68
Trogir, Yugo.	D3	24
Trögstad, Nor.	p29	14
Troisdorf, Ger.	C2	19
Trois-Pistoles, Que.	A8	74
Trois-Rivières, Que.	C5	74
Trois-Rivières-Ouest, Que.	C5	74
Trois-Saumons, Que.	B7	74
Troisvierges, Lux.	D9	17
Troitsk, Sov. Un.	D9	29
Troitskoye, Sov. Un.	B8	33
Trolldalen, Nor.	p28	14
Trollhättan, Swe.	H5	14
Trombetas, stm., Braz.	C3	59
Trombly, Mi., U.S.	B3	99
Tromper Wiek, b., Ger.	D7	15
Tromsö, Nor.	E5	82
Trona, Ca., U.S.	E5	82
Tronador, Monte, mtn., S.A.	E2	56
Trondheim, Nor.	F4	14
Trondheimsfjorden, Nor.	F4	14
Troon, Scot., U.K.	E4	13
Trooper, Pa., U.S.	*F11	115
Tropea, Italy	E5	23
Trophy Mountain, mtn., B.C.	D8	69
Tropic, Ut., U.S.	F3	121
Trosa, Swe.	u35	14
Trosky, Mn., U.S.	G2	100
Trossachs, Sask.	H3	75
Trostan, mtn., N. Ire., U.K.	B5	11
Trotters, N.D., U.S.	B2	111
Trotwood, Oh., U.S.	C1	112
Troup, Tx., U.S.	C5	120
Troup, co., Ga., U.S.	C1	87
Trousdale, Ks., U.S.	E4	93
Trousdale, co., Tn., U.S.	A5	119
Trousers Lake, l., N.B.	B3	71
Trout, La., U.S.	C3	95
Trout, stm., Alta.	A3	68
Trout, stm., Fl., U.S.	m8	86
Trout, stm., U.S.	B3	122
Trout Creek, Ont.	B5	73
Trout Creek, Mi., U.S.	n12	99
Trout Creek, Mt., U.S.	C1	103
Trout Creek, Ut., U.S.	D2	121
Trout Creek Pass, Co., U.S.	C5	83
Troutdale, Me., U.S.		
Troutdale, Or., U.S.	*B4	114
Trout Dale, Va., U.S.	D1	123
Trout Lake, Mi., U.S.	B6	99
Trout Lake, Wa., U.S.	D4	124
Trout Lake, l., B.C.	D9	69
Trout Lake, l., N.W. Ter.	D8	66
Trout Lake, l., Ont.	A5	73
Trout Lake, l., Ont.	o16	73
Trout Lake, l., Mn., U.S.	B6	100
Trout Lake, l., Wi., U.S.	B4	126
Troutman, Ga., U.S.	E2	87
Troutman, N.C., U.S.	B2	110
Trout Peak, mtn., Wy., U.S.	B3	127
Trout Run, Pa., U.S.	D7	115
Trouville [-sur-Mer], Fr.	C4	16
Trowbridge, Eng., U.K.	E5	10
Troy, Al., U.S.	D4	78
Troy, Id., U.S.	C2	89
Troy, Il., U.S.	E4	90
Troy, Ia., U.S.	H4	91
Troy, Ks., U.S.	D5	92
Troy, Mi., U.S.	o15	99
Troy, Mo., U.S.	C7	102
Troy, Ms., U.S.	A5	101
Troy, Mo., U.S.	C7	102
Troy, N.H., U.S.	E2	106
Troy, N.Y., U.S.	C7	109
Troy, N.C., U.S.	B3	110
Troy, Oh., U.S.	B1	112
Troy, Ok., U.S.	C5	113
Troy, Or., U.S.	B9	114
Troy, Pa., U.S.	C8	115
Troy, S.C., U.S.	D3	117
Troy, S.D., U.S.	B9	118
Troy, Tn., U.S.	A2	119
Troy, Vt., U.S.	B4	122
Troy, W.V., U.S.	B4	125
Troy Mills, Ia., U.S.	B6	92
Troy Grove, Il., U.S.	B4	90
Troy Peak, mtn., Nv., U.S.	E6	105
Troyan, Bul.	D5	24
Troyes, Fr.	D5	16
Troy (Ilion), hist., Tur.	C6	25
Troy International Airport, Micron.	Q18	52
Truk Lagoon, b., Micron.	Q18	52
Truman, Mn., U.S.	G4	100
Trumann, Ar., U.S.	B5	81
Trumansburg, N.Y., U.S.	C4	109
Trumbull, Ct., U.S.	E3	84
Trumbull, Ne., U.S.	D7	104
Trumbull, co., Oh., U.S.	A5	112
Trumbull, Mount, mtn., Az., U.S.	A2	80
Trun, Bul.	D6	24
Truro, N.S.	D6	71
Truro, Eng., U.K.	E4	10
Truro, Ia., U.S.	C4	92
Truscott, Tx., U.S.	C3	120
Truskmore, mtn., Ire.	C3	11
Trussville, Al., U.S.	B3	78
Trustom Pond, l., R.I., U.S.	G3	116
Trust Territory of the Pacific Islands see Pacific Islands, Trust Territory of the, dep., Oc.	F9	6
Truth or Consequences (Hot Springs), N.M., U.S.	D2	108
Trutnov, Czech.	C3	26
Truxton, Az., U.S.	B2	80
Truxton, Mo., U.S.	B6	102
Truxton, N.Y., U.S.	C4	109
Tryon, Ne., U.S.	C5	104
Tryon, N.C., U.S.	f10	110
Tryon, Ok., U.S.	B5	113
Trysil, Nor.	G5	14
Trzcianka, Pol.	B4	26
Trzebiatów, Pol.	A3	26
Trzebinia, Pol.	C5	26
Trzebnica, Pol.	C4	26
Tsagaan Tologoy Hiid, Mong.	C2	32
Tsaidam Basin see Qaidam Pendi, China	D3	31
Tsakir, Sov. Un.	A5	31
Tsaratanana, Madag.	g9	49
Tsast Bogd Mountain, mtn., Mong.	B3	31
Tsau, Bots.	B6	48
Tschetter Colony, S.D., U.S.	D8	118
Tselinograd, Sov. Un.	D10	29
Tsentralnyy, Sov. Un.	D26	8
Tsetserleg, Mong.	B5	31
Tshabong, Bots.	C3	49
Tshane, Bots.	B1	48
Tshela, Zaïre	B1	48
Tshikapa, Zaïre	C3	48
Tshilongo, Zaïre	D4	48
Tshimbo, Zaïre	B3	48
Tshofa, Zaïre	C4	48
Tshuapa, stm., Zaïre	B3	48
Tshwaane, Bots.	B3	49
Tsihombe, Madag.	i9	49
Tsimlyansk Reservoir, res., Sov. Un.	E7	29
Tsinan see Jinan, China	D8	31
Tsinghai see Qinghai, prov., China	D4	31
Tsingtao see Qingdao, China	D9	31
Tsintsabis, Nmb.	A2	49
Tsiroanomandidy, Madag.	g9	49
Tsitsihar see Qiqihar, China	B9	31
Tsivory, Madag.	h9	49
Tskhinvali, Sov. Un.	E2	28
Tsna, stm., Sov. Un.	E13	27
Tsodilo Hill, hill, Bots.	A3	49
Tsogttsetsiy, Mong.	C1	32
Tsu, Japan	I8	33
Tsuchiura, Japan	H10	33
Tsugaru Strait, strt., Japan	F10	33
Tsuken Island, i., Japan	O5	52
Tsulukidze, Sov. Un.	A14	40
Tsumeb, Nmb.	A2	49
Tsumis Park, Nmb.	B2	49
Tsun Wan, H.K.	*G7	31
Tsuruga, Japan	I8	33
Tsurugi, Mount, mtn., Japan	J7	33
Tsuruoka, Japan	G9	33
Tsushima, Japan	n15	33
Tsu Shima, is., Japan	E10	31
Tsushima, Japan	I6	33
Tsuyama, Japan	I6	33
Tua, stm., Port.	B2	22
Tual, Indon.	G8	34
Tualatin, Or., U.S.	*h12	114
Tualatin, stm., Or., U.S.	h11	114
Tuam, Ire.	D2	10
Tuamotu Archipelago, is., Fr. Poly.	H13	6
Tuangku, i., Indon.	K2	33
Tuapse, Sov. Un.	G16	8
Tuasivi, W. Sam.	F11	52
Tuasivi, Cape, c., W. Sam.	F11	52
Tuatapere, N.Z.	Q11	51
Tubac, Az., U.S.	F4	80
Tuba City, Az., U.S.	A4	80
Tubarão, Braz.	D3	56
Tūbās, Isr. Occ.	B7	41
Tuberose, Sask.	G1	75
Tübingen, Ger.	C6	20
Tubre, Italy	C6	20
Ṭubruq (Tobruk), Libya	C4	43
Tubuai Islands, is., Fr. Poly.	H13	6
Tucacas, Ven.	A4	60
Tucannon, stm., Wa., U.S.	C8	124
Tucannon Canyon, val., Wa., U.S.	C8	124
Tucano, Braz.	D3	57
Tuchola, Pol.	B4	26
Tuckahoe, N.J., U.S.	E3	107
Tuckahoe, N.Y., U.S.	h13	109
Tuckahoe, stm., N.J., U.S.	E3	107
Tuckahoe Creek, stm., Md., U.S.	C6	97
Tucker, Ar., U.S.	C4	81
Tucker, Ga., U.S.	h8	87
Tucker, Tx., U.S.	D5	120
Tucker, co., W.V., U.S.	B5	125
Tucker Island, i., N.J., U.S.	E4	107
Tuckerman, Ar., U.S.	B4	81
Tuckernuck Island, i., Ma., U.S.	D7	98
Tuckers Crossing, Ms., U.S.	D4	101
Tuckerton, N.J., U.S.	D4	107
Trujillo, Hond.	D7	63
Trujillo, Peru	C2	58
Trujillo, Spain	C3	22
Trujillo, Ven.	B3	60
Trujillo, state, Ven.	B3	60
Truk, is., Micron.	F9	6
Tucson, Az., U.S.	E5	80
Tucson Mountains, mts., Az., U.S.	E4	80
Tucumán, prov., Arg.	E2	55
Tucumcari, N.M., U.S.	B6	108
Tucumcari Mountain, mtn., N.M., U.S.	B6	108
Tucunaré, Braz.	B5	59
Tucupita, Ven.	C5	59
Tucuruí, Braz.	g10	28
Tuczno, Pol.	B5	26
Tudela, Spain	A5	22
Tudmur (Palmyra), Syria	E12	40
Tufi, Pap. N. Gui.	k12	50
Tuftonboro, N.H., U.S.	C4	106
Tugaloo Lake, res., U.S.	B1	117
Tugaske, Sask.	G2	75
Tug Fork, stm., U.S.	C2	125
Tuguegarao, Phil.	B6	34
Tuira, stm., Pan.	G9	62
Tukangbesi Islands, is., Indon.	G6	34
Tūkrah, Libya	C4	43
Tuktoyaktuk, N.W. Ter.	C6	66
Tukums, Sov. Un.	C4	27
Tukuyu, Tan.	C5	48
Tukwila, Wa., U.S.	f11	124
Tula, Mex.	C5	63
Tula, Sov. Un.	D6	29
Tula de Allende, Mex.	m14	63
Tulalip Indian Reservation, Wa., U.S.	A3	124
Tulancingo, Mex.	C5	63
Tulare, Ca., U.S.	D4	82
Tulare, S.D., U.S.	C7	118
Tulare, co., Ca., U.S.	D4	82
Tulare, Lake, l., Ca., U.S.	D4	82
Tularosa, N.M., U.S.	D3	108
Tularosa Mountains, mts., N.M., U.S.	D1	108
Tularosa Valley, val., N.M., U.S.	E3	108
Tulbagh, S. Afr.	D2	49
Tulcán, Ec.	A2	58
Tulcea, Rom.	C9	24
Tulchin, Sov. Un.	G7	27
Tulelake, Ca., U.S.	B3	82
Tule Lake Sump, sw., Ca., U.S.	B3	82
Tule River Indian Reservation, Ca., U.S.	E4	82
Tulia, Tx., U.S.	B2	120
Tulkarm, Isr. Occ.	B7	41
Tulla, Ire.	E3	11
Tullahassee, Ok., U.S.	B6	113
Tullahoma, Tn., U.S.	B5	119
Tullamore, Ire.	D3	10
Tulle, Fr.	E4	16
Tullins, Fr.	E6	16
Tulln, Aus.	D8	18
Tullow, Ire.	C5	11
Tullos, La., U.S.	C3	95
Tullytown, Pa., U.S.	T/C.Is.	8
Tulmaythah, Libya	F3	40
Tuloma, stm., Sov. Un.	B15	8
Tulot, Ar., U.S.	B5	81
Tulsā, Ar., U.S.	A6	113
Tulsa, co., Ok., U.S.	B6	113
Tulsequah, B.C.	E6	66
Tulsk, Ire.	D3	11
Tuluá, Col.	C2	60
Tulun, Sov. Un.	D13	29
Tulungagung, Indon.	G4	34
Tulu Welel, mtn., Eth.	D3	47
Tuma, stm., Nic.	D5	62
Tumacacori, Az., U.S.	F4	80
Tumacacori National Monument, Az., U.S.	F4	80
Tumaco, Col.	C2	60
Tumaco, Ensenada de, b., Col.	C2	60
Tumalo, Or., U.S.	C5	114
Tumba, Swe.	t35	14
Tumba, Lac, l., Zaïre	B2	48
Tumbarumba, Austl.	G7	51
Tumbaya, Arg.	A3	54
Tumbes, Peru	B1	58
Tumbes, dept., Peru	B1	58
Tumble Mountain, mtn., Mt., U.S.	E7	103
Tumbler Ridge, B.C.	B7	69
Tumbling Shoals, Ar., U.S.	B3	81
Tumen, China	C10	31
Tumen Jiang, stm., Asia	E4	33
Tumeremo, Ven.	B5	60
Tumkūr, India	F6	36
Tumnin, stm., Sov. Un.	A10	33
Tumon Bay, b., Guam	L10	52
Tumtum, Wa., U.S.	B8	124
Tumu, Ghana	D4	45
Tumuc-Humac Mountains, mts., S.A.	B3	59
Tumut, Austl.	G7	51
Tumwater, Wa., U.S.	B3	124
Tunapuna, Trin.	N23	65
Tunas de Zaza, Cuba	D4	64
Tunaycha, l., Sov. Un.	C11	33
Tunbridge, Vt., U.S.	D4	122
Tunbridge Wells see Royal Tunbridge Wells, Eng., U.K.	E7	10
Tunduru, Tan.	D6	48
Tundzha, stm., Eur.	D8	24
Tunga, stm., India	F6	36
Tungla, Nic.	D5	62
Tunga, prov., Ec.	B2	58
Tuni, India	I9	37
Tunica, La., U.S.	D4	95
Tunica, Ms., U.S.	A3	101
Tunica, co., Ms., U.S.	A3	101
Tunis, Tun.	B7	44
Tunis, Gulf of, b., Tun.	F3	23
Tunisia, ctry., Afr.	C6	44
Tunis Mills, Md., U.S.	C5	97
Tunja, Col.	B3	60
Tunkhannock, Pa., U.S.	C10	115
Tunk Lake, l., Me., U.S.	D4	96
Tunnel Hill, Ga., U.S.	B1	87
Tunnel Springs, Al., U.S.	D2	78
Tunnelton, In., U.S.	G5	91
Tunnelton, W.V., U.S.	B5	125
Tunø, i., Den.	C4	15
Tunp Range, mts., Wy., U.S.	D2	127
Tuntutuliak, Ak., U.S.	C7	79
Tununak, Ak., U.S.	C6	79
Tunuyán, Arg.	A3	54
Tunuyán, stm., Arg.	A3	54
Tunxi, China	F8	31
Tuolumne, Ca., U.S.	D3	82
Tuolumne, co., Ca., U.S.	C4	82
Tuolumne, stm., Ca., U.S.	D3	82
Tupã, Braz.	C2	56
Tupanciretã, Braz.	D2	56
Tupelo, Ar., U.S.	B4	81
Tupelo, Ms., U.S.	A5	101
Tupelo, Ok., U.S.	C5	113
Tupiza, Bol.	D2	55
Tupman, Ca., U.S.	E4	82
Tupper, B.C.	B7	69
Tupper Lake, N.Y., U.S.	A6	109
Tupper Lake, l., N.Y., U.S.	A6	109
Tuppers Plains, Oh., U.S.	C4	112
Tupperville, Ont.	E2	73
Tupungato, Arg.	A3	54
Tupungato, Cerro, mtn., S.A.	A3	54
Tuquan, China	B9	32
Túquerres, Col.	C2	60
Tura, India	E13	37
Tura, Sov. Un.	C13	29
Tura, stm., Sov. Un.	D8	28
Turabah, Sau. Ar.	A2	60
Turan Lowland, pl., Sov. Un.	E5	28
Turayf, Sau. Ar.	B2	42
Turbaco, Col.	A2	60
Turbat, Pak.	C3	36
Turbenthal, Switz.	B6	21
Turbeville, S.C., U.S.	D7	117
Turbo, Col.	B2	60
Turbotville, Pa., U.S.	D8	115
Turda, Rom.	B6	24
Turek, Pol.	B5	26
Turgay, Sov. Un.	E9	29
Turgay, stm., Sov. Un.	D8	28
Türgen Mountain, mtn., Mong.	B3	31
Türgovishte, Bul.	D8	24
Turgutlu, Tur.	C6	40
Turhal, Tur.	*B11	41
Turi, Sov. Un.	C5	27
Turiaçu, Braz.	B1	57
Turiaçu, stm., Braz.	B1	57
Turimiquire, Cerro, mtn., Ven.	A5	60
Turin, Alta.	E4	68
Turin see Torino, Italy	B1	23
Turin, Ga., U.S.	C2	87
Turin, Ia., U.S.	B2	92
Turin, N.Y., U.S.	B5	109
Turiy Rog, Sov. Un.	D5	33
Turka, Sov. Un.	G4	27
Turkestan, Sov. Un.	E9	29
Türkeve, Hung.	B4	24
Turkey, N.C., U.S.	C4	110
Turkey, Tx., U.S.	B2	120
Turkey, ctry., Asia	C10	40
Turkey, stm., Ia., U.S.	B6	92
Turkey Creek, La., U.S.	D3	95
Turkey Creek, stm., Ne., U.S.	D3	104
Turkey Creek, stm., Ok., U.S.	A3	113
Turkmen S.S.R., state, Sov. Un.	B5	97
Tuluá, Col.	C2	60
Tulun, Sov. Un.	D13	29
Tulungagung, Indon.	G4	34
Tulu Welel, mtn., Eth.	D3	47
Tuma, stm., Nic.	D5	62
Turnbull, Mount, mtn., Az., U.S.	D5	80
Turneffe Islands, is., Belize	D7	63
Turner, Ar., U.S.	C4	81
Turner, Me., U.S.	D2	96
Turner, Mi., U.S.	D7	99
Turner, Mt., U.S.	B8	103
Turner, Or., U.S.	C4	114
Turner, co., Ga., U.S.	E3	87
Turner, co., S.D., U.S.	D8	118
Turner Mountain, hill, Ct., U.S.	C1	84
Turners Falls, Ma., U.S.	A2	98
Turner Valley, Alta.	D3	68
Turney, Mo., U.S.	B3	102
Turnhout, Bel.	B6	16
Turnor Lake, l., Sask.	m7	75
Turnov, Czech.	C3	26
Turnu-Măgurele, Rom.	D7	24
Turočak, Sov. Un.	E26	8
Turon, Ks., U.S.	E5	93
Turpan, China	C2	31
Turpan Pendi, China	C2	31
Turpin, Ok., U.S.	e10	113
Turquino, Pico, mtn., Cuba	E5	64
Turrell, Ar., U.S.	B5	81
Turret Peak, mtn., Az., U.S.	C4	80
Turriff, Scot., U.K.	C6	13
Turshīz see Kāshmar, Iran	A10	42
Turtkul, Sov. Un.	E9	29
Turtle, stm., Ont.	E5	70
Turtle Creek, N.B.	D5	71
Turtle Creek, Pa., U.S.	k14	115
Turtle Flambeau Flowage, res., Wi., U.S.	B3	126
Turtleford, Sask.	D1	75
Turtle Lake, N.D., U.S.	B5	111
Turtle Lake, Wi., U.S.	C1	126
Turtle Lake, l., Sask.	D1	75
Turtle Mountain Indian Reservation, N.D., U.S.	A6	111
Turtle Mountains, hills, N.A.	A5	111
Turtle River, Mn., U.S.	C3	100
Turton, S.D., U.S.	B7	118
Turukhansk, Sov. Un.	C11	29
Turya, stm., Sov. Un.	F5	27
Tuscaloosa, Al., U.S.	B2	78
Tuscaloosa, co., Al., U.S.	B2	78
Tuscany (Toscana), prov., Italy	C3	23
Tuscarawas, co., Oh., U.S.	B4	112
Tuscarawas, stm., Oh., U.S.	B4	112
Tuscarora, Nv., U.S.	B5	105
Tuscarora Indian Reservation, N.Y., U.S.	B2	109
Tuscarora Mountain, mtn., Pa., U.S.	F6	115
Tuscarora Mountains, mts., Nv., U.S.	B5	105
Tuscola, Il., U.S.	D5	90
Tuscola, Ms., U.S.	C5	101
Tuscola, Tx., U.S.	C3	120
Tuscola, co., Mi., U.S.	E7	99
Tusculum, hist., Italy	h9	23
Tuscumbia, Al., U.S.	A2	78
Tuscumbia, Mo., U.S.	C5	102
Tushka, Ok., U.S.	C5	113
Tuskahoma, Ok., U.S.	C6	113
Tuskegee, Al., U.S.	C4	78
Tusket, N.S.	F4	71
Tusket, stm., N.S.	F4	71
Tustin, Ca., U.S.	*n13	82
Tustin, Mi., U.S.	D5	99
Tustumena Lake, l., Ak., U.S.	g16	79
Tutayev, Sov. Un.	C12	27
Tuthill, S.D., U.S.	D4	118
Tuticorin, India	G6	36
Tutrakan, Bul.	C8	24
Tuttle, N.D., U.S.	B6	111
Tuttle, Ok., U.S.	B4	113
Tuttle Creek, stm., Ks., U.S.	C7	93
Tuttle Creek Lake, res., Ks., U.S.	C7	93
Tuttlingen, Ger.	E4	18
Tutuala, Indon.	A5	49
Tutuban (Palmyra), Syria	E12	40
Tutuila, i., Am. Sam.	G13	52
Tutupaca, Volcán, vol., Peru	A3	54
Tututalak Mountain, mtn., Ak., U.S.	B7	79
Tutwiler, Ms., U.S.	A3	101
Tuvalu, ctry., Oc.	G10	6
Tuve, Swe.	A5	15
Tuvuca, i., Fiji	H16	52
Tuwayq, Jabal, mts., Sau. Ar.	D4	42
Tuxedo, N.C., U.S.	f10	110
Tuxedo Park, De., U.S.	i7	85
Tuxford, Sask.	G3	75
Tuxpan, Mex.	n12	63
Tuxpan, Mex.	C3	63
Tuxpan de Rodríguez Cano, Mex.	m15	63
Tuxtepec, Mex.	n15	63
Tuxtla Gutiérrez, Mex.	D6	63
Túy, Spain	A1	22
Tuyen Quang, Viet.	B6	35
Tuy Hoa, Viet.	F8	35
Tuymazy, Sov. Un.	D8	28
Tūysarkān, Iran	D4	39
Tuz, Lake, l., Tur.	C9	40
Tuzigoot National Monument, Az., U.S.	C3	80
Tūz Khurmātū, Iraq	E15	40
Tuzla, Yugo.	C4	24
Tver, Sov. Un.	C7	29
Tweed, Ont.	C7	73
Tweed, stm., U.K.	C5	10
Tweedsmuir Provincial Park, B.C.	C4	69
Tweedy Mountain, mtn., Mt., U.S.	E4	103
Twelve Mile, In., U.S.	C5	91
Twelve Mile Lake, l., Sask.	H2	75
Twelvepole Creek, East Fork, stm., W.V., U.S.	C2	125
Twelvepole Creek, West Fork, stm., W.V., U.S.	C2	125
Twentymile Creek, stm., U.S.	C3	125
Twentynine Palms, Ca., U.S.	E5	82
Twentynine Palms Base, Ca., U.S.	E5	82
Twentynine Palms Marine Corps Base, mil., Ca., U.S.	E5	82
Twiggs, co., Ga., U.S.	D3	87
Twillingate, Newf.	D4	72
Twin Bridges, Mt., U.S.	E4	103
Twin Brooks, S.D., U.S.	B9	118
Twin Buttes, Az., U.S.	C4	114
Twin Buttes Reservoir, res., Tx., U.S.	D2	120
Twin City, Ga., U.S.	D4	87
Twin Creek, stm., Oh., U.S.	C1	112
Twin Falls, Id., U.S.	G4	89
Twin Falls, co., Id., U.S.	G4	89
Twining, Mi., U.S.	D7	99
Twin Knolls, Az., U.S.	m9	80
Twin Lakes, Co., U.S.	B4	83
Twin Lakes, Ia., U.S.	F3	87
Twin Lakes, In., U.S.	B5	91
Twin Lakes, Wi., U.S.	F5	126
Twin Lakes, l., Ct., U.S.	A2	84
Twin Lakes, l., Ia., U.S.	B3	92
Twin Lakes, l., Me., U.S.	C4	96
Twin Lakes Mountain, mtn., N.Y., U.S.	B6	109
Twin Mountain, N.H., U.S.	B3	106
Twin Mountains, mts., Wy., U.S.	E7	127
Twin Peaks, mts., Id., U.S.	E4	89
Twin Rivers, Pa., U.S.	F4	115
Twinsburg, Oh., U.S.	A4	112
Twinton, Tn., U.S.	C8	119
Twin Valley, Mn., U.S.	C2	100
Twisp, Wa., U.S.	A5	124
Twist, Ar., U.S.	B5	81
Two Butte Creek, stm., Co., U.S.	D8	83
Two Buttes, Co., U.S.	D8	83
Two Creeks, Man.	D1	70
Twodot, Mt., U.S.	D6	103
Twoforks, stm., Sask.	C2	75
Two Harbors, Mn., U.S.	C7	100
Two Hills, Alta.	C5	68
Two Mile Beach, N.J., U.S.	F3	107
Two Prairie, Bayou, stm., Ar., U.S.	h11	81
Two Rivers, Wi., U.S.	D6	126
Two Rivers, North Branch, stm., Mn., U.S.	B2	100
Two Rivers, South Branch, stm., Mn., U.S.	B2	100
Tyachev, Sov. Un.	D7	26
Tyaskin, Md., U.S.	D6	97
Tybee Island, Ga., U.S.	D6	87
Tychy, Pol.	g9	26
Tye River, Va., U.S.	C4	123
Tygart Lake, res., W.V., U.S.	B5	125
Tygart River, Falls of the, wtfl., W.V., U.S.	k10	125
Tygarts Creek, stm., Ky., U.S.	B7	94
Tygart Valley, stm., W.V., U.S.	B4	125
Tyger, stm., S.C., U.S.	B4	117
Tygh Valley, Or., U.S.	B5	114
Tyler, Mn., U.S.	F2	100
Tyler, Tx., U.S.	C5	120
Tyler, co., Tx., U.S.	D5	120
Tyler, co., W.V., U.S.	B4	125
Tyler, Lake, res., Tx., U.S.	C5	120
Tyler Branch, stm., Vt., U.S.	B3	122
Tyler Heights, W.V., U.S.	m13	125
Tylersburg, Pa., U.S.	E7	115
Tylersville, Pa., U.S.	E7	115
Tylerton, Md., U.S.	D5	97
Tylertown, Ms., U.S.	D3	101
Tym, stm., Sov. Un.	C25	8
Tymochtee Creek, stm., Oh., U.S.	B2	112
Tynagh, Ire.	D3	11
Tyndall, Man.	D3	70
Tyndall, S.D., U.S.	E8	118
Tyndall Air Force Base, mil., Fl., U.S.	u16	86
Tyndinskiy, Sov. Un.	D15	29
Tyndrum, Scot., U.K.	D4	13
Tyne, stm., Eng., U.K.	C6	13
Tyne, stm., Scot., U.K.	E6	13
Tyne and Wear, co., Eng., U.K.	E7	13
Týnec, Czech.	o18	26
Tynemouth, Eng., U.K.	C6	10
Tyner, Sask.	G1	75
Tyner, Ky., U.S.	B5	91
Tyner, N.C., U.S.	A6	110
Tyner, Tn., U.S.	C8	71
Tyngsboro, Ma., U.S.	A5	98
Týn nad Vltavou, Czech.	F4	14
Tynset, Nor.	F4	14
Tyonek, Ak., U.S.	C9	79
Tyringham, Ma., U.S.	B1	98
Tyrma, Sov. Un.	A8	33
Tyro, Ks., U.S.	E8	93
Tyrone, Ky., U.S.	B5	94
Tyrone, N.M., U.S.	E1	108
Tyrone, Ok., U.S.	e9	113
Tyrone, Pa., U.S.	E5	115
Tyronza, Ar., U.S.	B5	81
Tyrrell, co., N.C., U.S.	B6	110
Tyrrell, Lake, l., Austl.	G4	51
Tysons Corner, Va., U.S.	*B5	123
Ty Ty, Ga., U.S.	E3	87
Ty Ty Creek, stm., Ga., U.S.	E3	87
Tyub-Karagan Peninsula, pen., Sov. Un.	B8	28
Tyukalinsk, Sov. Un.	D9	29
Tyuleniy Island, i., Sov. Un.	B12	33
Tyumen, Sov. Un.	D9	29
Tyuratam, Sov. Un.	E9	29
Tyvan, Sask.	G4	75
Tywyn, Wales, U.K.	B3	12
Tzaneen, S. Afr.	B5	49

U

Name	Map Ref.	Page
Uatumã, stm., Braz.	C3	59
Uaupés (Vaupés), stm., S.A.	C4	60
Ubá, Braz.	D7	57
Ubaira, Braz.	B3	57
Ubaitaba, Braz.	C4	57
Ubangi (Oubangui), stm., Afr.	A2	48
Ubaye, stm., Fr.	E2	20
Ubayyid, Wādī al, val., Asia	D7	41
Ube, Japan	E11	31
Úbeda, Spain	C4	22
Uberaba, Braz.	B3	57
Uberlândia, Braz.	E4	57
Überlingen, Ger.	E4	18
Ubiaja, Nig.	E8	45
Ubly, Mi., U.S.	E8	99
Ubombo, S. Afr.	m9	49
Ubon Ratchathani, Thai.	B2	34
Uborka, Sov. Un.	D6	27
Ubort, stm., Sov. Un.	F6	27
Ubrique, Spain	D3	22
Ubundu (Ponthierville), Zaïre	B4	48
Ucayali, dept., Peru	*C3	58
Ucayali, stm., Peru	C3	58
Uccle, Bel.	D10	23
Ucharal, Sov. Un.	E10	33
Uchinoura, b., Japan	C2	58
Uchiza, Peru	C3	56
Uchoa, Braz.	C3	56

Name	Map Ref.	Page
Uckange, Fr.	E6	17
Ucluelet, B.C.	E5	69
Ucon, Id., U.S.	F7	89
Udagamandalam, India	F6	36
Udaipur, India	D5	36
Udall, Ks., U.S.	E6	93
Udall, Mo., U.S.	E5	102
Udaquiola, Arg.	B5	54
Uddevalla, Swe.	H4	14
Uden, Neth.	C5	17
Udgīr, India	H6	37
Udhampur, India	B6	36
Udine, Italy	A4	23
Udon Thani, Thai.	B2	34
Udot, i., Micron.	Q18	52
Udu Point, c., Fiji	H16	52
Uecker, stm., Ger.	B6	18
Ueckermünde, Ger.	B6	18
Ueda, Japan	H9	33
Uehling, Ne., U.S.	C9	104
Uele, stm., Zaire	A3	48
Uelen, Sov. Un.	C21	29
Uelkal, Sov. Un.	C21	29
Uelsen, Ger.	B6	17
Uelzen, Ger.	B5	18
Ueno, Japan	o15	33
Uere, stm., Zaire	A4	48
Uesslingen, Switz.	A6	21
Uetendorf, Switz.	C4	21
Uetersen, Ger.	E3	15
Ufa, Sov. Un.	D8	29
Ufa, stm., Sov. Un.	B5	28
Uffenheim, Ger.	D5	19
Ugab, stm., Nmb.	B2	49
Ugalla, stm., Tan.	C5	48
Uganda, ctry., Afr.	A5	48
Ugashik, Ak., U.S.	D8	79
Ugashik Lakes, l., Ak., U.S.	D8	79
Ugep, Nig.	E6	45
Ugine, Fr.	D2	20
Uglegorsk, Sov. Un.	B13	31
Uglich, Sov. Un.	C12	27
Ugra, stm., Sov. Un.	D10	27
Ugūrchin, Bul.	D7	24
Uh, stm., Eur.	D7	26
Uherské Hradiště, Czech.	D4	26
Úhlava, stm., Czech.	D8	19
Ühlingen, Ger.	A5	21
Uhlman Lake, l., Man.	A2	70
Uhrichsville, Oh., U.S.	B4	112
Uhříněves, Czech.	n18	26
Uig, Scot., U.K.	B2	13
Uig, Scot., U.K.	C2	13
Uíge, Ang.	C2	48
Uíge, dept., Ang.	C2	48
Ŭijŏngbu, S. Kor.	H3	33
Uiju, N. Kor.	C9	31
Uil, Sov. Un.	D4	28
Uil, stm., Sov. Un.	D4	28
Uinkaret Plateau, plat., Az., U.S.	A2	80
Uinta, co., Wy., U.S.	E2	127
Uinta, stm., Ut., U.S.	*B4	121
Uintah, Ut., U.S.	D6	121
Uintah, co., Ut., U.S.	C5	121
Uintah and Ouray Indian Reservation, Ut., U.S.	C5	121
Uinta Mountains, mts., Ut., U.S.	C5	121
Uitenhage, S. Afr.	D4	49
Uithuizen, Neth.	A6	17
Uivak, Cape, c., Newf.	f9	72
Uji Islands, is., Japan	K4	33
Ujiji, Tan.	B4	48
Uji-yamada see Ise, Japan	I8	33
Ujjain, India	D6	36
Ujungpandang (Makasar), Indon.	G5	34
Uka, Japan	N6	52
Uka, Sov. Un.	D19	29
Ukerewe, i., Tan.	B5	48
Ukhta, Sov. Un.	C8	29
Ukiah, Ca., U.S.	C2	82
Ukiah, Or., U.S.	B8	114
Ukmerge, Sov. Un.	D5	27
Ukraine, state, Sov. Un.	E5	29
Uku, Ang.	D1	48
Ulaangom, Mong.	B3	31
Ulak Island, i., Ak., U.S.	E4	79
Ulan Bator (Ulaanbaatar), Mong.	B6	31
Ulan-Ude, Sov. Un.	D13	29
Ulba, Sov. Un.	E25	8
Ulchin, S. Kor.	H4	33
Ulcinj, Yugo.	E4	24
Uldza, stm., Asia	B7	31
Ulen, In., U.S.	D5	91
Ulen, Mn., U.S.	C2	100
Uleta, Fl., U.S.	*s13	86
Ulfborg, Den.	B2	14
Ulhāsnagar, India	*E5	36
Uliastay, Mong.	B4	31
Ulindi, stm., Zaire	B4	48
Ulla, Sov. Un.	D7	27
Ulla, stm., Spain	A1	22
Ulladulla, Austl.	G8	51
Ullapool, Scot., U.K.	B4	10
Ullared, Swe.	A6	15
Ullin, Il., U.S.	F4	90
Ullswater, l., Eng., U.K.	F6	13
Ullŭng Island, i., S. Kor.	H5	33
Ulm, Ger.	D4	18
Ulm, Ar., U.S.	C4	81
Ulm, Mt., U.S.	C5	103
Ulman, Mo., U.S.	C5	102
Ulongué, Moz.	E7	49
Ulricehamn, Swe.	I5	14
Ulsan, S. Kor.	I4	33
Ulster, Pa., U.S.	C9	115
Ulster, co., N.Y., U.S.	D6	109
Ulster, hist. reg., Eur.	C4	11
Ulúa, stm., Hond.	C3	62
Ulubat Lake, l., Tur.	B7	40
Uluborlu, Tur.	C8	40
Uludağ, mtn., Tur.	B7	40
Ulukışla, Tur.	D10	40
Ulungur He, stm., China	B2	31
Ulva, i., Scot., U.K.	D2	13
Ulverston, Eng., U.K.	G10	13
Ulverstone, Austl.	o15	50
Ulyanovsk, Sov. Un.	D7	29
Ulysses, Ks., U.S.	E2	93
Ulysses, Ne., U.S.	C8	104
Ulysses, Pa., U.S.	C6	115
Ulzburg, Ger.	E3	15
Uman, Sov. Un.	G8	27
Uman, i., Micron.	Q18	52
Umarkot, Pak.	C4	36
Umatac, Guam	M9	52
Umatac Bay, b., Guam	M9	52
Umatilla, Fl., U.S.	D5	86
Umatilla, Or., U.S.	B7	114
Umatilla, co., Or., U.S.	B8	114
Umatilla, stm., Or., U.S.	B7	114
Umatilla Indian Reservation, Or., U.S.	B8	114
Umba, Sov. Un.	D16	14
Umbagog Lake, l., U.S.	A4	106
Umboi, i., Pap. N. Gui.	k12	50
Umbria, prov., Italy	C4	23
Umbuzeiro, Braz.	C3	57
Umcolcus Lake, l., Me., U.S.	B4	96
Umeå, Swe.	F9	14
Umeälven, stm., Swe.	E8	14
Umhausen, Aus.	B6	20
Umlazi, S. Afr.	*C5	49
Umm el Faḥm, Isr.	B7	41
Umm Kaddādah, Sud.	C2	47
Umm Lajj, Sau. Ar.	C3	38
Umm Ruwābah, Sud.	C3	47
Umnak Island, i., Ak., U.S.	E6	79
Umniati, stm., Zimb.	A4	49
Umpire, Ar., U.S.	D1	81
Umpqua, stm., Or., U.S.	D3	114
Umpqua, Ne., U.S.	h12	104
Unadilla, Ga., U.S.	D3	87
Unadilla, Ne., U.S.	D9	104
Unadilla, N.Y., U.S.	C5	109
Unadilla, stm., N.Y., U.S.	C5	109
Unaí, Braz.	B5	56
Unaka Mountains, mts., U.S.	C11	119
Unalakleet, Ak., U.S.	C7	79
Unalaska Island, i., Ak., U.S.	E6	79
'Unayzah, Sau. Ar.	C4	38
Uncasville, Ct., U.S.	D7	84
Uncia, Bol.	C2	55
Uncompahgre, stm., Co., U.S.	C3	83
Uncompahgre Butte, mtn., Co., U.S.	C2	83
Uncompahgre Mountains, mts., Co., U.S.	C3	83
Uncompahgre Peak, mtn., Co., U.S.	C3	83
Uncompahgre Plateau, plat., Co., U.S.	C2	83
Underhill, Vt., U.S.	B3	122
Underhill Center, Vt., U.S.	B3	122
Underwood, Al., U.S.	B3	78
Underwood, Ia., U.S.	C2	92
Underwood, In., U.S.	G6	91
Underwood, Mn., U.S.	D3	100
Underwood, N.D., U.S.	B4	111
Underwood, Wa., U.S.	D4	124
Unecha, Sov. Un.	E9	27
Uneiuxi, stm., Braz.	D4	60
Unersee, Sov. Un.	F17	14
Ungaie, Austl.	F6	51
Ungava, Péninsule d', pen., Que.	g12	74
Ungava Bay, b., Can.	E19	64
Unggi, N. Kor.	C11	31
Unhošt', Czech.	n17	26
União, Braz.	B2	57
União da Victória, Braz.	D2	56
União dos Palmares, Braz.	C3	57
Unicoi, co., Tn., U.S.	C11	119
Unicoi Mountains, mts., U.S.	D9	119
Unije, i., Yugo.	C2	24
Unimak Island, i., Ak., U.S.	D7	79
Unimak Pass, strt., Ak., U.S.	E6	79
Unini, stm., Braz.	C2	59
Union, Arg.	B3	54
Union, Ar., U.S.	A4	81
Union, Ct., U.S.	B7	84
Union, Il., U.S.	A5	90
Union, In., U.S.	H3	91
Union, Ia., U.S.	k13	94
Union, Ky., U.S.	h10	95
Union, La., U.S.	C4	101
Union, Ms., U.S.	C4	101
Union, Ne., U.S.	D10	104
Union, N.H., U.S.	D4	106
Union, N.J., U.S.	*B4	107
Union, N.C., U.S.	A5	110
Union, N.D., U.S.	A8	111
Union, Oh., U.S.	*C1	112
Union, Or., U.S.	B9	114
Union, S.C., U.S.	B4	117
Union, Ut., U.S.	*C4	121
Union, W.V., U.S.	D4	125
Union, co., Ar., U.S.	D3	81
Union, co., Fl., U.S.	B4	86
Union, co., Ga., U.S.	B2	87
Union, co., Il., U.S.	F4	90
Union, co., In., U.S.	E8	91
Union, co., Ia., U.S.	C3	92
Union, co., Ky., U.S.	C2	94
Union, co., La., U.S.	B3	95
Union, co., Ms., U.S.	A4	101
Union, co., N.J., U.S.	B4	107
Union, co., N.M., U.S.	A6	108
Union, co., N.C., U.S.	B2	110
Union, co., Oh., U.S.	B2	112
Union, co., Or., U.S.	B8	114
Union, co., Pa., U.S.	E7	115
Union, co., S.C., U.S.	B4	117
Union, co., S.D., U.S.	E9	118
Union, co., Tn., U.S.	C10	119
Union, West Branch, stm., Me., U.S.	D4	96
Union Bay, B.C.	E5	69
Union Beach, N.J., U.S.	C4	107
Union Bridge, Md., U.S.	A3	97
Union Center, S.D., U.S.	C3	118
Union Center, Wi., U.S.	E3	126
Union Church, Ms., U.S.	D3	101
Union City, Ca., U.S.	h8	82
Union City, Ga., U.S.	C2	87
Union City, In., U.S.	D8	91
Union City, Mi., U.S.	F5	99
Union City, N.J., U.S.	h8	107
Union City, Oh., U.S.	B1	112
Union City, Ok., U.S.	B4	113
Union City, Pa., U.S.	C2	115
Union City, Tn., U.S.	A2	119
Union Creek, Or., U.S.	E4	114
Uniondale, In., U.S.	C7	91
Uniondale, N.Y., U.S.	*E7	109
Union Dale, Pa., U.S.	C10	115
Unión de Reyes, Cuba	C3	63
Unión de Tula, Mex.	n11	63
Union Flat Creek, stm., Wa., U.S.	C8	124
Union Furnace, Oh., U.S.	C3	112
Union Gap, Wa., U.S.	C5	124
Union Grove, Wi., U.S.	F5	126
Union Hall, Va., U.S.	C3	123
Union Island, i., St. Vin.	V26	65
Union Lake, Mi., U.S.	*o15	99
Union Lake, l., N.J., U.S.	E2	107
Union Mill, Hi., U.S.	C6	88
Union Mills, In., U.S.	B4	91
Union Mills, Md., U.S.	A3	97
Union Park, Fl., U.S.	D5	86
Union Pier, Mi., U.S.	G4	99
Union Point, Ga., U.S.	C3	87
Union Springs, Al., U.S.	C4	78
Union Springs, N.Y., U.S.	C4	109
Union Star, Mo., U.S.	B3	102
Uniontown, Al., U.S.	C2	78
Uniontown, Ks., U.S.	E9	93
Uniontown, Ky., U.S.	C2	94
Uniontown, Md., U.S.	A3	97
Uniontown, Oh., U.S.	B4	112
Uniontown, Pa., U.S.	G2	115
Uniontown, Wa., U.S.	C8	124
Union Village, R.I., U.S.	B3	116
Union Village, Vt., U.S.	D4	122
Union Village Reservoir, res., Vt., U.S.	C2	122
Unionville, Ont.	k15	73
Unionville, Ct., U.S.	B4	84
Unionville, Il., U.S.	F5	90
Unionville, In., U.S.	F5	91
Unionville, Ia., U.S.	D5	92
Unionville, Me., U.S.	D5	96
Unionville, Mi., U.S.	E7	99
Unionville, Mo., U.S.	A4	102
Unionville, Nv., U.S.	C3	105
Unionville, N.C., U.S.	B2	110
Unionville, Oh., U.S.	A5	112
Unionville, Tn., U.S.	B5	119
Unionville, Va., U.S.	B5	123
Unionville Center, Oh., U.S.	B2	112
Unisan, Phil.	p13	34
United Arab Emirates, ctry., Asia	C5	38
United Kingdom, ctry., Eur.	C5	10
United Nations Headquarters, N.Y., U.S.	h12	109
United Pueblos Indian Reservations, N.M., U.S.	A3	108
United States, ctry., N.A.	C8	76
United States Air Force Academy, mil., Co., U.S.	B6	83
United States Military Academy, mil., N.Y., U.S.	C6	109
United States Naval Academy, mil., Md., U.S.	C4	97
Unity, Sask.	E1	75
Unity, Il., U.S.	F4	90
Unity, Me., U.S.	D3	96
Unity, N.H., U.S.	D2	106
Unity, Or., U.S.	C8	114
Unity Pond, l., Me., U.S.	D3	96
Unity Reservoir, res., Or., U.S.	C8	114
Unityville, S.D., U.S.	D8	118
Universal, In., U.S.	E3	91
Universal City, Tx., U.S.	*E3	120
Universales, Montes, mts., Spain	B5	22
University, Fl., U.S.	*D4	86
University City, Mo., U.S.	C7	102
University Gardens, N.Y., U.S.	*n15	109
University Heights, Ia., U.S.	C6	92
University Heights, Oh., U.S.	h9	112
University Park, Ia., U.S.	C5	92
University Park, N.M., U.S.	E3	108
University Park, Tx., U.S.	n10	120
University Place, Wa., U.S.	f10	124
Unna, Ger.	B7	19
Unnen, I., Swe.	g10	10
Unst, i., Scot., U.K.	g10	10
Unstrut, stm., Ger.	B6	19
Unterwasser, Switz.	B7	21
Unuk, stm., N.A.	A2	69
Unuwhao, hill, N.Z.	K14	51
Unwin, Sask.	E1	75
Ünye, Tur.	B11	40
Unzha, stm., Sov. Un.	B2	28
Uozu, Japan	H8	33
Upata, Ven.	B5	60
Upatoi Creek, stm., Ga., U.S.	D2	87
Upemba, Lac, l., Zaire	C4	48
Upernavik, Grnld.	B15	61
Upham, N.D., U.S.	A5	111
Upía, stm., Col.	C3	60
Upington, S. Afr.	C3	49
Upland, Ca., U.S.	E5	82
Upland, In., U.S.	D7	91
Upland, Ne., U.S.	D7	104
Upolu, i., W. Sam.	G11	6
Upolu Point, c., Hi., U.S.	C6	88
Upper, prov., Ghana	D4	45
Upper Ammonoosuc, stm., N.H., U.S.	A4	106
Upper Arlington, Oh., U.S.	B2	112
Upper Arrow Lake, res., B.C.	D9	69
Upper Black Eddy, Pa., U.S.	E11	115
Upper Blackville, N.B.	C4	71
Upper Chichester Township, Pa., U.S.	*G11	115
Upperco, Md., U.S.	A4	97
Upper Darby, Pa., U.S.	G11	115
Upper Dublin Township, Pa., U.S.	*F11	115
Upper Fairmount, Md., U.S.	D6	97
Upper Fraser, B.C.	B7	69
Upper Frenchville, Me., U.S.	A4	96
Upper Gagetown, N.B.	D3	71
Upper Ganges Canal, India	C6	37
Upper Gloucester, Me., U.S.	E2	96
Upper Graniteville, Vt., U.S.	C4	122
Upper Greenwood Lake, N.J., U.S.	A4	107
Upper Humber, stm., Newf.	D3	72
Upper Indian Pond, l., Newf.	D3	72
Upper Iowa, stm., Ia., U.S.	A5	92
Upper Island Cove, Newf.	E5	72
Upper Jay, N.Y., U.S.	f11	109
Upper Kapuas Mountains, mts., Asia	E4	34
Upper Kent, N.B.	C2	71
Upper Klamath Lake, l., Or., U.S.	E4	114
Upper Manitou Lake, l., Ont.	E5	70
Upper Marlboro, Md., U.S.	C4	97
Upper Merion Township, Pa., U.S.	*F11	115
Upper Moreland Township, Pa., U.S.	*F11	115
Upper Musquodoboit, N.S.	D7	71
Upper New York Bay, b., U.S.	k8	107
Upper Providence Township, Pa., U.S.	*G11	115
Upper Red Lake, l., Mn., U.S.	B4	100
Upper Saddle River, N.J., U.S.	A4	107
Upper Saint Clair, Pa., U.S.	*F1	115
Upper Sandusky, Oh., U.S.	B2	112
Upper Sheila, N.B.	B5	71
Upper Silesia, hist. reg., Pol.	g9	26
Upper Southampton Township, Pa., U.S.	*F11	115
Upper Strasburg, Pa., U.S.	F6	115
Upper Tract, W.V., U.S.	B5	123
Upper Volta see Burkina Faso, ctry., Afr.	D4	45
Upper Wilson Pond, l., Me., U.S.	C3	96
Upper Woods Harbour, N.S.	F4	71
Uppsala, Swe.	H7	14
Upright, Cape, c., Ak., U.S.	C5	79
Upsala, Mn., U.S.	E4	100
Upsalquitch, N.B.	B3	71
Upsalquitch, stm., N.B.	B3	71
Upshur, co., Tx., U.S.	C5	120
Upshur, co., W.V., U.S.	C4	125
Upson, Wi., U.S.	B3	126
Upson, co., Ga., U.S.	D2	87
Upton, Que.	D5	74
Upton, Ky., U.S.	C4	94
Upton, Ma., U.S.	B4	98
Upton, Me., U.S.	D1	96
Upton, Wy., U.S.	B8	127
Upton, co., Tx., U.S.	D2	120
Urabá, Golfo de, b., Col.	B2	60
Uracoa, Ven.	B5	60
Urad Qianqi, China	D3	32
Ural, stm., Sov. Un.	E8	29
Ural Mountains, mts., Sov. Un.	D8	29
Urandi, Braz.	A4	56
Urania, La., U.S.	C3	95
Uranium City, Sask.	m7	75
Uraricoera, Braz.	B2	59
Uraricoera, stm., Braz.	B2	59
Urasoe, Japan	C5	52
Urawa, Japan	I9	33
Uravan, Co., U.S.	C2	83
Urbana, Ar., U.S.	i9	81
Urbana, Il., U.S.	C5	90
Urbana, In., U.S.	C6	91
Urbana, Md., U.S.	B3	97
Urbana, Mo., U.S.	D4	102
Urbana, Oh., U.S.	B2	112
Urbancrest, Oh., U.S.	m10	112
Urbandale, Ia., U.S.	C4	92
Urbank, Mn., U.S.	D3	100
Urbanna, Va., U.S.	C6	123
Urbino, Italy	C4	23
Urcos, Peru	D3	58
Urdaneta, Phil.	o13	34
Urdzhar, Sov. Un.	D10	28
Ure, stm., Eng., U.K.	F7	13
Ures, Mex.	B2	63
Urfa, Tur.	D12	40
Urga, Sov. Un.	E6	28
Urgench, Sov. Un.	E6	28
Uri, state, Switz.	C4	20
Uriah, Al., U.S.	D2	78
Uribia, Col.	A3	60
Urich, Mo., U.S.	C4	102
Urique, Mex.	B3	63
Uritsk (part of Leningrad), Sov. Un.	s31	14
Uruaçu, Braz.	A3	56
Uruana, Braz.	B3	56
Uruapan [del Progreso], Mex.	D4	63
Urubamba, Peru	D3	58
Urubamba, stm., Peru	C3	58
Urubu, stm., Braz.	C3	59
Urucará, Braz.	C2	57
Uruçuí, Braz.	C2	57
Urucuia, stm., Braz.	C3	59
Urucurituba, Braz.	C3	59
Uruguaiana, Braz.	D1	56
Uruguay, ctry., S.A.	E1	56
Uruguay (Uruguai), stm., S.A.	E1	56
Urumchi see Ürümqi, China	C2	31
Ürümqi (Urumchi), China	C2	31
Uruno Point, c., Guam	L10	52
Urusha, Sov. Un.	D15	29
Urutaí, Braz.	B3	56
Uryu, stm., Japan	D11	33
Uryupinsk, Sov. Un.	F14	27
Urziceni, Rom.	B20	8
Usak, Tur.	C7	40
Usakos, Nmb.	B2	49
Usedom, Ger.	E8	15
Usedom, i., Eur.	E8	15
Ushaki, Sov. Un.	s32	14
Ushibuka, Japan	J4	33
Ushtobe, Sov. Un.	D9	28
Ushuaia, Arg.	h12	54
Usingen, Ger.	B4	19
Usk, B.C.	B3	69
Usk, Wa., U.S.	A8	124
Uslar, Ger.	B4	19
Úslava, stm., Czech.	C2	19
Usman, Sov. Un.	E12	27
Usolye-Sibirskoye, Sov. Un.	D13	29
Uspenskiy, Sov. Un.	D8	28
Usquepaug, R.I., U.S.	F3	116
Ussel, Fr.	E5	16
Ussuri (Wusuli), stm., Asia	B11	31
Ussuriysk, Sov. Un.	E16	29
Ust-Bolsheretsk, Sov. Un.	D18	29
Uster, Switz.	B4	20
Ústica, i., Italy	*C3	23
Ústí nad Labem, Czech.	C3	26
Ustinov see Izhevsk, Sov. Un.	B8	28
Ust-Ishim, Sov. Un.	D8	28
Ustka, Pol.	A6	26
Ust-Kamchatsk, Sov. Un.	D19	29
Ust-Kamenogorsk, Sov. Un.	D10	28
Ust-Kut, Sov. Un.	D13	29
Ust-Maya, Sov. Un.	C16	29
Ust-Olenëk, Sov. Un.	B14	29
Ust-Shchugor, Sov. Un.	C9	28
Ust-Srednekan, Sov. Un.	C18	29
Ust-Tsilma, Sov. Un.	C8	29
Ust-Tym, Sov. Un.	B9	28
Ust-Urt Plateau, plat., Sov. Un.	E8	29
Ust-Usa, Sov. Un.	C8	29
Ustyuzhna, Sov. Un.	B11	27
Usu, China	C1	31
Usulután, El Sal.	D6	63
Usumacinta, stm., N.A.	D6	63
Utah, co., Ut., U.S.	C4	121
Utah, state, U.S.	D4	121
Utah Lake, l., Ut., U.S.	C4	121
Utajärvi, Fin.	E12	14
Ute, Ia., U.S.	B2	92
Ute Creek, stm., N.M., U.S.	A6	108
Ute Mountain Indian Reservation, U.S.	D2	83
Ute Park, N.M., U.S.	A4	108
Ute Reservoir, res., N.M., U.S.	B6	108
Utete, Tan.	C7	48
Uthai Thani, Thai.	B1	34
Utica, In., U.S.	H6	91
Utica, Ks., U.S.	D3	93
Utica, Ky., U.S.	C2	94
Utica, Mi., U.S.	F7	99
Utica, Ms., U.S.	C3	101
Utica, Mo., U.S.	B4	102
Utica, Ne., U.S.	D8	104
Utica, N.Y., U.S.	B5	109
Utica, Oh., U.S.	B3	112
Utica, Ok., U.S.	D5	113
Utica, Pa., U.S.	D2	115
Utica, S.D., U.S.	E8	118
Utiel, Spain	C5	22
Utikuma Lake, l., Alta.	B3	68
Utö, i., Swe.	u36	14
Utopia, Tx., U.S.	E3	120
Utopia, Lake, l., N.B.	D3	71
Utrata, stm., Pol.	m13	26
Utrecht, Neth.	A6	16
Utrecht, prov., Neth.	B5	17
Utrera, Spain	D3	22
Utsjoki, Fin.	C12	14
Utsunomiya, Japan	D12	31
Uttaradit, Thai.	B2	34
Uttar Pradesh, state, India	C6	36
Uttoxeter, Eng., U.K.	B6	12
Utuado, P.R.	B2	65
Utukok, stm., Ak., U.S.	B5	79
Utulei, Am. Sam.	F13	52
Uusikaupunki, Fin.	G9	14
Uva, stm., Col.	C3	60
Uvalda, Ga., U.S.	D4	87
Uvalde, Tx., U.S.	E3	120
Uvalde, co., Tx., U.S.	E3	120
Úvaly, Czech.	n18	26
Uvarovo, Sov. Un.	E14	27
Uvat, Sov. Un.	B7	28
Uverite Point, c., Fiji	H14	52
Uvinza, Tan.	C5	48
Uvira, Zaire	B4	48
Uvs Lake, l., Asia	A3	31
Uwajima, Japan	J6	33
Uwayl, Sud.	C2	47
'Uwaynāt, Jabal al, mtn., Afr.	E4	43
Uwharrie, stm., N.C., U.S.	B3	110
Uxbridge, Ont.	C5	73
Uxbridge (part of London), Eng., U.K.	k12	10
Uxbridge, Ma., U.S.	B4	98
Uxmal, hist., Mex.	C7	63
Uyar, Sov. Un.	D27	8
Uyo, Nig.	*E6	45
Uyuni, Bol.	D2	55
Uyuni, Salar de, pl., Bol.	D2	55
Uzbek S.S.R., state, Sov. Un.	E9	16
Uzès, Fr.	F7	17
Uzh, stm., Sov. Un.	G7	27
Uzhgorod, Sov. Un.	E11	27
Uzlovaya, Sov. Un.	D11	27
Uzunköprü, Tur.	B6	40
Uzwil, Switz.	B7	21
V		
Vaal, stm., S. Afr.	C4	49
Vaals, Neth.	D5	17
Vaasa, Fin.	F9	14
Vác, Hung.	B4	24
Vaca Key, i., Fl., U.S.	H5	86
Vacaria, Braz.	D2	56
Vacaville, Ca., U.S.	C3	82
Vacha, Ger.	C5	19
Vacherie, La., U.S.	h10	95
Vader, Wa., U.S.	C3	124
Vadis, W.V., U.S.	B4	125
Vadito, N.M., U.S.	A4	108
Vadnais Heights, Mn., U.S.	*m12	100
Vado, N.M., U.S.	E3	108
Vadodara, India	D5	36
Vadsö, Nor.	B13	14
Vaduz, Liech.	B7	21
Vagay, Sov. Un.	B7	28
Vaggeryd, Swe.	A8	15
Vagnhärad, Swe.	u35	14
Vagos, Port.	B1	22
Váh, stm., Czech.	D4	26
Vahsel Bay, b., Ant.	B9	7
Vaiden, Ms., U.S.	B4	101
Vaigai, stm., India	G6	36
Vaihingen, Ger.	E3	19
Vail, Az., U.S.	E5	80
Vail, Co., U.S.	B4	83
Vail, Ia., U.S.	B2	92
Vail Homes, N.J., U.S.	C3	107
Vails, N.J., U.S.	B2	107
Vaiteie Bay, b., W. Sam.	F12	52
Vakh, stm., Sov. Un.	C25	8
Vākhān, reg., Afg.	k17	39
Vakhrushev, Sov. Un.	B11	33
Valais, state, Switz.	C3	20
Valatie, N.Y., U.S.	C7	109
Valbarre, stm., Czech.	E12	27
Val-Barrette, Que.	C2	74
Val-Bélair, Que.	n17	74
Valcarrier-Village, Que.	C6	74
Valcheta, Arg.	E3	54
Valcourt, Que.	D5	74
Valdagno, Italy	D6	20
Valdai Hills, hills, Sov. Un.	C10	27
Val-David, Que.	C3	74
Valday, Sov. Un.	C10	27
Valdemorillo, Spain	o16	22
Valdepeñas, Spain	C4	22
Valderaduey, stm., Spain	A3	22
Valders, Wi., U.S.	D6	126
Valdés, Península, pen., Arg.	C4	54
Valdese, N.C., U.S.	B1	110
Valdez, Ak., U.S.	C10	79
Valdez, N.M., U.S.	A4	108
Valdilecha, Spain	p18	22
Valdivia, Chile	B2	54
Valdobbiadene, Italy	D7	20
Val-d'Or, Que.	k11	74
Valdosta, Ga., U.S.	F3	87
Vale, Nor.	p28	14
Vale, Or., U.S.	D9	114
Vale, S.D., U.S.	C2	118
Vale, Tn., U.S.	A3	119
Valeene, In., U.S.	H5	91
Valemount, B.C.	C8	69
Valença, Braz.	C4	56
Valença, Braz.	D3	57
Valença do Piauí, Braz.	C2	57
Valence, Fr.	E6	16
Valencia, Spain	C5	22
Valencia, Az., U.S.	m7	80
Valencia, Ca., U.S.	*E4	82
Valencia, Pa., U.S.	E2	115
Valencia, Ven.	A4	60
Valencia, co., N.M., U.S.	C3	108
Valencia, hist. reg., Spain	C5	22
Valencia [de Alcántara], Spain	C2	22
Valencia Heights, S.C., U.S.	D6	117
Valencia Island, i., Ire.	E1	10
Valenciennes, Fr.	B5	16
Valendas, Switz.	C7	21
Valentigney, Fr.	D7	16
Valentine, Az., U.S.	B2	80
Valentine, Ne., U.S.	B5	104
Valentine, Tx., U.S.	o12	120
Valera, Ven.	B3	60
Valhalla, N.Y., U.S.	D7	109
Valhermoso Springs, Al., U.S.	A3	78
Valier, Il., U.S.	E4	90
Valier, Mt., U.S.	B4	103
Valier, Pa., U.S.	E3	115
Valinda, Ca., U.S.	*m13	82
Valjevo, Yugo.	C4	24
Valka, Sov. Un.	C6	27
Valkeakoski, Fin.	G11	14
Valkenswaard, Neth.	C5	17
Valki, Sov. Un.	G10	27
Valladolid, Ec.	B2	58
Valladolid, Mex.	C7	63
Valladolid, Spain	B3	22
Vallākra, Swe.	C6	15
Vallauris, Fr.	F7	16
Vall de Uxó, Spain	C5	22
Vallecas, Spain	B4	22
Vallecito, Co., U.S.	D3	83
Vallecito Reservoir, res., Co., U.S.	D3	83
Vallecitos, N.M., U.S.	A3	108
Valle d'Aosta, prov., Italy	D2	20
Valle de la Pascua, Ven.	B4	60
Valle del Cauca, dept., Col.	C2	60
Valle de Santiago, Mex.	m13	63
Valledupar, Col.	A3	60
Vallée-Jonction, Que.	C7	74
Vallegrande, Bol.	C3	55
Vallejo, Ca., U.S.	C2	82
Vallenar, Chile	E1	55
Valletta, Malta	H11	8
Valle Vista, Ca., U.S.	*F5	82
Valley, Al., U.S.	*C4	78
Valley, Ne., U.S.	C9	104
Valley, Wa., U.S.	A8	124
Valley, co., Id., U.S.	E3	89
Valley, co., Mt., U.S.	B10	103
Valley, co., Ne., U.S.	C7	104
Valley, stm., Man.	D1	70
Valley Bend, W.V., U.S.	C5	125
Valley Center, Ks., U.S.	E6	93
Valley City, Il., U.S.	D3	90
Valley City, N.D., U.S.	C8	111
Valley City, Oh., U.S.	A4	112
Valley Cottage, N.Y., U.S.	g13	109
Valley Creek, stm., Al., U.S.	g6	78
Valley East, Ont.	p19	73
Valley Falls, Ks., U.S.	C8	93
Valley Falls, Or., U.S.	E6	114
Valley Falls, R.I., U.S.	B4	116
Valley Farms, Az., U.S.	E4	80
Valleyfield (part of Badger's Quay-Valleyfield-Pool's Island), Newf.	D5	72
Valleyford, Wa., U.S.	B8	124
Valley Forge, Pa., U.S.	o20	115
Valley Grove, W.V., U.S.	A4	125
Valley Head, Al., U.S.	A4	78
Valley Head, W.V., U.S.	C4	125
Valley Lee, Md., U.S.	D4	97
Valley Mills, Tx., U.S.	D4	120
Valley Park, Ms., U.S.	C3	101
Valley Park, Mo., U.S.	f12	102
Valley Ridge, Wa., U.S.	*B3	124
Valley Spring, Tx., U.S.	D3	120
Valley Springs, Ca., U.S.	A2	81
Valley Springs, S.D., U.S.	D9	118
Valley Station, Ky., U.S.	g11	94
Valley Stream, N.Y., U.S.	n15	109
Valleyview, Alta.	B2	68
Valley View, Ky., U.S.	C5	94
Valley View, Pa., U.S.	E8	115
Valley View, Tx., U.S.	C4	120
Valliant, Ok., U.S.	D6	113
Valli del Pasubio, Italy	D5	23
Vallonia, In., U.S.	G5	91
Vallorbe, Switz.	E3	18
Valls, Spain	B6	22
Vallscreek, W.V., U.S.	D3	125
Val Marie, Sask.	H2	75
Valmeyer, Il., U.S.	E3	90
Valmiera, Sov. Un.	C5	27
Valmont, Que.	h9	74
Valmontone, Italy	h9	23
Valmy, Nv., U.S.	C5	105
Valognes, Fr.	D6	16
Valona see Vlora, Alb.	B2	24
Valparaíso, Braz.	A4	56
Valparaíso, Chile	u15	54
Valparaíso, Mex.	C4	63
Valparaíso, Spain	H3	22
Valparaiso, Fl., U.S.	u15	86
Valparaiso, In., U.S.	B3	91
Valparaiso, Ne., U.S.	C9	104
Valparaíso, prov., Chile	D6	54
Valréas, Fr.	—	—
Vals, Cape, c., Indon.	G9	34
Val-Saint-Michel, Que.	n17	74
Valsetz, Or., U.S.	C3	114
Valtimo, Fin.	E12	14
Valtournanche, Italy	E4	21
Valujki, Sov. Un.	F12	27
Val Verde, Ut., U.S.	C4	121
Val Verde, co., Tx., U.S.	E2	120

Name	Map Ref.	Page
Valverde del Camino, Spain	D2	22
Vamdrup, Den.	C3	15
Vamori, Az., U.S.	F4	80
Van, Tur.	C14	40
Van, Tx., U.S.	C5	120
Van, W.V., U.S.	n12	125
Vanadium, N.M., U.S.	E1	108
Van Alstyne, Tx., U.S.	C4	120
Vananda, B.C.	E5	69
Van-Bruyssel, Que.	B5	74
Van Buren, Ar., U.S.	B1	81
Van Buren, In., U.S.	C6	91
Van Buren, Me., U.S.	A5	96
Van Buren, Mo., U.S.	E6	102
Van Buren, Oh., U.S.	A2	112
Van Buren, co., Ar., U.S.	B3	81
Van Buren, co., Ia., U.S.	D6	92
Van Buren, co., Mi., U.S.	F4	99
Van Buren, co., Tn., U.S.	D8	119
Vance, Ms., U.S.	A3	101
Vance, S.C., U.S.	E7	117
Vance, co., N.C., U.S.	A4	110
Vance Air Force Base, mil., Ok., U.S.	A3	113
Vanceboro, Me., U.S.	C5	96
Vanceboro, N.C., U.S.	B5	110
Vanceburg, Ky., U.S.	B6	94
Vancleave, Ms., U.S.	E5	101
Vancleve, Ky., U.S.	C6	94
Vancorum, Co., U.S.	C2	83
Vancouver, B.C.	E6	69
Vancouver, Wa., U.S.	D3	124
Vancouver Island, i., B.C.	E4	69
Vancouver Island Ranges, mts., B.C.	D4	69
Vandalia, Il., U.S.	E4	90
Vandalia, Mo., U.S.	B6	102
Vandalia, Mt., U.S.	B10	103
Vandalia, Oh., U.S.	*C1	112
Vandemere, N.C., U.S.	B6	110
Vandenberg Air Force Base, mil., Ca., U.S.	E3	82
Vandenberg Village, Ca., U.S.	*E3	82
Vander, N.C., U.S.	B4	110
Vanderbilt, Mi., U.S.	C6	99
Vanderbilt, Pa., U.S.	F2	115
Vanderbilt, Tx., U.S.	E4	120
Vanderbilt Peak, mtn., N.M., U.S.	E1	108
Vanderburgh, co., In., U.S.	H2	91
Vandercook Lake, Mi., U.S.	*F6	99
Vandergrift, Pa., U.S.	E2	115
Vanderhoof, B.C.	C5	69
Vanderpool, Tx., U.S.	E3	120
Vandervoort, Ar., U.S.	C1	81
Vanderwagen, N.M., U.S.	B1	108
Van Diemen, Cape, c., Austl.	B5	50
Van Diemen Gulf, b., Austl.	B5	50
Vandiver, Al., U.S.	B3	78
Vandling, Pa., U.S.	C11	115
Vanduser, Mo., U.S.	E8	102
Vandyne, Wi., U.S.	k9	126
Vanegas, Mex.	C4	63
Vänern, l., Swe.	H5	14
Vänersborg, Swe.	H5	14
Van Etten, N.Y., U.S.	C4	109
Vang, Mount, mtn., Ant.	B6	7
Vanga, Kenya	B6	48
Vangaindrano, Madag.	h9	49
Vanguard, Sask.	H2	75
Van Horn, Tx., U.S.	o12	120
Van Horne, Ia., U.S.	B5	92
Vanimo, Pap. N. Gui.	h11	50
Vanier, Ont.	h12	73
Vankleek Hill, Ont.	B10	73
Van Kull, strt., N.J., U.S.	k8	107
Van Lear, Ky., U.S.	C7	94
Vanleer, Tn., U.S.	A4	119
Vanlue, Oh., U.S.	B2	112
Van Meter, Ia., U.S.	C4	92
Vanna, Ga., U.S.	B3	87
Vanndale, Ar., U.S.	B5	81
Vannes, Fr.	D2	16
Vanoss, Ok., U.S.	C5	113
Van Phong Bay, b., Viet.	F8	35
Van Rees Mountains, mts., Indon.	F9	34
Vanrhynsdorp, S. Afr.	D2	49
Vansant, Va., U.S.	e9	123
Vanscoy, Sask.	E2	75
Vantaa (Vanda), Fin.	*G11	14
Vantage, Sask.	H2	75
Van Tassell, Wy., U.S.	D8	127
Vanua Balavu, i., Fiji	H16	52
Vanua Levu, i., Fiji	H15	52
Vanuatu, ctry., Oc.	H10	6
Vanua Vatu, i., Fiji	I16	52
Vanves, Fr.	g10	16
Van Vleck, Tx., U.S.	r14	120
Van Vleet, Ms., U.S.	B5	101
Van Wert, Ia., U.S.	C1	87
Van Wert, Oh., U.S.	B1	112
Van Wert, co., Oh., U.S.	B1	112
Van Wyck, S.C., U.S.	B6	117
Van Zandt, co., Tx., U.S.	C5	120
Vanzant, Mo., U.S.	E5	102
Varallo, Italy	D5	39
Värāmīn, Iran	D5	39
Vārānasi (Benares), India	C7	36
Varangerfjorden, Nor.	B14	14
Varano, Lake, b., Italy	D5	23
Varaždin, Yugo.	B3	24
Varazze, Italy	B2	23
Varberg, Swe.	I5	14
Vardaman, Ms., U.S.	B4	101
Vardar (Axiós), stm., Eur.	B4	40
Varde, Den.	C2	15
Varde Å, stm., Den.	C2	15
Vardenis, Sov. Un.	B15	41
Vardø, Nor.	B14	14
Varel, Ger.	B4	18
Varena, Sov. Un.	A8	26
Varennes, Que.	D4	74
Varennes, co., Pa., U.S.	C1	115
Vareš, Yugo.	C4	24
Varese, Italy	D3	23
Varese, Lake, l., Italy	E6	21
Varginha, Braz.	h11	25
Vári, Grc.	h11	25
Varina, Ia., U.S.	B3	92
Varina, Va., U.S.	C5	123
Varjão, Braz.	B4	56
Varkaus, Fin.	F12	14
Varkhān, stm., Afg.	E12	39
Varna (Stalin), Bul.	D8	24
Varna, Ont.	D3	73
Varna, Il., U.S.	B4	90
Varnado, La., U.S.	D6	95
Värnamo, Swe.	I6	14
Varney, Ont.	C3	73
Varnsdorf, Czech.	C3	26
Varnville, S.C., U.S.	F5	117
Värö, Swe.	A6	15
Várpalota, Hung.	B4	24
Vars, Ont.	h13	73
Varysburg, N.Y., U.S.	C2	109
Várzea, stm., Braz.	D2	56
Várzea da Palma, Braz.	A4	56
Várzea Grande, Braz.	B1	56
Varzi, Italy	E5	20
Varzuga, stm., Sov. Un.	D17	14
Vashon, Wa., U.S.	B3	124
Vashon, Point, c., Wa., U.S.	E11	124
Vashon Island, i., Wa., U.S.	f11	124
Vasilkov, Sov. Un.	F8	27
Vaslui, Rom.	B8	24
Vass, N.C., U.S.	B3	110
Vassalboro, Me., U.S.	*D3	96
Vassar, Man.	E4	70
Vassar, Ks., U.S.	D8	93
Vassar, Mi., U.S.	E7	99
Vassouras, Braz.	h6	56
Västerås, Swe.	H7	14
Västerhaninge, Swe.	t36	14
Västervik, Swe.	I7	14
Vasto, Italy	C5	23
Vasyugan, stm., Sov. Un.	B9	28
Vaternish Point, c., Scot., U.K.	C2	13
Vatican City, ctry., Eur.	D4	23
Vaticano, Cape, c., Italy	E5	23
Vatnajökull, ice, Ice.	n24	14
Vatomandry, Madag.	g9	49
Vatra Dornei, Rom.	B7	24
Vättern, l., Swe.	H6	14
Vatulele, i., Fiji	I14	52
Vatu Vara, i., Fiji	H16	52
Vaucluse, S.C., U.S.	D4	117
Vaucouleurs, Fr.	F5	17
Vaud, state, Switz.	C2	20
Vaudreuil, Que.	D3	74
Vaudreuil, co., Que.	D3	74
Vaughan, Ms., U.S.	C3	101
Vaughan, N.C., U.S.	A4	110
Vaughan, W.V., U.S.	m13	125
Vaughn, Mt., U.S.	C5	103
Vaughn, N.M., U.S.	C4	108
Vaughn, Or., U.S.	C3	114
Vaughnsville, Oh., U.S.	B1	112
Vaupés (Uaupés), stm., S.A.	C3	60
Vaupés, dept., Col.	C3	60
Vauvilliers, Fr.	B2	20
Vauxhall, Alta.	D4	68
Vavou, I.C.	E3	45
Vaxholm, Swe.	t36	14
Växjö, Swe.	I6	14
Våxtorp, Swe.	B7	15
Vaygach Island, i., Sov. Un.	C8	29
Váyia, Grc.	g10	25
Vazante, Braz.	B3	56
Vazealm, Tx., U.S.	C2	120
Veazie, Me., U.S.	D4	96
Veberöd, Swe.	C7	15
Veblen, S.D., U.S.	B8	118
Vechta, Ger.	F2	15
Veckholm, Swe.	t35	14
Vecsés, Hung.	B4	24
Veddige, Swe.	A6	15
Vedia, Arg.	A4	54
Veedersburg, In., U.S.	D3	91
Veendam, Neth.	A6	17
Veenendaal, Neth.	B1	20
Vega, i., Nor.	E4	14
Vega Alta, P.R.	B5	65
Vegreville, Alta.	C4	68
Veguita, N.M., U.S.	C3	108
Veinticinco de Mayo, Arg.	B3	54
Veinticinco de Mayo, Arg.	A3	54
Veinticinco de Mayo, Arg.	D3	54
Vejen, Den.	C3	15
Vejer [de la Frontera], Spain	D2	22
Vejle, Den.	J3	14
Vejle, Den.	C3	15
Vejprty, Czech.	C2	26
Vela, Cabo de la, c., Col.	A3	60
Velarde, N.M., U.S.	A4	108
Velas, Cabo, c., C.R.	E5	62
Velbert, Ger.	B2	19
Velda Rose Estates, Az., U.S.	D4	80
Velden, Ger.	A8	20
Velebit Mountains, mts., Yugo.	C2	24
Velestínon, Grc.	C4	25
Vélez, Col.	B3	60
Vélez Blanco, Spain	D4	22
Vélez-Málaga, Spain	D3	22
Vélez Rubio, Spain	D4	22
Velgast, Ger.	D6	15
Velhas, Rio das, stm., Braz.	B4	56
Velika Morava, stm., Yugo.	C4	24
Velikaya, stm., Sov. Un.	C7	27
Velikaya Lepetikha, Sov. Un.	H10	27
Velikiye Luki, Sov. Un.	D7	27
Velikiy Ustyug, Sov. Un.	C7	29
Veliko Tŭrnovo, Bul.	D7	24
Velingara, Sen.	D2	45
Velizh, Sov. Un.	D8	27
Velké Meziříčí, Czech.	D4	26
Velletri, Italy	D4	23
Vellinge, Swe.	C7	15
Vellore, India	F6	36
Velma, Ok., U.S.	C4	113
Velpen, In., U.S.	H3	91
Velsk, Sov. Un.	C7	29
Veltrusy, Czech.	n17	26
Velva, N.D., U.S.	A5	111
Velvary, Czech.	n17	26
Vemb, Den.	B2	15
Ven, i., Swe.	C6	15
Venado, Mex.	C2	23
Venaco, Fr.	C2	23
Venado Tuerto, Arg.	A4	54
Venango, Pa., U.S.	C1	115
Venango, co., Pa., U.S.	D2	115
Venceslau Brás, Braz.	G3	56
Venda, ctry., Afr.	B5	49
Vendôme, Fr.	D4	16
Venedocia, Oh., U.S.	B1	112
Venetia (Veneto), prov., Italy	A3	23
Venetie, Ak., U.S.	B10	79
Veneta, Or., U.S.	C3	114
Veneto, prov., Italy	D7	20
Venezuela, ctry., S.A.	B4	60
Venezuela, Golfo de, b., S.A.	A3	60
Veniaminof, Mount, mtn., Ak., U.S.	D8	79
Venice, Alta.	B4	68
Venice (Venezia), Italy	B4	23
Venice, Fl., U.S.	E4	86
Venice, Il., U.S.	E3	90
Venice, La., U.S.	E6	95
Venice, Ne., U.S.	g12	104
Venice, Ut., U.S.	E4	121
Venice, Gulf of, b., Eur.	B4	23
Venice Gardens, Fl., U.S.	*E4	86
Vénissieux, Fr.	E6	16
Venlo, Neth.	B7	16
Venn, Sask.	F3	75
Vennachar, Ont.	B7	73
Venø, i., Den.	B2	15
Vent, Aus.	C6	20
Venta, stm., Sov. Un.	C3	27
Ventana, Az., U.S.	E3	80
Ventimiglia, Italy	C1	23
Ventnor, Ont.	C9	73
Ventnor, Eng., U.K.	D6	12
Ventnor City, N.J., U.S.	E4	107
Ventry, Ire.	E1	11
Ventspils, Sov. Un.	C3	27
Ventuari, stm., Ven.	C4	60
Ventura (San Buenaventura), Ca., U.S.	E4	82
Ventura, Ia., U.S.	A4	92
Ventura, co., Ca., U.S.	E4	82
Venturia, N.D., U.S.	D6	111
Venus, Fl., U.S.	E5	86
Venus, Pa., U.S.	D2	115
Venustiano Carranza, Mex.	D6	63
Vera, Arg.	E3	55
Vera, Spain	D5	22
Vera, Ok., U.S.	A6	113
Vera, Tx., U.S.	C3	120
Vera Cruz, In., U.S.	C7	91
Veracruz, state, Mex.	C5	63
Veracruz [Llave], Mex.	C5	63
Veradale, Wa., U.S.	*B8	124
Veranópolis, Braz.	D2	56
Verbania, Italy	D4	20
Verbena, Al., U.S.	C3	78
Verda, Ky., U.S.	D6	94
Verde, stm., Braz.	B4	55
Verde, stm., Braz.	C2	56
Verde, stm., Braz.	B2	56
Verde, stm., Mex.	m14	63
Verde, stm., Mex.	m12	63
Verde, stm., Para.	D4	55
Verde, stm., Az., U.S.	C4	80
Verde, Point, c., Newf.	E4	72
Verde Island, i., Phil.	p13	34
Verde Island Passage, strt., Phil.	p13	34
Verdel, Ne., U.S.	B7	104
Verden, Ger.	B4	18
Verden, Ok., U.S.	B3	113
Verdi, Mn., U.S.	F2	100
Verdi, Nv., U.S.	D2	105
Verdigre, Ne., U.S.	B7	104
Verdigris, Ok., U.S.	A6	113
Verdigris, stm., U.S.	A6	113
Verdon, Ne., U.S.	D10	104
Verdon, S.D., U.S.	B7	118
Verdun, Fr.	C6	16
Verdun, Que.	q19	74
Verdun, Fr.	C6	16
Verdunville, W.V., U.S.	*D2	125
Vereeniging, S. Afr.	C4	49
Vereshchagino, Sov. Un.	D19	8
Vergara, Spain	A4	22
Vergara, Ur.	E2	56
Vergas, Mn., U.S.	D3	100
Vergennes, Il., U.S.	F4	90
Vergennes, Vt., U.S.	C2	122
Vergin, Sask.	F4	75
Verín, Spain	B2	22
Verísimo Sarmento see Camissombo, Ang.	C3	48
Veríssimo, Braz.	B3	56
Verkhnedvinsk, Sov. Un.	D7	27
Verkhneimbatsk, Sov. Un.	C26	8
Verkhnekolymsk, Sov. Un.	C18	29
Verkhneuralsk, Sov. Un.	E20	8
Verkhneusinskoye, Sov. Un.	E27	8
Verkhniy Baskunchak, Sov. Un.	D3	28
Verkhniy Ufaley, Sov. Un.	B6	28
Verkhnyaya Tura, Sov. Un.	D21	8
Verkhoyansk, Sov. Un.	C16	29
Verkhoyansk Mountains, mts., Sov. Un.	C15	29
Verlo, Sask.	G1	75
Vermilion, Alta.	C5	68
Vermilion, Oh., U.S.	A3	112
Vermilion, co., Il., U.S.	C6	90
Vermilion, co., La., U.S.	E3	95
Vermilion, stm., Alta.	C5	68
Vermilion, stm., Il., U.S.	C5	90
Vermilion, stm., La., U.S.	E3	95
Vermilion, stm., Oh., U.S.	A3	112
Vermilion Bay, Ont.	o16	73
Vermilion Bay, b., La., U.S.	E3	95
Vermilion Lake, l., Mn., U.S.	C6	100
Vermilion Pass, Can.	D2	68
Vermilion Range, hills, Mn., U.S.	C7	100
Vermillion, Ks., U.S.	C7	93
Vermillion, S.D., U.S.	E9	118
Vermillion, co., In., U.S.	E2	91
Vermillion, East Fork, stm., S.D., U.S.	C7	100
Vermillion Bluffs, clf., Co., U.S.	A2	83
Vermillion Creek, stm., Co., U.S.	A2	83
Vermont, Il., U.S.	C3	90
Vermont, state, U.S.	D3	122
Vermontville, Mi., U.S.	F5	99
Vernalis, Ca., U.S.	h10	82
Verndale, Mn., U.S.	D3	100
Verner, Ont.	A4	73
Verneuil, Fr.	C4	16
Verneukpan, pl., S. Afr.	D3	49
Vernon, B.C.	C4	16
Vernon, Al., U.S.	B1	78
Vernon, Az., U.S.	C6	80
Vernon, Co., U.S.	*B6	84
Vernon, Ct., U.S.	*B6	84
Vernon, Fl., U.S.	u16	86
Vernon, Il., U.S.	E4	90
Vernon, Gardens, Fl., U.S.	*G6	90
Vernon, Ok., U.S.	B6	113
Vernon, Tn., U.S.	B4	119
Vernon, Tx., U.S.	B3	120
Vernon, Ut., U.S.	C3	121
Vernon, Vt., U.S.	F3	122
Vernon, co., La., U.S.	C2	95
Vernon, co., Mo., U.S.	D3	102
Vernon, co., Wi., U.S.	E3	126
Vernon, Lake, l., Ont.	B5	73
Vernon Bridge, P.E.I.	C7	71
Vernon Center, Mn., U.S.	G4	100
Vernon Hill, Va., U.S.	D3	123
Vernon Hills, Va., U.S.	h9	90
Vernonia, Or., U.S.	B3	114
Vernon River, P.E.I.	C7	71
Vero Beach, Fl., U.S.	E6	86
Véroia, Grc.	B4	40
Verona, Ont.	C8	73
Verona, Italy	B3	23
Verona, Il., U.S.	B5	90
Verona, Ky., U.S.	k13	94
Verona, Ms., U.S.	A5	101
Verona, Mo., U.S.	E4	102
Verona, N.J., U.S.	B4	107
Verona, N.C., U.S.	C5	110
Verona, N.D., U.S.	C7	111
Verona, Oh., U.S.	C1	112
Verona, Pa., U.S.	k14	115
Verona, Wi., U.S.	F4	126
Verónica, Arg.	g8	54
Verret, N.B.	B1	71
Verret, Lake, l., La., U.S.	E4	95
Verrières-le-Buisson, Fr.	h10	16
Versailles, Fr.	C5	16
Versailles, Ct., U.S.	C7	84
Versailles, Il., U.S.	D3	90
Versailles, In., U.S.	F7	91
Versailles, Ky., U.S.	B5	94
Versailles, Mo., U.S.	C5	102
Versailles, Oh., U.S.	B1	112
Vershire, Vt., U.S.	D4	122
Versmold, Ger.	A3	19
Versoix, Switz.	C2	20
Vert, Cap, c., Sen.	E4	42
Verte, stm., Que.	B8	74
Verte, Île, i., Que.	A8	74
Verton, Fr.	D9	12
Vertou, Fr.	D3	16
Vertus, Fr.	F4	17
Verviers, Bel.	B6	16
Vervins, Fr.	C5	16
Verwall Group, mts., Aus.	B9	21
Verwood, Sask.	H3	75
Verzasca, stm., Switz.	D6	21
Verzenay, Fr.	C6	16
Veseleyville, N.D., U.S.	A8	111
Veselí nad Lužnicí, Czech.	D9	19
Veseloye, Sov. Un.	H10	27
Vesoul, Fr.	D7	16
Vesoul, Fr.	D7	16
Vesper, Ks., U.S.	C5	93
Vesper, Wi., U.S.	D4	126
Vesta, C.R.	F6	62
Vesta, Mn., U.S.	F3	100
Vestaburg, Mi., U.S.	E6	99
Vestal, N.Y., U.S.	C4	109
Vestal Center, N.Y., U.S.	C4	109
Vestavia Hills, Al., U.S.	g7	78
Vestby, Nor.	p28	14
Vesterålen, is., Nor.	C6	14
Vesterø Havn, Den.	A4	15
Vestervig, Den.	B2	15
Vesterøya, i., Nor.	p28	14
Vestfjorden, Nor.	D5	14
Vestmannaeyjar, Ice.	o22	14
Vestsjælland, co., Den.	C5	15
Vesuvius, Va., U.S.	C3	123
Vesuvius, vol., Italy	D5	23
Vesyegonsk, Sov. Un.	B11	27
Veszprém, Hung.	B3	24
Vesztő, Hung.	B5	24
Vetal, S.D., U.S.	D4	118
Veteran, Alta.	C5	68
Veteran, Wy., U.S.	E8	127
Vetlanda, Swe.	I6	14
Vetluga, stm., Sov. Un.	B3	28
Vetluzhskiy, Sov. Un.	B3	28
Vetovo, Bul.	D8	24
Vetren, Bul.	D7	24
Veurne, Bel.	C2	17
Vevay, In., U.S.	G7	91
Vevey, Switz.	E3	18
Veynes, Fr.	F2	121
Veyo, Ut., U.S.	F2	121
Vézelay-le-Lac, Fr.	E1	21
Vézère, stm., Fr.	E4	16
Vézirköprü, Tur.	B10	40
Viacha, Bol.	C2	55
Viadana, Italy	B3	23
Viamonte, Arg.	A4	54
Vian, Ok., U.S.	B7	113
Viana, Braz.	B2	57
Viana do Bollo, Spain	A2	22
Viana do Alentejo, Port.	C1	22
Viana do Castelo, Port.	B1	22
Vianen, Neth.	C5	17
Viangchan (Vientiane), Laos	B2	34
Vianópolis, Braz.	B3	56
Viar, stm., Spain	C3	23
Viareggio, Italy	C3	23
Viborg, Den.	B3	15
Viborg, S.D., U.S.	D8	118
Vibo Valentia, Italy	E6	23
Vic, Fr.	C6	16
Vicálvaro, Spain	p17	22
Vicco, Ky., U.S.	C6	94
Vicente, Point, c., Ca., U.S.	n12	82
Vicenza, Italy	D6	20
Viceroy, Sask.	H3	75
Vich, Spain	B7	22
Vichada, dept., Col.	C4	60
Vichada, stm., Col.	C4	60
Vichuga, Sov. Un.	C13	27
Vichuquén, Chile	A2	54
Vichy, Mo., U.S.	C6	102
Vick, Ar., U.S.	D3	81
Vick, La., U.S.	C3	95
Vickery, Oh., U.S.	A3	112
Vicksburg, In., U.S.	H3	91
Vicksburg, Mi., U.S.	F5	99
Vicksburg, Ms., U.S.	C3	101
Vicksburg National Military Park, Ms., U.S.	C3	101
Viçosa, Braz.	C4	56
Viçosa, Braz.	C4	56
Viçosa do Ceará, Braz.	B2	57
Vicosoprano, Switz.	D9	21
Vicovaro, Italy	g9	23
Vic [-sur-Seille], Fr.	F6	17
Victor, Co., U.S.	C5	83
Victor, Id., U.S.	F7	89
Victor, Ia., U.S.	C5	92
Victor, Mt., U.S.	D2	103
Victor, N.Y., U.S.	C3	109
Victor, S.D., U.S.	B9	118
Victor Harbor, Austl.	G6	50
Victoria, Arg.	A4	54
Victoria, B.C.	E6	69
Victoria, Newf.	E5	72
Victoria, P.E.I.	C6	71
Victoria, Chile	B2	54
Victoria, Gren.	C2	55
Victoria (Hong Kong), H.K.	G7	31
Victoria, Malay.	D5	34
Victoria, Phil.	o13	34
Victoria, Ks., U.S.	D4	93
Victoria, Ms., U.S.	A4	101
Victoria, Mo., U.S.	C7	102
Victoria, Tn., U.S.	D8	119
Victoria, Tx., U.S.	E4	120
Victoria, Va., U.S.	D4	123
Victoria, state, Austl.	G7	50
Victoria, co., N.B.	B2	71
Victoria, co., N.S.	C9	71
Victoria, co., Ont.	C6	73
Victoria, co., Tx., U.S.	E4	120
Victoria, stm., Austl.	C5	50
Victoria, Lake, l., Afr.	B5	48
Victoria, Lake, l., Austl.	F3	51
Victoria, Mount, mtn., Burma	D9	36
Victoria, Mount, mtn., Pap. N. Gui.	k12	50
Victoria Beach, Man.	D3	70
Victoria de Durango see Durango, Mex.	C4	63
Victoria de las Tunas, Cuba	D5	64
Victoria Falls, Zimb.	A4	49
Victoria Falls, wtfl., Afr.	A4	49
Victoria Harbour, Ont.	C5	73
Victoria Island, i., N.W. Ter.	B10	66
Victoria Lake, res., Newf.	D3	72
Victoria Land, reg., Ant.	B28	7
Victoria Peak, mtn., Belize	B3	62
Victoria Road, Ont.	C6	73
Victoria Strait, strt., N.W. Ter.	C12	66
Victoria West, S. Afr.	D3	49
Victoriaville, Que.	C6	74
Victorica, Arg.	B3	54
Victorino de la Plaza, Arg.	B4	54
Victorville, Ca., U.S.	E5	82
Victory, Ok., U.S.	C2	113
Victory, Wi., U.S.	E2	126
Vicuña, Chile	F1	55
Vicuña Mackenna, Arg.	A4	54
Vida, Mt., U.S.	C11	103
Vidal, Ca., U.S.	E6	82
Vidalia, Ga., U.S.	D4	87
Vidalia, La., U.S.	C4	95
Vidette, Ga., U.S.	C4	87
Vidin, Bul.	C6	24
Vidisha, India	F6	37
Vidor, Tx., U.S.	D5	120
Vidora, Sask.	H1	75
Viechtach, Ger.	D7	19
Viedma, Arg.	C4	54
Viedma, Lago, l., Arg.	D2	54
Vieja, Sierra, mts., U.S.	o12	120
Viejo, Cerro el, mtn., Col.	B3	60
Vielsalm, Bel.	B6	17
Vienenburg, Ger.	B5	19
Vienna (Wien), Aus.	D8	18
Vienna, Ont.	E4	73
Vienna, Ga., U.S.	D3	87
Vienna, Il., U.S.	F5	90
Vienna, La., U.S.	B3	95
Vienna, Md., U.S.	D6	97
Vienna, Mo., U.S.	C6	102
Vienna, S.D., U.S.	C8	118
Vienna, Va., U.S.	B5	123
Vienna, W.V., U.S.	B3	125
Vienne, Fr.	E6	16
Vienne, dept., Fr.	D4	16
Vienne, stm., Fr.	D4	16
Vientiane see Viangchan, Laos	B2	34
Vieques, P.R.	B5	65
Vieques, Isla de, i., P.R.	G12	64
Vieques, Pasaje de, strt., P.R.	B4	65
Vieques, Sonda de, strt., P.R.	B5	65
Viernheim, Ger.	D3	19
Viersen, Ger.	C6	17
Vierzon, Fr.	D5	16
Viesca, Mex.	C4	63
Vieste, Italy	D6	23
Vietnam, ctry., Asia	B3	34
Viet Tri, Viet.	B6	35
Vieux Desert, Lac, l., Wi., U.S.	B4	126
Vieux Fort, St. Luc.	J14	64
Vieux-Fort, Pointe du, c., Guad.	R8	65
View Park, Ca., U.S.	*m12	82
Vigan, Phil.	B1	34
Vigevano, Italy	E6	20
Vignola, Italy	B3	23
Vigo, Spain	B1	22
Vigo, co., In., U.S.	F3	91
Vigsø Bugt, b., Den.	A2	15
Vihowa, Pak.	E4	37
Vibank, Sask.	G4	75
Vik, Ice.	o23	14
Vikersund, Nor.	p27	14
Viking, Alta.	C5	68
Vila Bela da Santíssima Trindade, Braz.	B2	55
Vila da Maganja, Moz.	A6	49
Vila de Manica, Moz.	A5	49
Vila de Rei, Port.	C1	22
Vila de Sena, Moz.	A6	49
Vila do Conde, Port.	B1	22
Vila Fontes, Moz.	A6	49
Vilafranca del Penedés, Spain	C1	22
Vila Franca de Xira, Port.	C1	22
Vilalnoulos, Moz.	B3	49
Vila Nova de Foz Côa, Port.	A3	22
Vila Nova de Milfontes, Port.	D1	22
Vila Real, Port.	B2	22
Vila Real de Santo António, Port.	D2	22
Vilas, Co., U.S.	D8	83
Vilas, co., Wi., U.S.	B4	126
Vila São João, Braz.	C4	56
Vila Vasco da Gama, Moz.	D5	48
Viçosa, Braz.	C4	56
Vila Viçosa, Port.	C2	22
Vildbjerg, Den.	B2	15
Vildo, Pr.	B2	119
Vileyka, Sov. Un.	C7	27
Vilhelmina, Swe.	E7	14
Vilhena, Braz.	B3	55
Vilia, Grc.	g10	25
Viliya, stm., Sov. Un.	A8	26
Viljandi, Sov. Un.	B5	27
Vilkaviškis, Sov. Un.	A7	26
Vilkitsky, i., Sov. Un.	B7	128
Vilkovo, Sov. Un.	I7	27
Villa Abecia, Bol.	D2	55
Villa Adriana, hist., Italy	h9	23
Villa Ahumada, Mex.	m13	63
Villa Ángela, Arg.	E3	55
Villa Aroma, Bol.	C2	55
Villa Bella, Bol.	B2	55
Villacañas, Spain	C4	22
Villacarrillo, Spain	C4	22
Villach, Aus.	E6	21
Villacidro, Italy	A1	23
Villa Clara, prov., Cuba	C3	64
Villa Constitución, Arg.	A4	54
Villa Cuauhtémoc, Mex.	k15	63
Villa de Arriaga, Mex.	m13	63
Villa de Cura, Ven.	A3	60
Villa Delgado, El Sal.	*D3	62
Villa del Rosario, Arg.	A4	54
Villa de Méndez, Mex.	E3	63
Villa Dolores, Arg.	A3	54
Villadossola, Italy	D5	21
Villa Eufronio Viscarra, Bol.	C2	55
Villafamés, Spain	B5	22
Villafranca del Bierzo, Spain	A2	22
Villafranca de los Barros, Spain	C2	22
Villafranca [di Verona], Italy	B3	23
Villa Frontera, Mex.	C4	63
Villa García, Mex.	k13	63
Villagarcía, Spain	A1	22
Village, Ar., U.S.	D2	81
Village, Va., U.S.	C6	123
Village Creek, stm., Al., U.S.	f7	78
Village Springs, Al., U.S.	B3	78
Villa González, Mex.	C5	63
Villa Grove, Co., U.S.	C5	83
Villa Grove, Il., U.S.	D5	90
Villaguay, Arg.	A5	54
Villa Hayes, Para.	E4	55
Villahermosa, Mex.	D6	63
Villa Hills, Ky., U.S.	*A5	94
Villa Huidobro, Arg.	B4	54
Villa Iris, Arg.	B4	54
Villajoyosa, Spain	C5	22
Villalba, Spain	A2	22
Villalonga, Arg.	B4	54
Villalpando, Spain	B3	22
Villa María, Arg.	A4	54
Villa María Grande, Arg.	A5	54
Villamartín, Spain	D3	22
Villa Montes, Bol.	D3	55
Villami, Ec.	g5	58
Villanueva, Col.	A3	60
Villanueva, N.M., U.S.	B4	108
Villanueva de Córdoba, Spain	C3	22
Villanueva del Arzobispo, Spain	C4	22
Villanueva de la Serana, Spain	C3	22
Villanueva de los Infantes, Spain	C4	22
Villanueva [del Río y Minas], Spain	C4	22
Villanueva y Geltrú, Spain	B6	22
Villa Obregón (part of Mexico City), Mex.	h9	63
Villa Ocampo, Arg.	E3	55
Villa Ojo de Agua, Arg.	E3	55
Villa Oliva, Para.	E4	55
Villa Park, Ca., U.S.	*n13	82
Villa Park, Il., U.S.	k8	90
Villaputzu, Italy	E2	23
Villard, Mn., U.S.	E3	100
Villard-Bonnot, Fr.	E6	16
Villa Rica, Ga., U.S.	C2	87
Villa Ridge, Il., U.S.	F4	90
Villa Ridge, Mo., U.S.	C7	102
Villarreal, Spain	B5	22
Villarrica, Chile	B2	54
Villarrica, Para.	E4	55
Villarrobledo, Spain	C4	22
Villarrubia de los Ojos, Spain	C4	22
Villars-le-Terrior, Switz.	D3	21
Villars-les-Dombes, Fr.	E3	107
Villa San Martín (Loreto), Arg.	E3	55
Villa Unión, Arg.	E2	55
Villa Unión, Mex.	B4	63
Villa Unión, Mex.	B3	63
Villa Valeria, Arg.	A4	54
Villaverde, Spain	p17	22
Villavicencio, Col.	C3	60
Villaviciosa, Spain	A3	22
Villazón, Bol.	D2	55
Villebon, Que.	C2	74
Villedieu, Fr.	D3	12
Villefranche, Fr.	E5	16
Villefranche [-sur-Saône], Fr.	D6	16
Villegreen, Co., U.S.	D7	83
Villejuif, Fr.	g10	16
Ville Marie, Que.	G17	66
Villemomble, Fr.	g11	16
Villena, Spain	C5	22
Villeneuve-d'Ascq, Fr.	*B5	17
Villeneuve-le-Roi, Fr.	h10	16
Villeneuve [-lès-Avignon], Fr.	F6	16
Villeneuve-Saint-Georges, Fr.	h10	16
Villeneuve-sur-Lot, Fr.	E4	16
Villeneuve-sur-Yonne, Fr.	E5	16
Villepinte, Fr.	g11	16
Ville Platte, La., U.S.	D3	95
Villeroy, Que.	C6	74
Villers-Bretonneux, Fr.	C5	16
Villers-Cotterêts, Fr.	C5	16
Villersexel, Fr.	A1	21
Villers-Semeuse, Fr.	D3	17
Villerupt, Fr.	C6	17
Ville Saint-Georges, Que.	C7	74
Villeta, Para.	E4	55
Villeurbanne, Fr.	E6	16
Villingen-Schwenningen, Ger.	D3	18
Villisca, Ia., U.S.	D2	92
Villa, Alta.	C5	68
Vilnius, Sov. Un.	A8	26
Vilonia, Ar., U.S.	B3	81
Vilppula, Fin.	F11	14
Vils, stm., Ger.	D7	19
Vils, stm., Ger.	D6	19
Vilsbiburg, Ger.	D6	19
Vilseck, Ger.	D6	19
Vilshofen, Ger.	D7	19
Vilvoorde, Bel.	B6	17
Vilyuy, stm., Sov. Un.	C15	29
Vilyuysk, Sov. Un.	C15	29
Vimianzo, Spain	A1	22
Vimmerby, Swe.	I6	14
Vimperk, Czech.	D7	19
Vimy Ridge, Alta.	k10	81
Vina, Al., U.S.	A1	78
Vina, Ca., U.S.	C2	82
Viña del Mar, Chile	A2	54

Name	Map Ref.	Page
Vinalhaven, Me., U.S.	D4	96
Vinalhaven Island, i., Me., U.S.	D4	96
Vinaroz, Spain	B6	22
Vincennes, Fr.	g10	16
Vincennes, In., U.S.	G2	91
Vincennes Bay, b., Ant.	C23	7
Vincent, Al., U.S.	B3	78
Vincent, Ia., U.S.	B3	92
Vincent, Oh., U.S.	C4	112
Vincent, Tx., U.S.	C2	120
Vincentown, N.J., U.S.	D3	107
Vinces, Ec.	B2	58
Vinchina, Arg.	E2	55
Vinchina, stm., Arg.	E2	55
Vinco, Oh., U.S.	B4	113
Vindelälven, stm., Swe.	E8	14
Vindeln, Swe.	E8	14
Vinderup, Den.	B2	15
Vindhya Range, mts., India	D6	36
Vine Brook, stm., Ma., U.S.	g11	98
Vinegar Hill, mtn., Or., U.S.	C8	114
Vine Grove, Ky., U.S.	C4	94
Vineland, N.J., U.S.	E2	107
Vinemont, Al., U.S.	A3	78
Vineyard Haven, Ma., U.S.	D6	98
Vineyard Sound, strt., Ma., U.S.	D6	98
Vingåker, Swe.	t33	14
Vinh, Viet.	B3	34
Vinhais, Port.	B2	22
Vinh Long, Viet.	C3	34
Vining, Ks., U.S.	C6	93
Vining, Mn., U.S.	D3	100
Vinita, Ok., U.S.	A6	113
Vinkovci, Yugo.	C4	24
Vinland, Ks., U.S.	m15	93
Vinnitsa, Sov. Un.	E5	29
Vinson, Ok., U.S.	C2	113
Vinson Massif, mtn., Ant.	B4	7
Vinton, Ia., U.S.	B5	92
Vinton, La., U.S.	D2	95
Vinton, Oh., U.S.	D3	112
Vinton, Va., U.S.	C3	123
Vinton, co., Oh., U.S.	C3	112
Vintondale, Pa., U.S.	F4	115
Viola, Ar., U.S.	A4	81
Viola, De., U.S.	D3	85
Viola, Id., U.S.	C1	89
Viola, Il., U.S.	B3	90
Viola, Ks., U.S.	E6	93
Viola, N.Y., U.S.	*D6	109
Viola, Tn., U.S.	D8	119
Viola, Wi., U.S.	E3	126
Violet, La., U.S.	k12	95
Vipiteno, Italy	C7	23
Virden, Man.	E1	70
Virden, Il., U.S.	D4	90
Virden, N.M., U.S.	E1	108
Vire, Fr.	C3	16
Vire, stm., Fr.	C3	16
Viren, i., Swe.	t34	14
Virgem da Lapa, Braz.	B4	56
Vírgenes, Cabo, c., S.A.	E4	54
Virgil, N.Y., U.S.	C4	109
Virgil, S.D., U.S.	C7	118
Virgilina, Va., U.S.	D4	123
Virgin, Ut., U.S.	F2	121
Virgin, stm., U.S.	H13	27
Virgin Gorda, i., V.I. Br.	G12	64
Virginia, Ire.	D4	11
Virginia, S. Afr.	C4	49
Virginia, Al., U.S.	g6	78
Virginia, Il., U.S.	D3	90
Virginia, Mn., U.S.	C6	100
Virginia, Ne., U.S.	D9	104
Virginia, state, U.S.	C4	123
Virginia Beach, Va., U.S.	D7	123
Virginia City, Mt., U.S.	E5	103
Virginia City, Nv., U.S.	D2	105
Virginia Peak, mtn., Nv., U.S.	D2	105
Virgin Islands, dep., N.A.	G12	64
Virgin Islands, is., N.A.	B6	65
Virgin Mountains, mts., U.S.	A1	80
Virginópolis, Braz.	B4	56
Virgin Passage, strt., N.A.	B5	65
Virgolândia, Braz.	C3	56
Virochey, Camb.	g9	34
Viroflay, Fr.	g9	16
Viron, Grc.	*D4	25
Viroqua, Wi., U.S.	E3	126
Virovitica, Yugo.	C4	24
Virpazar, Yugo.	D4	24
Virrat, Fin.	F10	14
Virserum, Swe.	I6	14
Virton, Bel.	E5	17
Virú, Peru	C2	58
Vis, Yugo.	D3	24
Vis, i., Yugo.	D3	24
Visalia, Ca., U.S.	D4	82
Visalia, Ky., U.S.	k14	94
Visayan Sea, Phil.	C6	34
Visby, Swe.	I8	14
Visconde do Rio Branco, Braz.	F3	75
Viscount, Sask.	F3	75
Viscount Melville Sound, strt., N.W. Ter.	B11	66
Visé, Bel.	D5	17
Višegrad, Yugo.	D4	24
Viseu, Braz.	B1	57
Viseu, Port.	B2	22
Vishākhapatnam (Vizagapatam), India	E7	36
Vishera, stm., Sov. Un.	A5	28
Viskan, stm., Swe.	A6	15
Vislanda, Swe.	B8	15
Viso, Mount, mtn., Italy	B1	23
Visoko, Yugo.	D4	24
Visp, Switz.	E3	18
Vista, Man.	D1	70
Vista, Ca., U.S.	F5	82
Vista, Mo., U.S.	D4	102
Vista, Nv., U.S.	*D2	105
Vista Alegre, Braz.	C4	60
Vistonis, Lake, l., Grc.	B5	25
Vistula, stm., Eur.	A5	26
Vistula Lagoon, b., Eur.	A5	26
Vistula see Wisła, stm., Pol.	B5	26
Vit, stm., Bul.	D7	24
Vita, Man.	E3	70
Vitanovac, Yugo.	D5	24
Vitarte, Peru	D2	58
Vitebsk, Sov. Un.	D6	29
Viterbo, Italy	C4	23
Vitichi, Bol.	B1	56
Viti Levu, i., Fiji	H14	52
Viti Levu Bay, b., Fiji	H15	52
Vitim, Sov. Un.	D14	29
Vitim, stm., Sov. Un.	D14	29
Vitor, Peru	E3	58
Vitória, Braz.	C4	56
Vitória, Braz.	C4	59
Vitória, Braz.	A2	22
Vitória, Braz.	B2	22
Vitória da Conquista, Braz.	A4	56
Vitória [de Santo Antão], Braz.	C3	57
Vitória do Mearim, Braz.	B2	57
Vitória Quebrangulo, Braz.	k5	57
Vitré, Fr.	C3	16
Vitry-le-François, Fr.	C6	16
Vitry [-sur-Seine], Fr.	g10	16
Vittel, Fr.	C6	16
Vittoria, Ont.	E4	73
Vittoria, Italy	F5	23
Vittorio Veneto, Italy	B4	23
Vivero, Spain	A2	22
Vivian, La., U.S.	B1	95
Vivian, S.D., U.S.	D5	118
Vivian Park, Ut., U.S.	C4	121
Vivoratá, Arg.	B5	54
Viwa, i., Fiji	H14	52
Vize, Tur.	B6	40
Vizianagaram, India	E7	36
Vizille, Fr.	E6	16
Viziru, Rom.	C8	24
Vizzini, Italy	F5	23
Vjosa, stm., Eur.	B3	25
Vlaardingen, Neth.	B6	16
Vladikavkaz, Sov. Un.	E7	29
Vladimir, Sov. Un.	D7	29
Vladimiro-Aleksandrovskoye, Sov. Un.	C11	31
Vladimirovo, Sov. Un.	B12	33
Vladimir-Volynskiy, Sov. Un.	F5	27
Vladivostok, Sov. Un.	E16	29
Vlasenica, Yugo.	C4	24
Vlašim, Czech.	D9	19
Vlasotince, Yugo.	D6	24
Vlčany, Czech.	D4	19
Vlieland, i., Neth.	A6	16
Vlissingen, Neth.	B5	16
Vlkava, stm., Czech.	n18	26
Vlkava, stm., Czech.	n18	26
Vlora (Valona), Alb.	B2	40
Vlotho, Ger.	A3	19
Vltava, stm., Czech.	D3	26
Voca, Tx., U.S.	D3	120
Vodlozero, l., Sov. Un.	F17	14
Vodňany, Czech.	D9	19
Vohenstrauss, Ger.	D7	19
Vohibinany, Madag.	g9	49
Vohimarina, Madag.	f9	49
Vohipeno, Madag.	h9	49
Voi, Kenya	B6	48
Void, Fr.	F5	17
Voil, Loch, l., Scot., U.K.	D4	13
Voinjama, Lib.	E3	45
Voiron, Fr.	E6	16
Voisin, Lac, l., Sask.	C2	75
Voitsberg, Aus.	E7	18
Vojens, Den.	C3	15
Vokhma, Sov. Un.	B8	28
Volary, Czech.	E8	19
Volborg, Mt., U.S.	E11	103
Volcano, Hi., U.S.	D6	88
Volcano Island, i., Phil.	o13	34
Volcano Islands, is., Japan	E8	6
Volčansk, Sov. Un.	F11	27
Volga, Ia., U.S.	B6	92
Volga, S.D., U.S.	C9	118
Volga, W.V., U.S.	B4	125
Volga, stm., Sov. Un.	E7	29
Volga Plateau, plat., Sov. Un.	C3	28
Volgodonsk, Sov. Un.	H13	27
Volgograd (Stalingrad), Sov. Un.	E7	29
Volgograd Reservoir, res., Sov. Un.	D7	29
Volin, S.D., U.S.	E8	118
Volkach, Ger.	D5	19
Volkhov, Sov. Un.	B9	27
Volkhov, stm., Sov. Un.	B8	27
Völklingen, Ger.	D1	19
Volkovysk, Sov. Un.	E5	27
Vollenhove, Neth.	B5	17
Volney, Va., U.S.	f9	123
Volnovakha, Sov. Un.	H11	27
Volo, Il., U.S.	h8	90
Volochayevka Vtoraya, Sov. Un.	B7	33
Volochisk, Sov. Un.	G6	27
Volodarskiy (part of Leningrad), Sov. Un.	s31	14
Volodarskoye, Sov. Un.	D7	29
Vologda, Sov. Un.	C7	29
Vólos, Grc.	C4	40
Vólos, Gulf of see Pagasitikós Kólpos, b., Grc.		
Volsk, Sov. Un.	C8	28
Volta, prov., Ghana	E5	45
Volta, Lake, res., Ghana	E5	45
Volta Redonda, Braz.	C4	56
Volta Noire (Black Volta), stm., Afr.	D4	45
Volta Redonda, Braz.	C4	56
Volterra, Italy	C3	23
Voltri, Italy	B2	23
Volturno, stm., Italy	D5	23
Voluntown, Ct., U.S.	C8	84
Volusia, co., Fl., U.S.	C5	86
Völvi, Lake, l., Grc.	B4	25
Volzhskiy, Sov. Un.	G15	27
Vombsjön, l., Swe.	C7	15
Vona, Co., U.S.	B8	83
Vonda, Sask.	E2	75
Von Frank Mountain, mtn., Ak., U.S.	C9	79
Vónitsa, Grc.	C3	25
Vonore, Tn., U.S.	D9	119
Von Ormy, Tx., U.S.	k7	120
Vopnafjördur, Ice.	n25	14
Vorarlberg, state, Aus.	B5	20
Vorderrhein, stm., Switz.	C7	21
Vorderthal, Switz.	B6	21
Vordingborg, Den.	C3	15
Vorkuta, Sov. Un.	C9	29
Vorona, stm., Sov. Un.	E14	27
Voronezh, Sov. Un.	E5	28
Voronezh, stm., Sov. Un.	E12	27
Voronya, stm., Sov. Un.	C16	14
Vorterkaka Nunatak, mtn., Ant.	B15	7
Vosburg, S. Afr.	D3	49
Vosges, dept., Fr.	A2	20
Vosges, mts., Fr.	C7	16
Voskresensk, Sov. Un.	n18	27
Voss, Nor.	G2	14
Voss, N.D., U.S.	A8	111
Vostochnyy, Sov. Un.	B11	33
Vostok, sci., Ant.	B23	7
Vostok Island, i., Kir.	G12	6
Votaw, Tx., U.S.	D5	120
Votice, Czech.	D9	19
Votkinsk, Sov. Un.	B4	28
Vouga, stm., Port.	B1	22
Vouliagméni, Grc.	h11	25
Vouvray, Fr.	D4	16
Vouziers, Fr.	C6	16
Voyageurs National Park, Mn., U.S.	B5	100
Voyeykov Ice Shelf, ice, Ant.	C25	7
Vozhega, Sov. Un.	A13	27
Voznesensk, Sov. Un.	H8	27
Voznesenskoye, Sov. Un.	A8	33
Voznesenye, Sov. Un.	A10	27
Vrå, Den.	A3	15
Vranje, Yugo.	D5	24
Vratsa, Bul.	D6	24
Vrbas, Yugo.	C4	24
Vrbas, stm., Yugo.	C3	24
Vrchlabí, Czech.	C3	26
Vrede, S. Afr.	C4	49
Vreden, Ger.	A1	19
Vredenburgh, Al., U.S.	D2	78
Vreed en Hoop, Guy.	A3	59
Vrena, Swe.	u34	14
Vriezenveen, Neth.	B6	17
Vrigstad, Swe.	C7	21
Vrin, Switz.	C7	21
Vršac, Yugo.	C5	24
Vršovice (part of Prague), Czech.	n17	26
Vrútky, Czech.	D5	26
Vryburg, S. Afr.	C3	49
Vryheid, S. Afr.	C5	49
Všetaty, Czech.	n18	26
Vsetín, Czech.	D5	26
Vsevidof, Mount, mtn., Ak., U.S.	E6	79
Vsevolozhsk, Sov. Un.	r31	14
Vuaqava, i., Fiji	I16	52
Vúcha, stm., Bul.	E7	24
Vuda Point, c., Fiji	H14	52
Vukovar, Yugo.	C4	24
Vulcan, Alta.	D4	68
Vulcan, Mi., U.S.	C3	99
Vulcan, Mo., U.S.	D7	102
Vulcano, i., Italy	E5	23
Vůlchedrūma, Bul.	D6	24
Vung Tau, Viet.	G7	35
Vung Tau, Cape, c., Viet.	G7	35
Vunidawa, Fiji	H15	52
Vuoloyarvi, Sov. Un.	r31	14
Vuya Point, c., Fiji	H15	52
Vyartsilya, Sov. Un.	F14	14
Vyatka, stm., Sov. Un.	D7	29
Vyazemskiy, Sov. Un.	B4	28
Vyazma, Sov. Un.	D10	27
Vyazniki, Sov. Un.	C14	27
Vyborg, Sov. Un.	C5	29
Vychegda, stm., Sov. Un.	C18	8
Vygozero, l., Sov. Un.	F16	14
Vyksa, Sov. Un.	D14	27
Vyritsa, Sov. Un.	s31	14
Vyrovka, stm., Czech.	n19	26
Vyshniy Volochek, Sov. Un.	C10	27
Vyškov, Czech.	D4	26
Vysočany (part of Prague), Czech.	n17	26
Vysoká, Czech.	n18	26
Vysoké Mýto, Czech.	D4	26
Vyšší Brod, Czech.	E9	19
Vytegra, Sov. Un.	C6	29

W

Name	Map Ref.	Page
Wa, Ghana	D4	45
Waal, stm., Neth.	B6	16
Waalwijk, Neth.	C5	17
Waawaa, Puu, mtn., Hi., U.S.	D6	88
Wabamun, Alta.	C3	68
Wabamun Lake, l., Alta.	C3	68
Wabana (Bell Island), Newf.	E5	72
Wabasca, Alta.	B4	68
Wabasca, stm., Alta.	f1	68
Wabash, Ar., U.S.	C5	81
Wabash, In., U.S.	C6	91
Wabash, Ne., U.S.	h12	104
Wabash, co., Il., U.S.	E6	90
Wabash, co., In., U.S.	C6	91
Wabash, stm., U.S.	H2	91
Wabasha, Mn., U.S.	F6	100
Wabasha, co., Mn., U.S.	F6	100
Wabasso, Fl., U.S.	E6	86
Wabasso, Mn., U.S.	F3	100
Wabaunsee, Ks., U.S.	C7	93
Wabaunsee, co., Ks., U.S.	C7	93
Wabasseka, Ar., U.S.	C4	81
Wabeno, Wi., U.S.	C5	126
Wabigoon, Ont.	E5	70
Wabigoon Lake, l., Ont.	E5	70
Wabowden, Man.	B2	70
Wąbrzeźno, Pol.	B5	26
Wabush, Newf.	h8	72
Wabuska, Nv., U.S.	D2	105
Waccamaw, stm., U.S.	D9	117
Waccamaw, Lake, l., N.C., U.S.	C4	110
Waccasassa Bay, b., Fl., U.S.	C4	86
Wachapreague, Va., U.S.	C7	123
Wachusett Mountain, mtn., Ma., U.S.	B4	98
Wachusett Reservoir, res., Ma., U.S.	B4	98
Wacissa, Fl., U.S.	B3	86
Wacker, Il., U.S.	A3	90
Waco, Ga., U.S.	C1	87
Waco, Ks., U.S.	g12	93
Waco, Ne., U.S.	D8	104
Waco, N.C., U.S.	B1	110
Waco, Tx., U.S.	D4	120
Waco Lake, res., Tx., U.S.	D4	120
Waconda Lake, res., Ks., U.S.	C5	93
Waconia, Mn., U.S.	F5	100
Waddān, Libya	D3	43
Waddān, Jabal, Libya	D3	43
Waddell, N.C., U.S.	A6	110
Wadden Zee, Neth.	A6	16
Waddington, N.Y., U.S.	f9	109
Waddington, Mount, mtn., B.C.	D5	69
Waddy, Ky., U.S.	B4	94
Wade, N.C., U.S.	B4	110
Wade, Ok., U.S.	D5	113
Wade, Mount, mtn., Ant.	A32	7
Wade Hampton, S.C., U.S.	*B3	117
Wadena, Sask.	F4	75
Wadena, Ia., U.S.	B6	92
Wadena, Mn., U.S.	D3	100
Wadena, co., Mn., U.S.	D3	100
Wadesboro, N.C., U.S.	C2	110
Wadesville, In., U.S.	H2	91
Wadham Islands, is., Newf.	D5	72
Wadhwān see Surendranagar, India	F3	37
Wādī al Jayb (Ha Arava), val., Asia	m14	41
Wādī al Jöz (part of Jerusalem), Isr. Occ.	m14	41
Wading, stm., N.J., U.S.	D3	107
Wading, West Branch, stm., N.J., U.S.	D3	107
Wading River, N.J., U.S.	D4	107
Wading River, N.Y., U.S.	n16	109
Wadley, Al., U.S.	B4	78
Wadley, Ga., U.S.	D4	87
Wad Madanī, Sud.	C3	47
Wadowice, Pol.	F7	111
Wadsworth, Al., U.S.	D5	26
Wadsworth, Il., U.S.	h9	90
Wadsworth, Nv., U.S.	D2	105
Wadsworth, Oh., U.S.	A4	112
Waelder, Tx., U.S.	E4	120
Wagener, S.C., U.S.	D5	117
Wageningen, Sur.	A3	59
Wager Bay, b., N.W. Ter.	C15	66
Wagga, Sud.	B4	47
Wagga Wagga, Austl.	G8	50
Waggoner, Il., U.S.	D4	90
Waggoner, co., Ok., U.S.	B6	113
Wagner, Mt., U.S.	B8	103
Wagner, S.D., U.S.	D7	118
Wagners Lake, Ne., U.S.	*C8	104
Wagoner, Ok., U.S.	B6	113
Wagoner, co., Ok., U.S.	B6	113
Wagon Mound, N.M., U.S.	A5	108
Wagontire Mountain, mtn., Or., U.S.	D7	114
Wagram, N.C., U.S.	C3	110
Wagrowiec, Pol.	B4	26
Waha, Libya	D3	43
Wahai, Indon.	F7	34
Wah Cantonment, Pak.	*B5	36
Wahiawa, Hi., U.S.	B3	88
Wahiawa Reservoir, res., Hi., U.S.	g9	88
Wahkiakum, co., Wa., U.S.	C2	124
Wahkon, Mn., U.S.	D5	100
Wahlern, Switz.	C3	21
Wahoo, Ne., U.S.	C9	104
Wahoo Creek, stm., Ne., U.S.	g11	104
Wahpeton, N.D., U.S.	C9	111
Wah Wah Mountains, mts., Ut., U.S.	E2	121
Wahweap Creek, stm., Ut., U.S.	F4	121
Waialua, Hi., U.S.	B3	88
Waialua Bay, b., Hi., U.S.	B3	88
Waianae, Hi., U.S.	B3	88
Waianae Range, mts., Hi., U.S.	f9	88
Waiau, stm., N.Z.	O14	51
Waiawa Stream, stm., Hi., U.S.	g10	88
Waiblingen, Ger.	E4	19
Waidhofen [an der Thaya], Aus.	D7	18
Waidhofen [an der Ybbs], Aus.	E7	18
Waigeo, i., Indon.	F8	34
Waihee, Hi., U.S.	C5	88
Wai Islands, is., Camb.	H5	35
Waikabubak, Indon.	G5	34
Waikapu, Hi., U.S.	C5	88
Waikari, N.Z.	O14	51
Waikato, stm., N.Z.	L15	51
Waikawa, N.Z.	Q12	51
Waikelo, Indon.	G5	34
Waikiki Beach, Hi., U.S.	g10	88
Wailagi Lala, i., Fiji	H16	52
Wailea, Hi., U.S.	D6	88
Wailua, Hi., U.S.	C5	88
Wailuku, Hi., U.S.	C5	88
Wailuku, stm., Hi., U.S.	D6	88
Waimanalo, Hi., U.S.	B4	88
Waimanalo Bay, b., Hi., U.S.	g11	88
Waimate, N.Z.	P13	51
Waimea, Hi., U.S.	f9	88
Waimea, Hi., U.S.	B3	88
Wainganga, stm., India	D7	36
Waingapu, Indon.	G6	34
Waini Point, c., Guy.	A3	59
Wainunu Bay, b., Fiji	H15	52
Wainwright, Alta.	C5	68
Wainwright, Ak., U.S.	A7	79
Wainwright, Oh., U.S.	B4	112
Waiohinu, Hi., U.S.	D6	88
Waipahu, Hi., U.S.	B3	88
Waipara, N.Z.	O14	51
Waipawa, N.Z.	M16	51
Waipio Acres, Hi., U.S.	g9	88
Waipio Peninsula, pen., Hi., U.S.	g10	88
Waipukurau, N.Z.	N16	51
Wairau, stm., N.Z.	N14	51
Wairoa, N.Z.	M16	51
Waitaki, stm., N.Z.	P13	51
Waitara, N.Z.	M15	51
Waite, Me., U.S.	C5	96
Waite Park, Mn., U.S.	E4	100
Waiteville, W.V., U.S.	D4	125
Waits, stm., Vt., U.S.	C4	122
Waitsburg, Wa., U.S.	C7	124
Waitsfield, Vt., U.S.	C3	122
Waits River, Vt., U.S.	C4	122
Waitville, Sask.	E3	75
Waiwo, Indon.	F8	34
Wajima, Japan	H8	33
Wajir, Kenya	A7	48
Waka, Eth.	A3	48
Waka, Tx., U.S.	A2	120
Waka, Zaire	A4	48
Wakarusa, In., U.S.	A5	91
Wakarusa, Ks., U.S.	D8	93
Wakarusa, stm., Ks., U.S.	D8	93
Wakasa Bay, b., Japan	I7	33
Wakatipu, Lake, l., N.Z.	P12	51
Wakatomika Creek, stm., Oh., U.S.	B3	112
Wakaw, Sask.	E3	75
Wakaya, i., Fiji	H15	52
Wake, co., N.C., U.S.	B4	110
Wa Keeney, Ks., U.S.	C4	93
Wakefield, Eng., U.K.	A6	12
Wakefield, La., U.S.	D4	95
Wakefield, Ma., U.S.	B5	98
Wakefield, Mi., U.S.	n12	99
Wakefield, Ne., U.S.	B8	104
Wakefield, N.H., U.S.	C4	106
Wakefield, Oh., U.S.	D3	112
Wakefield, R.I., U.S.	F3	116
Wakefield, Va., U.S.	D6	123
Wake Forest, N.C., U.S.	B4	110
Wake Island, dep., Oc.	E10	6
Wake Island Air Force Base, mil., Wake I.	B2	52
Wake Lagoon, b., Wake I.	B2	52
Wakema, Burma	D1	35
Wakeman, Oh., U.S.	A3	112
Wakenda, Mo., U.S.	B4	102
Wakita, Ok., U.S.	A4	113
Wakkanai, Japan	B13	31
Wakkerstroom, S. Afr.	C5	49
Wakonda, S.D., U.S.	D8	118
Wakopa, Man.	E2	70
Wakpala, S.D., U.S.	B5	118
Wakuach, Lac, l., Que.	g8	72
Waku Kungo, Ang.	D2	48
Wakulla, Fl., U.S.	B2	86
Wakulla, co., Fl., U.S.	B2	86
Walachia, hist. reg., Rom.	C7	24
Walbourg, Fr.	F7	17
Walbridge, Oh., U.S.	e6	112
Wałbrzych (Waldenburg), Pol.	C7	20
Walchen Lake, l., Ger.	B7	20
Walcott, Ar., U.S.	A5	81
Walcott, Ia., U.S.	C7	92
Walcott, N.D., U.S.	C9	111
Walcott, Wy., U.S.	E6	127
Walcott, Lake, res., Id., U.S.	G5	89
Wałczz, Pol.	B5	26
Wald, Switz.	B4	21
Waldbröl, Ger.	C2	19
Waldeck, Ger.	G2	75
Walden, Ont.	A3	73
Walden, Co., U.S.	A4	83
Walden, N.Y., U.S.	D6	109
Walden, Vt., U.S.	C4	122
Waldenburg, Ar., U.S.	B5	81
Waldenburg see Wałbrzych, Pol.	C4	26
Walden Heights, Vt., U.S.	C4	122
Walden Pond, l., Ma., U.S.	g10	98
Walden Ridge, mtn., Tn., U.S.	D8	119
Waldheim, Sask.	E2	75
Waldkappel, Ger.	B4	19
Waldkirchen, Ger.	E8	19
Waldmünchen, Ger.	D7	19
Waldnaab, stm., Ger.	D6	18
Waldo, B.C.	E10	69
Waldo, Ar., U.S.	D2	81
Waldo, Fl., U.S.	C4	86
Waldo, Ks., U.S.	C5	93
Waldo, Oh., U.S.	B2	112
Waldo, co., Me., U.S.	D3	96
Waldoboro, Me., U.S.	D3	96
Waldo Lake, l., Ma., U.S.	h11	98
Waldo Lake, l., Or., U.S.	D4	114
Waldorf, Md., U.S.	C4	97
Waldport, Or., U.S.	C2	114
Waldron, Sask.	G4	75
Waldron, Ar., U.S.	C1	81
Waldron, In., U.S.	F6	91
Waldron, Mi., U.S.	G6	99
Waldron, Mo., U.S.	h10	102
Waldsassen, Ger.	C7	19
Waldshut, Ger.	E4	18
Waldwick, N.J., U.S.	A4	107
Walen, Lake, l., Switz.	B5	20
Walenstadt, Switz.	B7	21
Wales, Ak., U.S.	B6	79
Wales, Ma., U.S.	B3	98
Wales, N.D., U.S.	A7	111
Wales, Ut., U.S.	D5	121
Wales, ter., U.K.	D5	10
Waleska, Ga., U.S.	B2	87
Walford Station, Ont.	A2	73
Walgett, Austl.	E8	50
Walgreen Coast, Ant.	B2	7
Walhalla, Mi., U.S.	E4	99
Walhalla, N.D., U.S.	A8	111
Walhalla, S.C., U.S.	B2	117
Walhonding, stm., Oh., U.S.	B3	112
Walikale, Zaire	B5	48
Walker, Ia., U.S.	B6	92
Walker, La., U.S.	g10	95
Walker, Mi., U.S.	E5	99
Walker, Mn., U.S.	C4	100
Walker, Mo., U.S.	C3	102
Walker, co., Al., U.S.	B2	78
Walker, co., Ga., U.S.	B1	87
Walker, co., Tx., U.S.	D5	120
Walker, stm., Nv., U.S.	D3	105
Walker Lake, l., Man.	B3	70
Walker Lake, l., Nv., U.S.	E3	105
Walker Mill, Md., U.S.	*C4	97
Walker Mountain, mtn., Ga., U.S.	B3	87
Walker Mountain, mtn., Va., U.S.	C1	123
Walker River Indian Reservation, Nv., U.S.	D3	105
Walker Springs, Al., U.S.	D2	78
Walkersville, Md., U.S.	B3	97
Walkerton, Ont.	C3	73
Walkerton, In., U.S.	A5	91
Walkertown, N.C., U.S.	A2	110
Walkerville, Mi., U.S.	E4	99
Walkerville, Mt., U.S.	D4	103
Wall, S.D., U.S.	D3	118
Wallace, N.S.	D6	71
Wallace, Id., U.S.	B3	89
Wallace, In., U.S.	E3	91
Wallace, Ks., U.S.	C3	99
Wallace, Ne., U.S.	D4	104
Wallace, N.C., U.S.	C4	110
Wallace, S.D., U.S.	C8	118
Wallace, Va., U.S.	f9	123
Wallace, W.V., U.S.	B4	125
Wallace, co., Ks., U.S.	D2	93
Wallaceburg, Ont.	E2	73
Wallacetown, Ont.	E3	73
Wallagrass, Me., U.S.	A4	96
Walland, Tn., U.S.	D10	119
Wallaroo, Austl.	F6	50
Wallasey, Eng., U.K.	F5	12
Walla Walla, Wa., U.S.	C7	124
Walla Walla, co., Wa., U.S.	C7	124
Walldürn, Ger.	D4	19
Walled Lake, Mi., U.S.	o15	99
Wallen, In., U.S.	B7	91
Wallenpaupack, Lake, l., Pa., U.S.	D11	115
Wallen Ridge, mtn., Tn., U.S.	C10	119
Waller, Tx., U.S.	q14	120
Waller, co., Tx., U.S.	E5	120
Wallingford, Eng., U.K.	C6	12
Wallingford, Ct., U.S.	D4	84
Wallingford, Ia., U.S.	A3	92
Wallingford, Vt., U.S.	E3	122
Walling Mountain, mtn., Ma., U.S.	B1	98
Wallington, N.J., U.S.	h8	107
Wallis, Tx., U.S.	E5	120
Wallis and Futuna, dep., Oc.	G11	6
Wallis Sands, N.H., U.S.	D5	106
Wallkill, N.Y., U.S.	D6	109
Wallkill, stm., N.Y., U.S.	D6	109
Wall Lake, Ia., U.S.	B2	92
Walloomsac, stm., U.S.	F2	122
Walloon Lake, l., Mi., U.S.	C6	99
Wallowa, Or., U.S.	B9	114
Wallowa, co., Or., U.S.	B9	114
Wallowa Mountains, mts., Or., U.S.	B9	114
Wallpack Center, N.J., U.S.	A3	107
Walls, Ms., U.S.	A3	101
Wallsburg, Ut., U.S.	C4	121
Wallsend, Eng., U.K.	C6	10
Wallula, Wa., U.S.	C7	124
Wallula, Lake, res., U.S.	C7	124
Wallum Lake, res., U.S.	A1	116
Walney, Isle of, i., Eng., U.K.	C5	10
Walnut, Ca., U.S.	*m13	82
Walnut, Il., U.S.	B4	90
Walnut, Ia., U.S.	C2	92
Walnut, Ks., U.S.	E8	93
Walnut, Ms., U.S.	A5	101
Walnut, N.C., U.S.	f10	110
Walnut, co., Ks., U.S.	E6	93
Walnut Bottom, Pa., U.S.	F7	115
Walnut Canyon National Monument, Az., U.S.	B4	80
Walnut Cove, N.C., U.S.	A2	110
Walnut Creek, Ca., U.S.	h8	82
Walnut Creek, stm., Ks., U.S.	D4	93
Walnut Creek West, Ca., U.S.	*D2	82
Walnut Grove, Al., U.S.	A3	78
Walnut Grove, Ca., U.S.	F3	100
Walnut Grove, Ms., U.S.	C4	101
Walnut Grove, Mo., U.S.	D4	102
Walnut Hill, Fl., U.S.	u14	86
Walnut Hill, Me., U.S.	g7	96
Walnut Hill, hill, Ma., U.S.	A2	98
Walnut Mountain, hill, Ct., U.S.	B3	84
Walnut Park, Ca., U.S.	*n12	82
Walnutport, Pa., U.S.	E10	115
Walnut Ridge, Ar., U.S.	A5	81
Walpole, Sask.	H5	75
Walpole, Ma., U.S.	B5	98
Walpole, N.H., U.S.	D2	106
Walsall, Eng., U.K.	D6	10
Walsenburg, Co., U.S.	D6	83
Walsh, Alta.	E5	68
Walsh, Co., U.S.	D8	83
Walsh, co., N.D., U.S.	A8	111
Walsingham, Cape, c., N.W. Ter.	C20	66
Walsrode, Ger.	F3	15
Walterboro, S.C., U.S.	F6	117
Walter F. George Dam, U.S.	D4	78
Walter F. George Lake, res., U.S.	D4	78
Walterhill, Tn., U.S.	B5	119
Walters, La., U.S.	C4	95
Walters, Mn., U.S.	G5	100
Walters, Ok., U.S.	C3	113
Walters, Va., U.S.	D6	123
Walters Falls, Ont.	C4	73
Walthausen, Ger.	C5	19
Walterville, Or., U.S.	C4	114
Waltham, Ms., U.S.	D3	101
Waltham, Ma., U.S.	B5	98
Waltham, Mn., U.S.	G6	100
Waltham Station, Que.	B8	73
Walthall, Ne., U.S.	B9	104
Walthourville, Ga., U.S.	E5	87
Walton, N.S.	D6	71
Walton, Ont.	D3	73
Walton, Fl., U.S.	E6	86
Walton, In., U.S.	C5	91
Walton, Ks., U.S.	D6	93
Walton, N.Y., U.S.	C5	109
Walton, W.V., U.S.	C3	125
Walton, co., Fl., U.S.	u15	86
Walton, co., Ga., U.S.	C3	87
Waltonville, Il., U.S.	E4	90
Walvisbaai (Walvis Bay), S. Afr.	B1	49
Walvis Bay see Walvisbaai, S. Afr.		
Walworth, N.Y., U.S.	B3	109
Walworth, Wi., U.S.	F5	126
Walworth, co., S.D., U.S.	B5	118
Walworth, co., Wi., U.S.	F5	126
Wamac, Il., U.S.	E4	90
Wamba, Nig.	B5	91
Wamba, Zaire	A4	48
Wamba, stm., Afr.	C2	48
Wamego, Ks., U.S.	C7	93
Wamesit, Ma., U.S.	A5	98
Wamic, Or., U.S.	B5	114
Wampsville, N.Y., U.S.	B5	109
Wampum, Pa., U.S.	E1	115
Wamsutter, Wy., U.S.	E5	127
Wāna, Pak.	D2	36
Wanaka, N.Z.	P12	51
Wanaka, Lake, l., N.Z.	P12	51
Wanamie, Pa., U.S.	A6	109
Wanapitei, Lake, l., Ont.	A4	73
Wanapum Dam, Wa., U.S.	C6	124
Wanapum Lake, res., Wa., U.S.	B6	124
Wanaque, N.J., U.S.	A4	107
Wanaque Reservoir, res., N.J., U.S.	A4	107
Wanatah, In., U.S.	B4	91
Wanchese, N.C., U.S.	B7	110
Wandering River, Alta.	B4	68
Wando, S. Kor.	I3	33
Wando, stm., S.C., U.S.	F8	117
Wandoan, Austl.	C7	51
Wando Woods, S.C., U.S.	k11	117
Wandsworth (part of London), Eng., U.K.	m12	10
Wanette, Ok., U.S.	C4	113
Wang, stm., Thai.	D3	35

Name	Map Ref.	Page
Wanganui, N.Z.	M15	51
Wangaratta, Austl.	G8	50
Wangen [im Allgäu], Ger.	B5	20
Wangerooge, i., Ger.	B3	18
Wangkui, China	A12	32
Wangqing, China	C10	31
Wanham, Alta.	B1	68
Wanilla, Ms., U.S.	D3	101
Wanipigow, stm., Can.	D4	70
Wankie National Park, Zimb.	A4	49
Wann, Ne., U.S.	g12	104
Wann, Ok., U.S.	A6	113
Wannaska, Mn., U.S.	B3	100
Wanship, Ut., U.S.	C4	121
Wantage, Eng., U.K.	C6	12
Wantagh, N.Y., U.S.	*E7	109
Wanup, Ont.	A4	73
Wanxian, China	E6	31
Wanzai, China	J6	32
Wapakoneta, Oh., U.S.	B1	112
Wapanucka, Ok., U.S.	C5	113
Wapato, Wa., U.S.	C5	124
Wapawekka Hills, hills, Sask.	C3	75
Wapawekka Lake, l., Sask.	C3	75
Wapella, Sask.	G5	75
Wapella, Il., U.S.	C5	90
Wapello, Ia., U.S.	C6	92
Wapello, co., Ia., U.S.	C5	92
Wapisu Lake, l., Man.	B2	70
Wapiti, Wy., U.S.	B3	127
Wapiti, stm., Can.	B1	68
Wapiti Ridge, mtn., Wy., U.S.	B3	127
Wappapello, Mo., U.S.	E7	102
Wappapello Lake, res., Mo., U.S.	D7	102
Wappingers Falls, N.Y., U.S.	D7	109
Wapsipinicon, stm., Ia., U.S.	B5	92
Wapske, N.B.	C2	71
Wapus Lake, l., Sask.	A4	75
Wapwallopen, Pa., U.S.	D9	115
Wāqid, Eg.	D2	41
Waqqāṣ, Jord.	B7	41
Waquoit, Ma., U.S.	C6	98
War, W.V., U.S.	D3	125
Waramaug, Lake, l., Ct., U.S.	C2	84
Warangal, India	E6	36
Warba, Mn., U.S.	C5	100
Warburg, Alta.	C3	68
Warburg, Ger.	B4	19
Warburton, Austl.	H5	51
Warburton Creek, stm., Austl.	E6	50
Ward, Al., U.S.	C1	78
Ward, Ar., U.S.	B4	81
Ward, Co., U.S.	*A5	83
Ward, S.C., U.S.	D4	117
Ward, S.D., U.S.	C9	118
Ward, co., N.D., U.S.	A4	111
Ward, co., Tx., U.S.	D1	120
Ward, Mount, mtn., Ant.	B6	7
Wardell, Mo., U.S.	E8	102
Warden, Alta.	C4	68
Warden, Que.	D5	74
Warden, La., U.S.	B4	95
Warden, Wa., U.S.	B6	124
Wardensville, W.V., U.S.	B6	125
Warder, l., Ger.	E4	15
Wardha, India	D6	36
Wardha, stm., India	D6	36
Ward Hill, hill, Scot., U.K.	B5	13
Wardlow, Alta.	D5	68
Ward Mountain, mtn., Mt., U.S.	D2	103
Wardner, B.C.	E10	69
Wardner, Id., U.S.	B2	89
Wardsboro, Vt., U.S.	E3	122
Wardsville, Ont.	E3	73
Wardville, Ok., U.S.	C5	113
Ware, Ma., U.S.	B3	98
Ware, co., Ga., U.S.	E4	87
Ware, stm., Ma., U.S.	B3	98
War Eagle, W.V., U.S.	D3	125
War Eagle Creek, stm., Ar., U.S.	A2	81
War Eagle Mountain, mtn., Id., U.S.	G2	89
Wareham, Eng., U.K.	D5	12
Wareham, Ma., U.S.	C6	98
Warehouse Point, Ct., U.S.	B5	84
Waren, Ger.	B6	18
Waren, Indon.	F9	34
Warendorf, Ger.	B2	19
Waresboro, Ga., U.S.	E4	87
Waretown, N.J., U.S.	C4	107
Warfield, B.C.	E9	69
Warfield, Ky., U.S.	C7	94
Warfield, Va., U.S.	D5	123
Warfordsburg, Pa., U.S.	G5	115
Wargla, Alg.	C6	44
Warin, Indon.	E5	11
Waring, Tx., U.S.	E3	120
Wark, Eng., U.K.	E6	13
Warkworth, Ont.	C7	73
Warkworth, N.Z.	L15	51
Warley see Smethwick, Eng., U.K.	D5	10
Warman, Sask.	E2	75
Warman, Mn., U.S.	D5	100
Warmbad, Nmb.	C2	49
Warm Beach, Wa., U.S.	A3	124
Warminster, Eng., U.K.	C5	12
Warminster, Pa., U.S.	F11	115
Warm Lake, Id., U.S.	E3	89
Warm River, Id., U.S.	E7	89
Warm Springs, Ar., U.S.	A4	81
Warm Springs, Ga., U.S.	D2	87
Warm Springs, Nv., U.S.	E5	105
Warm Springs, Or., U.S.	C5	114
Warm Springs, Va., U.S.	B3	123
Warm Springs Indian Reservation, Or., U.S.	C5	114
Warm Springs Reservoir, res., Or., U.S.	D8	114
Warnemünde (part of Rostock), Ger.	A6	18
Warner, Alta.	E4	68
Warner, N.H., U.S.	D3	106
Warner, Oh., U.S.	C3	112
Warner, Ok., U.S.	B6	113
Warner, S.D., U.S.	B6	118
Warner, stm., N.H., U.S.	D3	106
Warner Mountain, mtn., Ma., U.S.	B1	98
Warner Mountains, mts., Ca., U.S.	B3	82
Warner Peak, mtn., Or., U.S.	E7	114
Warner Robins, Ga., U.S.	D3	87
Warner Springs, Ca., U.S.	F5	82
Warnes, Bol.	C3	55
Warnow, stm., Ger.	B2	18
Warpath, stm., Man.	C2	70
Warracknabeal, Austl.	H4	51
Warr Acres, Ok., U.S.	B4	113
Warragul, Austl.	I5	51
Warrego, stm., Austl.	E8	50
Warren, Austl.	E6	51
Warren, Ont.	A4	73
Warren, Ar., U.S.	D3	81
Warren, Ct., U.S.	C2	84
Warren, Id., U.S.	D3	89
Warren, Il., U.S.	A4	90
Warren, In., U.S.	C7	91
Warren, Me., U.S.	D3	96
Warren, Ma., U.S.	B3	98
Warren, Mi., U.S.	F7	99
Warren, Mn., U.S.	B2	100
Warren, N.H., U.S.	C3	106
Warren, N.Y., U.S.	C6	109
Warren, Oh., U.S.	A5	112
Warren, Ok., U.S.	C2	113
Warren, Or., U.S.	B4	114
Warren, Pa., U.S.	C3	115
Warren, R.I., U.S.	D5	116
Warren, Vt., U.S.	C3	122
Warren, co., Ga., U.S.	C4	87
Warren, co., Il., U.S.	C3	90
Warren, co., In., U.S.	D3	91
Warren, co., Ia., U.S.	C4	92
Warren, co., Ky., U.S.	C3	94
Warren, co., Ms., U.S.	C3	101
Warren, co., Mo., U.S.	C6	102
Warren, co., N.J., U.S.	B3	107
Warren, co., N.Y., U.S.	B7	109
Warren, co., N.C., U.S.	A4	110
Warren, co., Oh., U.S.	C1	112
Warren, co., Pa., U.S.	C3	115
Warren, co., Tn., U.S.	D8	119
Warren, co., Va., U.S.	B4	123
Warren, stm., U.S.	D5	116
Warren Center, Pa., U.S.	C9	115
Warrendale, Pa., U.S.	h13	115
Warren Park, In., U.S.	k10	91
Warren Peaks, mts., Wy., U.S.	B8	127
Warrenpoint, N. Ire., U.K.	C5	11
Warren Point, R.I., U.S.	F6	116
Warrens, Wi., U.S.	D3	126
Warrensburg, Il., U.S.	D4	90
Warrensburg, Mo., U.S.	C4	102
Warrensburg, N.Y., U.S.	B7	109
Warrensville, Pa., U.S.	D8	115
Warrensville Heights, Oh., U.S.	h9	112
Warrenton, S. Afr.	C3	49
Warrenton, Ga., U.S.	C4	87
Warrenton, Mo., U.S.	C6	102
Warrenton, N.C., U.S.	A4	110
Warrenton, Or., U.S.	A3	114
Warrenton, Va., U.S.	B5	123
Warrenville, Ct., U.S.	B7	84
Warrenville, Il., U.S.	k8	90
Warrenville, S.C., U.S.	D4	117
Warri, Nig.	E6	45
Warrick, co., In., U.S.	H3	91
Warrington, Eng., U.K.	D5	10
Warrington, Fl., U.S.	u14	86
Warrior, Al., U.S.	B3	78
Warrior Mountain, mtn., Md., U.S.	k13	97
Warrior Reservoir, res., Al., U.S.	C2	78
Warriors Mark, Pa., U.S.	E5	115
Warrnambool, Austl.	G7	50
Warroad, Mn., U.S.	B3	100
Warsaw, Ont.	C6	73
Warsaw (Warszawa), Pol.	B6	26
Warsaw, Il., U.S.	C2	90
Warsaw, In., U.S.	B6	91
Warsaw, Ky., U.S.	B5	94
Warsaw, Mo., U.S.	C4	102
Warsaw, N.Y., U.S.	C2	109
Warsaw, N.C., U.S.	B4	110
Warsaw, N.D., U.S.	A8	111
Warsaw, Oh., U.S.	B3	112
Warsaw, Va., U.S.	C6	123
Warspite, Alta.	B4	68
Warstein, Ger.	B3	19
Warta, Pol.	C5	26
Warta, stm., Pol.	B3	26
Wasatch, co., Ut., U.S.	C4	121
Wasatch Plateau, plat., Ut., U.S.	D4	121
Wasatch Range, mts., U.S.	B5	76
Wascana Creek, stm., Sask.	G3	75
Wasco, Ca., U.S.	E4	82
Wasco, Or., U.S.	B6	114
Wasco, co., Or., U.S.	B5	114
Waseca, Mn., U.S.	F5	100
Waseca, co., Mn., U.S.	F5	100
Waseca, Sask.	D1	75
Washademoak Lake, l., N.B.	D4	71
Washago, Ont.	C5	73
Washakie, co., Wy., U.S.	C4	127
Washakie Needles, mts., Wy., U.S.	C3	127
Washburn, Il., U.S.	C4	90
Washburn, Me., U.S.	B5	96
Washburn, Mo., U.S.	E4	102
Washburn, N.D., U.S.	B5	111
Washburn, Wi., U.S.	B3	126
Washburn, co., Wi., U.S.	C2	126
Washburn, Mount, mtn., Wy., U.S.	B2	127
Wāshīm, India	B4	36
Washington, D.C., U.S.	C3	97
Washington, Ga., U.S.	C4	87
Washington, Il., U.S.	C4	90
Washington, In., U.S.	G3	91
Washington, Ia., U.S.	C6	92
Washington, Ks., U.S.	C6	93
Washington, Ky., U.S.	B6	94
Washington, La., U.S.	D3	95
Washington, Mo., U.S.	C6	102
Washington, Ne., U.S.	g12	104
Washington, N.H., U.S.	D2	106
Washington, N.J., U.S.	B3	107
Washington, N.C., U.S.	B5	110
Washington, Ok., U.S.	B4	113
Washington, Pa., U.S.	F1	115
Washington, Tn., U.S.	D9	119
Washington, Ut., U.S.	F2	121
Washington, Vt., U.S.	C4	122
Washington, Va., U.S.	B4	123
Washington, W.V., U.S.	B3	125
Washington, co., Al., U.S.	D1	78
Washington, co., Ar., U.S.	A1	81
Washington, co., Co., U.S.	B7	83
Washington, co., Fl., U.S.	u16	86
Washington, co., Ga., U.S.	C4	87
Washington, co., Id., U.S.	E2	89
Washington, co., Il., U.S.	E4	90
Washington, co., In., U.S.	G5	91
Washington, co., Ia., U.S.	C6	92
Washington, co., Ks., U.S.	C6	93
Washington, co., Ky., U.S.	C4	94
Washington, co., La., U.S.	D5	95
Washington, co., Me., U.S.	D5	96
Washington, co., Md., U.S.	A2	97
Washington, co., Mn., U.S.	E6	100
Washington, co., Ms., U.S.	B3	101
Washington, co., Mo., U.S.	D7	102
Washington, co., Ne., U.S.	C9	104
Washington, co., N.Y., U.S.	B7	109
Washington, co., N.C., U.S.	B6	110
Washington, co., Oh., U.S.	C4	112
Washington, co., Ok., U.S.	A6	113
Washington, co., Or., U.S.	B3	114
Washington, co., Pa., U.S.	F1	115
Washington, co., R.I., U.S.	E2	116
Washington, co., Tn., U.S.	C11	119
Washington, co., Tx., U.S.	D4	120
Washington, co., Ut., U.S.	F2	121
Washington, co., Vt., U.S.	C3	122
Washington, co., Va., U.S.	f9	123
Washington, co., Wi., U.S.	E5	126
Washington, state, U.S.	B5	124
Washington, Cape, c., Fiji	I14	52
Washington, Lake, l., Fl., U.S.	D6	86
Washington, Lake, l., Mn., U.S.	E4	100
Washington, Lake, l., Ms., U.S.	B3	101
Washington, Lake, l., Wa., U.S.	e11	124
Washington, Mount, mtn., N.H., U.S.	B4	106
Washington Court House, Oh., U.S.	C2	112
Washington Crossing, N.J., U.S.	C3	107
Washington Depot, Ct., U.S.	C2	84
Washington Island, i., Wi., U.S.	C7	126
Washington Island see Teraina Island, i., Kir.	F12	6
Washington Park, Fl., U.S.	*F6	86
Washington Park, Il., U.S.	E3	90
Washington Terrace, Ut., U.S.	B4	121
Washington Township, N.J., U.S.	*B4	107
Washingtonville, Pa., U.S.	D8	115
Washita, co., Ok., U.S.	B2	113
Washita, stm., Ok., U.S.	C4	113
Washoe, co., Nv., U.S.	C2	105
Washoe City, Nv., U.S.	D2	105
Washougal, Wa., U.S.	D3	124
Washow Bay, b., Man.	D3	70
Washtenaw, co., Mi., U.S.	F7	99
Washtucna, Wa., U.S.	C7	124
Wasilków, Pol.	B7	26
Wasilla, Ak., U.S.	C10	79
Wasioja, Mn., U.S.	F6	100
Waskada, Man.	E1	70
Waskaganish, Que.	h11	74
Waskaiowaka Lake, l., Man.	A3	70
Waskatenau, Alta.	B4	68
Waskesiu Lake, l., Sask.	D2	75
Waskish, Mn., U.S.	B4	100
Waskom, Tx., U.S.	C5	120
Waspam, Nic.	C5	62
Wasque Point, c., Ma., U.S.	D7	98
Wassau Sound, strt., Ga., U.S.	E6	87
Wassenaar, Neth.	B4	17
Wasseralfingen, Ger.	E5	19
Wasserburg [am Inn], Ger.	D6	18
Wasserkuppe, mtn., Ger.	C4	19
Wass Lake, l., Man.	C4	70
Wasson, Il., U.S.	F5	90
Wassookeag, Lake, l., Me., U.S.	C3	96
Wassuk Range, mts., Nv., U.S.	E3	105
Wassy-sur-Blaise, Fr.	F4	17
Wasta, S.D., U.S.	C3	118
Wataga, Il., U.S.	B3	90
Watampone, Indon.	F6	34
Watapi Lake, l., Sask.	B6	68
Watauga, S.D., U.S.	B4	118
Watauga, Tn., U.S.	C11	119
Watauga, Tx., U.S.	*n9	120
Watauga, co., N.C., U.S.	A1	110
Watauga, stm., Tn., U.S.	C12	119
Watauga Lake, res., Tn., U.S.	C12	119
Watchaug Pond, l., R.I., U.S.	F2	116
Watchet, Eng., U.K.	C4	12
Watch Hill, R.I., U.S.	G1	116
Watch Hill Point, c., R.I., U.S.	G1	116
Watchung, N.J., U.S.	B4	107
Waterberg, mts., S. Afr.	—	—
Waterbury, Ct., U.S.	C3	84
Waterbury, Ne., U.S.	B9	104
Waterbury, Vt., U.S.	C3	122
Waterbury Center, Vt., U.S.	C3	122
Waterbury Reservoir, res., Vt., U.S.	C3	122
Waterdown, Ont.	D5	73
Wateree Lake, res., S.C., U.S.	C6	117
Waterflow, N.M., U.S.	A1	108
Waterford, Ont.	E4	73
Waterford, Ire.	D3	10
Waterford, P.E.I.	C5	71
Waterford, Va., U.S.	A5	123
Waterford, Wi., U.S.	F5	126
Waterford, co., Ire.	E4	11
Waterford Harbour, b., Ire.	E5	11
Waterford Mills, In., U.S.	A6	91
Waterford Works, N.J., U.S.	D3	107
Watergrasshill, Ire.	I3	11
Waterhen Lake, l., Man.	C2	70
Waterloo, Bel.	D4	17
Waterloo, Ont.	D4	73
Waterloo, Que.	D5	74
Waterloo, S.L.	G2	45
Waterloo, Al., U.S.	A1	78
Waterloo, Ar., U.S.	D2	81
Waterloo, Il., U.S.	E3	90
Waterloo, In., U.S.	A7	91
Waterloo, Ia., U.S.	B5	92
Waterloo, Ks., U.S.	C6	93
Waterloo, Mt., U.S.	E4	103
Waterloo, Ne., U.S.	g12	104
Waterloo, N.Y., U.S.	C4	109
Waterloo, Or., U.S.	C4	114
Waterloo, S.C., U.S.	C3	117
Waterloo, Wi., U.S.	E5	126
Waterloo, co., Ont.	D4	73
Waterman, Il., U.S.	B5	90
Waterman Four Corners, R.I., U.S.	C3	116
Waterman Reservoir, res., R.I., U.S.	B3	116
Waterport, N.Y., U.S.	B2	109
Waterproof, La., U.S.	C4	95
Waters, Mi., U.S.	D6	99
Watersmeet, Mi., U.S.	n12	99
Waterton, stm., N.A.	E4	68
Waterton-Glacier International Peace Park, N.A.	B3	103
Waterton Lakes National Park, Alta.	E3	68
Waterton Park, Alta.	E4	68
Watertown, Ct., U.S.	C3	84
Watertown, Fl., U.S.	B4	86
Watertown, Ma., U.S.	g11	98
Watertown, N.Y., U.S.	B5	109
Watertown, Oh., U.S.	C4	112
Watertown, S.D., U.S.	C8	118
Watertown, Tn., U.S.	A5	119
Watertown, Wi., U.S.	E5	126
Water Valley, Ky., U.S.	f9	94
Water Valley, Ms., U.S.	A4	101
Water View, Tx., U.S.	D2	120
Water Village, N.H., U.S.	C4	106
Waterville, N.S.	D5	71
Waterville, Ire.	F1	11
Waterville, Ks., U.S.	C7	93
Waterville, Me., U.S.	D3	96
Waterville, Ma., U.S.	A3	98
Waterville, Mn., U.S.	F5	100
Waterville, N.Y., U.S.	C5	109
Waterville, Oh., U.S.	A2	112
Waterville, Pa., U.S.	D7	115
Waterville, Vt., U.S.	B3	122
Waterville, Wa., U.S.	B5	124
Waterville Valley, N.H., U.S.	C3	106
Watervliet, Bel.	C3	17
Watervliet, Mi., U.S.	F4	99
Watervliet, N.Y., U.S.	C7	109
Watford, Ont.	E3	73
Watford, Eng., U.K.	k12	10
Watford City, N.D., U.S.	B2	111
Watha, N.C., U.S.	C5	110
Wathena, Ks., U.S.	C9	93
Watkins, Co., U.S.	B6	83
Watkins, Ia., U.S.	B6	92
Watkins, Mn., U.S.	E4	100
Watkins Glen, N.Y., U.S.	C4	109
Watkinsville, Ga., U.S.	C3	87
Watonga, Ok., U.S.	B3	113
Watonwan, co., Mn., U.S.	G4	100
Watonwan, stm., Mn., U.S.	G4	100
Watou, Bel.	D2	17
Watova, Ok., U.S.	A6	113
Watrous, Sask.	F3	75
Watrous, N.M., U.S.	B5	108
Watsa, Zaire	A4	48
Watseka, Il., U.S.	C6	90
Watson, Sask.	E3	75
Watson, In., U.S.	H6	91
Watson, La., U.S.	D4	95
Watson, Mn., U.S.	E3	100
Watson, Mo., U.S.	A2	102
Watson Chapel, Ar., U.S.	C3	81
Watson Lake, Yukon	D7	66
Watsontown, Pa., U.S.	D8	115
Watsonville, Ca., U.S.	D3	82
Watten, Fr.	D10	12
Watten, Loch, l., Scot., U.K.	B5	13
Wattenberg, Co., U.S.	A6	83
Wattensaw Bayou, stm., Ar., U.S.	C4	81
Watton, Mi., U.S.	B2	99
Wattrelos, Fr.	B5	16
Watts (part of Los Angeles), Ca., U.S.	n12	82
Watts, Ok., U.S.	A7	113
Watts Bar Dam, Tn., U.S.	D9	119
Watts Bar Lake, res., Tn., U.S.	D9	119
Wattsburg, Pa., U.S.	B2	115
Wattsville, Al., U.S.	B3	78
Wattsville, S.C., U.S.	B4	117
Wattwil, Switz.	B5	20
Watu, Zaire	B3	48
Watubela Islands, is., Indon.	F8	34
Watuppa Pond, l., Ma., U.S.	C5	98
Waubamik, Ont.	B4	73
Waubaushene, Ont.	C5	73
Waubay, S.D., U.S.	B8	118
Waubay Lake, l., S.D., U.S.	B8	118
Wauchope, Austl.	E9	51
Wauchope, Sask.	H5	75
Wauchula, Fl., U.S.	E5	86
Wauconda, Il., U.S.	A5	90
Wauconda, Wa., U.S.	A7	124
Waugh, Man.	E4	70
Waugh Mountain, mtn., Id., U.S.	D4	89
Waukau, Wi., U.S.	E5	126
Waukee, Ia., U.S.	C4	92
Waukegan, Il., U.S.	A6	90
Waukesha, Wi., U.S.	F5	126
Waukesha, co., Wi., U.S.	E5	126
Waukewan, Lake, l., N.H., U.S.	C3	106
Waukomis, Ok., U.S.	A4	113
Waukon, Ia., U.S.	A6	92
Wauna, Wa., U.S.	f10	124
Waunakee, Wi., U.S.	E4	126
Wauneta, Ne., U.S.	D4	104
Waupaca, Wi., U.S.	D4	126
Waupaca, co., Wi., U.S.	D5	126
Waupun, Wi., U.S.	E5	126
Wauregan, Ct., U.S.	C8	84
Waurika, Ok., U.S.	C4	113
Waurika Lake, res., Ok., U.S.	C3	113
Wausa, Ne., U.S.	B8	104
Wausau, Fl., U.S.	u16	86
Wausau, Wi., U.S.	D4	126
Wausaukee, Wi., U.S.	C6	126
Wauseon, Oh., U.S.	A1	112
Waushara, co., Wi., U.S.	D4	126
Wautoma, Wi., U.S.	D4	126
Wauwatosa, Wi., U.S.	m12	126
Wauzeka, Wi., U.S.	E3	126
Waveland, In., U.S.	E3	91
Waveland, Ms., U.S.	E4	101
Waveney, stm., Eng., U.K.	D7	10
Waverley, Austl.	*F9	51
Waverley, Austl.	*G8	50
Waverly, N.S.	E6	71
Waverly, Al., U.S.	C4	78
Waverly, Ga., U.S.	E5	87
Waverly, Il., U.S.	D4	90
Waverly, In., U.S.	C5	91
Waverly, Ia., U.S.	B5	92
Waverly, Ks., U.S.	D8	93
Waverly, Ky., U.S.	C2	94
Waverly, Mi., U.S.	*F6	99
Waverly, Mn., U.S.	E5	100
Waverly, Mo., U.S.	B4	102
Waverly, Ne., U.S.	D9	104
Waverly, N.Y., U.S.	C4	109
Waverly, Oh., U.S.	C3	112
Waverly, Tn., U.S.	A4	119
Waverly, Va., U.S.	C5	123
Waverly, W.V., U.S.	B3	125
Waverly Hall, Ga., U.S.	D2	87
Wawa, Ont.	o18	73
Wawa, Nig.	E5	45
Wāw, Sud.	D2	47
Wawanesa, Man.	E2	70
Wawasee, Lake, l., In., U.S.	B6	91
Wāw al Kabīr, Libya	D3	43
Wawayanda Lake, l., N.J., U.S.	A4	107
Wawayanda Mountain, mtn., N.J., U.S.	A4	107
Wawota, Sask.	H4	75
Waxahachie, Tx., U.S.	C4	120
Waxhaw, N.C., U.S.	C2	110
Waxweiler, Ger.	D6	17
Waya, i., Fiji	H14	52
Wayagamac, Lac, l., Que.	B5	74
Wayan, Id., U.S.	G7	89
Waycross, Ga., U.S.	E4	87
Wayland, Ia., U.S.	C6	92
Wayland, Ky., U.S.	C7	94
Wayland, Ma., U.S.	g10	98
Wayland, Mi., U.S.	F5	99
Wayland, Mo., U.S.	A6	102
Wayland, N.Y., U.S.	C3	109
Wayland Springs, Tn., U.S.	B4	119
Waylyn, S.C., U.S.	k12	117
Waymart, Pa., U.S.	C11	115
Wayne, Alta.	D4	68
Wayne, Mi., U.S.	p15	99
Wayne, Ne., U.S.	B8	104
Wayne, N.J., U.S.	B4	107
Wayne, N.Y., U.S.	C3	109
Wayne, Oh., U.S.	A2	112
Wayne, Pa., U.S.	F11	115
Wayne, W.V., U.S.	C2	125
Wayne, co., Ga., U.S.	E5	87
Wayne, co., Il., U.S.	E5	90
Wayne, co., In., U.S.	E7	91
Wayne, co., Ia., U.S.	D4	92
Wayne, co., Ky., U.S.	D5	94
Wayne, co., Mi., U.S.	F7	99
Wayne, co., Ms., U.S.	D5	101
Wayne, co., Mo., U.S.	D7	102
Wayne, co., Ne., U.S.	B8	104
Wayne, co., N.Y., U.S.	B3	109
Wayne, co., N.C., U.S.	B4	110
Wayne, co., Oh., U.S.	B4	112
Wayne, co., Pa., U.S.	C11	115
Wayne, co., Tn., U.S.	B4	119
Wayne, co., Ut., U.S.	E4	121
Wayne, co., W.V., U.S.	C2	125
Wayne City, Il., U.S.	E5	90
Waynesboro, Ga., U.S.	C4	87
Waynesboro, Ms., U.S.	D5	101
Waynesboro, Pa., U.S.	G6	115
Waynesboro, Tn., U.S.	B4	119
Waynesboro, Va., U.S.	B4	123
Waynesburg, Oh., U.S.	B4	112
Waynesburg, Pa., U.S.	G1	115
Waynesville, Ga., U.S.	E5	87
Waynesville, Mo., U.S.	D5	102
Waynesville, N.C., U.S.	f10	110
Waynesville, Oh., U.S.	C1	112
Waynetown, In., U.S.	D3	91
Waynewood, Va., U.S.	g12	123
Waynoka, Ok., U.S.	A3	113
Wayside, Ks., U.S.	E8	93
Wayside, Ms., U.S.	B2	101
Wayside, Wi., U.S.	h10	126
We, i., Indon.	J1	35
Weakley, co., Tn., U.S.	A3	119
Weare, N.H., U.S.	D3	106
Weatherford, Ok., U.S.	B3	113
Weatherford, Tx., U.S.	C4	120
Weatherly, Pa., U.S.	E10	115
Weatogue, Ct., U.S.	B4	84
Weaubleau, Mo., U.S.	D4	102
Weaver, Al., U.S.	B4	78
Weaver Lake, l., Man.	C3	70
Weaver Mountains, mts., Az., U.S.	C3	80
Weaverville, Ca., U.S.	B2	82
Weaverville, N.C., U.S.	f10	110
Webb, Sask.	G1	75
Webb, Al., U.S.	D4	78
Webb, Ms., U.S.	B3	101
Webb, co., Tx., U.S.	F3	120
Webb Air Force Base, mil., Tx., U.S.	C2	120
Webb City, Ar., U.S.	B2	81
Webb City, Mo., U.S.	D3	102
Webb City, Ok., U.S.	A5	113
Webber, Ks., U.S.	C5	93
Webber Lake, l., Man.	B5	70
Webbers Falls, Ok., U.S.	B6	113
Webberville, Mi., U.S.	F6	99
Webb Hill, hill, Ma., U.S.	B3	98
Webb Lake, l., Me., U.S.	D2	96
Webbville, Ky., U.S.	B7	94
Webbwood, Ont.	A3	73
Weber, co., Ut., U.S.	B4	121
Weber, Mount, mtn., B.C.	B3	69
Weber City, Va., U.S.	f9	123
Webster, Alta.	B1	68
Webster, Fl., U.S.	D4	86
Webster, In., U.S.	E8	91
Webster, Ia., U.S.	C5	92
Webster, Ma., U.S.	B4	98
Webster, Mn., U.S.	F5	100
Webster, N.H., U.S.	D3	106
Webster, N.Y., U.S.	B3	109
Webster, N.D., U.S.	A7	111
Webster, Pa., U.S.	F2	115
Webster, S.D., U.S.	B8	118
Webster, Tx., U.S.	r14	120
Webster, Wi., U.S.	C1	126
Webster, co., Ga., U.S.	D2	87
Webster, co., Ia., U.S.	B3	92
Webster, co., Ky., U.S.	C2	94
Webster, co., La., U.S.	B2	95
Webster, co., Ms., U.S.	B4	101
Webster, co., Mo., U.S.	D5	102
Webster, co., Ne., U.S.	D7	104
Webster, co., W.V., U.S.	C4	125
Webster City, Ia., U.S.	B4	92
Webster Groves, Mo., U.S.	f13	102
Webster Mills, Pa., U.S.	G5	115
Webster Reservoir, res., Ks., U.S.	C4	93
Webster Springs, W.V., U.S.	C4	125
Websterville, Vt., U.S.	C4	122
Wecota, S.D., U.S.	B6	118
Weda, Indon.	E7	34
Weddell Sea, Ant.	C9	7
Wedderburn, Or., U.S.	E2	114
Wedgefield, S.C., U.S.	D6	117
Wedgeport, N.S.	F4	71
Wedgewood, Mo., U.S.	f13	102
Wedowee, Al., U.S.	B4	78
Wedron, Il., U.S.	B5	90
Weed, Ca., U.S.	B2	82
Weed, N.M., U.S.	E4	108
Weed Heights, Nv., U.S.	E2	105
Weedon, Que.	D6	74
Weed Patch Hill, hill, In., U.S.	F5	91
Weedsport, N.Y., U.S.	B4	109
Weedville, Pa., U.S.	D5	115
Weehawken, N.J., U.S.	h8	107
Weekapaug, R.I., U.S.	G1	116
Weekes, Sask.	E4	75
Weeksbury, Ky., U.S.	C7	94
Weekstown, N.J., U.S.	D3	107
Weeksville, N.C., U.S.	A6	110
Weems, Va., U.S.	C6	123
Weener, Ger.	A7	17
Weeping Water, Ne., U.S.	D9	104
Weeping Water Creek, stm., Ne., U.S.	h12	104
Weert, Neth.	B6	16
Weesen, Switz.	B7	21
Weesp, Neth.	B5	17
Weferlingen, Ger.	A6	19
Wegdahl, Mn., U.S.	F3	100
Weggis, Switz.	B5	21
Wegorzewo, Pol.	A6	26
Węgrów, Pol.	B7	26
Wehr, Ger.	A4	21
Weichang, China	C8	31
Weida, Ger.	C7	19
Weiden, Ger.	D6	18
Weifang, China	D10	31
Weigelstown, Pa., U.S.	*G8	115
Weihai, China	D9	31
Wei He, stm., China	E6	31
Weilburg, Ger.	C3	19
Weiler, Ger.	A8	21
Weilheim, Ger.	E5	18
Weimar, Ger.	C5	18
Weimar, Tx., U.S.	E4	120
Weinan, China	E6	31
Weinböhla, Ger.	B5	19
Weiner, Ar., U.S.	B5	81
Weinert, Tx., U.S.	C3	120
Weinfelden, Switz.	A7	21
Weingarten, Ger.	A8	21
Weinheim, Ger.	D4	18
Weining, China	F5	31
Weinsberg, Ger.	D5	19
Weipa, Austl.	B7	50
Weippe, Id., U.S.	C3	89
Weir, Que.	D3	74
Weir, Ks., U.S.	E9	93
Weir, Ky., U.S.	C2	94
Weir, Ms., U.S.	B4	101
Weir, stm., Man.	A5	70
Weir, Lake, l., Fl., U.S.	C5	86
Weirdale, Sask.	D3	75
Weir River, Man.	A5	70
Weirsdale, Fl., U.S.	D5	86
Weirton, W.V., U.S.	A4	125
Weirwood, Va., U.S.	C7	123
Weiser, Id., U.S.	E2	89
Weiser, stm., Id., U.S.	E2	89
Weishan Lake, l., China	G7	31
Weishi, China	G6	32
Weisner Mountain, hill, Al., U.S.	A4	78
Weisse Elster, stm., Ger.	B7	19
Weissenberg, Ger.	D5	18
Weissenburg, Switz.	C3	21
Weissenfels, Ger.	B6	19
Weissenhorn, Ger.	A6	21
Weissert, Ne., U.S.	C6	104
Weisshorn, mtn., Switz.	C3	21
Weiss Lake, l., Al., U.S.	A4	78
Weisswasser, Ger.	B9	19
Weitra, Aus.	E9	21
Weixi, China	F4	31
Weizhou Dao, i., China	B8	35
Wejherowo, Pol.	A5	26
Wekiva Springs, Fl., U.S.	*D5	86
Wekusko Lake, l., Man.	B2	70
Welaka, Fl., U.S.	C5	86
Welch, Tx., U.S.	C1	120
Welch, W.V., U.S.	D3	125
Welches, Or., U.S.	B5	114
Welcome, La., U.S.	h10	95
Welcome, Mn., U.S.	G4	100
Welcome, S.C., U.S.	B3	117

Name	Map Ref.	Page
Weld, Me., U.S.	D2	96
Weld, co., Co., U.S.	A6	83
Welda, Ks., U.S.	D8	93
Weldon, Ger.	E5	19
Weldon, Sask.	D3	75
Weldon, Ar., U.S.	B4	81
Weldon, Ca., U.S.	C5	90
Weldon, Ia., U.S.	D4	92
Weldon, N.C., U.S.	A5	110
Weldon, Tx., U.S.	D5	120
Weldona, Co., U.S.	A7	83
Weldon Spring, Mo., U.S.	f12	102
Weleetka, Ok., U.S.	B5	113
Welega, prov., Eth.	D4	47
Welkom, S. Afr.	C4	49
Welland, Ont.	E5	73
Welland, stm., Eng., U.K.	D6	10
Wellandport, Ont.	D5	73
Wellborn, Fl., U.S.	B4	86
Wellborn, Tx., U.S.	D4	120
Wellersburg, Pa., U.S.	G4	115
Welles Harbor, b., Mid. Is.	K3	52
Wellesley, Ont.	D4	73
Wellesley, Ma., U.S.	B5	98
Wellesley Islands, is., Austl.	C6	50
Wellfleet, Ma., U.S.	C7	98
Wellfleet, Ne., U.S.	D5	104
Wellford, S.C., U.S.	B3	117
Wellin, Bel.	D5	17
Welling, Ok., U.S.	B7	113
Wellingborough, Eng., U.K.	B7	12
Wellington, Austl.	F7	51
Wellington, B.C.	f11	69
Wellington, Ont.	D7	73
Wellington, N.Z.	N15	51
Wellington, S. Afr.	D2	49
Wellington, Eng., U.K.	B5	12
Wellington, Al., U.S.	B4	78
Wellington, Co., U.S.	A5	83
Wellington, Il., U.S.	C6	90
Wellington, Ks., U.S.	E6	93
Wellington, Me., U.S.	C3	96
Wellington, Mo., U.S.	B4	102
Wellington, Newf.	E2	105
Wellington, Oh., U.S.	A3	112
Wellington, Tx., U.S.	B2	120
Wellington, Ut., U.S.	D5	121
Wellington, co., Ont.	D4	73
Wellington, Isla, i., Chile	D2	54
Wellington Channel, strt., N.W. Ter.	m33	66
Wellington Station, N.S.	E6	71
Wellington Station, P.E.I.	C5	71
Wellman, Ia., U.S.	C6	92
Wellman, Tx., U.S.	C1	120
Wellpinit, Wa., U.S.	B8	124
Wells, B.C.	C7	69
Wells, Eng., U.K.	C5	12
Wells, Ks., U.S.	C6	93
Wells, Me., U.S.	E2	96
Wells, Mi., U.S.	C3	99
Wells, Mn., U.S.	G5	100
Wells, Nv., U.S.	B7	105
Wells, N.Y., U.S.	B6	109
Wells, Tx., U.S.	D5	120
Wells, Vt., U.S.	E2	122
Wells, co., In., U.S.	C7	91
Wells, co., N.D., U.S.	B6	111
Wells, stm., Vt., U.S.	C4	122
Wells, Lake, l., Austl.	E3	50
Wells Beach, Me., U.S.	E2	96
Wellsboro, Pa., U.S.	B4	91
Wellsboro, Pa., U.S.	C7	115
Wellsburg, Ia., U.S.	B5	92
Wellsburg, N.Y., U.S.	C4	109
Wellsburg, W.V., U.S.	A4	125
Wellsford, Ks., U.S.	E4	93
Wells Gray Provincial Park, B.C.	C8	69
Wells Lake, l., Man.	A1	70
Wells-next-the-Sea, Eng., U.K.	D7	10
Wells River, Vt., U.S.	C4	122
Wells Tannery, Pa., U.S.	F5	115
Wellston, Mi., U.S.	D5	99
Wellston, Oh., U.S.	C3	112
Wellston, Ok., U.S.	B4	113
Wellsville, Ks., U.S.	D8	93
Wellsville, Mo., U.S.	B6	102
Wellsville, N.Y., U.S.	C3	109
Wellsville, Oh., U.S.	B5	112
Wellsville, Pa., U.S.	F8	115
Wellsville, Ut., U.S.	B4	121
Wells see Wells-next-the-Sea, Eng., U.K.	D7	10
Wellton, Az., U.S.	E1	80
Wellwood, Man.	D2	70
Welmlingen, Ger.	A4	21
Welo, prov., Eth.	C5	47
Wels, Aus.	D7	18
Welsford, N.B.	D3	71
Welsh, La., U.S.	D3	95
Welshpool, Wales, U.K.	D5	10
Welton, Ia., U.S.	C7	92
Welty, Ok., U.S.	B5	113
Welwitschia, Nmb.	B1	49
Welwyn, Sask.	G5	75
Welwyn Garden City, Eng., U.K.	k12	10
Welzow, Ger.	B9	19
Wem, Eng., U.K.	B5	12
Wema, Zaire	B5	48
Wembere, stm., Tan.	B5	48
Wembley, Alta.	B1	68
Wemding, Ger.	E5	19
Wemme, Or., U.S.	B5	114
Wenasoga, Ms., U.S.	A5	101
Wenatchee, Wa., U.S.	B5	124
Wenatchee, stm., Wa., U.S.	B5	124
Wenatchee Lake, l., Wa., U.S.	B5	124
Wenatchee Mountains, mts., Wa., U.S.	B5	124
Wenchang, China	C9	35
Wenchi, Ghana	E4	45
Wenchou see Wenzhou, China	F9	31
Wendel, Ca., U.S.	B3	82
Wendel, W.V., U.S.	k10	125
Wendell, Id., U.S.	G4	89
Wendell, Ma., U.S.	A3	98
Wendell, Mn., U.S.	D2	100
Wendell, N.H., U.S.	D2	106
Wendell, N.C., U.S.	B4	110
Wenden, Az., U.S.	D2	80
Wendeng, China	F10	32
Wendo, Eth.	D4	47
Wenji Gefersa, Eth.	*D4	47
Wenlock, stm., Austl.	B7	50
Wenona, Il., U.S.	B4	90
Wenona, Md., U.S.	D6	97
Wenonah, N.J., U.S.	D2	107
Wenshan, China	G5	31
Wentworth, Austl.	F7	50
Wentworth, N.S.	D6	71
Wentworth, N.H., U.S.	C3	106
Wentworth, N.C., U.S.	A3	110
Wentworth, S.D., U.S.	C8	118
Wentworth, Wi., U.S.	B2	126
Wentworth, co., Ont.	D4	73
Wentworth, Lake, l., N.H., U.S.	C4	106
Wentzville, Mo., U.S.	C7	102
Weohyakapka, Lake, l., Fl., U.S.	E5	86
Weott, Ca., U.S.	B2	82
Wepener, S. Afr.	C4	49
Wequetequock, Ct., U.S.	D8	84
Werdau, Ger.	C6	18
Werder, Ger.	A7	19
Werdohl, Ger.	B2	19
Werfen, Aus.	E6	18
Werl, Ger.	B2	19
Wernberg, Ger.	D6	18
Werne, Ger.	B2	19
Werneuchen, Ger.	B6	18
Wernigerode, Ger.	C5	18
Werra, stm., Eur.	C4	18
Wertach, stm., Ger.	D5	18
Wertheim, Ger.	D4	19
Wertingen, Ger.	E5	19
Wervik, Bel.	D3	17
Wesco, Mo., U.S.	D6	102
Wesel, Ger.	C3	18
Weser, stm., Ger.	B4	18
Weskan, Ks., U.S.	D2	93
Weslaco, Tx., U.S.	F4	120
Weslemkoon Lake, l., Ont.	C7	73
Wesley, Ar., U.S.	A2	81
Wesley, Ga., U.S.	A4	87
Wesley, Ia., U.S.	A3	92
Wesley, Me., U.S.	D5	96
Wesleyville, Newf.	D5	72
Wesleyville, Pa., U.S.	B2	115
Wessel Islands, is., Austl.	B6	50
Wesserunsett Lake, l., Me., U.S.	D3	96
Wessington, S.D., U.S.	C7	118
Wessington Springs, S.D., U.S.	C7	118
Wesson, Ar., U.S.	D3	81
Wesson, Ms., U.S.	D3	101
West, Ms., U.S.	B4	101
West, Tx., U.S.	D4	120
West, stm., P.E.I.	C6	71
West, stm., Ct., U.S.	D5	84
West, stm., Ma., U.S.	h9	98
West, stm., Vt., U.S.	E3	122
West Abington, Ma., U.S.	h12	98
West Acton, Ma., U.S.	g10	98
West Alexander, Pa., U.S.	F1	115
West Alexandria, Oh., U.S.	C1	112
West Allis, Wi., U.S.	m11	126
Westalton, Mo., U.S.	f13	102
West Alton, N.H., U.S.	C4	106
West Amityville, N.Y., U.S.	n15	109
West Andover, Ma., U.S.	A5	98
West Arichat, N.S.	D8	71
West Athens, Ca., U.S.	*n12	82
West Athens, Me., U.S.	D3	96
West Augusta, Va., U.S.	B3	123
West Babylon, N.Y., U.S.	*E7	109
West Baden Springs, In., U.S.	G4	91
West Baldwin, Me., U.S.	E2	96
Westbank, B.C.	E8	69
West Bank, ter., Isr. Occ.	B7	41
West Barnet, Vt., U.S.	C4	122
West Barnstable, Ma., U.S.	C7	98
West Barrington, R.I., U.S.	C5	116
West Baton Rouge, co., La., U.S.	D4	95
West Bay, Newf.	A3	72
West Bay, N.S.	D8	71
West Bay, Fl., U.S.	u16	86
West Bay, b., Fl., U.S.	u16	86
West Bay, b., N.C., U.S.	B6	110
West Bay, b., Tx., U.S.	r15	120
West Bay Shore, N.Y., U.S.	*n15	109
West Bend, Sask.	F4	75
West Bend, Ia., U.S.	B3	92
West Bend, Wi., U.S.	E5	126
West Bengal, state, India	F11	37
West Berkshire, Vt., U.S.	B3	122
West Berlin, N.J., U.S.	D3	107
West Berlin see Berlin (West), Ger.	B6	18
West Bethel, Me., U.S.	D2	96
West Billerica, Ma., U.S.	f10	98
West Blocton, Al., U.S.	B2	78
West Bloomfield, N.Y., U.S.	C3	109
West Bloomfield Township, Mi., U.S.	*F7	99
Westboro, Mo., U.S.	A2	102
Westboro, Wi., U.S.	C3	126
Westborough, Ma., U.S.	B4	98
West Bountiful, Ut., U.S.	C4	121
Westbourne, Man.	D2	70
West Bowdoin, Me., U.S.	f7	96
West Boylston, Ma., U.S.	B4	98
West Bradenton, Fl., U.S.	*E4	86
West Branch, Ia., U.S.	C6	92
West Branch, Mi., U.S.	D6	99
West Branch Reservoir, res., Ct., U.S.	B3	84
West Brentwood, N.H., U.S.	E5	106
West Bridgewater, Ma., U.S.	B5	98
West Bridgewater, Vt., U.S.	E3	122
West Bromwich, Eng., U.K.	D6	10
Westbrook, Ct., U.S.	D6	84
Westbrook, Me., U.S.	E2	96
Westbrook, Mn., U.S.	F3	100
Westbrook, Tx., U.S.	C2	120
West Brookfield, Ma., U.S.	B3	98
West Brooklyn, Il., U.S.	B4	90
Westbrookville, N.Y., U.S.	D6	109
West Burke, Vt., U.S.	B5	122
West Burlington, Ia., U.S.	D6	92
Westbury, N.Y., U.S.	*n15	109
West Buxton, Me., U.S.	E2	96
Westby, Wi., U.S.	E3	126
West Cache Creek, stm., Ok., U.S.	C3	113
West Caldwell, N.J., U.S.	B4	107
West Campton, N.H., U.S.	C3	106
West Canaan, N.H., U.S.	C2	106
West Canada Creek, stm., N.Y., U.S.	B6	109
West Cape Howe, c., Austl.	G2	50
West Cape May, N.J., U.S.	F3	107
West Carroll, co., La., U.S.	B4	95
West Carrollton, Oh., U.S.	C1	112
West Carry Pond, l., Me., U.S.	C2	96
West Carson, Ca., U.S.	*n12	82
West Carthage, N.Y., U.S.	B5	109
West Castleton, Vt., U.S.	D2	122
West Charleston, Vt., U.S.	B4	122
West Chatham, Ma., U.S.	C8	98
West Chazy, N.Y., U.S.	f11	109
Westchester, Fl., U.S.	*s13	86
Westchester, Il., U.S.	k9	90
West Chester, Ia., U.S.	C6	92
West Chester, Oh., U.S.	n13	112
West Chester, Pa., U.S.	G10	115
Westchester, co., N.Y., U.S.	D7	109
Westchester Station, N.S.	D6	71
West Chesterfield, N.H., U.S.	E1	106
West Chicago, Il., U.S.	k8	90
West Chop, c., Ma., U.S.	D6	98
West City, Il., U.S.	F5	90
Westcliffe, Co., U.S.	C5	83
West Coffeyville, Ks., U.S.	E8	93
West College Corner, In., U.S.	E8	91
West Columbia, S.C., U.S.	D5	117
West Columbia, Tx., U.S.	E5	120
West Compton, Ca., U.S.	*F4	82
West Concord, Ma., U.S.	*B5	98
West Concord, Mn., U.S.	F6	100
West Concord, N.C., U.S.	B2	110
Westconnaug Reservoir, res., R.I., U.S.	C2	116
West Cornwall, Ct., U.S.	B2	84
West Cote Blanche Bay, b., La., U.S.	E4	95
West Covina, Ca., U.S.	m13	82
West Creek, N.J., U.S.	D4	107
West Crossett, Ar., U.S.	D4	81
West Cumberland, Me., U.S.	E2	96
West Cummington, Ma., U.S.	B2	98
West Danby, N.Y., U.S.	C4	109
West Danville, Vt., U.S.	C4	122
West Decatur, Pa., U.S.	E5	115
West Demerara-Essequibo Coast, dept., Guy.	A3	59
West Dennis, Ma., U.S.	C7	98
West Des Moines, Ia., U.S.	C4	92
West Dover, Vt., U.S.	F3	122
West Dudley, Ma., U.S.	B4	98
West Dummerston, Vt., U.S.	F3	122
West Elk Mountains, mts., Co., U.S.	C3	83
West Elk Peak, mtn., Co., U.S.	C3	83
West Elkton, Oh., U.S.	C1	112
West Elmira, N.Y., U.S.	*C4	109
West Elwood, N.J., U.S.	D6	91
West Eminence, Mo., U.S.	D6	102
West Emma Creek, stm., Ks., U.S.	D6	93
West End, Bah.	A4	64
Westend, Ca., U.S.	E5	82
West End, N.C., U.S.	B3	110
West Enfield, Me., U.S.	C4	96
West Enosburg, Vt., U.S.	B3	122
West Epping, N.H., U.S.	D4	106
Westerkappeln, Ger.	A2	19
Westerland, Ger.	A4	18
Westerly, R.I., U.S.	F1	116
Western, Ne., U.S.	D8	104
Western, prov., Ghana	E4	45
Western, prov., Kenya	A5	48
Western, prov., Zam.	E3	48
Western Australia, state, Austl.	D3	50
Western Channel, strt., Asia	I4	33
Western Desert, des., Eg.	C2	38
Western Dvina (Daugava), stm., Sov. Un.	D7	27
Western Ghats, mts., India	E5	36
Western Grove, Ar., U.S.	A3	81
Western Head, c., Newf.	D2	72
Western Head, c., N.S.	F5	71
Western Hills, Co., U.S.	*B6	83
Western Island, i., Newf.	C4	72
Western Isles, prov., Scot., U.K.	B2	13
Westernport, Md., U.S.	m12	97
Westernport Reservoir, res., Md., U.S.	k12	97
Western Sahara, dep., Afr.	D2	44
Western Samoa, ctry., Oc.	G11	6
Western Shore, N.S.	E5	71
Western Springs, Il., U.S.	k9	90
Westerschelde, est., Neth.	B5	16
Westerstede, Ger.	A7	17
Westerville, Il., U.S.	D5	90
Westerville, Ne., U.S.	C6	104
Westerville, Oh., U.S.	B3	112
Westerwald, mts., Ger.	C4	18
West Fairlee, Vt., U.S.	D4	122
West Fairview, Pa., U.S.	*F8	115
Westfall, Ks., U.S.	D5	93
West Falmouth, Ma., U.S.	C6	98
West Fargo, N.D., U.S.	C9	111
West Farmington, Me., U.S.	D2	96
West Farmington, Oh., U.S.	A5	112
West Feliciana, co., La., U.S.	D4	95
Westfield, N.B.	D3	71
Westfield, Il., U.S.	D6	90
Westfield, In., U.S.	D5	91
Westfield, Ia., U.S.	B1	92
Westfield, Me., U.S.	B5	96
Westfield, Ma., U.S.	B2	98
Westfield, N.J., U.S.	B4	107
Westfield, N.Y., U.S.	C1	109
Westfield, N.D., U.S.	A2	110
Westfield, Pa., U.S.	C6	115
Westfield, Vt., U.S.	B4	122
Westfield, Wi., U.S.	E4	126
Westfield, stm., Ma., U.S.	B2	98
Westfield Center, Oh., U.S.	A4	112
Westfir, Or., U.S.	D4	114
West Flanders, prov., Bel.	C3	17
West Frankfort, Il., U.S.	F5	90
West Freehold, N.J., U.S.	*C4	107
West Friendship, Md., U.S.	B4	97
West Frisian Islands, is., Neth.	A6	16
Westgate, Fl., U.S.	F6	86
Westgate, Ia., U.S.	B6	92
West Gate, Va., U.S.	*B5	123
West Gate of Lomond, Va.		
West Glacier, Mt., U.S.	B3	103
West Glamorgan, co., Wales, U.K.	C4	12
West Glens Falls, N.Y., U.S.	*B7	109
West Glocester, R.I., U.S.	B1	116
West Glover, Vt., U.S.	B4	122
West Gorham, Me., U.S.	g7	96
West Goshen, Ct., U.S.	B2	84
West Gouldsboro, Me., U.S.	D4	96
West Granby, Ct., U.S.	B4	84
West Grand Lake, l., Me., U.S.	C5	96
West Granville, Ma., U.S.	B2	98
West Green, Ga., U.S.	E4	87
West Greene, Al., U.S.	C1	78
West Greenville, R.I., U.S.	B3	116
West Groton, Ma., U.S.	A4	98
West Grove, Ia., U.S.	D5	92
West Grove, Pa., U.S.	G10	115
West Halifax, Vt., U.S.	F3	122
West Hamlin, W.V., U.S.	C2	125
West Hampstead, N.H., U.S.	E4	106
Westhampton, Ma., U.S.	B2	98
West Hanover, Ma., U.S.	h12	98
West Harrison, In., U.S.	F8	91
West Hartford, Ct., U.S.	B4	84
West Hartford, Vt., U.S.	D4	122
West Hartland, Ct., U.S.	A4	84
West Hatfield, Ma., U.S.	B2	98
West Haven, Ct., U.S.	D4	84
West Haven, Or., U.S.	*B4	114
West Haverstraw, N.Y., U.S.	*D7	109
West Hazleton, Pa., U.S.	E9	115
West Helena, Ar., U.S.	C5	81
West Hempstead, N.Y., U.S.	*k13	109
West Hickory, Pa., U.S.	C3	115
West Hill Reservoir, res., Ma., U.S.	B4	98
Westhoff, Tx., U.S.	E4	120
West Hollywood, Ca., U.S.	*m12	82
Westhope, N.D., U.S.	A4	111
West Hopkinton, N.H., U.S.	D3	106
West Huntington, N.Y., U.S.	*n15	109
West Hyannisport, Ma., U.S.	C7	98
West Ice Shelf, ice, Ant.	C21	7
West Indies, is.	A3	53
West Island, i., Ma., U.S.	C6	98
West Islip, N.Y., U.S.	*E7	109
West Jefferson, N.C., U.S.	A1	110
West Jefferson, Oh., U.S.	C2	112
West Jersey, Il., U.S.	B4	90
West Jordan, Ut., U.S.	C4	121
Westkapelle (part of Knokke-Heist), Bel.	C3	17
Westkapelle, Neth.	C3	17
West Kennebunk, Me., U.S.	E2	96
West Kingston, R.I., U.S.	F3	116
West Lafayette, In., U.S.	D4	91
West Lafayette, Oh., U.S.	B4	112
Westlake, La., U.S.	D2	95
Westlake, Oh., U.S.	h9	112
Westlake, Or., U.S.	D2	114
Westlake Village, Ca., U.S.	*E4	82
Westland, Mi., U.S.	F7	99
West Laramie, Wy., U.S.	E7	127
West Lawn, Pa., U.S.	F10	115
West Lebanon, In., U.S.	D3	91
West Lebanon, Me., U.S.	E2	96
West Leisenring, Pa., U.S.	G2	115
West Leyden, N.Y., U.S.	B5	109
West Liberty, Il., U.S.	E5	90
West Liberty, Ia., U.S.	C6	92
West Liberty, Ky., U.S.	C6	94
West Liberty, Oh., U.S.	B2	112
West Liberty, W.V., U.S.	f8	125
West Lima, Wi., U.S.	E3	126
West Lincoln, Vt., U.S.	C2	122
Westline, Pa., U.S.	C4	115
West Linn, Or., U.S.	B4	114
West Loch Roag, b., Scot., U.K.	B2	13
West Loch Tarbert, b., Scot., U.K.	C1	13
West Loch Tarbert, b., Scot., U.K.	E3	13
Westlock, Alta.	B4	68
West Long Branch, N.J., U.S.	C4	107
West Lorne, Ont.	E3	73
West Louisville, Ky., U.S.	C2	94
West Manchester, Oh., U.S.	C1	112
West Mansfield, Ma., U.S.	B5	98
West Mansfield, Oh., U.S.	B2	112
West Marion, N.C., U.S.	f10	110
Westmeath, Ont.	B7	73
Westmeath, co., Ire.	D4	11
West Medway, Ma., U.S.	B5	98
West Melbourne, Fl., U.S.	*D6	86
West Memphis, Ar., U.S.	B5	81
Westmere, N.Y., U.S.	*C7	109
West Miami, Fl., U.S.	s13	86
West Middlesex, Pa., U.S.	D1	115
West Middleton, In., U.S.	D5	91
West Midlands, co., Eng., U.K.	*B6	12
West Mifflin, Pa., U.S.	F2	115
West Milan, N.H., U.S.	A4	106
West Milford, N.J., U.S.	A4	107
West Milton, Oh., U.S.	C1	112
West Milton, Pa., U.S.	D8	115
West Milwaukee, Wi., U.S.	m12	126
West Mineral, Ks., U.S.	E9	93
Westminster (part of London), Eng., U.K.	k12	10
Westminster, Ca., U.S.	n12	82
Westminster, Co., U.S.	B5	83
Westminster, Md., U.S.	A4	97
Westminster, Ma., U.S.	A4	98
Westminster, S.C., U.S.	B1	117
Westminster, Vt., U.S.	E4	122
West Modesto, Ca., U.S.	*D3	82
West Monroe, La., U.S.	B3	95
Westmont, Ca., U.S.	n12	82
Westmont, Il., U.S.	k9	90
Westmont, N.J., U.S.	D2	107
Westmont, Pa., U.S.	F4	115
Westmoreland, Ks., U.S.	C7	93
Westmoreland, N.H., U.S.	E2	106
Westmoreland, Tn., U.S.	A5	119
Westmoreland, co., Pa., U.S.	F2	115
Westmoreland, co., Va., U.S.	B6	123
Westmorland, Ca., U.S.	F6	82
Westmorland, co., N.B.	C5	71
West Mountain, mtn., Ar., U.S.	f7	81
West Mountain, mtn., N.Y., U.S.	B6	109
West Muncie, In., U.S.	D7	91
West Musquash Lake, l., Me., U.S.	C5	96
West Mystic, Ct., U.S.	D8	84
West Newbury, Ma., U.S.	A6	98
West Newbury, Vt., U.S.	C4	122
West Newfield, Me., U.S.	E2	96
West Newton, Pa., U.S.	F2	115
West New York, N.J., U.S.	h8	107
West Nicholson, Zimb.	F5	49
West Nishnabotna, stm., Ia., U.S.	C2	92
West Norriton, Pa., U.S.	o20	115
West Nottingham, N.H., U.S.	D4	106
West Nyack, N.Y., U.S.	*D7	109
West Olive, Mi., U.S.	F7	99
Weston (part of York), Ont.	m14	73
Weston, Co., U.S.	D6	83
Weston, Id., U.S.	G7	89
Weston, Me., U.S.	C5	96
Weston, Ma., U.S.	g10	98
Weston, Mo., U.S.	B3	102
Weston, Ne., U.S.	C9	104
Weston, Oh., U.S.	A2	112
Weston, Or., U.S.	B8	114
Weston, Vt., U.S.	E3	122
Weston, W.V., U.S.	B4	125
Weston, Wi., U.S.	D4	126
Weston, Wy., U.S.	B7	127
Weston, co., Wy., U.S.	C8	127
Weston-super-Mare, Eng., U.K.	E5	10
West Orange, N.J., U.S.	B4	107
West Ossipee, N.H., U.S.	C4	106
Westover, Al., U.S.	B3	78
Westover, Md., U.S.	D6	97
Westover, Pa., U.S.	E4	115
Westover, Tn., U.S.	B3	119
Westover, W.V., U.S.	B5	125
Westover Air Force Base, mil., Ma., U.S.	B2	98
West Palm Beach, Fl., U.S.	F6	86
West Paris, Me., U.S.	D2	96
West Park, N.Y., U.S.	D7	109
West Pasco, Wa., U.S.	*C6	124
West Paterson, N.J., U.S.	*B4	107
West Pawlet, Vt., U.S.	E2	122
West Pearl, stm., La., U.S.	D6	95
West Pelham, Ma., U.S.	*B2	98
West Pelzer, S.C., U.S.	B3	117
West Pembroke, Me., U.S.	D5	96
West Pensacola, Fl., U.S.	u14	86
West Peoria, Il., U.S.	C4	90
West Peru, Me., U.S.	D2	96
West Peterborough, N.H., U.S.	E3	106
Westphalia, In., U.S.	G3	91
Westphalia, Ks., U.S.	D8	93
Westphalia, Mi., U.S.	F6	99
Westphalia, Mo., U.S.	C5	102
Westphalia, hist. reg., Ger.	C3	17
West Pittsburg, Ca., U.S.	*g9	82
West Pittsburg, Pa., U.S.	E1	115
West Pittston, Pa., U.S.	m17	115
West Plains, Mo., U.S.	E6	102
West Plymouth, N.H., U.S.	C3	106
West Point, Al., U.S.	A3	78
West Point, Ca., U.S.	C3	82
West Point, Ga., U.S.	D1	87
West Point, Il., U.S.	C2	90
West Point, In., U.S.	D3	91
West Point, Ia., U.S.	C4	92
West Point, Ky., U.S.	C4	94
West Point, Ms., U.S.	B5	101
West Point, Ne., U.S.	C9	104
West Point, N.Y., U.S.	D7	109
West Point, Ut., U.S.	*B3	121
West Point, Va., U.S.	C6	123
West Point, mtn., Ak., U.S.	C11	79
West Point Lake, res., U.S.	C1	87
Westport, Newf.	D3	72
Westport, N.S.	E3	71
Westport, Ont.	C8	73
Westport, Ire.	C2	11
Westport, N.Z.	N13	51
Westport, Ct., U.S.	E2	84
Westport, In., U.S.	F6	91
Westport, Ky., U.S.	B4	94
Westport, Ma., U.S.	C5	98
Westport, Mn., U.S.	E3	100
Westport, N.H., U.S.	E2	106
Westport, N.Y., U.S.	A7	109
Westport, S.D., U.S.	B7	118
Westport, Tn., U.S.	B3	119
Westport, Wa., U.S.	C1	124
Westport Point, Ma., U.S.	C5	98
West Portsmouth, Oh., U.S.	D2	112
West Prairie, stm., Alta.	B2	68
West Puente Valley, Ca., U.S.	*m13	82
West Quoddy Head, c., Me., U.S.	D6	96
Westray, i., Scot., U.K.	A5	13
Westray Firth, strt., Scot., U.K.	A5	13
West Reading, Pa., U.S.	F10	115
West Redding, Ct., U.S.	D2	84
Westrhauderfehn, Ger.	A7	17
West Ridge, Ar., U.S.	B5	81
West Rindge, N.H., U.S.	E2	106
West River, Md., U.S.	C4	97
West Road, stm., B.C.	C5	69
West Rumney, N.H., U.S.	C3	106
West Rupert, Vt., U.S.	E2	122
West Rutland, Vt., U.S.	D2	122
West Rye, N.H., U.S.	D5	106
West Sacramento, Ca., U.S.	*C3	82
West Saint Modeste, Newf.	C3	72
West Saint Paul, Mn., U.S.	n12	100
West Salem, Il., U.S.	E5	90
West Salem, Oh., U.S.	B3	112
West Salem, Wi., U.S.	E2	126
West Salt Creek, stm., Co., U.S.	B2	83
West Sayville, N.Y., U.S.	*n15	109
West Scarborough, Me., U.S.	E2	96
West Seneca, N.Y., U.S.	C2	109
West Siberian Lowland, pl., Sov. Un.	C10	29
Westside, Ia., U.S.	B2	92
West Simsbury, Ct., U.S.	B4	84
West Slope, Or., U.S.	g12	114
West Spanish Peak, mtn., Co., U.S.	D6	83
West Spit, spit, Marsh Is.	S18	52
West Springfield, Ma., U.S.	B2	98
West Springfield, N.H., U.S.	D2	106
West Springfield, Va., U.S.	g12	123
West Stafford, Ct., U.S.	B6	84
West Stockbridge, Ma., U.S.	B1	98
West Suffield, Ct., U.S.	B5	84
West Sullivan, Me., U.S.	D4	96
West Sumner, Me., U.S.	D2	96
West Sussex, co., Eng., U.K.	E7	12
West Swanzey, N.H., U.S.	E2	106
West Terre Haute, In., U.S.	F3	91
West-Terschelling, Neth.	A5	16
West Thompson Lake, res., Ct., U.S.	B8	84
West Thornton, N.H., U.S.	C3	106
West Tisbury, Ma., U.S.	D6	98
West Topsham, Vt., U.S.	C4	122
West Townsend, Ma., U.S.	A4	98
West Townshend, Vt., U.S.	E3	122
West Union, Il., U.S.	D6	90
West Union, Ia., U.S.	B6	92
West Union, Oh., U.S.	D2	112
West Union, S.C., U.S.	B1	117
West Union, W.V., U.S.	B4	125
West Unity, Oh., U.S.	A1	112
West University Place, Tx., U.S.	r14	120
West Upton, Ma., U.S.	B4	98
Westvale, N.Y., U.S.	*B4	109
West Valley, N.Y., U.S.	C2	109
West Valley City, Ut., U.S.	C4	121
West Van Lear, Ky., U.S.	C7	94
West Vancouver, B.C.	f12	69
West View, Pa., U.S.	h13	115
Westville, Fl., U.S.	u16	86
Westville, Il., U.S.	C6	90
Westville, In., U.S.	A4	91
Westville, N.H., U.S.	E4	106
Westville, N.J., U.S.	D2	107
Westville, Oh., U.S.	B2	112
Westville, Ok., U.S.	A7	113
Westville, Pa., U.S.	D4	115
Westville, S.C., U.S.	C6	117
Westville Lake, res., Ma., U.S.	B3	98
West Virginia, state, U.S.	C4	125
West Walker, stm., U.S.	E2	105
West Wardsboro, Vt., U.S.	E3	122
West Wareham, Ma., U.S.	C6	98
West Warren, Ma., U.S.	B3	98
West Warwick, R.I., U.S.	D3	116
West Webster, N.Y., U.S.	*B3	109
Westwego, La., U.S.	k11	95
West Whittier, Ca., U.S.	*n12	82
West Willington, Ct., U.S.	B6	84
West Willow, Mi., U.S.	*F7	99
West Wilton, N.H., U.S.	E3	106
West Winfield, N.Y., U.S.	C5	109
West Winfield, Pa., U.S.	E2	115
Westwold, B.C.	D8	69
Westwood, Ca., U.S.	B3	82
Westwood, Ks., U.S.	k16	93
Westwood, Ky., U.S.	B7	94
Westwood, Ma., U.S.	B5	98
Westwood, Mi., U.S.	*F5	99
Westwood, N.J., U.S.	B4	107
Westwood Lakes, Fl., U.S.	s13	86
West Wyalong, Austl.	F8	50
West Wyoming, Pa., U.S.	n17	115
West Yarmouth, Ma., U.S.	C7	98
West Yellowstone, Mt., U.S.	F5	103
West York, Il., U.S.	D6	90
West York, Pa., U.S.	G8	115
West Yorkshire, co., Eng., U.K.	*G7	13
Wetar, i., Indon.	G7	34
Wetaskiwin, Alta.	C4	68
Wete, Tan.	C6	48
Wethersfield, Ct., U.S.	C5	84
Wetmore, Co., U.S.	C5	83
Wetmore, Ks., U.S.	C8	93
Wetmore, Mi., U.S.	B4	99
Wetmore, Or., U.S.	C7	114
Wet Mountains, mts., Co., U.S.	C5	83
Wetonka, S.D., U.S.	B7	118
Wettingen, Switz.	B4	20
Wetteren, Bel.	D3	17
Wetumka, Ok., U.S.	B5	113
Wetumpka, Al., U.S.	C3	78
Wetzel, co., W.V., U.S.	B4	125
Wetzikon, Switz.	B6	21
Wetzlar, Ger.	C4	18
Wevelgem, Bel.	D3	17
Wewahitchka, Fl., U.S.	B1	86
Wewak, Pap. N. Gui.	h11	50
Wewela, S.D., U.S.	D6	118
Wewoka, Ok., U.S.	B5	113
Wexford, Ire.	D5	10
Wexford, co., Mi., U.S.	D5	99
Wexford, co., Ire.	E5	11
Wexford Harbour, b., Ire.	E5	11
Weyakwin Lake, l., Sask.	C3	75
Weyauwega, Wi., U.S.	D5	126
Weyburn, Sask.	H4	75
Weyerhaeuser, Wi., U.S.	C2	126
Weyers Cave, Va., U.S.	B4	123
Weymouth, N.S.	E4	71
Weymouth, Ma., U.S.	B6	98
Weymouth, N.J., U.S.	D3	107
Weymouth [and Melcombe Regis], Eng., U.K.	E5	12
Weymouth Bay, b., Eng., U.K.	D5	12
Whakatane, N.Z.	L16	51
Whalan, Mn., U.S.	G7	100
Whales, Bay of, b., Ant.	B32	7
Whalesville, Md., U.S.	D7	97
Whalom, Ma., U.S.	A4	98
Whangarei, N.Z.	K15	51
Wharfe, stm., Eng., U.K.	D6	10
Wharton, N.J., U.S.	B3	107
Wharton, Oh., U.S.	B2	112
Wharton, Tx., U.S.	E4	120
Wharton, W.V., U.S.	n12	125
Wharton, co., Tx., U.S.	E4	120
Whataroa, N.Z.	O13	51
What Cheer, Ia., U.S.	C5	92
Whatcom, co., Wa., U.S.	A4	124
Whatcom, Lake, l., Wa., U.S.	A3	124
Whately, Ma., U.S.	B2	98
Wheatcroft, Ky., U.S.	C2	94
Wheatfield, In., U.S.	B3	91
Wheatland, Ca., U.S.	C3	82
Wheatland, Ia., U.S.	C7	92
Wheatland, Mo., U.S.	D4	102
Wheatland, N.D., U.S.	C8	111
Wheatland, Wy., U.S.	D8	127
Wheatland, co., Mt., U.S.	D7	103
Wheatland Reservoir, res., Wy., U.S.	E7	127
Wheatley, Ont.	E2	73
Wheatley, Ar., U.S.	C4	81
Wheaton, Il., U.S.	B5	90
Wheaton, Md., U.S.	B3	97
Wheaton, Mn., U.S.	E2	100
Wheaton, Mo., U.S.	E3	102
Wheat Ridge, Co., U.S.	B5	83
Wheelbarrow Peak, mtn., Nv., U.S.	F5	105
Wheeler, Ar., U.S.	A1	81
Wheeler, In., U.S.	B3	91
Wheeler, Mi., U.S.	E6	99
Wheeler, Ms., U.S.	A5	101
Wheeler, Or., U.S.	B3	114
Wheeler, Tx., U.S.	B2	120

Name	Map Ref.	Page
Wheeler, Wi., U.S.	C2	126
Wheeler, co., Ga., U.S.	D4	87
Wheeler, co., Ne., U.S.	C7	104
Wheeler, co., Or., U.S.	C6	114
Wheeler, co., Tx., U.S.	B2	120
Wheeler Air Force Base, mil., Hi., U.S.	g9	88
Wheeler Dam, Al., U.S.	A2	78
Wheeler Lake, res., Al., U.S.	A2	78
Wheeler Peak, mtn., Ca., U.S.	C4	82
Wheeler Peak, mtn., Nv., U.S.	E7	105
Wheeler Peak, mtn., N.M., U.S.	A4	108
Wheelersburg, Oh., U.S.	D3	112
Wheeling, Il., U.S.	h9	90
Wheeling, Mo., U.S.	B4	102
Wheeling, W.V., U.S.	A4	125
Wheeling Creek, stm., W.V., U.S.	f8	125
Wheelock, N.D., U.S.	A2	111
Wheelock, Vt., U.S.	B4	122
Wheelock Mountain, mtn., Vt., U.S.	B4	122
Wheelockville, Ma., U.S.	*B4	98
Wheelon, Ut., U.S.	*B3	121
Wheelwright, Ky., U.S.	C7	94
Wheelwright, Ma., U.S.	B3	98
Whelen Springs, Ar., U.S.	D2	81
Whernside, mtn., Eng., U.K.	F6	13
Whetstone, stm., U.S.	E2	100
Whickham, Eng., U.K.	F7	13
Whidbey Island, i., Wa., U.S.	A3	124
Whidbey Island Naval Air Station, mil., Wa., U.S.	A3	124
Whigham, Ga., U.S.	F2	87
Whigville, Ct., U.S.	C4	84
Whipholt, Mn., U.S.	C4	100
Whipple, W.V., U.S.	n13	125
Whiskey Gap, Alta.	E4	68
Whiskey Peak, mtn., Wy., U.S.	D5	127
Whiskeytown-Shasta-Trinity National Recreation Area, Ca., U.S.	B2	82
Whisky Chitto Creek, stm., La., U.S.	C2	95
Whistler, B.C.	D6	69
Whitacres, Ct., U.S.	A5	84
Whitakers, N.C., U.S.	A5	110
Whitbourne, Newf.	E5	72
Whitby, Ont.	D6	73
Whitby, Eng., U.K.	C6	10
Whitchurch, Eng., U.K.	B5	12
Whitchurch-Stouffville, Ont.	D5	73
Whitcombe, Mount, mtn., N.Z.	O13	51
Whitcomb Mountain, mtn., N.H., U.S.	A4	106
White, Ga., U.S.	B2	87
White, S.D., U.S.	C9	118
White, co., Ar., U.S.	B4	81
White, co., Ga., U.S.	B3	87
White, co., Il., U.S.	E5	90
White, co., In., U.S.	C4	91
White, co., Tn., U.S.	D8	119
White, stm., B.C.	D3	68
White, stm., U.S.	C4	81
White, stm., U.S.	D5	118
White, stm., U.S.	C7	121
White, stm., Az., U.S.	D5	80
White, stm., In., U.S.	H2	91
White, stm., Mi., U.S.	E4	99
White, stm., Nv., U.S.	E6	105
White, stm., Tx., U.S.	C2	120
White, stm., Vt., U.S.	D4	122
White, stm., Wa., U.S.	B5	124
White, stm., Wa., U.S.	B4	124
White, East Fork, stm., In., U.S.	G5	91
White, Lake, i., Austl.	D4	50
White Bay, b., Newf.	D3	72
White Bear, Sask.	G1	75
White Bear, stm., Newf.	E3	72
White Bear, stm., Newf.	B3	72
White Bear Islands, is., Newf.	A3	72
White Bear Lake, Mn., U.S.	E5	100
White Bear Lake, l., Newf.	A2	72
White Bear Lake, l., Sask.	H4	75
White Bird, Id., U.S.	D2	89
White Bluff, Tn., U.S.	A4	119
White Breast Creek, stm., Ia., U.S.	C4	92
White Butte, mtn., N.D., U.S.	C2	111
White Cap Mountain, mtn., Me., U.S.	C3	96
White Carpathians, mts., Czech.	D4	26
White Castle, La., U.S.	D4	95
White Center, Wa., U.S.	e11	124
White City, Fl., U.S.	C1	86
White City, Ks., U.S.	D7	93
White City, Or., U.S.	E4	114
White City, Ut., U.S.	*C4	121
Whiteclay, Ne., U.S.	B3	104
White Clay Creek, stm., U.S.	A3	104
White Clay Creek, stm., De., U.S.	B3	85
White Cliffs, Austl.	E4	51
White Cloud, Ks., U.S.	C8	93
White Cloud, Mi., U.S.	E5	99
White Coomb, mtn., Scot., U.K.	C5	10
Whitecourt, Alta.	B3	68
White Creek, stm., U.S.	E2	122
Whiteday, stm., W.V., U.S.	h10	125
White Deer, Pa., U.S.	D8	115
White Deer, Tx., U.S.	B2	120
White Earth, Mn., U.S.	C3	100
White Earth, N.D., U.S.	A3	111
White Earth Indian Reservation, Mn., U.S.	C3	100
White Earth Lake, l., Mn., U.S.	C3	100
Whiteface, Mn., U.S.	C1	100
Whiteface, stm., Mn., U.S.	C6	100
Whiteface Mountain, mtn., N.Y., U.S.	f10	109
White Face Mountain, mtn., Vt., U.S.	B3	122
White Fathers, N.Y., U.S.	f10	109
Whitefield, Me., U.S.	*D3	96
Whitefield, N.H., U.S.	B3	106
Whitefield, Ok., U.S.	C6	113
Whitefish, Mt., U.S.	B2	103
Whitefish Bay, Wi., U.S.	m12	126
Whitefish Bay, b., Mi., U.S.	B6	99
Whitefish Falls, Ont.	A3	73
Whitefish Lake, l., Alta.	B4	68
Whitefish Lake, l., Mn., U.S.	D4	100
Whitefish Point, Mi., U.S.	B6	99
Whitefish Range, mts., Mt., U.S.	B2	103
Whiteford, Md., U.S.	A5	97
White Fox, Sask.	D3	75
White Fox, stm., Sask.	D3	75
White Gull Creek, stm., Sask.	D3	75
Whitehall, Ire.	E4	11
White Hall, Al., U.S.	C3	78

White Hall, Ar., U.S.	C3	81
White Hall, Ga., U.S.	C3	87
White Hall, Il., U.S.	D3	90
Whitehall, La., U.S.	D5	95
Whitehall, Md., U.S.	A4	97
Whitehall, Mt., U.S.	E4	103
Whitehall, N.Y., U.S.	B7	109
Whitehall, Oh., U.S.	m11	112
Whitehall, Pa., U.S.	*E11	115
Whitehall, Pa., U.S.	*k14	115
Whitehall, S.C., U.S.	F6	117
White Hall, Wi., U.S.	D2	126
Whitehall Reservoir, res., Ma., U.S.	h9	98
Whitehaven, Eng., U.K.	C5	10
Whitehaven, Md., U.S.	D6	97
White Haven, Pa., U.S.	D10	115
Whitehead, N. Ire., U.K.	C6	11
White Heath, Il., U.S.	C5	90
Whitehorn, Point, c., Wa., U.S.	A3	124
Whitehorse, Yukon	D5	66
White Horse, N.J., U.S.	C3	107
Whitehorse, S.D., U.S.	B5	118
White Horse Beach, Ma., U.S.	C6	98
Whitehouse, Scot., U.K.	C6	13
Whitehouse, Oh., U.S.	A2	112
White House, Tn., U.S.	A5	119
White House Station, N.J., U.S.	B3	107
White Island, i., Ant.	C17	7
White Island, i., Ant.	f38	7
White Island Shores, Ma., U.S.	C6	98
White Knob Mountains, mts., Id., U.S.	F5	89
White Lake, Ont.	B8	73
White Lake, S.D., U.S.	D7	118
White Lake, Wi., U.S.	C5	126
White Lake, l., Ont.	B8	73
White Lake, l., La., U.S.	E3	95
Whitelaw, Alta.	A1	68
Whitelaw, Wi., U.S.	h10	126
Whiteman Air Force Base, mil., Mo., U.S.	C4	102
Whitemarsh Township, Pa., U.S.	*F11	115
White Meadow Lake, N.J., U.S.	B3	107
White Mesa Natural Bridge, Az., U.S.	A4	80
White Mills, Pa., U.S.	C11	115
White Mountain, Ak., U.S.	C7	79
White Mountain Peak, mtn., Ca., U.S.	D4	82
White Mountains, mts., U.S.	D4	82
White Mountains, mts., N.H., U.S.	B3	106
Whitemouth, Man.	E4	70
Whitemouth, stm., Man.	E4	70
Whitemouth Lake, l., Man.	E4	70
Whitemud, stm., Alta.	A2	68
White Nile (Al Baḥr al Abyaḍ), stm., Sud.	C3	47
White Nile Dam, Sud.	B3	47
White Oak, Ga., U.S.	E5	87
White Oak, N.C., U.S.	C4	110
White Oak, Oh., U.S.	o12	112
White Oak, Ok., U.S.	A6	113
White Oak, Pa., U.S.	*k14	115
White Oak, S.C., U.S.	C5	117
White Oak Creek, stm., Oh., U.S.	D2	112
Whiteoak Creek, stm., Tn., U.S.	A4	119
White Oak Lake, res., Ar., U.S.	D2	81
White Oak Mountain, mtn., Ar., U.S.	C2	81
Whitney, Mount, mtn., Ca., U.S.	D4	82
White Owl, S.D., U.S.	C3	118
White Pass, N.A.	D12	79
White Pigeon, Mi., U.S.	G5	99
White Pine, Mi., U.S.	m12	99
White Pine, Tn., U.S.	C10	119
White Pine, co., Nv., U.S.	D6	105
White Plains, Al., U.S.	B4	78
White Plains, Ga., U.S.	C3	87
White Plains, Ky., U.S.	C2	94
White Plains, Md., U.S.	C4	97
White Plains, N.Y., U.S.	D7	109
White Plains, N.C., U.S.	A2	110
White Pond, S.C., U.S.	E5	117
Whiteriver, Az., U.S.	D6	80
White River, S.D., U.S.	D5	118
White River Junction, Vt., U.S.	D4	122
White River Plateau, plat., Co., U.S.	B3	83
White Rock, B.C.	E6	69
White Rock, N.M., U.S.	*B3	108
White Rock, R.I., U.S.	F1	116
White Rock, S.C., U.S.	C5	117
White Rock, S.D., U.S.	B9	118
White Rock Creek, stm., Ks., U.S.	C5	93
Whiterocks, Ut., U.S.	C6	121
White Rocks, mtn., Ky., U.S.	D6	94
White Russia, see Byelorussia, state, Sov. Un.	D5	29
Whites, Ms., U.S.	B5	101
Whites, Wa., U.S.	B2	124
Whitesail Lake, l., B.C.	C4	69
White Salmon, Wa., U.S.	D4	124
White Salmon, stm., Wa., U.S.	C4	124
Whitesand Bay, b., Eng., U.K.	F4	75
Whitesand Bay, b., Eng., U.K.	D3	12
White Sands Missile Range, mil., N.M., U.S.	E3	108
White Sands National Monument, N.M., U.S.	E3	108
Whitesbog, N.J., U.S.	D3	107
Whitesboro, N.J., U.S.	E3	107
Whitesboro, N.Y., U.S.	B5	109
Whitesboro, Ok., U.S.	C7	113
Whitesboro, Tx., U.S.	C4	120
Whites Brook, N.B.	B2	71
Whitesburg, Ga., U.S.	C2	87
Whitesburg, Ky., U.S.	C7	94
Whites City, N.M., U.S.	E6	108
Whites Creek, stm., Tn., U.S.	g10	119
White Sea, Sov. Un.		
White Settlement, Tx., U.S.	*n9	120
Whiteshell Provincial Park, Man.	D4	70
Whiteshore Lake, l., Sask.	E1	75
Whiteside, Mo., U.S.	B6	102
Whiteside, Tn., U.S.	D8	119
Whiteside, co., Il., U.S.	B3	90
Whiteson, Or., U.S.	B3	114
White Springs, Fl., U.S.	B4	86
Whitestone, Ga., U.S.	B2	87
White Stone, Va., U.S.	C6	123
White Stone Lake, l., Man.	A3	70
Whitestown, In., U.S.	C5	91
White Sulphur Springs, Mt., U.S.	D6	103

White Sulphur Springs, W.V., U.S.	D4	125
Whitesville, De., U.S.	G4	85
Whitesville, Ky., U.S.	C3	94
Whitesville, N.Y., U.S.	C3	109
Whitesville, W.V., U.S.	D3	125
Whiteswan Lakes, l., Sask.	C3	75
Whitetail, Mt., U.S.	B11	103
White Tank Mountains, mts., Az., U.S.	k7	80
Whiteville, N.C., U.S.	C4	110
Whiteville, Tn., U.S.	B2	119
White Volta, stm., Afr.	D4	45
Whitewater, Man.	E1	70
Whitewater, Co., U.S.	C2	83
Whitewater, Ks., U.S.	E6	93
Whitewater, Mo., U.S.	D8	102
Whitewater, Mt., U.S.	B9	103
Whitewater, Wi., U.S.	F5	126
Whitewater, stm., U.S.	F7	91
Whitewater, stm., Ks., U.S.	E6	93
Whitewater, East Fork, stm., U.S.	E8	91
Whitewater, West Branch, stm., Ks., U.S.	g12	93
Whitewater Baldy, mtn., N.M., U.S.	D1	108
Whitewater Bay, b., Fl., U.S.	G6	86
White Woman Creek, stm., Ks., U.S.	D2	93
Whitewood, Sask.	G4	75
Whitewood, S.D., U.S.	C2	118
Whitewright, Tx., U.S.	C4	120
Whitfield, Al., U.S.	C1	78
Whitfield, co., Ga., U.S.	B2	87
Whitfield Estates, Fl., U.S.	q10	86
Whithorn, Scot., U.K.	C4	10
Whiting, In., U.S.	A3	91
Whiting, Ia., U.S.	B1	92
Whiting, Ks., U.S.	C8	93
Whiting, Me., U.S.	D5	96
Whiting, N.J., U.S.	D4	107
Whiting, Vt., U.S.	D2	122
Whiting, Wi., U.S.	D4	126
Whiting Bay, Scot., U.K.	E3	13
Whitingham, N.H., U.S.	F3	122
Whitinsville, Ma., U.S.	B4	98
Whitlow, Sask.	E2	75
Whitla, Alta.	E5	68
Whitlash, Mt., U.S.	B5	103
Whitley, co., In., U.S.	B6	91
Whitley, co., Ky., U.S.	D5	94
Whitley City, Ky., U.S.	D5	94
Whitlock, Tn., U.S.	A3	119
Whitman, Ma., U.S.	B6	98
Whitman, Ne., U.S.	B4	104
Whitman, N.D., U.S.	A7	111
Whitman, W.V., U.S.	D2	125
Whitman, co., Wa., U.S.	B8	124
Whitmans Pond, l., Ma., U.S.	h12	98
Whitman Square, N.J., U.S.	D2	107
Whitmell, Va., U.S.	D3	123
Whitmore, W.V., U.S.	C5	125
Whitmire, S.C., U.S.	B4	117
Whitmore Lake, Mi., U.S.	p14	99
Whitmore Mountains, mts., Ant.	A2	7
Whitmore Village, Hi., U.S.	f9	88
Whitney, Ont.	B6	73
Whitney, Id., U.S.	G7	89
Whitney, Pa., U.S.	F3	115
Whitney, S.C., U.S.	B4	117
Whitney, Tx., U.S.	D4	120
Whitney, Lake, res., Tx., U.S.	D4	120
Whitney, Mount, mtn., Ca., U.S.	D4	82
Whitney Point, N.Y., U.S.	C5	109
Whitney Point Lake, res., N.Y., U.S.	C5	109
Whitneyville, Me., U.S.	D5	96
Whitsett, N.C., U.S.	A3	110
Whitstable, Eng., U.K.	C9	12
Whitt, Tx., U.S.	C3	120
Whittemore, Ia., U.S.	A3	92
Whittemore, Mi., U.S.	D7	99
Whitten, Ia., U.S.	B4	92
Whittier, Ak., U.S.	C10	79
Whittier, Ca., U.S.	F4	82
Whittier, N.H., U.S.	C4	106
Whittier, N.C., U.S.	f9	110
Whittlesey, Eng., U.K.	B7	12
Whittlesey, Mount, hill, Wi., U.S.	B3	126
Whitwell, Tn., U.S.	D8	119
Wholdaia Lake, l., N.W. Ter.	D12	66
Whyalla, Austl.	F6	50
Whycocomagh, N.S.	D8	71
Wiarton, Ont.	C3	73
Wiau Lake, l., Alta.	B5	68
Wiawso, Ghana	E4	45
Wiay, i., Scot., U.K.	C1	13
Wibaux, Mt., U.S.	D12	103
Wibaux, co., Mt., U.S.	D12	103
Wiborg, Ky., U.S.	D5	94
Wichita, Ks., U.S.	E6	93
Wichita, co., Ks., U.S.	D2	93
Wichita, co., Tx., U.S.	B3	120
Wichita Falls, Tx., U.S.	C3	120
Wichita Mountains, mts., Ok., U.S.	C3	113
Wick, Scot., U.K.	A5	10
Wickatunk, N.J., U.S.	C4	107
Wickenburg, Az., U.S.	D3	80
Wickes, Ar., U.S.	C1	81
Wickes, Mt., U.S.	D4	103
Wickham, Que.	D5	74
Wickiup Reservoir, res., Or., U.S.	E5	114
Wickliffe, Ky., U.S.	f8	94
Wickliffe, Oh., U.S.	*A5	112
Wicklow, co., Ire.	I6	11
Wicklow Head, c., Ire.	E6	11
Wicklow Mountains, mts., Ire.	H6	11
Wico Sound, strt., Ant.	B5	7
Wicomico, co., Md., U.S.	D6	97
Wicomico, stm., Md., U.S.	C7	97
Widefield, Co., U.S.	C6	83
Widen, W.V., U.S.	C4	125
Widener, Ar., U.S.	B5	81
Widerøe, Mount, mtn., Ant.	B15	7
Wide Ruins, Az., U.S.	B6	80
Widnes, Eng., U.K.	A5	12
Wickox Playa, l., Az., U.S.	E5	80
Widuchowa, Pol.	B2	26
Wiebelskirchen, Ger.	D2	19
Wielen, N.Y., U.S.	C5	109
Wieliczka, Pol.	C6	26
Wieluń, Pol.	C5	26
Wiener Neustadt, Aus.	E8	18
Wieprz, stm., Pol.	C7	26
Wieprzanka, stm., Pol.	h10	26

Wiergate, Tx., U.S.	D6	120
Wiesau, Ger.	D7	19
Wiesbaden, Ger.	C4	18
Wiese, stm., Ger.	A4	21
Wiesenburg, Ger.	A7	19
Wiesental, Ger.	D3	19
Wiesloch, Ger.	D3	19
Wigan, Eng., U.K.	A5	12
Wiggins, Co., U.S.	A6	83
Wiggins, Ms., U.S.	E4	101
Wiggins Peak, mtn., Wy., U.S.	C3	127
Wight, Isle of, i., Eng., U.K.	E6	10
Wigton, Eng., U.K.	F5	13
Wigtown, Scot., U.K.	C4	10
Wigtown Bay, b., Scot., U.K.	C4	10
Wijhe, Neth.	B6	17
Wikieup, Az., U.S.	C2	80
Wikwemikong, Ont.	B3	73
Wil, Switz.	B5	20
Wilayah Persekutuan (Federal Territory), ter., Malay.	*K4	35
Wilbar, N.C., U.S.	A1	110
Wilbarger, co., Tx., U.S.	B3	120
Wilber, Ne., U.S.	D9	104
Wilberforce, Ont.	B6	73
Wilberforce, Oh., U.S.	C2	112
Wilbraham, Ma., U.S.	B3	98
Wilbur, Or., U.S.	D3	114
Wilbur, Wa., U.S.	B7	124
Wilburn, Ar., U.S.	B4	81
Wilburton, Ok., U.S.	C6	113
Wilcannia, Austl.	F7	50
Wilcox, Sask.	G3	75
Wilcox, Ne., U.S.	D6	104
Wilcox, Pa., U.S.	C4	115
Wilcox, co., Al., U.S.	D2	78
Wilcox, co., Ga., U.S.	E3	87
Wilcox, Mount, mtn., Ma., U.S.	B1	98
Wilczek, i., Sov. Un.	A8	128
Wild, stm., U.S.	B4	106
Wild Ammonoosuc, stm., N.H., U.S.	B3	106
Wild Branch, stm., Vt., U.S.	B4	122
Wildcat Creek, stm., In., U.S.	D4	91
Wildcat Creek, South Fork, stm., In., U.S.	D4	91
Wildcat Hill, hill, Sask.	D4	75
Wildcat Top, mtn., Tn., U.S.	D10	119
Wilder, Id., U.S.	F2	89
Wilder, Vt., U.S.	D4	122
Wilder Dam, U.S.	C2	106
Wildersville, Tn., U.S.	B3	119
Wildervank (part of Veendam), Neth.	A7	16
Wilderville, Or., U.S.	E3	114
Wildeshausen, Ger.	F2	15
Wildhaus, Switz.	B7	21
Wildhay, stm., Alta.	C2	68
Wildhorn, mtn., Switz.	D3	21
Wild Horse, Co., U.S.	C7	83
Wildhorse Creek, stm., Ok., U.S.	C4	113
Wild Horse Reservoir, res., Nv., U.S.	B6	105
Wildorado, Tx., U.S.	B1	120
Wild Rice, stm., Mn., U.S.	C2	100
Wild Rice, stm., N.D., U.S.	C8	111
Wild Rice, South Branch, stm., Mn., U.S.	C2	100
Wildrose, N.D., U.S.	A2	111
Wild Rose, Wi., U.S.	D4	126
Wildspitze, mtn., Aus.	C6	20
Wildsville, La., U.S.	C4	95
Wildwood, Alta.	C3	68
Wildwood, Fl., U.S.	D4	86
Wildwood, Il., U.S.	h9	90
Wildwood, N.J., U.S.	F3	107
Wildwood, Ut., U.S.	*C4	121
Wildwood Crest, N.J., U.S.	F3	107
Wiley, Co., U.S.	C8	83
Wiley, Wa., U.S.	C5	124
Wilhelm, Mount, mtn., Pap. N. Gui.	k12	50
Wilhelmina Gebergte, mts., Sur.	B3	59
Wilhelm-Pieck-Stadt Guben see Guben, Ger.	C7	18
Wilhelmshaven, Ger.	B4	18
Wilhoit, Az., U.S.	C3	80
Wilkau [-Hasslau], Ger.	C7	19
Wilkes, co., Ga., U.S.	C4	87
Wilkes, co., N.C., U.S.	A1	110
Wilkes-Barre, Pa., U.S.	D10	115
Wilkesboro, N.C., U.S.	A1	110
Wilkes Island, i., Wake I.	A1	52
Wilkes Land, reg., Ant.	B25	7
Wilkeson, Wa., U.S.	B3	124
Wilkesville, Oh., U.S.	C3	112
Wilkie, Sask.	E1	75
Wilkin, co., Mn., U.S.	D2	100
Wilkinsburg, Pa., U.S.	F2	115
Wilkinson, In., U.S.	E6	91
Wilkinson, Ms., U.S.	D2	101
Wilkinson, W.V., U.S.	D3	125
Wilkinson, co., Ga., U.S.	D3	87
Wilkinson, co., Ms., U.S.	D2	101
Wilkins Township, Pa., U.S.	*F2	115
Will, co., Il., U.S.	B6	90
Willacoochee, Ga., U.S.	E3	87
Willacy, co., Tx., U.S.	F4	120
Willamette, stm., Or., U.S.	C3	114
Willamette, Middle Fork, stm., Or., U.S.	D4	114
Willamette Pass, Or., U.S.	D4	114
Willamina, Or., U.S.	B3	114
Willapa, Austl.	E3	51
Willapa Bay, b., Wa., U.S.	C1	124
Willard, Ks., U.S.	C8	93
Willard, Ky., U.S.	B7	94
Willard, Mt., U.S.	D3	103
Willard, N.M., U.S.	C3	108
Willard, N.Y., U.S.	C4	109
Willard, Oh., U.S.	A3	112
Willard, Ut., U.S.	B3	121
Willard Bay, b., Ut., U.S.	B3	121
Willards, Md., U.S.	D7	97
Willard Stream, stm., Vt., U.S.	B5	122
Willcox, Az., U.S.	E6	80
Willcox Playa, l., Az., U.S.	E5	80
Willemstad, Neth.	C4	17
Willemstad, Neth. Ant.	H19	65
Willet, N.Y., U.S.	C5	109
Willette, Tn., U.S.	C8	119
William "Bill" Dannelly Reservoir, res., Al., U.S.	C2	78
William Lake, l., Man.	C2	70

William P. Lane, Jr. Memorial Bridge, Md., U.S.	B5	97
Williams, Az., U.S.	B3	80
Williams, Ca., U.S.	C2	82
Williams, In., U.S.	G4	91
Williams, Ia., U.S.	B4	92
Williams, Mn., U.S.	B4	100
Williams, S.C., U.S.	E6	117
Williams, co., N.D., U.S.	A2	111
Williams, co., Oh., U.S.	A1	112
Williams, stm., Vt., U.S.	E3	122
Williams, Cape, c., Ant.	B29	7
Williams Air Force Base, mil., Az., U.S.	D4	80
Williams Bay, Wi., U.S.	F5	126
Williamsburg, Ont.	C9	73
Williamsburg, Co., U.S.	*C5	83
Williamsburg, Ky., U.S.	D5	94
Williamsburg, Ia., U.S.	C5	92
Williamsburg, Ks., U.S.	D8	93
Williamsburg, Ma., U.S.	B2	98
Williamsburg, Mi., U.S.	D5	99
Williamsburg, N.M., U.S.	D2	108
Williamsburg, Oh., U.S.	C1	112
Williamsburg, Pa., U.S.	F5	115
Williamsburg, Va., U.S.	C6	123
Williamsburg, W.V., U.S.	D4	125
Williamsburg, co., S.C., U.S.	D8	117
Williamsfield, Il., U.S.	C3	90
Williams Fork, stm., Co., U.S.	A3	83
Williams Harbour, Newf.	B4	72
Williams Lake, B.C.	C6	69
Williams Mountain, mtn., Ok., U.S.	C7	113
Williamson, Ga., U.S.	C2	87
Williamson, Ia., U.S.	C4	92
Williamson, N.Y., U.S.	B3	109
Williamson, W.V., U.S.	D2	125
Williamson, co., Il., U.S.	F4	90
Williamson, co., Tn., U.S.	B5	119
Williamson, co., Tx., U.S.	D4	120
Williamson, Mount, mtn., Ca., U.S.	*D4	82
Williamson Head, c., Ant.	C28	7
Williamsport, Newf.	C3	72
Williamsport, In., U.S.	D3	91
Williamsport, Md., U.S.	A2	97
Williamsport, Oh., U.S.	C2	112
Williamsport, Pa., U.S.	D7	115
Williamsport, Tn., U.S.	B4	119
Williamston, Mi., U.S.	F6	99
Williamston, N.C., U.S.	B5	110
Williamston, S.C., U.S.	B3	117
Williamstown, Ont.	B10	73
Williamstown, Ks., U.S.	k15	93
Williamstown, Ky., U.S.	B5	94
Williamstown, Ma., U.S.	A1	98
Williamstown, Mo., U.S.	A6	102
Williamstown, N.J., U.S.	D3	107
Williamstown, N.Y., U.S.	B5	109
Williamstown, Pa., U.S.	E8	115
Williamstown, Vt., U.S.	C3	122
Williamstown, W.V., U.S.	B3	125
Williamsville, Il., U.S.	D4	90
Williamsville, Ms., U.S.	E3	101
Williamsville, Mo., U.S.	E7	102
Williamsville, N.Y., U.S.	C2	109
Williamsville, Vt., U.S.	F3	122
Williford, Ar., U.S.	A4	81
Willimantic, Ct., U.S.	C7	84
Willimantic, stm., Ct., U.S.	B6	84
Willimantic Reservoir, res., Ct., U.S.		
Willingboro, N.J., U.S.	C3	107
Willingdon, Alta.	C4	68
Willis, Ks., U.S.	C8	93
Willis, Mi., U.S.	p14	99
Willis, Tx., U.S.	D5	120
Willisburg, Ky., U.S.	C4	94
Willis Island, i., Newf.	D5	72
Williston, S. Afr.	C3	49
Williston, Fl., U.S.	C4	86
Williston, N.C., U.S.	C6	110
Williston, N.D., U.S.	A2	111
Williston, S.C., U.S.	E5	117
Williston, Tn., U.S.	B2	119
Williston, Vt., U.S.	C2	122
Williston Basin, U.S.	B2	111
Williston Lake, res., B.C.	B6	69
Willisville, Il., U.S.	F4	90
Willits, Ca., U.S.	C2	82
Willmar, Mn., U.S.	H4	75
Willmar, Mn., U.S.	E3	100
Willmore Wilderness Park, Alta.	C1	68
Willoughby, Austl.	*F9	50
Willoughby, Oh., U.S.	A4	112
Willoughby, Lake, l., Vt., U.S.	B4	122
Willoughby Hills, Oh., U.S.	A4	112
Willow, Ak., U.S.	g17	79
Willow, Ok., U.S.	B2	113
Willow, stm., B.C.	C6	69
Willowbrook, Sask.	F4	75
Willow Brook, Ca., U.S.	*n12	82
Willowbrook, Il., U.S.	*B6	89
Willow Bunch, Sask.	H3	75
Willow Bunch Lake, l., Sask.	A5	111
Willow City, N.D., U.S.	A5	111
Willow Creek, Mt., U.S.	E5	103
Willow Creek, stm., Alta.	D4	68
Willow Creek, stm., Nv., U.S.	C5	105
Willow Creek, stm., Ut., U.S.	D6	121
Willow Creek, stm., Wy., U.S.	C6	127
Willow Glen, Ca., U.S.	D3	85
Willow Grove, De., U.S.	F11	115
Willow Grove Naval Air Station, Pa., U.S.	F11	115
Willow Hill, Il., U.S.	E5	90
Willow Hill, Pa., U.S.	F6	115
Willow Lake, S.D., U.S.	C8	118
Willow Lake, l., N.W. Ter.	D7	66
Willowlake, stm., N.W. Ter.	D7	66
Willowmore, S. Afr.	D3	49
Willow Reservoir, res., Wi., U.S.	C3	126
Willow River, B.C.	B6	69
Willow Run, Mi., U.S.	p14	99
Willow Run, De., U.S.	i7	85
Willow Springs, Il., U.S.	k9	90

Willow Springs, Mo., U.S.	E6	102
Willsboro, N.Y., U.S.	f11	109
Wills Hill, hill, Ma., U.S.	f11	98
Willshire, Oh., U.S.	B1	112
Wills Mountain, mtn., U.S.	k13	97
Willston, Va., U.S.	B5	123
Wilmar, Ar., U.S.	D4	81
Wilmer, Al., U.S.	E1	78
Wilmer, Tx., U.S.	n10	120
Wilmerding, Pa., U.S.	k14	115
Wilmersdorf, Ger.	E7	15
Wilmette, Il., U.S.	A6	90
Wilmington, Austl.	F2	51
Wilmington, De., U.S.	B3	85
Wilmington, Il., U.S.	B5	90
Wilmington, Ma., U.S.	A5	98
Wilmington, N.Y., U.S.	f11	109
Wilmington, N.C., U.S.	C5	110
Wilmington, Oh., U.S.	C2	112
Wilmington, Vt., U.S.	F3	122
Wilmington Island, Ga., U.S.	*E5	87
Wilmington Manor, De., U.S.	i7	85
Wilmington Manor Gardens, De., U.S.	*B3	85
Wilmot, Mn., U.S.	G3	100
Wilmore, Ks., U.S.	E4	93
Wilmot, N.S.	E4	71
Wilmot, Ar., U.S.	D4	81
Wilmot, In., U.S.	B6	91
Wilmot, Ks., U.S.	E6	93
Wilmot, N.H., U.S.	D3	106
Wilmot, Oh., U.S.	B4	112
Wilmot, S.D., U.S.	B9	118
Wilmot Flat, N.H., U.S.	D3	106
Wilmslow, Eng., U.K.	A5	12
Wilno, Ont.	B7	73
Wilsall, Mt., U.S.	E6	103
Wilsey, Ks., U.S.	D7	93
Wilson, Ar., U.S.	B5	81
Wilson, Ks., U.S.	D5	93
Wilson, La., U.S.	D4	95
Wilson, Mi., U.S.	C3	99
Wilson, N.Y., U.S.	B2	109
Wilson, N.C., U.S.	B5	110
Wilson, Ok., U.S.	C4	113
Wilson, Pa., U.S.	E11	115
Wilson, Tx., U.S.	C2	120
Wilson, Ut., U.S.	B3	121
Wilson, Wy., U.S.	C2	127
Wilson, co., Ks., U.S.	E8	93
Wilson, co., N.C., U.S.	B5	110
Wilson, co., Tn., U.S.	A5	119
Wilson, co., Tx., U.S.	E3	120
Wilson, stm., Austl.	C4	51
Wilson, Mount, mtn., Az., U.S.	m12	82
Wilson, Mount, mtn., Ca., U.S.	m12	82
Wilson, Mount, mtn., Co., U.S.	D2	83
Wilson, Mount, mtn., Nv., U.S.	E7	105
Wilson, Mount, mtn., Or., U.S.	B5	114
Wilson Creek, Wa., U.S.	B6	124
Wilson Creek, stm., Wa., U.S.	B5	124
Wilson Creek, stm., Wa., U.S.	B5	124
Wilson Dam, Al., U.S.	A2	78
Wilson Lake, res., Al., U.S.	A2	78
Wilson Lake, res., Ks., U.S.	A6	93
Wilson Piedmont Glacier, ice, Ant.	e39	7
Wilsons, Va., U.S.	C5	123
Wilsons Beach, N.B.	E3	71
Wilsons Mills, Me., U.S.	D1	96
Wilsons Mills, N.C., U.S.	B4	110
Wilsons Promontory, c., Austl.	G8	50
Wilsonville, Al., U.S.	B3	78
Wilsonville, Ct., U.S.	A8	84
Wilsonville, Ne., U.S.	D4	90
Wilsonville, Or., U.S.	h12	114
Wilstedt, Ger.	E3	15
Wilster, Ger.	E3	15
Wilton, Al., U.S.	B3	78
Wilton, Ar., U.S.	D1	81
Wilton, Ct., U.S.	E2	84
Wilton, Ia., U.S.	C6	92
Wilton, Me., U.S.	D2	96
Wilton, Mn., U.S.	C3	100
Wilton, N.H., U.S.	E3	106
Wilton, N.Y., U.S.	B7	109
Wilton, N.D., U.S.	B5	111
Wilton, Wi., U.S.	E3	126
Wilton Center, N.H., U.S.	E3	106
Wilton Manors, Fl., U.S.	*r13	86
Wiltshire, co., Eng., U.K.	C6	12
Wiltz, Lux.	C6	16
Wiluna, Austl.	E3	50
Wimapedi, stm., Man.	B2	70
Wimauma, Fl., U.S.	E4	86
Wimbledon (part of London), Eng., U.K.	m12	12
Wimbledon, N.D., U.S.	B7	111
Wimborne, Alta.		
Wimborne Minster, Eng., U.K.	D6	12
Wimico, Lake, l., Fl., U.S.	C1	86
Winagami Lake, l., Alta.	B2	68
Winamac, In., U.S.	B4	91
Winburg, S. Afr.	C4	49
Winburne, Pa., U.S.	E5	115
Wincheck Pond, l., R.I., U.S.	E1	116
Winchell Mountain, mtn., Ma., U.S.	B2	98
Winchendon, Ma., U.S.	A3	98
Winchendon Springs, Ma., U.S.	A3	98
Winchester, Ont.	B9	73
Winchester, Eng., U.K.	E6	10
Winchester, Ar., U.S.	D4	81
Winchester, Id., U.S.	C2	89
Winchester, Il., U.S.	D3	90
Winchester, In., U.S.	D8	91
Winchester, Ks., U.S.	k15	93
Winchester, Ky., U.S.	C5	94
Winchester, Ma., U.S.	g11	98
Winchester, Nv., U.S.	D5	101
Winchester, N.H., U.S.	F2	106
Winchester, Tn., U.S.	B5	119
Winchester, Va., U.S.	A4	123
Winchester Bay, Or., U.S.	D2	114
Winchester Center, Ct., U.S.	B3	84
Wind, stm., Wa., U.S.	D4	124
Wind, stm., Wy., U.S.	C4	127
Wind Cave National Park, S.D., U.S.	D2	118
Wind Creek, stm., Wy., U.S.	C7	127
Windcrest, Tx., U.S.	*E3	120
Winder, Ga., U.S.	C3	87
Windermere, B.C.	D10	69
Windermere, Ont.	B5	73
Windermere, Fl., U.S.	D5	86
Windermere, l., Eng., U.K.	F6	13
Windfall, Alta.		
Windfall, In., U.S.	D6	91

Name	Map Ref.	Page
Windgap, Pa., U.S.	E11	115
Windham, Ct., U.S.	C7	84
Windham, Mt., U.S.	C6	103
Windham, N.Y., U.S.	C6	109
Windham, Oh., U.S.	A4	112
Windham, co., Ct., U.S.	B7	84
Windham, co., Vt., U.S.	F3	122
Windham Center, Me., U.S.	*E2	96
Windhoek, Nmb.	B2	49
Windigo, stm., Que.	B4	74
Winding Stair Mountain, mts., Ok., U.S.	C6	113
Wind Lake, Wi., U.S.	F5	126
Wind Lake, l., Wi., U.S.	n11	126
Windmill Point, c., Va., U.S.	D6	93
Windom, Ks., U.S.	D6	93
Windom, Mn., U.S.	G3	100
Windom Peak, mtn., Co., U.S.	D3	83
Window Rock, Az., U.S.	B6	80
Wind Point, Wi., U.S.	n12	126
Wind Ridge, Pa., U.S.	G1	115
Wind River Indian Reservation, Wy., U.S.	C4	127
Wind River Peak, mtn., Wy., U.S.	D3	127
Wind River Range, mts., Wy., U.S.	C3	127
Windsbach, Ger.	D5	19
Windsor, Newf.	D4	72
Windsor, N.S.	E5	71
Windsor, Ont.	E1	73
Windsor, Que.	D5	74
Windsor (New Windsor), Eng., U.K.	E6	10
Windsor, Co., U.S.	A6	83
Windsor, Ct., U.S.	B5	84
Windsor, Il., U.S.	D5	90
Windsor, Ma., U.S.	A1	98
Windsor, Mo., U.S.	C4	102
Windsor, N.J., U.S.	C3	107
Windsor, N.C., U.S.	B6	110
Windsor, N.D., U.S.	C6	111
Windsor, Pa., U.S.	G8	115
Windsor, S.C., U.S.	E4	117
Windsor, Vt., U.S.	E4	122
Windsor, Va., U.S.	D6	123
Windsor, co., Vt., U.S.	E3	122
Windsor Heights, Ia., U.S.	e8	92
Windsor Hills, Ca., U.S.	*n12	82
Windsor Locks, Ct., U.S.	B5	84
Windsorville, Ct., U.S.	B5	84
Windthorst, Sask.	G4	75
Windthorst, Tx., U.S.	C3	120
Windward Islands, is., N.A.	I14	64
Windward Passage, strt., N.A.	E7	64
Windygates, Man.	E2	70
Windy Hill, S.C., U.S.	C8	117
Windy Hills, De., U.S.	*B3	85
Windy Lake, l., Sask.	C4	75
Windy Peak, mtn., Wa., U.S.	A6	124
Windy Point, c., Newf.	C4	72
Winefred, stm., Alta.	B5	68
Winefred Lake, l., Alta.	B5	68
Winfall, N.C., U.S.	A6	110
Winfield, Alta.	C3	68
Winfield, Al., U.S.	B2	78
Winfield, Ia., U.S.	C6	92
Winfield, Ks., U.S.	E7	93
Winfield, Md., U.S.	B3	97
Winfield, Mo., U.S.	C7	102
Winfield, N.J., U.S.	k7	107
Winfield, Pa., U.S.	E8	115
Winfield, Tn., U.S.	C9	119
Winfield, W.V., U.S.	C3	125
Winfred, S.D., U.S.	D8	118
Wing, Al., U.S.	D3	78
Wing, Ar., U.S.	C2	81
Wing, N.D., U.S.	B5	111
Wing, stm., Mn., U.S.	D3	100
Wingate, In., U.S.	D3	91
Wingate, Md., U.S.	D5	97
Wingate, N.C., U.S.	C2	110
Winger, Mn., U.S.	C2	100
Wingham, Ont.	D3	73
Wingo, Ky., U.S.	I9	94
Winifreda, Arg.	C7	103
Winifrede, W.V., U.S.	B4	54
Winigan, Mo., U.S.	m12	125
Winisk, Ont.	A5	102
Winisk, stm., Ont.	n18	73
Winisk Lake, l., Ont.	n18	73
Wink, Tx., U.S.	n18	73
Winkelman, Az., U.S.	D1	120
Winkler, Man.	E5	80
Winkler, co., Tx., U.S.	E3	70
Winlaw, B.C.	D1	120
Winlock, Wa., U.S.	E9	69
Winn, Me., U.S.	C3	124
Winn, Mi., U.S.	C4	96
Winn, co., La., U.S.	E6	99
Winnabow, N.C., U.S.	C3	95
Winneba, Ghana	C4	110
Winnebago, Il., U.S.	E4	45
Winnebago, Mn., U.S.	A4	90
Winnebago, Ne., U.S.	G4	100
Winnebago, co., Il., U.S.	B9	104
Winnebago, co., Ia., U.S.	h8	126
Winnebago, co., Wi., U.S.	A4	90
Winnebago, stm., Ia., U.S.	D5	126
Winnebago, Lake, l., Wi., U.S.	A4	92
Winnebago Indian Reservation, Ne., U.S.	E5	126
Winneconne, Wi., U.S.	B9	104
Winnemucca, Nv., U.S.	D5	126
Winnemucca Lake, l., Nv., U.S.	C4	105
Winner, S.D., U.S.	C2	105
Winneshiek, co., Ia., U.S.	D6	118
Winnetka, Il., U.S.	A6	92
Winnetoon, Ne., U.S.	A6	90
Winnett, Mt., U.S.	B8	104
Winnfield, La., U.S.	C8	103
Winnibigoshish, Lake, l., Mn., U.S.	C3	95
Winnifred, Alta.	C4	100
Winnipeg, Man.	E5	68
Winnipeg, stm., Can.	E3	70
Winnipeg Beach, Man.	D4	70
Winnipegosis, Man.	C3	70
Winnipegosis, Lake, l., Man.	D3	70
Winnipesaukee, N.H., U.S.	C2	70
Winnipesaukee, Lake, l., N.H., U.S.	C4	106
Winnisquam, N.H., U.S.	C3	106
Winnisquam Lake, l., N.H., U.S.	C3	106
Winnsboro, La., U.S.	B4	95
Winnsboro, S.C., U.S.	C5	117
Winnsboro, Tx., U.S.	C5	120
Winnsboro Mills, S.C., U.S.	C5	117
Winona, Ks., U.S.	C2	93
Winona, Mi., U.S.	B2	99
Winona, Mn., U.S.	F7	100
Winona, Ms., U.S.	B4	101
Winona, Mo., U.S.	D6	102
Winona, N.H., U.S.	C3	106
Winona, Wa., U.S.	C8	124
Winona, W.V., U.S.	C4	125
Winona, co., Mn., U.S.	F7	100
Winona Lake, In., U.S.	B6	91
Winona Lake, l., Vt., U.S.	C2	122
Winooski, Vt., U.S.	C2	122
Winooski, stm., Vt., U.S.	C3	122
Winooski, North Branch, stm., Vt., U.S.	C3	122
Winschoten, Neth.	A7	16
Winsen, Ger.	E4	15
Winsford, Eng., U.K.	A5	12
Winside, Ne., U.S.	B8	104
Winslow, Az., U.S.	C5	80
Winslow, Ar., U.S.	B1	81
Winslow, Il., U.S.	A4	90
Winslow, In., U.S.	H3	91
Winslow, Me., U.S.	D3	96
Winslow, Ne., U.S.	C9	104
Winslow, N.J., U.S.	D3	107
Winsted, Ct., U.S.	B3	84
Winsted, Mn., U.S.	F4	100
Winston, Fl., U.S.	D4	86
Winston, Mo., U.S.	B3	102
Winston, Mt., U.S.	D5	103
Winston, N.M., U.S.	D2	108
Winston, Or., U.S.	D3	114
Winston, co., Al., U.S.	A2	78
Winston, co., Ms., U.S.	B4	101
Winston-Salem, N.C., U.S.	A2	110
Winstonville, Ms., U.S.	B3	101
Winsum, Neth.	A6	17
Winter, Sask.	E1	75
Winter, Wi., U.S.	C2	126
Winter Beach, Fl., U.S.	E6	86
Winterberg, Ger.	B3	19
Winter Garden, Fl., U.S.	D5	86
Winter Harbor, Me., U.S.	D4	96
Winter Harbour, B.C.	D3	69
Winter Haven, Fl., U.S.	D5	86
Wintering Lake, l., Man.	B3	70
Winter Park, Co., U.S.	B5	83
Winter Park, Fl., U.S.	D5	86
Winter Park, N.C., U.S.	C5	110
Winterport, Me., U.S.	D4	96
Winter Ridge, mtn., Or., U.S.	E6	114
Winters, Ca., U.S.	C2	82
Winters, Tx., U.S.	D3	120
Winterset, Ia., U.S.	C4	92
Winter Springs, Fl., U.S.	*D5	86
Winterswijk, Neth.	C6	17
Winterthur, Switz.	E14	18
Winterthur, De., U.S.	h7	85
Winterton, Newf.	E5	72
Winterville, Ga., U.S.	C3	87
Winterville, Me., U.S.	B4	96
Winterville, Ms., U.S.	B2	101
Winterville, N.C., U.S.	B5	110
Winthrop, Ar., U.S.	D1	81
Winthrop, Ct., U.S.	D5	84
Winthrop, Ia., U.S.	B6	92
Winthrop, Me., U.S.	D3	96
Winthrop, Ma., U.S.	B6	98
Winthrop, Mn., U.S.	F4	100
Winthrop, N.Y., U.S.	B2	102
Winthrop, Wa., U.S.	f10	109
Winthrop, Lake, l., Ma., U.S.	A5	124
Winthrop Harbor, Il., U.S.	h10	98
Winton, Austl.	A6	90
Winton, Bah.	D7	50
Winton, Mn., U.S.	m18	64
Winton, N.C., U.S.	C7	100
Winton, Lake, res., Oh., U.S.	A6	110
Wintzenheim, Fr.	o12	113
Winyah Bay, b., S.C., U.S.	A3	20
Wiota, Ia., U.S.	E9	117
Wīrātnagar, Nepal	C3	100
Wirksworth, Eng., U.K.	G11	36
Wirral, N.B.	C5	12
Wirt, co., W.V., U.S.	D3	71
Wirtz, Va., U.S.	B3	125
Wisbech, Eng., U.K.	C3	123
Wiscasset, Me., U.S.	B9	66
Wisconsin, state, U.S.	D3	96
Wisconsin, stm., Wi., U.S.	D4	126
Wisconsin, Lake, res., Wi., U.S.	E3	126
Wisconsin Dells, Wi., U.S.	E4	126
Wisconsin Rapids, Wi., U.S.	D4	126
Wisdom, Mt., U.S.	E3	103
Wise, N.C., U.S.	A4	110
Wise, Va., U.S.	f9	123
Wise, co., Tx., U.S.	C4	120
Wise, co., Va., U.S.	e9	123
Wiseman, Ak., U.S.	B9	79
Wise River, Mt., U.S.	E4	103
Wiseton, Sask.	F2	75
Wishart, Sask.	F3	75
Wishart, Mo., U.S.	D4	102
Wishaw, Scot., U.K.	E5	13
Wishek, N.D., U.S.	C6	111
Wishram, Wa., U.S.	D4	124
Wisła (Vistula), stm., Pol.	B5	26
Wisłok, stm., Pol.	C7	26
Wisłoka, stm., Pol.	D6	26
Wismar, Ger.	B5	18
Wismar Bucht, b., Ger.	B5	18
Wisner, La., U.S.	C4	95
Wisner, Ne., U.S.	C9	104
Wissant, Fr.	D9	12
Wissembourg, Fr.	C7	16
Wissota, Lake, res., Wi., U.S.	D2	126
Wister, Ok., U.S.	C7	113
Wister Lake, res., Ok., U.S.	C7	113
Witbank, S. Afr.	C4	49
Witchekan Lake, l., Sask.	D2	75
Witch Lake, Mi., U.S.	B3	99
Witham, Eng., U.K.	C8	12
Witham, stm., Eng., U.K.	A7	12
Withamsville, Oh., U.S.	C1	112
Withee, Wi., U.S.	D3	126
Witherbee, N.Y., U.S.	A7	109
Witherspoon, Mount, mtn., Ak., U.S.	g18	79
Withlacoochee, stm., U.S.	B3	86
Withlacoochee, stm., Fl., U.S.	C4	86
Withrow, Wa., U.S.	B6	124
Witless Bay, Newf.	E5	72
Witney, Eng., U.K.	C6	12
Witry-lès-Reims, Fr.	E4	17
Witt, Il., U.S.	D4	90
Witt, Tn., U.S.	C10	119
Witten, Ger.	B2	19
Witten, S.D., U.S.	D5	118
Witten, l., Ger.	D3	15
Wittenberg, Ger.	C6	18
Wittenberg, Wi., U.S.	D4	126
Wittenberge, Ger.	B5	18
Wittenheim, Fr.	B3	20
Wittingen, Ger.	B5	18
Wittlich, Ger.	D3	18
Wittman, Md., U.S.	C5	97
Wittmann, Az., U.S.	D3	80
Wittmund, Ger.	A7	17
Wittstock, Ger.	B5	18
Witu Islands, is., Pap. N. Gui.	h12	50
Witvlei, Nmb.	B2	49
Witzenhausen, Ger.	B4	19
Wiveliscombe, Eng., U.K.	C4	12
Wiwòn, N. Kor.	F3	33
Wixom, Mi., U.S.	o14	99
Wixom Lake, res., Mi., U.S.	E6	99
Wkra, stm., Pol.	B6	26
Władysławowo, Pol.	A5	26
Włocławek, Pol.	B5	26
Włodawa, Pol.	C7	26
Włoszczowa, Pol.	C5	26
Woburn, Que.	D7	74
Woburn, Ma., U.S.	B5	98
Woden, Ia., U.S.	A4	92
Wodzisław Śląski, Pol.	*C5	26
Woerden, Neth.	B4	17
Wohlen, Switz.	B5	21
Wohlthat Mountains, mts., Ant.	B14	7
Woito, Ont.	B7	73
Wokam, i., Indon.	G8	34
Woking, Alta.	B1	68
Woking, Eng., U.K.	m11	109
Wokingham, Eng., U.K.	C7	12
Wolbach, Ne., U.S.	C7	104
Wolcott, Co., U.S.	B4	83
Wolcott, Ct., U.S.	C4	84
Wolcott, In., U.S.	C3	91
Wolcott, N.Y., U.S.	B4	109
Wolcott, Vt., U.S.	B4	122
Wolcottville, In., U.S.	A7	91
Woldegk, Ger.	B5	18
Wolf, stm., Ms., U.S.	E7	15
Wolf, stm., Tn., U.S.	e9	119
Wolf, stm., Wi., U.S.	e9	119
Wolf, Isla, i., Ec.	C5	126
Wolf, North Fork, stm., Tn., U.S.	f5	58
Wolf, Volcán, vol., Ec.	B2	119
Wolfach, Ger.	f5	58
Wolf Creek, Mt., U.S.	G4	19
Wolf Creek, Or., U.S.	C4	103
Wolf Creek, stm., U.S.	E3	114
Wolf Creek, stm., Ia., U.S.	A2	113
Wolf Creek, stm., Mt., U.S.	B5	92
Wolf Creek, stm., W.V., U.S.	D7	99
Wolf Creek Pass, Co., U.S.	m13	125
Wolfe, co., Que.	D3	83
Wolfe, co., Ky., U.S.	D6	74
Wolfeboro, N.H., U.S.	C6	94
Wolfeboro Falls, N.H., U.S.	C4	106
Wolfe City, Tx., U.S.	C4	106
Wolfegg, Ger.	C4	120
Wolfen, Ger.	A8	21
Wolfenbüttel, Ger.	B7	19
Wolfenschiessen, Switz.	B5	18
Wolfhagen, Ger.	C5	21
Wolf Island, Mo., U.S.	B4	19
Wolflake, In., U.S.	E8	102
Wolf Lake, Il., U.S.	B7	91
Wolf Lake, Mi., U.S.	F4	90
Wolf Lake, l., Alta.	E4	99
Wolf Lake, l., Il., U.S.	B5	68
Wolf Mountain, mtn., Ak., U.S.	k9	90
Wolford, N.D., U.S.	B9	79
Wolf Point, Mt., U.S.	A6	111
Wolfratshausen, Ger.	B11	103
Wolfsberg, Aus.	B7	20
Wolfsburg, Ger.	E7	18
Wolfsville, Md., U.S.	A2	97
Wolf Swamp, sw., N.C., U.S.	C5	110
Wolf Trap, Va., U.S.	*B5	123
Wolfville, N.S.	D5	71
Wolgast, Ger.	A6	18
Wolhusen, Switz.	B4	20
Wolin, Pol.	B2	18
Wolin, i., Pol.	E8	15
Wollaston, Cape, c., N.W. Ter.	B9	66
Wollaston, Islas, is., Chile	k12	54
Wollaston Lake, l., Sask.	m8	75
Wollongong, Austl.	F9	50
Wolmaransstad, S. Afr.	C4	49
Wolmirstedt, Ger.	A6	19
Wołomin, Pol.	k14	26
Wołów, Pol.	C4	26
Wolseley, Sask.	G4	75
Wolsey, S.D., U.S.	C7	118
Wolsztyn, Pol.	*k8	90
Wolverhampton, Eng., U.K.	D5	10
Wolverine, Mi., U.S.	C6	99
Wolverton, Eng., U.K.	D6	10
Wolverton, Mn., U.S.	D2	100
Womack Hill, Al., U.S.	D1	78
Woman Lake, l., Mn., U.S.	D4	100
Womelsdorf, Pa., U.S.	F9	115
Wonalancet, N.H., U.S.	C4	106
Wonder Lake, Il., U.S.	A5	90
Wonderland, Ca., U.S.	B3	82
Wonewoc, Wi., U.S.	E3	126
Wŏnju, S. Kor.	H3	33
Wonotobo Vallen, wtfl., Sur.	A7	59
Wonowon, B.C.	A7	69
Wŏnsan, N. Kor.	D10	31
Wonthaggi, Austl.	G8	50
Wood, N.C., U.S.	A4	110
Wood, Pa., U.S.	F5	115
Wood, S.D., U.S.	D5	118
Wood, co., Oh., U.S.	A2	112
Wood, co., Tx., U.S.	C5	120
Wood, co., W.V., U.S.	B3	125
Wood, co., Wi., U.S.	D3	126
Wood, stm., B.C.	C8	69
Wood, stm., Sask.	H2	75
Wood, stm., R.I., U.S.	F2	116
Wood, stm., Wy., U.S.	C3	127
Wood, Mount, mtn., Mt., U.S.	E7	103
Woodall Mountain, mtn., Ms., U.S.	A5	101
Woodberry, Ar., U.S.	D3	81
Woodbine, Ga., U.S.	F5	87
Woodbine, Il., U.S.	A3	90
Woodbine, Ia., U.S.	C2	92
Woodbine, Ky., U.S.	D5	94
Woodbine, Md., U.S.	B3	97
Woodbine, N.J., U.S.	E3	107
Woodboro, Wi., U.S.	C4	126
Woodbourne, N.Y., U.S.	D6	109
Woodbourne, Oh., U.S.	*C1	112
Woodbridge, Eng., U.K.	B9	12
Woodbridge, N.J., U.S.	B4	107
Woodbridge, Va., U.S.	B5	123
Woodbridge [Township], N.J., U.S.	B4	107
Wood Buffalo National Park, Can.	E10	66
Woodburn, In., U.S.	B8	91
Wooldridge, Mo., U.S.	C5	102
Woodburn, Ia., U.S.	C4	92
Woodburn, Ky., U.S.	D3	94
Woodburn, Or., U.S.	B4	114
Woodbury, Ct., U.S.	C3	84
Woodbury, Ga., U.S.	D2	87
Woodbury, Ky., U.S.	C3	94
Woodbury, Mn., U.S.	F6	100
Woodbury, N.J., U.S.	D2	107
Woodbury, N.Y., U.S.	*E7	109
Woodbury, Pa., U.S.	F5	115
Woodbury, Tn., U.S.	B5	119
Woodbury, Vt., U.S.	C4	122
Woodbury, co., Ia., U.S.	B1	92
Woodbury Mountain, mtn., Vt., U.S.	C4	122
Woodcliff, Ga., U.S.	D5	87
Woodcliff Lake, N.J., U.S.	g8	107
Woodcliff Lake, l., N.J., U.S.	g8	107
Wood Dale, Il., U.S.	k9	90
Wood End, spit, Ma., U.S.	B7	98
Woodenhawk, De., U.S.	E3	85
Woodfibre, B.C.	E6	69
Woodfield, S.C., U.S.	C6	117
Woodford, Ire.	D3	11
Woodford, S.C., U.S.	D5	117
Woodford, co., Il., U.S.	C4	90
Woodford, co., Ky., U.S.	B5	94
Woodhaven, Mi., U.S.	*F7	99
Woodhull, Il., U.S.	B3	90
Woodhull, N.Y., U.S.	C3	109
Woodlake, Ca., U.S.	D4	82
Wood Lake, Mn., U.S.	F3	100
Wood Lake, Ne., U.S.	B5	104
Woodlake, Tx., U.S.	D5	120
Wood Lake, l., Sask.	B4	75
Woodland, Al., U.S.	B4	78
Woodland, Ca., U.S.	C3	82
Woodland, Ga., U.S.	D2	87
Woodland, Il., U.S.	C6	90
Woodland, Me., U.S.	C5	96
Woodland, Mi., U.S.	F5	99
Woodland, Ms., U.S.	B4	101
Woodland, N.C., U.S.	A5	110
Woodland, Pa., U.S.	D5	115
Woodland, Wa., U.S.	D3	124
Woodland Acres, Co., U.S.	D6	83
Woodland Beach, De., U.S.	C4	85
Woodland Mills, Tn., U.S.	A2	119
Woodland Park, Co., U.S.	C5	83
Woodlawn, Ont.	h11	73
Woodlawn, Il., U.S.	E4	90
Woodlawn, Ky., U.S.	e9	94
Woodlawn, Md., U.S.	g10	97
Woodlawn, Oh., U.S.	n13	112
Woodlawn, Va., U.S.	A4	119
Woodleaf, N.C., U.S.	B2	110
Woodlynne, N.J., U.S.	*D2	107
Woodman, N.H., U.S.	C5	106
Woodmere, N.Y., U.S.	*k13	109
Woodmont, Ct., U.S.	E4	84
Woodmoor, Md., U.S.	C5	97
Wood Mountain, Sask.	H2	75
Wood Mountain, mtn., Sask.	H2	75
Woodport, N.J., U.S.	B3	107
Woodridge, Man.	E3	70
Woodridge, Il., U.S.	k8	90
Wood-Ridge, N.J., U.S.	h8	107
Wood River, Il., U.S.	E3	90
Wood River Junction, R.I., U.S.	F2	116
Woodruff, Az., U.S.	C5	80
Woodruff, Ks., U.S.	C4	93
Woodruff, S.C., U.S.	B3	117
Woodruff, Ut., U.S.	B4	121
Woodruff, Wi., U.S.	C4	126
Woodruff, co., Ar., U.S.	B4	81
Woods, co., Ok., U.S.	A3	113
Woods, Lake, l., Austl.	C5	50
Woods, Lake, res., Tn., U.S.	B5	119
Woods Lake of the, l., N.A.	E4	70
Woodsboro, Md., U.S.	A3	97
Woodsboro, Tx., U.S.	E4	120
Woods Cross, Ut., U.S.	C4	121
Woodsdale, N.C., U.S.	A4	110
Woodsfield, Oh., U.S.	C4	112
Wood's Island, Newf.	D2	72
Woodson, Ar., U.S.	C3	81
Woodson, Il., U.S.	D3	90
Woodson, Tx., U.S.	C3	120
Woodson, co., Ks., U.S.	E8	93
Woodstock, N.B.	C2	71
Woodstock, Ont.	D4	73
Woodstock, Al., U.S.	B2	78
Woodstock, Ct., U.S.	B8	84
Woodstock, Ga., U.S.	B2	87
Woodstock, Il., U.S.	A5	90
Woodstock, Md., U.S.	B4	97
Woodstock, N.H., U.S.	C3	106
Woodstock, N.Y., U.S.	C6	109
Woodstock, Oh., U.S.	B2	112
Woodstock, Vt., U.S.	D3	122
Woodstock, Va., U.S.	B4	123
Woodstock Valley, Ct., U.S.	B7	84
Woodstown, N.J., U.S.	D2	107
Woodsville, N.J., U.S.	C3	107
Woodsville, Austl.	*F6	50
Woodville, Ont.	C5	73
Woodville, N.Z.	N15	51
Woodville, Fl., U.S.	B2	86
Woodville, Ga., U.S.	C3	87
Woodville, Id., U.S.	F6	89
Woodville, Ky., U.S.	e9	94
Woodville, Mi., U.S.	h9	98
Woodville, Ms., U.S.	D2	101
Woodville, Oh., U.S.	A2	112
Woodville, Tx., U.S.	D5	120
Woodville, Wi., U.S.	D1	126
Woodward, Al., U.S.	B3	78
Woodward, Ok., U.S.	A2	113
Woodward, co., Ok., U.S.	A2	113
Woodwards Cove, N.B.	E3	71
Woodway, Tx., U.S.	*D4	120
Woodworth, La., U.S.	C3	95
Woodworth, N.D., U.S.	B6	111
Woody, stm., Can.	C1	70
Wooler, Eng., U.K.	E6	13
Woolford, Md., U.S.	C5	97
Woollahra, Austl.	*F9	50
Woolmarket, Ms., U.S.	E5	101
Woolper Creek, stm., Ky., U.S.	h13	94
Woolrich, Pa., U.S.	D7	115
Woolsey Peak, mtn., Az., U.S.	D3	80
Woolstock, Ia., U.S.	B4	92
Woolwich, Me., U.S.	g8	96
Woomera, Austl.	F6	50
Woonsocket, R.I., U.S.	A3	116
Woonsocket, S.D., U.S.	C7	118
Woonsocket Reservoir Number Three, res., R.I., U.S.	B3	116
Wooster, Ar., U.S.	B3	81
Wooster, Oh., U.S.	B4	112
Woosung, Il., U.S.	B4	90
Wooqooyi Galbeed, prov., Som.	C4	47
Worb, Switz.	C4	21
Worbis, Ger.	B5	19
Worcester, S. Afr.	D2	49
Worcester, Eng., U.K.	D5	10
Worcester, Ma., U.S.	B4	98
Worcester, N.Y., U.S.	C6	109
Worcester, Vt., U.S.	C3	122
Worcester, co., Md., U.S.	D7	97
Worcester, co., Ma., U.S.	A3	98
Worcester Mountains, mts., Vt., U.S.	C3	122
Worden, Il., U.S.	E4	90
Worden, Mt., U.S.	E8	103
Worden, Or., U.S.	E5	114
Worden Pond, l., R.I., U.S.	F3	116
Wordsworth, Sask.	H4	75
Workington, Eng., U.K.	C5	10
Worksop, Eng., U.K.	A6	12
Workum, Neth.	B5	17
Worland, Wy., U.S.	B5	127
Worley, Id., U.S.	B2	89
Wormerveer, Neth.	B4	17
Worms, Ger.	D4	18
Worms, Ne., U.S.	C7	104
Worms Head, c., Wales, U.K.	C3	12
Woronoco, Ma., U.S.	B2	98
Worth, Il., U.S.	k9	90
Worth, Mo., U.S.	A3	102
Worth, co., Ga., U.S.	E3	87
Worth, co., Ia., U.S.	A4	92
Worth, co., Mo., U.S.	A3	102
Wortham, Tx., U.S.	D4	120
Worthing, Eng., U.K.	E6	10
Worthing, S.D., U.S.	D9	118
Worthington, In., U.S.	F4	91
Worthington, Ia., U.S.	B6	92
Worthington, Ky., U.S.	B7	94
Worthington, Mn., U.S.	G3	100
Worthington, Oh., U.S.	B2	112
Worthington, Pa., U.S.	E2	115
Worthington, W.V., U.S.	k10	125
Worthington Knob, mtn., Tn., U.S.	D8	119
Worthington Peak, mtn., Nv., U.S.	F6	105
Worthington Springs, Fl., U.S.	C4	86
Worthville, Ky., U.S.	B4	94
Worthville, N.C., U.S.	B3	110
Worton, Md., U.S.	B5	97
Wostok, Alta.	C4	68
Wotton, Que.	D6	74
Wounded Knee, S.D., U.S.	D3	118
Wouna, Nic.	E8	63
Wowoni, i., Indon.	F6	34
Woy Woy, Austl.	*F9	50
Woźniki, Pol.	f10	26
Wrangel Island, i., Sov. Un.	B21	29
Wrangell, Ak., U.S.	D13	79
Wrangell, Mount, mtn., Ak., U.S.	f19	79
Wrangell Island, i., Ak., U.S.	m24	79
Wrangell Mountains, mts., N.A.	D4	66
Wrangell Mountains, mts., Ak., N.A.	C11	79
Wrangell-Saint Elias National Park, Ak., U.S.	C11	79
Wrath, Cape, c., Scot., U.K.	A4	10
Wray, Co., U.S.	A8	83
Wray, Ga., U.S.	E3	87
Wren, Oh., U.S.	B1	102
Wrens, Ga., U.S.	C4	87
Wrenshall, Mn., U.S.	D6	100
Wrentham, Alta.	E4	68
Wrentham, Ma., U.S.	B5	98
Wrexham, Wales, U.K.	D5	10
Wriezen, Ger.	B7	18
Wright, Al., U.S.	A2	78
Wright, Ar., U.S.	C3	81
Wright, Fl., U.S.	*u15	86
Wright, Ks., U.S.	E4	93
Wright, Mn., U.S.	C5	92
Wright, co., Ia., U.S.	B4	92
Wright, co., Mn., U.S.	E5	100
Wright, co., Mo., U.S.	D5	102
Wright, Mount, mtn., Mt., U.S.	C3	106
Wright Brothers National Memorial, hist., N.C., U.S.	A7	110
Wright City, Mo., U.S.	C8	102
Wright City, Ok., U.S.	C6	113
Wright-Patterson Air Force Base, mil., Oh., U.S.	C1	112
Wrightson, Mount, mtn., Az., U.S.	F5	80
Wrightstown, N.J., U.S.	C3	107
Wrightstown, Wi., U.S.	D5	126
Wrightsville, Ar., U.S.	C3	81
Wrightsville, Ga., U.S.	D4	87
Wrightsville, Pa., U.S.	F8	115
Wrightsville Beach, N.C., U.S.	C5	110
Wrightsville Reservoir, res., Vt., U.S.	C3	122
Wrightwood, Ca., U.S.	E5	82
Wrigley, N.W. Ter.	D8	66
Wrigley Gulf, b., Ant.	B36	7
Wrocław (Breslau), Pol.	C4	26
Wrong Lake, l., Man.	C3	70
Wroxeter, Ont.	D3	73
Wroxham, Eng., U.K.	B9	12
Wroxton, Sask.	F5	75
Września, Pol.	B4	26
Wschowa, Pol.	D3	33
Wuchang, China	D3	33
Wuchow see Wuzhou, China	G7	31
Wuchuan, China	J3	32
Wuchuan, China	D4	31
Wuchuan, China	B9	35
Wuda, China	D6	31
Wudaoliang, China	D3	31
Wudu, China	D3	31
Wufeng, China	I4	32
Wugang, China	F7	31
Wuhai, China	E2	32
Wuhan, China	E7	31
Wuhe, China	H7	32
Wuhu, China	E8	31
Wu Jiang, stm., China	F6	31
Wukari, Nig.	E6	45
Wum, Cam.	D2	46
Wümme, stm., Ger.	E3	15
Wunsiedel, Ger.	C6	19
Wunstorf, Ger.	A4	19
Wupatki National Monument, Az., U.S.	B4	80
Wuppertal, Ger.	C3	18
Wurtsboro, N.Y., U.S.	D6	109
Wurtsmith Air Force Base, mil., Mi., U.S.	D7	99
Württemberg, hist. reg., Ger.	D4	18
Würzburg, Ger.	D4	18
Wurzen, Ger.	C6	18
Wushan, China	E8	31
Wusong, China	B2	70
Wusuli (Ussuri), stm., Asia	B11	31
Wutongqiao, China	F5	31
Wuwei, China	D5	31
Wuwei, China	I7	32
Wuxi, China	E9	31
Wuxing, China	E9	31
Wuyi, China	F6	32
Wuyiling, China	B10	31
Wuyuan, China	C6	31
Wuzhan, China	A2	33
Wuzhi Peak, mtn., China	B3	34
Wuzhong, China	F2	32
Wuzhou (Wuchow), China	G7	31
Wyaconda, Mo., U.S.	A6	102
Wyaconda, stm., Mo., U.S.	A6	102
Wyalusing, Pa., U.S.	C9	115
Wyandanch, N.Y., U.S.	*n15	109
Wyandot, co., Oh., U.S.	B2	112
Wyandotte, Mi., U.S.	F7	99
Wyandotte, Ok., U.S.	A7	113
Wyandotte, co., Ks., U.S.	C9	93
Wyandra, Austl.	C6	51
Wyanet, Il., U.S.	B4	90
Wyarno, Wy., U.S.	B6	127
Wyatt, In., U.S.	A5	91
Wyatt, Mo., U.S.	E8	102
Wyckoff, N.J., U.S.	*A4	107
Wyco, W.V., U.S.	D3	125
Wye, stm., U.K.	C5	12
Wyebridge, Ont.	C5	73
Wyevale, Ont.	C5	73
Wyeville, Wi., U.S.	D3	126
Wye Mills, Md., U.S.	C5	97
Wykoff, Mn., U.S.	G6	100
Wylie, Tx., U.S.	C4	120
Wylie, Lake, res., U.S.	A5	117
Wyman Lake, res., Me., U.S.	C3	96
Wymark, Sask.	G2	75
Wymondham, Eng., U.K.	B9	12
Wymore, Ne., U.S.	D9	104
Wyndham, Austl.	C4	50
Wyndmere, N.D., U.S.	C8	111
Wynnburg, Tn., U.S.	A2	119
Wynndel, B.C.	E9	69
Wynne, Ar., U.S.	B5	81
Wynnewood, Ok., U.S.	C4	113
Wynona, Ok., U.S.	A5	113
Wynoochee, stm., Wa., U.S.	B2	124
Wynot, Ne., U.S.	B8	104
Wynyard, Sask.	F3	75
Wyocena, Wi., U.S.	E4	126
Wyodak, Wy., U.S.	B7	127
Wyola, Mt., U.S.	E9	103
Wyoming, Ont.	E2	73
Wyoming, De., U.S.	D3	85
Wyoming, Il., U.S.	B4	90
Wyoming, Ia., U.S.	B6	92
Wyoming, Mi., U.S.	F5	99
Wyoming, Mn., U.S.	E6	100
Wyoming, N.Y., U.S.	C2	109
Wyoming, Oh., U.S.	o13	112
Wyoming, Pa., U.S.	n17	115
Wyoming, R.I., U.S.	E2	116
Wyoming, co., N.Y., U.S.	C2	109
Wyoming, co., Pa., U.S.	D9	115
Wyoming, co., W.V., U.S.	D3	125
Wyoming, state, U.S.	C5	127
Wyoming Peak, mtn., Wy., U.S.	D2	127
Wyoming Range, mts., Wy., U.S.	D2	127
Wyomissing, Pa., U.S.	F10	115
Wyrzysk, Pol.	B4	26
Wysocking Bay, b., N.C., U.S.	B7	110
Wysokie Mazowieckie, Pol.	B7	26
Wyszków, Pol.	B6	26
Wythe, co., Va., U.S.	D1	123
Wytheville, Va., U.S.	D1	123
Wytopitlock, Me., U.S.	C4	96
Wyvis, Ben, mtn., Scot., U.K.	C4	13

X

Xaafuun, Som.	C7	47
Xainza, China	B8	36
Xai-Xai (João Belo), Moz.	C5	49
Xalin, Som.	D6	47
Xambioá, Braz.	D5	59
Xangongo, Ang.	E1	48
Xánthi, Grc.	B5	40
Xapecó, stm., Braz.	D2	53
Xapuri, Braz.	B2	55
Xarardheere, Som.	E6	47
Xau, l., Bots.	B3	49
Xbonil, Mex.	D6	63
Xcalak, Mex.	D7	63
Xenia, Il., U.S.	E5	90
Xenia, Oh., U.S.	C2	112
Xiaguan, China	F5	31
Xiajiang, China	F8	31
Xiajin, China	F6	32
Xiamen (Amoy), China	G8	31
Xi'an (Sian), China	E6	31
Xiangfan, China	E7	31
Xiang Jiang, stm., China	J5	32
Xiangkhoang, Laos	B2	34
Xiangtan, China	F7	31
Xiangxiang, China	K5	32
Xiangyang, China	J6	32
Xianyang, China	E6	31
Xiao Hinggan Ling (Lesser Khingan Range), mts., China	B10	31
Xiapu, China	F9	31

Name	Map Ref.	Page
Xichang, China	F5	31
Xifeng, China	C11	32
Xigazê, China	C8	36
Xi Jiang, stm., China	G7	31
Xilitla, Mex.	m14	63
Xin Barag Zuoqi, China	B8	31
Xinbin, China	D11	31
Xincai, China	H6	32
Xingcheng, China	D9	31
Xinghua, China	H8	32
Xingkai Hu (Lake Khanka), l., Asia	B11	31
Xingtai, China	D7	31
Xingu, stm., Braz.	C4	59
Xinhua, China	K4	32
Xining, China	D5	31
Xinjiang, China	G4	31
Xinjiang Uygur, prov., China	C2	31
Xinjin, China	D9	31
Xinmin, China	C9	31
Xinning, China	K4	32
Xintai, China	*D8	31
Xinwen, China	G7	32
Xinxian, China	D7	31
Xinxiang, China	D7	31
Xinyang, China	E7	31
Xinye, China	H5	32
Xinyi He, stm., China	G8	32
Xinzhou, China	C8	35
Xique-Xique, Braz.	D2	57
Xishui, China	I6	32
Xi Ujimqin Qi, China	B7	32
Xiushui, China	J6	32
Xixabangma Mountain, mtn., Asia	C8	36
Xixian, China	F4	32
Xizang see Tibet, prov., China	E3	31
Xochimilco (part of Mexico City), Mex.	h9	63
Xuancheng, China	I8	32
Xuanhua, China	C8	31
Xuchang, China	E7	31
Xuddun, Som.	D6	47
Xuddur, Som.	E5	47
Xuguit Qi (Yakeshi), China	*B9	31
Xunhe, China	B4	33
Xunke, China	B4	33
Xupu, China	K4	32
Xuwen, China	B9	35
Xuyi, China	H8	32
Xuy Nong, is., Viet.	B7	35
Xuyong, China	F6	32
Xuzhou (Süchow), China	E8	31

Y

Ya'an, China	F5	31
Ya'bad, Isr. Occ.	B7	41
Yabassi, Cam.	E2	46
Yabbenohr Island, i., Marsh Is.	S17	52
Yablis, Nic.	C6	62
Yablonovy Mountains, mts., Sov. Un.	D14	29
Yabu, Japan	N5	52
Yabucoa, P.R.	B4	65
Yacata, i., Fiji	H16	52
Yacheng, China	B3	34
Yaco (Iaco), stm., S.A.	D3	58
Yacolt, Wa., U.S.	D3	124
Yacuiba, Bol.	D3	55
Yad Eli'ezer, Isr.	h10	41
Yadkin, co., N.C., U.S.	A2	110
Yadkin, stm., N.C., U.S.	A2	110
Yadkinville, N.C., U.S.	A2	110
Yad Mordekhay, Isr.	C6	41
Yadong, China	D12	37
Yadua, i., Fiji	H15	52
Yagasa Cluster, is., Fiji	I16	52
Yagoua, Cam.	C3	46
Yaguajay, Cuba	C4	64
Yaguas, stm., Peru	B3	58
Yahk, B.C.	E9	69
Yahuma, Zaire	A3	48
Yainax Butte, mtn., Or., U.S.	E5	114
Yaizu, Japan	o17	33
Yakima, Wa., U.S.	C5	124
Yakima, co., Wa., U.S.	C4	124
Yakima, stm., Wa., U.S.	C5	124
Yakima Indian Reservation, Wa., U.S.	C5	124
Yakima Ridge, mtn., Wa., U.S.	C5	124
Yakima Valley, val., Wa., U.S.	C5	124
Yako, Burkina	D4	45
Yakobi Island, i., Ak., U.S.	m21	79
Yakoma, Zaire	A3	48
Yaku Island, i., Japan	E11	31
Yakutat, Ak., U.S.	D12	79
Yakutat Bay, b., Ak., U.S.	D11	79
Yakutsk, Sov. Un.	C15	29
Yala, Thai.	D2	34
Yalaha, Fl., U.S.	D5	86
Yale, B.C.	E7	69
Yale, Il., U.S.	D5	90
Yale, Ia., U.S.	C3	92
Yale, Mi., U.S.	E8	99
Yale, Ok., U.S.	A5	113
Yale, S.D., U.S.	C8	118
Yale, Va., U.S.	D5	123
Yale, Mount, mtn., Co., U.S.	B4	83
Yale Lake, res., Wa., U.S.	D3	124
Yalinga, Cen. Afr. Rep.	D4	46
Yallahs Hill, hill, Jam.	F15	65
Yalobusha, co., Ms., U.S.	A4	101
Yalobusha, stm., Ms., U.S.	B4	101
Yalong Jiang, stm., China	F6	31
Yalova, Tur.	B7	40
Yalta, Sov. Un.	I10	27
Yalu, China	B9	31
Yalu Jiang, stm., Asia	C12	31
Yalutorovsk, Sov. Un.	B7	28
Yalvaç, Tur.	H14	40
Yama, Sov. Un.	q21	29
Yamachiche, Que.	C5	74
Yamagata, Japan	D13	31
Yamaguchi, Japan	I5	33
Yamal Peninsula, pen., Sov. Un.	B9	29
Yamantau, Mount, mtn. Sov. Un.	D8	28
Yamaska (Saint-Michel), Que.	C5	74
Yamaska, co., Que.	C5	74
Yambio, Sud.	E2	47
Yambol, Bul.	D8	24
Yamdena, i., Indon.	G8	34
Yamethin, Burma	D10	36
Yamhill, Or., U.S.	h11	114
Yamhill, co., Or., U.S.	B3	114
Yamkino, Sov. Un.	n18	27
Yamma Yamma, Lake, l., Austl.	E7	50
Yamoussoukro, I.C.		
Yampa, Co., U.S.	A4	83
Yampa, stm., Co., U.S.	A2	83

Yampa Plateau, plat., U.S.	A1	83
Yamparáez, Bol.	C2	55
Yamsay Mountain, mtn., Or., U.S.	E5	114
Yamsk, Sov. Un.	D18	29
Yamuna, stm., India	C7	36
Yamzho Yumco, l., China	C9	36
Yana, stm., Sov. Un.	C16	29
Yanac, Austl.	H3	51
Yanam, India	E7	36
Yan'an, China	D6	31
Yanaoca, Peru	D3	58
Yanaul, Sov. Un.	D20	8
Yanbu' al Bahr, Sau. Ar.	C3	38
Yancey, co., N.C., U.S.	f10	110
Yanceyville, N.C., U.S.	A3	110
Yancheng, China	*E9	31
Yancheng, China	H9	32
Yancheng, China	H5	32
Yanfolila, Mali	D3	45
Yangambi, Zaire	A3	48
Yangbajain, China	B13	37
Yangchou see Yangzhou, China	E8	31
Yangchun, China	G7	31
Yangdŏk, N. Kor.	G3	33
Yangiyul, Sov. Un.	G22	8
Yangjiang, China	G7	31
Yangquan, China	D7	31
Yangtze (Chang Jiang), stm., China	E8	31
Yangxian, China	H2	32
Yangyang, S. Kor.	G4	33
Yangzhou (Yangchou), China	E8	31
Yanji, China	C10	31
Yankeetown, Fl., U.S.	C4	86
Yanketown, In., U.S.	I3	91
Yankton, S.D., U.S.	E8	118
Yankton, co., S.D., U.S.	D8	118
Yankton Indian Reservation, S.D., U.S.	D8	118
Yanonge, Zaire	A3	48
Yanqi, China	C2	31
Yanshan, China	E7	32
Yanshi, China	G5	32
Yanshou, China	D4	33
Yantai, China	D9	31
Yantic, stm., Ct., U.S.	C7	84
Yantley, Al., U.S.	C1	78
Yantra, stm., Bul.	D7	24
Yanush, Ok., U.S.	C6	113
Yanzhou, China	D8	31
Yao, Chad	C3	46
Yao, Japan	*I7	33
Yaosca, Nic.	D5	62
Yaoundé, Cam.	E2	46
Yap, i., Micron.	F8	6
Yapen, i., Indon.	F9	34
Yaphank, N.Y., U.S.	*n16	109
Yaqeta, i., Fiji	H14	52
Yaque del Norte, stm., Dom. Rep.	E8	64
Yaqui, stm., Mex.	B3	63
Yar, Sov. Un.	B4	28
Yaracuy, state, Ven.	A4	60
Yaraka, Austl.	D7	50
Yardley, Pa., U.S.	F12	115
Yardville, N.J., U.S.	C3	107
Yarensk, Sov. Un.	C18	8
Yarí, stm., Col.	C3	60
Yarīm, Yemen	C5	47
Yaritagua, Ven.	A4	60
Yarker, Ont.	C8	73
Yarkovo, Sov. Un.	B7	28
Yarmouth, N.S.	F3	71
Yarmouth, la., U.S.	C6	92
Yarmouth, Me., U.S.	E2	96
Yarmouth, Ma., U.S.	C7	98
Yarmouth, co., N.S.	F4	71
Yarmouth Port, Ma., U.S.	*C7	98
Yarmūk, Nahr al, stm., Asia	B7	41
Yarnell, Az., U.S.	C3	80
Yarnema, Sov. Un.	F18	14
Yaroslavl, Sov. Un.	D6	27
Yarovskoye Marsh, sw., Sov. Un.	B8	28
Yarqah, Mayyat, well, Eg.	E5	41
Yarqon, stm., Isr.	C4	41
Yarram, Austl.	I6	51
Yarrow, B.C.	f13	69
Yarrowsburg, Md., U.S.	B2	97
Yartsevo, Sov. Un.	C27	8
Yartsevo, Sov. Un.	D9	27
Yarumal, Col.	B2	60
Yasawa, i., Fiji	H14	52
Yasawa Group, is., Fiji	H14	52
Yashi, Nig.	D6	45
Yasinovataya, Sov. Un.	q20	27
Yasinya, Sov. Un.	A7	24
Yasothon, Thai.	E6	35
Yass, Austl.	F8	50
Yata, Bol.	B2	55
Yates, co., N.Y., U.S.	C3	109
Yatesboro, Pa., U.S.	E3	115
Yates Center, Ks., U.S.	E8	93
Yates City, Il., U.S.	C3	90
Yatesville, Ga., U.S.	D2	87
Yathkyed Lake, l., N.W. Ter.	D13	66
Yatsuga, Mount, mtn., Japan	n17	33
Yatsushiro, Japan	J5	33
Yatsushiro Sea, Japan	J4	33
Yattah, Isr. Occ.	C7	41
Yauca, Peru	D3	58
Yauco, P.R.	B2	65
Yauco, Embalse de, res., P.R.	B2	65
Yauli, Peru	D2	58
Yaupi, Ec.	D3	58
Yauri, Peru	D3	58
Yautepec, Mex.	n14	63
Yauyos, Peru	D2	58
Yavapai, co., Az., U.S.	C3	80
Yavari (Javari), stm., S.A.	C3	58
Yavatmāl, India	C5	36
Yaví, Cerro, mtn., Ven.	B4	60
Yaviza, Pan.	F9	62
Yavne, Isr.	C6	41
Yavorov, Sov. Un.	A4	24
Yawatahama, Japan	J6	33
Yawgoog Pond, l., R.I., U.S.	E1	116
Yaxian, China	B3	34
Yazd (Yezd), Iran	B5	38
Yazoo, co., Ms., U.S.	C3	101
Yazoo, stm., Ms., U.S.	C3	101
Yazoo City, Ms., U.S.	C3	101
Ybbs, stm., Aus.	D7	20
Yding Skovhøj, hill, Den.	B3	15
Ye, Burma	E10	36
Yeadon, Pa., U.S.	p21	115
Yeager, Ok., U.S.	B5	113
Yeagertown, Pa., U.S.	E6	115
Yebbi Bou, Chad	A3	46
Yecla, Spain	C5	22
Yeddo, In., U.S.	D3	91
Yefremov, Sov. Un.	E12	27
Yegindybulak, Sov. Un.	D12	8
Yegoryevsk, Sov. Un.	D12	27
Yeguas, Punta, c., P.R.	B4	65

Yehud, Isr.	g10	41
Yei, Sud.	E3	47
Yekaterinoslavka, Sov. Un.	A4	33
Yelabuga, Sov. Un.	D19	8
Yelabuga, Sov. Un.	B7	33
Yelabuga, Sov. Un.	F14	27
Yelan, India	C7	36
Yelan-Kolenovskiy, Sov. Un.	F13	27
Yelanskoye, Sov. Un.	C15	29
Yelets, Sov. Un.	D6	29
Yélimané, Mali	C2	45
Yell, co., Ar., U.S.	B2	81
Yell, i., Scot., U.K.	g10	10
Yellandu, India	I8	37
Yellow, stm., U.S.	u15	86
Yellow, stm., Ga., U.S.	h8	87
Yellow, stm., In., U.S.	B4	91
Yellow, stm., Wi., U.S.	D3	126
Yellow, stm., Wi., U.S.	C3	126
Yellow Creek, Sask.	E3	75
Yellow Creek, Sask.	D3	75
Yellow Grass, Sask.	H3	75
Yellowhead Pass, Can.	C1	68
Yellow see Huang He, stm., China	D8	31
Yellow Jacket, Co., U.S.	D2	83
Yellowjacket Mountains, mts., Id., U.S.	D4	89
Yellowknife, N.W. Ter.	D10	66
Yellow Lake, l., Wi., U.S.	C1	126
Yellow Medicine, co., Mn., U.S.	F2	100
Yellow Pine, Al., U.S.	D1	78
Yellow Pine, Id., U.S.	E3	89
Yellow Sea, Asia	D9	31
Yellow Springs, Md., U.S.	B3	97
Yellow Springs, Oh., U.S.	C2	112
Yellowstone, co., Mt., U.S.	D8	103
Yellowstone, stm., U.S.	D10	103
Yellowstone, Clarks Fork, stm., U.S.	F7	103
Yellowstone Lake, l., Wy., U.S.	B2	127
Yellowstone National Park, Wy., U.S.	B2	127
Yellowstone National Park, co., Mt., U.S.	E6	103
Yellowstone National Park, U.S.	B2	127
Yellville, Ar., U.S.	A3	81
Yelm, Wa., U.S.	C3	124
Yelnya, Sov. Un.	D9	27
Yeltes, stm., Spain	B2	22
Yelverton Bay, b., N.W. Ter.	k35	66
Yelvington, Ky., U.S.	C3	94
Yelwa, Nig.	D5	45
Yemanzhelinsk, Sov. Un.	C6	28
Yemassee, S.C., U.S.	F6	117
Yemen, ctry., Asia	D4	38
Yen Bai, Viet.	D14	14
Yenakiyevo, Sov. Un.	G12	27
Yenangyat, Burma	B1	35
Yenangyaung, Burma	B1	35
Yenashimskiy Polkan, Mount, mtn., Sov. Un.	D12	29
Yenice, stm., Tur.	B9	40
Yenisey, stm., Sov. Un.	C11	29
Yenisey Ridge, mts., Sov. Un.	D27	8
Yeniseysk, Sov. Un.	D12	29
Yentna, stm., Ak., U.S.	f16	79
Yeo Lake, l., Austl.	E5	50
Yeoman, In., U.S.	C4	91
Yeotmal see Yavatmāl, India	C5	36
Yeovil, Eng., U.K.	E5	10
Yeppoon, Austl.	D9	50
Yerania Óri, mts., Grc.	g10	25
Yerevan, Sov. Un.	E7	29
Yerington, Nv., U.S.	E2	105
Yerington Indian Reservation, Nv., U.S.	D2	105
Yermakovskoye, Sov. Un.	E27	8
Yermentau, Sov. Un.	C8	28
Yermo, Ca., U.S.	E5	82
Yermolayevo, Sov. Un.	D19	8
Yerres, Fr.	h10	16
Yerres, stm., Fr.	F2	17
Yerseke, Neth.	C4	17
Yershov, Sov. Un.	C3	28
Yerupaja, Nevado, mtn., Peru	D2	58
Yeso, N.M., U.S.	C5	108
Yessentuki, Sov. Un.	G17	8
Yessey, Sov. Un.	C13	29
Yeste, Spain	C4	22
Yetter, Ia., U.S.	B3	92
Yeu, Île d', i., Fr.	D2	16
Yevlach, Sov. Un.	E3	28
Yevpatoriya, Sov. Un.	I9	27
Yexian, China	F8	32
Yeya, stm., Sov. Un.	H12	27
Yeysk, Sov. Un.	H12	27
Yezd see Yazd, Iran	B5	38
Yi, stm., Ur.	E1	56
Yiannitsá, Grc.	B4	25
Yíaros, i., Grc.	D5	25
Yibin, China	F5	31
Yichang, China	E7	31
Yicheng, China	I5	32
Yichuan, China	D7	31
Yichun, China	B10	31
Yidu, China	I4	32
Yidu, China	F8	32
Yigo, Guam	L10	52
Yilan, China	B10	31
Yiliang, China	G5	31
Yimianpo, China	D4	33
Yinchuan, China	D6	31
Yingcheng, China	G7	31
Ying He, stm., China	G6	32
Yingkou, China	C9	31
Yingshan, China	H7	32
Yingtan, China	F7	31
Yingxian, China	D7	32
Yining, China	E11	29
Yin Mountains, mts., China	D4	31
Yióura, i., Grc.	C5	25
Yirga Alem, Eth.	D3	47
Yirol, Sud.	D2	47
Yishan, China	G6	31
Yitong, China	C11	32
Yixian, China	D9	32
Yixing, China	I8	32
Yiyang, China	F7	31
Yŏju, S. Kor.	M10	52
Ylig Bay, Guam	D13	14
Ylikitka, l., Fin.	B16	12
Yli-ii, stm., Grnld.	E9	69
Ymir, B.C.	E4	120
Yoakum, Tx., U.S.	C1	120
Yoakum, co., Tx., U.S.	C4	101
Yockanookany, stm., Ms., U.S.	A4	101
Yocona, stm., Ms., U.S.		

Yoder, In., U.S.	C7	91
Yoder, Ks., U.S.	g11	93
Yoder, Wy., U.S.	E8	127
Yogyakarta, Indon.	G4	34
Yoho National Park, B.C.	D9	69
Yoichi, Japan	E10	33
Yojoa, Lago de, l., Hond.	C3	62
Yokadouma, Cam.	E2	46
Yokkaichi, Japan	E12	31
Yoko, Cam.	D2	46
Yokoate Island, i., Japan	L4	33
Yokohama, Japan	D12	31
Yokoshiba, Japan	n19	33
Yokosuka, Japan	D12	31
Yokote, Japan	G10	33
Yokum Seat, mtn., Ma., U.S.	B1	98
Yola, Nig.	E7	45
Yolo, co., Ca., U.S.	C2	82
Yolyn, W.V., U.S.	n12	125
Yom, stm., Thai.	B1	34
Yona, Guam	M10	52
Yonabaru, Japan	O5	52
Yonago, Japan	I6	33
Yonaha Mountain, hill, Japan	N6	52
Yoncalla, Or., U.S.	D3	114
Yonezawa, Japan	H10	33
Yong'an, China	F8	31
Yŏngan, N. Kor.	F4	33
Yonges Island, S.C., U.S.	F7	117
Yŏnghŭng, N. Kor.	G3	33
Yŏngil Bay, b., S. Kor.	H4	33
Yongji, China	G4	32
Yongnian, China	F6	32
Yongshou, China	G2	32
Yongshun, China	F6	31
Yongxiu, China	J6	32
Yonkers, N.Y., U.S.	E7	109
Yonne, stm., Fr.	D5	16
Yopal, Col.	B3	60
Yorba Linda, Ca., U.S.	*n13	82
York, Austl.	D5	73
York, Ont.	D5	73
York, Eng., U.K.	D6	10
York, Al., U.S.	C1	78
York, Ne., U.S.	D6	90
York, Il., U.S.	A8	91
York, In., U.S.	A8	91
York, Me., U.S.	E2	96
York, N.D., U.S.	A6	111
York, Ne., U.S.	D8	104
York, Pa., U.S.	G8	115
York, S.C., U.S.	A5	117
York, co., N.B.	C3	71
York, co., Ont.	D5	73
York, co., Me., U.S.	E2	96
York, co., Ne., U.S.	D8	104
York, co., Pa., U.S.	G8	115
York, co., S.C., U.S.	A5	117
York, stm., Ont.	B7	73
York, stm., Va., U.S.	C6	123
York, Cape, c., Grnld.	B14	61
York Beach, Me., U.S.	E2	96
Yorke Peninsula, pen., Austl.	F6	50
Yorketown, Austl.	*C4	107
York Factory, Man.	B6	68
York Harbor, Me., U.S.	E2	96
York Haven, Pa., U.S.	F8	115
Yorklyn, De., U.S.	A3	85
York Point, c., Newf.	C4	72
Yorkshire, N.Y., U.S.	C2	109
York Springs, Pa., U.S.	F7	115
Yorkton, Sask.	F4	75
Yorktown, Ar., U.S.	C4	81
Yorktown, In., U.S.	D7	91
Yorktown, Ia., U.S.	D2	92
Yorktown, N.J., U.S.	D2	107
Yorktown, N.Y., U.S.	*D7	109
Yorktown, Tx., U.S.	E4	120
Yorktown Heights, N.Y., U.S.	*D7	109
Yorktown Manor, R.I., U.S.	C3	116
Yorkville, Il., U.S.	B5	90
Yorkville, N.Y., U.S.	B5	109
Yorkville, Oh., U.S.	B5	112
Yorkville, Tn., U.S.	A2	119
Yoro, Hond.	C4	62
Yorosso, Mali	D4	45
Yoseki, Zaire	A3	48
Yosemite, Ky., U.S.	C5	94
Yosemite National Park, Ca., U.S.	D4	82
Yosemite National Park, Ca., U.S.	D3	82
Yoshkar-Ola, Sov. Un.	G9	34
Yost, Ut., U.S.	B2	121
Yost Lake, Ok., U.S.	A5	113
Yosu, S. Kor.	I3	33
Yotala, Bol.	E1	56
Yotvata, Isr.	E7	41
Youbou, B.C.	g11	69
Youghal, Ire.	D2	10
Youghal Bay, b., Ire.	E3	10
Youghiogheny, stm., U.S.	F2	115
Youghiogheny River Lake, res., U.S.	G3	115
You Jiang, stm., China	G6	31
Youkounkoun, Gui.	D2	45
Young, Austl.	G7	51
Young, Sask.	F3	75
Young, Az., U.S.	C5	80
Young, Ur.	E1	56
Young, co., Tx., U.S.	C3	120
Young America, In., U.S.	C5	91
Young Harris, Ga., U.S.	B3	87
Youngs Creek, In., U.S.	f11	124
Youngs Point, Ont.	C6	73
Youngstown, Alta.	D5	68
Youngstown, Fl., U.S.	B1	86
Youngstown, N.Y., U.S.	B1	109
Youngstown, Oh., U.S.	A5	112
Youngsville, La., U.S.	D3	95
Youngsville, N.M., U.S.	A3	108
Youngsville, N.C., U.S.	A4	110
Youngsville, Pa., U.S.	C3	115
Youngwood, Pa., U.S.	F2	115
Youssoufia, Mor.	B3	44
Youxi, China	K8	32
Youxian, China	I8	32
Youyang, China	F5	31
Youyang, China	C10	40
Ypacaraí, Para.	E4	55
Ypres see Ieper, Bel.	B5	16
Ypsilanti, Mi., U.S.	F7	99
Ypsilanti, N.D., U.S.	C7	111
Yreka, Ca., U.S.	B2	82
Yssingeaux, Fr.	E6	16
Ystad, Swe.	J5	14

Ythan, stm., Scot., U.K.	C6	13
Zákinthos (Zante), i., Grc.	D3	40
Zakopane, Pol.	D5	26
Zakroczym, Pol.	B6	26
Zala, stm., Hung.	B3	24
Zalaegerszeg, Hung.	B3	24
Zalamea de la Serana, Spain	C3	22
Zalamea la Real, Spain	D2	22
Zălau, Rom.	B6	24
Zaleski, Oh., U.S.	C3	112
Zalewo, Pol.	B5	26
Zalingei, Sud.	C1	47
Zalma, Mo., U.S.	D7	102
Zaltbommel, Neth.	C5	17
Zama, Ms., U.S.	C4	101
Zambales Mountains, mts., Phil.	o13	34
Zambezi (Balovale), Zam.	D3	48
Zambezi, stm., Afr.	H8	42
Zambézia, dept., Moz.	A6	49
Zambia, ctry., Afr.	D4	48
Zamboanga, Phil.	G5	105
Zambrano, Col.	B3	60
Zambrów, Pol.	B7	26
Zamora, Ec.	B2	58
Zamora, Spain	B2	58
Zamora, stm., Ec.	B2	58
Zamora-Chinchipe, prov., Ec.	B2	58
Zamora de Hidalgo, Mex.	D4	63
Zamość, Pol.	C7	26
Zamzam, Wādī, val., Libya	C2	43
Zanaga, Congo	B1	48
Zandvoort, Neth.	B4	17
Zanesville, In., U.S.	C7	91
Zanesville, Oh., U.S.	C4	112
Zanjān, Iran	A4	38
Zanpa Cape, c., Japan	O5	52
Zante see Zákinthos, i., Grc.	D3	40
Zanzibar, Tan.	C6	48
Zanzibar, i., Tan.	C6	48
Zaozhuang, China	G7	32
Zap, N.D., U.S.	B4	111
Zapadna Morava, stm., Yugo.	D5	24
Západočeský, prov., Czech.	D8	19
Zapala, Arg.	A3	54
Zapata, Tx., U.S.	F3	120
Zapata, co., Tx., U.S.	F3	120
Zapata, Peninsula de, pen., Cuba	C3	64
Zapatoca, Col.	B3	60
Zapopan, Mex.	m12	63
Zaporozhye, Sov. Un.	E6	29
Zapotillo, Ec.	B1	58
Zara, Tur.	C11	40
Zaragoza, Col.	B3	60
Zaragoza, Mex.	B4	63
Zaragoza, Mex.	k13	63
Zaragoza, Spain	B5	22
Zarand, Iran	B7	39
Zárate, Arg.	A5	54
Zaraysk, Sov. Un.	D12	27
Zaraza, Ven.	B4	60
Zard Kūh, mtn., Iran	C5	39
Zarembo Island, i., Ak., U.S.	m23	79
Zarephath, N.J., U.S.	B3	107
Zaria, Nig.	D6	45
Zarqā', Nahr az, stm., Jord.	B7	41
Zarrentin, Ger.	E4	15
Zarrīn Shahr, Iran	E5	39
Zaruma, Ec.	B1	58
Zarumilla, Peru	B1	58
Zaryevets, Sov. Un.	C7	44
Zarzis, Tun.	C7	44
Zasenbeck, Ger.	E4	15
Zasieki, Pol.	C3	26
Zásmuky, Czech.	o19	26
Zastava, Sov. Un.	A7	24
Zastron, S. Afr.	C4	49
Žatec, Czech.	C2	26
Zator, Pol.	h10	26
Zavala, co., Tx., U.S.	E3	120
Zavalla, Tx., U.S.	D5	120
Zavitinsk, Sov. Un.	D15	29
Zavodo-Petrovskiy, Sov. Un.	B7	28
Zawiercie, Pol.	C5	26
Zawīyat Masūs, Libya	C4	43
Zawr, Ra's az, c., Sau. Ar.	H4	39
Zbraslav, Czech.	B6	19
Ždʼár [nad Sázavou], Czech.	D2	19
Zdice, Czech.	o16	26
Zdolbunov, Sov. Un.	F6	27
Zduńska Wola, Pol.	C5	26
Zealandia, Sask.	F2	75
Zearing, Ia., U.S.	B4	92
Zeballos, B.C.	D4	69
Zebla, mtn., Tun.	F2	23
Zebrzydowice, Pol.	h9	26
Zebulon, Ga., U.S.	C2	87
Zebulon, Ky., U.S.	C7	94
Zebulon, N.C., U.S.	B4	110
Zeebrugge (part of Brugge), Bel.	B5	16
Zeeland, Mi., U.S.	F5	99
Zeeland, N.D., U.S.	D6	111
Zeeland, prov., Neth.	C3	17
Zeerust, S. Afr.	C4	49
Żefat (Safad), Isr.	F10	40
Zegrze, Pol.	k14	26
Zehdenick, Ger.	B6	18
Zeigler, Il., U.S.	F4	90
Zeil, Mount, mtn., Austl.	D5	50
Zeist, Neth.	A6	16
Zekiah Swamp Run, stm., Md., U.S.	C4	97
Zelechów, Pol.	C6	26
Zelenodolsk, Sov. Un.	B8	33
Zelenogorsk, Sov. Un.	A7	27
Zelenograd, Sov. Un.	C11	27
Železná Ruda, Czech.	D8	19
Zelienople, Pa., U.S.	E1	115
Zell, S.D., U.S.	C7	118
Zella-Mehlis, Ger.	E5	18
Zell am Ziller, Aus.	B7	20
Zeller Lake, l., Aus.	A7	20
Zelma, Sask.	F3	75
Zelzate, Bel.	B3	17
Zemaï, i., Tun.		
Zemetchino, Sov. Un.	E14	27
Zemio, Cen. Afr. Rep.	D5	46
Zenda, N.Y., U.S.	E5	93
Zendeh Jān, Afg.	D10	39
Zenica, Yugo.	C2	24
Zenith, Wa., U.S.	f11	124
Zenobia Peak, mtn., Co., U.S.	A2	83
Zenon Park, Sask.	D4	75
Zeona, S.D., U.S.	B3	118
Žepče, Yugo.	C2	24

Name	Map Ref.	Page
Zephyr, Tx., U.S.	D3	120
Zephyr Cove, Nv., U.S.	E2	105
Zephyrhills, Fl., U.S.	D4	86
Zerbst, Ger.	C6	18
Zereh, Gowd-e, depr., Afg.	C3	36
Zermatt, Switz.	C3	20
Zernez, Switz.	C6	20
Zeta, stm., Yugo.	D4	24
Zeulenroda, Ger.	C6	19
Zevenaar, Neth.	C6	17
Zevgolation, Grc.	D3	25
Zeya, Sov. Un.	D15	29
Zeya, stm., Sov. Un.	D15	29
Zeya Reservoir, res., Sov. Un.	D15	29
Zézere, stm., Port.	B2	22
Zgierz, Pol.	C5	26
Zgorzelec, Pol.	C3	26
Zhanatas, Sov. Un.	E7	28
Zhangbei, China	D6	32
Zhangiztobe, Sov. Un.	D10	28
Zhangjiakou, China	C7	31
Zhangwu, China	C10	32
Zhangye, China	D5	31
Zhangzhou (Changchou), China	G8	31
Zhanjiang, China	G7	31
Zhanyu, China	B10	32
Zhao'an, China	G8	31
Zhaodong, China	A11	32
Zhaoqing, China	G7	31
Zhaotong, China	F5	31
Zhaoxing, China	C5	33
Zhaoyuan, China	B11	32
Zhaozhou, China	D2	33
Zhari Namco, l., China	B8	36
Zharkamys, Sov. Un.	D5	28
Zhashui, China	H3	32
Zhaxigang, China	A7	37
Zhdanov see Mariupol, Sov. Un.	E6	29

Name	Map Ref.	Page
Zhecheng, China	G6	32
Zhejiang, prov., China	F9	31
Zhelaniya, Cape, c., Sov. Un.	B9	29
Zhen'an, China	H3	32
Zhenba, China	H2	32
Zheng'an, China	J2	32
Zhenglan Qi, China	C6	32
Zhengyangguan, China	H7	32
Zhengzhou (Chengchou), China	E7	31
Zhenjiang, China	E8	31
Zhenlai, China	B10	32
Zhenping, China	I3	32
Zhenyuan, China	K3	32
Zhidachov, Sov. Un.	D8	26
Zhidan, China	D6	31
Zhigansk, Sov. Un.	C15	29
Zhijiang, China	K3	32
Zhilaya Kosa, Sov. Un.	D4	28
Zhitomir, Sov. Un.	D5	29
Zhilevo, Sov. Un.	o18	27
Zhizdra, Sov. Un.	E10	27
Zhmerinka, Sov. Un.	G7	27
Zhob, Pak.	B4	36
Zhob, stm., Pak.	B2	37
Zhongba, China	C7	36
Zhongdian, China	F5	31
Zhongwei, China	D6	31
Zhongxian, China	E6	31
Zhongxiang, China	I5	32
Zhoukou, China	*E7	31
Zhoushan Qundao, is., China	E9	31
Zhuanghe, China	F8	32
Zhucheng, China	J9	32
Zhuji, China	H6	32
Zhumadian, China	E6	32
Zhuoxian, China	E7	31
Zhushan, China	F7	31
Zhuzhou, China		

Name	Map Ref.	Page
Zia Indian Reservation, N.M., U.S.	h7	108
Zia Pueblo, N.M., U.S.	*B3	108
Zibo, China	D8	31
Ziebach, co., S.D., U.S.	C4	118
Zielona Góra, Pol.	C3	26
Zierikzee, Neth.	C3	17
Ziesar, Ger.	A7	19
Ziftā, Eg.	D3	41
Zigazinskiy, Sov. Un.	C5	28
Zigey, Chad	C3	46
Zigong, China	F5	31
Zigui, China	E7	31
Ziguinchor, Sen.	D1	45
Zikhron Ya'aqov, Isr.	B6	41
Zile, Tur.	B10	40
Zilina, Czech.	D5	26
Zillah, Libya	D3	43
Zillah, Wa., U.S.	C5	124
Ziller, stm., Aus.	B7	20
Zilwaukee, Mi., U.S.	E7	99
Zima, Sov. Un.	D13	29
Zimapán, Mex.	C5	63
Zimba, Zam.	E4	48
Zimbabwe, ctry., Afr.	A5	49
Zimmerman, Mn., U.S.	E5	100
Zimnicea, Rom.	D7	24
Zin, Naḥal, val., Isr.	D7	41
Zinal, Switz.	D4	21
Zinc, Ar., U.S.	A3	81
Zincville, Ok., U.S.	A7	113
Zinder, Niger	D6	45
Zingst, Ger.	A6	19
Zion, Il., U.S.	C3	107
Zion, N.J., U.S.	C3	107
Zion, S.C., U.S.	C9	117
Zion Gate, hist., Isr. Occ.	m14	41
Zion National Park, Ut., U.S.	F3	121
Zion Reservoir, res., Az., U.S.	C6	80
Zionsville, In., U.S.	E5	91

Name	Map Ref.	Page
Zionville, N.C., U.S.	A1	110
Zipaquirá, Col.	B3	60
Zirándaro, Mex.	n13	63
Zirkel, Mount, mtn., Co., U.S.	A4	83
Zirndorf, Ger.	D5	19
Zistersdorf, Aus.	D8	18
Zitácuaro, Mex.	n13	63
Zittau, Ger.	C7	18
Ziwa Magharibi, prov., Tan.	B5	48
Ziway, Lake, l., Eth.	D4	47
Ziyang, China	E6	31
Ziyuan, China	K4	32
Zlatograd, Bul.	E7	24
Zlatoust, Sov. Un.	D9	29
Złoczew, Pol.	C5	26
Zlonice, Czech.	n17	26
Złotoryja, Pol.	C3	26
Złotów, Pol.	B4	26
Zlynka, Sov. Un.	E8	27
Zmeinogorsk, Sov. Un.	C10	28
Znamenka, Sov. Un.	G9	27
Żnin, Pol.	B4	26
Znojmo, Czech.	D4	26
Zoetermeer, Neth.	*B4	17
Zofingen, Switz.	B4	21
Zogno, Italy	E8	21
Zográfos, Grc.	*D4	25
Zohreh, stm., Iran	F5	39
Zolfo Springs, Fl., U.S.	E5	86
Zollikofen, Switz.	B3	21
Zollikon, Switz.	B6	21
Zolochev, Sov. Un.	G5	27
Zolotoy, Cape, c., Sov. Un.	B12	31
Zomba, Mwi.	E6	48
Zomergem, Bel.	C3	17
Zongo, Zaire	A2	48
Zonguldak, Tur.	B8	40

Name	Map Ref.	Page
Zörbig, Ger.	B7	19
Zorita, Spain	C3	22
Zorritos, Peru	B1	58
Zortman, Mt., U.S.	C8	103
Żory, Pol.	g9	26
Zossen, Ger.	B6	18
Zottegem, Bel.	D3	17
Zouar, Chad	A3	46
Zoutkamp, Neth.	A6	17
Zreïgat, Bir, well, Maur.	B3	45
Zrenjanin (Petrovgrad), Yugo.	C5	24
Zrmanja, stm., Yugo.	C2	24
Zschopau, Ger.	C8	19
Zuata, stm., Ven.	B4	60
Zubtsov, Sov. Un.	C10	27
Zuénoula, I.C.	E3	45
Zuera, Spain	B5	22
Zug, Switz.	E4	18
Zug, W. Sah.	E2	44
Zug, state, Switz.	B4	20
Zug, Lake, l., Switz.	E4	18
Zugdidi, Sov. Un.	A13	40
Zugspitze, mtn., Eur.	B6	20
Zuider Zee see IJsselmeer, l., Neth.	A6	16
Zulia, state, Ven.	B3	60
Zülpich, Ger.	C1	19
Zumbi, Ponta do, c., Braz.	B2	57
Zumbo, Moz.	A5	49
Zumbro, stm., Mn., U.S.	F6	100
Zumbro Falls, Mn., U.S.	F6	100
Zumbrota, Mn., U.S.	F6	100
Zumpango, Mex.	n14	63
Zungeru, Nig.	E6	45
Zunhua, China	C8	31
Zuni, N.M., U.S.	B1	108
Zuni, Va., U.S.	k14	123
Zuni, stm., U.S.	C6	80
Zuni Indian Reservation, N.M., U.S.	B1	108

Name	Map Ref.	Page
Zuni Mountains, mts., N.M., U.S.	B1	108
Zunyi, China	F6	31
Zuoquan, China	F5	32
Zuqar, i., Yemen	C5	47
Zurich, Ont.	D3	73
Zürich, Switz.	E4	18
Zurich, Ks., U.S.	C4	93
Zurich, Mt., U.S.	B7	103
Zürich, state, Switz.	B4	20
Zürich, Lake, l., Switz.	E4	18
Zuru, Nig.	D6	45
Zusam, stm., Ger.	E5	19
Zussdorf, Ger.	A7	21
Zutphen, Neth.	A7	16
Zuwārah, Libya	C2	43
Zuwayzā, Jord.	C7	41
Zuyevka, Sov. Un.	B4	28
Zvenigorodka, Sov. Un.	G8	27
Zvishavane, Zimb.	B5	49
Zvolen, Czech.	D5	26
Zvornik, Yugo.	C4	24
Zwartsluis, Neth.	B6	17
Zweibrücken, Ger.	D3	18
Zweisimmen, Switz.	C3	20
Zwenkau, Ger.	B7	19
Zwettl, Aus.	D7	18
Zwickau, Ger.	C6	18
Zwickauer Mulde, stm., Ger.	C7	19
Zwiesel, Ger.	D8	19
Zwingle, Ia., U.S.	B7	92
Zwischenahn, Ger.	A7	17
Zwolle, Neth.	A7	16
Zwolle, La., U.S.	C2	95
Żylks, La., U.S.	A1	95
Żyrardów, Pol.	B6	26
Zyryanovsk, Sov. Un.	D10	28
Żywiec, Pol.	D5	26